Classics

of

Western Philosophy

FIFTH EDITION

Edited by
STEVEN M. CAHN

HACKETT PUBLISHING COMPANY, INC.
INDIANAPOLIS/CAMBRIDGE

To Marilyn

First edition copyright © 1977
by Hackett Publishing Company, Inc.

Second edition copyright © 1985
by Hackett Publishing Company, Inc.

Third edition copyright © 1990
by Hackett Publishing Company, Inc.

Fourth edition copyright © 1995
by Hackett Publishing Company, Inc.

Fifth edition copyright © 1999
by Hackett Publishing Company, Inc.

05 04 03 02 01 00 99   1 2 3 4 5 6 7

Cover design by Brian Rak and John Pershing

For further information, please address

Hackett Publishing Company, Inc.
P.O. Box 44937
Indianapolis, Indiana 46244-0937

Library of Congress Cataloging-in-Publication Data

Classics of western philosophy
edited by Steven M. Cahn.
5th ed.
p.   cm.
Includes bibliographical references.
ISBN 0-87220-437-5 (hard.)
ISBN 0-87220-436-7 (pbk.)
1. Philosophy
I. Cahn, Steven M.
B29.C536 1999
190—dc21
98-47547
CIP

Contents

Preface

Here in one volume are the complete texts of twenty philosophical masterpieces, along with selections from nineteen others. Twenty-two of the world's greatest philosophers are represented, their writings spanning more than two millennia. Crucial fields of philosophy are explored in depth: metaphysics, epistemology, ethics, and philosophy of religion. An introduction to each author contains biographical data, philosophical commentary, and bilbiographical guides. Annotations are provided to clarify textual references.

What is the value of philosophy? Different philosophers have answered this question in different ways, but perhaps no reply is more inspirational, even to those who view it in part figuratively, than that provided by Bertrand Russell at the close of *The Problems of Philosophy*:

> Philosophy is to be studied, not for the sake of any definite answers to its questions, since no definite answers can, as a rule, be known to be true, but rather for the sake of the questions themselves; because these questions enlarge our conception of what is possible, enrich our intellectual imagination and diminish the dogmatic assurance which closes the mind against speculation; but above all because, through the greatness of the universe which philosophy contemplates, the mind also is rendered great, and becomes capable of that union with the universe which constitutes its highest good.*

• • •

The fifth edition contains seven major additions: selections from Books I and VII of Aristotle's *Metaphysics*, the section on personal identity from Hume's *Treatise*, major parts of Kant's *Critique of Pure Reason*, a section from Kierkegaard's *Concluding Unscientific Postscript*, two essays of Peirce, the first five chapters of Russell's *The Problems of Philosophy*, and Sartre's *The Humanism of Existentialism*. More of Plato's *Republic* has been included, and the materials from Aristotle's *On the Soul* and *Nicomachean Ethics*, Hobbes's *Leviathan*, and Locke's *Essay* have been somewhat altered. Mill's *On Liberty* has been abridged.

I very much appreciate the assistance of Israel Scheffler of Harvard University, Jonathan Vogel of Amherst College, and past and present faculty members at the University of Vermont: Charles Guignon, Patricia W. Kitcher (now of Columbia University), Philip S. Kitcher (now of Columbia University), William E. Mann, Derk Pereboom, and George Sher (now of Rice University). They have contributed most of the introductions, thereby providing expert commentary on the writings of each philosopher. Professor Guignon advised me on the selections from Hegel and Nietzsche and granted permission for use of his revision of J. B. Baillie's translation of Hegel. Professor Mann, with whom I consulted on a variety of editorial matters, furnished many of the translations of

---

The Problems of Philosophy (1912; rpt. New York: Oxford University Press, 1959), p. 161.

ix

Latin textual references. Professor Pereboom advised me on the selections from Berkeley, Kant, and Kierkegaard.

For suggestions regarding the contents of the book, I am also grateful to my friends of many years, John O'Connor, James Rachels, and David Rosenthal, as well as to the numerous philosophers who have taken the time and effort to write and offer counsel.

The production of the fifth edition was overseen by Meera Dash, Patty Cissna, Abigail Coyle, and Brian Rak. I am appreciative of their conscientiousness and sound judgment.

I also wish to thank Frances Hackett and Jay Hullett, who lead the Hackett Publishing Company and remain true to the values of its late founder, William H. Y. Hackett. Nearly a quarter century has passed since this work first appeared, and the kind reception it continues to enjoy is a testament to the power of William Hackett's publishing vision.

Steven M. Cahn
Professor of Philosophy
The Graduate School
The City University of New York

March 1999

Plato

Plato (427–347 B.C.) is surely the most famous of all philosophers. Little is known of his early life, except that he was born into a noble Athenian family and that at some time in his late teens, he came under the philosophical spell of Socrates (469–399 B.C.; valuable information about Socrates' life is contained in Plato's *Apology*). The events leading up to and culminating in the Athenian government's trial and execution of Socrates, when Plato was twenty-eight, soured Plato on the idea of embarking on a life in politics and resulted in his leaving Athens to travel in the Mediterranean region for a number of years. Plato returned to Athens in 387 and founded his school, the Academy, in the belief that such an educational institution was necessary for the training of political leaders who would be morally excellent. The Academy attracted many of the finest contemporary minds to it, including Aristotle. Plato twice visited Syracuse in a futile attempt to inculcate his moral and political ideals in Syracuse's young tyrant, Dionysius II.

Socrates wrote nothing: It is fortunate that his most illustrious follower did not follow his example. At least twenty-six of Plato's dialogues have survived, ranging in length from the brief *Crito* to the voluble *Laws,* which is longer than the *Republic.* It is customary to divide the dialogues into three periods of Plato's literary career: early, middle, and late. The early dialogues, of which the *Euthyphro, Apology,* and *Crito* are examples, are taken to be accurate if not verbatim portrayals of Socrates in philosophical action. The middle dialogues, represented here by the *Meno, Phaedo,* and *Republic,* display Plato at the height of his literary abilities, seeking to further the projects inspired by Socrates while at the same time introducing doctrines that are extremely unlikely to have been Socrates' own. The late dialogues are dialogues in name only, quite often technically demanding in nature. They appear to represent Plato's efforts to grapple with critical issues raised by the doctrines enunciated in the middle dialogues, issues most likely raised by others in the Academy.

As the *Apology* makes clear, Socrates professed to be ignorant of all matters philosophical although not disputing the Delphic oracle's pronouncement that he was the wisest of all men. He concluded that his "wisdom," compared to the pretenses of others, lay in knowing the extent of his ignorance. Taking his mission to be to show others the magnitude of their ignorance about the most important matters of their lives, Socrates relentlessly grilled his fellow Athenian citizens, using rigorous argumentation to demonstrate that uncritically accepted opinions about philosophically important matters could lead to logical catastrophe: The *Euthyphro* and the early pages of the *Meno* provide excellent examples of Socrates' technique.

Yet for all his professed ignorance, Socrates clung to several distinctive philosophical doctrines. First, one cannot have genuine knowledge about moral matters unless one can give a rationally defensible account of such notions as piety (*Euthyphro*), justice (*Republic*), and virtue or human excellence in general (*Meno*). Socrates thus pitted himself against the Sophists, a contemporary group of itinerant professional teachers, many of whom fostered the belief in their students that there was no objective knowledge to be had in ethics. Socrates believed that moral knowledge is possible but difficult to acquire, and that his method of exposing ignorance in others was a necessary first step to their acquiring it. Second, as the *Meno* intimates, in some way or other virtue (or excellence in humans) is knowledge. The remarkable corollary of this claim is the thesis that all wrongdoing is the result of ignorance. Third, as illustrated in the *Crito* and argued for in the *Republic,* Socrates believed that it is better for one to suffer injustice than to do injustice.

Plato came to believe that, if ethics is something more than the product of arbitrary convention, and if moral judgments are objective, then ethics must be grounded in objects that are unchanging in character and accessible to human minds. These objects are the Forms, the perfect, abstract objects discussed in the *Phaedo* and *Republic*. Humans can have knowledge of the Forms by recollection, a process that Plato describes in the *Meno*, alludes to in the *Phaedo*, and presupposes in the *Republic*. The importance Plato assigns to the Form of the Good in the *Republic* is designed to show how the acquisition of knowledge of the Forms provides one with the motivation to be virtuous. The doctrine of Recollection in turn presupposes that humans have existed before their present lives. From there it seems a small step to the thesis that the soul is immortal. In the *Phaedo*, whose dramatic setting is the day of Socrates' execution, Plato has Socrates present several arguments for the immortality of the soul. If the soul is immortal, then care for it should be more important than care for the body: One of the major themes of the *Republic* is that behaving justly is at least as valuable for the care of the soul, as well as for the care of the state, as physical health is for the care of the body.

The amount of excellent philosophical writings on Socrates and Plato is far too large to list here, but certainly includes the following. On Socrates in general, see Gregory Vlastos, *Socrates, Ironist and Moral Philosopher* (Ithaca: Cornell University Press, 1991); along with two collections of essays, Hugh Benson, ed., *Essays on the Philosophy of Socrates* (New York: Oxford University Press, 1992); and Gregory Vlastos, ed., *The Philosophy of Socrates* (Garden City: Doubleday, 1971). Two recent studies on early dialogues appearing here are C. D. C. Reeve, *Socrates in the Apology* (Indianapolis: Hackett Publishing Company, 1989); and, on the *Crito*, Richard Kraut, *Socrates and the State* (Princeton: Princeton University Press, 1984).

• • •

Although somewhat demanding, the following works on Plato are superb: R. E. Allen, ed., *Studies in Plato's Metaphysics* (London: Routledge & Kegan Paul, 1965); Terence Irwin, *Plato's Ethics* (New York: Oxford University Press, 1995); Richard Kraut, ed., *The Cambridge Companion to Plato* (Cambridge University Press, 1992); Gregory Vlastos, ed., *Plato: A Collection of Critical Essays: I: Metaphysics and Epistemology*, and *II: Ethics, Politics, and Philosophy of Art and Religion* (Garden City: Doubleday, 1970 and 1971); and Gregory Vlastos, *Platonic Studies*, second edition (Princeton: Princeton University Press, 1981). Two recent books devoted to the *Republic* are Julia Annas, *An Introduction to Plato's Republic* (Oxford: Clarendon Press, 1981); and Richard Kraut, ed., *Plato's Republic* (Lanham, Md.: Rowman & Littlefield, 1997).

W.E.M.

Meno

70 MENO: Can you tell me, Socrates, can virtue[1] be taught? Or is it not teachable but the result of practice, or is it neither of these, but men possess it by nature or in some other way?

SOCRATES: Before now, Meno, Thessalians had a high reputation among the Greeks and were admired for their horsemanship and their wealth, but *b* now, it seems to me, they are also admired for their wisdom, not least the fellow citizens of your friend Aristippus of Larissa. The responsibility for this reputation of yours lies with Gorgias,[2] for when he came to your city he found that the leading Aleuadae, your lover Aristippus among them, loved him for his wisdom, and so did the other leading Thessalians. In particular, he accustomed you to give a bold and grand answer to any question you may be asked, as *c* experts are likely to do. Indeed, he himself was ready to answer any Greek who wished to question him,

Reprinted from Plato's *Meno*, translated by G.M.A. Grube (Indianapolis: Hackett Publishing Company, 1976), by permission of the publisher. The translation follows Burnet's Oxford text. The only liberty taken is where the answers to Socrates' questions are very brief, merely indicating assent or the like. In such instances "he said," the so-frequent repetition of which reads awkwardly in English, has been replaced by a dash, to indicate a change of speaker.

1. [The Greek word is *aretē*. It can refer to specific virtues such as moderation, courage, etc.) but it is also used for *the* virtue or conglomeration of virtues that makes a man virtuous or good. In this dialogue it is mostly used in this more general sense. Socrates himself at times (e.g., 93b ff.) uses "good" as equivalent to virtuous—G.M.A.G.]

2. [Gorgias was perhaps the most famous of the earlier generation of Sophists, those traveling teachers who arose in the late fifth century to fill the need for higher education. They all taught rhetoric, or the art of speaking, but as Meno tells us, Gorgias concentrated on this more than the others and made fewer general claims for his teaching (95c). He visited Athens in 427 B.C., and his rhetorical devices gave him an immediate success. Plato named one of his dialogues after him. Fairly substantive fragments of his writings are extant.]

and every question was answered. But here in Athens, my dear Meno, the opposite is the case, as if there were a dearth of wisdom, and wisdom seems to have departed hence to go to you. If then you want to ask 71 one of us that sort of question, everyone will laugh and say: "Good stranger, you must think me happy indeed if you think I know whether virtue can be taught or how it comes to be; I am so far from knowing whether virtue can be taught or not that I do not even have any knowledge of what virtue itself is."

I myself, Meno, am as poor as my fellow citizens *b* in this matter, and I blame myself for my complete ignorance about virtue. If I do not know what something is, how could I know what qualities it possesses? Or do you think that someone who does not know at all who Meno is could know whether he is good-looking or rich or well-born, or the opposite of these? Do you think that is possible?

M: I do not; but, Socrates, do you really not know what virtue is? Are we to report this to the folk back *c* home about you?

S: Not only that, my friend, but also that, as I believe, I have never yet met anyone else who did know.

M: How so? Did you not meet Gorgias when he was here?

S: I did.

M: Did you then not think that he knew?

S: I do not altogether remember, Meno, so that I cannot tell you now what I thought then. Perhaps he does know; you know what he used to say, so you *d* remind me of what he said. You tell me yourself, if you are willing, for surely you share his views.—I do.

S: Let us leave Gorgias out of it, since he is not here. But Meno, by the gods, what do you yourself say that virtue is? Speak and do not begrudge us, so that I may have spoken a most unfortunate untruth when I said that I had never met anyone who knew, if you and Gorgias are shown to know.

M: It is not hard to tell you, Socrates. First, if *e* you want the virtue of a man, it is easy to say that a man's virtue consists of being able to manage public

3

affairs and in so doing to benefit his friends and harm his enemies and to be careful that no harm comes to himself; if you want the virtue of a woman, it is not difficult to describe: she must manage the home well, preserve its possessions, and be submissive to her husband; the virtue of a child, whether male or female, is different again, and so is that of an elderly man, if you want that, or if you want that of a free

72 man or a slave. And there are very many other virtues, so that one is not at a loss to say what virtue is. There is virtue for every action and every age, for every task of ours and every one of us — and Socrates, the same is true for wickedness.

S: I seem to be in great luck, Meno; while I am looking for one virtue, I have found you to have a whole swarm of them. But, Meno, to follow up the

b image of swarms, if I were asking you what is the nature of bees, and you said that they are many and of all kinds, what would you answer if I asked you: "Do you mean that they are many and varied and different from one another in so far as they are bees? Or are they no different in that regard, but in some other respect, in their beauty, for example, or their size or in some other such way?" Tell me, what would you answer if thus questioned?

M: I would say that they do not differ from one another in being bees.

S: If I went on to say: "Tell me, what is this very thing, Meno, in which they are all the same and do not

c differ from one another?" Would you be able to tell me?

M: I would.

S: The same is true in the case of the virtues. Even if they are many and various, all of them have one and the same form[3] which makes them virtues, and it is right to look to this when one is asked to make clear what virtue is. Or do you not understand

d what I mean?

M: I think I understand, but I certainly do not grasp the meaning of the question as fully as I want to.

S: I am asking whether you think it is only in the case of virtue that there is one for man, another for woman and so on, or is the same true in the case of health and size and strength? Do you think that there is one health for man and another for woman? Or, if it is health, does it have the same form everywhere, whether in man or in anything else whatever? e

M: The health of a man seems to me the same as that of a woman.

S: And so with size and strength? If a woman is strong, that strength will be the same and have the same form, for by "the same" I mean that strength is no different as far as being strength, whether in a man or a woman. Or do you think there is a difference?

M: I do not think so.

S: And will there be any difference in the case of virtue, as far as being virtue is concerned, whether it be in a child or an old man, in a woman or in a man? 73

M: I think, Socrates, that somehow this is no longer like those other cases.

S: How so? Did you not say that the virtue of a man consists of managing the city well,[4] and that of a woman of managing the household? — I did.

S: Is it possible to manage a city well, or a household, or anything else, while not managing it moderately and justly? — Certainly not.

S: Then if they manage justly and moderately, b they must do so with justice and moderation? — Necessarily.

S: So both the man and the woman, if they are to be good, need the same things, justice and moderation. — So it seems.

S: What about a child and an old man? Can they possibly be good if they are intemperate and unjust? — Certainly not.

---

3. [The Greek term is *eidos*, which Plato was to use for his separately existing eternal Forms. Its common meaning is stature or appearance. Socrates felt that if we apply the same name or epithet to a number of different things or actions, they must surely have a common characteristic to justify the use of the same term. A definition is then a description of this "form" or appearance, which it presents to the mind's eye. In the earlier dialogues however, as here, this form is not thought of as having a separate existence, but as immanent.]

4. [When discussing goodness or morality, social and political virtues would be more immediately present to the Greek mind than they are to ours. In both Plato and Aristotle a good man is above all a good citizen, whereas the modern mind thinks of goodness mainly in more individual terms, such as sobriety or sexual morals. An extreme example of this occurred in a contemporary judge's summation to the jury in the case of a woman of loose sexual behavior who was accused of murdering her husband. He actually said: "This is a case of murder, not of morals. The morals of the accused have nothing to do with it."]

S: But if they are moderate and just? — Yes.

c   S: So all human beings are good in the same way, for they become good by acquiring the same qualities. — It seems so.

S: And they would not be good in the same way if they did not have the same virtue. — They certainly would not be.

S: Since then the virtue of all is the same, try to tell me and to remember what Gorgias, and you with him, said that that same thing is.

d   M: What else but to be able to rule over people, if you are seeking one description to fit them all.

S: That is indeed what I am seeking, but Meno, is virtue the same in the case of a child or a slave, namely, for them to be able to rule over a master, and do you think that he who rules is still a slave? — I do not think so at all, Socrates.

S: It is not likely, my good man. Consider this further point: you say that virtue is to be able to rule. Shall we not add to this *justly and not unjustly?*

M: I think so, Socrates, for justice is virtue.

e   S: Is it virtue, Meno, or a virtue? — What do you mean?

S: As with anything else. For example, if you wish, take roundness, about which I would say that it is a shape, but not simply that it is shape. I would not so speak of it because there are other shapes.

M: You are quite right. So I too say that not only justice is a virtue but there are many other virtues.

74   S: What are they? Tell me, as I could mention other shapes to you if you bade me do so, so do you mention other virtues.

M: I think courage is a virtue, and moderation, wisdom, and munificence, and very many others.

S: We are having the same trouble again, Meno, though in another way; we have found many virtues while looking for one, but we cannot find the one which covers all the others.

b   M: I cannot yet find, Socrates, what you are looking for, one virtue for them all, as in the other cases.

S: That is likely, but I am eager, if I can, that we should make progress, for you understand that the same applies to everything. If someone asked you what I mentioned just now: "What is shape, Meno?" and you told him that it was roundness, and if then he said to you what I did: "Is roundness shape or a shape?" you would surely tell him that it is a shape? — I certainly would.

S: That would be because there are other c shapes? — Yes.

S: And if he asked you further what they were, you would tell him? — I would.

S: So too, if he asked you what color is, and you said it is white, and your questioner interrupted you, "Is white color or a color?" you would say that it is a color, because there are also other colors? — I would.

S: And if he bade you mention other colors, you would mention others that are no less colors than white is? — Yes.   d

S: Then if he pursued the argument as I did and said: "We always arrive at the many; do not talk to me in that way, but since you call all these many by one name, and say that no one of them is not a shape even though they are opposites, tell me what this is which applies as much to the round as to the straight and which you call shape, as you say the e round is as much a shape as the straight." Do you not say that? — I do.

S: When you speak like that, do you assert that the round is no more round than it is straight, and that the straight is no more straight than it is round?

M: Certainly not, Socrates.

S: Yet you say that the round is no more a shape than the straight is, nor the one more than the other. — That is true.

S: What then is this to which the name shape applies? Try to tell me. If then you answered the man who was questioning about shape or color: "I do not understand what you want, my man, nor what you 75 mean," he would probably wonder and say: "You do not understand that I am seeking that which is the same in all these cases?" Would you still have nothing to say, Meno, if one asked you: "What is this which applies to the round and the straight and the other things which you call shapes and which is the same in them all?" Try to say, that you may practice for your answer about virtue.

M: No, Socrates, but you tell me.   b

S: Do you want me to do you this favor?

M: I certainly do.

S: And you will then be willing to tell me about virtue?

M: I will.

S: We must certainly press on. The subject is worth it.

M: It surely is.

S: Come then, let us try to tell you what shape is. See whether you will accept that it is this: Let us say that shape is that which alone of existing things always follows color. Is that satisfactory to you, or do *c* you look for it in some other way? I should be satisfied if you defined virtue in this way.

M: But that is foolish, Socrates.

S: How do you mean?

M: That shape, you say, always follows color. Well then, if someone were to say that he did not know what color is, but that he had the same difficulty as he had about shape, what do you think your answer would be?

S: A true one, surely, and if my questioner was one of those clever and disputatious debaters, I would say to him: "I have given my answer; if it is wrong, it is your job to refute it." Then, if they are friends *d* as you and I are, and want to discuss with each other, they must answer in a manner more gentle and more proper to discussion. By this I mean that the answers must not only be true, but in terms admittedly known to the questioner. I too will try to speak in these terms. *e* Do you call something "the end?" I mean such a thing as a limit or boundary, for all those are, I say, the same thing. Prodicus[5] might disagree with us, but you surely call something "finished" or "completed"—that is what I want to express, nothing elaborate.

M: I do, and I think I understand what you mean.

76   S: Further, you call something a plane, and something else a solid, as in geometry?

M: I do.

S: From this you may understand what I mean by shape, for I say this of every shape, that a shape is that which limits a solid; in a word, a shape is the limit of a solid.

M: And what do you say color is, Socrates?

S: You are outrageous, Meno. You bother an *b* old man to answer questions, but you yourself are not willing to recall and to tell me what Gorgias says that virtue is.

M: After you have answered this, Socrates, I will tell you.

S: Even someone who was blindfolded would know from your conversation that you are handsome and still have lovers.

M: Why so?

S: Because you are forever giving orders in a discussion, as spoiled people do, who behave like tyrants as long as they are young. And perhaps you have recognized that I am at a disadvantage with handsome peo- *c* ple, so I will do you the favor of an answer.

M: By all means do me that favor.

S: Do you want me to answer after the manner of Gorgias, which you would most easily follow?

M: Of course I want that.

S: Do you both say there are effluvia of things, as Empedocles[6] does?—Certainly.

S: And that there are channels through which the effluvia make their way?—Definitely.

S: And some effluvia fit some of the channels, *d* while others are too small or too big?—That is so.

S: And there is something which you call sight?—There is.

S: From this, "comprehend what I state," as Pindar said; for color is an effluvium from shapes which fits the sight and is perceived.

M: That seems to me to be an excellent answer, Socrates.

S: Perhaps it was given in the manner to which you are accustomed. At the same time I think that you can deduce from this answer what sound is, and smell, and many such things.—Quite so.   *e*

S: It is a theatrical answer[7] so it pleases you, Meno, more than that about shape.—It does.

S: It is not better, son of Alexidemus, but I am convinced that the other is, and I think you would agree, if you did not have to go away before the

---

5. [Prodicus was a well-known Sophist who was especially keen on the exact meaning of words, and he was fond of making the proper distinctions between words of similar but not identical meanings. We see him in action in the *Protagoras* of Plato (especially 337a–c) where he appears with two other distinguished Sophists, Protagoras and Hippias. His insistence on the proper definition of words would naturally endear him to Socrates who, in Plato, always treats him with more sympathy than he does the other Sophists. The point here is that Prodicus would object to "end," "limit," and "boundary" being treated as "all the same thing."]

6. [Empedocles (c. 493–433 B.C.) of Acragas in Sicily was a famous physical philosopher. For him there were four eternal elements (earth, water, air, and fire), the intermingling and separation of which produced the physical phenomena. The reference here is to his theories of sense perception.]

7. [Theatrical because it brings in the philosophical theories of Empedocles and a quotation from Pindar, instead of being in simple terms such as Socrates' definition of shape.]

mysteries as you told me yesterday, but could remain and be initiated.

M: I would stay, Socrates, if you could tell me 77 many things like these.

S: I shall certainly not be lacking in eagerness to tell you such things, both for your sake and my own, but I may not be able to tell you many. Come now, you too try to fulfill your promise to me and tell me the nature of virtue as a whole and stop making many out of one, as jokers say whenever someone breaks something; but allow virtue to remain whole *b* and sound, and tell me what it is, for I have given you examples.

M: I think, Socrates, that virtue is, as the poet says, "to find joy in beautiful things and have power." So I say that virtue is to desire beautiful things and have the power to acquire them.

S: Do you mean that the man who desires beautiful things desires good things?—Most certainly.

S: Do you assume that there are people who *c* desire bad things, and others who desire good things? Do you not think, my good man, that all men desire good things?

M: I do not.

S: But some desire bad things?—Yes.

S: Do you mean that they believe the bad things to be good, or that they know they are bad and nevertheless desire them?—I think there are both kinds.

S: Do you think, Meno, that anyone, knowing that bad things are bad, nevertheless desires them?—I certainly do.

S: What do you mean by desiring? Is it to secure for oneself?—What else?

d S: Does he think that the bad things benefit him who possesses them, or does he know they harm him?

M: There are some who believe that the bad things benefit them, others who know that the bad things harm them.

S: And do you think that those who believe that bad things benefit them know that they are bad?

M: No, that I cannot altogether believe.

S: It is clear then that those who do not know *e* things to be bad do not desire what is bad, but they desire those things that they believe to be good but that are in fact bad. It follows that those who have no knowledge of these things and believe them to be good clearly desire good things. Is that not so?—It is likely.

S: Well then, those who you say desire bad things, believing that bad things harm their possessor, know that they will be harmed by them?—Necessarily.

S: And do they not think that those who are 78 harmed are miserable to the extent that they are harmed?—That too is inevitable.

S: And that those who are miserable are unhappy?—I think so.

S: Does anyone wish to be miserable and unhappy?—I do not think so, Socrates.

S: No one then wants what is bad, Meno, unless he wants to be such. For what else is being miserable but to desire bad things and secure them?

M: You are probably right, Socrates, and no one *b* wants what is bad.

S: Were you not saying just now that virtue is to desire good things and have the power to secure them?—Yes, I was.

S: The desiring part of this statement is common to everybody, and one man is no better than another in this?—So it appears.

S: Clearly then, if one man is better than another, he must be better at securing them.—Quite so.

S: This then is virtue according to your argument, the power of securing good things. *c*

M: I think, Socrates, that the case is altogether as you now understand it.

S: Let us see then whether what you say is true, for you may well be right. You say that the capacity to acquire good things is virtue?—I do.

S: And by good things you mean, for example, health and wealth?

M: Yes, and also to acquire gold and silver, also honors and offices in the city.

S: By good things you do not mean other goods than these?

M: No, but I mean all things of this kind.

S: Very well. According to Meno, the hereditary *d* guest friend of the Great King, virtue is the acquisition of gold and silver. Do you add to this acquiring, Meno, the words justly and piously, or does it make no difference to you but even if one secures these things unjustly, you call it virtue none the less?

M: Certainly not, Socrates.

S: You would then call it wickedness?—Indeed I would.

S: It seems then that the acquisition must be accompanied by justice or moderation or piety or *e* some other part of virtue; if it is not, it will not be virtue, even though it provides good things.

M: How could there be virtue without these?

S: Then failing to secure gold and silver, whenever it would not be just to do so, either for oneself or another, is not this failure to secure them also virtue?

M: So it seems.

79 S: Then to provide these goods would not be virtue any more than not to provide them, but apparently whatever is done with justice will be virtue, and what is done without anything of the kind is wickedness?

M: I think it must necessarily be as you say.

S: We said a little while ago that each of these things was a part of virtue, namely, justice and moderation and all such things? — Yes.

S: Then you are playing with me, Meno. — How so, Socrates?

S: Because I begged you just now not to break up or fragment virtue, and I gave examples of how you should answer. You paid no attention, but you b tell me that virtue is to be able to secure good things with justice, and this, you say, is a part of virtue.

M: I do.

S: It follows then from what you agree to, that to act in whatever you do with a part of virtue is virtue, for you say that justice is a part of virtue, as are all such qualities. Why do I say this? Because when I begged you to tell me about virtue as a whole, you are far from telling me what it is. Rather, you say that every action is virtue if it is performed with a part of virtue, as if c you had told me what virtue as a whole is, and I would already know that, even if you fragment it into parts.[8] I think you must face the same question from the beginning, my dear Meno, namely, what is virtue, if every action performed with a part of virtue is virtue? For that is what one is saying when he says that every action performed with justice is virtue. Do you not think you should face the same question again, or do you think one knows what a part of virtue is if one does not know virtue itself? — I do not think so.

d S: If you remember, when I was answering you about shape, we rejected the kind of answer that tried to answer in terms still being the subject of inquiry and not yet agreed upon. — And we were right to reject them.

8. [That is, Meno is including the term to be defined in the definition.]

S: Then surely, my good sir, you must not think, while the nature of virtue as a whole is still under inquiry, that by answering in terms of the parts of virtue you can make its nature clear to anyone or make anything else clear by speaking in this way, but only that the same question must be put to you again — what do e you take the nature of virtue to be when you say what you say? Or do you think there is no point in what I am saying? — I think what you say is right.

S: Answer me again then from the beginning: What do you and your friend say that virtue is?

M: Socrates, before I even met you I used to hear 80 that you are always in a state of perplexity and that you bring others to the same state, and now I think you are bewitching and beguiling me, simply putting me under a spell, so that I am quite perplexed. Indeed, if a joke is in order, you seem, in appearance and in every other way, to be like the broad torpedo fish, for it too makes anyone who comes close and touches it feel numb, and you now seem to have had that kind b of effect on me, for both my mind and my tongue are numb, and I have no answer to give you. Yet I have made many speeches about virtue before large audiences on a thousand occasions, very good speeches as I thought, but now I cannot even say what it is. I think you are wise not to sail away from Athens to go and stay elsewhere, for if you were to behave like this as a stranger in another city, you would be driven away for practising sorcery.

S: You are a rascal, Meno, and you nearly deceived me.

M: Why so particularly, Socrates?

S: I know why you drew this image of me.   c

M: Why do you think I did?

S: So that I should draw an image of you in return. I know that all handsome men rejoice in images of themselves; it is to their advantage, for I think that the images of beautiful people are also beautiful, but I will draw no image of you in turn. Now if the torpedo fish is itself numb and so makes others numb, then I resemble it, but not otherwise, for I myself do not have the answer when I perplex others, but I am more perplexed than anyone when I cause perplexity in others. So now I do not know what virtue is; perhaps you knew before you contacted me, but now you are certainly like one who does d not know. Nevertheless, I want to examine and seek together with you what it may be.

M: How will you look for it, Socrates, when you do not know at all what it is? How will you aim to search for something you do not know at all? If you should meet with it, how will you know that this is the thing that you did not know?

e S: I know what you want to say, Meno. Do you realize what a debater's argument you are bringing up, that a man cannot search either for what he knows or for what he does not know? He cannot search for what he knows—since he knows it, there is no need to search—nor for what he does not know, for he does not know what to look for.

M: Does that argument not seem sound to 81 you, Socrates?

S: Not to me.

M: Can you tell me why?

S: I can. I have heard wise men and women talk about divine matters. . . .

M: What did they say?

S: What was, I thought, both true and beautiful.

M: What was it, and who were they?

S: The speakers were among the priests and priestesses whose care it is to be able to give an ac-b count of their practices. Pindar too says it, and many others of the divine among our poets. What they say is this; see whether you think they speak the truth: They say that the human soul is immortal; at times it comes to an end, which they call dying, at times it is reborn, but it is never destroyed, and one must therefore live one's life as piously as possible:

Persephone will return to the sun above in the ninth year the souls of those from whom she will exact punish-
c ment for old miseries, and from these come noble kings, mighty in strength and greatest in wisdom, and for the rest of time men will call them sacred heroes.

As the soul is immortal, has been born often and has seen all things here and in the underworld, there is nothing which it has not learned; so it is in no way surprising that it can recollect the things it knew d before, both about virtue and other things. As the whole of nature is akin, and the soul has learned everything, nothing prevents a man, after recalling one thing only—a process men call learning—discovering everything else for himself, if he is brave and does not tire of the search, for searching and learning are, as a whole, recollection. We must, therefore, not believe that debater's argument, for it would

make us idle, and fainthearted men like to hear it, whereas my argument makes them energetic and e keen on the search. I trust that this is true, and I want to inquire along with you into the nature of virtue.

M: Yes, Socrates, but how do you mean that we do not learn, but that what we call learning is recollection? Can you teach me that this is so?

S: As I said just now, Meno, you are a rascal. You now ask me if I can teach you, when I say there 82 is no teaching but recollection, in order to show me up at once as contradicting myself.

M: No, by Zeus, Socrates, that was not my intention when I spoke, but just a habit. If you can somehow show me that things are as you say, please do so.

S: It is not easy, but I am nevertheless willing to do my best for your sake. Call one of these many b attendants of yours, whichever you like, that I may prove it to you in his case.

M: Certainly. You there, come forward.

S: Is he a Greek? Does he speak Greek?

M: Very much so. He was born in my household.

S: Pay attention then whether you think he is recollecting or learning from me.

M: I will pay attention.

S: Tell me now, boy, you know that a square figure is like this?—I do.

S: A square then is a figure in which all these c four sides are equal?—Yes indeed.

S: And it also has these lines through the middle equal?[9]—Yes.

S: And such a figure could be larger or smaller?—Certainly.

S: If then this side were two feet, and this other

9. [Socrates draws a square ABCD. The sides are of course equal, and the "lines through the middle" are the lines joining the middle points of these sides, which also go through the center of the square, namely EF and GH. He then assumes the sides to be two feet.]

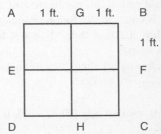

side two feet, how many feet would the whole be? Consider it this way: if it were two feet this way, and only one foot that way, the figure[10] would be once two feet?—Yes.

d   S: But if it is two feet also that way, it would surely be twice two feet?—Yes.

S: How many feet is twice two feet? Work it out and tell me.—Four, Socrates.

S: Now we could have another figure twice the size of this one, with the four sides equal like this one.—Yes.

S: How many feet will that be?—Eight.

S: Come now, try to tell me how long each side *e* of this will be. The side of this is two feet. What about each side of the one which is its double?—Obviously, Socrates, it will be twice the length.

S: You see, Meno, that I am not teaching the boy anything, but all I do is question him. And now he thinks he knows the length of the line on which an eight-foot figure is based. Do you agree?

M: I do.

S: And does he know?

M: Certainly not.

S: He thinks it is a line twice the length?

M: Yes.

S: Watch him now recollecting things in order, as one must recollect. Tell me, boy, do you say that 83 a figure double the size is based on a line double the length? Now I mean such a figure as this, not long on one side and short on the other, but equal in every direction like this one, and double the size, that is, eight feet. See whether you still believe that it will be based on a line double the length.—I do.

S: Now the line becomes double its length if we add another of the same length here?—Yes indeed.

S: And the eight-foot square will be based on it, if there are four lines of that length?—Yes.

b   S: Well, let us draw from it four equal lines, and surely that is what you say is the eight-foot square?—Certainly.

S: And within this figure are four squares, each of which is equal to the four-foot square?—Yes.

S: How big is it then? Is it not four times as big?—Of course.

S: Is this square then, which is four times as big, its double?—No, by Zeus.

10. [That is, the rectangle ABFE, which is obviously two square feet.]

S: How many times bigger is it?—Four times.

S: Then, my boy, the figure based on a line *c* twice the length is not double but four times as big?—You are right.

S: And four times four is sixteen, is it not?—Yes.

S: On how long a line should the eight-foot square be based? On *this* line we have a square that is four times bigger, do we not?—Yes.

S: Now this four-foot square is based on this line here, half the length?—Yes.

S: Very well. Is the eight-foot square not double this one and half that one?[11]—Yes.

S: Will it not be based on a line longer than this one and shorter than that one? Is that not so?—I *d* think so.

S: Good, you answer what you think. And tell me, was this one not two-feet long, and that one four feet?—Yes.

S: The line on which the eight-foot square is based must then be longer than this one of two feet, and shorter than that one of four feet?—It must be.

S: Try to tell me then how long a line you say *e* it is.—Three feet.

S: Then if it is three feet, let us add the half of this one, and it will be three feet? For these are two feet, and the other is one. And here, similarly, these are two feet and that one is one foot, and so the figure you mention comes to be?—Yes.

S: Now if it is three feet this way and three feet that way, will the whole figure be three times three feet?—So it seems.

S: How much is three times three feet?—Nine feet.

S: And the double square was to be how many feet?—Eight.

S: So the eight-foot figure cannot be based on the three-foot line?—Clearly not.

S: But on how long a line? Try to tell us exactly, 84 and if you do not want to work it out, show me from what line.—By Zeus, Socrates, I do not know.

S: You realize, Meno, what point he has reached

11. [That is, the eight-foot square is double the four-foot square and half the sixteen-foot square, double the square based on a line two feet long, and half the square based on a four-foot side, so it must be based on a line between two and four feet in length. The slave naturally suggests three feet, but that gives a nine-foot square, and is still wrong. (83e).]

in his recollection. At first he did not know what the basic line of the eight-foot square was; even now he does not yet know, but then he thought he knew, and answered confidently as if he did know, and he did not think himself at a loss, but now he does think

b himself at a loss, and as he does not know, neither does he think he knows.

M: That is true.

S: So he is now in a better position with regard to the matter he does not know?

M: I agree with that too.

S: Have we done him any harm by making him perplexed and numb as the torpedo fish does?

M: I do not think so.

S: Indeed, we have probably achieved something relevant to finding out how matters stand, for now, as he does not know, he would be glad to find out, whereas before he thought he could easily make many fine speeches to large audiences about the

c square of double size and said that it must have a base twice as long.

M: So it seems.

S: Do you think that before he would have tried to find out that which he thought he knew though he did not, before he fell into perplexity and realized he did not know and longed to know?

M: I do not think so, Socrates.

S: Has he then benefitted from being numbed?

M: I think so.

S: Look then how he will come out of his perplexity while searching along with me. I shall do nothing more than ask questions and not teach him.

d Watch whether you find me teaching and explaining things to him instead of asking for his opinion.

S: You tell me, is this not a four-foot figure? You understand? — I do.

S: We add to it this figure which is equal to it? — Yes.

S: And we add this third figure equal to each of them? — Yes.

S: Could we then fill in the space in the corner? — Certainly.[12]

S: So we have these four equal figures? — Yes.

S: Well then, how many times is the whole fig- e ure larger than this one?[13] — Four times.

S: But we should have had one that was twice as large, or do you not remember? — I certainly do.

S: Does not this line from one corner to the 85 other cut each of these figures in two?[14] — Yes.

S: So these are four equal lines which enclose this figure? — They are.

S: Consider now: how large is the figure? — I do not understand.

S: Within these four figures, each line cuts off half of each, does it not? — Yes.

S: How many of this size are there in this figure? — Four.

S: How many in this? — Two.

S: What is the relation of four to two? — Double. b

S: How many feet in this? — Eight.

S: Based on what line? — This one.

S: That is, on the line that stretches from corner to corner of the four-foot figure? — Yes. — Clever men call this the diagonal, so that if diagonal is its name, you say that the double figure would be that based on the diagonal? — Most certainly, Socrates.

S: What do you think, Meno? Has he, in his answers, expressed any opinion that was not his own? c

M: No, they were all his own.

S: And yet, as we said a short time ago, he did not know? — That is true.

S: So these opinions were in him, were they not? — Yes.

S: So the man who does not know has within himself true opinions about the things that he does not know? — So it appears.

S: These opinions have now just been stirred up like a dream, but if he were repeatedly asked these same questions in various ways, you know that in the d end his knowledge about these things would be as accurate as anyone's. — It is likely.

S: And he will know it without having been

12. [Socrates now builds up his sixteen-foot square by joining three four-foot squares. Filling "the space in the corner" will give another four-foot square, which completes the sixteen-foot square containing four four-foot squares.]

13. ["This one" is any one of the inside squares of four feet.]

14. [Socrates now draws the diagonals of the four inside squares, namely FH, HE, EG and GF, which together form the square GFHEG. We should note that Socrates here introduces a new element, which is not the result of a question but of his own knowledge, though the answer to the problem follows from questions. The new square contains four halves of a four-foot square, and is therefore eight feet.]

taught but only questioned, and find the knowledge within himself? — Yes.

S: And is not finding knowledge within oneself recollection? — Certainly.

S: Must he not either have at some time acquired the knowledge he now possesses, or else have always possessed it? — Yes.

S: If he always had it, he would always have
e known. If he acquired it, he cannot have done so in his present life. Or has someone taught him geometry? For he will perform in the same way about all geometry, and all other knowledge. Has someone taught him everything? You should know, especially as he has been born and brought up in your house.

M: But I know that no one has taught him.

S: Yet he has these opinions, or doesn't he?

M: That seems indisputable, Socrates.

86 S: If he has not acquired them in his present life, is it not clear that he had them and had learned them at some other time? — It seems so.

S: Then that was the time when he was not a human being? — Yes.

S: If then, during the time he exists and is not a human being he will have true opinions which, when stirred by questioning, become knowledge, will not his soul have learned during all time? For it is clear that during all time he exists, either as a man or not. — So it seems.

b S: Then if the truth about reality is always in our soul, the soul would be immortal so that you should always confidently try to seek out and recollect what you do not know at present — that is, what you do not recollect?[15]

M: Somehow, Socrates, I think that what you say is right.

S: I think so too, Meno. I do not insist that my argument is right in all other respects, but I would contend at all costs both in word and deed as far as I could that we will be better men, braver and less idle, if we believe that one must search for the things
c one does not know, rather than if we believe that it is not possible to find out what we do not know and that we must not look for it.

15. [This is what the whole passage on recollection with the slave is intended to prove, namely, that the sophism introduced by Meno — that one cannot find out what one does not know — is false.]

M: In this too I think you are right, Socrates.

S: Since we are of one mind that one should seek to find out what one does not know, shall we try to find out together what virtue is?

M: Certainly. But Socrates, I should be most pleased to investigate and hear your answer to my original question, whether we should try on the as- d sumption that virtue is something teachable, or is a natural gift, or in whatever way it comes to men.

S: If I were directing you, Meno, and not only myself, we would not have investigated whether virtue is teachable or not before we had investigated what virtue itself is. But because you do not even attempt to rule yourself, in order that you may be free, but you try to rule me and do so, I will agree with you — for what can I do? So we must, it appears, inquire into the qualities of something the nature of which e we do not yet know. However, please relax your rule a little bit for me and agree to investigate whether it is teachable or not by means of a hypothesis. I mean the way geometers often carry on their investigations. For example, if they are asked whether a specific area 87 can be inscribed in the form of a triangle within a given circle, one of them might say: "I do not yet know whether that area has that property, but I think I have, as it were, a hypothesis that is of use for the problem, namely this: If that area is such that when one has applied it as a rectangle to the given straight line in the circle it is deficient by a figure similar to b the very figure which is applied, then I think one alternative results, whereas another results if it is impossible for this to happen. So, by using this hypothesis, I am willing to tell you what results with regard to inscribing it in the circle — that is, whether it is impossible or not." So let us speak about virtue also, since we do not know either what it is or what qualities it possesses, and let us investigate whether it is teachable or not by means of a hypothesis, and say this: Among the things existing in the soul, of what sort is virtue, that it should be teachable or not? First, if it is another sort than knowledge, is it teachable or not, or, as we were just saying, recollectable? Let it c make no difference to us which term we use: is it teachable? Or is it plain to anyone that men cannot be taught anything but knowledge? — I think so.

S: But, if virtue is a kind of knowledge, it is clear that it could be taught. — Of course.

S: We have dealt with that question quickly, that

if it is of one kind it can be taught, if it is of a different kind, it cannot.—We have indeed.

S: The next point to consider seems to be *d* whether virtue is knowledge or something else.—That does seem to be the next point to consider.

S: Well now, do we say that virtue is itself something good, and will this hypothesis stand firm for us, that it is something good?—Of course.

S: If then there is anything else good that is different and separate from knowledge, virtue might well not be a kind of knowledge; but if there is nothing good that knowledge does not encompass, we would be right to suspect that it is a kind of knowledge.—That is so.

e S: Surely virtue makes us good?—Yes.

S: And if we are good, we are beneficent, for all that is good is beneficial. Is that not so?—Yes.

S: So virtue is something beneficial?

M: That necessarily follows from what has been agreed.

S: Let us then examine what kinds of things benefit us, taking them up one by one: health, we say, and strength, and beauty, and also wealth. We say that these things, and others of the same kind, benefit us, do we not?— We do.

S: Yet we say that these same things also some-*88* times harm one. Do you agree or not?—I do.

S: Look then, what directing factor determines in each case whether these things benefit or harm us? Is it not the right use of them that benefits us, and the wrong use that harms us?—Certainly.

S: Let us now look at the qualities of the soul. There is something you call moderation, and justice, courage, intelligence, memory, munificence, and all such things?—There is.

b S: Consider whichever of these you believe not to be knowledge but different from it; do they not at times harm us, at other times benefit us? Courage, for example, when it is not wisdom but like a kind of recklessness: when a man is reckless without understanding, he is harmed; when with understanding, he is benefitted.—Yes.

S: The same is true of moderation and mental quickness; when they are learned and disciplined with understanding they are beneficial, but without understanding they are harmful?—Very much so.

c S: Therefore, in a word, all that the soul undertakes and endures, if directed by wisdom, ends in happiness, but if directed by ignorance, it ends in the opposite?—That is likely.

S: If then virtue is something in the soul and it must be beneficial, it must be knowledge, since all the qualities of the soul are in themselves neither *d* beneficial nor harmful, but accompanied by wisdom or folly they become harmful or beneficial. This argument shows that virtue, being beneficial, must be a kind of wisdom.—I agree.

S: Furthermore, those other things we were mentioning just now, wealth and the like, are at times good and at times harmful. Just as for the rest of the soul the direction of wisdom makes things beneficial, but harmful if directed by folly, so in these cases, if the soul *e* uses and directs them right it makes them beneficial, but bad use makes them harmful?—Quite so.

S: The wise soul directs them right, the foolish soul wrongly?—That is so.

S: So one may say this about everything; all other human activities depend on the soul, and those of the soul itself depend on wisdom if they are to be good. *89* According to this argument the beneficial would be wisdom, and we say that virtue is beneficial?—Certainly.

S: Virtue then, as a whole or in part, is wisdom?

M: What you say, Socrates, seems to me quite right.

S: Then, if that is so, the good are not so by nature?—I do not think they are.

S: For if they were, this would follow: if the good *b* were so by nature, we would have people who knew which among the young were by nature good; we would take those whom they had pointed out and guard them in the Acropolis, sealing them up there much more carefully than gold so that no one could corrupt them, and when they reached maturity they would be useful to their cities.—Reasonable enough, Socrates.

S: Since the good are not good by nature, does *c* learning make them so?

M: Necessarily, as I now think, Socrates, and clearly, on our hypothesis, if virtue is knowledge, it can be taught.

S: Perhaps, by Zeus, but may it be that we were not right to agree to this?

M: Yet it seemed to be right at the time.

S: We should not only think it right at the time, but also now and in the future if it is to be at all sound.

d　M: What is the difficulty? What do you have in mind that you do not like about it and doubt that virtue is knowledge?

S: I will tell you, Meno. I am not saying that it is wrong to say that virtue is teachable if it is knowledge, but look whether it is reasonable of me to doubt whether it is knowledge. Tell me this: if not only virtue but anything whatever can be taught, should there not be of necessity people who teach it and people who learn it? — I think so.

e　S: Then again, if on the contrary there are no teachers or learners of something, we should be right to assume that the subject cannot be taught?

M: Quite so, but do you think that there are no teachers of virtue?

S: I have often tried to find out whether there were any teachers of it, but in spite of all my efforts I cannot find any. And yet I have searched for them with the help of many people, especially those whom I believed to be most experienced in this matter. And now, Meno, Anytus[16] here has opportunely come to sit down by us. Let us share our search with him. It 90 would be reasonable for us to do so, for Anytus, in the first place, is the son of Anthemion, a man of wealth and wisdom, who did not become rich automatically or as the result of a gift like Ismenias the Theban, who recently acquired the possessions of Polycrates, but through his own wisdom and efforts. Further, he did not seem to be an arrogant or puffed up or offensive citizen in other ways, but he was a *b* well-mannered and well-behaved man. Also he gave our friend here a good upbringing and education, as the majority of Athenians believe, for they are electing him to the highest offices. It is right then to look for the teachers of virtue with the help of men such as he, whether there are any and if so who they are. Therefore, Anytus, please join me and your guest friend Meno here, in our inquiry as to who are the teachers of virtue. Look at it in this way: if we wanted *c* Meno to become a good physician, to what teachers

would we send him? Would we not send him to the physicians?

A: Certainly.

S: And if we wanted him to be a good shoemaker, to shoemakers? — Yes.

S: And so with other pursuits? — Certainly.

S: Tell me again on this same topic, like this: we say that we would be right to send him to the physicians if we want him to become a physician; whenever we say that, we mean that it would be *d* reasonable to send him to those who practice the craft rather than to those who do not, and to those who exact fees for this very practice and have shown themselves to be teachers of anyone who wishes to come to them and learn. Is it not with this in mind that we would be right to send him? — Yes.

S: And the same is true about flute-playing and the other crafts? It would be very foolish for those *e* who want to make someone a flute-player to refuse to send him to those who profess to teach the craft and make money at it, but to send him to make trouble for others by seeking to learn from those who do not claim to be teachers or have a single pupil in that subject which we want the one we send to learn from them? Do you not think it very unreasonable to do so? — By Zeus I do, and also very ignorant.

S: Quite right. However, you can now deliberate with me about our guest friend Meno here. He has been telling me for some time, Anytus, that he longs 91 to acquire that wisdom and virtue which enables men to manage their households and their cities well, to take care of their parents, to know how to welcome and to send away both citizens and strangers as a good man should. Consider to whom we should be *b* right to send him to learn this virtue. Or is it obvious in view of what was said just now that we should send him to those who profess to be teachers of virtue and have shown themselves to be available to any Greek who wishes to learn, and for this fix a fee and exact it?

A: And who do you say these are, Socrates?

S: You surely know yourself that they are those whom men call sophists.

A: By Heracles, hush, Socrates. May no one of *c* my household or friends, whether citizen or stranger, be mad enough to go to these people and be harmed by them, for they clearly cause the ruin and corruption of their followers.

16. [Anytus was a successful democratic politician in Athens. His success must have come after the restoration of democratic government in Athens in 403 B.C., whereas Meno himself joined the expedition of Cyrus in 401 and never came back to Greece. So the conversation must have taken place about 402. Anytus was one of Socrates' accusers in 399, and Plato obviously expects his readers to have this in mind.]

S: How do you mean, Anytus? Are these people, alone of those who claim the knowledge to benefit one, so different from the others that they not only do not benefit what one entrusts to them but on the d contrary corrupt it, even though they obviously expect to make money from the process? I find I cannot believe you, for I know that one man, Protagoras, made more money from this knowledge of his than Phidias who made such notably fine works, and ten other sculptors. Surely what you say is extraordinary, if those who mend old sandals and restore clothes e would be found out within the month if they returned the clothes and sandals in a worse state than they received them; if they did this they would soon die of starvation, but the whole of Greece has not noticed for forty years that Protagoras corrupts those who frequent him and sends them away in a worse moral condition than he received them. I believe that he was nearly seventy when he died and had practiced his craft for forty years. During all that time to this very day his reputation has stood high; and not only Protagoras but a great many others, some born before 92 him and some still alive today. Are we to say that you maintain that they deceive and harm the young knowingly, or that they themselves are not aware of it? Are we to deem those whom some people consider the wisest of men to be so mad as that?

A: They are far from being mad, Socrates. It is much rather those among the young who pay their b fees who are mad, and even more the relatives who entrust their young to them and most of all the cities who allow them to come in and do not drive out any citizen or stranger who attempts to behave in this manner.

S: Has some sophist wronged you, Anytus, or why are you so hard on them?

A: No, by Zeus, I have never met one of them, nor would I allow any one of my people to do so.

S: Are you then altogether without any experience of these men?

A: And may I remain so.

c S: How then, my good sir, can you know whether there is any good in their instruction or not, if you are altogether without experience of it?

A: Easily, for I know who they are, whether I have experience of them or not.

S: Perhaps you are a wizard, Anytus, for I wonder, from what you yourself say, how else you know

about these things. However, let us not try to find d out who the men are whose company would make Meno wicked—let them be the sophists if you like— but tell us, and benefit your family friend here by telling him, to whom he should go in so large a city to acquire, to any worthwhile degree, the virtue I was just now describing.

A: Why did you not tell him yourself?

S: I did mention those whom I thought to be teachers of it, but you say I am wrong, and perhaps e you are right. You tell him in your turn to whom among the Athenians he should go. Tell him the name of anyone you want.

A: Why give him the name of one individual? Any Athenian gentleman he may meet, if he is willing to be persuaded, will make him a better man than the sophists would.

S: And have these gentlemen become virtuous automatically, without learning from anyone, and are 93 they able to teach others what they themselves never learned?

A: I believe that these men have learned from those who were gentlemen before them; or do you not think that there are many good men in this city?

S: I believe, Anytus, that there are many men here who are good at public affairs, and that there have been as many in the past, but have they been good teachers of their own virtue? That is the point we are discussing, not whether there are good men here or not, or whether there have been in the past, b but we have been investigating for some time whether virtue can be taught. And in the course of that investigation we are inquiring whether the good men of today and of the past knew how to pass on to another the virtue they themselves possessed, or whether a man cannot pass it on or receive it from another. This is what Meno and I have been investigating for some time. Look at it this way, from what you yourself have said. Would you not say that Themistocles was c a good man?—Yes. Even the best of men.

S: And therefore a good teacher of his own virtue if anyone was?

A: I think so, if he wanted to be.

S: But do you think he did not want some other people to be worthy men, and especially his own son? Or do you think he begrudged him this, and d deliberately did not pass on to him his own virtue? Have you not heard that Themistocles taught his son Cleophantus to be a good horseman? He could remain standing upright on horseback and shoot javelins from that position and do many other remarkable things which his father had him taught and made skillful at, all of which required good teachers. Have you not heard this from your elders?—I have.

S: So one could not blame the poor natural
e talents of the son for his failure in virtue?—Perhaps not.

S: But have you ever heard anyone, young or old, say that Cleophantus, the son of Themistocles, was a good and wise man at the same pursuits as his father?—Never.

S: Are we to believe that he wanted to educate his son in those other things but not to do better than his neighbors in that skill which he himself possessed, if indeed virtue can be taught?—Perhaps not, by Zeus.

S: And yet he was, as you yourself agree, among
94 the best teachers of virtue in the past. Let us consider another man, Aristides, the son of Lysimachus. Do you not agree that he was good?—I very definitely do.

S: He too gave his own son Lysimachus the best Athenian education in matters which are the business of teachers, and do you think he made him a better man than anyone else? For you have been in his
b company and seen the kind of man he is. Or take Pericles, a man of such magnificent wisdom. You know that he brought up two sons, Paralus and Xanthippus?—I know.

S: You also know that he taught them to be as good horsemen as any Athenian, that he educated them in the arts, in gymnastics, and in all else that was a matter of skill not to be inferior to anyone, but did he not want to make them good men? I think he did, but this could not be taught. And lest you think that only a few most inferior Athenians are incapable in this respect, reflect that Thucydides[17] too brought
c up two sons, Melesias and Stephanus, that he educated them well in all other things. They were the best wrestlers in Athens—he entrusted the one to Xanthias and the other to Eudorus, who were thought to be the best wrestlers of the day, or do you not remember?

A: I remember I have heard that said.

17. [Not the historian but Thucydides, the son of Melesias, an Athenian statesman who was an opponent of Pericles and who was ostracized in 440 B.C.]

S: It is surely clear that he would not have taught d his boys what it costs money to teach, but have failed to teach them what costs nothing—making them good men—if that could be taught? Or was Thucydides perhaps an inferior person who had not many friends among the Athenians and the allies? He belonged to a great house; he had great influence in the city and among the other Greeks, so that if virtue could be taught he would have found the man who could make his sons good men, be it a citizen or a stranger, if he himself did not have the time because e of his public concerns. But, friend Anytus, virtue can certainly not be taught.

A: I think, Socrates, that you easily speak ill of people. I would advise you, if you will listen to me, to be careful. Perhaps also in another city, and certainly here, it is easier to injure people than to benefit them. I think you know that yourself.   95

S: I think, Meno, that Anytus is angry, and I am not at all surprised. He thinks, to begin with, that I am slandering those men, and then he believes himself to be one of them. If he ever realizes what slander is, he will cease from anger, but he does not know it now. You tell me, are there not worthy men among your people?—Certainly.

S: Well now, are they willing to offer themselves b to the young as teachers? Do they agree they are teachers, and that virtue can be taught?

M: No, by Zeus, Socrates, but sometimes you would hear them say that it can be taught, at other times, that it cannot.

S: Should we say that they are teachers of this subject, when they do not even agree on this point?— I do not think so, Socrates.

S: Further, do you think that these sophists, who alone profess to be so, are teachers of virtue?

M: I admire this most in Gorgias, Socrates, that c you would never hear him promising this. Indeed, he ridicules the others when he hears them making this claim. He thinks one should make people clever speakers.

S: You do not think then that the sophists are teachers?

M: I cannot tell, Socrates; like most people, at times I think they are, at other times I think that they are not.

S: Do you know that not only you and the other public men at times think that it can be taught, at d other times that it cannot, but that the poet Theognis[18] says the same thing? — Where?

S: In his elegiacs: "Eat and drink with these men, and keep their company. Please those whose
e power is great, for you will learn goodness from the good. If you mingle with bad men you will lose even what wit you possess." You see that here he speaks as if virtue can be taught? — So it appears.

S: Elsewhere, he changes somewhat: "if this could be done" he says, "and intelligence could be instilled," somehow those who could do this "would collect large and numerous fees," and further: "Never would a bad son be born of a good father, for he
96 would be persuaded by wise words, but you will never make a bad man good by teaching." You realize that the poet is contradicting himself on the same subject? — He seems to be.

S: Can you mention any other subject of which those who claim to be teachers not only are not recognized to be teachers of others but are not recognized to have knowledge of it themselves, and are thought to
b be poor in the very matter which they profess to teach? Or any other subject of which those who are recognized as worthy teachers at one time say it can be taught and at other times that it cannot? Would you say that people who are so confused about a subject can be effective teachers of it? — No, by Zeus, I would not.

S: If then neither the sophists nor the worthy people themselves are teachers of this subject, clearly there would be no others? — I do not think there are.
c S: If there are no teachers, neither are there pupils? — As you say.

S: And we agreed that a subject that has neither teachers nor pupils is not teachable? — We have so agreed.

S: Now there seem to be no teachers of virtue anywhere? — That is so.

S: If there are no teachers, there are no learners? — That seems so.

S: Then virtue cannot be taught?
d M: Apparently not, if we have investigated this correctly. I certainly wonder, Socrates, whether there are no good men either, or in what way good men come to be.

18. [Theognis was a poet of mid-sixth century B.C. A collection of poems is extant (about twelve hundred lines), but the authenticity of a good deal of it is doubtful.]

S: We are probably poor specimens, you and I, Meno. Gorgias has not adequately educated you, nor Prodicus me. We must then at all costs turn our attention to ourselves and find someone who will in some way make us better. I say this in view of our e recent investigation, for it is ridiculous that we failed to see that it is not only under the guidance of knowledge that men succeed in their affairs, and that is perhaps why the knowledge of how good men come to be escapes us.

M: How do you mean, Socrates?

S: I mean this: we were right to agree that good men must be beneficent, and that this could not be otherwise. Is that not so? — Yes.

S: And that they will be beneficent if they give us correct guidance in our affairs. To this too we were right to agree? — Yes.   97

S: But that one cannot guide correctly if one does not have knowledge; to this our agreement is likely to be incorrect. — How do you mean?

S: I will tell you. A man who knew the way to Larissa, or anywhere else you like, and went there and guided others would surely lead them well and correctly? — Certainly.

S: What if someone had had a correct opinion b as to which was the way but had not gone there nor indeed had knowledge of it, would he not also lead correctly? — Certainly.

S: And as long as he has the right opinion about that of which the other has knowledge, he will not be a worse guide than the one who knows, as he has a true opinion, though not knowledge. — In no way worse.

S: So true opinion is in no way a worse guide to correct action than knowledge. It is this that we omitted in our investigation of the nature of virtue, c when we said that only knowledge can lead to correct action, for true opinion can do so also. — So it seems.

S: So correct opinion is no less useful than knowledge?

M: Yes, to this extent, Socrates. But the man who has knowledge will always succeed, whereas he who has true opinion will only succeed at times.

S: How do you mean? Will he who has the right opinion not always succeed, as long as his opinion is right?

M: That appears to be so of necessity, and it makes me wonder, Socrates, this being the case, why d

knowledge is prized far more highly than right opinion, and why they are different.

S: Do you know why you wonder, or shall I tell
you?—By all means tell me.

S: It is because you have paid no attention to
the statues of Daedalus, but perhaps there are none
in Thessaly.

M: What do you have in mind when you say this?

S: That they too run away and escape if one
e does not tie them down but remain in place if tied
down.—So what?

S: To acquire an untied work of Daedalus is not
worth much, like acquiring a runaway slave, for it
does not remain, but it is worth much if tied down,
for his works are very beautiful. What am I thinking
of when I say this? True opinions. For true opinions,
98 as long as they remain, are a fine thing and all they
do is good, but they are not willing to remain long,
and they escape from a man's mind, so that they are
not worth much until one ties them down by (giving)
an account of the reason why. And that, Meno my
friend, is recollection, as we previously agreed. After
they are tied down, in the first place they become
knowledge, and then they remain in place. That is
why knowledge is prized higher than correct opinion,
and knowledge differs from correct opinion in being
tied down.

M: Yes, by Zeus, Socrates, it seems to be something like that.

b   S: Indeed, I too speak as one who does not have
knowledge but is guessing. However, I certainly do
not think I am guessing that right opinion is a different
thing from knowledge. If I claim to know anything
else—and I would make that claim about few
things—I would put this down as one of the things
I know.—Rightly so, Socrates.

S: Well then, is it not correct that when true opinion guides the course of every action, it does no worse
than knowledge?—I think you are right in this too.

c   S: Correct opinion is then neither inferior to
knowledge nor less useful in directing actions, nor is
the man who has it less so than he who has knowledge.—That is so.

S: And we agreed that the good man is beneficent?—Yes.

S: Since then it is not only through knowledge
but also through right opinion that men are good, and
d beneficial to their cities when they are, and neither

knowledge nor true opinion come to men by nature
but are acquired—or do you think either of these
comes by nature?—I do not think so.

S: Then if they do not come by nature, men are
not so by nature either.—Surely not.

S: As goodness does not come by nature, we
inquired next whether it could be taught.—Yes.

S: We thought it could be taught, if it was knowledge?—Yes.

S: And that it was knowledge if it could be
taught?—Quite so.

S: And that if there were teachers of it, it could e
be taught, but if there were not, it was not teachable?—That is so.

S: And then we agreed that there were no teachers of it?—We did.

S: So we agreed that it was neither teachable
nor knowledge?—Quite so.

S: But we certainly agree that virtue is a good
thing?—Yes.

S: And that which guides correctly is both useful
and good?—Certainly.

S: And that only these two things, true belief 99
and knowledge, guide correctly, and that if a man
possesses these he gives correct guidance. The things
that turn out right by some chance are not due to
human guidance, but where there is correct human
guidance it is due to two things, true belief or knowledge.—I think that is so.

S: Now because it cannot be taught, virtue no
longer seems to be knowledge?—It seems not.

S: So one of the two good and useful things has b
been excluded, and knowledge is not the guide in
public affairs?—I do not think so.

S: So it is not by some kind of wisdom, or by
being wise, that such men lead their cities, those such
as Themistocles and those mentioned by Anytus just
now? That is the reason why they cannot make others
be like themselves, because it is not knowledge which
makes them what they are.

M: It is likely to be as you say, Socrates.

S: Therefore, if it is not through knowledge, the
only alternative is that it is through right opinion that c
statesmen follow the right course for their cities. As
regards knowledge, they are no different from soothsayers and prophets. They too say many true things
when inspired, but they have no knowledge of what
they are saying.—That is probably so.

S: And so, Meno, is it right to call divine these men who, without any understanding, are right in much that is of importance in what they say and do? — Certainly.

S: We should be right to call divine also those *d* soothsayers and prophets whom we just mentioned, and all the poets, and we should call no less divine and inspired those public men who are no less under the gods' influence and possession, as their speeches lead to success in many important matters, though they have no knowledge of what they are saying. — Quite so.

S: Women too, Meno, call good men divine, and the Spartans, when they eulogize someone, say "This man is divine."

e M: And they appear to be right, Socrates, though perhaps Anytus here will be annoyed with you for saying so.

S: I do not mind that; we shall talk to him again, but if we were right in the way in which we spoke and investigated in this whole discussion, virtue would be neither an inborn quality nor taught, but comes to those who possess it as a gift from the gods which is not accompanied by understanding, unless there *100* is someone among our statesmen who can make another into a statesman. If there were one, he could be said to be among the living as Homer said Teiresias was among the dead, namely, that "he alone retained his wits while the others flitted about like shadows." In the same manner such a man would, as far as virtue is concerned, here also be the only true reality compared, as it were, with shadows.

M: I think that is an excellent way to put it, Soc- *b* rates.

S: It follows from this reasoning, Meno, that virtue appears to be present in those of us who may possess it as a gift from the gods. We shall have clear knowledge of this when, before we investigate how it comes to be present in men, we first try to find out what virtue in itself is. But now the time has come for me to go. You convince your guest friend Anytus here of these very things of which you have yourself been convinced, in order that he may be more amenable. If you succeed, you will also confer a benefit upon the Athenians.

Euthyphro

2 EUTHYPHRO:[1]   What's new, Socrates, to make you leave your usual haunts in the Lyceum and spend your time here by the king-archon's court? Surely you are not prosecuting anyone before the king-archon as I am?

SOCRATES: The Athenians do not call this a prosecution but an indictment, Euthyphro.

b   E: What is this you say? Someone must have indicted you, for you are not going to tell me that you have indicted someone else.

S: No indeed.

E: But someone else has indicted you?

S: Quite so.

E: Who is he?

S: I do not really know him myself, Euthyphro. He is apparently young and unknown. They call him Meletus, I believe. He belongs to the Pitthean deme, if you know anyone from that deme called Meletus, with long hair, not much of a beard, and a rather aquiline nose.

E: I don't know him, Socrates. What charge does he bring against you?

c   S: What charge? A not ignoble one I think, for it is no small thing for a young man to have knowledge of such an important subject. He says he knows how our young men are corrupted and who corrupts them. He is likely to be wise, and when he sees my ignorance corrupting his contemporaries, he proceeds to accuse d me to the city as to their mother. I think he is the only one of our public men to start out the right way, for it is right to care first that the young should be as good as possible, just as a good farmer is likely to take care of the young plants first, and of the others later. So, too, Meletus first gets rid of us who corrupt 3 the young shoots, as he says, and then afterwards he will obviously take care of the older ones and become a source of great blessings for the city, as seems likely to happen to one who started out this way.

E: I could wish this were true, Socrates, but I fear the opposite may happen. He seems to me to start out by harming the very heart of the city by attempting to wrong you. Tell me, what does he say you do to corrupt the young?

S: Strange things, to hear him tell it, for he says b that I am a maker of gods, and on the ground that I create new gods while not believing in the old gods, he has indicted me for their sake, as he puts it.

E: I understand, Socrates. This is because you say that the divine sign keeps coming to you.[2] So he has written this indictment against you as one who makes innovations in religious matters, and he comes to court to slander you, knowing that such things are easily misrepresented to the crowd. The same is true in my case. Whenever I speak of divine matters in c the assembly and foretell the future, they laugh me down as if I were crazy; and yet I have foretold nothing that did not happen. Nevertheless, they envy all of us who do this. One need not worry about them, but meet them head on.

S: My dear Euthyphro, to be laughed at does not matter perhaps, for the Athenians do not mind anyone they think clever, as long as he does not teach his own wisdom, but if they think that he makes others to be like himself they get angry, whether through envy, as you say, or for some other reason.   d

E: I have certainly no desire to test their feelings towards me in this matter.

Reprinted from *The Trial and Death of Socrates*, translated by G.M.A. Grube (Indianapolis: Hackett Publishing Company, 1975), by permission of the publisher.

1. [We know nothing about Euthyphro except what we can gather from this dialogue. He is obviously a professional priest who considers himself an expert on ritual and on piety generally, and, it seems, is generally so considered. One Euthyphro is mentioned in Plato's *Cratylus* (396d) who is given to *enthousiasmos*, inspiration or possession, but we cannot be sure that it is the same person. — G.M.A.G.]

2. [In Plato, Socrates always speaks of his divine sign or voice as intervening to prevent him from doing or saying something (e.g., *Apology* 31d), but never positively. The popular view was that it enabled him to foretell the future, and Euthyphro here represents that view. Note, however, that Socrates dissociates himself from "you prophets" (3e).]

S: Perhaps you seem to make yourself but rarely available, and not be willing to teach your own wisdom, but I'm afraid that my liking for people makes them think that I pour out to anybody anything I have to say, not only without charging a fee but even glad to reward anyone who is willing to listen. If then they were intending to laugh at me, as you say they laugh at you, there would be nothing unpleasant in their spending their time in court laughing and jesting, but if they are going to be serious, the outcome e is not clear except to you prophets.

E: Perhaps it will come to nothing, Socrates, and you will fight your case as you think best, as I think I will mine.

S: What is your case, Euthyphro? Are you the defendant or the prosecutor?

E: The prosecutor.

S: Whom do you prosecute?

4 E: One whom I am thought crazy to prosecute.

S: Are you pursuing someone who will easily escape you?

E: Far from it, for he is quite old.

S: Who is it?

E: My father.

S: My dear sir! Your own father?

E: Certainly.

S: What is the charge? What is the case about?

E: Murder, Socrates.

S: Good heavens! Certainly, Euthyphro, most b men would not know how they could do this and be right. It is not the part of anyone to do this, but of one who is far advanced in wisdom.

E: Yes, by Zeus, Socrates, that is so.

S: Is then the man your father killed one of your relatives? Or is that obvious, for you would not prosecute your father for the murder of a stranger.

E: It is ridiculous, Socrates, for you to think that it makes any difference whether the victim is a stranger or a relative. One should only watch whether the killer acted justly or not; if he acted justly, let him go, but if not, one should prosecute, if, that is c to say, the killer shares your hearth and table. The pollution is the same if you knowingly keep company with such a man and do not cleanse yourself and him by bringing him to justice. The victim was a dependent of mine, and when we were farming in Naxos he was a servant of ours. He killed one of our household slaves in drunken anger, so my father

bound him hand and foot and threw him in a ditch, then sent a man here to inquire from the priest what d should be done. During that time he gave no thought or care to the bound man, as being a killer, and it was no matter if he died, which he did. Hunger and cold and his bonds caused his death before the messenger came back from the seer. Both my father and my other relatives are angry that I am prosecuting my father for murder on behalf of a murderer when he hadn't even killed him, they say, and even if he had, the dead man does not deserve a thought, since he was a killer. For, they say, it is impious for a son e to prosecute his father for murder. But their ideas of the divine attitude to piety and impiety are wrong, Socrates.

S: Whereas, by Zeus, Euthyphro, you think that your knowledge of the divine, and of piety and impiety, is so accurate that, when those things happened as you say, you have no fear of having acted impiously in bringing your father to trial?

E: I should be of no use, Socrates, and Euthyphro would not be superior to the majority of men, if I 5 did not have accurate knowledge of all such things.

S: It is indeed most important, my admirable Euthyphro, that I should become your pupil, and as regards this indictment challenge Meletus about these very things and say to him: that in the past too I considered knowledge about the divine to be most important, and that now that he says that I am guilty of improvising and innovating about the gods I have b become your pupil. I would say to him: "If, Meletus, you agree that Euthyphro is wise in these matters, consider me, too, to have the right beliefs and do not bring me to trial. If you do not think so, then prosecute that teacher of mine, not me, for corrupting the older men, me and his own father, by teaching me and by exhorting and punishing him." If he is not convinced, and does not discharge me or indict you instead of me, I shall repeat the same challenge in court.

E: Yes, by Zeus, Socrates, and, if he should try to indict me, I think I would find his weak spots and c the talk in court would be about him rather than about me.

S: It is because I realize this that I am eager to become your pupil, my dear friend. I know that other people as well as this Meletus do not even seem to notice you, whereas he sees me so sharply and clearly that he indicts me for ungodliness. So tell me now, by Zeus, what you just now maintained you clearly knew: what kind of thing do you say that godliness and ungodliness are, both as regards murder and other _d_ things; or is the pious not the same and alike in every action, and the impious the opposite of all that is pious and like itself, and everything that is to be impious presents us with one form[3] or appearance in so far as it is impious?

E: Most certainly, Socrates.

S: Tell me then, what is the pious, and what the impious, do you say?

E: I say that the pious is to do what I am doing now, to prosecute the wrongdoer, be it about murder or temple robbery or anything else, whether the _e_ wrongdoer is your father or your mother or anyone else; not to prosecute is impious. And observe, Socrates, that I can cite powerful evidence that the law is so. I have already said to others that such actions are right, not to favor the ungodly, whoever they are. These people themselves believe that Zeus is the best _6_ and most just of the gods, yet they agree that he bound his father because he unjustly swallowed his sons, and that he in turn castrated his father for similar reasons. But they are angry with me because I am prosecuting my father for his wrongdoing. They contradict themselves in what they say about the gods and about me.

S: Indeed, Euthyphro, this is the reason why I am a defendant in the case, because I find it hard to accept things like that being said about the gods, and it is likely to be the reason why I shall be told I do wrong. Now, however, if you, who have full knowl-_b_ edge of such things, share their opinions, then we must agree with them, too, it would seem. For what are we to say, we who agree that we ourselves have

no knowledge of them? Tell me, by the god of friendship, do you really believe these things are true?

E: Yes, Socrates, and so are even more surprising things, of which the majority has no knowledge.

S: And do you believe that there really is war among the gods, and terrible enmities and battles, and other such things as are told by the poets, and _c_ other sacred stories such as are embroidered by good writers and by representations of which the robe of the goddess is adorned when it is carried up to the Acropolis? Are we to say these things are true, Euthyphro?

E: Not only these, Socrates, but, as I was saying just now, I will, if you wish, relate many other things about the gods which I know will amaze you.

S: I should not be surprised, but you will tell me these at leisure some other time. For now, try to tell me more clearly what I was asking just now, for, my friend, you did not teach me adequately when I asked _d_ you what the pious was, but you told me that what you are doing now, in prosecuting your father for murder, is pious.

E: And I told the truth, Socrates.

S: Perhaps. You agree, however, that there are many other pious actions.

E: There are.

S: Bear in mind then that I did not bid you tell me one or two of the many pious actions but that form itself that makes all pious actions pious, for you agreed that all impious actions are impious and all pious actions pious through one form, or don't you re-_e_ member?

E: I do.

S: Tell me then what this form itself is, so that I may look upon it, and using it as a model, say that any action of yours or another's that is of that kind is pious, and if it is not that it is not.

E: If that is how you want it, Socrates, that is how I will tell you.

S: That is what I want.

E: Well then, what is dear to the gods is pious, _7_ what is not is impious.

S: Splendid, Euthyphro! You have now answered in the way I wanted. Whether your answer is true I do not know yet, but you will obviously show me that what you say is true.

E: Certainly.

S: Come then, let us examine what we mean.

---

3. [This is the kind of passage that makes it easier for us to follow the transition from Socrates' universal definitions to the Platonic theory of separately existent eternal universal Forms. The words _eidos_ and _idea_, the technical terms for the Platonic Forms, commonly mean physical stature or bodily appearance. As we apply a common epithet, in this case pious, to different actions or things, these must have a common characteristic, present a common appearance or form, to justify the use of the same term; but in the early dialogues, as here, it seems to be thought of as immanent in the particulars and without separate existence. The same is true of 6d where the word "Form" is also used.]

An action or a man dear to the gods is pious, but an action or a man hated by the gods is impious. They are not the same, but quite opposite, the pious and the impious. Is that not so?

E: It is indeed.

S: And that seems to be a good statement?

b E: I think so, Socrates.

S: We have also stated that the gods are in a state of discord, that they are at odds with each other, Euthyphro, and that they are at enmity with each other. Has that, too, been said?

E: It has.

S: What are the subjects of difference that cause hatred and anger? Let us look at it this way. If you and I were to differ about numbers as to which is the greater, would this difference make us enemies and angry with each other, or would we proceed to count c and soon resolve our difference about this?

E: We would certainly do so.

S: Again, if we differed about the larger and the smaller, we would turn to measurement and soon cease to differ.

E: That is so.

S: And about the heavier and the lighter, we would resort to weighing and be reconciled.

E: Of course.

S: What subject of difference would make us angry and hostile to each other if we were unable to come to a decision? Perhaps you do not have an d answer ready, but examine as I tell you whether these subjects are the just and the unjust, the beautiful and the ugly, the good and the bad. Are these not the subjects of difference about which, when we are unable to come to a satisfactory decision, you and I and other men become hostile to each other whenever we do?

E: That is the difference, Socrates, about those subjects.

S: What about the gods, Euthyphro? If indeed they have differences, will it not be about these same subjects?

E: It certainly must be so.

e S: Then according to your argument, my good Euthyphro, different gods consider different things to be just, beautiful, ugly, good, and bad, for they would not be at odds with one another unless they differed about these subjects, would they?

E: You are right.

S: And they like what each of them considers beautiful, good, and just, and hate the opposites of these?

E: Certainly.

S: But you say that the same things are considered just by some gods and unjust by others, and as they 8 dispute about these things they are at odds and at war with each other. Is that not so?

E: It is.

S: The same things then are loved by the gods and hated by the gods, and would be both god-loved and god-hated.

E: It seems likely.

S: And the same things would be both pious and impious, according to this argument?

E: I'm afraid so.

S: So you did not answer my question, you surprising man. I did not ask you what same thing is both pious and impious, and it appears that what is loved by the gods is also hated by them. So it is b in no way surprising if your present action, namely punishing your father, may be pleasing to Zeus but displeasing to Cronus and Uranus, pleasing to Hephaestus but displeasing to Hera, and so with any other gods who differ from each other on this subject.

E: I think, Socrates, that on this subject no gods would differ from one another, that whoever has killed anyone unjustly should pay the penalty.

S: Well now, Euthyphro, have you ever heard c any man maintaining that one who has killed or done anything else unjustly should not pay the penalty?

E: They never cease to dispute on this subject, both elsewhere and in the courts, for when they have committed many wrongs they do and say anything to avoid the penalty.

S: Do they agree they have done wrong, Euthyphro, and in spite of so agreeing do they nevertheless say they should not be punished?

E: No, they do not agree on that point.

S: So they do not say or do just anything. For they do not venture to say this, or dispute that they must not pay the penalty if they have done wrong, d but I think they deny doing wrong. Is that not so?

E: That is true.

S: Then they do not dispute that the wrongdoer must be punished, but they may disagree as to who the wrongdoer is, what he did and when.

E: You are right.

S: Do not the gods have the same experience, if indeed they are at odds with each other about the just and the unjust, as your argument maintains? Some assert that they wrong one another, while others deny it, but no one among gods or men ventures to

e say that the wrongdoer must not be punished.

E: Yes, that is true, Socrates, as to the main point.

S: And those who disagree, whether men or gods, dispute about each action, if indeed the gods disagree. Some say it is done justly, others unjustly. Is that not so?

E: Yes, indeed.

9   S: Come now, my dear Euthyphro, tell me, too, that I may become wiser, what proof you have that all the gods consider that man to have been killed unjustly who became a murderer while in your service, was bound by the master of his victim, and died in his bonds before the one who bound him found out from the seers what was to be done with him, and that it is right for a son to denounce and to prosecute his father on behalf of such a man. Come,

b try to show me a clear sign that all the gods definitely believe this action to be right. If you can give me adequate proof of this, I shall never cease to extol your wisdom.

E: This is perhaps no light task, Socrates, though I could show you very clearly.

S: I understand that you think me more dull-witted than the jury, as you will obviously show them that these actions were unjust and that all the gods hate such actions.

E: I will show it to them clearly, Socrates, if only they will listen to me.

c   S: They will listen if they think you show them well. But this thought came to me as you were speaking, and I am examining it, saying to myself: "If Euthyphro shows me conclusively that all the gods consider such a death unjust, to what greater extent have I learned from him the nature of piety and impiety? This action would then, it seems, be hated by the gods, but the pious and the impious were not thereby now defined, for what is hated by the gods has also been shown to be loved by them." So I will not insist on this point; let us assume, if you wish, that all the gods consider this unjust and that they

d all hate it. However, is this the correction we are making in our discussion, that what all the gods hate is impious, and what they all love is pious, and that

what some gods love and others hate is neither or both? Is that how you now wish us to define piety and impiety?

E: What prevents us from doing so, Socrates?

S: For my part nothing, Euthyphro, but you look whether on your part this proposal will enable you to teach me most easily what you promised.

E: I would certainly say that the pious is what all e the gods love, and the opposite, what all the gods hate, is the impious.

S: Then let us again examine whether that is a sound statement, or do we let it pass, and if one of us, or someone else, merely says that something is so, do we accept that it is so? Or should we examine what the speaker means?

E: We must examine it, but I certainly think that this is now a fine statement.

S: We shall soon know better whether it is. Con- 10 sider this: Is the pious being loved by the gods because it is pious, or is it pious because it is being loved by the gods?

E: I don't know what you mean, Socrates.

S: I shall try to explain more clearly: we speak of something carried[4] and something carrying, of something led and something leading, of something seen and something seeing, and you understand that these things are all different from one another and how they differ?

E: I think I do.

S: So there is also something loved and—a different thing—something loving.

E: Of course.

S: Tell me then whether the thing carried is a b

---

4. [This is the present participle form of the verb *pheromenon*, literally *being-carried*. The following passage is somewhat obscure, especially in translation, but the general meaning is clear. Plato points out that this participle simply indicates the object of an action of carrying, seeing, loving, etc. It follows from the action and adds nothing new, the action being prior to it, not following from it, and a thing is said to be loved because someone loves it, not vice versa. To say therefore that the pious is being loved by the gods says no more than that the gods love it. Euthyphro, however, also agrees that the pious is loved by the gods because of its nature (because it is pious), but the fact of its being loved by the gods does not define that nature, and as a definition is therefore unsatisfactory. It only indicates a quality or affect of the pious, and the pious is therefore still to be defined (11a7).]

carried thing because it is being carried, or for some other reason?

E: No, that is the reason.

S: And the thing led is so because it is being led, and the thing seen because it is being seen?

E: Certainly.

S: It is not being seen because it is a thing seen but on the contrary it is a thing seen because it is being seen; nor is it because it is something led that it is being led but because it is being led that it is something led; nor is something being carried because it is something carried, but it is something carried because it is being carried. Is what I want to say clear, Euthyphro? I want to say this, namely, that if anything is being changed or is being affected in any way, it is not being changed because it is something changed, but rather it is something changed because it is being changed; nor is it being affected because it is something affected, but it is something affected because it is being affected. Or do you not agree?

E: I do.

S: Is something loved either something changed or something affected by something?

E: Certainly.

S: So it is in the same case as the things just mentioned; it is not being loved by those who love it because it is something loved, but it is something loved because it is being loved by them?

E: Necessarily.

S: What then do we say about the pious, Euthyphro? Surely that it is being loved by all the gods, according to what you say?

E: Yes.

S: Is it being loved because it is pious, or for some other reason?

E: For no other reason.

S: It is being loved then because it is pious, but it is not pious because it is being loved?[5]

E: Apparently.

S: And yet it is something loved and god-loved because it is being loved by the gods?

E: Of course.

S: Then the god-loved is not the same as the pious, Euthyphro, nor the pious the same as the god-loved, as you say it is, but one differs from the other.

E: How so, Socrates?

S: Because we agree that the pious is being loved for this reason, that it is pious, but it is not pious because it is being loved. Is that not so?

E: Yes.

S: And that the god-loved, on the other hand, is so because it is being loved by the gods, by the very fact of being loved, but it is not being loved because it is god-loved.

E: True.

S: But if the god-loved and the pious were the same, my dear Euthyphro, then if the pious was being loved because it was pious, the god-loved would also be being loved because it was god-loved; and if the god-loved was god-loved because it was being loved by the gods, then the pious would also be pious because it was being loved by the gods. But now you see that they are in opposite cases as being altogether different from each other: the one is such as to be loved because it is being loved, the other is being loved because it is such as to be loved. I'm afraid, Euthyphro, that when you were asked what piety is, you did not wish to make its nature clear to me, but you told me an affect or quality of it, that the pious has the quality of being loved by all the gods, but you have not yet told me what the pious is. Now, if you will, do not hide things from me but tell me again from the beginning what piety is, whether being loved by the gods or having some other quality—we shall not quarrel about that—but be keen to tell me what the pious and the impious are.

E: But Socrates, I have no way of telling you what I have in mind, for whatever proposition we put forward goes around and refuses to stay put where we establish it.

5. [I quote an earlier comment of mine on this passage: "it gives in a nutshell a point of view from which Plato never departed. Whatever the gods may be, they must by their very nature love the right because it is right." They have no choice in the matter. "This separation of the dynamic power of the gods from the ultimate reality, this setting up of absolute values above the gods themselves was not as unnatural to a Greek as it would be to us ... The gods who ruled on Olympus ... were not creators but created beings. As in Homer, Zeus must obey the balance of Necessity, so the Platonic gods must conform to an eternal scale of values. They did not create them, cannot alter them, cannot indeed wish to do so." (*Plato's Thought*, Boston: Beacon Press, 1958, pp. 152–3.)]

S: Your statements, Euthyphro, seem to belong
c to my ancestor, Daedalus. If I were stating them and
putting them forward, you would perhaps be making
fun of me and say that because of my kinship with
him my conclusions in discussion run away and will
not stay where one puts them. As these propositions
are yours, however, we need some other jest, for they
will not stay put for you, as you say yourself.

E: I think the same jest will do for our discussion,
Socrates, for I am not the one who makes them go
round and not remain in the same place; it is you
d who are the Daedalus; for as far as I am concerned
they would remain as they were.

S: It looks as if I was cleverer than Daedalus in
using my skill, my friend, in so far as he could only
cause to move the things he made himself, but I can
make other people's move as well as my own. And
the smartest part of my skill is that I am clever without
wanting to be, for I would rather have your statements
e to me remain unmoved than possess the wealth of
Tantalus as well as the cleverness of Daedalus. But
enough of this. Since I think you are making unnecessary difficulties, I am as eager as you are to find a
way to teach me about piety, and do not give up
before you do. See whether you think all that is pious
is of necessity just.

E: I think so.

S: And is then all that is just pious? Or is all that
12 is pious just, but not all that is just pious, but some
of it is and some is not?

E: I do not follow what you are saying, Socrates.

S: Yet you are younger than I by as much as you
are wiser. As I say, you are making difficulties because
of your wealth of wisdom. Pull yourself together, my
dear sir, what I am saying is not difficult to grasp. I am
saying the opposite of what the poet said who wrote:

You do not wish to name Zeus, who had done it, and
who made all things grow, for where there is fear
b there is also shame.

I disagree with the poet. Shall I tell you why?

E: Please do.

S: I do not think that "where there is fear there
is also shame," for I think that many people who fear
disease and poverty and many other such things feel
fear, but are not ashamed of the things they fear. Do
you not think so?

E: I do indeed.

S: But where there is shame there is also fear.
For is there anyone who, in feeling shame and embar- c
rassment at anything, does not also at the same time
fear and dread a reputation for wickedness?

E: He is certainly afraid.

S: It is then not right to say "where there is fear
there is also shame," but that where there is shame
there is also fear, for fear covers a larger area than
shame. Shame is a part of fear just as odd is a part
of number, with the result that it is not true that
where there is number there is also oddness, but that
where there is oddness there is also number. Do you
follow me now?

E: Surely.

S: This is the kind of thing I was asking before,
whether where there is piety there is also justice, but
where there is justice there is not always piety, for d
the pious is a part of justice. Shall we say that, or do
you think otherwise?

E: No, but like that, for what you say appears to
be right.

S: See what comes next: if the pious is a part of
the just, we must, it seems, find out what part of the
just it is. Now if you asked me something of what we
mentioned just now, such as what part of number is
the even, and what number that is, I would say it is the
number that is divisible into two equal, not unequal,
parts. Or do you not think so?

E: I do.

S: Try in this way to tell me what part of the just e
the pious is, in order to tell Meletus not to wrong us
any more and not to indict me for ungodliness, since
I have learned from you sufficiently what is godly
and pious and what is not.

E: I think, Socrates, that the godly and pious is
the part of the just that is concerned with the care
of the gods, while that concerned with the care of
men is the remaining part of justice.

S: You seem to me to put that very well, but I
still need a bit of information. I do not know yet what 13
you mean by care, for you do not mean the care of
the gods in the same sense as the care of other things,
as, for example, we say, don't we, that not everyone
knows how to care for horses, but the horse
breeder does.

E: Yes, I do mean it that way.

S: So horse breeding is the care of horses.

E: Yes.

S: Nor does everyone know how to care for dogs, but the hunter does.

E: That is so.

S: So hunting is the care of dogs.

b E: Yes.

S: And cattle raising is the care of cattle.

E: Quite so.

S: While piety and godliness is the care of the gods, Euthyphro. Is that what you mean?

E: It is.

S: Now care in each case has the same effect; it aims at the good and the benefit of the object cared for, as you can see that horses cared for by horse breeders are benefited and become better. Or do you not think so?

E: I do.

S: So dogs are benefited by dog breeding, cattle *c* by cattle raising, and so with all the others. Or do you think that care aims to harm the object of its care?

E: By Zeus, no.

S: It aims to benefit the object of its care?

E: Of course.

S: Is piety then, which is the care of the gods, also to benefit the gods and make them better? Would you agree that when you do something pious you make some one of the gods better?

E: By Zeus, no.

S: Nor do I think that this is what you mean— far from it—but that is why I asked you what you *d* meant by the care of gods, because I did not believe you meant this kind of care.

E: Quite right, Socrates, that is not the kind of care I mean.

S: Very well, but what kind of care of the gods would piety be?

E: The kind of care, Socrates, that slaves take of their masters.

S: I understand. It is likely to be a kind of service of the gods.

E: Quite so.

S: Could you tell me to the achievement of what goal service to doctors tends? Is it not, do you think, to achieving health?

E: I think so.

e S: What about service to shipbuilders? To what achievement is it directed?

E: Clearly, Socrates, to the building of a ship.

S: And service to housebuilders to the building of a house?

E: Yes.

S: Tell me then, my good sir, to the achievement of what aim does service to the gods tend? You obviously know since you say that you, of all men, have the best knowledge of the divine.

E: And I am telling the truth, Socrates.

S: Tell me then, by Zeus, what is that excellent aim that the gods achieve, using us as their servants?

E: Many fine things, Socrates.

S: So do generals, my friend. Nevertheless you *14* could easily tell me their main concern, which is to achieve victory in war, is it not?

E: Of course.

S: The farmers too, I think, achieve many fine things, but the main point of their efforts is to produce food from the earth.

E: Quite so.

S: Well then, how would you sum up the many fine things that the gods achieve?

E: I told you a short while ago, Socrates, that it is a considerable task to acquire any precise knowl- *b* edge of these things, but, to put it simply, I say that if a man knows how to say and do what is pleasing to the gods at prayer and sacrifice, those are pious actions such as preserve both private houses and public affairs of state. The opposite of these pleasing actions are impious and overturn and destroy everything.

S: You could tell me in far fewer words, if you were willing, the sum of what I asked, Euthyphro, *c* but you are not keen to teach me, that is clear. You were on the point of doing so, but you turned away. If you had given that answer, I should now have acquired from you sufficient knowledge of the nature of piety. As it is, the lover of inquiry must follow his beloved wherever it may lead him. Once more then, what do you say that piety and the pious are? Are they a knowledge of how to sacrifice and pray?

E: They are.

S: To sacrifice is to make a gift to the gods, whereas to pray is to beg from the gods?

E: Definitely, Socrates.

S: It would follow from this statement that piety *d* would be a knowledge of how to give to, and beg from, the gods.

E: You understood what I said very well, Socrates.

S: That is because I am so desirous of your wisdom, and I concentrate my mind on it, so that no word of yours may fall to the ground. But tell me, what is this service to the gods? You say it is to beg from them and to give to them?

E: I do.

S: And to beg correctly would be to ask from them things that we need?

E: What else?

e   S: And to give correctly is to give them what they need from us, for it would not be skillful to bring gifts to anyone that are in no way needed.

E: True, Socrates.

S: Piety would then be a sort of trading skill between gods and men?

E: Trading yes, if you prefer to call it that.

S: I prefer nothing, unless it is true. But tell me, what benefit do the gods derive from the gifts they 15 receive from us? What they give us is obvious to all. There is for us no good that we do not receive from them, but how are they benefited by what they receive from us? Or do we have such an advantage over them in the trade that we receive all our blessings from them and they receive nothing from us?

E: Do you suppose, Socrates, that the gods are benefited by what they receive from us?

S: What could those gifts from us to the gods be, Euthyphro?

E: What else, do you think, than honor, reverence, and what I mentioned just now, gratitude.

b   S: The pious is then, Euthyphro, pleasing to the gods, but not beneficial or dear to them?

E: I think it is of all things most dear to them.

S: So the pious is once again what is dear to the gods.

E: Most certainly.

S: When you say this, will you be surprised if your arguments seem to move about instead of staying put? And will you accuse me of being Daedalus who makes them move, though you are yourself much more skillful than Daedalus and make them go round in a circle? Or do you not realize that our argument has moved around and come again to the same place? c You surely remember that earlier the pious and the god-loved were shown not to be the same but different from each other. Or do you not remember?

E: I do.

S: Do you then not realize now that you are saying that what is dear to the gods is the pious? Is this not the same as the god-loved? Or is it not?

E: It certainly is.

S: Either we were wrong when we agreed before, or, if we were right then, we are wrong now.

E: That seems to be so.

S: So we must investigate again from the beginning what piety is, as I shall not willingly give up before I learn this. Do not think me unworthy, but concentrate your attention and tell the truth. For you d know it, if any man does, and I must not let you go, like Proteus, before you tell me. If you had no clear knowledge of piety and impiety you would never have ventured to prosecute your old father for murder on behalf of a servant. For fear of the gods you would have been afraid to take the risk lest you should not be acting rightly, and would have been ashamed before men, but now I know well that you believe you have e clear knowledge of piety and impiety. So tell me, my good Euthyphro, and do not hide what you think it is.

E: Some other time, Socrates, for I am in a hurry now, and it is time for me to go.

S: What a thing to do, my friend! By going you have cast me down from a great hope I had, that I would learn from you the nature of the pious and the impious 16 and so escape Meletus' indictment by showing him that I had acquired wisdom in divine matters from Euthyphro, and my ignorance would no longer cause me to be careless and inventive about such things, and that I would be better for the rest of my life.

Apology[1]

17 I do not know, men of Athens, how my accusers affected you; as for me, I was almost carried away in spite of myself, so persuasively did they speak. And yet, hardly anything of what they said is true. Of the many lies they told, one in particular surprised me, namely that you should be careful not to be deceived b by an accomplished speaker like me. That they were not ashamed to be immediately proved wrong by the facts, when I show myself not to be an accomplished speaker at all, that I thought was most shameless on their part—unless indeed they call an accomplished speaker the man who speaks the truth. If they mean that, I would agree that I am an orator, but not after their manner, for indeed, as I say, practically nothing c they said was true. From me you will hear the whole truth, though not, by Zeus, gentlemen, expressed in embroidered and stylized phrases like theirs, but things spoken at random and expressed in the first words that come to mind, for I put my trust in the justice of what I say, and let none of you expect anything else. It would not be fitting at my age, as it might be for a young man, to toy with words when I appear before you.

One thing I do ask and beg of you, gentlemen: if you hear me making my defense in the same kind of language as I am accustomed to use in the market-place by the bankers' tables,[2] where many of you have heard me, and elsewhere, do not be surprised or d create a disturbance on that account. The position is this: this is my first appearance in a lawcourt, at the age of seventy; I am therefore simply a stranger to the manner of speaking here. Just as if I were really a stranger, you would certainly excuse me if I spoke in that dialect and manner in which I had been 18 brought up, so too my present request seems a just one, for you to pay no attention to my manner of speech—be it better or worse—but to concentrate your attention on whether what I say is just or not, for the excellence of a judge lies in this, as that of a speaker lies in telling the truth.

It is right for me, gentlemen, to defend myself first against the first lying accusations made against me and my first accusers, and then against the later accusations and the later accusers. There have been many who b have accused me to you for many years now, and none of their accusations are true. These I fear much more than I fear Anytus and his friends, though they too are formidable. These earlier ones, however, are more so, gentlemen; they got hold of most of you from childhood, persuaded you and accused me quite falsely, saying that there is a man called Socrates, a wise man, a student of all things in the sky and below the earth, who c makes the worse argument the stronger. Those who spread that rumor, gentlemen, are my dangerous accusers, for their hearers believe that those who study these things do not even believe in the gods. Moreover, these accusers are numerous, and have been at it a long time; also, they spoke to you at an age when you would most readily believe them, some of you being children and adolescents, and they won their case by default, as there was no defense.

What is most absurd in all this is that one cannot even know or mention their names unless one of them is a writer of comedies.[3] Those who maliciously d and slanderously persuaded you—who also, when persuaded themselves then persuaded others—all those are most difficult to deal with: one cannot bring one of them into court or refute him; one must simply fight with shadows, as it were, in making one's defense, and cross-examine when no one answers. I

Reprinted from *The Trial and Death of Socrates*, translated by G.M.A. Grube (Indianapolis: Hackett Publishing Company, 1975), by permission of the publisher.

1. [The word *apology* is a transliteration, not a translation, of the Greek *apologia* which means defense. There is certainly nothing apologetic about the speech.—G.M.A.G.]

2. [The bankers or money-changers had their counters in the marketplace. It seems that this was a favorite place for gossip.]

3. [This refers in particular to Aristophanes, whose comedy, *The Clouds*, produced in 425 B.C., ridiculed the (imaginary) school of Socrates.]

want you to realize too that my accusers are of two kinds: those who have accused me recently, and the old ones I mention; and to think that I must first defend myself against the latter, for you have also
e heard their accusations first, and to a much greater extent than the more recent.

Very well then. I must surely defend myself and
19 attempt to uproot from your minds in so short a time the slander that has resided there so long. I wish this may happen, if it is in any way better for you and me, and that my defense may be successful, but I think this is very difficult and I am fully aware of how difficult it is. Even so, let the matter proceed as the god may wish, but I must obey the law and make my defense.

Let us then take up the case from its beginning.
b What is the accusation from which arose the slander in which Meletus trusted when he wrote out the charge against me? What did they say when they slandered me? I must, as if they were my actual prose-cutors, read the affidavit they would have sworn. It goes something like this: Socrates is guilty of wrongdo-ing in that he busies himself studying things in the sky and below the earth; he makes the worse into the stronger argument, and he teaches these same things
c to others. You have seen this yourself in the comedy of Aristophanes, a Socrates swinging about there, say-ing he was walking on air and talking a lot of other nonsense about things of which I know nothing at all. I do not speak in contempt of such knowledge, if someone is wise in these things—lest Meletus bring more cases against me—but, gentlemen, I have no part in it, and on this point I call upon the majority of you as witnesses. I think it right that all those of
d you who have heard me conversing, and many of you have, should tell each other if anyone of you has ever heard me discussing such subjects to any extent at all. From this you will learn that the other things said about me by the majority are of the same kind.

Not one of them is true. And if you have heard from anyone that I undertake to teach people and
e charge a fee for it, that is not true either. Yet I think it a fine thing to be able to teach people as Gorgias of Leontini does, and Prodicus of Ceos, and Hippias of Elis.[4] Each of these men can go to any city and

persuade the young, who can keep company with anyone of their own fellow citizens they want without paying, to leave the company of these, to join with 20 themselves, pay them a fee, and be grateful to them besides. Indeed, I learned that there is another wise man from Paros who is visiting us, for I met a man who has spent more money on Sophists than every-body else put together, Callias, the son of Hipponicus. So I asked him—he has two sons—"Callias," I said, "if your sons were colts or calves, we could find and engage a supervisor for them who would make them excel in their proper qualities, some horse breeder b or farmer. Now since they are men, whom do you have in mind to supervise them? Who is an expert in this kind of excellence, the human and social kind? I think you must have given thought to this since you have sons. Is there such a person," I asked, "or is there not?" "Certainly there is," he said. "Who is he?" I asked, "What is his name, where is he from? and what is his fee?" "His name, Socrates, is Evenus, he comes from Paros, and his fee is five minas." I thought c Evenus a happy man, if he really possesses this art, and teaches for so moderate a fee. Certainly I would pride and preen myself if I had this knowledge, but I do not have it, gentlemen.

One of you might perhaps interrupt me and say: "But Socrates, what is your occupation? From where have these slanders come? For surely if you did not busy yourself with something out of the common, all these rumors and talk would not have arisen unless you did something other than most people. Tell us what it is, that we may not speak inadvisedly about d you." Anyone who says that seems to be right, and I will try to show you what has caused this reputation and slander. Listen then. Perhaps some of you will think I am jesting, but be sure that all that I shall say is true. What has caused my reputation is none other than a certain kind of wisdom. What kind of wisdom? Human wisdom, perhaps. It may be that I really pos-sess this, while those whom I mentioned just now are

---

4. [These were all well-known Sophists. Gorgias, after whom Plato named one of his dialogues, was a celebrated

rhetorician and teacher of rhetoric. He came to Athens in 427 B.C., and his rhetorical tricks took the city by storm. Two dialogues, the authenticity of which has been doubted, are named after Hippias, whose knowledge was encyclope-dic. Prodicus was known for his insistence on the precise meaning of words. Both he and Hippias are characters in the *Protagoras* (named after another famous Sophist).]

e wise with a wisdom more than human; else I cannot explain it, for I certainly do not possess it, and whoever says I do is lying and speaks to slander me. Do not create a disturbance, gentlemen, even if you think I am boasting, for the story I shall tell does not originate with me, but I will refer you to a trustworthy source. I shall call upon the god at Delphi as witness to the

21 existence and nature of my wisdom, if it be such. You know Chaerephon. He was my friend from youth, and the friend of most of you, as he shared your exile and your return. You surely know the kind of man he was, how impulsive in any course of action. He went to Delphi at one time and ventured to ask the oracle—as I say, gentlemen, do not create a disturbance—he asked if any man was wiser than I, and the Pythian replied that no one was wiser. Chaerephon is dead, but his brother will testify to you about this.

b Consider that I tell you this because I would inform you about the origin of the slander. When I heard of this reply I asked myself: "Whatever does the god mean? What is his riddle? I am very conscious that I am not wise at all; what then does he mean by saying that I am the wisest? For surely he does not lie; it is not legitimate for him to do so." For a long time I was at a loss as to his meaning; then I very reluctantly turned to some such investigation as this;

c I went to one of those reputed wise, thinking that there, if anywhere, I could refute the oracle and say to it: "This man is wiser than I, but you said I was." Then, when I examined this man—there is no need for me to tell you his name, he was one of our public men—my experience was something like this: I thought that he appeared wise to many people and especially to himself, but he was not. I then tried to

d show him that he thought himself wise, but that he was not. As a result he came to dislike me, and so did many of the bystanders. So I withdrew and thought to myself: "I am wiser than this man; it is likely that neither of us knows anything worthwhile, but he thinks he knows something when he does not, whereas when I do not know, neither do I think I know; so I am likely to be wiser than he to this small extent, that I do not think I know what I do not know." After this I approached another man, one of those

e thought to be wiser than he, and I thought the same thing, and so I came to be disliked both by him and by many others.

After that I proceeded systematically. I realized, to my sorrow and alarm, that I was getting unpopular, but I thought that I must attach the greatest importance to the god's oracle, so I must go to all those who had any reputation for knowledge to examine its meaning. And by the dog,[5] gentlemen of the jury— 22 for I must tell you the truth—I experienced something like this: in my investigation in the service of the god I found that those who had the highest reputation were nearly the most deficient, while those who were thought to be inferior were more knowledgeable. I must give you an account of my journeyings as if they were labors I had undertaken to prove the oracle irrefutable. After the politicians, I went to the poets, the writers of tragedies and dithyrambs and the others, *b* intending in their case to catch myself being more ignorant than they. So I took up those poems with which they seemed to have taken most trouble and asked them what they meant, in order that I might at the same time learn something from them. I am ashamed to tell you the truth, gentlemen, but I must. Almost all the bystanders might have explained the poems better than their authors could. I soon realized *c* that poets do not compose their poems with knowledge, but by some inborn talent and by inspiration, like seers and prophets who also say many fine things without any understanding of what they say. The poets seemed to me to have had a similar experience. At the same time I saw that, because of their poetry, they thought themselves very wise men in other respects, which they were not. So there again I withdrew, thinking that I had the same advantage over them as I had over the politicians.

Finally I went to the craftsmen, for I was conscious of knowing practically nothing, and I knew that I *d* would find that they had knowledge of many fine things. In this I was not mistaken; they knew things I did not know, and to that extent they were wiser than I. But, gentlemen of the jury, the good craftsmen seemed to me to have the same fault as the poets: each of them, because of his success at his craft, thought himself very wise in other most important pursuits, and this error of theirs overshadowed the *e* wisdom they had, so that I asked myself, on behalf of the oracle, whether I should prefer to be as I am,

5. [A curious oath, occasionally used by Socrates, it appears in a longer form in the *Gorgias* (482b) as "by the dog, the god of the Egyptians."]

with neither their wisdom nor their ignorance, or to have both. The answer I gave myself and the oracle was that it was to my advantage to be as I am.

As a result of this investigation, gentlemen of the jury, I acquired much unpopularity, of a kind that is hard to deal with and is a heavy burden; many slanders came from these people and a reputation for wisdom, for in each case the bystanders thought that I myself possessed the wisdom that I proved that my interlocutor did not have. What is probable, gentlemen, is that in fact the god is wise and that his oracular response meant that human wisdom is worth little or nothing, and that when he says this man, Socrates, he is using my name as an example, as if he said: "This man among you, mortals, is wisest who, like Socrates, understands that his wisdom is worthless." So even now I continue this investigation as the god bade me— and I go around seeking out anyone, citizen or stranger, whom I think wise. Then if I do not think he is, I come to the assistance of the god and show him that he is not wise. Because of this occupation, I do not have the leisure to engage in public affairs to any extent, nor indeed to look after my own, but I live in great poverty because of my service to the god.

Furthermore, the young men who follow me around of their own free will, those who have most leisure, the sons of the very rich, take pleasure in hearing people questioned; they themselves often imitate me and try to question others. I think they find an abundance of men who believe they have some knowledge but know little or nothing. The result is that those whom they question are angry, not with themselves but with me. They say: "That man Socrates is a pestilential fellow who corrupts the young." If one asks them what he does and what he teaches to corrupt them, they are silent, as they do not know, but, so as not to appear at a loss, they mention those accusations that are available against all philosophers, about "things in the sky and things below the earth," about "not believing in the gods" and "making the worse the stronger argument"; they would not want to tell the truth, I'm sure, that they have been proved to lay claim to knowledge when they know nothing. These people are ambitious, violent and numerous; they are continually and convincingly talking about me; they have been filling your ears for a long time with vehement slanders against me. From them Meletus attacked me, and Anytus and Lycon, Meletus

being vexed on behalf of the poets, Anytus on behalf of the craftsmen and the politicians, Lycon on behalf of the orators, so that, as I started out by saying, I should be surprised if I could rid you of so much slander in so short a time. That, gentlemen of the jury, is the truth for you. I have hidden or disguised nothing. I know well enough that this very conduct makes me unpopular, and this is proof that what I say is true, that such is the slander against me, and that such are its causes. If you look into this either now or later, this is what you will find.

Let this suffice as a defense against the charges of my earlier accusers. After this I shall try to defend myself against Meletus, that good and patriotic man, as he says he is, and my later accusers. As these are a different lot of accusers, let us again take up their sworn deposition. It goes something like this: Socrates is guilty of corrupting the young and of not believing in the gods in whom the city believes, but in other new spiritual things? Such is their charge. Let us examine it point by point.

He says that I am guilty of corrupting the young, but I say that Meletus is guilty of dealing frivolously with serious matters, of irresponsibly bringing people into court, and of professing to be seriously concerned with things about none of which he has ever cared, and I shall try to prove that this is so. Come here and tell me, Meletus. Surely you consider it of the greatest importance that our young men be as good as possible?[6]—Indeed I do.

Come then, tell the jury who improves them. You obviously know, in view of your concern. You say you have discovered the one who corrupts them, namely me, and you bring me here and accuse me to the jury. Come, inform the jury and tell them who it is. You see, Meletus, that you are silent and know not what to say. Does this not seem shameful to you and a sufficient proof of what I say, that you have not been concerned with any of this? Tell me, my good sir, who improves our young men?—The laws.

That is not what I am asking, but what person who has knowledge of the laws to begin with?—These jurymen, Socrates.

6. [Socrates here drops into his usual method of discussion by question and answer. This, no doubt, is what Plato had in mind, at least in part, when he made him ask the indulgence of the jury if he spoke "in his usual manner."]

How do you mean, Meletus? Are these able to educate the young and improve them?—Certainly.

All of them, or some but not others?—All of them.

Very good, by Hera. You mention a great abun-25 dance of benefactors. But what about the audience? Do they improve the young or not?—They do, too.

What about the members of Council?—The Councillors, also.

But, Meletus, what about the assembly? Do members of the assembly corrupt the young, or do they all improve them?—They improve them.

All the Athenians, it seems, make the young into fine good men, except me, and I alone corrupt them. Is that what you mean?—That is most definitely what I mean.

b   You condemn me to a great misfortune. Tell me: does this also apply to horses do you think? That all men improve them and one individual corrupts them? Or is quite the contrary true, one individual is able to improve them, or very few, namely, the horse breeders, whereas the majority, if they have horses and use them, corrupt them? Is that not the case, Meletus, both with horses and all other animals? Of course it is, whether you and Anytus say so or not. It would be a very happy state of affairs if only one person corrupted our youth, while the others improved them.

c   You have made it sufficiently obvious, Meletus, that you have never had any concern for our youth; you show your indifference clearly; that you have given no thought to the subjects about which you bring me to trial.

And by Zeus, Meletus, tell us also whether it is better for a man to live among good or wicked fellow citizens. Answer, my good man, for I am not asking a difficult question. Do not the wicked do some harm to those who are ever closest to them, whereas good people benefit them?—Certainly.

d   And does the man exist who would rather be harmed than benefited by his associates? Answer, my good sir, for the law orders you to answer. Is there any man who wants to be harmed?—Of course not.

Come now, do you accuse me here of corrupting the young and making them worse deliberately or unwillingly?—Deliberately.

What fellows, Meletus? Are you so much wiser at your age than I am at mine that you understand that wicked people always do some harm to their closest e neighbors while good people do them good, but I have reached such a pitch of ignorance that I do not realize this, namely that if I make one of my associates wicked I run the risk of being harmed by him so that I do such a great evil deliberately, as you say? I do not believe you, Meletus, and I do not think anyone else will. Either I do not corrupt the young or, if I 26 do, it is unwillingly, and you are lying in either case. Now if I corrupt them unwillingly, the law does not require you to bring people to court for such unwilling wrongdoings, but to get hold of them privately, to instruct them and exhort them; for clearly, if I learn better, I shall cease to do what I am doing unwillingly. You, however, have avoided my company and were unwilling to instruct me, but you bring me here, where the law requires one to bring those who are in need of punishment, not of instruction.

And so, gentlemen of the jury, what I said is clearly true: Meletus has never been at all concerned with b these matters. Nonetheless tell us, Meletus, how you say that I corrupt the young; or is it obvious from your deposition that it is by teaching them not to believe in the gods in whom the city believes but in other new spiritual things? Is this not what you say I teach and so corrupt them?—That is most certainly what I do say.

Then by those very gods about whom we are talking, Meletus, make this clearer to me and to the jury: c I cannot be sure whether you mean that I teach the belief that there are some gods—and therefore I myself believe that there are gods and am not altogether an atheist, nor am I guilty of that—not, however, the gods in whom the city believes, but others, and that this is the charge against me, that they are others. Or whether you mean that I do not believe in gods at all, and that this is what I teach to others.— This is what I mean, that you do not believe in gods at all.

You are a strange fellow, Meletus. Why do you say d this? Do I not believe, as other men do, that the sun and the moon are gods?—No, by Zeus, jurymen, for he says that the sun is stone, and the moon earth.

My dear Meletus, do you think you are prosecuting Anaxagoras? Are you so contemptuous of the jury and think them so ignorant of letters as not to know that the books of Anaxagoras[7] of Clazomenae are full of those theories, and further, that the young men learn e from me what they can buy from time to time for a drachma, at most, in the bookshops, and ridicule Socrates if he pretends that these theories are his own, especially as they are so absurd? Is that, by Zeus, what you think of me, Meletus, that I do not believe that there are any gods? — That is what I say, that you do not believe in the gods at all.

You cannot be believed, Meletus, even, I think, by yourself. The man appears to me, gentlemen of the jury, highly insolent and uncontrolled. He seems to 27 have made this deposition out of insolence, violence and youthful zeal. He is like one who composed a riddle and is trying it out: "Will the wise Socrates realize that I am jesting and contradicting myself, or shall I deceive him and others?" I think he contradicts himself in the affidavit, as if he said: "Socrates is guilty of not believing in gods but believing in gods," and surely that is the part of a jester!

Examine with me, gentlemen, how he appears to b contradict himself, and you, Meletus, answer us. Remember, gentlemen, what I asked you when I began, not to create a disturbance if I proceed in my usual manner.

Does any man, Meletus, believe in human activities who does not believe in humans? Make him answer, and not again and again create a disturbance. Does any man who does not believe in horses believe in horsemen's activities? Or in flute-playing activities but not in flute-players? No, my good sir, no man c could. If you are not willing to answer, I will tell you and the jury. Answer the next question, however. Does any man believe in spiritual activities who does not believe in spirits? — No one.

Thank you for answering, if reluctantly, when the jury made you. Now you say that I believe in spiritual things and teach about them, whether new or old, but at any rate spiritual things according to what you say, and to this you have sworn in your deposition. But if I believe in spiritual things I must quite inevitably

believe in spirits. Is that not so? It is indeed. I shall assume that you agree, as you do not answer. Do we d not believe spirits to be either gods or the children of gods? Yes or no? — Of course.

Then since I do believe in spirits, as you admit, if spirits are gods, this is what I mean when I say you speak in riddles and in jest, as you state that I do not believe in gods and then again that I do, since I do believe in spirits. If on the other hand the spirits are children of the gods, bastard children of the gods by nymphs or some other mothers, as they are said to be, what man would believe children of the gods to exist, but not gods? That would be just as absurd as to believe the young of horses and asses, namely mules, to exist, but e not to believe in the existence of horses and asses. You must have made this deposition, Meletus, either to test us or because you were at a loss to find any true wrongdoing of which to accuse me. There is no way in which you could persuade anyone of even small intelligence that it is possible for one and the same man to believe in spiritual but not also in divine things, and then again 28 for that same man to believe neither in spirits nor in gods nor in heroes.

I do not think, gentlemen of the jury, that it requires a prolonged defense to prove that I am not guilty of the charges in Meletus' deposition, but this is sufficient. On the other hand, you know that what I said earlier is true, that I am very unpopular with many people. This will be my undoing, if I am undone, not Meletus or Anytus but the slanders and envy of many people. This has destroyed many other good b men and will, I think, continue to do so. There is no danger that it will stop at me.

Someone might say: "Are you not ashamed, Socrates, to have followed the kind of occupation that has led to your being now in danger of death?" However, I should be right to reply to him: "You are wrong, sir, if you think that a man who is any good at all should take into account the risk of life or death; he should look to this only in his actions, whether what he does is right or wrong, whether he is acting like a good or a bad man." According to your view, all c the heroes who died at Troy were inferior people, especially the son of Thetis who was so contemptuous of danger compared with disgrace.[8] When he was

7. [Anaxagoras of Clazomenae, born about the beginning of the fifth century, came to Athens as a young man and spent time in the pursuit of natural philosophy. He claimed that the universe was directed by Nous (Mind), and that matter was indestructible but always combining in various ways. He left Athens after being prosecuted for impiety.]

8. [The scene between Thetis and Achilles is from the *Iliad* (18, 94ff.).]

eager to kill Hector, his goddess mother warned him, as I believe, in some such words as these: "My child, if you avenge the death of your comrade, Patroclus, and you kill Hector, you will die yourself, for your death is to follow immediately after Hector's." Hearing this, he despised death and danger and was much *d* more afraid to live a coward who did not avenge his friends. "Let me die at once," he said, "when once I have given the wrongdoer his deserts, rather than remain here, a laughingstock by the curved ships, a burden upon the earth." Do you think he gave thought to death and danger?

This is the truth of the matter, gentlemen of the jury: wherever a man has taken a position that he believes to be best, or has been placed by his commander, there he must I think remain and face danger, without a thought for death or anything else, *e* rather than disgrace. It would have been a dreadful way to behave, gentlemen of the jury, if, at Potidaea, Amphipolis and Delium, I had, at the risk of death, like anyone else, remained at my post where those you had elected to command had ordered me, and then, when the god ordered me, as I thought and believed, to live the life of a philosopher, to examine 29 myself and others, I had abandoned my post for fear of death or anything else. That would have been a dreadful thing, and then I might truly have justly been brought here for not believing that there are gods, disobeying the oracle, fearing death, and thinking I was wise when I was not. To fear death, gentlemen, is no other than to think oneself wise when one is not, to think one knows what one does not know. No one knows whether death may not be the greatest of all blessings for a man, yet men fear it as if they knew that it is the greatest of evils. And surely it is *b* the most blameworthy ignorance to believe that one knows what one does not know. It is perhaps on this point and in this respect, gentlemen, that I differ from the majority of men, and if I were to claim that I am wiser than anyone in anything, it would be in this, that, as I have no adequate knowledge of things in the underworld, so I do not think I have. I do know, however, that it is wicked and shameful to do wrong, to disobey one's superior, be he god or man. I shall never fear or avoid things of which I do not know, *c* whether they may not be good rather than things that I know to be bad. Even if you acquitted me now and did not believe Anytus, who said to you that either I should not have been brought here in the first place, or that now I am here, you cannot avoid executing me, for if I should be acquitted, your sons would practice the teachings of Socrates and all be thoroughly corrupted; if you said to me in this regard: "Socrates, we do not believe Anytus now; we acquit you, but only on condition that you spend no more time on this investigation and do not practice philosophy, and if you are caught doing so you will die;" if, *d* as I say, you were to acquit me on those terms, I would say to you: "Gentlemen of the jury, I am grateful and I am your friend, but I will obey the god rather than you, and as long as I draw breath and am able, I shall not cease to practice philosophy, to exhort you and in my usual way to point out to any one of you whom I happen to meet: Good Sir, you are an Athenian, a citizen of the greatest city with the greatest reputation for both wisdom and power; are you not ashamed of *e* your eagerness to possess as much wealth, reputation and honors as possible, while you do not care for nor give thought to wisdom or truth, or the best possible state of your soul?" Then, if one of you disputes this and says he does care, I shall not let him go at once or leave him, but I shall question him, examine him and test him, and if I do not think he has attained the goodness that he says he has, I shall reproach him because he attaches little importance to the most 30 important things and greater importance to inferior things. I shall treat in this way anyone I happen to meet, young and old, citizen and stranger, and more so the citizens because you are more kindred to me. Be sure that this is what the god orders me to do, and I think there is no greater blessing for the city than my service to the god. For I go around doing nothing but persuading both young and old among you not to care for your body or your wealth in preference to or as strongly as for the best possible state of *b* your soul, as I say to you: "Wealth does not bring about excellence, but excellence makes wealth and everything else good for men, both individually and collectively."

Now if by saying this I corrupt the young, this advice must be harmful, but if anyone says that I give different advice, he is talking nonsense. On this point I would say to you, gentlemen of the jury: "Whether you believe Anytus or not, whether you acquit me or not, do so on the understanding that this is my course *c* of action, even if I am to face death many times."

Do not create a disturbance, gentlemen, but abide by my request not to cry out at what I say but to listen, for I think it will be to your advantage to listen, and I am about to say other things at which you will perhaps cry out. By no means do this. Be sure that if you kill the sort of man I say I am, you will not harm me more than yourselves. Neither Meletus nor *d* Anytus can harm me in any way; he could not harm me, for I do not think it is permitted that a better man be harmed by a worse; certainly he might kill me, or perhaps banish or disfranchise me, which he and maybe others think to be great harm, but I do not think so. I think he is doing himself much greater harm doing what he is doing now, attempting to have a man executed unjustly. Indeed, gentlemen of the jury, I am far from making a defense now on my own behalf, as might be thought, but on yours, to prevent *e* you from wrongdoing by mistreating the god's gift to you by condemning me; for if you kill me you will not easily find another like me. I was attached to this city by the god—though it seems a ridiculous thing to say—as upon a great and noble horse which was somewhat sluggish because of its size and needed to be stirred up by a kind of gadfly. It is to fulfilll some such function that I believe the god has placed me in the city. I never cease to rouse each and every one *31* of you, to persuade and reproach you all day long and everywhere I find myself in your company.

Another such man will not easily come to be among you, gentlemen, and if you believe me you will spare me. You might easily be annoyed with me as people are when they are aroused from a doze, and strike out at me; if convinced by Anytus you could easily kill me, and then you could sleep on for the rest of your days, unless the god, in his care for you, sent you someone else. That I am the kind of person to be a gift of the god to the city you might realize from *b* the fact that it does not seem like human nature for me to have neglected all my own affairs and to have tolerated this neglect now for so many years while I was always concerned with you, approaching each one of you like a father or an elder brother to persuade you to care for virtue. Now if I profited from this by charging a fee for my advice, there would be some sense to it, but you can see for yourselves that, for all their shameless accusations, my accusers have not *c* been able in their impudence to bring forward a witness to say that I have ever received a fee or ever

asked for one. I, on the other hand, have a convincing witness that I speak the truth, my poverty.

It may seem strange that while I go around and give this advice privately and interfere in private affairs, I do not venture to go to the assembly and there advise the city. You have heard me give the reason for this in many places. I have a divine or spiritual sign which Meletus has ridiculed in his deposition. This began *d* when I was a child. It is a voice, and whenever it speaks it turns me away from something I am about to do, but it never encourages me to do anything. This is what has prevented me from taking part in public affairs, and I think it was quite right to prevent me. Be sure, gentlemen of the jury, that if I had long ago attempted to take part in politics, I should have died long ago, and benefited neither you nor myself. *e* Do not be angry with me for speaking the truth; no man will survive who genuinely opposes you or any other crowd and prevents the occurrence of many unjust and illegal happenings in the city. A man who *32* really fights for justice must lead a private, not a public, life if he is to survive for even a short time. ◄

I shall give you great proofs of this, not words but what you esteem, deeds. Listen to what happened to me, that you may know that I will not yield to any man contrary to what is right, for fear of death, even if I should die at once for not yielding. The things I shall tell you are commonplace and smack of the lawcourts, but they are true. I have never held any *b* other office in the city, but I served as a member of the Council, and our tribe Antiochis was presiding at the time when you wanted to try as a body the ten generals who had failed to pick up the survivors of the naval battle.[9] This was illegal, as you all recognized later. I was the only member of the presiding committee to oppose your doing something contrary to the laws, and I voted against it. The orators were

---

9. [This was the battle of Arginusae (south of Lesbos) in 406 B.C., the last Athenian victory of the war. A violent storm prevented the Athenian generals from rescuing their survivors. For this they were tried in Athens and sentenced to death by the assembly. They were tried in a body, and it is this to which Socrates objected in the Council's presiding committee which prepared the business of the assembly. He obstinately persisted in his opposition, in which he stood alone, and was overruled by the majority. Six generals who were in Athens were executed.]

ready to prosecute me and take me away, and your shouts were egging them on, but I thought I should c run any risk on the side of law and justice rather than join you, for fear of prison or death, when you were engaged in an unjust course.

This happened when the city was still a democracy. When the oligarchy was established, the Thirty[10] summoned me to the Hall, along with four others, and ordered us to bring Leon from Salamis, that he might be executed. They gave many such orders to many d people, in order to implicate as many as possible in their guilt. Then I showed again, not in words but in action, that, if it were not rather vulgar to say so, death is something I couldn't care less about, but that my whole concern is not to do anything unjust or impious. That government, powerful as it was, did not frighten me into any wrongdoing. When we left the Hall, the other four went to Salamis and brought in Leon, but I went home. I might have been put to e death for this, had not the government fallen shortly afterwards. There are many who will witness to these events.

Do you think I would have survived all these years if I were engaged in public affairs and, acting as a good man must, came to the help of justice and considered this the most important thing? Far from it, gentlemen of the jury, nor would any other man. 33 Throughout my life, in any public activity I may have engaged in, I am the same man as I am in private life. I have never come to an agreement with anyone to act unjustly, neither with anyone else nor with any one of those who they slanderously say are my pupils. I have never been anyone's teacher. If anyone, young or old, desires to listen to me when I am talking and dealing with my own concerns, I have never begrudged this to anyone, but I do not converse when b I receive a fee and not when I do not. I am equally ready to question the rich and the poor if anyone is willing to answer my questions and listen to what I say. And I cannot justly be held responsible for the good or bad conduct of these people, as I never promised to teach them anything and have not done so. If anyone says that he has learned anything from me,

or that he heard anything privately that the others did not hear, be assured that he is not telling the truth.

Why then do some people enjoy spending consid- c erable time in my company? You have heard why, gentlemen of the jury, I have told you the whole truth. They enjoy hearing those being questioned who think they are wise, but are not. And this is not unpleasant. To do this has, as I say, been enjoined upon me by the god, by means of oracles and dreams, and in every other way that a divine manifestation has ever ordered a man to do anything. This is true, gentlemen, and can easily be established.

If I corrupt some young men and have corrupted d others, then surely some of them who have grown older and realized that I gave them bad advice when they were young should now themselves come up here to accuse me and avenge themselves. If they were unwilling to do so themselves, then some of their kindred, their fathers or brothers or other relations should recall it now if their family had been harmed by me. I see many of these present here, first Crito, my contemporary and fellow demesman, the e father of Critobulus here; next Lysanias of Sphettus, the father of Aeschines here; also Antiphon the Cephisian, the father of Epigenes; and others whose brothers spent their time in this way; Nicostratus, the son of Theozotides, brother of Theodotus, and Theodotus has died so he could not influence him; Paralius here, son of Demodocus, whose brother was Theages; 34 there is Adeimantus, son of Ariston, brother of Plato here; Acantidorus, brother of Apollodorus here.

I could mention many others, some one of whom surely Meletus should have brought in as witness in his own speech. If he forgot to do so, then let him do it now; I will yield time if he has anything of the kind to say. You will find quite the contrary, gentlemen. These men are all ready to come to the help of the corruptor, the man who has harmed their b kindred, as Meletus and Anytus say. Now those who were corrupted might well have reason to help me, but the uncorrupted, their kindred who are older men, have no reason to help me except the right and proper one, that they know that Meletus is lying and that I am telling the truth.

Very well, gentlemen of the jury. This, and maybe other similar things, is what I have to say in my defense. Perhaps one of you might be angry as he c recalls that when he himself stood trial on a less

---

10. [This was the harsh oligarchy that was set up after the final defeat of Athens in 404 B.C. and that ruled Athens for some nine months in 404–403 before the democracy was restored.]

dangerous charge, he begged and implored the jury with many tears, that he brought his children and many of his friends and family into court to arouse as much pity as he could, but that I do none of these things, even though I may seem to be running the d ultimate risk. Thinking of this, he might feel resentful toward me and, angry about this, cast his vote in anger. If there is such a one among you—I do not deem there is, but if there is—I think it would be right to say in reply: My good sir, I too have a household and, in Homer's phrase, I am not born "from oak or rock" but from men, so that I have a family, indeed three sons, gentlemen of the jury, of whom one is an adolescent while two are children. Nevertheless, I will not beg you to acquit me by bringing them here. Why do I do none of these things? Not through e arrogance, gentlemen, nor through lack of respect for you. Whether I am brave in the face of death is another matter, but with regard to my reputation and yours and that of the whole city, it does not seem right to me to do these things, especially at my age and with my reputation. For it is generally believed, whether it be true or false, that in certain respects 35 Socrates is superior to the majority of men. Now if those of you who are considered superior, be it in wisdom or courage or whatever other virtue makes them so, are seen behaving like that, it would be a disgrace. Yet I have often seen them do this sort of thing when standing trial, men who are thought to be somebody, doing amazing things as if they thought it a terrible thing to die, and as if they were to be immortal if you did not execute them. I think these b men bring shame upon the city so that a stranger, too, would assume that those who are outstanding in virtue among the Athenians, whom they themselves select from themselves to fill offices of state and receive other honors, are in no way better than women. You should not act like that, gentlemen of the jury, those of you who have any reputation at all, and if we do, you should not allow it. You should make it very clear that you will more readily convict a man who performs these pitiful dramatics in court and so makes the city a laughingstock, than a man who keeps quiet.

Quite apart from the question of reputation, gentle-c men, I do not think it right to supplicate the jury and to be acquitted because of this, but to teach and persuade them. It is not the purpose of a juryman's office to give justice as a favor to whoever seems good to him, but to judge according to law, and this he has sworn to do. We should not accustom you to perjure yourselves, nor should you make a habit of it. This is irreverent conduct for either of us.

Do not deem it right for me, gentlemen of the jury, that I should act towards you in a way that I do d not consider to be good or just or pious, especially, by Zeus, as I am being prosecuted by Meletus here for impiety; clearly, if I convinced you by my supplication to do violence to your oath of office, I would be teaching you not to believe that there are gods, and my defense would convict me of not believing in them. This is far from being the case, gentlemen, for I do believe in them as none of my accusers do. I leave it to you and the god to judge me in the way that will be best for me and for you.

*[The jury now gives its verdict of guilty, and
Meletus asks for the penalty of death.]*

There are many other reasons for my not being e angry with you for convicting me, gentlemen of the jury, and what happened was not unexpected. I am 36 much more surprised at the number of votes cast on each side for I did not think the decision would be by so few votes but by a great many. As it is, a switch of only thirty votes would have acquitted me. I think myself that I have been cleared on Meletus' charges, b and not only this, but it is clear to all that, if Anytus and Lycon had not joined him in accusing me, he would have been fined a thousand drachmas for not receiving a fifth of the votes.

He assesses the penalty at death. So be it. What counter-assessment should I propose to you, gentlemen of the jury? Clearly it should be a penalty I deserve, and what do I deserve to suffer or to pay because I have deliberately not led a quiet life but have neglected what occupies most people: wealth, household affairs, the position of general or public orator or the other offices, the political clubs and factions that exist in the city? I thought myself too honest to survive if I occupied myself with those c things. I did not follow that path that would have made me of no use either to you or to myself, but I went to each of you privately and conferred upon him what I say is the greatest benefit, by trying to persuade him not to care for any of his belongings before caring that he himself should be as good and as wise as possible, not to care for the city's possessions more than for the city itself, and to care for other *d* things in the same way. What do I deserve for being such a man? Some good, gentlemen of the jury, if I must truly make an assessment according to my deserts, and something suitable. What is suitable for a poor benefactor who needs leisure to exhort you? Nothing is more suitable, gentlemen, than for such a man to be fed in the Prytaneum[11] much more suitable for him than for any one of you who has won a victory at Olympia with a pair or a team of *e* horses. The Olympian victor makes you think yourself happy; I make you be happy. Besides, he does not need food, but I do. So if I must make a just assessment *37* of what I deserve, I assess it as this: free meals in the Prytaneum.

When I say this you may think, as when I spoke of appeals to pity and entreaties, that I speak arrogantly, but that is not the case, gentlemen of the jury; rather it is like this: I am convinced that I never willingly wrong anyone, but I am not convincing you of this, for we have talked together but a short time. *b* If it were the law with us, as it is elsewhere, that a trial for life should not last one but many days, you would be convinced, but now it is not easy to dispel great slanders in a short time. Since I am convinced that I wrong no one, I am not likely to wrong myself, to say that I deserve some evil and to make some such assessment against myself. What should I fear? That I should suffer the penalty Meletus has assessed against me, of which I say I do not know whether it is good or bad? Am I then to choose in preference to this something that I know very well to be an evil *c* and assess the penalty at that? Imprisonment? Why should I live in prison, always subjected to the ruling magistrates, the Eleven? A fine, and imprisonment until I pay it? That would be the same thing for me, as I have no money. Exile? for perhaps you might accept that assessment.

I should have to be inordinately fond of life, gentlemen of the jury, to be so unreasonable as to suppose that other men will easily tolerate my company and *d* conversation when you, my fellow citizens, have been

unable to endure them, but found them a burden and resented them so that you are now seeking to get rid of them. Far from it, gentlemen. It would be a fine life at my age to be driven out of one city after another, for I know very well that wherever I go the young men will listen to my talk as they do here. If *e* I drive them away, they will themselves persuade their elders to drive me out; if I do not drive them away, their fathers and relations will drive me out on their behalf.

Perhaps someone might say: But Socrates, if you leave us will you not be able to live quietly, without talking? Now this is the most difficult point on which to convince some of you. If I say that it is impossible *38* for me to keep quiet because that means disobeying the god, you will not believe me and will think I am being ironical. On the other hand, if I say that it is the greatest good for a man to discuss virtue every day and those other things about which you hear me conversing and testing myself and others, for the unexamined life is not worth living for men, you will believe me even less.

What I say is true, gentlemen, but it is not easy to convince you. At the same time, I am not accustomed *b* to think that I deserve any penalty. If I had money, I would assess the penalty at the amount I could pay, for that would not hurt me, but I have none, unless you are willing to set the penalty at the amount I can pay, and perhaps I could pay you one mina of silver.[12] So that is my assessment.

Plato here, gentlemen of the jury, and Crito and Critobulus and Apollodorus bid me put the penalty at thirty minae, and they will stand surety for the money. Well then, that is my assessment, and they will be sufficient guarantee of payment.

[The jury now votes again and sentences Socrates to death.]

It is for the sake of a short time, gentlemen of the *c* jury, that you will acquire the reputation and the guilt, in the eyes of those who want to denigrate the city, of having killed Socrates, a wise man, for they

---

11. [The Prytaneum was the magistrates' hall or town hall of Athens in which public entertainments were given, particularly to Olympian victors on their return home.]

12. [One mina was 100 drachmas, equivalent to, say, twenty-five dollars, though in purchasing power probably five times greater. In any case, a ridiculously small sum under the circumstances.]

who want to revile you will say that I am wise even if I am not. If you had waited but a little while, this would have happened of its own accord. You see my age, that I am already advanced in years and close d to death. I am saying this not to all of you but to those who condemned me to death, and to these same jurors I say: Perhaps you think that I was convicted for lack of such words as might have convinced you, if I thought I should say or do all I could to avoid my sentence. Far from it. I was convicted because I lacked not words but boldness and shamelessness and the willingness to say to you what you would most gladly have heard from me, lamentations and tears and my e saying and doing many things that I say are unworthy of me but that you are accustomed to hear from others. I did not think then that the danger I ran should make me do anything mean, nor do I now regret the nature of my defense. I would much rather die after this kind of defense than live after making the other kind. Neither I nor any other man should, 39 on trial or in war, contrive to avoid death at any cost. Indeed it is often obvious in battle that one could escape death by throwing away one's weapons and by turning to supplicate one's pursuers, and there are many ways to avoid death in every kind of danger if one will venture to do or say anything to avoid it. It is not difficult to avoid death, gentlemen of the jury, b it is much more difficult to avoid wickedness, for it runs faster than death. Slow and elderly as I am, I have been caught by the slower pursuer, whereas my accusers, being clever and sharp, have been caught by the quicker, wickedness. I leave you now, condemned to death by you, but they are condemned by truth to wickedness and injustice. So I maintain my assessment, and they maintain theirs. This perhaps had to happen, and I think it is as it should be.

c   Now I want to prophesy to those who convicted me, for I am at the point when men prophesy most, when they are about to die. I say gentlemen, to those who voted to kill me, that vengeance will come upon you immediately after my death, a vengeance much harder to bear than that which you took in killing me. You did this in the belief that you would avoid giving an account of your life, but I maintain that quite the opposite will happen to you. There will be d more people to test you, whom I now held back, but you did not notice it. They will be more difficult to deal with as they will be younger and you will resent them more. You are wrong if you believe that by killing people you will prevent anyone from reproaching you for not living in the right way. To escape such tests is neither possible nor good, but it is best and easiest not to discredit others but to prepare oneself to be as good as possible. With this prophecy to you who convicted me, I part from you.

I should be glad to discuss what has happened with e those who voted for my acquittal during the time that the officers of the court are busy and I do not yet have to depart to my death. So, gentlemen, stay with me awhile, for nothing prevents us from talking to each other while it is allowed. To you, as being my 40 friends, I want to show the meaning of what has occurred. A surprising thing has happened to me, judges—you I would rightly call judges. At all previous times my familiar prophetic power, my spiritual manifestation, frequently opposed me, even in small matters, when I was about to do something wrong, but now that, as you can see for yourselves, I was faced with what one might think, and what is generally thought to be, the worst of evils, my divine sign has not opposed me, either when I left home at dawn, b or when I came into court, or at any time that I was about to say something during my speech. Yet in other talks it often held me back in the middle of my speaking, but now it has opposed no word or deed of mine. What do I think is the reason for this? I will tell you. What has happened to me may well be a good thing, and those of us who believe death to be an evil are certainly mistaken. I have convincing proof c of this, for it is impossible that my familiar sign did not oppose me if I was not about to do what was right.

Let us reflect in this way, too, that there is good hope that death is a blessing, for it is one of two things: either the dead are nothing and have no perception of anything, or it is, as we are told, a change and a relocating for the soul from here to another place. If d it is complete lack of perception, like a dreamless sleep, then death would be a great advantage. For I think that if one had to pick out that night during which a man slept soundly and did not dream, put beside it the other nights and days of his life, and then see how many days and nights had been better and more pleasant than that night, not only a private person but the great king would find them easy to count compared with the other days and nights. If e death is like this I say it is an advantage, for all eternity

would then seem to be no more than a single night. If, on the other hand, death is a change from here to another place, and what we are told is true and all who have died are there, what greater blessing
41 could there be, gentlemen of the jury? If anyone arriving in Hades will have escaped from those who call themselves judges here, and will find those true judges who are said to sit in judgment there, Minos and Rhadamanthus and Aeacus and Triptolemus and the other demi-gods who have been upright in their own life, would that be a poor kind of change? Again, what would one of you give to keep company with Orpheus and Musaeus, Hesiod and Homer? I am willing to die many times if that is true. It would be
b a wonderful way for me to spend my time whenever I met Palamedes and Ajax, the son of Telamon, and any other of the men of old who died through an unjust conviction, to compare my experience with theirs. I think it would be pleasant. Most important, I could spend my time testing and examining people there, as I do here, as to who among them is wise, and who thinks he is, but is not.

What would one not give, gentlemen of the jury, for the opportunity to examine the man who led
c the great expedition against Troy, or Odysseus, or Sisyphus, and innumerable other men and women one could mention. It would be an extraordinary happiness to talk with them, to keep company with them and examine them. In any case, they would certainly not put one to death for doing so. They are happier there than we are here in other respects, and for the rest of time they are deathless, if indeed what we are told is true.

You too must be of good hope as regards death, gentlemen of the jury, and keep this one truth in mind, that a good man cannot be harmed either in d life or in death, and that his affairs are not neglected by the gods. What has happened to me now has not happened of itself, but it is clear to me that it was better for me to die now and to escape from trouble. That is why my divine sign did not oppose me at any point. So I am certainly not angry with those who convicted me, or with my accusers. Of course that was not their purpose when they accused and convicted me, but they thought they were hurting me, and for this they deserve blame. This much I ask e from them: when my sons grow up, avenge yourselves by causing them the same kind of grief that I caused you, if you think they care for money or anything else more than they care for virtue, or if they think they are somebody when they are nobody. Reproach them as I reproach you, that they do not care for the right things and think they are worthy when they are not worthy of anything. If you do this, I shall have 42 been justly treated by you, and my sons also.

Now the hour to part has come. I go to die, you go to live. Which of us goes to the better lot is known to no one, except the god.

Crito

43 SOCRATES: Why have you come so early, Crito? Or is it not still early?

CRITO: It certainly is.

S: How early?

C: Early dawn.

S: I am surprised that the warder was willing to listen to you.

C: He is quite friendly to me by now, Socrates. I have been here often and I have given him something.

S: Have you just come, or have you been here for some time?

C: A fair time.

b S: Then why did you not wake me right away but sit there in silence?

C: By Zeus no, Socrates. I would not myself want to be in distress and awake so long. I have been surprised to see you so peacefully asleep. It was on purpose that I did not wake you, so that you should spend your time most agreeably. Often in the past throughout my life, I have considered the way you live happy, and especially so now that you bear your present misfortune so easily and lightly.

S: It would not be fitting at my age to resent the fact that I must die now.

c C: Other men of your age are caught in such misfortunes, but their age does not prevent them resenting their fate.

S: That is so. Why have you come so early?

C: I bring bad news, Socrates, not for you, apparently, but for me and all your friends the news is bad and hard to bear. Indeed, I would count it among the hardest.

d S: What is it? Or has the ship arrived from Delos, at the arrival of which I must die?

C: It has not arrived yet, but it will, I believe, arrive today, according to a message some men brought from Sunium, where they left it. This makes it obvious that it will come today, and that your life must end tomorrow.

S: May it be for the best. If it so please the gods, so be it. However, I do not think it will arrive today.

C: What indication have you of this? 44

S: I will tell you. I must die the day after the ship arrives.

C: That is what those in authority say.

S: Then I do not think it will arrive on this coming day, but on the next. I take to witness of this a dream I had a little earlier during this night. It looks as if it was the right time for you not to wake me.

C: What was your dream?

S: I thought that a beautiful and comely woman dressed in white approached me. She called me and said: "Socrates, may you arrive at fertile Phthia[1] on b the third day."

C: A strange dream, Socrates.

S: But it seems clear enough to me, Crito.

C: Too clear it seems, my dear Socrates, but listen to me even now and be saved. If you die, it will not be a single misfortune for me. Not only will I be deprived of a friend, the like of whom I shall never find again, but many people who do not know you or me very well will think that I could have saved c you if I were willing to spend money, but that I did not care to do so. Surely there can be no worse reputation than to be thought to value money more highly than one's friends, for the majority will not believe that you yourself were not willing to leave prison while we were eager for you to do so.

S: My good Crito, why should we care so much

---

1. [A quotation from the ninth book of the *Iliad* (363). Achilles has rejected all the presents of Agamemnon for him to return to the battle, and threatens to go home. He says his ships will sail in the morning, and with good weather he might arrive on the third day "in fertile Phthia" (which is his home). The dream means, obviously, that on the third day Socrates' soul, after death, will find its home. As always, counting the first member of a series, the third day is the day after tomorrow.—G.M.A.G.]

Reprinted from *The Trial and Death of Socrates*, translated by G.M.A. Grube (Indianapolis: Hackett Publishing Company, 1975), by permission of the publisher.

for what the majority think? The most reasonable people, to whom one should pay more attention, will believe that things were done as they were done.

d   C: You see, Socrates, that one must also pay attention to the opinion of the majority. Your present situation makes clear that the majority can inflict not the least but pretty well the greatest evils if one is slandered among them.

S: Would that the majority could inflict the greatest evils, for they would then be capable of the greatest good, and that would be fine, but now they cannot do either. They cannot make a man either wise or foolish, but they inflict things haphazardly.

e   C: That may be so. But tell me this, Socrates, are you anticipating that I and your other friends would have trouble with the informers if you escape from here, as having stolen you away, and that we should be compelled to lose all our property or pay
45 heavy fines and suffer other punishment besides? If you have any such fear, forget it. We would be justified in running this risk to save you, and worse, if necessary. Do follow my advice, and do not act differently.

S: I do have these things in mind, Crito, and also many others.

C: Have no such fear. It is not much money that some people require to save you and get you out of here. Further, do you not see that those informers are cheap, and that not much money would be needed to deal with them? My money is available and is, I think,
b sufficient. If, because of your affection for me, you feel you should not spend any of mine, there are those strangers here ready to spend money. One of them, Simmias the Theban, has brought enough for this very purpose. Cebes, too, and a good many others. So, as I say, do not let this fear make you hesitate to save yourself, nor let what you said in court trouble you, that you would not know what to do with yourself
c if you left Athens, for you would be welcomed in many places to which you might go. If you want to go to Thessaly, I have friends there who will greatly appreciate you and keep you safe, so that no one in Thessaly will harm you.

Besides, Socrates, I do not think that what you are doing is just, to give up your life when you can save it, and to hasten your fate as your enemies would hasten it, and indeed have hastened it in their wish to destroy you. Moreover, I think you are betraying
d your sons by going away and leaving them, when you could bring them up and educate them. You thus show no concern for what their fate may be. They will probably have the usual fate of orphans. Either one should not have children, or one should share with them to the end the toil of upbringing and education. You seem to me to choose the easiest path, whereas one should choose the path a good and courageous man would choose, particularly when one claims throughout one's life to care for virtue.

I feel ashamed on your behalf and on behalf of us, *e* your friends, lest all that has happened to you be thought due to cowardice on our part: the fact that your trial came to court when it need not have done so, the handling of the trial itself, and now this absurd ending which will be thought to have got beyond our control through some cowardice and unmanliness on *46* our part, since we did not save you, or you save yourself, when it was possible and could be done if we had been of the slightest use. Consider, Socrates, whether this is not only evil, but shameful, both for you and for us. Take counsel with yourself, or rather the time for counsel is past and the decision should have been taken, and there is no further opportunity, for this whole business must be ended tonight. If we delay now, then it will no longer be possible, it will be too late. Let me persuade you on every count, Socrates, and do not act otherwise.

S: My dear Crito, your eagerness is worth much *b* if it should have some right aim; if not, then the greater your keenness the more difficult it is to deal with. We must therefore examine whether we should act in this way or not, as not only now but at all times I am the kind of man who listens only to the argument that on reflection seems best to me. I cannot, now that this fate has come upon me, discard the arguments I used; they seem to me much the same. I value and *c* respect the same principles as before, and if we have no better arguments to bring up at this moment, be sure that I shall not agree with you, not even if the power of the majority were to frighten us with more bogeys, as if we were children, with threats of incarcerations and executions and confiscation of property. How should we examine this matter most reasonably? Would it be by taking up first your argument about the opinions of men, whether it is sound in every *d* case that one should pay attention to some opinions, but not to others? Or was that well-spoken before the necessity to die came upon me, but now it is clear

that this was said in vain for the sake of argument, that it was in truth play and nonsense? I am eager to examine together with you, Crito, whether this argument will appear in any way different to me in my present circumstances, or whether it remains the same, whether we are to abandon it or believe it. It was said on every occa-
e sion by those who thought they were speaking sensibly, as I have just now been speaking, that one should greatly value some people's opinions, but not others. Does that seem to you a sound statement?

You, as far as a human being can tell, are exempt from the likelihood of dying tomorrow, so the present
47 misfortune is not likely to lead you astray. Consider then, do you not think it a sound statement that one must not value all the opinions of men, but some and not others, nor the opinions of all men, but those of some and not of others? What do you say? Is this not well said?

C: It is.

S: One should value the good opinions, and not the bad ones?

C: Yes.

S: The good opinions are those of wise men, the bad ones those of foolish men?

C: Of course.

S: Come then, what of statements such as this:
b Should a man professionally engaged in physical training pay attention to the praise and blame and opinion of any man, or to those of one man only, namely a doctor or trainer?

C: To those of one only.

S: He should therefore fear the blame and welcome the praise of that one man, and not those of the many?

C: Obviously.

S: He must then act and exercise, eat and drink in the way the one, the trainer and the one who knows, thinks right, not all the others?

C: That is so.

c S: Very well. And if he disobeys the one, disregards his opinion and his praises while valuing those of the many who have no knowledge, will he not suffer harm?

C: Of course.

S: What is that harm, where does it tend, and what part of the man who disobeys does it affect?

C: Obviously the harm is to his body, which it ruins.

S: Well said. So with other matters, not to enumerate them all, and certainly with actions just and unjust, shameful and beautiful, good and bad, about which we are now deliberating, should we follow the d opinion of the many and fear it, or that of the one, if there is one who has knowledge of these things and before whom we feel fear and shame more than before all the others. If we do not follow his directions, we shall harm and corrupt that part of ourselves that is improved by just actions and destroyed by unjust actions. Or is there nothing in this?

C: I think there certainly is, Socrates.

S: Come now, if we ruin that which is improved by health and corrupted by disease by not following the opinions of those who know, is life worth living e for us when that is ruined? And that is the body, is it not?

C: Yes.

S: And is life worth living with a body that is corrupted and in bad condition?

C: In no way.

S: And is life worth living for us with that part of us corrupted that unjust action harms and just action benefits? Or do we think that part of us, whatever it is, that is concerned with justice and injustice, is inferior to the body?   48

C: Not at all.

S: It is more valuable?

C: Much more.

S: We should not then think so much of what the majority will say about us, but what he will say who understands justice and injustice, the one, that is, and the truth itself. So that, in the first place, you were wrong to believe that we should care for the opinion of the many about what is just, beautiful, good, and their opposites. "But," someone might say "the many are able to put us to death."

C: That too is obvious, Socrates, and someone b might well say so.

S: And, my admirable friend, that argument that we have gone through remains, I think, as before. Examine the following statement in turn as to whether it stays the same or not, that the most important thing is not life, but the good life.

C: It stays the same.

S: And that the good life, the beautiful life, and the just life are the same; does that still hold, or not?

C: It does hold.

S: As we have agreed so far, we must examine next whether it is just for me to try to get out of here when the Athenians have not acquitted me. If it is seen to be just, we will try to do so; if it is not, we will abandon the idea. As for those questions you raise about money, reputation, the upbringing of children, Crito, those considerations in truth belong to those people who easily put men to death and would bring them to life again if they could, without thinking; I mean the majority of men. For us, however, since our argument leads to this, the only valid consideration, as we were saying just now, is whether we should be acting rightly in giving money and gratitude to those who will lead me out of here, and ourselves helping with the escape, or whether in truth we shall do wrong in doing all this. If it appears that we shall be acting unjustly, then we have no need at all to take into account whether we shall have to die if we stay here and keep quiet, or suffer in another way, rather than do wrong.

C: I think you put that beautifully, Socrates, but see what we should do.

S: Let us examine the question together, my dear friend, and if you can make any objection while I am speaking, make it and I will listen to you, but if you have no objection to make, my dear Crito, then stop now from saying the same thing so often, that I must leave here against the will of the Athenians. I think it important to persuade you before I act, and not to act against your wishes. See whether the start of our inquiry is adequately stated, and try to answer what I ask you in the way you think best.

C: I shall try.

S: Do we say that one must never in any way do wrong willingly, or must one do wrong in one way and not in another? Is to do wrong never good or admirable, as we have agreed in the past, or have all these former agreements been washed out during the last few days? Have we at our age failed to notice for some time that in our serious discussions we were no different from children? Above all, is the truth such as we used to say it was, whether the majority agree or not, and whether we must still suffer worse things than we do now, or will be treated more gently, that nonetheless, wrongdoing is in every way harmful and shameful to the wrongdoer? Do we say so or not?

C: We do.

S: So one must never do wrong.

C: Certainly not.

S: Nor must one, when wronged, inflict wrong in return, as the majority believe, since one must never do wrong.

C: That seems to be the case.

S: Come now, should one injure anyone or not, Crito?

C: One must never do so.

S: Well then, if one is oneself injured, is it right, as the majority say, to inflict an injury in return, or is it not?

C: It is never right.

S: Injuring people is no different from wrongdoing.

C: That is true.

S: One should never do wrong in return, nor injure any man, whatever injury one has suffered at his hands. And Crito, see that you do not agree to this, contrary to your belief. For I know that only a few people hold this view or will hold it, and there is no common ground between those who hold this view and those who do not, but they inevitably despise each other's views. So then consider very carefully whether we have this view in common, and whether you agree, and let this be the basis of our deliberation, that neither to do wrong or to return a wrong is ever right, not even to injure in return for an injury received. Or do you disagree and do not share this view as a basis for discussion? I have held it for a long time and still hold it now, but if you think otherwise, tell me now. If, however, you stick to our former opinion, then listen to the next point.

C: I stick to it and agree with you. So say on.

S: Then I state the next point, or rather I ask you: when one has come to an agreement that is just with someone, should one fulfilll it or cheat on it?

C: One should fulfilll it.

S: See what follows from this: if we leave here without the city's permission, are we injuring people whom we should least injure? And are we sticking to a just agreement, or not?

C: I cannot answer your question, Socrates. I do not know.

S: Look at it this way. If, as we were planning to run away from here, or whatever one should call it, the laws and the state came and confronted us and asked: "Tell me, Socrates, what are you intending to do? Do you not by this action you are attempting *b* intend to destroy us, the laws, and indeed the whole city, as far as you are concerned? Or do you think it possible for a city not to be destroyed if the verdicts of its courts have no force but are nullified and set at naught by private individuals?" What shall we answer to this and other such arguments? For many things could be said, especially by an orator on behalf of this law we are destroying, which orders that the *c* judgments of the courts shall be carried out. Shall we say in answer, "The city wronged me, and its decision was not right." Shall we say that, or what?

C: Yes, by Zeus, Socrates, that is our answer.

S: Then what if the laws said: "Was that the agreement between us, Socrates, or was it to respect the judgments that the city came to?" And if we wondered at their words, they would perhaps add: "Socrates, do not wonder at what we say but answer, *d* since you are accustomed to proceed by question and answer. Come now, what accusation do you bring against us and the city, that you should try to destroy us? Did we not, first, bring you to birth, and was it not through us that your father married your mother and begat you? Tell you, do you find anything to criticize in those of us who are concerned with marriage?" And I would say that I do not criticize them. "Or in those of us concerned with the nurture of babies and the education that you too received? Were those assigned to that subject not right to instruct *e* your father to educate you in the arts and in physical culture?" And I would say that they were right. "Very well," they would continue, "and after you were born and nurtured and educated, could you, in the first place, deny that you are our offspring and servant, both you and your forefathers? If that is so, do you think that we are on an equal footing as regards the right, and that whatever we do to you it is right for you to do to us? You were not on an equal footing with your father as regards the right, nor with your *51* master if you had one, so as to retaliate for anything they did to you, to revile them if they reviled you, to beat them if they beat you, and so with many other things. Do you think you have this right to retaliation against your country and its laws? That if we undertake to destroy you and think it right to do so, you can undertake to destroy us, as far as you can, in return? And will you say that you are right to do so, you who truly care for virtue? Is your wisdom such as not to realize that your country is to be honored more than

your mother, your father and all your ancestors, that it is more to be revered and more sacred, and that it *b* counts for more among the gods and sensible men, that you must worship it, yield to it and placate its anger more than your father's? You must either persuade it or obey its orders, and endure in silence whatever it instructs you to endure, whether blows or bonds, and if it leads you into war to be wounded or killed, you must obey. To do so is right, and one must not give way or retreat or leave one's post, but both in war and in courts and everywhere else, one must obey the commands of one's city and country, *c* or persuade it as to the nature of justice. It is impious to bring violence to bear against your mother or father, it is much more so to use it against your country." What shall we say in reply, Crito, that the laws speak the truth, or not?

C: I think they do.

S: "Reflect now, Socrates," the laws might say "that if what we say is true, you are not treating us rightly by planning to do what you are planning. We have given you birth, nurtured you, educated you, we have given you and all other citizens a share of *d* all the good things we could. Even so, by giving every Athenian the opportunity, after he has reached manhood and observed the affairs of the city and us the laws, we proclaim that if we do not please him, he can take his possessions and go wherever he pleases. Not one of our laws raises any obstacle or forbids him, if he is not satisfied with us or the city, if one of you wants to go and live in a colony or wants to go anywhere else, and keep his property. We say, *e* however, that whoever of you remains, when he sees how we conduct our trials and manage the city in other ways, has in fact come to an agreement with us to obey our instructions. We say that the one who disobeys does wrong in three ways, first because in us he disobeys his parents, also those who brought him up, and because, in spite of his agreement, he neither obeys us nor, if we do something wrong, does *52* he try to persuade us to do better. Yet we only propose things, we do not issue savage commands to do whatever we order; we give two alternatives, either to persuade us or to do what we say. He does neither. We do say that you too, Socrates, are open to those charges if you do what you have in mind; you would be among, not the least, but the most guilty of the Athenians." And if I should say "Why so?" they might well be right to upbraid me and say that I am among the Athenians who most definitely came to that agree-b ment with them. They might well say: "Socrates, we have convincing proofs that we and the city were congenial to you. You would not have dwelt here most consistently of all the Athenians if the city had not been exceedingly pleasing to you. You have never left the city, even to see a festival, nor for any other reason except military service; you have never gone to stay in any other city, as people do; you have had c no desire to know another city or other laws; we and our city satisfied you.

"So decisively did you choose us and agree to be a citizen under us. Also, you have had children in this city, thus showing that it was congenial to you. Then at your trial you could have assessed your penalty at exile if you wished, and you are now attempting to do against the city's wishes what you could then have done with her consent. Then you prided yourself that you did not resent death, but you chose, as you said, death in preference to exile. Now, however, those words do not make you ashamed, and you pay d no heed to us, the laws, as you plan to destroy us, and you act like the meanest type of slave by trying to run away, contrary to your commitments and your agreement to live as a citizen under us. First then, answer us on this very point, whether we speak the truth when we say that you agreed, not only in words but by your deeds, to live in accordance with us." What are we to say to that, Crito? Must we not agree?

C: We must, Socrates.

S: "Surely," they might say, "you are breaking the commitments and agreements that you made with e us without compulsion or deceit, and under no pressure of time for deliberation. You have had seventy years during which you could have gone away if you did not like us, and if you thought our agreements 53 unjust. You did not choose to go to Sparta or to Crete, which you are always saying are well governed, nor to any other city, Greek or foreign. You have been away from Athens less than the lame or the blind or other handicapped people. It is clear that the city has been outstandingly more congenial to you than to other Athenians, and so have we, the laws, for what city can please without laws? Will you then not now stick to our agreements? You will, Socrates, if we can persuade you, and not make yourself a laughingstock by leaving the city.

"For consider what good you will do yourself or your friends by breaking our agreements and committing such a wrong? It is pretty obvious that your friends will themselves be in danger of exile, disfranchisement and loss of property. As for yourself, if you go b to one of the nearby cities—Thebes or Megara, both are well governed—you will arrive as an enemy to their government; all who care for their city will look on you with suspicion, as a destroyer of the laws. You will also strengthen the conviction of the jury that they passed the right sentence on you, for anyone c who destroys the laws could easily be thought to corrupt the young and the ignorant. Or will you avoid cities that are well governed and men who are civilized? If you do this, will your life be worth living? Will you have social intercourse with them and not be ashamed to talk to them? And what will you say? The same as you did here, that virtue and justice are man's most precious possession, along with lawful d behavior and the laws? Do you not think that Socrates would appear to be an unseemly kind of person? One must think so. Or will you leave those places and go to Crito's friends in Thessaly? There you will find the greatest license and disorder, and they may enjoy hearing from you how absurdly you escaped from prison in some disguise, in a leather jerkin or some other things in which escapees wrap themselves, thus altering your appearance. Will there be no one to say that you, likely to live but a short time more, were so greedy for life that you transgressed the most im- e portant laws? Possibly, Socrates, if you do not annoy anyone, but if you do, many disgraceful things will be said about you.

"You will spend your time ingratiating yourself with all men, and be at their beck and call. What will you do in Thessaly but feast, as if you had gone to a banquet in Thessaly? As for those conversations of yours about justice and the rest of virtue, where will they be? You say you want to live for the sake of your 54 children, that you may bring them up and educate them. How so? Will you bring them up and educate them by taking them to Thessaly and making strangers of them, that they may enjoy that too? Or not so, but they will be better brought up and educated here, while you are alive, though absent? Yes, your friends will look after them. Will they look after them if you go and live in Thessaly, but not if you go away to the underworld? If those who profess themselves your friends are any good at all, one must assume that they will.

b "Be persuaded by us who have brought you up, Socrates. Do not value either your children or your life or anything else more than goodness, in order that when you arrive in Hades you may have all this as your defense before the rulers there. If you do this deed, you will not think it better or more just or more pious here, nor will any one of your friends, nor will it be better for you when you arrive yonder. As it is, you depart, if you depart, after being wronged not by *c* us, the laws, but by men; but if you depart after shamefully returning wrong for wrong and injury for injury, after breaking your agreements and commitments with us, after injuring those you should injure least—yourself, your friends, your country and us—

we shall be angry with you while you are still alive, and our brothers, the laws of the underworld, will not receive you kindly, knowing that you tried to destroy us as far as you could. Do not let Crito persuade you, rather than us, to do what he says." *d*

Crito, my dear friend, be assured that these are the words I seem to hear, as the Corybants seem to hear the music of their flutes, and the echo of these words resounds in me, and makes it impossible for me to hear anything else. As far as my present beliefs go, if you speak in opposition to them, you will speak in vain. However, if you think you can accomplish anything, speak.

C: I have nothing to say, Socrates.

S: Let it be then, Crito, and let us act in this way, since this is the way the god is leading us. *e*

Phaedo

57 ECHECRATES: Were you with Socrates yourself, Phaedo,[1] on the day when he drank the poison in prison, or did someone else tell you about it?

PHAEDO: I was there myself, Echecrates.

E: What are the things he said before he died? And how did he die? I should be glad to hear this. Hardly anyone from Phlius[2] visits Athens nowadays, nor has b any stranger come from Athens for some time who could give us a clear account of what happened, except that he drank the poison and died, but nothing more.

58 P: Did you not even hear how the trial went?

E: Yes, someone did tell us about that, and we wondered that he seems to have died a long time after the trial took place. Why was that, Phaedo?

P: That was by chance, Echecrates. The day before the trial, as it happened, the prow of the ship that the Athenians send to Delos had been crowned with garlands.

E: What ship is that?

P: It is the ship in which, the Athenians say, Theseus once sailed to Crete, taking with him the b two lots of seven victims.[3] He saved them and was

himself saved. They vowed then to Apollo, so the story goes, that if they were saved they would send a mission to Delos every year. And from that time to this they send such an annual mission to the god. They have a law to keep the city pure while it lasts, and no execution may take place once the mission has begun until the ship has made its journey to Delos and returned to Athens, and this can sometimes take a long time if the winds delay it. The mission begins when the priest of Apollo crowns the prow of c the ship, and this happened, as I say, the day before Socrates' trial. That is why Socrates was in prison a long time between this trial and his execution.

E: What about his actual death, Phaedo? What did he say? What did he do? Who of his friends were with him? Or did the authorities not allow them to be present and he died with no friends present?

P: By no means. Some were present, in fact, a d good many.

E: Please be good enough to tell us all that occurred as fully as possible, unless you have some pressing business.

P: I have the time and I will try to tell you the whole story, for nothing gives me more pleasure than to call Socrates to mind, whether talking about him myself, or listening to someone else do so.

E: Your hearers will surely be like you in this, Phaedo. So do try to tell us every detail as exactly as you can.

P: I certainly found being there an astonishing experience. Although I was witnessing the death of e one who was my friend, I had no feeling of pity, for the man appeared happy both in manner and words as he died nobly and without fear, Echecrates, so that it struck me that even in going down to the underworld he was going with the gods' blessing and that 59 he would fare well when he got there, if anyone ever does. That is why I had no feeling of pity, such as would seem natural in my sorrow, nor indeed of pleasure, as we engaged in philosophical discussion as we were accustomed to do—for our arguments were of that sort—but I had a strange feeling, an

Reprinted from Plato's *Phaedo*, translated by G.M.A. Grube (Indianapolis: Hackett Publishing Company, 1977), by permission of the publisher. The translation follows Burnet's Oxford text except in rare instances. The only liberty taken is where the answers to Socrates' questions are very brief, merely indicating assent or the like. In such instances, "he said," the so-frequent repetition of which reads awkwardly in English, has been replaced by a dash, to indicate a change of speaker.

1. [Phaedo was a young friend of Socrates who later founded a school of philosophy at Elis.—G.M.A.G.]

2. [Phlius was a community in the northeastern part of the Peloponnesus where a Pythagorean society flourished about this time. We are told by Diogenes Laërtius (early third century A.D.) that Echecrates was a member of that society.]

3. [Legend says that Minos, king of Crete, compelled the Athenians to send seven youths and seven maidens every year to be sacrificed to the Minotaur until Theseus saved them and killed the monster.]

unaccustomed mixture of pleasure and pain at the same time as I reflected that he was just about to die. All of us present were affected in much the same way, sometimes laughing, then weeping; especially one of us, Apollodorus—you know the man and his ways.

b E: Of course I do.

P: He was quite overcome; but I was myself disturbed, and so were the others.

E: Who, Phaedo, were those present?

P: Among the local people there was Apollodorus, whom I mentioned, Critobulus and his father,[4] also Hermogenes, Epigenes, Aeschines and Antisthenes. Ctesippus of Paeania was there, Menexenus and some others. Plato, I believe, was ill.[5]

E: Were there some strangers present?

c P: Yes, Simmias from Thebes with Cebes and Phaedondes, and from Megara, Euclides and Terpsion.

E: What about Aristippus and Cleombrotus? Were they there?

P: No. They were said to be in Aegina.

E: Was there anyone else?

P: I think these were about all.

E: Well then, what do you say the conversation was about?

P: I will try to tell you everything from the beginning. On the previous days also both the others and

---

4. [The father of Critobulus is Crito, who in the dialogue named after him tries to persuade Socrates to escape from jail. He is also mentioned in *Apology* 33e and plays a prominent part in the death scene at the end of this dialogue. Several of the other friends of Socrates mentioned here also appear in other dialogues. Hermogenes is one of the speakers in the *Cratylus*. Epigenes is mentioned in *Apology* 33e, as is Aeschines. Aeschines was a writer of Socratic dialogues. Menexenus has a part in the *Lysis* and has a dialogue named after him. Simmias and Cebes are mentioned in the *Crito*, 45b, as having come to Athens with enough money to secure Socrates' escape.]

5. [It is interesting to note that Plato makes it clear that he was *not* present on the last day of Scorates' life, whereas in the *Apology* he twice mentions (34a and 38b) tht he *was* present at the trial. Whether this has any significance as regards the historical accuracy of the two works is anyone's guess. Probably it just happened to be so, but these are the only instances in which Plato mentions himself in all his works.]

I used to visit Socrates. We foregathered at daybreak d at the court where the trial took place, for it was close to the prison, and each day we used to wait around talking until the prison should open, for it did not open early. When it opened we used to go in to Socrates and spend most of the day with him. On this day we gathered rather early, because when we left the prison on the previous evening we were in- e formed that the ship from Delos had arrived, and so we told each other to come to the usual place as early as possible. When we arrived the gatekeeper who used to answer our knock came out and told us to wait and not go in until he told us to. "The Eleven,"[6] he said, "are freeing Socrates from his bonds and telling him how his death will take place today." After a short time he came and told us to go in. We found 60 Socrates recently released from his chains, and Xanthippe—you know her—sitting by him, holding their baby. When she saw us, she cried out and said the sort of thing that women usually say: "Socrates, this is the last time your friends will talk to you and you to them." Socrates looked at Crito. "Crito," he said, "let someone take her home." And some of Crito's people led her away lamenting and beating her breast. b

Socrates sat up on the bed, bent his leg and rubbed it with his hand, and as he rubbed he said: "What a strange thing that which men call pleasure seems to be, and how astonishing the relation it has with what is thought to be its opposite, namely pain! A man cannot have both at the same time. Yet if he pursues and catches the one, he is almost always bound to catch the other also, like two creatures with one head. I think that if Aesop had noted this he would have composed a fable that a god wished to reconcile their c opposition but could not do so, so he joined their two heads together, and therefore when a man has the one, the other follows later. This seems to be happening to me. My bonds caused pain in my leg, and now pleasure seems to be following."

Cebes intervened and said: "By Zeus, yes, Socrates, you did well to remind me. Evenus[7] asked me the day before yesterday, as others had done before, what d induced you to write poetry after you came to prison,

---

6. [The Eleven were the police commissioners of Athens.]

7. [Socrates refers to Evenus as a Sophist and teacher of the young in *Apology* 20a–b.]

you who had never composed any poetry before, putting the fables of Aesop into verse and composing the hymn to Apollo. If it is of any concern to you that I should have an answer to give to Evenus when he repeats his question, as I know he will, tell me what to say to him."

Tell him the truth, Cebes, he said, that I did not do this with the idea of rivalling him or his poems, for I knew that would not be easy, but I tried to find out the meaning of certain dreams and to satisfy my conscience in case it was this kind of art they were frequently bidding me to practice. The dreams were something like this: the same dream often came to me in the past, now in one shape now in another, but saying the same thing: "Socrates," it said, "practice and cultivate the arts." In the past I imagined that it was instructing and advising me to do what I was doing, such as those who encourage runners in a race, that the dream was thus bidding me do the very thing I was doing, namely, to practice the art of philosophy, this being the highest kind of art, and I was doing that.

But now, after my trial took place, and the festival of the god was preventing my execution, I thought that, in case my dream was bidding me to practice this popular art, I should not disobey it but compose poetry. I thought it safer not to leave here until I had satisfied by conscience by writing poems in obedience to the dream. So I first wrote in honor of the god of the present festival. After that I realized that a poet, if he is to be a poet, must compose fables, not arguments. Being no teller of fables myself, I took the stories I knew and had at hand, the fables of Aesop, and I versified the first ones I came across. Tell this to Evenus, Cebes, wish him well and bid him farewell, and tell him, if he is wise, to follow me as soon as possible. I am leaving today, it seems, as the Athenians so order it.

Said Simmias: "What kind of advice is this you are giving to Evenus, Socrates? I have met him many times, and from my observation he is not at all likely to follow it willingly."

How so, said he, is Evenus not a philosopher?

I think so, Simmias said.

Then Evenus will be willing, like every man who partakes worthily of philosophy. Yet perhaps he will not take his own life, for that, they say, is not right. As he said this, Socrates put his feet on the ground and remained in this position during the rest of the *d* conversation.

Then Cebes asked: "How do you mean Socrates, that it is not right to do oneself violence, and yet that the philosopher will be willing to follow one who is dying?"

Come now, Cebes, have you and Simmias, who keep company with Philolaus,[8] not heard about such things?

Nothing definite, Socrates.

Indeed, I too speak about this from hearsay, but I do not mind telling you what I have heard, for it is perhaps most appropriate for one who is about to depart yonder to tell and examine tales about what we believe that journey to be like. What else could *e* one do in the time we have until sunset?

But whatever is the reason, Socrates, for people to say that it is not right to kill oneself? As to your question just now, I have heard Philolaus say this when staying in Thebes and I have also heard it from others, but I have never heard anyone give a clear account of the matter.

Well, he said, we must do our best, and you may yet hear one. And it may well astonish you if this *62* subject, alone of all things, is simple, and it is never, as with everything else, better at certain times and for certain people to die than to live. And if this is so, you may well find it astonishing that those for whom it is better to die are wrong to help themselves, and that they must wait for someone else to benefit them.

And Cebes, lapsing into his own dialect, laughed quietly and said: "Zeus knows it is."

Indeed, said Socrates, it does seem unreasonable when put like that, but perhaps there is reason to it. *b* There is the explanation that is put in the language of the mysteries, that we men are in a kind of prison, and that one must not free oneself or run away. That seems to me an impressive doctrine and one not easy to understand fully. However, Cebes, this seems to

---

8. [Philolaus was a contemporary Pythagorean. The reference to him here, as well as the fact that the story is told to Echecrates at Phlius, gives the whole dialogue a Pythagorean background, and this seems a recognition on Plato's part of Pythagorean influence regarding the theories that follow, in particular, the theory of Forms and the purification of man's eternal soul through intellectual activity.]

me well expressed, that the gods are our guardians and that men are one of their possessions. Or do you not think so?

I do, said Cebes.

And would you not be angry if one of your posses-
c sions killed itself when you had not given any sign that you wished it to die, and if you had any punishment you could inflict, you would inflict it?

Certainly, he said.

Perhaps then, put in this way, it is not unreasonable that one should not kill oneself before a god had indicated some necessity to do so, like the necessity now put upon us.

That seems likely, said Cebes. As for what you were
d saying, that philosophers should be willing and ready to die, that seems strange, Socrates, if what we said just now is reasonable, namely, that a god is our protector and that we are his possessions. It is not logical that the wisest of men should not resent leaving this service in which they are governed by the best of masters, the gods, for a wise man cannot believe that he will look after himself better when he is free. A foolish man might easily think so, that he must
e escape from his master; he would not reflect that one must not escape from a good master but stay with him as long as possible, because it would be foolish to escape. But the sensible man would want always to remain with one better than himself. So, Socrates, the opposite of what was said before is likely to be true; the wise would resent dying, whereas the foolish would rejoice at it.

I thought that when Socrates heard this he was pleased by Cebes' argumentation. Glancing at us, he
63 said: "Cebes is always on the track of some arguments; he is certainly not willing to be at once convinced by what one says."

Said Simmias: "But actually, Socrates, I think myself that Cebes has a point now. Why should truly wise men want to avoid the service of masters better than themselves, and leave them easily? And I think Cebes is aiming his argument at you, because you are bearing leaving us so lightly, and leaving those good masters, as you say yourself, the gods."

b   You are both justified in what you say, and I think you mean that I must make a defense against this, as if I were in court.

You certainly must, said Simmias.

Come then, he said, let me try to make my defense

to you more convincing than it was to the jury. For, Simmias and Cebes, I should be wrong not to resent dying if I did not believe that I should go first to other wise and good gods, and then to men who have died and are better than men are here. Be assured that, as it is, I expect to join the company of good men. c This last I would not altogether insist on, but if I insist on anything at all in these matters, it is that I shall come to gods who are very good masters. That is why I am not so resentful, because I have good hope that some future awaits men after death, as we have been told for years, a much better future for the good than for the wicked.

Well now, Socrates, said Simmias, do you intend to keep this belief to yourself as you leave us, or would you share it with us? I certainly think it would be a d blessing for us too, and at the same time it would be your defense if you convince us of what you say.

I will try, he said, but first let us see what it is that Crito here has, I think, been wanting to say for quite a while.

What else, Socrates, said Crito, but what the man who is to give you the poison has been telling me for some time, that I should warn you to talk as little as possible. People get heated when they talk, he says, and one should not be heated when taking the poison, e as those who do must sometimes drink it two or three times.

Socrates replied: "Take no notice of him; only let him be prepared to administer it twice or, if necessary, three times."

I was rather sure you would say that, Crito said, but he has been bothering me for some time.

Let him be, he said. I want to make my argument before you, my judges, as to why I think that a man who has truly spent his life in philosophy is probably right to be of good cheer in the face of death and to be very hopeful that after death he will attain the greatest blessings yonder. I will try to tell you, Simmias 64 and Cebes, how this may be so. I am afraid that other people do not realize that the one aim of those who practice philosophy in the proper manner is to practice for dying and death. Now if this is true, if would be strange indeed if they were eager for this all their lives and then resent it when what they have wanted and practiced for a long time comes upon them.

Simmias laughed and said: "By Zeus, Socrates, you made me laugh, though I was in no laughing mood *b* just now. I think that the majority, on hearing this, will think that it describes the philosophers very well, and our people in Thebes would thoroughly agree that philosophers are nearly dead and that the majority of men is well aware that they deserve to be."

And they would be telling the truth, Simmias, except for their being aware. They are not aware of the way true philosophers are nearly dead, nor of the way *c* they deserve to be, nor of the sort of death they deserve. But never mind them, he said, let us talk among ourselves. Do we believe that there is such a thing as death?

Certainly, said Simmias.

Is it anything else than the separation of the soul from the body? Do we believe that death is this, namely, that the body comes to be separated by itself apart from the soul, and the soul comes to be separated by itself apart from the body? Is death anything else than that?

No, that is what it is, he said.

Consider then, my good sir, whether you share my opinion, for this will lead us to a better knowledge *d* of what we are investigating. Do you think it is the part of a philosopher to be concerned with such so-called pleasures as those of food and drink?

By no means.

What about the pleasures of sex?

Not at all.

What of the other pleasures concerned with the service of the body? Do you think such a man prizes them greatly, the acquisition of distinguished clothes and shoes and the other bodily ornaments? Do you think he values these or despises them, except in so *e* far as one cannot do without them?

I think the true philosopher despises them.

Do you not think, he said, that in general such a man's concern is not with the body but that, as far as he can, he turns away from the body towards the soul?

I do.

So in the first place, such things show clearly that *65* the philosopher more than other men frees the soul from association with the body as much as possible?

Apparently.

A man who finds no pleasure in such things and has no part in them is thought by the majority not to deserve to live and to be close to death; the man, that is, who does not care for the pleasures of the body.

What you say is certainly true.

Then what about the actual acquiring of knowledge? Is the body an obstacle when one associates with it in the search for knowledge? I mean, for exam- *b* ple, do men find any truth in sight or hearing, or are not even the poets[9] forever telling us that we do not see or hear anything accurately, and surely if those two physical senses are not clear or precise, our other senses can hardly be accurate, as they are all inferior to these. Do you not think so?

I certainly do, he said.

When then, he asked, does the soul grasp the truth? For whenever it attempts to examine anything with the body, it is clearly deceived by it.

True.   *c*

Is it not in reasoning if anywhere that any reality becomes clear to the soul?

Yes.

And indeed the soul reasons best when none of these senses troubles it, neither hearing nor sight, nor pain nor pleasure, but when it is most by itself, taking leave of the body and as far as possible having no contact or association with it in its search for reality.

That is so.

And it is then that the soul of the philosopher most disdains the body, flees from it and seeks to be *d* by itself?

It appears so.

What about the following, Simmias? Do we say that there is such a thing as the Just itself, or not?

We do say so, by Zeus.

And the Beautiful, and the Good?

Of course.

And have you ever seen any of these things with your eyes?

In no way, he said.

Or have you ever grasped them with any of your bodily senses? I am speaking of all things such as Size, Health, Strength and, in a word, the reality of all other things, that which each of them essentially is. Is what is most true in them contemplated through *e* the body, or is this the position: whoever of us prepares himself best and most accurately to grasp that thing

9. ["Even the poets" because poetry concerns itself with the world of sense and appeals to the passions and emotions of the lowest part of the soul (*Republic*, 595a ff.), whereas in the *Phaedo* passions and emotions are attributed to the body.]

itself which he is investigating will come closest to the knowledge of it?

Obviously.

Then he will do this most perfectly who approaches the object with thought alone, without associating 66 any sight with his thought, or dragging in any sense perception with his reasoning, but who, using pure thought alone, tries to track down each reality pure and by itself, freeing himself as far as possible from eyes and ears, and in a word, from the whole body, because the body confuses the soul and does not allow it to acquire truth and wisdom whenever it is associated with it. Will not that man reach reality, Simmias, if anyone does?

What you say, said Simmias, is indeed true.

b   All these things will necessarily make the true philosophers believe and say to each other something like this: "There is likely to be something such as a path to guide us out of our confusion, because as long as we have a body and our soul is fused with such an evil we shall never adequately attain what we desire, which we affirm to be the truth. The body keeps us busy in a thousand ways because of its need for nurture. Moreover, if certain diseases befall it, c they impede our search for the truth. It fills us with wants, desires, fears, all sorts of illusions and much nonsense, so that, as it is said, in truth and in fact no thought of any kind ever comes to us from the body. Only the body and its desires cause war, civil discord and battles, for all wars are due to the desire to acquire d wealth, and it is the body and the care of it, to which we are enslaved, which compel us to acquire wealth, and all this makes us too busy to practice philosophy. Worst of all, if we do get some respite from it and turn to some investigation, everywhere in our investigations the body is present and makes for confusion and fear, so that it prevents us from seeing the truth.

"It really has been shown to us that, if we are ever to have pure knowledge, we must escape from the e body and observe things in themselves with the soul by itself. It seems likely that we shall, only then, when we are dead, attain that which we desire and of which we claim to be lovers, namely, wisdom, as our argument shows, not while we live; for if it is impossible to attain any pure knowledge with the body, then one of two things is true: either we can never attain knowledge or we can do so after death. Then and 67 not before, the soul is by itself apart from the body.

While we live, we shall be closest to knowledge if we refrain as much as possible from association with the body and do not join with it more than we must, if we are not infected with its nature but purify ourselves from it until the god himself frees us. In this way we shall escape the contamination of the body's folly; we shall be likely to be in the company of people of the same kind, and by our own efforts we shall know all that is pure, which is presumably the truth, for it b is not permitted to the impure to attain the pure."

Such are the things, Simmias, that all those who love learning in the proper manner must say to one another and believe. Or do you not think so?

I certainly do, Socrates.

And if this is true, my friend, said Socrates, there is good hope that on arriving where I am going, if anywhere, I shall acquire what has been our chief preoccupation in our past life, so that the journey that is now ordered for me is full of good hope, as it c is also for any other man who believes that his mind has been prepared and, as it were, purified.

It certainly is, said Simmias.

And does purification not turn out to be what we mentioned in our argument some time ago, namely, to separate the soul as far as possible from the body and accustom it to gather itself and collect itself out of every part of the body and to dwell by itself as far as it can both now and in the future, freed, as it were, d from the bonds of the body?

Certainly, he said.

And that freedom and separation of the soul from the body is called death?

That is altogether so.

It is only those who practice philosophy in the right way, we say, who always most want to free the soul; and this release and separation of the soul from the body is the preoccupation of the philosophers?

So it appears.

Therefore, as I said at the beginning, it would be ridiculous for a man to train himself in life to live in a state as close to death as possible, and then to resent it when it comes?   e

Ridiculous, of course.

In fact, Simmias, he said, those who practice philosophy in the right way are in training for dying and they fear death least of all men. Consider it from this point of view: if they are altogether estranged from the body and desire to have their soul by itself, would

it not be quite absurd for them to be afraid and resentful when this happens? If they did not gladly set out for a place, where, on arrival, they may hope to attain that for which they had yearned during their
68 lifetime, that is, wisdom, and where they would be rid of the presence of that from which they are estranged?

Many men, at the death of their lovers, wives or sons, were willing to go to the underworld, driven by the hope of seeing there those for whose company they longed, and being with them. Will then a true lover of wisdom, who has a similar hope and knows that he will never find it to any extent except in Hades, be resentful of dying and not gladly undertake the journey thither? One must surely think so, my friend, if he is a true philosopher, for he is firmly
b convinced that he will not find pure knowledge anywhere except there. And if this is so, then, as I said just now, would it not be highly unreasonable for such a man to fear death?

It certainly would, by Zeus, he said.

Then you have sufficient indication, he said, that any man whom you see resenting death was not a
c lover of wisdom but a lover of the body, and also a lover of wealth or of honors, either or both.

It is certainly as you say.

And, Simmias, he said, does not what is called courage belong especially to men of this disposition?

Most certainly.

And the quality of moderation which even the majority call by that name, that is, not to get swept off one's feet by one's passions, but to treat them with disdain and orderliness, is this not suited only to those
d who most of all despise the body and live the life of philosophy?

Necessarily so, he said.

If you are willing to reflect on the courage and moderation of other people, you will find them strange.

In what way, Socrates?

You know that they all consider death a great evil?

Definitely, he said.

And the brave among them face death, when they do, for fear of greater evils?

That is so.

Therefore, it is fear and terror that make all men brave, except the philosophers. Yet it is illogical to be brave through fear and cowardice.
e   It certainly is.

What of the moderate among them? Is their experience not similar? Is it license of a kind that makes them moderate? We say this is impossible, yet their experience of this unsophisticated moderation turns out to be similar: they fear to be deprived of other pleasures which they desire, so they keep away from some pleasures because they are overcome by others. Now to be mastered by pleasure is what they call license, but what happens to them is that they master certain pleasures because they are mastered by others. 69 This is like what we mentioned just now, that in some way it is a kind of license that has made them moderate.

That seems likely.

My good Simmias, I fear this is not the right exchange to attain virtue, to exchange pleasures for pleasures, pains for pains, and fears for fears, the greater for the less like coins, but that the only valid currency for which all these things should be ex- b changed is wisdom. With this we have real courage and moderation and justice and, in a word, true virtue, with wisdom, whether pleasures and fears and all such things be present or absent. Exchanged for one another without wisdom such virtue is only an illusory appearance of virtue; it is in fact fit for slaves, without soundness or truth, whereas, in truth, moderation and courage and justice are a purging away of all such things, and wisdom itself is a kind of cleansing or c purification. It is likely that those who established the mystic rites for us were not inferior persons but were speaking in riddles long ago when they said that whoever arrives in the underworld uninitiated and unsanctified will wallow in the mire, whereas he who arrives there purified and initiated will dwell with the gods. There are indeed, as those concerned with the mysteries say, many who carry the thyrsus but the d Bacchants are few.[10] These latter are, in my opinion, no other than those who have practiced philosophy in the right way. I have in my life left nothing undone in order to be counted among these as far as possible, as I have been eager to be in every way. Whether my eagerness was right and we accomplished anything we shall, I think, know for certain in a short time, god willing, on arriving yonder.

This is my defense, Simmias and Cebes, that I am

---

10. [That is, the true worshippers of Dionysus, as opposed to those who only carry the external symbols of his worship.]

likely to be right to leave you and my masters here
e without resentment or complaint, believing that
there, as here, I shall find good masters and good
friends. If my defense is more convincing to you than
to the Athenian jury, it will be well.

When Socrates finished, Cebes intervened: Socrates, he said, everything else you said is excellent, I
70 think, but men find it very hard to believe what you
said about the soul. They think that after it has left
the body it no longer exists anywhere, but that it is
destroyed and dissolved on the day the man dies, as
soon as it leaves the body; and that, on leaving it, it
is dispersed like breath or smoke, has flown away and
gone and is no longer anything anywhere. If indeed
it gathered itself together and existed by itself and
escaped those evils you were recently enumerating,
there would then be much good hope, Socrates, that
b what you say is true; but to believe this requires a
good deal of faith and persuasive argument, to believe
that the soul still exists after a man has died and that
it still possesses some capability and intelligence.

What you say is true, Cebes, Socrates said, but
what shall we do? Do you want to discuss whether
this is likely to be true or not?

Personally, said Cebes, I should like to hear your
opinion on the subject.

I do not think, said Socrates, that anyone who heard
me now, not even a comic poet, could say that I am
c babbling and discussing things that do not concern
me, so we must examine the question thoroughly, if
you think we should do so. Let us examine it in some
such a manner as this: whether the souls of men who
have died exist in the underworld or not. We recall
an ancient theory that souls arriving there come from
here, and then again that they arrive here and are
born here from the dead. If that is true, that the living
come back from the dead, then surely our souls must
d exist there, for they could not come back if they did
not exist, and this is a sufficient proof that these things
are so if it truly appears that the living never come
from any other source than from the dead. If this is
not the case we should need another argument.

Quite so, said Cebes.

Do not, he said, confine yourself to humanity if
you want to understand this more readily, but take
all animals and all plants into account, and, in short,
e for all things which come to be, let us see whether they
come to be in this way, that is, from their opposites if

they have such, as the beautiful is the opposite of the
ugly and the just of the unjust, and a thousand other
things of the kind. Let us examine whether those that
have an opposite must necessarily come to be from
their opposite and from nowhere else, as for example
when something comes to be larger it must necessarily
become larger from having been smaller before.

Yes.

Then if something smaller comes to be, it will come
from something larger before, which became smaller? 71

That is so, he said.

And the weaker comes to be from the stronger,
and the swifter from the slower?

Certainly.

Further, if something worse comes to be, does it
not come from the better, and the juster from the
more unjust?

Of course.

So we have sufficiently established that all things
come to be in this way, opposites from opposites?

Certainly.

There is a further point, something such as this,
about these opposites: between each of those pairs of
opposites there are two processes: from the one to *b*
the other and then again from the other to the first;
between the larger and the smaller there is increase
and decrease, and we call the one increasing and the
other decreasing?

Yes, he said.

And so too there is separation and combination,
cooling and heating, and all such things, even if
sometimes we do not have a name for the process,
but in fact it must be everywhere that they come to
be from one another, and that there is a process of
becoming from each into the other?

Assuredly, he said.

Well then, is there an opposite to living, as sleeping
is the opposite of being awake?   *c*

Quite so, he said.

What is it?

Being dead, he said.

Therefore, if these are opposites, they come to be
from one another, and there are two processes of
generation between the two?

Of course.

I will tell you, said Socrates, one of the two pairs
I was just talking about, the pair itself and the two
processes, and you will tell me the other. I mean, to

sleep and to be awake; to be awake comes from sleep-
d ing, and to sleep comes from being awake. Of the
two processes one is going to sleep, the other is waking
up. Do you accept that, or not?

Certainly.

You tell me in the same way about life and death.
Do you not say that to be dead is the opposite of
being alive?

I do.

And they come to be from one another?

Yes.

What comes to be from being alive?

Being dead.

And what comes to be from being dead?

One must agree that it is being alive.

Then, Cebes, living creatures and things come to
be from the dead?

e   So it appears, he said.

Then our souls exist in the underworld?

That seems likely.

Then in this case one of the two processes of becoming is clear, for dying is clear enough, is it not?

It certainly is.

What shall we do then? Shall we not supply the
opposite process of becoming? Is nature to be lame in
this case? Or must we provide a process of becoming
opposite to dying?

We surely must.

And what is that?

Coming to life again.

72   Therefore, he said, if there is such a thing as coming
to life again, it would be a process of coming from
the dead to the living?

Quite so.

It is agreed between us then that the living come
from the dead in this way no less than the dead from
the living and, if that is so, it seems to be a sufficient
proof that the souls of the dead must be somewhere
whence they can come back again.

I think, Socrates, he said, that this follows from
what we have agreed on.

Consider in this way, Cebes, he said, that, as I
think, we were not wrong to agree. If the two processes
b of becoming did not always balance each other as if
they were going round in a circle, but generation
proceeded from one point to its opposite in a straight
line and it did not turn back again to the other opposite or take any turning, do you realize that all things

would ultimately have the same form, be affected in
the same way, and cease to become?

How do you mean? he said.

It is not hard to understand what I mean. If, for
example, there was such a process as going to sleep,
but no corresponding process of waking up, you realize that in the end everything would show the story
of Endymion[11] to have no meaning. There would be c
no point to it because everything would have the
same experience as he, be asleep. And if everything
were combined and nothing separated, the saying of
Anaxagoras[12] would soon be true, "that all things were
mixed together." In the same way, my dear Cebes,
if everything that partakes of life were to die and
remain in that state and not come to life again, would
not everything ultimately have to be dead and nothing d
alive? Even if the living came from some other source,
and all that lived died, how could all things avoid
being absorbed in death?

It could not be, Socrates, said Cebes, and I think
what you say is altogether true.

I think, Cebes, said he, that this is very definitely
the case and that we were not deceived when we
agreed on this: coming to life again in truth exists,
the living come to be from the dead, and the souls
of the dead exist.   e

Furthermore, Socrates, Cebes rejoined, such is also
the case if that theory is true that you are accustomed
to mention frequently, that for us learning is no other
than recollection. According to this, we must at some
previous time have learned what we now recollect.
This is possible only if our soul existed somewhere 73
before it took on this human shape. So according to
this theory too, the soul is likely to be something immortal.

⸺ Cebes, Simmias interrupted, what are the proofs
of this? Remind me, for I do not quite recall them
at the moment.

---

11. [Endymion was granted eternal sleep by Zeus, in some
versions at the request of Selene (the moon).]

12. [Anaxagoras of Clazomenae was born at the beginning
of the fifth century B.C. He came to Athens as a young man
and spent most of his life there in the study of natural philosophy. He is quoted later in the dialogue as claiming that the
universe is directed by Mind (Nous). See 97c ff. The reference here is to his statement that in the original state of the
world all its elements were thoroughly commingled.]

There is one excellent argument, said Cebes, namely that when men are interrogated in the right manner, they always give the right answer of their own accord, and they could not do this if they did not possess the knowledge and the right explanation b inside them. Then if one shows them a diagram or something else of that kind, this will show most clearly that such is the case.[13]

If this does not convince you, Simmias, said Socrates, see whether you agree if we examine it in some such way as this, for you doubt that what we call learning is recollection.

It is not that I doubt, said Simmias, but I want to experience the very thing we are discussing, recollection, and from what Cebes undertook to say, I am now remembering and am pretty nearly convinced. Nevertheless, I should like to hear now the way you were intending to explain it.

This way, he said. We surely agree that if anyone c recollects anything, he must have known it before.

Quite so, he said.

Do we not also agree that when knowledge comes to mind in this way, it is recollection? What way do I mean? Like this: when a man sees or hears or in some other way perceives one thing and not only knows that thing but also thinks of another thing of which the knowledge is not the same but different, are we not right to say that he recollects the second thing that comes into his mind?

d   How do you mean?

Things such as this: to know a man is surely a different knowledge from knowing a lyre.

Of course.

Well, you know what happens to lovers: whenever they see a lyre, a garment or anything else that their beloved is accustomed to use, they know the lyre, and the image of the boy to whom it belongs comes into their mind. This is recollection, just as someone, on seeing Simmias, often recollects Cebes, and there are thousands of other such occurrences.

Thousands indeed, said Simmias.

Is this kind of thing not recollection of a kind? he said, especially so when one experiences it about e things that one had forgotten, because one had not seen them for some time? — Quite so.

Further, he said, can a man seeing the picture of a horse or a lyre recollect a man, or seeing a picture of Simmias recollect Cebes? — Certainly.

Or seeing a picture of Simmias, recollect Simmias himself? — He certainly can.

In all these cases the recollection is occasioned by things that are similar, but it can also be occasioned 74 by things that are dissimilar? — It can.

When the recollection is caused by similar things, must one not of necessity also experience this: to consider whether the similarity to that which one recollects is deficient in any respect or complete? — One must.

Consider, he said, whether this is the case: we say that there is something that is equal. I do not mean a stick equal to a stick or a stone to a stone, or anything of that kind, but something else beyond all these, the Equal itself. Shall we say that this exists or not?

Indeed we shall, by Zeus, said Simmias, most defi- b nitely.

And do we know what this is? — Certainly.

Whence have we acquired the knowledge of it? Is it not from the things we mentioned just now, from seeing sticks or stones or some other things that are equal we come to think of that other which is different from them? Or doesn't it seem to you to be different? Look at it also this way: do not equal stones and sticks sometimes, while remaining the same, appear to one to be equal and to another to be unequal? — Certainly they do.

But what of the equals themselves?[14] Have they ever appeared unequal to you, or Equality to be In- c equality?

Never, Socrates.

13. [In the *Meno* Socrates does precisely that. By means of a geometrical diagram and merely by asking Meno's slave questions, he elicits from him the answer that the square on the diagonal of a square is double the original square. There, too, this is taken to prove that knowledge is recollection.]

14. [The plural is puzzling, as only the Form of Equality, on the one hand, and the (imperfectly) equal "sticks and stones" have been mentioned. Commentators suggest that the plural here refers to mathematical equals such as the angles at the base of an isosceles triangle. Plato must have something of the kind in mind, but it is hard to see how he expects a reader who could not be familiar with his later work to realize it, especially as the "equal things" in the next line again refer to the particulars.]

These equal things and the Equal itself are therefore not the same?

I do not think they are the same at all, Socrates.

But it is definitely from the equal things, though they are different from that Equal, that you have derived and grasped the knowledge of equality?

Very true, Socrates.

Whether it be like them or unlike them?

Certainly.

It makes no difference. As long as the sight of one thing makes you think of another, whether it be similar or dissimilar, this must of necessity be recol-*d* lection?

Quite so.

Well then, he said, do we experience something like this in the case of equal sticks and the other equal objects we just mentioned? Do they seem to us to be equal in the same sense as what is Equal itself? Is there some deficiency in their being such as the Equal, or is there not?

A considerable deficiency, he said.

Whenever someone, on seeing something, realizes that that which he now sees wants to be like some *e* other reality but falls short and cannot be like that other since it is inferior, do we agree that the one who thinks this must have prior knowledge of that to which he says it is like, but deficiently so?

Necessarily.

Well, do we also feel this about the equal objects and the Equal itself, or do we not?

Very definitely.

We must then possess knowledge of the Equal before that time when we first saw the equal objects *75* and realized that all these objects strive to be like the Equal but are deficient in this.

That is so.

Then surely we also agree that this conception of ours derives from seeing or touching or some other sense perception, and cannot come into our mind in any other way, for all these senses, I say, are the same.

They are the same, Socrates, at any rate in respect to that which our argument wishes to make plain.

b Our sense perceptions must surely make us realize that all that we perceive through them is striving to reach that which is Equal but falls short of it; or how do we express it?

Like that.

Then before we began to see or hear or otherwise perceive, we must have possessed knowledge of the Equal itself if we were about to refer our sense perceptions of equal objects to it, and realized that all of them were eager to be like it, but were inferior.

That follows from what has been said, Socrates.

But we began to see and hear and otherwise perceive right after birth?

Certainly.

We must then have acquired the knowledge of *c* equality before this.

Yes.

It seems then that we must have possessed it before birth.

It seems so.

Therefore, if we had this knowledge, we knew before birth and immediately after not only the Equal, but the Greater and the Smaller and all such things, for our present argument is no more about the Equal than about the Beautiful itself, the Good itself, the Just, the Pious and, as I say, about all those things to *d* which we can attach the word "itself," both when we are putting questions and answering them. So we must have acquired knowledge of them all before we were born.

That is so.

If, having acquired this knowledge in each case, we have not forgotten it, we remain knowing and have knowledge throughout our life, for to know is to acquire knowledge, keep it and not lose it. Do we not call the losing of knowledge forgetting?

Most certainly, Socrates, he said. *e*

But, I think, if we acquired this knowledge before birth, then lost it at birth, and then later by the use of our senses in connection with those objects we mentioned, we recovered the knowledge we had before, would not what we call learning be the recovery of our own knowledge, and we are right to call this recollection?

Certainly.

It was seen to be possible for someone to see or *76* hear or otherwise perceive something, and by this to be put in mind of something else which he had forgotten and which is related to it by similarity or difference. One of two things follows, as I say: either we were born with the knowledge of it, and all of us know it throughout life, or those who later, we say, are learning, are only recollecting, and learning would be recollection.

That is certainly the case, Socrates.

Which alternative do you choose, Simmias? That
b we are born with this knowledge or that we recollect
later the things of which we had knowledge previously?

I have no means of choosing at the moment, Socrates.

Well, can you make this choice? What is your
opinion about it? A man who has knowledge would
be able to give an account of what he knows, or would
he not?

He must certainly be able to do so, Socrates, he said.

And do you think everybody can give an account
of the things we were mentioning just now?

I wish they could, said Simmias, but I'm afraid it
is much more likely that by this time tomorrow there
will be no one left who can do so adequately.

c   So you do not think that everybody has knowledge
of those things?

No indeed.

So they recollect what they once learned?

They must.

When did our souls acquire the knowledge of
them? Certainly not since we were born as men.

Indeed no.

Before that then?

Yes.

So then, Simmias, our souls also existed apart from
the body before they took on human form, and they
had intelligence.

Unless we acquire the knowledge at the moment
of birth, Socrates, for that time is still left to us.

d   Quite so, my friend, but at what other time do we
lose it? We just now agreed that we are not born with
that knowledge. Do we then lose it at the very time
we acquire it, or can you mention any other time?

I cannot, Socrates. I did not realize that I was
talking nonsense.

So this is our position, Simmias? he said. If those
realities we are always talking about exist, the Beautiful and the Good and all that kind of reality, and
we refer all the things we perceive to that reality,
discovering that it existed before and is ours, and we
e compare these things with it, then, just as they exist,
so our soul must exist before we are born. If these
realities do not exist, then this argument is altogether
futile. Is this the position, that there is an equal necessity for those realities to exist, and for our souls to

exist before we were born? If the former do not exist,
neither do the latter?

I do not think, Socrates, said Simmias, that there
is any possible doubt that it is equally necessary for
both to exist, and it is opportune that our argument
comes to the conclusion that our soul exists before 77
we are born, and equally so that reality of which
you are now speaking. Nothing is so evident to me
personally as that all such things must certainly exist,
the Beautiful, the Good, and all those you mentioned
just now. I also think that sufficient proof of this has
been given.

Then what about Cebes? said Socrates, for we must
persuade Cebes also.

He is sufficiently convinced I think, said Simmias,
though he is the most difficult of men to persuade
by argument, but I believe him to be fully convinced
that our soul existed before we were born. I do not
think myself, however, that it has been proved that *b*
the soul continues to exist after death; the opinion
of the majority which Cebes mentioned still stands,
that when a man dies his soul is dispersed and this
is the end of its existence. What is to prevent the soul
coming to be and being constituted from some other
source, existing before it enters a human body and
then, having done so and departed from it, itself dying
and being destroyed?

You are right, Simmias, said Cebes. Half of what *c*
needed proof has been proved, namely, that our soul
existed before we were born, but further proof is
needed that it exists no less after we have died, if the
proof is to be complete.

It has been proved even now, Simmias and Cebes,
said Socrates, if you are ready to combine this argument with the one we agreed on before, that every
living thing must come from the dead. If the soul
exists before, it must, as it comes to life and birth,
come from nowhere else than death and being dead, *d*
so how could it avoid existing after death since it
must be born again? What you speak of has then even
now been proved. However, I think you and Simmias
would like to discuss the argument more fully. You
seem to have this childish fear that the wind would
really dissolve and scatter the soul, as it leaves the
body, especially if one happens to die in a high wind *e*
and not in calm weather.

Cebes laughed and said: "Assuming that we were
afraid, Socrates, try to change our minds, or rather

do not assume that we are afraid, but perhaps there is a child in us who has these fears; try to persuade him not to fear death like a bogey."

You should, said Socrates, sing a charm over him every day until you have charmed away his fears.

78 Where shall we find a good charmer for these fears, Socrates, he said, now that you are leaving us?

Greece is a large country, Cebes, he said, and there are good men in it; the tribes of foreigners are also numerous. You should search for such a charmer among them all, sparing neither trouble nor expense, for there is nothing on which you could spend your money to greater advantage. You must also search among yourselves, for you might not easily find people who could do this better than yourselves.

That shall be done, said Cebes, but let us, if it
b pleases you, go back to the argument where we left it.

Of course it pleases me.

Splendid, he said.

We must then ask ourselves something like this: what kind of thing is likely to be scattered? On behalf of what kind of thing should one fear this, and for what kind of thing should one not fear it? We should then examine to which class the soul belongs, and as a result either fear for the soul or be of good cheer.

What you say is true.

c Is not anything that is composite and a compound by nature liable to be split up into its component parts, and only that which is noncomposite, if anything, is not likely to be split up?

I think that is the case, said Cebes.

Are not the things that always remain the same and in the same state most likely not to be composite, whereas those that vary from one time to another and are never the same are composite?

I think that is so.

Let us then return to those same things with which
d we were dealing earlier, to that reality of whose existence we are giving an account in our questions and answers; are they ever the same and in the same state, or do they vary from one time to another; can the Equal itself, the Beautiful itself, each thing in itself, the real, ever be affected by any change whatever? Or does each of them that really is, being uniform by itself, remain the same and never in any way tolerate any change whatever?

It must remain the same, said Cebes, and in the same state, Socrates.

What of the many beautiful particulars, be they men, horses, clothes, or other such things, or the e many equal particulars, and all those which bear the same name as those others? Do they remain the same or, in total contrast to those other realities, one might say, never in any way remain the same as themselves or in relation to each other?

The latter is the case, they are never in the same state.

These latter you could touch and see and perceive 79 with the other senses, but those that always remain the same can only be grasped by the reasoning power of the mind? They are not seen but are invisible?

That is altogether true, he said.

Do you then want us to assume two kinds of existences, the visible and the invisible?

Let us assume this.

And the invisible always remains the same, whereas the visible never does?

Let us assume that too.

Now one part of ourselves is the body, another part b is the soul?

Quite so.

To which class of existence do we say the body is more alike and akin?

To the visible, as anyone can see.

What about the soul? Is it visible or invisible?

It is not visible to men, Socrates, he said.

Well, we meant visible and invisible to human eyes; or to any others, do you think?

To human eyes.

Then what do we say about the soul? Is it visible or not visible?

Not visible.

So it is invisible? —Yes.

So the soul is more like the invisible than the body, and the body more like the visible? —Without any c doubt, Socrates.

Haven't we also said some time ago that when the soul makes use of the body to investigate something, be it through hearing or seeing or some other sense— for to investigate something through the body is to do it through the senses—it is dragged by the body to the things that are never the same, and the soul itself strays and is confused and dizzy, as if it were drunk, in so far as it is in contact with that kind of thing?

Certainly.

d   But when the soul investigates by itself it passes into the realm of what is pure, ever existing, immortal and unchanging, and being akin to this, it always stays with it whenever it is by itself and can do so; it ceases to stray and remains in the same state as it is in touch with things of the same kind, and its experience then is what is called wisdom?

Altogether well said and very true, Socrates, he said.

Judging from what we have said before and what *e* we are saying now, to which of these two kinds do you think that the soul is more alike and more akin?

I think, Socrates, he said, that on this line of argument any man, even the dullest, would agree that the soul is altogether more like that which always exists in the same state rather than like that which does not.

What of the body?

That is like the other.

Look at it also this way: when the soul and the 80 body are together, nature orders the one to be subject and to be ruled, and the other to rule and be master. Then again, which do you think is like the divine and which like the mortal? Do you not think that the nature of the divine is to rule and to lead, whereas it is that of the mortal to be ruled and be subject?

I do.

Which does the soul resemble?

Obviously, Socrates, the soul resembles the divine, and the body resembles the mortal.

Consider then, Cebes, whether it follows from all that has been said that the soul is most like the divine, *b* deathless, intelligible, uniform, indissoluble, always the same as itself, whereas the body is most like that which is human, mortal, multiform, unintelligible, soluble and never consistently the same. Have we anything else to say to show, my dear Cebes, that this is not the case?

We have not.

Well then, that being so, is it not natural for the body to dissolve easily, and for the soul to be altogether indissoluble, or nearly so?

c   Of course.

You realize, he said, that when a man dies, the visible part, the body, which exists in the visible world, and which we call the corpse, whose natural lot it would be to dissolve, fall apart and be blown away, does not immediately suffer any of these things but remains for a fair time, in fact, quite a long time if the man dies with his body in a suitable condition and at a favorable season? If the body is emaciated or embalmed, as in Egypt, it remains almost whole for a remarkable length of time, and even if the body decays, some parts of it, namely bones and sinews and *d* the like, are nevertheless, one might say, deathless. Is that not so? — Yes.

Will the soul, the invisible part which makes its way to a region of the same kind, noble and pure and invisible, to Hades in fact, to the good and wise god whither, god willing, my soul must soon be going — will the soul, being of this kind and nature, be scattered and destroyed on leaving the body, as the majority of men say? Far from it, my dear Cebes and *e* Simmias, but what happens is much more like this: if it is pure when it leaves the body and drags nothing bodily with it, as it had no willing association with the body in life, but avoided it and gathered itself together by itself and always practiced this, which is no other than practising philosophy in the right way, 81 in fact, training to die easily. Or is this not training for death?

It surely is.

A soul in this state makes its way to the invisible, which is like itself, the divine and immortal and wise, and arriving there it can be happy, having rid itself of confusion, ignorance, fear, violent desires and the other human ills and, as is said of the initiates, truly spend the rest of time with the gods. Shall we say this, Cebes, or something different?

This, by Zeus, said Cebes.

But I think that if the soul is polluted and impure *b* when it leaves the body, having always been associated with it and served it, bewitched by physical desires and pleasures to the point at which nothing seems to exist for it but the physical, which one can touch and see or eat and drink or make use of for sexual enjoyment, and if that soul is accustomed to hate and fear and avoid that which is dim and invisible to the eyes but intelligible and to be grasped by philosophy — do you think such a soul will escape pure and by itself?

Impossible, he said.   *c*

It is, no doubt, permeated by the physical, which constant intercourse and association with the body, as well as considerable practice, has caused to become ingrained in it?

Quite so.

We must believe, my friend, that this bodily element is heavy, ponderous, earthy and visible. Through it, such a soul has become heavy and is dragged back to the visible region in fear of the unseen and of Hades. It wanders, as we are told, around *d* graves and monuments, where shadowy phantoms, images that such souls produce, have been seen, souls that have not been freed and purified but share in the visible, and are therefore seen.

That is likely, Socrates.

It is indeed, Cebes. Moreover, these are not the souls of good but of inferior men, which are forced to wander there, paying the penalty for their previous bad upbringing. They wander until their longing for *e* that which accompanies them, the physical, again imprisons them in a body, and they are then, as is likely, bound to such characters as they have practiced in their life.

What kind of characters do you say these are, Socrates?

Those, for example, who have carelessly practiced gluttony, violence and drunkenness are likely to join *82* a company of donkeys or of similar animals. Do you not think so?

Very likely.

Those who have esteemed injustice highly, and tyranny and plunder will join the tribes of wolves and hawks and kites, or where else shall we say that they go?

Certainly to those, said Cebes.

And clearly, the destination of the others will conform to the way in which they have behaved?

Clearly, of course.

The happiest of these, who will also have the best destination, are those who have practiced popular *b* and social virtue, which they call moderation and justice and which was developed by habit and practice, without philosophy or understanding?

How are they the happiest?

Because it is likely that they will again join a social and gentle group, either of bees or wasps or ants, and then again the same kind of human group, and so be moderate men.

That is likely.

No one may join the company of the gods who has not practiced philosophy and is not completely *c* pure when he departs from life, no one but the lover of learning. It is for this reason, my friends Simmias and Cebes, that those who practice philosophy in the right way keep away from all bodily passions, master them and do not surrender themselves to them; it is not at all for fear of wasting their substance and of poverty, which the majority and the money-lovers fear, nor for fear of dishonor and ill repute, like the ambitious and lovers of honors, that they keep away from them.

That would not be natural for them, Socrates, said Cebes.

By Zeus, no, he said. Those who care for their own *d* soul and do not live for the service of their body dismiss all these things. They do not travel the same road as those who do not know where they are going but, believing that nothing should be done contrary to philosophy and their deliverance and purification, they turn to this and follow wherever philosophy leads.

How so, Socrates?

I will tell you, he said. The lovers of learning know that when philosophy gets hold of their soul, it is imprisoned in and clinging to the body, and that it *e* is forced to examine other things through it as through a cage and not by itself, and that it wallows in every kind of ignorance. Philosophy sees that the worst feature of this imprisonment is that it is due to desires, so that the prisoner himself is contributing to his own incarceration most of all. As I say, the lovers of learning know that philosophy gets hold of their soul *83* when it is in that state, then gently encourages it and tries to free it by showing them that investigation through the eyes is full of deceit, as is that through the ears and the other senses. Philosophy then persuades the soul to withdraw from the senses in so far as it is not compelled to use them and bids the soul to gather itself together by itself, to trust only itself and whatever reality, existing by itself, the soul by *b* itself understands, and not to consider as true whatever it examines by other means, for this is different in different circumstances and is sensible and visible, whereas what the soul itself sees is intelligible and invisible. The soul of the true philosopher thinks that this deliverance must not be opposed and so keeps away from pleasures and desires and pains as far as he can; he reflects that violent pleasure or pain or passion does not cause merely such evils as one might expect, such as one suffers when one has been sick or extravagant through desire, but the greatest and *c* most extreme evil, though one does not reflect on this.

What is that, Socrates? asked Cebes.

That the soul of every man, when it feels violent pleasure or pain in connection with some object, inevitably believes at the same time that what causes such feelings must be very clear and very true, which it is not. Such objects are mostly visible, are they not?

Certainly.

d   And doesn't such an experience tie the soul to the body most completely?

How so?

Because every pleasure and every pain provides, as it were, another nail to rivet the soul to the body and to weld them together. It makes the soul corporeal, so that it believes that truth is what the body says it is. As it shares the beliefs and delights of the body, I think it inevitably comes to share its ways and manner of life and is unable ever to reach Hades in a pure state; it is always full of body when it departs, so that it soon falls back into another body and grows with it as if it had been sewn into it. Because of this, it can have no part in the company of the divine, the pure and uniform.

What you say is very true, Socrates, said Cebes.

This is why genuine lovers of learning are moderate and brave, or do you think it is for the reasons the majority says they are?

84   I certainly do not.

Indeed no. This is how the soul of a philosopher would reason: it would not think that while philosophy must free it, it should while being freed surrender itself to pleasures and pains and imprison itself again, thus laboring in vain like Penelope at her web. The soul of the philosopher achieves a calm from such emotions; it follows reason and ever stays with it contemplating the true, the divine, which is not the object of opinion. Nurtured by this, it believes that one should live in this manner as long as one is alive and, after death, arrive at what is akin and of the same kind, and escape from human evils. After such nurture there is no danger, Simmias and Cebes, that one should fear that, on parting from the body, the soul would be scattered and dissipated by the winds and no longer be anything anywhere.

c   When Socrates finished speaking there was a long silence. He appeared to be concentrating on what had been said, and so were most of us. But Cebes and Simmias were whispering to each other. Socrates observed them and questioned them. "Come," he said,

"do you think there is something lacking in my argument? There are still many doubtful points and many objections for anyone who wants a thorough discussion of these matters. If you are discussing some other subject, I have nothing to say, but if you have some difficulty about this one, do not hesitate to speak for yourselves and expound it if you think the argument could be improved, and if you think you will do better, take me along with you in the discussion."   d

I will tell you the truth, Socrates, said Simmias. Both of us have been in difficulty for some time, and each of us has been urging the other to question you because we wanted to hear what you would say, but we hesitated to bother you, lest it be displeasing to you in your present misfortune.

When Socrates heard this he laughed quietly and said: "Really, Simmias, it would be hard for me to persuade other people that I do not consider my e present fate a misfortune if I cannot persuade even you, and you are afraid that it is more difficult to deal with me than before. You seem to think me inferior to the swans in prophecy. They sing before too, but when they realize that they must die they sing most and most beautifully, as they rejoice that they are about to depart to join the god whose servants they 85 are. But men, because of their own fear of death, tell lies about the swans and say that they lament their death and sing in sorrow. They do not reflect that no bird sings when it is hungry or cold or suffers in any other way, neither the nightingale nor the swallow nor the hoopoe, though they do say that these sing laments when in pain. Nor do the swans, but I believe that as they belong to Apollo, they are prophetic, have b knowledge of the future and sing of the blessings of the underworld, sing and rejoice on that day beyond what they did before. As I believe myself to be a fellow servant with the swans and dedicated to the same god, and have received from my master a gift of prophecy not inferior to theirs, I am no more despondent than they on leaving life. Therefore, you must speak and ask whatever you want as long as the authorities allow it."

Well spoken, said Simmias. I will tell you my difficulty, and then Cebes will say why he does not accept what was said. I believe, as perhaps you do, that c precise knowledge on that subject is impossible or extremely difficult in our present life, but that it surely shows a very poor spirit not to examine thoroughly what is said about it, and to desist before one is exhausted by an all-round investigation. One should achieve one of these things: learn the truth about these things or find it for oneself, or, if that is impossible, adopt the best and most irrefutable of men's theories, and, borne upon this, sail through the dangers of life as upon a raft, unless someone should make that journey safer and less risky upon a firmer vessel of some divine doctrine. So even now, since you have said what you did, I will feel no shame at asking questions, and I will not blame myself in the future because I did not say what I think. As I examine what we said, both by myself and with Cebes, it does not seem to be adequate.

Said Socrates: "You may well be right, my friend, but tell me how it is inadequate."

In this way, as it seems to me, he said: "One might make the same argument about harmony, lyre and strings, that a harmony is something invisible, without body, beautiful and divine in the attuned lyre, whereas the lyre itself and its strings are physical, bodily, composite, earthy and akin to what is mortal. Then if someone breaks the lyre, cuts or breaks the strings and then insists, using the same argument as you, that the harmony must still exist and is not destroyed because it would be impossible for the lyre and the strings, which are mortal, still to exist when the strings are broken, and for the harmony, which is akin and of the same nature as the divine and immortal, to be destroyed before that which is mortal; he would say that the harmony itself still must exist and that the wood and the strings must rot before the harmony can suffer. And indeed Socrates, I think you must have this in mind, that we really do suppose the soul to be something of this kind; as the body is stretched and held together by the hot and the cold, the dry and the moist and other such things, and our soul is a mixture and harmony of those things when they are mixed with each other rightly and in due measure. If then the soul is a kind of harmony or attunement, clearly, when our body is relaxed or stretched without due measure by diseases and other evils, the soul must immediately be destroyed, even if it be most divine, as are the other harmonies found in music and all the works of artists, and the remains of each body last for a long time until they rot or are burned. Consider what we shall say in answer to one who deems the soul to be a mixture of bodily elements and to be the first to perish in the process we call death."

Socrates looked at us keenly, as was his habit, smiled and said: "What Simmias says is quite fair. If one of you is more resourceful than I am, why did he not answer him, for he seems to have handled the argument competently. However, I think that before we answer him, we should hear Cebes' objection, in order that we may have time to deliberate on an answer. When we have heard him we should either agree with them, if we think them in tune with us or, if not, defend our own argument. Come then, Cebes. What is troubling you?"

I tell you, said Cebes, the argument seems to me to be at the same point as before and open to the same objection. I do not deny that it has been very elegantly and, if it is not offensive to say so, sufficiently proved that our soul existed before it took on this present form, but I do not believe the same applies to its existing somewhere after our death. Not that I agree with Simmias' objection that the soul is not stronger and much more lasting than the body, for I think it is superior in all these respects. "Why then," the argument might say, "are you still unconvinced? Since you see that when the man dies, the weaker part continues to exist, do you not think that the more lasting part must be preserved during that time?" On this point consider whether what I say makes sense.

Like Simmias, I too need an image, for I think this argument is much as if one said at the death of an old weaver that the man had not perished but was safe and sound somewhere, and offered as proof the fact that the cloak the old man had woven himself and was wearing was still sound and had not perished. If one was not convinced, he would be asked whether a man lasts longer than a cloak which is in use and being worn, and if the answer was that a man lasts much longer, this would be taken as proof that the man was definitely safe and sound, since the more temporary thing had not perished. But Simmias, I do not think that is so, for consider what I say. Anybody could see that the man who said this was talking nonsense. That weaver had woven and worn out many such cloaks. He perished after many of them, but before the last. That does not mean that a man is inferior and weaker than a cloak. The image illustrates, I think, the relationship of the soul to the body, and anyone who says the same thing about them would appear to me to be talking sense, that the soul lasts a long time while the body is weaker and more short-lived. He might say that each soul wears out many bodies, especially if it lives many years. If the body were in a state of flux and perished while the man was still alive, and the soul wove afresh the

e body that is worn out, yet it would be inevitable that whenever the soul perished it would be wearing the last body it wove and perish only before this last. Then when the soul perished, the body would show the weakness of its nature by soon decaying and disappearing. So we cannot trust this argument and be confident that our soul continues to exist somewhere

88 after our death. For, if one were to concede, even more than you do, to a man using that argument, if one were to grant him not only that the soul exists in the time before we are born, but that there is no reason why the soul of some should not exist and continue to exist after our death, and thus frequently be born and die in turn; if one were to grant him that the soul's nature is so strong that it can survive many bodies, but if, having granted all this, one does not further agree that the soul is not damaged by its many births and is not, in the end, altogether de-stroyed in one of those deaths, he might say that no

b one knows which death and dissolution of the body brings about the destruction of the soul, since not one of us can be aware of this. And in that case, any man who faces death with confidence is foolish, unless he can prove that the soul is altogether immor-tal. If he cannot, a man about to die must of necessity always fear for his soul, lest the present separation of the soul from the body bring about the complete destruction of the soul.

c   When we heard what they said we were all de-pressed, as we told each other afterwards. We had been quite convinced by the previous argument, and they seemed to confuse us again, and to drive us to doubt not only what had already been said but also what was going to be said, lest we be worthless as critics or the subject itself admitted of no certainty.

ECHECRATES: By the gods, Phaedo, you have my sympathy, for as I listen to you now I find myself

d saying to myself: "What argument shall we trust? That of Socrates, which was extremely convincing, has now fallen into discredit; the statement that the soul is some kind of harmony has a remarkable hold on me, now and always, and when it was mentioned it

reminded me that I had myself previously thought so. And now I am again quite in need, as if from the beginning, of some other argument to convince me that the soul does not die along with the man. Tell me then, by Zeus, how Socrates tackled the argument. Was he obviously distressed, as you say you people were, or was he not, but quietly came to the rescue e of his argument, and did he do so satisfactorily or inadequately? Tell us everything as precisely as you can.

PHAEDO: I have certainly often admired Socrates, Echecrates, but never more than on this occasion. That he had a reply was perhaps not strange. What 89 I wondered at most in him was the pleasant, kind and admiring way he received the young men's argument, and how sharply he was aware of the effect the discus-sion had on us, and then how well he healed our distress and, as it were, recalled us from our flight and defeat and turned us around to join him in the examination of their argument.

E: How did he do this?

P: I will tell you. I happened to be sitting on his right by the couch on a low stool, so that he was sitting well above me. He stroked my head and pressed b the hair on the back of my neck, for he was in the habit of playing with my hair at times. "Tomorrow, Phaedo," he said, "you will probably cut this beauti-ful hair."

Likely enough, Socrates, I said.

Not if you take my advice, he said.

Why not? said I.

It is today, he said, that I shall cut my hair and you yours, if our argument dies on us, and we cannot revive it. If I were you, and the argument escaped c me, I would take an oath, as the Argives[15] did, not to let my hair grow before I fought again and defeated the argument of Simmias and Cebes.

But, I said, they say that not even Heracles could fight two people.

Then call on me as your Iolaus, as long as the daylight lasts.

I shall call on you, but in this case as Iolaus calling on Heracles.

---

15. [Herodotus (I, 82) tells us that after losing the city of Thyreae to the Spartans, the Argives swore not to let their hair grow again or their women wear golden ornaments until they had recaptured it.]

It makes no difference, he said, but first there is a certain experience we must be careful to avoid.

What is that? I asked.

d   That we should not become misologues, as people become misanthropes. There is no greater evil one can suffer than to hate reasonable discourse. Misology and misanthropy arise in the same way. Misanthropy comes when a man without knowledge or skill has placed great trust in someone and believes him to be altogether truthful, sound and trustworthy; then, a short time afterwards he finds him to be wicked and unreliable, and then this happens in another case; when one has frequently had that experience, espe-
e   cially with those whom one believed to be one's closest friends, then, in the end, after many such blows, one comes to hate all men and to believe that no one is sound in any way at all. Have you not seen this happen?

I surely have, I said.

This is a shameful state of affairs, he said, and obviously due to to an attempt to have human relations without any skill in human affairs, for such skill would lead one to believe, what is in fact true, that
90 the very good and the very wicked are both quite rare, and that most men are between those extremes.

How do you mean? said I.

The same as with the very tall and the very short, he said. Do you think anything is rarer than to find an extremely tall man or an extremely short one? Or a dog or any thing else whatever? Or again, one extremely swift or extremely slow, ugly or beautiful, white or black? Are you not aware that in all those cases the most extreme at either end are rare and few, but those in between are many and plentiful?

Certainly, I said.

b   Therefore, he said, if a contest of wickedness were established, there too the winners, you think, would be very few?

That is likely, said I.

Likely indeed, he said, but arguments are not like men in this particular. I was merely following your lead just now.[16] The similarity lies rather in this: it is as when one who lacks skill in arguments puts his trust in an argument as being true, then shortly afterwards

believes it to be false—as sometimes it is and sometimes it is not—and so with another argument and then another. You know how those in particular who spend their time studying contradiction in the end believe themselves to have become very wise and that c they alone have understood that there is no soundness or reliability in any object or in any argument, but that all that exists simply fluctuates up and down as if it were in the Euripus[17] and does not remain in the same place for any time at all.

What you say, I said, is certainly true.

It would be pitiable, Phaedo, he said, when there is a true and reliable argument and one that can be understood, if a man who has dealt with such d arguments as appear at one time true, at another time untrue, should not blame himself or his own lack of skill but, because of his distress, in the end gladly shift the blame away from himself to the arguments, and spend the rest of his life hating and reviling reasonable discussion and so be deprived of truth and knowledge of reality.

Yes, by Zeus, I said, that would be pitiable indeed.

This then is the first thing we should guard against, he said. We should not allow into our minds the e conviction that argumentation has nothing sound about it; much rather we should believe that it is we who are not yet sound and that we must take courage and be eager to attain soundness, you and the others for the sake of your whole life still to come, and I for 91 the sake of death itself. I am in danger at this moment of not having a philosophical attitude about this, but like those who are quite uneducated, I am eager to get the better of you in argument, for the uneducated, when they engage in argument about anything, give no thought to the truth about the subject of discussion but are only eager that those present will accept the position they have set forth. I differ from them only to this extent: I shall not be eager to get the agreement of those present that what I say is true, except incidentally, but I shall be very eager that I should myself be thoroughly convinced that things are so. For I am thinking—see in how contentious a spirit—that if what I say is true, it is a fine thing to be convinced; if, on the other hand, nothing exists after death, at b

16. [Socrates presumably means that there are plenty of very bad arguments. It is not clear where he was following Phaedo in the argument.]

17. [The Euripus was the name of the straits between Euboea and Boeotia; its currents were both violent and variable.]

least for this time before I die I shall distress those present less with lamentations and my folly will not continue to exist along with me—that would be a bad thing—but will come to an end in a short time. Thus prepared, Simmias and Cebes, he said, I come to deal with your argument. If you will take my advice, *c* you will give but little thought to Socrates but much more to the truth. If you think that what I say is true, agree with me; if not, oppose it with every argument and take care that in my eagerness I do not deceive myself and you and, like a bee, leave my sting in you when I go.

We must proceed, he said, and first remind me of what you said if I do not appear to remember it. Simmias, as I believe, is in doubt and fear that the soul, *d* though it is more divine and beautiful than the body, yet predeceases it, being a kind of harmony. Cebes, I thought, agrees with me that the soul lasts much longer than the body, but that no one knows whether the soul often wears out many bodies and then, on leaving its last body, is now itself destroyed. This then is death, the destruction of the soul, since the body is always being destroyed. Are these the questions, Simmias and Cebes, which we must investigate?

e They both agreed that they were.

Do you then, he asked, reject all our previous statements, or some but not others?

Some, they both said, but not others.

What, he said, about the statements we made that learning is recollection and that, if this was so, our 92 soul must of necessity exist elsewhere before us, before it was imprisoned in the body?

For myself, said Cebes, I was wonderfully convinced by it at the time and I stand by it now also, more than by any other statement.

That, said Simmias, is also my position, and I should be very surprised if I ever changed my opinion about this.

But you must change your opinion, my Theban friend, said Socrates, if you still believe that a harmony is a composite thing, and that the soul is a kind of harmony of the elements of the body in a state of tension, for surely you will not allow yourself to main- *b* tain that a composite harmony existed before those elements from which it had to be composed, or would you?

Never, Socrates, he said.

Do you realize, he said, that this is what you are

in fact saying when you state that the soul exists before it takes on the form and body of a man and that it is composed of elements which do not yet exist? A harmony is not like that to which you compare it; the lyre and the strings and the notes, though still unharmonized, exist; the harmony is composed last *c* of all, and is the first to be destroyed. How will you harmonize this statement with your former one?

In no way, said Simmias.

And surely, he said, a statement about harmony should do so more than any other.

It should, said Simmias.

So your statement is inconsistent? Consider which of your statements you prefer, that learning is recollection or that the soul is a harmony?

I much prefer the former, Socrates. I adopted the *d* latter without proof, because of a certain probability and plausibility, which is why it appeals to most men. I know that arguments of which the proof is based on probability are pretentious and, if one does not guard against them, they certainly deceive one, in geometry and everything else. The theory of recollection and learning, however, was based on an assumption worthy of acceptance, for our soul was said to exist also before it came into the body, just as the reality does that is of the kind that we qualify by the words "which truly is," and I convinced myself that I was quite correct to accept it. Therefore, I cannot *e* accept the theory that the soul is a harmony either from myself or anyone else.

What of this, Simmias? Do you think it natural for a harmony, or any other composite, to be in a different state from that of the elements of which it is composed? 93

Not at all, said Simmias.

Nor, as I think, can it act or be acted upon in a different way than its elements?

He agreed.

One must therefore suppose that a harmony does not direct its components, but is directed by them.

He accepted this.

A harmony is therefore far from making a movement, or uttering a sound, or doing anything else, in a manner contrary to that of its parts.

Far from it indeed, he said.

Does not the nature of each harmony depend on the way it has been harmonized?

I do not understand, he said.

Will it not, if it is more and more fully harmonized,

b be more and more fully a harmony, and if it is less and less fully harmonized, it will be less and less fully a harmony?

Certainly.

Can this be true about the soul, that one soul is more and more fully a soul than another, or is less and less fully a soul, even to the smallest extent?

Not in any way.

Come now, by Zeus, he said. One soul is said to have intelligence and virtue and to be good, another *c* to have folly and wickedness and to be bad. Are those things truly said?

They certainly are.

What will someone who holds the theory that the soul is a harmony say that those things are which reside in the soul, that is, virtue and wickedness? Are these some other harmony and disharmony? That the good soul is harmonized and, being a harmony, has within itself another harmony, whereas the evil soul is both itself a lack of harmony and has no other within itself?

I don't know what to say, said Simmias, but one who holds that assumption must obviously say something of that kind.

d We have previously agreed, he said, that one soul is not more and not less a soul than another, and this means that one harmony is not more and more fully, or less and less fully, a harmony than another. Is that not so?

Certainly.

Now that which is no more and no less a harmony is not more or less harmonized. Is that so?

It is.

Can that which is neither more nor less harmonized partake more or less of harmony, or does it do so equally?

Equally.

e Then if a soul is neither more nor less a soul than another, it has been harmonized to the same extent?

This is so.

If that is so, it would have no greater share of disharmony or of harmony?

It would not.

That being the case, could one soul have more wickedness or virtue than another, if wickedness is disharmony and virtue harmony?

It could not.

94 But rather, Simmias, according to correct reason-ing, no soul, if it is a harmony, will have any share of wickedness, for harmony is surely altogether this very thing, harmony, and would never share in disharmony.

It certainly would not.

Nor would a soul, being altogether this very thing, a soul, share in wickedness?

How could it, in view of what has been said?

So it follows from this argument that all the souls of all living creatures will be equally good, if souls are by nature equally this very thing, souls.

I think so, Socrates.

Does our argument seem right, he said, and does it seem that it should have come to this, if the hypothe- *b* sis that the soul is a harmony was correct?

Not in any way, he said.

Further, of all the parts of a man, can you mention any other part that rules him than his soul, especially if it is a wise soul?

I cannot.

Does it do so by following the affections of the body or by opposing them? I mean, for example, that when the body is hot and thirsty the soul draws him to the opposite, to not drinking; when the body is hungry, to not eating, and we see a thousand other examples of the soul opposing the affections of the *c* body. Is that not so?

It certainly is.

On the other hand we previously agreed that if the soul were a harmony, it would never be out of tune with the stress and relaxation and the striking of the strings or anything else done to its composing elements, but that it would follow and never direct them?

We did so agree, of course.

Well, does it now appear to do quite the opposite, ruling over all the elements of which one says it is *d* composed, opposing nearly all of them throughout life, directing all their ways, inflicting harsh and painful punishment on them, at times in physical culture and medicine, at other times more gently by threats and exhortations, holding converse with desires and passions and fears as if it were one thing talking to a different one, as Homer wrote somewhere in the *Odyssey* where he says that Odysseus "struck his breast and rebuked his heart saying,

'Endure, my heart, you have endured worse than this.'"

e Do you think that when he composed this the poet thought that his soul was a harmony, a thing to be directed by the affections of the body? Did he not rather regard it as ruling over them and mastering them, itself a much more divine thing than a harmony?

Yes, by Zeus, I think so, Socrates.

Therefore, my good friend, it is quite wrong for us 95 to say that the soul is a harmony, and in saying so we would disagree both with the divine poet Homer and with ourselves.

That is so, he said.

Very well, said Socrates. Harmonia of Thebes seems somehow reasonably propitious to us. How and by what argument, my dear Cebes, can we propitiate Cadmus?[18]

I think, Cebes said, that you will find a way. You dealt with the argument about harmony in a manner that was quite astonishing to me. When Simmias was *b* speaking of his difficulties I was very much wondering whether anyone would be able to deal with his argument, and I was quite dumbfounded when right away he could not resist your argument's first onslaught. I should not wonder therefore if that of Cadmus suffered the same fate.

My good sir, said Socrates, do not boast, lest some malign influence upset the argument we are about to make. However, we leave that to the care of the god, but let us come to grips with it in the Homeric fashion, to see if there is anything in what you say. The sum of your problem is this: you consider that the *c* soul must be proved to be immortal and indestructible before a philosopher on the point of death, who is confident that he will fare much better in the underworld than if he had led any other kind of life, can avoid being foolish and simple-minded in this confidence. To prove that the soul is strong, that it is divine, that it existed before we were born as men, all this, you say, does not show the soul to be immortal but only long-lasting. That it existed for a very long time before, that it knew much and acted much, *d* makes it no more immortal because of that; indeed, its very entering into a human body was the beginning

18. [Harmonia was in legend the wife of Cadmus, the founder of Thebes. Socrates' punning joke is simply that, having dealt with Harmonia (harmony), we must now deal with Cadmus (i.e., Cebes, the other Theban).]

of its destruction, like a disease; it would live that life in distress and would in the end be destroyed in what we call death. You say it makes no difference whether it enters a body once or many times as far as the fear of each of us is concerned, for it is natural for a man who is no fool to be afraid, if he does not know and cannot prove that the soul is immortal. This, I think, is what you maintain, Cebes; I deliberately repeat it often, in order that no point may escape us, and that *e* you may add or subtract something if you wish.

And Cebes said: "There is nothing that I want to add or subtract at the moment. That is what I say."

Socrates paused for a long time, deep in thought. He then said: "This is no unimportant problem that you raise, Cebes, for it requires a thorough investiga- 96 tion of the cause of generation and destruction. I will, if you wish, give you an account of my experience in these matters. Then if something I say seems useful to you, make use of it to persuade us of your position."

I surely do wish that, said Cebes.

Listen then, and I will, Cebes, he said. When I was a young man I was wonderfully keen on that wisdom which they call natural science, for I thought it splendid to know the causes of everything, why it comes to be, why it perishes and why it exists. I was often changing my mind in the investigation, in the *b* first instance, of questions such as these: Are living creatures nurtured when heat and cold produce a kind of putrefaction, as some say? Do we think with our blood, or air, or fire, or none of these, and does the brain provide our senses of hearing and sight and smell, from which come memory and opinion, and from memory and opinion which has become stable, comes knowledge? Then again, as I investigated how these things perish and what happens to things in the sky and on the earth, finally I became convinced that *c* I have no natural aptitude at all for that kind of investigation, and of this I will give you sufficient proof. This investigation made me quite blind even to those things which I and others thought that I clearly knew before, so that I unlearned what I thought I knew before, about many other things and specifically about how men grew. I thought before that it was obvious to anybody that men grew through *d* eating and drinking, for food adds flesh to flesh and bones to bones, and in the same way appropriate parts were added to all other parts of the body, so that the man grew from an earlier small bulk to a large bulk later, and so a small man became big. That is what I thought then. Do you not think it was reasonable?

I do, said Cebes.

Then further consider this: I thought my opinion was satisfactory, that when a large man stood by a *e* small one he was taller by a head, and so a horse was taller than a horse. Even clearer than this, I thought that ten was more than eight because two had been added, and that a two-cubit length is larger than a cubit because it surpasses it by half its length.

And what do you think now about those things?

That I am far, by Zeus, from believing that I know the cause of any of those things. I will not even allow myself to say that where one is added to one either the one to which it is added or the one that is added becomes two, or that the one added and the one to *97* which it is added become two because of the addition of the one to the other. I wonder that, when each of them is separate from the other, each of them is one, nor are they then two, but that, when they come near to one another, this is the cause of their becoming two, the coming together and being placed closer to one another. Nor can I any longer be persuaded that when one thing is divided, this division is the cause *b* of its becoming two, for just now the cause of becoming two was the opposite. At that time it was their coming close together and one was added to the other, but now it is because one is taken and separated from the other.

I do not any longer persuade myself that I know why a unit or anything else comes to be, or perishes or exists by the old method of investigation, and I do not accept it, but I have a confused method of my own. One day I heard someone reading, as he said, *c* from a book of Anaxagoras, and saying that it is Mind that directs and is the cause of everything. I was delighted with this cause and it seemed to me good, in a way, that Mind should be the cause of all. I thought that if this were so, the directing Mind would direct everything and arrange each thing in the way that was best. If then one wished to know the cause of each thing, why it comes to be or perishes or exists, *d* one had to find what was the best way for it to be, or to be acted upon, or to act. On these premises then it befitted a man to investigate only, about this and other things, what is best. The same man must inevitably also know what is worse, for that is part of the same knowledge. As I reflected on this subject I was glad to think that I had found in Anaxagoras a teacher about the cause of things after my own heart, and that he would tell me, first, whether the earth is *e* flat or round, and then would explain why it is so of necessity, saying which is better, and that it was better to be so. If he said it was in the middle of the universe, he would go on to show that it was better for it to be in the middle, and if he showed me those things I should be prepared never to desire any other kind of *98* cause. I was ready to find out in the same way about the sun and the moon and the other heavenly bodies, about their relative speed, their turnings and whatever else happened to them, how it is best that each should act or be acted upon. I never thought that Anaxagoras, who said that those things were directed by Mind, would bring in any other cause for them than that it was best for them to be as they are. Once he had *b* given the best for each as the cause for each and the general cause of all, I thought he would go on to explain the common good for all, and I would not have exchanged my hopes for a fortune. I eagerly acquired his books and read them as quickly as I could in order to know the best and the worst as soon as possible.

This wonderful hope was dashed as I went on reading and saw that the man made no use of Mind, nor gave it any responsibility for the management of things, but mentioned as causes air and ether and water and many other strange things. That seemed *c* to me much like saying that Socrates' actions are all due to his mind, and then in trying to tell the causes of everything I do, to say that the reason that I am sitting here is because my body consists of bones and sinews, because the bones are hard and are separated by joints, that the sinews are such as to contract and relax, that they surround the bones along with flesh and skin which hold them together, then as the bones *d* are hanging in their sockets, the relaxation and contraction of the sinews enable me to bend my limbs, and that is the cause of my sitting here with my limbs bent.

Again, he would mention other such causes for my talking to you: sounds and air and hearing, and a thousand other such things, but he would neglect to mention the true causes, that, after the Athenians decided it was better to condemn me, for this reason *e* it seemed best to me to sit here and more right to remain and to endure whatever penalty they ordered.

For by the dog, I think these sinews and bones could long ago have been in Megara or among the Boeo-
99 tians, taken there by my belief as to the best course, if I had not thought it more right and honorable to endure whatever penalty the city ordered rather than escape and run away. To call those things causes is too absurd. If someone said that without bones and sinews and all such things, I should not be able to do what I decided, he would be right, but surely to say that they are the cause of what I do, and not that I have chosen the best course, even though I act
b with my mind, is to speak very lazily and carelessly. Imagine not being able to distinguish the real cause from that without which the cause would not be able to act as a cause. It is what the majority appear to do, like people groping in the dark; they call it a cause, thus giving it a name that does not belong to it. That is why one man surrounds the earth with a vortex to make the heavens keep it in place, another
c makes the air support it like a wide lid. As for their capacity of being in the best place they could possibly be put, this they do not look for, nor do they believe it to have any divine force, but they believe that they will some time discover a stronger and more immortal Atlas to hold everything together more, and they do not believe that the truly good and "binding" binds and holds them together. I would gladly become the disciple of any man who taught the workings of that kind of cause. However, since I was deprived and could neither discover it myself nor learn it from
d another, do you wish me to give you an explanation of how, as a second best, I busied myself with the search for the cause, Cebes?

I would wish it above all else, he said.

After this, he said, when I had wearied of investigating things, I thought that I must be careful to avoid the experience of those who watch an eclipse of the sun, for some of them ruin their eyes unless they watch its reflection in water or some such material.
e A similar thought crossed my mind, and I feared that my soul would be altogether blinded if I looked at things with my eyes and tried to grasp them with each of my senses. So I thought I must take refuge in discussions and investigate the truth of things by means of words. However, perhaps this analogy is
100 inadequate, for I certainly do not admit that one who investigates things by means of words is dealing with images any more than one who looks at facts. How-

ever, I started in this manner: taking as my hypothesis in each case the theory that seemed to me the most compelling, I would consider as true, about cause and everything else, whatever agreed with this, and as untrue whatever did not so agree. But I want to put my meaning more clearly for I do not think that you understand me now.

No, by Zeus, said Cebes, not very well.

This, he said, is what I mean. It is nothing new, b but what I have never stopped talking about, both elsewhere and in the earlier part of our conversation. I am going to try to show you the kind of cause with which I have concerned myself. I turn back to those oft-mentioned things and proceed from them. I assume the existence of a Beautiful, itself by itself, of a Good and a Great and all the rest. If you grant me these and agree that they exist, I hope to show you the cause as a result, and to find the soul to be immortal.

Take it that I grant you this, said Cebes, and hasten c to your conclusion.

Consider then, he said, whether you share my opinion as to what follows, for I think that, if there is anything beautiful besides the Beautiful itself, it is beautiful for no other reason than that it shares in that Beautiful, and I say so with everything. Do you agree to this sort of cause? —I do.

I no longer understand or recognize those other sophisticated causes, and if someone tells me that a d thing is beautiful because it has a bright color or shape or any such thing, I ignore these other reasons— for all these confuse me—but I simply, naively and perhaps foolishly cling to this, that nothing else makes it beautiful other than the presence of, or the sharing in, or however you may describe its relationship to that Beautiful we mentioned, for I will not insist on the precise nature of the relationship, but that all beautiful things are beautiful by the Beautiful. That, I think, is the safest answer I can give myself or anyone e else. And if I stick to this I think I shall never fall into error. This is the safe answer for me or anyone else to give, namely, that it is through Beauty that beautiful things are made beautiful. Or do you not think so too? —I do.

And that it is through Bigness that big things are big and the bigger are bigger, and that smaller things are made small by Smallness? —Yes.

And you would not accept the statement that one

101 man is taller than another by a head[19] and the shorter man shorter by the same, but you would bear witness that you mean nothing else than that everything that is bigger is made bigger by nothing else than by Bigness, and that is the cause of its being bigger, and the smaller is made smaller only by Smallness and this is why it is smaller. I think you would be afraid that some opposite argument would confront you if you said that someone is bigger or smaller by a head, first, because the bigger is bigger and the smaller smaller by the same, then because the bigger is bigger
b by a head which is small, and this would be strange, namely, that someone is made bigger by something small. Would you not be afraid of this?

I certainly would, said Cebes, laughing.

Then you would be afraid to say that ten is more than eight by two, and that this is the cause of the excess, and not magnitude and because of magnitude, or that two cubits is bigger than one cubit by half and not by Bigness, for this is the same fear. — Certainly.

Then would you not avoid saying that when one
c is added to one it is the addition and when it is divided it is the division that is the cause of two? And you would loudly exclaim that you do not know how else each thing can come to be except by sharing in the particular reality in which it shares, and in these cases you do not know of any other cause of becoming two except by sharing in Twoness, and that the things that are to be two must share in this, as that which is to be one must share in Oneness, and you would dismiss these additions and divisions and other such subtleties, and leave them to those wiser than yourself to answer. But you, afraid, as they say, of your own
d shadow and your inexperience, would cling to the safety of your own hypothesis and give that answer. If someone then attacked your hypothesis itself, you would ignore him and would not answer until you had examined whether the consequences that follow from it agree with one another or contradict one another. And when you must give an account of your hypothesis itself you will proceed in the same way:

19. [This is very puzzling in English. In Greek the confusion is due to the double use of the dative, instrumental and causal, so that it could mean "because of a head," which is nonsense of course, but the ambiguity is there and makes the statement of Socrates possible.]

you will assume another hypothesis, the one which seems to you best of the higher ones until you come e to something acceptable, but you will not jumble the two as the debaters do by discussing the hypothesis and its consequences at the same time, if you wish to discover any truth. This they do not discuss at all nor give any thought to, but their wisdom enables them to mix everything up and yet to be pleased with themselves, but if you are a philosopher I think you 102 will do as I say.

What you say is very true, said Simmias and Cebes together.

ECHECRATES: Yes, by Zeus, Phaedo, and they were right, I think he made these things wonderfully clear to anyone of even small intelligence.

PHAEDO: Yes indeed, Echecrates, and all those present thought so too.

E: And so do we who were not present but hear of it now. What was said after that?

P: As I recall it, when the above had been accepted, and it was agreed that each of the Forms b existed, and that other things acquired their name by having a share in them, he followed this up by asking: If you say these things are so, when you then say that Simmias is taller than Socrates but shorter than Phaedo, do you not mean that there is in Simmias both tallness and shortness? — I do.

But, he said, do you agree that the words of the statement 'Simmias is taller than Socrates' do not express the truth of the matter? It is not, surely, the c nature of Simmias to be taller than Socrates because he is Simmias but because of the tallness he happens to have? Nor is he taller than Socrates because Socrates is Socrates, but because Socrates has smallness compared with the tallness of the other? — True.

Nor is he shorter than Phaedo because Phaedo is Phaedo, but because Phaedo has tallness compared with the shortness of Simmias? — That is so.

So then Simmias is called both short and tall, being between the two, presenting his shortness to be over- d come by the tallness of one, and his tallness to overcome the shortness of the other. He smilingly added, I seem to be going to talk like a book, but it is as I say. The other agreed.

My purpose is that you may agree with me. Now it seems to me that not only Tallness itself is never willing to be tall and short at the same time, but also

that the tallness in us[20] will never admit the short or be overcome, but one of two things happens: either
e it flees and retreats whenever its opposite, the short, approaches, or it is destroyed by its approach. It is not willing to endure and admit shortness and be other than it was, whereas I admit and endure shortness and still remain the same person and am this short man. But Tallness, being tall, cannot venture to be small. In the same way, the short in us is unwill-
103 ing to become or to be tall ever, nor does any other of the opposites become or be its opposite while still being what it was; either it goes away or is destroyed when that happens. — I altogether agree, said Cebes.

When he heard this, someone of those present— I have no clear memory of who it was—said: "By the gods, did we not agree earlier in our discussion[21] to the very opposite of what is now being said, namely, that the larger came from the smaller and the smaller from the larger, and that this simply was how opposites came to be, from their opposites, but now I think we are saying that this would never happen?"

On hearing this, Socrates inclined his head towards the speaker and said: "You have bravely reminded
b us, but you do not understand the difference between what is said now and what was said then, which was that an opposite thing came from an opposite thing; now we say that the opposite itself could never become opposite to itself, neither that in us nor that in nature. Then, my friend, we were talking of things that have opposite qualities and naming these after them, but now we say that these opposites themselves, from the presence of which in them things get their name, never can tolerate the coming to be from one
c another." At the same time he looked to Cebes and said: "Does anything of what this man says also disturb you?"

Not at the moment, said Cebes, but I do not deny that many things do disturb me.

We are altogether agreed then, he said, that an opposite will never be opposite to itself. — Entirely agreed.

20. [The "tallness in us" is not the Form, which is never immanent in the particular, nor need we imagine it to refer to another thing existing between the Form and the particular; it simply refers to the quality of tallness which is clearly inherent in the particulars. The expression could be used without reference to the theory of Forms at all.]

21. [The reference is to 70d–71a above.]

Consider then whether you will agree to this further point. There is something you call hot and something you call cold. — There is.

Are they the same as what you call snow and fire? — d By Zeus, no.

So the hot is something other than fire, and the cold is something other than snow? — Yes.

You think, I believe, that being snow it will not admit the hot, as we said before, and remain what it was and be both snow and hot, but when the hot approaches it will either retreat before it or be destroyed. — Quite so.

So fire, as the cold approaches, will either go away or be destroyed; it will never venture to admit coldness and remain what it was, fire and cold. — What you e say is true.

It is true then about some of these things that not only the Form itself deserves its own name for all time, but there is something else that is not the Form but has its character whenever it exists. Perhaps I can make my meaning clearer: the Odd must always be given this name we now mention. Is that not so? — Certainly.

Is it the only one of existing things to be called odd? — this is my question — or is there something 104 else than the Odd which one must nevertheless also always call odd, as well as by its own name, because it is such by nature as never to be separated from the Odd? I mean, for example, the number three and many others. Consider three: do you not think that it must always be called both by its own name and by that of the Odd, which is not the same as three? That is the nature of three, and of five, and of half of all the numbers; each of them is odd, but it is not b the Odd. Then again, two and four and the whole other column of numbers; each of them, while not being the same as the Even, is always even. Do you not agree? — Of course.

Look now. What I want to make clear is this: not only do those opposites not admit each other, but this is also true of those things which, while not being opposite to each other yet always contain the opposites, and it seems that these do not admit that Form which is opposite to that which is in them; when it approaches them, they either perish or give c way. Shall we not say that three will perish or undergo anything before, while remaining three, becoming even? — Certainly, said Cebes.

Yet surely two is not the opposite of three? — Indeed it is not.

It is then not only opposite Forms that do not admit each other's approach, but also some other things that do not admit the onset of opposites. — Very true.

Do you then want us, if we can, to define what these are? — I surely do.

d   Would they be the things that are compelled by whatever occupies them not only to contain that thing's Form but also always that of some opposite? — How do you mean?

As we were saying just now, you surely know that what the Form of three occupies must not only be three but also odd. — Certainly.

And we say that the opposite Form to the Form that achieves this result could never come to it. — It could not.

Now it is Oddness that has done this? — Yes.

And opposite to this is the Form of the Even? — Yes.

e   So then the Form of the Even will never come to three? — Never.

Then three has no share in the Even? — Never.

So three is uneven? — Yes.

As for what I said we must define, that is, what kind of things, while not being opposites to something, yet do not admit the opposite, as for example the triad, though it is not the opposite of the Even, yet does not admit it because it always brings along the opposite of 105 the Even, and so the dyad in relation to the Odd, fire to the Cold, and very many other things, see whether you would define it thus: Not only does the opposite not admit its opposite, but that which brings along some opposite into that which it occupies, that which brings this along will not admit the opposite to that which it brings along. Refresh your memory, it is no worse for being heard often. Five does not admit the form of the Even, nor will ten, which is twice five, admit the form of the Odd. It is the opposite of something else, yet it will not admit the form of the Odd. Nor do one-and-a-half and other such b   fractions admit the form of the Whole, nor will one-third, and so on, if you follow me and agree to this.

I certainly agree, he said, and I follow you.

Tell me again from the beginning, he said, and do not answer in the words of the question, but do as I do. I say that beyond that safe answer, which I spoke of first, I see another safe answer. If you should ask me what, coming into a body, makes it hot, my

reply would not be that safe and ignorant one, that c   it is heat, but our present argument provides a more sophisticated answer, namely, fire, and if you ask me what, on coming into a body, makes it sick, I will not say sickness but fever. Nor, if asked the presence of what in a number makes it odd, I will not say oddness but oneness, and so with other things. See if you now sufficiently understand what I want. — Quite sufficiently.

Answer me then, he said, what is it that, present in a body, makes it living? — A soul.

And is that always so? — Of course.   d

Whatever the soul occupies, it always brings life to it? — It does.

Is there, or is there not, an opposite to life? — There is.

What is it? — Death.

So the soul will never admit the opposite of that which it brings along, as we agree from what has been said?

Most certainly, said Cebes.

Well, and what do we call that which does not admit the form of the even? — The uneven.

What do we call that which will not admit the just and that which will not admit the musical?

The unmusical, and the other the unjust.   e

Very well, what do we call that which does not admit death?

The deathless, he said.

Now the soul does not admit death? — No.

So the soul is deathless? — It is.

Very well, he said. Shall we say that this has been proved, do you think?

Quite adequately proved, Socrates.

Well now, Cebes, he said, if the uneven were of necessity indestructible, surely three would be indestructible? — Of course.   106

And if the non-hot were of necessity indestructible, then whenever anyone brought heat to snow, the snow would retreat safe and unthawed, for it could not be destroyed, nor again could it stand its ground and admit the heat? — What you say is true.

In the same way, if the non-cold were indestructible, then when some cold attacked the fire, it would neither be quenched nor destroyed, but retreat safely. — Necessarily.

Must then the same not be said of the deathless? b   If the deathless is also indestructible, it is impossible for the soul to be destroyed when death comes upon it. For it follows from what has been said that it will not admit death or be dead, just as three, we said, will not be even nor will the odd; nor will fire be cold, nor the heat that is in the fire. But, someone might say, what prevents the odd, while not becoming c even as has been agreed, from being destroyed, and the even to come to be instead? We could not maintain against the man who said this that it is not destroyed, for the uneven is not indestructible. If we had agreed that it was indestructible we could easily have maintained that at the coming of the even, the odd and the three have gone away and the same would hold for fire and the hot and the other things. — Surely.

And so now, if we are agreed that the deathless is d indestructible, the soul, besides being deathless, is indestructible. If not, we need another argument.

— There is no need for one as far as that goes, for hardly anything could resist destruction if the deathless, which lasts forever, would admit destruction.

All would agree, said Socrates, that the god, and the Form of life itself, and anything that is deathless, are never destroyed. — All men would agree, by Zeus, to that, and the gods, I imagine, even more so.

e   If the deathless is indestructible, then the soul, if it is deathless, would also be indestructible? — Necessarily.

Then when death comes to man, the mortal part of him dies, it seems, but his deathless part goes away safe and indestructible, yielding the place to death. — So it appears.

Therefore the soul, Cebes, he said, is most certainly 107 deathless and indestructible and our souls will really dwell in the underworld.

— I have nothing more to say against that, Socrates, said Cebes, nor can I doubt your arguments. If Simmias here or someone else has something to say, he should not remain silent, for I do not know to what further occasion other than the present he could put it off if he wants to say or to hear anything on these subjects.

Certainly, said Simmias, I myself have no remaining grounds for doubt after what has been said; nevertheless, in view of the importance of our subject and my low opinion of human weakness, I am bound b still to have some private misgivings about what we have said.

You are not only right to say this, Simmias, Socrates said, but our first hypotheses require clearer examination, even though we find them convincing. And if you analyze them adequately, you will, I think, follow the argument as far as a man can and if the conclusion is clear, you will look no further. — That is true.

It is right to think then, gentlemen, that if the soul c is immortal, it requires our care not only for the time we call our life, but for the sake of all time, and that one is in terrible danger if one does not give it that care. If death were escape from everything, it would be a great boon to the wicked to get rid of the body and of their wickedness together with their soul. But now that the soul appears to be immortal, there is no escape from evil or salvation for it except by becom- d ing as good and wise as possible, for the soul goes to the underworld possessing nothing but its education and upbringing, which are said to bring the greatest benefit or harm to the dead right at the beginning of the journey yonder.

We are told that when each person dies, the guardian spirit who was allotted to him in life proceeds to lead him to a certain place, whence those who have been gathered together there must, after being judged, proceed to the underworld with the guide e who has been appointed to lead them thither from here. Having there undergone what they must and stayed there the appointed time, they are led back here by another guide after long periods of time. The journey is not as Aeschylus' Telephus[22] describes it. 108 He says that only one single path leads to Hades, but I think it is neither one nor simple, for then there would be no need of guides; one could not make any mistake if there were but one path. As it is, it is likely to have many forks and crossroads; and I base this judgment on the sacred rites and customs here.

The well-ordered and wise soul follows the guide and is not without familiarity with its surroundings, but the soul that is passionately attached to the body, as I said before, hovers around it and the visible world b for a long time, struggling and suffering much until it is led away by force and with difficulty by its appointed spirit. When the impure soul which has performed some impure deed joins the others after being involved in unjust killings, or committed other crimes

22. [The *Telephus* of Aeschylus is not extant, and little is known about it.]

which are akin to these and are actions of souls of this kind, everybody shuns it and turns away, unwilling to
c be its fellow traveller or its guide; such a soul wanders alone completely at a loss until a certain time arrives and it is forcibly led to its proper dwelling place. On the other hand, the soul that has led a pure and moderate life finds fellow travellers and gods to guide it, and each of them dwells in a place suited to it.

There are many strange places upon the earth, and the earth itself is not such as those who are used to discourse upon it believe it to be in nature or size, as someone has convinced me.
d Simmias said: "What do you mean, Socrates? I have myself heard many things said about the earth, but certainly not the things that convince you. I should be glad to hear them."

Indeed, Simmias, I do not think it requires the skill of Glaucus[23] to tell you what they are, but to prove them true requires more than that skill, and I should perhaps not be able to do so. Also, even if I had the knowledge, my remaining time would not
e be long enough to tell the tale. However, nothing prevents my telling you what I am convinced is the shape of the earth and what its regions are.

Even that is sufficient, said Simmias.

Well then, he said, the first thing of which I am
109 convinced is that if the earth is a sphere in the middle of the heavens, it has no need of air or any other force to prevent it from falling. The homogeneous nature of the heavens on all sides and the earth's own equipoise are sufficient to hold it, for an object balanced in the middle of something homogeneous will have no tendency to incline more in any direction than any other but will remain unmoved. This, he said, is the first point of which I am persuaded.

And rightly so, said Simmias.

Further, the earth is very large, and we live around
b the sea in a small portion of it between Phasis and the pillars of Heracles, like ants or frogs around a swamp; many other peoples live in many such parts of it. Everywhere about the earth there are numerous hollows of many kinds and shapes and sizes into which the water and the mist and the air have gathered. The earth itself is pure and lies in the pure sky

where the stars are situated, which the majority of those who discourse on these subjects call the ether. c The water and mist and air are the sediment of the ether and they always flow into the hollows of the earth. We, who dwell in the hollows of it, are unaware of this and we think that we live above, on the surface of the earth. It is as if someone who lived deep down in the middle of the ocean thought he was living on its surface. Seeing the sun and the other heavenly bodies through the water, he would think the sea to d be the sky; because he is slow and weak, he has never reached the surface of the sea or risen with his head above the water or come out of the sea to our region here, nor seen how much purer and more beautiful it is than his own region, nor has he ever heard of it from anyone who has seen it.

Our experience is the same: living in a certain hollow of the earth, we believe that we live upon its surface; the air we call the heavens, as if the stars made their way through it; this too is the same: because of our weakness and slowness we are not able to make our way to the upper limit of the air; if anyone got e to this upper limit, if anyone came to it or reached it on wings and his head rose above it, then just as fish on rising from the sea see things in our region, he would see things there and, if his nature could endure to contemplate them, he would know that there is the true heaven, the true light and the true earth, for the earth here, these stones and the whole 110 region, are spoiled and eaten away, just as things in the sea are by the salt water.

Nothing worth mentioning grows in the sea, nothing, one might say, is fully developed; there are caves and sand and endless slime and mud wherever there is earth—not comparable in any way with the beauties of our region. So those things above are in their turn far superior to the things we know. Indeed, if this is the moment to tell a tale, Simmias, it is worth hearing b about the nature of things on the surface of the earth under the heavens.

At any rate, Socrates, said Simmias, we should be glad to hear this story.

Well then, my friend, in the first place it is said that the earth, looked at from above, looks like those spherical balls made up of twelve pieces of leather; it is multi-colored, and of these colors those used by our painters give us an indication; up there the whole earth has these colors, but much brighter and purer c

23. [A proverbial expression meaning that a difficult task required the skill of Glaucus. Its origin is obscure, for there are several explanations given by the Scholiasts.]

than these; one part is sea-green and of marvelous beauty, another is golden, another is white, whiter than chalk or snow; the earth is composed also of the other colors, more numerous and beautiful than any we have seen. The very hollows of the earth, full of d water and air, gleaming among the variety of other colors, present a color of their own so that the whole is seen as a continuum of variegated colors. On the surface of the earth the plants grow with corresponding beauty, the trees and the flowers and the fruits, and so with the hills and the stones, more beautiful in their smoothness and transparency and color. Our precious stones here are but fragments, our cornelians, jaspers, emeralds and the rest. All stones there e are of that kind, and even more beautiful. The reason is that there they are pure, not eaten away or spoiled by decay and brine, or corroded by the water and air which have flowed into the hollows here and bring ugliness and disease upon earth, stones, the other animals and plants. The earth itself is adorned with 111 all these things, and also with gold and silver and other metals. These stand out, being numerous and massive and occurring everywhere, so that the earth is a sight for the blessed. There are many other living creatures upon the earth, and also men, some living inland, others at the edge of the air, as we live on the edge of the sea, others again live on islands surrounded by air close to the mainland. In a word, what b water and the sea are to us, the air is to them and the ether is to them what the air is to us. The climate is such that they are without disease, and they live much longer than people do here; their eyesight, hearing and intelligence and all such are as superior to ours as air is superior to water and ether to air in purity; they have groves and temples dedicated to the gods, in which the gods really dwell, and they c communicate with them by speech and prophecy and by the sight of them; they see the sun and moon and stars as they are, and in other ways their happiness is in accord with this.

This then is the nature of the earth as a whole and of its surroundings; around the whole of it there are many regions in the hollows; some are deeper and more open than that in which we live; others are deeper and have a narrower opening than ours, and d there are some that have less depth and more width. All these are connected with each other below the surface of the earth in many places by narrow and broader channels, and thus have outlets through which much water flows from one to another as into mixing bowls; huge rivers of both hot and cold water thus flow beneath the earth eternally, much fire and large rivers of fire, and many of wet mud, both more pure and more muddy, such as those flowing in ad- e vance of the lava and the stream of lava itself in Sicily. These streams then fill up every and all regions as the flow reaches each, and all these places move up and down with the oscillating movement of the earth. The natural cause of the oscillation is as follows: one of the hollows of the earth, which is also the biggest, 112 pierces through the whole earth; it is that which Homer mentioned when he said: "Far down where is the deepest pit below the earth . . . ," and which he elsewhere, and many other poets, call Tartarus; into this chasm all the rivers flow together, and again flow out of it, and each river is affected by the nature of the land through which it flows. The reason for b their flowing into and out of Tartarus is that this water has no bottom or solid base but it oscillates up and down in waves, and the air and wind about it do the same, for they follow it when it flows to this or that part of the earth. Just as when people breathe, the flow of air goes in and out, so here the air oscillates with the water and creates terrible winds as it goes in and out. Whenever the water retreats to what we c call the lower part of the earth, it flows into those parts and fills them up as if the water were pumped in; when it leaves that part for this, it fills these parts again, and the parts filled flow through the channels and through the earth and in each case arrive at the places to which the channels lead and create seas and marshes and rivers and springs. From there the waters flow under the earth again, some flowing d around larger and more numerous regions, some round smaller and shallower ones, then flow back into Tartarus, some at a point much lower than where they issued forth, others only a little way, but all of them at a lower point, some of them at the opposite side of the chasm, some on the same side; some flow in a wide circle round the earth once or many times like snakes, then go as far down as possible, then go back into the chasm of Tartarus. From each side it is possible to flow down as far as the center, but not e beyond, for this part that faces the river flow from either side is steep.

There are many other large rivers of all kinds, and

among these there are four of note; the biggest which flows on the outside (of the earth) in a circle is called Oceanus; opposite it and flowing in the opposite direction is the Acheron; it flows through many other 113 deserted regions and further underground makes its way to the Acherusian lake to which the souls of the majority come after death and, after remaining there for a certain appointed time, longer for some, shorter for others, they are sent back to birth as living creatures. The third river issues between the first two, and close to its source it falls into a region burning with b much fire and makes a lake larger than our sea, boiling with water and mud. From there it goes in a circle, foul and muddy, and winding on its way it comes, among other places, to the edge of the Acherusian lake but does not mingle with its waters; then, coiling many times underground it flows lower down into Tartarus; this is called the Pyriphlegethon, and its lava streams throw off fragments of it in various c parts of the earth. Opposite this the fourth river issues forth, which is called Stygion, and it is said to flow first into a terrible and wild region, all of it blue-gray in color, and the lake that this river forms by flowing into it is called the Styx. As its waters fall into the lake they acquire dread powers; then diving below and winding round it flows in the opposite direction from the Pyriphlegethon and into the opposite side of the Acherusian lake; its waters do not mingle with any other; it too flows in a circle and into Tartarus opposite the Pyriphlegethon. The name of that fourth river, the poets tell us, is Cocytus.

d   Such is the nature of these things. When the dead arrive at the place to which each has been led by his guardian spirit, they are first judged as to whether they have led a good and pious life. Those who have lived an average life make their way to the Acheron and embark upon such vessels as there are for them and proceed to the lake. There they dwell and are purified by penalties for any wrongdoing they may e have committed; they are also suitably rewarded for their good deeds as each deserves. Those who are deemed incurable because of the enormity of their crimes, having committed many great sacrileges or wicked and unlawful murders and other such wrongs—their fitting fate is to be hurled into Tartarus never to emerge from it. Those who are deemed to have committed great but curable crimes, such as doing violence to their father or mother in a fit of temper but who have felt remorse for the rest of their 114 lives, or who have killed someone in a similar manner, these must of necessity be thrown into Tartarus, but a year later the current throws them out, those who are guilty of murder by way of Cocytus, and those who have done violence to their parents by way of the Pyriphlegethon. After they have been carried along to the Acherusian lake, they cry out and shout, some for those they have killed, others for those they have maltreated, and calling them they then pray to them b and beg them to allow them to step out into the lake and to receive them. If they persuade them, they do step out and their punishment comes to an end; if they do not, they are taken back into Tartarus and from there into the rivers, and this does not stop until they have persuaded those they have wronged, for this is the punishment which the judges imposed on them.

Those who are deemed to have lived an extremely pious life are freed and released from the regions of c the earth as from a prison; they make their way up to a pure dwelling place and live on the surface of the earth. Those who have purified themselves sufficiently by philosophy live in the future altogether without a body; they make their way to even more beautiful dwelling places which it is hard to describe clearly, nor do we now have the time to do so. Because of the things we have enunciated, Simmias, one must make every effort to share in virtue and wisdom in one's life, for the reward is beautiful and the hope is great.

No sensible man would insist that these things are d as I have described them, but I think it is fitting for a man to risk the belief—for the risk is a noble one— that this, or something like this, is true about our souls and their dwelling places, since the soul is evidently immortal, and a man should repeat this to himself as if it were an incantation, which is why I have been prolonging my tale. That is the reason why a man should be of good cheer about his own soul, if during life he has ignored the pleasures of the body and its e ornamentation as of no concern to him and doing him more harm than good, but has seriously concerned himself with the pleasures of learning, and adorned his soul not with alien but with its own ornaments, namely, moderation, righteousness, courage, freedom 115 and truth, and in that state awaits his journey to the underworld.

Now you, Simmias, Cebes and the rest of you, Socrates continued, will each take that journey at some other time but my fated day calls me now, as a tragic character might say, and it is about time for me to have my bath, for I think it better to have it before I drink the poison and save the women the trouble of washing the corpse.

b When Socrates had said this Crito spoke. Very well, Socrates, what are your instructions to me and the others about your children or anything else? What can we do that would please you most?—Nothing new, Crito, said Socrates, but what I am always saying, that you will please me and mine and yourselves by taking good care of your own selves in whatever you do, even if you do not agree with me now, but if you neglect your own selves, and are unwilling to live *c* following the tracks, as it were, of what we have said now and on previous occasions, you will achieve nothing even if you strongly agree with me at this moment.

We shall be eager to follow your advice, said Crito, but how shall we bury you?

In any way you like, said Socrates, if you can catch me and I do not escape you. And laughing quietly, looking at us, he said: I do not convince Crito that I am this Socrates talking to you here and ordering *d* all I say, but he thinks that I am the thing which he will soon be looking at as a corpse, and so he asks how he shall bury me. I have been saying for some time and at some length that after I have drunk the poison I shall no longer be with you but will leave you to go and enjoy some good fortunes of the blessed, but it seems that I have said all this to him in vain in an attempt to reassure you and myself too. Give a pledge to Crito on my behalf, he said, the opposite pledge to that he gave the jury. He pledged that I *e* would stay, you must pledge that I will not stay after I die, but that I shall go away, so that Crito will bear it more easily when he sees my body being burned or buried and will not be angry on my behalf, as if I were suffering terribly, and so that he should not say at the funeral that he is laying out, or carrying out, or burying Socrates. For know you well, my dear Crito, that to express oneself badly is not only faulty as far as the language goes, but does some harm to the soul. You must be of good cheer, and say you are *116* burying my body, and bury it in any way you like and think most customary.

After saying this he got up and went to another room to take his bath, and Crito followed him and he told us to wait for him. So we stayed, talking among ourselves, questioning what had been said, and then again talking of the great misfortune that had befallen us. We all felt as if we had lost a father and would be orphaned for the rest of our lives. When *b* he had washed, his children were brought to him—two of his sons were small and one was older—and the women of his household came to him. He spoke to them before Crito and gave them what instructions he wanted. Then he sent the women and children away, and he himself joined us. It was now close to sunset, for he had stayed inside for some time. He came and sat down after his bath and conversed for a short while, when the officer of the Eleven came and stood by him and said: "I shall not reproach you *c* as I do the others, Socrates. They are angry with me and curse me when obeying the orders of my superiors, I tell them to drink the poison. During the time you have been here I have come to know you in other ways as the noblest, the gentlest and the best man who has ever come here. So now too I know that you will not make trouble for me; you know who is responsible and you will direct your anger against them. You know what message I bring. Fare you well, and try to endure what you must as easily as possible." *d* The officer was weeping as he turned away and went out. Socrates looked up at him and said: "Fare you well also, we shall do as you bid us." And turning to us he said: "How pleasant the man is! During the whole time I have been here he has come in and conversed with me from time to time, a most agreeable man. And how genuinely he now weeps for me. Come, Crito, let us obey him. Let someone bring the poison if it is ready; if not, let the man prepare it."

But Socrates, said Crito, I think the sun still shines *e* upon the hills and has not yet set. I know that others drink the poison quite a long time after they have received the order, eating and drinking quite a bit, and some of them enjoy intimacy with their loved ones. Do not hurry; there is still some time.

It is natural, Crito, for them to do so, said Socrates, for they think they derive some benefit from doing *117* this, but it is not fitting for me. I do not expect any benefit from drinking the poison a little later, except to become ridiculous in my own eyes for clinging to life, and be sparing of it when there is none left. So do as I ask and do not refuse me.

Hearing this, Crito nodded to the slave who was standing near him; the slave went out and after a time came back with the man who was to administer the poison, carrying it made ready in a cup. When Socrates saw him he said: "Well, my good man, you are an expert in this, what must one do?"—"Just drink

b it and walk around until your legs feel heavy, and then lie down and it will act of itself." And he offered the cup to Socrates who took it quite cheerfully, Echecrates, without a tremor or any change of feature or color, but looking at the man from under his eyebrows as was his wont, asked: "What do you say about pouring a libation from this drink? It is allowed?"—"We only mix as much as we believe will suffice," said the man.

c I understand, Socrates said, but one is allowed, indeed one must, utter a prayer to the gods that the journey from here to yonder may be fortunate. This is my prayer and may it be so.

And while he was saying this, he was holding the cup, and then drained it calmly and easily. Most of us had been able to hold back our tears reasonably well up till then, but when we saw him drinking it and after he drank it, we could hold them back no longer; my own tears came in floods against my will. So I covered my face. I was weeping for myself, not

d for him—for my misfortune in being deprived of such a comrade. Even before me, Crito was unable to restrain his tears and got up. Apollodorus had not ceased from weeping before, and at this moment his noisy tears and anger made everybody present break down, except Socrates. "What is this," he said, "you

strange fellows. It is mainly for this reason that I sent the women away, to avoid such unseemliness, for I e am told one should die in good omened silence. So keep quiet and control yourselves."

His words made us ashamed, and we checked our tears. He walked around, and when he said his legs were heavy he lay on his back as he had been told to do, and the man who had given him the poison touched his body, and after a while tested his feet and legs, pressed hard upon his foot and asked him if he felt this, and Socrates said no. Then he pressed 118 his calves, and made his way up his body and showed us that it was cold and stiff. He felt it himself and said that when the cold reached his heart he would be gone. As his belly was getting cold Socrates uncovered his head—he had covered it—and said—these were his last words—"Crito, we owe a cock to Asclepius;[24] make this offering to him and do not forget."— "It shall be done," said Crito, "tell us if there is anything else." But there was no answer. Shortly afterwards Socrates made a movement; the man uncovered him and his eyes were fixed. Seeing this Crito closed his mouth and his eyes.

Such was the end of our comrade, Echecrates, a man who, we would say, was of all those we have known the best, and also the wisest and the most upright.

24. [A cock was sacrificed to Asclepius by the sick people who slept in his temples, hoping for a cure. Socrates obviously means that death is a cure for the ills of life.]

Republic

Book I

327 I went down to the Piraeus yesterday with Glaucon, the son of Ariston. I wanted to say a prayer to the goddess,[1] and I was also curious to see how they would manage the festival, since they were holding it for the first time. I thought the procession of the local residents was a fine one and that the one conducted by the Thracians was no less outstanding. After we had said our prayer and seen the procession, we started
b back towards Athens. Polemarchus saw us from a distance as we were setting off for home and told his slave to run and ask us to wait for him. The slave caught hold of my cloak from behind: Polemarchus wants you to wait, he said. I turned around and asked where Polemarchus was. He's coming up behind you, he said, please wait for him. And Glaucon replied: All right, we will.

c Just then Polemarchus caught up with us. Adeimantus, Glaucon's brother,[2] was with him and so were Niceratus, the son of Nicias, and some others, all of whom were apparently on their way from the procession.

Polemarchus said: It looks to me, Socrates, as if you two are starting off for Athens.

It looks the way it is, then, I said.

Do you see how many we are? he said.

I do.

Well, you must either prove stronger than we are, or you will have to stay here.

Isn't there another alternative, namely, that we persuade you to let us go?

But could you persuade us, if we won't listen?

Certainly not, Glaucon said.

Well, we won't listen; you'd better make up your mind to that.

Don't you know, Adeimantus said, that there is to be a torch race on horseback for the goddess tonight? 328

On horseback? I said. That's something new. Are they going to race on horseback and hand the torches on in relays, or what?

In relays, Polemarchus said, and there will be an all-night festival that will be well worth seeing. After dinner, we'll go out to look at it. We'll be joined there by many of the young men, and we'll talk. So don't go; stay.

It seems, Glaucon said, that we'll have to stay.   b

If you think so, I said, then we must.

So we went to Polemarchus' house, and there we found Lysias and Euthydemus, the brothers of Polemarchus, Thrasymachus of Chalcedon, Charmantides of Paeania, and Clitophon the son of Aristonymus.[3] Polemarchus' father, Cephalus, was also there, and I thought he looked quite old, as I hadn't seen him for some time. He was sitting on a sort of cushioned c chair with a wreath on his head, as he had been offering a sacrifice in the courtyard. There was a circle of chairs, and we sat down by him.

As soon as he saw me, Cephalus welcomed me and said: Socrates, you don't come down to the Piraeus to see us as often as you should. If it were still easy for me to walk to town, you wouldn't have to come here; we'd come to you. But, as it is, you ought to come here more often, for you should know that as the d physical pleasures wither away, my desire for conversation and its pleasures grows. So do as I say: Stay with these young men now, but come regularly to see us, just as you would to friends or relatives.

Reprinted from *Plato: Republic*, translated by G.M.A. Grube, revised by C.D.C. Reeve (Indianapolis: Hackett Publishing Company, 1992) by permission of the publisher.

1. [The Thracian goddess Bendis, whose cult had recently been introduced in the Piraeus, the harbor area near Athens. — C.D.C.R.]

2. [Glaucon and Adeimantus were Plato's brothers. They are Socrates' chief interlocutors after Book I.]

3. [Lysias was a well-known writer of speeches for use in legal trials. Socrates discusses a speech attributed to him in the *Phaedrus*. Thrasymachus was a Sophist, a paid teacher of oratory and virtue. The few fragments of his writings that survive are translated in Freeman, *Ancilla to the Pre-Socratic Philosophers* (Cambridge: Harvard University Press, 1977). Charmantides is otherwise unknown.]

Indeed, Cephalus, I replied, I enjoy talking with the very old, for we should ask them, as we might ask those who have travelled a road that we too will

e probably have to follow, what kind of road it is, whether rough and difficult or smooth and easy. And I'd gladly find out from you what you think about this, as you have reached the point in life the poets call "the threshold of old age."[4] Is it a difficult time? What is your report about it?

By god, Socrates, I'll tell you exactly what I think.

329 A number of us, who are more or less the same age, often get together in accordance with the old saying.[5] When we meet, the majority complain about the lost pleasures they remember from their youth, those of sex, drinking parties, feasts, and the other things that go along with them, and they get angry as if they had been deprived of important things and had lived well then but are now hardly living at all. Some others moan about the abuse heaped on old people by their

b relatives, and because of this they repeat over and over that old age is the cause of many evils. But I don't think they blame the real cause, Socrates, for if old age were really the cause, I should have suffered in the same way and so should everyone else of my age. But as it is, I've met some who don't feel like that in the least. Indeed, I was once present when someone asked the poet Sophocles: "How are you as

c far as sex goes, Sophocles? Can you still make love with a woman?" "Quiet, man," the poet replied, "I am very glad to have escaped from all that, like a slave who has escaped from a savage and tyrannical master." I thought at the time that he was right, and I still do, for old age brings peace and freedom from all such things. When the appetites relax and cease to importune us, everything Sophocles said comes to pass, and we escape from many mad masters. In these

d matters and in those concerning relatives, the real cause isn't old age, Socrates, but the way people live. If they are moderate and contented, old age, too, is only moderately onerous; if they aren't, both old age and youth are hard to bear.

I admired him for saying that and I wanted him

e to tell me more, so I urged him on: When you say

things like that, Cephalus, I suppose that the majority of people don't agree, they think that you bear old age more easily not because of the way you live but because you're wealthy, for the wealthy, they say, have many consolations.

That's true; they don't agree. And there is something in what they say, though not as much as they think. Themistocles' retort is relevant here. When someone from Seriphus insulted him by saying that his high reputation was due to his city and not to 330 himself, he replied that, had he been a Seriphian, he wouldn't be famous, but neither would the other even if he had been an Athenian.[6] The same applies to those who aren't rich and find old age hard to bear: A good person wouldn't easily bear old age if he were poor, but a bad one wouldn't be at peace with himself even if he were wealthy.

Did you inherit most of your wealth, Cephalus, I asked, or did you make it for yourself?

What did I make for myself, Socrates, you ask. As a money-maker I'm in a sort of mean between my *b* grandfather and my father. My grandfather and namesake inherited about the same amount of wealth as I possess but multiplied it many times. My father, Lysanias, however, diminished that amount to even less than I have now. As for me, I'm satisfied to leave my sons here not less but a little more than I inherited.

The reason I asked is that you don't seem to love money too much. And those who haven't made their own money are usually like you. But those who have *c* made it for themselves are twice as fond of it as those who haven't. Just as poets love their poems and fathers love their children, so those who have made their own money don't just care about it because it's useful, as other people do, but because it's something they've made themselves. This makes them poor company, for they haven't a good word to say about anything except money.

That's true.

It certainly is. But tell me something else. What's

4. [Homer, *Iliad* 22.60, 24.487; *Odyssey* 25.246, 348, 23.212.]

5. ["God ever draws together like to like" (Homer, *Odyssey* 17.218). See Plato, *Lysis* 214a–215c.]

6. [Themistocles, a fifth-century Athenian statesman, was the chief architect of the Greek victory over Persia. By building up the navy, he secured Athens' future as a naval power and also paved the way for the increased political power of the poorer classes, from which sailors were largely drawn. Seriphus is a small island in the Cyclades.]

d the greatest good you've received from being very wealthy?

What I have to say probably wouldn't persuade most people. But you know, Socrates, that when someone thinks his end is near, he becomes frightened and concerned about things he didn't fear before. It's then that the stories we're told about Hades, about how people who've been unjust here must pay the penalty there—stories he used to make fun of—*e* twist his soul this way and that for fear they're true. And whether because of the weakness of old age or because he is now closer to what happens in Hades and has a clearer view of it, or whatever it is, he is filled with foreboding and fear, and he examines himself to see whether he has been unjust to anyone. If he finds many injustices in his life, he awakes from sleep in terror, as children do, and lives in anticipation of bad things to come. But someone who knows that 331 he hasn't been unjust has sweet good hope as his constant companion—a nurse to his old age, as Pindar[7] says, for he puts it charmingly, Socrates, when he says that when someone lives a just and pious life

> Sweet hope is in his heart,
> Nurse and companion to his age.
> Hope, captain of the ever-twisting
> Minds of mortal men.

How wonderfully well he puts that. It's in this connection that wealth is most valuable, I'd say, not for every man but for a decent and orderly one. Wealth can *b* do a lot to save us from having to cheat or deceive someone against our will and from having to depart for that other place in fear because we owe sacrifice to a god or money to a person. It has many other uses, but, benefit for benefit, I'd say that this is how it is most useful to a man of any understanding.

A fine sentiment, Cephalus, but, speaking of this *c* very thing itself, namely, justice,[8] are we to say uncon-

---

7. [Pindar (518–438 B.C.), a lyric poet from Boeotia, was most famous for his poems in celebration of the victors in the games, such as the Olympian and Pythian, held in various parts of Greece.]

8. [Unlike their usual equivalents "just" and "justice," the adjective *dikaios* and the noun *dikaiosunē* are often used in a wider sense, better captured by our words "right" or "correct." The opposite, *adikia*, then has the sense of general wrongdoing.]

ditionally that it is speaking the truth and paying whatever debts one has incurred? Or is doing these things sometimes just, sometimes unjust? I mean this sort of thing, for example: Everyone would surely agree that if a sane man lends weapons to a friend and then asks for them back when he is out of his mind, the friend shouldn't return them, and wouldn't be acting justly if he did. Nor should anyone be willing to tell the whole truth to someone who is out of his mind.

That's true.   *d*

Then the definition of justice isn't speaking the truth and repaying what one has borrowed.

It certainly is, Socrates, said Polemarchus, interrupting, if indeed we're to trust Simonides at all.[9]

Well, then, Cephalus said, I'll hand over the argument to you, as I have to look after the sacrifice.

So, Polemarchus said, am I then to be your heir in everything?

You certainly are, Cephalus said, laughing, and off he went to the sacrifice.

Then tell us, heir to the argument, I said, just what Simonides stated about justice that you consider *e* correct.

He stated that it is just to give to each what is owed to him. And it's a fine saying, in my view.

Well, now, it isn't easy to doubt Simonides, for he's a wise and godlike man. But what exactly does he mean? Perhaps you know, Polemarchus, but I don't understand him. Clearly, he doesn't mean what we said a moment ago, that it is just to give back whatever a person has lent to you, even if he's out of his mind when he asks for it. And yet what he has lent to you is surely something that's owed to him, isn't it?   332

Yes.

But it is absolutely not to be given to him when he's out of his mind?

That's true.

Then it seems that Simonides must have meant something different when he says that to return what is owed is just.

Something different indeed, by god. He means that friends owe it to their friends to do good for them, never harm.

---

9. [Simonides (c. 548–468 B.C.), a lyric and elegiac poet, was born in the Aegean island of Ceos.]

I follow you. Someone doesn't give a lender back what he's owed by giving him gold, if doing so would
b be harmful, and both he and the lender are friends. Isn't that what you think Simonides meant?

It is.

But what about this? Should one also give one's enemies whatever is owed to them?

By all means, one should give them what is owed to them. And in my view what enemies owe to each other is appropriately and precisely—something bad.

It seems then that Simonides was speaking in riddles—just like a poet!—when he said what justice is,
c for he thought it just to give to each what is appropriate to him, and this is what he called giving him what is owed to him.

What else did you think he meant?

Then what do you think he'd answer if someone asked him: "Simonides, which of the things that are owed or that are appropriate for someone or something to have does the craft[10] we call medicine give, and to whom or what does it give them?"

It's clear that it gives medicines, food, and drink to bodies.

And what owed or appropriate things does the craft we call cooking give, and to whom or what does it give them?
d   It gives seasonings to food.

Good. Now, what does the craft we call justice give, and to whom or what does it give it?

If we are to follow the previous answers, Socrates, it gives benefits to friends and does harm to enemies.

Simonides means, then, that to treat friends well and enemies badly is justice?

I believe so.

And who is most capable of treating friends well and enemies badly in matters of disease and health?

A doctor.
e   And who can do so best in a storm at sea?

A ship's captain.

What about the just person? In what actions and what work is he most capable of benefiting friends and harming enemies?

In wars and alliances, I suppose.

All right. Now, when people aren't sick, Polemarchus, a doctor is useless to them?

True.

And so is a ship's captain to those who aren't sailing?

Yes.

And to people who aren't at war, a just man is useless?

No, I don't think that at all.

Justice is also useful in peacetime, then?

It is.   333

And so is farming, isn't it?

Yes.

For getting produce?

Yes.

And shoemaking as well?

Yes.

For getting shoes, I think you'd say?

Certainly.

Well, then, what is justice useful for getting and using in peacetime?

Contracts, Socrates.

And by contracts do you mean partnerships, or what?

I mean partnerships.

Is someone a good and useful partner in a game of checkers because he's just or because he's a checkers player?   b

Because he's a checkers player.

And in laying bricks and stones, is a just person a better and more useful partner than a builder?

Not at all.

In what kind of partnership, then, is a just person a better partner than a builder or a lyre-player, in the way that a lyre-player is better than a just person at hitting the right notes?

In money matters, I think.

Except perhaps, Polemarchus, in using money, for whenever one needs to buy a horse jointly, I think a horse breeder is a more useful partner, isn't he?   c

Apparently.

And when one needs to buy a boat, it's a boatbuilder or a ship's captain?

Probably.

In what joint use of silver or gold, then, is a just person a more useful partner than the others?

10. [The Greek word translated as "craft" here is *technē*. It has the sort of connotation for Socrates and Plato that "science" has for us. Thus fifth-century doctors tried to show that medicine is a craft, much as contemporary psychoanalysts try to convince us that psychoanalysis is a science. For further discussion see Reeve, *Socrates in the Apology*, 37–45.]

When it must be deposited for safekeeping, Socrates.

You mean whenever there is no need to use them but only to keep them?

That's right.

Then it is when money isn't being used that justice is useful for it?

d I'm afraid so.

And whenever one needs to keep a pruning knife safe, but not to use it, justice is useful both in partnerships and for the individual. When you need to use it, however, it is skill at vine pruning that's useful?

Apparently.

You'll agree, then, that when one needs to keep a shield or a lyre safe and not to use them, justice is a useful thing, but when you need to use them, it is soldiery or musicianship that's useful?

Necessarily.

And so, too, with everything else, justice is useless when they are in use but useful when they aren't?

It looks that way.

In that case, justice isn't worth much, since it is *e* only useful for useless things. But let's look into the following point. Isn't the person most able to land a blow, whether in boxing or any other kind of fight, also most able to guard against it?

Certainly.

And the one who is most able to guard against disease is also most able to produce it unnoticed?

So it seems to me, anyway.

And the one who is the best guardian of an army is the very one who can steal the enemy's plans *334* and dispositions?

Certainly.

Whenever someone is a clever guardian, then, he is also a clever thief.

Probably so.

If a just person is clever at guarding money, therefore, he must also be clever at stealing it.

According to our argument, at any rate.

A just person has turned out then, it seems, to be a kind of thief. Maybe you learned this from Homer, for he's fond of Autolycus, the maternal grandfather *b* of Odysseus, whom he describes as better than everyone at lying and stealing.[11] According to you, Homer, and Simonides, then, justice seems to be some sort

of craft of stealing, one that benefits friends and harms enemies. Isn't that what you meant?

No, by god, it isn't. I don't know any more what I did mean, but I still believe that to benefit one's friends and harm one's enemies is justice.

Speaking of friends, do you mean those a person believes to be good and useful to him or those who *c* actually are good and useful, even if he doesn't think they are, and similarly with enemies?

Probably, one loves those one considers good and useful and hates those one considers bad and harmful.

But surely people often make mistakes about this, believing many people to be good and useful when they aren't, and making the opposite mistake about enemies?

They do indeed.

And then good people are their enemies and bad ones their friends?

That's right.

And so it's just to benefit bad people and harm good ones? *d*

Apparently.

But good people are just and able to do no wrong?

True.

Then, according to your account, it's just to do bad things to those who do no injustice.

No, that's not just at all, Socrates; my account must be a bad one.

It's just, then, is it, to harm unjust people and benefit just ones?

That's obviously a more attractive view than the other one, anyway.

Then, it follows, Polemarchus, that it is just for the many, who are mistaken in their judgment, to harm their friends, who are bad, and benefit their enemies, who are good. And so we arrive at a conclusion oppo- *e* site to what we said Simonides meant.

That certainly follows. But let's change our definition, for it seems that we didn't define friends and enemies correctly.

How did we define them, Polemarchus?

We said that a friend is someone who is believed to be useful.

And how are we to change that now?

Someone who is both believed to be useful and is useful is a friend; someone who is believed to be useful but isn't, is believed to be a friend but isn't. And the same for the enemy.   *335*

---

11. [The reference is to *Odyssey* 19.392–98.]

According to this account, then, a good person will be a friend and a bad one an enemy.

Yes.

So you want us to add something to what we said before about justice, when we said that it is just to treat friends well and enemies badly. You want us to add to this that it is just to treat well a friend who is good and to harm an enemy who is bad?

b Right. That seems fine to me.

Is it, then, the role of a just man to harm anyone?

Certainly, he must harm those who are both bad and enemies.

Do horses become better or worse when they are harmed?

Worse.

With respect to the virtue[12] that makes dogs good or the one that makes horses good?

The one that makes horses good.

And when dogs are harmed, they become worse in the virtue that makes dogs good, not horses?

Necessarily.

Then won't we say the same about human beings, *c* too, that when they are harmed they become worse in human virtue?

Indeed.

But isn't justice human virtue?

Yes, certainly.

Then people who are harmed must become more unjust?

So it seems.

Can musicians make people unmusical through music?

They cannot.

Or horsemen make people unhorsemanlike through horsemanship?

No.

Well, then, can those who are just make people unjust through justice? In a word, can those who are good make people bad through virtue?   *d*

They cannot.

It isn't the function of heat to cool things but of its opposite?

Yes.

Nor the function of dryness to make things wet but of its opposite?

Indeed.

Nor the function of goodness to harm but of its opposite?

Apparently.

And a just person is good?

Indeed.

Then, Polemarchus, it isn't the function of a just person to harm a friend or anyone else, rather it is the function of his opposite, an unjust person?

In my view that's completely true, Socrates.

If anyone tells us, then, that it is just to give to each what he's owed and understands by this that a *e* just man should harm his enemies and benefit his friends, he isn't wise to say it, since what he says isn't true, for it has become clear to us that it is never just to harm anyone?

I agree.

You and I shall fight as partners, then, against anyone who tells us that Simonides, Bias, Pittacus, or any of our other wise and blessedly happy men said this.[13]

I, at any rate, am willing to be your partner in the battle.

Do you know to whom I think the saying belongs that it is just to benefit friends and harm enemies? 336

Who?

I think it belongs to Periander, or Perdiccas, or Xerxes, or Ismenias of Corinth, or some other wealthy man who believed himself to have great power.[14]

---

12. [If something is a knife (say) or a man, its *aretē* or virtue as a knife or a man is that state or property of it that makes it a good knife or a good man. See *Charmides* 161a8–9; *Euthyphro* 6d6–e1; *Gorgias* 506d2–4; *Protagoras* 332b4–6; *Republic* 353d9–354a2. The *aretē* of a knife might include having a sharp blade; the *aretē* of a man might include being intelligent, well-born, just, or courageous. *Aretē* is thus broader than our notion of moral virtue. It applies to things (such as knives) which are not moral agents. And it applies to aspects of moral agents (such as intelligence or family status) which are not normally considered to be moral aspects of them. For these reasons it is sometimes more appropriate to render *aretē* as "excellence." But "virtue" remains the best overall translation, and once these few facts are borne in mind, it should seldom mislead.]

13. [Bias of Priene in Ionia (now the region of Turkey bordering on the eastern shore of the Aegean) and Pittacus of Mytilene (on the island of Lesbos in the eastern Aegean), both sixth century B.C., were two of the legendary seven sages of Greece.]

14. [Periander was tyrant of the city of Corinth (650–570 B.C.). Perdiccas is probably Perdiccas II, king of Macedon

That's absolutely true.

All right, since it has become apparent that justice and the just aren't what such people say they are, what else could they be?

While we were speaking, Thrasymachus had tried *b* many times to take over the discussion but was restrained by those sitting near him, who wanted to hear our argument to the end. When we paused after what I'd just said, however, he couldn't keep quiet any longer. He coiled himself up like a wild beast about to spring, and he hurled himself at us as if to tear us to pieces.

Polemarchus and I were frightened and flustered as he roared into our midst: What nonsense have you two been talking, Socrates? Why do you act like idiots *c* by giving way to one another? If you truly want to know what justice is, don't just ask questions and then refute the answers simply to satisfy your competitiveness or love of honor. You know very well that it is easier to ask questions than answer them. Give an answer yourself, and tell us what you say the just is. *d* And don't tell me that it's the right, the beneficial, the profitable, the gainful, or the advantageous, but tell me clearly and exactly what you mean; for I won't accept such nonsense from you.

His words startled me, and, looking at him, I was afraid. And I think that if I hadn't seen him before he stared at me, I'd have been dumbstruck. But as it was, I happened to look at him just as our discussion *e* began to exasperate him, so I was able to answer, and, trembling a little, I said: Don't be too hard on us, Thrasymachus, for if Polemarchus and I made an error in our investigation, you should know that we did so unwillingly. If we were searching for gold, we'd never willingly give way to each other, if by doing so we'd destroy our chance of finding it. So don't think that in searching for justice, a thing more valuable than even a large quantity of gold, we'd mindlessly give way to one another or be less than completely serious about finding it. You surely mustn't think that, but rather—as I do—that we're incapable of finding it. Hence it's surely far more appropriate for us to be

pitied by you clever people than to be given rough treatment.   337

When he heard that, he gave a loud, sarcastic laugh. By Heracles, he said, that's just Socrates' usual irony.[15] I knew, and I said so to these people earlier, that you'd be unwilling to answer and that, if someone questioned *you*, you'd be ironical and do anything rather than give an answer.

That's because you're a clever fellow, Thrasymachus. You knew very well that if you ask someone how much twelve is, and, as you ask, you warn him by saying "Don't tell me, man, that twelve is twice *b* six, or three times four, or six times two, or four times three, for I won't accept such nonsense," then you'll see clearly, I think, that no one could answer a question framed like that. And if he said to you: "What are you saying, Thrasymachus, am I not to give any of the answers you mention, not even if twelve happens to be one of those things? I'm amazed. Do you want me to say something other than the truth? Or do you mean something else?" What answer would you give him?   *c*

Well, so you think the two cases are alike?

Why shouldn't they be alike? But even if they aren't alike, yet seem so to the person you asked, do you think him any less likely to give the answer that seems right to him, whether we forbid him to or not?

Is that what you're going to do, give one of the forbidden answers?

I wouldn't be surprised—provided that it's the one that seems right to me after I've investigated the matter.

What if I show you a different answer about justice than all these—and a better one? What would you *d* deserve then?

What else than the appropriate penalty for one who doesn't know, namely, to learn from the one who does know? Therefore, that's what I deserve.

You amuse me, but in addition to learning, you must pay a fine.

(c. 450–413 B.C.), who is also mentioned in the *Gorgias* 471a–e. Xerxes was the king of Persia who invaded Greece in the second Persian war (begun in 480 B.C.). Ismenias is mentioned in the *Meno* 89e. All four are either notorious tyrants or men famous for their wealth.]

15. [The Greek word *eirōneia*, unlike its usual translation "irony," is correctly applied only to someone who intends to deceive. Thus Thrasymachus is not simply accusing Socrates of saying one thing while meaning another; he is accusing him of trying to deceive those present. See G. Vlastos, "Socratic Irony," *Classical Quarterly* 37 (1987): 79–96.]

I will as soon as I have some money.

He has some already, said Glaucon. If it's a matter of money, speak, Thrasymachus, for we'll all contribute for Socrates.

I know, he said, so that Socrates can carry on as *e* usual. He gives no answer himself, and then, when someone else does give one, he takes up the argument and refutes it.

How can someone give an answer, I said, when he doesn't know it and doesn't claim to know it, and when an eminent man forbids him to express the opinion he has? It's much more appropriate for you 338 to answer, since you say you know and can tell us. So do it as a favor to me, and don't begrudge your teaching to Glaucon and the others.

While I was saying this, Glaucon and the others begged him to speak. It was obvious that Thrasymachus thought he had a fine answer and that he wanted to earn their admiration by giving it, but he pretended that he wanted to indulge his love of victory by forcing me to answer. However, he agreed in the end, and *b* then said: There you have Socrates' wisdom; he himself isn't willing to teach, but he goes around learning from others and isn't even grateful to them.

When you say that I learn from others you are right, Thrasymachus, but when you say that I'm not grateful, that isn't true. I show what gratitude I can, but since I have no money, I can give only praise. But just how enthusiastically I give it when someone seems to me to speak well, you'll know as soon as you've answered, for I think that you will speak well.

Listen, then. I say that justice is nothing other than *c* the advantage of the stronger. Well, why don't you praise me? But then you'd do anything to avoid having to do that.

I must first understand you, for I don't yet know what you mean. The advantage of the stronger, you say, is just. What do you mean, Thrasymachus? Surely you don't mean something like this: Polydamus, the pancratist,[16] is stronger than we are; it is to his advantage to eat beef to build up his physical strength; therefore, this food is also advantageous and just for *d* us who are weaker than he is?

---

16. [*Pancration* was a mixture of boxing and wrestling combined with kicking and strangling. Biting and gouging were forbidden, but pretty well everything else, including breaking and dislocating limbs, was permitted.]

You disgust me, Socrates. Your trick is to take hold of the argument at the point where you can do it the most harm.

Not at all, but tell us more clearly what you mean.

Don't you know that some cities are ruled by a tyranny, some by a democracy, and some by an aristocracy?

Of course.

And in each city this element is stronger, namely, the ruler?

Certainly.

And each makes laws to its own advantage. Democracy makes democratic laws, tyranny makes tyrannical *e* laws, and so on with the others. And they declare what they have made—what is to their own advantage—to be just for their subjects, and they punish anyone who goes against this as lawless and unjust. This, then, is what I say justice is, the same in all cities, the advantage of the established rule. Since the established rule is surely stronger, anyone who reasons 339 correctly will conclude that the just is the same everywhere, namely, the advantage of the stronger.

Now I see what you mean. Whether it's true or not, I'll try to find out. But you yourself have answered that the just is the advantageous, Thrasymachus, whereas you forbade that answer to me. True, you've added "of the stronger" to it.

And I suppose you think that's an insignificant addition. *b*

It isn't clear yet whether it's significant. But it is clear that we must investigate to see whether or not it's true. I agree that the just is some kind of advantage. But you add that it's *of the stronger*. I don't know about that. We'll have to look into it.

Go ahead and look.

We will. Tell me, don't you also say that it is just to obey the rulers?

I do.

And are the rulers in all cities infallible, or are they liable to error? *c*

No doubt they are liable to error.

When they undertake to make laws, therefore, they make some correctly, others incorrectly?

I suppose so.

And a law is correct if it prescribes what is to the rulers' own advantage and incorrect if it prescribes what is to their disadvantage? Is that what you mean?

It is.

And whatever laws they make must be obeyed by their subjects, and this is justice?

Of course.

Then, according to your account, it is just to do d not only what is to the advantage of the stronger, but also the opposite, what is not to their advantage.

What are you saying?

The same as you. But let's examine it more fully. Haven't we agreed that, in giving orders to their subjects, the rulers are sometimes in error as to what is best for themselves, and yet that it is just for their subjects to do whatever their rulers order? Haven't we agreed to that much?

I think so.

Then you must also think that you have agreed e that it is just to do what is disadvantageous to the rulers and those who are stronger, whenever they unintentionally order what is bad for themselves. But you also say that it is just for the others to obey the orders they give. You're terribly clever, Thrasymachus, but doesn't it necessarily follow that it is just to do the opposite of what you said, since the weaker are then ordered to do what is disadvantageous to the stronger?

By god, Socrates, said Polemarchus, that's quite 340 clear.

If you are to be his witness anyway, said Clitophon, interrupting.

Who needs a witness? Polemarchus replied. Thrasymachus himself agrees that the rulers sometimes order what is bad for themselves and that it is just for the others to do it.

That, Polemarchus, is because Thrasymachus maintained that it is just to obey the orders of the rulers.

He also maintained, Clitophon, that the advantage b of the stronger is just. And having maintained both principles he went on to agree that the stronger sometimes gives orders to those who are weaker than he is—in other words, to his subjects—that are disadvantageous to the stronger himself. From these agreements it follows that what is to the advantage of the stronger is no more just than what is not to his advantage.

But, Clitophon responded, he said that the advantage of the stronger is what the stronger believes to be his advantage. This is what the weaker must do, and this is what he maintained the just to be.

That isn't what he said, Polemarchus replied.

It makes no difference, Polemarchus, I said. If Thrasymachus wants to put it that way now, let's c accept it. Tell me, Thrasymachus, is this what you wanted to say the just is, namely, what the stronger believes to be to his advantage, whether it is in fact to his advantage or not? Is that what we are to say you mean?

Not at all. Do you think I'd call someone who is in error stronger at the very moment he errs?

I did think that was what you meant when you agreed that the rulers aren't infallible but are liable to error.

That's because you are a false witness in arguments, Socrates. When someone makes an error in the treat- d ment of patients, do you call him a doctor in regard to that very error? Or when someone makes an error in accounting, do you call him an accountant in regard to that very error in calculation? I think that we express ourselves in words that, taken literally, do say that a doctor is in error, or an accountant, or a grammarian. But each of these, insofar as he is what we call him, never errs, so that, according to the e precise account (and you are a stickler for precise accounts), no craftsman ever errs. It's when his knowledge fails him that he makes an error, and in regard to that error he is no craftsman. No craftsman, expert, or ruler makes an error at the moment when he is ruling, even though everyone will say that a physician or a ruler makes errors. It's in this loose way that you must also take the answer I gave earlier. But the most precise answer is this. A ruler, insofar as he is a ruler, 341 never makes errors and unerringly decrees what is best for himself, and this his subject must do. Thus, as I said from the first, it is just to do what is to the advantage of the stronger.

All right, Thrasymachus, so you think I'm a false witness?

You certainly are.

And you think that I asked the questions I did in order to harm you in the argument?

I know it very well, but it won't do you any good. You'll never be able to trick me, so you can't harm b me that way, and without trickery you'll never be able to overpower me in argument.

I wouldn't so much as try, Thrasymachus. But in order to prevent this sort of thing from happening again, define clearly whether it is the ruler and stronger in the ordinary sense or in the precise sense whose advantage you said it is just for the weaker to promote as the advantage of the stronger.

I mean the ruler in the most precise sense. Now practice your harm-doing and false witnessing on that if you can—I ask no concessions from you—but you certainly won't be able to.

Do you think that I'm crazy enough to try to shave *c* a lion or to bear false witness against Thrasymachus?

You certainly tried just now, though you were a loser at that too.

Enough of this. Tell me: Is a doctor in the precise sense, whom you mentioned before, a money-maker or someone who treats the sick? Tell me about the one who is really a doctor.

He's the one who treats the sick.

What about a ship's captain? Is a captain in the precise sense a ruler of sailors or a sailor?

A ruler of sailors.

We shouldn't, I think, take into account the fact *d* that he sails in a ship, and he shouldn't be called a sailor for that reason, for it isn't because of his sailing that he is called a ship's captain, but because of his craft and his rule over sailors?

That's true.

And is there something advantageous to each of these, that is, to bodies and to sailors?

Certainly.

And aren't the respective crafts by nature set over them to seek and provide what is to their advantage?

They are.

And is there any advantage for each of the crafts themselves except to be as complete or perfect as possible?

e What are you asking?

This: If you asked me whether our bodies are sufficient in themselves, or whether they need something else, I'd answer: "They certainly have needs. And because of this, because our bodies are deficient rather than self-sufficient, the craft of medicine has now been discovered. The craft of medicine was developed to provide what is advantageous for a body." Do you think that I'm right in saying this or not?

You are right.

342   Now, is medicine deficient? Does a craft need some further virtue, as the eyes are in need of sight, and the ears of hearing, so that another craft is needed to

seek and provide what is advantageous to them?[17] Does a craft itself have some similar deficiency, so that each craft needs another, to seek out what is to its advantage? And does the craft that does the seeking need still another, and so on without end? Or does each seek out what is to its own advantage by itself? Or does it need neither itself nor another craft to seek *b* out what is advantageous to it, because of its own deficiencies? Or is it that there is no deficiency or error in any craft? That it isn't appropriate for any craft to seek what is to the advantage of anything except that of which it is the craft? And that, since it is itself correct, it is without either fault or impurity, as long as it is wholly and precisely the craft that it is? Consider this with the preciseness of language you mentioned. Is it so or not?

It appears to be so.

Medicine doesn't seek its own advantage, then, but that of the body?   *c*

Yes.

And horse-breeding doesn't seek its own advantage, but that of horses? Indeed, no other craft seeks its own advantage—for it has no further needs—but the advantage of that of which it is the craft?

Apparently so.

Now, surely, Thrasymachus, the crafts rule over and are stronger than the things of which they are the crafts?

Very reluctantly, he conceded this as well.

No kind of knowledge seeks or orders what is advantageous to itself, then, but what is advantageous to the weaker, which is subject to it.   *d*

He tried to fight this conclusion, but he conceded it in the end. And after he had, I said: Surely, then, no doctor, insofar as he is a doctor, seeks or orders what is advantageous to himself, but what is advantageous to his patient? We agreed that a doctor in the precise sense is a ruler of bodies, not a money-maker. Wasn't that agreed?

Yes.

17. [Sight is the virtue or excellence of the eyes (see 335b n. 12). Without it, the eyes cannot achieve what is advantageous to them, namely, sight. So eyes need some further virtue to seek and provide what is advantageous to them. But Socrates assumes throughout Book I that virtues are crafts (see 332d). Hence he can conclude that the eyes need a further craft to achieve what is advantageous to them.]

So a ship's captain in the precise sense is a ruler of sailors, not a sailor?

e   That's what we agreed.

Doesn't it follow that a ship's captain or ruler won't seek and order what is advantageous to himself, but what is advantageous to a sailor?

He reluctantly agreed.

So, then, Thrasymachus, no one in any position of rule, insofar as he is a ruler, seeks or orders what is advantageous to himself, but what is advantageous to his subjects; the ones of whom he is himself the craftsman. It is to his subjects and what is advantageous and proper to them that he looks, and everything he says and does he says and does for them.

When we reached this point in the argument, and 343 it was clear to all that his account of justice had turned into its opposite, instead of answering, Thrasymachus said: Tell me, Socrates, do you still have a wet nurse?

What's this? Hadn't you better answer *my* questions rather than asking *me* such things?

Because she's letting you run around with a snotty nose, and doesn't wipe it when she needs to! Why, for all she cares, you don't even know about sheep and shepherds.

Just what is it I don't know?

You think that shepherds and cowherds seek the b good of their sheep and cattle, and fatten them and take care of them, looking to something other than their master's good and their own. Moreover, you believe that rulers in cities—true rulers, that is— think about their subjects differently than one does about sheep, and that night and day they think of something besides their own advantage. You are so c far from understanding about justice and what's just, about injustice and what's unjust, that you don't realize that justice is really the good of another, the advantage of the stronger and the ruler, and harmful to the one who obeys and serves. Injustice is the opposite, it rules the truly simple and just, and those it rules do what is to the advantage of the other and stronger, and they make the one they serve happy, but themselves not at all. You must look at it as d follows, my most simple Socrates: A just man always gets less than an unjust one. First, in their contracts with one another, you'll never find, when the partnership ends, that a just partner has got more than an unjust one, but less. Second, in matters relating to the city, when taxes are to be paid, a just man pays

more on the same property, an unjust one less, but when the city is giving out refunds, a just man gets nothing, while an unjust one makes a large profit. e Finally, when each of them holds a ruling position in some public office, a just person, even if he isn't penalized in other ways, finds that his private affairs deteriorate because he has to neglect them, that he gains no advantage from the public purse because of his justice, and that he's hated by his relatives and acquaintances when he's unwilling to do them an unjust favor. The opposite is true of an unjust man in every respect. Therefore, I repeat what I said before: A person of great power outdoes everyone else.[18] Consider him if you want to figure out how much more 344 advantageous it is for the individual to be just rather than unjust. You'll understand this most easily if you turn your thoughts to the most complete injustice, the one that makes the doer of injustice happiest and the sufferers of it, who are unwilling to do injustice, most wretched. This is tyranny, which through stealth or force appropriates the property of others, whether sacred or profane, public or private, not little by little, but all at once. If someone commits only one part of injustice and is caught, he's punished and greatly b reproached—such partly unjust people are called temple-robbers,[19] kidnappers, housebreakers, robbers, and thieves when they commit these crimes. But when someone, in addition to appropriating their possessions, kidnaps and enslaves the citizens as well, instead of these shameful names he is called happy and blessed, not only by the citizens themselves, but c by all who learn that he has done the whole of injustice. Those who reproach injustice do so because they are afraid not of doing it but of suffering it. So, Socrates, injustice, if it is on a large enough scale, is stronger, freer, and more masterly than justice. And,

18. [Outdoing (*pleonektein*) is an important notion in the remainder of the *Republic*. It is connected to *pleonexia*, which is what one succumbs to when one always wants to outdo everyone else by getting and having more and more. *Pleonexia* is, or is the cause of, injustice (359c), since always wanting to outdo others leads one to try to get what belongs to them, what isn't *one's own*. It is contrasted with *doing or having one's own*, which is, or is the cause of, justice (434a, 441e).]

19. [The temples acted as public treasuries, so that a temple robber is the equivalent of a present-day bank robber.]

as I said from the first, justice is what is advantageous to the stronger, while injustice is to one's own profit and advantage.

Having emptied this great flood of words into our *d* ears all at once like a bath attendant, Thrasymachus intended to leave. But those present didn't let him and made him stay to give an account of what he had said. I too begged him to stay, and I said to him: After hurling such a speech at us, Thrasymachus, do you intend to leave before adequately instructing us or finding out whether you are right or not? Or do *e* you think it a small matter to determine which whole way of life would make living most worthwhile for each of us?

Is *that* what I seem to you to think? Thrasymachus said.

Either that, or else you care nothing for us and aren't worried about whether we'll live better or worse lives because of our ignorance of what you say you know. So show some willingness to teach it to us. It wouldn't be a bad investment for you to be the benefactor of a group as large as ours. For my own *345* part, I'll tell you that I am not persuaded. I don't believe that injustice is more profitable than justice, not even if you give it full scope and put no obstacles in its way. Suppose that there *is* an unjust person, and suppose he *does* have the power to do injustice, whether by trickery or open warfare; nonetheless, he doesn't persuade me that injustice is more profitable *b* than justice. Perhaps someone here, besides myself, feels the same as I do. So come now, and persuade us that we are wrong to esteem justice more highly than injustice in planning our lives.

And how am I to persuade you, if you aren't persuaded by what I said just now? What more can I do? Am I to take my argument and pour it into your very soul?

God forbid! Don't do that! But, first, stick to what you've said, and then, if you change your position, do it openly and don't deceive us. You see, Thrasymachus, that having defined the true doctor—to con-*c* tinue examining the things you said before—you didn't consider it necessary later to keep a precise guard on the true shepherd. You think that, insofar as he's a shepherd, he fattens sheep, not looking to what is best for the sheep but to a banquet, like a guest about to be entertained at a feast, or to a future sale, like a money-maker rather than a shepherd.

Shepherding is concerned only to provide what is best *d* for the things it is set over, and it is itself adequately provided with all it needs to be at its best when it doesn't fall short in any way of being the craft of shepherding. That's why I thought it necessary for us to agree before[20] that every kind of rule, insofar as it rules, doesn't seek anything other than what is best for the things it rules and cares for, and this is true both of public and private kinds of rule. But do you think that those who rule cities, the true rulers, *e* rule willingly?

I don't think it, by god, I know it.

But, Thrasymachus, don't you realize that in other kinds of rule no one wants to rule for its own sake, but they ask for pay, thinking that their ruling will benefit not themselves but their subjects? Tell me, doesn't every craft differ from every other in having *346* a different function? Please don't answer contrary to what you believe, so that we can come to some definite conclusion.

Yes, that's what differentiates them.

And each craft benefits us in its own peculiar way, different from the others. For example, medicine gives us health, navigation gives us safety while sailing, and so on with the others?

Certainly.

And wage-earning gives us wages, for this is its function? Or would you call medicine the same as *b* navigation? Indeed, if you want to define matters precisely, as you proposed, even if someone who is a ship's captain becomes healthy because sailing is advantageous to his health, you wouldn't for that reason call his craft medicine?

Certainly not.

Nor would you call wage-earning medicine, even if someone becomes healthy while earning wages?

Certainly not.

Nor would you call medicine wage-earning, even if someone earns pay while healing?

No.   *c*

We are agreed, then, that each craft brings its own peculiar benefit?

It does.

Then whatever benefit all craftsmen receive in common must clearly result from their joint practice of some additional craft that benefits each of them?

20. [See 341e–342e.]

So it seems.

And we say that the additional craft in question, which benefits the craftsmen by earning them wages, is the craft of wage-earning?

He reluctantly agreed.

Then this benefit, receiving wages, doesn't result *d* from their own craft, but rather, if we're to examine this precisely, medicine provides health, and wage-earning provides wages; house-building provides a house, and wage-earning, which accompanies it, provides a wage; and so on with the other crafts. Each of them does its own work and benefits the things it is set over. So, if wages aren't added, is there any benefit that the craftsman gets from his craft?

Apparently none.

But he still provides a benefit when he works for *e* nothing?

Yes, I think he does.

Then, it is clear now, Thrasymachus, that no craft or rule provides for its own advantage, but, as we've been saying for some time, it provides and orders for its subject and aims at its advantage, that of the weaker, not of the stronger. That's why I said just now, Thrasymachus, that no one willingly chooses to rule and to take other people's troubles in hand and straighten them out, but each asks for wages; for *347* anyone who intends to practice his craft well never does or orders what is best for himself—at least not when he orders as his craft prescribes—but what is best for his subject. It is because of this, it seems, that wages must be provided to a person if he's to be willing to rule, whether in the form of money or honor or a penalty if he refuses.

What do you mean, Socrates? said Glaucon. I know the first two kinds of wages, but I don't understand what penalty you mean or how you can call it a wage.

Then you don't understand the best people's kind of wages, the kind that moves the most decent to rule, when they are willing to rule at all. Don't you know *b* that the love of honor and the love of money are despised, and rightly so?

I do.

Therefore good people won't be willing to rule for the sake of either money or honor. They don't want to be paid wages openly for ruling and get called hired hands, nor to take them in secret from their rule and be called thieves. And they won't rule for the sake of honor, because they aren't ambitious honor-

lovers. So, if they're to be willing to rule, some com- *c* pulsion or punishment must be brought to bear on them—perhaps that's why it is thought shameful to seek to rule before one is compelled to. Now, the greatest punishment, if one isn't willing to rule, is to be ruled by someone worse than oneself. And I think that it's fear of this that makes decent people rule when they do. They approach ruling not as something good or something to be enjoyed, but as something necessary, since it can't be entrusted to anyone better *d* than—or even as good as—themselves. In a city of good men, if it came into being, the citizens would fight in order *not to rule*, just as they do now in order to rule. There it would be quite clear that anyone who is really a true ruler doesn't by nature seek his own advantage but that of his subjects. And everyone, knowing this, would rather be benefited by others than take the trouble to benefit them. So I can't at all agree with Thrasymachus that justice is the advantage of the stronger—but we'll look further into that another time. What Thrasymachus is now say- *e* ing—that the life of an unjust person is better than that of a just one—seems to be of far greater importance. Which life would you choose, Glaucon? And which of our views do you consider truer?

I certainly think that the life of a just person is more profitable.

Did you hear all of the good things Thrasymachus listed a moment ago for the unjust life?   *348*

I heard, but I wasn't persuaded.

Then, do you want us to persuade him, if we're able to find a way, that what he says isn't true?

Of course I do.

If we oppose him with a parallel speech about the blessings of the just life, and then he replies, and then we do, we'd have to count and measure the good things mentioned on each side, and we'd need a jury to decide the case. But if, on the other hand, *b* we investigate the question, as we've been doing, by seeking agreement with each other, we ourselves can be both jury and advocates at once.

Certainly.

Which approach do you prefer? I asked.

The second.

Come, then, Thrasymachus, I said, answer us from the beginning. You say that complete injustice is more profitable than complete justice?

I certainly do say that, and I've told you why.   *c*

Well, then, what do you say about this? Do you call one of the two a virtue and the other a vice?

Of course.

That is to say, you call justice a virtue and injustice a vice?

That's hardly likely, since I say that injustice is profitable and justice isn't.

Then, what exactly do you say?

The opposite.

That justice is a vice?

No, just very high-minded simplicity.

d   Then do you call being unjust being low-minded?

No, I call it good judgment.

You consider unjust people, then, Thrasymachus, to be clever and good?

Yes, those who are completely unjust, who can bring cities and whole communities under their power. Perhaps, you think I meant pickpockets? Not that such crimes aren't also profitable, if they're not found out, but they aren't worth mentioning by comparison to what I'm talking about.

I'm not unaware of what you want to say. But I

e wonder about this: Do you really include injustice with virtue and wisdom, and justice with their opposites?

I certainly do.

That's harder, and it isn't easy now to know what to say. If you had declared that injustice is more profitable, but agreed that it is a vice or shameful, as some others do, we could have discussed the matter on the basis of conventional beliefs. But now, obviously, you'll say that injustice is fine and strong and

349 apply to it all the attributes we used to apply to justice, since you dare to include it with virtue and wisdom.

You've divined my views exactly.

Nonetheless, we mustn't shrink from pursuing the argument and looking into this, just as long as I take you to be saying what you really think. And I believe that you aren't joking now, Thrasymachus, but are saying what you believe to be the truth.

What difference does it make to you, whether *I* believe it or not? It's *my account* you're supposed to be refuting.

It makes no difference. But try to answer this further

b question: Do you think that a just person wants to outdo[21] someone else who's just?

21. [*Pleon echein.* See 344a n. 18.]

Not at all, for he wouldn't then be as polite and innocent as he is.

Or to outdo someone who does a just action?

No, he doesn't even want to do that.

And does he claim that he deserves to outdo an unjust person and believe that it is just for him to do so, or doesn't he believe that?

He'd want to outdo him, and he'd claim to deserve to do so, but he wouldn't be able.

That's not what I asked, but whether a just person wants to outdo an unjust person but not a just one, thinking that this is what he deserves?   c

He does.

What about an unjust person? Does he claim that he deserves to outdo a just person or someone who does a just action?

Of course he does; he thinks he deserves to outdo everyone.

Then will an unjust person also outdo an *unjust* person or someone who does an *unjust* action, and will he strive to get the most he can for himself from everyone?

He will.

Then, let's put it this way: A just person doesn't outdo someone like himself but someone unlike himself, whereas an unjust person outdoes both like and unlike.   d

Very well put.

An unjust person is clever and good, and a just one is neither?

That's well put, too.

It follows, then, that an unjust person is like clever and good people, while the other isn't?

Of course that's so. How could he fail to be like them when he has their qualities, while the other isn't like them?

Fine. Then each of them has the qualities of the people he's like?

Of course.

All right, Thrasymachus. Do you call one person musical and another nonmusical?   e

I do.

Which of them is clever in music, and which isn't?

The musical one is clever, of course, and the other isn't.

And the things he's clever in, he's good in, and the things he isn't clever in, he's bad in?

Yes.

Isn't the same true of a doctor?

It is.

Do you think that a musician, in tuning his lyre and in tightening and loosening the strings, wants to outdo another musician, claiming that this is what he deserves?[22]

I do not.

But he does want to outdo a nonmusician?

Necessarily.

What about a doctor? Does he, when prescribing
350 food and drink, want to outdo another doctor or someone who does the action that medicine prescribes?

Certainly not.

But he does want to outdo a nondoctor?

Yes.

In any branch of knowledge or ignorance, do you think that a knowledgeable person would intentionally try to outdo other knowledgeable people or say something better or different than they do, rather than doing or saying the very same thing as those like him?

Well, perhaps it must be as you say.

And what about an ignorant person? Doesn't he want to outdo both a knowledgeable person and an
b ignorant one?

Probably.

A knowledgeable person is clever?

I agree.

And a clever one is good?

I agree.

Therefore, a good and clever person doesn't want to outdo those like himself but those who are unlike him and his opposite.

So it seems.

But a bad and ignorant person wants to outdo both his like and his opposite.

Apparently.

Now, Thrasymachus, we found that an unjust person tries to outdo those like him and those unlike him? Didn't you say that?

22. [Socrates' point may seem obscure, but what he has in mind is explained at 350a. All expert musicians try to get the same thing, perfect harmony, so they tighten and loosen their strings to exactly the same degree, namely, the one that will produce the right pitch. In the same way, all doctors who are masters of medicine prescribe the same diet for people with the same diseases, namely, the one that will best restore them to health.]

I did.

And that a just person won't outdo his like but his unlike? c

Yes.

Then, a just person is like a clever and good one, and an unjust is like an ignorant and bad one.

It looks that way.

Moreover, we agreed that each has the qualities of the one he resembles.

Yes, we did.

Then, a just person has turned out to be good and clever, and an unjust one ignorant and bad.

Thrasymachus agreed to all this, not easily as I'm telling it, but reluctantly, with toil, trouble, and— d since it was summer—a quantity of sweat that was a wonder to behold. And then I saw something I'd never seen before—Thrasymachus blushing. But, in any case, after we'd agreed that justice is virtue and wisdom and that injustice is vice and ignorance, I said: All right, let's take that as established. But we also said that injustice is powerful, or don't you remember that, Thrasymachus?

I remember, but I'm not satisfied with what you're now saying. I could make a speech about it, but, if I did, I know that you'd accuse me of engaging in oratory. So either allow me to speak, or, if you want e to ask questions, go ahead, and I'll say, "All right," and nod yes and no, as one does to old wives' tales.

Don't do that, contrary to your own opinion.

I'll answer so as to please you, since you won't let me make a speech. What else do you want?

Nothing, by god. But if that's what you're going to do, go ahead and do it. I'll ask my questions.

Ask ahead.

I'll ask what I asked before, so that we may proceed with our argument about justice and injustice in an 351 orderly fashion, for surely it was claimed that injustice is stronger and more powerful than justice. But, now, if justice is indeed wisdom and virtue, it will easily be shown to be stronger than injustice, since injustice is ignorance (no one could now be ignorant of that). However, I don't want to state the matter so unconditionally, Thrasymachus, but to look into it in some such way as this. Would you say that it is unjust for a city to b try to enslave other cities unjustly and to hold them in subjection when it has enslaved many of them?

Of course, that's what the best city will especially do, the one that is most completely unjust.

I understand that's your position, but the point I want to examine is this: Will the city that becomes stronger than another achieve this power without justice, or will it need the help of justice?

c If what you said a moment ago stands, and justice is cleverness or wisdom, it will need the help of justice, but if things are as I stated, it will need the help of injustice.

I'm impressed, Thrasymachus, that you don't merely nod yes or no but give very fine answers.

That's because I'm trying to please you.

You're doing well at it, too. So please me some more by answering this question: Do you think that a city, an army, a band of robbers or thieves, or any other tribe with a common unjust purpose would be able to achieve it if they were unjust to each other?

d No, indeed.

What if they weren't unjust to one another? Would they achieve more?

Certainly.

Injustice, Thrasymachus, causes civil war, hatred, and fighting among themselves, while justice brings friendship and a sense of common purpose. Isn't that so?

Let it be so, in order not to disagree with you.

You're still doing well on that front. So tell me this: If the effect of injustice is to produce hatred wherever it occurs, then, whenever it arises, whether among free men or slaves, won't it cause them to hate one another, engage in civil war, and prevent e them from achieving any common purpose?

Certainly.

What if it arises between two people? Won't they be at odds, hate each other, and be enemies to one another and to just people?

They will.

Does injustice lose its power to cause dissension when it arises within a single individual, or will it preserve it intact?

Let it preserve it intact.

Apparently, then, injustice has the power, first, to make whatever it arises in—whether it is a city, a family, an army, or anything else—incapable of 352 achieving anything as a unit, because of the civil wars and differences it creates, and, second, it makes that unit an enemy to itself and to what is in every way its opposite, namely, justice. Isn't that so?

Certainly.

And even in a single individual, it has by its nature the very same effect. First, it makes him incapable of achieving anything, because he is in a state of civil war and not of one mind; second, it makes him his own enemy, as well as the enemy of just people. Hasn't it that effect?

Yes.

And the gods too are just?

Let it be so.

So an unjust person is also an enemy of the gods, Thrasymachus, while a just person is their friend?   b

Enjoy your banquet of words! Have no fear, I won't oppose you. That would make these people hate me.

Come, then, complete the banquet for me by continuing to answer as you've been doing. We have shown that just people are cleverer and more capable of doing things, while unjust ones aren't even able to act together, for when we speak of a powerful c achievement by unjust men acting together, what we say isn't altogether true. They would never have been able to keep their hands off each other if they were completely unjust. But clearly there must have been some sort of justice in them that at least prevented them from doing injustice among themselves at the same time as they were doing it to others. And it was this that enabled them to achieve what they did. When they started doing unjust things, they were only halfway corrupted by their injustice (for those who are all bad and completely unjust are completely incapable of accomplishing anything). These are the things I understand to hold, not the ones you first maintained. We must now examine, as we proposed d before,[23] whether just people also live better and are happier than unjust ones. I think it's clear already that this is so, but we must look into it further, since the argument concerns no ordinary topic but the way we ought to live.

Go ahead and look.

I will. Tell me, do you think there is such a thing as the function of a horse?

I do.   e

And would you define the function of a horse or of anything else as that which one can do only with it or best with it?

I don't understand.

23. [See 347e.]

Let me put it this way: Is it possible to see with anything other than eyes?

Certainly not.

Or to hear with anything other than ears?

No.

Then, we are right to say that seeing and hearing are the functions of eyes and ears?

Of course.

What about this? Could you use a dagger or a 353 carving knife or lots of other things in pruning a vine?

Of course.

But wouldn't you do a finer job with a pruning knife designed for the purpose than with anything else?

You would.

Then shall we take pruning to be its function?

Yes.

Now, I think you'll understand what I was asking earlier when I asked whether the function of each thing is what it alone can do or what it does better than anything else.

I understand, and I think that this is the function b of each.

All right. Does each thing to which a particular function is assigned also have a virtue?[24] Let's go over the same ground again. We say that eyes have some function?

They do.

So there is also a virtue of eyes?

There is.

And ears have a function?

Yes.

So there is also a virtue of ears?

There is.

And all other things are the same, aren't they?

They are.

And could eyes perform their function well if they c lacked their peculiar virtue and had the vice instead?

How could they, for don't you mean if they had blindness instead of sight?

Whatever their virtue is, for I'm not now asking about that but about whether anything that has a function performs it well by means of its own peculiar virtue and badly by means of its vice?

That's true, it does.

So ears, too, deprived of their own virtue, perform their function badly?

24. [See 335b n. 12.]

That's right.

And the same could be said about everything else? d

So it seems.

Come, then, and let's consider this: Is there some function of a soul that you couldn't perform with anything else, for example, taking care of things, ruling, deliberating, and the like? Is there anything other than a soul to which you could rightly assign these, and say that they are its peculiar function?

No, none of them.

What of living? Isn't that a function of a soul?

It certainly is.

And don't we also say that there is a virtue of a soul?

We do.

Then, will a soul ever perform its function well, Thrasymachus, if it is deprived of its own peculiar e virtue, or is that impossible?

It's impossible.

Doesn't it follow, then, that a bad soul rules and takes care of things badly and that a good soul does all these things well?

It does.

Now, we agreed that justice is a soul's virtue, and injustice its vice?

We did.

Then, it follows that a just soul and a just man will live well, and an unjust one badly.

Apparently so, according to your argument.

And surely anyone who lives well is blessed and happy, and anyone who doesn't is the opposite.   354

Of course.

Therefore, a just person is happy, and an unjust one wretched.

So be it.

It profits no one to be wretched but to be happy.

Of course.

And so, Thrasymachus, injustice is never more profitable than justice.

Let that be your banquet, Socrates, at the feast of Bendis.

Given by you, Thrasymachus, after you became gentle and ceased to give me rough treatment. Yet I haven't had a fine banquet. But that's my fault not yours. I seem to have behaved like a glutton, snatching b at every dish that passes and tasting it before properly savoring its predecessor. Before finding the answer to our first inquiry about what justice is, I let that go and turned to investigate whether it is a kind of vice and ignorance or a kind of wisdom and virtue. Then an argument came up about injustice being more profitable than justice, and I couldn't refrain from abandoning the previous one and following up on that. Hence the result of the discussion, as far as I'm concerned, is that I know nothing, for when I don't know what justice is, I'll hardly know whether it is a kind of virtue or not, or whether a person who has it is happy or unhappy.

Book II

357 When I said this, I thought I had done with the discussion, but it turned out to have been only a prelude. Glaucon showed his characteristic courage on this occasion too and refused to accept Thrasymachus' abandonment of the argument. Socrates, he said, do you want to seem to have persuaded us that it is better in every way to be just than unjust, or do *b* you want truly to convince us of this?

I want truly to convince you, I said, if I can.

Well, then, you certainly aren't doing what you want. Tell me, do you think there is a kind of good we welcome, not because we desire what comes from it, but because we welcome it for its own sake—joy, for example, and all the harmless pleasures that have no results beyond the joy of having them?

Certainly, I think there are such things.

And is there a kind of good we like for its own sake *c* and also for the sake of what comes from it—knowing, for example, and seeing and being healthy? We welcome such things, I suppose, on both counts.

Yes.

And do you also see a third kind of good, such as physical training, medical treatment when sick, medicine itself, and the other ways of making money? We'd say that these are onerous but beneficial to us, and we wouldn't choose them for their own sakes, but for the sake of the rewards and other things that *d* come from them.

There is also this third kind. But what of it?

Where do you put justice?

I myself put it among the finest goods, as something 358 to be valued by anyone who is going to be blessed with happiness, both because of itself and because of what comes from it.

That isn't most people's opinion. They'd say that justice belongs to the onerous kind, and is to be practiced for the sake of the rewards and popularity that come from a reputation for justice, but is to be avoided because of itself as something burdensome.

I know that's the general opinion. Thrasymachus faulted justice on these grounds a moment ago and praised injustice, but it seems that I'm a slow learner.

Come, then, and listen to me as well, and see whether you still have that problem, for I think that *b* Thrasymachus gave up before he had to, charmed by you as if he were a snake. But I'm not yet satisfied by the argument on either side. I want to know what justice and injustice are and what power each itself has when it's by itself in the soul. I want to leave out of account their rewards and what comes from each of them. So, if you agree, I'll renew the argument of Thrasymachus. First, I'll state what kind of thing people consider justice to be and what its origins are. *c* Second, I'll argue that all who practice it do so unwillingly, as something necessary, not as something good. Third, I'll argue that they have good reason to act as they do, for the life of an unjust person is, they say, much better than that of a just one.

It isn't, Socrates, that I believe any of that myself. I'm perplexed, indeed, and my ears are deafened listening to Thrasymachus and countless others. But I've yet to hear anyone defend justice in the way I want, proving that it is better than injustice. I want *d* to hear it praised *by itself*, and I think that I'm most likely to hear this from you. Therefore, I'm going to speak at length in praise of the unjust life, and in doing so I'll show you the way I want to hear you praising justice and denouncing injustice. But see whether you want me to do that or not.

I want that most of all. Indeed, what subject could someone with any understanding enjoy discussing more often?

Excellent. Then let's discuss the first subject I mentioned—what justice is and what its origins are. *e*

They say that to do injustice is naturally good and to suffer injustice bad, but that the badness of suffering it so far exceeds the goodness of doing it that those who have done and suffered injustice and tasted both, but who lack the power to do it and avoid suffering it, decide that it is profitable to come to an agreement with each other neither to do injustice nor to suffer 359 it. As a result, they begin to make laws and covenants, and what the law commands they call lawful and just. This, they say, is the origin and essence of justice. It is intermediate between the best and the worst. The best is to do injustice without paying the penalty; the worst is to suffer it without being able to take revenge. Justice is a mean between these two extremes. People value it not as a good but because *b* they are too weak to do injustice with impunity. Someone who has the power to do this, however, and is a true man wouldn't make an agreement with anyone not to do injustice in order not to suffer it. For him that would be madness. This is the nature of justice, according to the argument, Socrates, and these are its natural origins.

We can see most clearly that those who practice justice do it unwillingly and because they lack the *c* power to do injustice, if in our thoughts we grant to a just and an unjust person the freedom to do whatever they like. We can then follow both of them and see where their desires would lead. And we'll catch the just person red-handed travelling the same road as the unjust. The reason for this is the desire to outdo others and get more and more.[1] This is what anyone's nature naturally pursues as good, but nature is forced by law into the perversion of treating fairness with respect.

The freedom I mentioned would be most easily realized if both people had the power they say the ancestor of Gyges of Lydia possessed. The story goes *d* that he was a shepherd in the service of the ruler of Lydia. There was a violent thunderstorm, and an earthquake broke open the ground and created a chasm at the place where he was tending his sheep. Seeing this, he was filled with amazement and went down into it. And there, in addition to many other wonders of which we're told, he saw a hollow bronze horse. There were windowlike openings in it, and, peeping in, he saw a corpse, which seemed to be of more than human size, wearing nothing but a gold *e* ring on its finger. He took the ring and came out of the chasm. He wore the ring at the usual monthly meeting that reported to the king on the state of the flocks. And as he was sitting among the others, he happened to turn the setting of the ring towards himself to the inside of his hand. When he did this, he

became invisible to those sitting near him, and they went on talking as if he had gone. He wondered at *360* this, and, fingering the ring, he turned the setting outwards again and became visible. So he experimented with the ring to test whether it indeed had this power—and it did. If he turned the setting inward, he became invisible; if he turned it outward, he became visible again. When he realized this, he at once arranged to become one of the messengers sent to report to the king. And when he arrived there, he seduced the king's wife, attacked the king with her help, killed him, and took over the kingdom.   *b*

Let's suppose, then, that there were two such rings, one worn by a just and the other by an unjust person. Now, no one, it seems, would be so incorruptible that he would stay on the path of justice or stay away from other people's property, when he could take whatever he wanted from the marketplace with impunity, go into people's houses and have sex with anyone he wished, kill or release from prison anyone he wished, and do all the other things that would make *c* him like a god among humans. Rather his actions would be in no way different from those of an unjust person, and both would follow the same path. This, some would say, is a great proof that one is never just willingly but only when compelled to be. No one believes justice to be a good when it is kept private, since, wherever either person thinks he can do injustice with impunity, he does it. Indeed, every man believes that injustice is far more profitable to himself than justice. And any exponent of this argument will *d* say he's right, for someone who didn't want to do injustice, given this sort of opportunity, and who didn't touch other people's property would be thought wretched and stupid by everyone aware of the situation, though, of course, they'd praise him in public, deceiving each other for fear of suffering injustice. So much for my second topic.

As for the choice between the lives we're discussing, we'll be able to make a correct judgment about that *e* only if we separate the most just and the most unjust. Otherwise we won't be able to do it. Here's the separation I have in mind. We'll subtract nothing from the injustice of an unjust person and nothing from the justice of a just one, but we'll take each to be complete in his own way of life. First, therefore, we must suppose that an unjust person will act as clever craftsmen

---

1. [*Pleonexian*. See 344a n. 18.—C.D.C.R.]

361 do: A first-rate captain or doctor, for example, knows the difference between what his craft can and can't do. He attempts the first but lets the second go by, and if he happens to slip, he can put things right. In the same way, an unjust person's successful attempts at injustice must remain undetected, if he is to be fully unjust. Anyone who is caught should be thought inept, for the extreme of injustice is to be believed to be just without being just. And our completely unjust person must be given complete injustice; nothing may be subtracted from it. We must allow that, while doing the greatest injustice, he has nonetheless provided himself with the greatest reputation for jus-
b tice. If he happens to make a slip, he must be able to put it right. If any of his unjust activities should be discovered, he must be able to speak persuasively or to use force. And if force is needed, he must have the help of courage and strength and of the substantial wealth and friends with which he has provided himself.

Having hypothesized such a person, let's now in our argument put beside him a just man, who is simple and noble and who, as Aeschylus says, doesn't want to be believed to be good but to be so.[2] We
c must take away his reputation, for a reputation for justice would bring him honor and rewards, so that it wouldn't be clear whether he is just for the sake of justice itself or for the sake of those honors and rewards. We must strip him of everything except justice and make his situation the opposite of an unjust person's. Though he does no injustice, he must have the greatest reputation for it, so that his justice may be tested full-strength and not diluted by wrongdoing and what comes from it. Let him stay like that un-
d changed until he dies—just, but all his life believed to be unjust. In this way, both will reach the extremes, the one of justice and the other of injustice, and we'll be able to judge which of them is happier.

Whew! Glaucon, I said, how vigorously you've scoured each of the men for our competition, just as you would a pair of statues for an art competition.

I do the best I can, he replied. Since the two are as I've described, in any case, it shouldn't be difficult to complete the account of the kind of life that awaits each of them, but it must be done. And if what I say sounds crude, Socrates, remember that it isn't I who *e* speak but those who praise injustice at the expense of justice. They'll say that a just person in such circumstances will be whipped, stretched on a rack, chained, blinded with fire, and, at the end, when he has suffered every kind of evil, he'll be impaled, and will realize then that one shouldn't want to be just but to be believed to be just. Indeed, Aeschylus' words 362 are far more correctly applied to unjust people than to just ones, for the supporters of injustice will say that a really unjust person, having a way of life based on the truth about things and not living in accordance with opinion, doesn't want simply to be believed to be unjust but actually to be so—

> Harvesting a deep furrow in his mind,
> Where wise counsels propagate.   *b*

He rules his city because of his reputation for justice; he marries into any family he wishes; he gives his children in marriage to anyone he wishes; he has contracts and partnerships with anyone he wants; and besides benefiting himself in all these ways, he profits because he has no scruples about doing injustice. In any contest, public or private, he's the winner and outdoes[3] his enemies. And by outdoing them, he becomes wealthy, benefiting his friends and harming his enemies. He makes adequate sacrifices to the gods and sets up magnificent offerings to them. He takes *c* better care of the gods, therefore, (and, indeed, of the human beings he's fond of) than a just person does. Hence it's likely that the gods, in turn, will take better care of him than of a just person. That's what they say, Socrates, that gods and humans provide a better life for unjust people than for just ones.

When Glaucon had said this, I had it in mind to respond, but his brother Adeimantus intervened: You *d* surely don't think that the position has been adequately stated?

Why not? I said.

The most important thing to say hasn't been said yet.

---

2. [In *Seven Against Thebes*, 592–94, it is said of Amphiaraus that "he did not wish to be believed to be the best but to be it." The passage continues with the words Glaucon quotes below at 362a–b.]

3. [*Pleonektein*. See 344a n. 18.]

Well, then, I replied, a man's brother must stand by him, as the saying goes.[4] If Glaucon has omitted something, you must help him. Yet what he has said is enough to throw me to the canvas and make me unable to come to the aid of justice.

Nonsense, he said. Hear what more I have to say, for we should also fully explore the arguments that are opposed to the ones Glaucon gave, the ones that *e* praise justice and find fault with injustice, so that what I take to be his intention may be clearer.

When fathers speak to their sons, they say that one must be just, as do all the others who have charge of anyone. But they don't praise justice itself, only the 363 high reputations it leads to and the consequences of being thought to be just, such as the public offices, marriages, and other things Glaucon listed. But they elaborate even further on the consequences of reputation. By bringing in the esteem of the gods, they are able to talk about the abundant good things that they themselves and the noble Hesiod and Homer say that the gods give to the pious,[5] for Hesiod says that the *b* gods make the oak trees

> Bear acorns at the top and bees in the middle
> And make fleecy sheep heavy laden with wool

for the just, and tells of many other good things akin to these. And Homer is similar:

> When a good king, in his piety,
> Upholds justice, the black earth bears
> Wheat and barley for him, and his
>   trees are heavy with fruit.
c
> His sheep bear lambs unfailingly,
>   and the sea yields up its fish.

Musaeus and his son make the gods give the just more headstrong goods than these.[6] In their stories, they lead the just to Hades, seat them on couches, provide them with a symposium of pious people, crown them with wreaths, and make them spend all

their time drinking—as if they thought drunkenness was the finest wage of virtue. Others stretch even *d* further the wages that virtue receives from the gods, for they say that someone who is pious and keeps his promises leaves his children's children and a whole race behind him. In these and other similar ways, they praise justice. They bury the impious and unjust in mud in Hades; force them to carry water in a sieve; bring them into bad repute while they're still alive, and all those penalties that Glaucon gave to the just person they give to the unjust. But they have nothing *e* else to say. This, then, is the way people praise justice and find fault with injustice.

Besides this, Socrates, consider another form of argument about justice and injustice employed both by private individuals and by poets. All go on repeating with one voice that justice and moderation are fine things, but hard and onerous, while licentiousness 364 and injustice are sweet and easy to acquire and are shameful only in opinion and law. They add that unjust deeds are for the most part more profitable than just ones, and, whether in public or private, they willingly honor vicious people who have wealth and other types of power and declare them to be happy. But they dishonor and disregard the weak and the poor, even though they agree that they are better than the others.   *b*

But the most wonderful of all these arguments concerns what they have to say about the gods and virtue. They say that the gods, too, assign misfortune and a bad life to many good people, and the opposite fate to their opposites. Begging priests and prophets frequent the doors of the rich and persuade them that they possess a god-given power founded on sacrifices and incantations. If the rich person or any of his ancestors has committed an injustice, they can *c* fix it with pleasant rituals. Moreover, if he wishes to injure some enemy, then, at little expense, he'll be able to harm just and unjust alike, for by means of spells and enchantments they can persuade the gods to serve them. And the poets are brought forward as witnesses to all these accounts. Some harp on the ease of vice, as follows:

> Vice in abundance is easy to get;
> The road is smooth and begins beside you,   *d*
> But the gods have put sweat between us and virtue,

---

4. [See Homer, *Odyssey* 16.97–98.]

5. [The two quotations which follow are from Hesiod, *Works and Days* 332–33, and Homer, *Odyssey* 19.109.]

6. [Musaeus was a legendary poet closely associated with the mystery religion of Orphism.]

and a road that is long, rough, and steep.[7] Others quote Homer to bear witness that the gods can be influenced by humans, since he said:

> The gods themselves can be swayed by prayer,
> And with sacrifices and soothing promises,
> Incense and libations, human beings turn
> e   them from their purpose
> When someone has transgressed and sinned.[8]

And they present a noisy throng of books by Musaeus and Orpheus, offspring as they say of Selene and the Muses, in accordance with which they perform their rituals.[9] And they persuade not only individuals but whole cities that the unjust deeds of the living or the dead can be absolved or purified through ritual 365 sacrifices and pleasant games. These initiations, as they call them, free people from punishment hereafter, while a terrible fate awaits those who have not performed the rituals.

When all such sayings about the attitudes of gods and humans to virtue and vice are so often repeated, Socrates, what effect do you suppose they have on the souls of young people? I mean those who are clever and are able to flit from one of these sayings to another, so to speak, and gather from them an impression of what sort of person he should be and of how best to travel the road of life. He would surely b ask himself Pindar's question, "Should I by justice or by crooked deceit scale this high wall and live my life guarded and secure?" And he'll answer: "The various sayings suggest that there is no advantage in my being just if I'm not also thought just, while the troubles and penalties of being just are apparent. But they tell me that an unjust person, who has secured for himself a reputation for justice, lives the life of a god. Since, then, 'opinion forcibly overcomes truth' c and 'controls happiness,' as the wise men say, I must surely turn entirely to it.[10] I should create a façade of illusory virtue around me to deceive those who come near, but keep behind it the greedy and crafty fox of the wise Archilochus."[11]

"But surely," someone will object, "it isn't easy for vice to remain always hidden." We'll reply that nothing great is easy. And, in any case, if we're to be happy, we must follow the path indicated in these d accounts. To remain undiscovered we'll form secret societies and political clubs. And there are teachers of persuasion to make us clever in dealing with assemblies and law courts. Therefore, using persuasion in one place and force in another, we'll outdo others[12] without paying a penalty.

"What about the gods? Surely, we can't hide from them or use violent force against them!" Well, if the gods don't exist or don't concern themselves with human affairs, why should we worry at all about hiding from them? If they do exist and do concern themselves with us, we've learned all we know about them e from the laws and the poets who give their genealogies—nowhere else. But these are the very people who tell us that the gods can be persuaded and influenced by sacrifices, gentle prayers, and offerings. Hence, we should believe them on both matters or neither. If we believe them, we should be unjust and offer sacrifices from the fruits of our injustice. If we are just, our only gain is not to be punished by the 366 gods, since we lose the profits of injustice. But if we are unjust, we get the profits of our crimes and transgressions and afterwards persuade the gods by prayer and escape without punishment.

"But in Hades won't we pay the penalty for crimes committed here, either ourselves or our children's children?" "My friend," the young man will say as he does his calculation, "mystery rites have great power and the gods have great power of absolution. The greatest cities tell us this, as do those children of the gods who have become poets and prophets." b

Why, then, should we still choose justice over the greatest injustice? Many eminent authorities agree

---

7. [*Works and Days* 287–89, with minor alterations.]

8. [*Iliad* 9.497–501, with minor alterations.]

9. [It is not clear whether Orpheus was a real person or a mythical figure. His fame in Greek myth rests on the poems in which the doctrines of the Orphic religion are set forth. These are discussed in W. Burkert, *Greek Religion* (Cambridge: Harvard University Press, 1985). Musaeus was a mythical singer closely related to Orpheus. Selene is the Moon.]

10. [The quotation is attributed to Simonides, whom Polemarchus cites in Book I.]

11. [Archilochus of Paros (c. 756–716 B.C.) was an iambic and elegiac poet who composed a famous fable about the fox and the hedgehog.]

12. [*Pleonektountes*. See 344a n. 18.]

that, if we practice such injustice with a false façade, we'll do well at the hands of gods and humans, living and dying as we've a mind to. So, given all that has been said, Socrates, how is it possible for anyone of c any power—whether of mind, wealth, body, or birth—to be willing to honor justice and not laugh aloud when he hears it praised? Indeed, if anyone can show that what we've said is false and has adequate knowledge that justice is best, he'll surely be full not of anger but of forgiveness for the unjust. He knows that, apart from someone of godlike character who is disgusted by injustice or one who has gained knowl- d edge and avoids injustice for that reason, no one is just willingly. Through cowardice or old age or some other weakness, people do indeed object to injustice. But it's obvious that they do so only because they lack the power to do injustice, for the first of them to acquire it is the first to do as much injustice as he can.

And all of this has no other cause than the one that led Glaucon and me to say to you: "Socrates, of all of you who claim to praise justice, from the original heroes of old whose words survive, to the men of the e present day, not one has ever blamed injustice or praised justice except by mentioning the reputations, honors, and rewards that are their consequences. No one has ever adequately described what each itself does of its own power by its presence in the soul of the person who possesses it, even if it remains hidden from gods and humans. No one, whether in poetry or in private conversations, has adequately argued that injustice is the worst thing a soul can have in it and that justice is the greatest good. If you had treated the subject in this way and persuaded us from youth, 367 we wouldn't now be guarding against one another's injustices, but each would be his own best guardian, afraid that by doing injustice he'd be living with the worst thing possible."

Thrasymachus or anyone else might say what we've said, Socrates, or maybe even more, in discussing justice and injustice—crudely inverting their powers, in my opinion. And, frankly, it's because I want to b hear the opposite from you that I speak with all the force I can muster. So don't merely give us a theoreti-cal argument that justice is stronger than injustice, but tell us what each itself does, because of its own powers, to someone who possesses it, that makes injus-tice bad and justice good. Follow Glaucon's advice, and don't take reputations into account, for if you

don't deprive justice and injustice of their true reputa-tions and attach false ones to them, we'll say that you are not praising them but their reputations and that you're encouraging us to be unjust in secret. In that c case, we'll say that you agree with Thrasymachus that justice is the good of another, the advantage of the stronger, while injustice is one's own advantage and profit, though not the advantage of the weaker.

You agree that justice is one of the greatest goods, the ones that are worth getting for the sake of what comes from them, but much more so for their own sake, such as seeing, hearing, knowing, being healthy, d and all other goods that are fruitful by their own nature and not simply because of reputation. There-fore, praise justice as a good of that kind, explaining how—because of its very self—it benefits its possessors and how injustice harms them. Leave wages and repu-tations for others to praise.

Others would satisfy me if they praised justice and blamed injustice in that way, extolling the wages of one and denigrating those of the other. But you, unless you order me to be satisfied, wouldn't, for you've spent your whole life investigating this and e nothing else. Don't, then, give us only a theoretical argument that justice is stronger than injustice, but show what effect each has because of itself on the person who has it—the one for good and the other for bad—whether it remains hidden from gods and human beings or not.

While I'd always admired the natures of Glaucon and Adeimantus, I was especially pleased on this occa- 368 sion, and I said: You are the sons of a great man, and Glaucon's lover began his elegy well when he wrote, celebrating your achievements at the battle of Megara,

Sons of Ariston, godlike offspring of a famous man.

That's well said in my opinion, for you must indeed be affected by the divine if you're not convinced that injustice is better than justice and yet can speak on its behalf as you have done. And I believe that you really are unconvinced by your own words. I infer b this from the way you live, for if I had only your words to go on, I wouldn't trust you. The more I trust you, however, the more I'm at a loss as to what to do. I don't see how I can be of help. Indeed, I believe I'm incapable of it. And here's my evidence. I thought what I said to Thrasymachus showed that justice is better than injustice, but you won't accept it from me. On the other hand, I don't see how I can refuse my help, for I fear that it may even be impious to have breath in one's body and the ability to speak and yet to stand idly by and not defend justice when c it is being prosecuted. So the best course is to give justice any assistance I can.

Glaucon and the others begged me not to abandon the argument but to help in every way to track down what justice and injustice are and what the truth about their benefits is. So I told them what I had in mind: The investigation we're undertaking is not an easy one but requires keen eyesight. Therefore, since d we aren't clever people, we should adopt the method of investigation that we'd use if, lacking keen eyesight, we were told to read small letters from a distance and then noticed that the same letters existed elsewhere in a larger size and on a larger surface. We'd consider it a godsend, I think, to be allowed to read the larger ones first and then to examine the smaller ones, to see whether they really are the same.

That's certainly true, said Adeimantus, but how is e this case similar to our investigation of justice?

I'll tell you. We say, don't we, that there is the justice of a single man and also the justice of a whole city?

Certainly.

And a city is larger than a single man?

It is larger.

Perhaps, then, there is more justice in the larger thing, and it will be easier to learn what it is. So, if you're willing, let's first find out what sort of thing 369 justice is in a city and afterwards look for it in the individual, observing the ways in which the smaller is similar to the larger.

That seems fine to me.

If we could watch a city coming to be in theory, wouldn't we also see its justice coming to be, and its injustice as well?

Probably so.

And when that process is completed, we can hope to find what we are looking for more easily?

b   Of course.

Do you think we should try to carry it out, then? It's no small task, in my view. So think it over.

We have already, said Adeimantus. Don't even consider doing anything else.

I think a city comes to be because none of us is self-sufficient, but we all need many things. Do you think that a city is founded on any other principle?

No.

And because people need many things, and because one person calls on a second out of one need c and on a third out of a different need, many people gather in a single place to live together as partners and helpers. And such a settlement is called a city.[13] Isn't that so?

It is.

And if they share things with one another, giving and taking, they do so because each believes that this is better for himself?

That's right.

Come, then, let's create a city in theory from its beginnings. And it's our needs, it seems, that will create it.

It is, indeed.

Surely our first and greatest need is to provide food to sustain life.   d

Certainly.

Our second is for shelter, and our third for clothes and such.

That's right.

How, then, will a city be able to provide all this? Won't one person have to be a farmer, another a builder, and another a weaver? And shouldn't we add a cobbler and someone else to provide medical care?

All right.

So the essential minimum for a city is four or five men?

Apparently.   e

And what about this? Must each of them contribute his own work for the common use of all? For example, will a farmer provide food for everyone, spending quadruple the time and labor to provide food to be shared by them all? Or will he not bother about that, producing one quarter the food in one quarter the time, and spending the other three quarters, one in 370 building a house, one in the production of clothes, and one in making shoes, not troubling to associate with the others, but minding his own business on his own?

---

13. [Notice that a city (*polis*) is a collection of people, not a collection of buildings.]

Perhaps, Socrates, Adeimantus replied, the way you suggested first would be easier than the other.

That certainly wouldn't be surprising, for, even as you were speaking it occurred to me that, in the first place, we aren't all born alike, but each of us differs somewhat in nature from the others, one being suited to one task, another to another. *b* Or don't you think so?

I do.

Second, does one person do a better job if he practices many crafts or—since he's one person himself—if he practices one?

If he practices one.

It's clear, at any rate, I think, that if one misses the right moment in anything, the work is spoiled.

It is.

That's because the thing to be done won't wait on the leisure of the doer, but the doer must of necessity pay close attention to his work rather than treating it *c* as a secondary occupation.

Yes, he must.

The result, then, is that more plentiful and better-quality goods are more easily produced if each person does one thing for which he is naturally suited, does it at the right time, and is released from having to do any of the others.

Absolutely.

Then, Adeimantus, we're going to need more than four citizens to provide the things we've mentioned, for a farmer won't make his own plough, not if it's to be a good one, nor his hoe, nor any of his other *d* farming tools. Neither will a builder—and he, too, needs lots of things. And the same is true of a weaver and a cobbler, isn't it?

It is.

Hence, carpenters, metal workers, and many other craftsmen of that sort will share our little city and make it bigger.

That's right.

Yet it won't be a huge settlement even if we add cowherds, shepherds, and other herdsmen in order *e* that the farmers have cows to do their ploughing, the builders have oxen to share with the farmers in hauling their materials, and the weavers and cobblers have hides and fleeces to use.

It won't be a small one either, if it has to hold all those.

Moreover, it's almost impossible to establish a city in a place where nothing has to be imported.

Indeed it is.

So we'll need yet further people to import from other cities whatever is needed.

Yes.

And if an importer goes empty-handed to another city, without a cargo of the things needed by the city from which he's to bring back what his own city needs, he'll come away empty-handed, won't he?   *371*

So it seems.

Therefore our citizens must not only produce enough for themselves at home but also goods of the right quality and quantity to satisfy the requirements of others.

They must.

So we'll need more farmers and other craftsmen in our city.

Yes.

And others to take care of imports and exports. And they're called merchants, aren't they?

Yes.

So we'll need merchants, too.

Certainly.

And if the trade is by sea, we'll need a good many others who know how to sail.   *b*

A good many, indeed.

And how will those in the city itself share the things that each produces? It was for the sake of this that we made their partnership and founded their city.

Clearly, they must do it by buying and selling.

Then we'll need a marketplace and a currency for such exchange.

Certainly.

If a farmer or any other craftsman brings some of his products to market, and he doesn't arrive at the *c* same time as those who want to exchange things with him, is he to sit idly in the marketplace, away from his own work?

Not at all. There'll be people who'll notice this and provide the requisite service—in well-organized cities they'll usually be those whose bodies are weakest and who aren't fit to do any other work. They'll stay around the market exchanging money for the goods *d* of those who have something to sell and then exchanging those goods for the money of those who want them.

Then, to fill this need there will have to be retailers in our city, for aren't those who establish themselves in the marketplace to provide this service of buying and selling called retailers, while those who travel between cities are called merchants?

That's right.

There are other servants, I think, whose minds *e* alone wouldn't qualify them for membership in our society but whose bodies are strong enough for labor. These sell the use of their strength for a price called a wage and hence are themselves called wage-earners. Isn't that so?

Certainly.

So wage-earners complete our city?

I think so.

Well, Adeimantus, has our city grown to completeness, then?

Perhaps it has.

Then where are justice and injustice to be found in it? With which of the things we examined did they come in?

I've no idea, Socrates, unless it was somewhere 372 in some need that these people have of one another.

You may be right, but we must look into it and not grow weary. First, then, let's see what sort of life our citizens will lead when they've been provided for in the way we have been describing. They'll produce bread, wine, clothes, and shoes, won't they? They'll build houses, work naked and barefoot in the summer, *b* and wear adequate clothing and shoes in the winter. For food, they'll knead and cook the flour and meal they've made from wheat and barley. They'll put their honest cakes and loaves on reeds or clean leaves, and, reclining on beds strewn with yew and myrtle, they'll feast with their children, drink their wine, and, crowned with wreaths, hymn the gods. They'll enjoy sex with one another but bear no more children than their resources allow, lest they fall into either poverty *c* or war.

It seems that you make your people feast without any delicacies, Glaucon interrupted.

True enough, I said, I was forgetting that they'll obviously need salt, olives, cheese, boiled roots, and vegetables of the sort they cook in the country. We'll give them desserts, too, of course, consisting of figs, chickpeas, and beans, and they'll roast myrtle and acorns before the fire,[14] drinking moderately. And so they'll live in peace and good health, and when they *d* die at a ripe old age, they'll bequeath a similar life to their children.

If you were founding a city for pigs, Socrates, he replied, wouldn't you fatten *them* on the same diet?

Then how should I feed these people, Glaucon? I asked.

In the conventional way. If they aren't to suffer hardship, they should recline on proper couches, dine at a table, and have the delicacies and desserts that people have nowadays.   *e*

All right, I understand. It isn't merely the origin of a city that we're considering, it seems, but the origin of a *luxurious* city. And that may not be a bad idea, for by examining it, we might very well see how justice and injustice grow up in cities. Yet the true city, in my opinion, is the one we've described, the healthy one, as it were. But let's study a city with a fever, if that's what you want. There's nothing to stop us. The things I mentioned earlier and the way of life I 373 described won't satisfy some people, it seems, but couches, tables, and other furniture will have to be added, and, of course, all sorts of delicacies, perfumed oils, incense, prostitutes, and pastries. We mustn't provide them only with the necessities we mentioned at first, such as houses, clothes, and shoes, but painting and embroidery must be begun, and gold, ivory, and the like acquired. Isn't that so?

Yes.   *b*

Then we must enlarge our city, for the healthy one is no longer adequate. We must increase it in size and fill it with a multitude of things that go beyond what is necessary for a city—hunters, for example, and artists or imitators, many of whom work with shapes and colors, many with music. And there'll be poets and their assistants, actors, choral dancers, contractors, and makers of all kinds of devices, including, among other things, those needed for the adornment of women. And so we'll need more servants, too. Or don't you think that we'll need tutors, wet *c* nurses, nannies, beauticians, barbers, chefs, cooks, and swineherds? We didn't need any of these in our

---

14. [It seems likely that a sexual pun is intended since myrtle (*murton*) and acorn (*phēgos*) are common slang terms for the female and male genitalia respectively.]

earlier city, but we'll need them in this one. And we'll also need many more cattle, won't we, if the people are going to eat meat?

Of course.

And if we live like that, we'll have a far greater
d need for doctors than we did before?

Much greater.

And the land, I suppose, that used to be adequate to feed the population we had then, will cease to be adequate and become too small. What do you think?

The same.

Then we'll have to seize some of our neighbors' land if we're to have enough pasture and ploughland. And won't our neighbors want to seize part of ours as well, if they too have surrendered themselves to the endless acquisition of money and have overstepped the limit of their necessities?

e   That's completely inevitable, Socrates.

Then our next step will be war, Glaucon, won't it?

It will.

We won't say yet whether the effects of war are good or bad but only that we've now found the origins of war. It comes from those same desires that are most of all responsible for the bad things that happen to cities and the individuals in them.

That's right.

Then the city must be further enlarged, and not just by a small number, either, but by a whole army, which will do battle with the invaders in defense of
374 the city's substantial wealth and all the other things we mentioned.

Why aren't the citizens themselves adequate for that purpose?

They won't be, if the agreement you and the rest of us made when we were founding the city was a good one, for surely we agreed, if you remember, that it's impossible for a single person to practice many crafts or professions well.

That's true.

Well, then, don't you think that warfare is a pro-
b fession?

Of course.

Then should we be more concerned about cobbling than about warfare?

Not at all.

But we prevented a cobbler from trying to be a farmer, weaver, or builder at the same time and said that he must remain a cobbler in order to produce

fine work. And each of the others, too, was to work all his life at a single trade for which he had a natural aptitude and keep away from all the others, so as not to miss the right moment to practice his own work well. Now, c isn't it of the greatest importance that warfare be practiced well? And is fighting a war so easy that a farmer or a cobbler or any other craftsman can be a soldier at the same time? Though no one can become so much as a good player of checkers or dice if he considers it only as a sideline and doesn't practice it from childhood. Or can someone pick up a shield or any other weapon or tool of war and immediately perform adequately in an infantry battle or any other kind? No other d tool makes anyone who picks it up a craftsman or champion unless he has acquired the requisite knowledge and has had sufficient practice.

If tools could make anyone who picked them up an expert, they'd be valuable indeed.

Then to the degree that the work of the guardians is most important, it requires most freedom from other e things and the greatest skill and devotion.

I should think so.

And doesn't it also require a person whose nature is suited to that way of life?

Certainly.

Then our job, it seems, is to select, if we can, the kind of nature suited to guard the city.

It is.

By god, it's no trivial task that we've taken on. But insofar as we are able, we mustn't shrink from it.

No, we mustn't.   375

Do you think that, when it comes to guarding, there is any difference between the nature of a pedigree young dog and that of a well-born youth?

What do you mean?

Well, each needs keen senses, speed to catch what it sees, and strength in case it has to fight it out with what it captures.

They both need all these things.

And each must be courageous if indeed he's to fight well.

Of course.

And will a horse, a dog, or any other animal be courageous, if he isn't spirited? Or haven't you noticed just how invincible and unbeatable spirit is, so that its pres- b ence makes the whole soul fearless and unconquerable?

I have noticed that.

The physical qualities of the guardians are clear, then.

Yes.

And as far as their souls are concerned, they must be spirited.

That too.

But if they have natures like that, Glaucon, won't they be savage to each other and to the rest of the citizens?

By god, it will be hard for them to be anything else.

c Yet surely they must be gentle to their own people and harsh to the enemy. If they aren't, they won't wait around for others to destroy the city but will do it themselves first.

That's true.

What are we to do, then? Where are we to find a character that is both gentle and high-spirited at the same time? After all, a gentle nature is the opposite of a spirited one.

Apparently.

If someone lacks either gentleness or spirit, he can't be a good guardian. Yet it seems impossible to combine *d* them. It follows that a good guardian cannot exist.

It looks like it.

I couldn't see a way out, but on reexamining what had gone before, I said: We deserve to be stuck, for we've lost sight of the analogy we put forward.

How do you mean?

We overlooked the fact that there *are* natures of the sort we thought impossible, natures in which these opposites are indeed combined.

Where?

You can see them in other animals, too, but especially in the one to which we compared the guardian, for you know, of course, that a pedigree dog naturally *e* has a character of this sort—he is gentle as can be to those he's used to and knows, but the opposite to those he doesn't know.

I do know that.

So the combination we want is possible after all, and our search for the good guardian is not contrary to nature.

Apparently not.

Then do you think that our future guardian, besides being spirited, must also be by nature philosophical?[15]

How do you mean? I don't understand.   376

It's something else you see in dogs, and it makes you wonder at the animal.

What?

When a dog sees someone it doesn't know, it gets angry before anything bad happens to it. But when it knows someone, it welcomes him, even if it has never received anything good from him. Haven't you ever wondered at that?

I've never paid any attention to it, but obviously that is the way a dog behaves.

Surely this is a refined quality in its nature and one that is truly philosophical.   *b*

In what way philosophical?

Because it judges anything it sees to be either a friend or an enemy, on no other basis than that it knows the one and doesn't know the other. And how could it be anything besides a lover of learning, if it defines what is its own and what is alien to it in terms of knowledge and ignorance?

It couldn't.

But surely the love of learning is the same thing as philosophy or the love of wisdom?

It is.

Then, may we confidently assume in the case of a human being, too, that if he is to be gentle toward his own and those he knows, he must be a lover of learning and wisdom?   *c*

We may.

Philosophy, spirit, speed, and strength must all, then, be combined in the nature of anyone who is to be a fine and good guardian of our city.

Absolutely.

The natural assets that a good guardian needs and the education he must have to develop them in the best possible way are the next topic. The appropriate basic education for future guardians, Socrates claims, is the traditional one consisting of music and poetry, on the one hand, and physical training, on the other. His discussion of it continues into Book III.

—S.M.C.

---

15. [The word *philosophos* is used here in its general sense to refer to intellectual curiosity or wanting to know things without ulterior motives. Plato is not suggesting (below) that pedigree dogs have the traits that he will attribute to full-blown philosophers in Books V–VII.]

Book III

412b All right, then what's the next thing we have to determine? Isn't it which of these same people will rule and which be ruled?

c Of course.

Now, isn't it obvious that the rulers must be older and the ruled younger?

Yes, it is.

And mustn't the rulers also be the best of them?

That, too.

And aren't the best farmers the ones who are best at farming?

Yes.

Then, as the rulers must be the best of the guardians, mustn't they be the ones who are best at guarding the city?

Yes.

Then, in the first place, mustn't they be knowledgeable and capable, and mustn't they care for the city?

d That's right.

Now, one cares most for what one loves.

Necessarily.

And someone loves something most of all when he believes that the same things are advantageous to it as to himself and supposes that if it does well, he'll do well, and that if it does badly, then he'll do badly too.

That's right.

Then we must choose from among our guardians those men who, upon examination, seem most of all *e* to believe throughout their lives that they must eagerly pursue what is advantageous to the city and be wholly unwilling to do the opposite.

Such people would be suitable for the job at any rate.

I think we must observe them at all ages to see whether they are guardians of this conviction and make sure that neither compulsion nor magic spells will get them to discard or forget their belief that they must do what is best for the city.

What do you mean by discarding?

I'll tell you. I think the discarding of a belief is either voluntary or involuntary—voluntary when one learns that the belief is false, involuntary in the case *413* of all true beliefs.

I understand voluntary discarding but not involuntary.

What's that? Don't you know that people are voluntarily deprived of bad things, but involuntarily deprived of good ones? And isn't being deceived about the truth a bad thing, while possessing the truth is good? Or don't you think that to believe the things that are is to possess the truth?

That's right, and I do think that people are involuntarily deprived of true opinions.

But can't they also be so deprived by theft, magic spells, and compulsion? *b*

Now, I don't understand again.

I'm afraid I must be talking like a tragic poet! By "the victims of theft" I mean those who are persuaded to change their minds or those who forget, because time, in the latter case, and argument, in the former, takes away their opinions without their realizing it. Do you understand now?

Yes.

By "the compelled" I mean those whom pain or suffering causes to change their mind.

I understand that, and you're right.

The "victims of magic," I think you'd agree, are those who change their mind because they are under *c* the spell of pleasure or fear.

It seems to me that everything that deceives does so by casting a spell.

Then, as I said just now, we must find out who are the best guardians of their conviction that they must always do what they believe to be best for the city. We must keep them under observation from childhood and set them tasks that are most likely to make them forget such a conviction or be deceived out of it, and we must select whoever keeps on remem- *d* bering it and isn't easily deceived, and reject the others. Do you agree?

Yes.

And we must subject them to labors, pains, and contests in which we can watch for these traits.

That's right.

Then we must also set up a competition for the third way in which people are deprived of their convictions, namely, magic. Like those who lead colts into noise and tumult to see if they're afraid, we must expose our young people to fears and pleasures, testing them more thoroughly than gold is tested by fire. If *e* someone is hard to put under a spell, is apparently gracious in everything, is a good guardian of himself and the music and poetry he has learned, and if he always shows himself to be rhythmical and harmonious, then he is the best person both for himself and for the city. Anyone who is tested in this way as a 414 child, youth, and adult, and always comes out of it untainted, is to be made a ruler as well as a guardian; he is to be honored in life and to receive after his death the most prized tombs and memorials. But anyone who fails to prove himself in this way is to be rejected. It seems to me, Glaucon, that rulers and guardians must be selected and appointed in some such way as this, though we've provided only a general pattern and not the exact details.

It also seems to me that they must be selected in this sort of way.

Then, isn't it truly most correct to call these people b complete guardians, since they will guard against external enemies and internal friends, so that the one will lack the power and the other the desire to harm the city? The young people we've hitherto called guardians we'll now call *auxiliaries* and supporters of the guardians' convictions.

I agree.

How, then, could we devise one of those useful falsehoods we were talking about a while ago, one c noble falsehood that would, in the best case, persuade even the rulers, but if that's not possible, then the others in the city?

What sort of falsehood?

Nothing new, but a Phoenician story which describes something that has happened in many places. At least, that's what the poets say, and they've persuaded many people to believe it too. It hasn't happened among us, and I don't even know if it could. It would certainly take a lot of persuasion to get people to believe it.

You seem hesitant to tell the story.

When you hear it, you'll realize that I have every reason to hesitate.

Speak, and don't be afraid.

I'll tell it, then, though I don't know where I'll get d the audacity or even what words I'll use. I'll first try to persuade the rulers and the soldiers and then the rest of the city that the upbringing and the education we gave them, and the experiences that went with them, were a sort of dream, that in fact they themselves, their weapons, and the other craftsmen's tools were at that time really being fashioned and nurtured e inside the earth, and that when the work was com-

pleted, the earth, who is their mother, delivered all of them up into the world. Therefore, if anyone attacks the land in which they live, they must plan on its behalf and defend it as their mother and nurse and think of the other citizens as their earthborn brothers.

It isn't for nothing that you were so shy about telling your falsehood.

Appropriately so. Nevertheless, listen to the rest of the story. "All of you in the city are brothers," we'll 415 say to them in telling our story, "but the god who made you mixed some gold into those who are adequately equipped to rule, because they are most valuable. He put silver in those who are auxiliaries and iron and bronze in the farmers and other craftsmen. For the most part you will produce children like yourselves, but, because you are all related, a silver child will occasionally be born from a golden parent, and vice b versa, and all the others from each other. So the first and most important command from the god to the rulers is that there is nothing that they must guard better or watch more carefully than the mixture of metals in the souls of the next generation. If an offspring of theirs should be found to have a mixture of iron or bronze, they must not pity him in any way, but give him the rank appropriate to his nature and drive him out to join the craftsmen and farmers. But c if an offspring of these people is found to have a mixture of gold or silver, they will honor him and take him up to join the guardians or the auxiliaries, for there is an oracle which says that the city will be ruined if it ever has an iron or a bronze guardian." So, do you have any device that will make our citizens believe this story?

I can't see any way to make them believe it themselves, but perhaps there is one in the case of their d sons and later generations and all the other people who come after them.

I understand pretty much what you mean, but even that would help to make them care more for the city and each other. However, let's leave this matter wherever tradition takes it. And let's now arm our earthborn and lead them forth with their rulers in charge. And as they march, let them look for the best place in the city to have their camp, a site from which they can most easily control those within, if anyone is unwilling to obey the laws, or repel any outside e enemy who comes like a wolf upon the flock. And when they have established their camp and made the requisite sacrifices, they must see to their sleeping quarters. What do you say?

I agree.

And won't these quarters protect them adequately both in winter and summer?

Of course, for it seems to me that you mean their housing.

Yes, but housing for soldiers, not for money-makers.

How do you mean to distinguish these from one an-
416 other?

I'll try to tell you. The most terrible and most shameful thing of all is for a shepherd to rear dogs as auxiliaries to help him with his flocks in such a way that, through licentiousness, hunger, or some other bad trait of character, they do evil to the sheep and become like wolves instead of dogs.

That's certainly a terrible thing.

Isn't it necessary, therefore, to guard in every way
b against our auxiliaries doing anything like that to the citizens because they are stronger, thereby becoming savage masters instead of kindly allies?

It is necessary.

And wouldn't a really good education endow them with the greatest caution in this regard?

But surely they have had an education like that.

Perhaps we shouldn't assert this dogmatically, Glaucon. What we can assert is what we were saying just now, that they must have the right education, whatever it is, if they are to have what will most make them gentle to each other and to those they
c are guarding.

That's right.

Now, someone with some understanding might say that, besides this education, they must also have the kind of housing and other property that will neither prevent them from being the best guardians nor en-
d courage them to do evil to the other citizens.

That's true.

Consider, then, whether or not they should live in some such way as this, if they're to be the kind of men we described. First, none of them should possess any private property beyond what is wholly necessary. Second, none of them should have a house or store-room that isn't open for all to enter at will. Third, whatever sustenance moderate and courageous war-rior-athletes require in order to have neither shortfall
e nor surplus in a given year they'll receive by taxation on the other citizens as a salary for their guardianship.

Fourth, they'll have common messes and live together like soldiers in a camp. We'll tell them that they always have gold and silver of a divine sort in their souls as a gift from the gods and so have no further need of human gold. Indeed, we'll tell them that it's impious for them to defile this divine possession by any admixture of such gold, because many impious deeds have been done that involve the currency used by ordinary people, while their own is pure. Hence, 417
for them alone among the city's population, it is un-lawful to touch or handle gold or silver. They mustn't be under the same roof as it, wear it as jewelry, or drink from gold or silver goblets. In this way they'd save both themselves and the city. But if they acquire private land, houses, and currency themselves, they'll be household managers and farmers instead of guard-ians—hostile masters of the other citizens instead of b
their allies. They'll spend their whole lives hating and being hated, plotting and being plotted against, more afraid of internal than of external enemies, and they'll hasten both themselves and the whole city to almost immediate ruin. For all these reasons, let's say that the guardians must be provided with housing and the rest in this way, and establish this as a law. Or don't you agree?

I certainly do, Glaucon said.

Book IV

Well, son of Ariston, your city might now be said to 427d
be established. The next step is to get an adequate light somewhere and to call upon your brother as well as Polemarchus and the others, so as to look inside it and see where the justice and the injustice might be in it, what the difference between them is, and which of the two the person who is to be happy should possess, whether its possession is unnoticed by all the gods and human beings or not.

You're talking nonsense, Glaucon said. You prom-ised to look for them yourself because you said it was impious for you not to come to the rescue of justice in every way you could.   e

That's true, and I must do what I promised, but you'll have to help.

We will.

I hope to find it in this way. I think our city, if indeed it has been correctly founded, is completely good.

Necessarily so.

Clearly, then, it is wise, courageous, moderate, and just.

Clearly.

Then, if we find any of these in it, what's left over will be the ones we haven't found?

428   Of course.

Therefore, as with any other four things, if we were looking for any one of them in something and recognized it first, that would be enough for us, but if we recognized the other three first, this itself would be sufficient to enable us to recognize what we are looking for. Clearly it couldn't be anything other than what's left over.

That's right.

Therefore, since there are four virtues, mustn't we look for them in the same way?

Clearly.

Now, the first thing I think I can see clearly in the city is wisdom, and there seems to be something odd
b about it.

What's that?

I think that the city we described is really wise. And that's because it has good judgment, isn't it?

Yes.

Now, this very thing, good judgment, is clearly some kind of knowledge, for it's through knowledge, not ignorance, that people judge well.

Clearly.

But there are many kinds of knowledge in the city.

Of course.

Is it because of the knowledge possessed by its carpenters, then, that the city is to be called wise and sound in judgment?

Not at all. It's called skilled in carpentry because
c of that.

Then it isn't to be called wise because of the knowledge by which it arranges to have the best wooden implements.

No, indeed.

What about the knowledge of bronze items or the like?

It isn't because of any knowledge of that sort.

Nor because of the knowledge of how to raise a harvest from the earth, for it's called skilled in farming because of that.

I should think so.

Then, is there some knowledge possessed by some of the citizens in the city we just founded that doesn't judge about any particular matter but about the city as a whole and the maintenance of good relations, both internally and with other cities?   d

There is indeed.

What is this knowledge, and who has it?

It is guardianship, and it is possessed by those rulers we just now called complete guardians.

Then, what does this knowledge entitle you to say about the city?

That it has good judgment and is really wise.

Who do you think that there will be more of in our city, metal-workers or these true guardians?   e

There will be far more metal-workers.

Indeed, of all those who are called by a certain name because they have some kind of knowledge, aren't the guardians the least numerous?

By far.

Then, a whole city established according to nature would be wise because of the smallest class and part in it, namely, the governing or ruling one. And to this class, which seems to be by nature the smallest, belongs a share of the knowledge that alone among 429 all the other kinds of knowledge is to be called wisdom.

That's completely true.

Then we've found one of the four virtues, as well as its place in the city, though I don't know how we found it.

Our way of finding it seems good enough to me.

And surely courage and the part of the city it's in, the part on account of which the city is called courageous, aren't difficult to see.

How is that?

Who, in calling the city cowardly or courageous, would look anywhere other than to the part of it that b fights and does battle on its behalf?

No one would look anywhere else.

At any rate, I don't think that the courage or cowardice of its other citizens would cause the city itself to be called either courageous or cowardly.

No, it wouldn't.

The city is courageous, then, because of a part of itself that has the power to preserve through everything its belief about what things are to be feared, namely, that they are the things and kinds of things c that the lawgiver declared to be such in the course of educating it. Or don't you call that courage?

I don't completely understand what you mean. Please, say it again.

I mean that courage is a kind of preservation.

What sort of preservation?

That preservation of the belief that has been inculcated by the law through education about what things and sorts of things are to be feared. And by preserving this belief "through everything," I mean preserving d it and not abandoning it because of pains, pleasures, desires, or fears. If you like, I'll compare it to something I think it resembles.

I'd like that.

You know that dyers, who want to dye wool purple, first pick out from the many colors of wool the one that is naturally white, then they carefully prepare this in various ways, so that it will absorb the color as well as possible, and only at that point do they apply the purple dye. When something is dyed in e this way, the color is fast—no amount of washing, whether with soap or without it, can remove it. But you also know what happens to material if it hasn't been dyed in this way, but instead is dyed purple or some other color without careful preparation.

I know that it looks washed out and ridiculous.

Then, you should understand that, as far as we could, we were doing something similar when we selected our soldiers and educated them in music 430 and physical training. What we were contriving was nothing other than this: That because they had the proper nature and upbringing, they would absorb the laws in the finest possible way, just like a dye, so that their belief about what they should fear and all the rest would become so fast that even such extremely effective detergents as pleasure, pain, fear, and desire wouldn't wash it out—and pleasure is much more b potent than any powder, washing soda, or soap. This power to preserve through everything the correct and law-inculcated belief about what is to be feared and what isn't is what I call courage, unless, of course, you say otherwise.

I have nothing different to say, for I assume that you don't consider the correct belief about these same things, which you find in animals and slaves, and which is not the result of education, to be inculcated by law, and that you don't call it courage but something else.

c   That's absolutely true.

Then I accept your account of courage.

Accept it instead as my account of *civic* courage, and you will be right. We'll discuss courage more fully some other time, if you like. At present, our inquiry concerns not it but justice. And what we've said is sufficient for that purpose.

You're quite right.

There are now two things left for us to find in the city, namely, moderation[1] and—the goal of our entire inquiry—justice.   d

That's right.

Is there a way we could find justice so as not to have to bother with moderation any further?

I don't know any, and I wouldn't want justice to appear first if that means that we won't investigate moderation. So if you want to please me, look for the latter first.

I'm certainly willing. It would be wrong not to be. e

Look, then.

We will. Seen from here, it is more like a kind of consonance and harmony than the previous ones.

In what way?

Moderation is surely a kind of order, the mastery of certain kinds of pleasures and desires. People indicate as much when they use the phrase "self-control" and other similar phrases. I don't know just what they mean by them, but they are, so to speak, like tracks or clues that moderation has left behind in language. Isn't that so?

Absolutely.

Yet isn't the expression "self-control" ridiculous? The stronger self that does the controlling is the same as the weaker self that gets controlled, so that only one person is referred to in all such expressions.   431

Of course.

Nonetheless, the expression is apparently trying to indicate that, in the soul of that very person, there is a better part and a worse one and that, whenever the naturally better part is in control of the worse, this is expressed by saying that the person is self-controlled or master of himself. At any rate, one praises someone by calling him self-controlled. But when, on the other hand, the smaller and better part is overpowered by

1. [The Greek term is *sōphrosunē*. It has a very wide meaning: self-control, good sense, reasonableness, temperance, and (in some contexts) chastity. Someone who keeps his head under pressure or temptation possesses *sōphrosunē*.—C.D.C.R.]

the larger, because of bad upbringing or bad com-
b pany, this is called being self-defeated or licentious
and is a reproach.

Appropriately so.

Take a look at our new city, and you'll find one
of these in it. You'll say that it is rightly called self-
controlled, if indeed something in which the better
rules the worse is properly called moderate and
self-controlled.

I am looking, and what you say is true.

Now, one finds all kinds of diverse desires, plea-
c sures, and pains, mostly in children, women, household slaves, and in those of the inferior majority who
are called free.

That's right.

But you meet with the desires that are simple,
measured, and directed by calculation in accordance
with understanding and correct belief only in the few
people who are born with the best natures and receive
the best education.

That's true.

Then, don't you see that in your city, too, the
desires of the inferior many are controlled by the
d wisdom and desires of the superior few?

I do.

Therefore, if any city is said to be in control of
itself and of its pleasures and desires, it is this one.

Absolutely.

And isn't it, therefore, also moderate because of
all this?

It is.

And, further, if indeed the ruler and the ruled in
e any city share the same belief about who should rule,
it is in this one. Or don't you agree?

I agree entirely.

And when the citizens agree in this way, in which
of them do you say moderation is located? In the
ruler or the ruled?

I suppose in both.

Then, you see how right we were to divine that
moderation resembles a kind of harmony?

How so?

Because, unlike courage and wisdom, each of
which resides in one part, making the city brave and
wise respectively, moderation spreads throughout the
432 whole. It makes the weakest, the strongest, and those
in between—whether in regard to reason, physical
strength, numbers, wealth, or anything else—all sing

the same song together. And this unanimity, this
agreement between the naturally worse and the naturally better as to which of the two is to rule both in
the city and in each one, is rightly called moderation.

I agree completely.   b

All right. We've now found, at least from the point
of view of our present beliefs, three out of the four
virtues in our city. So what kind of virtue is left,
then, that makes the city share even further in virtue?
Surely, it's clear that it is justice.

That is clear.

Then, Glaucon, we must station ourselves like
hunters surrounding a wood and focus our understanding, so that justice doesn't escape us and vanish
into obscurity, for obviously it's around here somewhere. So look and try eagerly to catch sight of it, c
and if you happen to see it before I do, you can tell
me about it.

I wish I could, but you'll make better use of me if
you take me to be a follower who can see things when
you point them out to him.

Follow, then, and join me in a prayer.

I'll do that, just so long as you lead.

I certainly will, though the place seems to be impenetrable and full of shadows. It is certainly dark
and hard to search though. But all the same, we must
go on.

Indeed we must.   d

And then I caught sight of something. Ah ha! Glaucon, it looks as though there's a track here, so it seems
that our quarry won't altogether escape us.

That's good news.

Either that, or we've just been stupid.

In what way?

Because what we are looking for seems to have
been rolling around at our feet from the very beginning, and we didn't see it, which was ridiculous of
us. Just as people sometimes search for the very thing
they are holding in their hands, so we didn't look in
the right direction but gazed off into the distance, e
and that's probably why we didn't notice it.

What do you mean?

I mean that, though we've been talking and hearing
about it for a long time, I think we didn't understand
what we were saying or that, in a way, we were talking
about justice.

That's a long prelude for someone who wants to
hear the answer.

Then listen and see whether there's anything in
433 what I say. Justice, I think, is exactly what we said must be established throughout the city when we were founding it—either that or some form of it. We stated, and often repeated, if you remember, that everyone must practice one of the occupations in the city for which he is naturally best suited.

Yes, we did keep saying that.

Moreover, we've heard many people say and have often said ourselves that justice is doing one's own
b work and not meddling with what isn't one's own.

Yes, we have.

Then, it turns out that this doing one's own work— provided that it comes to be in a certain way—is justice. And do you know what I take as evidence of this?

No, tell me.

I think that this is what was left over in the city when moderation, courage, and wisdom have been found. It is the power that makes it possible for them to grow in the city and that preserves them when
c they've grown for as long as it remains there itself. And of course we said that justice would be what was left over when we had found the other three.

Yes, that must be so.

And surely, if we had to decide which of the four will make the city good by its presence, it would be a hard decision. Is it the agreement in belief between the rulers and the ruled? Or the preservation among the soldiers of the law-inspired belief about what is to be feared and what isn't? Or the wisdom and guard-
d ianship of the rulers? Or is it, above all, the fact that every child, woman, slave, freeman, craftsman, ruler, and ruled each does his own work and doesn't meddle with what is other people's?

How could this fail to be a hard decision?

It seems, then, that the power that consists in every- one's doing his own work rivals wisdom, moderation,
e and courage in its contribution to the virtue of the city.

It certainly does.

And wouldn't you call this rival to the others in its contribution to the city's virtue justice?

Absolutely.

Look at it this way if you want to be convinced. Won't you order your rulers to act as judges in the city's courts?

Of course.

And won't their sole aim in delivering judgments

be that no citizen should have what belongs to another or be deprived of what is his own?

They'll have no aim but that.

Because that is just?

Yes.

Therefore, from this point of view also, the having and doing of one's own would be accepted as justice. 434

That's right.

Consider, then, and see whether you agree with me about this. If a carpenter attempts to do the work of a cobbler, or a cobbler that of a carpenter, or they exchange their tools or honors with one another, or if the same person tries to do both jobs, and all other such exchanges are made, do you think that does any great harm to the city?

Not much.

But I suppose that when someone, who is by nature a craftsman or some other kind of money-maker, is puffed up by wealth, or by having a majority of votes, or by his own strength, or by some other such thing, b and attempts to enter the class of soldiers, or one of the unworthy soldiers tries to enter that of the judges and guardians, and these exchange their tools and honors, or when the same person tries to do all these things at once, then I think you'll agree that these exchanges and this sort of meddling bring the city to ruin.

Absolutely.

Meddling and exchange between these three classes, then, is the greatest harm that can happen to the city and would rightly be called the worst thing someone could do to it.   c

Exactly.

And wouldn't you say that the worst thing that someone could do to his city is injustice?

Of course.

Then, that exchange and meddling is injustice. Or to put it the other way around: For the money-making, auxiliary, and guardian classes each to do its own work in the city, is the opposite. That's justice, isn't it, and makes the city just?

I agree. Justice is that and nothing else.   d

Let's not take that as secure just yet, but if we find that the same form, when it comes to be in each individual person, is accepted as justice there as well, we can assent to it. What else can we say? But if that isn't what we find, we must look for something else to be justice. For the moment, however, let's complete the present inquiry. We thought that, if we first tried to observe justice in some larger thing that possessed it, this would make it easier to observe in a single individual. We agreed that this larger thing is a city, and so we established the best city we could, e knowing well that justice would be in one that was good. So, let's apply what has come to light in the city to an individual, and if it is accepted there, all will be well. But if something different is found in the individual, then we must go back and test that on the city. And if we do this, and compare them 435 side by side, we might well make justice light up as if we were rubbing fire-sticks together. And, when it has come to light, we can get a secure grip on it for ourselves.

You're following the road we set, and we must do as you say.

Well, then, are things called by the same name, whether they are bigger or smaller than one another, like or unlike with respect to that to which that name applies?

Alike.

Then a just man won't differ at all from a just city b in respect to the form of justice; rather he'll be like the city.

He will.

But a city was thought to be just when each of the three natural classes within it did its own work, and it was thought to be moderate, courageous, and wise because of certain other conditions and states of theirs.

That's true.

Then, if an individual has these same three parts in his soul, we will expect him to be correctly called c by the same names as the city if he has the same conditions in them.

Necessarily so.

Then once again we've come upon an easy question, namely, does the soul have these three parts in it or not?

It doesn't look easy to me. Perhaps, Socrates, there's some truth in the old saying that everything fine is difficult.

Apparently so. But you should know, Glaucon, that, in my opinion, we will never get a precise answer d using our present methods of argument—although there is another longer and fuller road that does lead to such an answer. But perhaps we can get an answer that's up to the standard of our previous statements and inquiries.

Isn't that satisfactory? It would be enough for me at present.

In that case, it will be fully enough for me too.

Then don't weary, but go on with the inquiry.

Well, then, we are surely compelled to agree that each of us has within himself the same parts and e characteristics as the city? Where else would they come from? It would be ridiculous for anyone to think that spiritedness didn't come to be in cities from such individuals as the Thracians, Scythians, and others who live to the north of us who are held to possess spirit, or that the same isn't true of the love of learning, which is mostly associated with our part of the world, or of the love of money, which one might say is 436 conspicuously displayed by the Phoenicians and Egyptians.

It would.

That's the way it is, anyway, and it isn't hard to understand.

Certainly not.

But this *is* hard. Do we do these things with the same part of ourselves, or do we do them with three different parts? Do we learn with one part, get angry with another, and with some third part desire the pleasures of food, drink, sex, and the others that are closely akin to them? Or, when we set out after something, do we act with the whole of our soul, in each case? This is what's hard to determine in a way that's b up to the standards of our argument.

I think so too.

Well, then, let's try to determine in that way whether these parts are the same or different.

How?

It is obvious that the same thing will not be willing to do or undergo opposites in the same part of itself, in relation to the same thing, at the same time. So, if we ever find this happening in the soul, we'll know that we aren't dealing with one thing but many.   c

All right.

Then consider what I'm about to say.

Say on.

Is it possible for the same thing to stand still and move at the same time in the same part of itself?

Not at all.

Let's make our agreement more precise in order to avoid disputes later on. If someone said that a person who is standing still but moving his hands and head is moving and standing still at the same time, we wouldn't consider, I think, that he ought to put it like that. What he ought to say is that one part of the person is standing still and another part is moving.

d Isn't that so?

It is.

And if our interlocutor became even more amusing and was sophisticated enough to say that whole spinning tops stand still and move at the same time when the peg is fixed in the same place and they revolve, and that the same is true of anything else moving in a circular motion on the same spot, we wouldn't agree, because it isn't with respect to the same parts of themselves that such things both stand still and

e move. We'd say that they have an axis and a circumference and that with respect to the axis they stand still, since they don't wobble to either side, while with respect to the circumference they move in a circle. But if they do wobble to the left or right, front or back, while they are spinning, we'd say that they aren't standing still in any way.

And we'd be right.

No such statement will disturb us, then, or make us believe that the same thing can be, do, or undergo opposites, at the same time, in the same respect, and

437 in relation to the same thing.

They won't make me believe it, at least.

Nevertheless, in order to avoid going through all these objections one by one and taking a long time to prove them all untrue, let's hypothesize that this is corrrect and carry on. But we agree that if it should ever be shown to be incorrect, all the consequences we've drawn from it will also be lost.

We should agree to that.

Then wouldn't you consider all the following,

b whether they are doings or undergoings, as pairs of opposites: Assent and dissent, wanting to have something and rejecting it, taking something and pushing it away?

Yes, they are opposites.

What about these? Wouldn't you include thirst, hunger, the appetites as a whole, and wishing and

c willing somewhere in the class we mentioned? Wouldn't you say that the soul of someone who has an appetite for a thing wants what he has an appetite for and takes to himself what it is his will to have, and that insofar as he wishes something to be given

to him, his soul, since it desires this to come about, nods assent to it as if in answer to a question?

I would.

What about not willing, not wishing, and not having an appetite? Aren't these among the very opposites—cases in which the soul pushes and drives things away?

Of course.   d

Then won't we say that there is a class of things called appetites and that the clearest examples are hunger and thirst?

We will.

One of these is for food and the other for drink?

Yes.

Now, insofar as it is thirst, is it an appetite in the soul for more than that for which we say that it is the appetite? For example, is thirst thirst for hot drink or cold, or much drink or little, or, in a word, for drink of a certain sort? Or isn't it rather that, where heat is present as well as thirst, it causes the appetite to be for something cold as well, and where cold for e something hot, and where there is much thirst because of the presence of muchness, it will cause the desire to be for much, and where little for little? But thirst itself will never be for anything other than what it is in its nature to be for, namely, drink itself, and hunger for food.

That's the way it is, each appetite itself is only for its natural object, while the appetite for something of a certain sort depends on additions.

Therefore, let no one catch us unprepared or disturb us by claiming that no one has an appetite for 438 drink but rather good drink, nor food but good food, on the grounds that everyone after all has appetite for good things, so that if thirst is an appetite, it will be an appetite for good drink or whatever, and similarly with the others.[2]

All the same, the person who says that has a point.

But it seems to me that, in the case of all things that are related to something, those that are of a particular sort are related to a particular sort of thing, b while those that are merely themselves are related to a thing that is merely itself.

I don't understand.

2. [Plato is here laying the foundations for his rejection of the principle, espoused by Socrates in many earlier dialogues, that weakness of will is impossible.]

Don't you understand that the greater is such as to be greater than something?

Of course.

Than the less?

Yes.

And the much greater than the much less, isn't that so?

Yes.

And the once greater to the once less? And the going-to-be greater than the going-to-be less?

Certainly.

And isn't the same true of the more and the c fewer, the double and the half, heavier and lighter, faster and slower, the hot and the cold, and all other such things?

Of course.

And what about the various kinds of knowledge? Doesn't the same apply? Knowledge itself is knowledge of what can be learned itself (or whatever it is that knowledge is of), while a particular sort of knowledge is of a particular sort of thing. For example, when knowledge of building houses came to be, d didn't it differ from the other kinds of knowledge, and so was called knowledge of building?

Of course.

And wasn't that because it was a different sort of knowledge from all the others?

Yes.

And wasn't it because it was of a particular sort of thing that it itself became a particular sort of knowledge? And isn't this true of all crafts and kinds of knowledge?

It is.

Well, then, this is what I was trying to say—if you understand it now—when I said that of all things that are related to something, those that are merely themselves are related to things that are merely themselves, while those that are of a particular sort are related to things of a particular sort. However, I don't e mean that the sorts in question have to be the same for them both. For example, knowledge of health or disease isn't healthy or diseased, and knowledge of good and bad doesn't itself become good or bad. I mean that, when knowledge became, not knowledge of the thing itself that knowledge is of, but knowledge of something of a particular sort, the result was that it itself became a particular sort of knowledge, and this caused it to be no longer called knowledge without

qualification, but—with the addition of the relevant sort—medical knowledge or whatever.

I understand, and I think that that's the way it is.

Then as for thirst, wouldn't you include it among things that are related to something? Surely thirst is related to . . .   439

I know it's related to drink.

Therefore a particular sort of thirst is for a particular sort of drink. But thirst itself isn't for much or little, good or bad, or, in a word, for drink of a particular sort. Rather, thirst itself is in its nature only for drink itself.

Absolutely.

Hence the soul of the thirsty person, insofar as he's thirsty, doesn't wish anything else but to drink, and it wants this and is impelled towards it.   b

Clearly.

Therefore, if something draws it back when it is thirsting, wouldn't that be something different in it from whatever thirsts and drives it like a beast to drink? It can't be, we say, that the same thing, with the same part of itself, in relation to the same, at the same time, does opposite things.

No, it can't.

In the same way, I suppose, it's wrong to say of the archer that his hands at the same time push the bow away and draw it towards him. We ought to say that one hand pushes it away and the other draws it towards him.

Absolutely.   c

Now, would we assert that sometimes there are thirsty people who don't wish to drink?

Certainly, it happens often to many different people.

What, then, should one say about them? Isn't it that there is something in their soul, bidding them to drink, and something different, forbidding them to do so, that overrules the thing that bids?

I think so.

Doesn't that which forbids in such cases come into play—if it comes into play at all—as a result of rational calculation, while what drives and drags them to drink is a result of feelings and diseases?   d

Apparently.

Hence it isn't unreasonable for us to claim that they are two, and different from one another. We'll call the part of the soul with which it calculates the rational part and the part with which it lusts, hungers, thirsts, and gets excited by other appetites the irrational appetitive part, companion of certain indulgences and pleasures.

e   Yes. Indeed, that's a reasonable thing to think.

Then, let these two parts be distinguished in the soul. Now, is the spirited part by which we get angry a third part or is it of the same nature as either of the other two?

Perhaps it's like the appetitive part.

But I've heard something relevant to this, and I believe it. Leontius, the son of Aglaion, was going up from the Piraeus along the outside of the North Wall when he saw some corpses lying at the executioner's feet. He had an appetite to look at them but at the same time he was disgusted and turned away. For a time he struggled with himself and covered his face, but, finally, overpowered by the appetite, he pushed
440 his eyes wide open and rushed towards the corpses, saying, "Look for yourselves, you evil wretches, take your fill of the beautiful sight!"[3]

I've heard that story myself.

It certainly proves that anger sometimes makes war against the appetites, as one thing against another.

Besides, don't we often notice in other cases that when appetite forces someone contrary to rational calculation, he reproaches himself and gets angry
b with that in him that's doing the forcing, so that of the two factions that are fighting a civil war, so to speak, spirit allies itself with reason? But I don't think you can say that you've ever seen spirit, either in yourself or anyone else, ally itself with an appetite to do what reason has decided must not be done.

No, by god, I haven't.

What happens when a person thinks that he has
c done something unjust? Isn't it true that the nobler he is, the less he resents it if he suffers hunger, cold, or the like at the hands of someone whom he believes to be inflicting this on him justly, and won't his spirit, as I say, refuse to be aroused?

That's true.

But what happens if, instead, he believes that someone has been unjust to him? Isn't the spirit within him boiling and angry, fighting for what he believes to be just? Won't it endure hunger, cold, and the like and keep on till it is victorious, not ceasing from
d noble actions until it either wins, dies, or calms down,

called to heel by the reason within him, like a dog by a shepherd?

Spirit is certainly like that. And, of course, we made the auxiliaries in our city like dogs obedient to the rulers, who are themselves like shepherds of a city.

You well understand what I'm trying to say. But also reflect on this further point.

What?   *e*

The position of the spirited part seems to be the opposite of what we thought before. Then we thought of it as something appetitive, but now we say that it is far from being that, for in the civil war in the soul it aligns itself far more with the rational part.

Absolutely.

Then is it also different from the rational part, or is it some form of it, so that there are two parts in the soul — the rational and the appetitive — instead of three? Or rather, just as there were three classes in the city that held it together, the money-making, the *441* auxiliary, and the deliberative, is the spirited part a third thing in the soul that is by nature the helper of the rational part, provided that it hasn't been corrupted by a bad upbringing?

It must be a third.

Yes, provided that we can show it is different from the rational part, as we saw earlier it was from the appetitive one.

It isn't difficult to show that it is different. Even in small children, one can see that they are full of spirit right from birth, while as far as rational calculation is concerned, some never seem to get a share of it, while the majority do so quite late.   *b*

That's really well put. And in animals too one can see that what you say is true. Besides, our earlier quotation from Homer bears it out, where he says,

He struck his chest and spoke to his heart.[4]

For here Homer clearly represents the part that has calculated about better and worse as different from *c* the part that is angry without calculation.

That's exactly right.

Well, then, we've now made our difficult way through a sea of argument. We are pretty much agreed that the same number and the same kinds of classes as are in the city are also in the soul of each individual.

---

3. [Leontius' desire to look at the corpses is sexual in nature, for a fragment of contemporary comedy tells us that Leontius was known for his love of boys as pale as corpses.]

4. [*Odyssey* 20.27.]

That's true.

Therefore, it necessarily follows that the individual is wise in the same way and in the same part of himself as the city.

That's right.

And isn't the individual courageous in the same *d* way and in the same part of himself as the city? And isn't everything else that has to do with virtue the same in both?

Necessarily.

Moreover, Glaucon, I suppose we'll say that a man is just in the same way as a city.

That too is entirely necessary.

And we surely haven't forgotten that the city was just because each of the three classes in it was doing its own work.

I don't think we could forget that.

Then we must also remember that each one of us in whom each part is doing its own work will himself *e* be just and do his own.

Of course, we must.

Therefore, isn't it appropriate for the rational part to rule, since it is really wise and exercises foresight on behalf of the whole soul, and for the spirited part to obey it and be its ally?

It certainly is.

And isn't it, as we were saying, a mixture of music and poetry, on the one hand, and physical training, on the other, that makes the two parts harmonious, stretching and nurturing the rational part with fine words and learning, relaxing the other part through *442* soothing stories, and making it gentle by means of harmony and rhythm?

That's precisely it.

And these two, having been nurtured in this way, and having truly learned their own roles and been educated in them, will govern the appetitive part, which is the largest part in each person's soul and is by nature most insatiable for money. They'll watch over it to see that it isn't filled with the so-called pleasures of the body and that it doesn't become so big and strong that it no longer does its own work but attempts to enslave and rule over the classes it *b* isn't fitted to rule, thereby overturning everyone's whole life.

That's right.

Then, wouldn't these two parts also do the finest job of guarding the whole soul and body against external enemies—reason by planning, spirit by fighting, following its leader, and carrying out the leader's decisions through its courage?

Yes, that's true.

And it is because of the spirited part, I suppose, that we call a single individual courageous, namely, *c* when it preserves through pains and pleasures the declarations of reason about what is to be feared and what isn't.

That's right.

And we'll call him wise because of that small part of himself that rules in him and makes those declarations and has within it the knowledge of what is advantageous for each part and for the whole soul, which is the community of all three parts.

Absolutely.

And isn't he moderate because of the friendly and harmonious relations between these same parts, namely, when the ruler and the ruled believe in common that the rational part should rule and don't engage in civil war against it?   *d*

Moderation is surely nothing other than that, both in the city and in the individual.

And, of course, a person will be just because of what we've so often mentioned, and in that way.

Necessarily.

Well, then, is the justice in us at all indistinct? Does it seem to be something different from what we found in the city?

It doesn't seem so to me.

If there are still any doubts in our soul about this, we could dispel them altogether by appealing to ordinary cases.   *e*

Which ones?

For example, if we had to come to an agreement about whether someone similar in nature and training to our city had embezzled a deposit of gold or silver that he had accepted, who do you think would consider him to have done it rather than someone who isn't like him?   *443*

No one.

And would he have anything to do with temple robberies, thefts, betrayals of friends in private life or of cities in public life?

No, nothing.

And he'd be in no way untrustworthy in keeping an oath or other agreement.

How could he be?

And adultery, disrespect for parents, and neglect of the gods would be more in keeping with every other kind of character than his.

With every one.

And isn't the cause of all this that every part within *b* him does its own work, whether it's ruling or being ruled?

Yes, that and nothing else.

Then, are you still looking for justice to be something other than this power, the one that produces men and cities of the sort we've described?

No, I certainly am not.

Then the dream we had has been completely fulfilled—our suspicion that, with the help of some god, we had hit upon the origin and pattern of justice *c* right at the beginning in founding our city.[5]

Absolutely.

Indeed, Glaucon, the principle that it is right for someone who is by nature a cobbler to practice cobblery and nothing else, for the carpenter to practice carpentry, and the same for the others is a sort of image of justice—that's why it's beneficial.

Apparently.

And in truth justice is, it seems, something of this sort. However, it isn't concerned with someone's doing his own externally, but with what is inside him, *d* with what is truly himself and his own. One who is just does not allow any part of himself to do the work of another part or allow the various classes within him to meddle with each other. He regulates well what is really his own and rules himself. He puts himself in order, is his own friend, and harmonizes the three parts of himself like three limiting notes in a musical scale—high, low, and middle. He binds together those parts and any others there may be in between, and from having been many things he *e* becomes entirely one, moderate and harmonious. Only then does he act. And when he does anything, whether acquiring wealth, taking care of his body, engaging in politics, or in private contracts—in all of these, he believes that the action is just and fine that preserves this inner harmony and helps achieve it, and calls it so, and regards as wisdom the knowledge that oversees such actions. And he believes that the action that destroys this harmony is unjust, and calls it *444* so, and regards the belief that oversees it as ignorance.

5. [See 432c–433b.]

That's absolutely true, Socrates.

Well, then, if we claim to have found the just man, the just city, and what the justice is that is in them, I don't suppose that we'll seem to be telling a complete falsehood.

No, we certainly won't.

Shall we claim it, then?

We shall.

So be it. Now, I suppose we must look for injustice.

Clearly.

Surely, it must be a kind of civil war between the three parts, a meddling and doing of another's work, *b* a rebellion by some part against the whole soul in order to rule it inappropriately. The rebellious part is by nature suited to be a slave, while the other part is not a slave but belongs to the ruling class. We'll say something like that, I suppose, and that the turmoil and straying of these parts are injustice, licentiousness, cowardice, ignorance, and, in a word, the whole of vice.

That's what they are.

So, if justice and injustice are really clear enough to us, then acting justly, acting unjustly, and doing *c* injustice are also clear.

How so?

Because just and unjust actions are no different for the soul than healthy and unhealthy things are for the body.

In what way?

Healthy things produce health, unhealthy ones disease.

Yes.

And don't just actions produce justice in the soul and unjust ones injustice?   *d*

Necessarily.

To produce health is to establish the components of the body in a natural relation of control and being controlled, one by another, while to produce disease is to establish a relation of ruling and being ruled contrary to nature.

That's right.

Then, isn't to produce justice to establish the parts of the soul in a natural relation of control, one by another, while to produce injustice is to establish a relation of ruling and being ruled contrary to nature?

Precisely.

Virtue seems, then, to be a kind of health, fine

condition, and well-being of the soul, while vice is
e disease, shameful condition, and weakness.

That's true.

And don't fine ways of living lead one to the possession of virtue, shameful ones to vice?

Necessarily.

So it now remains, it seems, to inquire whether it
445 is more profitable to act justly, live in a fine way, and
be just, whether one is known to be so or not, or to
act unjustly and be unjust, provided that one doesn't
pay the penalty and become better as a result of punishment.

But, Socrates, this inquiry looks ridiculous to me
now that justice and injustice have been shown to
be as we have described. Even if one has every kind
of food and drink, lots of money, and every sort of
power to rule, life is thought to be not worth living
when the body's nature is ruined. So even if someone
b can do whatever he wishes, except what will free him
from vice and injustice and make him acquire justice
and virtue, how can it be worth living when his soul —
the very thing by which he lives — is ruined and in
turmoil?

Yes, it is ridiculous. Nevertheless, now that we've
come far enough to be able to see most clearly that
this is so, we mustn't give up.

That's absolutely the last thing we must do.

Then come here, so that you can see how many
c forms of vice there are, anyhow that I consider worthy
of examination.

I'm following you, just tell me.

Well, from the vantage point we've reached in our
argument, it seems to me that there is one form of
virtue and an unlimited number of forms of vice,
four of which are worth mentioning.

How do you mean?

It seems likely that there are as many types of soul
as there are specific types of political constitution.

How many is that?

d   Five forms of constitution and five of souls.

What are they?

One is the constitution we've been describing. And
it has two names. If one outstanding man emerges
among the rulers, it's called a kingship; if more than
one, it's called an aristocracy.

That's true.

Therefore, I say that this is one form of constitution.
Whether one man emerges or many, none of the

significant laws of the city would be changed, if they
followed the upbringing and education we described. e

Probably not.

Book V

This is the kind of city and constitution, then, that I 449
call good and correct, and so too is this kind of man.
And if indeed this is the correct kind, all the others —
whether as city governments or as organizations of
the individual soul — are bad and mistaken. Their
badness is of four kinds.

What are they? he said.

I was going to enumerate them and explain how
I thought they developed out of one another, but
Polemarchus, who was sitting a little further away
than Adeimantus, extended his hand and took hold b
of the latter's cloak by the shoulder from above. He
drew Adeimantus towards him, while he himself
leaned forward and said something to him. We overheard nothing of what he said except the words "Shall
we let it go, or what?"

We certainly won't let it go, Adeimantus said, now
speaking aloud.

And I asked: What is it that you won't let go?

You, he said.

For what reason in particular?   c

We think that you're slacking off and that you've
cheated us out of a whole important section of the
discussion in order to avoid having to deal with it.
You thought we wouldn't notice when you said — as
though it were something trivial — that, as regards
wives and children, anyone could see that the possessions of friends should be held in common.

But isn't that right, Adeimantus?

Yes it is. But this "right," like the other things we've
discussed, requires an explanation — in this case, an
explanation of the manner in which they are to be
held in common, for there may be many ways of doing
this. So don't omit telling us about the particular one d
you mean. We've been waiting for some time, indeed,
for you to tell us about the production of children —
how they'll be produced and, once born, how they'll
be brought up — and about the whole subject of having wives and children in common. We think that
this makes a considerable difference — indeed all the
difference — to whether a constitution is correct or
not. So now, since you are beginning to describe

another constitution before having adequately discussed these things, we are resolved, as you overheard, not to let you off until you explain all this as 450 fully as the rest.

Include me, Glaucon said, as a partner in this resolution.

In fact, Socrates, Thrasymachus added, you can take this as the resolution of all of us.

What a thing you've done, I said, in stopping me! What an argument you've started up again from the very beginning, as it were, about the constitution! I was delighted to think that it had already been described and was content to have these things accepted as they were stated before. You don't realize what a swarm of arguments you've stirred up by calling me to account now. I saw the swarm and passed the topic b by in order to save us a lot of trouble.

Well, said Thrasymachus, are we here to search for gold[1] or to listen to an argument?

The latter, I said, but within reason.

It's within reason, Socrates, Glaucon said, for people with any understanding to listen to an argument of this kind their whole life long. So don't mind about us, and don't get tired yourself. Rather, tell us at length what your thoughts are on the topic we inquired about, namely, what the common possession c of wives and children will amount to for the guardians and how the children will be brought up while they're still small, for the time between birth and the beginning of education seems to be the most difficult period of all. So try to tell us what the manner of this upbringing must be.

It isn't an easy subject to explain, for it raises even more incredulity than the topics we've discussed so far. People may not believe that what we say is possible or that, even if it could be brought about, it would be for the best. It's for this reason that I hesitated to bring it up, namely, that our argument might seem d to be no more than wishful thinking.

Then don't hesitate, for your audience isn't inconsiderate, incredulous, or hostile.

Are you trying to encourage me by saying that?

I am.

Well, you're doing the opposite. Your encouragement would be fine, if I could be sure I was speaking with knowledge, for one can feel both secure and confident when one knows the truth about the dearest and most important things and speaks about them among those who are themselves wise and dear friends. But to speak, as I'm doing, at a time when e one is unsure of oneself and searching for the truth, is a frightening and insecure thing to do. I'm not 451 afraid of being laughed at—that would be childish indeed. But I am afraid that, if I slip from the truth, just where it's most important not to, I'll not only fall myself but drag my friends down as well. So I bow to Adrastea[2] for what I'm going to say, for I suspect that it's a lesser crime to kill someone involuntarily than to mislead people about fine, good, and just institutions. Since it's better to run this risk among enemies than among friends, you've well and truly encouraged me! b

Glaucon laughed and said: Well, Socrates, if we suffer from any false note you strike in the argument, we'll release you and absolve you of any guilt as in a homicide case: your hands are clean, and you have not deceived us. So take courage and speak.

I will, for the law says that someone who kills involuntarily is free of guilt when he's absolved by the injured party.[3] So it's surely reasonable to think the same is true in my case as well.

With that as your defense, speak.

Then I'll have to go back to what should perhaps have been said in sequence, although it may be that c this way of doing things is in fact right and that after the completion of the male drama, so to speak, we should then go through the female one[4]—especially as you insist on it so urgently.

For men born and educated as we've described there is, in my opinion, no right way to acquire and use women and children other than by following the road

---

1. [Literally: to refine gold. A proverbial expression applied to those who neglect the task at hand for some more fascinating but less profitable pursuit. Thrasymachus seems to be reminding Socrates of his own words at 336e.—C.D.C.R.]

2. [Adrasteia was a kind of Nemesis, a punisher of pride and proud words. The "bow to Adrasteia" is therefore a kind of apology for the kind of act or statement that might otherwise spur her to take action.]

3. [See Plato, Laws 869e.]

4. [This may be an allusion to the mimes of Sophron of Syracuse (c. 470–400 B.C.), which were classified as male mimes and female mimes, because males were represented in the former, females in the latter.]

on which we started them. We attempted, in the argument, to set up the men as guardians of the herd.[5]

Yes.

Then let's give them a birth and rearing consistent
d with that and see whether it suits us or not.

How?

As follows: Do we think that the wives of our guardian watchdogs should guard what the males guard, hunt with them, and do everything else in common with them? Or should we keep the women at home, as incapable of doing this, since they must bear and rear the puppies, while the males work and have the entire care of the flock?

Everything should be in common, except that the
e females are weaker and the males stronger.

And is it possible to use any animals for the same things if you don't give them the same upbringing and education?

No, it isn't.

Therefore, if we use the women for the same things as the men, they must also be taught the same things.
452 Yes.

Now, we gave the men music and poetry and physical training.

Yes.

Then we must give these two crafts, as well as those having to do with warfare, to the women also to use in the same way as the men use them.

That seems to follow from what you say.

But perhaps much of what we are saying, since it is contrary to custom, would incite ridicule if it were carried out in practice as we've described.

It certainly would.

What is the most ridiculous thing that you see in it? Isn't it obviously the women exercising naked in the palestras[6] with the men? And not just the young women, but the older ones too—like old men in
b gymnasiums who, even though their bodies are wrinkled and not pleasant to look at, still love to do physical training.

Yes, that would look really ridiculous as things stand at present.

But surely, now that we've started to speak about this, we mustn't fear the various jokes that wits will make about this kind of change in music and poetry, physical training, and—last but not least—in bearing arms and riding horses.   c

You're right.

And now that we've begun to speak about this, we must move on to the tougher part of the law, begging these people not to be silly (though that is their own work!) but to take the matter seriously. They should remember that it wasn't very long ago that the Greeks themselves thought it shameful and ridiculous (as the majority of the barbarians still do) for even men to be seen naked and that when the Cretans and then the Lacedaemonians began the gymnasiums, the wits of those times could also have ridiculed it all. Or don't you think so?   d

I do.

But I think that, after it was found in practice to be better to strip than to cover up all those parts, then what was ridiculous to the eyes faded away in the face of what argument showed to be the best. This makes it clear that it's foolish to think that anything besides the bad is ridiculous or to try to raise a laugh at the sight of anything besides what's stupid or bad or (putting it the other way around) it's foolish to take seriously any standard of what is fine and beautiful e other than the good.

That's absolutely certain.

However, mustn't we first agree about whether our proposals are possible or not? And mustn't we give to anyone who wishes the opportunity to question us—whether in jest or in earnest—about whether female human nature *can* share all the tasks of that of the male, or none of them, or some but not others, 453 and to ask in which class the waging of war belongs? Wouldn't this, as the best beginning, also be likely to result in the best conclusion?

Of course.

Shall we give the argument against ourselves, then, on behalf of those who share these reservations, so that their side of the question doesn't fall by default?

There's no reason not to.   b

Then let's say this on their behalf: "Socrates and Glaucon, there's no need for others to argue with you, for you yourselves, when you began to found

5. [It is useful to contrast Plato's views on women with those of his contemporaries in Athens. The most reliable brief discussion of the latter is John Gould, "Law, Custom and Myth: Aspects of the Social Position of Women in Classical Athens," *Journal of Hellenic Studies* 100 (1980): 38–59.]

6. [A palestra is a wrestling school and training ground.]

your city, agreed that each must do his own work in accordance with his nature."

And I think we certainly did agree to that.

"Can you deny that a woman is by nature very different from a man?"

Of course not.

"And isn't it appropriate to assign different work to each in accordance with its nature?"

c   Certainly.

"How is it, then, that you aren't mistaken and contradicting yourselves when you say that men and women must do the same things, when their natures are so completely separate and distinct?"

Do you have any defense against that attack?

It isn't easy to think of one on the spur of the moment, so I'll ask you to explain the argument on our side as well, whatever it is.

This and many other such things, Glaucon, which I foresaw earlier, were what I was afraid of, so that I d hesitated to tackle the law concerning the possession and upbringing of women and children.

By god, it doesn't seem to be an easy topic.

It isn't. But the fact is that whether someone falls into a small diving pool or into the middle of the biggest ocean, he must swim all the same.

He certainly must.

Then we must swim too, and try to save ourselves from the sea of argument, hoping that a dolphin will pick us up or that we'll be rescued by some other desperate means.[7]

e   It seems so.

Come, then. Let's see if we can find a way out. We've agreed that different natures must follow different ways of life and that the natures of men and women are different. But now we say that those different natures must follow the same way of life. Isn't that the accusation brought against us?

That's it exactly.

Ah! Glaucon, great is the power of the craft of dispu-
454 tation.

Why is that?

Because many fall into it against their wills. They think they are having not a quarrel but a conversation, because they are unable to examine what has been said by dividing it up according to forms. Hence, they

pursue mere verbal contradictions of what has been said and have a quarrel rather than a conversation.

That does happen to lots of people, but it isn't happening to us at the moment, is it?

It most certainly is, for it looks to me, at any rate, as though we are falling into disputation against our will. b

How?

We're bravely, but in a quarrelsome and merely verbal fashion, pursuing the principle that natures that aren't the same must follow different ways of life. But when we assigned different ways of life to different natures and the same ones to the same, we didn't at all examine the form of natural difference and sameness we had in mind or in what regard we were distinguishing them.

No, we didn't look into that.

Therefore, we might just as well, it seems, ask ourselves whether the natures of bald and long-haired c men are the same or opposite. And, when we agree that they are opposite, then, if the bald ones are cobblers, we ought to forbid the long-haired ones to be cobblers, and if the long-haired ones are cobblers, we ought to forbid this to the bald ones.

That would indeed be ridiculous.

And aren't we in this ridiculous position because at that time we did not introduce every form of difference and sameness in nature, but focused on the one form of sameness and difference that was relevant to the particular ways of life themselves? We meant, for example, that a male and female doctor have souls d of the same nature. Or don't you think so?

I do.

But a doctor and a carpenter have different ones?

Completely different, surely.

Therefore, if the male sex is seen to be different from the female with regard to a particular craft or way of life, we'll say that the relevant one must be assigned to it. But if it's apparent that they differ only in this respect, that the females bear children while the males beget them, we'll say that there has been no kind of proof that women are different from men with respect to what we're talking about, and we'll continue to believe that our guardians and their wives e must have the same way of life.

And rightly so.

Next, we'll tell anyone who holds the opposite view to instruct us in this: With regard to what craft or way of life involved in the constitution of the city

7. [See Herodotus, *Histories* 1.23–24 for the story of Arion's rescue by the dolphin.]

455 are the natures of men and women not the same but different?

That's a fair question, at any rate.

And perhaps he'd say, just as you did a moment ago, that it isn't easy to give an immediate answer, but with enough consideration it should not be difficult.

Yes, he might say that.

Shall we ask the one who raises this objection to follow us and see whether we can show him that no b way of life concerned with the management of the city is peculiar to women?

Of course.

"Come, now," we'll say to him, "give us an answer: Is this what you meant by one person being naturally well suited for something and another being naturally unsuited? That the one learned it easily, the other with difficulty; that the one, after only a brief period of instruction, was able to find out things for himself, while the other, after much instruction, couldn't even remember what he'd learned; that the body of the one adequately served his thought, while the body of c the other opposed his. Are there any other things besides these by which you distinguished those who are naturally well suited for anything from those who are not?"

No one will claim that there are any others.

Do you know of anything practiced by human beings in which the male sex isn't superior to the female in all these ways? Or must we make a long story of it by mentioning weaving, baking cakes, and cooking vegetables, in which the female sex is believed to excel and in which it is most ridiculous of d all for it to be inferior?

It's true that one sex is much superior to the other in pretty well everything, although many women are better than many men in many things. But on the whole it is as you say.

Then there is no way of life concerned with the management of the city that belongs to a woman because she's a woman or to a man because he's a man, but the various natures are distributed in the same way in both creatures. Women share by nature in every way of life just as men do, but in all of them e women are weaker than men.

Certainly.

Then shall we assign all of them to men and none to women?

How can we?

We'll say, I suppose, that one woman is a doctor, another not, and that one is musical by nature, another not.

Of course.

And, therefore, won't one be athletic or warlike, while another is unwarlike and no lover of physical training?   456

I suppose so.

Further, isn't one woman philosophical or a lover of wisdom, while another hates wisdom? And isn't one spirited and another spiritless?

That too.

So one woman may have a guardian nature and another not, for wasn't it qualities of this sort that we looked for in the natures of the men we selected as guardians?

Certainly.

Therefore, men and women are by nature the same with respect to guarding the city, except to the extent that one is weaker and the other stronger.

Apparently.

Then women of this sort must be chosen along with men of the same sort to live with them and share b their guardianship, seeing that they are adequate for the task and akin to the men in nature.

Certainly.

And mustn't we assign the same way of life to the same natures?

We must.

We've come round, then, to what we said before and have agreed that it isn't against nature to assign an education in music, poetry, and physical training to the wives of the guardians.

Absolutely.

Then we're not legislating impossibilities or indulging in mere wishful thinking, since the law we estab- c lished is in accord with nature. It's rather the way things are at present that seems to be against nature.

So it seems.

Now, weren't we trying to determine whether our proposals were both possible and optimal?

Yes, we were.

And haven't we now agreed that they're possible?

Yes.

Then mustn't we next reach agreement about whether or not they're optimal?

Clearly.

Should we have one kind of education to produce

women guardians, then, and another to produce men, *d* especially as they have the same natures to begin with?

No.

Then, what do you think about this?

What?

About one man being better and another worse. Or do you think they're all alike?

Certainly not.

In the city we're establishing, who do you think will prove to be better men, the guardians, who receive the education we've described, or the cobblers, who are educated in cobblery?

Your question is ridiculous.

I understand. Indeed, aren't the guardians the best *e* of the citizens?

By far.

And what about the female guardians? Aren't they the best of the women?

They're by far the best.

Is there anything better for a city than having the best possible men and women as its citizens?

There isn't.

And isn't it music and poetry and physical training, lending their support in the way we described, that 457 bring this about?

Of course.

Then the law we've established isn't only possible; it is also optimal for a city?

Yes.

Then the guardian women must strip for physical training, since they'll wear virtue or excellence instead of clothes. They must share in war and the other guardians' duties in the city and do nothing else. But the lighter parts must be assigned to them because of the weakness of their sex. And the man who laughs at naked women doing physical training for the sake *b* of what is best is "plucking the unripe fruit"[8] of laughter and doesn't know, it seems, what he's laughing at or what he's doing, for it is and always will be the finest saying that the beneficial is beautiful, while the harmful is ugly.

Absolutely.

Can we say, then, that we've escaped one wave of criticism in our discussion of the law about women, that we haven't been altogether swept away by laying

8. [Plato is here adapting a phrase of Pindar, "plucking the unripe fruit of wisdom."]

it down that male and female guardians must share their entire way of life, and that our argument is *c* consistent when it states that this is both possible and beneficial?

And it's certainly no small wave that you've escaped.

You won't think that it's so big when you get a look at the next one.

Tell me about it, and I'll decide.

I suppose that the following law goes along with the last one and the others that preceded it.

Which one?

That all these women are to belong in common to all the men, that none are to live privately with any man, and that the children, too, are to be possessed in common, so that no parent will know his own off- *d* spring or any child his parent.

This wave is far bigger than the other, for there's doubt both about its possibility and about whether or not it's beneficial.

I don't think that its being beneficial would be disputed or that it would be denied that the common possession of women and children would be the greatest good, if indeed it is possible. But I think that there would be a lot of disagreement about whether or not it is possible.

There could very well be dispute about both.   *e*

You mean that I'll have to face a coalition of arguments. I thought I'd escape one of them, if you believed that the proposal was beneficial, and that I'd have only the one about whether or not it's possible left to deal with.

But you didn't escape unobserved, so you have to give an argument for both.

Well, then, I'll have to accept my punishment. But do me this favor. Let me, as if on a holiday, do what lazy people do who feast on their own thoughts when 458 out for a solitary walk. Instead of finding out how something they desire might actually come about, these people pass that over, so as to avoid tiring deliberations about what's possible and what isn't. They assume that what they desire is available and proceed to arrange the rest, taking pleasure in thinking through everything they'll do when they have what they want, thereby making their lazy souls even lazier. I'm getting soft myself at the moment, so I want to *b* delay consideration of the feasibility of our proposal until later. With your permission, I'll assume that it's feasible and examine how the rulers will arrange these matters when they come to pass. And I'll try to show that nothing could be more beneficial to the city and its guardians than those arrangements. These are the things I'll examine with you first, and I'll deal with the other question later, but only if you'll permit me to do it this way.

You have my permission, so carry on with your examination.

I suppose that our rulers and auxiliaries—if indeed they're worthy of the names—will be willing to com-
c mand and to obey respectively. In some cases, the rulers will themselves be obeying our laws, and in others, namely, the ones we leave to their discretion, they'll give directions that are in the spirit of our laws.

Probably so.

Then you, as their lawgiver, will select women just as you did men, with natures as similar to theirs as possible, and hand them over to the men. And since they have common dwellings and meals, rather than
d private ones, and live together and mix together both in physical training and in the rest of their upbringing, they will, I suppose, be driven by innate necessity to have sex with one another. Or don't you think we're talking about necessities here?

The necessities aren't geometrical but erotic, and they're probably better than the others at persuading and compelling the majority of people.

That's right. But the next point, Glaucon, is that promiscuity is impious in a city of happy people, and
e the rulers won't allow it.

No, for it isn't right.

Then it's clear that our next task must be to make marriage as sacred as possible. And the sacred marriages will be those that are most beneficial.

Absolutely.

How, then, will they be most beneficial? Tell me
459 this, Glaucon: I see that you have hunting dogs and quite a flock of noble fighting birds at home. Have you noticed anything about their mating and breeding?

Like what?

In the first place, although they're all noble, aren't there some that are the best and prove themselves to be so?

There are.

Do you breed them all alike, or do you try to breed from the best as much as possible?

I try to breed from the best.

And do you breed from the youngest or the oldest or from those in their prime?   b

From those in their prime.

And do you think that if they weren't bred in this way, your stock of birds and dogs would get much worse?

I do.

What about horses and other animals? Are things any different with them?

It would be strange if they were.

Dear me! If this also holds true of human beings, our need for excellent rulers is indeed extreme.

It does hold of them. But what of it?   c

Because our rulers will then have to use a lot of drugs. And while an inferior doctor is adequate for people who are willing to follow a regimen and don't need drugs, when drugs are needed, we know that a bolder doctor is required.

That's true. But what exactly do you have in mind?

I mean that it looks as though our rulers will have to make considerable use of falsehood and deception for the benefit of those they rule. And we said that all such falsehoods are useful as a form of drug.   d

And we were right.

Well, it seems we were right, especially where marriages and the producing of children are concerned.

How so?

It follows from our previous agreements, first, that the best men must have sex with the best women as frequently as possible, while the opposite is true of the most inferior men and women, and, second, that if our herd is to be of the highest possible quality, the former's offspring must be reared but not the latter's. And this must all be brought about without e being noticed by anyone except the rulers, so that our herd of guardians remains as free from dissension as possible.

That's absolutely right.

Therefore certain festivals and sacrifices will be established by law at which we'll bring the brides and grooms together, and we'll direct our poets to compose appropriate hymns for the marriages that take place. We'll leave the number of marriages for the rulers to decide, but their aim will be to keep the 460 number of males as stable as they can, taking into account war, disease, and similar factors, so that the city will, as far as possible, become neither too big nor too small.

That's right.

Then there'll have to be some sophisticated lotteries introduced, so that at each marriage the inferior people we mentioned will blame luck rather than the rulers when they aren't chosen.

There will.

And among other prizes and rewards the young men who are good in war or other things must be b given permission to have sex with the women more often, since this will also be a good pretext for having them father as many of the children as possible.

That's right.

And then, as the children are born, they'll be taken over by the officials appointed for the purpose, who may be either men or women or both, since our offices are open to both sexes.

Yes.

I think they'll take the children of good parents to c the nurses in charge of the rearing pen situated in a separate part of the city, but the children of inferior parents, or any child of the others that is born defective, they'll hide in a secret and unknown place, as is appropriate.[9]

It is, if indeed the guardian breed is to remain pure.

And won't the nurses also see to it that the mothers are brought to the rearing pen when their breasts have milk, taking every precaution to insure that no mother knows her own child and providing wet nurses d if the mother's milk is insufficient? And won't they take care that the mothers suckle the children for only a reasonable amount of time and that the care of sleepless children and all other such troublesome duties are taken over by the wet nurses and other attendants?

You're making it very easy for the wives of the guardians to have children.

And that's only proper. So let's take up the next thing we proposed. We said that the children's parents should be in their prime.

True.

Do you share the view that a woman's prime lasts e about twenty years and a man's about thirty?

Which years are those?

9. [There can be no doubt that Plato is recommending infanticide by exposure for these babies, a practice which was quite common in ancient Greece as a method of birth control.]

A woman is to bear children for the city from the age of twenty to the age of forty, a man from the time that he passes his peak as a runner until he reaches fifty-five.

At any rate, that's the physical and mental prime for both.   461

Then, if a man who is younger or older than that engages in reproduction for the community, we'll say that his offense is neither pious nor just, for the child he begets for the city, if it remains hidden, will be born in darkness, through a dangerous weakness of will, and without the benefit of the sacrifices and prayers offered at every marriage festival, in which the priests and priestesses, together with the entire city, ask that the children of good and beneficial parents may always prove themselves still better and more beneficial.   b

That's right.

The same law will apply if a man still of begetting years has a child with a woman of child-bearing age without the sanction of the rulers. We'll say that he brings to the city an illegitimate, unauthorized, and unhallowed child.

That's absolutely right.

However, I think that when women and men have passed the age of having children, we'll leave them free to have sex with whomever they wish, with these exceptions: For a man—his daughter, his mother, his daughter's children, and his mother's ancestors; for c a woman—her son and his descendants, her father and his ancestors. Having received these instructions, they should be very careful not to let a single fetus see the light of day, but if one is conceived and forces its way to the light, they must deal with it in the knowledge that no nurture is available for it.

That's certainly sensible. But how will they recognize their fathers and daughters and the others you mentioned?   d

They have no way of knowing. But a man will call all the children born in the tenth or seventh month after he became a bridegroom his sons, if they're male, and his daughters, if they're female, and they'll call him father. He'll call their children his grandchildren, and they'll call the group to which he belongs grandfathers and grandmothers. And those who were born at the same time as their mothers and fathers were having children they'll call their brothers and sisters. Thus, as we were saying, the relevant groups e will avoid sexual relations with each other. But the law will allow brothers and sisters to have sex with one another if the lottery works out that way and the Pythia[10] approves.

That's absolutely right.

This, then, Glaucon, is how the guardians of your city have their wives and children in common. We must now confirm that this arrangement is both consistent with the rest of the constitution and by far the best. Or how else are we to proceed?

462   In just that way.

Then isn't the first step towards agreement to ask ourselves what we say is the greatest good in designing the city—the good at which the legislator aims in making the laws—and what is the greatest evil? And isn't the next step to examine whether the system we've just described fits into the tracks of the good and not into those of the bad?

Absolutely.

Is there any greater evil we can mention for a city than that which tears it apart and makes it many instead of one? Or any greater good than that which
b binds it together and makes it one?

There isn't.

And when, as far as possible, all the citizens rejoice and are pained by the same successes and failures, doesn't this sharing of pleasures and pains bind the city together?

It most certainly does.

But when some suffer greatly, while others rejoice greatly, at the same things happening to the city or its people, doesn't this privatization of pleasures and
c pains dissolve the city?

Of course.

And isn't that what happens whenever such words as "mine" and "not mine" aren't used in unison? And similarly with "someone else's"?

Precisely.

Then, is the best-governed city the one in which most people say "mine" and "not mine" about the same things in the same way?

It is indeed.

What about the city that is most like a single person? For example, when one of us hurts his finger, the entire organism that binds body and soul together into a single system under the ruling part within it is aware of this, and the whole feels the pain together with the part that suffers. That's why we say that the man has a pain in his finger. And the same can be d said about any part of a man, with regard either to the pain it suffers or to the pleasure it experiences when it finds relief.

Certainly. And, as for your question, the city with the best government *is* most like such a person.

Then, whenever anything good or bad happens to a single one of its citizens, such a city above all others will say that the affected part is its own and will share in the pleasure or pain as a whole.   e

If it has good laws, that must be so.

It's time now to return to our own city, to look there for the features we've agreed on, and to determine whether it or some other city possesses them to the greatest degree.

Then that's what we must do.

What about those other cities? Aren't there rulers and people in them, as well as in ours?   463

There are.

Besides fellow citizens, what do the people call the rulers in those other cities?

In many they call them despots, but in democracies they are called just this—rulers.[11]

What about the people in our city? Besides fellow citizens, what do they call their rulers?

Preservers[12] and auxiliaries.   b

And what do they in turn call the people?

Providers of upkeep and wages.

What do the rulers call the people in other cities?

Slaves.

And what do the rulers call each other?

Co-rulers.

And ours?

Co-guardians.

Can you tell me whether a ruler in those other cities could address some of his co-rulers as his kinsmen and others as outsiders?

Yes, many could.

And doesn't he consider his kinsman to be his

10. [The priestess of Apollo at Delphi.]

11. [The Athenian democracy had nine *archontes*, or rulers, in Plato's time. These included the chief magistrates, the chief military leader, and an important authority in religious matters.]

12. [See 429c.]

own, and doesn't he address him as such, while he
c considers the outsider not to be his own?

He does.

What about your guardians? Could any of them consider a co-guardian as an outsider or address him as such?

There's no way he could, for when he meets any one of them, he'll hold that he's meeting a brother or sister, a father or mother, a son or daughter, or some ancestor or descendant of theirs.

You put that very well. But tell me this: Will your laws require them simply to use these kinship names or also to do all the things that go along with the d names? Must they show to their "fathers" the respect, solicitude, and obedience we show to our parents by law? Won't they fare worse at the hands of gods and humans, as people whose actions are neither pious nor just, if they do otherwise? Will these be the oracular sayings they hear from all the citizens from their childhood on, or will they hear something else about their fathers—or the ones they're told are their fathers—and other relatives?

The former. It would be absurd if they only mouthed kinship names without doing the things that e go along with them.

Therefore, in our city more than in any other, they'll speak in unison the words we mentioned a moment ago. When any one of them is doing well or badly, they'll say that "mine" is doing well or that "mine" is doing badly.

That's absolutely true.

Now, didn't we say that the having and expressing
464 of this conviction is closely followed by the having of pleasures and pains in common?

Yes, and we were right.

Then won't our citizens, more than any others, have the same thing in common, the one they call "mine"? And, having that in common, won't they, more than any others, have common pleasures and pains?

Of course.

And, in addition to the other institutions, the cause of this is the having of wives and children in common by the guardians?

That more than anything else is the cause.

But we agreed that the having of pains and pleasures in common is the greatest good for a city, and we characterized a well-governed city in terms of the body's reaction to pain or pleasure in any one of b its parts.

And we were right to agree.

Then, the cause of the greatest good for our city has been shown to be the having of wives and children in common by the auxiliaries.

It has.

And, of course, this is consistent with what we said before, for we said somewhere that, if they're going to be guardians, they mustn't have private houses, property, or possessions, but must receive their upkeep from the other citizens as a wage for their guard- c ianship and enjoy it in common.[13]

That's right.

Then isn't it true, just as I claimed, that what we are saying now, taken together with what we said before, makes even better guardians out of them and prevents them from tearing the city apart by not calling the same thing "mine"? If different people apply the term to different things, one would drag into his own house whatever he could separate from the others, and another would drag things into a different house to a different wife and children, and this would d make for private pleasures and pains at private things. But our people, on the other hand, will think of the same things as their own, aim at the same goal, and, as far as possible, feel pleasure and pain in unison.

Precisely.

And what about lawsuits and mutual accusations? Won't they pretty well disappear from among them, because they have everything in common except their own bodies? Hence they'll be spared all the dissension that arises between people because of the possession of money, children, and families.   e

They'll necessarily be spared it.

Nor could any lawsuits for insult or injury justly occur among them, for we'll declare that it's a fine and just thing for people to defend themselves against others of the same age, since this will compel them to stay in good physical shape.

That's right.

This law is also correct for another reason: If a spirited person vents his anger in this way, it will be 465 less likely to lead him into more serious disputes.

Certainly.

13. [See 416d ff.]

But an older person will be authorized to rule and punish all the younger ones.

Clearly.

And surely it's also obvious that a younger person won't strike or do any sort of violence to an older one or fail to show him respect in other ways, unless the rulers command it, for there are two guardians sufficient to prevent him from doing such things—shame and fear. Shame will prevent him from laying a hand on his parents, and so will the fear that the others would come to the aid of the victim, some as
b his sons, some as his brothers, and some as his fathers.

That's the effect they'll have.

Then, in all cases, won't the laws induce men to live at peace with one another?

Very much so.

And if there's no discord among the guardians, there's no danger that the rest of the city will break into civil war, either with them or among themselves.

Certainly not.

I hesitate to mention, since they're so unseemly, the pettiest of the evils the guardians would therefore escape: The poor man's flattery of the rich, the per-
c plexities and sufferings involved in bringing up children and in making the money necessary to feed the household, getting into debt, paying it off, and in some way or other providing enough money to hand over to their wives and household slaves to manage. All of the various troubles men endure in these matters are obvious, ignoble, and not worth discussing.

d   They're obvious even to the blind.

They'll be free of all these, and they'll live a life more blessedly happy than that of the victors in the Olympian games.

How?

The Olympian victors are considered happy on account of only a small part of what is available to our guardians, for the guardians' victory is even greater, and their upkeep from public funds more complete. The victory they gain is the preservation of the whole city, and the crown of victory that they and their children receive is their upkeep and all the necessities of life. They receive rewards from their own city while they live, and at their death they're
e given a worthy burial.

Those are very good things.

Do you remember that, earlier in our discussion, someone—I forget who—shocked us by saying that we hadn't made our guardians happy, that it was possible for them to have everything that belongs to the citizens, yet they had nothing? We said, I think, 466 that if this happened to come up at some point, we'd look into it then, but that our concern at the time was to make our guardians true guardians and the city the happiest we could, rather than looking to any one group within it and molding it for happiness.

I remember.

Well, then, if the life of our auxiliaries is apparently much finer and better than that of Olympian victors, is there any need to compare it to the lives of cobblers, farmers, or other craftsmen?   b

Not in my opinion.

Then it's surely right to repeat here what I said then: If a guardian seeks happiness in such a way that he's no longer a guardian and isn't satisfied with a life that's moderate, stable, and—as we say—best, but a silly, adolescent idea of happiness seizes him and incites him to use his power to take everything in the city for himself, he'll come to know the true wisdom c of Hesiod's saying that somehow "the half is worth more than the whole."[14]

If he takes my advice, he'll keep to his own life-style.

You agree, then, that the women and men should associate with one another in education, in things having to do with children, and in guarding the other citizens in the way we've described; that both when they remain in the city and when they go to war, they must guard together and hunt together like dogs and share in everything as far as possible; and that by d doing so they'll be doing what's best and not something contrary either to woman's nature as compared with man's or to the natural association of men and women with one another.

I agree.

Then doesn't it remain for us to determine whether it's possible to bring about this association among human beings, as it is among animals, and to say just how it might be done?

You took the words right out of my mouth.

As far as war is concerned, I think it's clear how they will wage it.   e

How so?

Men and women will campaign together. They'll

---

14. [*Works and Days* 40.]

take the sturdy children with them, so that, like the children of other craftsmen, they can see what they'll have to do when they grow up. But in addition to observing, they can serve and assist in everything to do with the war and help their mothers and fathers.

467 Haven't you noticed in the other crafts how the children of potters, for example, assist and observe for a long time before actually making any pots?

I have indeed.

And should these craftsmen take more care in training their children by appropriate experience and observation than the guardians?

Of course not; that would be completely ridiculous.

Besides, every animal fights better in the presence
b of its young.

That's so. But, Socrates, there's a considerable danger that in a defeat—and such things are likely to happen in a war—they'll lose their children's lives as well as their own, making it impossible for the rest of the city to recover.

What you say is true. But do you think that the first thing we should provide for is the avoidance of all danger?

Not at all.

Well, then, if people will probably have to face some danger, shouldn't it be the sort that will make them better if they come through it successfully?

Obviously.

And do you think that whether or not men who are going to be warriors observe warfare when they're still boys makes such a small difference that it isn't
c worth the danger of having them do it?

No, it does make a difference to what you're talking about.

On the assumption, then, that the children are to be observers of war, if we can contrive some way to keep them secure, everything will be fine, won't it?

Yes.

Well, then, in the first place, their fathers won't be ignorant, will they, about which campaigns are dangerous and which are not, but rather as knowledgeable about this as any human beings can
d be?

Probably so.

Then they'll take the children to some campaigns and not to others?

Correct.

And they'll put officers in charge of them whose

age and experience qualifies them to be leaders and tutors?

Appropriately so.

But, as we say, the unexpected often occurs.

Indeed.

With this in mind, we must provide the children with wings when they're small, so that they can fly away and escape.

What do you mean?   e

We must mount them on horses as early as possible—not on spirited or aggressive horses, but on very fast and manageable ones—and when they've learned to ride, they must be taken to observe a war. In this way, they'll get the best look at their own work and, if the need arises, make the securest possible escape to safety, following their older guides.

I think you're right.

What about warfare itself? What attitude should your soldiers have to each other and to the enemy? 468 Are my views about this right or not?

First, tell me what they are.

If one of them leaves his post or throws away his shield or does anything else of that sort through cowardice, shouldn't he be reduced to being a craftsman or farmer?

Certainly.

And shouldn't anyone who is captured alive be left to his captors as a gift to do with as they wish?

Absolutely.   b

But don't you think that anyone who distinguishes himself and earns high esteem should, while still on the campaign, first be crowned with wreaths by each of the adolescents and children who accompany the expedition?

I do.

And what about shaken by the right hand?

That too.

But I suppose that you wouldn't go this far?

Namely?

That he should kiss and be kissed by each of them.

That most of all. And I'd add this to the law: As long as the campaign lasts, no one he wants to kiss shall be allowed to refuse, for then, if one of them c happens to be in love with another, whether male or female, he'll be all the more eager to win the rewards of valor.

Excellent. And we've already stated that, since he's a good person, more marriages will be available to him, and he'll be selected for such things more frequently than the others, so that he'll beget as many children as possible.

Yes, we did say that.

Indeed, according to Homer too, it is just to honor in such ways those young people who are good, for he says that Ajax, when he distinguished himself in *d* battle, "was rewarded with the long cut off the backbone."[15] And that's an appropriate honor for a courageous young man, since it will both honor him and increase his strength.

That's absolutely right.

Then we'll follow Homer in these matters at least. And insofar as good people have shown themselves to be good, we'll honor them at sacrifices and all such occasions with hymns, "seats of honor, meats, and well-filled cups of wine,"[16] and in all the other ways we mentioned, so that, in addition to honoring *e* good men and women, we'll continue to train them.

That's excellent.

All right. And as for those who died on the campaign, won't we say, first of all, that, if their deaths were distinguished, they belong to the golden race?

That above all.

And won't we believe with Hesiod that, whenever any of that race die, they become

469   Sacred daemons living upon the earth,
        Noble spirits, protectors against evil,
            guardians of articulate mortals?[17]

We'll certainly believe that.

Then we'll inquire from the god what kind of distinguished funeral we should give to daemonic and godlike people, and we'll follow his instructions.

Of course.

And for the remainder of time, we'll care for their graves and worship at them as we would at those of daemons. And we'll follow the same rites for anyone *b* whom we judge to have lived an outstandingly good life, whether he died of old age or in some other way.

That is only just.

Now, what about enemies? How will our soldiers deal with them?

In what respect?

First, enslavement. Do you think it is just for Greeks to enslave Greek cities, or, as far as they can, should they not even allow other cities to do so, and make a habit of sparing the Greek race, as a precaution against being enslaved by the barbarians?   *c*

It's altogether and in every way best to spare the Greek race.

Then isn't it also best for the guardians not to acquire a Greek slave and to advise the other Greeks not to do so either?

Absolutely. In that way they'd be more likely to turn against the barbarians and keep their hands off one another.

What about despoiling the dead? Is it a good thing to strip the dead of anything besides their armor after a victory? Or don't cowards make this an excuse for not facing the enemy—as if they were doing some- *d* thing of vital importance in bending over a corpse? And haven't many armies been lost because of such plundering?

Indeed, they have.

Don't you think it's slavish and money-loving to strip a corpse? Isn't it small-minded and womanish to regard the body as your enemy, when the enemy himself has flitted away, leaving behind only the instrument with which he fought? Or do you think such behavior any different from that of dogs who get angry with the stone that hits them and leave the *e* thrower alone?

It's no different at all.

Then may our soldiers strip corpses or refuse the enemy permission to pick up their dead?

No, by god, they certainly may not.

Moreover, we won't take enemy arms to the temples as offerings, and if we care about the goodwill of other Greeks, we especially won't do this with *their* arms. Rather we'd be afraid of polluting[18] the temples 470 if we brought them such things from our own people, unless, of course, the god tells us otherwise.

That's absolutely right.

What about ravaging the land of the Greeks and

---

15. [*Iliad* 7.321.]

16. [*Iliad* 8.162.]

17. [*Works and Days* 122.]

18. [Greek views on pollution, which is now a foreign concept to us, are discussed in R. Parker, *Miasma* (Oxford: Clarendon Press, 1983).]

burning their houses? Will your soldiers do things of this sort to their enemies?

I'd like to hear *your* opinion about that.

Well, I think they should do neither of these things but destroy the year's harvest only. Do you want me b to tell you why?

Of course.

It seems to me that as we have two names, "war" and "civil war," so there are two things and the names apply to two kinds of disagreements arising in them. The two things I'm referring to are what is one's own and akin, on the one hand, and what's foreign and strange, on the other. The name "civil war" applies to hostilities with one's own, while "war" applies to hostilities with strangers.

That's certainly to the point.

Then see whether this is also to the point: I say c that the Greek race is its own and akin, but is strange and foreign to barbarians.

That's right.

Then when Greeks do battle with barbarians or barbarians with Greeks, we'll say that they're natural enemies and that such hostilities are to be called war. But when Greeks fight with Greeks, we'll say that they are natural friends and that in such circumstances Greece is sick and divided into factions and that such d hostilities are to be called civil war.

I, at any rate, agree to think of it that way.

Now, notice that, wherever something of the sort that's currently called civil war occurs and a city is divided, if either party ravages the land of the others and burns their houses, it's thought that this is abominable and that neither party loves their city, since otherwise they'd never have ravaged their very nurse and mother.[19] However, it *is* thought appropriate for the victors to carry off the harvest of the vanquished. Nonetheless, their attitude of mind should be that of e people who'll one day be reconciled and who won't always be at war.

This way of thinking is far more civilized than the other.

What about the city you're founding? It is Greek, isn't it?

It has to be.

Then, won't your citizens be good and civilized?

Indeed they will.

Then, won't they love Greece? Won't they consider Greece as their own and share the religion of the other Greeks?

Yes, indeed.

Then won't they consider their differences with Greeks—people who are their own—not as war but 471 as civil war?

Of course.

And won't they quarrel like people who know that one day they'll be reconciled?

Certainly.

Then they'll moderate their foes in a friendly spirit, not punish them with enslavement and destruction, for they're moderators, not enemies.

That's right.

And being Greeks, they won't ravage Greece or burn her houses, nor will they agree that in any of her cities all the inhabitants—men, women, and children—are their enemies, but that whatever differences arise are caused by the few enemies that any city inevitably contains. Because of this, because the majority are friendly, they won't ravage the country or destroy the houses, and they'll continue their quarrel only to the point at which those who caused it b are forced to pay the penalty by those who were its innocent victims.

I agree that this is the way our citizens must treat their enemies, and they must treat barbarians the way Greeks currently treat each other.

Then shall we also impose this law on the guardians: Neither ravage the country nor burn the houses? c

Consider it imposed. And let's also assume that this law and its predecessors are all fine. But I think, Socrates, that if we let you go on speaking about this subject, you'll never remember the one you set aside in order to say all this, namely, whether it's possible for this constitution to come into being and in what way it could be brought about. I agree that, if it existed, all the things we've mentioned would be good for the city in which they occurred. And I'll add some that you've left out. The guardians would be excellent fighters against an enemy because they'd be least likely to desert each other, since they know each other as brothers, fathers, and sons, and call each other by those names. Moreover, if their women joined their d campaigns, either in the same ranks or positioned in the rear to frighten the enemy and in case their help

19. [See 414e.]

should ever be needed, I know that this would make them quite unbeatable. And I also see all the good things that they'd have at home that you've omitted.
e Take it that I agree that all these things would happen, as well as innumerable others, if this kind of constitution came into being, and say no more on that subject. But rather let's now try to convince ourselves that it is possible and how it is possible, and let the rest go.

This is a sudden attack that you've made on my
472 argument, and you show no sympathy for my delay. Perhaps you don't realize that, just as I've barely escaped from the first two waves of objections, you're bringing the third—the biggest and most difficult one—down upon me. When you see and hear it, you'll surely be completely sympathetic, and recognize that it was, after all, appropriate for me to hesitate and be afraid to state and look into so paradoxical a view.

The more you speak like that, the less we'll let you off from telling us how it's possible for this constitution
b to come into being. So speak instead of wasting time.

Well, then, we must first remember that we got to this point while trying to discover what justice and injustice are like.

We must. But what of it?

Nothing. But if we discover what justice is like, will we also maintain that the just man is in no way different from the just itself, so that he is like justice in every respect? Or will we be satisfied if he comes
c as close to it as possible and participates in it far more than anyone else?

We'll be satisfied with that.

Then it was in order to have a model that we were trying to discover what justice itself is like and what the completely just man would be like, if he came into being, and what kind of man he'd be if he did, and likewise with regard to injustice and the most unjust man. We thought that, by looking at how their relationship to happiness and its opposite seemed to us, we'd also be compelled to agree about ourselves as well, that the one who was most like them would
d have a portion of happiness most like theirs. But we weren't trying to discover these things in order to prove that it's possible for them to come into being.

That's true.

Do you think that someone is a worse painter if, having painted a model of what the finest and most beautiful human being would be like and having

rendered every detail of his picture adequately, he could not prove that such a man could come into being?

No, by god, I don't.

Then what about our own case? Didn't we say that we were making a theoretical model of a good city?[20] e

Certainly.

So do you think that our discussion will be any less reasonable if we can't prove that it's possible to found a city that's the same as the one in our theory?

Not at all.

Then that's the truth of the matter. But if, in order to please you, I must also be willing to show how and under what conditions it would most be possible to found such a city, then you should agree to make the same concessions to me, in turn, for the purposes of this demonstration.

Which ones?

Is it possible to do anything in practice the same as in theory? Or is it in the nature of practice to grasp truth less well than theory does, even if some people don't think so? Will you first agree to this or not? 473

I agree.

Then don't compel me to show that what we've described in theory can come into being exactly as we've described it. Rather, if we're able to discover how a city could come to be governed in a way that most closely approximates our description, let's say that we've shown what you ordered us to show, namely, that it's possible for our city to come to be. Or wouldn't you be satisfied with that? *I* would be satisfied with it. b

So would I.

Then next, it seems, we should try to discover and point out what's now badly done in cities that keeps them from being governed in that way and what's the smallest change that would enable our city to reach our sort of constitution—one change, if possible, or if not one, two, and if not two, then the fewest in number and the least extensive.

That's absolutely right. c

There is one change we could point to that, in my opinion, would accomplish this. It's certainly neither small nor easy, but it is possible.

What is it?

20. [See 369a–c.]

Well, I've now come to what we likened to the greatest wave. But I shall say what I have to say, even if the wave is a wave of laughter that will simply drown me in ridicule and contempt. So listen to what I'm going to say.

Say on.

Until philosophers rule as kings or those who are now called kings and leading men genuinely and *d* adequately philosophize, that is, until political power and philosophy entirely coincide, while the many natures who at present pursue either one exclusively are forcibly prevented from doing so, cities will have no rest from evils, Glaucon, nor, I think, will the human race. And, until this happens, the constitution we've been describing in theory will never be born *e* to the fullest extent possible or see the light of the sun. It's because I saw how very paradoxical this statement would be that I hesitated to make it for so long, for it's hard to face up to the fact that there can be no happiness, either public or private, in any other city.

Socrates, after hurling a speech and statement like that at us, you must expect that a great many people (and not undistinguished ones either) will cast off their cloaks and, stripped for action, snatch any avail-
474 able weapon, and make a determined rush at you, ready to do terrible things. So, unless you can hold them off by argument and escape, you really will pay the penalty of general derision.

Well, you are the one that brought this on me.

And I was right to do it. However, I won't betray you, but rather defend you in any way I can—by goodwill, by urging you on, and perhaps by being able to give you more appropriate answers than someone else. So, with the promise of this assistance, try to show the unbelievers that things are as you say *b* they are.

I must try it, then, especially since you agree to be so great an ally. If we're to escape from the people you mention, I think we need to define for them who the philosophers are that we dare to say must rule. And once that's clear, we should be able to defend ourselves by showing that the people we mean are fitted by nature both to engage in philosophy and to rule in a city, while the rest are naturally fitted to *c* leave philosophy alone and follow their leader.

This would be a good time to give that definition.

Come, then, follow me, and we'll see whether or not there's some way to set it out adequately.

Lead on.

Do you need to be reminded or do you remember that, if it's rightly said that someone loves something, then he mustn't love one part of it and not another, but he must love all of it?[21]

I think you'll have to remind me, for I don't understand it at all.   *d*

That would be an appropriate response, Glaucon, for somebody else to make. But it isn't appropriate for an erotically inclined man to forget that all boys in the bloom of youth pique the interest of a lover of boys and arouse him and that all seem worthy of his care and pleasure. Or isn't that the way you people behave to fine and beautiful boys? You praise a snub-nosed one as cute, a hook-nosed one you say is regal, one in between is well proportioned, dark ones look manly, and pale ones are children of the gods. And as for a honey-colored boy, do you think that this very *e* term is anything but the euphemistic coinage of a lover who found it easy to tolerate sallowness, provided it was accompanied by the bloom of youth? In a word, you find all kinds of terms and excuses so as not to reject anyone whose flower is in bloom.   *475*

If you insist on taking me as your example of what erotically inclined men do, then, for the sake of the argument, I agree.

Further, don't you see wine-lovers behave in the same way? Don't they love every kind of wine and find any excuse to enjoy it?

Certainly.

And I think you see honor-lovers, if they can't be generals, be captains, and, if they can't be honored by people of importance and dignity, they put up with being honored by insignificant and inferior ones, for they desire the whole of honor.   *b*

Exactly.

Then do you agree to this or not? When we say that someone desires something, do we mean that he desires everything of that kind or that he desires one part of it but not another?

We mean he desires everything.

Then won't we also say that the philosopher doesn't desire one part of wisdom rather than another, but desires the whole thing?

Yes, that's true.

21. [Socrates here seems to be applying the principle he introduced at 438a–b. See 475c.]

And as for the one who's choosy about what he learns, especially if he's young and can't yet give an account of what is useful and what isn't, we won't
c say that he is a lover of learning or a philosopher, for we wouldn't say that someone who's choosy about his food is hungry or has an appetite for food or is a lover of food—instead, we'd say that he is a bad eater.

And we'd be right to say it.

But the one who readily and willingly tries all kinds of learning, who turns gladly to learning and is insatiable for it, is rightly called a philosopher, isn't he?

Then many strange people will be philosophers,
d for the lovers of sights seem to be included, since they take pleasure in learning things. And the lovers of sounds are very strange people to include as philosophers, for they would never willingly attend a serious discussion or spend their time that way, yet they run around to all the Dionysiac festivals, omitting none, whether in cities or villages, as if their ears were under contract to listen to every chorus. Are we to say that these people—and those who learn similar things or petty crafts—are philosophers?
e

No, but they are *like* philosophers.

And who are the true philosophers?

Those who love the sight of truth.

That's right, but what exactly do you mean by it?

It would not be easy to explain to someone else, but I think that you will agree to this.

To what?

Since the beautiful is the opposite of the ugly, they are two.

476 Of course.

And since they are two, each is one?

I grant that also.

And the same account is true of the just and the unjust, the good and the bad, and all the forms. Each of them is itself one, but because they manifest themselves everywhere in association with actions, bodies, and one another, each of them appears to be many.

That's right.

So, I draw this distinction: On one side are those you just now called lovers of sights, lovers of crafts, and practical people; on the other side are those we are arguing about and whom one would alone
b call philosophers.

How do you mean?

The lovers of sights and sounds like beautiful sounds, colors, shapes, and everything fashioned out of them, but their thought is unable to see and embrace the nature of the beautiful itself.

That's for sure.

In fact, there are very few people who would be able to reach the beautiful itself and see it by itself. Isn't that so?

Certainly.   c

What about someone who believes in beautiful things,[22] but doesn't believe in the beautiful itself and isn't able to follow anyone who could lead him to the knowledge of it? Don't you think he is living in a dream rather than a wakened state? Isn't this dreaming: whether asleep or awake, to think that a likeness is not a likeness but rather the thing itself that it is like?

I certainly think that someone who does that is dreaming.

But someone who, to take the opposite case, believes in the beautiful itself, can see both it and the things that participate in it and doesn't believe that the participants are it or that it itself is the participants—is d he living in a dream or is he awake?

He's very much awake.

So we'd be right to call his thought knowledge, since he knows, but we should call the other person's thought opinion, since he opines?

Right.

What if the person who has opinion but not knowledge is angry with us and disputes the truth of what we are saying? Is there some way to console him and e persuade him gently, while hiding from him that he isn't in his right mind?[23]

---

22. [Socrates may be referring here either to particular things that are beautiful or to the various beauties in them, which are properties or universals. The same is true later when Socrates speaks of "the many just things," "the many doubles," and the rest.]

23. [It is important to note that the argument that follows is intended to convince the lovers of sights and crafts that they have opinion rather than knowledge. Since these people are defined as being unable to countenance forms, the argument cannot achieve its purpose if it simply presupposes that there are forms or draws on the theory of forms, for the lovers of sights and crafts will not be convinced by an argument which appeals to something they are unable to accept.]

There must be.

Consider, then, what we'll say to him. Won't we question him like this? First, we'll tell him that nobody begrudges him any knowledge he may have and that we'd be delighted to discover that he knows something. Then we'll say: "Tell us, does the person who knows know something or nothing?" You answer for him.

He knows something.

Something that is or something that is not?[24]

Something that is, for how could something that is not be known?

477

Then we have an adequate grasp of this: No matter how many ways we examine it, what is completely is completely knowable and what is in no way is in every way unknowable?

A most adequate one.

Good. Now, if anything is such as to be and also not to be, won't it be intermediate between what purely is and what in no way is?

Yes, it's intermediate.

Then, as knowledge is set over what is, while ignorance is of necessity set over what is not, mustn't we find an intermediate between knowledge and ignorance to be set over what is intermediate between

b what is and what is not, if there is such a thing?

Certainly.

Do we say that opinion is something?

Of course.

A different power from knowledge or the same?

A different one.

Opinion, then, is set over one thing, and knowledge over another, according to the power of each.

Right.

Now, isn't knowledge by its nature set over what is, to know it as it is? But first maybe we'd better be a bit more explicit.

How so?

Powers are a class of the things that are that enable

c us—or anything else for that matter—to do whatever we are capable of doing. Sight, for example, and

hearing are among the powers, if you understand the kind of thing I'm referring to.

I do.

Here's what I think about them. A power has neither color nor shape nor any feature of the sort that many other things have and that I use to distinguish those things from one another. In the case of a power, I use only what it is set over and what it does, and d by reference to these I call each the power it is: What is set over the same things and does the same I call the same power; what is set over something different and does something different I call a different one. Do you agree?

I do.

Then let's back up. Is knowledge a power, or what class would you put it in?

It's a power, the strongest of them all.

And what about opinion, is it a power or some other kind of thing?   e

It's a power as well, for it is what enables us to opine.

A moment ago you agreed that knowledge and opinion aren't the same.

How could a person with any understanding think that a fallible power is the same as an infallible one?

Right. Then we agree that opinion is clearly different from knowledge.   478

It is different.

Hence each of them is by nature set over something different and does something different?

Necessarily.

Knowledge is set over what is, to know it as it is?

Yes.

And opinion opines?

Yes.

Does it opine the very thing that knowledge knows, so that the knowable and the opinable are the same, or is this impossible?

It's impossible, given what we agreed, for if a different power is set over something different, and opinion and knowledge are different powers, then the know- b able and the opinable cannot be the same.

Then, if what is is knowable, the opinable must be something other than what is?

It must.

Do we, then, opine what is not? Or is it impossible to opine what is not? Think about this. Doesn't someone who opines set his opinion over something? Or is it possible to opine, yet to opine nothing?

24. [Because of the ambiguity of the verb *einai* ("to be"), Socrates could be asking any or all of the following questions: (1) "Something that exists or something that does not exist?" (existential "is"); (2) "Something that is beautiful (say) or something that is not beautiful?" (predicative "is"); (3) "Something that is true or something that is not true?" (veridical "is").]

It's impossible.

But someone who opines opines some one thing?

Yes.

Surely the most accurate word for that which is
c not isn't "one thing" but "nothing"?

Certainly.

But we had to set ignorance over what is not and
knowledge over what is?

That's right.

So someone opines neither what is nor what is not?

How could it be otherwise?

Then opinion is neither ignorance nor knowledge?

So it seems.

Then does it go beyond either of these? Is it clearer
than knowledge or darker than ignorance?

No, neither.

Is opinion, then, darker than knowledge but clearer
than ignorance?

It is.
d   Then it lies between them?

Yes.

So opinion is intermediate between those two?

Absolutely.

Now, we said that, if something could be shown,
as it were, to be and not to be at the same time, it
would be intermediate between what purely is and
what in every way is not, and that neither knowledge
nor ignorance would be set over it, but something
intermediate between ignorance and knowledge?

Correct.

And now the thing we call opinion has emerged
as being intermediate between them?

It has.

Apparently, then, it only remains for us to find
e what participates in both being and not being and
cannot correctly be called purely one or the other,
in order that, if there is such a thing, we can rightly
call it the opinable, thereby setting the extremes over
the extremes and the intermediate over the intermediate. Isn't that so?

It is.

Now that these points have been established, I want
479 to address a question to our friend who doesn't believe
in the beautiful itself or any form of the beautiful
itself that remains always the same in all respects but
who does believe in the many beautiful things—the
lover of sights who wouldn't allow anyone to say that
the beautiful itself is one or that the just is one or

any of the rest: "My dear fellow," we'll say, "of all
the many beautiful things, is there one that will not
also appear ugly? Or is there one of those just things
that will not also appear unjust? Or one of those pious
things that will not also appear impious?"

There isn't one, for it is necessary that they appear
to be beautiful in a way and also to be ugly in a b
way, and the same with the other things you asked
about.

What about the many doubles? Do they appear
any the less halves than doubles?

Not one.

So, with the many bigs and smalls and lights and
heavies, is any one of them any more the thing someone says it is than its opposite?

No, each of them always participates in both opposites.

Is any one of the manys what someone says it is,
then, any more than it is not what he says it is?

No, they are like the ambiguities one is entertained
with at dinner parties or like the children's riddle
about the eunuch who threw something at a bat—
the one about what he threw at it and what it was c
in,[25] for they are ambiguous, and one cannot understand them as fixedly being or fixedly not being or
as both or as neither.

Then do you know how to deal with them? Or can
you find a more appropriate place to put them than
intermediate between being and not being? Surely,
they can't *be* more than what is or *not be* more than
what is not, for apparently nothing is darker than what
is not or clearer than what is.   d

Very true.

We've now discovered, it seems, that according to
the many conventions of the majority of people about
beauty and the others, they[26] are rolling around as

25. [The riddle seems to have been: A man who is not a
man saw and did not see a bird that was not a bird in a
tree (*xulon*) that was not a tree; he hit (*ballō*) and did not
hit it with a stone that was not a stone. The answer is that
a eunuch with bad eyesight saw a bat on a rafter, threw a
pumice stone at it and missed. "He saw a bird" is ambiguous
between "he saw what was actually a bird" and "he saw
what he took to be a bird," *xulon* means both "tree" and
"rafter" or "roof tree," and *ballō* means both "to throw" and
"to hit." The rest is obvious.]

26. [I.e., the many beautiful things, etc.]

intermediates between what is not and what purely is.[27]

We have.

And we agreed earlier that anything of that kind would have to be called the opinable, not the knowable—the wandering intermediate grasped by the intermediate power.

We did.

As for those who study the many beautiful things *e* but do not see the beautiful itself and are incapable of following another who leads them to it, who see many just things but not the just itself, and so with everything—these people, we shall say, opine everything but have no knowledge of anything they opine.

Necessarily.

What about the ones who in each case study the things themselves that are always the same in every respect? Won't we say that they know and don't opine?

That's necessary too.

Shall we say, then, that these people love and em-
480 brace the things that knowledge is set over, as the others do the things that opinion is set over? Remember we said that the latter saw and loved beautiful sounds and colors and the like but wouldn't allow the beautiful itself to be anything?

We remember, all right.

We won't be in error, then, if we call such people lovers of opinion rather than philosophers or lovers of wisdom and knowledge? Will they be angry with us if we call them that?

Not if they take my advice, for it isn't right to be angry with those who speak the truth.

As for those who in each case embrace the thing itself, we must call them philosophers, not lovers of opinion?

Most definitely.

Book VI

484 And so, Glaucon, I said, after a somewhat lengthy and difficult discussion, both the philosophers and the nonphilosophers have revealed who they are.

It probably wouldn't have been easy, he said, to have them do it in a shorter one.

Apparently not. But for my part, I think that the

matter would have been better illuminated if we had only it to discuss and not all the other things that remain to be treated in order to discover the difference between the just life and the unjust one.   *b*

What's our next topic?

What else but the one that's next in order? Since those who are able to grasp what is always the same in all respects are philosophers, while those who are not able to do so and who wander among the many things that vary in every sort of way are not philosophers, which of the two should be the leaders in a city?

What would be a sensible answer to that?

We should establish as guardians those who are clearly capable of guarding the laws and the ways of life of the city.   *c*

That's right.

And isn't it clear that the guardian who is to keep watch over everything should be keen-sighted rather than blind?

Of course it's clear.

Do you think, then, that there's any difference between the blind and those who are really deprived of the knowledge of each thing that is? The latter have no clear model in their souls, and so they cannot—in the manner of painters—look to what is most true, make constant reference to it, and study it as exactly as possible. Hence they cannot establish here on earth *d* conventions about what is fine or just or good, when they need to be established, or guard and preserve them, once they have been established.

No, by god, there isn't much difference between them.

Should we, then, make these blind people our guardians or rather those who know each thing that is and who are not inferior to the others, either in experience or in any other part of virtue?

It would be absurd to choose anyone but philosophers, if indeed they're not inferior in these ways, for the respect in which they are superior is pretty well the most important one.

Then shouldn't we explain how it is possible for someone to have both these sorts of qualities?   *485*

Certainly.

Then, as we said at the beginning of this discussion, it is necessary to understand the nature of philosophers first,[1] for I think that, if we can reach adequate

---

27. [See 484c–d, 493a ff.]

1. [See 474b–c.—C.D.C.R.]

agreement about that, we'll also agree that the same people *can* have both qualities and that no one but they should be leaders in cities.

How so?

Let's agree that philosophic natures always love the sort of learning that makes clear to them some feature b of the being that always is and does not wander around between coming to be and decaying.

And further, let's agree that, like the honor-lovers and erotically inclined men we described before,[2] they love all such learning and are not willing to give up any part of it, whether large or small, more valuable or less so.

That's right.

Consider next whether the people we're describing c must also have this in their nature.

What?

They must be without falsehood—they must refuse to accept what is false, hate it, and have a love for the truth.

That's a reasonable addition, at any rate.

It's not only reasonable, it's entirely necessary, for it's necessary for a man who is erotically inclined by nature to love everything akin to or belonging to the boy he loves.

That's right.

And could you find anything that belongs more to wisdom than truth does?

Of course not.

Then is it possible for the same nature to be a d philosopher—a lover of wisdom—and a lover of falsehood?

Not at all.

Then someone who loves learning must above all strive for every kind of truth from childhood on.

Absolutely.

Now, we surely know that, when someone's desires incline strongly for one thing, they are thereby weakened for others, just like a stream that has been partly diverted into another channel.

Of course.

Then, when someone's desires flow towards learning and everything of that sort, he'd be concerned, I suppose, with the pleasures of the soul itself by itself, and he'd abandon those pleasures that come through

the body—if indeed he is a true philosopher and not merely a counterfeit one.

That's completely necessary.   e

Then surely such a person is moderate and not at all a money-lover. It's appropriate for others to take seriously the things for which money and large expenditures are needed, but not for him.

That's right.

And of course there's also this to consider when you are judging whether a nature is philosophic or not. 486

What's that?

If it is at all slavish, you should not overlook that fact, for pettiness is altogether incompatible with a soul that is always reaching out to grasp everything both divine and human as a whole.

That's completely true.

And will a thinker high-minded enough to study all time and all being consider human life to be something important?

He couldn't possibly.

Then will he consider death to be a terrible thing? b

He least of all.

Then it seems a cowardly and slavish nature will take no part in true philosophy.

Not in my opinion.

And is there any way that an orderly person, who isn't money-loving, slavish, a boaster, or a coward, could become unreliable or unjust?

There isn't.

Moreover, when you are looking to see whether a soul is philosophic or not, you'll look to see whether it is just and gentle, from youth on, or savage and hard to associate with.

Certainly.

And here's something I think you won't leave out. c

What?

Whether he's a slow learner or a fast one. Or do you ever expect anyone to love something when it pains him to do it and when much effort brings only small return?

No, it couldn't happen.

And what if he could retain nothing of what he learned, because he was full of forgetfulness? Could he fail to be empty of knowledge?

How could he?

Then don't you think that, if he's laboring in vain, he'd inevitably come to hate both himself and that activity in the end?

2. [See 474c–475c.]

Of course.

Then let's never include a forgetful soul among those who are sufficiently philosophical for our pur-
d poses, but look for one with a good memory.

Absolutely.

Now, we'd certainly say that the unmusical and graceless element in a person's nature draws him to lack of due measure.

Of course.

And do you think that truth is akin to what lacks due measure or to what is measured?

To what is measured.

Then, in addition to those other things, let's look for someone whose thought is by nature measured and graceful and is easily led to the form of each thing that is.

Of course.

Well, then, don't you think the properties we've enumerated are compatible with one another and
e that each is necessary to a soul that is to have an adequate and complete grasp of that which is?

487   They're all completely necessary.

Is there any objection you can find, then, to a way of life that no one can adequately follow unless he's by nature good at remembering, quick to learn, high-minded, graceful, and a friend and relative of truth, justice, courage, and moderation?

Not even Momus[3] could find one.

When such people have reached maturity in age and education, wouldn't you entrust the city to them and to them alone?

And Adeimantus replied: No one would be able to contradict the things you've said, Socrates, but on each occasion that you say them, your hearers are
b affected in some such way as this. They think that, because they're inexperienced in asking and answering questions, they're led astray a little bit by the argument at every question and that, when these little bits are added together at the end of the discussion, great is their fall, as the opposite of what they said at the outset comes to light. Just as inexperienced checkers players are trapped by the experts in the end
c and can't make a move, so they too are trapped in the end and have nothing to say in this different kind of checkers, which is played not with disks but with

words. Yet the truth isn't affected by this outcome. I say this with a view to the present case, for someone might well say now that he's unable to oppose you as you ask each of your questions, yet he sees that of all those who take up philosophy—not those who merely dabble in it while still young in order to complete their upbringing and then drop it, but those who continue in it for a longer time—the greatest d number become cranks, not to say completely vicious, while those who seem completely decent are rendered useless to the city because of the studies you recommend.

When I'd heard him out, I said: Do you think that what these people say is false?

I don't know, but I'd be glad to hear what you think.

You'd hear that they seem to me to speak the truth.

How, then, can it be true to say that there will be no end to evils in our cities until philosophers— e people we agree to be useless—rule in them?

The question you ask needs to be answered by means of an image or simile.

And you, of course, aren't used to speaking in similes!

So! Are you making fun of me now that you've landed me with a claim that's so hard to establish? In any case, listen to my simile, and you'll appreciate all the more how greedy for images I am. What the 488 most decent people experience in relation to their city is so hard to bear that there's no other single experience like it. Hence to find an image of it and a defense for them, I must construct it from many sources, just as painters paint goat-stags by combining the features of different things. Imagine, then, that something like the following happens on a ship or on many ships. The shipowner is bigger and stronger than everyone else on board, but he's hard of hearing, a bit short-sighted, and his knowledge of seafaring is b equally deficient. The sailors are quarreling with one another about steering the ship, each of them thinking that he should be the captain, even though he's never learned the art of navigation, cannot point to anyone who taught it to him, or to a time when he learned it. Indeed, they claim that it isn't teachable and are ready to cut to pieces anyone who says that it is. They're always crowding around the shipowner, begging him and doing everything possible to get him to turn the rudder over to them. And sometimes, if c they don't succeed in persuading him, they execute

3. [Momus is a personification of blame or censure.]

the ones who do succeed or throw them overboard, and then, having stupefied their noble shipowner with drugs, wine, or in some other way, they rule the ship, using up what's in it and sailing in the way that people like that are prone to do. Moreover, they call the person who is clever at persuading or forcing the shipowner to let them rule a "navigator," a "captain,"

d and "one who knows ships," and dismiss anyone else as useless. They don't understand that a true captain must pay attention to the seasons of the year, the sky, the stars, the winds, and all that pertains to his craft, if he's really to be the ruler of a ship. And they don't believe there is any craft that would enable him to determine how he should steer the ship, whether

e the others want him to or not, or any possibility of mastering this alleged craft or of practicing it at the same time as the craft of navigation. Don't you think that the true captain will be called a real stargazer, a babbler, and a good-for-nothing by those who sail in ships governed in that way, in which such

489 things happen?

I certainly do.

I don't think that you need to examine the simile in detail to see that the ships resemble cities and their attitude to the true philosophers, but you already understand what I mean.

Indeed, I do.

Then first tell this simile to anyone who wonders why philosophers aren't honored in the cities, and try to persuade him that there would be far more

b cause for wonder if they were honored.

I will tell him.

Next tell him that what he says is true, that the best among the philosophers are useless to the majority. Tell him not to blame those decent people for this but the ones who don't make use of them. It isn't natural for the captain to beg the sailors to be ruled by him nor for the wise to knock at the doors of the rich—the man who came up with that wisecrack made a mistake.[4] The natural thing is for the sick person, rich or poor, to knock at the doctor's door,

c and for anyone who needs to be ruled to knock at the door of the one who can rule him. It isn't for the

ruler, if he's truly any use, to beg the others to accept his rule. Tell him that he'll make no mistake in likening those who rule in our cities at present to the sailors we mentioned just now, and those who are called useless stargazers to the true captains.

That's absolutely right.

Therefore, it isn't easy for the best ways of life to be highly esteemed by people who, as in these circumstances, follow the opposite ways. By far the greatest and most serious slander on philosophy, how-ever, results from those who profess to follow the

d philosophic way of life. I mean those of whom the prosecutor of philosophy declared that the greatest number are completely vicious and the most decent useless. And I admitted that what he said was true, didn't I?

Yes.

And haven't we explained why the decent ones are useless?

Yes, indeed.

Then, do you next want us to discuss why it's inevitable that the greater number are vicious and to try to show, if we can, that philosophy isn't responsible for this either?

e

Certainly.

Then, let's begin our dialogue by reminding our-selves of the point at which we began to discuss the nature that someone must have if he is to become a fine and good person. First of all, if you remember,

490 he had to be guided by the truth and always pursue it in every way, or else he'd really be a boaster, with no share at all in true philosophy.

That's what was said.

And isn't this view completely contrary to the opin-ions currently held about him?

It certainly is.

Then, won't it be reasonable for us to plead in his defense that it is the nature of the real lover of learning to struggle toward what is, not to remain with any of the many things that are believed to be, that, as he moves on, he neither loses nor lessens his erotic love

b until he grasps the being[5] of each nature itself with the part of his soul that is fitted to grasp it, because of its kinship with it, and that, once getting near what really is and having intercourse with it and having

4. [Aristotle, *Rhetoric* 1391a7–12, says that it was Simon-ides who, when asked whether it was better to be rich or wise, replied: "Rich—because the wise spend their time at the doors of the rich."]

5. [See 507b for an explanation of what "the being" (*ho estin*) of something is.]

begotten understanding and truth, he knows, truly
lives, is nourished, and—at that point, but not before—is relieved from the pains of giving birth?

That is the most reasonable defense possible.

Well, then, will such a person have any part in the
love of falsehood, or will he entirely hate it?

c   He'll hate it.

And if truth led the way, we'd never say, I suppose,
that a chorus of evils could ever follow in its train.

How could it?

But rather a healthy and just character, with moderation following it.

That's right.

What need is there, then, to marshal all over again
from the beginning the members of the philosophic
nature's chorus in their inevitable array? Remember
that courage, high-mindedness, ease in learning, and
a good memory all belong to it. Then you objected,
saying that anyone would be compelled to agree with
d   what we said, but that, if he abandoned the argument
and looked at the very people the argument is about,
he'd say that some of them were useless, while the
majority had every kind of vice. So we examined the
reason for this slander and have now arrived at the
point of explaining why the majority of them are bad.
And it's for this reason that we've again taken up the
nature of the true philosophers and defined what it
necessarily has to be.

e   That's true.

We must now look at the ways in which this nature
is corrupted, how it's destroyed in many people, while
a small number (the ones that are called useless rather
than bad) escape. After that, we must look in turn at
the natures of the souls that imitate the philosophic
nature and establish themselves in its way of life, so
491 as to see what the people are like who thereby arrive
at a way of life they are unworthy of and that is beyond
them and who, because they often strike false notes,
bring upon philosophy the reputation that you said
it has with everyone everywhere.

In what ways are they corrupted?

I'll try to enumerate them for you if I can. I suppose
that everyone would agree that only a few natures
possess all the qualities that we just now said were
essential to becoming a complete philosopher and
that seldom occur naturally among human beings.
b   Or don't you think so?

I certainly do.

Consider, then, the many important ways in which
these few can be corrupted.

What are they?

What will surprise you most, when you hear it, is
that each of the things we praised in that nature tends
to corrupt the soul that has it and to drag it away
from philosophy. I mean courage, moderation, and
the other things we mentioned.

That does sound strange.

Furthermore, all the things that are said to be good
also corrupt it and drag it away—beauty, wealth, phys- c
ical strength, relatives who are powerful in the city,
and all that goes with these. You understand what I
have in mind?

I do, and I'd be glad to learn even more about it.

If you correctly grasp the general point I'm after,
it will be clear to you, and what I've said before won't
seem so strange.

What do you want me to do?

We know that the more vigorous any seed, developing plant, or animal is, the more it is deficient in the d
things that are appropriate for it to have when it is
deprived of suitable food, season, or location.

For the bad is more opposed to the good than is
the merely not good.

Of course.

Then it's reasonable to say that the best nature fares
worse, when unsuitably nurtured, than an ordinary
one.

It is.

Then won't we say the same thing about souls too,
Adeimantus, that those with the best natures become e
outstandingly bad when they receive a bad upbringing? Or do you think that great injustices and pure
wickedness originate in an ordinary nature rather than
in a vigorous one that has been corrupted by its upbringing? Or that a weak nature is ever the cause of
either great good or great evil?

No, you're right.

Now, I think that the philosophic nature as we
defined it will inevitably grow to possess every virtue 492
if it happens to receive appropriate instruction, but
if it is sown, planted, and grown in an inappropriate
environment, it will develop in quite the opposite
way, unless some god happens to come to its rescue.
Or do you agree with the general opinion that certain
young people are actually corrupted by sophists—that
there are certain sophists with significant influence on

the young who corrupt them through private teaching? Isn't it rather the very people who say this who are the greatest sophists of all, since they educate most completely, turning young and old, men and *b* women, into precisely the kind of people they want them to be?

When do they do that?

When many of them are sitting together in assemblies, courts, theaters, army camps, or in some other public gathering of the crowd, they object very loudly and excessively to some of the things that are said or done and approve others in the same way, shouting and clapping, so that the very rocks and surroundings *c* echo the din of their praise or blame and double it. In circumstances like that, what is the effect, as they say, on a young person's heart? What private training can hold out and not be swept away by that kind of praise or blame and be carried by the flood wherever it goes, so that he'll say that the same things are beautiful or ugly as the crowd does, follow the same way of life as they do, and be the same sort of person as they are?

He will be under great compulsion to do so, Soc-*d* rates.

And yet we haven't mentioned the greatest compulsion of all.

What's that?

It's what these educators and sophists impose by their actions if their words fail to persuade. Or don't you know that they punish anyone who isn't persuaded, with disenfranchisement, fines, or death?

They most certainly do.

What other sophist, then, or what private conversations do you think will prevail in opposition to these?

e I don't suppose that any will.

No, indeed, it would be very foolish even to try to oppose them, for there isn't now, hasn't been in the past, nor ever will be in the future anyone with a character so unusual that he has been educated to virtue in spite of the contrary education he received from the mob—I mean, a human character; the divine, as the saying goes, is an exception to the rule. You should realize that if anyone is saved and becomes what he ought to be under our present constitu-*493* tions, he has been saved—you might rightly say—by a divine dispensation.

I agree.

Well, then, you should also agree to this.

What?

Not one of those paid private teachers, whom the people call sophists and consider to be their rivals in craft,[6] teaches anything other than the convictions that the majority express when they are gathered together. Indeed, these are precisely what the sophists call wisdom. It's as if someone were learning the moods and appetites of a huge, strong beast that he's rearing—how to approach and handle it, when it is *b* most difficult to deal with or most gentle and what makes it so, what sounds it utters in either condition, and what sounds soothe or anger it. Having learned all this through tending the beast over a period of time, he calls this knack wisdom, gathers his information together as if it were a craft,[7] and starts to teach it. In truth, he knows nothing about which of these convictions is fine or shameful, good or bad, just or unjust, but he applies all these names in accordance with how the beast reacts—calling what it enjoys good *c* and what angers it bad. He has no other account to give of these terms. And he calls what he is compelled to do just and fine, for he hasn't seen and cannot show anyone else how much compulsion and goodness really differ. Don't you think, by god, that someone like that is a strange educator?

I do indeed.

Then does this person seem any different from the one who believes that it is wisdom to understand the moods and pleasures of a majority gathered from all *d* quarters, whether they concern painting, music, or, for that matter, politics? If anyone approaches the majority to exhibit his poetry or some other piece of craftsmanship or his service to the city and gives them mastery over him to any degree beyond what's unavoidable, he'll be under Diomedean compulsion,[8]

6. [The craft in question is presumably that of teaching virtue.]

7. [See 332c n. 10. The distinction between a craft (*technē*) and a knack (*tribē, empeiria*) is explained in the *Gorgias* 462b ff.]

8. [The origin of the phrase is uncertain but a likely source is in the following story. Odysseus attempted to kill Diomedes when the two were returning from Troy to the Greek camp, but failed. Diomedes punished him by tying his arms together and driving him home with blows from the flat of his sword. But, whatever the source, the phrase refers to inescapable compulsion.]

as it's called, to do the sort of thing of which they approve. But have you ever heard anyone presenting an argument that such things are truly good and beautiful that wasn't absolutely ridiculous?

e   No, and I don't expect ever to hear one.

Keeping all this in mind, recall the following question: Can the majority in any way tolerate or accept the reality of the beautiful itself, as opposed to the many beautiful things, or the reality of each thing 494 itself, as opposed to the corresponding many?

Not in any way.

Then the majority cannot be philosophic.

They cannot.

Hence they inevitably disapprove of those who practice philosophy?

Inevitably.

And so do all those private individuals who associate with the majority and try to please them.

Clearly.

Then, because of all that, do you see any salvation for someone who is by nature a philosopher, to insure that he'll practice philosophy correctly to the end? Think about what we've said before. We agreed that b ease in learning, a good memory, courage, and high-mindedness belong to the philosophic nature.

Yes.

And won't someone with a nature like that be first among the children in everything, especially if his body has a nature that matches that of his soul?

How could he not be?

Then I suppose that, as he gets older, his family and fellow citizens will want to make use of him in connection with their own affairs.

Of course.

Therefore they'll pay court to him with their re-c quests and honors, trying by their flattery to secure for themselves ahead of time the power that is going to be his.

That's what usually happens, at any rate.

What do you think someone like that will do in such circumstances, especially if he happens to be from a great city, in which he's rich, well-born, good-looking, and tall? Won't he be filled with impractical expectations and think himself capable of managing the affairs, not only of the Greeks, but of the barbarians as well? And as a result, won't he exalt himself to great heights and be brimming

with pretension and pride that is empty and lacks d understanding?[9]

He certainly will.

And if someone approaches a young man in that condition and gently tells him the truth, namely, that that there's no understanding in him, that he needs it, and that it can't be acquired unless he works like a slave to attain it, do you think that it will be easy for him to listen when he's in the midst of so many evils?

Far from it.

And even if a young man of that sort somehow sees the point and is guided and drawn to philosophy because of his noble nature and his kinship with e reason, what do you think those people will do, if they believe that they're losing their use of him and his companionship? Is there anything they won't do or say to him to prevent him from being persuaded? Or anything they won't do or say about his persuader—whether plotting against him in private or publicly bringing him into court—to prevent him from such persuasion?

There certainly isn't.   495

Then, is there any chance that such a person will practice philosophy?

None at all.

Do you see, then, that we weren't wrong to say that, when someone with a philosophic nature is badly brought up, the very components of his nature—together with the other so-called goods, such as wealth and other similar advantages—are themselves in a way the cause of his falling away from the philosophic way of life?

I do, and what we said was right.

These, then, are the many ways in which the best nature—which is already rare enough, as we said—is destroyed and corrupted, so that it cannot follow the best way of life. And it is among these men that b we find the ones who do the greatest evils to cities and individuals and also—if they happen to be swept that way by the current[10]—the greatest good, for a

9. [It is widely believed that Plato has Alcibiades in mind here and in what follows. See Plato, *Symposium* 215d–216d. Alcibiades' extraordinary career is described in Thucydides, Books 6–8.]

10. [See 485d.]

petty nature will never do anything great, either to an individual or a city.

That's very true.

When these men, for whom philosophy is most *c* appropriate, fall away from her, they leave her desolate and unwed, and they themselves lead lives that are inappropriate and untrue. Then others, who are unworthy of her, come to her as to an orphan deprived of the protection of kinsmen and disgrace her. These are the ones who are responsible for the reproaches that you say are cast upon philosophy by those who revile her, namely, that some of those who consort with her are useless, while the majority deserve to suffer many bad things.

Yes, that is indeed what is said.

And it's a reasonable thing to say, for other little men—the ones who are most sophisticated at their own little crafts—seeing that this position, which is full of fine names and adornments, is vacated, leap *d* gladly from those little crafts to philosophy, like prisoners escaping from jail who take refuge in a temple. Despite her present poor state, philosophy is still more high-minded than these other crafts, so that many people with defective natures desire to possess her, even though their souls are cramped and spoiled by the mechanical nature of their work, in just the way that their bodies are mutilated by their crafts and *e* labors. Isn't that inevitable?

It certainly is.

Don't you think that a man of this sort looks exactly like a little bald-headed tinker who has come into some money and, having been just released from jail, has taken a bath, put on a new cloak, got himself up as a bridegroom, and is about to marry the boss's daughter because she is poor and abandoned?

496   They're exactly the same.

And what kind of children will that marriage produce? Won't they be illegitimate and inferior?

They have to be.

What about when men who are unworthy of education approach philosophy and consort with her unworthily? What kinds of thoughts and opinions are we to say they beget? Won't they truly be what are properly called sophisms, things that have nothing genuine about them or worthy of being called true wisdom?

That's absolutely right.

Then there remains, Adeimantus, only a very small group who consort with philosophy in a way that's worthy of her: A noble and well brought-up character, for example, kept down by exile, who remains with philosophy according to his nature because there is *b* no one to corrupt him, or a great soul living in a small city, who disdains the city's affairs and looks beyond them. A very few might be drawn to philosophy from other crafts that they rightly despise because they have good natures. And some might be held back by the bridle that restrains our friend Theages[11]—for he's in every way qualified to be tempted away from philosophy, but his physical illness restrains him by keeping him out of politics. Finally, my own case *c* is hardly worth mentioning—my daemonic sign[12]— because it has happened to no one before me, or to only a very few. Now, the members of this small group have tasted how sweet and blessed a possession philosophy is, and at the same time they've also seen the madness of the majority and realized, in a word, that hardly anyone acts sanely in public affairs and that there is no ally with whom they might go to the aid of justice and survive, that instead they'd perish before they could profit either their city or their *d* friends and be useless both to themselves and to others, just like a man who has fallen among wild animals and is neither willing to join them in doing injustice nor sufficiently strong to oppose the general savagery alone. Taking all this into account, they lead a quiet life and do their own work. Thus, like someone who takes refuge under a little wall from a storm of dust or hail driven by the wind, the philosopher—seeing others filled with lawlessness—is satisfied if he can somehow lead his present life free from injustice and impious acts and depart from it with good hope, blameless and content.   *e*

Well, that's no small thing for him to have accomplished before departing.   497

But it isn't the greatest either, since he didn't chance upon a constitution that suits him. Under a

---

11. [Theages figures in a Platonic dialogue named after him, which discusses the relationship between politics and philosophy. However, this dialogue is judged by many scholars to be of doubtful authenticity.]

12. [See Plato, *Apology* 31c–32a, where Socrates explains that his *daimonion* has kept him out of politics.]

suitable one, his own growth will be fuller, and he'll save the community as well as himself. It seems to me that we've now sensibly discussed the reasons why philosophy is slandered and why the slanderer is unjust—unless, of course, you have something to add.

I have nothing to add on that point. But which of our present constitutions do you think is suitable for philosophers?

None of them. That's exactly my complaint: None *b* of our present constitutions is worthy of the philosophic nature, and, as a result, this nature is perverted and altered, for, just as a foreign seed, sown in alien ground, is likely to be overcome by the native species and to fade away among them, so the philosophic nature fails to develop its full power and declines into *c* a different character. But if it were to find the best constitution, as it is itself the best, it would be clear that it is really divine and that other natures and ways of life are merely human. Obviously you're going to ask next what the best constitution is.

You're wrong there; I wasn't going to ask that, but whether it was the constitution we described when we were founding our city or some other one.

In the other respects, it is that one. But we said even then that there must always be some people in the city who have a theory of the constitution, the same one that guided you, the lawgiver, when you *d* made the laws.

We did say that.

Yes, but we didn't emphasize it sufficiently, for fear of what your objections have made plain, namely, that its proof would be long and difficult. And indeed what remains is by no means easy to go through.

What's that?

How a city can engage in philosophy without being destroyed, for all great things are prone to fall, and, as the saying goes, fine things are really hard to achieve.[13]

Nevertheless, to complete our discussion, we'll *e* have to get clear about this.

If anything prevents us from doing it, it won't be lack of willingness but lack of ability. At least you'll see how willing *I* am, for notice again how enthusiastically and recklessly I say that the manner in which a city ought to take up the philosophic way of life is the opposite of what it does at present.

13. [See Plato, *Hippias Major* 304b ff.]

How?

At present, those who study philosophy do so as young men who have just left childhood behind and have yet to take up household management and money-making. But just when they reach the hardest *498* part—I mean the part that has to do with giving a rational account—they abandon it and are regarded as fully trained in philosophy. In later life, they think they're doing well if they are willing to be in an invited audience when others are doing philosophy, for they think they should do this only as a sideline. And, with a few exceptions, by the time they reach old age, their eagerness for philosophy is quenched more thoroughly than the sun of Heraclitus, which is never rekindled.[14]   *b*

What should they do?

Entirely the opposite. As youths and children, they should put their minds to youthful education and philosophy and take care of their bodies at a time when they are growing into manhood, so as to acquire a helper for philosophy. As they grow older and their souls begin to reach maturity, they should increase their mental exercises. Then, when their strength begins to fail and they have retired from politics and military service, they should graze freely in the pastures of philosophy and do nothing else—I mean the ones who are to live happily and, in death, add a *c* fitting destiny in that other place to the life they have lived.

You seem to be speaking with true enthusiasm, Socrates. But I'm sure that most of your hearers, beginning with Thrasymachus, will oppose you with even greater enthusiasm and not be at all convinced.

Don't slander Thrasymachus and me just as we've become friends—not that we were enemies before. We won't relax our efforts until we either convince *d* him and the others or, at any rate, do something that may benefit them in a later incarnation, when, reborn, they happen upon these arguments again.

That's a short time you're talking about!

It's nothing compared to the whole of time. All the same, it's no wonder that the majority of people aren't convinced by our arguments, for they've never

14. [Aristotle (*Meteorologica* 355a14) reports Heraclitus as believing that "the sun is new every day." Hence the sun not only sets or is quenched at night, it actually ceases to exist, being replaced by a totally new sun the next morning.]

seen a *man* that fits our *plan* (and the rhymes of this sort they have heard are usually intended and not, like this one, the product of mere chance).[15] That is
e to say, they've never seen a man or a number of men who themselves rhymed with virtue, were assimilated to it as far as possible, and ruled in a city of the same
499 type. Or do you think they have?

I don't think so at all.

Nor have they listened sufficiently to fine and free arguments that search out the truth in every way for the sake of knowledge but that keep away from the sophistications and eristic quibbles that, both in public trials and in private gatherings, aim at nothing except reputation and disputation.

No, they haven't.

It was because of this, because we foresaw these difficulties, that we were afraid. Nonetheless, we were
b compelled by the truth to say that no city, constitution, or individual man will ever become perfect until either some chance event compels those few philosophers who aren't vicious (the ones who are now called useless) to take charge of a city, whether they want to or not, and compels the city to obey them, or until a god inspires the present rulers and kings or their offspring with a true erotic love for true philosophy. Now, it cannot be reasonably maintained, in my view,
c that either of these things is impossible, but if it could, we'd be justly ridiculed for indulging in wishful thinking. Isn't that so?

It is.

Then, if in the limitless past, those who were foremost in philosophy were forced to take charge of a city or if this is happening now in some foreign place far beyond our ken or if it will happen in the future,
d we are prepared to maintain our argument that, at whatever time the muse of philosophy controls a city, the constitution we've described will also exist at that time, whether it is past, present, or future. Since it is not impossible for this to happen, we are not speaking of impossibilities. That it is *difficult* for it to happen, however, we agree ourselves.

That's my opinion, anyway.

15. [Plato is mocking the rhetoricians, who were overfond of rhyme. Hence his own words, *ou gar pōpote eidon genomenon to nun legomenon*, which mean "they've never seen anything come into being which matches our account," exhibit the phenomenon he is mocking.]

But the majority don't share your opinion—is that what you are going to say?

They probably don't.

You should not make such wholesale charges against the majority, for they'll no doubt come to a different opinion, if instead of indulging your love of *e* victory at their expense, you soothe them and try to remove their slanderous prejudice against the love of learning, by pointing out what you mean by a philosopher and by defining the philosophic nature and way of life, as we did just now, so that they'll 500 realize that you don't mean the same people as they do. And if they once see it your way, even you will say that they'll have a different opinion from the one you just attributed to them and will answer differently. Or do you think that anyone who is gentle and without malice is harsh with someone who is neither irritable nor malicious? I'll anticipate your answer and say that a few people may have such a harsh character, but not the majority.

And, of course, I agree.

Then don't you also agree that the harshness the majority exhibit towards philosophy is caused by those *b* outsiders who don't belong and who've burst in like a band of revellers, always abusing one another, indulging their love of quarrels, and arguing about human beings in a way that is wholly inappropriate to philosophy?

I do indeed.

No one whose thoughts are truly directed towards the things that are, Adeimantus, has the leisure to look down at human affairs or to be filled with envy and hatred by competing with people. Instead, as he looks at and studies things that are organized and *c* always the same, that neither do injustice to one another nor suffer it, being all in a rational order, he imitates them and tries to become as like them as he can. Or do you think that someone can consort with things he admires without imitating them?

I do not. It's impossible.

Then the philosopher, by consorting with what is ordered and divine and despite all the slanders around that say otherwise, himself becomes as divine and ordered as a human being can.   *d*

That's absolutely true.

And if he should come to be compelled to put what he sees there into people's characters, whether into a single person or into a populace, instead of shaping only his own, do you think that he will be a poor craftsman of moderation, justice, and the whole of popular virtue?

He least of all.

And when the majority realize that what we are saying about the philosopher is true, will they be harsh with him or mistrust us when we say that the e city will never find happiness until its outline is sketched by painters who use the divine model?

They won't be harsh, if indeed they realize this. 501 But what sort of sketch do you mean?

They'd take the city and the characters of human beings as their sketching slate, but first they'd wipe it clean—which isn't at all an easy thing to do. And you should know that this is the plain difference between them and others, namely, that they refuse to take either an individual or a city in hand or to write laws, unless they receive a clean slate or are allowed to clean it themselves.

And they'd be right to refuse.

Then don't you think they'd next sketch the outline of the constitution?

Of course.

And I suppose that, as they work, they'd look often b in each direction, towards the natures of justice, beauty, moderation,[16] and the like, on the one hand, and towards those they're trying to put into human beings, on the other. And in this way they'd mix and blend the various ways of life in the city until they produced a human image based on what Homer too called "the divine form and image" when it occurred among human beings.[17]

That's right.

They'd erase one thing, I suppose, and draw in another until they'd made characters for human be-c ings that the gods would love as much as possible.

At any rate, that would certainly result in the finest sketch.

Then is this at all persuasive to those you said were straining to attack us—that the person we were praising is really a painter of constitutions? They were angry because we entrusted the city to him: Are they

any calmer, now that they've heard what we had to say?

They'll be much calmer, if they have any moderation.

Indeed, how could they possibly dispute it? Will they deny that philosophers are lovers of what is or d of the truth?

That would be absurd.

Or that their nature as we've described it is close to the best?

They can't deny that either.

Or that such a nature, if it follows its own way of life, isn't as completely good and philosophic as any other? Or that the people we excluded are more so?

Certainly not.   e

Then will they still be angry when we say that, until philosophers take control of a city, there'll be no respite from evil for either city or citizens, and the constitution we've been describing in theory will never be completed in practice?

They'll probably be less angry.

Then if it's all right with you, let's not say that they'll simply be less angry but that they'll become altogether gentle and persuaded, so that they'll be shamed into agreeing with us, if nothing else.   502

It's all right with me.

Let's assume, therefore, that they've been convinced on this point. Will anyone dispute our view that the offspring of kings or rulers could be born with philosophic natures?

No one would do that.

Could anyone claim that, if such offspring are born, they'll inevitably be corrupted? We agree ourselves that it's hard for them to be saved from corruption, but could anyone claim that in the whole of time not one of them could be saved?   b

How could he?

But surely one such individual would be sufficient to bring to completion all the things that now seem so incredible, provided that his city obeys him.

One would be sufficient.

If a ruler established the laws and ways of life we've described, it is surely not impossible that the citizens would be willing to carry them out.

Not at all.

And would it be either astonishing or impossible that others should think as we do?

I don't suppose it would.   c

---

16. [That is, the forms of justice, beauty, and moderation. See 476b, *Phaedo* 103b, *Parmenides* 132d, *Cratylus* 389a–390a.]

17. [See, for example, *Iliad* 1.131.]

But I think our earlier discussion was sufficient to show that these arrangements are best, if only they are possible.

Indeed it was.

Then we can now conclude that this legislation is best, if only it is possible, and that, while it is hard for it to come about, it is not impossible.

We can.

Now that this difficulty has been disposed of, we must deal with what remains, namely, how the saviors of our constitution will come to be in the city, what subjects and ways of life will cause them to come into *d* being, and at what ages they'll take each of them up.

Indeed we must.

It wasn't very clever of me to omit from our earlier discussion the troublesome topics of acquiring wives, begetting children, and appointing rulers, just because I knew that the whole truth would provoke resentment and would be hard to bring about in practice, for as it turned out, I had to go through these matters anyway. The subject of women and children has been adequately dealt with, but that of *e* the rulers has to be taken up again from the beginning. We said, if you remember, that they must show themselves to be lovers of their city when tested by pleasure *503* and pain and that they must hold on to their resolve through labors, fears, and all other adversities. Anyone who was incapable of doing so was to be rejected, while anyone who came through unchanged—like gold tested in a fire—was to be made ruler and receive prizes both while he lived and after his death. These were the sort of things we were saying while our argument, afraid of stirring up the very problems that *b* now confront us, veiled its face and slipped by.

That's very true; I do remember it.

We hesitated to say the things we've now dared to say anyway. So let's now also dare to say that those who are to be made our guardians in the most exact sense of the term must be philosophers.

Let's do it.

Then you should understand that there will probably be only a few of them, for they have to have the nature we described, and its parts mostly grow in separation and are rarely found in the same person.

c   What do you mean?

You know that ease of learning, good memory, quick wits, smartness, youthful passion, high-mindedness, and all the other things that go along with these

are rarely willing to grow together in a mind that will choose an orderly life that is quiet and completely stable, for the people who possess the former traits are carried by their quick wits wherever chance leads them and have no stability at all.

That's true.

On the other hand, people with stable characters, who don't change easily, who aren't easily frightened in battle, and whom one would employ because of their greater reliability, exhibit similar traits when it *d* comes to learning: They are as hard to move and teach as people whose brains have become numb, and they are filled with sleep and yawning whenever they have to learn anything.

That's so.

Yet we say that someone must have a fine and goodly share of both characters, or he won't receive the truest education, honors, or rule.

That's right.

Then, don't you think that such people will be rare?

Of course.

Therefore they must be tested in the labors, fears, and pleasures we mentioned previously. But they *e* must also be exercised in many other subjects—which we didn't mention but are adding now—to see whether they can tolerate the most important subjects or will shrink from them like the cowards who shrink from other tests.   *504*

It's appropriate to examine them like that. But what do you mean by the most important subjects?

Do you remember when we distinguished three parts in the soul, in order to help bring out what justice, moderation, courage, and wisdom each is?

If I didn't remember that, it wouldn't be just for me to hear the rest.

What about what preceded it?

What was that?

We said, I believe, that, in order to get the finest possible view of these matters, we would need to take *b* a longer road that would make them plain to anyone who took it but that it was possible to give demonstrations of what they are that would be up to the standard of the previous argument.[18] And you said that that would be satisfactory. So it seems to me that our discussion at that time fell short of exactness, but whether or not it satisfied you is for you to say.

18. [See 435d.]

I thought you gave us good measure and so, apparently, did the others.

Any measure of such things that falls short in any c way of that which is is not good measure, for nothing incomplete is the measure of anything, although people are sometimes of the opinion that an incomplete treatment is nonetheless adequate and makes further investigation unnecessary.

Indeed, laziness causes many people to think that.

It is a thought that a guardian of a city and its laws can well do without.

Probably so.

Well, then, he must take the longer road and put as much effort into learning as into physical training, for otherwise, as we were just saying, he will never d reach the goal of the most important subject and the most appropriate one for him to learn.

Aren't these virtues, then, the most important things? he asked. Is there anything even more important than justice and the other virtues we discussed?

There is something more important. However, even for the virtues themselves, it isn't enough to look at a mere sketch, as we did before, while neglecting the most complete account. It's ridiculous, isn't it, to strain every nerve to attain the utmost exactness and clarity about other things of little value and not to consider the most important things worthy of the e greatest exactness?

It certainly is. But do you think that anyone is going to let you off without asking you what this most important subject is and what it concerns?

No, indeed, and you can ask me too. You've certainly heard the answer often enough, but now either you aren't thinking or you intend to make trouble for me again by interrupting. And I suspect the latter, 505 for you've often heard it said that the form of the good is the most important thing to learn about and that it's by their relation to it that just things and the others become useful and beneficial. You know very well now that I am going to say this, and, besides, that we have no adequate knowledge of it. And you also know that, if we don't know it, even the fullest possible knowledge of other things is of no benefit to us, any more than if we acquire any possession without the good of it. Or do you think that it is any advantage to have every kind of possession without the good of b it? Or to know everything except the good, thereby knowing nothing fine or good?

No, by god, I don't.

Furthermore, you certainly know that the majority believe that pleasure is the good, while the more sophisticated believe that it is knowledge.

Indeed I do.

And you know that those who believe this can't tell us what sort of knowledge it is, however, but in the end are forced to say that it is knowledge of the good.

And that's ridiculous.

Of course it is. They blame us for not knowing the good and then turn around and talk to us as if we c did know it. They say that it is knowledge of the good—as if we understood what they're speaking about when they utter the word "good."

That's completely true.

What about those who define the good as pleasure? Are they any less full of confusion than the others? Aren't even they forced to admit that there are bad pleasures?

Most definitely.

So, I think, they have to agree that the same things are both good and bad. Isn't that true?

Of course.   d

It's clear, then, isn't it, why there are many large controversies about this?

How could it be otherwise?

And isn't this also clear? In the case of just and beautiful things, many people are content with what are believed to be so, even if they aren't really so, and they act, acquire, and form their own beliefs on that basis. Nobody is satisfied to acquire things that are merely believed to be good, however, but everyone wants the things that really *are* good and disdains mere belief here.

That's right.

Every soul pursues the good and does whatever it does for its sake. It divines that the good is something e but it is perplexed and cannot adequately grasp what it is or acquire the sort of stable beliefs it has about other things, and so it misses the benefit, if any, that even those other things may give. Will we allow the best people in the city, to whom we entrust everything, to be so in the dark about something of this kind and 506 of this importance?

That's the last thing we'd do.

I don't suppose, at least, that just and fine things will have acquired much of a guardian in someone who doesn't even know in what way they are good. And I divine that no one will have adequate knowledge of them until he knows this.

You've divined well.

But won't our constitution be perfectly ordered, if *b* a guardian who knows these things is in charge of it?

Necessarily. But, Socrates, you must also tell us whether you consider the good to be knowledge or pleasure or something else altogether.

What a man! It's been clear for some time that other people's opinions about these matters wouldn't satisfy you.

Well, Socrates, it doesn't seem right to me for you to be willing to state other people's convictions but not your own, especially when you've spent so much *c* time occupied with these matters.

What? Do you think it's right to talk about things one doesn't know as if one does know them?

Not as if one knows them, he said, but one ought to be willing to state one's opinions as such.

What? Haven't you noticed that opinions without knowledge are shameful and ugly things? The best of them are blind — or do you think that those who express a true opinion without understanding are any different from blind people who happen to travel the right road?

They're no different.

Do you want to look at shameful, blind, and crooked things, then, when you might hear illuminat- *d* ing and fine ones from other people?

By god, Socrates, Glaucon said, don't desert us with the end almost in sight. We'll be satisfied if you discuss the good as you discussed justice, moderation, and the rest.

That, my friend, I said, would satisfy me too, but I'm afraid that I won't be up to it and that I'll disgrace myself and look ridiculous by trying. So let's abandon the quest for what the good itself is for the time being, *e* for even to arrive at my own view about it is too big a topic for the discussion we are now started on. But I am willing to tell you about what is apparently an offspring of the good and most like it. Is that agreeable to you, or would you rather we let the whole matter drop?

It is. The story about the father remains a debt you'll pay another time.

I wish that I could pay the debt in full, and you *507* receive it instead of just the interest. So here, then,

is this child and offspring of the good. But be careful that I don't somehow deceive you unintentionally by giving you an illegitimate account of the child.[19]

We'll be as careful as possible, so speak on.

I will when we've come to an agreement and recalled some things that we've already said both here and many other times.

Which ones?   *b*

We say that there are many beautiful things and many good things, and so on for each kind, and in this way we distinguish them in words.

We do.

And beauty itself and good itself and all the things that we thereby set down as many, reversing ourselves, we set down according to a single form of each, believing that there is but one, and call it "the being" of each.[20]

That's true.

And we say that the many beautiful things and the rest are visible but not intelligible, while the forms are intelligible but not visible.

That's completely true.

With what part of ourselves do we see visible things? *c*

With our sight.

And so audible things are heard by hearing, and with our other senses we perceive all the other perceptible things.

That's right.

Have you considered how lavish the maker of our senses was in making the power to see and be seen?

I can't say I have.

Well, consider it this way. Do hearing and sound need another kind of thing in order for the former to hear and the latter to be heard, a third thing in whose absence the one won't hear or the other be heard?   *d*

No, they need nothing else.

And if there are any others that need such a thing, there can't be many of them. Can you think of one?

I can't.

You don't realize that sight and the visible have such a need?

---

19. [Throughout, Socrates is punning on the word *tokos*, which means either a child or the interest on capital.]

20. [The "being" of something is sometimes taken to refer to what we call its essence. Socrates would then be saying that the essence of the fineness present in many things is the form of the fine.]

How so?

Sight may be present in the eyes, and the one who has it may try to use it, and colors may be present in things, but unless a third kind of thing is present, which is naturally adapted for this very purpose, you e know that sight will see nothing, and the colors will remain unseen.

What kind of thing do you mean?

I mean what you call light.

You're right.

Then it isn't an insignificant kind of link that con-508 nects the sense of sight and the power to be seen— it is a more valuable link than any other linked things have got, if indeed light is something valuable.

And, of course, it's very valuable.

Which of the gods in heaven would you name as the cause and controller of this, the one whose light causes our sight to see in the best way and the visible things to be seen?

The same one you and others would name. Obviously, the answer to your question is the sun.

And isn't sight by nature related to that god in this way?

Which way?

Sight isn't the sun, neither sight itself nor that in b which it comes to be, namely, the eye.

No, it certainly isn't.

But I think that it is the most sunlike of the senses.

Very much so.

And it receives from the sun the power it has, just like an influx from an overflowing treasury.

Certainly.

The sun is not sight, but isn't it the cause of sight itself and seen by it?

That's right.

Let's say, then, that this is what I called the offspring of the good, which the good begot as its analogue. What the good itself is in the intelligible realm, in relation to understanding and intelligible things, the c sun is in the visible realm, in relation to sight and visible things.

How? Explain a bit more.

You know that, when we turn our eyes to things whose colors are no longer in the light of day but in the gloom of night, the eyes are dimmed and seem nearly blind, as if clear vision were no longer in them.

Of course.

Yet whenever one turns them on things illuminated

by the sun, they see clearly, and vision appears in those very same eyes?   d

Indeed.

Well, understand the soul in the same way: When it focuses on something illuminated by truth and what is, it understands, knows, and apparently possesses understanding, but when it focuses on what is mixed with obscurity, on what comes to be and passes away, it opines and is dimmed, changes its opinions this way and that, and seems bereft of understanding.

It does seem that way.

So that what gives truth to the things known and the power to know to the knower is the form of the e good. And though it is the cause of knowledge and truth, it is also an object of knowledge. Both knowledge and truth are beautiful things, but the good is other and more beautiful than they. In the visible realm, light and sight are rightly considered sunlike, but it is wrong to think that they are the sun, so here it is right to think of knowledge and truth as goodlike 509 but wrong to think that either of them is the good— for the good is yet more prized.

This is an inconceivably beautiful thing you're talking about, if it provides both knowledge and truth and is superior to them in beauty. You surely don't think that a thing like that could be pleasure.

Hush! Let's examine its image in more detail as follows.

How?   b

You'll be willing to say, I think, that the sun not only provides visible things with the power to be seen but also with coming to be, growth, and nourishment, although it is not itself coming to be.

How could it be?

Therefore, you should also say that not only do the objects of knowledge owe their being known to the good, but their being is also due to it, although the good is not being, but superior to it in rank and power.

And Glaucon comically said: By Apollo, what a daemonic superiority!   c

It's your own fault; you forced me to tell you my opinion about it.

And I don't want you to stop either. So continue to explain its similarity to the sun, if you've omitted anything.

I'm certainly omitting a lot.

Well, don't, not even the smallest thing.

I think I'll have to omit a fair bit, but, as far as is

possible at the moment, I won't omit anything voluntarily.

Don't.

Understand, then, that, as we said, there are these d two things, one sovereign of the intelligible kind and place, the other of the visible (I don't say "of heaven" so as not to seem to you to be playing the sophist with the name).[21] In any case, you have two kinds of thing, visible and intelligible.

Right.

It is like a line divided into two unequal sections.[22] Then divide each section—namely, that of the visible and that of the intelligible—in the same ratio as the line. In terms now of relative clarity and opacity, one subsection of the visible consists of images. And by images I mean, first, shadows, then reflections in e water and in all close-packed, smooth, and shiny ma-510 terials, and everything of that sort, if you understand.

I do.

In the other subsection of the visible, put the originals of these images, namely, the animals around us, all the plants, and the whole class of manufactured things.

21. [The play may be on the similarity of sound between *ouranou* ("of heaven") and *horatou* ("of the visible"). But it is more likely that Socrates is referring to the fact that *ouranou* seems to contain the word *nou*, the genitive case of *nous* ("understanding"), and relative of *noētou* ("of the intelligible"). Hence if he said that the sun was sovereign of heaven, he might be taken to suggest in sophistical fashion that it was sovereign of the intelligible and that there was no real difference between the good and the sun.]

22. [The line is illustrated below:]

Understanding (*noêsis*)

Thought (*dianoia*)

Belief (*pistis*)

Imagination (*eikasia*)

Consider them put.

Would you be willing to say that, as regards truth and untruth, the division is in this proportion: As the opinable is to the knowable, so the likeness is to the thing that it is like?

Certainly.   b

Consider now how the section of the intelligible is to be divided.

How?

As follows: In one subsection, the soul, using as images the things that were imitated before, is forced to investigate from hypotheses, proceeding not to a first principle but to a conclusion. In the other subsection, however, it makes its way to a first principle that is *not* a hypothesis, proceeding from a hypothesis but without the images used in the previous subsection, using forms themselves and making its investigation through them.

I don't yet fully understand what you mean.

Let's try again. You'll understand it more easily after the following preamble. I think you know that c students of geometry, calculation, and the like hypothesize the odd and the even, the various figures, the three kinds of angles, and other things akin to these in each of their investigations, as if they knew them. They make these their hypotheses and don't think it necessary to give any account of them, either to themselves or to others, as if they were clear to everyone. And going from these first principles through the remaining steps, they arrive in full agreement.   d

I certainly know that much.

Then you also know that, although they use visible figures and make claims about them, their thought isn't directed to them but to those other things that they are like. They make their claims for the sake of square itself and the diagonal itself, not the diagonal they draw, and similarly with the others. These figures that they make and draw, of which shadows and re- e flections in water are images, they now in turn use as images, in seeking to see those others themselves that one cannot see except by means of thought.   511

That's true.

This, then, is the kind of thing that, on the one hand, I said is intelligible, and, on the other, is such that the soul is forced to use hypotheses in the investigation of it, not travelling up to a first principle, since it cannot reach beyond its hypotheses, but using as images those very things of which images were made in the section below, and which, by comparison to their images, were thought to be clear and to be valued as such.

I understand that you mean what happens in geom-
b etry and related sciences.

Then also understand that, by the other subsection of the intelligible, I mean that which reason itself grasps by the power of dialectic. It does not consider these hypotheses as first principles but truly as hypotheses—but as stepping stones to take off from, enabling it to reach the unhypothetical first principle of every-thing. Having grasped this principle, it reverses itself and, keeping hold of what follows from it, comes down to a conclusion without making use of anything visible at all, but only of forms themselves, moving
c on from forms to forms, and ending in forms.

I understand, if not yet adequately (for in my opinion you're speaking of an enormous task), that you want to distinguish the intelligible part of that which is, the part studied by the science of dialectic, as clearer than the part studied by the so-called sciences, for which their hypotheses are first principles. And although those who study the objects of these sciences are forced to do so by means of thought rather than sense perception, still, because they do not go back
d to a genuine first principle, but proceed from hypotheses, you don't think that they understand them, even though, given such a principle, they are intelligible. And you seem to me to call the state of the geometers thought but not understanding, thought being intermediate between opinion and understanding.

Your exposition is most adequate. Thus there are four such conditions in the soul, corresponding to the four subsections of our line: Understanding for the highest, thought for the second, belief for the
e third, and imaging for the last. Arrange them in a ratio, and consider that each shares in clarity to the degree that the subsection it is set over shares in truth.

I understand, agree, and arrange them as you say.

Book VII

514 Next, I said, compare the effect of education and of the lack of it on our nature to an experience like this: Imagine human beings living in an underground, cavelike dwelling, with an entrance a long way up, which is both open to the light and as wide as the cave itself. They've been there since childhood, fixed

in the same place, with their necks and legs fettered, able to see only in front of them, because their bonds prevent them from turning their heads around. Light is provided by a fire burning far above and behind them. Also behind them, but on higher ground, there b is a path stretching between them and the fire. Imagine that along this path a low wall has been built, like the screen in front of puppeteers above which they show their puppets.

I'm imagining it.

Then also imagine that there are people along the wall, carrying all kinds of artifacts that project above it—statues of people and other animals, made out of stone, wood, and every material. And, as you'd expect, c some of the carriers are talking, and some are silent. 515

It's a strange image you're describing, and strange prisoners.

They're like us. Do you suppose, first of all, that these prisoners see anything of themselves and one another besides the shadows that the fire casts on the wall in front of them?

How could they, if they have to keep their heads motionless throughout life?   b

What about the things being carried along the wall? Isn't the same true of them?

Of course.

And if they could talk to one another, don't you think they'd suppose that the names they used applied to the things they see passing before them?[1]

They'd have to.

And what if their prison also had an echo from the wall facing them? Don't you think they'd believe that the shadows passing in front of them were talking whenever one of the carriers passing along the wall was doing so?

I certainly do.

Then the prisoners would in every way believe that the truth is nothing other than the shadows of c those artifacts.

They must surely believe that.

Consider, then, what being released from their bonds and cured of their ignorance would naturally be like, if something like this came to pass. When one of them was freed and suddenly compelled to

---

1. [Reading *parionta autous nomizein onomazein*. E.g., they would think that the name "human being" applied to the shadow of a statue of a human being.—C.D.C.R.]

stand up, turn his head, walk, and look up toward the light, he'd be pained and dazzled and unable to see the things whose shadows he'd seen before. What *d* do you think he'd say, if we told him that what he'd seen before was inconsequential, but that now—because he is a bit closer to the things that are and is turned towards things that are more—he sees more correctly? Or, to put it another way, if we pointed to each of the things passing by, asked him what each of them is, and compelled him to answer, don't you think he'd be at a loss and that he'd believe that the things he saw earlier were truer than the ones he was now being shown?

Much truer.

And if someone compelled him to look at the light *e* itself, wouldn't his eyes hurt, and wouldn't he turn around and flee towards the things he's able to see, believing that they're really clearer than the ones he's being shown?

He would.

And if someone dragged him away from there by force, up the rough, steep path, and didn't let him go until he had dragged him into the sunlight, wouldn't he be pained and irritated at being treated *516* that way? And when he came into the light, with the sun filling his eyes, wouldn't he be unable to see a single one of the things now said to be true?

He would be unable to see them, at least at first.

I suppose, then, that he'd need time to get adjusted before he could see things in the world above. At first, he'd see shadows most easily, then images of men and other things in water, then the things themselves. Of these, he'd be able to study the things in the sky and the sky itself more easily at night, looking at the light of the stars and the moon, than during *b* the day, looking at the sun and the light of the sun.

Of course.

Finally, I suppose, he'd be able to see the sun, not images of it in water or some alien place, but the sun itself, in its own place, and be able to study it.

Necessarily so.

And at this point he would infer and conclude that the sun provides the seasons and the years, governs everything in the visible world, and is in some way *c* the cause of all the things that he used to see.

It's clear that would be his next step.

What about when he reminds himself of his first dwelling place, his fellow prisoners, and what passed

for wisdom there? Don't you think that he'd count himself happy for the change and pity the others?

Certainly.

And if there had been any honors, praises, or prizes among them for the one who was sharpest at identifying the shadows as they passed by and who best remembered which usually came earlier, which later, and which simultaneously, and who could thus best *d* divine the future, do you think that our man would desire these rewards or envy those among the prisoners who were honored and held power? Instead, wouldn't he feel, with Homer, that he'd much prefer to "work the earth as a serf to another, one without possessions,"[2] and go through any sufferings, rather than share their opinions and live as they do?

I suppose he would rather suffer anything than live *e* like that.

Consider this too. If this man went down into the cave again and sat down in his same seat, wouldn't his eyes—coming suddenly out of the sun like that—be filled with darkness?

They certainly would.

And before his eyes had recovered—and the adjustment would not be quick—while his vision was still dim, if he had to compete again with the perpetual prisoners in recognizing the shadows, wouldn't he *517* invite ridicule? Wouldn't it be said of him that he'd returned from his upward journey with his eyesight ruined and that it isn't worthwhile even to try to travel upward? And, as for anyone who tried to free them and lead them upward, if they could somehow get their hands on him, wouldn't they kill him?

They certainly would.

This whole image, Glaucon, must be fitted together with what we said before. The visible realm should *b* be likened to the prison dwelling, and the light of the fire inside it to the power of the sun. And if you interpret the upward journey and the study of things above as the upward journey of the soul to the intelligible realm, you'll grasp what I hope to convey, since that is what you wanted to hear about. Whether it's true or not, only the god knows. But this is how I see it: In the knowable realm, the form of the good is the last thing to be seen, and it is reached only with

---

2. [*Odyssey* 11.489–90. The shade of the dead Achilles speaks these words to Odysseus, who is visiting Hades. Plato is, therefore, likening the cave dwellers to the dead.]

difficulty. Once one has seen it, however, one must conclude that it is the cause of all that is correct and
c beautiful in anything, that it produces both light and its source in the visible realm, and that in the intelligible realm it controls and provides truth and understanding, so that anyone who is to act sensibly in private or public must see it.

I have the same thought, at least as far as I'm able.

Come, then, share with me this thought also: It isn't surprising that the ones who get to this point are unwilling to occupy themselves with human affairs and that their souls are always pressing upwards, eager to spend their time above, for, after all, this is surely what we'd expect, if indeed things fit the image I
d described before.

It is.

What about what happens when someone turns from divine study to the evils of human life? Do you think it's surprising, since his sight is still dim, and he hasn't yet become accustomed to the darkness around him, that he behaves awkwardly and appears completely ridiculous if he's compelled, either in the courts or elsewhere, to contend about the shadows of justice or the statues of which they are the shadows and to dispute about the way these things are understood by people who have never seen justice
e itself?

That's not surprising at all.

No, it isn't. But anyone with any understanding
518 would remember that the eyes may be confused in two ways and from two causes, namely, when they've come from the light into the darkness *and* when they've come from the darkness into the light. Realizing that the same applies to the soul, when someone sees a soul disturbed and unable to see something, he won't laugh mindlessly, but he'll take into consideration whether it has come from a brighter life and is dimmed through not having yet become accustomed to the dark or whether it has come from greater ignorance into greater light and is dazzled by the increased brilliance. Then he'll declare the first soul happy in its experience and life, and he'll pity the
b latter—but even if he chose to make fun of it, at least he'd be less ridiculous than if he laughed at a soul that has come from the light above.

What you say is very reasonable.

If that's true, then here's what we must think about these matters: Education isn't what some people de-

clare it to be, namely, putting knowledge into souls that lack it, like putting sight into blind eyes.   c

They do say that.

But our present discussion, on the other hand, shows that the power to learn is present in everyone's soul and that the instrument with which each learns is like an eye that cannot be turned around from darkness to light without turning the whole body. This instrument cannot be turned around from that which is coming into being without turning the whole soul until it is able to study that which is and the brightest thing that is, namely, the one we call the good. Isn't that right?   d

Yes.

Then education is the craft concerned with doing this very thing, this turning around, and with how the soul can most easily and effectively be made to do it. It isn't the craft of putting sight into the soul. Education takes for granted that sight is there but that it isn't turned the right way or looking where it ought to look, and it tries to redirect it appropriately.

So it seems.

Now, it looks as though the other so-called virtues of the soul are akin to those of the body, for they really aren't there beforehand but are added later by habit and practice. However, the virtue of reason e seems to belong above all to something more divine, which never loses its power but is either useful and beneficial or useless and harmful, depending on the way it is turned. Or have you never noticed this about people who are said to be vicious but clever, how 519 keen the vision of their little souls is and how sharply it distinguishes the things it is turned towards? This shows that its sight isn't inferior but rather is forced to serve evil ends, so that the sharper it sees, the more evil it accomplishes.

Absolutely.

However, if a nature of this sort had been hammered at from childhood and freed from the bonds of kinship with becoming, which have been fastened to it by feasting, greed, and other such pleasures and which, like leaden weights, pull its vision down- b wards—if, being rid of these, it turned to look at true things, then I say that the same soul of the same person would see these most sharply, just as it now does the things it is presently turned towards.

Probably so.

And what about the uneducated who have no experience of truth? Isn't it likely—indeed, doesn't it follow necessarily from what was said before—that they will never adequately govern a city? But neither would those who've been allowed to spend their whole lives being educated. The former would fail because they c don't have a single goal at which all their actions, public and private, inevitably aim; the latter would fail because they'd refuse to act, thinking that they had settled while still alive in the faraway Isles of the Blessed.[3]

That's true.

It is our task as founders, then, to compel the best natures to reach the study we said before is the most important, namely, to make the ascent and see the good. But when they've made it and looked suffi- d ciently, we mustn't allow them to do what they're allowed to do today.

What's that?

To stay there and refuse to go down again to the prisoners in the cave and share their labors and honors, whether they are of less worth or of greater.

Then are we to do them an injustice by making them live a worse life when they could live a better one?

You are forgetting again that it isn't the law's con- e cern to make any one class in the city outstandingly happy but to contrive to spread happiness throughout the city by bringing the citizens into harmony with each other through persuasion or compulsion and by making them share with each other the benefits that each class can confer on the community.[4] The law produces such people in the city, not in order to 520 allow them to turn in whatever direction they want, but to make use of them to bind the city together.

That's true, I had forgotten.

Observe, then, Glaucon, that we won't be doing an injustice to those who've become philosophers in our city and that what we'll say to them, when we compel them to guard and care for the others, will be just. We'll say: "When people like you come to be in other cities, they're justified in not sharing in b their city's labors, for they've grown there spontaneously, against the will of the constitution. And what

grows of its own accord and owes no debt for its upbringing has justice on its side when it isn't keen to pay anyone for that upbringing. But we've made you kings in our city and leaders of the swarm, as it were, both for yourselves and for the rest of the city. You're better and more completely educated than the others and are better able to share in both types of c life.[5] Therefore each of you in turn must go down to live in the common dwelling place of the others and grow accustomed to seeing in the dark. When you are used to it, you'll see vastly better than the people there. And because you've seen the truth about fine, just, and good things, you'll know each image for what it is and also that of which it is the image. Thus, for you and for us, the city will be governed, not like the majority of cities nowadays, by people who fight over shadows and struggle against one another in order to rule—as if that were a great good—but by people who are awake rather than dreaming,[6] for the d truth is surely this: A city whose prospective rulers are least eager to rule must of necessity be most free from civil war, whereas a city with the opposite kind of rulers is governed in the opposite way."

Absolutely.

Then do you think that those we've nurtured will disobey us and refuse to share the labors of the city, each in turn, while living the greater part of their time with one another in the pure realm?

It isn't possible, for we'll be giving just orders to just people. Each of them will certainly go to rule as e to something compulsory, however, which is exactly the opposite of what's done by those who now rule in each city. This is how it is. If you can find a way of life that's better than ruling for the prospective rulers, your well-governed city will become a possibility, for only in it will the truly rich rule—not those 521 who are rich in gold but those who are rich in the wealth that the happy must have, namely, a good and rational life. But if beggars hungry for private goods go into public life, thinking that the good is there for the seizing, then the well-governed city is impossible, for then ruling is something fought over, and this civil and domestic war destroys these people and the rest of the city as well.

---

3. [A place where good people are said to live in eternal happiness, normally after death.]

4. [See 462a–466c.]

5. [That is, the practical life of ruling the city and the theoretical life of studying the good itself.]

6. [See 476c–d.]

That's very true.

Can you name any life that despises political rule
b besides that of the true philosopher?

No, by god, I can't.

But surely it is those who are not lovers of ruling who must rule, for if they don't, the lovers of it, who are rivals, will fight over it.

Of course.

Then who will you compel to become guardians of the city, if not those who have the best understanding of what matters for good government and who have other honors than political ones, and a better life as well?

No one.

The next step is the education of the philosopher-kings. (1) Their initial education is in music and poetry, physical training, and elementary mathematics. (2) This is followed by two or three years of compulsory physical training, rather like the military service that some countries still require. (3) Those who are most successful in these studies next receive ten years of education in mathematical science. (4) Those who are again most successful receive five years of training in dialectic. (5) Those who are still most successful receive fifteen years of practical political training. Finally, (6) those who are also successful in practical politics are "compelled to lift up the radiant light of their souls" to the good itself and are equipped to be philosopher-kings.

S.M.C.

Book VIII

The description of the kallipolis and of the man whose character resembles it—the philosopher-king—is now complete, and Socrates returns to the argument interrupted at the beginning of Book V. He describes four individual character types and the four types of constitutions that result when people who possess them rule in a city. He presents these as four stages in the increasing corruption or decline of the kallipolis, and he explains, by appeal to the mathematical myth of the geometrical number, why the kallipolis will decline. However, embedded in the myth is the serious philosophical suggestion that the kallipolis will decline because the philosopher-kings have to rely on sense perception in putting their eugenics policy into practice.

The first of the bad cities Socrates describes is a timocracy. It is ruled by people whose souls are themselves ruled by the spirited part of their soul, in which the desire for honor, victories, and good reputation are located. It is the second-best city to the kallipolis. The third-best city is an oligarchy. It is ruled by people whose souls are ruled by their necessary appetites. The fourth-best city is a democracy. It is ruled by people whose souls are ruled by unnecessary appetites. The worst city of all is a tyranny. It is ruled by someone whose soul is ruled by its lawless and unnecessary appetites.

Book IX

It remains, I said, to consider the tyrannical man 571 himself, how he evolves from a democrat, what he is like when he has come into being, and whether he is wretched or blessedly happy.

Yes, he said, he is the one who is still missing.

And do you know what else I think is still missing? What?

I don't think we have adequately distinguished the kinds and numbers of our desires, and, if that subject isn't adequately dealt with, our entire investigation will be less clear.   *b*

Well, isn't now as fine a time as any to discuss the matter?

It certainly is. Consider, then, what I want to know about our desires. It's this: Some of our unnecessary pleasures and desires seem to me to be lawless. They are probably present in everyone, but they are held in check by the laws and by the better desires in alliance with reason. In a few people, they have been eliminated entirely or only a few weak ones remain, while in others they are stronger and more numerous. *c*

What desires do you mean?

Those that are awakened in sleep, when the rest of the soul—the rational, gentle, and ruling part—slumbers. Then the beastly and savage part, full of food and drink, casts off sleep and seeks to find a way to gratify itself. You know that there is nothing it won't dare to do at such a time, free of all control by shame or reason. It doesn't shrink from trying to have sex with a mother, as it supposes, or with anyone else at all, whether man, god, or beast. It will commit *d* any foul murder, and there is no food it refuses to eat. In a word, it omits no act of folly or shamelessness.

That's completely true.

On the other hand, I suppose that someone who is healthy and moderate with himself goes to sleep only after having done the following: First, he rouses his rational part and feasts it on fine arguments and *e* speculations; second, he neither starves nor feasts his appetites, so that they will slumber and not disturb his best part with either their pleasure or their pain, 572 but they'll leave it alone, pure and by itself, to get on with its investigations, to yearn after and perceive something, it knows not what,[1] whether it is past, present, or future; third, he soothes his spirited part in the same way, for example, by not falling asleep with his spirit still aroused after an outburst of anger. And when he has quieted these two parts and aroused the third, in which reason resides, and so takes his rest, you know that it is then that he best grasps the truth and that the visions that appear in his dreams *b* are least lawless.

Entirely so.

However, we've been carried away from what we wanted to establish, which is this: Our dreams make it clear that there is a dangerous, wild, and lawless form of desire in everyone, even in those of us who seem to be entirely moderate or measured. See whether you think I'm talking sense and whether or not you agree with me.

I do agree.

Recall, then, what we said a democratic man is like. He was produced by being brought up from youth by a thrifty father who valued only those desires *c* that make money and who despised the unnecessary ones that aim at frivolity and display. Isn't that right?

Yes.

And by associating with more sophisticated men, who are full of the latter desires, he starts to indulge in every kind of insolence and to adopt their form of behavior, because of his hatred of his father's thrift. But, because he has a better nature than his corrupters, he is pulled in both directions and settles down in the middle between his father's way of life and theirs. And enjoying each in moderation, as he sup- *d* poses, he leads a life that is neither slavish nor lawless

and from having been oligarchic he becomes democratic.

That was and is our opinion about this type of man.

Suppose now that this man has in turn become older and that *he* has a son who is brought up in *his* father's ethos.

All right.

And further suppose that the same things that happened to his father now happen to him. First, he is led to all the kinds of lawlessness that those who are leading him call freedom. Then his father and the *e* rest of the household come to the aid of the middle desires, while the others help the other ones. Then, when those clever enchanters and tyrant-makers have no hope of keeping hold of the young man in any other way, they contrive to plant in him a powerful erotic love, like a great winged drone, to be the leader of those idle desires that spend whatever is at hand. Or do you think that erotic love is anything other 573 than an enormous drone in such people?

I don't think that it could be anything else.

And when the other desires—filled with incense, myrrh, wreaths, wine, and the other pleasures found in their company—buzz around the drone, nurturing it and making it grow as large as possible, they plant the sting of longing in it. Then this leader of the soul adopts madness as its bodyguard and becomes frenzied. If it finds any beliefs or desires in the man *b* that are thought to be good or that still have some shame, it destroys them and throws them out, until it's purged him of moderation and filled him with imported madness.

You've perfectly described the evolution of a tyrannical man.

Is this the reason that erotic love has long been called a tyrant?

It looks that way.

Then doesn't a drunken man have something of a tyrannical mind?												*c*

Yes, he has.

And a man who is mad and deranged attempts to rule not just human beings, but gods as well, and expects that he will be able to succeed.

He certainly does.

Then a man becomes tyrannical in the precise sense of the term when either his nature or his way of life or both of them together make him drunk, filled with erotic desire, and mad.

---

1. [Reading *skopein kai oregesthai tou kai aisthanesthai ho mē oiden.*—C.D.C.R.]

Absolutely.

This, then, it seems, is how a tyrannical man comes to be. But what way does he live?

No doubt *you're* going to tell *me*, just as posers of
d riddles usually do.

I am. I think that someone in whom the tyrant of erotic love dwells and in whom it directs everything next goes in for feasts, revelries, luxuries, girlfriends, and all that sort of thing.

Necessarily.

And don't many terrible desires grow up day and night beside the tyrannical one, needing many things to satisfy them?

Indeed they do.

Hence any income someone like that has is soon spent.

Of course.

Then borrowing follows, and expenditure of
e capital.

What else?

And when everything is gone, won't the violent crowd of desires that has nested within him inevitably shout in protest? And driven by the stings of the other desires and especially by erotic love itself (which leads all of them as its bodyguard), won't he become frenzied and look to see who possesses anything that he
574 could take, by either deceit or force?

He certainly will.

Consequently, he must acquire wealth from every source or live in great pain and suffering.

He must.

And just as the pleasures that are latecomers outdo the older ones and steal away their satisfactions, won't the man himself think that he deserves to outdo[2] his father and mother, even though he is younger than they are—to take and spend his father's wealth when he's spent his own share?

Of course.

And if they won't give it to him, won't he first try
b to steal it from them by deceitful means?

Certainly.

And if that doesn't work, wouldn't he seize it by force?

I suppose so.

And if the old man and woman put up a fight, would he be careful to refrain from acting like a tyrant?

I'm not very optimistic about their fate, if they do.

But, good god, Adeimantus, do you think he'd sacrifice his long-loved and irreplaceable mother for a recently acquired girlfriend whom he can do without? Or that for the sake of a newfound and replaceable boyfriend in the bloom of youth, he'd strike his c aged and irreplaceable father, his oldest friend? Or that he'd make his parents the slaves of these others, if he brought them under the same roof?

Yes, indeed he would.

It seems to be a very great blessing to produce a tyrannical son!

It certainly does!

What about when the possessions of his father and mother give out? With that great swarm of pleasures d inside him, won't he first try to break into someone's house or snatch someone's coat late at night? Then won't he try to loot a temple? And in all this, the old traditional opinions that he had held from childhood about what is fine or shameful—opinions that are accounted just—are overcome by the opinions, newly released from slavery, that are now the bodyguard of erotic love and hold sway along with it. When he himself was subject to the laws and his father and had e a democratic constitution within him, these opinions used only to be freed in sleep. Now, however, under the tyranny of erotic love, he has permanently become while awake what he used to become occasionally while asleep, and he won't hold back from any terrible murder or from any kind of food or act. But, rather, erotic love lives like a tyrant within him, in complete anarchy and lawlessness as his sole ruler, and drives 575 him, as if he were a city, to dare anything that will provide sustenance for itself and the unruly mob around it (some of whose members have come in from the outside as a result of his keeping bad company, while others have come from within, freed and let loose by his own bad habits). Isn't this the life that a tyrannical man leads?

It is indeed.

Now, if there are only a few such men in a city, and the rest of the people are moderate, this mob will leave the city in order to act as a bodyguard to some other tyrant or to serve as mercenaries if there b happens to be a war going on somewhere. But if they chance to live in a time of peace and quiet, they'll remain in the city and bring about lots of little evils.

What sort of evils do you mean?

2. [*Pleon echein.* See 344a n. 18.]

They steal, break into houses, snatch purses, steal clothes, rob temples, and sell people into slavery. Sometimes, if they are good speakers, they become sycophants and bear false witness and accept bribes.[3]

These evils *are* small, provided that there happen c to be only a few such people.

Yes, for small things are small by comparison to big ones. And when it comes to producing wickedness and misery in a city, all these evils together don't, as the saying goes, come within a mile of the rule of a tyrant. But when such people become numerous and conscious of their numbers, it is they—aided by the foolishness of the people—who create a tyrant. And he, more than any of them, has in his soul the greatest d and strongest tyrant of all.

Naturally, for he'd be the most tyrannical.

That's if the city happens to yield willingly, but if it resists him, then, just as he once chastised his mother and father, he'll now chastise his fatherland, if he can, by bringing in new friends and making his fatherland and his dear old motherland (as the Cretans call it) their slaves and keeping them that way, for this is surely the end at which such a man's desires are directed.

e   It most certainly is.

Now, in private life, before a tyrannical man attains power, isn't he this sort of person—one who associates primarily with flatterers who are ready to obey him in everything? Or if he himself happens to need anything from other people, isn't he willing to fawn on them and make every gesture of friendship, as if he were 576 dealing with his own family? But once he gets what he wants, don't they become strangers again?

Yes, they certainly do.

So someone with a tyrannical nature lives his whole life without being friends with anyone, always a master to one man or a slave to another and never getting a taste of either freedom or true friendship.

That's right.

---

3. [Athens had nothing corresponding to our public prosecutors. By and large, private citizens prosecuted each other. By the middle of the fifth century, some people began to make a profession of prosecuting others for financial, political, or personal reasons. These people were called sycophants. A vivid sense of their power and importance is conveyed in L. B. Carter, *The Quiet Athenian* (Oxford: Clarendon Press, 1986).]

Wouldn't we be right to call someone like that untrustworthy?

Of course.

And isn't he as unjust as anyone can be? If indeed what we earlier agreed about justice was right.   b

And it certainly was right.

Then, let's sum up the worst type of man: His waking life is like the nightmare we described earlier.[4]

That's right.

And he evolves from someone by nature most tyrannical who achieves sole rule. And the longer he remains tyrant, the more like the nightmare he becomes.

That's inevitable, said Glaucon, taking over the argument.

Well, then, I said, isn't the man who is clearly most vicious also clearly most wretched? And isn't the one who for the longest time is most of all a tyrant, most c wretched for the longest time? If, that is to say, truth rather than majority opinion is to settle these questions.

That much is certain, at any rate.

And isn't a tyrannical man like a city ruled by a tyrant, a democratic man like a city ruled by a democracy, and similarly with the others?

Of course.

And won't the relations between the cities with respect to virtue and happiness be the same as those between the men?

Certainly.   d

Then how does the city ruled by a tyrant compare to the city ruled by kings that we described first?

They are total opposites: one is the best, and the other the worst.

I won't ask you which is which, since it's obvious. But is your judgment the same with regard to their happiness and wretchedness? And let's not be dazzled by looking at one man—a tyrant—or at the few who surround him, but since it is essential to go into the city and study the whole of it, let's not give our opinion, till we've gone down and looked into every corner.   e

That's right, for it's clear to everyone that there is no city more wretched than one ruled by a tyrant and none more happy than one ruled by kings.

---

4. [See 571c–d.]

Would I be right, then, to make the same challenge about the individuals, assuming, first, that the person
577 who is fit to judge them is someone who in thought can go down into a person's character and examine it thoroughly, someone who doesn't judge from outside, the way a child does, who is dazzled by the façade that tyrants adopt for the outside world to see, but is able to see right through that sort of thing? And, second, that he's someone—since we'd all listen to him if he were—who is competent to judge, because he has lived in the same house with a tyrant and witnessed his behavior at home and his treatment of each member of his household when he is stripped of his theatrical façade, and has also seen how he
b behaves when in danger from the people? Shouldn't we ask the person who has seen all that to tell us how the tyrant compares to the others in happiness and wretchedness?

That's also right.

Then do you want us to pretend that we are among those who can give such a judgment and that we have already met tyrannical people, so that we'll have someone to answer our questions?

I certainly do.

Come, then, and look at it this way for me: Bearing
c in mind the resemblance between the city and the man, look at each in turn and describe its condition.

What kinds of things do you want me to describe?

First, speaking of the city, would you say that a tyrannical city is free or enslaved?

It is as enslaved as it is possible to be.

Yet you see in it people who are masters and free.

I do see a few like that, but the whole city, so to speak, and the most decent part of it are wretched, dishonored slaves.

Then, if man and city are alike, mustn't the same
d structure be in him too? And mustn't his soul be full of slavery and unfreedom, with the most decent parts enslaved and with a small part, the maddest and most vicious, as their master?

It must.

What will you say about such a soul then? Is it free or slave?

Slave, of course.

And isn't the enslaved and tyrannical city least likely to do what it wants?

Certainly.

Then a tyrannical soul—I'm talking about the whole soul—will also be least likely to do what it wants and, forcibly driven by the stings of a dronish gadfly, will be full of disorder and regret.   e

How could it be anything else?

Is a tyrannically ruled city rich or poor?

Poor.

Then a tyrannical soul, too, must always be poor and unsatisfiable.   578

That's right.

What about fear? Aren't a tyrannical city and man full of it?

Absolutely.

And do you think that you'll find more wailing, groaning, lamenting, and grieving in any other city?

Certainly not.

Then, are such things more common in anyone besides a tyrannical man, who is maddened by his desires and erotic loves?

How could they be?

It is in view of all these things, I suppose, and others like them, that you judged this to be the most b wretched of cities.

And wasn't I right?

Of course you were. But what do you say about a tyrannical man, when you look at these same things?

He's by far the most wretched of all of them.

There you're no longer right.

How is that?

I don't think that this man has yet reached the extreme of wretchedness.

Then who has?

Perhaps you'll agree that this next case is even more wretched.

Which one?

The one who is tyrannical but doesn't live a private life, because some misfortune provides him with the c opportunity to become an actual tyrant.

On the basis of what was said before, I assume that what you say is true.

Yes, but in matters of this sort, it isn't enough just to assume these things; one needs to investigate carefully the two men in question by means of argument, for the investigation concerns the most important thing, namely, the good life and the bad one.

That's absolutely right.

Then consider whether I'm talking sense or not, for I think our investigation will be helped by the following examples.   d

What are they?

We should look at all the wealthy private citizens in our cities who have many slaves, for, like a tyrant, they rule over many, although not over so many as he does.

That's right.

And you know that they're secure and do not fear their slaves.

What have they got to be afraid of?

Nothing. And do you know why?

Yes. It's because the whole city is ready to defend each of its individual citizens.

You're right. But what if some god were to lift one *e* of these men, his fifty or more slaves, and his wife and children out of the city and deposit him with his slaves and other property in a deserted place, where no free person could come to his assistance? How frightened would he be that he himself and his wife and children would be killed by the slaves?

Very frightened indeed.

And wouldn't he be compelled to fawn on some 579 of his own slaves, promise them lots of things, and free them, even though he didn't want to? And wouldn't he himself have become a panderer to slaves?

He'd have to or else be killed.

What if the god were to settle many other neighbors around him, who wouldn't tolerate anyone to claim that he was the master of another and who would inflict the worst punishments on anyone they caught doing it?

I suppose that he'd have even worse troubles, since *b* he'd be surrounded by nothing but vigilant enemies.

And isn't this the kind of prison in which the tyrant is held—the one whose nature is such as we have described it, filled with fears and erotic loves of all kinds? Even though his soul is really greedy for it, he's the only one in the whole city who can't travel abroad or see the sights that other free people want to see. Instead, he lives like a woman, mostly confined to his own house, and envying any other citizen who happens to travel abroad and see something worth-*c* while.

That's entirely so.

Then, isn't this harvest of evils a measure of the difference between a tyrannical man who is badly governed on the inside—whom you judged to be most wretched just now—and one who doesn't live

a private life but is compelled by some chance to be a tyrant, who tries to rule others when he can't even control himself. He's just like an exhausted body without any self-control, which, instead of living privately, is compelled to compete and fight with other bodies all its life.   *d*

That's exactly what he's like, Socrates, and what you say is absolutely true.

And so, Glaucon, isn't this a completely wretched condition to be in, and doesn't the reigning tyrant have an even harder life than the one you judged to be hardest?

He certainly does.

In truth, then, and whatever some people may think, a real tyrant is really a slave, compelled to engage in the worst kind of fawning, slavery, and pandering to the worst kind of people. He's so far from satisfying his desires in any way that it is clear— if one happens to know that one must study his whole *e* soul—that he's in the greatest need of most things and truly poor. And, if indeed his state is like that of the city he rules, then he's full of fear, convulsions, and pains throughout his life. And it is like it, isn't it?

Of course it is.

And we'll also attribute to the man what we mentioned before, namely, that he is inevitably envious, 580 untrustworthy, unjust, friendless, impious, host and nurse to every kind of vice, and that his ruling makes him even more so. And because of all these, he is extremely unfortunate and goes on to make those near him like himself.

No one with any understanding could possibly contradict you.

Come, then, and like the judge who makes the final decision,[5] tell me who among the five—the king, the timocrat, the oligarch, the democrat, and the tyrant—is first in happiness, who second, and so on *b* in order.

That's easy. I rank them in virtue and vice, in happiness and its opposite, in the order of their appearance, as I might judge choruses.

Shall we, then, hire a herald, or shall I myself announce that the son of Ariston has given as his verdict that the best, the most just, and the most happy is the most kingly, who rules like a king over *c*

---

5. [This probably refers to the way in which plays were judged at festivals.]

himself, and that the worst, the most unjust, and the most wretched is the most tyrannical, who most tyrannizes himself and the city he rules?

Let it be so announced.

And shall I add to the announcement that it holds, whether these things remain hidden from every god and human being or not?

Add it.

Good. Then that is one of our proofs. And there'd be a second, if you happen to think that there is d anything in this.

In what?

In the fact that the soul of each individual is divided into three parts, in just the way that a city is, for that's the reason I think that there is another proof.

What is it?

This: it seems to me that there are three pleasures corresponding to the three parts of the soul, one peculiar to each part, and similarly with desires and kinds of rule.

What do you mean?

The first, we say, is the part with which a person learns, and the second the part with which he gets angry. As for the third, we had no one special name for it, since it's multiform, so we named it after the e biggest and strongest thing in it. Hence we called it the appetitive part, because of the intensity of its appetites for food, drink, sex, and all the things associated with them, but we also called it the money-loving part, because such appetites are most easily 581 satisfied by means of money.

And rightly so.

Then, if we said that its pleasure and love are for profit, wouldn't that best determine its central feature for the purposes of our argument and insure that we are clear about what we mean when we speak of this part of the soul, and wouldn't we be right to call it money-loving and profit-loving?

That's how it seems to me, at least.

What about the spirited part? Don't we say that it is wholly dedicated to the pursuit of control, victory, and high repute?

b Certainly.

Then wouldn't it be appropriate for us to call it victory-loving and honor-loving?

It would be most appropriate.

Now, it is clear to everyone that the part with which

we learn is always wholly straining to know where the truth lies and that, of the three parts, it cares least for money and reputation.

By far the least.

Then wouldn't it be appropriate for us to call it learning-loving and philosophical?

Of course.

And doesn't this part rule in some people's souls, while one of the other parts—whichever it happens to be—rules in other people's? c

That's right.

And isn't that the reason we say that there are three primary kinds of people: philosophic, victory-loving, and profit-loving?

That's it precisely.

And also three forms of pleasure, one assigned to each of them?

Certainly.

And do you realize that, if you chose to ask three such people in turn to tell you which of their lives is most pleasant, each would give the highest praise to his own? Won't a money-maker say that the pleasure of being honored and that of learning are worth- d less compared to that of making a profit, if he gets no money from them?

He will.

What about an honor-lover? Doesn't he think that the pleasure of making money is vulgar and that the pleasure of learning—except insofar as it brings him honor—is smoke and nonsense?

He does.

And as for a philosopher, what do you suppose he thinks the other pleasures are worth compared to that of knowing where the truth lies and always being in e some such pleasant condition while learning? Won't he think that they are far behind? And won't he call them really necessary, since he'd have no need for them if they weren't necessary for life?

He will: we can be sure of that.

Then, since there's a dispute between the different forms of pleasure and between the lives themselves, not about which way of living is finer or more shameful or better or worse, but about which is more pleasant and less painful, how are we to know which of them is speaking most truly? 582

Don't ask me.

Look at it this way: How are we to judge things if

we want to judge them well? Isn't it by experience, reason, and argument? Or could anyone have better criteria than these?

How could he?

Consider, then: Which of the three men has most experience of the pleasures we mentioned? Does a profit-lover learn what the truth itself is like or acquire more experience of the pleasure of knowing it than *b* a philosopher does of making a profit?

There's a big difference between them. A philosopher has of necessity tasted the other pleasures since childhood, but it isn't necessary for a profit-lover to taste or experience the pleasure of learning the nature of the things that are and how sweet it is. Indeed, even if he were eager to taste it, he couldn't easily do so.

Then a philosopher is far superior to a profit-lover in his experience of both their pleasures.

c He certainly is.

What about an honor-lover? Has he more experience of the pleasure of knowing than a philosopher has of the pleasure of being honored?

No, for honor comes to each of them, provided that he accomplishes his aim. A rich man is honored by many people, so is a courageous one and a wise one, but the pleasure of studying the things that are cannot be tasted by anyone except a philosopher.

Then, as far as experience goes, he is the finest *d* judge of the three.

By far.

And he alone has gained his experience in the company of reason.

Of course.

Moreover, the instrument one must use to judge isn't the instrument of a profit-lover or an honor-lover but a philosopher.

What instrument is that?

Arguments, for didn't we say that we must judge by means of them?

Yes.

And argument is a philosopher's instrument most of all.

Of course.

Now, if wealth and profit were the best means of judging things, the praise and blame of a profit-lover *e* would necessarily be truest.

That's right.

And if honor, victory, and courage were the best means, wouldn't it be the praise and blame of an honor-lover?

Clearly.

But since the best means are experience, reason, and argument . . .

The praise of a wisdom-lover and argument-lover is necessarily truest.

Then, of the three pleasures, the most pleasant is that of the part of the soul with which we learn, 583 and the one in whom that part rules has the most pleasant life.

How could it be otherwise? A person with knowledge at least speaks with authority when he praises his own life.

To what life and to what pleasure does the judge give second place?

Clearly, he gives it to those of a warrior and honor-lover, since they're closer to his own than those of a money-maker.

Then the life and pleasure of a profit-lover come last, it seems.

Of course they do.

These, then, are two proofs in a row, and the just person has defeated the unjust one in both. The third *b* is dedicated in Olympic fashion to Olympian Zeus the Savior.[6] Observe then that, apart from those of a knowledgeable person, the other pleasures are neither entirely true nor pure but are like a shadow-painting, as I think I've heard some wise person say. And yet, if this were true, it would be the greatest and most decisive of the overthrows.

It certainly would. But what exactly do you mean?

I'll find out, if I ask the questions, and you answer. *c*

Ask, then.

Tell me, don't we say that pain is the opposite of pleasure?

Certainly.

And is there such a thing as feeling neither pleasure nor pain?

There is.

Isn't it intermediate between these two, a sort of

---

6. [The first toast at a banquet was to the Olympian Zeus, the third to Zeus the Savior. By combining the two aspects of Zeus in a single form of address, Plato seems to be emphasizing the importance of this final proof.]

calm of the soul by comparison to them? Or don't you think of it that way?

I do.

And do you recall what sick people say when they're ill?

Which saying of theirs do you have in mind?

That nothing gives more pleasure than being healthy, but that they hadn't realized that it was most *d* pleasant until they fell ill.

I do recall that.

And haven't you also heard those who are in great pain say that nothing is more pleasant than the cessation of their suffering?

I have.

And there are many similar circumstances, I suppose, in which you find people in pain praising, not enjoyment, but the absence of pain and relief from it as most pleasant.

That may be because at such times a state of calm becomes pleasant enough to content them.

And when someone ceases to feel pleasure, this *e* calm will be painful to him.

Probably so.

Then the calm we described as being intermediate between pleasure and pain will sometimes be both.

So it seems.

Now, is it possible for that which is neither to become both?

Not in my view.

Moreover, the coming to be of either the pleasant or the painful in the soul is a sort of motion, isn't it?

Yes.

And didn't what is neither painful nor pleasant *584* come to light just now as a calm state, intermediate between them?

Yes, it did.

Then, how can it be right to think that the absence of pain is pleasure or that the absence of pleasure is pain?

There's no way it can be.

Then it isn't right. But when the calm is next to the painful it appears pleasant, and when it is next to the pleasant it appears painful. However, there is nothing sound in these appearances as far as the truth about pleasure is concerned, only some kind of magic.

That's what the argument suggests, at any rate.

Take a look at the pleasures that don't come out *b* of pains, so that you won't suppose in their case also

that it is the nature of pleasure to be the cessation of pain or of pain to be the cessation of pleasure.

Where am I to look? What pleasures do you mean?

The pleasures of smell are especially good examples to take note of, for they suddenly become very intense without being preceded by pain, and when they cease they leave no pain behind. But there are plenty of other examples as well.

That's absolutely true.

Then let no one persuade us that pure pleasure is relief from pain or that pure pain is relief from *c* pleasure.

No, let's not.

However, most of the so-called pleasures that reach the soul through the body, as well as the most intense ones are of this form—they are some kind of relief from pain.

Yes, they are.

And aren't the pleasures and pains of anticipation, which arise from the expectation of future pleasures or pains, also of this form?

They are.

Do you know what kind of thing they are and what they most resemble?   *d*

No, what is it?

Do you believe that there is an up, a down, and a middle in nature?

I do.

And do you think that someone who was brought from down below to the middle would have any other belief than that he was moving upward? And if he stood in the middle and saw where he had come from, would he believe that he was anywhere other than the upper region, since he hasn't seen the one that is truly upper?

By god, I don't see how he could think anything else.

And if he was brought back, wouldn't he suppose that he was being brought down? And wouldn't he be right?   *e*

Of course.

Then wouldn't all this happen to him because he is inexperienced in what is really and truly up, down, and in the middle?

Clearly.

Is it any surprise, then, if those who are inexperienced in the truth have unsound opinions about lots of other things as well, or that they are so disposed to pleasure, pain, and the intermediate state that, when they descend to the painful, they believe truly and are really in pain, but that, when they ascend 585 from the painful to the intermediate state, they firmly believe that they have reached fulfilllment and pleasure? They are inexperienced in pleasure and so are deceived when they compare pain to painlessness, just as they would be if they compared black to gray without having experienced white.

No, by god, I wouldn't be surprised. In fact, I'd be very surprised if it were any other way.

Think of it this way: Aren't hunger, thirst, and the b like some sort of empty states of the body?

They are.

And aren't ignorance and lack of sense empty states of the soul?

Of course.

And wouldn't someone who partakes of nourishment or strengthens his understanding be filled?

Certainly.

Does the truer filling up fill you with that which is less or that which is more?

Clearly, it's with that which is more.

And which kinds partake more of pure being? Kinds of filling up such as filling up with bread or drink or delicacies or food in general? Or the kind of filling up that is with true belief, knowledge, understanding, and, in sum, with all of virtue? Judge it this way: That c which is related to what is always the same, immortal, and true, is itself of that kind, and comes to be in something of that kind—this is more, don't you think, than that which is related to what is never the same and mortal, is itself of that kind, and comes to be in something of that kind?

That which is related to what is always the same is far more.

And does the being of what is always the same participate more in being than in knowledge?

Not at all.

Or more than in truth?

Not that either.

And if less in truth, then less in being also?

Necessarily.

And isn't it generally true that the kinds of filling d up that are concerned with the care of the body share less in truth and being than those concerned with the care of the soul?

Yes, much less.

And don't you think that the same holds of the body in comparison to the soul?

Certainly.

And isn't that which is more, and is filled with things that are more, really more filled than that which is less, and is filled with things that are less?

Of course.

Therefore, if being filled with what is appropriate to our nature is pleasure, that which is more filled with things that are more enjoys more really and truly a more true pleasure, while that which partakes of e things that are less is less truly and surely filled and partakes of a less trustworthy and less true pleasure.

That's absolutely inevitable.

Therefore, those who have no experience of reason or virtue, but are always occupied with feasts and the 586 like, are brought down and then back up to the middle, as it seems, and wander in this way throughout their lives, never reaching beyond this to what is truly higher up, never looking up at it or being brought up to it, and so they aren't filled with that which really is and never taste any stable or pure pleasure. Instead, they always look down at the ground like cattle, and, with their heads bent over the dinner table, they feed, fatten, and fornicate. To outdo[7] others in these things, they kick and butt them with iron horns and hooves, killing each b other, because their desires are insatiable. For the part that they're trying to fill is like a vessel full of holes, and neither it nor the things they are trying to fill it with are among the things that are.

Socrates, you've exactly described the life of the majority of people, just like an oracle.

Then isn't it necessary for these people to live with pleasures that are mixed with pains, mere images and shadow-paintings of true pleasures? And doesn't the juxtaposition of these pleasures and pains make them appear intense, so that they give rise to mad erotic c passions in the foolish, and are fought over in just the way that Stesichorus tells us the phantom of Helen was fought over at Troy by men ignorant of the truth?[8]

Something like that must be what happens.

---

7. [*Pleonexias*. See 344a n.18.]

8. [According to the story, Stesichorus wrote a poem defaming Helen and was punished by being struck with blindness. His sight was restored when he added a verse to the poem in which he claimed that it was a phantom of Helen and not Helen herself who was at Troy. See *Phaedrus* 243a.]

And what about the spirited part? Mustn't similar things happen to someone who satisfies it? Doesn't his love of honor make him envious and his love of victory make him violent, so that he pursues the d satisfaction of his anger and of his desires for honors and victories without calculation or understanding?

Such things must happen to him as well.

Then can't we confidently assert that those desires of even the money-loving and honor-loving parts that follow knowledge and argument and pursue with their help those pleasures that reason approves will attain the truest pleasures possible for them, because they follow truth, and the ones that are most their own, e if indeed what is best for each thing is most its own?

And indeed it is best.

Therefore, when the entire soul follows the philosophic part, and there is no civil war in it, each part of it does its own work exclusively and is just, and in particular it enjoys its own pleasures, the best and 587 truest pleasures possible for it.

Absolutely.

But when one of the other parts gains control, it won't be able to secure its own pleasure and will compel the other parts to pursue an alien and untrue pleasure.

That's right.

And aren't the parts that are most distant from philosophy and reason the ones most likely to do this sort of compelling?

They're much more likely.

And isn't whatever is most distant from reason also most distant from law and order?

Clearly.

And didn't the erotic and tyrannical desires emerge b as most distant from these things?

By far.

And weren't the kingly and orderly ones least distant?

Yes.

Then I suppose that a tyrant will be most distant from a pleasure that is both true and his own and that a king will be least distant.

Necessarily.

So a tyrant will live most unpleasantly, and a king most pleasantly.

Necessarily.

Do you know how much more unpleasant a tyrant's life is than a king's?

I will if you tell me.

There are, it seems, three pleasures, one genuine and two illegitimate, and a tyrant is at the extreme end of the illegitimate ones, since he flees both law and reason and lives with a bodyguard of certain c slavish pleasures. But it isn't easy, all the same, to say just how inferior he is to a king, except perhaps as follows. A tyrant is somehow third from an oligarch, for a democrat was between them.

Yes.

Then, if what we said before is true, doesn't he live with an image of pleasure that is third from an oligarch's with respect to truth?[9]

He does.

Now, an oligarch, in turn, is third from a king,[10] if we identify a king and an aristocrat.   d

Yes, he's third.

So a tyrant is three times three times removed from true pleasure.

Apparently so.

It seems then, on the basis of the magnitude of its number, that the image of tyrannical pleasure is a plane figure.

Exactly.

But then it's clear that, by squaring and cubing it, we'll discover how far a tyrant's pleasure is from that of a king.

It is clear to a mathematician, at any rate.

Then, turning it the other way around, if someone wants to say how far a king's pleasure is from a tyrant's, he'll find, if he completes the calculation, that a e king lives seven hundred and twenty-nine times more pleasantly than a tyrant and that a tyrant is the same number of times more wretched.[11]

That's an amazing calculation of the difference

---

9. [Third because the Greeks always counted the first as well as the last member of a series, e.g., the day after tomorrow was the third day.]

10. [Because the timocrat is between them.]

11. [Socrates' mathematics is difficult to follow. He seems to have something like this in mind. The tyrant's image of pleasure is two-dimensional, whereas the true pleasure of the philosopher is three-dimensional. Hence, if a one-unit square represents the degree of closeness to true pleasure of an image nine times removed from it, true pleasure should be represented by a nine-unit cube. It follows that the king lives 729 times more pleasantly than the tyrant.

between the pleasure and pain of the two men, the
588 just and the unjust.

Yet it's a true one, and one appropriate to human
lives, if indeed days, nights, months, and years are
appropriate to them.

And of course they are appropriate.

Then, if a good and just person's life is that much
more pleasant than the life of a bad and unjust person,
won't its grace, fineness, and virtue be incalculably
greater?

By god, it certainly will.

All right, then. Since we've reached this point in
b the argument, let's return to the first things we said,
since they are what led us here. I think someone said
at some point that injustice profits a completely unjust
person who is believed to be just. Isn't that so?

It certainly is.

Now, let's discuss this with him, since we've agreed
on the respective powers that injustice and justice have.

How?

By fashioning an image of the soul in words, so
that the person who says this sort of thing will know
what he is saying.

c   What sort of image?

One like those creatures that legends tell us used
to come into being in ancient times, such as the
Chimera, Scylla, Cerberus,[12] or any of the multitude

However, in order to reach the number 729, which seems
to have been significant to Pythagoras and his followers
(there were, allegedly, 729 days and nights in the year, and
729 months in the "great year" recognized by the Pythagorean philosopher Philolaus), Socrates has made two fast
moves. First, he has illegitimately capitalized on the Greek
manner of counting series in order to count the oligarch
twice, once as the last term in his first series (tyrant, democrat, oligarch) and again as the first term in his second series
(oligarth, timocrat, king). Second, he has *multiplied* the
number of times the tyrant is removed from the oligarch
by the number of times the oligarch is removed from the
king, when he should have *added* them. The tyrant is therefore only five times removed from the king and lives only
125 times less pleasantly!]

12. [The Chimera was "lion in the front, serpent in the
back, and she-goat in the middle" (*Iliad* 6.181). Scylla had
six heads, each with three rows of teeth, and twelve feet
(see *Odyssey* 12.85 ff., 245 ff.). Cerberus was a huge dog
guarding the entrance to Hades; he had three heads and a
serpent's tail.]

of others in which many different kinds of things are
said to have grown together naturally into one.

Yes, the legends do tell us of such things.

Well, then, fashion a single kind of multicolored
beast with a ring of many heads that it can grow
and change at will—some from gentle, some from
savage animals.

That's work for a clever artist. However, since words
are more malleable than wax and the like, consider d
it done.

Then fashion one other kind, that of a lion, and
another of a human being. But make the first much
the largest and the other second to it in size.

That's easier—the sculpting is done.

Now join the three of them into one, so that that
they somehow grow together naturally.

They're joined.

Then, fashion around them the image of one of
them, that of a human being so that anyone who sees
only the outer covering and not what's inside will
think it is a single creature, a human being.   e

It's done.

Then, if someone maintains that injustice profits
this human being and that doing just things brings no
advantage, let's tell him that he is simply saying that it
is beneficial for him, first, to feed the multiform beast
well and make it strong, and also the lion and all that
pertains to him; second, to starve and weaken the human being within, so that he is dragged along wherever 589
either of the other two leads; and, third, to leave the
parts to bite and kill one another rather than accustoming them to each other and making them friendly.

Yes, that's absolutely what someone who praises
injustice is saying.

But, on the other hand, wouldn't someone who
maintains that just things are profitable be saying,
first, that all our words and deeds should insure that
the human being within this human being has the
most control; second, that he should take care of
the many-headed beast as a farmer does his animals, b
feeding and domesticating the gentle heads and preventing the savage ones from growing; and, third, that
he should make the lion's nature his ally, care for
the community of all his parts, and bring them up
in such a way that they will be friends with each
other and with himself?

Yes, that's exactly what someone who praises justice
is saying.

From every point of view, then, anyone who praises justice speaks truly, and anyone who praises injustice speaks falsely. Whether we look at the matter from the point of view of pleasure, good reputation, or *c* advantage, a praiser of justice tells the truth, while one who condemns it has nothing sound to say and condemns without knowing what he is condemning.

In my opinion, at least, he knows nothing about it.

Then let's persuade him gently—for he isn't wrong of his own will—by asking him these questions. Should we say that this is the original basis for the conventions about what is fine and what is shameful? Fine things are those that subordinate the beastlike parts of our nature to the human—or better, perhaps, *d* to the divine; shameful ones are those that enslave the gentle to the savage? Will he agree or what?

He will, if he takes my advice.

In light of this argument, can it profit anyone to acquire gold unjustly if, by doing so, he enslaves the best part of himself to the most vicious? If he got the gold by enslaving his son or daughter to savage and *e* evil men, it wouldn't profit him, no matter how much gold he got. How, then, could he fail to be wretched if he pitilessly enslaves the most divine part of himself to the most godless and polluted one and accepts golden gifts in return for a more terrible destruction 590 than Eriphyle's when she took the necklace in return for her husband's soul?[13]

A much more terrible one, Glaucon said. I'll answer for him.

And don't you think that licentiousness has long been condemned for just these reasons, namely, that because of it, that terrible, large, and multiform beast is let loose more than it should be?

Clearly.

And aren't stubbornness and irritability condemned because they inharmoniously increase and *b* stretch the lionlike and snakelike[14] part?

13. [Eriphyle was bribed by Polynices to persuade her husband, Amphiaraus, to take part in an attack on Thebes. He was killed, and she was murdered by her son in revenge. See *Odyssey* 11.326–7; Pindar, *Nemean* 9.37ff.]

14. [The snakelike part hasn't been previously mentioned, although it may be included in "all that pertains to" the lion (588e). It symbolizes some of the meaner components of the spirited part, such as irritability, which it would be unnatural to attribute to the noble lion.]

Certainly.

And aren't luxury and softness condemned because the slackening and loosening of this same part produce cowardice in it?

Of course.

And aren't flattery and slavishness condemned because they subject the spirited part to the moblike beast, accustoming it from youth on to being insulted for the sake of the money needed to satisfy the beast's insatiable appetites, so that it becomes an ape instead of a lion?

They certainly are.   *c*

Why do you think that the condition of a manual worker is despised? Or is it for any other reason than that, when the best part is naturally weak in someone, it can't rule the beasts within him but can only serve them and learn to flatter them?

Probably so.

Therefore, to insure that someone like that is ruled by something similar to what rules the best person, we say that he ought to be the slave of that best person who has a divine ruler within himself. It isn't to harm the slave that we say he must be ruled, which is what *d* Thrasymachus thought to be true of all subjects, but because it is better for everyone to be ruled by divine reason, preferably within himself and his own, otherwise imposed from without, so that as far as possible all will be alike and friends, governed by the same thing.

Yes, that's right.

This is clearly the aim of the law, which is the ally of everyone. But it's also our aim in ruling our children, we don't allow them to be free until we establish a constitution in them, just as in a city, and—by fostering their best part with our own— equip them with a guardian and ruler similar to our own to take our place. Then, and only then, we set 591 them free.

Clearly so.

Then how can we maintain or argue, Glaucon, that injustice, licentiousness, and doing shameful things are profitable to anyone, since, even though he may acquire more money or other sort of power from them, they make him more vicious?

There's no way we can.

Or that to do injustice without being discovered and having to pay the penalty is profitable? Doesn't the one who remains undiscovered become even more vicious, while the bestial part of the one who *b* is discovered is calmed and tamed and his gentle part freed, so that his entire soul settles into its best nature, acquires moderation, justice, and reason, and attains a more valuable state than that of having a fine, strong, healthy body, since the soul itself is more valuable than the body?

That's absolutely certain.

Then won't a person of understanding direct all c his efforts to attaining that state of his soul? First, he'll value the studies that produce it and despise the others.

Clearly so.

Second, he won't entrust the condition and nurture of his body to the irrational pleasure of the beast within or turn his life in that direction, but neither will he make health his aim or assign first place to being strong, healthy, and beautiful, unless he happens to acquire moderation as a result. Rather, it's clear that he will always cultivate the harmony of his d body for the sake of the consonance in his soul.

He certainly will, if indeed he's to be truly trained in music and poetry.

Will he also keep order and consonance in his acquisition of money, with that same end in view? Or, even though he isn't dazzled by the size of the majority into accepting their idea of blessed happiness, will he increase his wealth without limit and so have unlimited evils?

Not in my view.

Rather, he'll look to the constitution within him and guard against disturbing anything in it, either by e too much money or too little. And, in this way, he'll direct both the increase and expenditure of his wealth, as far as he can.

That's exactly what he'll do.

And he'll look to the same thing where honors are concerned. He'll willingly share in and taste those 592 that he believes will make him better, but he'll avoid any public or private honor that might overthrow the established condition of his soul.

If that's his chief concern, he won't be willing to take part in politics.

Yes, by the dog, he certainly will, at least in his own kind of city. But he may not be willing to do so in his fatherland, unless some divine good luck chances to be his.

I understand. You mean that he'll be willing to take part in the politics of the city we were founding and describing, the one that exists in theory, for I don't think it exists anywhere on earth.   b

But perhaps, I said, there is a model of it in heaven, for anyone who wants to look at it and to make himself its citizen on the strength of what he sees. It makes no difference whether it is or ever will be somewhere, for he would take part in the practical affairs of that city and no other.

Probably so, he said.

Aristotle

Aristotle (384–322 B.C.), born in the Ionian colony of Stagira in northern Greece, was the son of a physician to the Macedonian ruler. At eighteen he entered Plato's Academy in Athens, where he remained for two decades until Plato's death. He then taught outside Athens for a dozen years, including three as tutor to the young prince who later became known as Alexander the Great. In 335 Aristotle returned to Athens and founded his own school, the Lyceum, where he did his most productive research. On the death of Alexander in 323, an outbreak of anti-Macedonian feeling swept Athens, and Aristotle withdrew to the city of Calcis, "lest," he reportedly said, "the Athenians should sin twice against philosophy."

A distinguished historian of philosophy once referred to Aristotle as "the greatest mind produced by the Greeks"; even those who might not share this judgment would agree that his intellectual achievements were of enormous magnitude. Virtually singlehanded, he founded the study of logic. His philosophical treatises on metaphysics, ethics, politics, and aesthetics remain more than two thousand years later among the most profound works ever written on these subjects. His scientific studies produced groundbreaking results in biology, psychology, zoology, meteorology, and astronomy. Indeed, his later influence was so profound that during the Middle Ages he was often referred to simply as "the Philosopher."

As becomes clear in the *Categories,* a treatise on the structure of language with implications about the nature of reality, Aristotle rejected Plato's Theory of Forms, arguing that universals have no subsistence apart from particulars. For example, humanity or redness do not exist independently but only as common elements in specific substances. Thus, whereas Plato viewed knowledge as an a priori inquiry into Ideas, for Aristotle the acquisition of understanding involved an empirical investigation of essential structures shared by individual entities.

That every substance is a compound of form and matter is a position he maintained in his *Metaphysics*, so named since it came after the *Physics* in a first century B.C. edition of his works. In this treatise, after reviewing the opinions of his predecessors, he went on to investigate the study of "being *qua* being," what is true of all things that exist. He maintained that each particular is an embodied essence, a thing with an intelligible structure.

As regards the nature of persons, Aristotle rejected Plato's view of the soul as separate from the body, arguing in *On the Soul* that the soul is the body in action, just as sight is the activity of the eye. The soul, therefore, cannot exist apart from the body, for the processes of being, sensing, and knowing require an organism that lives, senses, and knows.

In the *Physics*, a study of the concepts used in physical science, Aristotle identified four causes or modes of explanation. These have come to be known as the material cause, formal cause, efficient cause, and final cause. In the case of a building, for example, its material cause may be bricks and mortar, its formal cause the architectural blueprints, its efficient cause the builders, and its final cause the providing of shelter. Aristotle stressed the importance of final causes in understanding the world, for in his view nature is teleological, exhibiting purposeful processes.

As to Aristotle's views on the purpose of human life, these are to be found in his *Nicomachean Ethics.* This work (named after Aristotle's son Nicomachus) is universally considered one of the great books of moral philosophy. It ranges from detailed analyses of such concepts as choosing, deliberating, and wishing, to a vision of the highest happiness as a life devoted to the exercise of pure reason. The book does possess some organizational difficulties; like other of Aristotle's treatises, it may consist partly of texts of his lectures as preserved in his students' notes. However, unity is provided by central themes, among which are the commitment to viewing the good as the fulfillment of human nature, the emphasis on a close relationship between ethics and the interests of society, and the need to distinguish moral from intellectual virtue.

This latter distinction provides Aristotle with an answer to the question, raised at the opening of Plato's *Meno,* as to the origin of virtue. According to Aristotle, moral virtue, which we might call "goodness of character," is formed by habit. One becomes good by doing good. Repeated acts of justice and self-control result in a just, self-controlled person who not only performs just and self-controlled actions but does so from a fixed character. Intellectual virtue, on the other hand, which we might refer to as "wisdom," is acquired by teaching and requires foresight and sophisticated intelligence.

In opposition to the Socratic doctrine that a person who knows the good will necessarily do the good, Aristotle insists on our acknowledging the phenomenon of moral weakness: the situation, so easy to recognize and yet so difficult to explain, in which individuals act contrary to what they believe to be for the best. Typically, he emphasizes that a theory which denies the existence of moral weakness is at variance with observed facts.

• • •

Helpful overviews of Aristotle's thought are John Herman Randall, Jr., *Aristotle* (1960; rpt. New York: Columbia University Press, 1962); volume six of W. K. C. Guthrie, *A History of Greek Philosophy* (Cambridge: Cambridge University Press, 1981); Jonathan Lear, *Aristotle: the Desire to Understand* (Cambridge: Cambridge University Press, 1988); and Terence Irwin, *Aristotle's First Principles* (New York: Oxford University Press, 1988). Detailed analyses of each of Aristotle's major works are provided in the standard commentary by W. D. Ross, *Aristotle: A Complete Exposition of His Works and Thought* (1923; rpt. Cleveland: Meridian Books, 1959). An incisive discussion of the *Physics* is Sarah Waterlow, *Nature, Change and Agency in Aristotle's Physics* (Oxford: Clarendon Press, 1982). Detailed studies of Aristotle's ethics include John M. Cooper, *Reason and Human Good in Aristotle* (rpt. Indianapolis: Hackett Publishing Company, 1986); Richard Kraut, *Aristotle on the Human Good* (Princeton: Princeton University Press, 1989); C. D. C. Reeve, *The Practices of Reason: Aristotle's Nicomachean Ethics* (Oxford: Clarendon Press, 1992); Nancy Sherman, *The Fabric of Character: Aristotle's Theory of Virtue* (Oxford: Clarendon Press, 1989); and Francis Sparshott, *Taking Life Seriously: A Study of the Argument of the Nicomachean Ethics* (Toronto: University of Toronto Press, 1994). Useful articles on the *Ethics* are collected in Amelie O. Rorty, ed., *Essays on Aristotle's Ethics* (Berkeley: University of California Press, 1980) and Nancy Sherman, ed., *Aristotle's Nicomachean Ethics* (Lanham, Md.: Rowman & Littlefield, 1999). A comprehensive guide to Aristotle's thought is Jonathan Barnes, ed., *The Cambridge Companion to Aristotle* (Cambridge: Cambridge University Press, 1995).

S.M.C.

Categories

Preliminary Explanations

DIFFERENT RELATIONS BETWEEN WORDS AND THINGS

1

1a1 If things have only a name in common and the account of the essence corresponding to the name is different for each, they are called homonymous. Both man and the painted animal, for instance, are animals [homonymously]; for these have only a name in common and the account corresponding to the name is different. For if someone says what being an animal
5 is for each of them, he will give a different account for each.

If things have the name in common and also have the same account of the essence corresponding to the name, they are called synonymous. Both man and ox, for instance, are animals synonymously, since each is called animal, by a common name, and the account of the essence is the same. For if someone
10 gives an account of each, saying what being an animal is for each of them, he will give the same account.

Things that are called what they are by having a name from something with a different inflexion are called paronymous; for example, the grammarian is
15 so called from grammar, and the brave person from bravery.

DIVISION OF THINGS SAID

2

Among things said, some involve combination, while others are without combination. Things involving combination are, e.g., man runs, man wins; things without combination are, e.g., man, ox, run, wins.

DIVISION OF BEINGS ACCORDING TO THEIR DIFFERENT RELATIONS TO A SUBJECT

Among beings some are said of a subject but are not 20 in any subject; man, e.g., is said of a subject, an individual man, but is not in any subject. Some are in a subject, but are not said of any subject. (By 'in a subject' I mean what belongs in something, not as a part, and cannot exist separately from what it is in.) 25 An individual [instance of] grammatical knowledge, for example, is in a subject, the soul, but is not said of any subject; and an individual [instance of] white is in a subject, the body (for all color is in body), but is not said of any subject. Some things are both said of a subject and in a subject; knowledge, e.g., is in a 1b subject, the soul, and is said of a subject, grammatical knowledge. Some things are neither in a subject nor said of a subject. This is true, for instance, of an individual man or horse; for nothing of this sort is 5 either in a subject or said of a subject.

Things that are individual and numerically one are, without exception, not said of any subject; but nothing prevents some of them from being in a subject; for an individual [instance of] grammatical knowledge is one of the things in a subject.

THE DIFFERENT RELATIONS TO THE SUBJECT EXPLAIN WHEN TRANSITIVE PREDICATIONS ARE LEGITIMATE

3

Whenever one thing is predicated of another as of a 10 subject, everything said of what is predicated is also said of the subject. Man, e.g., is predicated of an individual man, and animal of man; so animal will also be predicated of an individual man; for an indi- 15 vidual man is both man and animal.

Genera which are different and not subordinate to one another have differentiae that are different in species—e.g., the differentiae of animal and of knowledge. For footed, winged, aquatic, and biped are differentiae of animal, but none of them is a differentia

20 of knowledge; for one sort of knowledge is not differentiated from another by being biped. But if one genus is subordinate to another, nothing prevents them from having the same differentiae; for the higher genera are predicated of those below them, so that the subject will also have all the differentiae of the thing predicated.

THERE ARE TEN KINDS OF BEINGS

4

25 Of things said without combination, each signifies either substance or quantity or quality or relative or where or when or being in a position or having or acting on or being affected. To speak in outline, examples of substance are man, horse; of quantity: two feet long, three feet long; of quality: white, grammatical; of relative: double, half, larger; of where: in 2a the Lyceum, in the market place; of when: yesterday, last year; of being in a position: is lying; is sitting; of having: has shoes on, has armor on; of acting on: cutting, burning; of being affected: being cut, being burnt.

5   None of the things just mentioned is said all by itself in any affirmation; an affirmation results from the combination of these things with one another. For every affirmation seems to be either true or false, 10 whereas nothing said without combination—e.g. man, white, runs, wins—is either true or false.

Substance

PRIMARY AND SECONDARY SUBSTANCE

5

What is called substance most fully, primarily, and most of all, is what is neither said of any subject nor in any subject—e.g., an individual man or horse. The 15 species in which the things primarily called substances belong are called secondary substances, and so are their genera. An individual man, e.g., belongs in the species, man, and animal is the genus of the species; these things, then, e.g. man and animal, are called secondary substances.

DIFFERENCES BETWEEN THINGS SAID OF A SUBJECT AND THINGS IN A SUBJECT

It is evident from what has been said that if something is said of a subject, then both its name and its account 20 must be predicated of the subject. For instance, man is said of a subject, an individual man, and the name is predicated (since you will predicate man of an individual man); moreover, the account of man will also be predicated of an individual man (since an 25 individual man is also a man). And so both the name and the account will be predicated of the subject.

On the other hand, if something is in a subject, in most cases neither its name nor its account is predicated of the subject. In some cases, however, though nothing prevents the name from being predi- 30 cated of the subject, the account still cannot be predicated. White, e.g., is in a subject, body, and is predicated of body (for body is said to be white); but the account of white will never be predicated of body.

HOW OTHER THINGS DEPEND ON PRIMARY SUBSTANCES

All other things are either said of the primary sub- 35 stances as subjects, or are in them as subjects. This is evident if we examine particular cases. Animal, e.g., is predicated of man, and so also of an individual man; for if it is not predicated of any individual man, 2b neither is it predicated of man at all. Again, colour is in body, and so also in an individual body; for if it is not in any of the particular bodies, neither is it in body at all.

Hence all the other things are either said of the primary substances as subjects, or are in them as 5 subjects. If, then, the primary substances did not exist, neither could any of the other things exist. For all the other things are either said of these as subjects or are in these as subjects, so that if the primary substances did not exist, neither could any of the other things exist.

DIFFERENCES BETWEEN SECONDARY SUBSTANCES

Among secondary substances, the species is more a substance than the genus, since it is nearer to the primary substance; for if someone says what the primary substance is, it will be more informative and 10 more appropriate if he mentions the species than if he mentions the genus. It will be more informative, for instance, to say that an individual man is a man than to say that he is an animal, since man is more distinctive of an individual man, while animal is more common; and it will be more informative to say that an individual tree is a tree than that it is a plant.

15 Further, the primary substances are subjects for all the other things, and all the other things are predicated of them or are in them; and this is why they, most of all, are called substances. But as the primary substances are related to other things, so also is the
20 species related to the genus; for the species is a subject for the genus, since the genera are predicated of the species, whereas the species are not reciprocally predicated of the genera. And so for this reason too the species is more a substance than the genus.

Among species themselves, however—those that are not genera—one is no more a substance than another; for it is no more appropriate to say that an
25 individual man is a man than it is to say that an individual horse is a horse. And similarly, among primary substances one is no more a substance than another; for an individual man is no more a substance than an individual ox is.

Why Secondary Substances Are Substances

It is not surprising that, after the primary substances,
30 only their species and genera are said to be secondary substances; for they are the only things predicated that reveal the primary substance. For if one says what an individual man is, it will be appropriate to mention the species or the genus, though it will be more informative to mention man than animal. But it
35 would be inappropriate to mention anything else— e.g. white or runs or any other such thing. Hence it is not surprising that species and genera are the only other things said to be substances.

Further, it is because the primary substances are subjects for everything else that they are said to be
3a substances most fully. But as the primary substances are related to everything else, so also are the species and genera of primary substances related to all the other things; for all the other things are predicated of them. For you will call an individual man grammat-
5 ical, and hence you will call both man and animal grammatical; and the same is true in the other cases.

No Substance Is in a Subject

A feature common to every substance is not being in a subject; for a primary substance is neither said of nor in a subject. In this same way, it is evident that 10 neither are secondary substances in a subject; for man is said of a subject—an individual man—but is not in a subject, since man is not in an individual man. Similarly, animal is said of a subject—an individual man—but animal is not in an individual man.   15

Further, while things in a subject may sometimes have their name predicated of the subject, their account can never be predicated of it. Secondary substances, on the other hand, have both their account and their name predicated of the subject; for you will predicate both the account of man and the account 20 of animal, of an individual man. Hence no substance is in a subject.

This, however, is not distinctive of substance; the differentia is not in a subject either. For footed and biped are said of a subject—man—but are not in a subject, since neither footed nor biped is in man. 25 Again, the account of the differentia is predicated of whatever subject the differentia is said of; if footed is said of man, e.g., the account of footed will also be predicated of man, since man is footed.

We need not be worried that we will ever be compelled to say that the parts of substances, being in a 30 subject (the whole substance), are not substances. For when we spoke of things in a subject, we did not mean things belonging in something as parts.

Predication from a Substance is Synonymous

It is a feature of substances and differentiae that everything called from them is so called synonymously. For all the predications from these are predicated 35 either of the individuals or of the species. (For there is no predication from a primary substance—since it is not said of any subject—and among secondary substances the species is predicated of an individual, and the genus is predicated both of the species and of an individual. Similarly, differentiae are also predi- 3b cated both of the species and of the individuals.) Now the primary substances receive the account both of the species and of the genera, and the species receives the account of the genus; for whatever is said of what is predicated will also be said of the subject. Similarly, 5 both the species and the individuals receive the account of the differentiae; and we saw that synonymous things are those that both have the name in common and also have the same account. Hence everything called from substances and differentiae is so called synonymously.

Not Every Substance Is a This

10 Every substance seems to signify a this. In the case of primary substances, it is indisputably true that each of them signifies a this; for what is revealed is an individual and numerically one. In the case of secondary substances, however, it appears from the character of the name that they also signify a this, whenever 15 one speaks of man or animal; but this is not true. Rather, each signifies a quality; for the subject is not one, as the primary substance is, but man and animal are said of many things. But it does not simply signify a quality as white does; for white signifies nothing 20 other than quality, whereas the species and the genus demarcate the quality of substance—for they signify a substance of a certain quality. One demarcates a wider area with the genus than with the species; for in speaking of animal one encompasses a wider area than in speaking of man.

Substances Have no Contraries

It is also a feature of substances that nothing is contrary 25 to them. For what could be contrary to a primary substance? Nothing is contrary, for instance, to an individual man; nor is anything contrary to man or animal. This is not distinctive of substance, however, but is also true of many other things—e.g., of quantity, 30 since nothing is contrary to two feet long, nor to ten, nor to anything else of this kind. One might say that many is contrary to few, or large to small; but no definite quantity is contrary to any other.

Substance Does Not Admit of Degrees

Substance does not seem to admit of more or less. By this I do not mean that one substance is no more 35 a substance than another—for we have said that it is; rather, I mean that no substance is said to be more or less what it is. For example, if this substance is a man, it will not be more or less a man either than itself or than another. For one man is no more a man 4a than another, in the way that one white thing is whiter

than another, or one beautiful thing is more beautiful than another. In some cases a thing is called more or less something than itself—for example, the body which is white is said to be more white now than it was before, and the body which is hot is said to be more or less hot [than it was]. But substance is not 5 spoken of in this way; for a man is not said to be more a man now than before, nor is this said of any other substance. Thus substance does not admit of more or less.

Substance Individuals Are the Only Ones That Receive Contraries

It seems most distinctive of substance that numeri- 10 cally one and the same thing is able to receive contraries. In no other case could one cite something numerically one that is able to receive contraries. For example, the color that is numerically one and the same will not be pale and dark; nor will the action 15 which is numerically one and the same be bad and good; and the same is true of anything else that is not a substance. But a substance that is numerically one and the same is able to receive contraries. An individual man, for instance, being one and the same, becomes at one time pale, at another time dark, and 20 hot and cold, and bad and good; nothing of the sort appears in any other case.

An Alleged Counter-Example

Someone might object, however, that statements and beliefs are like this, since the same statement seems to be both true and false. If, e.g., the statement that 25 someone is seated is true, when he has stood up this same statement will be false. The same is true of belief; for if someone were to believe truly that someone is seated, he will believe falsely if he has the same belief about him when he has stood up.

But even if one were to accept this, even so the way in which these receive contraries is different. For in the case of substances, a thing is able to receive 30 contraries by itself changing; for it changed when it became cold from hot (since it altered), or dark from pale, or good from bad, and similarly in the other cases it is able to receive contraries by itself changing. Statements and beliefs, on the other hand, themselves 35 remain completely unmoved in every way; it is because the object [they are about] is moved that the contrary comes to be about them. For the statement that someone is seated remains the same, but it comes to be true at one time, and false at another time, when the object has been moved. The same is true of belief. Hence at least the way in which substance is able to receive contraries—by a change in itself— is distinctive of it, if indeed one were to concede that beliefs and statements are also able to receive contraries.

This, however, is not true. For it is not because they themselves receive something that a statement and a belief are said to be able to receive contraries, but because something else has been affected. For it is because the object is or is not some way that the statement is said to be true or false—not because the statement itself is able to receive contraries; for, without exception, no statement or belief is moved by anything. And so, since nothing comes to be in them, they are not able to receive contraries. But substance is said to be able to receive contraries, because it receives them itself. For it receives sickness and health, or paleness and darkness; and because it itself receives each thing of this sort, it is said to be able to receive contraries.

Hence it is distinctive of substance that numerically one and the same thing is able to receive contraries. So much, then, about substance.

Physics

BOOK II

Nature: An Internal Origin of Change

THE DIFFERENCE BETWEEN NATURAL AND
192b ARTIFICIAL OBJECTS

1

Among things that are, some are natural, others are
due to other causes. Those that are natural are animals
10 and their parts, plants, and the simple bodies, such
as earth, fire, air and water; for we say that these
things and things of this sort are natural. All these
things are evidently different from things not naturally
constituted; for each of them has in itself an origin
15 of change and stability, whether in place, or growth
and decay, or alteration.

Compare with these a bed or a cloak, or any other
such kind of thing [i.e. any artifact]. So described [as
bed etc.] and to the extent that they are products of
a craft, they have no innate impulse to change. But
20 insofar as they are coincidentally made of stone or
earth or a mixture of these, they have such an innate
impulse, and just to that extent. This is because nature
is a sort of origin and cause of change and stability,
in that to which it primarily belongs in itself and
not coincidentally.

(By 'not coincidentally' I mean the following:
Someone who is a doctor might come to be a cause
of health in himself. But still, it is not insofar as he
is being healed that he has the medical science;
25 rather, it is coincidental that the same person is a
doctor and is being healed, and that is why the two
[functions] are sometimes separated from each other.)

The same applies to everything else that is produced; for none of them has in itself the origin of
production. In some—e.g. a house and each of the

other products of handicraft—their origin is in other,
external things. In others, i.e. those that might come 30
to be coincidental causes for themselves, the origin
is in them, but is not in accord with what they are
in themselves.

WHATEVER HAS A NATURE IS A SUBSTANCE

Nature, then, is what we have said; and things have
a nature whenever they have this sort of origin. And
all these things are substance; for [substance] is a sort
of subject, and nature is always in a subject. The
things that accord with nature are both these, and 35
whatever belongs to them in themselves, as travelling 193a
upwards belongs to fire—for this neither is nor has
a nature, but is natural and accords with nature. We
have said, then, what nature is and what is natural
and accords with nature.

THERE IS NO DOUBT OF THE
EXISTENCE OF NATURE

An attempt to show that there is such a thing as nature
would be ridiculous. For it is evident that there are
many things of this sort; and to prove what is evident
from what is not is a mark of an inability to discriminate between what is known because of itself and 5
what is not. (It is clearly possible to suffer from this
inability; someone blind from birth would [have to]
make inferences about colours.) And so such people
are bound to argue about [mere] names, and understand nothing.

SOME THINK THAT NATURE IS MATTER

Some people think that the nature and substance of 10
a natural object is the primary constituent present in
it, but lacking any order in itself—in a bed, e.g., it
will be the wood, in a statue the bronze.

It is a sign of this, according to Antiphon,[1] that if

Reprinted by permission of the translators, Terence Irwin
and Gail Fine, from Aristotle, *Selections* (Indianapolis:
Hackett Publishing Company, 1995). The use of brackets
within the text indicates insertions not found in the manuscript. Headings are those of the translators.

1. [Antiphon (c. 479–411 B.C.) was an Athenian orator—S.M.C.]

you were to bury a bed, and the rotting residue were to become able to sprout, the result would be wood, not a bed; this, he thinks, is because the conventional arrangement, i.e. the craft [making the wood into a bed], is a [mere] coincident of the wood, whereas the substance is the wood that persists continuously while it is affected in these ways.

And if each of these things is related to something else in the same way (bronze and gold, e.g., to water; bones and wood to earth; and so on with anything else), that thing will also be their matter and substance.

This is why some say fire or earth or air or water is the nature of things that are; some say it is some among these, others that it is all of them. Whatever anyone supposed to persist in these cases—one thing or more than one—he takes this or these to be all the substance there is, and all the other things to be affections, states, and conditions of them; and these things are held to be everlasting, since they do not change from themselves, but the other things come to be and are destroyed an unlimited number of times.

This, then, is one way in which we speak of nature—as the primary matter that is subject for each thing that has in itself an origin of change and variation.

But Form Is Nature Too

In another way nature is the shape, i.e. the form, that accords with the account. For just as we speak of craftsmanship in what accords with craft and is crafted, so also we speak of nature in what accords with nature and is natural. But we would not yet speak of craftsmanship or of a product in accord with craft, if something were only potentially a bed and still lacked the form of a bed; nor would we say anything of the sort about whatever is naturally constituted. For what is only potentially flesh or bone neither has its nature nor is by nature until it acquires the form that accords with the account by which we define flesh or bone and say what it is.

In another way, then, nature is the shape and form of things having in themselves an origin of change; this form is not separable except in account. (What is composed of form and matter, e.g. man, is not nature, but is natural.)

Indeed, the form is nature more than the matter is.

(1) For something is called whatever it is [e.g. a bed or flesh] when it is actually so, more than when it is only potentially so.

(2) Further, a man comes to be from a man, but not a bed from a bed. Indeed, this is why some say that the nature of the bed is not the shape but the wood, because if it were to sprout the result would be wood, not a bed. But if this shows that the wood is nature, then the shape is also nature, since a man comes to be from a man.

(3) Further, nature spoken of as becoming is a road towards nature; for it is not like medical treatment, which is a road not towards medical science but towards health. For it is necessary that medical treatment proceeds *from* medical science, not *towards* medical science. But nature [as becoming] is not related to nature in this way; what is growing, insofar as it is growing, proceeds from something towards something. What is it, then, that grows? Not what it is growing from, but what it is growing into. Therefore, shape is nature.

Shape and nature are spoken of in two ways. For the privation is also form in a way. But we must consider later whether or not there is privation and a contrary in unqualified coming to be.

The Student of Nature, Unlike the Mathematician, Studies Matter

2

We have distinguished, then, the different ways in which we speak of nature. Next we should consider how the mathematician differs from the student of nature. [The difference is not obvious.] For natural bodies certainly have surfaces, solids, lengths, and points; and these are what the mathematician studies.

We should also consider whether astronomy is different from the study of nature, or a part of it. [Apparently it is a part of it;] for it would be absurd if the task of a student of nature were to know what the sun or moon is, but not to know any of the intrinsic coincidents—especially since students of nature evidently also discuss the shape of the sun and moon, particularly whether or not the earth and heaven are spherical.

Now these things are the concern of the mathematician as well as of the student of nature. But the mathematician is not concerned with them insofar as each is the limit of a natural body. Nor does he study the coincidents of a natural body insofar as they belong to a natural body. Hence he also separates them. For they are separable in thought from change, and his separating them makes no difference, since 35 no falsehood results.

Those who say there are ideas do not notice that they also do this; they separate natural objects, though 194a these are less separable than mathematical objects. This would become clear if one tried to state the definitions of both [ideas and mathematical objects]—of the things themselves and of their [intrinsic] coincidents. For odd and even, straight and curved, and also number, line, and point will not involve change, whereas flesh, bones, and man will— 5 we speak of them as we speak of the snub nose [as including matter], not as we speak of the curved.

This is also clear from the parts of mathematics more related to the study of nature—e.g., optics, harmonics, and astronomy. These are in a way the reverse 10 of geometry; for geometry investigates a natural line, but not insofar as it is natural, whereas optics investigates a mathematical line, but insofar as it is natural, not insofar as it is mathematical.

LIKE THE CRAFTSMAN, HOWEVER, HE STUDIES FORM AS WELL AS MATTER

But since we speak of nature in two ways—both as form and as matter—we should study it as though 15 we were investigating what snubness is, and hence we should study natural objects neither without their matter nor [simply] in accord with their matter. For indeed, since there are these two natures, there might be a puzzle about which one the student of nature should study. Perhaps the compound of the two? If so, then each one of them. Then is it the same or a different discipline that knows each one?

Judging by the early thinkers, the student of nature 20 would seem to study matter, since Empedocles[2] and Democritus[3] touched only slightly on form and essence. Grant, however, that craft imitates nature; and

2. [Regarding Empedocles, see Plato's *Meno*, n.6.]

3. [Democritus (c. 460–c. 370 B.C.) was a Greek philosopher who held that all things were composed of unchangeable atoms.]

grant that [in the crafts] it is the same science that knows the form and the matter up to a point—e.g. the doctor knows health, and also its constituents, bile and phlegm; and similarly the housebuilder knows both the form of the house and that its matter 25 is bricks and wood; and the same is true in the other cases. It follows that it is also a task for the study of nature to know both sorts of nature.

Moreover the same discipline studies both what something is for—i.e. the end—and whatever is for the end. Now nature is an end that something is for; for whenever a continuous change has some end, this 30 sort of terminus is also what the change is for. This is why it was a ludicrous remark when the poet said [of someone's death], 'He has reached the end he was born for.' It was ludicrous because what we mean by 'end' is not every terminus, but only one that is best.

For crafts [study both end and means, since they] produce their matter, some simply producing it, others making it suitable for their work; and we use all things as though they were for our sake, since we are 35 also an end in a way. (For the end that something is for is of two sorts, as we said in *On Philosophy*.)

There are two crafts that control the matter and involve knowledge: (a) the craft that uses [the matter], 194b and (b) the craft that directs this productive craft. Hence (a) the using craft also in a way directs, but with a difference, in that (b) the directing craft knows the form, whereas (a) the craft that directs by being productive knows the matter. For instance, (b) the 5 pilot knows what sort of form the rudder has, and he prescribes [its production], whereas (a) [the boatbuilder] knows what sort of wood and what sorts of changes are needed to make it. With products of a craft, then, we produce the matter for the sake of the product; with natural things, the matter is already present.

Further, matter is relative to something; for each 10 form has a different matter.

How much, then, must the student of nature know about form and essence? As much, perhaps, as the doctor knows about sinews, or the smith about bronze—enough to know what something is for. And he must confine himself to things that are separable in form, but are in matter—for a man is born from a man and the sun. But it is a task for first philosophy 15 [not for the study of nature] to determine what is separable and what it is like.

Cause and Chance

THE FOUR CAUSES

3

Now that we have determined these points, we should consider what sorts of causes, and how many, there are. For our inquiry aims at knowledge; and we think we have knowledge only when we find why something is so—i.e. when we find its primary cause. Clearly, 20 then, we must also do this for becoming, destruction, and every sort of natural change, so that when we know their origins we can try to refer to these in answering each of our questions.

THE MATERIAL CAUSE

In one way, then, that from which, as a constituent, an object comes into being is said to be its cause— 25 e.g. the bronze and silver, and their genera, are causes of the statue and bowl.

THE FORMAL CAUSE

In another way, the form—i.e. the pattern—is a cause. The form is the account [*logos*] of essence, and the genera of the account (e.g. of an octave, the ratio [*logos*] two to one; and in general number), and the parts that are in the account.

THE EFFICIENT CAUSE

Again, the source of the primary origin of change or stability is a cause; e.g. the adviser caused [the action], 30 and a father his child, and in general the producer causes the product and the initiator of the change causes what is changed.

THE FINAL CAUSE

Again, something's end—i.e. what it is for—is its cause, as health is of walking. For why does he walk? 35 We say, 'To be healthy'; and in saying this we think we have provided the cause. And the same is true of all the intermediate steps that advance the end, where 195a something else has initiated the change, as slimming, purging, drugs, or instruments, e.g. advance health; all of these are for the end, though they differ in that some are actions, some instruments.

We may take these, then, to be the ways we speak of causes.

THE SAME THING MAY HAVE MORE THAN ONE CAUSE

Since causes are spoken of in many ways, it follows 5 that there are many noncoincidental causes of the same thing. Both the sculpting craft and the bronze, e.g., are causes of the statue, not insofar as it is something else, but insofar as it is a statue. But they are not causes in the same way; the bronze is a cause as 10 matter, the sculpting craft as the source of the change. Some things are causes of each other—labour, e.g., is the cause of fitness, and fitness of labour. But they are not causes in the same way; fitness is the cause as end, and labour as the origin of change. Further, the same thing is the cause of contraries. For sometimes whatever is the cause of something by its presence is also held to be the cause of the contrary by its absence; e.g. we hold the absence of a pilot to have caused the wreck of the ship, when his presence would have caused its safety.

All the causes just mentioned are of four especially 15 evident types: (1) Letters are the cause of syllables, matter of artifacts, fire and such things of bodies, parts of the whole, and the assumptions of the conclusion, as that out of which. In these cases one thing—e.g. the parts—is cause as subject, while (2) the other 20 thing—the whole, the composition, and the form— is cause as essence. (3) The seed, the doctor, the adviser and, in general, the producer, are all the sources of the origin of change or stability. (4) Other things are causes as the end and the good of other things. For what the other things are for tends to be the best and their end (it does not matter whether 25 we call it the good or the apparent good). These, then, are how many kinds of causes there are.

WAYS IN WHICH CAUSES MAY BE CITED

Though there are many types of causes, they are fewer when they are arranged under heads. For causes are so called in many ways, and even among causes of the same kind some are prior and others posterior. 30 For example, the cause of health is the practitioner of the medical craft and the practitioner of a craft; the cause of an octave is the double and number;

and in every case the inclusive [and less specific causes are posterior] to the particular.

Further, some things and their genera are coincidental causes. Polycleitus[4] and the sculptor, e.g., are causes of the statue in different ways, because being 35 Polycleitus is coincidental to the sculptor. What includes the coincident is also a cause—if, e.g., the man, or, quite generally, the animal, is a cause of the statue. Some coincidental causes are more remote or more 195b proximate than others; e.g. if the pale man or the musician were said to be the cause of the statue [they would be more remote causes than Polycleitus is].

We may speak of any cause, either proper or coincidental, either as having a potentiality or as actualizing it; e.g. we may say either that the housebuilder, or 5 that the housebuilder actually building, is causing the house to be built.

Similar things may also be said about the things of which the causes are causes. For example, [we can speak of the cause] of this statue, or of a statue, or of an image in general; or of this bronze, or of bronze, or 10 of matter in general. The same is true of coincidents.

Further, we may speak in the same way of combinations [of proper and coincidental causes, and of proper and coincidental things caused]; e.g., instead of Polycleitus or a sculptor, Polycleitus the sculptor.

Still, all these ways amount to six, each spoken of in two ways. For there is (1) the particular and (2) the genus; (3) the coincident and (4) the genus of the coincident; and these may be spoken of either (5) in combination or (6) simply. And each of these 15 may be (i) actually or (ii) potentially operating. The difference is the following. (i) Causes that are actual and particular are and are not in being simultaneously with the things they cause—e.g. this one practising medicine with this one being made healthy; and in the same way, this one housebuilding with this thing 20 being built into a house. (ii) But this is not true of every cause referred to as potentially operating—for the house and the housebuilder are not destroyed simultaneously.

Here as elsewhere, we must always seek the most precise cause. A man, e.g., is building because he is a builder, and he is a builder insofar as he has his 25 building craft; his building craft, then, is the prior

4. [Polycleitus was a fifth century B.C. Greek sculptor.]

cause, and the same is true in all cases. Further, we must seek genera as causes of genera, and particulars as causes of particulars; a sculptor, e.g., is the cause of a statue, but this sculptor of this statue. And we must seek a potentiality as the cause of a potential effect, and something actualizing a potentiality as the cause of an actual effect.

This, then, is a sufficient determination of the number of causes, and of the ways they are causes. 30

LUCK AND CHANCE

4

Luck and chance are also said to be causes, and many things are said to be and to come to be because of them. We must investigate, then, in what way luck and chance are among the causes we have mentioned; whether luck is or is not the same as chance; and, in general, what they are. 35

DOUBTS ABOUT THE EXISTENCE OF LUCK

Some people even wonder whether there is any such thing as chance and luck. For, they say, nothing results from luck; everything said to result from 196a chance or luck has some definite cause—e.g. when as a result of luck someone comes to the marketplace and finds there the person he wanted to meet but did not expect, the cause is his wishing to go to market. The same is true of other things said to result 5 from luck; in every case, they say, it is possible to find some cause other than luck. For if there were such a thing as luck, it would appear truly strange and puzzling that none of the early philosophers who discussed the causes of coming into being and destruction ever determined anything about luck; in 10 fact they also would seem to have thought that nothing results from luck.

THESE DOUBTS ARE UNCONVINCING

But this too is surprising. For many things that come 15 into being and are in being result from luck and chance. Though people know perfectly well that everything that comes into being can be referred to some cause, as the old argument against luck says, still they all say that some of these things result from luck, and others do not.

Hence the early philosophers should have mentioned it in some way. But they certainly did not think luck was any of the causes they recognized—e.g. love or strife or mind or fire or any other such thing. Their position is strange, then, whether they supposed there was no such thing as luck, or thought there was, but omitted it—especially strange considering that they sometimes used it. Empedocles, for example, uses it 20 when he says that air is separated out on top, not always, but as luck has it; at least, he says in his cosmogony that it happened to run that way at that time, but often otherwise. And he says that most of the parts of animals result from luck.

Beliefs About Chance

25 There are some who also make chance the cause of our heaven and of all worlds. For they say that the vortex, and the motion that separated out and established everything in its present order, resulted from chance. And this is especially amazing. For animals and plants, they say, neither are nor come into being from luck, but rather, nature or mind or something of that sort is the cause, since it is not just any old thing that comes to be from each type of seed, but 30 an olive tree from one type, and a man from another; and yet they say that the heaven and the most divine of visible things result from chance, and that there is no cause of the sort that animals and plants have.

Now if this is so, it deserves attention; and something might well have been said about it. For in addition to the other strange aspects of what they say, it is still stranger to say all this when they see that nothing in the heavens results from chance, whereas 196b many things result from luck in the cases where [they suppose] nothing results from it. Surely the exact opposite would have been likely.

5   Some[5] indeed suppose that luck is a cause, but take it to be godlike and superhuman, and therefore obscure to the human mind.

So we must consider chance and luck—what each is, whether they are the same or different, and how they fit into the causes we have distinguished.

The Nature of Lucky Events

5

10 First, then, we see that some things always, others usually, come about in the same way. Evidently neither luck nor the result of luck is said to be the cause

5. [The reference is to Democritus.]

of these—neither of what is of necessity and always nor of what is usually. But besides these classes of things that come to be there is a third class, which everyone says results from luck; evidently, then, there 15 is such a thing as luck and chance, since we know that this third class results from luck, and that the results of luck belong to this class.

Further, some of the things that come to be come to be for something (some in accord with decision, others not, but both classes are for something), and some do not. Clearly, then, it is possible even for some 20 members of the third class—the neither necessary nor usual—to be for something. What is for something includes both the actions that result from thought and also the results of nature. This, then, is the sort of thing that we regard as a result of luck, whenever it comes about coincidentally.

['Coincidental' must be explained.] Just as some things are something in themselves, and others are 25 something coincidentally, so also it is possible for a cause to be of either sort. For example, the cause of a house is in itself the housebuilder, but coincidentally the pale or musical thing. Hence the cause in itself is determinate, but the coincidental cause is indeterminate, since one thing might have indefinitely many coincidents.

As has been said, then, whenever things that come to be for something have this coincidental cause, they are said to result from chance and luck. The difference between these should be defined later; we 30 may take it as evident for the moment that both are found in things that are for something.

An Example of a Lucky Event

[Suppose, for instance, that A wants to collect a debt from B; one day A comes to the market for some other reason, and meets B collecting subscriptions.] A would have come when B was collecting subscriptions, to recover the money from B, if A had known 35 [B would be there]. In fact, however, A did not come to do this; it was a coincidence that A came [when B was there], and did this [i.e. met B] to collect [the money]. And this is so when A frequents the place 197a [for that purpose] neither usually nor from necessity.

The end, the collection, is not a cause [of A's action] in A, but it is something he decides to do as a result of thought. And in this case A's coming is

said to result from luck; but if A always or usually frequented the place because he had decided to and
5 for the purpose of collecting the money, it would not result from luck.

How Luck Is a Cause: Explanation of Current Beliefs

Clearly, then, luck is a coincidental cause in things that are for something and in accord with decision. Hence thought—since decision requires thought—and luck concern the same things.

Now the causes whose results might be matters of luck are bound to be indeterminate. That is why luck also seems to be something indeterminate and obscure to a human being, and why it might seem
10 in one way that nothing results from luck. For, as we might reasonably expect, all these claims are correct.

(1) For in one way things do result from luck, since they are coincidental results, and luck is a coincidental cause. But luck is not the unqualified [and hence noncoincidental] cause of anything. The [unqualified] cause of a house, e.g., is a housebuilder, and
15 the coincidental cause a flute-player; and the man's coming and collecting the money, without having come to collect it, has an indefinite number of coincidental causes—he might have come because he wished to see someone, or was avoiding someone, or was going to see some sight.

(2) It is also correct to say that luck is something contrary to reason. For rational judgement tells us
20 what is always or usually the case; but luck is found in events that are neither.

(3) Hence, since causes of this sort are indeterminate, luck is also indeterminate.

Still, in some cases one might be puzzled about whether just anything might be a cause of luck. [Apparently not. Suppose someone's haircut exposes him to wind and sun, which are good for his health;] the wind or the sun's warmth, but not the haircut, might
25 be the cause of his health—for some coincidental causes are closer than others to what they cause.

How Luck Makes Someone Lucky or Unlucky

Luck is called good when something good results, bad when something bad results; we speak of being lucky and unlucky when the results are great. Hence one who just misses great evil or good is lucky or unlucky. For [though in fact he is no better or worse off than he was, he seems to be], because we think of him as already having [the great evil or good he just misses]—the short distance seems to us to be no distance. Further, it is reasonable that being lucky is unstable; for luck is unstable, since no result of luck can be either always or usually the case.
30

Both luck and chance are coincidental causes, then, as we have said, within the class of events that are capable of being neither exceptionless [i.e. always] nor usual, and specifically within the subclass of these that might be for something.

Luck Is Confined to Rational Agents

6

Chance, however, is not the same as luck, since it is 197b broader; for results of luck are also results of chance, but not all chance results result from luck. For luck and its results are found wherever it is possible to be lucky, and in general to act, and that is why luck must concern what is achievable by action. A sign of 5 this is the fact that being lucky seems to be the same, or nearly the same, as being happy, and being happy is a sort of action, since it is doing well in action. Hence what cannot act cannot do anything by luck either.

Hence neither an inanimate object nor a beast nor a child does anything by luck, because they do not have decision [which is needed for action]. Nor are they lucky or unlucky, except by a similarity—as Pro- 10 tarchus[6] said that the stones from which altars are made are lucky, because they are honored, while their fellows are trodden underfoot. Still, even these things are affected in a way by the results of luck, when an agent affects them by some lucky action; but otherwise not.

Chance, However, Is Also Found in Natural Objects

Chance, on the other hand, belongs to other animals than man and to many inanimate objects—e.g. we 15 say the horse came by chance since it was saved

---

6. [Protarchus was a student of Gorgias, regarding whom see Plato's *Meno*, n.2.]

because it came, although it did not come in order to be saved. And the tripod fell by chance, because it did not fall in order to be sat on, although it was set up in order to be sat on.

Hence it is evident that if an event is of the sort
20 that, speaking without qualification, is for something, (a) we say that it results from chance if it has an external cause and is not for the sake of its actual result; and (b) we say it results from luck if it results from chance and is an object of decision for an agent that makes decisions.

A sign of this is the fact that we say an event is pointless [*maten*] if it is [of the sort that is] for some result, but [in this case] is not for that result. If, e.g.,
25 walking is for evacuating the bowels, but when he walked [on this occasion] it was not for that reason, then we say that he walked pointlessly, and that his walking is pointless. Here we assume that an event is pointless if it is naturally for something else, but does not succeed in [being for] what it is naturally for. For if someone said that his washing was pointless because the sun was not eclipsed, he would be ridiculous, since washing is not for producing eclipses.

So also, then, an event happens by chance [*automaton*], as the name suggests, whenever it is pointless [*maten*]. For the stone did not fall in order to hit someone; it fell, then, by chance, because it might
30 have fallen because someone threw it to hit someone.

The separation of chance from luck is sharpest in natural events. For if an event is contrary to nature,
35 we regard it as a result of chance, not luck. But even this is different from [other cases of chance; the other cases] have an external cause, but [the natural cases] an internal.

How Luck and Chance Are Related to the Four Causes

We have said, then, what chance and luck are, and
198a how they differ. Each of them falls within the sort of cause that is the source of the origin of change. For they are in every case either among natural causes or among those resulting from thought; and the num-
5 ber of these is indefinite.

Chance and luck are causes of events that mind or nature might have caused, whenever they have some coincidental cause. Now nothing coincidental
10 is prior to anything that is in itself; hence clearly no

coincidental cause is prior to a cause in itself. Chance and luck are therefore posterior to mind and nature. And so however true it may be that chance is the cause of the heavens, still it is necessary for mind and nature to be prior causes of this universe and of many other things.

Connections Between the Four Causes

7

It is clear, then, that there are causes, and just the number we say there are; for that is the number of 15 answers to the question 'Why?'. For ultimately we refer the why (1) in the case of unchanging things, e.g. in mathematics, to the essence—for we refer ultimately to the definition of straight or commensurate or something else; or (2) to what first initiated change (e.g. why did they go to war?—because the 20 other side raided them); or (3) to what something is for (e.g. to be the rulers); or (4) with things that come to be, to the matter.

It is evident, then, that these are the causes, and that this is their number. Since there are four of them, it is a task for the student of nature to know them all. His answer to the question 'Why?' will be suitable to the study of nature if he refers to all of them—to the matter, the form, the initiator of change, and what something is for.

The last three often come to one; for what some- 25 thing is and what it is for are one, and the first source of the change is the same in kind as these—for man gives birth to man; and the same is true generally of things that initiate change by being changed.

Things that are changeless are outside the scope of the study of nature. For although they change things, they do not change them by having change or an origin of change within themselves, but they are unchanged. Hence there are three inquiries: one 30 about what is changeless; one about what is changed but imperishable; and one about what is perishable.

And so the why is given by referring to the matter, and to the essence, and to the first initiator of change. For in cases of coming to be, this is the normal way of examining the causes—by asking what comes to be after what, and what first acted or was affected, and so on in order in every case.   35

There are two sorts of origins that initiate change naturally. One of these origins is not itself natural, since it has no origin of change within itself; this is true of whatever initiates change without itself being 198b changed—e.g. what is completely changeless (i.e. the first of all beings) and also the essence (i.e. the form), since this is the end that something is for. So since nature is for something, this cause too must be known.

The why should be given in every way—e.g. this from this necessarily (from this without qualification 5 [i.e. always] or usually); and if this is to be (as the conclusion from the premises); and that this is the essence; and because it is better thus—not unqualifiedly better, but better in relation to the substance of each thing.

Teleology and Necessity in Nature

OBJECTION: APPARENT TELEOLOGY IN NATURE IS ONLY A CHANCE RESULT OF NECESSITY

8

10 We must first say why nature is among the causes that are for something, and then how necessity applies to natural things. For everyone refers to this cause, saying that since the hot, the cold and each element are naturally so, these other things are and come to 15 be from necessity. For indeed if they mention any other cause than necessity—as one thinker[7] mentions love or strife, and another[8] mentions mind—they just touch on it, then let it go.

Here, then, is a puzzle: why not suppose nature acts not for something or because it is better, but from necessity? Zeus's rain does not fall in order to make the grain grow, but from necessity; for it is necessary that what has been drawn up should cool, 20 and that what has cooled and become water should come down, and it is coincidental that this makes the grain grow. Similarly, if someone's grain is spoiled on the threshing-floor; it does not rain in order to spoil the grain, but it is coincidental that the rain spoils the grain.

Why not suppose, then, that the same is true of the parts of organisms in nature? It will be from necessity, e.g., that the front teeth come up sharp and

7. [The reference is to Empedocles.]

8. [The reference is to Anaxagoras, regarding whom see Plato's *Apology*, n.7.]

[coincidentally] suitable for biting, and the back ones 25 broad and useful for chewing food—since this [useful] result was coincidental, not what they came about for. And the same will be true of all the other parts when they seem to be for something.

On this view, then, whenever all the parts came about coincidentally as though for something, these animals survived, since their chance constitution 30 made them suitable for survival. Other animals, however, were differently constituted, and so were destroyed—indeed they are still being destroyed—as Empedocles says of the man-headed calves.

REPLY TO OBJECTION: NOT ALL NATURAL REGULARITIES HAPPEN BY CHANCE

This argument, then, and others like it, might puzzle someone. In fact, however, it is impossible for things to be like this. For these [teeth and other parts], and all natural things, come to be as they do either always 35 or usually, whereas no result of luck or chance does. For we do not regard frequent winter rain or a summer heatwave, but only summer rain or a winter heatwave, 199a as a result of luck or coincidence. If, then, these [teeth, etc.] seem to be either coincidental results or for something, and they cannot be coincidental or 5 chance results, it follows that they are for something. Now surely all such things are natural, as even those making these claims [about necessity] would agree. We find, then, that things are for something when they come into being and remain in being naturally.

ARGUMENTS FROM CRAFT TO NATURE SUPPORT NATURAL TELEOLOGY

Further, whenever a sequence has an end, the earlier action and the next in order are done for the end. Surely what is true for action is true for nature, and 10 what is true for nature is true for each action, if nothing prevents it. Now an action is done for something; what is natural, therefore, is for something. For example, if a house came into being naturally, it would do so just as it actually does by craft; and if 15 natural things came into being not only naturally but also by craft, they would come into being just as they do naturally; one thing, then, is for the other. In general, craft either completes the work that nature is unable to complete or imitates nature. If, then, what accords with craft is for something, then clearly what accords with nature is also for something; for there is the same relation of earlier stages to later both in sequences that accord with craft and in those that accord with nature.

20   This is most evident with animals other than man, since they use neither craft nor inquiry nor deliberation in their production [but nonetheless act for some end]—indeed this is why some are puzzled about whether spiders, ants, and other such things operate by understanding or in some other way. If we advance little by little in this way, it is evident that even in

25 plants things come to be that promote the end—leaves, e.g., grow for the protection of the fruit. If, then, it is both naturally and for some end that a swallow makes its nest and a spider its web, and if plants grow leaves for the sake of the fruit, and send roots down rather than up for nourishment, it evi-

30 dently follows that this sort of cause is found in things that come into being and remain in being naturally. And since nature is of two sorts, as matter and as form, and the form is the end, and since everything else is for the end, the form must be the cause that the other things are for.

THESE ARGUMENTS EXPLAIN APPARENT IRREGULARITIES IN NATURE

Errors occur even in what accords with craft—e.g. the grammarian writes incorrectly, and the doctor

35 gives the wrong medicine. And so clearly errors are

199b also possible in what accords with nature.

Now in some cases that accord with craft, the correct action is for something, and when errors occur, the attempt is for something, but misses the mark. It will be the same, then, in natural things; freaks will be errors missing the end they are for. Hence in

5 [Empedocles'] original formations of things, a defective origin would also have brought the [man-headed] calves into being, if they were unable to reach any definite term and end—as [freaks] come into being now when the seed is defective.

Further, it is necessary for the seed to come into being first, and not the animal right away; and in fact [Empedocles'] 'all-natured first' was seed.

Further, what is for something is present in plants as well as in animals, though it is less articulate. Then

10 what about plants [in Empedocles' beginning]? Did olive-headed vines keep coming into being, as he

says [man-headed] calves did? Surely not—that is absurd—but surely [mixed plants] would have to have come into being, if [mixed] animals did.

Further, [on Empedocles' view] coming into being would have to be mere luck among seeds also. But whoever says this entirely does away with nature and natural things. For things are natural when they are moved continuously from some origin in themselves and so arrive at some end; and from each origin 15 comes, not the same thing in each case, but not just any old thing either, and it always proceeds to the same [end] if nothing prevents it.

Not certainly the end that a process is for and the process that is for the end might also result from luck. We say, e.g., that the friend in the foreign country came by luck and paid the ransom and then went 20 away, if he does the action as though he had come to do it, but that was not in fact what he came to do. This [end is achieved] coincidentally—for luck is one of the coincidental causes, as we also said before. But whenever this [end] comes about always or usually, it is neither coincidental nor a result of luck. And 25 in natural things it is always so, unless something prevents it.

NOR DOES TELEOLOGY REQUIRE DELIBERATION

Besides, it is strange for people to think that no process comes about for something unless they see an agent who by deliberating has initiated the change. Even a craft does not deliberate. Moreover, if the shipbuilding craft were in the wood, it would produce a ship in the same way that nature would; and so if one thing is for another in craft, it is so in nature too. This 30 is clearest when a doctor applies medical treatment to himself—that is what nature is like.

It is evident, then, that nature is a cause as the end that something is for.

A COMMON MISCONCEPTION OF NATURAL NECESSITY

9

Is what is necessary necessary only given an assumption, or can it also be unconditional?

The current view is that there is [unconditional] 35 necessity in things that come to be. It is as though someone supposed that a wall has come into being from [unconditional] necessity, because heavy things naturally move downwards, and light things to the 200a surface, so that the stones and the foundations are below, while the earth is above because of its lightness, and the wooden logs are on the very top because they are lightest of all.

The Real Relation of
Necessity to Teleology

In fact, however, though the wall certainly requires these things, it did not come into being because of 5 them—except in the way something comes into being because of its matter—but to give shelter and protection.

The same is true in all other cases where something is for something; though they require things that have a necessary nature, they do not come about because of these things, except in the way that things come about because of their matter, but for something. For 10 instance, why is a saw this sort of thing? In order to do this, and for this [i.e. sawing]. But this end that the saw is for cannot come into being unless the saw is made of iron; it is necessary, then, for it to be made of iron if there is to be a saw performing its function. What is necessary, then, is so given the assumption [that the end is to be achieved], but not necessary as an end; for necessity is in the matter, whereas the 15 end that the process is for is in the account [containing the function of the saw].

Necessity in Nature and in Mathematics

Necessity is found both in mathematics and in things that come into being in accord with nature; and to some extent the two cases are similar. For instance, since the straight is [defined as] this, it is necessary for a triangle to have angles equal to two right angles. It is not true that since the triangle is so, the straight is so; if, however, the triangle is not so, the straight is not so either.

In things that come to be for something, it is reversed; if the end is or will be, then the previous 20 things are or will be too. Just as, in the mathematical case, if the conclusion [about the triangle] is not so, the origin [about the straight] will not be so either,

so also in nature if the previous things are not in being, the end that the process is for will not come about either.

[The analogy with mathematics is quite close.] For the end [like the mathematical origin] is also an origin; it is an origin not of action, but of reasoning [about how to achieve the end], and in the mathematical case, the origin is the origin of reasoning, since there is no action.

And so, if there is to be a house, it is necessary for 25 these things to come to be or to be present or, in general, for the matter that is for something to be there—bricks and stones, e.g., if there is to be a house. However, the end is not because of these things, except in the way something is because of its matter; nor will it come about because of them. In general, however, the end—the house or the saw—requires them—the stones or iron. Similarly, in the mathemat- 30 ical case, the origins require the triangle to have two right angles.

Both Matter and Teleology Concern
the Student of Nature

Evidently, then, what is necessary in natural things is what is spoken of as matter, and the changes of matter. The student of nature should mention both causes, but more especially what something is for, since this is the cause of the matter, whereas the matter is not the cause of the end. The end is what 35 something is for, and the origin is from the definition and the account [saying what something is for].

It is the same with things in accord with craft. For 200b instance, since a house is like this, these things must come to be and be present from necessity; and since health is this, these things must come to be and be present from necessity. In the same way, if a man is this, these things must [come to be and be present, from necessity]; and if these, then these.

But [we must not suppose that the account stating the end excludes necessity;] presumably necessity is also present in the account. Suppose, for instance, we define the function of sawing as this sort of cutting; 5 this sort of cutting requires a saw with teeth of this sort; and these require a saw made of iron. [Hence a saw is defined as being made of iron.] For some parts in the account are in it as matter of the account.

On the Soul

BOOK I

Introduction to the Study of the Soul

PROBLEMS OF METHOD

1

402a We suppose that knowing is fine and honorable, and that one type of knowing is finer and more honorable than another either because it is more exact or because it is concerned with better and more wonderful things. On both grounds, we might reasonably place 5 inquiry into the soul in the first rank. Moreover, knowledge of it seems to make an important contribution to [knowledge of] the truth as a whole, and especially to the [knowledge of] nature, since the soul is a sort of principle of animals. We seek to study and know the nature and essence of the soul, and then all of its coincidental properties; some of these seem to be distinctive attributes of the soul, while others also 10 seem to belong to animals because they have souls.

And yet it is altogether in every way a most difficult task to reach any conviction about the soul. For, as in many other areas of study, we are seeking the essence and the what-it-is; and so someone might perhaps think some single line of inquiry is appropriate for every case where we want to know the 15 substance—just as demonstration suits all coincidental properties that are distinctive of a given subject. On this view, then, we should seek this single line of inquiry. If, however, no single line of inquiry is suitable for the what-it-is, our task turns out to be still more difficult, since in that case we must discover how to study each area. But even if it is evident

whether demonstration or division or some further 20 line of inquiry is the right one, the question of where to begin our investigation causes many puzzles and confusions; for different things—for instance, numbers and surfaces—have different principles.

THE INITIAL QUESTIONS

First of all, presumably, we must determine the soul's genus and what it is. Is it, in other words, a this and a substance, or a quality, or a quantity, or something in one of the other predications that we have distin- 25 guished? Further, is it something potential or is it more of an actuality? That makes quite a bit of differ- 402b ence. We should also examine whether it is divisible into parts or has no parts. Do all souls belong to the same species or not? If not, do they differ in species, or in genus? As things are, those who discuss and inquire into the soul would seem to examine only the human soul. Nor should we forget to ask whether 5 there is just one account of the soul, as there is of animal, or a different account for each type of soul— for instance, of horse, dog, man, god—so that the universal animal either is nothing or else is posterior to these. The same will apply to any other common thing predicated.

Further, if there are not many types of soul, but [one type of soul with many] parts, must we begin 10 by inquiring into the whole soul, or by inquiring into the parts? It is also difficult to determine which parts differ in nature from each other and whether we should begin by inquiring into the parts or for their functions. Should we, for instance, begin with understanding, perceiving, and so on, or with the part that understands and the part that perceives? And if we should begin with the functions, we might be puzzled 15 anew about whether we should investigate the corresponding objects before the functions—the object of perception, for instance, before perceiving, and the object of understanding before understanding.

Reprinted by permission of the translators, Terence Irwin and Gail Fine, from Aristotle, *Selections* (Indianapolis: Hackett Publishing Company, 1995). The use of brackets within the text indicates insertions not found in the manuscript. Headings are those of the translators.

194

ESSENCE, COINCIDENT, AND DEFINITION

It would indeed seem useful to know the what-it-is, in order to study the causes of the coincidental properties of substances. In mathematics, for instance, it is useful to know what straight and curved are or 20 what a line and a surface are, in order to notice how many right angles the angles of a triangle are equal to. Conversely, however, the [knowledge of the] coincidental properties also is also very important for knowing the what-it-is. For we can state the essence best once we can describe how all or most of the 25 coincidental properties appear to be; for since the 403a what-it-is is the principle of all demonstration, a definition will clearly be dialectical and empty unless it results in knowledge, or at least in ready conjecture, about the coincidental properties.

THE RELATION OF PSYCHIC STATES TO THE BODY

A further puzzle arises about whether all the affections of the soul also belong to what has the soul or there 5 is also some affection that is distinctive of the soul itself. We must find the answer, but it is not easy.

In most cases (for instance, being angry or confident, having an appetite, or perceiving in general), it appears that without the body the soul neither is affected nor acts. Understanding, more than the other affections, would seem to be distinctive *of the soul*; but if it is also some sort of appearance or requires 10 appearance, then understanding also requires a body. And so if some function or affection of the soul is distinctive of it, then the soul would be separable; but if not, then it would not be separable. Similarly, the straight, insofar as it is straight, has many coincidental properties—for instance, that it touches a bronze sphere at a point—but if it is separated, it will 15 not touch the sphere in this way; for it is inseparable, given that in every case it requires some body.

In fact, all the affections of the soul—emotion, gentleness, fear, pity, confidence, and, further, joy, loving, and hating—would seem to require a body, since whenever we have them the body is affected in some way. An indication of this is the fact that 20 sometimes, though something severe and obvious affects us, we are not provoked or frightened; and sometimes we are moved by something small and faint, if the body is swelling and in the condition that accom-

panies anger. It is still more evident that sometimes, though nothing frightening is happening, people are affected just as a frightened person is.

If this is so, then clearly affections are forms that 25 involve matter. Hence the formulae will be, for instance: 'Being angry is a certain motion of this sort of body or part or capacity by this agency for this end'. Hence study of the soul—either every sort or this sort—turns out to be a task for the student of nature.

PROBLEMS OF DEFINITION

The student of nature and the dialectician would give different definitions of each of these affections—of anger, for instance. The dialectician would define it 30 as a desire to inflict pain in return for pain, or something of that sort, whereas the student of nature would define it as a boiling of the blood and of the hot [element] around the heart. The student of nature 403b describes the matter, whereas the dialectician describes the form and the account: for desire, for instance, is the form of the thing, but its existence requires this sort of matter. Similarly, the account of a house is of this sort—that it is a shelter preventing destruction by wind, rain, or heat; someone else will 5 say that it is stones, bricks, and timber; and someone else will say that it is the form in these [stones, for instance], for the sake of this end. Who, then, is the [real] student of nature—the one who is concerned with the matter but is ignorant of the account, or the one who is concerned only with the account? Or is the [real] student of nature more properly the one who mentions both form and matter? If so, then what is each of the first two?

Perhaps in fact there is no one who is concerned 10 with the inseparable affections of matter but not concerned with them insofar as they are separable. Rather, the student of nature is concerned with all the actions and affections of this sort of body and this sort of matter; what is not of this sort concerns someone else, perhaps a craftsman (for instance, a carpenter or a doctor). Inseparable affections, insofar as they 15 are not affections of this sort of body but [are considered] by abstraction, concern the mathematician; insofar as they are separated, they concern first philosophy.

We should return to where our discussion began.

We were saying, then, that the affections of the soul (for instance, emotion and fear) are, insofar as they are affections of the soul, inseparable (unlike surface and line) from the natural matter of animals.

BOOK II
Definition of the Soul

SUBSTANCES AS FORM, MATTER, AND COMPOUND

1

412a3 So much for the views on the soul that our predecessors have handed down. Let us now return and make
5 a new start, trying to determine what the soul is and what account of it best applies to all souls in common.

We say, then, that one kind of being is substance. One sort of substance is matter, which is not a this in its own right; another sort is shape or form, which makes [matter] a this; and the third sort is the com-
10 pound of matter and form. Matter is potentiality, and form is actuality; actuality is either, for instance, [the state of] knowing or [the activity of] attending [to what one knows].

NATURAL BODIES ARE SUBSTANCES
AS COMPOUNDS, SOULS AS FORM AND
FIRST ACTUALITY

What seem to be substances most of all are bodies, and especially natural bodies, since these are the sources of the others. Some natural bodies are alive and some are not—by 'life' I mean self-nourishment,
15 growth, and decay.

It follows that every living natural body is a substance and, [more precisely,] substance as compound. But since every such body is also this sort of body—i.e. the sort that is alive—the soul cannot be a body, since the body [is substance] as subject and matter and is not said
20 of a subject. The soul, then, must be substance as the form of a natural body that is potentially alive. Now, substance is actuality; hence the soul will be the actuality of this specific sort of body.

Actuality is spoken of in two ways—one corresponding to [the state of] knowing and the other to attending to [what one knows]. Evidently, then, the soul is the same sort of actuality that knowing is. For both being asleep and being awake require the
25 presence of the soul; being awake corresponds to

attending and being asleep to the state of inactive knowing. Moreover, in the same subject the state of knowing precedes the activity. Hence the soul is the first actuality of a natural body that is potentially alive.

The sort of natural body that is potentially alive is 412b an organic one. The parts of plants are also organs, though altogether simple ones; the leaf, for instance, is a shelter for the shell, and the shell for the fruit, and similarly the roots correspond to a mouth, since both draw in food. And so, if we must give an account common to every sort of soul, we will say that the 5 soul is the first actuality of a natural organic body.

Hence we need not ask whether the soul and body are one, any more than we need to ask this about the wax and the seal or, in general, about the matter and the thing of which it is the matter. For while one and being are spoken of in several ways, the actuality [and what it actualizes] are fully one.

We have said in general, then, that the soul is 10 substance that corresponds to the account; and this [sort of substance] is the essence of this sort of body. Suppose some instrument—an axe, for instance— were a natural body; then being an axe would be its substance, and its soul would also be this [i.e. being an axe]; and if this substance were separated from it, it would no longer be an axe, except homonymously. 15 In fact, however, it is an axe; for the soul is not the essence and form of this sort of body but of the specific sort of natural body that has in itself a principle of motion and rest.

We must also study this point by applying it to the parts [of living things]. If the eye, for instance, were an animal, sight would be its soul. For sight is the eye's substance that corresponds to the account, while 20 the eye is the matter of sight; if an eye loses its sight, it is no longer an eye, except homonymously, as a stone eye or a painted eye is. We must apply this point about the part to the whole living body; for what holds for the relation of part [of the faculty of perception] to part [of the body] holds equally for the relation of the whole *faculty of* perception to the whole perceptive body, insofar as it is perceptive. The 25 sort of body that is potentially alive is not the one that has lost its soul but the one that has it; and the seed or the fruit is potentially this sort of body.

Being awake, then, is a [second] actuality, corresponding to cutting or seeing. The soul is [a first] actuality, corresponding to [the faculty of] sight and 413a to the potentiality of the instrument [to cut]; and the body is potentially this. And as an eye is the pupil plus sight, so an animal is soul plus body.

SOME PARTS OF THE SOUL MAY BE SEPARABLE FROM THE BODY

It is clear, then, that the soul is not separable from the body. At least, some parts of it are not, if it is 5 divisible into parts; for the actuality of some [parts of the soul] is [the actuality] of the parts [of the body] themselves. Still, some [parts of the soul] might well not be actualities of any body and might therefore be separable. Moreover, it is still unclear whether the soul is the actuality of the body in the way a sailor is of a ship.

10   Let this, then, be our outline definition and sketch of the soul.

CRITERIA FOR A DEFINITION

2

Since what is perspicuous and better known from the point of view of reason emerges from what is less perspicuous but more evident, we must start again and apply this approach to the soul. For the defining account must not confine itself, as most definitions 15 do, to showing the fact; it must also contain and indicate its cause. The accounts that are customarily stated in formulae are like conclusions, so that if we ask, for instance, what squaring is, we are told that it is making an equilateral rectangle equal to an oblong rectangle. This sort of formula is an account of the conclusion, whereas the one that defines squaring as 20 the finding of the mean states the cause of the fact.

DIFFERENT FORMS OF LIFE

To begin our inquiry, then, we say that living is what distinguishes things with souls from things without souls. Living is spoken of in several ways—for instance, understanding, perception, locomotion and 25 rest, and also the motion involved in nourishment, and decay and growth. And so whatever has even one of these is said to be alive.

This is why all plants as well [as animals] seem to be alive, since they evidently have an internal potentiality and principle through which they both grow and decay in contrary directions. For they grow up and down and in all directions alike, not just up rather than down; they are continually nourished, and 30 they stay alive as long as they can absorb nourishment. This [sort of life] can be separated from the others, but in mortal things the others cannot be separated from it. This is evident in the case of plants, since they have no other potentiality of the soul.

This principle, then, is what makes something 413b alive. What makes something an animal is primarily perception; for whatever has perception, even without motion or locomotion, is said to be an animal, not simply to be alive. Touch is the primary type of perception belonging to all animals, and it can be sepa- 5 rated from the other senses, just as the nutritive [potentiality] can be separated from touch and the other senses.

THE PARTS OF THE SOUL

The part of the soul that belongs to plants as well as to animals is called nutritive; and all animals evidently have the sense of touch. Later we will state the expla- 10 nation of each of these facts. For now let us confine ourselves to saying that the soul is the principle of the [potentialities] we have mentioned—for nutrition, perception, understanding, and motion—and is defined by them.

Is each of these a soul or a part of a soul? And if a part, is it the sort that is separable only in account, 15 or is it also separable in place? In some cases the answer is easily seen, but some parts raise a puzzle. For some plants are evidently still alive when they are cut [from one plant] and are separated from each other; for, we assume, the soul in each plant is actually one but potentially more than one. And we see that the same is also true of other differentiae of the soul. 20 [This is clear] in the case of insects that are cut in two. For each part has both perception and locomotion; if it has perception, then it also has appearance and desire. For if it has perception, then it has pain and pleasure, and if it has these, then it necessarily also has appetite.

So far, however, nothing is evident about under- 25 standing and the potentiality for theoretical study. It would seem to be a different kind of soul, and the only part that can be separated, in the way in which the everlasting can be separated from the perishable.

It evidently follows, however, that the other parts

of the soul are not separable, as some say they are.
30 But they evidently differ in account; for perceiving is different from believing, and hence being the perceptive part is different from being the believing part, and so on for each of the other parts mentioned.

Further, animals are differentiated by the fact that some of them have all of these parts, some have
414a some of them, and some have only one; we should investigate the reason for this later. Practically the same is true of the senses; some animals have all of them, some have some of them, and some have only the most necessary one, touch.

ANOTHER APPROACH TO THE DEFINITION OF THE SOUL

5 When we say we live and perceive by something, we speak in two ways, just as we do when we say we know by something. For we say we know either by knowledge or by the soul, since we say we know by each of these; and similarly, we are healthy in one way by health, in another way by some part or the whole of the body. In these cases, knowledge or health is a sort of shape and form, i.e. an account and a
10 sort of actuality of what is receptive of knowledge or health; for the actuality of the agent seems to occur in the thing that is acted on and suitably disposed.

Now the soul is that by which we primarily live, perceive, and think, and so it will be an account and a
15 form, not matter and subject. For substance, as we said, is spoken of in three ways, as form, matter, and the compound of both; of these, matter is potentiality, form actuality. Since, therefore, the compound of body and soul is ensouled, body is not the actuality of soul, but the soul is the actuality of some sort of body.

THE RELATION OF SOUL TO BODY

This vindicates the view of those who think that the
20 soul is not a body but requires a body; for it is not a body, but it belongs to a body, and for that reason it is present in a body, and in this sort of body. Our predecessors were wrong, then, in trying to fit the soul into a body without further determining the proper sort of body, even though it appears that not
25 just any old thing receives any old thing. Our view, however, is quite reasonable, since a thing's actuality naturally comes to be in what has the potentiality for it, i.e. in the proper matter.

It is evident from this, then, that the soul is a certain sort of actuality and form of what has the potentiality to be of this sort.

THE DIFFERENT PARTS OF THE SOUL

3

As we said, some things have all the potentialities of the soul that were previously mentioned, while other 30 things have some of these potentialities, and others have only one. The potentialities we mentioned were those for nutrition, perception, desire, locomotion, and understanding. Now, plants have only the nutritive part. Other things have the nutritive part and also 414b the perceptive part, and if they have the perceptive part, they also have the desiring part. For desire includes appetite, emotion, and wish; but all animals have at least the sense of touch, and whatever has any perception has pleasure and pain and finds things 5 pleasant or painful. Whatever finds things pleasant and painful also has appetite, since appetite is desire for what is pleasant.

Further, animals have the perception of nourishment; for touch is perception of nourishment, since all living things are nourished by things that are dry and wet and hot and cold, and touch is the perception of these. Animals are nourished by other objects of perception only coincidentally, since neither sound 10 nor color nor smell contributes anything to nourishment, and flavor is an object of touch. Now, hunger and thirst are appetites for the dry and hot, and the wet and cold, respectively, while flavor is a sort of pleasant relish belonging to these.

We must make these points clear later on. For now let us confine ourselves to saying that living things that 15 have touch also have desire. Whether they all have appearance is not clear, and must be considered later.

Besides these parts, some things have the locomotive part. Other—human beings, for instance, and any thinking being that is different from, or superior to, a human being—also have the thinking part and intellect.

A COMPLETE ACCOUNT OF THE SOUL MUST DESCRIBE THESE PARTS

Clearly, then, soul will have one single account in 20 the same way that figure has; for just as figure is nothing besides the triangle and the figures that follow in order, so equally the soul is nothing besides those [potentialities] we have mentioned. Still, in the case of figures we can find a common account that fits all of them and is distinctive of none; the same is 25 true for the souls we have mentioned. It is ridiculous, then, in these and other such cases, to seek a common account that is not distinctive of any being and does not fit the proper and indivisible species, if we neglect 32 this [distinctive] account. Hence we must ask what the soul of each particular [kind of thing]—for instance, a 33 plant, a human being, or a beast—is.

What is true of the soul is similar to what is true 38 of figure; for in both cases the earlier is invariably present potentially in its successor—for instance, the triangle in the square, and the nutritive in the percep-415a tive. We must consider why they are in this order. For the perceptive part requires the nutritive, but in plants the nutritive is separated from the perceptive. Again, each of the other senses requires touch, 5 whereas touch is found without the other senses, since many animals lack sight, hearing, and smell. Among things that perceive, some but not all have the locomotive part. Finally and most rarely, some have reasoning and understanding. For perishable things that have reasoning also have all the other parts of the 10 soul; but not all of those that have each of the other parts also have reasoning—on the contrary, some animals lack appearance, while some live by appearance alone. Theoretical intellect requires a different account.

Clearly, then, the account of each of these parts of the soul is also the most proper account of [each type of] soul.

Nutrition and Generation

4

If we are to investigate these [parts of the soul] we 15 must find what each of them is and then inquire into the next questions and those that follow. And if we ought to say what, for instance, the understanding or the perceptive or the nutritive part is, we should first say what it is to understand or perceive, since actuali-20 ties and actions are prior in account to potentialities. If this is so, and if in addition the objects corresponding to the actualities are prior to them and so must be studied first, then we must, for the same reason, begin by determining the objects corresponding to

nutrition, sense, and understanding. And so we should first discuss nourishment and generation; for the nutritive soul belongs to other living things as well as [to plants], and it is the first and most widely shared 25 potentiality of the soul, the one that makes all living things alive.

Its functions are generation and the use of nourishment. For the most natural of all functions for a living thing, if it is complete and not defective and does not come to be by chance, is to produce another thing of the same sort as itself (an animal, if it is an animal, and a plant, if it is a plant), in order to share as far as it can in the everlasting and divine. For this 415b is the end they all strive for, and for its sake they do every action that accords with nature. (What something is for is of two types—the goal and the beneficiary.) These living things cannot share in the everlasting and divine by continuously existing, since no perishable thing can remain numerically one and the same; hence they share in it as far as they can, to 5 different degrees, and what remains is not the [parent] itself, but something else of the same sort as [the parent]—something that is specifically, not numerically, one with [the parent].

The Soul Is a Formal, Efficient, and Final Cause

The soul is the cause and principle of the living body. Now, causes are spoken of in many ways, and the soul is a cause in three of the ways distinguished— 10 as the source of motion, as what something is for, and as the substance of ensouled bodies.

It is clearly the cause as substance; for a thing's substance is the cause of its being, and the being of living things is their living, the cause and principle of which is soul. Moreover, the actuality is the form of what is potentiality.

The soul is evidently also a cause by being what 15 something is for. For just as productive thought aims at something, so does nature, and what it aims at is its end. In living things the natural end is the soul; for all natural bodies, of plants no less than of animals, are organs of the soul, since they are for the sake of 20 the soul. (The end for the sake of which is of two types, either the goal or the beneficiary.)

Moreover, the soul is also the source of locomotion, though not all living things have this potentiality.

Alteration and growth also depend on the soul; for
25 perception seems to be some kind of alteration, and
nothing that lacks a soul perceives. The same applies
to growth and decay; for nothing either decays or
grows naturally without being nourished, and nothing
that has no share of life is nourished.

Nutrition and Generation Show the Different Ways the Soul Is a Cause

Empedocles is wrong when he adds that plants grow
416a by putting down roots because earth naturally moves
downwards, and that plants grow by extending upwards because fire naturally moves upwards. His conception of up and down is wrong. For up and down
are not the same for each particular [sort of] thing
5 as they are for the universe as a whole; in fact, if we
ought to call organs the same or different in accordance with their functions, a plant's roots correspond
to an animal's head. Besides, what is it that holds
the fire and earth together when they are moving in
contrary directions? For they will be torn apart unless
something prevents it; whatever prevents it will be
the soul, the cause of growing and being nourished.
10   Some think the nature of fire is the unqualified
cause of nourishment and growth, since it is the only
body that is evidently nourished and grows, and hence
one might suppose that it also performs this function
in both plants and animals. In fact, however, fire is
15 a sort of joint cause, but not the unqualified cause;
it is the soul, rather than fire, that is the unqualified
cause. For while fire grows without limit, as long as
there is fuel, the size and growth of everything naturally constituted has a limit and form, which are
characteristic of soul, not of fire—i.e., of the form
rather than of the matter.

Different Accounts of Nutrition Turn out to Be Consistent

Since one and the same potentiality of the soul is
20 both nutritive and generative, we must first determine
the facts about nutrition; for this is the function that
distinguishes the nutritive potentiality from others.
    Contrary seems to nourish contrary, not in every
case, but only when they not only come to be but
also grow from each other; for many things come to
25 be from each other (healthy from sick, for instance)
without gaining any quantity. And not even those

contraries that grow seem to nourish each other in
the same way; water, for instance, nourishes fire, but
fire does not nourish water. It seems to be true, then,
of the simple bodies more than of other things, that
one thing nourishes and the other is nourished.

A puzzle arises: while some say that like nourishes 30
like, just as (they say) like grows by like, others, as
we have said, hold the opposite view, that contrary
nourishes contrary; for, they say, like is unaffected by
like, but nourishment changes and is digested, and
everything changes into its opposite or into the intermediate. Moreover, nourishment is affected by the 35
thing nourished, whereas the thing nourished is unaffected by the nourishment—just as the matter is af- 416b
fected by the carpenter, who is unaffected by it and
merely changes from inactivity to activity.

It matters for this question whether nourishment
is the first or last thing added. Perhaps it is both, if 5
undigested nourishment is added first, and digested
nourishment last. If so, then it would be possible to
speak of nourishment in both ways; for in so far as
nourishment is undigested, contrary nourishes contrary, and in so far as it has been digested, like nourishes like. Evidently, then, each view is in a way both
correct and incorrect.

Since nothing is nourished except what has a share
of life, the ensouled body, in so far as it is ensouled, 10
is what is nourished. Nourishment, therefore, is also
relative, not coincidentally, to an ensouled thing.
However, nourishing something is not the same as
making it grow; for an ensouled thing is caused to
grow in so far as it has some quantity, but it is nourished in so far as it is a this and a substance. For
it preserves its substance and exists as long as it is 15
nourished; and what it generates is not itself, but
something else of the same sort—for its own substance
already exists, and a thing does not generate, but
preserves, itself.

Hence this sort of principle in the soul is a potentiality of the sort that preserves the ensouled thing, in
so far as it is ensouled, and nourishment equips it
for its actuality; and so if it has been deprived of
nourishment it cannot exist. Further, since a thing's 23
end rightly determines what we should call it, and
in this case the end is the generation of another thing
of the same sort, this first soul will be the generative 25
soul, generating another thing of the same sort.

We must distinguish three things—what is nourished, what it is nourished by, and what nourishes. What nourishes is this first soul, what is nourished is the ensouled body, and what it is nourished by is the nourishment. What the soul nourishes by is of two types—just as what we steer by is both the hand and the rudder: The first both initiates motion and undergoes it, and the second simply undergoes it. Since all nourishment must be digestible and the hot element produces digestion, every ensouled thing contains heat.

30 This, then, is an outline of what nutrition is; we should describe it more clearly later in the discussions proper to it.

Perception

PERCEPTION AS MOTION

5

Now that we have determined this, let us discuss perception in general. Perception occurs in being moved and affected, as we have said, since it seems 35 to be a type of alteration. Some also say that like is 417a affected by like; we have said in our general discussion of acting and being affected how this is or is not possible.

A puzzle arises about why we do not perceive the senses themselves, and about why they do not produce perception without external objects, despite the pres- 5 ence of fire, earth, and the other elements, whose intrinsic or coincidental properties are the things that are perceived. Clearly, then, the perceptive part is [what it is] by merely potential, not actual, [perceiving], and so it does not perceive [without an external object]—just as what is combustible is not burnt all by itself without something to burn it, since otherwise it would burn itself with no need of actual fire.

10 We speak of perceiving in two ways; for we say that something sees or hears both in the case of something that has the potentiality for seeing or hearing, even though it is asleep at the time, and in the case of something that is actually seeing or hearing at the time. It follows that perception is also spoken of in two ways, as potential and as actual, and in the same way both what is potentially perceived and what is actually perceived are called objects of perception.

15 First, then, let us speak as though the actuality were the same as being affected and moved—for motion is in fact a sort of actuality, though an incomplete one, as we have said elsewhere. Now, everything is affected and moved by an agent that has the relevant property in actuality, so that in a way like is affected by like, and in a way unlike by unlike— for what is 20 being affected is unlike the agent, but when it has been affected it is like the agent.

DIFFERENT TYPES OF POTENTIALITY

We must also distinguish types of potentiality and actuality, since just now we were speaking of them without qualification. One way in which someone might know is the way we have in mind in saying that a man knows because man is a kind of thing that knows and has knowledge; another way is the 25 way we have in mind in saying that someone who has grammatical knowledge knows. These knowers have different sorts of potentiality—the first has a potentiality because he has the right sort of genus and matter, whereas the second has a potentiality because he has the potentiality to attend to something when he wishes, if nothing external prevents it. A third sort [of knower] is someone who is attending to something at the time, actualizing his knowledge and fully knowing (for instance) this A. In the first 30 and second case we pass from potentially to actually knowing; but in the first case we do so by being altered through learning, and by frequent changes from the contrary state, while in the second case—where we pass from having arithmetical or grammatical knowl- 417b edge without actualizing it, to actualizing it—we do so in another way.

Further, there is not just one way of being affected. On the contrary, one way of being affected is a destruction of contrary by contrary, while the other way is more properly preservation, not destruction, of a potential F by an actual F, when the potential F is [not contrary, but] like the actual F, in the way that a 5 potentiality is like its actuality. For the second case— where the possessor of knowledge comes to attend to what he knows—either is not a case of alteration at all (since the addition leads to [the knowledge] itself and to the actuality) or is a different kind of alteration. That is why we should not say that the intelligent subject is altered in exercising his intelligence, just as we should not say that the builder is altered in [actually] building.

10   First, then, when an understanding and intelligent subject is led from potentiality to actuality, we should not call this teaching but give it some other name. Again, if a subject with potential knowledge learns and acquires knowledge from a teacher with actual knowledge, then we should say either, as we said, that this is not a case of being affected, or that there
15 are two ways of being altered, one of which is a change into a condition of deprivation, and the other of which is a change into possession of a state and into [the fulfillment of the subject's] nature.

PERCEPTION AS POTENTIALITY AND ACTUALITY

In the perceiver, the first change is produced by its parent; and at birth it possesses perception corresponding to [the second type of] knowledge. We speak of actual perceiving in a way that corresponds to
20 attending, except that the visible, audible, and other perceptible objects that produce the actuality are external. This is because actual perception is of particulars, while knowledge is of universals, which are, in a way, in the soul itself; hence it is up to us to think
25 whenever we want to, but it is not up to us to perceive whenever we want to, since perception requires the presence of its object. The same is true for the types of knowledge that are about perceptible things, and for the same reason—namely that perceptible things are particulars and external.

There may be an opportunity to explain these
30 points more perspicuously another time, but for the moment let us be content with the distinctions we have made. There are different types of potentiality: One is what is meant in saying that a child is potentially a general. A second is what is meant in attributing the potentiality to someone of the right age, and
418a [this second type] applies to the perceptive part. Since the difference between these cases has no name, though our distinctions have shown that they are different, and in what ways, we have to use 'being affected' and 'being altered' as though they were the strictly correct names.

The perceiver is potentially what the perceptible
5 object actually is already, as we have said. When it is being affected, then, it is unlike the object; but when it has been affected it has been made like the object and has acquired its quality.

PROPER, COMMON, AND COINCIDENTAL OBJECTS OF PERCEPTION

6

We should first discuss the objects of perception, taking each sense in turn. An object of perception is spoken of in three ways: Two types are perceived intrinsically, and one coincidentally. One type of in-
10 trinsic object is proper to each sense, and the other type of intrinsic object is common to all the senses.

By 'proper object' I mean the one that cannot be perceived by another sense and about which we cannot be deceived. Sight, for instance, is of color; hearing of sound; taste of flavor; and touch has a number of different objects. At any rate, each sense discriminates
15 among its proper objects, and a sense is not deceived about whether, for instance, something is a color or a sound, but can be deceived about whether or where the colored or sounding thing is. These objects, then, are said to be proper to each sense.

Motion, rest, number, shape, and size are the common objects, since they are not proper to any one sense, but are common to them all—a certain sort of motion, for instance, is perceptible by both touch
20 and sight.

Something is said to be coincidentally perceptible if, for instance, the pale [thing] is the son of Diares. For we perceive the son of Diares coincidentally, since he coincides with the pale thing we perceive, and hence we are not affected at all by the perceptible object in so far as it is [the son of Diares].

Among the intrinsic objects of perception, the proper objects are most properly perceptible, and the
25 essence of each sense is by nature relative to these.

PERCEPTION REQUIRES SUITABLE ORGANS

11

. . . The objects of touch are the differentiae of body 423b27 in so far as it is body, i.e. those that distinguish the elements—hot, cold, dry, and wet; we have discussed these earlier in what we said about the elements. 30 Their tactile sense-organ, the primary seat of the sense called touch, is the part that has these qualities potentially. For perceiving is a way of being affected; hence 424a the agent causes the thing that is affected, which potentially has the quality that the agent has, to have that quality actually.

Hence we do not perceive anything that is as dry or wet, or hard or soft, [as the organ,] but only the excesses in either direction, because the sense is a 5 sort of intermediate condition between the contraries in objects of perception. And that is why a sense discriminates among its objects; for what is intermediate discriminates, since in relation to each extreme it becomes the other extreme. And just as what is going to perceive both pale and dark must be actually neither pale nor dark but potentially both, and simi-10 larly in the other cases, so also in the case of touch, [what is going to perceive the contraries] must be neither hot nor cold.

Further, just as we found that sight in a way per-ceives both the visible and the invisible, and similarly the other senses perceive the opposites, so also touch perceives the tangible and the intangible. What is intangible is either something that either has alto-gether very few of the differentiating properties of tangibles — air, for instance — or has an excess of tangi-15 ble qualities — for instance, things that destroy *the sense*.

We have spoken in outline, then, of the senses, one by one.

Perception Is Reception of Form without Matter

12

A general point to be grasped is that each sense re-ceives the perceptible forms without the matter. Wax, for instance, receives the design on a signet-ring with-20 out the iron or gold; it acquires the design in the gold or bronze, but not insofar as the design is gold or bronze. Similarly, each sense is affected by the thing that has color or flavor or sound, but not insofar as it is said to be that thing [for instance, a horse], but insofar as it has a given quality [for instance, color] and in accordance with the form [of the sense]. 25 The primary sense-organ is the seat of this sort of potentiality. Hence the organ and the capacity are one, but their being is different. For though [the sense-organ] that perceives is of some magnitude, being perceptive is not, and [so] the sense is not something with magnitude but is a [specific sort of] form and potentiality of the organ.

It is also evident from this why excesses in objects of perception destroy the sense-organs. For if the mo-30 tion is too strong for the sense-organ, then the form, i.e. the sense, is destroyed, just as the harmony and tension are destroyed if the strings of an instrument are struck heavily.

This also makes it evident why plants do not per-ceive, even though they have one part of soul, and are affected in some ways by objects of touch, since they are chilled and heated. The reason is that they 424b lack a [suitable] intermediate condition and a princi-ple suitable for receiving the form of perceptible things; instead, they are affected [by the form] with the matter.

A puzzle arises about whether something that can-not smell can be at all affected by odor, or something 5 that cannot see can be affected by color, and so on for the other cases. If the object of smell is odor, then anything produced by odor must be [the act of] smelling; hence nothing that is incapable of smelling anything can be affected by odor (the same applies to the other cases), and any such thing must be af-fected in so far as it is a perceiver. A further argument makes the same conclusion clear. For a body is af-10 fected neither by light and darkness nor by sound nor by odor, but only by their subject, as, for instance, the air that comes with the thunder splits the log.

On the other hand, tangible [qualities] and flavors affect bodies; otherwise, what would affect and alter soulless things? Then will the other objects of percep-tion also affect bodies? Perhaps not every body is liable to be affected by odor and sound, and those 15 that are affected are indefinite and impermanent — air, for instance, since it acquires an odor as though affected in some way.

Then what is there to smelling, besides being af-fected? Perhaps smelling is [not only being affected, but] also perceiving, while air that is affected [by odor], by contrast, soon becomes an object of percep-tion [not a perceiver].

BOOK III

Appearance

How We Perceive That We Perceive

2

Since we perceive that we are seeing and hearing, it 425b12 must be either sight or a different sense by which we perceive that we are seeing. [In the second case] the same sense will perceive both sight and the color that is the [external] subject, so that either there will be two senses perceiving the same thing, or else the sense 15 will perceive itself. Again, if the sense that perceives sight is different [from sight itself], then either it will go on without limit or there will be some sense that perceives itself, so that one ought to make this claim about the first sense.

Still, a puzzle arises. If perceiving by sight is seeing and if what we see is color or something colored, then if we are seeing, the first case of seeing will be colored.

20 It is evident, then, that perceiving by sight is not just one thing; for indeed, whenever we are not seeing, we discriminate light and darkness, but not in the same way. Moreover what sees is in fact colored in a way; for a sense-organ receives the object of perception without its matter. That is why, even when the objects of perception have gone away, perceptions 25 and appearances are still present in the sense-organs.

The Actuality of Perception Is the Same As the Actuality of Its Object

The actuality of the object of perception and of the sense are one and the same, but their being is not the same. I mean, for instance, that the actual sound and the actual hearing [are one and the same]; for 30 it is possible to have [the sense of] hearing without [actually] hearing, and what has sound is not always making a sound. But whenever what has the potentiality to hear is actually hearing, and what has the potentiality to sound is sounding, then actual hearing and actual sounding occur at the same time, so that we 426a would say that one thing is a case of hearing and the other a case of sounding.

If, then, the motion and the action are in the thing affected, both the sounding and the actual hearing must be in the [sense] that has the potentiality. For the actuality of what acts on something and initiates 5 motion in it comes to be in the thing affected—that is why what initiates motion need not be set in motion itself. Now, the actuality of what has the potentiality to sound is sound or sounding, while the actuality of what has a potentiality for hearing is hearing or listening for hearing is of two sorts, and so is sound.

The same account applies to the other senses and 10 their objects. For just as both acting on something

and being affected are in the thing affected, not in the thing acting on it, so also both the actuality of the object of perception and the actuality of the perceiver are in the perceiver. In some cases, however, the two actualities have different names, as sounding and hearing have, while in other cases one of them has no name; for the actuality of sight is called seeing, whereas the actuality of color has no name, and the 15 actuality of what has the potentiality to taste is called tasting, whereas the actuality of flavor has no name.

And since the actuality of the object of perception and of what has the potentiality of perceiving are one, but their being is different, it follows that hearing and sounding (spoken of in this way), flavor and tasting, and so on, must all perish or remain in being at the same time. But this is not necessary for the things said to have the relevant potentiality.

In fact the earlier naturalists were wrong on this 20 point, in supposing that nothing was pale or dark without sight, and that there was no flavor without taste. For in a way they were correct, but in a way incorrect. For perception and its object are spoken of in two ways, as potential and as actual; in the case 25 [of the actuality] what they say is correct, but in the case [of the potentiality] it is not. They, however, spoke without qualification about things that are not spoken of without qualification. . . .

Appearance Contrasted with Perception

3

. . . If appearance is that in virtue of which some 428a1 object appears to us, in contrast to what is so called metaphorically, then is it one of those potentialities or states in virtue of which we discriminate and attain truth or falsity? These are perception, belief, knowl- 5 edge, and understanding.

It is clear as follows that appearance is not the same as perception. For perception is either a potentiality, such as sight, or an actuality, such as seeing; but we have appearances when we have neither of these— in dreams, for instance. Moreover, perception is present in every [animal], but appearance is not. If they were the same in actuality, then it would be possible 10 for all beasts to have appearance, whereas in fact it does not seem possible [for all]; ants or bees, for instance, and grubs [do not have it]. Further, percep- tions are always true, whereas most appearances are false. Again, whenever we are actually perceiving accurately, we do not say that this appears to us [to be] a man; we are more inclined to say [that something 15 appears to be so] in cases where we do not see clearly whether something is true or false. Further, as we were saying before, sights appear to us even when we have our eyes closed.

APPEARANCE CONTRASTED WITH BELIEF

The remaining question is whether appearance is 20 belief; for belief may also be either true or false. Belief, however, implies conviction—since one cannot believe things if one does not find them convincing—whereas no beasts have conviction, though many have appearance. Further, belief implies conviction, conviction implies being persuaded, and persuasion implies reason, whereas no beasts have reason, though some have appearance.

25 It is evident, then, that appearance is neither belief that involves perception, nor belief that is produced through perception, nor a combination of belief and perception. This is so both for the reasons given and also because [on this view] belief will not be about anything other than the thing, if there is one, that is the object of perception.

I mean, for instance, that the combination of a belief about the pale and a perception of the pale 30 will turn out to be appearance; for surely it will not be the combination of a belief about the good and 428b a perception of the pale—for appearance will be having a belief non-coincidentally about the very thing one perceives. In fact, however, we sometimes have false appearances about the same things at the same time as we have a true supposition about them, as when, for instance, the sun appears a foot across, even though we are convinced that it is bigger than the inhabited world.

5 It turns out, then, [on the view being considered] that either we have lost the true belief we had, even though the thing still exists and we have neither forgotten our belief nor been persuaded to change it, or else, if we still have the true belief, the same belief must at the same time be both true and false. But in fact it could have become false only if the thing changed without our noticing it. It follows, then, that appearance cannot be any of these things, nor a product of them.

THE RELATION OF APPEARANCE TO PERCEPTION

It is possible, however, when one thing has been set 10 in motion, for a second thing to be set in motion by the first. Moreover, appearance seems to be a sort of motion, to involve perception, to be present in things that have perception, and to be about the objects of perception. Now, it is also possible for motion to result from actual perception, and this motion must be similar to the perception.

Hence this motion cannot occur without percep- 15 tion or in things that do not have perception. Things that have appearance act and are affected in many ways in accordance with it, and it can be either true or false. . . .

Thought

THOUGHT COMPARED WITH PERCEPTION

4

Now we must consider the part by which the soul 429a10 has knowledge and intelligence, and ask whether it is separable, or it is not separable in magnitude but only in account; and what its differentia is, and how understanding comes about.

Now, if understanding is like perceiving, it consists either in being affected by the object of intellect or in something else of the same sort. Hence the intellect 15 must be unaffected, but receptive of the form; it must have the quality [of the object] potentially, not actually; and it must be related to its object as the perceiving part is related to the objects of perception.

Hence the intellect, since it understands all things, must be unmixed, in order, as Anaxagoras says, to 'master' them (i.e. to know them); for the intrusion 20 of any foreign thing would hinder and obstruct it. And so it has no nature except this—that it is potential. Hence the part of the soul called intellect (by which I mean that by which the soul thinks and supposes) is not actually, before it understands, any of the things there are. It is also unreasonable, then, for intellect 25 to be mixed with the body, since it would then acquire some quality (for instance, hot or cold) or even, like the perceiving part, have some organ, whereas in fact it has none.

And so those who say that the soul is a place of forms are right, except that it is the intellectual soul, not the whole soul, which is—potentially, not actually—the forms.

30   The condition of the sense-organ and of the faculty of perception makes it evident that the perceiving part and the intellectual part are unaffected in differ-
429b   ent ways. For after a sense perceives something very perceptible, it cannot perceive; after hearing very loud sounds, for instance, it cannot hear sound, and after seeing vivid colors or smelling strong odors, it cannot see or smell. But whenever intellect understands something that is very intelligible, it understands
5   more, not less, about inferior objects; for intellect is separable, whereas the perceiving part requires a body.

When the intellect becomes each thing [that it understands], as it does when someone is said to have actual knowledge (this comes about whenever someone is able to actualize his knowledge through himself), even then it is still potential in a way, though not in the same way as before it learnt or discovered; and then it is capable of understanding itself.

The Objects of Thought

10   Magnitude is different from being magnitude and water from being water; and the same applies in many other cases too, though not in all, since in some cases the thing is the same as its being. It follows that to discriminate being flesh we use something different, or something in a different state, from what we use in discriminating flesh; for flesh requires matter, and,
15   like the snub, it is this [form] in this [matter]. Hence to discriminate the hot and the cold and the things of which flesh is some sort of form, we use the perceptive part; but to discriminate being flesh, we use something else that is either separable [from body] or related to it as a formerly bent line is related to the straight line it has become.

Further, if we turn to things whose being depends on abstraction, the straight is similar to the snub,
20   since it requires something continuous. But if being straight is different from the straight, then so is the essence of straight (duality, let us say) different from the straight, and therefore to discriminate it we use something different, or something in a different state. In general, then, the [separability] of intellect corresponds to the way in which objects are separable from matter.

Puzzles about Intellect and Thought

A puzzle arises. If intellect is simple and unaffected, having, as Anaxagoras says, nothing in common with anything, then how can it understand, if understand-
25   ing consists in being affected? For it seems that two things must have something in common if one is to affect the other. Again, is intellect itself an object of intellect? For if nothing other [than itself] makes it an object of intellect, and if all objects of intellect are one in species, then the other objects of intellect will also be intellect; alternatively, it will need something mixed into it, to make it an object of intellect in the same way as the other objects of intellect are.
30

On the other hand, our previous discussion of ways of being affected because of something in common has shown that the intellect is in a way potentially the objects of intellect, but before it understands them, it is none of them actually. Its potentiality is that of a
430a   writing tablet with nothing actually written on it— which is also true of intellect.

Further, intellect itself is an object of intellect in the same way as its objects are. For in the case of things without matter, the understanding part and its object are one, since actual knowledge and its object
5   are the same. (We should investigate why it is not [engaged in the activity of] understanding all the time.) In things that have matter, each object of intellect is potentially present; hence intellect will not be in them (since it is a potentiality for being such things without their matter), but it will be an object of intellect.

Passive Intellect and Productive Intellect

5

In the whole of nature each kind of thing has some-
10   thing as its matter, which is potentially all the things in the kind, and something else as the cause and producer, which produces them all—for instance, the craft in relation to its matter. These differences, then, must also be found in the soul. One sort of intellect corresponds to matter, since it becomes all things.
15   Another sort corresponds to the producer by producing all things in the way that a state, such as light, produces things—for in a way light makes potential colors into actual colors. This second sort of intellect

is separable, unaffected, and unmixed, since its essence is actuality.

For in every case the producer is more valuable than the thing affected, and the principle is more 20 valuable than the matter. Actual knowledge is the same as its object; potential knowledge is temporally prior in an individual [knower], but in general it is not even temporally prior. But [productive intellect] does not understand at one time and not at another.

Only when it has been separated is it precisely what it is, all by itself. And this alone is immortal and everlasting. But [when it is separated] we do not remember, because this [productive intellect] is 25 unaffected, whereas the intellect that is affected is perishable. And without this [productive intellect] nothing understands. . . .

Desire and Action

THE ROLE OF THOUGHT AND DESIRE IN PRODUCING ACTION

10

433*a*9 There are apparently two parts that move us—both 10 intellect and desire, if we take appearance to be a kind of understanding. For many people follow their appearances against their knowledge, and the other animals have appearance but lack understanding and reasoning. Both intellect and desire, then, move us from place to place. This is the intellect that reasons 15 for some goal and is concerned with action; its [concern with an] end distinguishes it from theoretical intellect. All desire also aims at some goal; for the object of desire is the starting point of intellect concerned with action, and the last stage [of our reasoning] is the starting point of action.

Hence it is reasonable to regard these two things—desire, and thought concerned with action—as the movers. For the object of desire moves us, and thought 20 moves us because its starting point is the object of desire. Moreover, whenever appearance moves us, it requires desire.

And so there is one mover, the desiring part. For if there were two—intellect and desire—they would move us insofar as they had a common form. In fact, however, intellect evidently does not move anything without desire, since wish is desire, and any motion in accordance with reasoning is in accordance with

wish; desire, on the other hand, also moves us against 25 reasoning, since appetite is a kind of desire. Now, intellect is always correct, but desire and appearance may be either correct or incorrect. Hence in every case the mover is the object of desire, but the object of desire is either the good or the apparent good— not every sort of good, but the good that is achievable in action. What is achievable in action admits of 30 being otherwise.

Evidently, then, the potentiality of the soul that moves us is the one called desire. People who divide 433*b* the soul into parts, if they divide it into separate parts corresponding to the different potentialities, will find very many of them—the nutritive, perceptive, intellectual, and deliberative parts, and, moreover, the desiring part; for the difference between these parts is wider than the one between the appetitive and emotional parts.

CONFLICTING DESIRES

Desires that are contrary to each other arise, however, 5 when reason and appetite are contrary, which happens in subjects that perceive time. For intellect urges us to draw back because of what is to come, while appetite [urges us on] because of what is present; for the pleasant thing that is present appears both unqualifiedly pleasant and unqualifiedly good, be- 10 cause we do not see what is to come.

Hence the mover is one in species—the desiring part, in so far as it is desiring. Indeed, the first mover of all is the object of desire, since it moves us without being moved, by being present to understanding or appearance. But the movers are numerically more than one.

HOW DESIRE RESULTS IN ACTION

We must distinguish three things—the mover, its instrument, and the subject moved. There are two types of movers: the unmoved mover and the moved 15 mover. The unmoved mover is the good achievable in action, and the moved mover is the desiring part; for the thing that is moved is moved insofar as it desires, and desire, insofar as it is actual, is a sort of motion. The thing moved is the animal. When we reach the instrument by which desire moves, we reach something bodily, and so we should study it when 20 we study the functions common to soul and body.

To summarize for the present: What moves something as an instrument is found where the same thing is both the starting point and the last stage. In the hinge-joint, for instance, the convex is last, and hence at rest, while the concave is the starting point, and 25 hence is moved. These are different in account, though they are spatially inseparable. For since everything is moved by pushing and pulling, something must remain at rest, as in a circle, and the motion must originate from this.

In general, then, as we have said, an animal moves itself insofar as it has desire. For desire it needs appearance; and appearance is either rational appearance 30 or the perceptual appearance that other animals share [with human beings].

The Connection between Desire and Appearance

11

We should also consider what it is that moves incom-434a plete animals, whose only form of perception is touch. Can they have appearance and appetite, or not? For they evidently have pleasure and pain; if they have these, they must have appetite. But how could they have appearance? Well, perhaps, just as they are 5 moved indeterminately, so also they have appearance and appetite, but have them indeterminately.

Rational and Non-rational Appearance

Now, the other animals as well [as man] also have perceptual appearance, as we have said, but [only] reasoning animals have deliberative appearance. For when we come to the question whether one is to do this or that, we come to a task for reasoning. And [in this case] one must measure by one [standard], since one pursues the greater [good]. And so one is able 10 to make one object of appearance out of many. And this is why [non-rational animals] do not seem to have belief; it is because they lack the [appearance] resulting from reasoning.

Conflicts between Desires

That is why desire lacks the deliberative part. And sometimes one desire overcomes and moves another, while sometimes the second overcomes and moves the first, like one sphere moving another, whenever incontinence occurs. By nature the [desire] that is 15 superior is dominant in every case and moves [the agent], and so it turns out that three motions are initiated [in the agent]. The part that has knowledge stays at rest and is not moved.

The Role of Different Types of Belief in Guiding Action

Now, one sort of supposition and statement is universal, while another is about what is particular; for the first says that this sort of agent ought to do this sort of thing, and the second says that this is this sort of thing and I am this sort of agent. Hence the second 20 belief, not the universal belief, initiates motion; or [rather] both initiate motion, but the first does so by being more at rest, in contrast to the second.

Metaphysics

BOOK I
The Science of First Causes

SCIENCE AND CRAFT GROW FROM SENSE-PERCEPTION, MEMORY, AND EXPERIENCE

1

980a21 All human beings by nature desire to know. A sign of this is our liking for the senses; for even apart from their usefulness we like them for themselves especially the sense of sight, since we choose seeing above practically all the others, not only as an aid to action, but also when we have no intention of acting. The reason 25 is that sight, more than any of the other senses, gives us knowledge of things and clarifies many differences between them.

Animals possess sense-perception by nature at birth. In some but not all of these, perception results in 980b memory, making them more intelligent and better at learning than those that cannot remember. Some animals that cannot hear sounds (for instance, bees and similar kinds of animal) are intelligent but do 25 not learn; those that both perceive sounds and have memory also learn.

Non-human animals live by appearances and memories but have little share in experience, whereas human beings also live by craft[1] and reasoning. In human beings experience results from memory, since 981a many memories of the same thing result in the capacity for a single experience.[2] Experience seems to be quite like science and craft, and indeed human beings attain science and craft through experience; for, as

---

Reprinted by permission of the translators, Terence Irwin and Gail Fine, from Aristotle, *Selections* (Indianapolis: Hackett Publishing Company, 1995). The use of brackets within the text indicates insertions not found in the manuscript. Headings are those of the translators.

1. craft. [Technē, like epistēmē, applies both to the state of having knowledge and to what someone in that state knows.—T.I. and G.F.]

2. [experience. See *Posterior Analytics* 100a3–6.]

Polus[3] correctly says, experience has produced craft, 5 but inexperience only luck.

A craft arises when many thoughts that arise from experience result in one universal judgment about similar things. For the judgment that in this illness this treatment benefited Callias, Socrates, and others, in many particular cases, is characteristic of experience, but the judgment that it benefited everyone of 10 a certain sort (marked out by a single kind) suffering from a certain disease (for instance, phlegmatic or bilious people when burning with fever) is characteristic of craft.

CRAFT IS SUPERIOR TO EXPERIENCE BECAUSE IT KNOWS CAUSES

For practical purposes, experience seems no worse than craft; indeed we even see that experienced people are actually more successful than those who have a rational account but lack experience. The reason 15 is that experience is cognition of particulars, whereas craft is cognition of universals. Moreover, each action and event concerns a particular; in medical treatment, for instance, we do not heal man (except coincidentally) but Callias or Socrates or some other individual 20 who is coincidentally a man.[4] If, then, someone has a rational account but lacks experience, and recognizes the universal but not the particular falling under it, he will often give the wrong treatment, since treatment is applied to the particular.

Nonetheless, we attribute knowing and compre- 25 hending to craft more than to experience, and we judge that craftsmen are wiser than experienced people, on the assumption that in every case knowledge, rather than experience, implies wisdom. This is because craftsmen know the cause, but [merely] experi-

---

3. [Polus. a rhetorical theorist of the mid-fifth century, a pupil of Gorgias. He is a character in Plato's *Gorgias*.]

4. [coincidentally a man: i.e. coincidentally from the point of view of healing. Aristotle does not mean that being a man is a COINCIDENTAL property of Socrates.]

enced people do not; for experienced people know the fact that something is so but not the reason why it is so, whereas craftsmen recognize the reason why, 30 i.e. the cause.

KNOWLEDGE OF CAUSES IS CHARACTERISTIC OF WISDOM

That is why we believe that the master craftsmen in a given craft are more honorable, know more, and 981b are wiser than the manual craftsmen, because they know the causes of what is produced. The manual craftsmen, we think, are like inanimate things that produce without knowing what they produce, in the way that, for instance, fire burns; the latter produce their products by a natural tendency, while the manual craftsmen produce theirs because of habit. We assume, then, that some craftsmen are wiser than 5 others not because they are better in practice, but because they have a rational account and recognize the causes.

And in general, a sign that distinguishes those who know from those who do not is their ability to teach. Hence we think craft, rather than experience, is 10 knowledge, since craftsmen can teach, while merely experienced people cannot.

Further, we do not think any of the senses is wisdom, even though they are the most authoritative ways of recognizing particulars. They do not tell us why anything is so; for instance, they do not tell us why fire is hot, but only that it is hot.

THEORETICAL WISDOM IS CHARACTERISTICALLY PURSUED FOR ITS OWN SAKE

It is not surprising, then, that in the earliest times 15 anyone who discovered any craft that went beyond the perceptions common to all was admired not only because he discovered something useful, but also for being a wise person, superior to others. Later on, as more crafts were discovered—some related to necessities, others to [leisuretime] pursuits—those who discovered these latter crafts were in every case judged 20 to be wiser than the others, because their sciences did not aim at practical utility. Hence, finally, after all these crafts had been established, the sciences that aim neither at pleasure nor at necessities were discovered, initially in the places where people had leisure. This is why mathematical crafts arose first in Egypt; for there the priestly class were allowed to be 25 at leisure.

The difference between craft and science and other similar sorts of things has been discussed in the Ethics.[5] The point of our present discussion is to show that in everyone's judgment any discipline deserving the name of wisdom must describe the first causes, i.e. the principles. And so, as we said earlier, the 30 experienced person seems to be wiser than those who have just any old perception; the craftsman seems to be wiser than those with nothing more than experi- 982a ence; the master craftsman wiser than the manual craftsman; and the purely theoretical sciences wiser than the productive sciences. It is clear, then, that wisdom is knowledge of certain sorts of principles and causes.

COMMON BELIEFS ABOUT WISDOM AND THE WISE PERSON

2

Since this is the science we are looking for, we should 5 consider what sorts of causes and principles wisdom is the science of. Perhaps this will become clearer if we consider our judgments about the wise person. First, we judge that he has knowledge about all things as far as possible, without, however, having it about 10 each particular [kind of thing]. Next, the one who is capable of knowing difficult things, i.e. things not easily known by human beings, is the wise person; for sense-perception is common to everyone, and that is why it is easy and not characteristic of wisdom. Further, someone is wiser in a given science if he is more exact, and a better teacher of the causes. Again, 15 if one of two sciences is choiceworthy for itself— [purely] for the sake of knowing it—and the other is choiceworthy [only] for the sake of its results, the first has a better claim to be wisdom than the second. Moreover, the superior science has a better claim than the subordinate science; for the wise person must give orders, not take them, and those who are 20 less wise must follow his orders, not he theirs. These, then, are our judgments about wisdom and wise people.

5. [the Ethics: See *Nicomachean Ethics* vi2.]

THE SCIENCE OF THE HIGHEST PRINCIPLES FITS THESE COMMON BELIEFS

Of these features, we judge that knowledge about everything necessarily belongs to the one who has the best claim to universal science; for he in a way knows everything that is a subject for a science. These most universal things are also just about the most difficult for human beings to know, since they are 25 furthest from perceptions.[6] Further, the most exact sciences are those that, more than the others, study the first things; for the sciences that are derived from fewer principles—for instance, arithmetic—are more exact than those—for instance, geometry—that require further principles. Moreover, the science that studies the causes is more of a teacher, since teachers 30 are those who state something's causes. Besides, knowledge and science for their own sake are most characteristic of the science of the most appropriate object of knowledge. For one who chooses knowledge 982b for its own sake will choose above all the science that is a science to the highest degree. This science is the science of the most appropriate objects of knowledge; these objects are the first things, i.e. the causes, since we know the subordinate things because of these and from these, not the other way round. Further, the 5 most superior science—the one that is superior to any subordinate science—is the one that knows the end for which a given thing should be done; this end is something's good, and in general the end is what is best in every sort of nature.

From everything that has been said, then, we find that the name under discussion, [i.e., 'wisdom'], applies to the same science; for we find that wisdom 10 must study the first principles and causes, and the good, the end, is one of the causes.

WISDOM IS THE RESULT OF WONDER, NOT OF NEED, AND IS PURSUED FOR ITS OWN SAKE, NOT FOR SOME FURTHER USE

The fact that this science is not productive is also clearer from those who first engaged in philosophy. For human beings originally began philosophy, as they do now, because of wonder, at first because they wondered at the strange things in front of them, and

later because, advancing little by little, they found greater things puzzling—what happens to the moon, 15 the sun and the stars, how the universe comes to be. Someone who wonders and is puzzled thinks he is ignorant (this is why the myth-lover is also a philosopher in a way, since myth is composed of wonders); 20 since, then, they engaged in philosophy to escape ignorance, they were evidently pursuing scientific knowledge [simply] for the sake of knowing, not for any further use.

What actually happened is evidence for this view. For it was only when practically everything required for necessities and for ease and [leisure-time] pursuits was supplied that they began to seek this sort of understanding; clearly, then, we do not seek it for some 25 further use. Just as we describe a free person as one who exists for his own sake and not for someone else's, so we also describe this as the only free science, since it is the only one that exists for its own sake.

IT IS THEREFORE A PREEMINENTLY DIVINE SCIENCE

Hence the possession of this science might justifiably be thought to be beyond human capacity. For in 30 many ways human nature is in slavery, so that, as Simonides says, 'the god alone would have this privilege', and it is unfitting for human beings to transgress their own level in their search for the science. If there actually is something in what the poets say, and the divine nature is spiteful, divine spite would be likely 983a in this case, and all those who go too far would suffer misfortunes. The divine nature, however, cannot be spiteful; as the proverb says, 'Poets tell many lies'.

Nor ought we to take any science to be more honorable than this one, since the most divine science is 5 also the most honorable, and this science that we are describing is the most divine. It alone is most divine in two ways: for the divine science [may be understood] as (i) the one that a god more than anyone else would be expected to have, or as (ii) the science of divine things. Only this science [of first causes] satisfies both conditions [for being divine]. For (i) the god seems to be among the causes of all things, and to be some sort of principle, and (ii) this is the sort of science that the god, alone or more than anyone 10 else, would be expected to have. Hence all the other sciences are more necessary than this one, but none is better.

6. [furthest from perceptions: See *Posterior Analytics* 72a1–5.]

Wisdom Both Arises from Wonder and Removes Wonder

However, the possession of this science must in a way leave us in a condition contrary to the one we were in when we began our search. For, as we said, everyone begins from wonder that something is the way it is, 15 as they wonder at toys that move spontaneously, or the turnings of the sun, or the incommensurability of the diagonal (for people who have not yet studied the cause are filled with wonder that there is something that is not measured by the smallest length). But we must end up in the contrary and (according to the proverb) the better state, the one that people 20 achieve by learning [the cause] in these other cases as well—for nothing would be more amazing to a geometer than if the diagonal turned out to be commensurable.

We have described, then, the nature of the science we are seeking, and the goal that our search and our whole line of inquiry must reach.

Survey of Previous Philosophers: The Presocratics

The Four Causes

3

It is evident, then, that we must acquire knowledge 25 of the original causes, since we say we know a thing whenever we think we recognize its primary cause. Causes are spoken of in four ways. One of these, we say, is the being and essence; for the reason why is traced back ultimately to the account, and the primary reason why is the cause and principle. Another is 30 the matter and subject. A third is the source of the principle of motion. The fourth is what something is for, i.e. the good—the opposite to the third cause, since it is the end of all coming to be and motion. 983b We have studied these causes adequately in our work on nature.[7] Still, let us also enlist those who previously took up the investigation of beings and pursued philosophical study about the truth; for it is clear that they also mention causes and principles of some sort. A discussion of their views, then, will ad- 5 vance our present line of inquiry; for either we shall

7. [on nature: See *Physics* ii 3.]

find some other kind of cause or we shall be more convinced about those we have just mentioned.

The Material Cause

Most of the first philosophers, then, thought that the only principles of all things were material. For, they say, there is some [subject] that all beings come from, the first thing they come to be from and the last thing they perish into, the substance remaining throughout 10 but changing in respect of its attributes. This, they say, is the element and the principle of beings. And for this reason they think that nothing either comes to be or is destroyed, on the assumption that this nature [that is the subject] persists in every change, just as we say that Socrates does not come to be without qualification when he comes to be good or musical, and that he is not destroyed when he loses 15 these states (because the subject, Socrates himself, remains)—so also they say that nothing else either comes to be or perishes without qualification (for there must be some nature, either one or more than one, that persists while everything else comes to be from it).

But they do not all agree about the number or type of this material principle. Thales, the originator of this sort of philosophy, says it is water (that is why he 20 also declared that the earth rests on water). Presumably he reached this judgment from seeing that what nourishes all things is wet and that the hot itself comes from the wet and is kept alive by it (and what all things come to be from is there principle). He also 25 reached this judgment because he thought that the seeds of all things have a wet nature (and water is the principle of the nature of wet things).

Some people think that even those who first gave accounts of the gods in very ancient times, long before the present, accepted this judgment about nature. For the ancients made Oceanus and Tethys the parents of 30 coming to be and described the oath of the gods as water, which they called Styx; for what is oldest is most honored, and what is most honored is the oath. It is perhaps unclear whether this belief about nature 984a is in fact old or even ancient, but at any rate this is what Thales is said to have declared about the first cause. (No one would think of including Hippon among these philosophers, given the triviality of his thought.) 5

Anaximenes and Diogenes take air to be both prior to water and also the primary principle of all the simple bodies, while Hippasus of Metapontium and Heraclitus of Ephesus say this about fire. Empedocles takes the four bodies to be principles, adding earth as a fourth to the ones mentioned. These, he says, 10 always remain and do not come to be, except in so far as they come to be more or fewer, being combined into one and dispersed from one into many.

Anaxagoras of Clazomenae, who was older than Empedocles but wrote later, says that the principles are unlimited; for he says that practically all the uniform things[8] (for instance, water or fire) come to be and are destroyed only in the ways we have men- 15 tioned, by being combined and dispersed; they do not come to be or get destroyed in any other way, but always remain.

THE MOVING CAUSE

If one went by these views, one might judge that the material cause is the only sort of cause. But as people thus advanced, reality itself showed them the way and 20 compelled them to search. For however true it might be that all coming to be and perishing is from one (or more than one) thing, still, why does this happen, and what is the cause? For certainly the subject does not produce change in itself. I mean, for instance, neither the wood nor the bronze causes itself to change, nor does the wood itself produce a bed, or 25 the bronze a statue, but something else causes the change. And to search for this is (in our view) to search for the second principle—the source of the principle of motion.

Those who were the very first to undertake this line of inquiry into nature, who said that the subject is one, were quite satisfied with this. But at least some 30 of those who said that the subject is one, as though defeated by this search [for an explanation of change], said that the one, i.e. nature as a whole, is immobile, not only as regards coming to be and perishing (that was an old belief agreed on by all), but also as regards every other sort of change. This view is distinctive 984b of them.

Of those who said that the universe is one element, none managed to notice this [second] cause, unless Parmenides did; he noticed it only in so far as he posited not only one cause, but also in a way two 5 causes. Indeed those who recognize more than one element—for instance, hot and cold, or fire and earth—make it easier to state [the cause that initiates motion], since they regard fire as having a nature that initiates motion, and water, earth, and other such things as having natures contrary to this.

After these sorts of principles were proposed by these people, other people found them inadequate to generate the nature of beings; once again, as we said, it was as though the truth itself compelled them, and so they began to search for the next sort of princi- 10 ple. For presumably it is unlikely that fire or earth or anything else of that sort would cause some things to be in a good and fine state and would cause other things to come to be in that state, and unlikely that people would think so; still, it was unsatisfactory to entrust so great a result to chance and luck. And so 15 when one of them said that mind is present (in nature just as in animals) as the cause of the world order and of all its arrangement, he seemed like a sober person, and his predecessors seemed like babblers in comparison. We know that Anaxagoras evidently made a start on giving such accounts, but an earlier 20 statement of them is ascribed to Hermotimus of Clazomenae. Those who held this view posited a principle of beings that is at once both the cause of things turning out well and the sort of cause that is the source of motion for beings.

EARLY GLIMPSES OF THE MOVING CAUSE

4

One might suspect that the first to search for this sort of cause was Hesiod and anyone else who counted desire or appetite among beings as a principle, as 25 Parmenides, for instance, also did. For he too, in describing the coming to be of the whole universe, says: 'Desire was the first of all the gods she devised'. And Hesiod says: 'Before everything else that came to be, there was chaos, and then the broad-fronted earth, and desire, preeminent among all the immortals.'[9] He assumes that there must be some cause 30

---

8. [uniform things: literally "things with parts similar to the wholes," *homoiomerē*.]

9. ["Before . . . immortals." An inaccurate quotation (probably, like many of Aristotle's quotations, from memory) of Hesiod, *Theogony* 116–20.]

among beings to initiate motion in things and to bring them together. Let us leave it till later to determine which of these people was the first [to discover this sort of cause].

Moreover, the contraries of good things (i.e. disorder and ugliness no less than order and beauty) were 985a also apparent in nature, and bad things were apparently more numerous than good things, and base things more numerous than beautiful things. For this reason someone else introduced love and strife so that each of them would be the cause of one of these two sorts of things. For if we follow Empedocles' argument, and do not confine ourselves to his mum-5 bling way of expressing it, but attend to what he has in mind, we will find that love is the cause of good things, and strife of bad. And so, if one were to claim that in a way Empedocles said—indeed was the first to say—that the good and the bad are principles, one would perhaps be right, if the cause of all goods is 10 the good itself.

These people, then, as we say, evidently made this much progress in fastening on two of the four causes that we distinguished in our work on nature—the matter and the principle of motion. But they did so dimly and not at all perspicuously. They were like unskilled boxers in fights, who, in the course of mov-15 ing around, often land good punches, but are not guided by knowledge; in the same way these thinkers would seem not to know what they are saying, since they evidently make practically no use of these causes, except to a slight degree.

Anaxagoras, for instance, uses mind[10] as an ad hoc 20 device[11] for the production of the universe; it is when he is puzzled about the cause of something's being necessarily as it is that he drags in mind, but in other cases he recognizes anything but mind as the cause of things that come to be. Empedocles, admittedly, uses these causes more than Anaxagoras does, but he too still makes insufficient use of them, and he does not suc-25 ceed in using them consistently. At any rate, he often makes love draw things apart, and strife draw them to-

gether. For whenever strife scatters the universe into its elements, all the fire is gathered into one, and so is each of the other elements; and whenever love brings things back together again into one, the parts from each element are necessarily scattered again.

Empedocles, then, went beyond his predecessors. 30 He was the first to distinguish this cause and to introduce it; he did not take the principle of motion to be one, but assumed different and contrary principles. Moreover, he was the first to say that there are four material elements. In fact, though, he does not use all four, but treats them as two, treating fire in its 985b own right as one nature, and its opposites—earth, air, and water—as together constituting another; this may be gathered from studying his poems. As we say, then, this is how many principles he recognized, and this is what he said about them.

Leucippus and his colleague Democritus, on the 5 other hand, say that the elements are the full and the empty, and that, of these, the full and solid is what is, and the empty is what is not. That is why they also say that what is no more of a being than what is not, because body is no more of a being than the empty is. They take these to be the material causes 10 of beings.

Those who take the substance that is the subject to be one explain how everything else comes to be by referring to the ways in which the subject is affected, taking the rare and the dense to be the principle of the ways it is affected. In the same way, Leucippus and Democritus take the differentiae[12] to be the causes of the other things. They say, however, that there are three of these differentiae—shape, order, and position. For they say that what is is differentiated only 15 by rhythm, touching, and turning.[13] Of these rhythm is shape, touching is order, and turning is position; for A differs from N in shape, AN from NA in order, 20 and Z from N in position. Like the other people, however, they were too lazy to take up the question about motion and to ask from what source and in what way it arises in beings.

---

10. [mind: nous.]

11. [ad hoc device: Literally "machine." Aristotle probably alludes to the theatrical device of the "god from the machine" (*deus ex machina*), brought out on a crane above the stage at the end of the play to provide an artificially tidy ending. Cf. *Poetics*, 1454a39–b3.]

12. [differentiae: i.e. of the atoms, the solid bodies referred to in general terms as the full.]

13. [rhythm, touching, and turning: These are the Atomists' own terms, which Aristotle explains; the illustration using letters (*stoicheia*, also translated "elements"; cf. 1041b15) is probably theirs too.]

This, then, would seem to be the extent, as we say, of the earlier thinkers' search for these two causes.

Criticisms of Plato

ORIGINS OF THE THEORY OF IDEAS

6

987a29 Plato's work came after the philosophical views we have mentioned;[14] it agreed with them in most ways,
30 but it also had distinctive features setting it apart from the philosophy of the Italians. For in his youth Plato first became familiar with Cratylus and with the Heraclitean beliefs that all perceptible things are always flowing and that there is no knowledge of them; he
987b held these views later too. Socrates, on the other hand, was concerned with ethics and not at all with nature as a whole; he was seeking the universal in ethics and was the first to turn his thought to definitions.
5 Plato agreed with Socrates, but because of his Heraclitean views he took these definitions to apply not to perceptible things but to other things; for, he thought, the common formula could not be of any of the perceptible things, since they are always changing. Beings of this sort [that definitions are of], then, he called Ideas, and he said that perceptible things are apart from these, and are all called after them, since the things with the same names as the Forms are
10 what they are[15] by participation in them.

In speaking of 'participation' he changed only the name; for the Pythagoreans say that things are what they are by imitating numbers, and Plato (changing the name) said they are what they are by participating [in Forms]. But they left it to others to investigate what it is to participate in or to imitate Forms.

IDEAS, MATHEMATICAL OBJECTS, AND NUMBERS

15 Further, he says that, apart from perceptible things and Forms, there are also mathematical objects in between. These differ from perceptible things in being everlasting and immobile; they differ from Forms

in that there are many of the same kind, whereas there is only one Form for each kind of thing.[16]

Since the Forms are the causes of other things, he thought that their elements are the elements of all beings. The great and the small, then, as matter, and the one, as substance, are principles; for Forms come 20 from these, by participating in the one. And yet he said, agreeing with the Pythagoreans, that the one is substance, and that it is not said to be one by being something else. He also agreed with them in saying 25 that numbers are the causes of the being of other things; but in positing a duality instead of treating the indeterminate as one, and in taking the great and small to constitute the indeterminate, he held a distinctive view of his own. Moreover, in his view numbers exist apart from perceptible things; whereas the Pythagoreans take the objects themselves to be numbers, and do not place mathematical objects between perceptible things and Forms.

His claim that the one and numbers exist apart 30 from the other objects (in contrast to the Pythagorean view) and his introduction of the Forms were the result of his investigation of arguments; for none of his predecessors engaged in dialectic. He made the other nature [besides the One] a duality because he thought that numbers (except the primes) could be neatly produced from the duality, as though from 988a something malleable.

What actually happens, though, is the contrary of this, and it is implausible to think it would happen in the way they [the Platonists] say. For in their view many things are made out of the matter, but the Form generates only once; in fact, however, only one table is apparently made out of one [bit of] matter, whereas the agent who applies the form, though he is one, makes many tables. Similarly, in the case of male 5 and female, the female is impregnated from one copulation, whereas the male impregnates many females. And yet these things are imitations of those principles [that they believe in].

PLATO CONSIDERED ONLY TWO OF THE FOUR CAUSES

This, then, was what Plato determined about the questions we are investigating. It is evident from what

14. [views we have mentioned: Aristotle has been discussing the Eleatics and Pythagoreans, whom he calls the "Italians."]

15. [are what they are: just "are," and hence perhaps literally, "exist" (and also in the rest of the paragraph).]

16. [there is only one Form for each kind of thing: Literally, "each Form itself is only one."]

has been said that he used only two causes, the cause
10 involving the what-it-is and the material cause; for
the Forms are causes of the what-it-is of the other
things, and the one is the cause of the what-it-is of
Forms. The nature of the matter that is the subject
for the Forms (in the case of perceptible things) and
for the one (in the case of Forms) is also evident: it
is the duality, the great and the small. Further, he
has assigned the cause of good and bad to the ele-
15 ments, one to each, as we say some earlier philosophers, such as Empedocles and Anaxagoras, also
sought to do.

THE IDEAS SIMPLY MULTIPLY THE NUMBER OF THINGS TO BE EXPLAINED

9

990a34 . . . As for those who posited Ideas, the first objection
is that in seeking to grasp the causes of the beings in
990b this world, they introduced different things, equal in
number to them. It is as though someone wanted to
count things and thought he could not do it if there
5 were fewer of them, but could do it if he added more.
For the Forms they resorted to in their search for the
causes of things in this world are practically equal in
number to—or at any rate are no fewer than—the
things in this world. For take each [kind of] thing
that has a one over many, both substances and non-
substances, both things in this world and everlasting
things; in each case there is some [one over many]
that has the same name [as the many].

THE ARGUMENTS FOR FORMS FAIL

Further, none of the proofs we[17] offer to show that
there are Forms appears to succeed; for some of them
10 are invalid, while some also yield Forms of things
that we think have no Forms. For the arguments from
the sciences yield Forms of all the things of which
there are sciences; the one over many yields Forms
15 even of negations; and the argument from thinking
about something that has perished yields Forms of

17. [we: Aristotle thinks of himself as one of the Platonic
school—though he does not endorse their position. In the
rest of this chapter "we" and "our" also refer to the Platonists,
not to Aristotle's independent views.]

things that perish, since there is an appearance[18] of
these. Further, among the more accurate arguments,
some produce Ideas of relatives, whereas we deny
that these are a kind of things that are in their own
right; others introduce the Third Man.

THE THEORY OF FORMS CONFLICTS WITH OTHER PLATONIST DOCTRINES

And in general the arguments for Forms undermine
the existence of things that matter more to us than
the existence of the Ideas does. For they imply that
number, not duality, is first and that what is relative 20
is prior to what is in its own right, and they lead to
all the other [unacceptable] conclusions that some
people have been led to believe by following the
beliefs about the Ideas, even though these beliefs
conflict with their own principles.

Further, the reasoning that leads us to say that there
are Ideas also yields Forms of many other things as
well as of substances. For a thought is one not only 25
in the case of substances but also in other cases; there
are sciences of other things as well as of substance;
and thousands of other such difficulties arise.

On the other hand, it is necessary, and follows from
the beliefs about Forms, that if things can participate
in Forms, only substances can have Ideas; for a thing
does not participate in a Form coincidentally, but 30
insofar as it is not said of a subject. (If, for instance,
something participates in the Double itself, it also
participates in the Everlasting, but coincidentally,
since it is coincidental that the Double is everlasting.)
Hence the Forms will be substances. But the same
things signify substances among the Forms as in this 991a
world—otherwise what will the claim that there is
something apart from these things, the one over many,
amount to? And if the Idea and the things participating in it have the same form, they will have something
in common—for why should [what it is to be] two
be one and the same thing in all the perishable twos
and in all of the many everlasting twos, but not one 5
and the same thing in the Two itself and in some
particular two? But if they do not have the same form,
they will be [merely] homonymous; it will be like
calling both Callias and a wooden [statue] a man,

18. [appearance: *phantasma*, usually rendered "object of
appearance."]

when one has observed no common [nature] that they share.

THE IDEAS CANNOT EXPLAIN PERCEPTIBLE THINGS

One might be especially puzzled about what on earth Forms contribute to perceptible things, either to those that are everlasting or to those that come to be and 10 perish; for they cause neither motion nor any change in them. Nor do they contribute to knowledge of other things, since they are not their substance—if they were, they would be in the other things. Nor do 15 they contribute to the being of other things, since Forms are not present in the things that participate in them. For if they were present, they might perhaps be thought to be causes, as white is if it is mixed in a white object. This argument was first stated by Anaxagoras and then by Eudoxus and certain others. It is easily upset, since it is easy to collect many 20 impossible consequences that challenge such a belief.

Nor can the other things be from Forms in any of the ways things are normally said to be from something. And to say that Forms are patterns and that other things participate in them is empty talk, mere poetic metaphors. For what is it that looks to the Ideas when it produces things? And it is possible for one thing to be, or to come to be, like another without 25 being copied from it, so that whether or not Socrates exists someone like Socrates might come to be; and clearly the same would be true even if Socrates were everlasting. Further, there will be many patterns of the same thing, hence many Forms; the Forms of man, for instance, will be Animal and Biped as well 30 as Man-itself. Further, the Forms will be patterns not only of perceptible things, but also of themselves— the genus, for instance, of its species—so that the 991b same thing will be both pattern and copy.

Further, it would seem impossible for a substance to be separate from what it is the substance of. How, then, if the Ideas are the substances of things, could they be separate from them?

According to the *Phaedo*,[19] the Forms are the causes 5 both of being and of coming to be. But what participates in the Forms does not come to be, even if the Forms exist, unless something initiates the motion.

19. [*Phaedo*: See Plato, *Phaedo* 100a–105c.]

And in addition to these [natural things], many things—for instance, a house or a ring—which in our view have no Forms, come to be. Hence it is clearly also possible for the [natural] things to be and to come to be because of causes of the sort just mentioned.

Further, if the Forms are numbers, how can they 10 be causes? Is it because beings are other numbers, so that one number, for instance, is man, another is Socrates, and another is Callias? If so, why are one lot of numbers causes of the other lot? It makes no difference if the Forms are everlasting and the other things are not. But if it is because things in this world—for instance, a harmony—are ratios of numbers, it is clear that the things of which they are ratios are some one [kind of] thing. But if there is this one thing, i.e. the matter, then evidently the numbers 15 themselves will also be ratios of one thing to another. If, for instance, Callias is a numerical ratio of fire, earth, water, and air, then his Idea will also be the number of certain other subjects. And Man-itself, even if it is in some way numerical, will nonetheless be a numerical ratio of certain things, not [properly] a number. This argument, then, does not show that 20 any Idea is a number.

THE PLATONISTS HAVE THE WRONG CONCEPTION OF A UNIVERSAL SCIENCE

. . . In general, it is impossible to find the elements 992b18 of beings without distinguishing the ways they are spoken of, since in fact beings are spoken of in many ways. It is especially impossible to find them if we 20 search in this way for the sorts of elements that compose beings. For what elements compose acting or being affected or the straight? Presumably these cannot be found; at most the elements of substances can be found. Hence it is incorrect either to seek the elements of all beings or to think one has found them.

And how could one even learn the elements of all things? For clearly one cannot begin with previous 25 cognition. If, for instance, we are learning geometry, we may have previous knowledge of other things [outside geometry], but we have no previous cognition about the subject matter of the science we are to learn about; the same is true in other cases. Hence if there is some science of all things, such as some say there is, we could not have previous cognition of 30

anything before we learn this science. And yet all learning, either through demonstration or through definitions, relies on previous cognition of either all or some things; for one must previously know the elements of the definition, and they must be well known; the same is true for learning through induc-
993a tion. Then is this science actually innate? If so, it is remarkable that we manage not to notice that we possess the supreme science.

Further, how is one to acquire recognition of the elements, and how is this knowledge to be made clear? For there is a puzzle here too, since our answers
5 might be disputed, as in the case of certain syllables; for some say that ZA is from S, D, and A, while others say it is a different sound, and none of the well-known ones.

Further, how could one recognize perceptible things without perception? And yet one would have to, if the elements composing all things are indeed the same, as complex sounds are [composed of] their
10 proper elements.

BOOK VII
The Study of Substance

SUBSTANCE IS THE PRIMARY TYPE OF BEING

1

1028a10 Being is spoken of in many ways, which we distinguished previously in the work on how many ways things are spoken of. For one [type of being] signifies what-it-is and a this; another signifies quality, or quantity, or any of the other things predicated in this way. But while being is spoken of in this many ways, it is evident that among these the primary being is the
15 what-it-is, which signifies substance. For whenever we say what quality this has, we call it good or bad, not six feet long or a man, whereas whenever we say what it is, we call it a man or a god, not pale or hot or six feet long; and the other things are called beings by belonging to this type of being—some as quantities, some as qualities, some as affections, some in
20 some other such way.

That is why someone might actually be puzzled about whether walking, flourishing, or sitting signifies a being, for none of these is in its own right nor is any of them capable of being separated from sub-

stance, but it is more true that the walking or sitting or flourishing thing is a being (if indeed it is a being). 25 This latter type of thing is apparently more of a being because it has some definite subject—the substance and the particular—which is discerned in such a predication; for this subject is implied in speaking of the good or sitting thing. Clearly, then, it is because of substance that each of those other things is also a 30 being, so that what is in the primary way—what is not something, but is without qualification a being— is substance.

HOW SUBSTANCE IS PRIMARY

Now the primary is so spoken of in many ways, but still, substance is primary in every way: in nature, in account, and in knowledge.[20] For none of the other things predicated is separable, but only substance. Substance is also primary in account, since its account is necessarily present in the account of each thing. 35 Moreover, we think we know a thing most of all whenever we know what, for instance, man or fire is, rather than when we know its quality or quantity or 1028b place; for indeed we know each of these only when we know *what* the quantity or the quality is.

THE OLD PUZZLE ABOUT BEING IS REALLY ABOUT SUBSTANCE

Indeed, the old question—always pursued from long ago till now, and always raising puzzles—'What is being?' is just the question 'What is substance?'. For 5 it is substance that some say is one and others say is more than one, some saying that it is limited in number, others that it is unlimited. And so we too must make it our main, our primary, indeed (we may say) our only, task to study what it is that is in this way.

CANDIDATES FOR SUBSTANCE

2

The most evident examples of substances seem to be 10 bodies. That is why we say that animals and plants and their parts are substances, and also natural bodies,

---

20. [in nature . . . knowledge: Read *kai phusei kai logō(i) kai gnōsei:* "in account, in knowledge, and in time." The next three sentences explain how substance is prior in each of the three ways just distinguished.]

such as fire, water, earth, and all such things, and whatever is either a part of these or composed of all or some of them—for instance, the universe and its parts, the stars, moon, and sun. But we ought to
15 consider: Are these the only substances there are, or are there also others? Or are only some of these things substances, or some of these and also some other things? Or are none of these things substances, but only some other things?

Some people think that the limits of a body—for instance, a surface, a line, a point, and a unit—are substances, and are so to a higher degree than a body and a solid. Further, some think there are no substances apart from perceptible things, while to others it seems that there are also everlasting substances, which are more numerous and are beings to a higher degree. Plato, for example, thinks that Forms
20 and mathematicals are two [types of] substances, and that the substance of perceptible bodies is a third [type]. Speusippus posits even more substances, beginning with the one, and posits a principle for each [type of] substance—one for numbers, another for magnitudes, and then another for soul; and in this way he multiplies the [types of] substances. Some say
25 that Forms and numbers have the same nature, and that everything else comes after them—lines, planes, and everything else, extending to the substance of the universe and to perceptible things.

We must consider, then, which of these views are correct or incorrect; what substances there are; whether or not there are any substances apart from perceptible substances, and in what way these percep-
30 tible substances are [substances]; and whether or not there is any separable substance apart from perceptible ones, and, if there is, why there is, and in what way it is [substance]. But before doing this, we must first sketch what substance is.

Substance as Subject

The Main Criteria for Substance

3

Substance is spoken of, if not in several ways, at any
35 rate in four main cases. For the essence, the universal and the genus seem to be the substance of a given thing, and the fourth of these cases is the subject.

Substance Is the First Subject

Now, the subject is that of which the other things are said, but which is not itself in turn said of any other thing, hence we must first determine what it 1029a is, since the primary subject seems to be substance most of all.

What is spoken of in this way [as the primary subject] is in one way the matter, in another way the form, and in a third way the thing composed of these. (By the matter I mean, for example, the bronze; by the form I mean the figure and character; and by the 5 thing composed of them I mean the statue, i.e., the compound.) And so if the form is prior to the matter, and more of a being, it will also, by the same argument, be prior to the thing composed of both.

We have now said in outline, then, what substance is: it is what is not said of a subject but has the other things said of it.

This Answer Seems to Make Matter the Only Substance

However, we must not confine ourselves to this answer. For it is inadequate: for, first, it is itself unclear; 10 and further, the matter turns out to be substance. For if the matter is not substance, it is hard to see what other substance there is; for when all the other things are removed, nothing [but the matter] evidently remains. For the other things are affections, products, and potentialities of bodies; and length, breadth, and depth are kinds of quantities but not substances (for 15 quantity is not substance), but the primary [subject] to which these belong is more of a substance than they are. But when length, breadth, and depth are abstracted, we see that nothing is left, except whatever is determined by these. And so, if we examine it in this way, the matter necessarily appears as the only substance.

By matter I mean what is spoken of in its own 20 right neither as being something, nor as having some quantity, nor as having any of the other things by which being is determined. For there is something of which each of these is predicated, something whose being is different from that of each of the things predicated; for the other things are predicated of the substance, and the substance is predicated of the matter. And so the last thing is in its own right neither something nor of some quantity nor any other [of the

25 things mentioned]; nor is it [in its own right] the negations of these, since what we have said implies that the negations as well [as the positive properties] belong to it [only] coincidentally.

But this Result Is Impossible, and Hence We Must Examine Form

And so, if we study it from this point of view, the result is that the matter is substance, but that is impossible. For being separable and being a this seem to belong to substance most of all; that is why the form and the [compound] of both [matter and form] would 30 seem to be substance more than the matter is.

And so the substance composed of both—I mean composed of the matter and the form—should be set aside, since it is posterior to the other two, and clear. The matter is also evident in a way. We must, then, consider the third type of substance, since it is the most puzzling.

1029b Since some of the perceptible substances are agreed to be substances, we should begin our search with these.

Substance as Essence

We Should Study Form by Studying Essence

4

Since we began by distinguishing the things by which we define substance and since essence seems to be one of these, we ought to study it. For it is useful to advance toward what is better known, since this is how anyone succeeds in learning, by advancing 5 through what is less well known, by nature to what is better known. In questions about action, our task is to advance from what is good to ourselves, and so to make what is good without reservation good to ourselves; in the same way, then, we should advance from what is better known to ourselves, and so make what is well known by nature well known to ourselves. Admittedly, what is well known and known first to 10 any given type of person is only slightly known and has little or no hold on being; still, we must begin from what is poorly known but known by us and try to come to know what is known without reservation,

by advancing, as has been said, through the very things that are known to us.

What Is Essence

First let us make some logical remarks about it. The essence of a thing is what the thing is said to be in its own right. For being you is not the same as being 15 a musician, since you are not a musician in your own right; hence your essence is what you are in your own right.

Nor indeed is your essence all of what you are in your own right. For a thing's essence is not what belongs to it in its own right in the way that pale belongs in its own right to a surface; for being a surface is not the same as being pale. But neither is a thing's essence the same as the combination of the thing and what belongs in its own right to it—for instance, being a pale surface, since here surface is added. It follows that the account of a thing's essence 20 is the account that describes but does not mention the thing; and so if being a pale surface is the same as being a smooth surface, being pale and being smooth are one and the same.

Do Composites Have Essences?

There are composites [not only among substances but] also in the other predications, since each of these (for instance, quality, quantity, when, where, and motion) has a subject; hence we should ask whether 25 there is an account of the essence of each of these composites, and whether an essence belongs to them—to a pale man, for instance—as well as to substances. Let us, then, call this composite 'cloak'. What is being a cloak?

One might object, however, that a cloak is not spoken of in its own right either. [We reply:] There are two ways in which we speak of what is not in its own right: one way is from addition, the other is not. 30 In the first case, something is said [not to be in its own right] because the thing to be defined is added to something else—if, for instance, one gave the account of pale man as a definition of pale. In the second case, something is said not to be in its own right because something else is added to it—if, for instance, 'cloak' signified a pale man, but one were to define cloak as pale. A pale man, then, is pale, but 1030a is not what being pale is.

Only Substances Have Essences in the Primary Way

But is being a cloak an essence at all? Perhaps not. For an essence is what something essentially is, but whenever one thing is said of another, the composite 5 of the two is not essentially a this; the pale man, for instance, is not essentially a this, since only a substance is a this. Hence the things that have an essence are those whose account is a definition. But the mere fact that a name and an account signify the same thing does not imply that the account is a definition. If it did, then all accounts would be formulae (since for every account, we can find a name that signifies 10 the same); so that even the *Iliad* would be a definition. Rather, an account is a definition [only] if it is of some primary thing; primary things are those that are spoken of in a way that does not consist in one thing's being said of another. Hence essence will belong only to species of a genus and to nothing else, since [only] these seem to be spoken of in a way that does not consist in one thing's participating in another, or in one thing's being an attribute or coincident of an- 15 other. Admittedly, everything else [besides members of a species], if it has a name, will also have an account saying what it signifies (i.e., that this belongs to this) or, instead of an unqualified account, a more exact one; but nothing else will have a definition or essence.

Nonsubstances Have Essences in a Secondary Way

Perhaps, however, definitions, like what-it-is, are spoken of in several ways. For in fact what-it-is in one 20 way signifies substance and a this, and in another way signifies each of the things predicated—quantity, quality, and all the rest. For just as being belongs to them all—not in the same way, but to substance primarily and to the other things derivatively—so also the what-it-is belongs without qualification to substance and derivatively to the other things. For we might ask what a quality is, so that quality is also a 25 what-it-is, though not without qualification; just as some people say, speaking logically, that not-being is (not that it is without qualification, but that it is not-being), so also we say what a quality is.

We must certainly consider what ought to be said about a particular question, but we must consider no less how things really are. That is why, in this case, since what is said is evident [we must consider how things are]. We find that essence, like what-it-is, be- 30 longs primarily and without qualification to sub-stance, and derivatively to the other things, where it will be the essence of quality or quantity, not the essence without qualification. For we must say that these [nonsubstances] are beings either homony-mously or by addition and substraction, as we say that what is not known is known [not to be known]. The right answer is that they are beings neither homony-mously nor in the same way. What is medical, for 35 instance, is spoken of with reference to one and the same thing, not by being one and the same thing, but not homonymously either—for a body, a proce- 1030b dure, and an instrument are called medical neither homonymously nor by having one [nature], but with reference to one thing. The same applies to beings.

It does not matter which alternative we accept: in 5 either case substances evidently have a definition and essence of the primary type, i.e., a definition and essence without qualification. Certainly other beings also have definitions and essences, but not primarily. For if we accept this view of definition, not every name that signifies the same as an account will neces-sarily have a definition corresponding to it; rather, in order to be a definition, the account must be of the right type, namely an account of something that is one—and something that is one not merely by conti-nuity (like the *Iliad*, or like things that are tied to-gether) but that is one in one of the ways in which 10 one is spoken of. Now, one is spoken of in the same ways as being, and one type of being signifies a this, another quantity, another quality. That is why there will also be an account and a definition of the pale man, but not in the way that there is of pale and of the substance.

The Relation of Subjects to Their Essences

6

We should investigate whether a thing is the same *1031a15* as or different from its essence. For this is useful for our investigation of substance; for a thing seems to be nothing other than its own substance, and some-thing's substance is said to be its essence.

In the case of things spoken of coincidentally, a 20 thing might seem to be different from its essence; a pale man, for instance, is different from being a pale man. For if it is the same, then being a man is the same as being a pale man; for, they say, a man is the same as a pale man, so that being a pale man is the same as being a man.

25 Perhaps, however, it is not necessary for things to be the same if one is a coincident of the other, since the extreme terms are not the same in the same way. But presumably it might seem to follow that the extremes, the coincidental things, turn out to be the same—for instance, being pale and being musical. In fact, however, it seems not to follow.

The Relation of Platonic Forms to Their Essences

But is it necessary for things spoken of in their own right to be the same as their essences? For instance,
30 what about substances of the sort some say Ideas are, ones that have no other substances or natures prior to them? If that the good itself [the Idea] is different from the essence of good, and the animal itself from the essence of animal, and the being itself from the
1031b essence of being, then there will be further substances, natures, and Ideas apart from those mentioned, and these will be prior substances and substances to a higher degree, if essence is substance.

If, then, [the Ideas and the essences] are severed from each other, it follows that [the Ideas] will not
5 be known and that [the essences] will not be beings. (By 'severed' I mean that the essence of good does not belong to the good itself, and being good does not belong to the essence of good.) For we know a thing whenever we know its essence. Further, what applies to good applies equally to the other essences, so that if the essence of good is not good, then neither will the essence of being be, nor the essence of one be one. But since all essences alike either are or are
10 not, it follows that, if not even the essence of being is a being, none of the other essences is a being either. Moreover, if the essence of good does not belong to a given thing, that thing is not good.

The good, then, is necessarily one with the essence of good, and the fine with the essence of fine. The same applies to all the primary things, those spoken of in their own right, not insofar as they belong to something else. For if this is true [i.e., that something is a primary being], it already implies [that the primary being is identical to its essence], even if it is not a Form—though presumably [the conclusion] is all the 15 more [necessary] if the thing is a Form.

Further, if the Ideas are what some people say they are, then clearly the subject will not be substance. For Ideas must be substances, but not by [being predicated] of a subject, since [if they were predicated of a subject], they would exist [only] by being participated in.

From these arguments, then, we find that a thing itself and its essence are noncoincidentally one and the same, and that knowing a thing is knowing its 20 essence; and so even isolating the Forms shows that a thing and its essence must be some one thing.

Things Spoken of in Their Own Right Are the Same as Their Essences

But because what is spoken of coincidentally—for instance, the musical or the pale—signifies two things, it is not true to say that it is the same as its essence. For the pale signifies both the subject of 25 which pale is a coincident and the coincident, and so in a way it is the same as its essence, and in a way it is not the same—for [the pale] is not the same as man or as pale man, but it is the same as the attribute.

We can also see that it is absurd [for something not to be the same as its essence], if we give a name to each essence; for apart from that essence there will be another essence as well—for instance, another essence 30 will be the essence of the essence of horse. But why not let some things be essences at once, going no further, since essence is substance? Moreover, not only is [a 1032a thing] one [with its essence], but their account is also the same; for one and being one are noncoincidentally one. Moreover, if there is another essence, the essences will go on to infinity; for one thing will be the essence of the one, and another will be the one, so that the same 5 argument will also apply in their case.

Clearly, then, in the case of the primary things, those spoken of in their own right, a thing and its essence are one and the same. And it is evident that the sophistical refutations aimed against this position are all resolved in the same way as is the puzzle of whether Socrates and being Socrates are the same; for there is no difference in the premises from which one would ask the questions or in the premises from which one would find a solution.   10

We have said, then, in what way something's essence is the same as the thing, and in what way it is not.

The Role of Form and Matter in Change

DIFFERENT TYPES OF COMING TO BE

7

Among things that come to be, some come to be by nature, some by craft, and some by chance, but they all come to be by some agent and from something, and come to be something. (By 'comes to be some-
15 thing' I mean something in any of the predications; for things come to be either this or of some quantity or quality or somewhere.) Things that have natural comings to be are those whose coming to be is from nature. What they come to be from is what we call matter; the agent is something that is by nature; and the something they come to be is a man or a plant or any-
20 thing of the sort we say are substances most of all.

Everything that comes to be by nature or craft has matter; for these things can both be and not be, and what has this potentiality is a thing's matter.

In general, both what something comes to be from and what it becomes is a nature; for what comes to be has a nature—a plant or an animal, for instance. Moreover, the agent is the nature that is spoken of with reference to form, and this nature is the same in form [as the nature of what comes to be], but it
25 is in another [particular], since a man generates a man. Things that come to be because of nature, then, come to be in this way.

The other comings to be are called productions; these are all from either craft or potentiality or thought. Some productions also come to be from
30 chance or luck, similarly to the way in which things come about from chance or luck among things that come to be from nature; for in the latter case too the same things that [usually] come to be from a seed also [sometimes] come to be without any seed. We must investigate these cases later.

THE ROLE OF FORM IN PRODUCTION

Things that come to be from craft are those whose
1032b form is in the soul. (By 'form' I mean a thing's essence and primary substance.) For even contraries have the same form in a way, since the substance of a privation is the substance opposed to it, so that health, for
5 instance, is the substance of disease because disease

results from the absence of health; and health is the account in the soul and the knowledge.

What is healthy comes into being when the producer has had the following sort of thought: since health is this, then if something is to be healthy, it must have this (for instance, a uniform condition of the body), and if it is to have this, it must have heat. This is how he thinks at each stage, until he leads the process back to the last thing, which is what he can produce himself; and then the motion from here on toward 10 health is called a production. And so it turns out that in a way health comes to be from health, and a house from a house—the one that has matter from the one without matter. For the medical or housebuilding [knowledge] is the form of health or house, and sub-stance without matter is what I call the essence.

One sort of coming to be and motion is called 15 thinking, another production. Thinking is the motion that proceeds from the principle, i.e., the form; and production is the motion that proceeds from the last stage of thinking. Each of the other things—those in between—comes to be in the same way. I mean, for instance, that if this [body] is to be healthy, its bodily condition must be made uniform. What, then, is it to be made uniform? This. [The body] will have this 20 if it is warmed. What is it to be warmed? This. But this is potentially present. And now he has reached what is up to himself.

If the motion toward health comes from craft, the producer that is its principle is the form in the soul; if it comes from chance, it comes from whatever is the principle of the production if the producer exercises a 25 craft. In medical treatment, for instance, the principle is presumably from warming, which the doctor pro-duces by rubbing; heat in the body, then, either is a part of health or is followed, directly or in several stages, by something that is part of health. This last thing producing the part [of health] is in a way itself also a part of health, just as the last thing (for instance, stones) is a part of the house, and part of the product in other cases. Hence, as is said, nothing can come to 30 be unless something is previously present. Evidently, 1033a then, some part will have to be present; for the matter is a part, since it is present in the product, and it comes to be the product.

But is [the matter] also one of the things in the account? We speak in both ways when we say what bronze circles are. For we speak of the matter when we say that the circle is bronze, and of the form when we say that it is this sort of shape; shape is the genus into which it is primarily placed. The bronze circle, then, has the matter in its account.

The Relation Between the Matter and the Product

Some things that come to be from matter, once they have come to be, are called not that, but of-that; the statue, for instance, is called of-stone, not stone, and similarly the healthy man is not called that from which he has come to be. The reason for this is that a thing comes to be from its privation, or from its subject which we call the matter. For instance, the man as well as the sick one comes to be healthy, but he is said to have come to be from the privation rather than the subject, so that he is said to have become healthy from having been sick, rather than from having been a man; that is why the healthy one is said to be a man, not to be sick, and the man is said to be healthy, [not sick]. But in cases where the privation—the privation of some definite shape in bronze, for instance, or of a house in bricks and timbers—is unclear and nameless, the product seems to come to be from this [matter], as in the first case [the man became healthy] from having been sick.

That is why, just as in the first case the product is not called by the name of that [privation] from which it came to be, so also in the second case the statue is not called wood, but rather the name is varied and the statue is called of-wood, not wood, or of-bronze, not bronze, or of-stone, not stone, and the house is of-bricks, not bricks. For if we look at it closely, we would not say without qualification, in this case any more than in the other, that a statue comes to be from wood, or a house from bricks; for that from which something comes to be must change and not remain when the thing comes to be. This, then, is why we speak in this way.

Both the Form and the Matter Must Exist Before Something Comes to Be

8

What comes to be, then, does so by some agent (i.e., the source of the principle of the coming to be) and from something (not the privation but the matter; we have now determined the sense in which we say

this) and becomes something (a sphere or a circle or whatever else it may be). And just as [the producer] does not produce the subject—the bronze—neither does he produce the sphere, unless he does so coincidentally, because he produces the bronze sphere and it is a sphere; for to produce a this is to produce a this from a subject in general.

Let me explain. To make the bronze round is not to produce the round or the sphere, but to produce one thing, this form, in another thing; for if someone produces the form, he must produce it from another thing, since another thing must have been the subject. For instance, he produces the bronze sphere, and this is so because he produces this, which is a sphere, from this subject, which is bronze; and if he also produces this form itself, i.e., sphere, clearly he will produce it in the same way, and then comings into being will go back to infinity.

Evidently, then, the form (or whatever the shape in the perceptible thing ought to be called) and the essence (i.e., what comes to be in something else by the agency of craft, nature, or potentiality) does not come into being and there is no coming to be of it. But the producer does make a bronze sphere to be; for he produces it from bronze and sphere—he produces this form in this subject, and the product is a bronze sphere.

If the essence of sphere in general is to have a coming to be, this essence will be something from something; for in each case what is coming to be must be divisible into this (i.e., matter) and this (i.e., form). Now, if the sphere is the figure whose circumference is everywhere equidistant from the center, one aspect of it is the matter that the product is in, the other is the form in that matter, and the whole thing—the bronze sphere, for instance—is what has come to be. It is evident, then, that what is called substance as form does not come to be, but the compound substance, which is called substance insofar as it is substance as form, does come to be. It is also evident that matter is present in everything that comes to be, and that one aspect of the product is this matter and the other is this form.

Platonic Ideas Are Useless for Explaining Coming to Be

Is there, then, some sphere apart from these [perceptible ones], or a house apart from bricks? If there were, then surely there could never have been any coming to be of any this. Rather, [sphere, for instance,] signifies this sort of thing; it is not a this and something definite. On the contrary, one produces or generates this sort of thing from this [matter], and when it has been generated, it is *this* thing of this sort. This whole 25 thing—for instance, Callias or Socrates—corresponds to this bronze sphere, while man and animal correspond to bronze sphere in general.

It is evident, then, that the forms, construed as some people habitually construe them, as things apart from particulars, are useless as causes, at any rate of comings to be and of substances; this role, at any rate, is no reason for these forms to be substances in their 30 own right.

In some cases, generator and generated are evidently also of the same sort, but they are not the same thing—they are one in form, not one in number. This is true of natural things (for instance, a man generates a man), except in cases where something contrary to nature comes about, so that a horse, for instance, generates a mule. And even in these cases something similar is true; for the nearest genus, what- 1034a ever is common to horse and ass, has no name, but is presumably both, as a mule is.

Evidently, then, there is no need to set up a form as a pattern. For if we sought such forms anywhere, it would be in natural generation, since natural things are substances most of all; but in fact the generator 5 is sufficient to produce the thing and to be the cause of the form in the matter. And the whole—this sort of form in this flesh and bones—is Callias or Socrates; and they differ because of matter, since their matter is different, but they are the same in form, since the form is indivisible.

How Things Come to Be by Chance as Well as by Craft

9

A puzzle might arise about why some things—for 10 instance, health—come to be both by craft and also from chance, while others—for instance, houses— do not. The reason is as follows. The matter that is the principle of production and coming to be from craft, and that has some part of the product present in it, in some cases can be moved by its own agency, and in other cases cannot. In some cases of the first sort, the matter can be moved [by its own agency] in a

particular way [required for a certain kind of product], and in other such cases it cannot; for many things 15 are capable of being moved by their own agency, but not in a particular way (for instance, dancing). Hence things with matter of this second sort—stones, for instance—cannot be moved in a particular way except by something else, but in another way they can be moved by their own agency. That is why in some cases the result requires a craftsman, but in other cases it does not; in these cases the movers will be agents that have no craft but can themselves be 20 moved, either by other agents that have no craft or from a part [of the eventual product].

It is also clear from what we have said that in a way every [product of craft] comes to be, just as natural things do, from something with the same name (for instance, a house from a house, insofar as it is produced by mind, since the craft [of building] is the form), or from a part with the same name, or from 25 something that has a part [of the product]. This is true if it does not come to be coincidentally; for the first cause in its own right of the production is a part of the product. Heat in the motion, for example, produces heat in the body, and this heat is either health or a part of it or is followed by a part of health or by health itself; that is why it is also said to produce [health], because it produces that on which health follows and in which it coincides. 30

And so, just as in deductions, substance is the principle of everything; for deductions begin from what-it-is, and comings to be are from this too.

Chance in Natural Coming to Be

Naturally constituted things are similar to the products of craft. For the seed produces in the same way as the efforts of craft do; for it has the form potentially, 1034b and in a way the parent providing the seed has the same name as the offspring. For one must not expect all offspring to come to be in the way a man comes to be from a man—even here, indeed, a female comes to be from a male. The offspring has the same name if it is not defective; hence a mule's parent is not a mule [since mules are defective].

Things that come to be by chance (just as in the 5 case of crafts) are those whose matter can on some occasions also be moved by its own agency with the motion that the seed [usually] initiates in it; unless this is true of the matter, things cannot come to be except from the parents.

The Coming to Be of Nonsubstances

Our argument not only shows that form cannot come to be in the case of substance, but it also applies equally to all the primary [genera]—to quantity, qual-
10 ity, and the other predications. For it is the bronze sphere, not sphere or bronze, that comes to be, and the same applies to bronze, if it comes to be; for in every case the matter and the form must previously exist. This is true both for what-it-is and also for quality, quantity, and each of the other predications; for what comes to be is not a quality, but wood of some
15 quality, and not a quantity, but wood or animal of some quantity.

However, a distinctive feature of substance may be noticed from these cases, that it must be produced by another actual substance preceding it (for instance, by an animal, if an animal comes to be), whereas a quality or quantity needs only a potential quality or quantity to precede it.

Substance, Form, and Universal

Can a Universal Be a Substance?

13

1038b Since we are investigating substance, let us return to it again. Just as the subject and the essence are said to be substance, so too is the universal. We have discussed the first two of these, namely essence and
5 subject; we have seen that something is a subject in one of two ways, either by being a this (as an animal is the subject for its attributes) or as matter is the subject for the actuality. But some also think that the universal is a cause and principle more than anything else is; that is why we should also discuss the universal.

A Universal Cannot Be the Substance of the Things It Is Predicated Of

For it would seem impossible for anything spoken of universally to be substance. For, first, the substance
10 of a thing is the substance that is distinctive of it, which does not belong to anything else, whereas the universal is common; for what is called universal is what naturally belongs to more than one thing. Then

which thing's substance will the universal be? For it must be the substance either of all or of none of them. It cannot be the substance of all; but if it is the substance of one of them, then the others will be this one too, since things that have one substance also have one essence and are themselves one. 15

Substance Is Subject, Hence Not Universal

Further, what is called substance is what is not said of a subject, whereas every universal is said of a subject.

If a Universal Is Substance, It Cannot Be a Component of Something's Essence

Now, suppose someone says: 'Admittedly, a universal cannot belong to something as its essence. Still, it is present in the essence, as animal is present in man and horse.' Surely it is clear that it will be some account of [the essence it is present in]. It does not matter even if it is not an account of everything in the substance; for this [universal] will still be the 20 substance of something, as man is of the man in which it is present. And so the result will be the same once again; for [the universal]—for instance, animal—will be the substance of whatever it is present in by being its distinctive property.

Further, it is both impossible and absurd for a this and substance, if it is composite, to be composed not 25 from substances and not from a this, but from a sort of thing; for it will follow that a nonsubstance, a sort of thing, will be prior* to substance, to a this. But that is impossible; for attributes cannot be prior to substance, either in account or in time or in knowledge—for if they were, they would also be separable.

Moreover, a substance will be present in [the substance] Socrates, so that [the universal] will be the 30 substance of two things.

In general, if a man and things spoken of in this way are substances, it follows that nothing in their account is the substance of any of them or exists separately from them or in anything else. I mean, for instance, that there is no animal, or anything else mentioned in the accounts, apart from the particular animals.

A Universal Cannot Be a This, and So Cannot Be a Substance

If we study them in this way, then, it is evident that 35 nothing that belongs universally is a substance and

1039a that what is predicated in common signifies this sort of thing, not a this. If it is a this, then many [difficulties] result, including the Third Man.

Our Distinction Between Actuality and Potentiality Explains Why Universals Cannot Be Substances

Further, our conclusion can also be made clear from the following points. Substance cannot be composed of substances that are actually present in it; for things 5 that are actually two in this way are never actually one, but if they are potentially two they are [actually] one. A double line, for instance, is composed of halves that are [only] potentially two things; for the actuality separates them. And so if substance is one, it will not be composed of substances that are actually present 10 in it. Democritus is right about actuality, when he says that one cannot come to be from two, or two from one; he says this because he regards the indivisible magnitudes as the substances. Clearly, then, the same will apply in the case of number if, as some say, number is a combination of units; for either the pair is not one or else a unit is not actually in it.

15 This conclusion, however, raises a puzzle. For if no substance can be composed of universals (because a universal signifies this sort of thing, not a this) and if no substance can be composed of substances actually present in it, then it follows that every substance will be incomposite, so that none will have any account. And yet, it seems to everyone, and we 20 have said much earlier, that substances alone, or most of all, have formulae, whereas now they too turn out not to have them. And so either nothing will have a definition or else in a way things will have definitions, and in a way they will not. What this means will be clearer from what follows.

The Impossibility of Separated Platonic Ideas

14

25 It is also evident from this what results for those who both say that the Ideas are separate substances and also, at the same time, take a Form to be composed of genus and differentiae. For if there are Forms, and if animal is in man and horse, then it is either numerically one and the same in both or numerically

different in each. (For clearly it is one in account; a statement of the account will state the same thing in 30 each case.) If, then, there is some man himself in his own right that is a this and separated, each of his components—for instance, animal and biped—must also signify a this and be separable and a substance; and so this is also true of animal.

A Generic Idea Cannot Be the Same in Different Species

If the animal in horse is one and the same as the animal in man, as you are one and the same as yourself, then how will this one thing that is in sepa- 1039b rate things be one, and why will this animal not be separate from itself as well?

Further, if it is to participate in two-footed and many-footed, then something impossible follows; for contraries will belong simultaneously to it, though it is one and a this. But if it is not to participate in them, what is meant by saying that animal is two- 5 footed or footed? Presumably [we might be told] they are combined and in contact or mixed; but all such answers are absurd.

Nor Can It Be Different in Different Species

Suppose, alternatively, that animal is different in each [species]; then there will be practically an unlimited number of things whose substance is animal, since man is noncoincidentally composed of animal.

Further, animal itself will be many things. For the 10 animal in each [species] is substance, because [the species] is not called [animal] by reference to anything else—if it were, then that other thing would be a component of man and would be its genus.

Further, all the elements composing man will be Ideas; but nothing will be the Idea of one thing and the substance of another (for that would be impossible). Hence animal itself will be each one of the animals in the different [species of] animals.

Further, what is that [animal in each species] composed of, and how will it be composed of animal 15 itself? Or how can the animal [in each species], whose substance is this animal itself, be something apart from animal itself?

There Are Even Worse Problems in the Relation of Ideas to Particulars

Further, in the case of perceptible things, these and even more absurd results follow. If, then, this cannot be how things are, clearly there are no Forms of perceptible things in the way some say there are.

Difficulties about Particular Substances

15

20 We have found that the compound and the form are different sorts of substance; I mean that the first sort of substance is substance by being the form, combined with matter, and the second sort is the form, without qualification. Now, all the substances spoken of as compounds perish, since all of them also come to be; but the form does not perish in such a way that it is ever [in the process of] perishing, since neither
25 is it ever [in the process of] coming to be. For it is the essence of this house, not the essence of house, that is [in the process of] coming to be, whereas forms are and are not without [any process of] coming to be and perishing, since we have shown that no one generates or produces them.

They Are Perishable and Hence Allow Neither Definition Nor Knowledge

For this reason there is neither definition nor demonstration about particular perceptible substances, because they have matter whose nature admits of both
30 being and not being; that is why all [perceptible] particulars are perishable.

Now, demonstrations and definitions that express knowledge, are of necessary things. And just as knowledge cannot be knowledge at one time and ignorance at another, but what admits of such variation is belief, so also neither demonstration nor definition admits
1040a of such variation; belief is what is concerned with what admits of being otherwise. It clearly follows that there will be neither definition nor demonstration of these [particular perceptible things]. For whenever perishing things pass from perception, they are unclear to those with knowledge, and though the accounts still remain in the souls of those with knowl-
5 edge, there will be neither definition nor demonstration [about perceptible things]. That is why, whenever anyone who looks for a formula is defining a particu-

lar, he ought to realize that the definition can in every case be undermined, since particulars cannot be defined.

Since Platonic Ideas Are Particulars, They Are Indefinable

Nor, indeed, can Ideas be defined. For Ideas are particulars, they say, and separable. But accounts 10 must be composed of names, and the definer will not make a [new] name (since it would be unknown); yet each of the established names is common to all [the particulars of a given kind], and so they must also belong to something else [as well as to a given particular]. If, for instance, someone defines you, he will say you are a thin or pale animal, or something else that belongs to something else as well as to you.

Someone might say: 'Even though each name [in the definition] belongs separately to many things, still 15 it is possible that all together belong only to this.' We should answer, first, that biped animal, for instance, belongs both to animal and to biped—indeed, this must be so with everlasting things, since they are prior to and parts of the composite thing. Moreover, they are also separable if man is separable; for either none of the three is separable or both animal and biped 20 are. And so if none of them is separable, the genus will not exist apart from the species; but if the genus is separable, so is the differentia. Moreover, [animal and biped] are prior in being [to biped animal], and therefore they are not destroyed when it is.

Further, if Ideas are composed of Ideas (for the things they are composed of are less composite), then the components of the Idea—for instance, animal and biped—will also have to be predicated of many things. If they are not, how will they be known? For 25 there will be an Idea which cannot be predicated of more than one thing. But that does not seem to be so; on the contrary, every Idea can, it seems, be participated in.

Difficulties in Defining Particulars

As has been said, then, we fail to notice that everlasting things [that are particulars] are indefinable. This is especially true in the case of those that are unique—for instance, the sun and the moon. For sometimes people not only go wrong by adding the sorts of things 30 (for instance, going around the earth, or being hidden at night) that can be removed from the sun without its ceasing to be the sun. (For [this sort of definition implies that] if it stops going around or shows at night, it will no longer be the sun; but that is absurd, since the sun signifies a certain substance.) They also [sometimes go wrong by mentioning only the features] that can be found in something else as well. If, for instance, something else of this sort comes to be, then clearly [according to the alleged definition],

1040b it will also have to be the sun, and in that case the account will be common [to the two]. But in fact the sun is a particular, as Cleon and Socrates are.

[These objections show why Ideas are indefinable.] For why does none of those [who believe in Ideas] present a formula of any Idea? If they tried to do so, the truth of what we have just said would become clear.

SOME APPARENT SUBSTANCES, BOTH PARTICULARS AND UNIVERSALS, LACK THE APPROPRIATE SORT OF UNITY

16

5 It is evident that even among the substances that are generally recognized to be such, most are potentialities. These include the parts of animals (for none of them is separated [as long as they remain parts of animals]; whenever they are separated, they all exist as matter), and also earth, fire, and air. For none of these is one, but each is a sort of heap, until they are worked up and some one thing comes to be from

10 them.

One would be most inclined to suppose that the parts of ensouled things that are closely [associated with] the soul are beings both in actuality and in potentiality; for they have principles of motion from some source in their joints, which is why some animals keep on living when they are divided. But none-

15 theless, all these things exist [only] in potentiality. They exist as long as they are one and continuous by nature, rather than by force or by growing together (that sort of thing is a deformity).

Now, one is spoken of in the same ways as being is; and the substance of one thing is one, and things whose substance is numerically one are numerically one. Evidently, then, neither one nor being can be the substance of things, just as being an element or being a principle cannot [be the substance of things];

20 rather, we ask 'What then is the principle?', so that

we may refer [the thing] to something better known. Among these things, then, being and one are substance to a higher degree than principle, element, and cause are; but even being and one are not substance, since nothing else common is substance either. For substance belongs only to itself and to what has it, the thing whose substance it is. Moreover, one 25 thing would not be in many places at once, but what is common exists in many places at once. Hence clearly no universal is found separately apart from particulars.

But those who say there are Forms are right in one way, in separating them, if they are indeed substances; but in another way they are wrong, because they say that the one over many is a Form. The reason is that 30 they cannot describe these imperishable substances apart from particular and perceptible substances, and so they make them the same in kind as perishable things (since these are the substances we know); they speak of man itself and horse itself, adding to perceptibles the word 'itself'.

And yet even if we had not seen the stars, nonethe- 1041a less, I think, they would have been everlasting substances apart from those we know; and so, as things are, it is equally true that even if we do not know what nonperceptible substances there are, there must presumably be some.

It is clear, then, that nothing said universally is a substance, and that no substance is composed of substances. 5

SUBSTANCE AS CAUSE AND ESSENCE

17

But let us make a sort of new beginning, and say over again what, and what sort of thing, substance should be said to be; for presumably our answer will also make things clear about the substance that is separated from perceptible substances. Since, then, substance is some sort of principle and cause, we should proceed from here. 10

In every case, we search for the reason why by asking why one thing belongs to another. For if we ask why a musical man is a musical man, either we are searching for what we have mentioned—for instance, why the man is musical—or else we are searching for something else. Now, to ask why something is itself is to search for nothing. For that [it is 15 so] and its being so—I mean, for instance, that the moon is eclipsed—must be clear already; and the answer 'because it is itself' is one account and one cause applying to every case, to why a man is a man or a musician a musician. Perhaps, however, someone might answer 'because each thing is indivisible from itself, since this is what it is to be one'. But this is a 20 short answer common to all cases.

We might, however, ask why a man is this sort of animal. Here, then, we are clearly not asking why something that is a man is a man. We are asking, then, why one thing belongs to another; that it does belong must already be clear, since otherwise we are searching for nothing. For instance, when we ask why 25 it thunders, we are asking why there is a noise in the clouds; here we ask why one thing belongs to another. Similarly, we ask why these things—for instance, bricks and stones—are a house.

Evidently, then, we are searching for the cause; and this is the essence, to speak from a logical point of view. In some cases—for instance, presumably, a house or a bed—the cause is the what something is 30 for; sometimes it is what first initiated the motion, since this is also a cause. We search for the latter type of cause in the case of coming to be and perishing; in the case of being as well [as in the case of coming to be] we search for the former type of cause.

ESSENCE IS SUBSTANCE AND FORM

What we are searching for is most easily overlooked when one thing is not said of another (as when we 1041b ask, for instance, what a man is), because we speak without qualification and do not specify that we are asking why these things are this thing. Instead of speaking without qualification, we must articulate our question before we search, since otherwise we will not have distinguished a genuine search from a search 5 for nothing. Since we must take it as given that the subject exists, clearly we search for why the matter is something. We ask, for instance, 'Why are these things a house?' Because the essence of house belongs to them. Similarly, a man is this, or rather is this body having this. Hence we search for the cause on account

of which the matter is something, i.e., for the form; and this cause is the substance.

Evidently, then, there is neither searching nor 10 teaching about incomposite things; the approach to them is different from searching.

THE FORM CANNOT BE ONE OF THE MATERIAL CONSTITUENTS OR COMPOSED OF THEM

Now, a composite is composed of something in such a way that the whole thing is one, not as a heap is, but as a syllable is. A syllable is not the same as its letters—for instance, B and A are not the same thing as BA, nor is flesh fire and earth. For when the components are dispersed, the flesh or syllable no longer 15 exists, though the letters or the fire and earth still do. Hence the syllable is something, and not only the vowel and the consonant but some further thing; and similarly, flesh is not only fire and earth, or the hot and cold, but some further thing.

Now suppose that this further thing must be either 20 an element or composed of elements. If it is an element, there will be the same argument over again; for flesh will be composed of this [new element], plus fire and earth, plus some further thing, so that it will go on without limit. If the further thing is composed of an element, it is clearly not composed of just one (otherwise it would itself be this one), but of more than one; and then we will repeat the same argument 25 about it as about flesh or a syllable.

It would seem, however, that this further thing is something, and not an element, and that it is the cause of one thing's being flesh and another thing's being a syllable, and similarly in the other cases.

SUBSTANCE IS FORM AND NATURE

Now this is the substance of a given thing; for this is the primary cause of the thing's being [what it is]. Some things are not substances, but the things that are substances are naturally constituted; hence this 30 nature—the one that is not an element but a principle—will apparently be substance. An element is what is present in something as the matter into which the thing is divided—for instance, the A and the B in the syllable.

Nicomachean Ethics

BOOK I

The Highest Good: Happiness

THE HIGHEST GOOD IS SUPREME IN THE HIERARCHY OF GOODS

1

1094a Every craft and every investigation, and likewise every action and decision, seems to aim at some good; hence the good has been well described as that at which everything aims.

However, there is an apparent difference among the ends aimed at. For the end is sometimes an activ-
5 ity, sometimes a product beyond the activity; and when there is an end beyond the action, the product is by nature better than the activity.

Since there are many actions, crafts and sciences, the ends turn out to be many as well; for health is the end of medicine, a boat of boatbuilding,
10 victory of generalship, and wealth of household management.

But whenever any of these sciences are subordinate to some one capacity—as e.g. bridlemaking and every other science producing equipment for horses is subordinate to horsemanship, while this and every action in warfare is in turn subordinate to generalship, and in the same way other sciences are subordinate to
15 further ones—in each of these the end of the ruling science is more choiceworthy than all the ends subordinate to it, since it is the end for which those ends are also pursued. And here it does not matter whether the ends of the actions are the activities themselves, or some product beyond them, as in the sciences we have mentioned.

Reprinted by permission of the translator, Terence Irwin, from Aristotle, *Nicomachean Ethics* (Indianapolis: Hackett Publishing Company, 1985). The use of brackets within the text indicates insertions not found in the manuscript. Headings are those of the translator.

THE RULING SCIENCE STUDYING HIGHEST GOOD IS POLITICAL SCIENCE

2

Suppose, then, that (a) there is some end of the things we pursue in our actions which we wish for because of itself, and because of which we wish for the other things; and (b) we do not choose everything because 20 of something else, since (c) if we do, it will go on without limit, making desire empty and futile; then clearly (d) this end will be the good, i.e. the best good.

Then surely knowledge of this good is also of great importance for the conduct of our lives, and if, like archers, we have a target to aim at, we are more likely to hit the right mark. If so, we should try to grasp, in 25 outline at any rate, what the good is, and which science or capacity is concerned with it.

It seems to concern the most controlling science, the one that, more than any other, is the ruling science. And political science apparently has this character.

(1) For it is the one that prescribes which of the 1094b sciences ought to be studied in cities, and which ones each class in the city should learn, and how far.

(2) Again, we see that even the most honoured capacities, e.g. generalship, household management, and rhetoric, are subordinate to it.

(3) Further, it uses the other sciences concerned 5 with action, and moreover legislates what must be done and what avoided.

Hence its end will include the ends of the other sciences, and so will be the human good.

[This is properly called political science;] for though admittedly the good is the same for a city as for an individual, still the good of the city is apparently a greater and more complete good to acquire and preserve. For while it is satisfactory to acquire and preserve the good even for an individual, it is finer 10 and more divine to acquire and preserve it for a people and for cities. And so, since our investigation aims at these [goods, for an individual and for a city], it is a sort of political science.

The Method of Political Inquiry

3

Our discussion will be adequate if its degree of clarity reflects the subject-matter; for we should not seek the same degree of exactness in all sorts of arguments alike, any more than in the products of different crafts.

15 Moreover, what is fine and what is just, the topics of inquiry in political science, differ and vary so much that they seem to rest on convention only, not on nature. Goods, however, also vary in the same sort of way, since they cause harm to many people; for it has happened that some people have been destroyed because of their wealth, others because of their bravery.

Since these, then, are the sorts of things we argue from and about, it will be satisfactory if we can indi-
20 cate the truth roughly and in outline; since [that is to say] we argue from and about what holds good usually [but not universally], it will be satisfactory if we can draw conclusions of the same sort.

Each of our claims, then, ought to be accepted in the same way [as claiming to hold good usually], since the educated person seeks exactness in each area to the extent that the nature of the subject allows;
25 for apparently it is just as mistaken to demand demonstrations from a rhetorician as to accept [merely] persuasive arguments from a mathematician.

1095a Further, each person judges well what he knows, and is a good judge about that; hence the good judge in a particular area is the person educated in that area, and the unconditionally good judge is the person educated in every area.

This is why a youth is not a suitable student of political science; for he lacks experience of the actions in life which political science argues from and about.
5 Moreover, since he tends to be guided by his feelings, his study will be futile and useless; for its end is action, not knowledge. And here it does not matter whether he is young in years or immature in character, since the deficiency does not depend on age, but results from being guided in his life and in each of his pursuits by his feelings; for an immature person, like an incontinent person, gets no benefit from his knowledge.
10 If, however, we are guided by reason in forming our desires and in acting, then this knowledge will be of great benefit.

These are the preliminary points about the student, about the way our claims are to be accepted, and about what we intend to do.

Common Beliefs about the Highest Good Are Inadequate

4

Let us, then, begin again. Since every sort of knowl- 15 edge and decision pursues some good, what is that good which we say is the aim of political science? What [in other words] is the highest of all the goods pursued in action?

As far as its name goes, most people virtually agree [about what the good is], since both the many and the cultivated call it happiness, and suppose that living well and doing well are the same as being happy. 20 But they disagree about what happiness is, and the many do not give the same answer as the wise.

For the many think it is something obvious and evident, e.g. pleasure, wealth or honour, some thinking one thing, others another; and indeed the same person keeps changing his mind, since in sickness he thinks it is health, in poverty wealth. And when they are conscious of their own ignorance, they admire 25 anyone who speaks of something grand and beyond them.

[Among the wise,] however, some used to think that besides these many goods there is some other good that is something in itself, and also causes all these goods to be goods.

Presumably, then, it is rather futile to examine all these beliefs, and it is enough to examine those that are most current or seem to have some argument 30 for them.

We must notice, however, the difference between arguments from origins and arguments towards origins. For indeed Plato was right to be puzzled about this, when he used to ask if [the argument] set out 1095b from the origins or led towards them—just as on a race course the path may go from the starting-line to the far end, or back again.

For while we should certainly begin from origins that are known, things are known in two ways; for some are known to us, some known unconditionally [but not necessarily known to us]. Presumably, then, the origin we should begin from is what is known to us.

This is why we need to have been brought up in 5

fine habits if we are to be adequate students of what is fine and just, and of political questions generally. For the origin we begin from is the belief that something is true, and if this is apparent enough to us, we will not, at this stage, need the reason why it is true in addition; and if we have this good upbringing, we have the origins to begin from, or can easily acquire
10 them. Someone who neither has them nor can acquire them should listen to Hesiod.[1] 'He who understands everything himself is best of all; he is noble also who listens to one who has spoken well; but he who neither understands it himself nor takes to heart what he hears from another is a useless man.'

THREE CONCEPTIONS OF THE BEST LIFE

5

But let us begin again from [the common beliefs] from which we digressed. For, it would seem, people
15 quite reasonably reach their conception of the good, i.e. of happiness, from the lives [they lead]; for there are roughly three most favoured lives—the lives of gratification, of political activity, and, third, of study.

The many, the most vulgar, seemingly conceive the good and happiness as pleasure, and hence they also like the life of gratification. Here they appear
20 completely slavish, since the life they decide on is a life for grazing animals; and yet they have some argument in their defence, since many in positions of power feel the same way as Sardanapallus[2] [and also choose this life].

The cultivated people, those active [in politics], conceive the good as honour, since this is more or less the end [normally pursued] in the political life. This, however, appears to be too superficial to be
25 what we are seeking, since it seems to depend more on those who honour than on the one honoured, whereas we intuitively believe that the good is something of our own and hard to take from us.

Further, their aim in pursuing honour is seemingly to convince themselves that they are good; at any rate, they seek to be honoured by intelligent people, among people who know them, and for virtue. It is

1. [Hesiod was an eighth-century B.C. Greek poet whose works are a rich source of mythology.—S.M.C.]

2. [According to legend, Sardanapallus was an Assyrian ruler who lived in great luxury.]

clear, then, that in the view of active people at least, virtue is superior [to honour].   30

Perhaps, indeed, one might conceive virtue more than honour to be the end of the political life. However, this also is apparently too incomplete [to be the good]. For, it seems, someone might possess virtue but be asleep or inactive throughout his life; or, further, he *1096a* might suffer the worst evils and misfortunes; and if this is the sort of life he leads, no one would count him happy, except to defend a philosopher's paradox. Enough about this, since it has been adequately discussed in the popular work also.

The third life is the life of study, which we will 5 examine in what follows.

The money-maker's life is in a way forced on him [not chosen for itself]; and clearly wealth is not the good we are seeking, since it is [merely] useful, [choiceworthy only] for some other end. Hence one would be more inclined to suppose that [any of] the goods mentioned earlier is the end, since they are liked for themselves. But apparently they are not [the end] either and many arguments have been presented 10 against them. Let us, then, dismiss them.

OUR OWN VIEW OF THE GOOD

But let us return once again to the good we are looking *1097a15* for, and consider just what it could be, since it is apparently one thing in one action or craft, and another thing in another; for it is one thing in medicine, another in generalship, and so on for the rest.

What, then, is the good in each of these cases? Surely it is that for the sake of which the other things are done; and in medicine this is health, in general- 20 ship victory, in housebuilding a house, in another case something else; but in every action and decision it is the end, since it is for the sake of the end that everyone does the other things.

And so, if there is some end of everything that is pursued in action, this will be the good pursued in action; and if there are more ends than one, these will be the goods pursued in action.

Our argument has progressed then, to the same conclusion [as before, that the highest end is the good]; but we must try to clarify this still more.   25

Though apparently there are many ends, we choose some of them, e.g. wealth, flutes and, in general,

instruments, because of something else; hence it is clear that not all ends are complete. But the best good is apparently something complete. Hence, if
30 only one end is complete, this will be what we are looking for; and if more than one are complete, the most complete of these will be what we are looking for.

An end pursued in itself, we say, is more complete than an end pursued because of something else; and an end that is never choiceworthy because of something else is more complete than ends that are choiceworthy both in themselves and because of this end; and hence an end that is always [choiceworthy, and also] choiceworthy in itself, never because of something else, is complete without reservation.

1097b   Now happiness more than anything else seems complete without reservation, since we always [choose it, and also] choose it because of itself, never because of something else.

Honour, pleasure, understanding and every virtue we certainly choose because of themselves, since we would choose each of them even if it had no further
5 result, but we also choose them for the sake of happiness, supposing that through them we shall be happy. Happiness, by contrast, no one ever chooses for their sake, or for the sake of anything else at all.

The same conclusion [that happiness is complete] also appears to follow from self-sufficiency, since the complete good seems to be self-sufficient.

Now what we count as self-sufficient is not what suffices for a solitary person by himself, living an
10 isolated life, but what suffices also for parents, children, wife and in general for friends and fellow-citizens, since a human being is a naturally political [animal]. Here, however, we must impose some limit; for if we extend the good to parents' parents and children's children and to friends of friends, we shall go on without limit, but we must examine this another time.

15   Anyhow, we regard something as self-sufficient when all by itself it makes a life choiceworthy and lacking nothing; and that is what we think happiness does.

Moreover, [the complete good is most choiceworthy, and] we think happiness is most choiceworthy of all goods, since it is not counted as one good among many. If it were counted as one among many, then, clearly, we think that the addition of the smallest of

goods would make it more choiceworthy; for [the smallest good] that is added becomes an extra quantity of goods [so creating a good larger than the original good], and the larger of two goods is always more 20 choiceworthy. [But we do not think any addition can make happiness more choiceworthy; hence it is most choiceworthy.]

Happiness, then, is apparently something complete and self-sufficient, since it is the end of the things pursued in action.

But presumably the remark that the best good is happiness is apparently something [generally] agreed, and what we miss is a clearer statement of what the best good is.

Well, perhaps we shall find the best good if we 25 first find the function of a human being. For just as the good, i.e. [doing] well, for a flautist, a sculptor, and every craftsman, and, in general, for whatever has a function and [characteristic] action, seems to depend on its function, the same seems to be true for a human being, if a human being has some function.

Then do the carpenter and the leatherworker have 30 their functions and actions, while a human being has none, and is by nature idle, without any function? Or, just as eye, hand, foot, and, in general, every [bodily] part apparently has its functions, may we likewise ascribe to a human being some function besides all of theirs?

What, then, could this be? For living is apparently shared with plants, but what we are looking for is the special function of a human being; hence we should 1098a set aside the life of nutrition and growth. The life next in order is some sort of life or sense-perception; but this too is apparently shared, with horse, ox and every animal. The remaining possibility, then, is some sort of life of action of the (part of the soul) that has reason.

Now this [part has two parts, which have reason in different ways], one as obeying the reason [in the other part], the other as itself having reason and think- 5 ing. [We intend both.] Moreover, life is also spoken of in two ways [as capacity and as activity], and we must take [a human being's special function to be] life as activity, since this seems to be called life to a fuller extent.

(a) We have found, then, that the human function is the soul's activity that expresses reason [as itself having reason] or requires reason [as obeying reason].

(b) Now the function of *F*, e.g. of a harpist, is the same in kind, so we say, as the function of an excellent
10 *F*, e.g. an excellent harpist. (c) The same is true without reservation in every case, when we add to the function the superior achievement that expresses the virtue; for a harpist's function, e.g., is to play the harp, and a good harpist's is to do it well. (d) Now we take the human function to be a certain kind of life, and take this life to be the soul's activity and actions that express reason. (e) [Hence by (c) and (d)] the excellent man's function is to do this finely
15 and well. (f) Each function is completed well when its completion expresses the proper virtue. (g) Therefore [by (d), (e) and (f)] the human good turns out to be the soul's activity that expresses virtue.

And if there are more virtues than one, the good will express the best and most complete virtue. Moreover, it will be in a complete life. For one swallow does not make a spring, nor does one day; nor simi-
20 larly, does one day or a short time make us blessed and happy.

DEFENCE OF THE ACCOUNT OF THE GOOD

This, then, is a sketch of the good; for, presumably, the outline must come first, to be filled in later. If the sketch is good, then anyone, it seems, can advance and articulate it, and in such cases time is a good discoverer or [at least] a good co-worker. That is also
25 how the crafts have improved, since anyone can add what is lacking [in the outline].

However, we must also remember our previous remarks, so that we do not look for the same degree of exactness in all areas, but the degree that suits the subject-matter in each area and is proper to the
30 investigation. For the carpenter's and the geometer's inquiries about the right angle are different also; the carpenter's is confined to the right angle's usefulness for his work, whereas the geometer's concerns what, or what sort of thing, the right angle is, since he studies the truth. We must do the same, then, in other areas too, [seeking the proper degree of exactness], so that digressions do not overwhelm our main task.
1098b   Nor should we make the same demand for an explanation in all cases. Rather, in some cases it is enough to prove that something is true without explaining why it is true. This is so, e.g. with origins, where the fact that something is true is the first principle, i.e. the origin.

Some origins are studied by means of induction, some by means of perception, some by means of some sort of habituation, and others by other means. In 5 each case we should try to find them out by means suited to their nature, and work hard to define them well. For they have a great influence on what follows; for the origin seems to be more than half the whole, and makes evident the answer to many of our questions.

DEFENCE OF THE ACCOUNT OF THE GOOD, FROM COMMON BELIEFS

8

However, we should examine the origin not only 10 from the conclusion and premises [of a deductive argument], but also from what is said about it; for all the facts harmonize with a true account, whereas the truth soon clashes with a false one.

Goods are divided, then, into three types, some called external, some goods of the soul, others goods of the body; and the goods of the soul are said to be 15 goods to the fullest extent and most of all, and the soul's actions and activities are ascribed to the soul. Hence the account [of the good] is sound, to judge by this belief anyhow—and it is an ancient belief agreed on by philosophers.

Our account is also correct in saying that some sort of actions and activities are the end; for then the end turns out to be a good of the soul, not an 20 external good.

The belief that the happy person lives well and does well in action also agrees with our account, since we have virtually said that the end is a sort of living well and doing well in action.

Further, all the features that people look for in happiness appear to be true of the end described in our account. For to some people it seems to be virtue; to others intelligence; to others some sort of wisdom; 25 to others again it seems to be these, or one of these, combined with pleasure or requiring its addition; and others add in external prosperity as well.

Some of these views are traditional, held by many, while others are held by a few reputable men; and it is reasonable for each group to be not entirely in error, but correct on one point at least, or even on most points.

First, our account agrees with those who say happi- 30

ness is virtue [in general] or some [particular] virtue; for activity expressing virtue is proper to virtue. Presumably, though, it matters quite a bit whether we suppose that the best good consists in possessing or in using, i.e. in a state or in an activity [that actualizes 1099a the state]. For while someone may be in a state that achieves no good, if, e.g., he is asleep or inactive in some other way, this cannot be true of the activity; for it will necessarily do actions and do well in them. And just as Olympic prizes are not for the finest and 5 strongest, but for contestants, since it is only these who win; so also in life [only] the fine and good people who act correctly win the prize.

Moreover, the life of these [active] people is also pleasant in itself. For being pleased is a condition of the soul, [hence included in the activity of the soul]. Further, each type of person finds pleasure in whatever he is called a lover of, or so that a horse, e.g. 10 pleases the horse-lover, a spectacle the lover of spectacles, and similarly what is just pleases the lover of justice, and in general what expresses virtue pleases the lover of virtue. Hence the things that please most people conflict, because they are not pleasant by nature, whereas the things that please lovers of what is fine are things pleasant by nature; and actions expressing virtue are pleasant in this way; and so they both please lovers of what is fine and are pleasant in them-15 selves.

Hence their life does not need pleasure to be added [to virtuous activity] as some sort of ornament; rather, it has its pleasure within itself. For besides the reasons already given, no one is good if he does not enjoy fine actions; for no one would call him just, e.g. if 20 he did not enjoy doing just actions, or generous if he did not enjoy generous actions, and similarly for the other virtues. If this is so, then actions expressing the virtues are pleasant in themselves.

Moreover, these actions are good and fine as well as pleasant; indeed, they are good, fine and pleasant more than anything else, since on this question the 25 excellent person has good judgement, and his judgement agrees with our conclusions.

Happiness, then, is best, finest and most pleasant, and these three features are not distinguished in the way suggested by the Delian inscription: 'What is most just is finest; being healthy is more beneficial; but it is most pleasant to win our heart's desire.' For 30 all three features are found in the best activities, and

happiness we say is these activities, or [rather] one of them, the best one.

Nonetheless, happiness evidently also needs external goods to be added [to the activity], as we said, since we cannot, or cannot easily, do fine actions if we lack the resources.

For, first of all, in many actions we use friends, wealth and political power just as we use instruments. 1099b Further, deprivation of certain [externals]—e.g. good birth, good children, beauty—mars our blessedness; for we do not altogether have the character of happiness if we look utterly repulsive or are ill-born, solitary or childless, and have it even less, presumably, if our 5 children or friends are totally bad, or were good but have died.

And so, as we have said, happiness would seem to need this sort of prosperity added also; that is why some people identify happiness with good fortune, while others [reacting from one extreme to the other] identify it with virtue.

The Place of Virtue and of External Goods in Happiness

9

This [question about the role of fortune] raises a puzzle: Is happiness acquired by learning, or habituation, or by some other form of cultivation? Or is it 10 the result of some divine fate, or even of fortune?

First, then, if the gods give any gift at all to human beings, it is reasonable for them to give happiness also; indeed, it is reasonable to give happiness more than any other human [good], in so far as it is the best of human [goods]. Presumably, however, this question is more suitable for a different inquiry.

But even if it is not sent by the gods, but instead 15 results from virtue and some sort of learning or cultivation, happiness appears to be one of the most divine things, since the prize and goal of virtue appears to be the best good, something divine and blessed.

Moreover [if happiness comes in this way] it will be widely shared; for anyone who is not deformed [in his capacity] for virtue will be able to achieve happiness through some sort of learning and attention. 20

And since it is better to be happy in this way than because of fortune, it is reasonable for this to be the way [we become] happy. For whatever is natural is naturally in the finest state possible, and so are the products of crafts and of every other cause, especially 25 the best cause; and it would be seriously inappropriate to entrust what is greatest and finest to fortune.

The answer to our question is also evident from our account [of happiness]. For we have said it is a certain sort of activity of the soul expressing virtue [, and hence not a product of fortune]; and some of the other goods are necessary conditions [of happiness], others are naturally useful and cooperative as instruments [but are not parts of it].

30   Further, this conclusion agrees with our opening remarks. For we took the goal of political science to be the best good; and most of its attention is devoted to the character of the citizens, to make them good people who do fine actions, [which is reasonable if happiness depends on virtue, not on fortune].

It is not surprising, then, that we regard neither ox nor horse nor any other kind of animal as happy, 1100a since none of them can share in this sort of activity. And for the same reason a child is not happy either, since his age prevents him from doing these sorts of actions; and if he is called happy, he is being congratulated because of anticipated blessedness, since, as we have said, happiness requires both com- 5 plete virtue and a complete life.

[Happiness needs a complete life.] For life includes many reversals of fortune, good and bad, and the most prosperous person may fall into a terrible disaster in old age, as the Trojan stories tell us about Priam,[3] but if someone has suffered these sorts of misfortunes and comes to a miserable end, no one counts him happy.

Introduction to the Account of Virtue

13

1102a5 Since happiness is an activity of the soul expressing complete virtue, we must examine virtue; for that will perhaps also be a way to study happiness better.

Moreover, the true politician seems to have spent more effort on virtue than on anything else, since he 10 wants to make the citizens good and law-abiding. We find an example of this in the Spartan and Cretan legislators and in any others with their concerns.

3. [Priam was the legendary king of Troy at the time of its destruction by the Greeks as related in Homer's *Iliad*.]

Since, then, the examination of virtue is proper for political science, the inquiry clearly suits our original decision [to pursue political science].

It is clear that the virtue we must examine is human virtue, since we are also seeking the human good and human happiness. And by human virtue we mean 15 virtue of the soul, not of the body, since we also say that happiness is an activity of the soul. If this is so, then it is clear the politician must acquire some knowledge about the soul, just as someone setting out to heal the eyes must acquire knowledge about 20 the whole body as well. This is all the more true to the extent that political science is better and more honourable than medicine — and even among doctors the cultivated ones devote a lot of effort to acquiring knowledge about the body. Hence the politician as well [as the student of nature] must study the soul.

But he must study it for the purpose [of inquiring into virtue], as far as suffices for what he seeks; for a more exact treatment would presumably take more 25 effort than his purpose requires. [We] have discussed the soul sufficiently [for our purposes] in [our] popular works as well [as our less popular], and we should use this discussion.

We have said, e.g., that one [part] of the soul is nonrational, while one has reason. Are these distinguished as parts of a body and everything divisible 30 into parts are? Or are they two only in account, and inseparable by nature, as the convex and the concave are in a surface? It does not matter for present purposes.

Consider the nonrational [part]. One [part] of it, i.e. the cause of nutrition and growth, is seemingly plant-like and shared [with other living things]: for 1102b we can ascribe this capacity of the soul to everything that is nourished, including embryos, and the same one to complete living things, since this is more reasonable than to ascribe another capacity to them.

Hence the virtue of this capacity is apparently shared, not [specifically] human. For this part and capacity more than others seem to be active in sleep, 5 and here the good and the bad person are least distinct, which is why happy people are said to be no better off than miserable people for half their lives.

And this lack of distinction is not surprising, since sleep is inactivity of the soul in so far as it is called excellent or base, unless to some small extent some movements penetrate [to our awareness], and in this

10 way the decent person comes to have better images [in dreams] than just any random person has. Enough about this, however, and let us leave aside the nutritive part, since by nature it has no share in human virtue.

Another nature in the soul seemingly is also nonrational, though in a way it shares in reason.

[Clearly it is nonrational.] For in the continent and the incontinent person we praise their reason, 15 i.e. the [part] of the soul that has reason, because it exhorts them correctly and towards what is best; but they evidently also have in them some other [part] that is by nature something besides reason, conflicting and struggling with reason.

For just as paralysed parts of a body, when we decide to move them to the right, do the contrary 20 and move off to the left, the same is true of the soul; for incontinent people have impulses in contrary directions. In bodies, admittedly, we see the part go astray, whereas we do not see it in the soul; nonetheless, presumably, we should suppose that the soul also 25 has a [part] besides reason, contrary to and countering reason. The [precise] way it is different does not matter.

However, this [part] as well [as the rational part] appears, as we said, to share in reason. At any rate, in the continent person it obeys reason; and in the temperate and the brave person it presumably listens still better to reason, since there it agrees with reason in everything.

The nonrational [part], then, as well [as the whole soul] apparently has two parts. For while the plant-30 like [part] shares in reason not at all, the [part] with appetites and in general desires shares in reason in a way, in so far as it both listens to reason and obeys it.

It listens in the way in which we are said to 'listen to reason' from father or friends, not in the way in which we ['give the reason'] in mathematics.

1103a The nonrational part also [obeys and] is persuaded in some way by reason, as is shown by hastening, and by every sort of reproof and exhortation.

If we ought to say, then, that this [part] also has reason, then the [part] that has reason, as well [as the nonrational part] will have two parts, one that has reason to the full extent by having it within itself, and another [that has it] by listening to reason as to a father.

The distinction between virtues also reflects this difference. For some virtues are called virtues of thought, other virtues of character; wisdom, compre-5 hension, and intelligence are called virtues of thought, generosity and temperance virtues of character.

For when we speak of someone's character we do not say that he is wise or has good comprehension, but that he is gentle or temperate. [Hence these are the virtues of character.] And yet, we also praise the wise person for his state, and the states that are praiseworthy are the ones we call virtues. [Hence wisdom 10 is also a virtue.]

BOOK II
Virtues of Character in General

How a Virtue of Character Is Acquired

1

Virtue, then, is of two sorts, virtue of thought and virtue of character. Virtue of thought arises and grows mostly from teaching, and hence needs experience 15 and time. Virtue of character [i.e. of *ethos*] results from habit [ethos]; hence its name 'ethical', slightly varied from '*ethos*'.

Hence it is also clear that none of the virtues of 20 character arises in us naturally.

For if something is by nature [in one condition], habituation cannot bring it into another condition. A stone, e.g., by nature moves downwards, and habituation could not make it move upwards, not even if you threw it up ten thousand times to habituate it; nor could habituation make fire move downwards, or bring anything that is by nature in one condition into another condition.

Thus the virtues arise in us neither by nature nor 25 against nature. Rather we are by nature able to acquire them, and reach our complete perfection through habit.

Further, if something arises in us by nature, we first have the capacity for it, and later display the activity. This is clear in the case of the senses; for we did not acquire them by frequent seeing or hearing, but already had them when we exercised them, and 30 did not get them by exercising them.

Virtues, by contrast, we acquire, just as we acquire crafts, by having previously activated them. For we learn a craft by producing the same product that we must produce when we have learned it, becoming builders, e.g. by building and harpists by playing the 1103b harp; so also, then, we become just by doing just actions, temperate by doing temperate actions, brave by doing brave actions.

What goes on in cities is evidence for this also. For the legislator makes the citizens good by habituating 5 them, and this is the wish of every legislator; if he fails to do it well he misses his goal. [The right] habituation is what makes the difference between a good political system and a bad one.

Further, just as in the case of a craft, the sources and means that develop each virtue also ruin it. For playing the harp makes both good and bad harpists, and it is analogous in the case of builders and all the 10 rest; for building well makes good builders, building badly, bad ones. If it were not so, no teacher would be needed, but everyone would be born a good or a bad craftsman.

It is the same, then, with the virtues. For actions in dealings with [other] human beings make some 15 people just, some unjust; actions in terrifying situations and the acquired habit of fear or confidence make some brave and others cowardly. The same is true of situations involving appetites and anger; for one or another sort of conduct in these situations 20 makes some people temperate and gentle, others intemperate and irascible.

To sum up, then, in a single account: A state [of character] arises from [the repetition of] similar activities. Hence we must display the right activities, since differences in these imply corresponding differences in the states. It is not unimportant, then, to acquire one sort of habit or another, right from our youth; 25 rather, it is very important, indeed all-important.

WHAT IS THE RIGHT SORT OF HABITUATION?

2

Our present inquiry does not aim, as our others do, at study; for the purpose of our examination is not to know what virtue is, but to become good, since otherwise the inquiry would be of no benefit to us. 30 Hence we must examine the right way to act, since, as we have said, the actions also control the character of the states we acquire.

First, then, actions should express correct reason. That is a common [belief], and let us assume it; later

we will say what correct reason is and how it is related to the other virtues.

But let us take it as agreed in advance that every 1104a account of the actions we must do has to be stated in outline, not exactly. As we also said at the start, the type of accounts we demand should reflect the subject-matter; and questions about actions and expediency, like questions about health, have no fixed [and invariable answers].

And when our general account is so inexact, the 5 account of particular cases is all the more inexact. For these fall under no craft or profession, and the agents themselves must consider in each case what the opportune action is, as doctors and navigators do.

The account we offer, then, in our present inquiry 10 is of this inexact sort; still, we must try to offer help.

First, then, we should observe that these sorts of states naturally tend to be ruined by excess and deficiency. We see this happen with strength and health, which we mention because we must use what is evident as a witness to what is not. For both excessive and deficient exercises ruin strength; and likewise, 15 too much or too little eating or drinking ruins health, while the proportionate amount produces, increases, and preserves it.

The same is true, then, of temperance, bravery and the other virtues. For if, e.g., someone avoids and is afraid of everything, standing firm against nothing, 20 he becomes cowardly, but if he is afraid of nothing at all and goes to face everything, he becomes rash. Similarly, if he gratifies himself with every pleasure and refrains from none, he becomes intemperate, but if he avoids them all, as boors do, he becomes some sort of insensible person. Temperance and bravery, 25 then, are ruined by excess and deficiency but preserved by the mean.

The same actions, then, are the sources and causes both of emergence and growth of virtues and of their ruin; but further, the activities of the virtues will be found in these same actions. For this is also true of 30 more evident cases, e.g. strength, which arises from eating a lot and from withstanding much hard labour, and it is the strong person who is most able to do these very things. It is the same with the virtues. Refraining from pleasures makes us become temperate, and when we have become temperate we are 35 most able to refrain from pleasures. And it is similar 1104b with bravery; habituation in disdaining what is fearful and in standing firm against it makes us become brave, and when we have become brave we shall be most able to stand firm.

PLEASURE AND PAIN ARE IMPORTANT IN HABITUATION

3

But [actions are not enough]; we must take as a sign of someone's state his pleasure or pain in consequence
5 of his action. For if someone who abstains from bodily pleasures enjoys the abstinence itself, then he is temperate, but if he is grieved by it, he is intemperate. Again, if he stands firm against terrifying situations and enjoys it, or at least does not find it painful, then he is brave, and if he finds it painful, he is cowardly.

[Pleasures and pains are appropriately taken as signs] because virtue of character is concerned with pleasures and pains.

10 (1) For it is pleasure that causes us to do base actions, and pain that causes us to abstain from fine ones. Hence we need to have had the appropriate upbringing—right from early youth, as Plato says—to make us find enjoyment or pain in the right things; for this is the correct education.

(2) Further, virtues are concerned with actions and feelings; but every feeling and every action implies
15 pleasure or pain; hence, for this reason too, virtue is concerned with pleasures and pains.

(3) Corrective treatment [if vicious actions] also indicates [the relevance of pleasure and pain], since it uses pleasures and pains; it uses them because such correction is a form of medical treatment, and medical treatment naturally operates through contraries.

(4) Further, as we said earlier, every state of soul is naturally related to and concerned with whatever
20 naturally makes it better or worse; and pleasures and pains make people worse, from pursuing and avoiding the wrong ones, at the wrong time, in the wrong ways, or whatever other distinctions of that sort are needed in an account.

These [bad effects of pleasure and pain] are the reason why people actually define the virtues as ways
25 of being unaffected and undisturbed [by pleasures and pains]. They are wrong, however, because they speak [of being unaffected] without specification, not

of being unaffected in the right or wrong way, at the right or wrong time, and the added specifications.

We assume, then, that virtue is the sort of state [with the appropriate specifications] that does the best actions concerned with pleasures and pains, and that vice is the contrary. The following points will also make it evident that virtue and vice are concerned 30 with the same things.

(5) There are three objects of choice—fine, expedient and pleasant—and three objects of avoidance—their contraries, shameful, harmful and painful. About all these, then, the good person is correct and the bad person is in error, and especially about pleasure. For pleasure is shared with animals, and implied 35 by every object of choice, since what is fine and what 1105a is expedient appear pleasant as well.

(6) Further, since pleasure grows up with all of us from infancy on, it is hard to rub out this feeling that is dyed into our lives; and we estimate actions as well [as feelings], some of us more, some less, by pleasure and pain. Hence, our whole inquiry must be about 5 these, since good or bad enjoyment or pain is very important for our actions.

(7) Moreover, it is harder to fight pleasure than to fight emotion, [though that is hard enough], as Heraclitus[4] says. Now both craft and virtue are concerned in every case with what is harder, since a good result is even better when it is harder. Hence, for this 10 reason also, the whole inquiry, for virtue and political science alike, must consider pleasures and pains; for if we use these well, we shall be good, and if badly, bad.

In short, virtue is concerned with pleasures and pains; the actions that are its sources also increase it 15 or, if they are done differently, ruin it; and its activity is concerned with the same actions that are its sources.

BUT OUR CLAIMS ABOUT HABITUATION RAISE A PUZZLE

4

However, someone might raise this puzzle: 'What do you mean by saying that to become just we must first do just actions and to become temperate we must

4. [Heraclitus (c. 535–c. 475 B.C.) was an influential pre-Socratic philosopher who viewed the world-order as a continuous flux and considered any claim to permanence an illusion of the human senses.]

first do temperate actions? For if we do what is grammatical or musical, we must already be grammarians 20 or musicians. In the same way, then, if we do what is just or temperate, we must already be just or temperate.'

But surely this is not so even with the crafts, for it is possible to produce something grammatical by chance or by following someone else's instructions. To be a grammarian, then, we must both produce something grammatical and produce it in the way in 25 which the grammarian produces it, i.e. expressing grammatical knowledge that is in us.

Moreover, in any case what is true of crafts is not true of virtues. For the products of a craft determine by their own character whether they have been produced well; and so it suffices that they are in the right state when they have been produced. But for actions ex- 30 pressing virtue to be done temperately or justly [and hence well] it does not suffice that they are themselves in the right state. Rather, the agent must also be in the right state when he does them. First, he must know [that he is doing virtuous actions]; second, he must decide on them, and decide on them for themselves; and, third, he must also do them from a firm and unchanging state.

1105b   As conditions for having a craft these three do not count, except for the knowing itself. As a condition for having a virtue, however, the knowing counts for nothing, or [rather] for only a little, whereas the other two conditions are very important, indeed all-impor- 5 tant. And these other two conditions are achieved by the frequent doing of just and temperate actions.

Hence, actions are called just or temperate when they are the sort that a just or temperate person would do. But the just and temperate person is not the one who [merely] does these actions, but the one who also does them in the way in which just or temperate people do them.

10   It is right, then, to say that a person comes to be just from doing just actions and temperate from doing temperate actions; for no one has even a prospect of becoming good from failing to do them.

The many, however, do not do these actions but take refuge in arguments, thinking that they are doing philosophy, and that this is the way to become excel- 15 lent people. In this they are like a sick person who listens attentively to the doctor, but acts on none of his instructions. Such a course of treatment will not improve the state of his body; any more than will the many's way of doing philosophy improve the state of their souls.

A Virtue of Character Is a State Intermediate Between Two Extremes, and Involving Decision

The Genus

5

Next we must examine what virtue is. Since there are three conditions arising in the soul—feelings, capacities and states—virtue must be one of these. 20

By feelings I mean appetite, anger, fear, confidence, envy, joy, love, hate, longing, jealousy, pity, in general whatever implies pleasure or pain.

By capacities I mean what we have when we are 25 said to be capable of these feelings—capable of, e.g., being angry or afraid or feeling pity.

By states I mean what we have when we are well or badly off in relation to feelings. If, e.g., our feeling is too intense or slack, we are badly off in relation to anger, but if it is intermediate, we are well off; and the same is true in the other cases.

First, then, neither virtues nor vices are feelings. 30 (a) For we are called excellent or base in so far as we have virtues or vices, not in so far as we have feelings. (b) We are neither praised nor blamed in so far as we have feelings; for we do not praise the angry or the frightened person, and do not blame the 1106a person who is simply angry but only the person who is angry in a particular way. But we are praised or blamed in so far as we have virtues or vices. (c) We are angry and afraid without decision; but the virtues are decisions of some kind, or [rather] require decision. (d) Besides, in so far as we have feelings, we are said to be moved; but in so far as we have virtues 5 or vices, we are said to be in some condition rather than moved.

For these reasons the virtues are not capacities either; for we are neither called good nor called bad in so far as we are simply capable of feelings. Further, while we have capacities by nature, we do not become 10 good or bad by nature; we have discussed this before.

If, then, the virtues are neither feelings nor capacities, the remaining possibility is that they are states. And so we have said what the genus of virtue is.

The Differentia

6

15 But we must say not only, as we already have, that it
is a state, but also what sort of state it is.

It should be said, then, that every virtue causes its
possessors to be in a good state and to perform their
functions well; the virtue of eyes, e.g., makes the eyes
and their functioning excellent, because it makes us
20 see well; and similarly, the virtue of a horse makes
the horse excellent, and thereby good at galloping,
at carrying its rider and at standing steady in the face
of the enemy. If this is true in every case, then the
virtue of a human being will likewise be the state
that makes a human being good and makes him
perform his function well.

25   We have already said how this will be true, and it
will also be evident from our next remarks, if we
consider the sort of nature that virtue has.

In everything continuous and divisible we can take
more, less and equal, and each of them either in the
object itself or relative to us; and the equal is some
intermediate between excess and deficiency.

By the intermediate in the object I mean what is
equidistant from each extremity; this is one and the
30 same for everyone. But relative to us the intermediate
is what is neither superfluous nor deficient; this is
not one, and is not the same for everyone.

If, e.g., ten are many and two are few, we take six
as intermediate in the object, since it exceeds [two]
35 and is exceeded [by ten] by an equal amount, [four];
1106b this is what is intermediate by numerical proportion.
But that is not how we must take the intermediate
that is relative to us. For if, e.g., ten pounds [of food]
are a lot for someone to eat, and two pounds a little,
it does not follow that the trainer will prescribe six,
since this might also be either a little or a lot for the
person who is to take it—for Milo[5] [the athlete] a
little, but for the beginner in gymnastics a lot; and
the same is true for running and wrestling. In this
5 way every scientific expert avoids excess and deficiency and seeks and chooses what is intermediate—
but intermediate relative to us, not in the object.

This, then, is how each science produces its product well, by focusing on what is intermediate and

making the product conform to that. This, indeed, 10
is why people regularly comment on well-made products that nothing could be added or subtracted, since
they assume that excess or deficiency ruins a good
[result] while the mean preserves it. Good craftsmen
also, we say, focus on what is intermediate when they
produce their product. And since virtue, like nature, 15
is better and more exact than any craft, it will also
aim at what is intermediate.

By virtue I mean virtue of character; for this [pur-
sues the mean because] it is concerned with feelings
and actions, and these admit of excess, deficiency
and an intermediate condition. We can be afraid,
e.g., or be confident, or have appetites, or get angry,
or feel pity, in general have pleasure or pain, both 20
too much and too little, and in both ways not well;
but [having these feelings] at the right times, about
the right things, towards the right people, for the right
end, and in the right way, is the intermediate and
best condition, and this is proper to virtue. Similarly,
actions also admit of excess, deficiency and the intermediate condition. Now virtue is concerned with
feelings and actions, in which excess and deficiency 25
are in error and incur blame, while the intermediate
condition is correct and wins praise, which are both
proper features of virtue. Virtue, then, is a mean, in
so far as it aims at what is intermediate.

Moreover, there are many ways to be in error since
badness is proper to what is unlimited, as the Pythagoreans pictured it, and good to what is limited; but 30
there is only one way to be correct. That is why error
is easy and correctness hard, since it is easy to miss
the target and hard to hit it. And so for this reason
also excess and deficiency are proper to vice, the
mean to virtue; 'for we are noble in only one way,
but bad in all sorts of ways.'

Virtue, then, is (a) a state that decides, (b) [consist-
ing] in a mean, (c) the mean relative to us, (d) which
is defined by reference to reason, (e) i.e., to the reason 1107a
by reference to which the intelligent person would
define it. It is a mean between two vices, one of excess
and one of deficiency.

It is a mean for this reason also: Some vices miss
what is right because they are deficient, others because they are excessive, in feelings or in actions, 5
while virtue finds and chooses what is intermediate.

Hence, as far as its substance and the account
stating its essence are concerned, virtue is a mean;

5. [Milo was a sixth-century B.C. Greek wrestler of legendary strength.]

but as far as the best [condition] and the good [result] are concerned, it is an extremity.

But not every action or feeling admits of the mean. For the names of some automatically include base-10 ness, e.g. spite, shamelessness, envy [among feelings], and adultery, theft, murder, among actions. All of these and similar things are called by these names because they themselves, not their excesses or deficiencies, are base.

Hence in doing these things we can never be correct, but must invariably be in error. We cannot do 15 them well or not well—e.g. by committing adultery with the right woman at the right time in the right way; on the contrary, it is true without reservation that to do any of them is to be in error.

[To think these admit of a mean], therefore, is like thinking that unjust or cowardly or intemperate action 20 also admits of a mean, an excess and a deficiency. For then there would be a mean of excess, a mean of deficiency, an excess of excess and a deficiency of deficiency.

Rather, just as there is no excess or deficiency of temperature or of bravery, since the intermediate is a sort of extreme [in achieving the good], so also 25 there is no mean of these [vicious actions] either, but whatever way anyone does them, he is in error. For in general there is no mean of excess or of deficiency, and no excess or deficiency of a mean.

THE DEFINITION OF VIRTUE AS A MEAN APPLIES TO THE INDIVIDUAL VIRTUES

7

However, we must not only state this general account 30 but also apply it to the particular cases. For among accounts concerning actions, though the general ones are common to more cases, the specific ones are truer, since actions are about particular cases, and our account must accord with these. Let us, then, find these from the chart.

1107b (1) First, in feelings of fear and confidence the mean is bravery. The excessively fearless person is nameless (and in fact many cases are nameless), while the one who is excessively confident is rash; the one who is excessively afraid and deficient in confidence is cowardly.

5 (2) In pleasures and pains, though not in all types, and in pains less than in pleasures, the mean is temperance and the excess intemperance. People deficient in pleasure are not often found, which is why they also lack even a name; let us call them insensible.

(3) In giving and taking money the mean is generos- 10 ity, the excess wastefulness and the deficiency ungenerosity. Here the vicious people have contrary excesses and defects; for the wasteful person spends to excess and is deficient in taking, whereas the ungenerous person takes to excess and is deficient in spending. At the moment we are speaking in outline and summary, and that suffices; later we shall define these 15 things more exactly.

(4) In questions of money there are also other conditions. Another mean is magnificence; for the magnificent person differs from the generous by being concerned with large matters, while the generous person is concerned with small. The excess is ostenta- 20 tion and vulgarity, and the deficiency niggardliness, and these differ from the vices related to generosity in ways we shall describe later.

(5) In honour and dishonour the mean is magnanimity, the excess something called a sort of vanity, and the deficiency pusillanimity.

(6) And just as we said that generosity differs from 25 magnificence in its concern with small matters, similarly there is a virtue concerned with small honors, differing in the same way from magnanimity, which is concerned with great honors. For honor can be desired either in the right way or more or less than is right. If someone desires it to excess, he is called an honor-lover, and if his desire is deficient he is 30 called indifferent to honor, but if he is intermediate he has no name. The corresponding conditions have no name either, except the condition of the honor-lover, which is called honor-loving.

This is why people at the extremes claim the intermediate area. Indeed, we also sometimes call the intermediate person an honor-lover, and sometimes call him indifferent to honor, and sometimes we praise the honor-lover, sometimes the person indifferent to honor. We will mention later the reason we 1108a do this; for the moment, let us speak of the other cases in the way we have laid down.

(7) Anger also admits of an excess, deficiency and mean. These are all practically nameless; but since 5 we call the intermediate person mild, let us call the mean mildness. Among the extreme people let the excessive person be irascible, and the vice be irascibil-

ity, and let the deficient person be a sort of inirascible person, and the deficiency be inirascibility.

10   There are three other means, somewhat similar to one another, but different. For they are all concerned with association in conversations and actions, but differ insofar as one is concerned with truth-telling in these areas, the other two with sources of pleasure, some of which are found in amusement, and the others in daily life in general. Hence we should also 15 discuss these states, so that we can better observe that in every case the mean is praiseworthy, while the extremes are neither praiseworthy nor correct, but blameworthy. Most of these cases are also nameless, and we must try, as in the other cases also, to make names ourselves, to make things clear and easy to follow.

20   (8) In truth-telling, then, let us call the intermediate person truthful, and the man truthfulness; pretence that overstates will be boastfulness, and the person who has it boastful; pretence that understates will be self-deprecation, and the person who has it self-deprecating.

(9) In sources of pleasure in amusements let us call the intermediate person witty, and the condition 25 wit; the excess buffoonery and the person who has it a buffoon; and the deficient person a sort of boor and the state boorishness.

(10) In the other sources of pleasure, those in daily life, let us call the person who is pleasant in the right way friendly, and the mean state friendliness. If someone goes to excess with no [further] aim he will be ingratiating; if he does it for his own advantage, 30 a flatterer. The deficient person, unpleasant in everything, will be a sort of quarrelsome and ill-tempered person.

(11) There are also means in feelings and concerned with feelings: shame, for instance, is not a virtue, but the person prone to shame as well as the virtuous person we have described receives praise. For here also one person is called intermediate, and another—the person excessively prone to shame, who is ashamed about everything—is called excessive; the 35 person who is deficient in shame or never feels shame 1108b at all is said to have no sense of disgrace; and the intermediate one is called prone to shame.

(12) Proper indignation is the mean between envy and spite; these conditions are concerned with pleasure and pain at what happens to our neighbors.

For the properly indignant person feels pain when someone does well undeservedly; the envious person 5 exceeds him by feeling pain when anyone does well, while the spiteful person is so deficient in feeling pain that he actually enjoys [other people's misfortunes].

There will also be an opportunity elsewhere to speak of these [means] that are not virtues.

We must consider justice after these other conditions, and, because it is not spoken of in one way only, we shall distinguish its two types and say how each of them is a mean.

Similarly, we must consider the virtues that belong 10 to reason.

BOOK III

The Preconditions of Virtue

VOLUNTARY ACTION

1

Virtue, then, is about feelings and actions; and these 1109b30 receive praise or blame when they are voluntary, but pardon, sometimes even pity, when they are involuntary. Hence, presumably, in examining virtue we must define the voluntary and the involuntary. This is also useful for legislators, both for honours and for correc- 35 tive treatments.

What comes about by force or because of ignorance 1110a seems to be involuntary. What is forced has an external origin, the sort of origin in which the agent or victim contributes nothing—if, e.g., a wind or human beings who control him were to carry him off.

But now consider actions done because of fear of greater evils, or because of something fine. Suppose, e.g., a tyrant tells you to do something shameful, 5 when he has control over your parents and children, and if you do it, they will live, but if not, they will die. These cases raise dispute about whether they are voluntary or involuntary.

However, the same sort of thing also happens with 10 throwing the cargo overboard in storms; for no one willingly throws cargo overboard, without restriction, but anyone with any sense throws cargo overboard to save himself and the others, [which is an added restriction].

These sorts of actions, then, are mixed. But they are seemingly more like voluntary actions. For at the

time they are done they are choiceworthy, and the goal of the action reflects the occasion; hence we should also call the action voluntary or involuntary
15 with reference to the time when he does it. Now in fact he does it willingly; for in these sorts of actions he has within him the origin of the movement of the limbs that are the instruments [of the action], and when the origin of the actions is in him, it is also up to him to do them or not to do them. Hence actions of this sort are voluntary, though presumably the actions without [the appropriate] restriction are involuntary, since no one would choose any action of this sort in itself.

For such [mixed] actions people are sometimes
20 actually praised, whenever they endure something shameful or painful as the price of great and fine results; and if they do the reverse, they are blamed, since it is a base person who endures what is most shameful for nothing fine or for only some moderately fine result.

In some cases there is no praise, but there is pardon,
25 whenever someone does a wrong action because of conditions that overtrain human nature, and that no one would endure. But presumably there are some things that we cannot be compelled to do, and rather than do them we should suffer the most terrible consequences and accept death; for the things that [allegedly] compelled Euripides' Alcmaeon to kill his mother appear ridiculous.[6]
30 It is sometimes hard, however, to judge what [goods] should be chosen at the price of what [evils], and what [evils] should be endured as the price of what [goods]. And it is even harder to abide by our judgment, since the results we expect [when we endure] are usually painful, and the actions we are compelled [to endure, when we choose] are usually shameful. That is why those who have been com-
1110b pelled or not compelled receive praise and blame.

What sorts of things, then, should we say are forced? Perhaps we should say that something is forced without restriction whenever its cause is external and the agent contributes nothing. Other things are involuntary in themselves, but choiceworthy on this occasion and as the price of these [goods], and their origin is

in the agent. These are involuntary in themselves, but, on this occasion and as the price of these [goods], voluntary. Still, they are seemingly more like volun- 5 tary actions, since actions are particulars, and these [particulars in mixed actions] are voluntary. But what sort of thing should be chosen as the price of what [good] is not easy to answer, since there are many differences in particular cases.

But suppose someone says that pleasant things and fine things force us, since they are outside us and compel us. It will follow that for him everything is forced, since everyone in every action aims at some- 10 thing fine or pleasant.

Moreover, if our action is forced and unwilling, we find it painful; but if something pleasant or fine is its cause, we do it with pleasure.

It is ridiculous, then, for [our opponent] to ascribe responsibility to external [causes] and not to himself, when he is easily snared by such things; and ridiculous 15 to take responsibility for fine actions himself, but to hold pleasant things responsible for his shameful actions.

What is forced, then, is seemingly what has its origin outside the person forced, who contributes nothing.

Everything caused by ignorance is non-voluntary, but what is involuntary also causes pain and regret. For if someone's action was caused by ignorance, but 20 he now has no objection to the action, he has done it neither willingly, since he did not know what it was, nor unwillingly, since he now feels no pain. Hence, among those who act because of ignorance, the agent who now regrets his action seems to be unwilling, while the agent with no regrets may be called non-willing, since he is another case — for since he is different, it is better if he has its own special name.

Further, action caused by ignorance is seemingly 25 different from action done in ignorance. For if the agent is drunk or angry, his action seems to be caused by drunkenness or anger, not by ignorance, though it is done in ignorance, not in knowledge.

[This ignorance does not make an action involuntary.] Certainly every vicious person is ignorant of the actions he must do or avoid, and this sort of error makes people unjust, and in general bad. But talk of 30 involuntary action is not meant to apply to [this] ignorance of what is beneficial.

6. [The play by the fifth-century B.C. Greek dramatist is not extant. According to Greek mythology, Alcmaeon killed his mother to avenge the death of his father.]

For the cause of involuntary action is not [this] ignorance in the decision, which causes vice; it is not [in other words] ignorance of the universal, since that
1111a is a cause for blame. Rather, the cause is ignorance of the particulars which the action consists in and is concerned with; but these allow both pity and pardon, since an agent acts involuntarily if he is ignorant of one of these.

Presumably, then, it is not a bad idea to define these particulars, and say what they are, and how many. They are: (1) who is doing it; (2) what he is doing; (3) about what or to what he is doing it; (4)
5 sometimes also what he is doing it with, e.g. the instrument; (5) for what result, e.g. safety; (6) in what way, e.g. gently or hard.

Now certainly someone could not be ignorant of *all* of these unless he were mad. Nor, clearly, (1) could he be ignorant of who is doing it, since he could hardly be ignorant of himself. But (2) he might be ignorant of what he is doing, as when someone says that [the secret] slipped out while he was speaking, or, as Aeschylus said about the mysteries, that he did not know it was forbidden to reveal it;[7] or, like the person
10 with the catapult, that he let it go when he [only] wanted to demonstrate it. (3) Again, he might think that his son is an enemy, as Merope did;[8] or (4) that the barbed spear has a button on it, or that the stone is pumice-stone. (5) By giving someone a drink to
15 save his life we might kill him; (6) and wanting to touch someone, as they do in sparring, we might wound him.

There is ignorance about all of these [particulars] that the action consists in. Hence someone who was ignorant of one of these seems to have done an action unwillingly, especially when he was ignorant of the most important of them; these seem to be (3) what he is doing it to, and (5) the result for which he does it.

Hence it is action called involuntary with refer-
20 ence to *this* sort of ignorance [that we meant when we said that] the agent must, in addition, feel pain and regret for his action.

Since, then, what is involuntary is what is forced

7. [The Greek dramatist is said to have been accused but then acquitted of revealing rites of a secret religious cult.]

8. [In a lost play of Euripides, Merope, not recognizing his son, nearly slays him.]

or is caused by ignorance, what is voluntary seems to be what has its origin in the agent himself when he knows the particulars that the action consists in.

[Our definition is sound.] For it is not correct to 25 say that action caused by emotion or appetite is involuntary.

For, first of all, on this view none of the other animals will ever act voluntarily; nor will children. [But clearly they do.]

Next, among all the actions caused by emotion or appetite do we do none of them voluntarily? Or do we do the fine actions voluntarily and the shameful involuntarily? Surely [the second answer] is ridiculous when one and the same thing [i.e. appetite or emotion] causes [both fine and shameful actions]. And presumably it is also absurd to say [as the first 30 answer implies] that things we ought to desire are involuntary; and in fact we ought both to be angry at some things and to have an appetite for some things, e.g., for health and learning.

Again, what is involuntary seems to be painful, whereas what reflects our appetite seems to be pleasant.

Moreover, how are errors that reflect emotion any less voluntary than those that reflect rational calculation? For both sorts of errors are to be avoided; and 1111b since nonrational feelings seem to be no less human [than rational calculation], actions resulting from emotion or appetite are also proper to a human being; it is absurd, then, to regard them as involuntary.

DECISION

2

Now that we have defined what is voluntary and 5 involuntary, the next task is to discuss decision; for it seems to be most proper to virtue, and to distinguish [good] characters [from bad] better than actions do.

Decision, then, is apparently voluntary, but not the same as what is voluntary, which extends more widely. For children and the other animals share in what is voluntary, but not in decision; and the actions we do on the spur of the moment are said to be voluntary, but not to express decision.   10

Those who say that decision is appetite or emotion or wish or some sort of belief are seemingly wrong.

For decision is not shared with non-rational [animals], but appetite and emotion are shared with them.

15 Further, the incontinent person acts on appetite, not on decision, but the continent person acts on decision, not on appetite.

Again, appetite is contrary to decision, but not to appetite.

Further, appetite's concern is what is pleasant and what is painful, but neither of these is the concern of decision.

Still less is emotion decision; for actions caused by emotion seem least of all to express decision.

20 But further, it is not wish either, though it is apparently close to it.

For, first, we do not decide to do what is impossible, and anyone claiming to decide to do it would seem a fool; but we do wish for what is impossible, e.g. never to die, as well [as for what is possible].

Further, we wish [not only for results we can achieve], but also for results that are [possible, but] not achievable through our own agency, e.g. victory 25 for some actor or competitor. But what we decide to do is never anything of that sort, but what we think would come about through our own agency.

Again, we wish for the end more [than for what promotes it], but we decide to do what promotes the end. We wish, e.g. to be healthy, but decide to do what will make us healthy; and we wish to be happy, and say so, but could not appropriately say we decide 30 to be happy, since in general, seemingly, what we decide to do is what is up to us.

Nor is it belief.

For, first, belief seems to be about everything, no less about what is eternal and what is impossible [for us] than about what is up to us.

Moreover, beliefs are divided into true and false, not into good and bad, but decisions are divided into good and bad more than into true and false.

1112a Now presumably no one even claims that decision is the same as belief in general. But it is not the same as any kind of belief either.

For it is our decisions to do what is good or evil, not our beliefs, that make the characters we have.

5 Again, we decide to take or avoid something good or evil. We believe what it is, whom it benefits or how; but we do not exactly believe to take or avoid.

Further, decision is praised more for deciding on what is right, whereas belief is praised for believing rightly.

Moreover, we decide on something [even] when

we know most completely that it is good; but [what] we believe [is] what we do not quite know.

Again, those who make the best decisions do not seem to be the same as those with the best beliefs; on the contrary, some seem to have better beliefs, 10 but to make the wrong decisions because of vice.

We can agree that decision follows or implies belief. But that is irrelevant, since it is not the question we are asking; our question is whether decision is the *same* as some sort of belief.

Then what, or what sort of thing, is decision, since it is none of the things mentioned? Well, apparently, it is voluntary, but not everything voluntary is decided. 15 Then perhaps what is decided is the result of prior deliberation. For decision is associated with reason and thought, and even the name itself seems to indicate that [what is decided, *prohaireton*] is chosen [*haireton*], before [*pro*] other things.

NOT EVERYTHING IS OPEN TO DELIBERATION

3

But do we deliberate about everything, and is everything open to deliberation, or is there no deliberation about some things? By 'open to deliberation', presum- 20 ably, we should mean what someone with some sense, not some fool or madman, might deliberate about.

Now no one deliberates about eternal things, e.g. about the universe, or that the sides and the diagonal are incommensurable; nor about things that are in movement but always come about the same way, 25 either from necessity or by nature or by some other cause, e.g. the solstices or the rising of the stars; nor about what happens different ways at different times, e.g. droughts and rains; nor about what results from fortune, e.g. the finding of a treasure. For none of 30 these results could be achieved through our agency.

We deliberate about what is up to us, i.e. about the actions we can do; and this is what is left [besides the previous cases]. For causes seem to include nature, necessity and fortune, but besides them mind and everything [operating] through human agency.

However, we do not deliberate about all human affairs; no Spartan, e.g., deliberates about how the Scythians might have the best political system. Rather, each type of human being deliberates about the actions *he* can do.

Now there is no deliberation about the sciences 1112b

that are exact and self-sufficient, e.g. about letters, since we are in no doubt about how to write them [in a word]. Rather, we deliberate about what results through our agency, but in different ways on different 5 occasions, e.g. about questions of medicine and money-making; more about navigation than about gymnastics, to the extent that it is less exactly worked out, and similarly with other [crafts]; and more about beliefs than about sciences, since we are more in doubt about them.

Deliberation concerns what is usually [one way rather than the other], where the outcome is unclear and the right way to act is undefined. And we enlist 10 partners in deliberation on large issues when we distrust our own ability to discern [the right answer].

We deliberate not about ends, but about what promotes ends; a doctor, e.g., does not deliberate about whether he will cure, or an orator about whether he will persuade, or a politician about whether he will 15 produce good order, or any other [expert] about the end [that his science aims at].

Rather, we first lay down the end, and then examine the ways and means to achieve it. If it appears that any of several [possible] means will reach it, we consider which of them will reach it most easily and most finely; and if only one [possible] means reaches it, we consider how that means will reach it, and how the means itself is reached, until we come to the first cause, the last thing to be discovered.

20 For a deliberator seemingly inquires and analyses in the way described, as though analysing a diagram. [The comparison is apt, since], apparently, all deliberation is inquiry, though not all inquiry, e.g. in mathematics, is deliberation. And seemingly the last thing [found] in the analysis is the first that comes to be.

25 If we encounter an impossible step—e.g. we need money but cannot raise it—we desist; but if the action appears possible, we undertake it. What is possible is what we could achieve through our agency, including what our friends could achieve for us; for what our friends achieve is, in a way, achieved through our agency, since the origin is in us. [In crafts] we sometimes look for instruments, sometimes [for the way] 30 to use them; so also in other cases we sometimes look for the means to the end, sometimes for the proper use of the means or for the means to that proper use.

As we have said, then, a human being, seemingly, originates action; deliberation is about the actions he

can do; and actions are for the sake of other things; hence we deliberate about what promotes an end, not about the end.

Nor do we deliberate about particulars, e.g. about 1113a whether this is a loaf or is cooked the right amount; for these are questions for perception, and if we keep on deliberating at each stage we will go on without end.

What we deliberate about is the same as what we decide to do, except that by the time we decide to do it, it is definite, for what we decide to do is what we have judged to be right as a result of deliberation. 5 For each of us stops inquiring how to act as soon as he traces the origin to himself, and within himself to the dominant part; for this is the part that decides. This is also clear from the ancient political systems represented by Homer; there the kings would first decide and then announce it to the people.

We have found, then, that what we decide to do 10 is whatever action among those up to us we deliberate about and desire to do. Hence also decision will be deliberative desire to do an action that is up to us; for when we have judged [that it is right] as a result of deliberation, our desire to do it expresses our wish.

So much, then, of an outline of the sort of thing that decision is about: it is about what promotes the end.

RATIONAL WISH FOR THE END

4

Wish, we have said, is for the end. But to some it 15 seems that wish is for the good, to others that it is for the apparent good.

If we say that the good is what is wished, it follows that what someone wishes if he chooses incorrectly is not wished at all. For if it is wished, then [on this view] it is good; but what he wishes is in fact evil, if 20 it turns out that way. [Hence what he wishes is not wished, which is self-contradictory.]

If, on the other hand, we say that the apparent good is wished, it follows that there is nothing wished by nature. To each person what is wished is what seems [good to him]; but different things, and indeed contrary things, if it turns out that way, appear good to different people. [Hence contrary things will be wished.]

If, then, these results do not satisfy us, should we say that, without restriction and in reality, what is wished is the good, but to each person what is wished is the apparent good?

25 To the excellent person, then, what is wished will be what is wished in reality, while to the base person what is wished is whatever it turns out to be [that appears to him]. Similarly in the case of bodies, really healthy things are healthy to people in good condition, while other things are healthy to sickly people, and the same is true of what is bitter, sweet, hot, heavy and so on.

30 For the excellent person judges each sort of thing correctly, and in each case what is true appears to him. For each state [of character] has its own special [view of] what is fine and pleasant, and presumably the excellent person is far superior because he sees what is true in each case, being a sort of standard and measure of what is fine and pleasant.

In the many, however, pleasure seemingly causes deception, since it appears good when it is not; at 1113b any rate, they choose what is pleasant because they assume it is good, and avoid pain because they assume it is evil.

Virtue and Vice Are in Our Power

5

We have found, then, that we wish for the end, and deliberate and decide about what promotes it; hence 5 the actions concerned with what promotes the end will be voluntary actions expressing decision. Now the activities of the virtues are concerned with [what promotes the end]; hence virtue is up to us, and so also is vice.

For when acting is up to us, so is not acting, and when No is up to us, so is Yes. Hence if acting, when 10 it is fine, is up to us, then not acting, when it is shameful, is also up to us; and if not acting, when it is fine, is up to us, then acting, when it is shameful, is also up to us. Hence if doing and likewise not doing, fine or shameful actions is up to us; and if, as we say, [doing or not doing them] is [what it is] to be a good or bad person; then it follows that being decent or base is up to us.

15 The claim that no one is willingly vicious or unwillingly blessed is, seemingly, partly true but partly false. For while certainly no one is unwillingly blessed, vice is voluntary. If it is not we must dispute the conclusion just reached, that a human being originates and fathers his own actions as he fathers his children. But if our conclusion appears true, and we cannot trace

[actions] back to other origins beyond those in ourselves, then it follows that whatever has its origin in us is itself up to us and voluntary. 20

Seemingly there is testimony to our views not only in what each of us does privately, but also in what legislators themselves do. For they impose corrective treatments and penalties on anyone who does vicious 25 actions, if he does them neither by force nor because of ignorance that he is not responsible for; and they honour anyone who does fine actions, on the assumption that they will encourage him and restrain the wrong doer. But they never encourage us to do anything that is not up to us and voluntary; they assume it is pointless to persuade us not to get hot or distressed or hungry or anything else of that sort, since persuasion will not stop it happening to us.

Indeed, they also impose corrective treatments on 30 someone for the ignorance itself if he seems to be responsible for the ignorance. A drunk, e.g., pays a double penalty; for the origin is in him, since he is in control of getting drunk, and his getting drunk is responsible for his ignorance.

They also impose corrective treatment on someone who [does a vicious action] in ignorance of some provision of law that he is required to know and that is not hard [to know]. And they impose it in other 1114a cases likewise for any other ignorance that seems to be caused by the agent's inattention; they assume it is up to him not to be ignorant, since he is in control of paying attention.

But presumably his character makes him inattentive. Still, he himself is responsible for having this character, by living carelessly, and similarly for being 5 unjust by cheating, or being intemperate by passing his time in drinking and the like; for each type of activity produces the corresponding character. This is clear from those who train for some contest or action, since they continually practise the appropriate activities. [Only] a totally insensible person would 10 not know that each type of activity is the source of the corresponding state; hence if someone does what he knows will make him unjust, he is willingly unjust.

Moreover, it is unreasonable for someone doing injustice not to wish to be unjust, or for someone doing intemperate action not to wish to be intemperate. This does not mean, however, that if he is unjust and wishes to stop, he will stop and will be just.

For neither does a sick person recover his health 15

[simply by wishing]; nonetheless, he is sick willingly, by living incontinently and disobeying the doctors, if that was how it happened. At that time, then, it was open to him not to be sick, though no longer open to him once he has let himself go, just as it was up to us to throw a stone, since the origin was in us, though we can no longer take it back once we have thrown it.

20 Similarly, then, the person who is [now] unjust or intemperate was originally free not to acquire this character, so that he has it willingly, though once he has acquired the character, he is no longer free not to have it [now].

It is not only vices of the soul that are voluntary; vices of the body are also voluntary for some people, who are those we actually censure. For we never censure someone if nature causes his ugliness; but if his lack of training or attention causes it, we do cen- 25 sure him. The same is true for weakness or maiming; for everyone would pity, not reproach someone if he were blind by nature or because of a disease or a wound, but would censure him if his heavy drinking or some other form of intemperance made him blind.

30 Hence bodily vices that are up to us are censured, while those not up to us are not censured. If so, then in the other cases also the vices that are censured will be up to us.

1114b But someone may say, 'Everyone aims at the apparent good, and does not control how it appears; on the contrary, his character controls how the end appears to him.'

First, then, if each person is in some way responsible for his own state [of character], then he is also himself in some way responsible for how [the end] appears.

If, on the other hand, he is not [responsible for his own state], he is not himself responsible for his own evil actions, but, on the contrary, does them because he is ignorant of the end, and thinks these are the way to reach the best [result] for himself. His aiming 5 at the end [he aims at] is not his own choice; rather, [to aim at the right end] he must by nature have a sort of inborn sense of sight to make him judge finely and choose what is really good.

Whoever has this fine aim by nature has a good nature. For this aim is the greatest and finest thing, 10 and he cannot learn it or acquire it from another; rather, its natural character [determines] the character of the aim he will have, and when it is naturally good and fine, that is true and complete good nature.

If all this is true, then, surely virtue will be no more voluntary than vice? For how the end appears is laid down, by nature or in whatever way, for the good and 15 the bad person alike, and they trace all the other things back to the end in doing whatever actions they do.

Suppose, then, that it is not nature that makes the end appear however it appears to each person, but something also depends on him; or, alternatively, suppose that [how] the end [appears] is natural, but virtue is voluntary because the virtuous person does the other things voluntarily. In either case vice will 20 be no less voluntary than virtue; for the bad person, no less than the good, is responsible for his own actions, even if not for [how] the end [appears].

Now the virtues, as we say, are voluntary, since in fact we are ourselves in a way jointly responsible for our states of character, and by having the characters we have we also make the end we lay down the sort of end it is. Hence the vices will also be voluntary, since the same is true of them. 25

We have now discussed the virtues in general. We have described their genus in outline; they are means, and they are states. Certain actions produce them, and they cause us to do these same actions, expressing the virtues themselves, in the way that correct reason prescribes. They are up to us and voluntary.

Actions and states, however, are not voluntary in 30 the same way. For we are in control of actions from the origin to the end, when we know the particulars. With states, however, we are in control of the origin, 1115a but do not know, any more than with sicknesses, what the cumulative effect of particular actions will be; none the less, since it was up to us to exercise a capacity either this way or another way, states are voluntary.

BOOK V

Justice

THE DEFINITION OF JUSTICE

1

The questions we must examine about justice and 1129a injustice are these: What sorts of actions are they concerned with? What sort of mean is justice? What are the extremes between which justice is intermedi- 5 ate? Let us examine them by the same type of investigation that we used in the topics discussed before.

We see that the state everyone means in speaking of justice is the state that makes us doers of just actions, that makes us do justice and wish what is just. In the same way they mean by injustice the state that makes us do injustice and wish what is unjust.
10 Let us also, then, [follow the common beliefs and] begin by assuming this in outline.

For what is true of sciences and capacities is not true of states. For while one and the same capacity or science seems to have contrary activities, a state that is a contrary has no contrary activities. Health, e.g., only makes us do healthy actions, not their con-
15 traries; for we say we are walking in a healthy way if [and only if] we are walking in the way a healthy person would.

Often one of a pair of contrary states is recognized from the other contrary; and often the states are recognized from their subjects. For if, e.g., the good state is evident, the bad state becomes evident too; and moreover the good state becomes evident from the
20 things that have it, and the things from the state. For if, e.g., the good state is thickness of flesh, then the bad state will necessarily be thinness of flesh, and the thing that produces the good state will be what produces thickness of flesh.

It follows, usually, that if one of a pair of contraries is spoken of in more ways than one, so is the other; if, e.g., what is just is spoken of in more ways than
25 one, so is what is unjust.

Now it would seem that justice and injustice are both spoken of in more ways than one, but since the different ways are closely related, their homonymy is unnoticed, and is less clear than it is with distant homonyms where the distance in appearance is wide (e.g., the bone below an animal's neck and what we
30 lock doors with are called keys homonymously).

Let us, then, find the number of ways an unjust person is spoken of. Both the lawless person and the greedy and unfair person seem to be unjust; and so, clearly, both the lawful and the fair person will be just. Hence what is just will be both what is lawful and what is fair, and what is unjust will be both what
1129b is lawless and what is unfair.

Since the unjust person is greedy, he will be concerned with goods—not with all goods, but only with those involved in good and bad fortune, goods which

are, [considered] unconditionally, always good, but for this or that person not always good. Though human beings pray for these and pursue them, they are 5 wrong; the right thing is to pray that what is good unconditionally will also be good for us; but to choose [only] what is good for us.

Now the unjust person [who chooses these goods] does not choose more in every case; in the case of what is bad unconditionally he actually chooses less. But since what is less bad also seems to be good in a way, 10 and greed aims at more of what is good, he seems to be greedy. In fact he is unfair; for unfairness includes [all these actions], and is a common feature [of his choice of the greater good and of the lesser evil].

GENERAL JUSTICE

2

Since, as we saw, the lawless person is unjustified and the lawful person is just, it clearly follows that whatever is lawful is in some way just; for the provisions of legislative science are lawful, and we say that each of them is just. Now in every matter they deal with the laws aim either at the common benefit of all, or at the benefit of 15 those in control, whose control rests on virtue or on some other such basis. And so in one way that we call just is whatever produces and maintains happiness and its parts for a political community.

Now the law instructs us to do the actions of a 20 brave person—not to leave the battle-line, e.g., or to flee, or to throw away our weapons; of a temperate person—not to commit adultery or wanton aggression; of a mild person—not to strike or revile another; and similarly requires actions that express the other virtues, and prohibits those that express the vices. The 25 correctly established law does this correctly, and the less carefully framed one does this worse.

This type of justice, then, is complete virtue, not complete virtue unconditionally, but complete virtue in relation to another. And this is why justice often seems to be supreme among the virtues, and 'neither the evening star nor the morning star is so marvellous',[9] and the proverb says 'And in justice all virtue 30 is summed up.'[10]

9. [The quotation is thought to be from Euripides' lost play *Melanippe*.]
10. [The quotation derives from the work of Theognis, a sixth-century B.C. poet from Megara.]

Moreover, justice is complete virtue to the highest degree because it is the complete exercise of complete virtue. And it is the complete exercise because the person who has justice is able to exercise virtue in relation to another, not only in what concerns himself; for many are able to exercise virtue in their own concerns but unable in what relates to another.

1130a   And hence Bias[11] seems to have been correct in saying that ruling will reveal the man, since a ruler is automatically related to another, and in a community. And for the same reason justice is the only virtue that seems to be another person's good, because it is 5 related to another; for it does what benefits another, either the ruler or the fellow-member of the community.

The worst person, therefore, is the one who exercises his vice towards himself and his friends as well [as towards others]. And the best person is not the one who exercises virtue [only] towards himself, but the one who [also] exercises it in relation to another, since this is a difficult task.

This type of justice, then, is the whole, not a part, of virtue, and the injustice contrary to it is the whole, 10 not a part, of vice.

At the same time our discussion makes clear the differences between virtue and this type of justice. For virtue is the same as justice, but what it is to be virtue is not the same as what it is to be justice. Rather, in so far as virtue is related to another, it is justice, and in so far as it is a certain sort of state unconditionally it is virtue.

BOOK VI

Virtues of Thought

THE DOCTRINE OF THE MEAN, CORRECT REASON, AND VIRTUES OF THOUGHT

1

1138b Since we have said previously that we must choose the intermediate condition, not the excess or the de-20 ficiency, and that the intermediate condition is as

11. [Bias of Priene was a sixth-century B.C. Ionian states-man, one of the Seven Wise Men of Greece, who distinguished themselves in public affairs. His most famous saying was, "Most men are bad."]

correct reason says, let us now determine this [i.e. what it says].

For in all the states of character we have mentioned, as well as in the others, there is a target which someone who has reason focusses on when he tightens and relaxes, and there is a definition of the means, which we take to be between excess and deficiency because they express correct reason.   25

To say this is admittedly true, but it is not at all clear. For in other pursuits directed by a science it is equally true that we must labour and be idle neither too much nor too little, but the intermediate amount prescribed by correct reason. But knowing only this, we would be none the wiser, e.g. about the medicines 30 to be applied to the body, if we were told we must apply as many as medical science instructs and in the way that the medical scientist applies them.

Similarly, then, our account of the states of the soul must not only be true up to this point; we must also determine what correct reason is, i.e. what its definition is.

After we divided the virtues of the soul we said that 35 some are virtues of character and some of thought. And so, having finished our discussion of the virtues of character, let us now discuss the others as follows, 1139a after first discussing the soul.

Previously, then, we said that there are two parts of the soul, one that has reason, and one non-rational. 5 Now we should divide in the same way the part that has reason.

Let us assume that there are two parts that have reason; one with which we study beings whose origins cannot be otherwise than they are, and one with which we study beings whose origins can be otherwise. For when the beings are of different kinds, the parts of the soul naturally suited to each of them 10 are also of different kinds, since the parts possess knowledge by being somehow similar and appropriate [to their objects].

Let us call one of these the scientific part, and the other the rationally calculating part, since deliberating is the same as rationally calculating, and no one deliberates about what cannot be otherwise. Hence 15 the rationally calculating part is one part of the soul that has reason.

Hence we should find the best state both of the scientific and of the rationally calculating part; for this state is the virtue of each of them. And since

something's virtue is relative to its own proper function [we must consider the function of each part].

THE VIRTUOUS PERSON HAS CORRECT DECISION

2

These are three [capacities] in the soul—perception,
understanding, desire—that control action and truth.
Of these three perception clearly originates no action,
20 since beasts have perception, but no share in action.

As assertion and denial are to thought, so pursuit
and avoidance are to desire. Now virtue of character
is a state that decides; and decision is a deliberative
desire. If, then, the decision is excellent, the reason
must be true and the desire correct, so that what
25 reason states is what desire pursues.

This, then, is thought and truth concerned with
action. By contrast, when thought is concerned with
study, not with action or production, its good or bad
state consists [simply] in being true or false. For truth
is the function of whatever thinks; but the function
of what thinks about action is truth agreeing with
30 correct desire.

Now the origin—the source, not the goal, of the
movement—is decision, and the origin of decision
is desire, and reason that aims at some goal. Hence
decision requires understanding and thought, and
35 also a state of character, since doing well or badly in
action requires both intellect and character.

Thought by itself, however, moves nothing; what
moves us is thought aiming at some goal and con-
1139b cerned with action. For this is the sort of thought
that also originates productive thought; for every producer in his production aims at some [further] goal,
and the unconditional goal is not the product, which
is only the [conditional] goal of some [production],
and aims at some [further] goal. [The unconditional
goal is] what we achieve in action, since doing well
in action is the goal.

Now desire is for the goal. Hence decision is either
understanding combined with desire or desire com-
5 bined with thought; and what originates movement
in this way is a human being.

We do not decide to do what is already past; no
one decides, e.g. to have sacked Troy. For neither do
we deliberate about what is past, but only about what
will be and admits [of being or not being]; and what
is past does not admit of not having happened. Hence

Agathon is correct to say 'Of this alone even a god is 10
deprived—to make what is all over to have never happened.[12]

Hence the function of each of the understanding
parts is truth; and so the virtue of each part will be
the state that makes that part grasp the truth most
of all.

SCIENTIFIC KNOWLEDGE

3

Then let us begin over again, and discuss these states 15
of the soul. Let us say, then, that there are five states
in which the soul grasps the truth in its affirmation
or denials. These are craft, scientific knowledge, intelligence, wisdom and understanding; for belief and
supposition admit of being false.

What science is is evident from the following, if
we must speak exactly and not be guided by
[mere] similarities.

For we all suppose that what we know scientifically 20
does not even admit of being otherwise; and whenever
what admits of being otherwise escapes observation,
we do not notice whether it is or is not, [and hence
we do not know about it]. Hence, what is known
scientifically is by necessity. Hence it is everlasting;
for the things that are by unqualified necessity are
all everlasting, and everlasting things are ingenerable
and indestructible.

Further, every science seems to be teachable, and 25
what is scientifically knowable is learnable. But all
teaching is from what is already known, as we also
say in the *Analytics*; for some teaching is through
induction, some by deductive inference, [which both
require previous knowledge].

Induction [reaches] the principle, i.e., the universal, while deductive inference proceeds from the universal. Hence deductive inference has principles from 30
which it proceeds, but which are not themselves
[reached] by deductive inference. Hence they are
[reached] by induction.

Scientific knowledge, then, is a demonstrative state,
and has all the other features that in the *Analytics*
we add to the definition. For someone has scientific
knowledge when he has the appropriate sort of confi-

---

12. [Agathon was a fifth-century B.C. Athenian poet.]

dence, and the principles are known to him; for if they are not better known to him than the conclusion, 35 he will have scientific knowledge only coincidentally.

So much for a definition of scientific knowledge.

INTELLIGENCE

5

1140a To grasp what intelligence is we should first study the sort of people we call intelligent.

It seems proper, then, to an intelligent person to be able to deliberate finely about what is good and beneficial for himself, not about some restricted area—e.g. about what promotes health or strength— but about what promotes living well as a whole [without restriction].

A sign of this is the fact that we call people intelligent about some [restricted area] whenever they cal-30 culate well to promote some excellent end, in an area where there is no craft. Hence where [living well] as a whole is concerned, the deliberative person will also be intelligent.

Now no one deliberates about what cannot be otherwise or about what cannot be achieved by his action. Hence, if science is associated with demonstration, but there is no demonstration of anything whose origin can be otherwise, since every such thing can itself 35 be otherwise; and if we cannot deliberate about what 1140b is by necessity; it follows that intelligence is neither a science nor a craft. It is not a science, because what is done in action can be otherwise; and it is not a craft, because action and production belong to different kinds.

The remaining possibility, then, is that intelligence 5 is a state grasping the truth, associated with reason, and concerned with action about what is good or bad for a human being.

For production has its end beyond it; but action does not, since its end is doing well itself, [and doing well is the concern of intelligence].

Hence Pericles[13] and such people are the ones whom we regard as intelligent, because they are able 10 to study what is good for themselves and for human

13. [Pericles (c. 495–429 B.C.), the eminent Athenian statesman, was renowned for his incorruptible character and the wisdom of his politics. He was a staunch defender of democracy and a patron of the arts.]

beings; and we think that household managers and politicians are such people.

This is also how we come to give temperance (sōphrosunē) its name, because we think that it preserves intelligence, (sōzousan tēn phronēsin). This is the sort of supposition that it preserves.

For the sort of supposition that is corrupted and perverted by what is pleasant or painful is not every sort—not, e.g., the supposition that the triangle does 15 or does not have two right angles—but a supposition about what is done in action.

For the origin of what is done in action is the goal it aims at; and if pleasure or pain has corrupted someone, the origin cannot appear to him. Hence it will not be apparent that this must be the goal and 20 cause of all his choice and action; for vice corrupts the origin.

Hence [since intelligence is what temperance preserves, and what temperance preserves is a true supposition about action], intelligence must be a state grasping the truth, associated with reason, and concerned with action about human goods.

Moreover, there is virtue [or vice in the use] of craft, but not in intelligence. Further, in a craft, someone who makes errors voluntarily is more choiceworthy; but with intelligence, as with the virtues, the reverse is true. Clearly, then, intelligence is a virtue, 25 not craft-knowledge.

There are two parts of the soul that have reason. Intelligence is a virtue of one of them, of the part that has belief; for belief is concerned, as intelligence is, with what admits of being otherwise.

Moreover, it is not only a state associated with reason. A sign of this is the fact that such a state is forgotten, but intelligence is not.

UNDERSTANDING

6

Scientific knowledge is supposition about universals, 30 things that are by necessity. Further, everything demonstrable and every science have principles, since scientific knowledge involves reason.

Hence there can be neither scientific knowledge or craft-knowledge nor intelligence about the principles of what is scientifically known. For what is scien- 35 tifically known is demonstrable, [but the principles are not]; and craft and intelligence are about what 1141a admits of being otherwise. Nor is wisdom [exclusively] about principles; for it is proper to the wise person to have a demonstration of some things.

5 [The states of the soul] by which we always grasp the truth and never make mistakes, about what can or cannot be otherwise, are scientific knowledge, intelligence, wisdom and understanding. But none of the first three — intelligence, scientific knowledge, wisdom — is possible about principles. The remaining possibility, then, is that we have understanding about principles.

Wisdom

7

10 We ascribe wisdom in crafts to the people who have the most exact [expertise] in the crafts, e.g. we call Pheidias a wise sculptor and Polycleitus a wise portrait-maker, signifying only that wisdom is excellence in a craft. But we also think some people are wise in general, not wise in some [restricted] area, or in some 15 other [specific] way, as Homer says in the *Margites*: 'The gods did not make him a digger or a ploughman or wise in anything.' Clearly, then, wisdom is the most exact [form] of scientific knowledge.

Hence the wise person must not only know what is derived from the origins of a science, but also grasp the truth about the origins. Therefore wisdom is understanding and scientific knowledge; it is scientific knowledge of the most honourable things that has received [understanding as] its coping-stone.

20 For it would be absurd for someone to think that political science or intelligence is the most excellent science, when the best thing in the universe is not a human being [and the most excellent science must be of the best things].

Moreover, what is good and healthy for human beings and for fish is not the same, but what is white or straight is always the same. Hence everyone would say that the content of wisdom is always the same, but the content of intelligence is not. For the agent 25 they would call intelligent is the one who studies well each question about his own [good], and he is the one to whom they would entrust such questions. Hence intelligence is also ascribed to some of the beasts, whenever they are evidently capable of forethought about their own life.

This also makes it evident that wisdom is not the same as political science. For if people are to say that [political science] about what is beneficial to themselves [as human beings] counts as wisdom, 30 there will be many types of wisdom [corresponding to the different species of animals]. For if there is no one medical science about all beings, there is no one [science] about the good of all animals, but a different [science] about each specific good. [Hence there will be many types of wisdom, contrary to our assumption that it has the best objects].

And it does not matter if human beings are the best among the animals. For there are other beings of a far more divine nature than human beings; e.g., the most evident are the beings composing the universe.   *1141b*

What we have said makes it clear that wisdom is both scientific knowledge and understanding about what is by nature most honourable. That is why people say that Anaxagoras[14] or Thales[15] or that sort of 5 person is wise, but not intelligent, when they see that he is ignorant of what benefits himself. And so they say that what he knows is extraordinary, amazing, difficult and divine, but useless, because it is not human goods that he looks for.

Intelligence Compared with the Other Virtues of Thought

Intelligence, by contrast, is about human concerns, 10 about what is open to deliberation. For we say that deliberating well is the function of the intelligent person more than anyone else; but no one deliberates about what cannot be otherwise, or about what lacks a goal that is a good achievable in action. The unconditionally good deliberator is the one whose aim expresses rational calculation in pursuit of the best good for a human being that is achievable in action.

14. [Anaxagoras (c. 500–428 B.C.) was a Greek philosopher who considered the world-order to have been produced by reason. His association with Pericles as teacher and friend led to his being brought to trial by Pericles' opponents on a charge of impiety. He was found guilty by the Athenian jury, but he escaped and retired to Ionia.]

15. [Thales (c. 636–546 B.C.) is traditionally considered the first of the Greek philosophers. According to legend, he fell into a well while gazing at the stars. He is credited, however, with predicting a solar eclipse and introducing geometry to the Greeks.]

15   Nor is intelligence about universals only. It must also come to know particulars, since it is concerned with action and action is about particulars. Hence in other areas also some people who lack knowledge but have experience are better in action than some with knowledge. For someone who knows that light meats
20 are digestible and healthy, but not which sorts of meats are light, will not produce health; the one who knows that bird meats are healthy will be better at producing health. And since intelligence is concerned with action, it must possess both [the universal and the particular knowledge] or the [particular] more [than the universal]. Here too, however, [as in medicine] there is a ruling [science].

INTELLIGENCE CONCERNS BOTH THE INDIVIDUAL AND THE COMMUNITY

8

Political science and intelligence are the same state, but their being is not the same.

One part of intelligence about the city is the ruling
25 part; this is legislative science.

The part concerned with particulars [often] monopolizes the name 'political science' that [properly] applies to both parts in common. This part is concerned with action and deliberation, since [it is concerned with decrees and] the decree is to be acted on as the last thing [reached in deliberation]. Hence these people are the only ones who are said to be politically active; for these are the only ones who practise [politics] in the way that handcraftsmen practise [their craft].
30   Now likewise intelligence concerned with the individual himself seems most of all to be counted as intelligence; and this [part of intelligence often] monopolizes the name 'intelligence' that [properly] applies [to all parts] in common. Of the other parts one is household science, another legislative, another political, one part of which is deliberative and another judicial.

In fact knowledge of what is [good] for oneself is one species [of intelligence]. But there is much difference [in opinions] about it.
1142a   Someone who knows about himself, and spends his time on his own concerns, seems to be intelligent, while politicians seem to be too active. Hence Euripides says, 'Surely I cannot be intelligent, when I could
5 have been inactive, numbered among all the many in the army, and have had an equal share. . . . For those who go too far and are too active. . . .'

For people seek what is good for themselves, and suppose that this [inactivity] is the action required [to achieve their good]. Hence this belief has led to the view that these are the intelligent people.

Presumably, however, one's own welfare requires 10 household management and a political system.

Moreover, [another reason for the difference of opinion is this]: it is unclear, and should be examined, how one must manage one's own affairs.

A sign of what has been said [about the unclarity of what intelligence requires] is the fact that whereas young people become accomplished in geometry and mathematics, and wise within these limits, intelligent young people do not seem to be found. The reason is that intelligence is concerned with particulars as well as universals, and particulars become known from experience, but a young person lacks experience, 15 since some length of time is needed to produce it.

Indeed [to understand the difficulty and importance of experience] we might consider why a boy can become accomplished in mathematics, but not in wisdom or natural science. Surely it is because mathematical objects are reached through abstraction, whereas the principles in these other cases are reached from experience. Young people, then, [lacking experience], have no real conviction in these 20 other sciences, but only say the words, whereas the nature of mathematical objects is clear to them.

Moreover [intelligence is difficult because it is deliberative and] deliberation may be in error about either the universal or the particular. For [we may wrongly suppose] either that all sorts of heavy water are bad or that this water is heavy.

Intelligence is evidently not scientific knowledge; 25 for, as we said, it concerns the last thing [i.e., the particular], since this is what is done in action. Hence it is opposed to understanding. For understanding is about the [first] terms, [those] that have no account of them; but intelligence is about the last thing, an object of perception, not of scientific knowledge.

This is not the perception of proper objects, but the sort by which we perceive that the last among mathematical objects is a triangle; for it will stop here too. This is another species [of perception than 30 perception of proper objects]; but it is still perception more than intelligence is.

Puzzles about Intelligence and Wisdom

12

1143b20 Someone might, however, be puzzled about what use they are.

For wisdom is not concerned with any sort of coming into being, and hence will not study any source of human happiness.

25 Admittedly intelligence will study this; but what do we need it for?

For knowledge of what is healthy or fit—i.e. of what results from the state, not of what produces it—makes us no readier to act appropriately if we are already healthy; for having the science of medicine or gymnastics makes us no readier to act appropriately. Similarly, intelligence is the science of what is just, fine and good for a human being; but this is what the good man does; and if we are already good, knowledge of them makes us no readier to act appropriately, since virtues are states activated in actions.

If we concede that intelligence is not useful for this, should we say it is useful for becoming good? 30 In that case it will be no use to those who are already excellent. Nor, however, will it be any use to those who are not. For it will not matter to them whether they have it themselves or take the advice of others who have it. The advice of others will be quite adequate for us, just as it is with health, when we wish to be healthy, but still do not learn medical science.

Besides, it would seem absurd for intelligence, inferior as it is to wisdom, to control it as a superior. [But 35 this will be the result,] since the science that produces also rules and prescribes about its product.

1144a We must discuss these questions; for so far we have only gone through the puzzles about them.

First of all, let us state that both intelligence and wisdom must be choiceworthy in themselves, even if neither produces anything at all; for each is the virtue of one of the two [rational] parts [of the soul].

Second, they do produce something. Wisdom produces happiness, not in the way that medical science 5 produces health, but in the way that health produces [health]. For since wisdom is a part of virtue as a whole, it makes us happy because it is a state that we possess and activate.

Further, we fulfil our function in so far as we have intelligence and virtue of character; for virtue makes the goal correct, and intelligence makes what pro-motes the goal [correct]. The fourth part of the soul, 10 the nutritive part, has no such virtue [related to our function], since no action is up to it to do or not to do.

The Relation of Virtue to Intelligence Is Clearer When We Distinguish Natural Virtue from Full Virtue

13

To answer the claim that intelligence will make us no readier to do fine and just actions, we must begin 15 from a little further back [in our discussion].

Here is where we begin. We say that some people who do just actions are not yet thereby just, if, e.g., they do the actions prescribed by the laws, either unwillingly because of ignorance, or because of some other end, not because of the actions themselves, even though they do the right actions, those that the excellent person ought to do. Equally, however, it is seemingly possible for someone to do each type of action in the state that makes him a good person, i.e. 20 because of decision and for the sake of the actions themselves.

Now virtue makes the decision correct; but the actions that are naturally to be done to fulfil the decision are the concern not of virtue, but of another capacity. We must get to know them more clearly before continuing our discussion.

There is a capacity, called cleverness, of the sort 25 that can do the actions that tend to promote the assumed goal, and can fully achieve them. If, then, the goal is fine, cleverness is praiseworthy, and if the goal is base, cleverness is unscrupulousness; hence both intelligent and unscrupulous people are called clever.

Intelligence is not the same as this capacity [of 30 cleverness], though it requires [cleverness]. Intelligence, this eye of the soul, cannot reach its fully developed state without virtue, as we have said and as is clear. For inferences about actions have an origin: 'Since the end and the best good is this sort of thing', whatever it actually is—let it be any old thing for the sake of argument. And this [best good] is apparent only to the good person; for vice perverts us and 35 produces false views about the origins of actions. 1144b

Evidently, then, we cannot be intelligent without being good.

We must, then, also examine virtue over again.

For virtue is similar [in this way] to intelligence; as intelligence is related to cleverness, not the same but similar, so natural virtue is related to full virtue.

5 For each of us seems to possess his type of character to some extent by nature, since we are just, brave, prone to temperance, or have another feature, immediately from birth. However, we still search for some other condition that will be fully good, and expect to possess these features in another way.

For these natural states belong to children and to beasts as well [as to adults], but without understanding 10 they are evidently harmful. At any rate, this much is seemingly clear; just as a heavy body moving around sightless suffers a heavy fall because it has no sight, so it is with virtue. [A naturally well-endowed person without understanding will harm himself.] But is someone acquires understanding, he improves in his action; and the state he now has, though still similar [to the natural one], will now be virtue to the full extent.

And so, just as there are two sorts of conditions, cleverness and intelligence, in the part of the soul 15 that has belief, so also there are two in the part that has character, natural virtue and full virtue. And full virtue is the one that we cannot acquire without intelligence.

This is why some say that all the virtues are [in-20 stances of] intelligence, and why Socrates' inquiries were in one way correct, and in another way in error. For since he thought all the virtues are [instances of] intelligence, he was in error; but since he thought they all require intelligence, he was right.

Here is a sign of this: Whenever people now define virtue, and have said what state it is and what it is related to, they all add that it is the state that expresses 25 correct reason. Now correct reason is reason that expresses intelligence; seemingly, then, they all in a way intuitively believe that the sort of state that is virtue is the state that expresses intelligence.

Here we must change direction a little. For it is not merely the state expressing correct reason, but the state associated with correct reason, that is virtue. And it is intelligence that is correct reason in this area. Socrates, then, thought that the virtues are [in-30 stances of] reason because he thought they are all [instances of] knowledge, whereas we think they are associated with reason.

What we have said, then, makes it clear that we cannot be fully good without intelligence, or intelligent without virtue of character.

In this way we can also solve the dialectical argument that someone might use to show that the virtues are separated from each other. For[, it is argued], since the same person is not naturally best suited for 35 all the virtues, someone will already have one virtue before he has got another.

This is indeed possible with the natural virtues. It is not possible, however, with [the full virtues], which 1145a15 someone must have to be called unconditionally good; for as soon as he has intelligence, which is a single state, he has all the virtues as well.

And clearly, even if intelligence were useless in action, we would need it because it is the virtue of this part of the soul, and because the decision will not be correct without intelligence or without virtue. 5 For virtue makes us reach the end in our action, while intelligence makes us reach what promotes the end.

Moreover, intelligence does not control wisdom or the better part of the soul, just as medical science does not control health. For it does not use health, but only aims to bring health into being; hence it prescribes for the sake of health, but does not prescribe to health. Besides, [saying that intelligence controls 10 wisdom] would be like saying that political science rules the gods because it prescribes about everything in the city.

BOOK VII

Continence and Incontinence

CONDITIONS SUPERIOR TO VIRTUE, INFERIOR TO VICE, AND BETWEEN VIRTUE AND VICE

1

Next we should make a new beginning, and say that 1145a15 there are three conditions of character to be avoided—vice, incontinence and bestiality. The contraries of two of these are clear; we call one virtue and the other continence.

The contrary to bestiality is most suitably called virtue superior to us, a heroic, indeed divine, sort of virtue. Thus Homer made Priam say that Hector was 20 remarkably good; 'nor did he look as though he were the child of a mortal man, but of a god.'[16] Moreover, so they say, human beings become gods because of exceedingly great virtue.

25 Clearly, then, this is the sort of state that would be opposite to the bestial state. For indeed, just as a beast has neither virtue nor vice, so neither does a god, but the god's state is more honourable than virtue, and the beast's belongs to some kind different from vice.

Now it is rare that a divine man exists. This is what the Spartans habitually call him; whenever they very 30 much admire someone, they say he is a divine man. Similarly, the bestial person is also rare among human beings. He is most often found in foreigners; but some bestial features also result from diseases and deformities. We also use this as a term of reproach for people whose vice exceeds the human level.

We must make some remarks about this condition 35 later. We have discussed vice earlier. We must now discuss incontinence, weakness and softness, softness and self indulgence, and also continence and resis-1145b tance; for we must not suppose that continence and incontinence are concerned with the same states as virtue and vice, or that they belong to a different kind.

As in the other cases we must set out the appearance, and firs of all go through the puzzles. In this 5 way we must prove the common beliefs about these ways of being affected—ideally, all the common beliefs, but if not all, then most of them, and the most important. For if the objections are solved, and the common beliefs are left, it will be an adequate proof.

COMMON BELIEFS ABOUT CONTINENCE AND INCONTINENCE

Continence and resistance seem to be good and praiseworthy conditions, while incontinence and weakness 10 seem to be base and blameworthy conditions.

The continent person seems to be the same as the one who abides by his rational calculation; and the incontinent person seems to be the same as the one who strays from it.

The incontinent person knows that his actions are base, but does them because of his feelings, while the continent person knows that his appetites are base, but because of reason does not follow them.

15 People think the temperate person is continent

16. [The quotation is from the *Iliad*.]

and resistant. Some think that every continent and resistant person is temperate, while others do not. Some people say the incontinent person is intemperate and the intemperate incontinent, with no distinction; others say they are different.

Sometimes it is said that an intelligent person cannot be incontinent; but sometimes it is said that some people are intelligent and clever, but still incontinent.

Further, people are called incontinent about emo- 20 tion, honour and gain.

PUZZLES ABOUT THE COMMON BELIEFS

2

We might be puzzled about the sort of correct supposition someone has when he acts incontinently.

First of all, some say he cannot have knowledge at the time. For it would be terrible, Socrates thought, for knowledge to be in someone, but mastered by something else, and dragged around like a slave. For 25 Socrates fought against the account [of incontinence] in general, in the belief that there is no incontinence; for no one, he thought, supposes while he acts that his action conflicts with what is best; our action conflicts with what is best only because we are ignorant [of the conflict].

This argument, then, contradicts things that appear clearly. If ignorance causes the incontinent person to be affected as he is, then we must look for the type of ignorance that it turns out to be; for it is evident, 30 at any rate, that before he is affected the person who acts incontinently does not think [he should do the action he eventually does].

Some people concede some of this, but reject some of it. For they agree that nothing is superior to knowledge, but deny that no one's action conflicts with what has seemed better to him. Hence they say that when the incontinent person is overcome by pleasure he has only belief, not knowledge. 35

In that case, however, if he has belief, not knowledge, and what resists is not a strong supposition, but only a mild one, such as people have when they are 1146a in doubt, we will pardon failure to abide by these beliefs against strong appetites. In fact, however, we do not pardon vice, or any other blameworthy condition [and incontinence is one of these].

Then is it intelligence that resists, since it is the 5 strongest? This is absurd. For on this view the same person will be both intelligent and incontinent; and no one would say that the intelligent person is the sort to do the worst actions willingly.

Besides, we have shown earlier that the intelligent person acts [on his knowledge], since he is concerned with the last things, [i.e. particulars], and that he has the other virtues.

10 Further, if the continent person must have strong and base appetites, the temperate person will not be continent nor the continent person temperate. For the temperate person is not the sort to have either excessive or base appetites; but [the continent person] must have both.

For if his appetites are good, the state that prevents him from following them must be base, so that not 15 all continence is excellent. If, on the other hand, the appetites are weak and not base, continence is nothing impressive; and if they are base and weak, it is nothing great.

Besides, if continence makes someone prone to abide by every belief, it is bad, if, e.g., it makes him abide by a false as well [as a true] belief.

And if incontinence makes someone prone to abandon every belief, there will be an excellent type of 20 incontinence. Neoptolemus, e.g., in Sophocles' *Philoctetes* is praiseworthy when, after being persuaded by Odysseus, he does not abide by [his resolve], because he feels pain at lying.

Besides, the sophistical argument is a puzzle. For [the sophists] wish to refute an [opponent, by showing] that his views have paradoxical results, so that they will be clever in encounters. Hence the inference that results in a puzzle; for thought is tied up, since 25 it does not want to stand still because the conclusion is displeasing, but it cannot advance because it cannot solve the argument.

A certain argument, then, concludes that foolishness associated with incontinence is virtue. For incontinence makes someone act contrary to what he supposes [is right]; but since he supposes that good things are evil and that it is wrong to do them, he will do 30 the good actions, not the evil.

Further, if someone acts to pursue what is pleasant because this is what he is persuaded and decides to do, he seems to be better than someone who acts not because of rational calculation, but because of incontinence.

For the first person is the easier to cure, because

he might be persuaded otherwise; but the incontinent person illustrates the proverb 'If water chokes us, what must we drink to wash it down?' For if he had been 35 persuaded to do the action he does, he would have stopped when he was persuaded to act otherwise; but 1146b in fact, though already persuaded to act otherwise, he still acts [wrongly].

Further, is there incontinence and continence about everything? If so, who is the simple incontinent? For no one has all the types of incontinence, but we say that some people are simply incontinent.

These, then, are the sorts of puzzles that arise. We 5 must undermine some of these claims, and leave others intact; for the solution of the puzzle is the discovery.

What Is the Scope of Incontinence?

3

First, then, we must examine whether the incontinent has knowledge or not, and in what way he has it. 10 Second, what should we take to be the incontinent and the continent person's area of concern—every pleasure and pain, or some definite subclass? Are the continent and the resistant person the same or different? Similarly we must deal with the other questions that are relevant to this study.

We begin the examination with this question: Are 15 the continent and the incontinent person distinguished [from others] (i) by their concerns, or (ii) by their attitudes to these? In other words, is the incontinent person incontinent (i) only by having these concerns, or instead (ii) by having this attitude; or instead (iii) by both?

[Surely (iii) is right.] For [(i) is insufficient] since the simple incontinent is not concerned with everything, but with the same things as the intemperate 20 person. Moreover, [(ii) is insufficient] since he is not incontinent simply by being inclined towards these things—that would make incontinence the same as intemperance. Rather [as (iii) implies], he is incontinent by being inclined towards them in this way. For the intemperate person acts on decision when he is led on, since he thinks it is right in every case to pursue the pleasant thing at hand; but the incontinent person thinks it is wrong to pursue it, yet still pursues it.

WHAT SORT OF KNOWLEDGE DOES THE INCONTINENT PERSON HAVE OR LACK?

25 It is claimed that the incontinent person's action conflicts with true belief, not with knowledge. But whether it is knowledge or belief that he has does not matter to the discussion. For some people with belief are in no doubt, but think they have exact knowledge.

If, then, it is the weakness of their conviction that makes people with belief, not people with knowledge, act in conflict with their supposition, it follows that 30 knowledge will be no different from belief; for, as Heraclitus makes clear, some people's convictions about what they believe are no weaker than other people's convictions about what they know.

But we speak of knowing in two ways, and ascribe it both to someone who has it without using it and to someone who is using it. Hence it will matter whether someone has the knowledge that his action is wrong, without attending to his knowledge, or he 35 both has and attends to it. For this second case seems extraordinary, but wrong action when he does not attend to his knowledge does not seem extraordinary.

1147a Besides, since there are two types of premises, someone's action may well conflict with his knowledge if he has both types of premises, but uses only the universal premise and not the partial premise. For [the partial premise states the particulars and] it is particular actions that are done.

Moreover, [in both types of premises] there are different types of universal, (a) one type referring to the agent himself, and (b) the other referring to the object. Perhaps, e.g., someone knows that (a1) dry things benefit every human being, and that (a2) he 5 himself is a human being, or that (b1) this sort of thing is dry; but he either does not have or does not activate the knowledge that (b2) this particular thing is of this sort.

Hence these ways [of knowing and not knowing] make such a remarkable difference that it seems quite intelligible [for someone acting against his knowledge] to have the one sort of knowledge [without (b2)], but astounding if he has the other sort [including (b2)].

10 Besides, human beings may have knowledge in a way different from those we have described. For we see that having without using includes different types

of having; hence some people, e.g. those asleep or mad or drunk, both have knowledge in a way and do not have it.

Moreover, this is the condition of those affected by strong feelings. For emotions, sexual appetites and some conditions of this sort clearly [both disturb 15 knowledge and] disturb the body as well, and even produce fits of madness in some people.

Clearly, then [since incontinents are also affected by strong feelings], we should say that they have knowledge in a way similar to these people.

Saying the words that come from knowledge is no sign [of fully having it]. For people affected in these ways even recite demonstrations and verses of Emped- 20 ocles. Further, those who have just learnt something do not yet know it, though they string the words together; for it must grow into them, and this needs time.

Hence we must suppose that incontinents say the words in the way that actors do.

Further, we may also look at the cause in the 25 following way, referring to [human] nature. One belief (a) is universal; the other (b) is about particulars, and because they are particulars perception controls them. And in the cases where these two beliefs result in (c) one belief, it is necessary in purely theoretical beliefs for the soul to affirm what has been concluded, and in beliefs about production (d) to act at once on what has been concluded.

If, e.g., (a) everything sweet must be tasted and (b) 30 this, some one particular thing, is sweet, it is necessary (d) for someone who is able and unhindered also to act on this at the same time.

Suppose, then, that someone has (a) the universal belief, and it hinders him from tasting; he has (b) the second belief, that everything sweet is pleasant and this is sweet, and this belief (b) is active; and he also has appetite. Hence the belief (c) yells him to avoid this, but appetite leads him on, since it is capa- 35 ble of moving each of the [bodily] parts.

The result, then, is that in a way reason and belief 1147b make him act incontinently. The belief (b) is contrary to correct reason (a), but only coincidentally, not in itself. For it is the appetite, not the belief, that is contrary [in itself to correct reason].

Hence beasts are not incontinent, because they have no universal supposition, but [only] appearance and memory of particulars. 5

How is the ignorance resolved, so that the incontinent person recovers his knowledge? The same account that applies to someone drunk or asleep applies here too, and is not special to this way of being affected. We must hear it from the natural scientists.

And since the last premise (b) is a belief about something perceptible, and controls action, this must 10 be what the incontinent person does not have when he is being affected. Or rather the way he has it is not knowledge of it, but, as we saw, [merely] saying the words, as the drunk says the words of Empedocles.

Further, since the last term does not seem to be universal, or expressive of knowledge in the same way 15 as the universal term, even the result Socrates was looking for seemingly comes about. For the knowledge that is present when someone is affected by incontinence, and that is dragged about because he is affected, is not the sort that seems to be knowledge to the full extent [in (c)], but only perceptual knowledge [in (b)].

So much, then, for knowing and not knowing, and for how it is possible to know and still to act incontinently.

BOOK X

Pleasure

HAPPINESS: FURTHER DISCUSSION

RECAPITULATION: HAPPINESS IS AN END IN ITSELF, CONSISTING IN VIRTUOUS ACTION

6

1176a30 We have now finished our discussion of the types of virtue; of friendship; and of pleasure. It remains for us to discuss happiness in outline, since we take this to be the end of human [aims]. Our discussion will be shorter if we first take up again what we said before.

We said, then, that happiness is not a state. For if it were, someone might have it and yet be asleep for 35 his whole life, living the life of a plant, or suffer the 1176b greatest misfortunes. If we do not approve of this, we count happiness as an activity rather than a state, as we said before.

Some activities are necessary, i.e. choiceworthy for some other end, while others are choiceworthy in themselves. Clearly, then, we should count happiness as one of those activities that are choiceworthy in themselves, not as one of those choiceworthy for some 5 other end. For happiness lacks nothing, but is self-sufficient; and an activity is choiceworthy in itself when nothing further beyond it is sought from it.

This seems to be the character of actions expressing virtue; for doing fine and excellent actions is choiceworthy for itself.

But pleasant amusements also [seem to be choiceworthy in themselves]. For they are not chosen for other ends, since they actually cause more harm than 10 benefit, by causing neglect of our bodies and possessions.

Moreover, most of the people congratulated for their happiness resort to these sorts of pastimes. Hence people who are witty [participants] in them have a good reputation with tyrants, since they offer them- 15 selves as pleasant [partners] in the tyrant's aims, and these are the sort of people the tyrant requires. And also these amusements seem to have the character of happiness because people in supreme power spend their leisure in them.

However, these sorts of people are presumably no evidence. For virtue and understanding, the sources of excellent activities do not depend on holding supreme power. Further, these powerful people have 20 had no taste of pure and civilized pleasure, and so they resort to bodily pleasures. But that is no reason to think these pleasures are most choiceworthy, since boys also think that what they honour is best. Hence, just as different things appear honourable to boys and to men, it is reasonable that in the same way different things appear honourable to base and to decent people.

As we have often said, then, what is honourable 25 and pleasant is what is so to the excellent person; and to each type of person the activity expressing his own proper state is most choiceworthy; hence the activity expressing virtue is most choiceworthy to the excellent person [and hence is most honourable and pleasant].

Happiness, then, is not found in amusement; for it would be absurd if the end were amusement, and our lifelong efforts and sufferings aimed at amusing 30 ourselves. For we choose practically everything for some other end—except for happiness, since it is [the] end; but serious work and toil aimed [only] at amusement appears stupid and excessively childish. Rather, it seems correct to amuse ourselves so that

we can do something serious; as Anacharsis says;[17] for amusement is seemingly relaxation, and it is because we cannot toil continuously that we require relax-
35 ation. Relaxation, then, is not [the] end, since we
1177a pursue it to prepare for activity.

Further, the happy life seems to be the life expressing virtue, which is a life involving serious actions, and not consisting in amusement.

Besides, we say that things to be taken seriously are better than funny things that provide amusement,
5 and that in each case the activity of the better part and the better person is more serious and excellent; and the activity of what is better is superior, and thereby has more the character of happiness.

Moreover, anyone at all, even a slave, no less than the best person, might enjoy bodily pleasures; but no one would allow that a slave shares in happiness, if one does not [also allow that the slave shares in the sort of] life [needed for happiness]. Happiness, then,
10 is found not in these pastimes, but in the activities expressing virtue, as we also said previously.

THEORETICAL STUDY IS THE SUPREME ELEMENT OF HAPPINESS

7

If happiness, then, is activity expressing virtue, it is reasonable for it to express the supreme virtue, which will be the virtue of the best thing.
15 The best is understanding, or whatever else seems to be the natural ruler and leader, and to understand what is fine and divine, by being itself either divine or the most divine element in us.

Hence complete happiness will be its activity expressing its proper virtue; and we have said that this activity is the activity of study. This seems to agree with what has been said before, and also with the truth.
20 For this activity is supreme, since understanding is the supreme element in us, and the objects of understanding are the supreme objects of knowledge.

Besides, it is the most continuous activity, since we are more capable of continuous study than of any continuous action.

We think pleasure must be mixed into happiness; and it is agreed that the activity expressing wisdom

is the pleasantest of the activities expressing virtue. 25 At any rate, philosophy seems to have remarkably pure and firm pleasures; and it is reasonable for those who have knowledge to spend their lives more pleasantly than those who seek it.

Moreover, the self-sufficiency we spoke of will be found in study above all.

For admittedly the wise person, the just person and the other virtuous people all need the goods necessary 30 for life. Still, when these are adequately supplied, the just person needs others as partners and recipients of his just actions; and the same is true of the temperate person and the brave person and each of the others.

But the wise person is able, and more able the wiser he is, to study even by himself; and though he presumably does it better with colleagues, even so he 1177b is more self-sufficient than any other [virtuous person].

Besides, study seems to be liked because of itself alone, since it has no result beyond having studied. But from the virtues concerned with action we try more or less to gain something beyond the action itself.

Happiness seems to be found in leisure, since we 5 accept trouble so that we can be at leisure, and fight wars so that we can be at peace. Now the virtues concerned with action have their activities in politics or war, and actions here seem to require trouble.

This seems completely true for actions in war, since no one chooses to fight a war, and no one continues it, for the sake of fighting a war; for someone would 10 have to be a complete murderer if he made his friends his enemies so that there could be battles and killings.

But the actions of the politician require trouble also. Beyond political activities themselves these actions seek positions of power and honours; or at least they seek happiness for himself and for his fellow- 15 citizens, which is something different from political science itself, and clearly is sought on the assumption that it is different.

Hence among sections expressing the virtues those in politics and war are preeminently fine and great; but they require trouble, aim at some [further] end, and are choiceworthy for something other than themselves.

But the activity of understanding, it seems, is supe- 20 rior in excellence because it is the activity of study; aims at no end beyond itself; has its own proper

17. [Anacharsis was a sixth-century B.C. Scythian prince of legendary wisdom.]

pleasure, which increases the activity; and is self-sufficient, leisure and unwearied, as far [as these are possible] for a human being. And whatever else is ascribed to the blessed person is evidently found in what expresses this activity.

25   Hence a human being's complete happiness will be this activity, if it receives a complete span of life, since nothing incomplete is proper to happiness.

Such a life would be superior to the human level. For someone will live it not in so far as he is a human being, but in so far as he has some divine element in him. And the activity of this divine element is as much superior to the activity expressing the rest of 30 virtue as this element is superior to the compound. Hence if understanding is something divine in comparison with a human being, so also will the life that expresses understanding be divine in comparison with human life.

We ought not to follow the proverb-writers, and 'think human, since you are human', or 'think mortal, since you are mortal'. Rather, as far as we can, we ought to be pro-immortal, and go to all lengths to live a life that expresses our supreme element; for 1178a however much this element may lack in bulk, by much more it surpasses everything in power and value.

Moreover, each person seems to be his understanding, if he is his controlling and better element; it would be absurd, then, if he were to choose not his own life, but something else's.

And what we have said previously will also apply 5 now. For what is proper to each thing's nature is supremely best and pleasantest for it; and hence for a human being the life expressing understanding will be supremely best and pleasantest, if understanding above all is the human being. This life, then, will also be happiest.

THE RELATION OF STUDY TO THE OTHER VIRTUES IN HAPPINESS

8

The life expressing the other kind of virtue [i.e. the kind concerned with action] is [happiest] in a secondary way because the activities expressing this virtue 10 are human.

For we do just and brave actions, and the others expressing the virtues, in relation to other people, by abiding by what fits each person in contracts, services, all types of actions, and also in feelings; and all these appear to be human conditions.

Indeed, some feelings actually seem to arise from the body; and in many ways virtue of character seems 15 to be proper to feelings.

Besides, intelligence is yoked together with virtue of character, and so is this virtue with intelligence. For the origins of intelligence express the virtues of character; and correctness in virtues of character expresses intelligence. And since these virtues are also connected to feelings, they are concerned with the compound. Since the virtues of the compound are 20 human virtues, the life and the happiness expressing these virtues is also human.

The virtue of understanding, however, is separated [from the compound]. Let us say no more about it, since an exact account would be too large a task for our present project.

Moreover, it seems to need external supplies very little, or [at any rate] less than virtue of character 25 needs them. For grant that they both need necessary goods, and to the same extent, since there will be only a very small difference even though the politician labours more about the body and suchlike. Still, there will be a large difference in [what is needed] for the [proper] activities [of each type of virtue].

For the generous person will need money for generous actions; and the just person will need it for paying debts, since wishes are not clear, and people who are 30 not just pretend to wish to do justice. Similarly, the brave person will need enough power, and the temperate person will need freedom [to do intemperate actions], if they are to achieve anything that the virtue requires. For how else will they, or any other virtuous people, make their virtue clear?

Moreover, it is disputed whether it is decision or 35 actions that is more in control of virtue, on the assumption that virtue depends on both. Well, certainly 1178b it is clear that what is complete depends on both; but for actions many external goods are needed, and the greater and finer the actions the more external goods are needed.

But someone who is studying needs none of these goods, for that activity at least; indeed, for study at least, we might say they are even hindrances.

In so far as he is a human being, however, and 5 [hence] lives together with a number of other human beings, he chooses to do the actions expressing virtue. Hence he will need the sorts of external goods [that are needed for the virtues], for living a human life.

In another way also it appears that complete happiness is some activity of study. For we traditionally
10 suppose that the gods more than anyone are blessed and happy; but what sorts of actions ought we to ascribe to them? Just actions? Surely they will appear ridiculous making contracts, returning deposits and so on. Brave actions? Do they endure what [they find] frightening and endure dangers because it is fine? Generous actions? Whom will they give to? And surely it would be absurd for them to have currency
15 or anything like that. What would their temperate actions be? Surely it is vulgar praise to say that they do not have base appetites. When we go through them all, anything that concerns actions appears trivial and unworthy of the gods.

However, we all traditionally suppose that they are
20 alive and active, since surely they are not asleep like Endymion.[18] Then if someone is alive, and action is excluded, and production even more, what is left but study? Hence the gods' activity that is superior in blessedness will be in study. And so the human activity that is most akin to the gods' will, more than any others, have the character of happiness.

A sign of this is the fact that other animals have no share in happiness, being completely deprived of
25 this activity of study. For the whole life of the gods is blessed, and human life is blessed to the extent that it has something resembling this sort of activity; but none of the other animals is happy, because none of them shares in study at all. Hence happiness extends just as far as study extends, and the more some-
30 one studies, the happier he is, not incidentally but in so far as he studies, since study is valuable in itself. And so [on this argument] happiness will be some kind of study.

However, the happy person is a human being, and so will need external prosperity also; for his nature is
35 not self-sufficient for study, but he needs a healthy body, and needs to have food and the other services provided.

18. [According to Greek mythology, Endymion was a remarkably beautiful young man who was placed into everlasting sleep by the Moon, so that she might embrace him each night.]

Still, even though no one can be blessed without *1179a* external goods, we must not think that to be happy we will need many large goods. For self-sufficiency and action do not depend on excess, and we can do fine actions even if we do not rule earth and sea; for even from moderate resources we can do the actions 5 expressing virtue. This is evident to see, when many private citizens seem to do decent actions no less than people in power—even more, in fact. It is enough if moderate resources are provided; for the life of someone whose activity expresses virtue will be happy.

Solon surely described the happy people well, 10 when he said they had been moderately supplied with external goods, had done what he regarded as the finest actions, and had lived their lives temperately. For it is possible to have moderate possessions and still to do the right actions.

And Anaxagoras seemingly supposed that the happy person was neither rich nor powerful, since he said he would not be surprised if the happy person appeared 15 an absurd sort of person to the many. For the many judge by externals, since these are all they perceive.

Hence the beliefs of the wise seemingly accord with our arguments; and so these also produce confidence.

The truth, however, in questions about action is 20 judged from what we do and how we live, since these are what control us. Hence we ought to examine what has been said by applying it to what we do and how we live; and if it harmonizes with what we do, we should accept it, but if it conflicts we should count it mere words.

The person whose activity expresses understanding and who takes care of understanding is seemingly in the best condition, and most loved by the gods. For if the gods pay some attention to human beings, as 25 they seem to, it would be reasonable for them to take pleasure in what is best and most akin to them, namely understanding; and reasonable for them to benefit in return those who most of all like and honour understanding, on the assumption that these people attend to what is beloved by the gods, and act correctly and finely.

Clearly, all this is true of the wise person more than anyone else; hence he is most loved by the gods. 30 And it is likely that this same person will be happiest; hence the wise person will be happier than anyone else in this way also.

Ethics, Moral Education, and Politics

We Must Study Moral Education to See How to Make People Virtuous

9

We have now said enough in outlines about happiness and the virtues, and about friendship and pleasure 35 also. Should we then think that our decision [to study 1179b these] has achieved its end? On the contrary, the aim of studies about action, as we say, is surely not to study and know about each thing, but rather to act on our knowledge. Hence knowing about virtue is not enough, but we must also try to possess and exercise virtue, or become good in any other way.

Now if arguments were sufficient by themselves to make people decent, the rewards they would com- 5 mand would justifiably have been many and large, as Theognis says, and rightly bestowed. In fact, however, arguments seem to have enough influence to stimulate and encourage the civilized ones among the young people, and perhaps to make virtue occupy a well-born character that truly loves what is fine; but they seem unable to stimulate the many towards being 10 fine and good.

For the many naturally obey fear, not shame; they avoid what is base because of the penalties, not because it is disgraceful. For since they live by their feelings, they pursue their proper pleasures and the 15 sources of them, and avoid the opposed pains, and have not even a notion of what is fine and [hence] truly pleasant, since they have had no taste of it.

What argument could reform people like these? For it is impossible, or not easy, to alter by argument what has long been absorbed by habit; but, presumably, we should be satisfied to achieve some share in virtue when we already have what we seem to need to become decent.

20   Some think it is nature that makes people good; some think it is habit; some that it is teaching.

The [contribution] of nature clearly is not up to us, but results from some divine cause in those who have it, who are the truly fortunate ones.

Arguments and teaching surely do not influence everyone, but the soul of the student needs to have 25 been prepared by habits for enjoying and hating finely, like ground that is to nourish seed. For someone whose life follows his feelings would not even listen to an argument turning him away, or comprehend it [even if he listened]; and in that state how could he be persuaded to change? And in general feelings seem to yield to force, not to argument.

Hence we must already in some way have a charac- 30 ter suitable for virtue, fond of what is fine and objecting to what is shameful.

Moral Education Requires Legislation

But it is hard for someone to be trained correctly for virtue from his youth if he has not been brought up under correct laws, since the many, especially the young, do not find it pleasant to live in a temperate and resistant way. Hence laws must prescribe their upbringing and practices; for they will not find these 35 things painful when they get used to them.

Presumably, however, it is not enough to get the 1180a correct upbringing and attention when they are young; rather, they must continue the same practices and be habituated to them when they become men. Hence we need laws concerned with these things also, and in general with all of life. For the many 5 yield to compulsion more than to argument, and to sanctions more than to what is fine.

This, some think, is why legislators should urge people towards virtue and exhort them to aim at what is fine, on the assumption that anyone whose good habits have prepared him decently will listen to them; but they should impose corrective treatments and penalties on anyone who disobeys or lacks the right nature, and completely expel an incurable. For the 10 decent person, it is assumed, will attend to reason because his life aims at what is fine, while the base person, since he desires pleasures, has to receive corrective treatment by pain, like a beast of burden; that is why it is said that the pains imposed must be those most contrary to the pleasures he likes.

As we have said, then, someone who is to be good 15 must be finely brought up and habituated, and then must live in decent practices, doing nothing base either willingly or unwillingly. And this will be true if his life follows some sort of understanding and correct order that has influence over him.

A father's instructions, however, lack this influence 20 and compelling power; and so in general do the instructions of an individual man, unless he is a king or someone like that. Law, however, has the power that compels; and law is reason that proceeds from a sort of intelligence and understanding. Besides, people become hostile to an individual human being who opposes their impulses even if he is correct in opposing them; whereas a law's prescription of what is decent is not burdensome.

25   And yet, only in Sparta or in a few other cities as well, does the legislator seem to have attended to upbringing and practices. In most other cities they are neglected, and each individual citizen lives as he wishes, 'laying down the rules for his children and wife', like Cyclops.[19]

It is best, then, if the community attends to upbring-
30 ing, and attends correctly. If, however, the community neglects it, it seems fitting for each individual to promote the virtue of his children and his friends — to be able to do it, or at least to decide to do it.

MORAL EDUCATION NEEDS LEGISLATIVE SCIENCE

From what we have said, however, it seems he will be better able to do it if he acquires legislative science.
35 For, clearly, attention by the community works through laws, and decent attention works through
1180b excellent laws; and whether the laws are written or unwritten, for the education of one or of many, seems unimportant, as it is in music, gymnastics and other practices. For just as in cities the provisions of law and the [prevailing] types of character have influence,
5 similarly a father's words and habits have influence, and all the more because of kinship and because of the benefits he does; for his children are already fond of him and naturally ready to obey.

Moreover, education adapted to an individual is actually better than a common education for everyone, just as individualized medical treatment is better. For though generally a feverish patient benefits from
10 rest and starvation, presumably some patient does not; nor does the boxing instructor impose the same way of fighting on everyone. Hence it seems that treatment in particular cases is more exactly right when each person gets special attention, since he then more often gets the suitable treatment.

19. [The reference is to Homer's *Odyssey*, in which the Cyclopes were portrayed as savage one-eyed giants living without government or laws.]

Nonetheless a doctor, a gymnastics trainer and everyone else will give the best individual attention if they also know universally what is good for all, or for 15 these sorts. For sciences are said to be, and are, of what is common [to many particular cases].

Admittedly someone without scientific knowledge may well attend properly to a single person, if his experience has allowed him to take exact note of what happens in each case, just as some people seem to be their own best doctors, though unable to help anyone else at all. None the less, presumably, it seems 20 that someone who wants to be an expert in a craft and a branch of study should progress to the universal, and come to know that, as far as possible; for that, as we have said, is what the sciences are about.

Then perhaps also someone who wishes to make people better by his attention, many people or few, should try to acquire legislative science, if we will 25 become good through laws. For not just anyone can improve the condition of anyone, or the person presented to him; but if anyone can it is the person with knowledge, just as in medical science and the others that require attention and intelligence.

Next, then, should we examine whence and how someone might acquire legislative science? Hence, 30 just as in other cases [we go to the practitioner], should we go to the politicians? For, as we saw, legislative science seems to be a part of political science.

But does the case of political science perhaps seem different from the other sciences and capacities? For in others the same people, e.g. doctors or painters, who transmit the capacity to others, actively practise it themselves. By contrast, those who advertise that 35 they teach politics are the sophists, and none of them practices it. Instead, those who practice it are the 1181a political activists, and they seem to act on some sort of capacity and experience rather than thought.

For evidently they neither write nor speak on such questions, though presumably it would be finer to do this than to compose speeches for the law courts or 5 the Assembly; nor have they made politicians out of their own sons or any other friends of theirs. And yet it would be reasonable for them to do this if they were able; for there is nothing better than the political capacity that they could leave to their cities, and nothing better that they could decide to produce in themselves, or, therefore, in their closest friends.

Certainly experience seemingly contributes quite 10

a lot; otherwise people would not have become better politicians by familiarity with politics. Hence those who aim to know about political science seemingly need experience as well.

By contrast, those of the sophists who advertise [that they teach political science] appear to be a long way from teaching; for they are altogether ignorant about the sort of thing political science is, and the sorts of things it is about. For if they had known what 15 it is, they would not have taken it to be the same as rhetoric, or something inferior to it, or thought it an easy task to assemble the laws with good reputations and then legislate. For they think they can select the best laws, as though the selection itself did not require comprehension, and as though correct judgement were not the most important thing, as it is in music.

20   It is those with experience in each area who judge the products correctly and who comprehend the method or way of completing them, and what fits with what; for if we lack experience, we must be satisfied with noticing that the product is well or badly 1181b made, as with painting. Now laws are seemingly the products of political science; how, then, could someone acquire legislative science, or judge which laws are best, from laws alone? For neither do we appear to become experts in medicine by reading textbooks.

And yet doctors not only try to describe the [recognized] treatments, but also distinguish different states, and try to say how each type of patient might be 5 cured and must be treated. And what they say seems to be useful to the experienced, though useless to the ignorant.

Similarly, then, collections of laws and political

systems[20] might also, presumably, be most useful if we are capable of studying them and of judging what is done finely or in the contrary way, and what sorts of [elements] fit with what. Those who lack the [proper] state [of experience] when they go through 10 these collections will not manage to judge finely, unless they can do it all by themselves [without training], though they might come to comprehend them better.

Since, then, our predecessors have left the area of legislation uncharted, it is presumably better to examine it ourselves instead, and indeed to examine political systems in general, and so to complete the 15 philosophy of human affairs, as far as we are able.

First, then, let us try to find out if our predecessors have made sound remarks on particular topics. Then let us study the collected political systems, to see from them what sorts of things preserve and destroy cities, 20 and each type of political system; and what causes some cities to conduct politics well, and some badly.

For when we have studied these questions, we will perhaps grasp better what sort of political system is best; how each political system should be organized so as to be best; and what habits and laws it should follow.

Let us discuss this, then, starting from the beginning.[21]

20. [Aristotle supervised a collection of the constitutional histories of one hundred fifty-eight Greek states, of which only one, the *Constitution of Athens*, is extant.]

21. [Here the *Nicomachean Ethics* ends, reminding us that for Aristotle the study of ethics is inseparable from the study of political philosophy.]

Epicurus

Epicurus (341–271 B.C.) was born of Athenian parents on the island of Samos, and was thus counted as an Athenian citizen. In order to fulfill his military obligations, he went to Athens in 323, the year in which Aristotle fled Athens, fearing anti-Macedonian sentiment after the death of Alexander the Great. However, even in Aristotle's absence Athens remained the center for philosophical activity, and Epicurus most certainly became familiar with Platonism and Aristotelianism. The death of Alexander brought about a good deal of political turmoil, some of which affected Epicurus directly. While he was in Athens, his family was evicted from Samos by the Macedonians, as were other Athenian colonists. It may be that Epicurus's evident antipathy to politics began with these events. In any case Epicureanism and the public life do not mix: the latter would upset the tranquillity required by the former.

Epicurus's family migrated to Colophon, in Asia Minor, and Epicurus rejoined them in 321. He spent the next ten years in Colophon, where he came under the tutelage of Nausiphanes, who espoused a version of atomism, a philosophy which had been founded by Leucippus (fifth century B.C.) and Democritus of Abdera (c. 460–c. 370 B.C.). Epicurus himself became a convert to atomism, but his atomism differed from that of his predecessors.

Epicurus's version of atomism contended that the universe is composed of only two kinds of things: bodies and the void. That bodies exist is a matter of observation. The existence of the void or empty space is necessary in order for bodies to move. Bodies of visible size are compounded out of bodies of invisible size, namely, atoms. It is impossible for anything to come into existence out of nothing, and it is impossible for anything to pass into nothingness. Therefore what exists always has existed and always will exist. Now many visible bodies are not everlasting; they can be cut up and disintegrated. But since it is impossible for anything to come out of or pass into nothingness, it must be that at least the ultimate parts or atoms of a visible body are not subject to creation, decomposition, or disintegration; that is, the atoms are everlasting. (Epicurus's arguments explaining why there should be ultimate parts at all and why, if they do exist, they are too small to be seen, are obscure.)

Epicurus's infinitely many atoms possess only three variable qualities. They can differ from each other in size, shape, and weight. Some atoms are larger than others, although none of them is big enough to be seen, and none is infinitely small. Some atoms are heavier than others, but the differences in weight do not result in differences in velocity among various atoms. In fact, all atoms move at exactly the same velocity as they fall directly downward through infinite space and infinite time. If all atoms followed parallel downward paths at the same speed, however, they would never interact with each other, and thus nothing would ever change. In order to avoid that difficulty, Epicurus claimed that the atoms occasionally swerve in a random way from their downward paths. When atoms swerve, they may strike other atoms, thus setting off whole series of collisions. Visible objects are the results of such collisions. These objects are systems of atoms which, for some time, display cohesiveness due to a kind of dynamic equilibrium. But, insisted Epicurus, such systems of atoms, no matter how large and well behaved, are the result of purely mechanical causes. There is no design or providence in the universe. Everything that exists can be explained in principle by the motions of atoms in empty space. Nor is the present world-order in which we find ourselves everlasting. It is, like every visible object in it, a collection of atoms which for the present time exists in a dynamic equilibrium, but which will eventually disperse.

Epicurus regarded his atomic theory as the key to his moral theory. The moral theory was epitomized in antiquity as follows: the gods are not to be feared, death is not to be feared, pleasure is easy to obtain, and it is easy to endure pain. The gods, who are also nothing more than collections of atoms, are not to be feared because they have utterly no concern for the affairs of humans. To have any concern would be to spoil their divine tranquillity. Death is not to be feared because it is simply the dissolution of the atomic structure which makes up the soul, and when that happens, one ceases to exist. Thus one can be confident that no pain will be experienced after death.

The pursuit of pleasure is natural in humans, according to Epicurus, and in fact, a person ought always to seek pleasure. But an Epicurean is not an epicure, one devoted to pleasing the senses. The pursuit of excessive or violent pleasures can only result in pain; thus, such pleasures should be avoided. Rather, the pleasure to be sought is best characterized as the absence of pain of any kind. The most pleasant condition, according to Epicurus, is that in which one is neither hungry, thirsty, nor apprehensive, yet confident that one will remain in that condition. In this condition, one's atomic structure is unperturbed. Thus, true pleasure for Epicurus does not require extravagance.

From the time Epicurus began teaching in Athens in 306 until his death, he and his followers lived an abstemious life together, but one which they regarded as approaching perfect pleasure. Once the Epicureans' concept of pleasure is understood, one can see why they thought that pleasure is easy to obtain.

Epicurus's attitude toward his own painful terminal illness illustrates the thesis that it is easy to endure pain. In a letter written to a disciple shortly before his death, he said that "there is set over against these pains the joy of my heart at the memory of our happy conversations in the past."

• • •

Although Epicurus was a prolific writer, few of his writings survive. His *Letter to Menoeceus* and *Principal Doctrines,* reprinted here, give us the rudiments of his moral theory. An important source of information about Epicureanism is the Roman poet Lucretius (c. 99–c. 55 B.C.), in *On the Nature of the Universe,* trans. R. E. Latham (Baltimore: Penguin Books, 1951). Important source material is topically arranged in A. A. Long and D. N. Sedley, eds., *The Hellenistic Philosophers* (Cambridge: University Press, 1987), two volumes (English translations in volume I). J. M. Rist, *Epicurus: An Introduction* (Cambridge: Cambridge University Press, 1972) is a well-balanced account. David J. Furley, *Two Studies in the Greek Atomists* (Princeton: Princeton University Press, 1967) is a more specialized but provocative work.

W.E.M.

Letter to Menoeceus

Epicurus to Menoeceus, greetings:

Let no one delay the study of philosophy while young nor weary of it when old. For no one is either too young or too old for the health of the soul. He who says either that the time for philosophy has not yet come or that it has passed is like someone who says that the time for happiness has not yet come or that it has passed. Therefore, both young and old must philosophize, the latter so that although old he may stay young in good things owing to gratitude for what has occurred, the former so that although young he too may be like an old man owing to his lack of fear of what is to come. Therefore, one must practise the things which produce happiness, since if that is present we have everything and if it is absent we do everything in order to have it.

Do and practise what I constantly told you to do, believing these to be the elements of living well. First, believe that god is an indestructible and blessed animal, in accordance with the general conception of god commonly held, and do not ascribe to god anything foreign to his indestructibility or repugnant to his blessedness. Believe of him everything which is able to preserve his blessedness and indestructibility. For gods do exist, since we have clear knowledge of them. But they are not such as the many believe them to be. For they do not adhere to their own views about the gods. The man who denies the gods of the many is not impious, but rather he who ascribes to the gods the opinions of the many. For the pronouncements of the many about the gods are not basic grasps but false suppositions. Hence come the greatest harm from the gods to bad men and the greatest benefits [to the good]. For the gods always welcome men who are like themselves, being congenial to their own virtues and considering that whatever is not such is uncongenial.

Get used to believing that death is nothing to us.

For all good and bad consists in sense-experience, and death is the privation of sense-experience. Hence, a correct knowledge of the fact that death is nothing to us makes the mortality of life a matter for contentment, not by adding a limitless time [to life] but by removing the longing for immortality. For there is nothing fearful in life for one who has grasped that there is nothing fearful in the absence of life. Thus, he is a fool who says that he fears death not because it will be painful when present but because it is painful when it is still to come. For that which while present causes no distress causes unnecessary pain when merely anticipated. So death, the most frightening of bad things, is nothing to us; since when we exist, death is not yet present, and when death is present, then we do not exist. Therefore, it is relevant neither to the living nor to the dead, since it does not affect the former, and the latter do not exist. But the many sometimes flee death as the greatest of bad things and sometimes choose it as a relief from the bad things of life. But the wise man neither rejects life nor fears death. For living does not offend him, nor does he believe not living to be something bad. And just as he does not unconditionally choose the largest amount of food but the most pleasant food, so he savours not the longest time but the most pleasant. He who advises the young man to live well and the old man to die well is simple-minded, not just because of the pleasing aspects of life but because the same kind of practice produces a good life and a good death. Much worse is he who says that it is good not to be born, "but when born to pass through the gates of Hades as quickly as possible."[1] For if he really believes what he says, why doesn't he leave life? For it is easy for him to do, if he has firmly decided on it. But if he is joking, he is wasting his time among men who don't welcome it. We must remember that what will happen is neither unconditionally within our power nor unconditionally outside our power, so

Reprinted from *Hellenistic Philosophy*, translated and edited by Brad Inwood and L. P. Gerson (Indianapolis: Hackett Publishing Company, 1988).

1. [Theognis 425, 427.—B.I. and L.P.G.]

that we will not unconditionally expect that it will occur nor despair of it as unconditionally not going to occur.

One must reckon that of desires some are natural, some groundless; and of the natural desires some are necessary and some merely natural; and of the necessary, some are necessary for happiness and some for freeing the body from troubles and some for life itself. The unwavering contemplation of these enables one to refer every choice and avoidance to the health of the body and the freedom of the soul from disturbance, since this is the goal of a blessed life. For we do everything for the sake of being neither in pain nor in terror. As soon as we achieve this state every storm in the soul is dispelled, since the animal is not in a passion to go after some need nor to seek something else to complete the good of the body and the soul. For we are in need of pleasure only when we are in pain because of the absence of pleasure, and when we are not in pain, then we no longer need pleasure.

And this is why we say that pleasure is the starting-point and goal of living blessedly. For we recognized this as our first innate good, and this is our starting point for every choice and avoidance and we come to this by judging every good by the criterion of feeling. And it is just because this is the first innate good, that we do not choose every pleasure; but sometimes we pass up many pleasures when we get a larger amount of what is uncongenial from them. And we believe many pains to be better than pleasures when a greater pleasure follows for a long while if we endure the pains. So every pleasure is a good thing, since it has a nature congenial [to us], but not every one is to be chosen. Just as every pain too is a bad thing, but not every one is such as to be always avoided. It is, however, appropriate to make all these decisions by comparative measurement and an examination of the advantages and disadvantages. For at some times we treat the good things as bad and conversely, the bad things as good.

And we believe that self-sufficiency is a great good, not in order that we might make do with few things under all circumstances, but so that if we do not have a lot we can make do with few, being genuinely convinced that those who least need extravagance enjoy it most; and that everything natural is easy to obtain and whatever is groundless is hard to obtain;

and that simple flavours provide a pleasure equal to that of an extravagant life-style when all pain from want is removed, and barley cakes and water provide the highest pleasure when someone in want takes them. Therefore, becoming accustomed to simple, not extravagant, ways of life makes one completely healthy, makes man unhesitant in the face of life's necessary duties, puts us in a better condition for the times of extravagance which occasionally come along, and makes us fearless in the face of chance. So when we say that pleasure is the goal we do not mean the pleasures of the profligate or the pleasures of consumption, as some believe, either from ignorance and disagreement or from deliberate misinterpretation, but rather the lack of pain in the body and disturbance in the soul. For it is not drinking bouts and continuous partying and enjoying boys and women, or consuming fish and the other dainties of an extravagant table, which produce the pleasant life, but sober calculation which searches out the reasons for every choice and avoidance and drives out the opinions which are the source of the greatest turmoil for men's souls.

Prudence is the principle of all these things and is the greatest good. That is why prudence is a more valuable thing than philosophy. For prudence is the source of all the other virtues, teaching that it is impossible to live pleasantly without living prudently, honourably, and justly, and impossible to live prudently, honourably, and justly without living pleasantly. For the virtues are natural adjuncts of the pleasant life and the pleasant life is inseparable from them.

For who do you believe is better than a man who has pious opinions about the gods, is always fearless about death, has reasoned out the natural goal of life and understands that the limit of good things is easy to achieve completely and easy to provide, and that the limit of bad things either has a short duration or causes little trouble?

As to [Fate], introduced by some as the mistress of all, [he is scornful, saying rather that some things happen of necessity,] others by chance and others by our own agency, and that he sees that necessity is not answerable [to anyone], that chance is unstable, while what occurs by our own agency is autonomous, and that it is to this that praise and blame are attached. For it would be better to follow the stories told about the gods than to be a slave to the fate of the natural philosophers. For the former suggests a hope of escaping bad things by honouring the gods, but the latter involves an inescapable and merciless necessity. And he [the wise man] believes that chance is not a god, as the many think, for nothing is done in a disorderly way by god; nor that it is an uncertain cause. For he does not think that anything good or bad with respect to living blessedly is given by chance to men, although it does provide the starting points of great good and bad things. And he thinks it better to be unlucky in a rational way than lucky in a senseless way; for it is better for a good decision not to turn out right in action than for a bad decision to turn out right because of chance.

Practise these and the related precepts day and night, by yourself and with a like-minded friend, and you will never be disturbed either when awake or in sleep, and you will live as a god among men. For a man who lives among immortal goods is in no respect like a mere mortal animal.

The Principal Doctrines

I. What is blessed and indestructible has no troubles itself, nor does it give trouble to anyone else, so that it is not affected by feelings of anger or gratitude. For all such things are a sign of weakness.[1]

II. Death is nothing to us. For what has been dissolved has no sense-experience, and what has no sense-experience is nothing to us.

III. The removal of all feeling of pain is the limit of the magnitude of pleasures. Wherever a pleasurable feeling is present, for as long as it is present, there is neither a feeling of pain nor a feeling of distress, nor both together.

IV. The feeling of pain does not linger continuously in the flesh; rather, the sharpest is present for the shortest time, while what merely exceeds the feeling of pleasure in the flesh lasts only a few days. And diseases which last a long time involve feelings of pleasure which exceed feelings of pain.

V. It is impossible to live pleasantly without living prudently, honourably, and justly and impossible to live prudently, honourably, and justly without living pleasantly. And whoever lacks this cannot live pleasantly.

VI. The natural good of public office and kingship is for the sake of getting confidence from [other] men, [at least] from those from whom one *is* able to provide this.

VII. Some men want to become famous and respected, believing that this is the way to acquire security against [other] men. Thus if the life of such men is secure, they acquire the natural good; but if it is not secure, they do not have that for the sake of which they strove from the beginning according to what is naturally congenial.

VIII. No pleasure is a bad thing in itself. But the things which produce certain pleasures bring troubles many times greater than the pleasures.

IX. If every pleasure were condensed and were present, both in time and in the whole compound [body and soul] or in the most important parts of our nature, then pleasures would never differ from one another.

X. If the things which produce the pleasures of profligate men dissolved the intellect's fears about the phenomena of the heavens and about death and pains and, moreover, if they taught us the limit of our desires, then we would not have reason to criticize them, since they would be filled with pleasures from every source and would contain no feeling of pain or distress from any source — and that is what is bad.

XI. If our suspicions about heavenly phenomena and about death did not trouble us at all and were never anything to us, and, moreover, if not knowing the limits of pains and desires did not trouble us, then we would have no need of natural science.

XII. It was impossible for someone ignorant about the nature of the universe but still suspicious about the subjects of the myths to dissolve his feelings of fear about the most important matters. So it was impossible to receive unmixed pleasures without knowing natural science.

XIII. It was useless to obtain security from men while the things above and below the earth and, generally, the things in the unbounded remained as objects of suspicion.

XIV. The purest security is that which comes from a quiet life and withdrawal from the many, although a certain degree of security from other men does come by means of the power to repel [attacks] and by means of prosperity.

XV. Natural wealth is both limited and easy to acquire. But wealth [as defined by] groundless opinions extends without limit.

XVI. Chance has a small impact on the wise man, while reasoning has arranged for, is arranging for, and will arrange for the greatest and most important matters throughout the whole of his life.

---

1. [Scholiast: "Elsewhere he says that the gods are contemplated by reason, and that some exist 'numerically' (i.e., are numerically distinct, each being unique in kind) while others are similar in form, because of a continuous flow of similar images to the same place; and that they are anthropomorphic." — B.I. and L.P.G.]

XVII. The just life is most free from disturbance, but the unjust life is full of the greatest disturbance.

XVIII. As soon as the feeling of pain produced by want is removed, pleasure in the flesh will not increase but is only varied. But the limit of mental pleasures is produced by a reasoning out of these very pleasures [of the flesh] and of the things related to these, which used to cause the greatest fears in the intellect.

XIX. Unlimited time and limited time contain equal [amounts of] pleasure, if one measures its limits by reasoning.

XX. The flesh took the limits of pleasure to be unlimited, and [only] an unlimited time would have provided it. But the intellect, reasoning out the goal and limit of the flesh and dissolving the fears of eternity, provided us with the perfect way of life and had no further need of unlimited time. But it [the intellect] did not flee pleasure, and even when circumstances caused an exit from life it did not die as though it were lacking any aspect of the best life.

XXI. He who has learned the limits of life knows that it is easy to provide that which removes the feeling of pain owing to want and makes one's whole life perfect. So there is no need for things which involve struggle.

XXII. One must reason about the real goal and every clear fact, to which we refer mere opinions. If not, everything will be full of indecision and disturbance.

XXIII. If you quarrel with all your sense-perceptions you will have nothing to refer to in judging even those sense-perceptions which you claim are false.

XXIV. If you reject unqualifiedly any sense-perception and do not distinguish the opinion about what awaits confirmation, and what is already present in the sense-perception, and the feelings, and every application of the intellect to presentations, you will also disturb the rest of your sense-perceptions with your pointless opinions; as a result you will reject every criterion. If, on the other hand, in your conceptions formed by opinion, you affirm everything that awaits confirmation as well as what does not, you will not avoid falsehood, so that you will be in the position of maintaining every disputable point in every decision about what is and is not correct.

XXV. If you do not, on every occasion, refer each of your actions to the goal of nature, but instead turn prematurely to some other [criterion] in avoiding or pursuing [things], your actions will not be consistent with your reasoning.

XXVI. The desires which do not bring a feeling of pain when not fulfilled are not necessary, but the desire for them is easy to dispel when they seem to be hard to achieve or to produce harm.

XXVII. Of the things which wisdom provides for the blessedness of one's whole life, by far the greatest is the possession of friendship.

XXVIII. The same understanding produces confidence about there being nothing terrible which is eternal or [even] long-lasting and has also realized that security amid even these limited [bad things] is most easily achieved through friendship.

XXIX. Of desires, some are natural and necessary, some natural and not necessary, and some neither natural nor necessary but occurring as a result of a groundless opinion.[2]

XXX. Among natural desires, those which do not lead to a feeling of pain if not fulfilled and about which there is an intense effort, these are produced by an groundless opinion and they fail to be dissolved not because of their own nature but because of the groundless opinions of mankind.

XXXI. The justice of nature is a pledge of reciprocal usefulness, [i.e.,] neither to harm one another nor be harmed.

XXXII. There was no justice or injustice with respect to all those animals which were unable to make pacts about neither harming one another nor being harmed. Similarly, [there was no justice or injustice] for all those nations which were unable or unwilling to make pacts about neither harming one another nor being harmed.

XXXIII. Justice was not a thing in its own right, but [exists] in mutual dealings in whatever places there [is] a pact about neither harming one another nor being harmed.

XXXIV. Injustice is not a bad thing in its own right, but [only] because of the fear produced by the

2. [Scholiast: "Epicurus thinks that those which liberate us from pains are natural and necessary, for example drinking in the case of thirst; natural and not necessary are those which merely provide variations of pleasure but do not remove the feeling of pain, for example expensive foods; neither natural nor necessary are, for example, crowns and the erection of statues."]

suspicion that one will not escape the notice of those assigned to punish such actions.

XXXV. It is impossible for someone who secretly does something which men agreed [not to do] in order to avoid harming one another or being harmed to be confident that he will escape detection, even if in current circumstances he escapes detection ten thousand times. For until his death it will be uncertain whether he will continue to escape detection.

XXXVI. In general outline justice is the same for everyone; for it was something useful in mutual associations. But with respect to the peculiarities of a region or of other [relevant] causes, it does not follow that the same thing is just for everyone.

XXXVII. Of actions believed to be just, that whose usefulness in circumstances of mutual associations is supported by the testimony [of experience] has the attribute of serving as just whether it is the same for everyone or not. And if someone passes a law and it does not turn out to be in accord with what is useful in mutual associations, this no longer possesses the nature of justice. And if what is useful in the sense of being just changes, but for a while fits our basic grasp [of justice], nevertheless it was just for that length of time, [at least] for those who do not disturb themselves with empty words but simply look to the facts.

XXXVIII. If objective circumstances have not changed and things believed to be just have been shown in actual practice not to be in accord with our basic grasp [of justice], then those things were not just. And if objective circumstances do change and the same things which had been just turn out to be no longer useful, then those things were just as long as they were useful for the mutual associations of fellow citizens; but later, when they were not useful, they were no longer just.

XXXIX. The man who has made the best arrangements for confidence about external threats is he who has made the manageable things akin to himself, and has at least made the unmanageable things not alien to himself. But he avoided all contact with things for which not even this could be managed and he drove out of his life everything which it profited him to drive out.

XL. All those who had the power to acquire the greatest confidence from [the threats posed by] their neighbours also thereby lived together most pleasantly with the surest guarantee; and since they enjoyed the fullest sense of belonging they did not grieve the early death of the departed, as though it called for pity.

Epictetus *Intro*

Stoicism as an organized philosophical movement flourished for a period of approximately five hundred years, from 300 B.C. to A.D. 180. The dates are, respectively, the approximate year in which the founder of Stoicism, Zeno of Citium (c. 344–c. 262 B.C.), began lecturing from a stoa, or porch, in the marketplace in Athens, and the year in which the last famous Stoic, the Roman emperor Marcus Aurelius, died. Although Stoic doctrine did not remain static in those five hundred years, the doctrinal differences between earlier and later Stoics appear for the most part to be minimal. What *is* remarkable is the difference in emphasis which Stoicism underwent. In the second and first centuries B.C., Stoicism was introduced into Roman intellectual circles. It found an audience so receptive that in the first and second centuries A.D., Stoicism was a powerful influence in the life of the Roman Empire, attracting such figures as Seneca (1–65), Epictetus (c. 50–c. 130), and Marcus Aurelius (121–180).

In the process of change, Stoicism became less of a philosophy and more of a guide to right conduct. The early Stoics had placed equal emphasis on Logic, Physics, and Ethics; but the Roman Stoics were concerned almost exclusively with the ethical and political aspects of Stoicism. It is easy to see why those aspects of Stoicism appealed to a Marcus Aurelius: the Stoic emphasis on duty and the Stoic belief that all people are citizens of one vast city dovetailed nicely with Roman imperialistic policy. But Stoicism also offered consolation to the less fortunate of the time, including Epictetus, a former slave, since it claimed that that which has ultimate value, namely, virtue, is equally open to all; and that such things as wealth, health, and honor are either of no value whatsoever or merely of instrumental value in the attainment of virtue.

The early Stoics saw the three areas of Logic, Physics, and Ethics as intimately related. These early Stoics made significant contributions to logical theory, with much of their work a departure from Aristotelian logic. For their physical theory the early Stoics looked back to what they took to be the teachings of a Pre-Socratic philosopher, Heraclitus of Ephesus, who flourished around 500 B.C. Heraclitus had taught that the universe is a continuously dynamic thing in which nothing remains strictly the same from one moment to the next. Heraclitus had used fire as a symbol for the ceaseless change occurring in the universe; he may also have intended to say that the universe is actually ruled and guided by fire, which would be the noblest kind of matter in nature. The early Stoics interpreted him in this way. Fire was also thought to be the source and seat of human intelligence; thus, if the universe is ruled by fire, the universe is itself intelligent. In fact, the Stoics believed the universe to be a vast rational being which exhibits, through the guidance of fire, order and law-governed behavior. The Stoics thus consciously appealed to a macrocosm-microcosm analogy: the universe is a rational animal writ large, and a person is or should be the universe writ small. This doctrine has four important repercussions for Stoic ethics.

First, since the source of human intelligence is a natural material element, fire, and since intelligence is the hallmark of what it is to be human, it followed for the Stoics that a person is a part of the natural physical universe, and not something over and above it. This belief fit very well with a doctrine that the Stoics adopted from the Cynics, namely, that all persons are "citizens of the world," which implied that all persons are radically equal. Stoic materialism thus provided a metaphysical underpinning for Stoic cosmopolitanism.

Second, if the universe itself is governed by certain laws and if a person is a microcosm of the universe, then it follows that a person is subject to the same laws as those which govern the universe.

The laws in question, moreover, were viewed not merely as *descriptive* but as *prescriptive:* they prescribe how things *ought* to behave. These laws might be at variance with the customs and legal conventions of a particular society, and if so, those customs and conventions are wrong. There is, in other words, a "natural law" which supersedes all customary law and which is binding on all persons. Natural Law theories in and after the Middle Ages have their roots in Stoicism.

Third, inasmuch as a person is a microcosm of an inherently rational world, a person ought to live a life in perfect conformity with nature, that is, a life in which reason dominates a person's actions and passions. The Stoic "wise man" will live his life so that he does only that which is in accord with nature; moreover, he will do it simply *because* it is in accord with nature. For the Stoic the value of an action resides not in the happiness or pleasure it may happen to bring about, but solely in the virtuous state of mind of the agent. In this respect Stoic ethics foreshadow the ethical theory of Immanuel Kant.

Finally, the Stoics' insistence on the law-governed nature of the universe committed them to determinism, the thesis that everything that happens is the outcome of the operation of unchangeable and all-pervasive laws. As their critics were quick to point out, this seemed to clash with their belief that humans are free, responsible agents. In order to meet this criticism the Stoics stressed that it is important to see what constitutes human freedom. Epictetus's *Encheiridion,* or "Handbook," reprinted here, besides giving a moving account of the Stoic view of life, attempts to resolve the contradiction between human freedom and determinism.

Not much is known of Epictetus's life. He was born in Hieropolis in Asia Minor, was for some time a slave, but was freed by his Roman master. He was educated by a Stoic philosopher and began to teach philosophy himself in Rome until he was banished by the emperor Domitian. Epictetus moved to Nicopolis, in northwestern Greece, where he taught and practiced Stoicism until his death. No written works survive: the *Encheiridion* was dictated to a disciple.

• • •

Important source material on Stoicism is topically arranged in A. A. Long and D. N. Sedley, eds., *The Hellenistic Philosophers* (Cambridge: Cambridge University Press, 1987), two volumes (English translations in volume I). F. H. Sandbach's *The Stoics* (New York: W. W. Norton, 1975) gives an elementary account. J. M. Rist, *Stoic Philosophy* (Cambridge: Cambridge University Press, 1969) deals topically with several major issues. Benson Mates, *Stoic Logic* (1953; rpt. Berkeley: University of California Press, 1961); Shmuel Sambursky, *Physics of the Stoics* (1959; rpt. London: Hutchinson, 1971); and Brad Inwood, *Ethics and Human Action in Early Stoicism* (Oxford: Clarendon Press, 1985) are excellent in their areas. There are important papers in A. A. Long, ed., *Problems in Stoicism* (London: Athlone Press, 1971) and John M. Rist, ed., *The Stoics* (Berkeley: University of California Press, 1978).

W.E.M.

Encheiridion

1

Some things are up to us and some are not up to us. Our opinions are up to us, and our impulses, desires, aversions—in short, whatever is our own doing. Our bodies are not up to us, nor are our possessions, our reputations, or our public offices, or, that is, whatever is not our own doing. The things that are up to us are by nature free, unhindered, and unimpeded; the things that are not up to us are weak, enslaved, hindered, not our own. So remember, if you think that things naturally enslaved are free or that things not your own are your own, you will be thwarted, miserable, and upset, and will blame both gods and men. But if you think that only what is yours is yours, and that what is not your own is, just as it is, not your own, then no one will ever coerce you, no one will hinder you, you will blame no one, you will not accuse anyone, you will not do a single thing unwillingly, you will have no enemies, and no one will harm you, because you will not be harmed at all.

As you aim for such great goals, remember that you must not undertake them by acting moderately,[1] but must let some things go completely and postpone others for the time being. But if you want both those great goals and also to hold public office and to be rich then you may perhaps not get even the latter just because you aim at the former too; and you certainly will fail to get the former, which are the only things that yield freedom and happiness.[2]

From the start, then, work on saying to each harsh appearance,[3] "You are an appearance, and not at all the thing that has the appearance." Then examine it and assess it by these yardsticks that you have, and first and foremost by whether it concerns the things that are up to us or the things that are not up to us. And if it is about one of the things that is not up to us, be ready to say, "You are nothing in relation to me."

2

Remember, what a desire proposes is that you gain what you desire, and what an aversion proposes is that you not fall into what you are averse to. Someone who fails to get what he desires is *un*fortunate, while someone who falls into what he is averse to has met *mis*fortune. So if you are averse only to what is against nature among the things that are up to you, then you will never fall into anything that you are averse to; but if you are averse to illness or death or poverty, you will meet misfortune. So detach your aversion from everything not up to us, and transfer it to what is against nature among the things that are up to us. And for the time being eliminate desire completely, since if you desire something that is not up to us, you are bound to be unfortunate, and at the same time none of the things that are up to us, which it would be good to desire, will be available to you. Make use only of impulse and its

---

Reprinted from *The Handbook of Epictetus*, translated, with introduction and annotations, by Nicholas White (Indianapolis: Hackett Publishing Company, 1983).

1. [This may mean simply that the proposed undertaking is difficult (Oldfather's translation suggests this), or it may mean (as I believe) that the aim cannot be achieved by the Aristotelian policy of pursuing a mean or middle course between extremes.—N.W.]

2. [Epictetus recommends aiming to have one's state of mind in accord with nature, in the sense explained in the previous paragraph and in c. 8. His point here is that if you aim for that and also simultaneously for certain "externals" like wealth, you will probably have neither and clearly will not have the former.]

3. [The word "appearance" translates *phantasia*, which some translators render by "impression" or "presentation." An appearance is roughly the immediate experience of sense or feeling, which may or may not represent an external state of affairs. (The Stoics held, against the Skeptics, that some appearances self-evidently do represent external states of affairs correctly.)]

contrary, rejection,[4] though with reservation, lightly, and without straining.

3

In the case of everything attractive or useful or that you are fond of, remember to say just what sort of thing it is, beginning with the least little things. If you are fond of a jug, say "I am fond of a jug!" For then when it is broken you will not be upset. If you kiss your child or your wife, say that you are kissing a human being; for when it dies you will not be upset.

4

When you are about to undertake some action, remind yourself what sort of action it is. If you are going out for a bath, put before your mind what happens at baths—there are people who splash, people who jostle, people who are insulting, people who steal. And you will undertake the action more securely if from the start you say of it, "I want to take a bath and to keep my choices in accord with nature;" and likewise for each action. For that way if something happens to interfere with your bathing you will be ready to say, "Oh, well, I wanted not only this but also to keep my choices in accord with nature, and I cannot do that if I am annoyed with things that happen."

5

What upsets people is not things themselves but their judgments about the things. For example, death is nothing dreadful (or else it would have appeared dreadful to Socrates), but instead the judgment about death that it is dreadful—*that* is what is dreadful. So when we are thwarted or upset or distressed, let us never blame someone else but rather ourselves, that is, our own judgments. An uneducated person accuses others when he is doing badly; a partly educated person accuses himself, an educated person accuses neither someone else nor himself.

4. [Impulse and rejection (*hormē* and *aphormē*) are, in Stoic terms, natural and non-rational psychological movements, so to speak, that are respectively toward or away from external objects.]

6

Do not be joyful about any superiority that is not your own. If the horse were to say joyfully, "I am beautiful," one could put up with it. But certainly you, when you say joyfully, "I have a beautiful horse," are joyful about the good of the horse. What, then, is your own? Your way of dealing with appearances. So whenever you are in accord with nature in your way of dealing with appearances, then be joyful, since then you are joyful about a good of your own.

7

On a voyage when your boat has anchored, if you want to get fresh water you may pick up a small shellfish and a vegetable by the way, but you must keep your mind fixed on the boat and look around frequently in case the captain calls. If he calls you must let all those other things go so that you will not be tied up and thrown on the ship like livestock. That is how it is in life too: if you are given a wife and a child instead of a vegetable and a small shellfish, that will not hinder you; but if the captain calls, let all those things go and run to the boat without turning back; and if you are old, do not even go very far from the boat, so that when the call comes you are not left behind.

8

Do not seek to have events happen as you want them to, but instead want them to happen as they do happen, and your life will go well.

9

Illness interferes with the body, not with one's faculty of choice,[5] unless that faculty of choice wishes it to. Lameness interferes with the limb, not with one's faculty of choice. Say this at each thing that happens to you, since you will find that it interferes with something else, not with you.

5. ["Faculty of choice" translates *proairesis*, which designates a rational faculty of the soul (cf. n. 4).]

10

At each thing that happens to you, remember to turn to yourself and ask what capacity you have for dealing with it. If you see a beautiful boy or woman, you will find the capacity of self-control for that. If hardship comes to you, you will find endurance. If it is abuse, you will find patience. And if you become used to this, you will not be carried away by appearances.

11

Never say about anything, "I have lost it," but instead, "I have given it back." Did your child die? It was given back. Did your wife die? She was given back. "My land was taken." So this too was given back. "But the person who took it was bad!" How does the way the giver[6] asked for it back concern you? As long as he gives it, take care of it as something that is not your own, just as travelers treat an inn.

12

If you want to make progress,[7] give up all considerations like these: "If I neglect my property I will have nothing to live on," "If I do not punish my slave boy he will be bad." It is better to die of hunger with distress and fear gone than to live upset in the midst of plenty. It is better for the slave boy to be bad than for you to be in a bad state. Begin therefore with little things. A little oil is spilled, a little wine is stolen: say, "This is the price of tranquillity; this is the price of not being upset." Nothing comes for free. When you call the slave boy, keep in mind that he is capable of not paying attention, and even if he does pay attention he is capable of not doing any of the things that you want him to. But he is not in such a good position that your being upset or not depends on him.

6. [The "giver" can be taken to be nature, or the natural order of the cosmos, or god, which the Stoics identified with each other.]

7. ["Making progress" (*prokoptein*) is the Stoic expression for movement in the direction of the ideal condition for a human being, embodied by the Stoic "sage" (cf. c. 15, n. 8).]

13

If you want to make progress, let people think you are a mindless fool about externals, and do not desire a reputation for knowing about them. If people think you amount to something, distrust yourself. Certainly it is not easy to be on guard both for one's choices to be in accord with nature and also for externals, and a person who concerns himself with the one will be bound to neglect the other.

14

You are foolish if you want your children and your wife and your friends to live forever, since you are wanting things to be up to you that are not up to you, and things to be yours that are not yours. You are stupid in the same way if you want your slave boy to be faultless, since you are wanting badness not to be badness but something else. But wanting not to fail to get what you desire—*this* you are capable of. A person's master is someone who has power over what he wants or does not want, either to obtain it or take it away. Whoever wants to be free, therefore, let him not want or avoid anything that is up to others. Otherwise he will necessarily be a slave.

15

Remember, you must behave as you do at a banquet. Something is passed around and comes to you: reach out your hand politely and take some. It goes by: do not hold it back. It has not arrived yet: do not stretch your desire out toward it, but wait until it comes to you. In the same way toward your children, in the same way toward your wife, in the same way toward public office, in the same way toward wealth, and you will be fit to share a banquet with the gods. But if when things are set in front of you, you do not take them but despise them, then you will not only share a banquet with the gods but also be a ruler along with them. For by acting in this way Diogenes and Heraclitus[8] and people like them were deservedly gods and were deservedly called gods.

8. [Diogenes the Cynic (the one who with his lantern looked for an honest man) and Heraclitus of Ephesus, the Pre-Socratic philosopher, were along with Socrates and Zeno people whom the Stoics said might possibly have reached the perfect condition of being sages, which the

16

When you see someone weeping in grief at the departure of his child or the loss of his property, take care not to be carried away by the appearance that the externals he is involved in are bad, and be ready to say immediately, "What weighs down on this man is not what has happened (since it does not weigh down on someone else), but his judgment about it." Do not hesitate, however, to sympathise with him verbally, and even to moan with him if the occasion arises; but be careful not to moan inwardly.

17

Remember that you are an actor in a play, which is as the playwright wants it to be: short if he wants it short, long if he wants it long. If he wants you to play a beggar, play even this part skillfully, or a cripple, or a public official, or a private citizen. What is yours is to play the assigned part well. But to choose it belongs to someone else.

18

When a raven gives an unfavorable sign by croaking,[9] do not be carried away by the appearance, but immediately draw a distinction to yourself and say, "None of these signs is for me, but only for my petty body or my petty property or my petty judgments or children or wife. For all signs are favorable if I wish, since it is up to me to be benefited by whichever of them turns out correct.

19

You can be invincible if you do not enter any contest in which victory is not up to you. See that you are not carried away by the appearance, in thinking that someone is happy when you see him honored ahead of you or very powerful or otherwise having a good reputation. For if the really good things are up to us, neither envy nor jealousy has a place, and you yourself will want neither to be a general or a magistrate or a consul, but to be free. And there is one road to this: despising what is not up to us.

20

Remember that what is insulting is not the person who abuses you or hits you, but the judgment about them that they *are* insulting. So when someone irritates you be aware that what irritates you is your own belief. Most importantly, therefore, try not to be carried away by appearance, since if you once gain time and delay you will control yourself more easily.

21

Let death and exile and everything that is terrible appear before your eyes every day, especially death; and you will never have anything contemptible in your thoughts or crave anything excessively.

22

If you crave philosophy prepare yourself on the spot to be ridiculed, to be jeered at by many people who will say, "Here he is again, all of a sudden turned philosopher on us!" and "Where did he get that high brow?" But don't *you* put on a high brow, but hold fast to the things that appear best to you, as someone assigned by god to this place. And remember that if you hold to these views, those who previously ridiculed you will later be impressed with you, but if you are defeated by them you will be doubly ridiculed.

23

If it ever happens that you turn outward to want to please another person, certainly you have lost your plan of life. Be content therefore in everything to be a philosopher, and if you want to seem to be one, make yourself appear so to yourself, and you will be capable of it.

Stoics took to be conceptually no different from the perfect condition of a god.]

9. [Most people in antiquity believed in fortune-telling of various kinds, involving bird-calls, the flight of birds, inspection of entrails, stars, and whatnot. Many Stoics, notably Chrysippus, believed in such things, not least because they saw in them manifestations of the order of the cosmos and the tight and intricate interconnections within it, and thus saw them as scientific rather than superstitious.]

24

Do not be weighed down by the consideration, "I shall live without any honor, everywhere a nobody!" For if lack of honors is something bad, I cannot be in a bad state because of another person any more than I can be in a shameful one. It is not your task[10] to gain political office, or be invited to a banquet, is it? Not at all. How then is that a lack of honor? And how will you be a nobody everywhere, if you need to be a somebody only in things that are up to you—in which it is open to you to be of the greatest worth? "But your friends will be without help!" What do you mean, "without help?" Well, they will be without a little cash from you, and you will not make them Roman citizens. Who told you, then, that these things are up to you and not the business of someone else? Who can give to someone else what he does not have himself? "Get money," someone says, "so that we may have some." If I can get it while keeping self-respect and trustworthiness and high-mindedness, show me the way and I will get it. But if you demand that I lose the good things that are mine so that you may acquire things that are not good, see for yourselves how unfair and inconsiderate you are. Which do you want more, money or a self-respecting and trustworthy friend? Then help me more toward this, and do not expect me to do things that will make me lose these qualities. "But my country," he says, "will be without help, in so far as it depends on me!" Again, what sort of "help" is this? So it will not have porticos and baths by your efforts. What does that amount to? For it does not have shoes because of the blacksmith or weapons because of the cobbler, but it is enough if each person fulfills his own task. And if you furnished for it another citizen who was trustworthy and self-respecting, would you in no way be helpful to it? "Yes, I would be." Then neither would you yourself be unhelpful to it. "Then what place," he says "will I have in the city?" The one you can have by preserving your trustworthiness and self-respect. And if while wanting to help it you throw away these things, what use will you be to it if you turn out shameless and untrustworthy?

10. [The word translated "task" here and below is *ergon*, which might also be translated by "function."]

25

Has someone been given greater honor than you at a banquet or in a greeting or by being brought in to give advice? If these things are good, you should be glad that he has got them. If they are bad, do not be angry that you did not get them. And remember, you cannot demand an equal share if you did not do the same things, with a view to getting things that are not up to us. For how can someone who does not hang around a person's door have an equal share with someone who does, or someone who does not escort him with someone who does, or someone who does not praise him with someone who does? You will be unjust and greedy, then, if you want to obtain these things for free when you have not paid the price for which they are bought. Well, what is the price of heads of lettuce? An obol, say. So if someone who has paid an obol takes the heads of lettuce, and you who do not pay do not take them, do not think that you are worse off than the one who did. For just as he has the lettuce, you have the obol that you did not pay. It is the same way in this case. You were not invited to someone's banquet? You did not give the host the price of the meal. He sells it for praise; he sells it for attention. Then give him the balance for which it is sold, if that is to your advantage. But you are greedy and stupid if you want both not to pay and also to take. Have you got nothing, then, in place of the meal? Indeed you do have something; you did not praise someone you did not wish to praise, and you did not have to put up with the people around his door.

26

It is possible to learn the will of nature from the things in which we do not differ from each other. For example, when someone else's little slave boy breaks his cup we are ready to say, "It's one of those things that just happen." Certainly, then, when your own cup is broken you should be just the way you were when the other person's was broken. Transfer the same idea to larger matters. Someone else's child is dead, or his wife. There is no one would not say, "It's the lot of a human being." But when one's own dies, immediately it is, "Alas! Poor me!" But we should have remembered how we feel when we hear of the same thing about others.

27

Just as a target is not set up to be missed, in the same way nothing bad by nature happens in the world.[11]

28

If someone turned your body over to just any person who happened to meet you, you would be angry. But are you not ashamed that you turn over your own faculty of judgment to whoever happens along, so that if he abuses you it is upset and confused?

29

For each action, consider what leads up to it and what follows it, and approach it in the light of that. Otherwise you will come to it enthusiastically at first, since you have not borne in mind any of what will happen next, but later when difficulties turn up you will give up disgracefully. You want to win an Olympic victory? I do too, by the gods, since that is a fine thing. But consider what leads up to it and what follows it, and undertake the action in the light of that. You must be disciplined, keep a strict diet, stay away from cakes, train according to strict routine at a fixed time in heat and in cold, not drink cold water, not drink wine when you feel like it, and in general you must have turned yourself over to your trainer as to a doctor, and then in the contest "dig in,"[12] sometimes dislocate your hand, twist your ankle, swallow a lot of sand, sometimes be whipped, and, after all that, lose. Think about that and then undertake training, if you want to. Otherwise you will be behaving the way children do, who play wrestlers one time, gladiators another time, blow trumpets another time, then act a play. In this way you too are now an athlete, now a gladiator, then an orator, then a philosopher,

yet you are nothing wholeheartedly, but like a monkey you mimic each sight that you see, and one thing after another is to your taste, since you do not undertake a thing after considering it from every side, but only randomly and half-heartedly.

In the same way when some people watch a philosopher and hear one speaking like Euphrates[13] (though after all who can speak like him?), they want to be philosophers themselves. Just you consider, as a human being, what sort of thing it is; then inspect your own nature and whether you can bear it. You want to do the pentathlon, or to wrestle? Look at your arms, your thighs, inspect your loins. Different people are naturally suited for different things. Do you think that if you do those things you can eat as you now do, drink as you now do, have the same likes and dislikes? You must go without sleep, put up with hardship, be away from your own people, be looked down on by a little slave boy, be laughed at by people who meet you, get the worse of it in everything, honor, public office, law course, every little thing. Think about whether you want to exchange these things for tranquillity, freedom, calm. If not, do not embrace philosophy, and do not like children be a philosopher at one time, later a tax-collector, then an orator, then a procurator of the emperor. These things do not go together. You must be one person, either good or bad. You must either work on your ruling principle,[14] or work on externals, practise the art either of what is inside or of what is outside, that is, play the role either of a philosopher or of a non-philosopher.

30

Appropriate actions[15] are in general measured by relationships. He is a father: that entails taking care of him, yielding to him in everything, putting up with

11. [According to the Stoic view, the universe as a whole is perfect and everything in it has a place in its overall design, so that nothing can exist or occur that is bad in its relation to that overall design.]

12. [Nobody knows just what this expression means in this context.]

13. [Euphrates was a Stoic lecturer noted for his eloquence.]

14. [The "ruling principle" (or "governing principle"), the *hēgemonikon*, in the rather complicated psychological theory adopted by the Stoics, is that central part of the soul that can understand what is good and decide to act on that understanding.]

15. ["Appropriate actions" are *kathēkonta*, which Cicero called *officia*, and are in English translations often called "duties," though the notion is actually somewhat different from that of duty. They are the actions that are of a type

him when he abuses you or strikes you. "But he is a bad father." Does nature then determine that you have a good father? No, only that you have a father.[16] My brother has done me wrong." Then keep your place in relation to him; do not consider his action, but instead consider what you can do to bring your own faculty of choice[17] into accord with nature. Another person will not do you harm unless you wish it; you will be harmed at just that time at which you take yourself to be harmed. In this way, then, you will discover the appropriate actions to expect from a neighbor, from a citizen, from a general, if you are in the habit of looking at relationships.

31

The most important aspect of piety toward the gods is certainly both to have correct beliefs about them, as beings that arrange the universe well and justly, and to set yourself to obey them and acquiesce in everything that happens and to follow it willingly, as something brought to completion by the best judgment. For in this way you will never blame the gods or accuse them of neglecting you. And this piety is impossible unless you detach the good and the bad from what is not up to us and attach it exclusively to what is up to us, because if you think that any of what is not up to us is good or bad, then when you fail to get what you want and fall into what you do not want, you will be bound to blame and hate those who cause this. For every animal by nature flees and turns away from things that are harmful and from what causes them, and pursues and admires things that are beneficial and what causes them. There is therefore no way for a person who thinks he is being harmed to enjoy what he thinks is harming him, just as it is impossible to enjoy the harm itself. Hence a son even abuses his father when the father does not give him a share of things that he thinks are good; and thinking that being a tyrant was a good thing is

what made enemies of Polyneices and Eteocles.[18] This is why the farmer too abuses the gods, and the sailor, and the merchant, and those who have lost their wives and children. For wherever someone's advantage lies, there he also shows piety. So whoever takes care to have desires and aversions as one should also in the same instance takes care about being pious. And it is always appropriate to make libations and sacrifices and give firstfruits according to the custom of one's forefathers, in a manner that is pure and neither slovenly nor careless, nor indeed cheaply nor beyond one's means.

32

When you make use of fortune-telling, remember that you do not know what will turn out and have gone to the fortune-teller to find out, but that if you really are a philosopher you have gone already knowing what sort of thing it is. For if it is one of the things that is not up to us, it is bound to be neither good nor bad. Therefore do not bring desire or aversion to the fortune-teller and do not approach him trembling but instead realizing that everything that turns out is indifferent[19] and nothing in relation to you, and that whatever sort of thing it may be, you will be able to deal with it well and no one will hinder that. So go confidently to the gods as advisers, and thereafter when some particular advice has been given to you remember who your advisers are and whom you will be disregarding if you disobey. Approach fortune-telling as Socrates thought a person should, in cases where the whole consideration has reference to the outcome, and no resource is available from reason or any other technique to find out about the matter. So, when it is necessary to share a danger with a friend or with your country, do not use fortune-telling about whether you should share the danger. For if the fortune-teller says that the omens are unfavorable, clearly death is signified or the injury of a part of your body or exile. But reason chooses to stand by your friend and to share danger with your country

---

generally in accord with nature, or with a particular sort of person's place in it.]

16. [The idea here is, roughly, that there are certain relationships of affinity established by the natural order, and that having a father represents one of them, but that having a good father is not entailed by it.]

17. [Cf. c. 9, n. 5, and c. 29, n. 14.]

18. [The story of the conflict between the brothers Polyneices and Eteocles is best known to modern readers from Sophocles' tragedy, *Antigone*.]

19. [Things that are "indifferent" in the Stoic view are all things that are external and not up to oneself (cf. c. 1, e.g.).]

even under these conditions. For this reason pay attention to the greater fortune-teller, Pythian Apollo, who threw out of the temple the man who did not help his brother when he was being murdered.[20]

33

Set up right now a certain character and pattern for yourself which you will preserve when you are by yourself and when you are with people. Be silent for the most part, or say what you have to in a few words. Speak rarely, when the occasion requires speaking, but not about just any topic that comes up, not about gladiators, horse-races, athletes, eating or drinking—the things that always come up; and especially if it is about people, talk without blaming or praising or comparing. Divert by your own talk, if you can, the talk of those with you to something appropriate. If you happen to be stranded among strangers, do not talk. Do not laugh a great deal or at a great many things or unrestrainedly. Refuse to swear oaths, altogether if possible, or otherwise as circumstances allow. Avoid banquets given by those outside philosophy. But if the appropriate occasion arises, take great care not to slide into their ways, since certainly if a person's companion is dirty the person who spends time with him, even if he happens to be clean, is bound to become dirty too. Take what has to do with the body to the point of bare need, such as food, drink, clothing, house, household slaves, and cut out everything that is for reputation or luxury. As for sex stay pure as far as possible before marriage, and if you have it do only what is allowable. But do not be angry or censorious toward those who do engage in it, and do not always be making an exhibition of the fact that you do not.

If someone reports back to you that so-and-so is saying bad things about you, do not reply to them but answer, "Obviously he didn't know my other bad characteristics, since otherwise he wouldn't just have mentioned these."

For the most part there is no need to go to public shows, but if ever the right occasion comes do not show your concern to be for anything but yourself;

20. [The idea is that one does not need a fortune-teller to tell one whether one should defend one's country or one's friends, and that this fact was recognized by the oracle of Apollo at Delphi.]

that is to say, wish to have happen only what does happen, and for the person to win who actually does win, since that way you will not be thwarted. But refrain completely from shouting or laughing at anyone or being very much caught up in it. After you leave, do not talk very much about what has happened, except what contributes to your own improvement, since that would show that the spectacle had impressed you.

Do not go indiscriminately or readily to people's public lectures, but when you do be on guard to be dignified and steady and at the same time try not to be disagreeable.

When you are about to meet someone, especially someone who seems to be distinguished, put to yourself the question, "What would Socrates or Zeno have done in these circumstances?" and you will not be at a loss as to how to deal with the occasion. When you go to see someone who is important, put to yourself the thought that you will not find him at home, that you will be shut out, that the door will be slammed, that he will pay no attention to you. If it is appropriate to go even under these conditions, go and put up with what happens, and never say to yourself, "It wasn't worth all that!" For that is the way of a non-philosopher, someone who is misled by externals.

In your conversations stay away from making frequent and longwinded mention of what you have done and the dangers that you have been in, since it is not as pleasant for others to hear about what has happened to you as it is for you to remember your own dangers.

Stay away from raising a laugh, since this manner slips easily into vulgarity and at the same time is liable to lessen your neighbors' respect for you. It is also risky to fall into foul language. So when anything like that occurs, if a good opportunity arises, go so far as to criticize the person who has done it, and otherwise by staying silent and blushing and frowning you will show that you are displeased by what has been said.

34

Whenever you encounter some kind of apparent pleasure, be on guard, as in the case of other appearances, not to be carried away by it, but let the thing wait for you and allow yourself to delay. Then bring before your mind two times, both the time when you enjoy the pleasure and the time when after enjoying it you later regret it and berate yourself; and set against these the way you will be pleased and will praise yourself if you refrain from it. But if the right occasion appears for you to undertake the action, pay attention so that you will not be overcome by its attractiveness and pleasantness and seductiveness, and set against it how much better it is to be conscious of having won this victory against it.

35

When you do something that you determine is to be done, never try not to be seen doing it, even if most people are likely to think something bad about it. If you are not doing it rightly, avoid the act itself; if you are doing it rightly, why do you fear those who will criticize you wrongly?

36

Just as the propositions "It is day" and "It is night" have their full value when disjoined [*sc.*, in "It is day *or* it is night"] but have negative value when conjoined [*sc.*, in "It is day *and* it is night"], in the same way, granted that taking the larger portion has value for one's body, it has negative value for preserving the fellowship of a banquet in the way one should.[21] So when you eat with another, remember not merely to see the value for your body of what lies in front of you, but also to preserve your respect for your host.

37

If you undertake some role beyond your capacity, you both disgrace yourself by taking it and also thereby neglect the role that you were unable to take.

21. [Very roughly, the idea is that the value of an action has to be judged from all features of the context. The parallel is that allegedly the meaningfulness of a sentence depends in a way on its context.]

38

Just as in walking about you pay attention so as not to step on a nail or twist your foot, pay attention in the same way so as not to harm your ruling principle.[22] And if we are on guard about this in every action, we shall set about it more securely.

39

The measure of possessions for each person is the body, as the foot is of the shoe. So if you hold to this principle you will preserve the measure; but if you step beyond it, you will in the end be carried as if over a cliff; just as in the case of the shoe, if you go beyond the foot, you get a gilded shoe, and then a purple embroidered one. For there is no limit to a thing once it is beyond its measure.

40

Women are called ladies by men right after they are fourteen. And so when they see that they have nothing else except to go to bed with men, they begin to make themselves up and place all their hopes in that. It is therefore worthwhile to pay attention so that they are aware that they are honored for nothing other than appearing modest and self-respecting.

41

It shows lack of natural talent to spend time on what concerns the body, as in exercising a great deal, eating a great deal, drinking a great deal, moving one's bowels or copulating a great deal. Instead you must do these things in passing, but turn your whole attention toward your faculty of judgment.[23]

22. [Cf. c. 29, n. 14.]
23. [Cf. c. 29, n. 14. The claim is in effect that one should be concerned wholly with the state of the ruling part of one's soul, and not with external states of affairs or with those aspects of the soul, such as one's affective feelings or desires, that are directly dependent on external states of affairs. One can see here the Stoic view, which seems paradoxical to many, that one's feelings and non-rational desires are in a crucial sense external to one's true self (cf. c. 6 and Introduction.).]

42

When someone acts badly toward you or speaks badly of you, remember that he does or says it in the belief that it is appropriate for him to do so. Accordingly he cannot follow what appears to you but only what appears to him, so that if things appear badly to him, he is harmed in as much as he has been deceived. For if someone thinks that a true conjunctive proposition[24] is false, the conjunction is not harmed but rather the one who is deceived. Starting from these considerations you will be gentle with the person who abuses you. For you must say on each occasion, "That's how it seemed to him."

43

Everything has two handles, one by which it may be carried and the other not. If your brother acts unjustly toward you, do not take hold of it by this side, that he has acted unjustly (since this is the handle by which it may not be carried), but instead by this side, that he is your brother and was brought up with you, and you will be taking hold of it in the way that it can be carried.

44

These statements are not valid inferences: "I am richer than you; therefore I am superior to you," or "I am more eloquent than you; therefore I am superior to you." But rather these are valid: "I am richer than you; therefore my property is superior to yours," or "I am more eloquent than you; therefore my speaking is superior to yours." But you are identical neither with your property nor with your speaking.

45

Someone takes a bath quickly; do not say that he does it badly but that he does it quickly. Someone drinks a great deal of wine; do not say that he does it badly but that he does a great deal of it. For until you have discerned what his judgment was, how do you know whether he did it badly? In this way it will

not turn out that you receive convincing appearances of some things but give assent to quite different ones.[25]

46

Never call yourself a philosopher and do not talk a great deal among non-philosophers about philosophical propositions, but do what follows from them. For example, at a banquet do not say how a person ought to eat, but eat as a person ought to. Remember that Socrates had so completely put aside ostentation that people actually went to him when they wanted to be introduced to philosophers, and he took them.[26] He was that tolerant of being overlooked. And if talk about philosophical propositions arises among non-philosophers, for the most part be silent, since there is a great danger of your spewing out what you have not digested. And when someone says to you that you know nothing and you are not hurt by it, then you know that you are making a start at your task. Sheep do not show how much they have eaten by bringing the feed to the shepherds, but they digest the food inside themselves, and outside themselves they bear wool and milk. So in your case likewise do not display propositions to non-philosophers but instead the actions that come from the propositions when they are digested.

47

When you have become adapted to living cheaply as far as your body is concerned, do not make a show of it, and if you drink water do not say at every opening that you drink water. If you wish to train yourself to hardship, do it for yourself and not for those outside.

25. [A "convincing appearance" is a *kataleptikē phantasia*, the sort of appearance that according to the Stoics is a self-evidently correct representation of the way things actually are (cf. n. 3). "Assent" is *synkatathesis*. Correct assent would of course be assent to self-evidently correct appearances. The line of thought here is, however, quite compressed, and the student will find it a difficult exercise to explain it.]

26. [The allusion is perhaps to the events in the early part of Plato's *Protagoras*.]

24. [Cf. c. 36. A proposition of this sort consists of two component propositions conjoined by "and."]

Do not throw your arms around statues.[27] Instead, when you are terribly thirsty, take cold water into your mouth, and spit it out, and do not tell anyone about it.

48

The position and character of a non-philosopher: he never looks for benefit or harm to come from himself but from things outside. The position and character of a philosopher: he looks for all benefit and harm to come from himself.

Signs of someone's making progress: he censures no one; he praises no one; he blames no one; he never talks about himself as a person who amounts to something or knows something. When he is thwarted or prevented in something, he accuses himself. And if someone praises him he laughs to himself at the person who has praised him; and if someone censures him he does not respond. He goes around like an invalid, careful not to move any of his parts that are healing before they have become firm. He has kept off all desire from himself, and he has transferred all aversion onto what is against nature among the things that are up to us. His impulses toward everything are diminished. If he seems foolish or ignorant, he does not care. In a single phrase, he is on guard against himself as an enemy lying in wait.

49

When someone acts grand because he understands and can expound the works of Chrysippus,[28] say to yourself, "If Chrysippus had not written unclearly, this man would have nothing to be proud of."

But what do *I* want? To learn to understand nature and follow it. So I try to find out who explains it. And I hear that Chrysippus does, and I go to him. But I do not understand the things that he has written, so I try to find the person who explains them. Up to this point there is nothing grand. But when I do find someone who explains them, what remains is to carry out what has been conveyed to me. This alone is grand. But if I am impressed by the explaining itself, what have I done but ended up a grammarian instead of a philosopher—except that I am explaining Chrysippus instead of Homer. Instead, when someone says to me, "Read me some Chrysippus," I turn red when I cannot exhibit actions that are similar to his words and in harmony with them.

50

Abide by whatever task is set before you as if it were a law, and as if you would be committing sacrilege if you went against it. But pay no attention to whatever anyone says about you, since that falls outside what is yours.

51

How long do you put off thinking yourself worthy of the best things, and never going against the definitive capacity of reason?[29] You have received the philosophical propositions that you ought to agree to and you have agreed to them. Then what sort of teacher are you still waiting for, that you put off improving yourself until he comes? You are not a boy any more, but already a full-grown man. If you now neglect things and are lazy and are always making delay after delay and set one day after another as the day for paying attention to yourself, then without realizing it you will make no progress but will end up a non-philosopher all through life and death. So decide now that you are worthy of living as a full-grown man who is making progress, and make everything that seems best be a law that you cannot go against. And if you meet with any hardship or anything pleasant or reputable or disreputable, then remember that the contest is *now* and the Olympic games are *now* and you cannot put things off any more and that your progress is made or destroyed by a single day and a single action. Socrates became fully perfect in this way, by not paying attention to anything but his reason in everything that he met with. You, even if you are not

27. [According to a story in Diogenes Laërtius 6.23, Diogenes, the Cynic did this nude in cold weather, to toughen himself. But the statues were outdoors, and Diogenes was a bit of a show-off (but cf. n. 8!).]

28. [Chrysippus was the third head of the Stoic school at Athens.]

29. [In brief, the capacity of reason here is that of distinguishing different things from each other and defining them.]

yet Socrates, ought to live as someone wanting to be Socrates.

52

The first and most necessary aspect of philosophy is that of dealing with philosophical propositions, such as "not to hold to falsehood." The second is that of demonstrations, for example, "How come one must not hold to falsehood?" The third is that of the confirmation and articulation of these, for example. "How come this is a demonstration? What is demonstration? What is entailment? What is conflict? What is truth? What is falsity?" Therefore the third is necessary because of the second, and the second because of the first; but the most necessary, and the one where one must rest, is the first. We, however, do it backwards, since we spend time in the third and all of our effort goes into it, and we neglect the first completely. Therefore we hold to falsehood, but we are ready to explain how it is demonstrated that one must not hold to falsehood.

53

On every occasion you must have these thoughts ready:

Lead me, Zeus, and you too, Destiny,
Wherever I am assigned by you;
I'll follow and not hesitate,
But even if I do not wish to,
Because I'm bad, I'll follow anyway.

Whoever has complied well with necessity
Is counted wise by us, and understands divine
  affairs.

Well, Crito, if it is pleasing to the gods this
  way, then let it happen this way.

Anytus and Meletus can kill me, but they
  can't harm me.[30]

---

30. [These four bits of poetry have the following origins. The first is by Cleanthes, who was head of the Stoic school at Athens between Zeno and Chrysippus. The second is a fragment of Euripides (fr. 965 Nauck). The third is Plato, *Crito* 43d, and the fourth is Plato, *Apology* 30c–d (slightly modified as compared with our manuscript texts), both purporting to be quotations from Socrates (cf. n. 8).]

Augustine

During the second through the fifth centuries or so of the Christian Era, Christian apologists began to graft the shoots of the New Testament onto the roots of Platonism, Aristotelianism, and Stoicism. Such husbandry was the work of the Fathers of the Church; hence, this part of the Christian Era is sometimes called the Patristic Era.

Indisputably the greatest of the Church Fathers was St. Augustine (A.D. 354–430). Born in the North African town of Thagaste (now Souk-Ahras, Algeria), Augustine was sent to Carthage in 370 to receive an education in rhetoric, preparatory to a career in law. Not only was Carthage then renowned for education in rhetoric and law, it was also, by Augustine's account, famous for its iniquity, in which he indulged himself freely. In Carthage Augustine first heard of Manicheanism, a dualistic Oriental religion he followed for some nine years. Augustine was attracted to the Manicheans by their swift solution to the problem of evil; that is, the problem of why an all-good, all-powerful God permits the existence of evil in the world. The Manicheans held that counterpoised to God is an all-powerful malignant force, and the world continually exhibits the endless strife between these two.

Following his education, Augustine taught rhetoric in Thagaste, Carthage, and Rome, and in 384 secured a position as a professor of rhetoric at Milan. His disenchantment with Manicheanism had been growing through the years, and by then it was complete; but still tormented by the problem of evil, he had settled for skepticism. While in Milan he encountered two influences which had a profound effect on his life: St. Ambrose, then bishop of Milan, and the writings of the Neoplatonists. Augustine heard many of the sermons given by Ambrose and was deeply moved by them. He also read, in Latin translation, some of the writings of such Neoplatonist philosophers as Plotinus (205–270), who claimed to be perfecting the philosophy of Plato. These two sources convinced him that his reservations about Christianity were ill founded. In particular, he now thought he saw a way out of the impasse created by the problem of evil: since everything that exists is created by God, and everything created by God is good, there could be no all-powerful, perfectly malign being continually thwarting God's efforts. It follows, then, according to Augustine, that evil is nonexistent. As Augustine would have it, evil is not the *presence* of something that exists, but rather the *absence* of something, namely, goodness. Augustine finally converted to Christianity in 386, and was baptized in Milan in the next year. After his conversion he returned to Africa, where he was ordained as priest in the city of Hippo. He rose rapidly in the ecclesiastical ranks to become the bishop of Hippo, a position he held until his death. He died in 430 as the Vandals were preparing to lay siege to Hippo.

Augustine's prodigious writings cover virtually every aspect of Christian experience, since he spent much of his adult life seeking to define Christianity and defend it not only from the attacks of nonbelievers but also from the challenges of several types of heretical Christians. For example, in addition to combating the Manicheans, Augustine also wrote several treatises against the members of a schismatic North African sect, the Donatists, who maintained that the sacraments, if administered by a sinful priest, had no validity. Augustine also took issue with the Pelagians, who denied the doctrine of original sin, claiming that Adam and Eve's sin was not transmitted to their descendants. The Pelagians believed that God's grace was not necessary for human salvation, a proposition vehemently denied by Augustine. His success against Christian heretics was so complete that subsequent Christian theologians generally consider it sufficient merely to cite his authority on many doctrinal issues. Indeed, his authority was so great that it was appealed to by both sides during the Reformation controversies.

It is commonly said that Augustine Platonized Christianity. This statement must be treated cautiously, for Augustine could not have read many, if any, of Plato's dialogues. In fact, he emphatically rejected many of Plato's most characteristic doctrines, including the doctrines of reincarnation (along with the associated Platonic thesis that the body is the prison of the soul, deserved because of the soul's transgressions in a previous life); recollection (which he replaced with a doctrine of divine illumination); and the denial of moral weakness. Nevertheless, there is a Platonic core to Augustine's thinking. Plato's Forms become for Augustine eternal ideas in God's mind; and, like Plato, Augustine makes a sharp distinction between the things that exist in space or time and that which is outside space and time, the latter being perfect, the former imperfect.

Augustine's most comprehensive treatment of the problems of time constitutes Book XI of his *Confessions,* which is reprinted here. The *Confessions* is a unique book, a work which is at once autobiographical, didactic, devotional, and philosophical. The first nine books give a detailed account of Augustine's life up to and including his conversion to Christianity. In Book XI, however, the issues are strictly theological and philosophical. Augustine begins with the question, "What was God doing before He created Heaven and Earth?" His treatment of this question leads him to consider the further question, "How is it possible to measure time?" which invokes the more general question, "What is time?" The honesty and evident self-perplexity with which he grapples with these difficult questions have attracted many contemporary philosophers to this book of the *Confessions.*

• • •

A serviceable biography of Augustine's life is Peter Brown, *Augustine of Hippo: A Biography* (Berkeley: University of California Press, 1967), which also contains information about English translations of Augustine's writings. Etienne Gilson, *The Christian Philosophy of Saint Augustine* (New York: Random House, 1960) provides a clear introduction to Augustine's philosophy. R. A. Markus, ed., *Augustine: A Collection of Critical Essays* (Garden City: Doubleday, 1972) and Gareth B. Matthews, *The Augustinian Tradition* (Berkeley: University of California Press, 1998) are valuable collections of papers on Augustine's philosophy. A recent study is Christopher Kirwan, *Augustine* (London: Routledge, 1989).

W.E.M.

Confessions

Book XI

In the Beginning God Created . . .

I

But, Lord, since You are in eternity, are You unaware of what I am saying to You? Or do you see in time what takes place in time? But if You *do see*, why am I giving You an account of all these things? Not, obviously, that You should learn them from me; but I excite my own love for You and the love of those who read what I write, that we all may say: *The Lord is great, and exceedingly to be praised*. I have said before and I will say again: "It is for love of Your love that I do it." We pray [for what we want], yet Truth Himself has said: *Your Father knows what is needful for you before you ask Him*. Thus we are laying bare our love for You in confessing to You our wretchedness and Your mercies towards us: that You may free us wholly as You have already freed us in part, so that we may cease to be miserable in ourselves and come to happiness in You. For You have called us to be poor in spirit, to be meek, to mourn, to hunger and thirst after justice, to be merciful and clean of heart and peacemakers.

Thus I have told You many things, with such power and will as I had, because You, O Lord my God, had first willed that I should confess to You: *for Thou art good and Thy mercy endureth forever*.

II

But when will the voice of my pen have power to tell all Your exhortations and all Your terrors, Your consolations and the guidance by which You have brought me to be to Your people a preacher of Your word and a dispenser of Your Sacrament? Even had

Reprinted from *Confessions of St. Augustine*, translated by F. J. Sheed (New York: Sheed & Ward, 1943), by permission of the publisher. The words in brackets are amplifications by the translator. The italicized words are Biblical quotations.

I the power to set down all these things duly, the drops of my time are too precious.

For a long time now I burn with the desire to meditate upon Your law, and to confess to You both my knowledge of it and my ignorance of it—the first beginnings of Your light and what remains of my own darkness—until my weakness shall be swallowed up in Your strength. And I do not want to see scattered and wasted upon other things such time as I find free from necessary care of the body, intellectual labour, and the service which either I owe men or do not owe but render all the same.

O Lord my God, be attentive to my prayer. Let Thy mercy grant my desire, since it does not burn for myself alone, but longs to serve the charity I have for my brethren: and in my heart Thou seest that it is so. Let me offer in sacrifice to Thee the service of my mind and my tongue, and do Thou give me what I may offer Thee. For I am needy and poor, *Thou art rich unto all who call upon Thee*. Thou art free from care for Thyself and full of care for us. Circumcise the lips of my mouth and lips of my mind of all rash speech and lying. May Thy Scriptures be for my chaste delight; let me not deceive others about them nor be myself deceived. O Lord, hearken and have mercy, O Lord my God, Light of the blind and Strength of the weak, but Light too of the clear of sight and Strength of the strong; hearken to my soul, hear it crying from the depths. Unless Thine ears are attentive to us in the abyss, whither shall we go? To whom shall we cry?

Thine is the day, and Thine is the night: at Thy will the moments flow and pass. Grant me, then, space for my meditations upon the hidden things of Thy law, nor close Thy law against me as I knock. Not for nothing hast Thou willed that the deep secrets of all those pages should be written, not for nothing have those woods their *stags*, which retire to them and are restored, walk in them and are fed, lie down in them and ruminate. Complete Thy work in me, O Lord, and open those pages to me. Thy voice is my joy, abounding above all joys. Grant me what I love, for I do love it. And this too is of Thy gift. Do not abandon what Thou hast given, nor scorn Thy grass that is athirst for Thee. Let me confess to thee whatsoever I shall find in Thy books, and *let me hear the voice of thy praise*, and drink of Thee and *consider the wondrous things of Thy law* from the first beginning, when Thou didst make heaven and earth, until our everlasting reign with Thee in Thy holy city.

O Lord have mercy on me and grant what I desire. For, as I think, my desire is not of earth, not of gold and silver and gems or fine raiment or power and glory or the lusts of the flesh or the necessities of my body and of this our earthly pilgrimage: *all these things shall be added unto us who seek the Kingdom of God and Thy justice.*

See, O my God, whence comes my desire. *The wicked have told me fables but not as Thy law.* That is the source of my desire. See, Father: gaze and see and approve: and may it be pleasing in the sight of Thy mercy that I should find grace before Thee, that the inner secret of Thy words may be laid open at my knock. I beseech it by our Lord Jesus Christ Thy Son, *the Man of Thy right hand, the Son of Man, whom Thou hast confirmed for Thyself* as Mediator between Thyself and us: by whom Thou didst seek us when we sought not Thee, didst seek us indeed that we might seek Thee: Thy Word, by which Thou hast made all things and me among them: The Only One, by whom Thou hast called the people of the faithful, and me among them, unto adoption. I beseech it by Him who sits at Thy right hand and makes intercession for us, *in whom are hidden all the treasures of wisdom and knowledge.* These treasures are what I seek in Thy books. Moses wrote of Him: this He says, who is Truth.

III

Grant me to hear and understand what is meant by *In the beginning You made heaven and earth.* For so Moses wrote, wrote and went his way: passed from this world to You and is no longer here before me. Were he here, I should lay hold of him, and ask him, and in Your name beg him, to explain the sense of those words to me; I should lend my bodily ear to the sounds that should issue from his mouth. If he spoke in Hebrew, his voice would beat upon my ear to no purpose, nothing of what it said would reach

my mind: if he spoke in Latin, I should know what he said. But how should I know that what he said was true? And if I did know it, would it be from him that I knew it? No: but within me, in the inner retreat of my mind, the Truth, which is neither Hebrew nor Greek, nor Latin, nor Barbarian, would tell me, without lips or tongue or sounded syllables: "He speaks truth:" and I (at once assured) would say to Your servant in all confidence: "You speak truth." Since, then, I cannot question him, I ask Thee, the Truth, filled with whom Moses spoke truth: I ask Thee, my God: pardon my sins, and as Thou didst grant to Thy servant to speak those words, grant me to understand them.

IV

We look upon the heavens and the earth, and they cry aloud that they were made. For they change and vary. (If anything was not made and yet exists, there is nothing in it that was not there before: and it is the essence of change and variation that something should be that was not there before.) They cry aloud, too, that they did not make themselves. "We exist, because we were made; but we did not exist before we existed to be able to give ourselves existence!" And their visible presence is itself the voice with which they speak.

It was You, Lord, who made them: for You are beautiful, and they are beautiful: You are good, and they are good: You are, and they are. But they neither are beautiful nor are good nor simply are as You their Creator: compared with You they are not beautiful and are not good and are not. These truths, thanks to You, we know; and our knowledge compared with Your knowledge is ignorance.

V

But *how* did You make heaven and earth? What instrument did You use for a work so mighty? You are not like an artist; for he forms one body from another as his mind chooses; his mind has the power to give external existence to the form it perceives within itself by its inner eye—and whence should it have that power unless You made it? It impresses that form upon a material already existent and having the capacity to be thus formed, such as clay or stone or wood or gold or such like. And how should these things have come to be unless You had made them to be? It was You who made the workman his body, and the mind that directs his limbs, the matter of which he makes what he makes, the intelligence by which he masters his art and sees inwardly what he is to produce exteriorly, the bodily sense by which he translates what he does from his mind to his material, and then informs the mind of the result of his workmanship, so that the mind may judge by that truth which presides within it whether the work is well done.

All these things praise You, the Creator of them all. But how do You create them? How, O God, did You create heaven and earth? Obviously it was not *in* heaven or on earth that You made heaven and earth; nor in the air nor in the waters, since these belong to heaven and earth; nor did You make the universe in the universe, because there was no place for it to be made in until it was made. Nor had You any material in Your hand when You were making heaven and earth: for where should You have got what You had not yet made to use as material? What exists, save because You exist? You spoke and heaven and earth were created; in Your word You created them.

VI

But *how* did You speak? Was it perhaps as when that voice sounded from the cloud saying: *This is my beloved Son?* That voice sounded and ceased to sound, had a beginning and an end. The syllables sounded and died away, the second after the first, the third after the second, and so in order, until the last after the rest, and silence after the last. From this it is clear beyond question that that voice was sounded by the movement of something created by You, a movement in time but serving Your eternal will.

These words were uttered in time and the bodily ear conveyed them to the understanding mind, whose spiritual ear is attuned to Your eternal Word. And the mind compared these words sounding in time with Your eternal Word and its silence: and it said: "It is other, far other. These words are far less than I, indeed they are not at all, for they pass away and are no more: but the Word of God is above me and endures for ever."

Thus, had it been by words sounding and passing away that You said "Let heaven and earth be made," and so created heaven and earth, there would have had to be some bodily creature before heaven and earth, by the movement of which in time that voice came and went in time.

But there was no bodily thing before heaven and earth: or if there were then certainly You did not use some still earlier utterance in time to produce it, that by it You might utter in time the decree that heaven and earth should be made. Whatever it may have been that produced such a voice, it must have been made by You, otherwise it would not have existed at all. But to produce the bodily thing capable of uttering those words, what word did You utter?

VII

Clearly You are calling us to the realization of that Word—God with You, God as You are God—which is uttered eternally and by which all things are uttered eternally.

For this is not an utterance in which what has been said passes away that the next thing may be said and so finally the whole utterance be complete: but all in one act, yet abiding eternally: otherwise it would be but time and change and no true eternity, no true immortality.

I know it, O my God, and I give You thanks. I know it, Lord, I confess it to You: and every man knows it as I do and praises You as I do who is not ungrateful for Your sure truth. We know, Lord, we know, that in the degree that anything is no longer what it was, and is now what it once was not, it is in the process of dying and beginning anew. But of Your Word nothing passes or comes into being, for it is truly immortal and eternal. Thus it is by a Word coeternal with Yourself that in one eternal act You say all that You say, and all things are made that You say are to be made. You create solely by thus saying. Yet all the things You create by saying are not brought into being in one act and from eternity.

VIII

Tell me, O Lord my God, how this can be? In a kind of way I see, but how to express it I do not know: save that whatever comes into being and ceases to be, begins at the moment and ends at the moment

when the eternal reason—which has in itself no beginning or ending—knows that it should begin or
end. That eternal reason is Your Word, *the Beginning
who also speaks unto us.* This He tells us in the Gospel
to our bodily ear, this He uttered exteriorly in the
ears of men: that we might believe in Him, and seek
Him within us and find Him in the eternal Truth,
where the one good Master teaches all His disciples.

There it is that I hear Your voice, Lord, telling me
that only one who teaches us is speaking to us, and
that whoever does not teach us may be speaking, but
not to us. Yet who teaches us save Truth unchanging?
When from changing creatures we learn anything,
we are led to Truth that does not change: and there
we truly learn, as we stand and hear Him and rejoice
with you for the voice of the bridegroom, returning
to the Source of our being. Thus it is that He is the
Beginning: unless He remained when we wandered
away, there should be no abiding place for our return.
But when we return from error, we return by realizing
the Truth; that we may realize it, He instructs us for
He is the *Beginning who also speaks unto us.*

IX

This then, O God, was the Beginning in which You
created Heaven and Earth: marvellously speaking and
marvellously creating in Your Word, Who is Your
Son and Your Strength and Your Wisdom and Your
Truth. Who shall understand this? Who shall relate
it? What is that light which shines upon me but
not continuously, and strikes upon my heart with no
wounding? I draw back in terror: I am on fire with
longing: terror in so far as I am different from it,
longing in the degree of my likeness to it. It is Wisdom,
Wisdom Itself, which in those moments shines upon
me, cleaving through my cloud. And the cloud returns to wrap me round once more as my strength is
beaten down under its darkness and the weight of
my sins: for *my strength is weakened through poverty,*
so that I can no longer support my good, until Thou,
Lord who art merciful to my iniquities, shall likewise
heal my weakness: redeeming my life from corruption
and crowning me with pity and compassion, and
filling my desire with good things: *my youth shall be
renewed like the eagle's. For we are saved by hope and
we wait with patience for Thy promises.*

Let him who can hear Thy voice speaking within

him; I, relying upon Thy inspired word, shall cry
aloud: *How great are Thy works, O Lord! Thou has
made all things in wisdom.* Wisdom is "the Beginning": and it is in that Beginning that You made
heaven and earth

X

Surely those are still in their ancient error who say
to us: "What was God doing before He made heaven
and earth?" If, they say, He was at rest and doing
nothing, why did He not continue to do nothing for
ever after as for ever before? If it was a new movement
and a new will in God to create something He had
never created before, how could that be a true eternity
in which a will should arise which did not exist before?
For the will of God is not a creature: it is prior to
every creature, since nothing would be created unless
the will of the Creator first so willed. The will of
God belongs to the very substance of God. Now if
something arose in the substance of God which was
not there before, that substance could not rightly be
called eternal; but if God's will that creatures should
be is from eternity, why are creatures not from
eternity?

XI

Those who speak thus do not yet understand You, O
Wisdom of God, Light of minds: they do not yet
understand how the things are made that are made
by You and in You. They strive for the savour of
eternity, but their mind is still tossing about in the
past and future movements of things, and is still vain.

Who shall lay hold upon their mind and hold it
still, that it may stand a little while, and a little while
glimpse the splendour of eternity which stands for
ever: and compare it with time whose moments never
stand, and see that it is not comparable. Then indeed
it would see that a long time is long only from the
multitude of movements that pass away in succession,
because they cannot co-exist: that in eternity nothing
passes but all is present, whereas time cannot be
present all at once. It would see that all the past is
thrust out by the future, and all the future follows
upon the past, and past and future alike are wholly
created and upheld in their passage by that which is
always present? Who shall lay hold upon the mind

of man, that it may stand and see that time with its past and future must be determined by eternity, which stands and does not pass, which has in itself no past or future. Could my hand have the strength [so to lay hold upon the mind of man] or could my mouth by its speaking accomplish so great a thing?

XII

I come now to answer the man who says: "What was God doing before He made Heaven and earth?" I do not give the jesting answer—said to have been given by one who sought to evade the force of the question—"He was getting Hell ready for people who pry too deep." To poke fun at a questioner is not to see the answer. My reply will be different. I would much rather say "I don't know," when I don't, than hold one up to ridicule who had asked a profound question and win applause for a worthless answer.

But, O my God, I say that You are the Creator of all creation, and if by the phrase heaven and earth we mean all creation, then I make bold to reply: Before God made heaven and earth, He did not make anything. For if He had made something, what would it have been but a creature? And I wish I knew all that it would be profitable for me to know, as well as I know that no creature was made before any creature was made.

XIII

But a lighter mind, adrift among images of time and its passing, might wonder that You, O God almighty and all-creating and all-conserving, Maker of heaven and earth, should have abstained from so vast a work for the countless ages that passed before You actually wrought it. Such a mind should awaken and realize how ill-grounded is his wonder.

How could countless ages pass when You, the Author and Creator of all ages, had not yet made them? What time could there be that You had not created? or how could ages pass, if they never were?

Thus, since You are the Maker of all times, if there actually was any time before You made heaven and earth, how can it be said that You were not at work? If there was time, You made it, for time could not pass before You made time. On the other hand, if before heaven and earth were made there was no time, then what is meant by the question "What were You doing *then?*" If there was not any time, there was not any "then."

It is not in time that You are before all time: otherwise You would not be before all time. You are before all the past by the eminence of Your ever-present eternity: and You dominate all the future in as much as it is still to be: and once it has come it will be past: but *Thou art always the self-same and Thy years shall not fail.* Your years neither go nor come: but our years come and go, that all may come. Your years abide all in one act of abiding: for they abide and the years that go are not thrust out by those that come, for none pass: whereas our years shall not be, till all are no more. Your years are as a single day; and Your day comes not daily but is today, a today which does not yield place to any tomorrow or follow upon any yesterday. In You today is eternity: thus it is that You begot one co-eternal with Yourself to whom you said: *Today have I begotten Thee.* You are the Maker of all time, and before all time You are, nor was there ever a time when there was no time!

XIV

At no time then had You not made anything, for time itself You made. And no time is co-eternal with You, for You stand changeless; whereas if time stood changeless, it would not be time. What then is time? Is there any short and easy answer to that? Who can put the answer into words or even see it in his mind? Yet what commoner or more familiar word do we use in speech than time? Obviously when we use it, we know what we mean, just as when we hear another use it, we know what he means.

What then *is* time? If no one asks me, I know; if I want to explain it to a questioner, I do not know. But at any rate this much I dare affirm I know: that if nothing passed there would be no past time; if nothing were approaching, there would be no future time; if nothing were, there would be no present time.

But the two times, past and future, how can they *be,* since the past is no more and the future is not yet? On the other hand, if the present were always present and never flowed away into the past, it would not be time at all, but eternity. But if the present is only time, because it flows away into the past, how can we say that it *is?* For it is, only because it will cease to be. Thus we can affirm that time *is* only in that it tends towards not-being.

XV

Yet we speak of a long time or a short time, applying these phrases only to past or future. Thus for example we call a hundred years ago a long time past, and a hundred years hence a long time ahead, and ten days ago a short time past, ten days hence a short time ahead. But in what sense can that which does not exist be long or short? The past no longer is, the future is not yet. Does this mean that we must not say: "It is long," but of the past "It was long," of the future "It will be long?"

O, my Lord, my Light, here too man is surely mocked by Your truth! If we say the past was long, was it long when it was already past or while it was still present? It could be long only while it was in existence to *be* long. But the past no longer exists; it cannot be long, because it is not at all.

Thus we must not say that the past was long: for we shall find nothing in it capable of being long, since, precisely because it is past, it is not at all. Let us say then that a particular time was long while it was present, because in so far as it was present, it was long. For it had not yet passed away and so become non-existent; therefore it still was something, and therefore capable of being long: though once it passed away, it ceased to be long by ceasing to be.

Let us consider, then, O human soul, whether present time can be long: for it has been given you to feel and measure time's spaces. What will you answer me?

Are the present hundred years a long time? But first see whether a hundred years *can* be present. If it is the first year of the hundred, then that year is present, but the other ninety-nine are still in the future, and so as yet are not: if we are in the second year, then one year is past, one year is present, the rest future. Thus whichever year of our hundred-year period we choose as present, those before it have passed away, those after it are still to come. Thus a hundred years cannot be present.

But now let us see if the chosen year is itself present. If we are in the first month, the others are still to come, if in the second, the first has passed away and the rest are not yet. Thus a year is not wholly present

while it runs, and if the whole of it is not present, then the year is not present. For a year is twelve months, and the month that happens to be running its course is the only one present, the others either are no longer or as yet are not. Even the current month is not present, but only one day of it: if that day is the first, the rest are still to come; if the last, the rest are passed away; if somewhere between, it has days past on one side and days still to come on the other.

Thus the present, which we have found to be the only time capable of being long, is cut down to the space of scarcely one day. But if we examine this one day, even it is not wholly present. A day is composed of twenty-four hours — day-hours, night-hours: the first hour finds the rest still to come, the last hour finds the rest passed away, any hour between has hours passed before it, hours to come after it. And that one hour is made of fleeing moments: so much of the hour as has fled away is past, what still remains is future. If we conceive of some point of time which cannot be divided into even the minutest parts of moments, that is the only point that can be called present: and that point flees at such lightning speed from being future to being past, that it has no extent of duration at all. For if it were so extended, it would be divisible into past and future: the present has no length.

Where, then, is there a time that can be called long? Is it the future? But we cannot say of the future "It is long" because as yet it is not at all and therefore is not long. We say "It will be long." By when will it be long? While it is still in the future, it will not be long, because it does not yet exist and so cannot be long. Suppose we say, then, that it is to be long only when, coming out of the future [which is not yet], it begins to be and is now present — and thus something, and thus capable of being long. But the present cries aloud, as we have just heard, that it cannot have length.

XVI

Yet, Lord, we are aware of periods of time; we compare one period with another and say that some are longer, some shorter. We measure how much one is longer than another and say that it is double, or triple, or single, or simply that one is as long as the other. But it is time actually passing that we measure by our awareness; who can measure times past which are now no more or times to come which are not yet, unless you are prepared to say that that which does not exist can be measured? Thus while time is passing, it can be perceived and measured; but when it has passed it cannot, for it *is* not.

XVII

I am seeking, Father, not saying: O, my God, aid me and direct me.

Perhaps it might be said that there are not three times, past, present and future, as we learnt in boyhood and have taught boys: but only present, because the other two do not exist. Or perhaps that these two do exist, but that time comes forth from some secret place when from future it becomes present, and departs into some secret place when from present it becomes past. For where have those who prophesied the future seen the future, if it does not yet exist? What does not exist cannot be seen. And those who describe the past could not describe it truly if they did not mentally see it: and if the past were totally without existence it would be totally impossible to see it. Hence both past and future must exist.

XVIII

Suffer me, Lord, to push my inquiry further; O my Hope, let not my purpose go awry.

If the future and the past exist, I want to know where they are. And if I cannot yet know this, at least I do know that wherever they are, they are there not as future or past, but present. If wherever they are they are future, then in that place they are not yet; if past, then they are there no more. Thus wherever they are and whatever they are, they *are* only as present. When we relate the past truly, it is not the things themselves that are brought forth from our memory— for these have passed away: but words conceived from the images of the things: for the things stamped their prints upon the mind as they passed through it by way of the senses. Thus for example my boyhood, which no longer exists, is in time past, which no longer exists; but the likeness of my boyhood, when I recall it and talk of it, I look upon in time present, because it is still present in my memory.

Whether the case is similar with prophecies of things to come—namely that images of things which are not yet are seen in advance as now existent—I confess, O my God, that I do not know. But this I do know, that we ordinarily consider our future actions in advance, and that this consideration is present, but the action we are thinking of does not yet exist, because it is future; when we have actually set about it and have begun to do what we planned, then that action will exist, because then it will not be future but present.

Whatever may be the mode of this mysterious foreseeing of things to come, unless the thing is it cannot be seen. But what now is, is not future but present. Therefore when we speak of seeing the future, obviously what is seen is not the things which are not yet because they are still to come, but their causes or perhaps the signs that foretell them, for these causes and signs do exist here and now. Thus to those who see them now, they are not future but present, and from them things to come are conceived by the mind and foretold. These concepts already exist, and those who foretell are gazing upon them, present within themselves.

Let me take one example from a vast number of such things.

I am looking at the horizon at dawn: I foretell that the sun is about to rise. What I am looking at is present, what I foretell is future—not the sun, of course, for it now is, but its rising which is not yet. But unless I could imagine the actual rising in my mind, as now when I speak of it, I could not possibly foretell it. But the dawn which I see in the sky is not the sunrise, although it precedes the sunrise; nor is the dawn the image of the sunrise that is in my mind. But both—the dawn and the image of the sunrise— are present and seen by me, so that the sunrise which is future can be told in advance. Thus the future is not yet; and if it is not yet, it is not; and if it is not, then it is totally impossible to see it. But it can be foretold from things present which now exist and are seen.

XIX

But You, O Ruler of Your creation, how is it that you can show souls things that are to come? For such things You have told Your prophets. In what manner do You show the future to man, for whom nothing future yet is? Or do You show only present signs of things to come? For what does not exist obviously cannot be shown. The means You use is altogether beyond my gaze; my eyes have not the strength; of myself I shall never be able to see so deep, but in You I shall be able, when you grant it, O lovely Light of the eyes of my spirit.

XX

At any rate it is now quite clear that neither future nor past actually exists. Nor is it right to say there are three times, past, present and future. Perhaps it would be more correct to say: there are three times, a present of things past, a present of things present, a present of things future. For these three exist in the mind, and I find them nowhere else: the present of things past is memory, the present of things present is sight, the present of things future is expectation. If we are allowed to speak thus, I see and admit that there are three times, that three times truly are.

By all means continue to say that there are three times, past, present and future; for, though it is incorrect, custom allows it. By all means say it. I do not mind, I neither argue nor object: provided that you understand what you are saying and do not think future or past now exists. There are few things that we phrase properly; most things we phrase badly: but what we are trying to say is understood.

XXI

I said a little while ago that we measure time in its passing, so that we are able to say that this period of time is to that as two to one, or that this is of the same duration as that, and can measure and describe any other proportions of time's parts.

Thus, as I said, we measure time *in its passing*. If you ask me how I know this, my answer is that I know it because we measure time, and we cannot measure what does not exist, and past and future do not exist. But how do we measure time present, since it has no extent? It is measured while it is passing; once it has passed, it cannot be measured, for then nothing exists to measure.

But where does time come from, and by what way does it pass, and where does it go, while we are measuring it? Where is it from?—obviously from the future. By what way does it pass?—by the present.

Where does it go?—into the past. In other words it passes from that which does not yet exist, by way of that which lacks extension, into that which is no longer.

But how are we measuring time unless in terms of some kind of duration? We cannot say single or double or triple or equal or proportioned in any other way, save of the duration of periods of time. But in what duration do we measure time while it is actually passing? In the future, from which it comes? But what does not yet exist cannot be measured. In the present, then, by which it passes? But that which has no space cannot be measured. In the past, to which it passes? But what no longer exists cannot be measured.

XXII

My mind burns to solve this complicated enigma. O Lord my God, O good Father, for Christ's sake I beseech Thee, do not shut off these obscure familiar problems from my longing, do not shut them off and leave them impenetrable but let them shine clear for me in the light of Thy mercy, O Lord. Yet whom shall I question about them? And to whom more fruitfully than to Thee shall I confess my ignorance: for Thou art not displeased at the zeal with which I am on fire for Thy Scriptures. Grant me what I love: for it is by Your gift that I love. Grant me this gift, Father, *who dost know how to give good gifts to Thy children*. Grant it because I have *studied that I might know and it is a labour in my sight* until Thou shalt open it to me. For Christ's sake I beseech Thee, in the name of Him who is the Holy of Holies, that no one prevent me. *I have believed, therefore have I spoken*. This is my hope; for this do I live, *that I may see the delight of the Lord. Behold Thou hast made my days old*, and they pass away: but how I know not.

We are forever talking of time and of times. "How long did he speak," "How long did it take him to do that," "For how long a time did I fail to see this," "This syllable is double the length of that." So we speak and so we hear others speak, and others understand us, and we them. They are the plainest and commonest of words, yet again they are profoundly obscure and their meaning still to be discovered.

XXIII

I once heard a learned man say that time is simply the movement of the sun and moon and stars. I did not agree. For why should not time rather be the movement of all bodies? Supposing the lights of heaven were to cease and the potter's wheel moved on, would there not be time by which we could measure its rotations and say that these were at equal intervals, or some slower, some quicker, some taking longer, some shorter? And if we spoke thus, should we not ourselves be speaking in time: would there not be in our words some syllables long, some short—because some would sound for a longer time, some for a shorter?

O God, grant unto men to see by some small example the elements in common between small things and great. There are stars and the lights of heaven *to be for signs and for seasons and for days and years.* This is evident; but just as I would not affirm that one turn of that little wooden wheel is a day, neither should my philosopher say that it is no time at all.

What I am trying to come at is the force and nature of time, by which we measure the movement of bodies and say for example that this movement is twice as long as that. A day means not only the length of time that the sun is above the earth—so that we distinguish day from night—but the time of the sun's whole circuit from east to east—as we say that so many days have passed, so many days being used to include their nights, for the nights are not reckoned separately. Thus, since a day is constituted by the movement of the sun and its completed circle from east to east, I wish to know whether a day is that movement itself, or simply the time the movement takes, or both.

If the movement of the sun through one complete circuit were the day, then it would be a day even if the sun sped through its course in a space of time equal to an hour. If the time the sun now takes to complete its circuit is the day, then it would not be a day if between one sunrise and the next there were only the space of an hour: the sun would have to go around twenty-four times to make one day. But if to constitute a day there is needed both the movement of the sun through one circuit and the time the sun now takes, then you would not have a day if the sun completed its whole circuit in an hour, nor again if the sun stood still and as much time passed as the sun normally takes to complete its journey from one morning to the next.

But I shall not at the moment pursue the question of what it is that we call a day. I shall continue to seek what time is, by which we measure the sun's journey: so that we should say that it had gone round in half its accustomed time, if it went round in a space of time equivalent to twelve hours. And comparing its normal time with this twelve-hour time, we should say that the latter was single, the former double; yet the sun would in the one case have made its journey from east to east in the shorter time, in the other in the longer (so that time is something independent of the sun's movement).

Let no one tell me that the movement of the heavenly bodies is time: when at the prayer of a man the sun stood still that he might complete his victory in battle, the sun stood still but time moved on. The battle was continued for the necessary length of time and was finished.

Therefore I see time as in some way extended. But do I see it? Or do I only seem to see it? Thou wilt show me, O Light, O Truth.

XXIV

Would You have me agree with one who said that time is the movement of a body? You would not: for I learn that no body moves save in time: You have said it. But I do not learn that the movement of the body is time: You have not said it. For when a body is in motion, it is by time that I measure how long it is in motion from the beginning of its movement till it ceases to move. And if I did not see when the movement began, and if it moved on without my seeing when it ceased, I should be able to measure only from the movement I began to look until the moment I stopped looking. If I looked for a long time, all I can say is that the time is long, but not how long it is, because when we say how long a time, we say it by comparison: as for example: this is as long as that, or this is twice that, and such like. But if we could note the point of space from which a body in motion comes or the point to which it goes, or could distinguish its parts if it is moving on its axis, we should be able to say how much time has elapsed for the movement of the body, or its part, from one place to another.

Thus since the movement of a body is not the same as our measurement of how long the movement takes, who can fail to see which of these is more deserving of the name of time? A body moves at different speeds, and sometimes stands still; but time enables us to measure not only its motion but its rest as well; and we say "It was at rest for the same length of time as it was in motion," or "It was at rest twice or thrice as long as it was in motion" or any other proportion, whether precisely measured or roughly estimated.

Therefore time is not the movement of a body.

XXV

I confess to You, Lord, that I still do not know what time is. And again I confess to You, Lord, that I know that I am uttering these things in time: I have been talking of time for a long time, and this long time would not be a long time unless time had passed. But how do I know this, since I do not know what time is? Or perhaps I do know, but simply do not know how to express what I know. Alas for me, I do not even know what I do not know! See me, O my God, I stand before You and I do not lie: as my speech is, so is my heart. *For Thou lightest my lamp, O Lord; O my God, enlighten my darkness.*

XXVI

Does not my soul speak truly to You when I say that I can measure time? For so it is, O Lord my God, I measure it and I do not know what it is that I am measuring. I measure the movement of a body, using time to measure it by. Do I not then measure time itself? Could I measure the movement of a body— its duration and how long it takes to move from place to place—if I could not measure the time in which it moves?

But if so, what do I use to measure time with? Do we measure a longer time by a shorter one, as we measure a beam in terms of cubits? Thus we say that the duration of a long syllable is measured by the space of a short syllable and is said to be double. Thus we measure the length of poems by the lengths of the lines, and the lengths of the lines by the lengths of the feet, and the lengths of the feet by the lengths of the syllables, and the lengths of long syllables by the lengths of short. We do not measure poems by pages, for that would be to measure space not time; we measure by the way the voice moves in uttering the poem, and we say: "It is a long poem, for it consists of so many lines; the lines are long for they

are composed of so many feet; the feet are long for they include so many syllables; this syllable is long for it is the double of a short syllable."

But not by all this do we arrive at an exact measure of time. It may well happen that a shorter line may take longer if it is recited slowly than a longer line hurried through. And the same is true of a poem or a foot or a syllable.

Thus it seems to me that time is certainly extendedness—but I do not know what it is extendedness of: probably of the mind itself. Tell me, O my God, what am I measuring, when I say either, with no aim at precision, that one period is longer than the other, or precisely, that one is double the other? That I measure time, I know. But I do not measure the future, for it is not yet; nor the present, for it is not extended in space; nor the past, which no longer exists. So what do I measure? Is it time in passage but not past? So I have already said.

XXVII

Persevere, O my soul, fix all the power of your gaze. *God is our helper. He made us, and not we ourselves.* Fix your gaze where truth is whitening toward the dawn.

Consider the example of a bodily voice. It begins to sound, it sounds and goes on sounding, then it ceases: and now there is silence, the sound has passed, the sound no longer is. It was future before it began to sound, and so could not be measured, for as yet it did not exist; and now it cannot be measured because now it exists no longer. Only while sounding could it be measured for then it was, and so was measurable. But even then it was not standing still; it was moving, and moving out of existence. Did this make it more measurable? Only in the sense that by its passing it was spread over a certain space of time which made it measurable: for the present occupies no space.

At any rate, let us grant that it could be measured. And now again imagine a voice. It begins to sound and goes on sounding continuously without anything to break its even flow. Let us measure it, while it is sounding. For when it has ceased to sound, it will be past and will no longer be measurable. Let us measure it then and say how long it is. But it is still sounding and can be measured only from its beginning when it began to sound to its end, when it ceased. For what we measure is the interval between some starting point and some conclusion. This means that a sound which is not yet over cannot be measured so that we may say how long or short it is, nor can it be said either to be equal to some other sound or single or double or any other proportion in relation to it. But when it *is* over, it will no longer be. Then how will it be possible to measure it? Yet we do measure time—not that which is not yet, nor that which is no longer, nor that which has no duration, nor that which lacks beginning and end. Thus it seems that we measure neither time future nor time past nor time present nor time passing: and yet we measure time.

Deus creator omnium:[1] This line is composed of eight syllables, short and long alternately: the four short syllables, the first, third, fifth, seventh are single in relation to the four long syllables, the second, fourth, sixth, eighth. Each long syllable has double the time of each short syllable. I pronounce them and I say that it is so, and so it is, as is quite obvious to the ear. As my ear distinguishes I measure a long syllable by a short and I perceive that it contains it twice. But since I hear a syllable only when the one before it has ceased—the one before being short and the one following long—how am I to keep hold of the short syllable, and how shall I set it against the long one to measure it and find that the long one is twice its length—given that the long syllable does not begin to sound until the short one has ceased? And again can I measure the long one while it is present, since I cannot measure it until it is completed? And its completion is its passing out of existence.

What then is it that I measure? Where is the short syllable by which I measure? Where is the long syllable which I measure? Both have sounded, have fled away, have gone into the past, are now no more: yet I do measure, and I affirm with confidence, in so far as a practised sense can be trusted, that one is single, the other double, in the length of time it occupies. And I could not do this unless they had both passed away and ended. Thus it is not the syllables themselves that I measure, for they are now no more, but something which remains engraved in my memory.

1. [God, the creator of all.—S.M.C.]

It is in you, O my mind, that I measure time. Do not bring against me, do not bring against yourself the disorderly throng of your impressions. In you, I say, I measure time. What I measure is the impress produced in you by things as they pass and abiding in you when they have passed: and it is present. I do not measure the things themselves whose passage produced the impress; it is the impress that I measure when I measure time. Thus either that is what time is, or I am not measuring time at all.

But when we measure silences, and say that some particular silence lasted as long as some particular phrase, do we not stretch our mind to measure the phrase as though it were actually sounded, so as to be able to form a judgment of the relation between the space of the silence and that space of time? For without voice or lips we can go through poems and verses and speeches in our minds, and we can allow for the time it takes for their movement, one part in relation to another, exactly as if we were reciting them aloud. If a man decides to utter a longish sound and settles in his mind how long the sound is to be, he goes through that space of time in silence, entrusts it to his memory, then begins to utter the sound, and it sounds until it reaches the length he had fixed for it. Or rather I should say [not that it sounds but] that it has sounded and will sound: for as much of it as has been uttered at a given moment has obviously sounded, and what remains will sound: and so he completes the sound: at every moment his attention, which is present, causes the future to make its way into the past, the future diminishing and the past growing, until the future is exhausted and everything is past.

XXVIII

But how is the future diminished or exhausted, since the future does not yet exist: or how does the past grow, since it no longer is? Only because, in the mind which does all this, there are three acts. For the mind expects, attends and remembers: what it expects passes, by way of what it attends to, into what it remembers. Would anyone deny that the future is as yet not existent? But in the mind there is already an expectation of the future. Would anyone deny that the past no longer exists? Yet still there is in the mind a memory of the past. Would anyone deny that the present time lacks extension, since it is but a point that passes on? Yet the attention endures, and by it that which is to be passes on its way to being no more. Thus it is not the future that is long, for the future does not exist: a long future is merely a long expectation of the future; nor is the past long since the past does not exist: a long past is merely a long memory of the past.

Suppose that I am about to recite a psalm that I know. Before I begin, my expectation is directed to the whole of it; but when I have begun, so much of it as I pluck off and drop away into the past becomes matter for my memory; and the whole energy of the action is divided between my memory, in regard to what I have said, and my expectation, in regard to what I am still to say. But there is a present act of attention, by which what was future passes on its way to becoming past. The further I go in my recitation, the more my expectation is diminished and my memory lengthened, until the whole of my expectation is used up when the action is completed and has passed wholly into my memory. And what is true of the whole psalm, is true for each part of the whole, and for each syllable: and likewise for any longer action, of which the canticle may be only a part: indeed it is the same for the whole life of man, of which all a man's actions are parts: and likewise for the whole history of the human race, of which all the lives of all men are parts.

XXIX

But *The mercy is better than lives*, and behold my life is but a scattering. *Thy right hand has held me up* in my Lord, the Son of Man who is the Mediator in many things and in divers manners—that *I may apprehend by Him in whom I am apprehended* and may be set free from what I once was, following your Oneness: *forgetting the things that are behind* and not poured out upon things to come and things transient, but *stretching forth to those that are before* (not by dispersal but by concentration of energy) *I press towards the prize of the supernal vocation*, where *I may hear the voice of Thy praise* and contemplate Thy delight which neither comes nor passes away.

But now my years are wasted in sighs, and Thou, O Lord, my eternal Father, art my only solace; but I am divided up in time, whose order I do not know,

and my thoughts and the deepest places of my soul are torn with every kind of tumult until the day when I shall be purified and melted in the fire of Thy love and wholly joined to Thee.

XXX

And I shall stand and be established in You, in my own true form, in Your truth. I shall no longer suffer the questions of men who, by a disease they have merited for their punishment, ever thirst for more than they can drink. Thus they ask: "What was God making before He made Heaven and earth?" "Or how did the idea of creating something come into His mind whereas He had never created anything before?"

Grant them, Lord, to think well what they are saying, and to realize that one cannot use the word "never" when there is no time. If you say that he "never" made anything, obviously this means that He did not make anything "at any time." Let them see then that there can be no time apart from creation, and let them cease to talk such nonsense. *Let them stretch forth to the things that are before*, and let them realize that before all times You are the Eternal Creator of all times, and that no times are co-eternal with You, nor is any creature, even if there were a creature above time.

XXXI

O Lord, My God, how deep is the abyss of Thy secret, and how far from it have the consequences of my sins held me? Cleanse my eyes and let me rejoice in Thy Light. Assuredly if there were a mind of such vast knowledge and fore-knowledge that all the past and all the future were as clearly known to it as some familiar canticle is known to me, such a mind would be marvellous beyond measure, would strike us silent with awe. For to such a mind nothing would be hidden of ages past or ages still to come, any more than when I am singing my canticle anything is unknown to me of what I have sung from the beginning, of what remains to me to sing to the end. Yet far from me be it to think that You, O Creator of the Universe, Creator of souls and bodies, had only such knowledge as that of the future and the past. Far more marvellously, far more mysteriously, do You hold Your knowledge. For when a man is singing a song he knows, or hearing a song he knows, his impressions vary and his senses are divided between the expectation of sounds to come and the memory of sounds already uttered. No such thing happens to You, the immutable and eternal, the eternal Creator of minds. In the beginning You knew heaven and earth without any element of change in your knowledge; and similarly in the beginning You created Heaven and earth without any element of change in Your action. Let him who understands praise You, and let him who does not understand praise You likewise. You are the highest, and the humble of heart are Your dwelling place. For You *lift up them that are cast down*, and those do not fall who have You for their high place.

Anselm

Although he is generally referred to as St. Anselm of Canterbury, Anselm (1033–1109) was not an Englishman by birth or education. He was born in the village of Aosta, in the Piedmont area of what is now Italy. Little is known of his early years, but in 1060 he entered the Benedictine monastery at Bec, in Normandy. Then under the mastership of Lanfranc, Bec had a reputation as an excellent school. When Lanfranc left Bec in 1063, his position fell to the evidently precocious Anselm, who eventually became abbot of the monastery. In the meantime Lanfranc followed William the Conqueror to England in 1066, serving as Archbishop of Canterbury until his death in 1089. William's son, William II, allowed the see of Canterbury to remain vacant for four years, after which time Anselm was made archbishop. He may have been chosen because it was thought that given his relatively advanced age and political inexperience, he would be not a bishop but a pawn in the hands of the king and the other bishops. He turned out to be anything but manipulatable.

Most of the disputes into which Anselm entered revolved around the conflicting claims of secular and spiritual authorities in a highly feudalized society; for example, whether a bishop was a feudal servant of the king, and whether the king had the right to invest bishops with the insignia of their office. Anselm's relations with William II and with William's successor, Henry I, were so fitful that he managed to get himself exiled during the reigns of both kings.

Anselm's philosophical and theological talents are so impressive that he has been called by some the "Father of Scholasticism." His careful, painstaking methods and his insistence on the importance of reason to the life of faith anticipate the works of the great thirteenth-century thinkers' teaching in the cathedral schools. Anselm did not write a magnum opus; his writings consist of several short works, almost all devoted to the philosophical investigation of a particular theological topic. Many of the titles reveal his dominant concerns and his willingness to probe a fairly narrow issue in depth: "On Truth," "On the Fall of the Devil," "Epistle Concerning the Incarnation of the Word," "Why God Became Man," "On the Virgin Conception and on Original Sin," "On the Harmony of Foreknowledge, Predestination, and the Grace of God with Free Will."

Although Anselm's writings may seem piecemeal, the vision which inspired and suffuses them is global. He was above all a believing Christian, but one who believed that mere belief was not enough. The task imposed by belief was to show that one's beliefs were rational. For Anselm there could be no genuine conflict between Christian faith and the findings of reason. Not to support the claims of Christian faith, however, by the use of cogent arguments would be a kind of intellectual laziness. His confidence in the power of reason—not only to show that Christian belief is *consistent* but to prove that the major tenets of Christianity are true—may strike us as absurdly extreme; even by the thirteenth century we find more cautious enunciations of the harmony of faith and reason.

Anselm's *Proslogion,* reprinted in this volume, is his most famous work. In rapid order Anselm argues for the existence of God and His traditionally ascribed divine attributes, such as omnipotence, justice, mercy, simplicity, and timelessness. He concludes by attempting to sketch how great the joy of the blessed will be.

Anselm's attempt to prove the existence of God has attracted the most attention. The argument, now called the ontological argument (a title bestowed on it by Immanuel Kant), is contained in Chapter 2 (some would include Chapter 3) of the *Proslogion.* The ontological argument has been scorned by some philosophers as the most naive of verbal conjuring tricks, and praised by others as sound. Aquinas, Hume, and Kant rejected it, while Descartes, Spinoza, and Leibniz accepted it. One can find contemporary philosophers on both sides. It is hard to think of any philosophical argument that has excited and agitated philosophers more than this one. For one thing, its sheer audacity is breathtaking. Anselm claims that the existence of God can be demonstrated simply by following out the logical implications of a certain characterization of God. Thus if Anselm's argument works, atheism does not just happen to be false; it is a logically impossible position. A second source of the argument's philosophical fascination is that in order either to defend or criticize it intelligently, one is forced to probe some controversial philosophical issues. As a contemporary philosopher puts it, "Many of the most knotty and difficult problems in philosophy meet in this argument." For example, how is it possible to deny the existence of something without presupposing the existence of the very thing whose existence is denied? Is existence a property of things? Are there genuinely different modes of existence, and if so, can the same thing exist in several modes?—and so on.

Recorded criticism of the ontological argument began almost before Anselm's quill had dried, with the monk Gaunilo's attack "on behalf of the fool." (Virtually nothing is known of Gaunilo's life.) The most tantalizing point made by Guanilo is the claim that the same argument Anselm uses to demonstrate the existence of a perfect being would, if sound, also demonstrate the existence of a perfect island. To ask whether Gaunilo's criticism is telling, and whether Anselm's reply to Gaunilo is adequate, is to embark on yet another philosophical inquiry.

• • •

For a brilliant and judicious account of Anselm's life and times, consult R. W. Southern, *Saint Anselm: A Portrait in a Landscape* (Cambridge: Cambridge University Press, 1990). Jasper Hopkins, *A Companion to the Study of St. Anselm* (Minneapolis: University of Minnesota Press, 1972) provides a knowledgeable discussion of virtually all Anselm's writings, with an informative emphasis on the theological issues with which Anselm was involved.

The literature on the ontological argument is vast. Two useful anthologies are Alvin Plantinga, ed., *The Ontological Argument* (Garden City: Doubleday, 1965) and John H. Hick and Arthur C. McGill, eds., *The Many-Faced Argument* (New York: Macmillan, 1967). The former includes many of the historically important reactions to the argument, along with contemporary assessments. The latter emphasizes the diversity of approaches that have been taken to Anselm's argument.

W.E.M.

Proslogion

Prologue

After I had published, at the urging of some of my brethren, a short work as a pattern for meditation on the rational basis of faith, adopting the role of someone who, by reasoning silently to himself, investigates things he does not know, I began to wonder, when I considered that it is constructed out of a chaining together of many arguments, whether it might be possible to find a single argument that needed nothing but itself alone for proof, that would by itself be enough to show that God really exists; that he is the supreme good, who depends on nothing else, but on whom all things depend for their being and for their well-being; and whatever we believe about the divine nature. And so I often turned my thoughts to this with great diligence. Sometimes I thought I could already grasp what I was looking for, and sometimes it escaped my mind completely. Finally, I gave up hope. I decided to stop looking for something that was impossible to find. But when I tried to stifle that thought altogether, lest by occupying my mind with useless speculation it should keep me from things I could actually accomplish, it began to hound me more and more, although I resisted and fought against it. Then one day, when my violent struggle against its hounding had worn me down, the thing I had despaired of finding presented itself in the very clash of my thoughts, so that I eagerly embraced the thought I had been taking such pains to drive away.

Therefore, thinking that what I had rejoiced to discover would please a reader if it were written down, I wrote about it and about a number of other things in the work that follows, adopting the role of someone trying to raise his mind to the contemplation of God and seeking to understand what he believes. Since I had judged that neither this work nor the one I

mentioned earlier deserved to be called a book, or to bear the name of an author, and yet I did not think they ought to be sent out without so much as a title by which they might induce someone who came across them to read them, I gave each a title. The first I called "A pattern for meditation on the rational basis of faith"; the second I called "Faith seeking understanding." But since both works had been transcribed under these titles by several readers, I was encouraged by a number of people (especially by Hugo, the Most Reverend Archbishop of Lyons, Apostolic Legate to France, who commanded me by his apostolic authority) to put my own name on these works. And so, in order to do so more suitably, I named the first *Monologion*, which means a speech made to oneself, and the second *Proslogion*, which means a speech made to another.

Chapter 1

A rousing of the mind to the contemplation of God

Come now, insignificant mortal. Leave behind your concerns for a little while, and retreat for a short time from your restless thoughts. Cast off your burdens and cares; set aside your labor and toil. Just for a little while make room for God and rest a while in him. "Enter into the chamber" (Matthew 6:6) of your mind, shut out everything but God and whatever helps you to seek him, and seek him "behind closed doors" (Matthew 6:6). Speak now, my whole heart: say to God, "I seek your face; your face, Lord, do I seek" (Psalm 27:8).

Come now, O Lord my God. Teach my heart where and how to seek you, where and how to find you. Lord, if you are not here, where shall I seek you, since you are absent? But if you are everywhere, why do I not see you, since you are present? Truly "you dwell in inaccessible light" (1 Timothy 6:16). And where is this "inaccessible light"? How am I to approach an inaccessible light? Who will lead to it, so that I can see you in it? And by what signs am I to seek you? Under what aspect? I have never seen you,

Translation by Thomas Williams. Copyright © 1995. Reprinted with permission. From Anselm, *Monologion and Proslogion*, trans. Thomas Williams (Indianapolis: Hackett Publishing Company, 1996). Reprinted with permission.

O Lord my God; I do not know your face. What shall he do, O Lord Most High? What shall he do, this distant exile from you? What shall your servant do, deeply troubled by his love for you and "banished far from your face"? (Psalm 51:11) He longs to see you, but your face is too far away from him. He desires to enter your presence, but your dwelling is inaccessible. He wants to find you, but he does not know where you are. He aspires to seek you, but he does not know your face. Lord, you are my God, and you are my Lord, but I have never seen you. You have made me and remade me, you have given me every good thing that is mine, and still I do not know you. I was created so that I might see you, but I have not yet done what I was created to do.

How wretched human beings are! They have lost the very thing for which they were created. Hard and terrible was their fall! Alas! Think what they have lost and what they have found; think what they left behind and what they kept. They have lost the happiness for which they were created and found an unhappiness for which they were not created. They left behind the only source of happiness and kept what brings nothing but misery. Once "human beings ate the bread of angels" (Psalm 78:25), for which they now hunger; now they "eat the bread of sorrows" (Psalm 127:2), which once they did not know. Alas for the common lamentation of human beings, the universal outcry of the children of Adam! He was satisfied to the full; we sigh with hunger. He had everything he needed; we go begging. He happily possessed those things and abandoned them in misery; we unhappily do without them and miserably desire them, but alas, we remain empty-handed. Why did he not preserve for us, as he could easily have done, what we so woefully lack? Why did he thus shut us out from the light and cover us with darkness? Why did he take away our life and inflict death upon us? What wretches we are! Think whence we have been cast out, whither we have been driven; thrown down from so great a height, and buried so deep. From our homeland into exile; from the vision of God into our blindness; from the joy of immortality into the bitterness and terror of death. What a wretched change! From such great good into such great evil! O woeful loss, woeful sorrow, all is woeful!

Alas, wretched man that I am, one of the wretched children of Eve, far from the presence of God. What have I undertaken, and what have I accomplished? Where was I heading, and where have I come to? What was I reaching toward, and what do I long for? "I have sought the good" (Psalm 122:9), and "behold, confusion!" (Jeremiah 14:19). I was heading for God but stumbled over myself. I sought rest in my solitude but "found trials and sorrows" (Psalm 116:3) deep within. I wanted to laugh as my mind rejoiced, but I am forced to "cry out as my heart weeps" (Psalm 38:8). Joy was hoped for, but look where the sighs are closing in.

"How long, O Lord?" (Psalm 6:3) "How long, O Lord, will you forget us? How long will you turn your face from us?" (Psalm 13:1) When will you look favorably upon us and hear us? When will you "enlighten our eyes" (Psalm 13:3) and "show us your face"? (Psalm 80:3, 7, 19) When will you give yourself to us again? Look favorably upon us, O Lord; hear us, enlighten us, show yourself to us. Give yourself to us again, that it might go well for us; for without you it goes so badly for us. Take pity upon our toils and strivings after you, for without you we can do nothing. You call us; come to our aid. I beseech you, Lord: let me not sigh in despair, but let me breathe hopefully again. I beseech you, Lord: my heart is made bitter with its desolation; sweeten it with your consolation. I beseech you, Lord: in my hunger I began to seek you; let me not depart from you empty. I have come to you starving; let me not leave unsatisfied. I have come as a beggar to one who is rich, as a pitiful wretch to one who has pity; let me not go back penniless and despised. If indeed "I sigh before I eat" (Job 3:24), grant that I might eat after I sigh. Lord, I am bent double; I can only look down. Raise me up so that I can turn my gaze upwards. "My sins are heaped up over my head" and entangle me; "like a heavy burden" they weigh me down (Psalm 38:4). Extricate me; lift my burdens, "lest like a pit they swallow me up" (Psalm 69:15). Let me look up at your light, whether from afar or from the depths. Teach me how to seek you, and show yourself to me when I seek. For I cannot seek you unless you teach me how, and I cannot find you unless you show yourself to me. Let me seek you in desiring you; let me desire you in seeking you. Let me find you in loving you; let me love you in finding you.

I acknowledge, Lord, and I thank you, that you have created in me this image of you so that I may remember you, think of you, and love you. Yet this image is so eroded by my vices, so clouded by the smoke of my sins, that it cannot do what it was created to do unless you renew and refashion it. I am not trying to scale your heights, Lord; my understanding is in no way equal to that. But I do long to understand your truth in some way, your truth which my heart believes and loves. For I do not seek to understand in order to believe; I believe in order to understand. For I also believe that "Unless I believe, I shall not understand."[1]

Chapter 2
That God truly exists

Therefore, Lord, you who grant understanding to faith, grant that, insofar as you know it is useful for me, I may understand that you exist as we believe you exist, and that you are what we believe you to be. Now we believe that you are something than which nothing greater can be thought. So can it be that no such being exists, since "The fool has said in his heart, 'There is no God'"? (Psalm 14:1; 53:1) But when this same fool hears me say "something than which nothing greater can be thought," he surely understands what he hears; and what he understands exists in his understanding,[2] even if he does not understand that it exists [in reality]. For it is one thing for an object to exist in the understanding and quite another to understand that the object exists [in reality]. When a painter, for example, thinks out in advance what he is going to paint, he has it in his understanding, but he does not yet understand that it exists, since he has not yet painted it. But once he has painted it, he both has it in his understanding and understands that it exists because he has now painted it. So even the fool must admit that something than which nothing greater can be thought exists at

---

1. [Anselm is here quoting St Augustine, who was fond of using this verse (which is an older translation of Isaiah 7:9) in explaining his views on the relationship between faith and reason. — T. W.]

2. The word here translated "understanding" is *"intellectus."* The text would perhaps read better if I translated it as "intellect," but this would obscure the fact that it is from the same root as the verb *"intelligere,"* "to understand." Some of what Anselm says makes a bit more sense if this fact is constantly borne in mind.

least in his understanding, since he understands this when he hears it, and whatever is understood exists in the understanding. And surely that than which a greater cannot be thought cannot exist only in the understanding. For if it exists only in the understanding, it can be thought to exist in reality as well, which is greater. So if that than which a greater cannot be thought exists only in the understanding, then that than which a greater *cannot* be thought is that than which a greater *can* be thought. But that is clearly impossible. Therefore, there is no doubt that something than which a greater cannot be thought exists both in the understanding and in reality.

Chapter 3
That he cannot be thought not to exist

This [being] exists so truly that it cannot be thought not to exist. For it is possible to think that something exists that cannot be thought not to exist, and such a being is greater than one that can be thought not to exist. Therefore, if that than which a greater cannot be thought can be thought not to exist, then that than which a greater cannot be thought is *not* that than which a greater cannot be thought; and this is a contradiction. So that than which a greater cannot be thought exists so truly that it cannot be thought not to exist.

And this is you, O Lord our God. You exist so truly, O Lord my God, that you cannot be thought not to exist. And rightly so, for if some mind could think something better than you, a creature would rise above the Creator and sit in judgment upon him, which is completely absurd. Indeed, everything that exists, except for you alone, can be thought not to exist. So you alone among all things have existence most truly, and therefore most greatly. Whatever else exists has existence less truly, and therefore less greatly. So then why did "the fool say in his heart, 'There is no God,'" when it is so evident to the rational mind that you of all beings exist most greatly? Why indeed, except because he is stupid and a fool?

Chapter 4
*How the fool said in his heart
what cannot be thought*

But how has he said in his heart what he could not think? Or how could he not think what he said in his heart, since to say in one's heart is the same as to think? But if he really—or rather, *since* he really—thought this, because he said it in his heart, and did not say it in his heart, because he could not think it, there must be more than one way in which something is 'said in one's heart' or 'thought'. In one sense of the word, to think a thing is to think the word that signifies that thing. But in another sense, it is to understand what exactly the thing is. God can be thought not to exist in the first sense, but not at all in the second sense. No one who understands what God is can think that God does not exist, although he may say these words in his heart with no signification at all, or with some peculiar signification. For God is that than which a greater cannot be thought. Whoever understands this properly, understands that this being exists in such a way that he cannot, even in thought, fail to exist. So whoever understands that God exists in this way cannot think that he does not exist.

Thanks be to you, my good Lord, thanks be to you. For what I once believed through your grace, I now understand through your illumination, so that even if I did not want to *believe* that you exist, I could not fail to *understand* that you exist.

Chapter 5
That God is whatever it is better to be than not to be; and that he alone exists through himself, and makes all other things from nothing

Then what are you, Lord God, than whom nothing greater can be thought? What are you, if not the greatest of all beings, who alone exists through himself and made all other things from nothing? For whatever is not this is less than the greatest that can be thought, but this cannot be thought of you. What good is missing from the highest good, through which every good thing exists? And so you are just, truthful, happy, and whatever it is better to be than not to be. For it is better to be just than unjust, and better to be happy than unhappy.

Chapter 6
How God can perceive even though he is not a body

Now it is better to be percipient, omnipotent, merciful, and impassible than not. But how can you perceive if you are not a body? How can you be omnipo-

tent if you cannot do everything? How can you be both merciful and impassible? If only corporeal things can perceive, because the senses exist in a body and are directed towards bodies, then how can you perceive? For you are not a body but the highest spirit, which is better than any body.

But if to perceive is just to know, or is aimed at knowledge—for whoever perceives knows according to the appropriate sense, as, for example, we know colors through sight and flavors through taste—then it is not inappropriate to say that whatever in some way knows also in some way perceives. Therefore, Lord, although you are not a body, you are indeed supremely percipient in the sense that you supremely know all things, not in the sense that an animal knows things through its bodily senses.

Chapter 7
In what sense God is omnipotent even though there are many things he cannot do

But how are you omnipotent if you cannot do everything?[3] And how can you do everything if you cannot be corrupted, or lie, or cause what is true to be false (as, for example, to cause what has been done not to have been done), or many other such things?

Or is the ability to do these things not power but weakness? For someone who can do these things can do what is not beneficial to himself and what he ought not to do. And the more he can do these things, the more power misfortune and wickedness have over him, and the less he has over them. So whoever can do these things can do them, not in virtue of his power, but in virtue of his weakness. So when we say that he "can" do these things, it is not because he has the power to do them, but because his weakness gives something else power over him. Or else it is some other manner of speaking, such as we often use

---

3. [This chapter is full of word play in the Latin that does not all come across in English. The words for "power" (*potentia*), "weakness" (*impotentia*), and various forms of the verb "can" (*posse*)—also translated here as "have power"—all share a common stem. And the word for omnipotent (*omnipotens*) means literally "able to do everything" (*omnia potens*).]

in speaking loosely. For example, we sometimes say 'to be' instead of 'not to be,' or 'to do' instead of 'not to do' or 'to do nothing.' For often when someone denies that something exists, we say "It is as you say it is"; but it would seem more correct to say "It is not as you say it is not." Again, we say "This man is sitting just as that man is doing" or "This man is resting just as that man is doing"; but to sit is not to do anything, and to rest is to do nothing. In the same way, then, when someone is said to have the "power" to do or suffer something that is not beneficial to himself or that he ought not to do, by 'power' we really mean 'weakness.' For the more he has this "power," the more power misfortune and wickedness have over him, and the less he has over them. Therefore, Lord God, you are all the more truly omnipotent because you can do nothing through weakness, and nothing has power over you.

Chapter 8
How God is both merciful and impassible

But how are you both merciful and impassible? For if you are impassible, you do not feel compassion, and if you do not feel compassion, your heart is not sorrowful out of compassion for sorrow; and that is what being merciful is. But if you are not merciful, how is it that you are such a comfort to the sorrowful?

So how, Lord, are you both merciful and not merciful? Is it not because you are merciful in relation to us but not in relation to yourself? You are indeed merciful according to what we feel, but not according to what you feel. For when you look with favor upon us in our sorrow, we feel the effect [*effectum*] of mercy, but you do not feel the emotion [*affectum*] of mercy. So you are merciful, because you save the sorrowful and spare those who sin against you; but you are also not merciful, because you are not afflicted with any feeling of compassion for sorrow.

Chapter 9
How the one who is completely and supremely just spares the wicked and justly has mercy on them

But how do you spare the wicked if you are completely and supremely just? For how does the one who is completely and supremely just do something that is

not just? And what sort of justice is it to give everlasting life to someone who deserves eternal death? How then, O good God, good to the good and to the wicked, how do you save the wicked if this is not just and you do not do anything that is not just?

Or, since your goodness is incomprehensible, does this lie hidden in the "inaccessible light where you dwell"? (1 Timothy 6:16) It is indeed in the highest and most secret place of your goodness that the spring is hidden whence the river of your mercy flows. For although you are totally and supremely just, you are nonetheless kind even to the wicked, since you are totally and supremely good. You would be less good if you were not kind to any wicked person. For it is better to be good both to the good and to the wicked than to be good only to the good, and it is better to be good to the wicked both in punishing and in sparing them than to be good only in punishing them. So it follows that you are merciful precisely because you are totally and supremely good. And while it may be easy to see why you repay the good with good and the evil with evil, one must certainly wonder why you, who are totally just and lack for nothing, give good things to your evil and guilty creatures. O God, how exalted is your goodness! We can see the source of your mercy, and yet we cannot discern it clearly. We know whence the river flows, but we do not see the spring from which it issues. For it is out of the fullness of goodness that you are kind to sinners, while the reason why you are lies hidden in the heights of goodness. True, out of goodness you repay the good with good and the evil with evil, but the very nature of justice seems to demand this. When you give good things to the wicked, however, one knows that he who is supremely good willed to do this, and yet one wonders why he who is supremely just could have willed such a thing.

O mercy, from what rich sweetness and sweet richness you flow forth for us! O immeasurable goodness of God, how intensely ought sinners to love you! You save the just whom justice commends and set free those whom justice condemns. The just are saved with the help of their merits, sinners despite their merits. The just are saved because you look upon the good things you have given them, sinners because you overlook the evil things you hate. O immeasurable goodness that thus "surpasses all understanding"! (Philippians 4:7) Let the mercy that proceeds from your great riches come upon me. Let that which flows forth from you flow over me. Spare me through your mercy, lest you exact retribution through your justice. For even if it is difficult to understand how your mercy coexists with your justice, one must nonetheless believe that it is in no way opposed to justice, because it flows out of your goodness, and there is no goodness apart from justice—indeed, goodness is actually in harmony with justice. In fact, if you are merciful because you are supremely good, and supremely good only because you are supremely just, then you are indeed merciful precisely because you are supremely just. Help me, O just and merciful God, whose light I seek, help me to understand what I am saying. You are indeed merciful because you are just.

So, then, is your mercy born of[4] your justice? Do you spare the wicked because of your justice? If it is so, Lord, if it is so, teach me how it is so. Is it because it is just for you to be so good that you cannot be understood to be better, and to act so powerfully that you cannot be thought to act more powerfully? For what could be more just than this? And this would certainly not be the case if you were good only in punishing and not in sparing, and if you made only those not yet good to be good and did not do this also for the wicked. And so it is in this sense just that you spare the wicked and make them good. And finally, what is not done justly should not be done, and what should not be done is done unjustly. So if it were not just for you to be merciful to the wicked, you should not be merciful; and if you should not be merciful, you would act unjustly in being merciful. But if it is wrong to say this, it is right to believe that you act justly in being merciful to the wicked.

Chapter 10

How God justly punishes and justly spares the wicked

But it is also just for you to punish the wicked. For what could be more just than for the good to receive good things and the wicked bad things? So how is it both just that you punish the wicked and just that you spare the wicked?

4. [Reading "*nascitur*" for "*noscitur*."]

Or do you justly punish the wicked in one way and justly spare them in another? For when you punish the wicked, this is just because it accords with their merits; but when you spare the wicked, this is just, not because it is in keeping with their merits, but because it is in keeping with your goodness. In sparing the wicked you are just in relation to yourself but not in relation to us, in the same way that you are merciful in relation to us but not in relation to yourself. Thus, in saving us whom you might justly destroy, you are merciful, not because you experience any emotion, but because we experience the effect of your mercy; and in the same way, you are just, not because you give us our due, but because you do what is fitting for you who are supremely good. And so in this way you justly punish and justly pardon without any inconsistency.

Chapter 11

How "all the ways of the Lord are mercy and truth," and yet "the Lord is just in all his ways"

But is it not also just in relation to yourself, O Lord, for you to punish the wicked? It is certainly just for you to be so just that you cannot be thought to be more just. And you would by no means be so just if you only repaid the good with good and did not repay the wicked with evil. For one who treats both the good and the wicked as they deserve is more just than one who does so only for the good. Therefore, O just and benevolent God, it is just in relation to you both when you punish and when you pardon. Thus indeed "all the ways of the Lord are mercy and truth" (Psalm 25:10), and yet "the Lord is just in all his ways" (Psalm 145:17). And there is no inconsistency here, for it is not just for those to be saved whom you will to punish, and it is not just for those to be condemned whom you will to spare. For only what you will is just, and only what you do not will is not just. Thus your mercy is born of your justice, since it is just for you to be so good that you are good even in sparing the wicked. And perhaps this is why the supremely Just One can will good things for the wicked. But even if one can somehow grasp why you can will to save the wicked, certainly no reasoning can comprehend why, from those who are alike in wickedness, you save some rather than others through your supreme goodness and condemn some rather than others through your supreme justice.

Thus you are indeed percipient, omnipotent, merciful, and impassible, just as you are living, wise, good, happy, eternal, and whatever it is better to be than not to be.

Chapter 12

That God is the very life by which he lives, and so on for similar attributes

But clearly, you are whatever you are, not through anything else, but through yourself. Therefore, you are the very life by which you live, the wisdom by which you are wise, and the very goodness by which you are good to the good and to the wicked, and so on for similar attributes.

Chapter 13

How he alone is unbounded and eternal, although other spirits are unbounded and eternal

Everything that is at all enclosed in a place or a time is less than that which is subject to no law of place or time. Therefore, since nothing is greater than you, you are not confined to any place or time; you exist everywhere and always. Since this can be said of you alone, you alone are unbounded and eternal. So how can other spirits also be said to be unbounded and eternal?

And indeed you alone are eternal, because you alone of all beings do not cease to exist, just as you do not begin to exist. But how are you alone unbounded? Is it that a created spirit is bounded compared to you but unbounded compared to a material object? Surely something is completely bounded if, when it is wholly in one place, it cannot at the same time be somewhere else. This is true only of material objects. On the other hand, something is unbounded if it is wholly everywhere at once, and this is true of you alone. But something is both bounded and unbounded if, when it is wholly in one place, it can at the same time be wholly in another place, but not everywhere; and this is true of created spirits. For if the whole soul were not present in each part of its

body, it would not as a whole sense each part. Therefore, Lord, you are uniquely unbounded and eternal, and yet other spirits are also unbounded and eternal.

Chapter 14

How and why God is both seen and not seen by those who seek him

Have you found what you were seeking, O my soul? You were seeking God, and you have found that he is the highest of all beings, than which nothing better can be thought; that he is life itself, light, wisdom, goodness, eternal happiness and happy eternity; and that he exists always and everywhere. If you have not found your God, how is he the one whom you have found, whom you have understood with such certain truth and true certainty? But if you have found him, why do you not perceive what you have found? Why does my soul not perceive you, O Lord God, if it has found you?

Or has it not found him whom it found to be light and truth? For how did it understand this, if not by seeing that light and truth? Could it have understood anything at all about you except by "your light and your truth"? (Psalm 43:3) Therefore, if it has seen the light and the truth, it has seen you. If it has not seen you, it has not seen the light or the truth. Or perhaps it was indeed the light and the truth that it saw, but it has not yet seen you, because it saw you only in part and did not "see you as you really are" (1 John 3:2).

O Lord my God, you who have fashioned and refashioned me, tell my longing soul what you are besides what it has seen, that it might see purely what it longs to see. It strives to see more, but beyond what it has already seen it sees nothing but darkness. Or rather, it does not see darkness, for "in you there is no darkness" (1 John 1:5); it sees that it cannot see more because of its own darkness. Why is this, Lord, why is this? Is its eye darkened by its own infirmity, or is it dazzled by your splendor? Surely it is both darkened in itself and dazzled by you. Indeed it is both obscured by its own littleness and overwhelmed by your vastness. Truly it is both pinched by its own narrowness and vanquished by your fullness. How great is that light, for from it flashes every truth that enlightens the rational mind! How full is that truth, for in it is everything that is true, and outside it is only nothingness and falsehood! How vast it is, for in one glance it sees everything that has been created, and it sees by whom and through whom and how it was all created from nothing! What purity, what simplicity, what certainty and splendor are there! Truly it is more than any creature can understand.

Chapter 15

That God is greater than can be thought

Therefore, Lord, you are not merely that than which a greater cannot be thought; you are something greater than can be thought. For since it is possible to think that such a being exists, then if you are not that being, it is possible to think something greater than you. But that is impossible.

Chapter 16

That this is the "inaccessible light where he dwells"

Truly, Lord, this is the "inaccessible light in which you dwell" (1 Timothy 6:16). For surely there is no other being that can penetrate this light so that it might see you there. Indeed, the reason that I do not see it is that it is too much for me. And yet whatever I do see, I see through it, just as a weak eye sees what it sees by the light of the sun, although it cannot look at that light directly in the sun itself. My understanding cannot see that light. It is too dazzling; my understanding does not grasp it, and the eye of my soul cannot bear to look into it for long. It is dazzled by its splendor, vanquished by its fullness, overwhelmed by its vastness, perplexed by its extent. O supreme and inaccessible light, O complete and blessed truth, how far you are from me while I am so close to you! How far you are from my sight while I am so present to yours! You are wholly present everywhere, and yet I do not see you. "In you I move and in you I have my being" (Acts 17:28), and yet I cannot come into your presence. You are within me and all around me, and yet I do not perceive you.

Chapter 17

That in God there is harmony, fragrance, savor, softness, and beauty in his own ineffable way

Still, O Lord, you are hidden from my soul in your light and happiness, and so it still lives in its darkness and misery. It looks around, but it does not see your beauty. It listens, but it does not hear your harmony. It smells, but it does not perceive your fragrance. It tastes, but it does not know your savor. It touches, but it does not sense your softness. For you have these qualities in you, O Lord God, in your own ineffable way; and you have given them in their own perceptible way to the things you created. But the senses of my soul have been stiffened, dulled, and obstructed by the long-standing weakness of sin.

Chapter 18

That there are no parts in God or in his eternity, which he himself is

Once again, "behold, confusion!" (Jeremiah 14:19) Behold, once again mourning and sorrow stand in the way of one seeking joy and happiness. My soul hoped for satisfaction, and once again it is overwhelmed by need. I tried to eat my fill, but I hunger all the more. I strove to rise to the light of God, but I fell back down into my own darkness. Indeed, I did not merely fall into it; I find myself entangled in it. I fell before "my mother conceived me" (Psalm 51:5). I was indeed conceived in darkness; I was born enshrouded in darkness. Truly, we all fell long ago in him "in whom we all sinned" (Romans 5:12). In him, who easily possessed it and wickedly lost it for himself and for us, we all lost what we desire to seek but do not know; what we seek but do not find; what we find but is not what we sought. Help me "because of your goodness, O Lord" (Psalm 25:7). "I have sought your face; your face, Lord, will I seek. Turn not your face from me" (Psalm 27:8–9). Lift me up from myself to you. Cleanse, heal, sharpen, "enlighten the eye" (Psalm 13:3) of my soul so that I may look upon you. Let my soul gather its strength, and let it once more strive with all its understanding to reach you, O Lord.

What are you, Lord, what are you? What shall my

heart understand you to be? Surely you are life, you are wisdom, you are truth, you are goodness, you are happiness, you are eternity, and you are every true good. These are many things; my narrow understanding cannot see so many things in one glance and delight in all of them at once. How then, Lord, are you all these things? Are they parts of you? Or rather, is not each of them all that you are? For whatever is composed of parts is not completely one. It is in some sense a plurality and not identical with itself, and it can be broken up either in fact or at least in the understanding. But such characteristics are foreign to you, than whom nothing better can be thought. Therefore there are no parts in you, Lord, and you are not a plurality. Instead, you are so much a unity, so much identical with yourself, that you are in no respect dissimilar to yourself. You are in fact unity itself; you cannot be divided by any understanding. Therefore, life and wisdom and the rest are not parts of you; they are all one. Each of them is all of what you are, and each is what the rest are. And since you have no parts, and neither does your eternity, which you yourself are, it follows that no part of you or of your eternity exists at a certain place or time. Instead, you exist as a whole in every place, and your eternity exists as a whole always.

Chapter 19

That God is not in a place or a time, but all things are in him

But if by your eternity you have been, and are, and will be, and if to have been is not the same as to be in the future, and to be is not the same as to have been or to be in the future, then how does your eternity exist as a whole always?

Is it that nothing of your eternity is in the past in such a way that it no longer exists, and nothing is in the future as if it did not exist already? So it is not the case that yesterday you were and tomorrow you will be; rather, yesterday, today, and tomorrow you *are*. In fact, it is not even the case that yesterday, today, and tomorrow you *are*; rather, you are simply outside time altogether. Yesterday, today, and tomorrow are merely in time. But you, although nothing exists without you, do not exist in a place or a time;

rather, all things exist in you. For nothing contains you, but you contain all things.

Chapter 20

That he is before and beyond even all eternal things

Therefore you fill and embrace all things; you are before and beyond all things. And indeed you are before all things, since "before they came into being, you already are" (Cf. Psalm 90:2). But how are you beyond all things? In what way are you beyond those things that will have no end?

Is it because they can in no way exist without you, whereas you do not exist any less even if they return to nothingness? For in this way you are in a certain sense beyond them. And is it also because they can be thought to have an end, whereas you cannot at all? Thus they do in one sense have an end, but you do not in any sense. And certainly what does not in any sense have an end is beyond, what does in some sense come to an end. And do you not also surpass even all eternal things in that both your and their eternity is wholly present to you, whereas they do not yet possess the part of their eternity that is yet to come, just as they no longer possess the part that is past? In this way you are indeed always beyond them, because you are always present somewhere they have not yet arrived—or because it is always present to you.

Chapter 21

Whether this is "the age of the age" or "the age of the ages"

So is this "the age of the age" or "the ages of the ages"?[5] For just as an age of time contains all temporal things, so your eternity contains even the very ages of time. This eternity is indeed "an age" because of its indivisible unity, but it is "ages" because of its boundless greatness. And although you are so great, Lord, that all things are full of you and are in you,

5. [That is, is it more correct to identify God's eternity as *"saeculum saeculi"* or as *"saecula saeculorum"*? Both expressions (usually translated into English as "world without end" or "for ever and ever") were found in Scripture and in the liturgy.]

nonetheless you have no spatial extension, so that there is no middle or half or any other part in you.

Chapter 22

That he alone is what he is and who he is

Therefore, you alone, Lord, are what you are; and you are who you are. For whatever is one thing as a whole and something else in its parts, and whatever has in it something changeable, is not entirely what it is. And whatever began to exist out of nonexistence and can be thought not to exist, and returns to nonexistence unless it subsists through some other being; and whatever has a past that no longer exists and a future that does not yet exist: that thing does not exist in a strict and absolute sense. But you are what you are, since whatever you are in any way or at any time, you are wholly and always that.

And you are the one who exists in a strict and absolute sense, because you have no past and no future but only a present, and you cannot be thought not to exist at any time. And you are life and light and wisdom and happiness and eternity and many such good things; and yet you are nothing other than the one supreme good, utterly self-sufficient, needing nothing, whom all things need for their being and their well-being.

Chapter 23

That this good is equally Father, Son, and Holy Spirit; and that this is the "one necessary thing," which is the complete, total, and only good

This good is you, O God the Father; it is your Word, that is to say, your Son. For there cannot be anything other than what you are, or anything greater or less than you, in the Word by which you utter yourself. For your Word is as true as you are truthful, and therefore he is the same truth that you are and no other. And you are so simple that nothing can be born of you that is other than what you are. And this good is the one love that is shared by you and your Son, that is, the Holy Spirit, who proceeds from you both. For this love is not unequal to you or to your Son, since you love yourself and him, and he loves

himself and you, as much as you and he *are*. Moreover, the one who is equal to both you and him is not other than you and he; nothing can proceed from the supreme simplicity that is other than that from which it proceeds. Thus, whatever each of you is individually, that is what the whole Trinity is at once, Father, Son, and Holy Spirit; for each of you individually is nothing other than the supremely simple unity and the supremely united simplicity, which cannot be multiplied or different from itself.

"Moreover, one thing is necessary" (Luke 10:42). And this is that one necessary thing, in which is all good—or rather, which is itself the complete, one, total, and unique good.

Chapter 24

A conjecture as to what sort of good this is, and how great it is

Bestir yourself, O my soul! Lift up your whole understanding, and consider as best you can what sort of good this is, and how great it is. For if particular goods are delightful, consider intently how delightful is that good which contains the joyfulness of all goods—and not such joyfulness as we have experienced in created things, but as different [from that] as the Creator differs from the creature. If created life is good, how good is the life that creates? If the salvation that has been brought about is joyful, how joyful is the salvation that brings about all salvation? If wisdom in the knowledge of created things is desirable, how desirable is the wisdom that created all things from nothing? In short, if there are many and great delights in delightful things, what kind and how great a delight is there in him who made those delightful things?

Chapter 25

What great goods there are for those who enjoy this good

O those who enjoy this good: what will be theirs, and what will not be theirs! Truly they will have everything they want and nothing they do not want. There will be such goods of both body and soul that "neither eye has seen nor ear heard nor the human heart" (1 Corinthians 2:9) conceived. So why are you wandering through many things, you insignificant mortal, seeking the goods of your soul and of your body? Love the one good, in which are all good things, and that is enough. Desire the simple good, which is the complete good, and that is enough. What do you love, O my flesh? What do you long for, O my soul? It is there; whatever you love, whatever you long for, it is there.

If it is beauty that delights you, "the righteous will shine like the sun" (Matthew 13:43). If it is swiftness or strength, or the freedom of a body that nothing can withstand, "they will be like the angels of God" (Matthew 22:30); for "it is sown an animal body, but it will rise a spiritual body" (1 Corinthians 15:44), with a power that is not from nature. If it is a long and healthy life, there is a healthy eternity and eternal health, for "the righteous will live for ever" (Wisdom 5:15) and "the salvation of the righteous is from the Lord" (Psalm 37:39). If it is satisfaction, "they will be satisfied when the glory of God has appeared" (Psalm 17:13). If it is drunkenness, "they will be drunk with the abundance of the house" (Psalm 36:8) of God. If it is music, there the choirs of angels sing unceasingly to God. If it is some pleasure, not impure but pure, God "will give them to drink from the torrent of his pleasure" (Psalm 36:8). If it is wisdom, the very wisdom of God will show itself to them. If it is friendship, they will love God more than themselves and one another as themselves, and God will love them more than they do themselves; for they will love God and themselves and one another through God, and God will love himself and them through himself. If it is concord, everyone will have but one will, for there will be no will among them but the will of God. If it is power, they will be omnipotent through their wills, just as God is through his. For just as God can do what he wills through himself, so they will be able to do what they will through God; for just as they will will only what God wills, so he will will whatever they will—and what he wills cannot fail to be. If it is wealth and honor, God will "set his good and faithful servants over many things" (Cf. Matthew 25:21, 23); indeed, they will be called, and will truly be, "sons of God" (Matthew 5:9) and "gods" (Psalm 82:6, John 10:34). Where his Son is, there they too will be, "heirs of God and joint-heirs with Christ" (Romans 8:17). If it is true security, they will be certain that they will never in any way lose this

security—or rather, this good; just as certain as they are that they will never give it up voluntarily, and that the loving God will never take it away against their will from those who love him, and that nothing more powerful than God will separate them from God against their will.

What great joy is there where so great a good is present! O human heart, O needy heart, heart that has known troubles, that is indeed overwhelmed by troubles: how greatly would you rejoice if you abounded in all these things! Ask your inmost self whether it can even comprehend its joy at such great happiness. And yet surely if someone else whom you loved in every respect as yourself had that same happiness, your joy would be doubled, for you would rejoice no less for him than for yourself. And if two or three or many more had that same happiness, you would rejoice as much for each of them as you would for yourself, if you loved each one as yourself. Therefore, in that perfect charity of countless happy angels and human beings, where no one will love anyone else less than he loves himself, each one will rejoice for each of the others just as he does for himself. If, then, the human heart will scarcely comprehend its own joy from so great a good, how will it be able to contain so many and such great joys? And indeed, since the more one loves someone, the more one rejoices in his good, it follows that, just as everyone in that perfect happiness will love God incomparably more than himself and all others with him, so everyone will rejoice inconceivably more in God's happiness than in his own, or in that of everyone else with him. But if they love God so much with "their whole heart, mind, and soul" (Matthew 22:37) that their whole heart, mind, and soul are too small for the greatness of their love, they will truly rejoice so much with their whole heart, mind, and soul that their whole heart, mind, and soul will be too small for the fullness of their joy.

Chapter 26

Whether this is the "fullness of joy" that the Lord promises

My God and my Lord, my hope and the joy of my heart, tell my soul whether this is that joy of which you tell us through your Son, "Ask and you shall receive, that your joy may be full" (John 16:24). For I have found a joy that is full and more than full. Indeed, when the heart, the mind, the soul, and the whole human being are filled with that joy, there will still remain joy beyond measure. The whole of that joy will therefore not enter into those who rejoice; instead, those who rejoice will enter wholly into that joy. Speak, Lord, tell your servant inwardly in his heart whether this is the joy into which your servants will enter who "enter into the joy of the Lord" (Matthew 25:21). But surely the joy with which your chosen ones will rejoice is something "no eye has seen, nor ear heard, nor has it entered into the heart of man" (1 Corinthians 2:9). Therefore, Lord, I have not yet expressed or conceived how greatly your blessed ones will rejoice. They will indeed rejoice as much as they love, and they will love as much as they know. How much will they know you then, Lord, and how much will they love you? Truly in this life "eye has not seen, nor has ear heard, nor has it entered into the heart of man" how much they will love and know you in that life.

O God, I pray that I will know and love you that I might rejoice in you. And if I cannot do so fully in this life, I pray that I might grow day by day until my joy comes to fullness. Let the knowledge of you grow in me here, and there let it be full. Let your love grow in me here, and there let it be full, so that my joy here is great in hope, and my joy there is full in reality. O Lord, by your Son you command us—or rather, you counsel us—to ask, and you promise that we will receive, "that our joy may be full." Lord, I ask what you counsel us through our "Wonderful Counselor" (Isaiah 9:6). Let me receive what you promise through your truth, "that my joy may be full." O truthful God, I ask that I may receive, "that my joy may be full." Until then, let my mind ponder on it, my tongue speak of it. Let my heart love it and my mouth proclaim it. Let my soul hunger for it, my flesh thirst for it, my whole being long for it, until I "enter into the joy of my Lord," who is God, Three in One, "blessed for ever. Amen" (Romans 1:25).

Gaunilo's Reply on Behalf of the Fool

Someone who either doubts or denies that there is any such being as that than which nothing greater can be thought is told that its existence is proved in the following way. First, the very person who denies or entertains doubts about this being has it in his understanding, since when he hears it spoken of he understands what is said. Further, what he understands must exist in reality as well, and not only in the understanding. The argument for this claim goes like this: to exist in reality is greater than to exist only in the understanding. Now if that being exists only in the understanding, then whatever also exists in reality is greater than it. Thus, that which is greater than everything else[1] will be less than something, and not greater than everything else, which is of course a contradiction. And so that which is greater than everything else, which has already been proved to exist in the understanding, must exist not only in the understanding but also in reality, since otherwise it could not be greater than everything else.

He can perhaps reply, "The only reason this is said to exist in my understanding is that I understand what is said. But in the same way, could I not also be said to have in my understanding any number of false things that have no real existence at all in themselves, since if someone were to speak of them I would understand whatever he said? Unless perhaps it is established that this being is such that it cannot be had in thought in the same way that any false or doubtful things can, and so I am not said to think of what I have heard or to have it in my thought, but to understand it and have it in my understanding, since I cannot think of it in any other way except

by understanding it, that is, by comprehending in genuine knowledge the fact that it actually exists.

"But first of all, if this were the case, there would be no distinction between having a thing in the understanding at one time and then later understanding that the thing exists, as there is in the case of a painting, which exists first in the mind of the painter and then in the finished work.

"Furthermore, it is nearly impossible to believe that this being, once someone had heard it spoken of, cannot be thought not to exist, in just the same way that even God can be thought not to exist. For if that were so, why bother with all this argument against someone who denies or doubts that such a being exists?

"Finally, it must be proved to me by some unassailable argument that this being merely needs to be thought in order for the understanding to perceive with complete certainty that it undoubtedly exists. It is not enough to tell me that it exists in my understanding, since I understand it when I hear about it. I still think I could likewise have any number of other doubtful or even false things in my understanding if I heard them spoken of by someone whose words I understand, and especially if I am so taken in by him that, as often happens, I believe him—as I still do not believe in that being.

"Accordingly, that example of the painter, who already has in his understanding the picture that he is going to paint, is not a close enough analogy to support this argument. For before that picture is painted, it is contained in the craft of the painter, and any such thing in the craft of a craftsman is nothing but a part of his intelligence. For, as Saint Augustine says, 'when a carpenter is about to make a chest in reality, he first has it in his craft. The chest that exists in reality is not a living thing, but the chest that exists in his craft is a living thing, since the soul of the craftsman, in which all those things exist before they

---

1. [Gaunilo regularly says "*maius omnibus*," which literally translated is "greater than everything." English idiom demands "greater than everything *else*," and I have translated it accordingly, but I thought it important to note the discrepancy.]

are produced, is alive.'[2] Now how can they be living things in the living soul of the craftsman unless they are nothing other than the knowledge or intelligence of his soul itself? By contrast, except for things that are recognized as belonging to the nature of the mind itself, when the intellect upon hearing or thinking of something perceives that it is true, that truth is undoubtedly distinct from the intellect that grasps it. So even if it is true that there is something than which a greater cannot be thought, that thing, when it is heard and understood, is not the same sort of thing as a picture that exists in the understanding of the painter before it is painted.

"There is a further argument, which I mentioned earlier. When I hear someone speak of that which is greater than everything else that can be thought (which, it is alleged, can be nothing other than God himself), I can no more think of it or have it in my understanding in terms of anything whose genus or species I already know, than I can think of God himself—and indeed, for this very reason I can also think of him as not existing. For I do not know the thing itself, and I cannot form an idea of it on the basis of something like it, since you yourself claim that it is so great that nothing else could be like it. Now if I heard something said about a man I do not know at all, whose very existence is unknown to me, I could think of him in accordance with that very thing that a man is, on the basis of that knowledge of genus or species by which I know what a man is or what men are. Nonetheless, it could happen that the one who spoke of this man was lying, and so the man whom I thought of would not exist. But I would still be thinking of him on the basis of a real thing: not what that particular man would be, but what any given man is.

"But when I hear someone speak of 'God' or 'something greater than everything else,' I cannot have it in my thought or understanding in the same way as this false thing. I was able to think of the false thing on the basis of some real thing that I actually knew. But in the case of God, I can think of him only on the basis of the word. And one can seldom or never think of any truth solely on the basis of a word. For

in thinking of something solely on the basis of a word, one does not think so much of the word itself (which is at least a real thing: the sound of letters or syllables) as of the meaning of the word that is heard. And in the present case, one does not do this as someone who knows what is customarily meant by the word and thinks of it on the basis of a thing that is real at least in thought. Instead, one thinks of it as someone who does not know the meaning of the word, who thinks only of the impression made on his mind by hearing the word and tries to imagine its meaning. It would be surprising if one ever managed to reach the truth about something in this way. Therefore, when I hear and understand someone saying that there exists something greater than everything else that can be thought, it is in this way, and this way only, that it is present in my understanding. So much, then, for the claim that that supreme nature already exists in my understanding.

"Then I am offered the further argument that this thing necessarily exists in reality, since if it did not, everything that exists in reality would be greater than it. And so this thing, which of course has been proved to exist in the understanding, would not be greater than everything else. To that argument I reply that if we are to say that something exists in the understanding that cannot even be thought on the basis of the true nature of anything whatever, then I shall not deny that even this thing exists in my understanding. But since there is no way to derive from this the conclusion that this thing also exists in reality, there is simply no reason for me to concede to him that this thing exists in reality until it is proved to me by some unassailable argument.

"And when he says that this thing exists because otherwise that which is greater than everything else would not be greater than everything else, he does not fully realize whom he is addressing. For I do not yet admit—indeed, I actually deny, or at least doubt—that this greater being is greater than any real thing. Nor do I concede that it exists at all, except in the sense that something exists (if you want to call it 'existence') when my mind tries to imagine some completely unknown thing solely on the basis of a word that it has heard. How, then, is the fact that this being has been proved to be greater than everything else supposed to show me that it exists in actual fact?

2. [*In Iohannem*, tractate 1, n. 17.]

For I continue to deny, or at least doubt, that this has been proved, so that I do not admit that this thing exists in my understanding or thought even in the way that many doubtful and uncertain things exist there. First I must become certain that this thing truly exists somewhere, and only then will the fact that it is greater than everything else show clearly that it also subsists in itself.

"For example, there are those who say that somewhere in the ocean is an island, which, because of the difficulty—or rather, impossibility—of finding what does not exist, some call 'the Lost Island.' This island (so the story goes) is more plentifully endowed than even the Isles of the Blessed with an indescribable abundance of all sorts of riches and delights. And because it has neither owner nor inhabitant, it is everywhere superior in its abundant riches to all the other lands that human beings inhabit. Suppose that someone tells me all this. The story is easily told and involves no difficulty, and so I understand it. But if this person went on to draw a conclusion, and say, 'You cannot any longer doubt that this island, more excellent than all others on earth, truly exists somewhere in reality. For you do not doubt that this island exists in your understanding, and since it is more excellent to exist not merely in the understanding, but also in reality, this island must also exist in reality. For if it did not, any land that exists in reality would be greater than it. And so this more excellent thing that you have understood would not in fact be more excellent.'—If, I say, he should try to convince me by this argument that I should no longer doubt whether the island truly exists, either I would think he was joking, or I would not know whom I ought to think more foolish: myself, if I grant him his conclusion, or him, if he thinks he can establish the existence of that island with any degree of certainty, without first showing that its excellence exists in my understanding as a thing that truly and undoubtedly exists and not in any way like something false or uncertain."

In this way the fool might meet the objections brought against him up to this point. The next asser-

tion is that this greater being is such that even in thought it cannot fail to exist, and that in turn rests entirely on the claim that otherwise this being would not be greater than everything else. To this argument he can make the very same response, and say, "When did I ever say that any such thing as that 'greater than everything else' exists in actual fact, so that on that basis I am supposed to accept the claim that it exists to such a degree that it cannot even be thought not to exist? Therefore you must first prove by some absolutely incontestable argument that there exists some superior being, i.e., one that is greater and better than all others that exist, so that from this we can also prove all of the qualities that that which is greater and better than all other things must necessarily possess." So instead of saying that the highest thing cannot be *thought* not to exist, perhaps it would be better to say that it cannot be *understood* not to exist, or even to be capable of not existing. For in the strict sense of the word, false things cannot be understood, even though they can of course be thought in the same way that the fool thought that God does not exist.

Furthermore, I know with absolute certainty that I myself exist, but nonetheless I also know that I can fail to exist. But I understand beyond all doubt that the highest being that exists, namely God, both exists and cannot fail to exist. Now I do not know whether I can think I do not exist even while I know with absolute certainty that I do exist. But if I can, why can I not do the same for anything else that I know with the same certainty? And if I cannot, it is not God alone who cannot be thought not to exist.

The rest of this book is argued so truly, so lucidly and magnificently, full of so much that is useful, and fragrant with the aroma of devout and holy feelings, that it should by no means be belittled on account of the claims made at the beginning, which are indeed accurately understood, but less compellingly argued. Rather, those claims should be demonstrated more solidly, and then the whole book can be accorded great honor and praise.

Anselm's Reply to Gaunilo

Since the one who takes me to task is not that fool against whom I was speaking in my book, but a Christian who is no fool, arguing on behalf of the fool, it will be enough for me to reply to the Christian.

You say—whoever you are who say that the fool could say these things—that something than which a greater cannot be thought is in the understanding no differently from that which cannot even be thought according to the true nature of anything at all. You also say that it does not follow (as I say it does) that that than which a greater cannot be thought exists in reality as well simply because it exists in the understanding, any more than it follows that the Lost Island most certainly exists simply because someone who hears it described in words has no doubt that it exists in his understanding. I, however, say this: if that than which a greater cannot be thought is neither understood nor thought, and exists neither in the understanding nor in thought, then either God is not that than which a greater cannot be thought, or else he is neither understood nor thought, and exists neither in the understanding nor in thought. I appeal to your own faith and conscience as the most compelling argument that this is false. Therefore, that than which a greater cannot be thought is indeed understood and thought, and exists in the understanding and in thought. So either the premises by which you attempt to prove the contrary are false, or else what you think follows from them does not in fact follow.

You think that from the fact that something than which a greater cannot be thought is understood, it does not follow that it exists in the understanding; nor does it follow that if it exists in the understanding, it therefore exists in reality. But I say with certainty that if it can be so much as thought to exist, it must necessarily exist. For that than which a greater cannot be thought cannot be thought of as beginning to exist. By contrast, whatever can be thought to exist, but does not in fact exist, can be thought of as beginning to exist. Therefore, it is not the case that that than which a greater cannot be thought can be thought to

exist, but does not in fact exist. If, therefore, it can be thought to exist, it does necessarily exist.

Furthermore, if it can be thought *at all*, it necessarily exists. For no one who denies or doubts that something than which a greater cannot be thought exists, denies or doubts that if it did exist, it would be unable to fail to exist either in reality or in the understanding, since otherwise it would not be that than which a greater cannot be thought. But whatever can be thought, but does not in fact exist, could (if it did exist) fail to exist either in reality or in the understanding. So if that than which a greater cannot be thought can be thought at all, it cannot fail to exist.

But let us assume instead that it does not exist, although it can be thought. Now something that can be thought but does not exist, would not, if it existed, be that than which a greater cannot be thought. And so, if it existed, that than which a greater cannot be thought would not be that than which a greater cannot be thought, which is utterly absurd. Therefore, if that than which a greater cannot be thought can be thought at all, it is false that it does not exist—and much more so if it can be understood and can exist in the understanding.

I shall say something more. If something does not exist everywhere and always, even if perhaps it does exist somewhere and sometimes, it can undoubtedly be thought not to exist anywhere or at any time, just as it does not exist in this particular place or at this particular time. For something that did not exist yesterday but does exist today can be conceived of as never existing in just the same way that it is understood as not existing yesterday. And something that does not exist here but does exist elsewhere can be thought not to exist anywhere in just the same way that it does not exist here. Similarly, when some parts of a thing do not exist in the same place or at the same time as other parts of that thing, all its parts—and therefore the thing as a whole—can be thought not to exist anywhere or at any time. Even if we say that time always exists and that the universe is everywhere, nevertheless, the whole of time does not always exist, and the whole of the universe is not everywhere. And just as some parts of time do not exist when others do, all of the parts can be thought not to exist at any time. And just as some parts of the universe do not exist where others do, all of the parts can be thought not to exist anywhere. Moreover, whatever is composed of parts can, at least in thought, be divided and fail to exist. Therefore, whatever does not exist as a whole in all places and at all times, even if it does exist, can be thought not to exist. But that than which a greater cannot be thought, if it exists, cannot be thought not to exist. For otherwise, even if it exists, it is not that than which a greater cannot be thought—which is absurd. Therefore, there is no time and no place in which it does not exist as a whole; it exists as a whole always and everywhere.

Do you think the being about whom these things are understood can in any way be thought or understood, or can exist in thought or in the understanding? If it cannot, these claims about it cannot be understood either. Perhaps you will say that it is not understood and does not exist in the understanding because it is not *fully* understood. But then you would have to say that someone who cannot gaze directly upon the purest light of the sun does not see the light of day, which is nothing other than the light of the sun. Surely that than which a greater cannot be thought is understood, and exists in the understanding, at least to the extent that these things about it are understood.

And so I said in the argument that you criticize, that when the fool hears someone utter the words "that than which a greater cannot be thought," he understands what he hears. Someone who does not understand it (if it is spoken in a language he knows) is rather feeble-minded, if indeed he has a mind at all.

Then I said that if it is understood, it exists in the understanding. Or does that which has been shown to exist necessarily in actual fact not exist in any understanding? But you will say that even if it exists in the understanding, it still does not follow that it is understood. Notice, however, that if it is understood, it does follow that it exists in the understanding. For when something is thought, it is thought by means of thinking; and what is thought by means of thinking exists in thinking just as it is thought. And in the same way, when something is understood, it is understood by means of the understanding; and what is understood by means of the understanding exists in the understanding, just as it is understood. What could be clearer than that?

After that I said that if it exists only in the understanding, it can be thought to exist in reality as well, which is greater. Therefore, if it exists only in the understanding, the very same thing is both that than which a greater *cannot* be thought and that than which a greater *can* be thought. Now I ask you, what could be more logical? For if it exists only in the understanding, can it not be thought to exist in reality as well? And if it can, does not the one who thinks it, think something greater than that thing is if it exists only in the understanding? So if that than which a greater *cannot* be thought exists only in the understanding, it is that than which a greater *can* be thought: what more logical conclusion could there be? But of course that than which a greater cannot be thought is not the same in anyone's understanding as that than which a greater can be thought. Does it not follow, therefore, that if that than which a greater cannot be thought exists in any understanding at all, it does not exist only in the understanding? For if it exists only in the understanding, it is that than which a greater can be thought, which is absurd.

But, you say, this is just the same as if someone were to claim that it cannot be doubted that a certain island in the ocean, surpassing all other lands in its fertility (which, from the difficulty—or rather, impossibility—of finding what does not exist, is called "the Lost Island"), exists in reality, because someone can easily understand it when it is described to him in words. I say quite confidently that if anyone can find for me something existing either in reality or only in thought to which he can apply this inference in my argument, besides that than which a greater cannot be thought, I will find and give to him that Lost Island, never to be lost again. In fact, however, it has already become quite clear that that than which a greater cannot be thought cannot be thought not to exist, since its existence is a matter of such certain truth. For otherwise it would not exist at all. Finally, if someone says that he thinks it does not exist, I say that when he thinks this, either he is thinking something than which a greater cannot be thought, or he is not. If he is not, then he is not thinking that it does not exist, since he is not thinking it at all. But if he is, he is surely thinking something that cannot be thought not to exist. For if it could be thought not to exist, it could be thought to have a beginning and an end, which is impossible. Therefore, someone who is thinking it, is thinking something that cannot be thought not to exist. And of course someone who is thinking this, does not think that that very thing does not exist. Otherwise he would be thinking something that cannot be thought. Therefore, that than which a greater cannot be thought cannot be thought not to exist.

When I say that this highest being cannot be *thought* not to exist, you reply that it would perhaps be better to say that it cannot be *understood* not to exist, or even to be capable of not existing. But in fact it was more correct to say that it cannot be *thought* not to exist. For if I had said that this thing cannot be understood not to exist, you (who say that in the strict sense of the word, false things cannot be understood) might well object that nothing that exists can be understood not to exist, since, after all, it is false that something that exists does not exist. Consequently, it is not God alone who cannot be understood not to exist. But if any of those things that most certainly exist can be understood not to exist, then other things that are certain can likewise be understood not to exist. If, however, we say 'thought' [rather than 'understood'] this objection will have no force if it is examined properly. For even if nothing that actually exists cannot be *understood* not to exist, everything can be *thought* not to exist, except for that which exists in the highest degree. Indeed, all and only those things that have a beginning or end, or are made up of parts, as well as whatever does not exist always and everywhere as a whole (as I discussed earlier), can be thought not to exist. The only thing that cannot be thought not to exist is that which has neither beginning nor end, and is not made up of parts, and which no thought discerns except as wholly present always and everywhere.

So you should realize that you can indeed *think* of yourself as not existing even while you know with absolute certainty that you exist. I am amazed that you said you did not know this. For we think of many things as not existing that we know exist, and we think of many things as existing that we know do not exist — not judging, but imagining, that things are as we are thinking of them. And so we can in fact think of something as not existing even while we know that it exists, since we can think the one thing and know

the other at the very same time. And yet we cannot think of something as not existing even while we know that it exists, since we cannot think of it as existing and not existing at the same time. So if someone distinguishes the two senses of this statement in this way, he will understand that in one sense nothing can be thought of as not existing when we know that it exists, and in another sense anything besides that than which a greater cannot be thought can be thought not to exist, even when we know that it exists. Thus God alone cannot be thought not to exist, but nonetheless it is also true that there are many things that cannot be thought not to exist while they actually exist. I think, however, that I adequately explained in my book the sense in which God is thought not to exist.

Now as for the other objections you raise against me on behalf of the fool, anyone with much sense at all can easily see through them, so I had judged it best not to bother proving this. But since I hear that some readers think they have some force against me, I will deal with them briefly. First, you repeatedly say that I argue that that which is greater than everything else exists in the understanding; and that if it exists in the understanding, it also exists in reality, for otherwise that which is greater than everything else would not be greater than everything else. Nowhere in anything I said can such an argument be found. For "that which is greater than everything else" and "that than which nothing greater can be thought" do not have the same force in proving that the thing spoken of exists in reality. For if someone says that that than which a greater cannot be thought is not something existing in reality, or is capable of not existing, or can be thought not to exist, he is easily refuted. For whatever does not exist is capable of not existing, and whatever is capable of not existing can be thought not to exist. Now whatever can be thought not to exist, if it does exist, is not that than which a greater cannot be thought. And if it does not exist, it would not be that than which a greater cannot be thought *even if it were to exist*. But it makes no sense to say that that than which a greater cannot be thought, if it exists, is not that than which a greater cannot be thought, and that if it [does not exist but] were to exist, it would not be that than which a greater cannot be thought. It is therefore evident that it exists, that it is not capable of not existing, and that it cannot be thought not to exist. For otherwise, if it exists, it is not the thing spoken of; and if it [does not exist but] were to exist, it would not be the thing spoken of.

This does not seem to be so easily proved with regard to what is said to be greater than everything else. For it is not as evident that something that can be thought not to exist is not that which is greater than everything else that exists, as it is that such a thing is not that than which a greater cannot be thought. Nor is it indubitable that if there is something greater than everything else, it is the same as that than which a greater cannot be thought, or that if such a thing were to exist, there would not exist another thing just like it. But these things are certainly true of what is called "that than which a greater cannot be thought." For what if someone were to say that something exists that is greater than everything else that exists, and yet that this very thing can be thought not to exist, and that something greater than it can be thought, although that greater thing does not actually exist? Can it be just as easily inferred in this case that it is not greater than everything else that exists, as it was perfectly certain in the previous case that it was not that than which a greater cannot be thought? In the second case we would need another premise, besides the mere fact that this being is said to be "greater than everything else," whereas in the first case there was no need for anything more than the expression "that than which a greater cannot be thought." Therefore, since "that than which a greater cannot be thought" proves things about itself and through itself that cannot be proved in the same way about what is said to be "greater than everything else," you have unjustly criticized me for saying things I did not say, when they differ greatly from what I actually said.

If, however, this can be proved through some further argument, you should not have criticized me for saying what can clearly be proved. And that it can in fact be proved should be easily perceived by anyone who knows that it can be proved for that than which a greater cannot be thought. For that than which a greater cannot be thought cannot be understood as anything other than the one thing that is greater than everything else. Therefore, just as that than which a greater cannot be thought is understood and exists in the understanding, and therefore is affirmed to exist in actual fact, even so that which is said to be

greater than everything else is with necessity inferred to be understood, to exist in the understanding, and consequently to exist in reality. So you see how right you were to compare me to that stupid man who was willing to affirm the existence of the Lost Island solely because the island would be understood if someone described it.

But you also raise the objection that all sorts of false or doubtful things can be understood, and exist in the understanding, in the very same way as the being I was talking about. I wonder what force you thought this objection could have against me. I was simply trying to prove something that was still in doubt, and for that it was enough for me to show that this being is understood, and exists in the understanding, in *some way or other*, since on that basis the argument would go on to determine whether it exists only in the understanding, like a false thing, or also in reality, like a real thing. For if false and doubtful things are understood, and exist in the understanding, in the sense that one who hears them spoken of understands what the speaker means, there is no reason that the being I was discussing could not be understood or exist in the understanding. But how can these two claims of yours be consistent: first, that if someone spoke of false things, you would understand whatever he said; and second, that if what you heard is not had in thought in the same way that false things are, you would not say that you think it and have it in your thought, but rather that you understand it and have it in your understanding, since you cannot think this thing without understanding it, that is, comprehending in genuine knowledge that it exists in reality? How, I ask, can these be consistent: that false things are understood in some sense, and that to understand is to comprehend in genuine knowledge that something exists? You should realize that this objection has no force against me. If false things can indeed be understood in some sense, and your definition of understanding applies not to all but only to some cases of understanding, then I should not have been criticized for saying that that than which a greater cannot be thought is understood and exists in the understanding even before it was certain that it exists in reality.

Next, you say that it is nearly impossible to believe that when this thing has been spoken of and heard, it cannot be thought not to exist in the way that even

God can be thought not to exist. Let those who have acquired even a meager knowledge of disputation and argument reply on my behalf. Is it rational for someone to deny [the existence of] what he understands, simply because it is said to be the same as something [whose existence] he denies because he does not understand it? Or if [its existence] is sometimes denied because it is only partly understood, and it is the same as something that is not understood at all, are not things in doubt more easily proved to be true of what exists in some understanding than of what exists in no understanding? Therefore, it is impossible to believe that someone would deny [the existence of] that than which a greater cannot be thought, which he understands to some extent when he hears of it, simply because he denies [the existence of] God, whose meaning he is not thinking of in any way. Or, if he also denies [the existence of] that than which a greater cannot be thought, because he does not fully understand it, is it not easier to prove [the existence of] what is understood to some extent than to prove what is not understood at all? So it was not irrational for me to prove against the fool that God exists by making use of the expression "that than which a greater cannot be thought," since he would understand that expression to some extent, whereas he might not understand "God" at all.

You go to some trouble to show that that than which a greater cannot be thought is not the same sort of thing as a picture, not yet painted, in the understanding of the painter, but your argument is not to the point. I did not bring up the picture that is thought out beforehand in order to claim that it was the same sort of thing as the being I was discussing, but merely so I could show that something exists in the understanding that would not be understood to exist [in reality].

Again, you say that when you hear "that than which a greater cannot be thought," you cannot think it in accordance with some thing that you know by genus or species, or have it in your understanding, since you do not know the thing itself and cannot infer it on the basis of something similar. But that is clearly wrong. For since every lesser good, insofar as it is good, is similar to a greater good, it is clear to every reasonable mind that by raising our thoughts from lesser goods to greater goods, we can infer a great deal about that than which a greater cannot be thought on the basis of those things than which a greater can be thought. Who, for example, is unable to think (even if he does not believe that what he thinks exists in reality) that if something that has a beginning and end is good, then something that has a beginning but never ceases to exist is much better? And that just as the latter is better than the former, so something that has neither beginning nor end is better still, even if it is always moving from the past through the present into the future? And that something that in no way needs or is compelled to change or move is far better even than that, whether any such thing exists in reality or not? Can such a thing not be thought? Can anything greater than this be thought? Or rather, is not this an example of inferring that than which a greater cannot be thought on the basis of those things than which a greater can be thought? So there is in fact a way to infer that than which a greater cannot be thought. And so in this way it is easy to refute a fool who does not accept the sacred authority, if he denies that one can infer that than which a greater cannot be thought on the basis of other things. But if an orthodox Christian were to deny this, he should recall that "since the creation of the world the invisible things of God—his everlasting power and divinity—have been clearly seen through the things that have been made" (Romans 1:20).

But even if it were true that that than which a greater cannot be thought cannot be thought or understood, it would not be false that [the expression] "that than which a greater cannot be thought" can be thought and understood. For just as one can use the word 'ineffable,' even though the thing that is said to be ineffable cannot be spoken of; and just as 'unthinkable' can be thought, even though the thing to which the word 'unthinkable' applies cannot be thought; in the same way, when someone says "that than which a greater cannot be thought," that which is heard can undoubtedly be thought and understood, even though the thing itself than which a greater cannot be thought cannot be thought or understood. For even if someone is foolish enough to say that something than which a greater cannot be thought does not exist, he will surely not be shameless enough to say that he cannot understand or think what he is saying. Or, if such a person does turn up, not only should his words be repudiated, but he himself should be ridiculed. So anyone who denies the existence of something than which a greater cannot be thought surely understands and thinks the denial that he is making. Now he cannot understand or think this denial without its parts. And one part of it is "that than which a greater cannot be thought." Therefore, whoever denies this, understands and thinks that than which a greater cannot be thought. Now it is quite clear that something that cannot fail to exist can be thought and understood in the same way. And one who thinks this is thinking something greater than is one who thinks something that can fail to exist. Therefore, if, while he is thinking that than which a greater cannot be thought, he thinks that it can fail to exist, he is not thinking that than which a greater cannot be thought. But it is not possible for the same thing at the same time both to be thought and not to be thought. Therefore, someone who thinks that than which a greater cannot be thought does not think that it can, but rather that it cannot, fail to exist. For this reason the thing that he is thinking exists necessarily, since whatever can fail to exist is not what he is thinking.

I believe I have now shown that my proof in the foregoing book that that than which a greater cannot be thought exists in reality was no weak argument, but a quite conclusive one, one that is not weakened by the force of any objection. For the meaning of this expression has such great force that, from the mere fact that it is understood or thought, what is said is necessarily proved both to exist in reality and to be whatever we ought to believe about the divine nature. Now we believe about the divine nature everything that can be thought, absolutely speaking, better for something to be than not to be. For example, it is better to be eternal than not eternal, good than not good, and indeed goodness itself, rather than not goodness itself. That than which something greater cannot be thought cannot fail to be anything of this sort. So one must believe that that than which a greater cannot be thought is whatever we ought to believe about the divine nature.

I am grateful for your kindness both in your criticisms and in your praise of my book. For since you lavished such great praise on the things you found worthy of acceptance, it is quite clear that you criticized the things that seemed weak to you, not from ill will but in a friendly spirit.

Thomas Aquinas

Aquinas (1225–1274) was born at the castle of Roccasecca, near Aquino, which lay between Rome and Naples. His well-to-do parents apparently intended an ecclesiastical career for him. He was sent to the Benedictine abbey at Monte Cassino for his early education; from there he went to the University of Naples in 1239.

While in Naples Aquinas came under the influence of the newly created Order of Preachers founded by St. Dominic (1170–1221). The Dominicans at the time were, like the Franciscans, mendicant, or begging, friars. Espousing absolute poverty, they saw their vocation as the spreading of the Gospel to the people, both by word and by living example. The apostolic zeal of the mendicant friars captured the imagination and admiration of many; both the Franciscans and the Dominicans were to become successful and powerful. To Aquinas's family, however, the Dominicans must have appeared an appalling bunch of rag-tag ne'er-do-wells, especially in comparison with the Benedictines, who had prestige, power, and corporate wealth. When Aquinas joined the Dominican order in 1243, his family reacted strongly, going so far as to lock him up in the castle. He remained unswayed, spending his time studying the Bible. Legend has it that his family even offered him the blandishments of a prostitute in order to change his mind. Legend also has it that he refused. After attaining his freedom, Aquinas went to Paris in about 1244 and to Cologne in 1248, to study philosophy and theology.

The Dominicans placed considerable value on intellectual pursuits, and Aquinas profited from the teaching of Albertus Magnus (Albert the Great), perhaps the first of a long line of outstanding Dominican intellects. In 1252 Aquinas returned to the University of Paris as a lecturer, receiving his doctorate in theology in 1256. The divinity faculty at Paris, however, was reluctant to confer the license to teach upon mendicant friars. Aquinas the Dominican and St. Bonaventure (1217–1274) the Franciscan argued their case before the Pope, and both were licensed in 1257. From 1259 to 1268 Aquinas taught at several Dominican monasteries in Italy. He then returned to Paris, only to go to Naples in 1272. Summoned to participate at the Council of Lyons in 1274, he died on the way at Fossanova, near the place of his birth.

Aquinas did not spend much of his adult life in any one place, but he managed to write a tremendous amount of material. Several of his works are commentaries on the works of Aristotle, a fact that requires some comment. Aristotle's major works had been lost to the non-Arabic West until the beginning of the thirteenth century. Their reappearance caused a good deal of intellectual ferment. To many, the world-view disclosed in Aristotle's writings seemed to be a pagan threat to Christianity. To others, including Aquinas, Aristotle's works provided an exhilarating cosmological, metaphysical, and epistemological framework on which to build a coherent and all-encompassing Christian world-view. However, although Aristotle was "the Philosopher," he was not infallible, and Aquinas felt free to reject those aspects of his philosophy which conflicted with Christian revelation.

Some of the most characteristic features of Aquinas's philosophy derived from Aristotle include the insistence on the primary role of the senses in the acquisition of natural knowledge, and the metaphysical analysis of things in terms of matter and form. On the other hand, while Aristotle had held out little chance for personal survival after death, Aquinas argued for personal immortality. Aristotle's "God," or unmoved mover, would appear not to care one whit about the world, whereas the God of Christianity, insisted Aquinas, must be a personal God.

Another difference between Aristotle and Aquinas served to illustrate Aquinas's views on the relation between reason and faith. Aristotle had asserted that the world was eternal—that is, it had always existed, a doctrine which ran contrary to the Christian doctrine that the world was created by God. Aquinas claimed that nothing in our natural knowledge of the world would force one to conclude either that the world was eternal or that it had been created. Aristotle's position, then, was neither confirmed nor refuted by the evidence of our senses and the operation of human reason. But it is refuted by Revelation, that body of knowledge which transcends our rational faculties and which God has chosen to reveal to us. As a result, the Christian will believe as an item of faith that the world was created by God. For Aquinas, reason is powerless to prove such articles of faith given by Revelation. But reason can operate to demonstrate the truth of propositions which are not themselves articles of faith, but are presupposed by the articles of faith. One such proposition is that God exists.

• • •

The greatest of Aquinas's philosophical writings in his monumental *Summa Theologica.* It is divided into three major parts, with each part divided into many questions, and each question into articles. The first two questions of the first part are reprinted here. In the first question Aquinas asks whether Christian theology is a science—a question which may seem peculiar until one finds out that by "science" Aquinas means nothing more than any body of knowledge which has first principles. In the second question Aquinas turns to the issue of God's existence. Here he criticizes Anselm's ontological argument but offers five arguments of his own to show that God exists. These "five ways" have attracted lavish philosophical attention through the centuries.

F. C. Copleston's *Aquinas* (Baltimore: Penguin Books, 1955) and Etienne Gilson's *The Christian Philosophy of St. Thomas Aquinas* (New York: Random House, 1956) are two good introductions to Aquinas's philosophy. Anthony Kenny, ed., *Aquinas: A Collection of Critical Essays* (Garden City: Doubleday, 1969) and Norman Kretzmann and Eleonore Stump, eds., *The Cambridge Companion to Aquinas* (Cambridge: Cambridge University Press, 1993) contain several important essays.

W.E.M.

Summa Theologica

Part One
GOD
Question I
The Nature and Domain of Sacred Doctrine
(In Ten Articles)

To place our purpose within definite limits, we must first investigate the nature and domain of sacred doctrine. Concerning this there are ten points of inquiry: —

(1) Whether sacred doctrine is necessary? (2) Whether it is a science? (3) Whether it is one or many? (4) Whether it is speculative or practical? (5) How it is compared with other sciences? (6) Whether it is a wisdom? (7) Whether God is its subject-matter? (8) Whether it is argumentative? (9) Whether it rightly employs metaphors and similes? (10) Whether the Sacred Scripture of this doctrine may be expounded in different senses?

First Article

Whether, Besides the Philosophical Sciences, Any Further Doctrine Is Required?

We proceed thus to the First Article: —

Objection 1. It seems that, besides the philosophical sciences, we have no need of any further knowledge. For man should not seek to know what is above reason: *Seek not the things that are too high for thee* (*Ecclus.* iii 22). But whatever is not above reason is sufficiently considered in the philosophical sciences. Therefore any other knowledge besides the philosophical sciences is superfluous.

Obj. 2. Further, knowledge can be concerned only with being, for nothing can be known, save the true,

Reprinted from *Basic Writings of St. Thomas Aquinas*, ed. Anton C. Pegis (New York: Random House, 1945), by permission of the publisher.

which is convertible with being. But everything that is, is considered in the philosophical sciences — even God Himself; so that there is a part of philosophy called theology, or the divine science, as is clear from Aristotle. Therefore, besides the philosophical sciences, there is no need of any further knowledge.

On the contrary, It is written (2 *Tim.* iii. 16): *All Scripture inspired of God is profitable to teach, to reprove, to correct, to instruct in justice.* Now Scripture, inspired by God, is not a part of the philosophical sciences discovered by human reason. Therefore it is useful that besides the philosophical sciences there should be another science — *i.e.*, inspired of God.

I answer that, It was necessary for man's salvation that there should be a knowledge revealed by God, besides the philosophical sciences investigated by human reason. First, because man is directed to God as to an end that surpasses the grasp of his reason: *The eye hath not seen, O God, besides Thee, what things Thou hast prepared for them that wait for Thee* (*Isa.* lxiv. 4). But the end must first be known by men who are to direct their thoughts and actions to the end. Hence it was necessary for the salvation of man that certain truths which exceed human reason should be made known to him by divine revelation. Even as regards those truths about God which human reason can investigate, it was necessary that man be taught by a divine revelation. For the truth about God, such as reason can know it, would only be known by a few, and that after a long time, and with the admixture of many errors; whereas man's whole salvation, which is in God, depends upon the knowledge of this truth. Therefore, in order that the salvation of men might be brought about more fitly and more surely, it was necessary that they be taught divine truths by divine revelation. It was therefore necessary that, besides the philosophical sciences investigated by reason, there should be a sacred science by way of revelation.

Reply Obj. 1. Although those things which are beyond man's knowledge may not be sought for by man through his reason, nevertheless, what is revealed by God must be accepted through faith. Hence the sacred text continues. *For many things are shown to thee above the understanding of man* (Ecclus. iii. 25). And in such things sacred science consists.

Reply Obj. 2. Sciences are diversified according to the diverse nature of their knowable objects. For the astronomer and the physicist both prove the same conclusion—that the earth, for instance is round: the astronomer by means of mathematics (*i.e.*, abstracting from matter), but the physicist by means of matter itself. Hence there is no reason why those things which are treated by the philosophical sciences, so far as they can be known by the light of natural reason, may not also be treated by another science so far as they are known by the light of the divine revelation. Hence the theology included in sacred doctrine differs in genus from that theology which is part of philosophy.

Second Article

Whether Sacred Doctrine Is a Science?

We proceed thus to the Second Article:—

Objection 1. It seems that sacred doctrine is not a science. For every science proceeds from self-evident principles. But sacred doctrine proceeds from articles of faith which are not self-evident, since their truth is not admitted by all: *For all men have not faith* (2 *Thess.* iii. 2). Therefore sacred doctrine is not a science.

Obj. 2. Further, science is not of individuals. But sacred doctrine treats of individual facts, such as the deeds of Abraham, Isaac and Jacob, and the like. Therefore sacred doctrine is not a science.

On the contrary, Augustine says that *to this science alone belongs that whereby saving faith is begotten, nourished, protected and strengthened*. But this can be said of no science except sacred doctrine. Therefore sacred doctrine is a science.

I answer that, Sacred doctrine is a science. We must bear in mind that there are two kinds of sciences. There are some which proceed from principles known by the natural light of the intellect, such as arithmetic and geometry and the like. There are also some which proceed from principles known by the light of a higher science: thus the science of optics proceeds from principles established by geometry, and music from principles established by arithmetic.

So it is that sacred doctrine is a science because it proceeds from principles made known by the light of a higher science, namely, the science of God and the blessed. Hence, just as music accepts on authority the principles taught by the arithmetician, so sacred science accepts the principles revealed by God.

Reply Obj. 1. The principles of any science are either in themselves self-evident, or reducible to the knowledge of a higher science; and such, as we have said, are the principles of sacred doctrine.

Reply Obj. 2. Individual facts are not treated in sacred doctrine because it is concerned with them principally; they are rather introduced as examples to be followed in our lives (as in the moral sciences), as well as to establish the authority of those men through whom the divine revelation, on which this sacred scripture or doctrine is based, has come down to us.

Third Article

Whether Sacred Doctrine Is One Science?

We proceed thus to the Third Article:—

Objection 1. It seems that sacred doctrine is not one science, for according to the Philosopher[1] *that science is one which treats only of one class of subjects*. But the creator and the creature, both of whom are treated in sacred doctrine, cannot be grouped together under one class of subjects. Therefore sacred doctrine is not one science.

Obj. 2. Further, in sacred doctrine we treat of angels, corporeal creatures and human morality. But these belong to separate philosophical sciences. Therefore sacred doctrine cannot be one science.

On the contrary, Holy Scripture speaks of it as one science: *Wisdom gave him the knowledge of holy things* (Wis. x. 10).

I answer that, Sacred doctrine is one science. The unity of a power or habit is to be gauged by its object, not indeed, in its material aspect, but as regards the formality under which it is an object. For example, man, ass, stone, agree in the one formality of being colored; and color is the formal object of sight. Therefore, because Sacred Scripture (as we have said) considers some things under the formality of being di-

---

1. [Aquinas often refers to Aristotle as "the Philosopher."—S.M.C.]

vinely revealed, all things which have been divinely revealed have in common the formality of the object of this science. Hence, they are included under sacred doctrine as under one science.

Reply Obj. 1. Sacred doctrine does not treat of God and creatures equally, but of God primarily, and of creatures only so far as they are referable to God as their beginning or end. Hence the unity of this science is not impaired.

Reply Obj. 2. Nothing prevents inferior powers or habits from being diversified by objects which yet agree with one another in coming together under a higher power or habit; because the higher power or habit regards its own object under a more universal formality. Thus, the object of the *common sense* is the sensible, including, therefore, whatever is visible or audible. Hence the *common sense*, although one power, extends to all the objects of the five senses. Similarly, objects which are the subject-matter of different philosophical sciences can yet be treated by this one single sacred science under one aspect, namely, in so far as they can be included in revelation. So that in this way sacred doctrine bears, as it were, the stamp of the divine science, which is one and simple, yet extends to everything.

Fourth Article

Whether Sacred Doctrine Is a Practical Science?

We proceed thus to the Fourth Article: —

Objection 1. It seems that sacred doctrine is a practical science, for a practical science is that which ends in action, according to the Philosopher. But sacred doctrine is ordained to action: *Be ye doers of the word, and not hearers only* (*Fas.* i. 22). Therefore sacred doctrine is a practical science.

Obj. 2. Further sacred doctrine is divided into the Old and the New Law. But law belongs to moral science, which is a practical science. Therefore sacred doctrine is a practical science.

On the contrary, Every practical science is concerned with the things man can do; as moral science is concerned with human acts, and architecture with buildings. But sacred doctrine is chiefly concerned with God, Who is rather the Maker of man. Therefore it is not a practical but a speculative science.

I answer that, Sacred doctrine, being one, extends

to things which belong to the different philosophical sciences, because it considers in each the same formal aspect, namely, so far as they can be known through the divine light. Hence, although among the philosophical sciences some are speculative and others practical, nevertheless, sacred doctrine includes both; as God, by one and the same science, knows both Himself and His works.

Still, it is more speculative than practical, because it is more concerned with divine things than with human acts; though even of these acts it treats inasmuch as man is ordained by them to the perfect knowledge of God, in which consists eternal beatitude.

This is a sufficient answer to the Objections.

Fifth Article

Whether Sacred Doctrine Is Nobler Than Other Sciences?

We proceed thus to the Fifth Article: —

Objection 1. It seems that sacred doctrine is not nobler than other sciences, for the nobility of a science depends on its certitude. But other sciences, the principles of which cannot be doubted, seem to be more certain than sacred doctrine; for its principles — namely, articles of faith — can be doubted. Therefore other sciences seem to be nobler.

Obj. 2. Further, it is the part of a lower science to draw upon a higher; as music draws upon arithmetic. But sacred doctrine does draw upon the philosophical sciences; for Jerome[2] observes, in his Epistle to Magnus, that *the ancient doctors so enriched their books with the doctrines and thoughts of the philosophers, that thou knowest not what more to admire in them, their profane erudition or their scriptural learning.* Therefore sacred doctrine is inferior to other sciences.

On the contrary, Other sciences are called the handmaidens of this one: *Wisdom sent her maids to invite to the tower* (*Prov.* ix. 3).

I answer that, Since this science is partly speculative and partly practical, it transcends all other sciences, speculative and practical. Now one speculative sci-

---

2. [Jerome (c.347–c.420), a Father of the Church, was the author of the Vulgate translation of the Bible, the official Latin version of the Roman Catholic Church.]

ence is said to be nobler than another either by reason of its greater certitude, or by reason of the higher dignity of its subject-matter. In both these respects this science surpasses other speculative sciences: in point of greater certitude, because other sciences derive their certitude from the natural light of human reason, which can err, whereas this derives its certitude from the light of the divine knowledge, which cannot err; in point of the higher dignity of its subject-matter, because this science treats chiefly of those things which by their sublimity transcend human reason, while other sciences consider only those things which are within reason's grasp. Of the practical sciences, that one is nobler which is ordained to a more final end, as political science is nobler than military science; for the good of the army is directed to the good of the state. But the purpose of this science, in so far as it is practical, is eternal beatitude, to which as to an ultimate end the ends of all the practical sciences are directed. Hence it is clear that from every standpoint it is nobler than other sciences.

Reply Obj. 1. It may well happen that what is in itself the more certain may seem to us the less certain because of the weakness of our intellect, *which is dazzled by the clearest objects of nature; as the owl is dazzled by the light of the sun.* Hence the fact that some happen to doubt about the articles of faith is not due to the uncertain nature of the truths, but to the weakness of the human intellect; yet the slenderest knowledge that may be obtained of the highest things is more desirable than the most certain knowledge obtained of the lowest things, as is said in *De Animalibus* xi.[3]

Reply Obj. 2. This science can draw upon the philosophical sciences, not as though it stood in need of them, but only in order to make its teaching clearer. For it accepts its principles, not from the other sciences, but immediately from God, by revelation. Therefore it does not draw upon the other sciences as upon its superiors, but uses them as its inferiors and handmaidens: even so the master sciences make use of subordinate sciences, as political science of military science. That it thus uses them is not due to its own defect or insufficiency, but to the defect of our intellect, which is more easily led by what is known through natural reason (from which proceed the other sciences), to that which is above reason, such as are the teachings of this science.

Sixth Article

Whether This Doctrine Is a Wisdom?

We proceed thus to the Sixth Article:—

Objection 1. It seems that this doctrine is not a wisdom. For no doctrine which borrows its principles is worthy of the name of wisdom, seeing that the wise man directs, and is not directed. But this doctrine borrows its principles. Therefore it is not a wisdom.

Obj. 2. Further, it is a part of wisdom to prove the principles of other sciences. Hence it is called the chief of sciences, as is clear in *Ethics* vi.[4] But this doctrine does not prove the principles of other sciences. Therefore it is not a wisdom.

Obj. 3. Further, this doctrine is acquired by study, whereas wisdom is acquired by God's inspiration, and is accordingly numbered among the gifts of the Holy Spirit (*Isa.* xi. 2). Therefore this doctrine is not a wisdom.

On the contrary, It is written (*Deut.* iv. 6): *This is your wisdom and understanding in the sight of nations.*

I answer that, This doctrine is wisdom above all human wisdoms not merely in any one order, but absolutely. For since it is the part of a wise man to order and to judge, and since lesser matters can be judged in the light of some higher cause, he is said to be wise in any genus who considers the highest cause in that genus. Thus in the realm of building, he who plans the form of the house is called wise and architect, in relation to the subordinate laborers who trim the wood and make ready the stones: thus it is said, *As a wise architect I have laid the foundation* (*1 Cor.* ii. 10). Again, in order of all human life, the prudent man is called wise, inasmuch as he directs his acts to a fitting end: thus it is said, *Wisdom is prudence to a man* (*Prov.* x. 23). Therefore, he who considers absolutely the highest cause of the whole universe, namely God, is most of all called wise. Hence wisdom is said to be the knowledge of divine things, as Augustine says. But sacred doctrine essentially treats of God viewed as the highest cause, for

---

3. [The reference is to a biological work by Aristotle.]

4. [The reference is to Aristotle's *Nicomachean Ethics*.]

it treats of Him not only so far as He can be known through creatures just as philosophers knew Him — *That which is known of God is manifest in them (Rom. i. 19)* — but also so far as He is known to Himself alone and revealed to others. Hence sacred doctrine is especially called a wisdom.

Reply Obj. 1. Sacred doctrine derives its principles, not from any human knowledge, but from the divine knowledge, by which, as by the highest wisdom, all our knowledge is ordered.

Reply Obj. 2. The principles of the other sciences either are evident and cannot be proved, or they are proved by natural reason in some other science. But the knowledge proper to this science comes through revelation, and not through natural reason. Therefore it is not its business to prove the principles of the other sciences, but only to judge them. For whatsoever is found in the other sciences contrary to the truth of this science must be condemned as false. Hence, it is said: *Destroying counsels and every height that exalteth itself against the knowledge of God (2 Cor. x. 4, 5).*

Reply Obj. 3. Since judgment pertains to wisdom, in accord with a twofold manner of judging there is a twofold wisdom. A man may judge in one way by inclination, as whoever has the habit of a virtue judges rightly of what is virtuous by his very inclination towards it. Hence it is the virtuous man, as we read,[5] who is the measure and rule of human acts. In another way, a man may judge by knowledge, just as a man learned in moral science might be able to judge rightly about virtuous acts, though he had not virtue. The first manner of judging divine things belongs to that wisdom which is numbered as a gift of the Holy Ghost: *The spiritual man judgeth all things (1 Cor. ii. 15).* And Dionysius says: *Hierotheus is taught not only as one learning, but also as experiencing divine things.* The second manner of judging belongs to this doctrine, inasmuch as it is acquired by study, though its principles are obtained by revelation.

Seventh Article

Whether God Is the Subject-Matter of This Science?

We proceed thus to the Seventh Article: —

Objection 1. It seems that God is not the subject-matter of this science. For, according to the Philoso-

pher, in every science the essence of its subject is presupposed. But this science cannot presuppose the essence of God, for Damascene says: *It is impossible to express the essence of God.* Therefore God is not the subject-matter of this science.

Obj. 2. Further, whatever conclusions are reached in any science must be comprehended under the subject-matter of that science. But in Holy Scripture we reach conclusions not only concerning God, but concerning many other things, such as creatures and human morality. Therefore God is not the subject-matter of this science.

On the contrary, The subject-matter of a science is that of which it principally treats. But in this science the treatment is mainly about God; for it is called theology, as treating of God. Therefore God is the subject-matter of this science.

I answer that, God is the subject-matter of this science. The relation between a science and its subject-matter is the same as that between a habit or a power and its object. Now properly speaking the object of a power or habit is that under whose formality all things are referred to that power or habit, as man and stone are referred to sight in that they are colored. Hence colored things are the proper object of sight. But in sacred doctrine all things are treated under the aspect of God, either because they are God Himself, or because they refer to God as to their beginning and end. Hence it follows that God is in very truth the subject-matter of this science. This is made clear also from the principles of this science, namely, the articles of faith, for faith is about God. The subject-matter of the principles and of the whole science must be the same, since the whole science is contained virtually in its principles.

Some, however, looking to what is treated in this science, and not to the aspect under which it is treated, have asserted the subject-matter of this science to be something other than God — that is, either things and signs, or the works of salvation, or the whole Christ, that is, the head and members. Of all these things, in truth, we treat in this science, but so far as they are ordered to God.

Reply Obj. 1. Although we cannot know in what consists the essence of God, nevertheless in this doctrine we make use of His effects, either of nature or of grace, in the place of a definition, in regard to whatever is treated in this doctrine concerning God;

---

5. [The reference is to Aristotle's *Nicomachean Ethics*.]

even as in some philosophical sciences we demonstrate something about a cause from its effect, by taking the effect in the place of a definition of the cause.

Reply Obj. 2. Whatever other conclusions are reached in this sacred science are comprehended under God, not as parts or species or accidents, but as in some way ordained to Him.

Eighth Article

Whether Sacred Doctrine Is Argumentative?

We proceed thus to the Eighth Article:—

Objection 1. It seems this doctrine is not argumentative. For Ambrose[6] says: *Put arguments aside where faith is sought.* But in this doctrine faith especially is sought: *But these things are written that you may believe* (*Fo.* xx. 31). Therefore sacred doctrine is not argumentative.

Obj. 2. Further, if it is argumentative, the argument is either from authority or from reason. If it is from authority, it seems unbefitting its dignity, for the proof from authority is the weakest form of proof according to Boethius.[7] But if from reason, this is unbefitting its end, because, according to Gregory,[8] *faith has no merit in those things of which human reason brings its own experience.* Therefore sacred doctrine is not argumentative.

On the contrary, The Scripture says that a bishop should *embrace that faithful word which is according to doctrine, that he may be able to exhort in sound doctrine and to convince the gainsayers* (*Tit.* i. 9).

I answer that, As the other sciences do not argue in proof of their principles, but argue from their principles to demonstrate other truths in these sciences, so this doctrine does not argue in proof of its principles, which are the articles of faith, but from them it goes

on to prove something else; as the Apostle[9] argues from the resurrection of Christ in proof of the general resurrection (*1 Cor.* xv, 12). However, it is to be borne in mind, in regard to the philosophical sciences, that the inferior sciences neither prove their principles nor dispute with those who deny them, but leave this to a higher science; whereas the highest of them, viz., metaphysics, can dispute with one who denies its principles, if only the opponent will make some concession; but if he concedes nothing, it can have no dispute with him, though it can answer his arguments. Hence Sacred Scripture, since it has no science above itself, disputes argumentatively with one who denies its principles only if the opponent admits some at least of the truths obtained through divine revelation. Thus, we can argue with heretics from texts in Holy Scripture, and against those who deny one article of faith we can argue from another. If our opponent believes nothing of divine revelation, there is no longer any means of proving the articles of faith by argument, but only of answering his objections— if he has any—against faith. Since faith rests upon infallible truth, and since the contrary of a truth can never be demonstrated, it is clear that the proofs brought against faith are not demonstrations, but arguments that can be answered.

Reply Obj. 1. Although arguments from human reason cannot avail to prove what belongs to faith, nevertheless, this doctrine argues from articles of faith to other truths.

Reply Obj. 2. It is especially proper to this doctrine to argue from authority, inasmuch as its principles are obtained by revelation; and hence we must believe the authority of those to whom the revelation has been made. Nor does this take away the dignity of this doctrine, for although the argument from authority based on human reason is the weakest, yet the argument from authority based on divine revelation is the strongest. But sacred doctrine also makes use of human reason, not, indeed, to prove faith (for thereby the merit of faith would come to an end), but to make clear other things that are set forth in this doctrine. Since therefore grace does not destroy nature, but perfects it, natural reason should minister to faith as the natural inclination of the will ministers to

6. [Ambrose (c.340–397) was bishop of Milan and a Father of the Church.]

7. [Boethius (c.480–524) was a Roman philosopher and statesman whose greatest work, *The Consolation of Philosophy*, was written while he was imprisoned prior to his execution on false charges ot treason.)

8. [Gregory I (c.540–604), a Father of the Church who served as pope, defended the view that the temporal powers of the emperor and the spiritual powers of the pope were each supreme within separate spheres.]

9. [Aquinas often refers to Paul as "the Apostle."]

charity. Hence the Apostle says: *Bringing into captivity every understanding unto the obedience of Christ* (2 *Cor.* x. 5). Hence it is that sacred doctrine makes use also of the authority of philosophers in those questions in which they were able to know the truth by natural reason, as Paul quotes a saying of Aratus:[10] *As some also of your own poets said: For we are also His offspring* (*Acts* xvii. 28). Nevertheless, sacred doctrine makes use of these authorities as extrinsic and probable arguments, but properly uses the authority of the canonical Scriptures as a necessary demonstration, and the authority of the doctors of the Church as one that may properly be used, yet merely as probable. For our faith rests upon the revelation made to the apostles and prophets, who wrote the canonical books, and not on the revelations (if any such there are) made to other doctors. Hence Augustine says: *Only those books of Scripture which are called canonical have I learned to hold in such honor as to believe their authors have not erred in any way in writing them. But other authors I so read as not to deem anything in their works to be true, merely because of their having so thought and written, whatever may have been their holiness and learning.*

Ninth Article

Whether Holy Scripture Should Use Metaphors?

We proceed thus to the Ninth Article:—

Objection 1. It seems that Holy Scripture should not use metaphors. For that which is proper to the lowest science seems not to befit this science, which holds the highest place of all. But to proceed by the aid of various similitudes and figures is proper to poetic, the least of all the sciences. Therefore it is not fitting that this science should make use of such similitudes.

Obj. 2. Further, this doctrine seems to be intended to make truth clear. Hence a reward is held out to those who manifest it: *They that explain me shall have life everlasting* (*Ecclus.* xxiv. 31). But by such similitudes truth is obscured. Therefore to put forward divine truths under the likeness of corporeal things does not befit this doctrine.

Obj. 3. Further, the higher creatures are, the nearer they approach to the divine likeness. If therefore any creature be taken to represent God, this representation ought chiefly to be taken from the higher creatures, and not from the lower; yet this is often found in the Scriptures.

On the contrary, It is written (*Osee* xxii. 10): *I have multiplied visions, and I have used similitudes by the ministry of the prophets*. But to put forward anything by means of similitudes is to use metaphors. Therefore sacred doctrine may use metaphors.

I answer that, It is befitting Holy Scripture to put forward divine and spiritual truths by means of comparisons with material things. For God provides for everything according to the capacity of its nature. Now it is natural to man to attain to intellectual truths through sensible things, because all our knowledge originates from sense. Hence in Holy Scripture spiritual truths are fittingly taught under the likeness of material things. This is what Dionysius[11] says: *We cannot be enlightened by the divine rays except they be hidden within the covering of many sacred veils*. It is also befitting Holy Scripture, which is proposed to all without distinction of persons—*To the wise and to the unwise I am a debtor* (*Rom.* i. 14)—that spiritual truths be expounded by means of figures taken from corporeal things, in order that thereby even the simple who are unable by themselves to grasp intellectual things may be able to understand it.

Reply Obj. 1. Poetry makes use of metaphors to produce a representation, for it is natural to man to be pleased with representations. But sacred doctrine makes use of metaphors as both necessary and useful.

Reply Obj. 2. The ray of divine revelation is not extinguished by the sensible imagery wherewith it is veiled, as Dionysius says; and its truth so far remains that it does not allow the minds of those to whom the revelation has been made, to rest in the likenesses, but raises them to the knowledge of intelligible truths; and through those to whom the revelation has been made others also may receive instruction in these matters. Hence those things that are taught metaphorically in one part of Scripture, in other parts are taught more openly. The very hiding of truth in figures is

---

10. [Aratus was a third-century B.C. Greek court poet.]

11. [Dionysius the Areopagite, who lived during the first century, was traditionally considered the first bishop of Athens.]

useful for the exercise of thoughtful minds, and as a defense against the ridicule of the unbelievers, according to the words, *Give not that which is holy to dogs* (*Matt.* vii. 6).

Reply Obj. 3. As Dionysius says, it is more fitting that divine truths should be expounded under the figure of less noble than of nobler bodies; and this for three reasons. First, because thereby men's minds are the better freed from error. For then it is clear that these things are not literal descriptions of divine truths, which might have been open to doubt had they been expressed under the figure of nobler bodies, especially in the case of those who could think of nothing nobler than bodies. Second, because this is more befitting the knowledge of God that we have in this life. For what He is not is clearer to us than what He is. Therefore similitudes drawn from things farthest away from God form within us a truer estimate that God is above whatsoever we may say or think of Him. Third, because thereby divine truths are the better hidden from the unworthy.

Tenth Article

Whether in Holy Scripture a Word May Have Several Senses?

We proceed thus to the Tenth Article:—

Objection 1. It seems that in Holy Scripture a word cannot have several senses, historical or literal, allegorical, tropological or moral, and anagogical. For many different senses in one text produce confusion and deception and destroy all force of argument. Hence no argument, but only fallacies, can be deduced from a multiplicity of propositions. But Holy Scripture ought to be able to state the truth without any fallacy. Therefore in it there cannot be several senses to a word.

Obj. 2. Further, Augustine says that *the Old Testament has a fourfold division: according to history, etiology, analogy, and allegory.* Now these four seem altogether different from the four divisions mentioned in the first objection. Therefore it does not seem fitting to explain the same word of Holy Scripture according to the four different senses mentioned above.

Obj. 3. Further, besides these senses, there is the parabolical, which is not one of these four.

On the contrary, Gregory says: *Holy Scripture by the manner of its speech transcends every science, because in one and the same sentence, while it describes a fact, it reveals a mystery.*

I answer that, The author of Holy Scripture is God, in Whose power it is to signify His meaning, not by words only (as man also can do), but also by things themselves. So, whereas in every other science things are signified by words, this science has the property that the things signified by the words have themselves also a signification. Therefore that first signification whereby words signify things belongs to the first sense, the historical or literal. That signification whereby things signified by words have themselves also a signification is called the spiritual sense, which is based on the literal, and presupposes it. Now this spiritual sense has a threefold division. For as the Apostle says (*Heb.* x. 1) the Old Law is a figure of the New Law, and Dionysius says *the New Law itself is a figure of future glory.* Again, the New Law, whatever our Head has done is a type of what we ought to do. Therefore, so far as the things of the Old Law signify the things of the New Law, there is the allegorical sense; so far as the things done in Christ, or so far as the things which signify Christ, are signs of what we ought to do, there is the moral sense. But so far as they signify what relates to eternal glory, there is the anagogical sense. Since the literal sense is that which the author intends, and since the author of Holy Scripture is God, Who by one act comprehends all things by His intellect, it is not unfitting, as Augustine says, if, even according to the literal sense, one word in Holy Scripture should have several senses.

Reply Obj. 1. The multiplicity of these senses does not produce equivocation or any other kind of multiplicity, seeing that these senses are not multiplied because one word signifies several things, but because the things signified by the words can be themselves signs of other things. Thus in Holy Scripture no confusion results, for all the senses are founded on one—the literal—from which alone can any argument be drawn, and not from those intended allegorically, as Augustine says. Nevertheless, nothing of Holy Scripture perishes because of this, since nothing necessary to faith is contained under the spiritual sense which is not elsewhere put forward clearly by the Scripture in its literal sense.

Reply Obj. 2. These three—history, etiology, analogy—are grouped under the literal sense. For it is called history, as Augustine expounds, whenever anything is simply related; it is called etiology when its cause is assigned, as when Our Lord gave the reason why Moses allowed the putting away of wives — namely, because of the hardness of men's hearts (*Matt.* xix. 8); it is called analogy whenever the truth of one text of Scripture is shown not to contradict the truth of another. Of these four, allegory alone stands for the three spiritual senses. Thus Hugh of St. Victor[12] includes the anagogical under the allegorical sense, laying down three senses only — the historical, the allegorical and the tropological.

Reply Obj. 3. The parabolical sense is contained in the literal, for by words things are signified properly and figuratively. Nor is the figure itself, but that which is figured, the literal sense. When Scripture speaks of God's arm, the literal sense is not that God has such a member, but only what is signified by this member, namely, operative power. Hence it is plain that nothing false can ever underlie the literal sense of Holy Scripture.

Question II
The Existence of God
(In Three Articles)

Because the chief aim of sacred doctrine is to teach the knowledge of God not only as He is in Himself, but also as He is the beginning of things and their last end, and especially of rational creatures, as is clear from what has been already said, therefore, in our endeavor to expound this science, we shall treat: (1) of God; (2) of the rational creature's movement towards God; (3) of Christ Who as man is our way to God.

In treating of God there will be a threefold division: —

For we shall consider (1) whatever concerns the divine essence. (2) Whatever concerns the distinctions of Persons. (3) Whatever concerns the procession of creatures from Him.

Concerning the divine essence, we must consider: —

(1) Whether God exists? (2) The manner of His existence, or, rather, what is *not* the manner of His existence. (3) Whatever concerns His operations — namely, His knowledge, will, power.

Concerning the first, there are three points of inquiry: —

(1) Whether the proposition *God exists* is self-evident? (2) Whether it is demonstrable? (3) Whether God exists?

First Article
Whether the Existence of God Is Self-Evident?

We proceed thus to the First Article: —

Objection 1. It seems that the existence of God is self-evident. For those things are said to be self-evident to us the knowledge of which exists naturally in us, as we can see in regard to first principles. But as Damascene[13] says, *the knowledge of God is naturally implanted in all*. Therefore the existence of God is self-evident.

Obj. 2. Further, those things are said to be self-evident which are known as soon as the terms are known, which the Philosopher says is true of the first principles of demonstration. Thus, when the nature of a whole and of a part is known, it is at once recognized that every whole is greater than its part. But as soon as the signification of the name *God* is understood, it is at once seen that God exists. For by this name is signified that thing than which nothing greater can be conceived. But that which exists actually and mentally is greater than that which exists only mentally. Therefore, since as soon as the name *God* is understood it exists mentally, it also follows that it exists actually. Therefore the proposition *God exists* is self-evident.

Obj. 3. Further, the existence of truth is self-evident. For whoever denies the existence of truth grants that truth does not exist: and, if truth does not exist, then the proposition *Truth does not exist* is true: and if there is anything true there must be truth. But God is truth itself: *I am the way, the truth, and the life* (*Fo.* xiv. 6). Therefore *God exists* is self-evident.

On the contrary, No one can mentally admit the opposite of what is self-evident, as the Philosopher states concerning the first principles of demonstration. But the opposite of the proposition *God is* can

---

12. [Hugh of St. Victor (1096–1141), born in Saxony, was a noted theologian who also wrote numerous mystical works.]

13. [John Damascene (c.675–c.749) was a Syrian theologian and Father of the Church.]

be mentally admitted: *The fool said in his heart, There is no God* (*Ps.* lii 1). Therefore, that God exists is not self-evident.

I answer that, A thing can be self-evident in either of two ways: on the one hand, self-evident in itself, though not to us; on the other, self-evident in itself, and to us. A proposition is self-evident because the predicate is included in the essence of the subject: *e.g., Man is an animal,* for animal is contained in the essence of man. If, therefore, the essence of the predicate and subject be known to all, the proposition will be self-evident to all; as is clear with regard to the first principles of demonstration, the terms of which are certain common notions that no one is ignorant of, such as being and non-being, whole and part, and the like. If, however, there are some to whom the essence of the predicate and subject is unknown, the proposition will be self-evident in itself, but not to those who do not know the meaning of the predicate and subject of the proposition. Therefore, it happens, as Boethius says, that there are some notions of the mind which are common and self-evident only to the learned, as that incorporeal substances are not in space. Therefore, I say that this proposition, *God exists,* of itself is self-evident, for the predicate is the same as the subject, because God is His own existence as will be hereafter shown. Now because we do not know the essence of God, the proposition is not self-evident to us, but needs to be demonstrated by things that are more known to us, though less known in their nature—namely, by His effects.

Reply Obj. 1. To know that God exists in a general and confused way is implanted in us by nature, inasmuch as God is man's beatitude. For man naturally desires happiness, and what is naturally desired by man is naturally known by him. This, however, is not to know absolutely that God exists; just as to know that someone is approaching is not the same as to know that Peter is approaching, even though it is Peter who is approaching; for there are many who imagine that man's perfect good, which is happiness, consists in riches, and others in pleasures, and others in something else.

Reply Obj. 2. Perhaps not everyone who hears this name *God* understands it to signify something than which nothing greater can be thought, seeing that some have believed God to be a body. Yet, granted that everyone understands that by this name *God* is signified something than which nothing greater can be thought, nevertheless, it does not therefore follow that he understands that what the name signifies exists actually, but only that it exists mentally. Nor can it be argued that it actually exists, unless it be admitted that there actually exists something than which nothing greater can be thought; and this precisely is not admitted by those who hold that God does not exist.

Reply Obj. 3. The existence of truth in general is self-evident, but the existence of a Primal Truth is not self-evident to us.

Second Article

Whether It Can Be Demonstrated That God Exists?

We proceed thus to the Second Article: —

Objection 1. It seems that the existence of God cannot be demonstrated. For it is an article of faith that God exists. But what is of faith cannot be demonstrated, because a demonstration produces scientific knowledge, whereas faith is of the unseen, as is clear from the Apostle (*Heb.* xi. 1). Therefore it cannot be demonstrated that God exists.

Obj. 2. Further, essence is the middle term of demonstration. But we cannot know in what God's essence consists, but solely in what it does not consist, as Damascene says. Therefore we cannot demonstrate that God exists.

Obj. 3. Further, if the existence of God were demonstrated, this could only be from His effects. But His effects are not proportioned to Him, since He is infinite and His effects are finite, and between the finite and infinite there is no proportion. Therefore, since a cause cannot be demonstrated by an effect not proportioned to it, it seems that the existence of God cannot be demonstrated.

On the contrary, the Apostle says: *The invisible things of Him are clearly seen, being understood by the things that are made* (*Rom.* i. 20). But this would not be unless the existence of God could be demonstrated through the things that are made; for the first thing we must know of anything is, whether it exists.

I answer that, Demonstration can be made in two ways: One is through the cause, and is called *propter quid,* and this is to argue from what is prior absolutely. The other is through the effect, and is called a demonstration *quia;* this is to argue from what is prior relatively only to us. When an effect is better known to us than its cause, from the effect we proceed to the knowledge of the cause. And from every effect the existence of its proper cause can be demonstrated, so long as its effects are better known to us; because, since every effect depends upon its cause, if the effect exists, the cause must pre-exist. Hence the existence of God, in so far as it is not self-evident to us, can be demonstrated from those of His effects which are known to us.

Reply Obj. 1. The existence of God and other like truths about God, which can be known by natural reason, are not articles of faith, but are preambles to the articles; for faith presupposes natural knowledge, even as grace presupposes nature and perfection the perfectible. Nevertheless, there is nothing to prevent a man, who cannot grasp a proof, from accepting, as a matter of faith, something which in itself is capable of being scientifically known and demonstrated.

Reply Obj. 2. When the existence of a cause is demonstrated from an effect, this effect takes the place of the definition of the cause in proving the cause's existence. This is especially the case in regard to God, because, in order to prove the existence of anything, it is necessary to accept as a middle term the meaning of the name, and not its essence, for the question of its essence follows on the question of its existence. Now the names given to God are derived from His effects, as will be later shown. Consequently, in demonstrating the existence of God from His effects, we may take for the middle term the meaning of the name *God*.

Reply Obj. 3. From effects not proportioned to the cause no perfect knowledge of that cause can be obtained. Yet from every effect the existence of the cause can be clearly demonstrated, and so we can demonstrate the existence of God from His effects; though from them we cannot know God perfectly as He is in His essence.

Third Article

Whether God Exists?

We proceed thus to the Third Article:—

Objection 1. It seems that God does not exist; because if one of two contraries be infinite, the other would be altogether destroyed. But the name *God* means that He is infinite goodness. If, therefore, God

existed, there would be no evil discoverable; but there is evil in the world. Therefore God does not exist.

Obj. 2. Further, it is superfluous to suppose that what can be accounted for by a few principles has been produced by many. But it seems that everything we see in the world can be accounted for by other principles, supposing God did not exist. For all natural things can be reduced to one principle, which is nature; and all voluntary things can be reduced to one principle, which is human reason, or will. Therefore there is no need to suppose God's existence.

On the contrary, It is said in the person of God: *I am Who am (Exod.* iii. 14).

I answer that, The existence of God can be proved in five ways.

The first and more manifest way is the argument from motion. It is certain, and evident to our senses, that in the world some things are in motion. Now whatever is moved is moved by another, for nothing can be moved except it is in potentiality to that towards which it is moved; whereas a thing moves inasmuch as it is in act. For motion is nothing else than the reduction of something from potentiality to actuality. But nothing can be reduced from potentiality to actuality, except by something in a state of actuality. Thus that which is actually hot, as fire, makes wood, which is potentially hot, to be actually hot, and thereby moves and changes it. Now it is not possible that the same thing should be at once in actuality and potentiality in the same respect, but only in different respects. For what is actually hot cannot simultaneously be potentially hot; but it is simultaneously potentially cold. It is therefore impossible that in the same respect and in the same way a thing should be both mover and moved, *i.e.*, that it should move itself. Therefore, whatever is moved must be moved by another. If that by which it is moved be itself moved, then this also must needs be moved by another, and that by another again. But this cannot go on to infinity, because then there would be no first mover, and, consequently, no other mover, seeing that subsequent movers move only inasmuch as they are moved by the first mover; as the staff moves only because it is moved by the hand. Therefore it is necessary to arrive at a first mover, moved by no other; and this everyone understands to be God.

The second way is from the nature of efficient cause. In the world of sensible things we find there is an order of efficient causes. There is no case known (neither is it, indeed, possible) in which a thing is found to be the efficient cause of itself; for so it would be prior to itself, which is impossible. Now in efficient causes it is not possible to go on to infinity, because in all efficient causes following in order, the first is the cause of the intermediate cause, and the intermediate is the cause of the ultimate cause, whether the intermediate cause be several, or one only. Now to take away the cause is to take away the effect. Therefore, if there be no first cause among efficient causes, there will be no ultimate, nor any intermediate, cause. But if in efficient causes it is possible to go on to infinity, there will be no first efficient cause, neither will there be an ultimate effect, nor any intermediate efficient causes; all of which is plainly false. Therefore it is necessary to admit a first efficient cause, to which everyone gives the name of God.

The third way is taken from possibility and necessity, and runs thus. We find in nature things that are possible to be and not to be, since they are found to be generated, and to be corrupted, and consequently, it is possible for them to be and not to be. But it is impossible for these always to exist, for that which can not-be at some time is not. Therefore, if everything can not-be, then at one time there was nothing in existence. Now if this were true, even now there would be nothing in existence, because that which does not exist begins to exist only through something already existing. Therefore, if at one time nothing was in existence, it would have been impossible for anything to have begun to exist; and thus even now nothing would be in existence—which is absurd. Therefore, not all beings are merely possible, but there must exist something the existence of which is necessary. But every necessary thing either has its necessity caused by another, or not. Now it is impossible to go on to infinity in necessary things which have their necessity caused by another, as has been already proved in regard to efficient causes. Therefore we cannot but admit the existence of some being having of itself its own necessity, and not receiving it from another, but rather causing in others their necessity. This all men speak of as God.

The fourth way is taken from the gradation to be found in things. Among beings there are some more

and some less good, true, noble, and the like. But *more* and *less* are predicated of different things according as they resemble in their different ways something which is the maximum, as a thing is said to be hotter according as it more nearly resembles that which is hottest; so that there is something which is truest, something best, something noblest, and consequently, something which is most being, for those things that are greatest in truth are greatest in being, as it is written in *Metaph* ii.[14] Now the maximum in any genus is the cause of all in that genus, as fire, which is the maximum of heat, is the cause of all hot things, as is said in the same book. Therefore there must also be something which is to all beings the cause of their being, goodness, and every other perfection; and this we call God.

The fifth way is taken from the governance of the world. We see that things which lack knowledge, such as natural bodies, act for an end, and this is evident from their acting always, or nearly always, in the same way, so as to obtain the best result. Hence it is plain that they achieve their end, not fortuitously, but designedly. Now whatever lacks knowledge cannot move towards an end, unless it be directed by some being endowed with knowledge and intelligence; as the arrow is directed by the archer. Therefore some intelligent being exists by whom all natural things are directed to their end; and this being we call God.

Reply Obj. 1. As Augustine says: *Since God is the highest good, He would not allow any evil to exist in His works, unless His omnipotence and goodness were such as to bring good even out of evil.* This is part of the infinite goodness of God, that He should allow evil to exist, and out of it produce good.

Reply Obj. 2. Since nature works for a determinate end under the direction of a higher agent, whatever is done by nature must be traced back to God as to its first cause. So likewise whatever is done voluntarily must be traced back to some higher cause other than human reason and will, since these can change and fail; for all things that are changeable and capable of defect must be traced back to an immovable and self-necessary first principle, as has been shown.

14. [The reference is to Aristotle's *Metaphysics*.]

René Descartes

René Descartes lived in an era of geniuses. In the year of his birth, 1596, Shakespeare was writing *Richard II* and *The Merchant of Venice*. When Descartes died in 1650, Newton was seven. Hobbes and Galileo were near-contemporaries.

Descartes was born in La Haye, now La Haye-Descartes, a small town in Touraine, France, and lived much of his life in virtual seclusion in Holland. His interests were extremely wide-ranging. He made major contributions to anatomy and physiology, optics, mathematics, and, of course, philosophy. At the center of his thought lies the view that each science is a branch of one unified science of the world, a science based on mathematics. Thus, Descartes was an early champion of Galileo's doctrine that "the book of nature is written in the language of mathematics." In addition to unifying other sciences through mathematics, Descartes effected a major unification within mathematics when he displayed the relation between the geometry of the ancients and the algebra he helped develop through the use of his Cartesian coordinate system.

The value of mathematics in studying natural science seems obvious to us today. How can mathematics advance the study of philosophy? Like Plato before him, Descartes believes that through training in mathematics the mind becomes capable of engaging in philosophical thought. In mathematics, we encounter absolute certainty, according to Descartes. We recognize that our conclusion cannot be mistaken, because our starting assumptions are obviously true and each step in the chain of reasoning is correct. Further, mathematics introduces us to knowledge gained through the understanding, or through reasoning, rather than through the senses. While children may originally come to accept that $1 + 1 = 2$ by counting cookies, the mature person's belief that $1 + 1 = 2$, always and with no exceptions, seems to have a different basis. Descartes believes that it rests on intellectual understanding: we grasp what a unit is and how the addition operation combines units. It is not mathematical results, but these two striking characteristics of mathematical knowledge, its certainty and its dependence on understanding rather than sensation, that provide illumination for philosophy. Descartes argues that, as with mathematics, certainty must be the touchstone of philosophical truth and the way to that truth must be through the understanding.

The *Meditations on First Philosophy,* reprinted here, is Descartes's most important philosophical treatise. It is an unusual work: rather than lecturing his readers on the virtues of his conclusions, Descartes invites us to come along with him on the journey of discovering those conclusions. What is required of readers is that we too reflect on the issues that intrigue Descartes, that we ask ourselves such questions as, "If I am thinking, is it possible for me to doubt that I exist?"

Recalling that Descartes wished to bring to philosophy the certainty he discerned in mathematics, it is hardly surprising that the First Meditation begins by attempting to doubt all claims. The doubting has two purposes. Descartes wants to show that beliefs based on sensory data are not certain, thereby establishing the superiority of the understanding in acquiring knowledge. He also wants to discover whether any of our beliefs is in fact immune to doubt. In the Second Meditation, Descartes and his readers come to understand through reasoning that there is a claim that cannot be doubted: when one contemplates one's existence, it is not possible to have the slightest doubt that one does in fact exist. This conclusion is neatly captured in the well-known phrase, *cogito, ergo sum,* or "I think, therefore I am" (although these words do not appear in the *Meditations*). It is crucially important to note that, for Descartes, the "I" in this claim does not refer to a physical person, but to an immaterial mind. "Cartesian dualism" is the view that the world consists of two fundamental types of entities: physical bodies and immaterial minds. Since only minds can think, the *cogito* can only be used to show that a mind exists.

Later in the *Meditations,* Descartes attempts to restore the beliefs that his method of doubt had cast aside, arguing that it is also certain that physical bodies exist. In the Third Meditation, he completes the *cogito* argument and lays the basis for the later arguments concerning the existence of the physical world, contending that any claim which cannot be doubted must actually be true because God exists and would not permit us to be deceived about anything which was completely obvious to us.

• • •

Vera Chappell has collected the best recent work on this topic in *Descartes' Meditations* (Lanham, Md.: Rowman & Littlefield, 1997). Anthony Kenny, *Descartes: A Study of His Philosophy* (New York: Random House, 1968) is designed as an introduction for students but also treats those aspects of Descartes's thought that are the most interesting to contemporary philosophers. Another helpful work on the introductory level is John Cottingham, *Descartes* (Oxford: Basil Blackwell, 1986). John Cottingham, ed., *The Cambridge Companion to Descartes* (Cambridge: Cambridge University Press, 1992) offers introductory essays on a variety of important topics. Harry Frankfurt, *Demons, Dreamers, and Madmen: The Defense of Reason in Descartes' Meditations* (Indianapolis: The Bobbs-Merrill Company, 1970) offers an excellent discussion of the first two meditations; E. M. Curley, *Descartes Against the Skeptics* (Cambridge, Mass.: Harvard University Press, 1978) provides a clear and interesting discussion of the first two meditations and of Descartes's relations to some of his contemporaries. Peter J. Markie, *Descartes's Gambit* (Ithaca and London: Cornell University Press, 1986) presents an incisive study of the strategy of Descartes's argumentation. When Descartes first published the *Meditations,* he included a series of objections by contemporaries and his replies to them, which is still a wonderful companion to the *Meditations.* These are available along with other major works of Descartes, including the *Discourse on Method,* the *Principles of Philosophy,* and *The Passions of the Soul,* in *The Philosophical Writings of Descartes,* 2 vols., trans. J. Cottingham, R. Stoothoff, and D. Murdock (Cambridge: Cambridge University Press, 1985). An influential contemporary critique of Descartes's position is Gilbert Ryle, *The Concept of Mind* (New York: Barnes and Noble, 1949).

P.W.K.

Meditations on First Philosophy

To those Most Wise and Distinguished Men,
the Dean and Doctors of the Faculty of Sacred Theology of Paris
René Descartes Sends Greetings

So right is the cause that impels me to offer this work to you, that I am confident you too will find it equally right and thus take up its defense, once you have understood the plan of my undertaking; so much is this the case that I have no better means of commending it here than to state briefly what I have sought to achieve in this work.

I have always thought that two issues—namely, God and the soul—are chief among those that ought to be demonstrated with the aid of philosophy rather than theology. For although it suffices for us believers to believe by faith that the human soul does not die with the body, and that God exists, certainly no unbelievers seem capable of being persuaded of any religion or even of almost any moral virtue, until these two are first proven to them by natural reason. And since in this life greater rewards are often granted to vices than to virtues, few would prefer what is right to what is useful, if they neither feared God nor anticipated an afterlife. Granted, it is altogether true that we must believe in God's existence because it is taught in the Holy Scriptures, and, conversely, that we must believe the Holy Scriptures because they have come from God. This is because, of course, since faith is a gift from God, the very same one who gives the grace that is necessary for believing the rest can also give the grace to believe that he exists. Nonetheless, this reasoning cannot be proposed to unbelievers because they would judge it to be circular. In fact, I have observed that not only do you and all other theologians affirm that one can prove the existence of God by natural reason, but also that one may infer from Sacred Scripture that the knowledge of him is easier to achieve than the many things we know about creatures, and is so utterly easy that those without this knowledge are blameworthy. For this is clear from *Wisdom*, Chapter 13, where it is said: "They are not to be excused, for if their capacity for knowing were so great that they could think well of this world, how is it that they did not find the Lord of it even more easily?" And in *Romans*, Chapter 1, it is said that they are "without excuse." And again in the same passage it appears we are being warned with the words: "What is known of God is manifest in them," that everything that can be known about God can be shown by reasons drawn exclusively from our own mind. For this reason, I did not think it unbecoming for me to inquire how this may be the case, and by what path God may be known more easily and with greater certainty than the things of this world.

And as to the soul, there are many who have regarded its nature as something into which one cannot easily inquire, and some have even gone so far as to say that human reasoning convinces them that the soul dies with the body, while it is by faith alone that they hold the contrary position. Nevertheless, because the Lateran Council[1] held under Leo X, in Session 8, condemned such people and expressly enjoined Christian philosophers to refute their arguments and to use all their powers to demonstrate the truth, I have not hesitated to undertake this task as well.

Moreover, I know that there are many irreligious people who refuse to believe that God exists and that the human mind is distinct from the body—for no

Reprinted by permission of the translator Donald A. Cress, from Descartes, *Meditations on First Philosophy*, 3rd ed. (Indianapolis: Hackett Publishing Company, 1993).

1. [The Council took place between 1512 and 1517.—S.M.C.]

other reason than their claim that up until now no one has been able to demonstrate these two things. By no means am I in agreement with these people; on the contrary, I believe that nearly all the arguments which have been brought to bear on these questions by great men have the force of a demonstration, when they are adequately understood, and I am convinced that hardly any arguments can be given that have not already been discovered by others. Nevertheless, I judge that there is no greater task to perform in philosophy than assiduously to seek out, once and for all, the best of all these arguments and to lay them out so precisely and plainly that henceforth all will take them to be true demonstrations. And finally, I was strongly urged to do this by some people who knew that I had developed a method for solving all sorts of problems in the sciences—not a new one, mind you, since nothing is more ancient than the truth, but one they had seen me use with some success in other areas. Accordingly, I took it to be my task to attempt something on this subject.

This treatise contains all that I have been able to accomplish. Not that I have attempted to gather together in it all the various arguments that could be brought forward as proof of the very same conclusions, for this does not seem worthwhile, except where no one proof is sufficiently certain. Rather, I have sought out the primary and chief arguments, so that I now make bold to propose these as most certain and evident demonstrations. Moreover, I will say in addition that these arguments are such that I believe there is no way open to the human mind whereby better ones could ever be found. For the urgency of the cause, as well as the glory of God, to which this entire enterprise is referred, compels me here to speak somewhat more freely on my own behalf than is my custom. But although I believe these arguments to be certain and evident, still I am not thereby convinced that they are suited to everyone's grasp. In geometry there are many arguments developed by Archimedes, Apollonius,[2] Pappus,[3] and others, which are taken by everyone to be evident and certain because they

contain absolutely nothing which, considered by itself, is not quite easily known, and in which what follows does not square exactly with what has come before. Nevertheless they are rather lengthy and require a particularly attentive reader; thus only a small handful of people understand them. Likewise, although the arguments I use here do, in my opinion, equal or even surpass those of geometry in certitude and obviousness, nevertheless I am fearful that many people will not be capable of adequately perceiving them, both because they too are a bit lengthy, with some of them depending on still others, and also because, first and foremost, they demand a mind that is quite free from prejudices and that can easily withdraw itself from association with the senses. Certainly there are not to be found in the world more people with an aptitude for metaphysical studies than those with an aptitude for geometry. Moreover, there is the difference that in geometry everyone is of a mind that usually nothing is put down in writing without there being a sound demonstration for it; thus the inexperienced more frequently err on the side of assenting to what is false, wanting as they do to give the appearance of understanding it, than on the side of denying what is true. But it is the reverse in philosophy: since it is believed that there is no issue that cannot be defended from either side, few look for the truth, and many more prowl about for a reputation for profundity by arrogantly challenging whichever arguments are the best.

And therefore, regardless of the force of my arguments, because they are of a philosophical nature I do not anticipate that what I will have accomplished through them will be very worthwhile unless you assist me with your patronage. Your faculty is held in such high esteem in the minds of all, and the name of the Sorbonne has such authority, that not only in matters of faith has no association, with the exception of the councils of the Church, been held in such high regard as yours, but even in human philosophy nowhere is there thought to be greater insightfulness and solidity, or greater integrity and wisdom in rendering judgments. Should you deign to show any interest in this work, I do not doubt that, first of all, its errors would be corrected by you (for I am mindful not only of my humanity but also, and most especially, of my ignorance, and thus do not claim that there are no errors in it); second, what is

2. [Apollonius of Perga (c.262–200 B.C.) was a Greek mathematician famed for his study of conic sections.]

3. [Pappus of Alexandria was a fourth-century Greek mathematician whose work exerted an influence on the revival of interest in geometry in the seventeenth century.]

lacking would be added, or what is not sufficiently complete would be perfected, or what is in need of further discussion would be expanded upon more fully, either by yourselves or at least by me, after you have given me your guidance; and finally, after the arguments contained in this work proving that God exists and that the mind is distinct from the body have been brought (as I am confident they can be) to such a level of lucidity that these arguments ought to be regarded as the most precise of demonstrations, you may be of a mind to make such a declaration and publicly attest to it. Indeed, should this come to pass, I have no doubt that all the errors that have ever been entertained regarding these issues would shortly be erased from the minds of men. For the truth itself will easily cause other men of intelligence and learning to subscribe to your judgment. Your authority will cause the atheists, who more often than not are dilettantes rather than men of intelligence and learning, to put aside their spirit of contrariness, and perhaps even to defend the arguments which they will come to know are regarded as demonstrations by all who are discerning, lest they appear not to understand them. And finally, everyone else will readily give credence to so many indications of support, and there will no longer be anyone in the world who would dare call into doubt either the existence of God or the real distinction between the soul and the body. Just how great the usefulness of this thing might be, you yourselves, in virtue of your singular wisdom, are in the best position of anyone to judge; nor would it behoove me to commend the cause of God and religion at any greater length to you, who have always been the greatest pillar of the Catholic Church.

Preface to the Reader

I have already touched briefly on the issues of God and the human mind in my *Discourse on the Method of Rightly Conducting One's Reason and Searching for Truth in the Sciences*, published in French in 1637. The intent there was not to provide a precise treatment of them, but only to offer a sample and to learn from the opinions of readers how these issues should be treated in the future. For they seemed to me to be so important that I judged they ought to be dealt with more than once. And the path I follow in order to explain them is so little trodden and so far

removed from the one commonly taken that I did not think it useful to hold forth at greater length in a work written in French and designed to be read indiscriminately by everyone, lest weaker minds be in a position to think that they too ought to set out on this path.

In the *Discourse* I asked everyone who might find something in my writings worthy of refutation to do me the favor of making me aware of it. As for what I touched on regarding these issues, only two objections were worth noting, and I will respond briefly to them here before undertaking a more precise explanation of them.

The first is that, from the fact that the human mind, when turned in on itself, does not perceive itself to be anything other than a thinking thing, it does not follow that its nature or *essence* consists only in its being a thinking thing, such that the word *only* excludes everything else that also could perhaps be said to belong to the nature of the soul. To this objection I answer that in that passage I did not intend my exclusion of those things to reflect the order of the truth of the matter (I was not dealing with it then), but merely the order of my perception. Thus what I had in mind was that I was aware of absolutely nothing that I knew belonged to my essence, save that I was a thinking thing, that is, a thing having within itself the faculty of thinking. Later on, however, I will show how it follows, from the fact that I know of nothing else belonging to my essence, that nothing else really does belong to it.

The second objection is that it does not follow from the fact that I have within me an idea of a thing more perfect than me, that this idea is itself more perfect than me, and still less that what is represented by this idea exists. But I answer that there is an equivocation here in the word "idea." For "idea" can be taken either materially, for an operation of the intellect (in which case it cannot be said to be more perfect than me), or objectively, for the thing represented by means of that operation. This thing, even if it is not presumed to exist outside the intellect, can nevertheless be more perfect than me by reason of its essence. I will explain in detail in the ensuing remarks how, from the mere fact that there is within me an idea of something more perfect than me, it follows that this thing really exists.

In addition, I have seen two rather lengthy treatises,

but these works, utilizing as they do arguments drawn from atheist commonplaces, focused their attack not so much on my arguments regarding these issues, as on my conclusions. Moreover, arguments of this type exercise no influence over those who understand my arguments, and the judgments of many people are so preposterous and feeble that they are more likely to be persuaded by the first opinions to come along, however false and contrary to reason they may be, than by a true and firm refutation of them which they hear subsequently. Accordingly, I have no desire to respond here to these objections, lest I first have to state what they are. I will only say in general that all the objections typically bandied about by the atheists to assail the existence of God always depend either on ascribing human emotions to God, or on arrogantly claiming for our minds such power and wisdom that we attempt to determine and grasp fully what God can and ought to do. Hence these objections will cause us no difficulty, provided we but remember that our minds are to be regarded as finite, while God is to be regarded as incomprehensible and infinite.

But now, after having, to some degree, conducted an initial review of the judgments of men, here I begin once more to treat the same questions about God and the human mind, together with the starting points of the whole of first philosophy, but not in a way that causes me to have any expectation of widespread approval or a large readership. On the contrary, I do not advise anyone to read these things except those who have both the ability and the desire to meditate seriously with me, and to withdraw their minds from the senses as well as from all prejudices. I know all too well that such people are few and far between. As to those who do not take the time to grasp the order and linkage of my arguments, but will be eager to fuss over statements taken out of context (as is the custom for many), they will derive little benefit from reading this work. Although perhaps they might find an occasion for quibbling in several places, still they will not find it easy to raise an objection that is either compelling or worthy of response.

But because I do not promise to satisfy even the others on all counts the first time around, and because I do not arrogantly claim for myself so much that I believe myself capable of anticipating all the difficulties that will occur to someone, I will first of all narrate in the *Meditations* the very thoughts by means of which I seem to have arrived at a certain and evident knowledge of the truth, so that I may determine whether the same arguments that persuaded me can be useful in persuading others. Next, I will reply to the objections of a number of very gifted and learned gentlemen, to whom these *Meditations* were forwarded for their examination prior to their being sent to press. For their objections were so many and varied that I have dared to hope that nothing will readily occur to anyone, at least nothing of importance, which has not already been touched upon by these gentlemen. And thus I earnestly entreat the readers not to form a judgment regarding the *Meditations* until they have deigned to read all these objections and the replies I have made to them.

Synopsis of the Following Six Meditations

In the First Meditation the reasons are given why we can doubt all things, especially material things, so long, that is, as, of course, we have no other foundations for the sciences than the ones which we have had up until now. Although the utility of so extensive a doubt is not readily apparent, nevertheless its greatest utility lies in freeing us of all prejudices, in preparing the easiest way for us to withdraw the mind from the senses, and finally, in making it impossible for us to doubt any further those things that we later discover to be true.

In the Second Meditation the mind, through the exercise of its own freedom, supposes the nonexistence of all those things about whose existence it can have even the least doubt. In so doing the mind realizes that it is impossible for it not to exist during this time. This too is of the greatest utility, since by means of it the mind easily distinguishes what things belong to it, that is, to an intellectual nature, from what things belong to the body. But because some people will perhaps expect to see proofs for the immortality of the soul in this Meditation, I think they should be put on notice here that I have attempted to write only what I have carefully demonstrated. Therefore the only order I could follow was the one typically used by geometers, which is to lay out everything on which a given proposition depends, before concluding anything about it. But the first and principal prerequisite for knowing that the soul is immortal is that we form a concept of the soul that is as lucid as possible and utterly distinct from every concept of a body. This is what has been done here. Moreover, there is the additional requirement that we know that everything that we clearly and distinctly understand is true, in exactly the manner in which we understand it; however, this could not have been proven prior to the Fourth Meditation. Moreover, we must have a distinct concept of corporeal nature, and this is formulated partly in the Second Meditation itself, and partly in the Fifth and Sixth Meditations. From all this one ought to conclude that all the things we clearly and distinctly conceive as different substances truly are substances that are really distinct from one another. (This, for example, is how mind and body are conceived.) This conclusion is arrived at in the Sixth Meditation. This same conclusion is also confirmed in this Meditation in virtue of the fact that we cannot understand a body to be anything but divisible, whereas we cannot understand the mind to be anything but indivisible. For we cannot conceive of half of a mind, as we can half of any body whatever, no matter how small. From this we are prompted to acknowledge that the natures of mind and body not only are different from one another, but even, in a manner of speaking, are contraries of one another. However, I have not written any further on the matter in this work, both because these considerations suffice for showing that the annihilation of the mind does not follow from the decaying of the body (and thus these considerations suffice for giving mortals hope in an afterlife), and also because the premises from which the immortality of the mind can be inferred depend upon an account of the whole of physics. First, we need to know that absolutely all substances, that is, things that must be created by God in order to exist, are by their very nature incorruptible, and can never cease to exist, unless, by the same God's denying his concurrence to them, they be reduced to nothingness. Second, we need to realize that body, taken in a general sense, is a substance and hence it too can never perish. But the human body, insofar as it differs from other bodies, is composed of merely a certain configuration of members, together with other accidents of the same sort. But the human mind is not likewise composed of any accidents, but is a pure substance. For even if all its accidents were

changed, so that it understands different things, wills different things, senses different things, and so on, the mind itself does not on that score become something different. On the other hand, the human body does become something different, merely as a result of the fact that a change in the shape of some of its parts has taken place. It follows from these considerations that a body can very easily perish, whereas the mind by its nature is immortal.

In the Third Meditation I have explained at sufficient length, it seems to me, my principal argument for proving the existence of God. Nevertheless, since my intent was to draw the minds of readers as far as possible from the senses, I had no desire to draw upon comparisons based upon corporeal things. Thus many obscurities may perhaps have remained; but these, I trust, will later be entirely removed in my Replies to the Objections. One such point of contention, among others, is the following: how can the idea that is in us of a supremely perfect being have so much objective reality that it can only come from a supremely perfect cause? This is illustrated in the Replies by a comparison with a very perfect machine, the idea of which is in the mind of some craftsman. For, just as the objective ingeniousness of this idea ought to have some cause (say, the knowledge possessed by the craftsman or by someone else from whom he received this knowledge), so too, the idea of God which is in us must have God himself as its cause.

In the Fourth Meditation it is proved that all that we clearly and distinctly perceive is true, and it is also explained what constitutes the nature of falsity. These things necessarily need to be known both to confirm what has preceded as well as to help readers understand what remains. (But here one should meanwhile bear in mind that in that Meditation there is no discussion whatsoever of sin, that is, the error committed in the pursuit of good and evil, but only the error that occurs in discriminating between what is true and what is false. Nor is there an examination of those matters pertaining to the faith or to the conduct of life, but merely of speculative truths known exclusively by means of the light of nature.)

In the Fifth Meditation, in addition to an explanation of corporeal nature in general, the existence of God is also demonstrated by means of a new proof. But again several difficulties may arise here; however, these are resolved later in my Replies to the Objections. Finally, it is shown how it is true that the certainty of even geometrical demonstrations depends upon the knowledge of God.

Finally, in the Sixth Meditation the understanding is distinguished from the imagination and the marks of this distinction are described. The mind is proved to be really distinct from the body, even though the mind is shown to be so closely joined to the body that it forms a single unit with it. All the errors commonly arising from the senses are reviewed; an account of the ways in which these errors can be avoided is provided. Finally, all the arguments on the basis of which we may infer the existence of material things are presented — not because I believe them to be very useful for proving what they prove, namely, that there really is a world, that men have bodies, and the like (things which no one of sound mind has ever seriously doubted), but rather because, through a consideration of these arguments, one realizes that they are neither so firm nor so evident as the arguments leading us to the knowledge of our mind and of God, so that, of all the things that can be known by the human mind, these latter are the most certain and the most evident. Proving this one thing was for me the goal of these Meditations. For this reason I will not review here the various issues that are also to be treated in these Meditations as the situation arises.

He rediculed Sartre

Belief that one person behaviour is responsible for another

Meditations on First Philosophy in Which the Existence of God and the Distinction Between the Soul and the Body Are Demonstrated

Meditation One: Concerning Those Things That Can Be Called into Doubt

Several years have now passed since I first realized how numerous were the false opinions that in my youth I had taken to be true, and thus how doubtful were all those that I had subsequently built upon them. And thus I realized that once in my life I had to raze everything to the ground and begin again from the original foundations, if I wanted to establish anything firm and lasting in the sciences. But the task seemed enormous, and I was waiting until I reached a point in my life that was so timely that no more suitable time for undertaking these plans of action would come to pass. For this reason, I procrastinated for so long that I would henceforth be at fault, were I to waste the time that remains for carrying out the project by brooding over it. Accordingly, I have today suitably freed my mind of all cares, secured for myself a period of leisurely tranquillity, and am withdrawing into solitude. At last I will apply myself earnestly and unreservedly to this general demolition of my opinions.

Yet to bring this about I will not need to show that all my opinions are false, which is perhaps something I could never accomplish. But reason now persuades me that I should withhold my assent no less carefully from opinions that are not completely certain and indubitable than I would from those that are patently false. For this reason, it will suffice for the rejection of all of these opinions, if I find in each of them some reason for doubt. Nor therefore need I survey each opinion individually, a task that would be endless. Rather, because undermining the foundations will cause whatever has been built upon them to crumble of its own accord, I will attack straightaway those principles which supported everything I once believed.

Surely whatever I had admitted until now as most true I received either from the senses or through the senses. However, I have noticed that the senses are sometimes deceptive; and it is a mark of prudence never to place our complete trust in those who have deceived us even once.

But perhaps, even though the senses do sometimes deceive us when it is a question of very small and distant things, still there are many other matters concerning which one simply cannot doubt, even though they are derived from the very same senses: for example, that I am sitting here next to the fire, wearing my winter dressing gown, that I am holding this sheet of paper in my hands, and the like. But on what grounds could one deny that these hands and this entire body are mine? Unless perhaps I were to liken myself to the insane, whose brains are impaired by such an unrelenting vapor of black bile that they steadfastly insist that they are kings when they are utter paupers, or that they are arrayed in purple robes when they are naked, or that they have heads made of clay, or that they are gourds, or that they are made of glass. But such people are mad, and I would appear no less mad, were I to take their behavior as an example for myself.

This would all be well and good, were I not a man who is accustomed to sleeping at night, and to experiencing in my dreams the very same things, or now and then even less plausible ones, as these insane people do when they are awake. How often does my evening slumber persuade me of such ordinary things as these: that I am here, clothed in my dressing gown, seated next to the fireplace—when in fact I am lying undressed in bed! But right now my eyes are certainly wide awake when I gaze upon this sheet of paper. This head which I am shaking is not heavy with sleep. I extend this hand consciously and deliberately, and I feel it. Such things would not be so distinct for someone who is asleep. As if I did not recall having been deceived on other occasions even by similar thoughts in my dreams! As I consider these matters more carefully, I see so plainly that there are no definitive signs by which to distinguish being awake from being asleep. As a result, I am becoming quite dizzy, and this dizziness nearly convinces me that I am asleep.

Let us assume then, for the sake of argument, that we are dreaming and that such particulars as these are not true: that we are opening our eyes, moving our head, and extending our hands. Perhaps we do not even have such hands, or any such body at all. Nevertheless, it surely must be admitted that the things seen during slumber are, as it were, like painted images, which could only have been produced in the likeness of true things, and that therefore at least these general things—eyes, head, hands, and the whole body—are not imaginary things, but are true and exist. For indeed when painters themselves wish to represent sirens and satyrs by means of especially bizarre forms, they surely cannot assign to them utterly new natures. Rather, they simply fuse together the members of various animals. Or if perhaps they concoct something so utterly novel that nothing like it has ever been seen before (and thus is something utterly fictitious and false), yet certainly at the very least the colors from which they fashion it ought to be true. And by the same token, although even these general things—eyes, head, hands and the like—could be imaginary, still one has to admit that at least certain other things that are even more simple and universal are true. It is from these components, as if from true colors, that all those images of things that are in our thought are fashioned, be they true or false.

This class of things appears to include corporeal nature in general, together with its extension; the shape of extended things; their quantity, that is, their size and number; as well as the place where they exist; the time through which they endure, and the like.

Thus it is not improper to conclude from this that physics, astronomy, medicine, and all the other disciplines that are dependent upon the consideration of composite things are doubtful, and that, on the other hand, arithmetic, geometry, and other such disciplines, which treat of nothing but the simplest and most general things and which are indifferent as to whether these things do or do not in fact exist, contain something certain and indubitable. For whether I am awake or asleep, two plus three make five, and a square does not have more than four sides. It does not seem possible that such obvious truths should be subject to the suspicion of being false.

Be that as it may, there is fixed in my mind a certain opinion of long standing, namely that there exists a God who is able to do anything and by whom I, such as I am, have been created. How do I know that he did not bring it about that there is no earth at all, no heavens, no extended thing, no shape, no size, no place, and yet bringing it about that all these things appear to me to exist precisely as they do now? Moreover, since I judge that others sometimes make mistakes in matters that they believe they know most perfectly, may I not, in like fashion, be deceived every time I add two and three or count the sides of a square, or perform an even simpler operation, if that can be imagined? But perhaps God has not willed that I be deceived in this way, for he is said to be supremely good. Nonetheless, if it were repugnant to his goodness to have created me such that I be deceived all the time, it would also seem foreign to that same goodness to permit me to be deceived even occasionally. But we cannot make this last assertion.

Perhaps there are some who would rather deny so powerful a God than believe that everything else is uncertain. Let us not oppose them; rather, let us grant that everything said here about God is fictitious. Now they suppose that I came to be what I am either by fate, or by chance, or by a connected chain of events, or by some other way. But because being deceived and being mistaken appear to be a certain imperfection, the less powerful they take the author of my origin to be, the more probable it will be that I am so imperfect that I am always deceived. I have nothing to say in response to these arguments. But eventually I am forced to admit that there is nothing among the things I once believed to be true which it is not permissible to doubt—and not out of frivolity or lack of forethought, but for valid and considered reasons. Thus I must be no less careful to withhold assent henceforth even from these beliefs than I would from those that are patently false, if I wish to find anything certain.

But it is not enough simply to have realized these things; I must take steps to keep myself mindful of them. For long-standing opinions keep returning,

[handwritten margin note: believe there a good god is]

and, almost against my will, they take advantage of my credulity, as if it were bound over to them by long use and the claims of intimacy. Nor will I ever get out of the habit of assenting to them and believing in them, so long as I take them to be exactly what they are, namely, in some respects doubtful, as has just now been shown, but nevertheless highly probable, so that it is much more consonant with reason to believe them than to deny them. Hence, it seems to me I would do well to deceive myself by turning my will in completely the opposite direction and pretend for a time that these opinions are wholly false and imaginary, until finally, as if with prejudices weighing down each side equally, no bad habit should turn my judgment any further from the correct perception of things. For indeed I know that meanwhile there is no danger or error in following this procedure, and that it is impossible for me to indulge in too much distrust, since I am now concentrating only on knowledge, not on action.

Accordingly, I will suppose not a supremely good God, the source of truth, but rather an evil genius, supremely powerful and clever, who has directed his entire effort at deceiving me. I will regard the heavens, the air, the earth, colors, shapes, sounds, and all external things as nothing but the bedeviling hoaxes of my dreams, with which he lays snares for my credulity. I will regard myself as not having hands, or eyes, or flesh, or blood, or any senses, but as nevertheless falsely believing that I possess all these things. I will remain resolute and steadfast in this meditation, and even if it is not within my power to know anything true, it certainly is within my power to take care resolutely to withhold my assent to what is false, lest this deceiver, however powerful, however clever he may be, have any effect on me. But this undertaking is arduous, and a certain laziness brings me back to my customary way of living. I am not unlike a prisoner who enjoyed an imaginary freedom during his sleep, but, when he later begins to suspect that he is dreaming, fears being awakened and nonchalantly conspires with these pleasant illusions. In just the same way, I fall back of my own accord into my old opinions, and dread being awakened, lest the toilsome wakefulness which follows upon a peaceful rest must be spent thenceforward not in the light but among the inextricable shadows of the difficulties now brought forward.

Meditation Two: Concerning the Nature of the Human Mind: That It Is Better Known Than the Body

Yesterday's meditation has thrown me into such doubts that I can no longer ignore them, yet I fail to see how they are to be resolved. It is as if I had suddenly fallen into a deep whirlpool; I am so tossed about that I can neither touch bottom with my foot, nor swim up to the top. Nevertheless I will work my way up and will once again attempt the same path I entered upon yesterday. I will accomplish this by putting aside everything that admits of the least doubt, as if I had discovered it to be completely false. I will stay on this course until I know something certain, or, if nothing else, until I at least know for certain that nothing is certain. Archimedes sought but one firm and immovable point in order to move the entire earth from one place to another. Just so, great things are also to be hoped for if I succeed in finding just one thing, however slight, that is certain and unshaken.

Therefore I suppose that everything I see is false. I believe that none of what my deceitful memory represents ever existed. I have no senses whatever. Body, shape, extension, movement, and place are all chimeras. What then will be true? Perhaps just the single fact that nothing is certain.

But how do I know there is not something else, over and above all those things that I have just reviewed, concerning which there is not even the slightest occasion for doubt? Is there not some God, or by whatever name I might call him, who instills these very thoughts in me? But why would I think that, since I myself could perhaps be the author of these thoughts? Am I not then at least something? But I have already denied that I have any senses and any body. Still I hesitate; for what follows from this? Am I so tied to a body and to the senses that I cannot exist without them? But I have persuaded myself that there is absolutely nothing in the world: no sky, no earth, no minds, no bodies. Is it then the case that I too do not exist? But doubtless I did exist, if I persuaded myself of something. But there is some deceiver or other who is supremely powerful and supremely sly and who is always deliberately deceiving me. Then too there is no doubt that I exist, if he is deceiving me. And let him do his best at deception, he will never

[handwritten margin notes along right edge: some times this is happening to me & will I find the right answer to a problem the thinking about & so on both]

bring it about that I am nothing so long as I shall think that I am something. Thus, after everything has been most carefully weighed, it must finally be established that this pronouncement "I am, I exist" is necessarily true every time I utter it or conceive it in my mind.

But I do not yet understand sufficiently what I am—I, who now necessarily exist. And so from this point on, I must be careful lest I unwittingly mistake something else for myself, and thus err in that very item of knowledge that I claim to be the most certain and evident of all. Thus, I will meditate once more on what I once believed myself to be, prior to embarking upon these thoughts. For this reason, then, I will set aside whatever can be weakened even to the slightest degree by the arguments brought forward, so that eventually all that remains is precisely nothing but what is certain and unshaken.

What then did I use to think I was? A man, of course. But what is a man? Might I not say a "rational animal"? No, because then I would have to inquire what "animal" and "rational" mean. And thus from one question I would slide into many more difficult ones. Nor do I now have enough free time that I want to waste it on subtleties of this sort. Instead, permit me to focus here on what came spontaneously and naturally into my thinking whenever I pondered what I was. Now it occurred to me first that I had a face, hands, arms, and this entire mechanism of bodily members: the very same as are discerned in a corpse, and which I referred to by the name "body." It next occurred to me that I took in food, that I walked about, and that I sensed and thought various things; these actions I used to attribute to the soul. But as to what this soul might be, I either did not think about it or else I imagined it a rarified I-know-not-what, like a wind, or a fire, or ether, which had been infused into my coarser parts. But as to the body I was not in any doubt. On the contrary, I was under the impression that I knew its nature distinctly. Were I perhaps tempted to describe this nature such as I conceived it in my mind, I would have described it thus: by "body," I understand all that is capable of being bounded by some shape, of being enclosed in a place, and of filling up a space in such a way as to exclude any other body from it; of being perceived by touch, sight, hearing, taste, or smell; of being moved in several ways, not, of course, by itself, but

by whatever else impinges upon it. For it was my view that the power of self-motion, and likewise of sensing or of thinking, in no way belonged to the nature of the body. Indeed I used rather to marvel that such faculties were to be found in certain bodies.

But now what am I, when I suppose that there is some supremely powerful and, if I may be permitted to say so, malicious deceiver who deliberately tries to fool me in any way he can? Can I not affirm that I possess at least a small measure of all those things which I have already said belong to the nature of the body? I focus my attention on them, I think about them, I review them again, but nothing comes to mind. I am tired of repeating this to no purpose. But what about those things I ascribed to the soul? What about being nourished or moving about? Since I now do not have a body, these are surely nothing but fictions. What about sensing? Surely this too does not take place without a body; and I seemed to have sensed in my dreams many things that I later realized I did not sense. What about thinking? Here I make my discovery: thought exists; it alone cannot be separated from me. I am; I exist—this is certain. But for how long? For as long as I am thinking; for perhaps it could also come to pass that if I were to cease all thinking I would then utterly cease to exist. At this time I admit nothing that is not necessarily true. I am therefore precisely nothing but a thinking thing; that is, a mind, or intellect, or understanding, or reason—words of whose meanings I was previously ignorant. Yet I am a true thing and am truly existing; but what kind of thing? I have said it already: a thinking thing.

What else am I? I will set my imagination in motion. I am not that concatenation of members we call the human body. Neither am I even some subtle air infused into these members, nor a wind, nor a fire, nor a vapor, nor a breath, nor anything I devise for myself. For I have supposed these things to be nothing. The assumption still stands; yet nevertheless I am something. But is it perhaps the case that these very things which I take to be nothing, because they are unknown to me, nevertheless are in fact no different from that "me" that I know? This I do not know, and I will not quarrel about it now. I can make a judgment only about things that are known to me. I know that I exist; I ask now who is this "I" whom I know? Most certainly, in the strict sense the knowledge of this "I" does not depend upon things of whose existence I do not yet have knowledge. Therefore it is not dependent upon any of those things that I simulate in my imagination. But this word "simulate"[4] warns me of my error. For I would indeed be simulating were I to "imagine" that I was something, because imagining is merely the contemplating of the shape or image of a corporeal thing. But I now know with certainty that I am and also that all these images—and, generally, everything belonging to the nature of the body—could turn out to be nothing but dreams. Once I have realized this, I would seem to be speaking no less foolishly were I to say: "I will use my imagination in order to recognize more distinctly who I am," than were I to say: "Now I surely am awake, and I see something true; but since I do not yet see it clearly enough, I will deliberately fall asleep so that my dreams might represent it to me more truly and more clearly." Thus I realize that none of what I can grasp by means of the imagination pertains to this knowledge that I have of myself. Moreover, I realize that I must be most diligent about withdrawing my mind from these things so that it can perceive its nature as distinctly as possible.

But what then am I? A thing that thinks. What is that? A thing that doubts, understands, affirms, denies, wills, refuses, and that also imagines and senses.

Indeed it is no small matter if all of these things belong to me. But why should they not belong to me? Is it not the very same "I" who now doubts almost everything, who nevertheless understands something, who affirms that this one thing is true, who denies other things, who desires to know more, who wishes not to be deceived, who imagines many things even against my will, who also notices many things which appear to come from the senses? What is there in all of this that is not every bit as true as the fact that I exist—even if I am always asleep or even if my creator makes every effort to mislead me? Which of these things is distinct from my thought? Which of them can be said to be separate from myself? For it is so obvious that it is I who doubt, I who understand, and I who will, that there is nothing by which it could be explained more clearly. But indeed it is also the same "I" who imagines; for although perhaps, as I

supposed before, absolutely nothing that I imagined is true, still the very power of imagining really does exist, and constitutes a part of my thought. Finally, it is this same "I" who senses or who is cognizant of bodily things as if through the senses. For example, I now see a light, I hear a noise, I feel heat. These things are false, since I am asleep. Yet I certainly do seem to see, hear, and feel warmth. This cannot be false. Properly speaking, this is what in me is called "sensing." But this, precisely so taken, is nothing other than thinking.

From these considerations I am beginning to know a little better what I am. But it still seems (and I cannot resist believing) that corporeal things—whose images are formed by thought, and which the senses themselves examine—are much more distinctly known than this mysterious "I" which does not fall within the imagination. And yet it would be strange indeed were I to grasp the very things I consider to be doubtful, unknown, and foreign to me more distinctly than what is true, what is known—than, in short, myself. But I see what is happening: my mind loves to wander and does not yet permit itself to be restricted within the confines of truth. So be it then; let us just this once allow it completely free rein, so that, a little while later, when the time has come to pull in the reins, the mind may more readily permit itself to be controlled.

Let us consider those things which are commonly believed to be the most distinctly grasped of all: namely the bodies we touch and see. Not bodies in general, mind you, for these general perceptions are apt to be somewhat more confused, but one body in particular. Let us take, for instance, this piece of wax. It has been taken quite recently from the honeycomb; it has not yet lost all the honey flavor. It retains some of the scent of the flowers from which it was collected. Its color, shape, and size are manifest. It is hard and cold; it is easy to touch. If you rap on it with your knuckle it will emit a sound. In short, everything is present in it that appears needed to enable a body to be known as distinctly as possible. But notice that, as I am speaking, I am bringing it close to the fire. The remaining traces of the honey flavor are disappearing; the scent is vanishing; the color is changing; the original shape is disappearing. Its size is increasing; it is becoming liquid and hot; you can hardly touch it. And now, when you rap on it, it no longer emits

---

4. [The Latin word *"effingo"* means "to form an image" or "imagine."]

Clothes doesn't say anything because it could be a woman dressed like a man [handwritten annotation]

any sound. Does the same wax still remain? I must confess that it does; no one denies it; no one thinks otherwise. So what was there in the wax that was so distinctly grasped? Certainly none of the aspects that I reached by means of the senses. For whatever came under the senses of taste, smell, sight, touch or hearing has now changed; and yet the wax remains.

Perhaps the wax was what I now think it is: namely that the wax itself never really was the sweetness of the honey, nor the fragrance of the flowers, nor the whiteness, nor the shape, nor the sound, but instead was a body that a short time ago manifested itself to me in these ways, and now does so in other ways. But just what precisely is this thing that I thus imagine? Let us focus our attention on this and see what remains after we have removed everything that does not belong to the wax: only that it is something extended, flexible, and mutable. But what is it to be flexible and mutable? Is it what my imagination shows it to be: namely, that this piece of wax can change from a round to a square shape, or from the latter to a triangular shape? Not at all; for I grasp that the wax is capable of innumerable changes of this sort, even though I am incapable of running through these innumerable changes by using my imagination. Therefore this insight is not achieved by the faculty of imagination. What is it to be extended? Is this thing's extension also unknown? For it becomes greater in wax that is beginning to melt, greater in boiling wax, and greater still as the heat is increased. And I would not judge correctly what the wax is if I did not believe that it takes on an even greater variety of dimensions than I could ever grasp with the imagination. It remains then for me to concede that I do not grasp what this wax is through the imagination; rather, I perceive it through the mind alone. The point I am making refers to this particular piece of wax, for the case of wax in general is clearer still. But what is this piece of wax which is perceived only by the mind? Surely it is the same piece of wax that I see, touch, and imagine; in short it is the same piece of wax I took it to be from the very beginning. But I need to realize that the perception of the wax is neither a seeing, nor a touching, nor an imagining. Nor has it ever been, even though it previously seemed so; rather it is an inspection on the part of the mind alone. This inspection can be imperfect and confused, as it was before, or clear and distinct, as it is now, depending on how closely I pay attention to the things in which the piece of wax consists.

But meanwhile I marvel at how prone my mind is to error. For although I am considering these things within myself silently and without words, nevertheless I seize upon words themselves and I am nearly deceived by the ways in which people commonly speak. For we say that we see the wax itself, if it is present, and not that we judge it to be present from its color or shape. Whence I might conclude straightaway that I know the wax through the vision had by the eye, and not through an inspection on the part of the mind alone. But then were I perchance to look out my window and observe men crossing the square, I would ordinarily say I see the men themselves just as I say I see the wax. But what do I see aside from hats and clothes, which could conceal automata? Yet I judge them to be men. Thus what I thought I had seen with my eyes, I actually grasped solely with the faculty of judgment, which is in my mind.

But a person who seeks to know more than the common crowd ought to be ashamed of himself for looking for doubt in common ways of speaking. Let us then go forward and inquire when it was that I perceived more perfectly and evidently what the piece of wax was. Was it when I first saw it and believed I knew it by the external sense, or at least by the so-called common sense, that is, the power of imagination? Or do I have more perfect knowledge now, when I have diligently examined both what the wax is and how it is known? Surely it is absurd to be in doubt about this matter. For what was there in my initial perception that was distinct? What was there that any animal seemed incapable of possessing? But indeed when I distinguish the wax from its external forms, as if stripping it of its clothing, and look at the wax in its nakedness, then, even though there can be still an error in my judgment, nevertheless I cannot perceive it thus without a human mind.

But what am I to say about this mind, that is, about myself? For as yet I admit nothing else to be in me over and above the mind. What, I ask, am I who seem to perceive this wax so distinctly? Do I not know myself not only much more truly and with greater certainty, but also much more distinctly and evidently? For if I judge that the wax exists from the fact that I see it, certainly from this same fact that I see the wax it follows much more evidently that I myself exist. For it could happen that what I see is not truly wax. It could happen that I have no eyes with which to see anything. But it is utterly impossible that, while I see or think I see (I do not now distinguish these two), I who think am not something. Likewise, if I judge that the wax exists from the fact that I touch it, the same outcome will again obtain, namely that I exist. If I judge that the wax exists from the fact that I imagine it, or for any other reason, plainly the same thing follows. But what I note regarding the wax applies to everything else that is external to me. Furthermore, if my perception of the wax seemed more distinct after it became known to me not only on account of sight or touch, but on account of many reasons, one has to admit how much more distinctly I am now known to myself. For there is not a single consideration that can aid in my perception of the wax or of any other body that fails to make even more manifest the nature of my mind. But there are still so many other things in the mind itself on the basis of which my knowledge of it can be rendered more distinct that it hardly seems worth enumerating those things which emanate to it from the body.

But lo and behold, I have returned on my own to where I wanted to be. For since I now know that even bodies are not, properly speaking, perceived by the senses or by the faculty of imagination, but by the intellect alone, and that they are not perceived through their being touched or seen, but only through their being understood, I manifestly know that nothing can be perceived more easily and more evidently than my own mind. But since the tendency to hang on to long-held beliefs cannot be put aside so quickly, I want to stop here, so that by the length of my meditation this new knowledge may be more deeply impressed upon my memory.

Meditation Three: Concerning God, That He Exists

I will now shut my eyes, stop up my ears, and withdraw all my senses. I will also blot out from my thoughts all images of corporeal things, or rather, since the latter is hardly possible, I will regard these images as empty, false and worthless. And as I converse with myself alone and look more deeply into myself, I will attempt to render myself gradually better known and

more familiar to myself. I am a thing that thinks, that is to say, a thing that doubts, affirms, denies, understands a few things, is ignorant of many things, wills, refrains from willing, and also imagines and senses. For as I observed earlier, even though these things that I sense or imagine may perhaps be nothing at all outside me, nevertheless I am certain that these modes of thinking, which are cases of what I call sensing and imagining, insofar as they are merely modes of thinking, do exist within me.

In these few words, I have reviewed everything I truly know, or at least what so far I have noticed that I know. Now I will ponder more carefully to see whether perhaps there may be other things belonging to me that up until now I have failed to notice. I am certain that I am a thinking thing. But do I not therefore also know what is required for me to be certain of anything? Surely in this first instance of knowledge, there is nothing but a certain clear and distinct perception of what I affirm. Yet this would hardly be enough to render me certain of the truth of a thing, if it could ever happen that something that I perceived so clearly and distinctly were false. And thus I now seem able to posit as a general rule that everything I very clearly and distinctly perceive is true.

Be that as it may, I have previously admitted many things as wholly certain and evident that nevertheless I later discovered to be doubtful. What sort of things were these? Why, the earth, the sky, the stars, and all the other things I perceived by means of the senses. But what was it about these things that I clearly perceived? Surely the fact that the ideas or thoughts of these things were hovering before my mind. But even now I do not deny that these ideas are in me. Yet there was something else I used to affirm, which, owing to my habitual tendency to believe it, I used to think was something I clearly perceived, even though I actually did not perceive it at all: namely, that certain things existed outside me, things from which those ideas proceeded and which those ideas completely resembled. But on this point I was mistaken; or rather, if my judgment was a true one, it was not the result of the force of my perception.

But what about when I considered something very simple and easy in the areas of arithmetic or geometry, for example that two plus three make five, and the like? Did I not intuit them at least clearly enough so as to affirm them as true? To be sure, I did decide later on that I must doubt these things, but that was only because it occurred to me that some God could perhaps have given me a nature such that I might be deceived even about matters that seemed most evident. But whenever this preconceived opinion about the supreme power of God occurs to me, I cannot help admitting that, were he to wish it, it would be easy for him to cause me to err even in those matters that I think I intuit as clearly as possible with the eyes of the mind. On the other hand, whenever I turn my attention to those very things that I think I perceive with such great clarity, I am so completely persuaded by them that I spontaneously blurt out these words: "let anyone who can do so deceive me; so long as I think that I am something, he will never bring it about that I am nothing. Nor will he one day make it true that I never existed, for it is true now that I do exist. Nor will he even bring it about that perhaps two plus three might equal more or less than five, or similar items in which I recognize an obvious contradiction." And certainly, because I have no reason for thinking that there is a God who is a deceiver (and of course I do not yet sufficiently know whether there even is a God), the basis for doubting, depending as it does merely on the above hypothesis, is very tenuous and, so to speak, metaphysical. But in order to remove even this basis for doubt, I should at the first opportunity inquire whether there is a God, and, if there is, whether or not he can be a deceiver. For if I am ignorant of this, it appears I am never capable of being completely certain about anything else.

However, at this stage good order seems to demand that I first group all my thoughts into certain classes, and ask in which of them truth or falsity properly resides. Some of these thoughts are like images of things; to these alone does the word "idea" properly apply, as when I think of a man, or a chimera, or the sky, or an angel, or God. Again there are other thoughts that take different forms: for example, when I will, or fear, or affirm, or deny, there is always something that I grasp as the subject of my thought, yet I embrace in my thought something more than the likeness of that thing. Some of these thoughts are called volitions or affects, while others are called judgments.

Now as far as ideas are concerned, if they are considered alone and in their own right, without being referred to something else, they cannot, properly speaking, be false. For whether it is a she-goat or a chimera that I am imagining, it is no less true that I imagine the one than the other. Moreover, we need not fear that there is falsity in the will itself or in the affects, for although I can choose evil things or even things that are utterly non-existent, I cannot conclude from this that it is untrue that I do choose these things. Thus there remain only judgments in which I must take care not to be mistaken. Now the principal and most frequent error to be found in judgments consists in the fact that I judge that the ideas which are in me are similar to or in conformity with certain things outside me. Obviously, if I were to consider these ideas merely as certain modes of my thought, and were not to refer them to anything else, they could hardly give me any subject matter for error.

Among these ideas, some appear to me to be innate, some adventitious, and some produced by me. For I understand what a thing is, what truth is, what thought is, and I appear to have derived this exclusively from my very own nature. But say I am now hearing a noise, or looking at the sun, or feeling the fire; up until now I judged that these things proceeded from certain things outside me, and finally, that sirens, hippogriffs, and the like are made by me. Or perhaps I can even think of all these ideas as being adventitious, or as being innate, or as fabrications, for I have not yet clearly ascertained their true origin.

But here I must inquire particularly into those ideas that I believe to be derived from things existing outside me. Just what reason do I have for believing that these ideas resemble those things? Well, I do seem to have been so taught by nature. Moreover, I do know from experience that these ideas do not depend upon my will, nor consequently upon myself, for I often notice them even against my will. Now, for example, whether or not I will it, I feel heat. It is for this reason that I believe this feeling or idea of heat comes to me from something other than myself, namely from the heat of the fire by which I am sitting. Nothing is more obvious than the judgment that this thing is sending its likeness rather than something else into me.

I will now see whether these reasons are powerful enough. When I say here "I have been so taught by nature," all I have in mind is that I am driven by a spontaneous impulse to believe this, and not that some light of nature is showing me that it is true. These are two very different things. For whatever is shown me by this light of nature, for example, that from the fact that I doubt, it follows that I am, and the like, cannot in any way be doubtful. This is owing to the fact that there can be no other faculty that I can trust as much as this light and which could teach that these things are not true. But as far as natural impulses are concerned, in the past I have often judged myself to have been driven by them to make the poorer choice when it was a question of choosing a good; and I fail to see why I should place any greater faith in them than in other matters.

Again, although these ideas do not depend upon my will, it does not follow that they necessarily proceed from things existing outside me. For just as these impulses about which I spoke just now seem to be different from my will, even though they are in me, so too perhaps there is also in me some other faculty, one not yet sufficiently known to me, which produces these ideas, just as it has always seemed up to now that ideas are formed in me without any help from external things when I am asleep.

And finally, even if these ideas did proceed from things other than myself, it does not therefore follow that they must resemble those things. Indeed it seems I have frequently noticed a vast difference in many respects. For example, I find within myself two distinct ideas of the sun. One idea is drawn, as it were, from the senses. Now it is this idea which, of all those that I take to be derived from outside me, is most in need of examination. By means of this idea the sun appears to me to be quite small. But there is another idea, one derived from astronomical reasoning, that is, it is elicited from certain notions that are innate in me, or else is fashioned by me in some other way. Through this idea the sun is shown to be several times larger than the earth. Both ideas surely cannot resemble the same sun existing outside me; and reason convinces me that the idea that seems to have emanated from the sun itself from so close is the very one that least resembles the sun.

All these points demonstrate sufficiently that up to this point it was not a well-founded judgment but only a blind impulse that formed the basis of my belief that things existing outside me send ideas or images of themselves to me through the sense organs or by some other means.

But still another way occurs to me for inquiring whether some of the things of which there are ideas in me do exist outside me: insofar as these ideas are merely modes of thought, I see no inequality among them; they all seem to proceed from me in the same manner. But insofar as one idea represents one thing and another idea another thing, it is obvious that they do differ very greatly from one another. Unquestionably, those ideas that display substances to me are something more and, if I may say so, contain within themselves more objective reality than those which represent only modes or accidents. Again, the idea that enables me to understand a supreme deity, eternal, infinite, omniscient, omnipotent, and creator of all things other than himself, clearly has more objective reality within it than do those ideas through which finite substances are displayed.

Now it is indeed evident by the light of nature that there must be at least as much [reality] in the efficient and total cause as there is in the effect of that same cause. For whence, I ask, could an effect get its reality, if not from its cause? And how could the cause give that reality to the effect, unless it also possessed that reality? Hence it follows that something cannot come into being out of nothing, and also that what is more perfect (that is, what contains in itself more reality) cannot come into being from what is less perfect. But this is manifestly true not merely for those effects whose reality is actual or formal, but also for ideas in which only objective reality is considered. For example, not only can a stone which did not exist previously not now begin to exist unless it is produced by something in which there is, either formally or eminently,[5] everything that is in the stone; nor heat be introduced into a subject which was not already hot unless it is done by something that is of at least as perfect an order as heat—and the same for the rest—but it is also true that there can be in me no idea of heat, or of a stone, unless it is placed in me by some cause that has at least as much reality as I conceive to be in the heat or in the stone. For although this cause conveys none of its actual or formal reality to my idea, it should not be thought for that reason that it must be less real. Rather, the very nature of an idea is such that of itself it needs no formal

5. [By "formal cause" Descartes means one as perfect as its effect; by "eminent cause" he means one more perfect.]

reality other than what it borrows from my thought, of which it is a mode. But that a particular idea contains this as opposed to that objective reality is surely owing to some cause in which there is at least as much formal reality as there is objective reality contained in the idea. For if we assume that something is found in the idea that was not in its cause, then the idea gets that something from nothing. Yet as imperfect a mode of being as this is by which a thing exists in the intellect objectively through an idea, nevertheless it is plainly not nothing; hence it cannot get its being from nothing.

Moreover, even though the reality that I am considering in my ideas is merely objective reality, I ought not on that account to suspect that there is no need for the same reality to be formally in the causes of these ideas, but that it suffices for it to be in them objectively. For just as the objective mode of being belongs to ideas by their very nature, so the formal mode of being belongs to the causes of ideas, at least to the first and preeminent ones, by their very nature. And although one idea can perhaps issue from another, nevertheless no infinite regress is permitted here; eventually some first idea must be reached whose cause is a sort of archetype that contains formally all the reality that is in the idea merely objectively. Thus it is clear to me by the light of nature that the ideas that are in me are like images that can easily fail to match the perfection of the things from which they have been drawn, but which can contain nothing greater or more perfect.

And the longer and more attentively I examine all these points, the more clearly and distinctly I know they are true. But what am I ultimately to conclude? If the objective reality of any of my ideas is found to be so great that I am certain that the same reality was not in me, either formally or eminently, and that therefore I myself cannot be the cause of the idea, then it necessarily follows that I am not alone in the world, but that something else, which is the cause of this idea, also exists. But if no such idea is found in me, I will have no argument whatsoever to make me certain of the existence of anything other than myself, for I have conscientiously reviewed all these arguments, and so far I have been unable to find any other.

Among my ideas, in addition to the one that displays me to myself (about which there can be no difficulty at this point), are others that represent God, corporeal and inanimate things, angels, animals, and finally other men like myself.

As to the ideas that display other men, or animals, or angels, I easily understand that they could be fashioned from the ideas that I have of myself, of corporeal things, and of God—even if no men (except myself), no animals, and no angels existed in the world.

As to the ideas of corporeal things, there is nothing in them that is so great that it seems incapable of having originated from me. For if I investigate them thoroughly and examine each one individually in the way I examined the idea of wax yesterday, I notice that there are only a very few things in them that I perceive clearly and distinctly: namely, size, or extension in length, breadth, and depth; shape, which arises from the limits of this extension; position, which various things possessing shape have in relation to one another; and motion, or alteration in position. To these can be added substance, duration, and number. But as for the remaining items, such as light and colors, sounds, odors, tastes, heat and cold and other tactile qualities, I think of these only in a very confused and obscure manner, to the extent that I do not even know whether they are true or false, that is, whether the ideas I have of them are ideas of things or ideas of non-things. For although a short time ago I noted that falsity properly so called (or "formal" falsity) is to be found only in judgments, nevertheless there is another kind of falsity (called "material" falsity) which is found in ideas whenever they represent a non-thing as if it were a thing. For example, the ideas I have of heat and cold fall so far short of being clear and distinct that I cannot tell from them whether cold is merely the privation of heat or whether heat is the privation of cold, or whether both are real qualities, or whether neither is. And because ideas can only be, as it were, of things, if it is true that cold is merely the absence of heat, then an idea that represents cold to me as something real and positive will not inappropriately be called false. The same holds for other similar ideas.

Assuredly I need not assign to these ideas an author distinct from myself. For if they were false, that is, if they were to represent non-things, I know by the light of nature that they proceed from nothing; that is, they are in me for no other reason than that something is lacking in my nature, and that my nature is not entirely perfect. If, on the other hand, these ideas are true, then because they exhibit so little reality to me that I cannot distinguish it from a non-thing, I see no reason why they cannot get their being from me.

As for what is clear and distinct in the ideas of corporeal things, it appears I could have borrowed some of these from the idea of myself: namely, substance, duration, number, and whatever else there may be of this type. For instance, I think that a stone is a substance, that is to say, a thing that is suitable for existing in itself; and likewise I think that I too am a substance. Despite the fact that I conceive myself to be a thinking thing and not an extended thing, whereas I conceive of a stone as an extended thing and not a thinking thing, and hence there is the greatest diversity between these two concepts, nevertheless they seem to agree with one another when considered under the rubric of substance. Furthermore, I perceive that I now exist and recall that I have previously existed for some time. And I have various thoughts and know how many of them there are. It is in doing these things that I acquire the ideas of duration and number, which I can then apply to other things. However, none of the other components out of which the ideas of corporeal things are fashioned (namely extension, shape, position, and motion) are contained in me formally, since I am merely a thinking thing. But since these are only certain modes of a substance, whereas I am a substance, it seems possible that they are contained in me eminently.

Thus there remains only the idea of God. I must consider whether there is anything in this idea that could not have originated from me. I understand by the name "God" a certain substance that is infinite, independent, supremely intelligent and supremely powerful, and that created me along with everything else that exists—if anything else exists. Indeed all these are such that, the more carefully I focus my attention on them, the less possible it seems they could have arisen from myself alone. Thus, from what has been said, I must conclude that God necessarily exists.

For although the idea of substance is in me by virtue of the fact that I am a substance, that fact is not sufficient to explain my having the idea of an infinite substance, since I am finite, unless this idea proceeded from some substance which really was infinite.

Nor should I think that I do not perceive the infinite by means of a true idea, but only through a negation of the finite, just as I perceive rest and darkness by means of a negation of motion and light. On the contrary, I clearly understand that there is more reality in an infinite substance than there is in a finite one. Thus the perception of the infinite is somehow prior in me to the perception of the finite, that is, my perception of God is prior to my perception of myself. For how would I understand that I doubt and that I desire, that is, that I lack something and that I am not wholly perfect, unless there were some idea in me of a more perfect being, by comparison with which I might recognize my defects?

Nor can it be said that this idea of God is perhaps materially false and thus can originate from nothing, as I remarked just now about the ideas of heat and cold, and the like. On the contrary, because it is the most clear and distinct and because it contains more objective reality than any other idea, no idea is in and of itself truer and has less of a basis for being suspected of falsehood. I maintain that this idea of a being that is supremely perfect and infinite is true in the highest degree. For although I could perhaps pretend that such a being does not exist, nevertheless I could not pretend that the idea of such a being discloses to me nothing real, as was the case with the idea of cold which I referred to earlier. It is indeed an idea that is utterly clear and distinct; for whatever I clearly and distinctly perceive to be real and true and to involve some perfection is wholly contained in that idea. It is no objection that I do not comprehend the infinite or that there are countless other things in God that I can in no way either comprehend or perhaps even touch with my thought. For the nature of the infinite is such that it is not comprehended by a being such as I, who am finite. And it is sufficient that I understand this very point and judge that all those things that I clearly perceive and that I know to contain some perfection—and perhaps even countless other things of which I am ignorant—are in God either formally or eminently. The result is that, of all the ideas that are in me, the idea that I have of God is the most true, the most clear and distinct.

But perhaps I am something greater than I myself understand. Perhaps all these perfections that I am attributing to God are somehow in me potentially, although they do not yet assert themselves and are not yet actualized. For I now observe that my knowledge is gradually being increased, and I see nothing standing in the way of its being increased more and more to infinity. Moreover, I see no reason why, with my knowledge thus increased, I could not acquire all the remaining perfections of God. And, finally, if the potential for these perfections is in me already, I see no reason why this potential would not suffice to produce the idea of these perfections.

Yet none of these things can be the case. First, while it is true that my knowledge is gradually being increased and that there are many things in me potentially that are not yet actual, nevertheless, none of these pertains to the idea of God, in which there is nothing whatever that is potential. Indeed this gradual increase is itself a most certain proof of imperfection. Moreover, although my knowledge may always increase more and more, nevertheless I understand that this knowledge will never by this means be actually infinite, because it will never reach a point where it is incapable of greater increase. On the contrary, I judge God to be actually infinite, so that nothing can be added to his perfection. Finally, I perceive that the objective being of an idea cannot be produced by a merely potential being (which, strictly speaking, is nothing), but only by an actual or formal being.

Indeed there is nothing in all these things that is not manifest by the light of nature to one who is conscientious and attentive. But when I am less attentive, and the images of sensible things blind the mind's eye, I do not so easily recall why the idea of a being more perfect than me necessarily proceeds from a being that really is more perfect. This being the case, it is appropriate to ask further whether I myself who have this idea could exist, if such a being did not exist.

From what source, then, do I derive my existence? Why, from myself, or from my parents, or from whatever other things there are that are less perfect than God. For nothing more perfect than God, or even as perfect as God, can be thought or imagined.

But if I got my being from myself, I would not doubt, nor would I desire, nor would I lack anything at all. For I would have given myself all the perfections of which I have some idea; in so doing, I myself would be God! I must not think that the things I lack could perhaps be more difficult to acquire than the ones I have now. On the contrary, it is obvious that it would have been much more difficult for me (that is, a thing or substance that thinks) to emerge out of nothing than it would be to acquire the knowledge of many things about which I am ignorant (these items of knowledge being merely accidents of that substance). Certainly, if I got this greater thing for myself, I would not have denied myself at least those things that can be had more easily. Nor would I have denied myself any of those other things that I perceive to be contained in the idea of God, for surely none of them seem to me more difficult to bring about. But if any of them were more difficult to bring about, they would certainly also seem more difficult to me, even if the remaining ones that I possess I got from myself, since it would be on account of them that I would experience that my power is limited.

Nor am I avoiding the force of these arguments, if I suppose that perhaps I have always existed as I do now, as if it then followed that no author of my existence need be sought. For because the entire span of one's life can be divided into countless parts, each one wholly independent of the rest, it does not follow from the fact that I existed a short time ago that I must exist now, unless some cause, as it were, creates me all over again at this moment, that is to say, which preserves me. For it is obvious to one who pays close attention to the nature of time that plainly the same force and action are needed to preserve anything at each individual moment that it lasts as would be required to create the same thing anew, were it not yet in existence. Thus conservation differs from creation solely by virtue of a distinction of reason; this too is one of those things that are manifest by the light of nature.

Therefore I must now ask myself whether I possess some power by which I can bring it about that I myself, who now exist, will also exist a little later on. For since I am nothing but a thinking thing—or at least since I am now dealing simply and precisely with that part of me which is a thinking thing—if such a power were in me, then I would certainly be aware of it. But I observe that there is no such power; and from this very fact I know most clearly that I depend upon some being other than myself.

But perhaps this being is not God, and I have been produced either by my parents or by some other causes less perfect than God. On the contrary, as I said before, it is obvious that there must be at least as much in the cause as there is in the effect. Thus, regardless of what it is that eventually is assigned as my cause, because I am a thinking thing and have within me a certain idea of God, it must be granted that what caused me is also a thinking thing and it too has an idea of all the perfections which I attribute to God. And I can again inquire of this cause whether it got its existence from itself or from another cause. For if it got its existence from itself, it is evident from what has been said that it is itself God, because, having the power of existing in and of itself, it unquestionably also has the power of actually possessing all the perfections of which it has in itself an idea — that is, all the perfections that I conceive to be in God. However, if it got its existence from another cause, I will once again inquire in similar fashion about this other cause: whether it got its existence from itself or from another cause, until finally I arrive at the ultimate cause, which will be God. For it is apparent enough that there can be no infinite regress here, especially since I am not dealing here merely with the cause that once produced me, but also and most especially with the cause that preserves me at the present time.

Nor can one fancy that perhaps several partial causes have concurred in bringing me into being, and that I have taken the ideas of the various perfections I attribute to God from a variety of causes, so that all of these perfections are found somewhere in the universe, but not all joined together in a single being — God. On the contrary, the unity, the simplicity, that is, the inseparability of all those features that are in God is one of the chief perfections that I understand to be in him. Certainly the idea of the unity of all his perfections could not have been placed in me by any cause from which I did not also get the ideas of the other perfections; for neither could some cause have made me understand them joined together and inseparable from one another, unless it also caused me to recognize what they were.

Finally, as to my parents, even if everything that I ever believed about them were true, still it is certainly not they who preserve me; nor is it they who in any way brought me into being, insofar as I am a thinking thing. Rather, they merely placed certain dispositions in the matter which I judged to contain me, that is, a mind, which now is the only thing I take myself to

be. And thus there can be no difficulty here concerning my parents. Indeed I have no choice but to conclude that the mere fact of my existing and of there being in me an idea of a most perfect being, that is, God, demonstrates most evidently that God too exists.

All that remains for me is to ask how I received this idea of God. For I did not draw it from the senses; it never came upon me unexpectedly, as is usually the case with the ideas of sensible things when these things present themselves (or seem to present themselves) to the external sense organs. Nor was it made by me, for I plainly can neither subtract anything from it nor add anything to it. Thus the only option remaining is that this idea is innate in me, just as the idea of myself is innate in me.

To be sure, it is not astonishing that in creating me, God should have endowed me with this idea, so that it would be like the mark of the craftsman impressed upon his work, although this mark need not be something distinct from the work itself. But the mere fact that God created me makes it highly plausible that I have somehow been made in his image and likeness, and that I perceive this likeness, in which the idea of God is contained, by means of the same faculty by which I perceive myself. That is, when I turn the mind's eye toward myself, I understand not only that I am something incomplete and dependent upon another, something aspiring indefinitely for greater and greater or better things, but also that the being on whom I depend has in himself all those greater things — not merely indefinitely and potentially, but infinitely and actually, and thus that he is God. The whole force of the argument rests on the fact that I recognize that it would be impossible for me to exist, being of such a nature as I am (namely, having in me the idea of God), unless God did in fact exist. God, I say, that same being the idea of whom is in me: a being having all those perfections that I cannot comprehend, but can somehow touch with my thought, and a being subject to no defects whatever. From these considerations it is quite obvious that he cannot be a deceiver, for it is manifest by the light of nature that all fraud and deception depend on some defect.

But before examining this idea more closely and at the same time inquiring into other truths that can be gathered from it, at this point I want to spend some time contemplating this God, to ponder his attributes and, so far as the eye of my darkened mind can take me, to gaze upon, to admire, and to adore the beauty of this immense light. For just as we believe by faith that the greatest felicity of the next life consists solely in this contemplation of the divine majesty, so too we now experience that from the same contemplation, although it is much less perfect, the greatest pleasure of which we are capable in this life can be perceived.

Meditation Four: Concerning the True and the False

Lately I have become accustomed to withdrawing my mind from the senses, and I have carefully taken note of the fact that very few things are truly perceived regarding corporeal things, although a great many more things are known regarding the human mind, and still many more things regarding God. The upshot is that I now have no difficulty directing my thought away from things that can be imagined to things that can be grasped only by the understanding and are wholly separate from matter. In fact the idea I clearly have of the human mind—insofar as it is a thinking thing, not extended in length, breadth or depth, and having nothing else from the body—is far more distinct than the idea of any corporeal thing. And when I take note of the fact that I doubt, or that I am a thing that is incomplete and dependent, there comes to mind a clear and distinct idea of a being that is independent and complete, that is, an idea of God. And from the mere fact that such an idea is in me, or that I who have this idea exist, I draw the obvious conclusion that God also exists, and that my existence depends entirely upon him at each and every moment. This conclusion is so obvious that I am confident that the human mind can know nothing more evident or more certain. And now I seem to see a way by which I might progress from this contemplation of the true God, in whom, namely, are hidden all the treasures of the sciences and wisdom, to the knowledge of other things.

To begin with, I acknowledge that it is impossible for God ever to deceive me, for trickery or deception is always indicative of some imperfection. And although the ability to deceive seems to be an indication of cleverness or power, the will to deceive undoubtedly attests to maliciousness or weakness. Accordingly, deception is incompatible with God.

Next I experience that there is in me a certain faculty of judgment, which, like everything else that is in me, I undoubtedly received from God. And since he does not wish to deceive me, he assuredly has not given me the sort of faculty with which I could ever make a mistake, when I use it properly.

No doubt regarding this matter would remain, but for the fact that it seems to follow from this that I am never capable of making a mistake. For if everything that is in me I got from God, and he gave me no faculty for making mistakes, it seems I am incapable of ever erring. And thus, so long as I think exclusively about God and focus my attention exclusively on him, I discern no cause of error or falsity. But once I turn my attention back on myself, I nevertheless experience that I am subject to countless errors. As I seek a cause of these errors, I notice that passing before me is not only a real and positive idea of God (that is, of a supremely perfect being), but also, as it were, a certain negative idea of nothingness (that is, of what is at the greatest possible distance from any perfection), and that I have been so constituted as a kind of middle ground between God and nothingness, or between the supreme being and non-being. Thus insofar as I have been created by the supreme being, there is nothing in me by means of which I might be deceived or be led into error; but insofar as I participate in nothingness or non-being, that is, insofar as I am not the supreme being and lack a great many things, it is not surprising that I make mistakes. Thus I certainly understand that error as such is not something real that depends upon God, but rather is merely a defect. And thus there is no need to account for my errors by positing a faculty given to me by God for this purpose. Rather, it just so happens that I make mistakes because the faculty of judging the truth, which I got from God, is not, in my case, infinite.

Still this is not yet altogether satisfactory; for error is not a pure negation, but rather a privation or a lack of some knowledge that somehow ought to be in me. And when I attend to the nature of God, it seems impossible that he would have placed in me a faculty that is not perfect in its kind or that is lacking some perfection it ought to have. For if it is true that the more expert the craftsman, the more perfect the works he produces, what can that supreme creator of all things make that is not perfect in all respects? No doubt God could have created me such that I never erred. No doubt, again, God always wills what is best. Is it then better that I should be in error rather than not?

As I mull these things over more carefully, it occurs to me first that there is no reason to marvel at the fact that God should bring about certain things the reasons for which I do not understand. Nor is his existence therefore to be doubted because I happen to experience other things of which I fail to grasp why and how he made them. For since I know now that my nature is very weak and limited, whereas the nature of God is immense, incomprehensible, and infinite, this is sufficient for me also to know that he can make innumerable things whose causes escape me. For this reason alone the entire class of causes which people customarily derive from a thing's "end," I judge to be utterly useless in physics. It is not without rashness that I think myself capable of inquiring into the ends of God.

It also occurs to me that whenever we ask whether the works of God are perfect, we should keep in view not simply some one creature in isolation from the rest, but the universe as a whole. For perhaps something might rightfully appear very imperfect if it were all by itself, and yet be most perfect, to the extent that it has the status of a part in the universe. And although subsequent to having decided to doubt everything, I have come to know with certainty only that I and God exist, nevertheless, after having taken note of the immense power of God, I cannot deny that many other things have been made by him, or at least could have been made by him. Thus I may have the status of a part in the universal scheme of things.

Next, as I focus more closely on myself and inquire into the nature of my errors (the only things that are indicative of some imperfection in me), I note that these errors depend on the simultaneous concurrence of two causes: the faculty of knowing that is in me and the faculty of choosing, that is, the free choice of the will, in other words, simultaneously on the intellect and will. Through the intellect alone I merely perceive ideas, about which I can render a judgment. Strictly speaking, no error is to be found in the intellect when properly viewed in this manner.

For although perhaps there may exist countless things about which I have no idea, nevertheless it must not be said that, strictly speaking, I am deprived of these ideas but only that I lack them in a negative sense. This is because I cannot adduce an argument to prove that God ought to have given me a greater faculty of knowing than he did. No matter how expert a craftsman I understand him to be, still I do not for that reason believe he ought to have bestowed on each one of his works all the perfections that he can put into some. Nor, on the other hand, can I complain that the will or free choice I have received from God is insufficiently ample or perfect, since I experience that it is limited by no boundaries whatever. In fact, it seems to be especially worth noting that no other things in me are so perfect or so great but that I understand that they can be still more perfect or greater. If, for example, I consider the faculty of understanding, I immediately recognize that in my case it is very small and quite limited, and at the very same time I form an idea of another much greater faculty of understanding—in fact, an understanding which is consummately great and infinite; and from the fact that I can form an idea of this faculty, I perceive that it pertains to the nature of God. Similarly, were I to examine the faculty of memory or imagination, or any of the other faculties, I would understand that in my case each of these is without exception feeble and limited, whereas in the case of God I understand each faculty to be boundless. It is only the will or free choice that I experience to be so great in me that I cannot grasp the idea of any greater faculty. This is so much the case that the will is the chief basis for my understanding that I bear a certain image and likeness of God. For although the faculty of willing is incomparably greater in God than it is in me, both by virtue of the knowledge and power that are joined to it and that render it more resolute and efficacious and by virtue of its object inasmuch as the divine will stretches over a greater number of things, nevertheless, when viewed in itself formally and precisely, God's faculty of willing does not appear to be any greater. This is owing to the fact that willing is merely a matter of being able to do or not do the same thing, that is, of being able to affirm or deny, to pursue or to shun; or better still, the will consists solely in the fact that when something is proposed to us by our intellect either to affirm or deny, to pursue or to shun, we are moved in such a way that we sense that we are determined to it by no external force. In order to be free I need not be capable of being moved in each direction; on the contrary, the more I am inclined toward one direction—either because I clearly understand that there is in it an aspect of the good and the true, or because God has thus disposed the inner recesses of my thought—the more freely do I choose that direction. Nor indeed does divine grace or natural knowledge ever diminish one's freedom; rather, they increase and strengthen it. However, the indifference that I experience when there is no reason moving me more in one direction than in another is the lowest grade of freedom; it is indicative not of any perfection in freedom, but rather of a defect, that is, a certain negation in knowledge. Were I always to see clearly what is true and good, I would never deliberate about what is to be judged or chosen. In that event, although I would be entirely free, I could never be indifferent.

But from these considerations I perceive that the power of willing, which I got from God, is not, taken by itself, the cause of my errors, for it is most ample as well as perfect in its kind. Nor is my power of understanding the cause of my errors. For since I got my power of understanding from God, whatever I understand I doubtless understand rightly, and it is impossible for me to be deceived in this. What then is the source of my errors? They are owing simply to the fact that, since the will extends further than the intellect, I do not contain the will within the same boundaries; rather, I also extend it to things I do not understand. Because the will is indifferent in regard to such matters, it easily turns away from the true and the good; and in this way I am deceived and I sin.

For example, during these last few days I was examining whether anything in the world exists, and I noticed that, from the very fact that I was making this examination, it obviously followed that I exist. Nevertheless, I could not help judging that what I understood so clearly was true; not that I was coerced into making this judgment because of some external force, but because a great light gave way to a great inclination in my will, and the less indifferent I was, the more spontaneously and freely did I believe it. But now, in addition to my knowing that I exist, insofar as I am a certain thinking thing, I also observe a certain idea of corporeal nature. It happens that I am in doubt as to whether the thinking nature which is in me, or rather which I am, is something different from this corporeal nature, or whether both natures are one and the same thing. And I assume that as yet no consideration has occurred to my intellect to convince me of the one alternative rather than the other. Certainly in virtue of this very fact I am indifferent about whether to affirm or to deny either alternative, or even whether to make no judgment at all in the matter.

Moreover, this indifference extends not merely to things about which the intellect knows absolutely nothing, but extends generally to everything of which the intellect does not have a clear enough knowledge at the very time when the will is deliberating on them. For although probable guesses may pull me in one direction, the mere knowledge that they are only guesses and not certain and indubitable proofs is all it takes to push my assent in the opposite direction. These last few days have provided me with ample experience on this point. For all the beliefs that I had once held to be most true I have supposed to be utterly false, and for the sole reason that I determined that I could somehow raise doubts about them.

But if I hold off from making a judgment when I do not perceive what is true with sufficient clarity and distinctness, it is clear that I am acting properly and am not committing an error. But if instead I were to make an assertion or a denial, then I am not using my freedom properly. Were I to select the alternative that is false, then obviously I will be in error. But were I to embrace the other alternative, it will be by sheer luck that I happen upon the truth; but I will still not be without fault, for it is manifest by the light of nature that a perception on the part of the intellect must always precede a determination on the part of the will. Inherent in this incorrect use of free will is the privation that constitutes the very essence of error: the privation, I say, present in this operation insofar as the operation proceeds for me, but not in the faculty given to me by God, nor even in its operation insofar as it depends upon him.

Indeed I have no cause for complaint on the grounds that God has not given me a greater power of understanding or a greater light of nature than he has, for it is of the essence of a finite intellect not to understand many things, and it is of the essence of a created intellect to be finite. Actually, instead of thinking that he has withheld from me or deprived me of those things that he has not given me, I ought to thank God, who never owed me anything, for what he has bestowed upon me.

Again, I have no cause for complaint on the grounds that God has given me a will that has a wider scope than my intellect. For since the will consists of merely one thing, something indivisible, as it were, it does not seem that its nature could withstand anything being removed from it. Indeed, the more ample the will is, the more I ought to thank the one who gave it to me.

Finally, I should not complain because God concurs with me in eliciting those acts of the will, that is those judgments, in which I am mistaken. For insofar as those acts depend on God, they are absolutely true and good; and in a certain sense, there is greater perfection in me in being able to elicit those acts than in not being able to do so. But privation, in which alone the defining characteristic of falsehood and wrong-doing is to be found, has no need whatever for God's concurrence, since a privation is not a thing, nor, when it is related to God as its cause, is it to be called a privation, but simply a negation. For it is surely no imperfection in God that he has given me the freedom to give or withhold my assent in those instances where he has not placed a clear and distinct perception in my intellect. But surely it is an imperfection in me that I do not use my freedom well and that I make judgments about things I do not properly understand. Nevertheless, I see that God could easily have brought it about that, while still being free and having finite knowledge, I should nonetheless never make a mistake. This result could have been achieved either by his endowing my intellect with a clear and distinct perception of everything about which I would ever deliberate, or by simply impressing the following rule so firmly upon my memory that I could never forget it: I should never judge anything that I do not clearly and distinctly understand. I readily understand that, considered as a totality, I would have been more perfect than I am now, had God made me that way. But I cannot therefore deny that it may somehow be a greater perfection in the universe as a whole that some of its parts are not immune to error, while others are, than if all of them were exactly alike. And I have no right to complain that the part God has wished me to play is not the principal and most perfect one of all.

Furthermore, even if I cannot abstain from errors in the first way mentioned above, which depends upon a clear perception of everything about which I must deliberate, nevertheless I can avoid error in the other way, which depends solely on my remembering to abstain from making judgments whenever the truth of a given matter is not apparent. For although I experience a certain infirmity in myself, namely that I am unable to keep my attention constantly focused on one and the same item of knowledge, nevertheless, by attentive and often repeated meditation, I can bring it about that I call this rule to mind whenever the situation calls for it, and thus I would acquire a certain habit of not erring.

Since herein lies the greatest and chief perfection of man, I think today's meditation, in which I investigated the cause of error and falsity, was quite profitable. Nor can this cause be anything other than the one I have described; for as often as I restrain my will when I make judgments, so that it extends only to those matters that the intellect clearly and distinctly discloses to it, it plainly cannot happen that I err. For every clear and distinct perception is surely something, and hence it cannot come from nothing. On the contrary, it must necessarily have God for its author: God, I say, that supremely perfect being to whom it is repugnant to be a deceiver. Therefore the perception is most assuredly true. Today I have learned not merely what I must avoid so as never to make a mistake, but at the same time what I must do to attain truth. For I will indeed attain it if only I pay enough attention to all the things that I perfectly understand, and separate them off from the rest, which I apprehend more confusedly and more obscurely. I will be conscientious about this in the future.

Meditation Five: Concerning the Essence of Material Things, and Again Concerning God, That He Exists

Several matters remain for me to examine concerning the attributes of God and myself, that is, concerning the nature of my mind. But perhaps I will take these up at some other time. For now, since I have noted what to avoid and what to do in order to attain the truth, nothing seems more pressing than that I try to free myself from the doubts into which I fell a few days ago, and that I see whether anything certain is to be had concerning material things.

Yet, before inquiring whether any such things exist outside me, I surely ought to consider the ideas of these things, insofar as they exist in my thought, and see which ones are distinct and which ones are confused.

I do indeed distinctly imagine the quantity that philosophers commonly call "continuous," that is, the extension of this quantity, or rather of the thing quantified in length, breadth and depth. I enumerate the various parts in it. I ascribe to these parts any sizes, shapes, positions, and local movements whatever; to these movements I ascribe any durations whatever.

Not only are these things manifestly known and transparent to me, viewed thus in a general way, but also, when I focus my attention on them, I perceive countless particulars concerning shapes, number, movement, and the like. Their truth is so open and so much in accord with my nature that, when I first discover them, it seems I am not so much learning something new as recalling something I knew beforehand. In other words, it seems as though I am noticing things for the first time that were in fact in me for a long while, although I had not previously directed a mental gaze upon them.

What I believe must be considered above all here is the fact that I find within me countless ideas of certain things, that, even if perhaps they do not exist anywhere outside me, still cannot be said to be nothing. And although, in a sense, I think them at will, nevertheless they are not something I have fabricated, rather they have their own true and immutable natures. For example, when I imagine a triangle, even if perhaps no such figure exists outside my thought anywhere in the world and never has, the triangle still has a certain determinate nature, essence, or form which is unchangeable and eternal, which I did not fabricate, and which does not depend on my mind. This is evident from the fact that various properties can be demonstrated regarding this triangle: namely, that its three angles are equal to two right angles, that its longest side is opposite its largest angle, and so on. These are properties I now clearly acknowledge, whether I want to or not, even if I previously had given them no thought whatever when I imagined

the triangle. For this reason, then, they were not fabricated by me.

It is irrelevant for me to say that perhaps the idea of a triangle came to me from external things through the sense organs because of course I have on occasion seen triangle-shaped bodies. For I can think of countless other figures, concerning which there can be no suspicion of their ever having entered me through the senses, and yet I can demonstrate various properties of these figures, no less than I can those of the triangle. All these properties are patently true because I know them clearly, and thus they are something and not merely nothing. For it is obvious that whatever is true is something, and I have already demonstrated at some length that all that I know clearly is true. And even if I had not demonstrated this, certainly the nature of my mind is such that nevertheless I cannot refrain from assenting to these things, at least while I perceive them clearly. And I recall that even before now, when I used to keep my attention glued to the objects of the senses, I always took the truths I clearly recognized regarding figures, numbers, or other things pertaining to arithmetic, geometry or, in general, to pure and abstract mathematics to be the most certain of all.

But if, from the mere fact that I can bring forth from my thought the idea of something, it follows that all that I clearly and distinctly perceive to belong to that thing really does belong to it, then cannot this too be a basis for an argument proving the existence of God? Clearly the idea of God, that is, the idea of a supremely perfect being, is one I discover to be no less within me than the idea of any figure or number. And that it belongs to God's nature that he always exists is something I understand no less clearly and distinctly than is the case when I demonstrate in regard to some figure or number that something also belongs to the nature of that figure or number. Thus, even if not everything that I have meditated upon during these last few days were true, still the existence of God ought to have for me at least the same degree of certainty that truths of mathematics had until now.

However, this point is not wholly obvious at first glance, but has a certain look of a sophism about it. Since in all other matters I have become accustomed to distinguishing existence from essence, I easily convince myself that it can even be separated from God's essence, and hence that God can be thought of as not existing. But nevertheless, it is obvious to anyone who pays close attention that existence can no more be separated from God's essence than its having three angles equal to two right angles can be separated from the essence of a triangle, or that that the idea of a valley can be separated from the idea of a mountain. Thus it is no less contradictory to think of God (that is, a supremely perfect being) lacking existence (that is, lacking some perfection) than it is to think of a mountain without a valley.

But granted I can no more think of God as not existing than I can think of a mountain without a valley, nevertheless it surely does not follow from the fact that I think of a mountain without a valley that a mountain exists in the world. Likewise, from the fact that I think of God as existing, it does not seem to follow that God exists, for my thought imposes no necessity on things. And just as one may imagine a winged horse, without there being a horse that has wings, in the same way perhaps I can attach existence to God, even though no God exists.

But there is a sophism lurking here. From the fact that I am unable to think of a mountain without a valley, it does not follow that a mountain or a valley exists anywhere, but only that, whether they exist or not, a mountain and a valley are inseparable from one another. But from the fact that I cannot think of God except as existing, it follows that existence is inseparable from God, and that for this reason he really exists. Not that my thought brings this about or imposes any necessity on anything; but rather the necessity of the thing itself, namely of the existence of God, forces me to think this. For I am not free to think of God without existence, that is, a supremely perfect being without a supreme perfection, as I am to imagine a horse with or without wings.

Further, it should not be said here that even though I surely need to assent to the existence of God once I have asserted that God has all perfections and that existence is one of these perfections, nevertheless that earlier assertion need not have been made. Likewise, I need not believe that all four-sided figures can be inscribed in a circle; but given that I posit this, it would then be necessary for me to admit that a rhombus can be inscribed in a circle. Yet this is obviously false. For although it is not necessary that I should ever happen upon any thought of God, nevertheless whenever I am of a mind to think of a being that is

first and supreme, and bring forth the idea of God as it were from the storehouse of my mind, I must of necessity ascribe all perfections to him, even if I do not at that time enumerate them all or take notice of each one individually. This necessity plainly suffices so that afterwards, when I realize that existence is a perfection, I rightly conclude that a first and supreme being exists. In the same way, there is no necessity for me ever to imagine a triangle, but whenever I do wish to consider a rectilinear figure having but three angles, I must ascribe to it those properties on the basis of which one rightly infers that the three angles of this figure are no greater than two right angles, even though I do not take note of this at the time. But when I inquire as to the figures that may be inscribed in a circle, there is absolutely no need whatever for my thinking that all four-sided figures are of this sort; for that matter, I cannot even fabricate such a thing, so long as I am of a mind to admit only what I clearly and distinctly understand. Consequently, there is a great difference between false assumptions of this sort and the true ideas that are inborn in me, the first and chief of which is the idea of God. For there are a great many ways in which I understand that this idea is not an invention that is dependent upon my thought, but is an image of a true and immutable nature. First, I cannot think of anything aside from God alone to whose essence existence belongs. Next, I cannot understand how there could be two or more Gods of this kind. Again, once I have asserted that one God now exists, I plainly see that it is necessary that he has existed from eternity and will endure for eternity. Finally, I perceive many other features in God, none of which I can remove or change.

But, whatever type of argument I use, it always comes down to the fact that the only things that fully convince me are those that I clearly and distinctly perceive. And although some of these things I thus perceive are obvious to everyone, while others are discovered only by those who look more closely and inquire carefully, nevertheless, once they have been discovered, they are considered no less certain than the others. For example, in the case of a right triangle, although it is not so readily apparent that the square of the hypotenuse is equal to the sum of the squares of the other two sides as it is that the hypotenuse is opposite the largest angle, nevertheless, once the former has been ascertained, it is no less believed. However, as far as God is concerned, if I were not overwhelmed by prejudices and if the images of sensible things were not besieging my thought from all directions, I would certainly acknowledge nothing sooner or more easily than him. For what, in and of itself, is more manifest than that a supreme being exists, that is, that God, to whose essence alone existence belongs, exists?

And although I needed to pay close attention in order to perceive this, nevertheless I now am just as certain about this as I am about everything else that seems most certain. Moreover, I observe also that certitude about other things is so dependent on this, that without it nothing can ever be perfectly known.

For I am indeed of such a nature that, while I perceive something very clearly and distinctly, I cannot help believing it to be true. Nevertheless, my nature is also such that I cannot focus my mental gaze always on the same thing, so as to perceive it clearly. Often the memory of a previously made judgment may return when I am no longer attending to the arguments on account of which I made such a judgment. Thus, other arguments can be brought forward that would easily make me change my opinion, were I ignorant of God. And thus I would never have true and certain knowledge about anything, but merely fickle and changeable opinions. Thus, for example, when I consider the nature of a triangle, it appears most evident to me, steeped as I am in the principles of geometry, that its three angles are equal to two right angles. And so long as I attend to its demonstration I cannot help believing this to be true. But no sooner do I turn the mind's eye away from the demonstration, than, however much I still recall that I had observed it most clearly, nevertheless, it can easily happen that I entertain doubts about whether it is true, were I ignorant of God. For I can convince myself that I have been so constituted by nature that I might occasionally be mistaken about those things I believe I perceive most evidently, especially when I recall that I have often taken many things to be true and certain, which other arguments have subsequently led me to judge to be false.

But once I perceived that there is a God, and also understood at the same time that everything else depends on him, and that he is not a deceiver, I then concluded that everything that I clearly and distinctly

perceive is necessarily true. Hence even if I no longer attend to the reasons leading me to judge this to be true, so long as I merely recall that I did clearly and distinctly observe it, no counter-argument can be brought forward that might force me to doubt it. On the contrary, I have a true and certain knowledge of it. And not just of this one fact, but of everything else that I recall once having demonstrated, as in geometry, and so on. For what objections can now be raised against me? That I have been made such that I am often mistaken? But I now know that I cannot be mistaken in matters I plainly understand. That I have taken many things to be true and certain which subsequently I recognized to be false? But none of these were things I clearly and distinctly perceived. But I was ignorant of this rule for determining the truth, and I believed these things perhaps for other reasons which I later discovered were less firm. What then remains to be said? That perhaps I am dreaming, as I recently objected against myself, in other words, that everything I am now thinking of is no truer than what occurs to someone who is asleep? Be that as it may, this changes nothing; for certainly, even if I were dreaming, if anything is evident to my intellect, then it is entirely true.

And thus I see plainly that the certainty and truth of every science depends exclusively upon the knowledge of the true God, to the extent that, prior to my becoming aware of him, I was incapable of achieving perfect knowledge about anything else. But now it is possible for me to achieve full and certain knowledge about countless things, both about God and other intellectual matters, as well as about the entirety of that corporeal nature which is the object of pure mathematics.

Meditation Six: Concerning the Existence of Material Things, and the Real Distinction between Mind and Body

It remains for me to examine whether material things exist. Indeed I now know that they can exist, at least insofar as they are the object of pure mathematics, since I clearly and distinctly perceive them. For no doubt God is capable of bringing about everything that I am capable of perceiving in this way. And I have never judged that God was incapable of something, except when it was incompatible with my perceiving it distinctly. Moreover, from the faculty of imagination, which I notice I use while dealing with material things, it seems to follow that they exist. For to anyone paying very close attention to what imagination is, it appears to be simply a certain application of the knowing faculty to a body intimately present to it, and which therefore exists.

To make this clear, I first examine the difference between imagination and pure intellection. So, for example, when I imagine a triangle, I not only understand that it is a figure bounded by three lines, but at the same time I also envisage with the mind's eye those lines as if they were present; and this is what I call "imagining." On the other hand, if I want to think about a chiliagon, I certainly understand that it is a figure consisting of a thousand sides, just as well as I understand that a triangle is a figure consisting of three sides, yet I do not imagine those thousand sides in the same way, or envisage them as if they were present. And although in that case—because of force of habit I always imagine something whenever I think about a corporeal thing—I may perchance represent to myself some figure in a confused fashion, nevertheless this figure is obviously not a chiliagon. For this figure is really no different from the figure I would represent to myself, were I thinking of a myriagon or any other figure with a large number of sides. Nor is this figure of any help in knowing the properties that differentiate a chiliagon from other polygons. But if the figure in question is a pentagon, I surely can understand its figure, just as was the case with the chiliagon, without the help of my imagination. But I can also imagine a pentagon by turning the mind's eye both to its five sides and at the same time to the area bounded by those sides. At this point I am manifestly aware that I am in need of a peculiar sort of effort on the part of the mind in order to imagine, one that I do not employ in order to understand. This new effort on the part of the mind clearly shows the difference between imagination and pure intellection.

Moreover, I consider that this power of imagining that is in me, insofar as it differs from the power of understanding, is not required for my own essence, that is, the essence of my mind. For were I to be lacking this power, I would nevertheless undoubtedly remain the same entity I am now. Thus it seems to follow that the power of imagining depends upon something distinct from me. And I readily understand that, were a body to exist to which a mind is so joined that it may apply itself in order, as it were, to look at it any time it wishes, it could happen that it is by means of this very body that I imagine corporeal things. As a result, this mode of thinking may differ from pure intellection only in the sense that the mind, when it understands, in a sense turns toward itself and looks at one of the ideas that are in it; whereas when it imagines, it turns toward the body, and intuits in the body something that conforms to an idea either understood by the mind or perceived by sense. To be sure, I easily understand that the imagination can be acutalized in this way, provided a body does exist. And since I can think of no other way of explaining imagination that is equally appropriate, I make a probable conjecture from this that a body exists. But this is only a probability. And even though I may examine everything carefully, nevertheless I do not yet see how the distinct idea of corporeal nature that I find in my imagination can enable me to develop an argument which necessarily concludes that some body exists.

But I am in the habit of imagining many other things, over and above that corporeal nature which is the object of pure mathematics, such as colors, sounds, tastes, pain, and the like, though not so distinctly. And I perceive these things better by means of the senses, from which, with the aid of the memory, they seem to have arrived at the imagination. Thus I should pay the same degree of attention to the senses, so that I might deal with them more appropriately. I must see whether I can obtain any reliable argument for the existence of corporeal things from those things that are perceived by the mode of thinking that I call "sense."

First of all, to be sure, I will review here all the things I previously believed to be true because I had perceived them by means of the senses and the causes I had for thinking this. Next I will assess the causes why I later called them into doubt. Finally, I will consider what I must now believe about these things.

So first, I sensed that I had a head, hands, feet, and other members that comprised this body which I viewed as part of me, or perhaps even as the whole of me. I sensed that this body was found among many other bodies, by which my body can be affected in various beneficial or harmful ways. I gauged what was opportune by means of a certain sensation of pleasure, and what was inopportune by a sensation of pain. In addition to pain and pleasure, I also sensed within me hunger, thirst, and other such appetites, as well as certain bodily tendencies toward mirth, sadness, anger, and other such affects. And externally, besides the extension, shapes, and motions of bodies, I also sensed their hardness, heat, and other tactile qualities. I also sensed light, colors, odors, tastes, and sounds, on the basis of whose variety I distinguished the sky, the earth, the seas, and the other bodies, one from the other. Now given the ideas of all these qualities that presented themselves to my thought, and which were all that I properly and immediately sensed, still it was surely not without reason that I thought I sensed things that were manifestly different from my thought, namely, the bodies from which these ideas proceeded. For I knew by experience that these ideas came upon me utterly without my consent, to the extent that, wish as I may, I could not sense any object unless it was present to a sense organ. Nor could I fail to sense it when it was present. And since the ideas perceived by sense were much more vivid and explicit and even, in their own way, more distinct than any of those that I deliberately and knowingly formed through meditation or that I found impressed on my memory, it seemed impossible that they came from myself. Thus the remaining alternative was that they came from other things. Since I had no knowledge of such things except from those same ideas themselves, I could not help entertaining the thought that they were similar to those ideas. Moreover, I also recalled that the use of the senses antedated the use of reason. And since I saw that the ideas that I myself fashioned were not as explicit as those that I perceived through the faculty of sense, and were for the most part composed of parts of the latter, I easily convinced myself that I had absolutely no idea in the intellect that I did not have beforehand in the sense faculty. Not without reason did I judge that this body, which by a certain special right I called "mine," belongs more to me than did any other. For I could never be separated from it in the same way I could be from other bodies. I sensed all appetites and feelings in and on behalf of it. Finally, I noticed pain and pleasurable excitement in its parts, but not in other bodies external to it. But why should a certain

sadness of spirit arise from some sensation or other of pain, and why should a certain elation arise from a sensation of excitement, or why should that peculiar twitching in the stomach, which I call hunger, warn me to have something to eat, or why should dryness in the throat warn me to take something to drink, and so on? I plainly had no explanation other than that I had been taught this way by nature. For there is no affinity whatsoever, at least none I am aware of, between this twitching in the stomach and the will to have something to eat, or between the sensation of something causing pain and the thought of sadness arising from this sensation. But nature also seems to have taught me everything else as well that I judged concerning the objects of the senses, for I had already convinced myself that this was how things were, prior to my assessing any of the arguments that might prove it.

Afterwards, however, many experiences gradually weakened any faith that I had in the senses. Towers that had seemed round from afar occasionally appeared square at close quarters. Very large statues mounted on their pedestals did not seem large to someone looking at them from ground level. And in countless other such instances I determined that judgments in matters of the external senses were in error. And not just the external senses, but the internal senses as well. For what can be more intimate than pain? But I had sometimes heard it said by people whose leg or arm had been amputated that it seemed to them that they still occasionally sensed pain in the very limb they had lost. Thus, even in my own case it did not seem to be entirely certain that some bodily member was causing me pain, even though I did sense pain in it. To these causes for doubt I recently added two quite general ones. The first was that everything I ever thought I sensed while awake I could believe I also sometimes sensed while asleep, and since I do not believe that what I seem to sense in my dreams comes to me from things external to me, I saw no reason why I should hold this belief about those things I seem to be sensing while awake. The second was that, since I was still ignorant of the author of my origin (or at least pretended to be ignorant of it), I saw nothing to prevent my having been so constituted by nature that I should be mistaken even about what seemed to me most true. As to the arguments that used to convince me of the truth of sensible things, I found no difficulty responding to them. For since I seemed driven by nature toward many things about which reason tried to dissuade me, I did not think that what I was taught by nature deserved much credence. And even though the perceptions of the senses did not depend on my will, I did not think that we must therefore conclude that they came from things distinct from me, since perhaps there is some faculty in me, as yet unknown to me, that produces these perceptions.

But now, having begun to have a better knowledge of myself and the author of my origin, I am of the opinion that I must not rashly admit everything that I seem to derive from the senses; but neither, for that matter, should I call everything into doubt.

First, I know that all the things that I clearly and distinctly understand can be made by God such as I understand them. For this reason, my ability clearly and distinctly to understand one thing without another suffices to make me certain that the one thing is different from the other, since they can be separated from each other, at least by God. The question as to the sort of power that might effect such a separation is not relevant to their being thought to be different. For this reason, from the fact that I know that I exist, and that at the same time I judge that obviously nothing else belongs to my nature or essence except that I am a thinking thing, I rightly conclude that my essence consists entirely in my being a thinking thing. And although perhaps (or rather, as I shall soon say, assuredly) I have a body that is very closely joined to me, nevertheless, because on the one hand I have a clear and distinct idea of myself, insofar as I am merely a thinking thing and not an extended thing, and because on the other hand I have a distinct idea of a body, insofar as it is merely an extended thing and not a thinking thing, it is certain that I am really distinct from my body, and can exist without it.

Moreover, I find in myself faculties for certain special modes of thinking, namely the faculties of imagining and sensing. I can clearly and distinctly understand myself in my entirety without these faculties, but not vice versa: I cannot understand them clearly and distinctly without me, that is, without a substance endowed with understanding in which they inhere, for they include an act of understanding in their formal concept. Thus I perceive them to be distinguished from me as modes from a thing. I also acknowledge that there are certain other faculties, such as those of moving from one place to another, of taking on various shapes, and so on, that, like sensing or imagining, cannot be understood apart from some substance in which they inhere, and hence without which they cannot exist. But it is clear that these faculties, if in fact they exist, must be in a corporeal or extended substance, not in a substance endowed with understanding. For some extension is contained in a clear and distinct concept of them, though certainly not any understanding. Now there clearly is in me a passive faculty of sensing, that is, a faculty for receiving and knowing the ideas of sensible things; but I could not use it unless there also existed, either in me or in something else, a certain active faculty of producing or bringing about these ideas. But this faculty surely cannot be in me, since it clearly presupposes no act of understanding, and these ideas are produced without my cooperation and often even against my will. Therefore the only alternative is that it is in some substance different from me, containing either formally or eminently all the reality that exists objectively in the ideas produced by that faculty, as I have just noted above. Hence this substance is either a body, that is, a corporeal nature, which contains formally all that is contained objectively in the ideas, or else it is God, or some other creature more noble than a body, which contains eminently all that is contained objectively in the ideas. But since God is not a deceiver, it is patently obvious that he does not send me these ideas either immediately by himself, or even through the mediation of some creature that contains the objective reality of these ideas not formally but only eminently. For since God has given me no faculty whatsoever for making this determination, but instead has given me a great inclination to believe that these ideas issue from corporeal things, I fail to see how God could be understood not to be a deceiver, if these ideas were to issue from a source other than corporeal things. And consequently corporeal things exist. Nevertheless, perhaps not all bodies exist exactly as I grasp them by sense, since this sensory grasp is in many cases very obscure and confused. But at least they do contain everything I clearly and distinctly understand—that is, everything, considered in a general sense, that is encompassed in the object of pure mathematics.

As far as the remaining matters are concerned,

which are either merely particular (for example, that the sun is of such and such a size or shape, and so on) or less clearly understood (for example, light, sound, pain, and the like), even though these matters are very doubtful and uncertain, nevertheless the fact that God is no deceiver (and thus no falsity can be found in my opinions, unless there is also in me a faculty given me by God for the purpose of rectifying this falsity) offers me a definite hope of reaching the truth even in these matters. And surely there is no doubt that all that I am taught by nature has some truth to it; for by "nature," taken generally, I understand nothing other than God himself or the ordered network of created things which was instituted by God. By my own particular nature I understand nothing other than the combination of all the things bestowed upon me by God.

There is nothing that this nature teaches me more explicitly than that I have a body that is ill-disposed when I feel pain, that needs food and drink when I suffer hunger or thirst, and the like. Therefore, I should not doubt that there is some truth in this.

By means of these sensations of pain, hunger, thirst and so on, nature also teaches not merely that I am present to my body in the way a sailor is present in a ship, but that I am most tightly joined and, so to speak, commingled with it, so much so that I and the body constitute one single thing. For if this were not the case, then I, who am only a thinking thing, would not sense pain when the body is injured; rather, I would perceive the wound by means of the pure intellect, just as a sailor perceives by sight whether anything in his ship is broken. And when the body is in need of food or drink, I should understand this explicitly, instead of having confused sensations of hunger and thirst. For clearly these sensations of thirst, hunger, pain, and so on are nothing but certain confused modes of thinking arising from the union and, as it were, the commingling of the mind with the body.

Moreover, I am also taught by nature that various other bodies exist around my body, some of which are to be pursued, while others are to be avoided. And to be sure, from the fact that I sense a wide variety of colors, sounds, odors, tastes, levels of heat, and grades of roughness, and the like, I rightly conclude that in the bodies from which these different perceptions of the senses proceed there are differences

corresponding to the different perceptions — though perhaps the latter do not resemble the former. And from the fact that some of these perceptions are pleasant while others are unpleasant, it is plainly certain that my body, or rather my whole self, insofar as I am comprised of a body and a mind, can be affected by various beneficial and harmful bodies in the vicinity.

Granted, there are many other things that I seem to have been taught by nature; nevertheless it was not really nature that taught them to me but a certain habit of making reckless judgments. And thus it could easily happen that these judgments are false: for example, that any space where there is absolutely nothing happening to move my senses is empty; or that there is something in a hot body that bears an exact likeness to the idea of heat that is in me; or that in a white or green body there is the same whiteness or greenness that I sense; or that in a bitter or sweet body there is the same taste, and so on; or that stars and towers and any other distant bodies have the same size and shape that they present to my senses, and other things of this sort. But to ensure that my perceptions in this matter are sufficiently distinct, I ought to define more precisely what exactly I mean when I say that I am "taught something by nature." For I am taking "nature" here more narrowly than the combination of everything bestowed on me by God. For this combination embraces many things that belong exclusively to my mind, such as my perceiving that what has been done cannot be undone, and everything else that is known by the light of nature. That is not what I am talking about here. There are also many things that belong exclusively to the body, such as that it tends to move downward, and so on. I am not dealing with these either, but only with what God has bestowed on me insofar as I am comprised of mind and body. Accordingly, it is this nature that teaches me to avoid things that produce a sensation of pain and to pursue things that produce a sensation of pleasure, and the like. But it does not appear that nature teaches us to conclude anything, besides these things, from these sense perceptions unless the intellect has first conducted its own inquiry regarding things external to us. For it seems to belong exclusively to the mind, and not to the composite of mind and body, to know the truth in these matters. Thus, although a star affects my eye no more than does the flame from a small torch, still there is no real or positive tendency in my eye toward believing that the star is no larger than the flame. Yet, ever since my youth, I have made this judgment without any reason for doing so. And although I feel heat as I draw closer to the fire, and I also feel pain upon drawing too close to it, there is not a single argument that persuades me that there is something in the fire similar to that heat, any more than to that pain. On the contrary, I am convinced only that there is something in the fire that, regardless of what it finally turns out to be, causes in us those sensations of heat or pain. And although there may be nothing in a given space that moves the senses, it does not therefore follow that there is no body in it. But I see that in these and many other instances I have been in the habit of subverting the order of nature. For admittedly I use the perceptions of the senses (which are properly given by nature only for signifying to the mind what things are useful or harmful to the composite of which it is a part, and to that extent they are clear and distinct enough) as reliable rules for immediately discerning what is the essence of bodies located outside us. Yet they signify nothing about that except quite obscurely and confusedly.

I have already examined in sufficient detail how it could happen that my judgments are false, despite the goodness of God. But a new difficulty now arises regarding those very things that nature shows me are either to be sought out or avoided, as well as the internal sensations where I seem to have detected errors, as for example, when someone is deluded by a food's pleasant taste to eat the poison hidden inside it. In this case, however, he is driven by nature only toward desiring the thing in which the pleasurable taste is found, but not toward the poison, of which he obviously is unaware. I can only conclude that this nature is not omniscient. This is not remarkable, since man is a limited thing, and thus only what is of limited perfection befits him.

But we not infrequently err even in those things to which nature impels us. Take, for example, the case of those who are ill and who desire food or drink that will soon afterwards be injurious to them. Perhaps it could be said here that they erred because their nature was corrupt. However, this does not remove our difficulty, for a sick man is no less a creature of God than a healthy one, and thus it seems no less inconsistent that the sick man got a deception-prone nature from God. And a clock made of wheels and counter-weights follows all the laws of nature no less closely when it has been badly constructed and does not tell time accurately than it does when it completely satisfies the wish of its maker. Likewise, I might regard a man's body as a kind of mechanism that is outfitted with and composed of bones, nerves, muscles, veins, blood and skin in such a way that, even if no mind existed in it, the man's body would still exhibit all the same motions that are in it now except for those motions that proceed either from a command of the will or, consequently, from the mind. I easily recognize that it would be natural for this body, were it, say, suffering from dropsy and experiencing dryness in the throat (which typically produces a thirst sensation in the mind), and also so disposed by its nerves and other parts to take something to drink, the result of which would be to exacerbate the illness. This is as natural as for a body without any such illness to be moved by the same dryness in the throat to take something to drink that is useful to it. And given the intended purpose of the clock, I could say that it deviates from its nature when it fails to tell the right time. And similarly, considering the mechanism of the human body in terms of its being equipped for the motions that typically occur in it, I may think that it too is deviating from its nature, if its throat were dry when having something to drink is not beneficial to its conservation. Nevertheless, I am well aware that this last use of "nature" differs greatly from the other. For this latter "nature" is merely a designation dependent on my thought, since it compares a man in poor health and a poorly constructed clock with the ideas of a healthy man and of a well-made clock, a designation extrinsic to the things to which it is applied. But by "nature" taken in the former sense, I understand something that is really in things, and thus is not without some truth.

When we say, then, in the case of the body suffering from dropsy, that its "nature" is corrupt, given the fact that it has a parched throat and yet does not need something to drink, "nature" obviously is merely an extrinsic designation. Nevertheless, in the case of the composite, that is, of a mind joined to such a body, it is not a pure designation, but a true error of nature that this body should be thirsty when having something to drink would be harmful to it. It therefore remains to inquire here how the goodness of God does not prevent "nature," thus considered, from being deceptive.

Now my first observation here is that there is a great difference between a mind and a body in that a body, by its very nature, is always divisible. On the other hand, the mind is utterly indivisible. For when I consider the mind, that is, myself insofar as I am only a thinking thing, I cannot distinguish any parts within me; rather, I understand myself to be manifestly one complete thing. Although the entire mind seems to be united to the entire body, nevertheless, were a foot or an arm or any other bodily part to be amputated, I know that nothing has been taken away from the mind on that account. Nor can the faculties of willing, sensing, understanding, and so on be called "parts" of the mind, since it is one and the same mind that wills, senses, and understands. On the other hand, there is no corporeal or extended thing I can think of that I may not in my thought easily divide into parts; and in this way I understand that it is divisible. This consideration alone would suffice to teach me that the mind is wholly diverse from the body, had I not yet known it well enough in any other way.

My second observation is that my mind is not immediately affected by all the parts of the body, but only by the brain, or perhaps even by just one small part of the brain, namely, by that part where the "common" sense is said to reside. Whenever this part of the brain is disposed in the same manner, it presents the same thing to the mind, even if the other parts of the body are able meanwhile to be related in diverse ways. Countless experiments show this, none of which need be reviewed here.

My next observation is that the nature of the body is such that whenever any of its parts can be moved by another part some distance away, it can also be moved in the same manner by any of the parts that lie between them, even if this more distant part is doing nothing. For example, in the cord ABCD, if the final part D is pulled, the first part A would be moved in exactly the same manner as it could be, if one of the intermediate parts B or C were pulled, while the end part D remained immobile. Likewise, when I feel a pain in my foot, physics teaches me that this sensation took place by means of nerves distributed throughout the foot, like stretched cords extending from the foot all the way to the brain.

When these nerves are pulled in the foot, they also pull on the inner parts of the brain to which they extend, and produce a certain motion in them. This motion has been constituted by nature so as to affect the mind with a sensation of pain, as if it occurred in the foot. But because these nerves need to pass through the skin, thigh, loins, back, and neck to get from the foot to the brain, it can happen that even if it is not the part in the foot but merely one of the intermediate parts that is being struck, the very same movement will occur in the brain that would occur were the foot badly injured. The inevitable result will be that the mind feels the same pain. The same opinion should hold for any other sensation.

My final observation is that, since any given motion occurring in that part of the brain immediately affecting the mind produces but one sensation in it, I can think of no better arrangement than that it produces the one sensation that, of all the ones it is able to produce, is most especially and most often conducive to the maintenance of a healthy man. Moreover, experience shows that all the sensations bestowed on us by nature are like this. Hence there is absolutely nothing to be found in them that does not bear witness to God's power and goodness. Thus, for example, when the nerves in the foot are agitated in a violent and unusual manner, this motion of theirs extends through the marrow of the spine to the inner reaches of the brain, where it gives the mind the sign to sense something, namely, the pain as if it is occurring in the foot. This provokes the mind to do its utmost to move away from the cause of the pain, since it is seen as harmful to the foot. But the nature of man could have been so constituted by God that this same motion in the brain might have indicated something else to the mind: for example, either the motion itself as it occurs in the brain, or in the foot, or in some place in between, or something else entirely different. But nothing else would have served so well the maintenance of the body. Similarly, when we need something to drink, a certain dryness arises in the throat that moves the nerves in the throat, and, by means of them, the inner parts of the brain. And this motion affects the mind with a sensation of thirst, because in this entire affair nothing is more useful for us to know than that we need something to drink in order to maintain our health; the same holds in the other cases.

From these considerations it is utterly apparent that, notwithstanding the immense goodness of God, the nature of man, insofar as it is composed of mind and body, cannot help being sometimes mistaken. For if some cause, not in the foot but in some other part through which the nerves extend from the foot to the brain, or perhaps even in the brain itself, were to produce the same motion that would normally be produced by a badly injured foot, the pain will be felt as if it were in the foot, and the senses will naturally be deceived. For since an identical motion in the brain can only bring about an identical sensation in the mind, and it is more frequently the case that this motion is wont to arise on account of a cause that harms the foot than on account of some other thing existing elsewhere, it is reasonable that the motion should always show pain to the mind as something belonging to the foot rather than to some other part. And if dryness in the throat does not arise, as is normal, because taking something to drink contributes to bodily health, but from a contrary cause, as happens in the case of someone with dropsy, then it is far better that it should deceive on that occasion than that it should always be deceptive when the body is in good health. The same holds for the other cases.

This consideration is most helpful, not only for my noticing all the errors to which my nature is liable, but also for enabling me to correct or avoid them without difficulty. To be sure, I know that all the senses set forth what is true more frequently than what is false regarding what concerns the welfare of the body. Moreover, I can nearly always make use of several of them in order to examine the same thing. Furthermore, I can use my memory, which connects current happenings with past ones, and my intellect, which now has examined all the causes of error.

Hence I should no longer fear that those things that are daily shown me by the senses are false. On the contrary, the hyperbolic doubts of the last few days ought to be rejected as ludicrous. This goes especially for the chief reason for doubting, which dealt with my failure to distinguish being asleep from being awake. For I now notice that there is a considerable difference between these two; dreams are never joined by the memory with all the other actions of life, as is the case with those actions that occur when one is awake. For surely, if, while I am awake, someone were suddenly to appear to me and then immediately disappear, as occurs in dreams, so that I see neither where he came from nor where he went, it is not without reason that I would judge him to be a ghost or a phantom conjured up in my brain, rather than a true man. But when these things happen, and I notice distinctly where they come from, where they are now, and when they come to me, and when I connect my perception of them without interruption with the whole rest of my life, I am clearly certain that these perceptions have happened to me not while I was dreaming but while I was awake. Nor ought I have even the least doubt regarding the truth of these things, if, having mustered all the senses, in addition to my memory and my intellect, in order to examine them, nothing is passed on to me by one of these sources that conflicts with the others. For from the fact that God is no deceiver, it follows that I am in no way mistaken in these matters. But because the need to get things done does not always permit us the leisure for such a careful inquiry, we must confess that the life of man is apt to commit errors regarding particular things, and we must acknowledge the infirmity of our nature.

Thomas Hobbes

Thomas Hobbes (1588–1679) was born in Malmesbury, Wiltshire, England. Raised by a well-to-do uncle, he entered Oxford at the age of fourteen and received his bachelor's degree in 1608. His early interests were largely classical. In 1629, however, on a visit to the continent his imagination was captured by the method of geometry, in which he saw a superior way of arriving at certain truths. In his masterpiece, *Leviathan*, Hobbes remarks that geometry is "the only science that it hath pleased God hitherto to bestow upon mankind." On another continental visit, from 1634 through 1637, Hobbes met Galileo in Italy, conversed frequently with eminent thinkers in Paris, and formulated the outlines of his own philosophical position. Returning to England in 1637, he became increasingly concerned about the impending civil war there. His support of monarchy and his fear of the parliamentarians led him to flee to Holland in 1640. Thereafter, Hobbes remained on the continent for eleven productive years, spending a part of this time tutoring the future Charles II. His final years in England, from 1650 on, were marked by continuing controversy over his views and by the banning of his books.

Hobbes's earlier works include the *Little Treatise*, a discussion of sensation (written between 1630 and 1637), and *Elements of Law* (1640), in which he argues for an undivided sovereignty. His masterpiece, *Leviathan* (1651), is a treatise on "the matter, forme, and power of a commonwealth, ecclesiasticall and civil." Among his other works are a trilogy: *De Cive* (1642), *De Corpore* (1655), and *De Homine* (1657); *Of Liberty and Necessity* (published without his consent in 1654); and a historical work, *Behemoth* (1668).

Although *Leviathan* is best known as a contribution to political philosophy, it is really a multifaceted work, containing important insights into metaphysics and psychology. Since Hobbes recognized that any adequate theory of government must grow out of a sound conception of the governed, he attempted to develop a comprehensive view of man from a mechanistic and materialistic base. *Leviathan* thus begins with the claim that sensation is nothing but motion in the appropriate bodily parts, and that the various forms of imagination which we call "memory," "dream," and "apparition" are all echoes of this initial motion. They are, in Hobbes's own vivid phrase, "decaying sense." Associations between thoughts are echoes of connections between past motions; and desire and aversion, the antecedents of action, are the "small beginnings of motion, within the body of man, before they appear in walking, speaking, striking, and other visible actions." Although the details of this materialistic account are crude, the views expressed are recognizable ancestors of views hotly debated today. Even Hobbes's particular brand of materialism, which identifies mental states with occurrences involving parts of physical objects rather than with those objects or parts themselves, continues to find favor.

Hobbes's political philosophy takes as its starting point an extremely pessimistic view of man's nature. According to Hobbes, the basic motivation of mankind is "a perpetual and restless desire of power after power, that ceaseth only in death." Given the universality of this desire for power, life in the state of nature, before the imposition of civil laws backed by sovereign force, must be a perpetual struggle for possessions, supremacy, and glory. In this state, the outcome of one's productive efforts is always uncertain, and life is "solitary, poor, nasty, brutish and short." To avoid this intolerable situation, the law of nature, which dictates self-preservation, commands men to surrender their liberty (although nor their ability to defend their lives or persons) to a single sovereign. By covenanting, or contracting, to lend their force to the sovereign's endeavors, they first create the conditions under which the enforcement of laws, and so too the institutions of property and justice, are possible. Thus is born Leviathan, the great artificial being of the commonwealth, whose very soul is sovereignty.

Hobbes's account does not point inevitably to any single form of government. He allows that the sovereignty may reside in a single ruler (monarchy), a group (aristocracy), or the entire population (democracy). He does insist, however, that whatever form the sovereign body takes, its power must be absolute. The reason for this is that the purpose of the original covenant is to create an authority strong enough to protect each member of the populace from the incursions of the others. Given this initial intent, any attempt to separate from the sovereign the abilities to tax, legislate, or deploy the military, to challenge or punish the sovereign's acts, or in any other way to limit his power, must violate the original agreement. There may be a risk that the sovereign will abuse his power; but for Hobbes (though not for Locke) this risk is far outweighed by the secure and orderly existence that that power makes possible.

• • •

For a good discussion of Hobbes's life and philosophy, see R. S. Peters, *Hobbes* (Baltimore: Penguin Books, 1956). A number of interesting shorter pieces are collected in Keith Brown, ed., *Hobbes Studies* (Cambridge, Mass: Harvard University Press, 1965). Two important works are Michael Oakshott, *Hobbes on Civil Association* (Berkeley: University of California Press, 1975), and Leo Strauss, *The Political Philosophy of Hobbes* (1936: rpt. Oxford: Oxford University Press, 1963). An influential study of Hobbes's political and moral philosophy is Howard Warrender, *The Political Philosophy of Thomas Hobbes* (Oxford: Oxford University Press, 1957). Hobbes's work is placed in its historical context in Jean Hampton, *Hobbes and the Social Contract Tradition* (New York: Cambridge University Press, 1986). Also noteworthy is Gregory S. Kavka, *Hobbesian Moral and Political Theory* (Princeton: Princeton University Press, 1986).

G.S.

Leviathan

THE INTRODUCTION

[1] Nature (the art whereby God hath made and governs the world) is by the *art* of man, as in many other things, so in this also imitated, that it can make an artificial animal. For seeing life is but a motion of limbs, the beginning whereof is in some principal part within, why may we not say that all *automata* (engines that move themselves by springs and wheels as doth a watch) have an artificial life? For what is the *heart*, but a *spring*; and the *nerves*, but so many *strings*; and the *joints*, but so many *wheels*, giving motion to the whole body, such as was intended by the artificer? *Art* goes yet further, imitating that rational and most excellent work of nature, *man*. For by art is created that great LEVIATHAN[1] called a COMMON-WEALTH, or STATE (in Latin CIVITAS), which is but an artificial man, though of greater stature and strength than the natural, for whose protection and defence it was intended; and in which the *sovereignty* is an artificial soul, as giving life and motion to the whole body; the *magistrates* and other *officers* of judicature and execution, artificial *joints*; *reward* and *punishment* (by which fastened to the seat of the sovereignty every joint and member is moved to perform his duty) are the *nerves*, that do the same in the body natural; the *wealth* and *riches* of all the particular members are the *strength*; *salus populi* (the people's safety) its *business*; *counsellors*, by whom all things needful for it to know are suggested unto it, are the *memory*; *equity* and *laws*, an artificial *reason* and *will*; *concord, health; sedition, sickness;* and *civil war, death.* Lastly, the *pacts* and *covenants* by which the parts of this body politic were at first made, set together, and united, resemble that *fiat*, or the *let us make man*, pronounced by God in the creation.

[2] To describe the nature of this artificial man, I will consider

First, the *matter* thereof, and the *artificer*, both which is *man*.

Secondly, *how* and by what *covenants* it is made; what are the *rights* and *just power* or *authority* of a *sovereign*; and what it is that *preserveth* and *dissolveth* it.

Thirdly, what is a *Christian commonwealth*.

Lastly, what is the *kingdom of darkness*.

[3] Concerning the first, there is a saying much usurped of late, that *wisdom* is acquired, not by reading of *books*, but of *men*. Consequently whereunto, those persons that for the most part can give no other proof of being wise take great delight to show what they think they have read in men, by uncharitable censures of one another behind their backs. But there is another saying not of late understood, by which they might learn truly to read one another, if they would take the pains; and that is, *nosce teipsum, read thy self*, which was not meant, as it is now used, to countenance either the barbarous state of men in power towards their inferiors, or to encourage men of low degree to a saucy behaviour towards their betters, but to teach us that for the similitude of the thoughts and passions of one man to the thoughts and passions of another, whosoever looketh into himself and considereth what he doth, when he does *think, opine, reason, hope, fear,* &c, and upon what grounds, he shall thereby read and know, what are the thoughts and passions of all other men upon the like occasions. I say the similitude of *passions*, which are the same in all men, *desire, fear, hope,* &c, not the similitude of the *objects* of the passions, which are the things *desired, feared, hoped,* &c; for these the constitution individual and particular education do so vary, and they are so easy to be kept from our knowledge, that the characters of man's heart, blotted and confounded as they are with dissembling, lying, counterfeiting, and erroneous doctrines, are legible only to him that searcheth hearts. And though by

Text edited by Edwin Curley. Copyright 1994 by Hackett Publishing Company. Reprinted with permission.

1. [The leviathan was a Biblical sea-monster.—S.M.C.]

men's actions we do discover their design sometimes, yet to do it without comparing them with our own, and distinguishing all circumstances by which the case may come to be altered, is to decipher without a key, and be for the most part deceived, by too much trust, or by too much diffidence, as he that reads is himself a good or evil man.

[4] But let one man read another by his actions never so perfectly, it serves him only with his acquaintance, which are but few. He that is to govern a whole nation must read in himself, not this or that particular man, but mankind, which though it be hard to do, harder than to learn any language or science, yet when I shall have set down my own reading orderly and perspicuously, the pains left another will be only to consider if he also find not the same in himself. For this kind of doctrine admitteth no other demonstration.

Part One
OF MAN
CHAPTER 1
Of Sense

[1] Concerning the thoughts of man, I will consider them first *singly*, and afterwards in *train*, or dependence upon one another. *Singly*, they are every one a *representation* or *appearance*, of some quality or other accident, of a body without us, which is commonly called an *object*. Which object worketh on the eyes, ears, and other parts of a man's body, and by diversity of working produceth diversity of appearances.

[2] The original of them all is that which we call SENSE. (For there is no conception in a man's mind which hath not at first, totally or by parts, been begotten upon the organs of sense.) The rest are derived from that original.

[3] To know the natural cause of sense is not very necessary to the business now in hand, and I have elsewhere written of the same at large. Nevertheless, to fill each part of my present method, I will briefly deliver the same in this place.

[4] The cause of sense is the external body, or object, which presseth the organ proper to each sense, either immediately, as in the taste and touch, or medi-

ately, as in seeing, hearing, and smelling; which pressure, by the mediation of nerves and other strings and membranes of the body, continued inwards to the brain and heart, causeth there a resistance, or counterpressure, or endeavour of the heart to deliver itself; which endeavour, because *outward*, seemeth to be some matter without. And this *seeming*, or *fancy*, is that which men call *sense*; and consisteth, as to the eye, in a *light* or *colour figured*; to the ear, in a *sound*; to the nostril, in an *odour*; to the tongue and palate, in a *savour*; and to the rest of the body, in *heat*, *cold*, *hardness*, *softness*, and such other qualities as we discern by *feeling*. All which qualities called *sensible* are in the object that causeth them but so many several motions of the matter, by which it presseth our organs diversely. Neither in us that are pressed are they anything else but divers motions (for motion produceth nothing but motion). But their appearance to us is fancy, the same waking that dreaming. And as pressing, rubbing, or striking the eye, makes us fancy a light, and pressing the ear, produceth a din, so do the bodies also we see, or hear, produce the same by their strong, though unobserved action. For if those colours and sounds were in the bodies, or objects, that cause them, they could not be severed from them, as by glasses, and in echoes by reflection, we see they are, where we know the thing we see is in one place, the appearance in another. And though at some certain distance the real and very object seem invested with the fancy it begets in us, yet still the object is one thing, the image or fancy is another. So that sense in all cases, is nothing else but original fancy, caused (as I have said) by the pressure, that is, by the motion, of external things upon our eyes, ears, and other organs thereunto ordained.

[5] But the philosophy-schools, through all the universities of Christendom, grounded upon certain texts of *Aristotle*, teach another doctrine, and say, for the cause of *vision*, that the thing seen sendeth forth on every side a *visible species* (in English, a *visible show*, *apparition*, or *aspect*, or a *being seen*), the receiving whereof into the eye is *seeing*. And for the cause of *hearing*, that the thing heard sendeth forth an *audible species*, that is, an *audible aspect*, or *audible being seen*, which entering at the ear maketh *hearing*. Nay for the cause of *understanding* also, they say the thing understood sendeth forth *intelligible species*, that is, an *intelligible being seen*, which coming into

the understanding makes us understand. I say not this as disapproving the use of universities; but because I am to speak hereafter of their office in a commonwealth, I must let you see on all occasions by the way, what things would be amended in them, amongst which the frequency of insignificant speech is one.

CHAPTER II

Of *Imagination*

[1] That when a thing lies still, unless somewhat else stir it, it will lie still for ever, is a truth that no man doubts of. But that when a thing is in motion, it will eternally be in motion, unless somewhat else stay it, though the reason be the same (namely, that nothing can change itself), is not so easily assented to. For men measure, not only other men, but all other things, by themselves; and because they find themselves subject after motion to pain and lassitude, think everything else grows weary of motion and seeks repose of its own accord, little considering whether it be not some other motion wherein that desire of rest they find in themselves consisteth. From hence it is that the schools say heavy bodies fall downwards out of an appetite to rest, and to conserve their nature in that place which is most proper for them, ascribing appetite and knowledge of what is good for their conservation (which is more than man has) to things inanimate, absurdly.

[2] When a body is once in motion, it moveth (unless something else hinder it) eternally; and whatsoever hindreth it, cannot in an instant, but in time and by degrees, quite extinguish it. And as we see in the water, though the wind cease, the waves give not over rolling for a long time after, so also it happeneth in that motion which is made in the internal parts of a man, then when he sees, dreams, &c. For after the object is removed, or the eye shut, we still retain an image of the thing seen, though more obscure than when we see it. And this is it, the Latins call *imagination*, from the image made in seeing, and apply the same, though improperly, to all the other senses. But the Greeks call it *fancy*, which signifies *appearance*, and is as proper to one sense as to another. IMAGINATION therefore is nothing but *decaying sense*, and is found in men and many other living creatures, as well sleeping as waking.

[3] The decay of sense in men waking is not the decay of the motion made in sense, but an obscuring of it, in such manner as the light of the sun obscureth the light of the stars; which stars do no less exercise their virtue, by which they are visible, in the day than in the night. But because amongst many strokes which our eyes, ears, and other organs receive from external bodies, the predominant only is sensible, therefore the light of the sun being predominant, we are not affected with the action of the stars. And any object being removed from our eyes, though the impression it made in us remain, yet other objects more present succeeding and working on us, the imagination of the past is obscured and made weak, as the voice of a man is in the noise of the day.

From whence it followeth that the longer the time is after the sight or sense of any object, the weaker is the imagination. For the continual change of man's body destroys in time the parts which in sense were moved, so that distance of time and of place hath one and the same effect in us. For as, at a great distance of place, that which we look at appears dim and without distinction of the smaller parts, and as voices grow weak and inarticulate, so also, after great distance of time, our imagination of the past is weak, and we lose (for example) of cities we have seen, many particular streets, and of actions, many particular circumstances. This *decaying sense*, when we would express the thing itself (I mean *fancy* itself), we call *imagination*, as I said before; but when we would express the *decay*, and signify that the sense is fading, old, and past, it is called *memory*. So that *imagination* and *memory* are but one thing, which for diverse considerations hath diverse names.

[4] Much memory, or memory of many things, is called *experience*. Again, imagination being only of those things which have been formerly perceived by sense, either all at once or by parts at several times, the former (which is the imagining the whole object, as it was presented to the sense) is *simple imagination*; as when one imagineth a man, or horse, which he hath seen before. The other is *compounded*; as when from the sight of a man at one time, and of a horse at another, we conceive in our mind a Centaur. So when a man compoundeth the image of his own person with the image of the actions of another man, as when a man imagines himself a *Hercules* or an *Alexander* (which happeneth often to them that are

much taken with reading of romances), it is a compound imagination, and properly but a fiction of the mind. There be also other imaginations that rise in men (though waking) from the great impression made in sense, as from gazing upon the sun, the impression leaves an image of the sun before our eyes a long time after; and from being long and vehemently attent upon geometrical figures, a man shall in the dark (though awake) have the images of lines and angles before his eyes, which kind of fancy hath no particular name, as being a thing that doth not commonly fall into men's discourse.

[5] The imaginations of them that sleep are those we call *dreams*. And these also (as all other imaginations) have been before, either totally or by parcels, in the sense. And because the brain and nerves, which are the necessary organs of sense, are so benumbed in sleep as not easily to be moved by the action of external objects, there can happen in sleep no imagination, and therefore no dream, but what proceeds from the agitation of the inward parts of man's body, which inward parts, for the connexion they have with the brain and other organs, when they be distempered, do keep the same in motion; whereby the imaginations there formerly made appear as if a man were waking, saving that the organs of sense being now benumbed, so as there is no new object which can master and obscure them with a more vigorous impression, a dream must needs be more clear, in this silence of sense, than are our waking thoughts. And hence it cometh to pass, that it is a hard matter, and by many thought impossible, to distinguish exactly between sense and dreaming. For my part, when I consider that in dreams I do not often, nor constantly, think of the same persons, places, objects, and actions that I do waking, nor remember so long a train of coherent thoughts dreaming as at other times, and because waking I often observe the absurdity of dreams, but never dream of the absurdities of my waking thoughts, I am well satisfied that being awake I know I dream not, though when I dream, I think myself awake.

[6] And seeing dreams are caused by the distemper of some of the inward parts of the body, diverse distempers must needs cause different dreams. And hence it is that lying cold breedeth dreams of fear and raiseth the thought and image of some fearful object (the motion from the brain to the inner parts, and from the inner parts to the brain, being reciprocal); and that as anger causeth heat in some parts of the body when we are awake, so when we sleep the overheating of the same parts causeth anger and raiseth up in the brain the imagination of an enemy. In the same manner as natural kindness, when we are awake, causeth desire, and desire makes heat in certain other parts of the body, so also too much heat in those parts, while we sleep, raiseth in the brain an imagination of some kindness shown. In sum, our dreams are the reverse of our waking imaginations, the motion when we are awake beginning at one end, and when we dream at another.

[7] The most difficult discerning of a man's dream from his waking thoughts is then, when by some accident we observe not that we have slept, which is easy to happen to a man full of fearful thoughts, and whose conscience is much troubled, and that sleepeth without the circumstances of going to bed, or putting off his clothes, as one that noddeth in a chair. For he that taketh pains, and industriously lays himself to sleep, in case any uncouth and exorbitant fancy come unto him, cannot easily think it other than a dream. We read of *Marcus Brutus* (one that had his life given him by *Julius Caesar*, and was also his favourite, and notwithstanding murdered him), how at *Philippi*, the night before he gave battle to *Augustus Caesar*, he saw a fearful apparition, which is commonly related by historians as a vision, but considering the circumstances, one may easily judge to have been but a short dream. For sitting in his tent, pensive and troubled with the horror of his rash act, it was not hard for him, slumbering in the cold, to dream of that which most affrighted him, which fear, as by degrees it made him wake, so also it must needs make the apparition by degrees to vanish; and having no assurance that he slept, he could have no cause to think it a dream, or anything but a vision. And this is no very rare accident; for even they that be perfectly awake, if they be timorous and superstitious, possessed with fearful tales and alone in the dark, are subject to the like fancies, and believe they see spirits and dead men's ghosts walking in churchyards; whereas it is either their fancy only, or else the knavery of such persons as make use of such superstitious fear to pass disguised in the night to places they would not be known to haunt.

[8] From this ignorance of how to distinguish

dreams and other strong fancies from vision and sense did arise the greatest part of the religion of the gentiles in times past, that worshipped satyrs, fawns, nymphs, and the like; and now-a-days the opinion that rude people have of fairies, ghosts, and goblins, and of the power of witches. For as for witches, I think not that their witchcraft is any real power, but yet that they are justly punished, for the false belief they have that they can do such mischief, joined with their purpose to do it if they can, their trade being nearer to a new religion than to a craft or science. And for fairies and walking ghosts, the opinion of them has I think been on purpose, either taught or not confuted, to keep in credit the use of exorcism, of crosses, of holy water, and other such inventions of ghostly men.

Nevertheless, there is no doubt but God can make unnatural apparitions. But that he does it so often as men need to fear such things more than they fear the stay or change of the course of nature, which he also can stay and change, is no point of Christian faith. But evil men, under pretext that God can do anything, are so bold as to say anything when it serves their turn, though they think it untrue; it is the part of a wise man to believe them no further than right reason makes that which they say appear credible. If this superstitious fear of spirits were taken away, and with it prognostics from dreams, false prophecies, and many other things depending thereon, by which crafty ambitious persons abuse the simple people, men would be much more fitted than they are for civil obedience.

[9] And this ought to be the work of the schools; but they rather nourish such doctrine. For (not knowing what imagination or the senses are) what they receive, they teach, some saying that imaginations rise of themselves and have no cause, others that they rise most commonly from the will, and that good thoughts are blown (inspired) into a man by God, and evil thoughts by the Devil, or that good thoughts are poured (infused) into a man by God, and evil ones by the Devil. Some say the senses receive the species of things and deliver them to the common sense, and the common sense delivers them over to the fancy, and the fancy to the memory, and the memory to the judgment, like handing of things from one to another, with many words making nothing understood.

[10] The imagination that is raised in man (or any other creature endued with the faculty of imagining) by words or other voluntary signs is that we generally call *understanding*, and is common to man and beast. For a dog by custom will understand the call or the rating of his master; and so will many other beasts. That understanding which is peculiar to man is the understanding not only his will, but his conceptions and thoughts, by the sequel and contexture of the names of things into affirmations, negations, and other forms of speech; and of this kind of understanding I shall speak hereafter [cf. v, 6].

CHAPTER III

Of the Consequence or *Train* of Imaginations

[1] By *Consequence*, or TRAIN of thoughts, I understand that succession of one thought to another which is called (to distinguish it from discourse in words) *mental discourse*.

[2] When a man thinketh on anything whatsoever, his next thought after, is not altogether so casual as it seems to be. Not every thought to every thought succeeds indifferently. But as we have no imagination whereof we have not formerly had sense, in whole or in parts, so we have no transition from one imagination to another whereof we never had the like before in our senses. The reason whereof is this. All fancies are motions within us, relics of those made in the sense; and those motions that immediately succeed one another in the sense continue also together after sense, insomuch as the former coming again to take place and be predominant, the latter followeth by coherence of the matter moved, in such manner as water upon a plain table is drawn which way any one part of it is guided by the finger. But because in sense, to one and the same thing perceived, sometimes one thing, sometimes another succeedeth, it comes to pass in time that in the imagining of anything there is no certainty what we shall imagine next; only this is certain, it shall be something that succeeded the same before, at one time or another.

[3] This train of thoughts, or mental discourse, is of two sorts. The first is *unguided, without design*, and inconstant, wherein there is no passionate thought to govern and direct those that follow to itself, as the end and scope of some desire or other passion; in which case the thoughts are said to wander, and seem

impertinent one to another, as in a dream. Such are commonly the thoughts of men that are not only without company, but also without care of anything, though even then their thoughts are as busy as at other times, but without harmony, as the sound which a lute out of tune would yield to any man, or in tune, to one that could not play. And yet in this wild ranging of the mind, a man may oft-times perceive the way of it, and the dependence of one thought upon another. For in a discourse of our present civil war, what could seem more impertinent than to ask (as one did) what was the value of a Roman penny? Yet the coherence to me was manifest enough. For the thought of the war introduced the thought of the delivering up the king to his enemies; the thought of that brought in the thought of the delivering up of Christ; and that again the thought of the 30 pence which was the price of that treason; and thence easily followed that malicious question; and all this in a moment of time, for thought is quick.

[4] The second is more constant, as being *regulated* by some desire, and design. For the impression made by such things as we desire or fear is strong and permanent, or (if it cease for a time) of quick return; so strong it is sometimes as to hinder and break our sleep. From desire ariseth the thought of some means we have seen produce the like of that which we aim at; and from the thought of that, the thought of means to that mean; and so continually, till we come to some beginning within our own power. And because the end, by the greatness of the impression, comes often to mind, in case our thoughts begin to wander, they are quickly again reduced into the way; which, observed by one of the seven wise men, made him give men this precept, which is now worn out, *Respice finem*, that is to say, in all your actions, look often upon what you would have, as the thing that directs all your thoughts in the way to attain it.

[5] The train of regulated thoughts is of two kinds: one, when of an effect imagined, we seek the causes, or means that produce it; and this is common to man and beast. The other is when, imagining anything whatsoever, we seek all the possible effects that can by it be produced; that is to say, we imagine what we can do with it, when we have it. Of which I have not at any time seen any sign, but in man only; for this is a curiosity hardly incident to the nature of any living creature that has no other passion but sensual,

such as are hunger, thirst, lust, and anger. In sum, the discourse of the mind, when it is governed by design, is nothing but *seeking*, or the faculty of invention, which the Latins called *sagacitas*, and *solertia*; a hunting out of the causes of some effect, present or past, or of the effects of some present or past cause. Sometimes a man seeks what he hath lost, and from that place and time wherein he misses it, his mind runs back, from place to place, and time to time, to find where and when he had it; that is to say, to find some certain and limited time and place in which to begin a method of seeking. Again, from thence his thoughts run over the same places and times, to find what action or other occasion might make him lose it. This we call *remembrance*, or calling to mind; the Latins call it *reminiscentia*, as it were a *re-conning* of our former actions.

[6] Sometimes a man knows a place determinate, within the compass whereof he is to seek; and then his thoughts run over all the parts thereof, in the same manner as one would sweep a room to find a jewel, or as a spaniel ranges the field till he find a scent, or as a man should run over the alphabet to start a rhyme.

[7] Sometimes a man desires to know the event of an action; and then he thinketh of some like action past, and the events thereof one after another, supposing like events will follow like actions. As he that foresees what will become of a criminal re-cons what he has seen follow on the like crime before, having this order of thoughts: the crime, the officer, the prison, the judge, and the gallows. Which kind of thoughts is called *foresight*, and *prudence*, or *providence*, and sometimes *wisdom*, though such conjecture, through the difficulty of observing all circumstances, be very fallacious. But this is certain: by how much one man has more experience of things past than another, by so much also he is more prudent, and his expectations the seldomer fail him. The *present* only has a being in nature; things *past* have a being in the memory only; but things *to come* have no being at all, the *future* being but a fiction of the mind, applying the sequels of actions past to the actions that are present; which with most certainty is done by him that has most experience, but not with certainty enough. And though it be called prudence when the event answereth our expectation, yet in its own nature it is but presumption. For the foresight

of things to come, which is providence, belongs only to him by whose will they are to come. From him only, and supernaturally, proceeds prophecy. The best prophet naturally is the best guesser; and the best guesser, he that is most versed and studied in the matters he guesses at, for he hath most *signs* to guess by.

[8] A *sign* is the event antecedent of the consequent, and contrarily, the consequent of the antecedent, when the like consequences have been observed before; and the oftener they have been observed, the less uncertain is the sign. And therefore he that has most experience in any kind of business has most signs whereby to guess at the future time, and consequently is the most prudent; and so much more prudent than he that is new in that kind of business, as not to be equalled by any advantage of natural and extemporary wit, though perhaps many young men think the contrary.

[9] Nevertheless it is not prudence that distinguisheth man from beast. There be beasts that at a year old observe more, and pursue that which is for their good more prudently, than a child can do at ten.

[10] As prudence is a *presumption* of the *future*, contracted from the *experience* of time *past*, so there is a presumption of things past taken from other things (not future but) past also. For he that hath seen by what courses and degrees a flourishing state hath first come into civil war and then to ruin, upon the sight of the ruins of any other state will guess the like war and the like courses have been there also. But this conjecture has the same uncertainty almost with the conjecture of the future, both being grounded only upon experience.

[11] There is no other act of man's mind that I can remember, naturally planted in him so as to need no other thing to the exercise of it but to be born a man, and live with the use of his five senses. Those other faculties of which I shall speak by and by, and which seem proper to man only, are acquired and increased by study and industry, and of most men learned by instruction and discipline, and proceed all from the invention of words and speech. For besides sense, and thoughts, and the train of thoughts, the mind of man has no other motion, though by the help of speech and method the same faculties may be improved to such a height as to distinguish men from all other living creatures.

[12] Whatsoever we imagine is *finite*. Therefore there is no idea or conception of anything we call *infinite*. No man can have in his mind an image of infinite magnitude, nor conceive infinite swiftness, infinite time, or infinite force, or infinite power. When we say anything is infinite, we signify only that we are not able to conceive the ends and bounds of the thing named, having no conception of the thing, but of our own inability. And therefore the name of *God* is used, not to make us conceive him (for he is *incomprehensible*, and his greatness and power are unconceivable), but that we may honour him. Also because whatsoever (as I said before) we conceive has been perceived first by sense, either all at once or by parts, a man can have no thought representing anything not subject to sense. No man therefore can conceive anything, but he must conceive it in some place, and endued with some determinate magnitude, and which may be divided into parts; nor that anything is all in this place, and all in another place at the same time; nor that two or more things can be in one and the same place at once; for none of these things ever have, or can be, incident to sense, but are absurd speeches, taken upon credit (without any signification at all) from deceived philosophers, and deceived or deceiving schoolmen.[2]

CHAPTER VI

Of the Interiour Beginnings of Voluntary Motions Commonly Called the *Passions*, and the Speeches by Which They Are Expressed

[1] There be in animals two sorts of *motions* peculiar to them: one called *vital*, begun in generation and continued without interruption through their whole life, such as are the *course* of the *blood*, the *pulse*, the *breathing*, the *concoction*, *nutrition*, *excretion*, &c, to which motions there needs no help of imagination; the other is *animal motion*, otherwise called *voluntary motion* as to go, to *speak*, to *move* any of our limbs, in such manner as is first fancied in our minds. That sense is motion in the organs and interior parts of man's body, caused by the action of

2. [The term "schoolmen" was applied to medieval theologians and philosophers, often with a connotation of pedantry.]

the things we see, hear, &c, and that fancy is but the relics of the same motion, remaining after sense, has been already said in the first and second chapters. And because *going*, *speaking*, and the like voluntary motions depend always upon a precedent thought of *whither*, *which way*, and *what*, it is evident that the imagination is the first internal beginning of all voluntary motion. And although unstudied men do not conceive any motion at all to be there, where the thing moved is invisible, or the space it is moved in is (for the shortness of it) insensible, yet that doth not hinder, but that such motions are. For let a space be never so little, that which is moved over a greater space whereof that little one is part must first be moved over that. These small beginnings of motion within the body of man, before they appear in walking, speaking, striking, and other visible actions, are commonly called ENDEAVOUR.

[2] This endeavour, when it is toward something which causes it, is called APPETITE or DESIRE, the latter being the general name, and the other oftentimes restrained to signify the desire of food, namely *hunger* and *thirst*. And when the endeavour is fromward something, it is generally called AVERSION. These words, *appetite* and *aversion*, we have from the *Latins*, and they both of them signify the motions, one of approaching, the other of retiring. So also do the Greek words for the same, which are *horme* and *aphorme*. For nature itself does often press upon men those truths which afterwards, when they look for somewhat beyond nature, they stumble at. For the Schools find in mere appetite to go, or move, no actual motion at all; but because some motion they must acknowledge, they call it metaphorical motion, which is but an absurd speech; for though words may be called metaphorical, bodies and motions cannot.

[3] That which men desire they are also said to LOVE, and to HATE those things for which they have aversions. So that desire and love are the same thing, save that by desire we always signify the absence of the object; by love, most commonly the presence of the same. So also by aversion we signify the absence, and by hate, the presence of the object.

[4] Of appetites and aversions some are born with men, as appetite of food, appetite of excretion and exoneration (which may also and more properly be called aversions from somewhat they feel in their bodies) and some other appetites, not many. The rest, which are appetites of particular things, proceed from experience and trial of their effects upon themselves or other men. For of things we know not at all, or believe not to be, we can have no further desire than to taste and try. But aversion we have for things, not only which we know have hurt us, but also that we do not know whether they will hurt us or not.

[5] Those things which we neither desire nor hate we are said to *contemn*, CONTEMPT being nothing else but an immobility or contumacy of the heart in resisting the action of certain things, and proceeding from that the heart is already moved otherwise, by other more potent objects, or from want of experience of them.

[6] And because the constitution of a man's body is in continual mutation, it is impossible that all the same things should always cause in him the same appetites and aversions; much less can all men consent in the desire of almost any one and the same object.

[7] But whatsoever is the object of any man's appetite or desire that is it which he for his part calleth *good*; and the object of his hate and aversion, *evil*; and of his contempt, *vile* and *inconsiderable*. For these words of good, evil, and contemptible are ever used with relation to the person that useth them, there being nothing simply and absolutely so, nor any common rule of good and evil to be taken from the nature of the objects themselves, but from the person of the man (where there is no commonwealth), or (in a commonwealth) from the person that representeth it, or from an arbitrator or judge whom men disagreeing shall by consent set up, and make his sentence the rule thereof.

[8] The Latin tongue has two words whose significations approach to those of good and evil, but are not precisely the same; and those are *pulchrum* and *turpe*. Whereof the former signifies that which by some apparent signs promiseth good; and the latter, that which promiseth evil. But in our tongue we have not so general names to express them by. But for *pulchrum* we say, in some things, *fair*; in others, *beautiful*, or *handsome*, or *gallant*, or *honourable*, or *comely*, or *amiable*, and for *turpe*, foul, *deformed*, *ugly*, *base*, *nauseous*, and the like, as the subject shall require; all which words, in their proper places, signify nothing else but the *mien*, or countenance, that promiseth good and evil. So that of good there be three

kinds: good in the promise, that is *pulchrum*; good in effect, as the end desired, which is called *jucundum, delightful*; and good as the means, which is called *utile, profitable*; and as many of evil; for *evil* in promise is that they call *turpe*; evil in effect and end is *molestum, unpleasant, troublesome*; and evil in the means *inutile, unprofitable, hurtful*.

[9] As in sense that which is really within us is (as I have said before) only motion caused by the actin of external objects (but in appearance, to the sight, light and colour, to the ear, sound, to the nostril, odour, &c.), so when the action of the same object is continued from the eyes, ears, and other organs to the heart, the real effect there is nothing but motion or endeavour, which consisteth in appetite or aversion, to or from the object moving. But the appearance, or sense of that motion, is that we either call DELIGHT, or TROUBLE OF MIND.

[10] This motion which is called appetite, and for the appearance of it *delight* and *pleasure*, seemeth to be a corroboration of vital motion, and a help thereunto; and therefore such things as caused delight were not improperly called *jucunda* (*a juvando*, from helping or fortifying); and the contrary, *molesta, offensive*, from hindering and troubling the motion vital.

[11] *Pleasure*, therefore, or *delight*, is the appearance, or sense, of good; and *molestation* or *displeasure*, the appearance, or sense, of evil. And consequently all appetite, desire, and love is accompanied with some delight more or less; and all hatred and aversion, with more or less displeasure and offence.

[12] Of pleasures or delights, some arise from the sense of an object present, and those may be called *pleasures of sense* (the word *sensual*, as it is used by those only that condemn them, having no place till there be laws). Of this kind are all onerations and exonerations of the body, as also all that is pleasant in the *sight, hearing, smell, taste, or touch*. Others arise from the expectation that proceeds from foresight of the end or consequence of things, whether those things in the sense please or displease. And these are *pleasures of the mind* of him that draweth those consequences, and are generally called JOY. In the like manner displeasures are some in the sense, and called PAIN; others in the expectation of consequences, and are called GRIEF.

[13] These simple passions, called *appetite, desire, love, aversion, hate, joy*, and *grief*, have their names

for diverse considerations diversified. As first, when they one succeed another, they are diversely called from the opinion men have of the likelihood of attaining what they desire. Secondly, from the object loved or hated. Thirdly, from the consideration of many of them together. Fourthly, from the alteration or succession itself.

[14] For *appetite* with an opinion of attaining is called HOPE.

[15] The same without such opinion, DESPAIR.

[16] *Aversion* with opinion of *hurt* from the object, FEAR.

[17] The same with hope of avoiding that hurt by resistance, COURAGE.

[18] Sudden *courage*, ANGER.

[19] Constant *hope*, CONFIDENCE of ourselves.

[20] Constant *despair*, DIFFIDENCE of ourselves.

[21] *Anger* for great hurt done to another, when we conceive the same to be done by injury, INDIGNATION.

[22] *Desire* of good to another, BENEVOLENCE, GOOD WILL, CHARITY. If to man generally, GOOD NATURE.

[23] *Desire* of riches, COVETOUSNESS, a name used always in signification of blame, because men contending for them are displeased with one another's attaining them, though the desire in itself be to be blamed or allowed, according to the means by which those riches are sought.

[24] *Desire* of office or precedence, AMBITION, a name used also in the worse sense, for the reason before mentioned.

[25] *Desire* of things that conduce but a little to our ends, and fear of things that are but of little hindrance, PUSILLANIMITY.

[26] *Contempt* of little helps and hindrances, MAGNANIMITY.

[27] *Magnanimity* in danger of death or wounds, VALOUR, FORTITUDE.

[28] *Magnanimity* in the use of riches, LIBERALITY.

[29] *Pusillanimity*, in the same, WRETCHEDNESS, MISERABLENESS, or PARSIMONY; as it is liked or disliked.

[30] *Love* of persons for society, KINDNESS.

[31] *Love* of persons for pleasing the sense only, NATURAL LUST.

[32] *Love* of the same, acquired from rumination, that is, imagination of pleasure past, LUXURY.

[33] *Love* of one singularly, with desire to be singu-

larly beloved, THE PASSION OF LOVE. The same, with fear that the love is not mutual, JEALOUSY.

[34] *Desire*, by doing hurt to another, to make him condemn some fact of his own, REVENGEFULNESS.

[35] *Desire* to know why, and how, CURIOSITY, such as is in no living creature but *man*, so that man is distinguished, not only by his reason, but also by this singular passion from other *animals*, in whom the appetite of food and other pleasures of sense by predominance take away the care of knowing causes, which is a lust of the mind that by a perseverance of delight in the continual and indefatigable generation of knowledge exceedeth the short vehemence of any carnal pleasure.

[36] *Fear* of power invisible, feigned by the mind, or imagined from tales publicly allowed, RELIGION; not allowed, SUPERSTITION. And when the power imagined is truly such as we imagine, TRUE RE-LIGION.

[37] *Fear* without the apprehension of why or what, PANIC TERROR, called so from the fables, that make *Pan* the author of them; whereas in truth there is always in him that so feareth first, some apprehension of the cause, though the rest run away by example, every one supposing his fellow to know why. And therefore this passion happens to none but in a throng, or multitude of people.

[38] *Joy* from apprehension of novelty, ADMIRA-TION; proper to man, because it excites the appetite of knowing the cause.

[39] *Joy* arising from imagination of a man's own power and ability is that exultation of the mind which is called GLORYING; which, if grounded upon the experience of his own former actions, is the same with *confidence*; but if grounded on the flattery of others, or only supposed by himself, for delight in the consequences of it, is called VAINGLORY; which name is properly given, because a well grounded *confidence* begetteth attempt, whereas the supposing of power does not, and is therefore rightly called *vain*.

[40] *Grief* from opinion of want of power is called DEJECTION of mind.

[41] The *vain-glory* which consisteth in the feigning or supposing of abilities in ourselves (which we know are not) is most incident to young men, and nourished by the histories or fictions of gallant persons; and is corrected oftentimes by age and employment.

[42] *Sudden glory* is the passion which maketh those *grimaces* called LAUGHTER, and is caused either by some sudden act of their own that pleaseth them, or by the apprehension of some deformed thing in another, by comparison whereof they suddenly applaud themselves. And it is incident most to them that are conscious of the fewest abilities in themselves, who are forced to keep themselves in their own favour by observing the imperfections of other men. And therefore much laughter at the defects of others is a sign of pusillanimity. For of great minds one of the proper works is to help and free others from scorn, and compare themselves only with the most able.

[43] On the contrary, *sudden dejection* is the passion that causeth WEEPING, and is caused by such accidents as suddenly take away some vehement hope, or some prop of their power; and they are most subject to it that rely principally on helps external, such as are women and children. Therefore some weep for the loss of friends; others for their unkindness; others for the sudden stop made to their thoughts of revenge, by reconciliation. But in all cases, both laughter and weeping are sudden motions, custom taking them both away. For no man laughs at old jests, or weeps for an old calamity.

[44] *Grief* for the discovery of some defect of ability is SHAME, or the passion that discovereth itself in BLUSHING, and consisteth in the apprehension of some thing dishonourable; and in young men is a sign of the love of good reputation and commendable; in old men it is a sign of the same, but because it comes too late, not commendable.

[45] The *contempt* of good reputation is called IMPUDENCE.

[46] *Grief* for the calamity of another is PITY, and ariseth from the imagination that the like calamity may befall himself; and therefore is called also COM-PASSION, and in the phrase of this present time a FELLOW-FEELING; and therefore for calamity arriving from great wickedness, the best men have the least pity; and for the same calamity, those have least pity that think themselves least obnoxious to the same.

[47] *Contempt*, or little sense, of the calamity of others is that which men called CRUELTY, proceeding from security of their own fortune. For, that any man should take pleasure in other men's great harms without other end of his own I do not conceive it possible.

[48] *Grief* for the success of a competitor in wealth,

honour, or other good, if it be joined with endeavour to enforce our own abilities to equal or exceed him, is called EMULATION; but joined with endeavour to supplant or hinder a competitor, ENVY.

[49] When in the mind of man appetites and aversions, hopes and fears, concerning one and the same thing arise alternately, and diverse good and evil consequences of the doing or omitting the thing propounded come successively into our thoughts, so that sometimes we have an appetite to it, sometimes an aversion from it, sometimes hope to be able to do it, sometimes despair or fear to attempt it, the whole sum of desires, aversions, hopes and fears, continued till the thing be either done or thought impossible, is what we call DELIBERATION.

[50] Therefore of things past, there is no *deliberation*, because manifestly impossible to be changed; nor of things known to be impossible, or thought so, because men know or think such deliberation vain. But of things impossible which we think possible, we may deliberate, not knowing it is in vain. And it is called *deliberation*, because it is a putting an end to the *liberty* we had of doing or omitting, according to our own appetite or aversion.

[51] This alternate succession of appetites, aversions, hopes and fears is no less in other living creatures than in man; and therefore beasts also deliberate.

[52] Every *deliberation* is then said to *end*, when that whereof they deliberate is either done or thought impossible, because till then we retain the liberty of doing or omitting, according to our appetite or aversion.

[53] In deliberation, the last appetite or aversion immediately adhering to the action, or to the omission thereof, is that we call the WILL, the act (not the faculty) of *willing*. And beasts that have *deliberation* must necessarily also have *will*. The definition of the *will* given commonly by the Schools, that it is a *rational appetite*, is not good. For if it were, then could there be no voluntary act against reason. For a *voluntary act* is that which proceedeth from the *will*, and no other. But if instead of a rational appetite, we shall say an appetite resulting from a precedent deliberation, then the definition is the same that I have given here. *Will* therefore *is the last appetite in deliberating.* And though we say in common discourse, a man had a will once to do a thing, that nevertheless he forbore to do, yet that is properly but an inclination, which

makes no action voluntary; because the action depends not of it, but of the last inclination or appetite. For if the intervenient appetites make any action voluntary, then by the same reason all intervenient aversions should make the same action involuntary; and so one and the same action should be both voluntary and involuntary.

[54] By this it is manifest that not only actions that have their beginning from covetousness, ambition, lust, or other appetites to the thing propounded, but also those that have their beginning from aversion or fear of those consequences that follow the omission are *voluntary actions*.

[55] The forms of speech by which the passions are expressed are partly the same and partly different from those by which we express our thoughts. And first, generally all passions may be expressed *indicatively*, as *I love, I fear, I joy, I deliberate, I will, I command*; but some of them have particular expressions by themselves, which nevertheless are not affirmations (unless it be when they serve to make other inferences besides that of the passion they proceed from). Deliberation is expressed *subjunctively*, which is a speech proper to signify suppositions, with their consequences, as *if this be done, then this will follow*, and differs not from the language of reasoning, save that reasoning is in general words, but deliberation for the most part is of particulars. The language of desire and aversion is *imperative*, as *do this, forbear that*, which, when the party is obliged to do or forbear, is *command*; otherwise *prayer*, or else *counsel*. The language of vain-glory, of indignation, pity and revengefulness, *optative*; but of the desire to know there is a peculiar expression, called *interrogative*, as *what is it, when shall it, how is it done*, and *why so?* other language of the passions I find none; for cursing, swearing, reviling, and the like, do not signify as speech, but as the actions of a tongue accustomed.

[56] These forms of speech, I say, are expressions, or voluntary significations, of our passions; but certain signs they be not, because they may be used arbitrarily, whether they that use them have such passions or not. The best signs of passions present are in the countenance, motions of the body, actions, and ends or aims which we otherwise know the man to have.

[57] And because in deliberation the appetites and aversions are raised by foresight of the good and evil consequences and sequels of the action whereof we

deliberate, the good or evil effect thereof dependeth on the foresight of a long chain of consequences, of which very seldom any man is able to see to the end. But for so far as a man seeth, if the good in those consequences be greater than the evil, the whole chain is that which writers call *apparent* or *seeming good*. And contrarily, when the evil exceedeth the good, the whole is *apparent* or *seeming evil*; so that he who hath by experience or reason the greatest and surest prospect of consequences deliberates best himself, and is able, when he will, to give the best counsel unto others.

[58] *Continual success* in obtaining those things which a man from time to time desireth, that is to say, continual prospering, is that men call FELICITY; I mean the felicity of this life. For there is no such thing as perpetual tranquillity of mind, while we live here; because life itself is but motion, and can never be without desire, nor without fear, no more than without sense. What kind of felicity God hath ordained to them that devoutly honour Him, a man shall no sooner know than enjoy, being joys that now are as incomprehensible as the word of school-men *beatifical vision* is unintelligible.

[59] The form of speech whereby men signify their opinion of the goodness of anything is PRAISE. That whereby they signify the power and greatness of anything is MAGNIFYING. And that whereby they signify the opinion they have of a man's felicity is by the Greeks called *makarismos*, for which we have no name in our tongue. And thus much is sufficient for the present purpose, to have been said of the PASSIONS.

CHAPTER XI

Of the Difference of *Manners*

[1] By *manners* I mean not here decency of behaviour, as how one man should salute another, or how a man should wash his mouth or pick his teeth before company, and such other points of the *small morals*, but those qualities of mankind that concern their living together in peace and unity. To which end we are to consider that the felicity of this life consisteth not in the repose of a mind satisfied. For there is no such *Finis ultimus* (utmost aim) nor *Summum Bonum* (greatest good) as is spoken of in the books of the old moral philosophers. Nor can a man any more live, whose desires are at an end, than he whose senses and imaginations are at a stand. Felicity is a continual progress of the desire, from one object to another, the attaining of the former being still but the way to the latter. The cause whereof is that the object of man's desire is not to enjoy once only, and for one instant of time, but to assure forever the way of his future desire. And therefore the voluntary actions and inclinations of all men tend, not only to the procuring, but also to the assuring of a contented life, and differ only in the way; which ariseth partly from the diversity of passions in divers men, and partly from the difference of the knowledge or opinion each one has of the causes which produce the effect desired.

[2] So that in the first place, I put for a general inclination of all mankind, a perpetual and restless desire of power after power, that ceaseth only in death. And the cause of this is not always that a man hopes for a more intensive delight than he has already attained to, or that he cannot be content with a moderate power, but because he cannot assure the power and means to live well which he hath present, without the acquisition of more. And from hence it is that kings, whose power is greatest, turn their endeavours to the assuring it at home by laws or abroad by wars; and when that is done, there succeedeth a new desire, in some of fame from new conquest, in others of ease and sensual pleasure, in others of admiration or being flattered for excellence in some art or other ability of the mind.

[3] Competition of riches, honour, command, or other power, inclineth to contention, enmity, and war; because the way of one competitor to the attaining of his desire is to kill, subdue, supplant, or repel the other. Particularly, competition of praise inclineth to a reverence of antiquity. For men contend with the living, not with the dead, to these ascribing more than due, that they may obscure the glory of the other.

[4] Desire of ease and sensual delight disposeth men to obey a common power, because by such desires a man doth abandon the protection might be hoped for from his own industry and labour. Fear of death and wounds disposeth to the same, and for the same reason. On the contrary, needy men, and hardy, not contented with their present condition, as also all men that are ambitious of military command, are inclined to continue the causes of war, and to stir up

trouble and sedition; for there is no honour military but by war, nor any such hope to mend an ill game as by causing a new shuffle.

[5] Desire of knowledge, and arts of peace, inclineth men to obey a common power. For such desire containeth a desire of leisure, and consequently protection from some other power than their own.

[6] Desire of praise disposeth to laudable actions, such as please them whose judgment they value; for of those men whom we contemn, we contemn also the praises. Desire of fame after death does the same. And though after death there be no sense of the praise given us on earth, as being joys that are either swallowed up in the unspeakable joys of Heaven, or extinguished in the extreme torments of hell, yet is not such fame vain, because men have a present delight therein, from the foresight of it and of the benefit that may redound thereby to their posterity, which though they now see not, yet they imagine; and anything that is pleasure in the sense, the same also is pleasure in the imagination.

CHAPTER XIII

Of the *Natural Condition* of *Mankind*, As Concerning Their Felicity, and Misery

[1] Nature hath made men so equal in the faculties of body and mind as that, though there be found one man sometimes manifestly stronger in body or of quicker mind than another, yet when all is reckoned together the difference between man and man is not so considerable as that one man can thereupon claim to himself any benefit to which another may not pretend as well as he. For as to the strength of body, the weakest has strength enough to kill the strongest, either by secret machination, or by confederacy with others that are in the same danger with himself.

[2] And as to the faculties of the mind—setting aside the arts grounded upon words, and especially that skill of proceeding upon general and infallible rules called science (which very few have, and but in few things), as being not a native faculty (born with us), nor attained (as prudence) while we look after somewhat else—I find yet a greater equality amongst men than that of strength. For prudence is but experience, which equal time equally bestows on all men in those things they equally apply themselves

unto. That which may perhaps make such equality incredible is but a vain conceit of one's own wisdom, which almost all men think they have in a greater degree than the vulgar, that is, than all men but themselves and a few others whom, by fame or for concurring with themselves, they approve. For such is the nature of men that howsoever they may acknowledge many others to be more witty, or more eloquent, or more learned, yet they will hardly believe there be many so wise as themselves. For they see their own wit at hand, and other men's at a distance. But this proveth rather that men are in that point equal, than unequal. For there is not ordinarily a greater sign of the equal distribution of anything than that every man is contented with his share.

[3] From this equality of ability ariseth equality of hope in the attaining of our ends. And therefore, if any two men desire the same thing, which nevertheless they cannot both enjoy, they become enemies; and in the way to their end, which is principally their own conservation, and sometimes their delectation only, endeavour to destroy or subdue one another. And from hence it comes to pass that, where an invader hath no more to fear than another man's single power, if one plant, sow, build, or possess a convenient seat, others may probably be expected to come prepared with forces united, to dispossess and deprive him, not only of the fruit of his labour, but also of his life or liberty. And the invader again is in the like danger of another.

[4] And from this diffidence of one another, there is no way for any man to secure himself so reasonable as anticipation, that is, by force or wiles to master the persons of all men he can, so long till he see no other power great enough to endanger him. And this is no more than his own conservation requireth, and is generally allowed. Also, because there be some that taking pleasure in contemplating their own power in the acts of conquest, which they pursue farther than their security requires, if others (that otherwise would be glad to be at ease within modest bounds) should not by invasion increase their power, they would not be able, long time, by standing only on their defence, to subsist. And by consequence, such augmentation of dominion over men being necessary to a man's conservation, it ought to be allowed him.

[5] Again, men have no pleasure, but on the contrary a great deal of grief, in keeping company where

there is no power able to over-awe them all. For every man looketh that his companion should value him at the same rate he sets upon himself, and upon all signs of contempt, or undervaluing, naturally endeavours, as far as he dares (which amongst them that have no common power to keep them in quiet, is far enough to make them destroy each other), to extort a greater value from his contemners, by damage, and from others, by the example.

[6] So that in the nature of man we find three principal causes of quarrel: first, competition; secondly, diffidence; thirdly, glory.

[7] The first maketh men invade for gain; the second, for safety; and the third, for reputation. The first use violence to make themselves masters of other men's persons, wives, children, and cattle; the second, to defend them; the third, for trifles, as a word, a smile, a different opinion, and any other sign of undervalue, either direct in their persons, or by reflection in their kindred, their friends, their nation, their profession, or their name.

[8] Hereby it is manifest that during the time men live without a common power to keep them all in awe, they are in that condition which is called war, and such a war as is of every man against every man. For WAR consisteth not in battle only, or the act of fighting, but in a tract of time wherein the will to contend by battle is sufficiently known. And therefore, the notion of *time* is to be considered in the nature of war, as it is in the nature of weather. For as the nature of foul weather lieth not in a shower or two of rain, but in an inclination thereto of many days together, so the nature of war consisteth not in actual fighting, but in the known disposition thereto during all the time there is no assurance to the contrary. All other time is PEACE.

[9] Whatsoever therefore is consequent to a time of war, where every man is enemy to every man, the same is consequent to the time wherein men live without other security than what their own strength and their own invention shall furnish them withal. In such condition there is no place for industry, because the fruit thereof is uncertain, and consequently, no culture of the earth, no navigation, nor use of the commodities that may be imported by sea, no commodious building, no instruments of moving and removing such things as require much force, no knowledge of the face of the earth, no account of

time, no arts, no letters, no society, and which is worst of all, continual fear and danger of violent death, and the life of man, solitary, poor, nasty, brutish, and short.

[10] It may seen strange, to some man that has not well weighed these things, that nature should thus dissociate, and render men apt to invade and destroy one another. And he may, therefore, not trusting to this inference made from the passions, desire perhaps to have the same confirmed by experience. Let him therefore consider with himself—when taking a journey, he arms himself, and seeks to go well accompanied; when going to sleep, he locks his doors; when even in his house, he locks his chests; and this when he knows there be laws, and public officers, armed, to revenge all injuries shall be done him— what opinion he has of his fellow subjects, when he rides armed; of his fellow citizens, when he locks his doors; and of his children and servants, when he locks his chests. Does he not there as much accuse mankind by his actions, as I do by my words? But neither of us accuse man's nature in it. The desires and other passions of man are in themselves no sin. No more are the actions that proceed from those passions, till they know a law that forbids them—which till laws be made they cannot know. Nor can any law be made, till they have agreed upon the person that shall make it.

[11] It may peradventure be thought, there was never such a time nor condition of war as this; and I believe it was never generally so, over all the world. But there are many places where they live so now. For the savage people in many places of *America* (except the government of small families, the concord whereof dependeth on natural lust) have no government at all, and live at this day in that brutish manner as I said before. Howsoever, it may be perceived what manner of life there would be where there were no common power to fear, by the manner of life which men that have formerly lived under a peaceful government use to degenerate into, in a civil war.

[12] But though there had never been any time wherein particular men were in a condition of war one against another, yet in all times kings and persons of sovereign authority, because of their independency, are in continual jealousies and in the state and posture of gladiators, having their weapons pointing and their eyes fixed on one another, that is, their forts, garrisons, and guns upon the frontiers of their kingdoms, and

continual spies upon their neighbours, which is a posture of war. But because they uphold thereby the industry of their subjects, there does not follow from it that misery which accompanies the liberty of particular men.

[13] To this war of every man against every man, this also is consequent: that nothing can be unjust. The notions of right and wrong, justice and injustice, have there no place. Where there is no common power, there is no law; where no law, no injustice. Force and fraud are in war the two cardinal virtues. Justice and injustice are none of the faculties neither of the body, nor mind. If they were, they might be in a man that were alone in the world, as well as his senses and passions. They are qualities that relate to men in society, not in solitude. It is consequent also to the same condition that there be no propriety, no dominion, no *mine* and *thine* distinct, but only that to be every man's that he can get, and for so long as he can keep it. And thus much for the ill condition which man by mere nature is actually placed in, though with a possibility to come out of it, consisting partly in the passions, partly in his reason.

[14] The passions that incline men to peace are fear of death, desire of such things as are necessary to commodious living, and a hope by their industry to obtain them. And reason suggesteth convenient articles of peace, upon which men may be drawn to agreement. These articles are they which otherwise are called the Laws of Nature, whereof I shall speak more particularly in the two following chapters.

CHAPTER XIV

Of the First and Second *Natural Laws* and of *Contracts*

[1] The RIGHT OF NATURE, which writers commonly call *jus naturale*, is the liberty each man hath to use his own power, as he will himself, for the preservation of his own nature, that is to say, of his own life, and consequently of doing anything which, in his own judgment and reason, he shall conceive to be the aptest means thereunto.

[2] By LIBERTY is understood, according to the proper signification of the word, the absence of external impediments, which impediments may oft take away part of a man's power to do what he would, but

cannot hinder him from using the power left him, according as his judgment and reason shall dictate to him.

[3] A LAW OF NATURE (*lex naturalis*) is a precept or general rule, found out by reason, by which a man is forbidden to do that which is destructive of his life or taketh away the means of preserving the same, and to omit that by which he thinketh it may be best preserved. For though they that speak of this subject use to confound *jus* and *lex* (*right* and *law*), yet they ought to be distinguished, because RIGHT consisteth in liberty to do or to forbear, whereas LAW determineth and bindeth to one of them; so that law and right differ as much as obligation and liberty, which in one and the same matter are inconsistent.

[4] And because the condition of man (as hath been declared in the precedent chapter) is a condition of war of everyone against everyone (in which case everyone is governed by his own reason and there is nothing he can make use of that may not be a help unto him in preserving his life against his enemies), it followeth that in such a condition every man has a right to everything, even to one another's body. And therefore, as long as this natural right of every man to everything endureth, there can be no security to any man (how strong or wise soever he be) of living out the time which nature ordinarily alloweth men to live. And consequently it is a precept, or general rule of reason *that every man ought to endeavour peace, as far as he has hope of obtaining it, and when he cannot obtain it, that he may seek and use all helps and advantages of war*. The first branch of which rule containeth the first and fundamental law of nature, which is *to seek peace, and follow it*. The second, the sum of the right of nature, which is *by all means we can, to defend ourselves*.

[5] From this fundamental law of nature, by which men are commanded to endeavour peace, is derived this second law: *that a man be willing, when others are so too, as far-forth as for peace and defence of himself he shall think it necessary, to lay down this right to all things, and be contented with so much liberty against other men, as he would allow other men against himself*. For as long as every man holdeth this right of doing anything he liketh, so long are all men in the condition of war. But if other men will not lay down their right as well as he, then there is no reason for anyone to divest himself of his; for that were to

expose himself to prey (which no man is bound to), rather than to dispose himself to peace. This is that law of the Gospel: "whatsoever you require that others should do to you, that do ye to them." And that law of all men: *quod tibi fieri non vis, alteri ne feceris.*

[6] To *lay down* a man's *right* to anything is to *divest* himself of the *liberty* of hindering another of the benefit of his own right to the same. For he that renounceth or passeth away his right giveth not to any other man a right which he had not before (because there is nothing to which every man had not right by nature), but only standeth out of his way, that he may enjoy his own original right without hindrance from him, not without hindrance from another. So that the effect which redoundeth to one man by another man's defect of right is but so much diminution of impediments to the use of his own right original.

[7] Right is laid aside either by simply renouncing it or by transferring it to another. By *simply* RENOUNCING, when he cares not to whom the benefit thereof redoundeth. By TRANSFERRING, when he intendeth the benefit thereof to some certain person or persons. And when a man hath in either manner abandoned or granted away his right, then is he said to be OBLIGED or BOUND not to hinder those to whom such right is granted or abandoned from the benefit of it; and [it is said] that he *ought*, and it is his DUTY, not to make void that voluntary act of his own, and that such hindrance is INJUSTICE, and INJURY, as being *sine jure* [without right], the right being before renounced or transferred. So that *injury* or *injustice*, in the controversies of the world, is somewhat like to that which in the disputations of scholars is called absurdity. For as it is there called an *absurdity* to contradict what one maintained in the beginning, so in the world it is called injustice and injury voluntarily to undo that which from the beginning he had voluntarily done.

The way by which a man either simply renounceth or transferreth his right is a declaration, or signification by some voluntary and sufficient sign or signs, that he doth so renounce or transfer, or hath so renounced or transferred the same, to him that accepteth it. And these signs are either words only, or actions only, or (as it happeneth most often) both words and actions. And the same are the BONDS by which men are bound and obliged, bonds that have

their strength, not from their own nature (for nothing is more easily broken than a man's word) but from fear of some evil consequence upon the rupture.

[8] Whensoever a man transferreth his right or renounceth it, it is either in consideration of some right reciprocally transferred to himself or for some other good he hopeth for thereby. For it is a voluntary act, and of the voluntary acts of every man the object is some *good to himself.* And therefore there be some rights which no man can be understood by any words or other signs to have abandoned or transferred. As, first, a man cannot lay down the right of resisting them that assault him by force, to take away his life, because he cannot be understood to aim thereby at any good to himself. [Second], the same may be said of wounds, and chains, and imprisonment, both because there is no benefit consequent to such patience (as there is to the patience of suffering another to be wounded or imprisoned), as also because a man cannot tell, when he seeth men proceed against him by violence, whether they intend his death or not. [Third], and lastly, the motive and end for which this renouncing and transferring of right is introduced, is nothing else but the security of a man's person, in his life and in the means of so preserving life as not to be weary of it. And therefore if a man by words or other signs seem to despoil himself of the end for which those signs were intended, he is not to be understood as if he meant it, or that it was his will, but that he was ignorant of how such words and actions were to be interpreted.

[9] The mutual transferring of right is that which men call CONTRACT.

[10] There is difference between transferring of right to the thing and transferring (or tradition, that is, delivery) of the thing itself. For the thing may be delivered together with the translation of the right (as in buying and selling with ready money, or exchange of goods or lands); and it may be delivered some time after.

[11] Again, one of the contractors may deliver the thing contacted for on his part, and leave the other to perform his part at some determinate time after (and in the meantime be trusted); and then the contract on his part is called PACT, or COVENANT; or both parts may contract now, to perform hereafter, in which cases he that is to perform in time to come, being trusted, his performance is called *keeping of*

promise, or *faith*, and the failing of performance (if it be voluntary) *violation of faith*.

[12] When the transferring of right is not mutual, but one of the parties transferreth in hope to gain thereby friendship or service from another (or from his friends), or in hope to gain the reputation of charity or magnanimity, or to deliver his mind from the pain of compassion, or in hope of reward in heaven, this is not contract, but GIFT, FREE-GIFT, GRACE, which words signify one and the same thing.

[13] Signs of contract are either *express* or *by inference*. Express are words spoken with understanding of what they signify; and such words are either of the time *present* or *past* (as, *I give, I grant, I have given, I have granted, I will that this be yours*), or of the future (as, *I will give, I will grant*), which words of the future are called PROMISE.

[14] Signs by inference are: sometimes the consequence of words, sometimes the consequence of silence; sometimes the consequence of actions, sometimes the consequence of forbearing an action; and generally a sign by inference of any contract is whatsoever sufficiently argues the will of the contractor.

[15] Words alone, if they be of the time to come, and contain a bare promise, are an insufficient sign of a free-gift, and therefore not obligatory. For if they be of the time to come (as, *tomorrow I will give*), they are a sign I have not given yet, and consequently that my right is not transferred, but remaineth till I transfer it by some other act. But if the words be of the time present or past (as, *I have given, or do give to be delivered tomorrow*), then is my tomorrow's right given away today; and that by the virtue of the words, though there were no other argument of my will. And there is a great difference in the signification of these words: *volo hoc tuum esse cras* and *cras dabo* (that is, between *I will that this be thine tomorrow* and *I will give it thee tomorrow*); for the word *I will* in the former manner of speech signifies an act of the will present, but in the latter it signifies a promise of an act of the will to come; and therefore the former words, being of the present, transfer a future right; the latter, that be of the future, transfer nothing.

But if there be other signs of the will to transfer a right besides words, then though the gift be free, yet may the right be understood to pass by words of the future (as, if a man propound a prize to him that comes first to the end of a race, the gift is free, and though the words be of the future, yet the right passeth; for if he would not have his words so be understood, he should not have let them run).

[16] In contracts the right passeth, not only where the words are of the time present or past, but also where they are of the future, because all contract is mutual translation, or change of right; and therefore he that promiseth only (because he hath already received the benefit for which he promiseth) is to be understood as if he intended the right should pass; for unless he had been content to have his words so understood, the other would not have performed his part first. And for that cause, in buying and selling, and other acts of contract, a promise is equivalent to a covenant, and therefore obligatory.

[17] He that performeth first in the case of a contract is said to MERIT that which he is to receive by the performance of the other, and he hath it as *due*. Also when a prize is propounded to many, which is to be given to him only that winneth (or money is thrown amongst many, to be enjoyed by them that catch it), though this be a free gift, yet so to win (or so to catch) is to *merit*, and to have it as DUE. For the right is transferred in the propounding of the prize (and in throwing down the money), though it be not determined to whom but by the event of the contention.

But there is between these two sorts of merit, this difference: that in contract I merit by virtue of my own power, and the contractor's need; but in this case of free gift, I am enabled to merit only by the benignity of the giver; in contract I merit at the contractor's hand that he should depart with his right; in this case of gift, I merit not that the giver should part with his right, but that when he has parted with it, it should be mine rather than another's.

And this I think to be the meaning of that distinction of the Schools between *meritum congrui* and *meritum condigni*.[3] For God Almighty having promised Paradise to those men (hoodwinked with carnal desires) that can walk through this world according to the precepts and limits prescribed by him, they say: he that shall so walk shall merit Paradise *ex congruo*. But because no man can demand a right to it, by his own righteousness or any other power in himself, but by the free grace of God only, they say: no

---

3. [Merit by coincidence and merit deserved.]

man can merit Paradise *ex condigno*. This, I say, I think is the meaning of that distinction; but because disputers do not agree upon the signification of their own terms of art longer than it serves their turn, I will not affirm anything of their meaning. Only this I say: when a gift is given indefinitely, as a prize to be contended for, he that winneth meriteth, and may claim the prize as due.

[18] If a covenant be made wherein neither of the parties perform presently, but trust one another, in the condition of mere nature (which is a condition of war of every man against every man) upon any reasonable suspicion it is void; but if there be a common power set over them both, with right and force sufficient to compel performance, it is not void. For he that performeth first has no assurance the other will perform after, because the bonds of words are too weak to bridle men's ambition, avarice, anger, and other passions, without the fear of some coercive power; which in the condition of mere nature, where all men are equal and judges of the justness of their own fears, cannot possibly be supposed. And therefore, he which performeth first does but betray himself to his enemy, contrary to the right (he can never abandon) of defending his life and means of living.

[19] But in a civil estate, where there is a power set up to constrain those that would otherwise violate their faith, that fear is no more reasonable; and for that cause, he which by the covenant is to perform first is obliged so to do.

[20] The cause of fear which maketh such a covenant invalid must be always something arising after the covenant made (as some new fact or other sign of the will not to perform), else it cannot make the covenant void. For that which could not hinder a man from promising, ought not to be admitted as a hindrance of performing.

[21] He that transferreth any right transferreth the means of enjoying it, as far as lieth in his power. As he that selleth land is understood to transfer the herbage and whatsoever grows upon it; nor can he that sells a mill turn away the stream that drives it. And they that give to a man the right of government in sovereignty are understood to give him the right of levying money to maintain soldiers, and of appointing magistrates for the administration of justice.

[22] To make covenants with brute beasts is impossible because, not understanding our speech, they understand not, nor accept of, any translation of right, nor can translate any right to another; and without mutual acceptation, there is no covenant.

[23] To make covenant with God is impossible, but by mediation of such as God speaketh to (either by revelation supernatural or by his lieutenants that govern under him, and in his name); for otherwise we know not whether our covenants be accepted or not. And therefore, they that vow anything [OL: to God] contrary to any law of nature vow in vain, as being a thing unjust to pay such vow. And if it be a thing commanded by the law of nature, [OL: they vow in vain;] it is not the vow, but the law that binds them.

[24] The matter or subject of a covenant is always something that falleth under deliberation (for to covenant is an act of the will; that is to say an act, and the last act, of deliberation) and is therefore always understood to be something to come, and which is judged possible for him that covenanteth to perform.

[25] And therefore, to promise that which is known to be impossible is no covenant. But if that prove impossible afterwards which before was thought possible, the covenant is valid and bindeth, though not to the thing itself, yet to the value; or, if that also be impossible, to the unfeigned endeavour of performing as much as is possible (for to more no man can be obliged).

[26] Men are freed of their covenants two ways: by performing or by being forgiven. For performance is the natural end of obligation; and forgiveness, the restitution of liberty (as being a retransferring of that right in which the obligation consisted).

[27] Covenants entered into by fear, in the condition of mere nature, are obligatory. For example, if I covenant to pay a ransom, or service, for my life, to an enemy, I am bound by it. For it is a contract wherein one receiveth the benefit of life; the other is to receive money, or service, for it; and consequently, where no other law (as in the condition of mere nature) forbiddeth the performance, the covenant is valid. Therefore prisoners of war, if trusted with the payment of their ransom, are obliged to pay it; and if a weaker prince make a disadvantageous peace with a stronger, for fear, he is bound to keep it, unless (as hath been said before [¶20]) there ariseth some new and just cause of fear, to renew the war. And even in commonwealths, if I be forced to redeem myself from a thief by promising him money, I am bound to

pay it, till the civil law discharge me. For whatsoever I may lawfully do without obligation, the same I may lawfully covenant to do through fear; and what I lawfully covenant, I cannot lawfully break.

[28] A former covenant makes void a later. For a man that hath passed away his right to one man today, hath it not to pass tomorrow to another; and therefore the later promise passeth no right, but is null.

[29] A covenant not to defend myself from force by force is always void. For (as I have showed before) no man can transfer or lay down his right to save himself from death, wounds, and imprisonment (the avoiding whereof is the only end of laying down any right), and therefore the promise of not resisting force in no covenant transferreth any right, nor is obliging. For though a man may covenant thus *unless I do so, or so, kill me*, he cannot covenant thus *unless I do so, or so, I will not resist you, when you come to kill me*. For man by nature chooseth the lesser evil, which is danger of death in resisting, rather than the greater, which is certain and present death in not resisting. And this is granted to be true by all men, in that they lead criminals to execution and prison with armed men, notwithstanding that such criminals have consented to the law by which they are condemned.

[30] A covenant to accuse oneself, without assurance of pardon, is likewise invalid. For in the condition of nature, where every man is judge, there is no place for accusation; and in the civil state the accusation is followed with punishment, which being force, a man is not obliged not to resist. The same is also true of the accusation of those by whose condemnation a man falls into misery (as, of a father, wife, or benefactor). For the testimony of such an accuser, if it be not willingly given, is presumed to be corrupted by nature, and therefore not to be received; and where a man's testimony is not to be credited, he is not bound to give it. Also accusations upon torture are not to be reputed as testimonies. For torture is to be used but as means of conjecture and light in the further examination and search of truth; and what is in that case confessed tendeth to the ease of him that is tortured, not to the informing of the torturers, and therefore ought not to have the credit of a sufficient testimony; for whether he deliver himself by true or false accusation, he does it by the right of preserving his own life.

[31] The force of words being (as I have formerly noted) too weak to hold men to the performance of their covenants, there are in man's nature but two imaginable helps to strengthen it. And those are either a fear of the consequence of breaking their word, or a glory or pride in appearing not to need to break it. This latter is a generosity too rarely found to be presumed on, especially in the pursuers of wealth, command, or sensual pleasure (which are the greatest part of mankind).

The passion to be reckoned upon is fear, whereof there be two very general objects: one, the power of spirits invisible; the other, the power of those men they shall therein offend. Of these two, though the former be the greater power, yet the fear of the latter is commonly the greater fear. The fear of the former is in every man his own religion, which hath place in the nature of man before civil society. The latter hath not so, at least not place enough to keep men to their promises, because in the condition of mere nature the inequality of power is not discerned but by the event of battle.

So that before the time of civil society, or in the interruption thereof by war, there is nothing can strengthen a covenant of peace agreed on, against the temptations of avarice, ambition, lust, or other strong desire, but the fear of that invisible power which they every one worship as God and fear as a revenger of their perfidy. All therefore that can be done between two men not subject to civil power is to put one another to swear by the God he feareth; which *swearing*, or OATH, is a *form of speech, added to a promise, by which he that promiseth signifieth that unless he perform, he renounceth the mercy of his God, or calleth to him for vengeance on himself.* Such was the heathen form *Let* Jupiter *kill me else, as I kill this beast.* So is our form *I shall do thus, and thus, so help me God.* And this, with the rites and ceremonies which everyone useth in his own religion, that the fear of breaking faith might be the greater.

[32] By this it appears that an oath taken according to any other form or rite than his that sweareth is in vain, and no oath, and that there is no swearing by anything which the swearer thinks not God. For though men have sometimes used to swear by their kings, for fear or flattery, yet they would have it thereby understood they attributed to them divine honour. And that swearing unnecessarily by God is but prophaning of his name, and swearing by other things, as men do in com-

mon discourse, is not swearing, but an impious custom, gotten by too much vehemence of talking.

[33] It appears also that the oath adds nothing to the obligation. For a covenant, if lawful, binds in the sight of God without the oath as much as with it; if unlawful, bindeth not at all, though it be confirmed with an oath.

CHAPTER XV

Of Other Laws of Nature

[1] From that law of nature by which we are obliged to transfer to another such rights as, being retained, hinder the peace of mankind, there followeth a third, which is this *that men perform their covenants made*, without which covenants are in vain, and but empty words, and the right of all men to all things remaining, we are still in the condition of war.

[2] And in this law of nature consisteth the fountain and original of JUSTICE. For where no covenant hath preceded, there hath no right been transferred, and every man has right to everything; and consequently, no action can be unjust. But when a covenant is made, then to break it is *unjust*; and the definition of INJUSTICE is no other than *the not performance of covenant*. And whatsoever is not unjust, is *just*.

[3] But because covenants of mutual trust where there is a fear of not performance on either part (as hath been said in the former chapter [xiv, 18–20]) are invalid, though the original of justice be the making of covenants, yet injustice actually there can be none till the cause of such fear be taken away, which, while men are in the natural condition of war, cannot be done. Therefore, before the names of just and unjust can have place, there must be some coercive power to compel men equally to the performance of their covenants, by the terror of some punishment greater than the benefit they expect by the breach of their covenant, and to make good that propriety which by mutual contract men acquire, in recompense of the universal right they abandon; and such power there is none before the erection of a commonwealth. And this is also to be gathered out of the ordinary definition of justice in the Schools; for they say that *justice is the constant will of giving to every man his own*. And therefore where there is no *own*, that is, no propriety,

there in no injustice; and where there is no coercive power erected, that is, where there is no commonwealth, there is no propriety, all men having right to all things; therefore where there is no commonwealth, there nothing is unjust. So that the nature of justice consisteth in keeping of valid covenants; but the validity of covenants begins not but with the constitution of a civil power sufficient to compel men to keep them; and then it is also that propriety begins.

[4] The fool hath said in his heart: "there is no such thing as justice"; and sometimes also with his tongue, seriously alleging that: "every man's conservation and contentment being committed to his own care, there could be no reason why every man might not do what he thought conduced thereunto, and therefore also to make or not make, keep or not keep, covenants was not against reason, when it conduced to one's benefit." He does not therein deny that there be covenants, and that they are sometimes broken, sometimes kept, and that such breach of them may be called injustice, and the observance of them justice; but he questioneth whether injustice, taking away the fear of God (for the same fool hath said in his heart there is no God), may not sometimes stand with that reason which dictateth to every man his own good; and particularly then, when it conduceth to such a benefit as shall put a man in a condition to neglect, not only the dispraise and revilings, but also the power of other men.

"The kingdom of God is gotten by violence; but what if it could be gotten by unjust violence? were it against [OL: right] reason so to get it, when it is impossible to receive hurt by it [OL: but only the supreme good]? and if it be not against reason, it is not against justice; or else justice is not to be approved for good."

From such reasoning as this, successful wickedness hath obtained the name of virtue, and some that in all other things have disallowed the violation of faith, yet have allowed it when it is for the getting of a kingdom. And the heathen that believed that *Saturn* was deposed by his son *Jupiter* believed nevertheless the same *Jupiter* to be the avenger of injustice, somewhat like to a piece of law in *Coke's* Commentaries on *Littleton*,[4] where he says: if the right heir of the

---

4. [Edward Coke (1552–1634) was an eminent English jurist who defended common law against encroachments

crown be attainted of treason, yet the crown shall descend to him, and *eo instante* [immediately] the attainder be void; from which instances a man will be very prone to infer that "when the heir apparent of a kingdom shall kill him that is in possession, though his father, you may call it injustice, or by what other name you will, yet it can never be against reason, seeing all the voluntary actions of men tend to the benefit of themselves, and those actions are most reasonable that conduce most to their ends." This specious reasoning is nevertheless false.

[5] For the question is not of promises mutual where there is no security of performance on either side (as when there is no civil power erected over the parties promising), for such promises are no covenants, but either where one of the parties has performed already, or where there is a power to make him perform, there is the question whether it be against reason, that is, against the benefit of the other to perform or not. And I say it is not against reason. For the manifestation whereof we are to consider: first, that when a man doth a thing which, notwithstanding anything can be foreseen and reckoned on, tendeth to his own destruction (howsoever some accident which he could not expect, arriving, may turn it to his benefit), yet such events do not make it reasonably or wisely done. Secondly, that in a condition of war wherein every man to every man (for want of a common power to keep them all in awe) is an enemy, there is no man can hope by his own strength or wit to defend himself from destruction without the help of confederates (where everyone expects the same defence by the confederation that anyone else does); and therefore, he which declares he thinks it reason to deceive those that help him can in reason expect no other means of safety than what can be had from his own single power. He, therefore, that breaketh his covenant, and consequently declareth that he thinks he may with reason do so, cannot be received into any society that unite themselves for peace and defence but by the error of them that receive him; nor when he is received, be retained in it without seeing the danger of their error; which errors a man

cannot reasonably reckon upon as the means of his security; and therefore, if he be left or cast out of society, he perisheth; and if he live in society, it is by the errors of other men, which he could not foresee nor reckon upon; and consequently [he has acted] against the reason of his preservation, and so as all men that contribute not to his destruction forbear him only out of ignorance of what is good for themselves.

[6] As for the instance of gaining the secure and perpetual felicity of heaven by any way, it is frivolous, there being but one way imaginable, and that is not breaking, but keeping of covenant.

[7] And for the other instance of attaining sovereignty by rebellion, it is manifest that, though the event follow, yet because it cannot reasonably be expected (but rather the contrary), and because (by gaining it so) others are taught to gain the same in like manner, the attempt thereof is against reason. Justice, therefore, that is to say, keeping of covenant, is a rule of reason by which we are forbidden to do anything destructive to our life, and consequently a law of nature.

[8] There be some that proceed further, and will not have the law of nature to be those rules which conduce to the preservation of man's life on earth, but to the attaining of an eternal felicity after death, to which they think the breach of covenant may conduce, and consequently be just and reasonable (such are they that think it a work of merit to kill, or depose, or rebel against the sovereign power constituted over them by their own consent.) But because there is no natural knowledge of man's estate after death, much less of the reward that is then to be given to breach of faith, but only a belief grounded upon other men's saying that they know it supernaturally, or that they know those that knew them that knew others that knew it supernaturally, breach of faith cannot be called a precept of reason or nature.

[9] Others, that allow for a law of nature the keeping of faith, do nevertheless make exception of certain persons (as heretics and such as use not to perform their covenant to others); and this also is against reason. For if any fault of a man be sufficient to discharge our covenant made, the same ought in reason to have been sufficient to have hindered the making of it.

[10] The names of just and unjust, when they are attributed to men, signify one thing; and when they are attributed to actions, another. When they are

---

by the crown. Thomas Littleton (c. 1442–1481), an English barrister and judge, wrote a work on property law which in an edition expanded by Coke was the standard text on the subject until the nineteenth century.]

attributed to men, they signify conformity or inconformity of manners to reason. But when they are attributed to actions, they signify the conformity or inconformity to reason, not of manners or manner of life, but of particular actions. A just man, therefore, is he that taketh all the care he can that his actions may be all just; and an unjust man is he that neglecteth it. And such men are more often in our language styled by the names of righteous and unrighteous, than just and unjust, though the meaning be the same. Therefore a righteous man does not lose that title by one or a few unjust actions that proceed from sudden passion or mistake of things or persons; nor does an unrighteous man lose his character for such actions as he does or forbears to do for fear, because his will is not framed by the justice, but by the apparent benefit of what he is to do. That which gives to human actions the relish of justice is a certain nobleness or gallantness of courage (rarely found) by which a man scorns to be beholden for the contentment of his life to fraud or breach of promise. This justice of the manners is that which is meant where justice is called a virtue, and injustice a vice.

[11] But the justice of actions denominates men, not just, but *guiltless*; and the injustice of the same (which is also called injury) gives them but the name of *guilty*.

[12] Again, the injustice of manners is the disposition or aptitude to do injury, and is injustice before it proceed to act and without supposing any individual person injured. But the injustice of an action (that is to say injury) supposeth an individual person injured, namely, him to whom the covenant was made; and therefore, many times the injury is received by one man, when the damage redoundeth to another. As when the master commandeth his servant to give money to a stranger; if it be not done, the injury is done to the master, whom he had before covenanted to obey, but the damage redoundeth to the stranger, to whom he had no obligation, and therefore could not injure him. And so also in commonwealths, private men may remit to one another their debts, but not robberies or other violences whereby they are endamaged; because the detaining of debt is an injury to themselves, but robbery and violence are injuries to the person of the commonwealth.

[13] Whatsoever is done to a man conformable to his own will, signified to the doer, is no injury to him. For if he that doeth it hath not passed away his original right to do what he please by some antecedent covenant, there is no breach of covenant, and therefore no injury done him. And if he have, then his will [i.e., that of the person acted on] to have it done being signified, is a release of that covenant; and so again there is no injury done him.

[14] Justice of actions is by writers divided into *commutative* and *distributive*; and the former they say consisteth in proportion arithmetical; the latter, in proportion geometrical. Commutative, therefore, they place in the equality of value of the things contracted for; and distributive, in the distribution of equal benefit to men of equal merit (as if it were injustice to sell dearer than we buy, or to give more to a man than he merits). The value of all things contracted for is measured by the appetite of the contractors; and therefore the just value is that which they be contented to give. And merit (besides that which is by covenant, where the performance on one part meriteth the performance of the other part, and falls under justice commutative, not distributive) is not due by justice, but is rewarded of grace only.

And therefore, this distinction, in the sense wherein it useth to be expounded, is not right. To speak properly, commutative justice is the justice of a contractor, that is, a performance of covenant (in buying and selling, hiring and letting to hire, lending and borrowing, exchanging, bartering, and other acts of contract).

[15] And distributive justice [is] the justice of an arbitrator, that is to say, the act of defining what is just. Wherein (being trusted by them that make him arbitrator) if he perform his trust, he is said to distribute to every man his own; and this is indeed just distribution, and may be called (though improperly) distributive justice (but more properly, equity, which also is a law of nature, as shall be shown in due place [¶24]).

[16] As justice dependeth on antecedent covenant, so does GRATITUDE depend on antecedent grace, that is to say, antecedent free-gift; and is the fourth law of nature, which may be conceived in this form *that a man which receiveth benefit from another of mere grace endeavour that he which giveth it have no reasonable cause to repent him of his good will.* For no man giveth but with intention of good to himself, because gift is voluntary, and of all voluntary acts the object is to every man his own good; of which, if men see

they shall be frustrated, there will be no beginning of benevolence or trust; nor, consequently, of mutual help, nor of reconciliation of one man to another; and therefore they are to remain still in the condition of war, which is contrary to the first and fundamental law of nature, which commandeth men to *seek peace*. The breach of this law is called *ingratitude*, and hath the same relation to grace that injustice hath to obligation by covenant.

[17] A fifth law of nature is COMPLAISANCE, that is to say, *that every man strive to accommodate himself to the rest*. For the understanding whereof we may consider that there is, in men's aptness to society, a diversity of nature rising from their diversity of affections, not unlike to that we see in stones brought together for building of an edifice. For as that stone which (by the asperity and irregularity of figure) takes more room from others than itself fills, and (for the hardness) cannot be easily made plain, and thereby hindereth the building, is by the builders cast away as unprofitable and troublesome, so also a man that (by asperity of nature) will strive to retain those things which to himself are superfluous and to others necessary, and (for the stubbornness of his passions) cannot be corrected, is to be left or cast out of society as cumbersome thereunto. For seeing every man, not only by right, but also by necessity of nature, is supposed to endeavour all he can to obtain that which is necessary for his conservation, he that shall oppose himself against it for things superfluous is guilty of the war that thereupon is to follow; and, therefore, doth that which is contrary to the fundamental law of nature, which commandeth *to seek peace*. The observers of this law may be called SOCIABLE (the Latins call them *commodi*); the contrary, *stubborn, insociable, froward, intractable*.

[18] A sixth law of nature is this *that upon caution of the future time, a man ought to pardon the offences past of them that, repenting, desire it*. For PARDON is nothing but granting of peace, which (though granted to them that persevere in their hostility be not peace but fear, yet) not granted to them that give caution of the future time is sign of an aversion to peace; and therefore contrary to the law of nature.

[19] A seventh is *that in revenges* (that is, retribution of evil for evil) *men look not at the greatness of the evil past, but the greatness of the good to follow*. Whereby we are forbidden to inflict punishment with

any other design than for correction of the offender, or direction of others. For this law is consequent to the next before it, that commandeth pardon upon security of the future time. Besides, revenge without respect to the example and profit to come is a triumph, or glorying, in the hurt of another, tending to no end (for the end is always somewhat to come); and glorying to no end is vainglory, and contrary to reason; and to hurt without reason tendeth to the introduction of war, which is against the law of nature, and is commonly styled by the name of *cruelty*.

[20] And because all signs of hatred or contempt provoke to fight, insomuch as most men choose rather to hazard their life than not to be revenged, we may in the eighth place, for a law of nature, set down this precept *that no man by deed, word, countenance, or gesture, declare hatred or contempt of another*. The breach of which law is commonly called *contumely*.

[21] The question 'who is the better man?' has no place in the condition of mere nature, where (as has been shewn before) all men are equal. The inequality that now is, has been introduced by the laws civil. I know that *Aristotle* (in the first book of his Politics [ch. iii–vii], for a foundation of his doctrine) maketh men by nature, some more worthy to command (meaning the wiser sort, such as he thought himself to be for his philosophy), others to serve (meaning those that had strong bodies, but were not philosophers as he), as if master and servant were not introduced by consent of men, but by difference of wit; which is not only against reason, but also against experience. For there are very few so foolish that had not rather govern themselves than be governed by others; nor when the wise in their own conceit contend by force with them who distrust their own wisdom, do they always, or often, or almost at any time, get the victory. If nature therefore have made men equal, that equality is to be acknowledged; or if nature have made men unequal, yet because men that think themselves equal will not enter into conditions of peace but upon equal terms, such equality must be admitted. And therefore for the ninth law of nature, I put this *that every man acknowledge other for his equal by nature*. The breach of this precept is *pride*.

[22] On this law dependeth another: *that at the entrance into conditions of peace, no man require to reserve to himself any right which he is not content should be reserved to every one of the rest*. As it is

necessary, for all men that seek peace, to lay down certain rights of nature (that is to say, not to have liberty to do all they list), so is it necessary, for man's life, to retain some (as, right to govern their own bodies, [right to] enjoy air, water, motion, ways to go from place to place, and all things else without which a man cannot live, or not live well). If in this case, at the making of peace, men require for themselves that which they would not have to be granted to others, they do contrary to the precedent law, that commandeth the acknowledgment of natural equality, and therefore also against the law of nature. The observers of this law are those we call *modest*, and the breakers *arrogant* men. The Greeks call the violation of this law *pleonexia*, that is, a desire of more than their share.

[23] Also *if a man be trusted to judge between man and man*, it is a precept of the law of nature that *he deal equally between them*. For without that, the controversies of men cannot be determined but by war. He, therefore, that is partial in judgment doth what in him lies to deter men from the use of judges and arbitrators; and consequently (against the fundamental law of nature), is the cause of war.

[24] The observance of this law (from the equal distribution to each man of that which in reason belongeth to him) is called EQUITY, and (as I have said before) distributive justice; the violation [is called] *acception of persons (prosopolepsia)*.

[25] And from this followeth another law: *that such things as cannot be divided be enjoyed in common, if it can be; and if the quantity of the thing permit, without stint; otherwise proportionably to the number of them that have right.* For otherwise the distribution is unequal, and contrary to equity.

[26] But some things there be that can neither be divided nor enjoyed in common. Then the law of nature which prescribeth equity requireth *that the entire right (or else, making the use alternate, the first possession) be determined by lot*. For equal distribution is of the law of nature, and other means of equal distribution cannot be imagined.

[27] Of *lots* there be two sorts: *arbitrary* and *natural*. Arbitrary is that which is agreed on by the competitors; natural is either *primogeniture* (which the Greek calls *kleronomia*, which signifies, *given by lot*) or *first seizure*.

[28] And therefore those things which cannot be enjoyed in common, nor divided, ought to be adjudged to the first possessor; and in some cases to the firstborn, as acquired by lot.

[29] It is also a law of nature *that all men that mediate peace be allowed safe conduct*. For the law that commandeth peace, as the *end*, commandeth intercession, as the *means*; and to intercession the means is safe conduct.

[30] And because (though men be never so willing to observe these laws) there may nevertheless arise questions concerning a man's action (first, whether it were done or not done; secondly, if done, whether against the law or not against the law; the former whereof is called a question *of fact*; the latter a question *of right*), therefore unless the parties to the question covenant mutually to stand to the sentence of another, they are as far from peace as ever. This other to whose sentence they submit is called an ARBITRATOR. And therefore it is of the law of nature *that they that are at controversy, submit their right to the judgment of an arbitrator*.

[31] And seeing every man is presumed to do all things in order to his own benefit, *no man is a fit arbitrator in his own cause*; and if he were never so fit, yet (equity allowing to each party equal benefit) if one be admitted to judge, the other is to be admitted also; and so the controversy, that is, the cause of war, remains, against the law of nature.

[32] For the same reason no man in any cause ought to be received for arbitrator, to whom greater profit, or honour, or pleasure apparently ariseth out of the victory of one party, than of the other; for he hath taken (though an unavoidable bribe, yet) a bribe; and no man can be obliged to trust him. And thus also the controversy, and the condition of war remaineth, contrary to the law of nature.

[33] And in a controversy of *fact* the judge (being to give no more credit to one [litigant] than to the other, if there be no other arguments) must give credit to a third [a non-litigant witness], or to a third and fourth; or more; for else the question is undecided, and left to force, contrary to the law of nature.

[34] These are the laws of nature dictating peace for a means of the conservation of men in multitudes; and which only concern the doctrine of civil society. There be other things tending to the destruction of particular men (as drunkenness and all other parts of intemperance), which may therefore also be reckoned

amongst those things which the law of nature hath forbidden; but are not necessary to be mentioned, nor are pertinent enough to this place.

[35] And though this may seem too subtle a deduction of the laws of nature to be taken notice of by all men (whereof the most part are too busy in getting food, and the rest too negligent, to understand), yet to leave all men inexcusable they have been contracted into one easy sum, intelligible even to the meanest capacity, and that is *Do not that to another, which thou wouldst not have done to thyself*; which sheweth him that he has no more to do in learning the laws of nature but (when, weighing the actions of other men with his own, they seem too heavy) to put them into the other part of the balance, and his own into their place, that his own passions and self-love may add nothing to the weight; and then there is none of these laws of nature that will not appear unto him very reasonable.

[36] The laws of nature oblige *in foro interno*, that is to say, they bind to a desire they should take place; but *in foro externo*, that is, to the putting them in act, not always. For he that should be modest and tractable, and perform all he promises, in such time and place where no man else should do so, should but make himself a prey to others, and produce his own certain ruin, contrary to the ground of all laws of nature, which tend to nature's preservation. And again, he that having sufficient security that others shall observe the same laws towards him, observes them not himself, seeketh not peace, but war, and consequently the destruction of his nature by violence.

[37] And whatsoever laws bind *in foro interno* may be broken, not only by a fact contrary to the law, but also by a fact according to it, in case a man think it contrary. For though his action in this case be according to the law, yet his purpose was against the law, which, where the obligation is *in foro interno*, is a breach.

[38] The laws of nature are immutable and eternal; for injustice, ingratitude, arrogance, pride, iniquity, acception of persons, and the rest, can never be made lawful. For it can never be that war shall preserve life, and peace destroy it.

[39] The same laws, because they oblige only to a desire and endeavour (I mean an unfeigned and constant endeavour) are easy to be observed. For in that they require nothing but endeavour, he that endeavoureth their performance fulfilleth them; and he that fulfilleth the law is just.

[40] And the science of them [the laws of nature] is the true and only moral philosophy. For moral philosophy is nothing else but the science of what is *good* and *evil* in the conversation and society of mankind. *Good* and *evil* are names that signify our appetites and aversions, which in different tempers, customs, and doctrines of men are different; and divers men differ not only in their judgment on the senses (of what is pleasant and unpleasant to the taste, smell, hearing, touch, and sight), but also of what is conformable or disagreeable to reason in the actions of common life. Nay, the same man in divers times differs from himself, and one time praiseth (that is, calleth good) what another time he dispraiseth (and calleth evil); from whence arise disputes, controversies, and at last war. And therefore so long a man is in the condition of mere nature (which is a condition of war) as private appetite is the measure of good and evil; and consequently, all men agree on this, that peace is good; and therefore also the way or means of peace (which, as I have shewed before, are *justice, gratitude, modesty, equity, mercy*, and the rest of the laws of nature) are good (that is to say, *moral virtues*), and their contrary vices, evil.

Now the science of virtue and vice is moral philosophy; and therefore the true doctrine of the laws of nature is the true moral philosophy. But the writers of moral philosophy, though they acknowledge the same virtues and vices, yet not seeing wherein consisted their goodness, nor that they come to be praised as the means of peaceable, sociable, and comfortable living, place them in a mediocrity of passions (as if not the cause, but the degree of daring, made fortitude; or not the cause, but the quantity of a gift, made liberality).

[41] These dictates of reason men use to call by the name of laws, but improperly; for they are but conclusions or theorems concerning what conduceth to the conservation and defence of themselves, whereas law, properly, is the word of him that by right hath command over others. But yet if we consider the same theorems, as delivered in the word of God, that by right commandeth all things; then are they properly called laws.

Part Two
OF COMMONWEALTH
CHAPTER XVII

Of the Causes, Generation, and Definition of a *Commonwealth*

[1] The final cause, end, or design of men (who naturally love liberty and dominion over others) in the introduction of that restraint upon themselves in which we see them live in commonwealths is the foresight of their own preservation, and of a more contented life thereby; that is to say, of getting themselves out from that miserable condition of war, which is necessarily consequent (as hath been shown [ch. xiii]) to the natural passions of men, when there is no visible power to keep them in awe, and tie them by fear of punishment to the performance of their covenants and observation of those laws of nature set down in the fourteenth and fifteenth chapters.

[2] For the laws of nature (as *justice, equity, modesty, mercy,* and (in sum) *doing to others as we would be done to*) of themselves, without the terror of some power to cause them to be observed, are contrary to our natural passions, that carry us to partiality, pride, revenge, and the like. And covenants without the sword are but words, and of no strength to secure a man at all. Therefore notwithstanding the laws of nature (which every one hath then kept, when he has the will to keep them, when he can do it safely), if there be no power erected, or not great enough for our security, every man will, and may lawfully rely on his own strength and art, for caution against all other men. And in all places where men have lived by small families, to rob and spoil one another has been a trade, and so far from being reputed against the law of nature that the greater spoils they gained, the greater was their honour; and men observed no other laws therein but the laws of honour, that is, to abstain from cruelty, leaving to men their lives and instruments of husbandry. And as small families did then, so now do cities and kingdoms (which are but greater families) for their own security enlarge their dominions upon all pretences of danger and fear of invasion or assistance that may be given to invaders, [and] endeavour as much as they can to subdue or weaken their neighbours, by open force and secret arts for want of other caution, justly (and are remembered for it in after ages with honour).

[3] Nor is it the joining together of a small number of men that gives them this security; because in small numbers, small additions on the one side or the other make the advantage of strength so great as is sufficient to carry the victory; and therefore gives encouragement to an invasion. The multitude sufficient to confide in for our security is not determined by any certain number, but by comparison with the enemy we fear, and is then sufficient, when the odds of the enemy is not of so visible and conspicuous moment, to determine the event of war, as to move him to attempt.

[4] And be there never so great a multitude, yet if their actions be directed according to their particular judgments and particular appetites, they can expect thereby no defence, nor protection, neither against a common enemy, nor against the injuries of one another. For being distracted in opinions concerning the best use and application of their strength, they do not help, but hinder one another, and reduce their strength by mutual opposition to nothing; whereby they are easily, not only subdued by a very few that agree together, but also when there is no common enemy, they make war upon each other, for their particular interests. For if we could suppose a great multitude of men to consent in the observation of justice and other laws of nature without a common power to keep them all in awe, we might as well suppose all mankind to do the same; and then there neither would be, nor need to be, any civil government or commonwealth at all, because there would be peace without subjection.

[5] Nor is it enough for the security, which men desire should last all the time of their life, that they be governed and directed by one judgment for a limited time, as in one battle or one war. For though they obtain a victory by their unanimous endeavour against a foreign enemy, yet afterwards, when either they have no common enemy, or he that by one part is held for an enemy is by another part held for a friend, they must needs by the difference of their interests dissolve, and fall again into a war amongst themselves.

[6] It is true that certain living creatures (as bees and ants) live sociably one with another (which are therefore by *Aristotle* numbered amongst political creatures), and yet have no other direction than their

particular judgments and appetites, nor speech whereby one of them can signify to another what he thinks expedient for the common benefit; and therefore some man may perhaps desire to know why mankind cannot do the same. To which I answer,

[7] First, that men are continually in competition for honour and dignity, which these creatures are not; and consequently, amongst men there ariseth, on that ground, envy and hatred, and finally war; but amongst these not so.

[8] Secondly, that amongst these creatures the common good differeth not from the private; and being by nature inclined to their private, they procure thereby the common benefit. But man, whose joy consisteth in comparing himself with other men, can relish nothing but what is eminent.

[9] Thirdly, that these creatures (having not, as man, the use of reason) do not see, nor think they see, any fault in the administration of their common business; whereas amongst men there are very many that think themselves wiser, and abler to govern the public, better than the rest; and these strive to reform and innovate, one this way, another that way; and thereby bring it into distraction and civil war.

[10] Fourthly, that these creatures, though they have some use of voice (in making known to one another their desires and other affections), yet they want that art of words by which some men can represent to others that which is good in the likeness of evil, and evil in the likeness of good, and augment or diminish the apparent greatness of good and evil, discontenting men, and troubling their peace at their pleasure.

[11] Fifthly, irrational creatures cannot distinguish between *injury* and *damage*; and therefore, as long as they be at ease, they are not offended with their fellows, whereas man is then most troublesome, when he is most at ease; for then it is that he loves to shew his wisdom, and control the actions of them that govern the commonwealth.

[12] Lastly, the agreement of these creatures is natural; that of men is by covenant only, which is artificial; and therefore, it is no wonder if there be somewhat else required (besides covenant) to make their agreement constant and lasting, which is a common power to keep them in awe, and to direct their actions to the common benefit.

[13] The only way to erect such a common power as may be able to defend them from the invasion of foreigners and the injuries of one another, and thereby to secure them in such sort as that by their own industry, and by the fruits of the earth, they may nourish themselves and live contentedly, is to confer all their power and strength upon one man, or upon one assembly of men, that may reduce all their wills, by plurality of voices, unto one will, which is as much as to say, to appoint one man or assembly of men to bear their person, and every one to own and acknowledge himself to be author of whatsoever he that so beareth their person shall act, or cause to be acted, in those things which concern the common peace and safety, and therein to submit their wills, every one to his will, and their judgments, to his judgment. This is more than consent, or concord; it is a real unity of them all, in one and the same person, made by covenant of every man with every man, in such manner as if every man should say to every man *I authorize and give up my right of governing myself to this man, or to this assembly of men, on this condition, that thou give up thy right to him, and authorize all his actions in like manner*. This done, the multitude so united in one person is called a COMMONWEALTH, in Latin CIVITAS. This is the generation of that great LEVIATHAN, or rather (to speak more reverently) of that *Mortal God* to which we owe, under the *Immortal God*, our peace and defence. For by this authority, given him by every particular man in the commonwealth, he hath the use of so much power and strength conferred on him that by terror thereof he is enabled to conform the wills of them all to peace at home and mutual aid against their enemies abroad. And in him consisteth the essence of the commonwealth, which (to define it) is *one person, of whose acts a great multitude, by mutual covenants one with another, have made themselves every one the author, to the end he may use the strength and means of them all, as he shall think expedient, for their peace and common defence*.

[14] And he that carrieth this person is called SOVEREIGN, and said to have *Sovereign Power*; and every one besides, his SUBJECT.

[15] The attaining to this sovereign power is by two ways. One, by natural force, as when a man maketh his children to submit themselves and their children to his government, as being able to destroy them if they refuse, or by war subdueth his enemies

to his will, giving them their lives on that condition. The other is when men agree amongst themselves to submit to some man, or assembly of men, voluntarily, on confidence to be protected by him against all others. This latter may be called a political commonwealth, or commonwealth by *institution*, and the former, a commonwealth by *acquisition*. And first, I shall speak of a commonwealth by institution.

CHAPTER XVIII

Of the *Rights* of Sovereigns by Institution

[1] A *commonwealth* is said to be *instituted*, when a *multitude* of men do agree and *covenant, every one with every one*, that to whatsoever *man* or *assembly of men* shall be given by the major part the *right* to *present* the person of them all (that is to say, to be their *representative*) every one, as well he that *voted for it* as he that *voted against it*, shall *authorize* all the actions and judgments of that man or assembly of men, in the same manner as if they were his own, to the end, to live peaceably amongst themselves and be protected against other men.

[2] From this institution of a commonwealth are derived all the *rights* and *faculties* of him, or them, on whom the sovereign power is conferred by the consent of the people assembled.

[3] First, because they covenant, it is to be understood they are not obliged by former covenant to anything repugnant hereunto. And consequently they that have already instituted a commonwealth, being thereby bound by covenant to own the actions and judgments of one, cannot lawfully make a new covenant amongst themselves to be obedient to any other, in any thing whatsoever, without his permission. And therefore, they that are subjects to a monarch cannot without his leave cast off monarchy and return to the confusion of a disunited multitude, nor transfer their person from him that beareth it to another man, or other assembly of men; for they are bound, every man to every men, to own, and be reputed author of, all that he that already is their sovereign shall do and judge fit to be done; so that, any one man dissenting, all the rest should break their covenant made to that man, which is injustice. And they have also every man given the sovereignty to him that beareth their person; and therefore if they depose him, they take

from him that which is his own, and so again it is injustice. Besides, if he that attempteth to depose his sovereign be killed, or punished by him for such attempt, he is author of his own punishment, as being, by the institution, author of all his sovereign shall do; and because it is injustice for a man to do anything for which he may be punished by his own authority, he is also, upon that title, unjust.

And whereas some men have pretended for their disobedience to their sovereign a new covenant, made (not with men, but) with God, this also is unjust; for there is no covenant with God but by mediation of somebody that representeth God's person, which none doth but God's lieutenant, who hath the sovereignty under God. But this pretence of covenant with God is so evident a lie, even in the pretenders' own consciences, that it is not only an act of an unjust, but also of a vile and unmanly disposition.

[4] Secondly, because the right of bearing the person of them all is given to him they make sovereign by covenant only of one to another, and not of him to any of them, there can happen no breach of covenant on the part of the sovereign; and consequently none of his subjects, by any pretence of forfeiture, can be freed from his subjection.

That he which is made sovereign maketh no covenant with his subjects beforehand is manifest, because either he must make it with the whole multitude, as one party to the covenant, or he must make a several covenant with every man. With the whole, as one party, it is impossible, because as yet they are not one person; and if he make so many several covenants as there be men, those covenants after he hath the sovereignty are void, because what act soever can be pretended by any one of them for breach thereof is the act both of himself and of all the rest, because done in the person and by the right of every one of them in particular.

Besides, if any one (or more) of them pretend a breach of the covenant made by the sovereign at his institution, and others (or one other) of his subjects (or himself alone) pretend there was no such breach, there is in this case no judge to decide the controversy; it returns therefore to the sword again; and every man recovereth the right of protecting himself by his own strength, contrary to the design they had in the institution. It is therefore in vain to grant sovereignty by way of precedent covenant.

The opinion that any monarch receiveth his power by covenant, that is to say, on condition, proceedeth from want of understanding this easy truth, that covenants, being but words and breath, have no force to oblige, contain, constrain, or protect any man, but what it has from the public sword, that is, from the united hands of that man or assembly of men that hath the sovereignty, and whose actions are avouched by them all, and performed by the strength of them all, in him united. But when an assembly of men is made sovereign, then no man imagineth any such covenant to have passed in the institution; for no man is so dull as to say, for example, the people of *Rome* made a covenant with the Romans, to hold the sovereignty on such or such conditions, which not performed, the Romans might lawfully depose the Roman people. That men see not the reason to be alike in a monarchy and in a popular government proceedeth from the ambition of some that are kinder to the government of an assembly, whereof they may hope to participate, than of monarchy, which they despair to enjoy.

[5] Thirdly, because the major part hath by consenting voices declared a sovereign, he that dissented must now consent with the rest, that is, be contented to avow all the actions he shall do, or else justly be destroyed by the rest. For if he voluntarily entered into the congregation of them that were assembled, he sufficiently declared thereby his will (and therefore tacitly covenanted) to stand to what the major part should ordain; and therefore, if he refuse to stand thereto, or make protestation against any of their decrees, he does contrary to his covenant, and therefore unjustly. And whether he be of the congregation or not, and whether his consent be asked or not, he must either submit to their decrees or be left in the condition of war he was in before, wherein he might without injustice be destroyed by any man whatsoever.

[6] Fourthly, because every subject is by this institution author of all the actions and judgments of the sovereign instituted, it follows that, whatsoever he doth, it can be no injury to any of his subjects, nor ought he to be by any of them accused of injustice. For he that doth anything by authority from another doth therein no injury to him by whose authority he acteth; but by this institution of a commonwealth every particular man is author of all the sovereign doth; and consequently he that complaineth of injury from his sovereign complaineth of that whereof he himself is author, and therefore ought not to accuse any man but himself; no nor himself of injury, because to do injury to one's self is impossible. It is true that they that have sovereign power may commit iniquity, but not injustice, or injury in the proper signification.

[7] Fifthly, and consequently to that which was said last, no man that hath sovereign power can justly be put to death, or otherwise in any manner by his subjects punished. For seeing every subject is author of the actions of his sovereign, he punisheth another for the actions committed by himself.

[8] And because the end of this institution is the peace and defence of them all, and whosoever has right to the end has right to the means, it belongeth of right to whatsoever man or assembly that hath the sovereignty, to be judge both of the means of peace and defence, and also of the hindrances and disturbances of the same, and to do whatsoever he shall think necessary to be done, both beforehand (for the preserving of peace and security, by prevention of discord at home and hostility from abroad) and, when peace and security are lost, for the recovery of the same. And therefore,

[9] Sixthly, it is annexed to the sovereignty to be judge of what opinions and doctrines are averse, and what conducing, to peace; and consequently, on what occasions, how far, and what men are to be trusted withal, in speaking to multitudes of people, and who shall examine the doctrines of all books before they be published. For the actions of men proceed from their opinions, and in the well-governing of opinions consisteth the well-governing of men's actions, in order to their peace and concord. And though in matter of doctrine nothing ought to be regarded but the truth, yet this is not repugnant to regulating of the same by peace. For doctrine repugnant to peace can no more be true than peace and concord can be against the law of nature. It is true that in a commonwealth where (by the negligence of unskillfulness of governors and teachers) false doctrines are by time generally received, the contrary truths may be generally offensive. Yet the most sudden and rough bustling in of a new truth that can be does never break the peace, but only sometimes awake the war. For those men that are so remissly governed that they dare take up arms to defend or introduce an opinion are still

in war, and their condition not peace, but only a cessation of arms for fear of one another; and they live, as it were, in the precincts of battle continually. It belongeth therefore to him that hath the sovereign power to be judge (or constitute all judges) of opinions and doctrines, as a thing necessary to peace, thereby to prevent discord and civil war.

[10] Seventhly, is annexed to the sovereignty the whole power of prescribing the rules whereby every man may know what goods he may enjoy, and what actions he may do, without being molested by any of his fellow-subjects; and this is it men call *propriety*. For before constitution of sovereign power (as hath already been shown) all men had right to all things, which necessarily causeth war; and therefore, this propriety, being necessary to peace, and depending on sovereign power, is the act of that power, in order to the public peace. These rules of propriety (or *meum* and *tuum*) and of *good, evil, lawful,* and *unlawful* in the actions of subjects are the civil laws; that is to say, the laws of each commonwealth in particular (though the name of civil law be now restrained to the ancient civil laws of the city of *Rome*, which being the head of a great part of the world, her laws at that time were in these parts the civil law).

[11] Eighthly, is annexed to the sovereignty the right of judicature, that is to say, of hearing and deciding all controversies which may arise concerning law (either civil or natural) or concerning fact. For without the decision of controversies there is no protection of one subject against the injuries of another, the laws concerning *meum* and *tuum* are in vain, and to every man remaineth, from the natural and necessary appetite of his own conservation, the right of protecting himself by his private strength, which is the condition of war, and contrary to the end for which every commonwealth is instituted.

[12] Ninthly, is annexed to the sovereignty the right of making war and peace with other nations and commonwealths, that is to say, of judging when it is for the public good, and how great forces are to be assembled, armed, and paid for that end, and to levy money upon the subjects to defray the expenses thereof. For the power by which the people are to be defended consisteth in their armies; and the strength of an army, in the union of their strength under one command; which command the sovereign instituted therefore hath, because the command of the *militia*, without other institution, maketh him that hath it sovereign. And therefore, whosoever is made general of an army, he that hath the sovereign power is always generalissimo.

[13] Tenthly, is annexed to the sovereignty the choosing of all counsellors, ministers, magistrates, and officers, both in peace and war. For seeing the sovereign is charged with the end, which is the common peace and defence, he is understood to have power to use such means as he shall think most fit for his discharge.

[14] Eleventhly, to the sovereign is committed the power of rewarding with riches or honour, and of punishing with corporal or pecuniary punishment or with ignominy, every subject according to the law he hath formerly made (or if there be no law made, according as he shall judge most to conduce to the encouraging of men to serve the commonwealth, or deterring of them from doing disservice to the same).

[15] Lastly, considering what values men are naturally apt to set upon themselves, what respect they look for from others, and how little they value other men, from whence continually arise amongst them emulation, quarrels, factions, and at last war, to the destroying of one another, and diminution of their strength against a common enemy, it is necessary that there be laws of honour and a public rate of the worth of such men as have deserved (or are able to deserve) well of the commonwealth, and that there be force in the hands of some or other to put those laws in execution. But it hath already been shown that not only the whole *militia*, or forces of the commonwealth, but also the judicature of all controversies is annexed to the sovereignty. To the sovereign therefore it belongeth also to give titles of honour, and to appoint what order of place and dignity each man shall hold, and what signs of respect, in public or private meetings, they shall give to one another.

[16] These are the rights which make the essence of sovereignty, and which are the marks whereby a man may discern in what man, or assembly of men, the sovereign power is placed and resideth. For these are incommunicable and inseparable. The power to coin money, to dispose of the estate and persons of infant heirs, to have preemption in markets, and all other statute prerogatives may be transferred by the sovereign, and yet the power to protect his subjects be retained. But if he transfer the *militia*, he retains

the judicature in vain, for want of execution of the laws; or if he grant away the power of raising money, the *militia* is in vain; or if he give away the government of doctrines, men will be frightened into rebellion with the fear of spirits. And so if we consider any one of the said rights, we shall presently see, that the holding of all the rest will produce no effect, in the conservation of peace and justice, the end for which all commonwealths are instituted. And this division is it, whereof it is said *a kingdom divided in itself cannot stand*; for unless this division precede, division into opposite armies can never happen. If there had not first been an opinion received of the greatest part of *England*, that these powers were divided between the King, and the Lords, and the House of Commons, the people had never been divided and fallen into this civil war, first between those that disagreed in politics, and after between the dissenters about the liberty of religion, which have so instructed men in this point of sovereign right that there be few now (in *England*) that do not see that these rights are inseparable, and will be so generally acknowledged at the next return of peace; and so continue, till their miseries are forgotten, and no longer, except the vulgar be better taught than they have hitherto been.

[17] And because they are essential and inseparable rights, it follows necessarily that in whatsoever words any of them seem to be granted away, yet if the sovereign power itself be not in direct terms renounced, and the name of sovereign no more given by the grantees to him that grants them, the grant is void; for when he has granted all he can, if we grant back the sovereignty, all is restored, as inseparably annexed thereunto.

[18] This great authority being indivisible, and inseparably annexed to the sovereignty, there is little ground for the opinion of them that say of sovereign kings, though they be *singulis majores*, of greater power than every one of their subjects, yet they be *universis minores*, of less power than them all together. For if by *all together* they mean not the collective body as one person, then *all together*, and *every one*, signify the same; and the speech is absurd. But if by *all together* they understand them as one person (which person the sovereign bears), then the power of all together is the same with the sovereign's power; and so again the speech is absurd; which absurdity they see

well enough when the sovereignty is in an assembly of the people; but in a monarch they see it not; and yet the power of sovereignty is the same in whomsoever it be placed.

[19] And as the power, so also the honour of the sovereign ought to be greater than that of any or all the subjects. For in the sovereignty is the fountain of honour. The dignities of lord, earl, duke, and prince are his creatures. As in the presence of the master, the servants are equal, and without any honour at all, so are the subjects in the presence of the sovereign. And though they shine, some more, some less, when they are out of his sight, yet in his presence they shine no more than the stars in [the] presence of the sun.

[20] But a man may here object that the condition of subjects is very miserable, as being obnoxious to the lusts and other irregular passions of him or them that have so unlimited a power in their hands. And commonly, they that live under a monarch think it the fault of monarchy, and they that live under the government of democracy or other sovereign assembly attribute all the inconvenience to that form of commonwealth (whereas the power in all forms, if they be perfect enough to protect them, is the same), not considering that the estate of man can never be without some incommodity or other, and that the greatest that in any form of government can possibly happen to the people in general is scarce sensible, in respect of the miseries and horrible calamities that accompany a civil war (or that dissolute condition of masterless men, without subjection to laws and a coercive power to tie their hands from rapine and revenge), nor considering that the greatest pressure of sovereign governors proceedeth not from any delight or profit they can expect in the damage or weakening of their subjects (in whose vigour consisteth their own strength and glory), but in the restiveness of themselves that, unwillingly contributing to their own defence, make it necessary for their governors to draw from them what they can in time of peace, that they may have means on any emergent occasion, or sudden need, to resist or take advantage on their enemies. For all men are by nature provided of notable multiplying glasses (that is their passions and self-love), through which every little payment appeareth a great grievance, but are destitute of those prospective glasses (namely moral and civil science), to see afar

off the miseries that hang over them, and cannot without such payments be avoided.

CHAPTER XX

Of Dominion *Paternal* and *Despotical*

[1] A *commonwealth by acquisition* is that where the sovereign power is acquired by force; and it is acquired by force when men singly (or many together by plurality of voices) for fear of death or bonds do authorize all the actions of that man or assembly that hath their lives and liberty in his power.

[2] And this kind of dominion or sovereignty differeth from sovereignty by institution only in this, that men who choose their sovereign do it for fear of one another, and not of him whom they institute; but in this case they subject themselves to him they are afraid of. In both cases they do it for fear, which is to be noted by them that hold all such covenants as proceed from fear of death or violence void; which, if it were true, no man in any kind of commonwealth could be obliged to obedience. It is true that in a commonwealth once instituted or acquired, promises proceeding from fear of death or violence are no covenants, nor obliging, when the thing promised is contrary to the laws; but the reason is not, because it was made upon fear, but because he that promiseth hath no right in the thing promised. Also, when he may lawfully perform and doth not, it is not the invalidity of the covenant that absolveth him, but the sentence of the sovereign. Otherwise, whensoever a man lawfully promiseth, he unlawfully breaketh; but when the sovereign, who is the actor, acquitteth him, then he is acquitted by him that extorted the promise, as by the author of such absolution.

[3] But the rights and consequences of sovereignty are the same in both. His power cannot, without his consent, be transferred to another; he cannot forfeit it; he cannot be accused by any of his subjects of injury; he cannot be punished by them; he is judge of what is necessary for peace, and judge of doctrines; he is sole legislator, and supreme judge of controversies, and of the times and occasions of war and peace; to him it belongeth to choose magistrates, counsellors, commanders, and all other officers and ministers, and to determine of rewards and punishments, honour and order. The reasons whereof are the same which are alleged in the precedent chapter for the same rights and consequence of sovereignty by institution.

[4] Dominion is acquired two ways: by generation and by conquest. The right of dominion by generation is that which the parent hath over his children, and is called PATERNAL. And is not so derived from the generation as if therefore the parent had dominion over his child because he begat him, but from the child's consent, either express or by other sufficient arguments declared. For as to the generation, God hath ordained to man a helper, and there be always two that are equally parents; the dominion therefore over the child should belong equally to both, and he be equally subject to both, which is impossible; for no man can obey two masters. And whereas some have attributed the dominion to the man only, as being of the more excellent sex, they misreckon in it. For there is not always that difference of strength or prudence between the man and the woman as that the right can be determined without war. In commonwealths this controversy is decided by the civil law, and for the most part (but not always) the sentence is in favour of the father, because for the most part commonwealths have been erected by the fathers, not by the mothers of families.

But the question lieth now in the state of mere nature, where there are supposed no laws of matrimony, no laws for the education of children, but the law of nature, and the natural inclination of the sexes, one to another, and to their children. In this condition of mere nature either the parents between themselves dispose of the dominion over the child by contract, or do not dispose thereof at all. If they dispose thereof, the right passeth according to the contract. We find in history that the *Amazons*[5] contracted with the men of the neighbouring countries, to whom they had recourse for issue, that the issue male should be sent back, but the female remain with themselves, so that the dominion of the females was in the mother.

[5] If there be no contract, the dominion is in the mother. For in the condition of mere nature, where there are no matrimonial laws, it cannot be known who is the father unless it be declared by the mother;

---

5. [According to Greek mythology, the Amazons were a tribe of warlike women.]

and therefore the right of dominion over the child dependeth on her will, and is consequently hers. Again, seeing the infant is first in the power of the mother, so as she may either nourish or expose it, if she nourish it, it oweth its life to the mother, and is therefore obliged to obey her rather than any other, and by consequence the dominion over it is hers. But if she expose it, and another find and nourish it, the dominion is in him that nourisheth it. For it ought to obey him by whom it is preserved, because preservation of life being the end for which one man becomes subject to another, every man is supposed to promise obedience to him in whose power it is to save or destroy him.

[6] If the mother be the father's subject, the child is in the father's power; and if the father be the mother's subject (as when a sovereign queen marrieth one of her subjects), the child is subject to the mother, because the father also is her subject.

[7] If a man and woman, monarchs of two several kingdoms, have a child, and contract concerning who shall have the dominion of him, the right of the dominion passeth by the contract. If they contract not, the dominion followeth the dominion of the place of his [sc. the child's] residence. For the sovereign of each country hath dominion over all that reside therein.

[8] He that hath the dominion over the child hath dominion also over the children of the child, and over their children's children. For he that hath dominion over the person of a man hath dominion over all that is his, without which dominion were but a title, without the effect.

[9] The right of succession to paternal dominion proceedeth in the same manner as doth the right of succession to monarchy, of which I have already sufficiently spoken in the precedent chapter.

[10] Dominion acquired by conquest, or victory in war, is that which some writers call DESPOTICAL, from *despotes*, which signifieth a *lord* or *master*, and is the dominion of the master over his servant. And this dominion is then acquired to the victor when the vanquished, to avoid the present stroke of death, covenanteth either in express words, or by other sufficient signs of the will, that so long as his life and the liberty of his body is allowed him, the victor shall have the use thereof, at his pleasure. And after such covenant made, the vanquished is a SERVANT, and not before; for by the word *servant* (whether it be derived from *servire*, to serve, or from *servare*, to save, which I leave to grammarians to dispute) is not meant a captive (which is kept in prison or bonds till the owner of him that took him, or bought him of one that did, shall consider what to do with him; for such men, commonly called slaves, have no obligation at all, but may break their bonds or the prison, and kill or carry away captive their master, justly), but one that, being taken, hath corporal liberty allowed him, and upon promise not to run away, nor to do violence to his master, is trusted by him.

[11] It is not therefore the victory that giveth the right of dominion over the vanquished, but his own covenant. Nor is he obliged because he is conquered (that is to say, beaten, and taken or put to flight), but because he cometh in, and submitteth to the victor; nor is the victor obliged by an enemy's rendering himself (without promise of life) to spare him for this his yielding to discretion, which obliges not the victor longer than in his own discretion he shall think fit.

[12] And that which men do, when they demand (as it is now called) *quarter* (which the Greeks called *zogria, taking alive*) is to evade the present fury of the victor by submission, and to compound for their life with ransom or service; and therefore he that hath quarter hath not his life given, but deferred till farther deliberation; for it is not an yielding on condition of life, but to discretion. And then only is his life in security, and his service due, when the victor hath trusted him with his corporal liberty. For slaves that work in prisons, or fetters, do it not of duty, but to avoid the cruelty of their task-masters.

[13] The master of the servant is master also of all he hath, and may exact the use thereof; that is to say, of his goods, of his labour, of his servants, and of his children, as often as he shall think fit. For he holdeth his life of his master, by the covenant of obedience, that is, of owning and authorizing whatsoever the master shall do. And in case the master, if he refuse, kill him, or cast him into bonds, or otherwise punish him for his disobedience, he is himself the author of the same, and cannot accuse him of injury.

[14] In sum, the rights and consequences of both *paternal* and *despotical* dominion are the very same with those of a sovereign by institution, and for the

same reasons, which reasons are set down in the precedent chapter. So that for a man that is monarch of divers nations, whereof he hath, in one the sovereignty by institution of the people assembled, and in another by conquest (that is by the submission of each particular, to avoid death or bonds), to demand of one nation more than of the other from the title of conquest, as being a conquered nation, is an act of ignorance of the rights of sovereignty. For the sovereign is absolute over both alike, or else there is no sovereignty at all (and so every man may lawfully protect himself, if he can, with his own sword, which is the condition of war).

Baruch Spinoza

Baruch Spinoza (1632–1677) was born in Amsterdam, his parents Jewish refugees from the Spanish Inquisition. Educated in the traditional religious studies of his people, he absorbed a profound knowledge of the Bible and Hebrew, later mastering Latin, the language in which he wrote.

Spinoza not only kept abreast of the scientific and philosophical developments of his own time, but as a result of his dissatisfaction with anthropomorphism and mysticism, also studied the works of the important Jewish medieval philosophers who had grappled with these issues—men such as Maimonides (1135–1204), Gersonides (1288–1344), and Crescas (1340–1410). When questioned by a tribunal of his congregation, Spinoza was unwilling to disavow his heterodox theological opinions. Subsequently, the Jewish community of Holland, not at that time entitled to citizenship and fearful of reprisals for permitting such heresies, excommunicated him at the age of twenty-four. For the next four years he stayed in Amsterdam, pursuing his studies while earning a living grinding and polishing lenses. He then moved to the small village of Rijnsburg, near Leyden, and later to Voorburg, outside The Hague, continuing his lonely life as a scholar and lens-grinder. He was offered a chair of philosophy at the University of Heidelberg, but refused it, fearful of losing his freedom of expression. He died at forty-four, the victim of tuberculosis, his frail constitution weakened by arduous labor as well as by the glass dust he had inhaled while practicing his vocation. He was regarded as a person of great courtesy, unusual modesty, and equanimity.

Only two books by Spinoza appeared during his lifetime: *The Principles of Descartes' Philosophy*, an expository volume in geometrical form; and the anonymously published *Theological-Political Treatise*. The latter is perhaps the earliest example of what two centuries later became known as "higher criticism," the study of the Bible as a historical document open to rational interpretation. His posthumous works included an unfinished Hebrew grammar, intended to support his scientific approach to Scriptural exegesis; the *Short Treatise on God, Man, and His Well-Being*, an early, partial draft of his philosophical system; the fragmentary *Treatise on the Correction of the Understanding*, an introduction to his methodology; the incomplete *Political Treatise*, which stresses the value of individual liberty and religious toleration, as well as supporting democracy against the claims of monarchy and aristocracy; and his masterpiece, the *Ethics, Demonstrated in Geometrical Order*, one of the most majestic of all philosophical works.

Spinoza viewed the world as possessing an intelligible structure according to which every event was in principle comprehensible as a necessary part of the whole. The logical order of that whole was to be understood only "through itself" and was variously termed "substance," "Nature," or "God." The geometric format of the *Ethics* illustrates this central thesis, since the propositions, corollaries, and notes are all intended as deductions from the initial definitions and axioms, which are presented as self-explanatory.

Part I contains Spinoza's detailed demonstration of the essence of God. In Part II he offers his solution to the traditional philosophical problem of the relation between mind and body, regarding these not, as Descartes had, as two separate substances, but rather as two aspects of the one Substance. The remainder of the *Ethics* (not reprinted here) contains Spinoza's moral theory and his view of the ideal life. The terms "good" and "bad" are, according to Spinoza, merely words we use to express our own desires. In order to achieve salvation, we need to free ourselves from the bondage of these emotions and strive through reason to achieve knowledge of and identification with the order of the universe, thus coming to possess "the intellectual love of God" which is "blessedness." By thus reinterpreting the concept of God and imparting spirituality to the study of nature, Spinoza fused his commitment to the scientific model of knowledge with the monotheistic version of his religious heritage.

• • •

Helpful overviews of Spinoza's thought are Stuart Hampshire, *Spinoza* (Middlesex: Penguin Books, 1951) and Henry E. Allison, *Benedict de Spinoza: An Introduction*, Revised Edition (New Haven: Yale University Press, 1987). An incisive presentation of Spinoza's philosophical perspective is chapter five of John Herman Randall, Jr., *The Career of Philosophy: From the Middle Ages to the Enlightenment* (1962; rpt. New York: Columbia University Press, 1970). Also useful as a concise presentation of the major themes in Spinoza's system is the essay by P. H. Nidditch in D. J. O'Connor, ed., *A Critical History of Western Philosophy* (Glencoe: The Free Press, 1964). Two detailed examinations of the *Ethics* are Jonathan Bennett, *A Study of Spinoza's ETHICS* (Indianapolis: Hackett Publishing Company, 1984) and Edwin Curley, *Behind the Geometrical Method: A Reading of Spinoza's Ethics* (Princeton: Princeton University Press, 1988). A detailed study of Spinoza's view of God is Richard Mason, *The God of Spinoza: A Philosophical Study* (Cambridge: Cambridge University Press, 1997). A useful collections of essays is Derk Pereboom, ed., *The Rationalists: Descartes, Spinoza, Leibniz* (Lanham, Md.: Rowman & Littlefield, 1999). An especially fine essay that penetrates to the heart of Spinoza's thought is the text of a lecture by Frederick J. F. Woodbridge, delivered at Columbia University in 1933 and reprinted in the edition of the *Ethics* edited by James Gutmann (New York: Hafner, 1957). The classic study of the *Ethics* from a historical point of view, exhibiting in immense detail its connections to the work of Aristotle, Descartes, and others, is Harry Austryn Wolfson, *The Philosophy of Spinoza* (1934; rpt. Cleveland: Meridian Books, 1958). A comprehensive guide to Spinoza's thought is Don Garrett, ed., *The Cambridge Companion to Spinoza* (Cambridge: Cambridge University Press, 1996).

S.M.C.

The Ethics

Part I
CONCERNING GOD

DEFINITIONS

1. By that which is self-caused I mean that whose essence involves existence; or that whose nature can be conceived only as existing.

2. A thing is said to be finite in its own kind [*in suo genere finita*] when it can be limited by another thing of the same nature. For example, a body is said to be finite because we can always conceive of another body greater than it. So, too, a thought is limited by another thought. But body is not limited by thought, nor thought by body.

3. By substance I mean that which is in itself and is conceived through itself; that is, that the conception of which does not require the conception of another thing from which it has to be formed.

4. By attribute I mean that which the intellect perceives of substance as constituting its essence.

5. By mode I mean the affections of substance, that is, that which is in something else and is conceived through something else.

6. By God I mean an absolutely infinite being, that is, substance consisting of infinite attributes, each of which expresses eternal and infinite essence.

Explication

I say 'absolutely infinite,' not 'infinite in its kind.' For if a thing is only infinite in its kind, one may deny that it has infinite attributes. But if a thing is absolutely infinite, whatever expresses essence and does not involve any negation belongs to its essence.

Reprinted by permission of the translator, Samuel Shirley, from Spinoza, *The Ethics and Selected Letters* (Indianapolis: Hackett Publishing Company, 1992).

7. That thing is said to be free [*liber*] which exists solely from the necessity of its own nature, and is determined to action by itself alone. A thing is said to be necessary [*necessarius*] or rather, constrained [*coactus*], if it is determined by another thing to exist and to act in a definite and determinate way.

8. By eternity I mean existence itself insofar as it is conceived as necessarily following solely from the definition of an eternal thing.

Explication

For such existence is conceived as an eternal truth, just as is the essence of the thing, and therefore cannot be explicated through duration or time, even if duration be conceived as without beginning and end.

AXIOMS

1. All things that are, are either in themselves or in something else.

2. That which cannot be conceived through another thing must be conceived through itself.

3. From a given determinate cause there necessarily follows an effect; on the other hand, if there be no determinate cause, it is impossible that an effect should follow.

4. The knowledge of an effect depends on, and involves, the knowledge of the cause.

5. Things which have nothing in common with each other cannot be understood through each other; that is, the conception of the one does not involve the conception of the other.

6. A true idea must agree with that of which it is the idea [*ideatum*].

7. If a thing can be conceived as not existing, its essence does not involve existence.

PROPOSITION 1

Substance is by nature prior to its affections.

Proof

This is evident from Defs. 3 and 5.

PROPOSITION 2

Two substances having different attributes have nothing in common.

Proof

This too is evident from Def. 3; for each substance must be in itself and be conceived through itself; that is, the conception of the one does not involve the conception of the other.

PROPOSITION 3

When things have nothing in common, one cannot be the cause of the other.

Proof

If things have nothing in common, then (Ax. 5) they cannot be understood through one another, and so (Ax. 4) one cannot be the cause of the other.

PROPOSITION 4

Two or more distinct things are distinguished from one another either by the difference of the attributes of the substances or by the difference of the affections of the substances.

Proof

All things that are, are either in themselves or in something else (Ax. 1); that is (Defs. 3 and 5), nothing exists external to the intellect except substances and their affections. Therefore, there can be nothing external to the intellect through which several things can be distinguished from one another except substances or (which is the same thing) (Def. 4) the attributes and the affections of substances.

PROPOSITION 5

In the universe there cannot be two or more substances of the same nature or attribute.

Proof

If there were several such distinct substances, they would have to be distinguished from one another either by a difference of attributes or by a difference of affections (Pr. 4). If they are distinguished only by a difference of attributes, then it will be granted that there cannot be more than one substance of the same attribute. But if they are distinguished by a difference of affections, then, since substance is by nature prior to its affections (Pr. 1), disregarding therefore its affections and considering substance in itself, that is (Def. 3 and Ax. 6) considering it truly, it cannot be conceived as distinguishable from another substance. That is (Pr. 4), there cannot be several such substances but only one.

PROPOSITION 6

One substance cannot be produced by another substance.

Proof

In the universe there cannot be two substances of the same attribute (Pr. 5), that is (Pr. 2), two substances having something in common. And so (Pr. 3) one cannot be the cause of the other; that is, one cannot be produced by the other.

Corollary

Hence it follows that substance cannot be produced by anything else. For in the universe there exists nothing but substances and their affections, as is evident from Ax. 1 and Defs. 3 and 5. But, by Pr. 6, it cannot be produced by another substance. Therefore, substance cannot be produced by anything else whatsoever.

Another Proof

This can be proved even more readily by the absurdity of the contradictory. For if substance could be produced by something else, the knowledge of substance would have to depend on the knowledge of its cause (Ax. 4), and so (Def. 3) it would not be substance.

PROPOSITION 7

Existence belongs to the nature of substance.

Proof

Substance cannot be produced by anything else (Cor. Pr. 6) and is therefore self-caused [*causa sui*]; that is (Def. 1), its essence necessarily involves existence; that is, existence belongs to its nature.

PROPOSITION 8

Every substance is necessarily infinite.

Proof

There cannot be more than one substance having the same attribute (Pr. 5), and existence belongs to the nature of substance (Pr. 7). It must therefore exist either as finite or as infinite. But it cannot exist as finite, for (Def. 2) it would have to be limited by another substance of the same nature, and that substance also would have to exist (Pr. 7). And so there would exist two substances of the same attribute, which is absurd (Pr. 5). Therefore, it exists as infinite.

Scholium 1

Since in fact to be finite is in part a negation and to be infinite is the unqualified affirmation of the existence of some nature, it follows from Proposition 7 alone that every substance must be infinite.

Scholium 2

I do not doubt that for those who judge things confusedly and are not accustomed to know things through their primary causes it is difficult to grasp the proof of Proposition 7. Surely, this is because they neither distinguish between the modification of substances and substances themselves, nor do they know how things are produced. And so it comes about that they ascribe to substances a beginning which they see natural things as having; for those who do not know the true causes of things confuse everything. Without any hesitation they imagine trees as well as men talking and stones as well as men being formed from seeds; indeed, any forms whatsoever are imagined to change into any other forms. So too, those who confuse the divine nature with human nature easily ascribe to God human emotions, especially so long as they are ignorant of how the latter are produced in the mind. But if men were to attend to the nature of substance, they would not doubt at all the truth of Proposition 7; indeed, this Proposition would be an axiom to all and would be ranked among universally accepted truisms. For by substance they would understand that which is in itself and is conceived through itself; that is, that the knowledge of which does not require the knowledge of any other thing. By modifications they would understand that which is in another thing, and whose conception is formed from the thing in which they are. Therefore, in the case of nonexistent modifications we can have true ideas of them since their essence is included in something else, with the result that they can be conceived through that something else, although they do not exist in actuality externally to the intellect. However, in the case of substances, because they are conceived only through themselves, their truth external to the intellect is only in themselves. So if someone were to say that he has a clear and distinct—that is, a true—idea of substance and that he nevertheless doubts whether such a substance exists, this would surely be just the same as if he were to declare that he has a true idea but nevertheless suspects that it may be false (as is obvious to anyone who gives his mind to it). Or if anyone asserts that substance is created, he at the same time asserts that a false idea has become true, than which nothing more absurd can be conceived. So it must necessarily be admitted that the existence of substance is as much an eternal truth as is its essence.

From here we can derive in another way that there cannot be but one [substance] of the same nature, and I think it worthwhile to set out the proof here. Now to do this in an orderly fashion I ask you to note:

1. The true definition of each thing involves and expresses nothing beyond the nature of the thing defined. Hence it follows that—

2. No definition involves or expresses a fixed number of individuals, since it expresses nothing but the nature of the thing defined. For example, the

definition of a triangle expresses nothing other than simply the nature of a triangle, and not a fixed number of triangles.

3. For each individual existent thing there must necessarily be a definite cause for its existence.

4. The cause for the existence of a thing must either be contained in the very nature and definition of the existent thing (in effect, existence belongs to its nature) or must have its being independently of the thing itself.

From these premises it follows that if a fixed number of individuals exist in Nature, there must necessarily be a cause why those individuals and not more or fewer exist. If, for example, in Nature twenty men were to exist (for the sake of greater clarity I suppose that they exist simultaneously and that no others existed in Nature before them), in order to account for the existence of these twenty men, it will not be enough for us to demonstrate the cause of human nature in general; it will furthermore be necessary to demonstrate the cause why not more or fewer than twenty men exist, since (Note 3) there must necessarily be a cause for the existence of each one. But this cause (Notes 2 and 3) cannot be contained in the nature of man, since the true definition of man does not involve the number twenty. So (Note 4) the cause of the existence of these twenty men, and consequently of each one, must necessarily be external to each one, and therefore we can reach the unqualified conclusion that whenever several individuals of a kind exist, there must necessarily be an external cause for their existence. Now since existence belongs to the nature of substance (as has already been shown in this Scholium) the definition of substance must involve necessary existence, and consequently the existence of substance must be concluded solely from its definition. But the existence of several substances cannot follow from the definition of substance (as I have already shown in Notes 2 and 3). Therefore, from the definition of substance it follows necessarily that there exists only one substance of the same nature, as was proposed.

PROPOSITION 9

The more reality or being a thing has, the more attributes it has.

Proof

This is evident from Definition 4.

PROPOSITION 10

Each attribute of one substance must be conceived through itself.

Proof

For an attribute is that which intellect perceives of substance as constituting its essence (Def. 4), and so (Def. 3) it must be conceived through itself.

Scholium

From this it is clear that although two attributes be conceived as really distinct, that is, one without the help of the other, still we cannot deduce therefrom that they constitute two entities, or two different substances. For it is in the nature of substance that each of its attributes be conceived through itself, since all the attributes it possesses have always been in it simultaneously, and one could not have been produced by another; but each expresses the reality or being of substance. So it is by no means absurd to ascribe more than one attribute to one substance. Indeed, nothing in Nature is clearer than that each entity must be conceived under some attribute, and the more reality or being it has, the more are its attributes which express necessity, or eternity, and infinity. Consequently, nothing can be clearer than this, too, that an absolutely infinite entity must necessarily be defined (Def. 6) as an entity consisting of infinite attributes, each of which expresses a definite essence, eternal and infinite. Now if anyone asks by what mark can we distinguish between different substances, let him read the following Propositions, which show that in Nature there exists only one substance, absolutely infinite. So this distinguishing mark would be sought in vain.

PROPOSITION 11

God, or substance consisting of infinite attributes, each of which expresses eternal and infinite essence, necessarily exists.

Proof

If you deny this, conceive, if you can, that God does not exist. Therefore (Ax. 7), his essence does not involve existence. But this is absurd (Pr. 7). Therefore, God necessarily exists.

Second Proof

For every thing a cause or reason must be assigned either for its existence or for its nonexistence. For example, if a triangle exists, there must be a reason, or cause, for its existence. If it does not exist, there must be a reason or cause which prevents it from existing, or which annuls its existence. Now this reason or cause must either be contained in the nature of the thing or be external to it. For example, the reason why a square circle does not exist is indicated by its very nature, in that it involves a contradiction. On the other hand, the reason for the existence of substance also follows from its nature alone, in that it involves existence (Pr. 7). But the reason for the existence or nonexistence of a circle or a triangle does not follow from their nature, but from the order of universal corporeal Nature. For it is from this latter that it necessarily follows that either the triangle necessarily exists at this moment or that its present existence is impossible. This is self-evident, and therefrom it follows that a thing necessarily exists if there is no reason or cause which prevents its existence. Therefore if there can be no reason or cause which prevents God from existing or which annuls his existence, we are bound to conclude that he necessarily exists. But if there were such a reason or cause, it would have to be either within God's nature or external to it; that is, it would have to be in another substance of another nature. For if it were of the same nature, by that very fact it would be granted that God exists. But a substance of another nature would have nothing in common with God (Pr. 2), and so could neither posit nor annul his existence. Since therefore there cannot be external to God's nature a reason or cause that would annul God's existence, then if indeed he does not exist, the reason or cause must necessarily be in God's nature, which would therefore involve a contradiction. But to affirm this of a Being absolutely infinite and in the highest degree perfect is absurd. Therefore neither in God nor external to God is there

any cause or reason which would annul his existence. Therefore, God necessarily exists.

A Third Proof

To be able to not exist is weakness; on the other hand, to be able to exist is power, as is self-evident. So if what now necessarily exists is nothing but finite entities, then finite entities are more potent than an absolutely infinite Entity—which is absurd. Therefore either nothing exists, or an absolutely infinite Entity necessarily exists, too. But we do exist, either in ourselves or in something else which necessarily exists (Ax. 1 and Pr. 7). Therefore, an absolutely infinite Entity—that is (Def. 6), God—necessarily exists.

Scholium

In this last proof I decided to prove God's existence *a posteriori* so that the proof may be more easily perceived, and not because God's existence does not follow *a priori* from this same basis. For since the ability to exist is power, it follows that the greater the degree of reality that belongs to the nature of a thing, the greater amount of energy it has for existence. So an absolutely infinite Entity or God will have from himself absolutely infinite power to exist, and therefore, exists absolutely.

But perhaps many will not readily find this proof convincing because they are used to considering only such things as derive from external causes. Of these things they observe that those which come quickly into being—that is, which readily exist—likewise readily perish, while things which they conceive as more complex they regard as more difficult to bring into being—that is, not so ready to exist. However, to free them from these misconceptions I do not need at this point to show what measure of truth there is in the saying, "Quickly come, quickly go," neither need I raise the question whether or not everything is equally easy in respect of Nature as a whole. It is enough to note simply this, that I am not here speaking of things that come into being through external causes, but only of substances, which (Pr. 6) cannot be produced by any external cause. For whether they consist of many parts or few, things that are brought about by external causes owe whatever degree of perfection or reality they possess entirely to the power of the external cause, and so their existence has its origin solely in the perfection of the external cause, and not in their own perfection. On the other hand, whatever perfection substance possesses is due to no external cause; therefore its existence, too, must follow solely from its own nature, and is therefore nothing else but its essence. So perfection does not annul a thing's existence: on the contrary, it posits it; whereas imperfection annuls a thing's existence. So there is nothing of which we can be more certain than the existence of an absolutely infinite or perfect Entity; that is, God. For since his essence excludes all imperfection and involves absolute perfection, it thereby removes all reason for doubting his existence and affords the utmost certainty of it. This, I think, must be quite clear to all who give a modicum of attention to the matter.

PROPOSITION 12

No attribute of substance can be truly conceived from which it would follow that substance can be divided.

Proof

The parts into which substance thus conceived would be divided will either retain the nature of substance or they will not. In the first case each part will have to be infinite (Pr. 8) and self-caused (Pr. 6) and consist of a different attribute (Pr. 5); and so several substances could be formed from one substance, which is absurd (Pr. 6). Furthermore, the parts would have nothing in common with the whole (Pr. 2), and the whole could exist and be conceived without its parts (Def. 4 and Pr. 10), the absurdity of which none can doubt. But in the latter case in which the parts will not retain the nature of substance—then when the whole substance would have been divided into equal parts it would lose the nature of substance and would cease to be. This is absurd (Pr. 7).

PROPOSITION 13

Absolutely infinite substance is indivisible.

Proof

If it were divisible, the parts into which it would be divided will either retain the nature of absolutely infinite substance, or not. In the first case, there would therefore be several substances of the same nature,

which is absurd (Pr. 5). In the second case, absolutely infinite substance can cease to be, which is also absurd (Pr. 11).

Corollary

From this it follows that no substance, and consequently no corporeal substance, insofar as it is substance, is divisible.

Scholium

The indivisibility of substance can be more easily understood merely from the fact that the nature of substance can be conceived only as infinite, and that a part of substance can mean only finite substance, which involves an obvious contradiction (Pr. 8).

PROPOSITION 14

There can be, or be conceived, no other substance but God.

Proof

Since God is an absolutely infinite being of whom no attribute expressing the essence of substance can be denied (Def. 6) and since he necessarily exists (Pr. 11), if there were any other substance but God, it would have to be explicated through some attribute of God, and so there would exist two substances with the same attribute, which is absurd (Pr. 5). So there can be no substance external to God, and consequently no such substance can be conceived. For if it could be conceived, it would have to be conceived necessarily as existing; but this is absurd (by the first part of this proof). Therefore, no substance can be or be conceived external to God.

Corollary 1

Hence it follows quite clearly that God is one: that is (Def. 6), in the universe there is only one substance, and this is absolutely infinite, as I have already indicated in Scholium Pr. 10.

Corollary 2

It follows that the thing extended and the thing thinking are either attributes of God or (Ax. 1) affections of the attributes of God.

PROPOSITION 15

Whatever is, is in God, and nothing can be or be conceived without God.

Proof

Apart from God no substance can be or be conceived (Pr. 14), that is (Def. 3), something which is in itself and is conceived through itself. Now modes (Def. 5) cannot be or be conceived without substance; therefore, they can be only in the divine nature and can be conceived only through the divine nature. But nothing exists except substance and modes (Ax. 1). Therefore, nothing can be or be conceived without God.

Scholium

Some imagine God in the likeness of man, consisting of mind and body, and subject to passions. But it is clear from what has already been proved how far they stray from the true knowledge of God. These I dismiss, for all who have given any consideration to the divine nature deny that God is corporeal. They find convincing proof of this in the fact that by body we understand some quantity having length, breadth, and depth, bounded by a definite shape; and nothing more absurd than this can be attributed to God, a being absolutely infinite.

At the same time, however, by other arguments which they try to prove their point, they show clearly that in their thinking corporeal or extended substance is set completely apart from the divine nature, and they assert that it is created by God. But they have no idea from what divine power it could have been created, which clearly shows that they don't know what they are saying. Now I have clearly proved—at any rate, in my judgment (Cor. Pr. 6 and Sch. 2 Pr. 8)—that no substance can be produced or created by anything else. Furthermore, in Proposition 14 we showed that apart from God no substance can be or be conceived, and hence we deduced that extended substance is one of God's infinite attributes.

However, for a fuller explanation I will refute my opponents' arguments, which all seem to come down to this. Firstly, they think that corporeal substance, insofar as it is substance, is made up of parts, and so they deny that it can be infinite, and consequently that it can pertain to God. This they illustrate with many examples, of which I will take one or two. They say that if corporeal substance is infinite, suppose it to be divided into two parts. Each of these parts will be either finite or infinite. If the former, then the infinite is made up of two finite parts, which is absurd. If the latter, then there is an infinite which is twice as great as another infinite, which is also absurd.

Again, if an infinite length is measured in feet, it will have to consist of an infinite number of feet; and if it is measured in inches, it will consist of an infinite number of inches. So one infinite number will be twelve times greater than another infinite number.

Lastly, if from one point in an infinite quantity two lines, AB and AC, be drawn of fixed and determinate length, and thereafter be produced to infinity, it is clear that the distance between B and C continues to increase and finally changes from a determinate distance to an indeterminate distance.

As these absurdities follow, they think, from supposing quantity to be infinite, they conclude that corporeal substance must be finite and consequently cannot pertain to God's essence.

The second argument is also drawn from God's consummate perfection. Since God, they say, is a supremely perfect being, he cannot be that which is acted upon. But corporeal substance, being divisible, can be acted upon. It therefore follows that corporeal substance does not pertain to God's essence.

These are the arguments I find put forward by writers who thereby seek to prove that corporeal substance is unworthy of the divine essence and cannot pertain to it. However, the student who looks carefully into these arguments will find that I have already replied to them, since they are all founded on the same supposition that material substance is composed of parts, and this I have already shown to be absurd (Pr. 12 and Cor. Pr. 13). Again, careful reflection will show that all those alleged absurdities (if indeed they are absurdities, which is not now under discussion) from which they seek to prove that extended substance is finite do not at all follow from the supposition that quantity is infinite, but that infinite quantity is measurable and is made up of finite parts. Therefore, from the resultant absurdities no other conclusion can be reached but that infinite quantity is not measurable and cannot be made up of finite parts. And this is exactly what we have already proved (Pr. 12). So the weapon they aimed at us is in fact turned against themselves. If therefore from this 'reductio ad absurdum' argument of theirs they still seek to deduce that extended substance must be finite, they are surely just like one who, having made the supposition that a circle has the properties of a square, deduces therefrom that a circle does not have a center from which all lines drawn to the circumference are equal. For corporeal substance, which can be conceived only as infinite, one, and indivisible (Prs. 8, 5, and 12), they conceive as made up of finite parts, multiplex, and divisible, so as to deduce that it is finite. In the same way others, too, having supposed that a line is composed of points, can find many arguments to prove that a line cannot be infinitely divided. Indeed, it is just as absurd to assert that corporeal substance is composed of bodies or parts as that a body is composed of surfaces, surfaces of lines, and lines of points. This must be admitted by all who know clear reason to be infallible, and particularly those who say that a vacuum cannot exist. For if corporeal substance could be so divided that its parts were distinct in reality, why could one part not be annihilated while the others remain joined together as before? And why should all the parts be so fitted together as to leave no vacuum? Surely, in the case of things which are in reality distinct from one another, one can exist without the other and remain in its original state. Since therefore there is no vacuum in Nature (of which [more] elsewhere) and all its parts must so harmonize that there is no vacuum, it also follows that the parts cannot be distinct in reality; that is, corporeal substance, insofar as it is substance, cannot be divided.

If I am now asked why we have this natural inclination to divide quantity, I reply that we conceive quantity in two ways, to wit, abstractly, or superficially—in other words, as represented in the imagination—or as substance, which we do only through the intellect. If therefore we consider quantity insofar as we represent it in the imagination—and this is what we more frequently and readily do—we find it to be finite, divisible, and made up of parts. But if we consider it intellectually and conceive it insofar as it is substance—and this is very difficult—then it will be found to be infinite, one, and indivisible, as we have already sufficiently proved. This will be quite clear to those who can distinguish between the imagination and the intellect, especially if this point also is stressed, that matter is everywhere the same, and there are no distinct parts in it except insofar as we conceive matter as modified in various ways. Then its parts are distinct, not really but only modally. For example, we conceive water to be divisible and to have separate parts insofar as it is water, but not insofar as it is material substance. In this latter respect it is not capable of separation or division. Furthermore, water, qua water, comes into existence and goes out of existence; but qua substance it does not come into existence nor go out of existence [*corrumpitur*].

I consider that in the above I have also replied to the second argument, since this too is based on the supposition that matter, insofar as it is substance, is divisible and made up of parts. And even though this were not so, I do not know why matter should be unworthy of the divine nature, since (Pr. 14) there can be no substance external to God by which it can be acted upon. All things, I repeat, are in God, and all things that come to pass do so only through the laws of God's infinite nature and follow through the necessity of his essence (as I shall later show). Therefore, by no manner of reasoning can it be said that God is acted upon by anything else or that extended substance is unworthy of the divine nature, even though it be supposed divisible, as long as it is granted to be eternal and infinite.

But enough of this subject for the present.

PROPOSITION 16

From the necessity of the divine nature there must follow infinite things in infinite ways [modis], *(that is, everything that can come within the scope of infinite intellect).*

Proof

This proposition should be obvious to everyone who will but consider this point, that from the given definition of any one thing the intellect infers a number of properties which necessarily follow in fact from the definition (that is, from the very essence of the thing), and the more reality the definition of the thing expresses (that is, the more reality the essence of the thing defined involves), the greater the number of its properties. Now since divine nature possesses absolutely infinite attributes (Def. 6), of which each one also expresses infinite essence in its own kind, then there must necessarily follow from the necessity of the divine nature an infinity of things in infinite ways (that is, everything that can come within the scope of the infinite intellect).

Corollary 1: Hence it follows that God is the efficient cause of all things that can come within the scope of the infinite intellect.

Corollary 2: Secondly, it follows that God is the cause through himself, not however *per accidens.*

Corollary 3: Thirdly, it follows that God is absolutely the first cause.

PROPOSITION 17

God acts solely from the laws of his own nature, constrained by none.

Proof

We have just shown that an infinity of things follow, absolutely, solely from the necessity of divine nature, or—which is the same thing—solely from the laws of that same nature (Pr. 16); and we have proved (Pr. 15) that nothing can be or be conceived without God, but that everything is in God. Therefore, there can be nothing external to God by which he can be determined or constrained to act. Thus God acts solely from the laws of his own nature and is constrained by none.

Corollary 1

Hence it follows, firstly, that there is no cause, except the perfection of his nature, which either extrinsically or intrinsically moves God to act.

Corollary 2

It follows, secondly, that God alone is a free cause. For God alone exists solely from the necessity of his own nature (Pr. 11 and Cor. 1 Pr. 14) and acts solely from the necessity of his own nature (Pr. 17). So he alone is a free cause (Def. 7).

Scholium

Others take the view that God is a free cause because—so they think—he can bring it about that those things which we have said follow from his nature—that is, which are within his power—should not come about; that is, they should not be produced by him. But this is as much as to say that God can bring it about that it should not follow from the nature of a triangle that its three angles are equal to two right angles, or that from a given cause the effect should not follow, which is absurd.

Furthermore, I shall show later on without the help of this proposition that neither intellect nor will pertain to the nature of God. I know indeed that there are many who think they can prove that intellect in the highest degree and free will belong to the nature of God; for they say they know of nothing more perfect which they may attribute to God than that which is the highest perfection in us. Again, although they conceive of God as having in actuality intellect in the highest degree, they yet do not believe he can bring about the existence of everything which in actuality he understands, for they think they would thereby be nullifying God's power. If, they say, he had created everything that is within his intellect, then he would not have been able to create anything more; and this they regard as inconsistent with God's omnipotence. So they have preferred to regard God as indifferent to everything and as creating nothing but what he has decided, by some absolute exercise of will, to create. However, I think I have shown quite clearly (Pr. 16) that from God's supreme power or infinite nature an infinity of things in infinite ways— that is, everything—has necessarily flowed or is always following from that same necessity, just as from the nature of a triangle it follows from eternity to eternity that its three angles are equal to two right angles. Therefore, God's omnipotence has from eternity been actual and will remain for eternity in the same actuality. In this way, I submit, God's omnipotence is established as being far more perfect. Indeed my opponents—let us speak frankly—seem to be denying God's omnipotence. For they are obliged to admit that God understands an infinite number of creatable things which nevertheless he can never create. If this were not so, that is, if he were to create all the things that he understands, he would exhaust his omnipotence, according to them, and render himself imperfect. Thus, to affirm God as perfect they are reduced to having to affirm at the same time that he cannot bring about everything that is within the bounds of his power. I cannot imagine anything more absurd than this, or more inconsistent with God's omnipotence.

Furthermore, I have something here to say about the intellect and will that is usually attributed to God. If intellect and will do indeed pertain to the eternal essence of God, one must understand in the case of both these attributes something very different from the meaning widely entertained. For the intellect and will that would constitute the essence of God would have to be vastly different from human intellect and will, and would have no point of agreement except the name. They could be no more alike than the celestial constellation of the Dog and the dog that barks. This I will prove as follows. If intellect does pertain to the divine nature, it cannot, like man's intellect, be posterior to (as most thinkers hold) or simultaneous with the objects of understanding, since God is prior in causality to all things (Cor. 1 Pr. 16). On the contrary, the truth and formal essence of things is what it is because it exists as such in the intellect of God as an object of thought. Therefore, God's intellect, insofar as it is conceived as constituting God's essence, is in actual fact the cause of things, in respect both of their essence and their existence. This seems to have been recognized also by those who have asserted that God's intellect, will, and power are one and the same. Since therefore God's intellect is the one and only cause of things, both of their essence and their existence, as we have shown, it must necessarily be different from them both in respect of essence and existence. For that which is caused differs from its cause precisely in what it has from its cause. For example, a man is the cause of the existence of another man, but not of the other's essence; for the essence is an eternal truth. So with regard to their essence the two men can be in full agreement, but they must differ with regard to existence; and for that reason if the existence of the one should cease, the existence of the other would not thereby cease. But if the essence of the one could be destroyed and rendered false, so too would the essence of the other. Therefore, a thing which is the cause of the essence and existence of some effect must differ from that effect both in respect of essence and existence. But

God's intellect is the cause of the essence and existence of man's intellect. Therefore, God's intellect, insofar as it is conceived as constituting the divine essence, differs from man's intellect both in respect of essence and existence, and cannot agree with it in any respect other than name—which is what I sought to prove. In the matter of will, the proof is the same, as anyone can readily see.

PROPOSITION 18

God is the immanent, not the transitive, cause of all things.

Proof

All things that are, are in God, and must be conceived through God (Pr. 15), and so (Cor. 1 Pr. 16) God is the cause of the things that are in him, which is the first point. Further, there can be no substance external to God (Pr. 14); that is (Def. 3), a thing which is in itself external to God—which is the second point. Therefore, God is the immanent, not the transitive, cause of all things.

PROPOSITION 19

God [is eternal], that is, all the attributes of God are eternal.

Proof

God is substance (Def. 6) which necessarily exists (Pr. 11); that is, (Pr. 7) a thing to whose nature it pertains to exist, or—and this is the same thing—a thing from whose definition existence follows; and so (Def. 8) God is eternal. Further, by the attributes of God must be understood that which expresses the essence of the Divine substance (Def. 4), that is, that which pertains to substance. It is this, I say, which the attributes themselves must involve. But eternity pertains to the nature of substance (as I have shown in Pr. 7). Therefore, each of the attributes must involve eternity, and so they are all eternal.

Scholium

This proposition is also perfectly clear from the manner in which I proved the existence of God (Pr. 11). From this proof, I repeat, it is obvious that God's existence is, like his essence, an eternal truth. Again, I have also proved God's eternity in another way in

Proposition 19 of my *Descartes's Principles of Philosophy*, and there is no need here to go over that ground again.

PROPOSITION 20

God's existence and his essence are one and the same.

Proof

God and all his attributes are eternal (Pr. 19); that is, each one of his attributes expresses existence (Def. 8). Therefore, the same attributes of God that explicate his eternal essence (Def. 4) at the same time explicate his eternal existence; that is, that which constitutes the essence of God at the same time constitutes his existence, and so his existence and his essence are one and the same.

Corollary 1

From this it follows, firstly, that God's existence, like his essence, is an eternal truth.

Corollary 2

It follows, secondly, that God is immutable; that is, all the attributes of God are immutable. For if they were to change in respect of existence, they would also have to change in respect of essence (Pr. 10); that is—and this is self-evident—they would have to become false instead of true, which is absurd.

PROPOSITION 21

All things that follow from the absolute nature of any attribute of God must have existed always, and as infinite; that is, through the said attribute they are eternal and infinite.

Proof

Suppose this proposition be denied and conceive, if you can, that something in some attribute of God, following from its absolute nature, is finite and has a determinate existence or duration; for example, the idea of God in Thought. Now Thought, being assumed to be an attribute of God, is necessarily infinite by its own nature (Pr. 11). However, insofar as it has the idea of God, it is being supposed as finite. Now (Def. 2) it cannot be conceived as finite unless it is

determined through Thought itself. But it cannot be determined through Thought itself insofar as Thought constitutes the idea of God, for it is in that respect that Thought is supposed to be finite. Therefore, it is determined through Thought insofar as Thought does not constitute the idea of God, which Thought must nevertheless necessarily exist (Pr. 11). Therefore, there must be Thought which does not constitute the idea of God, and so the idea of God does not follow necessarily from its nature insofar as it is absolute Thought. (For it is conceived as constituting and as not constituting the idea of God.) This is contrary to our hypothesis. Therefore, if the idea of God in Thought, or anything in some attribute of God (it does not matter what is selected, since the proof is universal), follows from the necessity of the absolute nature of the attribute, it must necessarily be infinite. That was our first point.

Furthermore, that which thus follows from the necessity of the nature of some attribute cannot have a determinate existence, or duration. If this be denied, suppose that there is in some attribute of God a thing following from the necessity of the nature of the attribute, for example, the idea of God in Thought, and suppose that this thing either did not exist at some time, or will cease to exist in the future. Now since Thought is assumed as an attribute of God, it must necessarily exist, and as immutable (Pr. 11 and Cor. 2 Pr. 20). Therefore, outside the bounds of the duration of the idea of God (for this idea is supposed at some time not to have existed, or will at some point cease to exist) Thought will have to exist without the idea of God. But this is contrary to the hypothesis, for it is supposed that when Thought is granted the idea of God necessarily follows. Therefore, the idea of God in Thought, or anything that necessarily follows from the absolute nature of some attribute of God, cannot have a determinate existence, but is eternal through that same attribute. That was our second point. Note that the same holds for anything in an attribute of God which necessarily follows from the absolute nature of God.

PROPOSITION 22

Whatever follows from some attribute of God, insofar as the attribute is modified by a modification that exists necessarily and as infinite through that same attribute, must also exist both necessarily and as infinite.

Proof

This proposition is proved in the same way as the preceding one.

PROPOSITION 23

Every mode which exists necessarily and as infinite must have necessarily followed either from the absolute nature of some attribute of God or from some attribute modified by a modification which exists necessarily and as infinite.

Proof

A mode is in something else through which it must be conceived (Def. 5); that is (Pr. 15), it is in God alone and can be conceived only through God. Therefore, if a mode is conceived to exist necessarily and to be infinite, both these characteristics must necessarily be inferred or perceived through some attribute of God insofar as that attribute is conceived to express infinity and necessity of existence, or (and by Def. 8 this is the same) eternity; that is (Def. 6 and Pr. 19), insofar as it is considered absolutely. Therefore, a mode which exists necessarily and as infinite must have followed from the absolute nature of some attribute of God, either directly (Pr. 21) or through the mediation of some modification which follows from the absolute nature of the attribute; that is (Pr. 22), which exists necessarily and as infinite.

PROPOSITION 24

The essence of things produced by God does not involve existence.

Proof

This is evident from Def. 1. For only that whose nature (considered in itself) involves existence is self-caused and exists solely from the necessity of its own nature.

Corollary

Hence it follows that God is the cause not only of the coming into existence of things but also of their continuing in existence, or, to use a scholastic term, God is the cause of the being of things [*essendi rerum*]. For whether things exist or do not exist, in reflecting on their essence we realize that this essence involves neither existence nor duration. So it is not their essence which can be the cause of either their existence or their duration, but only God, to whose nature alone existence pertains (Cor. 1 Pr. 14).

PROPOSITION 25

God is the efficient cause not only of the existence of things but also of their essence.

Proof

If this is denied, then God is not the cause of the essence of things, and so (Ax. 4) the essence of things can be conceived without God. But this is absurd (Pr. 15). Therefore, God is also the cause of the essence of things.

Scholium

This proposition follows more clearly from Pr. 16; for from that proposition it follows that from the given divine nature both the essence and the existence of things must be inferred. In a word, in the same sense that God is said to be self-caused he must also be said to be the cause of all things. This will be even clearer from the following Corollary.

Corollary

Particular things are nothing but affections of the attributes of God, that is, modes wherein the attributes of God find expression in a definite and determinate way. The proof is obvious from Pr. 15 and Def. 5.

PROPOSITION 26

A thing which has been determined to act in a particular way has necessarily been so determined by God; and a thing which has not been determined by God cannot determine itself to act.

Proof

That by which things are said to be determined to act in a particular way must necessarily be something positive (as is obvious). So God, from the necessity of his nature, is the efficient cause both of its essence and its existence (Prs. 25 and 16)—which was the first point. From this the second point quite clearly follows as well. For if a thing which has not been determined by God could determine itself, the first part of this proposition would be false, which, as I have shown, is absurd.

PROPOSITION 27

A *thing which has been determined by God to act in a particular way cannot render itself undetermined.*

Proof

This proposition is evident from Axiom 3.

PROPOSITION 28

Every individual thing, i.e., anything whatever which is finite and has a determinate existence, cannot exist or be determined to act unless it be determined to exist and to act by another cause which is also finite and has a determinate existence, and this cause again cannot exist or be determined to act unless it be determined to exist and to act by another cause which is also finite and has a determinate existence, and so ad infinitum.

Proof

Whatever is determined to exist and to act has been so determined by God (Pr. 26 and Cor. Pr. 24). But that which is finite and has a determinate existence cannot have been produced by the absolute nature of one of God's attributes, for whatever follows from the absolute nature of one of God's attributes is infinite and eternal (Pr. 21). It must therefore have followed from God or one of his attributes insofar as that is considered as affected by some mode; for nothing exists but substance and its modes (Ax. 1 and Defs. 3 and 5), and modes (Cor. Pr. 25) are nothing but affections of God's attributes. But neither could a finite and determined thing have followed from God or one of his attributes insofar as that is affected by a modification which is eternal and infinite (Pr. 22). Therefore, it must have followed, or been determined to exist and to act, by God or one of his attributes insofar as it was modified by a modification which is finite and has a determinate existence. That was the first point. Then again this cause or this mode (the reasoning is the same as in the first part of this proof) must also have been determined by another cause, which is also finite and has a determinate

existence, and again this last (the reasoning is the same) by another, and so *ad infinitum*.

Scholium

Since some things must have been produced directly by God (those things, in fact, which necessarily follow from his absolute nature) and others through the medium of these primary things (which other things nevertheless cannot be or be conceived without God), it follows, firstly, that God is absolutely the proximate cause of things directly produced by him. I say 'absolutely' [*absolute*], and not 'in its own kind' [*suo genere*], as some say. For the effects of God can neither be nor be conceived without their cause (Pr. 15 and Cor. Pr. 24). It follows, secondly, that God cannot properly be said to be the remote cause of individual things, unless perchance for the purpose of distinguishing these things from things which he has produced directly, or rather, things which follow from his absolute nature. For by 'remote cause' we understand a cause which is in no way conjoined with its effect. But all things that are, are in God, and depend on God in such a way that they can neither be nor be conceived without him.

PROPOSITION 29

Nothing in nature is contingent, but all things are from the necessity of the divine nature determined to exist and to act in a definite way.

Proof

Whatever is, is in God (Pr. 15). But God cannot be termed a contingent thing, for (Pr. 11) he exists necessarily, not contingently. Again, the modes of the divine nature have also followed from it necessarily, not contingently (Pr. 16), and that, too, whether insofar as the divine nature is considered absolutely (Pr. 21) or insofar as it is considered as determined to act in a definite way (Pr. 27). Furthermore, God is the cause of these modes not only insofar as they simply exist (Cor. Pr. 24), but also insofar as they are considered as determined to a particular action (Pr. 26). Now if they are not determined by God (Pr. 26), it is an impossibility, not a contingency, that they should determine themselves. On the other hand (Pr. 27), if they are determined by God, it is an impossibility, not a contingency, that they should render themselves undetermined. Therefore, all things are determined from the necessity of the divine nature not only to exist but also to exist and to act in a definite way. Thus, there is no contingency.

Scholium

Before I go any further, I wish to explain at this point what we must understand by 'Natura naturans' and 'Natura naturata.' I should perhaps say not 'explain,' but 'remind the reader,' for I consider that it is already clear from what has gone before that by 'Natura naturans' we must understand that which is in itself and is conceived through itself; that is, the attributes of substance that express eternal and infinite essence; or (Cor. 1 Pr. 14 and Cor. 2 Pr. 17), God insofar as he is considered a free cause. By 'Natura naturata' I understand all that follows from the necessity of God's nature, that is, from the necessity of each one of God's attributes; or all the modes of God's attributes insofar as they are considered as things which are in God and can neither be nor be conceived without God.

PROPOSITION 30

The finite intellect in act or the infinite intellect in act must comprehend the attributes of God and the affections of God, and nothing else.

Proof

A true idea must agree with its object [*ideatum*] (Ax. 6); that is (as is self-evident), that which is contained in the intellect as an object of thought must necessarily exist in Nature. But in Nature (Cor. 1 Pr. 14) there is but one substance—God—and no other affections (Pr. 15) than those which are in God and that can neither be nor be conceived (Pr. 15) without God. Therefore, the finite intellect in act or the infinite intellect in act must comprehend the attributes of God and the affections of God, and nothing else.

PROPOSITION 31

The intellect in act, whether it be finite or infinite, as also will, desire, love etc., must be related to Natura naturata, not to Natura naturans.

Proof

By intellect (as is self-evident) we do not understand absolute thought, but only a definite mode of thinking which differs from other modes such as desire, love, etc., and so (Def. 5) must be conceived through absolute thought—that is (Pr. 15 and Def. 6), an attribute of God which expresses the eternal and infinite essence of thought—in such a way that without this attribute it can neither be nor be conceived; and therefore (Sch. Pr. 29) it must be related to Natura naturata, not to Natura naturans, just like the other modes of thinking.

Scholium

The reason for my here speaking of the intellect in act is not that I grant there can be any intellect in potentiality, but that, wishing to avoid any confusion, I want to confine myself to what we perceive with the utmost clarity, to wit, the very act of understanding, than which nothing is more clearly apprehended by us. For we can understand nothing that does not lead to a more perfect cognition of the understanding.

PROPOSITION 32

Will cannot be called a free cause, but only a necessary cause.

Proof

Will, like intellect, is only a definite mode of thinking, and so (Pr. 28) no single volition can exist or be determined to act unless it is determined by another cause, and this cause again by another, and so *ad infinitum*. Now if will be supposed infinite, it must also be determined to exist and to act by God, not insofar as he is absolutely infinite substance, but insofar as he possesses an attribute which expresses the infinite and eternal essence of Thought (Pr. 23). Therefore, in whatever way will is conceived, whether finite or infinite, it requires a cause by which it is determined to exist and to act; and so (Def. 7) it cannot be said to be a free cause, but only a necessary or constrained cause.

Corollary 1

Hence it follows, firstly, that God does not act from freedom of will.

Corollary 2

It follows, secondly, that will and intellect bear the same relationship to God's nature as motion-and-rest and, absolutely, as all natural phenomena that must be determined by God (Pr. 29) to exist and to act in a definite way. For will, like all the rest, stands in need of a cause by which it may be determined to exist and to act in a definite manner. And although from a given will or intellect infinite things may follow, God cannot on that account be said to act from freedom of will any more than he can be said to act from freedom of motion-and-rest because of what follows from motion-and-rest (for from this, too, infinite things follow). Therefore, will pertains to God's nature no more than do other natural phenomena. It bears the same relationship to God's nature as does motion-and-rest and everything else that we have shown to follow from the necessity of the divine nature and to be determined by that divine nature to exist and to act in a definite way.

PROPOSITION 33

Things could not have been produced by God in any other way or in any other order than is the case.

Proof

All things have necessarily followed from the nature of God (Pr. 16) and have been determined to exist and to act in a definite way from the necessity of God's nature (Pr. 29). Therefore, if things could have been of a different nature or been determined to act in a different way so that the order of Nature would have been different, then God's nature, too, could have been other than it now is, and therefore (Pr. 11) this different nature, too, would have had to exist, and consequently there would have been two or more Gods, which (Cor. 1, Pr. 14) is absurd. Therefore, things could not have been produced by God in any other way or in any other order than is the case.

Scholium 1

Since I have here shown more clearly than the midday sun that in things there is absolutely nothing by virtue of which they can be said to be 'contingent,' I now wish to explain briefly what we should understand by 'contingent'; but I must first deal with 'necessary' and 'impossible.' A thing is termed 'necessary' either by reason of its essence or by reason of its cause. For a thing's existence necessarily follows either from its essence and definition or from a given efficient cause. Again, it is for these same reasons that a thing is termed 'impossible'—that is, either because its essence or definition involves a contradiction or because there is no external cause determined to bring it into existence. But a thing is termed 'contingent' for no other reason than the deficiency of our knowledge. For if we do not know whether the essence of a thing involves a contradiction, or if, knowing full well that its essence does not involve a contradiction, we still cannot make any certain judgment as to its existence because the chain of causes is hidden from us, then that thing cannot appear to us either as necessary or as impossible. So we term it either 'contingent' or 'possible.'

Scholium 2

It clearly follows from the above that things have been brought into being by God with supreme perfection, since they have necessarily followed from a most perfect nature. Nor does this imply any imperfection in God, for it is his perfection that has constrained us to make this affirmation. Indeed, from its contrary it would clearly follow (as I have just shown) that God is not supremely perfect, because if things had been brought into being in a different way by God, we should have to attribute to God another nature different from that which consideration of a most perfect Being has made us attribute to him.

However, I doubt not that many will ridicule this view as absurd and will not give their minds to its examination, and for this reason alone, that they are in the habit of attributing to God another kind of freedom very different from that which we (Def. 7) have assigned to him, that is, an absolute will. Yet I do not doubt that if they were willing to think the matter over and carefully reflect on our chain of proofs they would in the end reject the kind of freedom which they now attribute to God not only as nonsensical but as a serious obstacle to science. It is needless for me here to repeat what was said in the Scholium to Proposition 17. Yet for their sake I shall proceed to show that, even if it were to be granted that will pertains to the essence of God, it would nevertheless follow from his perfection that things could not have been created by God in any other way or in any other order. This will readily be shown if we first consider—as they themselves grant—that on God's decree and will alone does it depend that each thing is what it is. For otherwise God would not be the cause of all things. Further, there is the fact that all God's decrees have been sanctioned by God from eternity, for otherwise he could be accused of imperfection and inconstancy. But since the eternal does not admit of 'when' or 'before' or 'after,' it follows merely from God's perfection that God can never decree otherwise nor ever could have decreed otherwise; in other words, God could not have been prior to his decrees nor can he be without them. "But," they will say, "granted the supposition that God had made a different universe, or that from eternity he had made a different decree concerning Nature and her order, no imperfection in God would follow therefrom." But if they say this, they will be granting at the same time that God can change his decrees. For if God's decrees had been different from what in fact he has decreed regarding Nature and her order—that is, if he had willed and conceived differently concerning Nature—he would necessarily have had a different intellect and a different will from that which he now has. And if it is permissible to attribute to God a different intellect and a different will without any change in his essence and perfection, why should he not now be able to change his decrees concerning created things, and nevertheless remain equally perfect? For his intellect and will regarding created things and their order have the same relation to his essence and perfection, in whatever manner it be conceived.

Then again, all philosophers whom I have read grant that in God there is no intellect in potentiality but only intellect in act. Now since all of them also grant that his intellect and will are not distinct from his essence, it therefore follows from this, too, that if God had had a different intellect in act and a different will, his essence too would necessarily have been different. Therefore—as I deduced from the beginning—if things had been brought into being by God so as to be different from what they now are, God's intellect and will—that is (as is granted), God's essence—must have been different, which is absurd. Therefore, since things could not have been brought

into being by God in any other way or order—and it follows from God's supreme perfection that this is true—surely we can have no sound reason for believing that God did not wish to create all the things that are in his intellect through that very same perfection whereby he understands them.

"But," they will say, "there is in things no perfection or imperfection; that which is in them whereby they are perfect or imperfect, and are called good or bad, depends only on the will of God. Accordingly, if God had so willed it he could have brought it about that that which is now perfection should be utmost imperfection, and vice versa." But what else is this but an open assertion that God, who necessarily understands that which he wills, can by his will bring it about that he should understand things in a way different from the way he understands them—and this, as I have just shown, is utterly absurd. So I can turn their own argument against them, as follows. All things depend on the power of God. For things to be able to be otherwise than as they are, God's will, too, would necessarily have to be different. But God's will cannot be different (as we have just shown most clearly from the consideration of God's perfection). Therefore, neither can things be different.

I admit that this view which subjects everything to some kind of indifferent will of God and asserts that everything depends on his pleasure diverges less from the truth than the view of those who hold that God does everything with the good in mind. For these people seem to posit something external to God that does not depend upon him, to which in acting God looks as if it were a model, or to which he aims, as if it were a fixed target. This is surely to subject God to fate; and no more absurd assertion can be made about God, whom we have shown to be the first and the only free cause of both the essence and the existence of things. So I need not spend any more time in refuting this absurdity.

PROPOSITION 34

God's power is his very essence.

Proof

From the sole necessity of God's essence it follows that God is self-caused (Pr. 11) and the cause of all things (Pr. 16 and Cor.). Therefore, God's power, whereby he and all things are and act, is his very essence.

PROPOSITION 35

Whatever we conceive to be within God's power necessarily exists.

Proof

Whatever is within God's power must be so comprehended in his essence (Pr. 34) that it follows necessarily from it, and thus necessarily exists.

PROPOSITION 36

Nothing exists from whose nature an effect does not follow.

Proof

Whatever exists expresses God's nature or essence in a definite and determinate way (Cor. Pr. 25); that is (Pr. 34), whatever exists expresses God's power, which is the cause of all things, in a definite and determinate way, and so (Pr. 16) some effect must follow from it.

APPENDIX

I have now explained the nature and properties of God: that he necessarily exists, that he is one alone, that he is and acts solely from the necessity of his own nature, that he is the free cause of all things and how so, that all things are in God and are so dependent on him that they can neither be nor be conceived without him, and lastly, that all things have been predetermined by God, not from his free will or absolute pleasure, but from the absolute nature of God, his infinite power. Furthermore, whenever the opportunity arose I have striven to remove prejudices that might hinder the apprehension of my proofs. But since there still remain a considerable number of prejudices, which have been, and still are, an obstacle—indeed, a very great obstacle—to the acceptance of the concatenation of things in the manner which I have expounded, I have thought it proper at this point to bring these prejudices before the bar of reason.

Now all the prejudices which I intend to mention here turn on this one point, the widespread belief among men that all things in Nature are like themselves in acting with an end in view. Indeed, they hold it as certain that God himself directs everything to a fixed end; for they say that God has made everything for man's sake and has made man so that he should worship God. So this is the first point I shall consider, seeking the reason why most people are victims of this prejudice and why all are so naturally disposed to accept it. Secondly, I shall demonstrate its falsity; and lastly I shall show how it has been the source of misconceptions about good and bad, right and wrong, praise and blame, order and confusion, beauty and ugliness, and the like.

However, it is not appropriate here to demonstrate the origin of these misconceptions from the nature of the human mind. It will suffice at this point if I take as my basis what must be universally admitted, that all men are born ignorant of the causes of things, that they all have a desire to seek their own advantage, a desire of which they are conscious. From this it follows, firstly, that men believe that they are free, precisely because they are conscious of their volitions and desires; yet concerning the causes that have determined them to desire and will they do not think, not even dream about, because they are ignorant of them. Secondly, men act always with an end in view, to wit, the advantage that they seek. Hence it happens that they are always looking only for the final causes of things done, and are satisfied when they find them, having, of course, no reason for further doubt. But if they fail to discover them from some external source, they have no recourse but to turn to themselves, and to reflect on what ends would normally determine them to similar actions, and so they necessarily judge other minds by their own. Further, since they find within themselves and outside themselves a considerable number of means very convenient for the pursuit of their own advantage—as, for instance, eyes for seeing, teeth for chewing, cereals and living creatures for food, the sun for giving light, the sea for breeding fish—the result is that they look on all the things of Nature as means to their own advantage. And realizing that these were found, not produced by them, they come to believe that there is someone else who produced these means for their use. For looking on things as means, they could not believe them to be self-created, but on the analogy of the means which they are accustomed to produce for themselves, they were bound to conclude that there was some governor or governors of Nature, endowed with human freedom, who have attended to all their needs and made everything for their use. And having no information on the subject, they also had to estimate the character of these rulers by their own, and so they asserted that the gods direct everything for man's use so that they may bind men to them and be held in the highest honor by them. So it came about that every individual devised different methods of worshipping God as he thought fit in order that God should love him beyond others and direct the whole of Nature so as to serve his blind cupidity and insatiable greed. Thus it was that this misconception developed into superstition and became deep-rooted in the minds of men, and it was for this reason that every man strove most earnestly to understand and to explain the final causes of all things. But in seeking to show that Nature does nothing in vain—that is, nothing that is not to man's advantage—they seem to have shown only this, that Nature and the gods are as crazy as mankind.

Consider, I pray, what has been the upshot. Among so many of Nature's blessings they were bound to discover quite a number of disasters, such as storms, earthquakes, diseases, and so forth, and they maintained that these occurred because the gods were angry at the wrongs done to them by men, or the faults committed in the course of their worship. And although daily experience cried out against this and showed by any number of examples that blessings and disasters befall the godly and the ungodly alike without discrimination, they did not on that account abandon their ingrained prejudice. For they found it easier to regard this fact as one among other mysteries they could not understand and thus maintain their innate condition of ignorance rather than to demolish in its entirety the theory they had constructed and devise a new one. Hence they made it axiomatic that the judgment of the gods is far beyond man's understanding. Indeed, it is for this reason, and this reason only, that truth might have evaded mankind forever had not Mathematics, which is concerned not with ends but only with the essences and properties of figures, revealed to men a different standard of truth. And there are other causes too—there is no need to mention them here—which could have made men aware of these widespread misconceptions and brought them to a true knowledge of things.

I have thus sufficiently dealt with my first point. There is no need to spend time in going on to show that Nature has no fixed goal and that all final causes are but figments of the human imagination. For I think that this is now quite evident, both from the basic causes from which I have traced the origin of this misconception and from Proposition 16 and the Corollaries to Proposition 32, and in addition from the whole set or proofs I have adduced to show that all things in Nature proceed from all eternal necessity and with supreme perfection. But I will make this additional point, that this doctrine of Final Causes turns Nature completely upside down, for it regards as an effect that which is in fact a cause, and vice versa. Again, it makes that which is by nature first to be last; and finally, that which is highest and most perfect is held to be the most imperfect. Omitting the first two points as self-evident, Propositions 21, 22, and 23 make it clear that that effect is most perfect which is directly produced by God, and an effect is the less perfect in proportion to the number of intermediary causes required for its production. But if the things produced directly by God were brought about to enable him to attain an end, then of necessity the last things for the sake of which the earlier things were brought about would excel all others. Again, this doctrine negates God's perfection; for if God acts with an end in view, he must necessarily be seeking something that he lacks. And although theologians and metaphysicians may draw a distinction between a purpose arising from want and an assimilative purpose, they still admit that God has acted in all things for the sake of himself, and not for the sake of the things to be created. For prior to creation they are not able to point to anything but God as a purpose for God's action. Thus they have to admit that God lacked and desired those things for the procurement of which he willed to create the means—as is self-evident.

I must not fail to mention here that the advocates of this doctrine, eager to display their talent in assigning purpose to things, have introduced a new style of argument to prove their doctrine, i.e., a reduction, not to the impossible, but to ignorance, thus revealing the lack of any other argument in its favor. For example, if a stone falls from the roof on somebody's head and kills him, by this method of arguing they will prove that the stone fell in order to kill the man; for if it had not fallen for this purpose by the will of God, how could so many circumstances (and there are often many coinciding circumstances) have chanced to concur? Perhaps you will reply that the event occurred because the wind was blowing and the man was walking that way. But they will persist in asking why the wind blew at that time and why the man was walking that way at that very time. If you again reply that the wind sprang up at that time because on the previous day the sea had begun to toss after a period of calm and that the man had been invited by a friend, they will again persist—for there is no end to questions—"But why did the sea toss, and why was the man invited for that time?" And so they will go on and on asking the causes of causes, until you take refuge in the will of God—that is, the sanctuary of ignorance. Similarly, when they consider the structure of the human body, they are astonished, and being ignorant of the causes of such skillful work they conclude that it is fashioned not by mechanical art but by divine or supernatural art, and is so arranged that no one part shall injure another.

As a result, he who seeks the true causes of miracles and is eager to understand the works of Nature as a scholar, and not just to gape at them like a fool, is universally considered an impious heretic and denounced by those to whom the common people bow down as interpreters of Nature and the gods. For these people know that the dispelling of ignorance would entail the disappearance of that astonishment, which is the one and only support for their argument and for safeguarding their authority. But I will leave this subject and proceed to the third point that I proposed to deal with.

When men become convinced that everything that is created is created on their behalf, they were bound to consider as the most important quality in every individual thing that which was most useful to them, and to regard as of the highest excellence all those things by which they were most benefited. Hence they came to form these abstract notions to explain the natures of things: Good, Bad, Order, Confusion, Hot, Cold, Beauty, Ugliness; and since they believe that they are free, the following abstract notions came into being: Praise, Blame, Right, Wrong. The latter I shall deal with later on after I have treated of human nature; at this point I shall briefly explain the former.

All that conduces to well being and to the worship of God they call Good, and the contrary, Bad. And since those who do not understand the nature of things, but only imagine things, make no affirmative judgments about things themselves and mistake their imagination for intellect, they are firmly convinced that there is order in things, ignorant as they are of things and of their own nature. For when things are in such arrangement that, being presented to us through our senses, we can readily picture them and thus readily remember them, we say that they are well arranged; if the contrary, we say that they are ill arranged, or confused. And since those things we can readily picture we find pleasing compared with other things, men prefer order to confusion, as though order were something in Nature other than what is relative to our imagination. And they say that God has created all things in an orderly way, without realizing that they are thus attributing human imagination to God—unless perchance they mean that God, out of consideration for the human imagination, arranged all things in the way that men could most easily imagine. And perhaps they will find no obstacle in the fact that there are any number of things that far surpass our imagination, and a considerable number that confuse the imagination because of its weakness.

But I have devoted enough time to this. Other notions, too, are nothing but modes of imagining whereby the imagination is affected in various ways, and yet the ignorant consider them as important attributes of things because they believe—as I have said—that all things were made on their behalf, and they call a thing's nature good or bad, healthy or rotten and corrupt, according to its effect on them. For instance, if the motion communicated to our nervous system by objects presented through our eyes is conducive to our feeling of well being, the objects which are its cause are said to be beautiful, while the objects which provoke a contrary motion are called ugly. Those things that we sense through the nose are called fragrant or fetid; through the tongue, sweet or bitter, tasty or tasteless; those that we sense by touch are called hard or soft, rough or smooth, and so on. Finally, those that we sense through our ears are said to give forth noise, sound, or harmony, the last of which has driven men to such madness that they used to believe that even God delights in harmony. There are philosophers who have convinced themselves that the motions of the heavens give rise to harmony. All this goes to show that everyone's judgment is a function of the disposition of his brain, or rather, that he mistakes for reality the way his imagination is affected. Hence it is no wonder—as we should note in passing—that we find so many controversies arising among men, resulting finally in skepticism. For although human bodies agree in many respects, there are very many differences, and so one man thinks good what another thinks bad; what to one man is well ordered, to another is confused; what to one is pleasing, to another is displeasing, and so forth. I say no more here because this is not the place to treat at length of this subject, and also because all are well acquainted with it from experience. Everybody knows those sayings: "So many heads, so many opinions," "everyone is wise in his own sight," "brains differ as much as palates," all of which show clearly that men's judgment is a function of the disposition of the brain, and they are guided by imagination rather than intellect. For if men understood things, all that I have put forward would be found, if not attractive, at any rate convincing, as Mathematics attests.

We see therefore that all the notions whereby the common people are wont to explain Nature are merely modes of imagining, and denote not the nature of any thing but only the constitution of the imagination. And because these notions have names as if they were the names of entities existing independently of the imagination I call them 'entities of imagination' [*entia imaginationis*] rather than 'entities of reason' [*entia rationis*]. So all arguments drawn from such notions against me can be easily refuted. For many are wont to argue on the following lines: If everything has followed from the necessity of God's most perfect nature, why does Nature display so many imperfections, such as rottenness to the point of putridity, nauseating ugliness, confusion, evil, sin, and so on? But, as I have just pointed out, they are easily refuted. For the perfection of things should be measured solely from their own nature and power; nor are things more or less perfect to the extent that they please or offend human senses, serve or oppose human interests. As to those who ask why God did not create men in such a way that they should be governed solely by reason, I make only this reply, that he lacked not material for creating all things from the highest to the lowest degree of perfection; or, to speak more accurately, the laws of his nature were

so comprehensive as to suffice for the production of everything that can be conceived by an infinite intellect, as I proved in Proposition 16.

These are the misconceptions which I undertook to deal with at this point. Any other misconception of this kind can be corrected by everyone with a little reflection.

Part II
OF THE NATURE AND ORIGIN OF THE MIND

I now pass on to the explication of those things that must necessarily have followed from the essence of God, the eternal and infinite Being; not indeed all of them—for we proved in Proposition 16 Part I that from his essence there must follow infinite things in infinite ways—but only those things that can lead us as it were by the hand to the knowledge of the human mind and its utmost blessedness.

DEFINITIONS

1. By 'body' I understand a mode that expresses in a definite and determinate way God's essence insofar as he is considered as an extended thing. (See Cor. Pr. 25, I)

2. I say that there pertains to the essence of a thing that which, when granted, the thing is necessarily posited, and by the annulling of which the thing is necessarily annulled; or that without which the thing can neither be nor be conceived, and, vice versa, that which cannot be or be conceived without the thing.

3. By idea I understand a conception of the Mind which the Mind forms because it is a thinking thing.

Explication

I say 'conception' rather than 'perception' because the term perception seems to indicate that the Mind is passive to its object, whereas conception seems to express an activity of the Mind.

4. By an adequate idea I mean an idea which, insofar as it is considered in itself without relation to its

object, has all the properties—that is, intrinsic characteristics—of a true idea [*ideatum*].

Explication

I say 'intrinsic' so as to exclude the extrinsic characteristic—to wit, the agreement of the idea with that of which it is an idea.

5. Duration is the indefinite continuance of existing.

Explication

I say 'indefinite' because it can in no wise be determined through the nature of the existing thing, nor again by the thing's efficient cause which necessarily posits, but does not annul, the existence of the thing.

6. By reality and perfection I mean the same thing.

7. By individual things [*res singulares*] I mean things that are finite and have a determinate existence. If several individual things concur in one act in such a way as to be all together the simultaneous cause of one effect, I consider them all, in that respect, as one individual.

AXIOMS

1. The essence of man does not involve necessary existence; that is, from the order of Nature it is equally possible that a certain man exists or does not exist.

2. Man thinks.

3. Modes of thinking such as love, desire, or whatever emotions are designated by name, do not occur unless there is in the same individual the idea of the thing loved, desired, etc. But the idea can be without any other mode of thinking.

4. We feel a certain body to be affected in many ways.

5. We do not feel or perceive any individual things except bodies and modes of thinking. [N.B.: For Postulates, see after Proposition 13.]

PROPOSITION 1

Thought is an attribute of God; i.e., God is a thinking thing.

Proof

Individual thoughts, or this and that thought, are modes expressing the nature of God in a definite and determinate way (Cor. Pr. 25, I). Therefore there belongs to God (Def. 5, I) an attribute the conception of which is involved in all individual thoughts, and through which they are conceived. Thought, therefore, is one of God's infinite attributes, expressing the eternal and infinite essence of God (Def. 6, I); that is, God is a thinking thing.

Scholium

This Proposition is also evident from the fact that we can conceive of an infinite thinking being. For the more things a thinking being can think, the more reality or perfection we conceive it to have. Therefore a being that can think infinite things in infinite ways is by virtue of its thinking necessarily infinite. Since therefore by merely considering Thought we conceive an infinite being, Thought is necessarily one of the infinite attributes of God (Defs. 4 and 6, I), as we set out to prove.

PROPOSITION 2

Extension is an attribute of God; i.e., God is an extended thing.

Proof

This Proposition is proved in the same way as the preceding proposition.

PROPOSITION 3

In God there is necessarily the idea both of his essence and of everything that necessarily follows from his essence.

Proof

For God can (Pr. 1, II) think infinite things in infinite ways, or (what is the same thing, by Pr. 16, I) can form the idea of his own essence and of everything that necessarily follows from it. But all that is in God's power necessarily exists (Pr. 35, I). Therefore such an idea necessarily exists, and only in God (Pr. 15, I).

Scholium

By God's power the common people understand free will and God's right over all things that are, which things are therefore commonly considered as contingent. They say that God has power to destroy everything and bring it to nothing. Furthermore, they frequently compare God's power with that of kings. But this doctrine we have refuted in Cors. 1 and 2, Pr. 32, I; and in Pr. 16, I, we proved that God acts by the same necessity whereby he understands himself; that is, just as it follows from the necessity of the divine nature (as is universally agreed) that God understands himself, by that same necessity it also follows that God acts infinitely in infinite ways. Again, we showed in Pr. 34, I that God's power is nothing but God's essence in action, and so it is as impossible for us to conceive that God does not act as that God does not exist. Furthermore, if one wished to pursue the matter, I could easily show here that the power that common people assign to God is not only a human power (which shows that they conceive God as a man or like a man) but also involves negation of power. But I am reluctant to hold forth so often on the same subject. I merely request the reader most earnestly to reflect again and again on what we said on this subject in Part I from Proposition 16 to the end. For nobody will rightly apprehend what I am trying to say unless he takes great care not to confuse God's power with a king's human power or right.

PROPOSITION 4

The idea of God, from which infinite things follow in infinite ways, must be one, and one only.

Proof

Infinite intellect comprehends nothing but the attributes of God and his affections (Pr. 30, I). But God is one, and one only (Cor. 1, Pr. 14, I). Therefore the idea of God, from which infinite things follow in infinite ways, must be one, and one only.

PROPOSITION 5

The formal being of ideas recognizes God as its cause only insofar as he is considered as a thinking thing, and not insofar as he is explicated by any other attribute; that is, the ideas both of God's attributes and of individual things recognize as their efficient cause not the things of which they are ideas,—that is, the things perceived,—but God himself insofar as he is a thinking thing.

Proof

This is evident from Pr. 3, II. For there our conclusion that God can form the idea of his own essence and of everything that necessarily follows therefrom was inferred solely from God's being a thinking thing, and not from his being the object of his own idea. Therefore the formal being of ideas recognizes God as its cause insofar as he is a thinking thing. But there is another proof, as follows. The formal being of ideas is a mode of thinking (as is self-evident); that is (Cor. Pr. 25, I), a mode which expresses in a definite manner the nature of God insofar as he is a thinking thing, and so does not involve (Pr. 10, I) the conception of any other attribute of God. Consequently (Ax. 4, I), it is the effect of no other attribute but Thought; and so the formal being of ideas recognizes God as its cause only insofar as he is considered as a thinking thing.

PROPOSITION 6

The modes of any attribute have God for their cause only insofar as he is considered under that attribute, and not insofar as he is considered under any other attribute.

Proof

Each attribute is conceived through itself independently of any other (Pr. 10, I). Therefore the modes of any attribute involve the conception of their own attribute, and not that of any other. Therefore they have God for their cause only insofar as he is considered under the attribute of which they are modes, and not insofar as he is considered under any other attribute (Ax. 4, I).

Corollary

Hence it follows that the formal being of things that are not modes of thinking does not follow from the nature of God by reason of his first having known them; rather, the objects of ideas follow and are inferred from their own attributes in the same way and by the same necessity as we have shown ideas to follow from the attribute of Thought.

PROPOSITION 7

The order and connection of ideas is the same as the order and connection of things.

Proof

This is evident from Ax. 4, I; for the idea of what is caused depends on the knowledge of the cause of which it is the effect.

Corollary

Hence it follows that God's power of thinking is coextensive with his actualized power of acting. That is, whatever follows formally from the infinite nature of God, all this follows from the idea of God as an object of thought in God according to the same order and connection.

Scholium

At this point, before proceeding further, we should recall to mind what I have demonstrated above—that whatever can be perceived by infinite intellect as constituting the essence of substance pertains entirely to the one sole substance. Consequently, thinking substance and extended substance are one and the same substance, comprehended now under this attribute, now under that. So, too, a mode of Extension and the idea of that mode are one and the same thing, expressed in two ways. This truth seems to have been glimpsed by some of the Hebrews,[1] who hold that God, God's intellect, and the things understood by God are one and the same. For example, a circle existing in Nature and the idea of the existing circle—which is also in God—are one and the same thing,

1. [The reference is most likely to Moses Maimonides, *The Guide of The Perplexed*, Part 1, Chapter 68.—S.S.]

explicated through different attributes. And so, whether we conceive Nature under the attribute of Extension or under the attribute of Thought or under any other attribute, we find one and the same order, or one and the same connection of causes—that is, the same things following one another. When I said that God is the cause, e.g., of the idea of a circle only insofar as he is a thinking thing, and of a circle only insofar as he is an extended thing, my reason was simply this, that the formal being of the idea of a circle can be perceived only through another mode of thinking as its proximate cause, and that mode through another, and so *ad infinitum*, with the result that as long as things are considered as modes of thought, we must explicate the order of the whole of Nature, or the connection of causes, through the attribute of Thought alone; and insofar as things are considered as modes of Extension, again the order of the whole of Nature must be explicated through the attribute of Extension only. The same applies to other attributes. Therefore God, insofar as he consists of infinite attributes, is in fact the cause of things as they are in themselves. For the present, I cannot give a clearer explanation.

PROPOSITION 8

The ideas of nonexisting individual things or modes must be comprehended in the infinite idea of God in the same way as the formal essences of individual things or modes are contained in the attributes of God.

Proof

This proposition is obvious from the preceding one, but may be understood more clearly from the preceding Scholium.

Corollary

Hence it follows that as long as individual things do not exist except insofar as they are comprehended in the attributes of God, their being as objects of thought—that is, their ideas—do not exist except insofar as the infinite idea of God exists; and when individual things are said to exist not only insofar as they are comprehended in the attributes of God but also insofar as they are said to have duration, their ideas also will involve the existence through which they are said to have duration.

Scholium

Should anyone want an example for a clearer understanding of this matter, I can think of none at all that would adequately explicate the point with which I am here dealing, for it has no parallel. Still, I shall try to illustrate it as best I can. The nature of a circle is such that the rectangles formed from the segments

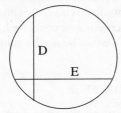

of its intersecting chords are equal. Hence an infinite number of equal rectangles are contained in a circle, but none of them can be said to exist except insofar as the circle exists, nor again can the idea of any one of these rectangles be said to exist except insofar as it is comprehended in the idea of the circle. Now of this infinite number of intersecting chords let two, E and D, exist. Now indeed their ideas also exist not only insofar as they are merely comprehended in the idea of the circle but also insofar as they involve the existence of those rectangles, with the result that they are distinguished from the other ideas of the other rectangles.

PROPOSITION 9

The idea of an individual thing existing in actuality has God for its cause not insofar as he is infinite but insofar as he is considered as affected by another idea of a thing existing in actuality, of which God is the cause insofar as he is affected by a third idea, and so ad infinitum.

Proof

The idea of an individual actually existing thing is an individual mode of thinking distinct from other modes (Cor. and Sch. Pr. 8, II), and so (Pr. 6, II) it has God as its cause only insofar as he is a thinking thing. But not (Pr. 28, I) insofar as he is a thinking

thing absolutely, but insofar as he is considered as affected by another definite mode of thinking. And of this latter God is also the cause insofar as he is affected by another definite mode of thinking, and so *ad infinitum*. But the order and connection of ideas is the same as the order and connection of causes (Pr. 7, II). Therefore an individual idea is caused by another idea; i.e., God insofar as he is considered as affected by another idea. And this last idea is caused by God, insofar as he is affected by yet another idea, and so *ad infinitum*.

Corollary

Whatsoever happens in the individual object of any idea, knowledge of it is in God only insofar as he has the idea of that object.

Proof

Whatsoever happens in the object of any idea, the idea of it is in God (Pr. 3, II) not insofar as he is infinite, but insofar as he is considered as affected by another idea of an individual thing (preceding Pr.). But the order and connection of ideas is the same as the order and connection of things (Pr. 7, II). Therefore the knowledge of what happens in an individual object is in God only insofar as he has the idea of that object.

PROPOSITION 10

The being of substance does not pertain to the essence of man; i.e., substance does not constitute the form [forma] of man.

Proof

The being of substance involves necessary existence (Pr. 7, I). So if the being of substance pertained to the essence of man, man would necessarily be granted together with the granting of substance (Def. 2, II), and consequently man would necessarily exist, which is absurd (Ax. 1, II). Therefore . . . etc.

Scholium

This Proposition is also proved from Pr. 5, I, which states that there cannot be two substances of the same nature. Now since many men can exist, that which constitutes the form of man is not the being of substance. This Proposition is furthermore evident from the other properties of substance—that substance is by its own nature infinite, immutable, indivisible, etc., as everyone can easily see.

Corollary

Hence it follows that the essence of man is constituted by definite modifications of the attributes of God.

Proof

For the being of substance does not pertain to the essence of man (preceding Pr.), which must therefore (Pr. 15, I) be something that is in God, and which can neither be nor be conceived without God; i.e., an affection or mode (Cor. Pr. 25, I) which expresses the nature of God in a definite and determinate way.

Scholium

All must surely admit that nothing can be or be conceived without God. For all are agreed that God is the sole cause of all things, both of their essence and their existence; that is, God is the cause of things not only in respect of their coming into being [*secundum fieri*], as they say, but also in respect of their being. But at the same time many assert that that without which a thing can neither be nor be conceived pertains to the essence of the thing, and so they believe that either the nature of God pertains to the essence of created things or that created things can either be or be conceived without God; or else, more probably, they hold no consistent opinion. I think that the reason for this is their failure to observe the proper order of philosophical enquiry. For the divine nature, which they should have considered before all else— it being prior both in cognition and in Nature—they have taken to be last in the order of cognition, and the things that are called objects of sense they have taken as prior to everything. Hence it has come about that in considering natural phenomena, they have completely disregarded the divine nature. And when thereafter they turned to the contemplation of the divine nature, they could find no place in their thinking for those fictions on which they had built their natural science, since these fictions were of no avail in attaining knowledge of the divine nature. So it is

little wonder that they have contradicted themselves on all sides.

But I pass over these points, for my present purpose is restricted to explaining why I have not said that that without which a thing can neither be nor be perceived pertains to the essence of the thing. My reason is that individual things can neither be nor be conceived without God, and yet God does not pertain to their essence. But I did say that that necessarily constitutes the essence of a thing which, when posited, posits the thing, and by the annulling of which the thing is annulled; i.e., that without which the thing can neither be nor be conceived, and vice versa, that which can neither be nor be conceived without the thing.

PROPOSITION 11

That which constitutes the actual being of the human mind is basically nothing else but the idea of an individual actually existing thing.

Proof

The essence of man (Cor. Pr. 10, II) is constituted by definite modes of the attributes of God, to wit (Ax. 2, II), modes of thinking. Of all these modes the idea is prior in nature (Ax. 3, II), and when the idea is granted, the other modes—modes to which the idea is prior by nature—must be in the same individual (Ax. 3, II). And so the idea is that which basically constitutes the being of the human mind. But not the idea of a nonexisting thing; for then (Cor. Pr. 8, II) the idea itself could not be said to exist. Therefore, it is the idea of an actually existing thing. But not the idea of an infinite thing, for an infinite thing (Prs. 21 and 22, I) must always necessarily exist, and this is absurd (Ax. 1, II). Therefore that which first constitutes the actual being of the human mind is the idea of an individual actually existing thing.

Corollary

Hence it follows that the human mind is part of the infinite intellect of God; and therefore when we say that the human mind perceives this or that, we are saying nothing else but this: that God—not insofar as he is infinite but insofar as he is explicated through the nature of the human mind, that is, insofar as he constitutes the essence of the human mind—has this or that idea. And when we say that God has this or that idea not only insofar as he constitutes the essence of the human mind but also insofar as he has the idea of another thing simultaneously with the human mind, then we are saying that the human mind perceives a thing partially or inadequately.

Scholium

At this point our readers will no doubt find themselves in some difficulty and will think of many things that will give them pause. So I ask them to proceed slowly step by step with me, and to postpone judgment until they have read to the end.

PROPOSITION 12

Whatever happens in the object of the idea constituting the human mind is bound to be perceived by the human mind; i.e., the idea of that thing will necessarily be in the human mind. That is to say, if the object of the idea constituting the human mind is a body, nothing can happen in that body without its being perceived by the mind.

Proof

Whatever happens in the object of any idea, knowledge thereof is necessarily in God (Cor. Pr. 9, II) insofar as he is considered as affected by the idea of that object; that is, (Pr. 11, II) insofar as he constitutes the mind of some thing. So whatever happens in the object of the idea constituting the human mind, knowledge thereof is necessarily in God insofar as he constitutes the nature of the human mind; that is (Cor. Pr. 11, II), knowledge of that thing is necessarily in the mind; i.e., the mind perceives it.

Scholium

This Proposition is also obvious, and is more clearly understood from Sch. Pr. 7, II, q.v.

PROPOSITION 13

The object of the idea constituting the human mind is the body—i.e., a definite mode of extension actually existing, and nothing else.

Proof

If the body were not the object of the human mind, the ideas of the affections of the body would not be in God (Cor. Pr. 9, II) insofar as he constitutes our mind, but insofar as he constitutes the mind of another thing; that is, (Cor. Pr. 11, II) the ideas of the affections of the body would not be in our mind. But (Ax. 4, II) we do have ideas of the affections of a body. Therefore the object of the idea constituting the human mind is a body, a body actually existing (Pr. 11, II). Again, if there were another object of the mind apart from the body, since nothing exists from which some effect does not follow (Pr. 36, I), there would necessarily have to be in our mind the idea of some effect of it (Pr. 12, II). But (Ax. 5, II) there is no such idea. Therefore the object of our mind is an existing body, and nothing else.

Corollary

Hence it follows that man consists of mind and body, and the human body exists according as we sense it.

Scholium

From the above we understand not only that the human Mind is united to the Body but also what is to be understood by the union of Mind and Body. But nobody can understand this union adequately or distinctly unless he first gains adequate knowledge of the nature of our body. For what we have so far demonstrated is of quite general application, and applies to men no more than to other individuals, which are all animate, albeit in different degrees. For there is necessarily in God an idea of each thing whatever, of which idea God is the cause in the same way as he is the cause of the idea of the human body. And so whatever we have asserted of the idea of the human body must necessarily be asserted of the idea of each thing. Yet we cannot deny, too, that ideas differ among themselves as do their objects, and that one is more excellent and contains more reality than another, just as the object of one idea is more excellent than that of another and contains more reality. Therefore, in order to determine the difference between the human mind and others and in what way it surpasses them, we have to know the nature of its object, (as we have said); that is, the nature of the human body. Now I cannot here explain this nature, nor is it essential for the points that I intend to demonstrate. But I will make this general assertion, that in proportion as a body is more apt than other bodies to act or be acted upon simultaneously in many ways, so is its mind more apt than other minds to perceive many things simultaneously; and in proportion as the actions of one body depend on itself alone and the less that other bodies concur with it in its actions, the more apt is its mind to understand distinctly. From this we can realise the superiority of one mind over others, and we can furthermore see why we have only a very confused knowledge of our body, and many other facts which I shall deduce from this basis in what follows. Therefore I have thought it worthwhile to explicate and demonstrate these things more carefully. To this end there must be a brief preface concerning the nature of bodies.

Axiom 1

All bodies are either in motion or at rest.

Axiom 2

Each single body can move at varying speeds.

Lemma 1

Bodies are distinguished from one another in respect of motion and rest, quickness and slowness, and not in respect of substance.

Proof

The first part of this Lemma I take to be self-evident. As to bodies not being distinguished in respect of substance, this is evident from both Pr. 5 and Pr. 8, Part I, and still more clearly from Sch. Pr. 15, Part I.

Lemma 2

All bodies agree in certain respects.

Proof

All bodies agree in this, that they involve the conception of one and the same attribute (Def. 1, II), and also in that they may move at varying speeds, and may be absolutely in motion or absolutely at rest.

Lemma 3

A body in motion or at rest must have been determined to motion or rest by another body, which likewise has been determined to motion or rest by another body, and that body by another, and so *ad infinitum*.

Proof

Bodies are individual things (Def. 1, II) which are distinguished from one another in respect of motion and rest (Lemma 1), and so (Pr. 28, I) each body must have been determined to motion or rest by another individual thing, namely, another body (Pr. 6, II), which is also in motion or at rest (Ax. 1). But this body again—by the same reasoning—could not have been in motion or at rest unless it had been determined to motion or rest by another body, and this body again—by the same reasoning—by another body, and so on, *ad infinitum*.

Corollary

Hence it follows that a body in motion will continue to move until it is determined to rest by another body, and a body at rest continues to be at rest until it is determined to move by another body. This, too, is self-evident; for when I suppose, for example, that a body A is at rest and I give no consideration to other moving bodies, I can assert nothing about body A but that it is at rest. Now if it should thereafter happen that body A is in motion, this surely could not have resulted from the fact that it was at rest; for from that fact nothing else could have followed than that body A should be at rest. If on the other hand A were supposed to be in motion, as long as we consider only A, we can affirm nothing of it but that it is in motion. If it should thereafter happen that A should be at rest, this surely could not have resulted from its previous motion; for from its motion nothing else could have followed but that A was in motion. So this comes about from a thing that was not in A, namely, an external cause by which the moving body A was determined to rest.

Axiom 1

All the ways in which a body is affected by another body follow from the nature of the affected body together with the nature of the body affecting it, so that one and the same body may move in various ways in accordance with the various natures of the bodies causing its motion; and, on the other hand, different bodies may be caused to move in different ways by one and the same body.

Axiom 2

When a moving body collides with a body at rest and is unable to cause it to move, it is reflected so as to continue its motion, and the angle between the line of motion of the reflection and the plane of the body at rest with which it has collided is equal to the angle between the line of incidence of motion and the said plane.

So far we have been discussing the simplest bodies, those which are distinguished from one another solely by motion and rest, quickness and slowness. Now let us advance to composite bodies.

Definition

When a number of bodies of the same or different magnitude form close contact with one another through the pressure of other bodies upon them, or if they are moving at the same or different rates of speed so as to preserve an unvarying relation of movement among themselves, these bodies are said to be united with one another and all together to form one body or individual thing, which is distinguished from other things through this union of bodies.

Axiom 3

The degree of difficulty with which the parts of an individual thing or composite body can be made to change their position and consequently the degree of difficulty with which the individual takes on different shapes, is proportional to the extent of the surface areas along which they are in close contact. Hence bodies whose parts maintain close contact along large areas of their surfaces I term hard; those whose parts maintain contact along small surface areas I term soft; while those whose parts are in a state of motion among themselves I term liquid.

Lemma 4

If from a body, or an individual thing composed of a number of bodies, certain bodies are separated, and at the same time a like number of other bodies of the same nature take their place, the individual thing will retain its nature as before, without any change in its form [*forma*].

Proof

Bodies are not distinguished in respect of substance (Lemma 1). That which constitutes the form of the individual thing consists in a union of bodies (preceding definition). But this union, by hypothesis, is retained in spite of the continuous change of component bodies. Therefore the individual thing will retain its own nature as before, both in respect of substance and of mode.

Lemma 5

If the parts of an individual thing become greater or smaller, but so proportionately that they all preserve the same mutual relation of motion-and-rest as before, the individual thing will likewise retain its own nature as before without any change in its form.

Proof

The reasoning is the same as in the preceding Lemma.

Lemma 6

If certain bodies composing an individual thing are made to change the existing direction of their motion, but in such a way that they can continue their motion and keep the same mutual relation as before, the individual thing will likewise preserve its own nature without any change of form.

Proof

This is self-evident; for, by hypothesis, the individual thing retains all that we, in defining it, asserted as constituting its form.

Lemma 7

Furthermore, the individual thing so composed retains its own nature, whether as a whole it is moving or at rest, and in whatever direction it moves, provided that each constituent part retains its own motion and continues to communicate this motion to the other parts.

Proof

This is evident from its definition, which you will find preceding Lemma 4.

Scholium

We thus see how a composite individual can be affected in many ways and yet preserve its nature. Now hitherto we have conceived an individual thing composed solely of bodies distinguished from one another only by motion-and-rest and speed of movement; that is, an individual thing composed of the simplest bodies. If we now conceive another individual thing composed of several individual things of different natures, we shall find that this can be affected in many other ways while still preserving its nature. For since each one of its parts is composed of several bodies, each single part can therefore (preceding Lemma), without any change in its nature, move with varying degrees of speed and consequently communicate its own motion to other parts with varying degrees of speed. Now if we go on to conceive a third kind of individual things composed of this second kind, we shall find that it can be affected in many other ways without any change in its form. If we thus continue to infinity, we shall readily conceive the whole of Nature as one individual whose parts—that is, all the constituent bodies—vary in infinite ways without any change in the individual as a whole.

If my intention had been to write a full treatise on body, I should have had to expand my explications and demonstrations. But I have already declared a different intention, and the only reason for my dealing with this subject is that I may readily deduce therefrom what I have set out to prove.

POSTULATES

1. The human body is composed of very many individual parts of different natures, each of which is extremely complex.

2. Of the individual components of the human body, some are liquid, some are soft, and some are hard.

3. The individual components of the human body, and consequently the human body itself, are affected by external bodies in a great many ways.

4. The human body needs for its preservation a great many other bodies, by which, as it were [quasi], it is continually regenerated.

5. When a liquid part of the human body is determined by an external body to impinge frequently on another part which is soft, it changes the surface of that part and impresses on it certain traces of the external body acting upon it.

6. The human body can move external bodies and dispose them in a great many ways.

PROPOSITION 14

The human mind is capable of perceiving a great many things, and this capacity will vary in proportion to the variety of states which its body can assume.

Proof

The human body (Posts. 3 and 6) is affected by external bodies in a great many ways and is so structured that it can affect external bodies in a great many ways. But the human mind must perceive all that happens in the human body (Pr. 12, II). Therefore the human mind is capable of perceiving very many things, and . . . etc.

PROPOSITION 15

The idea which constitutes the formal being of the human mind is not simple, but composed of very many ideas.

Proof

The idea which constitutes the formal being of the human mind is the idea of the body (Pr. 13, II), which is composed of a great number of very composite individual parts (Postulate 1). But in God there is necessarily the idea of every individual component part (Cor. Pr. 8, II). Therefore (Pr. 7, II) the idea of the human body is composed of these many ideas of the component parts.

PROPOSITION 16

The idea of any mode wherein the human body is affected by external bodies must involve the nature of the human body together with the nature of the external body.

Proof

All the modes wherein a body is affected follow from the nature of the body affected together with the nature of the affecting body (Ax. 1 after Cor. Lemma 3). Therefore the idea of these modes will necessarily involve the nature of both bodies (Ax. 4, I). So the idea of any mode wherein the human body is affected by an external body involves the nature of the human body and the external body.

Corollary 1

Hence it follows that the human mind perceives the nature of very many bodies along with the nature of its own body.

Corollary 2

Secondly, the ideas that we have of external bodies indicate the constitution of our own body more than the nature of external bodies. This I have explained with many examples in Appendix, Part I.

PROPOSITION 17

If the human body is affected in a way [modo] *that involves the nature of some external body, the human mind will regard that same external body as actually existing, or as present to itself, until the human body undergoes a further modification which excludes the existence or presence of the said body.*

Proof

This is evident; for as long as the human body is thus affected, so long will the human mind (Pr. 12, II) regard this affection of the body; that is (by the preceding Proposition), so long will it have the idea of a mode existing in actuality, an idea involving the nature of an external body; that is, an idea which does not exclude but posits the existence or presence of the nature of the external body. So the mind (Cor.1 of the preceding Proposition) will regard the external body as actually existing, or as present, until . . . etc.

Corollary

The mind is able to regard as present external bodies by which the human body has been once affected, even if they do not exist and are not present.

Proof

When external bodies so determine the fluid parts of the human body that these frequently impinge on the softer parts, they change the surfaces of these softer parts (Post.5). Hence it comes about (Ax.2 after Cor. Lemma 3) that the fluid parts are reflected therefrom in a manner different from what was previously the case; and thereafter, again coming into contact with the said changed surfaces in the course of their own spontaneous motion, they are reflected in the same way as when they were impelled towards those surfaces by external bodies. Consequently, in continuing this reflected motion they affect the human body in the same manner, which manner will again be the object of thought in the mind (Pr. 12, II); that is (Pr. 17, II), the mind will again regard the external body as present. This will be repeated whenever the fluid parts of the human body come into contact with those same surfaces in the course of their own spontaneous motion. Therefore, although the external bodies by which the human body has once been affected may no longer exist, the mind will regard them as present whenever this activity of the body is repeated.

Scholium

So we see how it can come about that we regard as present things which are not so, as often happens. Now it is possible that there are other causes for this fact, but it is enough for me at this point to have indicated one cause through which I can explicate the matter just as if I had demonstrated it through its true cause. Yet I do not think that I am far from the truth, since all the postulates that I have assumed contain scarcely anything inconsistent with experience; and after demonstrating that the human body exists just as we sense it (Cor. Pr. 13, II), we may not doubt experience.

In addition (preceding Cor. and Cor. 2 Pr. 16, II), this gives a clear understanding of the difference between the idea, e.g., of Peter which constitutes the essence of Peter's mind, and on the other hand the idea of Peter which is in another man, say Paul. The former directly explicates the essence of Peter's body, and does not involve existence except as long as Peter exists. The latter indicates the constitution of Paul's body rather than the nature of Peter; and so, while that constitution of Paul's body continues to be, Paul's mind will regard Peter as present to him although Peter may not be in existence. Further, to retain the usual terminology, we will assign the word 'images' [*imagines*] to those affections of the human body the ideas of which set forth external bodies as if they were present to us, although they do not represent shapes. And when the mind regards bodies in this way, we shall say that it 'imagines' [*imaginari*].

At this point, to begin my analysis of error, I should like you to note that the imaginations of the mind, looked at in themselves, contain no error; i.e., the mind does not err from the fact that it imagines, but only insofar as it is considered to lack the idea which excludes the existence of those things which it imagines to be present to itself. For if the mind, in imagining nonexisting things to be present to it, knew at the same time that those things did not exist in fact, it would surely impute this power of imagining not to the defect but to the strength of its own nature, especially if this faculty of imagining were to depend solely on its own nature; that is, (Def. 7, I) if this faculty of imagining were free.

PROPOSITION 18

If the human body has once been affected by two or more bodies at the same time, when the mind afterwards imagines one of them, it will straightway remember the others too.

Proof

The mind imagines (preceding Cor.) any given body for the following reason, that the human body is affected and conditioned by the impressions of an external body in the same way as it was affected when certain of its parts were acted upon by the external body. But, by hypothesis, the human mind was at that time conditioned in such a way that the mind imagined two bodies at the same time. Therefore it will now also imagine two bodies at the same time, and the mind, in imagining one of them, will straightway remember the other as well.

Scholium

Hence we clearly understand what memory is. It is simply a linking of ideas involving the nature of things outside the human body, a linking which occurs in the mind parallel to the order and linking of the affections of the human body. I say, firstly, that it is only the linking of those ideas that involve the nature of things outside the human body, not of those ideas that explicate the nature of the said things. For they are in fact (Pr. 16, II) ideas of the affections of the human body which involve the nature both of the human body and of external bodies. Secondly, my purpose in saying that this linking occurs in accordance with the order and linking of the affections of the human body is to distinguish it from the linking of ideas in accordance with the order of the intellect whereby the mind perceives things through their first causes, and which is the same in all men.

Furthermore, from this we clearly understand why the mind, from thinking of one thing, should straightway pass on to thinking of another thing which has no likeness to the first. For example, from thinking of the word 'pomum' [apple] a Roman will straightway fall to thinking of the fruit, which has no likeness to that articulated sound nor anything in common with it other than that the man's body has often been affected by them both; that is, the man has often heard the word 'pomum' while seeing the fruit. So everyone will pass on from one thought to another according as habit in each case has arranged the images in his body. A soldier, for example, seeing the tracks of a horse in the sand will straightway pass on from thinking of the horse to thinking of the rider, and then thinking of war, and so on. But a peasant, from thinking of a horse, will pass on to thinking of a plough, and of a field, and so on. So every person will pass on from thinking of one thing to thinking of another according as he is in the habit of joining together and linking the images of things in various ways.

PROPOSITION 19

The human mind has no knowledge of the body, nor does it know it to exist, except through ideas of the affections by which the body is affected.

Proof

The human mind is the very idea or knowledge of the human body (Pr. 13, II), and this idea is in God (Pr. 9, II) insofar as he is considered as affected by another idea of a particular thing; or, since (Post. 4) the human body needs very many other bodies by which it is continually regenerated, and the order and connection of ideas is the same (Pr. 7, II) as the order and connection of causes, this idea is in God insofar as he is considered as affected by the ideas of numerous particular things. Therefore God has the idea of the human body, or knows the human body, insofar as he is affected by numerous other ideas, and not insofar as he constitutes the nature of the human mind; that is, (Cor. Pr. 11, II), the human mind does not know the human body. But the ideas of the affections of the body are in God insofar as he does constitute the nature of human mind; i.e., the human mind perceives these affections (Pr. 12, II) and consequently perceives the human body (Pr. 16, II), and perceives it as actually existing (Pr. 17, II). Therefore, it is only to that extent that the human mind perceives the human body.

PROPOSITION 20

There is also in God the idea or knowledge of the human mind, and this follows in God and is related to God in the same way as the idea or knowledge of the human body.

Proof

Thought is an attribute of God (Pr. 1, II), and so (Pr. 3, II) the idea of both Thought and its affections—and consequently of the human mind as well—must necessarily be in God. Now this idea or knowledge of the mind does not follow in God insofar as he is infinite, but insofar as he is affected by another idea of a particular thing (Pr. 9, II). But the order and connection of ideas is the same as the order and connection of causes (Pr. 7, II). Therefore, the idea or knowledge of the mind follows in God and is related to God in the same way as the idea or knowledge of the body.

PROPOSITION 21

This idea of the mind is united to the mind in the same way as the mind is united to the body.

Proof

That the mind is united to the body we have shown from the fact that the body is the object of the mind (Prs. 12 and 13, II), and so by the same reasoning the idea of the mind must be united to its object—that is, to the mind itself—in the same way as the mind is united to the body.

Scholium

This proposition is understood far more clearly from Sch. Pr. 7, II. There we showed that the idea of the body and the body itself—that is, (Pr. 13, II) mind and body—are one and the same individual thing, conceived now under the attribute of Thought and now under the attribute of Extension. Therefore, the idea of the mind and the mind itself are one and the same thing, conceived under one and the same attribute, namely, Thought. The idea of the mind, I repeat, and the mind itself follow in God by the same necessity and from the same power of thought. For in fact the idea of the mind—that is, the idea of an idea—is nothing other than the form [*forma*] of the idea insofar as the idea is considered as a mode of thinking without relation to its object. For as soon as anyone knows something, by that very fact he knows that he knows, and at the same time he knows that he knows that he knows, and so on *ad infinitum*. But I will deal with this subject later.

PROPOSITION 22

The human mind perceives not only the affections of the body but also the ideas of these affections.

Proof

The ideas of ideas of affections follow in God and are related to God in the same way as ideas of affections, which can be proved in the same manner as Pr. 20, II. But the ideas of affections of the body are in the human mind (Pr. 12, II); that is (Cor. Pr. 11, II), in God insofar as he constitutes the essence of the human mind. Therefore the ideas of these ideas will be in God insofar as he has knowledge or the idea of the human mind; that is (Pr. 21, II), they will be in the human mind itself, which therefore perceives not only the affections of the body but also the ideas of these affections.

PROPOSITION 23

The mind does not know itself except insofar as it perceives ideas of affections of the body.

Proof

The idea or knowledge of the mind (Pr. 20, II) follows in God and is related to God in the same way as the idea or knowledge of the body. But since (Pr. 19, II) the human mind does not know the human body—that is, (Cor. Pr. 11, II) since the knowledge of the human body is not related to God insofar as he constitutes the nature of the human mind—therefore neither is knowledge of the mind related to God insofar as he constitutes the essence of the human mind. And so (Cor. Pr. 11, II) the human mind to that extent does not know itself. Again, the ideas of the affections by which the body is affected involve the nature of the human body (Pr. 16, II); that is, (Pr. 13, II) they are in agreement [*conveniunt*] with the nature of the mind. Therefore, the knowledge of these ideas will necessarily involve knowledge of the mind. But (preceding Pr.) the knowledge of these ideas is in the human mind. Therefore, the human mind knows itself only to that extent.

PROPOSITION 24

The human mind does not involve an adequate knowledge of the component parts of the human body.

Proof

The component parts of the human body do not pertain to the essence of the body itself save insofar as they preserve an unvarying relation of motion with one another (Def. after Cor. Lemma 3), and not insofar as they can be considered as individual things apart from their relation to the human body. For the parts of the human body (Post. 1) are very composite individual things, whose parts can be separated from the human body (Lemma 4) without impairing in any way its nature and specific reality [*forma*], and can establish a quite different relation of motion with other bodies (Ax. 1 after Lemma 3). Therefore (Pr. 3, II), the idea or knowledge of any component part will be in God, and will be so (Pr. 9, II) insofar as he is considered as affected by another idea of a particular thing, a particular thing which is prior in Nature's order to the part itself (Pr. 7, II). Further, the same holds good of any part of an individual component part of the human body, and so of any component part of the human body there is knowledge in God insofar as he is affected by very many ideas of things, and not insofar as he has the idea only of the human body, that is (Pr. 13, II), the idea that constitutes the nature of the human mind. So (Cor. Pr. 11, II) the human mind does not involve adequate knowledge of the component parts of the human body.

PROPOSITION 25

The idea of any affection of the human body does not involve an adequate knowledge of an external body.

Proof

We have shown that the idea of an affection of the human body involves the nature of an external body insofar as the external body determines the human body in some definite way (Pr. 16, II). But insofar as the external body is an individual thing that is not related to the human body, the idea or knowledge of it is in God (Pr. 9, II) insofar as God is considered as affected by the idea of another thing which is (Pr. 7, II) prior in nature to the said external body. Therefore, an adequate knowledge of the external body is not in God insofar as he has the idea of an affection of the human body; i.e., the idea of an affection of the human body does not involve an adequate knowledge of an external body.

PROPOSITION 26

The human mind does not perceive any external body as actually existing except through the ideas of affections of its own body.

Proof

If the human body is not affected in any way by an external body, then (Pr. 7, II) neither is the idea of the human body—that is (Pr. 13, II), the human mind—affected in any way by the idea of the existence of that body; i.e., it does not in any way perceive the existence of that external body. But insofar as the human body is affected in some way by an external body, to that extent it perceives the external body (Pr. 16, II, with Cor.1).

Corollary

Insofar as the human mind imagines [*imaginatur*] an external body, to that extent it does not have an adequate knowledge of it.

Proof

When the human mind regards external bodies through the ideas of affections of its own body, we say that it imagines [*imaginatur*] (see Sch. Pr. 17, II), and in no other way can the mind imagine external bodies as actually existing (preceding Pr.). Therefore, insofar as the mind imagines external bodies (Pr. 25, II), it does not have adequate knowledge of them.

PROPOSITION 27

The idea of any affection of the human body does not involve adequate knowledge of the human body.

Proof

Any idea whatsoever of any affection of the human body involves the nature of the human body only to the extent that the human body is considered to be affected in some definite way (Pr. 16, II). But insofar as the human body is an individual thing that can be affected in many other ways, the idea . . . etc. (See Proof Pr. 25, II).

PROPOSITION 28

The ideas of the affections of the human body, insofar as they are related only to the human mind, are not clear and distinct, but confused.

Proof

The ideas of the affections of the human body involve the nature both of external bodies and of the human body itself (Pr. 16, II), and must involve the nature not only of the human body but also of its parts. For affections are modes in which parts of the human body (Post. 3), and consequently the body as a whole, is affected. But (Prs. 24 and 25, II) an adequate knowledge of external bodies, as also of the component parts of the human body, is not in God insofar as he is considered as affected by the human mind, but insofar as he is considered as affected by other ideas. Therefore, these ideas of affections, insofar as they are related only to the human mind, are like conclusions without premises; that is, as is self-evident, confused ideas.

Scholium

The idea that constitutes the nature of the human mind is likewise shown, when considered solely in itself, not to be clear and distinct, as is also the idea of the human mind and the ideas of affections of the human body insofar as they are related only to the human mind, as everyone can easily see.

PROPOSITION 29

The idea of the idea of any affection of the human body does not involve adequate knowledge of the human mind.

Proof

The idea of an affection of the human body (Pr. 27, II) does not involve adequate knowledge of the body itself; in other words, it does not adequately express the nature of the body; that is (Pr. 13, II), it does not adequately agree [*convenit*] with the nature of the mind. So (Ax. 6, I) the idea of this idea does not adequately express the nature of the human mind; i.e., it does not involve an adequate knowledge of it.

Corollary

Hence it follows that whenever the human mind perceives things after the common order of nature, it does not have an adequate knowledge of itself, nor of its body, nor of external bodies, but only a confused and fragmentary knowledge. For the mind does not know itself save insofar as it perceives ideas of the affections of the body (Pr. 23, II). Now it does not perceive its own body (Pr. 19, II) except through ideas of affections of the body, and also it is only through these affections that it perceives external bodies (Pr. 26, II). So insofar as it has these ideas, it has adequate knowledge neither of itself (Pr. 29, II) nor of its own body (Pr. 27, II) nor of external bodies (Pr. 25, II), but only a fragmentary [*multilatam*] and confused knowledge (Pr. 28, II and Sch.).

Scholium

I say expressly that the mind does not have an adequate knowledge, but only a confused and fragmentary knowledge, of itself, its own body, and external bodies whenever it perceives things from the common order of nature, that is, whenever it is determined externally—namely, by the fortuitous run of circumstance—to regard this or that, and not when it is determined internally, through its regarding several things at the same time, to understand their agreement, their differences, and their opposition. For whenever it is conditioned internally in this or in another way, then it sees things clearly and distinctly, as I shall later show.

PROPOSITION 30

We can have only a very inadequate knowledge of the duration of our body.

Proof

The duration of our body does not depend on its essence (Ax. 1, II), nor again on the absolute nature of God (Pr. 21, I), but (Pr. 28, I) it is determined to exist and to act by causes which are also determined by other causes to exist and to act in a definite and determinate way, and these again by other causes, and so *ad infinitum*. Therefore, the duration of our body depends on the common order of nature and the structure of the universe. Now there is in God adequate knowledge of the structure of the universe insofar as he has ideas of all the things in the universe, and not insofar as he has only the idea of the human body (Cor. Pr. 9, II). Therefore, knowledge of the duration of our body is very inadequate in God insofar

as he is considered only to constitute the nature of the human mind. That is (Cor. Pr. 11, II), this knowledge is very inadequate in the human mind.

PROPOSITION 31

We can have only a very inadequate knowledge of the duration of particular things external to us.

Proof

Each particular thing, just like the human body, must be determined by another particular thing to exist and to act in a definite and determinate way, and this latter thing again by another, and so on *ad infinitum* (Pr. 28, I). Now since we have shown in the preceding Proposition that from this common property of particular things we can have only a very inadequate knowledge of the duration of the human body, in the case of the duration of particular things we have to come to the same conclusion: that we can have only a very inadequate knowledge thereof.

Corollary

Hence it follows that all particular things are contingent and perishable. For we can have no adequate knowledge of their duration (preceding Pr.), and that is what is to be understood by contingency and perishability (Sch. I, Pr. 33, I). For apart from this there is no other kind of contingency (Pr. 29, I).

PROPOSITION 32

All ideas are true insofar as they are related to God.

Proof

All ideas, which are in God, agree completely with the objects of which they are ideas (Cor. Pr. 7, II), and so they are all true. (Ax. 6, I)

PROPOSITION 33

There is nothing positive in ideas whereby they can be said to be false.

Proof

If this be denied, conceive, if possible, a positive mode of thinking which constitutes the form [*forma*] of error or falsity. This mode of thinking cannot be in God (preceding Pr.), but neither can it be or be conceived externally to God (Pr. 15, I). Thus there can be nothing positive in ideas whereby they can be called false.

PROPOSITION 34

Every idea which in us is absolute, that is, adequate and perfect, is true.

Proof

When we say that there is in us an adequate and perfect idea, we are saying only this (Cor. Pr. 11, II), that there is an adequate and perfect idea in God insofar as he constitutes the essence of our mind. Consequently we are saying only this, that such an idea is true (Pr. 32, II).

PROPOSITION 35

Falsity consists in the privation of knowledge which inadequate ideas, that is, fragmentary and confused ideas, involve.

Proof

There is nothing positive in ideas which constitutes the form [*forma*] of falsity (Pr. 33, II). But falsity cannot consist in absolute privation (for minds, not bodies, are said to err and be deceived), nor again in absolute ignorance, for to be ignorant and to err are different. Therefore it consists in that privation of knowledge which inadequate knowledge, that is, inadequate and confused ideas, involves.

Scholium

In Sch. Pr. 17, II I explained how error consists in the privation of knowledge, but I will give an example to enlarge on this explanation. Men are deceived in thinking themselves free, a belief that consists only in this, that they are conscious of their actions and ignorant of the causes by which they are determined. Therefore, the idea of their freedom is simply the ignorance of the cause of their actions. As to their saying that human actions depend on the will, these are mere words without any corresponding idea. For none of them knows what the will is and how it moves the body, and those who boast otherwise and make up stories of dwelling places and habitations of the soul provoke either ridicule or disgust.

As another example, when we gaze at the sun, we see it as some two hundred feet distant from us. The error does not consist in simply seeing the sun in this way but in the fact that while we do so we are not aware of the true distance and the cause of our seeing it so. For although we may later become aware that the sun is more than six hundred times the diameter of the earth distant from us, we shall nevertheless continue to see it as close at hand. For it is not our ignorance of its true distance that causes us to see the sun to be so near; it is that the affection of our body involves the essence of the sun only to the extent that the body is affected by it.

PROPOSITION 36

Inadequate and confused ideas follow by the same necessity as adequate, or clear and distinct, ideas.

Proof

All ideas are in God (Pr. 15, I), and insofar as they are related to God, they are true (Pr. 32, II) and adequate (Cor. Pr. 7, II). So there are no inadequate or confused ideas except insofar as they are related to the particular mind of someone (see Prs. 24 and 28, II). So all ideas, both adequate and inadequate, follow by the same necessity (Cor. Pr. 6, II).

PROPOSITION 37

That which is common to all things (see Lemma 2 above) and is equally in the part as in the whole, does not constitute the essence of any one particular thing.

Proof

If this be denied, conceive, if possible, that it does constitute the essence of one particular thing, B. Therefore it can neither be nor be conceived without B (Def. 2, II). But this is contrary to our hypothesis. Therefore, it does not pertain to B's essence, nor does it constitute the essence of any other particular thing.

PROPOSITION 38

Those things that are common to all things and are equally in the part as in the whole, can be conceived only adequately.

Proof

Let A be something common to all bodies, and equally in the part of any body as in the whole. I say that A can be conceived only adequately. For its idea (Cor. Pr. 7, II) will necessarily be in God both insofar as he has the idea of the human body and insofar as he has the ideas of affections of the human body, affections which partly involve the natures of both the human body and external bodies (Prs. 16, 25 and 27, II). That is (Prs. 12 and 13, II), this idea will necessarily be adequate in God insofar as he constitutes the human mind; that is, insofar as he has the ideas which are in the human mind. Therefore, the mind (Cor. Pr. 11, II) necessarily perceives A adequately, and does so both insofar as it perceives itself and insofar as it perceives its own body or any external body; nor can A be perceived in any other way.

Corollary

Hence it follows that there are certain ideas or notions common to all men. For (by Lemma 2) all bodies agree in certain respects, which must be (preceding Pr.) conceived by all adequately, or clearly and distinctly.

PROPOSITION 39

Of that which is common and proper to the human body and to some external bodies by which the human body is customarily affected, and which is equally in the part as well as in the whole of any of these bodies, the idea also in the mind will be adequate.

Proof

Let A be that which is common and proper to the human body and to some external bodies and which is equally in the human body as in those same external bodies, and which is finally equally in the part of any external body as in the whole. There will be in God an adequate idea of A (Cor. Pr. 7, II) both insofar as he has the idea of the human body and insofar as he

has ideas of those posited external bodies. Let it now be supposed that the human body is affected by an external body through that which is common to them both, that is, A. The idea of this affection will involve the property A (Pr. 16, II), and so (Cor. Pr. 7, II) the idea of this affection, insofar as it involves the property A, will be adequate in God insofar as he is affected by the idea of the human body; that is (Pr. 13, II), insofar as he constitutes the nature of the human mind. So this idea will also be adequate in the human mind (Cor. Pr. 11, II).

Corollary

Hence it follows that the mind is more capable of perceiving more things adequately in proportion as its body has more things in common with other bodies.

PROPOSITION 40

Whatever ideas follow in the mind from ideas that are adequate in it are also adequate.

Proof

This is evident. For when we say that an idea follows in the human mind from ideas that are adequate in it, we are saying no more than that there is in the divine intellect an idea of which God is the cause, not insofar as he is infinite nor insofar as he is affected by ideas of numerous particular things, but only insofar as he constitutes the essence of the human mind.

Scholium 1

I have here set forth the cause of those notions that are called 'common,' and which are the basis of our reasoning processes. Now certain axioms or notions have other causes which it would be relevant to set forth by this method of ours; for thus we could establish which notions are more useful compared with others, and which are of scarcely any value. And again, we could establish which notions are common to all, which ones are clear and distinct only to those not laboring under prejudices [*praejudiciis*] and which ones are ill-founded. Furthermore, this would clarify the origin of those notions called 'secondary'— and consequently the axioms which are based on them—as well as other related questions to which I have for some time given thought. But I have decided not to embark on these questions at this point because I have set them aside for another treatise,[2] and also to avoid wearying the reader with too lengthy a discussion of this subject. Nevertheless, to omit nothing that it is essential to know, I shall briefly deal with the question of the origin of the so-called 'transcendental terms,' such as 'entity,' 'thing,' 'something' [*ens, res, aliquid*].

These terms originate in the following way. The human body, being limited, is capable of forming simultaneously in itself only a certain number of distinct images. (I have explained in Sch. Pr. 17, II what an image is.) If this number be exceeded, these images begin to be confused, and if the number of distinct images which the body is capable of forming simultaneously in itself be far exceeded, all the images will be utterly confused with one another. This being so, it is evident from Cor. Pr. 17 and Pr. 18, II that the human mind is able to imagine simultaneously and distinctly as many bodies as there are images that can be formed simultaneously in its body. But when the images in the body are utterly confused, the mind will also imagine all the bodies confusedly without any distinction, and will comprehend them, as it were, under one attribute, namely, that of entity, thing, etc. This conclusion can also be reached from the fact that images are not always equally vivid, and also from other causes analogous to these, which I need not here explicate. For it all comes down to this, that these terms signify ideas confused in the highest degree.

Again, from similar causes have arisen those notions called 'universal,' such as 'man,' 'horse,' 'dog,' etc; that is to say, so many images are formed in the human body simultaneously (e.g., of man) that our capacity to imagine them is surpassed, not indeed completely, but to the extent that the mind is unable to imagine the unimportant differences of individuals (such as the complexion and stature of each, and their exact number) and imagines distinctly only their common characteristic insofar as the body is affected by them. For it was by this that the body was affected most repeatedly, by each single individual. The mind expresses this by the word 'man,' and predicates this

word of an infinite number of individuals. For, as we said, it is unable to imagine the determinate number of individuals.

But it should be noted that not all men form these notions in the same way; in the case of each person the notions vary according as that thing varies whereby the body has more frequently been affected, and which the mind more readily imagines or calls to mind. For example, those who have more often regarded with admiration the stature of men will understand by the word 'man' an animal of upright stature, while those who are wont to regard a different aspect will form a different common image of man, such as that man is a laughing animal, a featherless biped, or a rational animal. Similarly, with regard to other aspects, each will form universal images according to the conditioning of his body. Therefore, it is not surprising that so many controversies have arisen among philosophers who have sought to explain natural phenomena through merely the images of these phenomena.

Scholium 2

From all that has already been said it is quite clear that we perceive many things and form universal notions:

1. From individual objects presented to us through the senses in a fragmentary [*mutilate*] and confused manner without any intellectual order (see Cor. Pr. 29, II); and therefore I call such perceptions 'knowledge from casual experience.'

2. From symbols. For example, from having heard or read certain words we call things to mind and we form certain ideas of them similar to those through which we imagine things (Sch. Pr. 18, II). Both these ways of regarding things I shall in future refer to as 'knowledge of the first kind,' 'opinion' or 'imagination.'

3. From the fact that we have common notions and adequate ideas of the properties of things (see Cor. Pr. 38 and 39 with its Cor., and Pr. 40, II). I shall refer to this as 'reason' and 'knowledge of the second kind.'

Apart from these two kinds of knowledge there is, as I shall later show, a third kind of knowledge, which

2. [This is Spinoza's incomplete essay, *On The Improvement of the Understanding.*]

I shall refer to as 'intuition.' This kind of knowledge proceeds from an adequate idea of the formal essence of certain attributes of God to an adequate knowledge of the essence of things. I shall illustrate all these kinds of knowledge by one single example. Three numbers are given; it is required to find a fourth which is related to the third as the second to the first. Tradesmen have no hesitation in multiplying the second by the third and dividing the product by the first, either because they have not yet forgotten the rule they learnt without proof from their teachers, or because they have in fact found this correct in the case of very simple numbers, or else from the force of the proof of Proposition 19 of the Seventh Book of Euclid, to wit, the common property of proportionals. But in the case of very simple numbers, none of this is necessary. For example, in the case of the given numbers 1, 2, 3, everybody can see that the fourth proportional is 6, and all the more clearly because we infer in one single intuition the fourth number from the ratio we see the first number bears to the second.

PROPOSITION 41

Knowledge of the first kind is the only cause of falsity; knowledge of the second and third kind is necessarily true.

Proof

In the preceding Scholium we asserted that all those ideas which are inadequate and confused belong to the first kind of knowledge; and thus (Pr. 35, II), this knowledge is the only cause of falsity. Further, we asserted that to knowledge of the second and third kind there belong those ideas which are adequate. Therefore (Pr. 34, II), this knowledge is necessarily true.

PROPOSITION 42

Knowledge of the second and third kind, and not knowledge of the first kind, teaches us to distinguish true from false.

Proof

This Proposition is self-evident. For he who can distinguish the true from the false must have an adequate idea of the true and the false; that is (Sch. 2 Pr. 40,

II) he must know the true and the false by the second or third kind of knowledge.

PROPOSITION 43

He who has a true idea knows at the same time that he has a true idea, and cannot doubt its truth.

Proof

A true idea in us is one which is adequate in God insofar as he is explicated through the nature of the human mind (Cor. Pr. 11, II). Let us suppose, then, that there is in God, insofar as he is explicated through the nature of the human mind, an adequate idea, A. The idea of this idea must also necessarily be in God, and is related to God in the same way as the idea A (Pr. 20, II, the proof being of general application). But by our supposition the idea A is related to God insofar as he is explicated through the nature of the human mind. Therefore, the idea of the idea A must be related to God in the same way; that is (Cor. Pr. 11, II), this adequate idea of the idea A will be in the mind which has the adequate idea A. So he who has an adequate idea, that is, he who knows a thing truly (Pr. 34, II), must at the same time have an adequate idea, that is, a true knowledge of his knowledge; that is, (as is self-evident) he is bound at the same time to be certain.

Scholium

I have explained in the Scholium to Pr. 21, II what is an idea of an idea; but it should be noted that the preceding proposition is sufficiently self-evident. For nobody who has a true idea is unaware that a true idea involves absolute certainty. To have a true idea means only to know a thing perfectly, that is, to the utmost degree. Indeed, nobody can doubt this, unless he thinks that an idea is some dumb thing like a picture on a tablet, and not a mode of thinking, to wit, the very act of understanding. And who, pray, can know that he understands some thing unless he first understands it? That is, who can know that he is certain of something unless he is first certain of it? Again, what standard of truth can there be that is clearer and more certain than a true idea? Indeed, just as light makes manifest both itself and darkness, so truth is the standard both of itself and falsity.

I think I have thus given an answer to those questions which can be stated as follows: If a true idea is distinguished from a false one only inasmuch as it is said to correspond with that of which it is an idea, then a true idea has no more reality or perfection than a false one (since they are distinguished only by an extrinsic characteristic) and consequently neither is a man who has true ideas superior to one who has only false ideas. Secondly, how do we come to have false ideas? And finally, how can one know for certain that one has ideas which correspond with that of which they are ideas? I have now given an answer, I repeat, to these problems. As regards the difference between a true and a false idea, it is clear from Pr. 35, II that the former is to the latter as being to non-being. The causes of falsity I have quite clearly shown from Propositions 19 to 35 with the latter's Scholium, from which it is likewise obvious what is the difference between a man who has true ideas and one who has only false ideas. As to the last question, how can a man know that he has an idea which corresponds to that of which it is an idea, I have just shown, with abundant clarity, that this arises from the fact that he does have an idea that corresponds to that of which it is an idea; that is, truth is its own standard. Furthermore, the human mind, insofar as it perceives things truly, is part of the infinite intellect of God (Cor. Pr. 11, II), and thus it is as inevitable that the clear and distinct ideas of the mind are true as that God's ideas are true.

PROPOSITION 44

It is not in the nature of reason to regard things as contingent, but as necessary.

Proof

It is in the nature of reason to perceive things truly (Pr. 41, II), to wit, (Ax. 6, I) as they are in themselves; that is (Pr. 29, I), not as contingent, but as necessary.

Corollary 1

Hence it follows that it solely results from imagination [*imaginatio*] that we regard things, both in respect of the past and of the future, as contingent.

Scholium

I shall explain briefly how this comes about. We have shown above (Pr. 17, II and Cor.) that although things may not exist, the mind nevertheless always imagines them as present unless causes arise which exclude their present existence. Further, we have shown (Pr. 18, II) that if the human body has once been affected by two external bodies at the same time, when the mind later imagines one of them, it will straightway call the other to mind as well; that is, it will regard both as present to it unless other causes arise which exclude their present existence. Furthermore, nobody doubts that time, too, is a product of the imagination, and arises from the fact that we see some bodies move more slowly than others, or more quickly, or with equal speed. Let us therefore suppose that yesterday a boy saw Peter first of all in the morning, Paul at noon, and Simon in the evening, and that today he again sees Peter in the morning. From Pr. 18, II it is clear that as soon as he sees the morning light, forthwith he will imagine the sun as traversing the same tract of sky as on the previous day, that is, he will imagine a whole day, and he will imagine Peter together with morning, Paul with midday, and Simon with evening; that is, he will imagine the existence of Paul and Simon with reference to future time. On the other hand, on seeing Simon in the evening he will refer Paul and Peter to time past by imagining them along with time past. This train of events will be the more consistent the more frequently he sees them in that order. If it should at some time befall that on another evening he sees James instead of Simon, then the following morning he will imagine along with evening now Simon, now James, but not both together. For we are supposing that he has seen only one of them in the evening, not both at the same time. Therefore, his imagination will waver, and he will imagine, along with a future evening, now one, now the other; that is, he will regard neither of them as going to be there for certain, but both of them contingently. This wavering of the imagination occurs in the same way if the imagination be of things which we regard with relation to past or present time, and consequently we shall imagine things, as related both to present and past or future time, as contingent.

Corollary 2

It is in the nature of reason to perceive things in the light of eternity [*sub quadam specie aeternitatis*].

Proof

It is in the nature of reason to regard things as necessary, not as contingent (previous Pr.). Now it perceives this necessity truly (Pr. 41, II); that is, as it is in itself (Ax. 6, I). But (Pr. 16, I) this necessity is the very necessity of God's eternal nature. Therefore, it is in the nature of reason to regard things in this light of eternity. Furthermore, the basic principles of reason are those notions (Pr. 38, II) which explicate what is common to all things, and do not explicate (Pr. 37, II) the essence of any particular thing, and therefore must be conceived without any relation to time, but in the light of eternity.

PROPOSITION 45

Every idea of any body or particular thing existing in actuality necessarily involves the eternal and infinite essence of God.

Proof

The idea of a particular thing actually existing necessarily involves both the essence and the existence of the thing (Cor. Pr. 8, II). But particular things cannot be conceived without God (Pr. 15, I). Now since they have God for their cause (Pr. 6, II) insofar as he is considered under that attribute of which the things themselves are modes, their ideas (Ax. 4, I) must necessarily involve the conception of their attribute; that is (Def. 6, I), the eternal and infinite essence of God.

Scholium

Here by existence I do not mean duration, that is, existence insofar as it is considered in the abstract as a kind of quantity. I am speaking of the very nature of existence, which is attributed to particular things because they follow in infinite numbers in infinite ways from the eternal necessity of God's nature (Pr. 16, I). I am speaking, I repeat, of the very existence of particular things insofar as they are in God. For although each particular thing is determined by an-

other particular thing to exist in a certain manner, the force by which each perseveres in existing follows from the eternal necessity of God's nature. See Cor. Pr. 24, I.

PROPOSITION 46

The knowledge of the eternal and infinite essence of God which each idea involves is adequate and perfect.

Proof

The proof of the preceding proposition is universally valid, and whether a thing be considered as a part or a whole, its idea, whether of whole or part, involves the eternal and infinite essence of God (preceding Pr.). Therefore, that which gives knowledge of the eternal and infinite essence of God is common to all things, and equally in the part as in the whole. And so this knowledge will be adequate (Pr. 38, II).

PROPOSITION 47

The human mind has an adequate knowledge of the eternal and infinite essence of God.

Proof

The human mind has ideas (Pr. 22, II) from which (Pr. 23, II) it perceives itself, its own body (Pr. 19, II) and external bodies (Cor. 1, Pr. 16 and Pr. 17, II) as actually existing, and so it has an adequate knowledge of the eternal and infinite essence of God (Prs. 45 and 46, II).

Scholium

Hence we see that God's infinite essence and his eternity are known to all. Now since all things are in God and are conceived through God, it follows that from this knowledge we can deduce a great many things so as to know them adequately and thus to form that third kind of knowledge I mentioned in Sch. 2 Pr. 40, II, of the superiority and usefulness of which we shall have occasion to speak in Part V. That men do not have as clear a knowledge of God as they do of common notions arises from the fact that they are unable to imagine God as they do bodies, and that they have connected the word 'God' with the images of things which they commonly see; and this they can scarcely avoid, being affected continually by external bodies. Indeed, most errors result solely from the incorrect application of words to things. When somebody says that the lines joining the center of a circle to its circumference are unequal, he surely understands by circle, at least at that time, something different from what mathematicians understand. Likewise, when men make mistakes in arithmetic, they have different figures in mind from those on paper. So if you look only to their minds, they indeed are not mistaken; but they seem to be wrong because we think that they have in mind the figures on the page. If this were not the case, we would not think them to be wrong, just as I did not think that person to be wrong whom I recently heard shouting that his hall had flown into his neighbour's hen, for I could see clearly what he had in mind. Most controversies arise from this, that men do not correctly express what is in their mind, or they misunderstand another's mind. For, in reality, while they are hotly contradicting one another, they are either in agreement or have different things in mind, so that the apparent errors and absurdities of their opponents are not really so.

PROPOSITION 48

In the mind there is no absolute, or free, will. The mind is determined to this or that volition by a cause, which is likewise determined by another cause, and this again by another, and so ad infinitum.

Proof

The mind is a definite and determinate mode of thinking (Pr. 11, II), and thus (Cor. 2, Pr. 17, I) it cannot be the free cause of its actions: that is, it cannot possess an absolute faculty of willing and non-willing. It must be determined to will this or that (Pr. 28, I) by a cause, which likewise is determined by another cause, and this again by another, etc.

Scholium

In the same way it is proved that in the mind there is no absolute faculty of understanding, desiring, loving, etc. Hence it follows that these and similar faculties are either entirely fictitious or nothing more than metaphysical entities or universals which we are wont

to form from particulars. So intellect and will bear the same relation to this or that idea, this or that volition, as stoniness to this or that stone, or man to Peter and Paul. As to the reason why men think they are free, we explained that in the Appendix to Part I.

But before proceeding further, it should here be noted that by the will I mean the faculty of affirming and denying, and not desire. I mean, I repeat, the faculty whereby the mind affirms or denies what is true or what is false, not the desire whereby the mind seeks things or shuns them. But now that we have proved that these faculties are universal notions which are not distinct from the particulars from which we form them, we must inquire whether volitions themselves are anything more than ideas of things. We must inquire, I say, whether there is in the mind any other affirmation and denial apart from that which the idea, insofar as it is an idea, involves. On this subject see the following proposition and also Def. 3, II, lest thought becomes confused with pictures. For by ideas I do not mean images such as are formed at the back of the eye — or, if you like, in the middle of the brain — but conceptions of thought.

PROPOSITION 49

There is in the mind no volition, that is, affirmation and negation, except that which an idea, insofar as it is an idea, involves.

Proof

There is in the mind (preceding Pr.) no absolute faculty of willing and non-willing, but only particular volitions, namely, this or that affirmation, and this or that negation. Let us therefore conceive a particular volition, namely, a mode of thinking whereby the mind affirms that the three angles of a triangle are equal to two right angles. This affirmation involves the conception, or idea, of a triangle; that is, it cannot be conceived without the idea of a triangle. For to say that A must involve the conception of B is the same as to say that A cannot be conceived without B. Again, this affirmation (Ax. 3, II) cannot even be without the idea of a triangle. Therefore, this idea can neither be nor be conceived without the idea of a triangle. Furthermore, this idea of a triangle must involve this same affirmation, namely, that its three angles are equal to two right angles. Therefore, vice versa, this idea of a triangle can neither be nor be conceived without this affirmation, and so (Def. 2, II) this affirmation belongs to the essence of the idea of a triangle, and is nothing more than the essence itself. And what I have said of this volition (for it was arbitrarily selected) must also be said of every volition, namely, that it is nothing but an idea.

Corollary

Will and intellect are one and the same thing.

Proof

Will and intellect are nothing but the particular volitions and ideas (Pr. 48, II and Sch.). But a particular volition and idea are one and the same thing (preceding Pr.). Therefore will and intellect are one and the same thing.

Scholium

By this means we have removed the cause to which error is commonly attributed. We have previously shown that falsity consists only in the privation that fragmentary and confused ideas involve. Therefore, a false idea, insofar as it is false, does not involve certainty. So when we say that a man acquiesces in what is false and has no doubt thereof, we are not thereby saying that he is certain, but only that he does not doubt, or that he acquiesces in what is false because there is nothing to cause his imagination to waver. On this point see Sch. Pr. 44, II. So however much we suppose a man to adhere to what is false, we shall never say that he is certain. For by certainty we mean something positive (Pr. 43, II and Sch.), not privation of doubt. But by privation of certainty we mean falsity.

But for a fuller explanation of the preceding proposition some things remain to be said. Then, again, there is the further task of replying to objections that may be raised against this doctrine of ours. Finally, to remove every shred of doubt, I have thought it worthwhile to point out certain advantages of this doctrine. I say certain advantages, for the most important of them will be better understood from what we have to say in Part V.

I begin, then, with the first point, and I urge my readers to make a careful distinction between an idea—i.e., a conception of the mind—and the images of things that we imagine. Again, it is essential to distinguish between ideas and the words we use to signify things. For since these three—images, words, and ideas—have been utterly confused by many, or else they fail to distinguish between them through lack of accuracy, or, finally, through lack of caution, our doctrine of the will, which it is essential to know both for theory and for the wise ordering of life, has never entered their minds. For those who think that ideas consist in images formed in us from the contact of external bodies are convinced that those ideas of things whereof we can form no like image are not ideas, but mere fictions fashioned arbitrarily at will. So they look on ideas as dumb pictures on a tablet, and misled by this preconception they fail to see that an idea, insofar as it is an idea, involves affirmation or negation. Again, those who confuse words with idea, or with the affirmation which an idea involves, think that when they affirm or deny something merely by words contrary to what they feel, they are able to will contrary to what they feel. Now one can easily dispel these misconceptions if one attends to the nature of thought, which is quite removed from the concept of extension. Then one will clearly understand that an idea, being a mode of thinking, consists neither in the image of a thing nor in words. For the essence of words and images is constituted solely by corporeal motions, far removed from the concept of thought. With these few words of warning, I turn to the aforementioned objections.

The first of these rests on the confident claim that the will extends more widely than the intellect, and therefore is different from it. The reason for their belief that the will extends more widely than the intellect is that they find—so they say—that they do not need a greater faculty of assent, that is, of affirming and denying, than they already possess, in order to assent to an infinite number of other things that we do not perceive, but that we do need an increased faculty of understanding. Therefore will is distinct from intellect, the latter being finite and the former infinite.

Second, it may be objected against us that experience appears to tell us most indisputably that we are able to suspend judgment so as not to assent to things that we perceive, and this is also confirmed by the fact that nobody is said to be deceived insofar as he perceives something, but only insofar as he assents or dissents. For instance, he who imagines a winged horse does not thereby grant that there is a winged horse; that is, he is not thereby deceived unless at the same time he grants that there is a winged horse. So experience appears to tell us most indisputably that the will, that is, the faculty of assenting, is free, and different from the faculty of understanding.

Third, it may be objected that one affirmation does not seem to contain more reality than another; that is, we do not seem to need greater power in order to affirm that what is true is true than to affirm that what is false is true. On the other hand, we do perceive that one idea has more reality or perfection than another. For some ideas are more perfect than others in proportion as some objects are superior to others. This, again, is a clear indication that there is a difference between will and intellect.

Fourthly, it may be objected that if man does not act from freedom of will, what would happen if he should be in a state of equilibrium like Buridan's ass? Will he perish of hunger and thirst? If I were to grant this, I would appear to be thinking of an ass or a statue, not of a man. If I deny it, then the man will be determining himself, and consequently will possess the faculty of going and doing whatever he wants.

Besides these objections there may possibly be others. But since I am not obliged to stress every objection that can be dreamed up, I shall make it my task to reply to these objections only, and as briefly as possible.

To the first objection I reply that, if by the intellect is meant clear and distinct ideas only, I grant that the will extends more widely than the intellect, but I deny that the will extends more widely than perceptions, that is, the faculty of conceiving. Nor indeed do I see why the faculty of willing should be termed infinite any more than the faculty of sensing. For just as by the same faculty of willing we can affirm an infinite number of things (but in succession, for we cannot affirm an infinite number of things simultaneously), so also we can sense or perceive an infinite number of bodies (in succession) by the same faculty of sensing. If my objectors should say that there are an infinite number of things that we cannot sense, I retort that we cannot grasp them by any amount of thought, and consequently by any amount of willing.

But, they say, if God wanted to bring it about that we should perceive these too, he would have had to give us a greater faculty of perceiving, but not a greater faculty of willing than he has already given us. This is the same as saying that if God wishes to bring it about that we should understand an infinite number of other entities, he would have to give us a greater intellect than he already has, so as to encompass these same infinite entities, but not a more universal idea of entity. For we have shown that the will is a universal entity, or the idea whereby we explicate all particular volitions; that is, that which is common to all particular volitions. So if they believe that this common or universal idea of volitions is a faculty, it is not at all surprising that they declare this faculty to extend beyond the limits of the intellect to infinity. For the term 'universal' is applied equally to one, to many, and to an infinite number of individuals.

To the second objection I reply by denying that we have free power to suspend judgment. For when we say that someone suspends judgment, we are saying only that he sees that he is not adequately perceiving the thing. So suspension of judgment is really a perception, not free will. To understand this more clearly, let us conceive a boy imagining a winged horse and having no other perception. Since this imagining involves the existence of a horse (Cor. Pr. 17, II), and the boy perceives nothing to annul the existence of the horse, he will regard the horse as present and he will not be able to doubt its existence, although he is not certain of it. We experience this quite commonly in dreams, nor do I believe there is anyone who thinks that while dreaming he has free power to suspend judgment regarding the contents of his dream, and of bringing it about that he should not dream what he dreams that he sees. Nevertheless, it does happen that even in dreams we suspend judgment, to wit, when we dream that we are dreaming. Furthermore, I grant that nobody is deceived insofar as he has a perception; that is, I grant that the imaginings of the mind, considered in themselves, involve no error (see Sch. Pr. 17, II). But I deny that a man makes no affirmation insofar as he has a perception. For what else is perceiving a winged horse than affirming wings of a horse? For if the mind were to perceive nothing apart from the winged horse, it would regard the horse as present to it, and would have no cause to doubt the existence of the horse, nor would it have any faculty of dissenting, unless the imagining of the winged horse were joined to an idea which annuls the existence of the said horse, or unless the mind perceives that the idea which it has of the winged horse is inadequate. Then it will either necessarily deny the existence of the said horse or it will necessarily doubt it.

In the above I think I have also answered the third objection by my assertion that the will is a universal term predicated of all ideas and signifying only what is common to all ideas, namely, affirmation, the adequate essence of which, insofar as it is thus conceived as an abstract term, must be in every single idea, and the same in all in this respect only. But not insofar as it is considered as constituting the essence of the idea, for in that respect particular affirmations differ among themselves as much as do ideas. For example, the affirmation which the idea of a circle involves differs from the affirmation which the idea of a triangle involves as much as the idea of a circle differs from the idea of a triangle. Again, I absolutely deny that we need an equal power of thinking to affirm that what is true is true as to affirm that what is false is true. For these two affirmations, if you look to their meaning and not to the words alone, are related to one another as being to non-being. For there is nothing in ideas that constitutes the form of falsity (see Pr. 35, II with Sch. and Sch. Pr. 47, II). Therefore, it is important to note here how easily we are deceived when we confuse universals with particulars, and mental constructs [entia rationis] and abstract terms with the real.

As to the fourth objection, I readily grant that a man placed in such a state of equilibrium (namely, where he feels nothing else but hunger and thirst and perceives nothing but such-and-such food and drink at equal distances from him) will die of hunger and thirst. If they ask me whether such a man is not to be reckoned an ass rather than a man, I reply that I do not know, just as I do not know how one should reckon a man who hangs himself, or how one should reckon babies, fools, and madmen.

My final task is to show what practical advantages accrue from knowledge of this doctrine, and this we shall readily gather from the following points:

1. It teaches that we act only by God's will, and that we share in the divine nature, and all the more as our actions become more perfect and as we understand God more and more. Therefore this doctrine, apart from giving us complete tranquillity of mind, has the further advantage of teaching us wherein lies our greatest happiness or blessedness, namely, in the knowledge of God alone, as a result of which we are induced only to such actions as are urged on us by love and piety. Hence we clearly understand how far astray from the true estimation of virtue are those who, failing to understand that virtue itself and the service of God is happiness itself and utmost freedom, expect God to bestow on them the highest rewards in return for their virtue and meritorious actions as if in return for the basest slavery.

2. It teaches us what attitude we should adopt regarding fortune, or the things that are not in our power, that is, the things that do not follow from our nature; namely, to expect and to endure with patience both faces of fortune. For all things follow from God's eternal decree by the same necessity as it follows from the essence of a triangle that its three angles are equal to two right angles.

3. This doctrine assists us in our social relations, in that it teaches us to hate no one, despise no one, ridicule no one, be angry with no one, envy no one. Then again, it teaches us that each should be content with what he has and should help his neighbor, not from womanish pity, or favour, or superstition, but solely from the guidance of reason as occasion and circumstance require. This I shall demonstrate in Part IV.

4. Finally, this doctrine is also of no small advantage to the commonwealth, in that it teaches the manner in which citizens should be governed and led; namely, not so as to be slaves, but so as to do freely what is best.

And thus I have completed the task I undertook in this Scholium, and thereby I bring to an end Part II, in which I think I have explained the nature of the human mind and its properties at sufficient length and as clearly as the difficult subject matter permits, and that from my account can be drawn many excellent lessons, most useful and necessary to know, as will partly be disclosed in what is to follow.

Gottfried Leibniz

Leibniz was born in 1646 in Leipzig, in what is now Germany, the son of a professor of moral philosophy. He studied at the University of Leipzig from 1661 until 1666 and then at the University of Altdorf from 1666 to 1667, earning degrees in law and philosophy. After graduating, he rejected an academic offer from the University of Leipzig, and instead entered the service of the Elector of Mainz. In 1672 he travelled to Paris as a diplomat, where he stayed until 1676. There, benefitting from the guidance of Christian Huygens, one of the most important physicists of the time, he became thoroughly acquainted with modern science and philosophy. In Paris he also developed the calculus, independently of Newton, who developed it around the same time. After his years in Paris, Leibniz travelled to England and then to the Netherlands, where he met Spinoza. When he returned to Germany he became a counselor at the court in Hanover, which was to be his principal residence until his death in 1716.

In Hanover, Leibniz wrote numerous philosophical works, many of which were not published until after his death. In several of these works, the *Discourse on Metaphysics* (1686), the *New System of Nature* (1695), and the *Monadology* (1714), he displays his metaphysical system in outline form. Leibniz's philosophical views on physics are set out in the *Specimen of Dynamics* (1698), *On Nature Itself* (1697), and in his correspondence with De Volder (1699–1706) and with Samuel Clarke, Newton's friend (1715–16). Theology is treated at length in the *Theodicy,* published in 1710, and in his correspondence with Antoine Arnauld (1686–90). In 1704 Leibniz finished a substantial commentary of Locke's *Essay,* entitled *New Essays on Human Understanding.*

At the center of Leibniz's system is the notion of a *monad,* which is an immaterial, simple, mind-like entity, modelled on the Cartesian soul. In Leibniz's view, monads are the only substances that exist. Matter, therefore, is not among the fundamental constituents of reality, but is rather an appearance of systems of monads: Matter is *phenomenal.* Hence physics is a study of appearances, and not of ultimately real things. Metaphysics, by contrast, since it has monads in its purview, is about ultimately real things.

In Leibniz's conception, monads are *windowless,* that is, they do not have any real causal relations with other monads. All causal relations among different created things are merely phenomenal. God gives each monad its own internal program which consists of various perceptions, none of which involve real interactions with other monads. However, God does set up all of the monads in pre-established harmony, so that, for example, when the monad that is you has a perception of speaking to me, God has set up my monad so that at the same time I will have a perception of you speaking to me, despite the fact that you are not *really* interacting with me at all. Leibniz's idea comes partly from his view that all relations, like *speaking to* and *being next to* must, in the end, be reducible to *intrinsic* properties, properties that are not relational at all, and thus make no reference to any entity other than the thing that possesses it. In his analysis of Leibniz, Kant points out that the Cartesian soul provides a model of a substance all of whose properties—thoughts or perceptions—are intrinsic to it, and that this is why Leibniz believes that all substances are like Cartesian souls.

In Leibniz's view, all of the monads *express* the entire universe: Each of them has perceptions of everything that has occurred, is occurring, and will occur in the universe. In this respect, all monads are the very same. But each of them differs from every other in the *point of view* from which it expresses the universe. This is partly a matter of which perceptions are clear and distinct, and which

461

are more confused and obscure. Certain perceptions may be conscious and clear in you, for example, perceptions of what you did in the last hour, but merely unconscious and confused in me. Some monads, such as those that provide the metaphysical foundations of rocks and buildings, lack any conscious perceptions at all.

Leibniz was a determinist in that he held that, in virtue of choosing the best of all possible worlds, God determines every event that occurs, including each of our actions. One of Leibniz's great philosophical struggles involved attempting to show that human moral responsibility is compatible with this divine determinism. He devised several solutions to this problem, one of which involves the renowned formulation that in our choices, God inclines our souls without necessitating them.

● ● ●

For a classic account of Leibniz's philosophical system, see Bertrand Russell, *A Critical Exposition of the Philosophy of Leibniz* (London, 1900). Nicholas Rescher's *The Philosophy of Leibniz* (Englewood Cliffs: Prentice-Hall, 1967) provides a good introduction to Leibniz's views. Important critical studies include Robert M. Adams, *Leibniz: Determinist, Theist, Idealist* (Oxford: Oxford University Press, 1994); Nicholas Jolley, *Leibniz and Locke* (Oxford: Oxford University Press, 1984); Robert McRae, *Leibniz: Perception, Apperception, and Thought* (Toronto: University of Toronto Press, 1976); Robert Sleigh, *Leibniz and Arnauld* (New Haven: Yale University Press, 1990); and Catherine Wilson, *Leibniz's Metaphysics: A Comparative and Historical Study* (Princeton: Princeton University Press, 1989). Some collections of essays on Leibniz are Harry Frankfurt, ed., *Leibniz: A Collection of Critical Essays* (Garden City: Doubleday, 1972); Michael Hooker, ed., *Leibniz: Critical and Interpretive Essays* (Minneapolis: University of Minnesota Press, 1982); R. S. Woolhouse, ed., *Leibniz: Metaphysics and Philosophy of Science* (Oxford: Oxford University Press, 1981); and Derk Pereboom, ed., *The Rationalists: Descartes, Spinoza, Leibniz* (Lanham, Md.: Rowman & Littlefield, 1999).

D.P.

Discourse on Metaphysics

1. *On divine perfection, and that God does everything in the most desirable way.* The most widely accepted and meaningful notion we have of God is expressed well enough in these words, that God is an absolutely perfect being; yet the consequences of these words are not sufficiently considered. And, to penetrate more deeply into this matter, it is appropriate to remark that there are several entirely different perfections in nature, that God possesses all of them together, and that each of them belongs to him in the highest degree.

We must also know what a perfection is. A fairly sure test for being a perfection is that forms or natures that are not capable of a highest degree are not perfections, as for example, the nature of number or figure. For the greatest of all numbers (or even the number of all numbers), as well as the greatest of all figures, imply a contradiction, but the greatest knowledge and omnipotence do not involve any impossibility. Consequently, power and knowledge are perfections, and, insofar as they belong to God, they do not have limits.

Whence it follows that God, possessing supreme and infinite wisdom, acts in the most perfect manner, not only metaphysically, but also morally speaking, and that, with respect to ourselves, we can say that the more enlightened and informed we are about God's works, the more we will be disposed to find them excellent and in complete conformity with what we might have desired.

2. *Against those who claim that there is no goodness in God's works, or that the rules of goodness and beauty are arbitrary.* Thus I am far removed from the opinion of those who maintain that there are no rules of goodness and perfection in the nature of things or in the ideas God has of them and who say that the works of God are good solely for the formal reason that God has made them.[1] For, if this were so, God, knowing that he is their author, would not have had to consider them afterwards and find them good, as is testified by the Sacred Scriptures — which seem to have used such anthropomorphic expressions only to make us understand that the excellence of God's works can be recognized by considering them in themselves, even when we do not reflect on this empty external denomination which relates them to their cause. This is all the more true, since it is by considering his works that we can discover the creator. His works must therefore carry his mark in themselves. I confess that the contrary opinion seems to me extremely dangerous and very near to the opinion of the recent innovators[2] who hold that the beauty of the universe and the goodness we attribute to the works of God are but the chimeras of those who conceive of God in terms of themselves. Thus, in saying that things are not good by virtue of any rule of goodness but solely by virtue of the will of God, it seems to me that we unknowingly destroy all of God's love and all of his glory. For why praise him for what he has done if he would be equally praiseworthy in doing the exact contrary? Where will his justice and wisdom reside if there remains only a certain despotic power, if will holds the place of reason, and if, according to the definition of tyrants, justice consists in whatever pleases the most powerful? Besides, it seems that all acts of will presuppose a reason for willing and that this reason is naturally prior to the act of will. That is why I also find completely strange the expression of some other philosophers who say that the eternal truths of metaphysics and geometry and consequently also the rules of goodness, justice, and perfection are merely the effects of the will of God; instead, it seems to me, they are only the consequences of his understanding, which, assuredly, does not depend on his will, any more than does his essence.

3. *Against those who believe that God might have made things better.* Nor can I approve of the opin-

Reprinted from Leibniz, *Philosophical Essays*, edited and translated by Roger Ariew and Daniel Garber (Indianapolis: Hackett Publishing Company, 1989).

1. [This is Descartes's view. — R.A. and D.G.]

2. [Spinoza, and by extension, Descartes.]

ion of some moderns who maintain boldly that what God has made is not of the highest perfection and that he could have done much better.[3] For it seems to me that the consequences of this opinion are wholly contrary to the glory of God: as a lesser evil is relatively good, so a lesser good is relatively evil. And to act with less perfection than one could have is to act imperfectly. To show that an architect could have done better is to find fault with his work. This opinion is also contrary to the Sacred Scripture, which assure us of the goodness of God's works. For, if their view were sufficient, then since the series of imperfections descends to infinity, God's works would always have been good in comparison with those less perfect, no matter how he created them but something is hardly praiseworthy if it can be praised only in this way. I also believe that a great many passages from Sacred Scripture and the holy fathers will be found favoring my opinion, but scarcely any will be found favoring the opinion of these moderns, an opinion which is, in my judgment, unknown to all antiquity and which is based only on the inadequate knowledge we have of the general harmony of the universe and of the hidden reasons for God's conduct. This enables us to judge audaciously that many things could have been rendered better. Besides, these moderns insist on certain dubious subtleties, for they imagine that nothing is so perfect that there is not something more perfect—this is an error.

They also believe that in this way they are able to safeguard God's freedom, as though it were not freedom of the highest sort to act in perfection following sovereign reason. For to believe that God does something without having any reason for his will—overlooking the fact that this seems impossible—is an opinion that conforms little to his glory. Let us assume, for example, that God chooses between A and B and that he takes A without having any reason to prefer it to B. I say that this action of God is at the very least not praiseworthy; for all praise must be based on some reason, and by hypothesis there is none here. Instead I hold that God does nothing for which he does not deserve to be glorified.

4. *That the love of God requires our complete satisfaction and acquiescence with respect to what he has* done without our being quietists as a result. The general knowledge of this great truth, that God acts always in the most perfect and desirable way possible, is, in my judgment, the foundation of the love that we owe God in all things, since he who loves seeks his satisfaction in the happiness or perfection of the object loved and in his actions. To will the same and dislike the same is true friendship. And I believe that it is difficult to love God well when we are not disposed to will what God wills, when we might have the power to change it. In fact, those who are not satisfied with what God does seem to me like dissatisfied subjects whose attitudes are not much different from those of rebels.

I hold, therefore, that, according to these principles, in order to act in accordance with the love of God, it is not sufficient to force ourselves to be patient; rather, we must truly be satisfied with everything that has come to us according to his will. I mean this acquiescence with respect to the past. As for the future, we must not be quietists[4] and stand ridiculously with arms folded, awaiting that which God will do, according to the sophism that the ancients called *logon aergon*, the lazy reason. But we must act in accordance with what we presume to be the *will of God*, insofar as we can judge it, trying with all our might to contribute to the general good and especially to the embellishment and perfection of that which affects us or that which is near us, that which is, so to speak, in our grasp. For, although the outcome might perhaps demonstrate that God did not wish our good will to have effect at present, it does not follow that he did not wish us to act as we have. On the contrary, since he is the best of all masters, he never demands more than the right intention, and it is for him to know the proper hour and place for letting the good designs succeed.

5. *What the rules of the perfection of divine conduct consist in, and that the simplicity of the ways is in balance with the richness of the effects.* Therefore it is sufficient to have the confidence that God does everything for the best and that nothing can harm

---

3. [Malebranche's *Traité* seems to be one of the main targets of this essay.]

4. [The quietists were followers of Miguel de Molinos (ca. 1640–97), author of the *Guida spirituale* (1675), and others, who stressed passive contemplation and complete resignation to the will of God.]

those who love him. But to know in detail the reasons that could have moved him to choose this order of the universe—to allow sins, to dispense his saving grace in a certain way—surpasses the power of a finite mind, especially when it has not yet attained the enjoyment of the vision of God.

However, we can make some general remarks concerning the course of providence in the governance of things. We can therefore say that one who acts perfectly is similar to an excellent geometer who can find the best constructions for a problem; or to a good architect who makes use of his location and the funds set aside for a building in the most advantageous manner, allowing nothing improper or lacking in the beauty of which it is capable; or to a good householder, who makes use of his holdings in such a way that there remains nothing uncultivated and sterile; or to a skilled machinist who produces his work in the least difficult way possible; or to a learned author who includes the greatest number of truths [*realités*] in the smallest possible volume. Now, the most perfect of all beings, those that occupy the least volume, that is, those that least interfere with one another, are minds, whose perfections consist in their virtues. That is why we mustn't doubt that the happiness of minds is the principal aim of God and that he puts this into practice to the extent that general harmony permits it. We shall say more about this below.

As for the simplicity of the ways of God, this holds properly with respect to his means, as opposed to the variety, richness, and abundance, which holds with respect to his ends or effects. And the one must be in balance with the others, as are the costs of a building and the size and beauty one demands of it. It is true that nothing costs God anything—even less than it costs a philosopher to build the fabric of his imaginary world out of hypotheses—since God has only to make decrees in order that a real world come into being. But in matters of wisdom, decrees or hypotheses take the place of expenditures to the extent that they are more independent of one another, because reason requires that we avoid multiplying hypotheses or principles, in somewhat the same way that the simplest system is always preferred in astronomy.

6. *God does nothing which is not orderly and it is not even possible to imagine events that are not regular.* The volitions or acts of God are commonly divided into ordinary or extraordinary. But it is good to consider that God does nothing which is not orderly. Thus, what passes for extraordinary is extraordinary only with some particular order established among creatures; for everything is in conformity with respect to the universal order. This is true to such an extent that not only does nothing completely irregular occur in the world, but we would not even be able to imagine such a thing. Thus, let us assume, for example, that someone jots down a number of points at random on a piece of paper, as do those who practice the ridiculous art of geomancy.[5] I maintain that it is possible to find a geometric line whose notion is constant and uniform, following a certain rule, such that this line passes through all the points in the same order in which the hand jotted them down.

And if someone traced a continuous line which is sometimes straight, sometimes circular, and sometimes of another nature, it is possible to find a notion, or rule, or equation common to all the points of this line, in virtue of which these very changes must occur. For example, there is no face whose contours are not part of a geometric line and cannot be traced in one stroke by a certain regular movement. But, when a rule is extremely complex, what is in conformity with it passes for irregular.

Thus, one can say, in whatever manner God might have created the world, it would always have been regular and in accordance with a certain general order. But God has chosen the most perfect world, that is, the one which is at the same time the simplest in hypotheses and the richest in phenomena, as might be a line in geometry whose construction is easy and whose properties and effects are extremely remarkable and widespread. I use these comparisons to sketch an imperfect likeness of divine wisdom and to point out something that can at least elevate our minds to conceive in some way what cannot be sufficiently expressed. But I do not claim to explain in this way the great mystery upon which the entire universe depends.

7. *That miracles conform to the general order, even though they may be contrary to the subordinate maxims; and about what God wills or permits by a*

5. [Geomancy is the art of divination by means of lines or figures.]

general or particular volition. Now, since nothing can happen which is not in the order, one can say that miracles are as much within the order as are natural operations, operations which are called natural because they are in conformity with certain subordinate maxims that we call the nature of things. For one can say that this nature is only God's custom, with which he can dispense for any stronger reason than the one which moved him to make use of these maxims.

As for the general or particular volitions, depending upon how the matter is understood, we can say that God does everything following his most general will, which is in conformity with the most perfect order he has chosen, but we can also say that he has particular volitions which are exceptions to these aforementioned subordinate maxims. For the most general of God's laws, the one that rules the whole course of the universe, is without exception.

We can say also that God wills everything that is an object of his particular volition. But we must make a distinction with respect to the objects of his general volition, such as the actions of other creatures, particularly the actions of those that are reasonable, actions with which God wishes to concur. For, if the action is good in itself, we can say that God wills it and sometimes commands it, even when it does not take place. But if the action is evil in itself and becomes good only by accident, because the course of things (particularly punishment and atonement) corrects its evilness and repays the evil with interest in such a way that in the end there is more perfection in the whole sequence than if the evil had not occurred, then we must say that God permits this but does not will it, even though he concurs with it because of the laws of nature he has established and because he knows how to draw a greater good from it.

8. *To distinguish the actions of God from those of creatures we explain the notion of an individual substance.* It is rather difficult to distinguish the actions of God from those of creatures; for some believe that God does everything, while others imagine that he merely conserves the force he has given to creatures. What follows will let us see the extent to which we can say the one or the other. And since actions and passions properly belong to individual substances [*actiones sunt suppositorum*],[6] it will be necessary to explain what such an individual substance is.

It is indeed true that when several predicates are attributed to a single subject and this subject is attributed to no other, it is called an individual substance; but this is not sufficient, and such an explanation is merely nominal. We must therefore consider what it is to be attributed truly to a certain subject.

Now it is evident that all true predication has some basis in the nature of things and that, when a proposition is not an identity, that is, when the predicate is not explicitly contained in the subject, it must be contained in it virtually. That is what the philosophers call *in-esse*, when they say that the predicate is in the subject. Thus the subject term must always contain the predicate term, so that one who understands perfectly the notion of the subject would also know that the predicate belongs to it.

Since this is so, we can say that the nature of an individual substance or of a complete being is to have a notion so complete that it is sufficient to contain and to allow us to deduce from it all the predicates of the subject to which this notion is attributed. An accident, on the other hand, is a being whose notion does not include everything that can be attributed to the subject to which the notion is attributed. Thus, taken in abstraction from the subject, the quality of being a king which belongs to Alexander the Great is not determinate enough to constitute an individual and does not include the other qualities of the same subject, nor does it include everything that the notion of this prince includes. On the other hand, God, seeing Alexander's individual notion or haecceity,[7] sees in it at the same time the basis and reason for all the predicates which can be said truly of him, for example, that he vanquished Darius and Porus; he even knows *a priori* (and not by experience) whether he died a natural death or whether he was poisoned,

---

6. [Leibniz is making use of Scholastic logical terminology: a *suppositum* is an individual subsistent substance; *actiones sunt suppositorum* therefore means that actions are of individual subsistent substances.]

7. [The word *haecceitas* (or *heccéité*, what we are translating as "haecceity") was coined by John Duns Scotus (ca. 1270–1308) to refer to an individual essence or "thisness"— what *haecceitas* means literally.]

something we can know only through history. Thus when we consider carefully the connection of things, we can say that from all time in Alexander's soul there are vestiges of everything that has happened to him and marks of everything that will happen to him and even traces of everything that happens in the universe, even though God alone could recognize them all.

9. *That each singular substance expresses the whole universe in its own way, and that all its events, together with all their circumstances and the whole sequence of external things, are included in its notion.* Several notable paradoxes follow from this; among others, it follows that it is not true that two substances can resemble each other completely and differ only in number [*solo numero*], and that what Saint Thomas asserts on this point about angels or intelligences (that here every individual is a lowest species)[8] is true of all substances, provided that one takes the specific difference as the geometers do with respect to their figures. It also follows that a substance can begin only by creation and end only by annihilation; that a substance is not divisible into two; that one substance cannot be constructed from two; and that thus the number of substances does not naturally increase and decrease, though they are often transformed.

Moreover, every substance is like a complete world and like a mirror of God or of the whole universe, which each one expresses in its own way, somewhat as the same city is variously represented depending upon the different positions from which it is viewed. Thus the universe is in some way multiplied as many times as there are substances, and the glory of God is likewise multiplied by as many entirely different representations of his work. It can even be said that every substance bears in some way the character of God's infinite wisdom and omnipotence and imitates him as much as it is capable. For it expresses, however confusedly, everything that happens in the universe, whether past, present, or future — this has some resemblance to an infinite perception or knowledge. And since all other substances in turn express this substance and accommodate themselves to it, one can

8. [See St. Thomas Aquinas, *Summa Theologica* I, q. 50, art. 4.]

say that it extends its power over all the others, in imitation of the creator's omnipotence.

10. *That the belief in substantial forms has some basis, but that these forms do not change anything in the phenomena and must not be used to explain particular effects.* It seems that the ancients, as well as many able men accustomed to deep meditation who have taught theology and philosophy some centuries ago (some of whom are respected for their saintliness) have had some knowledge of what we have just said; this is why they introduced and maintained the substantial forms which are so decried today. But they are not so distant from the truth nor so ridiculous as the common lot of our new philosophers imagines.

I agree that the consideration of these forms serves no purpose in the details of physics and must not be used to explain particular phenomena. That is where the Scholastics failed, as did the physicians of the past who followed their example, believing that they could account for the properties of bodies by talking about forms and qualities without taking the trouble to examine their manner of operation. It is as if we were content to say that a clock has a quality of clockness derived from its form without considering in what all of this consists; that would be sufficient for the person who buys the clock, provided that he turns over its care to another.

But this misunderstanding and misuse of forms must not cause us to reject something whose knowledge is so necessary in metaphysics that, I hold, without it one cannot properly know the first principles or elevate our minds sufficiently well to the knowledge of incorporeal natures and the wonders of God.

However, just as a geometer does not need to burden his mind with the famous labyrinth of the composition of the continuum, there is no need for any moral philosopher and even less need for a jurist or statesman to trouble himself with the great difficulties involved in reconciling free will and God's providence, since the geometer can achieve all his demonstrations and the statesman can complete all his deliberations without entering into these discussions, discussions that remain necessary and important in philosophy and theology. In the same way, a physicist can explain some experiments, at times using previous simpler experiments and at times using geometric and mechanical demonstrations, without needing general considerations from another sphere. And if he uses God's concourse, or else a soul, animating force [*archée*], or something else of this nature, he is raving just as much as the person who, in the course of an important practical deliberation, enters into a lofty discussion concerning the nature of destiny and the nature of our freedom. In fact, people often commit this fault without thinking when they encumber their minds with the consideration of fatalism and sometimes are even diverted from a good resolution or a necessary duty in this way.

11. *That the thoughts of the theologians and philosophers who are called Scholastics are not entirely to be disdained.*   I know that I am advancing a great paradox by attempting to rehabilitate the old philosophy in some fashion and to restore the almost banished substantial forms to their former place. But perhaps I will not be condemned so easily when it is known that I have long meditated upon the modern philosophy, that I have given much time to experiments in physics and demonstrations in geometry, and that I had long been persuaded about the futility of these beings, which I finally was required to embrace in spite of myself and, as it were, by force, after having myself carried out certain studies. These studies made me recognize that our moderns do not give enough credit to Saint Thomas and to the other great men of his time and that there is much more solidity than one imagines in the opinions of the Scholastic philosophers and theologians, provided that they are used appropriately and in their proper place. I am even convinced that, if some exact and thoughtful mind took the trouble to clarify and summarize their thoughts after the manner of the analytic geometers, he would find there a great treasure of extremely important and wholly demonstrative truths.

12. *That the notions involved in extension contain something imaginary and cannot constitute the substance of body.*   But, to resume the thread of our discussion, I believe that anyone who will meditate about the nature of substance, as I have explained it above, will find that the nature of body does not consist merely in extension, that is, in size, shape, and motion, but that we must necessarily recognize in body something related to souls, something we commonly call substantial form, even though it makes no change in the phenomena, any more than do the souls of animals, if they have any. It is even possible to demonstrate that the notions of size, shape, and motion are not as distinct as is imagined and that they contain something imaginary and relative to our perception, as do (though to a greater extent) color, heat, and other similar qualities, qualities about which one can doubt whether they are truly found in the nature of things outside ourselves. That is why qualities of this kind cannot constitute any substance. And if there were no other principle of identity in body other than the one just mentioned, a body could not subsist for more than a moment.

Yet the souls and substantial forms of other bodies are entirely different from intelligent souls, which alone know their actions. Not only don't intelligent souls perish naturally, but they also always preserve the basis for the knowledge of what they are; this is what renders them alone susceptible to punishment and reward and makes them citizens of the republic of the universe, whose monarch is God. It also follows that all other creatures must serve them—something which we will later discuss more fully.

13. *Since the individual notion of each person includes once and for all everything that will ever happen to him, one sees in it the* a priori *proofs of the truth of each event, or, why one happened rather than another. But these truths, however certain, are nevertheless contingent, being based on the free will of God or of his creatures, whose choice always has its reasons, which incline without necessitating.* But before going further, we must attempt to resolve a great difficulty that can arise from the foundations we have set forth above. We have said that the notion of an individual substance includes once and for all everything that can ever happen to it and that, by considering this notion, one can see there everything that can truly be said of it, just as we can see in the nature of a circle all the properties that can be deduced from it. But it seems that this would eliminate the difference between contingent and necessary truths, that there would be no place for human freedom, and that an absolute fatalism would rule all our actions as well as all the other events of the world. To this I reply that we must distinguish between what is certain and what is necessary. Everyone grants that

future contingents are certain, since God foresees them, but we do not concede that they are necessary on that account. But (someone will say) if a conclusion can be deduced infallibly from a definition or notion, it is necessary. And it is true that we are maintaining that everything that must happen to a person is already contained virtually in his nature or notion, just as the properties of a circle are contained in its definition; thus the difficulty still remains. To address it firmly, I assert that connection or following [*consécution*] is of two kinds. The one whose contrary implies a contradiction is absolutely necessary; this deduction occurs in the eternal truths, for example, the truths of geometry. The other is necessary only *ex hypothesi* and, so to speak, accidentally, but it is contingent in itself, since its contrary does not imply a contradiction. And this connection is based not purely on ideas and God's simple understanding, but on his free decrees and on the sequence of the universe.

Let us take an example. Since Julius Caesar will become perpetual dictator and master of the republic and will overthrow the freedom of the Romans, this action is contained in his notion, for we assume that it is the nature of such a perfect notion of a subject to contain everything, so that the predicate is included in the subject, *ut possit inesse subjecto*.[9] It could be said that it is not in virtue of this notion or idea that he must perform this action, since it pertains to him only because God knows everything. But someone might insist that his nature or form corresponds to this notion, and, since God has imposed this personality on him, it is henceforth necessary for him to satisfy it. I could reply by citing future contingents, since they have no reality as yet, save in God's understanding and will, and, because God gave them this form in advance, they must in the same way correspond to it.

But I much prefer to overcome difficulties rather than to excuse them by giving some other similar difficulties, and what I am about to say will illuminate the one as well as the other. It is here, then, that we must apply the distinction concerning connections, and I say that whatever happens in conformity with these predeterminations [*avances*] is certain but not

9. [The Latin is an approximate paraphrase of the preceding clause.]

necessary, and if one were to do the contrary, he would not be doing something impossible in itself, even though it would be impossible [*ex hypothesi*] for this to happen. For if someone were able to carry out the whole demonstration by virtue of which he could prove this connection between the subject, Caesar, and the predicate, his successful undertaking, he would in fact be showing that Caesar's future dictatorship is grounded in his notion or nature, that there is a reason why he crossed the Rubicon rather than stopped at it and why he won rather than lost at Pharsalus and that it was reasonable, and consequently certain, that this should happen. But this would not show that it was necessary in itself nor that the contrary implies a contradiction. It is reasonable and certain in almost the same way that God will always do the best, even though what is less perfect does not imply a contradiction.

For it will be found that the demonstration of this predicate of Caesar is not as absolute as those of numbers or of geometry, but that it supposes the sequence of things that God has freely chosen, a sequence based on God's first free decree always to do what is most perfect and on God's decree with respect to human nature, following out of the first decree, that man will always do (although freely) that which appears to be best. But every truth based on these kinds of decrees is contingent, even though it is certain; for these decrees do not change the possibility of things, and, as I have already said, even though it is certain that God always chooses the best, this does not prevent something less perfect from being and remaining possible in itself, even though it will not happen, since it is not its impossibility but its imperfection which causes it to be rejected. And nothing is necessary whose contrary is possible.

We will therefore be in a position to satisfy these sorts of difficulties, however great they may appear (and in fact they are not made any the less pressing by considering the other thinkers who have ever treated this matter), as long as we recognize that all contingent propositions have reasons to be one way rather than another or else (what comes to the same thing) that they have *a priori* proofs of their truth which render them certain and which show that the connection between subject and predicate of these propositions has its basis in the natures of both. But they do not have necessary demonstrations, since these reasons are based only on the principle of contingency or the principle of the existence of things, that is, based on what is or appears to be best from among several equally possible things. On the other hand, necessary truths are based on the principle of contradiction and on the possibility or impossibility of essences themselves, without regard to the free will of God or his creatures.

14. *God produces various substances according to the different views he has of the universe, and through God's intervention the proper nature of each substance brings it about that what happens to one corresponds with what happens to all the others, without their acting upon one another directly.* After having seen, in some way, what the nature of substances consists in, we must try to explain the dependence they have upon one another and their actions and passions. Now, first of all, it is very evident that created substances depend upon God, who preserves them and who even produces them continually by a kind of emanation, just as we produce our thoughts. For God, so to speak, turns on all sides and in all ways the general system of phenomena which he finds it good to produce in order to manifest his glory, and he views all the faces of the world in all ways possible, since there is no relation that escapes his omniscience. The result of each view of the universe, as seen from a certain position, is a substance which expresses the universe in conformity with this view, should God see fit to render his thought actual and to produce this substance. And since God's view is always true, our perceptions are always true; it is our judgments, which come from ourselves, that deceive us.

Now we said above, and it follows from what we have just said, that each substance is like a world apart, independent of all other things, except for God; thus all our phenomena, that is, all the things that can ever happen to us, are only consequences of our being. And since these phenomena maintain a certain order in conformity with our nature or, so to speak, in conformity with the world which is in us, an order which enables us to make useful observations to regulate our conduct, observations justified by the success of future phenomena, an order which thus allows us often to judge the future from the past without error, this would be sufficient to enable us to say that these phenomena are true without bothering with whether they are outside us and whether others also perceive them. Nevertheless, it is very true that the perceptions or expressions of all substances mutually correspond in such a way that each one, carefully following certain reasons or laws it has observed, coincides with others doing the same—in the same way that several people who have agreed to meet in some place at some specified time can really do this if they so desire. But although they all express the same phenomena, it does not follow that their expressions are perfectly similar; it is sufficient that they are proportional. In just the same way, several spectators believe that they are seeing the same thing and agree among themselves about it, even though each sees and speaks in accordance with his view.

And God alone (from whom all individuals emanate continually and who sees the universe not only as they see it but also entirely differently from all of them) is the cause of this correspondence of their phenomena and makes that which is particular to one of them public to all of them; otherwise, there would be no interconnection. We could therefore say in some way and properly speaking, though not in accordance with common usage, that one particular substance never acts upon another particular substance nor is acted upon by it, if we consider that what happens to each is solely a consequence of its complete idea or notion alone, since this idea already contains all its predicates or events and expresses the whole universe. In fact, nothing can happen to us except thoughts and perceptions, and all our future thoughts and perceptions are merely consequences, though contingent, of our preceding thoughts and perceptions, in such a way that, if I were capable of considering distinctly everything that happens or appears to me at this time, I could see in it everything that will ever happen or appear to me. This would never fail, and it would happen to me regardless, even if everything outside of me were destroyed, provided there remained only God and me. But since we attribute what we perceive in a certain way to other things as causes acting on us, we must consider the basis for this judgment and the element of truth there is in it.

15. *The action of one finite substance on another consists only in the increase of degree of its expression*

together with the diminution of the expression of the other, insofar as God requires them to accommodate themselves to one another. But, without entering into a long discussion, in order to reconcile the language of metaphysics with practice, it is sufficient for now to remark that we ascribe to ourselves — and with reason — the phenomena that we express most perfectly and that we attribute to other substances the phenomena that each expresses best. Thus a substance, which is of infinite extension insofar as it expresses everything, becomes limited in proportion to its more or less perfect manner of expression. This, then, is how one can conceive that substances impede or limit each other, and consequently one can say that, in this sense, they act upon one another and are required, so to speak, to accommodate themselves to one another. For it can happen that a change that increases the expression of one diminishes that of another. Now, the efficacy [*vertu*] a particular substance has is to express well the glory of God, and it is by doing this that it is less limited. And whenever something exercises its efficacy or power, that is, when it acts, it improves and extends itself insofar as it acts. Therefore, when a change takes place by which several substances are affected (in fact every change affects all of them), I believe one may say that the substance which immediately passes to a greater degree of perfection or to a more perfect expression exercises its power and *acts*, and the substance which passes to a lesser degree shows its weakness and is *acted upon* [*pâtit*]. I also hold that every action of a substance which has perfection involves some *pleasure*, and every passion some *pain* and vice versa. However, it can happen that a present advantage is destroyed by a greater evil in what follows, whence one can sin in acting, that is, in exercising one's power and finding pleasure.

16. *God's extraordinary concourse is included in that which our essence expresses, for this expression extends to everything. But this concourse surpasses the powers of our nature or of our distinct expression, which is finite and follows certain subordinate maxims.* It now only remains to explain how God can sometimes influence men and other substances by an extraordinary and miraculous concourse, since it seems that nothing extraordinary and supernatural can happen to them, given that all their events are only consequences of their nature. But we must remember what we have said above concerning miracles in the universe — that they are always in conformity with the universal law of the general order, even though they may be above the subordinate maxims. And to the extent that every person or substance is like a small world expressing the large world, we can say equally that the extraordinary action of God on this substance does not fail to be miraculous, despite the fact that it is included in the general order of the universe insofar as it is expressed by the essence or individual notion of this substance. That is why, if we include in our nature everything that it expresses, nothing is supernatural to it, for our nature extends everywhere, since an effect always expresses its cause and God is the true cause of substances. But what our nature expresses more perfectly belongs to it in a particular way, since it is in this that its power consists. But since it is limited, as I have just explained, there are many things that surpass the powers of our nature and even surpass the powers of all limited natures. Thus, to speak more clearly, I say that God's miracles and extraordinary concourse have the peculiarity that they cannot be foreseen by the reasoning of any created mind, no matter how enlightened, because the distinct comprehension of the general order surpasses all of them. On the other hand, everything that we call natural depends on the less general maxims that creatures can understand. Thus, in order that my words may be as irreproachable as my meaning, it would be good to connect certain ways of speaking with certain thoughts. We could call that which includes everything we express our essence or idea; since this expresses our union with God himself, it has no limits and nothing surpasses it. But that which is limited in us could be called our nature or our power; and in that sense, that which surpasses the natures of all created substances is supernatural.

17. *An example of a subordinate maxim or law of nature; in which it is shown, against the Cartesians and many others, that God always conserves the same force but not the same quantity of motion.* I have already mentioned the subordinate maxims or laws of nature often enough, and it seems appropriate to give an example of one. Our new philosophers commonly make use of the famous rule that God always conserves the same quantity of motion in the

world. In fact, this rule is extremely plausible, and, in the past, I held it as indubitable. But I have since recognized what is wrong with it. It is that Descartes and many other able mathematicians have believed that the quantity of motion, that is, the speed multiplied by the size of the moving body, coincides exactly with the moving force, or, to speak geometrically, that the forces are proportional to the product of the speeds and [sizes of] bodies. Now, it is extremely reasonable that the same force is always conserved in the universe. Also, when we attend to the phenomena, we see that there is no perpetual mechanical motion, because then the force of a machine, which is always diminished somewhat by friction and which must sooner or later come to an end, would restore itself, and consequently would increase by itself without any new external impulsion. We observe also that the force of a body is diminished only in proportion to the force it imparts to some bodies contiguous to it or to its own parts, insofar as they have separate motion.

Thus they believed that what can be said about force can also be said about the quantity of motion. But to show the difference between them, I assume that a body falling from a certain height acquires the force to rise up that height, if its direction carries it that way, at least, if there are no impediments. For example, a pendulum would rise again exactly to the height from which it descended if the resistance of the air and some other small obstacles did not diminish its acquired force a little.

I *assume* also that as much force is required to elevate A, a body of one pound, to CD, a height of four fathoms, as to elevate B, a body of four pounds, to EF, a height of one fathom. All this is admitted by our new philosophers.

It is therefore evident that, having fallen from height CD, body A acquired exactly as much force as did body B, which fell from height EF; for since body (B) reached F and acquired the force to rise to E (by the first assumption), it has the force to carry a body of four pounds, that is, itself, to EF, the height of one fathom; similarly, since body (A) reached D and acquired the force to rise to C, it has the force to carry a body of one pound, that is, itself, to CD, a height of four fathoms. Therefore (by the second assumption), the force of these two bodies is equal.

Let us now see whether the quantity of motion is also the same in each. But here we will be surprised to

find a very great difference. For Galileo demonstrated that the speed acquired by the fall CD is twice the speed acquired by the fall EF, even though the one height is four times the other. Let us therefore multiply body A, proportional to 1, with its speed, proportional to 2; the product or quantity of motion will be proportional to 2. On the other hand, let us multiply body B, proportional to 4, by its speed, proportional to 1; the product or quantity of motion will be proportional to 4. Therefore the quantity of motion of body (A) at point D is half of the quantity of motion of body (B) at point F; yet their forces are equal. Hence, there is a great difference between quantity of motion and force — which is what needed to be proved.

Thus we see that force must be calculated from the quantity of the effect it can produce, for example, by the height to which a heavy body of a certain size and kind can be raised; this is quite different from the speed that can be imparted to it. And to give it double the speed, it must be given more than double the force.

Nothing is simpler that this proof. Descartes fell into error here only because he had too much confidence in his own thoughts, even when they were not sufficiently ripe. But I am surprised that his followers have not since then discovered this mistake; and I fear that they are beginning, little by little, to imitate some of the Peripatetics, whom they ridicule, like them gradually acquiring the habit of consulting their master's writings rather than reason and nature.

18. *The distinction between force and quantity of motion is important, among other reasons, for judging that one must have recourse to metaphysical considerations distinct from extension in order to explain the phenomena of bodies.* This consideration, the distinction between force and quantity of motion, is rather important, not only in physics and mechanics, in order to find the true laws of nature and rules of motion and even to correct the several errors of practice which have slipped into the writings of some able mathematicians, but also in metaphysics, in order to understand the principles better. For if we consider only what motion contains precisely and formally, that is, change of place, motion is not something entirely real, and when several bodies change position among themselves, it is not possible to determine, merely from a consideration of these changes, to which body we should attribute motion or rest, as I could show geometrically, if I wished to stop and do this now.

But the force or proximate cause of these changes is something more real, and there is sufficient basis to attribute it to one body more than to another. Also, it is only in this way that we can know to which body the motion belongs. Now, this force is something different from size, shape, and motion, and one can therefore judge that not everything conceived in body consists solely in extension and in its modifications, as our moderns have persuaded themselves. Thus we are once again obliged to reestablish some beings or forms they have banished. And it becomes more and more apparent that, although all the particular phenomena of nature can be explained mathematically or mechanically by those who understand them, nevertheless the general principles of corporeal nature and of mechanics itself are more metaphysical than geometrical, and belong to some indivisible forms or natures as the causes of appearances, rather than to corporeal mass or extension. This is a reflection capable of reconciling the mechanical philosophy of the moderns with the caution of some intelligent and well-intentioned persons who fear, with some reason, that we are withdrawing too far from immaterial beings, to the disadvantage of piety.

19. *The utility of final causes in physics.* Since I do not like to judge people wrongly, I do not accuse our new philosophers, who claim to banish final causes from physics.[10] But I am nevertheless obliged to confess that the consequences of this opinion appear dangerous to me, especially if I combine it with the one I refuted at the beginning of this discourse, which seems to go so far as to eliminate final causes altogether, as if God proposed no end or good in acting or as if the good were not the object of his will. As for myself, I hold, on the contrary, that it is here we must seek the principle of all existences and laws of nature, because God always intends the best and most perfect.

I am quite willing to admit that we are subject to deception when we wish to determine God's ends or counsels. But this is only when we try to limit them to some particular design, believing that he had only one thing in view, when instead he regards everything at the same time. For instance, it is a great mistake to believe that God made the world only for us, although it is quite true that he made it in its entirety for us and that there is nothing in the universe which does not affect us and does not also accommodate itself in accordance with his regard for us, following the principles set forth above. Thus when we see some good effect or perfection occurring or ensuing from God's works, we can say with certainty that God had proposed it. For he does nothing by chance and is not like us, who sometimes fail to do the good. That is why, far from being able to fall into error in this, as do extreme politicians who imagine too much subtlety in the designs of princes or as do commentators who look for too much erudition in their author, we cannot attribute too much reflection to this infinite wisdom, and there is no subject in which error is to be feared less, provided we limit ourselves to affirmations and avoid negative propositions that limit God's designs.

Anyone who sees the admirable structure of animals will find himself forced to recognize the wisdom of the author of things. And I advise those who have any feelings of piety and even feelings of true philosophy to keep away from the phrases of certain would-

10. [The "new philosophers" Leibniz has in mind include Descartes and Spinoza, who explain everything mechanically and reject final causes.]

be free thinkers who say that we see because it happens that we have eyes and not that eyes were made for seeing. When one seriously holds these opinions ascribing everything to the necessity of matter or to some chance (even though both must appear ridiculous to those who understand what we have explained above), it is difficult to recognize an intelligent author of nature. For the effect must correspond to its cause; indeed, the effect is best recognized through a knowledge of the cause. Moreover, it is unreasonable to introduce a supreme intelligence as orderer of things and then, instead of using his wisdom, use only the properties of matter to explain the phenomena. This is as if, in order to account for the conquest of an important place by a great prince, a historian were to claim that it occurred because the small particles of gunpowder, set off by the contact of a spark, escaped with sufficient speed to push a hard and heavy body against the walls of the place, while the little particles that make up the brass of the cannon were so firmly interlaced that this speed did not separate them, instead of showing how the foresight of the conqueror enabled him to choose the suitable means and times and how his power overcame all obstacles.

20. *A noteworthy passage by Socrates in Plato against the philosophers who are overly materialistic.* This reminds me of a beautiful passage by Socrates in Plato's *Phaedo.* This passage agrees marvelously with my opinions on this point and seems to be directed expressly against our overly materialistic philosophers. Thus I have been tempted to translate this account, even though it is a little long; perhaps this sample will give an incentive to some of us to share in many of the other beautiful and solid thoughts which can be found in the writings of this famous author.[11]

21. *If mechanical rules depended only on geometry without metaphysics, the phenomena would be entirely different.* Now, since we have always recognized God's wisdom in the detail of the mechanical structure of some particular bodies, it must also be displayed in the general economy of the world and

in the constitution of the laws of nature. This is true to such an extent that one can observe the counsels of this wisdom in the laws of motion in general. For if there were nothing in bodies but extended mass and nothing in motion but change of place and if everything should and could be deduced solely from these definitions by geometrical necessity, it would follow, as I have shown elsewhere, that, upon contact, the smallest body would impart its own speed to the largest body without losing any of this speed; and we would have to accept a number of such rules which are completely contrary to the formation of a system. But the decree of divine wisdom always to conserve the same total force and the same total direction has provided for this.

I even find that several effects of nature can be demonstrated doubly, that is, by considering first the efficient cause and then by considering the final cause, making use, for example, of God's decree always to produce his effect by the easiest and most determinate ways, as I have shown elsewhere in accounting for the rules of catoptrics and dioptrics;[12] I shall say more about this soon.

22. *Reconciliation of two ways of explaining things, by final causes and by efficient causes, in order to satisfy both those who explain nature mechanically and those who have recourse to incorporeal natures.* It is appropriate to make this remark in order to reconcile those who hope to explain mechanically the formation of the first tissue of an animal and the whole machinery of its parts, with those who account for this same structure using final causes. Both ways are good and both can be useful, not only for admiring the skill of the Great Worker, but also for discovering something useful in physics and in medicine. And the authors who follow these different routes should not malign each other.

For I see that those who apply themselves to explaining the beauty of the divine anatomy laugh at others who imagine that a movement of certain fluids that seems fortuitous could have produced such a beautiful variety of limbs, and call these people rash and profane. And the latter, on the other hand, call

11. Leibniz's marginal note: "The passage from Plato's *Phaedo* where Socrates ridicules Anaxagoras, who introduces mind but does not make use of it, is to be inserted."

12. [The reference is to the "Unicum Opticae, Catoptricae et Dioptricae Principium, Autore G. G. L.," from the *Acta Eridutorum* (June 1682).]

the former simple and superstitious, comparing them to the ancients who regarded physicists as impious when they maintained that it is not Jupiter that thunders, but some matter present in the clouds. It would be best to join together both considerations, for if it is permitted to use a humble comparison I recognize and praise the skill of a worker not only by showing his designs in making the parts of his machine, but also by explaining the instruments he used in making each part, especially when these instruments are simple and cleverly contrived. *And God is a skillful enough artisan* to produce a machine which is a thousand times more ingenious than that of our body, while using only some very simple fluids explicitly concocted in such a way that only the ordinary laws of nature are required to arrange them in the right way to produce so admirable an effect; but it is also true that this would not happen at all unless God were the author of nature.

However, I find that the way of efficient causes, which is in fact deeper and in some sense more immediate and *a priori*, is, on the other hand, quite difficult when one comes to details, and I believe that, for the most part, our philosophers are still far from it. But the way of final causes is easier, and is not infrequently of use in divining important and useful truths which one would be a long time in seeking by the other, more physical way; anatomy can provide significant examples of this. I also believe that Snell, who first discovered the rules of refraction, would have waited a long time before discovering them if he first had to find out how light is formed. But he apparently followed the method which the ancients used for catoptrics, which is in fact that of final causes. For, by seeking the easiest way to lead a ray from a given point to another point given by reflection on a given plane (assuming that this is nature's design), they discovered the equality of angles of incidence and angles of reflection, as can be seen in a little treatise by Heliodorus of Larissa, and elsewhere.[13] That is what, I believe, Snell and Fermat after him (though without knowing anything about Snell) have most ingeniously applied to refraction. For when, in the same media, rays observe the same proportion between sines (which is proportional to the resistances of the media), this happens to be the easiest or, at least, the most determinate way to pass from a given point in a medium to a given point in another. And the demonstration Descartes attempted to give of this same theorem by way of efficient causes is not nearly as good. At least there is room for suspicion that he would never have found the law in this way, if he had learned nothing in Holland of Snell's discovery.[14]

23. *To return to immaterial substances, we explain how God acts on the understanding of minds and whether we always have the idea of that about which we think.* I found it appropriate to insist a bit on these considerations of final causes, incorporeal natures, and an intelligent cause with respect to bodies, in order to show their use even in physics and mathematics: on the one hand, to purge the mechanical philosophy of the impiety with which it is charged and, on the other hand, to elevate the minds of our philosophers from material considerations alone to nobler meditations. It is now appropriate to return from bodies to immaterial natures, in particular to minds, and to say something of the means God uses to enlighten them and act on them. In this matter, too, we must not doubt that there are certain laws of nature, of which I could speak more fully elsewhere. But for now it will be sufficient to touch somewhat on ideas, whether we see all things in God and how God is our light.

It may be appropriate to observe that the improper use of ideas gives rise to several errors. For when we reason about something, we imagine ourselves to have the idea of that thing; and that is the foundation upon which certain ancient and new philosophers have built a certain extremely imperfect demonstration of God. For, they say, I must have an idea of God or of a perfect being since I think of him, and one cannot think without an idea. Now, the idea of this being

13. [Heliodorus of Larissa, or Damianos, was a Greek mathematician who flourished after Ptolemy.]

14. [The law of refraction was first published in the second discourse of Descartes's *Dioptrics*. Descartes does indeed attempt to derive the law from hypotheses about the nature of light. Snell discovered the same laws at roughly the same time as Descartes, and there was (and continues to be) a lively dispute about who discovered the law first, and whether Descartes actually discovered the law or learned it from Snell. Leibniz seems to favor Snell.]

contains all perfections, and existence is a perfection, so consequently he exists. But since we often think of impossible chimeras—for example, of the highest degree of speed, of the greatest number, of the intersection of the conchoid with its base or rule—this reasoning is insufficient. It is therefore in this sense that we can say that there are true and false ideas, depending upon whether the thing in question is possible or not. And it is only when we are certain of its possibility that we can boast of having an idea of the thing. Thus the argument above proves, at least, that God exists necessarily, if he is possible. It is indeed a prerogative of divine nature, one that surpasses all others, that divine nature needs only its possibility or essence in order actually to exist, and it is precisely this that is called *ens a se*.

24. *What is clear or obscure, distinct or confused, adequate and intuitive or suppositive knowledge; nominal, real, causal, and essential definition.*   In order to understand better the nature of ideas, we must to some extent touch on the varieties of knowledge. When I can recognize a thing from among others without being able to say what its differences or properties consist in, the knowledge is *confused*. It is in this way that we sometimes know something *clearly*, without being in any doubt whether a poem or a picture is done well or badly, simply because it has a certain something, I know not what, that satisfies or offends us. But when I can explain the marks which I have, the knowledge is called *distinct*. And such is the knowledge of an assayer, who discerns the true from the false by means of certain tests or marks which make up the definition of gold.

But distinct knowledge has degrees, for ordinarily the notions that enter into the definition would themselves need definition and are known only confusedly. But when everything that enters into a distinct definition or distinct knowledge is known distinctly, down to the primitive notions, I call this knowledge *adequate*. And when my mind understands all the primitive ingredients of a notion at once and distinctly, it has *intuitive* knowledge of it; this is extremely rare, since the greater part of human knowledge is only confused or *suppositive*.

It is also good to distinguish nominal and real definitions. I call a definition *nominal* when one can still doubt whether the notion defined is possible, as,

for example, if I say that an endless helix is a solid line whose parts are congruent or can be superimposed on one another; anyone who does not know from elsewhere what an endless helix is could doubt whether such a line is possible, even though having such congruent parts is in fact one of the reciprocal properties of the endless helix, for other lines whose parts are congruent (which are only the circumference of a circle and the straight line) are planar, that is, they can be inscribed on a plane. This shows that any reciprocal property can serve as a nominal definition; but when the property makes known the possibility of the thing, it constitutes a real definition. As long as we have only a nominal definition, we cannot be certain of the consequences we derive, for if it concealed some contradiction or impossibility, the opposite conclusions could be derived from it. That is why truths do not depend upon names and are not arbitrary, as some new philosophers have believed.[15]

Furthermore, there are still great differences between the kinds of real definitions. For when possibility is proved only by experience, as in the definition of quicksilver, whose possibility we know because we know that there actually is such a body which is an extremely heavy but rather volatile fluid, the definition is merely real and nothing more; but when the proof of the possibility is *a priori*, the definition is both real and *causal*, as when it contains the possible generation of the thing. And when a definition pushes the analysis back to the primitive notions without assuming anything requiring an *a priori* proof of its possibility, it is perfect or *essential*.

25. *In what case our knowledge is joined to the contemplation of the idea.*   Now, it is evident that we have no idea of a notion when it is impossible. And in the case where knowledge is only *suppositive*, even when we have the idea, we do not contemplate it, for such a notion is only known in the way in which we know notions involving a hidden impossibility [*occultement impossibles*]; and if a notion is possible, we do not learn its possibility in this way. For example, when I think of a thousand or of a chiliagon, I often do this without contemplating the idea—as when I

15. [Leibniz probably has Hobbes in mind here.]

say that a thousand is ten times a hundred without bothering to think of what 10 and 100 are because I *suppose* I know it and do not believe I need to stop now and conceive it. Thus, it could happen, as in fact it often happens, that I am mistaken with respect to a notion I suppose or believe that I understand, although in fact the notion is impossible, or at least incompatible with those to which I join it. And whether I am mistaken or not, this suppositive way of conceiving remains the same. Therefore, only in confused notions when our knowledge is *clear* or in distinct notions when it is *intuitive* do we see the entire idea in them.

26. *That we have all ideas in us; and of Plato's doctrine of reminiscence.* In order properly to conceive what an idea is, we must prevent an equivocation. For some take the idea to be the form or difference of our thoughts, and thus we have an idea in the mind only insofar as we think of it; every time we think of it again, we have other ideas of the same thing, though similar to the preceding ideas. But it seems that others take the idea as an immediate object of thought or as some permanent form that remains when we are not contemplating it. And, in fact, our soul always has in it the quality of representing to itself any nature or form whatsoever, when the occasion to think of it presents itself. And I believe that this quality of our soul, insofar as it expresses some nature, form, or essence, is properly the idea of the thing, which is in us and which is always in us, whether we think of it or not. For our soul expresses God, the universe, and all essences, as well as all existences.

This agrees with my principles, for nothing ever enters into our mind naturally from the outside; and we have a bad habit of thinking of our soul as if it received certain species as messengers and as if it has doors and windows. We have all these forms in our mind; we even have forms from all time, for the mind always expresses all its future thoughts and already thinks confusedly about everything it will ever think about distinctly. And nothing can be taught to us whose idea we do not already have in our mind, an idea which is like the matter of which that thought is formed.

This is what Plato so excellently recognized when he proposed his doctrine of reminiscence, a very solid doctrine, provided that it is taken rightly and purged

of the error of preexistence and provided that we do not imagine that at some earlier time the soul must already have known and thought distinctly what it learns and thinks now. Plato also strengthened his view by way of a fine experiment, introducing a little boy, whom he leads insensibly to extremely difficult truths of geometry concerning incommensurables without teaching him anything, merely by asking appropriate questions in proper order.[16] This demonstrates that our soul knows all these things virtually and requires only *attention* to recognize truths, and that, consequently, it has, at very least, the ideas upon which these truths depend. One can even say that it already possesses these truths, if they are taken as relations of ideas.

27. *How our soul can be compared to empty tablets and how our notions come from the senses.* Aristotle preferred to compare our soul to tablets that are still blank, where there is room for writing,[17] and he maintained that nothing is in our understanding that does not come from the senses. That agrees better with the popular notions, as is Aristotle's way, but Plato goes deeper. However, these kinds of doxologies or practicologies may be acceptable in ordinary usage, much as we see that those who follow Copernicus do not stop saying that the sun rises and sets. I even find that they can be given a good sense, a sense according to which they have nothing false in them, just as I have already noted how one can truly say that particular substances act on one another. In this same way, one can also say that we receive knowledge from the outside by way of the senses, because some external things contain or express more particularly the reasons that determine our soul to certain thoughts. But when we are concerned with the exactness of metaphysical truths, it is important to recognize the extent and independence of our soul, which

16. [This is a reference to Plato's *Meno*, 82b *et seq.*, where, in a familiar passage, Socrates leads a young slave boy through some geometrical arguments.]

17. [Aristotle, *De Anima*, Book II, chap. 4. The doctrine that nothing is in the intellect that was not first in the senses, attributed to Aristotle by the Scholastics, does not actually occur in Aristotle; perhaps it is a rendering of *Posterior Analytics*, Book II, chap. 19, or *Nicomachean Ethics*, Book VI, chap. 3, sec. 3.]

goes infinitely further than is commonly thought, though in ordinary usage in life we attribute to it only what we perceive most manifestly and what belongs to us most particularly, for it serves no purpose to go any further.

However, it would be good to choose terms proper to each conception [*sens*] in order to avoid equivocation. Thus, the expressions in our soul, whether we conceive them or not, can be called *ideas*, but those we conceive or form can be called *notions, concepts* [*conceptus*]. But however we take these expressions, it is always false to say that all our notions come from the external senses, for the notions I have of myself and of my thoughts, and consequently of being, substance, action, identity, and of many others, arise from an internal experience.

28. *God alone is the immediate object of our perceptions, which exist outside of us, and he alone is our light.*   Now, in rigorous metaphysical truth, there is no external cause acting on us except God alone, and he alone communicates himself to us immediately in virtue of our continual dependence. From this it follows that there is no other external object that touches our soul and immediately excites our perception. Thus we have ideas of everything in our soul only by virtue of God's continual action on us, that is to say, because every effect expresses its cause, and thus the essence of our soul is a certain expression, imitation or image of the divine essence, thought, and will, and of all the ideas comprised in it. It can then be said that God is our immediate external object and that we see all things by him. For example, when we see the sun and the stars, it is God who has given them to us and who conserves the ideas of them in us, and it is God who determines us really to think of them by his ordinary concourse while our senses are disposed in a certain manner, according to the laws he has established. God is the sun and the light of souls, the light that lights every man that comes into this world,[18] and this is not an opinion new to our times. After Holy Scripture and the Church Fathers, who have always preferred Plato to Aristotle, I remember having previously noted that from the time of the Scholastics, several believed that God is the

light of the soul and, in their way of speaking, the active intellect of the rational soul. The Averroists gave the sense of this a bad turn,[19] but others, among whom was, I believe, William of St. Amour, and several mystical theologians, have taken it in a manner worthy of God and capable of elevating the soul to the knowledge of its good.

29. *Yet we think immediately through our own ideas and not through those of God.*   However, I am not of the opinion of certain able philosophers who seem to maintain that our very ideas are in God and not at all in us.[20] In my opinion, this arises from the fact that they have not yet considered sufficiently either what we have just explained about substances or the full extent and independence of our soul, which makes it contain everything that happens to us and makes it express God and, with him, all possible and actual beings, just as an effect expresses its cause. Also, it is inconceivable that I think through the ideas of others. The soul must actually be affected in a certain way when it thinks of something, and it must already have in itself not only the passive power of being able to be affected in this way (which is already wholly determined) but also an active power, a power by virtue of which there have always been in its nature marks of the future production of this thought and dispositions to produce it in its proper time. And all this already involves the idea included in this thought.

30. *How God inclines our soul without necessitating it; that we do not have the right to complain and that we must not ask why Judas sins but only why Judas the sinner is admitted to existence in preference to some other possible persons. On original imperfection before sin and on the degrees of grace.*   There are a number of considerations with respect to the action of God on human will which are so difficult that it would be inordinately lengthy to pursue them here. Roughly speaking, however,

18. [John 1:9.]

19. [Averroists were Christian followers of Averroes (or Ibn Ruschd — 1126–98), the great Arabic commentator on Aristotle, who held that the active intellect in each man is part of a single active intellect. The doctrine of a single world-soul was condemned as heresy.]

20. [Malebranche, again, is Leibniz's primary target, as above in sec. 23.]

here is what can be said. In concurring with our actions, God ordinarily does no more than follow the laws he has established, that is, he continually conserves and produces our being in such a way that thoughts come to us spontaneously or freely in the order that the notion pertaining to our individual substance contains them, a notion in which they could be foreseen from all eternity. Moreover, in virtue of his decree that the will always tend toward the apparent good, expressing or imitating his will in certain particular respects (so that this apparent good always has some truth in it), God determines our will to choose what seems better, without, however, necessitating it. For, absolutely speaking, the will is in a state of indifference, as opposed to one of necessity, and it has the power to do otherwise or even to suspend its action completely; these two alternatives are possible and remain so.

Therefore the soul must guard itself against deceptive appearances [*les surprises des apparences*] through a firm will to reflect and neither to act nor to judge in certain circumstances except after having deliberated fully. But it is true, and it is even assured from all eternity, that a certain soul will not make use of this power in such a situation. But who is to blame? Can the soul complain about anything other than itself? All these complaints after the fact are unjust, if they would have been unjust before the fact. Now, could this soul, a little before sinning, complain about God in good faith, as if God determined it to sin? Since God's determinations in these matters cannot be foreseen, how does the soul know that it is determined to sin, unless it is actually sinning already? It is only a matter of not willing, and God could not put forth an easier and more just condition; thus judges do not seek the reasons which have disposed a man to have a bad will, but only stop to consider the extent to which this particular will is bad. But perhaps it is certain from all eternity that I shall sin? Answer this question for yourself: perhaps not; and without considering what you cannot know and what can give you no light, act according to your duty, which you do know.

But someone else will say, why is it that this man will assuredly commit this sin? The reply is easy: otherwise he would not be this man. For God sees from all time that there will be a certain Judas whose notion or idea (which God has) contains this free and future action. Therefore only this question remains, why does such a Judas, the traitor, who is merely possible in God's idea, actually exist? But no reply to this question is to be expected on earth, except that, in general, one must say that, since God found it good that he should exist, despite the sin that God foresaw, it must be that this sin is paid back with interest in the universe, that God will derive a greater good from it, and that it will be found that, in sum, the sequence of things in which the existence of that sinner is included is the most perfect among all the possible sequences. But we cannot always explain the admirable economy of this choice while we are travellers in this world; it is enough to know it without understanding it. And here is the occasion to recognize the *altitudinem divitarum*, the depth and abyss of divine wisdom, without seeking a detail that involves infinite considerations.[21]

Yet one sees clearly that God is not the cause of evil. For not only did original sin take possession of the soul after the innocence of men had been lost, but even before this, there was an original imperfection or limitation connatural to all creatures, which makes them liable to sin or capable of error. Thus, the supralapsarians[22] raise no more problems than the others do. And it is to this, in my view, that we must reduce the opinion of Saint Augustine and other authors, the opinion that the root of evil is in nothingness, that is to say, in the privation or limitation of creatures, which God graciously remedies by the degree of perfection it pleases him to give. This grace of God, whether ordinary or extraordinary, has its degrees and its measures; in itself, it is always efficacious in producing a certain proportionate effect, and, further, it is always sufficient, not only to secure us from sin, but even to produce salvation, assuming that man unites himself to it by what derives from him. But it is not always sufficient to overcome man's inclinations, for otherwise he would have nothing more to strive for; this is reserved solely for the absolutely efficacious grace which is always victorious, whether it is so by itself or by way of appropriate circumstances.

---

21. [The Latin translates: "depth of riches," a reference to Romans 11:33.]

22. [Calvinists who held that God's decrees of election and reprobation preceded the fall.]

31. *On the motives of election, on faith foreseen, on middle knowledge, on the absolute decree and that it all reduces to the reason why God has chosen for existence such a possible person whose notion includes just such a sequence of graces and free acts; this puts an end to all difficulties at once.* Finally, God's graces are wholly pure graces, upon which creatures have no claim. However, just as it is not sufficient to appeal to God's absolute or conditional foresight into the future actions of men in order to account for his choice in the dispensation of these graces, we also must not imagine absolute decrees that have no reasonable motive. As for God's foreknowledge of faith or good works, it is very true that he has elected only those whose faith and charity he foresaw, whom he foreknew he would endow with faith. But the same question returns, why will God give the grace of faith or of good works to some rather than to others? And as for this knowledge God has, which is the foresight not of faith and good works, but of their grounds [*matière*] and predisposition, that is, foresight of what a man would contribute to them on his side (for it is true that there are differences among men whenever there are differences in grace and that, in fact, although a man needs to be stimulated to the good and be converted, he must also act in that direction afterward), it seems to several people that one could say that God, seeing what a man would do without grace or extraordinary assistance, or at least seeing the sort of person he is, leaving grace aside, might resolve to give grace to those whose natural dispositions were better or, at least, less imperfect or less bad. But even if that were the case, one can say that these natural dispositions, insofar as they are good, are still the effect of grace, although ordinary grace, since God has favored some more than others. And since he knows that these natural advantages he gives will serve as motives for grace or extraordinary assistance, is it not true, according to this doctrine, that in the end everything is completely reduced to his mercy?

Since we do not know how much and in what way God takes account of natural dispositions in the dispensation of grace, I believe, then, that the most exact and surest thing to say, according to our principles, as I have already noted, is that among the possible beings there must be the person of Peter or John, whose notion or idea contains this entire sequence of ordinary and extraordinary graces and all the rest of these events with

their circumstances, and that it pleased God to choose him for actual existence from among an infinity of equally possible persons. After this it seems that there is nothing more to ask and that all difficulties vanish.

For, with respect to this single great question, why it pleased God to choose him from among so many other possible persons, one would have to be very unreasonable not to be content with the general reasons we have given, reasons whose details lie beyond us. Thus, instead of having recourse to an absolute decree which is unreasonable, since it is without reason, or to reasons which do not solve the difficulty completely and are in need of further reasons, it would be best to say with Saint Paul, that God here followed certain great reasons of wisdom or appropriateness, unknown to mortals and based on the general order, whose aim is the greatest perfection of the universe. It is to this that the motives of the glory of God and the manifestation of his justice are reduced, as well as of his mercy and generally of his perfections and finally the immense depth of his riches, with which the soul of Saint Paul was enraptured.

32. *The utility of these principles in matters of piety and religion.* For the rest, it seems that the thoughts we have just explained, particularly the great principle of the perfection of the operations of God and the principle that the notion of a substance contains all its events with all their circumstances, far from harming, serve to confirm religion, to dispel enormous difficulties, to enflame souls with a divine love, and to elevate minds to the knowledge of incorporeal substances, much more than hypotheses we have seen until now. For one sees clearly that all other substances depend on God, in the same way as thoughts emanate from our substance, that God is all in all, and that he is intimately united with all creatures, in proportion to their perfection, that it is he alone who determines them from the outside by his influence, and, if to act is to determine immediately, it can be said in this sense, in the language of metaphysics, that God alone operates on me, and God alone can do good or evil to me; the other substances contribute only by reason of these determinations, because God, having regard for all, shares his blessings and requires them to accommodate themselves to one another. Hence God alone brings about the connection and communication among substances, and it is through

him that the phenomena of any substance meet and agree with those of others and consequently, that there is reality in our perceptions. But, in practice, one ascribes an action to particular reasons in the sense that I have explained above, because it is not necessary always to mention the universal cause in particular cases.

We also see that every substance has a perfect spontaneity (which becomes freedom in intelligent substances), that everything that happens to it is a consequence of its idea or of its being, and that nothing determines it, except God alone. And that is why a person of very exalted mind, revered for her saintliness, was in the habit of saying that the soul must often think as if there were nothing but God and itself in the world.[23]

Now, nothing gives us a stronger understanding of immortality than the independence and extent of the soul in question here, which shelters it absolutely from all external things, since the soul alone makes up its whole world and is sufficient to itself with God. And it is as impossible that it should perish without annihilation, as it is that the world (of which it is a perpetual living expression) should destroy itself; hence, it is impossible that the changes in this extended mass called our body should do anything to the soul or that the dissolution of this body should destroy what is indivisible.

33. *Explanation of the union of soul and body, a matter which has been considered as inexplicable or miraculous, and on the origin of confused perceptions.* We also see the unexpected illumination of this great mystery of the union of the soul and the body, that is, how it happens that the passions and actions of the one are accompanied by the actions and passions, or by the corresponding phenomena, of the other. For there is no way to conceive that the one has any influence on the other, and it is unreasonable simply to appeal to the extraordinary operation of the universal cause in an ordinary and particular thing. But here is the true reason: we have said that everything that happens to the soul and to each substance follows from its notion, and therefore the very idea or essence of the soul carries with it the

fact that all its appearances or perceptions must arise spontaneously from its own nature and precisely in such a way that they correspond by themselves to what happens in the whole universe. But they correspond more particularly and more perfectly to what happens in the body assigned to it, because the soul expresses the state of the universe in some way and for some time, according to the relation other bodies have to its own body. This also allows us to know how our body belongs to us, without, however, being attached to our essence. And I believe that persons who can meditate will judge our principles favorably, because they will be able to see easily what the connection between the soul and the body consists in, a connection which seems inexplicable in any other way.

We also see that the perceptions of our senses, even when they are clear, must necessarily contain some confused feelings [*sentiment*], for our body receives the impression of all other bodies, since all the bodies of the universe are in sympathy, and, even though our senses are related to everything, it is impossible for our soul to attend to everything in particular; that is why our confused sensations are the result of a truly infinite variety of perceptions. This is almost like the confused murmur coming from the innumerable set of breaking waves heard by those who approach the seashore. Now, if from several perceptions (which do not come together to make one), there is none which stands out before the others and if they make impressions that are almost equally strong or equally capable of gaining the attention of the soul, the soul can only perceive them confusedly.

34. *On the difference between minds and other substances, souls or substantial forms, and that the immortality required includes memory.* Assuming that the bodies that make up an *unum per se*, as does man, are substances, that they have substantial forms, and that animals have souls, we must admit that these souls and these substantial forms cannot entirely perish, no more than atoms or the ultimate parts of matter can, on the view of other philosophers. For no substance perishes, although it can become completely different. They also express the whole universe, although more imperfectly than minds do. But the principal difference is that they do not know what they are nor what they do, and consequently, since they do not reflect on themselves, they cannot dis-

---

23. [Leibniz probably had St. Theresa in mind here.]

cover necessary and universal truths. It is also because they lack reflection about themselves that they have no moral qualities. As a result, though they may pass through a thousand transformations, like those we see when a caterpillar changes into a butterfly, yet from the moral or practical point of view, the result is as if they had perished; indeed, we may even say that they have perished physically, in the sense in which we say that bodies perish through their corruption. But the intelligent soul, knowing what it is—having the ability to utter the word "I," a word so full of meaning—does not merely remain and subsist metaphysically, which it does to a greater degree than the others, but also remains the same morally and constitutes the same person. For it is memory or the knowledge of this self that renders it capable of punishment or reward. Thus the immortality required in morality and religion does not consist merely in this perpetual subsistence common to all substances, for without the memory of what one has been, there would be nothing desirable about it. Suppose that some person all of a sudden becomes the king of China, but only on the condition that he forgets what he has been, as if he were born anew; practically, or as far as the effects could be perceived, wouldn't that be the same as if he were annihilated and a king of China created at the same instant in his place? That is something this individual would have no reason to desire.

35. *The excellence of minds and that God considers them preferable to other creatures. That minds express God rather than the world, but that the other substances express the world rather than God.* But so that we may judge by natural reasons that God will always preserve not only our substance, but also our person, that is, the memory and knowledge of what we are (though distinct knowledge is sometimes suspended during sleep and fainting spells), we must join morals to metaphysics, that is, we must not only consider God as the principle and cause of all substances and all beings, but also as the leader of all persons or intelligent substances and as the absolute monarch of the most perfect city or republic, which is what the universe composed of all minds together is, God himself being the most perfect of all minds and the greatest of all beings. For certainly minds are the most perfect beings and best express divinity. And

since the whole nature, end, virtue, and function of substance is merely to express God and the universe, as has been sufficiently explained, there is no reason to doubt that the substances which express the universe with the knowledge of what they are doing and which are capable of knowing great truths about God and the universe, express it incomparably better than do those natures, which are either brutish and incapable of knowing truths or completely destitute of sensation and knowledge. And the difference between intelligent substances and substances that have no intelligence at all is just as great as the difference between a mirror and someone who sees.

Since God himself is the greatest and wisest of all minds, it is easy to judge that the beings with whom he can, so to speak, enter into conversation, and even into a society—by communicating to them his views and will in a particular manner and in such a way that they can know and love their benefactor—must be infinitely nearer to him than all other things, which can only pass for the instruments of minds. So we see that all wise persons value a man infinitely more than any other thing, no matter how precious it is, and it seems that the greatest satisfaction that a soul, content in other ways, can have is to see itself loved by others. With respect to God, though, there is the difference that his glory and our worship cannot add anything to his satisfaction, since knowledge of creatures is only a consequence of his supreme and perfect happiness—far from contributing to it or being its partial cause. However, what is good and reasonable in finite minds is found preeminently in him, and, just as we would praise a king who would prefer to preserve the life of a man rather than the most precious and rarest of his animals, we should not doubt that the most enlightened and most just of all monarchs is of the same opinion.

36. *God is the monarch of the most perfect republic, composed of all minds, and the happiness of this city of God is his principal purpose.* Indeed, minds are the most perfectible substances, and their perfections are peculiar in that they interfere with each other the least, or rather they aid one another the most, for only the most virtuous can be the most perfect friends. Whence it obviously follows that God, who always aims for the greatest perfection in general, will pay the greatest attention to minds and will give

them the greatest perfection that universal harmony can allow, not only in general, but to each of them in particular.

One can even say that God, insofar as he is a mind, is the originator of existences; otherwise, if he lacked the will to choose the best, there would be no reason for a possible thing to exist in preference to others. Thus the quality that God has of being a mind himself takes precedence over all the other considerations he can have toward creatures; only minds are made in his image and are, as it were, of his race or like children of his household, since they alone can serve him freely and act with knowledge in imitation of the divine nature; a single mind is worth a whole world, since it does not merely express the world but it also knows it and it governs itself after the fashion of God. In this way we may say that, although all substances express the whole universe, nevertheless the other substances express the world rather than God, while minds express God rather than the world. And this nature of minds, so noble that it brings them as near to divinity as it is possible for simple creatures, has the result that God draws infinitely more glory from them than from all other beings, or rather the other beings only furnish minds the matter for glorifying him.

That is why this moral quality God has, which makes him the lord or monarch of minds, relates to him, so to speak, personally and in a quite singular manner. It is because of this that he humanizes himself, that he is willing to allow anthropomorphism, and that he enters into society with us, as a prince with his subjects; and this consideration is so dear to him that the happy and flourishing state of his empire, which consists in the greatest possible happiness of its inhabitants, becomes the highest of his laws. For happiness is to people what perfection is to beings. And if the first principle of the existence of the physical world is the decree to give it the greatest perfection possible, the first intent of the moral world or the City of God, which is the noblest part of the universe, must be to diffuse in it the greatest possible happiness.

Therefore we must not doubt that God has ordered everything in such a way that minds not only may live always, which is certain, but also that they may always preserve their moral quality, so that the city does not lose a single person, just as the world does not lose any substance. And consequently they will always know what they are, otherwise they would not be susceptible to reward or punishment, something, however, essential to a republic, but above all essential to the most perfect republic, in which nothing can be neglected.

Finally, since God is at the same time the most just and most good-natured of monarchs and since he demands only a good will, as long as it is sincere and serious, his subjects cannot wish for a better condition, and, to make them perfectly happy, he wants only for them to love him.

37. *Jesus Christ has revealed to men the mystery and admirable laws of the kingdom of heaven and the greatness of the supreme happiness that God prepares for those who love him.* The ancient philosophers knew very little of these important truths; Jesus Christ alone has expressed them divinely well and in a manner so clear and familiar that the coarsest of minds have grasped them. Thus his gospel has entirely changed the course of human affairs; he has brought us to know the kingdom of heaven, or that perfect republic of minds which deserves the title of City of God, whose admirable laws he has disclosed to us. He alone has made us see how much God loves us and with what exactitude he has provided for everything that concerns us; that, caring for sparrows, he will not neglect the rational beings which are infinitely more dear to him; that all the hairs on our head are numbered; that heaven and earth will perish rather than the word of God and what pertains to the economy of our salvation; that God has more regard for the least of the intelligent souls than for the whole machinery of the world; that we must not fear those who can destroy bodies but cannot harm souls, because God alone can make souls happy or unhappy; and that the souls of the just, in his hands, are safe from all the upheavals of the universe, God alone being able to act upon them; that none of our actions are forgotten; that everything is taken account of, even idle words or a spoonful of water well used; finally, that everything must result in the greatest welfare of those who are good; that the just will be like suns; and that neither our senses nor our mind has ever tasted anything approaching the happiness that God prepares for those who love him.

Monadology

1. The monad, which we shall discuss here, is nothing but a simple substance that enters into composites—simple, that is, without parts.

2. And there must be simple substances, since there are composites; for the composite is nothing more than a collection, or *aggregate*, of simples.

3. But where there are no parts, neither extension, nor shape, nor divisibility is possible. These monads are the true atoms of nature and, in brief, the elements of things.

4. There is also no dissolution to fear, and there is no conceivable way in which a simple substance can perish naturally.

5. For the same reason, there is no conceivable way a simple substance can begin naturally, since it cannot be formed by composition.

6. Thus, one can say that monads can only begin or end all at once, that is, they can only begin by creation and end by annihilation, whereas composites begin or end through their parts.

7. There is also no way of explaining how a monad can be altered or changed internally by some other creature, since one cannot transpose anything in it, nor can one conceive of any internal motion that can be excited, directed, augmented, or diminished within it, as can be done in composites, where there can be change among the parts. The monads have no windows through which something can enter or leave. Accidents cannot be detached, nor can they go about outside of substances, as the sensible species of the Scholastics once did. Thus, neither substance nor accident can enter a monad from without.

8. However, monads must have some qualities, otherwise they would not even be beings. And if simple substances did not differ at all in their qualities, there would be no way of perceiving any change in things, since what there is in a composite can only come from its simple ingredients; and if the monads

Reprinted from Leibniz, *Philosophical Essays*, edited and translated by Roger Ariew and Daniel Garber (Indianapolis: Hackett Publishing Company, 1989).

had no qualities, they would be indiscernible from one another, since they also do not differ in quantity. As a result, assuming a plenum, in motion, each place would always receive only the equivalent of what it already had, and one state of things would be indistinguishable from another.

9. It is also necessary that each monad be different from each other. For there are never two beings in nature that are perfectly alike, two beings in which it is not possible to discover an internal difference, that is, one founded on an intrinsic denomination.

10. I also take for granted that every created being, and consequently the created monad as well, is subject to change, and even that this change is continual in each thing.

11. It follows from what we have just said that the monad's natural changes come from an *internal principle*, since no external cause can influence it internally.

12. But, besides the principle of change, there must be *diversity* [*un détail*] *in that which changes*, which produces, so to speak, the specification and variety of simple substances.

13. This diversity must involve a multitude in the unity or in the simple. For, since all natural change is produced by degrees, something changes and something remains. As a result, there must be a plurality of properties [*affections*] and relations in the simple substance, although it has no parts.

14. The passing state which involves and represents a multitude in the unity or in the simple substance is nothing other than what one calls *perception*, which should be distinguished from apperception, or consciousness, as will be evident in what follows. This is where the Cartesians have failed badly, since they took no account of the perceptions that we do not apperceive. This is also what made them believe that minds alone are monads and that there are no animal souls or other entelechies. With the common people, they have confused a long stupor with death, properly speaking, which made them fall again into the Scholastic prejudice of completely separated souls, and

they have even confirmed unsound minds in the belief in the mortality of souls.

15. The action of the internal principle which brings about the change or passage from one perception to another can be called *appetition*; it is true that the appetite cannot always completely reach the whole perception toward which it tends, but it always obtains something of it, and reaches new perceptions.

16. We ourselves experience a multitude in a simple substance when we find that the least thought we ourselves apperceive involves variety in its object. Thus, all those who recognize that the soul is a simple substance should recognize this multitude in the monad; and Mr. Bayle should not find any difficulty in this as he has done in his *Dictionary* article, "Rorarius."[1]

17. Moreover, we must confess that the *perception*, and what depends on it, is *inexplicable in terms of mechanical reasons*, that is, through shapes and motions. If we imagine that there is a machine whose structure makes it think, sense, and have perceptions, we could conceive it enlarged, keeping the same proportions, so that we could enter into it, as one enters into a mill. Assuming that, when inspecting its interior, we will only find parts that push one another, and we will never find anything to explain a perception. And so, we should seek perception in the simple substance and not in the composite or in the machine. Furthermore, this is all one can find in the simple substance—that is, perception and their changes. It is also in this alone that all the *internal actions* of simple substances can consist.

18. One can call all simple substances or created monads entelechies, for they have in themselves a certain perfection (*echousi to enteles*); they have a sufficiency (*autarkeia*) that makes them the sources of their internal actions, and, so to speak, incorporeal automata.

1. [Leibniz's *Theodicy* was, to a large extent, an attempt to answer the skeptical arguments, from Bayle's *Historical and Critical Dictionary*, regarding the impossibility of reconciling faith with reason. "Rorarius," an article of the *Dictionary*, was Bayle's occasion for a discussion of the problem of the souls of animals: Jerome Rorarius (1485–1566) wrote a treatise maintaining that men are less rational than the lower animals. In "Rorarius" Bayle criticizes Leibniz's views.—R.A. and D.G.]

19. If we wish to call *soul* anything that has *perceptions* and *appetites* in the general sense I have just explained, then all simple substances or created monads can be called souls. But, since sensation is something more than a simple perception, I think that the general name of monad and entelechy is sufficient for simple substances which only have perceptions, and that we should only call those substances *souls* where perception is more distinct and accompanied by memory.

20. For we experience within ourselves a state in which we remember nothing and have no distinct perception; this is similar to when we faint or when we are overwhelmed by a deep, dreamless sleep. In this state the soul does not differ sensibly from a simple monad; but since this state does not last, and since the soul emerges from it, our soul is something more.

21. And it does not at all follow that in such a state the simple substance is without any perception. This is not possible for the previous reasons; for it cannot perish, and it also cannot subsist without some property [*affection*], which is nothing other than its perception. But when there is a great multitude of small perceptions in which nothing is distinct, we are stupefied. This is similar to when we continually spin in the same direction several times in succession, from which arises a dizziness that can make us faint and does not allow us to distinguish anything. Death can impart this state to animals for a time.

22. And since every present state of a simple substance is a natural consequence of its preceding state, the present is pregnant with the future.

23. Therefore, since on being awakened from a stupor we apperceive our perceptions, it must be the case that we had some perceptions immediately before, even though we did not apperceive them; for a perception can only come naturally from another perception, as a motion can only come naturally from a motion.

24. From this we see that if, in our perceptions, we had nothing distinct or, so to speak, in relief and stronger in flavor, we would always be in a stupor. And this is the state of bare monads.

25. We also see that nature has given heightened perceptions to animals from the care she has taken to furnish them organs that collect several rays of light or several waves of air, in order to make them

more effectual by bringing them together. There is something similar to this in odor, taste, and touch, and perhaps in many other senses which are unknown to us. I will soon explain how what occurs in the soul represents what occurs in the organs.

26. Memory provides a kind of sequence in souls, which imitates reason, but which must be distinguished from it. We observe that when animals have the perception of something which strikes them, and when they previously had a similar perception of that thing, then, through a representation in their memory, they expect that which was attached to the thing in the preceding perception, and are led to have sensations similar to those they had before. For example, if we show dogs a stick, they remember the pain that it caused them and they flee.

27. And the strong imagination that strikes and moves them comes from the magnitude or the multitude of the preceding perceptions. For often a strong impression produces, all at once, the effect produced by a long *habit* or by many lesser, reiterated perceptions.

28. Men act like beasts insofar as the sequence of their perceptions results from the principle of memory alone; they resemble the empirical physicians who practice without theory. We are all mere Empirics in three fourths of our actions. For example, when we expect that the day will dawn tomorrow, we act like an Empiric,[2] because until now it has always been thus. Only the astronomer judges this by reason.

29. But the knowledge of eternal and necessary truths is what distinguishes us from simple animals and furnishes us with *reason* and the sciences, by raising us to a knowledge of ourselves and of God. And that is what we call the rational soul, or *mind*, in ourselves.

30. It is also through the knowledge of necessary truths and through their abstractions that we rise to *reflective acts*, which enable us to think of that which is called "I" and enable us to consider that this or that is in us. And thus, in thinking of ourselves, we think of being, or substance, of the simple and of the composite, of the immaterial and of God himself, by conceiving that that which is limited in us is limitless in him. And these reflective acts furnish the principal objects of our reasonings.

31. Our reasonings are based on *two great principles, that of contradiction*, in virtue of which we judge that which involves a contradiction to be false, and that which is opposed or contradictory to the false to be true.

32. And *that of sufficient reason*, by virtue of which we consider that we can find no true or existent fact, no true assertion, without there being a sufficient reason why it is thus and not otherwise, although most of the time these reasons cannot be known to us.

33. There are also two kinds of *truths*, those of *reasoning* and those of *fact*. The truths of reasoning are necessary and their opposite is impossible; the truths of fact are contingent, and their opposite is possible. When a truth is necessary, its reason can be found by analysis, resolving it into simpler ideas and simpler truths until we reach the primitives.

34. This is how the speculative *theorems* and practical *canons* of mathematicians are reduced by analysis to *definitions*, *axioms*, and *postulates*.

35. And there are, finally, *simple ideas*, whose definition cannot be given. There are also axioms and postulates, in brief, *primitive principles*, which cannot be proved and which need no proof. And these are *identical propositions*, whose opposite contains an explicit contradiction.

36. But there must also be a *sufficient reason* in *contingent truths*, or *truths of fact*, that is, in the series of things distributed throughout the universe of creatures, where the resolution into particular reasons could proceed into unlimited detail because of the immense variety of things in nature and because of the division of bodies to infinity. There is an infinity of past and present shapes and motions that enter into the efficient cause of my present writing, and there is an infinity of small inclinations and dispositions of my soul, present and past, that enter into its final cause.

37. And since all this *detail* involves nothing but other prior or more detailed contingents, each of which needs a similar analysis in order to give its reason, we do not make progress in this way. It must be the case that the sufficient or ultimate reason is outside the sequence or *series* of this multiplicity of contingencies, however infinite it may be.

2. [The Empirics were a sect of physicians before Galen (c. A.D. 150). In later times, the epithet "Empiric" was given to physicians who despised theoretical study and trusted tradition and their own experience.]

38. And that is why the ultimate reason of things must be in a necessary substance in which the diversity of changes is only eminent, as in its source. This is what we call *God*.

39. Since this substance is a sufficient reason for all this diversity, which is utterly interconnected, *there is only one God, and this God is sufficient.*

40. We can also judge that this supreme substance which is unique, universal, and necessary must be incapable of limits and must contain as much reality as is possible, insofar as there is nothing outside it which is independent of it, and insofar as it is a simple consequence of its possible existence.

41. From this it follows that God is absolutely perfect—*perfection* being nothing but the magnitude of positive reality considered as such, setting aside the limits or bounds in the things which have it. And here, where there are no limits, that is, in God, perfection is absolutely infinite.

42. It also follows that creatures derive their perfections from God's influence, but that they derive their imperfections from their own nature, which is incapable of being without limits. For it is in this that they are distinguished from God.

43. It is also true that God is not only the source of existences, but also that of essences insofar as they are real, that is, or the source of that which is real in possibility. This is because God's understanding is the realm of eternal truths or that of the ideas on which they depend; without him there would be nothing real in possibles, and not only would nothing exist, but also nothing would be possible.

44. For if there is reality in essences or possibles, or indeed, in eternal truths, this reality must be grounded in something existent and actual, and consequently, it must be grounded in the existence of the necessary being, in whom essence involves existence, that is, in whom possible being is sufficient for actual being.

45. Thus God alone (or the necessary being) has this privilege, that he must exist if he is possible. And since nothing can prevent the possibility of what is without limits, without negation, and consequently without contradiction, this by itself is sufficient for us to know the existence of God *a priori*. We have also proved this by the reality of the eternal truths. But we have also just proved it *a posteriori* since there are contingent beings, which can only have their final

or sufficient reason in the necessary being, a being that has the reason of its existence in itself.

46. However, we should not imagine, as some do, that since the eternal truths depend on God, they are arbitrary and depend on his will, as Descartes appears to have held, and after him Mr. Poiret.[3] This is true only of contingent truths, whose principle is *fitness* [*convenance*] or the choice of the *best*. But necessary truths depend solely on his understanding, and are its internal object.

47. Thus God alone is the primitive unity or the first [*originaire*] simple substance; all created or derivative monads are products, and are generated, so to speak, by continual fulgurations of the divinity from moment to moment, limited by the receptivity of the creature, to which it is essential to be limited.

48. God has *power*, which is the source of everything, *knowledge*, which contains the diversity of ideas, and finally *will*, which brings about changes or products in accordance with the principle of the best. And these correspond to what, in created monads, is the subject or the basis, the perceptive faculty and the appetitive faculty. But in God these attributes are absolutely infinite or perfect, while in the created monads or in entelechies (or *perfectihabies*, as Hermolaus Barbarus translated that word)[4] they are only imitations of it, in proportion to the perfection that they have.

49. The creature is said to *act* externally insofar as it is perfect, and *to be acted upon* [*patir*] by another, insofar as it is imperfect. Thus we attribute *action* to a monad insofar as it has distinct perceptions, and *passion*, insofar as it has confused perceptions.

50. And one creature is more perfect than another insofar as one finds in it that which provides an *a priori* reason for what happens in the other; and this is why we say that it acts on the other.

3. [Pierre Poiret (1646–1719) was initially one of Descartes's followers; he published a book of reflections on God, soul and evil, *Cogitationum rationalium de Deo, anima, et malo libri quattuor* (1677), which was attacked by Bayle.]

4. [Hermolaus Barbarus (1454–93) was an Italian scholar who attempted, through retranslations of Aristotle, to recover Aristotle's original doctrine from under the layers of Scholastic interpretations. His works include popular compendia of ethics and natural philosophy, drawn from the writings of Aristotle.]

51. But in simple substances the influence of one monad over another can only be ideal, and can only produce its effect through God's intervention, when in the ideas of God a monad reasonably asks that God take it into account in regulating the others from the beginning of things. For, since a created monad cannot have an internal physical influence upon another, this is the only way in which one can depend on another.

52. It is in this way that actions and passions among creatures are mutual. For God, comparing two simple substances, finds in each reasons that require him to adjust the other to it; and consequently, what is active in some respects is passive from another point of view: *active* insofar as what is known distinctly in one serves to explain what happens in another; and *passive* insofar as the reason for what happens in one is found in what is known distinctly in another.

53. Now, since there is an infinity of possible universes in God's ideas, and since only one of them can exist, there must be a sufficient reason for God's choice, a reason which determines him towards one thing rather than another.

54. And this reason can only be found in *fitness*, or in the degree of perfection that these worlds contain, each possible world having the right to claim existence in proportion to the perfection it contains.

55. And this is the cause of the existence of the best, which wisdom makes known to God, which his goodness makes him choose, and which his power makes him produce.

56. This interconnection or accommodation of all created things to each other, and each to all the others, brings it about that each simple substance has relations that express all the others, and consequently, that each simple substance is a perpetual, living mirror of the universe.

57. Just as the same city viewed from different directions appears entirely different and, as it were, multiplied perspectively, in just the same way it happens that, because of the infinite multitude of simple substances, there are, as it were, just as many different universes, which are, nevertheless, only perspectives on a single one, corresponding to the different points of view of each monad.

58. And this is the way of obtaining as much variety as possible, but with the greatest order possible, that is, it is the way of obtaining as much perfection as possible.

59. Moreover, this is the only hypothesis (which I dare say is demonstrated) that properly enhances God's greatness. Mr. Bayle recognized this when, in his *Dictionary* (article "Rorarius"), he set out objections to it; indeed, he was tempted to believe that I ascribed too much to God, more than is possible. But he was unable to present any reason why this universal harmony, which results in every substance expressing exactly all the others through the relations it has to them, is impossible.

60. Furthermore, in what I have just discussed, we can see the *a priori* reasons why things could not be otherwise. Because God, in regulating the whole, had regard for each part, and particularly for each monad, and since the nature of the monad is representative, nothing can limit it to represent only a part of things. However, it is true that this representation is only confused as to the detail of the whole universe, and can only be distinct for a small portion of things, that is, either for those that are closest, or for those that are greatest with respect to each monad, otherwise each monad would be a divinity. Monads are limited, not as to their objects, but with respect to the modifications of their knowledge of them. Monads all go confusedly to infinity, to the whole; but they are limited and differentiated by the degrees of their distinct perceptions.

61. In this respect, composites are analogous to simples. For everything is a plenum, which makes all matter interconnected. In a plenum, every motion has some effect on distant bodies, in proportion to their distance. For each body is affected, not only by those in contact with it, and in some way feels the effects of everything that happens to them, but also, through them, it feels the effects of those in contact with the bodies with which it is itself immediately in contact. From this it follows that this communication extends to any distance whatsoever. As a result, every body is affected by everything that happens in the universe, to such an extent that he who sees all can read in each thing what happens everywhere, and even what has happened or what will happen, by observing in the present what is remote in time as well as in space. "All things conspire [*sympnoia panta*]," said Hippocrates. But a soul can read in itself only what is distinctly represented there; it cannot unfold all its folds at once, because they go to infinity.

62. Thus, although each created monad represents the whole universe, it more distinctly represents the body which is particularly affected by it, and whose entelechy it constitutes. And just as this body expresses the whole universe through the interconnection of all matter in the plenum, the soul also represents the whole universe by representing this body, which belongs to it in a particular way.

63. The body belonging to a monad (which is the entelechy or soul of that body) together with an entelechy constitutes what may be called a *living being*, and together with a soul constitutes what is called an *animal*. Now, the body of a living being or an animal is always organized; for, since every monad is a mirror of the universe in its way, and since the universe is regulated in a perfect order, there must also be an order in the representing being, that is, in the perceptions of the soul, and consequently, in the body in accordance with which the universe is represented therein.

64. Thus each organized body of a living being is a kind of divine machine or natural automaton, which infinitely surpasses all artificial automata. For a machine constructed by man's art is not a machine in each of its parts. For example, the tooth of a brass wheel has parts or fragments which, for us, are no longer artificial things, and no longer have any marks to indicate the machine for whose use the wheel was intended. But natural machines, that is, living bodies, are still machines in their least parts, to infinity. That is the difference between nature and art, that is, between divine art and our art.

65. And the author of nature has been able to practice this divine and infinitely marvelous art, because each portion of matter is not only divisible to infinity, as the ancients have recognized, but is also actually subdivided without end, each part divided into parts having some motion of their own; otherwise, it would be impossible for each portion of matter to express the whole universe.

66. From this we see that there is a world of creatures, of living beings, of animals, of entelechies, of souls in the least part of matter.

67. Each portion of matter can be conceived as a garden full of plants, and as a pond full of fish. But each branch of a plant, each limb of an animal, each drop of its humors, is still another such garden or pond.

68. And although the earth and air lying between the garden plants, or the water lying between the fish of the pond, are neither plant nor fish, they contain yet more of them, though of a subtleness imperceptible to us, most often.

69. Thus there is nothing fallow, sterile, or dead in the universe, no chaos and no confusion except in appearance, almost as it looks in a pond at a distance, where we might see the confused and, so to speak, teeming motion of the fish in the pond, without discerning the fish themselves.

70. Thus we see that each living body has a dominant entelechy, which in the animal is the soul; but the limbs of this living body are full of other living beings, plants, animals, each of which also has its entelechy, or its dominant soul.

71. But we must not imagine, as some who have misunderstood my thought do, that each soul has a mass or portion of matter of its own, always proper to or allotted by it, and that it consequently possesses other lower living beings, forever destined to serve it. For all bodies are in a perpetual flux, like rivers, and parts enter into them and depart from them continually.

72. Thus the soul changes body only little by little and by degrees, so that it is never stripped at once of all its organs. There is often metamorphosis in animals, but there is never metempsychosis nor transmigration of souls; there are also no completely *separated souls*, nor spirits [*Génies*] without bodies. God alone is completely detached from bodies.

73. That is why there is never total generation nor, strictly speaking, perfect death, death consisting in the separation of the soul. And what we call *generations* are developments and growths, as what we call deaths are enfoldings and diminutions.

74. Philosophers have been greatly perplexed about the origin of forms, entelechies, or souls. But today, when exact inquiries on plants, insects, and animals have shown us that organic bodies in nature are never produced from chaos or putrefaction, but always through seeds in which there is, no doubt, some *preformation*, it has been judged that, not only the organic body was already there before conception, but there was also a soul in this body; in brief, the animal itself was there, and through conception this animal was merely prepared for a great transformation, in order to become an animal of another kind.

Something similar is seen outside generation, as when worms become flies, and caterpillars become butterflies.

75. Those *animals*, some of which are raised by conception to the level of the larger animals, can be called *spermatic*. But those of them that remain among those of their kind, that is, the majority, are born, multiply, and are destroyed, just like the larger animals. There are but a small number of Elect that pass onto a larger stage [*théatre*].

76. But this was only half the truth. I have, therefore, held that if the animal never begins naturally, it does not end naturally, either; and not only will there be no generation, but also no complete destruction, nor any death, strictly speaking. These *a posteriori* reasonings, derived from experience, agree perfectly with my principles deduced *a priori*, as above.

77. Thus one can state that not only is the soul (mirror of an indestructible universe) indestructible, but so is the animal itself, even though its mechanism often perishes in part, and casts off or puts on its organic coverings.

78. These principles have given me a way of naturally explaining the union, or rather the conformity of the soul and the organic body. The soul follows its own laws and the body also follows its own; and they agree in virtue of the harmony pre-established between all substances, since they are all representations of a single universe.

79. Souls act according to the laws of final causes, through appetitions, ends, and means. Bodies act according to the laws of efficient causes or of motions. And these two kingdoms, that of efficient causes and that of final causes, are in harmony with each other.

80. Descartes recognized that souls cannot impart a force to bodies because there is always the same quantity of force in matter. However, he thought that the soul could change the direction of bodies. But that is because the law of nature, which also affirms the conservation of the same total direction in matter, was not known at that time. If he had known it, he would have hit upon my system of pre-established harmony.

81. According to this system, bodies act as if there were no souls (though this is impossible); and souls act as if there were no bodies; and both act as if each influenced the other.

82. As for *minds* or rational souls, I find that, at

bottom, what we just said holds for all living beings and animals, namely that animals and souls begin only with the world and do not end any more than the world does. However, rational animals have this peculiarity, that their little spermatic animals, as long as they only remain in this state, have only ordinary or sensitive souls. But that as soon as the Elect among them, so to speak, attain human nature by actual conception, their sensitive souls are elevated to the rank of reason and to the prerogative of minds.

83. Among other differences which exist between ordinary souls and minds, some of which I have already noted, there are also the following: that souls, in general, are living mirrors or images of the universe of creatures, but that minds are also images of the divinity itself, or of the author of nature, capable of knowing the system of the universe, and imitating something of it through their schematic representations [*échantillons architectoniques*] of it, each mind being like a little divinity in its own realm.

84. That is what makes minds capable of entering into a kind of society with God, and allows him to be, in relation to them, not only what an inventor is to his machine (as God is in relation to the other creatures) but also what a prince is to his subjects, and even what a father is to his children.

85. From this it is easy to conclude that the collection of all minds must make up the city of God, that is, the most perfect possible state under the most perfect of monarchs.

86. This city of God, this truly universal monarchy, is a moral world within the natural world, and the highest and most divine of God's works. The glory of God truly consists in this city, for he would have none if his greatness and goodness were not known and admired by minds. It is also in relation to this divine city that God has goodness, properly speaking, whereas his wisdom and power are evident everywhere.

87. Since earlier we established a perfect harmony between two natural kingdoms, the one of efficient causes, the other the final causes, we ought to note here yet another harmony between the physical kingdom of nature and the moral kingdom of grace, that is, between God considered as the architect of the mechanism of the universe, and God considered as the monarch of the divine city of minds.

88. This harmony leads things to grace through

the very path of nature. For example, this globe must be destroyed and restored by natural means at such times as the governing of minds requires it, for the punishment of some and the reward of others.

89. It can also be said that God the architect pleases in every respect God the legislator, and, as a result, sins must carry their penalty with them by the order of nature, and even in virtue of the mechanical structure of things. Similarly, noble actions will receive their rewards through mechanical means with regard to bodies, even though this cannot, and must not, always happen immediately.

90. Finally, under this perfect government, there will be no good action that is unrewarded, no bad action that goes unpublished, and everything must result in the well-being of the good, that is, of those who are not dissatisfied in this great state, those who trust in providence, after having done their duty, and who love and imitate the author of all good, as they should, finding pleasure in the consideration of his perfections according to the nature of genuinely *pure love*, which takes pleasure in the happiness of the beloved. This is what causes wise and virtuous persons to work for all that appears to be in conformity with the presumptive or antecedent divine will, and nevertheless, to content themselves with what God brings about by his secret, consequent, or decisive will, since they recognize that if we could understand the order of the universe well enough, we would find that it surpasses all the wishes of the wisest, and that it is impossible to make it better than it is.[5] This is true not only for the whole in general, but also for ourselves in particular, if we are attached, as we should be, to the author of the whole, not only as the architect and efficient cause of our being, but also as to our master and final cause; he ought to be the whole aim of our will, and he alone can make us happy.

---

5. [The distinction between God's antecedent and consequent will can be found in Thomas Aquinas, *Summa Theologica* I, q. 23, art. 2, ad 1.]

John Locke

John Locke was born in Wrington, England, a town near Bristol, in 1632. He was raised in a Puritan household, and there he received an elementary education, as well as instruction in theology and politics. He entered Westminster school in 1647, and from there he was elected to a scholarship at Christ Church, Oxford. Locke was to make Oxford his home for about thirty years. For his bachelor's and master's degrees he studied metaphysics, logic, rhetoric, and classical languages. The philosophy taught at Oxford at the time was Aristotelian, and his lack of enthusiasm for that system was to be reflected in his mature views. During this period he developed an interest in medicine, which he pursued with an eye toward understanding the methodology of experimental science. Consideration of this methodology, as well as his friendships with the chemist Robert Boyle and the physicist Isaac Newton, was to influence his philosophical views profoundly. From 1675 to 1679, he went to France due to his poor health, where he devoted his time to his studies. For many years Locke served as physician and later also as secretary and advisor to Lord Ashley, later Earl of Shaftesbury. In 1683, because of his connections with Shaftesbury's anti-Stuart politics, he felt compelled to flee to the Netherlands. Here he was able to finish his two greatest works, *Two Treatises of Government* (1690) and *An Essay Concerning Human Understanding* (1690). Another work he completed during this time is *A Letter Concerning Toleration* (1689). Locke returned to England in 1689 with William of Orange, who, together with his wife Mary, assumed the British throne in the Glorious Revolution. He then retired to Oates in Essex, the home of his friend Lady Masham and her husband, where he spent the remainder of his life. Works published in this final period include *Some Thoughts Concerning Education* (1693) and *The Reasonableness of Christianity* (1695). Locke died in 1704.

In *An Essay Concerning Human Understanding* Locke develops an empiricist account of science and of knowledge. In his view, all of our ideas and all of our knowledge have their origin in sensory experience. Locke contrasts this position with the rationalist claim that some of our ideas and consequently some of our knowledge are *innate,* that is, part of the structure of the mind from birth. By contrast, Locke argues that all human ideas and knowledge derive either from sensation of the external world or from reflection, a kind of sensation of the elements of one's mind: "All those sublime thoughts, which tower above the clouds, and reach as high as heaven itself, take their rise and footing here: In all that great extent wherein the mind wanders, in those remote speculations, it may seem to be elevated with, it stirs not one jot beyond those ideas, which sense or reflection have offered for its contemplation" (*Essay* 2.1.24).

Locke associates his empiricist view with a degree of pessimism about the extent of our ability to acquire knowledge. Human beings have only a limited range of sensory capacities, and our understanding is limited in its operations to the ideas it can acquire by means of these capacities. And further, our understanding is limited in its power, so that, for example, it cannot apprehend the relations among all of its ideas at once.

In the *Essay,* Locke also develops views about the central issues that faced the emerging modern scientific conception of the physical world. He criticizes Descartes's claim that the essence of matter consists solely in extension—spatial three-dimensionality—on the grounds that it leads to unacceptable results, such as the indistinguishability of matter and space and the inconceivability of a vacuum. In Locke's view, the essence of matter does not consist simply in extension, but also in solidity or impenetrability—the physical force that hinders the approach of two bodies when they are moving toward each other. His view is akin to the *dynamical* views of matter of Leibniz and Kant, according to which its essence consists primarily in force.

Siding with Galileo and Descartes, Locke also argues that the real characteristics of matter are the primary qualities, such as extension and motion, and that by contrast with the Aristotelian view, matter has no qualities that resemble secondary-quality ideas, such as the ideas of color, shape, sound, taste, odor, and temperature. Locke presents a much-discussed *perceptual relativity* argument for claims of this sort: If one hand is initially warm, and the other cold, and both are placed in the same bowl of water, it will feel cooler to one hand than the other. Since the water couldn't have a quality that resembles the temperature sensations of each of the hands, one should conclude that the water really has no such quality at all. Nevertheless Locke does want to maintain the commonsensical view that physical objects really have secondary qualities, and accordingly he characterizes a secondary quality as a power that an object has in virtue of its primary qualities to produce a secondary-quality idea in a perceiver. Redness, therefore, is not a quality in a physical object that resembles one's sensation of red, but rather a power that an object has in virtue of its primary qualities—perhaps in virtue of its surface texture—to produce sensations of red in perceivers.

A further feature of the *Essay* is Locke's attack on Aristotelian science, which he thought to be on the wrong track, since its primary concerns seemed to him to involve characterizing natural kinds by merely superficial definitions of their essences. According to his own account, inspired by the revival of the ancient Greek atomism, natural kinds have "corpuscular" real essences, consisting of arrangements of unobservable particles, from which their observable primary qualities result. Yet Locke does not think that we can gain any genuine knowledge of real essences of material substances. He also denies that we can come to know the nature of the connections between the real essences of material substances and the secondary-quality ideas they produce in us. The only hypothesis we can grasp on this issue, he claims, is that this connection is established by God. Locke does, however, argue that we can acquire knowledge of real essences in geometry and in morality.

Locke believes in dualism of body and mind—that the body is material while the mind is immaterial—but he does not think that this view can be firmly established, since the hypothesis that God annexes thought to a purely material system cannot be ruled out. What makes us the same persons over time, he argues, is continuity of consciousness or memory. Locke also claims that the existence of God can be established with "mathematical certainty." His religion is in a sense rationalist, since he maintains that beliefs based solely on revelation are inferior to beliefs supported by reasoned argument. In this respect, Locke's religion is a forerunner of the deism that was to become so influential in the eighteenth century.

• • •

Important scholarly books on Locke include Peter Alexander, *Ideas, Qualities, and Corpuscles: Locke and Boyle on the External World* (Cambridge: Cambridge University Press, 1985); Michael R. Ayers, *Locke* (London: Routledge and Kegan Paul, 1991); Jonathan Bennett, *Locke, Berkeley, Hume: Central Themes* (Oxford: Oxford University Press, 1971); Nicholas Jolley, *Leibniz and Locke* (Oxford: Oxford University Press, 1984); J. L. Mackie, *Problems from Locke* (Oxford: Oxford University Press, 1971); R. S. Woolhouse, *Locke* (Brighton: Harvester Press, 1983). Good collections of essays are C. B. Martin and D. M. Armstrong, eds., *Locke and Berkeley: A Collection of Critical Essays* (Garden City: Doubleday, 1968) and Margaret Atherton, ed., *The Empiricists: Locke, Berkeley, Hume* (Lanham, Md.: Rowman & Littlefield, 1998).

D.P.

An Essay Concerning Human Understanding

INTRODUCTION

1. *An Inquiry into the Understanding pleasant and useful.* Since it is the *understanding* that sets man above the rest of sensible beings, and gives him all the advantage and dominion which he has over them; it is certainly a subject, even for its nobleness, worth our labour to inquire into. The understanding, like the eye, whilst it makes us see and perceive all other things, takes no notice of itself; and it requires art and pains to set it at a distance and make it its own object. But whatever be the difficulties that lie in the way of this inquiry; whatever it be that keeps us so much in the dark to ourselves; sure I am that all the light we can let in upon our minds, all the acquaintance we can make with our own understandings, will not only be very pleasant, but bring us great advantage, in directing our thoughts in the search of other things.

2. *Design.* This, therefore, being my purpose — to inquire into the original, certainty, and extent of *human knowledge*, together with the grounds and degrees of *belief, opinion,* and *assent;* — I shall not at present meddle with the physical consideration of the mind; or trouble myself to examine wherein its essence consists; or by what motions of our spirits or alterations of our bodies we come to have any *sensation* by our organs, or any *ideas* in our understandings; and whether those ideas do in their formation, any or all of them, depend on matter or not. These are speculations which, however curious and entertaining, I shall decline, as lying out of my way in the design I am now upon. It shall suffice to my present purpose, to consider the discerning faculties of a man, as they are employed about the objects which they have to do with. And I shall imagine I have not wholly misemployed myself in the thoughts I shall have on this occasion, if, in this historical, plain method, I can give any account of the ways whereby our understandings come to attain those notions of things we have; and can set down any measures of the certainty of our knowledge; or the grounds of those persuasions which are to be found amongst men, so various, different, and wholly contradictory; and yet asserted somewhere or other with such assurance and confidence, that he that shall take a view of the opinions of mankind, observe their opposition, and at the same time consider the fondness and devotion wherewith they are embraced, the resolution and eagerness wherewith they are maintained, may perhaps have reason to suspect, that either there is no such thing as truth at all, or that mankind hath no sufficient means to attain a certain knowledge of it.

3. *Method.* It is therefore worth while to search out the bounds between opinion and knowledge; and examine by what measures, in things whereof we have no certain knowledge, we ought to regulate our assent and moderate our persuasion. In order whereunto I shall pursue this following method: —

First, I shall inquire into the original of those *ideas,* notions, or whatever else you please to call them, which a man observes, and is conscious to himself he has in his mind; and the ways whereby the understanding comes to be furnished with them.

Secondly, I shall endeavour to show what *knowledge* the understanding hath by those ideas; and the certainty, evidence, and extent of it.

Thirdly, I shall make some inquiry into the nature and grounds of *faith* or *opinion:* whereby I mean that assent which we give to any proposition as true, of whose truth yet we have no certain knowledge. And here we shall have occasion to examine the reasons and degrees of *assent.*

8. *What Idea stands for.* Before I proceed on to what I have thought on this subject, I must here in the entrance beg pardon of my reader for the frequent use of the word *idea,* which he will find in the following treatise. It being that term which, I think, serves best to stand for whatsoever is the *object* of the understanding when a man thinks, I have used it to express whatever is meant by *phantasm, notion, species,* or

whatever it is which the mind can be employed about in thinking; and I could not avoid frequently using it.

I presume it will be easily granted me, that there are such *ideas* in men's minds: every one is conscious of them in himself; and men's words and actions will satisfy him that they are in others.

BOOK I

NEITHER PRINCIPLES NOR IDEAS ARE INNATE

Chapter I

NO INNATE SPECULATIVE PRINCIPLES

1. *The way shown how we come by any knowledge, sufficient to prove it not innate.* It is an established opinion amongst some men, that there are in the understanding certain *innate principles*; some primary notions, κοιναὶ ἔννοιαι, characters, as it were, stamped upon the mind of man; which the soul receives in its very first being, and brings into the world with it. It would be sufficient to convince unprejudiced readers of the falseness of this supposition, if I should only show (as I hope I shall in the following parts of this Discourse) how men, barely by the use of their natural faculties, may attain to all the knowledge they have, without the help of any innate impressions; and may arrive at certainty, without any such original notions or principles. For I imagine any one will easily grant that it would be impertinent to suppose the ideas of colours innate in a creature to whom God hath given sight, and a power to receive them by the eyes from external objects; and no less unreasonable would it be to attribute several truths to the impressions of nature, and innate characters, when we may observe in ourselves faculties fit to attain as easy and certain knowledge of them as if they were originally imprinted on the mind.

But because a man is not permitted without censure to follow his own thoughts in the search of truth, when they lead him ever so little out of the common road, I shall set down the reasons that made me doubt of the truth of that opinion, as an excuse for my mistake, if I be in one; which I leave to be considered by those who, with me, dispose themselves to embrace truth wherever they find it.

2. *General Assent the great Argument.* There is nothing more commonly taken for granted than that there are certain *principles*, both *speculative* and *practical*, (for they speak of both), universally agreed upon by all mankind: which therefore, they argue, must needs be the constant impressions which the souls of men receive in their first beings, and which they bring into the world with them, as necessarily and really as they do any of their inherent faculties.

3. *Universal Consent proves nothing innate.* This argument, drawn from universal consent, has this misfortune in it, that if it were true in matter of fact, that there were certain truths wherein all mankind agreed, it would not prove them innate, if there can be any other way shown how men may come to that universal agreement, in the things they do consent in, which I presume may be done.

4. *'What is, is,' and 'It is impossible for the same Thing to be and not to be,' not universally assented to.* But, which is worse, this argument of universal consent which is made use of to prove innate principles, seems to me a demonstration that there are none such: because there are none to which all mankind give an universal assent. I shall begin with the speculative, and instance in those magnified principles of demonstration, 'Whatsoever is, is,' and 'It is impossible for the same thing to be and not to be'; which, of all others, I think have the most allowed title to innate. These have so settled a reputation of maxims universally received, that it will no doubt be thought strange if any one should seem to question it. But yet I take liberty to say, that these propositions are so far from having an universal assent, that there are a great part of mankind to whom they are not so much as known.

5. *Not on the Mind naturally imprinted, because not known to Children, Idiots, &c.* For, first, it is evident, that all children and idiots have not the least apprehension or thought of them. And the want of that is enough to destroy that universal assent which must needs be the necessary concomitant of all innate truths: it seeming to me near a contradiction to say, that there are truths imprinted on the soul, which it perceives or understands not: imprinting, if it signify anything, being nothing else but the making certain

truths to be perceived. For to imprint anything on the mind without the mind's perceiving it, seems to me hardly intelligible. If therefore children and idiots have souls, have minds, with those impressions upon them, *they* must unavoidably perceive them, and necessarily know and assent to these truths; which since they do not, it is evident that there are no such impressions. For if they are not notions naturally imprinted, how can they be innate? and if they are notions imprinted, how can they be unknown? To say a notion is imprinted on the mind, and yet at the same time to say, that the mind is ignorant of it, and never yet took notice of it, is to make this impression nothing. No proposition can be said to be in the mind which it never yet knew, which it was never yet conscious of. For if any one may, then, by the same reason, all propositions that are true, and the mind is capable ever of assenting to, may be said to be in the mind, and to be imprinted: since, if any one can be said to be in the mind, which it never yet knew, it must be only because it is capable of knowing it; and so the mind is of all truths it ever shall know. Nay, thus truths may be imprinted on the mind which it never did, nor ever shall know; for a man may live long, and die at last in ignorance of many truths which his mind was capable of knowing, and that with certainty. So that if the capacity of knowing be the natural impression contended for, all the truths a man ever comes to know will, by this account, be every one of them innate; and this great point will amount to no more, but only to a very improper way of speaking; which, whilst it pretends to assert the contrary, says nothing different from those who deny innate principles. For nobody, I think, ever denied that the mind was capable of knowing several truths. The capacity, they say, is innate; the knowledge acquired. But then to what end such contest for certain innate maxims? If truths can be imprinted on the understanding without being perceived, I can see no difference there can be between any truths the mind is *capable* of knowing in respect of their original: they must all be innate or all adventitious: in vain shall a man go about to distinguish them. He therefore that talks of innate notions in the understanding, cannot (if he intend thereby any distinct sort of truths) mean such truths to be in the understanding as it never perceived, and is yet wholly ignorant of. For if these words 'to be in the understanding' have any propriety, they signify to

be understood. So that to be in the understanding, and not to be understood; to be in the mind and never to be perceived, is all one as to say anything is and is not in the mind or understanding. If therefore these two propositions, 'Whatsoever is, is,' and 'It is impossible for the same thing to be and not to be,' are by nature imprinted, children cannot be ignorant of them: infants, and all that have souls, must necessarily have them in their understandings, know the truth of them, and assent to it.

BOOK II
OF IDEAS

Chapter I

OF IDEAS IN GENERAL, AND THEIR ORIGINAL

1. *Idea is the Object of Thinking.*   Every man being conscious to himself that he thinks; and that which his mind is applied about whilst thinking being the *ideas* that are there, it is past doubt that men have in their minds several ideas,—such as are those expressed by the words *whiteness, hardness, sweetness, thinking, motion, man, elephant, army, drunkenness,* and others: it is in the first place then to be inquired, *How he comes by them?*

I know it is a received doctrine, that men have native ideas, and original characters, stamped upon their minds in their very first being. This opinion I have at large examined already; and, I suppose what I have said in the foregoing Book will be much more easily admitted, when I have shown whence the understanding may get all the ideas it has; and by what ways and degrees they may come into the mind;— for which I shall appeal to every one's own observation and experience.

2. *All Ideas come from Sensation or Reflection.* Let us then suppose the mind to be, as we say, white paper, void of all characters, without any ideas:— How comes it to be furnished? Whence comes it by that vast store which the busy and boundless fancy of man has painted on it with an almost endless variety? Whence has it all the *materials* of reason and knowledge? To this I answer, in one word, from EXPERIENCE. In that all our knowledge is founded;

and from that it ultimately derives itself. Our observation employed either, about external sensible objects, or about the internal operations of our minds perceived and reflected on by ourselves, is that which supplies our understandings with all the *materials* of thinking. These two are the fountains of knowledge, from whence all the ideas we have, or can naturally have, do spring.

3. *The Objects of Sensation and Source of Ideas.* First, our Senses, conversant about particular sensible objects, do convey into the mind several distinct perceptions of things, according to those various ways wherein those objects do affect them. And thus we come by those *ideas* we have of *yellow, white, heat, cold, soft, hard, bitter, sweet,* and all those which we call sensible qualities; which when I say the senses convey into the mind, I mean, they from external objects convey into the mind what produces there those perceptions. This great source of most of the ideas we have, depending wholly upon our senses, and derived by them to the understanding, I call our senses, and derived by them to the understanding, I call SENSATION.

4. *The Operations of our Minds, the other Source of them.* Secondly, the other fountain from which experience furnisheth the understanding with ideas is, — the perception of the operations of our own mind within us, as it is employed about the ideas it has got; — which operations, when the soul comes to reflect on and consider, do furnish the understanding with another set of ideas, which could not be had from things without. And such are *perception, thinking, doubting, believing, reasoning, knowing, willing,* and all the different actings of our own minds; — which we being conscious of, and observing in ourselves, do from these receive into our understandings as distinct ideas as we do from bodies affecting our senses. This source of ideas every man has wholly in himself; and though it be not sense, as having nothing to do with external objects, yet it is very like it, and might properly enough be called *internal sense.* But as I call the other Sensation, so I call this REFLECTION, the ideas it affords being such only as the mind gets by reflecting on its own operations within itself. By reflection then, in the following part of this discourse, I would be understood to mean, that notice which the mind takes of its own operations, and the manner of them, by reason whereof there come to be ideas of these operations in the understanding. These two, I say, viz. external material things, as the objects of SENSATION, and the operations of our own minds within, as the objects of REFLECTION, are to me the only originals from whence all our ideas take their beginnings. The term *operations* here I use in a large sense, as comprehending not barely the actions of the mind about its ideas, but some sort of passions arising sometimes from them, such as is the satisfaction or uneasiness arising from any thought.

5. *All our Ideas are of the one or the other of these.* The understanding seems to me not to have the least glimmering of any ideas which it doth not receive from one of these two. *External objects* furnish the mind with the ideas of sensible qualities, which are all those different perceptions they produce in us; and *the mind* furnishes the understanding with ideas of its own operations.

These, when we have taken a full survey of them, and their several modes, combinations, and relations, we shall find to contain all our whole stock of ideas; and that we have nothing in our minds which did not come in one of these two ways. Let any one examine his own thoughts, and thoroughly search into his understanding; and then let him tell me, whether all the original ideas he has there, are any other than of the objects of his senses, or of the operations of his mind, considered as objects of his reflection. And how great a mass of knowledge soever he imagines to be lodged there, he will, upon taking a strict view, see that he has not any idea in his mind but what one of these two have imprinted; — though perhaps, with infinite variety compounded and enlarged by the understanding, as we shall see hereafter.

10. *The Soul thinks not always; for this wants Proofs.* But whether the soul be supposed to exist antecedent to, or coeval with, or some time after the first rudiments of organization, or the beginnings of life in the body, I leave to be disputed by those who have better thought of that matter. I confess myself to have one of those dull souls, that doth not perceive itself always to contemplate ideas; nor can conceive it any more necessary for the soul always to think, than for the body always to move: the perception of ideas

being (as I conceive) to the soul, what motion is to the body; not its essence, but one of its operations. And therefore, though thinking be supposed never so much the proper action of the soul, yet it is not necessary to suppose that it should be always thinking, always in action. That, perhaps, is the privilege of the infinite Author and Preserver of all things, who 'never slumbers nor sleeps'; but is not competent to any finite being, at least not to the soul of man. We know certainly, by experience, that we *sometimes* think; and thence draw this infallible consequence, — that there is something in us that has a power to think. But whether that substance *perpetually* thinks or no, we can be no further assured than experience informs us. For, to say that actual thinking is essential to the soul, and inseparable from it, is to beg what is in question, and not to prove it by reason; — which is necessary to be done, if it be not a self-evident proposition. But whether this, 'That the soul always thinks,' be a self-evident proposition, that everybody assents to at first hearing, I appeal to mankind. It is doubted whether I thought at all last night or no. The question being about a matter of fact, it is begging it to bring, as a proof for it, an hypothesis, which is the very thing in dispute: by which way one may prove anything, and it is but supposing that all watches, whilst the balance beats, think, and it is sufficiently proved, and past doubt, that my watch thought all last night. But he that would not deceive himself, ought to build his hypothesis on matter of fact, and make it out by sensible experience, and not presume on matter of fact, because of his hypothesis, that is, because he supposes it to be so; which way of proving amounts to this, that I must necessarily think all last night, because another supposes I always think, though I myself cannot perceive that I always do so.

But men in love with their opinions may not only suppose what is in question, but allege wrong matter of fact. How else could any one make it an inference of mine, that a thing is not, because we are not sensible of it in our sleep? I do not say there is no *soul* in a man, because he is not sensible of it in his sleep; but I do say, he cannot *think* at any time, waking or sleeping, without being sensible of it. Our being sensible of it is not necessary to anything but to our thoughts; and to them it is; and to them it always will be necessary, till we can think without being conscious of it.

Chapter II

OF SIMPLE IDEAS

1. *Uncompounded Appearances.* The better to understand the nature, manner, and extent of our knowledge, one thing is carefully to be observed concerning the ideas we have; and that is, that some of them are *simple* and some *complex.*

Though the qualities that affect our senses are, in the things themselves, so united and blended, that there is no separation, no distance between them; yet it is plain, the ideas they produce in the mind enter by the senses simple and unmixed. For, though the sight and touch often take in from the same object, at the same time, different ideas; — as a man sees at once motion and colour; the hand feels softness and warmth in the same piece of wax: yet the simple ideas thus united in the same subject, are as perfectly distinct as those that come in by different senses. The coldness and hardness which a man feels in a piece of ice being as distinct ideas in the mind as the smell and whiteness of a lily; or as the taste of sugar, and smell of a rose. And there is nothing can be plainer to a man than the clear and distinct perception he has of those simple ideas; which, being each in itself uncompounded, contains in it nothing but *one uniform appearance, or conception in the mind,* and is not distinguishable into different ideas.

2. *The Mind can neither make nor destroy them.* These simple ideas, the materials of all our knowledge, are suggested and furnished to the mind only by those two ways above mentioned, viz. sensation and reflection. When the understanding is once stored with these simple ideas, it has the power to repeat, compare, and unite them, even to an almost infinite variety, and so can make at pleasure new complex ideas. But it is not in the power of the most exalted wit, or enlarged understanding, by any quickness or variety of thought, to *invent* or *frame* one new simple idea in the mind, not taken in by the ways before mentioned: nor can any force of the understanding *destroy* those that are there. The dominion of man, in this little world of his own understanding being much what the same as it is in the great world of visible things; wherein his power, however managed by art and skill, reaches no farther than to compound and divide the materials that are made to his

hand; but can do nothing towards the making the least particle of new matter, or destroying one atom of what is already in being. The same inability will every one find in himself, who shall go about to fashion in his understanding one simple idea, not received in by his senses from external objects, or by reflection from the operations of his own mind about them. I would have any one try to fancy any taste which had never affected his palate; or frame the idea of a scent he had never smelt: and when he can do this, I will also conclude that a blind man hath ideas of colours, and a deaf man true distinct notions of sounds.

Chapter III

OF SIMPLE IDEAS OF SENSE

1. *Division of simple Ideas.* The better to conceive the ideas we receive from sensation, it may not be amiss for us to consider them, in reference to the different ways whereby they make their approaches to our minds, and make themselves perceivable by us.

First, then, There are some which come into our minds *by one sense only*.

Secondly, There are others that convey themselves into the mind *by more senses than one*.

Thirdly, Others that are had from *reflection only*.

Fourthly, There are some that make themselves way, and are suggested to the mind *by all the ways of sensation and reflection*.

We shall consider them apart under these several heads.

Ideas of one Sense. — There are some ideas which have admittance only through one sense, which is peculiarly adapted to receive them. Thus light and colours, as white, red, yellow, blue, with their several degrees or shades and mixtures, as green, scarlet, purple, sea-green, and the rest, come in only by the eyes. All kinds of noises, sounds, and tones, only by the ears. The several tastes and smells, by the nose and palate. And if these organs, or the nerves which are the conduits to convey them from without to their audience in the brain, — the mind's presence-room (as I may so call it) — are any of them so disordered

as not to perform their functions, they have no postern to be admitted by; no other way to bring themselves into view, and be perceived by the understanding.

The most considerable of those belonging to the touch, are heat and cold, and solidity: all the rest, consisting almost wholly in the sensible configuration, as smooth and rough; or else, more or less firm adhesion of the parts, as hard and soft, tough and brittle, are obvious enough.

2. *Few simple Ideas have Names.* I think it will be needless to enumerate all the particular simple ideas belonging to each sense. Nor indeed is it possible if we would; there being a great many more of them belonging to most of the senses than we have names for. The variety of smells, which are as many almost, if not more, than species of bodies in the world, do most of them want names. Sweet and stinking commonly serve our turn for these ideas, which in effect is little more than to call them pleasing or displeasing; though the smell of a rose and violet, both sweet, are certainly very distinct ideas. Nor are the different tastes, that by our palates we receive ideas of, much better provided with names. Sweet, bitter, sour, harsh, and salt are almost all the epithets we have to denominate that numberless variety of relishes, which are to be found distinct, not only in almost every sort of creatures, but in the different parts of the same plant, fruit, or animal. The same may be said of colours and sounds. I shall, therefore, in the account of simple ideas I am here giving, content myself to set down only such as are most material to our present purpose, or are in themselves less apt to be taken notice of though they are very frequently the ingredients of our complex ideas; amongst which, I think, I may well account solidity, which therefore I shall treat of in the next chapter.

Chapter IV

IDEA OF SOLIDITY

1. *We receive this Idea from Touch.* The idea of *solidity* we receive by our touch: and it arises from the resistance which we find in body to the entrance of any other body into the place it possesses, till it has left it. There is no idea which we receive more constantly from sensation than solidity. Whether we move or rest, in what posture soever we are, we always

feel something under us that supports us, and hinders our further sinking downwards; and the bodies which we daily handle make us perceive that, whilst they remain between them, they do, by an insurmountable force, hinder the approach of the parts of our hands that press them. *That which thus hinders the approach of two bodies, when they are moved one towards another, I call solidity.* I will not dispute whether this acceptation of the word solid be nearer to its original signification than that which mathematicians use it in. It suffices that I think the common notion of solidity will allow, if not justify, this use of it; but if any one think it better to call it *impenetrability*, he has my consent. Only I have thought the term solidity the more proper to express this idea, not only because of its vulgar use in that sense, but also because it carries something more of positive in it than impenetrability; which is negative, and is perhaps more a consequence of solidity, than solidity itself. This, of all other, seems the idea most intimately connected with, and essential to body; so as nowhere else to be found or imagined, but only in matter. And though our senses take no notice of it, but in masses of matter, of a bulk sufficient to cause a sensation in us: yet the mind, having once got this idea from such grosser sensible bodies, traces it further, and considers it, as well as figure, in the minutest particle of matter that can exist; and finds it inseparably inherent in body, wherever or however modified.

2. *Solidity fills Space.* This is the idea which belongs to body, whereby we conceive it to fill space. The idea of which filling of space is,—that where we imagine any space taken up by a solid substance, we conceive it so to possess it, that it excludes all other solid substances; and will for ever hinder any other two bodies, that move towards one another in a straight line, from coming to touch one another, unless it removes from between them in a line not parallel to that which they move in. This idea of it, the bodies which we ordinarily handle sufficiently furnish us with.

6. *What Solidity is.* If any one asks me, *What this solidity is,* I send him to his senses to inform him. Let him put a flint or a football between his hands, and then endeavour to join them, and he will know. If he thinks this not a sufficient explication of solidity,

what it is, and wherein it consists; I promise to tell him what it is, and wherein it consists, when he tells me what thinking is, or wherein it consists; or explains to me what extension or motion is, which perhaps seems much easier. The simple ideas we have, are such as experience teaches them us; but if, beyond that, we endeavour by words to make them clearer in the mind, we shall succeed no better than if we went about to clear up the darkness of a blind man's mind by talking; and to discourse into him the ideas of light and colours. The reason of this I shall show in another place.

Chapter V

OF SIMPLE IDEAS OF DIVERS SENSES

Ideas received both by seeing and touching. The ideas we get by more than one sense are, of *space* or *extension, figure, rest,* and *motion.* For these make perceivable impressions, both on the eyes and touch; and we can receive and convey into our minds the ideas of the extension, figure, motion, and rest of bodies, both by seeing and feeling. But having occasion to speak more at large of these in another place, I here only enumerate them.

Chapter VI

OF SIMPLE IDEAS OF REFLECTION

1. *Simple Ideas are the Operations of Mind about its other Ideas.* The mind receiving the ideas mentioned in the foregoing chapters from without, when it turns its view inward upon itself, and observes its own actions about those ideas it has, takes from thence other ideas, which are as capable to be the objects of its contemplation as any of those it received from foreign things.

2. *The Idea of Perception, and Idea of Willing, we have from Reflection.* The two great and principal actions of the mind, which are most frequently considered, and which are so frequent that every one that pleases may take notice of them in himself, are these two:—

> *Perception,* or *Thinking*; and
> *Volition,* or *Willing.*

The power of thinking is called the *Understanding*, and the power of volition is called the *Will*; and these two powers or abilities in the mind are denominated faculties.

Of some of the *modes* of these simple ideas of reflection, such as are *remembrance, discerning, reasoning, judging, knowledge, faith*, &c., I shall have occasion to speak hereafter.

Chapter VII

OF SIMPLE IDEAS OF BOTH SENSATION AND REFLECTION

1. *Ideas of Pleasure and Pain.*   There be other simple ideas which convey themselves into the mind by all the ways of sensation and reflection, viz, *pleasure* or *delight*, and its opposite, *pain*, or *uneasiness; power, existence; unity.*

2. *Mix with almost all our other Ideas.*   Delight or uneasiness, one or other of them, join themselves to almost all our ideas both of sensation and reflection: and there is scarce any affection of our senses from without, any retired thought of our mind within, which is not able to produce in us pleasure or pain. By pleasure and pain, I would be understood to signify, whatsoever delights or molests us; whether it arises from the thoughts of our minds, or anything operating on our bodies. For, whether we call it satisfaction, delight, pleasure, happiness, &c., on the one side, or uneasiness, trouble, pain, torment, anguish, misery, &c., on the other, they are still but different degrees of the same thing, and belong to the ideas of pleasure and pain, delight or uneasiness; which are the names I shall most commonly use for those two sorts of ideas.

7. *Ideas of Existence and Unity.* *Existence* and *Unity* are two other ideas that are suggested to the understanding by every object without, and every idea within. When ideas are in our minds, we consider them as being actually there, as well as we consider things to be actually without us; — which is, that they exist, or have existence. And whatever we can consider as one thing, whether a real being or idea, suggests to the understanding the idea of unity.

8. *Idea of Power.*   Power also is another of those simple ideas which we receive from sensation and reflection. For, observing in ourselves that we do and can think, and that we can at pleasure move several parts of our bodies which were at rest; the effects, also, that natural bodies are able to produce in one another, occurring every moment to our senses, — we both these ways get the idea of power.

9. *Idea of Succession.*   Besides these there is another idea, which, though suggested by our senses, yet is more constantly offered to us by what passes in our minds; and that is the idea of *succession*. For if we look immediately into ourselves, and reflect on what is observable there, we shall find our ideas always, whilst we are awake, or have any thought, passing in train, one going and another coming, without intermission.

10. *Simple Ideas the materials of all our Knowledge.*   These, if they are not all, are at least (as I think) the most considerable of those simple ideas which the mind has, and out of which is made all its other knowledge; all which it receives only by the two forementioned ways of sensation and reflection.

Nor let any one think these too narrow bounds for the capacious mind of man to expatiate in, which takes its flight further than the stars, and cannot be confined by the limits of the world; that extends its thoughts often even beyond the utmost expansion of Matter, and makes excursions into that incomprehensible Inane. I grant all this, but desire any one to assign any *simple idea* which is not received from one of those inlets before mentioned, or any *complex idea* not made out of those simple ones. Nor will it be so strange to think these few simple ideas sufficient to employ the quickest thought, or largest capacity; and to furnish the materials of all that various knowledge, and more various fancies and opinions of all mankind, if we consider how many words may be made out of the various composition of twenty-four letters; or if, going one step further, we will but reflect on the variety of combinations that may be made with barely one of the above-mentioned ideas, viz. number, whose stock is inexhaustible and truly infinite: and what a large and immense field doth extension alone afford the mathematicians?

Chapter VIII

SOME FURTHER CONSIDERATIONS CONCERNING OUR SIMPLE IDEAS OF SENSATION

7. *Ideas in the Mind, Qualities in Bodies.*   To discover the nature of our *ideas* the better, and to discourse of them intelligibly, it will be convenient to distinguish them *as they are ideas or perceptions in our minds*; and *as they are modifications of matter in the bodies that cause such perceptions in us*: that so we may not think (as perhaps usually is done) that they are exactly the images and resemblances of something inherent in the subject; most of those of sensation being in the mind no more the likeness of something existing without us, than the names that stand for them are the likeness of our ideas, which yet upon hearing they are apt to excite in us.

8. *Our Ideas and the Qualities of Bodies.*   Whatsoever the mind perceives *in itself*, or is the immediate object of perception, thought, or understanding, that I call *idea*; and the power to produce any idea in our mind, I call *quality* of the subject wherein that power is. Thus a snowball having the power to produce in us the ideas of white, cold, and round,—the power to produce those ideas in us, as they are in the snowball, I call qualities; and as they are sensations or perceptions in our understandings, I call them ideas; which *ideas*, if I speak of sometimes as in the things themselves, I would be understood to mean those qualities in the objects which produce them in us.

9. *Primary Qualities of Bodies.*   Qualities thus considered in bodies are,

First, such as are utterly inseparable from the body, in what state soever it be; and such as in all the alterations and changes it suffers, all the force can be used upon it, it constantly keeps; and such as sense constantly finds in every particle of matter which has bulk enough to be perceived; and the mind finds inseparable from every particle of matter, though less than to make itself singly be perceived by our senses: v.g. Take a grain of wheat, divide it into two parts; each part has still solidity, extension, figure, and mobility: divide it again, and it retains still the same qualities; and so divide it on, till the parts become insensible; they must retain still each of them all those qualities.

For division (which is all that a mill, or pestle, or any other body, does upon another, in reducing it to insensible parts) can never take away either solidity, extension, figure or mobility from any body, but only makes two or more distinct separate masses of matter, of that which was but one before; all which distinct masses, reckoned as so many distinct bodies, after division, make a certain number. These I call *original* or *primary qualities* of body, which I think we may observe to produce simple ideas in us, viz. solidity, extension, figure, motion or rest, and number.

10. *Secondary Qualities of Bodies.*   *Secondly*, such qualities which in truth are nothing in the objects themselves but powers to produce various sensations in us by their primary qualities, i.e. by the bulk, figure, texture, and motion of their insensible parts, as colours, sounds, tastes, &c. These I call *secondary qualities*. To these might be added a *third* sort, which are allowed to be barely powers; though they are as much real qualities in the subject as those which I, to comply with the common way of speaking, call qualities, but for distinction, secondary qualities. For the power in fire to produce a new colour, or consistency, in *wax* or *clay*,—by its primary qualities, is as much a quality in fire, as the power it has to produce in *me* a new idea or sensation of warmth or burning, which I felt not before,—by the same primary qualities, viz. the bulk, texture, and motion of its insensible parts.

11. *How Bodies produce Ideas in us.*   The next thing to be considered is, how bodies produce ideas in us; and that is manifestly by impulse, the only way which we can conceive bodies to operate in.

12. *By motions, external, and in our organism.*   If then external objects be not united to our minds when they produce ideas therein; and yet we perceive these *original* qualities in such of them as singly fall under our senses, it is evident that some motion must be thence continued by our nerves, or animal spirits, by some parts of our bodies, to the brains or the seat of sensation, there to produce in our minds the particular ideas we have of them. And since the extension, figure, number, and motion of bodies of an observable bigness, may be perceived at a distance by the sight, it is evident some singly imperceptible

bodies must come from them to the eyes, and thereby convey to the brain some motion; which produces these ideas which we have of them in us.

13. *How secondary Qualities produce their ideas.* After the same manner that the ideas of these original qualities are produced in us, we may conceive that the ideas of *secondary* qualities are also produced, viz. by the operation of insensible particles on our senses. For, it being manifest that there are bodies and good store of bodies, each whereof are so small, that we cannot by any of our senses discover either their bulk, figure, or motion,—as is evident in the particles of the air and water, and others extremely smaller than those; perhaps as much smaller than the particles of air and water, as the particles of air and water are smaller than peas or hail-stones;—let us suppose at present that the different motions and figures, bulk and number, of such particles, affecting the several organs of our senses, produce in us those different sensations which we have from the colours and smells of bodies; v.g. that a violet, by the impulse of such insensible particles of matter, of peculiar figures and bulks, and in different degrees and modifications of their motions, causes the ideas of the blue colour, and sweet scent of that flower to be produced in our minds. It being no more impossible to conceive that God should annex such ideas to such motions, with which they have no similitude, than that he should annex the idea of pain to the motion of a piece of steel dividing our flesh, with which that idea hath no resemblance.

14. *They depend on the primary Qualities.* What I have said concerning colours and smells may be understood also of tastes and sounds, and other the like sensible qualities; which, whatever reality we by mistake attribute to them, are in truth nothing in the objects themselves, but powers to produce various sensations in us; and depend on those primary qualities, viz. bulk, figure, texture, and motion of parts as I have said.

15. *Ideas of primary Qualities are Resemblances; of secondary, not.* From whence I think it easy to draw this observation,—that the ideas of primary qualities of bodies are resemblances of them, and their patterns do really exist in the bodies themselves, but

the ideas produced in us by these secondary qualities have no resemblance of them at all. There is nothing like our ideas, existing in the bodies themselves. They are, in the bodies we denominate from them, only a power to produce those sensations in us; and what is sweet, blue, or warm in idea, is but the certain bulk, figure, and motion of the insensible parts, in the bodies themselves, which we call so.

16. *Examples.* Flame is denominated hot and light; snow, white and cold; and manna, white and sweet, from the ideas they produce in us. Which qualities are commonly thought to be the same in those bodies that those ideas are in us, the one the perfect resemblance of the other, as they are in a mirror, and it would by most men be judged very extravagant if one should say otherwise. And yet he that will consider that the same fire that, at one distance produces in us the sensation of warmth, does, at a nearer approach, produce in us the far different sensation of pain, ought to bethink himself what reason he has to say—that this idea of warmth, which was produced in him by the fire, is *actually in the fire*; and his idea of pain, which the same fire produced in him the same way, is *not* in the fire. Why are whiteness and coldness in snow, and pain not, when it produces the one and the other idea in us; and can do neither, but by the bulk, figure, number, and motion of its solid parts?

17. *The ideas of the Primary alone really exist.* The particular bulk, number, figure, and motion of the parts of fire or snow are really in them,—whether any one's senses perceive them or no: and therefore they may be called *real* qualities, because they really exist in those bodies. But light, heat, whiteness, or coldness, are no more really in them than sickness or pain is in manna. Take away the sensation of them; let not the eyes see light or colours, nor the ears hear sounds; let the palate not taste, nor the nose smell, and all colours, tastes, odours, and sounds, *as they are such particular ideas*, vanish and cease, and are reduced to their causes, i.e. bulk, figure, and motion of parts.

18. *The secondary exist in things only as modes of the primary.* A piece of manna of a sensible bulk is able to produce in us the idea of a round or square

figure; and by being removed from one place to another, the idea of motion. This idea of motion represents it as it really is in manna moving: a circle or square are the same, whether in idea or existence, in the mind or in the manna. And this, both motion and figure, are really in the manna, whether we take notice of them or no: this everybody is ready to agree to. Besides, manna, by the bulk, figure, texture, and motion of its parts, has a power to produce the sensations of sickness, and sometimes of acute pains or gripings in us. That these ideas of sickness and pain are *not* in the manna, but effects of its operations on us, and are nowhere when we feel them not; this also every one readily agrees to. And yet men are hardly to be brought to think that sweetness and whiteness are not really in manna; which are but the effects of the operations of manna, by the motion, size, and figure of its particles, on the eyes and palate: as the pain and sickness caused by manna are confessedly nothing but the effects of its operations on the stomach and guts, by the size, motion, and figure of its insensible parts, (for by nothing else can a body operate, as has been proved): as if it could not operate on the eyes and palate, and thereby produce in the mind particular distinct ideas, which in itself it has not, as well as we allow it can operate on the guts and stomach, and thereby produce distinct ideas, which in itself it has not. These ideas, being all effects of the operations of manna on several parts of our bodies, by the size, figure, number, and motion of its parts; — why those produced by the eyes and palate should rather be thought to be really in the manna, than those produced by the stomach and guts; or why the pain and sickness, ideas that are the effect of manna, should be thought to be nowhere when they are not felt; and yet the sweetness and whiteness, effects of the same manna on other parts of the body, by ways equally as unknown, should be thought to exist in the manna, when they are not seen or tasted, would need some reason to explain.

19. *Examples.*   Let us consider the red and white colours in porphyry. Hinder light from striking on it, and its colours vanish; it no longer produces any such ideas in us: upon the return of light it produces these appearances on us again. Can any one think any real alterations are made in the porphyry by the presence or absence of light; and that those ideas of whiteness and redness are really in porphyry in the light, when it is plain *it has no colour in the dark*? It has, indeed, such a configuration of particles, both night and day, as are apt, by the rays of light rebounding from some parts of that hard stone, to produce in us the idea of redness, and from others the idea of whiteness; but whiteness or redness are not in it at any time, but such a texture that hath the power to produce such a sensation in us.

20. Pound an almond, and the clear white colour will be altered into a dirty one, and the sweet taste into an oily one. What real alteration can the beating of the pestle make in any body, but an alteration of the texture of it?

21. *Explains how water felt as cold by one hand may be warm to the other.*   Ideas being thus distinguished and understood, we may be able to give an account how the same water, at the same time, may produce the idea of cold by one hand and of heat by the other: whereas it is impossible that the same water, if those ideas were really in it, should at the same time be both hot and cold. For, if we imagine *warmth*, as it is in our hands, to be nothing but a certain sort and degree of motion in the minute particles of our nerves or animal spirits, we may understand how it is possible that the same water may, at the same time, produce the sensations of heat in one hand and cold in the other; which yet *figure* never does, that never producing the idea of a square by one hand which has produced the idea of a globe by another. But if the sensation of heat and cold be nothing but the increase or diminution of the motion of the minute parts of our bodies, caused by the corpuscles of any other body, it is easy to be understood, that if that motion be greater in one hand than in the other; if a body be applied to the two hands, which has in its minute particles a greater motion than in those of one of the hands, and a less than in those of the other, it will increase the motion of the one hand and lessen it in the other; and so cause the different sensations of heat and cold that depend thereon.

23. *Three Sorts of Qualities in Bodies.*   The qualities, then, that are in bodies, rightly considered, are of three sorts: —

First, The bulk, figure, number, situation, and motion or rest of their solid parts. Those are in them, whether we perceive them or not; and when they are of that size that we can discover them, we have by these an idea of the thing as it is in itself; as is plain in artificial things. These I call *primary qualities*.

Secondly, The power that is in any body, by reason of its insensible primary qualities, to operate after a peculiar manner on any of our senses, and thereby produce in *us* the different ideas of several colours, sounds, smells, tastes, &c. These are usually called *sensible qualities*.

Thirdly, The power that is in any body, by reason of the particular constitution of its primary qualities, to make such a change in the bulk, figure, texture, and motion of *another body*, as to make it operate on our senses differently from what it did before. Thus the sun has a power to make wax white, and fire to make lead fluid. These are usually called *powers*.

The first of these, as has been said, I think may be properly called real, original, or primary qualities; because they are in the things themselves, whether they are perceived or not: and upon their different modifications it is that the secondary qualities depend.

The other two are only powers to act differently upon other things: which powers result from the different modifications of those primary qualities.

24. *The first are Resemblances; the second thought to be Resemblances, but are not; the third neither are, nor are thought so.*   But, though the two latter sorts of qualities are powers barely, and nothing but powers, relating to several other bodies, and resulting from the different modifications of the original qualities, yet they are generally otherwise thought of. For the *second* sort, viz. the powers to produce several ideas in us, by our senses, are looked upon as real qualities in the things thus affecting us: but the *third* sort are called and esteemed barely powers. v.g. The idea of heat or light, which we receive by our eyes, or touch, from the sun, are commonly thought real qualities existing in the sun, and something more than mere powers in it. But when we consider the sun in reference to wax, which it melts or blanches, we look on the whiteness and softness produced in

the wax, not as qualities in the sun, but effects produced by powers in it. Whereas, if rightly considered, these qualities of light and warmth, which are perceptions in me when I am warmed or enlightened by the sun, are no otherwise in the sun, than the changes made in the wax, when it is blanched or melted, are in the sun. They are all of them equally *powers in the sun, depending on its primary qualities*; whereby it is able, in the one case, so to alter the bulk, figure, texture, or motion of some of the insensible parts of my eyes or hands, as thereby to produce in me the idea of light or heat; and in the other, it is able so to alter the bulk, figure, texture, or motion of the insensible parts of the wax, as to make them fit to produce in me the distinct ideas of white and fluid.

Chapter IX

OF PERCEPTION

1. *Perception the first simple Idea of Reflection.* PERCEPTION, as it is the first faculty of the mind exercised about our ideas; so it is the first and simplest idea we have from reflection, and is by some called thinking in general. Though thinking, in the propriety of the English tongue, signifies that sort of operation in the mind about its ideas, wherein the mind is active; where it, with some degree of voluntary attention, considers anything. For in bare naked perception, the mind is, for the most part, only passive; and what it perceives, it cannot avoid perceiving.

2. *Reflection alone can give us the idea of what perception is.*   What perception is, every one will know better by reflecting on what he does himself, when he sees, hears, feels, &c., or thinks, than by any discourse of mine. Whoever reflects on what passes in his own mind cannot miss it. And if he does not reflect, all the words in the world cannot make him have any notion of it.

3. *Arises in sensation only when the mind notices the organic impression.*   This is certain, that whatever alterations are made in the body, if they reach not the mind; whatever impressions are made on the outward parts, if they are not taken notice of within, there is no perception. Fire may burn our bodies with no other effect than it does a billet, unless the motion

be continued to the brain, and there the sense of heat, or idea of pain, be produced in the mind; wherein consists actual perception.

4. *Impulse on the organ insufficient.* How often may a man observe in himself, that whilst his mind is intently employed in the contemplation of some objects, and curiously surveying some ideas that are there, it takes no notice of impressions of sounding bodies made upon the organ of hearing, with the same alteration that uses to be for the producing the idea of sound? A sufficient impulse there may be on the organ; but it not reaching the observation of the mind, there follows no perception: and though the motion that uses to produce the idea of sound be made in the ear, yet no sound is heard. Want of sensation, in this case, is not through any defect in the organ, or that the man's ears are less affected than at other times when he does hear: but that which uses to produce the idea, though conveyed in by the usual organ, not being taken notice of in the understanding, and so imprinting no idea in the mind, there follows no sensation. So that wherever there is sense or perception, there some idea is actually produced, and present in the understanding.

8. *Sensations often changed by the Judgment.* We are further to consider concerning perception, that the ideas we receive by sensation are often, in grown people, altered by the judgment, without our taking notice of it. When we set before our eyes a round globe of any uniform colour, v.g. gold, alabaster, or jet, it is certain that the idea thereby imprinted on our minds is of a flat circle, variously shadowed, with several degrees of light and brightness coming to our eyes. But we having, by use, been accustomed to perceive what kind of appearance convex bodies are wont to make in us; what alterations are made in the reflections of light by the difference of the sensible figures of bodies;—the judgment presently, by an habitual custom, alters the appearances into their causes. So that from that which is truly variety of shadow or colour, collecting the figure, it makes it pass for a mark of figure, and frames to itself the perception of a convex figure and an uniform colour; when the idea we receive from thence is only a plane variously coloured, as is evident in painting. To which purpose I shall here insert a problem of that very ingenious and studious promoter of real knowledge, the learned and worthy Mr. Molineux,[1] which he was pleased to send me in a letter some months since; and it is this:—'Suppose a man *born* blind, and now adult, and taught by his *touch* to distinguish between a cube and a sphere of the same metal, and nighly of the same bigness, so as to tell, when he felt one and the other, which is the cube, which the sphere. Suppose then the cube and sphere placed on a table, and the blind man be made to see: *quaere*, whether *by his sight, before he touched them,* he could now distinguish and tell which is the globe, which the cube?' To which the acute and judicious proposer answers, 'Not. For, though he has obtained the experience of how a globe, how a cube affects his touch, yet he has not yet obtained the experience, that what affects his touch so or so, must affect his sight so or so; or that a protuberant angle in the cube, that pressed his hand unequally, shall appear to his eye as it does in the cube.'—I agree with this thinking gentleman, whom I am proud to call my friend, in his answer to this problem; and am of opinion that the blind man, at first sight, would not be able with certainty to say which was the globe, which the cube, whilst he only saw them; though he could unerringly name them by his touch, and certainly distinguish them by the difference of their figures felt. This I have set down, and leave with my reader, as an occasion for him to consider how much he may be beholden to experience, improvement, and acquired notions, where he thinks he had not the least use of, or help from them. And the rather, because this observing gentleman further adds, that 'having, upon the occasion of my book, proposed this to divers very ingenious men, he hardly ever met with one that at first gave the answer to it which he thinks true, till by hearing his reasons they were convinced.'

Chapter X
OF RETENTION

1. *Contemplation.* The next faculty of the mind, whereby it makes a further progress towards knowledge, is that which I call *retention*; or the keeping of

1. [William Molineux (1656–1698), a Dubliner who was a Member of Parliament and who published a work on optics, entered into correspondence with Locke, and the two became close friends. The letter Locke refers to was

those simple ideas which from sensation or reflection it hath received. This is done two ways.

First, by keeping the idea which is brought into it, for some time actually in view, which is called *contemplation*.

2. *Memory.* The other way of retention is, the power to revive again in our minds those ideas which, after imprinting, have disappeared, or have been as it were laid aside out of sight. And thus we do, when we conceive heat or light, yellow or sweet,—the object being removed. This is *memory*, which is as it were the storehouse of our ideas. For, the narrow mind of man not being capable of having many ideas under view and consideration at once, it was necessary to have a repository, to lay up those ideas which, at another time, it might have use of. But, our *ideas* being nothing but actual perceptions in the mind, which cease to be anything when there is no perception of them; this laying up of our ideas in the repository of the memory signifies no more but this,—that the mind has a power in many cases to revive perceptions which it has once had, with this additional perception annexed to them, that *it has had them before*. And in this sense it is that our ideas are said to be in our memories, when indeed they are actually nowhere;—but only there is an ability in the mind when it will to revive them again, and as it were paint them anew on itself, though some with more, some with less difficulty; some more lively, and other more obscurely. And thus it is, by the assistance of this faculty, that we are said to have all those ideas in our understandings which, though we do not actually contemplate, yet we *can* bring in sight, and make appear again, and be the objects of our thoughts, without the help of those sensible qualities which first imprinted them there.

7. *In Remembering, the Mind is often active.* In this secondary perception, as I may so call it, or viewing again the ideas that are lodged in the memory, the mind is oftentimes more than barely passive; the appearance of those dormant pictures depending sometimes on the *will*. The mind very often sets itself on work in search of some hidden idea, and turns as

it were the eye of the soul upon it; though sometimes too they start up in our minds of their own accord, and offer themselves to the understanding; and very often are roused and tumbled out of their dark cells into open daylight, by turbulent and tempestuous passions; our affections bringing ideas to our memory, which had otherwise lain quiet and unregarded. This further is to be observed, concerning ideas lodged in the memory, and upon occasion revived by the mind, that they are not only (as the word *revive* imports) none of them new ones, but also that the mind takes notice of them as of a former impression, and renews its acquaintance with them, as with ideas it had known before. So that though ideas formerly imprinted are not all constantly in view, yet in remembrance they are constantly known to be such as have been formerly imprinted; i.e. in view, and taken notice of before, by the understanding.

Chapter XI

OF DISCERNING, AND OTHER OPERATIONS OF THE MIND

1. *No Knowledge without Discernment.* Another faculty we may take notice of in our minds is that of *discerning* and *distinguishing* between the several ideas it has. It is not enough to have a confused perception of something in general. Unless the mind had a distinct perception of different objects and their qualities, it would be capable of very little knowledge, though the bodies that affect us were as busy about us as they are now, and the mind were continually employed in thinking. On this faculty of distinguishing one thing from another depends the evidence and certainty of several, even very general, propositions, which have passed for innate truths;—because men, overlooking the true cause why those propositions find universal assent, impute it wholly to native uniform impressions; whereas it in truth depends upon this clear discerning faculty of the mind, whereby it *perceives* two ideas to be the same, or different. But of this more hereafter.

4. *Comparing.* The COMPARING them one with another, in respect of extent, degrees, time, place, or any other circumstances, is another operation of the mind about its ideas, and is that upon which depends all that large tribe of ideas comprehended under *rela-*

---

sent in 1693, and the discussion of Molineux's problem was added to the *Essay* in its second edition (1694).—S.M.C.]

tion; which, of how vast an extent it is, I shall have occasion to consider hereafter.

6. *Compounding..*   The next operation we may observe in the mind about its ideas is COMPOSITION; whereby it puts together several of those simple ones it has received from sensation and reflection, and combines them into complex ones. Under this of composition may be reckoned also that of *enlarging*, wherein, though the composition does not so much appear as in more complex ones, yet it is nevertheless a putting several ideas together, though of the same kind. Thus, by adding several units together, we make the idea of a dozen; and putting together the repeated ideas of several perches, we frame that of a furlong.

8. *Naming.*   When children have, by repeated sensations, got ideas fixed in their memories, they begin by degrees to learn the use of signs. And when they have got the skill to apply the organs of speech to the framing of articulate sounds, they begin to make use of words, to signify their ideas to others. These verbal signs they sometimes borrow from others, and sometimes make themselves, as one may observe among the new and unusual names children often give to things in the first use of language.

9. *Abstraction.*   The use of words then being to stand as outward marks of our internal ideas, and those ideas being taken from particular things, if every particular idea that we take in should have a distinct name, names must be endless. To prevent this, the mind makes the particular ideas received from particular objects to become general; which is done by considering them as they are in the mind such appearances,—separate from all other existences, and the circumstances of real existence, as time, place, or any other concomitant ideas. This is called ABSTRACTION, whereby ideas taken from particular beings become general representatives of all of the same kind; and their names general names, applicable to whatever exists conformable to such abstract ideas. Such precise, naked appearances in the mind, without considering how, whence, or with what others they came there, the understanding lays up (with names commonly annexed to them) as the standards to rank real existences into sorts, as they agree with these patterns, and to denominate them accordingly. Thus the same

colour being observed to-day in chalk or snow, which the mind yesterday received from milk, it considers that appearance alone, makes it a representative of all of that kind; and having given it the name *whiteness*, it by that sound signifies the same quality wheresoever to be imagined or met with; and thus universals, whether ideas or terms, are made.

10. *Brutes abstract not.*   If it may be doubted whether beasts compound and enlarge their ideas that way to any degree; this, I think, I may be positive in,—that the power of abstracting is not at all in them; and that the having of general ideas is that which puts a perfect distinction betwixt man and brutes, and is an excellency which the faculties of brutes do by no means attain to. For it is evident we observe no footsteps in them of making use of general signs for universal ideas; from which we have reason to imagine that they have not the faculty of abstracting, or making general ideas, since they have no use of words, or any other general signs.

11. *Brutes abstract not, yet are not bare machines.* Nor can it be imputed to their want of fit organs to frame articulate sounds, that they have no use or knowledge of general words; since many of them, we find, can fashion such sounds, and pronounce words distinctly enough, but never with any such application. And, on the other side, men who, through some defect in the organs, want words, yet fail not to express their universal ideas by signs, which serve them instead of general words, a faculty which we see beasts come short in. And, therefore, I think, we may suppose, that it is in this that the species of brutes are discriminated from man: and it is that proper difference wherein they are wholly separated, and which at last widens to so vast a distance. For if they have any ideas at all, and are not bare machines, (as some would have them,[2]) we cannot deny them to have some reason. It seems as evident to me, that they do reason, as that they have sense; but it is only in particular ideas, just as they received them from their senses. They are the best of them tied up within those narrow bounds, and have not (as I think) the faculty to enlarge them by any kind of abstraction.

2. [Descartes, for example.]

15. *The true Beginning of Human Knowledge.* And thus I have given a short, and, I think, true *history of the first beginnings of human knowledge*;—whence the mind has its first objects; and by what steps it makes it progress to the laying in and storing up those ideas, out of which is to be framed all the knowledge it is capable of: wherein I must appeal to experience and observation whether I am in the right: the best way to come to truth being to examine things as really they are, and not to conclude they are, as we fancy of ourselves, or have been taught by others to imagine.

17. *Dark Room.* I pretend not to teach, but to inquire; and therefore cannot but confess here again,—that external and internal sensation are the only passages I can find of knowledge to the understanding. These alone, as far as I can discover, are the windows by which light is let into this *dark room*. For, methinks, the understanding is not much unlike a closet wholly shut from light, with only some little openings left, to let in external visible resemblances, or ideas of things without: would the pictures coming into such a dark room but stay there, and lie so orderly as to be found upon occasion, it would very much resemble the understanding of a man, in reference to all objects of sight, and the ideas of them.

These are my guesses concerning the means whereby the understanding comes to have and retain simple ideas, and the modes of them, with some other operations about them.

I proceed now to examine some of these simple ideas and their modes a little more particularly.

Chapter XII

OF COMPLEX IDEAS

1. *Made by the Mind out of simple Ones.* We have hitherto considered those ideas, in the reception whereof the mind is only passive, which are those simple ones received from sensation and reflection before mentioned, whereof the mind cannot make one to itself, nor have any idea which does not wholly consist of them. But as the mind is wholly passive in the reception of all its simple ideas, so it exerts several acts of its own, whereby out of its simple ideas, as the materials and foundations of the rest, the others are framed. The acts of the mind, wherein it exerts its power over its simple ideas, are chiefly these three:

(1) Combining several simple ideas into one compound one; and thus all *complex ideas* are made. (2) The second is bringing two ideas, whether simple or complex, together, and setting them by one another, so as to take a view of them at once, without uniting them into one; by which way it gets all its *ideas of relations*. (3) The third is separating them from all other ideas that accompany them in their real existence: this is called abstraction: and thus all its *general ideas* are made. This shows man's power, and its ways of operation, to be much the same in the material and intellectual world. For the materials in both being such as he has no power over, either to make or destroy, all that man can do is either to unite them together, or to set them by one another, or wholly separate them. I shall here begin with the first of these in the consideration of complex ideas, and come to the other two in their due places. As simple ideas are observed to exist in several combinations united together, so the mind has a power to consider several of them united together as one idea; and that not only as they are united in external objects, but as itself has joined them together. Ideas thus made up of several simple ones put together, I call *complex*;—such as are beauty, gratitude, a man, an army, the universe; which, though complicated of various simple ideas, or complex ideas made up of simple ones, yet are, when the mind pleases, considered each by itself, as one entire thing, and signified by one name.

2. *Made voluntarily.* In this faculty of repeating and joining together its ideas, the mind has great power in varying and multiplying the objects of its thoughts, infinitely beyond what sensation or reflection furnished it with: but all this still confined to those simple ideas which it received from those two sources, and which are the ultimate materials of all its compositions. For simple ideas are all from things themselves, and of these the mind *can* have no more, nor other than what are suggested to it. It can have no other ideas of sensible qualities than what come from without by the senses; nor any ideas of other kind of operations of a thinking substance, than what it finds in itself. But when it has once got these simple ideas, it is not confined barely to observation, and what offers itself from without; it can, by its own power, put together those ideas it has, and make new complex ones, which it never received so united.

3. *Complex ideas are either of Modes, Substances, or Relations. Complex ideas,* however compounded and decompounded, though their number be infinite, and the variety endless, wherewith they fill and entertain the thoughts of men; yet I think they may be all reduced under these three heads: —

    1. Modes.

    2. Substances.

    3. Relations.

4. *Ideas of Modes.*   First, *Modes* I call such complex ideas which, however compounded, contain not in them the supposition of subsisting by themselves, but are considered as dependences on, or affections of substances; — such as are the ideas signified by the words triangle, gratitude, murder, &c. And if in this I use the word mode in somewhat a different sense from its ordinary signification, I beg pardon; it being unavoidable in discourses, differing from the ordinary received notions, either to make new words, or to use old words in somewhat a new signification; the later whereof, in our present case, is perhaps the more tolerable of the two.

5. *Simple and mixed Modes of simple ideas.*   Of these *modes,* there are two sorts which deserve distinct consideration: —

    First, there are some which are only variations, or different combinations of the same simple idea, without the mixture of any other; — as a dozen, or score; which are nothing but the ideas of so many distinct units added together, and these I call *simple modes* as being contained within the bounds of one simple idea.

    Secondly, there are others compounded of simple ideas of several kinds, but together to make one complex one; — v.g. beauty, consisting of a certain composition of colour and figure, causing delight to the beholder; theft, which being the concealed change of the possession of anything, without the consent of the proprietor, contains, as is visible, a combination of several ideas of several kinds: and these I call *mixed modes.*

6. *Ideas of Substances, single or collective.*   Secondly, the ideas of *substances* are such combinations of simple ideas as are taken to represent distinct *particular* things subsisting by themselves; in which the supposed or confused idea of substance, such as it is, is always the first and chief. Thus if to substance be joined the simple idea of a certain dull whitish colour, with certain degrees of weight, hardness, ductility, and fusibility, we have the idea of lead; and a combination of the ideas of a certain sort of figure, with the powers of motion, thought and reasoning, joined to substance, make the ordinary idea of a man. Now of substances also, there are two sorts of ideas: — one of *single* substances, as they exist separately, as of a man or a sheep; the other of several of those put together, as an army of men, or flock of sheep — which *collective* ideas of several substances thus put together are as much each of them one single idea as that of a man or an unit.

7. *Ideas of Relation.*   Thirdly, the last sort of complex ideas is that we call *relation,* which consists in the consideration and comparing one idea with another.

    Of these several kinds we shall treat in their order.

Chapter XXI

OF POWER

1. *This Idea, how got.*   The mind being every day informed, by the senses, of the alteration of those simple ideas it observes in things without; and taking notice how one comes to an end, and ceases to be, and another begins to exist which was not before; reflecting also on what passes within itself, and observing a constant change of its ideas, sometimes by the impression of outward objects on the senses, and sometimes by the determination of its own choice; and concluding from what it has so constantly observed to have been, that the like changes will for the future be made in the same things, by like agents, and by the like ways, — considers in one thing the possibility of having any of its simple ideas changed, and in another the possibility of making that change; and so comes by the idea which we call *power.* Thus we say, Fire has a power to melt gold, i.e. to destroy the consistency of its insensible parts, and consequently its hardness, and make it fluid; and gold has a power to be melted; that the sun has a power to

blanch wax, and wax a power to be blanched by the sun, whereby the yellowness is destroyed, and whiteness made to exist in its room. In which, and the like cases, the power we consider is in reference to the change of perceivable ideas. For we cannot observe any alteration to be made in, or operation upon anything, but by the observable change of its sensible ideas; nor conceive any alteration to be made, but by conceiving a change of some of its ideas.

2. *Power, active and passive.* Power thus considered is two-fold, viz. as able to make, or able to receive any change. The one may be called *active*, and the other *passive* power. Whether matter be not wholly destitute of active power, as its author, God, is truly above all passive power; and whether the intermediate state of created spirits be not that alone which is capable of both active and passive power, may be worth consideration. I shall not now enter into that inquiry, my present business being not to search into the original of power, but how we come by the *idea* of it. But since active powers make so great a part of our complex ideas of natural substances, (as we shall see hereafter,) and I mention them as such, according to common apprehension; yet they being not, perhaps, so truly *active* powers as our hasty thoughts are apt to represent them, I judge it not amiss, by this intimation, to direct our minds to the consideration of God and spirits, for the clearest idea of *active* power.

4. *The clearest Idea of active Power had from Spirit.* We are abundantly furnished with the idea of *passive* power by almost all sorts of sensible things. In most of them we cannot avoid observing their sensible qualities, nay, their very substances, to be in a continual flux. And therefore with reason we look on them as liable still to the same change. Nor have we of *active* power (which is the more proper signification of the word power) fewer instances. Since whatever change is observed, the mind must collect a power somewhere able to make that change, as well as a possibility in the thing itself to receive it. But yet, if we will consider it attentively, bodies, by our senses, do not afford us so clear and distinct an idea of active power, as we have from reflection on the operations of our minds. For all power relating to action, and there being but two sorts of action whereof we have an idea, viz. thinking and motion, let us

consider whence we have the clearest ideas of the powers which produce these actions. (1) Of thinking, body affords us no idea at all; it is only from reflection that we have that. (2) Neither have we from body any idea of the beginning of motion. A body at rest affords us no idea of any active power to move; and when it is set in motion itself, that motion is rather a passion than an action in it. For, when the ball obeys the motion of a billiard-stick, it is not any action of the ball, but bare passion. Also when by impulse it sets another ball in motion that lay in its way, it only communicates the motion it had received from another, and loses in itself so much as the other received: which gives us but a very obscure idea of an *active* power of moving in body, whilst we observe it only to *transfer*, but not *produce* any motion. For it is but a very obscure idea of power which reaches not the production of the action, but the continuation of the passion. For so is motion in a body impelled by another; the continuation of the alteration made in it from rest to motion being little more an action, than the continuation of the alteration of its figure by the same blow is an action. The idea of the *beginning* of motion we have only from reflection on what passes in ourselves; where we find by experience, that, barely by willing it, barely by a thought of the mind, we can move the parts of our bodies, which were before at rest. So that it seems to me, we have, from the observation of the operation of bodies by our senses, but a very imperfect obscure idea of *active* power; since they afford us not any idea in themselves of the power to begin any action, either motion or thought.

5. *Will and Understanding two Powers in Mind or Spirit.* This, at least, I think evident, — That we find in ourselves a power to begin or forbear, continue or end several actions of our minds, and motions of our bodies, barely by a thought or preference of the mind ordering, or as it were commanding, the doing or not doing such or such a particular action. This power which the mind has thus to order the consideration of any idea, or the forebearing to consider it; or to prefer the motion of any part of the body to its rest, and *vice versa*, in any particular instance, is that which we call the *Will*. The actual exercise of that power, by directing any particular action, or its forbearance, is that which we call *volition* or *willing*. The forbear-

ance of that action, consequent to such order or command of the mind, is called *voluntary*. And whatsoever action is performed without such a thought of the mind, is called *involuntary*. The power of perception is that which we call the *Understanding*. Perception, which we make the act of the understanding, is of three sorts: — 1. The perception of ideas in our minds. 2. The perception of the signification of signs. 3. The perception of the connexion or repugnancy, agreement or disagreement, that there is between any of our ideas. All these are attributed to the understanding, or perceptive power, though it be the two latter only that use allows us to say we understand.

7. *Whence the idea of liberty and necessity.*   Everyone, I think, finds in himself a power to begin or forbear, continue or put an end to several actions in himself. From the consideration of the extent of this power of the mind over the actions of the man, which everyone finds in himself, arise the ideas of liberty and necessity.

8. *Liberty, what.*   All the actions that we have any idea of reducing themselves, as has been said, to these two, viz. thinking and motion; so far as a man has power to think or not to think, to move or not to move, according to the preference or direction of his own mind, so far is a man *free*. Whenever any performance or forbearance are not equally in a man's power; wherever doing or not doing will not equally *follow* upon the preference of his mind directing it, there he is not free, though perhaps the action may be voluntary. So, that the idea of *liberty* is, the idea of a power in any agent to do or forbear any particular action, according to the determination or thought of the mind, whereby either of them is preferred to the other: where either of them is not in the power of the agent to be produced by him according to his volition, there he is not at liberty; that agent is under *necessity*. So that liberty cannot be where there is no thought, no volition, no will; but there may be thought, there may be will, there may be volition, where there is no liberty. A little consideration of an obvious instance or two may make this clear.

9. *Supposes Understanding and Will.*   A tennis-ball, whether in motion by the stroke of a racket, or lying still at rest, is not by any one taken to be a free

agent. If we inquire into the reason, we shall find it is because we conceive not a tennis-ball to think, and consequently not to have any volition, or *preference* of motion to rest, or *vice versâ*; and therefore has not liberty, is not a free agent; but all its both motion and rest come under our idea of necessary, and are so called. Likewise a man falling into the water, (a bridge breaking under him,) has not herein liberty, is not a free agent. For though he has volition, though he prefers his not falling to falling; yet the forbearance of that motion not being in his power, the stop or cessation of that motion follows not upon his volition; and therefore herein he is not free. So a man striking himself, or his friend, by a convulsive motion of his arm, which it is not in his power, by volition or the direction of his mind, to stop or forbear, nobody thinks he has in this liberty; every one pities him, as acting by necessity and constraint.

10. *Belongs not to Volition.*   Again: suppose a man be carried, whilst fast asleep, into a room where is a person he longs to see and speak with; and be there locked fast in, beyond his power to get out: he awakes, and is glad to find himself in so desirable company, which he stays willingly in, i.e. prefers his stay to going away. I ask, is not this stay voluntary? I think nobody will doubt it: and yet, being locked fast in, it is evident he is not at liberty not to stay, he has not freedom to be gone. So that liberty is not an idea belonging to volition, or preferring; but to the person having the power of doing, or forbearing to do, according as the mind shall choose or direct. Our idea of liberty reaches as far as that power, and no farther. For wherever restraint comes to check that power, or compulsion takes away that indifferency of ability to act, or to forbear acting, there liberty, and our notion of it, presently ceases.

11. *Voluntary opposed to involuntary, not to necessary.*   We have instances enough, and often more than enough, in our own bodies. A man's heart beats, and the blood circulates, which it is not in his power by any thought or volition to stop; and therefore in respect of these motions, where rest depends not on his choice, nor would follow the determination of his mind, if it should prefer it, he is not a free agent. Convulsive motions agitate his legs, so that though he wills it ever so much, he cannot by any power of

his mind stop their motion, (as in that odd disease called *chorea sancti viti*), but he is perpetually dancing; he is not at liberty in this action, but under as much necessity of moving, as a stone that falls, or a tennis-ball struck with a racket. On the other side, a palsy or the stocks hinder his legs from obeying the determination of his mind, if it would thereby transfer his body to another place. In all these there is want of freedom; though the sitting still, even of a paralytic, whilst he prefers it to a removal, is truly voluntary. Voluntary, then, is not opposed to necessary, but to involuntary. For a man may prefer what he can do, to what he cannot do; the state he is in, to its absence or change; though necessity has made it in itself unalterable.

12. *Liberty, what.* As it is in the motions of the body, so it is in the thoughts of our minds: where any one is such, that we have power to take it up, or lay it by, according to the preference of the mind, there we are at liberty. A waking man, being under the necessity of having some ideas constantly in his mind, is not at liberty to think or not to think; no more than he is at liberty, whether his body shall touch any other or no: but whether he will remove his contemplation from one idea to another is many times in his choice; and then he is, in respect of his ideas, as much at liberty as he is in respect of bodies he rests on; he can at pleasure remove himself from one to another. But yet some ideas to the mind, like some motions to the body, are such as in certain circumstances it cannot avoid, nor obtain their absence by the utmost effort it can use. A man on the rack is not at liberty to lay by the idea of pain, and divert himself with other contemplations: and sometimes a boisterous passion hurries our thoughts, as a hurricane does our bodies, without leaving us the liberty of thinking on other things, which we would rather choose. But as soon as the mind regains the power to stop or continue, begin or forbear, any of these motions of the body without, or thoughts within, according as it thinks fit to prefer either to the other, we then consider the man as a *free agent* again.

13. *Necessity, what.* Wherever thought is wholly wanting, or the power to act or forbear according to the direction of thought, there necessity takes place. This, in an agent capable of volition, when the beginning or continuation of any action is contrary to that preference of his mind, is called compulsion; when the hindering or stopping any action is contrary to his volition, it is called restraint. Agents that have no thought, no volition at all, are in everything *necessary agents.*

14. *Liberty belongs not to the Will.* If this be so, (as I imagine it is,) I leave it to be considered, whether it may not help to put an end to that long agitated, and, I think, unreasonable, because unintelligible question, viz. *Whether man's will be free or no?* For if I mistake not, it follows from what I have said, that the question itself is altogether improper; and it is as insignificant to ask whether man's *will* be free, as to ask whether his sleep be swift, or his virtue square: liberty being as little applicable to the will, as swiftness of motion is to sleep, or squareness to virtue. Every one would laugh at the absurdity of such a question as either of these: because it is obvious that the modifications of motion belong not to sleep, nor the difference of figure to virtue; and when any one well considers it, I think he will as plainly perceive that liberty, which is but a power, belongs only to *agents*, and cannot be an attribute or modification of the will, which is also but a power.

15. *Volition.* Such is the difficulty of explaining and giving clear notions of internal actions by sounds, that I must here warn my reader, that *ordering, directing, choosing, preferring*, &c., which I have made use of, will not distinctly enough express volition, unless he will reflect on what he himself does when he wills. For example, preferring, which seems perhaps best to express the act of volition, does it not precisely. For though a man would prefer flying to walking, yet who can say he ever wills it? Volition, it is plain, is an act of the mind knowingly exerting that dominion it takes itself to have over any part of the man, by employing it in, or withholding it from, any particular action. And what is the will, but the faculty to do this? And is that faculty anything more in effect than a power; the power of the mind to determine its thought, to the producing, continuing, or stopping any action, as far as it depends on us? For can it be denied that whatever agent has a power to think on its own actions, and to prefer their doing or omission either to other, has that faculty called will? *Will*, then,

is nothing but such a power. *Liberty*, on the other side, is the power a *man* has to do or forbear doing any particular action according as its doing or forbearance has the actual preference in the mind; which is the same thing as to say, according as he himself wills it.

16. *Powers belonging to Agents.* It is plain then that the will is nothing but one power or ability, and *freedom* another power or ability so that, to ask, whether the will has freedom, is to ask whether one power has another power, one ability another ability; a question at first sight too grossly absurd to make a dispute, or need an answer. For, who is it that sees not that powers belong only to agents, and are attributes only of substances, and not of powers themselves? So that this way of putting the question (viz. whether the will be free) is in effect to ask, whether the will be a substance, an agent, or at least to suppose it, since freedom can properly be attributed to nothing else. If freedom can with any propriety of speech be applied to power, it may be attributed to the power that is in a man to produce, or forbear producing, motion in parts of his body, by choice or preference; which is that which denominates him free, and is freedom itself. But if any one should ask, whether freedom were free, he would be suspected not to understand well what he said; and he would be thought to deserve Midas's ears,[3] who, knowing that rich was a denomination for the possession of riches, should demand whether riches themselves were rich.

21. *But to the Agent or Man.* To return, then, to the inquiry about liberty, I think the question is not proper, *whether the will be free*, but *whether a man be free*. Thus, I think.

First, That so far as any one can, by the direction or choice of his mind, preferring the existence of any action to the non-existence of that action, and *vice versa*, make *it* to exist or not exist, so far *he* is free. For if I can, by a thought directing the motion of my finger, make it move when it was at rest, or *vice versa*, it is evident, that in respect of that I am free: and if

3. [According to Greek mythology, King Midas argued that Apollo, the god of music, had lost a musical contest, and Apollo then punished Midas by turning his ears into those of an ass.]

I can, by a like thought of my mind, preferring one to the other, produce either words or silence, I am at liberty to speak or hold my peace: and as far as this power reaches, of acting or not acting, by the determination of his own thought preferring either, so far is a man free. For how can we think any one freer, than to have the power to do what he will? And so far as any one can, by preferring any action to its not being, or rest to any action, produce that action or rest, so far can he do what he will. For such a preferring of action to its absence, is the willing of it: and we can scarce tell how to imagine any being freer, than *to be able to do what he wills*. So that in respect of actions within the reach of such a power in him, a man seems as free as it is possible for freedom to make him.

22. *In respect of willing, a Man is not free.* But the inquisitive mind of man, willing to shift off from himself, as far as he can, all thoughts of guilt, though it be by putting himself into a worse state than that of fatal necessity, is not content with this: freedom, unless it reaches further than this, will not serve the turn: and it passes for a good plea, that a man is not free at all, if he be not as *free to will* as he is to *act what he wills*. Concerning a man's liberty, there yet, therefore, is raised this further question, *Whether a man be free to will?* which I think is what is meant, when it is disputed whether the will be free. And as to that I imagine.

23. *How a man cannot be free to will.* Secondly, That willing, or volition, being an action, and freedom consisting in a power of acting or not acting, a man in respect of willing or the act of volition, when any action in his power is once proposed to his thoughts, as presently to be done, cannot be free. The reason whereof is very manifest. For, it being unavoidable that the action depending on his will should exist or not exist, and its existence or not existence following perfectly the determination and preference of his will, he cannot avoid willing the existence or non-existence of that action; it is absolutely necessary that he will the one or the other; i.e., prefer the one to the other: since one of them must necessarily follow; and that which does follow follows by the choice and determination of his mind; that is, by his willing it: for if he did not will it, it would not be. So that, in respect of

the act of willing, a man in such a case is not free: liberty consisting in a power to act or not to act; which, in regard of volition, a man, upon such a proposal, has not. For it is unavoidably necessary to prefer the doing or forbearance of an action in a man's power, which is once so proposed to his thoughts; a man must necessarily will the one or the other of them; upon which preference or volition, the action or its forbearance certainly follows, and is truly voluntary. But the act of volition, or preferring one of the two, being that which he cannot avoid, a man, in respect of that act of willing, is under a necessity, and so cannot be free; unless necessity and freedom can consist together, and a man can be free and bound at once. Besides to make a man free after this manner, by making the action of willing to depend on his will, there must be another antecedent will, to determine the acts of this will, and another to determine that, and so *in infinitum*: for wherever one stops, the actions of the last will cannot be free. Nor is any being, as far I can comprehend beings above, capable of such a freedom of will, that it can forbear to will, i.e. to prefer the being or not being of anything in its power, which it has once considered as such.

24. *Liberty is freedom to execute what is willed.* This, then, is evident. That *a man is not at liberty to will, or not to will, anything in his power that he once considers of*: liberty consisting in a power to act or to forbear acting, and in that only. For a man that sits still is said yet to be at liberty; because he can walk if he wills it. A man that walks is at liberty also, not because he walks or moves; but because he can stand still if he wills it. *But if a man sitting still has not a power to remove himself, he is not at liberty*; so likewise a man falling down a precipice, though in motion, is not at liberty, because he cannot stop that motion if he would. This being so, it is plain that a man that is walking, to whom it is proposed to give off walking, is not at liberty, whether he will determine himself to walk, or give off walking or not: he must necessarily prefer one or the other of them; walking or not walking. And so it is in regard of all other actions in our power so proposed, which are the far greater number. For, considering the vast number of voluntary actions that succeed one another every moment that we are awake in the course of our lives, there are but few of them that are thought on

or proposed to the will, till the time they are to be done; and in all such actions, as I have shown, the mind, in respect of willing, has not a power to act or not to act, wherein consists liberty. The mind, in that case, has not a power to forbear *willing*; it cannot avoid some determination concerning them, let the consideration be as short, the thought as quick as it will, it either leaves the man in the state he was before thinking, or changes it; continues the action, or puts an end to it. Whereby it is manifest, that *it* orders and directs one, in preference to, or with neglect of the other, and thereby either the continuation or change becomes *unavoidably* voluntary.

25. *The Will determined by something without it.* Since then it is plain that, in most cases, a man is not at liberty, whether he will nor no, (for, when an action in his power is proposed to his thoughts, he *cannot* forbear volition; he *must* determine one way or the other;) the next thing demanded is,—*Whether a man be at liberty to will which of the two he pleases, motion or rest?* This question carries the absurdity of it so manifestly in itself, that one might thereby sufficiently be convinced that liberty concerns not the will. For, to ask whether a man be at liberty to will either motion or rest, speaking or silence, which he pleases, is to ask whether a man can will what he wills, or be pleased with what he is pleased with? A question which, I think, needs no answer: and they who can make a question of it must suppose one will to determine the acts of another, and another to determine that, and so on *in infinitum*.

26. *The ideas of* liberty *and* volition *must be defined.* To avoid these and the like absurdities, nothing can be of greater use than to establish in our minds determined ideas of the things under consideration. If the ideas of liberty and volition were well fixed in our understandings, and carried along with us in our minds, as they ought, through all the questions that are raised about them, I suppose a great part of the difficulties that perplex men's thoughts, and entangle their understandings, would be much easier resolved; and we should perceive where the confused signification of terms, or where the nature of the thing caused the obscurity.

27. *Freedom.* First, then, it is carefully to be remembered, That freedom consists in the dependence

of the existence, or not existence of any *action*, upon our *volition* of it; and not in the dependence of any action, or its contrary, on our *preference*. A man standing on a cliff, is at liberty to leap twenty yards downwards into the sea, not because he has a power to do the contrary action, which is to leap twenty yards upwards, for that he cannot do; but he is therefore free, because he has a power to leap or not to leap. But if a greater force than his, either holds him fast, or tumbles him down, he is no longer free in that case; because the doing or forbearance of that particular action is no longer in his power. He that is a close prisoner in a room twenty feet square, being at the north side of his chamber, is at liberty to walk twenty feet southward, because he can walk or not walk it; but is not, at the same time, at liberty to do the contrary, i.e. to walk twenty feet northward.

In this, then, consists freedom, viz. in our being able to act or not to act, according as we shall choose or will.

28. *What Volition and action mean.* Secondly, we must remember, that *volition* or *willing* is an act of the mind directing its thought to the production of any action, and thereby exerting its power to produce it. To avoid multiplying of words, I would crave leave here, under the word *action*, to comprehend the forbearance too of any action proposed: sitting still, or holding one's peace, when walking or speaking are proposed, though mere forbearances, requiring as much the determination of the will, and being as often weighty in their consequences, as the contrary actions, may, on that consideration, well enough pass for actions too: but this I say, that I may not be mistaken, if (for brevity's sake) I speak thus.

29. *What determines the Will.* Thirdly, the will being nothing but a power in the mind to direct the operative faculties of a man to motion or rest, as far as they depend on such direction; to the question, What is it determines the will? the true and proper answer is, The mind. For that which determines the general power of directing, to this or that particular direction, is nothing but the agent itself exercising the power it has that particular way. If this answer satisfies not, it is plain the meaning of the question, What determines the will? is this,—What moves the mind, in every particular instance, to determine its general power of directing, to this or that particular motion or rest? And to this I answer,—*The motive for continuing in the same state or action, is only the present satisfaction in it; the motive to change is always some uneasiness*: nothing setting us upon the change of state, or upon any new action, but some uneasiness. This is the great motive that works on the mind to put it upon action, which for shortness' sake we will call determining of the will, which I shall more at large explain.

48. *The Power to suspend the Prosecution of any Desire makes way for Consideration.* There being in us a great many uneasinesses, always soliciting and ready to determine the will, it is natural, as I have said, that the greatest and most pressing should determine the will to the next action; and so it does for the most part, but not always. For, the mind having in most cases, as is evident in experience, a power to *suspend* the execution and satisfaction of any of its desires; and so all, one after another; is at liberty to consider the objects of them, examine them on all sides, and weigh them with others. In this lies the liberty man has; and from the not·using of it right comes all that variety of mistakes, errors, and faults which we run into in the conduct of our lives, and our endeavours after happiness; whilst we precipitate the determination of our wills, and engage too soon, before due examination. To prevent this, we have a power to suspend the prosecution of this or that desire; as every one daily may experiment in himself. This seems to me the source of all liberty; in this seems to consist that which is (as I think improperly) called *free-will*. For, during this suspension of any desire, before the will be determined to action, and the action (which follows that determination) done, we have opportunity to examine, view, and judge of the good or evil of what we are going to do; and when, upon due examination, we have judged, we have done our duty, all that we can, or ought to do, in pursuit of our happiness; and it is not a fault, but a perfection of our nature, to desire, will, and act according to the last result of a fair examination.

73. *Recapitulation—Liberty of indifferency.* To conclude this inquiry into *human liberty*, which, as it stood before, I myself from the beginning fearing, and a very judicious friend of mine, since the publication, suspecting to have some mistake in it, though he could not particularly show it me, I was put upon a stricter review of this chapter. Wherein lighting upon a very easy and scarce observable slip I had

made, in putting one seemingly indifferent word for another that discovery opened to me this present view, which here, in this second edition, I submit to the learned world, and which, in short, is this: *Liberty* is a power to act or not to act, according as the mind directs. A power to direct the operative faculties to motion or rest in particular instances is that which we call the *will*. That which in the train of our voluntary actions determines the will to any change of operation is *some present uneasiness*, which is, or at least is always accompanied with that of *desire*. Desire is always moved by evil, to fly it: because a total freedom from pain always makes a necessary part of our happiness: but every good, nay, every greater good, does not constantly move desire, because it may not make, or may not be taken to make, any necessary part of our happiness. For all that we desire, is only to be happy. But, though this general desire of happiness operates constantly and invariably, yet the satisfaction of any particular desire *can be suspended* from determining the will to any subservient action, till we have maturely examined whether the particular apparent good which we then desire makes a part of our real happiness, or be consistent or inconsistent with it. The result of our judgment upon that examination is what ultimately determines the man; who could not be *free* if his will were determined by anything but his own desire, guided by his own judgment. I know that liberty, by some, is placed in an indifference of the man; antecedent to the determination of his will. I wish they who lay so much stress on such an antecedent indifference, as they call it, had told us plainly, whether this supposed indifference be antecedent to the thought and judgment of the understanding, as well as to the decree of the will. For it is pretty hard to state it between them, i.e. immediately *after* the judgment of the understanding, and *before* the determination of the will: because the determination of the will immediately follows the judgment of the understanding: and to place liberty in an indifference, antecedent to the thought and judgment of the understanding, seems to me to place liberty in a state of darkness, wherein we can neither see nor say anything of it; at least it places it in a subject incapable of it, no agent being allowed capable of liberty, but in consequence of thought and judgment. I am not nice about phrases, and therefore consent to say with those that love to speak so, that

liberty is placed in indifferency; but it is an indifferency which remains after the judgment of the understanding, yea, even after the determination of the will: and that is an indifferency not of the *man*, (for after he has once judged which is best, viz. to do or forbear, he is no longer indifferent,) but an indifferency of *the operative powers of the man*, which remaining equally able to operate or to forbear operating after as before the decree of the will, are in a state, which, if one pleases, may be called indifferency; and as far as this indifferency reaches, a man is free, and no further: v.g. I have the ability to move my hand, or to let it rest; that operative power is indifferent to move or not to move my hand. I am then, in that respect perfectly free; my will determines that operative power to rest: I am yet free, because the indifferency of that my operative power to act, or not to act, still remains; the power of moving my hand is not at all impaired by the determination of my will, which at present orders rest; the indifferency of that power to act, or not to act, is just as it was before, as will appear, if the will puts it to the trial, by ordering the contrary. But if, during the rest of my hand, it be seized with a sudden palsy, the indifferency of that operative power is gone, and with it my liberty; I have no longer freedom in that respect, but am under a necessity of letting my hand rest. On the other side, if my hand be put into motion by a convulsion, the indifferency of that operative faculty is taken away by that motion; and my liberty in that case is lost, for I am under a necessity of having my hand move. I have added this, to show in what sort of indifferency liberty seems to me to consist, and not in any other, real or imaginary.

74. *Active and passive power, in motions and in thinking.* Before I close this chapter, it may perhaps be to our purpose, and help to give us clearer conceptions about *power*, if we make our thoughts take a little more exact survey of *action*. I have said above, that we have ideas but of two sorts of action, viz. motion and thinking. These, in truth, though called and counted actions, yet, if nearly considered, will not be found to be always perfectly so. For, if I mistake not, there are instances of both kinds, which, upon due consideration, will be found rather passions than actions; and consequently so far the effects barely of *passive powers* in those subjects, which yet on their

accounts are thought agents. For, in these instances, the substance that hath motion or thought receives the impression, whereby it is put into that action, purely from without, and so acts merely by the capacity it has to receive such an impression from some external agent; and such a power is not properly an active power, but a mere passive capacity in the subject. Sometimes the substance or agent puts itself into action by its own power, and this is properly *active power*. Whatsoever modification a substance has, whereby it produces any effect, that is called action: v.g. a solid substance, by motion, operates on or alters the sensible ideas of another substance, and therefore this modification of motion we call action. But yet this motion in that solid substance is, when rightly considered, but a passion, if it received it only from some external agent. So that the active power of motion is in no substance which cannot begin motion in itself or in another substance when at rest. So likewise in thinking, a power to receive ideas or thoughts from the operation of any external substance is called a power of thinking: but this is but a passive power, or capacity., But to be able to bring into view ideas out of sight at one's own choice, and to compare which of them one thinks fit, this is an active power. This reflection may be of some use to preserve us from mistakes about powers and actions, which grammar, and the common frame of languages, may be apt to lead us into. Since what is signified by verbs that grammarians call active, does not always signify action: v.g. this proposition: I *see* the moon, or a star, or I *feel* the heat of the sun, though expressed by a verb active, does not signify any action in me, whereby I operate on those substances, but only the reception of the ideas of light, roundness, and heat; wherein I am not active, but barely passive, and cannot, in that position of my eyes or body, avoid receiving them. But when I turn my eyes another way, or remove my body out of the sunbeams, I am properly active; because of my own choice, by a power within myself, I put myself into that motion. Such an action is the product of active power.

Chapter XXIII

OF OUR COMPLEX IDEAS OF SUBSTANCES

1. *Ideas of particular Substances, how made.*   The mind being, as I have declared, furnished with a great number of the simple ideas, conveyed in by the senses as they are found in exterior things, or by reflection on its own operations, takes notice also that a certain number of these simple ideas go constantly together; which being presumed to belong to one thing, and words being suited to common apprehensions, and made use of for quick dispatch, are called, so united in one subject, by one name; which, by inadvertency, we are apt afterward to talk of and consider as one simple idea, which indeed is a complication of many ideas together: because, as I have said, not imaging how these simple ideas *can* subsist by themselves, we accustom ourselves to suppose some *substratum* wherein they do subsist, and from which they do result, which therefore we call *substance*.

2. *Our obscure Idea of Substance is general.*   So that if any one will examine himself concerning his notion of pure substance in general, he will find he has no other idea of it at all, but only a supposition of he knows not what *support* of such qualities which are capable of producing simple ideas in us; which qualities are commonly called accidents. If any one should be asked, what is the subject wherein colour or weight inheres, he would have nothing to say, but the solid extended parts; and if he were demanded, what is it that solidity and extension adhere in, he would not be in a much better case than the Indian before mentioned who, saying that the world was supported by a great elephant, was asked what the elephant rested on; to which his answer was—a great tortoise: but being again pressed to know what gave support to the broad-backed tortoise, replied—*something, he knew not what*. And thus here, as in all other cases where we use words without having clear and distinct ideas, we talk like children: who, being questioned what such a thing is, which they know not, readily give this satisfactory answer, that it is *something*: which in truth signifies no more, when so used, either by children or men, but that they know not what; and that the thing they pretend to know, and talk of, is what they have no distinct idea of at all, and so are perfectly ignorant of it, and in the dark. The idea then we have, to which we give the *general* name substance, being nothing but the supposed, but unknown, support of those qualities we find existing, which we imagine cannot subsist *sine re substante*, without something to support them, we call that sup-

port *substantia*; which, according to the true import of the word, is, in plain English, standing under or upholding.

3. *Of the Sorts of Substances.* An obscure and relative idea of *substance in general* being thus made we come to have the ideas of *particular sorts of substances*, by collecting *such* combinations of simple ideas as are, by experience and observation of men's senses, taken notice of to exist together; and are therefore supposed to flow from the particular internal constitution, or unknown essence of that substance. Thus we come to have the ideas of a man, horse, gold, water, &c.; of which substances, whether any one has any other *clear* idea, further than of certain simple ideas coexistent together, I appeal to every one's own experience. It is the ordinary qualities observable in iron, or a diamond, put together, that make the true complex idea of those substances, which a smith or a jeweller commonly knows better than a philosopher; who, whatever *substantial forms* he may talk of, has no other idea of those substances, than what is framed by a collection of those simple ideas which are to be found in them: only we must take notice, that our complex ideas of substances, besides all those simple ideas they are made up of, have always the confused idea of something to which they belong, and in which they subsist: and therefore when we speak of any sort of substance, we say it is a thing having such or such qualities; as body is a thing that is extended, figured, and capable of motion; spirit, a thing capable of thinking; and so hardness, friability, and power to draw iron, we say, are qualities to be found in a loadstone. These, and the like fashions of speaking, intimate that the substance is supposed always *something besides* the extension, figure, solidity, motion, thinking, or other observable ideas, though we know not what it is.

4. *No clear or distinct idea of Substance in general.* Hence, when we talk or think of any particular sort of corporeal substances, as horse, stone, &c., though the idea we have of either of them be but the complication or collection of those several simple ideas of sensible qualities, which we used to find united in the thing called horse or stone; yet, *because we cannot conceive how they should subsist alone, nor one in another*, we suppose them existing in and supported

by some common subject; which support we denote by the name substance, though it be certain we have no clear or distinct idea of that thing we suppose a support.

5. *As clear an Idea of spiritual substance as of corporeal substance.* The same thing happens concerning the operations of the mind, viz. thinking, reasoning, fearing, &c., which we concluding not to subsist of themselves, nor apprehending how they can belong to body, or be produced by it, we are apt to think these the actions of some other *substance*, which we call *spirit*; whereby yet it is evident that, having no other idea or notion of matter, but something wherein those many sensible qualities which affect our senses do subsist; by supposing a substance wherein thinking, knowing, doubting, and a power of moving, &c., do subsist, we have as clear a notion of the substance of spirit, as we have of body; the one being supposed to be (without knowing what it is) the *substratum* to those simple ideas we have from without; and the other supposed (with a like ignorance of what it is) to be the *substratum* to those operations we experiment in ourselves within. It is plain then, that the idea of *corporeal substance* in matter is as remote from our conceptions and apprehensions, as that of *spiritual substance*, or spirit: and therefore, from our not having any notion of the substance of spirit, we can no more conclude its non-existence, than we can, for the same reason, deny the existence of body; it being as rational to affirm there is no body, because we have no clear and distinct idea of the substance of matter, as to say there is no spirit, because we have no clear and distinct idea of the substance of a spirit.

6. *Our ideas of particular Sorts of Substances.* Whatever therefore be the secret abstract nature of substance in general, all the ideas we have of particular distinct sorts of substances are nothing but several combinations of simple ideas, co-existing in such, though unknown, cause of their union, as makes the whole subsist of itself. It is by such combinations of simple ideas, and nothing else, that we represent particular sorts of substances to ourselves; such are the ideas we have of their several species in our minds; and such only do we, by their specific names, signify to others, v.g. man, horse, sun, water, iron: upon hearing which words, every one who understands the

language, frames in his mind a combination of those several simple ideas which he has usually observed, or fancied to exist together under that denomination; all which he supposes to rest in and be, as it were, adherent to that unknown common subject, which inheres not in anything else. Though, in the meantime, it be manifest, and every one, upon inquiry into his own thoughts, will find, that he has no other idea of any substance, v.g. let it be gold, horse, iron, man, vitriol, bread, but what he has barely of those sensible qualities, which he supposes to inhere; with a supposition of such a *substratum* as gives, as it were, a support to those qualities or simple ideas, which he has observed to exist united together. Thus, the idea of the sun,—what is it but an aggregate of those several simple ideas, bright, hot, roundish, having a constant regular motion, at a certain distance from us, and perhaps some other: as he who thinks and discourses of the sun has been more or less accurate in observing those sensible qualities, ideas, or properties, which are in that thing which he calls the sun.

9. *Three sorts of Ideas make our complex ones of Corporeal Substances.* The ideas that make our complex ones of corporeal substances, are of these three sorts. First, the ideas of the primary qualities of things, which are discovered by our senses, and are in them even when we perceive them not; such are the bulk, figure, number, situation, and motion of the parts of bodies; which are really in them, whether we take notice of them or not. Secondly, the sensible secondary qualities, which, depending on these, are nothing but the powers those substances have to produce several ideas in us by our senses; which ideas are not in the things themselves, otherwise than as anything in its cause. Thirdly, the aptness we consider in any substance, to give or receive such alterations of primary qualities, as that the substance so altered should produce in us different ideas from what it did before; these are called active and passive powers: all which powers, as far as we have any notice or notion of them, terminate only in sensible simple ideas. For whatever alteration a loadstone has the power to make in the minute particles of iron, we should have no notion of any power it had at all to operate on iron, did not its sensible motion discover it: and I doubt not, but there are a thousand changes, that bodies we daily handle have a power to cause in one another,

which we never suspect, because they never appear in sensible effects.

10. *Powers thus make a great Part of our complex Ideas of particular Substances.* Powers therefore justly make a great part of our complex ideas of substances. He that will examine his complex idea of gold, will find several of its ideas that make it up to be only powers; as the power of being melted, but of not spending itself in the fire; of being dissolved in *aqua regia*, are ideas as necessary to make up our complex idea of gold, as its colour and weight: which, if duly considered, are also nothing but different powers. For, to speak truly, yellowness is not actually in gold, but is a power in gold to produce that idea in us by our eyes, when placed in a due light: and the heat, which we cannot leave out of our ideas of the sun, is no more really in the sun, than the white colour it introduced into wax. These are both equally powers in the sun, operating, by the motion and figure of its sensible parts, so on a man, as to make him have the idea of heat; and so on wax, as to make it capable to produce in a man the idea of white.

11. *The now secondary Qualities of Bodies would disappear, if we could discover the primary ones of their minute Parts.* Had we senses acute enough to discern the minute particles of bodies, and the real constitution on which their sensible qualities depend, I doubt not but they would produce quite different ideas in us: and that which is now the yellow colour of gold, would then disappear, and instead of it we should see an admirable texture of parts, of a certain size and figure. This microscopes plainly discover to us; for what to our naked eyes produces a certain colour, is, by thus augmenting the acuteness of our senses, discovered to be quite a different thing; and the thus altering, as it were, the proportion of the bulk of the minute parts of a coloured object to our usual sight, produces different ideas from what it did before. Thus, sand or pounded glass, which is opaque, and white to the naked eye, is pellucid in a microscope; and a hair seen in this way, loses its former colour, and is, in a great measure, pellucid, with a mixture of some bright sparkling colours, such as appear from the refraction of diamonds, and other pellucid bodies. Blood, to the naked eye, appears all red; but by a good microscope, wherein its lesser

parts appear, shows only some few globules of red, swimming in a pellucid liquor, and how these red globules would appear, if glasses could be found that could yet magnify them a thousand or ten thousand times more, is uncertain.

14. *Our specific Ideas of Substances.* But to return to the matter in hand,—the ideas we have of substances, and the ways we come by them. I say, our *specific* ideas of substances are nothing else but *a collection of a certain number of simple ideas, considered as united in one thing.* These ideas of substances, though they are commonly simple apprehensions, and the names of them simple terms, yet in effect are complex and compounded. Thus the idea which an Englishman signifies by the name swan, is white colour, long neck, red beak, black legs, and whole feet, and all these of a certain size, with a power of swimming in the water, and making a certain kind of noise, and perhaps, to a man who has long observed this kind of birds, some other properties: which all terminate in sensible simple ideas, all united in one common subject.

15. *Our Ideas of spiritual Substances, as clear as of bodily Substances.* Besides the complex ideas we have of material sensible substances, of which I have last spoken,—by the simple ideas we have taken from those operations of our own minds, which we experiment daily in ourselves, as thinking, understanding, willing, knowing, and power of beginning motion, &c., co-existing in some substance, we are able to frame the *complex idea of an immaterial spirit.* And thus, by putting together the ideas of thinking, perceiving, liberty, and power of moving themselves and other things, we have as clear a perception and notion of immaterial substances as we have of material. For putting together the ideas of thinking and willing, or the power of moving or quieting corporeal motion, joined to substance, of which we have no distinct idea, we have the idea of an immaterial spirit; and by putting together the ideas of coherent solid parts, and a power of being moved, joined with substance, of which likewise we have no positive idea, we have the idea of matter. The one is as clear and distinct an idea as the other: the idea of thinking, and moving a body, being as clear and distinct ideas as the ideas of extension, solidity, and being moved. For our idea of substance is equally obscure, or none at all, in both: it is but a supposed I know not what, to support those ideas we call accidents. It is for want of reflection that we are apt to think that our senses show us nothing but material things. Every act of sensation, when duly considered, gives us an equal view of both parts of nature, the corporeal and spiritual. For whilst I know, by seeing or hearing, &c., that there is some corporeal being without me, the object of that sensation, I do more certainly know, that there is some spiritual being within me that sees and hears. This, I must be convinced, cannot be the action of bare insensible matter; nor ever could be, without an immaterial thinking being.

16. *No Idea of abstract Substance either in Body or Spirit.* By the complex idea of extended, figured, coloured, and all other sensible qualities, which is all that we know of it, we are as far from the idea of the substance of body, as if we knew nothing at all: nor after all the acquaintance and familiarity which we imagine we have with matter, and the many qualities men assure themselves they perceive and know in bodies, will it perhaps upon examination be found, that they have any more or clearer primary ideas belonging to body, than they have belonging to immaterial spirit.

17. *Cohesion of solid parts and Impulse, the primary ideas peculiar to Body.* The primary ideas we have *peculiar to body*, as contradistinguished to spirit, are the *cohesion of solid, and consequently separable, parts*, and a *power of communicating motion by impulse.* These, I think, are the original ideas proper and peculiar to body; for figure is but the consequence of finite extension.

18. *Thinking and Motivity.* The ideas we have belonging and *peculiar to spirit*, are *thinking*, and *will*, or *a power of putting body into motion by thought, and, which is consequent to it, liberty.* For, as body cannot but communicate its motion by impulse to another body, which it meets with at rest, so the mind can put bodies into motion, or forbear to do so, as it pleases. The ideas of *existence, duration*, and *mobility*, are common to them both.

37. *Recapitulation.* And thus we have seen what kind of ideas we have of *substances of all kinds*, wherein they consist, and how we came by them. From whence, I think, it is very evident,

First, That all our ideas of the several *sorts* of substances are nothing but collections of simple ideas: with a supposition of *something* to which they belong, and in which they subsist: though of this supposed something we have no clear distinct idea at all.

Secondly, That all the simple ideas, that thus united in one common *substratum*, make up our complex ideas of several *sorts* of substances, are no other but such as we have received from sensation or reflection. So that even in those which we think we are most intimately acquainted with, and that come nearest the comprehension of our most enlarged conceptions, we cannot go beyond those simple ideas. And even in those which seem most remote from all we have to do with, and do infinitely surpass anything we can perceive in ourselves by reflection; or discover by sensation in other things, we can attain to nothing but those simple ideas, which we originally received from sensation or reflection; as is evident in the complex ideas we have of angels, and particularly of God himself.

Thirdly, That most of the simple ideas that make up our complex ideas of substances, when truly considered, are only *powers*, however we are apt to take them for positive qualities; v.g. the greatest part of the ideas that make our complex idea of *gold* are yellowness, great weight, ductility, fusibility, and solubility in *aqua regia*, &c., all united together in an unknown *substratum*: all which ideas are nothing else but so many relations to other substances; and are not really in the gold, considered barely in itself, though they depend on those real and primary qualities of its internal constitution, whereby it has a fitness differently to operate, and be operated on by several other substances.

Chapter XXVII

OF IDENTITY AND DIVERSITY

1. *Wherein Identity consists.* Another occasion the mind often takes of comparing, is the very being of things, when, considering *anything as existing at any determined time and place*, we compare it with *itself existing at another time*, and thereon form the ideas of *identity* and *diversity*. When we see anything to be in any place in any instant of time, we are sure (be it what it will) that it is that very thing, and not another which at that same time exists in another place, how like and undistinguishable soever it may be in all other respects: and in this consists *identity*, when the ideas it is attributed to vary not at all from what they were that moment wherein we consider their former existence, and to which we compare the present. For we never finding, nor conceiving it possible, that two things of the same kind should exist in the same place at the same time, we rightly conclude, that, whatever exists anywhere at any time, excludes all of the same kind, and is there itself alone. When therefore we demand whether anything be the *same* or no, it refers always to something that existed such a time in such a place, which it was certain, at that instant, was the same with itself, and no other. From whence it follows, that one thing cannot have two beginnings of existence, nor two things one beginning; it being impossible for two things of the same kind to be or exist in the same instant, in the very same place; or one and the same thing in different places. That, therefore, that had one beginning, is the same thing; and that which had a different beginning in time and place from that, is not the same, but divers. That which has made the difficulty about this relation has been the little care and attention used in having precise notions of the things to which it is attributed.

2. *Identity of Substances and of Modes.* We have the ideas but of three sorts of substances: 1. *God.* 2. *Finite intelligences.* 3. *Bodies.*

First, *God* is without beginning, eternal, unalterable, and everywhere, and therefore concerning his identity there can be no doubt.

Secondly, *Finite spirits* having had each its determinate time and place of beginning to exist, the relation to that time and place will always determine to each of them its identity, as long as it exists.

Thirdly, The same will hold of every *particle of matter*, to which no addition or substraction of matter being made, it is the same. For, though these three sorts of substances, as we term them, do not exclude one another out of the same place, yet we cannot conceive but that they must necessarily each of them exclude any of the same kind out of the same place: or else the notions and names of identity and diversity would be in vain, and there could be no such distinctions of substances, or anything else one from another. For example: could two bodies be in the same place at the same time; then those two parcels of matter must be one and the same, take them great or little; nay, all bodies must be one and the same. For, by the same reason that two particles of matter may be in one place, all bodies may be in one place: which, when it can be supposed, takes away the distinction of identity and diversity of one and more, and renders it ridiculous. But it being a contradiction that two or more should be one, identity and diversity are relations and ways of comparing well founded, and of use to the understanding. All other things being but modes or relations ultimately terminated in substances, the identity and diversity of each particular existence of them too will be by the same way determined: only as to things whose existence is in succession, such as are the actions of finite beings, v.g. *motion* and *thought*, both which consist in a continued train of succession, concerning *their* diversity there can be no question: because each perishing the moment it begins, they cannot exist in different times, or in different places, as permanent beings can at different times exist in distant places; and therefore no motion or thought, considered as at different times, can be the same, each part thereof having a different beginning of existence.

3. *Principium Individuationis.* From what has been said, it is easy to discover what is so much inquired after, the *principium individuationis*; and that, it is plain, is existence itself; which determines a being of any sort to a particular time and place, incommunicable to two beings of the same kind. Thus, though it seems easier to conceive in simple substances or modes; yet, when reflected on, is not more difficult in compound ones, if care be taken to what it is applied: v.g. let us suppose an atom, i.e. a continued body under one immutable superficies, existing in a determined time and place; it is evident, that, considered in any instant of its existence, it is in that instant the same with itself. For, being at that instant what it is, and nothing else, it is the same, and so must continue as long as its existence is continued; for so long it will be the same, and no other. In

like manner, if two or more atoms be joined together into the same mass, every one of those atoms will be the same, by the foregoing rule: and whilst they exist united together, the mass, consisting of the same atoms, must be the same mass, or the same body, let the parts be ever so differently jumbled. But if one of these atoms be taken away, or one new one added, it is no longer the same mass or the same body. In the state of living creatures, their identity depends not on a mass of the same particles, but on something else. For in them the variation of great parcels of matter alters not the identity: an oak growing from a plant to a great tree, and then lopped, is still the same oak; and a colt grown up to a horse, sometimes fat, sometimes lean, is all the while the same horse: though, in both these cases, there may be a manifest change of the parts; so that truly they are not either of them the same masses of matter, though they be truly one of them the same oak, and the other the same horse. The reason whereof is, that, in these two cases—a *mass of matter* and a *living body*—identity is not applied to the same thing.

4. *Identity of Vegetables.* We must therefore consider wherein an oak differs from a mass of matter, and that seems to me to be in this, that the one is only the cohesion of particles of matter any how united, the other such a disposition of them as constitutes the parts of an oak; and such an organization of those parts as is fit to receive and distribute nourishment, so as to continue and frame the wood, bark, and leaves, &c., of an oak, in which consists the vegetable life. That being then one plant which has such an organization of parts in one coherent body, partaking of one common life, it continues to be the same plant as long as it partakes of the same life, though that life be communicated to new particles of matter vitally united to the living plant, in a like continued organization conformable to that sort of plants. For this organization, being at any one instant in any one collection of matter, is in that particular concrete distinguished from all other, and *is* that individual life, which existing constantly from that moment both forwards and backwards, in the same continuity of insensibly succeeding parts united to the living body of the plant, it has that identity which makes the same plant, and all the parts of it, parts of the same plant, during all the time that they exist united in that

continued organization, which is fit to convey that common life to all the parts so united.

5. *Identity of Animals.* The case is not so much different in *brutes* but that any one may hence see what makes an animal and continues it the same. Something we have like this in machines, and may serve to illustrate it. For example, what is a watch? It is plain it is nothing but a fit organization or construction of parts to a certain end, which, when a sufficient force is added to it, it is capable to attain. If we would suppose this machine one continued body, all whose organized parts were repaired, increased, or diminished by a constant addition or separation of insensible parts, with one common life, we should have something very much like the body of an animal; with this difference, That, in an animal the fitness of the organization, and the motion wherein life consists, begin together, the motion coming from within; but in machines the force coming sensibly from without, is often away when the organ is in order, and well fitted to receive it.

6. *The Identity of Man.* This also shows wherein the identity of the same *man* consists; viz. in nothing but a participation of the same continued life, by constantly fleeting particles of matter, in succession vitally united to the same organized body. He that shall place the identity of man in anything else, but, like that of other animals, in one fitly organized body, taken in any one instant, and from thence continued, under one organization of life, in several successively fleeting particles of matter united to it, will find it hard to make an embryo, one of years, mad and sober, the *same* man, by any supposition, that will not make it possible for Seth, Ismael, Socrates, Pilate, St. Austin, and Caesar Borgia, to be the same man. For if the identity of *soul alone* makes the same *man*; and there be nothing in the nature of matter why the same individual spirit may not be united to different bodies, it will be possible that those men, living in distant ages, and of different tempers, may have been the same man: which way of speaking must be from a very strange use of the word man, applied to an idea out of which body and shape are excluded. And that way of speaking would agree yet worse with the notions of those philosophers who allow of transmigration, and are of opinion that the souls of men may,

for their miscarriages, be detruded into the bodies of beasts, as fit habitations, with organs suited to the satisfaction of their brutal inclinations. But yet I think nobody, could he be sure that the *soul* of Heliogabalus were in one of his hogs, would yet say that hog were a *man* or *Heliogabalus*.

9. *Personal Identity.* This being premised, to find wherein personal identity consists, we must consider what *person* stands for;—which, I think, is a thinking intelligent being, that has reason and reflection, and can consider itself as itself, the same thinking thing, in different times and places; which it does only by that consciousness which is inseparable from thinking, and, as it seems to me, essential to it: it being impossible for any one to perceive without *perceiving* that he does perceive. When we see, hear, smell, taste, feel, meditate, or will anything, we know that we do so. Thus it is always as to our present sensations and perceptions: and by this every one is to himself that which he calls *self*:—it not being considered, in this case, whether the same self be continued in the same or divers substances. For, since consciousness always accompanies thinking, and it is that which makes everyone to be what he calls self, and thereby distinguishes himself from all other thinking things, in this alone consists personal identity, i.e. the sameness of a rational being: and as far as this consciousness can be extended backwards to any past action or thought, so far reaches the identity of that person; it is the same self now it was then; and it is by the same self with this present one that now reflects on it, that that action was done.

10. *Consciousness makes personal Identity.* But it is further inquired, whether it be the same identical substance. This few would think they had reason to doubt of, if these perceptions, with their consciousness, always remained present in the mind, whereby the same thinking thing would be always consciously present, and, as would be thought, evidently the same to itself. But that which seems to make the difficulty is this, that this consciousness being interrupted always by forgetfulness, there being no moment of our lives wherein we have the whole train of all our past actions before our eyes in one view, but even the best memories losing the sight of one part whilst they are viewing another; and we sometimes, and that the

greatest part of our lives, not reflecting on our past selves, being intent on our present thoughts, and in sound sleep having no thoughts at all, or at least none with that consciousness which remarks our waking thoughts,—I say, in all these cases, our consciousness being interrupted, and we losing the sight of our past selves, doubts are raised whether we are the same thinking thing, i.e., the same *substance* or no. Which, however reasonable or unreasonable, concerns not *personal* identity at all. The question being what makes the same person, and not whether it be the same identical substance, which always thinks in the same person, which, in this case, matters not at all: different substances, by the same consciousness (where they do partake in it) being united into one person, as well as different bodies by the same life are united into one animal, whose identity is preserved in that change of substances by the unity of one continued life. For, it being the same consciousness that makes a man be himself to himself, personal identity depends on that only, whether it be annexed solely to one individual substance, or can be continued in a succession of several substances. For as far as any intelligent being *can* repeat the idea of any past action with the same consciousness it had of it at first, and with the same consciousness it has of any present action; so far it is the same personal self. For it is by the consciousness it has of its present thoughts and actions, that it is *self to itself* now, and so will be the same self, as far as the same consciousness can extend to actions past or to come; and would be by distance of time, or change of substance, no more two persons, than a man be two men by wearing other clothes today than he did yesterday, with a long or a short sleep between: the same consciousness uniting those distant actions into the same person, whatever substances contributed to their production.

16. *Consciousness alone unites actions into the same Person.* But though the same immaterial substance or soul does not alone, wherever it be, and in whatsoever state, make the same *man*; yet it is plain, consciousness, as far as ever it can be extended—should it be to ages past—unites existences and actions very remote in time into the same *person*, as well as it does the existences and actions of the immediately preceding moment: so that whatever has the consciousness of present and past actions, is the same

person to whom they both belong. Had I the same consciousness that I saw the ark and Noah's flood, as that I saw an overflowing of the Thames last winter, or as that I write now, I could no more doubt that I who write this now, that saw the Thames overflowed last winter, and that viewed the flood at the general deluge, was the same *self*,—place that self in what *substance* you please—than that I who write this am the same *myself* now while I write (whether I consist of all the same substance, material or immaterial, or no) that I was yesterday. For as to this point of being the same self, it matters not whether this present self be made up of the same or other substances—I being as much concerned, and as justly accountable for any action that was done a thousand years since, appropriated to me now by this self-consciousness, as I am for what I did the last moment.

17. *Self depends on Consciousness, not on Substance.* Self is that conscious thinking thing,—whatever substance made up of, (whether spiritual or material, simple or compounded, it matters not)—which is sensible or conscious of pleasure and pain, capable of happiness or misery, and so is concerned for itself, as far as that consciousness extends. Thus every one finds that, whilst comprehended under that consciousness, the little finger is as much a part of himself as what is most so. Upon separation of this little finger, should this consciousness go along with the little finger, and leave the rest of the body, it is evident the little finger would be the person, the same person; and self then would have nothing to do with the rest of the body. As in this case it is the consciousness that goes along with the substance, when one part is separate from another, which makes the same person, and constitutes this inseparable self: so it is in reference to substances remote in time. That with which the consciousness of this present thinking thing *can* join itself, makes the same person, and is one self with it, and with nothing else; and so attributes to itself, and owns all the actions of that thing, as its own, as far as that consciousness reaches, and no further; as every one who reflects will perceive.

18. *Persons, not Substances, the Objects of Reward and Punishment.* In this personal identity is

founded all the right and justice of reward and punishment; happiness and misery being that for which every one is concerned for *himself*, and not mattering what becomes of any *substance*, not joined to, or affected with that consciousness. For, as it is evident in the instance I gave but now, if the consciousness went along with the little finger when it was cut off, that would be the same self which was concerned for the whole body yesterday, as making part of itself, whose actions then it cannot but admit as its own now. Though, if the same body should still live, and immediately from the separation of the little finger have its own peculiar consciousness, whereof the little finger knew nothing, it would not at all be concerned for it, as a part of itself, or could own any of its actions, or have any of them imputed to him.

20. *Absolute oblivion separates what is thus forgotten from the person, but not from the man.* But yet possibly it will still be objected,—Suppose I wholly lose the memory of some parts of my life, beyond a possibility of retrieving them, so that perhaps I shall never be conscious of them again; yet am I not the same person that did those actions, had those thoughts that I once was conscious of, though I have now forgot them? To which I answer, that we must here take notice what the word *I* is applied to; which, in this case, is the *man* only. And the same man being presumed to be the same person, I is easily here supposed to stand also for the same person. But if it be possible for the same man to have distinct incommunicable consciousness at different times, it is past doubt the same man would at different times make different persons; which, we see, is the sense of mankind in the solemnest declaration of their opinions, human laws not punishing the mad man for the sober man's actions, nor the sober man for what the mad man did,—thereby making them two persons: which is somewhat explained by our way of speaking in English when we say such an one is 'not himself,' or is 'beside himself'; in which phrases it is insinuated, as if those who now, or at least first used them, thought that self was changed; the self-same person was no longer in that man.

22. But is not a man drunk and sober the same person? Why else is he punished for the fact he commits when drunk, though he be never afterwards

conscious of it? Just as much the same person as a man that walks, and does other things in his sleep, is the same person, and is answerable for any mischief he shall do in it. Human laws punish both, with a justice suitable to *their* way of knowledge;—because, in these cases, they cannot distinguish certainly what is real, what counterfeit: and so the ignorance in drunkenness or sleep is not admitted as a plea. For, though punishment be annexed to personality, and personality to consciousness, and the drunkard perhaps be not conscious of what he did, yet human judicatures justly punish him; because the fact is proved against him, but want of consciousness cannot be proved for him. But in the Great Day, wherein the secrets of all hearts shall be laid open, it may be reasonable to think, no one shall be made to answer for what he knows nothing of; but shall receive his doom, his conscience accusing or excusing him.

25. *Consciousness unites substances, material or spiritual, with the same personality.* I agree, the more probable opinion is, that this consciousness is annexed to, and the affection of, one individual immaterial substance.

But let men, according to their diverse hypotheses, resolve of that as they please. This every intelligent being, sensible of happiness or misery, must grant—that there is something that is *himself*, that he is concerned for, and would have happy; that this self has existed in a continued duration more than one instant, and therefore it is possible may exist, as it has done, months and years to come, without any certain bounds to be set to its duration; and may be the same self, by the same consciousness continued on for the future. And thus, by this consciousness he finds himself to be the same self which did such and such an action some years since, by which he comes to be happy or miserable now. In all which account of self, the same numerical *substance* is not considered as making the same self; but the same continued *consciousness*, in which several substances may have been united, and again separated from it, which, whilst they continued in a vital union with that wherein this consciousness then resided, made a part of that same self. Thus any part of our bodies, vitally united to that which is conscious in us, makes a part of ourselves: but upon separation from the vital union by which that consciousness is communicated, that which a moment since was part of ourselves, is now no more so than a part of another man's self is a part of me: and it is not impossible but in a little time may become a real part of another person. And so we have the same numerical substance become a part of two different persons; and the same person preserved under the change of various substances. Could we suppose any spirit wholly stripped of all its memory or consciousness of past actions, as we find our minds always are of a great part of ours, and sometimes of them all; the union or separation of such a spiritual substance would make no variation of personal identity, any more than that of any particle of matter does. Any substance vitally united to the present thinking being is a part of that very same self which now is; anything united to it by a consciousness of former actions, makes also a part of the same self, which is the same both then and now.

BOOK III
OF WORDS

Chapter II

OF THE SIGNIFICATION OF WORDS

1. *Words are sensible Signs, necessary for Communication of Ideas.*   Man, though he have great variety of thoughts, and such from which others as well as himself might receive profit and delight; yet they are all within his own breast, invisible and hidden from others, nor can of themselves be made to appear. The comfort and advantage of society not being to be had without communication of thoughts, it was necessary that man should find out some external sensible signs, whereof those invisible ideas, which his thoughts are made up of, might be made known to others. For this purpose nothing was so fit, either for plenty or quickness, as those articulate sounds, which with so much ease and variety he found himself able to make. Thus we may conceive how *words*, which were by nature so well adapted to that purpose, came to be made use of by men as the signs of their ideas; not by any natural connexion that there is between particular articulate sounds and certain ideas, for then there would be but one language amongst all men; but by a voluntary imposition,

whereby such a word is made arbitrarily the mark of such an idea. The use, then, of words, is to be sensible marks of ideas; and the ideas they stand for are their proper and immediate signification.

3. *Examples of this.*   This is so necessary in the use of language, that in this respect the knowing and the ignorant, the learned and the unlearned, use the words they speak (with any meaning) all alike. They, in every man's mouth, stand for the ideas he has, and which he would express by them. A child having taken notice of nothing in the metal he hears called *gold*, but the bright shining yellow colour, he applies the word gold only to his own idea of that colour, and nothing else; and therefore calls the same colour in a peacock's tail gold. Another that hath better observed, adds to shining yellow great weight: and then the sound gold, when he uses it, stands for a complex idea of a shining yellow and a very weighty substance. Another adds to those qualities fusibility: and then the word gold signifies to him a body, bright, yellow, fusible, and very heavy. Another adds malleability. Each of these uses equally the word gold, when they have occasion to express the idea which they have applied it to: but it is evident that each can apply it only to his own idea; nor can be make it stand as a sign of such a complex idea as he has not.

Chapter III

OF GENERAL TERMS

1. *The greatest Part of Words are general terms.* All things that exist being particulars, it may perhaps be thought reasonable that words, which ought to be conformed to things, should be so too,—I mean in their signification: but yet we find quite the contrary. The far greatest part of the words that make all languages are general terms: which has not been the effect of neglect or chance, but of reason and necessity.

2. *That every particular Thing should have a Name for itself is impossible.*   First, It is impossible that every particular thing should have a distinct peculiar name. For, the signification and use of words depending on that connexion which the mind makes between its ideas and the sounds it uses as signs of them, it is necessary, in the application of names to things,

that the mind should have distinct ideas of the things, and retain also the particular name that belongs to every one, with its peculiar appropriation to that idea. But it is beyond the power of human capacity to frame and retain distinct ideas of all the particular things we meet with: every bird and beast men saw; every tree and plant that affected the senses, could not find a place in the most capacious understanding. If it be looked on as an instance of a prodigious memory, that some generals have been able to call every soldier in their army by his proper name, we may easily find a reason why men have never attempted to give names to each sheep in their flock, or crow that flies over their heads; much less to call every leaf of plants, or grain of sand that came in their way, by a peculiar name.

3. *And would be useless, if it were possible.*   Secondly, If it were possible, it would yet be useless; because it would not serve to the chief end of language. Men would in vain heap up names of particular things, that would not serve them to communicate their thoughts. Men learn names, and use them in talk with others, only that they may be understood: which is then only done when, by use or consent, the sound I make by the organs of speech, excites in another man's mind who hears it, the idea I apply it to in mine, when I speak it. This cannot be done by names applied to particular things; whereof I alone having the ideas in my mind, the names of them could not be significant or intelligible to another, who was not acquainted with all those very particular things which had fallen under my notice.

4. *A distinct name for every particular thing, not fitted for enlargement of knowledge.*   Thirdly, But yet, granting this also feasible, (which I think is not,) yet a distinct name for every particular thing would not be of any great use for the improvement of knowledge: which, though founded in particular things, enlarges itself by general views; to which things reduced into sorts, under general names, are properly subservient. These, with the names belonging to them, come within some compass, and do not multiply every moment, beyond what either the mind can contain, or use requires. And therefore, in these, men have for the most part stopped: but yet not so as to hinder themselves from distinguishing particular

things by appropriated names, where convenience demands it. And therefore in their own species, which they have most to do with, and wherein they have often occasion to mention particular persons, they make use of proper names; and there distinct individuals have distinct denominations.

5. *What things have proper Names and why.*   Besides persons, countries also, cities, rivers, mountains, and other the like distinctions of place have usually found peculiar names, and that for the same reason; they being such as men have often an occasion to mark particularly, and, as it were, set before others in their discourses with them. And I doubt not but, if we had reason to mention particular horses as often as we have to mention particular men, we should have proper names for the one, as familiar as for the other, and Bucephalus would be a word as much in use as Alexander. And therefore we see that, amongst jockeys, horses have their proper names to be known and distinguished by, as commonly as their servants: because, amongst them, there is often occasion to mention this or that particular horse when he is out of sight.

6. *How general words are made.*   The next thing to be considered is, — How general words come to be made. For, since all things that exist are only particulars, how come we by general terms; or where find we those general natures they are supposed to stand for? Words become general by being made the signs of general ideas: and ideas become general, by separating from them the circumstances of time and place, and any other ideas that may determine them to this or that particular existence. By this way of abstraction they are made capable of representing more individuals than one; each of which having in it a conformity to that abstract idea, is (as we call it) of that sort.

7. *Shown by the way we enlarge our complex ideas from infancy.*   But, to deduce this a little more distinctly, it will not perhaps be amiss to trace our notions and names from their beginning, and observe by what degrees we proceed, and by what steps we enlarge our ideas from our first infancy. There is nothing more evident, than that the ideas of the persons children converse with (to instance in them alone) are like

the persons themselves, only particular. The ideas of the nurse and the mother are well framed in their minds; and, like pictures of them there, represent only those individuals. The names they first gave to them are confined to these individuals; and the names of *nurse* and *mamma*, the child uses, determine themselves to those persons. Afterwards, when time and a larger acquaintance have made them observe that there are a great many other things in the world, that in some common agreements of shape, and several other qualities, resemble their father and mother, and those persons they have been used to, they frame an idea, which they find those many particulars do partake in; and to that they give, with others, the name *man*, for example. And thus they come to have a general name, and a general idea. Wherein they make nothing new; but only leave out of the complex idea they had of Peter and James, Mary and Jane, that which is peculiar to each, and retain only what is common to them all.

8. *And further enlarge our complex ideas, by still leaving out properties contained in them.* By the same way that they come by the general name and idea of *man*, they easily advance to more general names and notions. For, observing that several things that differ from their idea of man, and cannot therefore be comprehended under that name, have yet certain qualities wherein they agree with man, by retaining only those qualities, and uniting them into one idea, they have again another and more general idea; to which having given a name they make a term of a more comprehensive extension: which new idea is made, not by any new addition, but only as before, by leaving out the shape, and some other properties signified by the name man, and retaining only a body, with life, sense, and spontaneous motion, comprehended under the name *animal*.

9. *General natures are nothing but abstract and partial ideas of more complex ones.* That this is the way whereby men first formed general ideas, and general names to them, I think is so evident, that there needs no other proof of it but the considering of a man's self, or others, and the ordinary proceedings of their minds in knowledge. And he that thinks *general natures* or *notions* are anything else but such abstract and partial ideas of more complex ones, taken

at first from particular existences, will, I fear, be at a loss where to find them. For let any one effect, and then tell me, wherein does his idea of *man* differ from that of *Peter* and *Paul*, or his idea of *horse* from that of *Bucephalus*, but in the leaving out something that is peculiar to each individual, and retaining so much of those particular complex ideas of several particular existences as they are found to agree in? Of the complex ideas signified by the names *man* and *horse*, leaving out but those particulars wherein they differ, and retaining only those wherein they agree, and of those making a new distinct complex idea, and giving the name *animal* to it, one has a more general term, that comprehends with man several other creatures. Leave out of the idea of *animal*, sense and spontaneous motion, and the remaining complex idea, made up of the remaining simple ones of body, life, and nourishment, becomes a more general one, under the more comprehensive term, *vivens*. And, not to dwell longer upon this particular, so evident in itself; by the same way the mind proceeds to *body, substance,* and at last to *being, thing,* and such universal terms, which stand for any of our ideas whatsoever. To conclude: this whole mystery of genera and species, which make such a noise in the schools, and are with justice so little regarded out of them, is nothing else but *abstract ideas*, more or less comprehensive, with names annexed to them. In all which this is constant and unvariable, that every more general term stands for such an idea, and is but a part of any of those contained under it.

10. *Why the Genus is ordinarily made Use of in Definitions.* This may show us the reason why, in the defining of words, which is nothing but declaring their signification, we make use of the *genus*, or next general word that comprehends it. Which is not out of necessity, but only to save the labour of enumerating the several simple ideas which the next general word or *genus* stands for; or, perhaps, sometimes the shame of not being able to do it. But though defining by *genus* and *differentia* (I crave leave to use these terms of art, though originally Latin, since they most properly suit those notions they are applied to), I say, though defining by the *genus* be the shortest way, yet I think it may be doubted whether it be the best. This I am sure, it is not the only, and so not absolutely necessary. For, definition being nothing but making

another understand by words what idea the term defined stands for, a definition is best made by enumerating those simple ideas that are combined in the signification of the term defined: and, if, instead of such an enumeration, men have accustomed themselves to use the next general term, it has not been out of necessity, or for greater clearness, but for quickness and dispatch sake. For I think that, to one who desired to know what idea the word *man* stood for; if it should be said, that man was a solid extended substance, having life, sense, spontaneous motion, and the faculty of reasoning, I doubt not but the meaning of the term man would be as well understood, and the idea it stands for be at least as clearly made known, as when it is defined to be a rational animal: which, by the several definitions of *animal, vivens*, and *corpus*, resolves itself into those enumerated ideas. I have, in explaining the term *man*, followed here the ordinary definition of the schools; which, though perhaps not the most exact, yet serves well enough to my present purpose. And one may, in this instance, see what gave occasion to the rule, that a definition must consist of *genus* and *differentia*; and it suffices to show us the little necessity there is of such a rule, or advantage in the strict observing of it. For, definitions, as has been said, being only the explaining of one word by several others, so that the meaning or idea it stands for may be certainly known; languages are not always so made according to the rules of logic, that every term can have its signification exactly and clearly expressed by two others. Experience sufficiently satisfies us to the contrary; or else those who have made this rule have done ill, that they have given us so few definitions conformable to it. But of definitions more in the next chapter.

11. *General and Universal are Creatures of the Understanding, and belong not to the Real Existence of things.*   To return to general words: it is plain, by what has been said, that *general* and *universal* belong not to the real existence of things; but are the inventions and creatures of the understanding, made by it for its own use, and concern only signs, whether words or ideas. Words are general, as has been said, when used for signs of general ideas, and so are applicable indifferently to many particular things; and ideas are general when they are set up as the representatives of many particular things: but universality belongs not to things themselves, which are all of them particular in their existence, even those words and ideas which in their signification are general. When therefore we quit particulars, the generals that rest are only creatures of our own making; their general nature being nothing but the capacity they are put into, by the understanding, of signifying or representing many particulars. For the signification they have is nothing but a relation that, by the mind of man, is added to them.

12. *Abstract Ideas are the Essences of Genera and Species.*   The next thing therefore to be considered is, What kind of signification it is that general words have. For, as it is evident that they do not signify barely one particular thing; for then they would not be general terms, but proper names, so, on the other side, it is as evident they do not signify a plurality; for *man* and *men* would then signify the same; and the distinction of numbers (as the grammarians call them) would be superfluous and useless. That then which general words signify is a *sort* of things; and each of them does that, by being a sign of an abstract idea in the mind; to which idea, as things existing are found to agree, so they come to be ranked under that name, or, which is all one, be of that sort. Whereby it is evident that the *essences* of the sorts, or, if the Latin word pleases better, *species* of things, are nothing else but these abstract ideas. For the having the essence of any species, being that which makes anything to be of that species; and the conformity to the idea to which the name is annexed being that which gives a right to that name; the having the essence, and the having that conformity, must needs be the same thing: since to be of any species, and to have a right to the name of that species, is all one. As, for example, to be a *man*, or of the *species* man, and to have right to the *name* man, is the same thing, Again, to be a man, or of the species man, and have the *essence* of a man, is the same thing, Now, since nothing can be a man, or have a right to the name man, but what has a conformity to the abstract idea the name man stands for, nor anything be a man, or have a right to the species man, but what has the essence of that species; it follows, that the abstract idea for which the name stands, and the essence of the species, is one and the same. From whence it is easy to observe, that the essences of the sorts of things,

and, consequently, the sorting of things, is the workmanship of the understanding that abstracts and makes those general ideas.

13. *They are the Workmanship of the Understanding, but have their Foundation in the Similitude of Things.* I would not here be thought to forget, much less to deny, that Nature, in the production of things, makes several of them alike: there is nothing more obvious, especially in the races of animals, and all things propagated by seed. But yet I think we may say, *the sorting of them under names is the workmanship of the understanding, taking occasion, from the similitude it observes amongst them, to make abstract general ideas,* and set them up in the mind, with names annexed to them, as patterns or forms, (for, in that sense, the word *form* has a very proper signification,) to which as particular things existing are found to agree, so they come to be of that species, have that denomination, or are put into that *classis.* For when we say this is a man, that a horse; this justice, that cruelty; this a watch, that a jack; what do we else but rank things under different specific names, as agreeing to those abstract ideas, of which we have made those names the signs? And what are the essences of those species set out and marked by names, but those abstract ideas in the mind; which are, as it were, the bonds between particular things that exist, and the names they are to be ranked under? And when general names have any connexion with particular beings, these abstract ideas are the medium that unites them: so that the essences of species, as distinguished and denominated by us, neither are nor can be anything but those precise abstract ideas we have in our minds. And therefore the supposed real essences of substances, if different from our abstract ideas, cannot be the essences of the species *we* rank things into. For two species may be one, as rationally as two different essences be the essence of one species: and I demand what are the alterations [which] may, or may not be made in a *horse* or *lead,* without making either of them to be of another species? In determining the species of things by *our* abstract ideas, this is easy to resolve, but if any one will regulate himself herein by supposed *real* essences, he will, I suppose, be at a loss: and he will never be able to know when anything precisely cease to be of the species of a *horse* or *lead.*

14. *Each distinct abstract Idea is a distinct Essence.* Nor will any one wonder that I say these essences, or abstract ideas (which are the measures of name, and the boundaries of species) are the workmanship of the understanding, who considers that at least the complex ones are often, in several men, different collections of simple ideas; and therefore that is *covetousness* to one man, which is not so to another. Nay, even in substances, where their abstract ideas seem to be taken from the things themselves, they are not constantly the same; no, not in that species which is most familiar to us, and with which we have the most intimate acquaintance: it having been more than once doubted, whether the *foetus* born of a woman were a *man,* even so far as that it hath been debated, whether it were or were not to be nourished and baptized: which could not be, if the abstract idea or essence to which the name man belonged were of nature's making; and were not the uncertain and various collection of simple ideas, which the understanding put together, and then, abstracting it, affixed a name to it. So that, in truth, every distinct abstract idea is a distinct essence; and the names that stand for such distinct ideas are the names of things essentially different. Thus a circle is as essentially different from an oval as a sheep from a goat; and rain is as essentially different from snow as water from earth: that abstract idea which is the essence of one being impossible to be communicated to the other. And thus any two abstract ideas, that in any part vary one from another, with two distinct names annexed to them, constitute two distinct sorts, or, if you please, *species,* as essentially different as any two of the most remote or opposite in the world.

15. *Several significations of the word Essence.* But since the essences of things are thought by some (and not without reason) to be wholly unknown, it may not be amiss to consider the several significations of the word *essence.*

First, Essence may be taken for the very being of anything, whereby it is what it is. And thus the real internal, but generally (in substances) unknown constitution of things, whereon their discoverable qualities depend, may be called their essence. This is the proper original signification of the word, as is evident from the formation of it; *essentia,* in its primary notation, signifying properly, being. And in this sense it is still used, when we speak of the essence of *particular* things, without giving them any name.

Secondly, The learning and disputes of the schools having been much busied about *genus* and *species*, the word *essence* has almost lost its primary signification: and, instead of the real constitution of things, has been almost wholly applied to the artificial constitution of *genus* and *species*. It is true, there is ordinarily supposed a real constitution of the sorts of things; and it is past doubt there must be some real constitution, on which any collection of simple ideas co-existing must depend. But, it being evident that things are ranked under names into sorts or species, only as they agree to certain abstract ideas, to which we have annexed those names, the essence of each *genus*, or sort, comes to be nothing but that abstract idea which the general, or sortal (if I may have leave so to call it from sort, as I do general from genus,) name stands for. And this we shall find to be that which the word essence imports in its most familiar use.

These two sorts of essences, I suppose, may not unfitly be termed, the one the *real*, the other *nominal essence*.

16. *Constant Connexion between the Name and nominal Essence.*
Between the *nominal essence* and the *name* there is so near a connexion, that the name of any sort of things cannot be attributed to any particular being but what has this essence, whereby it answers that abstract idea whereof that name is the sign.

17. *Supposition, that Species are distinguished by their real Essences useless.*
Concerning the *real essences* of corporeal substances (to mention these only) there are, if I mistake not, two opinions. The one is of those who, using the word essence for they know not what, suppose a certain number of those essences, according to which all natural things are made, and wherein they do exactly every one of them partake, and so become of this or that species. The other and more rational opinion is of those who look on all natural things to have a real, but unknown, constitution of their insensible parts; from which flow those sensible qualities which serve us to distinguish them one from another, according as we have occasion to rank them into sorts, under common denominations. The former of these opinions, which supposes these essences as a certain number of forms or moulds,

wherein all natural things that exist are cast, and do equally partake, has, I imagine, very much perplexed the knowledge of natural things. The frequent productions of monsters, in all the species of animals, and of changelings, and other strange issues of human birth, carry with them difficulties, not possible to consist with this hypothesis; since it is as impossible that two things partaking exactly of the same real essence should have different properties, as that two figures partaking of the same real essence of a circle should have different properties. But were there no other reason against it, yet the supposition of essences that cannot be known; and the making of them, nevertheless, to be that which distinguishes the species of things, is so wholly useless and unserviceable to any part of our knowledge, that that alone were sufficient to make us lay it by, and content ourselves with such essences of the sorts or species of things as come within the reach of our knowledge: which, when seriously considered, will be found, as I have said, to be nothing else but, those *abstract* complex ideas to which we have annexed distinct general names.

18. *Real and nominal Essence, the same in simple Ideas and Modes, different in Substances.*
Essences being thus distinguished into nominal and real, we may further observe, that, in the species of simple ideas and modes, they are always the same; but in substances always quite different. Thus, a figure including a space between three lines, is the real as well as nominal essence of a triangle; it being not only the abstract idea to which the general name is annexed, but the very *essentia* or being of the thing itself; that foundation from which all its properties flow, and to which they are all inseparably annexed. But it is far otherwise concerning that parcel of matter which makes the ring on my finger; wherein these two essences are apparently different. For, it is the real constitution of its insensible parts, on which depend all those properties of colour, weight, fusibility, fixedness, &c., which are to be found in it; which constitution we know not, and so, having no particular idea of, having no name that is the sign of it. But yet it is its colour, weight, fusibility, fixedness, &c., which makes it to be gold, or gives it a right to that name, which is therefore its nominal essence. Since nothing can be called gold but what has a conformity of qualities to that abstract complex idea to which that

name is annexed. But this distinction of essences, belonging particularly to substances, we shall, when we come to consider their names, have an occasion to treat of more fully.

19. *Essences ingenerable and incorruptible.* That such abstract ideas, with names to them, as we have been speaking of are essences, may further appear by what we are told concerning essences, viz. that they are all ingenerable and incorruptible. Which cannot be true of the real constitutions of things, which begin and perish with them. All things that exist, besides their Author, are all liable to change; especially those things we are acquainted with, and have ranked into bands under distinct names or ensigns. Thus, that which was grass to-day is to-morrow the flesh of a sheep; and, within a few days after, becomes part of a man: in all which and the like changes, it is evident their real essence—i.e. that constitution whereon the properties of these several things depended—is destroyed, and perishes with them. But essences being taken for ideas established in the mind, with names annexed to them, they are supposed to remain steadily the same, whatever mutations the particular substances are liable to. For, whatever becomes of *Alexander* and *Bucephalus*, the ideas to which *man* and *horse* are annexed, are supposed nevertheless to remain the same; and so the essences of those species are preserved whole and undestroyed, whatever changes happen to any or all of the individuals of those species. By this means the essence of a species rests safe and entire, without the existence of so much as one individual of that kind. For, were there now no circle existing anywhere in the world, (as perhaps that figure exists not anywhere exactly marked out,) yet the idea annexed to that name would not cease to be what it is; nor cease to be as a pattern to determine which of the particular figures we meet with have or have not a right to the *name* circle, and so to show which of them, by having that essence, was of that species. And though there neither were nor had been in nature such a beast as *unicorn*, or such a fish as a *mermaid*; yet, supposing those names to stand for complex abstract ideas that contained no inconsistency in them, the essence of a mermaid is as intelligible as that of a man; and the idea of an unicorn as certain, steady, and permanent as that of a horse. From what has been said, it is evident, that the doctrine of the immu-

tability of essences proves them to be only abstract ideas; and is founded on the relation established between them and certain sounds as signs of them; and will always be true, as long as the same name can have the same signification.

20. *Recapitulation.* To conclude. This is that which in short I would say, viz. that all the great business of *genera* and *species*, and their *essences*, amounts to no more but this:—That men making abstract ideas, and settling them in their minds with names annexed to them, do thereby enable themselves to consider things, and discourse of them, as it were in bundles, for the easier and readier improvement and communication of their knowledge, which would advance but slowly were their words and thoughts confined only to particulars.

Chapter IV

OF SIMPLE IDEAS

5. *If all names were definable, it would be a Process* in infinitum. I will not here trouble myself to prove that all terms are not definable, from that progress *in infinitum*, which it will visibly lead us into, if we should allow that all names could be defined. For, if the terms of one definition were still to be defined by another, where at last should we stop? But I shall, from the nature of our ideas, and the signification of our words, show *why some names can, and others cannot be defined*; and *which they are*.

6. *What a Definition is.* I think it is agreed, that a *definition* is nothing else but *the showing the meaning of one word by several other not synonymous terms*. The meaning of words being only the ideas they are made to stand for by him that uses them, the meaning of any term is then showed, or the word is defined, when, by other words, the idea it is made the sign of, and annexed to, in the mind of the speaker, is as it were represented, or set before the view of another; and thus its signification ascertained. This is the only use and end of definitions; and therefore the only measure of what is, or is not a good definition.

7. *Simple Ideas, why undefinable.* This being premised, I say that the *names of simple ideas, and*

those only, are incapable of being defined. The reason whereof is this, That the several terms of a definition, signifying several ideas, they can all together by no means represent an idea which has no composition at all: and therefore a definition, which is properly nothing but the showing the meaning of one word by several others not signifying each the same thing, can in the names of simple ideas have no place.

Chapter VI

OF THE NAMES OF SUBSTANCES

1. *The common Names of Substances stand for Sorts.* The common names of substances, as well as other general terms, stand for *sorts*: which is nothing else but the being made signs of such complex ideas wherein several particular substances do or might agree, by virtue of which they are capable of being comprehended in one common conception, and signified by one name. I say do or might agree: for though there be but one sun existing in the world, yet the idea of it being abstracted, so that more substances (if there were several) might each agree in it, it is as much a sort as if there were as many suns as there are stars. They want not their reasons who think there are, and that each fixed star would answer the idea the name sun stands for, to one who was placed in a due distance: which, by the way, may show us how much the sorts, or, if you please, *genera* and *species* of things (for those Latin terms signify to me no more than the English word sort) depend on such collections of ideas as men have made, and not on the real nature of things; since it is not impossible but that, in propriety of speech, that might be a sun to one which is a star to another.

2. *The Essence of each Sort of substance is our abstract Idea to which the name is annexed.* The measure and boundary of each sort or species, whereby it is constituted that particular sort, and distinguished from others, is that we call its *essence*, which is nothing but that abstract idea to which the name is annexed; so that everything contained in that idea is essential to that sort. This, though it be all the essence of natural substances that *we* know, or by which we distinguish them into sorts, yet I call it by a peculiar name, the *nominal essence*, to distinguish it from the real constitution of substances, upon which

depends this nominal essence, and all the properties of that sort; which, therefore, as has been said, may be called the *real essence*: v.g. the nominal essence of gold is that complex idea the word gold stands for, let it be, for instance, a body yellow, of a certain weight, malleable, fusible, and fixed. But the real essence is the constitution of the insensible parts of that body, on which those qualities and all the other properties of gold depend. How far these two are different, though they are both called essence, is obvious at first sight to discover.

3. *The nominal and real Essence different.* For, though perhaps voluntary motion, with sense and reason, joined to a body of a certain shape, be the complex idea to which I and others annex the name *man*, and so be the nominal essence of the species so called: yet nobody will say that complex idea is the real essence and source of all those operations which are to be found in any individual of that sort. The foundation of all those qualities which are the ingredients of our complex idea, is something quite different: and had we such a knowledge of that constitution of man, from which his faculties of moving, sensation, and reasoning, and other powers flow, and on which his so regular shape depends, as it is possible angels have, and it is certain his Maker has, we should have a quite other idea of his essence than what now is contained in our definition of that species, be it what it will: and our idea of any individual man would be as far different from what it is now, as is his who knows all the springs and wheels and other contrivances within of the famous clock at Strasburg, from that which a gazing countryman has of it, who barely sees the motion of the hand, and hears the clock strike, and observes only some of the outward appearances.

4. *Nothing essential to Individuals.* That *essence*, in the ordinary use of the word, relates to sorts, and that it is considered in particular beings no further than as they are ranked into sorts, appears from hence: that, take but away the abstract ideas by which we sort individuals, and rank them under common names, and then the thought of anything essential to any of them instantly vanishes: we have no notion of the one without the other, which plainly shows their relation. It is necessary for me to be as I am; God and nature has made me so: but there is nothing I

have is essential to me. An accident or disease may very much alter my colour or shape; a fever or fall may take away my reason or memory, or both; and an apoplexy leave neither sense, nor understanding, no, nor life. Other creatures of my shape may be made with more and better, or fewer and worse faculties than I have; and others may have reason and sense in a shape and body very different from mine. None of these are essential to the one or the other, or to any individual whatever, till the mind refers it to some sort of species of things; and then presently, according to the abstract idea of that sort, something is found essential. Let any one examine his own thoughts, and he will find that as soon as he supposes or speaks of essential, the consideration of some species, or the complex idea signified by some general name, comes into his mind; and it is in reference to that that this or that quality is said to be essential. So that if it be asked, whether it be essential to me or any other particular corporeal being, to have reason? I say, no; no more than it is essential to this white thing I write on to have words in it. But if that particular being be to be counted of the sort *man*, and to have the name *man* given it, then reason is essential to it; supposing reason to be a part of the complex idea the name man stands for: as it is essential to this thing I write on to contain words, if I will give it the name *treatise*, and rank it under that species. So that essential and not essential relate only to our abstract ideas, and the names annexed to them; which amounts to no more than this, that whatever particular thing has not in it those qualities which are contained in the abstract idea which any general term stands for, cannot be ranked under that species, nor be called by that name; since that abstract idea is the very essence of that species.

5. *The only essences perceived by us in individual substances are those qualities which entitle them to receive their names.*   Thus, if the idea of *body* with some people be bare extension or space, then solidity is not essential to body: if others make the idea to which they give the name *body* to be solidity and extension, then solidity is essential to body. That therefore, and that alone, is considered as essential, which makes a part of the complex idea the name of a sort stands for; without which no particular thing can be reckoned of that sort, nor be entitled to that

name. Should there be found a parcel of matter that had all the other qualities that are in iron, but wanted obedience to the loadstone, and would neither be drawn by it nor receive direction from it, would any one question whether it wanted anything essential? It would be absurd to ask, Whether a thing really existing wanted anything essential to it. Or could it be demanded, Whether this made an essential or specific difference or no, since *we* have no other measure of essential or specific but our abstract ideas? And to talk of specific differences in *nature*, without reference to general ideas in names, is to talk unintelligibly. For I would ask for any one, What is sufficient to make an essential difference in nature between any two particular beings, without any regard had to some abstract idea, which is looked upon as the essence and standard of a species? All such patterns and standards being quite laid aside, particular beings, considered barely in themselves, will be found to have all their qualities equally essential; and everything in each individual will be essential to it; or, which is more, nothing at all. For, though it may be reasonable to ask, Whether obeying the magnet be essential to iron? yet I think it is very improper and insignificant to ask, whether it be essential to the particular parcel of matter I cut my pen with; without considering it under the name *iron*, or as being of a certain species. And if, as has been said, our abstract ideas, which have names annexed to them, are the boundaries of species, nothing can be essential but what is contained in those ideas.

6. *Even the real essences of individual substances imply potential sorts.*   It is true, I have often mentioned a *real essence*, distinct in substances from those abstract ideas of them, which I call their nominal essence. By this real essence I mean, that real constitution of anything, which is the foundation of all those properties that are combined in, and are constantly found to co-exist with the nominal essence; that particular constitution which everything has within itself, without any relation to anything without it. But essence, even in this sense, *relates to a sort, and supposes a species.* For, being that real constitution on which the properties depend, it necessarily supposes a sort of things, properties belonging only to species, and not to individuals: v.g. supposing the nominal essence of gold to be a body of such a peculiar colour and

weight, with malleability and fusibility, the real essence is that constitution of the parts of matter on which these qualities and their union depend; and is also the foundation of its solubility in *aqua regia* and other properties, accompanying that complex idea. Here are essences and properties, but all upon supposition of a sort or general abstract idea, which is considered as immutable; but there is no individual parcel of matter to which any of these qualities are so annexed as to be essential to it or inseparable from it. That which is essential belongs to it as a condition whereby it is of this or that sort: but take away the consideration of its being ranked under the name of some abstract idea, and then there is nothing necessary to it, nothing inseparable from it. Indeed, as to the real essences of substances, we only suppose their being, without precisely knowing what they are; but that which annexes them still to the species is the nominal essence, of which they are the supposed foundation and cause.

7. *The nominal Essence bounds the Species for us.* The next thing to be considered is, by which of those essences it is that substances are determined into sorts or species; and that, it is evident, is by the nominal essence. For it is that alone that the name, which is the mark of the sort, signifies. It is impossible, therefore, that anything should determine the sorts of things, which *we* rank under general names, but that idea which that name is designed as a mark for; which is that, as has been shown, which we call nominal essence. Why do we say this is a horse, and that a mule; this is an animal, that an herb? How comes any particular thing to be of this or that sort, but because it has that nominal essence; or, which is all one, agrees to that abstract idea, that name is annexed to? And I desire any one but to reflect on his own thoughts, when he fears or speaks any of those or other names of substances, to know what sort of essences they stand for.

8. *The nature of Species, as formed by us.* And that the species of things to us are nothing but the ranking them under distinct names, according to the complex ideas in *us*, and not according to precise, distinct, real essences in *them*, is plain from hence: — That we find many of the individuals that are ranked into one sort, called by one common name, and so

received as being of one species, have yet qualities, depending on their real constitutions, as far different one from another as from others from which they are accounted to differ specifically. This, as it is easy to be observed by all who have to do with natural bodies, so chemists especially are often, by sad experience, convinced of it, when they, sometimes in vain, seek for the same qualities in one parcel of sulphur, antimony, or vitriol, which they have found in others. For, though they are bodies of the same species, having the same nominal essence, under the same name, yet do they often, upon severe ways of examination, betray qualities so different one from another, as to frustrate the expectation and labour of very wary chemists. But if things were distinguished into species, according to their real essences, it would be as impossible to find different properties in any two individual substances of the same species, as it is to find different properties in two circles, or two equilateral triangles. That is properly the essence to *us*, which determines every particular to this or that *classis*; or, which is the same thing, to this or that general name: and what can that be else, but that abstract idea to which that name is annexed; and so has, in truth, a reference, not so much to the being of particular things, as to their general denominations?

9. *Not the real Essence, or texture of parts, which we know not.* Nor indeed can we rank and sort things, and consequently (which is the end of sorting) denominate them, by their real essences; because we know them not. Our faculties carry us no further towards the knowledge and distinction of substances, than a collection of *those sensible ideas which we observe in them*; which, however made with the greatest diligence and exactness we are capable of, yet is more remote from the true internal constitution from which those qualities flow, than, as I said, a countryman's idea is from the inward contrivance of that famous clock at Strasburg, whereof he only sees the outward figure and motions. There is not so contemptible a plant or animal, that does not confound the most enlarged understanding. Though the familiar use of things about us take off our wonder, yet it cures not our ignorance. When we come to examine the stones we tread on, or the iron we daily handle, we presently find we know not their make; and can give no reason of the different qualities we find in them.

It is evident the internal constitution, whereon their properties depend, is unknown to us: for to go no further than the grossest and most obvious we can imagine amongst them, What is that texture of parts, that real essence, that makes lead and antimony fusible, wood and stones not? What makes lead and iron malleable, antimony and stones not? And yet how infinitely these come short of the fine contrivances and inconceivable real essences of plants or animals, every one knows. The workmanship of the all-wise and powerful God in the great fabric of the universe, and every part thereof, further exceeds the capacity and comprehension of the most inquisitive and intelligent man, than the best contrivance of the most ingenious man doth the conceptions of the most ignorant of rational creatures. Therefore we in vain pretend to range things into sorts, and dispose them into certain classes under names, by their real essences, that are so far from our discovery or comprehension. A blind man may as soon sort things by their colours, and he that has lost his smell as well distinguish a lily and a rose by their odours, as by those internal constitutions which he knows not. He that thinks he can distinguish sheep and goats by their real essences, that are unknown to him, may be pleased to try his skill in those species called *cassiowary* and *querechinchio*; and by their internal real essences determine the boundaries of those species, without knowing the complex idea of sensible qualities that each of those names stand for, in the countries where those animals are to be found.

13. *The Nominal Essence that of the Species, as conceived by us, proved from Water and Ice.* But to return to the species of corporeal substances. If I should ask any one whether ice and water were two distinct species of things, I doubt not but I should be answered in the affirmative: and it cannot be denied but he that says they are two distinct species is in the right. But if an Englishman bred in Jamaica, who perhaps had never seen nor heard of ice, coming into England in the winter, find the water he put in his basin at night in a great part frozen in the morning, and, not knowing any peculiar name it had, should call it hardened water; I ask whether this would be a new species to him, different from water? And I think it would be answered here, It would not be to him a new species, no more than congealed jelly,

with it is cold, is a distinct species from the same jelly fluid and warm; or than liquid gold in the furnace is a distinct species from hard gold in the hands of a workman. And if this be so, it is plain that *our distinct species* are *nothing but distinct complex ideas, with distinct names annexed to them.* It is true every substance that exists has its peculiar constitution, whereon depend those sensible qualities and powers we observe in it; but the ranking of things into species (which is nothing but sorting them under several titles) is done by us according to the ideas that *we* have of them: which, though sufficient to distinguish them by names, so that we may be able to discourse of them when we have them not present before us; yet if we suppose it to be done by their real internal constitutions, and that things existing are distinguished by nature into species, by real essences, according as we distinguish them into species by names, we shall be liable to great mistakes.

14. *Difficulties in the supposition of a certain number of real Essences.* To distinguish substantial being into species, according to the usual supposition, that there are certain precise essences of forms of things, whereby all the individuals existing are, by nature distinguished into species, these things are necessary:—

15. *A crude supposition.* First, To be assured that nature, in the production of things, always designs them to partake of certain regulated established essences, which are to be the models of all things to be produced. This, in that crude sense it is usually proposed, would need some better explication, before it can fully be assented to.

16. *Monstrous births.* Secondly, It would be necessary to know whether nature always attains that essence it designs in the production of things. The irregular and monstrous births, that in divers sorts of animals have been observed, will always give us reason to doubt of one or both of these.

17. *Are monsters really a distinct species?* Thirdly, It ought to be determined whether those we call monsters be really a distinct species, according to the scholastic notion of the word species; since it is certain that everything that exists has its particular

constitution. And yet we find that some of these monstrous productions have few or none of those qualities which are supposed to result from, and accompany, the essence of that species from whence they derive their originals, and to which, by their descent, they seem to belong.

18. *Men can have no ideas of Real Essences.* Fourthly, The real essences of those things which we distinguish into species, and as so distinguished we name, ought to be known; i.e. we ought to have ideas of them. But since we are ignorant in these four points, the supposed real essences of things stand *us* not in stead for the distinguishing substances into species.

19. *Our Nominal Essences of Substances not perfect collections of the properties that flow from their Real Essences.* Fifthly, The only imaginable help in this case would be, that, having framed perfect complex ideas of the properties of things flowing from their different real essences, we should thereby distinguish them into species. But neither can this be done. For, being ignorant of the real essence itself, it is impossible to know all those properties that flow from it, and are so annexed to it, that any one of them being away, we may certainly conclude that that essence is not there, and so the thing is not of that species. We can never know what is the precise number of properties depending on the real essence of gold, any one of which failing, the real essence of gold, and consequently gold, would not be there, unless we knew the real essence of gold itself, and by that determined that species. By the word *gold* here, I must be understood to design a particular piece of matter; v.g. the last guinea that was coined. For, if it should stand here, in its ordinary signification, for that complex idea which I or any one else calls gold, i.e. for the nominal essence of gold, it would be jargon. So hard is it to show the various meaning and imperfection of words, when we have nothing else but words to do it by.

20. *Hence names independent of Real Essences.* By all which it is clear, that our distinguishing substances into species by names, is not at all founded on their real essences; nor can we pretend to range and determine them exactly into species, according to internal essential differences.

21. *But stand for such a collection of simple ideas as we have made the Name stand for.* But since, as has been remarked, we have need of *general* words, though we know not the real essences of things; all we can do is, to collect such a number of simple ideas as, by examination, we find to be united together in things existing, and thereof to make one complex idea. Which, though it be not the real essence of any substance that exists, is yet the specific essence to which our name belongs, and is convertible with it; by which we may at least try the truth of these nominal essences. For example: there be that say that the essence of body is *extension*; if it be so, we can never mistake in putting the essence of anything for the thing itself. Let us then in discourse put extension for body, and when we would say that body moves, let us say that extension moves, and see how ill it will look. He that should say that one extension by impulse moves another extension, would, by the bare expression, sufficiently show the absurdity of such a notion. The essence of anything in respect of us, is the whole complex idea comprehended and marked by that name; and in substances, besides the several distinct simple ideas that make them up, the confused one of substance, or of an unknown support and cause of their union, is always a part: and therefore the essence of body is not bare extension, but an extended solid thing; and so to say, an extended solid thing moves, or impels another, is all one, and as intelligible, as to say, *body* moves or impels. Likewise, to say that a rational animal is capable of conversation, is all one as to say a man; but no one will say that rationality is capable of conversation, because it makes not the whole essence to which we give the name man.

22. *Our Abstract Ideas are to us the Measures of the Species we make: instance in that of Man.* There are creatures in the world that have shapes like ours, but are hairy, and want language and reason. There are naturals amongst us that have perfectly our shape, but want reason, and some of them language too. There are creatures, as it is said, (*sit fides penes authorem,* but there appears no contradiction that there should be such,) that, with language and reason and a shape in other things agreeing with ours, have

hairy tails; others where the males have no beards, and others where the females have. If it be asked whether these be all *men* or no, all of human species? it is plain, the question refers only to the nominal essence: for those of them to whom the definition of the word man, or the complex idea signified by that name, agrees, are men, and the other not. But if the inquiry be made concerning the supposed real essence; and whether the internal constitution and frame of these several creatures be specifically different, it is wholly impossible for us to answer, no part of that going into our specific idea: only we have reason to think, that where the faculties or outward frame so much differs, the internal constitution is not exactly the same. But what difference in the real internal constitution makes a specific difference it is in vain to inquire; whilst our measures of species be, as they are, only our abstract ideas, which we know; and not that internal constitution, which makes no part of them. Shall the difference of hair only on the skin be a mark of a different internal specific constitution between a changeling and a drill, when they agree in shape, and want of reason and speech? And shall not the want of reason and speech be a sign to us of different real constitutions and species between a changeling and a reasonable man? And so of the rest, if we pretend that distinction of species or sorts is fixedly established by the real frame and secret constitutions of things.

25. *The specific Essences that are commonly made by Men.* But supposing that the *real* essences of substances were discoverable by those that would severely apply themselves to that inquiry, yet we could not reasonably think that the ranking of things under general names was regulated by those internal real constitutions, or anything else but their *obvious* appearances; since languages, in all countries, have been established long before sciences. So that they have not been philosophers or logicians, or such who have troubled themselves about forms and essences, that have made the general names that are in use amongst the several nations of men: but those more or less comprehensive terms have, for the most part, in all languages, received their birth and signification from ignorant and illiterate people, who sorted and denominated things by those sensible qualities they found in them; thereby to signify them, when absent, to others, whether they had an occasion to mention a sort or a particular thing.

26. *Therefore very various and uncertain in the ideas of different men.* Since then it is evident that we sort and name substances by their nominal and not by their real essences, the next thing to be considered is how, and by whom these essences come to be made. As to the latter, it is evident they are made by the mind, and not by nature: for were they Nature's workmanship, they could not be so various and different in several men as experience tells us they are. For if we will examine it, we shall not find the nominal essence of any one species of substances in all men the same: no, not of that which of all others we are the most intimately acquainted with. It could not possibly be that the abstract idea to which the name *man* is given should be different in several men, if it were of Nature's making; and that to one it should be *animal rationale*, and to another, *animal implume bipes latis unguibus*. He that annexes the name man to a complex idea, made up of sense and spontaneous motion, joined to a body of such a shape, has thereby one essence of the species man; and he that, upon further examination, adds rationality, has another essence of the species he calls man: by which means the same individual will be a true man to the one which is not so to the other. I think there is scarce any one will allow this upright figure, so well known, to be the essential difference of the species man; and yet how far men determine of the sorts of animals rather by their shape than descent, is very visible; since it has been more than once debated, whether several human foetuses should be preserved or received to baptism or no, only because of the difference of their outward configuration from the ordinary make of children, without knowing whether they were not as capable of reason as infants cast in another mould: some whereof, though of an approved shape, are never capable of as much appearance of reason all their lives as is to be found in an ape, or an elephant, and never give any signs of being acted by a rational soul. Whereby it is evident, that the outward figure, which only was found wanting, and not the faculty of reason, which nobody could know would be wanting in its due season, was made essential to the human species. The learned divine and lawyer must, on such occasions, renounce his sacred definition of *animal ratio-*

nale, and substitute some other essence of the human species. Monsieur Menage[4] furnishes us with an example worth the taking notice of on this occasion: 'When the abbot of Saint Martin,' says he, 'was born, he had so little of the figure of a man, that it bespake him rather a monster. It was for some time under deliberation, whether he should be baptized or no. However, he was baptized, and declared a man provisionally till time should show what he would prove. Nature had moulded him so untowardly, that he was called all his life the Abbot Malotru; i.e. ill-shaped. He was of Caen.' (*Menagiana*, 278, 430.) This child, we see, was very near being excluded out of the species of man, barely by his shape. He escaped very narrowly as he was; and it is certain, a figure a little more oddly turned had cast him, and he had been executed, as a thing not to be allowed to pass for man. And yet there can be no reason given why, if the lineaments of his face had been a little altered, a rational soul could not have been lodged in him; why a visage somewhat longer, or a nose flatter, or a wider mouth, could not have consisted, as well as the rest of his ill figure, with such a soul, such parts, as made him, disfigured as he was, capable to be a dignitary in the church.

27. *Nominal Essences of particular substances are undetermined by nature, and therefore various as men vary.* Wherein, then, would I gladly know, consist the precise and unmovable boundaries of that species? It is plain, if we examine, there is no such thing made by Nature, and established by her amongst men. The real essence of that or any other sort of substances, it is evident, we know not; and therefore are so undetermined in our nominal essences, which we make ourselves, that, if several men were to be asked concerning some oddly-shaped *foetus*, as soon as born, whether it were a *man* or no, it is past doubt one should meet with different answers. Which could not happen, if the nominal essences whereby we limit and distinguish the species of substances, were not made by man with some liberty; but were exactly copied from precise boundaries set by nature, whereby it distinguished all substances into certain species. Who would undertake to resolve what species

that monster was of which is mentioned by Licetus (lib. i. c. 3),[5] with a man's head and hog's body? Or those other which to the bodies of men had the heads of beasts, as dogs, horses, &c. If any of these creatures had lived, and could have spoke, it would have increased the difficulty. Had the upper part to the middle been of human shape, and all below swine, had it been murder to destroy it? Or must the bishop have been consulted, whether it were man enough to be admitted to the font or no? As I have been told it happened in France some years since, in somewhat a like case. So uncertain are the boundaries of species of animals to us, who have no other measures than the complex ideas of our own collecting: and so far are we from certainly knowing what a *man* is; though perhaps it will be judged great ignorance to make any doubt about it. And yet I think I may say, that the certain boundaries of that species are so far from being determined, and the precise number of simple ideas which make the nominal essence so far from being settled and perfectly known, that very material doubts may still arise about it. And I imagine none of the definitions of the word *man* which we yet have, nor descriptions of that sort of animal, are so perfect and exact as to satisfy a considerate inquisitive person; much less to obtain a general consent, and to be that which men would everywhere stick by, in the decision of cases, and determining of life and death, baptism or no baptism, in productions that might happen.

28. *But not so arbitrary as Mixed Modes.* But though these nominal essences of substances are made by the mind, they are not yet made so arbitrarily as those of mixed modes. To the making of any nominal essence, it is necessary, First, that the ideas whereof it consists have such a union as to make but one idea, how compounded soever. Secondly, that the particular ideas so united be exactly the same, neither more nor less. For if two abstract complex ideas differ either in number or sorts of their component parts, they make two different, and not one and the same essence. In the first of these, the mind, in making its complex ideas of substances, only follows nature; and puts none together which are not sup-

4. [Giles Menage (1613–1690) was a French philologist and critic.]

5. [Fortunato Liceto (1577–1657) was an Italian physician. The reference is to his *De Monstrorum Causis* (Of the Causes of Monsters).]

posed to have a union in nature. Nobody joins the voice of a sheep with the shape of a horse; nor the colour of lead with the weight and fixedness of gold, to be the complex ideas of any real substances; unless he has a mind to fill his head with chimeras, and his discourse with unintelligible words. Men observing certain qualities always joined and existing together, therein copied nature; and of ideas so united made their complex ones of substances. For, though men may make what complex ideas they please, and give what names to them they will; yet, if they will be understood *when they speak of things really existing*, they must in some degree conform their ideas to the things they would speak of; or else men's language will be like that of Babel,[6] and every man's words, being intelligible only to himself, would no longer serve to conversation and the ordinary affairs of life, if the ideas they stand for be not some way answering the common appearances and agreement of substances as they really exist.

29. *Our Nominal Essences of substances usually consist of a few obvious qualities observed in things.* Secondly, Though the mind of man, in making its complex ideas of substances, never puts any together that do not really, or are not supposed to, co-exist; and so it truly borrows that union from nature: yet the number it combines depends upon the various care, industry, or fancy of him that makes it. Men generally content themselves with some few sensible obvious qualities; and often, if not always, leave out others as material and as firmly united as those that they take. Of sensible substances there are two sorts: one of organized bodies, which are propagated by seed; and in these the *shape* is that which to us is the leading quality, and most characteristical part, that determines the species. And therefore in vegetables and animals, an extended solid substance of such a certain figure usually serves the turn. For however some men seem to prize their definition of *animal rationale*, yet should there a creature be found that

had language and reason, but partaked not of the usual shape of a man, I believe it would hardly pass for a man, how much soever it were *animal rationale*. And if Balaam's ass[7] had all his life discoursed as rationally as he did once with his master, I doubt yet whether any one would have thought him worthy the name man, or allowed him to be of the same species with himself. As in vegetables and animals it is the shape, so in most other bodies, not propagated by seed, it is the *colour* we most fix on, and are most led by. Thus where we find the colour of gold, we are apt to imagine all the other qualities comprehended in our complex idea to be there also: and we commonly take these two obvious qualities, viz. shape and colour, for so presumptive ideas of several species, that in a good picture, we readily say, this is a lion, and that a rose; this is a gold, and that a silver goblet, only by the different figures and colours represented to the eye by the pencil.

30. *Yet, imperfect as they thus are, they serve for common converse.* But though this serves well enough for gross and confused conceptions, and inaccurate ways of talking and thinking; yet *men are far enough from having agreed on the precise number of simple ideas or qualities belonging to any sort of things, signified by its name.* Nor is it a wonder; since it requires much time, pains, and skill, strict inquiry, and long examination to find out what, and how many, those simple ideas are, which are constantly and inseparably united in nature, and are always to be found together in the same subject. Most men, wanting either time, inclination, or industry enough for this, even to some tolerable degree, content themselves with some few obvious and outward appearances of things, thereby readily to distinguish and sort them for the common affairs of life: and so, without further examination, give them names, or take up the names already in use. Which, though in common conversation they pass well enough for the signs of some few obvious qualities co-existing, are yet far enough from comprehending, in a settled signification, a precise number of simple ideas, much less all those which are united in nature. He that shall

6. [The reference is to a Biblical story related in the Book of Genesis, according to which, at a time when all people spoke the same language, they attempted to build a tower that reached to heaven, but they were prevented from doing so by God, who confounded their language so they could not understand one another.]

7. [The reference is to a Biblical story related in the Book of Numbers, according to which God gave the power of speech to the prophet Balaam's ass.]

consider, after so much stir about genus and species, and such a deal of talk of specific differences, how few words we have yet settled definitions of, may with reason imagine, that those *forms* which there hath been so much noise made about are only chimeras, which give us no light into the specific natures of things. And he that shall consider how far the names of substances are from having significations wherein all who use them do agree, will have reason to conclude that, though the nominal essences of substances are all supposed to be copied from nature, yet they are all, or most of them, very imperfect. Since the composition of those complex ideas are, in several men, very different: and therefore that these boundaries of species are as men, and not as Nature, makes them, if at least there are in nature any such prefixed bounds. It is true that many particular substances are so made by Nature, that they have agreement and likeness one with another, and so afford a foundation of being ranked into sorts. But the sorting of things by us, or the making of determinate species, being in order to naming and comprehending them under general terms, I cannot see how it can be properly said, that Nature sets the boundaries of the species of things: or, if it be so, our boundaries of species are not exactly conformable to those in nature. For we, having need of general names for present use, stay not for a perfect discovery of all those qualities which would *best* show us their most material differences and agreements; but we ourselves divide them, by certain obvious appearances, into species, that we may the easier under general names communicate our thoughts about them. For, having no other knowledge of any substance but of the simple ideas that are united in it; and observing several particular things to agree with others in several of those simple ideas; we make that collection our specific idea, and give it a general name; that in recording our thoughts, and in our discourse with others, we may in one short word designate all the individuals that agree in that complex idea, without enumerating the simple ideas that make it up; and so not waste our time and breath in tedious descriptions: which we see they are fain to do who would discourse of any new sort of things they have not yet a name for.

31. *Essences of Species under the same Name very different in different minds.*   But however these spe-

cies of substances pass well enough in ordinary conversation, it is plain that this complex idea, wherein they observe several individuals to agree, is by different men made very differently; by some more, and others less accurately. In some, this complex idea contains a greater, and in others a smaller number of qualities; and so is apparently such as the mind makes it. The yellow shining colour makes gold to children; others add weight, malleableness, and fusibility; and others yet other qualities, which they find joined with that yellow colour, as constantly as its weight and fusibility. For in all these and the like qualities, one has as good a right to be put into the complex idea of that substance wherein they are all joined as another. And therefore different men, leaving out or putting in several simple ideas which others do not, according to their various examination, skill, or observation of that subject, have different essences of gold, which must make therefore be of their own and not of nature's making.

32. *The more general our Ideas of Substances are, the more incomplete and partial they are.*   If the number of simple ideas that make the nominal essence of the lowest species, or first sorting, of individuals, depends on the mind of man, variously collecting them, it is much more evident that they do so in the more comprehensive classes, which, by the masters of logic, are called *genera*. These are complex ideas designedly imperfect: and it is visible at first sight, that several of those qualities that are to be found in the things themselves are purposely left out of generical ideas. For, as the mind, to make general ideas comprehending several particulars, leaves out those of time and place, and such other, that make them incommunicable to more than one individual; so to make other yet more general ideas, that may comprehend different sorts, it leaves out those qualities that distinguish them, and puts into its new collection only such ideas as are common to several sorts. The same convenience that made men express several parcels of yellow matter coming from Guinea and Peru under one name, sets them also upon making of one name that may comprehend both gold and silver, and some other bodies of different sorts. This is done by leaving out those qualities, which are peculiar to each sort, and retaining a complex idea made up of those that are common to them all. To which

the name *metal* being annexed, there is a genus constituted; the essence whereof being that abstract idea, containing only malleableness and fusibility, with certain degrees of weight and fixedness, wherein some bodies of several kinds agree, leaves out the colour and other qualities peculiar to gold and silver, and the other sorts comprehended under the name metal. Whereby it is plain that men follow not exactly the patterns set them by nature, when they make their general ideas of substances; since there is no body to be found which has barely malleableness and fusibility in it, without other qualities as inseparable as those. But men, in making their general ideas, seeking more the convenience of language, and quick dispatch by short and comprehensive signs, that the true and precise nature of things as they exist, have, in the framing their abstract ideas, chiefly pursued that end; which was to be furnished with store of general and variously comprehensive names. So that in this whole business of genera and species, the genus, or more comprehensive, is but a partial conception of what is in the species; and the species but a partial idea of what is to be found in each individual. If therefore any one will think that a man, and a horse, and an animal, and a plant, &c., are distinguished by real essences made by nature, he must think nature to be very liberal of these real essences, making one for body, another for an animal, and another for a horse; and all these essences liberally bestowed upon Bucephalus. But if we would rightly consider what is done in all these genera and species, or sorts, we should find that there is no new thing made, but only more or less comprehensive signs, whereby we may be enabled to express in a few syllables great numbers of particular things, as they agree in more or less general conceptions, which we have framed to that purpose. In all which we may observe, that the more general term is always the name of a less complex idea; and that each genus is but a partial conception of the species comprehended under it. So that if these abstract general ideas be thought to be complete, it can only be in respect of a certain established relation between them and certain names which are made use of to signify them; and not in respect of anything existing, as made by nature.

33. *This all accommodated to the end of Speech.* This is adjusted to the true end of speech, which is

to be the easiest and shortest way of communicating our notions. For thus he that would discourse of things, as they agreed in the complex idea of extension and solidity, needed but use the word *body* to denote all such. He that to these would join others, signified by the words life, sense, and spontaneous motion, needed but use the word *animal* to signify all which partaked of those ideas, and he that had made a complex idea of a body, with life, sense, and motion, with the faculty of reasoning, and a certain shape joined to it, needed but use the short monosyllable *man*, to express all particulars that correspond to that complex idea. This is the proper business of genus and species: and this men do without any consideration of real essences, or substantial forms; which come not within the reach of our knowledge when we think of those things, nor within the signification of our words when we discourse with others.

34. *Instance in Cassowaries.* Were I to talk with any one of a sort of birds I lately saw in St. James's Park, about three or four feet high, with a covering of something between feathers and hair, of a dark brown colour, without wings, but in the place thereof two or three little branches coming down like sprigs of Spanish broom, long great legs, with feet only of three claws, and without a tail; I must make this description of it, and so may make others understand me. But when I am told that the name of it is *cassuaris*, I may then use that word to stand in discourse for all my complex idea mentioned in that description; though by that word, which is now become a specific name, I know no more of the real essence or constitution of that sort of animals than I did before; and knew probably as much of the nature of that species of birds before I learned the name, as many Englishmen do of swans or herons, which are specific names, very well known, of sorts of birds common in England.

35. *Men determine the Sorts of Substances, which may be sorted variously.* From what has been said, it is evident that *men* make sorts of things. For, it being different essences alone that make different species, it is plain that they who make those abstract ideas which are the nominal essences do thereby make the species, or sort. Should there be a body found, having all the other qualities of gold except malleableness, it would no doubt be made a question

whether it were gold or not, i.e. whether it were of that species. This could be determined only by that abstract idea to which every one annexed the name gold: so that it would be true gold to him, and belong to that species, who included not malleableness in his nominal essence, signified by the sound gold; and on the other side it would not be true gold, or of that species, to him who included malleableness in his specific idea. And how, I pray, is it that makes these diverse species, even under one and the same name, but men that make two different abstract ideas, consisting not exactly of the same collection of qualities? Nor is it a mere supposition to imagine that a body may exist wherein the other obvious qualities of gold may be without malleableness; since it is certain that gold itself will be sometimes so eager, (as artists call it,) that it will as little endure the hammer as glass itself. What we have said of the putting in, or leaving out of malleableness, in the complex idea the name gold is by any one annexed to, may be said of its peculiar weight, fixedness, and several other the like qualities: for whatever is left out, or put in, it is still the complex idea to which that name is annexed that makes the species: and as any particular parcel of matter answers that idea, so the name of the sort belongs truly to it; and it is of that species. And thus anything is true gold, perfect metal. All which determination of the species, it is plain, depends on the understanding of man, making this or that complex idea.

36. *Nature makes the Similitudes of Substances.* This, then, in short, is the case: Nature makes many *particular things*, which do agree one with another in many sensible qualities, and probably too in their internal frame and constitution: but it is not this real essence that distinguishes them into species; it is men who, taking occasion from the qualities they find united in them, and wherein they observe often several individuals to agree, range them into sorts, in order to their naming, for the convenience of comprehensive signs; under which individuals, according to their conformity to this or that abstract idea, come to be ranked as under ensigns: so that this is of the blue, that the red regiment; this is a man, that a drill: and in this, I think, consists the whole business of genus and species.

BOOK IV
OF KNOWLEDGE AND PROBABILITY

Chapter I

OF KNOWLEDGE IN GENERAL

1. *Our Knowledge conversant about our Ideas only.* Since the mind, in all its thoughts and reasonings, hath no other immediate object but its own ideas, which it alone does or can contemplate, it is evident that our knowledge is only conversant about them.

2. *Knowledge is the Perception of the Agreement or Disagreement of two Ideas.* *Knowledge* then seems to me to be nothing but *the perception of the connexion of and agreement, or disagreement and repugnancy of any of our ideas.* In this alone it consists. Where this perception is, there is knowledge, and where it is not, there, though we may fancy, guess, or believe, yet we always come short of knowledge. For when we know that white is not black, what do we else but perceive, that these two ideas do not agree? When we possess ourselves with the utmost security of the demonstration, that the three angles of a triangle are equal to two right ones, what do we more but perceive, that equality to two right ones does necessarily agree to, and is inseparable from, the three angles of a triangle.

3. *This Agreement or Disagreement may be any of four sorts.* But to understand a little more distinctly wherein this agreement or disagreement consists, I think we may reduce it all to these four sorts:

I. *Identity,* or *diversity.*

II. *Relation.*

III. *Co-existence,* or *necessary connexion.*

IV. *Real existence.*

4. *First, Of Identity, or Diversity in ideas.* As to the first sort of agreement or disagreement, viz. *identity* or *diversity.* It is the first act of the mind, when it has any sentiments or ideas at all, to perceive its ideas; and so far as it perceives them, to know each what

it is, and thereby also to perceive their difference, and that one is not another. This is so absolutely necessary, that without it there could be no knowledge, no reasoning, no imagination, no distinct thoughts at all. By this the mind clearly and infallibly perceives each idea to agree with itself, and to be what it is; and all distinct ideas to disagree, i.e. the one not to be the other: and this it does without pains, labour, or deduction; but at first view, by its natural power of perception and distinction. And though men of art have reduced this into those general rules, *What is, is,* and *It is impossible for the same thing to be and not to be,* for ready application in all cases, wherein there may be occasion to reflect on it: yet it is certain that the first exercise of this faculty is about particular ideas. A man infallibly knows, as soon as ever he has them in his mind, that the ideas he calls *white* and *round* are the very ideas they are; and that they are not other ideas which he calls *red* or *square.* Nor can any maxim or proposition in the world make him know it clearer or surer than he did before, and without any such general rule. This then is the first agreement or disagreement which the mind perceives in its ideas; which it always perceives at first sight: and if there ever happen any doubt about it, it will always be found to be about the names, and not the ideas themselves, whose identity and diversity will always be perceived, as soon and clearly as the ideas themselves are; nor can it possibly be otherwise.

5. *Secondly, Of abstract Relations between ideas.* The next sort of agreement or disagreement the mind perceives in any of its ideas may, I think, be called *relative,* and is nothing but the perception of the *relation* between any two ideas, of what kind soever, whether substances, modes, or any other. For, since all distinct ideas must eternally be known not to be the same, and so be universally and constantly denied one of another, there could be no room for any positive knowledge at all, if we could not perceive any relation between our ideas, and find out the agreement or disagreement they have one with another, in several ways the mind takes of comparing them.

6. *Thirdly, Of their necessary Co-existence in Substances.* The third sort of agreement or disagreement to be found in our ideas, which the perception of the mind is employed about, is *co-existence* or *non-co-existence* in the *same subject*; and this belongs particularly to substances. Thus when we pronounce concerning gold, that it is fixed, our knowledge of this truth amounts to no more but this, that fixedness, or a power to remain in the fire unconsumed, is an idea that always accompanies and is joined with that particular sort of yellowness, weight, fusibility, malleableness, and solubility in *aqua regia,* which make our complex idea signified by the word gold.

7. *Fourthly, Of real Existence agreeing to any idea.* The fourth and last sort is that of *actual real existence* agreeing to any idea.

Within these four sorts of agreement or disagreement is, I suppose, contained all the knowledge we have, or are capable of. For all the inquiries we can make concerning any of our ideas, all that we know or can affirm concerning any of them, is, That it is, or is not, the same with some other; that it does or does not always co-exist with some other idea in the same subject; that it has this or that relation with some other idea; or that it has a real existence without the mind. Thus, 'blue is not yellow,' is of identity. 'Two triangles upon equal bases between two parallels are equal,' is of relation. 'Iron is susceptible of magnetical impressions,' is of co-existence. 'God is,' is of real existence. Though identity and co-existence are truly nothing but relations, yet they are such peculiar ways of agreement or disagreement of our ideas, that they deserve well to be considered as distinct heads, and not under relation in general; since they are so different grounds of affirmation and negation, as will easily appear to any one, who will but reflect on what is said in several places of this *Essay.*

Chapter II

OF THE DEGREES OF OUR KNOWLEDGE

1. *Of the degrees, or differences in clearness, of our Knowledge: I. Intuitive.* All our knowledge consisting, as I have said, in the view the mind has of its own ideas, which is the utmost light and greatest certainty we, with our faculties, and in our way of knowledge, are capable of, it may not be amiss to consider a little the degrees of its evidence. The different clearness of our knowledge seems to me to lie in the different way of perception the mind has of the

agreement or disagreement of any of its ideas. For if we will reflect on our own ways of thinking, we will find, that sometimes the mind perceives the agreement or disagreement of two ideas *immediately by themselves*, without the intervention of any other: and this I think we may call *intuitive knowledge*. For in this the mind is at no pains of proving or examining, but perceives the truth as the eye doth light, only by being directed towards it. Thus the mind perceives that *white* is not *black*, that a *circle* is not a *triangle*, that *three* are more than *two* and equal to *one and two*. Such kinds of truths the mind perceives at the first sight of the ideas together, by bare intuition; without the intervention of any other idea: and this kind of knowledge is the clearest and most certain that human frailty is capable of. This part of knowledge is irresistible, and, like bright sunshine, forces itself immediately to be perceived, as soon as ever the mind turns its view that way; and leaves no room for hesitation, doubt, or examination, but the mind is presently filled with the clear light of it. *It is on this intuition that depends all the certainty and evidence of all our knowledge*; which certainty every one finds to be so great, that he cannot imagine, and therefore not require a greater: for a man cannot conceive himself capable of a greater certainty than to know that any idea in his mind is such as he perceives it to be; and that two ideas, wherein he perceives a difference, are different and not precisely the same. He that demands a greater certainty than this, demands he knows not what, and shows only that he has a mind to be a sceptic, without being able to be so. Certainty depends so wholly on this intuition, that, in the next degree of knowledge which I call demonstrative, this intuition is necessary in all the connexions of the intermediate ideas, without which we cannot attain knowledge and certainty.

2. *II. Demonstrative.*   The next degree of knowledge is, where the mind perceives the agreement or disagreement of any ideas, but not immediately. Though wherever the mind perceives the agreement or disagreement of any of its ideas, there be certain knowledge; yet it does not always happen, that the mind sees that agreement or disagreement, which there is between them, even where it is discoverable; and in that case remains in ignorance, and at most gets no further than a probable conjecture. The rea-

son why the mind cannot always perceive presently the agreement or disagreement of two ideas, is, because those ideas, concerning whose agreement or disagreement the inquiry is made, cannot by the mind be so put together as to show it. In this case then, when the mind cannot so bring its ideas together as by their immediate comparison, and as it were juxtaposition or application one to another, to perceive their agreement or disagreement, it is fain, *by the intervention of other ideas* (one or more, as it happens) to discover the agreement or disagreement which it searches; and this is that which we call *reasoning*. Thus, the mind being willing to know the agreement or disagreement in bigness between the three angles of a triangle and two right ones, cannot by an immediate view and comparing them do it: because the three angles of a triangle cannot be brought at once, and be compared with any other one, or two, angles; and so of this the mind has no immediate, no intuitive knowledge. In this case the mind is fain to find out some other angles, to which the three angles of a triangle have an equality; and, finding those equal to two right ones, comes to know their equality to two right ones.

7. *Each Step in Demonstrated knowledge must have Intuitive Evidence.*   Now, in every step reason makes in demonstrative knowledge, there is an intuitive knowledge of that agreement or disagreement it seeks with the next intermediate idea which it uses as a proof: for if it were not so, that yet would need a proof; since without the perception of such agreement or disagreement, there is no knowledge produced: if it be perceived by itself, it is intuitive knowledge: if it cannot be perceived by itself, there is need of some intervening idea, as a common measure, to show their agreement or disagreement. By which it is plain, that every step in reasoning that produces knowledge, has intuitive certainty; which when the mind perceives, there is no more required but to remember it, to make the agreement or disagreement of the ideas concerning which we inquire visible and certain. So that to make anything a demonstration, it is necessary to perceive the immediate agreement of the intervening ideas, whereby the agreement or disagreement of the two ideas under examination (whereof the one is always the first, and the other the last in the account) is found. This intuitive perception

of the agreement or disagreement of the intermediate ideas, in each step and progression of the demonstration, must also be carried exactly in the mind, and a man must be sure that no part is left out: which, because in long deductions, and the use of many proofs, the memory does not always so readily and exactly retain; therefore it comes to pass, that this is more imperfect than intuitive knowledge, and men embrace often falsehood for demonstrations.

14. *III. Sensitive Knowledge of the particular Existence of finite beings without us.*   These two, viz. intuition and demonstration, are the degrees of our *knowledge*; whatever cones short of one of these, with what assurance soever embraced, is but *faith*, or *opinion*, but not knowledge, at least in all general truths. There is, indeed, another perception of the mind, employed about *the particular existence of finite beings without us*, which, going beyond bare probability, and yet not reaching perfectly to either of the foregoing degrees of certainty, passes under the name of *knowledge*. There can be nothing more certain than that the idea we receive from an external object is in our minds: this is intuitive knowledge. But whether there be anything more than barely that idea in our minds; whether we can thence certainly infer the existence of anything without us, which corresponds to that idea, is that whereof some men think there may be a question made; because men may have such ideas in their minds, when no such thing exists, no such object affects their senses. But yet here I think we are provided with an evidence that puts us past doubting. For I ask any one, Whether he be not invincibly conscious to himself of a different perception, when he looks on the sun by day, and thinks on it by night; when he actually tastes wormwood, or smells a rose, or only thinks on that savour or odour? We as plainly find the difference there is between any idea revived in our minds by our own memory, and actually coming into our minds by our senses, as we do between any two distinct ideas. If any one say, a dream may do the same thing, and all these ideas may be produced in us without any external objects; he may please to dream that I make him this answer: — 1. That it is no great matter, whether I remove his scruple or no: where all is but dream, reasoning and arguments are of no use, truth and knowledge nothing. 2. That I believe he will allow

a very manifest difference between dreaming of being in the fire, and being actually in it. But yet if he be resolved to appear so sceptical as to maintain, that what I call being actually in the fire is nothing but a dream; and that we cannot thereby certainly know, that any such thing as fire actually exists without us: I answer, That we certainly finding that pleasure or pain follows upon the application of certain objects to us, whose existence we perceive, or dream that we perceive, by our senses; this certainty is as great as our happiness or misery, beyond which we have no concernment to know or to be. So that, I think, we may add to the two former sorts of knowledge this also, of the existence of particular external objects, by that perception and consciousness we have of the actual entrance of ideas from them, and allow these three degrees of knowledge, viz. *intuitive*, *demonstrative*, and *sensitive*: in each of which there are different degrees and ways of evidence and certainty.

Chapter III

OF THE EXTENT OF HUMAN KNOWLEDGE

1. *First, it extends no further than we have Ideas.*   Knowledge, as has been said, lying in the perception of the agreement or disagreement of any of our ideas, it follows from hence, That,

First, we can have knowledge no further than we have *ideas*.

2. *It extends no further than we can perceive their Agreement or Disagreement.*   Secondly, That we can have no knowledge further than we can have *perception* of that agreement or disagreement. Which perception being: 1. Either by *intuition*, or the immediate comparing any two ideas; or, 2. By *reason*, examining the agreement or disagreement of two ideas, by the intervention of some others; or, 3. By *sensation*, perceiving the existence of particular things: hence it also follows:

3. *Intuitive Knowledge extends itself not to all the relations of all our Ideas.*   Thirdly, That we cannot have an *intuitive knowledge* that shall extend itself to all our ideas, and all that we would know about them; because we cannot examine and perceive all the relations they have one to another, by juxta-position, or

an immediate comparison one with another. Thus, having the ideas of an obtuse and an acute angled triangle, both drawn from equal bases, and between parallels, I can, by intuitive knowledge, perceive the one not to be the other, but cannot that way know whether they be equal or no; because their agreement or disagreement in equality can never be perceived by an immediate comparing them: the difference of figure makes their parts incapable of an exact immediate application; and therefore there is need of some intervening qualities to measure them by, which is demonstration, or rational knowledge.

4. *Nor does Demonstrative Knowledge.* Fourthly, It follows, also, from what is above observed, that our *rational knowledge* cannot reach to the whole extent of our ideas: because between two different ideas we would examine, we cannot always find such mediums as we can connect one to another with an intuitive knowledge in all the parts of the deduction; and wherever that fails, we come short of knowledge and demonstration.

5. *Sensitive Knowledge narrower than either.*
Fifthly, *Sensitive knowledge* reaching no further than the existence of things actually present to our senses, is yet much narrower than either of the former.

6. *Our Knowledge, therefore, narrower than our Ideas.* Sixthly, From all which it is evident, that the *extent of our knowledge* comes not only short of the reality of things, but even of the extent of our own ideas. Though our knowledge be limited to our ideas, and cannot exceed them either in extent or perfection; and though these be very narrow bounds, in respect of the extent of All-being, and far short of what we may justly imagine to be in some even created understandings, not tied down to the dull and narrow information that is to be received from some few, and not very acute, ways of perception, such as are our senses; yet it would be well with us if our knowledge were but as large as our ideas, and there were not many doubts and inquiries *concerning the ideas we have*, whereof we are not, nor I believe ever shall be in this world resolved. Nevertheless, I do not question but that human knowledge, under the present circumstances of our beings and constitutions, may be carried much further than it has hitherto been, if men would

sincerely, and with freedom of mind, employ all that industry and labour of thought, in improving the means of discovering truth, which they do for the colouring or support of falsehood, to maintain a system, interest, or party they are once engaged in. But yet after all, I think I may, without injury to human perfection, be confident, that our knowledge would never reach to all we might desire to know concerning those ideas we have; nor be able to surmount all the difficulties, and resolve all the questions that might arise concerning any of them. We have the ideas of a *square*, a *circle*, and *equality*; and yet, perhaps, shall never be able to find a circle equal to a square, and certainly know that it is so. We have the ideas of *matter* and *thinking*, but possibly shall never be able to know whether any mere material being thinks or no; it being impossible for us, by the contemplation of our own ideas, without revelation, to discover whether Omnipotency has not given to some systems of matter, fitly disposed, a power to perceive and think, or else joined and fixed to matter, so disposed, a thinking immaterial substance: it being, in respect of our notions, not much more remote from our comprehension to conceive that GOD can, if he pleases, superadd to matter a *faculty of thinking*, than that he should superadd to it *another substance with a faculty of thinking*; since we know not wherein thinking consists, nor to what sort of substances the Almighty has been pleased to give that power, which cannot be in any created being, but merely by the good pleasure and bounty of the Creator. For I see no contradiction in it, that the first Eternal thinking Being, or Omnipotent Spirit, should, if he pleased, give to certain systems of created senseless matter, put together as he thinks fit, some degrees of sense, perception, and thought: though, as I think I have proved, lib iv. ch. 10, § 14, &c., it is no less than a contradiction to suppose matter (which is evidently in its own nature void of sense and thought) should be that Eternal first-thinking Being. What certainty of knowledge can any one have, that some perceptions, such as, v.g., pleasure and pain, should not be in some bodies themselves, after a certain manner modified and moved, as well as that they should be in an immaterial substance, upon the motion of the parts of the body: Body, as far as we can conceive, being able only to strike and affect body, and motion, according to the utmost reach of our ideas, being able to produce nothing but motion; so that when we allow it to produce pleasure or pain, or the idea of a colour or sound, we are fain to quit our reason, go beyond our ideas, and attribute it wholly to the good pleasure of our Maker. For, since we must allow He has annexed effects to motion which we can no way conceive motion able to produce, what reason have we to conclude that He could not order them as well to be produced in a subject we cannot conceive capable of them, as well as in a subject we cannot conceive the motion of matter can any way operate upon?

But to return to the argument in hand: our knowledge, I say, is not only limited to the paucity and imperfections of the ideas we have, and which we employ it about, but even comes short of that too: but how far it reaches, let us now inquire.

7. *How far our Knowledge reaches.* The affirmations or negations we make concerning the ideas we have, may, as I have before intimated in general, be reduced to these four sorts, viz. identity, co-existence, relation, and real existence. I shall examine how far our knowledge extends in each of these:

8. *Firstly, Our Knowledge of Identity and Diversity in ideas extends as far as our Ideas themselves.* First, as to *identity* and *diversity*. In this way of agreement or disagreement of our ideas, our intuitive knowledge is as far extended as our ideas themselves: and there can be no idea in the mind, which it does not, presently, by an intuitive knowledge, perceive to be what it is, and to be different from any other.

9. *Secondly, Of their Co-existence, extends only a very little way.* As to the second sort, which is the agreement or disagreement of our ideas in *co-existence*, in this our knowledge is very short; though in this consists the greatest and most material part of our knowledge concerning substances. For our ideas of the species of substances being, as I have showed, nothing but certain collections of simple ideas united in one subject, and so co-existing together; v.g. our idea of flame is a body hot, luminous, and moving upward; of gold, a body heavy to a certain degree, yellow, malleable, and fusible: for these, or some such complex ideas as these, in men's minds, do these two names of the different substances, flame and gold, stand for. When we would know anything further

concerning these, or any other sort of substances, what do we inquire, but what *other* qualities or powers these substances have or have not? Which is nothing else but to know what *other* simple ideas do, or do not, co-exist with those that make up that complex idea?

10. *Because the Connexion between simple Ideas in substances is for the most part unknown.* This, how weighty and considerable a part soever of human science, is yet very narrow, and scarce any at all. The reason whereof is, that the simple ideas whereof our complex ideas of substances are made up are, for the most part, such as carry with them, in their own nature, no *visible necessary* connexion or inconsistency with any other simple ideas, whose co-existence with them we would inform ourselves about.

11. *Especially of the secondary Qualities of Bodies.* The ideas that our complex ones of substances are made up of, and about which our knowledge concerning substances is most employed, are those of their secondary qualities; which depending all (as has been shown) upon the primary qualities of their minute and insensible parts; or, if not upon them, upon something yet more remote from our comprehension; it is impossible we should know which have a *necessary* union or inconsistency one with another. For, not knowing the root they spring from, not knowing what size, figure, and texture of parts they are, on which depend, and from which result those qualities which make our complex idea of gold, it is impossible we should know what *other* qualities result from, or are incompatible with, the same constitution of the insensible parts of gold; and so consequently must always co-exist with that complex idea we have of it, or else are inconsistent with it.

12. *Because necessary Connexion between any secondary and the primary Qualities is undiscoverable by us.* Besides this ignorance of the primary qualities of the insensible parts of bodies, on which depend all their secondary qualities, there is yet another and more incurable part of ignorance, which sets us more remote from a certain knowledge of the co-existence or *inco-existence* (if I may so say) of different ideas in the same subject; and that is, that there is no discoverable connexion between any secondary quality and those primary qualities which it depends on.

13. *We have no perfect knowledge of their Primary Qualities.*   That the size, figure, and motion of one body should cause a change in the size, figure, and motion of another body, is not beyond our conception; the separation of the parts of one body upon the intrusion of another; and the change from rest to motion upon impulse; these and the like seem to have *some connexion* one with another. And if we knew these primary qualities of bodies, we might have reason to hope we might be able to know a great deal more of these operations of them one upon another: but our minds not being able to discover any connexion betwixt these primary qualities of bodies and the sensations that are produced in us by them, we can never be able to establish certain and undoubted rules of the *consequence* or *co-existence* of any secondary qualities, though we could discover the size, figure, or motion of those invisible parts which immediately produce them. We are so far from knowing *what* figure, size, or motion of parts produce a yellow colour, a sweet taste, or a sharp sound, that we can by no means conceive how *any* size, figure, or motion of any particles, can possibly produce in us the idea of any colour, taste, or sound whatsoever: there is no conceivable connexion between the one and the other.

14. *And seek in vain for certain and universal knowledge of unperceived qualities in substances.* In vain, therefore, shall we endeavour to discover by our ideas (the only true way of certain and universal knowledge) what other ideas are to be found constantly joined with that of *our* complex idea of any substance: since we neither know the real constitution of the minute parts on which their qualities do depend; nor, did we know them, could we discover any necessary connexion between them and any of the secondary qualities: which is necessary to be done before we can certainly know their necessary co-existence. So, that, let our complex idea of any species of substances be what it will, we can hardly, from the simple ideas contained in it, certainly determine the necessary co-existence of any other quality whatsoever. Our knowledge in all these inquiries reaches very little further than our experience. Indeed some few of the primary qualities have a necessary dependence and visible connexion one with another, as figure necessarily supposes extension; receiving or

communicating motion by impulse, supposes solidity. But, though these, and perhaps some others of our ideas have: yet there are so few of them that have a visible connexion one with another, that we can by intuition or demonstration discover the co-existence of very few of the qualities that are to be found united in substances: and we are left only to the assistance of our senses to make known to us what qualities they contain. For of all the qualities that are co-existent in any subject, without this dependence and evident connexion of their ideas one with another, we cannot know certainly any two to co-exist, any further than experience, by our senses, informs us. Thus, though we see the yellow colour, and, upon trial, find the weight, malleableness, fusibility, and fixedness that are united in a piece of gold; yet, because no one of these ideas has any evident dependence or necessary connexion with the other, we cannot certainly know that where any four of these are, the fifth will be there also, how highly probable soever it may be; because the highest probability amounts not to certainty, without which there can be no true knowledge. For this co-existence can be no further known than it is perceived; and it cannot be perceived but either in particular subjects, by the observation of our senses, or, in general, by the necessary connexion of the ideas themselves.

18. *Thirdly, Of Relations between abstracted ideas it is not easy to say how far our knowledge extends.* As to the third sort of our knowledge, viz. the agreement or disagreement of any of our ideas in any other relation: this, as it is the largest field of our knowledge, so it is hard to determine how far it may extend: because the advances that are made in this part of knowledge, depending on our sagacity in finding intermediate ideas, that may show the relations and habitudes of ideas whose coexistence is not considered, it is a hard matter to tell when we are at an end of such discoveries; and when reason has all the helps it is capable of, for the finding of proofs, or examining the agreement or disagreement of remote ideas. They that are ignorant of Algebra cannot imagine the wonders in this kind are to be done by it: and what further improvements and helps advantageous to other parts of knowledge the sagacious mind of man may yet find out, it is not easy to determine. This at least I believe, that the *ideas of quantity* are not those alone

that are capable of demonstration and knowledge; and that other, and perhaps more useful, parts of contemplation, would afford us certainty, if vices, passions, and domineering interest did not oppose or menace such endeavours.

21. *Fourthly, Of the three real Existences of which we have certain knowledge.* As to the fourth sort of our knowledge, viz. of the *real actual existence of things*, we have an intuitive knowledge of *our own existence*, and a demonstrative knowledge of the existence of a *God*: of the existence of *anything else*, we have no other but a sensitive knowledge; which extends not beyond the objects present to our senses.

Chapter IV

OF THE REALITY OF KNOWLEDGE

1. *Objection. 'Knowledge placed in our Ideas may be all unreal or chimerical.'* I doubt not but my reader, by this time, may be apt to think that I have been all this while only building a castle in the air; and be ready to say to me: —

'To what purpose all this stir? Knowledge, say you, is only the perception of the agreement or disagreement of our own ideas: but who knows what those ideas may be? Is there anything so extravagant as the imaginations of men's brains? Where is the head that has no chimeras in it? Or if there be a sober and a wise man, what difference will there be, by your rules, between his knowledge and that of the most extravagant fancy in the world? They both have their ideas, and perceive their agreement and disagreement one with another. If there be any difference between them, the advantage will be on the warm-headed man's side, as having the more ideas, and the more lively. And so, by your rules, he will be the more knowing. If it be true, that all knowledge lies only in the perception of the agreement or disagreement of our own ideas, the visions of an enthusiast and the reasonings of a sober man will be equally certain. It is no matter how things are: so a man observe but the agreement of his own imaginations, and talk conformably, it is all truth, all certainty. Such castles in the air will be as strongholds of truth, as the demonstrations of Euclid. That an harpy is not a centaur is by this way as certain knowledge, and as much a truth, as that a square is not a circle.

'But of what use is all this fine knowledge of *men's own imaginations*, to a man that inquires after the reality of things? It matters not what men's fancies are, it is the knowledge of things that is only to be prized: it is this alone gives a value to our reasonings, and preference to one man's knowledge over another's, that it is of things as they really are, and not of dreams and fancies.'

2. *Answer. Not so, where Ideas agree with Things.* To which I answer, That if our knowledge of our ideas terminate in them, and reach no further, where there is something further intended, our most serious thoughts will be of little more use than the reveries of a crazy brain; and the truths built thereon of no more weight than the discourses of a man who sees things clearly in a dream, and with great assurance utters them. But I hope, before I have done, to make it evident, that this way of certainty, by the knowledge of our own ideas, goes a little further than bare imagination: and I believe it will appear that all the certainty of general truths a man has lies in nothing else.

3. *But what shall be the criterion of this agreement?* It is evident the mind knows not things immediately, but only by the intervention of the ideas it has of them. Our knowledge, therefore, is real only so far as there is a *conformity* between our ideas and the reality of things. But what shall be here the criterion? How shall the mind, when it perceives nothing but its own ideas, know that they agree with things themselves? This, though it seems not to want difficulty, yet, I think, there be two sorts of ideas that we may be assured agree with things.

4. *As, First, All Simple Ideas are really conformed to Things.* The first are simple ideas, which since the mind, as has been showed, can by no means make to itself, must necessarily be the product of things operating on the mind, in a natural way, and producing therein those perceptions which by the Wisdom and Will of our Maker they are ordained and adapted to. From whence it follows, that simple ideas are not fictions of our fancies, but the natural and regular productions of things without us, really operating upon us; and so carry with them all the conformity which is intended; or which our state requires: for they represent to us things under those appearances

which they are fitted to produce in us: whereby we are enabled to distinguish the sorts of particular substances, to discern the states they are in, and so to take them for our necessities, and apply them to our uses. Thus, the idea of whiteness, or bitterness, as it is in the mind, exactly answering that power which is in any body to produce it there, has all the real conformity it can or ought to have, with things without us. And this conformity between our simple ideas and the existence of things, is sufficient for real knowledge.

5. *Secondly, All Complex Ideas, except ideas of Substances, are their own archetypes.* Secondly, All our complex ideas, *except those of substances*, being archetypes of the mind's own making, not intended to be the copies of anything, nor referred to the existence of anything, as to their originals, cannot want any conformity necessary to real knowledge. For that which is not designed to represent anything but itself, can never be capable of a wrong representation, nor mislead us from the true apprehension of anything, by its dislikeness to it: and such, excepting those of substances, are all our complex ideas. Which, as I have showed in another place, are combinations of ideas, which the mind, by its free choice, puts together, without considering any connexion they have in nature. And hence it is, that in all these sorts the ideas themselves are considered as the archetypes, and things no otherwise regarded, but as they are conformable to them. So that we cannot but be infallibly certain, that all the knowledge we attain concerning these ideas is real, and reaches things themselves. Because in all our thoughts, reasonings, and discourses of this kind, we intend things no further than as they are conformable to our ideas. So that in these we cannot miss of a certain and undoubted reality.

6. *Hence the reality of Mathematical Knowledge.* I doubt not but it will be easily granted, that the knowledge we have of mathematical truths is not only certain, but real knowledge; and not the bare empty vision of vain, insignificant chimeras of the brain: and yet, if we will consider, we shall find that it is only of our own ideas. The mathematician considers the truth and properties belonging to a rectangle or circle only as they are an idea in his own mind. For it is possible he never found either of them existing mathematically, i.e. precisely true, in his life. But yet the knowledge he has of any truths or properties belonging to a circle, or any other mathematical figure, are nevertheless true and certain, even of real things existing: because real things are no further concerned, nor intended to be meant by any such propositions, than as things really agree to those archetypes in his mind. Is it true of the *idea* of a triangle, that its three angles are equal to two right ones? It is true also of a triangle, wherever it *really exists*. Whatever other figure exists, that it is not exactly answerable to that idea of a triangle in his mind, is not at all concerned in that proposition. And therefore he is certain all his knowledge concerning such ideas is real knowledge: because, intending things no further than they agree with those his ideas, he is sure what he knows concerning those figures, when they have *barely an ideal existence* in his mind, will hold true of them also when they have *a real existence* in matter: his consideration being barely of those figures, which are the same wherever or however they exist.

7. *And of Moral.* And hence it follows that moral knowledge is as capable of real certainty as mathematics. For certainty being but the perception of the agreement or disagreement of our ideas, and demonstration nothing but the perception of such agreement, by the intervention of other ideas or mediums; our moral ideas, as well as mathematical, being archetypes themselves, and so adequate and complete ideas; all the agreement or disagreement which we shall find in them will produce real knowledge, as well as in mathematical figures.

11. *Thirdly, Our complex Ideas of Substances have their Archetypes without us; and here knowledge comes short.* Thirdly, There is another sort of complex ideas, which, being referred to archetypes without us, may differ from them, and so our knowledge about them may come short of being real. Such are our ideas of substances, which, consisting of a collection of simple ideas, supposed taken from the works of nature, may yet vary from them; by having more or different ideas united in them than are to be found united in the things themselves. From whence it comes to pass, that they may, and often do, fail of being exactly conformable to things themselves.

18. *Recapitulation.* Wherever we perceive the agreement or disagreement of any of our ideas, there is certain knowledge: and wherever we are sure those ideas agree with the reality of things, there is certain real knowledge. Of which agreement of our ideas with the reality of things, having here given the marks, I think, I have shown *wherein it is that certainty, real certainty, consists.* Which, whatever it was to others, was, I confess, to me heretofore, one of those desiderata which I found great want of.

Chapter VI

OF UNIVERSAL PROPOSITIONS: THEIR TRUTH AND CERTAINTY

1. *Treating of Words necessary to Knowledge.* Though the examining and judging of ideas by themselves, their names being quite laid aside, be the best and surest way to clear and distinct knowledge: yet, through the prevailing custom of using sounds for ideas, I think it is very seldom practised. Every one may observe how common it is for names to be made use of, instead of the ideas themselves, even when men think and reason within their own breasts; especially if the ideas be very complex, and made up of a great collection of simple ones. This makes the consideration of *words* and *propositions* so necessary a part of the Treatise of Knowledge, that it is very hard to speak intelligibly of the one, without explaining the other.

2. *General Truths hardly to be understood, but in verbal Propositions.* All the knowledge we have, being only of particular or general truths, it is evident that whatever may be done in the former of these, the latter, which is that which with reason is most sought after, can never be well made known, and is very seldom apprehended, but as conceived and expressed in words. It is not, therefore, out of our way, in the examination of our knowledge, to inquire into the truth and certainty of universal propositions.

3. *Certainty twofold — of Truth and of Knowledge.* But that we may not be misled in this case by that which is the danger everywhere, I mean by the doubt-

fulness of terms, it is fit to observe that certainty is twofold; *certainty of truth* and *certainty of knowledge.* Certainty of truth is, when words are so put together in propositions as exactly to express the agreement or disagreement of the ideas they stand for, as really it is. Certainty of knowledge is to perceive the agreement or disagreement of ideas, as expressed in any proposition. This we usually call knowing, or being certain of the truth of any proposition.

4. *No Proposition can be certainly known to be true, where the real Essence of each Species mentioned is not known.* Now, because we cannot be certain of the truth of any general proposition, unless we know the precise bounds and extent of the species its terms stand for, it is necessary we should know the essence of each species, which is that which constitutes and bounds it.

This, in all simple ideas and modes, is not hard to do. For in these the real and nominal essence being the same, or, which is all one, the abstract idea which the general term stands for being the sole essence and boundary that is or can be supposed of the species, there can be no doubt how far the species extends, or what things are comprehended under each term; which, it is evident, are all that have an exact conformity with the idea it stands for, and no other.

But in substances, wherein a real essence, distinct from the nominal, is supposed to constitute, determine, and bound the species, the extent of the general word is very uncertain; because, not knowing this real essence, we cannot know what is, or what is not of that species; and, consequently, what may or may not with certainty be affirmed of it. And thus, speaking of a *man,* or *gold,* or any other species of natural substances, as supposed constituted by a precise and real essence which nature regularly imparts to every individual of that kind, whereby it is made to be of that species, we cannot be certain of the truth of any affirmation or negation made of it. For man or gold, taken in this sense, and used for species of things constituted by real essences, different from the complex idea in the mind of the speaker, stand for we know not what; and the extent of these species, with such boundaries, are so unknown and undetermined, that it is impossible with any certainty to affirm, that all men are rational, or that all gold is yellow. But where the nominal essence is kept to, as the boundary of each species, and men extend the application of any general term no further than to the particular things in which the complex idea it stands for is to be found, there they are in no danger to mistake the bounds of each species, nor can be in doubt, on this account, whether any proposition be true or not. I have chosen to explain this uncertainty of propositions in this scholastic way, and have made use of the terms of *essences*, and *species*, on purpose to show the absurdity and inconvenience there is to think of them as of any other sort of realities, than barely abstract ideas with names to them. To suppose that the species of things are anything but the sorting of them under general names, according as they agree to several abstract ideas of which we make those names the signs, is to confound truth, and introduce uncertainty into all general propositions that can be made about them. Though therefore these things might, to people not possessed with scholastic learning, be treated of in a better and clearer way; yet those wrong notions of essences or species having got root in most people's minds who have received any tincture from the learning which has prevailed in this part of the world, are to be discovered and removed, to make way for that use of words which should convey certainty with it.

5. *This more particularly concerns Substances.* The names of substances, then, whenever made to stand for species which are supposed to be constituted by real essences which we know not, are not capable to convey certainty to the understanding. Of the truth of general propositions made up of such terms we cannot be sure. The reason whereof is plain: for how can we be sure that this or that quality is in gold, when we know not what is or is not gold? Since in this way of speaking, nothing is gold but what partakes of an essence, which we, not knowing, cannot know where it is or is not, and so cannot be sure that any parcel of matter in the world is or is not in this sense gold; being incurably ignorant whether *it* has or has not that which makes anything to be called gold; i.e. that real essence of gold whereof we have no idea at all. This being as impossible for us to know as it is for a blind man to tell in what flower the colour of a pansy is or is not to be found, whilst he has no idea of the colour of a pansy at all. Or if we could (which is impossible) certainly know where a real essence, which we know not, is, v.g. in what parcels of matter

the real essence of gold is, yet could we not be sure that this or that quality could with truth be affirmed of gold; since it is impossible for us to know that this or that quality or idea has a necessary connexion with a real essence of which we have no idea at all, whatever species that supposed real essence may be imagined to constitute.

6. *The Truth of few universal Propositions concerning Substances is to be known.* On the other side, the names of substances, when made use of as they should be, for the ideas men have in their minds, though they carry a clear and determinate signification with them, will not yet serve us to make many universal propositions of whose truth we can be certain. Not because in this use of them we are uncertain what things are signified by them, but because the complex ideas they stand for are such combinations of simple ones as carry not with them any discoverable connexion or repugnancy, but with a very few other ideas.

7. *Because necessary Co-existence of simple Ideas in Substances can in few Cases be known.* The complex ideas that our names of the species of substances properly stand for, are collections of such qualities as have been observed to co-exist in an unknown substratum, which we call substance; but what other qualities necessarily co-exist with such combinations, we cannot certainly know, unless we can discover their natural dependence; which, in their primary qualities, we can go but a very little way in; and in all their secondary qualities we can discover no connexion at all: for the reasons mentioned, chap. iii. Viz. I. Because we know not the real constitutions of substances, on which each secondary quality particularly depends. 2. Did we know that, it would serve us only for experimental (not universal) knowledge; and reach with certainty no further than that bare instance: because our understandings can discover no conceivable connexion between any secondary quality and any modification whatsoever of any of the primary ones. And therefore there are very few general propositions to be made concerning substances, which can carry with them undoubted certainty.

8. *Instances in Gold.* 'All gold is fixed,' is a proposition whose truth we cannot be certain of, how univer-

sally soever it be believed. For if, according to the useless imagination of the Schools, any one supposes the term gold to stand for a species of things set out by nature, by a real essence belonging to it, it is evident he knows not what particular substances are of that species; and so cannot with certainty affirm anything universally of gold. But if he makes gold stand for a species determined by its nominal essence, let the nominal essence, for example, be the complex idea of a body of a certain yellow colour, malleable, fusible, and heavier than any other known;—in this proper use of the word gold, there is no difficulty to know what is or is not gold. But yet no other quality can with certainty be universally affirmed or denied of gold, but what hath a *discoverable* connexion or inconsistency with that nominal essence. Fixedness, for example, having no necessary connexion that we can discover, with the colour, weight, or any other simple idea of our complex one, or with the whole combination together; it is impossible that we should certainly know the truth of this proposition, that all gold is fixed.

9. *No discoverable necessary connexion between nominal essence of gold and other simple ideas.* As there is no discoverable connexion between fixedness and the colour, weight, and other simple ideas of that nominal essence of gold; so, if we make our complex idea of gold, a body yellow, fusible, ductile, weighty, and fixed, we shall be at the same uncertainty concerning solubility in *aqua regia*, and for the same reason. Since we can never, from consideration of the ideas themselves, with certainty affirm or deny of a body whose complex idea is made up of yellow, very weighty, ductile, fusible, and fixed, that it is soluble in *aqua regia*: and so on of the rest of its qualities. I would gladly meet with one general affirmation concerning any quality of gold, that any one can certainly know is true. It will, no doubt, be presently objected, Is not this an universal proposition, *All gold is malleable*? To which I answer, It is a very certain proposition, if malleableness be a part of the complex idea the word gold stands for. But then here is nothing affirmed of gold, but that that sound stands for an idea in which malleableness is contained: and such a sort of truth and certainty as this it is, to say a centaur is four-footed. But if malleableness make not a part of the specific essence the name of gold

stands for, it is plain, *all gold is malleable*, is not a certain proposition. Because, let the complex idea of gold be made up of whichsoever of its other qualities you please, malleableness will not appear to depend on that complex idea, nor follow from any simple one contained in it: the connexion that malleableness has (if it has any) with those other qualities being only by the intervention of the real constitution of its insensible parts; which, since we know not, it is impossible we should perceive that connexion, unless we could discover that which ties them together.

10. *As far as any such Co-existence can be known, so far Universal Propositions may be certain. But this will go but a little way.* The more, indeed, of these coexisting qualities we unite into one complex idea, under one name, the more precise and determinate we make the signification of that word; but never yet make it thereby more capable of universal certainty, *in respect of other qualities not contained in our complex idea*: since we perceive not their connexion or dependence on one another; being ignorant both of that real constitution in which they are all founded, and also how they flow from it. For the chief part of our knowledge concerning substances is not, as in other things, barely of the relation of two ideas that may exist separately; but is of the necessary connexion and co-existence of several distinct ideas in the same subject, or of their repugnancy so to co-exist. Could we begin at the other end, and discover what it was wherein that colour consisted, what made a body lighter or heavier, what texture of parts made it malleable, fusible, and fixed, and fit to be dissolved in this sort of liquor, and not in another;—if, I say, we had such an idea as this of bodies, and could perceive therein all sensible qualities originally consist, and how they are produced; we might frame such abstract ideas of them as would furnish us with matter of more general knowledge, and enable us to make universal propositions, that should carry general truth and certainty with them. But whilst our complex ideas of the sorts of substances are so remote from that internal real constitution on which their sensible qualities depend, and are made up of nothing but an imperfect collection of those apparent qualities our senses can discover, there can be few general propositions concerning substances of whose real truth we can be certainly assured; since there are but few sim-

ple ideas of whose real truth we can be certainly assured; since there are but few simple ideas of whose connexion and necessary co-existence we can have certain and undoubted knowledge. I imagine, amongst all the secondary qualities of substances, and the powers relating to them, there cannot any two be named, whose necessary co-existence, or repugnance to co-exist, can certainly be known; unless in those of the same sense, which necessarily exclude one another, as I have elsewhere showed. No one, I think, by the colour that is in any body, can certainly know what smell, taste, sound, or tangible qualities it has, nor what alterations it is capable to make or receive on or from other bodies. The same may be said of the sound or taste, &c. Our specific names of substances standing for any collections of such ideas, it is not to be wondered that we can with them make very few general propositions of undoubted real certainty. But yet so far as any complex idea of any sort of substances contains in it any simple idea, whose *necessary* co-existence with any other *may* be discovered, so far universal propositions may with certainty be made concerning it: v.g. could any one discover a necessary connexion between malleableness and the colour or weight of gold, or any other part of the complex idea signified by that name, he might make a certain universal proposition concerning gold in this respect; and the real truth of this proposition, that *all gold is malleable*, would be as certain as of this, *the three angles of all right-lined triangles are all equal to two right ones*.

Chapter IX

OF OUR THREEFOLD KNOWLEDGE OF EXISTENCE

1. *General Propositions that are certain concern not Existence.* Hitherto we have only considered the essences of things; which being only abstract ideas, and thereby removed in our thoughts from particular existence, (that being the proper operation of the mind, in abstraction, to consider an idea under no other existence but what it has in the understanding,) gives us no knowledge of real existence at all. Where, by the way, we may take notice, that universal propositions of whose truth or falsehood we can have certain knowledge concern not existence: and further, that all particular affirmations or negations that would

not be certain if they were made general, are only concerning existence; they declaring only the accidental union or separation of ideas in things existing, which, in their abstract natures, have no known necessary union or repugnancy.

2. *A threefold Knowledge of Existence.* But, leaving the nature of propositions, and different ways of predication to be considered more at large in another place, let us proceed now to inquire concerning our knowledge of the *existence of things*, and how we come by it. I say, then, that we have the knowledge of *our own* existence by intuition; of the existence of God by demonstration; and of *other things* by sensation.

3. *Our Knowledge of our own Existence is Intuitive.* As for *our own existence*, we perceive it so plainly and so certainly, that it neither needs nor is capable of any proof. For nothing can be more evident to us than our own existence. I think, I reason, I feel pleasure and pain: can any of these be more evident to me than my own existence? If I doubt of all other things, that very doubt makes me perceive my own existence, and will not suffer me to doubt of that. For if I know I feel pain, it is evident I have as certain perception of my own existence, as of the existence of the pain I feel: or if I know I doubt, I have as certain perception of the existence of the thing doubting, as of that thought which I *call doubt*. Experience then convinces us, that we have an *intuitive knowledge* of our own existence, and an internal infallible perception that we are. In every act of sensation, reasoning, or thinking, we are conscious to ourselves of our own being; and, in this matter, come not short of the highest degree of certainty.

Chapter X

OF OUR KNOWLEDGE OF THE EXISTENCE OF A GOD

1. *We are capable of knowing certainly that there is a God.* Though God has given us no innate ideas of himself; though he has stamped no original characters on our minds, wherein we may read his being; yet having furnished us with those faculties our minds are endowed with, he hath not left himself without witness: since we have sense, perception, and

reason, and cannot want a clear proof of him, as long as we carry *ourselves* about us. Nor can we justly complain of our ignorance in this great point; since he has so plentifully provided us with the means to discover and know him; so far as is necessary to the end of our being, and the great concernment of our happiness. But, though this be the most obvious truth that reason discovers, and though its evidence be (if I mistake not) equal to mathematical certainty; yet it requires thought and attention; and the mind must apply itself to a regular deduction of it from some part of our intuitive knowledge, or else we shall be as uncertain and ignorant of this as of other propositions, which are in themselves capable of clear demonstration. To show, therefore, that we are capable of *knowing*, i.e. *being certain* that there is a God, and *how we may come by* this certainty, I think we need go no further than *ourselves*, and that undoubted knowledge we have of our own existence.

2. *For Man knows that he himself exists.* I think it is beyond question, that man has a clear idea of his own being; he knows certainly he exists, and that he is something. He that can doubt whether he be anything or no, I speak not to; no more than I would argue with pure nothing, or endeavour to convince nonentity that it were something. If any one pretends to be so sceptical as to deny his own existence, (for really to doubt of it is manifestly impossible,) let him for me enjoy his beloved happiness of being nothing, until hunger or some other pain convince him of the contrary. This, then, I think I may take for a truth, which every one's certain knowledge assures him of, beyond the liberty of doubting, viz. that he is *something that actually exists.*

3. *He knows also that Nothing cannot produce a Being; therefore Something must have existed from Eternity.* In the next place, man knows, by an intuitive certainty, that bare *nothing can no more produce any real being, than it can be equal to two right angles.* If a man knows not that nonentity, or the absence of all being, cannot be equal to two right angles, it is impossible he should know any demonstration in Euclid. If, therefore, we know there is some real being, and that nonentity cannot produce any real being, it is an evident demonstration, that *from eternity there has been something*; since what was not from

eternity had a beginning; and what had a beginning must be produced by something else.

4. *And that eternal Being must be most powerful.* Next, it is evident, that what had its being and beginning from another, must also have all that which is in and belongs to its being from another too. All the powers it has must be owing to and received from the same source. This eternal source, then, of all being must also be the source and original of all power; and so *this eternal Being must be also the most powerful.*

5. *And most knowing.* Again, a man finds in *himself* perception and knowledge. We have then got one step further; and we are certain now that there is not only some being, but some knowing, intelligent being in the world. There was a time, then, when there was no knowing being, and when knowledge began to be; or else there had been also *a knowing being from eternity*. If it be said, there was a time when no being had any knowledge, when that eternal being was void of all understanding; I reply, that then it was impossible there should ever have been any knowledge: it being as impossible that things wholly void of knowledge, and operating blindly, and without any perception, should produce a knowing being, as it is impossible that a triangle should make itself three angles bigger than two right ones. For it is as repugnant to the idea of senseless matter, that it should put into itself sense, perception, and knowledge, as it is repugnant to the idea of a triangle, that it should put into itself greater angles than two right ones.

6. *And therefore God.* Thus, from the consideration of ourselves, and what we infallibly find in our own constitutions, our reason leads us to the knowledge of this certain and evident truth, — *That there is an eternal, most powerful, and most knowing Being*; which whether any one will please to call God, it matters not. The thing is evident; and from this idea duly considered, will easily be deduced all those other attributes, which we ought to ascribe to this eternal Being. If, nevertheless, any one should be found to senselessly arrogant, as to suppose man alone knowing and wise, but yet the product of mere ignorance and chance; and that all the rest of the universe acted only by that blind haphazard; I shall leave with him

that very rational and emphatical rebuke of Tully[8] (1. ii. De Leg.), to be considered at his leisure: 'What can be more sillily arrogant and misbecoming, than for a man to think that he has a mind and understanding in him, but yet in all the universe beside there is no such thing? Or that those things, which with the utmost stretch of his reason he can scarce comprehend, should be moved and managed without any reason at all?' *Quid est enim verius, quam neminem esse oportere tam stulte arrogantem, ut in se mentem et rationem putet inesse, in caelo mundoque non putet? Aut ea quae vix summa ingenii ratione comprehendat, nulla ratione moveri putet?*

From what has been said, it is plain to me we have a more certain knowledge of the existence of a God, than of anything our senses have not immediately discovered to us. Nay, I presume I may say, that we more certainly know that there is a God, than that there is anything else without us. When I say we *know*, I mean there is such a knowledge within our reach which we cannot miss, if we will but apply our minds to that, as we do to several other inquiries.

Chapter XI

OF OUR KNOWLEDGE OF THE EXISTENCE OF OTHER THINGS

1. *Knowledge of the existence of other Finite Beings is to be had only by actual Sensation.* The knowledge of our own being we have by intuition. The existence of a God, reason clearly makes known to us, as has been shown.

The knowledge of the existence of *any other thing* we can have only by *sensation*: for there being no necessary connexion of real existence with any *idea* a man hath in his memory; nor of any other existence but that of God with the existence of any particular man: no particular man can know the existence of any other being, but only when, by actual operating upon him, it makes itself perceived by him. For, the having the idea of anything in our mind, no more proves the existence of that thing, than the picture of a man evidences his being in the world, or the visions of a dream make thereby a true history.

8. [Marcus Tullius Cicero (106–43 B.C.), the statesman and philosopher, was considered the greatest Roman orator. Locke's reference is to *De Legibus*, a political dialogue.]

2. *Instance: Whiteness of this Paper.* It is therefore the *actual receiving* of ideas from without that gives us notice of the existence of other things, and makes us know, that something doth exist at that time without us, which causes that idea in us; though perhaps we neither know nor consider how it does it. For it takes not from the certainty of our sense, and the ideas we receive by them, that we know not the manner wherein they are produced: v.g. whilst I write this, I have, by the paper affecting my eyes, that idea produced in my mind, which, whatever object causes, I call *white*; by which I know that that quality or accident (i.e. whose appearance before my eyes always causes that idea) doth really exist, and hath a being without me. And of this, the greatest assurance I can possibly have, and to which my faculties can attain, is the testimony of my eyes, which are the proper and sole judges of this thing; whose testimony I have reason to rely on as so certain, that I can no more doubt, whilst I write this, that I see white and black, and that something really exists that causes that sensation in me, than that I write or move my hand; which is a certainty as great as human nature is capable of, concerning the existence of anything, but a man's self alone, and of God.

3. *This notice by our Senses, though not so certain as Demonstration, yet may be called Knowledge, and proves the Existence of Things without us.* The notice we have by our senses of the existing of things without us, though it be not altogether so certain as our intuitive knowledge, or the deductions of our reason employed about the clear abstract ideas of our own minds; yet it is an assurance that deserves the name of *knowledge*. If we persuade ourselves that our faculties act and inform us right concerning the existence of those objects that affect them, it cannot pass for an ill-grounded confidence: for I think nobody can, in earnest, be so sceptical as to be uncertain of the existence of those things which he sees and feels. At least, he that can doubt so far, (whatever he may have with his own thoughts,) will never have any controversy with me; since he can never be sure I say anything contrary to his own opinion. As to myself, I think God has given me assurance enough of the existence of things without me: since, by their different application, I can produce in myself both pleasure and pain, which is one great concernment of my

present state. This is certain: the confidence that our faculties do not herein deceive us, is the greatest assurance we are capable of concerning the existence of material beings. For we cannot act anything but by our faculties; nor talk of knowledge itself, but by the help of those faculties which are fitted to apprehend even what knowledge is.

But besides the assurance we have from our senses themselves, that they do not err in the information they give us of the existence of things without us, when they are affected by them, we are further confirmed in this assurance by other concurrent reasons: —

4. *Confirmed by concurrent reasons:* — *First, Because we cannot have ideas of Sensation but by the Inlet of the Senses.* I. It is plain those perceptions are produced in us by exterior causes affecting our senses: because those that want the *organs* of any sense, never can have the ideas belonging to that sense produced in their minds. This is too evident to be doubted: and therefore we cannot but be assured that they come in by the organs of that sense, and no other way. The organs themselves, it is plain, do not produce them: for then the eyes of a man in the dark would produce colours, and his nose smell roses in the winter: but we see nobody gets the relish of a pineapple, till he goes to the Indies, where it is, and tastes it.

5. *Secondly, Because we find that an Idea from actual Sensation, and another from Memory, are very distinct Perceptions.* II. Because sometimes I find that *I cannot avoid the having those ideas produced in my mind.* For though, when my eyes are shut, or windows fast, I can at pleasure recall to my mind the ideas of light, or the sun, which former sensations had lodged in my memory; so I can at pleasure lay by *that* idea, and take into my view that of the smell of a rose, or taste sugar. But, if I turn my eyes at noon towards the sun, I cannot avoid the ideas which the light or sun then produces in me. So that there is a manifest difference between the ideas laid up in my memory, (over which, if they were there only, I should have constantly the same power to dispose of them, and lay them by at pleasure,) and those which force themselves upon me, and I cannot avoid having. And therefore it must needs be some exterior cause, and the brisk acting of

some objects without me, whose efficacy I cannot resist, that produces those ideas in my mind, whether I will or no. Besides, there is nobody who doth not perceive the difference in himself between contemplating the sun, as he hath the idea of it in his memory, and actually looking upon it: of which two, his perception is so distinct, that few of his ideas are more distinguishable one from another. And therefore he hath certain knowledge that they are not *both* memory, or the actions of his mind, and fancies only within him; but that actual seeing hath a cause without.

6. *Thirdly, Because Pleasure or Pain, which accompanies actual Sensation, accompanies not the returning of those Ideas without the external Objects.* III. Add to this, that many of those ideas are *produced in us with pain,* which afterwards we remember without the least offence. Thus, the pain of heat or cold, when the idea of it is revived in our minds, gives us no disturbance; which, when felt, was very troublesome; and is again, when actually repeated: which is occasioned by the disorder the external object causes in our bodies when applied to them: and we remember the pains of hunger, thirst, or the headache, without any pain at all; which would either never disturb us, or else constantly do it, as often as we thought of it, were there nothing more but ideas floating in our minds, and appearances entertaining our fancies, without the real existence of things affecting us from abroad. The same may be said of *pleasure,* accompanying several actual sensations. And though mathematical demonstration depends not upon sense, yet the examining them by diagrams gives great credit to the evidence of our sight, and seems to give it a certainty approaching to that of demonstration itself. For, it would be very strange, that a man should allow it for an undeniable truth, that two angles of a figure, which he measures by lines and angles of a diagram, should be bigger one than the other, and yet doubt of the existence of those lines and angles, which by looking on he makes use of to measure that by.

7. *Fourthly, Because our Senses assist one another's Testimony of the Existence of outward Things, and enable us to predict.* IV. Our *senses* in many cases *bear witness to the truth of each other's report,* concerning the existence of sensible things without us. He that *sees* a fire, may, if he doubt whether it be anything

more than a bare fancy, *feel* it too; and be convinced, by putting his hand in it. Which certainly could never be put into such exquisite pain by a bare idea or phantom, unless that the pain be a fancy too: which yet he cannot, when the burn is well, by raising the idea of it, bring upon himself again.

Thus I see, whilst I write this, I can change the appearance of the paper; and by designing the letters, tell *beforehand* what new idea it shall exhibit the very next moment, by barely drawing my pen over it: which will neither appear (let me fancy as much as I will) if my hands stand still; or though I move my pen, if my eyes be shut: nor, when those characters are once made on the paper, can I choose afterwards but see them as they are; that is, have the ideas of such letters as I have made. Whence it is manifest, that they are not barely the sport and play of my own imagination, when I find that the characters that were made at the pleasure of my own thoughts, do not obey them; nor yet cease to be, whenever I shall fancy it, but continue to affect my senses constantly and regularly, according to the figures I made them. To which if we will add, that the sight of those shall, from another man, draw such sounds as I beforehand design they shall stand for, there will be little reason left to doubt that those words I write do really exist without me, when they cause a long series of regular sounds to affect my ears, which could not be the effect of my imagination, nor could my memory retain them in that order.

8. *This Certainty is as great as our Condition needs.* But yet, if after all this any one will be so sceptical as to distrust his senses, and to affirm that all we see and hear, feel and taste, think and do, during our whole being, is but the series and deluding appearances of a long dream, whereof there is no reality; and therefore will question the existence of all things, or our knowledge of anything: I must desire him to consider, that, if all be a dream, then he doth but dream that he makes the question, and so it is not much matter that a waking man should answer him. But yet, if he pleases, he may dream that I make him this answer, That the certainty of things existing in *rerum natura* when we have the testimony of our senses for it is not only as great as our frame can attain to, but as our condition needs. For, our faculties being suited not to the full extent of being, nor to a perfect, clear, comprehensive knowledge of things

free from all doubt and scruple; but to the preservation of us, in whom they are; and accommodated to the use of life: they serve to our purpose well enough, if they will but give us certain notice of those things, which are convenient or inconvenient to us. For he that sees a candle burning, and hath experimented the force of its flame by putting his finger in it, will little doubt that this is something existing without him, which does him harm, and puts him to great pain: which is assurance enough, when no man requires greater certainty to govern his actions by than what is as certain as his actions themselves. And if our dreamer pleases to try whether the glowing heat of a glass furnace be barely a wandering imagination in a drowsy man's fancy, by putting his hand into it, he may perhaps be wakened into a certainty greater than he could wish, that it is something more than bare imagination. So that this evidence is as great as we can desire, being as certain to us as our pleasure or pain, i.e. happiness or misery; beyond which we have no concernment, either of knowing or being. Such an assurance of the existence of things without us is sufficient to direct us in the attaining the good and avoiding the evil which is caused by them, which is the important concernment we have of being made acquainted with them.

9. *But reaches no further than actual Sensation.* In fine, then, when our senses do actually convey into our understandings any idea, we cannot but be satisfied that there doth something *at that time* really exist without us, which doth affect our senses, and by them give notice of itself to our apprehensive faculties, and actually produce that idea which we then perceive: and we cannot so far distrust their testimony, as to doubt that such *collections* of simple ideas as we have observed by our senses to be united together, do really exist together. But this knowledge extends as far as the present testimony of our senses, employed about particular objects that do then affect them, and no further. For if I saw such a collection of simple ideas as is wont to be called *man*, existing together one minute since, and am now alone, I cannot be certain that the same man exists now, since there is no *necessary connexion* of his existence a minute since with his existence now: by a thousand ways he may cease to be, since I had the testimony of my senses for his existence. And if I cannot be

certain that the man I saw last to-day is now in being, I can less be certain that he is so who hath been longer removed from my senses, and I have not seen since yesterday, or since the last year: and much less can I be certain of the existence of men that I never saw. And, therefore, though it be highly probable that millions of men do now exist, yet, whilst I am alone, writing this, I have not that certainty of it which we strictly call knowledge; though the great likelihood of it puts me past doubt, and it be reasonable for me to do several things upon the confidence that there are men (and men also of my acquaintance, with whom I have to do) now in the world: but this is but probability, not knowledge.

12. *The Existence of other finite Spirits not knowable, and rests on Faith.*   What ideas we have of spirits, and how we come by them, I have already shown. But though we have those ideas in our minds, and know we have them there, the having the ideas of spirits does not make us know that any such things do exist without us, or that there are any finite spirits, or any other spiritual beings, but the Eternal God. We have ground from revelation, and several other reasons, to believe with assurance that there are such creatures: but our senses not being able to discover them, we want the means of knowing their particular existences. For we can no more know that there are finite spirits really existing, by the idea we have of such beings in our minds, than by the ideas any one has of fairies or centaurs, he can come to know that things answering those ideas do really exist.

And therefore concerning the existence of finite spirits, as well as several other things, we must content ourselves with the evidence of faith; but universal, certain propositions concerning this matter are beyond our reach. For however true it may be, v.g., that all the intelligent spirits that God ever created do still exist, yet it can never make a part of our certain knowledge. These and the like propositions we may assent to, as highly probable, but are not, I fear, in this state capable of knowing. We are not, then, to put others upon demonstrating, nor ourselves upon search of universal certainty in all those matters; wherein we are not capable of any other knowledge, but what our senses give us in this or that particular.

13. *Only particular Propositions concerning concrete Existences are knowable.*   By which it appears that there are two sorts of propositions:—(1) There is one sort of propositions concerning the *existence* of anything answerable to such an idea: as having the idea of an elephant, phoenix, motion, or an angel, in my mind, the first and natural inquiry is, Whether such a thing does anywhere exist? And this knowledge is only of particulars. No existence of anything without us, but only of God, can certainly be known further than our senses inform us. (2) There is another sort of propositions, wherein is expressed the agreement or disagreement of *our abstract ideas*, and their dependence on one another. Such propositions may be universal and certain. So, having the idea of God and myself, of fear and obedience, I cannot but be sure that God is to be feared and obeyed by me: and this proposition will be certain, concerning man in general, if I have made an abstract idea of such a species, whereof I am one particular. But yet this proposition, how certain soever, that 'men ought to fear and obey God' proves not to me the *existence of men* in the world; but will be true of all such creatures, whenever they do exist: which certainty of such general propositions depends on the agreement or disagreement to be discovered in those abstract ideas.

14. *And all general Propositions that are known to be true concern abstract Ideas.*   In the former case, our knowledge is the consequence of the existence of things, producing ideas in our minds by our senses: in the latter, knowledge is the consequence of the ideas (be they what they will) that are in our minds, producing there general certain propositions. Many of these are called *aeternae veritates*, and all of them indeed are so; not from being written, all or any of them, in the minds of all men; or that they were any of them propositions in any one's mind, till he, having got the abstract ideas, joined or separated them by affirmation or negation. But wheresoever we can suppose such a creature as man is, endowed with such faculties, and thereby furnished with such ideas as we have, we must conclude, he must needs, when he applies his thoughts to the consideration of his ideas, know the truth of certain propositions that will arise from the agreement or disagreement which he will perceive in his own ideas. Such propositions are therefore called *eternal truths*, not because they are eternal propositions actually formed, and antecedent to the understanding that at any time makes them;

nor because they are imprinted on the mind from any patterns that are anywhere out of the mind, and existed before: but because, being once made about abstract ideas, so as to be true, they will, whenever they can be supposed to be made again at any time, past or to come, by a mind having those ideas, always actually be true. For names being supposed to stand perpetually for the same ideas, and the same ideas having immutably the same habitudes one to another, propositions concerning any abstract ideas that are once true must needs be *eternal verities*.

George Berkeley

George Berkeley was born in Kilkenny, Ireland, in 1685. He studied at Trinity College, Dublin, where he received his B.A. in 1704 and his M.A. in 1707. Subsequently, he joined the faculty at Trinity, where he stayed until 1712. During this time at Trinity, Berkeley wrote his most important philosophical works, *An Essay Towards a New Theory of Vision* (1709), *A Treatise Concerning the Principles of Human Knowledge* (the *Principles*) (1710), and *Three Dialogues between Hylas and Philonous* (the *Dialogues*) (1713). In this period he also became an Anglican clergyman. For several years, beginning in 1713, he lived in London, where he associated with the literati of the time. In 1721, the year he published *De Motu*, a book on the philosophy of physics, he returned to Trinity, where he remained until 1724. From 1724 until 1728 he promoted a plan to establish a college in Bermuda for sons of settlers and native Americans. In 1728 he married Anne Forster and then sailed to Newport, Rhode Island, where he waited in vain until 1731 for the promised government subsidy for the college. The college was never established, and in 1731 he returned to London. During his stay in America, he wrote *Alciphron: or, the Minute Philosopher* (1734), a defense of Christianity. Around this time he also wrote *The Theory of Vision* (1733) and two books on the philosophy of mathematics, *The Analyst* (1734) and a *Defense of Free Thinking in Mathematics* (1735), and he published the third edition of the *Principles* (1734), which incorporates certain significant revisions. While in London, Berkeley was made bishop of Cloyne, a diocese in Ireland, where he lived from 1734 until 1752. In this period he produced an unusual work, *Siris: a Chain of Philosophical Reflections and Inquiries Concerning the Virtues of Tar-water, and Divers Other Subjects* (1744). In 1752 he moved his family to Oxford because his son George, one of his five children, was to study there, and in the next year, 1753, he died.

Berkeley is best known for his immaterialism, his view that there is no matter in the universe, and all that exists are minds (*spirits*) and their states. Matter, in his view, is by definition stuff external to any mind. Berkeley did not deny that there are objects such as books and trees, but he held that such physical objects exist only in minds, wholly constituted of ideas. A tree, for example, consists entirely of certain ideas in the mind of a perceiver—ideas of, for example, size, shape, weight, resistance, and color.

In both the *Principles* and the *Dialogues* the most prominent place is given to a series of arguments against the existence of matter. Berkeley's most basic anti-materialistic intuition is that, when we consider carefully what it means for a physical object to exist, we will see that it is just that its various qualities are perceived—its color is seen, its texture felt, its odor smelled, and its flavor tasted. For physical things, as Berkeley puts it, their *esse* is *percipi*, that is, for them *to be* is *to be perceived*. Beyond this basic consideration, Berkeley advances two types of argument against the existence of matter. In one sort, Berkeley contends that we would never come to know the existence of material objects. All we directly perceive are sensations, and indirectly, by means of inference from the sensations we directly perceive, we could never conclude that material objects exist, because we have no explanation of how material objects can cause sensations in immaterial minds.

The second sort of argument is devoted to the claim that matter cannot even be conceived by us. We cannot conceive of matter by forming an idea that resembles a material object, because ideas cannot resemble material objects—they can resemble only other ideas. But further, when I attempt to conceive of a material object by forming an idea of a physical object that is external to any mind, I do not succeed, because the physical object is nevertheless in *my* mind, the mind of the conceiver. Perhaps Berkeley's most important consideration against the existence of matter involves his attack on the supposed mind-independence of primary qualities. In the tradition of Galileo, Descartes, and Locke, we can form a conception of mind-independent physical things by forming an idea of entities possessing only primary qualities—for example, extension, size, shape, motion, location, and duration. By contrast, secondary qualities such as color, taste, odor, and temperature do not provide us with a conception of mind-independent physical things. This is partly because perception of secondary qualities varies with the state or nature of the perceptual organs. For example, a bowl of water can feel warmer or cooler depending on the initial temperature of the hand one is feeling the water with, and thus, temperature is perception- or mind-dependent. Berkeley argues that perception of primary qualities varies in the very same way and that consequently primary qualities are as mind-dependent as the secondary qualities are.

Berkeley's universe is a community of immaterial spirits. God is the greatest of the spirits, and he sends the other spirits sensations in an orderly way, giving rise to a physical world consisting wholly of sensations and governed by laws of nature. Despite the incredulity with which Berkeley's claims are often received, he nevertheless argued that his views are commonsensical, and that those of the materialists are mere philosophers' inventions. Berkeley's legacy remains in a creative alternative to commonly held metaphysical views, in resourceful and important challenges to the modern understanding of matter.

• • •

Important studies of Berkeley's views include Margaret Atherton, *Berkeley's Revolution in Vision* (Ithaca: Cornell University Press, 1990); A. A. Luce, *The Dialectic of Immaterialism: An Account of the Making of Berkeley's Principles* (London: Hodder and Stoughton, 1963); Robert Muehlmann, *Berkeley's Ontology* (Indianapolis: Hackett, 1992); George Pitcher, *Berkeley* (London: Routledge & Kegan Paul, 1977); I. C. Tipton, *Berkeley: The Philosophy of Immaterialism* (London: Methuen, 1974); and Kenneth P. Winkler, *Berkeley: An Interpretation* (Oxford: Oxford University Press, 1989). Some of the best collections of critical essays are C. B. Martin and D. M. Armstrong, eds., *Locke and Berkeley: A Collection of Critical Essays* (Garden City: Doubleday, 1968); Ernest Sosa, ed., *Essays on the Philosophy of George Berkeley* (Dordrecht: D. Reidel, 1987); Colin Turbayne, ed., *Berkeley: Critical and Interpretive Essays* (Minneapolis: University of Minnesota Press, 1987); and Margaret Atherton, ed., *The Empiricists: Locke, Berkeley, Hume* (Lanham, Md.: Rowman & Littlefield, 1998).

D.P.

A Treatise Concerning the
Principles of Human Knowledge

PREFACE

What I make public here has, after a long and scrupulous inquiry, seemed to me evidently true and not unuseful to be known—particularly to those who are tainted with skepticism or want a demonstration of the existence and immateriality of God or the natural immortality of the soul. Whether it is so or not, I am content the reader should impartially examine, since I do not think myself any further concerned for the success of what I have written than as it is agreeable to *truth*. But to the end *this* may not suffer, I make it my request that the reader suspend his judgment until he has, *at least*, once read the whole through with that degree of attention and thought which the subject matter shall seem to deserve. For as there are some passages that, taken by themselves, are very liable to gross misinterpretation (nor could it be remedied), and to be charged with most absurd consequences, which, nevertheless, upon an entire perusal will appear not to follow from them; so likewise, though the whole should be read over, yet if this is done transiently, it is very probable my sense may be mistaken, but to a thinking reader, I flatter myself, it will be throughout clear and obvious. As for the characters of novelty and singularity, which some of the following notions may seem to bear, it is, I hope, needless to make any apology on that account. He must surely be either very weak or very little acquainted with the sciences, who shall reject a truth that is capable of demonstration, for no other reason but because it is newly known and contrary to the prejudices of mankind. This much I thought fit to premise in order to prevent, if possible, the hasty censures of a sort of men who are too apt to condemn an opinion before they rightly comprehend it.

From *The Works of George Berkeley*, ed. G. N. Wright (London, 1843), 2 vols., English, modified.

INTRODUCTION

1. Philosophy being nothing else but the study of wisdom and truth, it may with reason be expected that those who have spent most time and pains in it should enjoy a greater calm and serenity of mind, a greater clearness and evidence of knowledge, and be less disturbed with doubts and difficulties than other men. Yet so it is, we see the illiterate bulk of mankind who walk the high road of plain, common sense, and are governed by the dictates of nature, for the most part easy and undisturbed. To them nothing that is familiar appears unaccountable or difficult to comprehend. They do not complain of any want of evidence in their senses, and are out of all danger of becoming skeptics. But no sooner do we depart from sense and instinct to follow the light of a superior principle, to reason, meditate, and reflect on the nature of things, but a thousand scruples spring up in our minds concerning those things which before we seemed fully to comprehend. Prejudices and errors of sense do from all parts discover themselves to our view, and, endeavoring to correct these by reason, we are insensibly drawn into uncouth paradoxes, difficulties, and inconsistencies, which multiply and grow upon us as we advance in speculation, until at length, having wandered through many intricate mazes, we find ourselves just where we were, or, which is worse, sit down in a forlorn skepticism.

2. The cause of this is thought to be the obscurity of things or the natural weakness and imperfection of our understandings. It is said the faculties we have are few and those designed by nature for the support and comfort (pleasure) of life and not to penetrate into the inward essence and constitution of things. Besides, the mind of man being finite, when it treats of things which partake of infinity, it is not to be wondered at if it runs into absurdities and contradictions, out of which it is impossible it should ever extricate itself, it being of the nature of infinite not to be comprehended by that which is finite.

3. But, perhaps, we may be too partial to ourselves in placing the fault originally in our faculties and not rather in the wrong use we make of them. It is a hard thing to suppose that right deductions from true principles should ever end in consequences which cannot be maintained or made consistent. We should believe that God has dealt more bountifully with the sons of men than to give them a strong desire for that knowledge which he had placed quite out of their reach. This would not be agreeable to the accustomed indulgent methods of Providence, which, whatever appetites it may have implanted in the creatures, does usually furnish them with such means as, if rightly made use of, will not fail to satisfy them. Upon the whole I am inclined to think that the far greater part, if not all, of those difficulties which have up to now amused philosophers and blocked up the way to knowledge are entirely owing to ourselves—that we have first raised a dust and then complain we cannot see.

4. My purpose, therefore, is to try if I can discover what those principles are which have introduced all that doubtfulness and uncertainty, those absurdities and contradictions into the several sects of philosophy, inasmuch as the wisest men have thought our ignorance incurable, conceiving it to arise from the natural dullness and limitation of our faculties. And surely it is a work well deserving our pains to make a strict inquiry concerning the first principles of human knowledge, to sift and examine them on all sides, especially since there may be some grounds to suspect that those obstacles and difficulties which stay and embarrass the mind in its search after truth do not spring from any darkness and intricacy in the objects or natural defect in the understanding so much as from false principles which have been insisted on and might have been avoided.

5. However difficult and discouraging this attempt may seem when I consider how many great and extraordinary men have gone before me in the same designs, yet I am not without some hopes, upon the consideration that the largest views are not always the clearest, and that he who is shortsighted will be obliged to draw the object nearer, and may, perhaps, by a close and narrow survey discern that which had escaped far better eyes.

6. In order to prepare the mind of the reader for the easier conceiving what follows it is proper to premise somewhat, by way of introduction, concerning the nature and abuse of language. But unraveling this matter leads me in some measure to anticipate my design by taking notice of what seems to have had a chief part in rendering speculation intricate and perplexed and to have occasioned innumerable errors and difficulties in almost all parts of knowledge. And that is the opinion that the mind has a power of framing *abstract ideas* or notions of things. He who is not a perfect stranger to the writings and disputes of philosophers must necessarily acknowledge that no small part of them are spent about abstract ideas. These are in a more especial manner thought to be the object of those sciences which go by the name of *logic* and *metaphysics* and of all that which passes under the notion of the most abstracted and sublime learning, in all of which one shall scarce find any question handled in such a manner as does not suppose their existence in the mind and that it is well acquainted with them.

7. It is agreed on all hands that the qualities or modes of things never do really exist each of them apart by itself and separated from all others, but are mixed, as it were, and blended together, several in the same object. But we are told the mind, being able to consider each quality singly or abstracted from those other qualities with which it is united, does by that means frame abstract ideas to itself. For example, there is perceived by sight an object extended, colored, and moved; this mixed or compound idea the mind resolving into its simple, constituent parts, and viewing each by itself, exclusive of the rest, does frame the abstract ideas of extension, color, and motion. Not that it is possible for color or motion to exist without extension, but only that the mind can frame to itself by *abstraction* the idea of color exclusive of extension and of motion exclusive of both color and extension.

8. Again, the mind having observed that, in the particular extensions perceived by sense, there is something common and alike in all, and some other things peculiar as this or that figure or magnitude, which distinguish them one from another, it considers apart or singles out by itself that which is common, making thereof a most abstract idea of extension, which is neither line, surface, nor solid, nor has any figure or magnitude, but is an idea entirely prescinded from all these. So likewise the mind, by leaving out

of the particular colors perceived by sense that which distinguishes them one from another and retaining that only which is common to all, makes an idea of color in abstract which is neither red, nor blue, nor white, nor any other determinate color. And, in like manner, by considering motion abstractly not only from the body moved, but likewise from the figure it describes and all particular directions and velocities, the abstract idea of motion is framed—which equally corresponds to all particular motions whatsoever that may be perceived by sense.

9. And as the mind frames to itself abstract ideas of qualities or modes, so it does, by the same precision or mental separation, attain abstract ideas of the more compounded beings, which include several coexistent qualities. For example, the mind, having observed that *Peter, James,* and *John* resemble each other in certain common agreements of shape and other qualities, leaves out of the complex or compounded idea it has of *Peter, James,* and any other particular man that which is peculiar to each, retaining only what is common to all, and so makes an abstract idea in which all the particulars equally partake, abstracting entirely from and cutting off all those circumstances and differences which might determine it to any particular existence. And after this manner it is said we come by the abstract idea of *man* or, if you please, humanity or human nature, in which it is true there is included color, because there is no man but has some color; but then it can be neither white, nor black, nor any particular color, because there is no one particular color in which all men partake. So likewise there is included stature, but then it is neither tall stature nor short stature, nor yet middle stature, but something abstracted from all these. And so of the rest. Moreover, there being a great variety of other creatures that partake in some parts, but not all, of the complex idea of *man,* the mind, leaving out those parts which are peculiar to men and retaining those only which are common to all the living creatures, frames the idea of *animal* which abstracts not only from all particular men, but also all birds, beasts, fishes, and insects. The constituent parts of the abstract idea of animal are body, life, sense, and spontaneous motion. By *body* is meant body without any particular shape or figure, there being no one shape or figure common to all animals without covering either of hair or feathers, or scales, etc., nor yet na-

ked—hair, feathers, scales, and nakedness being the distinguishing properties of particular animals, and, for that reason, left out of the *abstract idea.* Upon the same account the spontaneous motion must be neither walking, nor flying, nor creeping; it is nevertheless a motion, but what that motion is, it is not easy to conceive.

10. Whether others have this wonderful faculty of *abstracting their ideas* they best can tell, for myself I find indeed I have a faculty of imagining, or representing to myself the ideas of those particular things I have perceived and of variously compounding and dividing them. I can imagine a man with two heads or the upper parts of a man joined to the body of a horse. I can consider the hand, the eye, the nose, each by itself abstracted or separated from the rest of the body. But then whatever hand or eye I imagine, it must have some particular shape and color. Likewise the idea of man that I frame to myself must be either of a white or a black or a tawny, a straight or a crooked, a tall or a short or a middle-sized man. I cannot by any effort of thought conceive the abstract idea above described. And it is equally impossible for me to form the abstract idea of motion distinct from the body moving, and which is neither swift nor slow, curvilinear nor rectilinear; and the like may be said of all other abstract general ideas whatsoever. To be plain, I admit myself able to abstract in one sense, as when I consider some particular parts or qualities separated from others with which, though they are united in some object, yet it is possible they may really exist without them. But I deny that I can abstract one from another or conceive separately those qualities which it is impossible should exist so separated or that I can frame a general notion by abstracting from particulars in the manner aforesaid—which two last are the proper meanings of *abstraction.* And there are grounds to think most men will acknowledge themselves to be in my case. The generality of men which are simple and illiterate never pretend to *abstract notions.* It is said they are difficult and not to be attained without pains and study. We may therefore reasonably conclude that if there are such, they are confined only to the learned.

11. I proceed to examine what can be alleged in defense of the doctrine of abstraction and try if I can discover what it is that inclines the men of speculation to embrace an opinion so remote from common sense

as that seems to be. There has been a late deservedly esteemed philosopher[1] who, no doubt, has given it very much countenance by seeming to think that having abstract general ideas is what puts the widest difference in point of understanding between man and beast.—

> The having of general ideas, (he says) is that which puts a perfect distinction between man and brutes, and is an excellency which the faculties of brutes do by no means attain unto. For it is evident we observe no footsteps in them of making use of general signs for universal ideas, from which we have reason to imagine that they do not have the faculty of *abstracting* or making general ideas, since they have no use of words or any other general signs.

And a little after:

> Therefore, I think, we may suppose that it is in this that the species of brutes are discriminated from men, and it is that proper difference in which they are wholly separated, and which at last widens to so wide a distance. For if they have any ideas at all, and are not bare machines (as some would have them), we cannot deny them to have some reason. It seems as evident to me that they do some of them in certain instances reason as that they have sense, but it is only in particular ideas, just as they receive them from their senses. They are the best of them tied up within those narrow bounds, and have not (as I think) the faculty to enlarge them by any kind of *abstraction*. *Essay on Human Understanding* II, chap. 9, sec. 10, 11.

I readily agree with this learned author that the faculties of brutes can by no means attain to *abstraction*. But then if this is made the distinguishing property of that sort of animals, I fear a great many of those that pass for men must be reckoned into their number. The reason that is here assigned why we have no grounds to think brutes have abstract general ideas is that we observe in them no use of words or any other general signs, which is built on this supposition, namely, that the making use of words implies the having general ideas. From this it follows

that men who use language are able to abstract or generalize their ideas. That this is the sense and argument of the author will further appear by his answering the question he puts in another place. "Since all things that exist are only particulars, how do we come by general terms?" His answer is, "Words become general by being made the signs of general ideas."[2] *Essay on Human Understanding* III, chap. 3, sec. 6. But to this I cannot assent, for it seems that a word becomes general by being made the sign, not of an abstract general idea, but of several particular ideas, any one of which it indifferently suggests to the mind. For example, when it is said *the change of motion is proportional to the impressed force*, or that *whatever has extension is divisible*, these propositions are to be understood of motion and extension in general, and nevertheless it will not follow that they suggest to my thoughts an idea of motion without a body moved or any determinate direction and velocity, or that I must conceive an abstract general idea of extension, which is neither line, surface, nor solid, neither great nor small, black, white, nor red, nor of any other determinate color. It is only implied that whatever motion I consider, whether it is swift or slow, perpendicular, horizontal, or oblique, or in whatever object, the axiom concerning it holds equally true. As does the other of every particular extension, it does not matter whether line, surface, or solid, whether of this or that magnitude or figure.

12. By observing how ideas become general, we may the better judge how words are made so. And here it is to be noted that I do not deny absolutely there are general ideas, but only that there are any *abstract general ideas*, for, in the passages above quoted, in which there is mention of general ideas, it is always supposed that they are formed by abstraction, after the manner set forth in sec. 8 and 9. Now, if we will annex a meaning to our words and speak only of what we can conceive, I believe we shall acknowledge that an idea, which considered in itself is particular, becomes general by being made to represent or stand for all other particular ideas of the same sort. To make this plain by an example, suppose a geometrician is demonstrating the method of cutting a line in two equal parts. He draws, for instance, a

---

1. [The reference is to John Locke. The two subsequent quotations are from *An Essay Concerning Human Understanding*, Bk. II, ch. XI, secs. 10–11.—S.M.C.]

2. [The quotation is from Locke's *Essay*, Bk. III, ch. III, sec. 6.]

black line of an inch in length; this, which in itself is a particular line, is nevertheless with regard to its signification general, since, as it is used there, it represents all particular lines whatsoever, so that what is demonstrated of it is demonstrated of all lines or, in other words, of a line in general. And as that particular line becomes general by being made a sign, so the name *line*, which, taken absolutely, is particular, by being a sign is made general. And as the former owes its generality not to its being the sign of an abstract or general line, but of all particular right lines that may possibly exist, so the latter must be thought to derive its generality from the same cause, namely, the various particular lines which it indifferently denotes.

13. To give the reader a yet clearer view of the nature of abstract ideas and the uses they are thought necessary to, I shall add one more passage out of the *Essay on Human Understanding*, which is as follows.

"*Abstract ideas* are not so obvious or easy to children or the yet unexercised mind as particular ones. If they seem so to grown men, it is only because by constant and familiar use they are made so. For when we nicely reflect upon them, we shall find that general ideas are fictions and contrivances of the mind that carry difficulty with them, and do not so easily offer themselves as we are apt to imagine. For example, does it not require some pains and skill to form the general idea of a triangle? (which is yet none of the most abstract, comprehensive, and difficult) for it must be neither oblique nor rectangle, neither equilateral, isosceles, nor scalene, but *all and none* of these at once. In effect, it is something imperfect that cannot exist, an idea in which some parts of several different and *inconsistent* ideas are put together. It is true the mind in this imperfect state has need of such ideas, and makes all the haste to them it can, for the convenience of communication and enlargement of knowledge, to both which it is naturally very much inclined. But yet one has reason to suspect such ideas are marks of our imperfection. At least this is enough to show that the most abstract and general ideas are not those that the mind is first and most easily acquainted with, nor such as its earliest knowledge is conversant about." IV, chap. 7, sec. 9.[3]

If any man has the faculty of framing in his mind such an idea of a triangle as is here described, it is

in vain to pretend to dispute him out of it, nor would I go about it. All I desire is that the reader would fully and certainly inform himself whether he has such an idea or not. And this, I think, can be no hard task for anyone to perform. What is more easy than for anyone to look a little into his own thoughts and there try whether he has, or can attain to have, an idea that shall correspond with the description that is here given of the general idea of a triangle, which is *neither oblique, nor rectangle, equilateral, isosceles, nor scalene, but all and none of these at once?*

14. Much is here said of the difficulty that abstract ideas carry with them and the pains and skill requisite to the forming them. And it is on all hands agreed that there is need of great toil and labor of the mind to emancipate our thoughts from particular objects and raise them to those sublime speculations that are conversant about abstract ideas, from all of which the natural consequence should seem to be that so difficult a thing as the forming abstract ideas was not necessary for *communication*, which is so easy and familiar to all sorts of men. But, we are told, if they seem obvious and easy to grown men, *it is only because by constant and familiar use they are made so.* Now I would gladly know at what time it is men are employed in surmounting that difficulty and furnishing themselves with those necessary helps for discourse. It cannot be when they are grown up, for then it seems they are not conscious of any such pains-taking; it remains, therefore, to be the business of their childhood. And surely the great and multiplied labor of framing abstract notions will be found a hard task for that tender age. Is it not a hard thing to imagine that a couple of children cannot chatter together about their sugarplums, and rattles, and the rest of their little trinkets, until they have first tacked together countless inconsistencies and so framed in their minds *abstract general ideas* and annexed them to every common name they make use of?

15. Nor do I think them a whit more needful for the *enlargement of knowledge* than for *communication*. It is, I know, a point much insisted on, that all knowledge and demonstration are about universal notions, to which I fully agree, but then it does not appear to me that those notions are formed by *abstraction* in the manner premised; *universality*, so far as I can comprehend, not consisting in the absolute, positive nature or conception of anything, but in the

3. [Bk. IV, ch. VII, sec. 9.]

relation it bears to the particulars signified or represented by it, by virtue of which it is the case that things, names, or notions, being in their own nature *particular*, are rendered *universal*. Thus, when I demonstrate any proposition concerning triangles, it is to be supposed that I have in view the universal idea of a triangle, which ought not be understood as if I could frame an idea of a triangle which was neither equilateral, nor scalene, nor isosceles, but only that the particular triangle I consider—whether of this or that sort it does not matter—does equally stand for and represent all rectilinear triangles whatsoever, and is in that sense *universal*. All this seems very plain and not to include any difficulty in it.

16. But here it will be demanded how we can know any proposition to be true of all particular triangles, except we have first seen it demonstrated of the abstract idea of a triangle which equally agrees to all? For, because a property may be demonstrated to agree to some one particular triangle, it will not then follow that it equally belongs to any other triangle which in all respects is not the same with it. For example, having demonstrated that the three angles of an isosceles rectangular triangle are equal to two right ones, I cannot therefore conclude this affection agrees to all other triangles, which have neither a right angle nor two equal sides. It seems therefore that to be certain this proposition is universally true we must either make a particular demonstration for every particular triangle, which is impossible, or once and for all demonstrate it of the *abstract idea of a triangle*, in which all the particulars do indifferently partake and by which they are all equally represented. To which I answer that, though the idea I have in view while I make the demonstration is, for instance, that of an isosceles rectangular triangle whose sides are of a determinate length, I may nevertheless be certain it extends to all other rectilinear triangles of whatever sort or bigness—and that because neither the right angle, nor the equality, nor determinate length of the sides are at all concerned in the demonstration. It is true the diagram I have in view includes all these particulars, but then there is not the least mention made of them in the proof of the proposition. It is not said the three angles are equal to two right ones because one of them is a right angle or because the sides comprehending it are of the same length. This sufficiently shows that the right angle might have

been oblique and the sides unequal, and for all that the demonstration has held good. And for this reason it is that I conclude that to be true of any obliquangular or scalene, which I had demonstrated of a particular right-angled, isosceles triangle, and not because I demonstrated the proposition of the abstract idea of a triangle. And here it must be acknowledged that a man may consider a figure merely as triangular, without attending to the particular qualities of the angles or relations of the sides. So far he may abstract, but this will never prove that he can frame an abstract general inconsistent idea of a triangle. In like manner we may consider *Peter* insofar as he is a man or insofar as he is an animal without framing the aforementioned abstract idea either of man or of animal inasmuch as all that is perceived is not considered.

17. It would be an endless as well as a useless thing, to trace the *schoolmen*,[4] those great masters of abstraction, through all the manifold, inextricable labyrinths of error and dispute which their doctrine of abstract natures and notions seems to have led them into. What bickerings and controversies, and what a learned dust has been raised about those matters, and what mighty advantage has been derived to mankind from this, are things at this day too clearly known to need being insisted on. And it had been well if the ill effects of that doctrine were confined to those only who make the most avowed profession of it. When men consider the great pains, industry, and parts that have, for so many ages, been laid out on the cultivation and advancement of the sciences, and that notwithstanding all this the far greater part of them remain full of darkness and uncertainty, and disputes that are likely never to have an end, and even those that are thought to be supported by the most clear and cogent demonstrations, contain in them paradoxes which are perfectly irreconcilable to the understandings of men, and that, taking all together, a small portion of them does supply any real benefit to mankind, otherwise than by being an innocent diversion and amusement—I say, the consideration of all this is apt to throw them into a despondency and perfect contempt of all study. But this may perhaps cease, upon a view of the false principles that have obtained in the world, among

4. [Regarding the term "schoolmen," see Hobbes's *Leviathan*, n. 2.]

all of which there is none, I think, has a more wide influence over the thoughts of speculative men than this of abstract general ideas.

18. I come now to consider the *source* of this prevailing notion, and that seems to me to be language. And surely nothing of less extent than reason itself could have been the source of an opinion so universally received. The truth of this appears as from other reasons so also from the plain confession of the ablest patrons of abstract ideas, who acknowledge that they are made in order to naming—from which it is a clear consequence that if there had been no such thing as speech or universal signs, there never had been any thought of abstraction. See book III, chap. 6, sec. 39, and elsewhere, of the *Essay on Human Understanding*. Let us therefore examine the manner in which words have contributed to the origin of that mistake. First, then, it is thought that every name has, or ought to have, only one precise and settled signification, which inclines men to think there are certain *abstract, determinate ideas*, which constitute the true and only immediate signification of each general name. And that it is by the mediation of these abstract ideas that a general name comes to signify any particular thing. Whereas, in truth, there is no such thing as one precise and definite signification annexed to any general name, they all signifying indifferently a great number of particular ideas—all of which does evidently follow from what has been already said and will clearly appear to anyone by a little reflection. To this it will be objected that every name that has a definition is thereby restrained to one certain signification. For example, a *triangle* is defined to be a *plain surface comprehended by three right lines*, by which that name is limited to denote one certain idea and no other. To this I answer that in the definition it is not said whether the surface is great or small, black or white, nor whether the sides are long or short, equal or unequal, nor with what angles they are inclined to each other, in all of which there may be great variety, and consequently there is no one settled idea which limits the signification of the word *triangle*. It is one thing to keep a name constantly to the same definition and another to make it stand everywhere for the same idea—the one is necessary, the other useless and impracticable.

19. Secondly, but to give a further account how words came to produce the doctrine of abstract ideas,

it must be observed that it is a received opinion that language has no other end but the communicating of our ideas and that every significant name stands for an idea. This being so, and it being in addition certain that names which yet are not thought altogether insignificant do not always mark out particular conceivable ideas, it is straightway concluded that they stand for abstract notions. That there are many names in use among speculative men which do not always suggest to others determinate particular ideas is what nobody will deny. And a little attention will discover that it is not necessary (even in the strictest reasonings) that significant names which stand for ideas should, every time they are used, excite in the understanding the ideas they are made to stand for—in reading and discoursing, names being for the most part used as letters are in *algebra*, in which, though a particular quantity is marked by each letter, yet to proceed right it is not requisite that in every step each letter suggest to your thoughts that particular quantity it was appointed to stand for.

20. Besides, the communicating of ideas marked by words is not the chief and only end of language, as is commonly supposed. There are other ends such as the raising of some passion, the exciting to or deterring from an action, the putting the mind in some particular disposition—to which the former is in many cases barely subservient, and sometimes entirely omitted, when these can be obtained without it, as I think does not infrequently happen in the familiar use of language. I entreat the reader to reflect with himself and see if it does not often happen either in hearing or reading a discourse that the passions of fear, love, hatred, admiration, disdain, and the like, arise immediately in his mind upon the perception of certain words without any ideas coming between. At first, indeed, the words might have occasioned ideas that were fit to produce those emotions; but, if I am not mistaken, it will be found that when language is once grown familiar, the hearing of the sounds or sight of the characters is often immediately attended with those passions which at first were accustomed to be produced by the intervention of ideas that are now quite omitted. May we not, for example, be affected with the promise of a *good thing*, though we do not have an idea of what it is? Or is not being threatened with danger sufficient to excite a dread, though we do not think of any particular evil likely

to befall us, nor yet frame to ourselves an idea of danger in abstract? If anyone shall join ever so little reflection of his own to what has been said, I believe it will evidently appear to him that general names are often used in the propriety of language without the speaker's designing them for marks of ideas in his own which he would have them raise in the mind of the hearer. Even proper names themselves do not seem always spoken with a design to bring into our view the ideas of those individuals that are supposed to be marked by them. For example, when a school-man tells me "Aristotle has said it," all I conceive he means by it is to dispose me to embrace his opinion with the deference and submission which custom has annexed to that name. And this effect may be so instantly produced in the minds of those who are accustomed to resign their judgment to the authority of that philosopher, as it is impossible any idea either of his person, writings, or reputation should go before. Innumerable examples of this kind may be given, but why should I insist on those things which everyone's experience will, I do not doubt, plentifully suggest unto him?

21. We have, I think, shown the impossibility of *abstract ideas*. We have considered what has been said for them by their ablest patrons, and endeavored to show they are of no use for those ends to which they are thought necessary. And lastly, we have traced them to the source from which they flow, which appears to be language. It cannot be denied that words are of excellent use in that by their means all that stock of knowledge which has been purchased by the joint labors of inquisitive men in all ages and nations may be drawn into the view and made the possession of one single person. But at the same time it must be admitted that most parts of knowledge have been strangely perplexed and darkened by the abuse of words and general ways of speech in which they are delivered. Since, therefore, words are so apt to impose on the understanding whatever ideas I consider, I shall endeavor to take them bare and naked into my view, keeping out of my thoughts, so far as I am able, those names which long and constant use has so strictly united with them—from which I may expect to derive the following advantages:

22. First, I shall be sure to get clear of all controversies purely verbal—the springing up of which weeds in almost all the sciences has been a main hindrance

to the growth of true and sound knowledge. Secondly, this seems to be a sure way to extricate myself out of that fine and subtle net of *abstract ideas* which has so miserably perplexed and entangled the minds of men; and that with this peculiar circumstance, that by how much the finer and more curious was the wit of any man, by so much the deeper was he like to be ensnared and faster held there. Thirdly, so long as I confine my thoughts to my own ideas divested of words, I do not see how I can be easily mistaken. The objects I consider I clearly and adequately know. I cannot be deceived in thinking I have an idea which I do not have. It is not possible for me to imagine that any of my own ideas are alike or unlike that are not truly so. To discern the agreements or disagreements that are between my ideas, to see what ideas are included in any compound idea and what not, there is nothing more requisite than an attentive perception of what passes in my own understanding.

23. But the attainment of all these advantages does presuppose an entire deliverance from the deception of words, which I dare hardly promise myself—so difficult a thing it is to dissolve a union so early begun and confirmed by so long a habit as that between words and ideas. This difficulty seems to have been very much increased by the doctrine of *abstraction*. For so long as men thought abstract ideas were annexed to their words, it does not seem strange that they should use words for ideas, it being found an impracticable thing to lay aside the word and retain the abstract idea in the mind, which in itself was perfectly inconceivable. This seems to me the principal cause why those men who have so emphatically recommended to others the laying aside all use of words in their meditations and contemplating their bare ideas have yet failed to perform it themselves. Of late many have been very sensible of the absurd opinions and insignificant disputes which grow out of the abuse of words. And in order to remedy these evils they advise well that we attend to the ideas signified and draw off our attention from the words which signify them. But however good this advice may be they have given others, it is plain they could not have a due regard to it themselves so long as they thought the only immediate use of words was to signify ideas and that the immediate signification of every general name was a *determinate, abstract idea*.

24. But, these being known to be mistakes, a man

may with greater ease prevent his being imposed on by words. He who knows he has no other than *particular* ideas will not puzzle himself in vain to find out and conceive the *abstract* idea annexed to any name. And he who knows names do not always stand for ideas will spare himself the labor of looking for ideas where there are none to be had. It is, therefore, to be wished that everyone would use his utmost endeavors to obtain a clear view of the ideas he would consider, separating from them all that dress and encumbrance of words which so much contribute to blind the judgment and divide the attention. In vain do we extend our view into the heavens and pry into the entrails of the earth, in vain do we consult the writings of learned men and trace the dark footsteps of antiquity; we need only draw the curtain of words to behold the fairest tree of knowledge, whose fruit is excellent and within the reach of our hand.

25. Unless we take care to clear the first principles of knowledge from the embarrassment and delusion of words, we may make infinite reasonings upon them to no purpose; we may draw consequences from consequences and be never the wiser. The further we go, we shall only lose ourselves the more irrecoverably and be the deeper entangled in difficulties and mistakes. Whoever, therefore, designs to read the following sheets, I entreat him to make my words the occasion of his own thinking and endeavor to attain the same train of thoughts in reading that I had in writing them. By this means it will be easy for him to discover the truth or falsity of what I say. He will be out of all danger of being deceived by my words and I do not see how he can be led into an error by considering his own naked, undisguised ideas.

Part I

1. It is evident to anyone who takes a survey of the objects of human knowledge that they are either ideas actually imprinted on the senses or else such as are perceived by attending to the passions and operations of the mind or, lastly, ideas formed by help of memory and imagination, either compounding, dividing, or barely representing those originally perceived in the aforesaid ways. By sight I have the ideas of light and colors with their several degrees and variations. By touch I perceive, for example, hard and soft, heat and cold, motion and resistance, and of all these more

and less either as to quantity or degree. Smelling furnishes me with odors, the palate with tastes, and hearing conveys sounds to the mind in all their variety of tone and composition. And as several of these are observed to accompany each other, they come to be marked by one name, and so to be reputed as one thing. Thus, for example, a certain color, taste, smell, figure, and consistency having been observed to go together are accounted one distinct thing and signified by the name *apple*. Other collections of ideas constitute a stone, a tree, a book, and the like sensible things—which as they are pleasing or disagreeable excite the passions of love, hatred, joy, grief, and so forth.

2. But, besides all that endless variety of ideas or objects of knowledge, there is likewise something which knows or perceives them and exercises various operations as willing, imagining, remembering about them. This perceiving, active being is what I call *mind, spirit, soul,* or *myself,* by which words I do not denote any one of my ideas, but a thing entirely distinct from them, in which they exist or, which is the same thing, by which they are perceived—for the existence of an idea consists in being perceived.

3. That neither our thoughts, nor passions, nor ideas formed by the imagination exist without the mind is what everybody will allow. And (to me) it seems no less evident that the various sensations or ideas imprinted on the sense, however blended or combined together (that is, whatever objects they compose), cannot exist otherwise than in a mind perceiving them. I think an intuitive knowledge may be obtained of this by anyone who shall attend to what is meant by the term *exist* when applied to sensible things. The table I write on, I say, exists; that is, I see and feel it; and if I were out of my study, I should say it existed—meaning by that that if I was in my study I might perceive it, or that some other spirit actually does perceive it. There was an odor; that is, it was smelled; there was a sound, that is to say, it was heard; a color or figure, and it was perceived by sight or touch. This is all that I can understand by these and the like expressions. For as to what is said of the absolute existence of unthinking things without any relation to their being perceived that seems perfectly unintelligible. Their *esse* is *percipi*, nor is it possible they should have any existence out of the minds or thinking things which perceive them.

4. It is indeed an opinion strangely prevailing among men that houses, mountains, rivers, and, in a word, sensible objects have an existence, natural or real, distinct from their being perceived by the understanding. But with however great an assurance and acquiescence this principle may be entertained in the world, yet whoever shall find in his heart to call it in question may, if I am not mistaken, perceive it to involve a manifest contradiction. For what are the aforementioned objects but the things we perceive by sense? And what do we perceive besides our own ideas or sensations? And is it not plainly repugnant that any one of these or any combination of them should exist unperceived?

5. If we thoroughly examine this tenet, it will, perhaps, be found at bottom to depend on the doctrine of *abstract ideas*. For can there be a nicer strain of abstraction than to distinguish the existence of sensible objects from their being perceived, so as to conceive them existing unperceived? Light and colors, heat and cold, extension and figures—in a word, the things we see and feel—what are they but so many sensations, notions, ideas, or impressions on the sense? And is it possible to separate, even in thought, any of these from perception? For my part I might as easily divide a thing from itself. I may indeed divide in my thoughts or conceive apart from each other those things which, perhaps, I never perceived by sense so divided. Thus I imagine the trunk of a human body without the limbs or conceive the smell of a rose without thinking of the rose itself. So far I will not deny I can abstract, if that may properly be called *abstraction* which extends only to the conceiving separately such objects as it is possible may really exist or be actually perceived asunder. But my conceiving or imagining power does not extend beyond the possibility of real existence or perception. Hence, as it is impossible for me to see or feel anything without an actual sensation of that thing, so is it impossible for me to conceive in my thoughts any sensible thing or object distinct from the sensation or perception of it. In truth, the object and the sensation are the same thing and cannot therefore be abstracted from each other.

6. Some truths are so near and obvious to the mind that a man need only open his eyes to see them. Such I take this important one to be, namely, that all the choir of heaven and furniture of the earth, in a word,

all those bodies which compose the mighty frame of the world, do not have any subsistence without a mind—that their being [*esse*] is to be perceived or known, that consequently so long as they are not actually perceived by me or do not exist in my mind or that of any other created spirit, they must either have no existence at all or else subsist in the mind of some eternal spirit—it being perfectly unintelligible and involving all the absurdity of abstraction to attribute to any single part of them an existence independent of a spirit. To be convinced of this, the reader need only reflect and try to separate in his own thoughts the being of a sensible thing from its being perceived.

7. From what has been said it follows there is not any other substance than *spirit*, or that which perceives. But for the fuller proof of this point, let it be considered the sensible qualities are color, figure, motion, smell, taste, and qualities of a similar kind—that is, the ideas perceived by sense. Now for an idea to exist in an unperceiving thing is a manifest contradiction, for to have an idea is all one has to perceive; that, therefore, in which color, figure, and the like qualities exist must perceive them; hence it is clear there can be no unthinking substance or *substratum* of those ideas.

8. But, you say, though the ideas themselves do not exist without the mind, yet there may be things like them of which they are copies or resemblances, which things exist without the mind in an unthinking substance. I answer, an idea can be like nothing but an idea; a color or figure can be like nothing but another color or figure. If we look but ever so little into our thoughts, we shall find it impossible for us to conceive a likeness except only between our ideas. Again, I ask whether those supposed originals or external things of which our ideas are the pictures or representations are themselves perceivable or not? If they are, then they are ideas and we have gained our point; but if you say they are not, I appeal to anyone whether it makes sense to assert a color is like something which is invisible; hard or soft, like something which is intangible; and so of the rest.

9. There are some who make a distinction between *primary* and *secondary* qualities.[5] By the former they

5. [Locke, for example. See his *Essay*, Bk. II, ch. VIII.]

mean extension, figure, motion, rest, solidity or impenetrability, and number; by the latter they denote all other sensible qualities, as colors, sounds, tastes, and so forth. The ideas we have of these they acknowledge not to be the resemblances of anything existing without the mind or unperceived, but they will have our ideas of the primary qualities to be patterns or images of things which exist without the mind, in an unthinking substance which they call matter. By matter therefore we are to understand an inert, senseless substance, in which extension, figure, and motion do actually subsist. But it is evident from what we have already shown that extension, figure, and motion are only ideas existing in the mind, and that an idea can be like nothing but another idea, and that consequently neither they nor their archetypes can exist in an unperceiving substance. Hence it is plain that the very notion of what is called matter, or corporeal substance, involves a contradiction in it.

10. Those who assert that figure, motion, and the rest of the primary or original qualities do exist without the mind in unthinking substances do at the same time acknowledge that colors, sounds, heat, cold, and secondary qualities of a similar kind do not—which they tell us are sensations existing in the mind alone that depend on and are occasioned by the different size, texture, and motion of the minute particles of matter. This they take for an undoubted truth which they can demonstrate beyond all exception. Now, if it is certain that those original qualities are inseparably united with the other sensible qualities and not, even in thought, capable of being abstracted from them, it plainly follows that they exist only in the mind. But I desire anyone to reflect and try whether he can, by any abstraction of thought, conceive the extension and motion of a body without all other sensible qualities. For my own part, I see evidently that it is not in my power to frame an idea of a body extended and moved, but I must in addition give it some color or other sensible quality which is acknowledged to exist only in the mind. In short, extension, figure, and motion, abstracted from all other qualities, are inconceivable. Where, therefore, the other sensible qualities are, these must be also, namely, in the mind and nowhere else.

11. Again, *great* and *small*, *swift* and *slow*, are allowed to exist nowhere without the mind, being entirely relative, and changing as the frame or position of the organs of sense varies. The extension, therefore, which exists without the mind is neither great nor small, the motion neither swift nor slow—that is, they are nothing at all. But, you say, they are extension in general and motion in general; thus we see how much the tenet of extended, moveable substances existing without the mind depends on that strange doctrine of *abstract ideas*. And here I cannot but remark how nearly the vague and indeterminate description of matter or corporeal substance which the modern philosophers are run into by their own principles resembles that antiquated and so much ridiculed notion of *materia prima*, to be met with in *Aristotle* and his followers. Without extension solidity cannot be conceived; since, therefore, it has been shown that extension exists not in an unthinking substance, the same must also be true of solidity.

12. That number is entirely the creature of the mind, even though the other qualities are allowed to exist without, will be evident to whoever considers that the same thing bears a different denomination of number as the mind views it with different respects. Thus, the same extension is one, or three, or thirty-six, according as the mind considers it with reference to a yard, a foot, or an inch. Number is so visibly relative and dependent on men's understanding that it is strange to think how anyone should give it an absolute existence without the mind. We say one book, one page, one line; all these are equally units, though some contain several of the others. And in each instance it is plain the unit relates to some particular combination of ideas arbitrarily put together by the mind.

13. Unity, I know, some[6] will have to be a simple or uncompounded idea accompanying all other ideas into the mind. That I have any such idea answering the word *unity* I do not find; and if I had, I think I could not miss finding it; on the contrary, it should be the most familiar to my understanding, since it is said to accompany all other ideas and to be perceived by all the ways of sensation and reflection. To say no more, it is an *abstract idea*.

14. I shall further add that, after the same manner as modern philosophers prove certain sensible qualities to have no existence in matter, or without the

6. [Locke, for one.]

mind, the same thing may be likewise proved of all other sensible qualities whatsoever. Thus, for instance, it is said that heat and cold are affections only of the mind and not at all patterns of real beings, existing in the corporeal substances which excite them for that the same body which appears cold to one hand seems warm to another. Now, why may we not as well argue that figure and extension are not patterns or resemblances of qualities existing in matter, because to the same eye at different stations, or eyes of a different texture at the same station, they appear various and cannot, therefore, be the images of anything settled and determinate without the mind? Again, it is proved that sweetness is not really in the said thing, because, the thing remaining unaltered, the sweetness is changed into bitter as in case of a fever or otherwise vitiated palate. Is it not as reasonable to say that motion is not without the mind, since if the succession of ideas in the mind becomes swifter, the motion, it is acknowledged, shall appear slower without any alteration in any external object?

15. In short, let anyone consider those arguments which are thought manifestly to prove that colors and tastes exist only in the mind, and he shall find they may with equal force be brought to prove the same thing of extension, figure, and motion. Though it must be confessed this method of arguing does not so much prove that there is no extension or color in an outward object as that we do not know by sense which is the true extension or color of the object. But the previous arguments plainly show it to be impossible that any color or extension at all, or other sensible quality whatsoever, should exist in an unthinking subject without the mind or, in truth, that there should be any such thing as an outward object.

16. But let us examine a little the received opinion. It is said extension is a mode or accident of matter, and that matter is the *substratum* that supports it. Now I desire that you would explain what is meant by matter's *supporting* extension; you say, I have no idea of matter and, therefore, cannot explain it. I answer, though you have no positive, yet if you have any meaning at all, you must at least have a relative idea of matter; though you do not know what it is, yet you must be supposed to know what relation it bears to accidents, and what is meant by its supporting them. It is evident *support* cannot here be taken in its usual or literal sense, as when we say that pillars support a building; in what sense therefore must it be taken?

17. If we inquire into what the most accurate philosophers[7] declare themselves to mean by *material substance*, we shall find them acknowledge they have no other meaning annexed to those sounds but the idea of being in general together with the relative notion of its supporting accidents. The general idea of being appears to me the most abstract and incomprehensible of all others; and as for its supporting accidents, this, as we have just now observed, cannot be understood in the common sense of those words; it must, therefore, be taken in some other sense, but what that is they do not explain. So that when I consider the two parts or branches which make the signification of the words *material substance*, I am convinced there is no distinct meaning annexed to them. But why should we trouble ourselves any further in discussing this material *substratum* or support of figure and motion and other sensible qualities? Does it not suppose they have an existence without the mind? And is not this a direct repugnance and altogether inconceivable?

18. But though it is possible that solid, figured, moveable substances may exist without the mind corresponding to the ideas we have of bodies, yet how is it possible for us to know this? Either we must know it by sense or by reason. As for our senses, by them we have knowledge only of our sensations, ideas, or those things that are immediately perceived by sense, call them what you will; but they do not inform us that things exist without the mind, or unperceived, like those which are perceived. This the materialists themselves acknowledge. It remains, therefore, that if we have any knowledge at all of external things, it must be by reason, inferring their existence from what is immediately perceived by sense. But what reason can induce us to believe the existence of bodies without the mind from what we perceive, since the very patrons of matter themselves do not pretend there is any necessary connection between them and our ideas? I say it is granted on all hands (and what happens in dreams, frenzies, and the like, puts it beyond dispute) that it is possible we might be affected with all the ideas we have now, though no bodies

7. [The reference is again to Locke. See his *Essay*, Bk. II, ch. XXIII, sec. 2.]

resembling them existed without. Hence it is evident the supposition of external bodies is not necessary for the producing our ideas, since it is granted they are produced sometimes and might possibly be produced always in the same order we see them in at present without their concurrence.

19. But though we might possibly have all our sensations without them, yet perhaps it may be thought easier to conceive and explain the manner of their production by supposing external bodies in their likeness rather than otherwise; and so it might be at least probable there are such things as bodies that excite their ideas in our minds. But neither can this be said, for though we give the materialists their external bodies, they by their own confession are never the nearer knowing how our ideas are produced, since they admit themselves unable to comprehend in what manner body can act upon spirit or how it is possible it should imprint any idea in the mind. Hence it is evident the production of ideas or sensations in our minds can be no reason why we should suppose matter or corporeal substances, since that is acknowledged to remain equally inexplicable with or without this supposition. If, therefore, it were possible for bodies to exist without the mind, yet to hold they do so must necessarily be a very precarious opinion, since it is to suppose, without any reason at all, that God has created innumerable beings that are entirely useless and serve to no manner of purpose.

20. In short, if there were external bodies, it is impossible we should ever come to know it; and if there were not, we might have the very same reasons to think there were that we have now. Suppose—what no one can deny possible—an intelligence, without the help of external bodies, to be affected with the same train of sensations or ideas that you are, imprinted in the same order and with like vividness in his mind. I ask whether that intelligence does not have all the reason to believe the existence of corporeal substances, represented by his ideas and exciting them in his mind, that you can possibly have for believing the same thing? Of this there can be no question—this one consideration is enough to make any reasonable person suspect the strength of whatever arguments he may think himself to have for the existence of bodies without the mind.

21. Were it necessary to add any further proof against the existence of matter after what has been said, I could instance several of those errors and difficulties (not to mention impieties) which have sprung from that tenet. It has occasioned countless controversies and disputes in philosophy, and not a few of greater moment in religion. But I shall not enter into the detail of them in this place as well because I think arguments *a posteriori* are unnecessary for confirming what has been, if I am not mistaken, sufficiently demonstrated *a priori*, as because I shall find occasion to say something about them below.

22. I am afraid I have given cause to think me needlessly prolix in handling this subject. For to what purpose is it to dilate on that which may be demonstrated with the utmost evidence in a line or two to anyone who is capable of the least reflection? It is but looking into your own thoughts and so trying whether you can conceive it possible for a sound, or figure, or motion, or color, to exist without the mind or unperceived. This easy trial may make you see that what you contend for is a downright contradiction. Inasmuch as I am content to put the whole upon this issue, if you can but conceive it possible for one extended, moveable substance, or in general, for any one idea, or anything like an idea, to exist otherwise than in a mind perceiving it, I shall readily give up the cause; and as for all that *compages* of external bodies which you contend for, I shall grant you its existence, though you cannot either give me any reason why you believe it exists or assign any use to it when it is supposed to exist. I say the bare possibility of your opinion's being true shall pass for an argument that it is so.

23. But, you say, surely there is nothing easier than to imagine trees, for instance, in a park or books existing in a closet and nobody nearby to perceive them. I answer: you may so, there is no difficulty in it; but what is all this, I beseech you, more than framing in your mind certain ideas which you call *books* and *trees* and at the same time omitting to frame the idea of anyone that may perceive them? But do not you yourself perceive or think of them all the while? This, therefore, is nothing to the purpose; it only shows you have the power of imagining or forming ideas in your mind, but it does not show that you can conceive it possible that the objects of your thought may exist without the mind. To make this out, it is necessary that you conceive them existing unconceived or unthought of, which is a manifest

repugnance. When we do our utmost to conceive the existence of external bodies, we are all the while only contemplating our own ideas. But the mind, taking no notice of itself, is deluded to think it can and does conceive bodies existing unthought of or without the mind, though at the same time they are apprehended by or exist in itself. A little attention will discover to anyone the truth and evidence of what is said here and make it unnecessary to insist on any other proofs against the existence of material substance.

24. It is very obvious, upon the least inquiry into our own thoughts, to know whether it is possible for us to understand what is meant by the *absolute existence of sensible objects in themselves or without the mind*. To me it is evident those words mark out either a direct contradiction or else nothing at all. And to convince others of this, I know no readier or fairer way than to entreat they would calmly attend to their own thoughts; and if by this attention the emptiness or repugnance of those expressions does appear, surely nothing more is requisite for their conviction. It is on this, therefore, that I insist, namely, that "the absolute existence of unthinking things" are words without a meaning or which include a contradiction. This is what I repeat and inculcate, and earnestly recommend to the attentive thoughts of the reader.

25. All our ideas, sensations, or the things which we perceive, by whatever names they may be distinguished, are visibly inactive—there is nothing of power or agency included in them. So that one idea or object of thought cannot produce or make any alteration in another. To be satisfied of the truth of this, there is nothing else requisite but a bare observation of our ideas. For since they and every part of them exist only in the mind, it follows that there is nothing in them but what is perceived. But whoever shall attend to his ideas, whether of sense or reflection, will not perceive in them any power or activity; there is, therefore, no such thing contained in them. A little attention will discover to us that the very being of an idea implies passiveness and inertness in it, inasmuch as it is impossible for an idea to do anything or, strictly speaking, to be the cause of anything; neither can it be the resemblance or pattern of any active being, as is evident from sec. 8. From this it plainly follows that extension, figure, and motion cannot be the cause of our sensations. To say, there-

fore, that these are the effects of powers resulting from the configuration, number, motion, and size of corpuscles must certainly be false.

26. We perceive a continual succession of ideas; some are excited anew, others are changed or totally disappear. There is, therefore, some cause of these ideas on which they depend and which produces and changes them. That this cause cannot be any quality or idea or combination of ideas is clear from the preceding section. It must, therefore, be a substance; but it has been shown that there is no corporeal or material substance. It remains, therefore, that the cause of ideas is an incorporeal active substance or spirit.

27. A spirit is one simple, undivided, active being; as it perceives ideas it is called the *understanding*, and as it produces or otherwise operates about them it is called the *will*. Hence there can be no idea formed of a soul or spirit; for all ideas whatever, being passive and inert (see sec. 25), they cannot represent unto us, by way of image or likeness, that which acts. A little attention will make it plain to anyone that to have an idea which shall be like that active principle of motion and change of ideas is absolutely impossible. Such is the nature of *spirit*, or that which acts, that it cannot be of itself perceived but only by the effects which it produces. If any man shall doubt of the truth of what is here delivered, let him but reflect and try if he can frame the idea of any power or active being, and whether he has ideas of two principal powers marked by the names *will* and *understanding*, distinct from each other as well as from a third idea of substance or being in general, with a relative notion of its supporting or being the subject of the aforesaid powers—which is signified by the name *soul* or *spirit*. This is what some hold; but, so far as I can see, the words *will, soul, spirit* do not stand for different ideas or, in truth, for any idea at all, but for something which is very different from ideas, and which, being an agent, cannot be like or represented by any idea whatsoever—though it must be admitted at the same time that we have some notion of soul, spirit, and the operations of the mind, such as willing, loving, hating, inasmuch as we know or understand the meaning of those words.

28. I find I can excite ideas in my mind at pleasure and vary and shift the scene as often as I think fit. It is no more than willing and straightway this or that

idea arises in my fancy; and by the same power it is obliterated and makes way for another. This making and unmaking of ideas does very properly denominate the mind active. This much is certain and grounded on experience, but when we talk of unthinking agents or of exciting ideas exclusive of volition, we only amuse ourselves with words.

29. But whatever power I may have over my own thoughts, I find the ideas actually perceived by sense do not have a like dependence on my will. When in broad daylight I open my eyes, it is not in my power to choose whether I shall see or not, or to determine what particular objects shall present themselves to my view; and so likewise as to the hearing and other senses—the ideas imprinted on them are not creatures of my will. There is, therefore, some other will or spirit that produces them.

30. The ideas of sense are more strong, lively, and distinct than those of the imagination; they have likewise a steadiness, order, and coherence and are not excited at random as those which are the effects of human wills often are, but in a regular train or series, the admirable connection of which sufficiently testifies to the wisdom and benevolence of its author. Now the set rules or established methods in which the mind we depend on excites in us the ideas of sense are called the *laws of nature*; and these we learn by experience, which teaches us that such and such ideas are attended with such and such other ideas in the ordinary course of things.

31. This gives us a sort of foresight which enables us to regulate our actions for the benefit of life. And without this we should be eternally at a loss; we could not know how to do anything that might procure us the least pleasure or remove the least pain of sense. That food nourishes, sleep refreshes, and fire warms us; that to sow in the seedtime is the way to reap in the harvest; and, in general, that to obtain such or such ends, such or such means are conducive—all this we know, not by discovering any necessary connection between our ideas, but only by the observa-tion of the settled laws of nature, without which we should be all in uncertainty and confusion and a grown man would no more know how to manage himself in the affairs of life than an infant just born.

32. And yet this consistent, uniform working which so evidently displays the goodness and wisdom of that governing Spirit whose will constitutes the laws of nature is so far from leading our thoughts to him that it rather sends them wandering after second causes. For when we perceive certain ideas of sense constantly followed by other ideas and we know this is not of our own doing, we immediately attribute power and agency to the ideas themselves and make one the cause of another, than which nothing can be more absurd and unintelligible. Thus, for example, having observed that when we perceive by sight a certain round luminous figure, we at the same time perceive by touch the idea or sensation called *heat*, we do conclude from this the sun to be the cause of heat. And in like manner perceiving the motion and collision of bodies to be attended with sound, we are inclined to think the latter an effect of the former.

33. The ideas imprinted on the senses by the author of nature are called *real things*; and those excited in the imagination, being less regular, vivid, and constant, are more properly termed *ideas*, or *images of things* which they copy and represent. But then our sensations, be they never so vivid and distinct, are nevertheless *ideas*; that is, they exist in the mind or are perceived by it as truly as the ideas of its own framing. The ideas of sense are allowed to have more reality in them, that is, to be more strong, orderly, and coherent than the creatures of the mind, but this is no argument that they exist without the mind. They are also less dependent on the spirit, or thinking substance which perceives them in that they are excited by the will of another and more powerful spirit, yet still they are *ideas*; and certainly no *idea*, whether faint or strong, can exist otherwise than in a mind perceiving it.

Three Dialogues

Between
Hylas and Philonous,
in Opposition to Skeptics and Atheists

THE FIRST DIALOGUE

PHILONOUS: Good morning, Hylas; I did not expect to find you up so early.

HYLAS: It is indeed something unusual, but my thoughts were so taken up with a subject I was discoursing of last night that, finding I could not sleep, I resolved to rise and take a turn in the garden.

P: It happened well to let you see what innocent and agreeable pleasures you lose every morning. Can there be a pleasanter time of the day, or a more delightful season of the year? That purple sky, those wild but sweet notes of birds, the fragrant bloom upon the trees and flowers, the gentle influence of the rising sun, these and a thousand nameless beauties of nature inspire the soul with secret transports; its faculties too being at this time fresh and lively are fit for these meditations, which the solitude of a garden and tranquillity of the morning naturally dispose us to. But I am afraid I interrupt your thoughts, for you seemed very intent on something.

H: It is true, I was, and shall be obliged to you if you will permit me to go on in the same vein; not that I would by any means deprive myself of your company, for my thoughts always flow more easily in conversation with a friend than when I am alone, but my request is that you would allow me to impart my reflections to you.

P: With all my heart, it is what I should have requested myself, if you had not prevented me.

H: I was considering the odd fate of those men who have in all ages, through an affectation of being distinguished from the vulgar — or some unaccount-

able turn of thought — pretended either to believe nothing at all or to believe the most extravagant things in the world. This, however, might be borne, if their paradoxes and skepticism did not draw after them some consequences of general disadvantage to mankind. But the mischief lies here, that when men of less leisure see them who are supposed to have spent their whole time in the pursuits of knowledge, professing an entire ignorance of all things or advancing such notions as are repugnant to plain and commonly received principles, they will be tempted to entertain suspicions concerning the most important truths, which they had up to now held sacred and unquestionable.

P: I entirely agree with you as to the ill tendency of the affected doubts of some philosophers and fantastic conceits of others. I am even so far gone of late in this way of thinking that I have discarded several of the sublime notions I had got in their schools for vulgar opinions. And I give it you on my word, since this revolt from metaphysical notions to the plain dictates of nature and common sense, I find my understanding strangely enlightened so that I can now easily comprehend a great many things which before were all mystery and riddle.

H: I am glad to find there was nothing in the accounts I heard of you.

P: Pray, what were those?

H: You were represented in last night's conversation as one who maintained the most extravagant opinion that ever entered into the mind of man, namely, that there is no such thing as *material substance* in the world.

P: That there is no such thing as what philosophers call *material substance*, I am seriously persuaded, but if I were made to see anything absurd or

From *The Works of George Berkeley*, ed. G. N. Wright (London, 1843), 2 vols., English, modified.

skeptical in this, I should then have the same reason to renounce this, that I imagine I have now to reject the contrary opinion.

H: What! Can anything be more fantastic, more repugnant to common sense, or a more manifest piece of skepticism, than to believe there is no such thing as *matter*?

P: Softly, good Hylas. What if it should prove that you, who hold there is, are by virtue of that opinion a greater skeptic and maintain more paradoxes and repugnancies to common sense than I who believe no such thing?

H: You may as soon persuade me the part is greater than the whole, as that, in order to avoid absurdity and skepticism, I should ever be obliged to give up my opinion in this point.

P: Well then, are you content to admit that opinion for true which upon examination shall appear most agreeable to common sense and remote from skepticism?

H: With all my heart. Since you are for raising disputes about the plainest things in nature, I am content for once to hear what you have to say.

P: Pray, Hylas, what do you mean by a *skeptic*?

H: I mean what all men mean, one that doubts of everything.

P: He then who entertains no doubt concerning some particular point, with regard to that point, cannot be thought a *skeptic*.

H: I agree with you.

P: Whether doubting consists in embracing the affirmative or negative side of a question?

H: In neither; for whoever understands English cannot but know that *doubting* signifies a suspense between both.

P: He then who denies any point can no more be said to doubt of it than he who affirms it with the same degree of assurance.

H: True.

P: And, consequently, in this case his denial is no more to be esteemed *skeptical* than the other.

H: I acknowledge it.

P: How does it come to pass then, Hylas, that you pronounce me a *skeptic*, because I deny what you affirm, namely, the existence of matter? Since, for all you can tell, I am as peremptory in my denial as you in your affirmation.

H: Hold on, Philonous, I have been a little out in my definition, but every false step a man makes in discourse is not to be insisted on. I said, indeed, that a *skeptic* was one who doubted of everything, but I should have added: or who denies the reality and truth of things.

P: What things? Do you mean the principles and theorems of sciences? But these you know are universal intellectual notions and consequently independent of matter; the denial of this therefore does not imply denying them.

H: I grant it. But are there no other things? What do you think of distrusting the senses, of denying the real existence of sensible things, or pretending to know nothing of them? Is not this sufficient to call a man a *skeptic*?

P: Shall we therefore examine which of us it is that denies the reality of sensible things or professes the greatest ignorance of them, since, if I take you rightly, he is to be esteemed the greatest *skeptic*?

H: That is what I desire.

P: What do you mean by sensible things?

H: Those things which are perceived by the senses. Can you imagine that I mean anything else?

P: Pardon me, Hylas, if I am desirous clearly to apprehend your notions, since this may much shorten our inquiry. Allow me then to ask you this further question. Are those things only perceived by the senses which are perceived immediately? Or may those things properly be said to be *sensible* which are perceived mediately or not without the intervention of others?

H: I do not sufficiently understand you.

P: In reading a book, what I immediately perceive are the letters, but mediately, or by means of these, are suggested to my mind the notions of God, virtue, truth, etc. Now that the letters are truly sensible things, or perceived by sense, there is no doubt; but I would like to know whether you take the things suggested by them to be so too.

H: No, certainly, it would be absurd to think *God* or *virtue* sensible things, though they may be signified and suggested to the mind by sensible marks with which they have an arbitrary connection.

P: It seems then, that by *sensible things* you mean those only which can be perceived immediately by sense.

H: Right.

P: Does it not follow from this that though I see one part of the sky red, and another blue, and that my reason does then evidently conclude there must be some cause of that diversity of colors, yet that cause cannot be said to be a sensible thing or perceived by the sense of seeing?

H: It does.

P: In like manner, though I hear a variety of sounds, yet I cannot be said to hear the causes of those sounds.

H: You cannot.

P: And when by my touch I perceive a thing to be hot and heavy, I cannot say with any truth or propriety that I feel the cause of its heat or weight.

H: To prevent any more questions of this kind, I tell you once and for all that by *sensible things* I mean those only which are perceived by sense and that in truth the senses perceive nothing which they do not perceive immediately, for they make no inferences. The deducing therefore of causes or occasions from effects and appearances, which alone are perceived by sense, entirely relates to reason.

P: This point then is agreed between us—that *sensible things are those only which are immediately perceived by sense*. You will further inform me whether we immediately perceive by sight anything besides light, and colors, and figures; or by hearing anything but sounds; by the palate, anything besides tastes; by the smell, besides odors; or by the touch, more than tangible qualities.

H: We do not.

P: It seems, therefore, that if you take away all sensible qualities, there remains nothing sensible.

H: I grant it.

P: Sensible things therefore are nothing else but so many sensible qualities or combinations of sensible qualities.

H: Nothing else.

P: Heat then is a sensible thing.

H: Certainly.

P: Does the reality of sensible things consist in being perceived? Or, is it something distinct from their being perceived and that bears no relation to the mind?

H: To *exist* is one thing and to be *perceived* is another.

P: I speak with regard to sensible things only; and of these I ask whether by their real existence you mean a subsistence exterior to the mind and distinct from their being perceived?

H: I mean a real absolute being, distinct from and without any relation to their being perceived.

P: Heat, therefore, if it is allowed a real being, must exist without the mind.

H: It must.

P: Tell me, Hylas, is this real existence equally compatible to all degrees of heat which we perceive, or is there any reason why we should attribute it to some and deny it others? And if there is, pray let me know that reason.

H: Whatever degree of heat we perceive by sense, we may be sure the same exists in the object that occasions it.

P: What! The greatest as well as the least?

H: I tell you, the reason is plainly the same in respect of both: They are both perceived by sense; no, the greater degree of heat is more sensibly perceived and, consequently, if there is any difference, we are more certain of its real existence than we can be of the reality of a lesser degree.

P: But is not the most vehement and intense degree of heat a very great pain?

H: No one can deny it.

P: And is any unperceiving thing capable of pain or pleasure?

H: No certainly.

P: Is your material substance a senseless being or a being endowed with sense and perception?

H: It is senseless without doubt.

P: It cannot therefore be the subject of pain.

H: By no means.

P: Nor consequently of the greatest heat perceived by sense, since you acknowledge this to be no small pain.

H: I grant it.

P: What shall we say then of your external object; is it a material substance or not?

H: It is a material substance with the sensible qualities inhering in it.

P: How then can a great heat exist in it, since you admit it cannot in a material substance? I desire you would clear this point.

H: Hold on, Philonous, I fear I was wrong in yielding intense heat to be a pain. It should seem rather that pain is something distinct from heat and the consequence or effect of it.

P: Upon putting your hand near the fire, do you perceive one simple uniform sensation or two distinct sensations?

H: But one simple sensation.

P: Is not the heat immediately perceived?

H: It is.

P: And the pain?

H: True.

P: Seeing therefore they are both immediately perceived at the same time and the fire affects you only with one simple or uncompounded idea, it follows that this same simple idea is both the intense heat immediately perceived and the pain, and, consequently, that the intense heat immediately perceived is nothing distinct from a particular sort of pain.

H: It seems so.

P: Again, try in your thoughts, Hylas, if you can conceive a vehement sensation to be without pain or pleasure.

H: I cannot.

P: Or can you frame to yourself an idea of sensible pain or pleasure in general, abstracted from every particular idea of heat, cold, tastes, smells, etc.?

H: I do not find that I can.

P: Does it not therefore follow that sensible pain is nothing distinct from those sensations or ideas in an intense degree?

H: It is undeniable, and, to speak the truth, I begin to suspect a very great heat cannot exist but in a mind perceiving it.

P: What! Are you then in that *skeptical* state of suspense between affirming and denying?

H: I think I may be positive in the point. A very violent and painful heat cannot exist without the mind.

P: It does not, therefore, according to you, have any real being.

H: I admit it.

P: Is it therefore certain that there is no body in nature really hot?

H: I have not denied there is any real heat in bodies. I only say there is no such thing as an intense real heat.

P: But did you not say before that all degrees of heat were equally real or, if there was any difference, that the greater would be more undoubtedly real than the lesser?

H: True, but it was because I did not then con-sider the ground there is for distinguishing between them which I now plainly see. And it is this: Because intense heat is nothing else but a particular kind of painful sensation and pain cannot exist but in a perceiving being, it follows that no intense heat can really exist in an unperceiving corporeal substance. But this is no reason why we should deny heat in an inferior degree to exist in such a substance.

P: But how shall we be able to discern those degrees of heat which exist only in the mind, from those which exist without it?

H: That is no difficult matter. You know the least pain cannot exist unperceived; therefore, whatever degree of heat is a pain exists only in the mind. But as for all other degrees of heat nothing obliges us to think the same of them.

P: I think you granted before that no unperceiving being was capable of pleasure any more than of pain.

H: I did.

P: And is not warmth, or a more gentle degree of heat than what causes uneasiness, a pleasure?

H: What then?

P: Consequently, it cannot exist without the mind in any unperceiving substance or body.

H: So it seems.

P: Since, therefore, those degrees of heat that are not painful as well as those that are can exist only in a thinking substance, may we not conclude that external bodies are absolutely incapable of any degree of heat whatsoever?

H: On second thought, I do not think it so evident that warmth is a pleasure as that a great degree of heat is a pain.

P: I do not pretend that warmth is as great a pleasure as heat is a pain. But if you grant it to be even a small pleasure, it serves to make good my conclusion.

H: I could rather call it an *indolence*. It seems to be nothing more than a privation of both pain and pleasure. And that such a quality or state as this may agree to an unthinking substance, I hope you will not deny.

P: If you are resolved to maintain that warmth, or a gentle degree of heat, is no pleasure, I do not know how to convince you otherwise than by appealing to your own sense. But what do you think of cold?

H: The same that I do of heat. An intense degree

of cold is a pain, for to feel a very great cold is to perceive a great uneasiness; it cannot, therefore, exist without the mind, but a lesser degree of cold may as well as a lesser degree of heat.

P: Those bodies, therefore, upon whose application to our own we perceive a moderate degree of heat, must be concluded to have a moderate degree of heat or warmth in them; and those, upon whose application we feel a like degree of cold, must be thought to have cold in them.

H: They must.

P: Can any doctrine be true that necessarily leads a man into an absurdity?

H: Without doubt it cannot.

P: Is it not an absurdity to think that the same thing should be at the same time both cold and warm?

H: It is.

P: Suppose now one of your hands hot, and the other cold, and that they are both at once put into the same vessel of water in an intermediate state; will not the water seem cold to one hand and warm to the other?

H: It will.

P: Ought we not therefore by your principles conclude: It is really both cold and warm at the same time, that is, according to your own concession, believe an absurdity?

H: I confess it seems so.

P: Consequently, the principles themselves are false, since you have granted that no true principle leads to an absurdity.

H: But, after all, can anything be more absurd than to say *there is no heat in the fire?*

P: To make the point still clearer, tell me whether in two cases exactly alike we ought not make the same judgment?

H: We ought.

P: When a pin pricks your finger, does it not rend and divide the fibers of your flesh?

H: It does.

P: And when a coal burns your finger, does it do so any more?

H: It does not.

P: Since, therefore, you neither judge the sensation itself occasioned by the pin, nor anything like it to be in the pin, you should not, conformably to what you have now granted, judge the sensation occasioned by the fire, or anything like it, to be in the fire.

H: Well, since it must be so, I am content to yield this point and acknowledge that heat and cold are only sensations existing in our minds, but there still remain qualities enough to secure the reality of external things.

P: But what will you say, Hylas, if it shall appear that the case is the same with regard to all other sensible qualities and that they can no more be supposed to exist without the mind than heat and cold?

H: Then indeed you will have done something to the purpose, but that is what I despair of seeing proved.

P: Let us examine them in order. What think you of tastes—do they exist without the mind or not?

H: Can any man in his senses doubt whether sugar is sweet or wormwood bitter?

P: Inform me, Hylas. Is a sweet taste a particular kind of pleasure or pleasant sensation, or is it not?

H: It is.

P: And is not bitterness some kind of uneasiness or pain?

H: I grant it.

P: If therefore sugar and wormwood are unthinking corporeal substances existing without the mind, how can sweetness and bitterness, that is, pleasure and pain, agree to them?

H: Hold on, Philonous, I now see what deluded me all this time. You asked whether heat and cold, sweetness and bitterness, were not particular sorts of pleasure and pain—to which I answered simply that they were. Whereas I should have distinguished thus: Those qualities, as perceived by us, are pleasures or pains, but not as existing in the external objects. We must not, therefore, conclude absolutely that there is no heat in the fire or sweetness in the sugar, but only that heat or sweetness, as perceived by us, is not in the fire or sugar. What do you say to this?

P: I say it is nothing to the purpose. Our discourse proceeded altogether concerning sensible things, which you defined to be the things we *immediately perceive by our senses.* Therefore, whatever other qualities you speak of as distinct from these, I know nothing of them, nor do they at all belong to the point in dispute. You may indeed pretend to have discovered certain qualities which you do not perceive and assert those insensible qualities exist in fire and sugar. But what use can be made of this to your present purpose, I am at a loss to conceive. Tell me then once more—

do you acknowledge that heat and cold, sweetness and bitterness (meaning those qualities which are perceived by the senses), do not exist without the mind?

H: I see it is to no purpose to hold out, so I give up the cause as to those mentioned qualities. Though I profess it sounds odd to say that sugar is not sweet.

P: But for your further satisfaction, take this along with you: That which at other times seems sweet shall to a distempered palate appear bitter. And nothing can be plainer than that various persons perceive different tastes in the same food, since that which one man delights in, another abhors. And how could this be, if the taste was something really inherent in the food?

H: I acknowledge I do not know how.

P: In the next place, odors are to be considered. And with regard to these, I would gladly know whether what has been said of tastes does not exactly agree to them? Are they not so many pleasing or displeasing sensations?

H: They are.

P: Can you then conceive it possible that they should exist in an unperceiving thing?

H: I cannot.

P: Or can you imagine that filth and garbage affect those brute animals that feed on them out of choice with the same smells which we perceive in them?

H: By no means.

P: May we not therefore conclude of smells, as of the other aforementioned qualities, that they cannot exist in any but a perceiving substance or mind?

H: I think so.

P: Then as to sounds, what must we think of them—are they accidents really inherent in external bodies or not?

H: That they do not inhere in the sonorous bodies is plain from this: because a bell struck in the exhausted receiver of an air pump sends forth no sound. The air, therefore, must be thought the subject of sound.

P: What reason is there for that, Hylas?

H: Because, when any motion is raised in the air, we perceive a greater or lesser sound in proportion to the air's motion, but without some motion in the air we never hear any sound at all.

P: And granting that we never hear a sound but when some motion is produced in the air, yet I do not see how you can infer from this that the sound itself is in the air.

H: It is this very motion in the external air that produces in the mind the sensation of *sound*. For striking on the drum of the ear, it causes a vibration, which, being communicated to the brain by the auditory nerves, then affects the soul with the sensation called sound.

P: What! Is sound then a sensation?

H: I tell you, as perceived by us, it is a particular sensation in the mind.

P: And can any sensation exist without the mind?

H: No, certainly.

P: How then can sound, being a sensation, exist in the air if by the air you mean a senseless substance existing without the mind.

H: You must distinguish, Philonous, between sound as it is perceived by us and as it is in itself, or (which is the same thing) between the sound we immediately perceive and that which exists without us. The former indeed is a particular kind of sensation, but the latter is merely a vibrational or undulatory motion in the air.

P: I thought I had already obviated that distinction by the answer I gave when you were applying it in a like case before. But, to say no more of that, are you sure then that sound is really nothing but motion?

H: I am.

P: Whatever therefore agrees to real sound may with truth be attributed to motion.

H: It may.

P: It is then good sense to speak of *motion*, as of a thing that is *loud, sweet, acute,* or *grave*.

H: I see you are resolved not to understand me. Is it not evident those accidents or modes belong only to sensible sound, or *sound* in the common meaning of the word, but not to *sound* in the real and philosophic sense, which, as I just now told you, is nothing but a certain motion of the air?

P: It seems then there are two sorts of sound, the one vulgar, or that which is heard, the other philosophical and real.

H: Even so.

P: And the latter consists in motion.

H: I told you so before.

P: Tell me, Hylas, to which of the senses, do you think, the idea of motion belongs—to the hearing?

H: No, certainly, but to the sight and touch.

P: It should follow then, that according to you, real sounds may possibly be *seen* or *felt*, but never *heard*.

H: Look, Philonous, you may if you please make a jest of my opinion, but that will not alter the truth of things. I admit, indeed, the inferences you draw me into sound something odd, but common language, you know, is framed by and for the use of the vulgar. We must not therefore wonder if expressions adapted to exact philosophic notions seem uncouth and out of the way.

P: Is it come to that? I assure you, I imagine myself to have gained no small point, since you make so light of departing from common phrases and opinions, it being a main part of our inquiry to examine whose notions are widest of the common road and most repugnant to the general sense of the world. But can you think it no more than a philosophical paradox to say that *real sounds are never heard* and that the idea of them is obtained by some other sense. And is there nothing in this contrary to nature and the truth of things?

H: To deal ingenuously, I do not like it. And after the concessions already made, I granted as well that sounds too have no real being without the mind.

P: And I hope you will make no difficulty to acknowledge the same of colors.

H: Pardon me, the case of colors is very different. Can anything be plainer than that we see them on the objects?

P: The objects you speak of are, I suppose, corporeal substances existing without the mind.

H: They are.

P: And have true and real colors inhering in them?

H: Each visible object has that color which we see in it.

P: How! Is there anything visible but what we perceive by sight?

H: There is not.

P: And do we perceive anything by sense which we do not perceive immediately?

H: How often must I be obliged to repeat the same thing? I tell you, we do not.

P: Have patience, good Hylas, and tell me once more whether there is anything immediately perceived by the senses except sensible qualities. I know

you asserted there was not, but I would now be informed whether you still persist in the same opinion.

H: I do.

P: Pray, is your corporeal substance either a sensible quality or made up of sensible qualities?

H: What a question that is! Who ever thought it was?

P: My reason for asking was because in saying *each visible object has that color which we see in it*, you make visible objects be corporeal substances, which implies either that corporeal substances are sensible qualities or else that there is something besides sensible qualities perceived by sight; but as this point was formerly agreed between us and is still maintained by you, it is a clear consequence that your corporeal substance is nothing distinct from sensible qualities.

H: You may draw as many absurd consequences as you please and endeavor to perplex the plainest things, but you shall never persuade me out of my senses. I clearly understand my own meaning.

P: I wish you would make me understand it too. But since you are unwilling to have your notion of corporeal substance examined, I shall urge that point no further. Only be pleased to let me know whether the same colors which we see exist in external bodies or some other.

H: The very same.

P: What! Are then the beautiful red and purple we see on yonder clouds really in them? Or do you imagine they have in themselves any other form than that of a dark mist or vapor?

H: I must admit, Philonous, those colors are not really in the clouds as they seem to be at this distance. They are only apparent colors.

P: *Apparent* call you them? How shall we distinguish these apparent colors from real?

H: Very easily. Those are to be thought apparent which, appearing only at a distance, vanish upon a nearer approach.

P: And those, I suppose, are to be thought real which are discovered by the most near and exact survey.

H: Right.

P: Is the nearest and most exact survey made by the help of a microscope or by the naked eye?

H: By a microscope, doubtless.

P: But a microscope often discovers colors in an

object different from those perceived by the unassisted sight. And in case we had microscopes magnifying to any assigned degree, it is certain that no object whatsoever viewed through them would appear in the same color which it exhibits to the naked eye.

H: And what will you conclude from all this? You cannot argue that there are really and naturally no colors on objects because they may be altered or made to vanish by artificial managements.

P: I think it may evidently be concluded from your own concessions that all the colors we see with our naked eyes are only apparent as those on the clouds, since they vanish upon a more close and accurate inspection, which is afforded us by a microscope. Then as to what you say by way of prevention, I ask you whether the real and natural state of an object is better discovered by a very sharp and piercing sight or by one which is less sharp.

H: By the former without doubt.

P: Is it not plain from *Dioptrics* that microscopes make the sight more penetrating and represent objects as they would appear to the eye, in case it were naturally endowed with a most exquisite sharpness?

H: It is.

P: Consequently, the microscopic representation is to be thought that which best sets forth the real nature of the thing or what it is in itself. The colors therefore perceived by it are more genuine and real than those perceived otherwise.

H: I confess there is something in what you say.

P: Besides, it is not only possible but manifest that there actually are animals whose eyes are by nature framed to perceive those things which by reason of their minuteness escape our sight. What do you think of those inconceivably small animals perceived by glasses? Must we suppose they are all stark blind? Or, in case they see, can it be imagined their sight does not have the same use in preserving their bodies from injuries which appears in that of all other animals? And if it does, is it not evident they must see particles less than their own bodies, which will present them with a far different view in each object from that which strikes our senses? Even our own eyes do not always represent objects to us after the same manner. With *jaundice*, everyone knows that all things seem yellow. Is it not therefore highly probable that those animals in whose eyes we discern a very different texture from that of ours and whose

bodies abound with different humors, do not see the same colors in every object that we do? From all of which, should it not seem to follow that all colors are equally apparent and that none of those which we perceive are really inherent in any outward object?

H: It should.

P: The point will be past all doubt if you consider that in case colors were real properties or affections inherent in external bodies, they could admit of no alteration without some change made in the very bodies themselves. But is it not evident from what has been said that upon the use of microscopes, upon a change happening in the humors of the eye, or a variation of distance, without any manner of real alteration in the thing itself, the colors of any object are either changed or totally disappear? No, all other circumstances remaining the same, change but the situation of some objects and they shall present different colors to the eye. The same thing happens upon viewing an object in various degrees of light. And what is more known than that the same bodies appear differently colored by candlelight from what they do in the open day? Add to these the experiment of a prism which, separating the heterogeneous rays of light, alters the color of any object and will cause the whitest to appear of a deep blue or red to the naked eye. And now tell me whether you are still of the opinion that every body has its true, real color inhering in it; and if you think it has, I would gladly know further from you what certain distance and position of the object, what peculiar texture and formation of the eye, what degree or kind of light is necessary for ascertaining that true color and distinguishing it from apparent ones.

H: I admit myself entirely satisfied that they are all equally apparent and that there is no such thing as color really inhering in external bodies, but that it is altogether in the light. And what confirms me in this opinion is that, in proportion to the light, colors are still more or less vivid, and if there is no light, then there are no colors perceived. Besides, allowing there are colors on external objects, yet how is it possible for us to perceive them? For no external body affects the mind unless it acts first on our organs of sense. But the only action of bodies is motion, and motion cannot be communicated otherwise than by impulse. A distant object, therefore, cannot act on the eye, nor consequently make itself or its properties perceivable to the soul. From this it plainly follows that it is immediately some contiguous substance which, operating on the eye, occasions a perception of colors—and such is light.

P: How! Is light then a substance?

H: I tell you, Philonous, external light is nothing but a thin fluid substance whose minute particles, being agitated with a brisk motion and in various manners reflected from the different surfaces of outward objects to the eyes, communicate different motions to the optic nerves, which being propagated to the brain, cause various impressions in it; and these are attended with the sensations of red, blue, yellow, etc.

P: It seems, then, the light does no more than shake the optic nerves.

H: Nothing else.

P: And, consequent to each particular motion of the nerves, the mind is affected with a sensation, which is some particular color.

H: Right.

P: And these sensations have no existence without the mind.

H: They do not.

P: How then do you affirm that colors are in the light, since by light you understand a corporeal substance external to the mind?

H: Light and colors, as immediately perceived by us, I grant cannot exist without the mind. But in themselves they are only the motions and configurations of certain insensible particles of matter.

P: Colors then, in the vulgar sense, or taken for the immediate objects of sight, cannot agree to any but a perceiving substance.

H: That is what I say.

P: Well then, since you give up the point as to those sensible qualities which are alone thought colors by all mankind besides, you may hold what you please with regard to those invisible ones of the philosophers. It is not my business to dispute about them; only I would advise you to envision yourself, whether, considering the inquiry we are upon, it would be prudent for you to affirm: *The red and blue which we see are not real colors, but certain unknown motions and figures which no man ever did or can see are truly so.* Are not these shocking notions, and are not they subject to as many ridiculous inferences as those you were obliged to renounce before in the case of sounds?

H: I frankly admit, Philonous, that it is in vain to stand out any longer. Colors, sounds, tastes, in a word, all those termed *secondary qualities*, have certainly no existence without the mind. But by this acknowledgment I must not be supposed to derogate anything from the reality of matter or external objects, seeing it is no more than several philosophers maintain who nevertheless are the furthest imaginable from denying matter. For the clearer understanding of this you must know sensible qualities are by philosophers divided into *primary* and *secondary*.[1] The former are extension, figure, solidity, gravity, motion, and rest. And these they hold exist really in bodies. The latter are those above enumerated or, briefly, all sensible qualities besides the primary, which they assert are only so many sensations or ideas existing nowhere but in the mind. But all this, I do not doubt, you are already apprised of. For my part, I have been a long time sensible there was such an opinion current among philosophers, but was never thoroughly convinced of its truth until now.

P: You are still then of the opinion that extension and figures are inherent in external unthinking substances.

H: I am.

P: But what if the same arguments which are brought against secondary qualities will hold proof against these also?

H: Why then I shall be obliged to think they too exist only in the mind.

P: Is it your opinion that the very figure and extension which you perceive by sense exist in the outward object or material substance?

H: It is.

P: Have all other animals as good grounds to think the same of the figure and extension which they see and feel?

H: Without doubt, if they have any thought at all.

P: Answer me, Hylas. Do you think the senses were bestowed upon all animals for their preservation and well being in life? Or were they given to men alone for this end?

H: I make no question but they have the same use in all other animals.

P: If so, is it not necessary they should be enabled

----

1. [See Locke's Essay, Bk. II, ch. VIII—S.M.C.]

by them to perceive their own limbs and those bodies which are capable of harming them?

H: Certainly.

P: A mite therefore must be supposed to see his own foot, and things equal or even less than it, as bodies of some considerable dimension, though at the same time they appear to you scarce discernible or at best as so many visible points.

H: I cannot deny it.

P: And to creatures less than the mite they will seem yet larger.

H: They will.

P: To the extent that what you can hardly discern will to another extremely minute animal appear as some huge mountain.

H: All this I grant.

P: Can one and the same thing be at the same time in itself of different dimensions?

H: That would be absurd to imagine.

P: But from what you have laid down it follows that both the extension perceived by you and that perceived by the mite itself, as likewise all those perceived by lesser animals, are each of them the true extension of the mite's foot—that is to say, by your own principles you are led into an absurdity.

H: There seems to be some difficulty in the point.

P: Again, have you not acknowledged that no real inherent property of any object can be changed without some change in the thing itself?

H: I have.

P: But as we approach to or recede from an object, the visible extension varies, being at one distance ten or a hundred times greater than at another. Does it not therefore follow from this, likewise, that it is not really inherent in the object?

H: I admit I am at a loss what to think.

P: Your judgment will soon be determined if you will venture to think as freely concerning this quality as you have done concerning the rest. Was it not admitted as a good argument that neither heat nor cold was in the water because it seemed warm to one hand and cold to the other?

H: It was.

P: Is it not the very same reasoning to conclude there is no extension or figure in an object because to one eye it shall seem little, smooth, and round, when at the same time it appears to the other, great, uneven, and angular?

H: The very same. But does this latter fact ever happen?

P: You may at any time make the experiment by looking with one eye bare and with the other through a microscope.

H: I do not know how to maintain it, and yet I am loath to give up *extension*; I see so many odd consequences following upon such a concession.

P: Odd, you say? After the concessions already made, I hope you will stick at nothing for its oddness. But on the other hand should it not seem very odd if the general reasoning which includes all other sensible qualities did not also include extension? If it is allowed that no idea nor anything like an idea can exist in an unperceiving substance, then surely it follows that no figure or mode of extension, which we can either perceive or imagine or have any idea of, can be really inherent in matter—not to mention the peculiar difficulty there must be in conceiving a material substance, prior to and distinct from extension, to be the *substratum* of extension. Whatever the sensible quality is, figure, or sound, or color, it seems equally impossible it should subsist in that which does not perceive it.

H: I give up the point for the present, reserving still a right to retract my opinion, in case I shall hereafter discover any false step in my progress to it.

P: That is a right you cannot be denied. Figures and extension being dispatched, we proceed next to *motion*. Can a real motion in any external body be at the same time both very swift and very slow?

H: It cannot.

P: Is not the motion of a body swift in a reciprocal proportion to the time it takes up in describing any given space? Thus a body that describes a mile in an hour moves three times faster than it would in case it described only a mile in three hours.

H: I agree with you.

P: And is not time measured by the succession of ideas in our minds?

H: It is.

P: And is it not possible ideas should succeed one another twice as fast in your mind as they do in mine or in that of some spirit of another kind?

H: I admit it.

P: Consequently, the same body may to another seem to perform its motion over any space in half the time that it does to you. And the same reasoning will hold as to any other proportion—that is to say, according to your principles (since the motions perceived are both really in the object) it is possible one and the same body shall be really moved the same way at once, both very swift and very slow. How is this consistent either with common sense or with what you just now granted?

H: I have nothing to say to it.

P: Then as for *solidity*, either you do not mean any sensible quality by that word, and so it is beside our inquiry, or if you do, it must be either hardness or resistance. But both the one and the other are plainly relative to our senses, it being evident that what seems hard to one animal may appear soft to another who has greater force and firmness of limbs. Nor is it less plain that the resistance I feel is not in the body.

H: I admit the very sensation of resistance, which is all you immediately perceive, is not in the *body*, but the cause of that sensation is.

P: But the causes of our sensations are not things immediately perceived, and, therefore, not sensible. This point I thought had been already determined.

H: I admit it was, but you will pardon me if I seem a little embarrassed; I do not know how to quit my old notions.

P: To help you out, do but consider that if extension is once acknowledged to have no existence without the mind, the same must necessarily be granted of motion, solidity, and gravity, since they all evidently suppose extension. It is therefore superfluous to inquire particularly concerning each of them. In denying extension, you have denied them all to have any real existence.

H: I wonder, Philonous, if what you say is true, why those philosophers who deny the secondary qualities any real existence should yet attribute it to the primary. If there is no difference between them, how can this be accounted for?

P: It is not my business to account for every opinion of the philosophers. But among other reasons which may be assigned for this, it seems probable that pleasure and pain being annexed to the former rather than the latter may be one. Heat and cold, tastes and smells, have something more vividly pleasing or disagreeable than the ideas of extension, figure, and motion affect us with. And it being too visibly absurd to hold that pain or pleasure can be in an unperceiv-

ing substance, men are more easily weaned from believing the external existence of the secondary than the primary qualities. You will be satisfied there is something in this if you recollect the difference you made between an intense and more moderate degree of heat, allowing the one a real existence, while you denied it to the other. But after all, there is no rational ground for that distinction, for surely an indifferent sensation is as truly *a sensation* as one more pleasing or painful, and consequently should not any more than they be supposed to exist in an unthinking subject.

H: It has just come into my head, Philonous, that I have somewhere heard of a distinction between absolute and sensible extension. Now though it is acknowledged that great and small, consisting merely in the relation which other extended beings have to the parts of our own bodies, do not really inhere in the substances themselves, yet nothing obliges us to hold the same with regard to *absolute extension*, which is something abstracted from *great* and *small*, from this or that particular magnitude or figure. So likewise as to motion, *swift* and *slow* are altogether relative to the succession of ideas in our own minds. But it does not follow, because those modifications of motion do not exist without the mind, that absolute motion abstracted from them therefore does not.

P: Pray what is it that distinguishes one motion or one part of extension from another? Is it not something sensible, as some degree of swiftness or slowness, some certain magnitude or figure peculiar to each?

H: I think so.

P: These qualities, therefore, stripped of all sensible properties, are without all specific and numerical differences, as the schools call them.

H: They are.

P: That is to say, they are extension in general and motion in general.

H: Let it be so.

P: But it is a universally received maxim that *everything which exists is particular*. How then can motion in general or extension in general exist in any corporeal substance?

H: I will take time to solve your difficulty.

P: But I think the point may be speedily decided. Without doubt you can tell whether you are able to frame this or that idea. Now I am content to put our dispute on this issue. If you can frame in your thoughts a distinct abstract idea of motion or extension, divested of all those sensible modes as swift and slow, great and small, round and square, and the like, which are acknowledged to exist only in the mind, I will then yield the point you contend for. But if you cannot, it will be unreasonable on your side to insist any longer upon what you have no notion of.

H: To confess ingenuously, I cannot.

P: Can you even separate the ideas of extension and motion from the ideas of all those qualities which they who make the distinction term *secondary*?

H: What! Is it not an easy matter to consider extension and motion by themselves, abstracted from all other sensible qualities? Pray how do the mathematicians treat of them?

P: I acknowledge, Hylas, it is not difficult to form general propositions and reasonings about those qualities without mentioning any other and in this sense to consider or treat of them abstractly. But how does it follow that because I can pronounce the word *motion* by itself, I can form the idea of it in my mind exclusive of body? Or because theorems may be made of extension and figures without any mention of *great* or *small*, or any other sensible mode or quality, that therefore it is possible such an abstract idea of extension without any particular size or figure, or sensible quality, should be distinctly formed and apprehended by the mind? Mathematicians treat of quantity without regarding what other sensible qualities it is attended with, as being altogether indifferent to their demonstrations. But when, laying aside the words, they contemplate the bare ideas, I believe you will find they are not the pure abstracted ideas of extension.

H: But what do you say to *pure intellect*? May not abstracted ideas be framed by that faculty?

P: Since I cannot frame abstract ideas at all, it is plain I cannot frame them by the help of *pure intellect*, whatever faculty you understand by those words. Besides, not to inquire into the nature of pure intellect and its spiritual objects, as *virtue, reason, God*, or the like—this much seems manifest—that sensible things are only to be perceived by sense or represented by the imagination. Figures, therefore, and extension, being originally perceived by sense, do not belong to pure intellect. But for your further satisfaction, try if you can frame the idea of any figure abstracted from all particularities of size or even from other sensible qualities.

H: Let me think a little—I do not find that I can.

P: And can you think it possible that what implies a repugnance in its conception should really exist in nature?

H: By no means.

P: Since, therefore, it is impossible even for the mind to disunite the ideas of extension and motion from all other sensible qualities, does it not follow that where the one exists, there necessarily the other exists likewise?

H: It should seem so.

P: Consequently, the very same arguments which you admitted as conclusive against the secondary qualities are without any further application of force against the primary too. Besides, if you will trust your senses, is it not plain all sensible qualities coexist or appear to them as being in the same place? Do they ever represent a motion, or figure, as being divested of all other visible and tangible qualities?

H: You need say no more on this head. I am free to admit, if there is no secret error or oversight in our proceedings up to now, that all sensible qualities are alike to be denied existence without the mind. But my fear is that I have been too liberal in my former concessions or overlooked some fallacy or other. In short, I did not take time to think.

P: For that matter, Hylas, you may take what time you please in reviewing the progress of our inquiry. You are at liberty to recover any slips you might have made or offer whatever you have omitted, which makes for your first opinion.

H: One great oversight I take to be this: that I did not sufficiently distinguish the *object* from the *sensation*. Now though this latter may not exist without the mind, yet it will not follow from this that the former cannot.

P: What object do you mean? The object of the senses?

H: The same.

P: It is then immediately perceived?

H: Right.

P: Make me understand the difference between what is immediately perceived and a sensation.

H: The sensation I take to be an act of the mind perceiving, besides which there is something perceived, and this I call the *object*. For example, there is red and yellow on that tulip. But then the act of perceiving those colors is in me only, and not in the tulip.

P: What tulip do you speak of? Is it that which you see?

H: The same.

P: And what do you see besides color, figure, and extension?

H: Nothing.

P: What you would say then is that the red and yellow are coexistent with the extension; is it not?

H: That is not all. I would say they have a real existence without the mind in some unthinking substance.

P: That the colors are really in the tulip, which I see, is manifest. Neither can it be denied that this tulip may exist independent of your mind or mine; but that any immediate object of the senses, that is, any idea or combination of ideas, should exist in an unthinking substance or exterior to all minds, is in itself an evident contradiction. Nor can I imagine how this follows from what you said just now, namely, that the red and yellow were on the tulip *you saw*, since you do not pretend to see that unthinking substance.

H: You have an artful way, Philonous, of diverting our inquiry from the subject.

P: I see you have no mind to be pressed that way. To return then to your distinction between *sensation* and *object*; if I take you right, you distinguish in every perception two things, the one an action of the mind, the other not.

H: True.

P: And this action cannot exist in or belong to any unthinking thing, but whatever besides is implied in a perception, may.

H: That is my meaning.

P: So that if there was a perception without any act of the mind, it was possible such a perception should exist in an unthinking substance.

H: I grant it. But it is impossible there should be such a perception.

P: When is the mind said to be active?

H: When it produces, puts an end to, or changes anything.

P: Can the mind produce, discontinue, or change anything but by an act of the will?

H: It cannot.

P: The mind therefore is to be accounted active in its perceptions, insofar as volition is included in them.

H: It is.

P: In plucking this flower I am active, because I do it by the motion of my hand, which was consequent upon my volition—so likewise in applying it to my nose. But is either of these smelling?

H: No.

P: I act too in drawing the air through my nose, because my breathing so rather than otherwise is the effect of my volition. But neither can this be called *smelling*, for if it were, I should smell every time I breathed in that manner.

H: True.

P: Smelling then is somewhat consequent to all this.

H: It is.

P: But I do not find my will concerned any further. Whatever more there is, as that I perceive such a particular smell or any smell at all, this is independent of my will and I am altogether passive in this. Do you find it otherwise with you, Hylas?

H: No, the very same.

P: Then as to seeing, is it not in your power to open your eyes or keep them shut, to turn them this or that way?

H: Without doubt.

P: But does it in like manner depend on your will that, in looking on this flower, you perceive *white* rather than any other color? Or directing your open eyes towards that part of the heaven beyond, can you avoid seeing the sun? Or is light or darkness the effect of your volition?

H: No, certainly.

P: You are then in these respects altogether passive.

H: I am.

P: Tell me now, whether *seeing* consists in perceiving light and colors or in opening and turning the eyes?

H: Without doubt, in the former.

P: Since, therefore, you are in the very perception of light and colors altogether passive, what has become of that action you were speaking of as an ingredient in every sensation? And does it not follow from your own concessions that the perception of light and colors, including no action in it, may exist in an unperceiving substance? And is this not a plain contradiction?

H: I do not know what to think of it.

P: Besides, since you distinguish the *active* and *passive* in every perception, you must do it in that of pain. But how is it possible that pain — let it be as little active as you please — should exist in an unperceiving substance? In short, do but consider the point and then confess ingenuously whether light and colors, tastes, sounds, etc., are not all equally passions or sensations in the soul. You may indeed call them *external objects* and give them in words what subsistence you please. But examine your own thoughts and then tell me whether it is not as I say?

H: I acknowledge, Philonous, that upon a fair observation of what passes in my mind, I can discover nothing else but that I am a thinking being, affected with variety of sensations; neither is it possible to conceive how a sensation should exist in an unperceiving substance. But then, on the other hand, when I look on sensible things in a different view, considering them as so many modes and qualities, I find it necessary to suppose a material *substratum*, without which they cannot be conceived to exist.

P: *Material substratum* call you it? Pray, by which of your senses did you become acquainted with that being?

H: It is not itself sensible, its modes and qualities only being perceived by the senses.

P: I presume, then, it was by reflection and reason you obtained the idea of it.

H: I do not pretend to any proper positive idea of it. However, I conclude it exists, because qualities cannot be conceived to exist without a support.

P: It seems then you have only a relative notion of it, or that you conceive it not otherwise than by conceiving the relation it bears to sensible qualities.

H: Right.

P: Be pleased, therefore, to let me know in what that relation consists.

H: Is it not sufficiently expressed in the term *substratum* or *substance*?

P: If so, the word *substratum* should import that it is spread under the sensible qualities or accidents.

H: True.

P: And consequently under extension.

H: I admit it.

P: It is therefore somewhat in its own nature entirely distinct from extension.

H: I tell you extension is only a mode, and matter is something that supports modes. And is it not evident the thing supported is different from the thing supporting?

P: So that something distinct from and exclusive of extension is supposed to be the *substratum* of extension.

H: Just so.

P: Answer me, Hylas. Can a thing be spread without extension? Or is not the idea of extension necessarily included in *spreading*?

H: It is.

P: Whatever, therefore, you suppose spread under anything must have in itself an extension distinct from the extension of that thing under which it is spread.

H: It must.

P: Consequently, every corporeal substance being the *substratum* of extension must have in itself another extension by which it is qualified to be a *substratum*, and so on to infinity. And I ask whether this is not absurd in itself and repugnant to what you granted just now, namely, that the *substratum* was something distinct from and exclusive of extension.

H: Yes, but, Philonous, you take me wrong. I do not mean that matter is *spread* in a gross literal sense under extension. The word *substratum* is used only to express in general the same thing with *substance*.

P: Well then, let us examine the relation implied in the term *substance*. Is it not that it stands under accidents?

H: The very same.

P: But that one thing may stand under or support another, must it not be extended?

H: It must.

P: Is not therefore this supposition liable to the same absurdity with the former?

H: You still take things in a strict literal sense; that is not fair, Philonous.

P: I am not for imposing any sense on your words; you are at liberty to explain them as you please. Only I beseech you, make me understand something by them. You tell me matter supports or stands under accidents. How? Is it as your legs support your body?

H: No; that is the literal sense.

P: Pray let me know any sense, literal or not

literal, that you understand it in. How long must I wait for an answer, Hylas?

H: I declare I do not know what to say. I once thought I understood well enough what was meant by matter's supporting accidents. But now the more I think on it, the less can I comprehend it; in short, I find that I know nothing of it.

P: It seems then you have no idea at all, neither relative nor positive, of matter; you know neither what it is in itself nor what relation it bears to accidents.

H: I acknowledge it.

P: And yet you asserted that you could not conceive how qualities or accidents should really exist without conceiving at the same time a material support of them.

H: I did.

P: That is to say, when you conceive the real existence of qualities, you do in addition conceive something which you cannot conceive.

H: It was wrong, I admit. But still I fear there is some fallacy or other. Pray what do you think of this? It has just come into my head that the ground of all our mistake lies in your treating of each quality by itself. Now, I grant that each quality cannot singly subsist without the mind. Color cannot exist without extension, neither can figure without some other sensible quality. But as the several qualities united or blended together form entire sensible things, nothing hinders why such things may not be supposed to exist without the mind.

P: Either, Hylas, you are jesting or have a very bad memory. Though indeed we went through all the qualities by name one after another, yet my arguments, or rather your concessions, nowhere tended to prove that the secondary qualities did not subsist each alone by itself, but that they were not *at all* without the mind. Indeed in treating of figure and motion, we concluded they could not exist without the mind because it was impossible even in thought to separate them from all secondary qualities so as to conceive them existing by themselves. But then this was not the only argument made use of upon that occasion. But (to pass by all that has been said up to now, and reckon it for nothing, if you will have it so) I am content to put the whole upon this issue. If you can conceive it possible for any mixture or combination of qualities or any sensible object whatever to exist without the mind, then I will grant it actually to be so.

H: If it comes to that, the point will soon be decided. What is more easy than to conceive a tree or house existing by itself, independent of, and unperceived by any mind whatsoever? I do at this present time conceive them existing after that manner.

P: What are you saying, Hylas—can you see a thing which is at the same time unseen?

H: No, that would be a contradiction.

P: Is it not as great a contradiction to talk of *conceiving* a thing which is *unconceived*?

H: It is.

P: The tree or house, therefore, which you think of is conceived by you.

H: How should it be otherwise?

P: And what is conceived is surely in the mind.

H: Without question, that which is conceived is in the mind.

P: How then did you come to say you conceived a house or tree existing independent and out of all minds whatsoever?

H: That was, I admit, an oversight; but stay, let me consider what led me into it. It is a pleasant mistake enough. As I was thinking of a tree in a solitary place where no one was present to see it, I thought that was to conceive a tree as existing unperceived or unthought of, not considering that I myself conceived it all the while. But now I plainly see that all I can do is to frame ideas in my own mind. I may indeed conceive in my own thoughts the idea of a tree, or a house, or a mountain, but that is all. And this is far from proving that I can conceive them *existing out of the minds of all spirits*.

P: You acknowledge then that you cannot possibly conceive how any one corporeal sensible thing should exist otherwise than in a mind.

H: I do.

P: And yet you will earnestly contend for the truth of that which you cannot so much as conceive.

H: I profess I do not know what to think, but still some scruples remain with me. Is it not certain I see things at a distance? Do we not perceive the stars and moon, for example, to be a great way off? Is this not, I say, manifest to the senses?

P: Do you not in a dream too perceive those or the like objects?

H: I do.

P: And do they not then have the same appearance of being distant?

H: They have.

P: But you do not then conclude the apparitions in a dream to be without the mind?

H: By no means.

P: You ought not therefore conclude that sensible objects are without the mind from their appearance or manner in which they are perceived.

H: I acknowledge it. But does not my sense deceive me in those cases?

P: By no means. Of the idea or thing which you immediately perceive, neither sense nor reason informs you that it actually exists without the mind. By sense you only know that you are affected with such certain sensations of light and colors, etc. And these you will not say are without the mind.

H: True, but besides all that, do you not think the sight suggests something of *outness* or *distance*?

P: Upon approaching a distant object, do the visible size and figure change perpetually or do they appear the same at all distances?

H: They are in a continual change.

P: Sight, therefore, does not suggest or in any way inform you that the visible object you immediately perceive exists at a distance or will be perceived when you advance further onward, there being a continued series of visible objects succeeding each other during the whole time of your approach.

H: It does not; but still I know, upon seeing an object, what object I shall perceive after having passed over a certain distance—no matter whether it be exactly the same or no—there is still something of distance suggested in the case.

P: Good Hylas, do but reflect a little on the point and then tell me whether there is any more in it than this: From the ideas you actually perceive by sight, you have by experience learned to collect what other ideas you will (according to the standing order of nature) be affected with, after such a certain succession of time and motion.

H: Upon the whole, I take it to be nothing else.

P: Now is it not plain that if we suppose a man born blind was suddenly made to see, he could at first have no experience of what may be suggested by sight?

H: It is.

P: He would not then, according to you, have any notion of distance annexed to the things he saw; but would take them for a new set of sensations existing only in his mind.

H: It is undeniable.

P: But to make it still more plain: is not *distance* a line turned endwise to the eye?

H: It is.

P: And can a line so situated be perceived by sight?

H: It cannot.

P: Does it not therefore follow that distance is not properly and immediately perceived by sight?

H: It should seem so.

P: Again, is it your opinion that colors are at a distance?

H: It must be acknowledged they are only in the mind.

P: But do not colors appear to the eye as coexisting in the same place with extension and figures?

H: They do.

P: How can you then conclude from sight that figures exist without, when you acknowledge colors do not, the sensible appearance being the very same with regard to both?

H: I do not know what to answer.

P: But allowing that distance was truly and immediately perceived by the mind, yet it would not then follow it existed out of the mind. For whatever is immediately perceived is an idea; and can any idea exist out of the mind?

H: To suppose that would be absurd, but inform me, Philonous, can we perceive or know nothing besides our ideas?

P: As for the rational deducing of causes from effects, that is besides our inquiry. And by the senses you can best tell whether you perceive anything which is not immediately perceived. And I ask you whether the things immediately perceived are other than your own sensations or ideas? You have indeed more than once, in the course of this conversation, declared yourself on those points; but you seem, by this last question, to have departed from what you then thought.

H: To speak the truth, Philonous, I think there are two kinds of objects, the one perceived immediately, which are likewise called ideas, the other are real things or external objects perceived by the mediation of ideas, which are their images and representations. Now I admit ideas do not exist without the mind, but the latter sort of object does. I am sorry I did not think of this distinction sooner; it would probably have cut short your discourse.

P: Are those external objects perceived by sense or by some other faculty?

H: They are perceived by sense.

P: How! Is there anything perceived by sense which is not immediately perceived?

H: Yes, Philonous, in some sort there is. For example, when I look on a picture or statue of Julius Caesar, I may be said, after a manner, to perceive him (though not immediately) by my senses.

P: It seems then you will have our ideas, which alone are immediately perceived, to be pictures of external things, and that these also are perceived by sense inasmuch as they have a conformity or resemblance to our ideas.

H: That is my meaning.

P: And in the same way that Julius Caesar, in himself invisible, is nevertheless perceived by sight; real things, in themselves imperceptible, are perceived by sense.

H: In the very same.

P: Tell me, Hylas, when you behold the picture of Julius Caesar, do you see with your eyes any more than some colors and figures, with a certain symmetry and composition of the whole?

H: Nothing else.

P: And would not a man who had never known anything of Julius Caesar see as much?

H: He would.

P: Consequently, he has his sight and the use of it in as perfect a degree as you.

H: I agree with you.

P: From where does it come then that your thoughts are directed to the Roman emperor and his are not? This cannot proceed from the sensations or ideas of sense by you then perceived, since you acknowledge you have no advantage over him in that respect. It should seem therefore to proceed from reason and memory, should it not?

H: It should.

P: Consequently, it will not follow from that instance that anything is perceived by sense which is not immediately perceived. Though I grant we may in one meaning be said to perceive sensible things mediately by sense, that is, when, from a frequently perceived connection, the immediate perception of ideas by one sense suggests to the mind others perhaps belonging to another sense which are accustomed to be connected with them. For instance, when I hear a coach drive along the streets, immediately I perceive only the sound; but, from the experience I have had that such a sound is connected with a coach, I am said to hear the coach. It is nevertheless evident that, in truth and strictness, nothing can be *heard* but *sound*, and the coach is not then properly perceived by sense, but suggested from experience. So likewise when we are said to see a red-hot bar of iron, the solidity and heat of the iron are not the objects of sight, but suggested to the imagination by the color and figure, which are properly perceived by that sense. In short, those things alone are actually and strictly perceived by any sense which would have been perceived in case that same sense had then been first conferred on us. As for other things, it is plain they are only suggested to the mind by experience grounded on former perceptions. But to return to your comparison of Caesar's picture, it is plain, if you keep to that, you must hold that the real things or archetypes of our ideas are not perceived by sense, but by some internal faculty of the soul as reason or memory. I would therefore gladly know what arguments you can draw from reason for the existence of what you call *real things* or *material objects*, or whether you remember to have seen them formerly as they are in themselves, or if you have heard or read of anyone who did.

H: I see, Philonous, you are disposed to raillery, but that will never convince me.

P: My aim is only to learn from you the way to come at the knowledge of *material beings*. Whatever we perceive is perceived either immediately or mediately, by sense, or by reason and reflection. But as you have excluded sense, pray show me what reason you have to believe their existence, or what *medium* you can possibly make use of to prove it, either to mine or your own understanding.

H: To deal ingenuously, Philonous, now that I consider the point, I do not find I can give you any good reason for it. But this much seems pretty plain — that it is at least possible such things may really exist, and as long as there is no absurdity in supposing them, I am resolved to believe as I did, until you bring good reasons to the contrary.

P: What! Has it come to this that you only believe the existence of material objects and that your belief is founded barely on the possibility of its being true? Then you will have me bring reasons against it, though another would think it reasonable the proof should lie on him who holds the affirmative. And after all, this very point which you are now resolved to maintain without any reason is, in effect, what you have more than once during this discourse seen good reason to give up. But to pass over all this — if I understand you rightly, you say our ideas do not exist without the mind, but that they are copies, images, or representations of certain originals that do.

H: You take me right.

P: They are then like external things.

H: They are.

P: Have those things a stable and permanent nature independent of our senses, or are they in a perpetual change upon our producing any motions in our bodies, suspending, exerting, or altering our faculties or organs of sense?

H: Real things, it is plain, have a fixed and real nature, which remains the same, notwithstanding any change in our senses or in the posture and motion of our bodies, which indeed may affect the ideas in our minds, but it would be absurd to think they had the same effect on things existing without the mind.

P: How then is it possible that things perpetually fleeting and variable as our ideas should be copies or images of anything fixed and constant? Or, in other words, since all sensible qualities, as size, figure, color, etc., that is, our ideas, are continually changing upon every alteration in the distance, medium, or instruments of sensation, how can any determinate material objects be properly represented or painted forth by several distinct things, each of which is so different from and unlike the rest? Or if you say it resembles some one only of our ideas, how shall we be able to distinguish the true copy from all the false ones?

H: I profess, Philonous, I am at a loss. I do not know what to say to this.

P: But neither is this all. Which are material objects in themselves — perceptible or imperceptible?

H: Properly and immediately nothing can be perceived but ideas. All material things, therefore, are in themselves insensible and to be perceived only by their ideas.

P: Ideas then are sensible, and their archetypes or originals insensible.

H: Right.

P: But how can that which is sensible be like that which is insensible? Can a real thing in itself *invisible* be like a *color*; or a real thing which is not *audible* be like a *sound*? In a word, can anything be like a sensation or idea but another sensation or idea?

H: I must admit, I think not.

P: Is it possible there should be any doubt in the point? Do you not perfectly know your own ideas?

H: I know them perfectly, since what I do not perceive or know can be no part of my idea.

P: Consider, therefore, and examine them, and then tell me if there is anything in them which can exist without the mind or if you can conceive anything like them existing without the mind.

H: Upon inquiry, I find it is impossible for me to conceive or understand how anything but an idea can be like an idea. And it is most evident that *no idea can exist without the mind*.

P: You are, therefore, by your principles forced to deny the reality of sensible things, since you made it to consist in an absolute existence exterior to the mind. That is to say, you are a downright *skeptic*. So I have gained my point, which was to show your principles led to skepticism.

H: For the present I am, if not entirely convinced, at least silenced.

P: I would gladly know what more you would require in order to have a perfect conviction. Have you not had the liberty of explaining yourself all manner of ways? Were any little slips in discourse laid hold and insisted on? Or were you not allowed to retract or reinforce anything you had offered, as best served your purpose? Has not everything you could say been heard and examined with all the fairness imaginable? In a word, have you not in every point been convinced out of your own mouth? And if you can at present discover any flaw in any of your former concessions, or think of any remaining subterfuge, any new distinction, color, or comment whatsoever, why do you not produce it?

H: A little patience, Philonous. I am at present so amazed to see myself ensnared, and as it were imprisoned in the labyrinths you have drawn me into, that on the sudden it cannot be expected I should find my way out. You must give me time to look about me and recollect myself.

P: Listen, is not this the college bell?

H: It rings for prayers.

P: We will go in then if you please, and meet here again tomorrow morning. In the meantime you may employ your thoughts on this morning's discourse, and try if you can find any fallacy in it, or invent any new means to extricate yourself.

H: Agreed.

THE SECOND DIALOGUE

HYLAS: I beg your pardon, Philonous, for not meeting you sooner. All this morning my head was so filled with our late conversation that I had not leisure to think of the time of the day, or indeed of anything else.

PHILONOUS: I am glad you were so intent upon it, in hopes if there were any mistakes in your concessions or fallacies in my reasonings from them, you will now discover them to me.

H: I assure you, I have done nothing ever since I saw you but search after mistakes and fallacies— and, with that view, have minutely examined the whole series of yesterday's discourse—but all in vain, for the notions it led me into, upon review, appear still more clear and evident, and the more I consider them, the more irresistibly do they force my assent.

P: And is this not, you think, a sign that they are genuine, that they proceed from nature and are conformable to right reason? Truth and beauty are in this alike, that the strictest survey sets them both off to advantage. While the false luster of error and disguise cannot endure being reviewed or too nearly inspected.

H: I admit there is a great deal in what you say. Nor can anyone be more entirely satisfied of the truth of those odd consequences so long as I have in view the reasonings that lead to them. But when these are out of my thoughts, there seems, on the other hand, something so satisfactory, so natural and intelligible in the modern way of explaining things that I profess I do not know how to reject it.

P: I do not know what way you mean.

H: I mean the way of accounting for our sensations or ideas.

P: How is that?

H: It is supposed the soul makes her residence in some part of the brain from which the nerves take their rise and are thus extended to all parts of the body, and that outward objects, by the different impressions they make on the organs of sense, communicate certain vibrational motions to the nerves, and these being filled with spirits, propagate them to the brain or seat of the soul, which, according to the various impressions or traces thereby made in the brain, is variously affected with ideas.

P: And do you call this an explication of the manner whereby we are affected with ideas?

H: Why not, Philonous? Have you anything to object against it?

P: I would first know whether I rightly understand your hypothesis. You make certain traces in the brain to be the causes or occasions of our ideas. Pray tell me whether by the *brain* you mean any sensible thing?

H: What else do you think I could mean?

P: Sensible things are all immediately perceivable; and those things which are immediately perceivable are ideas; and these exist only in the mind. This much you have, if I am not mistaken, long since agreed to.

H: I do not deny it.

P: The brain therefore you speak of, being a sensible thing, exists only in the mind. Now, I would gladly know whether you think it reasonable to suppose that one idea or thing existing in the mind occasions all other ideas. And if you think so, pray how do you account for the origin of that primary idea or brain itself?

H: I do not explain the origin of our ideas by that brain which is perceivable to sense, this being itself only a combination of sensible ideas, but by another which I imagine.

P: But are not things imagined as truly *in the mind* as things perceived?

H: I must confess they are.

P: It comes, therefore, to the same thing, and you have been all this while accounting for ideas by certain motions or impressions in the brain, that is, by some alterations in an idea—whether sensible or imaginable, it does not matter.

H: I begin to suspect my hypothesis.

P: Beside spirits, all that we know or conceive are our own ideas. When, therefore, you say all ideas are occasioned by impressions in the brain, do you conceive this brain or not? If you do, then you talk of ideas imprinted in an idea causing that same idea, which is absurd. If you do not conceive it, you talk unintelligibly instead of forming a reasonable hypothesis.

H: I now clearly see it was a mere dream. There is nothing in it.

P: You need not be much concerned at it; for, after all, this way of explaining things, as you called it, could never have satisfied any reasonable man. What connection is there between a motion in the nerves and the sensations of sound or color in the mind? Or how is it possible these should be the effect of that?

H: But I could never think it had so little in it as now it seems to have.

P: Well then, are you at length satisfied that no sensible things have a real existence, and that you are in truth a thoroughgoing *skeptic*?

H: It is too plain to be denied.

P: Look! Are not the fields covered with a delightful greenery? Is there not something in the woods and groves, in the rivers and clear springs, that soothes, that delights, that transports the soul? At the prospect of the wide and deep ocean, or some huge mountain whose top is lost in the clouds, or of an old gloomy forest, are not our minds filled with a pleasing horror? Even in rocks and deserts, is there not an agreeable wildness? How sincere a pleasure is it to behold the natural beauties of the earth! To preserve and renew our relish for them, is not the veil of night alternately drawn over her face, and does she not change her dress with the seasons? How aptly are the elements disposed! What variety and use in the meanest production of nature! What delicacy, what beauty, what contrivance in animal and vegetable bodies! How exquisitely are all things suited as well to their particular ends as to constitute opposite parts of the whole! And while they mutually aid and support, do they not also set off and illustrate each other! Raise now your thoughts from this ball of earth to all those glorious luminaries that adorn the high arch of heaven. The motion and situation of the planets, are they not admirable for use and order? Were those (miscalled *erratic*) globes ever known to stray in their repeated journeys through the pathless void? Do they not measure areas round the sun ever proportioned to the times? So fixed, so immutable, are the laws by which the unseen Author of nature actuates the universe. How vivid and radiant is the luster of the fixed stars! How magnificent and rich that negligent profusion with which they appear to be scattered throughout the whole azure vault! Yet if you take the telescope, it brings into your sight a new host of stars that escape the naked eye. Here they seem contiguous and minute, but to a nearer view immense orbs of light at various distances, far sunk in the abyss of space. Now you must call imagination to your aid. The feeble narrow sense cannot ascertain innumerable worlds revolving round the central fires, and in those worlds the energy of an all-perfect mind displayed in endless forms. But neither sense nor imagination is big enough to comprehend the boundless extent with all its glittering furniture. Though the laboring mind exerts and strains each power to its utmost reach, there still stands out ungrasped an immeasurable surplus. Yet all the vast bodies that compose this mighty frame, however distant and remote, are by some secret mechanism, some divine art and force, linked in a mutual dependence and intercourse with each other, even with this earth, which was almost slipped from my thoughts and lost in the crowd of worlds. Is not the whole system immense, beautiful, glorious beyond expression and beyond thought? What treatment then do those philosophers deserve who would deprive these noble and delightful scenes of all reality? How should those principles be entertained that lead us to think all the visible beauty of the creation a false imaginary glare? To be plain, can you expect this skepticism of yours will not be thought extravagantly absurd by all men of sense?

H: Other men may think as they please, but for your part you have nothing to reproach me with. My comfort is you are as much a skeptic as I am.

P: There, Hylas, I must beg leave to differ from you.

H: What! Have you all along agreed to the premises, and do you now deny the conclusion and leave me to maintain these paradoxes which you led me into by myself? This surely is not fair.

P: I deny that I agreed with you in those notions that led to skepticism. You indeed said the reality of sensible things consisted in an *absolute existence* out of the minds of spirits or distinct from their being perceived. And, pursuant to this notion of reality, you are obliged to deny sensible things any real existence, that is, according to your own definition, you profess yourself a *skeptic*. But I neither said nor thought the reality of sensible things was to be defined after that manner. To me it is evident, for the reasons you allow of, that sensible things cannot exist otherwise than in a mind or spirit. From this I conclude, not that they have no real existence, but that, seeing they do not depend on my thought, and have an existence distinct from being perceived by me, *there must be some other mind in which they exist.* As sure, therefore, as the sensible world really exists, so sure is there an infinite, omnipresent Spirit who contains and supports it.

H: What! This is no more than I and all Christians hold — no, and all others too who believe there is a God and that he knows and comprehends all things.

P: Yes, but here lies the difference. Men commonly believe that all things are known or perceived by God because they believe the being of a God, whereas I, on the other side, immediately and necessarily conclude the being of a God because all sensible things must be perceived by him.

H: But so long as we all believe the same thing, what matter is it how we come by that belief?

P: But neither do we agree in the same opinion. For philosophers, though they acknowledge all corporeal beings to be perceived by God, yet they attribute to them an absolute subsistence distinct from their being perceived by any mind whatever, which I do not. Besides, is there no difference between saying *there is a God, therefore he perceives all things,* and saying *sensible things do really exist — and if they really exist, they are necessarily perceived by an infinite mind — therefore there is an infinite mind, or God?* This furnishes you with a direct and immediate demonstration, from a most evident principle, of the *being of a God.* Theologians and philosophers had proved beyond all controversy, from the beauty and usefulness of the several parts of the creation, that it was the workmanship of God. But that — setting aside all help of astronomy and natural philosophy, all contemplation of the contrivance, order, and adjustment of things — an infinite mind should be necessarily inferred from the bare existence of the sensible world is an advantage peculiar to them only who have made this easy reflection: that the sensible world is that which we perceive by our several senses; and that nothing is perceived by the senses besides ideas; and that no idea or archetype of an idea can exist otherwise than in a mind. You may now, without any laborious search into the sciences, without any subtlety of reason or tedious length of discourse, oppose and baffle the most strenuous advocate for atheism. Those miserable refuges, whether in an eternal succession of un-

thinking causes and effects or in a fortuitous concourse of atoms — those wild imaginations of Vanini,[2] Hobbes, and Spinoza, in a word, the whole system of atheism — is it not entirely overthrown by this single reflection on the repugnance included in supposing the whole or any part, even the most rude and shapeless, of the visible world to exist without a mind? Let anyone of those abettors of impiety but look into his own thoughts and there try if he can conceive how so much as a rock, a desert, a chaos, or confused jumble of atoms, how anything at all, either sensible or imaginable, can exist independent of a mind, and he need go no further to be convinced of his folly. Can anything be fairer than to put a dispute on such an issue and leave it to a man himself to see if he can conceive, even in thought, what he holds to be true in fact, and to allow it a real existence from a notion?

H: It cannot be denied, there is something highly serviceable to religion in what you advance. But do you not think it looks very like a notion entertained by some eminent moderns,[3] of *seeing all things in God?*

P: I would gladly know that opinion; pray explain it to me.

H: They conceive that the soul, being immaterial, is incapable of being united with material things so as to perceive them in themselves, but that she perceives them by her union with the substance of God, which, being spiritual, is therefore purely intelligible or capable of being the immediate object of a spirit's thought. Besides, the divine essence contains in it perfections correspondent to each created being, and which are, for that reason, proper to exhibit or represent them to the mind.

P: I do not understand how our ideas, which are things altogether passive and inert, can be the essence or any part (or like any part) of the essence or substance of God, who is an impassive, indivisible, purely

2. [Giulio Cesare Lucilio Vanini (1585–1619) was an Italian philosopher burned at the stake at Toulouse, France on charges of atheism and witchcraft.]

3. [The reference is to Nicholas Malebranche (1638–1715), one of the occasionalists, who maintained that no interaction occurs between mental and physical events nor among events in either realm. The appearance of interaction was ascribed to the intervention of God, whose actions were said to produce regularities.]

active being. Many more difficulties and objections occur at first view against this hypothesis, but I shall only add that it is liable to all the absurdities of the common hypotheses in making a created world exist otherwise than in the mind of a spirit. Besides all which, it has this peculiar to itself that it makes that material world serve to no purpose. And if it passes for a good argument against other hypotheses in the sciences that they suppose nature or the Divine Wisdom to make something in vain or do by tedious round-about methods what might have been performed in a much more easy and compendious way, what shall we think of that hypothesis which supposes the whole world made in vain?

H: But what do you say, are not you too of the opinion that we see all things in God? If I am not mistaken, what you advance comes near it.

P: Few men think, yet all will have opinions. Hence men's opinions are superficial and confused. It is nothing strange that tenets which in themselves are ever so different should nevertheless be confounded with each other by those who do not consider them attentively. I shall not therefore be surprised if some men imagine that I run into the enthusiasm of Malebranche, though in truth I am very remote from it. He builds on the most abstract general ideas, which I entirely disclaim. He asserts an absolute external world, which I deny. He maintains that we are deceived by our senses and do not know the real natures or the true forms and figures of extended beings—to all of which I hold the direct contrary. So that, upon the whole, there are no principles more fundamentally opposite than his and mine. It must be admitted I entirely agree with what the Holy Scripture says that "in God we live, and move, and have our being"[4] (Acts 17:28). But that we see things in his essence, after the manner above set forth, I am far from believing. Take here in brief my meaning. It is evident that the things I perceive are my own ideas and that no idea can exist unless it be in a mind. Nor is it less plain that these ideas, or things perceived by me, either themselves or their archetypes, exist independently of my mind, since I do not know myself to be their author, it being out of my power to determine at pleasure what particular ideas I shall be affected

with upon opening my eyes or ears. They must therefore exist in some other mind, whose will it is they should be exhibited to me. The things, I say, immediately perceived, are ideas or sensations, call them which you will. But how can any idea or sensation exist in, or be produced by, anything but a mind or spirit? This indeed is inconceivable, and to assert that which is inconceivable is to talk nonsense, is it not?

H: Without doubt.

P: But, on the other hand, it is very conceivable that they should exist in and be produced by a spirit, since this is no more than I daily experience in myself—inasmuch as I perceive numberless ideas and, by an act of my will, can form a great variety of them and raise them up in my imagination, though it must be confessed, these creatures of the fancy are not altogether so distinct, so strong, vivid, and permanent, as those perceived by my senses, which latter are called *real things*. From all which I conclude *there is a mind which affects me every moment with all the sensible impressions I perceive*. And from the variety, order, and manner of these, I conclude the author of them to be *wise, powerful, and good beyond comprehension*. Mark it well: I do not say I see things by perceiving that which represents them in the intelligible substance of God. This I do not understand; but I say the things perceived by me are known by the understanding and produced by the will of an infinite Spirit. And is not all this most plain and evident? Is there any more in it than what a little observation of our own minds, and that which passes in them, not only enables us to conceive but also obliges us to acknowledge?

H: I think I understand you very clearly and admit the proof you give of a Deity seems no less evident than it is surprising. But allowing that God is the supreme and universal cause of all things, yet may not there be still a third nature besides spirits and ideas? May we not admit a subordinate and limited cause of our ideas? In a word, may there not for all that be *matter*?

P: How often must I inculcate the same thing? You allow the things immediately perceived by sense to exist nowhere without the mind, but there is nothing perceived by sense which is not perceived immediately. Therefore, there is nothing sensible that exists without the mind. The matter, therefore, which you still insist on is something intelligible, I suppose,

4. [The quotation is from Acts 17:28.]

something that may be discovered by reason and not by sense.

H: You are in the right.

P: Pray let me know what reasoning your belief of matter is grounded on, and what this matter is in your present sense of it.

H: I find myself affected with various ideas of which I know I am not the cause; neither are they the cause of themselves or of one another, or capable of subsisting by themselves, as being altogether inactive, fleeting, dependent beings. They have therefore some cause distinct from me and them, of which I pretend to know no more than that it is *the cause of my ideas*. And this thing, whatever it is, I call matter.

P: Tell me, Hylas, has everyone a liberty to change the current proper signification annexed to a common name in any language? For example, suppose a traveler should tell you that in a certain country men might pass unhurt through the fire, and, upon explaining himself, you found he meant by the word *fire* that which others call *water*, or if he should assert there are trees which walk upon two legs, meaning men by the term *trees*. Would you think this reasonable?

H: No, I should think it very absurd. Common custom is the standard of propriety in language. And for any man to affect speaking improperly is to pervert the use of speech and can never serve to a better purpose than to protract and multiply disputes where there is no difference in opinion.

P: And does not *matter*, in the common current meaning of the word, signify an extended, solid, moveable, unthinking, inactive substance?

H: It does.

P: And has it not been made evident that no such substance can possibly exist? And though it should be allowed to exist, yet how can that which is *inactive* be a *cause* or that which is *unthinking* be a *cause of thought*? You may, indeed, if you please, annex to the word *matter* a contrary meaning to what is vulgarly received, and tell me you understand by it an unextended, thinking, active being, which is the cause of our ideas. But what else is this than to play with words and run into that very fault you just now condemned with so much reason? I do by no means find fault with your reasoning, in that you collect a cause from the *phenomena*, but I deny that the cause deducible by reason can properly be termed matter.

H: There is indeed something in what you say. But I am afraid you do not thoroughly comprehend my meaning. I would by no means be thought to deny that God, or an infinite spirit, is the supreme cause of all things. All I contend for is that subordinate to the supreme agent there is a cause of a limited and inferior nature, which concurs in the production of our ideas, not by any act of will or spiritual efficiency, but by that kind of action which belongs to matter, namely *motion*.

P: I find you are at every turn relapsing into your old exploded conceit of a moveable and consequently an extended substance existing without the mind. What! Have you already forgot you were convinced, or are you willing I should repeat what has been said on that head? In truth this is not fair dealing in you still to suppose the being of that which you have so often acknowledged to have no being. But not to insist further on what has been so largely handled, I ask whether all your ideas are not perfectly passive and inert, including nothing of action in them?

H: They are.

P: And are sensible qualities anything else but ideas?

H: How often have I acknowledged that they are not?

P: But is not motion a sensible quality?

H: It is.

P: Consequently, it is no action.

H: I agree with you. And indeed it is very plain that when I stir my finger, it remains passive, but my will which produced the motion is active.

P: Now I desire to know, in the first place, whether motion being allowed to be no action, you can conceive any action besides volition; and, in the second place, whether to say something and conceive nothing is not to talk nonsense; and, lastly, whether having considered the premises, you do not perceive that to suppose any efficient or active cause of our ideas other than *spirit* is highly absurd and unreasonable?

H: I give up the point entirely. But though matter may not be a cause, yet what hinders its being an *instrument* subservient to the supreme agent in the production of our ideas?

P: An instrument, you say; pray what may be the figure, springs, wheels, and motions of that instrument?

H: Those I pretend to determine nothing of, both the substance and its qualities being entirely unknown to me.

P: What? You are then of the opinion, it is made up of unknown parts, that it has unknown motions, and an unknown shape.

H: I do not believe it has any figure or motion at all, being already convinced that no sensible qualities can exist in an unperceiving substance.

P: But what notion is it possible to frame of an instrument void of all sensible qualities, even extension itself?

H: I do not pretend to have any notion of it.

P: And what reason do you have to think this unknown, this inconceivable somewhat does exist? Is it that you imagine God cannot act as well without it or that you find by experience the use of some such thing when you form ideas in your own mind?

H: You are always teasing me for reasons of my belief. Pray what reasons do you have not to believe it?

P: It is to me a sufficient reason not to believe the existence of anything if I see no reason for believing it. But, not to insist on reasons for believing, you will not so much as let me know what it is you would have me believe, since you say you have no manner of notion of it. After all, let me entreat you to consider whether it is like a philosopher, or even like a man of common sense, to pretend to believe you do not know what and you do not know why.

H: Hold on, Philonous. When I tell you matter is an *instrument*, I do not mean altogether nothing. It is true, I do not know the particular kind of instrument, but, however, I have some notion of *instrument in general*, which I apply to it.

P: But what if it should prove that there is something, even in the most general notion of *instrument*, as taken in a distinct sense from *cause*, which makes the use of it inconsistent with the divine attributes?

H: Make that appear and I shall give up the point.

P: What do you mean by the general nature or notion of *instrument*?

H: That which is common to all particular instruments composes the general notion.

P: Is it not common to all instruments that they are applied to the doing those things only which cannot be performed by the mere act of our wills? Thus, for instance, I never use an instrument to move my finger because it is done by a volition. But I should use one if I were to remove part of a rock or tear up a tree by the roots. Are you of the same mind? Or can you show any example where an instrument is made use of in producing an effect immediately depending on the will of the agent?

H: I admit I cannot.

P: How, therefore, can you suppose that an all-perfect Spirit, on whose will all things have an absolute and immediate dependence, should need an instrument in his operations or, not needing it, make use of it? Thus it seems to me that you are obliged to admit the use of a lifeless inactive instrument to be incompatible with the infinite perfection of God— that is, by your own confession to give up the point.

H: It does not readily occur what I can answer you.

P: But I think you should be ready to admit the truth when it has been fairly proved to you. We, indeed, who are beings of finite powers, are forced to make use of instruments. And the use of an instrument shows the agent to be limited by rules of another's prescription and that he cannot obtain his end, but in such a way and by such conditions. From this it seems a clear consequence that the supreme unlimited agent uses no tool or instrument at all. The will of an omnipotent Spirit is no sooner exerted than executed, without the application of means, which, if they are employed by inferior agents, it is not upon account of any real efficacy that is in them or necessary aptitude to produce any effect, but merely in compliance with the laws of nature or those conditions prescribed to them by the first cause, who is himself above all limitation or prescription whatsoever.

H: I will no longer maintain that matter is an instrument. However, I would not be understood to give up its existence either, since, notwithstanding what has been said, it may still be an *occasion*.

P: How many shapes is your matter to take? Or how often must it be proved not to exist before you are content to part with it? But to say no more of this (though by all the laws of disputation I may justly blame you for so frequently changing the signification of the principal term) I would gladly know what you mean by affirming that matter is an occasion, having already denied it to be a cause. And when you have shown in what sense you understand *occasion*, pray, in the next place, be pleased to show me what reason induces you to believe there is such an occasion of our ideas.

H: As to the first point: By *occasion* I mean an inactive, unthinking being, at the presence of which God excites ideas in our minds.

P: And what may be the nature of that inactive, unthinking being?

H: I know nothing of its nature.

P: Proceed then to the second point and assign some reason why we should allow an existence to this inactive, unthinking, unknown thing.

H: When we see ideas produced in our minds after an orderly and constant manner, it is natural to think they have some fixed and regular occasions at the presence of which they are excited.

P: You acknowledge then God alone to be the cause of our ideas and that he causes them at the presence of those occasions.

H: That is my opinion.

P: Those things which you say are present to God, without doubt he perceives.

H: Certainly. Otherwise they could not be to him an occasion of acting.

P: Not to insist now on your making sense of this hypothesis or answering all the puzzling questions and difficulties it is liable to: I only ask whether the order and regularity observable in the series of our ideas, or the course of nature, are not sufficiently accounted for by the wisdom and power of God, and whether it does not derogate from those attributes to suppose he is influenced, directed, or put in mind, when and how he is to act, by any unthinking substance. And, lastly, whether in case I granted all you contend for, it would make anything to your purpose, it not being easy to conceive how the external or absolute existence of an unthinking substance, distinct from its being perceived, can be inferred from my allowing that there are certain things perceived by the mind of God which are to him the occasion of producing ideas in us.

H: I am perfectly at a loss what to think, this notion of *occasion* seeming now altogether as groundless as the rest.

P: Do you not at length perceive that in all these different meanings of *matter*, you have been only supposing you do not know what, for no manner of reason, and to no kind of use?

H: I freely admit myself less fond of my notions since they have been so accurately examined. But still, I think I have some confused perception that there is such a thing as *matter*.

P: Either you perceive the being of matter immediately or mediately. If immediately, pray inform me by which of the senses you perceive it. If mediately, let me know by what reasoning it is inferred from those things which you perceive immediately. So much for the perception. Then for the matter itself, I ask whether it is object, *substratum*, cause, instrument, or occasion? You have already pleaded for each of these, shifting your notions and making matter to appear sometimes in one shape, then in another. And what you have offered has been disapproved and rejected by yourself. If you have anything new to advance, I would gladly hear it.

H: I think I have already offered all I had to say on those heads. I am at a loss what more to urge.

P: And yet you are loath to part with your old prejudice. But to make you quit it more easily, I desire that, besides what has been suggested up to now, you will further consider whether, upon the supposition that matter exists, you can possibly conceive how you should be affected by it? Or, supposing it did not exist, whether it is not evident you might for all that be affected with the same ideas you now are, and consequently have the very same reasons to believe its existence that you now can have?

H: I acknowledge it is possible we might perceive all things just as we do now, though there was no matter in the world; neither can I conceive, if there is matter, how it should produce any idea in our minds. And I do further grant you have entirely satisfied me that it is impossible there should be such a thing as matter in any of the foregoing senses. But still I cannot help supposing that there is *matter* in some sense or other. What that is I do not indeed pretend to determine.

P: I do not expect you should define exactly the nature of that unknown being. Only be pleased to tell me whether it is a substance, and if so, whether you can suppose a substance without accidents, or in case you suppose it to have accidents or qualities, I desire you will let me know what those qualities are, at least what is meant by matter's supporting them.

H: We have already argued on those points. I have no more to say to them. But to prevent any further questions, let me tell you, I at present understand by *matter* neither substance nor accident, thinking nor extended being, neither cause, instrument, nor occasion, but something entirely unknown, distinct from all these.

P: It seems then you include in your present notion of matter nothing but the general abstract of idea of *entity*.

H: Nothing else, save only that I superadd to this general idea the negation of all those particular things, qualities, or ideas that I perceive, imagine, or in any way apprehend.

P: Pray where do you suppose this unknown matter to exist?

H: Oh Philonous! Now you think you have entangled me; for if I say it exists in place, then you will infer that it exists in the mind, since it is agreed that place or extension exists only in the mind, but I am not ashamed to admit my ignorance. I do not know where it exists; only I am sure it does not exist in place. There is a negative answer for you and you must expect no other to all the questions you put for the future about matter.

P: Since you will not tell me where it exists, be pleased to inform me after what manner you suppose it to exist or what you mean by its existence.

H: It neither thinks nor acts, neither perceives, nor is perceived.

P: But what is there positive in your abstracted notion of its existence?

H: Upon a nice observation, I do not find I have any positive notion or meaning at all. I tell you again I am not ashamed to admit my ignorance. I do not know what is meant by its *existence* or how it exists.

P: Continue, good Hylas, to act the same ingenuous part and tell me sincerely whether you can frame a distinct idea of entity in general, prescinded from and exclusive of all thinking and corporeal beings, all particular things whatsoever.

H: Hold on, let me think a little—I profess, Philonous, I do not find that I can. At first glance I thought I had some dilute and airy notion of pure entity in abstract, but upon closer attention it has quite vanished out of sight. The more I think on it, the more am I confirmed in my prudent resolution of giving none but negative answers and not pretending to the least degree of any positive knowledge or conception of matter, its *where*, its *how*, its *entity*, or anything belonging to it.

P: When, therefore, you speak of the existence of matter, you do not have any notion in your mind.

H: None at all.

P: Pray tell me if the case does not stand thus: At first, from a belief in material substance, you would have it that the immediate objects existed without the mind; then, that they are archetypes; then causes; next instruments; then occasions; lastly, *something in general*, which being interpreted proves *nothing*. So matter comes to nothing. What do you think, Hylas? Is not this a fair summary of your whole proceeding?

H: Be that as it will, yet I still insist upon it that our not being able to conceive a thing is no argument against its existence.

P: That from a cause, effect, operation, sign, or other circumstance, there may reasonably be inferred the existence of a thing not immediately perceived, and that it would be absurd for any man to argue against the existence of that thing from his having no direct and positive notion of it, I freely admit. But where there is nothing of all this; where neither reason nor revelation induces us to believe the existence of a thing; where we have not even a relative notion of it; where an abstraction is made from perceiving and being perceived, from spirit and idea; lastly, where there is not so much as the most inadequate or faint idea pretended to, I will not, indeed, then conclude against the reality of any notion or existence of anything, but my inference shall be that you mean nothing at all, that you imply words to no manner of purpose, without any design or signification whatsoever. And I leave it to you to consider how mere jargon should be treated.

H: To deal frankly with you, Philonous, your arguments seem in themselves unanswerable, but they do not have so great an effect on me as to produce that entire conviction, that hearty acquiescence which attends demonstration. I find myself still relapsing into an obscure surmise of I do not know what—*matter*.

P: But are you not sensible, Hylas, that two things must concur to take away all scruple and work a plenary assent in the mind? Let a visible object be set in never so clear a light, yet, if there is any imperfection in the sight, or if the eye is not directed towards it, it will not be distinctly seen. And though a demonstration be never so well grounded and fairly proposed, yet, if there is in addition a stain of prejudice or a wrong bias on the understanding, can it be expected on a sudden to perceive clearly and adhere firmly to the truth? No, there is need of time and pains; the attention must be awakened and detained by a frequent repetition of the same thing placed often in the same, often in different lights. I have said it already, and find I must still repeat and inculcate, that it is an unaccountable license you take in pretending to maintain you do not know what, you do not know for what reason, you do not know to what purpose. Can this be paralleled in any art or science, any sect or profession of men? Or is there anything so barefacedly groundless and unreasonable to be met with even in the lowest of common conversation? But perhaps you will still say, matter may exist, though at the same time you neither know what is meant by *matter*, nor by its *existence*. This indeed is surprising, and the more so because it is altogether voluntary, you not being led to it by any one reason; for I challenge you to show me that thing in nature which needs matter to explain or account for it.

H: The reality of things cannot be maintained without supposing the existence of matter. And is not this, you think, a good reason why I should be earnest in its defense?

P: The reality of things! What things, sensible or intelligible?

H: Sensible things.

P: My glove, for example?

H: That or any other thing perceived by the senses.

P: But to fix on some particular thing, is it not a sufficient evidence to me of the existence of this *glove* that I see it, and feel it, and wear it? Or if this will not do, how is it possible I should be assured of the reality of this thing, which I actually see in this place, by supposing that some unknown thing, which I never did or can see, exists after an unknown manner, in an unknown place, or in no place at all? How can the supposed reality of that which is intangible be a proof that anything tangible really exists? Or of that which is invisible, that any visible thing, or in general of anything which is imperceptible, that a perceptible exists? Do but explain this and I shall think nothing too hard for you.

H: Upon the whole, I am content to admit the existence of matter is highly improbable; but the di-

rect and absolute impossibility of it does not appear to me.

P: But granting matter to be possible, yet, upon that account merely, it can have no more claim to existence than a golden mountain or a centaur.

H: I acknowledge it, but still you do not deny it is possible; and that which is possible, for all you know, may actually exist.

P: I deny it to be possible, and have, if I am not mistaken, evidently proved from your own concessions that it is not. In the common meaning of the word *matter*, is there any more implied than an extended, solid, figured, moveable substance, existing without the mind? And have not you acknowledged over and over that you have seen evident reason for denying the possibility of such a substance?

H: True, but that is only one sense of the term *matter*.

P: But is it not the only proper genuine received sense? And if matter in such a sense is proved impossible, may it not be thought with good grounds absolutely impossible? How else could anything be proved impossible? Or indeed how could there be any proof at all one way or the other to a man who takes the liberty to unsettle and change the common signification of words?

H: I thought philosophers might be allowed to speak more accurately than the vulgar and were not always confined to the common meaning of a term.

P: But this now mentioned is the common received sense among philosophers themselves. But not to insist on that, have you not been allowed to take matter in what sense you pleased? And have you not used this privilege in the utmost extent, sometimes entirely changing, at others leaving out or putting into the definition of it whatever for the present best served your design, contrary to all the known rules of reason and logic? And has not this shifting, unfair method of yours spun out our dispute to an unnecessary length, matter having been particularly examined and by your own confession refuted in each of those senses? And can any more be required to prove the absolute impossibility of a thing than the proving it impossible in every particular sense that either you or anyone else understands it in?

H: But I am not so thoroughly satisfied that you have proved the impossibility of matter in the last most obscure, abstracted, and indefinite sense.

P: When is a thing shown to be impossible?

H: When a repugnance is demonstrated between the ideas comprehended in its definition.

P: But where there are no ideas, there no repugnance can be demonstrated between ideas.

H: I agree with you.

P: Now, in that which you call the obscure, indefinite sense of the word matter, it is plain, by your own confession, there was included no idea at all, no sense except an unknown sense, which is the same thing as none. You are not, therefore, to expect I should prove a repugnance between ideas where there are no ideas, or the impossibility of matter taken in an *unknown* sense—that is, no sense at all. My business was only to show you meant *nothing*, and this you were brought to admit. So that in all your various senses, you have been shown either to mean nothing at all or, if anything, an absurdity. And if this is not sufficient to prove the impossibility of a thing, I desire you will let me know what is.

H: I acknowledge you have proved that matter is impossible; nor do I see what more can be said in defense of it. But, at the same time that I give up this, I suspect all my other notions. For surely none could be more seemingly evident than this once was, and yet it now seems as false and absurd as ever it did true before. But I think we have discussed the point sufficiently for the present. The remaining part of the day I would willingly spend in running over in my thoughts the several heads of this morning's conversation, and tomorrow shall be glad to meet you here again about the same time.

P: I will not fail to attend you.

THE THIRD DIALOGUE

PHILONOUS: Tell me, Hylas, what are the fruits of yesterday's meditation? Has it confirmed you in the same mind you were in at parting? Or have you since seen cause to change your opinion?

HYLAS: Truly my opinion is that all our opinions are alike vain and uncertain. What we approve today, we condemn tomorrow. We keep a stir about knowledge and spend our lives in the pursuit of it, when, alas, we know nothing all the while; nor do I think it possible for us ever to know anything in this life. Our faculties are too narrow and too few. Nature certainly never intended us for speculation.

P: What! You say we can know nothing, Hylas?

H: There is not that single thing in the world of which we can know the real nature, or what it is in itself.

P: Will you tell me I do not really know what fire or water is?

H: You may indeed know that fire appears hot and water fluid, but this is no more than knowing what sensations are produced in your own mind, upon the application of fire and water to your organs of sense. Their internal constitution, their true and real nature, you are utterly in the dark as to *that*.

P: Do I not know this to be a real stone that I stand on and that which I see before my eyes to be a real tree?

H: *Know?* No, it is impossible you or any man alive should know it. All you know is that you have such a certain idea or appearance in your own mind. But what is this to the real tree or stone? I tell you that color, figure, and hardness, which you perceive, are not the real natures of those things or in the least like them. The same may be said of all other real things or corporeal substances which compose the world. They have, none of them, anything in themselves like those sensible qualities perceived by us. We should not, therefore, pretend to affirm or know anything of them as they are in their own nature.

P: But surely, Hylas, I can distinguish gold, for example, from iron, and how could this be, if I knew not what either truly was?

H: Believe me, Philonous, you can only distinguish between your own ideas. That yellowness, that weight, and other sensible qualities, do you think they are really in the gold? They are only relative to the senses and have no absolute existence in nature. And in pretending to distinguish the species of real things by the appearances in your mind, you may perhaps act as wisely as he who should conclude two men were of a different species because their clothes were not of the same color.

P: It seems, then, we are altogether put off with the appearances of things, and those false ones too. The very meat I eat and the cloth I wear have nothing in them like what I see and feel.

H: Even so.

P: But is it not strange the whole world should be thus imposed on and so foolish as to believe their senses? And yet I do not know how it is, but men eat, and drink, and sleep, and perform all the offices of life as comfortably and conveniently as if they really knew the things they are conversant about.

H: They do so, but you know ordinary practice does not require a nicety of speculative knowledge. Hence the vulgar retain their mistakes, and for all that make a shift to bustle through the affairs of life. But philosophers know better things.

P: You mean, they know that they *know nothing*.

H: That is the very top and perfection of human knowledge.

P: But are you all this while in earnest, Hylas; and are you seriously persuaded that you know nothing real in the world? Suppose you are going to write, would you not call for pen, ink, and paper, like another man; and do you not know what it is you call for?

H: How often must I tell you that I do not know the real nature of any one thing in the universe? I may, indeed, upon occasion, make use of pen, ink, and paper. But what any one of them is in its own true nature, I declare positively I do not know. And the same is true with regard to every other corporeal thing. And, what is more, we are not only ignorant of the true and real nature of things, but even of their existence. It cannot be denied that we perceive such certain appearances or ideas; but it cannot be concluded from this that bodies really exist. No, now I think on it, I must, agreeably to my former concessions, further declare that it is impossible any real corporeal thing should exist in nature.

P: You amaze me. Was anything ever more wild and extravagant than the notions you now maintain, and is it not evident you are led into all these extravagances by the belief of *material substance*? This makes you dream of those unknown natures in everything. It is this which occasions your distinguishing between the reality and sensible appearances of things. It is to this you are indebted for being ignorant of what everybody else knows perfectly well. Nor is this all: you are not only ignorant of the true nature of everything, but you do not know whether anything really exists or whether there are any true natures at all. For as much as you attribute to your material beings an absolute or external existence, in which you suppose their reality consists, and as you are forced, in the end, to acknowledge such an existence means either a direct repugnance or nothing at all, it follows that you are obliged to pull down your own hypothesis of material substance and positively to deny the real existence of any part of the universe. And so you are plunged into the deepest and most deplorable *skepticism* that ever man was. Tell me, Hylas, is it not as I say?

H: I agree with you. *Material substance* was no more than an hypothesis, and a false and groundless one too. I will no longer spend my breath in defense of it. But whatever hypothesis you advance, or whatever scheme of things you introduce in its stead, I do not doubt it will appear every whit as false; let me but be allowed to question you upon it. That is, allow me to serve you in your own kind and I warrant it shall conduct you through as many perplexities and contradictions to the very same state of skepticism that I myself am in at present.

P: I assure you, Hylas, I do not pretend to frame any hypothesis at all. I am of a vulgar cast, simple enough to believe my senses and leave things as I find them. To be plain, it is my opinion that the real things are those very things I see and feel and perceive by my senses. These I know, and, finding they answer all the necessities and purposes of life, have no reason to be solicitous about any other unknown beings. A piece of sensible bread, for instance, would stay my stomach better than ten thousand times as much of that insensible, unintelligible, real bread you speak of. It is likewise my opinion that colors and other sensible qualities are in the objects. I cannot for my life help thinking that snow is white and fire hot. You indeed, who by *snow* and *fire* mean certain external, unperceived, unperceiving substances, are in the right to deny whiteness or heat to be affections inherent in them. But I, who understand by those words the things I see and feel, am obliged to think like other folks. And as I am no skeptic with regard to the nature of things, so neither am I as to their existence. That a thing should be really perceived by my senses and at the same time not really exist is to me a plain contradiction, since I cannot prescind or abstract, even in thought, the existence of a sensible thing from its being perceived. Wood, stones, fire, water, flesh, iron, and the like things, which I name and discourse of, are things that I know. And I should not have known them but that I perceived them by my senses; and things perceived by the senses are immediately perceived; and things immediately perceived are ideas; and ideas cannot exist without the mind; their existence, therefore, consists in being perceived;

when, therefore, they are actually perceived, there can be no doubt of their existence. Away then with all that skepticism, all those ridiculous philosophical doubts. What a jest is it for a philosopher to question the existence of sensible things until he has it proved to him from the veracity of God or to pretend our knowledge in this point falls short of intuition or demonstration! I might as well doubt of my own being as of the being of those things I actually see and feel.

H: Not so fast, Philonous; you say you cannot conceive how sensible things should exist without the mind. Do you not?

P: I do.

H: Supposing you were annihilated, cannot you conceive it possible that things perceivable by sense may still exist?

P: I can; but then it must be in another mind. When I deny sensible things an existence out of the mind, I do not mean my mind in particular, but all minds. Now it is plain they have an existence exterior to my mind, since I find them by experience to be independent of it. There is, therefore, some other mind in which they exist during the intervals between the times of my perceiving them, as likewise they did before my birth and would do after my supposed annihilation. And as the same is true with regard to all other finite created spirits, it necessarily follows there is an *omnipresent, eternal Mind* which knows and comprehends all things, and exhibits them to our view in such a manner and according to such rules as he himself has ordained and are by us termed the *laws of nature.*

H: Answer me, Philonous. Are all our ideas perfectly inert beings? Or do they have any agency included in them?

P: They are altogether passive and inert.

H: And is not God an agent, a being purely active?

P: I acknowledge it.

H: No idea, therefore, can be like or represent the nature of God.

P: It cannot.

H: Since, therefore, you have no idea of the mind of God, how can you conceive it possible that things should exist in his mind? Or, if you can conceive the mind of God without having an idea of it, why may I not be allowed to conceive the existence of matter, notwithstanding that I have no idea of it?

P: As to your first question, I admit I have properly no idea, either of God or any other spirit; for these, being active, cannot be represented by things perfectly inert as our ideas are. I do nevertheless know that I, who am a spirit or thinking substance, exist as certainly as I know my ideas exist. Further, I know what I mean by the terms *I* and *myself*; and I know this immediately, or intuitively, though I do not perceive it as I perceive a triangle, a color, or a sound. The mind, spirit, or soul, is that indivisible, unextended thing, which thinks, acts, and perceives. I say *indivisible*, because unextended, and *unextended*, because extended, figured, moveable things are ideas; and that which perceives ideas, which thinks and wills, is plainly itself no idea, nor like an idea. Ideas are things inactive and perceived, and spirits a sort of beings altogether different from them. I do not therefore say my soul is an idea or like an idea. However, taking the word *idea* in a large sense, my soul may be said to furnish me with an idea, that is, an image or likeness of God, though indeed extremely inadequate. For all the notion I have of God is obtained by reflecting on my own soul, heightening its powers and removing its imperfections. I have, therefore, though not an inactive idea, yet in myself some sort of an active thinking image of the Deity. And though I do not perceive him by sense, yet I have a notion of him or know him by reflection and reasoning. My own mind and my own ideas I have an immediate knowledge of, and, by the help of these, do mediately apprehend the possibility of the existence of other spirits and ideas. Further, from my own being and from the dependency I find in myself and my ideas, I do by an act of reason necessarily infer the existence of a God and of all created things in the mind of God. So much for your first question. For the second, I suppose by this time you can answer it yourself. For you neither perceive matter objectively, as you do an inactive being or idea, nor know it, as you do yourself, by a reflective act—neither do you mediately apprehend it by similitude of the one or the other, nor yet collect it by reasoning from that which you know immediately—all of which makes the case of *matter* widely different from that of the *Deity.*

H: You say your own soul supplies you with some sort of an idea or image of God. But at the same time you acknowledge you have, properly speaking, no idea of your own soul. You even affirm that spirits are a sort of beings altogether different from ideas, consequently, that no idea can be like a spirit. We have, therefore, no idea of any spirit. You admit nevertheless that there is spiritual substance, although you have no idea of it, while you deny there can be such a thing as material substance, because you have no notion or idea of it. Is this fair dealing? To act consistently, you must either admit matter or reject spirit. What do you say to this?

P: I say, in the first place, that I do not deny the existence of material substance merely because I have no notion of it, but because the notion of it is inconsistent or, in other words, because it is repugnant that there should be a notion of it. Many things, for all I know, may exist, of which neither I nor any other man has or can have any idea or notion whatsoever. But then those things must be possible; that is, nothing inconsistent must be included in their definition. I say, secondly, that, although we believe things to exist which we do not perceive, yet we may not believe that any particular thing exists without some reason for such belief, but I have no reason for believing the existence of matter. I have no immediate intuition of this; neither can I mediately from my sensations, ideas, notions, actions, or passions infer an unthinking, unperceiving, inactive substance, either by probable deduction or necessary consequence, whereas the being of myself, that is, my own soul, mind, or thinking principle, I evidently know by reflection. You will forgive me if I repeat the same things in answer to the same objections. In the very notion or definition of material substance, there is included a manifest repugnance and inconsistency. But this cannot be said of the notion of spirit. That ideas should exist in what does not perceive, or be produced by what does not act, is repugnant. But it is no repugnance to say that a perceiving thing should be the subject of ideas or an active thing the cause of them. It is granted we have neither an immediate evidence nor a demonstrative knowledge of the existence of other finite spirits, but it will not then follow that such spirits are on a foot with material substances, if to suppose the one is inconsistent and it is not inconsistent to suppose the other; if the one can be inferred by no argument, and there is a probability for the other; if we see signs and effects indicating distinct finite agents like ourselves, and see no sign or symptom whatever that leads to a rational belief of matter. I say, lastly, that

I have a notion of spirit, though I do not have, strictly speaking, an idea of it. I do not perceive it as an idea or by means of an idea, but know it by reflection.

H: Notwithstanding all you have said, it seems to me that, according to your own way of thinking, and in consequence of your own principles, it should follow that you are only a system of floating ideas without any substance to support them. Words are not to be used without a meaning. And as there is no more meaning in spiritual substance than in material substance, the one is to be exploded as well as the other.

P: How often must I repeat that I know or am conscious of my own being and that I myself am not my ideas, but something else, a thinking, active principle that perceives, knows, wills, and operates about ideas? I know that I, one and the same self, perceive both colors and sounds; that a color cannot perceive a sound nor a sound a color; that I am therefore one individual principle, distinct from color and sound, and, for the same reason, from all other sensible things and inert ideas. But I am not in like manner conscious of either the existence or the essence of matter. On the contrary, I know that nothing inconsistent can exist and that the existence of matter implies an inconsistency. Further, I know what I mean when I affirm that there is a spiritual substance or support of ideas, that is, that a spirit knows and perceives ideas. But I do not know what is meant when it is said that an unperceiving substance has inherent in it and supports either ideas or the archetypes of ideas. There is, therefore, upon the whole no parity of case between spirit and matter.

H: I admit myself satisfied in this point. But do you in earnest think the real existence of sensible things consists in their being actually perceived? If so, how does it come that all mankind distinguishes between them? Ask the first man you meet, and he shall tell you, *to be perceived* is one thing and *to exist* is another.

P: I am content, Hylas, to appeal to the common sense of the world for the truth of my notion. Ask the gardener why he thinks the cherry tree over there exists in the garden, and he shall tell you because he sees and feels it—in a word, because he perceives it by his senses. Ask him why he thinks an orange tree is not there, and he shall tell you because he does not perceive it. What he perceives by sense, that he terms a real being and says it *is*, or *exists*; but that which is not perceivable, the same, he says, has no being.

H: Yes, Philonous, I grant the existence of a sensible thing consists in being perceivable, but not in being actually perceived.

P: And what is perceivable but an idea? And can an idea exist without being actually perceived? These are points long since agreed between us.

H: But be your opinion never so true, yet surely you will not deny it is shocking and contrary to the common sense of men. Ask the fellow, whether tree over there has an existence out of his mind, what answer, do you think, he would make?

P: The same that I should myself, namely, that it does exist out of his mind. But then to a Christian it cannot surely be shocking to say the real tree existing without his mind is truly known and comprehended by (that is, *exists in*) the infinite mind of God. Probably he may not at first glance be aware of the direct and immediate proof there is of this, inasmuch as the very being of a tree or any other sensible thing implies a mind in which it is. But the point itself he cannot deny. The question between the materialists and me is not whether things have a real existence out of the mind of this or that person, but whether they have an absolute existence, distinct from being perceived by God and exterior to all minds. This, indeed, some heathens and philosophers have affirmed, but whoever entertains notions of the Deity suitable to the Holy Scriptures will be of another opinion.

H: But, according to your notions, what difference is there between real things and chimeras formed by the imagination or the visions of a dream, since they are all equally in the mind?

P: The ideas formed by the imagination are faint and indistinct; they have, besides, an entire dependence on the will. But the ideas perceived by sense, that is, real things, are more vivid and clear, and, being imprinted on the mind by a spirit distinct from us, have not a like dependence on our will. There is, therefore, no danger of confounding these with the foregoing, and there is as little of confounding them with the visions of a dream, which are dim, irregular, and confused. And though they should happen to be never so lively and natural, yet, by their not being connected and of a piece with the preceding

and subsequent transactions of our lives, they might easily be distinguished from realities. In short, by whatever method you distinguish *things* from *chimeras* on your own scheme, the same, it is evident, will hold also upon mine. For it must be, I presume, by some perceived difference, and I am not for depriving you of any one thing that you perceive.

H: But still, Philonous, you hold there is nothing in the world but spirits and ideas. And this, you must necessarily acknowledge, sounds very odd.

P: I admit the word *idea*, not being commonly used for *thing*, sounds something out of the way. My reason for using it was because a necessary relation to the mind is understood to be implied by that term and it is now commonly used by philosophers to denote the immediate objects of the understanding. But however odd the proposition may sound in words, yet it includes nothing so very strange or shocking in its sense, which in effect amounts to no more than this, namely, that there are only things perceiving and things perceived; or that every unthinking being is necessarily and from the very nature of its existence perceived by some mind, if not by any finite created mind, yet certainly by the infinite mind of God, in whom "we live, and move, and have our being" (Acts 17:28). Is this as strange as to say the sensible qualities are not in the objects or that we cannot be sure of the existence of things, or know anything of their real natures, though we both see and feel them and perceive them by all our senses?

H: And, in consequence of this, must we not think there are no such things as physical or corporeal causes, but that a spirit is the immediate cause of all the *phenomena* in nature? Can there be anything more extravagant than this?

P: Yes, it is infinitely more extravagant to say a thing which is inert operates on the mind and a thing which is unperceiving is the cause of our perceptions. Besides, that which to you, I do not know for what reason, seems so extravagant is no more than the Holy Scriptures assert in a hundred places. In them God is represented as the sole and immediate author of all those effects which some heathens and philosophers are accustomed to ascribe to nature, matter, fate, or the like unthinking principle. This is so much the constant language of Scripture that it would be needless to confirm it by citations.

H: You are not aware, Philonous, that in making

God the immediate author of all the motions in nature, you make him the author of murder, sacrilege, adultery, and the like heinous sins.

P: In answer to that I observe, first, that the imputation of guilt is the same whether a person commits an action with or without an instrument. In case, therefore, you suppose God to act by the mediation of an instrument or occasion called *matter*, you as truly make him the author of sin as I, who think him the immediate agent in all those operations vulgarly ascribed to nature. I further observe that sin or moral turpitude does not consist in the outward physical action or motion, but in the internal deviation of the will from the laws of reason and religion. This is plain, in that the killing an enemy in a battle, or putting a criminal legally to death, is not thought sinful, though the outward acts are the very same with that in the case of murder. Since, therefore, sin does not consist in the physical action, making God an immediate cause of all such actions is not making him the author of sin. Lastly, I have nowhere said that God is the only agent who produces all the motions in bodies. It is true I have denied there are any other agents besides spirits, but this is very consistent with allowing to thinking, rational beings, in the production of motions, the use of limited powers ultimately indeed derived from God, but immediately under the direction of their own wills, which is sufficient to entitle them to all the guilt of their actions.

H: But denying matter, Philonous, or corporeal substance—there is the point. You can never persuade me that this is not repugnant to the universal sense of mankind. Were our dispute to be determined by most voices, I am confident you would give up the point without gathering the votes.

P: I wish both our opinions were fairly stated and submitted to the judgment of men who had plain common sense without the prejudices of a learned education. Let me be represented as one who trusts his senses, who thinks he knows the things he sees and feels and entertains no doubts of their existence, and you fairly set forth with all your doubts, your paradoxes, and your skepticism about you, and I shall willingly acquiesce in the determination of any indifferent person. That there is no substance in which ideas can exist besides spirit is evident to me. And that the objects immediately perceived are ideas is

agreed on all hands. And that sensible qualities are objects immediately perceived no one can deny. It is therefore evident there can be no *substratum* of those qualities but spirit, in which they exist, not by way of mode or property, but as a thing perceived in that which perceives it. I deny, therefore, that there is any unthinking *substratum* of the objects of sense and, in that meaning, that there is any material substance. But if by *material substance* is meant only sensible body, that which is seen and felt (and the unphilosophical part of the world, I dare say, mean no more), then I am more certain of matter's existence than you or any other philosopher pretend to be. If there is anything which makes the generality of mankind averse from the notions I espouse, it is a misapprehension that I deny the reality of sensible things, but as it is you who are guilty of that and not I, it follows that in truth their aversion is against your notions and not mine. I do therefore assert that I am as certain of my own being as that there are bodies or corporeal substances (meaning the things I perceive by my senses), and that, granting this, the bulk of mankind will take no thought about, nor think themselves at all concerned in the fate of those unknown natures and philosophical quiddities, which some men are so fond of.

H: What do you say to this? Since, according to you, men judge of the reality of things by their senses, how can a man be mistaken in thinking the moon a plain lucid surface about a foot in diameter; or a square tower, seen at a distance, round; or an oar, with one end in the water, crooked?

P: He is not mistaken with regard to the ideas he actually perceives, but in the inferences he makes from his present perceptions. Thus, in the case of the oar, what he immediately perceives by sight is certainly crooked, and so far he is in the right. But if he then concludes that upon taking the oar out of the water he shall perceive the same crookedness, or that it would affect his touch as crooked things are accustomed to do, in that he is mistaken. In like manner, if he should conclude from what he perceives in one station, that, in case he advances toward the moon or tower, he should still be affected with the like ideas, he is mistaken. But his mistake does not lie in what he perceives immediately and at present (it being a manifest contradiction to suppose he should err in respect of that), but in the wrong judgment he makes concerning the ideas he apprehends to be connected with those immediately perceived, or concerning the ideas that, from what he perceives at present, he imagines would be perceived in other circumstances. The case is the same with regard to the Copernican system. We do not here perceive any motion of the earth, but it would be erroneous to conclude from this that, in case we were placed at as great a distance from that as we are now from the other planets, we should not then perceive its motion.

H: I understand you and must necessarily admit you say things plausible enough, but give me leave to put you in mind of one thing. Pray, Philonous, were you not formerly as positive that matter existed as you are now that it does not?

P: I was. But here lies the difference. Before, my positiveness was founded without examination, upon prejudice; but now, after inquiry, upon evidence.

H: After all, it seems our dispute is rather about words than things. We agree in the thing, but differ in the name. That we are affected with ideas from without is evident; and it is no less evident that there must be (I will not say archetypes, but) powers outside the mind corresponding to those ideas. And as these powers cannot subsist by themselves, there is some subject of them necessarily to be admitted, which I call *matter* and you call *spirit*. This is all the difference.

P: Pray, Hylas, is that powerful being, or subject of powers, extended?

H: It has not extension; but it has the power to raise in you the idea of extension.

P: It is therefore itself unextended.

H: I grant it.

P: Is it not also active?

H: Without doubt; otherwise, how could we attribute powers to it?

P: Now let me ask you two questions: *First*, whether it is agreeable to the usage either of philosophers or others to give the name *matter* to an unextended active being? And *secondly*, whether it is not ridiculously absurd to misapply names contrary to the common use of language?

H: Well then, let it not be called matter, since you will have it so, but some *third nature* distinct from matter and spirit. For what reason is there why you should call it spirit? Does not the notion of spirit imply that it is thinking as well as active and unextended?

P: My reason is this: Because I have a mind to have some notion or meaning in what I say, but I have no notion of any action distinct from volition, neither can I conceive volition to be anywhere but in a spirit; therefore, when I speak of an active being, I am obliged to mean a spirit. Besides, what can be plainer than that a thing which has no ideas in itself cannot impart them to me; and if it has ideas, surely it must be a spirit. To make you comprehend the point still more clearly, if it is possible, I assert as well as you that since we are affected from without, we must allow powers to be without in a being distinct from ourselves. So far we are agreed. But then we differ as to the kind of this powerful being. I will have it to be spirit, you matter or I do not know what (I may add too, you do not know what) third nature. Thus I prove it to be spirit. From the effects I see produced, I conclude there are actions; and because actions, volitions; and because there are volitions, there must be a will. Again, the things I perceive must have an existence, they or their archetypes, out of my mind, but, being ideas, neither they nor their archetypes can exist otherwise than in an understanding; there is therefore an understanding. But will and understanding constitute in the strictest sense a mind or spirit. The powerful cause, therefore, of my ideas is in strict propriety of speech a *spirit*.

H: And now I warrant you think you have made the point very clear, little suspecting that what you advance leads directly to a contradiction. Is it not an absurdity to imagine any imperfection in God?

P: Without doubt.

H: To suffer pain is an imperfection.

P: It is.

H: Are we not sometimes affected with pain and uneasiness by some other being?

P: We are.

H: And have you not said that being is a spirit, and is not that spirit God?

P: I grant it.

H: But you have asserted that whatever ideas we perceive from without are in the mind which affects us. The ideas, therefore, of pain and uneasiness are in God; or in other words, God suffers pain — that is to say, there is an imperfection in the divine nature, which you acknowledged was absurd. So you are caught in a plain contradiction.

P: That God knows or understands all things and

that he knows among other things what pain is, even every sort of painful sensation, and what it is for his creatures to suffer pain, I make no question. But that God, though he knows and sometimes causes painful sensations in us, can himself suffer pain, I positively deny. We, who are limited and dependent spirits, are liable to impressions of sense, the effects of an external agent, which, being produced against our wills, are sometimes painful and uneasy. But God, whom no external being can affect, who perceives nothing by sense as we do, whose will is absolute and independent, causing all things and liable to be thwarted or resisted by nothing, it is evident such a being as this can suffer nothing, nor be affected with any painful sensation, or indeed any sensation at all. We are chained to a body, that is to say, our perceptions are connected with corporeal motions. By the law of our nature we are affected upon every alteration in the nervous parts of our sensible body—which sensible body rightly considered is nothing but a complexion of such qualities or ideas as have no existence distinct from being perceived by a mind—so that this connection of sensations with corporeal motions means no more than a correspondence in the order of nature between two sets of ideas or things immediately perceivable. But God is a pure spirit, disengaged from all such sympathy or natural ties. No corporeal motions are attended with the sensations of pain or pleasure in his mind. To know everything knowable is certainly a perfection; but to endure, or suffer, or feel anything by sense, is an imperfection. The former, I say, agrees to God, but not the latter. God knows or has ideas, but his ideas are not conveyed to him by sense as ours are. Your not distinguishing where there is so manifest a difference makes you fancy you see an absurdity where there is none.

H: But all this while you have not considered that the quantity of matter has been demonstrated to be proportioned to the gravity of bodies. And what can withstand demonstration?

P: Let me see how you demonstrate that point.

H: I lay it down for a principle that the moments or quantities of motion in bodies are in a direct compounded reason of the velocities and quantities of matter contained in them. Hence, where the velocities are equal, it follows the moments are directly as the quantity of matter in each. But it is found by experience that all bodies (bating the small inequalities arising from the resistance of the air) descend with an equal velocity; the motion therefore of descending bodies, and consequently their gravity, which is the cause or principle of that motion, is proportional to the quantity of matter—which was to be demonstrated.

P: You lay it down as a self-evident principle that the quantity of motion in any body is proportional to the velocity and *matter* taken together; and this is made use of to prove a proposition from which the existence of *matter* is inferred. Pray is not this arguing in a circle?

H: In the premise I only mean that the motion is proportional to the velocity, jointly with the extension and solidity.

P: But allowing this to be true, yet it will not then follow that gravity is proportional to *matter* in your philosophic sense of the word, except you take it for granted that unknown *substratum*, or whatever else you call it, is proportional to those sensible qualities—which to suppose is plainly begging the question. That there is magnitude and solidity, or resistance, perceived by sense, I readily grant, as likewise that gravity may be proportional to those qualities, I will not dispute. But that either these qualities as perceived by us or the powers producing them do exist in a *material substratum*; this is what I deny and you indeed affirm, but notwithstanding your demonstration have not yet proved.

H: I shall insist no longer on that point. Do you think, however, you shall persuade me that natural philosophers have been dreaming all this while? Pray what becomes of all their hypotheses and explications of the *phenomena* which suppose the existence of matter?

P: What do you mean, Hylas, by the *phenomena*?

H: I mean the appearances which I perceive by my senses.

P: And the appearances perceived by sense, are they not ideas?

H: I have told you so a hundred times.

P: Therefore, to explain the *phenomena* is to show how we come to be affected with ideas, in that manner and order in which they are imprinted on our senses. Is it not?

H: It is.

P: Now if you can prove that any philosopher has explained the production of any one idea in our minds by the help of *matter*, I shall forever acquiesce and look on all that has been said against it as nothing, but if you cannot, it is in vain to urge the explication of *phenomena*. That a being endowed with knowledge and will should produce or exhibit ideas is easily understood. But that a being which is utterly destitute of these faculties should be able to produce ideas, or in any sort to affect an intelligence, this I can never understand. This I say, though we had some positive conception of matter, though we knew its qualities and could comprehend its existence, would yet be so far from explaining things that it is itself the most inexplicable thing in the world. And yet for all this, it will not follow that philosophers have been doing nothing; for by observing and reasoning upon the connection of ideas, they discover the laws and methods of nature, which is a part of knowledge both useful and entertaining.

H: After all, can it be supposed God would deceive all mankind? Do you imagine he would have induced the whole world to believe the being of matter if there was no such thing?

P: That every epidemic opinion arising from prejudice, or passion, or thoughtlessness, may be imputed to God, as the author of it, I believe you will not affirm. Whatever opinion we father on him, it must be either because he has discovered it to us by supernatural revelation or because it is so evident to our natural faculties, which were framed and given us by God, that it is impossible we should withhold our assent from it. But where is the revelation or where is the evidence that extorts the belief of matter? No, how does it appear that matter, taken for something distinct from what we perceive by our senses, is thought to exist by all mankind, or indeed by any except a few philosophers who do not know what they would be at? Your question supposes these points are clear; and when you have cleared them, I shall think myself obliged to give you another answer. In the meantime let it suffice that I tell you I do not suppose God has deceived mankind at all.

H: But the novelty, Philonous, the novelty! There lies the danger. New notions should always be discountenanced; they unsettle men's minds and nobody knows where they will end.

P: Why rejecting a notion that has no foundation either in sense or in reason or in divine authority should be thought to unsettle the belief of such opinions as are grounded on all or any of these, I cannot imagine. That innovations in government and religion are dangerous and ought to be discountenanced, I freely admit. But is there the like reason why they should be discouraged in philosophy? Making anything known which was unknown before is an innovation in knowledge, and if all such innovations had been forbidden, men would [not] have made a notable progress in the arts and sciences. But it is none of my business to plead for novelties and paradoxes. That the qualities we perceive are not in the objects; that we must not believe our senses; that we know nothing of the real nature of things and can never be assured even of their existence; that real colors and sounds are nothing but certain unknown figures and motions; that motions are in themselves neither swift nor slow; that there are in bodies absolute extensions, without any particular magnitude or figure; that a thing stupid, thoughtless, and inactive operates on a spirit; that the least particle of a body contains innumerable extended parts. These are the novelties, these are the strange notions which shock the genuine uncorrupted judgment of all mankind, and, being once admitted, embarrass the mind with endless doubts and difficulties. And it is against these and the like innovations I endeavor to vindicate common sense. It is true, in doing this, I may perhaps be obliged to use some *ambages* and ways of speech not common. But if my notions are once thoroughly understood, that which is most singular in them will in effect be found to amount to no more than this: that it is absolutely impossible and a plain contradiction to suppose that any unthinking being should exist without being perceived by a mind. And if this notion is singular, it is a shame it should be so at this time of day and in a Christian country.

H: As for the difficulties other opinions may be liable to, those are out of the question. It is your business to defend your own opinion. Can anything be plainer than that you are for changing all things into ideas? You, I say, who are not ashamed to charge me with *skepticism*. This is so plain there is no denying it.

P: You mistake me. I am not for changing things into ideas, but rather ideas into things, since those immediate objects of perception, which, according to you, are only appearances of things, I take to be the real things themselves.

H: Things! You may pretend what you please, but it is certain you leave us nothing but the empty forms of things, the outside only which strikes the senses.

P: What you call the empty forms and outside of things seems to me the very things themselves. Nor are they empty or incomplete otherwise than upon your supposition that matter is an essential part of all corporeal things. We both, therefore, agree in this: that we perceive only sensible forms, but we differ in this: You will have them to be empty appearances; I, real beings. In short, you do not trust your senses; I do.

H: You say you believe your senses and seem to applaud yourself that in this you agree with the vulgar. According to you, therefore, the true nature of a thing is discovered by the senses. If so, where does that disagreement come from? Why is not the same figure and other sensible qualities perceived all manner of ways? And why should we use a microscope, the better to discover the true nature of a body, if it were discoverable to the naked eye?

P: Strictly speaking, Hylas, we do not see the same object that we feel; neither is the same object perceived by the microscope which was by the naked eye. But in case every variation was thought sufficient to constitute a new kind or individual, the endless number or confusion of names would render language impracticable. Therefore, to avoid this as well as other inconveniences which are obvious upon a little thought, men combine together several ideas, apprehended by various senses, or by the same sense at different times, or in different circumstances, but observed, however, to have some connection in nature, either with respect to coexistence or succession; all which they refer to one name and consider as one thing. Hence it follows that when I examine by my other senses a thing I have seen, it is not in order to understand better the same object which I had perceived by sight, the object of one sense not being perceived by the other senses. And when I look through a microscope, it is not that I may perceive more clearly what I perceived already with my bare eyes, the object perceived by the glass being quite different from the former. But in both cases my aim is only to know what ideas are connected together; and the more a man knows of the connection of ideas, the more he is said to know of the nature of things. What, therefore, if our ideas are variable?

What if our senses are not in all circumstances affected with the same appearances? It will not then follow they are not to be trusted, or that they are inconsistent either with themselves or anything else, except with your preconceived notion of (I do not know what) one single, unchanged, unperceivable, real nature, marked by each name, which prejudice seems to have taken its rise from not rightly understanding the common language of men speaking of several distinct ideas as united into one thing by the mind. And, indeed, there is cause to suspect several erroneous conceits of the philosophers are owing to the same original: while they began to build their schemes, not so much on notions as words which were framed by the vulgar merely for convenience and dispatch in the common actions of life, without any regard to speculation.

H: I think I apprehend your meaning.

P: It is your opinion the ideas we perceive by our senses are not real things, but images or copies of them. Our knowledge, therefore, is no further real than as our ideas are the true representations of those originals. But as these supposed originals are in themselves unknown, it is impossible to know how far our ideas resemble them or whether they resemble them at all. We cannot, therefore, be sure we have any real knowledge. Further, as our ideas are perpetually varied, without any change in the supposed real things, it necessarily follows they cannot all be true copies of them, or, if some are and others are not, it is impossible to distinguish the former from the latter. And this plunges us yet deeper in uncertainty. Again, when we consider the point, we cannot conceive how any idea, or anything like an idea, should have an absolute existence out of a mind, nor consequently, according to you, how there should be any real thing in nature. The result of all this is that we are thrown into the most hopeless and abandoned *skepticism*. Now give me leave to ask you, *first*, whether your referring ideas to certain absolutely existing unperceived substances, as their originals, is not the source of all this *skepticism? Secondly*, whether you are informed, either by sense or reason, of the existence of those unknown originals? And in case you are not, whether it is not absurd to suppose them? *Thirdly*, whether upon inquiry, you find there is anything distinctly conceived or meant by the *absolute or external existence of unperceiving substances? Lastly,* whether, the premises considered, it is not the wisest way to follow nature, trust your senses, and laying aside all anxious thought about unknown natures or substances, admit with the vulgar those for real things which are perceived by the senses?

H: For the present, I have no inclination to the answering part. I would much rather see how you can get over what follows. Pray, are not the objects perceived by the senses of one likewise perceivable to others present? If there were a hundred more here, they would all see the garden, the trees, and flowers as I see them. But they are not in the same manner affected with the ideas I frame in my imagination. Does not this make a difference between the former sort of objects and the latter?

P: I grant it does. Nor have I ever denied a difference between the objects of sense and those of imagination. But what would you infer from this? You cannot say that sensible objects exist unperceived because they are perceived by many.

H: I admit I can make nothing of that objection, but it has led me into another. Is it not your opinion that by our senses we perceive only the ideas existing in our minds?

P: It is.

H: But the same idea which is in my mind cannot be in yours or in any other mind. Does it not, therefore, follow from your principles that no two can see the same thing? And is not this highly absurd?

P: If the term *same* be taken in the vulgar meaning, it is certain (and not at all repugnant to the principles I maintain) that different persons may perceive the same thing, or the same thing or idea exist in different minds. Words are of arbitrary imposition; and since men are accustomed to apply the word *same* where no distinction or variety is perceived, and I do not pretend to alter their perceptions, it follows that, as men have said before, *several saw the same thing,* so they may upon like occasions, still continue to use the same phrase without any deviation either from propriety of language or the truth of things. But if the term *same* is used in the meaning of philosophers who pretend to an abstracted notion of identity, then, according to their sundry definitions of this notion (for it is not yet agreed in what that philosophic identity consists), it may or may not be possible for various persons to perceive the same thing. But whether philosophers shall think fit to call a thing

the *same* or not, is, I conceive, of small importance. Let us suppose several men together, all endowed with the same faculties, and consequently affected in like sort by their senses, and who had yet never known the use of language; they would without question agree in their perceptions. Though perhaps, when they came to the use of speech, some regarding the uniformity of what was perceived might call it the *same* thing; others, especially regarding the diversity of persons who perceived, might choose the denomination of different things. But who does not see that all the dispute is about a word—namely, whether what is perceived by different persons may yet have the term *same* applied to it? Or suppose a house whose walls or outward shell remaining unaltered, the chambers are all pulled down, and new ones built in their place, and that you should call this the *same,* and I should say it was not the *same* house—would we not for all this perfectly agree in our thoughts of the house considered in itself? And would not all the difference consist in a sound? If you should say we differ in our notions, for that you superadded to your idea of the house the simple abstracted idea of identity, whereas I did not; I would tell you I do not know what you mean by that *abstracted idea of identity*; and I should desire you to look into your own thoughts and be sure you understood yourself.—Why so silent, Hylas? Are you not yet satisfied that men may dispute about identity and diversity without any real difference in their thoughts and opinions abstracted from names? Take this further reflection with you, that whether matter be allowed to exist or not, the case is exactly the same as to the point in hand. For the materialists themselves acknowledge what we immediately perceive by our senses to be our own ideas. Your difficulty, therefore, that no two see the same thing makes equally against the materialists and me.

H: But they suppose an external archetype to which, referring their several ideas, they may truly be said to perceive the same thing.

P: And (not to mention your having discovered those archetypes) so may you suppose an external archetype on my principles—*external,* I mean, to your own mind, though indeed it must be supposed to exist in that mind which comprehends all things; but then this serves all the ends of identity as well as if it existed out of a mind. And I am sure you yourself will not say it is less intelligible.

H: You have indeed clearly satisfied me, either that there is no difficulty at bottom in this point or if there is, it counts equally against both opinions.

P: But that which counts equally against two contradictory opinions can be a proof against neither.

H: I acknowledge it. But, after all, Philonous, when I consider the substance of what you advance against *skepticism*, it amounts to no more than this: We are sure that we really see, hear, feel—in a word, that we are affected with sensible impressions.

P: And how are we concerned any further? I see this *cherry*, I feel it, I taste it—and I am sure *nothing* cannot be seen or felt or tasted—it is therefore *real*. Take away the sensations of softness, moisture, redness, tartness, and you take away the *cherry*. Since it is not a being distinct from sensations, a *cherry*, I say, is nothing but a congeries of sensible impressions or ideas perceived by various senses, which ideas are united into one thing (or have one name given them) by the mind because they are observed to attend each other. Thus, when the palate is affected with such a particular taste, the sight is affected with a red color, the touch with roundness, softness, etc. Hence, when I see and feel and taste in sundry certain manners, I am sure the *cherry* exists or is real, its reality being in my opinion nothing abstracted from those sensations. But if by the word *cherry* you mean an unknown nature distinct from all those sensible qualities, and by its existence something distinct from its being perceived, then indeed I admit neither you nor I nor anyone else can be sure it exists.

H: But what would you say, Philonous, if I should bring the very same reasons against the existence of sensible things in a mind which you have offered against their existing in a material *substratum*?

P: When I see your reasons, you shall hear what I have to say to them.

H: Is the mind extended or unextended?

P: Unextended, without doubt.

H: Do you say the things you perceive are in your mind?

P: They are.

H: Again, have I not heard you speak of sensible impressions?

P: I believe you may.

H: Explain to me now, O Philonous, how it is possible there should be room for all those trees and houses to exist in your mind. Can extended things

be contained in that which is unextended? Or are we to imagine impressions made on a thing void of all solidity? You cannot say objects are in your mind as books in your study or that things are imprinted on it as the figure of a seal upon wax. In what sense, therefore, are we to understand those expressions? Explain this to me, if you can, and I shall then be able to answer all those queries you formerly put to me about my *substratum*.

P: Look you, Hylas, when I speak of objects as existing in the mind or imprinted on the senses, I would not be understood in the gross literal sense, as when bodies are said to exist in a place or a seal to make an impression upon wax. My meaning is only that the mind comprehends or perceives them and that it is affected from without or by some being distinct from itself. This is my explication of your difficulty, and how it can serve to make your tenet of an unperceiving material *substratum* intelligible, I would gladly know.

H: No, if that be all, I confess I do not see what use can be made of it. But are you not guilty of some abuse of language in this?

P: None at all, it is no more than common custom, which you know is the rule of language, has authorized, nothing being more usual than for philosophers to speak of the immediate objects of the understanding as things existing in the mind. Nor is there anything in this, but what is conformable to the general analogy of language, most part of the mental operations being signified by words borrowed from sensible things—as is plain in the terms *comprehend*, *reflect*, *discourse*, etc., which being applied to the mind, must not be taken in their gross original sense.

H: You have, I admit, satisfied me in this point. But there still remains one great difficulty, which I do not know how you will get over. And, indeed, it is of such importance that if you could solve all others, without being able to find a solution for this, you must never expect to make me a proselyte to your principles.

P: Let me know this mighty difficulty.

H: The Scripture account of the creation is what appears to me utterly irreconcilable with your notions. Moses tells us of a creation,[5] a creation of what? of

---

5. [This and subsequent references are to the first chapter of the Book of Genesis.]

ideas? No, certainly, but of things, of real things, solid corporeal substances. Bring your principles to agree with this and I shall perhaps agree with you.

P: Moses mentions the sun, moon, and stars, earth and sea, plants and animals—that all these do really exist and were in the beginning created by God, I make no question. If by *ideas* you mean fictions and fancies of the mind, then these are no ideas. If by *ideas* you mean immediate objects of the understanding, or sensible things which cannot exist unperceived, or out of a mind, then these things are ideas. But whether you do or do not call them *ideas*, it matters little. The difference is only about a name. And whether that name is retained or rejected, the sense, the truth, and reality of things continues the same. In common talk, the objects of our senses are not termed *ideas*, but *things*. Call them so still, provided you do not attribute to them any absolute external existence, and I shall never quarrel with you for a word. The creation, therefore, I allow to have been a creation of things, of *real* things. Neither is this in the least inconsistent with my principles, as is evident from what I have now said, and would have been evident to you without this, if you had not forgotten what had been so often said before. But as for solid corporeal substances, I desire you to show where Moses makes any mention of them, and if they should be mentioned by him or any other inspired writer, it would still be incumbent on you to show those words were not taken in the vulgar meaning, for things falling under our senses, but in the philosophic meaning, for matter, or an unknown quiddity, with an absolute existence. When you have proved these points, then (and not until then) may you bring the authority of Moses into our dispute.

H: It is in vain to dispute about a point so clear. I am content to refer it to your own conscience. Are you not satisfied there is some peculiar repugnance between the Mosaic account of the creation and your notions?

P: If all possible sense which can be put on the first chapter of Genesis may be conceived as consistently with my principles as any other, then it has no peculiar repugnance with them. But there is no sense you may not as well conceive, believing as I do. Since, besides spirits, all you conceive are ideas, and the existence of these I do not deny. Neither do you pretend they exist without the mind.

H: Pray let me see any sense you can understand it in.

P: Why I imagine that if I had been present at the creation, I should have seen things produced into being, that is, become perceptible, in the order described by the sacred historian. I ever before believed the Mosaic account of the creation and now find no alteration in my manner of believing it. When things are said to begin or end their existence, we do not mean this with regard to God, but his creatures. All objects are eternally known by God, or, which is the same thing, have an eternal existence in his mind, but when things, before imperceptible to creatures, are by a decree of God made perceptible to them, then are they said to begin a relative existence with respect to created minds. Upon reading therefore the Mosaic account of the creation, I understand that the several parts of the world became gradually perceivable to finite spirits, endowed with proper faculties, so that, whoever such were present, they were in truth perceived by them. This is the literal, obvious sense suggested to me by the words of the Holy Scripture, in which is included no mention or no thought, either of *substratum*, instrument, occasion, or absolute existence. And upon inquiry, I do not doubt it will be found that most plain, honest men, who believe the creation, never think of those things any more than I. What metaphysical sense you may understand it in, you only can tell.

H: But, Philonous, you do not seem to be aware that you allow created things in the beginning only a relative, and, consequently, hypothetical being— that is to say, upon supposition there were men to perceive them, without which they have no actuality of absolute existence in which creation might terminate. Is it not, therefore, according to you, plainly impossible that the creation of any inanimate creatures should precede that of man? And is not this directly contrary to the Mosaic account?

P: In answer to that, I say, *first*, created beings might begin to exist in the mind of other created intelligences besides men. You will not, therefore, be able to prove any contradiction between Moses and my notions unless you first show there was no other order of finite created spirits in being before man. I say further—in case we conceive the creation as we should at this time a parcel of plants or vegetables of all sorts produced by an invisible power in a desert where nobody was present—that this way of explaining or conceiving it is consistent with my principles, since they deprive you of nothing, either sensible or imaginable; that it exactly suits with the common, natural, undebauched notions of mankind; that it manifests the dependence of all things on God, and consequently has all the good effect or influence which it is possible that important article of our faith should have in making men humble, thankful, and resigned to their Creator. I say, moreover, that in this naked conception of things, divested of words, there will not be found any notion of what you call the *actuality of absolute existence*. You may indeed raise a dust with those terms and so lengthen our dispute to no purpose. But I entreat you calmly to look into your own thoughts and then tell me if they are not a useless and unintelligible jargon.

H: I admit I have no very clear notion annexed to them. But what do you say to this? Do you not make the existence of sensible things consist in their being in a mind? And were not all things eternally in the mind of God? Did they not therefore exist from all eternity, according to you? And how could that which was eternal be created in time? Can anything be clearer or better connected than this?

P: And are not you too of the opinion that God knew all things from eternity?

H: I am.

P: Consequently, they always had a being in the divine intellect.

H: This I acknowledge.

P: By your own confession, therefore, nothing is new, or begins to be, in respect of the mind of God. So we are agreed in that point.

H: What shall we make then of the creation?

P: May we not understand it to have been entirely in respect of finite spirits, so that things with regard to us may properly be said to begin their existence, or be created, when God decreed they should become perceptible to intelligent creatures in that order and manner which he then established and we now call the laws of nature? You may call this a *relative*, or *hypothetical existence* if you please. But so long as it supplies us with the most natural, obvious, and literal sense of the Mosaic history of the creation—so long as it answers all the religious ends of that great article—in a word, so long as you can assign no other sense or meaning in its stead, why should we

reject this? Is it to comply with a ridiculous skeptical humor of making everything nonsense and unintelligible? I am sure you cannot say it is for the glory of God. For allowing it to be a thing possible and conceivable that the corporeal world should have an absolute subsistence extrinsic to the mind of God, as well as to the minds of all created spirits, yet how could this set forth either the immensity or omniscience of the Deity or the necessary and immediate dependence of all things on him? No, would it not rather seem to derogate from those attributes?

H: Well, but as to this decree of God's for making things perceptible, what do you say, Philonous, is it not plain God did either execute that decree from all eternity or at some certain time began to will what he had not actually willed before, but only designed to will? If the former, then there could be no creation or beginning of existence in finite things. If the latter, then we must acknowledge something new to befall the Deity, which implies a sort of change; and all change argues imperfection.

P: Pray consider what you are doing. Is it not evident this objection concludes equally against a creation in any sense, no, against every other act of the Deity discoverable by the light of nature? None of which can we conceive otherwise than as performed in time and having a beginning. God is a being of transcendent and unlimited perfections; his nature, therefore, is incomprehensible to finite spirits. It is not, therefore, to be expected that any man, whether *materialist* or *immaterialist*, should have exactly just notions of the Deity, his attributes, and ways of operation. If then you would infer anything against me, your difficulty must not be drawn from the inadequateness of our conceptions of the divine nature, which is unavoidable on any scheme, but from the denial of matter, of which there is not one word directly or indirectly in what you have now objected.

H: I must acknowledge the difficulties you are concerned to clear are such only as arise from the nonexistence of matter and are peculiar to that notion. So far you are in the right. But I cannot by any means bring myself to think there is no such peculiar repugnance between the creation and your opinion, though indeed where to fix it I do not distinctly know.

P: What would you have? Do I not acknowledge a twofold state of things, the one ectypal or natural, the other archetypal and eternal? The former was created in time, the latter existed from everlasting in the mind of God. Is not this agreeable to the common notions of theologians? Or is any more than this necessary in order to conceive the creation? But you suspect some peculiar repugnance, though you do not know where it lies. To take away all possibility of scruple in the case, do but consider this one point. Either you are not able to conceive the creation on any hypothesis whatsoever, and if so, there is no ground for dislike or complaint against my particular opinion on that score, or you are able to conceive it, and if so, why not on my principles, since nothing conceivable is taken away by that means? You have all along been allowed the full scope of sense, imagination, and reason. Whatever, therefore, you could before apprehend, either immediately or mediately by your senses, or by ratiocination from your senses, whatever you could perceive, imagine, or understand remains still with you. If, therefore, the notion you have of the creation by other principles is intelligible, you have it still upon mine; if it is not intelligible, I conceive it to be no notion at all, and so there is no loss of it. And, indeed, it seems to me very plain that the supposition of matter, that is, a thing perfectly unknown and inconceivable, cannot serve to make us conceive anything. And I hope it does not need to be proved to you that if the existence of matter does not make the creation conceivable, the creation's being without it inconceivable can be no objection against its nonexistence.

H: I confess, Philonous, you have almost satisfied me in this point of the creation.

P: I would gladly know why you are not quite satisfied. You tell me indeed of a repugnance between the Mosaic history and immaterialism, but you do not know where it lies. Is this reasonable, Hylas? Can you expect I should solve a difficulty without knowing what it is? But to pass by all that, would not a man think you were assured there is no repugnance between the received notions of materialists and the inspired writings?

H: And so I am.

P: Ought the historical part of Scripture to be understood in a plain, obvious sense, or in a sense which is metaphysical and out of the way?

H: In the plain sense, doubtless.

P: When Moses speaks of herbs, earth, water, etc., as having been created by God, do you not think the sensible things, commonly signified by those words, are suggested to every unphilosophical reader?

H: I cannot help thinking so.

P: And are not all ideas, or things perceived by sense, to be denied a real existence by the doctrine of the materialists?

H: This I have already acknowledged.

P: The creation, therefore, according to them, was not the creation of sensible things, which have only a relative being, but of certain unknown natures, which have an absolute being in which creation might terminate.

H: True.

P: Is it not, therefore, evident the asserters of matter destroy the plain obvious sense of Moses, with which their notions are utterly inconsistent, and instead of it obtrude on us I do not know what, something equally unintelligible to themselves and me.

H: I cannot contradict you.

P: Moses tells us of a creation. A creation of what? Of unknown quiddities, of occasions, or *substratums*? No, certainly; but of things obvious to the senses. You must first reconcile this with your notions if you expect I should be reconciled to them.

H: I see you can assault me with my own weapons.

P: Then as to *absolute existence*, was there ever known a more jejune notion than that? Something it is, so abstracted and unintelligible, that you have frankly owned you could not conceive it, much less explain anything by it. But allowing matter to exist and the notion of absolute existence to be as clear as light, yet was this ever known to make the creation more credible? No, has it not furnished the *atheists* and *infidels* of all ages with the most plausible argument against a creation? That a corporeal substance, which has an absolute existence without the minds of spirits, should be produced out of nothing by the mere will of a spirit has been looked upon as a thing so contrary to all reason, so impossible and absurd that not only the most celebrated among the ancients, but even various modern and Christian philosophers have thought matter coeternal with the Deity. Lay these things together and then judge whether materialism disposes men to believe the creation of things.

H: I admit, Philonous, I think it does not. This of the *creation* is the last objection I can think of, and I must necessarily admit it has been sufficiently answered as well as the rest. Nothing now remains to be overcome but a sort of unaccountable backwardness that I find in myself toward your notions.

P: When a man is swayed to one side of a question, he does not know why; can this, do you think, be anything else but the effect of prejudice, which never fails to attend old and rooted notions? And indeed in this respect I cannot deny the belief of matter to have very much the advantage over the contrary opinion with men of a learned education.

H: I confess it seems to be as you say.

P: As a balance, therefore, to this weight of prejudice, let us throw into the scale the great advantages that arise from the belief of immaterialism, both in regard to religion and human learning. The being of a God and incorruptibility of the soul, those great articles of religion, are they not proved with the clearest and most immediate evidence? When I say the being of a *God*, I do not mean an obscure, general cause of things, of which we have no conception, but *God* in the strict and proper sense of the word. A being whose spirituality, omnipresence, providence, omniscience, infinite power, and goodness are as conspicuous as the existence of sensible things, of which (notwithstanding the fallacious pretenses and affected scruples of *skeptics*) there is no more reason to doubt than of our own being. Then with relation to human sciences: In natural philosophy, what intricacies, what obscurities, what contradictions, has the belief of matter led men into! To say nothing of the numberless disputes about its extent, continuity, homogeneity, gravity, divisibility, etc., do they not pretend to explain all things by bodies operating on bodies, according to the laws of motion? And yet, are they able to comprehend how any one body should move another? No, admitting there was no difficulty in reconciling the notion of an inert being with a cause or in conceiving how an accident might pass from one body to another, yet by all their strained thoughts and extravagant suppositions, have they been able to reach the mechanical production of any one animal or vegetable body? Can they account, by the laws of motion, for sounds, tastes, smells, or colors, or for the regular course of things? Have they accounted, by physical principles, for the aptitude and contrivance even of the most inconsiderable parts of the universe? But laying aside matter and corporeal causes and admitting only the efficiency of an all-perfect mind, are not all the effects of nature easy and intelligible? If the *phenomena* are nothing else but *ideas*, God is a *spirit*, but matter an unintelligent, unperceiving being. If they demonstrate an unlimited power in their cause, God is active and omnipotent, but matter an inert mass. If the order, regularity, and usefulness of them can never be sufficiently admired, God is infinitely wise and provident, but matter destitute of all contrivance and design. These surely are great advantages in *physics*. Not to mention that the apprehension of a distant Deity naturally disposes men to a negligence in their *moral* actions, which they would be more cautious of in case they thought him immediately present and acting on their minds without the interposition of matter or unthinking second causes. Then in *metaphysics*; what difficulties concerning entity in abstract, substantial forms, hylarchic principles, plastic natures, substance and accident, principle of individuation, possibility of matter's thinking, origin of ideas, the manner how two independent substances, so widely different as *spirit* and *matter*, should mutually operate on each other! What difficulties, I say, and endless disquisitions concerning these and innumerable other like points, do we escape by supposing only spirits and ideas? Even *mathematics* itself, if we take away the absolute existence of extended things, becomes much more clear and easy, the most shocking paradoxes and intricate speculations in those sciences depending on the infinite divisibility of finite extension, which depends on that supposition. But what need is there to insist on the particular sciences? Is not that opposition to all science whatsoever, that frenzy of the ancient and modern *skeptics*, built on the same foundation? Or can you produce so much as one argument against the reality of corporeal things, or in behalf of that avowed utter ignorance of their natures which does not suppose their reality to consist in an external absolute existence? Upon this supposition indeed the objections from the change of colors in a pigeon's neck or the appearances of a broken oar in the water must be allowed to have weight. But those and the like objections vanish if we do not maintain the being of absolute external originals, but place the reality of things in ideas, fleeting indeed, and changeable, however, not changed at random, but according to the fixed order of nature. For in this consists that constancy and truth of things which secures all the concerns of life and distinguishes that which is *real* from the irregular visions of the fancy.

H: I agree to all you have now said and must admit that nothing can incline me to embrace your opinion more than the advantages I see it is attended with. I am by nature lazy and this would be a mighty abridgment in knowledge. What doubts, what hypotheses, what labyrinths of amusement, what fields of disputation, what an ocean of false learning may be avoided by that single notion of *immaterialism*?

P: After all, is there anything further remaining to be done? You may remember you promised to embrace that opinion which upon examination should appear most agreeable to common sense and remote from *skepticism*. This, by your own confession, is that which denies matter or the absolute existence of corporeal things. Nor is this all; the same notion has been proved several ways, viewed in different lights, pursued in its consequences, and all objections against it cleared. Can there be a greater evidence of its truth? Or is it possible it should have all the marks of a true opinion and yet be false?

H: I admit myself entirely satisfied for the present in all respects. But what security can I have that I shall still continue the same full assent to your opinion and that no unthought-of objection or difficulty will occur hereafter?

P: Pray, Hylas, do you in other cases, when a point is once evidently proved, withhold your assent on account of objections or difficulties it may be liable to? Are the difficulties that attend the doctrine of incommensurable quantities, of the angle of contact, of the asymptotes to curves, or the like, sufficient to make you hold out against mathematical demonstration? Or will you disbelieve the providence of God because there may be some particular things which you do not know how to reconcile with it? If there are difficulties attending immaterialism, there are at the same time direct and evident proofs for it. But for the existence of matter there is not one proof and far more numerous and insurmountable objections lie against it. But where are those mighty difficulties you insist on? Alas, you do not know where or what they are—something which may possibly occur later. If this is a sufficient pretense for withholding your full assent, you should never yield it to any proposition, however free from exceptions, however clearly and solidly demonstrated.

H: You have satisfied me, Philonous.

P: But to arm you against all future objections, do but consider that what bears equally hard on two contradictory opinions can be a proof against neither. Whenever, therefore, any difficulty occurs, try if you can find a solution for it on the hypothesis of the *materialists*. Be not deceived by words, but sound your own thoughts. And in case you cannot conceive it easier by the help of *materialism*, it is plain it can be no objection against *immaterialism*. Had you proceeded all along by this rule, you would probably have spared yourself abundance of trouble in objecting, since of all your difficulties I challenge you to show one that is explained by matter, no, which is not more unintelligible with than without that supposition, and consequently makes rather *against* than *for* it. You should consider, in each particular, whether the difficulty arises from the *nonexistence of matter*. If it does not, you might as well argue from the infinite divisibility of extension against divine foreknowledge as from such a difficulty against *immaterialism*. And yet, upon recollection, I believe you will find this to have been often if not always the case. You should likewise take heed not to argue on a *petitio principii*. One is apt to say the unknown substances ought to be esteemed real things rather than the ideas in our minds; and who can tell but the unthinking external substance may concur as a cause or instrument in the production of our ideas? But is not this proceeding on a supposition that there are such external substances? And to suppose this, is it not begging the question? But, above all things, you should beware of imposing on yourself by that vulgar sophism, which is called *ignoratio elenchi*. You talked often as if you thought I maintained the nonexistence of sensible things, whereas in truth no one can be more thoroughly assured of their existence than I am, and it is you who doubt—I should have said, positively deny it. Everything that is seen, felt, heard, or any way perceived by the senses is, on the principles I embrace, a real being, but not on yours. Remember, the matter you contend for is an unknown somewhat (if indeed it may be termed *somewhat*), which is quite stripped of all sensible qualities, and can be neither perceived by sense, nor apprehended by the mind. Remember, I say that it is not any object which is hard or soft, hot or cold, blue or white, round or square, etc. For all these things I affirm do exist.

Though, indeed, I deny they have existence distinct from being perceived or that they exist out of all minds whatsoever. Think on these points; let them be attentively considered and still kept in view. Otherwise you will not comprehend the state of the question—without which your objections will always be wide of the mark and, instead of mine, may possibly be directed (as more than once they have been) against your own notions.

H: I must necessarily admit, Philonous, nothing seems to have kept me from agreeing with you more than this same *mistaking the question*. In denying matter, at first glimpse I am tempted to imagine you deny the things we see and feel, but, upon reflection, find there is no ground for it. What do you think, therefore, of retaining the name *matter* and applying it to sensible things? This may be done without any change in your sentiments, and, believe me, it would be a means of reconciling them to some persons who may be more shocked at an innovation in words than in opinion.

P: With all my heart, retain the word *matter* and apply it to the objects of sense, if you please, provided you do not attribute to them any subsistence distinct from their being perceived. I shall never quarrel with you for an expression. *Matter* or *material substance* are terms introduced by philosophers, and, as used by them, imply a sort of independence or a subsistence distinct from being perceived by a mind, but are never used by common people, or if ever, it is to signify the immediate objects of sense. One would think, therefore, so long as the names of all particular things, with the terms *sensible, substance, body, stuff,* and the like, are retained, the word *matter* should be never missed in common talk. And in philosophical discourses it seems the best way to leave it quite out, since there is not perhaps any one thing that has more favored and strengthened the depraved bent of the mind toward atheism than the use of that general confused term.

H: Well, but, Philonous, since I am content to give up the notion of an unthinking substance exterior to the mind, I think you ought not deny me the privilege of using the word *matter* as I please and annexing it to a collection of sensible qualities subsisting only in the mind. I freely admit there is no other substance in a strict sense than *spirit*. But I have been so long accustomed to the term *matter* that I do not

know how to part with it. To say there is no *matter* in the world is still shocking to me. Whereas to say there is no *matter*, if by that term is meant an unthinking substance existing without the mind, but if by *matter* is meant some sensible thing whose existence consists in being perceived, then there is *matter*—this distinction gives it quite another turn—and men will come into your notions with small difficulty when they are proposed in that manner. For, after all, the controversy about *matter* in the strict meaning of it lies altogether between you and the philosophers, whose principles, I acknowledge, are not near so natural or so agreeable to the common sense of mankind and Holy Scripture as yours. There is nothing we either desire or shun but as it makes or is apprehended to make some part of our happiness or misery. But what has happiness or misery, joy or grief, pleasure or pain, to do with absolute existence or with unknown entities, abstracted from all relation to us? It is evident, things regard us only as they are pleasing or displeasing, and they can please or displease only insofar as they are perceived. Further, therefore, we are not concerned; and thus far you leave things as you found them. Yet still there is something new in this doctrine. It is plain, I do not now think with the philosophers, nor yet altogether with the vulgar. I would like to know how the case stands in that respect, precisely what you have added to or altered in my former notions.

P: I do not pretend to be a setter-up of *new notions*. My endeavors tend only to unite and place in a clearer light that truth which was before shared between the vulgar and the philosophers—the former being of opinion that *those things they immediately perceive are the real things* and the latter that *the things immediately perceived are ideas which exist only in the mind*—which two notions put together do in effect constitute the substance of what I advance.

H: I have been a long time distrusting my senses; I thought I saw things by a dim light and through false glasses. Now the glasses are removed and a new light breaks in upon my understanding. I am clearly convinced that I see things in their native forms and am no longer in pain about their unknown natures or absolute existence. This is the state I find myself in at present, though, indeed, the course that brought me to it I do not yet thoroughly comprehend. You set out upon the same principles that Academics,

Cartesians, and the like sects usually do; and for a long time it looked as if you were advancing their philosophical *skepticism*; but, in the end, your conclusions are directly opposite to theirs.

P: You see, Hylas, the water of the fountain over there, how it is forced upwards in a round column to a certain height, at which it breaks and falls back into the basin from which it rose, its ascent as well as descent proceeding from the same uniform law or principle of *gravitation*. Just so, the same principles which, at first view, lead to *skepticism*, pursued to a certain point, bring men back to common sense.

David Hume

David Hume was born in 1711 in Edinburgh. At the age of fifteen he had completed his education at Edinburgh University, and he began to study law. Three years later, convinced that he had made a major philosophical discovery, he abandoned his legal studies to devote his entire attention to philosophy. In 1739, Hume published his *Treatise of Human Nature* which, in his own words, "fell deadborn from the press." Disappointed by his failure to obtain an audience for his ideas, Hume decided that the style of the *Treatise* was at fault, and in 1748 he published an abbreviated version of Book I of the *Treatise*. This later work, *An Enquiry Concerning Human Understanding*, is reprinted here, along with a piece of the *Treatise* that has no counterpart in the *Enquiry*, Hume's famous dismissal of personal identity.

Hume continued to write on philosophical topics, publishing his *Enquiry Concerning the Principles of Morals* in 1751. He also wrote works on political theory, as well as a history of England; in his lifetime, his fame rested chiefly on these nonphilosophical writings. A sociable and witty man, he had numerous friends and, at his death in 1776, was widely mourned. The *Dialogues Concerning Natural Religion* was published posthumously.

Hume's official aim in the *Enquiry* is to investigate the powers of human reason. Yet from its first page, the work has a very definite thrust. A vigorous opponent of superstition, Hume is interested in disclosing the pretensions of traditional metaphysics, which he regards as providing cover for dogmatism and prejudice.

An important weapon in Hume's attack is his distinction between "relations of ideas" and "matter of fact." In some areas of inquiry, says Hume, we establish our conclusions by reasoning deductively from first principles, but these merely record the meanings we have given to our terms. Arithmetic and geometry are prime examples of sciences in which, according to Hume's theory, we work out the logical consequences of our definitions. However, not all our knowledge is founded on definition and deduction. The laws of nature cannot be deduced from definitions, but are established by experiment and observation. Hume points out that we are not able to deduce these laws from statements which record our observations. Rather, our acceptance of them is based on a kind of inference which is more risky than deduction. In a deductive argument the truth of the premises guarantees the truth of the conclusion. But, as Hume notes, our belief that the sun will rise every morning is founded on our past experience; and even though it may be true that the sun has risen every morning of our lives, that evidence does not guarantee the truth of the thesis that the sun will always rise.

Hume poses for us the problem of how we can reasonably accept statements about the entire course of nature. What justifies us in generalizing, from our own limited experience, about principles which allegedly hold true throughout the universe? Hume offers a simple and devastating argument in response: we cannot find any a priori guarantee for the orderliness of the universe and we can appeal to past experience to support the idea that nature is regular only by arguing in a circle since past experience is a good indicator of the future only if we assume the orderliness of nature.

Hume's own solution to this problem is to claim that no rational justifications can be given for our ordinary nondeductive inferences. We make these inferences through the operation of habit, or, as Hume calls it, custom. A similar operation is at work when we make causal judgments. Hume argues that such judgments have a complex logical structure. Custom determines us to expect a regular succession in which an earlier event, which we call the cause, is followed by events of the type of the effect. Hume then applies this analysis of causation to the issue of human freedom. He argues that once we have a clear understanding of what is involved in causation, and once we know what is meant by human freedom, we will recognize that there is no inconsistency between the thesis that all human actions are caused and the claim that humans sometimes act freely.

In the passage taken from the *Treatise*, Hume turns his formidable critical powers on a question even closer to home: What justifies us in believing that we preserve our identity as persons through time? When he looks inward, he can find no simple and continuing self. The weakness of previous philosophical arguments for a self leads him to the startling claim that the identity of persons is a fiction. In the *Dialogues Concerning Natural Religion* Hume's principal aim is to show that religious debates are futile. Since we cannot reason deductively to conclusions about the nature and existence of God, our reasoning in this area must be nondeductive. That is, we must examine the evidence of the creation to look for clues about the Creator. As Hume notes, however, the evidence is morally ambiguous. Since both good and bad things happen, how is an inference to an all-good Creator to be justified?

● ● ●

David Fate Norton, ed., *The Cambridge Companion to Hume* (Cambridge: Cambridge University Press, 1993) offers accessible essays on important topics. Don J. Garrett's *Cognition of Commitment* (Oxford: Oxford University Press, 1997) is a clear, recent account of central themes in Hume's philosophy. An older, but widely influential survey of Hume's entire philosophy is Norman Kemp Smith, *The Philosophy of David Hume* (1941; rpt. London: Macmillan, 1964). Helpful anthologies are V. C. Chappell, ed., *Hume: A Collection of Essays* (Garden City: Doubleday, 1966) and Margaret Atherton, ed., *The Empiricists: Locke, Berkeley, Hume* (Lanham, Md.: Rowman & Littlefield, 1998). Barry Stroud's *Hume* (London: Routledge, 1978) provides a systematic and illuminating discussion of Hume's epistemology.

P.S.K.
P.W.K.

An Enquiry Concerning Human Understanding

SECTION I
Of the Different Species of Philosophy.

Moral philosophy,[1] or the science of human nature, may be treated after two different manners, each of which has its peculiar merit and may contribute to the entertainment, instruction, and reformation of mankind. The one considers man chiefly as born for action and as influenced in his measures by taste and sentiment, pursuing one object and avoiding another according to the value which these objects seem to possess and according to the light in which they present themselves. As virtue, of all objects, is allowed to be the most valuable, this species of philosophers paint her in the most amiable colors, borrowing all help from poetry and eloquence and treating their subject in an easy and obvious manner, and such as is best fitted to please the imagination and engage the affections. They select the most striking observations and instances from common life, place opposite characters in a proper contrast, and, alluring us into

the paths of virtue by the views of glory and happiness, direct our steps in these paths by the soundest precepts and most illustrious examples. They make us *feel* the difference between vice and virtue; they excite and regulate our sentiments; and so they can but bend our hearts to the love of probity and true honor, they think, that they have fully attained the end of all their labors.

The other species of philosophers consider man in the light of a reasonable rather than an active being and endeavor to form his understanding more than cultivate his manners. They regard human nature as a subject of speculation and, with a narrow scrutiny, examine it in order to find those principles which regulate our understanding, excite our sentiments, and make us approve or blame any particular object, action, or behavior. They think it a reproach to all literature that philosophy should not yet have fixed, beyond controversy, the foundation of morals, reasoning, and criticism, and should forever talk of truth and falsehood, vice and virtue, beauty and deformity, without being able to determine the source of these distinctions. While they attempt this arduous task, they are deterred by no difficulties; but proceeding from particular instances to general principles, they still push on their inquiries to principles more general and rest not satisfied until they arrive at those original principles by which, in every science, all human curiosity must be bounded. Though their speculations seem abstract and even unintelligible to common readers, they aim at the approbation of the learned and the wise and think themselves sufficiently compensated for the labor of their whole lives, if they can discover some hidden truths which may contribute to the instruction of posterity.

It is certain that the easy and obvious philosophy will always, with the generality of mankind, have the preference above the accurate and abstruse, and by many will be recommended not only as more agreeable, but more useful than the other. It enters more into common life, molds the heart and affections, and, by touching those principles which actuate men,

From *The Philosophical Works of David Hume*, T. H. Green and T. H. Grose, eds. (London: Longman's, Green, and Co., 1948), 4 vols., English, modified, taking into account variations from numerous editions. Notes reprinted from Hume's *An Enquiry Concerning Human Understanding* (Indianapolis: Hackett Publishing Company, 1977), by permission of the publisher.

1. [Hume employs the term "moral" in three different senses throughout his writings. In the present case, "moral philosophy" does not mean, as it might for us today, merely the study of our obligations, standards of right and wrong conduct, and the meaning of ethical concepts, but rather includes all those subjects which have a relation to human nature—politics, history, and ethics are typical examples. In this sense, moral philosophy is opposed to natural philosophy or physical science. In addition to the second contemporary sense noted above, Hume often employs "moral" to mean "based on experience or matters of fact," thereby contrasting "moral" with "demonstrative" or "intuitive." For examples of the last sense, see pp. 604, 634, and 655—E.S.]

reforms their conduct and brings them nearer to that model of perfection which it describes. On the contrary, the abstruse philosophy, being founded on a turn of mind which cannot enter into business and action, vanishes when the philosopher leaves the shade and comes into open day, nor can its principles easily retain any influence over our conduct and behavior. The feelings of our heart, the agitation of our passions, the vehemence of our affections, dissipate all its conclusions and reduce the profound philosopher to a mere plebeian.

This also must be confessed that the most durable as well as most just fame has been acquired by the easy philosophy and that abstract reasoners seem up to now to have enjoyed only a momentary reputation from the caprice or ignorance of their own age, but have not been able to support their renown with more equitable posterity. It is easy for a profound philosopher to commit a mistake in his subtle reasonings; and one mistake is the necessary parent of another, while he pushes on his consequences and is not deterred from embracing any conclusion by its unusual appearance or its contradiction to popular opinion. But a philosopher whose only purpose is to represent the common sense of mankind in more beautiful and more engaging colors, if by accident he falls into error, goes no further, but, renewing his appeal to common sense and the natural sentiments of the mind, returns into the right path and secures himself from any dangerous illusions. The fame of Cicero[2] flourishes at present, but that of Aristotle is utterly decayed. La Bruyère[3] passes the seas and still maintains his reputation. But the glory of Malebranche[4] is confined to his own nation and to his own age. And Addison,[5] perhaps, will be read with pleasure when Locke shall be entirely forgotten.

The mere philosopher is a character which is commonly but little acceptable in the world, as being supposed to contribute nothing either to the advantage or pleasure of society, while he lives remote from communication with mankind and is wrapped up in principles and notions equally remote from their comprehension. On the other hand, the mere ignorant is still more despised, nor is anything deemed a surer sign of an illiberal genius in an age and nation where the sciences flourish than to be entirely destitute of all relish for those noble entertainments. The most perfect character is supposed to lie between those extremes: retaining an equal ability and taste for books, company, and business; preserving in conversation that discernment and delicacy which arise from polite letters, and in business that probity and accuracy which are the natural result of a just philosophy. In order to diffuse and cultivate so accomplished a character, nothing can be more useful than compositions of the easy style and manner which do not draw too much from life, require no deep application or retreat to be comprehended, and send back the student among mankind full of noble sentiments and wise precepts applicable to every exigency of human life. By means of such compositions virtue becomes amiable, science agreeable, company instructive, and retirement entertaining.

Man is a reasonable being and, as such, receives from science his proper food and nourishment. But so narrow are the bounds of human understanding that little satisfaction can be hoped for in this particular, either from the extent or security of his acquisitions. Man is a sociable no less than a reasonable being. But neither can he always enjoy company agreeable and amusing or preserve the proper relish for them. Man is also an active being and, from that disposition, as well as from the various necessities of human life, must submit to business and occupation. But the mind requires some relaxation and cannot always support its bent to care and industry. It seems, then, that nature has pointed out a mixed kind of life as most suitable to human race and secretly admonished them to allow none of these biases to *draw* too much, so as to incapacitate them for other occupations and entertainments. Indulge your passion for science, she says, but let your science be human and such as may have a direct reference to action and society. Abstruse thought and profound researches I prohibit and will severely punish by the pensive melancholy which they introduce, by the endless uncertainty in which they involve you and by the cold reception which your pretended discoveries shall

2. [See Locke's *Essay*, n. 8.]

3. [A French author of character sketches and maxims, Jean de La Bruyère (1645–1696) was also a literary critic.]

4. [See Berkeley's *Three Dialogues*, n. 3.]

5. [Joseph Addison (1672–1719) was an English poet, essayist, and critic.]

meet with, when communicated. Be a philosopher, but, amid all your philosophy, be still a man.[6]

Were the generality of mankind contented to prefer the easy philosophy to the abstract and profound, without throwing any blame or contempt on the latter, it might not be improper, perhaps, to comply with this general opinion and allow every man to enjoy, without opposition, his own taste and sentiment. But as the matter is often carried further, even to the absolute rejecting of all profound reasonings, or what is commonly called *metaphysics*, we shall now proceed to consider what can reasonably be pleaded in their behalf.

We may begin with observing that one considerable advantage which results from the accurate and abstract philosophy is its subservience to the easy and humane, which, without the former, can never attain a sufficient degree of exactness in its sentiments, precepts, or reasonings. All polite letters are nothing but pictures of human life in various attitudes and situations, and inspire us with different sentiments of praise or blame, admiration or ridicule, according to the qualities of the object which they set before us. An artist must be better qualified to succeed in this undertaking who, besides a delicate taste and a quick apprehension, possesses an accurate knowledge of the internal fabric, the operations of the understanding, the workings of the passions, and the various species of sentiment which discriminate vice and virtue. However painful this inward search or inquiry may

appear, it becomes in some measure requisite to those who would describe with success the obvious and outward appearances of life and manners. The anatomist presents to the eye the most hideous and disagreeable objects, but his science is useful to the painter in delineating even a Venus or a Helen. While the latter employs all the richest colors of his art and gives his figures the most graceful and engaging airs, he must still carry his attention to the inward structure of the human body, the position of the muscles, the fabric of the bones, and the use and figure of every part or organ. Accuracy is, in every case, advantageous to beauty, and just reasoning to delicate sentiment. In vain would we exalt the one by depreciating the other.

Besides, we may observe, in every art or profession, even those which most concern life or action, that a spirit of accuracy, however acquired, carries all of them nearer their perfection and renders them more subservient to the interests of society. And though a philosopher may live remote from business, the genius of philosophy, if carefully cultivated by several, must gradually diffuse itself throughout the whole society and bestow a similar correctness on every art and calling. The politician will acquire greater foresight and subtlety in the subdividing and balancing of power, the lawyer more method and finer principles in his reasonings, and the general more regularity in his discipline and more caution in his plans and operations. The stability of modern governments above the ancient and the accuracy of modern philosophy have improved, and probably will still improve, by similar gradations.

Were there no advantage to be reaped from these studies beyond the gratification of an innocent curiosity, yet ought not even this be despised as being one accession to those few safe and harmless pleasures which are bestowed on human race. The sweetest and most inoffensive path of life leads through the avenues of science and learning; and whoever can either remove any obstructions in this way or open up any new prospect ought so far to be esteemed a benefactor to mankind. And though these researches may appear painful and fatiguing, it is with some minds as with some bodies, which, being endowed with vigorous and florid health, require severe exercise, and reap a pleasure from what, to the generality of mankind, may seem burdensome and laborious.

---

6. [The preceding two sentences might well refer to Hume himself, as he concuded Book I of the *Treatise of Human Nature*. "But before I launch out into those immense depths of philosophy, which lie before me, I find myself inclined to stop a moment in my present station, and to ponder that voyage, which I have undertaken . . . I am first affrighted and confounded with that forlorn solitude, in which I am placed in my philosophy, and fancy myself some strange uncouth monster, who not being able to mingle and unite in society, has been expelled all human commerce, and left utterly abandoned and disconsolate . . . I have exposed myself to the enmity of all metaphysicians, logicians and mathematicians, and even theologians; and can I wonder at the insults I must suffer. I have declared my disapprobation of their systems; and can I be surprised, if they should express a hatred of mine and of my person." Hume's personal agony was not alleviated by the book's icy reception.]

Obscurity, indeed, is painful to the mind as well as to the eye, but to bring light from obscurity, by whatever labor, must necessarily be delightful and rejoicing.

But this obscurity in the profound and abstract philosophy is objected to, not only as painful and fatiguing, but as the inevitable source of uncertainty and error. Here indeed lies the most just and most plausible objection against a considerable part of metaphysics that they are not properly a science, but arise either from the fruitless efforts of human vanity, which would penetrate into subjects utterly inaccessible to the understanding, or from the craft of popular superstitions, which, being unable to defend themselves on fair ground, raise these entangling brambles to cover and protect their weakness. Chased from the open country, these robbers fly into the forest and lie in wait to break in upon every unguarded avenue of the mind and overwhelm it with religious fears and prejudices. The stoutest antagonist, if he remits his watch a moment, is oppressed. And many, through cowardice and folly, open the gates to the enemies and willingly receive them with reverence and submission as their legal sovereigns.

But is this a sufficient reason why philosophers should desist from such researches and leave superstition still in possession of her retreat? Is it not proper to draw an opposite conclusion and perceive the necessity of carrying the war into the most secret recesses of the enemy? In vain do we hope that men, from frequent disappointment, will at last abandon such airy sciences and discover the proper province of human reason. For, besides the fact that many persons find too sensible an interest in perpetually recalling such topics—besides this, I say, the motive of blind despair can never reasonably have place in the sciences, since, however unsuccessful former attempts may have proved, there is still room to hope that the industry, good fortune, or improved sagacity of succeeding generations may reach discoveries unknown to former ages. Each adventurous genius will still leap at the arduous prize and find himself stimulated, rather than discouraged by the failures of his predecessors, while he hopes that the glory of achieving so hard an adventure is reserved for him alone. The only method of freeing learning at once from these abstruse questions is to inquire seriously into the nature of human understanding and show, from

an exact analysis of its powers and capacity, that it is by no means fitted for such remote and abstruse subjects. We must submit to this fatigue in order to live at ease ever after[7] and must cultivate true metaphysics with some care in order to destroy the false and adulterate. Indolence, which to some persons affords a safeguard against this deceitful philosophy, is, with others, overbalanced by curiosity; and despair, which at some moments prevails, may give place afterwards to sanguine hopes and expectations. Accurate and just reasoning is the only catholic remedy fitted for all persons and all dispositions and is alone able to subvert that abstruse philosophy and metaphysical jargon which, being mixed up with popular superstition, renders it in a manner impenetrable to careless reasoners and gives it the air of science and wisdom.

Besides this advantage of rejecting, after deliberate inquiry, the most uncertain and disagreeable part of learning, there are many positive advantages which result from an accurate scrutiny into the powers and faculties of human nature. It is remarkable concerning the operations of the mind that, though most intimately present to us, yet, whenever they become the object of reflection, they seem involved in obscurity, nor can the eye readily find those lines and boundaries which discriminate and distinguish them. The objects are too fine to remain long in the same aspect or situation and must be apprehended in an instant by a superior penetration derived from nature and improved by habit and reflection. It becomes, therefore, no inconsiderable part of science barely to know the different operations of the mind, to separate them from each other, to class them under their

---

7. [The preceding two sentences are almost a paraphrase of John Locke's remarks in the Introduction to his *Essay Concerning Human Understanding* (1690): "If by this inquiry into the nature of the understanding, I can discover the powers thereof; how far they reach; to what things they are in any degree proportionate; and where they fail us, I suppose it may be of use to prevail with the busy mind of man to be more cautious in meddling with things exceeding its comprehension; to stop when it is at the utmost extent of its tether and to sit down in a quiet ignorance of those things which, upon examination, are found to be beyond the reach of our capacities."]

proper heads, and to correct all that seeming disorder in which they lie involved when made the object of reflection and inquiry. This task of ordering and distinguishing, which has no merit when performed with regard to external bodies, the objects of our senses, rises in its value when directed towards the operations of the mind in proportion to the difficulty and labor which we meet with in performing it. And if we can go no further than this mental geography or delineation of the distinct parts and powers of the mind, it is at least a satisfaction to go so far;[8] and the more obvious this science may appear (and it is by no means obvious), the more contemptible still must the ignorance of it be esteemed in all pretenders to learning and philosophy.

Nor can there remain any suspicion that this science is uncertain and chimerical, unless we should entertain such a skepticism as is entirely subversive of all speculation and even action. It cannot be doubted that the mind is endowed with several powers and faculties, that these powers are distinct from each other, that what is really distinct to immediate perception may be distinguished by reflection, and consequently that there is a truth and falsehood in all propositions on this subject, and a truth and falsehood which does not lie beyond the compass of human understanding. There are many obvious distinctions of this kind, such as those between the will and understanding, the imagination and passions, which fall within the comprehension of every human creature; and the finer and more philosophical distinctions are no less real and certain, though more difficult to be comprehended. Some instances, especially late ones, of success in these inquiries[9] may give us a more just

notion of the certainty and solidity of this branch of learning. And shall we esteem it worthy the labor of a philosopher to give us a true system of the planets and adjust the position and order of those remote bodies, while we affect to overlook those who, with so much success, delineate the parts of the mind in which we are so intimately concerned?

But may we not hope that philosophy, if cultivated with care and encouraged by the attention of the public, may carry its researches still further and discover, at least in some degree, the secret springs and principles by which the human mind is actuated in its operations? Astronomers had long contented themselves with proving, from the phenomena, the true motions, order, and magnitude of the heavenly bodies, until a philosopher at last arose[10] who seems, from the happiest reasoning, to have also determined the laws and forces by which the revolutions of the planets are governed and directed. The like has been performed with regard to other parts of nature. And there is no reason to despair of equal success in our inquiries concerning the mental powers and economy, if prosecuted with equal capacity and caution. It is probable that one operation and principle of the mind depends on another, which again may be resolved into one more general and universal. And how far these researches may possibly be carried, it will be difficult for us, before or even after a careful trial, exactly to determine.[11] This much is certain — that attempts of this kind are made every day even by those who philosophize the most negligently. And nothing can be more requisite than to enter upon the enterprise with thorough care and attention that, if it lies within the compass of human understanding, it may at last be happily achieved; if not, it may, however, be rejected with some confidence and security. This last conclusion, surely, is not desirable nor ought it be embraced too rashly. For how much must

---

8. [Hume had been more optimistic in the Introduction to the *Treatise of Human Nature:* "In pretending, therefore, to explain the principles of human nature, we in effect propose a complete system of the sciences, built on a foundation almost entirely new, and the only one upon which they can stand with any security." For a further illustration of the more subdued tone of the *Enquiry* and its more moderate claims, see footnote 11.]

9. [In the Introduction to the *Treatise of Human Nature*, Hume had cited John Locke (1632–1704), Francis Bacon (1561–1626), Joseph Butler (1692–1752), Francis Hutcheson (1694–1746), Bernard Mandeville (1670–1733), and Lord Shaftesbury (1671–1713) among those who "have begun to put the science of man on a new footing."]

10. [Sir Isaac Newton (1642–1721).]

11. [Cf. *Treatise of Human Nature*, Introduction, ". . . we must endeavor to render all our principles as universal as possible, by tracing up our experiments to the utmost, and explaining all effects from the simplest and fewest causes . . . Where experiments of this kind are judiciously collected and compared, we may hope to establish on them a science, which will not be inferior in certainty, and will be much superior in utility to any other of human comprehension."]

we diminish from the beauty and value of this species of philosophy upon such a supposition? Moralists have been accustomed up to now, when they considered the vast multitude and diversity of those actions that excite our approbation or dislike, to search for some common principle on which this variety of sentiments might depend. And though they have sometimes carried the matter too far, by their passion for some one general principle, it must, however, be confessed that they are excusable in expecting to find some general principles into which all the vices and virtues were justly to be resolved. The like has been the endeavor of critics, logicians, and even politicians; nor have their attempts been wholly unsuccessful, though perhaps longer time, greater accuracy, and more ardent application may bring these sciences still nearer their perfection. To throw up at once all pretensions of this kind may justly be deemed more rash, precipitate, and dogmatic than even the boldest and most affirmative philosophy that has ever attempted to impose its crude dictates and principles on mankind.

What? Though these reasonings concerning human nature seem abstract and of difficult comprehension, this affords no presumption of their falsehood. On the contrary, it seems impossible that what has escaped so many wise and profound philosophers up to now can be very obvious and easy. And whatever pains these researches may cost us, we may think ourselves sufficiently rewarded, not only in point of profit but of pleasure, if, by that means, we can make any addition to our stock of knowledge in subjects of such unspeakable importance.

But as, after all, the abstractedness of these speculations is no recommendation, but rather a disadvantage to them, and as this difficulty may perhaps be surmounted by care and art and the avoiding of all unnecessary detail, we have, in the following inquiry, attempted to throw some light upon subjects from which uncertainty has deterred the wise up to now, and obscurity the ignorant. Happy if we can unite the boundaries of the different species of philosophy by reconciling profound inquiry with clearness and truth with novelty! And still more happy if, reasoning in this easy manner, we can undermine the foundations of an abstruse philosophy which seems to have up to now served only as a shelter to superstition and a cover to absurdity and error!

SECTION II
Of the Origin of Ideas.

Everyone will readily allow that there is a considerable difference between the perceptions of the mind when a man feels the pain of excessive heat or the pleasure of moderate warmth and when he afterwards recalls to his memory this sensation or anticipates it by his imagination. These faculties may mimic or copy the perceptions of the senses, but they never can entirely reach the force and vivacity of the original sentiment. The utmost we say of them, even when they operate with greatest vigor, is that they represent their object in so lively a manner that we could *almost* say we feel or see it: But, unless the mind is disordered by disease or madness, they never can arrive at such a pitch of vivacity as to render these perceptions altogether indistinguishable. All the colors of poetry, however splendid, can never paint natural objects in such a manner as to make the description be taken for a real landscape. The most lively thought is still inferior to the dullest sensation.

We may observe a like distinction to run through all the other perceptions of the mind. A man in a fit of anger is actuated in a very different manner from one who only thinks of that emotion. If you tell me that any person is in love, I easily understand your meaning and form a just conception of his situation, but never can mistake that conception for the real disorders and agitations of the passion. When we reflect on our past sentiments and affections, our thought is a faithful mirror and copies its objects truly, but the colors which it employs are faint and dull in comparison of those in which our original perceptions were clothed. It requires no nice discernment or metaphysical head to mark the distinction between them.

Here, therefore, we may divide all the perceptions of the mind into two classes or species which are distinguished by their different degrees of force and vivacity. The less forcible and lively are commonly denominated thoughts or ideas. The other species want a name in our language and in most others, I suppose, because it was not requisite for any but philosophical purposes to rank them under a general term or appellation. Let us, therefore, use a little freedom and call them impressions, employing that word in a sense somewhat different from the usual.[12] By the term *impression*, then, I mean all our more lively perceptions, when we hear, or see, or feel, or love, or hate, or desire, or will. And impressions are distinguished from ideas, which are the less lively perceptions of which we are conscious when we reflect on any of those sensations or movements above mentioned.

Nothing, at first view, may seem more unbounded than the thought of man, which not only escapes all human power and authority, but is not even restrained within the limits of nature and reality. To form monsters and join incongruous shapes and appearances costs the imagination no more trouble than to conceive the most natural and familiar objects. And while the body is confined to one planet, along which it creeps with pain and difficulty, the thought can in an instant transport us into the most distant regions of the universe or even beyond the universe into the unbounded chaos where nature is supposed to lie in total confusion. What never was seen or heard of, may yet be conceived, nor is anything beyond the power of thought except what implies an absolute contradiction.

But though our thought seems to possess this unbounded liberty, we shall find upon a nearer examination that it is really confined within very narrow limits and that all this creative power of the mind amounts to no more than the faculty of compounding, transposing, augmenting, or diminishing the materials afforded us by the senses and experience. When we think of a golden mountain, we only join two consistent ideas, *gold* and *mountain*, with which we were formerly acquainted. A virtuous horse we can conceive, because, from our own feeling, we can conceive virtue; and this we may unite to the figure and shape

of a horse, which is an animal familiar to us. In short, all the materials of thinking are derived either from our outward or inward sentiment. The mixture and composition of these belongs alone to the mind and will. Or, to express myself in philosophical language, all our ideas or more feeble perceptions are copies of our impressions or more lively ones.

To prove this, the two following arguments will, I hope, be sufficient. *First*, when we analyze our thoughts or ideas, however compounded or sublime, we always find that they resolve themselves into such simple ideas as were copied from a precedent feeling or sentiment. Even those ideas which at first view seem the most wide of this origin are found, upon a nearer scrutiny, to be derived from it. The idea of God, as meaning an infinitely intelligent, wise, and good being, arises from reflecting on the operations of our own mind and augmenting, without limit, those qualities of goodness and wisdom. We may prosecute this inquiry to what length we please; where we shall always find that every idea which we examine is copied from a similar impression. Those who would assert that this position is not universally true, nor without exception, have only one method, and an easy one at that, of refuting it by producing that idea which, in their opinion, is not derived from this source. It will then be incumbent on us, if we would maintain our doctrine, to produce the impression or lively perception which corresponds to it.

Secondly, if it happens, from a defect of the organ, that a man is not susceptible of any species of sensation, we always find that he is as little susceptible of the correspondent ideas. A blind man can form no notion of colors, a deaf man of sounds. Restore either of them that sense in which he is deficient by opening this new inlet for his sensations, you also open an inlet for the ideas and he finds no difficulty in conceiving these objects. The case is the same if the object proper for exciting any sensation has never been applied to the organ. A Laplander or Negro has no notion of the relish of wine. And though there are few or no instances of a like deficiency in the mind where a person has never felt or is wholly incapable of a sentiment or passion that belongs to his species, yet we find the same observation to take place in a less degree. A man of mild manners can form no idea of inveterate revenge or cruelty, nor can a selfish heart easily conceive the heights of friendship and

12. [In Hume's time, the term "impression" was commonly employed to refer to a copy or effect produced on the senses or mind by external causes or objects. In this respect, Hume's use is new. For he claims to be employing the term to refer to perceptions, independent of their origin or causal implications concerning their production — "By the term of impression I would not be understood to express the manner in which our lively perceptions are produced in the soul, but merely the perceptions, themselves." (*Treatise* I, 1.1. note). Because of this new usage, even things which have no representative character, such as emotions and volitions, are included under the heading of impressions.]

generosity. It is readily allowed that other beings may possess many senses of which we can have no conception, because the ideas of them have never been introduced to us in the only manner by which an idea can have access to the mind, namely, by the actual feeling and sensation.

There is, however, one contradictory phenomenon which may prove that it is not absolutely impossible for ideas to arise independent of their correspondent impressions. I believe it will readily be allowed that the several distinct ideas of color which enter by the eye or those of sound which are conveyed by the ear are really different from each other, though at the same time resembling. Now if this is true of different colors, it must be no less so of the different shades of the same color; and each shade produces a distinct idea, independent of the rest. For if this should be denied, it is possible, by the continual gradation of shades, to run a color insensibly into what is most remote from it; and if you will not allow any of the means to be different, you cannot without absurdity deny the extremes to be the same. Suppose, therefore, a person to have enjoyed his sight for thirty years and to have become perfectly acquainted with colors of all kinds, except one particular shade of blue, for instance, which it never has been his fortune to meet with. Let all the different shades of that color, except that single one, be placed before him, descending gradually from the deepest to the lightest, it is plain that he will perceive a blank where that shade is wanting, and will be sensible that there is a greater distance in that place between the contiguous colors than in any other. Now I ask whether it is possible for him, from his own imagination, to supply this deficiency and raise up to himself the idea of that particular shade, though it had never been conveyed to him by his senses? I believe there are few but will be of the opinion that he can. And this may serve as a proof that the simple ideas are not always, in every instance, derived from the correspondent impressions, though this instance is so singular that it is scarcely worth our observing and does not merit that for it alone we should alter our general maxim.

Here, therefore, is a proposition which not only seems in itself simple and intelligible, but, if a proper use were made of it, might render every dispute equally intelligible and banish all that jargon, which has so long taken possession of metaphysical reasonings and drawn disgrace upon them. All ideas, especially abstract ones, are naturally faint and obscure. The mind has but a slender hold of them. They are apt to be confounded with other resembling ideas; and when we have often employed any term, though without a distinct meaning, we are apt to imagine that it has a determinate idea annexed to it. On the contrary, all impressions, that is, all sensations either outward or inward, are strong and vivid. The limits between them are more exactly determined; nor is it easy to fall into any error or mistake with regard to them. When we entertain, therefore, any suspicion that a philosophical term is employed without any meaning or idea (as is but too frequent), we need but inquire *from what impression is that supposed idea derived*? And if it is impossible to assign any, this will serve to confirm our suspicion. By bringing ideas into so clear a light, we may reasonably hope to remove all dispute which may arise concerning their nature and reality.[13]

13. It is probable that no more was meant by those, who denied innate ideas, than that all ideas were copies of our impressions; though it must be confessed, that the terms, which they employed, were not chosen with such caution, nor so exactly defined, as to prevent all mistakes about their doctrine. For what is meant by *innate*? If innate be equivalent to natural, then all the perceptions and ideas of the mind must be allowed to be innate or natural, in whatever sense we take the latter word, whether in opposition to what is uncommon, artificial, or miraculous. If by innate be meant, cotemporary to our birth, the dispute seems to be frivolous; nor is it worth while to enquire at what time thinking begins, whether before, at, or after our birth. Again, the word *idea*, seems to be commonly taken in a very loose sense, by *Locke* and others: as standing for any of our perceptions, our sensations and passions, as well as thoughts. Now in this sense, I should desire to know, what can be meant by asserting, that self-love, or resentment of injuries, or the passion between the sexes is not innate?

But admitting these terms, *impressions* and *ideas*, in the sense above explained, and understanding by *innate*, what is original or copied from no precedent perception, then may we assert, that all our impressions are innate, and our ideas not innate.

To be ingenuous, I must own it to be my opinion, that Locke was betrayed into this question by the schoolmen, who, making use of undefined terms, draw out their disputes to a tedious length, without ever touching the point in question. A like ambiguity and circumlocution seem to run

SECTION III
Of the Association of Ideas.

It is evident that there is a principle of connection between the different thoughts or ideas of the mind and that, in their appearance to the memory or imagination, they introduce each other with a certain degree of method and regularity. In our more serious thinking or discourse this is so observable that any particular thought which breaks in upon the regular tract or chain of ideas is immediately remarked and rejected. And even in our wildest and most wandering reveries, no, in our very dreams, we shall find, if we reflect, that the imagination did not run altogether at adventures, but that there was still a connection upheld among the different ideas which succeeded each other. Were the loosest and freest conversation to be transcribed, there would immediately be observed something which connected it in all its transitions. Or where this is wanting, the person who broke the thread of discourse might still inform you that there had secretly revolved in his mind a succession of thought which had gradually led him from the subject of conversation. Among different languages, even where we cannot suspect the least connection or communication, it is found that the words expressive of ideas the most compounded do yet nearly correspond to each other—certain proof that the simple ideas comprehended in the compound ones were bound together by some universal principle which had an equal influence on all mankind.

Though it is too obvious to escape observation that different ideas are connected together, I do not find that any philosopher has attempted to enumerate or class all the principles of association—a subject, however, that seems worthy of curiosity. To me there appear to be only three principles of connection among ideas, namely, *resemblance, contiguity* in time or place, and *cause* or *effect*.

That these principles serve to connect ideas will not, I believe, be much doubted. A picture naturally

leads our thoughts to the original.[14] The mention of one apartment in a building naturally introduces an inquiry or discourse concerning the others;[15] and if we think of a wound, we can scarcely forbear reflecting on the pain which follows it.[16] But that this enumeration is complete, and that there are no other principles of association except these, may be difficult to prove to the satisfaction of the reader or even to a man's own satisfaction. All we can do, in such cases, is to run over several instances and examine carefully the principle which binds the different thoughts to each other, never stopping until we render the principle as general as possible.[17] The more instances we examine and the more care we employ, the more assurance shall we acquire that the enumeration, which we form from the whole, is complete and entire.

SECTION IV
Skeptical Doubts Concerning the Operations of the Understanding.

Part I.

All the objects of human reason or inquiry may naturally be divided into two kinds, namely, *relations of ideas* and *matters of fact*. Of the first kind are the sciences of geometry, algebra, and arithmetic, and, in short, every affirmation which is either intuitively or demonstratively certain. *That the square of the hypotenuse is equal to the squares of the two sides* is a proposition which expresses a relation between these figures. *That three times five is equal to the half of thirty* expresses a relation between these numbers. Propositions of this kind are discoverable by the mere operation of thought, without dependence on what is anywhere existent in the universe. Though there never were a circle or triangle in nature, the truths

---

through that great philosopher's reasonings on this as well as most other subjects.

[In Book I of the *Essay Concerning Human Understanding*, Locke had attacked the theory of innate ideas and contended that the mind is a *tabula rasa* or blank slate at birth.]

14. Resemblance.

15. Contiguity.

16. Cause and Effect.

17. For instance, *Contrast* or *Contrariety* is also a connexion among ideas: But it may, perhaps, be considered as a mixture of *Causation* and *Resemblance*. Where two objects are contrary, the one destroys the other; that is, the cause of its annihilation, and the idea of the annihilation of an object, implies the idea of its former existence.

demonstrated by Euclid would forever retain their certainty and evidence.

Matters of fact, which are the second objects of human reason, are not ascertained in the same manner; nor is our evidence of their truth, however great, of a like nature with the foregoing. The contrary of every matter of fact is still possible, because it can never imply a contradiction and is conceived by the mind with the same facility and distinctness, as if ever so conformable to reality. *That the sun will not rise tomorrow* is no less intelligible a proposition and implies no more contradiction than the affirmation that *it will rise*. We should in vain, therefore, attempt to demonstrate its falsehood. Were it demonstratively false, it would imply a contradiction and could never be distinctly conceived by the mind.[18]

It may, therefore, be a subject worthy of curiosity to inquire what is the nature of that evidence which assures us of any real existence and matter of fact beyond the present testimony of our senses or the records of our memory. This part of philosophy, it is observable, has been little cultivated either by the ancients or moderns, and, therefore, our doubts and errors in the prosecution of so important an inquiry may be the more excusable, while we march through such difficult paths without any guide or direction. They may even prove useful by exciting curiosity and destroying that implicit faith and security which is the bane of all reasoning and free inquiry. The discovery of defects in the common philosophy, if there are any, will not, I presume, be a discouragement, but rather an incitement, as is usual, to attempt something more full and satisfactory than has yet been proposed to the public.

All reasonings concerning matter of fact seem to be founded on the relation of *cause and effect*. By means of that relation alone we can go beyond the evidence of our memory and senses. If you were to ask a man why he believes any matter of fact which is absent—for instance, that his friend is in the country or in France—he would give you a reason, and this reason would be some other fact: as a letter received from him or the knowledge of his former resolutions and promises. A man finding a watch or any other machine on a desert island would conclude that there had once been men on that island. All our reasonings concerning fact are of the same nature. And here it is constantly supposed that there is a connection between the present fact and that which is inferred from it. Were there nothing to bind them together, the inference would be entirely precarious. The hearing of an articulate voice and rational discourse in the dark assures us of the presence of some person. Why? Because these are the effects of the human make and fabric, and closely connected with it. If we anatomize all the other reasonings of this nature, we shall find that they are founded on the relation of cause and effect and that this relation is either near or remote, direct or collateral. Heat and light are collateral effects of fire and the one effect may justly be inferred from the other.

If we would satisfy ourselves, therefore, concerning the nature of that evidence which assures us of matters of fact, we must inquire how we arrive at the knowledge of cause and effect.

I shall venture to affirm, as a general proposition which admits of no exception, that the knowledge of this relation is not, in any instance, attained by reasonings *a priori*, but arises entirely from experience when we find that any particular objects are constantly conjoined with each other. Let an object be presented to a man of ever so strong natural reason and abilities; if that object is entirely new to him, he will not be able, by the most accurate examination of its sensible qualities, to discover any of its causes or effects. Adam, though his rational faculties are supposed entirely

18. [Compare the distinction between "relations of ideas" and "matters of fact" with the distinction between two kinds of relations discussed in the *Treatise* I, 3. 1. "Relations may be divided into two classes; into such as depend entirely on the ideas, which we compare together, and such as may be changed without any change in the ideas. 'Tis from the idea of a triangle, that we discover the relation of equality, which its three angles bear to two right ones; and this relation is invariable, as long as our idea remains the same. On the contrary, the relations of *contiguity* and *distance* betwixt two objects may be changed merely by an alteration of their place, without any change on the objects themselves or on their ideas." It is significant to note that although geometry is included in the list of disciplines dealing with "relations of ideas", in editions of the *Enquiry* prior to 1756, the following footnote appeared in Section XII: "In general, we may pronounce, that the ideas of *greater*, *less*, or *equal*, which are the chief objects of geometry, are far from being so exact or determinate as to be the foundation of such extraordinary inferences. . . ."]

perfect at the very first, could not have inferred from the fluidity and transparency of water that it would suffocate him, or from the light and warmth of fire that it would consume him. No object ever discovers, by the qualities which appear to the senses, either the causes which produced it or the effects which will arise from it; nor can our reason, unassisted by experience, ever draw any inference concerning real existence and matter of fact.

This proposition, *that causes and effects are discoverable, not by reason but by experience*, will readily be admitted with regard to such objects as we remember to have once been altogether unknown to us, since we must be conscious of the utter inability which we then lay under of foretelling what would arise from them. Present two smooth pieces of marble to a man who has no tincture of natural philosophy; he will never discover that they will adhere together in such a manner as to require great force to separate them in a direct line, while they make so small a resistance to a lateral pressure. Such events as bear little analogy to the common course of nature are also readily confessed to be known only by experience, nor does any man imagine that the explosion of gunpowder or the attraction of a lodestone could ever be discovered by *a priori* arguments. In like manner, when an effect is supposed to depend upon an intricate machinery or secret structure of parts, we make no difficulty in attributing all our knowledge of it to experience. Who will assert that he can give the ultimate reason why milk or bread is proper nourishment for a man, not for a lion or a tiger?

But the same truth may not appear at first sight to have the same evidence with regard to events which have become familiar to us from our first appearance in the world, which bear a close analogy to the whole course of nature, and which are supposed to depend on the simple qualities of objects without any secret structure of parts. We are apt to imagine that we could discover these effects by the mere operation of our reason without experience. We fancy that were we brought, all of the sudden, into this world, we could at first have inferred that one billiard ball would communicate motion to another upon impulse and that we did not need to have waited for the event in order to pronounce with certainty concerning it. Such is the influence of custom that where it is strongest

it not only covers our natural ignorance, but even conceals itself and seems not to take place, merely because it is found in the highest degree.

But to convince us that all the laws of nature and all the operations of bodies without exception are known only by experience, the following reflections may perhaps suffice. Were any object presented to us and were we required to pronounce concerning the effect which will result from it without consulting past observation, after what manner, I beseech you, must the mind proceed in this operation? It must invent or imagine some event which it ascribes to the object as its effect and it is plain that this invention must be entirely arbitrary. The mind can never possibly find the effect in the supposed cause by the most accurate scrutiny and examination. For the effect is totally different from the cause and consequently can never be discovered in it. Motion in the second billiard ball is a quite distinct event from motion in the first, nor is there anything in the one to suggest the smallest hint of the other. A stone or piece of metal raised into the air and left without any support immediately falls. But to consider the matter *a priori*, is there anything we discover in this situation which can beget the idea of a downward rather than an upward or any other motion in the stone or metal?

And as the first imagination or invention of a particular effect in all natural operations is arbitrary where we do not consult experience, so must we also esteem the supposed tie or connection between the cause and effect which binds them together and renders it impossible that any other effect could result from the operation of that cause. When I see, for instance, a billiard ball moving in a straight line towards another, even suppose motion in the second ball should by accident be suggested to me as the result of their contact or impulse, may I not conceive that a hundred different events might as well follow from that cause? May not both these balls remain at absolute rest? May not the first ball return in a straight line or leap off from the second in any line or direction? All these suppositions are consistent and conceivable. Why then should we give the preference to one which is no more consistent or conceivable than the rest? All our reasonings *a priori* will never be able to show us any foundation for this preference.

In a word, then, every effect is a distinct event from

its cause. It could not, therefore, be discovered in the cause and the first invention or conception of it, *a priori*, must be entirely arbitrary. And even after it is suggested, the conjunction of it with the cause must appear equally arbitrary, since there are always many other effects which, to reason, must seem fully as consistent and natural. In vain, therefore, should we pretend to determine any single event or infer any cause or effect without the assistance of observation and experience.

Hence we may discover the reason why no philosopher who is rational and modest has ever pretended to assign the ultimate cause of any natural operation or to show distinctly the action of that power which produces any single effect in the universe. It is confessed that the utmost effort of human reason is to reduce the principles productive of natural phenomena to a greater simplicity and to resolve the many particular effects into a few general causes by means of reasonings from analogy, experience, and observation. But as to the causes of these general causes,[19] we should in vain attempt their discovery, nor shall we ever be able to satisfy ourselves by any particular explication of them. These ultimate springs and principles are totally shut up from human curiosity and inquiry. Elasticity, gravity, cohesion of parts, communication of motion by impulse—these are probably the ultimate causes and principles which we shall ever discover in nature; and we may esteem ourselves sufficiently happy if, by accurate inquiry and reasoning, we can trace up the particular phenomena to, or near to, these general principles. The most perfect philosophy of the natural kind only staves off our ignorance a little longer, as perhaps the most perfect philosophy of the moral or metaphysical kind serves only to discover larger portions of it. Thus the observation of human blindness and weakness is the result of all philosophy and meets us at every turn in spite of our endeavors to elude or avoid it.

Nor is geometry, when taken into the assistance of natural philosophy, ever able to remedy this defect or lead us into the knowledge of ultimate causes by all that accuracy of reasoning for which it is so justly celebrated. Every part of mixed mathematics[20] proceeds upon the supposition that certain laws are established by nature in her operations and abstract reasonings are employed either to assist experience in the discovery of these laws or to determine their influence in particular instances where it depends upon any precise degree of distance and quantity. Thus, it is a law of motion, discovered by experience, that the moment or force of any body in motion is in the compound ratio or proportion of its solid contents and its velocity, and consequently that a small force may remove the greatest obstacle or raise the greatest weight if, by any contrivance or machinery, we can increase the velocity of that force so as to make it an overmatch for its antagonist. Geometry assists us in the application of this law by giving us the just dimensions of all the parts and figures which can enter into any species of machine, but still the discovery of the law itself is owing merely to experience and all the abstract reasonings in the world could never lead us one step towards the knowledge of it. When we reason *a priori* and consider merely any object or cause as it appears to the mind, independent of all observation, it never could suggest to us the notion of any distinct object, such as its effect, much less show us the inseparable and inviolable connection between them. A man must be very sagacious who could discover by reasoning that crystal is the effect of heat, and ice of cold, without being previously acquainted with the operation of these qualities.

Part II.

But we have not yet attained any tolerable satisfaction with regard to the question first proposed. Each solution still gives rise to a new question as difficult as the foregoing and leads us on to further inquiries. When it is asked, *What is the nature of all our reasonings concerning matter of fact?* the proper answer seems to be that they are founded on the relation of cause and effect. When again it is asked, *What is the foundation of all our reasonings and conclusions concerning that relation?* it may be replied in one word, experience. But if we still carry on our sifting

19. [Compare with Sect. V, Pt. I.]
20. [For Hume, "mixed mathematics" is equivalent to what would today be called "applied mathematics", or the application of mathematics or mathematical principles to the physical world and experience, as, for instance, in astronomy, surveying, or the calculation of probabilities.]

humor and ask, *What is the foundation of all conclusions from experience?* this implies a new question which may be of more difficult solution and explication. Philosophers who give themselves airs of superior wisdom and sufficiency have a hard task when they encounter persons of inquisitive dispositions, who push them from every corner to which they retreat, and who are sure at last to bring them to some dangerous dilemma. The best expedient to prevent this confusion is to be modest in our pretensions and even to discover the difficulty ourselves before it is objected to us. By this means we may make a kind of merit of our very ignorance.

I shall content myself in this section with an easy task and shall pretend only to give a negative answer to the question here proposed. I say, then, that even after we have experience of the operations of cause and effect, our conclusions from that experience are not founded on reasoning or any process of the understanding. This answer we must endeavor both to explain and to defend.

It must certainly be allowed that nature has kept us at a great distance from all her secrets and has afforded us only the knowledge of a few superficial qualities of objects, while she conceals from us those powers and principles on which the influence of these objects entirely depends. Our senses inform us of the color, weight, and consistency of bread, but neither sense nor reason can ever inform us of those qualities which fit it for the nourishment and support of a human body. Sight or feeling conveys an idea of the actual motion of bodies, but as to that wonderful force or power which would carry on a moving body forever in a continued change of place and which bodies never lose but by communicating it to others, of this we cannot form the most distant conception. But notwithstanding this ignorance of natural powers[21] and principles, we always presume when we see like sensible qualities that they have like secret powers and expect that effects similar to those which we have experienced will follow from them. If a body of like color and consistency with that bread which we have formerly eaten is presented to us, we make no scruple of repeating the experiment and foresee with certainty

like nourishment and support. Now this is a process of the mind or thought of which I would willingly know the foundation. It is allowed on all hands that there is no known connection between the sensible qualities and the secret powers, and consequently that the mind is not led to form such a conclusion concerning their constant and regular conjunction by anything which it knows of their nature. As to past *experience*, it can be allowed to give *direct* and *certain* information of those precise objects only and that precise period of time which fell under its cognizance. But why this experience should be extended to future times and to other objects which, for all we know, may be only similar in appearance; this is the main question on which I would insist. The bread which I formerly ate nourished me—that is, a body of such sensible qualities was, at that time, endowed with such secret powers. But does it follow that other bread must also nourish me at another time and that like sensible qualities must always be attended with like secret powers? The consequence seems in no way necessary. At least, it must be acknowledged that there is here a consequence drawn by the mind that there is a certain step taken, a process of thought, and an inference which wants to be explained. These two propositions are far from being the same: *I have found that such an object has always been attended with such an effect*, and *I foresee that other objects which are similar in appearance will be attended with similar effects*. I shall allow, if you please, that the one proposition may justly be inferred from the other; I know in fact that it always is inferred. But if you insist that the inference is made by a chain of reasoning, I desire you to produce that reasoning. The connection between these propositions is not intuitive. There is required a medium which may enable the mind to draw such an inference, if indeed it is drawn by reasoning and argument. What that medium is, I must confess, passes my comprehension; and it is incumbent on those to produce it who assert that it really exists and is the origin of all our conclusions concerning matter of fact.

This negative argument must certainly, in process of time, become altogether convincing if many penetrating and able philosophers shall turn their inquiries this way and no one is ever able to discover any connecting proposition or intermediate step which supports the understanding in this conclusion. But

---

21. ["Power" is used loosely, in a popular sense. A more detailed explanation of the word would lend strength to the argument. See Section VII.]

as the question is yet new, every reader may not trust so far to his own penetration as to conclude that, because an argument escapes his inquiry, therefore it does not really exist. For this reason it may be requisite to venture upon a more difficult task, and, enumerating all the branches of human knowledge, endeavor to show that none of them can afford such an argument.

All reasonings may be divided into two kinds, namely, demonstrative reasoning, or that concerning relations of ideas, and moral reasoning, or that concerning matter of fact and existence. That there are no demonstrative arguments in the case seems evident, since it implies no contradiction that the course of nature may change and that an object, seemingly like those which we have experienced, may be attended with different or contrary effects. May I not clearly and distinctly conceive that a body, falling from the clouds and which in all other respects resembles snow, has yet the taste of salt or feeling of fire? Is there any more intelligible proposition than to affirm that all the trees will flourish in December and January and decay in May and June? Now, whatever is intelligible and can be distinctly conceived implies no contradiction and can never be proved false by any demonstrative argument or abstract reasoning *a priori*.

If we are, therefore, engaged by arguments to put trust in past experience and make it the standard of our future judgment, these arguments must be probable only, or such as regard matter of fact and real existence according to the division above mentioned. But that there is no argument of this kind must appear if our explication of that species of reasoning is admitted as solid and satisfactory. We have said that all arguments concerning existence are founded on the relation of cause and effect, that our knowledge of that relation is derived entirely from experience, and that all our experimental conclusions proceed upon the supposition that the future will be conformable to the past. To endeavor, therefore, the proof of this last supposition by probable arguments, or arguments regarding existence, must be evidently going in a circle and taking that which is the very point in question for granted.

In reality, all arguments from experience are founded on the similarity which we discover among natural objects and by which we are induced to expect effects similar to those which we have found to follow from such objects. And though none but a fool or madman will ever pretend to dispute the authority of experience or to reject that great guide of human life, it may surely be allowed a philosopher to have so much curiosity at least as to examine the principle of human nature which gives this mighty authority to experience and makes us draw advantage from that similarity which nature has placed among different objects. From causes which appear *similar*, we expect similar effects. This is the sum of all our experimental conclusions. Now it seems evident that, if this conclusion were formed by reason, it would be as perfect at first, and upon one instance, as after ever so long a course of experience. But the case is far otherwise. Nothing so like as eggs, yet no one, on account of this appearing similarity, expects the same taste and relish in all of them. It is only after a long course of uniform experiments in any kind that we attain a firm reliance and security with regard to a particular event. Now where is that process of reasoning which, from one instance, draws a conclusion so different from that which it infers from a hundred instances that are in no way different from that single one? This question I propose as much for the sake of information as with an intention of raising difficulties. I cannot find, I cannot imagine any such reasoning. But I keep my mind still open to instruction, if anyone will vouchsafe to bestow it on me.

Should it be said that, from a number of uniform experiments, we *infer* a connection between the sensible qualities and the secret powers? This, I must confess, seems the same difficulty couched in different terms. The question still recurs: on what process of argument this *inference* is founded? Where is the medium, the interposing ideas which join propositions so very wide of each other? It is confessed that the color, consistency, and other sensible qualities of bread do not appear of themselves to have any connection with the secret powers of nourishment and support. For otherwise we could infer these secret powers from the first appearance of these sensible qualities without the aid of experience, contrary to the sentiment of all philosophers and contrary to plain matter of fact. Here, then, is our natural state of ignorance with regard to the powers and influence of all objects. How is this remedied by experience? It only shows us a number of uniform effects resulting from certain objects and teaches us that those particu-

Skepticism

lar objects, at that particular time, were endowed with such powers and forces. When a new object endowed with similar sensible qualities is produced, we expect similar powers and forces and look for a like effect. From a body of like color and consistency with bread, we expect like nourishment and support. But this surely is a step or progress of the mind which wants to be explained. When a man says, *I have found, in all past instances, such sensible qualities conjoined with such secret powers*: And when he says, *Similar sensible qualities will always be conjoined with similar secret powers*; he is not guilty of a tautology, nor are these propositions in any respect the same. You say that the one proposition is an inference from the other. But you must confess that the inference is not intuitive, neither is it demonstrative. Of what nature is it then? To say it is experimental is begging the question. For all inferences from experience suppose as their foundation that the future will resemble the past and that similar powers will be conjoined with similar sensible qualities. If there is any suspicion that the course of nature may change, and that the past may be no rule for the future, all experience becomes useless and can give rise to no inference or conclusion. It is impossible, therefore, that any arguments from experience can prove this resemblance of the past to the future, since all these arguments are founded on the supposition of that resemblance. Let the course of things be allowed up to now ever so regular, that alone, without some new argument or inference, does not prove that for the future it will continue so. In vain do you pretend to have learned the nature of bodies from your past experience. Their secret nature and, consequently, all their effects and influence may change without any change in their sensible qualities. This happens sometimes and with regard to some objects. Why may it not happen always and with regard to all objects? What logic, what process of argument secures you against this supposition? My practice, you say, refutes my doubts. But you mistake the purport of my question. As an agent, I am quite satisfied in the point; but as a philosopher who has some share of curiosity—I will not say skepticism—I want to learn the foundation of this inference. No reading, no inquiry has yet been able to remove my difficulty or give me satisfaction in a matter of such importance. Can I do better than propose the difficulty to the public, even

though, perhaps, I have small hopes of obtaining a solution? We shall at least, by this means, be sensible of our ignorance, if we do not augment our knowledge.

I must confess that a man is guilty of unpardonable arrogance who concludes, because an argument has escaped his own investigation, that therefore it does not really exist. I must also confess that, though all the learned for several ages should have employed themselves in fruitless search upon any subject, it may still, perhaps, be rash to conclude positively that the subject must therefore pass all human comprehension. Even though we examine all the sources of our knowledge and conclude them unfit for such a subject, there may still remain a suspicion that the enumeration is not complete or the examination not accurate. But with regard to the present subject, there are some considerations which seem to remove all this accusation of arrogance or suspicion of mistake.

It is certain that the most ignorant and stupid peasants, no infants, no even brute beasts, improve by experience and learn the qualities of natural objects by observing the effects which result from them. When a child has felt the sensation of pain from touching the flame of a candle, he will be careful not to put his hand near any candle, but will expect a similar effect from a cause which is similar in its sensible qualities and appearance. If you assert, therefore, that the understanding of the child is led into this conclusion by any process of argument or ratiocination, I may justly require you to produce that argument, nor have you any pretense to refuse so equitable a demand. You cannot say that the argument is abstruse and may possibly escape your inquiry, since you confess that it is obvious to the capacity of a mere infant. If you hesitate therefore a moment or if, after reflection, you produce any intricate or profound argument, you, in a manner, give up the question and confess that it is not reasoning which engages us to suppose the past resembling the future and to expect similar effects from causes which are similar to appearance. This is the proposition which I intended to enforce in the present section. If I am right, I pretend not to have made any mighty discovery. And if I am wrong, I must acknowledge myself to be indeed a very backward scholar, since I cannot now discover an argument which, it seems, was perfectly familiar to me long before I was out of my cradle.

Section V
Skeptical Solution of These Doubts.
Part I.

The passion for philosophy, like that for religion, seems liable to this inconvenience that, though it aims at the correction of our manners and extirpation of our vices, it may only serve, by imprudent management, to foster a predominant inclination and push the mind, with more determined resolution, towards that side which already *draws* too much by the bias and propensity of the natural temper. It is certain that, while we aspire to the magnanimous firmness of the philosophic sage and endeavor to confine our pleasures altogether within our own minds, we may, at last, render our philosophy like that of Epictetus and other *Stoics*,[22] only a more refined system of selfishness, and reason ourselves out of all virtue as well as social enjoyment. While we study with attention the vanity of human life and turn all our thoughts towards the empty and transitory nature of riches and honors, we are, perhaps, all the while flattering our natural indolence which, hating the bustle of the world and drudgery of business, seeks a pretense of reason to give itself a full and uncontrolled indulgence. There is, however, one species of philosophy which seems little liable to this inconvenience, and that because it strikes in with no disorderly passion of the human mind, nor can mingle itself with any natural affection or propensity; and that is the Academic or skeptical philosophy.[23] The academics always talk of doubt and suspense of judgment, of danger in hasty determinations, of confining to very narrow bounds the inquiries of the understanding, and of renouncing all speculations which do not lie within the limits of common life and practice. Nothing, therefore, can be more contrary than such a philosophy to the supine indolence of the mind, its rash arrogance, its lofty pretensions, and its superstitious credulity. Every passion is mortified by it except the love of truth; and that passion never is nor can be carried to too high a degree. It is surprising, therefore, that this philosophy, which in almost every instance must be harmless and innocent, should be the subject of so much groundless reproach and blame. But, perhaps, the very circumstance which renders it so innocent is what chiefly exposes it to the public hatred and resentment. By flattering no irregular passion, it gains few partisans. By opposing so many vices and follies, it raises to itself abundance of enemies who stigmatize it as libertine, profane, and irreligious.

Nor need we fear that this philosophy, while it endeavors to limit our inquiries to common life, should ever undermine the reasonings of common life and carry its doubts so far as to destroy all action as well as speculation. Nature will always maintain her rights and prevail in the end over any abstract reasoning whatsoever. Though we should conclude, for instance, as in the foregoing section that, in all reasonings from experience, there is a step taken by the mind which is not supported by any argument or process of the understanding, there is no danger that these reasonings, on which almost all knowledge

22. [Stoicism, the school of philosophy that spanned at least five centuries, from the third century B.C. to the second century A.D., had as its main ethical tenet that man must live in harmony with nature; nature is construed as inherently rational and man must be rational as well. Epictetus (c. A.D.50–c. 130), an illustrious later Stoic, maintained that living in harmony with nature is a matter of distinguishing those things within our power from those which are not, and seeking to control only the former. This involves purging oneself of desires and strong feelings concerning the latter. As Epictetus noted, "Men are disturbed not by things, but by the view which they take of things" (*Encheiridion* V).]

23. [Academical or skeptical philosophy, the title of Section XII of the *Enquiry*, refers to the philosophy of the Greek Academy founded by Plato, more specifically, to the philosophy of the Academy in the second and third centuries

B.C., in which a form of moderate skepticism reputedly was espoused. For example, Carneades (c.213–128 B.C.), one of the leading members of the school, is said to have challenged Stoic doctrines concerning the infallibility of our perceptions and claimed that no perception is infallible or an object of knowledge. All we can be sure of is the nature of the "appearances". Still, the academic skeptics, unlike the Pyrrhonians (see footnote 84), formulated a theory of credible belief according to which some things are more probable than others, and did not advocate a suspension of judgment on all things. Hume is often taken to be advocating a theory of academic or moderate skepticism in the *Enquiry*. For a further discussion of this topic, see Richard H. Popkin, "David Hume: His Pyrrhonism and his Critique of Pyrrhonism" in *Hume*, edited by V.C. Chappell (South Bend, Ind.: 1968).]

depends, will ever be affected by such a discovery. If the mind is not engaged by argument to make this step, it must be induced by some other principle of equal weight and authority and that principle will preserve its influence as long as human nature remains the same. What that principle is may well be worth the pains of inquiry.

Suppose a person, though endowed with the strongest faculties of reason and reflection, to be brought on a sudden into this world; he would, indeed, immediately observe a continual succession of objects and one event following another, but he would not be able to discover anything further. He would not at first, by any reasoning, be able to reach the idea of cause and effect, since the particular powers by which all natural operations are performed never appear to the senses; nor is it reasonable to conclude, merely because one event in one instance precedes another, that therefore the one is the cause, the other the effect. Their conjunction may be arbitrary and casual. There may be no reason to infer the existence of one from the appearance of the other. And in a word, such a person without more experience could never employ his conjecture or reasoning concerning any matter of fact or be assured of anything beyond what was immediately present to his memory and senses.

Suppose again that he has acquired more experience and has lived so long in the world as to have observed similar objects or events to be constantly conjoined together—what is the consequence of this experience? He immediately infers the existence of one object from the appearance of the other. Yet he has not, by all his experience, acquired any idea or knowledge of the secret power by which the one object produces the other, nor is it by any process of reasoning he is engaged to draw this inference. But still he finds himself determined to draw it. And though he should be convinced that his understanding has no part in the operation, he would nevertheless continue in the same course of thinking. There is some other principle which determines him to form such a conclusion.

This principle is *custom* or *habit*. For wherever the repetition of any particular act or operation produces a propensity to renew the same act or operation without being impelled by any reasoning or process of the understanding, we always say that this propensity is the effect of *custom*. By employing that word we pre-

tend not to have given the ultimate reason of such a propensity. We only point out a principle of human nature which is universally acknowledged and which is well known by its effects. Perhaps we can push our inquiries no further or pretend to give the cause of this cause, but must rest contented with it as the ultimate principle which we can assign of all our conclusions from experience. It is sufficient satisfaction that we can go so far without repining at the narrowness of our faculties because they will carry us no further. And it is certain we here advance a very intelligible proposition at least, if not a true one, when we assert that after the constant conjunction of two objects, heat and flame, for instance, or weight and solidity, we are determined by custom alone to expect the one from the appearance of the other. This hypothesis seems even the only one which explains the difficulty why we draw, from a thousand instances, an inference which we are not able to draw from one instance that is in no respect different from them. Reason is incapable of any such variation. The conclusions which it draws from considering one circle are the same which it would form upon surveying all the circles in the universe. But no man, having seen only one body move after being impelled by another, could infer that every other body will move after a like impulse. All inferences from experience, therefore, are effects of custom, not of reasoning.[24]

Custom, then, is the great guide of human life. It is that principle alone which renders our experience useful to us and makes us expect, for the future, a similar train of events with those which have appeared in the past. Without the influence of custom we should be entirely ignorant of every matter of fact

---

24. Nothing is more usual than for writers, even on *moral*, *political*, or *physical* subjects, to distinguish between *reason* and *experience*, and to suppose, that these species of argumentation are entirely different from each other. The former are taken for the mere result of our intellectual faculties, which, by considering *a priori* the nature of things, and examining the effects, that must follow from their operation, establish particular principles of science and philosophy. The latter are supposed to be derived entirely from sense and observation, by which we learn what has actually resulted from the operation of particular objects, and are thence able to infer, what will, for the future, result from them. Thus, for instance, the limitations and restraints of

beyond what is immediately present to the memory and senses. We should never know how to adjust means to ends or to employ our natural powers in the production of any effect. There would be an end at once of all action as well as of the chief part of speculation.

---

civil government, and a legal constitution, may be defended, either from *reason*, which reflecting on the great frailty and corruption of human nature, teaches, that no man can safely be trusted with unlimited authority; or from *experience* and history, which inform us of the enormous abuses, that ambition, in every age and country, has been found to make of so imprudent a confidence.

The same distinction between reason and experience is maintained in all our deliberations concerning the conduct of life; while the experienced statesman, general, physician, or merchant is trusted and followed; and the unpractised novice, with whatever natural talents endowed, neglected and despised. Though it be allowed, that reason may form very plausible conjectures with regard to the consequences of such a particular conduct in such particular circumstances; it is still supposed imperfect, without the assistance of experience, which is alone able to give stability and certainty to the maxims, derived from study and reflection.

But notwithstanding that this distinction be thus universally received, both in the active and speculative scenes of life, I shall not scruple to pronounce, that it is, at bottom, erroneous, at least, superficial.

If we examine those arguments which, in any of the sciences above-mentioned, are supposed to be the mere effects of reasoning and reflection, they will be found to terminate, at last, in some general principle or conclusion, for which we can assign no reason but observation and experience. The only difference between them and those maxims, which are vulgarly esteemed the result of pure experience, is, that the former cannot be established without some process of thought, and some reflection on what we have observed, in order to distinguish its circumstances, and trace its consequences: Whereas in the latter, the experienced event is exactly and fully similar to that which we infer as the result of any particular situation. The history of a Tiberius or a Nero makes us dread a like tyranny, were our monarchs freed from the restraints of laws and senates: But the observation of any fraud or cruelty in private life is sufficient, with the aid of a little thought, to give us the same apprehension; while it serves as an instance of the general curruption of human nature, and shows us the danger which we must incur by reposing an entire confidence in mankind. In both cases, it is experience which is ultimately the foundation of our inference and conclusion.

There is no man so young and unexperienced, as not

But here it may be proper to remark that though our conclusions from experience carry us beyond our memory and senses and assure us of matters of fact, which happened in the most distant places and most remote ages, yet some fact must always be present to the senses or memory from which we may first proceed in drawing these conclusions. A man who should find in a desert country the remains of pompous buildings would conclude that the country had, in ancient times, been cultivated by civilized inhabitants, but did nothing of this nature occur to him, he could never form such an inference. We learn the events of former ages from history, but then we must peruse the volumes in which this instruction is contained and from this carry up our inferences from one testimony to another, until we arrive at the eyewitnesses and spectators of these distant events. In a word, if we proceed not upon some fact present to the memory or senses, our reasonings would be merely hypothetical; and however the particular links might be connected with each other, the whole chain of inferences would have nothing to support it, nor could we ever, by its means, arrive at the knowledge of any real existence. If I ask, why you believe any particular matter of fact which you relate, you must tell me some reason; and this reason will be some other fact connected with it. But as you cannot proceed after this manner *in infinitum*, you must at last terminate in some fact which is present to your memory or

---

to have formed, from observation, many general and just maxims concerning human affairs and the conduct of life; but it must be confessed, that when a man comes to put these in practice, he will be extremely liable to error, till time and farther experience both enlarge these maxims, and teach him their proper use and application. In every situation or incident, there are many particular and seemingly minute circumstances, which the man of greatest talents is, at first, apt to overlook, though on them the justness of his conclusions, and consequently the prudence of his conduct, entirely depend. Not to mention, that, to a young beginner, the general observations and maxims occur not always on the proper occasions, nor can be immediately applied with due calmness and distinction. The truth is, an unexperienced reasoner could be no reasoner at all, were he absolutely unexperienced; and when we assign that character to any one, we mean it only in a comparative sense, and suppose him possessed of experience, in a smaller and more imperfect degree.

senses or must allow that your belief is entirely without foundation.

What then is the conclusion of the whole matter? A simple one, though it must be confessed, pretty remote from the common theories of philosophy. All belief of matter of fact or real existence is derived merely from some object present to the memory or senses and a customary conjunction between that and some other object. Or, in other words, having found in many instances that any two kinds of objects, flame and heat, snow and cold, have always been conjoined together, if flame or snow is presented anew to the senses, the mind is carried by custom to expect heat or cold and to *believe* that such a quality does exist and will discover itself upon a nearer approach. This belief is the necessary result of placing the mind in such circumstances. It is an operation of the soul when we are so situated, as unavoidable as feeling the passion of love, when we receive benefits—or hatred, when we meet with injuries. All these operations are a species of natural instincts which no reasoning or process of the thought and understanding is able either to produce or to prevent.

At this point, it would be very allowable for us to stop our philosophical researches. In most questions we can never make a single step further; and in all questions, we must terminate here at last, after our most restless and curious inquiries. But still our curiosity will be pardonable, perhaps commendable, if it carry us on to still further researches and make us examine more accurately the nature of this *belief* and of the *customary conjunction* from which it is derived. By this means we may meet with some explications and analogies that will give satisfaction, at least to such as love the abstract sciences and can be entertained with speculations which, however accurate, may still retain a degree of doubt and uncertainty. As to readers of a different taste, the remaining part of this section is not calculated for them and the following inquiries may well be understood, though it is neglected.

Part II.

Nothing is more free than the imagination of man, and though it cannot exceed that original stock of ideas furnished by the internal and external senses, it has unlimited power of mixing, compounding, separating, and dividing these ideas, in all the varieties of fiction and vision. It can feign a train of events with all the appearance of reality, ascribe to them a particular time and place, conceive them as existent, and paint them out to itself with every circumstance that belongs to any historical fact which it believes with the greatest certainty. In what, therefore, consists the difference between such a fiction and belief? It lies not merely in any peculiar idea which is annexed to such a conception as commands our assent and which is wanting to every known fiction. For as the mind has authority over all its ideas, it could voluntarily annex this particular idea to any fiction and consequently be able to believe whatever it pleases; contrary to what we find by daily experience. We can, in our conception, join the head of a man to the body of a horse, but it is not in our power to believe that such an animal has ever really existed.

It follows, therefore, that the difference between *fiction* and *belief* lies in some sentiment or feeling which is annexed to the latter, not to the former, and which depends not on the will, nor can be commanded at pleasure. It must be excited by nature like all other sentiments and must arise from the particular situation in which the mind is placed at any particular juncture. Whenever any object is presented to the memory or senses, it immediately, by the force of custom, carries the imagination to conceive that object which is usually conjoined to it; and this conception is attended with a feeling or sentiment different from the loose reveries of the fancy. In this consists the whole nature of belief. For as there is no matter of fact which we believe so firmly that we cannot conceive the contrary, there would be no difference between the conception assented to and that which is rejected were it not for some sentiment which distinguishes the one from the other. If I see a billiard ball moving towards another on a smooth table, I can easily conceive it to stop upon contact. This conception implies no contradiction, but still it feels very differently from that conception by which I represent to myself the impulse and the communication of motion from one ball to another.

Were we to attempt a *definition* of this sentiment, we should, perhaps, find it a very difficult, if not an impossible task; in the same manner as if we should endeavor to define the feeling of cold, or passion of anger, to a creature who never had any experience of these sentiments. Belief is the true and proper name of this feeling, and no one is ever at a loss to know the meaning of that term, because every man is every moment conscious of the sentiment represented by it. It may not, however, be improper to attempt a *description* of this sentiment, in hopes we may by that means arrive at some analogies which may afford a more perfect explication of it. I say then that belief is nothing but a more vivid, lively, forcible, firm, steady conception of an object than what the imagination alone is ever able to attain. This variety of terms, which may seem so unphilosophical, is intended only to express that act of the mind which renders realities, or what is taken for such, more present to us than fictions, causes them to weigh more in the thought, and gives them a superior influence on the passions and imagination. Provided we agree about the thing, it is needless to dispute about the terms. The imagination has the command over all its ideas and can join and mix and vary them in all the ways possible. It may conceive fictitious objects with all the circumstances of place and time. It may set them in a manner before our eyes, in their true colors, just as they might have existed. But as it is impossible that this faculty of imagination can ever, of itself, reach belief, it is evident that belief consists not in the peculiar nature or order of ideas, but in the *manner* of their conception and in their *feeling* to the mind. I confess that it is impossible perfectly to explain this feeling or manner of conception. We may make use of words which express something near it. But its true and proper name, as we observed before, is *belief*, which is a term that everyone suffi-ciently understands in common life. And in philosophy we can go no further than assert that *belief* is something felt by the mind which distinguishes the ideas of the judgment from the fictions of the imagination. It gives them more weight and influence, makes them appear of greater importance, enforces them in the mind, and renders them the governing principle of our actions. I hear at present, for instance, a person's voice with whom I am acquainted and the sound comes as from the next room. This impression of my senses immediately conveys my thought to the person, together with all the surrounding objects. I paint them out to myself as existing at present with the same qualities and relations of which I formerly knew them possessed. These ideas take faster hold of my mind

than ideas of an enchanted castle. They are very different to the feeling and have a much greater influence of every kind, either to give pleasure or pain, joy or sorrow.

Let us, then, take in the whole compass of this doctrine and allow that the sentiment of belief is nothing but a conception more intense and steady than what attends the mere fictions of the imagination and that this *manner* of conception arises from a customary conjunction of the object with something present to the memory or senses. I believe that it will not be difficult, upon these suppositions, to find other operations of the mind analogous to it and to trace up these phenomena to principles still more general.

We have already observed that nature has established connections among particular ideas and that no sooner one idea occurs to our thoughts than it introduces its correlative and carries our attention towards it by a gentle and insensible movement. These principles of connection or association we have reduced to three, namely, *resemblance, contiguity,* and *causation*; these are the only bonds that unite our thoughts together and beget that regular train of reflection or discourse which, in a greater or less degree, takes place among all mankind. Now here arises a question on which the solution of the present difficulty will depend. Does it happen in all these relations that when one of the objects is presented to the senses or memory the mind is not only carried to the conception of the correlative, but reaches a steadier and stronger conception of it than what otherwise it would have been able to attain? This seems to be the case with that belief which arises from the relation of cause and effect. And if the case is the same with the other relations or principles of association, this may be established as a general law which takes place in all the operations of the mind.

We may, therefore, observe, as the first experiment to our present purpose, that upon the appearance of the picture of an absent friend, our idea of him is evidently enlivened by the *resemblance*, and that every passion which that idea occasions, whether of joy or sorrow, acquires new force and vigor. In producing this effect there concur both a relation and a present impression. Where the picture bears him no resemblance, at least was not intended for him, it never so much as conveys our thought to him. And where it is absent, as well as the person, though the mind may pass from the thought of the one to that of the other, it feels its idea to be rather weakened than enlivened by that transition. We take a pleasure in viewing the picture of a friend when it is set before us; but when it is removed, rather choose to consider him directly than by reflection in an image which is equally distant and obscure.

The ceremonies of the Roman Catholic religion may be considered as instances of the same nature. The devotees of that superstition usually plead in excuse for the mummeries with which they are upbraided that they feel the good effect of those external motions, and postures, and actions in enlivening their devotion and quickening their fervor, which otherwise would decay, if directed entirely to distant and immaterial objects. We shadow out the objects of our faith, they say, in sensible types and images, and render them more present to us by the immediate presence of these types than it is possible for us to do merely by an intellectual view and contemplation. Sensible objects have always a greater influence on the fancy than any other, and this influence they readily convey to those ideas to which they are related and which they resemble. I shall only infer from these practices and this reasoning that the effect of resemblance in enlivening the ideas is very common; and as in every case a resemblance and a present impression must concur, we are abundantly supplied with experiments to prove the reality of the foregoing principle.

We may add force to these experiments by others of a different kind, in considering the effects of *contiguity* as well as of *resemblance*. It is certain that distance diminishes the force of every idea and that, upon our approach to any object, though it does not discover itself to our senses, it operates upon the mind with an influence which imitates an immediate impression. The thinking on any object readily transports the mind to what is contiguous; but it is only the actual presence of an object that transports it with a superior vivacity. When I am a few miles from home, whatever relates to it touches me more nearly than when I am two hundred leagues distant, though even at that distance the reflecting on anything in the neighborhood of my friends or family naturally produces an idea of them. But, as in this latter case, both the objects of the mind are ideas, notwithstanding there is an easy transition between them; that

transition alone is not able to give a superior vivacity to any of the ideas, for want of some immediate impression.[25]

No one can doubt but causation has the same influence as the other two relations of resemblance and contiguity. Superstitious people are fond of the relics of saints and holy men, for the same reason that they seek after types or images in order to enliven their devotion and give them a more intimate and strong conception of those exemplary lives which they desire to imitate. Now it is evident that one of the best relics which a devotee could procure would be the handiwork of a saint; and if his clothes and furniture are ever to be considered in this light, it is because they were once at his disposal and were moved and affected by him; in this respect they are to be considered as imperfect effects and as connected with him by a shorter chain of consequences than any of those by which we learn the reality of his existence.

Suppose that the son of a friend who had been long dead or absent were presented to us; it is evident that this object would instantly revive its correlative idea and recall to our thoughts all past intimacies and familiarities in more lively colors than they would otherwise have appeared to us. This is another phenomenon which seems to prove the principle above mentioned.

We may observe that in these phenomena the belief of the correlative object is always presupposed, with-

---

25. [The reference is to Cicero, *de Finibus*, Lib. v.2: "Should I say that we came by it naturally, he said, or is it because of some delusion that we are more moved when we see those places in which we have heard that many noteworthy people spent their time, than if we were hearing of their deeds or reading one of their writings? And in fact I am myself moved at this moment; for Plato comes to my mind, who was the first, we are told, to make a habit of holding discussions here. And it is not just his memory which those little gardens bring to me—they seem to set the man himself before my eyes. Here is Speusippus, here is Xenocrates, and over there his pupil Polemo—that chair we are looking at was actually Polemo's. Even our own senate house—I mean the Hostilia, not the new one, which seems smaller to me since it was enlarged—I used to look at it and imagine Scipio, Cato, Laelius, and of course my own grandfather most of all. Such is the power of suggestion in places. It is not without good reason that the training of the memory is launched upon this basis."]

out which the relation could have no effect. The influence of the picture supposes that we *believe* our friend to have once existed. Contiguity to home can never excite our ideas of home unless we *believe* that it really exists. Now I assert that this belief, where it reaches beyond the memory or senses, is of a similar nature and arises from similar causes with the transition of thought and vivacity of conception here explained. When I throw a piece of dry wood into a fire, my mind is immediately carried to conceive that it augments, not extinguishes, the flame. This transition of thought from the cause to the effect does not proceed from reason. It derives its origin altogether from custom and experience. And as it first begins from an object present to the senses, it renders the idea or conception of flame more strong and lively than any loose, floating reverie of the imagination. That idea arises immediately. The thought moves instantly towards it and conveys to it all that force of conception which is derived from the impression present to the senses. When a sword is leveled at my breast, does not the idea of wound and pain strike me more strongly than when a glass of wine is presented to me, even though by accident this idea should occur after the appearance of the latter object? But what is there in this whole matter to cause such a strong conception except only a present object and a customary transition to the idea of another object which we have been accustomed to conjoin with the former? This is the whole operation of the mind in all our conclusions concerning matter of fact and existence; and it is a satisfaction to find some analogies by which it may be explained. The transition from a present object does in all cases give strength and solidity to the related idea.

Here, then, is a kind of preestablished harmony[26]

between the course of nature and the succession of our ideas; and though the powers and forces by which the former is governed are wholly unknown to us, yet our thoughts and conceptions have still, we find, gone on in the same train with the other works of nature. Custom is that principle by which this correspondence has been effected, so necessary to the subsistence of our species and the regulation of our conduct in every circumstance and occurrence of human life. Had not the presence of an object instantly excited the idea of those objects commonly conjoined with it, all our knowledge must have been limited to the narrow sphere of our memory and senses and we should never have been able to adjust means to ends or employ our natural powers either to the producing of good or avoiding of evil. Those who delight in the discovery and contemplation of *final causes*[27] have here ample subject to employ their wonder and admiration.

I shall add, for a further confirmation of the foregoing theory, that as this operation of the mind by which we infer like effects from like causes, and *vice versa*, is so essential to the subsistence of all human creatures, it is not probable that it could be trusted to the fallacious deductions of our reason, which is slow in its operations, does not appear, in any degree, during the first years of infancy, and at best is in every age and period of human life extremely liable to error and mistake. It is more conformable to the ordinary wisdom of nature to secure so necessary an act of the mind by some instinct or mechanical tendency which may be infallible in its operations, may discover itself at the first appearance of life and thought, and may be independent of all the labored deductions of the understanding. As nature has taught us the use of our limbs without giving us the knowledge of the muscles and nerves by which they are actuated, so has she implanted in us an instinct which carries forward the thought in a correspondent course to that which she

26. [In the philosophy of Leibniz (1646–1716), "pre-established harmony" refers to the fact that as there can be no interaction between one entity or substance and another, whether in perception or action, God must create each entity in the universe so that its states arise from itself and yet in complete harmony or conformity with the states of all other things. Leibniz illustrated this notion by using the example of two clocks. They can be in perfect agreement, not because they mutually influence each other, nor because they are continually adjusted, but because they are manufactured so skillfully that keeping the same time is guaranteed.]

27. [In the philosophy of Aristotle (384–322 B.C.), a final cause is a structure common to members of a species, which helps to make intelligible the changes of the members and which answers the question: What is the end or goal of the thing? The concept was frequently applied to the universe itself, and it was maintained that the universe had an end state or goal toward which it was heading. See *Enquiry*, Section XI.]

has established among external objects, though we are ignorant of those powers and forces on which this regular course and succession of objects totally depends.

SECTION VI
Of Probability.[28]

Though there is no such thing as *chance* in the world, our ignorance of the real cause of any event has the same influence on the understanding and begets a like species of belief or opinion.

There is certainly a probability which arises from a superiority of chances on any side and, according as this superiority increases and surpasses the opposite chances, the probability receives a proportional increase and begets still a higher degree of belief or assent to that side in which we discover the superiority. If a die were marked with one figure or number of spots on four sides, and with another figure or number of spots on the two remaining sides, it would be more probable that the former would turn up than the latter, though, if it had a thousand sides marked in the same manner and only one side different, the probability would be much higher and our belief or expectation of the event more steady and secure. This process of the thought or reasoning may seem trivial and obvious, but to those who consider it more narrowly, it may, perhaps, afford matter for curious speculation.

It seems evident that when the mind looks forward to discover the event which may result from the throw of such a die, it considers the turning up of each particular side as alike probable and it is the very nature of chance to render all the particular events comprehended in it entirely equal. But finding a greater number of sides concur in the one event than in the other, the mind is carried more frequently to that event and meets it more often in revolving the various possibilities or chances on which the ultimate result depends. This concurrence of several views in one particular event begets immediately, by an inexplicable contrivance of nature, the sentiment of belief and gives that event the advantage over its antagonist which is supported by a smaller number of views and recurs less frequently to the mind. If we allow that belief is nothing but a firmer and stronger conception of an object than what attends the mere fictions of the imagination, this operation may, perhaps, in some measure be accounted for. The concurrence of these several views or glimpses imprints the idea more strongly on the imagination, gives it superior force and vigor, renders its influence on the passions and affections more sensible, and, in a word, begets that reliance or security which constitutes the nature of belief and opinion.

The case is the same with the probability of causes as with that of chance. There are some causes which are entirely uniform and constant in producing a particular effect and no instance has ever yet been found of any failure or irregularity in their operation. Fire has always burned, and water suffocated, every human creature. The production of motion by impulse and gravity is a universal law which has up to now admitted of no exception. But there are other causes which have been found more irregular and uncertain; nor has rhubarb always proved a purge, or opium a soporific, to everyone who has taken these medicines. It is true, when any cause fails of producing its usual effect, philosophers do not ascribe this to any irregularity in nature, but suppose that some secret causes in the particular structure of parts have prevented the operation. Our reasonings, however, and conclusions concerning the event are the same as if this principle had no place. Being determined by custom to transfer the past to the future in all our inferences, where the past has been entirely regular and uniform, we expect the event with the greatest assurance and leave no room for any contrary supposition. But where different effects have been found to follow from causes which are to *appearance* exactly similar, all these various effects must occur to the mind in transferring the past to the future and enter into our consideration when we determine the probability of the event. Though we give the preference to that which has been found most usual and believe that this effect will exist, we must not overlook the

---

28. Mr. Locke divides all arguments into demonstrative and probable. In this view, we must say, that it is only probable all men must die, or that the sun will rise tomorrow. But to conform our language more to common use, we ought to divide arguments into *demonstrations*, *proofs*, and *probabilities*. By proofs meaning such arguments from experience as leave no room for doubt or opposition. [For Hume's explanation of "opposition," see Section X.]

other effects, but must assign to each of them a particular weight and authority in proportion as we have found it to be more or less frequent. It is more probable, in almost every country of Europe, that there will be frost sometime in January than that the weather will continue open throughout that whole month, though this probability varies according to the different climates and approaches to a certainty in the more northern kingdoms. Here, then, it seems evident that when we transfer the past to the future in order to determine the effect which will result from any cause, we transfer all the different events in the same proportion as they have appeared in the past and conceive one to have existed a hundred times, for instance, another ten times, and another once. As a great number of views do here concur in one event, they fortify and confirm it to the imagination, beget that sentiment which we call *belief*, and give its object the preference above the contrary event which is not supported by an equal number of experiments and does not recur so frequently to the thought in transferring the past to the future. Let anyone try to account for this operation of the mind upon any of the received systems of philosophy and he will be sensible of the difficulty. For my part, I shall think it sufficient if the present hints excite the curiosity of philosophers and make them sensible how defective all common theories are in treating of such curious and such sublime subjects.

SECTION VII
Of the Idea of Necessary Connection.
Part I.

The great advantage of the mathematical sciences above the moral consists in this, that the ideas of the former, being sensible, are always clear and determinate, the smallest distinction between them is immediately perceptible, and the same terms are still expressive of the same ideas without ambiguity or variation. An oval is never mistaken for a circle, nor an hyperbola for an ellipsis. The isosceles and scalene are distinguished by boundaries more exact than vice and virtue, right and wrong. If any term is defined in geometry, the mind readily, of itself, substitutes on all occasions the definition for the term defined. Or

even when no definition is employed, the object itself may be presented to the senses and by that means be steadily and clearly apprehended. But the finer sentiments of the mind, the operations of the understanding, the various agitations of the passions, though really in themselves distinct, easily escape us when surveyed by reflection; nor is it in our power to recall the original object as often as we have occasion to contemplate it. Ambiguity, by this means, is gradually introduced into our reasonings. Similar objects are readily taken to be the same and the conclusion becomes at last very wide of the premises.

One may safely, however, affirm that if we consider these sciences in a proper light, their advantages and disadvantages nearly compensate each other and reduce both of them to a state of equality. If the mind, with greater facility, retains the ideas of geometry clear and determinate, it must carry on a much longer and more intricate chain of reasoning and compare ideas much wider of each other in order to reach the more abstruse truths of that science. And if moral ideas are apt, without extreme care, to fall into obscurity and confusion, the inferences are always much shorter in these disquisitions and the intermediate steps which lead to the conclusion much fewer than in the sciences which treat of quantity and number. In reality, there is scarcely a proposition in Euclid so simple as not to consist of more parts than are to be found in any moral reasoning which runs not into chimera and conceit. Where we trace the principles of the human mind through a few steps, we may be very well satisfied with our progress, considering how soon nature throws a bar to all our inquiries concerning causes and reduces us to an acknowledgment of our ignorance. The chief obstacle, therefore, to our improvement in the moral or metaphysical sciences is the obscurity of the ideas and ambiguity of the terms. The principal difficulty in mathematics is the length of inferences and compass of thought requisite to the forming of any conclusion. And, perhaps, our progress in natural philosophy is chiefly retarded by the want of proper experiments and phenomena which are often discovered by chance and cannot always be found when requisite, even by the most diligent and prudent inquiry. As moral philosophy seems up to now to have received less improvement than either geometry or physics, we may conclude that if there is any difference in this respect among these sciences, the difficulties which obstruct the progress of the former require superior care and capacity to be surmounted.

There are no ideas which occur in metaphysics more obscure and uncertain than those of *power, force, energy,* or *necessary connection,* of which it is every moment necessary for us to treat in all our disquisitions. We shall, therefore, endeavor in this section to fix, if possible, the precise meaning of these terms and thereby remove some part of that obscurity which is so much complained of in this species of philosophy.

It seems a proposition which will not admit of much dispute that all our ideas are nothing but copies of our impressions, or, in other words, that it is impossible for us to *think* of anything which we have not antecedently *felt* either by our external or internal senses. I have endeavored[29] to explain and prove this proposition, and have expressed my hopes that by a proper application of it men may reach a greater clearness and precision in philosophical reasonings than what they have up to now been able to attain. Complex ideas may, perhaps, be well known by definition, which is nothing but an enumeration of those parts or simple ideas that compose them. But when we have pushed up definitions to the most simple ideas and find still some ambiguity and obscurity, what resource are we then possessed of? By what invention can we throw light upon these ideas and render them altogether precise and determinate to our intellectual view? Produce the impressions or original sentiments from which the ideas are copied. These impressions are all strong and sensible. They do not admit of ambiguity. They are not only placed in a full light themselves, but may throw light on their correspondent ideas, which lie in obscurity. And by this means we may, perhaps, attain a new microscope or species of optics by which, in the moral sciences, the most minute and most simple ideas may be so enlarged as to fall readily under our apprehension and be equally known with the grossest and most sensible ideas that can be the object of our inquiry.

To be fully acquainted, therefore, with the idea of power or necessary connection, let us examine its impression and, in order to find the impression with greater certainty, let us search for it in all the sources from which it may possibly be derived.

When we look about us towards external objects and consider the operation of causes, we are never able, in a single instance, to discover any power or necessary connection, any quality which binds the effect to the cause and renders the one an infallible consequence of the other. We only find that the one does actually in fact follow the other. The impulse of one billiard ball is attended with motion in the second. This is the whole that appears to the *outward* senses. The mind feels no sentiment or *inward* impression from this succession of objects. Consequently, there is not, in any single particular instance of cause and effect, anything which can suggest the idea of power or necessary connection.

From the first appearance of an object we never can conjecture what effect will result from it. But were the power or energy of any cause discoverable by the mind, we could foresee the effect, even without experience, and might, at first, pronounce with certainty concerning it by the mere dint of thought and reasoning.

In reality, there is no part of matter that ever does, by its sensible qualities, discover any power or energy or give us ground to imagine that it could produce anything or be followed by any other object which we could denominate its effect. Solidity, extension, motion—these qualities are all complete in themselves and never point out any other event which may result from them. The scenes of the universe are continually shifting and one object follows another in an uninterrupted succession; but the power or force which actuates the whole machine is entirely concealed from us and never discovers itself in any of the sensible qualities of body. We know that, in fact, heat is a constant attendant of flame, but what is the connection between them we have no room so much as to conjecture or imagine. It is impossible, therefore, that the idea of power can be derived from the contemplation of bodies in single instances of their operation, because no bodies ever discover any power which can be the original of this idea.[30]

---

29. Section II. Of the Origin of Ideas.

30. Mr. Locke, in his chapter of power, says, that, finding from experience, that there are several new productions in matter, and concluding that there must somewhere be a

Since, therefore, external objects as they appear to the senses give us no idea of power or necessary connection by their operation in particular instances, let us see whether this idea is derived from reflection on the operations of our own minds and is copied from any internal impression. It may be said that we are every moment conscious of internal power, while we feel that, by the simple command of our will, we can move the organs of our body or direct the faculties of our mind. An act of volition produces motion in our limbs or raises a new idea in our imagination. This influence of the will we know by consciousness. Hence we acquire the idea of power or energy and are certain that we ourselves and all other intelligent beings are possessed of power. This idea, then, is an idea of reflection, since it arises from reflecting on the operations of our own mind and on the command which is exercised by will, both over the organs of the body and faculties of the mind.

We shall proceed to examine this pretension and, first, with regard to the influence of volition over the organs of the body. This influence, we may observe, is a fact which, like all other natural events, can be known only by experience and can never be foreseen from any apparent energy or power in the cause which connects it with the effect and renders the one an infallible consequence of the other. The motion of our body follows upon the command of our will. Of this we are every moment conscious. But the means by which this is effected, the energy by which the will performs so extraordinary an operation, of this we are so far from being immediately conscious that it must forever escape our most diligent inquiry.

For *first*, is there any principle in all nature more mysterious than the union of soul with body, by which a supposed spiritual substance acquires such an influence over a material one that the most refined thought is able to actuate the grossest matter? Were we empowered by a secret wish to remove mountains or control the planets in their orbit, this extensive authority would not be more extraordinary, nor more

beyond our comprehension. But if by consciousness we perceived any power or energy in the will, we must know this power; we must know its connection with the effect; we must know the secret union of soul and body, and the nature of both these substances by which the one is able to operate in so many instances upon the other.

Secondly, we are not able to move all the organs of the body with a like authority, though we cannot assign any reason besides experience for so remarkable a difference between one and the other. Why has the will an influence over the tongue and fingers, not over the heart or liver? This question would never embarrass us were we conscious of a power in the former case, not in the latter. We should then perceive, independent of experience, why the authority of will over the organs of the body is circumscribed within such particular limits. Being in that case fully acquainted with the power or force by which it operates, we should also know why its influence reaches precisely to such boundaries, and no further.

A man suddenly struck with a palsy in the leg or arm or who had newly lost those members frequently endeavors, at first, to move them and employ them in their usual offices. Here he is as much conscious of power to command such limbs as a man in perfect health is conscious of power to actuate any member which remains in its natural state and condition. But consciousness never deceives. Consequently, neither in the one case nor in the other are we ever conscious of any power. We learn the influence of our will from experience alone. And experience only teaches us how one event constantly follows another, without instructing us in the secret connection which binds them together and renders them inseparable.

Thirdly, we learn from anatomy that the immediate object of power in voluntary motion is not the member itself which is moved, but certain muscles and nerves and animal spirits[31] and, perhaps, something still more minute and more unknown through which the motion is successively propagated before it reaches the member itself whose motion is the immediate object of volition. Can there be a more certain

power capable of producing them, we arrive at last by this reasoning at the idea of power. But no reasoning can ever give us a new, original, simple idea; as this philosopher himself confesses. This, therefore, can never be the origin of that idea. [The reference is to Locke's *Essay*, Bk. II, ch. XXI.]

31. [Fluids or currents in the nerves produced by the warming of the blood. "Animal spirits" was a major concept in seventeenth- and eighteenth-century attempts to explain sensation, bodily motion, and voluntary behavior.]

proof that the power by which this whole operation is performed, so far from being directly and fully known by an inward sentiment or consciousness, is to the last degree mysterious and unintelligible? Here the mind wills a certain event. Immediately another event, unknown to ourselves and totally different from the one intended, is produced. This event produces another, equally unknown, until at last, through a long succession the desired event is produced. But if the original power was felt, it must be known. If it was known, its effect must also be known, since all power is relative to its effect. And *vice versa*, if the effect is not known, the power cannot be known nor felt. How indeed can we be conscious of a power to move our limbs when we have no such power, but only that to move certain animal spirits which, though they produce at last the motion of our limbs, yet operate in such a manner as is wholly beyond our comprehension?

We may, therefore, conclude from the whole, I hope, without any temerity, though with assurance, that our idea of power is not copied from any sentiment or consciousness of power within ourselves when we give rise to animal motion or apply our limbs to their proper use and office. That their motion follows the command of the will is a matter of common experience, like other natural events. But the power or energy by which this is effected, like that in other natural events, is unknown and inconceivable.[32]

32. [It may be pretended, that the resistance which we meet with in bodies, obliging us frequently to exert our force, and call up all our power, this gives us the idea of force and power. It is this *nisus* or strong endeavour, of which we are conscious, that is the original impression from which this idea is copied. But, first, we attribute power to a vast number of objects, where we never can suppose this resistance or exertion of force to take place; to the Supreme Being, who never meets with any resistance; to the mind in its command over its ideas and limbs, in common thinking and motion, where the effect follows immediately upon the will, without any exertion or summoning up of force; to inanimate matter, which is not capable of this sentiment. *Secondly*, This sentiment of an endeavour to overcome resistance has no known connexion with any event: What follows it, we know by experience; but could not know it *a priori*. It must, however, be confessed, that the animal *nisus*, which we experience, though it can afford no accurate precise idea of power, enters very much into that vulgar, inaccurate idea, which is formed of it.]

Shall we then assert that we are conscious of a power or energy in our own minds when, by an act or command of our will, we raise up a new idea, fix the mind to the contemplation of it, turn it on all sides, and at last dismiss it for some other idea when we think that we have surveyed it with sufficient accuracy? I believe the same arguments will prove that even this command of the will gives us no real idea of force or energy.

First, it must be allowed that when we know a power, we know that very circumstance in the cause by which it is enabled to produce the effect, for these are supposed to be synonymous. We must, therefore, know both the cause and effect and the relation between them. But do we pretend to be acquainted with the nature of the human soul and the nature of an idea or the aptitude of the one to produce the other? This is a real creation, a production of something out of nothing, which implies a power so great that it may seem, at first sight, beyond the reach of any being less than infinite. At least it must be admitted that such a power is not felt, nor known, nor even conceivable by the mind. We only feel the event, namely, the existence of an idea consequent to a command of the will. But the manner in which this operation is performed, the power by which it is produced, is entirely beyond our comprehension.

Secondly, the command of the mind over itself is limited, as well as its command over the body; and these limits are not known by reason or any acquaintance with the nature of cause and effect, but only by experience and observation, as in all other natural events and in the operation of external objects. Our authority over our sentiments and passions is much weaker than that over our ideas; and even the latter authority is circumscribed within very narrow boundaries. Will anyone pretend to assign the ultimate reason of these boundaries or show why the power is deficient in one case, not in another?

Thirdly, this self-command is very different at different times. A man in health possesses more of it than one languishing with sickness. We are more master of our thoughts in the morning than in the evening—fasting, than after a full meal. Can we give any reason for these variations except experience? Where, then, is the power of which we pretend to be conscious? Is there not here, either in a spiritual or material substance or both, some secret mechanism or structure of parts upon which the effect depends and which, being entirely unknown to us, renders the power or energy of the will equally unknown and incomprehensible?

Volition is surely an act of the mind with which we are sufficiently acquainted. Reflect upon it. Consider it on all sides. Do you find anything in it like this creative power by which it raises from nothing a new idea and, with a kind of fiat, imitates the omnipotence of its Maker—if I may be allowed so to speak—who called forth into existence all the various scenes of nature? So far from being conscious of this energy in the will, it requires as certain experience as that of which we are possessed to convince us that such extraordinary effects do ever result from a simple act of volition.

The generality of mankind never find any difficulty in accounting for the more common and familiar operations of nature, such as the descent of heavy bodies, the growth of plants, the generation of animals, or the nourishment of bodies by food. But suppose that in all these cases they perceive the very force or energy of the cause by which it is connected with its effect and is forever infallible in its operation. They acquire, by long habit, such a turn of mind that upon the appearance of the cause they immediately expect with assurance its usual attendant and hardly conceive it possible that any other event could result from it. It is only on the discovery of extraordinary phenomena, such as earthquakes, pestilence, and prodigies of any kind, that they find themselves at a loss to assign a proper cause and to explain the manner in which the effect is produced by it. It is usual for men, in such difficulties, to have recourse to some invisible intelligent principle[33] as the immediate cause of that event which surprises them and which they think cannot be accounted for from the common powers of nature. But philosophers, who carry their scrutiny a little further, immediately perceive that, even in the most familiar events, the energy of the cause is as unintelligible as in the most unusual and that we only learn by experience the frequent conjunction of objects, without being ever able to comprehend anything like connection between them.

Here, then, many philosophers[34] think themselves obliged by reason to have recourse, on all occasions, to the same principle which the vulgar never appeal to but in cases that appear miraculous and supernatural. They acknowledge mind and intelligence to be not only the ultimate and original cause of all things, but the immediate and sole cause of every event which appears in nature. They pretend that those objects which are commonly denominated *causes* are in reality nothing but *occasions*; and that the true and direct principle of every effect is not any power or force in nature, but a volition of the Supreme Being, who wills that such particular objects should forever be conjoined with each other. Instead of saying that one billiard ball moves another by a force which it has derived from the author of nature, it is the Deity himself, they say, who, by a particular volition, moves the second ball, being determined to this operation by the impulse of the first ball, in consequence of those general laws which he has laid down to himself in the government of the universe. But philosophers advancing still in their inquiries, discover that as we are totally ignorant of the power on which depends the mutual operation of bodies, we are no less ignorant of that power on which depends the operation of mind on body or of body on mind; nor are we able, either from our senses or consciousness, to assign the ultimate principle in one case more than in the other. The same ignorance, therefore, reduces them to the same conclusion. They assert that the Deity is the immediate cause of the union between soul and body and that they are not the organs of sense which, being agitated by external objects, produce sensations in the mind, but that it is a particular volition of our omnipotent Maker which excites such a sensation in consequence of such a motion in the organ. In like manner, it is not any energy in the will that produces local motion in our members. It is God himself, who is pleased to second our will, in itself impotent, and to command that motion which we erroneously attribute to our own power and efficacy. Nor do philosophers stop at this conclusion. They[35] sometimes ex-

33. [In Latin, *"deus ex machina"*: In Greek and Roman plays, a deity brought in by stage machinery to intervene in the action or resolve a situation.]

34. [The remainder of this paragraph is a discussion of the views of the "occasionalists," followers of Descartes (1596–1650), whose most famous representative was Nicolas Malebranche (1638–1715).]

35. [Malebranche, for example.]

tend the same inference to the mind itself in its internal operations. Our mental vision or conception of ideas is nothing but a revelation made to us by our Maker. When we voluntarily turn our thoughts to any object and raise up its image in the fancy, it is not the will which creates that idea, it is the universal Creator who discovers it to the mind and renders it present to us.

Thus, according to these philosophers, every thing is full of God. Not content with the principle that nothing exists but by his will, that nothing possesses any power but by his concession, they rob nature and all created beings of every power in order to render their dependence on the Deity still more sensible and immediate. They do not consider that by this theory they diminish, instead of magnifying, the grandeur of those attributes which they affect so much to celebrate. It argues surely more power in the Deity to delegate a certain degree of power to inferior creatures than to produce everything by his own immediate volition. It argues more wisdom to contrive at first the fabric of the world with such perfect foresight that, of itself and by its proper operation, it may serve all the purposes of providence than if the great Creator were obliged every moment to adjust its parts and animate by his breath all the wheels of that stupendous machine.

But if we would have a more philosophical confutation of this theory, perhaps the two following reflections may suffice.

First, it seems to me that this theory of the universal energy and operation of the Supreme Being is too bold ever to carry conviction with it to a man sufficiently apprised of the weakness of human reason and the narrow limits to which it is confined in all its operations. Though the chain of arguments which conduct to it were ever so logical, there must arise a strong suspicion, if not an absolute assurance, that it has carried us quite beyond the reach of our faculties when it leads to conclusions so extraordinary and so remote from common life and experience. We arrived in fairyland long before we have reached the last steps of our theory; and *there* we have no reason to trust our common methods of argument or to think that our usual analogies and probabilities have any authority. Our line is too short to fathom such immense abysses. And however we may flatter ourselves that we are guided, in every step which we take, by a kind

of verisimilitude and experience, we may be assured that this fancied experience has no authority when we thus apply it to subjects that lie entirely out of the sphere of experience. But on this we shall have occasion to touch afterwards.[36]

Secondly, I cannot perceive any force in the arguments on which this theory is founded. We are ignorant, it is true, of the manner in which bodies operate on each other. Their force or energy is entirely incomprehensible. But are we not equally ignorant of the manner or force by which a mind, even the supreme mind, operates either on itself or on body? From where, I beseech you, do we acquire any idea of it? We have no sentiment or consciousness of this power in ourselves. We have no idea of the Supreme Being but what we learn from reflection on our own faculties. Were our ignorance, therefore, a good reason for rejecting anything, we should be led into that principle of denying all energy in the Supreme Being as much as in the grossest matter. We surely comprehend as little the operations of one as of the other. Is it more difficult to conceive that motion may arise from impulse than that it may arise from volition? All we know is our profound ignorance in both cases.[37]

36. [Section XII.]

37. I need not examine at length the *vis inertiae* which is so much talked of in the new philosophy, and which is ascribed to matter. We find by experience, that a body at rest or in motion continues for ever in its present state, till put from it by some new cause: And that a body impelled takes as much motion from the impelling body as it acquires itself. These are facts. When we call this a *vis inertiae*, we only mark these facts, without pretending to have any idea of the inert power; in the same manner as, when we talk of gravity, we mean certain effects without comprehending that active power. It was never the meaning of Sir Isaac Newton to rob second causes of all force or energy; though some of his followers have endeavoured to establish that theory upon his authority. On the contrary, that great philosopher had recourse to an ethereal active fluid to explain his universal attraction; though he was so cautious and modest as to allow, that it was a mere hypothesis, not to be insisted on, without more experiments. I must confess, that there is something in the fate of opinions a little extraordinary. Des Cartes insinuated that doctrine of the universal and sole efficacy of the Deity, without insisting on it. Malebranche and other Cartesians made it the foundation of all their philosophy. It had, however, no authority in England. Locke, Clarke [Samuel Clarke (1675–1729)], and Cud-

Part II.

But to hasten to a conclusion of this argument, which is already drawn out to too great a length. We have sought in vain for an idea of power or necessary connection in all the sources from which we could suppose it to be derived. It appears that in single instances of the operation of bodies we never can, by our utmost scrutiny, discover anything but one event following another, without being able to comprehend any force or power by which the cause operates or any connection between it and its supposed effect. The same difficulty occurs in contemplating the operations of mind on body, where we observe the motion of the latter to follow upon the volition of the former, but are not able to observe or conceive the tie which binds together the motion and volition, or the energy by which the mind produces this effect. The authority of the will over its own faculties and ideas is not a whit more comprehensible, so that, upon the whole, there does not appear, throughout all nature, any one instance of connection which is conceivable by us. All events seem entirely loose and separate. One event follows another, but we never can observe any tie

worth [Ralph Cudworth (1617–1688)], never so much as take notice of it, but supposed all along that matter has a real, though subordinate and derived power. By what means has it become so prevalent among our modern metaphysicians?

[The "new philosophy" is Newtonianism. The followers of Newton who might satisfy Hume's description and were also known to him include: George Cheyne (1671–1743), author of *Philosophical Principles of Religion: Natural and Revealed* (1715), and who some think was Hume's physician as a young man; Colin Maclaurin (1698–1746), who taught mathematics at the University of Edinburgh when Hume was a student there, and who wrote *An Account of Sir Isaac Newton's Philosophical Discoveries* (1748); and William Whiston (1667–1752), Newton's successor at Cambridge, and author of *A New Theory of the Earth* (1696). For a discussion of the relation between Hume and Newton see: James Noxon, *Hume's Philosophical Development: a Study of his Methods* (Oxford: 1973); Robert H. Hurlbutt III, *Hume, Newton, and the Design Argument* (Lincoln, Neb.: 1965); and Nicholas Capaldi, *David Hume: The Newtonian Philosopher* (Boston: 1975). One "modern metaphysician" would be George Berkeley, who maintained that since objects are merely collections of passive ideas, no agency is to be found in them.]

between them. They seem *conjoined*, but never *connected*. And as we can have no idea of anything which never appeared to our outward sense or inward sentiment, the necessary conclusion *seems* to be that we have no idea of connection or power at all and that these words are absolutely without any meaning when employed either in philosophical reasonings or common life.

But there still remains one method of avoiding this conclusion and one source which we have not yet examined. When any natural object or event is presented, it is impossible for us, by any sagacity or penetration to discover, or even conjecture, without experience, what event will result from it, or to carry our foresight beyond that object which is immediately present to the memory and senses. Even after one instance or experiment where we have observed a particular event to follow upon another, we are not entitled to form a general rule or foretell what will happen in like cases, it being justly esteemed an unpardonable temerity to judge of the whole course of nature from one single experiment, however accurate or certain. But when one particular species of event has always, in all instances, been conjoined with another, we make no longer any scruple of foretelling one upon the appearance of the other and of employing that reasoning which can alone assure us of any matter of fact or existence. We then call the one object *cause*, the other *effect*. We suppose that there is some connection between them, some power in the one by which it infallibly produces the other and operates with the greatest certainty and strongest necessity.

It appears, then, that this idea of a necessary connection among events arises from a number of similar instances which occur, of the constant conjunction of these events, nor can that idea ever be suggested by any one of these instances surveyed in all possible lights and positions. But there is nothing in a number of instances, different from every single instance, which is supposed to be exactly similar, except only that after a repetition of similar instances the mind is carried by habit, upon the appearance of one event, to expect its usual attendant and to believe that it will exist. This connection, therefore, which we *feel* in the mind, this customary transition of the imagination from one object to its usual attendant, is the sentiment or impression from which we form the idea of power or necessary connection. Nothing further is in the case. Contemplate the subject on all sides, you will never find any other origin of that idea. This is the sole difference between one instance, from which we can never receive the idea of connection, and a number of similar instances by which it is suggested. The first time a man saw the communication of motion by impulse, as by the shock of two billiard balls, he could not pronounce that the one event was *connected*, but only that it was *conjoined* with the other. After he has observed several instances of this nature, he then pronounces them to be *connected*. What alteration has happened to give rise to this new idea of *connection*? Nothing but that he now *feels* these events to be *connected* in his imagination and can readily foretell the existence of one from the appearance of the other. When we say, therefore, that one object is connected with another, we mean only that they have acquired a connection in our thought and give rise to this inference by which they become proofs of each other's existence—a conclusion, which is somewhat extraordinary, but which seems founded on sufficient evidence. Nor will its evidence be weakened by any general diffidence of the understanding or skeptical suspicion concerning every conclusion which is new and extraordinary. No conclusions can be more agreeable to skepticism than such as make discoveries concerning the weakness and narrow limits of human reason and capacity.

And what stronger instance can be produced of the surprising ignorance and weakness of the understanding than the present? For surely, if there is any relation among objects which it imports to us to know perfectly, it is that of cause and effect. On this are founded all our reasonings concerning matter of fact or existence. By means of it alone we attain any assurance concerning objects which are removed from the present testimony of our memory and senses. The only immediate utility of all sciences is to teach us how to control and regulate future events by their causes. Our thoughts and inquiries are, therefore, every moment employed about this relation; yet so imperfect are the ideas which we form concerning it that it is impossible to give any just definition of cause, except what is drawn from something extraneous and foreign to it. Similar objects are always conjoined with similar. Of this we have experience. Suitably to this experience, therefore, we may define a

cause to be *an object followed by another and where all the objects similar to the first are followed by objects similar to the second*. Or, in other words, *where, if the first object had not been, the second never had existed*. The appearance of a cause always conveys the mind, by a customary transition, to the idea of the effect. Of this also we have experience. We may, therefore, suitably to this experience, form another definition of cause, and call it *an object followed by another and whose appearance always conveys the thought to that other*. But though both these definitions are drawn from circumstances foreign to the cause, we cannot remedy this inconvenience or attain any more perfect definition which may point out that circumstance in the cause which gives it a connection with its effect. We have no idea of this connection, nor even any distinct notion what it is we desire to know when we endeavor at a conception of it. We say, for instance, that the vibration of this string is the cause of this particular sound. But what do we mean by that affirmation? We either mean that *this vibration is followed by this sound, and that all similar vibrations have been followed by similar sounds*: Or that *this vibration is followed by this sound and that upon the appearance of one, the mind anticipates the senses and forms immediately an idea of the other*. We may consider the relation of cause and effect in either of these two lights; but beyond these, we have no idea of it.[38]

To recapitulate, therefore, the reasonings of this

38. According to these explications and definitions, the idea of *power* is relative as much as that of *cause*; and both have a reference to an effect, or some other event constantly conjoined with the former. When we consider the *unknown* circumstance of an object, by which the degree or quantity of its effect is fixed and determined, we call that its power: And accordingly, it is allowed by all philosophers, that the effect is the measure of the power. But if they had any idea of power, as it is in itself, why could not they measure it in itself? The dispute whether the force of a body in motion be as its velocity, or the square of its velocity; this dispute, I say, needed not be decided by comparing its effects in equal or unequal times; but by a direct mensuration and comparison.

As to the frequent use of the words, Force, Power, Energy, etc. which every where occur in common conversation, as well as in philosophy; that is no proof, that we are acquainted, in any instance, with the connecting principle between cause and effect, or can account ultimately for section: Every idea is copied from some preceding impression or sentiment; and where we cannot find any impression, we may be certain that there is no idea. In all single instances of the operation of bodies or minds, there is nothing that produces any impression, nor consequently can suggest any idea of power or necessary connection. But when many uniform instances appear and the same object is always followed by the same event, we then begin to entertain the notion of cause and connection. We then *feel* a new sentiment or impression, namely, a customary connection in the thought or imagination between one object and its usual attendant and this sentiment is the original of that idea which we seek for. For as this idea arises from a number of similar instances and not from any single instance, it must arise from that circumstance in which the number of instances differ from every individual instance. But this customary connection or transition of the imagination is the only circumstance in which they differ. In every other particular they are alike. The first instance which we saw of motion communicated by the shock of two billiard balls (to return to this obvious illustration) is exactly similar to any instance that may, at present, occur to us, except only that we could not at first *infer* one event from the other, which we are enabled to do at present, after so long a course of uniform experience. I do not know whether the reader will readily apprehend this reasoning. I am afraid that, should I multiply words about it or throw it into a greater variety of lights, it would only become more

obscure and intricate. In all abstract reasonings, there is one point of view which, if we can happily hit, we shall go further towards illustrating the subject than by all the eloquence and copious expression in the world. This point of view we should endeavor to reach, and reserve the flowers of rhetoric for subjects which are more adapted to them.

Section VIII
Of Liberty and Necessity.
Part I.

It might reasonably be expected in questions which have been canvassed and disputed with great eagerness since the first origin of science and philosophy that the meaning of all the terms, at least, should have been agreed upon among the disputants, and our inquiries, in the course of two thousand years, been able to pass from words to the true and real subject of the controversy. For how easy may it seem to give exact definitions of the terms employed in reasoning and make these definitions, not the mere sound of words, the object of future scrutiny and examination? But if we consider the matter more narrowly, we shall be apt to draw a quite opposite conclusion. From this circumstance alone that a controversy has been long kept on foot and remains still undecided, we may presume that there is some ambiguity in the expression and that the disputants affix different ideas to the terms employed in the controversy. For as the faculties of the mind are supposed to be naturally alike in every individual—otherwise nothing could be more fruitless than to reason or dispute together—it would be impossible, if men affix the same ideas to their terms, that they could so long form different opinions of the same subject, especially when they communicate their views and each party turn themselves on all sides in search of arguments which may give them the victory over their antagonists. It is true that if men attempt the discussion of questions which lie entirely beyond the reach of human capacity, such as those concerning the origin of worlds or the economy of the intellectual system or region of spirits, they may long beat the air in their fruitless contests and never arrive at any determinate conclusion. But if the question regards any subject of common life and experience, nothing, one would

---

the production of one thing by another. These words, as commonly used, have very loose meanings annexed to them; and their ideas are very uncertain and confused. No animal can put external bodies in motion without the sentiment of a *nisus* or endeavour; and every animal has a sentiment or feeling from the stroke or blow of an external object, that is in motion. These sensations, which are merely animal, and from which we can *a priori* draw no inference, we are apt to transfer to inanimate objects, and to suppose, that they have some such feelings, whenever they transfer or receive motion. With regard to energies, which are exerted, without our annexing to them any idea of communicated motion, we consider only the constant experienced conjunction of the events; and as we *feel* a customary connexion between the ideas, we transfer that feeling to the objects; as nothing is more usual than to apply to external bodies every internal sensation, which they occasion.

think, could preserve the dispute so long undecided, but some ambiguous expressions which keep the antagonists still at a distance and hinder them from grappling with each other.

This has been the case in the long disputed question concerning liberty and necessity and to so remarkable a degree that, if I am not much mistaken, we shall find that all mankind, both learned and ignorant, have always been of the same opinion with regard to this subject and that a few intelligible definitions would immediately have put an end to the whole controversy. I admit that this dispute has been so much canvassed on all hands and has led philosophers into such a labyrinth of obscure sophistry that it is no wonder if a sensible reader indulge his ease so far as to turn a deaf ear to the proposal of such a question from which he can expect neither instruction nor entertainment. But the state of the argument here proposed may, perhaps, serve to renew his attention, as it has more novelty, promises at least some decision of the controversy, and will not much disturb his ease by any intricate or obscure reasoning.

I hope, therefore, to make it appear that all men have ever agreed in the doctrine both of necessity and of liberty, according to any reasonable sense which can be put on these terms, and that the whole controversy has up to now turned merely upon words. We shall begin with examining the doctrine of necessity.

It is universally allowed that matter, in all its operations, is actuated by a necessary force and that every natural effect is so precisely determined by the energy of its cause that no other effect, in such particular circumstances, could possibly have resulted from it. The degree and direction of every motion are, by the laws of nature, prescribed with such exactness that a living creature may as soon arise from the shock of two bodies as motion in any other degree or direction than what is actually produced by it. Would we, therefore, form a just and precise idea of *necessity*, we must consider from where that idea arises when we apply it to the operation of bodies.

It seems evident that, if all the scenes of nature were continually shifted in such a manner that no two events bore any resemblance to each other, but every object was entirely new, without any similitude to whatever had been seen before, we should never, in that case, have attained the least idea of necessity or of a connection among these objects. We might say, upon such a supposition, that one object or event has followed another, not that one was produced by the other. The relation of cause and effect must be utterly unknown to mankind. Inference and reasoning concerning the operations of nature would, from that moment, be at an end; and the memory and senses remain the only canals by which the knowledge of any real existence could possibly have access to the mind. Our idea, therefore, of necessity and causation arises entirely from the uniformity observable in the operations of nature, where similar objects are constantly conjoined together and the mind is determined by custom to infer the one from the appearance of the other. These two circumstances form the whole of that necessity which we ascribe to matter. Beyond the constant *conjunction* of similar objects and the consequent *inference* from one to the other, we have no notion of any necessity or connection.

If it appears, therefore, that all mankind have ever allowed, without any doubt or hesitation, that these two circumstances take place in the voluntary actions of men and in the operations of mind, it must follow that all mankind have ever agreed in the doctrine of necessity and that they have up to now disputed merely for not understanding each other.

As to the first circumstance, the constant and regular conjunction of similar events, we may possibly satisfy ourselves by the following considerations. It is universally acknowledged that there is a great uniformity among the actions of men in all nations and ages and that human nature remains still the same in its principles and operations. The same motives always produce the same actions. The same events follow from the same causes. Ambition, avarice, self-love, vanity, friendship, generosity, public spirit—these passions, mixed in various degrees and distributed through society, have been, from the beginning of the world, and still are the source of all the actions and enterprises which have ever been observed among mankind. Would you know the sentiments, inclinations, and course of life of the Greeks and Romans? Study well the temper and actions of the French and English. You cannot be much mistaken in transferring to the former *most* of the observations which you have made with regard to the latter. Mankind are so much the same, in all times and places, that history informs us of nothing new or strange in this particular. Its chief use is only to discover the constant and universal principles of human nature by showing men in all varieties of circumstances and situations and furnishing us with materials from which we may form our observations and become acquainted with the regular springs of human action and behavior. These records of wars, intrigues, factions, and revolutions are so many collections of experiments by which the politician or moral philosopher fixes the principles of his science, in the same manner as the physician or natural philosopher becomes acquainted with the nature of plants, minerals, and other external objects by the experiments which he forms concerning them. Nor are the earth, water, and other elements examined by Aristotle and Hippocrates[39] more like to those which at present lie under our observation than the men described by Polybius[40] and Tacitus[41] are to those who now govern the world.

Should a traveler, returning from a far country, bring us an account of men, wholly different from any with whom we were ever acquainted, men, who were entirely divested of avarice, ambition, or revenge, who knew no pleasure but friendship, generosity, and public spirit, we should immediately, from these circumstances, detect the falsehood and prove him a liar with the same certainty as if he had stuffed his narration with stories of centaurs and dragons, miracles and prodigies. And if we would explode any forgery in history, we cannot make use of a more convincing argument than to prove that the actions ascribed to any person are directly contrary to the course of nature and that no human motives, in such circumstances, could ever induce him to such a conduct. The veracity of Quintus Curtius[42] is as much to be suspected when he describes the supernatural courage of Alexander by which he was hurried on singly to attack multitudes, as when he describes his supernatural force and activity by which he was able to resist them. So readily and universally do we acknowledge a uniformity in human motives and actions as well as in the operations of body.

Hence, likewise, the benefit of that experience acquired by long life and a variety of business and company, in order to instruct us in the principles of human nature and regulate our future conduct as well as speculation. By means of this guide we mount up to the knowledge of men's inclinations and motives from their actions, expressions, and even gestures, and again descend to the interpretation of their actions from our knowledge of their motives and inclinations. The general observations, treasured up by a course of experience, give us the clue of human nature and teach us to unravel all its intricacies. Pretexts and appearances no longer deceive us. Public declarations pass for the specious coloring of a cause. And though virtue and honor are allowed their proper weight and authority, that perfect disinterestedness, so often pretended to, is never expected in multitudes and parties, seldom in their leaders, and scarcely even in individuals of any rank or station. But were there no uniformity in human actions and were every experiment which we could form of this kind irregular and anomalous, it would be impossible to collect any general observations concerning mankind and no experience, however accurately digested by reflection, would ever serve to any purpose. Why is the aged husband more skillful in his calling than the young beginner, but because there is a certain uniformity in the operation of the sun, rain, and earth towards the production of vegetables, and experience teaches the old practitioner the rules by which this operation is governed and directed?

We must not, however, expect that this uniformity of human actions should be carried to such a length as that all men, in the same circumstances, will always act precisely in the same manner, without making any allowance for the diversity of characters, prejudices, and opinions. Such a uniformity in every particular is found in no part of nature. On the contrary, from observing the variety of conduct in different men, we are enabled to form a greater variety of maxims which still suppose a degree of uniformity and regularity.

Are the manners of men different in different ages and countries? We learn from this the great force of

---

39. [Hippocrates (c. 460–c. 30 B.C.), a Greek physician, became known as "The Father of Medicine."]

40. [Polybius (c. 201–120 B.C.), a Greek historian, wrote of the rise of Rome.]

41. [Tacitus (55–c. 117), a Roman historian, wrote about the Germanic tribes and about the luxurious habits of Romans, which he criticized sharply.]

42. [Quintus Curtius Rufus, a first-century Roman author, wrote a history of Alexander the Great.]

custom and education which mold the human mind from its infancy and form it into a fixed and established character. Is the behavior and conduct of the one sex very unlike that of the other? It is from this we become acquainted with the different characters which nature has impressed upon the sexes and which she preserves with constancy and regularity. Are the actions of the same person much diversified in the different periods of his life from infancy to old age? This affords room for many general observations concerning the gradual change of our sentiments and inclinations and the different maxims which prevail in the different ages of human creatures. Even the characters which are peculiar to each individual have a uniformity in their influence; otherwise our acquaintance with the persons and our observation of their conduct could never teach us their dispositions or serve to direct our behavior with regard to them.

I grant it possible to find some actions which seem to have no regular connection with any known motives and are exceptions to all the measures of conduct which have ever been established for the government of men. But if we would willingly know what judgment should be formed of such irregular and extraordinary actions, we may consider the sentiments commonly entertained with regard to those irregular events which appear in the course of nature and the operations of external objects. All causes are not conjoined to their usual effects with like uniformity. An artificer who handles only dead matter may be disappointed of his aim as well as the politician who directs the conduct of sensible and intelligent agents.

The vulgar, who take things according to their first appearance, attribute the uncertainty of events to such an uncertainty in the causes as makes the latter often fail of their usual influence, though they meet with no impediment in their operation. But philosophers, observing that almost in every part of nature there is contained a vast variety of springs and principles which are hid by reason of their minuteness or remoteness, find that it is at least possible the contrariety of events may not proceed from any contingency in the cause but from the secret operation of contrary causes. This possibility is converted into certainty by further observation, when they remark that, upon an exact scrutiny, a contrariety of effects always betrays a contrariety of causes and proceeds from their mutual opposition. A peasant can give no better reason for

the stopping of any clock or watch than to say that it does not commonly go right. But an artist easily perceives that the same force in the spring or pendulum always has the same influence on the wheels, but fails of its usual effect, perhaps by reason of a grain of dust which puts a stop to the whole movement. From the observation of several parallel instances, philosophers form a maxim that the connection between all causes and effects is equally necessary and that its seeming uncertainty in some instances proceeds from the secret opposition of contrary causes.

Thus, for instance, in the human body, when the usual symptoms of health or sickness disappoint our expectation, when medicines do not operate with their wonted powers, when irregular events follow from any particular cause, the philosopher and physician are not surprised at the matter, nor are ever tempted to deny, in general, the necessity and uniformity of those principles by which the animal economy is conducted. They know that a human body is a mighty complicated machine, that many secret powers lurk in it which are altogether beyond our comprehension, that to us it must often appear very uncertain in its operations, and that therefore the irregular events which outwardly discover themselves can be no proof that the laws of nature are not observed with the greatest regularity in its internal operations and government.

The philosopher, if he is consistent, must apply the same reasoning to the actions and volitions of intelligent agents. The most irregular and unexpected resolutions of men may frequently be accounted for by those who know every particular circumstance of their character and situation. A person of an obliging disposition gives a peevish answer; but he has a toothache or has not dined. A stupid fellow discovers an uncommon alacrity in his carriage; but he has met with a sudden piece of good fortune. Or even when an action, as sometimes happens, cannot be particularly accounted for either by the person himself or by others, we know, in general, that the characters of men are to a certain degree inconstant and irregular. This is, in a manner, the constant character of human nature, though it is applicable in a more particular manner to some persons who have no fixed rule for their conduct, but proceed in a continued course of caprice and inconstancy. The internal principles and motives may operate in a uniform manner, notwithstanding these seeming irregularities—in the same manner as the winds, rain, clouds, and other variations of the weather are supposed to be governed by steady principles, though not easily discoverable by human sagacity and inquiry.

Thus, it appears not only that the conjunction between motives and voluntary actions is as regular and uniform as that between the cause and effect in any part of nature, but also that this regular conjunction has been universally acknowledged among mankind and has never been the subject of dispute either in philosophy or common life. Now, as it is from past experience that we draw all inferences concerning the future and as we conclude that objects will always be conjoined together which we find to have always been conjoined, it may seem superfluous to prove that this experienced uniformity in human actions is a source from which we draw *inferences* concerning them. But in order to throw the argument into a greater variety of lights, we shall also insist, though briefly, on this latter topic.

The mutual dependence of men is so great in all societies that scarcely any human action is entirely complete in itself or is performed without some reference to the actions of others, which are requisite to make it answer fully the intention of the agent. The poorest artificer who labors alone expects at least the protection of the magistrate to ensure him the enjoyment of the fruits of his labor. He also expects that, when he carries his goods to market and offers them at a reasonable price, he shall find purchasers and shall be able, by the money he acquires, to engage others to supply him with those commodities which are requisite for his subsistence. In proportion as men extend their dealings and render their intercourse with others more complicated, they always comprehend in their schemes of life a greater variety of voluntary actions which they expect, from the proper motives, to cooperate with their own. In all these conclusions they take their measures from past experience in the same manner as in their reasonings concerning external objects, and firmly believe that men as well as all the elements are to continue in their operations the same that they have ever found them. A manufacturer reckons upon the labor of his servants for the execution of any work as much as upon the tools which he employs and would be equally sur-

prised were his expectations disappointed. In short, this experimental inference and reasoning concerning the actions of others enters so much into human life that no man, while awake, is ever a moment without employing it. Have we not reason, therefore, to affirm that all mankind have always agreed in the doctrine of necessity, according to the foregoing definition and explication of it?

Nor have philosophers ever entertained a different opinion from the people in this particular. For not to mention that almost every action of their life supposes that opinion, there are even few of the speculative parts of learning to which it is not essential. What would become of *history* had we not a dependence on the veracity of the historian, according to the experience which we have had of mankind? How could *politics* be a science, if laws and forms of government had not a uniform influence upon society? Where would be the foundation of *morals*, if particular characters had no certain or determinate power to produce particular sentiments and if these sentiments had no constant operation on actions? And with what pretense could we employ our *criticism* upon any poet or polite author, if we could not pronounce the conduct and sentiments of his actors either natural or unnatural to such characters and in such circumstances? It seems almost impossible, therefore, to engage either in science or action of any kind without acknowledging the doctrine of necessity and this *inference* from motives to voluntary actions, from characters to conduct.

And indeed, when we consider how aptly *natural* and *moral* evidence link together and form only one chain of argument, we shall make no scruple to allow that they are of the same nature and derived from the same principles. A prisoner who has neither money nor interest discovers the impossibility of his escape as well when he considers the obstinacy of the jailer as the walls and bars with which he is surrounded and in all attempts for his freedom chooses to work upon the stone and iron of the one rather than upon the inflexible nature of the other. The same prisoner, when conducted to the scaffold, foresees his death as certainly from the constancy and fidelity of his guards as from the operation of the ax or wheel. His mind runs along a certain train of ideas: the refusal of the soldiers to consent to his escape; the action of the executioner; the separation of the head and body; bleeding, convulsive motions, and death. Here is a connected chain of natural causes and voluntary actions, but the mind feels no difference between them in passing from one link to another, nor is less certain of the future event than if it were connected with the objects present to the memory or senses by a train of causes cemented together by what we are pleased to call a *physical* necessity. The same experienced union has the same effect on the mind, whether the united objects are motives, volition, and actions, or figure and motion. We may change the names of things, but their nature and their operation on the understanding never change.

Were a man whom I know to be honest and opulent and with whom I live in intimate friendship to come into my house where I am surrounded with my servants, I rest assured that he is not to stab me before he leaves it in order to rob me of my silver standish; and I no more suspect this event than the falling of the house itself which is new and solidly built and founded. — *But he may have been seized with a sudden and unknown frenzy.* — So may a sudden earthquake arise, and shake and tumble my house about my ears. I shall therefore change the suppositions. I shall say that I know with certainty that he is not to put his hand into the fire and hold it there until it is consumed. And this event I think I can foretell with the same assurance as that, if he threw himself out at the window and met with no obstruction, he will not remain a moment suspended in the air. No suspicion of an unknown frenzy can give the least possibility to the former event which is so contrary to all the known principles of human nature. A man who at noon leaves his purse full of gold on the pavement at Charing Cross may as well expect that it will fly away like a feather as that he will find it untouched an hour after. Over one half of human reasonings contain inferences of a similar nature, attended with more or less degrees of certainty, proportioned to our experience of the usual conduct of mankind in such particular situations.

I have frequently considered what could possibly be the reason why all mankind, though they have ever, without hesitation, acknowledged the doctrine of necessity in their whole practice and reasoning, have yet discovered such a reluctance to acknowledge it in words and have rather shown a propensity, in all ages, to profess the contrary opinion. The matter,

I think, may be accounted for after the following manner. If we examine the operations of body and the production of effects from their causes, we shall find that all our faculties can never carry us further in our knowledge of this relation than barely to observe that particular objects are *constantly conjoined* together and that the mind is carried, by a *customary transition*, from the appearance of one to the belief of the other. But though this conclusion concerning human ignorance is the result of the strictest scrutiny of this subject, men still entertain a strong propensity to believe that they penetrate further into the powers of nature and perceive something like a necessary connection between the cause and the effect. When again they turn their reflections towards the operations of their own minds and *feel* no such connection of the motive and the action, they are apt to suppose from this that there is a difference between the effects which result from material force and those which arise from thought and intelligence. But being once convinced that we know nothing further of causation of any kind than merely the *constant conjunction* of objects and the consequent *inference* of the mind from one to another and finding that these two circumstances are universally allowed to have place in voluntary actions, we may be more easily led to admit the same necessity common to all causes. And though this reasoning may contradict the systems of many philosophers in ascribing necessity to the determinations of the will, we shall find, upon reflection, that they dissent from it in words only, not in their real sentiment. Necessity, according to the sense in which it is here taken, has never yet been rejected, nor can ever, I think, be rejected by any philosopher. It may only, perhaps, be pretended that the mind can perceive in the operations of matter some further connection between the cause and effect and a connection that has no place in the voluntary actions of intelligent beings. Now whether it is so or not can only appear upon examination, and it is incumbent on these philosophers to make good their assertion by defining or describing that necessity and pointing it out to us in the operations of material causes.

It would seem, indeed, that men begin at the wrong end of this question concerning liberty and necessity when they enter upon it by examining the faculties of the soul, the influence of the understanding, and the operations of the will. Let them first discuss a more simple question, namely, the operations of body and of brute unintelligent matter, and try whether they can there form any idea of causation and necessity, except that of a constant conjunction of objects and subsequent inference of the mind from one to another. If these circumstances form, in reality, the whole of that necessity which we conceive in matter and if these circumstances are also universally acknowledged to take place in the operations of the mind, the dispute is at an end—at least must be admitted to be merely verbal thereafter. But as long as we will rashly suppose that we have some further idea of necessity and causation in the operations of external objects, at the same time that we can find nothing further in the voluntary actions of the mind, there is no possibility of bringing the question to any determinate issue while we proceed upon so erroneous a supposition. The only method of undeceiving us is to mount up higher, to examine the narrow extent of science when applied to material causes, and to convince ourselves that all we know of them is the constant conjunction and inference above mentioned. We may, perhaps, find that it is with difficulty we are induced to fix such narrow limits to human understanding. But we can afterwards find no difficulty when we come to apply this doctrine to the actions of the will. For as it is evident that these have a regular conjunction with motives and circumstances and characters and as we always draw inferences from one to the other, we must be obliged to acknowledge in words that necessity which we have already avowed in every deliberation of our lives and in every step of our conduct and behavior.[43]

43. The prevalence of the doctrine of liberty may be accounted for, from another cause, *viz.* a false sensation or seeming experience which we have, or may have, of liberty or indifference, in many of our actions. The necessity of any action, whether of matter or of mind, is not, properly speaking, a quality in the agent, but in any thinking or intelligent being, who may consider the action; and it consists chiefly in the determination of his thoughts to infer the existence of that action from some preceding objects; as liberty, when opposed to necessity, is nothing but the want of that determination, and a certain looseness or indifference, which we feel, in passing, or not passing, from the idea of one object to that of any succeeding one. Now we may observe, that, though, in *reflecting* on human actions, we seldom feel such a looseness or indifference, but are

But to proceed in this reconciling project with regard to the question of liberty and necessity—the most contentious question of metaphysics, the most contentious science—it will not require many words to prove that all mankind have ever agreed in the doctrine of liberty as well as in that of necessity, and that the whole dispute, in this respect also, has been up to now merely verbal. For what is meant by liberty when applied to voluntary actions? We cannot surely mean that actions have so little connection with motives, inclinations, and circumstances that one does not follow with a certain degree of uniformity from the other and that one affords no inference by which we can conclude the existence of the other. For these are plain and acknowledged matters of fact. By liberty, then, we can only mean *a power of acting or not acting according to the determinations of the will*—that is, if we choose to remain at rest, we may; if we choose to move, we also may. Now this hypothetical liberty is universally allowed to belong to everyone who is not a prisoner and in chains. Here then is no subject of dispute.

Whatever definition we may give of liberty, we

commonly able to infer them with considerable certainty from their motives, and from the dispositions of the agent; yet it frequently happens, that, in *performing* the actions themselves, we are sensible of something like it: And as all resembling objects are readily taken for each other, this has been employed as a demonstrative and even intuitive proof of human liberty. We feel, that our actions are subject to our will, on most occasions; and imagine we feel, that the will itself is subject to nothing, because, when by a denial of it we are provoked to try, we feel, that it moves easily every way, and produces an image of itself, (or a *Velleïty*, as it is called in the schools) even on that side, on which it did not settle. This image, or faint motion, we persuade ourselves, could, at that time, have been completed into the thing itself; because, should that be denied, we find, upon a second trial, that, at present, it can. We consider not, that the fantastical desire of showing liberty, is here the motive of our actions. And it seems certain, that, however we may imagine we feel a liberty within ourselves, a spectator can commonly infer our actions from our motives and character; and even where he cannot, he concludes in general, that he might, were he perfectly acquainted with every circumstance of our situation and temper, and the most secret springs of our complexion and disposition. Now this is the very essence of necessity, according to the foregoing doctrine.

should be careful to observe two requisite circumstances: *first*, that it is consistent with plain matter of fact; *secondly*, that it is consistent with itself. If we observe these circumstances and render our definition intelligible, I am persuaded that all mankind will be found of one opinion with regard to it.

It is universally allowed that nothing exists without a cause of its existence, and that chance, when strictly examined, is a mere negative word and does not mean any real power which has anywhere a being in nature. But it is pretended that some causes are necessary, some not necessary. Here then is the advantage of definitions. Let anyone *define* a cause without comprehending, as a part of the definition, a *necessary connection* with its effect, and let him show distinctly the origin of the idea expressed by the definition, and I shall readily give up the whole controversy. But if the foregoing explication of the matter is received, this must be absolutely impracticable. Had not objects a regular conjunction with each other, we should never have entertained any notion of cause and effect and this regular conjunction produces that inference of the understanding which is the only connection that we can have any comprehension of. Whoever attempts a definition of cause exclusive of these circumstances will be obliged either to employ unintelligible terms or such as are synonymous to the term which he endeavors to define.[44] And if the definition above mentioned is admitted, liberty, when opposed to necessity, not to constraint, is the same thing with chance, which is universally allowed to have no existence.

Part II.

There is no method of reasoning more common and yet none more blamable than in philosophical disputes to endeavor the refutation of any hypothesis by

44. Thus, if a cause be defined, *that which produces any thing*; it is easy to observe, that *producing* is synonymous to *causing*. In like manner, if a cause be defined, *that by which anything exists*; this is liable to the same objection. For what is meant by these words, *by which*? Had it been said, that a cause is *that* after which *anything constantly exists*; we should have understood the terms. For this is, indeed, all we know of the matter. And this constancy forms the very essence of necessity, nor have we any other idea of it.

a pretense of its dangerous consequences to religion and morality. When any opinion leads to absurdities, it is certainly false; but it is not certain that an opinion is false because it is of dangerous consequence. Such topics, therefore, ought entirely to be forborne, as serving nothing to the discovery of truth, but only to make the person of an antagonist odious. This I observe in general, without pretending to draw any advantage from it. I frankly submit to an examination of this kind and shall venture to affirm that the doctrines both of necessity and of liberty, as above explained, are not only consistent with morality, but are absolutely essential to its support.

Necessity may be defined two ways, conformably to the two definitions of cause of which it makes an essential part. It consists either in the constant conjunction of like objects or in the inference of the understanding from one object to another. Now necessity, in both these senses, (which, indeed, are at bottom the same) has universally, though tacitly, in the schools, in the pulpit, and in common life been allowed to belong to the will of man and no one has ever pretended to deny that we can draw inferences concerning human actions and that those inferences are founded on the experienced union of like actions with like motives, inclinations, and circumstances. The only particular in which anyone can differ is that either, perhaps, he will refuse to give the name of necessity to this property of human actions—but as long as the meaning is understood I hope the word can do no harm—or that he will maintain it possible to discover something further in the operations of matter. But this, it must be acknowledged, can be of no consequence to morality or religion, whatever it may be to natural philosophy or metaphysics. We may here be mistaken in asserting that there is no idea of any other necessity or connection in the actions of body. But surely we ascribe nothing to the actions of the mind but what everyone does and must readily allow of. We change no circumstance in the received orthodox system with regard to the will, but only in that with regard to material objects and causes. Nothing, therefore, can be more innocent at least than this doctrine.

All laws being founded on rewards and punishments, it is supposed as a fundamental principle that these motives have a regular and uniform influence on the mind and both produce the good and prevent the evil actions. We may give to this influence what name we please; but, as it is usually conjoined with the action, it must be esteemed a *cause* and be looked upon as an instance of that necessity which we would here establish.

The only proper object of hatred or vengeance is a person or creature endowed with thought and consciousness, and when any criminal or injurious actions excite that passion, it is only by their relation to the person or connection with him. Actions are, by their very nature, temporary and perishing, and where they do not proceed from some cause in the character and disposition of the person who performed them, they can neither redound to his honor if good, nor infamy if evil. The actions themselves may be blamable; they may be contrary to all the rules of morality and religion. But the person is not answerable for them and, as they proceeded from nothing in him that is durable and constant and leave nothing of that nature behind them, it is impossible he can, upon their account, become the object of punishment or vengeance. According to the principle, therefore, which denies necessity and consequently causes that a man is as pure and untainted after having committed the most horrid crime as at the first moment of his birth, nor is his character any way concerned in his actions, since they are not derived from it, and the wickedness of the one can never be used as a proof of the depravity of the other.

Men are not blamed for such actions as they perform ignorantly and casually, whatever may be the consequences. Why? But because the principles of these actions are only momentary and terminate in them alone. Men are less blamed for such actions as they perform hastily and unpremeditatedly than for such as proceed from deliberation. For what reason? But because a hasty temper, though a constant cause or principle in the mind, operates only by intervals and does not infect the whole character. Again, repentance wipes off every crime, if attended with a reformation of life and manners. How is this to be accounted for? But by asserting that actions render a person criminal merely as they are proofs of criminal principles in the mind; and when, by an alteration of these principles, they cease to be just proofs, they likewise cease to be criminal. But, except upon the doctrine of necessity, they never were just proofs and consequently never were criminal.

It will be equally easy to prove, and from the same arguments, that *liberty*, according to that definition above mentioned, in which all men agree, is also essential to morality and that no human actions, where it is wanting, are susceptible of any moral qualities or can be the objects either of approbation or dislike. For as actions are objects of our moral sentiment only so far as they are indications of the internal character, passions, and affections, it is impossible that they can give rise either to praise or blame where they do not proceed from these principles, but are derived altogether from external violence.

I do not pretend to have obviated or removed all objections to this theory with regard to necessity and liberty. I can foresee other objections derived from topics which have not here been treated of. It may be said, for instance, that if voluntary actions are subjected to the same laws of necessity with the operations of matter, there is a continued chain of necessary causes, preordained and predetermined, reaching from the original cause of all to every single volition of every human creature. No contingency anywhere in the universe, no indifference, no liberty. While we act, we are at the same time acted upon. The ultimate Author of all our volitions is the Creator of the world, who first bestowed motion on this immense machine and placed all beings in that particular position from which every subsequent event, by an inevitable necessity, must result. Human actions, therefore, either can have no moral turpitude at all, as proceeding from so good a cause, or if they have any turpitude, they must involve our Creator in the same guilt, while he is acknowledged to be their ultimate cause and author. For as a man who fired a mine is answerable for all the consequences, whether the train he employed is long or short, so wherever a continued chain of necessary causes is fixed, that Being, either finite or infinite, who produces the first is likewise the author of all the rest and must both bear the blame and acquire the praise which belong to them. Our clear and unalterable ideas of morality establish this rule upon unquestionable reasons when we examine the consequences of any human action and these reasons must still have greater force when applied to the volitions and intentions of a Being infinitely wise and powerful. Ignorance or impotence may be pleaded for so limited a creature as man, but those imperfections have no place in our Creator. He foresaw, he ordained, he intended all those actions of men which we so rashly pronounce criminal. And we must therefore conclude either that they are not criminal or that the Deity, not man, is accountable for them. But as either of these positions is absurd and impious, it follows that the doctrine from which they are deduced cannot possibly be true, as being liable to all the same objections. An absurd consequence, if necessary, proves the original doctrine to be absurd in the same manner as criminal actions render criminal the original cause, if the connection between them is necessary and inevitable.

This objection consists of two parts, which we shall examine separately: *First,* that if human actions can be traced up, by a necessary chain, to the Deity, they can never be criminal, on account of the infinite perfection of that Being from whom they are derived and who can intend nothing but what is altogether good and laudable. Or, *secondly,* if they are criminal, we must retract the attribute of perfection which we ascribe to the Deity and must acknowledge him to be the ultimate author of guilt and moral turpitude in all his creatures.

The answer to the first objection seems obvious and convincing. There are many philosophers who, after an exact scrutiny of all the phenomena of nature, conclude that the whole, considered as one system, is, in every period of its existence, ordered with perfect benevolence, and that the utmost possible happiness will, in the end, result to all created beings without any mixture of positive or absolute ill and misery. Every physical ill, they say, makes an essential part of this benevolent system and could not possibly be removed, even by the Deity himself, considered as a wise agent, without giving entrance to greater ill or excluding greater good which will result from it. From this theory some philosophers, and the ancient *Stoics* among the rest, derived a topic of consolation under all afflictions, while they taught their pupils that those ills under which they labored were in reality goods to the universe and that to an enlarged view which could comprehend the whole system of nature every event became an object of joy and exultation. But though this topic is specious and sublime, it was soon found in practice weak and ineffectual. You would surely more irritate than appease a man lying under the racking pains of gout by preaching up to him the rectitude of those general laws which produced the malignant humors in his body and led them through the proper canals to the sinews and nerves, where they now excite such acute torments. These enlarged views may, for a moment, please the imagination of a speculative man who is placed in ease and security, but neither can they dwell with constancy on his mind, even though undisturbed by the emotions of pain or passion, much less can they maintain their ground when attacked by such powerful antagonists. The affections take a narrower and more natural survey of their object, and, by an economy more suitable to the infirmity of human minds, regard alone the beings around us, and are actuated by such events as appear good or ill to the private system.

The case is the same with *moral* as with *physical* ill. It cannot reasonably be supposed that those remote considerations which are found of so little efficacy with regard to one will have a more powerful influence with regard to the other. The mind of man is so formed by nature that, upon the appearance of certain characters, dispositions, and actions, it immediately feels the sentiment of approbation or blame; nor are there any emotions more essential to its frame and constitution. The characters which engage our approbation are chiefly such as contribute to the peace and security of human society, as the characters which excite blame are chiefly such as tend to public detriment and disturbance. From this it may reasonably be presumed that the moral sentiments arise, either mediately or immediately, from a reflection of these opposite interests. What though philosophical meditations establish a different opinion or conjecture that everything is right with regard to the whole, and that the qualities which disturb society are, in the main, as beneficial and are as suitable to the primary intention of nature as those which more directly promote its happiness and welfare? Are such remote and uncertain speculations able to counterbalance the sentiments which arise from the natural and immediate view of the objects? A man who is robbed of a considerable sum, does he find his vexation for the loss any way diminished by these sublime reflections? Why then should his moral resentment against the crime be supposed incompatible with them? Or why should not the acknowledgment of a real distinction between vice and virtue be reconcilable to all speculative systems of philosophy, as well as that of a real distinction between personal beauty and deformity?

Both these distinctions are founded in the natural sentiments of the human mind. And these sentiments are not to be controlled or altered by any philosophical theory or speculation whatsoever.

The *second* objection does not admit of so easy and satisfactory an answer, nor is it possible to explain distinctly how the Deity can be the mediate cause of all the actions of men without being the author of sin and moral turpitude. These are mysteries which mere natural and unassisted reason is very unfit to handle; and whatever system she embraces, she must find herself involved in inextricable difficulties, and even contradictions, at every step which she takes with regard to such subjects. To reconcile the indifference and contingency of human actions with prescience or to defend absolute decrees and yet free the Deity from being the author of sin has been found up to now to exceed all the power of philosophy. Happy, if she is sensible of her temerity from there, when she pries into these sublime mysteries, and, leaving a scene so full of obscurities and perplexities, returns with suitable modesty to her true and proper province, the examination of common life, where she will find difficulties enough to employ her inquiries without launching into so boundless an ocean of doubt, uncertainty, and contradiction!

SECTION IX
Of the Reason of Animals.

All our reasonings concerning matter of fact are founded on a species of analogy which leads us to expect from any cause the same events which we have observed to result from similar causes. Where the causes are entirely similar, the analogy is perfect and the inference drawn from it is regarded as certain and conclusive. Nor does any man ever entertain a doubt where he sees a piece of iron that it will have weight and cohesion of parts, as in all other instances which have ever fallen under his observation. But where the objects do not have so exact a similarity, the analogy is less perfect and the inference is less conclusive, though still it has some force in proportion to the degree of similarity and resemblance. The anatomical observations formed upon one animal are, by this species of reasoning, extended to all animals; and it is certain that, when the circulation of the

blood, for instance, is clearly proved to have place in one creature, as a frog, or fish, it forms a strong presumption that the same principle has place in all. These analogical observations may be carried further, even to this science of which we are now treating, and any theory by which we explain the operations of the understanding or the origin and connection of the passions in man will acquire additional authority, if we find that the same theory is requisite to explain the same phenomena in all other animals. We shall make trial of this with regard to the hypothesis by which we have, in the foregoing discourse, endeavored to account for all experimental reasoning and it is hoped that this new point of view will serve to confirm all our former observations.

First, it seems evident that animals, as well as men, learn many things from experience and infer that the same events will always follow from the same causes. By this principle they become acquainted with the more obvious properties of external objects and gradually, from their birth, treasure up a knowledge of the nature of fire, water, earth, stones, heights, depths, etc., and of the effects which result from their operation. The ignorance and inexperience of the young are here plainly distinguishable from the cunning and sagacity of the old, who have learned, by long observation, to avoid what hurt them and to pursue what gave ease or pleasure. A horse that has been accustomed to the field becomes acquainted with the proper height which he can leap, and will never attempt what exceeds his force and ability. An old greyhound will trust the more fatiguing part of the chase to the younger and will place himself so as to meet the hare in her doubles; nor are the conjectures which he forms on this occasion founded in anything but his observation and experience.

This is still more evident from the effects of discipline and education on animals who, by the proper application of rewards and punishments, may be taught any course of action the most contrary to their natural instincts and propensities. Is it not experience which renders a dog apprehensive of pain when you menace him or lift up the whip to beat him? Is it not even experience which makes him answer to his name and infer, from such an arbitrary sound, that you mean him rather than any of his fellows and intend to call him when you pronounce it in a certain manner and with a certain tone and accent?

In all these cases we may observe that the animal infers some fact beyond what immediately strikes his senses and that this inference is altogether founded on past experience, while the creature expects from the present object the same consequences which it has always found in its observation to result from similar objects.

Secondly, it is impossible that this inference of the animal can be founded on any process of argument or reasoning by which he concludes that like events must follow like objects and that the course of nature will always be regular in its operations. For if there are in reality any arguments of this nature, they surely lie too abstruse for the observation of such imperfect understandings, since it may well employ the utmost care and attention of a philosophic genius to discover and observe them. Animals, therefore, are not guided in these inferences by reasoning. Neither are children. Neither are the generality of mankind in their ordinary actions and conclusions. Neither are philosophers themselves, who, in all the active parts of life, are in the main the same with the vulgar and are governed by the same maxims. Nature must have provided some other principle, of more ready and more general use and application; nor can an operation of such immense consequence in life as that of inferring effects from causes be trusted to the uncertain process of reasoning and argumentation. Were this doubtful with regard to men, it seems to admit of no question with regard to the brute creation; and the conclusion being once firmly established in the one, we have a strong presumption, from all the rules of analogy, that it ought to be universally admitted without any exception or reserve. It is custom alone which engages animals from every object that strikes their senses to infer its usual attendant and carries their imagination from the appearance of the one to conceive the other in that particular manner which we denominate *belief*. No other explication can be given of this operation, in all the higher as well as lower classes of sensitive beings which fall under our notice and observation.[45]

---

45. Since all reasonings concerning facts or causes is derived merely from custom, it may be asked how it happens, that men so much surpass animals in reasoning, and one man so much surpasses another? Has not the same custom the same influence on all?

But though animals learn many parts of their knowledge from observation, there are also many parts of it which they derive from the original hand of nature, which much exceed the share of capacity they possess on ordinary occasions and in which they

---

We shall here endeavour briefly to explain the great difference in human understandings: After which the reason of the difference between men and animals will easily be comprehended.

1. When we have lived any time, and have been accustomed to the uniformity of nature, we acquire a general habit, by which we always transfer the known to the unknown, and conceive the latter to resemble the former. By means of this general habitual principle, we regard even one experiment as the foundation of reasoning, and expect a similar event with some degree of certainty, where the experiment has been made accurately, and free from all foreign circumstances. It is therefore considered as a matter of great importance to observe the consequences of things; and as one man may very much surpass another in attention and memory and observation, this will make a very great difference in their reasoning.

2. Where there is a complication of causes to produce any effect, one mind may be much larger than another, and better able to comprehend the whole system of objects, and to infer justly their consequences.

3. One man is able to carry on a chain of consequences to a greater length than another.

4. Few men can think long without running into a confusion of ideas, and mistaking one for another; and there are various degrees of this infirmity.

5. The circumstance, on which the effect depends, is frequently involved in other circumstances, which are foreign and extrinsic. The separation of it often requires great attention, accuracy, and subtilty.

6. The forming of general maxims from particular observation is a very nice operation; and nothing is more usual, from haste or a narrowness of mind, which sees not on all sides, than to commit mistakes in this particular.

7. When we reason from analogies, the man, who has the greater experience or the greater promptitude of suggesting analogies, will be the better reasoner.

8. Biases from prejudice, education, passion, party, etc. hang more upon one mind than another.

9. After we have acquired a confidence in human testimony, books and conversation enlarge much more the sphere of one man's experience and thought than those of another.

It would be easy to discover many other circumstances that make a difference in the understandings of men.

improve little or nothing by the longest practice and experience. These we denominate instincts and are so apt to admire as something very extraordinary and inexplicable by all the disquisitions of human understanding. But our wonder will perhaps cease or diminish when we consider that the experimental reasoning itself which we possess in common with beasts and on which the whole conduct of life depends is nothing but a species of instinct or mechanical power that acts in us unknown to ourselves and in its chief operations is not directed by any such relations or comparisons of ideas as are the proper objects of our intellectual faculties. Though the instinct is different, yet still it is an instinct which teaches a man to avoid the fire, as much as that which teaches a bird, with such exactness, the art of incubation and the whole economy and order of its nursery.

SECTION X
Of Miracles.[46]
Part I.

There is, in Dr. Tillotson's writings,[47] an argument against the *real presence*[48] which is as concise and elegant and strong as any argument can possibly be supposed against a doctrine so little worthy of a serious refutation. It is acknowledged on all hands, says that learned prelate, that the authority either of the Scripture or of tradition is founded merely in the testimony of the Apostles who were eyewitnesses to those mira-

cles of our Savior by which he proved his divine mission. Our evidence, then, for the truth of the *Christian* religion is less than the evidence for the truth of our senses, because even in the first authors of our religion it was no greater; and it is evident it must diminish in passing from them to their disciples, nor can anyone rest such confidence in their testimony as in the immediate object of his senses. But a weaker evidence can never destroy a stronger; and, therefore, were the doctrine of the real presence ever so clearly revealed in scripture, it would be directly contrary to the rules of just reasoning to give our assent to it. It contradicts sense, though both the Scripture and tradition, on which it is supposed to be built, do not carry such evidence with them as sense, when they are considered merely as external evidences and are not brought home to everyone's breast by the immediate operation of the Holy Spirit.

Nothing is so convenient as a decisive argument of this kind, which must at least *silence* the most arrogant bigotry and superstition and free us from their impertinent solicitations. I flatter myself that I have discovered an argument of a like nature which, if just, will, with the wise and learned, be an everlasting check to all kinds of superstitious delusion and consequently will be useful as long as the world endures. For so long, I presume, will the accounts of miracles and prodigies be found in all history, sacred and profane.

Though experience is our only guide in reasoning concerning matters of fact, it must be acknowledged that this guide is not altogether infallible, but in some cases is apt to lead us into errors. One who in our climate should expect better weather in any week of June than in one of December would reason justly and conformably to experience, but it is certain that he may happen, in the event, to find himself mistaken. However, we may observe that in such a case he would have no cause to complain of experience, because it commonly informs us beforehand of the uncertainty by that contrariety of events which we may learn from a diligent observation. All effects do not follow with like certainty from their supposed causes. Some events are found, in all countries and all ages, to have been constantly conjoined together. Others are found to have been more variable and sometimes to disappoint our expectations, so that in our reasonings concerning matter of fact there are all imaginable degrees

46. [A draft of this section was extant as early as 1737; although Hume had apparently entertained the idea of including it in the *Treatise*, evidence suggests that he withheld it for fear of displeasing Joseph Butler, whose approval of the work he sought. The essay was first published as part of the *Enquiry* and is thought by many to be a direct reply to two influential works, one by Thomas Sherlock (1678–1761), Bishop of London, *Tryal of the Witnesses of the Resurrection of Jesus* (1729); the other was Zachary Pearce's (1690–1774) *Miracles of Jesus Vindicated* (1729).]

47. [John Tillotson (1630–1694), a Presbyterian theologian who became Archbishop of Canterbury in 1691, argued in *Rule of Faith* (1676) and *A Doctrine Against Transubstantiation* (1684) that transubstantiation could never be established as part of Christian doctrine.]

48. [The presence of the body and blood of Christ in the bread and wine of the Eucharist.]

of assurance from the highest certainty to the lowest species of moral evidence.

A wise man, therefore, proportions his belief to the evidence. In such conclusions as are founded on an infallible experience, he expects the event with the last degree of assurance and regards his past experience as a full *proof* of the future existence of that event. In other cases he proceeds with more caution. He weighs the opposite experiments. He considers which side is supported by the greater number of experiments—to that side he inclines with doubt and hesitation; and when at last he fixes his judgment, the evidence does not exceed what we properly call *probability*. All probability, then, supposes an opposition of experiments and observations where the one side is found to overbalance the other and to produce a degree of evidence proportioned to the superiority. A hundred instances or experiments on one side and fifty on another afford a doubtful expectation of any event, though a hundred uniform experiments with only one that is contradictory reasonably beget a pretty strong degree of assurance. In all cases we must balance the opposite experiments where they are opposite and deduct the smaller number from the greater in order to know the exact force of the superior evidence.

To apply these principles to a particular instance, we may observe that there is no species of reasoning more common, more useful, and even necessary to human life than that which is derived from the testimony of men and the reports of eyewitnesses and spectators. This species of reasoning, perhaps, one may deny to be founded on the relation of cause and effect. I shall not dispute about a word. It will be sufficient to observe that our assurance in any argument of this kind is derived from no other principle than our observation of the veracity of human testimony and of the usual conformity of facts to the reports of witnesses. It being a general maxim that no objects have any discoverable connection together and that all the inferences which we can draw from one to another are founded merely on our experience of their constant and regular conjunction, it is evident that we ought not make an exception to this maxim in favor of human testimony whose connection with any event seems in itself as little necessary as any other. Were not the memory tenacious to a certain degree, had not men commonly an inclination to

truth and a principle of probity, were they not sensible to shame when detected in a falsehood, were not these, I say, discovered by *experience* to be qualities inherent in human nature, we should never repose the least confidence in human testimony. A man delirious or noted for falsehood and villainy has no manner of authority with us.

And as the evidence derived from witnesses and human testimony is founded on past experience, so it varies with the experience and is regarded either as a *proof* or a *probability*, according as the conjunction between any particular kind of report and any kind of object has been found to be constant or variable. There are a number of circumstances to be taken into consideration in all judgments of this kind; and the ultimate standard by which we determine all disputes that may arise concerning them is always derived from experience and observation. Where this experience is not entirely uniform on any side, it is attended with an unavoidable contrariety in our judgments and with the same opposition and mutual destruction of argument as in every other kind of evidence. We frequently hesitate concerning the reports of others. We balance the opposite circumstances which cause any doubt or uncertainty; and when we discover a superiority on any side, we incline to it, but still with a diminution of assurance in proportion to the force of its antagonist.

This contrariety of evidence, in the present case, may be derived from several different causes: from the opposition of contrary testimony, from the character or number of the witnesses, from the manner of their delivering their testimony, or from the union of all these circumstances. We entertain a suspicion concerning any matter of fact when the witnesses contradict each other, when they are but few or of a doubtful character, when they have an interest in what they affirm, when they deliver their testimony with hesitation or, on the contrary, with too violent affirmations. There are many other particulars of the same kind which may diminish or destroy the force of any argument derived from human testimony.

Suppose, for instance, that the fact which the testimony endeavors to establish partakes of the extraordinary and the marvelous—in that case, the evidence resulting from the testimony admits of a diminution, greater or less in proportion as the fact is more or less unusual. The reason why we place any credit in witnesses and historians is not derived from any *connection* which we perceive *a priori* between testimony and reality, but because we are accustomed to find a conformity between them. But when the fact attested is such a one as has seldom fallen under our observation, here is a contest of two opposite experiences, of which the one destroys the other as far as its force goes and the superior can only operate on the mind by the force which remains. The very same principle of experience which gives us a certain degree of assurance in the testimony of witnesses gives us also, in this case, another degree of assurance against the fact which they endeavor to establish—from which contradiction there necessarily arises a counterpoise and mutual destruction of belief and authority.

I should not believe such a story were it told me by Cato[49] was a proverbial saying in Rome, even during the lifetime of that philosophical patriot.[50] The incredibility of a fact, it was allowed, might invalidate so great an authority.

The Indian prince[51] who refused to believe the first relations concerning the effects of frost reasoned justly, and it naturally required very strong testimony to engage his assent to facts that arose from a state of nature with which he was unacquainted and which bore so little analogy to those events of which he had had constant and uniform experience. Though they were not contrary to his experience, they were not conformable to it.[52]

But in order to increase the probability against the testimony of witnesses, let us suppose that the fact which they affirm, instead of being only marvelous, is really miraculous, and suppose also that the testimony, considered apart and in itself, amounts to an entire proof—in that case, there is proof against proof, of which the strongest must prevail, but still with a diminution of its force in proportion to that of its antagonist.

A miracle is a violation of the laws of nature; and as a firm and unalterable experience has established these laws, the proof against a miracle, from the very nature of the fact, is as entire as any argument from experience can possibly be imagined. Why is it more than probable that all men must die, that lead cannot of itself remain suspended in the air, that fire consumes wood and is extinguished by water, unless it is that these events are found agreeable to the laws of nature and there is required a violation of these laws or, in other words, a miracle to prevent them? Nothing is esteemed a miracle if it ever happen in the common course of nature. It is no miracle that a man, seemingly in good health, should die all of a sudden, because such a kind of death, though more unusual than any other, has yet been frequently observed to happen. But it is a miracle that a dead man should come to life, because that has never been observed in any age or country. There must, therefore, be a uniform experience against every miraculous

---

49. [The reference is to Marcus Porcius Cato (Cato the Younger) (95–46 B.C.), a Roman statesman and philosopher.]

50. Plutarch in *Vita Catonis*. [Plutarch (c. 46–c. 120) was a Greek biographer who vividly portrayed the lives of noted Greeks and Romans. The reference here is to his *Life of Cato*.

51. [A variation of this story appears in Locke's *Essay Concerning Human Understanding* IV. 15., as a story about the King of Siam and a Dutch ambassador. An account closer to Hume's is mentioned by Butler in the Introduction to his *Analogy of Religion, Natural and Revealed, to the Constitution and Course of Nature* (1736).]

52. No Indian, it is evident, could have experience that water did not freeze in cold climates. This is placing nature in a situation quite unknown to him; and it is impossible for him to tell *a priori* what will result from it. It is making a new experiment, the consequence of which is always

uncertain. One may sometimes conjecture from analogy what will follow; but still this is but conjecture. And it must be confessed, that, in the present case of freezing, the event follows contrary to the rules of analogy, and is such as a rational Indian would not look for. The operations of cold upon water are not gradual, according to the degrees of cold; but whenever it comes to the freezing point, the water passes in a moment, from the utmost liquidity to perfect hardness. Such an event, therefore, may be denominated *extraordinary*, and requires a pretty strong testimony, to render it credible to people in a warm climate: But still it is not *miraculous*, nor contrary to uniform experience of the course of nature in cases where all the circumstances are the same. The inhabitants of Sumatra have always seen water fluid in their own climate, and the freezing of their rivers ought to be deemed a prodigy: But they never saw water in Muscovy during the winter; and therefore they cannot reasonably be positive what would there be the consequence.

event; otherwise the event would not merit that appellation. And as a uniform experience amounts to a proof, there is here a direct and full *proof*, from the nature of the fact, against the existence of any miracle, nor can such a proof be destroyed or the miracle rendered credible but by an opposite proof which is superior.[53]

The plain consequence is (and it is a general maxim worthy of our attention): that no testimony is sufficient to establish a miracle, unless the testimony is of such a kind that its falsehood would be more miraculous than the fact which it endeavors to establish; and even in that case there is a mutual destruction of arguments and the superior only gives us an assurance suitable to that degree of force which remains after deducting the inferior. When anyone tells me that he saw a dead man restored to life, I immediately consider with myself whether it is more probable that this person should either deceive or be deceived or that the fact which he relates should really have happened. I weigh the one miracle against the other and, according to the superiority which I discover, I pronounce my decision and always reject the greater miracle. If the falsehood of his testimony would be more miraculous than the event which he relates,

then, and not until then, can he pretend to command my belief or opinion.

Part II.

In the foregoing reasoning we have supposed that the testimony upon which a miracle is founded may possibly amount to an entire proof and that the falsehood of that testimony would be a real prodigy. But it is easy to show that we have been a great deal too liberal in our concession and that there never was a miraculous event established on so full an evidence.

For *first*, there is not to be found, in all history, any miracle attested by a sufficient number of men of such unquestioned good sense, education, and learning, as to secure us against all delusion in themselves; of such undoubted integrity as to place them beyond all suspicion of any design to deceive others; of such credit and reputation in the eyes of mankind as to have a great deal to lose in case of their being detected in any falsehood, and at the same time attesting facts performed in such a public manner and in so celebrated a part of the world as to render the detection unavoidable — all which circumstances are requisite to give us a full assurance in the testimony of men.

Secondly, we may observe in human nature a principle which, if strictly examined, will be found to diminish extremely the assurance which we might, from human testimony, have in any kind of prodigy. The maxim by which we commonly conduct ourselves in our reasonings is that the objects of which we have no experience resemble those of which we have; that what we have found to be most usual is always most probable; and that where there is an opposition of arguments, we ought to give the preference to such as are founded on the greatest number of past observations. But though, in proceeding by this rule, we readily reject any fact which is unusual and incredible in an ordinary degree, yet in advancing further, the mind does not observe always the same rule; but when anything is affirmed utterly absurd and miraculous, it rather the more readily admits of such a fact upon account of that very circumstance which ought to destroy all its authority. The passion of *surprise* and *wonder*, arising from miracles, being an agreeable emotion, gives a sensible tendency towards the belief of those events from which it is

---

53. Sometimes an event may not, *in itself, seem* to be contrary to the laws of nature, and yet, if it were real, it might, by reason of some circumstances, be denominated a miracle; because, in *fact*, it is contrary to these laws. Thus if a person, claiming a divine authority, should command a sick person to be well, a healthful man to fall down dead, the clouds to pour rain, the winds to blow, in short, should order many natural events, which immediately follow upon his command; these might justly be esteemed miracles, because they are really, in this case, contrary to the laws of nature. For if any suspicion remain, that the event and command concurred by accident, there is no miracle, and a transgression of these laws; because nothing can be more contrary to nature than that the voice or command of a man should have such an influence. A miracle may be accurately defined, *a transgression of a law of nature by a particular volition of the Deity, or by the interposition of some invisible agent.* A miracle may either be discoverable by men or not. This alters not its nature and essence. The raising of a house or ship into the air is a visible miracle. The raising of a feather, when the wind wants ever so little of a force requisite for that purpose, is as real a miracle, though not so sensible with regard to us.

derived. And this goes so far that even those who cannot enjoy this pleasure immediately, nor can believe those miraculous events of which they are informed, yet love to partake of the satisfaction at secondhand or by rebound, and place a pride and delight in exciting the admiration of others.

With what greediness are the miraculous accounts of travelers received, their descriptions of sea and land monsters, their relations of wonderful adventures, strange men, and uncouth manners? But if the spirit of religion joins itself to the love of wonder, there is an end of common sense and human testimony in these circumstances loses all pretensions to authority. A religionist may be an enthusiast and imagine he sees what has no reality. He may know his narrative to be false and yet persevere in it with the best intentions in the world, for the sake of promoting so holy a cause. Or even where this delusion does not have place, vanity, excited by so strong a temptation, operates on him more powerfully than on the rest of mankind in any other circumstances, and self-interest with equal force. His auditors may not have and commonly do not have sufficient judgment to canvass his evidence. What judgment they have, they renounce by principle in these sublime and mysterious subjects. Or if they were ever so willing to employ it, passion and a heated imagination disturb the regularity of its operations. Their credulity increases his impudence and his impudence overpowers their credulity.

Eloquence, when at its highest pitch, leaves little room for reason or reflection, but, addressing itself entirely to the fancy or the affections, captivates the willing hearers and subdues their understanding. Happily, this pitch it seldom attains. But what a Tully[54] or a Demosthenes[55] could scarcely effect over a Roman or Athenian audience, every Capuchin,[56] every itinerant or stationary teacher can perform over the generality of mankind, and in a higher degree by touching such gross and vulgar passions.

The many instances of forged miracles and prophecies and supernatural events, which, in all ages, have

either been detected by contrary evidence or which detect themselves by their absurdity, prove sufficiently the strong propensity of mankind to the extraordinary and the marvelous and ought reasonably to beget a suspicion against all relations of this kind. This is our natural way of thinking, even with regard to the most common and most credible events. For instance, there is no kind of report which rises so easily and spreads so quickly, especially in country places and provincial towns, as those concerning marriages, inasmuch that two young persons of equal condition never see each other twice, but the whole neighborhood immediately join them together. The pleasure of telling a piece of news so interesting, of propagating it, and of being the first reporters of it spreads the intelligence. And this is so well known that no man of sense gives attention to these reports until he finds them confirmed by some greater evidence. Do not the same passions, and others still stronger, incline the generality of mankind to believe and report with the greatest vehemence and assurance all religious miracles?

Thirdly, it forms a strong presumption against all supernatural and miraculous relations that they are observed chiefly to abound among ignorant and barbarous nations; or if a civilized people has ever given admission to any of them that people will be found to have received them from ignorant and barbarous ancestors, who transmitted them with that inviolable sanction and authority which always attend received opinions. When we peruse the first histories of all nations, we are apt to imagine ourselves transported into some new world where the whole frame of nature is disjointed and every element performs its operations in a different manner from what it does at present. Battles, revolutions, pestilence, famine, and death are never the effect of those natural causes which we experience. Prodigies, omens, oracles, judgments quite obscure the few natural events that are intermingled with them. But as the former grow thinner every page, in proportion as we advance nearer the enlightened ages, we soon learn that there is nothing mysterious or supernatural in the case, but that all proceeds from the usual propensity of mankind towards the marvelous, and that, though this inclination may at intervals receive a check from sense and learning, it can never be thoroughly extirpated from human nature.

---

54. [Regarding Tully (Cicero), see Locke's *Essay*, n. 8.]

55. [Demosthenes (c. 384–322 B.C.) was a famous Greek orator.]

56. [The Capuchins, founded in the sixteenth century, were Franciscan friars who did extensive preaching and missionary work.]

It is strange, a judicious reader is apt to say, upon the perusal of these wonderful historians, that *such prodigious events never happen in our days*. But it is nothing strange, I hope, that men should lie in all ages. You must surely have seen instances enough of that frailty. You have yourself heard many such marvelous relations started which, being treated with scorn by all the wise and judicious, have at last been abandoned even by the vulgar. Be assured that those renowned lies which have spread and flourished to such a monstrous height arose from like beginnings, but being sown in a more proper soil, shot up at last into prodigies almost equal to those which they relate.

It was a wise policy in that false prophet Alexander, who, though now forgotten, was once so famous, to lay the first scene of his impostures in Paphlagonia, where, as Lucian tells us,[57] the people were extremely ignorant and stupid and ready to swallow even the grossest delusion. People at a distance, who are weak enough to think the matter at all worth inquiry, have no opportunity of receiving better information. The stories come magnified to them by a hundred circumstances. Fools are industrious in propagating the imposture, while the wise and learned are contented, in general, to deride its absurdity, without informing themselves of the particular facts by which it may be distinctly refuted. And thus the impostor above mentioned was enabled to proceed from his ignorant Paphlagonians to the enlisting of votaries, even among the Greek philosophers and men of the most eminent rank and distinction in Rome—No, could engage the attention of that sage emperor Marcus Aurelius[58] so far as to make him trust the success of a military expedition to his delusive prophecies.

The advantages are so great of starting an imposture among an ignorant people that, even though the delusion should be too gross to impose on the generality of them (*which, though seldom, is sometimes the case*),

it has a much better chance for succeeding in remote countries than if the first scene had been laid in a city renowned for arts and knowledge. The most ignorant and barbarous of these barbarians carry the report abroad. None of their countrymen have a large correspondence or sufficient credit and authority to contradict and beat down the delusion. Men's inclination to the marvelous has full opportunity to display itself. And thus a story which is universally exploded in the place where it was first started shall pass for certain at a thousand miles distance. But had Alexander fixed his residence at Athens, the philosophers of that renowned mart of learning had immediately spread throughout the whole Roman empire their sense of the matter, which, being supported by so great authority and displayed by all the force of reason and eloquence, had entirely opened the eyes of mankind. It is true, Lucian, passing by chance through, had an opportunity of performing this good office. But, though much to be wished, it does not always happen that every Alexander meets with a Lucian, ready to expose and detect his impostures.

I may add, as a *fourth* reason which diminishes the authority of prodigies, that there is no testimony for any, even those which have not been expressly detected, that is not opposed by an infinite number of witnesses, so that not only the miracle destroys the credit of testimony, but the testimony destroys itself. To make this the better understood, let us consider that in matters of religion whatever is different is contrary and that it is impossible the religions of ancient Rome, of Turkey, of Siam, and of China should all of them be established on any solid foundation. Every miracle, therefore, pretended to have been wrought in any of these religions (and all of them abound in miracles), as its direct scope is to establish the particular system to which it is attributed, so it has the same force, though more indirectly, to overthrow every other system. In destroying a rival system, it likewise destroys the credit of those miracles on which that system was established, so that all the prodigies of different religions are to be regarded as contrary facts and the evidences of these prodigies, whether weak or strong, as opposite to each other. According to this method of reasoning, when we believe any miracle of Mahomet or his successors, we have for our warrant the testimony of a few barbarous Arabians. And, on the other hand, we are to regard the authority

---

57. [In *Alexander, the False Prophet*, the Greek author Lucian (born c. 120) relates how Alexander of Abonoteichos was hailed as an oracle because of a hoax perpetrated on the people of Paphlagonia, whereby he made it appear that the god Asclepius was being born in the form of a serpent from a goose's egg. Paphlagonia was an ancient country in Asia Minor located in what is now Turkey.]

58. [Marcus Aurelius (121–180) was a Roman Emperor and a major Stoic philosopher.]

of Titus Livius,[59] Plutarch, Tacitus, and, in short, of all the authors and witnesses, Greek, Chinese, and Roman Catholic, who have related any miracle in their particular religion—I say, we are to regard their testimony in the same light as if they had mentioned that Mahometan miracle and had in express terms contradicted it with the same certainty as they have for the miracle they relate. This argument may appear over subtle and refined, but is not in reality different from the reasoning of a judge who supposes that the credit of two witnesses maintaining a crime against anyone is destroyed by the testimony of two others who affirm him to have been two hundred leagues distant at the same instant when the crime is said to have been committed.

One of the best attested miracles in all profane history is that which Tacitus reports of Vespasian,[60] who cured a blind man in Alexandria by means of his spittle and a lame man by the mere touch of his foot, in obedience to a vision of the god Serapis, who had enjoined them to have recourse to the Emperor for these miraculous cures. The story may be seen in that fine historian,[61] where every circumstance seems to add weight to the testimony, and might be displayed at large with all the force of argument and eloquence, if anyone were now concerned to enforce the evidence of that exploded and idolatrous superstition: the gravity, solidity, age, and probity of so great an emperor, who, through the whole course of his life, conversed in a familiar manner with his friends and courtiers and never affected those extraordinary airs of divinity assumed by Alexander and Demetrius;[62] the historian, a contemporary writer noted for candor and veracity, and in addition the greatest and most penetrating genius perhaps of all antiquity, and so free from any tendency to credulity that he even lies under the contrary imputation of atheism and profaneness; the persons from whose authority he related the miracle of established character for judgment and veracity, as we may well presume; eyewitnesses of the fact, and confirming their testimony after the Flavian family[63] was despoiled of the empire and could no longer give any reward as the price of a lie. *Utrumque, qui interfuere, nunc quoque memorant, postquam nullum mendacio pretium.*[64] To which, if we add the public nature of the facts, as related, it will appear that no evidence can well be supposed stronger for so gross and so palpable a falsehood.

There is also a memorable story related by Cardinal de Retz,[65] which may well deserve our consideration. When that intriguing politician fled into Spain to avoid the persecution of his enemies, he passed through Saragossa, the capital of Arragon, where he was shown, in the cathedral, a man who had served seven years as a doorkeeper and was well known to everybody in town who had ever paid his devotions at that church. He had been seen for so long a time wanting a leg, but recovered that limb by the rubbing of holy oil upon the stump; and when the Cardinal examined it, he found it to be a true natural leg like the other. This miracle was vouched by all the canons of the church; and the whole company in town were appealed to for a confirmation of the fact, whom the cardinal found, by their zealous devotion, to be thorough believers of the miracle. Here the relater was also contemporary to the supposed prodigy, of an incredulous and libertine character, as well as of great genius; the miracle of so *singular* a nature as could scarcely admit of a counterfeit, and the witnesses very numerous, and all of them, in a manner, spectators of the fact to which they gave their testimony. And what adds mightily to the force of the evidence and may double our surprise on this occa-

---

59. [Titus Livius (59 B.C.—A.D. 17), commonly known as Livy, was a Roman historian; his major work, the 142-book *History of Rome*, covered Rome's beginnings until his own time.]

60. [Vespasian (9–79) was emperor of Rome and founder of the Flavian dynasty which ruled from 69 to 96.]

61. Hist. Bk. IV, Chap. 81. Suetonius gives nearly the same account in VESP. 7. [The reference to Suetonius is found in *Lives of the Twelve Caesars*, Book VIII. The story is not found in Tacitus exactly as Hume describes it, for Tactitus, himself, seems to have doubted that the cure was "miraculous."]

62. [Demetrius I (c. 336–283 B.C.), ruler of Macedonia.]

63. [The family that ruled the Roman Empire A.D. 69–96 and included the emperor Vespasian and his sons Titus (40–81) and Domitian (51–96).]

64. [Of each event, those who were present, even now keep speaking, though they get no reward for lying.]

65. [Cardinal de Retz (1613–1679), a French political leader. His memoirs (1717) provide insight into the court life of his time.]

sion is that the Cardinal himself, who relates the story, does not seem to give any credit to it and, consequently, cannot be suspected of any concurrence in the holy fraud. He considered justly that it was not requisite, in order to reject a fact of this nature, to be able accurately to disprove the testimony and to trace its falsehood through all the circumstances of knavery and credulity which produced it. He knew that, as this was commonly altogether impossible at any small distance of time and place, so was it extremely difficult, even where one was immediately present, by reason of the bigotry, ignorance, cunning, and roguery of a great part of mankind. He therefore concluded, like a just reasoner, that such an evidence carried falsehood upon the very face of it and that a miracle supported by any human testimony was more properly a subject of derision than of argument.

There surely never was a greater number of miracles ascribed to one person than those which were lately said to have been wrought in France upon the tomb of Abbé Paris, the famous Jansenist, with whose sanctity the people were so long deluded. The curing of the sick, giving hearing to the deaf and sight to the blind, were everywhere talked of as the usual effects of that holy sepulcher. But what is more extraordinary, many of the miracles were immediately proved upon the spot, before judges of unquestioned integrity, attested by witnesses of credit and distinction, in a learned age, and on the most eminent theater that is now in the world. Nor is this all: A relation of them was published and dispersed everywhere, nor were the *Jesuits*, though a learned body supported by the civil magistrate and determined enemies to those opinions in whose favor the miracles were said to have been wrought, ever able distinctly to refute or detect them.[66] Where shall we find such

66. This book was writ by Mons. Montgerron, counsellor or judge of the parliament of Paris, a man of figure and character, who was also a martyr to the cause, and is now said to be somewhere in a dungeon on account of his book.

There is another book in three volumes (called *Recueil des Miracles de l'Abbé* Paris) giving an account of many of these miracles, and accompanied with prefatory discourses, which are very well written. There runs, however, through the whole of these a ridiculous comparison between the miracles of our Saviour and those of the Abbé; wherein it is asserted, that the evidence for the latter is equal to that for the former: As if the testimony of men could ever be

a number of circumstances agreeing to the corroboration of one fact? And what have we to oppose to such a cloud of witnesses but the absolute impossibility or miraculous nature of the events which they relate?

----

put in the balance with that of God himself, who conducted the pen of the inspired writers. If these writers, indeed, were to be considered merely as human testimony, the French author is very moderate in his comparison: since he might, with some appearance of reason, pretend, that the Jansenist miracles much surpass the other in evidence and authority. The following circumstances are drawn from authentic papers, inserted in the above-mentioned book.

Many of the miracles of Abbé Paris were proved immediately by witnesses before the officiality or bishop's court at Paris, under the eye of cardinal Noailles, whose character for integrity and capacity was never contested even by his enemies.

His successor in the archbishopric was an enemy to the Jansenists, and for that reason promoted to the see by the court. Yet 22 rectors or *curés* of Paris, with infinite earnestness, press him to examine those miracles, which they assert to be known to the whole world, and undisputably certain: But he wisely forbore.

The Molinist party had tried to discredit these miracles in one instance, that of Madamoiselle le Franc. But, besides that their proceedings were in many respects the most irregular in the world, particularly in citing only a few of the Jansenist witnesses, whom they tampered with: Besides this, I say, they soon found themselves overwhelmed by a cloud of new witnesses, one hundred and twenty in number, most of them persons of credit and substance in Paris, who gave oath for the miracle. This was accompanied with a solemn and earnest appeal to the parliament. But the parliament were forbidden by authority to meddle in the affair. It was at last observed, that where men are heated by zeal and enthusiasm, there is no degree of human testimony so strong as may not be procured for the greatest absurdity: And those who will be so silly as to examine the affair by that medium, and seek particular flaws in the testimony, are almost sure to be confounded. It must be a miserable imposture, indeed, that does not prevail in that contest. [The Molinists were Jesuits who followed the teachings of Luis de Molina (1535–1600). Molina's main tenet concerned the problem of reconciling divine grace and human freedom; he claimed that although God has infallible knowledge of whether or not an individual will accept grace, this foreknowledge does not determine the action of the individual. Hence, the efficacy of grace is not a matter of God's will, but of His knowledge, and, ultimately, therefore, a matter of man's acceptance.]

All who have been in France about that time have heard of the reputation of Mons. Heraut, the *lieutenant de Police*,

And this, surely, in the eyes of all reasonable people, will alone be regarded as a sufficient refutation.

Is the consequence just, because some human testimony has the utmost force and authority in some cases, when it relates the battle of Philippi or Pharsalia,[67] for instance, that therefore all kinds of testimony must in all cases have equal force and authority? Suppose that the Caesarean and Pompeian factions

whose vigilance, penetration, activity, and extensive intelligence have been much talked of. This magistrate, who by the nature of his office is almost absolute, was invested with full powers, on purpose to suppress or discredit these miracles; and he frequently seized immediately, and examined the witnesses and subjects of them: But never could reach any thing satisfactory against them.

In the case of Madamoiselle Thibaut he sent the famous De Sylva to examine her; whose evidence is very curious. The physician declares, that it was impossible she could have been so ill as was proved by witnesses; because it was impossible she could, in so short a time, have recovered so perfectly as he found her. He reasoned, like a man of sense, from natural causes; but the opposite party told him, that the whole was a miracle, and that his evidence was the very best proof of it.

The Molinists were in a sad dilemma. They durst not assert the absolute insufficiency of human evidence, to prove a miracle. They were obliged to say, that these miracles were wrought by witchcraft and the devil. But they were told, that this was the resource of the Jews of old.

No Jansenist was ever embarrassed to account for the cessation of the miracles, when the church-yard was shut up by the king's edict. It was the touch of the tomb, which produced these extraordinary effects; and when no one could approach the tomb, no effects could be expected. God, indeed, could have thrown down the walls in a moment; but he is master of his own graces and works, and it belongs not to us to account for them. He did not throw down the walls of every city like those of Jericho, on the sounding of the rams' horns, nor break up the prison of every apostle, like that of St. Paul.

No less a man, than the Duc de Chatillon, a duke and peer of France, of the highest rank and family, gives evidence of a miraculous cure, performed upon a servant of his, who had lived several years in his house with a visible and palpable infirmity.

I shall conclude with observing, that no clergy are more celebrated for strictness of life and manners than the secular clergy of France, particularly the rectors or curés of Paris, who bear testimony to these impostures.

The learning, genius, and probity of the gentlemen, and the austerity of the nuns of Port-Royal, have been much celebrated all over Europe. [Port Royal was the name of a famous Jansenist monastery located not far from Paris and, derivatively, the Jansenist movement associated with the school. Jansenism was a Roman Catholic movement based on the teachings of Cornelius Jansen (1585–1638), a Dutch theologian. Jansen denied freedom of the will and maintained predestination and the infallible efficacy of Divine grace needed for salvation. Blaise Pascal (1623–1662), Jean Racine (1639–1699), Antoine Arnauld (1612–1694), and Pierre Nicole (1625–1695) all were affiliated with the movement. Pascal, Arnauld, and Nicole wrote tracts for the Jansenists and the latter two co-authored the *Logique ou l'art de Penser* (1662), known as the Port Royal Logic. Racine was a student at the monastery and wrote the *Abrégé de l'histoire de Port-Royal* (1742 and 1747), to which Hume refers in this footnote. In addition, Pascal's sister was a nun at the monastery and Arnauld's sister an abess.] Yet they all give evidence for a miracle, wrought on the niece of the famous Pascal, whose sanctity of life, as well as extraordinary capacity, is well known. The famous Racine gives an account of this miracle in his famous history of Port-Royal, and fortifies it with all the proofs, which a multitude of nuns, priests, physicians, and men of the world, all of them of undoubted credit, could bestow upon it. Several men of letters, particularly the bishop of Tournay, thought this miracle so certain, as to employ it in the refutation of atheists and free-thinkers. The queen-regent of France, who was extremely prejudiced against the Port-Royal, sent her own physician to examine the miracle, who returned an absolute convert. In short, the supernatural cure was so uncontestable, that it saved, for a time, that famous monastery from the ruin with which it was threatened by the Jesuits. Had it been a cheat, it had certainly been detected by such sagacious and powerful antagonists, and must have hastened the ruin of the contrivers. Our divines, who can build up a formidable castle from such despicable materials; what a prodigious fabric could they have reared from these and many other circumstances, which I have not mentioned! How often would the great names of Pascal, Racine, Arnaud, Nicole, have resounded in our ears? But if they be wise, they had better adopt the miracle, as being more worth, a thousand times, than all the rest of their collection. Besides, it may serve very much to their purpose. For that miracle was really performed by the touch of an authentic holy prickle of the holy thorn, which composed the holy crown, which, &c.

67. [Philippi was a city in eastern Macedonia and the scene of the two battles in 42 B.C. at which Antony and Octavian (Augustus), allies of the slain Caesar, defeated Cassius and Brutus, former supporters of Pompey. Pharsalia was a city in Thessaly in Greece where a battle was fought in 48

had, each of them, claimed the victory in these battles, and that the historians of each party had uniformly ascribed the advantage to their own side, how could mankind, at this distance, have been able to determine between them? The contrariety is equally strong between the miracles related by Herodotus[68] or Plutarch and those delivered by Mariana, Bede, or any monkish historian.

The wise lend a very academic faith to every report which favors the passion of the reporter, whether it magnifies his country, his family, or himself, or in any other way strikes in with his natural inclinations and propensities. But what greater temptation than to appear a missionary, a prophet, an ambassador from heaven? Who would not encounter many dangers and difficulties in order to attain so sublime a character? Or if, by the help of vanity and a heated imagination, a man has first made a convert of himself and entered seriously into the delusion, who ever scruples to make use of pious frauds in support of so holy and meritorious a cause?

The smallest spark may here kindle into the greatest flame, because the materials are always prepared for it. The *avidum genus auricularum*,[69] the gazing populace, receive greedily, without examination, whatever soothes superstition and promotes wonder.

How many stories of this nature have, in all ages, been detected and exploded in their infancy? How many more have been celebrated for a time and have afterwards sunk into neglect and oblivion? Where such reports, therefore, fly about, the solution of the phenomenon is obvious and we judge in conformity to regular experience and observation when we account for it by the known and natural principles of credulity and delusion. And shall we, rather than

have a recourse to so natural a solution, allow of a miraculous violation of the most established laws of nature?

I need not mention the difficulty of detecting a falsehood in any private or even public history at the place where it is said to happen, much more when the scene is removed to ever so small a distance. Even a court of judicature, with all the authority, accuracy, and judgment, which they can employ, find themselves often at a loss to distinguish between truth and falsehood in the most recent actions. But the matter never comes to any issue, if trusted to the common method of altercation and debate and flying rumors, especially when men's passions have taken part on either side.

In the infancy of new religions, the wise and learned commonly esteem the matter too inconsiderable to deserve their attention or regard. And when afterwards they would willingly detect the cheat in order to undeceive the deluded multitude, the season is now past and the records and witnesses which might clear up the matter have perished beyond recovery.

No means of detection remain but those which must be drawn from the very testimony itself of the reporters. And these, though always sufficient with the judicious and knowing, are commonly too fine to fall under the comprehension of the vulgar.

Upon the whole, then, it appears that no testimony for any kind of miracle has ever amounted to a probability, much less to a proof; and that, even supposing it amounted to a proof, it would be opposed by another proof derived from the very nature of the fact which it would endeavor to establish. It is experience only which gives authority to human testimony and it is the same experience which assures us of the laws of nature. When, therefore, these two kinds of experience are contrary, we have nothing to do but subtract the one from the other and embrace an opinion either on one side or the other with that assurance which arises from the remainder. But according to the principle here explained, this subtraction with regard to all popular religions amounts to an entire annihilation and, therefore, we may establish it as a maxim that no human testimony can have such force as to prove a miracle and make it a just foundation for any such system of religion.

I beg the limitations here made may be remarked, when I say that a miracle can never be proved so as

---

B.C. in which Julius Caesar (102–44 B.C.) triumphed over Pompey (106–48 B.C.).]

68. [Herodotus (c. 484–c. 425 B.C.), was a Greek historian often referred to as "The Father of History." He wrote *The Persian Wars*. Juan de Mariana (c. 1536–c. 1623), a Spanish Jesuit and historian, wrote a history of Spain. Bede (673–735), an English historian and Benedictine monk, wrote an ecclesiastical history of England.]

69. [Literally, "a gossip-hungry race"; this is an adaptation or misquotation of *Humanum genus est avidum nimus auricularum* "the human race is too gossip-hungry" (Lucretius, *De Rerum Natura*, iv. 594).]

to be the foundation of a system of religion. For I admit that otherwise there may possibly be miracles or violations of the usual course of nature of such a kind as to admit of proof from human testimony; though perhaps it will be impossible to find any such in all the records of history. Thus, suppose all authors, in all languages, agree that from the first of January 1600 there was a total darkness over the whole earth for eight days; suppose that the tradition of this extraordinary event is still strong and lively among the people—that all travelers who return from foreign countries bring us accounts of the same tradition without the least variation or contradiction—it is evident that our present philosophers, instead of doubting the fact, ought to receive it as certain and ought to search for the causes from which it might be derived. The decay, corruption, and dissolution of nature is an event rendered probable by so many analogies that any phenomenon which seems to have a tendency towards that catastrophe comes within the reach of human testimony, if that testimony is very extensive and uniform.

But suppose that all the historians who treat of England should agree that on the first of January 1600, Queen Elizabeth died; that both before and after her death she was seen by her physicians and the whole court, as is usual with persons of her rank; that her successor was acknowledged and proclaimed by the parliament; and that, after being interred a month, she again appeared, resumed the throne, and governed England for three years—I must confess that I should be surprised at the concurrence of so many odd circumstances, but should not have the least inclination to believe so miraculous an event. I should not doubt of her pretended death and of those other public circumstances that followed it; I should only assert it to have been pretended, and that it neither was nor possibly could be real. You would in vain object to me the difficulty and almost impossibility of deceiving the world in an affair of such consequence; the wisdom and solid judgment of that renowned queen, with the little or no advantage which she could reap from so poor an artifice—all this might astonish me, but I would still reply that the knavery and folly of men are such common phenomena that I should rather believe the most extraordinary events to arise from their concurrence than admit of so signal a violation of the laws of nature.

But should this miracle be ascribed to any new system of religion, men in all ages have been so much imposed on by ridiculous stories of that kind that this very circumstance would be a full proof of a cheat and sufficient, with all men of sense, not only to make them reject the fact, but even reject it without further examination. Though the Being to whom the miracle is ascribed is in this case Almighty, it does not, upon that account, become a whit more probable, since it is impossible for us to know the attributes or actions of such a Being otherwise than from the experience which we have of his productions in the usual course of nature. This still reduces us to past observation and obliges us to compare the instances of the violation of truth in the testimony of men with those of the violation of the laws of nature by miracles, in order to judge which of them is most likely and probable. As the violations of truth are more common in the testimony concerning religious miracles than in that concerning any other matter of fact, this must diminish very much the authority of the former testimony and make us form a general resolution, never to lend any attention to it, with whatever specious pretense it may be covered.

Lord Bacon seems to have embraced the same principles of reasoning. "We ought," says he, "make a collection or particular history of all monsters and prodigious births or productions and, in a word, of everything new, rare, and extraordinary in nature. But this must be done with the most severe scrutiny, lest we depart from truth. Above all, every relation must be considered as suspicious which depends in any degree upon religion, as the prodigies of Livy. And no less so, everything that is to be found in the writers of natural magic or alchemy or such authors who seem, all of them, to have an unconquerable appetite for falsehood and fable."[70]

I am the better pleased with the method of reasoning here delivered, as I think it may serve to confound those dangerous friends or disguised enemies to the *Christian Religion* who have undertaken to defend it by the principles of human reason. Our most holy

70. *Novum Organum* lib. ii. aph. 29. [Francis Bacon (1561–1626) was an English philosopher and statesman who stressed the importance of scientific methodology in the acquisition of knowledge, and according to Hume first applied "experimental philosophy to natural subjects."]

religion is founded on Faith, not on reason; and it is a sure method of exposing it to put it to such a trial as it is by no means fitted to endure. To make this more evident, let us examine those miracles related in Scripture and, not to lose ourselves in too wide a field, let us confine ourselves to such as we find in the *Pentateuch*,[71] which we shall examine according to the principles of these pretended Christians, not as the word or testimony of God himself, but as the production of a mere human writer and historian. Here then we are first to consider a book presented to us by a barbarous and ignorant people, written in an age when they were still more barbarous, and in all probability long after the facts which it relates, corroborated by no concurring testimony, and resembling those fabulous accounts which every nation gives of its origin. Upon reading this book we find it full of prodigies and miracles. It gives an account of a state of the world and of human nature entirely different from the present: of our fall from that state; of the age of man extended to near a thousand years; of the destruction of the world by a deluge; of the arbitrary choice of one people as the favorites of heaven, and that people the countrymen of the author; of their deliverance from bondage by prodigies the most astonishing imaginable: I desire anyone to lay his hand upon his heart and, after a serious consideration, declare whether he thinks that the falsehood of such a book, supported by such a testimony, would be more extraordinary and miraculous than all the miracles it relates — which is, however, necessary to make it be received according to the measures of probability above established.

What we have said of miracles may be applied without any variation to prophecies; and, indeed, all prophecies are real miracles and as such only can be admitted as proofs of any revelation. If it did not exceed the capacity of human nature to foretell future events, it would be absurd to employ any prophecy as an argument for a divine mission or authority from heaven. So that, upon the whole, we may conclude that the Christian religion not only was at first attended with miracles, but even at this day cannot be believed by any reasonable person without one. Mere

reason is insufficient to convince us of its veracity. And whoever is moved by faith to assent to it is conscious of a continued miracle in his own person which subverts all the principles of his understanding and gives him a determination to believe what is most contrary to custom and experience.

Section XI
Of a Particular Providence and of a Future State.

I was lately engaged in conversation with a friend who loves skeptical paradoxes, where, though he advanced many principles of which I can by no means approve, yet as they seem to be curious and to bear some relation to the chain of reasoning carried on throughout this inquiry, I shall here copy them from my memory as accurately as I can in order to submit them to the judgment of the reader.

Our conversation began with my admiring the singular good fortune of philosophy, which, as it requires entire liberty above all other privileges and chiefly flourishes from the free opposition of sentiments and argumentation, received its first birth in an age and country of freedom and toleration, and was never cramped, even in its most extravagant principles, by any creeds, confessions, or penal statutes. For, except the banishment of Protagoras[72] and the death of Socrates, which last event proceeded partly from other motives, there are scarcely any instances to be met with, in ancient history, of this bigoted jealousy with which the present age is so much infested. Epicurus lived at Athens to an advanced age in peace and tranquillity. Epicureans[73] were even admitted to receive the sacerdotal character and to officiate at the altar in the most sacred rites of the established religion. And the public encouragement[74] of pensions and salaries was afforded equally by the wisest of all

---

71. [The Pentateuch, the Five Books of Moses, is the first five books of the Bible: Genesis, Exodus, Leviticus, Numbers, and Deuteronomy.]

72. [Protagoras of Abdera (490(?)–421(?) B.C.), outstanding member of the group of philosophers known as the Sophists, was exiled from Athens because of his religious views, which were said to be impious.]

73. Luciani συμπ. ἢ λαπίθαι. 9. [*The Carousel or the Lapiths.*]

74. Luciani ευνοῦχος. 3. [*The Eunuch.*]

the Roman emperors[75] to the professors of every sect of philosophy. How requisite such kind of treatment was to philosophy, in her early youth, will easily be conceived, if we reflect that even at present, when she may be supposed more hardy and robust, she bears with much difficulty the inclemency of the seasons and those harsh winds of calumny and persecution which blow upon her.

You admire, says my friend, as the singular good fortune of philosophy what seems to result from the natural course of things and to be unavoidable in every age and nation. This pertinacious bigotry, of which you complain as so fatal to philosophy, is really her offspring who, after allying with superstition, separates himself entirely from the interest of his parent and becomes her most inveterate enemy and persecutor. Speculative dogmas of religion, the present occasions of such furious dispute, could not possibly be conceived or admitted in the early ages of the world, when mankind, being wholly illiterate, formed an idea of religion more suitable to their weak apprehension and composed their sacred tenets of such tales chiefly as were the objects of traditional belief more than of argument or disputation. After the first alarm, therefore, was over, which arose from the new paradoxes and principles of the philosophers, these teachers seem ever after, during the ages of antiquity, to have lived in great harmony with the established superstition and to have made a fair partition of mankind between them — the former claiming all the learned and wise, the latter possessing all the vulgar and illiterate.

It seems then, I say, that you leave politics entirely out of the question and never suppose that a wise magistrate can justly be jealous of certain tenets of philosophy, such as those of Epicurus, which, denying a divine existence and consequently a providence and a future state, seem to loosen in a great measure the ties of morality and may be supposed, for that reason, pernicious to the peace of civil society.

I know, he replied, that in fact these persecutions never, in any age, proceeded from calm reason or from experience of the pernicious consequences of philosophy, but arose entirely from passion and prejudice. But what if I should advance further and assert that, if Epicurus had been accused before the people

by any of the *sycophants* or informers of those days, he could easily have defended his cause and proved his principles of philosophy to be as salutary as those of his adversaries who endeavored with such zeal to expose him to the public hatred and jealousy?

I wish, I said, you would try your eloquence upon so extraordinary a topic and make a speech for Epicurus which might satisfy, not the mob of Athens, if you will allow that ancient and polite city to have contained any mob, but the more philosophical part of his audience, such as might be supposed capable of comprehending his arguments.

The matter would not be difficult upon such conditions, he replied; and if you please, I shall suppose myself Epicurus for a moment and make you stand for the Athenian people, and shall deliver you such an harangue as will fill all the urn with white beans and leave not a black one to gratify the malice of my adversaries.[76]

Very well. Pray proceed upon these suppositions.

I come here, O you Athenians, to justify in your assembly what I maintained in my school and I find myself impeached by furious antagonists, instead of reasoning with calm and dispassionate inquirers. Your deliberations, which of right should be directed to questions of public good and the interest of the commonwealth, are diverted to the disquisitions of speculative philosophy, and these magnificent, but perhaps fruitless inquiries take place of your more familiar, but more useful occupations. But so far as in me lies I will prevent this abuse. We shall not here dispute concerning the origin and government of worlds. We shall only inquire how far such questions concern the public interest. And if I can persuade you that they are entirely indifferent to the peace of society and security of government, I hope that you will presently send us back to our schools, there to examine at leisure the question, the most sublime, but, at the same time, the most speculative of all philosophy.

The religious philosophers, not satisfied with the tradition of your forefathers and doctrine of your priests (in which I willingly acquiesce), indulge a rash curiosity in trying how far they can establish

75. Id. & Dio. [*The Eunuch* and Dio Cassius (c. 150– c. 235), *History of Rome*, Bk. LXXII.]

76. [In Athens, beans were used for balloting: white beans signified assent or agreement; black ones, dissent or disagreement. For an examination of the argument, see Hume's *Dialogues Concerning Natural Religion*.]

religion upon the principles of reason; and they thereby excite, instead of satisfying, the doubts which naturally arise from a diligent and scrutinous inquiry. They paint in the most magnificent colors the order, beauty, and wise arrangement of the universe and then ask if such a glorious display of intelligence could proceed from the fortuitous concourse of atoms or if chance could produce what the greatest genius can never sufficiently admire. I shall not examine the justness of this argument. I shall allow it to be as solid as my antagonists and accusers can desire. It is sufficient if I can prove, from this very reasoning, that the question is entirely speculative, and that, when, in my philosophical disquisitions, I deny a providence and a future state, I do not undermine the foundations of society, but advance principles which they themselves, upon their own topics, if they argue consistently, must allow to be solid and satisfactory.

You then, who are my accusers, have acknowledged that the chief or sole argument for a divine existence (which I never questioned) is derived from the order of nature, where there appear such marks of intelligence and design that you think it extravagant to assign for its cause either chance or the blind and unguided force of matter. You allow that this is an argument drawn from effects to causes. From the order of the work you infer that there must have been project and forethought in the workman. If you cannot make out this point, you allow that your conclusion fails and you do not pretend to establish the conclusion in a greater latitude than the phenomena of nature will justify. These are your concessions. I desire you to mark the consequences.

When we infer any particular cause from an effect, we must proportion the one to the other and can never be allowed to ascribe to the cause any qualities but what are exactly sufficient to produce the effect. A body of ten ounces raised in any scale may serve as a proof that the counterbalancing weight exceeds ten ounces, but can never afford a reason that it exceeds a hundred. If the cause assigned for any effect is not sufficient to produce it, we must either reject that cause or add to it such qualities as will give it a just proportion to the effect. But if we ascribe to it further qualities or affirm it capable of producing other effects, we can only indulge the license of conjecture and arbitrarily suppose the existence of qualities and energies without reason or authority.

The same rule holds whether the cause assigned is brute unconscious matter or a rational intelligent being. If the cause is known only by the effect, we never ought to ascribe to it any qualities beyond what are precisely requisite to produce the effect; nor can we, by any rules of just reasoning, return back from the cause and infer other effects from it, beyond those by which alone it is known to us. No one, merely from the sight of one of Zeuxis's[77] pictures, could know that he was also a statuary or architect and was an artist no less skillful in stone and marble than in colors. The talents and taste displayed in the particular work before us—these we may safely conclude the workman to be possessed of. The cause must be proportioned to the effect; and if we exactly and precisely proportion it, we shall never find in it any qualities that point further or afford an inference concerning any other design or performance. Such qualities must be somewhat beyond what is merely requisite for producing the effect which we examine.

Allowing, therefore, the gods to be the authors of the existence or order of the universe, it follows that they possess that precise degree of power, intelligence, and benevolence which appears in their workmanship, but nothing further can ever be proved, except we call in the assistance of exaggeration and flattery to supply the defects of argument and reasoning. So far as the traces of any attributes at present appear, so far may we conclude these attributes to exist. The supposition of further attributes is mere hypothesis, much more the supposition that in distant regions of space or periods of time there has been or will be a more magnificent display of these attributes and a scheme of administration more suitable to such imaginary virtues. We can never be allowed to mount up from the universe, the effect, to Jupiter, the cause, and then descend downwards to infer any new effect from that cause, as if the present effects alone were not entirely worthy of the glorious attributes which we ascribe to that deity. The knowledge of the cause being derived solely from the effect, they must be exactly adjusted to each other and the one can never refer to anything further or be the foundation of any new inference and conclusion.

You find certain phenomena in nature. You seek

---

77. [Zeuxis was a fifth-century B.C. Greek painter.]

a cause or author. You imagine that you have found him. You afterwards become so enamored of this offspring of your brain that you imagine it impossible but he must produce something greater and more perfect than the present scene of things, which is so full of ill and disorder. You forget that this superlative intelligence and benevolence are entirely imaginary or, at least, without any foundation in reason and that you have no ground to ascribe to him any qualities but what you see he has actually exerted and displayed in his productions. Let your gods, therefore, O philosophers, be suited to the present appearances of nature and do not presume to alter these appearances by arbitrary suppositions in order to suit them to the attributes which you so fondly ascribe to your deities.

When priests and poets, supported by your authority, O Athenians, talk of a golden or silver age which preceded the present state of vice and misery, I hear them with attention and with reverence. But when philosophers who pretend to neglect authority and to cultivate reason hold the same discourse, I do not pay them, I admit, the same obsequious submission and pious deference. I ask: Who carried them into the celestial regions, who admitted them into the councils of the gods, who opened to them the book of fate that they thus rashly affirm that their deities have executed or will execute any purpose beyond what has actually appeared? If they tell me that they have mounted on the steps or by the gradual ascent of reason and by drawing inferences from effects to causes, I still insist that they have aided the ascent of reason by the wings of imagination; otherwise they could not thus change their manner of inference and argue from causes to effects, presuming that a more perfect production than the present world would be more suitable to such perfect beings as the gods and forgetting that they have no reason to ascribe to these celestial beings any perfection or any attribute but what can be found in the present world.

Hence all the fruitless industry to account for the ill appearances of nature and save the honor of the gods, while we must acknowledge the reality of that evil and disorder with which the world so much abounds. The obstinate and intractable qualities of matter, we are told, or the observance of general laws, or some such reason, is the sole cause which controlled the power and benevolence of Jupiter and obliged him to create mankind and every sensible

creature so imperfect and so unhappy. These attributes, then, are, it seems, beforehand taken for granted in their greatest latitude. And upon that supposition, I admit that such conjectures may, perhaps, be admitted as plausible solutions of the ill phenomena. But still I ask: Why take these attributes for granted or why ascribe to the cause any qualities but what actually appear in the effect? Why torture your brain to justify the course of nature upon suppositions which, for all you know, may be entirely imaginary and of which there are to be found no traces in the course of nature?

The religious hypothesis, therefore, must be considered only as a particular method of accounting for the visible phenomena of the universe. But no just reasoner will ever presume to infer from it any single fact and alter or add to the phenomena in any single particular. If you think that the appearances of things prove such causes, it is allowable for you to draw an inference concerning the existence of these causes. In such complicated and sublime subjects, everyone should be indulged in the liberty of conjecture and argument. But here you ought to rest. If you come backward and, arguing from your inferred causes, conclude that any other fact has existed or will exist in the course of nature which may serve as a fuller display of particular attributes I must admonish you that you have departed from the method of reasoning attached to the present subject and have certainly added something to the attributes of the cause beyond what appears in the effect; otherwise you could never, with tolerable sense or propriety, add anything to the effect in order to render it more worthy of the cause.

Where, then, is the odiousness of that doctrine which I teach in my school, or rather, which I examine in my gardens? Or what do you find in this whole question in which the security of good morals or the peace and order of society are in the least concerned?

I deny a providence, you say, and supreme governor of the world who guides the course of events and punishes the vicious with infamy and disappointment, and rewards the virtuous with honor and success in all their undertakings. But surely I do not deny the course itself of events, which lies open to everyone's inquiry and examination. I acknowledge that, in the present order of things, virtue is attended with more peace of mind than vice and meets with a more favorable reception from the world. I am sensible that, according to the past experience of mankind, friendship is the chief joy of human life and moderation the only source of tranquillity and happiness. I never balance between the virtuous and the vicious course of life, but am sensible that, to a well-disposed mind, every advantage is on the side of the former. And what can you say more, allowing all your suppositions and reasonings? You tell me, indeed, that this disposition of things proceeds from intelligence and design. But whatever it proceeds from, the disposition itself, on which depends our happiness or misery and consequently our conduct and deportment in life, is still the same. It is still open for me, as well as you, to regulate my behavior by my experience of past events. And if you affirm that, while a divine providence is allowed, and a supreme distributive justice in the universe, I ought to expect some more particular reward of the good and punishment of the bad beyond the ordinary course of events, I here find the same fallacy which I have before endeavored to detect. You persist in imagining that, if we grant that divine existence for which you so earnestly contend, you may safely infer consequences from it and add something to the experienced order of nature by arguing from the attributes which you ascribe to your gods. You do not seem to remember that all your reasonings on this subject can only be drawn from effects to causes and that every argument deduced from causes to effects must of necessity be a gross sophism, since it is impossible for you to know anything of the cause but what you have antecedently not inferred, but discovered to the full in the effect.

But what must a philosopher think of those vain reasoners who, instead of regarding the present scene of things as the sole object of their contemplation, so far reverse the whole course of nature as to render this life merely a passage to something further—a porch which leads to a greater and vastly different building, a prologue which serves only to introduce the piece and give it more grace and propriety? From where, do you think, can such philosophers derive their idea of the gods? From their own conceit and imagination surely. For if they derived it from the present phenomena, it would never point to anything further, but must be exactly adjusted to them. That the divinity may *possibly* be endowed with attributes which we have never seen exerted, may be governed by principles of action which we cannot discover to

be satisfied. All this will freely be allowed. But still this is mere *possibility* and hypothesis. We never can have reason to *infer* any attributes or any principles of action in him, but so far as we know them to have been exerted and satisfied.

Are there any marks of a distributive justice in the world? If you answer in the affirmative, I conclude that, since justice here exerts itself, it is satisfied. If you reply in the negative, I conclude that you have then no reason to ascribe justice, in our sense of it, to the gods. If you hold a medium between affirmation and negation, by saying that the justice of the gods at present exerts itself in part, but not in its full extent, I answer that you have no reason to give it any particular extent, but only so far as you see it, *at present*, exert itself.

Thus I bring the dispute, O Athenians, to a short issue with my antagonists. The course of nature lies open to my contemplation as well as to theirs. The experienced train of events is the great standard by which we all regulate our conduct. Nothing else can be appealed to in the field or in the senate. Nothing else ought ever to be heard of in the school or in the closet. In vain would our limited understanding break through those boundaries which are too narrow for our fond imagination. While we argue from the course of nature and infer a particular intelligent cause which first bestowed and still preserves order in the universe, we embrace a principle which is both uncertain and useless. It is uncertain because the subject lies entirely beyond the reach of human experience. It is useless because our knowledge of this cause being derived entirely from the course of nature, we can never, according to the rules of just reasoning, return back from the cause with any new inference or, making additions to the common and experienced course of nature, establish any new principles of conduct and behavior.

I observe (I said, finding he had finished his harangue) that you do not neglect the artifice of the demagogues of old and as you were pleased to make me stand for the people, you insinuate yourself into my favor by embracing those principles to which, you know, I have always expressed a particular attachment. But allowing you to make experience (as indeed I think you ought) the only standard of our judgment concerning this and all other questions of fact, I do not doubt but, from the very same experience to which you appeal, it may be possible to refute this reasoning which you have put into the mouth of Epicurus. If you saw, for instance, a half-finished building surrounded with heaps of brick and stone and mortar and all the instruments of masonry, could you not *infer* from the effect that it was a work of design and contrivance? And could you not return again, from this inferred cause, to infer new additions to the effect and conclude that the building would soon be finished and receive all the further improvements which art could bestow upon it? If you saw upon the seashore the print of one human foot, you would conclude that a man had passed that way and that he had also left the traces of the other foot, though effaced by the rolling of the sands or inundation of the waters. Why then do you refuse to admit the same method of reasoning with regard to the order of nature? Consider the world and the present life only as an imperfect building from which you can infer a superior intelligence and, arguing from that superior intelligence which can leave nothing imperfect, why may you not infer a more finished scheme or plan which will receive its completion in some distant point of space or time? Are not these methods of reasoning exactly similar? And under what pretense can you embrace the one while you reject the other?

The infinite difference of the subjects, he replied, is a sufficient foundation for this difference in my conclusions. In works of human art and contrivance, it is allowable to advance from the effect to the cause, and, returning back from the cause, to form new inferences concerning the effect and examine the alterations which it has probably undergone or may still undergo. But what is the foundation of this method of reasoning? Plainly this: that man is a being whom we know by experience, whose motives and designs we are acquainted with, and whose projects and inclinations have a certain connection and coherence according to the laws which nature has established for the government of such a creature. When, therefore, we find that any work has proceeded from the skill and industry of man, as we are otherwise acquainted with the nature of the animal, we can draw a hundred inferences concerning what may be expected from him; and these inferences will all be founded in experience and observation. But did we know man only from the single work or production which we examine, it would be impossible for us to argue in this manner, because our knowledge of all the qualities which we ascribe to him, being in that case derived from the production, it is impossible they could point to anything further or be the foundation of any new inference. The print of a foot in the sand can only prove, when considered alone, that there was some figure adapted to it by which it was produced. But the print of a human foot proves likewise, from our other experience, that there was probably another foot which also left its impression, though effaced by time or other accidents. Here we mount from the effect to the cause, and, descending again from the cause, infer alterations in the effect; but this is not a continuation of the same simple chain of reasoning. We comprehend in this case a hundred other experiences and observations concerning the *usual* figure and members of that species of animal without which this method of argument must be considered as fallacious and sophistical.

The case is not the same with our reasonings from the works of nature. The Deity is known to us only by his productions and is a single being in the universe, not comprehended under any species or genus, from whose experienced attributes or qualities we can, by analogy, infer any attribute or quality in him. As the universe shows wisdom and goodness, we infer wisdom and goodness. As it shows a particular degree of these perfections, we infer a particular degree of them precisely adapted to the effect which we examine. But further attributes or further degrees of the same attributes we can never be authorized to infer or suppose by any rules of just reasoning. Now, without some such license of supposition, it is impossible for us to argue from the cause or infer any alteration in the effect beyond what has immediately fallen under our observation. Greater good produced by this Being must still prove a greater degree of goodness. A more impartial distribution of rewards and punishments must proceed from a greater regard to justice and equity. Every supposed addition to the works of nature makes an addition to the attributes of the Author of nature, and, consequently, being entirely unsupported by any reason or argument, can never be admitted but as mere conjecture and hypothesis.[78]

78. [In general, it may, I think, be established as a maxim, that where any cause is known only by its particular effects, it must be impossible to infer any new effects from that

The great source of our mistake in this subject and of the unbounded license of conjecture which we indulge is that we tacitly consider ourselves as in the place of the Supreme Being and conclude that he will, on every occasion, observe the same conduct which we ourselves, in his situation, would have embraced as reasonable and eligible. But, besides that the ordinary course of nature may convince us that almost everything is regulated by principles and maxims very different from ours—besides this, I say, it must evidently appear contrary to all rules of analogy to reason from the intentions and projects of men to those of a Being so different and so much superior. In human nature there is a certain experienced coherence of designs and inclinations, so that when, from any fact, we have discovered one intention of any man, it may often be reasonable, from experience, to infer another and draw a long chain of conclusions concerning his past or future conduct. But this method of reasoning can never have place with regard to a Being so remote and incomprehensible, who bears much less analogy to any other being in the universe than the sun to a waxen taper, and who discovers himself only by some faint traces or outlines beyond which we have no authority to ascribe to him any attribute or perfection. What we imagine to be a superior perfection may really be a defect. Or were it ever so much a perfection, the ascribing of it to

_____

cause; since the qualities, which are requisite to produce these new effects along with the former, must either be different, or superior, or of more extensive operation, than those which simply produced the effect, whence alone the cause is supposed to be known to us. We can never, therefore, have any reason to suppose the existence of these qualities. To say, that the new effects proceed only from a continuation of the same energy, which is already known from the first effects, will not remove the difficulty. For even granting this to be the case (which can seldom be supposed), the very continuation and exertion of a like energy (for it is impossible it can be absolutely the same), I say, this exertion of a like energy, in a different period of space and time, is a very arbitrary supposition, and what there cannot possibly be any traces of in the effects, from which all our knowledge of the cause is originally derived. Let the *inferred* cause be exactly proportioned (as it should be) to the known effect; and it is impossible that it can possess any qualities, from which new or different effects can be *inferred*.]

the Supreme Being, where it does not appear to have been really exerted to the full in his works, savors more of flattery and panegyric than of just reasoning and sound philosophy. All the philosophy, therefore, in the world and all the religion, which is nothing but a species of philosophy, will never be able to carry us beyond the usual course of experience or give us measures of conduct and behavior different from those which are furnished by reflections on common life. No new fact can ever be inferred from the religious hypothesis, no event foreseen or foretold, no reward or punishment expected or dreaded beyond what is already known by practice and observation. So that my apology for Epicurus will still appear solid and satisfactory, nor have the political interests of society any connection with the philosophical disputes concerning metaphysics and religion.

There is still one circumstance, I replied, which you seem to have overlooked. Though I should allow your premises, I must deny your conclusion. You conclude that religious doctrines and reasonings *can* have no influence on life because they *ought* to have no influence, never considering that men reason not in the same manner you do, but draw many consequences from the belief of a divine Existence and suppose that the Deity will inflict punishments on vice and bestow rewards on virtue beyond what appear in the ordinary course of nature. Whether this reasoning of theirs is just or not is no matter. Its influence on their life and conduct must still be the same. And those who attempt to disabuse them of such prejudices may, for all I know, be good reasoners, but I cannot allow them to be good citizens and politicians, since they free men from one restraint upon their passions and make the infringement of the laws of society in one respect more easy and secure.

After all, I may perhaps agree to your general conclusion in favor of liberty, though upon different premises from those on which you endeavor to found it. I think that the state ought to tolerate every principle of philosophy, nor is there an instance that any government has suffered in its political interests by such indulgence. There is no enthusiasm among philosophers; their doctrines are not very alluring to the people and no restraint can be put upon their reasonings but what must be of dangerous consequence to the sciences and even to the state, by paving the way for persecution and oppression in points where the generality of mankind are more deeply interested and concerned.

But there occurs to me (I continued) with regard to your main topic a difficulty which I shall just propose to you, without insisting on it, lest it lead into reasonings of too nice and delicate a nature. In a word, I much doubt whether it is possible for a cause to be known only by its effect (as you have all along supposed) or to be of so singular and particular a nature as to have no parallel and no similarity with any other cause or object that has ever fallen under our observation. It is only when two species of objects are found to be constantly conjoined that we can infer the one from the other; and were an effect presented which was entirely singular and could not be comprehended under any known species, I do not see that we could form any conjecture or inference at all concerning its cause. If experience and observation and analogy are, indeed, the only guides which we can reasonably follow in inferences of this nature, both the effect and cause must bear a similarity and resemblance to other effects and causes which we know, and which we have found in many instances to be conjoined with each other. I leave it to your own reflection to pursue the consequences of this principle. I shall just observe that, as the antagonists of Epicurus always suppose the universe, an effect quite singular and unparalleled, to be the proof of a Deity, a cause no less singular and unparalleled, your reasonings upon that supposition seem, at least, to merit our attention. There is, I admit, some difficulty how we can ever return from the cause to the effect and, reasoning from our ideas of the former, infer any alteration on the latter or any addition to it.

Section XII
Of the Academic or Skeptical Philosophy.
Part I.

There is not a greater number of philosophical reasonings displayed upon any subject than those which prove the existence of a Deity and refute the fallacies of atheists; and yet the most religious philosophers still dispute whether any man can be so blinded as to be a speculative atheist. How shall we reconcile these contradictions? The knights-errant who wandered about to clear the world of dragons and giants never entertained the least doubt with regard to the existence of these monsters.

The *skeptic* is another enemy of religion, who naturally provokes the indignation of all divines and graver philosophers, though it is certain that no man ever met with any such absurd creature or conversed with a man who had no opinion or principle concerning any subject, either of action or speculation. This begets a very natural question: What is meant by a skeptic? And how far it is possible to push these philosophical principles of doubt and uncertainty?

There is a species of skepticism, *antecedent* to all study and philosophy, which is much inculcated by Descartes[79] and others as a sovereign preservative against error and precipitate judgment. It recommends a universal doubt not only of all our former opinions and principles, but also of our very faculties, of whose veracity, they say, we must assure ourselves by a chain of reasoning deduced from some original principle which cannot possibly be fallacious or deceitful. But neither is there any such original principle which has a prerogative above others that are self-evident and convincing. Or if there were, could we advance a step beyond it but by the use of those very faculties of which we are supposed to be already diffident. The Cartesian doubt, therefore, were it ever possible to be attained by any human creature (as it plainly is not) would be entirely incurable and no reasoning could ever bring us to a state of assurance and conviction upon any subject.

It must, however, be confessed that this species of skepticism, when more moderate, may be understood in a very reasonable sense and is a necessary prepara-

---

79. [In the *Discourse on Method* (1637) and the *Meditations* (1641), Descartes advocated a form of provisional doubt or skepticism in which "as far as the opinions which I had been receiving since my birth were concerned, I could not do better than to reject them completely for once in my lifetime, and to resume them afterwards, or perhaps accept better ones in their place, when I had determined how they fitted into a rational scheme . . . In this I did not wish to imitate the sceptics, who doubted only for the sake of doubting and intended to remain always irresolute; on the contrary, my whole purpose was to achieve greater certainty and to reject the loose earth and sand in favor of rock and clay" (*Discourse on Method* II and III).]

tive to the study of philosophy by preserving a proper impartiality in our judgments and weaning our mind from all those prejudices which we may have imbibed from education or rash opinion. To begin with clear and self-evident principles, to advance by timorous and sure steps, to review frequently our conclusions and examine accurately all their consequences—though by these means we shall make both a slow and a short progress in our systems—are the only methods by which we can ever hope to reach truth and attain a proper stability and certainty in our determinations.

There is another species of skepticism, *consequent* to science and inquiry, when men are supposed to have discovered either the absolute fallaciousness of their mental faculties or their unfitness to reach any fixed determination in all those curious subjects of speculation about which they are commonly employed. Even our very senses are brought into dispute by a certain species of philosophers and the maxims of common life are subjected to the same doubt as the most profound principles or conclusions of metaphysics and theology. As these paradoxical tenets (if they may be called tenets) are to be met with in some philosophers, and the refutation of them in several, they naturally excite our curiosity and make us inquire into the arguments on which they may be founded.

I need not insist upon the more trite topics employed by the skeptics in all ages against the evidence of *sense* such as those which are derived from the imperfection and fallaciousness of our organs on numberless occasions: the crooked appearance of an oar in water, the various aspects of objects according to their different distances, the double images which arise from the pressing one eye, with many other appearances of a like nature. These skeptical topics, indeed, are only sufficient to prove that the senses alone are not implicitly to be depended on, but that we must correct their evidence by reason and by considerations derived from the nature of the medium, the distance of the object, and the disposition of the organ, in order to render them, within their sphere, the proper *criteria* of truth and falsehood. There are other more profound arguments against the senses which do not admit of so easy a solution.

It seems evident that men are carried by a natural instinct or prepossession to repose faith in their senses, and that without any reasoning, or even almost before the use of reason, we always suppose an external universe which does not depend on our perception, but would exist though we and every sensible creature were absent or annihilated. Even the animal creation are governed by a like opinion and preserve this belief of external objects, in all their thoughts, designs, and actions.

It seems also evident that when men follow this blind and powerful instinct of nature they always suppose the very images presented by the senses to be the external objects and never entertain any suspicion that the one are nothing but representations of the other. This very table which we see white and which we feel hard is believed to exist independent of our perception and to be something external to our mind which perceives it. Our presence does not bestow being on it. Our absence does not annihilate it. It preserves its existence uniform and entire, independent of the situation of intelligent beings who perceive or contemplate it.

But this universal and primary opinion of all men is soon destroyed by the slightest philosophy which teaches us that nothing can ever be present to the mind but an image or perception, and that the senses are only the inlets through which these images are conveyed, without being able to produce any immediate intercourse between the mind and the object. The table which we see seems to diminish as we remove further from it. But the real table which exists independent of us suffers no alteration. It was, therefore, nothing but its image which was present to the mind. These are the obvious dictates of reason and no man who reflects ever doubted that the existences which we consider when we say *this house* and *that tree* are nothing but perceptions in the mind and fleeting copies or representations of other existences which remain uniform and independent.

So far, then, are we necessitated by reasoning to contradict or depart from the primary instincts of nature and to embrace a new system with regard to the evidence of our senses. But here philosophy finds herself extremely embarrassed when she would justify this new system and obviate the cavils and objections of the skeptics. She can no longer plead the infallible and irresistible instinct of nature, for that led us to a quite different system which is acknowledged fallible and even erroneous. And to justify this pretended philosophical system by a chain of clear and convincing argument, or even any appearance of argument, exceeds the power of all human capacity.

By what argument can it be proved that the perceptions of the mind must be caused by external objects entirely different from them, though resembling them (if that is possible), and could not arise either from the energy of the mind itself, or from the suggestion of some invisible and unknown spirit, or from some other cause still more unknown to us? It is acknowledged that in fact many of these perceptions arise not from anything external, as in dreams, madness, and other diseases. And nothing can be more inexplicable than the manner in which body should so operate upon mind as ever to convey an image of itself to a substance supposed of so different and even contrary a nature.

It is a question of fact whether the perceptions of the senses are produced by external objects resembling them; how shall this question be determined? By experience surely as all other questions of a like nature. But here experience is and must be entirely silent. The mind never has anything present to it but the perceptions and cannot possibly reach any experience of their connection with objects. The supposition of such a connection is, therefore, without any foundation in reasoning.

To have recourse to the veracity of the supreme Being in order to prove the veracity of our senses is surely making a very unexpected circuit. If his veracity were at all concerned in this matter, our senses would be entirely infallible, because it is not possible that he can ever deceive. Not to mention that, if the external world is once called in question, we shall be at a loss to find arguments by which we may prove the existence of that Being or any of his attributes.

This is a topic, therefore, in which the profounder and more philosophical skeptics will always triumph when they endeavor to introduce a universal doubt into all subjects of human knowledge and inquiry. Do you follow the instincts and propensities of nature, may they say, in assenting to the veracity of sense? But these lead you to believe that the very perception or sensible image is the external object. Do you disclaim this principle in order to embrace a more rational opinion that the perceptions are only representations of something external? You here depart from your natural propensities and more obvious sentiments and yet are not able to satisfy your reason, which can never find any convincing argument from experience to prove that the perceptions are connected with any external objects.

There is another skeptical topic of a like nature, derived from the most profound philosophy, which might merit our attention were it requisite to dive so deep in order to discover arguments and reasonings which can so little serve to any serious purpose. It is universally allowed by modern inquirers that all the sensible qualities of objects, such as hard, soft, hot, cold, white, black, etc., are merely secondary and do not exist in the objects themselves, but are perceptions of the mind, without any external archetype or model which they represent. If this is allowed with regard to secondary qualities, it must also follow with regard to the supposed primary qualities of extension and solidity, nor can the latter be any more entitled to that denomination than the former. The idea of extension is entirely acquired from the senses of sight and feeling and if all the qualities perceived by the senses are in the mind, not in the object, the same conclusion must reach the idea of extension which is wholly dependent on the sensible ideas or the ideas of secondary qualities.[80] Nothing can save us from this conclusion but the asserting that the ideas of those primary qualities are attained by *abstraction*; an opinion which, if we examine it accurately, we shall find to be unintelligible and even absurd. An extension that is neither tangible nor visible cannot possibly be conceived; and a tangible or visible extension which is neither hard nor soft, black nor white, is equally beyond the reach of human conception. Let any man try to conceive a triangle in general which is neither *isosceles* nor *scalene*, nor has any particular length or proportion of sides, and he will soon perceive the

---

80. [The distinction between primary and secondary qualities was first made by Robert Boyle (1627–1691), although the basis for the distinction goes back to ancient philosophy and is implicit in the writings of Galileo (1564–1642) and Descartes. The primary qualities are commonly understood to be those qualities of our ideas which truly characterize (or are in) the object; the secondary, those qualities of our ideas which do not truly characterize (or are not in) the object, and are, thus, merely perceptions of the mind.]

absurdity of all the scholastic notions with regard to abstraction and general ideas.[81]

Thus the first philosophical objection to the evidence of sense or to the opinion of external existence consists in this, that such an opinion, if rested on natural instinct, is contrary to reason and, if referred to reason, is contrary to natural instinct and at the same time carries no rational evidence with it to convince an impartial inquirer. The second objection goes further and represents this opinion as contrary to reason, at least, if it is a principle of reason that all sensible qualities are in the mind, not in the object. Deprive matter of all its intelligible qualities, both primary and secondary, you in a manner annihilate it and leave only a certain unknown, inexplicable *something* as the cause of our perceptions—a notion so imperfect that no skeptic will think it worthwhile to contend against it.

Part II.

It may seem a very extravagant attempt of the skeptics to destroy *reason* by argument and ratiocination, yet is this the grand scope of all their inquiries and disputes. They endeavor to find objections both to our abstract reasonings and to those which regard matter of fact and existence.

The chief objection against all *abstract* reasonings is derived from the ideas of space and time—ideas which, in common life and to a careless view, are very clear and intelligible, but when they pass through the scrutiny of the profound sciences (and they are the chief object of these sciences) afford principles which seem full of absurdity and contradiction. No

priestly *dogmas* invented on purpose to tame and subdue the rebellious reason of mankind ever shocked common sense more than the doctrine of the infinite divisibility of extension, with its consequences, as they are pompously displayed by all geometers and metaphysicians with a kind of triumph and exultation. A real quantity, infinitely less than any finite quantity, containing quantities infinitely less than itself, and so on *in infinitum*; this is an edifice so bold and prodigious that it is too weighty for any pretended demonstration to support because it shocks the clearest and most natural principles of human reason.[82] But what renders the matter more extraordinary is that these seemingly absurd opinions are supported by a chain of reasoning, the clearest and most natural, nor is it possible for us to allow the premises without admitting the consequences. Nothing can be more convincing and satisfactory than all the conclusions concerning the properties of circles and triangles, and yet, when these are once received, how can we deny that the angle of contact between a circle and its tangent is infinitely less than any rectilinear angle— that as you may increase the diameter of the circle *in infinitum*, this angle of contact becomes still less, even *in infinitum*, and that the angle of contact between other curves and their tangents may be infinitely less than those between any circle and its tangent, and so on, *in infinitum*? The demonstration of these principles seems as unexceptionable as that which proves the three angles of a triangle to be equal to two right ones, though the latter opinion is natural and easy and the former big with contradiction and absurdity. Reason here seems to be thrown into a kind of amazement and suspense which, without the suggestions of any skeptic, gives her a diffidence of herself and of the ground on which she treads. She

---

81. This argument is drawn from Dr. Berkeley [*A Treatise Concerning the Principles of Human Knowledge*, Introduction]; and indeed most of the writings of that very ingenious author form the best lessons of scepticism, which are to be found either among the ancient or modern philosophers, Bayle not excepted. He professes, however, in his title-page (and undoubtedly with great truth) to have composed his book against the sceptics as well as against the atheists and free-thinkers. But that all his arguments, though otherwise intended, are, in reality, merely sceptical, appears from this, *that they admit of no answer and produce no conviction.* Their only effect is to cause that momentary amazement and irresolution and confusion, which is the result of scepticism.

82. Whatever disputes there may be about mathematical points, we must allow that there are physical points; that is, parts of extension, which cannot be divided or lessened, either by the eye or imagination. These images, then, which are present to the fancy or senses, are absolutely indivisible, and consequently must be allowed by mathematicians to be infinitely less than any real part of extension; and yet nothing appears more certain to reason, than that an infinite number of them composes an infinite extension. How much more an infinite number of those infinitely small parts of extension, which are still supposed infinitely divisible?

sees a full light which illuminates certain places, but that light borders upon the most profound darkness. And between these she is so dazzled and confounded that she scarcely can pronounce with certainty and assurance concerning any one object.

The absurdity of these bold determinations of the abstract sciences seems to become, if possible, still more palpable with regard to time than extension. An infinite number of real parts of time, passing in succession and exhausted one after another, appears so evident a contradiction that no man, one should think, whose judgment is not corrupted, instead of being improved by the sciences, would ever be able to admit of it.

Yet still reason must remain restless and unquiet, even with regard to that skepticism to which she is driven by these seeming absurdities and contradictions. How any clear, distinct idea can contain circumstances contradictory to itself, or to any other clear, distinct idea, is absolutely incomprehensible and is, perhaps, as absurd as any proposition which can be formed — so that nothing can be more skeptical or more full of doubt and hesitation than this skepticism itself which arises from some of the paradoxical conclusions of geometry or the science of quantity.[83]

83. It seems to me not impossible to avoid these absurdities and contradictions, if it be admitted, that there is no such thing as abstract or general ideas, properly speaking; but that all general ideas are, in reality, particular ones, attached to a general term, which recalls, upon occasion, other particular ones, that resemble, in certain circumstances, the idea, present to the mind. Thus when the term Horse, is pronounced, we immediately figure to ourselves the idea of a black or a white animal, of a particular size or figure: But as that term is also usually applied to animals of other colours, figures and sizes, these ideas, though not actually present to the imagination, are easily recalled; and our reasoning and conclusion proceed in the same way, as if they were actually present. If this be admitted (as seems reasonable) it follows that all the ideas of quantity, upon which mathematicians reason, are nothing but particular, and such as are suggested by the senses and imagination, and consequently, cannot be infinitely divisible. It is sufficient to have dropped this hint at present, without prosecuting it any farther. It certainly concerns all lovers of science not to expose themselves to the ridicule and contempt of the ignorant by their conclusions; and this seems the readiest solution of these difficulties.

The skeptical objections to *moral* evidence or to the reasonings concerning matter of fact are either *popular* or *philosophical*. The popular objections are derived from the natural weakness of human understanding: the contradictory opinions which have been entertained in different ages and nations; the variations of our judgment in sickness and health, youth and old age, prosperity and adversity; the perpetual contradiction of each particular man's opinions and sentiments with many other topics of that kind. It is needless to insist further on this head. These objections are but weak. For, as in common life, we reason every moment concerning fact and existence and cannot possibly subsist without continually employing this species of argument, any popular objections derived from this must be insufficient to destroy that evidence. The great subverter of *Pyrrhonism*,[84] or the excessive principles of skepticism, is action, and employment, and the occupations of common life. These principles may flourish and triumph in the schools, where it is indeed difficult, if not impossible, to refute them. But as soon as they leave the shade and by the presence of the real objects which actuate our passions and sentiments are put in opposition to the more powerful principles of our nature, they vanish like smoke and leave the most determined skeptic in the same condition as other mortals.

The skeptic, therefore, had better keep within his proper sphere and display those *philosophical* objec-

84. [A form of extreme skepticism named after its first exponent, Pyrrho of Elis (c. 360–c. 270 B.C.). Unlike the Academic skeptics (see footnote 23), who are represented as having claimed that some things are more credible than others, even if nothing is certain, the Pyrrhonians are typically represented as being skeptical of that and all other doctrines, as recommending suspension of judgment on all things, and in lieu of knowledge, that one live according to nature, custom, or the laws of his country. Michel de Montaigne (1533–1592) presents a graphic view of the Pyrrhonians in his *Apology for Raimond Sebond* (1576): "They do their work with everything. If they win, your proposition is lame; if you win, theirs is. If they lose, they confirm ignorance; if you lose, you confirm it . . . They use their reason to inquire and debate, but not to conclude and choose. Whoever will imagine a perpetual confession of ignorance, a judgment without leaning or inclination, on any occasion whatever, he has a conception of Pyrrhonism."]

tions which arise from more profound researches. Here he seems to have ample matter of triumph, while he justly insists that all our evidence for any matter of fact which lies beyond the testimony of sense or memory is derived entirely from the relation of cause and effect; that we have no other idea of this relation than that of two objects which have been frequently *conjoined* together; that we have no argument to convince us that objects which have, in our experience, been frequently conjoined, will likewise, in other instances, be conjoined in the same manner; and that nothing leads us to this inference but custom or a certain instinct of our nature which it is indeed difficult to resist, but which, like other instincts, may be fallacious and deceitful. While the skeptic insists upon these topics, he shows his force, or rather, indeed, his own and our weakness, and seems, for the time at least, to destroy all assurance and conviction. These arguments might be displayed at greater length, if any durable good or benefit to society could ever be expected to result from them.

For here is the chief and most confounding objection to *excessive* skepticism, that no durable good can ever result from it while it remains in its full force and vigor. We need only ask such a skeptic *What his meaning is? And what he proposes by all these curious researches?* He is immediately at a loss and does not know what to answer. A Copernican or Ptolemaist who each supports his different system of astronomy may hope to produce a conviction which will remain constant and durable with his audience. A Stoic or Epicurean displays principles which may not only be durable, but which have an effect on conduct and behavior. But a Pyrrhonian cannot expect that his philosophy will have any constant influence on the mind or, if it had, that its influence would be beneficial to society. On the contrary, he must acknowledge, if he will acknowledge anything, that all human life must perish, were his principles universally and steadily to prevail. All discourse, all action would immediately cease and men would remain in a total lethargy until the necessities of nature, unsatisfied, put an end to their miserable existence. It is true—so fatal an event is very little to be dreaded. Nature is always too strong for principle. And though a Pyrrhonian may throw himself or others into a momentary amazement and confusion by his profound reasonings, the first

and most trivial event in life will put to flight all his doubts and scruples and leave him the same, in every point of action and speculation, with the philosophers of every other sect or with those who never concerned themselves in any philosophical researches. When he awakes from his dream, he will be the first to join in the laugh against himself and to confess that all his objections are mere amusement and can have no other tendency than to show the whimsical condition of mankind, who must act and reason and believe, though they are not able, by their most diligent inquiry, to satisfy themselves concerning the foundation of these operations or to remove the objections which may be raised against them.

Part III.

There is, indeed, a more *mitigated* skepticism or *academic* philosophy which may be both durable and useful and which may, in part, be the result of this Pyrrhonism or *excessive* skepticism when its undistinguished doubts are in some measure corrected by common sense and reflection. The greater part of mankind are naturally apt to be affirmative and dogmatic in their opinions and while they see objects only on one side and have no idea of any counterpoising argument, they throw themselves precipitately into the principles to which they are inclined, nor have they any indulgence for those who entertain opposite sentiments. To hesitate or balance perplexes their understanding, checks their passion, and suspends their action. They are, therefore, impatient until they escape from a state which to them is so uneasy and they think that they can never remove themselves far enough from it by the violence of their affirmations and obstinacy of their belief. But could such dogmatic reasoners become sensible of the strange infirmities of human understanding, even in its most perfect state and when most accurate and cautious in its determinations, such a reflection would naturally inspire them with more modesty and reserve, and diminish their fond opinion of themselves and their prejudice against antagonists. The illiterate may reflect on the disposition of the learned who, amid all the advantages of study and reflection, are commonly still diffident in their determinations. And if any of the learned are inclined, from their natural temper, to haughtiness and obstinacy, a small tincture of Pyrrhonism might abate their pride by showing them that the few advantages which they may have attained over their fellows are but inconsiderable, if compared with the universal perplexity and confusion which is inherent in human nature. In general, there is a degree of doubt and caution and modesty which, in all kinds of scrutiny and decision, ought forever accompany a just reasoner.

Another species of *mitigated* skepticism which may be of advantage to mankind and which may be the natural result of the Pyrrhonian doubts and scruples is the limitation of our inquiries to such subjects as are best adapted to the narrow capacity of human understanding. The *imagination* of man is naturally sublime, delighted with whatever is remote and extraordinary, and running without control into the most distant parts of space and time in order to avoid the objects which custom has rendered too familiar to it. A correct *judgment* observes a contrary method and, avoiding all distant and high inquiries, confines itself to common life and to such subjects as fall under daily practice and experience, leaving the more sublime topics to the embellishment of poets and orators or to the arts of priests and politicians. To bring us to so salutary a determination, nothing can be more serviceable than to be once thoroughly convinced of the force of the Pyrrhonian doubt and of the impossibility that anything but the strong power of natural instinct could free us from it. Those who have a propensity to philosophy will still continue their researches, because they reflect that, besides the immediate pleasure attending such an occupation, philosophical decisions are nothing but the reflections of common life, methodized and corrected. But they will never be tempted to go beyond common life so long as they consider the imperfection of those faculties which they employ, their narrow reach, and their inaccurate operations. While we cannot give a satisfactory reason why we believe, after a thousand experiments, that a stone will fall or fire burn, can we ever satisfy ourselves concerning any determination which we may form with regard to the origin of worlds and the situation of nature from and to eternity?

This narrow limitation, indeed, of our inquiries is in every respect so reasonable that it suffices to make the slightest examination into the natural powers of the hu-

man mind and to compare them with their objects, in order to recommend it to us. We shall then find what are the proper subjects of science and inquiry.

It seems to me that the only objects of the abstract sciences or of demonstration are quantity and number and that all attempts to extend this more perfect species of knowledge beyond these bounds are mere sophistry and illusion. As the component parts of quantity and number are entirely similar, their relations become intricate and involved and nothing can be more curious, as well as useful, than to trace, by a variety of mediums, their equality or inequality through their different appearances. But as all other ideas are clearly distinct and different from each other, we can never advance further, by our utmost scrutiny, than to observe this diversity and, by an obvious reflection, pronounce one thing not to be another. Or if there is any difficulty in these decisions, it proceeds entirely from the indeterminate meaning of words, which is corrected by more just definitions. That *the square of the hypotenuse is equal to the squares of the other two sides* cannot be known, let the terms be ever so exactly defined, without a train of reasoning and inquiry. But to convince us of this proposition, *that where there is no property there can be no injustice*, it is only necessary to define the terms and explain injustice to be a violation of property. This proposition is, indeed, nothing but a more imperfect definition. It is the same case with all those pretended syllogistic reasonings which may be found in every other branch of learning except the sciences of quantity and number; and these may safely, I think, be pronounced the only proper objects of knowledge and demonstration.

All other inquiries of men regard only matter of fact and existence and these are evidently incapable of demonstration. Whatever *is* may *not be*. No negation of a fact can involve a contradiction. The nonexistence of any being, without exception, is as clear and distinct an idea as its existence.[85] The proposition which affirms it not to be, however false, is no less conceivable and intelligible than that which affirms it to be. The case is different with the sciences, properly so called. Every proposition which is not true is

85. [Cf. *Treatise* I.2.6: "The idea of existence, then, is the very same with the idea of what we conceive to be existent.

there confused and unintelligible. That the cube root of 64 is equal to the half of 10 is a false proposition and can never be distinctly conceived. But that Caesar, or the angel Gabriel, or any being never existed may be a false proposition, but still is perfectly conceivable, and implies no contradiction.

The existence, therefore, of any being can only be proved by arguments from its cause or its effect and these arguments are founded entirely on experience. If we reason *a priori*, anything may appear able to produce anything. The falling of a pebble may, for all we know, extinguish the sun or the wish of a man control the planets in their orbits. It is only experience which teaches us the nature and bounds of cause and effect and enables us to infer the existence of one object from that of another.[86] Such is the foundation

---

To reflect on any thing simply, and to reflect on it as existent, are nothing different from each other. That idea, when conjoined with the idea of any object, makes no addition to it. Whatever we conceive, we conceive to be existent. Any idea we please to form is the idea of a being; and the idea of a being is any idea we please to form."—and Descartes, *Meditations* V: "It is certain that I . . . find the idea of God in my consciousness . . . and I know with not less clearness and distinctness that an actual and eternal existence pertains to his nature, than that all which is demonstrable of any figure or number really belongs to the nature of that figure or number."]

86. That impious maxim of the ancient philosophy, *Ex nihilo, nihil fit* [From nothing, nothing comes], by which the creation of matter was excluded, ceases to be a maxim, according to this philosophy. Not only the will of the supreme Being may create matter; but, for aught we know *a priori*, the will of any other being might create it, or any other cause, that the most whimsical imagination can assign.

of moral reasoning, which forms the greater part of human knowledge and is the source of all human action and behavior.

Moral reasonings are either concerning particular or general facts. All deliberations in life regard the former, as also all disquisitions in history, chronology, geography, and astronomy.

The sciences which treat of general facts are politics, natural philosophy, physics, chemistry, etc., where the qualities, causes, and effects of a whole species of objects are inquired into.

Divinity or theology, as it proves the existence of a Deity and the immortality of souls, is composed partly of reasonings concerning particular, partly concerning general facts. It has a foundation in *reason* so far as it is supported by experience. But its best and most solid foundation is *faith* and divine revelation.

Morals and criticism are not so properly objects of the understanding as of taste and sentiment. Beauty, whether moral or natural, is felt more properly than perceived. Or if we reason concerning it and endeavor to fix its standard, we regard a new fact, namely, the general taste of mankind or some such fact which may be the object of reasoning and inquiry.

When we run over libraries, persuaded of these principles, what havoc must we make? If we take in our hand any volume—of divinity or school metaphysics, for instance—let us ask: *Does it contain any abstract reasoning concerning quantity or number?* No. *Does it contain any experimental reasoning concerning matter of fact and existence?* No. Commit it then to the flames, for it can contain nothing but sophistry and illusion.

A Treatise of Human Nature

Of Personal Identity

There are some philosophers who imagine we are every moment intimately conscious of what we call our self, that we feel its existence and its continuance in existence, and are certain beyond the evidence of a demonstration both of its perfect identity and simplicity. The strongest sensation, the most violent passion, they say, instead of distracting us from this view, only fix it the more intensely and make us consider their influence on *self* either by their pain or pleasure. To attempt a further proof of this would be to weaken its evidence, since no proof can be derived from any fact of which we are so intimately conscious, nor is there anything of which we can be certain if we doubt of this.

Unluckily all these positive assertions are contrary to that very experience which is pleaded for them, nor have we any idea of *self* after the manner it is here explained. For from what impression could this idea be derived? This question it is impossible to answer without a manifest contradiction and absurdity, and yet it is a question which must necessarily be answered, if we would have the idea of self pass for clear and intelligible. It must be some one impression that gives rise to every real idea. But self or person is not any one impression, but that to which our several impressions and ideas are supposed to have a reference. If any impression gives rise to the idea of self, that impression must continue invariably the same through the whole course of our lives, since self is supposed to exist after that manner. But there is no impression constant and invariable. Pain and pleasure, grief and joy, passions and sensations succeed each other and never all exist at the same time. It cannot, therefore, be from any of these impressions or from any other that the idea of self is derived, and, consequently, there is no such idea.

From *The Philosophical Works of David Hume*, T. H. Green and T. H. Grose, eds. (London: Longman's, Green, and Co., 1898), 4 vols., English, modified.

But further, what must become of all our particular perceptions upon this hypothesis? All these are different, and distinguishable, and separable from each other, and may be separately considered, and may exist separately, and have no need of anything to support their existence. After what manner therefore do they belong to self and how are they connected with it? For my part, when I enter most intimately into what I call *myself*, I always stumble on some particular perception or other, of heat or cold, light or shade, love or hatred, pain or pleasure. I never can catch *myself* at any time without a perception and never can observe anything but the perception. When my perceptions are removed for any time, as by sound sleep, so long am I insensible of myself and may truly be said not to exist. And were all my perceptions removed by death and could I neither think, nor feel, nor see, nor love, nor hate after the dissolution of my body, I should be entirely annihilated, nor do I conceive what is further requisite to make me a perfect nonentity. If anyone, upon serious and unprejudiced reflection, thinks he has a different notion of *himself*, I must confess I can reason no longer with him. All I can allow him is that he may be in the right as well as I and that we are essentially different in this particular. He may, perhaps, perceive something simple and continued which he calls *himself*, though I am certain there is no such principle in me.

But setting aside some metaphysicians of this kind, I may venture to affirm of the rest of mankind that they are nothing but a bundle or collection of different perceptions which succeed each other with an inconceivable rapidity and are in a perpetual flux and movement. Our eyes cannot turn in their sockets without varying our perceptions. Our thought is still more variable than our sight and all our other senses and faculties contribute to this change; nor is there any single power of the soul which remains unalterably the same perhaps for one moment. The mind is a kind of theater where several perceptions successively make their appearance, pass, repass, glide away, and mingle in an infinite variety of postures and situations.

There is properly no *simplicity* in it at one time nor *identity* in different, whatever natural propensity we may have to imagine that simplicity and identity. The comparison of the theater must not mislead us. They are the successive perceptions only that constitute the mind, nor have we the most distant notion of the place where these scenes are represented or of the materials of which it is composed.

What, then, gives us so great a propensity to ascribe an identity to these successive perceptions and to suppose ourselves possessed of an invariable and uninterrupted existence through the whole course of our lives? In order to answer this question we must distinguish between personal identity as it regards our thought or imagination and as it regards our passions or the concern we take in ourselves. The first is our present subject and to explain it perfectly we must take the matter pretty deep and account for that identity which we attribute to plants and animals, there being a great analogy between it and the identity of a self or person.

We have a distinct idea of an object that remains invariable and uninterrupted through a supposed variation of time and this idea we call that of *identity* or *sameness*. We have also a distinct idea of several different objects existing in succession and connected together by a close relation, and this, to an accurate view, affords as perfect a notion of *diversity* as if there was no manner of relation among the objects. But though these two ideas of identity and a succession of related objects be in themselves perfectly distinct and even contrary, yet it is certain that, in our common way of thinking, they are generally confounded with each other. That action of the imagination by which we consider the uninterrupted and invariable object and that by which we reflect on the succession of related objects are almost the same to the feeling, nor is there much more effort of thought required in the latter case than in the former. The relation facilitates the transition of the mind from one object to another and renders its passage as smooth as if it contemplated one continued object. This resemblance is the cause of the confusion and mistake and makes us substitute the notion of identity instead of that of related objects. However at one instant we may consider the related succession as variable or interrupted, we are sure the next to ascribe to it a perfect identity and regard it as invariable and uninter-

rupted. Our propensity to this mistake is so great from the resemblance above mentioned that we fall into it before we are aware, and though we incessantly correct ourselves by reflection and return to a more accurate method of thinking, yet we cannot long sustain our philosophy or take off this bias from the imagination. Our last resource is to yield to it and boldly assert that these different related objects are in effect the same, however interrupted and variable. In order to justify to ourselves this absurdity, we often feign some new and unintelligible principle that connects the objects together and prevents their interruption or variation. Thus we feign the continued existence of the perceptions of our senses to remove the interruption and run into the notion of a *soul*, and *self*, and *substance* to disguise the variation. But, we may further observe that where we do not give rise to such a fiction, our propensity to confound identity with relation is so great that we are apt to imagine something unknown and mysterious, connecting the parts, besides their relation, and this I take to be the case with regard to the identity we ascribe to plants and vegetables. And even when this does not take place, we still feel a propensity to confound these ideas, though we are not able fully to satisfy ourselves in that particular nor find anything invariable and uninterrupted to justify our notion of identity.

Thus the controversy concerning identity is not merely a dispute of words. For when we attribute identity, in an improper sense, to variable or interrupted objects, our mistake is not confined to the expression, but is commonly attended with a fiction, either of something invariable and uninterrupted, or of something mysterious and inexplicable, or at least with a propensity to such fictions. What will suffice to prove this hypothesis to the satisfaction of every fair inquirer is to show from daily experience and observation that the objects which are variable or interrupted, and yet are supposed to continue the same, are such only as consist of a succession of parts, connected together by resemblance, contiguity, or causation. For as such a succession answers evidently to our notion of diversity, it can only be by mistake we ascribe to it an identity, and as the relation of parts, which leads us into this mistake, is really nothing but a quality which produces an association of ideas and an easy transition of the imagination from one to another, it can only be from the resemblance which this act of the mind bears to that by which we contemplate one continued object that the error arises. Our chief business, then, must be to prove that all objects to which we ascribe identity without observing their invariableness and uninterruptedness are such as consist of a succession of related objects.

In order to [see] this, suppose any mass of matter of which the parts are contiguous and connected to be placed before us. It is plain we must attribute a perfect identity to this mass, provided all the parts continue uninterruptedly and invariably the same, whatever motion or change of place we may observe either in the whole or in any of the parts. But supposing some very *small* or *inconsiderable* part to be added to the mass or subtracted from it, though this absolutely destroys the identity of the whole, strictly speaking, yet as we seldom think so accurately, we scruple not to pronounce a mass of matter the same where we find so trivial an alteration. The passage of the thought from the object before the change to the object after it is so smooth and easy that we scarce perceive the transition and are apt to imagine that it is nothing but a continued survey of the same object.

There is a very remarkable circumstance that attends this experiment, which is that though the change of any considerable part in a mass of matter destroys the identity of the whole, yet we must measure the greatness of the part, not absolutely, but by its *proportion* to the whole. The addition or diminution of a mountain would not be sufficient to produce a diversity in a planet, though the change of a very few inches would be able to destroy the identity of some bodies. It will be impossible to account for this but by reflecting that objects operate upon the mind and break or interrupt the continuity of its actions not according to their real greatness, but according to their proportion to each other, and therefore, since this interruption makes an object cease to appear the same, it must be the uninterrupted progress of the thought which constitutes the imperfect identity.

This may be confirmed by another phenomenon. A change in any considerable part of a body destroys its identity, but it is remarkable that where the change is produced *gradually* and *insensibly* we are less apt to ascribe to it the same effect. The reason can plainly be no other than that the mind, in following the successive changes of the body, feels an easy passage from surveying its condition in one moment to view-

ing of it in another and at no particular time perceives any interruption in its actions—from which continued perception it ascribes a continued existence and identity to the object.

But whatever precaution we may use in introducing the changes gradually and making them proportional to the whole, it is certain that where the changes are at last observed to become considerable, we make a scruple of ascribing identity to such different objects. There is, however, another artifice by which we may induce the imagination to advance a step further, and that is by producing a reference of the parts to each other and a combination to some *common end* or purpose. A ship of which a considerable part has been changed by frequent repairs is still considered as the same, nor does the difference of the materials hinder us from ascribing an identity to it. The common end, in which the parts conspire, is the same under all their variations and affords an easy transition of the imagination from one situation of the body to another.

But this is still more remarkable when we add a *sympathy* of parts to their *common end* and suppose that they bear to each other the reciprocal relation of cause and effect in all their actions and operations. This is the case with all animals and vegetables, where not only the several parts have a reference to some general purpose, but also a mutual dependence on and connection with each other. The effect of so strong a relation is that though everyone must allow that in a very few years both vegetables and animals endure a *total* change, yet we still attribute identity to them, while their form, size, and substance are entirely altered. An oak that grows from a small plant to a large tree is still the same oak, though there is not one particle of matter or figure of its parts the same. An infant becomes a man and is sometimes fat, sometimes lean without any change in his identity.

We may also consider the two following phenomena, which are remarkable in their kind. The first is that though we are commonly able to distinguish pretty exactly between numerical and specific identity, yet it sometimes happens that we confound them and in our thinking and reasoning employ the one for the other. Thus, a man who hears a noise that is frequently interrupted and renewed says it is still the same noise, though it is evident the sounds have only a specific identity or resemblance and there is nothing numerically the same but the cause which produced them. In like manner it may be said without breach of the propriety of language that such a church, which was formerly of brick, fell to ruin and that the parish rebuilt the same church of freestone and according to modern architecture. Here neither the form nor materials are the same, nor is there anything common to the two objects but their relation to the inhabitants of the parish. Yet this alone is sufficient to make us denominate them the same. But we must observe that in these cases the first object is in a manner annihilated before the second comes into existence, by which means we are never presented in any one point of time with the idea of difference and multiplicity and, for that reason, are less scrupulous in calling them the same.

Secondly, we may remark that though in a succession of related objects it is in a manner requisite that the change of parts are not sudden nor entire in order to preserve the identity, yet where the objects are in their nature changeable and inconstant, we admit of a more sudden transition than would otherwise be consistent with that relation. Thus, as the nature of a river consists in the motion and change of parts, though in less than twenty-four hours these are totally altered, this does not hinder the river from continuing the same during several ages. What is natural and essential to anything is, in a manner, expected, and what is expected makes less impression and appears of less moment than what is unusual and extraordinary. A considerable change of the former kind seems really less to the imagination than the most trivial alteration of the latter and, by breaking less the continuity of the thought, has less influence in destroying the identity.

We now proceed to explain the nature of *personal identity*, which has become so great a question in philosophy, especially of late years, in *England*, where all the more abstruse sciences are studied with a peculiar ardor and application. And here it is evident the same method of reasoning must be continued which has so successfully explained the identity of plants and animals, and ships and houses, and of all the compounded and changeable productions either of art or nature. The identity which we ascribe to the mind of man is only a fictitious one and of a like kind with that which we ascribe to vegetables and animal bodies. It cannot, therefore, have a different origin, but must proceed from a like operation of the imagination upon like objects.

But lest this argument should not convince the reader, though in my opinion perfectly decisive, let him weigh the following reasoning, which is still closer and more immediate. It is evident that the identity which we attribute to the human mind, however perfect we may imagine it to be, is not able to run the several different perceptions into one and make them lose their characters of distinction and difference which are essential to them. It is still true that every distinct perception which enters into the composition of the mind is a distinct existence, and is different, and distinguishable, and separable from every other perception, either contemporary or successive. But as, notwithstanding this distinction and separability, we suppose the whole train of perceptions to be united by identity, a question naturally arises concerning this relation of identity, whether it is something that really binds our several perceptions together or only associates their ideas in the imagination, that is, in other words, whether, in pronouncing concerning the identity of a person, we observe some real bond among his perceptions or only feel one among the ideas we form of them. This question we might easily decide if we would recollect what has been already proved at large, namely, that the understanding never observes any real connection among objects and that even the union of cause and effect, when strictly examined, resolves itself into a customary association of ideas. For from this it evidently follows that identity is nothing really belonging to these different perceptions and uniting them together but rather is merely a quality which we attribute to them because of the union of their ideas in the imagination when we reflect upon them. Now, the only qualities which can give ideas a union in the imagination are these three relations above mentioned. These are the uniting principles in the ideal world, and without them every distinct object is separable by the mind, and may be separately considered, and appears not to have any more connection with any other object than if disjoined by the greatest difference and remoteness. It is, therefore, on some of these three relations of resemblance, contiguity, and causation that identity depends, and as the very essence of these relations consists in their producing an easy transition of ideas, it follows that our notions of personal identity proceed entirely from the smooth and uninterrupted progress of the thought along a train of connected ideas, according to the principles above explained.

The only question, therefore, which remains is by what relations this uninterrupted progress of our thought is produced when we consider the successive existence of a mind or thinking person. And here it is evident we must confine ourselves to resemblance and causation and must drop contiguity, which has little or no influence in the present case.

To begin with *resemblance*: Suppose we could see clearly into the breast of another and observe that succession of perceptions which constitutes his mind or thinking principle, and suppose that he always preserves the memory of a considerable part of past perceptions, it is evident that nothing could more contribute to bestowing a relation on this succession amid all its variations. For what is the memory but a faculty by which we raise up the images of past perceptions? And as an image necessarily resembles its object, must not the frequent placing of these resembling perceptions in the chain of thought convey the imagination more easily from one link to another and make the whole seem like the continuance of one object? In this particular, then, the memory not only discovers the identity, but also contributes to its production by producing the relation of resemblance among the perceptions. The case is the same whether we consider ourselves or others.

As to *causation*, we may observe that the true idea of the human mind is to consider it as a system of different perceptions or different existences which are linked together by the relation of cause and effect, and mutually produce, destroy, influence, and modify each other. Our impressions give rise to their correspondent ideas, and these ideas, in their turn, produce other impressions. One thought chases another and draws after it a third by which it is expelled in its turn. In this respect, I cannot compare the soul more properly to anything than to a republic or commonwealth in which the several members are united by the reciprocal ties of government and subordination and give rise to other persons who propagate the same republic in the incessant changes of its parts. And as the same individual republic may not only change its members, but also its laws and constitutions, in like manner the same person may vary his character and disposition as well as his impressions and ideas without losing his identity. Whatever changes he en-

dures, his several parts are still connected by the relation of causation. And in this view our identity with regard to the passions serves to corroborate that with regard to the imagination by making our distant perceptions influence each other and by giving us a present concern for our past or future pains or pleasures.

As memory alone acquaints us with the continuance and extent of this succession of perceptions, it is to be considered upon that account chiefly as the source of personal identity. Had we no memory, we never should have any notion of causation nor consequently of that chain of causes and effects which constitute our self or person. But having once acquired this notion of causation from the memory, we can extend the same chain of causes and consequently the identity of our persons beyond our memory and can comprehend times, circumstances, and actions which we have entirely forgotten, but suppose in general to have existed. For how few of our past actions are there of which we have any memory? Who can tell me, for instance, what were his thoughts and actions on the 1st of January 1715, the 11th of March 1719, and the 3rd of August 1733? Or will he affirm, because he has entirely forgotten the incidents of these days, that the present self is not the same person with the self of that time, and by that means overturn all the most established notions of personal identity? In this view, therefore, memory does not so much *produce* as *discover* personal identity by showing us the relation of cause and effect among our different perceptions. It will be incumbent on those who affirm that memory produces entirely our personal identity to give a reason why we can thus extend our identity beyond our memory.

The whole of this doctrine leads us to a conclusion which is of great importance in the present affair, namely that all the nice and subtle questions concerning personal identity can never possibly be decided and are to be regarded rather as grammatical than as philosophical difficulties. Identity depends on the relations of ideas, and these relations produce identity by means of that easy transition they occasion. But as the relations and the easiness of the transition may diminish by insensible degrees, we have no just standard by which we can decide any dispute concerning the time when they acquire or lose a title to the name of identity. All the disputes concerning the identity of connected objects are merely verbal, except so far as the relation of parts gives rise to some fiction or imaginary principle of union as we have already observed.

What I have said concerning the first origin and uncertainty of our notion of identity, as applied to the human mind, may be extended with little or no variation to that of *simplicity*. An object whose different coexistent parts are bound together by a close relation operates upon the imagination after much the same manner as one perfectly simple and indivisible and does not require a much greater stretch of thought in order to [form] its conception. From this similarity of operation we attribute a simplicity to it and feign a principle of union as the support of this simplicity and the center of all the different parts and qualities of the object.

Thus we have finished our examination of the several systems of philosophy, both of the intellectual and moral world; and, in our miscellaneous way of reasoning, have been led into several topics, which will either illustrate and confirm some preceding part of this discourse, or prepare the way for our following opinions. It is now time to return to a more close examination of our subject, and to proceed in the accurate anatomy of human nature, having fully explained the nature of our judgment and understanding.

Dialogues Concerning Natural Religion

Pamphilus to Hermippus

It has been remarked, my Hermippus, that, though the ancient philosophers conveyed most of their instruction in the form of dialogue, this method of composition has been little practiced in later ages, and has seldom succeeded in the hands of those who have attempted it. Accurate and regular argument, indeed, such as is now expected of philosophical inquirers, naturally throws a man into the methodical and didactic manner; where he can immediately, without preparation, explain the point at which he aims; and thence proceed, without interruption, to deduce the proofs on which it is established. To deliver a *system* in conversation scarcely appears natural; and while the dialogue writer desires, by departing from the direct style of composition, to give a freer air to his performance, and avoid the appearance of *author* and *reader*, he is apt to run into a worse inconvenience and convey the image of *pedagogue* and *pupil*. Or if he carries on the dispute in the natural spirit of good company, by throwing in a variety of topics and preserving a proper balance among the speakers, he often loses so much time in preparations and transitions that the reader will scarcely think himself compensated, by all the graces of dialogue, for the order, brevity, and precision, which are sacrificed to them.

There are some subjects, however, to which dialogue-writing is peculiarly adapted, and where it is still preferable to the direct and simple method of composition.

Any point of doctrine which is so *obvious* that it scarcely admits of dispute, but at the same time so *important* that it cannot be too often inculcated, seems to require some such method of handling it; where the novelty of the manner may compensate the triteness of the subject, where the vivacity of conversation may enforce the precept, and where the variety of lights, presented by various personages and characters, may appear neither tedious nor redundant.

Any question of philosophy, on the other hand, which is so *obscure* and *uncertain* that human reason can reach no fixed determination with regard to it— if it should be treated at all—seems to lead us naturally into the style of dialogue and conversation. Reasonable men may be allowed to differ where no one can reasonably be positive: Opposite sentiments, even without any decision, afford an agreeable amusement; and if the subject be curious and interesting, the book carries us, in a manner, into company, and unites the two greatest and purest pleasures of human life— study and society.

Happily, these circumstances are all to be found in the subject of *natural religion*. What truth so obvious, so certain, as the *being* of a God, which the most ignorant ages have acknowledged, for which the most refined geniuses have ambitiously striven to produce new proofs and arguments? What truth so important as this, which is the ground of all our hopes, the surest foundation of morality, the firmest support of society, and the only principle which ought never to be a moment absent from our thoughts and meditations? But, in treating of this obvious and important truth, what obscure questions occur concerning the *nature* of that Divine Being; his attributes, his decrees, his plan of providence? These have been always subjected to the disputations of men: Concerning these, human reason has not reached any certain determination. But these are topics so interesting that we cannot restrain our restless inquiry with regard to them; though nothing but doubt, uncertainty, and contradiction have as yet been the result of our most accurate researches.

This I had lately occasion to observe, while I passed, as usual, part of the summer season with Cleanthes, and was present at those conversations of his with Philo and Demea, of which I gave you lately some imperfect account. Your curiosity, you then told me, was so excited that I must, of necessity, enter into a more exact detail of their reasonings, and display those various systems which they advanced with regard to so delicate a subject as that of natural religion. The remarkable contrast in their characters still further raised your expectations; while you opposed the accurate philosophical turn of Cleanthes to the careless scepticism of Philo, or compared either of their dispositions with the rigid inflexible orthodoxy of Demea. My youth rendered me a mere auditor of their disputes; and that curiosity, natural to the early season of life, has so deeply imprinted in my memory the whole chain and connection of their arguments, that, I hope, I shall not omit or confound any considerable part of them in the recital.

Part I

After I joined the company, whom I found sitting in Cleanthes' library, Demea paid Cleanthes some compliments on the great care which he took of my education, and on his unwearied perseverance and constancy in all his friendships. The father of Pamphilus, said he, was your intimate friend; the son is your pupil, and may indeed be regarded as your adopted son, were we to judge by the pains which you bestow in conveying to him every useful branch of literature and science. You are no more wanting, I am persuaded, in prudence than in industry. I shall, therefore, communicate to you a maxim which I have observed with regard to my own children, that I may learn how far it agrees with your practice. The method I follow in their education is founded on the saying of an ancient, *"That students of philosophy ought first to learn logics, then ethics, next physics, last of all the nature of the gods."*[1] This science of natural theology, according to him, being the most profound and abstruse of any, required the maturest judgment in its students; and none but a mind enriched with all the other sciences can safely be entrusted with it.

Are you so late, says Philo, in teaching your children the principles of religion? Is there no danger of their neglecting or rejecting altogether those opinions of which they have heard so little during the whole course of their education? It is only as a science,

1. Chrysippus *apud* Plut., *De repug. Stoicorum* [Chrysippus (c.279–c.206 B.C.), third leader of the Stoic school, is said to have been one of the greatest logicians of ancient times. Regarding Plutarch, see Hume's *Enquiry*, n.50. The work referred to is *Of the Inconsistencies of the Stoics.* — S.M.C.]

replied Demea, subjected to human reasoning and disputation, that I postpone the study of natural theology. To season their minds with early piety is my chief care; and by continual precept and instruction and I hope too, by example, I imprint deeply on their tender minds an habitual reverence for all the principles of religion. While they pass through every other science, I still remark the uncertainty of each part; the eternal disputations of men; the obscurity of all philosophy; and the strange, ridiculous conclusions which some of the greatest geniuses have derived from the principles of mere human reason. Having thus tamed their minds to a proper submission and self-diffidence, I have no longer any scruple of opening to them the greatest mysteries of religion, nor apprehend any danger from that assuming arrogance of philosophy, which may lead them to reject the most established doctrines and opinions.

Your precaution, says Philo, of seasoning your children's minds early with piety is certainly very reasonable, and no more than is requisite in this profane and irreligious age. But what I chiefly admire in your plan of education is your method of drawing advantage from the very principles of philosophy and learning which, by inspiring pride and self-sufficiency, have commonly, in all ages, been found so destructive to the principles of religion. The vulgar, indeed, we may remark, who are unacquainted with science and profound inquiry, observing the endless disputes of the learned, have commonly a thorough contempt for philosophy; and rivet themselves the faster, by that means, in the great points of theology which have been taught them. Those who enter a little into study and inquiry, finding many appearances of evidence in doctrines the newest and most extraordinary, think nothing too difficult for human reason; and, presumptuously breaking through all fences, profane the inmost sanctuaries of the temple. But Cleanthes will, I hope, agree with me that, after we have abandoned ignorance, the surest remedy, there is still one expedient left to prevent this profane liberty. Let Demea's principles be improved and cultivated: Let us become thoroughly sensible of the weakness, blindness, and narrow limits of human reason: Let us duly consider its uncertainty and endless contrarieties, even in subjects of common life and practice: Let the errors and deceits of our very senses be set before us; the insuperable difficulties which attend first principles in all systems; the contradictions which adhere to the very ideas of matter, cause and effect, extension, space, time, motion; and, in a word, quantity of all kinds, the object of the only science that can fairly pretend to any certainty or evidence. When these topics are displayed in their full light, as they are by some philosophers and almost all divines, who can retain such confidence in this frail faculty of reason as to pay any regard to its determinations in points so sublime, so abstruse, so remote from common life and experience? When the coherence of the parts of a stone, or even that composition of parts which renders it extended; when these familiar objects, I say, are so inexplicable, and contain circumstances so repugnant and contradictory; with what assurance can we decide concerning the origin of worlds or trace their history from eternity to eternity?

While Philo pronounced these words, I could observe a smile in the countenance both of Demea and Cleanthes. That of Demea seemed to imply an unreserved satisfaction in the doctrines delivered; but in Cleanthes' features I could distinguish an air of finesse, as if he perceived some raillery or artificial malice in the reasonings of Philo.

You propose then, Philo, said Cleanthes, to erect religious faith on philosophical scepticism; and you think that, if certainty or evidence be expelled from every other subject of inquiry, it will all retire to these theological doctrines, and there acquire a superior force and authority. Whether your scepticism be as absolute and sincere as you pretend, we shall learn by and by, when the company breaks up; we shall then see whether you go out at the door or the window, and whether you really doubt if your body has gravity or can be injured by its fall, according to popular opinion derived from our fallacious senses and more fallacious experience. And this consideration, Demea, may, I think, fairly serve to abate our ill-will to this humorous sect of the sceptics. If they be thoroughly in earnest, they will not long trouble the world with their doubts, cavils, and disputes; if they be only in jest, they are, perhaps, bad railers, but can never be very dangerous, either to the state, to philosophy, or to religion.

In reality, Philo, continued he, it seems certain that, though a man in a flush of humor, after intense reflection on the many contradictions and imperfections of human reason, may entirely renounce all belief and opinion, it is impossible for him to perse-

vere in this total scepticism or make it appear in his conduct for a few hours. External objects press in upon him: Passions solicit him: His philosophical melancholy dissipates; and even the utmost violence upon his own temper will not be able, during any time, to preserve the poor appearance of scepticism. And for what reason impose on himself such a violence? This is a point in which it will be impossible for him ever to satisfy himself, consistently with his sceptical principles. So that, upon the whole, nothing could be more ridiculous than the principles of the ancient Pyrrhonians;[2] if, in reality, they endeavored, as is pretended, to extend throughout the same scepticism which they had learned from the declamations of their schools, and which they ought to have confined to them.

In this view, there appears a great resemblance between the sects of the Stoics and Pyrrhonians, though perpetual antagonists; and both of them seem founded on this erroneous maxim: that what a man can perform sometimes, and in some dispositions, he can perform always and in every disposition. When the mind, by Stoical reflections, is elevated into a sublime enthusiasm of virtue and strongly smit with any *species* of honor or public good, the utmost bodily pain and sufferings will not prevail over such a high sense of duty; and it is possible, perhaps, by its means, even to smile and exult in the midst of tortures. If this sometimes may be the case in fact and reality, much more may a philosopher, in his school or even in his closet, work himself up to such an enthusiasm, and support, in imagination, the acutest pain or most calamitous event which he can possibly conceive. But how shall he support this enthusiasm itself? The bent of his mind relaxes and cannot be recalled at pleasure; avocations lead him astray; misfortunes attack him unawares; and the *philosopher* sinks, by degrees, into the *plebeian*.

I allow of your comparison between the Stoics and Sceptics, replied Philo. But you may observe, at the same time, that though the mind cannot, in Stoicism, support the highest flights of philosophy, yet, even when it sinks lower, it still retains somewhat of its former disposition; and the effects of the Stoic's reasoning will appear in his conduct in common life, and

2. [The reference is to followers of Pyrrho, regarding whom see Hume's *Enquiry*, n. 84.]

through the whole tenor of his actions. The ancient schools, particularly that of Zeno,[3] produced examples of virtue and constancy which seem astonishing to present times.

> Vain Wisdom all and false Philosophy.
> Yet with a pleasing sorcery could charm
> Pain, for a while, or anguish; and excite
> Fallacious Hope, or arm the obdurate breast
> With stubborn Patience, as with triple steel.[4]

In like manner, if a man has accustomed himself to sceptical considerations on the uncertainty and narrow limits of reason, he will not entirely forget them when he turns his reflection on other subjects; but in all his philosophical principles and reasoning, I dare not say, in his common conduct, he will be found different from those who either never formed any opinions in the case or have entertained sentiments more favorable to human reason.

To whatever length anyone may push his speculative principles of scepticism, he must act, I own, and live, and converse like other men; and for this conduct he is not obliged to give any other reason than the absolute necessity he lies under of so doing. If he ever carries his speculations farther than this necessity constrains him, and philosophizes either on natural or moral subjects, he is allured by a certain pleasure and satisfaction which he finds in employing himself after that manner. He considers, besides, that everyone, even in common life, is constrained to have more or less of this philosophy; that from our earliest infancy we make continual advances in forming more general principles of conduct and reasoning; that the larger experience we acquire, and the stronger reason we are endued with, we always render our principles the more general and comprehensive; and that what we call *philosophy* is nothing but a more regular and methodical operation of the same kind. To philosophize on such subjects is nothing essentially different from reasoning on common life, and we may only expect greater stability, if not greater truth, from our

3. [Zeno of Citium (c.334–c.262 B.C.), a Greek philosopher who had studied under the Cynics, was the founder of Stoicism. He is not to be confused with Zeno of Elea (c.490–430 B.C.), creator of the immortal paradoxes.]

4. [The quotation is from John Milton's *Paradise Lost*.]

philosophy on account of its exacter and more scrupulous method of proceeding.

But when we look beyond human affairs and the properties of the surrounding bodies—when we carry our speculations into the two eternities, before and after the present state of things; into the creation and formation of the universe; the existence and properties of spirits; the powers and operations of one universal Spirit existing without beginning and without end, omnipotent, omniscient, immutable, infinite, and incomprehensible—we must be far removed from the smallest tendency to scepticism not to be apprehensive that we have here got quite beyond the reach of our faculties. So long as we confine our speculations to trade, or morals, or politics, or criticism, we make appeals, every moment, to common sense and experience, which strengthen our philosophical conclusions and remove (at least in part) the suspicion, which we so justly entertain with regard to every reasoning, that is very subtle and refined. But in theological reasonings, we have not this advantage; while at the same time we are employed upon objects which, we must be sensible, are too large for our grasp, and of all others, require most to be familiarized to our apprehension. We are like foreigners in a strange country to whom everything must seem suspicious, and who are in danger every moment of transgressing against the laws and customs of the people with whom they live and converse. We know not how far we ought to trust our vulgar methods of reasoning in such a subject, since, even in common life, and in that province which is peculiarly appropriated to them, we cannot account for them and are entirely guided by a kind of instinct or necessity in employing them.

All sceptics pretend that, if reason be considered in an abstract view, it furnishes invincible arguments against itself, and that we could never retain any conviction or assurance, on any subject, were not the sceptical reasonings so refined and subtile that they are not able to counterpoise the more solid and more natural arguments derived from the senses and experience. But it is evident, whenever our arguments lose this advantage and run wide of common life, that the most refined scepticism comes to be upon a footing with them, and is able to oppose and counterbalance them. The one has no more weight than the other. The mind must remain in suspense between them;

and it is that very suspense or balance which is the triumph of scepticism.

But I observe, says Cleanthes, with regard to you, Philo, and all speculative sceptics that your doctrine and practice are as much at variance in the most abstruse points of theory as in the conduct of common life. Wherever evidence discovers itself, you adhere to it, notwithstanding your pretended scepticism; and I can observe, too, some of your sect to be as decisive as those who make greater professions of certainty and assurance. In reality, would not a man be ridiculous who pretended to reject Newton's explication of the wonderful phenomenon of the rainbow because that explication gives a minute anatomy of the rays of light—a subject, forsooth, too refined for human comprehension? And what would you say to one who, having nothing particular to object to the arguments of Copernicus and Galileo for the motion of the earth, should withhold his assent on that general principle that these subjects were too magnificent and remote to be explained by the narrow and fallacious reason of mankind?

There is indeed a kind of brutish and ignorant scepticism, as you well observed, which gives the vulgar a general prejudice against what they do not easily understand, and makes them reject every principle which requires elaborate reasoning to prove and establish it. This species of scepticism is fatal to knowledge, not to religion; since we find that those who make greatest profession of it give often their assent, not only to the great truths of theism and natural theology, but even to the most absurd tenets which a traditional superstition has recommended to them. They firmly believe in witches, though they will not believe nor attend to the most simple proposition of Euclid. But the refined and philosophical sceptics fall into an inconsistence of an opposite nature. They push their researches into the most abstruse corners of science, and their assent attends them in every step, proportioned to the evidence which they meet with. They are even obliged to acknowledge that the most abstruse and remote objects are those which are best explained by philosophy. Light is in reality anatomized; the true system of the heavenly bodies is discovered and ascertained. But the nourishment of bodies by food is still an inexplicable mystery; the cohesion of the parts of matter is still incomprehensible. These sceptics, therefore, are obliged, in every question, to consider each particular evidence apart, and proportion their assent to the precise degree of evidence which occurs. This is their practice in all natural, mathematical, moral, and political science. And why not the same, I ask, in the theological and religious? Why must conclusions of this nature be alone rejected on the general presumption of the insufficiency of human reason, without any particular discussion of the evidence? Is not such an unequal conduct a plain proof of prejudice and passion?

Our senses, you say, are fallacious; our understanding erroneous; our ideas, even of the most familiar objects—extension, duration, motion—full of absurdities and contradictions. You defy me to solve the difficulties or reconcile the repugnancies which you discover in them. I have not capacity for so great an undertaking: I have not leisure for it: I perceive it to be superfluous. Your own conduct, in every circumstance, refutes your principles, and shows the firmest reliance on all the received maxims of science, morals, prudence, and behavior.

I shall never assent to so harsh an opinion as that of a celebrated writer,[5] who says that the Sceptics are not a sect of philosophers: they are only a sect of liars. I may, however, affirm (I hope without offence) that they are a sect of jesters or railers. But for my part, whenever I find myself disposed to mirth and amusement, I shall certainly choose my entertainment of a less perplexing and abstruse nature. A comedy, a novel, or, at most, a history seems a more natural recreation than such metaphysical subtilties and abstractions.

In vain would the sceptic make a distinction between science and common life, or between one science and another. The arguments employed in all, if just, are of a similar nature and contain the same force and evidence. Or if there be any difference among them, the advantage lies entirely on the side of theology and natural religion. Many principles of mechanics are founded on very abstruse reasoning; yet no man who has any pretensions to science, even no speculative sceptic, pretends to entertain the least doubt with regard to them. The Copernican system

5. *L'art de penser.* [This work, the influential *Port-Royal Logic,* was coauthored by Pierre Nicole (1625–1695), a French theologian, and Antoine Arnauld, regarding whom see Hume's *Enquiry,* n. 66.]

contains the most surprising paradox, and the most contrary to our natural conceptions, to appearances, and to our very senses; yet even monks and inquisitors are now constrained to withdraw their opposition to it. And shall Philo, a man of so liberal a genius and extensive knowledge, entertain any general undistinguished scruples with regard to the religious hypothesis, which is founded on the simplest and most obvious arguments and, unless it meets with artificial obstacles, has such easy access and admission into the mind of man?

And here we may observe, continued he, turning himself towards Demea, a pretty curious circumstance in the history of the sciences. After the union of philosophy with the popular religion, upon the first establishment of Christianity, nothing was more usual, among all religious teachers, than declamations against reason, against the senses, against every principle derived merely from human research and inquiry. All the topics of the ancient Academics[6] were adopted by the Fathers, and thence propagated for several ages in every school and pulpit throughout Christendom. The Reformers embraced the same principles of reasoning or rather declamation; and all panegyrics on the excellence of faith were sure to be interlarded with some severe strokes of satire against natural reason. A celebrated prelate, too,[7] of the Romish communion, a man of the most extensive learning, who wrote a demonstration of Christianity, has also composed a treatise which contains all the cavils of the boldest and most determined Pyrrhonism. Locke seems to have been the first Christian who ventured openly to assert that *faith* was nothing but a species of *reason*; that religion was only a branch of philosophy; and that a chain of arguments, similar to that which established any truth in morals, politics, or physics, was always employed in discovering all the principles of theology, natural and revealed. The ill use which Bayle and other libertines made of the philosophical scepticism of the Fathers and first Reformers still further propagated the judicious sentiment of Mr. Locke. And it is now in a manner avowed, by all pretenders to reasoning and philosophy, that

atheist and sceptic are almost synonymous. And as it is certain that no man is in earnest when he professes the latter principle, I would fain hope that there are as few who seriously maintain the former.

Don't you remember, said Philo, the excellent saying of Lord Bacon[8] on this head? That a little philosophy, replied Cleanthes, makes a man an atheist; a great deal converts him to religion. That is a very judicious remark, too, said Philo. But what I have in my eye is another passage, where, having mentioned David's fool, who said in his heart there is no God, this great philosopher observes that the atheists nowadays have a double share of folly; for they are not contented to say in their hearts there is no God, but they also utter that impiety with their lips, and are thereby guilty of multiplied indiscretion and imprudence. Some people, though they were ever so much in earnest, cannot, methinks, be very formidable.

But though you should rank me in this class of fools, I cannot forbear communicating a remark that occurs to me from the history of the religious and irreligious scepticism with which you have entertained us. It appears to me that there are strong symptoms of priestcraft in the whole progress of this affair. During ignorant ages, such as those which followed the dissolution of the ancient schools, the priests perceived that atheism, deism, or heresy of any kind, could only proceed from the presumptuous questioning of received opinions, and from a belief that human reason was equal to everything. Education had then a mighty influence over the minds of men, and was almost equal in force to those suggestions of the senses and common understanding by which the most determined sceptic must allow himself to be governed. But at present, when the influence of education is much diminished and men, from a more open commerce of the world, have learned to compare the popular principles of different nations and ages, our sagacious divines have changed their whole system of philosophy and talk the language of Stoics, Platonists, and Peripatetics,[9] not that of Pyrrhonians and Academics. If we distrust human reason we have now no other principle to lead us into religion. Thus sceptics

6. [Regarding the Academy, see Hume's *Enquiry*, n. 23.]

7. Mons. Huet. [The reference is to Peter Daniel Huet (1630–1721), a renowned French scholar who was bishop of Avranches.]

8. [Regarding Francis Bacon, see Hume's *Enquiry*, n. 70.]

9. [The term "Peripatetics," derived from a Greek word meaning "walking about," is applied to the followers of Aristotle, since he is said to have taught in this manner.]

in one age, dogmatists in another—whichever system best suits the purpose of these reverend gentlemen in giving them an ascendant over mankind—they are sure to make it their favorite principle and established tenet.

It is very natural, said Cleanthes, for men to embrace those principles by which they find they can best defend their doctrines, nor need we have any recourse to priestcraft to account for so reasonable an expedient. And surely, nothing can afford a stronger presumption that any set of principles are true and ought to be embraced than to observe that they tend to the confirmation of true religion, and serve to confound the cavils of atheists, libertines, and freethinkers of all denominations.

Part II

I must own, Cleanthes, said Demea, that nothing can more surprise me than the light in which you have all along put this argument. By the whole tenor of your discourse, one would imagine that you were maintaining the Being of a God against the cavils of atheists and infidels, and were necessitated to become a champion for that fundamental principle of all religion. But this, I hope, is not by any means a question among us. No man; no man, at least of common sense, I am persuaded, ever entertained a serious doubt with regard to a truth so certain and self-evident. The question is not concerning the *being* but the *nature of God*. This I affirm, from the infirmities of human understanding, to be altogether incomprehensible and unknown to us. The essence of that supreme mind, his attributes, the manner of his existence, the very nature of his duration—these and every particular which regards so divine a being are mysterious to men. Finite, weak, and blind creatures, we ought to humble ourselves in his august presence, and, conscious of our frailties, adore in silence his infinite perfections which eye hath not seen, ear hath not heard, neither hath it entered into the heart of man to conceive. They are covered in a deep cloud from human curiosity; it is profaneness to attempt penetrating through these sacred obscurities; and, next to the impiety of denying his existence, is the temerity of prying into his nature and essence, decrees and attributes.

But lest you should think that my *piety* has here got the better of my *philosophy*, I shall support my opinion, if it needs any support, by a very great authority. I might cite all the divines, almost from the foundation of Christianity, who have ever treated of this or any other theological subject; but I shall confine myself, at present, to one equally celebrated for piety and philosophy. It is Father Malebranche who, I remember, thus expresses himself.[10] "One ought not so much (says he) to call God a spirit in order to express positively what he is, as in order to signify that he is not matter. He is a Being infinitely perfect—of this we cannot doubt. But in the same manner as we ought not to imagine, even supposing him corporeal, that he is clothed with a human body, as the anthropomorphites asserted, under color that that figure was the most perfect of any, so neither ought we to imagine that the spirit of God has human ideas or bears any resemblance to our spirit, under color that we know nothing more perfect than a human mind. We ought rather to believe that as he comprehends the perfections of matter without being material . . . he comprehends also the perfections of created spirits without being spirit, in the manner we conceive spirit: That his true name is *He that is*, or, in other words, Being without restriction, All Being, the Being infinite and universal."

After so great an authority, Demea, replied Philo, as that which you have produced, and a thousand more which you might produce, it would appear ridiculous in me to add my sentiment or express my approbation of your doctrine. But surely, where reasonable men treat these subjects, the question can never be concerning the *being* but only the *nature* of the Deity. The former truth, as you well observe, is unquestionable and self-evident. Nothing exists without a cause; and the original cause of this universe (whatever it be) we call *God*, and piously ascribe to him every species of perfection. Whoever scruples this fundamental truth deserves every punishment which can be inflicted among philosophers, to wit, the greatest ridicule, contempt, and disapprobation. But as all perfection is entirely relative, we ought never to imagine that we comprehend the attributes of this divine Being, or to suppose that his perfections have any analogy or likeness to the perfections of a

10. *Recherche de la Vérité*, liv. 3, cap. 9. [Regarding Malebranche, see Berkeley's *Three Dialogues*, n. 3. The work referred to is *The Search for Truth.*]

human creature. Wisdom, thought, design, knowledge—these we justly ascribe to him because these words are honorable among men, and we have no other language or other conceptions by which we can express our adoration of him. But let us beware lest we think that our ideas anywise correspond to his perfections, or that his attributes have any resemblance to these qualities among men. He is infinitely superior to our limited view and comprehension; and is more the object of worship in the temple than of disputation in the schools.

In reality, Cleanthes, continued he, there is no need of having recourse to that affected scepticism so displeasing to you in order to come at this determination. Our ideas reach no farther than our experience: We have no experience of divine attributes and operations. I need not conclude my syllogism: You can draw the inference yourself. And it is a pleasure to me (and I hope to you, too) that just reasoning and sound piety here concur in the same conclusion, and both of them establish the adorably mysterious and incomprehensible nature of the Supreme Being.

Not to lose any time in circumlocutions, said Cleanthes, addressing himself to Demea, much less in replying to the pious declamations of Philo, I shall briefly explain how I conceive this matter. Look round the world: Contemplate the whole and every part of it: You will find it to be nothing but one great machine, subdivided into an infinite number of lesser machines, which again admit of subdivisions to a degree beyond what human senses and faculties can trace and explain. All these various machines, and even their most minute parts, are adjusted to each other with an accuracy which ravishes into admiration all men who have ever contemplated them. The curious adapting of means to ends, throughout all nature, resembles exactly, though it much exceeds, the productions of human contrivance—of human design, thought, wisdom, and intelligence. Since therefore the effects resemble each other, we are led to infer, by all the rules of analogy, that the causes also resemble, and that the Author of Nature is somewhat similar to the mind of man, though possessed of much larger faculties, proportioned to the grandeur of the work which he has executed. By this argument *a posteriori*, and by this argument alone, do we prove at once the existence of a Deity and his similarity to human mind and intelligence.

I shall be so free, Cleanthes, said Demea, as to tell you that from the beginning I could not approve of your conclusion concerning the similarity of the Deity to men, still less can I approve of the mediums by which you endeavor to establish it. What! No demonstration of the Being of God! No abstract arguments! No proofs *a priori!* Are these which have hitherto been so much insisted on by philosophers all fallacy, all sophism? Can we reach no farther in this subject than experience and probability? I will say not that this is betraying the cause of a Deity; but surely, by this affected candor, you give advantages to atheists which they never could obtain by the mere dint of argument and reasoning.

What I chiefly scruple in this subject, said Philo, is not so much that all religious arguments are by Cleanthes reduced to experience, as that they appear not to be even the most certain and irrefragable of that inferior kind. That a stone will fall, that fire will burn, that the earth has solidity, we have observed a thousand and a thousand times; and when any new instance of this nature is presented, we draw without hesitation the accustomed inference. The exact similarity of the cases gives us a perfect assurance of a similar event, and a stronger evidence is never desired nor sought after. But wherever you depart, in the least, from the similarity of the cases, you diminish proportionably the evidence; and may at last bring it to a very weak *analogy*, which is confessedly liable to error and uncertainty. After having experienced the circulation of the blood in human creatures, we make no doubt that it takes place in Titius and Maevius; but from its circulation in frogs and fishes it is only a presumption, though a strong one, from analogy that it takes place in men and other animals. The analogical reasoning is much weaker when we infer the circulation of the sap in vegetables from our experience that the blood circulates in animals; and those who hastily followed that imperfect analogy are found, by more accurate experiments, to have been mistaken.

If we see a house, Cleanthes, we conclude, with the greatest certainty, that it had an architect or builder because this is precisely that species of effect which we have experienced to proceed from that species of cause. But surely you will not affirm that the universe bears such a resemblance to a house that we can with the same certainty infer a similar cause, or that the analogy is here entire and perfect. The dissimilitude is so striking that the utmost you can here pretend to is a guess, a conjecture, a presumption concerning a similar cause; and how that pretension will be received in the world, I leave you to consider.

It would surely be very ill received, replied Cleanthes; and I should be deservedly blamed and detested did I allow that the proofs of a Deity amounted to no more than a guess or conjecture. But is the whole adjustment of means to ends in a house and in the universe so slight a resemblance? the economy of final causes? the order, proportion, and arrangement of every part? Steps of a stair are plainly contrived that human legs may use them in mounting; and this inference is certain and infallible. Human legs are also contrived for walking and mounting; and this inference, I allow, is not altogether so certain because of the dissimilarity which you remark; but does it, therefore, deserve the name only of presumption or conjecture?

Good God! cried Demea, interrupting him, where are we? Zealous defenders of religion allow that the proofs of a Deity fall short of perfect evidence! And you, Philo, on whose assistance I depended in proving the adorable mysteriousness of the Divine Nature, do you assent to all these extravagant opinions of Cleanthes? For what other name can I give them? or, why spare my censure when such principles are advanced, supported by such an authority, before so young a man as Pamphilus?

You seem not to apprehend, replied Philo, that I argue with Cleanthes in his own way, and, by showing him the dangerous consequences of his tenets, hope at last to reduce him to our opinion. But what sticks most with you, I observe, is the representation which Cleanthes has made of the argument *a posteriori*; and, finding that that argument is likely to escape your hold and vanish into air, you think it so disguised that you can scarcely believe it to be set in its true light. Now, however much I may dissent, in other respects, from the dangerous principle of Cleanthes, I must allow that he has fairly represented that argument, and I shall endeavor so to state the matter to you that you will entertain no further scruples with regard to it.

Were a man to abstract from everything which he knows or has seen, he would be altogether incapable, merely from his own ideas, to determine what kind of scene the universe must be, or to give the preference to one state or situation of things above another. For as nothing which he clearly conceives could be esteemed impossible or implying a contradiction, every chimera of his fancy would be upon an equal footing; nor could he assign just reason why he adheres to one idea or system, and rejects the others which are equally possible.

Again, after he opens his eyes and contemplates the world as it really is, it would be impossible for him at first to assign the cause of any one event, much less the whole of things, or of the universe. He might set his fancy a rambling, and she might bring him in an infinite variety of reports and representations. These would all be possible; but, being all equally possible, he would never of himself give a satisfactory account for his preferring one of them to the rest. Experience alone can point out to him the true cause of any phenomenon.

Now, according to this method of reasoning, Demea, it follows (and is, indeed, tacitly allowed by Cleanthes himself) that order, arrangement, or the adjustment of final causes, is not of itself any proof of design, but only so far as it has been experienced to proceed from that principle. For aught we can know *a priori*, matter may contain the source or spring of order originally within itself, as well as mind does; and there is no more difficulty in conceiving that the several elements, from an internal unknown cause, may fall into the most exquisite arrangement, than to conceive that their ideas, in the great universal mind, from a like internal unknown cause, fall into that arrangement. The equal possibility of both these suppositions is allowed. But, by experience, we find (according to Cleanthes) that there is a difference between them. Throw several pieces of steel together, without shape or form, they will never arrange themselves so as to compose a watch. Stone and mortar and wood, without an architect, never erect a house. But the ideas in a human mind, we see, by an unknown, inexplicable economy, arrange themselves so as to form the plan of a watch or house. Experience, therefore, proves that there is an original principle of order in mind, not in matter. From similar effects we infer similar causes. The adjustment of means to ends is alike in the universe, as in a machine of human contrivance. The causes, therefore, must be resembling.

I was from the beginning scandalized, I must own,

with this resemblance which is asserted between the Deity and human creatures, and must conceive it to imply such a degradation of the Supreme Being as no sound theist could endure. With your assistance, therefore, Demea, I shall endeavor to defend what you justly call the adorable mysteriousness of the Divine Nature, and shall refute this reasoning of Cleanthes, provided he allows that I have made a fair representation of it.

When Cleanthes had assented, Philo, after a short pause, proceeded in the following manner.

That all inferences, Cleanthes, concerning fact are founded on experience, and that all experimental reasonings are founded on the supposition that similar causes prove similar effects, and similar effects similar causes, I shall not at present much dispute with you. But observe, I entreat you, with what extreme caution all just reasoners proceed in the transferring of experiments to similar cases. Unless the cases be exactly similar, they repose no perfect confidence in applying their past observation to any particular phenomenon. Every alteration of circumstances occasions a doubt concerning the event; and it requires new experiments to prove certainly that the new circumstances are of no moment or importance. A change in bulk, situation, arrangement, age, disposition of the air, or surrounding bodies—any of these particulars may be attended with the most unexpected consequences. And unless the objects be quite familiar to us, it is the highest temerity to expect with assurance, after any of these changes, an event similar to that which before fell under our observation. The slow and deliberate steps of philosophers here, if anywhere, are distinguished from the precipitate march of the vulgar, who, hurried on by the smallest similitude, are incapable of all discernment or consideration.

But can you think, Cleanthes, that your usual phlegm and philosophy have been preserved in so wide a step as you have taken when you compared to the universe houses, ships, furniture, machines; and, from their similarity in some circumstances, inferred a similarity in their causes? Thought, design, intelligence, such as we discover in men and other animals, is no more than one of the springs and principles of the universe, as well as heat or cold, attraction or repulsion, and a hundred others which fall under daily observation. It is an active cause by which some particular parts of nature, we find, pro-

duce alterations on other parts. But can a conclusion, with any propriety, be transferred from parts to the whole? Does not the great disproportion bar all comparison and inference? From observing the growth of a hair, can we learn anything concerning the generation of a man? Would the manner of a leaf's blowing, even though perfectly known, afford us any instruction concerning the vegetation of a tree?

But allowing that we were to take the *operations* of one part of nature upon another for the foundation of our judgment concerning the *origin* of the whole (which never can be admitted), yet why select so minute, so weak, so bounded a principle as the reason and design of animals is found to be upon this planet? What peculiar privilege has this little agitation of the brain which we call *thought*, that we must thus make it the model of the whole universe? Our partiality in our own favor does indeed present it on all occasions, but sound philosophy ought carefully to guard against so natural an illusion.

So far from admitting, continued Philo, that the operations of a part can afford us any just conclusion concerning the origin of the whole, I will not allow any one part to form a rule for another part if the latter be very remote from the former. Is there any reasonable ground to conclude that the inhabitants of other planets possess thought, intelligence, reason, or anything similar to these faculties in men? When nature has so extremely diversified her manner of operation in this small globe, can we imagine that she incessantly copies herself throughout so immense a universe? And if thought, as we may well suppose, be confined merely to this narrower corner and has even there so limited a sphere of action, with what propriety can we assign it for the original cause of all things? The narrow views of a peasant who makes his domestic economy the rule for the government of kingdoms is in comparison a pardonable sophism.

But were we ever so much assured that a thought and reason resembling the human were to be found throughout the whole universe, and were its activity elsewhere vastly greater and more commanding than it appears in this globe; yet I cannot see why the operations of a world constituted, arranged, adjusted, can with any propriety be extended to a world which is in its embryo-state, and is advancing towards that constitution and arrangement. By observation we know somewhat of the economy, action, and nourishment of a finished animal; but we must transfer with great caution that observation to the growth of a foetus in the womb, and still more to the formation of an animalcule in the loins of its male parent. Nature, we find, even from our limited experience, possesses an infinite number of springs and principles which incessantly discover themselves on every change of her position and situation. And what new and unknown principles would actuate her in so new and unknown a situation as that of the formation of a universe, we cannot, without the utmost temerity, pretend to determine.

A very small part of this great system, during a very short time, is very imperfectly discovered to us; and do we thence pronounce decisively concerning the origin of the whole?

Admirable conclusion! Stone, wood, brick, iron, brass, have not, at this time, in this minute globe of earth, an order or arrangement without human art and contrivance; therefore, the universe could not originally attain its order and arrangement without something similar to human art. But is a part of nature a rule for another part very wide of the former? Is it a rule for the whole? Is a very small part a rule for the universe? Is nature in one situation a certain rule for nature in another situation vastly different from the former?

And can you blame me, Cleanthes, if I here imitate the prudent reserve of Simonides,[11] who, according to the noted story, being asked by Hiero,[12] *What God was?* desired a day to think of it, and then two days more; and after that manner continually prolonged the term, without ever bringing in his definition or description? Could you even blame me if I had answered, at first, *that I did not know,* and was sensible that this subject lay vastly beyond the reach of my faculties? You might cry out sceptic and railer, as much as you pleased; but, having found in so many other subjects much more familiar the imperfections and even contradictions of human reason, I never should expect any success from its feeble conjectures in a subject so sublime and so remote from the sphere of our observation. When two *species* of objects have

11. [Simonides of Ceos (c.356–c.468 B.C.) was a Greek poet.]
12. [The reference is to Hiero I, a fifth-century B.C. ruler of Syracuse noted as a patron of literature.]

always been observed to be conjoined together, I can *infer,* by custom, the existence of one wherever I *see* the existence of the other; and this I call an argument from experience. But how this argument can have place where the objects, as in the present case, are single, individual, without parallel or specific resemblance, may be difficult to explain. And will any man tell me with a serious countenance that an orderly universe must arise from some thought and art like the human because we have experience of it? To ascertain this reasoning it were requisite that we had experience of the origin of the worlds; and it is not sufficient, surely, that we have seen ships and cities arise from human art and contrivance . . .

Philo was proceeding in this vehement manner, somewhat between jest and earnest, as it appeared to me, when he observed some signs of impatience in Cleanthes, and then immediately stopped short. What I had to suggest, said Cleanthes, is only that you would not abuse terms, or make use of popular expressions to subvert philosophical reasonings. You know that the vulgar often distinguish reason from experience, even where the question relates only to matter of fact and existence, though it is found, where that *reason* is properly analyzed, that it is nothing but a species of experience. To prove by experience the origin of the universe from mind is not more contrary to common speech than to prove the motion of the earth from the same principle. And a caviller might raise all the same objections to the Copernican system which you have urged against my reasonings. Have you other earths, might he say, which you have seen to move? Have . . .

Yes! cried Philo, interrupting him, we have other earths. Is not the moon another earth, which we see to turn round its center? Is not Venus another earth, where we observe the same phenomenon? Are not the revolutions of the sun also a confirmation, from analogy, of the same theory? All the planets, are they not earths which revolve about the sun? Are not the satellites moons which move round Jupiter and Saturn, and along with these primary planets round the sun? These analogies and resemblances, with others which I have not mentioned, are the sole proofs of the Copernican system; and to you it belongs to consider whether you have any analogies of the same kind to support your theory.

In reality, Cleanthes, continued he, the modern

system of astronomy is now so much received by all inquirers, and has become so essential a part even of our earliest education, that we are not commonly very scrupulous in examining the reasons upon which it is founded. It is now become a matter of mere curiosity to study the first writers on that subject who had the full force of prejudice to encounter, and were obliged to turn their arguments on every side in order to render them popular and convincing. But if we peruse Galileo's famous *Dialogues*[13] concerning the system of the world, we shall find that that great genius, one of the sublimest that ever existed, first bent all his endeavors to prove that there was no foundation for the distinction commonly made between elementary and celestial substances. The schools, proceeding from the illusions of sense, had carried this distinction very far; and had established the latter substances to be ingenerable, incorruptible, unalterable, impassible; and had assigned all the opposite qualities to the former. But Galileo, beginning with the moon, proved its similarity in every particular to the earth: its convex figure, its natural darkness when not illuminated, its density, its distinction into solid and liquid, the variations of its phases, the mutual illuminations of the earth and moon, their mutual eclipses, the inequalities of the lunar surface, etc. After many instances of this kind, with regard to all the planets, men plainly saw that these bodies became proper objects of experience, and that the similarity of their nature enabled us to extend the same arguments and phenomena from one to the other.

In this cautious proceeding of the astronomers you may read your own condemnation, Cleanthes; or rather may see that the subject in which you are engaged exceeds all human reason and inquiry. Can you pretend to show any such similarity between the fabric of a house and the generation of a universe? Have you ever seen nature in any such situation as resembles the first arrangement of the elements? Have worlds ever been formed under your eye, and have you had leisure to observe the whole progress of the phenomenon, from the first appearance of order to its final consummation? If you have, then cite your experience and deliver your theory.

13. [The reference is to Galileo's *Dialogue Concerning the Two Chief World Systems* (1632).]

Part III

How the most absurd argument, replied Cleanthes, in the hands of a man of ingenuity and invention, may acquire an air of probability! Are you not aware, Philo, that it became necessary for Copernicus and his first disciples to prove the similarity of the terrestrial and celestial matter because several philosophers, blinded by old systems and supported by some sensible appearances, had denied this similarity; but that it is by no means necessary that theists should prove the similarity of the works of nature to those of art, because this similarity is self-evident and undeniable? The same matter, a like form; what more is requisite to show an analogy between their causes, and to ascertain the origin of all things from a divine purpose and intention? Your objections, I must freely tell you, are no better than the abstruse cavils of those philosophers who denied motion, and ought to be refuted in the same manner—by illustrations, examples, and instances rather than by serious argument and philosophy.

Suppose, therefore, that an articulate voice were heard in the clouds, much louder and more melodious than any which human art could ever reach; suppose that this voice were extended in the same instant over all nations and spoke to each nation in its own language and dialect; suppose that the words delivered not only contain a just sense and meaning, but convey some instruction altogether worthy of a benevolent Being superior to mankind—could you possibly hesitate a moment concerning the cause of this voice, and must you not instantly ascribe it to some design or purpose? Yet I cannot see but all the same objections (if they merit that appellation) which lie against the system of theism may also be produced against this inference.

Might you not say that all conclusions concerning fact were founded on experience; that, when we hear an articulate voice in the dark and thence infer a man, it is only the resemblance of the effects which leads us to conclude that there is a like resemblance in the cause; but that this extraordinary voice, by its loudness, extent, and flexibility to all languages, bears so little analogy to any human voice that we have no reason to suppose any analogy in their causes; and, consequently, that a rational, wise, coherent speech proceeded, you know not whence, from some accidental whistling of the winds, not from any divine reason or intelligence? You see clearly your own objections in these cavils; and I hope too, you see clearly that they cannot possibly have more force in the one case than in the other.

But to bring the case still nearer the present one of the universe, I shall make two suppositions which imply not any absurdity or impossibility. Suppose that there is a natural, universal, invariable language, common to every individual of human race, and that books are natural productions which perpetuate themselves in the same manner with animals and vegetables, by descent and propagation. Several expressions of our passions contain a universal language: All brute animals have a natural speech, which, however limited, is very intelligible to their own species. And as there are infinitely fewer parts and less contrivance in the finest composition of eloquence than in the coarsest organized body, the propagation of an *Iliad* or *Aeneid* is an easier supposition than that of any plant or animal.

Suppose, therefore, that you enter into your library thus peopled by natural volumes containing the most refined reason and most exquisite beauty; could you possibly open one of them and doubt that its original cause bore the strongest analogy to mind and intelligence? When it reasons and discourses; when it expostulates, argues, and enforces its views and topics; when it applies sometimes to the pure intellect, sometimes to the affections; when it collects, disposes, and adorns every consideration suited to the subject; could you persist in asserting that all this, at the bottom, had really no meaning, and that the first formation of this volume in the loins of its original parent proceeded not from thought and design? Your obstinacy, I know, reaches not that degree of firmness; even your sceptical play and wantonness would be abashed at so glaring an absurdity.

But if there be any difference, Philo, between this supposed case and the real one of the universe, it is all to the advantage of the latter. The anatomy of an animal affords many stronger instances of design than the perusal of Livy or Tacitus;[14] and any objection which you start in the former case, by carrying me back to so unusual and extraordinary a scene as the first formation of worlds, the same objection has place on the supposition of our vegetating library. Choose, then, your party, Philo, without ambiguity or evasion; assert either that a rational volume is no proof of a rational cause or admit of a similar cause to all the works of nature.

Let me here observe, too, continued Cleanthes, that this religious argument, instead of being weakened by that scepticism so much affected by you, rather acquires force from it and becomes more firm and undisputed. To exclude all argument or reasoning of every kind is either affectation or madness. The declared profession of every reasonable sceptic is only to reject abstruse, remote, and refined arguments; to adhere to common sense and the plain instincts of nature; and to assent, wherever any reasons strike him with so full a force that he cannot, without the greatest violence, prevent it. Now the arguments for natural religion are plainly of this kind; and nothing but the most perverse, obstinate metaphysics can reject them. Consider, anatomize the eye; survey its structure and contrivance, and tell me, from your own feeling, if the idea of a contriver does not immediately flow in upon you with a force like that of sensation. The most obvious conclusion, surely, is in favor of design; and it requires time, reflection, and study, to summon up those frivolous though abstruse objections which can support infidelity. Who can behold the male and female of each species, the correspondence of their parts and instincts, their passions and whole course of life before and after generation, but must be sensible that the propagation of the species is intended by nature? Millions and millions of such instances present themselves through every part of the universe, and no language can convey a more intelligible, irresistible meaning than the curious adjustment of final causes. To what degree, therefore, of blind dogmatism must one have attained to reject such natural and such convincing arguments?

Some beauties in writing we may meet with which seem contrary to rules, and which gain the affections and animate the imagination in opposition to all the precepts of criticism and to the authority of the established masters of art. And if the argument for theism be, as you pretend, contradictory to the principles of logic, its universal, its irresistible influence proves clearly that there may be arguments of a like irregular

14. [Regarding Livy, see Hume's *Enquiry*, n. 59. Regarding Tacitus, see Hume's *Enquiry*, n. 41.]

nature. Whatever cavils may be urged, an orderly world, as well as a coherent, articulate speech, will still be received as an incontestable proof of design and intention.

It sometimes happens, I own, that the religious arguments have not their due influence on an ignorant savage and barbarian; not because they are obscure and difficult, but because he never asks himself any question with regard to them. Whence arises the curious structure of an animal? From the copulation of its parents. And these whence? From *their* parents? A few removes set the objects at such a distance that to him they are lost in darkness and confusion; nor is he actuated by any curiosity to trace them farther. But this is neither dogmatism nor scepticism, but stupidity: a state of mind very different from your sifting, inquisitive disposition, my ingenious friend. You can trace causes from effects; you can compare the most distant and remote objects; and your greatest errors proceed not from barrenness of thought and invention, but from too luxuriant a fertility which suppresses your natural good sense by a profusion of unnecessary scruples and objections.

Here I could observe, Hermippus, that Philo was a little embarrassed and confounded; but, while he hesitated in delivering an answer, luckily for him, Demea broke in upon the discourse and saved his countenance.

Your instance, Cleanthes, said he, drawn from books and language, being familiar, has, I confess, so much more force on that account; but is there not some danger, too, in this very circumstance, and may it not render us presumptuous, by making us imagine we comprehend the Deity and have some adequate idea of his nature and attributes? When I read a volume, I enter into the mind and intention of the author; I become him, in a manner, for the instant, and have an immediate feeling and conception of those ideas which revolved in his imagination while employed in that composition. But so near an approach we never surely can make to the Deity. His ways are not our ways. His attributes are perfect but incomprehensible. And this volume of nature contains a great and inexplicable riddle, more than any intelligible discourse or reasoning.

The ancient Platonists, you know, were the most religious and devout of all the pagan philosophers; yet many of them, particularly Plotinus,[15] expressly declare that intellect or understanding is not to be ascribed to the Deity, and that our most perfect worship of him consists, not in acts of veneration, reverence, gratitude, or love, but in a certain mysterious self-annihilation or total extinction of all our faculties. These ideas are, perhaps, too far stretched; but still it must be acknowledged that, by representing the Deity as so intelligible and comprehensible, and so similar to a human mind, we are guilty of the grossest and most narrow partiality, and make ourselves the model of the whole universe.

All the *sentiments* of the human mind, gratitude, resentment, love, friendship, approbation, blame, pity, emulation, envy, have a plain reference to the state and situation of man, and are calculated for preserving the existence and promoting the activity of such a being in such circumstances. It seems, therefore, unreasonable to transfer such sentiments to a supreme existence or to suppose him actuated by them; and the phenomena, besides, of the universe will not support us in such a theory. All our *ideas* derived from the senses are confessedly false and illusive, and cannot therefore be supposed to have place in a supreme intelligence. And as the ideas of internal sentiment, added to those of the external senses, compose the whole furniture of human understanding, we may conclude that none of the *materials* of thought are in any respect similar in the human and in the divine intelligence. Now, as to the *manner* of thinking, how can we make any comparison between them or suppose them anywise resembling? Our thought is fluctuating, uncertain, fleeting, successive, and compounded; and were we to remove these circumstances, we absolutely annihilate its essence, and it would in such a case be an abuse of terms to apply to it the name of thought or reason. At least, if it appear more pious and respectful (as it really is) still to retain these terms when we mention the Supreme Being, we ought to acknowledge that their meaning, in that case, is totally incomprehensible; and that the infirmities of our nature do not permit us to reach any ideas which in the least correspond to the ineffable sublimity of the Divine attributes.

15. [Plotinus (205–270), born in Egypt, developed a complex philosophical system referred to as Neo-Platonism which fused elements of Platonism and mysticism.]

Part IV

It seems strange to me, said Cleanthes, that you, Demea, who are so sincere in the cause of religion, should still maintain the mysterious, incomprehensible nature of the Deity, and should insist so strenuously that he has no manner of likeness or resemblance to human creatures. The Deity, I can readily allow, possesses many powers and attributes of which we can have no comprehension; but, if our ideas, so far as they go, be not just and adequate and correspondent to his real nature, I know not what there is in this subject worth insisting on. Is the name, without any meaning, of such mighty importance? Or how do you *mystics*, who maintain the absolute incomprehensibility of the Deity, differ from sceptics or atheists, who assert that the first cause of all is unknown and unintelligible? Their temerity must be very great if, after rejecting the production by a mind—I mean a mind resembling the human (for I know of no other)—they pretend to assign, with certainty, any other specific intelligible cause; and their conscience must be very scrupulous, indeed, if they refuse to call the universal unknown cause a God or Deity, and to bestow on him as many sublime eulogies and unmeaning epithets as you shall please to require of them.

Who could imagine, replied Demea, that Cleanthes, the calm philosophical Cleanthes, would attempt to refute his antagonists by affixing a nickname to them; and, like the common bigots and inquisitors of the age, have recourse to invective and declamation instead of reasoning? Or does he not perceive that these topics are easily retorted, and that *anthropomorphite* is an appellation as invidious, and implies as dangerous consequences, as the epithet of *mystic* with which he has honored us? In reality, Cleanthes, consider what it is you assert when you represent the Deity as similar to a human mind and understanding. What is the soul of man? A composition of various faculties, passions, sentiments, ideas—united, indeed, into one self or person, but still distinct from each other. When it reasons, the ideas which are the parts of its discourse arrange themselves in a certain form or order which is not preserved entire for a moment, but immediately gives place to another arrangement. New opinions, new passions, new affections, new feelings arise which continually diversify the mental scene and produce in it the greatest variety and most rapid succession imaginable. How is this compatible with that perfect immutability and simplicity which all true theists ascribe to the Deity? By the same act, say they, he sees past, present, and future; his love and hatred, his mercy and justice, are one individual operation; he is entire in every point of space, and complete in every instant of duration. No succession, no change, no acquisition, no diminution. What he is implies not in it any shadow of distinction or diversity. And what he is this moment he ever has been and ever will be, without any new judgment, sentiment, or operation. He stands fixed in one simple, perfect state; nor can you ever say, with any propriety, that this act of his is different from that other, or that this judgment or idea has been lately formed and will give place, by succession, to any different judgment or idea.

I can readily allow, said Cleanthes, that those who maintain the perfect simplicity of the Supreme Being, to the extent in which you have explained it, are complete *mystics*, and chargeable with all the consequences which I have drawn from their opinion. They are, in a word, *atheists*, without knowing it. For though it be allowed that the Deity possesses attributes of which we have no comprehension, yet ought we never to ascribe to him any attributes which are absolutely incompatible with that intelligent nature essential to him. A mind whose acts and sentiments and ideas are not distinct and successive, one that is wholly simple and totally immutable, is a mind which has no thought, no reason, no will, no sentiment, no love, no hatred; or, in a word, is no mind at all. It is an abuse of terms to give it that appellation, and we may as well speak of limited extension without figure, or of number without composition.

Pray consider, said Philo, whom you are at present inveighing against. You are honoring with the appellation of *atheist* all the sound, orthodox divines, almost, who have treated of this subject; and you will at last be, yourself, found, according to your reckoning, the only sound theist in the world. But if idolaters be atheists, as, I think, may justly be asserted, and Christian theologians the same, what becomes of the argument, so much celebrated, derived from the universal consent of mankind?

But, because I know you are not much swayed by names and authorities, I shall endeavor to show you, a little more distinctly, the inconveniences of that anthropomorphism which you have embraced, and shall prove that there is no ground to suppose a plan of the world to be formed in the Divine mind, consisting of distinct ideas, differently arranged, in the same manner as an architect forms in his head the plan of a house which he intends to execute.

It is not easy, I own, to see what is gained by this supposition, whether we judge of the matter by *reason* or by *experience*. We are still obliged to mount higher in order to find the cause of this cause which you had assigned as satisfactory and conclusive.

If *reason* (I mean abstract reason derived from inquiries *a priori*) be not alike mute with regard to all questions concerning cause and effect, this sentence at least it will venture to pronounce: that a mental world or universe of ideas requires a cause as much as does a material world or universe of objects; and, if similar in its arrangement, must require a similar cause. For what is there in this subject which should occasion a different conclusion or inference? In an abstract view, they are entirely alike; and no difficulty attends the one supposition which is not common to both of them.

Again, when we will needs force *experience* to pronounce some sentence, even on these subjects which lie beyond her sphere, neither can she perceive any material difference in this particular between these two kinds of worlds, but finds them to be governed by similar principles, and to depend upon an equal variety of causes in their operations. We have specimens in miniature of both of them. Our own mind resembles the one; a vegetable or animal body the other. Let experience, therefore, judge from these samples. Nothing seems more delicate, with regard to its causes, than thought; and as these causes never operate in two persons after the same manner, so we never find two persons who think exactly alike. Nor indeed does the same person think exactly alike at any two different periods of time. A difference of age, of the disposition of his body, of weather, of food, of company, of books, of passions—any of these particulars, or others more minute, are sufficient to alter the curious machinery of thought and communicate to it very different movements and operations. As far as we can judge, vegetables and animal bodies are not more delicate in their motions, nor depend upon a greater variety or more curious adjustment of springs and principles.

How, therefore, shall we satisfy ourselves concerning the cause of that Being whom you suppose the Author of Nature, or, according to your system of anthropomorphism, the ideal world into which you trace the material? Have we not the same reason to trace that ideal world into another ideal world or new intelligent principle? But if we stop and go no farther, why go so far—why not stop at the material world? How can we satisfy ourselves without going on *in infinitum*? And, after all, what satisfaction is there in that infinite progression? Let us remember the story of the Indian philosopher and his elephant. It was never more applicable than to the present subject. If the material world rests upon a similar ideal world, this ideal world must rest upon some other, and so on without end. It were better, therefore, never to look beyond the present material world. By supposing it to contain the principle of its order within itself, we really assert it to be God; and the sooner we arrive at that Divine Being, so much the better. When you go one step beyond the mundane system, you only excite an inquisitive humor which it is impossible ever to satisfy.

To say that the different ideas which compose the reason of the Supreme Being fall into order of themselves and by their own nature is really to talk without any precise meaning. If it has a meaning, I would fain know why it is not as good sense to say that the parts of the material world fall into order of themselves and by their own nature. Can the one opinion be intelligible, while the other is not so?

We have, indeed, experience of ideas which fall into order of themselves and without any *known* cause. But, I am sure, we have a much larger experience of matter which does the same, as in all instances of generation and vegetation where the accurate analysis of the cause exceeds all human comprehension. We have also experience of particular systems of thought and of matter which have no order; of the first in madness, of the second in corruption. Why, then, should we think that order is more essential to one than the other? And if it requires a cause in both, what do we gain by your system, in tracing the universe of objects into a similar universe of ideas? The first step which we make leads us on forever. It were, therefore, wise in us to limit all our inquiries to the present world, without looking farther. No satisfaction can ever be attained by these speculations which so far exceed the narrow bounds of human understanding.

It was usual with the Peripatetics, you know, Cleanthes, when the cause of any phenomenon was demanded, to have recourse to their *faculties* or *occult qualities*, and to say, for instance, that bread nourished by its nutritive faculty, and senna purged by its purgative. But it has been discovered that this subterfuge was nothing but the disguise of ignorance, and that these philosophers, though less ingenuous, really said the same thing with the sceptics or the vulgar who fairly confessed that they knew not the cause of these phenomena. In like manner, when it is asked, what cause produces order in the ideas of the Supreme Being, can any other reason be assigned by you, anthropomorphites, than that it is a *rational* faculty, and that such is the nature of the Deity? But why a similar answer will not be equally satisfactory in accounting for the order of the world, without having recourse to any such intelligent creator as you insist on, may be difficult to determine. It is only to say that *such* is the nature of material objects, and that they are all originally possessed of a *faculty* of order and proportion. These are only more learned and elaborate ways of confessing our ignorance; nor has the one hypothesis any real advantage above the other, except in its greater conformity to vulgar prejudices.

You have displayed this argument with great emphasis, replied Cleanthes: You seem not sensible how easy it is to answer it. Even in common life, if I assign a cause for any event, is it any objection, Philo, that I cannot assign the cause of that cause, and answer every new question which may incessantly be started? And what philosophers could possibly submit to so rigid a rule?—philosophers who confess ultimate causes to be totally unknown, and are sensible that the most refined principles into which they trace the phenomena are still to them as inexplicable as these phenomena themselves are to the vulgar. The order and arrangement of nature, the curious adjustment of final causes, the plain use and intention of every part and organ—all of these bespeak in the clearest language an intelligent cause or author. The heavens and the earth join in the same testimony: The whole chorus of nature raises one hymn to the praises of its Creator. You alone, or almost alone, disturb this general harmony. You start abstruse doubts, cavils, and objections; you ask me what is the cause of this cause? I know not; I care not; that concerns not me. I have found a Deity; and here I stop my inquiry. Let those go farther who are wiser or more enterprising.

I pretend to be neither, replied Philo; and for that very reason I should never, perhaps, have attempted to go so far, especially when I am sensible that I must at least be contented to sit down with the same answer which, without further trouble, might have satisfied me from the beginning. If I am still to remain in utter ignorance of causes and can absolutely give an explication of nothing, I shall never esteem it any advantage to shove off for a moment a difficulty which you acknowledge must immediately, in its full force, recur upon me. Naturalists, indeed, very justly explain particular effects by more general causes, though these general causes themselves should remain in the end totally inexplicable; but they never surely thought it satisfactory to explain a particular effect by a particular cause which was no more to be accounted for than the effect itself. An ideal system, arranged of itself, without a precedent design, is not a whit more explicable than a material one which attains its order in a like manner; nor is there any more difficulty in the latter supposition than in the former.

Part V

But to show you still more inconveniences, continued Philo, in your anthropomorphism, please to take a new survey of your principles. *Like effects prove like causes.* This is the experimental argument; and this, you say too, is the sole theological argument. Now it is certain that the liker the effects are which are seen and the liker the causes which are inferred, the stronger is the argument. Every departure on either side diminishes the probability and renders the experiment less conclusive. You cannot doubt of the principle; neither ought you to reject its consequences.

All the new discoveries in astronomy which prove the immense grandeur and magnificence of the works of nature are so many additional arguments for a Deity, according to the true system of theism; but, according to your hypothesis of experimental theism, they become so many objections, by removing the effect still farther from all resemblance to the effects of human art and contrivance. For if Lucretius,[16] even following the old system of the world, could exclaim:

> Quis regere immensi summam, quis habere
>   profundi
> Indu manu validas potis est moderanter habenas?
> Quis pariter coelos omnes convertere? et omnes
> Ignibus aetheriis terras suffire feraces?
> Omnibus inque locis esse omni tempore
>   praesto?[17]

If Tully[18] esteemed this reasoning so natural as to put it into the mouth of his Epicurean:

> Quibus enim oculis animi intueri potuit vester Plato fabricam illam tanti operis, qua construi a Deo atque aedificari mundum facit? quae molitio? quae ferramenta? qui vectes? quae machinae? qui ministri tanti muneris fuerunt? quemadmodum autem obedire et parere voluntati architecti aer, ignis, aqua, terra potuerunt?[19]

If this argument, I say, had any force in former ages, how much greater must it have at present when the

16. [Lucretius (c.99 B.C.–c.55 B.C.), a Roman poet and philosopher who espoused the Epicurean view that the universe is composed of everlasting atoms that move in a void, the whole exhibiting beauty and majesty but without purpose or divine providence.]

17. Lib. xi. 1094. [The quotation is from *On the Nature of the Universe.* "Who is able to rule the whole of the immeasurable; who is able, with control, to hold in hand the strong reins of the boundless? Who equally is able to turn all the heavens? And who is able to warm all fertile grounds with ethereal fire? Who is able to be present in all places at every time?" (The translation is by William E. Mann.)]

18. [Regarding Tully (Cicero), see Locke's *Essay*, n. 8.]

19. *De Nat. Deor.*, lib. i. [The quotation is from *On the Nature of the Gods.* "For with which of the soul's eyes has your [master] Plato been able to contemplate that fabrication of such great labor, by which he establishes that the universe is furnished and even constructed by God? What preparation [was involved]? What tools? What levers? What machines? What agents were there for such a great enterprise? Moreover, how were air, fire, water, and earth able to obey and to come forth at the will of the architect?" (The translation is by William E. Mann, whose amplifications are in brackets.)]

bounds of nature are so infinitely enlarged and such a magnificent scene is opened to us? It is still more unreasonable to form our idea of so unlimited a cause from our experience of the narrow productions of human design and invention.

The discoveries by microscopes, as they open a new universe in miniature, are still objections, according to you; arguments, according to me. The further we push our researches of this kind, we are still led to infer the universal cause of all to be vastly different from mankind, or from any object of human experience and observation.

And what say you to the discoveries in anatomy, chemistry, botany? . . . These surely are no objections, replied Cleanthes; they only discover new instances of art and contrivance. It is still the image of mind reflected on us from innumerable objects. Add a mind *like the human*, said Philo. I know of no other, replied Cleanthes. And the liker, the better, insisted Philo. To be sure, said Cleanthes.

Now, Cleanthes, said Philo, with an air of alacrity and triumph, mark the consequences. *First*, by this method of reasoning you renounce all claim to infinity in any of the attributes of the Deity. For, as the cause ought only to be proportioned to the effect, and the effect, so far as it falls under our cognizance, is not infinite, what pretensions have we, upon your suppositions, to ascribe that attribute to the divine Being? You will still insist that, by removing him so much from all similarity to human creatures, we give in to the most arbitrary hypothesis, and at the same time weaken all proofs of his existence.

Secondly, you have no reason, on your theory, for ascribing perfection to the Deity, even in his finite capacity; or for supposing him free from every error, mistake, or incoherence, in his undertakings. There are many inexplicable difficulties in the works of nature which, if we allow a perfect author to be proved *a priori*, are easily solved, and become only seeming difficulties from the narrow capacity of man, who cannot trace infinite relations. But according to your method of reasoning, these difficulties become all real; and, perhaps, will be insisted on as new instances of likeness to human art and contrivance. At least, you must acknowledge that it is impossible for us to tell, from our limited views, whether this system contains any great faults or deserves any considerable praise if compared to other possible and even real systems. Could a peasant, if the *Aeneid* were read to him, pronounce that poem to be absolutely faultless, or even assign to it its proper rank among the productions of human wit, he who had never seen any other production?

But were this world ever so perfect a production, it must still remain uncertain whether all the excellences of the work can justly be ascribed to the workman. If we survey a ship, what an exalted idea must we form of the ingenuity of the carpenter who framed so complicated, useful, and beautiful a machine? And what surprise must we feel when we find him a stupid mechanic who imitated others, and copied an art which, through a long succession of ages, after multiplied trials, mistakes, corrections, deliberations, and controversies, had been gradually improving? Many worlds might have been botched and bungled, throughout an eternity, ere this system was struck out; much labor lost; many fruitless trials made; and a slow but continued improvement carried on during infinite ages in the art of world-making. In such subjects, who can determine where the truth, nay, who can conjecture where the probability lies, amidst a great number of hypotheses which may be proposed, and a still greater which may be imagined?

And what shadow of an argument, continued Philo, can you produce from your hypothesis to prove the unity of the Deity? A great number of men join in building a house or ship, in rearing a city, in framing a commonwealth; why may not several deities combine in contriving and framing a world? This is only so much greater similarity to human affairs. By sharing the work among several, we may so much further limit the attributes of each, and get rid of that extensive power and knowledge which must be supposed in one deity, and which, according to you, can only serve to weaken the proof of his existence. And if such foolish, such vicious creatures as man can yet often unite in framing and executing one plan, how much more those deities or demons, whom we may suppose several degrees more perfect?

To multiply causes without necessity is indeed contrary to true philosophy, but this principle applies not to the present case. Were one deity antecedently proved by your theory who were possessed of every attribute requisite to the production of the universe, it would be needless, I own (though not absurd), to suppose any other deity existent. But while it is still

a question whether all these attributes are united in one subject or dispersed among several independent beings; by what phenomena in nature can we pretend to decide the controversy? Where we see a body raised in a scale, we are sure that there is in the opposite scale, however concealed from sight, some counterpoising weight equal to it; but it is still allowed to doubt whether that weight be an aggregate of several distinct bodies or one uniform united mass. And if the weight requisite very much exceeds anything which we have ever seen conjoined in any single body, the former supposition becomes still more probable and natural. An intelligent being of such vast power and capacity as is necessary to produce the universe — or, to speak in the language of ancient philosophy, so prodigious an animal — exceeds all analogy and even comprehension.

But further, Cleanthes, men are mortal, and renew their species by generation; and this is common to all living creatures. The two great sexes of male and female, says Milton, animate the world. Why must this circumstance, so universal, so essential, be excluded from those numerous and limited deities? Behold, then, the theogeny of ancient times brought back upon us.

And why not become a perfect anthropomorphite? Why not assert the deity or deities to be corporeal, and to have eyes, a nose, mouth, ears, etc? Epicurus maintained that no man had ever seen reason but in a human figure; therefore, the gods must have a human figure. And this argument, which is deservedly so much ridiculed by Cicero, becomes, according to you, solid and philosophical.

In a word, Cleanthes, a man who follows your hypothesis is able, perhaps, to assert or conjecture that the universe sometime arose from something like design; but beyond that position he cannot ascertain one single circumstance, and is left afterwards to fix every point of his theology by the utmost license of fancy and hypothesis. This world, for aught he knows, is very faulty and imperfect, compared to a superior standard; and was only the first rude essay of some infant deity who afterwards abandoned it, ashamed of his lame performance; it is the work only of some dependent, inferior deity, and is the object of derision to his superiors; it is the production of old age and dotage in some superannuated deity; and ever since his death has run on at adventures, from the first impulse and active force which it received from him. You justly give signs of horror, Demea, at these strange suppositions; but these, and a thousand more of the same kind, are Cleanthes' suppositions, not mine. From the moment the attributes of the Deity are supposed finite, all these have place. And I cannot, for my part, think that so wild and unsettled a system of theology is, in any respect, preferable to none at all.

These suppositions I absolutely disown, cried Cleanthes; they strike me, however, with no horror, especially when proposed in that rambling way in which they drop from you. On the contrary, they give me pleasure when I see that, by the utmost indulgence of your imagination, you never get rid of the hypothesis of design in the universe, but are obliged at every turn to have recourse to it. To this concession I adhere steadily; and this I regard as a sufficient foundation for religion.

Part VI

It must be a slight fabric, indeed, said Demea, which can be erected on so tottering a foundation. While we are uncertain whether there is one deity or many, whether the deity or deities, to whom we owe our existence, be perfect or imperfect, subordinate or supreme, dead or alive, what trust or confidence can we repose in them? What devotion or worship address to them? What veneration or obedience pay them? To all the purposes of life the theory of religion becomes altogether useless; and even with regard to speculative consequences its uncertainty, according to you, must render it totally precarious and unsatisfactory.

To render it still more unsatisfactory, said Philo, there occurs to me another hypothesis which must acquire an air of probability from the method of reasoning so much insisted on by Cleanthes. That like effects arise from like causes—this principle he supposes the foundation of all religion. But there is another principle of the same kind, no less certain and derived from the same source of experience, that, where several known circumstances are observed to be similar, the unknown will also be found similar. Thus, if we see the limbs of a human body, we conclude that it is also attended with a human head, though hid from us. Thus, if we see, through a chink in a wall, a small part of the sun, we conclude that were the wall removed we should see the whole body. In short, this method of

reasoning is so obvious and familiar that no scruple can ever be made with regard to its solidity.

Now, if we survey the universe, so far as it falls under our knowledge, it bears a great resemblance to an animal or organized body, and seems actuated with a like principle of life and motion. A continual circulation of matter in it produces no disorder; a continual waste in every part is incessantly repaired; the closest sympathy is perceived throughout the entire system; and each part or member, in performing its proper offices, operates both to its own preservation and to that of the whole. The world, therefore, I infer, is an animal; and the Deity is the *soul* of the world, actuating it, and actuated by it.

You have too much learning, Cleanthes, to be at all surprised at this opinion which, you know, was maintained by almost all the theists of antiquity, and chiefly prevails in their discourses and reasonings. For though sometimes the ancient philosophers reason from final causes, as if they thought the world the workmanship of God, yet it appears rather their favorite notion to consider it as his body whose organization renders it subservient to him. And it must be confessed that, as the universe resembles more a human body than it does the works of human art and contrivance, if our limited analogy could ever, with any propriety, be extended to the whole of nature, the inference seems juster in favor of the ancient than the modern theory.

There are many other advantages, too, in the former theory which recommended it to the ancient theologians. Nothing more repugnant to all their notions—because nothing more repugnant to common experience—than mind without body; a mere spiritual substance which fell not under their senses nor comprehension, and of which they had not observed one single instance throughout all nature. Mind and body they knew because they felt both; an order, arrangement, organization, or internal machinery, in both they likewise knew, after the same manner; and it could not but seem reasonable to transfer this experience to the universe, and to suppose the divine mind and body to be also coeval and to have, both of them, order and arrangement naturally inherent in them and inseparable from them.

Here, therefore, is a new species of *anthropomorphism*, Cleanthes, on which you may deliberate; and a theory which seems not liable to any considerable difficulties. You are too much superior, surely, to *systematical prejudices* to find any more difficulty in supposing an animal body to be, originally, of itself or from unknown causes, possessed of order and organization, than in supposing a similar order to belong to mind. But the *vulgar prejudice* that body and mind ought always to accompany each other ought not, one should think, to be entirely neglected; since it is founded on *vulgar experience*, the only guide which you profess to follow in all these theological inquiries. And if you assert that our limited experience is an unequal standard by which to judge of the unlimited extent of nature, you entirely abandon your own hypothesis, and must thenceforward adopt our mysticism, as you call it, and admit of the absolute incomprehensibility of the Divine Nature.

This theory, I own, replied Cleanthes, has never before occurred to me, though a pretty natural one; and I cannot readily, upon so short an examination and reflection, deliver any opinion with regard to it. You are very scrupulous, indeed, said Philo; were I to examine any system of yours, I should not have acted with half that caution and reserve, in starting objections and difficulties to it. However, if anything occur to you, you will oblige us by proposing it.

Why then, replied Cleanthes, it seems to me that, though the world does, in many circumstances, resemble an animal body, yet is the analogy also defective in many circumstances the most material: no organ of sense, no seat of thought or reason; no one precise origin of motion and action. In short, it seems to bear a stronger resemblance to a vegetable than to an animal, and your inference would be so far inconclusive in favor of the soul of the world.

But, in the next place, your theory seems to imply the eternity of the world; and that is a principle which, I think, can be refuted by the strongest reasons and probabilities. I shall suggest an argument to this purpose which, I believe, has not been insisted on by any writer. Those who reason from the late origin of arts and sciences, though their inference wants not force, may perhaps be refuted by considerations derived from the nature of human society, which is in continual revolution between ignorance and knowledge, liberty and slavery, riches and poverty; so that it is impossible for us, from our limited experience, to foretell with assurance what events may or may not be expected. Ancient learning and history seem

to have been in great danger of entirely perishing after the inundation of the barbarous nations; and had these convulsions continued a little longer, or been a little more violent, we should not probably have now known what passed in the world a few centuries before us. Nay, were it not for the superstition of the popes, who preserved a little jargon of Latin in order to support the appearance of an ancient and universal church, that tongue must have been utterly lost; in which case the Western world, being totally barbarous, would not have been in a fit disposition for receiving the Greek language and learning, which was conveyed to them after the sacking of Constantinople. When learning and books had been extinguished, even the mechanical arts would have fallen considerably to decay; and it is easily imagined that fable or tradition might ascribe to them a much later origin than the true one. This vulgar argument, therefore, against the eternity of the world seems a little precarious.

But here appears to be the foundation of a better argument. Lucullus was the first that brought cherry-trees from Asia to Europe; though that tree thrives so well in many European climates that it grows in the woods without any culture. Is it possible that, throughout a whole eternity, no European had ever passed into Asia and thought of transplanting so delicious a fruit into his own country? Or if the tree was once transplanted and propagated, how could it ever afterwards perish? Empires may rise and fall; liberty and slavery succeed alternately; ignorance and knowledge give place to each other; but the cherry-tree will still remain in the woods of Greece, Spain, and Italy, and will never be affected by the revolutions of human society.

It is not two thousand years since vines were transplanted into France, though there is no climate in the world more favorable to them. It is not three centuries since horses, cows, sheep, swine, dogs, corn, were known in America. Is it possible that during the revolutions of a whole eternity there never arose a Columbus who might open the communication between Europe and that continent? We may as well imagine that all men would wear stockings for ten thousand years, and never have the sense to think of garters to tie them. All these seem convincing proofs of the youth or rather infancy of the world, as being founded on the operation of principles more constant and steady than those by which human society is governed and directed. Nothing less than a total convulsion of the elements will ever destroy all the European animals and vegetables which are now to be found in the Western world.

And what argument have you against such convulsions? replied Philo. Strong and almost incontestable proofs may be traced over the whole earth that every part of this globe has continued for many ages entirely covered with water. And though order were supposed inseparable from matter, and inherent in it; yet may matter be susceptible of many and great revolutions, through the endless periods of eternal duration. The incessant changes to which every part of it is subject seem to intimate some such general transformations; though, at the same time, it is observable that all the changes and corruptions of which we have ever had experience are but passages from one state of order to another; nor can matter ever rest in total deformity and confusion. What we see in the parts, we may infer in the whole; at least, that is the method of reasoning on which you rest your whole theory. And were I obliged to defend any particular system of this nature, which I never willingly should do, I esteem none more plausible than that which ascribes an eternal, inherent principle of order to the world, though attended with great and continual revolutions and alterations. This at once solves all difficulties; and if the solution, by being so general, is not entirely complete and satisfactory, it is at least a theory that we must sooner or later have recourse to, whatever system we embrace. How could things have been as they are, were there not an original inherent principle of order somewhere, in thought or in matter? And it is very indifferent to which of these we give the preference. Chance has no place, on any hypothesis, sceptical or religious. Everything is surely governed by steady, inviolable laws. And were the inmost essence of things laid open to us, we should then discover a scene of which, at present, we can have no idea. Instead of admiring the order of natural beings, we should clearly see that it was absolutely impossible for them, in the smallest article, ever to admit of any other disposition.

Were anyone inclined to revive the ancient pagan theology which maintained, as we learn from Hesiod,[20] that this globe was governed by 30,000 deities,

who arose from the unknown powers of nature, you would naturally object, Cleanthes, that nothing is gained by this hypothesis; and that it is as easy to suppose all men and animals, beings more numerous but less perfect, to have sprung immediately from a like origin. Push the same inference a step further, and you will find a numerous society of deities as explicable as one universal deity who possesses within himself the powers and perfections of the whole society. All these systems, then, of scepticism, polytheism, and theism, you must allow, on your principles, to be on a like footing, and that no one of them has any advantage over the others. You may thence learn the fallacy of your principles.

Part VII

But here, continued Philo, in examining the ancient system of the soul of the world there strikes me, all of a sudden, a new idea which, if just, must go near to subvert all your reasoning, and destroy even your first inferences on which you repose such confidence. If the universe bears a greater likeness to animal bodies and to vegetables than to the works of human art, it is more probable that its cause resembles the cause of the former than that of the latter, and its origin ought rather to be ascribed to generation or vegetation than to reason or design. Your conclusion, even according to your own principles, is therefore lame and defective.

Pray open up this argument a little further, said Demea, for I do not rightly apprehend it in that concise manner in which you have expressed it.

Our friend Cleanthes, replied Philo, as you have heard, asserts that since no question of fact can be proved otherwise than by experience, the existence of a Deity admits not of proof from any other medium. The world, says he, resembles the works of human contrivance; therefore its cause must also resemble that of the other. Here we may remark that the operation of one very small part of nature, to wit, man, upon another very small part, to wit, that inanimate matter lying within his reach, is the rule by which Cleanthes judges of the origin of the whole; and he measures objects, so widely disproportioned, by the same individual standard. But to waive all objections drawn from this topic, I affirm that there are other parts of the universe (besides the machines of human

20. [Regarding Hesiod, see Aristotle's *Ethics*, n. 1.]

invention) which bear still a greater resemblance to the fabric of the world, and which, therefore, afford a better conjecture concerning the universal origin of this system. These parts are animals and vegetables. The world plainly resembles more an animal or a vegetable than it does a watch or a knitting-loom. Its cause, therefore, it is more probable, resembles the cause of the former. The cause of the former is generation or vegetation. The cause, therefore, of the world we may infer to be something similar or analogous to generation or vegetation.

But how is it conceivable, said Demea, that the world can arise from anything similar to vegetation or generation?

Very easily, replied Philo. In like manner as a tree sheds its seed into the neighboring fields and produces other trees; so the great vegetable, the world, or this planetary system, produces within itself certain seeds which, being scattered into the surrounding chaos, vegetate into new worlds. A comet, for instance, is the seed of a world; and after it has been fully ripened, by passing from sun to sun, and star to star, it is at last tossed into the unformed elements which everywhere surround this universe, and immediately sprouts up into a new system.

Or if, for the sake of variety (for I see no other advantage) we should suppose this world to be an animal; a comet is the egg of this animal; and in like manner as an ostrich lays its egg in the sand, which, without any further care, hatches the egg and produces a new animal, so . . . I understand you, says Demea: But what wild, arbitrary suppositions are these? What *data* have you for such extraordinary conclusions? And is the slight, imaginary resemblance of the world to a vegetable or an animal sufficient to establish the same inference with regard to both? Objects which are in general so widely different; ought they to be a standard for each other?

Right, cries Philo: This is the topic on which I have all along insisted. I have still asserted that we have no *data* to establish any system of cosmogony. Our experience, so imperfect in itself and so limited both in extent and duration, can afford us no probable conjecture concerning the whole of things. But if we must needs fix on some hypothesis, by what rule, pray, ought we to determine our choice? Is there any other rule than the great similarity of the objects compared? And does not a plant or an animal, which

springs from vegetation or generation, bear a stronger resemblance to the world than does any artificial machine, which arises from reason and design?

But what is this vegetation and generation of which you talk? said Demea. Can you explain their operations, and anatomize that fine internal structure on which they depend?

As much, at least, replied Philo, as Cleanthes can explain the operations of reason, or anatomize that internal structure on which *it* depends. But without any such elaborate disquisitions, when I see an animal, I infer that it sprang from generation; and that with as great certainty as you conclude a house to have been reared by design. These words *generation, reason* mark only certain powers and energies in nature whose effects are known, but whose essence is incomprehensible; and one of these principles, more than the other, has no privilege for being made a standard to the whole of nature.

In reality, Demea, it may reasonably be expected that the larger the views are which we take of things, the better will they conduct us in our conclusions concerning such extraordinary and such magnificent subjects. In this little corner of the world alone, there are four principles, *reason, instinct, generation, vegetation,* which are similar to each other, and are the causes of similar effects. What a number of other principles may we naturally suppose in the immense extent and variety of the universe could we travel from planet to planet, and from system to system, in order to examine each part of this mighty fabric? Any one of these four principles above mentioned (and a hundred others which lie open to our conjecture) may afford us a theory by which to judge of the origin of the world; and it is a palpable and egregious partiality to confine our view entirely to that principle by which our own minds operate. Were this principle more intelligible on that account, such a partiality might be somewhat excusable; but reason, in its internal fabric and structure, is really as little known to us as instinct or vegetation; and, perhaps, even that vague, undeterminate word *nature* to which the vulgar refer everything is not at the bottom more inexplicable. The effects of these principles are all known to us from experience; but the principles themselves and their manner of operation are totally unknown; nor is it less intelligible or less conformable to experience to say that the world arose by vegetation, from a seed shed by another world, than to say that it arose from a divine reason or contrivance, according to the sense in which Cleanthes understands it.

But methinks, said Demea, if the world had a vegetative quality and could sow the seeds of new worlds into the infinite chaos, this power would be still an additional argument for design in its author. For whence could arise so wonderful a faculty but from design? Or how can order spring from anything which perceives not that order which it bestows?

You need only look around you, replied Philo, to satisfy yourself with regard to this question. A tree bestows order and organization on that tree which springs from it, without knowing the order; an animal in the same manner on its offspring; a bird on its nest; and instances of this kind are even more frequent in the world than those of order which arise from reason and contrivance. To say that all this order in animals and vegetables proceeds ultimately from design is begging the question; nor can that great point be ascertained otherwise than by proving, *a priori*, both that order is, from its nature, inseparably attached to thought, and that it can never of itself or from original unknown principles belong to matter.

But further, Demea, this objection which you urge can never be made use of by Cleanthes, without renouncing a defence which he has already made against one of my objections. When I inquired concerning the cause of that supreme reason and intelligence into which he resolves everything, he told me that the impossibility of satisfying such inquiries could never be admitted as an objection in any species of philosophy. *We must stop somewhere,* says he; *nor is it ever within the reach of human capacity to explain ultimate causes or show the last connections of any objects. It is sufficient if any steps, so far as we go, are supported by experience and observation.* Now, that vegetation and generation, as well as reason, are experienced to be principles of order in nature is undeniable. If I rest my system of cosmogony on the former, preferably to the latter, it is at my choice. The matter seems entirely arbitrary. And when Cleanthes asks me what is the cause of my great vegetative or generative faculty, I am equally entitled to ask him the cause of his great reasoning principle. These questions we have agreed to forbear on both sides; and it is chiefly his interest on the present occasion to stick to this agreement. Judging by our limited and imperfect experience, generation has some privileges above reason; for we see every day the latter arise from the former, never the former from the latter.

Compare, I beseech you, the consequences on both sides. The world, say I, resembles an animal; therefore it is an animal, therefore it arose from generation. The steps, I confess, are wide; yet there is some small appearance of analogy in each step. The world, says Cleanthes, resembles a machine; therefore it is a machine, therefore it arose from design. The steps are here equally wide, and the analogy less striking. And if he pretends to carry on *my* hypothesis a step further, and to infer design or reason from the great principle of generation on which I insist, I may, with better authority, use the same freedom to push further *his* hypothesis, and infer a divine generation or theogony from his principle of reason. I have at least some faint shadow of experience, which is the utmost that can ever be attained in the present subject. Reason, in innumerable instances, is observed to arise from the principle of generation, and never to arise from any other principle.

Hesiod and all the ancient mythologists were so struck with this analogy that they universally explained the origin of nature from an animal birth, and copulation. Plato, too, so far as he is intelligible, seems to have adopted some such notion in his *Timaeus.*

The Brahmins[21] assert that the world arose from an infinite spider, who spun this whole complicated mass from his bowels, and annihilates afterwards the whole or any part of it, by absorbing it again and resolving it into his own essence. Here is a species of cosmogony which appears to us ridiculous because a spider is a little contemptible animal whose operations we are never likely to take for a model of the whole universe. But still here is a new species of analogy, even in our globe. And were there a planet wholly inhabited by spiders (which is very possible), this inference would there appear as natural and irrefragable as that which in our planet ascribes the origin of all things to design and intelligence, as explained by Cleanthes. Why an orderly system may not be spun from the belly as well as from the brain, it will be difficult for him to give a satisfactory reason.

---

21. [Brahmins are members of the highest Hindu caste.]

I must confess, Philo, replied Cleanthes, that, of all men living, the task which you have undertaken, of raising doubts and objections, suits you best and seems, in a manner, natural and unavoidable to you. So great is your fertility of invention that I am not ashamed to acknowledge myself unable, on a sudden, to solve regularly such out-of-the-way difficulties as you incessantly start upon me; though I clearly see, in general, their fallacy and error. And I question not, but you are yourself, at present, in the same case, and have not the solution so ready as the objection; while you must be sensible that common sense and reason are entirely against you, and that such whimsies as you have delivered may puzzle but never can convince us.

Part VIII

What you ascribe to the fertility of my invention, replied Philo, is entirely owing to the nature of the subject. In subjects adapted to the narrow compass of human reason there is commonly but one determination which carries probability or conviction with it; and to a man of sound judgment all other suppositions but that one appear entirely absurd and chimerical. But in such questions as the present, a hundred contradictory views may preserve a kind of imperfect analogy, and invention has here full scope to exert itself. Without any great effort of thought, I believe that I could, in an instant, propose other systems of cosmogony which would have some faint appearance of truth; though it is a thousand, a million to one if either yours or any one of mine be the true system.

For instance, what if I should revive the old Epicurean hypothesis? This is commonly, and I believe justly, esteemed the most absurd system that has yet been proposed; yet I know not whether, with a few alterations, it might not be brought to bear a faint appearance of probability. Instead of supposing matter infinite, as Epicurus did, let us suppose it finite. A finite number of particles is only susceptible of finite transpositions, and it must happen, in an eternal duration, that every possible order or position must be tried an infinite number of times. This world, therefore, with all its events, even the most minute, has before been produced and destroyed, and will again be produced and destroyed, without any bounds and limitations. No one who has a conception of the powers of infinite, in comparison of finite, will ever scruple this determination.

But this supposes, said Demea, that matter can acquire motion without any voluntary agent or first mover.

And where is the difficulty, replied Philo, of that supposition? Every event, before experience, is equally difficult and incomprehensible; and every event, after experience, is equally easy and intelligible. Motion, in many instances, from gravity, from elasticity, from electricity, begins in matter, without any known voluntary agent; and to suppose always, in these cases, an unknown voluntary agent is mere hypothesis—and hypothesis attended with no advantages. The beginning of motion in matter itself is as conceivable *a priori* as its communication from mind and intelligence.

Besides, why may not motion have been propagated by impulse through all eternity, and the same stock of it, or nearly the same, be still upheld in the universe? As much as is lost by the composition of motion, as much is gained by its resolution. And whatever the causes are, the fact is certain that matter is and always has been in continual agitation, as far as human experience or tradition reaches. There is not probably, at present, in the whole universe, one particle of matter at absolute rest.

And this very consideration, too, continued Philo, which we have stumbled on in the course of the argument suggests a new hypothesis of cosmogony that is not absolutely absurd and improbable. Is there a system, an order, an economy of things, by which matter can preserve that perpetual agitation which seems essential to it, and yet maintain a constancy in the forms which it produces? There certainly is such an economy, for this is actually the case with the present world. The continual motion of matter, therefore, in less than infinite transpositions, must produce this economy or order; and, by its very nature, that order, when once established, supports itself for many ages if not to eternity. But wherever matter is so poised, arranged, and adjusted, as to continue in perpetual motion, and yet preserve a constancy in the forms, its situation must, of necessity, have all the same appearance of art and contrivance which we observe at present. All the parts of each form must have a relation to each other and to the whole; and the whole itself must have a relation to the other parts of the universe, to the element in which the form subsists, to the materials with which it repairs its waste and decay, and to every other form which is hostile or friendly. A defect in any of these particulars destroys the form; and the matter of which it is composed is again set loose, and is thrown into irregular motions and fermentations till it unite itself to some other regular form. If no such form be prepared to receive it, and if there be a great quantity of this corrupted matter in the universe, the universe itself is entirely disordered, whether it be the feeble embryo of a world in its first beginnings that is thus destroyed or the rotten carcass of one languishing in old age and infirmity. In either case, a chaos ensues till finite though innumerable revolutions produce, at last, some forms whose parts and organs are so adjusted as to support the forms amidst a continued succession of matter.

Suppose (for we shall endeavor to vary the expression) that matter were thrown into any position by a blind, unguided force; it is evident that this first position must, in all probability, be the most confused and most disorderly imaginable, without any resemblance to those works of human contrivance which, along with a symmetry of parts, discover an adjustment of means to ends and a tendency to self-preservation. If the actuating force cease after this operation, matter must remain forever in disorder, and continue an immense chaos, without any proportion or activity. But suppose that the actuating force, whatever it be, still continues in matter, this first position will immediately give place to a second which will likewise, in all probability, be as disorderly as the first, and so on through many successions of changes and revolutions. No particular order or position ever continues a moment unaltered. The original force, still remaining in activity, gives a perpetual restlessness to matter. Every possible situation is produced, and instantly destroyed. If a glimpse or dawn of order appears for a moment, it is instantly hurried away and confounded by that never-ceasing force which actuates every part of matter.

Thus the universe goes on for many ages in a continued succession of chaos and disorder. But is it not possible that it may settle at last, so as not to lose its motion and active force (for that we have supposed inherent in it), yet so as to preserve a uniformity of appearance, amidst the continual motion and fluctuation of its parts? This we find to be the case with the universe at present. Every individual is perpetually changing, and every part of every individual; and yet the whole remains, in appearance, the same. May we not hope for such a position or rather be assured of it from the eternal revolutions of unguided matter; and may not this account for all the appearing wisdom and contrivance which is in the universe? Let us contemplate the subject a little, and we shall find this adjustment if attained by matter of a seeming stability in the forms, with a real and perpetual revolution or motion of parts, affords a plausible, if not a true, solution of the difficulty.

It is in vain, therefore, to insist upon the uses of the parts in animals or vegetables, and their curious adjustment to each other. I would fain know how an animal could subsist unless its parts were so adjusted? Do we not find that it immediately perishes whenever this adjustment ceases, and that its matter, corrupting, tries some new form? It happens indeed that the parts of the world are so well adjusted that some regular form immediately lays claim to this corrupted matter; and if it were not so, could the world subsist? Must it not dissolve, as well as the animal, and pass through new positions and situations till in great but finite succession it fall, at last, into the present or some such order?

It is well, replied Cleanthes, you told us that this hypothesis was suggested on a sudden, in the course of the argument. Had you had leisure to examine it, you would soon have perceived the insuperable objections to which it is exposed. No form, you say, can subsist unless it possess those powers and organs requisite for its subsistence; some new order or economy must be tried, and so on, without intermission, till at last some order which can support and maintain itself is fallen upon. But according to this hypothesis, whence arise the many conveniences and advantages which men and all animals possess? Two eyes, two ears are not absolutely necessary for the subsistence of the species. Human race might have been propagated and preserved without horses, dogs, cows, sheep, and those innumerable fruits and products which serve to our satisfaction and enjoyment. If no camels had been created for the use of man in the sandy deserts of Africa and Arabia, would the world have been dissolved? If no loadstone had been framed to give that wonderful and useful direction to the needle, would human society and the human kind have been immediately extinguished? Though the maxims of nature be in general very frugal, yet instances of this kind are far from being rare; and any one of them is sufficient proof of design—and of a benevolent design—which gave rise to the order and arrangement of the universe.

At least, you may safely infer, said Philo, that the foregoing hypothesis is so far incomplete and imperfect, which I shall not scruple to allow. But can we ever reasonably expect greater success in any attempts of this nature? Or can we ever hope to erect a system of cosmogony that will be liable to no exceptions, and will contain no circumstance repugnant to our limited and imperfect experience of the analogy of nature? Your theory itself cannot surely pretend to any such advantage; even though you have run into *anthropomorphism*, the better to preserve a conformity to common experience. Let us once more put it to trial. In all instances which we have ever seen, ideas are copied from real objects, and are ectypal, not archetypal, to express myself in learned terms. You reserve this order and give thought the precedence. In all instances which we have ever seen, thought has no influence upon matter except where that matter is so conjoined with it as to have an equal reciprocal influence upon it. No animal can move immediately anything but the members of its own body; and, indeed, the equality of action and reaction seems to be an universal law of nature; but your theory implies a contradiction to this experience. These instances, with many more which it were easy to collect (particularly the supposition of a mind or system of thought that is eternal or, in other words, an animal ingenerable and immortal)—these instances, I say, may teach all of us sobriety in condemning each other, and let us see that no system of this kind ought ever to be received from a slight analogy, so neither ought any to be rejected on account of a small incongruity. For that is an inconvenience from which we can justly pronounce no one to be exempted.

All religious systems, it is confessed, are subject to great and insuperable difficulties. Each disputant triumphs in his turn, while he carries on an offensive war, and exposes the absurdities, barbarities, and pernicious tenets of his antagonist. But all of them, on the whole, prepare a complete triumph for the *sceptic*, who tells them that no system ought ever to be embraced with regard to such subjects; for this plain reason, that no absurdity ought ever to be assented to with regard to any subject. A total suspense of judgment is here our only reasonable resource. And if every attack, as is commonly observed, and no defence among theologians is successful, how complete must be *his* victory who remains always, with all mankind, on the offensive, and has himself no fixed station or abiding city which he is ever, on any occasion, obliged to defend?

Part IX

But if so many difficulties attend the argument *a posteriori*, said Demea, had we not better adhere to that simple and sublime argument *a priori* which, by offering to us infallible demonstration, cuts off at once all doubt and difficulty? By this argument, too, we may prove the *infinity* of the Divine attributes, which, I am afraid, can never be ascertained with certainty from any other topic. For how can an effect which either is finite or, for aught we know, may be so—how can such an effect, I say, prove an infinite cause? The unity, too, of the Divine Nature it is very difficult, if not absolutely impossible, to deduce merely from contemplating the works of nature; nor will the uniformity alone of the plan, even were it allowed, give us any assurance of that attribute. Whereas the argument *a priori* . . .

You seem to reason, Demea, interposed Cleanthes, as if those advantages and conveniences in the abstract argument were full proofs of its solidity. But it is first proper, in my opinion, to determine what argument of this nature you choose to insist on; and we shall afterwards, from itself, better than from its *useful* consequences, endeavor to determine what value we ought to put upon it.

The argument, replied Demea, which I would insist on is the common one. Whatever exists must have a cause or reason of its existence, it being absolutely impossible for anything to produce itself or be the cause of its own existence. In mounting up, therefore, from effects to causes, we must either go on in tracing an infinite succession, without any ultimate cause at all, or must at last have recourse to some ultimate cause that is *necessarily* existent. Now, that the first supposition is absurd may be thus proved. In the infinite chain or succession of causes and effects, each single effect is determined to exist by the power and efficacy of that cause which immediately preceded; but the whole eternal chain or succession, taken together, is not determined or caused by anything; and yet it is evident that it requires a cause or reason, as much as any particular object which begins to exist in time. The question is still reasonable why this particular succession of causes existed from eternity, and not any other succession or no succession at all. If there be no necessarily existent being, any supposition which can be formed is equally possible; nor is there any more absurdity in nothing's having existed from eternity than there is in that succession of causes which constitutes the universe. What was it, then, which determined something to exist rather than nothing, and bestowed being on a particular possibility, exclusive of the rest? *External causes*, there are supposed to be none. *Chance* is a word without meaning. Was it *nothing*? But that can never produce anything. We must, therefore, have recourse to a necessarily existent Being who carries the *reason* of his existence in himself; and who cannot be supposed not to exist, without an express contradiction. There is, consequently, such a Being—that is, there is a Deity.

I shall not leave it to Philo, said Cleanthes (though I know that the starting objections is his chief delight), to point out the weakness of this metaphysical reasoning. It seems to me so obviously ill-grounded, and at the same time of so little consequence to the cause of true piety and religion, that I shall myself venture to show the fallacy of it.

I shall begin with observing that there is an evident absurdity in pretending to demonstrate a matter of fact, or to prove it by any arguments *a priori*. Nothing is demonstrable unless the contrary implies a contradiction. Nothing that is distinctly conceivable implies a contradiction. Whatever we conceive as existent, we can also conceive as non-existent. There is no being, therefore, whose non-existence implies a contradiction. Consequently there is no being whose existence is demonstrable. I propose this argument as entirely decisive, and am willing to rest the whole controversy upon it.

It is pretended that the Deity is a necessarily existent being; and this necessity of his existence is attempted to be explained by asserting that, if we knew his whole essence or nature, we should perceive it to be as impossible for him not to exist, as for twice two not

to be four. But it is evident that this can never happen, while our faculties remain the same as at present. It will still be possible for us, at any time, to conceive the non-existence of what we formerly conceived to exist; nor can the mind ever lie under a necessity of supposing any object to remain always in being; in the same manner as we lie under a necessity of always conceiving twice two to be four. The words, therefore, *necessary existence* have no meaning; or, which is the same thing, none that is consistent.

But further, why may not the material universe be the necessarily existent Being, according to this pretended explication of necessity? We dare not affirm that we know all the qualities of matter; and, for aught we can determine, it may contain some qualities which, were they known, would make its non-existence appear as great a contradiction as that twice two is five. I find only one argument employed to prove that the material world is not the necessarily existent Being; and this argument is derived from the contingency both of the matter and the form of the world. "Any particle of matter," it is said, "may be *conceived* to be annihilated, and any form may be *conceived* to be altered. Such an annihilation or alteration, therefore, is not impossible."[22] But it seems a great partiality not to perceive that the same argument extends equally to the Deity, so far as we have any conception of him; and that the mind can at least imagine him to be non-existent, or his attributes to be altered. It must be some unknown, inconceivable qualities which can make his non-existence appear impossible or his attributes unalterable: And no reason can be assigned why these qualities may not belong to matter. As they are altogether unknown and inconceivable, they can never be proved incompatible with it.

Add to this that in tracing an eternal succession of objects it seems absurd to inquire for a general cause or first author. How can anything that exists from eternity have a cause, since that relation implies a priority in time and in a beginning of existence?

In such a chain, too, or succession of objects, each part is caused by that which preceded it, and causes that which succeeds it. Where then is the difficulty?

---

22. Dr. Clark. [The quotation is from *A Demonstration of the Being and Attributes of God* by Samuel Clarke, regarding whom see Hume's *Enquiry*, n. 37.]

But the *whole*, you say, wants a cause. I answer that the uniting of these parts into a whole, like the uniting of several distinct countries into one kingdom, or several distinct members into one body, is performed merely by an arbitrary act of the mind, and has no influence on the nature of things. Did I show you the particular causes of each individual in a collection of twenty particles of matter, I should think it very unreasonable should you afterwards ask me what was the cause of the whole twenty. This is sufficiently explained in explaining the cause of the parts.

Though the reasonings which you have urged, Cleanthes, may well excuse me, said Philo, from starting any further difficulties; yet I cannot forbear insisting still upon another topic. It is observed by arithmeticians that the products of 9 compose always either 9 or some lesser product of 9 if you add together all the characters of which any of the former products is composed. Thus, of 18, 27, 36, which are products of 9, you make 9 by adding 1 to 8, 2 to 7, 3 to 6. Thus 369 is a product also of 9; and if you add 3, 6, and 9, you make 18, a lesser product of 9.[23] To a superficial observer so wonderful a regularity may be admired as the effect either of chance or design; but a skilful algebrist immediately concludes it to be the work of necessity, and demonstrates that it must forever result from the nature of these numbers. Is it not probable, I ask, that the whole economy of the universe is conducted by a like necessity, though no human algebra can furnish a key which solves the difficulty? And instead of admiring the order of natural beings, may it not happen that, could we penetrate into the intimate nature of bodies, we should clearly see why it was absolutely impossible they could ever admit of any other disposition? So dangerous is it to introduce this idea of necessity into the present question! and so naturally does it afford an inference directly opposite to the religious hypothesis!

But dropping all these abstractions, continued Philo, and confining ourselves to more familiar topics,

23. *République des Lettres*, Août 1685. [The reference is to the *Nouvelles de la république des lettres*, a journal edited in Holland by Pierre Bayle (1647–1706), a French sceptical philosopher. The article cited by Hume appeared not in the August issue, as he stated, but in the September issue and was written by Bernard le Bovier de Fontenelle (1657–1757), a French scientist and man of letters.]

I shall venture to add an observation that the argument *a priori* has seldom been found very convincing, except to people of a metaphysical head who have accustomed themselves to abstract reasoning, and who, finding from mathematics that the understanding frequently leads to truth through obscurity, and contrary to first appearances, have transferred the same habit of thinking to subjects where it ought not to have place. Other people, even of good sense and the best inclined to religion, feel always some deficiency in such arguments, though they are not perhaps able to explain distinctly where it lies—a certain proof that men ever did and ever will derive their religion from other sources than from this species of reasoning.

Part X

It is my opinion, I own, replied Demea, that each man feels, in a manner, the truth of religion within his own breast; and, from a consciousness of his imbecility and misery rather than from any reasoning, is led to seek protection from that Being on whom he and all nature are dependent. So anxious or so tedious are even the best scenes of life that futurity is still the object of all our hopes and fears. We incessantly look forward and endeavor, by prayers, adoration, and sacrifice, to appease those unknown powers whom we find, by experience, so able to afflict and oppress us. Wretched creatures that we are! What resource for us amidst the innumerable ills of life did not religion suggest some methods of atonement, and appease those terrors with which we are incessantly agitated and tormented?

I am indeed persuaded, said Philo, that the best and indeed the only method of bringing everyone to a due sense of religion is by just representations of the misery and wickedness of men. And for that purpose a talent of eloquence and strong imagery is more requisite than that of reasoning and argument. For is it necessary to prove what everyone feels within himself? It is only necessary to make us feel it, if possible, more intimately and sensibly.

The people, indeed, replied Demea, are sufficiently convinced of this great and melancholy truth. The miseries of life, the unhappiness of man, the general corruptions of our nature, the unsatisfactory enjoyment of pleasures, riches, honors—these phrases have become almost proverbial in all languages. And who can doubt of what all men declare from their own immediate feeling and experience?

In this point, said Philo, the learned are perfectly agreed with the vulgar; and in all letters, *sacred* and *profane*, the topic of human misery has been insisted on with the most pathetic eloquence that sorrow and melancholy could inspire. The poets, who speak from sentiment, without a system, and whose testimony has therefore the more authority, abound in images of this nature. From Homer down to Dr. Young,[24] the whole inspired tribe have ever been sensible that no other representation of things would suit the feeling and observation of each individual.

As to authorities, replied Demea, you need not seek them. Look round this library of Cleanthes. I shall venture to affirm that, except authors of particular sciences, such as chemistry or botany, who have no occasion to treat of human life, there is scarce one of those innumerable writers from whom the sense of human misery has not, in some passage or other, extorted a complaint and confession of it. At least, the chance is entirely on that side; and no one author has ever, so far as I can recollect, been so extravagant as to deny it.

There you must excuse me, said Philo: Leibniz has denied it, and is perhaps the first[25] who ventured upon so bold and paradoxical an opinion; at least, the first who made it essential to his philosophical system.

And by being the first, replied Demea, might he not have been sensible of his error? For is this a subject in which philosophers can propose to make discoveries especially in so late an age? And can any man hope by a simple denial (for the subject scarcely admits of reasoning) to bear down the united testimony of mankind, founded on sense and consciousness?

And why should man, added he, pretend to an exemption from the lot of all other animals? The whole earth, believe me, Philo, is cursed and polluted.

A perpetual war is kindled amongst all living creatures. Necessity, hunger, want stimulate the strong and courageous; fear, anxiety, terror agitate the weak and infirm. The first entrance into life gives anguish to the new-born infant and to its wretched parent; weakness, impotence, distress attend each stage of that life, and it is, at last, finished in agony and horror.

Observe, too, says Philo, the curious artifices of nature in order to embitter the life of every living being. The stronger prey upon the weaker and keep them in perpetual terror and anxiety. The weaker, too, in their turn, often prey upon the stronger, and vex and molest them without relaxation. Consider that innumerable race of insects, which either are bred on the body of each animal or, flying about, infix their stings in him. These insects have others still less than themselves which torment them. And thus on each hand, before and behind, above and below, every animal is surrounded with enemies which incessantly seek his misery and destruction.

Man alone, said Demea, seems to be, in part, an exception to this rule. For by combination in society he can easily master lions, tigers, and bears, whose greater strength and agility naturally enable them to prey upon him.

On the contrary, it is here chiefly, cried Philo, that the uniform and equal maxims of nature are most apparent. Man, it is true, can, by combination, surmount all his *real* enemies and become master of the whole animal creation; but does he not immediately raise up to himself *imaginary* enemies, the demons of his fancy, who haunt him with superstitious terrors and blast every enjoyment of life? His pleasure, as he imagines, becomes in their eyes a crime; his food and repose give them umbrage and offence; his very sleep and dreams furnish new materials to anxious fear; and even death, his refuge from every other ill, presents only the dread of endless and innumerable woes. Nor does the wolf molest more the timid flock than superstition does the anxious breast of wretched mortals.

Besides, consider, Demea: This very society by which we surmount those wild beasts, our natural enemies, what new enemies does it not raise to us? What woe and misery does it not occasion? Man is the greatest enemy of man. Oppression, injustice, contempt, contumely, violence, sedition, war, calumny, treachery, fraud—by these they mutually tor-

24. [The reference is to Edward Young (1683–1765), an English poet.]

25. That sentiment had been maintained by Dr. King and some few others before Leibniz, though by none of so great fame as that German philosopher. [The reference is to William King (1650–1729), an Irish clergyman who wrote *De Origine Mali* (Of the Origin of Evil).]

ment each other, and they would soon dissolve that society which they had formed were it not for the dread of still greater ills which must attend their separation.

But though these external insults, said Demea, from animals, from men, from all the elements, which assault us form a frightful catalogue of woes, they are nothing in comparison of those which arise within ourselves, from the distempered condition of our mind and body. How many lie under the lingering torment of diseases? Hear the pathetic enumeration of the great poet.

> Intestine stone and ulcer, colic-pangs,
> Demoniac frenzy, moping melancholy,
> And moon-struck madness, pining atrophy,
> Marasmus, and wide-wasting pestilence.
> Dire was the tossing, deep the groans: *Despair*
> Tended the sick, busiest from couch to couch.
> And over them triumphant *Death* his dart
> Shook: but delay'd to strike, though oft invok'd
> With vows, as their chief good and final hope.[26]

The disorders of the mind, continued Demea, though more secret, are not perhaps less dismal and vexatious. Remorse, shame, anguish, rage, disappointment, anxiety, fear, dejection, despair—who has ever passed through life without cruel inroads from these tormentors? How many have scarcely ever felt any better sensations? Labor and poverty, so abhorred by everyone, are the certain lot of the far greater number; and those few privileged persons who enjoy ease and opulence never reach contentment or true felicity. All the goods of life united would not make a very happy man, but all the ills united would make a wretch indeed; and any one of them almost (and who can be free from every one), nay, often the absence of one good (and who can possess all) is sufficient to render life ineligible.

Were a stranger to drop on a sudden into this world, I would show him, as a specimen of its ills, a hospital full of diseases, a prison crowded with malefactors and debtors, a field of battle strewed with carcasses, a fleet foundering in the ocean, a nation languishing under tyranny, famine, or pestilence. To turn the gay side of life to him and give him a notion of its pleasures—whither should I conduct him? To a ball, to an opera, to court? He might justly think that I was only showing him a diversity of distress and sorrow.

There is no evading such striking instances, said Philo, but by apologies which still further aggravate the charge. Why have all men, I ask, in all ages, complained incessantly of the miseries of life? . . . They have no just reason, says one: These complaints proceed only from their discontented, repining, anxious disposition . . . And can there possibly, I reply, be a more certain foundation of misery than such a wretched temper?

But if they were really as unhappy as they pretend, says my antagonist, why do they remain in life? . . .

Not satisfied with life, afraid of death.

This is the secret chain, say I, that holds us. We are terrified, not bribed to the continuance of our existence.

It is only a false delicacy, he may insist, which a few refined spirits indulge, and which has spread these complaints among the whole race of mankind . . . And what is this delicacy, I ask, which you blame? Is it anything but a greater sensibility to all the pleasures and pains of life? And if the man of a delicate, refined temper, by being so much more alive than the rest of the world, is only so much more unhappy, what judgment must we form in general of human life?

Let men remain at rest, says our adversary, and they will be easy. They are willing artificers of their own misery. . . . No! reply I: An anxious languor follows their repose; disappointment, vexation, trouble, their activity and ambition.

I can observe something like what you mention in some others, replied Cleanthes; but I confess I feel little or nothing of it in myself, and hope that it is not so common as you represent it.

If you feel not human misery yourself, cried Demea, I congratulate you on so happy a singularity. Others, seemingly the most prosperous, have not been ashamed to vent their complaints in the most melancholy strains. Let us attend to the great, the fortunate emperor, Charles V,[27] when, tired with human gran-

---

26. [The quotation is from John Milton's *Paradise Lost*.]

27. [Charles V (1500–1588) was king of Spain for forty years.]

deur, he resigned all his extensive dominions into the hands of his son. In the last harangue which he made on that memorable occasion, he publicly avowed *that the greatest prosperities which he had ever enjoyed had been mixed with so many adversities that he might truly say he had never enjoyed any satisfaction or contentment.* But did the retired life in which he sought for shelter afford him any greater happiness? If we may credit his son's account, his repentance commenced the very day of his resignation.

Cicero's fortune, from small beginnings, rose to the greatest luster and renown; yet what pathetic complaints of all ills of life do his familiar letters, as well as philosophical discourses, contain? And suitably to his own experience, he introduces Cato,[28] the great, the fortunate Cato protesting in his old age that had he a new life in his offer he would reject the present.

As yourself, ask any of your acquaintance, whether they would live over again the last ten or twenty years of their life. No! but the next twenty, they say, will be better:

> And from the dregs of life, hope to receive
> What the first sprightly running could not give.[29]

Thus, at last, they find (such is the greatness of human misery, it reconciles even contradictions) that they complain at once of the shortness of life and of its vanity and sorrow.

And is it possible, Cleanthes, said Philo, that after all these reflections, and infinitely more which might be suggested, you can still persevere in your anthropomorphism, and assert the moral attributes of the Deity, his justice, benevolence, mercy, and rectitude, to be of the same nature with these virtues in human creatures? His power, we allow, is infinite; whatever he wills is executed; but neither man nor any other animal is happy; therefore, he does not will their happiness. His wisdom is infinite; he is never mistaken in choosing the means to any end; but the course of nature tends not to human or animal felicity; therefore, it is not established for that purpose. Through

the whole compass of human knowledge there are no inferences more certain and infallible than these. In what respect, then, do his benevolence and mercy resemble the benevolence and mercy of men?

Epicurus' old questions are yet unanswered.

Is he willing to prevent evil, but not able? then is he impotent. Is he able, but not willing? then is he malevolent. Is he both able and willing? whence then is evil?

You ascribe, Cleanthes (and I believe justly), a purpose and intention to nature. But what, I beseech you, is the object of that curious artifice and machinery which she has displayed in all animals—the preservation alone of individuals, and propagation of the species? It seems enough for her purpose, if such a rank be barely upheld in the universe, without any care or concern for the happiness of the members that compose it. No resource for this purpose: no machinery in order merely to give pleasure or ease: no fund of pure joy and contentment: no indulgence without some want or necessity accompanying it. At least, the few phenomena of this nature are overbalanced by opposite phenomena of still greater importance.

Our sense of music, harmony, and indeed beauty of all kinds, gives satisfaction, without being absolutely necessary to the preservation and propagation of the species. But what racking pains, on the other hand, arise from gouts, gravels, megrims, toothaches, rheumatisms, where the injury to the animal machinery is either small or incurable? Mirth, laughter, play, frolic seem gratuitous satisfactions which have no further tendency; spleen, melancholy, discontent, superstition are pains of the same nature. How then does the divine benevolence display itself, in the sense of you anthropomorphites? None but we mystics, as you were pleased to call us, can account for this strange mixture of phenomena, by deriving it from attributes infinitely perfect but incomprehensible.

And have you, at last, said Cleanthes smiling, betrayed your intentions, Philo? Your long agreement with Demea did indeed a little surprise me, but I find you were all the while erecting a concealed battery against me. And I must confess that you have now fallen upon a subject worthy of your noble spirit of opposition and controversy. If you can make out the present point, and prove mankind to be unhappy or corrupted, there is an end at once of all religion.

---

28. [The reference is to Marcus Porcius Cato the Elder (234–149 B.C.), a Roman statesman.]

29. [The quotation is from John Dryden's *Aurengzebe*.]

For to what purpose establish the natural attributes of the Deity, while the moral are still doubtful and uncertain?

You take umbrage very easily, replied Demea, at opinions the most innocent and the most generally received, even amongst the religious and devout themselves; and nothing can be more surprising than to find a topic like this—concerning the wickedness and misery of man—charged with no less than atheism and profaneness. Have not all pious divines and preachers who have indulged their rhetoric on so fertile a subject; have they not easily, I say, given a solution of any difficulties which may attend it? This world is but a point in comparison of the universe; this life but a moment in comparison of eternity. The present evil phenomena, therefore, are rectified in other regions, and in some future period of existence. And the eyes of men, being then opened to larger views of things, see the whole connection of general laws, and trace, with adoration, the benevolence and rectitude of the Deity through all the mazes and intricacies of his providence.

No! replied Cleanthes, no! These arbitrary suppositions can never be admitted, contrary to matter of fact, visible and uncontroverted. Whence can any cause be known but from its known effects? Whence can any hypothesis be proved but from the apparent phenomena? To establish one hypothesis upon another is building entirely in the air; and the utmost we ever attain by these conjectures and fictions is to ascertain the bare possibility of our opinion, but never can we, upon such terms, establish its reality.

The only method of supporting divine benevolence—and it is what I willingly embrace—is to deny absolutely the misery and wickedness of man. Your representations are exaggerated; your melancholy views mostly fictitious; your inferences contrary to fact and experience. Health is more common than sickness; pleasure than pain; happiness than misery. And for one vexation which we meet with, we attain, upon computation, a hundred enjoyments.

Admitting your position, replied Philo, which yet is extremely doubtful, you must at the same time allow that, if pain be less frequent than pleasure, it is infinitely more violent and durable. One hour of it is often able to outweigh a day, a week, a month of our common insipid enjoyments; and how many days, weeks, and months are passed by several in

the most acute torments? Pleasure, scarcely in one instance, is ever able to reach ecstasy and rapture; and in no one instance can it continue for any time at its highest pitch and altitude. The spirits evaporate, the nerves relax, the fabric is disordered, and the enjoyment quickly degenerates into fatigue and uneasiness. But pain often, good God, how often! rises to torture and agony; and the longer it continues, it becomes still more genuine agony and torture. Patience is exhausted, courage languishes, melancholy seizes us, and nothing terminates our misery but the removal of its cause or another event which is the sole cure of all evil, but which, from our natural folly, we regard with still greater horror and consternation.

But not to insist upon these topics, continued Philo, though most obvious, certain, and important, I must use the freedom to admonish you, Cleanthes, that you have put the controversy upon a most dangerous issue, and are unawares introducing a total scepticism into the most essential articles of natural and revealed theology. What! no method of fixing a just foundation for religion unless we allow the happiness of human life, and maintain a continued existence even in this world, with all our present pains, infirmities, vexations, and follies, to be eligible and desirable! But this is contrary to everyone's feeling and experience; it is contrary to an authority so established as nothing can subvert. No decisive proofs can ever be produced against this authority; nor is it possible for you to compute, estimate, and compare all the pains and all the pleasures in the lives of all men and of all animals; and thus, by your resting the whole system of religion on a point which, from its very nature, must forever be uncertain, you tacitly confess that that system is equally uncertain.

But allowing you what never will be believed, at least, what you never possibly can prove, that animal or, at least, human happiness in this life exceeds its misery, you have yet done nothing; for this is not, by any means, what we expect from infinite power, infinite wisdom, and infinite goodness. Why is there any misery at all in the world? Not by chance, surely. From some cause then. Is it from the intention of the Deity? But he is perfectly benevolent. Is it contrary to his intention? But he is almighty. Nothing can shake the solidity of this reasoning, so short, so clear, so decisive, except we assert that these subjects exceed all human capacity, and that our common measures

of truth and falsehood are not applicable to them —
a topic which I have all along insisted on, but which
you have, from the beginning, rejected with scorn
and indignation.

But I will be contented to retire still from this
intrenchment, for I deny that you can ever force
me in it. I will allow that pain or misery in man is
compatible with infinite power and goodness in the
Deity, even in your sense of these attributes: what
are you advanced by all these concessions? A mere
possible compatibility is not sufficient. You must *prove*
these pure, unmixed and uncontrollable attributes
from the present mixed and confused phenomena,
and from these alone. A hopeful undertaking! Were
the phenomena ever so pure and unmixed, yet, being
finite, they would be insufficient for that purpose.
How much more, where they are also so jarring
and discordant!

Here, Cleanthes, I find myself at ease in my argument. Here I triumph. Formerly, when we argued
concerning the natural attributes of intelligence and
design, I needed all my sceptical and metaphysical
subtilty to elude your grasp. In many views of the
universe and of its parts, particularly the latter, the
beauty and fitness of final causes strike us with such
irresistible force that all objections appear (what I
believe they really are) mere cavils and sophisms; nor
can we then imagine how it was ever possible for us
to repose any weight on them. But there is no view
of human life or of the condition of mankind from
which, without the greatest violence, we can infer
the moral attributes or learn that infinite benevolence,
conjoined with infinite power and infinite wisdom,
which we must discover by the eyes of faith alone.
It is your turn now to tug the laboring oar, and to
support your philosophical subtilties against the dictates of plain reason and experience.

Part XI

I scruple not to allow, said Cleanthes, that I have
been apt to suspect the frequent repetition of the
word *infinite*, which we meet with in all theological
writers, to savor more of panegyric than of philosophy,
and that any purposes of reasoning, and even of religion, would be better served were we to rest contented
with more accurate and more moderate expressions.
The terms *admirable*, *excellent*, *superlatively great*,

wise, and *holy* — these sufficiently fill the imaginations
of men, and anything beyond, besides that it leads
into absurdities, has no influence on the affections
or sentiments. Thus, in the present subject, if we
abandon all human analogy, as seems your intention,
Demea, I am afraid we abandon all religion and retain
no conception of the great object of our adoration.
If we preserve human analogy, we must forever find
it impossible to reconcile any mixture of evil in the
universe with infinite attributes; much less can we
ever prove the latter from the former. But supposing
the Author of Nature to be finitely perfect, though
far exceeding mankind, a satisfactory account may
then be given of natural and moral evil, and every
untoward phenomenon be explained and adjusted.
A less evil may then be chosen in order to avoid a
greater; inconveniences be submitted to in order to
reach a desirable end; and, in a word, benevolence,
regulated by wisdom and limited by necessity, may
produce just such a world as the present. You, Philo,
who are so prompt at starting views and reflections
and analogies, I would gladly hear, at length, without
interruption, your opinion of this new theory; and if
it deserves our attention, we may afterwards, at more
leisure, reduce it into form.

My sentiments, replied Philo, are not worth being
made a mystery of; and, therefore, without any cere-
mony, I shall deliver what occurs to me with regard
to the present subject. It must, I think, be allowed
that, if a very limited intelligence whom we shall
suppose utterly unacquainted with the universe were
assured that it were the production of a very good,
wise, and powerful being, however finite, he would,
from his conjectures, form *beforehand* a different notion of it from what we find it to be by experience;
nor would he ever imagine, merely from these attributes of the cause of which he is informed, that the
effect could be so full of vice and misery and disorder,
as it appears in this life. Supposing now that this
person were brought into the world, still assured that
it was the workmanship of such a sublime and benevolent being, he might, perhaps, be surprised at the
disappointment, but would never retract his former
belief if founded on any very solid argument, since
such a limited intelligence must be sensible of his
own blindness and ignorance, and must allow that
there may be many solutions of those phenomena
which will forever escape his comprehension. But

supposing, which is the real case with regard to man, that this creature is not antecedently convinced of a supreme intelligence, benevolent, and powerful, but is left to gather such a belief from the appearances of things—this entirely alters the case, nor will he ever find any reason for such a conclusion. He may be fully convinced of the narrow limits of his understanding, but this will not help him in forming an inference concerning the goodness of superior powers, since he must form that inference from what he knows, not from what he is ignorant of. The more you exaggerate his weakness and ignorance, the more diffident you render him, and give him the greater suspicion that such subjects are beyond the reach of his faculties. You are obliged, therefore, to reason with him merely from the known phenomena, and to drop every arbitrary supposition or conjecture.

Did I show you a house or palace where there was not one apartment convenient or agreeable; where the windows, doors, fires, passages, stairs, and the whole economy of the building were the source of noise, confusion, fatigue, darkness, and the extremes of heat and cold, you would certainly blame the contrivance, without any further examination. The architect would in vain display his subtilty, and prove to you that, if this door or that window were altered, greater ills would ensue. What he says may be strictly true: The alteration of one particular, while the other parts of the building remain, may only augment the inconveniences. But still you would assert in general that, if the architect had had skill and good intentions, he might have formed such a plan of the whole, and might have adjusted the parts in such a manner as would have remedied all or most of these inconveniences. His ignorance, or even your own ignorance of such a plan, will never convince you of the impossibility of it. If you find any inconveniences and deformities in the building, you will always, without entering into any detail, condemn the architect.

In short, I repeat the question: Is the world, considered in general and as it appears to us in this life, different from what a man or such a limited being would, *beforehand*, expect from a very powerful, wise, and benevolent Deity? It must be strange prejudice to assert the contrary. And from thence I conclude that, however consistent the world may be, allowing certain suppositions and conjectures with the idea of such a Deity, it can never afford us an inference

concerning his existence. The consistency is not absolutely denied, only the inference. Conjectures, especially where infinity is excluded from the divine attributes, may perhaps be sufficient to prove a consistency, but can never be foundations for any inference.

There seem to be *four* circumstances on which depend all or the greatest part of the ills that molest sensible creatures; and it is not impossible but all these circumstances may be necessary and unavoidable. We know so little beyond common life, or even of common life, that, with regard to the economy of a universe, there is no conjecture, however wild, which may not be just; nor any one, however plausible, which may not be erroneous. All that belongs to human understanding, in this deep ignorance and obscurity, is to be sceptical or at least cautious, and not to admit of any hypothesis whatever, much less of any which is supported by no appearance of probability. Now this I assert to be the case with regard to all the causes of evil and the circumstances on which it depends. None of them appear to human reason in the least degree necessary or unavoidable, nor can we suppose them such, without the utmost license of imagination.

The *first* circumstance which introduces evil is that contrivance or economy of the animal creation by which pains, as well as pleasures, are employed to excite all creatures to action, and make them vigilant in the great work of self-preservation. Now pleasure alone, in its various degrees, seems to human understanding sufficient for this purpose. All animals might be constantly in a state of enjoyment; but when urged by any of the necessities of nature, such as thirst, hunger, weariness; instead of pain, they might feel a diminution of pleasure by which they might be prompted to seek that object which is necessary to their subsistence. Men pursue pleasure as eagerly as they avoid pain; at least, they might have been so constituted. It seems, therefore, plainly possible to carry on the business of life without any pain. Why then is any animal ever rendered susceptible of such a sensation? If animals can be free from it an hour, they might enjoy a perpetual exemption from it, and it required as particular a contrivance of their organs to produce that feeling as to endow them with sight, hearing, or any of the senses. Shall we conjecture that such a contrivance was necessary, without any appearance of reason; and shall we build on that conjecture as on the most certain truth?

But a capacity of pain would not alone produce pain were it not for the *second* circumstance, viz., the conducting of the world by general laws; and this seems nowise necessary to a very perfect being. It is true, if everything were conducted by particular volitions, the course of nature would be perpetually broken, and no man could employ his reason in the conduct of life. But might not other particular volitions remedy this inconvenience? In short, might not the Deity exterminate all ill, wherever it were to be found, and produce all good, without any preparation or long progress of causes and effects?

Besides, we must consider that, according to the present economy of the world, the course of nature, though supposed exactly regular, yet to us appears not so, and many events are uncertain, and many disappoint our expectations. Health and sickness, calm and tempest, with an infinite number of other accidents whose causes are unknown and variable, have a great influence both on the fortunes of particular persons and on the prosperity of public societies; and indeed all human life, in a manner, depends on such accidents. A being, therefore, who knows the secret springs of the universe might easily, by particular volitions, turn all these accidents to the good of mankind and render the whole world happy, without discovering himself in any operation. A fleet whose purposes were salutary to society might always meet with a fair wind; good princes enjoy sound health and long life; persons born to power and authority be framed with good tempers and virtuous dispositions. A few such events as these, regularly and wisely conducted, would change the face of the world; and yet would no more seem to disturb the course of nature or confound human conduct than the present economy of things where the causes are secret and variable and compounded. Some small torches given to Caligula's[30] brain in his infancy might have converted him into a Trajan.[31] One wave, a little higher than the rest, by burying Caesar and his fortune in the bottom of the ocean, might have restored liberty to a consider-

able part of mankind. There may, for aught we know, be good reasons why Providence interposes not in this manner, but they are unknown to us; and, though the mere supposition that such reasons exist may be sufficient to *save* the conclusion concerning the divine attributes, yet surely it can never be sufficient to *establish* that conclusion.

If everything in the universe be conducted by general laws, and if animals be rendered susceptible of pain, it scarcely seems possible but some ill must arise in the various shocks of matter and the various concurrence and opposition of general laws; but this ill would be very rare were it not for the *third* circumstance which I proposed to mention, viz., the great frugality with which all powers and faculties are distributed to every particular being. So well adjusted are the organs and capacities of all animals, and so well fitted to their preservation, that, as far as history or tradition reaches, there appears not to be any single species which has yet been extinguished in the universe. Every animal has the requisite endowments, but these endowments are bestowed with so scrupulous an economy that any considerable diminution must entirely destroy the creature. Wherever one power is increased, there is a proportional abatement in the other. Animals which excel in swiftness are commonly defective in force. Those which possess both are either imperfect in some of their senses or are oppressed with the most craving wants. The human species, whose chief excellence is reason and sagacity, is of all others the most necessitous, and the most deficient in bodily advantages, without clothes, without arms, without food, without lodging, without any convenience of life, except what they owe to their own skill and industry. In short, nature seems to have formed an exact calculation of the necessities of her creatures; and, like a *rigid master,* has afforded them little more powers or endowments than what are strictly sufficient to supply those necessities. An *indulgent parent* would have bestowed a large stock in order to guard against accidents, and secure the happiness and welfare of the creature in the most unfortunate concurrence of circumstances. Every course of life would not have been so surrounded with precipices that the least departure from the true path, by mistake or necessity, must involve us in misery and ruin. Some reserve, some fund, would have been provided to ensure happiness, nor would the powers

---

30. [Caligula (12–41) was a Roman emperor renowned for his cruelty.]

31. [Trajan (c.53–117) was a Roman emperor who pursued benevolent social policies.]

and the necessities have been adjusted with so rigid an economy. The Author of Nature is inconceivably powerful; his force is supposed great, if not altogether inexhaustible; nor is there any reason, as far as we can judge, to make him observe this strict frugality in his dealings with his creatures. It would have been better, were his power extremely limited, to have created fewer animals, and to have endowed these with more faculties for their happiness and preservation. A builder is never esteemed prudent who undertakes a plan beyond what his stock will enable him to finish.

In order to cure most of the ills of human life, I require not that man should have the wings of the eagle, the swiftness of the stag, the force of the ox, the arms of the lion, the scales of the crocodile or rhinoceros; much less do I demand the sagacity of an angel or cherubim. I am contented to take an increase in one single power or faculty of his soul. Let him be endowed with a greater propensity to industry and labor, a more vigorous spring and activity of mind, a more constant bent to business and application. Let the whole species possess naturally an equal diligence with that which many individuals are able to attain by habit and reflection, and the most beneficial consequences, without any allay of ill, is the immediate and necessary result of this endowment. Almost all the moral as well as natural evils of human life arise from idleness; and were our species, by the original constitution of their frame, exempt from this vice or infirmity, the perfect cultivation of land, the improvement of arts and manufactures, the exact execution of every office and duty, immediately follow; and men at once may fully reach that state of society which is so imperfectly attained by the best regulated government. But as industry is a power, and the most valuable of any, nature seems determined, suitably to her usual maxims, to bestow it on men with a very sparing hand; and rather to punish him severely for his deficiency in it than to reward him for his attainments. She has so contrived his frame that nothing but the most violent necessity can oblige him to labor; and she employs all his other wants to overcome, at least in part, the want of diligence, and to endow him with some share of a faculty of which she has thought fit naturally to bereave him. Here our demands may be allowed very humble, and therefore the more reasonable. If we required the endowments of superior

penetration and judgment, of a more delicate taste of beauty, of a nicer sensibility to benevolence and friendship, we might be told that we impiously pretend to break the order of nature, that we want to exalt ourselves into a higher rank of being, that the presents which we require, not being suitable to our state and condition, would only be pernicious to us. But it is hard, I dare to repeat it, it is hard that, being placed in a world so full of wants and necessities, where almost every being and element is either our foe or refuses its assistance . . . we should also have our own temper to struggle with, and should be deprived of that faculty which can alone fence against these multiplied evils.

The *fourth* circumstance whence arises the misery and ill of the universe is the inaccurate workmanship of all the springs and principles of the great machine of nature. It must be acknowledged that there are few parts of the universe which seem not to serve some purpose, and whose removal would not produce a visible defect and disorder in the whole. The parts hang all together, nor can one be touched without affecting the rest, in a greater or less degree. But at the same time, it must be observed that none of these parts or principles, however useful, are so accurately adjusted as to keep precisely within those bounds in which their utility consists; but they are, all of them, apt, on every occasion, to run into the one extreme or the other. One would imagine that this grand production had not received the last hand of the maker—so little finished is every part, and so coarse are the strokes with which it is executed. Thus the winds are requisite to convey the vapors along the surface of the globe, and to assist men in navigation; but how often, rising up to tempests and hurricanes, do they become pernicious? Rains are necessary to nourish all the plants and animals of the earth; but how often are they defective? how often excessive? Heat is requisite to all life and vegetation, but is not always found in the due proportion. On the mixture and secretion of the humors and juices of the body depend the health and prosperity of the animal; but the parts perform not regularly their proper function. What more useful than all the passions of the mind, ambition, vanity, love, anger? But how often do they break their bounds and cause the greatest convulsions in society? There is nothing so advantageous in the universe but what frequently becomes pernicious, by its excess or defect; nor has nature guarded, with the requisite accuracy, against all disorder or confusion. The irregularity is never perhaps so great as to destroy any species, but is often sufficient to involve the individuals in ruin and misery.

On the concurrence, then, of these *four* circumstances does all or the greatest part of natural evil depend. Were all living creatures incapable of pain, or were the world administered by particular volitions, evil never could have found access into the universe; and were animals endowed with a large stock of powers and faculties, beyond what strict necessity requires, or were the several springs and principles of the universe so accurately framed as to preserve always the just temperament and medium, there must have been very little ill in comparison of what we feel at present. What then shall we pronounce on this occasion? Shall we say that these circumstances are not necessary, and that they might easily have been altered in the contrivance of the universe? This decision seems too presumptuous for creatures so blind and ignorant. Let us be more modest in our conclusions. Let us allow that, if the goodness of the Deity (I mean a goodness like the human) could be established on any tolerable reasons *a priori*, these phenomena, however untoward, would not be sufficient to subvert that principle, but might easily, in some unknown manner, be reconcilable to it. But let us still assert that, as this goodness is not antecedently established but must be inferred from the phenomena, there can be no grounds for such an inference while there are so many ills in the universe, and while these ills might so easily have been remedied, as far as human understanding can be allowed to judge on such a subject. I am sceptic enough to allow that the bad appearances, notwithstanding all my reasonings, may be compatible with such attributes as you suppose, but surely they can never prove these attributes. Such a conclusion cannot result from scepticism, but must arise from the phenomena, and from our confidence in the reasonings which we deduce from these phenomena.

Look round this universe. What an immense profusion of beings, animated and organized, sensible and active! You admire this prodigious variety and fecundity. But inspect a little more narrowly these living existences, the only beings worth regarding. How hostile and destructive to each other! How insufficient all of them for their own happiness! How contemptible or odious to the spectator! The whole presents nothing but the idea of a blind nature, impregnated by a great vivifying principle, and pouring forth from her lap, without discernment or parental care, her maimed and abortive children!

Here the Manichaean[32] system occurs as a proper hypothesis to solve the difficulty; and, no doubt, in some respects it is very specious and has more probability than the common hypothesis, by giving a plausible account of the strange mixture of good and ill which appears in life. But if we consider, on the other hand, the perfect uniformity and agreement of the parts of the universe, we shall not discover in it any marks of the combat of a malevolent with a benevolent being. There is indeed an opposition of pains and pleasures in the feelings of sensible creatures; but are not all the operations of nature carried on by an opposition of principles, of hot and cold, moist and dry, light and heavy? The true conclusion is that the original source of all things is entirely indifferent to all these principles, and has no more regard to good above ill than to heat above cold, or to drought above moisture, or to light above heavy.

There may *four* hypotheses be framed concerning the first causes of the universe: that they are endowed with perfect goodness; that they have perfect malice; that they are opposite and have both goodness and malice; that they have neither goodness nor malice. Mixed phenomena can never prove the two former unmixed principles; and the uniformity and steadiness of general laws seem to oppose the third. The fourth, therefore, seems by far the most probable.

What I have said concerning natural evil will apply to moral with little or no variation; and we have no more reason to infer that the rectitude of the Supreme Being resembles human rectitude than that his benevolence resembles the human. Nay, it will be thought that we have still greater cause to exclude from him moral sentiments, such as we feel them, since moral evil, in the opinion of many, is much more predominant above moral good than natural evil above natural good.

---

32. [Manichaeism, a religion founded by the Persian Mani (c.216–c.276), strongly influenced the development of Christianity. Basic to the Manichaean outlook is the doctrine that the universe is the scene of an eternal struggle between two antagonistic powers, Light and Darkness (or Good and Evil).]

But even though this should not be allowed, and though the virtue which is in mankind should be acknowledged much superior to the vice; yet, so long as there is any vice at all in the universe, it will very much puzzle you anthropomorphites how to account for it. You must assign a cause for it, without having recourse to the first cause. But as every effect must have a cause, and that cause another, you must either carry on the progression *in infinitum* or rest on that original principle, who is the ultimate cause of all things. . . .

Hold! hold! cried Demea: Whither does your imagination hurry you? I joined in alliance with you in order to prove the incomprehensible nature of the Divine Being, and refute the principles of Cleanthes, who would measure everything by human rule and standard. But I now find you running into all the topics of the greatest libertines and infidels, and betraying that holy cause which you seemingly espoused. Are you secretly, then, a more dangerous enemy than Cleanthes himself?

And are you so late in perceiving it? replied Cleanthes. Believe me, Demea, your friend Philo, from the beginning, has been amusing himself at both our expense; and it must be confessed that the injudicious reasoning of our vulgar theology has given him but too just a handle of ridicule. The total infirmity of human reason, the absolute incomprehensibility of the Divine Nature, the great and universal misery, and still greater wickedness of men — these are strange topics, surely, to be so fondly cherished by orthodox divines and doctors. In ages of stupidity and ignorance, indeed, these principles may safely be espoused; and perhaps no views of things are more proper to promote superstition than such as encourage the blind amazement, the diffidence, and melancholy of mankind. But at present . . .

Blame not so much, interposed Philo, the ignorance of these reverend gentlemen. They know how to change their style with the times. Formerly, it was a most popular theological topic to maintain that human life was vanity and misery, and to exaggerate all the ills and pains which are incident to men. But of late years, divines, we find, begin to retract this position and maintain, though still with some hesitation, that there are more goods than evils, more pleasures than pains, even in this life. When religion stood entirely upon temper and education, it was thought proper to encourage melancholy; as indeed, mankind never have recourse to superior powers so readily as in that disposition. But as men have now learned to form principles and to draw consequences, it is necessary to change the batteries, and to make use of such arguments as will endure at least some scrutiny and examination. This variation is the same (and from the same causes) with that which I formerly remarked with regard to scepticism.

Thus Philo continued to the last his spirit of opposition, and his censure of established opinions. But I could observe that Demea did not at all relish the latter part of the discourse; and he took occasion soon after, on some pretence or other, to leave the company.

Part XII

After Demea's departure, Cleanthes and Philo continued the conversation in the following manner. Our friend, I am afraid, said Cleanthes, will have little inclination to revive this topic of discourse while you are in company; and to tell the truth, Philo, I should rather wish to reason with either of you apart on a subject so sublime and interesting. Your spirit of controversy, joined to your abhorrence of vulgar superstition, carries you strange lengths when engaged in an argument; and there is nothing so sacred and venerable, even in your own eyes, which you spare on that occasion.

I must confess, replied Philo, that I am less cautious on the subject of Natural Religion than on any other; both because I know that I can never, on that head, corrupt the principles of any man of common sense and because no one, I am confident, in whose eyes I appear a man of common sense will ever mistake my intentions. You, in particular, Cleanthes, with whom I live in unreserved intimacy; you are sensible that, notwithstanding the freedom of my conversation and my love of singular arguments, no one has a deeper sense of religion impressed on his mind, or pays more profound adoration to the Divine Being, as he discovers himself to reason in the inexplicable contrivance and artifice of nature. A purpose, an intention, a design strikes everywhere the most careless, the most stupid thinker; and no man can be so hardened in absurd systems as at all times to reject it. *That nature does nothing in vain* is a maxim established in all the schools, merely from the contemplation of the works of nature, without any religious purpose; and, from a firm conviction of its truth, an anatomist who had observed a new organ or canal would never be satisfied till he had also discovered its use and intention. One great foundation of the Copernican system is the maxim *that nature acts by the simplest methods, and chooses the most proper means to any end*; and astronomers often, without thinking of it, lay this strong foundation of piety and religion. The same thing is observable in other parts of philosophy; and thus all the sciences almost lead us insensibly to acknowledge a first intelligent Author; and their authority is often so much the greater as they do not directly profess that intention.

It is with pleasure I hear Galen[33] reason concerning the structure of the human body. The anatomy of a man, says he, discovers above 600 different muscles; and whoever duly considers these will find that, in each of them, nature must have adjusted at least ten different circumstances in order to attain the end which she proposed: proper figure, just magnitude, right disposition of the several ends, upper and lower position of the whole, the due insertion of the several nerves, veins, and arteries; so that, in the muscles alone, above 6000 several views and intentions must have been formed and executed. The bones he calculates to be 284; the distinct purposes aimed at in the structure of each, above forty. What a prodigious display of artifice, even in these simple and homogeneous parts! But if we consider the skin, ligaments, vessels, glandules, humors, the several limbs and members of the body, how must our astonishment rise upon us, in proportion to the number and intricacy of the parts so artificially adjusted! The further we advance in these researches, we discover new scenes of art and wisdom; but descry still, at a distance, further scenes beyond our reach; in the fine internal structure of the parts, in the economy of the brain, in the fabric of the seminal vessels. All these artifices are repeated in every different species of animal, with wonderful variety, and with exact propriety, suited to the different

intentions of nature in framing each species. And if the infidelity of Galen, even when these natural sciences were still imperfect, could not withstand such striking appearances, to what pitch of pertinacious obstinacy must a philosopher in this age have attained who can now doubt of a Supreme Intelligence!

Could I meet with one of this species (who, I thank God, are very rare), I would ask him: Supposing there were a God who did not discover himself immediately to our senses, were it possible for him to give stronger proofs of his existence than what appear on the whole face of nature? What indeed could such a Divine Being do but copy the present economy of things, render many of his artifices so plain that no stupidity could mistake them, afford glimpses of still greater artifices which demonstrate his prodigious superiority above our narrow apprehensions, and conceal altogether a great many from such imperfect creatures? Now, according to all rules of just reasoning, every fact must pass for undisputed when it is supported by all the arguments which its nature admits of, even though these arguments be not, in themselves, very numerous or forcible: How much more in the present case where no human imagination can compute their number, and no understanding estimate their cogency.

I shall further add, said Cleanthes, to what you have so well urged, that one great advantage of the principle of theism is that it is the only system of cosmogony which can be rendered intelligible and complete, and yet can throughout preserve a strong analogy to what we every day see and experience in the world. The comparison of the universe to a machine of human contrivance is so obvious and natural, and is justified by so many instances of order and design in nature, that it must immediately strike all unprejudiced apprehensions and procure universal approbation. Whoever attempts to weaken this theory cannot pretend to succeed by establishing in its place any other that is precise and determinate: It is sufficient for him if he start doubts and difficulties; and, by remote and abstract views of things reach that suspense of judgment which is here the utmost boundary of his wishes. But, besides that this state of mind is in itself unsatisfactory, it can never be steadily maintained against such striking appearances as continually engage us into the religious hypothesis. A

33. *De Formatione Foetus.* [Galen (c.130–c.200) was a Greek physician and devotee of philosophy who served at the court of Marcus Aurelius (regarding whom, see Hume's *Enquiry*, n. 58) and wrote prolifically, most notably in the fields of anatomy and physiology.]

false, absurd system, human nature, from the force of prejudice, is capable of adhering to with obstinacy and perseverance; but no system at all, in opposition to a theory supported by strong and obvious reason, by natural propensity, and by early education, I think it absolutely impossible to maintain or defend.

So little, replied Philo, do I esteem this suspense of judgment in the present case to be possible that I am apt to suspect there enters somewhat of a dispute of words into this controversy, more than is usually imagined. That the works of nature bear a great analogy to the productions of art is evident; and, according to all the rules of good reasoning, we ought to infer, if we argue at all concerning them, that their causes have a proportional analogy. But as there are also considerable differences, we have reason to suppose a proportional difference in the causes, and, in particular, ought to attribute a much higher degree of power and energy to the supreme cause than any we have ever observed in mankind. Here, then, the existence of a *Deity* is plainly ascertained by reason; and if we make it a question whether, on account of these analogies, we can properly call him a *mind* or *intelligence*, notwithstanding the vast difference which may reasonably be supposed between him and human minds; what is this but a mere verbal controversy? No man can deny the analogies between the effects: to restrain ourselves from inquiring concerning the causes is scarcely possible. From this inquiry the legitimate conclusion is that the causes have also an analogy; and if we are not contented with calling the first and supreme cause a *God* or *Deity*, but desire to vary the expression, what can we call him but *Mind* or *Thought*, to which he is justly supposed to bear a considerable resemblance?

All men of sound reason are disgusted with verbal disputes, which abound so much in philosophical and theological inquiries; and it is found that the only remedy for this abuse must arise from clear definitions, from the precision of those ideas which enter into any argument, and from the strict and uniform use of those terms which are employed. But there is a species of controversy which, from the very nature of language and of human ideas, is involved in perpetual ambiguity, and can never, by any precaution or any definitions, be able to reach a reasonable certainty or precision. These are the controversies concerning the degrees of any quality or circum-

stance. Men may argue to all eternity whether Hannibal be a great, or a very great, or a superlatively great man, what degree of beauty Cleopatra possessed, what epithet of praise Livy or Thucydides[34] is entitled to, without bringing the controversy to any determination. The disputants may here agree in their sense and differ in the terms, or *vice versa*, yet never be able to define their terms so as to enter into each other's meaning; because the degrees of these qualities are not, like quantity or number, susceptible of any exact mensuration, which may be the standard in the controversy. That the dispute concerning theism is of this nature, and consequently is merely verbal, or, perhaps, if possible, still more incurably ambiguous, will appear upon the slightest inquiry. I ask the theist if he does not allow that there is a great and immeasurable, because incomprehensible, difference between the *human* and the *divine* mind: The more pious he is, the more readily will he assent to the affirmative, and the more will he be disposed to magnify the difference; he will even assert that the difference is of a nature which cannot be too much magnified. I next turn to the atheist, who, I assert, is only nominally so and can never possibly be in earnest, and I ask him whether, from the coherence and apparent sympathy in all the parts of this world, there be not a certain degree of analogy among all the operations of nature, in every situation and in every age; whether the rotting of a turnip, the generation of an animal, and the structure of human thought, be not energies that probably bear some remote analogy to each other. It is impossible he can deny it: He will readily acknowledge it. Having obtained this concession, I push him still further in his retreat, and I ask him if it be not probable that the principle which first arranged and still maintains order in this universe bears not also some remote inconceivable analogy to the other operations of nature and, among the rest, to the economy of human mind and thought. However reluctant, he must give his assent. Where then, cry I to both these antagonists, is the subject of your dispute? The theist allows that the original intelligence is very different from human reason; the atheist allows that the original principle of order bears some remote analogy to it. Will you quarrel, Gentle-

34. [Thucydides (c.460–400 B.C.) was the noted Greek historian who authored the *History of the Peloponnesian War*.]

men, about the degrees, and enter into a controversy which admits not of any precise meaning, nor consequently of any determination? If you should be so obstinate, I should not be surprised to find you insensibly change sides; while the theist, on the one hand, exaggerates the dissimilarity between the Supreme Being and frail, imperfect, variable, fleeting, and mortal creatures; and the atheist, on the other, magnifies the analogy among all the operations of nature, in every period, every situation, and every position. Consider then where the real point of controversy lies; and if you cannot lay aside your disputes, endeavor, at least, to cure yourselves of your animosity.

And here I must also acknowledge, Cleanthes, that, as the works of nature have a much greater analogy to the effects of *our* art and contrivance than to those of *our* benevolence and justice, we have reason to infer that the natural attributes of the Deity have a greater resemblance to those of men than his moral have to human virtues. But what is the consequence? Nothing but this, that the moral qualities of man are more defective in their kind than his natural abilities. For, as the Supreme Being is allowed to be absolutely and entirely perfect, whatever differs most from him departs the farthest from the supreme standard of rectitude and perfection.[35]

These, Cleanthes, are my unfeigned sentiments on this subject; and these sentiments, you know, I have ever cherished and maintained. But in proportion to my veneration for true religion is my abhorrence of vulgar superstitions; and I indulge a peculiar pleasure, I confess, in pushing such principles sometimes into

absurdity, sometimes into impiety. And you are sensible that all bigots, notwithstanding their great aversion to the latter above the former, are commonly equally guilty of both.

My inclination, replied Cleanthes, lies, I own, a contrary way. Religion, however corrupted, is still better than no religion at all. The doctrine of a future state is so strong and necessary a security to morals that we never ought to abandon or neglect it. For if finite and temporary rewards and punishments have so great an effect, as we daily find, how much greater must be expected from such as are infinite and eternal?

How happens it then, said Philo, if vulgar superstition be so salutary to society, that all history abounds so much with accounts of its pernicious consequences on public affairs? Factions, civil wars, persecutions, subversions of government, oppression, slavery—these are the dismal consequences which always attend its prevalence over the minds of men. If the religious spirit be ever mentioned in any historical narration, we are sure to meet afterwards with a detail of the miseries which attend it. And no period of time can be happier or more prosperous than those in which it is never regarded or heard of.

The reason of this observation, replied Cleanthes, is obvious. The proper office of religion is to regulate the hearts of men, humanize their conduct, infuse the spirit of temperance, order, and obedience; and, as its operation is silent and only enforces the motives of morality and justice, it is in danger of being overlooked and confounded with these other motives. When it distinguishes itself, and acts as a separate principle over men, it has departed from its proper sphere and has become only a cover to faction and ambition.

And so will all religion, said Philo, except the philosophical and rational kind. Your reasonings are more easily eluded than my facts. The inference is not just—because finite and temporary rewards and punishments have so great influence that therefore such as are infinite and eternal must have so much greater. Consider, I beseech you, the attachment which we have to present things, and the little concern which we discover for objects so remote and uncertain. When divines are declaiming against the common behavior and conduct of the world, they always represent this principle as the strongest imaginable (which

---

35. It seems evident that the dispute between the sceptics and dogmatists is entirely verbal, or, at least, regards only the degrees of doubt and assurance which we ought to indulge with regard to all reasoning; and such disputes are commonly, at the bottom, verbal and admit not of any precise determination. No philosophical dogmatist denies that there are difficulties both with regard to the senses and to all science, and that these difficulties are, in a regular, logical method, absolutely insolvable. No sceptic denies that we lie under an absolute necessity, notwithstanding these difficulties, of thinking, and believing, and reasoning, with regard to all kinds of subjects, and even of frequently assenting with confidence and security. The only difference, then, between these sects, if they merit that name, is that the sceptic, from habit, caprice, or inclination, insists most on the difficulties, the dogmatist, for like reasons, on the necessity.

indeed it is), and describe almost all human kind as lying under the influence of it, and sunk into the deepest lethargy and unconcern about their religious interests. Yet these same divines, when they refute their speculative antagonists, suppose the motives of religion to be so powerful that, without them, it were impossible for civil society to subsist; nor are they ashamed of so palpable a contradiction. It is certain, from experience, that the smallest grain of natural honesty and benevolence has more effect on men's conduct than the most pompous views suggested by theological theories and systems. A man's natural inclination works incessantly upon him; it is forever present to the mind, and mingles itself with every view and consideration; whereas religious motives, where they act at all, operate only by starts and bounds; and it is scarcely possible for them to become altogether habitual to the mind. The force of the greatest gravity, say the philosophers, is infinitely small, in comparison of that of the least impulse, yet it is certain that the smallest gravity will, in the end, prevail above a great impulse because no strokes or blows can be repeated with such constancy as attraction and gravitation.

Another advantage of inclination: It engages on its side all the wit and ingenuity of the mind, and, when set in opposition to religious principles, seeks every method and art of eluding them; in which it is almost always successful. Who can explain the heart of man, or account for those strange salvos and excuses with which people satisfy themselves when they follow their inclinations in opposition to their religious duty? This is well understood in the world; and none but fools ever repose less trust in a man because they hear that, from study and philosophy, he has entertained some speculative doubts with regard to theological subjects. And when we have to do with a man who makes a great profession of religion and devotion, has this any other effect upon several who pass for prudent than to put them on their guard, lest they be cheated and deceived by him?

We must further consider that philosophers, who cultivate reason and reflection, stand less in need of such motives to keep them under the restraint of morals; and that the vulgar, who alone may need them, are utterly incapable of so pure a religion as represents the Deity to be pleased with nothing but virtue in human behavior. The recommendations to the Divinity are generally supposed to be either frivolous observances or rapturous ecstasies or a bigoted credulity. We need not run back into antiquity or wander into remote regions to find instances of this degeneracy. Amongst ourselves, some have been guilty of that atrociousness, unknown to the Egyptian and Grecian superstitions, of declaiming, in express terms, against morality, and representing it as a sure forfeiture of the divine favor if the least trust or reliance be laid upon it.

But even though superstition or enthusiasm should not put itself in direct opposition to morality, the very diverting of the attention, the raising up a new and frivolous species of merit, the preposterous distribution which it makes of praise and blame, must have the most pernicious consequences, and weaken extremely men's attachment to the natural motives of justice and humanity.

Such a principle of action likewise, not being any of the familiar motives of human conduct, acts only by intervals on the temper, and must be roused by continual efforts in order to render the pious zealot satisfied with his own conduct and make him fulfil his devotional task. Many religious exercises are entered into with seeming fervor where the heart, at the time, feels cold and languid. A habit of dissimulation is by degrees contracted, and fraud and falsehood become the predominant principle. Hence the reason of that vulgar observation that the highest zeal in religion and the deepest hypocrisy, so far from being inconsistent, are often or commonly united in the same individual character.

The bad effects of such habits, even in common life, are easily imagined; but, where the interests of religion are concerned, no morality can be forcible enough to bind the enthusiastic zealot. The sacredness of the cause sanctifies every measure which can be made use of to promote it.

The steady attention alone to so important an interest as that of eternal salvation is apt to extinguish the benevolent affections, and beget a narrow, contracted selfishness. And when such a temper is encouraged, it easily eludes all the general precepts of charity and benevolence.

Thus the motives of vulgar superstition have no great influence on general conduct, nor is their operation favorable to morality, in the instances where they predominate.

Is there any maxim in politics more certain and infallible than that both the number and authority of priests should be confined within very narrow limits, and that the civil magistrate ought, for ever, to keep his *fasces* and *axes*[36] from such dangerous hands? But if the spirit of popular religion were so salutary to society, a contrary maxim ought to prevail. The greater number of priests and their greater authority and riches will always augment the religious spirit. And though the priests have the guidance of this spirit, why may we not expect a superior sanctity of life and greater benevolence and moderation from persons who are set apart for religion, who are continually inculcating it upon others, and who must themselves imbibe a greater share of it? Whence comes it then that, in fact, the utmost a wise magistrate can propose with regard to popular religions is, as far as possible, to make a saving game of it, and to prevent their pernicious consequences with regard to society? Every expedient which he tries for so humble a purpose is surrounded with inconveniences. If he admits only one religion among his subjects, he must sacrifice, to an uncertain prospect of tranquillity, every consideration of public liberty, science, reason, industry, and even his own independence. If he gives indulgence to several sects, which is the wiser maxim, he must preserve a very philosophical indifference to all of them and carefully restrain the pretensions of the prevailing sect; otherwise he can expect nothing but endless disputes, quarrels, factions, persecutions, and civil commotions.

True religion, I allow, has no such pernicious consequences; but we must treat of religion as it has commonly been found in the world, nor have I anything to do with that speculative tenet of theism which, as it is a species of philosophy, must partake of the beneficial influence of that principle, and, at the same time, must lie under a like inconvenience of being always confined to very few persons.

Oaths are requisite in all courts of judicature, but it is a question whether their authority arises from any popular religion. It is the solemnity and importance of the occasion, the regard to reputation, and the reflecting on the general interests of society, which are the chief restraints upon mankind. Customhouse oaths and political oaths are but little regarded even by some who pretend to principles of honesty and religion; and a Quaker's asseveration is with us justly put upon the same footing with the oath of any other person. I know that Polybius[37] ascribes the infamy of Greek faith to the prevalence of the Epicurean philosophy; but I know also that Punic faith had as bad a reputation in ancient times as Irish evidence has in modern, though we cannot account for these vulgar observations by the same reason. Not to mention that Greek faith was infamous before the rise of the Epicurean philosophy; and Euripides,[38] in a passage which I shall point out to you, has glanced a remarkable stroke of satire against his nation, with regard to this circumstance.

Take care, Philo, replied Cleanthes, take care; push not matters too far, allow not your zeal against false religion to undermine your veneration for the true. Forfeit not this principle—the chief, the only great comfort in life and our principal support amidst all the attacks of adverse fortune. The most agreeable reflection which it is possible for human imagination to suggest is that of genuine theism, which represents us as the workmanship of a Being perfectly good, wise, and powerful; who created us for happiness; and who, having implanted in us immeasurable desires of good, will prolong our existence to all eternity, and will transfer us into an infinite variety of scenes, in order to satisfy those desires and render our felicity complete and durable. Next to such a Being himself (if comparison be allowed), the happiest lot which we can imagine is that of being under his guardianship and protection.

These appearances, said Philo, are most engaging and alluring; and, with regard to the true philosopher, they are more than appearances. But it happens here, as in the former case, that, with regard to the greater part of mankind, the appearances are deceitful, and that the terrors of religion commonly prevail above its comforts.

It is allowed that men never have recourse to devotion so readily as when dejected with grief or depressed with sickness. Is not this a proof that the

36. [Rods and axes, a Roman symbol of authority.]

37. Lib. vi, cap. 54 [The reference is to the *Histories* of Polybius, regarding whom see Hume's *Enquiry*, n. 40.]

38. *Iphigenia in Tauride.*

religious spirit is not so nearly allied to joy as to sorrow?

But men, when afflicted, find consolation in religion, replied Cleanthes. Sometimes, said Philo; but it is natural to imagine that they will form a notion of those unknown beings, suitable to the present gloom and melancholy of their temper, when they betake themselves to the contemplation of them. Accordingly, we find the tremendous images to predominate in all religions, and we ourselves, after having employed the most exalted expression in our descriptions of the Deity, fall into the flattest contradiction in affirming that the damned are infinitely superior in number to the elect.

I shall venture to affirm that there never was a popular religion which represented the state of departed souls in such a light as would render it eligible for human kind that there should be such a state. These fine models of religion are the mere product of philosophy. For as death lies between the eye and the prospect of futurity, that event is so shocking to nature that it must throw a gloom on all the regions which lie beyond it; and suggest to the generality of mankind the idea of Cerberus[39] and Furies, devils, and torrents of fire and brimstone.

It is true, both fear and hope enter into religion because both these passions, at different times, agitate the human mind, and each of them forms a species of divinity suitable to itself. But when a man is in a cheerful disposition, he is fit for business, or company, or entertainment of any kind; and he naturally applies himself to these and thinks not of religion. When melancholy and dejected, he has nothing to do but brood upon the terrors of the invisible world, and to plunge himself still deeper in affliction. It may indeed happen that, after he has, in this manner, engraved the religious opinions deep into his thought and imagination, there may arrive a change of health or circumstances which may restore his good humor and, raising cheerful prospects of futurity, make him run into the other extreme of joy and triumph. But still it must be acknowledged that, as terror is the primary principle of religion, it is the passion which always predominates in it, and admits but of short intervals of pleasure.

Not to mention that these fits of excessive, enthusiastic joy, by exhausting the spirits, always prepare the way for equal fits of superstitious terror and dejection, nor is there any state of mind so happy as the calm and equable. But this state it is impossible to support where a man thinks that he lies in such profound darkness and uncertainty, between an eternity of happiness and an eternity of misery. No wonder that such an opinion disjoints the ordinary frame of mind and throws it into the utmost confusion. And though that opinion is seldom so steady in its operation as to influence all the actions; yet it is apt to make a considerable breach in the temper, and to produce that gloom and melancholy so remarkable in all devout people.

It is contrary to common sense to entertain apprehensions or terrors upon account of any opinion whatsoever, or to imagine that we run any risk hereafter, by the freest use of our reason. Such a sentiment implies both an *absurdity* and an *inconsistency*. It is an absurdity to believe that the Deity has human passions, and one of the lowest human passions, a restless appetite for applause. It is an inconsistency to believe that, since the Deity has this human passion, he has not others also; and, in particular, a disregard to the opinions of creatures so much inferior.

To know God, says Seneca,[40] *is to worship him.* All other worship is indeed absurd, superstitious, and even impious. It degrades him to the low condition of mankind, who are delighted with entreaty, solicitation, presents, and flattery. Yet is this impiety the smallest of which superstition is guilty. Commonly, it depresses the Deity far below the condition of mankind, and represents him as a capricious demon who exercises his power without reason and without humanity! And were that Divine Being disposed to be offended at the vices and follies of silly mortals, who are his own workmanship, ill would it surely fare with the votaries of most popular superstitions. Nor would any of human race merit his *favor* but a very few, the philosophical theists, who entertain or rather indeed

39. [According to Greek mythology, Cerberus was the monstrous dog who guarded the entrance to the underworld.]

40. [Lucius Annaeus Seneca (c.3 B.C.–A.D. 65), born in Córdoba, Spain, was a Stoic philosopher who tutored the young Nero and became his political adviser, although later, having left the court, he was accused of conspiracy against the Emperor and forced to commit suicide.]

endeavor to entertain suitable notions of his divine perfections. As the only persons entitled to his *compassion* and *indulgence* would be the philosophical sceptics, a sect almost equally rare, who, from a natural diffidence of their own capacity, suspend or endeavor to suspend all judgment with regard to such sublime and such extraordinary subjects.

If the whole of natural theology, as some people seem to maintain, resolves itself into one simple, though somewhat ambiguous, at least undefined, proposition, *That the cause or causes of order in the universe probably bear some remote analogy to human intelligence*—if this proposition be not capable of extension, variation, or more particular explication; if it affords no inference that affects human life, or can be the source of any action or forbearance; and if the analogy, imperfect as it is, can be carried no further than to the human intelligence, and cannot be transferred, with any appearance of probability, to the other qualities of the mind; if this really be the case, what can the most inquisitive, contemplative, and religious man do more than give a plain, philosophical assent to the proposition, as often as it occurs, and believe that the arguments on which it is established exceed the objections which lie against it? Some astonishment, indeed, will naturally arise from the greatness of the object: Some melancholy from its obscurity: Some contempt of human reason that it

can give no solution more satisfactory with regard to so extraordinary and magnificent a question. But believe me, Cleanthes, the most natural sentiment which a well-disposed mind will feel on this occasion is a longing desire and expectation that heaven would be pleased to dissipate, at least alleviate, this profound ignorance by affording some more particular revelation to mankind, and making discoveries of the nature, attributes, and operations of the divine object of our faith. A person, seasoned with a just sense of the imperfections of natural reason, will fly to revealed truth with the greatest avidity; while the haughty dogmatist, persuaded that he can erect a complete system of theology by the mere help of philosophy, disdains any further aid and rejects this adventitious instructor. To be a philosophical sceptic is, in a man of letters, the first and most essential step towards being a sound, believing Christian—a proposition which I would willingly recommend to the attention of Pamphilus; and I hope Cleanthes will forgive me for interposing so far in the education and instruction of his pupil.

Cleanthes and Philo pursued not this conversation much further; and as nothing ever made greater impression on me than all the reasonings of that day, so I confess that, upon a serious review of the whole, I cannot but think that Philo's principles are more probable than Demea's, but that those of Cleanthes approach still nearer to the truth.

Immanuel Kant

Born in Königsburg, East Prussia, in 1724, Immanuel Kant is widely regarded as the most important figure in philosophy after Aristotle. His novel approaches to questions of knowledge, metaphysics, morality, art, politics, science, and mathematics have dominated many subsequent generations. This influence has sometimes produced intellectual rebellion, only to be followed a generation or two later by another "back to Kant" movement. Kant's principal doctrines are contained in his three great critiques—*Critique of Pure Reason* (1781/87), *Critique of Practical Reason* (1787), and *Critique of Judgment* (1790).

Although the *Critique of Pure Reason* is famous for being difficult to read, its central topics can be captured in two questions: What can we know and how can we know it? What can't we know and why can't we know these things? Kant's highly original answer to the first question is best understood in the context of his empiricist predecessors. The empiricists claimed that all knowledge came from the senses: Nothing is in the mind that was not first in the senses. Kant's rationalist predecessor Leibniz had offered an important modification of this position: Nothing is in the mind that was not first in the senses, *except the mind itself*. In a sense, Kant's view is an elaborate and detailed extension of this cryptic claim from Leibniz. Kant regarded knowledge as the joint product of sensory evidence and the mind's ways of combining those data into usable form.

To illustrate Kant's view, consider two highly general claims: "The shortest distance between two points is a straight line" and "All events have causes." Like Descartes, Kant believes that mathematical claims such as the preceding statement about straight lines have a peculiar status: It is impossible for them to be false. In contrast to Descartes, he does not believe that this is due to their being known by some mysterious process of intellectual insight. Kant stands firmly with the empiricists in believing that all knowledge has to originate in the evidence of the senses. If all knowledge has to come from the senses, however, then how can anyone ever amass enough evidence to show that the shortest distance between two points is *always* a straight line? Kant's novel suggestion is that the claim is true—and can be known to be true—because it reflects the mind's own ways of combining sensory data in usable form. By considering widely shared assumptions about the evidence available to the senses, Kant thinks it is possible to determine the mind's own contribution to knowledge. In particular, Kant argues that the mind transforms all sensory data into representations of Euclidean space. If Kant is right about this necessary transformation performed by the mind, then, in the world as we represent it, it will be true that the shortest distance between two points is always a straight line.

Kant offers a similar explanation for the unusual status of some metaphysical claims, most famous among them, "All events have causes." David Hume had argued that there was no way to show that every event must have a cause. Kant accepts Hume's point that this claim can hardly be established by looking at each and every event. Once again, however, Kant believes that he can establish that this claim cannot be false, by showing that the mind cannot make any sense of the data it receives unless it interprets those data as representing causally interacting objects.

Kant's answer to the second, negative question is briefer, but equally influential: Many traditional questions of metaphysics, such as the nature of the soul and the existence of God, can never be resolved, because we lack any sensory evidence for such claims. The central positive arguments of the *Critique of Pure Reason* are contained in the excerpts presented below.

Although the *Critique of Practical Reason* was intended to be Kant's most systematic treatment of morality, the *Grounding for the Metaphysics of Morals* (reprinted below) has been far more influential. Kant begins this treatise with an investigation of our ordinary views about morality. This study yields a surprising and worrying result. According to our ordinary ways of thinking, an action has moral worth only if it is free of any ulterior motive. People cannot be bribed or or threatened into behaving morally. To be moral, an action must be done just because it is the right thing to do—and for no other reason. This insight raises a serious question: How, then, is morality possible? Kant's answer emerges in his three different formulations of the moral law (which he calls the "categorical imperative"): Morality is possible because people are capable of forming universal rules of conduct for themselves and others, which they act on out of respect for this very ability to create a morally ordered world—a world in which virtue is rewarded and vice punished, unlike the natural world, where strength and luck predominate.

• • •

Patricia Kitcher, ed., *Kant's Critique of Pure Reason* (Lanham, Md., Rowman & Littlefield, 1998) is a collection of the best recent essays on the topic. Paul Guyer, ed., *The Cambridge Companion to Kant* (Cambridge: Cambridge University Press, 1992) contains broad and clear essays on many of Kant's central themes. Henry Allison, *Kant's Transcendental Idealism* (New Haven: Yale University Press, 1983) offers many detailed and illuminating discussions of difficult passages. Patricia Kitcher, *Kant's Transcendental Psychology* (New York: Oxford University Press, 1990) tries to relate Kant's doctrines to contemporary projects, such as cognitive science's efforts to fathom the structure of the mind. Peter Strawson, *The Bounds of Sense* (London: Methuen, 1966) remains an extremely influential reading of the first critique. Paul Guyer, ed., *Kant's Groundwork of the Metaphysics of Morals* (Lanham, Md., Rowman & Littlefield, 1998) is a collection of the best recent essays on this topic. Christine Korsgaard, *Creating the Kingdom of Ends* (Cambridge: Cambridge University Press, 1996); Barbara Herman, *The Practice of Moral Judgment* (Cambridge, Mass.: Harvard University Press, 1993); and Onora O'Neill's *Constructions of Reason* (New York: Cambridge University Press, 1990) are useful book-length treatments of Kant's ethics.

P.W.K.

Critique of Pure Reason

Preface
[Second Edition]

Whether someone's treatment of the cognitions pertaining to reason's business does or does not follow the secure path of a science — this we can soon judge from the result. If, after many preparations and arrangements have been made, the treatment falters as soon as it turns to its purpose; or if, in order to reach that purpose, it repeatedly has to retrace its steps and enter upon a different path; or, again, if the various collaborators cannot be brought to agree on the manner in which their common aim is to be achieved — then we may rest assured that such an endeavor is still far from having entered upon the secure path of a science, but is a mere groping about. We shall indeed be rendering a service to reason if we can possibly discover that path, even if we should have to give up as futile much that was included in the purpose which we had previously adopted without deliberation.

Bviii   *Logic* has been following that secure path from the earliest times. This is evident from the fact that since *Aristotle* it has not needed to retrace a single step, unless perhaps removing some of its dispensable subtleties, or setting it forth in a more distinct and determinate way, were to be counted as improvements of logic, even though they pertain more to the elegance of that science than to its being secure. Another remarkable fact about logic is that thus far it also has not been able to advance a single step, and hence is to all appearances closed and completed. It is true that some of the more recent [philosophers] have meant to expand logic. Some of them have inserted into it *psychological* chapters on the different cognitive powers (e.g., on our power of imagination, or on ingenuity). Others have inserted *metaphysical* chap-

Reprinted from Immanuel Kant, *Critique of Pure Reason*, trans. Werner S. Pluhar (Indianapolis: Hackett Publishing Company, 1996), by permission of the publisher.

ters on the origin of cognition, or the origin of the different kinds of certainty according to the difference in the objects (i.e., chapters on idealism, skepticism, etc.). Still others have inserted into logic *anthropological* chapters on prejudices (as well as their causes and remedies). But all these attempts to expand logic are the result of ignorance concerning the peculiar nature of this science. We do not augment sciences, but corrupt them, if we allow their boundaries to overlap. But the boundary of logic is determined quite precisely by the fact that logic is a science that provides nothing but a comprehensive exposition and Bix strict proof of the formal rules of all thought. (Such thought may be a priori or empirical, may have any origin or object whatsoever, and may encounter in our minds obstacles that are accidental or natural.)

That logic has been so successful in following the secure path of a science is an advantage that it owes entirely to its limitations. They entitle it, even obligate it, to abstract from all objects of cognition and their differences; hence in logic the understanding deals with nothing more than itself and its form. Reason naturally had to find it far more difficult to enter upon the secure path of science when dealing not just with itself, but also with objects. By the same token, logic is a propaedeutic and forms, as it were, only the vestibule of the sciences; and when knowledge is at issue, while for the judging of such knowledge we do indeed presuppose a logic, yet for its acquisition we must look to what are called sciences properly and objectively.

Now insofar as there is to be reason in these sciences, something in them must be cognized a priori. Moreover, reason's cognition can be referred to the object of that cognition in two ways: either in order merely to *determine* the object and its concept (which Bx must be supplied from elsewhere), or in order to *make it actual* as well. The first is reason's *theoretical*, the second its *practical cognition*. In both the pure part, i.e., the part in which reason determines its object entirely a priori, must be set forth all by itself beforehand, no matter how much or how little it may contain. We must not mix with this part what comes from other sources. For we follow bad economic procedures if we blindly spend what comes in and are afterwards unable, when the procedure falters, to distinguish which part of the income can support the expenditure and which must be cut from it.

Two [sciences involving] theoretical cognitions by reason are to determine their *objects* a priori: they are *mathematics* and *physics*. In mathematics this determination is to be entirely pure; in physics it is to be at least partly pure, but to some extent also in accordance with sources of cognition other than reason.

Mathematics has been following the secure path of a science since the earliest times to which the history of human reason extends; it did so already among that admirable people, the Greeks. But we must not think that it was as easy for mathematics to Bxi hit upon that royal road—or, rather, to build it on its own—as it was for logic, where reason deals only with itself. Rather, I believe that for a long time (above all, it was still so among the Egyptians) mathematics did no more than grope about, and that its transformation into a science was due to a *revolution* brought about by the fortunate idea that occurred to one man during an experiment. From that time onward, the route that mathematics had to take could no longer be missed, and the secure path of a science had been entered upon and traced out for all time and to an infinite distance. This revolution in the way of thinking was much more important than the discovery of the passage around the celebrated Cape.[1] Its history, and that of the fortunate man who brought this revolution about, is lost to us. But *Diogenes Laërtius*[2] always names the reputed authors of even the minutest elements of geometrical demonstration, elements that

1. [The Cape of Good Hope—W.S.P.]

2. [Author of the only extant continuous account of the lives and doctrines of the main Greek philosophers. He is thought to have flourished (where is not clear) in the early part of the third century A.D. His work is known under various titles, such as *The Lives of Philosophers*, *Lives and Opinions of Famous Philosophers*, and several others.]

in ordinary people's judgment do not even stand in need of proof; and Diogenes hands down to us a story concerning the change that was brought about by the first indication of this new path's discovery. This story shows that the memory of this change must have seemed exceedingly important to mathematicians, and thus became indelible. When the *isosceles triangle* was first demonstrated, something dawned on the man who did so. (He may have been called *Thales*,[3] or by some other name.) He found that what he Bxii needed to do was not to investigate what he saw in the figure, nor—for that matter—to investigate the mere concept of that figure, and to let that inform him, as it were, of the figure's properties. He found, rather, that he must bring out (by constructing the figure) the properties that the figure had by virtue of what he himself was, according to concepts, thinking into it a priori and exhibiting. And he found that in order for him to know anything a priori and with certainty about the figure, he must attribute to this thing nothing but what follows necessarily from what he has himself put into it in accordance with his concept.

Natural science took much longer to hit upon the high road of science. For only about a century and a half have passed since the ingenious *Bacon*, Baron Verulam,[4] made the proposal that partly prompted this road's discovery, and partly—insofar as some were already on the trial of this discovery—invigorated it further. This discovery, too, can be explained only by a sudden revolution in people's way of thinking. I shall here take account of natural science only insofar as it is founded on *empirical* principles.

Something dawned on all investigators of nature when *Galileo* let balls, of a weight chosen by himself, roll down his inclined plane; or when *Torricelli*[5] made

3. [Thales of Miletus (in Asia Minor), who was considered one of the Seven Wise Men of ancient Greece, flourished around 585 B.C. He has been regarded, since early antiquity, as the founder of the Ionian school of natural philosophy, and is generally credited with having introduced geometry to Greece.]

4. [Francis Bacon (1561–1626), Baron Verulam, Viscount St. Albans, lord chancellor of England, philosopher, and man of letters.]

5. [Evangelista Torricelli (1608–1647), Italian physicist and mathematician. He was first to create a sustained vacuum, and he invented the barometer.]

the air carry a weight that he had judged beforehand to be equal to the weight of a water column known to Bxiii him; or when, in more recent times, *Stahl*[6] converted metals into calx and that in turn into metal, by withdrawing something[7] from the metals and then restoring it to them.[8] What all these investigators of nature comprehended[9] was that reason has insight only into what it itself produces according to its own plan; and that reason must not allow nature by itself to keep it in leading strings, as it were, but reason must—using principles that underlie its judgments—proceed according to constant laws and compel nature to answer reason's own questions. For otherwise our observations, made without following any plan outlined in advance, are contingent, i.e., they have no coherence at all in terms of a necessary law—even though such a law is what reason seeks and requires. When approaching nature, reason must hold in one hand its principles, in terms of which alone concordant appearances can count as laws, and in the other hand the experiment that it has devised in terms of those principles. Thus reason must indeed approach nature in order to be instructed by it; yet it must do so not in the capacity of a pupil who lets the teacher tell him whatever the teacher wants, but in the capacity of an appointed judge who compels the witnesses to answer the question that he puts to them. Thus even Bxiv physics owes that very advantageous revolution in its

6. [Georg Ernst Stahl (1660–1734), German physician and chemist. He developed the phlogiston theory of combustion, which offered the first comprehensive explanation of combustion and of such related biological processes as respiration, fermentation, and decay. The theory dominated chemical thought for almost a century, until its replacement by Lavoisier's oxidation theory of combustion.]

7. [The "something" was thought to be phlogiston. On the phlogiston theory of combustion (cf. previous note), the processes involved are these: Metals, when heated, lose phlogiston and become calces (or calx, in the singular), kinds of ashy powder now known to be oxides. Calces, when heated with charcoal, reabsorb phlogiston and become metals again. (The original phlogiston having been scattered and lost, the new phlogiston absorbed by the calx comes from the charcoal, which is especially rich in phlogiston.)]

8. I am not here following with precision the course of the history of the experimental method; indeed, the first beginnings of that history are not well known.

9. [As a result of the mentioned experiments.]

way of thinking to this idea: the idea that we must, in accordance with what reason itself puts into nature, seek in nature (not attribute to it fictitiously) whatever reason must learn from nature and would know nothing of on its own. This is what put natural science, for the very first time, on the secure path of a science, after it had for so many centuries been nothing more than a mere groping about.

Metaphysics is a speculative cognition by reason that is wholly isolated and rises entirely above being instructed by experience. It is cognition through mere concepts (not, like mathematics, cognition through the application of concepts to intuition), so that here reason is to be its own pupil. But although metaphysics is older than all the other sciences, and would endure even if all the others were to be engulfed utterly in the abyss of an all-annihilating barbarism, fate thus far has not favored it to the point of enabling it to enter upon the secure path of a science. For in metaphysics reason continually falters, even when the laws into which it seeks to gain (as it pretends) a priori insight are those that are confirmed by the commonest experience. Countless times, in metaphysics, we have to retrace our steps, because we find that our path does not lead us where we want to go. As regards agreement in the assertions made by its Bxv devotees, metaphysics is very far indeed from such agreement. It is, rather, a combat arena which seems to be destined quite specifically for practicing one's powers in mock combat, and in which not one fighter has ever been able to gain even the smallest territory and to base upon his victory a lasting possession. There can be no doubt, therefore, that the procedure of metaphysics has thus far been a mere groping about, and—worst of all—a groping about among mere concepts.

Why is it, then, that in metaphysics we have thus far been unable to find the secure path of science? Might this path be impossible here? Why, then, has nature inflicted on reason, as one of reason's most important concerns, the restless endeavor to discover that path? What is more: how little cause have we to place confidence in our reason, when in one of the most important matters where we desire knowledge reason not merely forsakes us, but puts us off with mere pretenses and in the end betrays us! Or if we have only missed the path thus far, what indication do we have that if we renew our search, we may hope to be more fortunate than others before us have been?

I would think that the examples of mathematics and natural science, which have become what they Bxvi now are by a revolution accomplished all at once, are sufficiently remarkable to [suggest that we should] reflect on the essential component in that revolution, viz., the transformation of the way of thinking that became so advantageous for them; and as far as is permitted by the fact that they, as rational cognitions, are analogous to metaphysics, we should [there] imitate them with regard to that transformation, at least by way of an experiment. Thus far it has been assumed that all our cognition must conform to objects. On that presupposition, however, all our attempts to establish something about them a priori, by means of concepts through which our cognition would be expanded, have come to nothing. Let us, therefore, try to find out by experiment whether we shall not make better progress in the problems of metaphysics if we assume that objects must conform to our cognition. — This assumption already agrees better with the demanded possibility of an a priori cognition of objects — i.e., a cognition that is to ascertain something about them before they are given to us. The situation here is the same as was that of *Copernicus* when he first thought of explaining the motions of celestial bodies.[10] Having found it difficult to make progress there when he assumed that the entire host of stars revolved around the spectator, he tried to find out by experiment whether he might not be more successful if he had the spectator revolve and the stars remain at rest. Now, we can try a similar experiment in meta-Bxvii physics, with regard to our *intuition* of objects. If our intuition had to conform to the character of its objects, then I do not see how we could know anything a priori about that character. But I can quite readily conceive of this possibility if the object (as object of the senses) conforms to the character of our power of intuition. However, if these intuitions are to become

cognitions, I cannot remain with them but must refer them, as presentations, to something or other as their object, and must determine this object by means of them. [Since for this determination I require concepts, I must make one of two assumptions.] I can assume that the *concepts* by means of which I bring about this determination likewise conform to the object;[11] and in that case I am again in the same perplexity as to how I can know anything a priori about that object. Or else I assume that the objects, or — what amounts to the same[12] — the *experience* in which alone they (as objects that are given to us) can be cognized, conform to those concepts. On this latter assumption, I immediately see an easier way out. For experience is itself a way of cognizing for which I need understanding. But understanding has its rule, a rule that I must presuppose within me even before objects are given to me, and hence must presuppose a priori; and that rule is expressed in a priori concepts. Hence all objects of experience must necessarily conform Bxviii to these concepts and agree with them. Afterwards, however, we must also consider objects insofar as they can merely be thought, though thought necessarily, but cannot at all be given in experience (at least not in the way in which reason thinks them). Our attempts to think these objects (for they must surely be thinkable) will afterwards provide us with a splendid touchstone of what we are adopting as the changed method in our way of thinking, viz., that all we cognize a priori about things is what we ourselves put into them.[13]

10. [Nicolaus Copernicus (1473–1543), the Polish astronomer, reinvented the heliocentric hypothesis. The hypothesis had been advanced previously by Aristarchus, a Greek astronomer of the third century B.C. But his work was lost a few decades after he wrote it, and we know about it only through other writers' testimony that itself was not recovered until long after the time of Copernicus.]

11. [As do the intuitions.]

12. [Because the objects under discussion are objects of our experience, i.e., objects as experienced (objects given to us in experience).]

13 [This method, then, which imitates that of the investigator of nature, consists in searching for the elements of pure reason in what can be *confirmed or refuted by an experiment*. Now the propositions of pure reason, especially if they venture beyond all bounds of possible experience, cannot be tested by doing (as we do in natural science) an experiment with their *objects*. Hence testing such propositions will be feasible only by doing an experiment with *concepts* and *principles* that we assume a priori. In that experiment we must arrange [to use] these concepts and principles in such a way that the same objects can be contemplated from two different standpoints: *on the one hand*, for the sake of experience, as objects of the senses and of the understanding; yet *on the other hand*, for the sake of isolated reason

This experiment is as successful as was desired. It promises that metaphysics will be on the secure path of a science in its first part, viz., the part where it deals with those a priori concepts for which corresponding Bxix objects adequate to these concepts can be given in experience. For on the changed way of thinking we can quite readily explain how a priori cognition is possible; what is more, we can provide satisfactory proofs for the laws that lie a priori at the basis of nature considered as the sum of objects of experience. Neither of these accomplishments was possible on the kind of procedure used thus far. On the other hand, this deduction — provided in the first part of metaphysics — of our power to cognize a priori[14] produces a disturbing result that seems highly detrimental to the whole purpose of metaphysics as dealt with in the second part: viz., that with this power to cognize a priori we shall never be able to go beyond the boundary of possible experience, Bxx even though doing so is precisely the most essential concern of this science. Yet this very [situation permits] the experiment that will countercheck the truth of the result that we obtained from the first assessment of our a priori rational cognition: viz., that our rational cognition applies only to appearances, and leaves the thing in itself uncognized by us, even though inherently actual. For what necessarily impels us to go beyond the boundary of experience and of all appearances is the *unconditioned* that reason demands in things in themselves; reason — necessarily and quite rightfully — demands this unconditioned for everything conditioned, thus demanding that the series of conditions be completed by means of that unconditioned. Suppose, now, we find that the unconditioned *cannot be thought at all without contradiction* if we assume that our experiential cognition conforms to objects as things in themselves, yet that *the contradiction vanishes* if we assume that our presentation of things, as these are given to us, does not conform to them as things in themselves, but

that these objects are, rather, appearances that conform to our way of presenting. Suppose that we find, consequently, that the unconditioned is not to be met with in things insofar as we are acquainted with them (i.e., insofar as they are given to us), but is to be met with in them [only] insofar as we are not acquainted with them, viz., insofar as they are things in themselves. If this is what we find, it will show that what we assumed initially only by way of an experiment[15] does in fact Bxxi have a foundation.[16] Now, once we have denied that speculative reason can make any progress in that realm of the suprasensible,[17] we still have an option available to us. We can try to discover whether perhaps in reason's practical cognition data can be found that would allow us to determine reason's transcendent concept of the unconditioned.[18] Perhaps in this way our a priori cognition, though one that is possible only from a practical point of view, would still allow us to get beyond the boundary of all possible experience, as is the wish of metaphysics. Moreover, when we follow this kind of procedure,[19] still speculative reason has at least provided us with room for such an expansion [of our cognition], even if it had to leave that room empty. And hence there is as yet nothing to keep us from filling in that room, if we can, with practical *data* of reason; indeed, reason summons us to do so.[20]   Bxxii

15. [Viz., that our power of a priori cognition can inform us only about appearances, but can never take us beyond the boundary of possible experience and allow us to cognize the thing in itself.]

16. This experiment of pure reason is very similar to that done in *chemistry*, which is called sometimes the experiment of *reduction*, but generally the *synthetic procedure*. The *analysis* of the *metaphysician* has divided pure a priori cognition into two very heterogeneous elements, viz., such cognition of things as appearances, and of things in themselves. The [metaphysician's] *dialectic* recombines the two so as to yield *agreement* with reason's necessary idea of the *unconditioned*, and finds that this agreement can never be obtained except through that distinction, which is therefore [a] true one.

17. [I.e., the realm of objects considered as things in themselves rather than as objects of sense.]

18. [I.e., make the concept determinate, give it content by means of attributes or "determinations."]

19. [I.e., the use of practical reason.]

20. In the same way [as Kant has just described in the case of metaphysics] the central laws governing the motions of the celestial bodies provided with established certainty what

that strives to transcend all bounds of experience, as objects that we merely think. Now if it turns out that contemplating things from that twofold point of view results in harmony with the principle of reason, but that doing so from one and the same point of view puts reason into an unavoidable conflict with itself, then the experiment decides in favor of the correctness of distinguishing the two points of view.

14. [I.e., legitimation of the claim that we have such a power.]

The task, then, of this critique of pure speculative reason consists in the described attempt to transform the procedure previously followed in metaphysics, by subjecting metaphysics to a complete revolution, thus following the example set by the geometricians and investigators of nature. The critique is a treatise on the method [of the science of metaphysics], not a system of the science itself. Yet it does set down the Bxxiii entire outline of metaphysics, including the bounds of this science as well as its entire internal structure. For pure speculative reason has a twofold peculiarity. First, it both can and ought to measure what its own ability is according to the different ways in which it selects objects for its thought. For in a priori cognition nothing can be attributed to objects except what the thinking subject takes from itself. Second, pure speculative reason also can and ought to enumerate completely and on its own the various ways it has of posing problems to itself, and thus to set down in advance the entire outline for a system of metaphysics. For, as regards its cognitive principles, it is an entirely separate, self-subsistent unity in which, as in an organized body, each member exists for the sake of all the others, and all exist for the sake of each one. In this unity no principle can safely be taken in *one* reference unless we have also investigated it in [its] *thoroughgoing* reference to our entire pure use of reason. But [as a consequence of this unity of pure speculative reason] metaphysics is also exceptionally fortunate in a way that is denied to all other rational sciences dealing with objects (as distinguished from

---

Copernicus had initially assumed only as a hypothesis, and at the same time provided proof of the invisible force (*New-tonian* attraction) that links together the world edifice. That force would have remained forever undiscovered if Coperni-cus had not dared, in a manner that conflicted with the senses but yet was true, to seek the observed motions not in the celestial objects but in the spectator. The transforma-tion in the way of thinking [in metaphysics] which I set forth in the *Critique* is analogous to the Copernician hypoth-esis. Here in the preface I likewise put it forth only as a hypothesis, even though in the treatise itself it will be proved, not hypothetically but apodeictically, from the character of our presentations of space and time and from the elementary concepts [i.e., the categories] of the understanding. Here I put it forth as a hypothesis in order merely to draw attention to the first attempts at such a transformation; and such attempts are always hypothetical.

logic, which deals only with the form of thought as such): Once metaphysics has been brought by this cri-tique onto the secure path of a science, it is able to encompass completely the entire realm of the cogni-tions pertaining to it. Hence it can complete its work Bxxiv and put it aside for the use of posterity, as capital that can never be increased. What enables metaphysics to complete its work is that it deals merely with principles, and with the restrictions on their use as determined by these principles themselves. Moreover, being a basic science, it is also obligated to achieve this complete-ness; regarding metaphysics we must be able to say: *nil actum reputans, si quid superesset agendum.*[21]

But, it will be asked, what sort of treasure is this that we mean to bequeath to posterity, in leaving them a metaphysics that has been purified by critique, though thereby also made durable? A cursory survey of this work will leave one with the impression that such a metaphysics benefits us only *negatively,* viz., by instructing us that in [using] speculative reason we must never venture beyond the boundary of experi-ence; and this instruction is indeed its primary benefit. But this benefit becomes *positive* as soon as we be-come aware that the principles with which speculative reason ventures beyond its boundary do not in fact *expand* our use of reason; they unfailingly *narrow* it, as we find when we examine them more closely. For these principles, which properly pertain to sensibility, do actually threaten[22] to expand the bounds of sensi-bility until they include everything, thus threatening Bxxv even to displace the pure (practical) use of reason. Hence a critique that restricts speculative reason is, to that extent, indeed *negative.* But because, by doing so, the critique also removes an obstacle that re-stricts—or even threatens to annihilate—the practical

---

21. ["Thinking that nothing was done as long as anything remained to be done." The quote is from the (unfinished) *De bello civili* (*On the Civil War*) by the Roman poet Lucan (Marcus Annaeus Lucanus, A.D. 39–65), ii, 657. The poem, which is also called *Pharsalia* (after the battle of Pharsalos described in Book vii), deals with the contest between Julius Caesar and the Senate, and the person referred to in the quote is Caesar. Actually, instead of *reputans* (thinking) the original has *credens* (believing), and instead of *si* it has *dum* or possibly *cum* (a switch that does not affect the meaning here).]

22. [If used in the way described.]

use of reason, its benefit is in fact *positive* and very important. We see this as soon as we become convinced that there is a use of pure reason which is practical and absolutely necessary (viz., its moral use). When used practically, pure reason inevitably expands and reaches beyond the bounds of sensibility; and although it does not require for this any help from speculative pure reason, it must still be assured against interference from it in order not to fall into contradiction with itself. To deny that this service rendered by the critique has a *positive* benefit would be like saying that the police provides no positive benefit; after all, one might say, the main task of the police is only to put a stop to the violence on whose account citizens must fear each other, in order that everyone may carry on his business calmly and safely. Now in the analytic part of the critique I shall prove that space and time are only forms of our sensible intuition and hence are only conditions of the existence of things as appearances, and that, furthermore, we have no concepts of understanding, and hence Bxxvi also no elements whatever for the cognition of things, except insofar as intuition can be given corresponding to these concepts. That will prove, consequently, that we cannot have [speculative] cognition of any object as thing in itself, but can have such cognition only insofar as the object is one of sensible intuition, i.e., an appearance. And from this it does indeed follow that any possible speculative cognition of reason is restricted to mere objects of *experience*. On the other hand, it must be noted carefully that this [conclusion] is always subject to this reservation: that we must be able at least to *think*, even if not [speculatively] *cognize*, the same objects also as things in themselves.[23]

23. In order for me to *cognize* an object I must be able to prove its [real] possibility (either from its actuality as attested by experience, or a priori by means of reason). But I can *think* whatever I want to, even if I am unable to commit myself to there being, in the sum of all [logical] possibilities, an object corresponding to the concept. All that is required in order for me to think something is that I do not contradict myself, i.e., that my concept be a [logically] possible thought. But I require something further in order to attribute objective reality to a concept (i.e., real possibility, as distinguished from the merely logical possibility just mentioned). However—and this is my point—this something further need not be sought in theoretical sources of cognition, but may also lie in practical ones.

For otherwise an absurd proposition would follow, Bxxvii viz., that there is appearance without anything that appears. Now let us suppose that the distinction, necessitated by our critique, between objects of experience and these same objects as things in themselves, had not been made at all. In that case the principle of causality, and hence nature's mechanism as governing the determination of [the exercise of] that causality, would definitely have to hold for all things as such[24] [construed] as efficient causes. Hence I could not, without manifest contradiction, say of the same being, for example the human soul, that its will is free and yet is subject to natural necessity, i.e., not free. For I would be taking the soul *in the same sense* in the two propositions, viz., as a thing as such (thing in itself); nor, without prior critique, could I help taking it so. Suppose, on the other hand, that the *Critique* is not in error when it teaches us to take the object in *two different senses*, viz., as appearance and as thing in itself: and that the deduction of the *Critique's* concepts of understanding is correct, so that the principle of causality applies to things only in the first sense, viz., insofar as they are objects of experience, but that these same objects are not subject to that principle when taken in the second sense.[25] On these suppositions, no contradiction arises when we Bxxviii think the same will in both these ways: in its appearance (i.e., in its visible acts), as conforming necessarily to natural law and as to that extent *not free*; yet on the other hand, *qua* belonging to a thing in itself,[26] as not subject to that law, and hence as *free*. Now as regards my soul when considered from this second standpoint, I cannot *cognize* it through any [use of] speculative reason (let alone through empirical observation); nor, therefore, can I in this way cognize freedom as the property of a being to which I attribute effects in the world of sense. For otherwise I would have to cognize such a being as a being determined with regard to its existence and yet as not determined in time (which is impossible, because I cannot base such a concept on any intuition). Nevertheless, [although I cannot in this way cognize my freedom,] I can still *think* freedom. I.e., at least my presentation

24. [I.e., including things in themselves.]

25. [I.e., as things in themselves.]

26. [A soul.]

of freedom contains no contradiction, if we make our critical distinction between the two ways of presenting (sensible and intellectual), and restrict accordingly the pure concepts of understanding and hence also the principles that flow from them. Now let us suppose that morality necessarily presupposes freedom (in the strictest sense) as a property of our will; for morality adduces a priori, as *data* of reason, original practical principles residing in reason, and these prin- Bxxix ciples would be absolutely impossible without the presupposition of freedom. But then suppose that speculative reason had proved that freedom cannot be thought at all.[27] In that case the moral presupposition[28] would have to yield to the other [supposition].[29] For this other [supposition]'s opposite involves a manifest contradiction[30] (whereas the opposite of freedom and morality involves no contradiction, unless freedom has already been presupposed).[31] Hence *freedom*, and with it morality, would have to give way to the *mechanism of nature*. But in fact the situation is different. All I need for morality is that freedom does not contradict itself and hence can at least be thought; I do not need to have any further insight into it. In other words, all I need is that freedom [in my act] puts no obstacle whatever in the way of the natural mechanism [that governs] the same act (when the act is taken in a different reference). Thus the doctrine of morality maintains its own place, and so does natural science. But this would not have happened if the

27. [Viz., as ruled out by the necessary mechanism of nature.]

28. [Of freedom, as presupposed by morality.]

29. [That freedom cannot be thought.]

30. [Which would thus prove the original supposition, viz., that freedom cannot be thought. The opposite (or denial) of this supposition is that freedom *can* be thought, which would contradict a necessary mechanism that (as would have been proved by speculative reason) rules out freedom.]

31. [Here the opposite (or denial) is that there is no freedom and hence no (possibility of) morality, which would not contradict a necessary mechanism, obviously not even one that ruled out freedom. Hence here the opposite or denial cannot prove the original supposition, viz., of freedom as presupposed by morality. A contradiction would arise only if we had already presupposed freedom: freedom would contradict both its own denial and that of (the possibility of) morality.]

critique had not instructed us beforehand about our unavoidable ignorance regarding things in themselves, restricting to mere appearances what we can *cognize* theoretically. This same exposition of the positive benefit found in critical principles of pure reason can be produced again in regard to the concept of *God* and of the *simple nature* of our *soul*; but for the sake of brevity I shall omit it. Thus[32] I cannot even *assume God, freedom*, and *immortality*, [as I must] for Bxxx the sake of the necessary practical use of my reason, if I do not at the same time *deprive* speculative reason of its pretensions to transcendent insight. For in order to reach God, freedom, and immortality, speculative reason must use principles that in fact extend merely to objects of possible experience; and when these principles are nonetheless applied to something that cannot be an object of experience, they actually do always transform it into an appearance, and thus they declare all *practical expansion* of reason to be impossible. I therefore had to annul *knowledge* in order to make room for *faith*. And the true source of all the lack of faith which conflicts with morality—and is always highly dogmatic—is dogmatism in metaphysics, i.e., the prejudice according to which we can make progress in metaphysics without a [prior] critique of pure reason.

Although, therefore, it cannot be difficult to leave to posterity the bequest of a metaphysics drawn up systematically in accordance with a critique of pure reason, yet such a metaphysics is a gift that is not to be despised. For consider merely how reason is cultivated generally by pursuing the secure path of a science, as compared to its baseless groping and careless roaming-about when there is no critique. Con- Bxxxi sider also our youth with their desire for knowledge, who can then make better use of their time than they can under the usual dogmatism. That dogmatism encourages them quite early and strongly to reason with ease about things of which they understand nothing and into which, moreover, neither they nor anyone else in the world will ever have any insight. It may even encourage them to seek to invent new ideas and opinions and thus to neglect the study of well-founded sciences. Above all, however, [we see the value of] such a metaphysics if we take into ac-

32. [By the same reasoning that has just been used.]

count the inestimable advantage of putting an end, for all future time, to all objections against morality and religion, and of doing so in the *Socratic* manner, viz., by the clearest proof of the opponents' ignorance. For there has always been some metaphysics in the world; and some metaphysics will presumably continue to be found in it, but with it also a dialectic of pure reason, because a dialectic is natural to pure reason. Hence the primary and most important concern of philosophy is to deprive metaphysics, once and for all, of its detrimental influence, by obstructing the source of its errors.

Despite this important change in the realm of the sciences and the *loss* that speculative reason must suffer in what it has thus far imagined to be its posses-Bxxxii sion, the situation remains entirely as favorable as ever with regard to the universal human concern, and with regard to the benefit that the world has thus far obtained from the teachings of pure reason. The loss affects only the *monopoly of the schools*; in no way does it affect the *interests of the people*. Let me ask the most adamant dogmatist whether any of the following proofs have ever been able, after emerging from the schools, to reach the public and exert the slightest influence on its conviction: the one that proves our soul's continuance after death from the simplicity of substance; or the one that proves the freedom of the will as opposed to universal mechanism by means of subtle but ineffectual distinctions between subjective and objective practical necessity; or the one that proves the existence of God from the concept of a maximally real being ([or] from the contingency of what is changeable and the necessity of a prime mover). I take it that these proofs have never reached the public and influenced it in that way; nor can they ever be expected to do so, because the common human understanding is unfit for such subtle speculation. Rather, the conviction spreading to the public, insofar as it rests on rational grounds, has had to arise from quite different causes. As regards the soul's continuance after death, the hope for a *future life* arose solely from a predisposition discernible to every human being in his [own] nature, viz., the inability ever to be satisfied by what is temporal (and thus is inadequate for the predispositions of his whole vocation). As regards the freedom of the will, the consciousness of *freedom* arose from nothing but the clear exhibition of duties in their opposition to

all claims of the inclinations. Finally, as regards the Bxxxiii existence of God, the faith in [the existence of] a wise and great *author of the world* arose solely from the splendid order, beauty, and provisions manifested everywhere in nature. Indeed, not only does this possession [of convictions held by the public] remain undisturbed, but it even gains further authority through what the schools are [here] being told: viz., that on a point dealing with the universal human concern they should not claim to have a higher and more extensive insight than that which can be attained just as readily by the great multitude (most worthy of our respect); and that they should therefore confine themselves solely to the cultivation of these universally comprehensible and for moral aims sufficient bases of proof. Hence the change[33] affects merely the arrogant claims of the schools, who would like to be considered in these matters (as they are rightly considered in many other matters) as the sole experts and guardians for truths whose key they keep to themselves, telling the public only how to use them (*quod mecum nescit, solus vult scire videri*).[34] On the other hand, a more legitimate claim of the speculative phi- Bxxxiv losopher is nonetheless being taken care of here. He remains always the exclusive trustee of a science that is useful to the public without its knowing this: viz., the critique of reason. For that critique can never become popular; nor does it need to be. For just as finely spun arguments for useful truths never make it into the heads of the people, so do the equally subtle objections against those arguments never occur to them. The school, on the other hand, inevitably gets involved in both the arguments and the objections, as does anyone who advances to [the point where he can] speculate. Hence the school is obligated to investigate thoroughly the rights of speculative reason, in order to forestall once and for all the scandal that sooner or later must become apparent, even to the people, from [all] the controversies—the controversies in which, when there is no critique,

33. [In the realm of the sciences.]

34. ["What he is as ignorant of as I am he wants to appear to be the only one to understand." I am grateful to Francis E. Sparshott for identifying this quote (and to Geoffrey Payzant for knowing whom to ask). It is from Horace's *Epistles*, II, i, 87. The original text actually has *ignorat* instead of (the synonymous) *nescit*.]

metaphysicians (and, as such, finally also the clergy) inevitably become entangled, and which thereafter even corrupt their teachings. Solely by means of critique can we cut off, at the very root, *materialism, fatalism, atheism,* freethinking *lack of faith, fanaticism,* and *superstition,* which can become harmful universally; and, finally, also *idealism* and *skepticism,* which are dangerous mainly to the schools and cannot Bxxxv easily cross over to the public. If governments do indeed think it proper to occupy themselves with the concerns of scholars, they should promote the freedom for such critique, by which alone the works of reason can be put on a firm footing. Promoting such freedom would conform much better to their wise care for both sciences and people than does supporting the ridiculous despotism of the schools. The schools raise a loud cry about danger to the public if one tears up the webs they have spun, even though in fact the public has never taken notice of these webs and hence can never feel the loss of them.

Critique does not stand in contrast to the *dogmatic procedure* that reason follows in its pure cognitions; for that procedure is science (and science must always be dogmatic, i.e., it must always do strict proofs from secure a priori principles). Rather, critique stands in contrast to *dogmatism.* Dogmatism is the pretension that we can make progress[35] by means of no more than a pure cognition from concepts (i.e., philosophical cognition) in accordance with principles—such concepts and principles as reason has been using for a long time—without inquiring into the manner and the right by which reason has arrived at them. Hence dogmatism is the dogmatic procedure followed by reason *without prior critique of its own ability.* The contrast, therefore, is not one that is meant to support Bxxxvi a garrulous shallowness with claims to the name of popularity; let alone one to support skepticism, which makes short work of all metaphysics. Rather, critique is the preliminary operation necessary for promoting a metaphysics that is well-founded and [thus] a science. Such a metaphysics must necessarily be carried out dogmatically, and systematically according to the strictest demand, and hence carried out in a way that complies with school standards (rather than in a popular way). For this demand cannot be remitted

because metaphysics promises to carry out its task entirely a priori, and therefore to the complete satisfaction of speculative reason. Hence in carrying out some day the plan prescribed by the critique, i.e., in [composing] the future system of metaphysics, we shall have to follow the strict method of the illustrious *Wolff,* the greatest among all the dogmatic philosophers.[36] He was first to provide the example (through which he became the originator of the—not yet extinct—spirit of thoroughness in Germany) as to how one is to take the secure path of a science: viz., by establishing principles in a law-governed way, determining concepts distinctly, trying for strictness in proofs, and avoiding bold leaps in inferences. He was, by the same token, superbly suited to transfer into that secure state such a science as metaphysics is— provided it had occurred to him to prepare the ground in advance by a critique of the organ,[37] viz., pure Bxxxvii reason itself. His failure to do so must be imputed not so much to him as rather to the dogmatic way of thinking [characteristic] of his age; and for this failure neither the philosophers of his own period, nor those of all the previous ones, have any [grounds] to reproach one another. Those who reject Wolff's method and yet simultaneously also the procedure of the critique of pure reason can have in mind nothing but [the aim of] shaking off the fetters of *Science* altogether, thus converting work into play, certainty into opinion, and philosophy into philodoxy.[38]

As regards this second edition, I wanted, as is proper, to seize this opportunity in order to remedy as much as possible any difficulties and obscurity, from which many of the misinterpretations may have arisen that acute men—perhaps not without my fault—have hit upon in judging this book. I have not found anything to change in the propositions themselves and in the bases used for proving them, nor in the form and completeness of the plan. This is due partly to the long examination to which I had subjected them

---

35. [In metaphysics.]

36. [Baron Christian von Wolff (1679–1754), German mathematician, natural scientist, and, above all, rationalist philosopher of the enlightenment. He is the author of numerous writings. Although his work follows the tradition of Descartes and Leibniz, he developed his own philosophical system within that tradition.]

37. [I.e., instrument. See B86.]

38. [Pursuit of a creed.]

before submitting the book to the public, and partly to the character of the matter itself, i.e., the nature of a pure speculative reason. For pure speculative reason has a true structure. In such a structure everything is an organ, i.e., everything is there for the sake of each member, and each individual member is Bxxxviii there for the sake of all, and hence even the slightest defect,[39] whether it be a mistake (error) or an omission, must inevitably betray itself when we use that plan or system. I hope, moreover, that this system will continue to maintain itself in this unchangeable state. What entitles me to this confidence is not self-conceit, but merely the fact that this [unchangeable state of the system] is evident from the following experiment: We obtain the same result whether we proceed from the minutest elements all the way to the whole of pure reason, or proceed backward to each part when starting from the whole (for this whole also is given by itself, through reason's final aim in the practical sphere); and the result is the same because any attempt to alter even the smallest part immediately gives rise to contradictions, not merely in the system, but in human reason in general. On the other hand, much remains to be done as regards the [manner of] *exposition*, and in this regard I have tried to make improvements by providing this new edition. Some of these improvements are meant to remedy the misunderstanding concerning the Aesthetic, especially the concept of time; others, the obscurity in the deduction of the concepts of understanding. Yet other improvements are meant to remedy the supposed lack of sufficient evidence in the proofs of the principles of pure understanding; and others still, finally, to remedy the misinterpretation of the paralogisms advanced against rational psychology. That is how far the alterations extend that I have made in the manner of exposition. (I.e., they extend only to Bxxxix the end of the first chapter of the Transcendental Bxl Dialectic.)[40] I did not extend them further because there was not enough time, and also because with

39. [In the plan displaying that systematic structure.]

40. Only one of my alterations could I call, properly speaking, an addition, and even it concerns only the kind of proof I offer. It consists—see p. [B] 275—in a new refutation of psychological *idealism*, and a strict proof (also, I believe, the only possible proof) of the objective reality of outer intuition. However innocuous idealism may be considered

regard to the remainder I had not come upon any misunderstanding by competent and impartial critics. Bxli Although I cannot name these critics and praise them Bxlii as they deserve, they will doubtless find on their own the places where I have taken their suggestions into

to be (without in fact being so) as regards the essential purposes of metaphysics, there always remains this scandal for philosophy and human reason in general [if we accept idealism]: that we have to accept merely on faith the existence of things outside us (even though they provide us with all the material we have for cognitions, even for those of our inner sense); and that, if it occurs to someone to doubt their existence, we have no satisfactory proof with which to oppose him. Since there is some obscurity in the expressions I used in that proof, from the third to the sixth line. I request that the passage be changed to the following: *"But this permanent something cannot be an intuition within me. For all bases determining my existence that can be encountered within me are presentations; and, being presentations, they themselves require something permanent distinct from them, by reference to which their variation, and hence my existence in the time in which they vary, can be determined."* I suppose some will object to this proof by saying: But all I am conscious of directly is what is within me, i.e., my *presentation* of external things, and hence we still have not established whether or not there is anything corresponding to it outside me. However, through inner *experience* I am Bxl conscious of *my existence in time* (and hence also of its determinability in time), and that is more than to be conscious merely of my presentation. But this consciousness of my existence (and of its determinability) in time is the same thing as *empirical consciousness of my existence*, and that can be determined only by reference to something linked with my existence that is *outside me.* Therefore this consciousness of my existence in time is linked, by way of identity, with the consciousness of a relation to something outside me; and hence what inseparably connects what is outside me with my inner sense is experience rather than invention, [outer] sense rather than my power of imagination. For outer sense is in itself already the referring of intuition to something actual outside me; and the reality of outer sense, as distinguished from imagination, rests only on our linking outer sense inseparably, as we are doing here, with inner experience itself, viz., as the condition of the possibility of inner experience. [This empirical consciousness of my existence contrasts with] the *intellectual consciousness* of my existence that I have in the conception I am, which accompanies all my judgments and acts of understanding; if with that intellectual consciousness of my existence I could at the same time link a determination of my existence through intellectual intuition, then this account.[41] The improvements do, however, involve a small loss for the reader, a loss that I could not prevent without making the book rather too voluminous: I had to omit or abbreviate various materials that, while not required essentially for the completeness of the whole, will yet be missed by many readers as possibly useful for some other aim. I had to do this in order

determination would not include necessarily the consciousness of a relation to something outside me. But in fact I am unable to do so. That intellectual consciousness of my existence does indeed lead the way; but the inner intuition in which alone my existence can be determined is sensible intuition, and is tied to the condition of time. But this [kind of] determination [of my existence], and hence inner experience itself, depends on something permanent to which I must regard myself as related by way of contrast; and anything permanent is not within me and hence is to be found only in something outside me. Hence the reality of outer sense is linked necessarily with the reality of inner sense, and this [link] makes experience as such possible. In other words, I am conscious with just as much certainty that there are things outside me that have reference to my sense, as I am conscious that I myself exist as determined in time. On the other hand, for which of my given intuitions there actually are objects outside me that correspond to them, objects that must hence be attributed not to the power of imagination but to outer *sense*, as belonging to it, must be established in each particular case. It must be established—and here the proposition that there actually is outer experience must always lie at the basis—in accordance with the rules by which experience as such (even inner experience) is distinguished from imagination. We may add to this a comment: The presentation of something *permanent* in one's existence is not the same thing as a *permanent presentation*. For although—like all our presentations, even those of matter—the presentation of something permanent may be quite mutable and may vary greatly, it yet refers to something permanent. Hence this permanent something must be a thing that is distinct from all my presentations and is external. The existence of this thing is included necessarily in the *determination* of my own existence, and [together] with it amounts to only a single experience; and this experience would not take place even inwardly if it were not (in part) outer at the same time. As to how this occurs, we cannot explain that any further, just as in general we cannot explain further how what is constant is thought by us [as constant] in time, with the concept of change arising from the simultaneity of what is constant with what varies.

41. [In making the alterations I mentioned above.]

to make room for my new exposition, which, as I hope, is more comprehensible now. Basically, my exposition changes absolutely nothing in the propositions or even in the bases used for proving them. But now and then the way in which it departs from my previous method of setting forth the material is such that I could not have accomplished this exposition by means of mere interpolations. I hope that this small loss, which anyone who so wishes can make up anyway by comparing this edition with the first one, is more than made up by the fact that the new version is more comprehensible. I have been pleased and gratified by what I have seen in various published writings (including reviews of some books, as well as separate treatises). I saw there that the spirit of thoroughness in Germany has not faded away, but has only been drowned out for a short time by the tone in vogue, whereby people employ in their thinking a freedom that befits [only] a genius. And I saw that courageous and bright minds have gained mastery of my *Critique* despite its thorny paths—paths that lead to a science of pure reason which complies with school standards, but which as such is the only science that lasts, and hence is exceedingly necessary. These worthy men have that happy combination of thorough insight with a talent for lucid exposition (the very talent that I am not aware of in myself), and I leave it to them to perfect my treatment of the material, which here and there may still be deficient as regards lucidity of exposition. For although there is in this case no danger of my being refuted, there certainly is a danger of my not being understood. As for myself, although I shall from now on be unable to enter into controversy, I shall pay careful attention to all suggestions, whether from friends or opponents, in order to use them in the future when I carry out the system of metaphysics in accordance with this propaedeutic. In the course of these labors, I have advanced considerably in age (this month I reach my sixty-fourth year). I must therefore spend my time frugally, if I want to carry out my plan of providing the metaphysics both of nature and of morals, and thus confirm the correctness of my critique of both speculative and practical reason. Hence I must rely on the help of those worthy men who have made this work their own, expecting them to clear up the obscurities in it that could hardly have been avoided initially, as well as to defend it as a whole. Any philo-

Bxli

Bxliii

Bxliv

sophical treatise can be tweaked in individual places (for it cannot come forward in all the armor worn by mathematical treatises), while yet the structure of the system, considered as a unity, is not in the slightest danger. Few people have the intellectual agility to survey such a system when it is new, but fewer still have the inclination to do so, because they find all innovation inconvenient. Again, in any work that for the most part uses language freely, we can easily dig up seeming contradictions if we tear individual passages from their contexts and compare them with one another. In the eyes of those who rely on the judgment of others, such seeming contradictions cast an unfavorable light on the work; but they are quite easily resolved by someone who has gained command of the idea as a whole. Moreover, if a theory is internally stable, then any action and reaction that initially portend great danger will in time serve only to smooth away the theory's unevenness; and in a short time they will even provide the theory with the requisite elegance, if those who deal with it are men of impartiality, insight, and true popularity.

Königsberg, in the month of April, 1787.

Introduction
[Second Edition]

I. On the Distinction between Pure and Empirical Cognition

There can be no doubt that all our cognition begins with experience. For what else might rouse our cognitive power to its operation if objects stirring our senses did not do so? In part these objects by themselves bring about presentations. In part they set in motion our understanding's activity, by which it compares these presentations, connects or separates them, and thus processes the raw material of sense impressions into a cognition of objects that is called experience. *In terms of time,* therefore, no cognition in us precedes experience, and all our cognition begins with experience.

But even though all our cognition starts **with** experience, that does not mean that all of it arises **from** experience. For it might well be that even our experiential cognition is composite, consisting of what we receive through impressions and what our own cognitive power supplies from itself (sense impressions merely prompting it to do so). If our cognitive power does make such an addition, we may not be able to distinguish it from that basic material until long B2 practice has made us attentive to it and skilled in separating it from the basic material.

This question, then, whether there is such a cognition that is independent of experience and even of all impressions of the senses, is one that cannot be disposed of as soon as it comes to light, but that at least still needs closer investigation. Such cognitions are called *a priori cognitions;* they are distinguished from empirical cognitions, whose sources are a posteriori, namely, in experience.

But that expression, [viz., *a priori,*] is not yet determinate enough to indicate adequately the full meaning of the question just posed. For it is customary, I suppose, to say of much cognition derived from experiential sources that we can or do partake of it a priori. We say this because we derive the cognition not directly from experience but from a universal rule, even though that rule itself was indeed borrowed by us from experience. Thus if someone has undermined the foundation of his house, we say that he could have known a priori that the house would cave in, i.e., he did not have to wait for the experience of its actually caving in. And yet he could not have known this completely a priori. For he did first have to find out through experience that bodies have weight and hence fall when their support is withdrawn.

In what follows, therefore, we shall mean by a priori cognitions not those that occur independently of this B3 or that experience, but those that occur *absolutely* independently of all experience. They contrast with empirical cognitions, which are those that are possible only a posteriori, i.e., through experience. But we call a priori cognitions *pure* if nothing empirical whatsoever is mixed in with them. Thus, e.g., the proposition, Every change has its cause, is an a priori proposition; yet it is not pure, because change is a concept that can be obtained only from experience.

II. We Are in Possession of Certain A Priori Cognitions, and Even Common Understanding Is Never without Them

What matters here is that we find a characteristic by which we can safely distinguish a pure cognition from empirical ones. Now, experience does indeed teach us that something is thus or thus, but not that it cannot be otherwise. **First,** then, if we find a proposition such that in thinking it we think at the same time its *necessity,* then it is an a priori judgment; and if, in addition, it is not derived from any proposition except one that itself has the validity of a necessary proposition, then it is absolutely a priori. **Second,** experience never provides its judgments with true or strict *universality,* but only (through induction) with assumed and comparative universality; hence [there] we should, properly speaking, say [merely] that as far as we have B4 observed until now, no exception is to be found to this or that rule. If, therefore, a judgment is thought with strict universality, i.e., thought in such a way that no exception whatever is allowed as possible, then the judgment is not derived from experience, but is valid absolutely a priori. Hence empirical universality is only [the result of] our choosing to upgrade validity from one that holds in most cases to one that holds in all, as, e.g., in the proposition. All bodies have weight. But when universality is strict and belongs to a judgment essentially, then it points to a special cognitive source for the judgment, viz., a power of a priori cognition. Hence necessity and strict universality are safe indicators of a priori cognition, and they do moreover belong together inseparably. It is nevertheless advisable to make separate use of the two criteria, even though each is infallible by itself. For, in using them, there are times when showing the empirical limitedness of a cognition is easier than showing the contingency of the judgments based on it; and there are times when showing the unlimited universality that we attribute to a judgment is more convincing than is showing the judgment's necessity.

Now, it is easy to show that in human cognition there actually are such judgments [as we are looking for, viz.], judgments that are necessary and in the strictest sense universal, and hence are pure a priori judgments. If we want an example from the sciences, we need only B5 look to all the propositions of mathematics; if we want one from the most ordinary use of understanding, then we can use the proposition that all change must have a cause. Indeed, in this latter proposition the very concept of a cause so manifestly contains the concept of a necessity in [the cause's] connection with an effect, and of a strict universality of the rule [governing that connection], that the concept of a cause would get lost entirely if we derived it as *Hume* did: viz., from a repeated association of what happens with what precedes, and from our resulting habit[42] of connecting pre-

sentations (hence from a merely subjective necessity). But we do not need such examples[43] in order to prove that pure a priori principles actual[ly exist] in our cognition. We could, alternatively, establish that these principles are indispensable for the possibility of experience as such, and hence establish [their existence] a priori. For where might even experience get its certainty if all the rules by which it proceeds were always in turn[44] empirical and hence contingent, so that they could hardly be considered first principles? But here we may settle for having established as a matter of fact [that there is a] pure use of our cognitive power, and to have established what its indicators are. However, we can see such an a priori origin not merely in judgments, but even in some concepts. If from your experiential concept of a *body* you gradually omit everything that is empirical in a body—the color, the hardness or softness, the weight, even the impenetrability—there yet remains the *space* that was occupied by the body (which has now entirely vanished), and this space you cannot omit [from the concept]. B6 Similarly, if from your empirical concept of any object whatever, corporeal or incorporeal, you omit all properties that experience has taught you, you still cannot take away from the concept the property through which you think the object either as a *substance* or as *attaching* to a substance (even though this concept of substance is more determinate than that of an object as such[45]). Hence you must, won over by the necessity with which this concept of substance forces itself upon you, admit that this concept resides a priori in your cognitive power.

III. Philosophy Needs a Science That Will Determine the Possibility, the Principles, and the Range of All A Priori Cognitions

Much more significant yet than all the preceding[46] is the fact that there are certain cognitions that [not only extend to but] even leave the realm of all possible

42. [Or "custom": *Enquiry Concerning Human Understanding.* V, Pt. I, and cf. VII, Pt. II. Cf. also below, B 19–20, 127. Kant knew Hume's *Treatise of Human Nature* only indirectly, through citations (translated into German) from James Beattie's *Essay on the Nature and Immutability of Truth*, of 1770.]

43. [Examples from the sciences or from ordinary understanding.]

44. [I.e., even the higher-order rules.]

45. [The concept of an object as such does not include even (the property or "determination" of) permanence.]

46. [I.e., than the fact that we have a priori cognitions as described.]

experiences. These cognitions, by means of concepts to which no corresponding object can be given in experience at all, appear to expand the range of our judgments beyond all bounds of experience.

And precisely in these latter cognitions, which go beyond the world of sense, where experience cannot provide us with any guide or correction, reside our B7 reason's inquiries. We regard these inquiries as far superior in importance, and their final aim as much more sublime, than anything that our understanding can learn in the realm of appearances. Indeed, we would sooner dare anything, even at the risk of error, than give up such treasured inquiries [into the unavoidable problems of reason], whether on the ground that they are precarious somehow, or from disdain and indifference. These unavoidable problems of reason themselves are *God, freedom, and immortality*. But the science whose final aim, involving the science's entire apparatus, is in fact directed solely at solving these problems is called *metaphysics*. Initially, the procedure of metaphysics is *dogmatic*: i.e., [metaphysics], without first examining whether reason is capable or incapable of so great an enterprise, confidently undertakes to carry it out.

Now, suppose that we had just left the terrain of experience. Would we immediately erect an edifice by means of what cognitions we have, though we do not know from where? Would we erect it on credit, i.e., on principles whose origin is unfamiliar to us? It does seem natural that we would not, but that we would first seek assurance through careful inquiries that the foundation had been laid. In other words, it does seem natural that we would, rather, long since have raised the question as to just how our understanding could arrive at all these a priori cognitions, and what might be their range, validity, and value. And in fact nothing would be more natural, if by the term *natural* we mean what properly and reasonably B8 ought to happen. If, on the other hand, we mean by this term what usually happens, then nothing is more natural and comprehensible than the fact that for a long time this inquiry had to remain unperformed. For, one part of these [a priori] cognitions, viz., the mathematical ones, possess long-standing reliability, and thereby raise favorable expectations concerning other [a priori] cognitions as well, even though these may be of a quite different nature. Moreover, once we are beyond the sphere of experience, we are assured

of not being refuted by experience. The appeal of expanding our cognitions is so great that nothing but hitting upon a clear contradiction can stop our progress. On the other hand, we can avoid such contradiction by merely being cautious in our inventions—even though they remain nonetheless inventions. Mathematics provides us with a splendid example of how much we can achieve, independently of experience, in a priori cognition. Now, it is true that mathematics deals with objects and cognitions only to the extent that they can be exhibited in intuition. But this detail is easily overlooked because that intuition can itself be given a priori and hence is rarely distinguished from a mere pure concept. Captivated by such a proof of reason's might, our urge to expand [our cognitions] sees no boundaries. When the light dove parts the air in free flight and feels the air's resistance, it might come to think that it would do much better still in space devoid of air. In the B9 same way *Plato* left the world of sense because it sets such narrow limits to our understanding; on the wings of the ideas, he ventured beyond that world and into the empty space of pure understanding. He did not notice that with all his efforts he made no headway. He failed to make headway because he had no resting point against which—as a foothold, as it were—he might brace himself and apply his forces in order to set the understanding in motion. But [Plato is no exception]: it is human reason's usual fate, in speculation, to finish its edifice as soon as possible, and not to inquire until afterwards whether a good foundation has in fact been laid for it. Then all sorts of rationalizations are hunted up in order to reassure us that the edifice is sturdy, or, preferably, even to reject altogether so late and risky an examination of it. But what keeps us, while we are building, free from all anxiety and suspicion, and flatters us with a seeming thoroughness, is the following. A large part—perhaps the largest—of our reason's business consists in dissecting what concepts of objects we already have. This [procedure] supplies us with a multitude of cognitions. And although these cognitions are nothing more than clarifications or elucidations of what has already been thought in our concepts (although thought as yet in a confused way), they are yet rated equal to new insights at least in form, even though in matter or content they do not expand the concepts we have B10 but only spell them out. Now since this procedure yields actual a priori cognition that progresses in a safe and useful way, reason uses this pretense, though without itself noticing this, to lay claim surreptitiously to assertions of a quite different kind. In these assertions, reason adds to given concepts others quite foreign to them, doing so moreover a priori. Yet how reason arrived at these concepts is not known; indeed, such a question is not even thought of. Hence I shall deal at the very outset with the distinction between these two kinds of cognition.

IV. ON THE DISTINCTION BETWEEN ANALYTIC AND SYNTHETIC JUDGMENTS

In all judgments in which we think the relation of a subject to the predicate (I here consider affirmative judgments only, because the application to negative judgments is easy afterwards), this relation is possible in two ways. Either the predicate B belongs to the subject A as something that is (covertly) contained in this concept A; or B, though connected with concept A, lies quite outside it. In the first case I call the judgment *analytic*; in the second, *synthetic*. Hence (affirmative) analytic judgments are those in which the predicate's connection with the subject is thought by [thinking] identity, whereas those judgments in which this connection is thought without [thinking] B11 identity are to be called synthetic. Analytic judgments could also be called *elucidatory*. For they do not through the predicate add anything to the concept of the subject; rather, they only dissect the concept, breaking it up into its component concepts which had already been thought in it (although thought confusedly). Synthetic judgments, on the other hand, could also be called *expansive*. For they do add to the concept of the subject a predicate that had not been thought in that concept at all and could not have been extracted from it by any dissection. For example, if I say: All bodies are extended—then this is an analytic judgment. For I do not need to go beyond the concept that I link with the word body in order to find that extension is connected with it. All I need to do in order to find this predicate in the concept is to dissect the concept, i.e., become conscious of the manifold that I always think in it. Hence the judgment is analytic. By contrast, if I say: All bodies are heavy—then the predicate is something quite different from what I think in the mere concept

of a body as such. Hence adding such a predicate yields a synthetic judgment.

Experiential judgments, as such, are one and all synthetic. For to base an analytic judgment on experience would be absurd, because in its case I can formulate my judgment without going outside my concept, and hence do not need for it any testimony of experience. Thus the [analytic] proposition that bodies are extended is one that holds a priori and is not an experiential judgment. For before I turn to experi- B12 ence, I already have in the concept [of body] all the conditions required for my judgment. I have only to extract from it, in accordance with the principle of contradiction, the predicate [of extension]; in doing so, I can at the same time become conscious of the judgment's necessity, of which experience would not even inform me. On the other hand, though in the concept of a body as such I do not at all include the predicate of heaviness, yet the concept designates an object of experience by means of part of this experience; hence I can [synthetically] add to this part further parts, of the same experience, in addition to those that belonged to the concept of a body as such. I can begin by cognizing the concept of a body *analytically* through the characteristics of extension, impenetrability, shape, etc., all of which are thought in this concept. But then I expand my cognition: by looking back to the experience from which I have abstracted this concept of body, I also find heaviness to be always connected with the above characteristics; and so I add it, as a predicate, to that concept *synthetically*. Hence experience is what makes possible the synthesis of the predicate of heaviness with the concept of body. For although neither of the two concepts is contained in the other, yet they belong to each other, though only contingently, as parts of a whole; that whole is experience, which is itself a synthetic combination of intuitions.

In synthetic judgments that are a priori, however, this remedy[47] is entirely lacking. If I am to go beyond B13 the concept A in order to cognize another concept B as combined with it, I rely on something that makes the synthesis possible: what is that something, considering that here I do not have the advantage of looking around for it in the realm of experience? Take the

47. [I.e., experience.]

proposition: Everything that happens has its cause. — In the concept of something that happens I do indeed think an existence preceded by a time, etc., and from this one can obtain analytic judgments. But the concept of a cause lies quite outside that earlier concept and indicates something different from what happens; hence it is not part of what is contained in this latter presentation. In speaking generally of what happens, how can I say about it something quite different from it, and cognize as belonging to it — indeed, belonging to it necessarily — the concept of cause, even though this concept is not contained in the concept of what happens? What is here the unknown = X on which the understanding relies when it believes that it discovers, outside the concept A, a predicate B that is foreign to concept A but that the understanding considers nonetheless to be connected with that concept? This unknown cannot be experience. For in adding the presentation of cause to the presentation of what happens, the above principle does so not only with greater universality than experience can provide, but also with the necessity's being expressed; hence it does so entirely a priori and on the basis of mere concepts. Now, on such synthetic, i.e., expansive, principles depends the whole final aim of our speculative a priori cognition. For, analytic principles are indeed B14 exceedingly important and needed, but only for attaining that distinctness in concepts which is required for a secure and extensive synthesis that, as such, will actually be a new acquisition [of cognition].

V. All Theoretical Sciences of Reason Contain Synthetic A Priori Judgments as Principles

1. *Mathematical judgments are one and all synthetic.* Although this proposition is incontestably certain and has very important consequences, it seems thus far to have escaped the notice of those who have analyzed human reason; indeed, it seems to be directly opposed to all their conjectures. For they found that all the inferences made by mathematicians proceed (as the nature of all apodeictic certainty requires) according to the principle of contradiction; and thus they came to be persuaded that the principle of contradiction is also the basis on which we recognize the principles [of mathematics]. In this they were mistaken. For though we can indeed gain insight into a synthetic

proposition according to the principle of contradiction, we can never do so [by considering] that proposition by itself, but can do so only by presupposing another synthetic proposition from which it can be deduced.

We must note, first of all, that mathematical propositions, properly so called, are always a priori judgments rather than empirical ones; for they carry with them necessity, which we could never glean from experience. But if anyone refuses to grant that all B15 such propositions are a priori — all right: then I restrict my assertion to *pure mathematics*, in the very concept of which is implied that it contains not empirical but only pure a priori cognition.

It is true that one might at first think that the proposition 7 + 5 = 12 is a merely analytic one that follows, by the principle of contradiction, from the concept of a sum of seven and five. Yet if we look more closely, we find that the concept of the sum of 7 and 5 contains nothing more than the union of the two numbers into one; but in [thinking] that union we are not thinking in any way at all what that single number is that unites the two. In thinking merely that union of seven and five, I have by no means already thought the concept of twelve; and no matter how long I dissect my concept of such a possible sum, still I shall never find in it that twelve. We must go beyond these concepts and avail ourselves of the intuition corresponding to one of the two: e.g., our five fingers, or (as *Segner* does in his *Arithmetic*[48]) five dots. In this way we must gradually add, to the concept of seven, the units of the five given in intuition. For I start by taking the number 7. Then, for the concept of the 5, I avail myself of the fingers of my hand as intuition. Thus, in that image of mine, I gradually add to the number 7 the units that I previously gathered B16 together in order to make up the number 5. In this way I see the number 12 arise. That 5 *were to be added* to 7, this I had indeed already thought in the concept of a sum = 7+5, but not that this sum is

---

48. [Johann Andreas von Segner (1704–1777). German physicist and mathematician at Jena, Gottingen, and Halle. He is the author of several significant works, and introduced the concept of the surface tension of liquids. The work mentioned here, as translated from the Latin, is his *Anfangsgründe der Arithmetik* (*Elements of Arithmetic*). See the second edition (Halle/Saale: Renger, 1773), pp. 27, 79.]

equal to the number 12. Arithmetic propositions are therefore always synthetic. We become aware of this all the more distinctly if we take larger numbers. For then it is very evident that, no matter how much we twist and turn our concepts, we can never find the [number of the] sum by merely dissecting our concepts, i.e., without availing ourselves of intuition.

Just as little are any principles of pure geometry analytic. That the straight line between two points is the shortest is a synthetic proposition. For my concept of *straight* contains nothing about magnitude, but contains only a quality. Therefore the concept of shortest is entirely added to the concept of a straight line and cannot be extracted from it by any dissection. Hence we must here avail ourselves of intuition; only by means of it is the synthesis possible.

It is true that a few propositions presupposed by geometricians are actually analytic and based on the principle of contradiction. But, like identical propositions, they serve not as principles but only [as links in] the chain of method. Examples are a=a; the whole is equal to itself; or (a+b)>a, i.e., the whole is greater than its part. And yet even these principles, although they hold according to mere concepts, are admitted in mathematics only because they can be exhibited in intuition. [As for mathematics generally,] what commonly leads us to believe that the predicate of its apodeitic judgments is contained in our very concept, and that the judgment is therefore analytic, is merely the ambiguity with which we express ourselves. For we say that we *are to* add in thought a certain predicate to a given concept, and this necessity adheres indeed to the very concepts. But here the question is not what we *are to* add in thought to the given concept, but what we *actually* think in the concept, even if only obscurely; and there we find that, although the predicate does indeed adhere necessarily to such concepts, yet it does so not as something thought in the concept itself, but by means of an intuition that must be added to the concept.

2. *Natural science (physica) contains synthetic a priori judgments as principles.* Let me cite as examples just a few propositions: e.g., the proposition that in all changes in the corporeal world the quantity of matter remains unchanged; or the proposition that in all communication of motion, action and reaction must always be equal to each other. Both propositions are clearly not only necessary, and hence of a priori

origin, but also synthetic. For in the concept of matter I do not think permanence, but think merely the matter's being present in space insofar as it occupies space. Hence I do actually go beyond the concept of matter, in order to add to it a priori in thought something that I have not thought *in it*. Hence the proposition is thought not analytically but synthetically and yet a priori, and the same occurs in the remaining propositions of the pure part of natural science.

3. *Metaphysics is to contain synthetic a priori cognitions.* This holds even if metaphysics is viewed as a science that thus far has merely been attempted, but that because of the nature of human reason is nonetheless indispensable. Metaphysics is not at all concerned merely to dissect concepts of things that we frame a priori, and thereby to elucidate them analytically. Rather, in metaphysics we want to expand our a priori cognition. In order to do this, we must use principles which go beyond the given concept and which add to it something that was not contained in it; and, by means of such synthetic a priori judgments, we must presumably go so far beyond such concepts that even experience[49] can no longer follow us; as in the proposition: The world must have a first beginning—and others like that. And hence metaphysics consists, at least *in terms of its purpose*, of nothing but synthetic a priori propositions.

VI. The General Problem of Pure Reason   B19

Much is gained already when we can bring a multitude of inquiries under the formula of a single problem. For we thereby facilitate not only our own business by defining it precisely, but also—for anyone else who wants to examine it—the judgment as to whether or not we have carried out our project adequately. Now the proper problem of pure reason is contained in this question:

How are synthetic judgments possible a priori?

That metaphysics has thus far remained in such a shaky state of uncertainty and contradictions is attributable to a sole cause: the fact that this problem, and perhaps even the distinction between *analytic* and

---

49. [Actual *or possible* experience.]

synthetic judgments, has not previously occurred to anyone.[50] Whether metaphysics stands or falls depends on the solution of this problem, or on an adequate proof that the possibility which metaphysics demands to see explained[51] does not exist at all. *David Hume* at least came closer to this problem than any other philosopher. Yet he did not think of it nearly determinately enough and in its universality, but merely remained with the synthetic proposition about the connection of an effect with its causes (*principium* B20 *causalitatis*).[52] He believed he had discovered that such a proposition is quite impossible a priori. Thus, according to his conclusions, everything that we call metaphysics would amount to no more than the delusion of a supposed rational insight into what in fact is merely borrowed from experience and has, through habit, acquired a seeming necessity. This assertion, which destroys all pure philosophy, would never have entered Hume's mind if he had envisaged our problem in its universality. For he would then have seen

that by his argument there could be no pure mathematics either, since it certainly does contain synthetic a priori propositions: and from such an assertion his good sense would surely have saved him.

In solving the above problem we solve at the same time another one, concerning the possibility of the pure use of reason in establishing and carrying out all sciences that contain theoretical a priori cognition of objects; i.e., we also answer these questions:

How is pure mathematics possible?
How is pure natural science possible?

Since these sciences are actually given [as existent], it is surely proper for us to ask **how** they are possible; for that they must be possible is proved by their being actual.[53] As regards *metaphysics*, however, there are B21 grounds on which everyone must doubt its possibility: its progress thus far has been poor; and thus far not a single metaphysics has been put forth of which we can say, as far as the essential purpose of metaphysics is concerned, that it is actually at hand.

Yet in a certain sense this *kind of cognition* must likewise be regarded as given; and although metaphysics is not actual as a science, yet it is actual as a natural predisposition (i.e., as a *metaphysica naturalis*[54]). For human reason, impelled by its own need rather than moved by the mere vanity of gaining a lot of knowledge, proceeds irresistibly to such questions as cannot be answered by any experiential use of reason and any principles taken from such use. And thus all human beings, once their reason has expanded to [the point where it can] speculate, actually have always had in them, and always will have in them, some metaphysics. Now concerning it, too, there is this question:

50. [The problem, roughly, is this: In the case of *analytic* judgments (judgments whose truth depends solely on the meanings of their terms, i.e., on the content of the concepts involved) it is easy to see how such judgments can (by which Kant means "can legitimately") be made a priori (independently of experience). But the truth of *synthetic* (nonanalytic) judgments depends on *more* than their meaning (conceptual content). An example is the judgment (see B 17) that in all changes in the corporeal world the quantity of matter remains unchanged. This judgment is clearly not analytic, but asserts something (not merely conceptual) about the world (and hence about any possible experience that we may have of it). How then can we make such judgments a priori? Kant's answer lies in his "Copernican revolution" (B xvi–xviii). We can make synthetic judgments a priori insofar as objects of experience (which are the same thing as object-experiences) must conform a priori to what we contribute to experience (and hence to them), instead of experience's conforming a priori to totally independent objects (things in themselves) by means of some preestablished harmony. By the same token, as Kant will show in the Transcendental Dialectic, synthetic a priori judgments that go *beyond* all possible experience (make assertions about things in themselves) cannot be justified (legitimated) theoretically at all (though they may still be justifiable *morally-practically*).]

51. [I.e., how synthetic judgments are possible a priori.]

52. [Principle of causality.]

53. This actuality may still be doubted by some in the case of pure natural science. Yet we need only examine the propositions that are to be found at the beginning of physics proper (empirical physics), such as those about the permanence of the quantity of matter, about inertia, about the equality of action and reaction, etc., in order to soon be convinced that these propositions themselves amount to a *physica pura* (or *physica rationalis*). Such a physics, as a science in its own right, surely deserves to be put forth separately and in its whole range, whether this range be narrow or broad.

54. [Natural metaphysics.]

How is metaphysics as a natural
B22   predisposition possible?

i.e., how, from the nature of universal human reason, do the questions arise that pure reason poses to itself and is impelled, by its own need, to answer as best it can?

Thus far, however, all attempts to answer these natural questions—e.g., whether the world has a beginning or has been there from eternity, etc.—have met with unavoidable contradictions. Hence we cannot settle for our mere natural predisposition for metaphysics, i.e., our pure power of reason itself, even though some metaphysics or other (whichever it might be) always arises from it. Rather, it must be possible, by means of this predisposition[55] to attain certainty either concerning our knowledge or lack of knowledge of the objects [of metaphysics], i.e., either concerning a decision about the objects that its questions deal with, or certainty concerning the ability or inability of reason to make judgments about these objects. In other words, it must be possible to expand our pure reason in a reliable way, or to set for it limits that are determinate and safe. This last question, which flows from the general problem above,[56] may rightly be stated thus:

How is metaphysics as science possible?

Ultimately, therefore, critique of pure reason leads necessarily to science; the dogmatic use of pure reason without critique, on the other hand, to baseless asser-
B23 tions that can always be opposed by others that seem equally plausible, and hence to *skepticism.*

This science, moreover, cannot be overly, forbiddingly voluminous. For it deals not with objects of reason, which are infinitely diverse, but merely with [reason] itself. [Here reason] deals with problems that issue entirely from its own womb; they are posed to it not by the nature of things distinct from it, but by its own nature. And thus, once it has become completely acquainted with its own ability regarding the objects that it may encounter in experience, reason must find it easy to determine, completely and

safely, the range and the bounds of its use [when] attempted beyond all bounds of experience.

Hence all attempts that have been made thus far to bring a metaphysics about *dogmatically* can and must be regarded as if they had never occurred. For whatever is analytic in one metaphysics or another, i.e., is mere dissection of the concepts residing a priori in our reason, is only a prearrangement for metaphysics proper, and is not yet its purpose at all. That purpose is to expand our a priori cognition synthetically, and for this purpose the dissection of reason's a priori concepts is useless. For it shows merely what is contained in these concepts; it does not show how we arrive at such concepts a priori, so that we could then also determine the valid use of such concepts in regard to the objects of all cognition B24 generally. Nor do we need much self-denial to give up all these claims;[57] for every metaphysics put forth thus far has long since been deprived of its reputation by the fact that it gave rise to undeniable, and in the dogmatic procedure indeed unavoidable, contradictions of reason with itself. A different treatment, completely opposite to the one used thus far, must be given to metaphysics—a science, indispensable to human reason, whose every new shoot can indeed be lopped off but whose root cannot be eradicated. We shall need more perseverance in order to keep from being deterred—either from within by the difficulty of this science or from without by people's resistance to it—from thus finally bringing it to a prosperous and fruitful growth.

VII. IDEA AND DIVISION OF A SPECIAL SCIENCE UNDER THE NAME OF CRITIQUE OF PURE REASON

From all of the above we arrive at the idea of a special science that may be called the *critique of pure reason.* For reason is the power that provides us with the *principles* of a priori cognition. Hence pure reason is that reason which contains the principles for cognizing something absolutely a priori. An *organon* of pure reason would be the sum of those principles by which B25 all pure a priori cognitions can be acquired and actually brought about. Comprehensive application of such an organon would furnish us with a system of

---

55. [I.e., our power of reason.]

56. [The problem as to how (in general) synthetic judgments are possible a priori: B 19.]

57. [Of dogmatic metaphysics.]

pure reason. Such a system, however, is a tall order; and it remains to be seen whether indeed an expansion of our cognition is possible here at all, and in what cases it is possible. Hence a science that merely judges pure reason, its sources, and its bounds may be regarded as the *propaedeutic* to the system of pure reason. Such a propaedeutic would have to be called not a *doctrine* but only a *critique* of pure reason. Its benefit, in regard to speculation, would actually only be negative. For such a critique would serve only to purify our reason, not to expand it, and would keep our reason free from errors, which is a very great gain already. I call *transcendental* all cognition that deals not so much with objects as rather with our way of cognizing objects in general insofar as that way of cognizing is to be possible a priori. A *system* of such concepts[58] would be called *transcendental philosophy*. But, once again, this [system of] transcendental philosophy is too much for us as yet, here at the beginning. For since such a science would have to contain both analytic cognition and synthetic a priori cognition, in their completeness, it has too broad a range as far as our aim is concerned. For we need to carry the analysis only as far as it is indispensably necessary for gaining insight, in their entire range, into the principles of a priori synthesis, which is all that we B26 are concerned with. What we are now dealing with is [not such a science, but only] this inquiry, which properly speaking can be called only a transcendental critique, not a doctrine. For its aim is not to expand the cognitions themselves, but only to correct them; and it is to serve as the touchstone of the value, or lack of value, of all a priori cognitions. Accordingly, such a critique is a preparation; if possible, for an organon of those [cognitions]; or, should the [attempt to produce an] organon be unsuccessful, at least for a canon of them. Such a canon would, at any rate, some day allow us to exhibit, analytically as well as synthetically, the complete system of the philosophy of pure reason, whether that system were to consist in expanding the cognition of pure reason or merely in setting boundaries for it. That such a system is possible—and, indeed, that it cannot be overly wide-ranging, so that we may hope to complete it entirely—can be gathered even in advance from the

following: What here constitutes the object[59] is not the nature of things, which is inexhaustible, but the understanding that makes judgments about the nature of things, and even this understanding, again, only in regard to its a priori cognition. Moreover, the understanding's supply of a priori cognition cannot be hidden from us, because, after all, we need not search for it outside the understanding; and we may indeed suppose that supply to be small enough in order for us to record it completely, judge it for its value or lack of value, and make a correct assessment of it. B27 [But my readers must not expect to find in this critique more than the mentioned preparation.] Still less must they expect here a critique of books and systems of pure reason, but should expect the critique of our power of pure reason itself. Only if we use that critique as our basis do we have a reliable touchstone for assessing the philosophical content of old and new works in this field. Without such critique, unqualified historians and judges pass judgment on other people's baseless assertions by means of their own, which are just as baseless.

Transcendental philosophy is the idea of a science for which the critique of pure reason is to outline the entire plan *architectonically*, i.e., from principles, with full guarantee of the completeness and reliability of all the components that make up this edifice. Transcendental philosophy is the system of all principles of pure reason. That this critique is not itself already called transcendental philosophy is due solely to this: in order for this critique to be a complete system, it would have to include a comprehensive analysis of the whole of human a priori cognition. Now, it is indeed true that our critique must also put before us a complete enumeration of all the root concepts that make up that pure cognition. Yet the critique refrains, and properly so, from providing either the comprehensive analysis of these concepts themselves, or the complete review of the concepts derived from them. [There are two reasons for this.] First, this dissection of concepts would not serve our purpose; for it lacks B28 that precariousness which we find in synthesis, [the precariousness] on account of which the whole critique is in fact there. Second, taking on the responsibility for the completeness of such an analysis and

---

58. [I.e., a system of a priori concepts of objects in general.]

59. [Of our inquiry.]

derivation (a responsibility from which we could, after all, have been exempted in view of our aim) would go against the unity of our plan. On the other hand, this completeness in the dissection of the a priori concepts yet to be supplied, as well as in the derivation [of other concepts] from them, can easily be added later: provided that first of all these [concepts] are there, as comprehensive principles of synthesis, and nothing is lacking as regards this essential aim.[60]

Accordingly, the critique of pure reason [in a way] includes everything that makes up transcendental philosophy; it is the complete idea of transcendental philosophy. But the critique is not yet that science itself, because it carries the analysis [of a priori concepts] only as far as is required for making a complete judgment about synthetic a priori cognition.

The foremost goal in dividing such a science is this: no concepts whatever containing anything empirical must enter into this science; or, differently put, the goal is that the a priori cognition in it be completely pure.[61] Hence, although the supreme principles and basic concepts of morality are a priori cognitions, they still do not belong in transcendental philosophy. For B29 they do of necessity also bring [empirical concepts] into the formulation of the system of pure morality:[62] viz., the concepts of pleasure and displeasure, of desires and inclinations, etc., all of which are of empirical origin. Although the supreme principles and basic

concepts of morality do not lay these empirical concepts themselves at the basis of their precepts, they must still bring in such pleasure and displeasure, desires and inclinations, etc. in [formulating] the concept of duty: viz., as an obstacle to be overcome, or as a stimulus that is not to be turned into a motive. Hence transcendental philosophy is a philosophy of merely speculative pure reason. For everything practical, insofar as it contains incentives, refers to feelings, and these belong to the empirical sources of cognition.

If, then, the division of the science being set forth here is to be performed in terms of the general viewpoint of a system as such, then this science must contain in the first place a *doctrine of elements*, and in the second a *doctrine of method*, of pure reason. Each of these two main parts would be subdivided; but the bases on which that subdivision would be made cannot yet be set forth here. Only this much seems to be needed here by way of introduction or advance notice: Human cognition has two stems, viz., *sensibility* and *understanding*, which perhaps spring from a common root, though one unknown to us. Through sensibility objects are *given* to us; through understanding they are *thought*. Now if sensibility were to contain a priori presentations constituting the B30 condition under which objects are given to us, it would to that extent belong to transcendental philosophy. And since the conditions under which alone the objects of human cognition are given to us precede the conditions under which these objects are thought, the transcendental doctrine of sense[63] would have to belong to the *first* part of the science of elements.

60. [Of supplying these concepts, as such principles.]

61. [For the distinction between "a priori" and "pure," see B 3.]

62. ["Whereupon the system is *no longer* pure, though it is still a priori.]

63. [I.e., in effect, of sensibility.]

PART I

TRANSCENDENTAL AESTHETIC

§ 1

In whatever way and by whatever means a cognition may refer to objects, still *intuition* is that by which a cognition refers to objects directly, and at which all thought aims as a means.[64] Intuition, however, takes place only insofar as the object is given to us; but that, in turn, is possible only — for us human beings, at any rate — by the mind's being affected in a certain manner. The capacity (a receptivity) to acquire presentations as a result of the way in which we are affected by objects is called **sensibility**. Hence by means of sensibility objects are *given* to us, and it alone supplies us with *intuitions*. Through understanding, on the other hand, objects are *thought*, and from it arise *concepts*. But all thought must, by means of certain characteristics, refer ultimately to intuitions, whether it does so straightforwardly (*directe*) or circuitously (*indirecte*); and hence it must, in us [human beings], refer ultimately to sensibility, because no object can be given to us in any other manner than through sensibility.

B34 The effect of an object on our capacity for presentation, insofar as we are affected by the object, is *sensation*. Intuition that refers to the object through sensation is called *empirical* intuition. The undetermined object of an empirical intuition is called *appearance*.

Whatever in an appearance corresponds to sensation I call its *matter*; but whatever in an appearance brings about the fact that the manifold of the appearance can be ordered in certain relations I call the *form* of appearance. Now, that in which alone sensations can be ordered and put into a certain form cannot itself be sensation again. Therefore, although the matter of all appearance is given to us only a

posteriori, the form of all appearance must altogether lie ready for the sensations a priori in the mind; and hence that form must be capable of being examined apart from all sensation.

All presentations in which nothing is found that belongs to sensation I call *pure* (in the transcendental sense of the term). Accordingly, the pure form of sensible intuitions generally, in which everything manifold in experience is intuited in certain relations, will be found in the mind a priori. This pure form of sensibility will also itself be called *pure intuition*. B35 Thus, if from the presentation of a body I separate what the understanding thinks in it, such as substance, force, divisibility, etc., and if I similarly separate from it what belongs to sensation in it, such as impenetrability, hardness, color, etc., I am still left with something from this empirical intuition, namely, extension and shape. These belong to pure intuition, which, even if there is no actual object of the senses or of sensation, has its place in the mind a priori, as a mere form of sensibility.

There must, therefore, be a science of all principles of a priori sensibility. I call such a science *transcenden-* B36 *tal aesthetic*. It constitutes the first part of the transcendental doctrine of elements, and stands in contrast to that [part of the] transcendental doctrine of elements which contains the principles of pure thought and is called transcendental logic.

Hence in the transcendental aesthetic we shall, first of all, *isolate* sensibility, by separating from it everything that the understanding through its concepts thinks [in connection] with it, so that nothing other than empirical intuition will remain.[65] Second,

64. [I.e., as a means to such cognition.]

65. The Germans are the only people who have come to use the word *aesthetic*[s] to designate what others call the critique of taste. They are doing so on the basis of a false hope conceived by that superb analyst, *Baumgarten* [Alexander Gottlieb Baumgarten (1714–1762), philosopher in the Leibnizian tradition and disciple of Wolff. He introduced the term "aesthetics" in a sense close to the modern one. Kant himself later found a way to base the critique of taste on a priori principles; his aesthetic theory forms the first part of

we shall also segregate from sensibility everything that belongs to sensation, so that nothing will remain but pure intuition and the mere form of appearances, which is all that sensibility can supply a priori. In the course of that inquiry it will be found that there are two pure forms of sensible intuition, which are principles for a priori cognition: viz., space and time. We now proceed to the task of examining these.

B37
TRANSCENDENTAL AESTHETIC

Section I
Space

§2

METAPHYSICAL EXPOSITION[66] OF THIS CONCEPT

By means of outer sense (a property of our mind) we present objects as outside us, and present them one and all in space. In space their shape, magnitude,

---

the third *Critique*, published in 1790. Kant there reacts to the aesthetic theories prevalent at the time, including that of Baumgarten.], who hoped to bring one critical judging of the beautiful under rational principles, and to raise the rules for such judging to the level of a science. Yet that endeavor is futile. For, as regards their principal sources, those rules or criteria are merely empirical. Hence they can never serve as determinate a priori laws to which our judgment of taste would have to conform; it is, rather, our judgment of taste which constitutes the proper touchstone for the correctness of those rules or criteria. Because of this it is advisable to follow either of two alternatives. One of these is to let this new name *aesthetic*[s] become extinct again, and to reserve the name *aesthetic* for the doctrine that is true science. (In doing so we would also come closer to the language of the ancients and its meaning: among the ancients the division of cognition into αἰσθητά καὶ νοητά [the sensible and the intelligible] was quite famous. The other alternative would be for the new aesthetic[s] to share the name with speculative philosophy; we would then take the name partly in its transcendental sense, and partly in the psychological meaning.

66. [The metaphysical exposition investigates the nature of the presentation of space and shows that this presentation is given a priori. The transcendental exposition of space (in § 3) shows that and how from the a priori presentation of space something else that is a priori follows — viz., synthetic a priori cognitions (propositions of geometry). Cf. B 133–34.]

and relation to one another are determined or determinable. By means of inner sense the mind intuits itself, or its inner state. Although inner sense provides no intuition of the soul itself as an object, yet there is a determinate form under which alone [as condition] we can intuit the soul's inner state. [That form is time.] Thus everything belonging to our inner determinations is presented in relations of time. Time cannot be intuited outwardly, any more than space can be intuited as something within us. What, then, are space and time? Are they actual beings? Are they only determinations of things, or, for that matter, relations among them? If so, are they at least determinations or relations that would belong to things intrinsically also, i.e., even if these things were not intuited? Or are they determinations and relations that adhere only to the form of the intuition and hence to the subjective character of our mind, so that apart from B38 that character these predicates cannot be ascribed to any thing at all? In order to inform ourselves on these points, let us first of all give an exposition of the concept of space. Now, by *exposition* (*expositio*) I mean clear (even if not comprehensive) presentation of what belongs to a concept; and such exposition is *metaphysical* if it contains what exhibits the concept as *given a priori*.

1. Space is not an empirical concept that has been abstracted from outer experiences. For the presentation of space must already lie at the basis in order for certain sensations to be referred to something outside me (i.e., referred to something in a location of space other than the location in which I am). And it must similarly already lie at the basis in order for me to be able to present [the objects of] these sensations as outside and *alongside* one another, and hence to present them not only as different but as being in different locations. Accordingly, the presentation of space cannot be one that we take from the relations of outer appearance by means of experience; rather, only through the presentation of space is that outer experience possible in the first place.

2. Space is a necessary a priori presentation that underlies all outer intuitions. We can never have a presentation of there being no space, even though we are quite able to think of there being no objects B39 encountered in it. Hence space must be regarded as the condition for the possibility of appearances, and not as a determination dependent on them. Space

is an a priori presentation that necessarily underlies outer appearances.

3. Space is not a discursive or, as we say, universal concept of things as such; rather, it is a pure intuition. For, first, we can present only one space; and when we speak of many spaces, we mean by that only parts of one and the same unique space. Nor, second, can these parts precede the one all-encompassing space, as its constituents, as it were (from which it can be assembled); rather, they can be thought only as *in it*. Space is essentially one; the manifold in it, and hence also the universal concept of spaces as such, rests solely on [our bringing in] limitations. It follows from this that, as far as space is concerned, an a priori intuition of it (i.e., one that is not empirical) underlies all concepts of space. By the same token, no geometric principles—e.g., the principle that in a triangle two sides together are greater than the third—are ever derived from universal concepts of *line* and *triangle*; rather, they are all derived from intuition, and are derived from it moreover a priori, with apodeictic certainty.

4. We present space as an infinite *given* magnitude. Now it is true that every concept must be thought as B40 a presentation that is contained in an infinite multitude of different possible presentations (as their common characteristic) and hence the concept contains these presentations *under itself*. But no concept, as such, can be thought as containing an infinite multitude of presentations *within itself*. Yet that is how we think space (for all parts of space, *ad infinitum*, are simultaneous). Therefore the original presentation of space is an a priori *intuition*, not a *concept*.[67]

§3

Transcendental Exposition of the Concept of Space

By a *transcendental exposition* I mean the explication of a concept as a principle that permits insight into the possibility of other synthetic a priori cognitions. Such explication requires (1) that cognitions of that

sort do actually flow from the given concept, and (2) that these cognitions are possible only on the presupposition of a given way of explicating that concept.

Geometry is a science that determines the properties of space synthetically and yet a priori. What, then, must the presentation of space be in order for such cognition of space to be possible? Space must originally be intuition. For from a mere concept one B41 cannot obtain propositions that go beyond the concept; but we do obtain such propositions in geometry (Introduction, V). This intuition must, however, be encountered in us a priori, i.e., prior to any perception of an object; hence this intuition must be pure rather than empirical. For geometric propositions are one and all apodeictic, i.e., linked with the consciousness of their necessity—e.g., the proposition that space has only three dimensions. But propositions of that sort cannot be empirical judgments or judgments of experience; nor can they be inferred from such judgments (Introduction, II).

How, then, can the mind have an outer intuition which precedes the objects themselves, and in which the concept of these objects can be determined a priori? Obviously, this can be so only insofar as this intuition resides merely in the subject, as the subject's formal character of being affected by objects and of thereby acquiring from them *direct presentation*, i.e., *intuition*, and hence only as form of outer *sense* in general.

Our explication of the concept of space is, therefore, the only one that makes comprehensible the *possibility of geometry* as a [kind of] synthetic a priori cognition. Any way of explicating the concept that fails to make this possibility comprehensible, even if it should otherwise seem to have some similarity to ours, can be distinguished from it most safely by these criteria.[68]

Conclusions from the Above Concepts   B42

(a) Space represents no property whatever of any things in themselves, nor does it represent things in themselves in their relation to one another.[69] That is,

---

67. [But, as Kant has indicated, from this original intuition of space concepts can be formed, including such concepts as those of empirical space, relative space, Euclidean space, mathematical space.]

68. [The criteria numbered (1) and (2) at the beginning of this subsection.]

69. [As Leibniz claimed when he said that space involves nothing but the relations among the monads (things in themselves).]

space represents no determination of such things, no determination that adheres to objects themselves and that would remain even if we abstracted from all subjective conditions of intuition. For determinations, whether absolute or relative, cannot be intuited prior to the existence of the things to which they belong, and hence cannot be intuited a priori.

(b) Space is nothing but the mere form of all appearances of outer senses; i.e., it is the subjective condition of sensibility under which alone outer intuition is possible for us. Now, the subject's receptivity for being affected by objects precedes necessarily all intuitions of these objects. Thus we can understand how the form of all appearances can be given in the mind prior to all actual perceptions, and hence given a priori; and we can understand how this form, as a pure intuition in which all objects must be determined, can contain, prior to all experience, principles for the relations among these objects.

Only from the human standpoint, therefore, can we speak of space, of extended beings, etc. If we depart from the subjective condition under which alone we can — viz., as far as we may be affected by objects — acquire outer intuition, then the presenta-
B43 tion of space means nothing whatsoever. This predicate is ascribed to things only insofar as they appear to us, i.e., only insofar as they are objects of sensibility. The constant form of this receptivity which we call sensibility is a necessary condition of all relations in which objects are intuited as outside us; and if we abstract from these objects, then the form of that receptivity is a pure intuition that bears the name of space. We cannot make the special conditions of sensibility to be conditions of the possibility of things, but only of the possibility of their appearances. Hence we can indeed say that space encompasses all things that appear to us externally, but not that it encompasses all things in themselves, intuited or not, or intuited by whatever subject. For we can make no judgment at all about the intuitions of other thinking beings, as to whether they are tied to the same conditions that limit our intuition and that are valid for us universally. If the limitation on a judgment is added to the concept of the subject [term], then the judgment holds unconditionally. The proposition, All things are side by side in space, holds under the limitation: if these things are taken as objects of our sensible intuition. If I here add the condition to the concept and

say, All things considered as outer appearances are side by side in space, then this rule holds universally and without limitation. Accordingly, our exposition B44 teaches that space is *real* (i.e., objectively valid) in regard to everything that we can encounter externally as object, but teaches at the same time that space is *ideal* in regard to things when reason considers them in themselves, i.e., without taking into account the character of our sensibility. Hence we assert that space is *empirically real* (as regards all possible outer experience), despite asserting that space is *transcendentally ideal*, i.e., that it is nothing as soon as we omit [that space is] the condition of the possibility of all experience and suppose space to be something underlying things in themselves.

Besides space, on the other hand, no other subjective presentation that is referred to something external could be called an a priori objective presentation. For from none of them can we derive synthetic a priori propositions, as we can from intuition in space (§3). Hence, strictly speaking, ideality does not apply to them, even though they agree with the presentation of space inasmuch as they belong merely to the subjective character of the kind of sense involved. They may belong, e.g., to the sense of sight, of hearing, or of touch, by [being] sensations of colors, sounds, or heat. Yet because they are mere sensations rather than intuitions, they do not allow us to cognize any object at all, let alone a priori.

The only aim of this comment is to forestall an error: it might occur to someone to illustrate the B45 ideality of space asserted above by means of examples such as colors or taste, etc. These are thoroughly insufficient for this, because they are rightly regarded not as properties of things, but merely as changes in ourselves as subjects, changes that may even be different in different people. For in this case, something that originally is itself only appearance — e.g., a rose — counts as a thing in itself in the empirical meaning of this expression, a thing in itself that in regard to color can nonetheless appear differently to every eye. The transcendental concept of appearances in space, on the other hand, is a critical reminder. It reminds us that nothing whatever that is intuited in space is a thing in itself, and that space is not a form of things, one that might belong to them as they are in themselves. Rather, what we call external objects are nothing but mere presentations of our sensibility. The form of this sensibility is space; but its true correlate, i.e., the thing in itself, is not cognized at all through these presentations, and cannot be. Nor, on the other hand, is the thing in itself ever at issue in experience.

B46 TRANSCENDENTAL AESTHETIC

Section II
Time

§4

METAPHYSICAL EXPOSITION OF THE CONCEPT OF TIME

1. Time is not an empirical concept that has been abstracted from any experience. For simultaneity or succession would not even enter our perception if the presentation of time did not underlie them a priori. Only on the presupposition of this presentation can we present this and that as being at one and the same time (simultaneously) or at different times (sequentially).

2. Time is a necessary presentation that underlies all intuitions. As regards appearances in general, we cannot annul time itself, though we can quite readily remove appearances from time. Hence time is given a priori. All actuality of appearances is possible only in time. Appearances, one and all, may go away; but time itself (as the universal condition of their possibility) cannot be annulled.

B47   3. This a priori necessity, moreover, is the basis for the possibility of apodeictic principles about relations of time, or for the possibility of axioms about time in general. Time has only one dimension; different times are not simultaneous but sequential (just as different spaces are not sequential but simultaneous). These principles cannot be obtained from experience. For experience would provide neither strict universality nor apodeictic certainty; we could say only that common perception teaches us that it is so, but not that it must be so. These principles hold as rules under which alone experiences are possible at all; and they instruct us prior to experience, not through it.

4. Time is not a discursive or, as it is called, universal concept; rather it is a pure form of sensible intuition. Different times are only parts of one and the

same time; and the kind of presentation that can be given only through a single object is intuition. Moreover, the proposition that different times cannot be simultaneous could not be derived from a universal concept. The proposition is synthetic, and [therefore] cannot arise from concepts alone. Hence it is contained directly in the intuition and presentation of time.

5. To say that time is infinite means nothing more than that any determinate magnitude of time is possi- B48 ble only through limitations [put] on a single underlying time. Hence the original presentation *time* must be given as unlimited. But if something is such that its parts themselves and any magnitude of an object in it can be presented determinately only through limitation, then the whole presentation of it cannot be given through concepts (for they contain only partial presentations), but any such presentation must be based on direct intuition.

§5

TRANSCENDENTAL EXPOSITION OF THE CONCEPT OF TIME

I may refer for this exposition to No. 3, where, for the sake of brevity, I put among the items of the metaphysical exposition what in fact is transcendental. Let me add here that the concept of change, and with it the concept of motion (as change of place), is possible only through and in the presentation of time; and that if this presentation were not (inner) a priori intuition, no concept whatsoever could make comprehensible the possibility of a change, i.e., of a combination, in one and the same object, of contradictory opposed predicates (e.g., one and the same thing's being in a place and not being in that same place). Only in time can both of two contradictorily opposed determinations be met with in one thing: B49 viz., *sequentially*. Hence our concept of time explains the possibility of all that synthetic a priori cognition which is set forth by the—quite fertile—general theory of motion.

§6

CONCLUSIONS FROM THESE CONCEPTS

(a) Time is not something that is self-subsistent or that attaches to things as an objective determination, and that hence would remain if one abstracted from all subjective conditions of our intuition of it. For if time were self-sufficient, then it would be something that without there being an actual object would yet be actual.[70] But if, on the second alternative, time were a determination or order attaching to things themselves,[71] then it could not precede the objects as their condition, and could not a priori be cognized through synthetic propositions and intuited. But this a priori cognition and intuition can take place quite readily if time is nothing but the subjective condition under which alone any intuition can take place in us. For in that case this form of inner intuition can be presented prior to the objects, and hence presented a priori.

(b) Time is nothing but the form of inner sense, i.e., of the intuiting we do of ourselves and of our inner state. For time cannot be a determination of B50 outer appearances, [because] it does not belong to any shape or position, etc., but rather determines the relation of presentations in our inner state. And precisely because this inner intuition gives us no shape, do we try to make up for this deficiency by means of analogies. We present time sequence by a line progressing *ad infinitum,* a line in which the manifold constitutes a series of only one dimension. And from the properties of that line we infer all the properties of time, except for the one difference that the parts of the line are simultaneous whereas the parts of time are always sequential. This fact, moreover, that all relations of time can be expressed by means of outer intuition, shows that the presentation of time is itself intuition.

(c) Time is the formal a priori condition of all appearances generally. Space is the pure form of all outer appearances; as such it is limited, as an a priori condition, to just outer appearances. But all presentations, whether or not they have outer things as their objects, do yet in themselves, as determinations of the mind, belong to our inner state; and this inner state is subject to the formal condition of inner intuition, and hence to the condition of time. Therefore time is an a priori condition of all appearance generally: it is the direct condition of inner appearances

(of our souls), and precisely thereby also, indirectly, B51 a condition of outer appearances. If I can say a priori that all outer appearances are in space and are determined a priori according to spatial relations, then the principle of inner sense allows me to say, quite universally, that all appearances generally, i.e., all objects of the senses, are in time and stand necessarily in relations of time.

If we take objects as they may be in themselves— i.e., if we abstract from the way in which we intuit ourselves inwardly, and in which by means of this intuition we also take into our power of presentation all outer intuitions—then time is nothing. Time has objective validity only with regard to appearances, because these are already things considered as *objects of our senses.* But time is no longer objective if we abstract from the sensibility of our intuition, and hence from the way of presenting peculiar to us, and speak of *things as such.* Hence time is merely a subjective condition of our (human) intuition (an intuition that is always sensible—i.e., inasmuch as we are affected by objects); in itself, i.e., apart from the subject, time is nothing. Nevertheless, time is necessarily objective in regard to all appearances, and hence also in regard to all things that we can encounter in experience. We cannot say that all things [as such] are in time; for in the concept of things as such B52 we abstract from all ways of intuiting them, while yet this intuition is the very condition under which[72] time belongs in the presentation of objects. If now we add the condition to the concept, and say that all things as appearances (objects of sensible intuition) are in time, then this principle has all its objective correctness and a priori universality.

Hence the doctrine we are asserting is that time is *empirically real,* i.e., objectively valid in regard to all objects that might ever be given to our senses. And since our intuition is always sensible, no object that is not subject to the condition of time can ever be given to us in experience. On the other hand, we dispute that time has any claim to absolute reality; i.e., we dispute any claim whereby time would, quite without taking into account the form of our sensible intuition, attach to things absolutely, as a condition or property. Nor indeed can such properties, properties

70. [As in the case of Newton's absolute space.]

71. [As in the case of Leibniz, who held that time involves nothing but relations among the monads (things in themselves).]

72. [As added to the concept of a thing as such.]

belonging to things in themselves, ever be given to us through the senses. In this, then, consists the *transcendental ideality* of time. According to this view,[73] if we abstract from the subjective conditions of sensible intuition, then time is nothing, and cannot be included among objects in themselves (apart from their relation to our intuition) either as subsisting [as such B53 an object] or as inhering [in one]. But this ideality of time is not to be compared, any more than is the ideality of space, with the subreptions of sensations.[74] For in their case we presuppose that the appearance itself in which these predicates[75] [allegedly] inhere has objective reality.[76] In the case of time, such objective reality is entirely absent,[77] except insofar as this reality is merely empirical, i.e., except insofar as we regard the object itself as merely appearance. See, on this, the above comment, in SECTION 1.[78]

§7

ELUCIDATION

Against this theory, which grants that time is empirically real but disputes that it is real absolutely and transcendentally, I have heard men of insight raise quite unanimously an objection. I gather from this great unanimity that the objection must occur naturally to every reader who is not accustomed to contemplations such as these. The objection is the following. Changes are actual. (This is proved by the variation on the part of our own presentations—even if one were to deny all outer appearances, along with their changes.) Now changes are possible only in time. Therefore time is something actual. There is no difficulty in replying to the objection. I concede the whole

73. [The transcendental idealism of time, properly speaking.]

74. [I.e., (instances of) their surreptitious substitution for, and thus confusion with, something in the object, as discussed above: B 44–45.]

75. [I.e., the colors, sounds, etc., surreptitiously treated as properties of the object.]

76. [Whereas the colors, sounds, etc., do not.]

77. [And is here treated as such, subreption thus being precluded.]

78. [See the end of the section on space: B 44–45.]

argument. Time is indeed something actual, viz., the actual form of inner intuition. It therefore has subjective reality in regard to inner experience; i.e., I actu- B54 ally have the presentation of time and of my determinations in time. Hence time is to be regarded as actual, though not as an object but as the way of presenting that I myself have as an object. Suppose, on the other hand, that I could intuit myself without being subject to this condition of sensibility, or that another being could so intuit me; in that case the very same determinations that we now present as changes would provide a cognition in which the presentation of time, and hence also that of change, would not occur at all. Hence time retains its empirical reality as condition of all our experiences. Only absolute reality must, by the reasons adduced above, be denied to time. Time is nothing but the form of our inner intuition.[79] If we take away from time [the qualification that it is] the special condition of our sensibility, then the concept of time vanishes as well; time attaches not to objects themselves, but merely to the subject intuiting them.

But what causes this objection to be raised so unanimously, and raised, moreover, by those who nonetheless cannot think of any plausible objection against B55 the doctrine that space is ideal, is the following. They had no hope of establishing apodeictically that space is real absolutely; for they are confronted by idealism, according to which the actuality of external objects is incapable of strict proof. By contrast, the actuality of the object of our inner sense (the actuality of myself and of my state) is directly evident through consciousness. External objects might be a mere illusion; but the object of inner sense is, in their opinion, undeniably something actual. They failed to bear in mind, however, that both of them, though their actuality as presentations is indisputable, still belong only to appearance. Appearance always has two sides. One is the side where the object is regarded in itself (without regard to the way in which it is intuited, which is

79. I can indeed say: My presentations follow one another. But that means only that we are conscious of them as being in a time sequence—in accordance, i.e., with the form of inner sense. Time is not, on that account, something in itself, nor is it a determination attaching to things objectively.

precisely why its character always remains problematic).[80] The other is the side where we take account of the form of the intuition of this object. This form must be sought not in the object in itself, but in the subject to whom the object appears. Yet this form belongs to the appearance of this object actually and necessarily.

Time and space are, accordingly, two sources of cognition. From these sources we can draw a priori different synthetic cognitions — as is shown above all by the splendid example that pure mathematics provides in regard to our cognitions of space and its relations. For time and space, taken together, are pure forms of all sensible intuition, and thereby make synthetic propositions possible a priori. But precisely thereby (i.e., by being merely conditions of sensibility), these a priori sources of cognition determine their own bounds; viz., they determine that they apply to objects merely insofar as these are regarded as appearances, but do not exhibit things in themselves. Appearances are the sole realm where these a priori sources of cognition are valid; if we go outside that realm, there is no further objective use that can be made of them. This [limited] reality of space and time leaves the reliability of experiential cognition otherwise untouched; for we have equal certainty in that cognition, whether these forms necessarily attach to things in themselves or only to our intuition of these things. Those, on the other hand, who assert that space and time — whether they assume these as subsistent or as only inherent — are real absolutely must be at variance with the principles of experience itself.[81] For suppose they decide to assume space and time as subsistent (thus taking what is usually the side of the mathematical investigators of nature): then they must assume two eternal and infinite self-subsistent nonentities (space and time), which exist (yet without there being anything actual) only in order to encompass everything actual. Or suppose they assume space and time as only inherent (thus taking the side to which some metaphysical natural scientists belong).

Here space and time count for them as relations of appearances (occurring concurrently or sequentially) — relations abstracted from experience but, as thus separated, presented confusedly. If they take this second side, then they must dispute that the mathematical a priori doctrines are valid for actual things (e.g., things in space), or at least that they are apodeictically certain. For a posteriori there is no such certainty at all. According to this second opinion, the a priori concepts of space and time are only creatures of the imagination, and their source must actually be sought in experience: the relations[82] are abstracted from experience; and the imagination has made from them something that, while containing what is universal in these relations, yet cannot occur without the restrictions that nature has connected with them. Those who assume space and time as [real absolutely and] subsistent do gain this much: they make the realm of appearances free[83] for mathematical assertions. On the other hand, these very conditions[84] create great confusion for them when the understanding wants to go beyond the realm of appearances. Those, on the other hand, who assume space and time as [real absolutely but as] only inherent gain on this latter point. I.e., they do not find the presentations of space and time getting in their way when they want to judge objects not as appearances but merely as they relate to the understanding. But they can neither indicate a basis for the possibility of mathematical a priori cognitions (since they lack a true and objectively valid a priori intuition[85]), nor bring the propositions of experience into necessary agreement with those a priori mathematical assertions. Our theory of the true character of these two original forms of sensibility provides the remedy for both [sets of] difficulties.

Finally, transcendental aesethetic cannot contain more than these two elements, i.e., space and time. This is evident from the fact that all other concepts

80. [For Kant's view that things in themselves are (thought of as) what appears, see B xxvii.]

81. [For Kant's discussion of these two alternatives, representing (respectively) the Newtonian and the Leibnizian views, cf. the beginning of the preceding subsection, B 49.]

82. [Of space and time.]

83. [Which on the opposing view just mentioned it was not.]

84. [The self-subsistent space and time as being eternal and infinite.]

85. [To which to appeal.]

belonging to sensibility presuppose something empirical. This holds even for the concept of motion, which unites the two components.[86] For [the concept of] motion presupposes the perception of something movable.[87] But in space, considered in itself, there is nothing movable; therefore the movable must be something that we find *in space only through experience*, and hence must be an empirical datum. Similarly, transcendental aesthetic cannot include among its a priori data the concept of change. For time itself does not change; rather, what changes is something that is in time. Therefore the concept of change requires the perception of some existent and of the succession of its determinations; hence it requires experience.

B59

§8

GENERAL COMMENTS ON TRANSCENDENTAL AESTHETIC

I. In order to forestall any misinterpretation of our opinion regarding the basic character of sensible cognition as such, we must first explain as distinctly as possible what that opinion is.

What we have tried to say, then, is the following. All our intuition is nothing but the presentation of appearance. The things that we intuit are not in themselves what we intuit them as being. Nor do their relations in themselves have the character that they appear to us as having. And if we annul ourselves as subject, or even annul only the subjective character of the senses generally, then this entire character of objects and all their relations in space and time — indeed, even space and time themselves — would vanish; being appearances, they cannot exist in themselves, but can exist only in us. What may be the case regarding objects in themselves and apart from all this receptivity of our sensibility remains to us entirely unknown. All we know is the way in which we perceive them. That way is peculiar to us and does not necessarily have to apply to all beings, even though it applies necessarily to all human beings. Solely with B60 that way of perceiving are we dealing here. Space

and time are its pure forms; sensation as such as its matter. Only that way of perceiving can we cognize a priori, i.e., prior to all actual perception, and that is why it is called pure intuition. Sensation, on the other hand, is that component in our cognition on whose account it is called a posteriori cognition, i.e., empirical intuition. The forms [of intuition] attach to our sensibility with absolute necessity, no matter of what kind our sensations may be; the sensations can differ very much. Even if we could bring this institution of ours to the highest degree of distinctness, that would still not get us closer to the character of objects in themselves. For what we would cognize, and cognize completely, would still be only our way of intuiting, i.e., our sensibility; and we would always cognize it only under the conditions attaching to the subject originally: space and time. What objects may be in themselves would still never become known to us, not even through the most enlightened cognition of what alone is given to us, viz., their appearance.

Hence we must reject the view[88] that our entire sensibility is nothing but our confused presentation of things, a presentation that contains solely what belongs to them in themselves, but contains it only by way of an accumulation of characteristics and partial presentations that we do not consciously discriminate. For this view falsifies the concept of sensibility and of appearance, thus rendering the entire doctrine of sensibility useless and empty. The distinction between an indistinct and a distinct presentation B61 is merely logical and does not concern the content. No doubt the concept of *rightness* as employed by common sense contains just the same as can be extricated from it by the most subtle speculation, except that in its common and practical use one is not conscious of the diverse presentations contained in that thought. But that does not entitle us to say that the common concept is sensible and contains a mere appearance. For rightness cannot be an appearance at all; rather, its concept lies in the understanding,[89] and we present by it a character of acts (their moral character) which belongs to them in themselves. On the other hand, when a *body* is presented in intuition,

---

86. [Space and time.]
87. [Namely, matter.]

88. [Held by Leibniz.]
89. [And not in intuition.]

this presentation contains nothing whatever that could belong to an object in itself. It contains, rather, merely the appearance of something, and the way we are affected by that something. This receptivity of our cognitive capacity is called sensibility; and even if we were to see through that appearance and to its very bottom, yet this receptivity remains as different as day and night from cognition of the object in itself.

Hence the philosophy of Leibniz and Wolff, by considering the distinction between what is sensible and what is intellectual as a merely logical one, has imposed an entirely wrong point of view on all investigations about the nature and origin of our cognitions. For plainly the distinction is transcendental, and does not concern merely the forms of these cognitions, B62 i.e., their distinctness or indistinctness, but concerns their origin and content. Hence sensibility does not merely fail to provide us with a distinct cognition of the character of things in themselves; it provides us with none whatsoever. And once we remove our subjective character, then the presented object, along with the properties contributed to it by sensible intuition, is not to be found anywhere at all; nor can it possibly be found, because this subjective character is precisely what determines the form of that object as appearance.[90]

It is true that we commonly make this distinction about appearances: we distinguish what attaches to their intuition essentially and holds for the sense of every human being in general, from what belongs to that intuition only contingently by being valid only for a special position of this or that sense, or for the special organization of that sense, but not valid for the relation of [the intuition to] sensibility in general. We then speak of the first kind of cognition as presenting the object in itself, and of the second as presenting only its appearance. This distinction, however, is only empirical. If (as is commonly done) we fail to go beyond it and do not (as we ought to do) regard that empirical intuition in turn as mere appearance, in which nothing whatever belonging to some thing in itself is to be found, then our transcendental distinction is lost. We then believe after all that we cognize B63 things in themselves, even though in the world of

sense, however deeply we explore its objects, we deal with nothing whatever but appearances. Thus it is true, e.g., that when during a rain accompanied by sunshine we see a rainbow, we will call it a mere appearance, while calling the rain the thing in itself. And this is indeed correct, provided that we here take the concept of a thing in itself as meaning only something physical. We then mean by it something that in general experience, and in all its different positions in relation to the senses, is yet determined thus, and not otherwise, in intuition. But suppose that we take this empirical something as such, and that—without being concerned about its being the same for the sense of every human being—we ask whether it presents also an object in itself (not whether it presents the rain drops, for these, as appearances, will already be empirical objects). In that case our question about the presentation's relation to the object is transcendental, and the answer is: Not only are these drops mere appearances; rather, even their round shape, and indeed even the space in which they fall, are nothing in themselves. They are, rather, mere modifications, or foundations, of our sensible intuition. The transcendental object, however, remains unknown to us.

Our second important concern in this transcendental aesthetic is that it should not merely gain some favor as a plausible hypothesis, but should be as certain and indubitable as can possibly be demanded of a theory that is to serve as an organon. In order to make this certainty fully evident, let us select some case that can render the validity of this organon obvi- B64 ous and can serve to clarify further what has been set forth in §3.

Suppose, then, that space and time are in themselves objective, and are conditions of the possibility of things in themselves. We then find, in the first place, that we encounter a large number of synthetic a priori propositions about both space and time— above all about space, which we shall therefore investigate here as our prime example. The propositions of geometry are cognized synthetically a priori and with apodeictic certainty. And so I ask: From where do you obtain such propositions, and on what does the understanding rely in order to arrive at such absolutely necessary and universally valid truths? There is no other way [to arrive at truths] than through concepts

90. [This is exactly what is involved in Kant's Copernican revolution. See B xvi–xvii.]

or through intuition. But these concepts and intuitions are both given either a priori or a posteriori. The a posteriori ones, i.e., empirical concepts as well as the empirical intuition on which they are based, can yield only such synthetic propositions as are likewise merely empirical, i.e., propositions of experience. As such, these propositions can never contain necessity and absolute universality; yet these are what characterize all geometric propositions. The first and sole means of arriving at such cognitions is a priori, through mere concepts or through intuitions. From mere concepts, however, we clearly can obtain no

B65 synthetic cognition at all, but only analytic cognition. Just take the proposition that two straight lines cannot enclose any space and hence do not permit [construction of] any figure, and try to derive it from the concept of straight lines and of the number two. Or take the proposition that three straight lines permit [construction of] a figure, and try similarly to derive it from these mere concepts. All your endeavor is futile, and you find yourselves compelled to have recourse to intuition, as indeed geometry always does. Hence you give yourselves an object in intuition. But of which kind is this intuition? Is it a pure a priori intuition or an empirical one? If it were an empirical intuition, then it could never turn into a universally valid proposition, let alone an apodeictic one; for experience can never supply anything like that. Hence you must give your object to yourselves a priori in intuition, and base your synthetic proposition on this object. Now suppose that there did not lie within you a power to intuit a priori; that this subjective condition were not, as regards its form, at the same time the universal a priori condition under which alone the object of this (outer) intuition is itself possible; and that the object (the triangle) were something in itself, even apart from any relation to yourselves as subject. If that were so, how could you say that what necessarily lies in [or belongs to] your subjective conditions for constructing a triangle must also belong necessarily to the triangle itself? For, after all, you could not add to your concepts (of three lines) anything new (the

B66 figure) that would therefore have to be met with necessarily in the object, since this object would be given prior to your cognition rather than through it. Hence you could not synthetically a priori establish anything whatsoever about external objects if space

(and similarly time) were not a mere form of your intuition, an intuition that a priori contains conditions under which alone things can be external objects for you—these objects being nothing in themselves, apart from these subjective conditions. Therefore the following is not merely possible—or probable, for that matter—but indubitably certain: Space and time, as the necessary conditions of all (outer and inner) experience, are merely subjective conditions of all our intuition. Hence in relation to these conditions all objects are mere appearances, and are not given to us in this way on their own. And that is why much can be said a priori about these objects as regards their form, but not the least can ever be said about the thing in itself that may underlie these appearances.

II. This theory, according to which both outer and inner sense are ideal and hence all objects of the senses are mere appearances, can be confirmed superbly by the following observation. Whatever in our cognition belongs to intuition (excluding, therefore, what are not cognitions at all, i.e., both the feeling of pleasure and displeasure and the will) contains nothing but mere relations; of places in an intuition B67 (extension), of change of places (motion), and of laws according to which this change is determined (motive forces). But what is present in that place, or what effect—besides the change of place—it produces in the things themselves, is not given to us by [what belongs to intuition]. Now through mere relations we do not, of course, cognize a thing in itself. Hence our judgment must surely be this: since through outer sense we are given nothing but mere relational presentations, outer sense can, by the same token, contain in its presentation only the relation of an object to the subject, but not the intrinsic character belonging to the object in itself. The same applies to inner intuition. For not only does the proper material in it, with which we occupy our mind, consist in presentations of *outer senses*; but the time in which we place these presentations, and which itself precedes the consciousness of them in experience and underlies, as formal condition, the way in which we place them within the mind, already contains relations: of succession, of simultaneity, and of what is simultaneous with succession (the permanent). Now, presentation that can precede all acts of thinking anything is intuition; and if this intuition contains nothing but relations then it is the form of intuition. But this form does not present anything except insofar as something is being placed within the mind. Therefore this form B68 can be nothing but the way in which the mind is affected by its own activity—viz., this placing of its presentation—and hence affected by itself; i.e., it is an inner sense insofar as that sense's form is concerned. Whatever is presented through a sense is, to that extent, always appearance. Hence either we must not grant that there is an inner sense at all; or we must grant that the subject who is the object of this sense can be presented through it only as appearance, and not as he would judge himself if his intuition were self-activity only, i.e., if it were intellectual intuition. What underlies this whole difficulty is this: how can a subject inwardly intuit himself? But this difficulty is shared by every theory. The consciousness of oneself (apperception) is the simple presentation of the *I*; and if through this consciousness by itself all the manifold in the subject were given *self-actively,* then the inner intuition would be intellectual. But in man this consciousness requires also inner perception of the manifold given in the subject beforehand; and the way in which this manifold is given in the mind— viz., without spontaneity—must, for the sake of marking this distinction, be called sensibility. If the power to become conscious of oneself is to locate (apprehend) what lies in the mind, then it must affect the mind; and only in that way can it produce an intuition of itself. But the form of this intuition lies at the basis B69 beforehand in the mind; and this form determines, in the presentation of time, the way in which the manifold is [placed] together in the mind. And thus this power does not intuit itself as it would if it presented itself directly and self-actively; rather, it intuits itself according to the way in which it is affected from within, and hence intuits itself as it appears to itself, not as it is.

III. I am saying, then, that the intuition of external objects and the self-intuition of the mind both present these objects and the mind, in space and in time, as they affect our senses, i.e., as they appear. But I do not mean by this that these objects are a mere *illusion.* For when we deal with appearance, the objects, and indeed even the properties that we ascribe to them, are always regarded as something actually given— except that insofar as the object's character depends only on the subject's way of intuiting this given object in its relation to him, we do also distinguish this object as *appearance* from the same object as object *in itself.*[91] Thus when I posit both bodies and my soul as being in accordance with the quality of space and time, as condition of their existence, I do indeed assert that this quality lies in my way of intuiting and not in those objects in themselves. But in asserting this I am not saying that the bodies merely *seem* to be outside me, or that my soul only *seems* to be given in my self-consciousness. It would be my own fault if I turned into mere illusion what I ought to class with appearance.[92] This is not, however, what happens B70 if we follow our principle that all our sensible intuitions are ideal. On the contrary: it is when we attribute *objective reality* to those forms of presentation that we cannot prevent everything from being thereby transformed into mere *illusion.* For suppose that we regard space and time as properties that, as far as their very possibility is concerned, must be found in things in themselves. And now reflect on the absurdities in which we then become entangled, inasmuch as [we then have] two infinite things that must not be substances nor anything actually inhering in substances, but that yet must be something existent—indeed, B71 must be the necessary condition for the existence of

---

91. [In Kant's usual (transcendental) sense of this expression, rather than in its empirical sense (found, e.g., at B 45 and B 62).]

92. The predicates of the appearance can be ascribed to the object itself in relation to our sense: e.g., to the rose, the red color or the scent. But what is mere illusion can never be ascribed as predicate to an object, precisely because illusion ascribes to the object taken *by itself* what belongs to it only in relation to the senses or in general to the subject—an example being the two handles initially ascribed to Saturn. If something is not to be met with at all in the object in itself, but is always to be met with in the object's relation to the subject and is inseparable from the presentation of the object, then it is appearance. And thus the predicates of space and time are rightly ascribed to objects of the senses, as such; and in this there is no illusion. Illusion first arises if, by contrast, I ascribe the redness to the rose *in itself,* or the handles to Saturn, or extension to all external objects *in themselves,* without taking account of—and limiting my judgment to—a determinate relation of these objects to the subject.

all things—and must moreover remain even if all existing things are annulled. If we thus reflect on this supposition, then we can hardly blame the good *Berkeley* for downgrading bodies to mere illusion. Indeed, even our own existence, which would in this way be made dependent on the self-subsistent reality of a nonentity such as time would be, would be transformed along with this time into nothing but illusion—an absurdity of which no one thus far has made himself guilty.

IV. In natural theology we think an object [viz., God] that not only cannot possibly be an object of intuition for us, but that cannot in any way be an object of sensible intuition even to itself. [When we think of God in this way,] we take great care to remove the conditions of time and space from all his intuition. (All his cognition must be intuition rather than *thought*, which always manifests limits.) But what right do we have to do this if we have beforehand turned space and time into forms of things in themselves—such forms, moreover, as are a priori conditions of the existence of things and hence would remain even if we had annulled the things themselves? For as conditions of all existence in general, they would have to be conditions also of the existence of God. If we are not to make space and time objective
B72 forms of all things, then we are left with only one alternative: we must make them subjective forms of our kind of intuition, inner and outer. Our kind of intuition is called sensible[93] because it is *not original.* I.e., it is not such that through this intuition itself the existence of its object is given (the latter being a kind of intuition that, as far as we can see, can belong only to the original being). Rather, our kind of intuition is dependent on the existence of the object, and hence is possible only by the object's affecting the subject's capacity to present.

93. [Rather than intellectual.]

There is, moreover, no need for us to limit this kind of intuition—intuition in space and time—to the sensibility of man. It may be (though we cannot decide this) that any finite thinking being must necessarily agree with man in this regard. Yet even if this kind of intuition were thus universally valid, it would not therefore cease to be sensibility. It would remain sensibility precisely because it is derivative (*intuitus derivativus*) rather than original (*intuitus originarius*), and hence is not intellectual intuition. For the reason just set forth, intellectual intuition seems to belong solely to the original being, and never to a being that is dependent as regards both its existence and its intuition (an intuition that determines that being's existence by reference to given objects). This last remark, however, must be considered as included in our aesthetic theory only as an illustration, not as a basis of proof.

CONCLUDING THE TRANSCENDENTAL AESTHETIC   *B73*

Thus in our pure a priori intuitions, space and time, we now have one of the components required for solving the general problem of transcendental philosophy: *How are synthetic propositions possible a priori?* When in an a priori judgment about space and time we want to go beyond the given concept, we encounter[94] what cannot be discovered a priori in the given concept, but can indeed be so discovered in the intuition corresponding to that concept and can be combined with it synthetically. Because of this,[95] however, such judgments can never reach beyond objects of the senses, and can hold only for objects of possible experience.

94. [In the a priori intuition.]
95. [The judgment's dependence on intuition and the merely synthetic connection to the concept.]

PART II

TRANSCENDENTAL LOGIC
Introduction
Idea of a Transcendental Logic

I

ON LOGIC AS SUCH

Our cognition arises from two basic sources of the mind. The first is [our ability] to receive presentations (and is our receptivity for impressions); the second is our ability to cognize an object through these presentations (and is the spontaneity of concepts[96]). Through receptivity an object is *given* to us; through spontaneity an object is *thought* in relation to that [given] presentation (which [otherwise][97] is a mere determination of the mind). Intuition and concepts, therefore, constitute the elements of all our cognition. Hence neither concepts without an intuition corresponding to them in some way or other, nor intuition without concepts can yield cognition. Both intuition and concepts are either pure or empirical. They are *empirical* if they contain sensation (sensation presupposes the actual presence of the object); they are *pure* if no sensation is mixed in with the presentation.[98] Sensation may be called the matter of sensible cogni-
B75 tion. Hence pure intuition contains only the form under which something is intuited, and a pure concept contains solely the form of the thought of an object as such. Only pure intuitions or concepts are possible a priori; empirical ones are possible only a posteriori.

Let us give the name *sensibility* to our mind's recep-

tivity, [i.e., to its ability] to receive presentations insofar as it is affected in some manner. *Understanding*, on the other hand, is our ability to produce presentations ourselves, i.e., our *spontaneity* of cognition. Our *intuition*, by our very nature, can never be other than *sensible* intuition;[99] i.e., it contains only the way in which we are affected by objects. *Understanding*, on the other hand, is our ability to *think* the object of sensible intuition. Neither of these properties is to be preferred to the other. Without sensibility no object would be given to us; and without understanding no object would be thought. Thoughts without content are empty; intuitions without concepts are blind. Hence it is just as necessary that we make our concepts sensible (i.e., that we add the object to them in intuition) as it is necessary that we make our intuitions understandable (i.e., that we bring them under concepts). Moreover, this capacity and this ability[100] cannot exchange their functions. The understanding cannot intuit anything,[101] and the senses cannot think anything. Only from their union can cognition arise. B76 This fact, however, must not lead us to confuse their respective contributions;[102] it provides us, rather, with a strong reason for carefully separating and distinguishing sensibility and understanding from each other. Hence we distinguish the science of the rules of sensibility as such, i.e., aesthetic, from the science of the rules of the understanding as such, i.e., logic.

Now logic, in turn, can be done from two points of view, either as logic of the understanding's general use or as logic of its special use. The logic of the understanding's general use contains the absolutely necessary rules of thought without which the understanding cannot be used at all. Hence it deals with the understanding without regard to the difference among the objects to which the understanding may

---

96. [I.e., the self-activity (cf. B 68) of using concepts in thought and cognition and of expanding them to frame new ones.]

97. [I.e., apart from that thought, whereby this determination enters into our cognition of the object.]

98. [I.e., the intuition or concept.]

99. [Only an intuitive understanding (ours is discursive, i.e., conceptual) can have *intellectual* intuition. See B 72.]

100. [I.e., sensibility and understanding.]

101. [See n. 99, just above.]

102. [To cognition.]

be directed. This logic may be called elementary logic. The logic of the understanding's special use, which may be called the organon of this or that science, contains the rules for thinking correctly about a certain kind of objects. The schools usually make this logic a preface to the sciences, using it as a propaedeutic, even though in terms of the progression of human reason it comes last: reason does not arrive at this logic until long after the science is done and needs only finishing touches that will correct and B77 perfect it. For if we are to state the rule as to how a [particular] science can be brought about, then the objects of that science must already be familiar to us to a fairly high degree.

Now general logic is either pure or applied logic. In general logic we abstract from all empirical conditions under which we exercise our understanding. We abstract, e.g., from the influence of the senses, from the play of imagination, from the laws of memory, from the force of habit, from inclination, etc.; hence we abstract also from the sources of prejudices, and indeed from all causes generally that give rise, or may be alleged to give rise, to such and such cognitions. For these empirical conditions concern the understanding only as applied under certain circumstances, and becoming acquainted with these circumstances requires experience. Hence a logic that is *general* but also *pure* deals with nothing but a priori principles. Such a logic is a *canon of understanding* and of reason, but only as regards what is formal in our use of them—i.e., we disregard what the content may be (whether it is empirical or transcendental). A *general logic* is called *applied*, on the other hand, if it is concerned with the rules of the understanding as used under the subjective empirical conditions taught us by psychology. Hence such a logic has empirical principles, although it is general insofar as it deals with our use of the understanding without distinguishing the understanding's objects. That is also the reason why applied general logic is neither a canon of the understanding as such nor an organon B78 of special sciences, but solely a cathartic for the common understanding.[103] In general logic, therefore, the part that is to constitute the pure doctrine of reason must be separated entirely from the part that is to constitute applied (though still general) logic. Only

the first of these parts[104] is, properly speaking, a science, although it is brief and dry and thus is such as the exposition of a doctrine of the understanding's elements is required to be in order to comply with school standards. In such pure general logic, therefore, the logicians must always have in mind two rules:

1. As general logic, it abstracts from all content of the cognition of understanding and from the difference among the objects of that cognition, and deals with nothing but the mere form of thought.

2. As pure logic, it has no empirical principles. Hence it does not (as people have sometimes come to be persuaded) take anything from psychology; and therefore psychology has no influence whatever on the canon of the understanding. Pure general logic is demonstrated doctrine, and everything in it must be certain completely a priori.

What I call applied logic is a presentation of the understanding and of the rules governing its necessary use *in concreto*, viz., its use under the contingent conditions attaching to the subject, conditions that B79 can impede or promote this use and that are, one and all, given only empirically. (This definition of applied logic is contrary to the ordinary meaning of the expression, according to which applied logic should contain certain exercises for which pure logic gives the rule). On my definition, applied logic deals with attention; attention's being impeded and the consequences thereof; the origin of error; the states of doubt, of having scruples, of conviction, etc. Pure general logic relates to applied general logic as pure morality relates to the doctrine proper of virtue. Pure morality contains merely the moral laws of a free will as such; the doctrine of virtue examines these laws as impeded by the feelings, inclinations, and passions to which human beings are more or less subject. The doctrine of virtue can never serve as true and demonstrated science; for, just like applied logic, it requires empirical and psychological principles.

II

On Transcendental Logic

General logic, as we have shown, abstracts from all content of cognition, i.e., from all reference of cogni-

---

103. [I.e., common sense.]

104. [Pure general logic.]

tion to its object. It examines only the logical form in the relation that cognitions have to one another, i.e., only the form of thought as such. But (as the Transcendental Aesthetic establishes) there are both pure and empirical intuitions; and hence we might B80 well find it appropriate to distinguish also between pure and empirical thought of objects. In that case there would be a logic in which we would not abstract from all content of cognition. For a logic containing merely the rules governing the pure thought of an object would only exclude all those cognitions that have empirical content. Such a logic, moreover, would also deal with the origin of our cognitions of objects insofar as that origin cannot be attributed to the objects, whereas general logic has nothing to do with the origin of cognition. Rather, general logic examines presentations, whether these have their basic origin a´ priori in ourselves, or are given only empirically; and it examines these presentations merely in terms of the laws according to which the understanding, when it thinks, uses them in their relation to one another. Hence general logic deals only with that form of the understanding which can be imparted to the presentations, whatever their origin may be irrespective of that form.

And here I shall make a comment; it extends its influence to all subsequent contemplations, and hence must be remembered carefully. We must not call just any a priori cognition transcendental, but must call transcendental (i.e., concerning the a priori possibility or the a priori use of cognition) only that a priori cognition whereby we cognize that—and how—certain presentations (intuitions or concepts) B81 are applied, or are possible, simply a priori. Hence neither space nor any a priori geometric determination of it is a transcendental presentation. Rather, we may call transcendental only the cognition that these presentations are not at all of empirical origin, and the possibility whereby they can nonetheless refer a priori to objects of experience. Similarly, the use of space regarding objects in general[105] would also be transcendental. But if the use of space is limited to objects of the senses only, then it is called empirical. The distinction between the transcendental and the empirical belongs, therefore, only to the critique of

cognitions, and does not concern the reference of these cognitions to their object.

We shall expect, then, that there may perhaps be concepts referring a priori to objects. Not being pure or sensible intuitions, but being merely acts of pure thought, they would be concepts, but such concepts as originate neither empirically nor aesthetically.[106] In this expectation, then, we frame in advance the idea of a science of pure understanding and of rational cognition, whereby we think objects completely a priori. Such a science would determine the origin, the range, and the objective validity of such rational cognitions. It would have to be called *transcendental logic.* For it deals merely with the laws of understanding and of reason; yet it does so only insofar as this B82 logic is referred a priori to objects—unlike general logic, which is referred indiscriminately to empirical as well as pure rational cognitions.

III

On the Division of General Logic into Analytic and Dialectic

What is truth? is the ancient and famous question with which people meant to drive logicians into a corner, trying to get them to the point where either they must let themselves be caught in a pitiful circle, or they must confess their ignorance and hence admit the futility of their whole art. In asking logicians this question, these people took for granted, and they presupposed, the explication of the name *truth,*[107] viz., that truth is the agreement of cognition with its object. They demanded to know, instead, what is the universal and safe criterion of the truth of any cognition. [They failed to see, however, the absurdity of their own question.]

To know what question one should, reasonably, ask is already a great and necessary proof of one's sagacity and insight. For if the question is in itself absurd and demands answers that are unnecessary, then it not only embarrasses the person raising it, but sometimes has the further disadvantage of misleading the incautious listener: it may prompt him to give

---

105. [Objects of experience (which includes sensation) and objects of pure geometry.]

106. [I.e., concepts originating neither from empirical intuition nor from intuition generally.]

107. [I.e., in effect, the definition.]

B83 absurd answers and to provide us with the ridiculous spectacle where (as the ancients said) one person milks the ram[108] while the other holds a sieve underneath.

Thus if truth consists in the agreement of a cognition with its object, then this object must here be distinguished from others. For if a cognition does not agree with the object to which it is referred then it is false, even if it contains something that might well hold for other objects. Now a universal criterion of truth would be one that is valid for all cognitions, without distinction of their objects. But while in such a universal criterion of truth we thus abstract from all content of cognition (i.e., from its reference to its object), yet truth concerns this very content. Clearly, therefore, asking questions about a mark for the truth of this content of cognitions is quite impossible and absurd; and hence one cannot possibly give an indicator of truth that is sufficient and yet universal at the same time. Now we have already earlier called the content of a cognition its matter. Hence we shall have to say that no universal indicator can be demanded for the truth of cognition in terms of its matter, because such an indicator would be intrinsically contradictory.

As regards cognition in terms of its mere form (setting aside all content), on the other hand, and thus as regards a logic insofar as it puts forth the universal and B84 necessary rules of the understanding, it is equally clear that such a logic must in these very rules set down criteria of truth. For whatever contradicts these rules is false, because the understanding is then in conflict with its own universal rules of thought, and hence with itself. These criteria, however, concern only the form of truth, i.e., the truth of thought as such, and are to that extent quite correct. But they are not sufficient. For even if a cognition accorded completely with logical form, i.e., even if it did not contradict itself, it could still contradict its object. Therefore the merely logical criterion of truth, viz., a cognition's agreement with the universal and formal laws of understanding and reason, is indeed the *conditio sine qua non*,[109] and hence the negative condition, of all truth. But logic cannot go any farther than this; it has no touchstone by which it can discover an error that concerns content rather than form.

Now general logic analyzes the whole formal business of understanding and reason into its elements, and exhibits these elements as principles governing all logical judging of our cognition. Hence this part of logic may be called an analytic. This analytic is at least the negative touchstone of truth, precisely because all cognition must first of all be tested and assessed, in terms of its form, by these rules;[110] this must be done before we examine these rules themselves in terms of their content in order to establish whether they contain positive truth as regards their B85 object. On the other hand, the mere form of cognition, however much it may agree with logical laws, is far from being sufficient to establish that a cognition is true objectively (materially). Hence with mere logic no one can venture to make judgments about objects and assert anything about them. Rather, we must first go outside logic to obtain well-based information about objects, in order then to attempt merely employing this information and connecting it in a coherent whole in accordance with logical laws, or—better yet—in order only to test the information by these laws. Yet there is something very tempting about possessing so plausible an art, whereby we give to all our cognitions the form of our understanding—even though we may still be very empty-handed and poor as regards the cognition's content. So great is this temptation that this general logic, which is merely a *canon* for judging, has been used—like an *organon*, as it were—for the actual production of at least deceptive objective assertions, and thus has in fact been misused. Now general logic, when used as supposed organon, is called *dialectic*.

Although the ancients used this name *dialectic*, as standing for a science or art, in quite different senses, still from their actual use of the name we can safely glean that dialectic was for them nothing other than B86 the *logic of illusion*. I.e., it was the sophistical art of giving an air of truth to one's ignorance, and indeed even to one's deliberate deceptions; this was done by imitating the method of thoroughness prescribed by logic as such, and by employing the topic of

---

108. [Reference works characterize this saying as a Greco-Roman proverb quoted (e.g.) in Samuel Hieron, *Works* (1616), i, 586; and in John Hales, *Several Tracts* (1656), 40. Milking of rams is mentioned also in Vergil's *Eclogues*, iii, 91.]

109. [Indispensable (or necessary) condition.]

110. [I.e., the principles just mentioned.]

logic[111] to paint over any empty pretense. Now we may note (as a sure and useful warning) that general logic, when *regarded as an organon*, is always a logic of illusion, i.e., it is always dialectical. For general logic teaches us nothing whatever about the content of cognition; it teaches us merely the formal conditions for the agreement [of cognition] with the understanding, and these conditions are wholly inconsequential otherwise, i.e., as regards the [cognition's] objects. Hence the impudent use of general logic as an instrument (organon), in order (at least allegedly) to broaden and expand one's knowledge, comes down to nothing but idle chatter, where anything one wishes is—with some semblance of plausibility—asserted or, for that matter, challenged at will.

Such instruction is in no way compatible with the dignity of philosophy. For this reason the name *dialectic* has been [redefined so that a dialectic is] included with logic as a *critique* of *dialectical illusion*; and this is how we want it to be understood here as well.

_{B87}

IV

ON THE DIVISION OF TRANSCENDENTAL LOGIC INTO TRANSCENDENTAL ANALYTIC AND DIALECTIC

In a transcendental logic we isolate the understanding (just as in the transcendental aesthetic above we isolated sensibility), and we select from our cognition merely that part of thought which has its origin solely in the understanding. The use of this pure cognition rests on the condition, however, that objects to which it can be applied are given to us in intuition. For without intuition, all our cognition lacks objects, and thus remains completely empty. That part, then, of transcendental logic which sets forth the elements of understanding's pure cognition, as well as the principles without which no object can be thought at all, is transcendental analytic. It is at the same time a logic of truth. For no cognition can contradict it

without at the same time losing all content, i.e., all reference to any object, and hence without losing all truth. On the other hand, there is great enticement and temptation to employ these pure cognitions of understanding and these principles by themselves, and to do so even beyond the bounds of experience, even though only experience can provide us with B88 the matter (objects) to which those pure concepts of understanding can be applied. As a consequence, the understanding runs the risk that, by idly engaging in subtle reasoning, it will put the merely formal principles of pure understanding to a material use, and will make judgments indiscriminately even about objects that are not given, or indeed about objects that perhaps cannot be given in any way at all. Properly, then, transcendental analytic should be only a canon for judging the empirical use.[112] Hence we misuse transcendental analytic if we accept it as the organon of a universal and unlimited use, and if with pure understanding alone we venture to judge, assert, and decide anything synthetically about objects as such. Hence[113] the use of pure understanding would then be dialectical. Therefore the second part of transcendental logic must be a critique of this dialectical illusion, and is called transcendental dialectic. It is to be regarded not as an art of dogmatically creating such illusion (an art that is unfortunately quite prevalent in diverse cases of metaphysical jugglery), but as a critique of understanding and reason as regards their hyperphysical use. We need such a critique in order to uncover the deceptive illusion in the baseless pretensions of understanding and reason; and we need it in order to downgrade reason's claim that it discovers and expands [cognition]—which it supposedly accomplishes by merely using transcendental principles—[to the claim that it] merely judges pure understanding and guards it against sophistical deceptions.

TRANSCENDENTAL LOGIC _{B89}
Division I
TRANSCENDENTAL ANALYTIC

Transcendental analytic consists in the dissection of our entire a priori cognition into the elements of

111. [The topic (or topics) of (general) logic is the art, developed above all by Aristotle in his *Topics*, of discovering plausible (though not demonstrative) arguments to establish or refute a given position. This discovery is accomplished by means of general argument forms that, being prepared in advance, serve as the "places" (Greek τόποι [*tópoi*], Latin *topica*) or headings to which the more specific arguments are referred.]

112. [Of the understanding; similarly for "universal and unlimited use" just below.]

113. [I.e., as such a misuse.]

understanding's pure cognition. The following points are what matters in this dissection: (1) The concepts must be pure rather than empirical. (2) They must belong not to intuition and sensibility, but to thought and understanding. (3) They must be elementary concepts, and must be distinguished carefully from concepts that are either derivative or composed of such elementary concepts. (4) Our table of these concepts must be complete, and the concepts must occupy fully the whole realm of pure understanding. Now, this completeness [characteristic] of a science cannot be assumed reliably by gauging an aggregate of concepts that was brought about merely through trials. Hence this completeness is possible only by means of an *idea of the whole* of understanding's a priori cognition, and through the division, determined by that idea, of the concepts amounting to that cognition; and hence this completeness is possible only through the *coherence* of these concepts *in a system*. Pure understanding differentiates itself fully not only from everything empirical, but even from all sensibility [generally].[114] Therefore it is a unity that is self-sub-
B90 sistent, sufficient to itself, and that cannot be augmented by supplementing it with any extrinsic additions. Hence the sum of pure understanding's cognition will constitute a system that can be encompassed and determined by an idea. The system's completeness and structure can at the same time serve as a touchstone of the correctness and genuineness of whatever components of cognition fit into the system. This entire part of the Transcendental Logic[115] consists, however, of two *books*; one of these contains the *concepts*, the other the *principles*, of pure understanding.

Transcendental Analytic
Book I
Analytic of Concepts

By *analytic of concepts* I do not mean the analysis of concepts, i.e., the usual procedure in philosophical inquiries of dissecting already available concepts in terms of their content and bringing them to distinctness; rather, I mean the hitherto rarely attempted

dissection[116] *of the power of understanding itself*. The purpose of this dissection is to explore the possibility of a priori concepts, by locating them solely in the understanding, as their birthplace, and by analyzing the understanding's pure use as such. For this exploration is the proper task of a transcendental philosophy; B91 the rest[117] is the logical treatment of concepts in philosophy generally. Hence we shall trace the pure concepts all the way to their first seeds and predispositions in the human understanding, where these concepts lie prepared until finally, on the occasion of experience, they are developed and are exhibited by that same understanding in their purity, freed from the empirical conditions attaching to them.

Analytic of Concepts

Chapter I
On the Guide for the Discovery of All Pure Concepts of Understanding

When we bring into play a cognitive power, then, depending on the various ways in which we may be prompted to do so, different concepts come to the fore that allow us to recognize this power. These concepts can be collected[118] in an essay that will be more or less comprehensive, once the concepts have been observed fairly long or with significant mental acuity. But by this—as it were, mechanical—procedure we can never reliably determine at what point that inquiry will be completed. Moreover, if concepts are discovered only on given occasions, then they reveal themselves in no order or systematic unity; B92 instead they are ultimately only paired according to similarities, and arranged in series according to the quantity of their content, from the simple concepts on to the more composite. The way in which these series are brought about, despite being methodical in a certain manner, is anything but systematic.

Transcendental philosophy has the advantage, but also the obligation, of locating its concepts according to a principle. For these concepts arise, pure and unmixed, from the understanding, which is an abso-

114. [I.e., even from a priori intuition.]
115. [Viz., the Transcendental Analytic.]

116. [I.e., analysis.]
117. [The analysis of concepts mentioned above.]
118. [And set forth.]

lute unity; and hence these concepts themselves must cohere with each other according to one concept or idea. Such coherence, however, provides us with a rule by which we can determine a priori the proper place for each pure concept of understanding, and the completeness of all of them taken together—whereas otherwise all of this would be subject to one's own discretion or to chance.

Transcendental Guide for the Discovery of All Pure Concepts of Understanding

Section I
On the Understanding's Logical Use As Such

The understanding was explicated merely negatively above, viz., as a non-sensible cognitive power. And since independently of sensibility we cannot partake of any intuition, it follows that the understanding is not a power of intuition. Apart from intuition, how-B93 ever, there is only one way of cognizing, viz., through concepts. Hence the cognition of any understanding, or at least of the human understanding, is a cognition through concepts; it is not intuitive, but discursive. All our intuitions, as sensible, rest on our being affected; concepts, on the other hand, rest on functions. By *function* I mean the unity of the act of arranging various presentations under one common presentation. Hence concepts[119] are based on the spontaneity of thought, whereas sensible intuitions are based on the receptivity for impressions. Now the only use that the understanding can make of these concepts is to judge by means of them. But in such judging, a concept is never referred directly to an object, because the only kind of presentation that deals with its object directly is intuition. Instead the concept is referred directly to some other presentation of the object (whether that presentation be an intuition or itself already a concept). Judgment, therefore, is the indirect cognition of an object, viz., the presentation of a presentation of it. In every judgment there is a concept that [comprises and thus] holds for many [presentations], and, among them, comprises also a

given presentation that is referred directly to the object. E.g., in the judgment, *All bodies are divisible*, the concept of the divisible refers to various other concepts; but, among these, it is here referred specifically to the concept of body, and the concept of body is referred in turn to certain appearances that we B94 encounter. Hence these objects are presented indirectly through the concept of divisibility. Accordingly, all judgments are functions of unity among our presentations. For instead of cognizing the object by means of a direct presentation, we do so by means of a higher presentation comprising both this direct presentation and several other presentations; and we thereby draw many possible cognitions together into one. Now since all acts of the understanding can be reduced to judgments, the *understanding* as such can be presented as a *power of judgment*. For, according to what we said above, the understanding is a power of thought. But thought is cognition through concepts; and concepts, as predicates of possible judgments, refer to some presentation of an as yet undetermined object. Thus the concept of body signifies something—e.g., metal—that can be cognized through that concept. Hence it is a concept only because there are contained under it other presentations by means of which it can refer to objects. Therefore the concept of body is the predicate for a possible judgment, e.g., the judgment that every metal is a body. Therefore we can find all of the functions of the understanding if we can exhibit completely the functions of unity in judgments. This, however, can be accomplished quite readily, as the following section will show.

[Transcendental] Guide for the Discovery of All Pure Concepts B95 of Understanding

Section II

§ 9

On the Understanding's Logical Function in Judgments

If we abstract from all content of a judgment as such and pay attention only to the mere form of understanding in it, then we find that the function of

---

119. [Inasmuch as they involve such an act.]

thought in judgment can be brought under four headings, each containing under it three moments. They can conveniently be presented in the following table.

1
Quantity of Judgments
Universal
Particular
Singular

2   3
Quality   *Relation*
Affirmative   Categorical
Negative   Hypothetical
Infinite   Disjunctive

4
Modality
Problematic
Assertoric
Apodeictic

B96   Since this division departs in some respects, even though not in essential ones, from the customary technical apparatus used by logicians, there will be some point in my offering the following safeguards against the worrisome possibility of its being misunderstood.

1. Logicians are right in saying that, when judgments are used in syllogisms, singular judgments can be treated like universal ones. For precisely because singular judgments have no range at all, any predicate of them cannot be referred to some part of what is contained under the concept of the subject and be excluded from some other part of it. Hence the predicate of a singular judgment holds for the subject concept without exception, just as if this concept were a generally valid[120] one and the predicate held for the whole denotation within the concept's range. On the other hand, if[121] a singular judgment is compared in terms of quantity with a generally valid one merely as [two kinds of] cognition[122], then the singular judgment relates to the generally valid one as unity relates

to infinity, and hence is in itself essentially distinct from it. Suppose, therefore, that I assess a singular judgment (*iudicium singulare*) not merely in terms of its intrinsic validity but also as cognition as such, and assess it in terms of the quantity that it has by comparison with other cognitions. In that case the singular judgment is indeed distinct from generally valid judgments (*iudicia communia*); and hence it then deserves a separate place in a complete table of the moments of thought as such (although it does indeed not deserve a separate place in the logic that B97 is limited to the use of judgments merely in relation to one another).

2. Similarly, in a transcendental logic we must distinguish from *affirmative* judgments [not only negative ones but] also *infinite judgments*, even though in general logic they are rightly included with affirmative ones and do not constitute a separate member in the division of judgments. For general logic abstracts from all content of the predicate (even if the predicate is negative), and has regard only for whether the predicate is being ascribed to the subject or is being opposed to it. But transcendental logic considers the judgment also in terms of what value or content there is in this logical affirmation made by means of a merely negative predicate, and in terms of what gain for cognition as a whole is provided by this affirmation. If in speaking of the soul I had said, It is not mortal, then by this negative judgment I would at least have avoided an error. Now if I say instead, The soul is nonmortal, then I have indeed, in terms of logical form, actually affirmed something; for I have posited the soul in the unlimited range of nonmortal beings. Now what is mortal comprises one part of the whole range of possible beings, and what is nonmortal comprises the other. Hence my proposition[123] says nothing more than that the soul is one of the infinite multitude of things that remain if I take away whatever is mortal. But to say that is only to limit the infinite sphere of all that is possible, viz., to limit it to the extent that what is mortal is separated from it and the B98 soul is posited in the remaining space of the sphere's range.[124] But despite this exclusion [of what is mortal

---

120. [I.e., in effect, universal.]

121. [As is done in transcendental logic (as distinguished from general logic).]

122. [I.e., as two kinds of judgments (propositions), rather than as parts of a syllogism.]

123. [That the soul is nonmortal.]

124. [I.e., the space (of the sphere's range) that includes whatever is nonmortal.]

from it], this space still remains infinite; and even if we take away from it still more parts, this does not in the least increase the concept of the soul and determine it affirmatively. Hence although such judgments[125] are infinite as regards logical range, they are actually merely limitive as regards the content of cognition as such. In view of this, they must not be omitted from the transcendental table of all moments of the thought occurring in judgments, because the function that the understanding performs in these infinite judgments may perhaps be important in the realm of the understanding's pure a priori cognition.

3. The following are all the relations of thought in judgments: (a) the relation of the predicate to the subject; (b) the relation of the ground to its consequence; (c) the relation, in a divided cognition, of all of the division's members to one another. In these three kinds of judgments we consider, in relation to one another: in the first kind of judgments, two concepts only; in the second, two judgments; in the third, several judgments. To illustrate the second kind, take a hypothetical proposition: If there is a perfect justice, then the persistently evil person is punished. This proposition in fact contains the relation of two propositions: There is a perfect justice; and, The persistently evil person is punished. Whether these two propositions are in themselves true remains undecided here; only the implication is thought through this hypothetical judgment. Finally, to illustrate the third kind: a B99 disjunctive judgment contains a relation of two, or of several, propositions to one another. But this relation is not one of sequence. Rather, it is a relation of logical opposition, insofar as the sphere of the one proposition excludes the sphere of the other; yet it is at the same time a relation of community, insofar as the two propositions together occupy the sphere of the proper cognition involved. Hence the relation of the propositions in a disjunctive judgment is a relation of the parts of a cognition's sphere. For the sphere of each part complements the sphere of the other part, to yield the whole sum of the divided cognition. Take this judgment, e.g.: The world exists either through blind chance, or through internal necessity, or through an external cause. Each of these propositions occupies a part of the sphere of possible cogni-

tion concerning the existence of a world as such; all of them together occupy the whole sphere. To remove the cognition from one of these spheres means placing it into one of the other spheres; and, on the other hand, to place it into one sphere means to remove it from the others. Hence in a disjunctive judgment there is a certain community of cognitions. This community consists in the fact that the cognitions reciprocally exclude one another, and yet as a *whole* determine thereby the true cognition; for, taken together, they constitute the whole content of a single given cognition. And this, moreover, is all that I here need to point out in view of what follows.

4. The modality of judgments is a very special function of them. What distinguishes this function is the fact that it contributes nothing to the judgment's B100 content (for besides quantity, quality, and relation there is nothing else to constitute a judgment's content). Rather, modality concerns only the value that the copula has in reference to thought as such. *Problematic* judgments are those where the affirmation or negation is taken as merely *possible* (optional); *assertoric* ones are those where the affirmation or negation is considered as *actual* (true); *apodeictic* ones are those in which it is regarded as *necessary*.[126] Thus the two judgments (*antecedens* and *consequens*) whose relation constitutes the hypothetical judgment, and similarly the judgments (members of the division) in whose interaction the disjunctive judgment consists, are one and all problematic only. In the above example, the proposition, There is a perfect justice, is not uttered assertorically, but is thought only as an optional judgment, i.e., one that it is possible for someone to assume; only the implication is assertoric. This is also the reason why such optional judgments, even if manifestly false, can still, when taken problematically, be conditions for the cognition of truth. Thus in the disjunctive judgment used above, the judgment *The world exists through blind chance* has only problematic meaning; viz., to the effect that someone might perhaps assume this proposition for an instant. B101 And yet it serves us in finding the true proposition

125. [As the judgment that the soul is nonmortal.]

126. Just as if thought were a function of the *understanding* in the case of problematic judgments, of our *power of judgment* in the case of assertoric ones, and of *reason* in the case of apodeictic judgments. This remark must wait for its clarification until later.

(just as indicating the wrong road serves us in finding the right one among the number of all the roads that one can take). Hence a problematic proposition is one that expresses only logical possibility (which is not objective possibility). I.e., it expresses a free choosing to let such a proposition stand—a mere electing to admit it into the understanding. An assertoric proposition speaks of logical actuality or truth; thus in a hypothetical syllogism, e.g., the antecedent occurs problematically in the major premise but assertorically in the minor premise. And the assertoric proposition indicates that it is already linked with the understanding in accordance with the understanding's law. An apodeictic proposition thinks the assertoric one as determined by these laws of the understanding themselves, and hence thinks it as maintaining [this or that] a priori; and in this way it expresses logical necessity. Thus everything is incorporated in the understanding by degrees: at first we judge something problematically; then perhaps we also accept it assertorically as true; and finally we maintain it as linked inseparably with the understanding, i.e., as necessary and apodeictic. And hence these three functions of modality may also be called so many moments of thought as such.

[Transcendental] Guide for
B102   **the Discovery of All Pure Concepts of Understanding**

Section III

§ 10

ON THE PURE CONCEPTS OF UNDERSTANDING, OR CATEGORIES

General logic, as we have said several times already, abstracts from all content of cognition. It expects presentations to be given to it from somewhere else— no matter where—in order then to transform these presentations into concepts in the first place. This it does analytically. Transcendental logic, on the other hand, has lying before it a manifold of a priori sensibility, offered to it by transcendental aesthetic. Transcendental aesthetic offers it this manifold in order to provide it with a material for the pure concepts of

understanding. Without this material, transcendental logic would have no content, and hence would be completely empty. Now space and time contain a manifold of pure a priori intuition. But they belong nonetheless to the conditions of our mind's receptivity under which alone the mind can receive presentations of objects, and which, by the same token, must always affect the concept of these objects. Yet the spontaneity of our thought requires that this manifold, in order to be turned into a cognition, must first be gone through, taken up, and combined in a certain manner. This act I call synthesis.

By *synthesis*, in the most general sense of the term, B103 I mean the act of putting various presentations with one another and of comprising their manifoldness in one cognition. Such synthesis is *pure* if the manifold is given not empirically but a priori (as is the manifold in space and time). Before any analysis of our presentations can take place, these presentations must first be given, and hence in terms of *content* no concepts can originate analytically. Rather, synthesis of a manifold (whether this manifold is given empirically or a priori) is what first gives rise to a cognition. Although this cognition may still be crude and confused at first and hence may require analysis, yet synthesis is what in fact gathers the elements for cognition and unites them to [form] a certain content. Hence if we want to make a judgment about the first origin of our cognition, then we must first direct our attention to synthesis.

Synthesis as such, as we shall see hereafter, is the mere effect produced by the imagination, which is a blind but indispensable function of the soul without which we would have no cognition whatsoever, but of which we are conscious only very rarely. Bringing this synthesis to *concepts*, on the other hand, is a function belonging to the understanding; and it is through this function that the understanding first provides us with cognition in the proper meaning of the term.

Now *pure synthesis, conceived of generally,* yields B104 the pure concept of understanding. By pure synthesis I mean the synthesis that rests on a basis of synthetic a priori unity. E.g., our act of counting (as is more noticeable primarily with larger numbers) is a *synthesis according to concepts*, because it is performed according to a common basis of unity (such as the decimal system). Hence under this concept the unity of the manifold's synthesis becomes necessary.

Bringing various presentations *under* a concept (a task dealt with by general logic) is done analytically. But bringing, not presentations but the *pure synthesis* of presentations, *to* concepts is what transcendental logic teaches. The first [thing] that we must be given a priori in order to cognize any object is the *manifold* of pure intuition. The second [thing] is the *synthesis* of this manifold by the imagination. But this synthesis does not yet yield cognition. The third [thing we need] in order to cognize an object that we encounter is the concepts which give *unity* to this pure synthesis and which consist solely in the presentation of this necessary synthetic unity. And these concepts rest on the understanding.

The same function that gives unity to the various presentations *in a judgment* also gives unity to the

B105 mere synthesis of various presentations *in an intuition*. This unity—speaking generally—is called pure concept of understanding. Hence the same understanding—and indeed through the same acts whereby it brought about, in concepts, the logical form of a judgment by means of analytic unity—also brings into its presentations a transcendental content, by means of the synthetic unity of the manifold in intuition as such; and because of this, these presentations are called pure concepts of understanding applying a priori to objects. Bringing such a transcendental content into these presentations is something that general logic cannot accomplish.

Thus there arise precisely as many pure concepts of understanding applying a priori to objects of intuition as such, as in the preceding table there were logical functions involved in all possible judgments. For these functions of the understanding are completely exhaustive and survey its power entirely. Following Aristotle, we shall call these functions *categories*. For our aim is fundamentally the same as his, even though it greatly deviates from his in its execution.

This, then, is the list of all the original pure concepts of synthesis that the understanding contains a priori. Indeed, it is a pure understanding only because of these concepts; for through them alone can it understand something in the manifold of intuition, i.e., think an object of intuition. This division of the categories has been generated systematically from a common princi-

TABLE OF CATEGORIES

B106

1
OF QUANTITY
Unity
Plurality
Allness

2
OF QUALITY
Reality
Negation
Limitation

3
OF RELATION
of *Inherence* and Subsistence
(*substantia et accidens*)
of *Causality* and Dependence
(Cause and Effect)
of *Community* (Interaction
between Agent and Patient)

4
OF MODALITY
Possibility—Impossibility
Existence—Nonexistence
Necessity—Contingency

ple, viz., our ability to judge (which is equivalent to our ability to think). It has not been generated rhapsodically, by locating pure concepts haphazardly, where B107 we can never be certain that the enumeration of the concepts is complete. For we then infer the division only by induction, forgetting that in this way we never gain insight into why precisely these concepts, rather than others, reside in the pure understanding. Locating these basic concepts was a project worthy of an acute man like Aristotle. But having no principle,[127] he snatched them up as he came upon them. He hunted up ten of them at first, and called them *categories* (predicaments).[128] He later believed that he had discovered five more categories, and added them under the name of postpredicaments.[129] But his table remained deficient even then. Moreover, we also find in it some modes of pure sensibility (*quando, ubi, situs,* and *prius,*

127. [For locating these concepts.]

128. [Substance, quantity, quality, relation, place, time, posture, state, action, undergoing.]

129. [The five relational categories, of doubtful authenticity, found in chs. 10–15 of the *Categories*: opposition, priority, simultaneity, motion, having.]

simul),[130] as well as an empirical mode (motus),[131] none of which belong at all in this register of the root [concepts] of the understanding. Again, derivative concepts (actio, passio)[132] are also included among the original concepts,[133] while some of the original concepts[134] are missing entirely.

Hence for the sake of [distinguishing] the original concepts, we must note also that the categories, as the true *root concepts* of pure understanding, have also their equally pure *derivative concepts*. In a complete system of transcendental philosophy these derivative concepts can by no means be omitted. In a merely critical essay, on the other hand, I can settle for merely mentioning them.

B108   Let me call these pure but derivative concepts of understanding the *predicables* of pure understanding (in contrast to the predicaments[135]). Once we have the original and primitive concepts, we can easily add the derivative and subsidiary ones and thus depict completely the genealogical tree of pure understanding. Since I am here concerned with the completeness not of the system but only of the principles for a system, I am reserving that complementary work for another enterprise.[136] We can, however, come close to achieving that aim of completing the tree if we pick up a textbook on ontology and subordinate the predicables to the categories: e.g., to the category of causality, the predicables of force, action, undergoing; to the category of community, the predicables of presence, resistance; to the predicaments of modality, the predicables of arising, passing away, change; and so on. When the categories are combined either with the modes of pure sensibility or with one another, they yield a great multitude of derivative a priori concepts. Mentioning these concepts and, if possible, listing them completely would be a useful and not disagreeable endeavor, but one that we can here dispense with.

130. [Respectively, when (time), where (place), posture, prior (priority), simultaneous (simultaneity).]

131. [Motion.]

132. [Action, passion (undergoing).]

133. [On Aristotle's list.]

134. [I.e., as contained in Kant's own table of categories.]

135. [I.e., categories.]

136. [Presumably the activity of producing a metaphysics of nature. Cf. above, B xliii.]

In this treatise I deliberately refrain from offering definitions of these categories, even though I may possess them. I shall hereafter dissect the concepts only to a degree adequate for the doctrine of method that I here produce. Whereas definitions of the catego- B109 ries could rightly be demanded of me in a system of pure reason, here they would only make us lose sight of the main point of the inquiry. For they would give rise to doubts and charges that we may readily relegate to another activity without in any way detracting from our essential aim. Still, from what little I have mentioned about this, we can see distinctly that a complete lexicon with all the requisite explications not only is possible but could easily be brought about. The compartments are now at hand. They only need to be filled in; and a systematic [transcendental] topic, such as the present one, will make it difficult to miss the place where each concept properly belongs, and at the same time will make it easy to notice any place that is still empty.

§ 11

Concerning this table of categories one can make nice observations that might perhaps have important consequences regarding the scientific form of all rational cognitions. For in the theoretical part of philosophy this table is exceedingly useful—indeed, indispensable—for drawing up completely *the plan for a science as a whole* insofar as this science rests on a priori concepts, and for *dividing* it systematically *according to determinate principles*. This is self-evident already from these facts: The table lists completely all the elementary concepts of understanding; indeed, it contains even the form of a system of them residing in the human understanding. Consequently B110 the table directs us to all the *moments* of a projected speculative science—indeed, even to their *order*. In fact, a sample of their so directing us has already been provided by me elsewhere. Here now are some of those comments that can be made about the table of categories.

The *first comment* is that this table containing four classes of concepts of understanding can be broken up, initially, into two divisions. The concepts in the first division are directed to objects of intuition (both pure and empirical), while those in the second are directed to the existence of these objects (these objects being referred either to each other or to the understanding).

The first division I would call that of the *mathematical* categories, the second, that of the *dynamical* categories. The first division of categories, as we can see by inspecting the table, has no correlates; only in the second division do we find correlates. This distinction must surely have a basis in the nature of the understanding.

The *second comment* to be made about the table is that the number of categories in each class is equal everywhere, viz., three; this, too, calls for meditation, because normally all a priori division by concepts must be dichotomous. Add to this, moreover, the fact that in each case the third category of the class arises from the combination of the second category with the first of the same class.

B111   Thus *allness* (totality) is nothing but plurality considered as unity; *limitation* is nothing but reality combined with negation; *community* is the causality of a substance reciprocally determining [and being determined by] another substance; *necessity*, finally, is nothing but the existence that is given through possibility itself. This fact, however, must by no means lead us to think that the third category is a mere derivative concept, rather than a root concept, of pure understanding. For combining the first and second categories, in order to produce the third concept, requires that the understanding perform a special act that is not the same as the act it performs in the case of the first and second concepts. Thus the concept of a *number* (which belongs to the category of allness) is not possible in every case where we have the concepts of multitude and unity (e.g., it is not possible in the presentation of infinity). Again, combining the two concepts of a *cause* and of a *substance* does not yet provide me with an immediate understanding of *influence*, i.e., understanding of how a substance can become the cause of something in another substance. This shows that a special act of the understanding is required;[137] and thus it is with the remaining classes of categories.

The *third comment* to be made about the table of categories concerns the category of *community*, which is to be found under the third heading. This is the one category whose agreement with the form corresponding to it in the table of logical functions — viz.,

B112   the form of a disjunctive judgment — is not so obvious as in the case of the others.

In order to assure ourselves of this agreement, we must note the following: In all disjunctive judgments the sphere (the multitude of everything contained under the judgment) is presented as a whole divided into parts (the subordinate concepts). And because the parts cannot be contained one under another, they are thought as *coordinated* with rather than as *subordinated* to one another, so that they determine one another not *unilaterally* as in a *series*, but *reciprocally* as in an *aggregate* wherein, when one member of the division is posited, all the rest are excluded, and conversely).

Now a similar connection is thought in [thinking] a *whole* of *things*. In such a whole, one thing is not *subordinated*, as effect, to another as cause of its existence; rather, it is simultaneously and reciprocally *coordinated* with others, as cause regarding their determination (as, e.g., in a body whose parts reciprocally attract — or, for that matter, repel — one another). This kind of connection is entirely different from the one found in the mere relation of cause to effect (ground to consequence), where the consequence does not in turn reciprocally determine the ground and hence does not together with it constitute a whole (e.g., the world together with its creator does not constitute a whole). When the understanding presents the sphere of a divided concept, it follows a certain procedure; B113 it observes that same procedure when it thinks a thing as divisible. And in the divided concept the members of the division exclude one another and yet are combined in one sphere; in the same way, the understanding[138] presents the thing's parts as being such that while the existence of each part also belongs to it alone (as a substance) to the exclusion of the others, yet the parts are combined in one whole.

§ 12

In the transcendental philosophy of the ancients, however, we find an additional chapter containing pure concepts of understanding. Although these concepts are not there included among the categories, yet according to the ancients they were to count as a priori concepts of objects. In that case, however, these concepts would in fact increase the number

---

137. [To produce the category of community.]

138. [In thinking a thing as divisible.]

of categories—which cannot be. These additional concepts are set forth in this proposition, so famous among the scholastics: *quodlibet ens est unum verum, bonum*.[139] Now it is true that the use of this principle turned out to permit only very meager inferences (yielding nothing but tautological propositions); by the same token, in more recent times the principle has come to receive little more than honorable mention in metaphysics. Yet whenever a thought—no matter how empty it seems to be—has maintained itself for such a long time, then it deserves an inquiry into its origin, and entitles us to conjecture that it has its basis in some rule of the understanding that, as often happens, has only been wrongly interpreted.

B114 But in fact these supposedly transcendental predicates of *things* are nothing but logical requirements and criteria for all *cognition* of *things* in general; and they lay at the basis of such cognition the categories of quantity, viz., those of *unity*, *plurality*, and *allness*. These categories, however, should properly be taken materially, as belonging to the possibility of things themselves. Those [philosophers], on the other hand, used them in fact only in their formal meaning, as belonging to the logical demands concerning any cognition; yet, through carelessness, they still turned these criteria of thought into properties of things in themselves. Let me explain. In every cognition there are three components. First, there is *unity* of the concept; we may call it *qualitative unity*, provided that in [thinking] it we think only the unity in the collating of the manifold of cognitions: e.g., the unity of the topic in a play, a speech, or a story. Second, in every cognition there is *truth* as regards the consequences. The more true consequences arise from a given concept, the more indicators there are of its objective reality. We might call this the *qualitative plurality* of the characteristics that belong to a concept as their common ground (rather than are thought, in the concept, as a quantity). Finally, third, in every cognition there is *perfection*; it consists in the fact that the plurality together leads back again to the unity of the concept, and that it agrees fully with this and with no other concept. This perfection may be

B115 called *qualitative completeness* (totality). This shows that these logical criteria for the possibility of cognition as such only transform the three categories of

quantity. In these categories, the unity in the production of the quantum must be assumed as homogeneous throughout. Here, however, they are only transformed, in order to connect components of cognition—even *heterogeneous* ones—in one consciousness, using as principle for this connection the quality of a cognition. Thus the criterion for the possibility of a concept (rather than for the possibility of the concept's object) is the concept's definition; in it the *unity* of the concept, the *truth* of everything that may be derived from it initially, and finally the *completeness* of what has been extracted from it constitute what the whole concept requires for its construction. Or, again, the *criterion of a hypothesis* is the understandability of the assumed *basis of explanation*, or, i.e.: its *unity* (without an auxiliary hypothesis); the *truth* of the consequences derivable from it (their agreement with one another and with experience); and, finally, the *completeness* of the basis for the explanation of these consequences—which means that these consequences point back to no more and no less than was assumed in the hypothesis, and that they analytically a posteriori bring back and agree with what was thought synthetically a priori in the hypothesis. Therefore by adding the concepts of unity, truth, and perfection to the transcendental table of categories we do not at all complement that table— as if perhaps it were deficient. Rather, while setting aside entirely the relation of these concepts to ob- B116 jects[140] we bring the procedure used with these concepts under general logical rules governing the agreement of cognition with itself.

Analytic of Concepts
Chapter II
On the Deduction of
the Pure Concept of Understanding

Section I

§ 13

ON THE PRINCIPLES OF A TRANSCENDENTAL DEDUCTION AS SUCH

When teachers of law talk about rights and claims, they distinguish in a legal action the question regard-

---

139. [Any being is one, true, good.]

140. [I.e., the relation implied in the categories.]

ing what is legal (*quid iuris*) from the question concerning fact (*quid facti*), and they demand proof of both.[141] The first proof, which is to establish the right, or for that matter the legal entitlement, they call the *deduction*. [This term also applies to philosophy.] We employ a multitude of empirical concepts without being challenged by anyone. And we consider ourselves justified, even without having offered a deduction, to assign to these empirical concepts a meaning and imagined signification, because we always have experience available to us to prove their objective reality. But there are also concepts that we usurp, as, e.g., *fortune, fate*. And although these concepts run loose, with our almost universal forbearance, yet they are sometimes confronted by the question [of their legality], *quid iuris*. This question then leaves us in considerable perplexity regarding the deduction[142] of these concepts; for neither from experience nor from reason can we adduce any distinct legal basis from which the right to use them emerges distinctly.

B117

But there are, among the various concepts making up the highly mixed fabric of human cognition, some that are determined for pure a priori use as well (i.e., for a use that is completely independent of all experience and their right to be so used always requires a deduction. For proofs based on experience are insufficient to establish the legitimacy of using them in that way; yet we do need to know how these concepts can refer to objects even though they do not take these objects from any experience. Hence when I explain in what way concepts can refer to objects a priori, I call that explanation the *transcendental deduction* of these concepts. And I distinguish transcendental deduction from *empirical* deduction, which indicates in what way a concept has been acquired through experience and through reflection upon experience, and which therefore concerns not the concept's legitimacy but only the fact whereby we came to possess it.

B118

We already have, at this point, two types of concepts that, while being wholly different in kind, do yet agree inasmuch as both of them refer to objects completely a priori: viz., on the one hand, the concepts of space and time as forms of sensibility; and, on the other

hand, the categories as concepts of understanding. To attempt an empirical deduction of these two types of concepts would be a futile job. For what is distinctive in their nature is precisely the fact that they refer to their objects without having borrowed anything from experience in order to present these objects. Hence if a deduction of these concepts is needed, then it must always be transcendental.

But even for these concepts, as for all cognition, we can locate in experience, if not the principle of their possibility, then at least the occasioning causes of their production. Thus the impressions of the senses first prompt [us] to open up the whole cognitive power in regard to them, and to bring about experience. Experience contains two quite heterogeneous elements: viz., a *matter* for cognition, taken from the senses; and a certain *form* for ordering this matter, taken from the inner source of pure intuition and thought. It is on the occasion of the impressions of the senses that pure intuition and thought are first brought into operation and produce concepts. Such exploration of our cognitive power's first endeavors to ascend from singular perceptions to universal concepts is doubtless highly beneficial, and we are indebted to the illustrious *Locke* for first opening up the path to it.[143] Yet such exploration can never yield a *deduction*[144] of the pure a priori concepts, which does not lie on that path at all. For in view of these concepts' later use, which is to be wholly independent of experience, they must be able to display a birth certificate quite different from that of descent from experiences. The attempted[145] physiological derivation concerns a *quaestio facti*,[146] and therefore cannot properly be called a deduction at all. Hence I shall name it the explanation of our *possession* of a pure cognition. Clearly, then, the only possible deduction of this pure cognition is a transcendental and by no means an empirical one, and empirical deductions regarding the pure a priori concepts are nothing but futile attempts—attempts that only those can engage

B119

141. [Legality and factuality.]

142. [I.e., legitimation.]

143. [See *An Essay Concerning Human Understanding*, Bk. II.]

144. [I.e., legitimation.]

145. [By philosophers such as Locke.]

146. [Question of fact (rather than of legality or legitimation).]

in who have not comprehended the quite peculiar nature of these cognitions.

Yet even if it be granted that the only possible kind of deduction of pure a priori cognition is one along the transcendental path, that still does not show that this deduction is inescapably necessary. We did earlier trace the concepts of space and time to their sources by means of a transcendental deduction, and B120 we explained and determined their a priori objective validity. Yet geometry, using nothing but a priori cognitions, follows its course securely without needing to ask philosophy for a certificate of the pure and legitimate descent of geometry's basic concept of space. On the other hand, the use of the concept of space in this science does apply only to the external world of sense. Space is the pure form of the intuition of that world. In that world, therefore, all geometric cognition is directly evident, because it is based on a priori intuition; and, through cognition itself, objects are (as regards their form) given a priori in intuition. With the *pure concepts of understanding*, on the other hand, begins the inescapable requirement to seek a transcendental deduction—not only of these concepts themselves, but also of space. For these concepts speak of objects through predicates of pure a priori thought, not through predicates of intuition and sensibility; hence they refer to objects universally, i.e., apart from all conditions of sensibility. They are, then, concepts that are not based on experience; and in a priori intuition, too, they cannot display any object on which they might, prior to all experience, base their synthesis. Hence these concepts not only arouse suspicion concerning the objective validity and limits of their use, but they also make ambiguous B121 the *concept of space*; for they tend to use it even beyond the conditions of sensible intuition—and this indeed is the reason why a transcendental deduction of this concept was needed above. I must therefore convince the reader, before he has taken a single step in the realm of pure reason, that such a deduction is inescapably necessary. For otherwise he proceeds blindly, and after manifold wanderings must yet return to the ignorance from which he started. But the reader must also distinctly see in advance the inevitable difficulty of providing such a deduction. For otherwise he might complain of obscurity when in fact the matter itself is deeply shrouded, or might be too quickly discouraged during the removal of

obstacles. For we either must entirely abandon all claims to pure rational insights into the realm that we care about most, viz., the realm beyond the bounds of all possible experience, or else must bring this critical inquiry to completion.

We had little trouble above in making comprehensible how the concepts of space and time, despite being a priori cognitions, must yet refer necessarily to objects, and how they make possible, independently of any experience, a synthetic cognition of objects. For only by means of such pure forms of sensibility can an object appear to us, i.e., can it be an object of empirical intuition. Hence space and B122 time are pure intuitions containing a priori the condition for the possibility of objects as appearances, and the synthesis in space and time has objective validity.

The categories of understanding, on the other hand, do not at all present to us the conditions under which objects are given in intuition. Therefore objects can indeed appear to us without having to refer necessarily to functions of understanding, and hence without the understanding's containing a priori the conditions of these objects. Thus we find here a difficulty that we did not encounter in the realm of sensibility: viz., how *subjective conditions of thought* could have *objective validity*, i.e., how they could yield conditions for the possibility of all cognition of objects. For appearances can indeed be given in intuition without functions of understanding. Let me take, e.g., the concept of cause. This concept signifies a special kind of synthesis where upon [the occurrence of] something, A, something quite different, B, is posited according to a rule. Why appearances should contain anything like that is not evident a priori. (I say *a priori* because experience cannot be adduced as proof, since we must be able to establish this concept's objective validity a priori.) Hence there is doubt a priori whether perhaps such a concept might not even be empty and encounter no object at all among appearances. For while it is evident that objects of sensible intuition must conform to the formal conditions of B123 sensibility lying a priori in the mind, since otherwise they would not be objects for us, it is not so easy to see the inference whereby they must in addition conform to the conditions that the understanding requires for the synthetic unity of thought. For, I suppose, appearances might possibly be of such a character that the understanding would not find them to conform at all to the conditions of its unity. Everything might then be so confused that, e.g., the sequence of appearances would offer us nothing providing us with a rule of synthesis and thus corresponding to the concept of cause and effect, so that this concept would then be quite empty, null, and without signification. But appearances would nonetheless offer objects to our intuition; for intuition in no way requires the functions of thought.

Suppose that we planned to extricate ourselves from these troublesome inquiries by saying that examples of such regularity among appearances are offered to us incessantly by experience, and that these examples give us sufficient prompting to isolate from them the concept of cause and thus to verify at the same time the objective validity of such a concept. In that case we would be overlooking the fact that the concept of cause cannot arise in that way at all; rather, it either must have its basis completely a priori in the B124 understanding, or must be given up entirely as a mere chimera. For this concept definitely requires that something, A, be of such a kind that something else, B, follows from it *necessarily* and according to an *absolutely universal rule*. Although appearances do provide us with cases from which we can obtain a rule whereby something usually happens, they can never provide us with a rule whereby the result is *necessary*. This is, moreover, the reason why the synthesis of cause and effect is imbued with a dignity that cannot at all be expressed empirically: viz., that the effect is not merely added to the cause, but is posited *through* the cause and results *from* it. And the strict universality of the rule is indeed no property whatever of empirical rules; empirical rules can, through induction, acquire none but comparative universality, i.e., extensive usability. But if we treated the pure concepts of understanding as merely empirical products, then our use of them would change entirely.

§ 14

TRANSITION TO THE TRANSCENDENTAL
DEDUCTION OF THE CATEGORIES

Only two cases are possible where synthetic presentation and its objects can concur, can necessarily refer to each other, and can—as it were—meet each other:

viz., either if the object makes the presentation possible, or if the presentation alone makes the object possible. If the object makes the presentation possible, B125 then the reference is only empirical and the presentation is never possible a priori. This is what happens in the case of appearances, as regards what pertains to sensation in them. But suppose that the presentation alone makes the object possible. In that case, while presentation in itself does not produce its object *as regards existence* (for the causality that presentation has by means of the will is not at issue here at all), yet presentation is a priori determinative in regard to the object if *cognizing* something *as an object* is possible only through it. Now there are two conditions under which alone there can be cognition of an object. The first condition is *intuition*; through it the object is given, though only as appearance. The second condition is the *concept*; through it an object is thought that corresponds to this intuition. Now it is evident from the above that the first condition, viz., the condition under which alone objects can be intuited, does indeed, as far as their form is concerned, underlie objects a priori in the mind. Hence all appearances necessarily agree with this formal condition of sensibility, because only through it can they appear, i.e., be empirically intuited and given. Now the question arises whether concepts do not also a priori precede [objects], as conditions under which alone something can be, if not intuited, yet thought as object as such. For in that case all empirical cognition of ob- B126 jects necessarily conforms to such concepts, because nothing is possible as *object of experience* unless these concepts are presupposed. But all experience, besides containing the senses' intuition through which something is given, does also contain a *concept* of an object that is given in intuition, or that appears. Accordingly, concepts of objects as such presumably underlie all experiential cognition as its a priori conditions. Hence presumably the objective validity of the categories, as a priori concepts, rests on the fact that through them alone is experience possible (as far as the form of thought in it is concerned). For in that case the categories refer to objects of experience necessarily and a priori, because only by means of them can any experiential object whatsoever be thought at all.

Hence the transcendental deduction of all a priori concepts has a principle to which the entire investigation must be directed: viz., the principle that these concepts must be cognized as a priori conditions for the possibility of experience (whether the possibility of the intuition found in experience, or the possibility of the thought). If concepts serve as the objective basis for the possibility of experience, then—precisely because of this—they are necessary. But to unfold the experience in which these concepts are found is not to deduce them (but is only to illustrate them); for otherwise they would, after all, be only contingent.

B127 Without that original reference of these concepts to possible experience wherein all objects of cognition occur, their reference to any object whatever would be quite incomprehensible.

The illustrious **Locke**, not having engaged in this contemplation, and encountering pure concepts of understanding in experience, also derived them from experience. Yet he proceeded so *inconsistently* that he dared to try using these concepts for cognitions that go far beyond any boundary of experience. **David Hume** recognized that in order for us to be able to do this, the origin of these concepts must be a priori. But he was quite unable to explain how it is possible that concepts not in themselves combined in the understanding should nonetheless have to be thought by it as necessarily combined in the object. Nor did it occur to him that perhaps the understanding itself might, through these concepts, be the author of the experience wherein we encounter the understanding's objects. Thus, in his plight, he derived these concepts from experience (viz., from *habit*, a subjective necessity that arises in experience through repeated association and that ultimately is falsely regarded as objective). But he proceeded quite consistently after that, for he declared that we cannot use these concepts and the principles that they occasion in order to go beyond the boundary of experi-

B128 ence. Yet the *empirical* derivation of these concepts which occurred to both[147] cannot be reconciled with the scientific a priori cognitions that we actually have, viz., our a priori cognitions of *pure mathematics* and *universal natural science*, and hence this empirical derivation is refuted by that fact.

Of these two illustrious men, Locke left the door wide open for *fanaticism*; for once reason has gained possession of such rights, it can no longer be kept within limits by indefinite exhortations to moderation.

Hume, believing that he had uncovered so universal a delusion—regarded as reason—of our cognitive power, surrendered entirely to *skepticism*. We are now about to try to find out whether we cannot provide for human reason safe passage between these two cliffs, assign to it determinate bounds, and yet keep open for it the entire realm of its appropriate activity.

The only thing that I still want to do before we start is to *explicate the categories:* they are concepts of an object as such whereby the object's intuition is regarded as *determined* in terms of one of the logical functions in judging. Thus the function of the *categorical* judgment—i.e., All bodies are divisible—is that of the relation of subject to predicate. But the understanding's merely logical use left undetermined to which of the two concepts we want to give the func- B129 tion of the subject, and to which the function of the predicate. For we can also say, Something divisible is a body. If, on the other hand, I bring the concept of a body under the category of substance, then through this category is determined the fact that the body's empirical intuition in experience must be considered always as subject only, never as mere predicate. And similarly in all the remaining categories.

Deduction of the Pure Concepts of Understanding

Section II
[Second Edition]
Transcendental Deduction of the Pure Concepts of Understanding

§ 15

ON THE POSSIBILITY OF A COMBINATION AS SUCH

The [uncombined] manifold of presentations can be given in an intuition that is merely sensible, i.e., nothing but receptivity,[148] and the form of this intuition can lie a priori in our power of presentation without being anything but the way in which the subject is affected. But a manifold's *combination (coniunctio)* as such can never come to us through the senses; nor, therefore, can it already be part of what

---

147. [Locke and Hume.]

148. [In contrast to an intellectual intuition. See B 72.]

B130 is contained in the pure form of sensible intuition. For this combination is an act of spontaneity by the power of presentation; and this power must be called understanding, in order to be distinguished from sensibility. Hence all combination is an act of understanding—whether or not we become conscious of such combination; whether it is a combination of the manifold of intuition or of the manifold of various concepts; and whether, in the case of intuition, it is a combination of sensible or of nonsensible intuition. I would assign to this act of understanding the general name *synthesis*, in order to point out at the same time: that we cannot present anything as combined in the object without ourselves' having combined it beforehand; and that, among all presentations, *combination* is the only one that cannot be given through objects, but—being an act of the subject's self-activity—can be performed only by the subject himself. We readily become aware here that this act of synthesis must originally be a single act and must hold equally for all combination; and that resolution or *analysis*, which seems to be its opposite yet always presupposes it. For where the understanding has not beforehand combined anything, there it also cannot resolve anything, because only *through the understanding* could the power of presentation have been given something as combined.

But the concept of combination carries with it, besides the concept of the manifold and of its synthesis, also the concept of the manifold's unity. Combina-
B131 tion is presentation of the *synthetic* unity of the manifold.[149] Hence the presentation of this unity cannot arise from the combination; rather, by being added to the presentation of the manifold, it makes possible the concept of combination in the first place. This unity, which thus precedes a priori all concepts of combination, is by no means the category of unity mentioned earlier (in § 10[150]). For all categories are

149. We need not here consider whether the [manifold] presentations themselves are identical, so that one can be thought analytically through the other: the *consciousness* of the one presentation can nonetheless, insofar as we are talking about the manifold, always be distinguished from the consciousness of the other presentation; and what matters here is solely the synthesis of this (possible) consciousness.

150. [Specifically, B 106.]

based on logical functions occurring in judgments; but in these functions combination, and hence unity of given concepts, is already thought. Hence a category already presupposes combination. We must therefore search for this unity (which is qualitative unity; see § 12[151]) still higher up, viz., in what itself contains the basis for the unity of different concepts in judgments, and hence contains the basis for the possibility of understanding, even as used logically.

§ 16

On the Original Synthetic Unity of Apperception

The *I think* must be *capable* of accompanying all my presentations. For otherwise something would be presented to me that could not be thought at all—which B132 is equivalent to saying that the presentation either would be impossible, or at least would be nothing to me. Presentation that can be given prior to all thought is called *intuition*. Hence everything manifold in intuition has a necessary reference to the *I think* in the same subject in whom this manifold is found. But this presentation [i.e., the *I think*] is an act of spontaneity; i.e., it cannot be regarded as belonging to sensibility. I call it *pure apperception*, in order to distinguish it from *empirical* apperception. Or, again, I call it *original apperception*; for it is the self-consciousness which, because it produces the presentation *I think* that must be capable of accompanying all other presentations[,] and [because it] is one and the same in all consciousness, cannot be accompanied by any further presentation. I also call the *unity* of this apperception the *transcendental* unity of self-consciousness, in order to indicate that a priori cognition can be obtained from it. For the manifold presentations given in a certain intuition would not one and all be *my* presentations, if they did not one and all belong to one self-consciousness. I.e., as my presentations (even if I am not conscious of them as being mine), they surely must conform necessarily to the condition under which alone they *can* stand together in one universal self-consciousness, since otherwise they would not thoroughly belong to me. And B133 from this original combination much can be inferred.

This same thoroughgoing identity of the appercep-

151. [Specifically, B 114.]

tion of a manifold given in intuition contains a synthesis of presentations, and is possible only through the consciousness of this synthesis. For the empirical consciousness that accompanies different presentations is intrinsically sporadic and without any reference to the subject's identity. Hence this reference comes about not through my merely accompanying each presentation with consciousness, but through my *adding* one presentation to another and being conscious of their synthesis. Hence only because I can combine a manifold of given presentations *in one consciousness,* is it possible for me to present the *identity itself of the consciousness in these presentations.*[152] I.e., the *analytic* unity of apperception is possible only under
B134 the presupposition of some *synthetic* unity of apperception.[153] The thought that these presentations given in intuition belong one and all to me is, accordingly, tantamount to the thought that I unite them, or at least can unite them, in one self-consciousness. And although that thought itself is not yet the consciousness of the *synthesis* of the presentations, it still presupposes the possibility of that synthesis. I.e., only because I can comprise the manifold of the presentations in one consciousness, do I call them one and all *my* presentations. For otherwise I would have a self as many-colored and varied as I have presentations that I am conscious of. Hence synthetic unity of the manifold of intuitions, as given a priori, is the basis of the identity itself of apperception, which

precedes a priori all *my* determinate thought. But combination does not lie in objects, and can by no means be borrowed from them by perception and thus be taken up only then into the understanding. It is, rather, solely something performed by the under- B135
standing; and understanding itself is nothing more than the power to combine a priori and to bring the manifold of given intuitions under the unity of apperception—the principle of this unity being the supreme principle in all of human cognition.

Now, it is true that this principle of the necessary unity of apperception is itself merely an identical[154] and hence an analytic proposition. Yet it does declare as necessary a synthesis of the manifold given in an intuition, a synthesis without which that thoroughgoing identity of self-consciousness cannot be thought. For through the *I,* as simple presentation, nothing manifold is given; only in intuition, which is distinct from this presentation, can a manifold be given, and only through *combination* can it be thought in one consciousness. An understanding wherein through self-consciousness alone everything manifold would at the same time be given would be an understanding that *intuits.*[155] Our understanding can only *think,* and must seek intuition in the senses. I am, then, conscious of the self as identical, as regards the manifold of the presentations given to me in an intuition, because I call them one and all *my* presentations that make up one presentation. That, however, is tantamount to saying that I am conscious of a necessary a priori synthesis of them. This synthesis is called the original synthetic unity of apperception. All presentations given to me are subject to this unity; but they B136
must also be brought under it through a synthesis.

§ 17

THE PRINCIPLE OF THE SYNTHETIC UNITY OF APPERCEPTION IS THE SUPREME PRINCIPLE FOR ALL USE OF THE UNDERSTANDING

The supreme principle for the possibility of all intuition in reference to sensibility was, according to the

152. [I.e., across these presentations.]

153. The analytic unity of consciousness attaches to all concepts that are, and inasmuch as they are, common [to several presentations.] E.g., in thinking *red* as such, I present a property that can be found (as a characteristic) in something or other or can be combined with other presentations; hence only by virtue of a possible synthetic unity that I think beforehand can I present the analytic unity. A presentation that is to be thought as common to different presenta-
B134 tions is regarded as belonging to presentations that, besides having it, also have something *different* about them. Consequently it must beforehand be thought in synthetic unity with other presentations (even if only possible ones). Only then can I think in it the analytic unity of consciousness that makes the presentation a *conceptus communis.* And thus the synthetic unity of apperception is the highest point, to which we must attach all use of the understanding, even the whole of logic, and in accordance with it transcendental philosophy; indeed, this power is the understanding itself.

154. [I.e., based, for its truth, on identity.]
155. [On intuitive understanding and its (intellectual) intuition, see above, B 72.]

Transcendental Aesthetic, that everything manifold in intuition is subject to the formal conditions of space and time. The supreme principle for the possibility of all intuition in reference to understanding is that everything manifold in intuition is subject to conditions of the original synthetic unity of apperception.[156] All manifold presentations of intuition are subject to the first principle insofar as they are *given* to us. They are subject to the second principle insofar as they B137 must be capable of being *combined* in one consciousness. For without that combination, nothing can be thought or cognized through such presentations, because the given presentations do then not have in common the act of apperception, *I think*, and thus would not be collated[157] in one self-consciousness.

Understanding—speaking generally—is the power of *cognitions*. Cognitions consist in determinate reference of given presentations to an object. And an *object* is that in whose concept the manifold of a given intuition is *united*. But all unification of presentations requires that there be unity of consciousness in the synthesis of them. Consequently the reference of presentations to an object consists solely in this unity of consciousness, and hence so does their objective validity and consequently their becoming cognitions. On this unity, consequently, rests the very possibility of the understanding.

Hence the principle of the original *synthetic* unity of apperception is the primary pure cognition of understanding, on which the entire remaining use of

the understanding is based; and this cognition is at the same time entirely independent of all conditions of sensible intuition. Thus the mere form of outer sensible intuition, i.e., space, is as yet no cognition at all; it provides only the manifold of a priori intuition for a possible cognition. Rather, in order to cognize something or other—e.g., a line—in space, I must *draw* it; and hence I must bring about synthetically B138 a determinate combination of the given manifold, so that the unity of this act[158] is at the same time the unity of consciousness (in the concept of a line), and so that an object (a determinate space) is thereby first cognized. The synthetic unity of consciousness is, therefore, an objective condition of all cognition. Not only do I myself need this condition in order to cognize an object, but every intuition must be subject to it *in order to become an object for me.* For otherwise, and without that synthesis, the manifold would *not* unite in one consciousness.

Although this last proposition makes the synthetic unity [of consciousness] a condition of all thought, it is—as I have said—itself analytic. For it says no more than that all *my* presentations in some given intuition must be subject to the condition under which alone I can ascribe them—as *my* presentations—to the identical self, and hence under which alone I can collate them, as combined synthetically in one apperception, through the universal expression *I think.*

On the other hand, this principle is not one for every possible understanding as such, but is a principle only for that [kind of] understanding through whose pure apperception, in the presentation *I think*, nothing manifold whatever is yet given. An alternative [kind of] understanding would be that understanding through whose self-consciousness the manifold of intuition would at the same time be given—i.e., an B139 understanding through whose presentation the objects of this presentation would at the same time exist.[159] Such an understanding would not require, for the unity of consciousness, a special act of synthesis of the manifold. The human understanding, which merely thinks but does not intuit, does need that

---

156. Space and time, and all their parts, are *intuitions*; hence they, with the manifold that they contain, are singular presentations. (See the Transcendental Aesthetic.)[a] Hence space and time are not mere concepts, through which the very same consciousness is encountered as contained in many presentations. They are, rather, [presentations through which] many presentations are encountered as contained in one presentation and in the consciousness thereof, and hence [they are presentations] encountered as composite; and consequently the unity of this consciousness is encountered as *synthetic*, but yet as original. This *singularity* of [intuition] is important when applied [to specific contexts]. (See § 25.[b])

[a][Although Kant did not there use the term 'singular,' the reference seems to be to ¶ numbers 3 and 4 (A 24–25/B 39), and § 4, numbers 4 and 5 (A 31–2/B 47).]

[b][Below, B 157–59.]

157. [I.e., arranged and held together.]

158. [Of synthesis.]

159. [This would be an intuitive understanding, and its intuition would be intellectual. See above B 72.]

synthesis. But still, for the human understanding the principle[160] is unavoidably the first principle. And thus our understanding cannot even frame the slightest concept of a different possible understanding—whether of an understanding that itself would intuit; or of an understanding that would indeed have lying at its basis a sensible intuition, yet one of a different kind from that in space and time.

§ 18

What Objective Unity of Self-Consciousness Is

The *transcendental unity* of apperception is the unity whereby everything manifold given in an intuition is united in a concept of the object. Hence this unity is called *objective*, and must be distinguished from *subjective* unity of consciousness, which is a *determination of inner sense* whereby that manifold of intuition for such [objective] combination is given empirically. Whether I can be conscious *empirically* of the manifold as simultaneous or as sequential depends B140 on circumstances or empirical conditions. Hence empirical unity of consciousness, through association of presentations, itself concerns an appearance and is entirely contingent. On the other hand, the pure form of intuition in time, merely as intuition as such containing a given manifold, is subject to the original unity of consciousness. It is subject to that unity solely through the necessary reference of the manifold of intuition to the one [self], i.e., to the *I think*, and hence through the understanding's pure synthesis that lies a priori at the basis of the empirical synthesis. Only the original unity of consciousness is valid objectively. The empirical unity of apperception, which we are not examining here and which moreover is only derived from the original unity under given conditions *in concreto*, has only subjective validity. One person will link the presentation of a certain word with one thing, another with some other thing; and the unity of consciousness in what is empirical is not, as regards what is given, necessary and universally valid.

160. [Of the synthetic unity of apperception.]

§ 19

The Logical Form of All Judgments Consists in the Objective Unity of Apperception of the Concepts Contained in Them

I have never been able to settle for the explication that logicians give of a judgment as such. A judgment, they say, is the presentation of a relation between two concepts. Now, I shall not here quarrel with them B141 about one respect in which this explication is defective (although this oversight has given rise to many irksome consequences for logic): viz., that it fits at most *categorical* judgments only, but not hypothetical and disjunctive ones (since these contain a relation not of concepts but of further judgments).[161] I shall point out only that this explication of a judgment leaves undetermined wherein this *relation*[162] consists.

But suppose that I inquire more precisely into the [relation or] reference of given cognitions in every judgment, and that I distinguish it, as belonging to the understanding, from the relation in terms of laws of the reproductive imagination (a relation that has only subjective validity). I then find that a judgment is nothing but a way of bringing given cognitions to the objective unity of apperception. This is what the little relational word *is* in judgments intends [to indi- B142 cate], in order to distinguish the objective unity of given presentations from the subjective one. For this word indicates the reference of the presentations to original apperception and its *necessary unity*. The reference to this necessary unity is there even if the judgment itself is empirical and hence contingent—e.g., Bodies are heavy. By this I do not mean that

161. The voluminous doctrine of the four syllogistic figures concerns only categorical syllogisms. Now, this doctrine is nothing more than the art of surreptitiously creating, by concealing immediate inferences (*consequentiae immediatae*) among the premises of a pure syllogism, the illusion that there are more kinds of inference than that of the first figure. Still, the doctrine would not on account of that illusion alone have met with special fortune, had it not also succeeded in procuring for categorical judgments an exclusive reputation, viz. as judgments to which all others must be capable of being referred [as their basis]—which, however, is false by § 9.

162. [Between the concepts.]

these presentations belong *necessarily to one another* in the empirical intuition. Rather, I mean that they belong to one another *by virtue of the necessary unity* of apperception in the synthesis of intuitions; i.e., they belong to one another according to principles of the objective determination of all presentations insofar as these presentations can become cognition—all of these principles being derived from the principle of the transcendental unity of apperception. Only through this [reference to original apperception and its necessary unity] does this relation [among presentations] become a *judgment,* i.e., a relation that is *valid objectively* and can be distinguished adequately from a relation of the same presentations that would have only subjective validity—e.g., a relation according to laws of association. According to these laws, all I could say is: When I support a body, then I feel a pressure of heaviness. I could not say: It, the body, is heavy—which amounts to saying that these two presentations are not merely together in perception (no matter how often repeated), but are combined in the object, i.e., combined independently of what the subject's state is.

§ 20

All Sensible Intuitions Are Subject to the Categories, Which Are Conditions under Which Alone Their Manifold Can Come Together in One Consciousness

The manifold given [which is found] in a sensible intuition is subject necessarily to the original synthetic unity of apperception; for solely through this unity is the *unity* of intuition possible. (§ 17.) But the act of understanding whereby the manifold of given presentations (whether intuitions or concepts) are brought under one apperception as such is the logical function of judgments. (§ 19.) Therefore everything manifold, insofar as it is given in one empirical intuition, is *determined* in regard to one of the logical functions of judging, inasmuch as through this function it is brought to one consciousness as such. The *categories,* however, are indeed nothing but precisely these functions of judging insofar as the manifold of a given intuition is determined in regard to them. (§ 13.) Hence, by the same token, the manifold in a given intuition is subject necessarily to the categories.

§ 21   B144

Comment

Through the synthesis of understanding, a manifold contained in an intuition that I call mine is presented as belonging to the *necessary* unity of self-consciousness, and this presenting is done by means of the category.[163] Hence the category indicates that the empirical consciousness of a given manifold of one intuition is just as subject to a pure a priori self-consciousness, as empirical intuition is subject to a pure sensible intuition that likewise takes place a priori. Hence in the above proposition[164] I have made the beginning of a *deduction* of the pure concepts of understanding. Since the categories are *independent of sensibility* and arise in the understanding alone, I must still abstract, in this deduction, from the way in which the manifold for an empirical intuition is given, in order to take account solely of the unity that the understanding contributes to the intuition by means of the category. Afterwards (§ 26) I shall show, from the way in which the empirical intuition is given in sensibility, that the intuition's unity is none other than the unity that (by § 20, above) the category prescribes to the manifold of a given intuition as such; and that hence by my explaining the category's a priori validity regarding all objects of our senses, the deduction's aim will first be fully attained.

From one point, however, I could not abstract in the above proof: viz., from the fact that the manifold for the intuition must be given still prior to the understanding's synthesis, and independently of it; but how it is given remains undetermined here. For if I were to think of an understanding[165] that itself intuited[166]

---

163. The basis of proof for this rests on the presented *unity of intuition,* through which an *object*[a] is given. That unity always implies[b] a synthesis of the manifold given[c] for an intuition, and already contains this manifold given's reference to unity of apperception.

  [a][Emphasis added.]

  [b][Or 'includes': *in sich schließ.*]

  [c][Here again 'manifold' is an adjective, and 'given' is a participle that is about to be construed as a noun. Cf. above, B 143.]

164. [The proposition at the beginning of § 21.]

165. [Other than our own.]

166. [See above, B 72.]

(as, e.g., a divine understanding that did not present given objects[167] but through whose presentation the objects would at the same time be given or produced), then in regard to such cognition the categories would have no signification whatever. The categories are only rules for an understanding whose entire power consists in thought, i.e., in the act of bringing to the unity of apperception the synthesis of the manifold that has, in intuition, been given to it from elsewhere. Hence such an understanding by itself cognizes nothing whatever, but only combines and orders the material for cognition, i.e., the intuition, which must be given to it by the object. But why our understanding has this peculiarity, that it a priori brings about unity B146 of apperception only by means of the categories, and only by just this kind and number of them—for this no further reason can be given, just as no reason can be given as to why we have just these and no other functions in judging, or why time and space are the only forms of our possible intuition.

§ 22

A Category Cannot Be Used for Cognizing Things Except When It Is Applied to Objects of Experience

Thinking an object and *cognizing* an object are, then, not the same. For cognition involves two components: first, the concept (the category), through which an object as such is thought; and second, the intuition, through which the object is given. For if no intuition corresponding to the concept could be given at all, then in terms of its form the concept would indeed be a thought; but it would be a thought without any object, and no cognition at all of any thing whatsoever would be possible by means of it. For as far as I would know, there would be nothing, and could be nothing, to which my thought could be applied. Now, all intuition that is possible for us is sensible (see the Transcendental Aesthetic). Hence in us, thinking an object as such by means of a pure concept of understanding can become cognition only insofar as this concept is referred to objects of the senses. Sensible B147 intuition is either pure intuition (space and time)

---

167. [As does our understanding, which presents objects given outside of itself, viz., in sensible intuition.]

or empirical intuition of what, through sensation, is presented directly as actual in space and time. By determining pure intuition we can (in mathematics) acquire a priori cognition of objects as appearances, but only in terms of their form; that, however, still leaves unestablished whether there can be things that must be intuited in this form. Consequently all mathematical concepts are, by themselves, no cognitions—except insofar as one presupposes that there are things that can be exhibited to us only in accordance with the form of that pure sensible intuition. But *things in space and time* are given only insofar as they are perceptions (i.e., presentations accompanied by sensation), and hence are given only through empirical presentation. Consequently the pure concepts of understanding, even when they are (as in mathematics) applied to a priori intuitions, provide cognition only insofar as these intuitions—and hence, by means of them, also the concepts of understanding—can be applied to empirical intuitions. Consequently the categories also do not supply us, by means of intuition, with any cognition of things, except through their possible application to *empirical* intuition. I.e., the categories serve only for the possibility of *empirical cognition*. Such cognition, however, is called *experience*. Consequently the categories cannot be used for B148 cognizing things except insofar as these things are taken as objects of possible experience.

§ 23

The last proposition above is of the greatest importance. For it determines the bounds for the use of the pure concepts of understanding in regard to objects just as much as the Transcendental Aesthetic determined the bounds for the use of the pure form of our sensible intuition. Space and time, as conditions for the possibility as to how objects can be given to us, hold no further than for objects of the senses, and hence hold for objects of experience only. Beyond these bounds, space and time present nothing whatsoever; for they are only in the senses and have no actuality apart from them. The pure concepts of understanding are free from this limitation and extend to objects of intuition as such, whether this intuition is similar to ours or not, as long as it is sensible rather than intellectual. But this further extension of the concepts beyond *our* sensible intuition is of no benefit to us whatsoever. For they are then empty concepts of objects, i.e., concepts through which we cannot judge at all whether or not these objects are so much as possible. I.e., the pure concepts of understanding are then mere forms of thought, without objective reality; for we then have available no intuition to which the synthetic unity of apperception—which is all that those concepts contain—could be applied so B149 that the concepts could determine an object. Solely *our* sensible and empirical intuition can provide them with meaning and significance.

Hence if we suppose an object of a *nonsensible* intuition[168] as given, then we can indeed present it through all the predicates that are already contained in the presupposition *that the object has as a property nothing belonging to sensible intuition:* hence we can present that it is not extended or in space, that its duration is not a time, that no change (i.e., succession of determinations in time) is to be found in it, etc. But yet I have no proper cognition if I merely indicate how the intuition of the object is *not*, without being able to say what the intuition does contain. For I have not then presented the possibility of there being an object for my pure concept of understanding, since I was unable to give an intuition corresponding to the concept, but was able only to say that our intuition does not hold for it. However, the foremost point here is that to such a something not even one single category could be applied. E.g., one could not apply to it the concept of a substance, i.e., the concept of something that can exist as subject but never as mere predicate. For I do not know at all, concerning this concept, whether there can be anything whatever corresponding to this conceptual determination [of substance], unless empirical intuition gives me the instance for applying it. But more about this later.

B150
§ 24

On Applying the Categories to Objects of the Senses As Such

The pure concepts of understanding refer, through mere understanding, to objects of intuition as such — i.e., we leave undetermined whether this intuition is ours or some other, although it must be sensible

intuition. But the concepts are, precisely because of this, mere *forms of thought*, through which as yet no determinate object is cognized. We saw that the synthesis or combination of the manifold in them referred merely to the unity of apperception, and was thereby the basis for the possibility of a priori cognition insofar as such cognition rests on the understanding; and hence this synthesis was not just transcendental but was also purely intellectual only. But there lies at the basis in us a priori a certain form of sensible intuition, a form that is based on the receptivity of our capacity to present (i.e., based on our sensibility). Hence the understanding (as spontaneity) can, by means of the manifold of given presentations, determine inner sense in accordance with the synthetic unity of apperception; and thus it can think synthetic unity of the apperception of the manifold of a priori *sensible intuition*—this unity being the condition to which all objects of our (i.e., human) intuition must necessarily be subject. And thereby the categories, as themselves mere forms of thought, acquire objective reality. I.e., they acquire application to objects that B151 can be given to us in intuition. But they apply to these objects only as appearances; for only of appearances are we capable of having a priori intuition.

This *synthesis* of the manifold of sensible intuition, which is a priori possible and necessary, may be called *figurative* synthesis (*synthesis speciosa*). This serves to distinguish it from the synthesis that would be thought in the mere category, in regard to the manifold of an intuition as such;[169] this latter synthesis is called combination of understanding (*synthesis intellectualis*). Both these syntheses are *transcendental*, not just because they themselves proceed a priori, but because they also are the basis for the possibility of other a priori cognition.

However, when the figurative synthesis concerns merely the original synthetic unity of apperception, i.e., merely this transcendental unity thought in the categories, then it must be called the *transcendental synthesis of imagination*, to distinguish it from the merely intellectual combination.[170] **Imagination** is the power of presenting an object in intuition even *without the object's being present*. Now, all our intu-

168. [I.e., intellectual intuition. See above, B 72.]

169. [I.e., sensible or intellectual.]
170. [Of understanding.]

ition is sensible; and hence the imagination, because of the subjective condition under which alone it can give to the concepts of understanding a corresponding intuition, belongs to *sensibility*. Yet the synthesis of imagination is an exercise of spontaneity, which is B152 determinative, rather than merely determinable, as is sense; hence this synthesis can a priori determine sense in terms of its form in accordance with the unity of apperception. To this extent, therefore, the imagination is a power of determining sensibility a priori; and its synthesis of intuitions *in accordance with the categories* must be the transcendental synthesis of *imagination*. This synthesis is an action of the understanding upon sensibility, and is the understanding's first application (and at the same time the basis of all its other applications) to objects of the intuition that is possible for us. As figurative, this synthesis is distinct from the intellectual synthesis, which proceeds without any imagination but merely through understanding. Now insofar as the imagination is spontaneity, I sometimes also call it the *productive* imagination, thereby distinguishing it from the *reproductive* imagination. The synthesis of the reproductive imagination is subject solely to empirical laws, viz., to the laws of association. Therefore this synthesis contributes nothing to the explanation of the possibility of a priori cognition, and hence belongs not in transcendental philosophy but in psychology.

———————————

Now, this is the place to clarify something paradoxical that must have struck everyone in reading the exposition of the form of inner sense (§ 6): viz., how this sense exhibits to consciousness even ourselves B153 only as we appear to ourselves, not as we are in ourselves. For we intuit ourselves only as we are inwardly *affected*; and this seems contradictory, because we [despite being active] would then have to relate to ourselves as passive.[171] And this is the reason why people in their systems of psychology usually prefer to pass *inner sense* off as being the same as the power of *apperception* (which we carefully distinguish from inner sense).

However, what determines inner sense is the understanding and its original power of combining the

manifold of intuition, i.e., the power of bringing that manifold under one apperception (on which apperception the understanding's possibility itself rests). Now in us human beings the understanding is not itself a power of intuitions; and even if an intuition were already given in sensibility, the understanding cannot take it up *into itself*, in order—as it were—to combine the manifold of [what would then be] *its own* intuition. Hence when the understanding is considered by itself alone, then its synthesis is nothing but the unity of the understanding's act: the act of which the understanding is conscious as an act even apart from sensibility, but through which the understanding itself is able to determine sensibility inwardly as regards the manifold that may, in accordance with the form of sensibility's intuition, be given to the understanding. Hence it is understanding which performs, on the *passive* subject whose *power* it is, that act—under the name of a *transcendental synthesis of imagination*—of which we rightly say that inner sense B154 is affected by it. Apperception and its synthetic unity is so far from being the same as inner sense that, as the source of all combination, it applies rather to the manifold of *intuitions as such*,[172] and—under the name of the categories—applies, prior to all sensible intuition, to objects as such. Inner sense, on the other hand, contains the mere *form* of intuition, but without combination of the manifold in this form, and hence contains as yet no *determinate* intuition at all. Determinate intuition is possible only through the consciousness of the manifold's determination by the transcendental act of imagination (i.e., by the synthetic influence of understanding on inner sense)—the act that I have called figurative synthesis.

This [need for figurative synthesis], moreover, we always perceive in ourselves. We cannot think a line without *drawing* it in thought. We cannot think a circle without *describing* it.[173] We cannot at all present the three dimensions of space without *placing* three lines perpendicularly to one another from the same point. And even time we cannot present except inasmuch as, in *drawing* a straight line (meant to be the externally figurative presentation[174] of time), we attend

———————————

171. [I.e., even though as intuiting we would be active, as *being intuited* we (the same subject) would simultaneously be passive.]

172. [Sensible or intellectual.]

173. [I.e., without tracing it in thought.]

174. [I.e., the presentation that is figurative in the external way.]

merely to the act of the manifold's synthesis whereby we successively determine inner sense, and thereby attend to the succession of this determination in inner sense. Indeed, what first produces the concept of

B155 succession is motion, taken as act of the subject (rather than as a determination of an object)[175] and consequently as the synthesis of the manifold in space, if we abstract from this manifold and attend merely to the act whereby we determine *inner sense* according to its form. Hence by no means does the understanding already find in inner sense such a combination of the manifold; rather, the understanding *produces it,* inasmuch as the understanding *affects* that sense. But how (inasmuch as in addition to sensible intuition I can present, at least as possible, a different kind of intuition) can the *I* who thinks be distinct from the *I* that intuits itself,[176] and yet be the same as it by being the same subject? And hence how can I say: I, as intelligence and *thinking* subject, cognize *myself* as an object that is *thought,* viz., I so cognize myself insofar as in addition[177] I am also given to myself in intuition—except that I cognize myself, as I do other phenomena, not as I am to the understanding, but as I appear to myself? This question involves neither more nor less difficulty than does the question as to how I can be an object to myself at all, viz., an object

B156 of intuition and of inner perceptions. Yet so it must actually be, as we can easily establish if space is already accepted as being merely a pure form of the appearances of outer senses. For as regards time, which after

---

175. Motion of an *object* in space does not belong in a pure science, and consequently not in geometry. For the fact that something is movable cannot be cognized a priori, but can be cognized only through experience. But motion taken as the *describing* [i.e., outlining] of a space is a pure act of the successive synthesis, by productive imagination, of the manifold in outer intuition as such, and belongs not only to geometry but even to transcendental philosophy.

176. [The point of the parenthetical remark may be that this distinctness combined with sameness seems even *more* problematic if we consider intuition *as such*—including, i.e., the intellectual intuition of an intuitive understanding—than if we consider sensible intuition, which at least is not the intuition of an understanding. Or perhaps Kant is saying merely that this issue of distinctness arises because in our case intuition and understanding are *not* united.]

177. [To being thought.]

all is not an object of outer intuition at all, we cannot present it to ourselves except under the image of a line insofar as we draw that line; without exhibiting time in this way, we could not cognize the singleness of its dimension. Likewise, in seeking for all inner perceptions the determination of length of time, or again of time positions, we must always get this determination from what changeable features are exhibited to us by outer things. Consequently the determinations of inner sense must be arranged by us as appearances in time in precisely the same way as the determinations of the outer senses are arranged by us in space. Hence if concerning the determinations of the outer senses we grant that we cognize objects through them only insofar as we are outwardly affected, then we must also concede concerning inner sense that we intuit ourselves through it only as we are inwardly affected *by ourselves*; i.e., we must concede that, as far as inner intuition is concerned, our own [self as] subject is cognized by us only as appearance, but not in terms of what it is in itself.[178]

§ 25   B157

By contrast, in the transcendental synthesis of the manifold of presentations as such, and hence in the synthetic original unity of apperception, I am not conscious of myself as I appear to myself, nor as I am in myself, but am conscious only that I am. This *presentation* is a *thought,* not an *intuition.* Now *cognition* of ourselves requires not only the act of thought that brings the manifold of every possible intuition to the unity of apperception, but requires in addition a definite kind of intuition whereby this manifold is given. Hence although my own existence is not appearance (still less mere illusion), determination B158

---

178. I fail to see how one can find so many difficulties in the view that inner sense is affected by ourselves—of which every act of *attention* can provide us with an example. In such acts the understanding always determines inner sense, in accordance with the combination that the understanding thinks, turning it into the inner intuition that corresponds to the manifold in the understanding's synthesis. Everyone will be able to perceive in himself how much the mind is commonly affected by this.

of my existence[179] can occur only in conformity with the form of inner sense and according to the particular way in which the manifold that I combine is given in inner intuition. Accordingly I have no *cognition* of myself as I am but merely cognition of how I appear to myself. Hence consciousness of oneself is far from being a cognition of oneself, regardless of all the categories, which make up the thought of an *object as such* through the combination of the manifold in one apperception. We saw that in order for me to cognize an object different from myself, I not only require the thinking (which I have in the category) of an object as such, but do also require an intuition whereby I determine that universal concept. In the same way, in order to cognize myself, too, I not only require the consciousness of myself or the fact that I think myself, but require also an intuition of the manifold in me whereby I determine this thought. And I exist as an intelligence. This intelligence is

B159 conscious solely in its power of combination. But as regards the manifold that it is to combine, this intelligence is subjected to a limiting condition (which it calls inner sense). As subjected to this condition, it can make that combination intuitable only in terms of time relations, which lie wholly outside the concepts of understanding, properly so called.[180] And hence this intelligence can still cognize itself only as, in regard to an intuition (one that cannot be

179. The *I think* expresses the act of determining my existence. Hence the existence [of myself] is already given through this *I think*; but there is not yet given through it the way in which I am to determine that existence, i.e., posit the manifold belonging to it. In order for that manifold to be given, self-intuition is required; and at the basis of this self-intuition lies a form given a priori, viz., time, which is sensible and belongs to the ability to receive the determin-

B158 able. Now unless I have in addition a different [viz., intellectual] self-intuition that gives, prior to the act of *determination*, the *determinative* in me (only of its spontaneity am I in fact conscious) just as time so gives the determinable, then I cannot determine my existence as that of a self-active being; instead I present only the spontaneity of my thought, i.e., of the [act of] determination, and my existence remains determinable always only sensibly, i.e., as the existence of an appearance. But it is on account of this spontaneity that I call myself an *intelligence*.

180. [I.e., unschematized.]

intellectual and given by the understanding itself), it merely appears to itself; it cannot cognize itself as it would if its *intuition* were intellectual.

§ 26

TRANSCENDENTAL DEDUCTION OF THE UNIVERSALLY POSSIBLE USE IN EXPERIENCE OF THE PURE CONCEPTS OF UNDERSTANDING

In the *metaphysical deduction*[181] we established the a priori origin of the categories as such through their complete concurrence with the universal logical functions of thought. But in the *transcendental deduction* we exhibited the possibility of them[182] as a priori cognitions of objects of an intuition as such (§§ 20, 21). We must now explain how it is possible, through *categories*, to cognize a priori whatever objects *our senses may encounter*—to so cognize them as regards not the form of their intuition, but the laws of their combination—and hence, as it were, to prescribe laws to nature, and even to make nature possible. For B160 without this suitability of the categories,[183] one would fail to see how everything that our senses may encounter would have to be subject to the laws that arise a priori from the understanding alone.

First of all, let me point out that by *synthesis of apprehension* I mean that combination of the manifold in an empirical intuition whereby perception, i.e., empirical consciousness of the intuition (as appearance), becomes possible.

We have a priori, in the presentations of space and time, *forms* of both outer and inner sensible intuition; and to these forms the synthesis of apprehension of the manifold of appearance must always conform, because that synthesis itself can take place only according to this form. But space and time are presented a priori not merely as *forms* of sensible intuition, but as themselves *intuitions* (containing a manifold), and hence are presented with the determination[184] of the *unity* of this manifold in them (see the Transcenden- B161

181. [B 90–116. Kant did not there use this name.]

182. [The categories as such.]

183. [For such cognition and prescription.]

184. [I.e., here, property.]

tal Aesthetic).[185] Therefore even *unity of synthesis* of the manifold outside or within us, and hence also a *combination* to which everything that is to be presented determinately in space or time must conform, is already given a priori as condition of the synthesis of all *apprehension*—given along with (not in) these intuitions. This synthetic unity, however, can be none other than the unity of the combination, conforming to the categories but applied to our *sensible intuition*, of the manifold of a given *intuition as such* in an original consciousness. Consequently all synthesis, the synthesis through which even perception becomes possible, is subject to the categories; and since experience is cognition through connected perceptions, the categories are conditions of the possibility of experience and hence hold a priori also for all objects of experience.

B162 Hence, e.g., when I turn the empirical intuition of a house into a perception by apprehending the intuition's manifold, then in this apprehension I use as a basis the *necessary unity* of space and of outer sensible intuition as such; and I draw, as it were, the house's shape in conformity with this synthetic unity of the manifold in space. But this same unity, if I abstract from the form of space, resides in the understanding, and is the category of the synthesis of the homogeneous in an intuition as such, i.e., the category of

185. Space, presented as *object* (as we are actually required to present it in geometry), contains more than mere form of intuition; viz., it contains also *combination*, of the manifold given[a] according to the form of sensibility, into an *intuitive*[b] presentation—so that the *form of intuition* gives us merely a manifold, but *formal intuition* gives us unity of presentation. In the Transcendental Aesthetic I had merely included
B161 this unity with sensibility, wanting only to point out that it precedes any concept. But in fact this unity presupposes a synthesis; this synthesis does not belong to the senses, but through it do all concepts of space and time first become possible. For through this unity (inasmuch as understanding determines sensibility) space or time are first *given* as intuitions, and hence the unity of this a priori intuition belongs to space and time, and not to the concept of understanding (see § 24).
a[*Des mannigfaltigen . . . Gegebenen.* I.e., 'manifold' is an adjective, and 'given' is a participle functioning as a noun.]
b[*anschaulich.*]

magnitude.[186] Hence the synthesis of apprehension, i.e., perception,[187] must conform throughout to that category.[188]

When (to take a different example) I perceive the freezing of water, then I apprehend two states (fluidity and solidity) as states that stand to each other in a relation of time. Since the appearance is inner *intuition*, I lay time at its basis. But in time I necessarily present B163 synthetic *unity* of the manifold; without this unity, that relation[189] could not be given *determinately* (as regards time sequence) in an intuition. However, this synthetic unity, as a priori condition under which I combine the manifold of an *intuition as such*, is—if I abstract from the constant form of *my* inner intuition, i.e., from time—the category of *cause*; through this category, when I apply it to my sensibility, *everything that happens is, in terms of its relation, determined* by me *in time as such.* Therefore apprehension in such an event, and hence the event itself, is subject—as regards possible perception—to the concept of the *relation of effects and causes*; and thus it is in all other cases.

Categories are concepts that prescribe laws a priori to appearances, and hence to nature regarded as the sum of all appearances (*natura materialiter spectata*).[190] And now this question arises: Since the categories are not derived from nature and do not conform to it as their model (for then they would be merely empirical), how are we to comprehend the fact that nature must conform to the categories, i.e., how can the categories determine a priori the combination of nature's manifold without gleaning that combination from nature? Here now is the solution of this puzzle.

186. [I.e., quantity.]
187. [Not apprehension but the synthesis of apprehension is being equated with perception.]
188. In this way we prove that the synthesis of apprehension, which is empirical, must conform necessarily to the synthesis of apperception, which is intellectual and is contained wholly a priori in the category. The spontaneity that brings combination into the manifold of intuition is one and the same in the two cases: in apprehension it does so under the name of power of imagination; in apperception it does so under the name of understanding.
189. [Of time.]
190. [Nature considered materially.]

B164 How it is that the laws of appearances in nature must agree with the understanding and its a priori form, i.e., with the understanding's power to combine the manifold as such, is not any stranger than how it is that appearances themselves must agree with the form of a priori sensible intuition. For just as appearances exist not in themselves but only relatively to the subject in whom the appearances inhere insofar as the subject has senses, so the laws exist not in the appearances but only relatively to that same being insofar as that being has understanding. Things in themselves would have their law-governedness necessarily, even apart from an understanding that cognizes them. But appearances are only presentations of things that exist uncognized as regards what they may be in themselves. As mere appearances, however, they are subject to no law of connection whatever except the one prescribed by the connecting power. Now what connects the manifold of sensible intuition is imagination; and imagination depends on understanding as regards the unity of its intellectual synthesis, and on sensibility as regards the manifoldness of apprehension. Now all possible perception depends on this synthesis of apprehension; but it itself, this empirical synthesis, depends on transcendental synthesis and hence on the categories. Therefore all possible perceptions, and hence also everything what-
B165 ever that can reach empirical consciousness, i.e., all appearances of nature, must in regard to their combination be subject to the categories. Nature (regarded merely as nature as such) depends (as *natura formaliter spectata*)[191] on the categories as the original basis of its necessary law-governedness. But even the pure power of understanding does not suffice for prescribing a priori to appearances, through mere categories, more laws than those underlying a *nature as such* considered as law-governedness of appearances in space and time. Particular laws, because they concern appearances that are determined empirically, are not *derivable completely* from those laws,[192] although the particular laws are one and all subject to the categories. Experience must be added in order for us to become acquainted with particular laws *at all*; but the a priori laws alone give us information about

experience as such and about what can be cognized as an object of that experience.

§ 27

RESULT OF THIS DEDUCTION OF THE CONCEPTS OF UNDERSTANDING

We cannot *think* an object except through categories; we cannot cognize an object thought by us except through intuitions corresponding to those concepts. Now all our intuitions are sensible, and this [sensible] cognition is empirical insofar as its object is given. B166 Empirical cognition, however, is experience. *Consequently no cognition is possible for us a priori except solely of objects of possible experience.*[193]

But this cognition, which is limited to just objects of experience, is not therefore all taken from experience. Rather, as far as pure intuitions as well as pure concepts of understanding are concerned, they are elements of cognition that are found in us a priori. Now, there are only two ways in which one can conceive of a *necessary* agreement of experience with the concepts of its objects: either experience makes these concepts possible, or these concepts make experience possible. The first alternative is not what happens as B167 regards the categories (nor as regards pure sensible intuition). For they are a priori concepts and hence are independent of experience. (To assert that their origin is empirical would be to assert a kind of *generatio aequivoca*).[194] There remains, consequently, only

193. In order to keep my readers from being troubled prematurely by the worrisome detrimental consequences of this proposition, let me just remind them that in our *thinking* the categories are not limited by the conditions of our sensible intuition, but have an unbounded realm. Intuition is required only for *cognizing* what we think, i.e., only for determining the object. Thus if intuition is lacking, the thought of the object can otherwise still have its true and useful consequences for the subject's *use of reason*. But because the use of reason is not always directed to the determination of the object and hence to cognition, but is sometimes directed also to the determination of the subject and his volition, it cannot yet be set forth here. [Kant is here referring to the practical use of pure reason in the realm of morality.]

194. [A generation of something by something so different from it that such generation would be an absurdity.]

191. [Nature considered formally.]

192. [The a priori laws underlying a nature as such.]

the second alternative (a system[195] of *epigenesis*, as it were, of pure reason):[196] viz., that the categories contain the bases, on the part of the understanding, of the possibility of all experience as such. But as to how the categories make experience possible, and as to what principles of the possibility of experience they provide us with when applied to appearances, more information will be given in the following chapter on the transcendental use of our power of judgment.

Someone might want to propose, in addition to the two sole ways mentioned above, a middle course between them: viz., that the categories are neither *self-thought* a priori first principles of our cognition, nor again are drawn from experience, but are subjective predispositions for thinking that are implanted in us [and given to us] simultaneously with our existence; and that they were so arranged by our originator that their use harmonizes exactly with the laws of nature governing the course of experience (this theory would be a kind of *preformation system* of pure reason).[197] If such a middle course were proposed, the following would decide against it (apart from the fact that with such a hypothesis one can see no end to B168 how far the presupposition of predetermined predispositions to future judgments might be carried): viz., that the categories would in that case lack the *necessity* which belongs essentially to the concept of them. For, the concept of cause, e.g., which asserts the necessity of a result under a presupposed condition, would be false if it rested only on an arbitrary subjective necessity, implanted in us, to link certain empirical presentations according to such a rule of relation. I could then not say that the effect is connected with the cause in the object (i.e., connected with it necessarily), but could say only that I am so equipped that I cannot think this presentation otherwise than as thus connected. And this is just what the skeptic most longs [to hear]. For then all our insight, achieved through the supposed objective validity of our judgments, is nothing but sheer illusion; and there would also be no lack of people who would not concede

this subjective necessity (which must be felt) in themselves. At the very least one could not quarrel with anyone about something that rests merely on the way in which his [self as] subject is organized.

Brief Sketch of This Deduction

This deduction is the exhibition of the pure concepts of understanding (and, with them, of all theoretical a priori cognition) as principles of the possibility of experience; the exhibition of these principles, however, as the *determination* of appearances in space B169 and time *as such*; and the exhibition, finally, of this determination as arising from the *original* synthetic unity of apperception, this unity being the form of understanding as referred to space and time, the original forms of sensibility.

———————

Only up to this point do I consider the division into subsections to be necessary, because we have been dealing with the elementary concepts. Now that we want to present to ourselves the use of these concepts, the treatise may go on without such division, cohering in terms of continuity.

B
Second Analogy

Principle of Temporal Succession According to the Law of Causality

All changes occur according to the law of the connection of cause and effect.

Proof

(The previous principle has established that all appearances [forming part] of the temporal succession[198] are one and all only *changes*;[199] i.e., they are a successive being and not-being of the determinations of substance, which itself is permanent. The principle has established, therefore, that there is no such thing as the being of substance itself as succeeding its not-being, or its not-being as succeeding its existence; B233 in other words, there is no such thing as the arising

---

195. [Or, i.e., theory.]

196. [I.e., a system of pure reason whereby experience comes about by epigenesis.]

197. [I.e., a system of pure reason whereby experience is formed in advance.]

198. [And hence all variation (cf. the restatement of the principle, just below).]

199. [Of substance.]

or passing away of substance itself. The principle could also have been expressed thus: *All variation (succession) on the part of appearances is only change*; for an arising or passing away of substance would not be changes of it, because the concept of change presupposes the same subject as existing, and hence as being permanent, with two opposite determinations. After this preliminary reminder, there now follows the proof.)

I perceive that appearances succeed one another, i.e., that at one time there is a state of things whose opposite was there in the things' previous state. Hence I am in fact connecting two perceptions in time. Now connection is not the work of mere sense and intuition, but is here the product of a synthetic ability of our imagination which determines inner sense in regard to time relation. But imagination can link those two states in two ways, so that either the one or the other state precedes in time. For time cannot in itself be perceived, and what precedes or follows cannot be determined by reference to it in the object—empirically, as it were. I am, therefore, conscious only that my imagination places one state before and the other after, but not that the one state B234 precedes the other in the object. In other words, mere perception leaves indeterminate the *objective relation* of the appearances following one another. Now in order for this objective relation to be cognized as determinate, the relation between the two states must be thought as being such that it determines as necessary which of the states must be placed before and which after, rather than vice versa. But a concept carrying with it a necessity of synthetic unity can only be a pure concept of understanding, which therefore does not reside in perception. Here this concept is that of the *relation of cause and effect*; of these two, the cause is what determines the effect in time, and determines it as the consequence, rather than as something that [as occurring] merely in imagination might [instead] precede (or might not even be perceived at all). Therefore experience itself—i.e., empirical cognition of appearances—is possible only inasmuch as we subject the succession of appearances, and hence all change, to the law of causality. Hence appearances themselves, taken as objects of experience, are possible only in accordance with this law.

Apprehension of the manifold of appearances is always successive. The presentations of the parts suc-

ceed one another. Whether they also follow one another in the object is a second point for reflection which is not already contained in the first point.[200] Now it is true that anything, even every presentation insofar as one is conscious of it, can be called an object. Yet what this word might signify in the case B235 of appearances, not insofar as they (as presentations) are objects but insofar as they only designate an object, calls for deeper investigation. Insofar as appearances, taken only as presentations, are simultaneously objects of consciousness, they are not at all distinct from apprehension, i.e., from the taking up into the synthesis of imagination; and we must say, therefore, that the manifold of appearances is always produced in the mind successively. If appearances were things in themselves, then no human being could gather[201] from the succession of presentations how their manifold is combined in the object. For we deal, after all, only with our presentations; how things may be in themselves (i.e., apart from taking account of presentations whereby they affect us), is entirely outside our sphere of cognition. Appearances, then, are indeed not things in themselves; but they are all that can be given to us for cognition. And now, whereas the presentation [as such] of the manifold in apprehension is always successive, I am to indicate what sort of combination in time belongs to the manifold in appearances themselves. Thus, e.g., the apprehension of the manifold in the appearance of a house standing before me is successive. Now the question is whether the manifold of this house itself is successive intrinsically as well; and this, to be sure, no one will grant. B236 But once I raise my concepts of an object to the level of transcendental signification, the house is not at all a thing in itself, but is only an appearance, i.e., a presentation, whose transcendental object is unknown. What, then, do I mean by the question as to how the manifold may be combined in appearance itself (which, after all, is nothing in itself)? Here what lies in the successive apprehension is regarded as presentation; but the appearance that is given to me, despite being nothing more than a sum of these pre-

200. [The first point being that the presentations of the parts succeed one another.]

201. [Human beings lack the intellectual intuition (viz., of things in themselves) that an intuitive understanding would have. See B 72.]

sentations, is regarded as their object, with which the concept that I obtain from the presentations of apprehension is to agree. We soon see that, since agreement of cognition with the object is truth, the question can only be inquiring after the formal conditions of empirical truth; and we see that appearance, as contrasted with the presentations of apprehension, can be presented as an object distinct from them only if it is subject to a rule that distinguishes it from any other apprehension and that makes necessary one kind of combination of the manifold. That [element] in the appearance which contains the condition of this necessary rule of apprehension is the object.

Let us now proceed to our problem. That something occurs, i.e., that something, or a state that was not there before, comes to be cannot be perceived B237 empirically[202] unless it is preceded by an appearance that does not contain this state. For an actuality succeeding an empty time, i.e., an arising not preceded by any state of things, cannot be apprehended any more than empty time itself. Hence any apprehension of an event is a perception succeeding another perception. But because, as I showed above by reference to the appearance of a house, this is so in all synthesis of apprehension, the apprehension of an event is not yet distinguished thereby from other apprehensions. Yet I also observe that if, in an appearance containing an occurrence, I call A the preceding state of the perception and B the succeeding state, then B can in apprehension only succeed A, and similarly perception A cannot succeed B but can only precede it. For example, I see a ship floating down the river. My perception of its position lower down in the course of the river succeeds the perception of its position higher up, and there is no possibility that in the apprehension of this appearance the ship should be perceived first lower down and afterwards higher up in the river. Hence the order in the perceptions' succession in apprehension is here determinate, and apprehension is tied to this order. In the previous example of a house my perceptions could, in appre-
B238 hension, start from the house's top and end at the bottom, but they could also start from below and end above; and they could likewise apprehend the manifold of the empirical intuition by proceeding

either to the right or to the left. Hence in the series of these perceptions there was no determinate order making necessary the point in apprehension where I must begin in order to combine the manifold empirically. In the perception of what occurs,[203] however, this rule[204] is always to be found, and through it the order of the perceptions succeeding one another (in the apprehension of this appearance) is made *necessary*.

In our case,[205] therefore, I shall have to derive the *subjective succession* of apprehension from the *objective succession* of appearances; for otherwise the subjective succession is entirely indeterminate and fails to distinguish any one appearance from some other appearance. The subjective succession by itself, being entirely arbitrary, proves nothing about the connection of the manifold in the object. Hence the objective succession will consist in the order of the manifold of appearance whereby the apprehension of the one item (viz. what occurs) succeeds the apprehension of the other (viz., what precedes) *according to a rule*. This alone can entitle me to say of the appearance itself, and not merely of my apprehension, that a succession is to be found in it—which means the same as that I cannot perform the apprehension except in precisely this succession.[206]

In accordance with such a rule, therefore, what precedes an event as such must contain the condition B239 for a rule whereby this event always and necessarily follows. But I cannot go, conversely, from the event backward and determine (through apprehension) what precedes. For no appearance goes back from the succeeding point of time to the previous one, although it does refer *to some previous one*. The progression from a given time to the determinate following time, on the other hand, is necessary. Hence because it[207] is, after all, something that follows, I must necessarily refer it to something else as such that precedes it and that it succeeds according to a rule, i.e., necessarily. Thus the event, as the conditioned, directs us reliably to some condition, while this condition determines the event.

---

202. [As Kant uses the term 'perceive,' 'empirically' is actually redundant.]

203. [As in the case of the ship floating down the river.]
204. [As to where I must begin.]
205. [I.e., the case of an event.]
206. [Or "sequence."]
207. [I.e., the event.]

Suppose that an event is not preceded by anything that it must succeed according to a rule. Then all succession of perception would be determined solely in apprehension, i.e., merely subjectively; but this would not at all determine objectively which item in fact precedes in perception and which follows. We would in that way have only a play of presentations that would not refer to any object whatever; i.e., our perception would not at all distinguish one appearance from all others in terms of time relation. For the succession in apprehending is in that case everywhere the same, and hence there is in appearance B240 nothing determining this succession so that a certain[208] succession is, as objective, made necessary by it. Hence I shall in that case not say that two states succeed each other in appearance. Rather, I shall say only that one apprehension succeeds the other; and this is merely something *subjective* and determines no object, and hence cannot count as cognition of any object (not even of an object in [the realm of] appearance).

Hence when we experience that something occurs, then in doing so we always presuppose that it is preceded by something or other that it succeeds according to a rule. Otherwise I would not say of the object that it succeeds; for the mere succession in my apprehension, if it is not determined by a rule by reference to something preceding it, justifies no [assumption of a] succession in the object. Hence it is always on account of a rule that I make my subjective synthesis (of apprehension) objective, viz., a rule according to which appearances in their succession, i.e., as they occur, are determined by the previous state. And the experience itself of something that occurs is possible solely and exclusively under this presupposition.

It is true that this seems to contradict all the remarks that people have always made about the course taken by our understanding. According to those remarks, it is only by perceiving and comparing the agreeing successions of events that follow upon preceding appearances that we are first led to discover a rule B241 whereby certain events always succeed certain appearances, and only thereby we are first prompted to frame the concept of cause. This concept would, on such

a basis, be merely empirical. And the rule whereby everything that occurs has a cause, as this concept provides it, would be just as contingent as the experience itself.[209] The rule's universality and necessity would then be attributed to it only fictitiously and would have no true universal validity, because they would be based not on anything a priori, but only on induction. But the case with this rule is the same as that with other pure a priori presentations (e.g., space and time): we can extract them as clear concepts from experience solely because we have put them into experience and hence have brought experience about through them in the first place. To be sure, this presentation of a rule determining the series of events, as a concept of cause, can have logical clarity only once we have made use of it in experience. Yet [our] taking account of this presentation, [viz.,] as a condition of the synthetic unity in time of appearances, was nonetheless the basis of the experience itself, and hence the experience was preceded a priori by this condition.

Hence we must show, in the example [of an event], that even in experience we never attribute succession (in the case of an event—where something occurs that was not there before) to the object and we never distinguish this succession from the subjective one B242 in our apprehension, except when there lies at the basis a rule that compels us to observe this order of perceptions rather than some other order; indeed, we must show that this compulsion is what in fact makes the presentation of a succession in the object possible in the first place.

We have within us presentations of which we can also become conscious. But no matter how far this consciousness[210] may extend and how accurate and punctilious it may be, they still remain forever only presentations, i.e., inner determinations of our mind in this or that time relation. How is it, then, that we posit an object for these presentations; or how is it that in addition to the subjective reality that they have as modifications [of the mind], we also attribute to them who knows what sort of objective reality? Their objective signification cannot consist in the reference

---

208. [I.e., specific or particular.]

209. [On which it is based.]
210. [Of our presentations.]

to another presentation (of what one would want to call object). For otherwise the question returns: how does this other presentation, in turn, go beyond itself and acquire objective signification in addition to the subjective one that it possesses by being a determination of the mental state? Suppose that we inquire what new character is given to our presentations by the *reference to an object*, and what is the dignity that they thereby obtain. We then find that this reference does nothing beyond making necessary the presentations' being combined[211] in a certain way and being B243 subjected to a rule; and we find, conversely, that only through the necessity of a certain order in the time relation of our presentations is objective signification conferred on them.

In the synthesis of appearances the manifold of presentations is always successive. Now, through this succession no object whatever is presented; for through this succession, which is common to all apprehensions, nothing is distinguished from anything else. But once I perceive, or assume in advance, that there is in this succession a reference to the preceding state, upon which the presentation follows according to a rule, then something presents itself as an event, or as something that occurs. I.e., I then cognize an object that I must posit in a certain determinate position in time—a position that in view of the preceding state cannot be assigned to it differently. Hence when I perceive that something occurs, then this presentation contains, first, [the presupposition] that something precedes; for precisely by reference to this preceding something does the appearance acquire its time relation, viz., its existing after a preceding time in which it was not. But, second, it can obtain its determinate time position in this relation only inasmuch as in the preceding state something is presupposed that it succeeds always, i.e., succeeds according to a rule. And from this results, first, that I cannot reverse the series, taking what occurs and putting it ahead of what it succeeds; and, second, that if the state that precedes is posited, then this specific event B244 succeeds unfailingly and necessarily. Thus it is that among our presentations there comes to be an order in which what is present directs us (insofar as it has

come to be) to some preceding state as a correlate of the happening that is given. And although this correlate is still indeterminate, it does refer determinatively to this happening as its consequence and in the time series connects it with itself necessarily.

Suppose, then, that it is a necessary law of our sensibility, and hence a *formal condition* of all perceptions, that the previous time necessarily determines the following one (inasmuch as I cannot arrive at the following time except through the preceding one). If this is so, then it is also an indispensable *law of empirical presentation* of the time series that the appearances of past time determine every existent in the following time; and that these existents, as events, do not take place except insofar as their existence is determined in time—i.e., fixed in time according to a rule—by those appearances of past time. For *only in appearances can we cognize empirically this continuity in the coherence of times.*

Understanding is required for all experience and for its possibility. And the first thing that understanding does for these is not that of making the presentation of objects distinct, but that of making the presentation of an object possible at all. Now, this is done B245 through the understanding's transferring the time order to the appearances and to their existence, by allotting to each appearance, as consequence, a position in time determined a priori with regard to the preceding appearances; without this position in time the appearance would not agree with time itself, which a priori determines for all its parts their position. Now this determination of an appearance's position cannot be taken from the relation of appearances toward absolute time (for absolute time is not an object of perception). Rather, conversely, the appearances must themselves determine for one another their positions in time, and must make these positions necessary in the time order; i.e., what follows or occurs must succeed what was contained in the previous state and must do so according to a universal rule. This results in a series of appearances that, by means of the understanding, produces and makes necessary in the series of possible perceptions the same order and steady coherence that is found a priori in the form of inner intuition (i.e., in time), in which all [such] perceptions would have to have their position.

211. [Or "linked": *Verbindang.*]

Hence that something occurs is a perception belonging to a possible experience. This experience becomes actual when I view the appearance as determined as regards its position in time, and hence view it as an object that in the coherence of perceptions can always be found according to a rule. This rule, B246 however, for determining something in regard to temporal succession, is that the condition under which an event always (i.e., necessarily) follows is to be found in what precedes the event. Hence the principle of sufficient basis[212] is the basis of possible experience, i.e., of objective cognition of appearances with regard to their relation in time sequence.

The basis for proving this proposition, however, rests solely on the following moments. All empirical cognition involves the synthesis of the manifold by the imagination. This synthesis is always successive, i.e., in it the presentations always succeed one another. In the imagination itself, however, the sequence is not at all determined as regards order (i.e., as to what must precede and what must follow), and the series of the presentations following one another can be taken as proceeding backward just as well as forward. But if this synthesis is a synthesis of apprehension (of the manifold of a given appearance), then the order is determined in the object, or—to speak more accurately—there is in this apprehension an order of successive synthesis that determines an object; and according to this order something must necessarily precede, and when this something is posited then the other event must necessarily follow. Hence if my perception is to contain the cognition of an event, i.e., of something's actually occurring, then it must be an empirical judgment in which we think B247 of the consequence as determined, i.e., as presupposing in terms of time another appearance that it succeeds necessarily, or according to a rule. Otherwise, if I posited what precedes and the event did not succeed it necessarily, then I would have to regard this event as only a subjective play of my imaginings; and if I still presented by it something objective, then I would have to call it a mere dream. Therefore

212. [Kant is reinterpreting, in accordance with the second analogy, the principle of sufficient reason used by Leibniz and later broadened by Wolff (to include not only the contingent).]

the relation of appearances (as possible perceptions) whereby what follows (occurs) is with regard to its existence determined in time, necessarily and according to a rule, by something preceding it—in other words, the relation of cause to effect—is the condition of the objective validity of our empirical judgments as regards the series of perceptions, and hence is the condition of these judgments' empirical truth and therefore of experience. The principle of the causal relation in the succession of appearances holds, therefore, also for all objects of experience ([insofar as they are] under the conditions of succession), because it is itself the basis of the possibility of such experience.

Here, however, emerges a perplexity that must still be removed. The principle of the causal connection among appearances is, in our formulation, limited to their [occurring in] sequence. Yet in using the principle we find that it fits also the case of their concomitance, and that cause and effect can be simultaneous. E.g., there is heat in the room which is not found in the open air. I look around for the cause, B248 and discover a heated stove. Now this stove, as cause, is simultaneous with its effect, the room's heat. Hence here there is between cause and effect no sequence in terms of time. They are, rather, simultaneous; and yet the law of cause and effect does hold. The majority of efficient causes in nature are simultaneous with their effects, and the temporal succession of the effects is due only to the fact that the cause cannot accomplish its entire effect in one instant. But at the instant when the effect first arises, it is always simultaneous with the causality of its cause. For if the cause had ceased to be an instant before, then the effect would not have arisen at all. It must be noted carefully, here, that what we are considering is the *order* of time, not the *lapse* of time; the relation remains even if no time has elapsed. The time between the causality of the cause and the cause's direct effect may be *vanishingly brief*, but yet the relation of the cause to the effect always remains determinable in terms of time. If I consider as cause a [lead] ball that lies on a stuffed cushion and makes an indentation in it, then this cause is simultaneous with the effect. But I nonetheless distinguish the two by the time relation of their dynamical connection. For if I lay the ball on the cushion, then the previous smooth shape of the cushion is succeeded by the indentation; but if the cushion

B249 has an indentation (no matter from where), then this is not succeeded by a lead ball.[213]

Hence temporal succession is indeed an effect's sole empirical criterion in reference to the causality of the cause preceding it. The [totally filled] tumbler is the cause of the water's rising above the horizontal plane [at the top] of the tumbler, although the two appearances are simultaneous. For as soon as water is scooped from a larger vessel with [an empty] tumbler, there ensues this: the horizontal level that the water had in the larger vessel changes to a concave level in the [partially filled] tumbler.

This causality leads to the concept of action; action leads to the concept of force and thereby to the concept of substance. Since my critical project deals solely with the sources of synthetic a priori cognition and I do not want to mingle with it dissections [of concepts], which concern merely the elucidation (rather than the expansion) of concepts, I leave the detailed exposition of these concepts to a future system of pure reason—although such an analysis can also be found in abundance in the textbooks of this kind that are already familiar. What I must, however, touch upon is the empirical criterion of a substance insofar as it seems to manifest itself not through the permanence of appearance but better and more easily through action.

B250   Where there is action and hence activity and force, there is also substance, and in substance alone must be sought the seat of that fertile source of appearances. That is nicely said; but if we are to explain what we mean by substance and want to avoid the fallacy of circular reasoning, then the answer is not so easy. How, from action on something, are we to infer at once *the agent's permanence*—this permanence being, after all, so essential and peculiar a characteristic of substance ([as] *phaenomenon*[214]). Yet according to our previous remarks, solving the question is not so difficult after all, even though the question would be quite insoluble according to the usual way (of proceeding with one's concepts, viz., merely analyti-

cally). Action already means the relation of the causality's subject to the effect. Now any effect consists in what occurs, and hence in the mutable that designates time in terms of succession. Therefore the ultimate subject of the mutable is the *permanent* as the substratum of everything that varies, i.e., substance. For according to the principle of causality actions are always the first basis of all variation by appearances; hence actions cannot reside in a subject that itself varies, since otherwise other actions and another subject determining that variation would be required. By virtue of this does action prove, as a sufficient empirical criterion, the substantiality of a subject, without my B251 needing first of all to search for the subject's permanence by perceptions that I have compared. Nor could proving this substantiality along this path of comparison be accomplished as comprehensively as is required by the magnitude and strict universality of the concept of substance. For, that the first subject of the causality of all arising and passing away cannot itself arise and pass away (in the realm of appearances) is a safe inference that issues in empirical necessity and permanence in existence, and hence in the concept of a substance as appearance.

When something occurs then the mere arising, even if we take no account of what arises, is in itself already an object of inquiry. The transition itself from a state's not-being to this state, even supposing that this state contained no quality in [the realm] of appearance, already calls for inquiry. This arising, as was shown in the First Analogy, concerns not substance (for substance does not arise) but its state. Hence arising is only change, and not origination from nothing. For if this origination from nothing is regarded as effect of an extraneous cause, then it is called creation; and creation cannot be admitted as an event among appearances, because its very possibility would already annul the unity of experience. If, on the other hand, I regard all things not as phenomena but as things in themselves and as objects merely of understanding, then despite their being substances B252 they can still be regarded as being dependent, in terms of their existence, on an extraneous cause. That alternative, however, would then entail quite different significations of the words, and would not fit appearances, as possible objects of experience.

Now, we do not a priori have the least concept as

213. [Kant's point is that temporal succession decides empirically what is the cause and what is the effect. The indentation did not cause the lead ball, because it is not succeeded by the lead ball.]

214. [I.e., substance ([taken as] phenomenal).]

to how anything can be changed at all, i.e., how it is possible that one state occurring at one point of time can be succeeded by an opposite state occurring at another point of time. This [concept of how change is possible] requires knowledge of actual forces—e.g., knowledge of the motive forces, or, which is the same, of certain successive appearances (as motions) indicating such forces—and such knowledge can be given only empirically. But we can nonetheless examine a priori, according to the law of causality and the conditions of time, the form of every change, i.e., the condition under which alone, as an arising of a different state, change can take place (no matter what may be its content, i.e., the state being changed); and hence we can so examine the succession itself of the states (i.e., the occurrence).[215]

B253   When a substance passes from one state, a, to another, b, then the point of time of the second state is different from the point of time of the first, and follows it. In the same way, too, the second state as reality (in [the realm of] appearance) differs from the first, in which this reality was not, as b differs from zero; i.e., even if state b were to differ from state a only in magnitude, the change is [still] an arising of b–a;[216] which in the previous state was not and in regard to which that state = 0.

The question, therefore, is how a thing passes from one state, = a, to another, = b. Between two instants there is always a time, and between two states at those instants there is always a difference that has a magnitude (for all parts of appearances are always magnitudes in turn). Hence any transition from one state to another occurs in a time that is contained between two instants, the first instant determining the state that the thing leaves and the second instant determining the state that it enters. Both instants, therefore, are bounds of the time of a change and hence bounds of the intermediate state between the two states, and as such belong also to the entire change. Now every change has a cause that manifests its causality in the entire time wherein the

change takes place. Hence this cause produces its change not suddenly (i.e., all at once, or in one instant), B254 but in a time; so that, as the time increases from its initial instant (a) up to its completion (in b), the reality's magnitude (b–a) is also produced through all the smaller degrees contained between the first degree and the last. Hence all change is possible only through a continuous action of the causality; this action, insofar as it is uniform, is called a moment. Change does not consist of these moments, but is produced by them as their effect.

This, then, is the law of the continuity of all change. The basis of this law is this fact: that neither time nor, for that matter, appearance in time consists of parts that are the smallest; and that nonetheless, as a thing changes, its state passes through all these parts, as elements, to the thing's second state. *No difference of the real in [the realm of] appearance is the smallest*, just as no difference in the magnitude of times is the smallest. And thus the reality's new state grows, starting from the first state, in which it was not, through all the infinite degrees of this reality; and the differences of the degrees from one another are all smaller than the difference between 0 and a.

What benefit this principle may have for the investigation of nature is of no concern to us here. But how is such a principle, which thus seems to expand our cognition of nature, possible completely a priori? This question very much requires our examination, even though what the principle says is [so] obviously actual and correct that we might believe ourselves to be B255 exempted from the question as to how the principle was possible. For there is such a variety of unfounded claims about our cognition's expansion by pure reason, that we must adopt as a universal principle [the resolve] to be throughout distrustful on that account, and not to believe or assume anything of the sort, even upon the clearest dogmatic proof, without documentation that can provide a well-founded deduction.

All increase of empirical cognition and any progress of perception—no matter what the objects may be, whether appearances or pure intuitions—is nothing but an expansion of the determination of inner sense, i.e., a progression in time. This progression in time determines everything and is in itself determined through nothing further. I.e., the progression's parts are given only in time and through the synthesis of

---

215. It should be noted carefully that I am talking not about the change of certain relations as such, but about change of a state. Thus if a body moves uniformly then it does not change its state (of motion) at all; but it does change its state if its motion increases or decreases.

216. [I.e., b minus a.]

time; they are not given prior to the synthesis. Because of this, every transition in perception to something that follows in time is a determination of time through the production of this perception; and since time is always and in all its parts a magnitude, every such transition is the production of a perception as a magnitude that goes through all degrees, none of which is the smallest, from zero onward up to the perception's determinate degree. From this, then, is evident the possibility of cognizing a priori a law governing B256 changes as regards their form. For we only anticipate our own apprehension, whose formal condition, since it resides in ourselves prior to all given appearance, must indeed be capable of being cognized a priori.

We have seen that time contains the sensible a priori condition for the possibility of a continuous progression of what exists to what follows. In the same way the understanding, by means of the unity of apperception, is the a priori condition for the possibility of a continuous determination, through the series of causes and effects, of all positions for appearances in this time—the causes entailing unfailingly the existence of the effects, and thereby making the empirical cognition of time relations valid for every time (i.e., universally) and hence valid objectively.

Refutation of Idealism

Idealism (I mean *material* idealism) is the theory that declares the existence of objects in space outside us either to be merely doubtful and *unprovable*, or to be *false* and *impossible*. The *first* is the *problematic* idealism of *Descartes*; it declares only one empirical assertion (*assertio*) to be indubitable, viz.: *I am*. The *second* is the *dogmatic* idealism of Berkeley; it declares space, with all the things to which space attaches as inseparable condition, to be something that is in itself impossible, and hence also declares the things in space to be mere imaginings. Dogmatic idealism is unavoidable if one regards space as a property that is to belong to things in themselves; for then space, with everything that space serves as condition, is a nonentity. However, the basis for this idealism has already been removed by us in the Transcendental Aesthetic. Problematic idealism, which asserts noth-
B275 ing about this but only alleges that we are unable to prove by direct experience an existence apart from

our own, is reasonable and is in accordance with a thorough philosophical way of thinking—viz., in permitting no decisive judgment before a sufficient proof has been found. The proof it demands must, therefore, establish that regarding external things we have not merely *imagination* but also *experience*. And establishing this surely cannot be done unless one can prove that even our *inner* experience, indubitable for Descartes, is possible only on the presupposition of *outer* experience.

Theorem

The mere, but empirically determined, consciousness of my own existence proves the existence of objects in space outside me.

Proof

I am conscious of my existence as determined in time. All time determination presupposes something *permanent* in perception. But this permanent something cannot be something within me, precisely because my existence can be determined in time only by this permanent something. Therefore perception of this permanent something is possible only through a *thing* outside me and not through mere *presentation* of a thing outside me. Hence determination of my existence in time is possible only through the existence of actual things that I perceive outside me. Now B276 consciousness of my existence in time is necessarily linked with consciousness of the possibility of this time determination; therefore it is necessarily linked also with the existence of things outside me, as condition of the time determination. I.e., the consciousness of my own existence is simultaneously a direct consciousness of the existence of other things outside me.

Comment 1. In the preceding proof one becomes aware that the game that idealism played is being turned around and against it—and more rightly so. Idealism assumed that the only direct experience is inner experience and that from it we only *infer* external things; but[217] we infer them only unreliably, as happens whenever we infer *determinate* causes from given effects, because the cause of the presentations

217. [Or "*definite* [or *specific*] causes," as distinguished from inferring *some* cause or other.]

that we ascribe—perhaps falsely—to external things may also reside in ourselves. Yet here we have proved *B277* that outer experience is in fact direct,[218] and that only by means of it can there be inner experience—i.e., not indeed consciousness of our own existence, but yet determination of that existence in time. To be sure, the presentation *I am*, which expresses the consciousness that can accompany all thinking, is what directly includes the existence of a subject; but it is not yet a *cognition* of that subject, and hence is also no empirical cognition—i.e., experience—of it. For such experience involves, besides the thought of something existent, also intuition, and here specifically inner intuition, in regard to which—viz., time—the subject must be determined; and this determination definitely requires external objects. Thus, consequently, inner experience is itself only indirect and is possible only through outer experience.

Comment 2. Now, all experiential use that we make of our cognitive power in determining time agrees completely with this view. Not only can we perceive any time determination solely through the variation

---

218. In the preceding theorem, the *direct* consciousness of the existence of external things is not presupposed but proved, whether or not we have insight into the possibility of this consciousness. The question concerning that possibility would be whether we have only an inner sense, and no outer sense but merely outer imagination. Clearly, however, in order for us even to imagine something—i.e., exhibit it to sense in intuition—as external, we must already have an outer sense, and must thereby distinguish directly the mere receptivity of an outer intuition from the spontaneity that characterizes all imagining. For if even outer sense were merely imagined, this would annul our very power of intuition which is to be determined by the imagination.

in external relations (i.e., through motion) by reference to the permanent in space (e.g., the sun's motion with respect to the earth's objects); but except merely *B278* for *matter* we do not even have anything permanent on which, as intuition, we could base the concept of a substance. And even this permanence is not drawn from outer experience, but is presupposed a priori as necessary condition of all time determination, and hence presupposed also as determination of inner sense, with regard to our own existence, through the existence of external things. The consciousness that I have of myself in the presentation *I* is not an intuition at all, but is a merely *intellectual* presentation of a thinking subject's self-activity. Hence this *I* also does not have the least predicate of intuition that, as *permanent*, could serve as correlate for the time determination in inner sense—as, say, *impenetrability* is such a predicate of *empirical* intuition in matter.

Comment 3. It does not follow, from the fact that the existence of external objects is required for the possibility of a determinate consciousness of ourselves, that every intuitive presentation of external things implies also these things' existence; for the presentation may very well be (as it is in dreams as well as in madness) the mere effect of the imagination. Yet it is this effect merely through the reproduction of former outer perceptions; and these, as has been shown, are possible only through the actuality of external objects. What was here to be proved is only that inner experience as such is possible only through *B279* outer experience as such. Whether this or that supposed experience is not perhaps a mere imagining must be ascertained by reference to its particular determinations and by holding it up to the criteria of all actual experience.

Grounding for the Metaphysics of Morals

PREFACE

Ancient Greek philosophy was divided into three sciences: physics, ethics, and logic. This division is perfectly suitable to the nature of the subject, and the only improvement that can be made in it is perhaps only to supply its principle so that there will be a possibility on the one hand of insuring its completeness and on the other of correctly determining its necessary subdivisions.

All rational knowledge is either material and concerned with some object, or formal and concerned only with the form of understanding and of reason themselves and with the universal rules of thought in general without regard to differences of its objects. Formal philosophy is called logic. Material philosophy, however, has to do with determinate objects and with the laws to which these objects are subject; and such philosophy is divided into two parts, because these laws are either laws of nature or laws of freedom. The science of the former is called physics, while that of the latter is called ethics; they are also called doctrine of nature and doctrine of morals respectively.

Logic cannot have any empirical part, i.e., a part in which the universal and necessary laws of thought would be based on grounds taken from experience; for in that case it would not be logic, i.e., a canon for understanding and reason, which is valid for all thinking and which has to be demonstrated.[1] Natural and moral philosophy, on the contrary, can each have an empirical part. The former has to because it must determine the laws of nature as an object of experience, and the latter because it must determine the will of man insofar as the will is affected by nature. The laws of the former are those according to which everything does happen, while the laws of the latter are those according to which everything ought to happen, although these moral laws also consider the conditions under which what ought to happen frequently does not.

All philosophy insofar as it is founded on experience may be called empirical, while that which sets forth its doctrines as founded entirely on a priori principles may be called pure. The latter, when merely formal, is called logic; but when limited to determinate objects of the understanding, it is called metaphysics.

In this way there arises the idea of a twofold metaphysics: a metaphysics of nature and a metaphysics of morals.[2] Physics will thus have its empirical part, but also a rational one. Ethics will too, though here the empirical part might more specifically be called practical anthropology,[3] while the rational part might properly be called morals.

All industries, crafts, and arts have gained by the division of labor, viz., one man does not do everything, but each confines himself to a certain kind of work that is distinguished from all other kinds by the treatment it requires, so that the work may be done with the highest perfection and with greater ease. Where work is not so distinguished and divided, where everyone is a jack of all trades, there industry remains sunk in the greatest barbarism. Whether or not pure philosophy in all its parts requires its own special man might well be in itself a subject worthy of consideration. Would not the whole of this learned industry be better off if those who are accustomed, as the public taste demands, to purvey a mixture of the empirical with the rational in all sorts of proportions unknown even to themselves and who style themselves independent thinkers, while giving the name of hair-splitters to those who apply themselves to the purely rational part, were to be given warning about

Reprinted by permission of the translator, James W. Ellington, from Kant, *Grounding for the Metaphysics of Morals* (Indianapolis: Hackett Publishing Company, 1981).

1. [Kant's *Logic* was first published in 1800 in a version edited by Gottlob Benjamin Jäsche, who was one of Kant's students. — J.W.E.]

2. [*The Metaphysical Foundations of Natural Science* was published in 1786. *The Metaphysics of Morals* appeared in 1797.]

3. [*Anthropology from a Pragmatic Point of View* first appeared in 1798.]

pursuing simultaneously two jobs which are quite different in their technique, and each of which perhaps requires a special talent that when combined with the other talent produces nothing but bungling? But I only ask here whether the nature of science does not require that the empirical part always be carefully separated from the rational part. Should not physics proper (i.e., empirical physics) be preceded by a metaphysics of nature, and practical anthropology by a metaphysics of morals? Both of these meta-

389 physics must be carefully purified of everything empirical in order to know how much pure reason can accomplish in each case and from what sources it draws its a priori teaching, whether such teaching be conducted by all moralists (whose name is legion) or only by some who feel a calling thereto.

Since I am here primarily concerned with moral philosophy, the foregoing question will be limited to a consideration of whether or not there is the utmost necessity for working out for once a pure moral philosophy that is wholly cleared of everything which can only be empirical and can only belong to anthropology. That there must be such a philosophy is evident from the common idea of duty and of moral laws. Everyone must admit that if a law is to be morally valid, i.e., is to be valid as a ground of obligation, then it must carry with it absolute necessity. He must admit that the command, "Thou shalt not lie," does not hold only for men, as if other rational beings had no need to abide by it, and so with all the other moral laws properly so called; and he must concede that the ground of obligation here must therefore be sought not in the nature of man nor in the circumstances of the world in which man is placed, but must be sought a priori solely in the concepts of pure reason; he must grant that every other precept which is founded on principles of mere experience—even a precept that may in certain respects be universal—insofar as it rests in the least on empirical grounds—perhaps only in its motive—can indeed be called a practical rule, but never a moral law.

Thus not only are moral laws together with their principles essentially different from every kind of practical cognition in which there is anything empirical, but all moral philosophy rests entirely on its pure part. When applied to man, it does not in the least borrow from acquaintance with him (anthropology) but gives a priori laws to him as a rational being. To

be sure, these laws require, furthermore, a power of judgment sharpened by experience, partly in order to distinguish in what cases they are applicable, and partly to gain for them access to the human will as well as influence for putting them into practice. For man is affected by so many inclinations that, even though he is indeed capable of the idea of a pure practical reason, he is not so easily able to make that idea effective *in concreto* in the conduct of his life.

A metaphysics of morals is thus indispensably nec- 390 essary, not merely because of motives of speculation regarding the source of practical principles which are present a priori in our reason, but because morals themselves are liable to all kinds of corruption as long as the guide and supreme norm for correctly estimating them are missing. For in the case of what is to be morally good, that it conforms to the moral law is not enough; it must also be done for the sake of the moral law. Otherwise that conformity is only very contingent and uncertain, since the non-moral ground may now and then produce actions that conform with the law but quite often produces actions that are contrary to the law. Now the moral law in its purity and genuineness (which is of the utmost concern in the practical realm) can be sought nowhere but in a pure philosophy. Therefore, pure philosophy (metaphysics) must precede; without it there can be no moral philosophy at all. That philosophy which mixes pure principles with empirical ones does not deserve the name of philosophy (for philosophy is distinguished from ordinary rational knowledge by its treatments in a separate science of what the latter comprehends only confusedly). Still less does it deserve the name of moral philosophy, since by this very confusion it spoils even the purity of morals and counteracts its own ends.

There must be no thought that what is required here is already contained in the propaedeutic that precedes the celebrated Wolff's moral philosophy, i.e., in what he calls *Universal Practical Philosophy*,[4] and that hence there is no need to break entirely new ground. Just because his work was to be a universal practical philosophy, it has not taken into consider-

---

4. [This work of Christian Wolff was published in 1738–39; this and other of his works served for many years as the standard philosophy textbooks in German universities. Wolff's philosophy was founded on that of Leibniz.]

ation any special kind of will, such as one determined solely by a priori principles without any empirical motives and which could be called a pure will, but has considered volition in general, together with all the actions and conditions belonging to it under this general signification. And thereby does his propaedeutic differ from a metaphysics of morals in the same way that general logic, which expounds the acts and rules of thinking in general, differs from transcendental philosophy, which treats merely of the particular acts and rules of pure thinking, i.e., of that thinking whereby objects are cognized completely a priori. For the metaphysics of morals has to investigate the idea and principles of a possible pure will and not the

391 actions and conditions of human volition as such, which are for the most part drawn from psychology. Moral laws and duty are discussed in this universal practical philosophy (though quite improperly), but this is no objection to what has been said about such philosophy. For the authors of this science remain true to their idea of it on the following point also: they do not distinguish the motives which, as such, are presented completely a priori by reason alone and are properly moral, from the empirical motives which the understanding raises to general concepts merely by the comparison of experiences. Rather, they consider motives irrespective of any difference in their source; and inasmuch as they regard all motives as being homogeneous, they consider nothing but their relative strength or weakness. In this way they frame their concept of obligation, which is certainly not moral, but is all that can be expected from a philosophy which never decides regarding the origin of all possible practical concepts whether they are a priori or merely a posteriori.

I intend some day to publish a metaphysics of morals,[5] but as a preliminary to that I now issue this *Grounding* [1785]. Indeed there is properly no other foundation for such a metaphysics than a critical examination of pure practical reason, just as there is properly no other foundation for a metaphysics [of nature] than the critical examination of pure speculative reason, which has already been published.[6] But,

in the first place, the former critique is not so absolutely necessary as the latter one, because human reason can, even in the most ordinary mind, be easily brought in moral matters to a high degree of correctness and precision, while on the other hand in its theoretical but pure use it is wholly dialectical. In the second place, if a critical examination of pure practical reason is to be complete, then there must, in my view, be the possibility at the same time of showing the unity of practical and speculative reason in a common principle; for in the final analysis there can be only one and the same reason, which is to be differentiated solely in its application. But there is no possibility here of bringing my work to such completeness, without introducing considerations of an entirely different kind and without thereby confusing the reader. Instead of calling the present work a *Critique of Pure Practical Reason*, I have, therefore, adopted the title *Grounding for the Metaphysics of Morals* [*Grundlegung zur Metaphysik der Sitten.*][7]

But, in the third place, since a metaphysis of morals, despite the forbidding title, is nevertheless capable of a high degree of popularity and adaptation to the ordinary understanding, I find it useful to separate from the aforementioned metaphysics this preliminary work on its foundation [*Grundlage*] in order later to have no need to introduce unavoidable subtleties into doctrines that are easier to grasp. 392

The present *Grounding* [*Grundlegung*] is, however, intended for nothing more than seeking out and establishing the supreme principle of morality. This constitutes by itself a task which is complete in its purpose and should be kept separate from every other moral inquiry. The application of this supreme principle to the whole ethical system would, to be sure, shed much light on my conclusions regarding this central question, which is important but has not heretofore been at all satisfactorily discussed; and the adequacy manifested by the principle throughout such application would provide strong confirmation for the principle. Nevertheless, I must forego this advantage, which after all would be more gratifying for myself than helpful for others, since ease of use and apparent adequacy of a principle do not provide any certain

---

5. [This appeared in 1797.]

6. [The first edition of the *Critique of Pure Reason* appeared in 1781, while the second edition appeared in 1787. The *Critique of Practical Reason* was published in 1788.]

7. [This might be translated as *Laying the Foundation for the Metaphysics of Morals*. But for the sake of brevity *Grounding for the Metaphysics of Morals* has been chosen.]

proof of its soundness, but do awaken, rather, a certain bias which prevents any rigorous examination and estimation of it for itself, without any regard to its consequences.

The method adopted in this work is, I believe, one that is most suitable if we proceed analytically from ordinary knowledge to a determination of the supreme principle and then back again synthetically from an examination of this principle and its sources to ordinary knowledge where its application is found. Therefore, the division turns out to be the following:

1. *First Section*. Transition from the Ordinary Rational Knowledge of Morality to the Philosophical.

2. *Second Section*. Transition from Popular Moral Philosophy to a Metaphysics of Morals.

3. *Third Section*. Final Step from a Metaphysics of Morals to a Critique of Pure Practical Reason.

FIRST SECTION

393

Transition from the Ordinary Rational Knowledge of Morality to the Philosophical

There is no possibility of thinking of anything at all in the world, or even out of it, which can be regarded as good without qualification, except, a *good will*. Intelligence, wit, judgment, and whatever talents of the mind one might want to name are doubtless in many respects good and desirable, as are such qualities of temperament as courage, resolution, perseverance. But they can also become extremely bad and harmful if the will, which is to make use of these gifts of nature and which in its special constitution is called character, is not good. The same holds with gifts of fortune; power, riches, honor, even health, and that complete well-being and contentment with one's condition which is called happiness make for pride and often hereby even arrogance, unless there is a good will to correct their influence on the mind and herewith also to rectify the whole principle of action and make it universally conformable to its end. The sight of a being who is not graced by any touch of a pure and good will but who yet enjoys an uninterrupted prosperity can never delight a rational and impartial spectator. Thus a good will seems to consti-

tute the indispensable condition of being even worthy of happiness.

Some qualities are even conducive to this good will itself and can facilitate is work. Nevertheless, they have no intrinsic unconditional worth; but they always presuppose, rather, a good will, which restricts the high esteem in which they are otherwise rightly held, and does not permit them to be regarded as absolutely good. Moderation in emotions and passions, self-control, and calm deliberation are not only good in many respects but even seem to constitute part of the intrinsic worth of a person. But they are far from being rightly called good without qualification (however unconditionally they were commended by the ancients). For without the principles of a good will, they can become extremely bad; the coolness of a villain makes him not only much more dangerous but also immediately more abominable in our eyes than he would have been regarded by us without it.

A good will is good not because of what it effects or accomplishes, nor because of its fitness to attain some proposed end; it is good only through its willing, i.e., it is good in itself. When it is considered in itself, then it is to be esteemed very much higher than anything which it might ever bring about merely in order to favor some inclination, or even the sum total of all inclinations. Even if, by some especially unfortunate fate or by the niggardly provision of stepmotherly nature, this will should be wholly lacking in the power to accomplish its purpose; if with the greatest effort it should yet achieve nothing, and only the good will should remain (not, to be sure, as a mere wish but as the summoning of all the means in our power), yet would it, like a jewel, still shine by its own light as something which has its full value in itself. Its usefulness or fruitlessness can neither augment nor diminish this value. Its usefulness would be, as it were, only the setting to enable us to handle it in ordinary dealings or to attract to it the attention of those who are not yet experts, but not to recommend it to real experts or to determine its value.

But there is something so strange in this idea of the absolute value of a mere will, in which no account is taken of any useful results, that in spite of all the agreement received even from ordinary reason, yet there must arise the suspicion that such an idea may perhaps have as its hidden basis merely some highflown fancy, and that we may have misunderstood

the purpose of nature in assigning to reason the gov-
395 erning of our will. Therefore, this idea will be examined from this point of view.

In the natural constitution of an organized being,
i.e., one suitably adapted to the purpose of life, let
there be taken as a principle that in such a being no
organ is to be found for any end unless it be the most
fit and the best adapted for that end. Now if that
being's preservation, welfare, or in a word its happiness, were the real end of nature in the case of a
being having reason and will, then nature would have
hit upon a very poor arrangement in having the reason
of the creature carry out this purpose. For all the
actions which such a creature has to perform with
this purpose in view, and the whole rule of his conduct
would have been prescribed much more exactly by
instinct; and the purpose in question could have been
attained much more certainly by instinct than it ever
can be by reason. And if in addition reason had been
imparted to this favored creature, then it would have
had to serve him only to contemplate the happy constitution of his nature, to admire that nature, to rejoice
in it, and to feel grateful to the cause that bestowed
it; but reason would not have served him to subject
his faculty of desire to its weak and delusive guidance
nor would it have served him to meddle incompe-
tently with the purpose of nature. In a word, nature
would have taken care that reason did not strike out
into a practical use nor presume, with its weak insight,
to think out for itself a plan for happiness and the
means for attaining it. Nature would have taken upon
herself not only the choice of ends but also that of
the means, and would with wise foresight have entrusted both to instinct alone.

And, in fact, we find that the more a cultivated
reason devotes itself to the aim of enjoying life and
happiness, the further does man get away from true
contentment. Because of this there arises in many
persons, if only they are candid enough to admit it,
a certain degree of misology, i.e., hatred of reason.
This is especially so in the case of those who are the
most experienced in the use of reason, because after
calculating all the advantages they derive, I say not
from the invention of all the arts of common luxury,
but even from the sciences (which in the end seem
to them to be also a luxury of the understanding),
they yet find that they have in fact only brought
396 more trouble on their heads than they have gained

in happiness. Therefore, they come to envy, rather
than despise, the more common run of men who are
closer to the guidance of mere natural instinct and
who do not allow their reason much influence on
their conduct. And we must admit that the judgment
of those who would temper, or even reduce below
zero, the boastful eulogies on behalf of the advantages
which reason is supposed to provide as regards the
happiness and contentment of life is by no means
morose or ungrateful to the goodness with which the
world is governed. There lies at the root of such
judgments, rather, the idea that existence has another
and much more worthy purpose, for which, and not
for happiness, reason is quite properly intended, and
which must, therefore, be regarded as the supreme
condition to which the private purpose of men must,
for the most part, defer.

Reason, however, is not competent enough to
guide the will safely as regards its objects and the
satisfaction of all our needs (which it in part even
multiplies); to this end would an implanted natural
instinct have led much more certainly. But inasmuch
as reason has been imparted to us as a practical faculty,
i.e., as one which is to have influence on the will,
its true function must be to produce a will which is
not merely good as a means to some further end, but
is good in itself. To produce a will good in itself
reason was absolutely necessary, inasmuch as nature
in distributing her capacities has everywhere gone to
work in a purposive manner. While such a will may
not indeed be the sole and complete good, it must,
nevertheless, be the highest good and the condition
of all the rest, even of the desire for happiness. In
this case there is nothing inconsistent with the wisdom
of nature that the cultivation of reason, which is requisite for the first and unconditioned purpose, may in
many ways restrict, at least in this life, the attainment
of the second purpose, viz., happiness, which is always
conditioned. Indeed happiness can even be reduced
to less than nothing, without nature's failing thereby
in her purpose; for reason recognizes as its highest
practical function the establishment of a good will,
whereby in the attainment of this end reason is capable only of its own kind of satisfaction, viz., that of
fulfilling a purpose which is in turn determined only
by reason, even though such fulfillment should often
interfere with the purposes of inclination.

The concept of a will estimable in itself and good 397

without regard to any further end must now be developed. This concept already dwells in the natural sound understanding and needs not so much to be taught as merely to be elucidated. It always holds first place in estimating the total worth of our actions and constitutes the condition of all the rest. Therefore, we shall take up the concept of *duty*, which includes that of a good will, though with certain subjective restrictions and hindrances, which far from hiding a good will or rendering it unrecognizable, rather bring it out by contrast and make it shine forth more brightly.

I here omit all actions already recognized as contrary to duty, even though they may be useful for this or that end; for in the case of these the question does not arise at all as to whether they might be done from duty, since they even conflict with duty. I also set aside those actions which are really in accordance with duty, yet to which men have no immediate inclination, but perform them because they are impelled thereto by some other inclination. For in this [second] case to decide whether the action which is in accord with duty has been done from duty or from some selfish purpose is easy. This difference is far more difficult to note in the [third] case where the action accords with duty and the subject has in addition an immediate inclination to do the action. For example,[8] that a dealer should not overcharge an inexperienced purchaser certainly accords with duty; and where there is much commerce, the prudent merchant does not overcharge but keeps to a fixed price for everyone in general, so that a child may buy from him just as well as everyone else may. Thus customers are honestly served, but this is not nearly enough for making us believe that the merchant has acted this way from duty and from principles of honesty; his own advantage required him to do it. He cannot, however, be assumed to have in addition [as in the third case] an immediate inclination toward his buyers, causing him, as it were, out of love to give no one as far as price is concerned any advantage over another. Hence the action was done neither from duty nor from immediate inclination, but merely for a selfish purpose.

8. [The ensuing example provides an illustration of the second case.]

On the other hand,[9] to preserve one's life is a duty; and, furthermore, everyone has also an immediate inclination to do so. But on this account the often anxious care taken by most men for it has no intrinsic worth, 398 and the maxim of their action has no moral content. They preserve their lives, to be sure, in accordance with duty, but not from duty. On the other hand,[10] if adversity and hopeless sorrow have completely taken away the taste for life, if an unfortunate man, strong in soul and more indignant at his fate than despondent or dejected, wishes for death and yet preserves his life without loving it — not from inclination or fear, but from duty — then his maxim indeed has a moral content.[11]

To be beneficent where one can is a duty; and

9. [This next example illustrates the third case.]

10. [The ensuing example illustrates the fourth case.]

11. [Four different cases have been distinguished in the two foregoing paragraphs. Case 1 involves those actions which are contrary to duty (lying, cheating, stealing, etc.). Case 2 involves those which accord with duty but for which a person perhaps has no immediate inclination, though he does have a mediate inclination thereto (one pays his taxes not because he likes to but in order to avoid the penalties set for delinquents, one treats his fellows well not because he really likes them but because he wants their votes when at some future time he runs for public office, etc.). A vast number of so-called "morally good" actions actually belong to this case 2 — they accord with duty because of self-seeking inclinations. Case 3 involves those which accord with duty and for which a person does have an immediate inclination (one does not commit suicide because all is going well with him, one does not commit adultery because he considers his wife to be the most desirable creature in the whole world, etc.). Case 4 involves those actions which accord with duty but are contrary to some immediate inclination (one does not commit suicide even when he is in dire distress, one does not commit adultery even though his wife has turned out to be an impossible shrew, etc.). Now case 4 is the crucial test case of the will's possible goodness — but Kant does not claim that one should lead his life in such a way as to encounter as many such cases as possible in order constantly to test his virtue (deliberately marry a shrew so as to be able to resist the temptation to commit adultery). Life itself forces enough such cases upon a person without his seeking them out. But when there is a conflict between duty and inclination, duty should always be followed. Case 3 makes for the easiest living and the greatest contentment, and anyone would wish that life might present him with far more of these cases than with cases 2 or 4.

besides this, there are many persons who are so sympathetically constituted that, without any further motive of vanity or self-interest, they find an inner pleasure in spreading joy around them and can rejoice in the satisfaction of others as their own work. But I maintain that in such a case an action of this kind, however dutiful and amiable it may be, has nevertheless no true moral worth.[12] It is on a level with such actions as arise from other inclinations, e.g., the inclination for honor, which if fortunately directed to what is in fact beneficial and accords with duty and is thus honorable, deserves praise and encouragement, but not esteem; for its maxim lacks the moral content of an action done not from inclination but from duty. Suppose then the mind of this friend of mankind to be clouded over with his own sorrow so that all sympathy with the lot of others is extinguished, and suppose him still to have the power to benefit others in distress, even though he is not touched by their trouble because he is sufficiently absorbed with his own; and now suppose that, even though no inclination moves him any longer, he nevertheless tears himself from this deadly insensibility and performs the action without any inclination at all, but solely from duty—then for the first time his action has genuine moral worth.[13] Further still, if nature has put little sympathy in this or that man's heart, if (while being an honest man in other respects) he is by temperament cold and indifferent to the sufferings of others, perhaps because as regards his own sufferings he is endowed with the special gift of patience and fortitude and expects or even requires that others should have the same; if such a man (who would truly not be nature's worst product) had not been exactly fashioned by her to be a philanthropist, would he not yet find in himself a

source from which he might give himself a worth far higher than any that a good-natured temperament might have? By all means, because just here does the 399 worth of the character come out; this worth is moral and incomparably the highest of all, viz., that he is beneficent, not from inclination, but from duty.[14]

To secure one's own happiness is a duty (at least indirectly); for discontent with one's condition under many pressing cares and amid unsatisfied wants might easily become a great temptation to transgress one's duties. But here also do men of themselves already have, irrespective of duty, the strongest and deepest inclination toward happiness, because just in this idea are all inclinations combined into a sum total.[15] But the precept of happiness is often so constituted as greatly to interfere with some inclinations, and yet men cannot form any definite and certain concept of the sum of satisfaction of all inclinations that is called happiness. Hence there is no wonder that a single inclination which is determinate both as to what it promises and as to the time within which it can be satisfied may outweigh a fluctuating idea; and there is no wonder that a man, e.g., a gouty patient, can choose to enjoy what he likes and to suffer what he may, since by his calculation he has here at least not sacrificed the enjoyment of the present moment to some possibly groundless expectations of the good fortune that is supposed to be found in health. But even in this case, if the universal inclination to happiness did not determine his will and if health, at least for him, did not figure as so necessary an element in his calculations; there still remains here, as in all other cases, a law, viz., that he should promote his happiness not from inclination but from duty, and thereby for the first time does his conduct have real moral worth.[16]

Undoubtedly in this way also are to be understood those passages of Scripture which command us to love our neighbor and even our enemy. For love as an inclination cannot be commanded; but beneficence from duty, when no inclination impels us[17] and even

---

But yet one should not arrange his life in such a way as to avoid case 4 at all costs and to seek out case 3 as much as possible (become a recluse so as to avoid the possible rough and tumble involved with frequent association with one's fellows, avoid places where one might encounter the sick and the poor so as to spare oneself the pangs of sympathy and the need to exercise the virtue of benefiting those in distress, etc.). For the purpose of philosophical analysis Kant emphasizes case 4 as being the test case of the will's possible goodness, but he is not thereby advocating puritanism.]

12. [This is an example of case 3.]

13. [This is an example of case 4.]

14. [This is an even more extreme example of case 4.]

15. [This is an example of case 3.]

16. [This example is a weak form of case 4; the action accords with duty but is not contrary to some immediate inclination.]

17. [This is case 4 in its weak form.]

when a natural and unconquerable aversion opposes such beneficence,[18] is practical, and not pathological, love. Such love resides in the will and not in the propensities of feeling, in principles of action and not in tender sympathy; and only this practical love can be commanded.

The second proposition[19] is this: An action done from duty has its moral worth, not in the purpose that is to be attained by it, but in the maxim according to which the action is determined. The moral worth depends, therefore, not on the realization of the object
400 of the action, but merely on the principle of volition according to which, without regard to any objects of the faculty of desire, the action has been done. From what has gone before it is clear that the purposes which we may have in our actions, as well as their effects regarded as ends and incentives of the will, cannot give to actions any unconditioned and moral worth. Where, then, can this worth lie if it is not to be found in the will's relation to the expected effect? Nowhere but in the principle of the will, with no regard to the ends that can be brought about through such action. For the will stands, as it were, at a cross-roads between its a priori principle, which is formal, and its a posteriori incentive, which is material; and since it must be determined by something, it must be determined by the formal principle of volition, if the action is done from duty—and in that case every material principle is taken away from it.

The third proposition, which follows from the other two, can be expressed thus: Duty is the necessity of an action done out of respect for the law. I can indeed have an inclination for an object as the effect of my proposed action; but I can never have respect for such an object, just because it is merely an effect and is not an activity of the will. Similarly, I can have no respect for inclination as such, whether my own or that of another. I can at most, if my own inclination, approve it; and, if that of another, even love it, i.e., consider it to be favorable to my own advantage. An object of respect can only be what is connected with my will solely as ground and never as effect—some-thing that does not serve my inclination but, rather, outweighs it, or at least excludes it from consideration when some choice is made—in other words, only the law itself can be an object of respect and hence can be a command. Now an action done from duty must altogether exclude the influence of inclination and therewith every object of the will. Hence there is nothing left which can determine the will except objectively the law and subjectively pure respect for this practical law, i.e., the will can be subjectively determined by the maxim[20] that I should follow such a law even if all my inclinations are thereby thwarted. 401

Thus the moral worth of an action does not lie in the effect expected from it nor in any principle of action that needs to borrow its motive from this expected effect. For all these effects (agreeableness of one's condition and even the furtherance of other people's happiness) could have been brought about also through other causes and would not have required the will of a rational being, in which the highest and unconditioned good can alone be found. Therefore, the pre-eminent good which is called moral can consist in nothing but the representation of the law in itself, and such a representation can admittedly be found only in a rational being insofar as this representation, and not some expected effect, is the determining ground of the will. This good is already present in the person who acts according to this representation, and such good need not be awaited merely from the effect.[21]

18. [This is case 4 in its strong form.]

19. [The first proposition of morality says that an action must be done from duty in order to have any moral worth. It is implicit in the preceding examples but was never explicitly stated.]

20. A maxim is the subjective principle of volition. The objective principle (i.e., one which would serve all rational beings also subjectively as a practical principle if reason had full control over the faculty of desire) is the practical law. [See below Kant's footnote at Ak. 420–21.]

21. There might be brought against me here an objection that I take refuge behind the word "respect" in an obscure feeling, instead of giving a clear answer to the question by means of a concept of reason. But even though respect is a feeling, it is not one received through any outside influence but is, rather, one that is self-produced by means of a rational concept; hence it is specifically different from all feelings of the first kind, which can all be reduced to inclination or fear. What I recognize immediately as a law for me, I recognize with respect; this means merely the consciousness of the subordination of my will to a law without the mediation of other influences upon my sense. The immediate determination of the will by the law, and

402   But what sort of law can that be the thought of which must determine the will without reference to any expected effect, so that the will can be called absolutely good without qualification? Since I have deprived the will of every impulse that might arise for it from obeying any particular law, there is nothing left to serve the will as principle except the universal conformity of its actions to law as such, i.e., I should never act except in such a way that I can also will that my maxim should become a universal law.[22] Here mere conformity to law as such (without having as its basis any law determining particular actions) serves the will as principle and must so serve it if duty is not to be a vain delusion and a chimerical concept. The ordinary reason of mankind in its practical judgments agrees completely with this, and always has in view the aforementioned principle.

For example, take this question. When I am in distress, may I make a promise with the intention of not keeping it? I readily distinguish here the two meanings which the question may have; whether making a false promise conforms with prudence or with duty. Doubtless the former can often be the case. Indeed I clearly see that escape from some present difficulty by means of such a promise is not enough. In addition I must carefully consider whether from this lie there may later arise far greater inconvenience for me than from what I now try to escape. Furthermore, the consequences of my false promise are not easy to forsee, even with all my supposed cunning; loss of confidence in me might prove to be far more disadvantageous than the misfortune which I now try to avoid. The more prudent way might be to act according to a universal maxim and to make it a habit not to promise anything without intending to keep it. But that such a maxim is, nevertheless, always based on nothing but a fear of consequences becomes clear to me at once. To be truthful from duty is, however, quite different from being truthful from fear of disadvantageous consequences; in the first case the concept of the action itself contains a law for me, while in the second I must first look around elsewhere to see what are the results for me that might be connected with the action. For to deviate from the principle of duty is quite certainly bad; but to abandon my 403 maxim of prudence can often be very advantageous for me, though to abide by it is certainly safer. The most direct and infallible way, however, to answer the question as to whether a lying promise accords with duty is to ask myself whether I would really be content if my maxim (of extricating myself from difficulty by means of a false promise) were to hold as a universal law for myself as well as for others, and could I really say to myself that everyone may promise falsely when he finds himself in a difficulty from which he can find no other way to extricate himself. Then I immediately become aware that I can indeed will the lie but can not at all will a universal law to lie. For by such a law there would really be no promises at all, since in vain would my willing future actions be professed to other people who would not believe what I professed, or if they over-hastily did believe, then they would pay me back in like coin. Therefore, my maxim would necessarily destroy itself just as soon as it was made a universal law.[23]

Therefore, I need no far-reaching acuteness to discern what I have to do in order that my will may be morally good. Inexperienced in the course of the world and incapable of being prepared for all its

---

the consciousness thereof, is called respect, which is hence regarded as the effect of the law upon the subject and not as the cause of the law. Respect is properly the representation of a worth that thwarts my self-love. Hence respect is something that is regarded as an object of neither inclination nor fear, although it has at the same time something analogous to both. The object of respect is, therefore, nothing but the law—indeed that very law which we impose on ourselves and yet recognize as necessary in itself. As law, we are subject to it without consulting self-love; as imposed on us by ourselves, it is a consequence of our will. In the former aspect, it is analogous to fear; in the latter, to inclination. All respect for a person is properly only respect for the law (of honesty, etc.) of which the person provides an example. Since we regard the development of our talents as a duty, we think of a man of talent as being also a kind of example of the law (the law of becoming like him by practice), and that is what constitutes our respect for him. All so-called moral interest consists solely in respect for the law.

22. [This is the first time in the *Grounding* that the categorical imperative is stated.]

23. [This means that when you tell a lie, you merely take exception to the general rule that says everyone should always tell the truth and believe that what you are saying is true. When you lie, you do not thereby will that everyone else lie and not believe that what you are saying is true, because in such a case your lie would never work to get you what you want.]

contingencies, I only ask myself whether I can also will that my maxim should become a universal law. If not, then the maxim must be rejected, not because of any disadvantage accruing to me or even to others, but because it cannot be fitting as a principle in a possible legislation of universal law, and reason exacts from me immediate respect for such legislation. Indeed I have as yet no insight into the grounds of such respect (which the philosopher may investigate). But I at least understand that respect is an estimation of a worth that far outweighs any worth of what is recommended by inclination, and that the necessity of acting from pure respect for the practical law is what constitutes duty, to which every other motive must give way because duty is the condition of a will good in itself, whose worth is above all else.

Thus within the moral cognition of ordinary human reason we have arrived at its principle. To be sure, such reason does not think of this principle abstractly in its universal form, but does always have it actually in view and does use it as the standard of 404 judgment. It would here be easy to show how ordinary reason, with this compass in hand, is well able to distinguish, in every case that occurs, what is good or evil, in accord with duty or contrary to duty, if we do not in the least try to teach reason anything new but only make it attend, as Socrates did, to its own principle—and thereby do we show that neither science nor philosophy is needed in order to know what one must do to be honest and good, and even wise and virtuous. Indeed we might even have conjectured beforehand that cognizance of what every man is obligated to do, and hence also to know, would be available to every man, even the most ordinary. Yet we cannot but observe with admiration how great an advantage the power of practical judgment has over the theoretical in ordinary human understanding. In the theoretical, when ordinary reason ventures to depart from the laws of experience and the perceptions of sense, it falls into sheer inconceivabilities and self-contradictions, or at least into a chaos of uncertainty, obscurity, and instability. In the practical, however, the power of judgment first begins to show itself to advantage when ordinary understanding excludes all sensuous incentives from practical laws. Such understanding then becomes even subtle, whether in quibbling with its own conscience or with other claims regarding what is to be called right, or whether in

wanting to determine correctly for its own instruction the worth of various actions. And the most extraordinary thing is that ordinary understanding in this practical case may have just as good a hope of hitting the mark as that which any philosopher may promise himself. Indeed it is almost more certain in this than even a philosopher is, because he can have no principle other than what ordinary understanding has, but he may easily confuse his judgment by a multitude of foreign and irrelevant considerations and thereby cause it to swerve from the right way. Would it not, therefore, be wiser in moral matters to abide by the ordinary rational judgment or at most to bring in philosophy merely for the purpose of rendering the system of morals more complete and intelligible and of presenting its rules in a way that is more convenient for use (especially in disputation), but not for the purpose of leading ordinary human understanding away from its happy simplicity in practical matters and of bringing it by means of philosophy into a new path of inquiry and instruction?

Innocence is indeed a glorious thing; but, unfortu- 405 nately, it does not keep very well and is easily led astray. Consequently, even wisdom—which consists more in doing and not doing than in knowing—needs science, not in order to learn from it, but in order that wisdom's precepts may gain acceptance and permanence. Man feels within himself a powerful counterweight to all the commands of duty, which are presented to him by reason as being so pre-eminently worthy of respect; this counterweight consists of his needs and inclinations, whose total satisfaction is summed up under the name of happiness. Now reason irremissibly commands its precepts, without thereby promising the inclinations anything; hence it disregards and neglects these impetuous and at the same time so seemingly plausible claims (which do not allow themselves to be suppressed by any command). Hereby arises a natural dialectic, i.e., a propensity to quibble with these strict laws of duty, to cast doubt upon their validity, or at least upon their purity and strictness, and to make them, where possible, more compatible with our wishes and inclinations. Thereby are such laws corrupted in their very foundations and their whole dignity is destroyed—something which even ordinary practical reason cannot in the end call good.

Thus is ordinary human reason forced to go outside

its sphere and take a step into the field of practical philosophy, not by any need for speculation (which never befalls such reason so long as it is content to be mere sound reason) but on practical grounds themselves. There it tries to obtain information and clear instruction regarding the source of its own principle and the correct determination of this principle in its opposition to maxims based on need and inclination, so that reason may escape from the perplexity of opposite claims and may avoid the risk of losing all genuine moral principles through the ambiguity into which it easily falls. Thus when ordinary practical reason cultivates itself, there imperceptibly arises in it a dialectic which compels it to seek help in philosophy. The same thing happens in reason's theoretical use; in this case, just as in the other, peace will be found only in a thorough critical examination of our reason.

406 SECOND SECTION

Transition from Popular Moral Philosophy to a Metaphysics of Morals

If we have so far drawn our concept of duty from the ordinary use of our practical reason, one is by no means to infer that we have treated it as a concept of experience. On the contrary, when we pay attention to our experience of the way human beings act, we meet frequent and—as we ourselves admit—justified complaints that there cannot be cited a single certain example of the disposition to act from pure duty; and we meet complaints that although much may be done that is in accordance with what duty commands, yet there are always doubts as to whether what occurs has really been done from duty and so has moral worth. Hence there have always been philosophers who have absolutely denied the reality of this disposition in human actions and have ascribed everything to a more or less refined self-love. Yet in so doing they have not cast doubt upon the rightness of the concept of morality. Rather, they have spoken with sincere regret as to the frailty and impurity of human nature, which they think is noble enough to take as its precept an idea so worthy of respect but yet is too weak to follow this idea: reason, which should legislate for human nature, is used only to look after the interest of inclinations, whether singly or, at best, in their greatest possible harmony with one another.

In fact there is absolutely no possibility by means 407 of experience to make out with complete certainty a single case in which the maxim of an action that may in other respects conform to duty has rested solely on moral grounds and on the representation of one's duty. It is indeed sometimes the case that after the keenest self-examination we can find nothing except the moral ground of duty that could have been strong enough to move us to this or that good action and to such great sacrifice. But there cannot with certainty be at all inferred from this that some secret impulse of self-love, merely appearing as the idea of duty, was not the actual determining cause of the will. We like to flatter ourselves with the false claim to a more noble motive; but in fact we can never, even by the strictest examination, completely plumb the depths of the secret incentives of our actions. For when moral value is being considered, the concern is not with the actions, which are seen, but rather with their inner principles, which are not seen.

Moreover, one cannot better serve the wishes of those who ridicule all morality as being a mere phantom of human imagination getting above itself because of self-conceit than by conceding to them that the concepts of duty must be drawn solely from experience (just as from indolence one willingly persuades himself that such is the case as regards all other concepts as well). For by so conceding, one prepares for them a sure triumph. I am willing to admit out of love for humanity that most of our actions are in accordance with duty; but if we look more closely at our planning and striving, we everywhere come upon the dear self, which is always turning up, and upon which the intent of our actions is based rather than upon the strict command of duty (which would often require self-denial). One need not be exactly an enemy of virtue, but only a cool observer who does not take the liveliest wish for the good to be straight off its realization, in order to become doubtful at times whether any true virtue is actually to be found in the world. Such is especially the case when years increase and one's power of judgment is made shrewder by experience and keener in observation. Because of these things nothing can protect us from a complete falling away from our ideas of duty and preserve in the soul a well-grounded respect for duty's law except

408 the clear conviction that, even if there never have been actions springing from such pure sources, the question at issue here is not whether this or that has happened but that reason of itself and independently of all experience commands what ought to happen. Consequently, reason unrelentingly commands actions of which the world has perhaps hitherto never provided an example and whose feasibility might well be doubted by one who bases everything upon experience; for instance, even though there might never yet have been a sincere friend, still pure sincerity in friendship is nonetheless required of every man, because this duty, prior to all experience, is contained as duty in general in the idea of a reason that determines the will by means of a priori grounds.

There may be noted further that unless we want to deny to the concept of morality all truth and all reference to a possible object, we cannot but admit that the moral law is of such widespread significance that it must hold not merely for men but for all rational beings generally, and that it must be valid not merely under contingent conditions and with exceptions but must be absolutely necessary. Clearly, therefore, no experience can give occasion for inferring even the possibility of such apodeictic laws. For with what right could we bring into unlimited respect as a universal precept for every rational nature what is perhaps valid only under the contingent conditions of humanity? And how could laws for the determination of our will be regarded as laws for the determination of a rational being in general and of ourselves only insofar as we are rational beings, if these laws were merely empirical and did not have their source completely a priori in pure, but practical, reason?

Moreover, worse service cannot be rendered morality than that an attempt be made to derive it from examples. For every example of morality presented to me must itself first be judged according to principles of morality in order to see whether it is fit to serve as an original example, i.e., as a model. But in no way can it authoritatively furnish the concept of morality. Even the Holy One of the gospel must first be compared with our ideal of moral perfection before he is recognized as such. Even he says of himself,
409 "Why do you call me (whom you see) good? None is good (the archetype of the good) except God only (whom you do not see)." But whence have we the concept of God as the highest good? Solely from the idea of moral perfection, which reason frames a priori and connects inseparably with the concept of a free will. Imitation has no place at all in moral matters. And examples serve only for encouragement, i.e., they put beyond doubt the feasibility of what the law commands and they make visible what the practical rule expresses more generally. But examples can never justify us in setting aside their true original, which lies in reason, and letting ourselves be guided by them.

If there is then no genuine supreme principle of morality that must rest merely on pure reason, independently of all experience, I think it is unnecessary even to ask whether it is a good thing to exhibit these concepts generally (in abstracto), which, along with the principles that belong to them, hold a priori, so far as the knowledge involved is to be distinguished from ordinary knowledge and is to be called philosophical. But in our times it may well be necessary to do so. For if one were to take a vote as to whether pure rational knowledge separated from everything empirical, i.e., metaphysics of morals, or whether popular practical philosophy is to be preferred, one can easily guess which side would be preponderant.

This descent to popular thought is certainly very commendable once the ascent to the principles of pure reason has occurred and has been satisfactorily accomplished. That would mean that the doctrine of morals has first been grounded on metaphysics and that subsequently acceptance for morals has been won by giving it a popular character after it has been firmly established. But it is quite absurd to try for popularity in the first inquiry, upon which depends the total correctness of the principles. Not only can such a procedure never lay claim to the very rare merit of a true philosophical popularity, inasmuch as there is really no art involved at all in being generally intelligible if one thereby renounces all basic insight, but such a procedure turns out a disgusting mishmash of patchwork observations and half-reasoned principles in which shallowpates revel because all this is something quite useful for the chitchat of everyday life. Persons of insight, on the other hand, feel confused by all this and turn their eyes away with a dissatisfaction which they nevertheless cannot cure. Yet philosophers, who quite see through the delusion, 410 get little hearing when they summon people for a time from this pretended popularity in order that they may be rightfully popular only after they have attained definite insight.

One need only look at the attempts to deal with morality in the way favored by popular taste. What he will find in an amazing mixture is at one time the particular constitution of human nature (but along with this also the idea of a rational nature in general), at another time perfection, at another happiness; here moral feeling, and there the fear of God; something of this, and also something of that. But the thought never occurs to ask whether the principles of morality are to be sought at all in the knowledge of human nature (which can be had only from experience). Nor does the thought occur that if these principles are not to be sought here but to be found, rather, completely a priori and free from everything empirical in pure rational concepts only, and are to be found nowhere else even to the slightest extent—then there had better be adopted the plan of undertaking this investigation as a separate inquiry, i.e., as pure practical philosophy or (if one may use a name so much decried) as a metaphysics[24] of morals. It is better to bring this investigation to full completeness entirely by itself and to bid the public, which demands popularity, to await the outcome of this undertaking.

But such a completely isolated metaphysics of morals, not mixed with any anthropology, theology, physics, or hyperphysics, and still less with occult qualities (which might be called hypophysical), is not only an indispensable substratum of all theoretical and precisely defined knowledge of duties, but is at the same time a desideratum of the highest importance for the actual fulfillment of their precepts. For the pure thought of duty and of the moral law generally, unmixed with any extraneous addition of empirical inducements, has by the way of reason alone (which first becomes aware hereby that it can of itself be practical) an influence on the human heart so much

more powerful than all other incentives[25] which may *411* be derived from the empirical field that reason in the consciousness of its dignity despises such incentives and is able gradually to become their master. On the other hand, a mixed moral philosophy, compounded both of incentives drawn from feelings and inclinations and at the same time of rational concepts, must make the mind waver between motives that cannot be brought under any principle and that can only by accident lead to the good but often can also lead to the bad.

It is clear from the foregoing that all moral concepts have their seat and origin completely a priori in reason, and indeed in the most ordinary human reason just as much as in the most highly speculative. They cannot be abstracted from any empirical, and hence merely contingent, cognition. In this purity of their origin lies their very worthiness to serve us as supreme practical principles; and to the extent that something empirical is added to them, just so much is taken away from their genuine influence and from the absolute worth of the corresponding actions. Moreover, it is not only a requirement of the greatest necessity from a theoretical point of view, when it is a question of speculation, but also of the greatest practical importance, to draw these concepts and laws from pure reason, to present them pure and unmixed, and indeed to determine the extent of this entire practical

---

24. Pure philosophy of morals (metaphysics) may be distinguished from the applied (viz., applied to human nature) just as pure mathematics is distinguished from applied mathematics and pure logic from applied logic. By this designation one is also immediately reminded that moral principles are not grounded on the peculiarities of human nature but must subsist a priori of themselves, and that from such principles practical rules must be derivable for every rational nature, and accordingly for human nature.

25. I have a letter from the late excellent Sulzer [Johann Georg Sulzer (1720–1779), an important Berlin savant, who translated Hume's *Enquiry Concerning the Principles of Morals* into German in 1755] in which he asks me why it is that moral instruction accomplishes so little, even though it contains so much that is convincing to reason. My answer was delayed so that I might make it complete. But it is just that the teachers themselves have not purified their concepts: since they try to do too well by looking everywhere for motives for being morally good, they spoil the medicine by trying to make it really strong. For the most ordinary observation shows that when a righteous act is represented as being done with a steadfast soul and sundered from all view to any advantage in this or another world, and even under the greatest temptations of need or allurement, it far surpasses and eclipses any similar action that was in the least affected by any extraneous incentive; it elevates the soul and inspires the wish to be able to act in this way. Even moderately young children feel this impression, and duties should never be represented to them in any other way.

and pure rational cognition, i.e., to determine the 412 whole faculty of pure practical reason. The principles should not be made to depend on the particular nature of human reason, as speculative philosophy may permit and even sometimes finds necessary; but, rather, the principles should be derived from the universal concept of a rational being in general, since moral laws should hold for every rational being as such. In this way all morals, which require anthropology in order to be applied to humans, must be entirely expounded at first independently of anthropology as pure philosophy, i.e., as metaphysics (which can easily be done in such distinct kinds of knowledge). One knows quite well that unless one is in possession of such a metaphysics, then the attempt is futile. I shall not say to determine exactly for speculative judgment the moral element of duty in all that accords with duty, but that the attempt is impossible, even in ordinary and practical usage, especially in that of moral instruction, to ground morals on their genuine principles and thereby to produce pure moral dispositions and engraft them on men's minds for the promotion of the highest good in the world.

In this study we must advance by natural stages not merely from ordinary moral judgment (which is here ever so worthy of respect) to philosophical judgment, as has already been done, but also from popular philosophy, which goes no further than it can get by groping about with the help of examples, to metaphysics (which does not permit itself to be held back any longer by what is empirical, and which, inasmuch as it must survey the whole extent of rational knowledge of this kind, goes right up to ideas, where examples themselves fail us). In order to make such an advance, we must follow and clearly present the practical faculty of reason from its universal rules of determination to the point where the concept of duty springs from it.

Everything in nature works according to laws. Only a rational being has the power to act according to his conception of laws, i.e., according to principles, and thereby has he a will. Since the derivation of actions from laws requires reason, the will is nothing but practical reason. If reason infallibly determines the will, then in the case of such a being actions which are recognized to be objectively necessary are also subjectively necessary, i.e., the will is a faculty of choosing only that which reason, independently of

inclination, recognizes as being practically necessary, i.e., as good. But if reason of itself does not sufficiently determine the will, and if the will submits also to subjective conditions (certain incentives) which do 413 not always agree with objective conditions; in a word, if the will does not in itself completely accord with reason (as is actually the case with men), the actions which are recognized as objectively necessary are subjectively contingent, and the determination of such a will according to objective laws is necessitation. That is to say that the relation of objective laws to a will not thoroughly good is represented as the determination of the will of a rational being by principles of reason which the will does not necessarily follow because of its own nature.

The representation of an objective principle insofar as it necessitates the will is called a command (of reason), and the formula of the command is called an imperative.

All imperatives are expressed by an *ought* and thereby indicate the relation of an objective law of reason to a will that is not necessarily determined by this law because of its subjective constitution (the relation of necessitation). Imperatives say that something would be good to do or to refrain from doing, but they say it to a will that does not always therefore do something simply because it has been represented to the will as something good to do. That is practically good which determines the will by means of representations of reason and hence not by subjective causes, but objectively, i.e., on grounds valid for every rational being as such. It is distinguished from the pleasant as that which influences the will only by means of sensation from merely subjective causes, which hold only for this or that person's senses but do not hold as a principle of reason valid for everyone.[26]

26. The dependence of the faculty of desire on sensations is called inclination, which accordingly always indicates a need. The dependence of a contingently determinable will on principles of reason, however, is called interest. Therefore an interest is found only in a dependent will which is not of itself always in accord with reason; in the divine will no interest can be thought. But even the human will can take an interest in something without thereby acting from interest. The former signifies practical interest in the action, while the latter signifies pathological interest in the object of the action. The former indicates only dependence of the will on principles of reason by itself, while the latter indicates

414 A perfectly good will would thus be quite as much subject to objective laws (of the good), but could not be conceived as thereby necessitated to act in conformity with law, inasmuch as it can of itself, according to its subjective constitution, be determined only by the representation of the good. Therefore no imperatives hold for the divine will, and in general for a holy will; the *ought* is here out of place, because the *would* is already of itself necessarily in agreement with the law. Consequently, imperatives are only formulas for expressing the relation of objective laws of willing in general to the subjective imperfection of the will of this or that rational being, e.g., the human will.

Now all imperatives command either hypothetically or categorically. The former represent the practical necessity of a possible action as a means for attaining something else that one wants (or may possibly want). The categorical imperative would be one which represented an action as objectively necessary in itself, without reference to another end.

Every practical law represents a possible action as good and hence as necessary for a subject who is practically determinable by reason; therefore all imperatives are formulas for determining an action which is necessary according to the principle of a will that is good in some way. Now if the action would be good merely as a means to something else, so is the imperative hypothetical. But if the action is represented as good in itself, and hence as necessary in a will which of itself conforms to reason as the principle of the will, then the imperative is categorical.

An imperative thus says what action possible by me would be good, and it presents the practical rule in relation to a will which does not forthwith perform an action simply because it is good, partly because the subject does not always know that the action is good and partly because (even if he does know it is good) his maxims might yet be opposed to the objective principles of practical reason.

A hypothetical imperative thus says only that an 415 action is good for some purpose, either possible or actual. In the first case it is a problematic practical principle; in the second case an assertoric one. A categorical imperative, which declares an action to be of itself objectively necessary without reference to any purpose, i.e., without any other end, holds as an apodeictic practical principle.

Whatever is possible only through the powers of some rational being can be thought of as a possible purpose of some will. Consequently, there are in fact infinitely many principles of action insofar as they are represented as necessary for attaining a possible purpose achievable by them. All sciences have a practical part consisting of problems saying that some end is possible for us and of imperatives telling us how it can be attained. These can, therefore, be called in general imperatives of skill. Here there is no question at all whether the end is reasonable and good, but there is only a question as to what must be done to attain it. The prescriptions needed by a doctor in order to make his patient thoroughly healthy and by a poisoner in order to make sure of killing his victim are of equal value so far as each serves to bring about its purpose perfectly. Since there cannot be known in early youth what ends may be presented to us in the course of life, parents especially seek to have their children learn many different kinds of things, and they provide for skill in the use of means to all sorts of arbitrary ends, among which they cannot determine whether any one of them could in the future become an actual purpose for their ward, though there is always the possibility that he might adopt it. Their concern is so great that they commonly neglect to form and correct their children's judgment regarding the worth of things which might be chosen as ends.

There is, however, one end that can be presupposed as actual for all rational beings (so far as they are dependent beings to whom imperatives apply); and thus there is one purpose which they not merely can have but which can certainly be assumed to be such that they all do have by a natural necessity, and this is happiness. A hypothetical imperative which represents the practical necessity of an action as means for the promotion of happiness is assertoric. It may be

---

the will's dependence on principles of reason for the sake of inclination, i.e., reason merely gives the practical rule for meeting the need of inclination. In the former case the action interests me, while in the latter case what interests me is the object of the action (so far as this object is pleasant for me). In the First Section we have seen that in the case of an action done from duty regard must be given not to the interest in the object, but only to interest in the action itself and in its rational principle (viz., the law).

416 expounded not simply as necessary to an uncertain, merely possible purpose, but as necessary to a purpose which can be presupposed a priori and with certainty as being present in everyone because it belongs to his essence. Now skill in the choice of means to one's own greatest well-being can be called prudence[27] in the narrowest sense. And thus the imperative that refers to the choice of means to one's own happiness, i.e., the precept of prudence, still remains hypothetical; the action is commanded not absolutely but only as a means to a further purpose.

Finally, there is one imperative which immediately commands a certain conduct without having as its condition any other purpose to be attained by it. This imperative is categorical. It is not concerned with the matter of the action and its intended result, but rather with the form of the action and the principle from which it follows; what is essentially good in the action consists in the mental disposition, let the consequences be what they may. This imperative may be called that of morality.

Willing according to these three kinds of principles is also clearly distinguished by dissimilarity in the necessitation of the will. To make this dissimilarity clear I think that they are most suitably named in their order when they are said to be either *rules of skill, counsels of prudence,* or *commands (laws) of morality.* For law alone involves the concept of a necessity that is unconditioned and indeed objective and hence universally valid, and commands are laws which must be obeyed, i.e., must be followed even in opposition to inclination. Counsel does indeed involve necessity, but involves such necessity as is valid only under a subjectively contingent condition, viz., whether this or that man counts this or that as belonging to his happiness. On the other hand, the categorical imperative is limited by no condition, and can quite properly be called a command since it is

absolutely, though practically, necessary. The first kind of imperatives might also be called technical (belonging to art), the second kind pragmatic[28] (belonging to welfare), the third kind moral (belonging 417 to free conduct as such, i.e., to morals).

The question now arises: how are all of these imperatives possible?[29] This question does not seek to know how the fulfillment of the action commanded by the imperative can be conceived, but merely how the necessitation of the will expressed by the imperative in setting a task can be conceived. How an imperative of skill is possible requires no special discussion. Whoever wills the end, wills (so far as reason has decisive influence on his actions) also the means that are indispensably necessary to his actions and that lie in his power. This proposition, as far as willing is concerned, is analytic. For in willing an object as my effect there is already thought the causality of myself as an acting cause, i.e., the use of means. The imperative derives the concept of actions necessary to this end from the concept of willing this end. (Synthetic propositions are indeed required for determining the means to a proposed end; but such propositions are concerned not with the ground, i.e., the act of the will, but only with the way to realize the object of the will.) Mathematics teaches by nothing but synthetic propositions that in order to bisect a line according to a sure principle I must from each of its extremities draw arcs such that they intersect. But when I know that the proposed result can come about only by means of such an action, then the proposition (if I fully will the effect, then I also will the action required for it) is analytic. For it is one and the same thing to conceive of something as an effect that is possible in a certain way through me and to conceive of myself as acting in the same way with regard to the aforesaid effect.

---

27. The word "prudence" is used in a double sense: firstly, it can mean worldly wisdom, and, secondly, private wisdom. The former is the skill of someone in influencing others so as to use them for his own purposes. The latter is the sagacity to combine all these purposes for his own lasting advantage. The value of the former is properly reduced to the latter, and it might better be said of one who is prudent in the former sense but not in the latter that he is clever and cunning, but on the whole imprudent.

28. It seems to me that the proper meaning of the word "pragmatic" could be defined most accurately in this way. For those sanctions are called pragmatic which properly flow not from the law of states as necessary enactments but from provision for the general welfare. A history is pragmatically written when it teaches prudence, i.e., instructs the world how it can provide for its interests better than, or at least as well as, has been done in former times.
29. [That is, why should one let his actions be determined at various times by one or the other of these three kinds of imperatives?]

If it were only as easy to give a determinate concept
418 of happiness, then the imperatives of prudence would exactly correspond to those of skill and would be likewise analytic. For there could be said in this case just as in the former that whoever wills the end also wills (necessarily according to reason) the sole means thereto which are in his power. But, unfortunately, the concept of happiness is such an indeterminate one that even though everyone wishes to attain happiness, yet he can never say definitely and consistently what it is that he really wishes and wills. The reason for this is that all the elements belonging to the concept of happiness are unexceptionally empirical, i.e., they must be borrowed from experience, while for the idea of happiness there is required an absolute whole, a maximum of well-being in my present and in every future condition. Now it is impossible for the most insightful and at the same time most powerful, but nonetheless finite, being to frame here a determinate concept of what it is that he really wills. Does he want riches? How much anxiety, envy, and intrigue might he not thereby bring down upon his own head! Or knowledge and insight? Perhaps these might only give him an eye that much sharper for revealing that much more dreadfully evils which are at present hidden but are yet unavoidable, or such an eye might burden him with still further needs for the desires which already concern him enough. Or long life? Who guarantees that it would not be a long misery? Or health at least? How often has infirmity of the body kept one from excesses into which perfect health would have allowed him to fall, and so on? In brief, he is not able on any principle to determine with complete certainty what will make him truly happy, because to do so would require omniscience. Therefore, one cannot act according to determinate principles in order to be happy, but only according to empirical counsels, e.g., of diet, frugality, politeness, reserve, etc., which are shown by experience to contribute on the average the most to well-being. There follows from this that imperatives of prudence, strictly speaking, cannot command at all, i.e., present actions objectively as practically necessary. They are to be taken as counsels (*consilia*) rather than as commands (*praecepta*) of reason. The problem of determining certainly and universally what action will promote the happiness of a rational being is completely insoluble. Therefore, regarding such action no imperative that

in the strictest sense could command what is to be done to make one happy is possible, inasmuch as happiness is not an ideal of reason but of imagination. 419 Such an ideal rests merely on empirical grounds; in vain can there be expected that such grounds should determine an action whereby the totality of an infinite series of consequences could be attained. This imperative of prudence would, nevertheless, be an analytic practical proposition if one assumes that the means of happiness could with certainty be assigned; for it differs from the imperative of skill only in that for it the end is given while for the latter the end is merely possible. Since both, however, command only the means to what is assumed to be willed as an end, the imperative commanding him who wills the end to will likewise the means thereto is in both cases analytic. Hence there is also no difficulty regarding the possibility of an imperative of prudence.

On the other hand, the question as to how the imperative of morality is possible is undoubtedly the only one requiring a solution. For it is not at all hypothetical; and hence the objective necessity which it presents cannot be based on any presupposition, as was the case with the hypothetical imperatives. Only there must never here be forgotten that no example can show, i.e., empirically, whether there is any such imperative at all. Rather, care must be taken lest all imperatives which are seemingly categorical may nevertheless be covertly hypothetical. For instance, when it is said that you should not make a false promise, the assumption is that the necessity of this avoidance is no mere advice for escaping some other evil, so that it might be said that you should not make a false promise lest you ruin your credit when the falsity comes to light. But when it is asserted that an action of this kind must be regarded as bad in itself, then the imperative of prohibition is therefore categorical. Nevertheless, it cannot with certainty be shown by means of an example that the will is here determined solely by the law without any other incentive, even though such may seem to be the case. For it is always possible that secretly there is fear of disgrace and perhaps also obscure dread of other dangers; such fear and dread may have influenced the will. Who can prove by experience that a cause is not present? Experience only shows that a cause is not perceived. But in such a case the so-called moral imperative, which as such appears to be categorical and unconditioned, would actually be only a pragmatic precept which makes us pay attention to our own advantage and merely teaches us to take such advantage into consideration.

We shall, therefore, have to investigate the possibility of a categorical imperative entirely a priori, inasmuch as we do not here have the advantage of having 420 its reality given in experience and consequently of thus being obligated merely to explain its possibility rather than to establish it. In the meantime so much can be seen for now: the categorical imperative alone purports to be a practical law, while all the others may be called principles of the will but not laws. The reason for this is that whatever is necessary merely in order to attain some arbitrary purpose can be regarded as in itself contingent, and the precept can always be ignored once the purpose is abandoned. Contrariwise, an unconditioned command does not leave the will free to choose the opposite at its own liking. Consequently, only such a command carries with it that necessity which is demanded from a law.

Secondly, in the case of this categorical imperative, or law of morality, the reason for the difficulty (of discerning its possibility) is quite serious. The categorical imperative is an a priori synthetic practical proposition;[30] and since discerning the possibility of propositions of this sort involves so much difficulty in theoretic knowledge, there may readily be gathered that there will be no less difficulty in practical knowledge.

In solving this problem, we want first to inquire whether perhaps the mere concept of a categorical imperative may not also supply us with the formula containing the proposition that can alone be a categorical imperative. For even when we know the purport of such an absolute command, the question

as to how it is possible will still require a special and difficult effort, which we postpone to the last section.[31]

If I think of a hypothetical imperative in general, I do not know beforehand what it will contain until its condition is given. But if I think of a categorical imperative, I know immediately what it contains. For since, besides the law, the imperative contains only the necessity that the maxim[32] should accord with 421 this law, while the law contains no condition to restrict it, there remains nothing but the universality of a law as such with which the maxim of the action should conform. This conformity alone is properly what is represented as necessary by the imperative.

Hence there is only one categorical imperative and it is this: Act only according to that maxim whereby you can at the same time will that it should become a universal law.[33]

Now if all imperatives of duty can be derived from this one imperative as their principle, then there can at least be shown what is understood by the concept of duty and what it means, even though there is left undecided whether what is called duty may not be an empty concept.

The universality of law according to which effects are produced constitutes what is properly called nature in the most general sense (as to form), i.e., the existence of things as far as determined by universal laws. Accordingly, the universal imperative of duty may be expressed thus: Act as if the maxim of your action were to become through your will a universal law of nature.[34]

We shall now enumerate some duties, following the usual division of them into duties to ourselves

---

31. [See below Ak. 446–63.]

32. A maxim is the subjective principle of acting and must be distinguished from the objective principle, viz., the practical law. A maxim contains the practical rule which reason determines in accordance with the conditions of the subject (often his ignorance or his inclinations) and is thus the principle according to which the subject does act. But the law is the objective principle valid for every rational being, and it is the principle according to which he ought to act, i.e., an imperative.

33. [This formulation of the categorical imperative is often referred to as the formula of universal law.]

34. [This is often called the formula of the law of nature.]

---

30. I connect a priori, and therefore necessarily, the act with the will without presupposing any condition taken from some inclination (though I make such a connection only objectively, i.e., under the idea of a reason having full power over all subjective motives). Hence this is a practical proposition which does not analytically derive the willing of an action from some other willing already presupposed (for we possess no such perfect will) but which connects the willing of an action immediately with the concept of the will of a rational being as something which is not contained in this concept.

and to others and into perfect and imperfect duties.[35]

422 1. A man reduced to despair by a series of misfortunes feels sick of life but is still so far in possession of his reason that he can ask himself whether taking his own life would not be contrary to his duty to himself.[36] Now he asks whether the maxim of his action could become a universal law of nature. But his maxim is this: from self-love I make as my principle to shorten my life when its continued duration threatens more evil than it promises satisfaction. There only remains the question as to whether this principle of self-love can become a universal law of nature. One sees at once a contradiction in a system of nature whose law would destroy life by means of the very same feeling that acts so as to stimulate the furtherance of life, and hence there could be no existence as a system of nature. Therefore, such a maxim cannot possibly hold as a universal law of nature and is, consequently, wholly opposed to the supreme principle of all duty.

2. Another man in need finds himself forced to borrow money. He knows well that he won't be able to repay it, but he sees also that he will not get any loan unless he firmly promises to repay it within a fixed time. He wants to make such a promise, but he still has conscience enough to ask himself whether it is not permissible and is contrary to duty to get out of difficulty in this way. Suppose, however, that he decides to do so. The maxim of his action would then be expressed as follows: when I believe myself to be in need of money, I will borrow money and promise

to pay it back, although I know that I can never do so. Now this principle of self-love or personal advantage may perhaps be quite compatible with one's entire future welfare, but the question is now whether it is right.[37] I then transform the requirement of self-love into a universal law and put the question thus: how would things stand if my maxim were to become a universal law? He then sees at once that such a maxim could never hold as a universal law of nature and be consistent with itself, but must necessarily be self-contradictory. For the universality of a law which says that anyone believing himself to be in difficulty could promise whatever he pleases with the intention of not keeping it would make promising itself and the end to be attained thereby quite impossible, inasmuch as no one would believe what was promised him but would merely laugh at all such utterances as being vain pretenses.

3. A third finds in himself a talent whose cultivation could make him a man useful in many respects. But he finds himself in comfortable circumstances and 423 prefers to indulge in pleasure rather than to bother himself about broadening and improving his fortunate natural aptitudes. But he asks himself further whether his maxim of neglecting his natural gifts, besides agreeing of itself with his propensity to indulgence, might agree also with what is called duty.[38] He then sees that a system of nature could indeed always subsist according to such a universal law, even though every man (like South Sea Islanders) should let his talents rust and resolve to devote his life entirely to idleness, indulgence, propagation, and, in a word, to enjoyment. But he cannot possibly will that this should become a universal law of nature or be implanted in us as such a law by a natural instinct. For as a rational being he necessarily wills that all his faculties should be developed, inasmuch as they are given him for all sorts of possible purposes.

4. A fourth man finds things going well for himself but sees others (whom he could help) struggling with great hardships; and he thinks: what does it matter to me? Let everybody be as happy as Heaven wills or as he can make himself; I shall take nothing from

35. There should be noted here that I reserve the division of duties for a future *Metaphysics of Morals* [in Part II of the *Metaphysics of Morals*, entitled *The Metaphysical Principles of Virtue*, Ak. 417–474]. The division presented here stands as merely an arbitrary one (in order to arrange my examples). For the rest, I understand here by a perfect duty one which permits no exception in the interest of inclination. Accordingly, I have perfect duties which are external [to others], while other ones are internal [to oneself]. This classification runs contrary to the accepted usage of the schools, but I do not intend to justify it here, since there is no difference for my purpose whether this classification is accepted or not.

36. [Not committing suicide is an example of a perfect duty to oneself. See *Metaphysical Principles of Virtue*, Ak. 422–24.]

37. [Keeping promises is an example of a perfect duty to others. See *ibid.*, Ak. 423–31.]

38. [Cultivating one's talents is an example of an imperfect duty to oneself. See *ibid.*, Ak. 444–46.]

him nor even envy him; but I have no desire to contribute anything to his well-being or to his assistance when in need. If such a way of thinking were to become a universal law of nature, the human race admittedly could very well subsist and doubtless could subsist even better than when everyone prates about sympathy and benevolence and even on occasions exerts himself to practice them but, on the other hand, also cheats when he can, betrays the rights of man, or otherwise violates them. But even though it is possible that a universal law of nature could subsist in accordance with that maxim, still it is impossible to will that such a principle should hold everywhere as a law of nature.[39] For a will which resolved in this way would contradict itself, inasmuch as cases might often arise in which one would have need of the love and sympathy of others and in which he would deprive himself, by such a law of nature springing from his own will, of all hope of the aid he wants for himself.

424   These are some of the many actual duties, or at least what are taken to be such, whose derivation from the single principle cited above is clear. We must be able to will that a maxim of our action become a universal law; this is the canon for morally estimating any of our actions. Some actions are so constituted that their maxims cannot without contradiction even be thought as a universal law of nature, much less be willed as what should become one. In the case of others this internal impossibility is indeed not found, but there is still no possibility of wiling that their maxim should be raised to the universality of a law of nature, because such a will would contradict itself. There is no difficulty in seeing that the former kind of action conflicts with strict or narrow [perfect] (irremissible) duty, while the second kind conflicts only with broad [imperfect] (meritorious) duty.[40] By means of these examples there has thus been fully set forth how all duties depend as regards the kind of obligation (not the object of their action) upon the one principle.

If we now attend to ourselves in any transgression of a duty, we find that we actually do not will that our maxim should become a universal law—because

this is impossible for us—but rather that the opposite of this maxim should remain a law universally.[41] We only take the liberty of making an exception to the law for ourselves (or just for this one time) to the advantage of our inclination. Consequently, if we weighed up everything from one and the same standpoint, namely, that of reason, we would find a contradiction in our own will, viz., that a certain principle be objectively necessary as a universal law and yet subjectively not hold universally but should admit of exceptions. But since we at one moment regard our action from the standpoint of a will wholly in accord with reason and then at another moment regard the very same action from the standpoint of a will affected by inclination, there is really no contradiction here. Rather, there is an opposition (*antagonismus*) of inclination to the precept of reason, whereby the universality (*universalitas*) of the principle is changed into a mere generality (*generalitas*) so that the practical principle of reason may meet the maxim halfway. Although this procedure cannot be justified in our own impartial judgment, yet it does show that we actually acknowledge the validity of the categorical imperative and (with all respect for it) merely allow ourselves a few exceptions which, as they seem to us, are unimportant and forced upon us.

We have thus at least shown that if duty is a concept 425 which is to have significance and real legislative authority for our actions, then such duty can be expressed only in categorical imperatives but not at all in hypothetical ones. We have also—and this is already a great deal—exhibited clearly and definitely for every application what is the content of the categorical imperative, which must contain the principle of all duty (if there is such a thing at all). But we have not yet advanced far enough to prove a priori that there actually is an imperative of this kind, that there is a practical law which of itself commands absolutely and without any incentives, and that following this law is duty.

In order to attain this proof there is the utmost

---

39. [Benefiting others is an example of an imperfect duty to others. See *ibid*., Ak. 452–54.]

40. [Compare *ibid*., Ak. 390–94, 410–11, 421–51.]

41. [This is to say, for example, that when you tell a lie, you do so on the condition that others are truthful and believe that what you are saying is true, because otherwise your lie will never work to get you what you want. When you tell a lie, you simply take exception to the general rule that says everyone should always tell the truth.]

importance in being warned that we must not take it into our mind to derive the reality of this principle from the special characteristics of human nature. For duty has to be a practical, unconditioned necessity of action; hence it must hold for all rational beings (to whom alone an imperative is at all applicable) and for this reason only can it also be a law for all human wills. On the other hand, whatever is derived from the special natural condition of humanity, from certain feelings and propensities, or even, if such were possible, from some special tendency peculiar to human reason and not holding necessarily for the will of every rational being—all of this can indeed yield a maxim valid for us, but not a law. This is to say that such can yield a subjective principle according to which we might act if we happen to have the propensity and inclination, but cannot yield an objective principle according to which we would be directed to act even though our every propensity, inclination, and natural tendency were opposed to it. In fact, the sublimity and inner worth of the command are so much the more evident in a duty, the fewer subjective causes there are for it and the more they oppose it; such causes do not in the least weaken the necessitation exerted by the law or take away anything from its validity.

Here philosophy is seen in fact to be put in a precarious position, which should be firm even though there is neither in heaven nor on earth anything upon which it depends or is based. Here philosophy must show its purity as author of its laws, and not as the herald of such laws as are whispered to it by an implanted sense or by who knows what tutelary nature. Such laws may be better than nothing at all, but they can never give us principles dictated by 426 reason. These principles must have an origin that is completely a priori and must at the same time derive from such origin their authority to command. They expect nothing from the inclination of men but, rather, expect everything from the supremacy of the law and from the respect owed to the law. Without the latter expectation, these principles condemn man to self-contempt and inward abhorrence.

Hence everything empirical is not only quite unsuitable as a contribution to the principle of morality, but is even highly detrimental to the purity of morals. For the proper and inestimable worth of an absolutely good will consists precisely in the fact that the princi-

ple of action is free of all influences from contingent grounds, which only experience can furnish. This lax or even mean way of thinking which seeks its principle among empirical motives and laws cannot too much or too often be warned against, for human reason in its weariness is glad to rest upon this pillow. In a dream of sweet illusions (in which not Juno but a cloud is embraced) there is substituted for morality some bastard patched up from limbs of quite varied ancestry and looking like anything one wants to see in it but not looking like virtue to him who has once beheld her in her true form.[42]

Therefore, the question is this: is it a necessary law for all rational beings always to judge their actions according to such maxims as they can themselves will that such should serve as universal laws? If there is such a law, then it must already be connected (completely a priori) with the concept of the will of a rational being in general. But in order to discover this connection we must, however reluctantly, take a step into metaphysics, although into a region of it different from speculative philosophy, i.e., we must enter the metaphysics of morals. In practical philosophy the concern is not with accepting grounds for 427 what happens but with accepting laws of what ought to happen, even though it never does happen—that is, the concern is with objectively practical laws. Here there is no need to inquire into the reasons as to why something pleases or displeases, how the pleasure of mere sensation differs from taste, and whether taste differs from a general satisfaction of reason, upon what does the feeling of pleasure and displeasure rest, and how from this feeling desires and inclinations arise, and how, finally, from these there arise maxims through the cooperation of reason. All of this belongs to an empirical psychology, which would constitute the second part of the doctrine of nature, if this doctrine is regarded as the philosophy of nature insofar as this philosophy is grounded on empirical laws. But here the concern is with objectively practical laws,

---

42. To behold virtue in her proper form is nothing other than to present morality stripped of all admixture of what is sensuous and of every spurious adornment of reward or self-love. How much she then eclipses all else that appears attractive to the inclinations can be easily seen by everyone with the least effort of his reason, if it be not entirely ruined for all abstraction.

and hence with the relation of a will to itself insofar as it is determined solely by reason. In this case everything related to what is empirical falls away of itself, because if reason entirely by itself determines conduct (and the possibility of such determination we now wish to investigate), then reason must necessarily do so a priori.

The will is thought of as a faculty of determining itself to action in accordance with the representation of certain laws, and such a faculty can be found only in rational beings. Now what serves the will as the objective ground of its self-determination is an end; and if this end is given by reason alone, then it must be equally valid for all rational beings. On the other hand, what contains merely the ground of the possibility of the action, whose effect is an end, is called the means. The subjective ground of desire is the incentive; the objective ground of volition is the motive. Hence there arises the distinction between subjective ends, which rest on incentives, and objective ends, which depend on motives valid for every rational being. Practical principles are formal when they abstract from all subjective ends; they are material, however, when they are founded upon subjective ends, and hence upon certain incentives. The ends which a rational being arbitrarily proposes to himself as effects of this action (material ends) are all merely relative, for only their relation to a specially constituted faculty of desire in the subject gives them their worth. Consequently, such worth cannot provide any universal principles, which are valid and necessary

428 for all rational beings and, furthermore, are valid for every volition, i.e., cannot provide any practical laws. Therefore, all such relative ends can be grounds only for hypothetical imperatives.

But let us suppose that there were something whose existence has in itself an absolute worth, something which as an end in itself could be a ground of determinate laws. In it, and in it alone, would there be the ground of a possible categorical imperative, i.e., of a practical law.

Now I say that man, and in general every rational being, exists as an end in himself and not merely as a means to be arbitrarily used by this or that will. He must in all his actions, whether directed to himself or to other rational beings, always be regarded at the same time as an end. All the objects of inclinations have only a conditioned value; for if there were not

these inclinations and the needs founded on them, then their object would be without value. But the inclinations themselves, being sources of needs, are so far from having an absolute value such as to render them desirable for their own sake that the universal wish of every rational being must be, rather, to be wholly free from them. Accordingly, the value of any object obtainable by our action is always conditioned. Beings whose existence depends not on our will but on nature have, nevertheless, if they are not rational beings, only a relative value as means and are therefore called things. On the other hand, rational beings are called persons inasmuch as their nature already marks them out as ends in themselves, i.e., as something which is not to be used merely as means and hence there is imposed thereby a limit on all arbitrary use of such beings, which are thus objects of respect. Persons are, therefore, not merely subjective ends, whose existence as an effect of our actions has a value for us; but such beings are objective ends, i.e., exist as ends in themselves. Such an end is one for which there can be substituted no other end to which such beings should serve merely as means, for otherwise nothing at all of absolute value would be found anywhere. But if all value were conditioned and hence contingent, then no supreme practical principle could be found for reason at all.

If then there is to be a supreme practical principle and, as far as the human will is concerned, a categorical imperative, then it must be such that from the conception of what is necessarily an end for everyone because this end is an end in itself it constitutes an objective principle of the will and can hence serve as a practical law. The ground of such a principle is this: rational nature exists as an end in itself. In this 429 way man necessarily thinks of his own existence; thus far is it a subjective principle of human actions. But in this way also does every other rational being think of his existence on the same rational ground that holds also for me;[43] hence it is at the same time an objective principle, from which, as a supreme practical ground, all laws of the will must be able to be derived. The practical imperative will therefore be the following: Act in such a way that you treat

43. This proposition I here put forward as a postulate. The grounds for it will be found in the last section. [See below Ak. 446–63.]

humanity, whether in your own person or in the person of another, always at the same time as an end and never simply as a means.[44] We now want to see whether this can be carried out in practice.

Let us keep to our previous examples.[45]

First, as regards the concept of necessary duty to oneself, the man who contemplates suicide will ask himself whether his action can be consistent with the idea of humanity as an end in itself. If he destroys himself in order to escape from a difficult situation, then he is making use of his person merely as a means so as to maintain a tolerable condition till the end of his life. Man, however, is not a thing and hence is not something to be used merely as a means; he must in all his actions always be regarded as an end in himself. Therefore, I cannot dispose of man in my own person by mutilating, damaging, or killing him. (A more exact determination of this principle so as to avoid all misunderstanding, e.g., regarding the amputation of limbs in order to save oneself, or the exposure of one's life to danger in order to save it, and so on, must here be omitted; such questions belong to morals proper.)

Second, as concerns necessary or strict duty to others, the man who intends to make a false promise will immediately see that he intends to make use of another man merely as a means to an end which the latter does not likewise hold. For the man whom I 430 want to use for my own purposes by such a promise cannot possibly concur with my way of acting toward him and hence cannot himself hold the end of this action. This conflict with the principle of duty to others becomes even clearer when instances of attacks on the freedom and property of others are considered. For then it becomes clear that a transgressor of the rights of men intends to make use of the persons of others merely as a means, without taking into consideration that, as rational beings, they should always be esteemed at the same time as ends, i.e., be esteemed only as beings who must themselves be able to hold the very same action as an end.[46]

Third, with regard to contingent (meritorious) duty to oneself, it is not enough that the action does not conflict with humanity in our own person as an end in itself; the action must also harmonize with this end. Now there are in humanity capacities for greater perfection which belong to the end that nature has in view as regards humanity in our own person. To neglect these capacities might perhaps be consistent with the maintenance of humanity as an end in itself, but would not be consistent with the advancement of this end.

Fourth, concerning meritorious duty to others, the natural end that all men have is their own happiness. Now humanity might indeed subsist if nobody contributed anything to the happiness of others, provided he did not intentionally impair their happiness. But this, after all, would harmonize only negatively and not positively with humanity as an end in itself, if everyone does not also strive, as much as he can, to further the ends of others. For the ends of any subject who is an end in himself must as far as possible be my ends also, if that conception of an end in itself is to have its full effect in me.

This principle of humanity and of every rational 431 nature generally as an end in itself is the supreme limiting condition of every man's freedom of action. This principle is not borrowed from experience, first, because of its universality, inasmuch as it applies to all rational beings generally, and no experience is capable of determining anything about them; and, secondly, because in experience (subjectively) humanity is not thought of as the end of men, i.e., as an object that we of ourselves actually make our end which as a law ought to constitute the supreme limiting condition of all subjective ends (whatever they may be); and hence this principle must arise from pure reason [and not from experience]. That is to say that the ground of all practical legislation lies

---

44. [This oft-quoted version of the categorical imperative is usually referred to as the formula of the end in itself.]

45. [See above Ak. 422–23.]

46. Let it not be thought that the trivial *quod tibi non vis fieri, etc.* [do not do to others what you do not want done to yourself] can here serve as a standard or principle. For

it is merely derived from our principle, although with several limitations. It cannot be a universal law, for it contains the ground neither of duties to oneself nor of duties of love toward others (for many a man would gladly consent that others should not benefit him, if only he might be excused from benefiting them). Nor, finally, does it contain the ground of strict duties toward others, for the criminal would on this ground be able to dispute with the judges who punish him; and so on.

objectively in the rule and in the form of universality, which (according to the first principle) makes the rule capable of being a law (say, for example, a law of nature). Subjectively, however, the ground of all practical legislation lies in the end; but (according to the second principle) the subject of all ends is every rational being as an end in himself. From this there now follows the third practical principle of the will as the supreme condition of the will's conformity with universal practical reason, viz., the idea of the will of every rational being as a will that legislates universal law.[47]

According to this principle all maxims are rejected which are not consistent with the will's own legislation of universal law. The will is thus not merely subject to the law but is subject to the law in such a way that it must be regarded also as legislating for itself and only on this account as being subject to the law (of which it can regard itself as the author).

In the previous formulations of imperatives, viz., that based on the conception of the conformity of actions to universal law in a way similar to a natural order and that based on the universal prerogative of rational beings as ends in themselves, these imperatives just because they were thought of as categorical excluded from their legislative authority all admixture of any interest as an incentive. They were, however, only assumed to be categorical because such an assumption had to be made if the concept of duty was to be explained. But that there were practical propositions which commanded categorically could not itself be proved, nor can it be proved anywhere in this section. But one thing could have been done, viz., to indicate that in willing from duty the renunciation of all interest is the specific mark distinguishing a categorical imperative from a hypothetical one and that such renunciation was expressed in the imperative itself by means of some determination contained 432 in it. This is done in the present (third) formulation of the principle, namely, in the idea of the will of every rational being as a will that legislates universal law.

When such a will is thought of, then even though a will which is subject to law may be bound to this law by means of some interest, nevertheless a will that is itself a supreme lawgiver is not able as such to depend on any interest. For a will which is so dependent would itself require yet another law restricting the interest of its self-love to the condition that such interest should itself be valid as a universal law.

Thus the principle that every human will as a will that legislates universal law in all its maxims,[48] provided it is otherwise correct, would be well suited to being a categorical imperative in the following respect: just because of the idea of legislating universal law such an imperative is not based on any interest, and therefore it alone of all possible imperatives can be unconditional. Or still better, the proposition being converted, if there is a categorical imperative (i.e., a law for the will of every rational being), then it can only command that everything be done from the maxim of such a will as could at the same time have as its object only itself regarded as legislating universal law. For only then are the practical principle and the imperative which the will obeys unconditional, inasmuch as the will can be based on no interest at all.

When we look back upon all previous attempts that have been made to discover the principle of morality, there is no reason now to wonder why they one and all had to fail. Man was viewed as bound to laws by his duty; but it was not seen that man is subject only to his own, yet universal, legislation and that he is bound only to act in accordance with his own will, which is, however, a will purposed by nature to legislate universal laws. For when man is thought as being merely subject to a law (whatever it might be), then the law had to carry with it some interest 433 functioning as an attracting stimulus or as a constraining force for obedience, inasmuch as the law did not arise as a law from his own will. Rather, in order that his will conform with law, it had to be necessitated by something else to act in a certain way. By this absolutely necessary conclusion, however, all the labor spent in finding a supreme ground for duty was irretrievably lost; duty was never discovered, but only the necessity of acting from a certain interest. This might be either one's own interest or another's, but

47. [This is usually called the formula of autonomy.]

48. I may here be excused from citing instances to elucidate this principle inasmuch as those which were first used to elucidate the categorical imperative and its formula can all serve the same purpose here. [See above Ak. 421–23, 429–30.]

either way the imperative had to be always conditional and could never possibly serve as a moral command. I want, therefore, to call my principle the principle of the autonomy of the will, in contrast with every other principle, which I accordingly count under heteronomy.

The concept of every rational being as one who must regard himself as legislating universal law by all his will's maxims, so that he may judge himself and his actions from this point of view, leads to another very fruitful concept, which depends on the aforementioned one, viz., that of a kingdom of ends.

By "kingdom" I understand a systematic union of different rational beings through common laws. Now laws determine ends as regards their universal validity; therefore, if one abstracts from the personal differences of rational beings and also from all content of their private ends, then it will be possible to think of a whole of all ends in systematic connection (a whole both of rational being as ends in themselves and also of the particular ends which each may set for himself); that is, one can think of a kingdom of ends that is possible on the aforesaid principles.

For all rational beings stand under the law that each of them should treat himself and all others never merely as means but always at the same time as an end in himself. Hereby arises a systematic union of rational beings through common objective laws, i.e., a kingdom that may be called a kingdom of ends (certainly only an ideal), inasmuch as these laws have in view the very relation of such beings to one another as ends and means.[49]

A rational being belongs to the kingdom of ends as a member when he legislates in it universal laws while also being himself subject to these laws. He belongs to it as sovereign, when as legislator he is himself subject to the will of no other.

434 A rational being must always regard himself as legislator in a kingdom of ends rendered possible by freedom of the will, whether as member or as sovereign. The position of the latter can be maintained not merely through the maxims of his will but only if he is a completely independent being without needs and with unlimited power adequate to his will.

Hence morality consists in the relation of all action to that legislation whereby alone a kingdom of ends is possible. This legislation must be found in every rational being and must be able to arise from his will, whose principle then is never to act on any maxim except such as can also be a universal law and hence such as the will can thereby regard itself as at the same time the legislator of universal law. If now the maxims do not by their very nature already necessarily conform with this objective principle of rational beings as legislating universal laws, then the necessity of acting on that principle is called practical necessitation, i.e., duty. Duty does not apply to the sovereign in the kingdom of ends, but it does apply to every member and to each in the same degree.

The practical necessity of acting according to this principle, i.e., duty, does not rest at all on feelings, impulses, and inclinations, but only on the relation of rational beings to one another, a relation in which the will of a rational being must always be regarded at the same time as legislative, because otherwise he could not be thought of as an end in himself. Reason, therefore, relates every maxim of the will as legislating universal laws to every other will and also to every action toward oneself; it does so not on account of any other practical motive or future advantage but rather from the idea of the dignity of a rational being who obeys no law except what he at the same time enacts himself.

In the kingdom of ends everything has either a price or a dignity. Whatever has a price can be replaced by something else as its equivalent; on the other hand, whatever is above all price, and therefore admits of no equivalent, has a dignity.

Whatever has reference to general human inclinations and needs has a market price; whatever, without presupposing any need, accords with a certain taste, i.e., a delight in the mere unpurposive play of our mental powers,[50] has an affective price; but that which constitutes the condition under which alone some- 435 thing can be an end in itself has not merely a relative worth, i.e., a price, but has an intrinsic worth, i.e., dignity.

Now morality is the condition under which alone a rational being can be an end in himself, for only thereby can he be a legislating member in the king-

49. [This is usually called the formula of the kingdom of ends.]

50. [See Kant, *Critique of Aesthetic Judgment*, §'s 1–5.]

dom of ends. Hence morality and humanity, insofar as it is capable of morality, alone have dignity. Skill and diligence in work have market price; wit, lively imagination, and humor have an affective price; but fidelity to promises and benevolence based on principles (not on instinct) have intrinsic worth. Neither nature nor art contain anything which in default of these could be put in their place; for their worth consists, not in the effects which arise from them, nor in the advantage and profit which they provide, but in mental dispositions, i.e., in the maxims of the will which are ready in this way to manifest themselves in action, even if they are not favored with success. Such actions also need no recommendation from any subjective disposition or taste so as to meet with immediate favor and delight; there is no need of any immediate propensity or feeling toward them. They exhibit the will performing them as an object of immediate respect; and nothing but reason is required to impose them upon the will, which is not to be cajoled into them, since in the case of duties such cajoling would be a contradiction. This estimation, therefore, lets the worth of such a disposition be recognized as dignity and puts it infinitely beyond all price, with which it cannot in the least be brought into competition or comparison without, as it were, violating its sanctity,

What then is it that entitles the morally good disposition, or virtue, to make such lofty claims? It is nothing less than the share which such a disposition affords the rational being of legislating universal laws, so that he is fit to be a member in a possible kingdom of ends, for which his own nature has already determined him as an end in himself and therefore as a legislator in the kingdom of ends. Thereby is he free as regards all laws of nature, and he obeys only those laws which he gives to himself. Accordingly, his maxims can belong to a universal legislation to which he at the 436 same time subjects himself. For nothing can have any worth other than what the law determines. But the legislation itself which determines all worth must for that very reason have dignity, i.e., unconditional and incomparable worth; and the word "respect" alone provides a suitable expression for the esteem which a rational being must have for it. Hence autonomy is the ground of the dignity of human nature and of every rational nature.

The aforementioned three ways of representing the principle of morality are at bottom only so many formulas of the very same law: one of them by itself contains a combination of the other two. Nevertheless, there is a difference in them, which is subjectively rather than objectively practical, viz., it is intended to bring an idea of reason closer to intuition (in accordance with a certain analogy) and thereby closer to feeling. All maxims have, namely,

1. A form, which consists in universality; and in this respect the formula of the moral imperative is expressed thus: maxims must be so chosen as if they were to hold as universal laws of nature.

2. A matter, viz., an end; and here the formula says that a rational being, inasmuch as he is by his very nature an end and hence an end in himself, must serve in every maxim as a condition limiting all merely relative and arbitrary ends.

3. A complete determination of all maxims by the formula that all maxims proceeding from his own legislation ought to harmonize with a possible kingdom of ends as a kingdom of nature.[51] There is a progression here through the categories of the *unity* of the form of the will (its universality), the *plurality* of its matter (its objects, i.e., its ends), and the *totality* of completeness of its system of ends. But one does better if in moral judgment he follows the rigorous method and takes as his basis the universal formula of the categorical imperative: Act according to that 437 maxim which can at the same time make itself a universal law. But if one wants also to secure acceptance for the moral law, it is very useful to bring one and the same action under the three aforementioned concepts and thus, as far as possible, to bring the moral law nearer to intuition.

We can now end where we started in the beginning, viz., the concept of an unconditionally good will.

51. Teleology considers nature as a kingdom of ends; morals regards a possible kingdom of ends as a kingdom of nature. In the former the kingdom of ends is a theoretical idea for explaining what exists. In the latter it is a practical idea for bringing about what does not exist but can be made actual by our conduct, i.e., what can be actualized in accordance with this very idea.

That will is absolutely good which cannot be evil, i.e., whose maxim, when made into a universal law, can never conflict with itself. This principle is therefore also its supreme law: Act always according to that maxim whose universality as a law you can at the same time will. This is the only condition under which a will can never be in conflict with itself, and such an imperative is categorical. Inasmuch as the validity of the will as a universal law for possible actions is analogous to the universal connection of the existence of things in accordance with universal laws, which is the formal aspect of nature in general, the categorical imperative can also be expressed thus: Act according to maxims which can at the same time have for their object themselves as universal laws of nature. In this way there is provided the formula for an absolutely good will.

Rational nature is distinguished from the rest of nature by the fact that it sets itself an end. This end would be the matter of every good will. But in the idea of an absolutely good will—good without any qualifying condition (of attaining this or that end)—complete abstraction must be made from every end that has to come about as an effect (since such would make every will only relatively good). And so the end must here be conceived, not as an end to be effected, but as an independently existing end. Hence it must be conceived only negatively, i.e., as an end which should never be acted against and therefore as one which in all willing must never be regarded merely as means but must always be esteemed at the same time as an end. Now this end can be nothing but the subject of all possible ends themselves, because this subject is at the same time the subject of a possible absolutely good will; for such a will cannot without contradiction be subordinated to any other object.

438 The principle: So act in regard to every rational being (yourself and others) that he may at the same time count in your maxim as an end in himself, is thus basically the same as the principle: Act on a maxim which at the same time contains in itself its own universal validity for every rational being. That in the use of means for every end my maxim should be restricted to the condition of its universal validity as a law for every subject says just the same as that a subject of ends, i.e., a rational being himself, must be made the ground for all maxims of actions and

must thus be used never merely as means but as the supreme limiting condition in the use of all means, i.e., always at the same time as an end.

Now there follows incontestably from this that every rational being as an end in himself must be able to regard himself with reference to all laws to which he may be subject as being at the same time the legislator of universal law, for just this very fitness of his maxims for the legislation of universal law distinguishes him as an end in himself. There follows also that his dignity (prerogative) of being above all the mere things of nature implies that his maxims must be taken from the viewpoint that regards himself, as well as every other rational being, as being legislative beings (and hence are they called persons). In this way there is possible a world of rational beings (*mundus intelligibilis*) as a kingdom of ends, because of the legislation belonging to all persons as members. Therefore, every rational being must so act as if he were through his maxim always a legislating member in the universal kingdom of ends. The formal principle of these maxims is this: So act as if your maxims were to serve at the same time as a universal law (for all rational beings). Thus a kingdom of ends is possible only on the analogy of a kingdom of nature; yet the former is possible only through maxims, i.e., self-imposed rules, while the latter is possible only through laws of efficient causes necessitated from without. Regardless of this difference and even though nature as a whole is viewed as a machine, yet insofar as nature stands in a relation to rational beings as its ends, it is on this account given the name of a kingdom of nature. Such a kingdom of ends would actually be realized through maxims whose rule is prescribed to all rational beings by the categorical imperative, if these maxims were universally obeyed. But even if a rational being himself strictly obeys such a maxim, he cannot for that reason count on everyone else's being true to it, nor can he expect the kingdom of nature and its purposive order to be in harmony with him as a fitting member of a kingdom of ends made possible by himself, i.e., he cannot expect the kingdom of nature to favor his expectation of happi- 439 ness. Nevertheless, the law: Act in accordance with the maxims of a member legislating universal laws for a merely possible kingdom of ends, remains in full force, since it commands categorically. And just in this lies the paradox that merely the dignity of humanity as rational nature without any further end or advantage to be thereby gained—and hence respect for a mere idea—should yet serve as an inflexible precept for the will; and that just this very independence of the maxims from all such incentives should constitute the sublimity of maxims and the worthiness of every rational subject to be a legislative member in the kingdom of ends, for otherwise he would have to be regarded as subject only to the natural law of his own needs. And even if the kingdom of nature as well as the kingdom of ends were thought of as both united under one sovereign so that the latter kingdom would thereby no longer remain a mere idea but would acquire true reality, then indeed the kingdom of ends would gain the addition of a strong incentive, but never any increase in its intrinsic worth. For this sole absolute legislator must, in spite of all this, always be thought of as judging the worth of rational beings solely by the disinterested conduct prescribed to themselves by means of this idea alone. The essence of things is not altered by their external relations; and whatever without reference to such relations alone constitutes the absolute worth of man is also what he must be judged by, whoever the judge may be, even the Supreme Being. Hence morality is the relation of actions to the autonomy of the will, i.e., to the possible legislation of universal law by means of the maxims of the will. That action which is compatible with the autonomy of the will is permitted; that which is not compatible is forbidden. That will whose maxims are necessarily in accord with the laws of autonomy is a holy, or absolutely good, will. The dependence of a will which is not absolutely good upon the principle of autonomy (i.e., moral necessitation) is obligation, which cannot therefore be applied to a holy will. The objective necessity of an action from obligations is called duty.

From what has just been said, there can now easily be explained how it happens that, although in the concept of duty we think of subjection to the law, 440 yet at the same time we thereby ascribe a certain dignity and sublimity to the person who fulfills all his duties. For not insofar as he is subject to the moral law does he have sublimity, but rather has it only insofar as with regard to this very same law he is at the same time legislative, and only thereby is he subject to

the law. We have also shown above[52] how neither fear nor inclination, but solely respect for the law, is the incentive which can give an action moral worth. Our own will, insofar as it were to act only under the condition of its being able to legislate universal law by means of its maxims—this will, ideally possible for us, is the proper object of respect. And the dignity of humanity consists just in its capacity to legislate universal law, though with the condition of humanity's being at the same time itself subject to this very same legislation.

Autonomy of the Will As the Supreme Principle of Morality

Autonomy of the will is the property that the will has of being a law to itself (independently of any property of the objects of volition). The principle of autonomy is this: Always choose in such a way that in the same volition the maxims of the choice are at the same time present as universal law. That this practical rule is an imperative, i.e., that the will of every rational being is necessarily bound to the rule as a condition, cannot be proved by merely analyzing the concepts contained in it, since it is a synthetic proposition. For proof one would have to go beyond cognition of objects to a critical examination of the subject, i.e. go to a critique of pure practical reason, since this synthetic proposition which commands apodeictically must be capable of being cognized completely a priori. This task, however, does not belong to the present section. But that the above principle of autonomy is the sole principle of morals can quite well be shown by mere analysis of the concepts of morality; for thereby the principle of morals is found to be necessarily a categorical imperative, which commands nothing more nor less than this very autonomy.

Heteronomy of the Will As the Source of All   441 Spurious Principles of Morality

If the will seeks the law that is to determine it anywhere but in the fitness of its maxims for its own legislation of universal laws, and if it thus goes outside

52. [Ak. 400–402.]

of itself and seeks this law in the character of any of its objects, then heteronomy always results. The will in that case does not give itself the law, but the object does so because of its relation to the will. This relation, whether it rests on inclination or on representations of reason, admits only of hypothetical imperatives: I ought to do something because I will something else. On the other hand, the moral, and hence categorical, imperative says that I ought to act in this way or that way, even though I did not will something else. For example, the former says that I ought not to lie if I would maintain my reputation; the latter says that I ought not to lie even though lying were to bring me not the slightest discredit. The moral imperative must therefore abstract from every object to such an extent that no object has any influence at all on the will, so that practical reason (the will) may not merely minister to an interest not belonging to it but may merely show its own commanding authority as the supreme legislation. Thus, for example, I ought to endeavor to promote the happiness of others, not as though its realization were any concern of mine (whether by immediate inclination or by any satisfaction indirectly gained through reason), but merely because a maxim which excludes it cannot be comprehended as a universal law in one and the same volition.

Classification of All Possible Principles of Morality Founded upon the Assumed Fundamental Concept of Heteronomy

Here as elsewhere human reason in its pure use, so long as it lacks a critical examination, first tried every possible wrong way before it succeeded in finding the only right way.

442   All principles that can be taken from this point of view are either empirical or rational. The first kind, drawn from the principle of happiness, are based upon either physical or moral feeling. The second kind, drawn from the principle of perfection, are based upon either the rational concept of perfection as a possible effect of our will or else upon the concept of an independent perfection (the will of God) as a determining cause of our will.

Empirical principles are wholly unsuited to serve as the foundation for moral laws. For the universality

with which such laws ought to hold for all rational beings without exception (the unconditioned practical necessity imposed by moral laws upon such beings) is lost if the basis of these laws is taken from the particular constitution of human nature or from the accidental circumstances in which such nature is placed. But the principle of one's own happiness is the most objectionable. Such is the case not merely because this principle is false and because experience contradicts the supposition that well-being is always proportional to well-doing, nor yet merely because this principle contributes nothing to the establishment of morality, inasmuch as making a man happy is quite different from making him good and making him prudent and sharp-sighted for his own advantage quite different from making him virtuous. Rather, such is the case because this principle of one's own happiness bases morality upon incentives that undermine it rather than establish it and that totally destroy its sublimity, inasmuch as motives to virtue are put in the same class as motives to vice and inasmuch as such incentives merely teach one to become better at calculation, while the specific difference between virtue and vice is entirely obliterated. On the other hand, moral feeling, this alleged special sense,[53] remains closer to morality than does the aforementioned principle of one's own happiness. Yet the appeal to the principle of moral feeling is superficial, since men who cannot think believe that they will be helped out by feeling, even when the question is solely one of universal laws. They do so even though feelings naturally differ from one another by an infinity of degrees, so that feelings are not capable of providing a uniform measure of good and evil; furthermore, they do so even though one man cannot by

---

53. I count the principle of moral feeling under that of happiness, because every empirical interest promises to contribute to our well-being through the amenity afforded by something, whether immediately and without any reference to advantage or with reference to advantage. Similarly, the principle of sympathy for the happiness of others must with Hutcheson be counted along with the principle of moral sense as adopted by him. [Francis Hutcheson (1694–1747) was Professor of Moral Philosophy in the University of Glasgow, Scotland. He was the main proponent of the doctrine of moral sense.]

his feeling judge validly at all for other men. Nevertheless, the principle of moral feeling is closer to morality and its dignity than is the principle of one's own happiness inasmuch as the former principle pays 443 virtue the honor of ascribing to her directly the satisfaction and esteem that is held for her, and does not, as it were, tell her to her face that our attachment to her rests not on her beauty but only on our advantage.

Among the rational principles of morality (or those arising from reason rather than from feeling) there is the ontological concept of perfection. It is empty, indeterminate, and hence is no use for finding in the immeasurable field of possible reality the maximum sum suitable for us. Furthermore, in attempting to distinguish specifically between the reality just mentioned and every other, it exhibits an inevitable tendency for turning about in a circle and cannot avoid tacitly presupposing the morality that it has to explain. Nevertheless, it is better than the theological concept, whereby morality is derived from a divine and most perfect will. It is better not merely because we cannot intuit divine perfection but can only derive it from our own concepts, among which morality is foremost; but also because if it is not so derived (and being thus derived would involve a crudely circular explanation), then the only remaining concept of God's will is drawn from such characteristics as desire for glory and dominion combined with such frightful representations as those of might and vengeance. Any system of morals based on such notions would be directly opposed to morality.

But if I had to choose between the concept of moral sense and that of perfection in general (both of which at least do not weaken morality, even though they are not at all capable of serving as its foundation), I would decide for the latter because it at least withdraws the decision of the question from sensibility and brings it to the court of pure reason, though it does not even here get any decision. Furthermore, I would choose the concept of perfection in general because it preserves the indeterminate idea (of a will good in itself) free from falsity until it can be more precisely determined.

For the rest, I believe that I may be excused from a lengthy refutation of all these doctrines. Such a refutation would be merely superfluous labor, since it is so easy and is presumably so well understood even by those whose office requires them to declare themselves for one of these theories (since their hearers would not tolerate suspension of judgment). But what interests us more here is to know that these principles never lay down anything but heteronomy of the will as the first ground of morality and that they must, consequently, necessarily fail in their purpose.

In every case where an object of the will must be 444 laid down as the foundation for prescribing a rule to determine the will, there the rule is nothing but heteronomy. The imperative is then conditioned, viz., if or because one wills this object, one should act thus or so. Hence the imperative can never command morally, i.e., categorically. Now the object may determine the will by means of inclination, as in the case of the principle of one's own happiness, or by means of reason directed to objects of our volition in general, as in the case of the principle of perfection. Yet in both cases the will never determines itself immediately by the thought of an action, but only by the incentive that the anticipated effect of the action has upon the will: I ought to do something because I will something else. And here must yet another law be assumed in me the subject, whereby I necessarily will this something else; this other law in turn requires an imperative to restrict this maxim. For the impulse which the representation of an object that is possible by means of our powers is to exert upon the will of a subject in accordance with his natural constitution belongs to the nature of the subject, whether to his sensibility (his inclination and taste) or to his understanding and reason, whose employment on an object is by the particular arrangement of their nature attended with satisfaction; consequently, the law would, properly speaking, be given by nature. This law, insofar as it is a law of nature, must be known and proved through experience and is therefore in itself contingent and hence is not fit to be an apodeictic practical rule, such as a moral rule must be. The law of nature under discussion is always merely heteronomy of the will; the will does not give itself the law, but a foreign impulse gives the law to the will by means of the subject's nature, which is adapted to receive such an impulse.

An absolutely good will, whose principle must be a categorical imperative, will therefore be indeterminate as regards all objects and will contain merely the form of willing; and indeed that form is autonomy. This is to say that the fitness of the maxims of every good will to make themselves universal laws is itself the only law that the will of every rational being imposes on itself, without needing to assume any incentive or interest as a basis.

How such a synthetic practical a priori proposition is possible and why it is necessary are problems whose solution does not lie any longer within the bounds of a metaphysics of morals. Furthermore, we have not here asserted the truth of this proposition, much 445 less professed to have within our power a proof of it. We simply showed by developing the universally accepted concept of morality that autonomy of the will is unavoidably bound up with it, or rather is its very foundation. Whoever, then, holds morality to be something real, and not a chimerical idea without any truth, must also admit the principle here put forward. Hence this section, like the first, was merely analytic. To show that morality is not a mere phantom of the brain, which morality cannot be if the categorical imperative, and with it the autonomy of the will, is true and absolutely necessary as an a priori principle, we require a possible synthetic use of pure practical reason. But we must not venture on this use without prefacing it with a critical examination of this very faculty of reason. In the last section we shall give the main outlines of this critical examination as far as sufficient for our purpose.[54]

446   **THIRD SECTION**

Transition from a Metaphysics of Morals
to a Critique of Pure Practical Reason

The Concept of Freedom Is the Key for an Explanation of the Autonomy of the Will

The will is a kind of causality belonging to living beings insofar as they are rational; freedom would be the property of this causality that makes it effective independent of any determination by alien causes. Similarly, natural necessity is the property of the causality of all non-rational beings by which they are determined to activity through the influence of alien causes.

The foregoing explanation of freedom is negative and is therefore unfruitful for attaining an insight regarding its essence; but there arises from it a positive concept, which as such is richer and more fruitful. The concept of causality involves that of laws according to which something that we call cause must entail something else — namely, the effect. Therefore freedom is certainly not lawless, even though it is not a property of will in accordance with laws of nature. It must, rather, be a causality in accordance with immutable laws, which, to be sure, is of a special kind; otherwise a free will would be something absurd. As we have already seen [in the preceding paragraph], natural necessity is a heteronomy of efficient causes, 447 inasmuch as every effect is possible only in accordance with the law that something else determines the efficient cause to exercise its causality. What else, then, can freedom of the will be but autonomy, i.e., the property that the will has of being a law to itself? The proposition that the will is in every action a law to itself expresses, however, nothing but the principle of acting according to no other maxim than that which can at the same time have itself as a universal law for its object. Now this is precisely the formula of the categorical imperative and is the principle of morality. Thus a free will and a will subject to moral laws are one and the same.

Therefore if freedom of the will is presupposed, morality (together with its principle) follows by merely analyzing the concept of freedom. However, the principle of morality is, nevertheless, a synthetic proposition: viz., an absolutely good will is one whose maxim can always have itself as content when such maxim is regarded as a universal law; it is synthetic because this property of the will's maxim can never be found by analyzing the concept of an absolutely good will. Now such synthetic propositions are possible only as follows — two cognitions are bound together through their connection with a third in which both of them are to be found. The positive concept of freedom furnishes this third cognition, which cannot, as is the case with physical causes, be the nature

54. [The ensuing Third Section is difficult to grasp. Kant expressed himself more clearly regarding the topics discussed there in the *Critique of Practical Reason*, Part I, Book I ("Analytic of Pure Practical Reason").]

of the world of sense (in whose concept is combined the concept of something as cause in relation to something else as effect). We cannot here yet show straight away what this third cognition is which freedom indicates to us and of which we have an a priori idea, nor can we as yet conceive of the deduction of the concept of freedom from pure practical reason and therewith also the possibility of a categorical imperative. Rather, we require some further preparation.

Freedom Must Be Presupposed as a Property of the Will of All Rational Beings

It is not enough to ascribe freedom to our will, on whatever ground, if we have not also sufficient reason for attributing it to all rational beings. For inasmuch as morality serves as a law for us only insofar as we are rational beings, it must also be valid for all rational beings. And since morality must be derived solely from the property of freedom, one must show that freedom is also the property of the will of all rational 448 beings. It is not enough to prove freedom from certain alleged experiences of human nature (such a proof is indeed absolutely impossible, and so freedom can be proved only a priori). Rather, one must show that freedom belongs universally to the activity of rational beings endowed with a will. Now I say that every being who cannot act in any way other than under the idea of freedom is for this very reason free from a practical point of view. This is to say that for such a being all the laws that are inseparably bound up with freedom are valid just as much as if the will of such a being could be declared to be free in itself for reasons that are valid for theoretical philosophy.[55] Now I claim that we must necessarily attribute to every rational being which has a will also the idea of freedom, under which only can such a being act. For in such a being we think of a reason that is practical,

i.e., that has causality in reference to its objects. Now we cannot possibly think of a reason that consciously lets itself be directed from outside as regards its judgments; for in that case the subject would ascribe the determination of his faculty of judgment not to his reason, but to an impulse. Reason must regard itself as the author of its principles independent of foreign influences. Therefore as practical reason or as the will of a rational being must reason regard itself as free. This is to say that the will of a rational being can be a will of its own only under the idea of freedom, and that such a will must therefore, from a practical point of view, be attributed to all rational beings.

Concerning the Interest Attached to the Ideas of Morality

We have finally traced the determinate concept of morality back to the idea of freedom, but we could not prove freedom to be something actual in ourselves and in human nature. We saw merely that we must 449 presuppose it if we want to think of a being as rational and as endowed with consciousness of its causality as regards actions, i.e., as endowed with a will. And so we find that on the very same ground we must attribute to every being endowed with reason and a will this property of determining itself to action under the idea of its own freedom.

Now there resulted from the presupposition of this idea of freedom also the consciousness of a law of action: that the subjective principles of actions, i.e., maxims, must always be so adopted that they can also be valid objectively, i.e., universally, as principles, and can therefore serve as universal laws of our own legislation. But why, then, should I subject myself to this principle simply as a rational being and by so doing also subject to this principle all other beings endowed with reason? I am willing to grant that no interest impels me to do so, because this would not give a categorical imperative. But nonetheless I must necessarily take an interest in it and discern how this comes about, for this *ought* is properly a *would* which is valid for every rational being, provided that reason is practical for such a being without hindrances. In the case of beings who, like ourselves, are also affected by sensibility, i.e., by incentives of a kind other than the purely rational, and who do not always act as reason by itself would act, this necessity of action is

---

55. I adopt this method of assuming as sufficient for our purpose that freedom is presupposed merely as an idea by rational beings in their actions in order that I may avoid the necessity of having to prove freedom from a theoretical point of view as well. For even if this latter problem is left unresolved, the same laws that would bind a being who was really free are valid equally for a being who cannot act otherwise than under the idea of its own freedom. Thus we can relieve ourselves of the burden which presses on the theory.

expressed only as an *ought*, and the subjective necessity is to be distinguished from the objective.

It therefore seems as if we have in the idea of freedom actually only presupposed the moral law, namely, the principle of the autonomy of the will, and as if we could not prove its reality and objective necessity independently. In that case we should indeed still have gained something quite considerable by at least determining the genuine principle more exactly than had previously been done. But as regards its validity and the practical necessity of subjecting oneself to it, we would have made no progress. We could give no satisfactory answer if asked the following questions: why must the universal validity of our maxim taken as a law be a condition restricting our actions; upon what do we base the worth that we assign to this way of acting—a worth that is supposed to be so great that there can be no higher interest; 450 how does it happen that by this alone does man believe that he feels his own personal worth, in comparison with which that of an agreeable or disagreeable condition is to be regarded as nothing.

Indeed we do sometimes find that we can take an interest in a personal characteristic which involves no interest in any [external] condition but only makes us capable of participating in the condition in case reason were to effect the allotment. This is to say that the mere worthiness of being happy can of itself be of interest even without the motive of participating in this happiness. This judgment, however, is in fact only the result of the importance that we have already presupposed as belonging to moral laws (when by the idea of freedom we divorce ourselves from all empirical interest). However, in this way we are not as yet able to have any insight into why it is that we should divorce ourselves from such interest, i.e., that we should consider ourselves as free in action and yet hold ourselves as subject to certain laws so as to find solely in our own person a worth that can compensate us for the loss of everything that gives worth to our condition. We do not see how this is possible and hence how the moral law can obligate us.

One must frankly admit that there is here a sort of circle from which, so it seems, there is no way to escape. In the order of efficient causes we assume that we are free so that we may think of ourselves as subject to moral laws in the order of ends. And we then think of ourselves as subject to these laws because

we have attributed to ourselves freedom of the will. Freedom and self-legislation of the will are both autonomy and are hence reciprocal concepts. Since they are reciprocal, one of them cannot be used to explain the other or to supply its ground, but can at most be used only for logical purposes to bring seemingly different conceptions of the same object under a single concept (just as different fractions of the same value are reduced to lowest terms).

However, one recourse still remains open to us, namely, to inquire whether we do not take one point of view when by means of freedom we think of ourselves as a priori efficient causes, and another point of view when we represent ourselves with reference to our actions as effects which we see before our eyes.

No subtle reflection is required for the following observation, which even the commonest understanding may be supposed to make, though it does so in its own fashion through some obscure discrimination of the faculty of judgment which it calls feeling: all representations that come to us without our choice 451 (such as those of the senses) enable us to know objects only as they affect us; what they may be in themselves remains unknown to us. Therefore, even with the closest attention and the greatest clarity that the understanding can bring to such representations, we can attain to a mere knowledge of appearances but never to knowledge of things in themselves. Once this distinction is made (perhaps merely as a result of observing the difference between representations which are given to us from without and in which we are passive from those which we produce entirely from ourselves and in which we show our own activity); then there follows of itself that we must admit and assume that behind the appearances there is something else which is not appearance, namely, things in themselves. Inasmuch as we can never cognize them except as they affect us [through our senses], we must admit that we can never come any nearer to them nor ever know what they are in themselves. This must provide a distinction, however crude, between a world of sense and a world of understanding; the former can vary considerably according to the difference of sensibility [and sense impressions] in various observers, while the latter, which is the basis of the former, remains always the same. Even with regard to himself, a man cannot presume to know what he is in himself by means of the acquaintance which he has through internal sensation. For since he does not, as it were, create himself and since he acquires the concept of himself not a priori but empirically, it is natural that he can attain knowledge even about himself only through inner sense and therefore only through the appearance of his nature and the way in which his consciousness is affected. But yet he must necessarily assume that beyond his own subject's constitution as composed of nothing but appearances there must be something else as basis, namely, his ego as constituted in itself. Therefore with regard to mere perception and the receptivity of sensations, he must count himself as belonging to the world of sense; but with regard to whatever there may be in him of pure activity (whatever reaches consciousness immediately and not through affecting the senses) he must count himself as belonging to the intellectual world, of which he has, however, no further knowledge.

Such a conclusion must be reached by a reflective man regarding all the things that may be presented 452 to him. It is presumably to be found even in the most ordinary understanding, which, as is well known, is quite prone to expect that behind objects of the senses there is something else invisible and acting of itself. But such understanding spoils all this by making the invisible again sensible, i.e., it wants to make the invisible an object of intuition; and thereby does it become not a bit wiser.

Now man really finds in himself a faculty which distinguishes him from all other things and even from himself insofar as he is affected by objects. That faculty is reason, which as pure spontaneity is elevated even above understanding. For although the latter is also spontaneous and does not, like sense, merely contain representations that arise only when one is affected by things (and is therefore passive), yet understanding can produce by its activity no other concepts than those which merely serve to bring sensuous representations [intuitions] under rules and thereby to unite them in one consciousness. Without this use of sensibility, understanding would think nothing at all. Reason, on the other hand, shows such a pure spontaneity in the case of what are called ideas that it goes far beyond anything that sensibility can offer and shows its highest occupation in distinguishing the world of sense from the world of understanding, thereby prescribing limits to the understanding itself.

Therefore a rational being must regard himself qua intelligence (and hence not from the side of his lower powers) as belonging not to the world of sense but to the world of understanding. Therefore he has two standpoints from which he can regard himself and know laws of the use of his powers and hence of all his actions; first, insofar as he belongs to the world of sense subject to laws of nature (heteronomy); secondly, insofar as he belongs to the intelligible world subject to laws which, independent of nature, are not empirical but are founded only on reason.

As a rational being and hence as belonging to the intelligible world, can man never think of the causality of his own will except under the idea of freedom; for independence from the determining causes of the world of sense (an independence which reason must always attribute to itself) is freedom. Now the idea of freedom is inseparably connected with the concept of autonomy, and this in turn with the universal principle of morality, which ideally is the ground of all 453 actions of rational beings, just as natural law is the ground of all appearances.

The suspicion that we raised earlier is now removed, viz., that there might be a hidden circle involved in our inference from freedom to autonomy, and from this to the moral law — this is to say that we had perhaps laid down the idea of freedom only for the sake of the moral law in order subsequently to infer this law in its turn from freedom, and that we had therefore not been able to assign any ground at all for this law but had only assumed it by begging a principle which well-disposed souls would gladly concede us but which we could never put forward as a demonstrable proposition. But now we see that when we think of ourselves as free, we transfer ourselves into the intelligible world as members and know the autonomy of the will together with its consequence, morality; whereas when we think of ourselves as obligated, we consider ourselves as belonging to the world of sense and yet at the same time to the intelligible world.

How Is a Categorical Imperative Possible?

The rational being counts himself, qua intelligence, as belonging to the intelligible world, and only insofar as he is an efficient cause belonging to the intelligible world does he call his causality a will. But on the other side, he is conscious of himself as being also a part of the world of sense, where his actions are found as mere appearances of that causality. The possibility of these actions cannot, however, be discerned through such causality, which we do not know; rather, these actions as belonging to the world of sense must be viewed as determined by other appearances, namely, desires and inclinations. Therefore, if I were solely a member of the intelligible world, then all my actions would perfectly conform to the principle of the autonomy of a pure will; if I were solely a part of the world of sense, my actions would have to be taken as in complete conformity with the natural law of desires and inclinations, i.e., with the heteronomy of nature. (My actions would in the first case rest on the supreme principle of morality, in the second case on that of happiness.) But the intelligible world contains the ground of the world of sense and therefore also the ground of its laws; consequently, the intelligible world is (and must be thought of as) directly legislative for my will (which belongs wholly to the intelligible world). Therefore, even though on the one hand I must regard myself as a being belonging to the world of sense, yet on the other hand shall I have to know myself as an intelligence and as subject 454 to the law of the intelligible world, i.e., to reason, which contains this law in the idea of freedom, and hence to know myself as subject to the autonomy of the will. Consequently, I must regard the laws of the intelligible world as imperatives for me, and the actions conforming to this principle as duties.

And thus are categorical imperatives possible because the idea of freedom makes me a member of an intelligible world. Now if I were a member of only that world, all my actions *would* always accord with autonomy of the will. But since I intuit myself at the same time as a member of the world of sense, my actions *ought* so to accord. This categorical *ought* presents a synthetic a priori proposition, whereby in addition to my will as affected by sensuous desires there is added further the idea of the same will, but as belonging to the intelligible world, pure and practical of itself, and as containing the supreme condition of the former will insofar as reason is concerned. All this is similar to the way in which concepts [categories] of the understanding, which of themselves signify nothing but the form of law in general, are added to intuitions of the world of sense and thus make possible synthetic a priori propositions, upon which all knowledge of nature rests.

The practical use of ordinary human reason bears out the correctness of this deduction. There is no one, not even the meanest villain, provided only that he is otherwise accustomed to the use of reason, who, when presented with examples of honesty of purpose, of steadfastness in following good maxims, and of sympathy and general benevolence (even when involved with great sacrifices of advantages and comfort) does not wish that he might also possess these qualities. Yet he cannot attain these in himself only because of his inclinations and impulses; but at the same time he wishes to be free from such inclinations which are a burden to him. He thereby proves that by having a will free of sensuous impulses he transfers himself in thought into an order of things entirely different from that of his desires in the field of sensibility. Since he cannot expect to obtain by the aforementioned wish any gratification of his desires or any condition that would satisfy any of his actual or even conceivable inclinations (inasmuch as through such an expectation the very idea that elicited the wish would be deprived of its preeminence) he can only expect a greater intrinsic worth of his own person. This better person he believes himself to be when he transfers himself to the standpoint of a member of the intelligi- 455 ble world, to which he is involuntarily forced by the idea of freedom, i.e., of being independent of determination by causes of the world of sense. From this standpoint he is conscious of having a good will, which by his own admission constitutes the law for the bad will belonging to him as a member of the world of sense — a law whose authority he acknowledges even while he transgresses it. The moral *ought* is, therefore, a necessary *would* insofar as he is a member of the intelligible world, and is thought by him as an *ought* only insofar as he regards himself as being at the same time a member of the world of sense.

Concerning the Extreme Limit of All Practical Philosophy

All men think of themselves as free as far as their will is concerned. Hence arise all judgments upon actions as being such as ought to have been done, even though they were not done. But this freedom is not a concept of experience, nor can it be such, since it always holds, even though experience shows the opposite of those requirements represented as necessary under the presupposition of freedom. On the other hand, it is just as necessary that whatever happens should be determined without any exception according to laws of nature; and this necessity of nature is likewise no concept of experience, just because it involves the concept of necessity and thus of a priori knowledge. But this concept of nature is confirmed by experience and must inevitably be presupposed if there is to be possible experience, which is coherent knowledge of the objects of sense in accordance with universal laws. Freedom is, therefore, only an idea of reason whose objective reality is in itself questionable; but nature is a concept of the understanding, which proves, and necessarily must prove, its reality by examples from experience.

There arises from this a dialectic of reason, since the freedom attributed to the will seems to contradict the necessity of nature. And even though at this parting of the ways reason for speculative purposes finds the road of natural necessity much better worn and more serviceable than that of freedom, yet for practi-456 cal purposes the footpath of freedom is the only one upon which it is possible to make use of reason in our conduct. Therefore, it is just as impossible for the most subtle philosophy as for the most ordinary human reason to argue away freedom. Hence philosophy must assume that no real contradiction will be found between freedom and natural necessity in the same human actions, for it cannot give up the concept of nature any more than that of freedom.

Nevertheless, even though one might never be able to comprehend how freedom is possible, yet this apparent contradiction must at least be removed in a convincing manner. For if the thought of freedom contradicts itself or nature, which is equally necessary, then freedom would have to be completely given up in favor of natural necessity.

It would, however, be impossible to escape this contradiction if the subject, deeming himself free, were to think of himself in the same sense or in the very same relationship when he calls himself free as when he assumes himself subject to the law of nature regarding the same action. Therefore, an unavoidable problem of speculative philosophy is at least to show that its illusion regarding the contradiction rests on our thinking of man in a different sense and relation when we call him free from when we regard him as being a part of nature and hence as subject to the laws of nature. Hence it must show not only that both can coexist very well, but that both must be thought of as necessarily united in the same subject; for otherwise no explanation could be given as to why reason should be burdened with an idea which involves us in a perplexity that is solely embarrassing to reason in its theoretic use, even though it may without contradiction be united with another idea that is sufficiently established. This duty, however, is incumbent solely on speculative philosophy in order that it may clear the way for practical philosophy. Thus the philosopher has no option as to whether he will remove the apparent contradiction or leave it untouched; for in the latter case the theory regarding this could be *bonum vacans*,[56] into the possession of which the fatalist can justifiably enter and chase all morality out of its supposed property as occupying it without title.

Nevertheless, one cannot here say as yet that the boundary of practical philosophy begins. For the settlement of the controversy does not belong to practical philosophy; the latter only requires speculative reason 457 to put an end to the dissension in which it is entangled as regards theoretical questions in order that practical reason may have rest and security from external attacks that might make disputable the ground upon which it wants to build.

The just claim to freedom of the will made even by ordinary human reason is founded on the consciousness and the admitted presupposition that reason is independent of mere subjective determination by causes which together make up what belongs only to sensation and comes under the general designation of sensibility. Regarding himself in this way as intelligence, man thereby puts himself into another order of things. And when he thinks of himself as intelligence endowed with a will and consequently with causality, he puts himself into relation with determining grounds of a kind altogether different from the kind when he perceives himself as a phenomenon in the world of sense (as he really is also) and subjects his causality to external determination according to laws of nature. Now he soon realizes that both can—and indeed must—hold good at the same time. For there is not the slightest contradiction involved in saying

56. [Vacant property.]

that a thing as appearance (belonging to the world of sense) is subject to certain laws, while it is independent of those laws when regarded as a thing or being in itself. That man must represent and think of himself in this twofold way rests, on the one hand, upon the consciousness of himself as an object affected through the senses and, on the other hand, upon the consciousness of himself as intelligence, i.e., as independent of sensuous impulses in his use of reason (and hence as belonging to the intelligible world).

And hence man claims that he has a will which reckons to his account nothing that belongs merely to his desires and inclinations, and which, on the contrary, thinks of actions that can be performed only by disregarding all desires and sensuous incitements as being possible and as indeed being necessary for him. The causality of such actions lies in man as intelligence and lies in the laws of such effects and actions as are in accordance with principles of an intelligible world, of which he knows nothing more than that in such a world reason alone, and indeed pure reason independent of sensibility, gives the law. Furthermore, since he is in such a world his proper self only as intelligence (whereas regarded as a human being he is merely an appearance of himself), those laws apply to him immediately and categorically. Consequently, incitements from inclinations and impulses (and hence from the whole nature of the world of senses) cannot impair the laws of his willing insofar 458 as he is intelligence. Indeed he does not even hold himself responsible for such inclinations and impulses or ascribe them to his proper self, i.e., his will, although he does ascribe to his will any indulgence which he might extend to them if he allowed them any influence on his maxims to the detriment of the rational laws of his will.

When practical reason thinks itself into an intelligible world, it does not in the least thereby transcend its limits, as it would if it tried to enter it by intuition or sensation. The thought of an intelligible world is merely negative as regards the world of sense. The latter world does not give reason any laws for determining the will and is positive only in this single point, viz., it simultaneously combines freedom as negative determination with a positive faculty and even a causality of reason. This causality is designated as a will to act in such a way that the principle of actions may accord with the essential character of a rational cause, i.e., with the condition that the maxim of these actions have universal validity as a law. But if practical reason were to bring in an object of the will, i.e., a motive of action, from the intelligible world, then it would overstep its boundaries and pretend to be acquainted with something of which it knows nothing. The concept of an intelligible world is thus only a point of view which reason sees itself compelled to take outside of appearances in order to think of itself as practical. If the influences of sensibility were determining for man, reason would not be able to take this point of view, which is nonetheless necessary if he is not to be denied the consciousness of himself as intelligence and hence as a rational cause that is active through reason, i.e., free in its operation. This thought certainly involves the idea of an order and a legislation different from that of the mechanism of nature which applies to the world of sense; and it makes necessary the concept of an intelligible world (i.e., the whole of rational beings as things in themselves). But it makes not the slightest claim to anything more than to think of such a world as regards merely its formal condition—i.e., the universality of the will's maxims as laws and thus the will's autonomy, which alone is consistent with freedom. On the contrary, all laws determined by reference to an object yield heteronomy, which can be found only in laws of nature and can apply only to the world of sense.

But reason would overstep all its bounds if it under- 459 took to explain how pure reason can be practical. This is exactly the same problem as explaining how freedom is possible.

For we can explain nothing but what we can reduce to laws whose object can be given in some possible experience. But freedom is a mere idea, whose objective reality can in no way be shown in accordance with laws of nature and consequently not in any possible experience. Therefore, the idea of freedom can never admit of comprehension or even of insight, because it cannot by any analogy have an example falling under it. It holds only as a necessary presupposition of reason in a being who believes himself conscious of a will, i.e., of a faculty distinct from mere desire (namely, a faculty of determining himself to action as intelligence and hence in accordance with laws of reason independently of natural instincts). But where determination according to laws of nature ceases, there likewise ceases all explanation and nothing remains but defense, i.e., refutation of the objections of those who profess to have seen deeper into the essence of things and thereupon boldly declare freedom to be impossible. One can only show them that their supposed discovery of a contradiction lies nowhere but here: in order to make the law of nature applicable to human actions, they have necessarily had to regard man as an appearance; and now when they are required to think of man qua intelligence as thing in himself as well, they still persist in regarding him as appearance. In that case, to be sure, the exemption of man's causality (i.e., his will) from all the natural laws of the world of sense would, as regards one and the same subject, give rise to a contradiction. But this disappears if they would but bethink themselves and admit, as is reasonable, that behind appearances there must lie as their ground also things in themselves (though hidden) and that the laws of their operations cannot be expected to be the same as those that govern their appearances.

460   The subjective impossibility of explaining freedom of the will is the same as the impossibility of discovering and explaining an interest[57] which man can take in moral laws. Nevertheless, he does indeed take such an interest, the basis of which in us is called moral feeling. Some people have falsely construed this feeling to be the standard of our moral judgment, whereas it must rather be regarded as the subjective effect that the law exercises upon the will, while reason alone furnishes the objective grounds of such moral feeling.

57. Interest is that by which reason becomes practical, i.e., a cause determining the will. Therefore one says of rational beings only that they take an interest in something; nonrational creatures feel only sensuous impulses. Reason takes an immediate interest in the action only when the universal validity of the maxim of the action is a sufficient determining ground of the will. Such an interest alone is pure. But when reason is able to determine the will only by means of another object of desire or under the presupposition of some special feeling in the subject, then reason takes only a mediate interest in the action. And since reason of itself alone without the help of experience can discover neither objects of the will nor a special feeling underlying the will, the latter interest would be only empirical and not a pure rational interest. The logical interest of reason (viz., to extend its insights) is never immediate, but presupposes purposes for which reason might be used.

In order to will what reason alone prescribes as an *ought* for sensuously affected rational beings, there certainly must be a power of reason to infuse a feeling of pleasure or satisfaction in the fulfillment of duty, and hence there has to be a causality of reason to determine sensibility in accordance with rational principles. But it is quite impossible to discern, i.e., to make a priori conceivable, how a mere thought which itself contains nothing sensuous can produce a sensation of pleasure or displeasure. For here is a special kind of causality regarding which, as with all causality, we can determine nothing a priori but must consult experience alone. However, experience can provide us with no relation of cause and effect except between two objects of experience. But in this case pure reason by means of mere ideas (which furnish no object at all for experience) is to be the cause of an effect that admittedly lies in experience. Consequently, there is for us men no possibility at all for an explanation as to how and why the universality of a maxim as a law, and hence morality, interests us. This much only is certain: the moral law is valid for us not because it interests us (for this is heteronomy and the dependence of practical reason on sensibility, viz., on an underlying feeling whereby reason could 461 never be morally legislative); but, rather, the moral law interests us because it is valid for us as men, since it has sprung from our will as intelligence and hence from our proper self. But what belongs to mere appearance is necessarily subordinated by reason to the nature of the thing in itself.

Thus the question as to how a categorical imperative is possible can be answered to the extent that there can be supplied the sole presupposition under which such an imperative is alone possible — namely, the idea of freedom. The necessity of this presupposition is discernible, and this much is sufficient for the practical use of reason, i.e., for being convinced as to the validity of this imperative, and hence also of the moral law; but how this presupposition itself is possible can never be discerned by any human reason. However, on the presupposition of freedom of the will of an intelligence, there necessarily follows the will's autonomy as the formal condition under which alone the will can be determined. To presuppose this freedom of the will (without involving any contradiction with the principle of natural necessity in the connection of appearances in the world of sense) is not only quite possible (as speculative philosophy can show), but is without any further condition also necessary for a rational being conscious of his causality through reason and hence conscious of a will (which is different from desires) as he makes such freedom in practice, i.e., in idea, the underlying condition of all his voluntary actions. But how pure reason can be practical by itself without other incentives taken from whatever source—i.e., how the mere principle of the universal validity of all reason's maxims as laws (which would certainly be the form of a pure practical reason) can by itself, without any matter (object) of the will in which some antecedent interest might be taken, furnish an incentive and produce an interest which could be called purely moral; or, in other words, how pure reason could be practical: to explain all this is quite beyond the power of human reason, and all the effort and work of seeking such an explanation is wasted.

It is just the same as if I tried to find out how freedom itself is possible as causality of a will. For I
462 thereby leave the philosophical basis of explanation, and I have no other basis. Now I could indeed flutter about in the world of intelligences, i.e., in the intelligible world still remaining to me. But even though I have an idea of such a world—an idea which has its own good grounds—yet I have not the slightest acquaintance with such a world and can never attain such acquaintance by all the efforts of my natural faculty of reason. This intelligible world signifies only a something that remains over when I have excluded from the determining grounds of my will everything that belongs to the world of sense, so as to restrict the principle of having all motives come from the field of sensibility. By so doing I set bounds to this field and show that it does not contain absolutely everything within itself but that beyond it there is still something more, regarding which, however, I have no further acquaintance. After the exclusion of all matter, i.e., cognition of objects, from pure reason which thinks this ideal, nothing remains over for me except such reason's form, viz., the practical law of the universal validity of maxims; and in conformity with this law I think of reason in its relation to a pure intelligible world as a possible efficient cause, i.e., as a cause determining the will. An incentive must in this case be wholly absent; this idea of an intelligible world would here have to be itself the incentive or

have to be that in which reason originally took an interest. But to make this conceivable is precisely the problem that we cannot solve.

Here then is the extreme limit of all moral inquiry. To determine this limit is of great importance for the following considerations. On the one hand, reason should not, to the detriment of morals, search around in the world of sense for the supreme motive and for some interest that is conceivable but is nonetheless empirical. On the other hand, reason should not flap its wings impotently, without leaving the spot, in a space that for it is empty, namely, the space of transcendent concepts that is called the intelligible world, and thereby lose itself among mere phantoms of the brain. Furthermore, the idea of a pure intelligible world regarded as a whole of all intelligences to which we ourselves belong as rational beings (even though we are from another standpoint also members of the world of sense) remains always a useful and permissible idea for the purpose of a rational belief, although all knowledge ends at its boundary. This idea produces in us a lively interest in the moral law by means of the splendid ideal of a universal kingdom of ends in themselves (rational beings), to which we can be- 463 long as members only if we carefully conduct ourselves according to maxims of freedom as if they were laws of nature.

Concluding Remark

The speculative use of reason with regard to nature leads to the absolute necessity of some supreme cause of the world. The practical use of reason with reference to freedom leads also to absolute necessity, but only to the necessity of the laws of the actions of a rational being as such. Now it is an essential principle of all use of our reason to push its knowledge to a consciousness of its necessity (for without necessity there would be no rational knowledge). But there is an equally essential restriction of the same reason that it cannot have insight into the necessity either of what is or what does happen or of what should happen, unless there is presupposed a condition under which it is or does happen or should happen. In this way, however, the satisfaction of reason is only further and further postponed by the continual inquiry after the condition. Reason, therefore, restlessly seeks the unconditionally necessary and sees itself compelled to assume this without having any means of making such necessity conceivable; reason is happy enough if only it can find a concept which is compatible with this assumption. Hence there is no fault in our deduction of the supreme principle of morality, but rather a reproach which must be made against human reason generally, involved in the fact that reason cannot render conceivable the absolute necessity of an unconditioned practical law (such as the categorical imperative must be). Reason cannot be blamed for not being willing to explain this necessity by means of a condition, namely, by basing it on some underlying interest, because in that case the law would no longer be moral, i.e., a supreme law of freedom. And so even though we do not indeed grasp the practical unconditioned necessity of the moral imperative, we do nevertheless grasp its inconceivability. This is all that can be fairly asked of a philosophy which strives in its principles to reach the very limit of human reason.

G.W.F. Hegel

G.W.F. Hegel was born in Stuttgart, Germany, in 1770. He studied at the University of Tübingen, where he became close friends with the poet Hölderlin. His early thought was influenced by Kant, Fichte, and Schelling, but also by his studies of Spinoza, Greek philosophy, and the New Testament. From 1801 to 1806 Hegel taught at the University of Jena, where he completed his *Phenomenology of Mind* as Napoleon's forces were bombing the city. After eight years as rector at a Gymnasium in Nuremberg and two years at the University of Heidelberg, the taught at the University of Berlin until his death in 1831. His words include *Phenomenology* (1807), *Science of Logic* (1812–16), *Encyclopedia of the Philosophical Sciences* (1817), and *Philosophy of Right* (1820).

Hegel's philosophy is called "Absolute Idealism," the view that all reality is shaped and constituted by the mind. But it is important to see that this kind of idealism is quite different from the subjective idealism of someone like Berkeley. First, the German word for "mind," *Geist*, refers not just to individual minds, but to something that is essentially shared and is realized in what people *do*. It is closer to what we mean by "spirit" when we speak of the "spirit on campus" or a team's "fighting spirit." And, second, instead of denying the existence of matter, Hegel's idealism holds that mind needs a material world in order to be able to express and fulfill itself in a concrete form. In this respect, the "ideas" in this idealism are more like the ordering Ideas in Plato's philosophy than like Berkeley's mental ideas. To say that mind constitutes reality, then, is to say that there is a rational order underlying all reality. Or, as Hegel puts it, "the real is rational and the rational is real."

Hegel's philosophy grows out of Kant's theory in *Critique of Pure Reason*. Kant argued that reality is not something that is simply "out there" waiting for us to try to grasp it, but is instead something that is constituted through our cognitive activity as knowers. This idea is summed up in Kant's "supreme principle," which says that "the conditions of the *possibility of experience* in general are likewise conditions of the *possibility of the objects of experience*." The point here is that "transcendental apperception," the pure subject, confers form on reality through pure intuition and, most important for Hegel, through the synthesizing power of its concepts. Since our conceptualizing makes possible the objective world we encounter in our experience, we can have knowledge only of "phenomena," that is, things as they appear to us through our concepts.

Hegel draws from Kant the idea that the pure conceptualizing subject (or, as he calls it, the "concept") is the source of the necessary and universal structure permeating all reality. But he rejects Kant's claim that we can never know reality as it is in itself. If we can talk about a reality that is supposedly beyond our comprehension, Hegel says, then we have already comprehended it, and so it *is* known. Thus, there is no room for the notion of a reality that is alien to or totally distinct from the mind. Moreover, Hegel rejects Kant's uncritical assumption that the Newtonian science of his own day was the highest truth to which science could aspire. In Hegel's view, any science that regards the world as consisting of natural kinds simply "out there" in the world is only a temporary stage on the way to true science. Such a view, which Hegel calls "Understanding," will have to give way to "Reason," a more holistic science that grasps the fact that the nature of anything is defined by its relation to what it is not—its "other" or "negation"—within the systematic whole constituted by *Geist*. At the level of Reason, all dualistic oppositions—including those of subject and object, mind and matter, self and others—will be seen for what they are: only partial and distorted manifestations of *Geist*.

The *Phenomenology of Mind* is supposed to lead us to true science and its recognition of the identity of thinking and being. The book's Introduction begins with a critique of the assumption, fundamental to traditional epistemology, that we are at the most basic levels *minds* attempting to correctly represent an ultimate *reality* (the "Truth," the "Absolute," or the "in itself") presumed to exist totally independent of our minds. Given this subject/object model of our situation, Hegel believes, skepticism is inevitable, for once subject and object are separated, there is no way to find out whether our knowing (regarded as an active tool or a passive medium) is giving us an accurate picture of reality. Despite this problem, however, scientific inquiry keeps making important advances in knowledge, and this seems to suggest that what is problematic is not science, but the uncritical presuppositions built into epistemology's subject/object model.

In order to overcome the subject/object model, it is necessary to work within the confines of science as it is today, within what Hegel calls "apparent science," and to get that science to recognize that it is inadequate by its own criteria. Hegel's conception of knowledge as an appearing, a phenomenon, displays his profound insight into the *historical* nature of knowledge. In his view, history has been characterized by a series of different "shapes" (*Gestalten*) of consciousness, what we today might call "worldviews" or "paradigms," which have evolved from the most elementary models to the most sophisticated ones in our contemporary world. What leads consciousness to move from more primitive models to more sophisticated ones is the discovery of internal inconsistencies within the earlier outlooks. This "dialectical" movement will continue, Hegel thinks, until consciousness goes through all possible models of knowledge and arrives at absolute truth (the unity of all reality under the Concept, which he calls the "Idea").

• • •

The most readable discussion of Hegel is Robert C. Solomon, *In the Spirit of Hegel* (Oxford: Oxford University Press, 1983). Charles Taylor, *Hegel* (Cambridge: Cambridge University Press, 1975) provides a valuable overview of Hegel. Werner Marx, *Hegel's Phenomenology of Spirit* (New York: Harper & Row, 1975) is an excellent analysis of the Introduction to the *Phenomenology*. Alasdair MacIntyre, *Hegel: A Collection of Critical Essays* (New York: Doubleday, 1972), and Michael Inwood, *Hegel* (Oxford: Oxford University Press, 1985) are good collections.

C.G.

Phenomenology of Mind

INTRODUCTION

It is natural to suppose that, before philosophy enters upon its subject proper—namely, the actual knowledge of what truly is—it is first necessary to come to an understanding concerning knowledge, which is looked upon as the instrument by which to take possession of the Absolute, or as the medium through which one gets in touch with it. The concern seems legitimate, partly because there are various kinds of knowledge, among which one might be better adapted than another for the attainment of our purpose, so that a wrong choice of means is possible; partly, again, because knowing is a faculty of a definite kind and with a determinate range, so that, without the more precise determination of its nature and limits, we might take hold of clouds of error instead of the heaven of truth.

This apprehensiveness is sure to develop into the conviction that the whole enterprise which sets out to secure for consciousness by means of knowledge what exists in itself, is in its very nature absurd, and that between knowledge and the Absolute there lies a boundary which completely cuts off the one from the other. For if knowledge is the instrument for gaining access to absolute Reality, the suggestion immediately occurs that the application of an instrument to anything does *not* leave it as it is for itself, but rather entails a molding and alteration of it. Or, again, if knowledge is not an instrument we actively employ, but is instead a kind of passive medium through which the light of the truth reaches us, then here, too, we do not receive the truth as it is in itself, but only as it is through and in this medium. In either case, we employ a means that immediately brings about the very opposite of its own end; or, rather, the absurdity lies in making use of any means at all.

It seems indeed open to us to find a remedy for this parlous state by gaining knowledge of the way the *instrument* operates. For it would thereby become possible to remove from the result the part which, in our idea of the Absolute received through that instrument, belongs to the instrument, and thus to get the truth in its purity. But this "improvement" would as a matter of fact, only bring us back to the point where we were before. If we take away from a definitely formed thing that which the instrument has done in the shaping of it, then the thing (in this case, the Absolute) stands before us once more just as it was previous to all this trouble, which as we now see, was superfluous. If the Absolute were only to be brought on the whole nearer to us by this agency, without any change being wrought in it, like a bird caught by a limestick, it would certainly scorn a trick of that sort, if it were not in and for itself, and by its own will, with us from the start. For a trick is what knowledge in such a case would be, since by all its busy toil and trouble it gives itself the air of doing something quite different from bringing about a relation that is merely immediate, and so a waste of time to establish. Or, again, if the examination of knowledge, which we represent as a *medium*, is supposed to make us acquainted with the law of its refraction, it is likewise useless to eliminate this effect from the result. For knowledge is not the refraction of the ray, but the ray itself by which the truth becomes accessible to us, and if this be removed, then only a bare direction or the empty place would be indicated.

Meanwhile, if the fear of falling into error introduces an element of distrust into science, which without any scruples of that sort goes to work and actually does know, it is not easy to understand why, conversely, a distrust should not be placed in this very distrust itself, and we should be concerned that the fear of error is already the error itself. As a matter of fact, this fear presupposes something, indeed a great deal, as truth, and supports its scruples and inferences on what should itself be examined beforehand to see whether it is truth. To be precise, it starts with ideas about knowledge as an instrument, and as a medium, and it presupposes a *distinction between ourselves and this knowledge.* More especially, it takes for granted that the Absolute stands *on one side*, and that *knowledge stands on the other side*, by itself and cut off from the Absolute, though still something real. In other words, it presupposes that knowledge, which, by being outside the Absolute, is certainly also outside the truth, is nevertheless true—a position which, while calling itself fear of error, shows itself rather as fear of the truth.

This conclusion comes from the fact that the Absolute alone is true, or that the True is alone absolute. One may set it aside by saying that a knowledge which does not indeed know the Absolute as science wants to do, is nonetheless true too; and that knowledge in general, though it may possibly be incapable of grasping the Absolute, can still be capable of truth of another kind. But we shall see as we proceed that random talk like this leads in the long run to a confused distinction between an absolute truth and a truth of some other sort, and that "absolute," "knowledge," and so on, are words which presuppose a meaning that first has to be found.

With such useless ideas and expressions about knowledge, as that it is an instrument to take hold of the Absolute, or a medium through which we have a glimpse of truth, and so on (external relations to which all these ideas of a knowledge which is separated from the Absolute and an Absolute separated from knowledge in the last resort lead), we need not concern ourselves. Nor need we trouble about the excuses which create the incapacity of science out of the presupposition of such relations, in order at once to be rid of the toil of science, and to assume the air of serious and zealous effort about it. Instead of being troubled with giving answers to all these, they may be straight away rejected as adventitious and arbitrary ideas; and the use which is here made of words like "absolute," "knowledge," as also "objective" and "subjective," and innumerable others, whose meaning is assumed to be familiar to everyone, might well be regarded as so much deception. For to give the impression that their significance is universally familiar, and that everyone indeed possesses their concept, looks rather like an attempt to dispense with the only important matter, which is just to provide this concept. With better right, on the contrary, we might spare ourselves the trouble of taking any notice at all of such ideas and ways of talking which would have

the effect of warding off science altogether, for they make a mere empty show of knowledge, which vanishes at once when science comes on the scene.

But science, in the very fact that it comes on the scene, is itself an appearance; its "coming on the scene" is not yet *itself* carried out in all the length and breadth of its truth. In this regard, it is a matter of indifference whether we consider that science is the appearance because it comes on the scene *alongside another* kind of knowledge, or call that other untrue knowledge its process of appearing. Science, however, must liberate itself from this semblance, and it can do so only by turning against it. For science cannot simply reject an untrue form of knowledge and treat it as a common view of things, and then assure us that it itself is an entirely different kind of knowledge, for which the other is of no account at all; nor can it appeal to the fact that in this other there are presages of a better. By giving that *assurance*, it would declare its force and value to lie in its bare *existence*; but the untrue knowledge also appeals to the fact that it *is*, and assures us that to it *science* is nothing. One barren assurance, however, is of just as much value as another. Still less can science appeal to the presages of something better that is to be found in the untrue knowledge, to the signs that point the way toward science. For it would, on the one hand, be appealing again in the same way to the mere fact of its existence; on the other hand, it would only be appealing to itself, to the way it exists in untrue knowledge. In other words, it would be appealing to a bad form of its own existence, to its appearance rather than to what it is in and for itself. For this reason we shall here undertake the presentation of knowledge as an appearance.

Now because this presentation has for its object only apparent knowledge, the presentation itself seems not to be science, free and self-moving in the shape proper to itself. But the presentation may, from this point of view, be taken as the pathway of natural consciousness which is pressing forward to true knowledge. Or it may be regarded as the path of the soul, which is traversing the series of its own forms of embodiment, like stages appointed for it by its own nature, that it may rise to the level of the Spirit when, through the complete experience of its own self, it arrives at the knowledge of what it is in itself.

Natural consciousness will prove itself to be only

a concept of knowledge, or not real knowledge. Since, however, it immediately takes itself to be the real and genuine knowledge, this pathway has a negative significance for it, and what is actually the realization of the concept means for it rather the ruin and over-throw of itself, for on this road it loses its own truth. Because of that, the road can be looked on as the path of *doubt*, or more properly a highway of despair. For what happens there is not what is usually under-stood by doubting: a jostling against this or that sup-posed truth, the outcome of which is a dispelling of the doubt and a return to the former truth, so that at the end the matter is taken as it was before. Instead, this pathway is the conscious insight into the untruth of apparent knowledge, for which what is most real is, after all, only the unrealized concept. On that account, too, this thoroughgoing skepticism is not that with which an earnest zeal for truth and science fancies it has prepared and equipped itself for these purposes, namely, the *resolve*, in science, not to de-liver oneself over to the thoughts of others on their mere authority, but to examine everything for oneself, and only follow one's own conviction, or, still better, to produce everything oneself, and hold only one's own act for truth.

The series of shapes, which consciousness traverses on this road, is instead the detailed history of the *education* of consciousness itself to the level of sci-ence. That resolve presents this mental education in the simple form of something immediately finished and complete, as having already taken place; this pathway of natural consciousness, in contrast, is, as opposed to this untruth, the actual fulfillment of that process. To follow one's own conviction is certainly more than to hand oneself over to authority; but by the conversion of opinion held on authority into opinion held out of personal conviction, the content of what is held is not necessarily altered, and truth has not thereby taken the place of error. The only difference between sticking to a system of opinion and prejudice on the authority of others and holding to one based on personal conviction is the conceit inherent in the latter. Skepticism, directed to the whole compass of apparent consciousness, in contrast, makes the mind for the first time qualified to test what truth is, since it brings about a despair regarding what are called natural views, thoughts, and opinions, whether these are called personal or belonging to others. If the con-sciousness proceeds *straight away* to the examination and is still filled and hampered with these views, it as a matter of fact is incapable of what it wants to undertake.

The *completeness* of the forms of unreal conscious-ness will be brought about precisely through the necessity of the advance and the necessity of their connection with one another. To make this compre-hensible we may remark by way of a preliminary that the exposition of untrue consciousness in its untruth is not a merely *negative* process. Such a one-sided view of it is what the natural consciousness generally adopts, and a knowledge which makes this one-sided-ness its essence is one of those shapes assumed by incomplete consciousness that occurs along the way and will present itself. This view is skepticism, which always sees in the result only *pure nothingness*, and abstracts from the fact that this nothingness is determi-nate, that it is the nothingness of *that out of which it results*. Nothingness, however, is in fact only the true result when taken as the nothing of what it comes from; it is then a *determinate* nothingness and has a *content*. The skepticism which ends with the abstrac-tion "nothing" or "emptiness" can advance from this not a step farther, but must wait and see whether there is possibly anything new offered, and what that is—in order to cast it into the same empty abyss. When, in contrast, the result is apprehended as it truly is, as *determinate* negation, a new form has thereby immediately arisen, and in the negation the transition is made by which the progress through the complete succession of forms comes about of itself.

The *goal*, however, is fixed for knowledge just as necessarily as the succession in the process. The ter-minus is at that point where knowledge is no longer compelled to go beyond itself, where it finds its own self, and the concept corresponds to the object and the object to the concept. The progress towards this goal consequently is without a halt and at no earlier stage is satisfaction to be found. That which is con-fined to a life of nature is unable of itself to go beyond its immediate existence; but it is forced beyond that by something other than itself, and this uprooting is its *death*. Consciousness, however, is to itself its own *concept*; hence, it immediately transcends what is limited, and, since this limitedness belongs to it, con-sciousness transcends its own self. Along with the particular there is at the same time set up the "beyond," even if this is only *beside* what is limited, as in the case of spatial intuition. Consciousness, therefore, suffers this violence at its own hands; it destroys its own limited satisfaction. Feeling this violence, anxiety may well withdraw from the truth, and struggle to preserve for itself what is in danger of being lost. But it can find no rest. Should it wish to remain in unthinking indolence, thought will agitate the thoughtlessness, and its restlessness will disturb that indolence. Or if it takes its stand in a form of sentimentality, which assures us it finds everything *good in its kind*, this assurance likewise will suffer violence at the hands of reason, which finds something *not* good just because and in so far as it is a *kind*. Or, again, fear of the truth may conceal itself from itself and others behind the pretense that it is its burning zeal for the truth that makes it so difficult, nay impossible, to find any other truth except that of which alone vanity is capable—that of being ever so much more clever than any thoughts that one gets from oneself or others. This sort of conceit, which understands how to belittle every truth and turn away from it back into itself, and gloats over this its own private understanding, which always knows how to dissipate every possible thought, and to find, instead of all the content, merely the barren "I"—this is a satisfaction which must be left to itself, for it flees the universal and seeks only an isolated being-for-itself.

As the foregoing has been stated, provisionally and in general, concerning the manner and the necessity of the process of the inquiry, it may also be of further service to make some observations regarding the *method* of carrying this out. This exposition, viewed as a relation of *science* to *apparent* knowledge, and as an *inquiry* and *critical examination into the reality of knowing*, does not seem able to be effected without some presupposition which is laid down as an ultimate *criterion*. For an examination consists in applying an accepted standard, and, on the final agreement or disagreement therewith of what is tested, deciding whether what is examined is right or wrong; the standard in general, and science as well, were this the criterion, is thereby accepted as the *essence* or *in itself*. But here, where science first appears on the scene, neither science nor any sort of standard has justified itself as the essence or ultimate in itself; and without this, no examination seems able to be instituted.

This contradiction and its removal will become more distinct if, to begin with, we call to mind the abstract determinations of knowledge and of truth as they are found in consciousness. Consciousness, we find, *distinguishes* from itself something, to which at the same time it *relates* itself; or, to use the current expression, there is something *for* consciousness. And the determinate form of this process of *relating*, or of there *being* something *for* a consciousness, is *knowledge*. But from this being for another we distinguish *being in itself*; what is related to knowledge is likewise distinguished from it, and posited as also *existing* outside this relation. The aspect of being in itself is called *Truth*. What really lies in these determinations does not further concern us here; for since the object of our inquiry is apparent knowledge, its determinations are also taken up, in the first instance, as they are immediately offered to us. And they are offered to us very much in the way we have just stated.

If now our inquiry deals with the truth of knowledge, it appears that we are inquiring what knowledge is *in itself*. But in this inquiry knowledge is *our* object, it is *for us*. Thus, its essential nature [*Ansich*], were this to come to light, would be rather its being for *us*. Whatever we should assert to be its essence would rather be, not the truth of knowledge, but only our knowledge of it. The essence or the criterion would lie in us, and what was to be compared with this standard, and decided upon as a result of this comparison, would not necessarily have to recognize that criterion.

But the nature of the object which we are examining surmounts this separation, or semblance of separation, and its presupposition. Consciousness furnishes its own criterion in itself, and the inquiry will therefore be a comparison of itself with its own self; for the distinction just made falls inside itself. In consciousness, there is one element *for* an other, that is, consciousness in general, contains the specific character of the moment of knowledge. At the same time, this "other" is to consciousness not merely *for it*, but is also outside this relation, or has a being *in itself*, that is, there is the moment of truth. Thus, in what consciousness inside itself declares to be the in itself or truth, we have the criterion which it itself sets up, and by which we are to measure its knowledge. Suppose we call *knowledge* the *concept*, and call the essence or *truth* the entity or the *object*, then the examination consists in seeing whether the concept corresponds with the object. But if we call the *essence* or the in itself *of the object* the *concept*, and, on the other side, understand by the *object* the object as *object*, that is, the way the it is *for an other*, then the examination consists in our seeing whether the object corresponds to its concept. It is clear, of course, that both of these processes are the same. The essential fact to be borne in mind throughout the whole inquiry, however, is that both these moments, *concept* and *object*, "*being for another*" and "*being in itself*," themselves fall within that knowledge which we are examining. Consequently we do not require to bring criteria with us, nor to apply *our* fancies and thoughts in the inquiry. And just by our leaving these aside we are enabled to treat and address the subject as it actually is *in itself* and *for itself*.

But not only in this respect, that concept and object, the criterion and what is to be tested, are ready to hand in consciousness itself, is any addition of ours superfluous, but we are also spared the trouble of comparing these two moments and of making an *examination* in the strict sense of the term. In this respect, since consciousness tests and examines itself, all we are left to do is simply and solely *to look on*. For consciousness is, on the one hand, consciousness of the object, and, on the other, consciousness of itself; it is consciousness of what to it is true, and consciousness of its knowledge of that truth. Since both are *for the same consciousness*, consciousness is itself their comparison: it is the same consciousness that decides and knows whether the knowledge of the object corresponds with this object or not. The object, it is true, appears only to be in such wise for consciousness as consciousness knows it. Consciousness does not seem able to get, so to say, behind it, to get at it as it is *not for consciousness* but *in itself*, and consequently seems also unable to test knowledge by it. But just because consciousness has, in general, knowledge of an object, there is already present the distinction that what the object is *in itself* is one thing *to* consciousness, while knowledge, or the being of the object *for* consciousness, is *to it* another moment. Upon this distinction, which is present as a fact, the examination turns. Should both moments, when thus compared, not correspond, then consciousness seems bound to alter its knowledge in order to make it fit the object. But in the alteration of the knowledge, the object itself also, in point of fact, is altered. For

the knowledge which existed was essentially a knowledge of the object: with a change in the knowledge, the object also becomes different, since it belonged essentially to this knowledge. Hence consciousness comes to find that what formerly to it was the *in itself* is not what is in itself or what was *in itself* was so only *for consciousness*. Since, then, in the case of its object consciousness finds its knowledge not corresponding with this object, the object likewise fails to hold out. Or, alternatively, the criterion for examining is altered when that, whose criterion this was to be, does not hold its ground in the course of the examination. Thus the examination is not only an examination of knowledge, but also of the criterion used in the process.

This *dialectical* process that consciousness executes on itself—on its knowledge as well as on its object— *insofar as the new and true object arises out of it*, is precisely what is termed *experience*. In this connection, there is a moment in the process just mentioned which should be brought into more decided prominence, and by which a new light is cast on the scientific aspect of the following exposition. Consciousness knows *something*; this something is the essence or what is *in itself*. This object, however, is also the *in itself* for consciousness. Hence arises the ambiguity of this truth. Consciousness, as we see, now has two objects: one is the first *in itself*, the second is the existence *for consciousness of this in itself*. The last object appears at first sight to be merely the reflection of consciousness into itself, that is, an idea not of an object, but solely of its knowledge of that first object. But as was already indicated, by that very process the first object is altered; it ceases to be what is in itself and becomes consciously something which is *in itself* only *for consciousness*. Consequently, then, what this in itself is *for consciousness* is the truth. This means, however, that this is the *essence*, or the *object* which consciousness has. This new object contains the nothingness of the first; it is the experience resulting from that first object.

In this presentation of the course of experience, there is an element in virtue of which it does not seem to be in agreement with what is ordinarily understood by experience. This is the transition from the first object and the knowledge of it to the other object, in regard to which we say we have had experience. This was so stated that the knowledge of the first object, the existence *for consciousness* of the first in itself, is itself to be the second object. But it usually seems that we learn by experience the untruth of our first concept by appealing *to some other object* which we may happen to find by chance and externally, so that in general what we have is merely the bare and simple *apprehension* of what is in and for itself. On the view given above, however, the new object is seen to have come about by a *reversal of consciousness* itself. This way of looking at the matter is *our* doing, what *we* contribute; by its means the series of experiences through which consciousness passes is lifted into a scientifically constituted sequence, but this does not exist for the consciousness we observe and consider.

We have here, however, the same sort of circumstance of which we spoke a short time ago when dealing with the relation of this presentation to skepticism, namely, that the result which at any time comes about in the case of an untrue mode of knowledge cannot possibly collapse into an empty nothingness, but must necessarily be taken as the negation of *that of which it is a result*—a result which contains what truth the preceding mode of knowledge has in it. What we have here is presented to us in this form: since what at first appeared as object is reduced, when it passes into consciousness, to what knowledge takes it to be, and the *in itself becomes* what this entity *in itself* is *for consciousness*, this latter is the new object. And with this there appears also a new shape of consciousness, of which the essence is something other than that of the preceding mode. It is this circumstance which carries forward the whole succession of the shapes of consciousness in their own necessity. It is only this necessity, this *origination* of the new object, which offers itself to consciousness without consciousness knowing how it comes by it, that to us, who watch the process, is to be seen as going on, so to speak, behind its back. Thereby there enters into its process a moment of being *in itself* and of being *for us*, which is not expressly presented to that consciousness which is in the grip of experience itself. The *content*, however, of what we see arising exists *for it*, and we comprehend merely its formal character, that is, its *pure* origination. *For consciousness*, what has thus arisen has merely the character of object, while *for us* it appears at the same time as a process and coming into being.

In virtue of that necessity, this pathway to science is itself already a *science*, and is, moreover as regards its content, a science of the *experience of consciousness*.

The experience which consciousness has concerning itself can, by its essential concept, embrace nothing less than the entire system of consciousness, the whole realm of the truth of mind, and in such a way that the moments of truth are set forth in the specific and peculiar character they here possess—not as abstract pure moments, but as they are for consciousness, or as consciousness itself comes forward in its relation to them, and in virtue of which they are moments of the whole of the *shapes of consciousness*. In pressing forward to its true form of existence, consciousness will come to a point at which it lays aside its semblance of being hampered with what is foreign to it, with what is only *for* it and exists as an other. It will reach a position where its appearance becomes identical with its essence, where in consequence, its exposition coincides with just this very point, this very stage of the authentic science of mind. And finally, when it grasps this its own essence, it will indicate the nature of absolute knowledge itself.

I. SENSE CERTAINTY— THE "THIS" AND MEANING

The knowledge, which is at the start or immediately our object, can be nothing else than just that which is *immediate* knowledge, knowledge of the *immediate*, of what *is*. We have, in dealing with it, to proceed, too, in an immediate way, to accept what is given, not altering anything in it as it is presented to us, and keeping mere apprehension (*Auffassen*) free from conceptual comprehension (*Begreifen*).

The concrete content that *sense certainty* furnishes makes this immediately appear to be the *richest* kind of knowledge, to be even a knowledge of endless wealth—a wealth to which we can as little find any limit when we traverse its *extent* in space and time, where that content is presented before us, as when we take a fragment out of the abundance it offers us and by dividing seek to penetrate its *intent*. Besides that, it seems to be the *truest*, the most authentic knowledge, for it has not as yet left out anything from the object; it has the object before itself in its entirety and completeness.

This bare fact of *certainty*, however, is really and admittedly the *most abstract* and the *poorest* kind of *truth*. It merely says regarding what it knows: it *is*; and its truth contains solely the *being* of the fact it knows. Consciousness, on its part, in the case of this form of certainty, takes the shape merely of pure "*I.*" In other words, *I*, in such a case, am merely *qua* pure *This*, and the object likewise is merely *qua* pure *This*. I, *this* particular conscious I, am *certain* of *this* fact before me, not because I *qua* consciousness have developed myself in connection with it and in manifold ways set thought to work about it: and not, again, because the fact, the thing, of which I am certain, in virtue of its having a multitude of distinct qualities, was replete with possible modes of relation and a variety of connections with other things. Neither of these has anything to do with the truth of sense certainty: neither the I nor the thing has here the meaning of a manifold relation with a variety of other things, of mediation in a variety of ways. The I does not contain or imply a manifold of ideas or thoughts, nor does the thing mean what has a multiplicity of qualities. Rather the thing, the fact, *is*; and it *is* merely because it *is*. It *is* — that is the essential point for sense-knowledge, and that bare fact of *being*, that simple immediacy, constitutes its *truth*. In the same way the certainty *qua relation*, the certainty "*of*" something, is an *immediate* pure relation; consciousness is *I* and nothing more, a pure *This*; the *individual* consciousness knows a pure *This*, or knows what is *individual*.

But, when we look closely, there is a good deal more implied in that bare *pure being* that constitutes the kernel of this form of certainty, and is given out by it as its truth. A concrete actual certainty of sense is not merely this pure immediacy, but an *example*, an *instance* [*Beispiel*, or "play of two"], of that immediacy. Among the innumerable distinctions that come to light here, we find in all cases the fundamental difference, namely, that in sense experience, pure being at once breaks up into the two "*Thises*," as we have called them, one this as *I*, and one as *object*. When we reflect on this distinction, it is seen that neither the one nor the other is merely *immediate*, merely *is* in sense certainty, but is at the same time *mediated*. I have the certainty *through* the other, namely, through the actual fact; and this again exists in that certainty *through* an other, namely, through the I.

It is not only we who make this distinction of essence and example, immediacy and mediation; we *find* it in sense certainty itself, and it has to be taken up in the form in which it exists there, not as we have just determined it. In sense certainty, one This is put forward as existing in simple immediacy, as the essential reality, the *object*. The other, however, is put forward as the non-essential, as *mediated*, something which is not in itself in the certainty, but there through an other "I," *a state of knowledge* which only knows the object because the object is, and which can as well be as not be. The object, however, is the real truth, and is the essential reality; it *is*, quite independently of whether it is known or not. It remains and stands even though it is not known, whereas the knowledge does not exist if the object is not there.

We have thus to consider, as to the object, whether in point of fact it does exist in sense certainty itself as such an essential reality as that certainty gives it out to be; whether its concept, which is to be essential reality, corresponds to the way it is present in that certainty. We have for that purpose not to reflect about it and ponder what it might be in truth, but to deal with it merely as sense certainty contains it.

Sense certainty itself has thus to be asked: *What is the This?* If we take it in the two-fold form of its existence, as the *Now* and as the *Here*, the dialectic it has in it will take a form as intelligible as the This itself. To the question, *What is the Now?* we reply, for example, *The Now is night-time*. To test the truth of this certainty of sense, a simple experiment is all we need: we write that truth down. A truth cannot lose anything by being written down, and just as little by our preserving and keeping it. If we look again at the truth we have written down, look at it *now*, *at this noon-time*, however, we shall have to say it has turned stale and become out of date.

The Now that is night is kept fixed, that is, it is treated as what it is given out to be, as something which *is*; but it proves to be rather a something which is *not*. The Now itself no doubt maintains itself, but as what is *not* night; similarly in its relation to the day which the Now is at present, it maintains itself as something that is also not day, or as altogether something *negative*. This self-maintaining Now is therefore not something immediate, but something mediated, for, *qua* something that remains and preserves itself, it is determined through and *by means* of the fact that something else, namely, day and night, is *not*. Thereby it is just as much as ever, *Now*, and in being this simple fact, it is indifferent to what is still associated with it. Just as little as night or day is its being, it is just as truly *also* day and night; it is not in the least affected by this otherness through which it is what it is. A simple entity of this sort, which is by and through negation, which is neither this nor that, which is a *not-this*, and with equal indifference this as well as that—a thing of this kind we call a *universal*. The universal is therefore in point of fact the truth of sense certainty.

It is as a universal, too, that we *give utterance* to the sensory. What we say is: *"This,"* that is, the *universal this*; or we say: *"it is,"* that of *being in general*. Of course, we do not thereby *think* the universal this or being in general, but we *utter* what is universal; in other words, we do not actually and absolutely say what in this sense certainty we really *mean*. Language, however, as we see, is the more truthful: in it we ourselves refute directly and at once our own *meaning*, and since universality is the real truth of sense certainty, and language merely expresses this truth, it is not possible at all for us even to express in words any sensory being that we *mean*.

The same will be the case when we take the *Here*, the other form of the *This*. *Here*, for example, is the *tree*. I turn around and this truth has disappeared and has changed round into its opposite: *Here is not a tree*, but *a house*. The Here itself does not disappear; it *is* and remains in the disappearance of the house, tree, and so on, and is indifferently house, tree. The *This* is shown thus again to be *mediated simplicity*, in other words, to be *universality*.

Pure being, then, remains as the essential element for this sense certainty, since sense certainty in its very nature proves the universal to be the truth of its object. But that pure being is not in the form of something immediate, but of something in which the process of negation and mediation is essential. Consequently it is not what we *intend* or *mean* by *being*, but is *being* with the *determination* that it is an abstraction, the purely universal. And *our* intended meaning, which takes the truth of sense certainty to be *not* something universal, is alone left standing in contrast to this empty, indifferent Now and Here.

If we compare the relation in which *knowledge* and the *object* first stood with the relation they have come to assume in this result, it is found to be just the reverse of what first appeared. The object, which professed to be the essential reality, is now the non-essential element of sense certainty, for the universal, which the object has come to be, is no longer such as the object essentially was to be for sense certainty. The certainty is now found to lie in the opposite element, namely, in knowledge, which formerly was the nonessential factor. Its truth lies in the object as my (*meinem*) object, or lies in the *meaning* (*meinen*), in which I mean; it *is*, because *I* know it. Sense certainty is thus indeed banished from the object, but it is not yet thereby done away with; it is merely forced back into the I. We have still to see what experience reveals regarding its reality in this sense.

The force of sense certainty's truth thus lies now in the *I*, in the immediate fact of my being conscious of seeing, hearing, and so on; the disappearance of the particular Now and Here that we mean is prevented by the fact that I hold on to them. The Now is daytime, because *I* see it; the Here is a tree for a similar reason. Sense certainty, however, goes through, in this connection, the same dialectic process as in the former case. I, *this* I, see the tree and assert the tree to be Here; *another* I, however, sees the house and maintains the Here is not a tree but a house. Both truths have the same verification—the immediacy of seeing—and the certainty and assurance both have as to their specific way of knowing, but the one certainty disappears in the other.

In all this, what does not disappear is the *I qua universal*, whose seeing is neither the seeing of this tree nor of this house, but just seeing *simpliciter*, which is mediated through the negation of this house, and so forth, and, in being so, is all the same simple and indifferent to what is associated with it, the house, the tree, and so on. I is merely universal, like Now, Here, or This in general. No doubt I mean an *individual I*, but just as little as I am able to say what I mean by Now, Here, so it is impossible in the case of the I too. By saying "this Here," "this Now," "an individual thing," I say *all* Thises, Heres, Nows, or Individuals. In the same way when I say "I," "this individual I," I say quite generally *"all I's"*—everyone is what I say, everyone is "I," this individual I. When philosophy is requested, by way of putting it to a crucial test— a test which it could not possibly sustain—to "deduce," to "construe," "to find a priori," or however it is put a so-called *this thing*, or *this particular man*, it is quite fair to ask that this demand should say *what* "this thing," or *what* "this I" it means. But to say this is quite impossible.

Sense certainty discovers by experience, therefore, that its essential nature lies neither in the object nor in the I, and that the immediacy peculiar to it is neither an immediacy of the one nor of the other. For in the case of both, what I mean is rather something nonessential, and the object and the I are universals, in which that Now and Here and I, that I mean do not hold out, do not exist. We arrive in this way at the result that we have to posit the *whole* sense certainty itself, which persists therein as *immediacy*, and in consequence excludes from itself all the opposition which in the foregoing had a place there.

This pure immediacy, then, has nothing more to do with the fact of otherness, with Here in the form of a tree passing into a Here that is not a tree, with Now in the sense of day-time changing into a Now that is night-time, or with there being an other I to which something else is object. Its truth stands fast as a self-identical relation making no distinction of essential and nonessential, between I and object, and into which, therefore, in general, no distinction can find its way. I, *this* I, assert, then, the Here as tree, and do not turn around so that for me Here might become *not* a tree, and I take no notice of the fact that another I finds the Here as not-tree, or that I myself at some other time take the Here as not-tree, the Now as not-day. I am pure intuition and nothing more. For myself I stand by the fact that the Now is day-time, or, again, by the fact that Here is a tree, and again, I do not compare Here and Now themselves with one another; I take my stand on *one* immediate relation: the Now is day.

Since, then, this certainty will cease to exist if we direct its attention to a Now that is night or an I to whom it is night, let us go to it and try to point to the Now that is asserted. We must let ourselves *point it out*, for the truth of this immediate relation is the truth of *this I* which restricts itself to a Now or a Here. Were we to examine this truth afterwards, or stand at a distance from it, it would have no meaning at all, for that would do away with the immediacy, which is of its essence. We have therefore to enter the same point of time or of space, indicate them, show them to ourselves, that is, turn ourselves into

the very same I, the very same This, which is the subject knowing with certainty. Let us, then, see how that immediate that is pointed out to us is constituted.

The Now is pointed out; *this* Now. "Now"—as soon as it is pointed out it is gone. The Now that *is*, is other than the one pointed out, and we see that the Now is just this—to be no longer the very time when it is. The Now as it is shown to us is one that *has been*, and that is its truth; it does not have the truth of being, of something that *is*. No doubt this is true, that it *has* been, but what *has been* is in point of fact not genuinely real, it *is not*—and what is, of course, was the point in question.

In thus pointing out the Now, we thus see merely a process which takes the following course: *First*, I point out the Now, and it is asserted to be the truth. I point it out, however, as something that *has been*, or as something canceled and done away with. Having thus annulled and passed beyond that first truth, I, *second*, now assert as the second truth that it *has* been, that it is superseded. But, *thirdly*, what *has* been *is not*; I then supersede its *having* been, the fact of its being annulled, the second truth, negating thereby the negation of the Now and returning thereby to the first position: that *Now is*. The Now and pointing out the Now are thus so constituted that neither the one nor the other is an immediate simple fact, but a process with diverse moments in it. A *This* is posited, but it is instead an *other* that is posited; the *This* is superseded. And this otherness, this canceling of the former, is itself again annulled, and so turned back to the first. But the This, reflected thus into itself, is not exactly the same as it was to begin with, namely, something immediate. Rather, it is a *something reflected-into-self*, a simple entity, which remains in its otherness: a Now which is any number of Nows. And that is the genuinely true Now: the Now is simple day-time which has many Nows within it—hours. A Now of that sort, again—an hour—is similarly many minutes, and this Now—a minute—is in the same way many Nows, and so on. Showing, indicating, pointing out [the Now] is thus itself the very process which expresses what the Now in truth really *is*, namely, a result, or a plurality of Nows all taken together. And the pointing out is the way of getting to know, of experiencing, that Now is a *universal*.

The Here *pointed out*, which I keep hold of, is likewise a *this* Here which, in fact, is *not this* Here, but a Before and Behind, an Above and Below, a Right and Left. The Above is itself likewise this manifold otherness—Above, Below, etc. The Here, which was to be pointed out, disappears in other Heres, and these disappear similarly. What is pointed out, held fast, and is permanent, is a *negative This*, which only is so when the Heres are taken as they should be, but therein cancel one another. It is a simple complex of many Heres. The Here that is meant would be the point, but a point does not exist. Rather, when it is pointed out as *being*, as having existence, that very act of pointing out proves it to be not immediate knowledge, but a process, a movement, from the Here meant through a plurality of Heres to the universal Here, which is a simple plurality of Heres, just as day is a simple plurality of Nows.

It is clear from all this that the dialectical process involved in sense certainty is nothing else than the simple history of its process—of its experience—and that sense certainty itself is nothing else than just this history. The natural consciousness, too, for that reason, is of itself always coming to this result, which is the real truth in this case, and is always having experience of it. But it is always forgetting it again, and beginning the process all over. It is therefore astonishing when, in defiance of this experience, it is announced as "universal experience"—nay, even as a philosophical doctrine, the outcome in fact of skepticism—that the reality or being of external things in the sense of "Thises," sensory particulars, has absolute validity and truth for consciousness. One who makes such an assertion really does not know what he is saying, does not know that he is stating the opposite of what he wants to say. The truth for consciousness of a sensuous "This" is said to be universal experience—but the very opposite is universal experience. Every consciousness of itself cancels again, as soon as made, such a truth as, for example, Here is a tree, or Now is noon, and expresses the very opposite: Here is *not* a tree, but *instead* a house. And similarly, it straightaway cancels again the assertion that here cancels the first, and that is also just an assertion of a sensuous This. And in all sense certainty, what we find by experience is in truth merely, as we have seen, that "This" is a *universal*, the very opposite of what that assertion maintained to be universal experience.

We may be permitted here, in this appeal to universal experience, to anticipate a reference to the practi-

cal sphere. In this connection we may answer those who thus insist on the truth and certainty of the reality of objects of sense by saying that they had better be sent back to the most elementary school of wisdom, the ancient Eleusinian mysteries of Ceres and Bacchus;[1] they have not yet learnt the inner secret of the eating of bread and the drinking of wine. For those who are initiated into these mysteries not only come to doubt the being of things of sense, but get into a state of despair about them altogether; they themselves partly bring about the nothingness of those things, and partly they see those things accomplish their own nothingness. Even animals are not shut off from this wisdom, but show they are deeply initiated into it. For they do not stand stock still before things of sense as if these were things in themselves; they despair of this reality altogether and in complete assurance of the nothingness of things, they set to without more ado and eat them up. And all nature proclaims as animals do these open secrets, these mysteries revealed to all, which teach the truth of sensory things.

Those who put forward such assertions really themselves say, if we bear in mind what we remarked before, the direct opposite of what they mean—a fact which is perhaps best able to bring them to reflect on the nature of the certainty of sense experience. They speak of the existence of *external* objects, which can be more precisely characterized as *actual*, absolutely *particular, wholly personal, individual* things, each of them not like anything or anyone else; this is the existence they say has absolute certainty and truth. They mean *this* bit of paper I am writing on, or rather *have* written on, but they do not say what they mean. If they really wanted to *say* this bit of paper that they mean, and they *wanted* to say so, that is impossible, because the This of sense, which is meant, *cannot be reached* by language, which belongs to consciousness, that is, to what is inherently universal. In the very attempt to say it, it would, therefore, crumble in their hands. Those who began to describe it would not be able to finish doing so: they would

---

1. [The Eleusinian mysteries were the most famous Greek religious rites, perhaps originated as part of an early agrarian festival in the city of Eleusis, and held in honor of Ceres (or, in Greek mythology, Demeter), the goddess of agriculture, and involving Bacchus (or, in Greek mythology, Dionysus), the god of wine.—S.M.C.]

have to hand it over to others, who would themselves in the last resort have to confess to speaking about a thing that has no being. They indeed mean *this* bit of paper here, which is quite different from that bit over there. But they speak of actual *things, external or sensible objects, absolutely individual* being, and so on; that is, they say about them what is simply *universal.*

Consequently, what is called inexpressible is nothing else than what is untrue, irrational, something barely and simply meant. If nothing is said of a thing except that it is *an actual thing,* an *external object,* this only asserts that it is the most universal of all possible things, and thereby we express its *likeness,* its identity, with everything, rather than its difference from everything else. When I say "an individual thing," I at once state it to be really a universal, for everything is an individual thing. And in the same way, "this thing" is everything and anything we like. More precisely, as this bit of paper, each and every paper is a "this bit of paper," and I have thus said all the while what is universal. If I want, however, to help out speech—which has the divine nature of directly turning the mere "meaning" right round about, making it into something else, and so not letting it ever come the length of words at all—by *pointing out* this bit of paper, then I get the experience of what is, in point of fact, the real truth of sense certainty. I point it out as a Here, which is a Here among other Heres, or is in itself simply many Heres together, that is, a universal. I take it up, then, as in truth it is, and instead of knowing something immediate, I "take something truly," I *perceive* [*nehme wahr*].

Søren Kierkegaard

Søren Kierkegaard was born in Copenhagen, Denmark, in 1813, the youngest child of a large family. He was raised in a wealthy middle-class home, with the strictest devotion to church and religion. His father was a successful merchant and an avid reader of theology, and his mother had been his father's servant before she became his second wife. Kierkegaard had a hunchback, and this, according to some, is the "thorn in his flesh" he often mentions in his writings. He viewed his life as governed by a deep melancholy, which he self-consciously attempted to hide with wit and gaiety. An event of crucial importance for Kierkegaard was his breaking of his engagement to Regine Olsen in 1841. His reason for this action is an important but unsolved mystery. First educated at home, he began university as a student of theology, but soon turned to literature and philosophy. Kierkegaard was especially steeped in the philosophy of Hegel, which he studied in Berlin. A dominant theme in his life was his opposition to official state Christianity, seen by him as encumbered by a passionless conformity to bourgeois respectability and stability. Instead, Kierkegaard advocated a life of intense religious commitment, free from superficiality and empty formalism. His works include *Either/Or* (1843), *Fear and Trembling* (1843), *Philosophical Fragments* (1844), *Concluding Unscientific Postscript* (1846), *The Sickness Unto Death* (1849), *Training in Christianity* (1851), and *The Attack Upon "Christendom"* (1854–55). His writings were largely ignored outside of Denmark until the twentieth century, when they became very influential. Kierkegaard died in 1855, at the age of 42, after collapsing while carrying the last of his inheritance from the bank.

The overriding concern in Kierkegaard's religious and philosophical writings is to provide insight into meaning and fulfillment in human life. Achieving meaning in life, in his view, is not something simply given to us, but it is accomplished through our decisions. But Kierkegaard does not believe that we are ultimately on our own in making the best possible choice for our lives. His final recommendations are religious, and he argues that the best decision we can make is one in which we are dependent on God.

Kierkegaard claims that human existence involves a profound tension or conflict between two dimensions. A self is a tension between the finite and the infinite, between the temporal and the eternal. The notion of the temporal signifies the events of our lives considered as separate and particular moments, immediate and distinct from one another. As temporal beings, we are no different from the other animals, which also have sensations and try to satisfy desires. The notion of the eternal, by contrast, signifies the overarching unity that these events can have just for humans. Though we are beings governed by basic passions and desires, aiming at momentary satisfactions, we are also beings who can make life something more coherent and unified, something more than just a series of fragmented projects aimed at transitory enjoyments.

One can come to understand Kierkegaard's views by considering his threefold classification of the ways we humans can attempt to achieve fulfillment. For him there are three main "spheres of existence" or modes of life: the aesthetic, the ethical, and the religious. The most fundamental characteristic of the person living the aesthetic life is that his purposes are exhausted by the satisfaction of desires for momentary or short-term fulfillments. Kierkegaard believes that the aesthetic option will always fail as a route to meaning in life. An aesthetic person aims at the satisfaction of desires for momentary pleasures. Both the attraction and the failure of the aesthetic life can be explained by the fact that it expresses only one side of the self, the temporal aspect.

Kierkegaard believes that the expression of the eternal side can be achieved only by means of a decisive, continuously renewed choice which produces an overarching unity among the disparate moments in one's experience. This choice calls for a commitment, a "leap," that will unify one's life. Such a commitment might be ethical, for example, a commitment to another person in marriage; or religious, a commitment to God. The mark of the ethical life is a constantly renewed decision, made by one's own will alone, to live in accord with ethical duty. By continuously renewing this commitment, one can attempt to provide a unity to the various moments in one's life that expresses one's eternal nature. But Kierkegaard describes striving to express the eternal through one's own will alone as the most agonizing, albeit the highest form of despair.

Kierkegaard maintains that there is a better solution to be found in the religious life, in part because in making a religious commitment one need not rely on oneself. His most thorough work on religion, the *Concluding Unscientific Postscript*, poses the claim that *truth is subjectivity*. Yet Kierkegaard does not mean to deny that there are objective facts. Rather, "truth is subjectivity" means that, when meaning in one's life is at stake, one's attitude toward the object of one's concerns takes precedence over the issue of whether one is actually right about some fact. In Kierkegaard's view, what is especially important for meaning in life is one's attitude in a relationship with a person or thing, by contrast with merely having true beliefs about that person or thing.

For example, someone might master all of the true sentences about something that is genuinely important, while maintaining a detached, theoretical stance. Imagine, for example, a psychologist who develops a theory about human relationships so accurate and insightful that it has changed the lives of many people. But suppose further that as a scientist she has developed so detached an attitude that she is unable to live in accordance with her theory in her own relationships, with the result that her life is very empty and unfulfilled. Such a person possesses the truth objectively, but not subjectively. By contrast, another person might deeply and passionately live her relationships in accord with her insights. She would be in the truth subjectively.

In Kierkegaard's view, what is most important in the search for meaning and fulfillment for one's life is the nature of one's relationship. If one is attempting to relate oneself to God, the infinite being, the appropriate kind of relationship is one of infinite intensity. To illustrate these claims about truth, Kierkegaard argues that a pagan praying with infinite passion, "although his eyes rest on the image of an idol," has a more appropriate relationship to the truth, or is more "in the truth," than someone who has fewer false beliefs and more true beliefs about religion, but holds them without deep feeling.

• • •

Significant studies of Kierkegaard's philosophy include C. Stephen Evans, *Kierkegaard's Fragments and Postscript: The Religious Philosophy of Johannes Climacus* (Atlantic Highlands, N.J.: Humanities Press, 1983), and Louis Mackey, *Kierkegaard: A Kind of Poet* (Philadelphia: University of Pennsylvania Press, 1971). Two important essays on Kierkegaard, both by Robert Adams, are "Truth and Subjectivity," in Eleonore Stump, ed., *Reasoned Faith: Essays in Philosophical Theology in Honor of Norman Kretzmann* (Ithaca: Cornell University Press, 1993) and "The Knight of Truth," *Faith and Philosophy*, 7 (October 1990). An important collection of essays is Alastair Hannay and Gordon Marino, eds., *The Cambridge Companion to Kierkegaard* (Cambridge: Cambridge University Press, 1997).

D.P.

Concluding Unscientific Postscript

(abridged)

The Subjective Truth, Inwardness, Truth Is Subjectivity

. . . The way of objective reflection makes the subject accidental, and thereby transforms existence into something indifferent, something vanishing. Away from the subject the objective way of reflection leads to the objective truth, and while the subject and his subjectivity become indifferent, the truth also becomes indifferent, and this indifference is precisely its objective validity; for all interest, like all decisiveness, is rooted in subjectivity. The way of objective reflection leads to abstract thought, to mathematics, to historical knowledge of different kinds; and always it leads away from the subject, whose existence or non-existence, and from the objective point of view quite rightly, becomes infinitely indifferent. Quite rightly, since as Hamlet says,[1] existence and non-existence have only subjective significance. At its maximum this way will arrive at a contradiction, and in so far as the subject does not become wholly indifferent to himself, this merely constitutes a sign that his objective striving is not objective enough. At its maximum this way will lead to the contradiction that only the objective has come into being, while the subjective has gone out; that is to say, the existing subjectivity has vanished, in that it has made an attempt to become what in the abstract sense is called subjectivity, the mere abstract form of an abstract objectivity. And yet, the objectivity which has thus come into being is, from the subjective point of view at the most, either an hypothesis or an approximation, because all eternal decisiveness is rooted in subjectivity.

However, the objective way deems itself to have a security which the subjective way does not have (and, of course, existence and existing cannot be thought in combination with objective security); it thinks to escape a danger which threatens the subjective way, and this danger is at its maximum: madness. In a merely subjective determination of the truth, madness and truth become in the last analysis indistinguishable, since they may both have inwardness.[2] Nevertheless, perhaps I may here venture to offer a little remark, one which would seem to be not wholly superfluous in an objective age. The absence of inwardness is also madness. The objective truth as such, is by no means adequate to determine that whoever utters it is sane; on the contrary, it may even betray the fact that he is mad, although what he says may be entirely true, and especially objectively true. I shall here permit myself to tell a story, which without any sort of adaptation on my part comes direct from an asylum. A patient in such an institution seeks to escape, and actually succeeds in effecting his purpose by leaping out of a window, and prepares to start on the road to freedom, when the thought strikes him (shall I say sanely enough or madly enough?): "When you come to town you will be recognized, and you will at once be brought back here again; hence you need to prepare yourself fully to convince everyone by the objective truth of what you say, that all is in order as far as your sanity is concerned." As he walks

1. [Act III, Scene I.—W.L.]

2. Even this is not really true, however, for madness never has the specific inwardness of the infinite. Its fixed idea is precisely some sort of objectivity, and the contradiction of madness consists in embracing this with passion. The critical point in such madness is thus again not the subjective, but the little finitude which has become a fixed idea, which is something that can never happen to the infinite.

along and thinks about this, he sees a ball lying on the ground, picks it up, and puts it into the tail pocket of his coat. Every step he takes the ball strikes him, politely speaking, on his hinder parts, and every time it thus strikes him he says: "Bang, the earth is round." He comes to the city, and at once calls on one of his friends; he wants to convince him that he is not crazy, and therefore walks back and forth, saying continually: "Bang, the earth is round!" But is not the earth round? Does the asylum still crave yet another sacrifice for this opinion, as in the time when all men believed it to be flat as a pancake? Or is a man who hopes to prove that he is sane, by uttering a generally accepted and generally respected objective truth, insane? And yet it was clear to the physician that the patient was not yet cured; though it is not to be thought that the cure would consist in getting him to accept the opinion that the earth is flat. But all men are not physicians, and what the age demands seems to have a considerable influence upon the question of what madness is. Aye, one could almost be tempted sometimes to believe that the modern age, which has modernized Christianity, has also modernized the question of Pontius Pilate,[3] and that its urge to find something in which it can rest proclaims itself in the question: What is madness? When a *Privatdocent*, every time his scholastic gown reminds him that he ought to say something, says *de omnibus dubitandum est*,[4] and at the same time writes away at a system which offers abundant internal evidence in every other sentence that the man has never doubted anything at all: he is not regarded as mad.

Don Quixote[5] is the prototype for a subjective madness, in which the passion of inwardness embraces a particular finite fixed idea. But the absence of inwardness gives us on the other hand the prating madness, which is quite as comical; and it might be a very desirable thing if an experimental psychologist would delineate it by taking a handful of such philosophers and bringing them together. In the type of madness which manifests itself as an aberrant inwardness, the tragic and the comic is that the something which is of such infinite concern to the unfortunate individual is a particular fixation which does not really concern anybody. In the type of madness which consists in the absence of inwardness, the comic is that though the something which the happy individual knows really is the truth, the truth which concerns all men, it does not in the slightest degree concern the much respected prater. This type of madness is more inhuman than the other. One shrinks from looking into the eyes of a madman of the former type lest one be compelled to plumb there the depths of his delirium; but one dares not look at a madman of the latter type at all, from fear of discovering that he has eyes of glass and hair made from carpet-rags; that he is, in short, an artificial product. If you meet someone who suffers from such a derangement of feeling, the derangement consisting in his not having any, you listen to what he says in a cold and awful dread, scarcely knowing whether it is a human being who speaks, or a cunningly contrived walking stick in which a talking machine has been concealed. It is always unpleasant for a proud man to find himself unwittingly drinking a toast of brotherhood with the public hangman;[6] but to find oneself engaged in rational and philosophical conversation with a walking stick is almost enough to make a man lose his mind.

The subjective reflection turns its attention inwardly to the subject, and desires in this intensification of inwardness to realize the truth. And it proceeds in such fashion that, just as in the preceding objective reflection, when the objectivity had come into being, the subjectivity had vanished, so here the subjectivity of the subject becomes the final stage, and objectivity a vanishing factor. Not for a single moment is it forgotten that the subject is an existing individual, and that existence is a process of becoming, and that therefore the notion of the truth as identity of thought and being is a chimera of abstraction, in its truth only an expectation of the creature; not because the truth is not such an identity, but because the knower is an existing individual for whom the truth cannot be such

3. [The first-century Roman governor of Judea who, according to the New Testament, officiated at the trial of Jesus. — S.M.C.]

4. [Everything is to be doubted.]

5. [In the remarkable novel of that name by the Spanish writer Miguel de Cervantes Saavedra (1547–1616), Don Quixote is a country gentleman who sets forth on a series of adventures in which he has difficulty distinguishing reality from illusion.]

6. [Like Geert Westphaler in Scene 8 of the comedy of that name.]

an identity as long as he lives in time. Unless we hold fast to this, speculative philosophy will immediately transport us into the fantastic realism of the I-am-I,[7] which modern speculative thought has not hesitated to use without explaining how a particular individual is related to it; and God knows, no human being is more than such a particular individual.

If an existing individual were really able to transcend himself, the truth would be for him something final and complete; but where is the point at which he is outside himself? The I-am-I is a mathematical point which does not exist, and in so far there is nothing to prevent everyone from occupying this standpoint; the one will not be in the way of the other. It is only momentarily that the particular individual is able to realize existentially a unity of the infinite and the finite which transcends existence. This unity is realized in the moment of passion. Modern philosophy has tried anything and everything in the effort to help the individual to transcend himself objectively, which is a wholly impossible feat; existence exercises its restraining influence, and if philosophers nowadays had not become mere scribblers in the service of a fantastic thinking and its preoccupation, they would long ago have perceived that suicide was the only tolerable practical interpretation of its striving. But the scribbling modern philosophy holds passion in contempt; and yet passion is the culmination of existence for an existing individual — and we are all of us existing individuals. In passion the existing subject is rendered infinite in the eternity of the imaginative representation, and yet he is at the same time most definitely himself. The fantastic I-am-I is not an identity of the infinite and the finite, since neither the one nor the other is real; it is a fantastic rendezvous in the clouds,[8] an unfruitful embrace, and the relationship of the individual self to this mirage is never indicated.

All essential knowledge relates to existence, or only such knowledge as has an essential relationship to existence is essential knowledge. All knowledge which does not inwardly relate itself to existence, in the reflection of inwardness, is, essentially viewed, accidental knowledge; its degree and scope is essentially indifferent. That essential knowledge is essentially related to existence does not mean the above-mentioned identity which abstract thought postulates between thought and being; nor does it signify, objectively, that knowledge corresponds to something existent as its object. But it means that knowledge has a relationship to the knower, who is essentially an existing individual, and that for this reason all essential knowledge is essentially related to existence. Only ethical and ethico-religious knowledge has an essential relationship to the existence of the knower.

Mediation is a mirage, like the I-am-I. From the abstract point of view everything is and nothing comes into being. Mediation can therefore have no place in abstract thought, because it presupposes *movement*. Objective knowledge may indeed have the existent for its object; but since the knowing subject is an existing individual, and through the fact of his existence in process of becoming, philosophy must first explain how a particular existing subject is related to a knowledge of mediation. It must explain what he is in such a moment, if not pretty nearly *distrait*; where he is, if not in the moon? There is constant talk of mediation and mediation; is mediation then a man, as Peter Deacon[9] believes that *Imprimatur* is a man? How does a human being manage to become something of this kind? Is this dignity, this great *philosophicum*, the fruit of study, or does the magistrate give it away, like the office of deacon or grave-digger? Try merely to enter into these and other such plain questions of a plain man, who would gladly become mediation if it could be done in some lawful and honest manner, and not either by saying abracadabra, or by forgetting that he is himself an existing human being, for whom existence is therefore something essential, and an ethico-religious existence a suitable *quantum satis*.[10] A speculative philosopher may perhaps find it in bad taste to ask such questions. But it is important not to direct the polemic to the wrong

7. [The reference is to the thought of Johann Gottlieb Fichte (1762–1814), the German idealist philosopher who, maintaining that the essence of the I lies in self-awareness, provided a transition from the philosophy of Kant to that of Hegel.]

8. [As when Axion sought to embrace Juno and found that he was embracing a cloud.]

9. [As in Holberg's comedy *Erasmus Montanus*, Act III, Scene 3.]

10. [Sufficiency.]

point, and hence not to begin in a fantastic objective manner to discuss *pro* and *contra* whether there is a mediation or not, but to hold fast what it means to be a human being.

In an attempt to make clear the difference of way that exists between an objective and a subjective reflection, I shall now proceed to show how a subjective reflection makes its way inwardly in inwardness. Inwardness in an existing subject culminates in passion; corresponding to passion in the subject the truth becomes a paradox; and the fact that the truth becomes a paradox is rooted precisely in its having a relationship to an existing subject. Thus the one corresponds to the other. By forgetting that one is an existing subject, passion goes by the board and the truth is no longer a paradox; the knowing subject becomes a fantastic entity rather than a human being, and the truth becomes a fantastic object for the knowledge of this fantastic entity.

When the question of truth is raised in an objective manner, reflection is directed objectively to the truth, as an object to which the knower is related. Reflection is not focussed upon the relationship, however, but upon the question of whether it is the truth to which the knower is related. If only the object to which he is related is the truth, the subject is accounted to be in the truth. When the question of the truth is raised subjectively, reflection is directed subjectively to the nature of the individual's relationship; if only the mode of this relationship is in the truth, the individual is in the truth even if he should happen to be thus related to what is not true.[11] Let us take as an example the knowledge of God. Objectively, reflection is directed to the problem of whether this object is the true God; subjectively, reflection is directed to the question whether the individual is related to a something *in such a manner* that his relationship is in truth a God-relationship. On which side is the truth now to be found? Ah, may we not here resort to a mediation, and say: It is on neither side, but in the mediation of both? Excellently well said, provided we might have it explained how an existing individual manages to be in a state of mediation. For to be in a state of mediation is to be finished, while to exist is to become. Nor can an existing individual be in two places at the same time—he cannot be an identity of subject and object. When he is nearest to being in two places at the same time he is in passion; but passion is momentary, and passion is also the highest expression of subjectivity.

The existing individual who chooses to pursue the objective way enters upon the entire approximation-process by which it is proposed to bring God to light objectively. But this is in all eternity impossible, because God is a subject, and therefore exists only for subjectivity in inwardness. The existing individual who chooses the subjective way apprehends instantly the entire dialectical difficulty involved in having to use some time, perhaps a long time, in finding God objectively; and he feels this dialectical difficulty in all its painfulness, because every moment is wasted in which he does not have God.[12] That very instant he has God, not by virtue of any objective deliberation, but by virtue of the infinite passion of inwardness. The objective inquirer, on the other hand, is not embarrassed by such dialectical difficulties as are involved in devoting an entire period of investigation to finding God—since it is possible that the inquirer may die tomorrow; and if he lives he can scarcely regard God as something to be taken along if convenient, since God is precisely that which one takes *a tout prix*,[13] which in the understanding of passion constitutes the true inward relationship to God.

It is at this point, so difficult dialectically, that the way swings off for everyone who knows what it means to think, and to think existentially; which is something very different from sitting at a desk and writing about what one has never done, something very different from writing *de omnibus dubitandum* and at the same

---

11. The reader will observe that the question here is about essential truth, or about the truth which is essentially related to existence, and that it is precisely for the sake of clarifying it as inwardness or as subjectivity that this contrast is drawn.

12. In this manner God certainly becomes a postulate, but not in the otiose manner in which this word is commonly understood. It becomes clear rather that the only way in which an existing individual comes into relation with God, is when the dialectical contradiction brings his passion to the point of despair, and helps him to embrace God with the "category of despair" (faith). Then the postulate is so far from being arbitrary that it is precisely a life-necessity. It is then not so much that God is a postulate, as that the existing individual's postulation of God is a necessity.

13. [At any cost.]

time being as credulous existentially as the most sensuous of men. Here is where the way swings off, and the change is marked by the fact that while objective knowledge rambles comfortably on by way of the long road of approximation without being impelled by the urge of passion, subjective knowledge counts every delay a deadly peril, and the decision so infinitely important and so instantly pressing that it is as if the opportunity had already passed.

Now when the problem is to reckon up on which side there is most truth, whether on the side of one who seeks the true God objectively, and pursues the approximate truth of the God-idea; or on the side of one who, driven by the infinite passion of his need of God, feels an infinite concern for his own relationship to God in truth (and to be at one and the same time on both sides equally, is as we have noted not possible for an existing individual, but is merely the happy delusion of an imaginary I-am-I): the answer cannot be in doubt for anyone who has not been demoralized with the aid of science. If one who lives in the midst of Christendom goes up to the house of God, the house of the true God, with the true conception of God in his knowledge, and prays, but prays in a false spirit; and one who lives in an idolatrous community prays with the entire passion of the infinite, although his eyes rest upon the image of an idol: where is there most truth? The one prays in truth to God though he worships an idol; the other prays falsely to the true God, and hence worships in fact an idol.

When one men investigates objectively the problem of immortality, and another embraces an uncertainty with the passion of the infinite: where is there most truth, and who has the greater certainty? The one has entered upon a never-ending approximation, for the certainty of immortality lies precisely in the subjectivity of the individual; the other is immortal, and fights for his immortality by struggling with the uncertainty. Let us consider Socrates.[14] Nowadays everyone dabbles in a few proofs; some have several such proofs, others fewer. But Socrates! He puts the question objectively in a problematic manner: *if* there is an immortality. He must therefore be accounted

a doubter in comparison with one of our modern thinkers with the three proofs? By no means. On this "if" he risks his entire life, he has the courage to meet death, and he has with the passion of the infinite so determined the pattern of his life that it must be found acceptable — *if* there is an immortality. Is any better proof capable of being given for the immortality of the soul? But those who have the three proofs do not at all determine their lives in conformity therewith; if there is an immortality it must feel disgust over their manner of life: can any better refutation be given of the three proofs? The bit of uncertainty that Socrates had, helped him because he himself contributed the passion of the infinite; the three proofs that the others have do not profit them at all, because they are dead to spirit and enthusiasm, and their three proofs, in lieu of proving anything else, prove just this. A young girl may enjoy all the sweetness of love on the basis of what is merely a weak hope that she is beloved, because she rests everything on this weak hope; but many a wedded matron more than once subjected to the strongest expressions of love, has in so far indeed had proofs, but strangely enough has not enjoyed *quod erat demonstrandum.*[15] The Socratic ignorance, which Socrates held fast with the entire passion of his inwardness, was thus an expression for the principle that the eternal truth is related to an existing individual, and that this truth must therefore be a paradox for him as long as he exists; and yet it is possible that there was more truth in the Socratic ignorance as it was in him, than in the entire objective truth of the System, which flirts with what the times demand and accommodates itself to *Privatdocents.*

The objective accent falls on WHAT is said, the subjective accent on HOW it is said. This distinction holds even in the aesthetic realm, and receives definite expression in the principle that what is in itself true may in the mouth of such and such a person become untrue. In these times this distinction is particularly worthy of notice, for if we wish to express in a single sentence the difference between ancient times and our own, we should doubtless have to say: "In ancient times only an individual here and there knew the truth; now all know it, except that the inwardness of its appropriation stands in an inverse

---

14. [The reference is doubtless to Plato's *Apology* and to his *Phaedrus*, though in neither is to be found exactly what S.K. says here.]

15. [What was to be demonstrated.]

relationship to the extent of its dissemination."[16] Aesthetically the contradiction that truth becomes untruth in this or that person's mouth, is best construed comically: In the ethico-religious sphere, accent is again on the "how." But this is not to be understood as referring to demeanor, expression, or the like; rather it refers to the relationship sustained by the existing individual, in his own existence, to the content of his utterance. Objectively the interest is focussed merely on the thought-content, subjectively on the inwardness. At its maximum this inward "how" is the passion of the infinite, and the passion of the infinite is the truth. But the passion of the infinite is precisely subjectivity, and thus subjectivity becomes the truth. Objectively there is no infinite decisiveness, and hence it is objectively in order to annul the difference between good and evil, together with the principle of contradiction, and therewith also the infinite difference between the true and the false. Only in subjectivity is there decisiveness, to seek objectivity is to be in error. It is the passion of the infinite that is the decisive factor and not its content, for its content is precisely itself. In this manner subjectivity and the subjective "how" constitute the truth.

But the "how" which is thus subjectively accentuated precisely because the subject is an existing individual, is also subject to a dialectic with respect to time. In the passionate moment of decision, where the road swings away from objective knowledge, it seems as if the infinite decision were thereby realized. But in the same moment that existing individual finds himself in the temporal order, and the subjective "how" is transformed into a striving, a striving which receives indeed its impulse and a repeated renewal from the decisive passion of the infinite, but is nevertheless a striving.

When subjectivity is the truth, the conceptual determination of the truth must include an expression for the antithesis to objectivity, a memento of the fork in the road where the way swings off; this expression will at the same time serve as an indication of the tension of the subjective inwardness. Here is such a definition of truth: *An objective uncertainty held fast in an appropriation-process of the most passionate inwardness is the truth*, the highest truth attainable for an *existing* individual. At the point where the way swings off (and where this is cannot be specified objectively, since it is a matter of subjectivity), there objective knowledge is placed in abeyance. Thus the subject merely has, objectively, the uncertainty; but it is this which precisely increases the tension of that infinite passion which constitutes his inwardness. The truth is precisely the venture which chooses an objective uncertainty with the passion of the infinite. I contemplate the order of nature in the hope of finding God, and I see omnipotence and wisdom; but I also see much else that disturbs my mind and excites anxiety. The sum of all this is an objective uncertainty. But it is for this very reason that the inwardness becomes as intense as it is, for it embraces this objective uncertainty with the entire passion of the infinite. In the case of a mathematical proposition the objectivity is given, but for this reason the truth of such a proposition is also an indifferent truth.

But the above definition of truth is an equivalent expression for faith. Without risk there is no faith. Faith is precisely the contradiction between the infinite passion of the individual's inwardness and the objective uncertainty. If I am capable of grasping God objectively, I do not believe, but precisely because I cannot do this I must believe. If I wish to preserve myself in faith I must constantly be intent upon holding fast the objective uncertainty, so as to remain out upon the deep, over seventy thousand fathoms of water, still preserving my faith.

16. *Stages on Life's Way*, Note on p. 426. Though ordinarily not wishing an expression of opinion on the part of reviewers, I might at this point almost desire it, provided such opinions, so far from flattering me, amounted to an assertion of the daring truth that what I say is something that everybody knows, even every child, and that the cultured know infinitely much better. If it only stands fast that everyone knows it, my standpoint is in order, and I shall doubtless make shift to manage with the unity of the comic and the tragic. If there were anyone who did not know it I might perhaps be in danger of being dislodged from my position of equilibrium by the thought that I might be in a position to communicate to someone the needful preliminary knowledge. It is just this which engages my interest so much, this that the cultured are accustomed to say: that everyone knows what the highest is. This was not the case in paganism, nor in Judaism, nor in the seventeen centuries of Christianity. Hail to the nineteenth century! Everyone knows it. What progress has been made since the time when only a few knew it. To make up for this, perhaps, we must assume that no one nowadays does it.

John Stuart Mill

John Stuart Mill (1806–1873) was born in London, the son of a well-known philosopher, James Mill. He was extremely well educated by his father, beginning his studies of Greek and Latin at the ages of three and eight, and subsequently reading widely in the classics, history, philosophy, logic, and mathematics. In 1826, at the age of twenty, he underwent a period of acute depression: his ability to feel emotion, he believed, had been weakened by his intensive analytic training. He responded to this crisis by turning to the arts, taking special solace in the poetry of Wordsworth. Eventually he recovered fully. Hired as a clerk by the East India Company in 1823, he supported himself by working for this concern in various capacities until his retirement in 1858. In 1831 he met Harriet Taylor, a merchant's wife with whom he fell in love. Mill and Harriet Taylor were close and constant friends for many years, collaborating on many literary enterprises and finally marrying in 1851 after her husband's death. In his later years, Mill served a term in Parliament (1865–1868).

Mill's contributions to philosophy and social thoughts are varied. *A System of Logic* (1843) and *An Examination of Sir William Hamilton's Philosophy* (1865) deal with questions of logic and epistemology. *On Liberty* (1859) is a well known discussion of the extent to which society may interfere with individuals' liberties. In *Utilitarianism* (first published in *Fraser's Magazine*, 1861), Mill expounds his own version of utilitarian ethics. Other topics of social importance are discussed in *Principles of Political Economy* (1848), *Considerations on Representative Government* (1861), *August Comte and Positivism* (1865), and *The Subjection of Women* (1869). His *Autobiography* (1873) presents a fascinating picture of his life.

Like the earlier empiricists, Mill believed that sensation and the mind's awareness of its own activity are the sole sources of all knowledge. However, his empiricism differs from earlier versions on a number of important issues, among them the nature of ordinary objects and the role of induction. Mill accepted Berkeley's contention that ordinary objects are collections of sense-impressions but rejected his contention that the continuous existence of these objects is due mainly to God's continuing perception of them. Rather, Mill argued, the continuous existence of tables, chairs, and other objects resides entirely in the fact that we *could* perceive them at any moment. Ordinary objects are just "permanent possibilities of sensation." Concerning induction, or reasoning which extrapolates from known regularities to conclusions about what is likely to happen in unknown instances, Mill did not share Hume's skepticism. Inductive reasoning, he argued, is licensed by a general axiom of nature's uniformity (itself arrived at inductively), and is the fundamental element in all forms of inference, including deductive inference. Even the truths of mathematics and geometry, generally held to be known a priori, are actually determined by generalizing from past experience.

Mill's moral philosophy is known as utilitarianism. Its fundamental principle is that we should always perform those acts which will bring the most happiness or, failing that, the least unhappiness to the most people. This "greatest happiness principle" did not originate with Mill but was pioneered by Jeremy Bentham (1748–1832), the English philosopher and social reformer. However, Mill's essay *Utilitarianism* is the principle's best-known formulation. In support of the greatest happiness principle, Mill argued that "the sole evidence it is possible to produce that anything is desirable is that people do actually desire it"; and that, as a matter of fact, happiness is the one and only thing that people desire. When they seem to desire other things, such as wealth or virtue, it is always because these things are either means to their happiness or "part of their happiness." Given this reasoning, Mill naturally differed with Bentham over the values of different types of pleasure. Bentham had held that the intensity of a pleasure is the only criterion of its worth. For him, sublime moments of intellect or sentiment were worth no more than equally intense moments of animal gratification. For Mill, however, pleasures of equal intensity could differ in worth. Anyone who has experienced both the pleasures of the brute and the pleasures of the civilized person will prefer the latter to the former; and so, according to Mill, the civilized pleasures must be preferable.

At first glance, Mill's greatest-happiness principle may seem to imply that society should interfere with people's liberties whenever such interference will maximize overall happiness. However, Mill did not take any such position. Rather, he argued in *On Liberty* that "the only purpose for which power can be rightfully exercised over any member of a civilised community, against his will, is to prevent harm to others. His own good, either physical or moral, is not a sufficient warrant." In support of this principle, Mill cited the varied benefits of liberty in self-regarding actions. Such liberty, he argued, leads to the discovery of useful new truths and modes of life; confirms and strengthens the insights we already possess; and promotes the happiness of each individual more surely than any enforced and uniform standard can. In this and other ways, Mill attempted to reconcile his utilitarianism with the plurality of values which we possess.

• • •

For general discussion of Mill's work, see R. P. Anschutz, *The Philosophy of John Stuart Mill* (Oxford: Oxford University Press, 1953), Alan Ryan, *J. S. Mill* (London: Routledge & Kegan Paul, 1974), John Skorupski, *John Stuart Mill* (London and New York: Routledge, 1989), and David Lyons, *Rights, Welfare, and Mill's Moral Theory* (Oxford: Clarendon, 1994). For shorter essays, see J. P. Schneewind, ed., *Mill: A Collection of Critical Essays* (Garden City: Doubleday, 1968); Peter Radcliff, ed., *Limits of Liberty* (Belmont, Calif.: Wadsworth, 1966); Samuel Gorovitz, ed., *Utilitarianism with Critical Essays* (Indianapolis: Bobbs-Merrill, 1971), David Lyons, ed., *Mill's Utilitarianism* (Lanham, Md.: Rowman & Littlefield, 1997), Gerald Dworkin, ed., *Mill's On Liberty* (Lanham, Md: Rowman & Littlefield, 1997), and John Skorupski, ed., *The Cambridge Companion to Mill* (Cambridge: Cambridge University Press, 1998). A clear general discussion of utilitarianism can be found in J. J. C. Smart and Bernard Williams, *Utilitarianism: For and Against* (Cambridge: Cambridge University Press, 1973).

G.S.

Utilitarianism

CHAPTER I
General Remarks

There are few circumstances among those which make up the present condition of human knowledge more unlike what might have been expected, or more significant of the backward state in which speculation on the most important subjects still lingers, than the little progress which has been made in the decision of the controversy respecting the criterion of right and wrong. From the dawn of philosophy, the question concerning the *summum bonum*, or, what is the same thing, concerning the foundation of morality, has been accounted the main problem in speculative thought, has occupied the most gifted intellects and divided them into sects and schools carrying on a vigorous warfare against one another. And after more than two thousand years the same discussions continue, philosophers are still ranged under the same contending banners, and neither thinkers nor mankind at a large seem nearer to being unanimous on the subject than when the youth Socrates listened to the old Protagoras[1] and asserted (if Plato's dialogue be grounded on a real conversation) the theory of utilitarianism against the popular morality of the so-called sophist.

It is true that similar confusion and uncertainty and, in some cases, similar discordance exist respecting the first principles of all the sciences, not excepting that which is deemed the most certain of them — mathematics, without much impairing, generally indeed without impairing at all, the trustworthiness of the conclusions of those sciences. An apparent anomaly, the explanation of which is that the detailed doctrines of a science are not usually deduced from, nor depend for their evidence upon, what are called its first principles. Were it not so, there would be no science more precarious, or whose conclusions were more insufficiently made out, than algebra, which derives none of its certainty from what are commonly taught to learners as its elements, since these, as laid down by some of its most eminent teachers, are as full of fictions as English law, and of mysteries as theology. The truths which are ultimately accepted as the first principles of a science are really the last results of metaphysical analysis practiced on the elementary notions with which the science is conversant; and their relation to the science is not that of foundations to an edifice, but of roots to a tree, which may perform their office equally well though they be never dug down to and exposed to light. But though in science the particular truths precede the general theory, the contrary might be expected to be the case with a practical art, such as morals or legislation. All action is for the sake of some end, and rules of action, it seems natural to suppose, must take their whole character and color from the end to which they are subservient. When we engage in pursuit, a clear and precise conception of what we are pursuing would seem to be the first thing we need, instead of the last we are to look forward to. A test of right and wrong must be the means, one would think, of ascertaining what is right or wrong, and not a consequence of having already ascertained it.

The difficulty is not avoided by having recourse to the popular theory of a natural faculty, a sense of instinct, informing us of right and wrong. For — besides that the existence of such a moral instinct is itself one of the matters in dispute — those believers in it who have any pretensions to philosophy have been obliged to abandon the idea that it discerns what is right or wrong in the particular case in hand, as our other senses discern the sight or sound actually present. Our moral faculty, according to all those of its interpreters who are entitled to the name of thinkers, supplies us only with the general principles of moral judgments; it is a branch of our reason, not of our sensitive faculty, and must be looked to for the abstract doctrines of morality, not for perception of it in the concrete. The intuitive, no less than what may be termed the inductive, school of ethics insists on the necessity of general laws. They both agree that the

---

1. [Regarding Protagoras, see Hume's *Enquiry*, n. 72. — S.M.C.]

morality of an individual action is not a question of direct perception, but of the application of a law to an individual case. They recognize also, to a great extent, the same moral laws, but differ as to their evidence and the source from which they derive their authority. According to the one opinion, the principles of morals are evident *a priori*, requiring nothing to command assent except that the meaning of the terms be understood. According to the other doctrine, right and wrong, as well as truth and falsehood, are questions of observation and experience. But both hold equally that morality must be deduced from principles; and the intuitive school affirm as strongly as the inductive that there is a science of morals. Yet they seldom attempt to make out a list of the *a priori* principles which are to serve as the premises of the science; still more rarely do they make any effort to reduce those various principles to one first principle or common ground of obligation. They either assume the ordinary precepts of morals as of *a priori* authority, or they lay down as the common groundwork of those maxims some generality much less obviously authoritative than the maxims themselves, and which has never succeeded in gaining popular acceptance. Yet to support their pretensions there ought either to be some one fundamental principle or law at the root of all morality, or, if there be several, there should be a determinate order of precedence among them; and the one principle, or the rule for deciding between the various principles when they conflict, ought to be self-evident.

To inquire how far the bad effects of this deficiency have been mitigated in practice, or to what extent the moral beliefs of mankind have been vitiated or made uncertain by the absence of any distinct recognition of an ultimate standard, would imply a complete survey and criticism of past and present ethical doctrine. It would, however, be easy to show that whatever steadiness or consistency these moral beliefs have attained has been mainly due to the tacit influence of a standard not recognized. Although the non-existence of an acknowledged first principle has made ethics not so much a guide as a consecration of men's actual sentiments, still, as men's sentiments, both of favor and of aversion, are greatly influenced by what they suppose to be the effects of things upon their happiness, the principle of utility, or, as Bentham latterly called it, the greatest happiness principle, has

had a large share in forming the moral doctrines even of those who most scornfully reject its authority. Nor is there any school of thought which refuses to admit that the influence of actions on happiness is a most material and even predominant consideration in many of the details of morals, however unwilling to acknowledge it as the fundamental principle of morality and the source of moral obligation. I might go much further and say that to all those *a priori* moralists who deem it necessary to argue at all, utilitarian arguments are indispensable. It is not my present purpose to criticize these thinkers; but I cannot help referring, for illustration, to a systematic treatise by one of the most illustrious of them, the *Metaphysics of Ethics* by Kant. This remarkable man, whose system of thought will long remain one of the landmarks in the history of philosophical speculation, does, in the treatise in question, lay down a universal first principle as the origin and ground of moral obligation; it is this: "So act that the rule on which thou actest would admit of being adopted as a law by all rational beings." But when he begins to deduce from this precept any of the actual duties of morality, he fails, almost grotesquely, to show that there would be any contradiction, any logical (not to say physical) impossibility, in the adoption by all rational beings of the most outrageously immoral rules of conduct. All he shows is that the *consequences* of their universal adoption would be such as no one would choose to incur.

On the present occasion, I shall, without further discussion of the other theories, attempt to contribute something toward the understanding and appreciation of the "utilitarian" or "happiness" theory, and toward such proof as it is susceptible of. It is evident that this cannot be proof in the ordinary and popular meaning of the term. Questions of ultimate ends are not amenable to direct proof. Whatever can be proved to be good must be so by being shown to be a means to something admitted to be good without proof. The medical art is proved to be good by its conducing to health; but how is it possible to prove that health is good? The art of music is good, for the reason, among others, that it produces pleasure; but what proof is it possible to give that pleasure is good? If, then, it is asserted that there is a comprehensive formula, including all things which are in themselves good, and that whatever else is good is not so as an end but as a means, the formula may be accepted or rejected, but is not a subject of what is commonly understood by proof. We are not, however, to infer that its acceptance or rejection must depend on blind impulse or arbitrary choice. There is a larger meaning of the word "proof," in which this question is as amenable to it as any other of the disputed questions of philosophy. The subject is within the cognizance of the rational faculty; and neither does that faculty deal with it solely in the way of intuition. Considerations may be presented capable of determining the intellect either to give or withhold its assent to the doctrine; and this is equivalent to proof.

We shall examine presently of what nature are these considerations; in what manner they apply to the case, and what rational grounds, therefore, can be given for accepting or rejecting the utilitarian formula. But it is a preliminary condition of rational acceptance or rejection that the formula should be correctly understood. I believe that the very imperfect notion ordinarily formed of its meaning is the chief obstacle which impedes its reception, and that, could it be cleared even from only the grosser misconceptions, the question would be greatly simplified and a large proportion of its difficulties removed. Before, therefore, I attempt to enter into the philosophical grounds which can be given for assenting to the utilitarian standard, I shall offer some illustrations of the doctrine itself, with the view of showing more clearly what it is, distinguishing it from what it is not, and disposing of such of the practical objections to it as either originate in, or are closely connected with, mistaken interpretations of its meaning. Having thus prepared the ground, I shall afterwards endeavor to throw such light as I can call upon the question considered as one of philosophical theory.

CHAPTER II

What Utilitarianism Is

A passing remark is all that needs be given to the ignorant blunder of supposing that those who stand up for utility as the test of right and wrong use the term in that restricted and merely colloquial sense in which utility is opposed to pleasure. An apology is due to the philosophical opponents of utilitarianism for even the momentary appearance of confounding them with anyone capable of so absurd a misconception; which is the more extraordinary, inasmuch as the contrary accusation, of referring everything to pleasure, and that, too, in its grossest form, is another of the common charges against utilitarianism: and, as has been pointedly remarked by an able writer, the same sort of persons, and often the very same persons, denounce the theory "as impracticably dry when the word 'utility' precedes the word 'pleasure,' and as too practically voluptuous when the word 'pleasure' precedes the word 'utility.'" Those who know anything about the matter are aware that every writer, from Epicurus to Bentham, who maintained the theory of utility meant by it, not something to be contradistinguished from pleasure, but pleasure itself, together with exemption from pain; and instead of opposing the useful to the agreeable or the ornamental, have always declared that the useful means these, among other things. Yet the common herd, including the herd of writers, not only in newspapers and periodicals, but in books of weight and pretension, are perpetually falling into this shallow mistake. Having caught up the word "utilitarian," while knowing nothing whatever about it but its sound, they habitually express by it the rejection or the neglect of pleasure in some of its forms: of beauty, of ornament, or of amusement. Nor is the term thus ignorantly misapplied solely in disparagement, but occasionally in compliment, as though it implied superiority to frivolity and the mere pleasures of the moment. And this perverted use is the only one in which the word is popularly known, and the one from which the new generation are acquiring their sole notion of its meaning. Those who introduced the word, but who had for many years discontinued it as a distinctive appellation, may well feel themselves called upon to resume it if by doing so they can hope to contribute anything toward rescuing it from this utter degradation.[2]

2. The author of this essay has reason for believing himself to be the first person who brought the word "utilitarian" into use. He did not invent it, but adopted it from a passing expression in Mr. Galt's *Annals of the Parish*. [John Galt (1779–1839) was a Scottish novelist.] After using it as a designation for several years, he and others abandoned it from a growing dislike to anything resembling a badge or watchword of sectarian distinction. But as a name for one single opinion, not a set of opinions—to denote the recognition of utility as a standard, not any particular way of applying it—the term supplies a want in the language, and offers,

The creed which accepts as the foundation of morals "utility" or the "greatest happiness principle" holds that actions are right in proportion as they tend to promote happiness; wrong as they tend to produce the reverse of happiness. By happiness is intended pleasure and the absence of pain; by unhappiness, pain and the privation of pleasure. To give a clear view of the moral standard set up by the theory, much more requires to be said; in particular, what things it includes in the ideas of pain and pleasure, and to what extent this is left an open question. But these supplementary explanations do not affect the theory of life on which this theory of morality is grounded—namely, that pleasure and freedom from pain are the only things desirable as ends; and that all desirable things (which are as numerous in the utilitarian as in any other scheme) are desirable either for pleasure inherent in themselves or as means to the promotion of pleasure and the prevention of pain.

Now such a theory of life excites in many minds, and among them in some of the most estimable in feeling and purpose, inveterate dislike. To suppose that life has (as they express it) no higher end than pleasure—no better and nobler object of desire and pursuit—they designate as utterly mean and groveling, as a doctrine worthy only of swine, to whom the followers of Epicurus were, at a very early period, contemptuously likened; and modern holders of the doctrine are occasionally made the subject of equally polite comparisons by its German, French, and English assailants.

When thus attacked, the Epicureans have always answered that it is not they, but their accusers, who represent human nature in a degrading light, since the accusation supposes human beings to be capable of no pleasures except those of which swine are capable. If this supposition were true, the charge could not be gainsaid, but would then be no longer an imputation; for if the sources of pleasure were precisely the same to human beings and to swine, the rule of life which is good enough for the one would be good enough for the other. The comparison of the Epicurean life to that of beasts is felt as degrading, precisely because a beast's pleasures do not satisfy a human being's conceptions of happiness. Human

beings have faculties more elevated than the animal appetites and, when once made conscious of them, do not regard anything as happiness which does not include their gratification. I do not indeed, consider the Epicureans to have been by any means faultless in drawing out their scheme of consequences from the utilitarian principle. To do this in any sufficient manner, many Stoic, as well as Christian, elements require to be included. But there is no known Epicurean theory of life which does not assign to the pleasures of the intellect, of the feelings and imagination, and of the moral sentiments a much higher value as pleasures than to those of mere sensation. It must be admitted, however, that utilitarian writers in general have placed the superiority of mental over bodily pleasures chiefly in the greater permanency, safety, uncostliness, etc., of the former—that is, in their circumstantial advantages rather than in their intrinsic nature. And on all these points utilitarians have fully proved their case; but they might have taken the other and, as it may be called, higher ground with entire consistency. It is quite compatible with the principle of utility to recognize the fact that some kinds of pleasure are more desirable and more valuable than others. It would be absurd that, while in estimating all other things quality is considered as well as quantity, the estimation of pleasure should be supposed to depend on quantity alone.

If I am asked what I mean by difference of quality in pleasures, or what makes one pleasure more valuable than another, merely as a pleasure, except its being greater in amount, there is but one possible answer. Of two pleasures, if there be one to which all or almost all who have experience of both give a decided preference, irrespective of any feeling of moral obligation to prefer it, that is the more desirable pleasure. If one of the two is, by those who are competently acquainted with both, placed so far above the other that they prefer it, even though knowing it to be attended with a greater amount of discontent, and would not resign it for any quantity of the other pleasure which their nature is capable of, we are justified in ascribing to the preferred enjoyment a superiority in quality so far outweighing quantity as to render it, in comparison, of small account.

Now it is an unquestionable fact that those who are equally acquainted with and equally capable of appreciating and enjoying both do give a most marked

---

in many cases, a convenient mode of avoiding tiresome circumlocutions.

preference to the manner of existence which employs their higher faculties. Few human creatures would consent to be changed into any of the lower animals for a promise of the fullest allowance of a beast's pleasure; no intelligent human being would consent to be a fool, no instructed person would be an ignoramus, no person of feeling and conscience would be selfish and base, even though they should be persuaded that the fool, the dunce, or the rascal is better satisfied with his lot than they are with theirs. They would not resign what they possess more than he for the most complete satisfaction of all the desires which they have in common with him. If they ever fancy they would, it is only in cases of unhappiness so extreme that to escape from it they would exchange their lot for almost any other, however undesirable in their own eyes. A being of higher faculties requires more to make him happy, is capable probably of more acute suffering, and certainly accessible to it at more points, than one of an inferior type; but in spite of these liabilities, he can never really wish to sink into what he feels to be a lower grade of existence. We may give what explanation we please of this unwillingness; we may attribute it to pride, a name which is given indiscriminately to some of the most and to some of the least estimable feelings of which mankind are capable; we may refer it to the love of liberty and personal independence, an appeal to which was with the Stoics one of the most effective means for the inculcation of it; to the love of power or to the love of excitement, both of which do really enter into and contribute to it; but its most appropriate appellation is a sense of dignity, which all human beings possess in one form or other, and in some, though by no means in exact, proportion to their higher faculties, and which is so essential a part of the happiness of those in whom it is strong that nothing which conflicts with it could be otherwise than momentarily an object of desire to them. Whoever supposes that this preference takes place at a sacrifice of happiness—that the superior being, in anything like equal circumstances, is not happier than the inferior—confounds the two very different ideas of happiness and content. It is indisputable that the being whose capacities of enjoyment are low has the greatest chance of having them fully satisfied; and a highly endowed being will always feel that any happiness which he can look for, as the

world is constituted, is imperfect. But he can learn to bear its imperfections, if they are at all bearable; and they will not make him envy the being who is indeed unconscious of the imperfections, but only because he feels not at all the good which those imperfections qualify. It is better to be a human being dissatisfied than a pig satisfied; better to be Socrates dissatisfied than a fool satisfied. And if the fool, or the pig, are of a different opinion, it is because they only know their own side of the question. The other party to the comparison knows both sides.

It may be objected that many who are capable of the higher pleasures occasionally, under the influence of temptation, postpone them to the lower. But this is quite compatible with a full appreciation of the intrinsic superiority of the higher. Men often, from infirmity of character, make their election for the nearer good, though they know it to be the less valuable; and this no less when the choice is between two bodily pleasures than when it is between bodily and mental. They pursue sensual indulgences to the injury of health, though perfectly aware that health is the greater good. It may be further objected that many who begin with youthful enthusiasm for everything noble, as they advance in years, sink into indolence and selfishness. But I do not believe that those who undergo this very common change voluntarily choose the lower description of pleasures in preference to the higher. I believe that, before they devote themselves exclusively to the one, they have already become incapable of the other. Capacity for other nobler feelings is in most natures a very tender plant, easily killed, not only by hostile influences, but by mere want of sustenance; and in the majority of young persons it speedily dies away if the occupations to which their position in life has devoted them, and the society into which it has thrown them, are not favorable to keeping that higher capacity in exercise. Men lose their high aspirations as they lose their intellectual tastes, because they have not time or opportunity for indulging them; and they addict themselves to inferior pleasures, not because they deliberately prefer them, but because they are either the only ones to which they have access or the only ones which they are any longer capable of enjoying. It may be questioned whether anyone who has remained equally susceptible to both classes of pleasures ever knowingly and calmly preferred the lower, though many, in all ages, have broken down in an ineffectual attempt to combine both.

From this verdict of the only competent judges, I apprehend there can be no appeal. On a question which is the best worth having of two pleasures, or which of two modes of existence is the most grateful to the feelings, apart from its moral attributes and from its consequences, the judgment of those who are qualified by knowledge of both, or, if they differ, that of the majority among them, must be admitted as final. And there needs be the less hesitation to accept this judgment respecting the quality of pleasures, since there is no other tribunal to be referred to even on the question of quantity. What means are there of determining which is the acutest of two pains, or the intensest of two pleasurable sensations, except the general suffrage of those who are familiar with both? Neither pains nor pleasures are homogeneous, and pain is always heterogeneous with pleasure. What is there to decide whether a particular pleasure is worth purchasing at the cost of a particular pain, except the feelings and judgment of the experienced? When, therefore, those feelings and judgment declare the pleasures derived from the higher faculties to be preferable *in kind*, apart from the question of intensity, to those of which the animal nature, disjoined from the higher faculties, is susceptible, they are entitled on this subject to the same regard.

I have dwelt on this point as being a necessary part of a perfectly just conception of utility or happiness considered as the directive rule of human conduct. But it is by no means an indispensable condition to the acceptance of the utilitarian standard; for that standard is not the agent's own greatest happiness, but the greatest amount of happiness altogether; and if it may possibly be doubted whether a noble character is always the happier for its nobleness, there can be no doubt that it makes other people happier, and that the world in general is immensely a gainer by it. Utilitarianism, therefore, could only attain its end by the general cultivation of nobleness of character, even if each individual were only benefited by the nobleness of others, and his own, so far as happiness is concerned, were a sheer deduction from the benefit. But the bare enunciation of such an absurdity as this last renders refutation superfluous.

According to the greatest happiness principle, as above explained, the ultimate end, with reference to and for the sake of which all other things are desirable—whether we are considering our own good or that of other people—is an existence exempt as far as possible from pain, and as rich as possible in enjoyments, both in point of quantity and quality; the test of quality and the rule of measuring it against quantity being the preference felt by those who, in their opportunities of experience, to which must be added their habits of self-consciousness and self-observation, are best furnished with the means of comparison. This, being according to the utilitarian opinion the end of human action, is necessarily also the standard of morality, which may accordingly be defined "the rules and precepts for human conduct," by the observance of which an existence such as has been described might be, to the greatest extent possible, secured to all mankind; and not to them only, but, so far as the nature of things admits, to the whole sentient creation.

Against this doctrine, however, arises another class of objectors who say that happiness, in any form, cannot be the rational purpose of human life and action; because, in the first place, it is unattainable; and they contemptuously ask, What right hast thou to be happy?—a question which Mr. Carlyle[3] clinches by the addition, What right, a short time ago, hadst thou even *to be?* Next they say that men can do *without* happiness; that all noble human beings have felt this, and could not have become noble but by learning the lesson of *Entsagen*, or renunciation; which lesson, thoroughly learned and submitted to, they affirm to be the beginning and necessary condition of all virtue.

The first of these objections would go to the root of the matter were it well founded; for if no happiness is to be had at all by human beings, the attainment of it cannot be the end of morality or of any rational conduct. Though, even in that case, something might still be said for the utilitarian theory, since utility includes not solely the pursuit of happiness, but the prevention or mitigation of unhappiness; and if the

3. [Thomas Carlyle (1795–1881) was a Scottish author and social critic who wrote a multivolume history of the French Revolution. His theistic view stressed the essential spirituality of the world and its leaders.]

former aim be chimerical, there will be all the greater scope and more imperative need for the latter, so long at least as mankind think fit to live and do not take refuge in the simultaneous act of suicide recommended under certain conditions by Novalis.[4] When, however, it is thus positively asserted to be impossible that human life should be happy, the assertion, if not something like a verbal quibble, is at least an exaggeration. If by happiness be meant a continuity of highly pleasurable excitement, it is evident enough that this is impossible. A state of exalted pleasure lasts only moments or in some cases, and with some intermissions, hours or days, and is the occasional brilliant flash of enjoyment, not its permanent and steady flame. Of this the philosophers who have taught that happiness is the end of life were as fully aware as those who taunt them. The happiness which they meant was not a life of rapture, but moments of such, in an existence made up of few and transitory pains, many and various pleasures, with a decided predominance of the active over the passive, and having as the foundation of the whole not to expect more from life than it is capable of bestowing. A life thus composed, to those who have been fortunate enough to obtain it, has always appeared worthy of the name of happiness. And such an existence is even now the lot of many during some considerable portion of their lives. The present wretched education and wretched social arrangements are the only real hindrance to its being attainable by almost all.

The objectors perhaps may doubt whether human beings, if taught to consider happiness as the end of life, would be satisfied with such a moderate share of it. But great numbers of mankind have been satisfied with much less. The main constituents of a satisfied life appear to be two, either of which by itself is often found sufficient for the purpose: tranquility and excitement. With much tranquillity, many find that they can be content with very little pleasure; with much excitement, many can reconcile themselves to a considerable quantity of pain. There is assuredly no inherent impossibility of enabling even the mass of mankind to unite both, since the two are so far from being incompatible that they are in natural alliance, the prolongation of either being a preparation

for, and exciting a wish for, the other. It is only those in whom indolence amounts to a vice that do not desire excitement after an interval of repose; it is only those in whom the need of excitement is a disease that feel the tranquillity which follows excitement dull and insipid, instead of pleasurable in direct proportion to the excitement which preceded it. When people who are tolerably fortunate in their outward lot do not find in life sufficient enjoyment to make it valuable to them, the cause generally is caring for nobody but themselves. To those who have neither public nor private affections, the excitements of life are much curtailed, and in any case dwindle in value as the time approaches when all selfish interests must be terminated by death; while those who leave after them objects of personal affection, and especially those who have also cultivated a fellow-feeling with the collective interests of mankind, retain as lively an interest in life on the eve of death as in the vigor of youth and health. Next to selfishness, the principal cause which makes life unsatisfactory is want of mental cultivation. A cultivated mind—I do not mean that of a philosopher, but any mind to which the fountains of knowledge have been opened, and which has been taught, in any tolerable degree, to exercise its faculties—finds sources of inexhaustible interest in all that surrounds it: in the objects of nature, the achievements of art, the imaginations of poetry, the incidents of history, the ways of mankind, past and present, and their prospects in the future. It is possible, indeed, to become indifferent to all this, and that too without having exhausted a thousandth part of it, but only when one has had from the beginning no moral or human interest in these things and has sought in them only the gratification of curiosity.

Now there is absolutely no reason in the nature of things why an amount of mental culture sufficient to give an intelligent interest in these objects of contemplation should not be the inheritance of everyone born in a civilized country. As little is there an inherent necessity that any human being should be a selfish egotist, devoid of every feeling or care but those which center in his own miserable individuality. Something far superior to this is sufficiently common even now, to give ample earnest of what the human species may be made. Genuine private affections and a sincere interest in the public good are possible, though in unequal degrees, to every rightly brought up human

4. [Pseudonym of Friedrich Leopold Freiherr von Hardenberg (1771–1801), a German romantic poet.]

being. In a world in which there is so much to interest, so much to enjoy, and so much also to correct and improve, everyone who has this moderate amount of moral and intellectual requisites is capable of an existence which may be called enviable; and unless such a person, through bad laws or subjection to the will of others, is denied the liberty to use the sources of happiness within his reach, he will not fail to find this enviable existence, if he escapes the positive evils of life, the great sources of physical and mental suffering—such as indigence, disease, and the unkindness, worthlessness, or premature loss of objects of affection. The main stress of the problem lies, therefore, in the contest with these calamities from which it is a rare good fortune entirely to escape; which, as things now are, cannot be obviated, and often cannot be in any material degree mitigated. Yet no one whose opinion deserves a moment's consideration can doubt that most of the great positive evils of the world are in themselves removable, and will, if human affairs continue to improve, be in the end reduced within narrow limits. Poverty, in any sense implying suffering, may be completely extinguished by the wisdom of society combined with the good sense and providence of individuals. Even that most intractable of enemies, disease, may be indefinitely reduced in dimensions by good physical and moral education and proper control of noxious influences, while the progress of science holds out a promise for the future of still more direct conquests over this detestable foe. And every advance in that direction relieves us from some, not only of the chances which cut short our own lives, but, what concerns us still more, which deprive us of those in whom our happiness is wrapt up. As for vicissitudes of fortune and other disappointments connected with worldly circumstances, these are principally the effect either of gross imprudence, of ill-regulated desires, or of bad or imperfect social institutions. All the grand sources, in short, of human suffering are in a great degree, many of them almost entirely, conquerable by human care and effort; and though their removal is grievously slow—though a long succession of generations will perish in the breach before the conquest is completed, and this world becomes all that, if will and knowledge were not wanting, it might easily be made—yet every mind sufficiently intelligent and generous to bear a part, however small and inconspicuous, in the endeavor will draw a noble enjoyment from the contest itself, which he would not for any bribe in the form of selfish indulgence consent to be without.

And this leads to the true estimation of what is said by the objectors concerning the possibility and the obligation of learning to do without happiness. Unquestionably it is possible to do without happiness; it is done involuntarily by nineteen-twentieths of mankind, even in those parts of our present world which are least deep in barbarism; and it often has to be done voluntarily by the hero or the martyr, for the sake of something which he prizes more than his individual happiness. But this something, what is it, unless the happiness of others or some of the requisites of happiness? It is noble to be capable of resigning entirely one's own portion of happiness, or chances of it; but, after all, this self-sacrifice must be for some end; it is not its own end; and if we are told that its end is not happiness but virtue, which is better than happiness, I ask, would the sacrifice be made if the hero or martyr did not believe that it would earn for others immunity from similar sacrifices? Would it be made if he thought that his renunciation of happiness for himself would produce no fruit for any of his fellow creatures, but to make their lot like his and place them also in the condition of persons who have renounced happiness? All honor to those who can abnegate for themselves the personal enjoyment of life when by such renunciation they contribute worthily to increase the amount of happiness in the world; but he who does it or professes to do it for any other purpose is no more deserving of admiration than the ascetic mounted on his pillar. He may be an inspiring proof of what men *can* do, but assuredly not an example of what they *should*.

Though it is only in a very imperfect state of the world's arrangements that anyone can best serve the happiness of others by the absolute sacrifice of his own, yet, so long as the world is in that imperfect state, I fully acknowledge that the readiness to make such a sacrifice is the highest virtue which can be found in man. I will add that in this condition of the world, paradoxical as the assertion may be, the conscious ability to do without happiness gives the best prospect of realizing such happiness as is attainable. For nothing except that consciousness can raise a person above the chances of life by making him feel that, let fate and fortune do their worst, they have not power to subdue him; which, once felt, frees him from excess of anxiety concerning the evils of life and enables him, like many a Stoic in the worst times of the Roman Empire, to cultivate in tranquillity the sources of satisfaction accessible to him, without concerning himself about the uncertainty of their duration any more than about their inevitable end.

Meanwhile, let utilitarians never cease to claim the morality of self-devotion as a possession which belongs by as good a right to them as either to the Stoic or to the Transcendentalist.[5] The utilitarian morality does recognize in human beings the power of sacrificing their own greatest good for the good of others. It only refuses to admit that the sacrifice is itself a good. A sacrifice which does not increase or tend to increase the sum total of happiness, it considers as wasted. The only self-renunciation which it applauds is devotion to the happiness, or to some of the means of happiness, of others, either of mankind collectively or of individuals within the limits imposed by the collective interests of mankind.

I must again repeat what the assailants of utilitarianism seldom have the justice to acknowledge, that the happiness which forms the utilitarian standard of what is right in conduct is not the agent's own happiness but that of all concerned. As between his own happiness and that of others, utilitarianism requires him to be as strictly impartial as a disinterested and benevolent spectator. In the golden rule of Jesus of Nazareth, we read the complete spirit of the ethics of utility. "To do as you would be done by," and "to love your neighbor as yourself," constitute the ideal perfection of utilitarian morality. As the means of making the nearest approach to this ideal, utility would enjoin, first, that laws and social arrangements should place the happiness or (as, speaking practically, it may be called) the interest of every individual as nearly as possible in harmony with the interest of the whole; and, secondly, that education and opinion, which have so vast a power over human character, should so use that power as to establish in the mind of every

individual an indissoluble association between his own happiness and the good of the whole, especially between his own happiness and the practice of such modes of conduct, negative and positive, as regard for the universal happiness prescribes; so that not only he may be unable to conceive the possibility of happiness to himself, consistently with conduct opposed to the general good, but also that a direct impulse to promote the general good may be in every individual one of the habitual motives of action, and the sentiments connected therewith may fill a large and prominent place in every human being's sentient existence. If the impugners of the utilitarian morality represented it to their own minds in this its true character, I know not what recommendation possessed by any other morality they could possibly affirm to be wanting to it; what more beautiful or more exalted developments of human nature any other ethical system can be supposed to foster, or what springs of action, not accessible to the utilitarian, such systems rely on for giving effect to their mandates.

The objectors to utilitarianism cannot always be charged with representing it in a discreditable light. On the contrary, those among them who entertain anything like a just idea of its disinterested character sometimes find fault with its standard as being too high for humanity. They say it is exacting too much to require that people shall always act from the inducement of promoting the general interests of society. But this is to mistake the very meaning of a standard of morals and confound the rule of action with the motive of it. It is the business of ethics to tell us what are our duties, or by what test we may know them; but no system of ethics requires that the sole motive of all we do shall be a feeling of duty; on the contrary, ninety-nine hundredths of all our actions are done from other motives, and rightly so done if the rule of duty does not condemn them. It is the more unjust to utilitarianism that this particular misapprehension should be made a ground of objection to it, inasmuch as utilitarian moralists have gone beyond almost all others in affirming that the motive has nothing to do with the morality of the action, though much with the worth of the agent. He who saves a fellow creature from drowning does what is morally right, whether his motive be duty or the hope of being paid for his trouble; he who betrays the friend that trusts him is guilty of a crime, even if his object

5. [Transcendentalism was a literary and philosophical movement that flourished in New England from about 1835 to 1860. It emphasized intuition as the source of knowledge and enlightened individualism as the basis of ethics. Its leading spokesmen were Ralph Waldo Emerson (1803–1882) and Henry David Thoreau (1817–1862).]

be to serve another friend to whom he is under greater obligations.[6] But to speak only of actions done from the motive of duty, and in direct obedience to principle: it is a misapprehension of the utilitarian mode of thought to conceive it as implying that people should fix their minds upon so wide a generality as the world, or society at large. The great majority of good actions are intended not for the benefit of the world, but for that of individuals, of which the good

6. An opponent, whose intellectual and moral fairness it is a pleasure to acknowledge (the Rev. J. Llewellyn Davies), has objected to this passage, saying, "Surely the rightness or wrongness of saving a man from drowning does depend very much upon the motive with which it is done. Suppose that a tyrant, when his enemy jumped into the sea to escape from him, saved him from drowning simply in order that he might inflict upon him more exquisite tortures, would it tend to clearness to speak of that rescue as 'a morally right action'? Or suppose again, according to one of the stock illustrations of ethical inquiries, that a man betrayed a trust received from a friend, because the discharge of it would fatally injure that friend himself or someone belonging to him, would utilitarianism compel one to call the betrayal 'a crime' as much as if it had been done from the meanest motive?"

I submit that he who saves another from drowning in order to kill him by torture afterwards does not differ only in motive from him who does the same thing from duty or benevolence; the act itself is different. The rescue of the man is, in the case supposed, only the necessary first step of an act far more atrocious than leaving him to drown would have been. Had Mr. Davies said, "The rightness or wrongness of saving a man from drowning does depend very much"—not upon the motive, but—"upon the *intention*," no utilitarian would have differed from him. Mr. Davies, by an oversight too common not to be quite venial, has in this case confounded the very different ideas of Motive and Intention. There is no point which utilitarian thinkers (and Bentham pre-eminently) have taken more pains to illustrate than this. The morality of the action depends entirely upon the intention—that is, upon what the agent *wills to do*. But the motive, that is, the feeling which makes him will so to do, if it makes no difference in the act, makes none in the morality: though it makes a great difference in our moral estimation of the agent, especially if it indicates a good or a bad habitual *disposition*—a bent of character from which useful, or from which hurtful actions are likely to arise.

[This note appeared in the second edition of *Utilitarianism* but not in subsequent ones.]

of the world is made up; and the thoughts of the most virtuous man need not on these occasions travel beyond the particular persons concerned, except so far as is necessary to assure himself that in benefiting them he is not violating the rights, that is, the legitimate and authorized expectations, of anyone else. The multiplication of happiness is, according to the utilitarian ethics, the object of virtue: the occasions on which any person (except one in a thousand) has it in his power to do this on an extended scale—in other words, to be a public benefactor—are but exceptional; and on these occasions alone is he called on to consider public utility; in every other case, private utility, the interest or happiness of some few persons, is all he has to attend to. Those alone the influence of whose actions extends to society in general need concern themselves habitually about so large an object. In the case of abstinences indeed—of things which people forbear to do from moral considerations, though the consequences in the particular case might be beneficial—it would be unworthy of an intelligent agent not to be consciously aware that the action is of a class which, if practiced generally, would be generally injurious, and that this is the ground of the obligation to abstain from it. The amount of regard for the public interest implied in this recognition is no greater than is demanded by every system of morals, for they all enjoin to abstain from whatever is manifestly pernicious to society.

The same considerations dispose of another reproach against the doctrine of utility, founded on a still grosser misconception of the purpose of a standard of morality and of the very meaning of the words "right" and "wrong." It is often affirmed that utilitarianism renders men cold and unsympathizing; that it chills their moral feelings toward individuals; that it makes them regard only the dry and hard consideration of the consequences of actions, not taking into their moral estimate the qualities from which those actions emanate. If the assertion means that they do not allow their judgment respecting the rightness or wrongness of an action to be influenced by their opinion of the qualities of the person who does it, this is a complaint not against utilitarianism, but against any standard or morality at all; for certainly no known ethical standard decides an action to be good or bad because it is done by a good or bad man, still less because done by an amiable, a brave, or a benevolent man, or the contrary. These considerations are relevant, not to the estimation of actions, but of persons; and there is nothing in the utilitarian theory inconsistent with the fact that there are other things which interest us in persons besides the rightness and wrongness of their actions. The Stoics, indeed, with the paradoxical misuse of language which was part of their system, and by which they strove to raise themselves above all concern about anything but virtue, were fond of saying that he who has that has everything; that he, and only he, is rich, is beautiful, is a king. But no claim of this description is made for the virtuous man by the utilitarian doctrine. Utilitarians are quite aware that there are other desirable possessions and qualities besides virtue, and are perfectly willing to allow to all of them their full worth. They are also aware that a right action does not necessarily indicate a virtuous character, and that actions which are blamable often proceed from qualities entitled to praise. When this is apparent in any particular case, it modifies their estimation, not certainly of the act, but of the agent. I grant that they are, notwithstanding, of opinion that in the long run the best proof of a good character is good actions; and resolutely refuse to consider any mental disposition as good of which the predominant tendency is to produce bad conduct. This makes them unpopular with many people, but it is an unpopularity which they must share with everyone who regards the distinction between right and wrong in a serious light; and the reproach is not one which a conscientious utilitarian need be anxious to repel.

If no more be meant by the objection than that many utilitarians look on the morality of actions, as measured by the utilitarian standards, with too exclusive a regard, and do not lay sufficient stress upon the other beauties of character which go toward making a human being lovable or admirable, this may be admitted. Utilitarians who have cultivated their moral feelings, but not their sympathies, nor their artistic perceptions, do fall into this mistake; and so do all other moralists under the same conditions. What can be said in excuse for other moralists is equally available for them, namely, that, if there is to be any error, it is better that it should be on that side. As a matter of fact, we may affirm that among utilitarians, as among adherents of other systems, there is every imaginable degree of rigidity and of laxity in the applica-

tion of their standard; some are even puritanically rigorous, while others are as indulgent as can possibly be desired by sinner or by sentimentalist. But on the whole, a doctrine which brings prominently forward the interest that mankind have in the repression and prevention of conduct which violates the moral law is likely to be inferior to no other in turning the sanctions of opinion against such violations. It is true, the question "What does violate the moral law?" is one on which those who recognize different standards of morality are likely now and then to differ. But difference of opinion on moral questions was not first introduced into the world by utilitarianism, while that doctrine does supply, if not always an easy, at all events a tangible and intelligible, mode of deciding such differences.

It may not be superfluous to notice a few more of the common misapprehensions of utilitarian ethics, even those which are so obvious and gross that it might appear impossible for any person of candor and intelligence to fall into them; since persons, even of considerable mental endowment, often give themselves so little trouble to understand the bearings of any opinion against which they entertain a prejudice, and men are in general so little conscious of this voluntary ignorance as a defect that the vulgarest misunderstandings of ethical doctrines are continually met with in the deliberate writings of persons of the greatest pretensions both to high principle and to philosophy. We not uncommonly hear the doctrine of utility inveighed against as a *godless* doctrine. If it be necessary to say anything at all against so mere an assumption, we may say that the question depends upon what idea we have formed of the moral character of the Deity. If it be a true belief that God desires, above all things, the happiness of his creatures, and that this was his purpose in their creation, utility is not only not a godless doctrine, but more profoundly religious than any other. If it be meant that utilitarianism does not recognize the revealed will of God as the supreme law of morals, I answer that a utilitarian who believes in the perfect goodness and wisdom of *God* necessarily believes that whatever God has thought fit to reveal on the subject of morals must fulfill the requirements of utility in a supreme degree. But others besides utilitarians have been of opinion that the Christian revelation was intended, and is fitted, to inform the hearts and minds of mankind with a spirit which should enable them to find for themselves what is right, and incline them to do it when found, rather than to tell them, except in a very general way, what it is; and that we need a doctrine of ethics, carefully followed out, to *interpret* to us the will of God. Whether this opinion is correct or not, it is superfluous here to discuss; since whatever aid religion, either natural or revealed, can afford to ethical investigation is as open to the utilitarian moralist as to any other. He can use it as the testimony of God to the usefulness or hurtfulness of any given course of action by as good a right as others can use it for the indication of a transcendental law having no connection with usefulness or with happiness.

Again, utility is often summarily stigmatized as an immoral doctrine by giving it the name of "expediency," and taking advantage of the popular use of that term to contrast it with principle. But the expedient, in the sense in which it is opposed to the right, generally means that which is expedient for the particular interest of the agent himself; as when a minister sacrifices the interests of his country to keep himself in place. When it means anything better than this, it means that which is expedient for some immediate object, some temporary purpose, but which violates a rule whose observance is expedient in a much higher degree. The expedient, in this sense, instead of being the same thing with the useful, is a branch of the hurtful. Thus it would often be expedient, for the purpose of getting over some momentary embarrassment, or attaining some object immediately useful to ourselves or others, to tell a lie. But inasmuch as the cultivation in ourselves of a sensitive feeling on the subject of veracity is one of the most useful, and the enfeeblement of that feeling one of the most hurtful, things to which our conduct can be instrumental; and inasmuch as any, even unintentional, deviation from truth does that much toward weakening the trustworthiness of human assertion, which is not only the principal support of all present social well-being, but the insufficiency of which does more than any one thing that can be named to keep back civilization, virtue, everything on which human happiness on the largest scale depends—we feel that the violation, for a present advantage, of a rule of such transcendent expediency is not expedient, and that he who, for the sake of convenience to himself or to some other individual, does what depends on him to deprive mankind of the good, and inflict upon them the evil, involved in the greater or less reliance which they can place in each other's word, acts the part of one of their worst enemies. Yet that even this rule, sacred as it is, admits of possible exceptions is acknowledged by all moralists; the chief of which is when the withholding of some fact (as of information from a malefactor, or of bad news from a person dangerously ill) would save an individual (especially an individual other than oneself) from great and unmerited evil, and when the withholding can only be effected by denial. But in order that the exception may not extend itself beyond the need, and may have the least possible effect in weakening reliance on veracity, it ought to be recognized and, if possible, its limits defined; and, if the principle of utility is good for anything, it must be good for weighing these conflicting utilities against one another and marking out the region within which one or the other preponderates.

Again, defenders of utility often find themselves called upon to reply to such objections as this—that there is not time, previous to action, for calculating and weighing the effects of any line of conduct on the general happiness. This is exactly as if anyone were to say that it is impossible to guide our conduct by Christianity because there is not time, on every occasion on which anything has to be done, to read through the Old and New Testaments. The answer to the objection is that there has been ample time, namely, the whole past duration of the human species. During all that time mankind have been learning by experience the tendencies of actions; on which experience all the prudence as well as all the morality of life are dependent. People talk as if the commencement of this course of experience had hitherto been put off, and as if, at the moment when some man feels tempted to meddle with the property or life of another, he had to begin considering for the first time whether murder and theft are injurious to human happiness. Even then I do not think that he would find the question very puzzling; but, at all events, the matter is now done to his hand. It is truly a whimsical supposition that, if mankind were agreed in considering utility to be the test of morality, they would remain without any agreement as to what *is* useful, and would take no measures for having their notions on the subject taught to the young and enforced by law and opinion. There is no difficulty in proving any ethical standard whatever to work ill if we suppose universal idiocy to be conjoined with it; but on any hypothesis short of that, mankind must by this time have acquired positive beliefs as to the effects of some actions on their happiness; and the beliefs which have thus come down are the rules of morality for the multitude, and for the philosopher until he has succeeded in finding better. That philosophers might easily do this, even now, on many subjects; that the received code of ethics is by no means of divine right; and that mankind have still much to learn as to the effects of actions on the general happiness, I admit or rather earnestly maintain. The corollaries from the principle of utility, like the precepts of every practical art, admit of indefinite improvement, and, in a progressive state of the human mind, their improvement is perpetually going on. But to consider the rules of morality as improvable is one thing; to pass over the intermediate generalization entirely and endeavor to test each individual action directly by the first principle is another. It is a strange notion that the acknowledgment of a first principle is inconsistent with the admission of secondary ones. To inform a traveler respecting the place of his ultimate destination is not to forbid the use of landmarks and direction-posts on the way. The proposition that happiness is the end and aim of morality does not mean that no road ought to be laid down to that goal, or that persons going thither should not be advised to take one direction rather than another. Men really ought to leave off talking a kind of nonsense on this subject, which they would neither talk nor listen to on other matters of practical concernment. Nobody argues that the art of navigation is not founded on astronomy because sailors cannot wait to calculate the Nautical Almanac. Being rational creatures, they go to sea with it ready calculated; and all rational creatures go out upon the sea of life with their minds made up on the common questions of right and wrong, as well as on many of the far more difficult questions of wise and foolish. And this, as long as foresight is a human quality, it is to be presumed they will continue to do. Whatever we adopt as the fundamental principle of morality, we require subordinate principles to apply it by; the impossibility of doing without them, being common to all systems, can afford no argument against any one in particular; but gravely to argue as if no such secondary principles could be had, and as if mankind had remained till

now, and always must remain, without drawing any general conclusions from the experience of human life is as high a pitch, I think, as absurdity has ever reached in philosophical controversy.

The remainder of the stock arguments against utilitarianism mostly consist in laying to its charge the common infirmities of human nature, and the general difficulties which embarrass conscientious persons in shaping their course through life. We are told that a utilitarian will be apt to make his own particular case an exception to moral rules, and, when under temptation, will see a utility in the breach of a rule, greater than he will see in its observance. But is utility the only creed which is able to furnish us with excuses for evil-doing and means of cheating our own conscience? They are afforded in abundance by all doctrines which recognize as a fact in morals the existence of conflicting considerations, which all doctrines do that have been believed by sane persons. It is not the fault of any creed, but of the complicated nature of human affairs, that rules of conduct cannot be so framed as to require no exceptions, and that hardly any kind of action can safely be laid down as either always obligatory or always condemnable. There is no ethical creed which does not temper the rigidity of its laws by giving a certain latitude, under the moral responsibility of the agent, for accommodation to peculiarities of circumstances; and under every creed, at the opening thus made, self-deception and dishonest casuistry get in. There exists no moral system under which there do not arise unequivocal cases of conflicting obligation. These are the real difficulties, the knotty points both in the theory of ethics and in the conscientious guidance of personal conduct. They are overcome practically, with greater or with less success, according to the intellect and virtue of the individual; but it can hardly be pretended that anyone will be the less qualified for dealing with them, from possessing an ultimate standard to which conflicting rights and duties can be referred. If utility is the ultimate source of moral obligations, utility may be invoked to decide between them when their demands are incompatible. Though the application of the standard may be difficult, it is better than none at all; while in other systems, the moral laws all claiming independent authority, there is no common umpire entitled to interfere between them; their claims to precedence one over another rest on little better than sophistry, and, unless determined, as they generally are, by the unacknowledged influence of consideration of utility, afford a free scope for the action of personal desires and partialities. We must remember that only in these cases of conflict between secondary principles is it requisite that first principles should be appealed to. There is no case of moral obligation in which some secondary principle is not involved; and if only one, there can seldom be any real doubt which one it is, in the mind of any person by whom the principle itself is recognized.

CHAPTER III

Of the Ultimate Sanction
of the Principle of Utility

The question is often asked, and properly so, in regard to any supposed moral standard—What is its sanction? what are the motives to obey? or, more specifically, what is the source of its obligation? whence does it derive its binding force? It is a necessary part of moral philosophy to provide the answer to this question, which, though frequently assuming the shape of an objection to the utilitarian morality, as if it had some special applicability to that above others, really arises in regard to all standards. It arises, in fact, whenever a person is called on to *adopt* a standard, or refer morality to any basis on which he has not been accustomed to rest it. For the customary morality, that which education and opinion have consecrated, is the only one which presents itself to the mind with the feeling of being *in itself* obligatory; and when a person is asked to believe that this morality *derives* its obligation from some general principle round which custom has not thrown the same halo, the assertion is to him a paradox; the supposed corollaries seem to have a more binding force than the original theorem; the superstructure seems to stand better without than with what is represented as its foundation. He says to himself, I feel that I am bound not to rob or murder, betray or deceive; but why am I bound to promote the general happiness? If my own happiness lies in something else, why may I not give that the preference?

If the view adopted by the utilitarian philosophy of the nature of the moral sense be correct, this difficulty will always present itself until the influences which form moral character have taken the same hold of the principle which they have taken of some of the consequences—until, by the improvement of education, the feeling of unity with our fellow creatures shall be (what it cannot be denied that Christ intended it to be) as deeply rooted in our character, and to our own consciousness as completely a part of our nature, as the horror of crime is in an ordinarily well-brought up young person. It the meantime, however, the difficulty has no peculiar application to the doctrine of utility, but is inherent in every attempt to analyze morality and reduce it to principles; which, unless the principle is already in men's minds invested with as much sacredness as any of its applications, always seems to divest them of a part of their sanctity.

The principle of utility either has, or there is no reason why it might not have, all the sanctions which belong to any other system of morals. Those sanctions are either external or internal. Of the external sanctions it is not necessary to speak at any length. They are the hope of favor and the fear of displeasure from our fellow creatures or from the Ruler of the universe, along with whatever we may have of sympathy or affection for them, or of love and awe of Him, inclining us to do His will independently of selfish consequences. There is evidently no reason why all these motives for observance should not attach themselves to the utilitarian morality as completely and as powerfully as to any other. Indeed, those of them which refer to our fellow creatures are sure to do so, in proportion to the amount of general intelligence; for whether there be any other ground of moral obligation than the general happiness or not, men do desire happiness; and however imperfect may be their own practice, they desire and commend all conduct in others toward themselves by which they think their happiness is promoted. With regard to the religious motive, if men believe, as most profess to do, in the goodness of God, those who think that conduciveness to the general happiness is the essence or even only the criterion of good must necessarily believe that it is also that which God approves. The whole force therefore of external reward and punishment, whether physical or moral, and whether proceeding from God or from our fellow men, together with all that the capacities of human nature admit of disinterested devotion to either, become available to enforce the utilitarian morality, in proportion as that morality is recognized; and the more powerfully, the more the appliances of education and general cultivation are bent to the purpose.

So far as to external sanctions. The internal sanction of duty, whatever our standard of duty may be, is one and the same—a feeling in our own mind; a pain, more or less intense, attendant on violation of duty, which in properly cultivated moral natures rises, in the more serious cases, into shrinking from it as an impossibility. This feeling, when disinterested and connecting itself with the pure idea of duty, and not with some particular form of it, or with any of the merely accessory circumstances, is the essence of conscience; though in that complex phenomenon as it actually exists, the simple fact is in general all encrusted over with collateral associations derived from sympathy, from love, and still more from fear; from all the forms of religious feeling; from the recollections of childhood and of all our past life; from self-esteem, desire of the esteem of others, and occasionally even self-abasement. This extreme complication is, I apprehend, the origin of the sort of mystical character which, by a tendency of the human mind of which there are many other examples, is apt to be attributed to the idea of moral obligation, and which leads people to believe that the idea cannot possibly attach itself to any other objects than those which, by a supposed mysterious law, are found in our present experience to excite it. Its binding force, however, consists in the existence of a mass of feeling which must be broken through in order to do what violates our standard of right, and which, if we do nevertheless violate that standard, will probably have to be encountered afterwards in the form of remorse. Whatever theory we have of the nature or origin of conscience, this is what essentially constitutes it.

The ultimate sanction, therefore, of all morality (external motives apart) being a subjective feeling in our own minds, I see nothing embarrassing to those whose standard is utility in the question, What is the sanction of that particular standard? We may answer, the same as of all other moral standards—the conscientious feelings of mankind. Undoubtedly this sanction has no binding efficacy on those who do not possess the feelings it appeals to; but neither will these persons be more obedient to any other moral principle than to the utilitarian one. On them morality of any kind has no hold but through the external

sanctions. Meanwhile the feelings exist, a fact in human nature, the reality of which, and the great power with which they are capable of acting on those in whom they have been duly cultivated, are proved by experience. No reason has even been shown why they may not be cultivated to as great intensity in connection with the utilitarian as with any other rule of morals.

There is, I am aware, a disposition to believe that a person who sees in moral obligation a transcendental fact, an objective reality belonging to the province of "things in themselves," is likely to be more obedient to it than one who believes it to be entirely subjective, having its seat in human consciousness only. But whatever a person's opinion may be on this point of ontology, the force he is really urged by is his own subjective feeling, and is exactly measured by its strength. No one's belief that duty is an objective reality is stronger than the belief that God is so; yet the belief in God, apart from the expectation of actual reward and punishment, only operates on conduct through and in proportion to, the subjective religious feeling. The sanction, so far as it is disinterested, is always in the mind itself; and the notion, therefore, of the transcendental moralists must be that this sanction will not exist *in* the mind unless it is believed to have its root out of the mind; and that if a person is able to say to himself, "That which is restraining me and which is called my conscience is only a feeling in my own mind," he may possibly draw the conclusion that when the feeling ceases the obligation ceases, and that if he find the feeling inconvenient, he may disregard it and endeavor to get rid of it. But is this danger confined to the utilitarian morality? Does the belief that moral obligation has its seat outside the mind make the feeling of it too strong to get rid it? The fact is so far otherwise that all moralists admit and lament the ease with which, in the generality of minds, conscience can be silenced or stifled. The question, "Need I obey my conscience?" is quite as often put to themselves by persons who never heard of the principle of utility as by its adherents. Those whose conscientious feelings are so weak as to allow of their asking this question, if they answer it affirmatively, will not do so because they believe in the transcendental theory, but because of the external sanctions.

It is not necessary, for the present purpose, to decide

whether the feeling of duty is innate or implanted. Assuming it to be innate, it is an open question to what objects it naturally attaches itself; for the philosophic supporters of that theory are now agreed that the intuitive perception is of principles of morality and not of the details. If there be anything innate in the matter, I see no reason why the feeling which is innate should not be that of regard to the pleasures and pains of others. If there is any principle of morals which is intuitively obligatory, I should say it must be that. If so, the intuitive ethics would coincide with the utilitarian, and there would be no further quarrel between them. Even as it is, the intuitive moralists, though they believe that there are other intuitive moral obligations, do already believe this to be one; for they unanimously hold that a large *portion* of morality turns upon the consideration due to the interests of our fellow creatures. Therefore, if the belief in the transcendental origin of moral obligation gives any additional efficacy to the internal sanction, it appears to me that the utilitarian principle has already the benefit of it.

On the other hand, if, as is my own belief, the moral feelings are not innate but acquired, they are not for that reason the less natural. It is natural to man to speak, to reason, to build cities, to cultivate the ground, though these are acquired faculties. The moral feelings are not indeed a part of our nature in the sense of being in any perceptible degree present in all of us; but this, unhappily, is a fact admitted by those who believe the most strenuously in their transcendental origin. Like the other acquired capacities above referred to, the moral faculty, if not a part of our nature, is a natural outgrowth from it; capable, like them, in a certain small degree, of springing up spontaneously; and susceptible of being brought by cultivation to a high degree of development. Unhappily it is also susceptible, by a sufficient use of the external sanctions and of the force of early impressions, of being cultivated in almost any direction, so that there is hardly anything so absurd or so mischievous that it may not, by means of these influences, be made to act on the human mind with all the authority of conscience. To doubt that the same potency might be given by the same means to the principle of utility, even if it had no foundation in human nature, would be flying in the face of all experience.

But moral associations which are wholly of artificial creation, when the intellectual culture goes on, yield by degrees to the dissolving force of analysis; and if the feeling of duty, when associated with utility, would appear equally arbitrary; if there were no leading department of our nature, no powerful class of sentiments, with which that association would harmonize, which would make us feel congenial and incline us not only to foster it in others (for which we have abundant interested motives), but also to cherish it in ourselves — if there were not, in short, a natural basis of sentiment for utilitarian morality, it might well happen that this association also, even after it had been implanted by education, might be analyzed away.

But there *is* this basis of powerful natural sentiment; and that it is which, when once the general happiness is recognized as the ethical standard, will constitute the strength of the utilitarian morality. This firm foundation is that of the social feelings of mankind — the desire to be in unity with our fellow creatures, which is already a powerful principle in human nature, and happily one of those which tend to become stronger, even without express inculcation, from the influences of advancing civilization. The social state is at once so natural, so necessary, and so habitual to man, that, except in some unusual circumstances or by an effort of voluntary abstraction, he never conceives himself otherwise than as a member of a body; and this association is riveted more and more, as mankind are further removed from the state of savage independence. Any condition, therefore, which is essential to a state of society becomes more and more an inseparable part of every person's conception of the state of things which he is born into, and which is the destiny of a human being. Now society between human beings, except in the relation of master and slave, is manifestly impossible on any other footing than that the interests of all are to be consulted. Society between equals can only exist on the understanding that the interests of all are to be regarded equally. And since in all states of civilization, every person, except an absolute monarch, has equals, everyone is obliged to live on these terms with somebody; and in every age some advance is made toward a state in which it will be impossible to live permanently on other terms with anybody. In this way people grow up unable to conceive as possible to them a state of total disregard of other people's interests. They are under a necessity of conceiving themselves as at least abstaining from all the grosser injuries, and (if only for their own protection) living in a state of constant protest against them. They are also familiar with the fact of co-operating with others and proposing to themselves a collective, not an individual, interest as the aim (at least for the time being) of their actions. So long as they are co-operating, their ends are identified with those of others; there is at least a temporary feeling that the interests of others are their own interests. Not only does all strengthening of social ties, and all healthy growth of society, give to each individual a stronger personal interest in practically consulting the welfare of others, it also leads him to identify his *feelings* more and more with their good, or at least with an even greater degree of practical consideration for it. He comes, as though instinctively, to be conscious of himself as a being who *of course* pays regard to others. The good of others becomes to him a thing naturally and necessarily to be attended to, like any of the physical conditions of our existence. Now, whatever amount of this feeling a person has, he is urged by the strongest motives both of interest and of sympathy to demonstrate it, and to the utmost of his power encourage it in others; and even if he has none of it himself, he is as greatly interested as anyone else that others should have it. Consequently, the smallest germs of the feeling are laid hold of and nourished by the contagion of sympathy and the influences of education; and a complete web of corroborative association is woven round it by the powerful agency of the external sanctions. This mode of conceiving ourselves and human life, as civilization goes on, is felt to be more and more natural. Every step in political improvement renders it more so, by removing the sources of opposition of interest and leveling those inequalities of legal privilege between individuals or classes, owing to which there are large portions of mankind whose happiness it is still practicable to disregard. In an improving state of the human mind, the influences are constantly on the increase which tend to generate in each individual a feeling of unity with all the rest; which, if perfect, would make him never think of, or desire, any beneficial condition for himself in the benefits of which they are not included. If we now suppose this feeling of unity to be taught as a religion, and the whole force of eduction, of institutions, and of opinion directed,

as it once was in the case of religion, to make every person grow up from infancy surrounded on all sides both by the profession and the practice of it, I think that no one who can realize this conception will feel any misgiving about the sufficiency of the ultimate sanction for the happiness morality. To any ethical student who finds the realization difficult, I recommend, as a means of facilitating it, the second of M. Comte's two principal works, the *Traité de politique positive.*[7] I entertain the strongest objections to the system of politics and morals set forth in that treatise, but I think it has superabundantly shown the possibility of giving to the service of humanity, even without the aid of belief in a Providence, both the psychological power and the social efficacy of a religion, making it take hold of human life, and color all thought, feeling, and action in a manner of which the greatest ascendancy ever exercised by any religion may be but a type and foretaste; and of which the danger is, not that it should be insufficient, but that it should be so excessive as to interfere unduly with human freedom and individuality.

Neither is it necessary to the feeling which constitutes the binding force of the utilitarian morality on those who recognize it to wait for those social influences which would make its obligation felt by mankind at large. In the comparatively early state of human advancement in which we now live, a person cannot, indeed, feel that entireness of sympathy with all others which would make any real discordance in the general direction of their conduct in life impossible, but already a person in whom the social feeling is at all developed cannot bring himself to think of the rest of his fellow creatures as struggling rivals with him for the means of happiness, whom he must desire to see defeated in their object in order that he may succeed in his. The deeply rooted conception which every individual even now has of himself as a social being tends to make him feel it one of his natural wants that there should be harmony between his feel-

7. [Auguste Comte (1798–1857) was the French philosopher who founded positivism, a view that denies the sense of speculative metaphysics and stresses the role of scientific observation in achieving understanding. As a social reformer he called for a moral order in which all people and nations could live in harmony. The work referred to is his *Treatise of Positive Polity.*]

ings and aims and those of his fellow creatures. If differences of opinion and of mental culture make it impossible for him to share many of their actual feelings—perhaps make him denounce and defy those feelings—he still needs to be conscious that his real aim and theirs do not conflict; that he is not opposing himself to what they really wish for, namely, their own good, but is, on the contrary, promoting it. This feeling in most individuals is much inferior in strength to their selfish feelings, and is often wanting altogether. But to those who have it, it possesses all the characters of a natural feeling. It does not present itself to their minds as a superstition of education or a law despotically imposed by the power of society, but as an attribute which it would not be well for them to be without. This conviction is the ultimate sanction of the greatest happiness morality. This it is which makes any mind of well-developed feelings work with, and not against, the outward motives to care for others, afforded by what I have called the external sanctions; and, when those sanctions are wanting or act in an opposite direction, constitutes in itself a powerful internal binding force, in proportion to the sensitiveness and thoughtfulness of the character, since few but those whose mind is a moral blank could bear to lay out their course of life on the plan of paying no regard to others except so far as their own private interest compels.

CHAPTER IV

Of What Sort of Proof the Principle of Utility Is Susceptible

It has already been remarked that questions of ultimate ends do not admit of proof, in the ordinary acceptation of the term. To be incapable of proof by reasoning is common to all first principles, to the first premises of our knowledge, as well as to those of our conduct. But the former, being matters of fact, may be the subject of a direct appeal to the faculties which judge of fact—namely, our senses and our internal consciousness. Can an appeal be made to the same faculties on questions of practical ends? Or by what other faculty is cognizance taken of them?

Questions about ends are, in other words, questions what things are desirable. The utilitarian doctrine is that happiness is desirable, and the only thing desirable, as an end; all other things being only desirable as means to that end. What ought to be required of this doctrine, what conditions is it requisite that the doctrine should fulfill—to make good its claim to be believed?

The only proof capable of being given that an object is visible is that people actually see it. The only proof that a sound is audible is that people hear it; and so of the other sources of our experience. In like manner, I apprehend, the sole evidence it is possible to produce that anything is desirable is that people do actually desire it. If the end which the utilitarian doctrine proposes to itself were not, in theory and in practice, acknowledged to be an end, nothing could ever convince any person that it was so. No reason can be given why the general happiness is desirable, except that each person, so far as he believes it to be attainable, desires his own happiness. This, however, being a fact, we have not only all the proof which the case admits of, but all which it is possible to require, that happiness is a good, that each person's happiness is a good to that person, and the general happiness, therefore, a good to the aggregate of all persons. Happiness has made out its title as *one* of the ends of conduct and, consequently, one of the criteria of morality.

But it has not, by this alone, proved itself to be the sole criterion. To do that, it would seem, by the same rule, necessary to show, not only that people desire happiness, but that they never desire anything else. Now it is palpable that they do desire things which, in common language, are decidedly distinguished from happiness. They desire, for example, virtue and the absence of vice no less really than pleasure and the absence of pain. The desire of virtue is not as universal, but it is as authentic a fact as the desire of happiness. And hence the opponents of the utilitarian standard deem that they have a right to infer that there are other ends of human action besides happiness, and that happiness is not the standard of approbation and disapprobation.

But does the utilitarian doctrine deny that people desire virtue, or maintain that virtue is not a thing to be desired? The very reverse. It maintains not only that virtue is to be desired, but that it is to be desired disinterestedly, for itself. Whatever may be the opinion of utilitarian moralists as to the original conditions by which virtue is made virtue, however they may believe (as they do) that actions and dispositions are only virtuous because they promote another end than virtue, yet this being granted, and it having been decided, from considerations of this description, what *is* virtuous, they not only place virtue at the very head of the things which are good as means to the ultimate end, but they also recognize as a psychological fact the possibility of its being, to the individual, a good in itself, without looking to any end beyond it; and hold that the mind is not in a right state, not in a state conformable to utility, not in the state most conducive to the general happiness, unless it does love virtue in this manner—as a thing desirable in itself, even although, in the individual instance, it should not produce those other desirable consequences which it tends to produce, and on account of which it is held to be virtue. This opinion is not, in the smallest degree, a departure from the happiness principle. The ingredients of happiness are very various, and each of them is desirable in itself, and not merely when considered as swelling an aggregate. The principle of utility does not mean that any given pleasure, as music, for instance, or any given exemption from pain, as for example health, is to be looked upon as means to a collective something termed happiness, and to be desired on that account. They are desired and desirable in and for themselves; besides being means, they are a part of the end. Virtue, according to the utilitarian doctrine, is not naturally and originally part of the end, but it is capable of becoming so; and in those who live it disinterestedly it has become so, and is desired and cherished, not as a means to happiness, but as a part of their happiness.

To illustrate this further, we may remember that virtue is not the only thing originally a means, and which if it were not a means to anything else would be and remain indifferent, but which by association with what it is a means to comes to be desired for itself, and that too with the utmost intensity. What, for example, shall we say of the love of money? There is nothing originally more desirable about money than about any heap of glittering pebbles. Its worth is solely that of the things which it will buy; the desires for other things than itself, which it is a means of gratifying. Yet the love of money is not only one of the strongest moving forces of human life, but money is, in many cases, desired in and for itself; the desire

to possess it is often stronger than the desire to use it, and goes on increasing when all the desires which point to ends beyond it, to be compassed by it, are falling off. It may, then, be said truly that money is desired not for the sake of an end, but as part of the end. From being a means to happiness, it has come to be itself a principal ingredient of the individual's conception of happiness. The same may be said of the majority of the great objects of human life: power, for example, or fame, except that to each of these there is a certain amount of immediate pleasure annexed, which has at least the semblance of being naturally inherent in them—a thing which cannot be said of money. Still, however, the strongest natural attraction, both of power and of fame, is the immense aid they give to the attainment of our other wishes; and it is the strong association thus generated between them and all our objects of desire which gives to the direct desire of them the intensity it often assumes, so as in some characters to surpass in strength all other desires. In these cases the means have become a part of the end, and a more important part of it than any of the things which they are means to. What was once desired as an instrument for the attainment of happiness has come to be desired for its own sake. In being desired for its own sake it is, however, desired as *part* of happiness. The person is made, or thinks he would be made, happy by its mere possession; and is made unhappy by failure to obtain it. The desire of it is not a different thing from the desire of happiness any more than the love of music or the desire of health. They are included in happiness. They are some of the elements of which the desire of happiness is made up. Happiness is not an abstract idea but a concrete whole; and these are some of its parts. And the utilitarian standard sanctions and approves their being so. Life would be a poor thing, very ill provided with sources of happiness, if there were not this provision of nature by which things originally indifferent, but conducive to, or otherwise associated with, the satisfaction of our primitive desires, become in themselves sources of pleasure more valuable than the primitive pleasures, both in permanency, in the space of human existence that they are capable of covering, and even in intensity.

Virtue, according to the utilitarian conception, is a good of this description. There was no original desire of it, or motive to it, save its conduciveness to pleasure, and especially to protection from pain. But through the association thus formed it may be felt a good in itself, and desired as such with as great intensity as any other good; and with this difference between it and the love of money, of power, or of fame—that all of these may, and often do, render the individual noxious to the other members of the society to which he belongs, whereas there is nothing which makes him so much a blessing to them as the cultivation of the disinterested love of virtue. And consequently, the utilitarian standard, while it tolerates and approves those other acquired desires, up to the point beyond which they would be more injurious to the general happiness than promotive of it, enjoins and requires the cultivation of the love of virtue up to the greatest strength possible, as being above all things important to the general happiness.

It results from the preceding considerations that there is in reality nothing desired except happiness. Whatever is desired otherwise than as a means to some end beyond itself, and ultimately to happiness, is desired as itself a part of happiness, and is not desired for itself until it has become so. Those who desire virtue for its own sake desire it either because the consciousness of it is a pleasure, or because the consciousness of being without it is a pain, or for both reasons united; as in truth the pleasure and pain seldom exist separately, but almost always together—the same person feeling pleasure in the degree of virtue attained, and pain in not having attained more. If one of these gave him no pleasure, and the other no pain, he would not love or desire virtue, or would desire it only for the other benefits which it might produce to himself or to persons whom he cared for.

We have now, then, an answer to the question, of what sort of proof the principle of utility is susceptible. If the opinion which I have now stated is psychologically true—if human nature is so constituted as to desire nothing which is not either a part of happiness or a means of happiness—we can have no other proof, and we require no other, that these are the only things desirable. If so, happiness is the sole end of human action, and the promotion of it the test by which to judge of all human conduct; from whence it necessarily follows that it must be the criterion of morality, since a part is included in the whole.

And now to decide whether this is really so, whether mankind do desire nothing for itself but that which is a pleasure to them, or of which the absence is a pain, we have evidently arrived at a question of fact and experience, dependent, like all similar questions, upon evidence. It can only be determined by practiced self-consciousness and self-observation, assisted by observation of others. I believe that these sources of evidence, impartially consulted, will declare that desiring a thing and finding it pleasant, aversion to it and thinking of it as painful, are phenomena entirely inseparable or, rather, two parts of the same phenomenon—in strictness of language, two different modes of naming the same psychological fact; that to think of an object as desirable (unless for the sake of its consequences) and to think of it as pleasant are one and the same thing; and that to desire anything except in proportion as the idea of it is pleasant is a physical and metaphysical impossibility.

So obvious does this appear to me that I expect it will hardly be disputed; and the objection made will be, not that desire can possibly be directed to anything ultimately except pleasure and exemption from pain, but that the will is a different thing from desire; that a person of confirmed virtue or any other person whose purposes are fixed carries out his purposes without any thought of the pleasure he has in contemplating them or expects to derive from their fulfillment, and persists in acting on them, even though these pleasures are much diminished by changes in his character or decay of his passive sensibilities, or are outweighed by the pains which the pursuit of the purposes may bring upon him. All this I fully admit and have stated it elsewhere as positively and emphatically as anyone. Will, the active phenomenon, is a different thing from desire, the state of passive sensibility, and, though originally an offshoot from it, may in time take root and detach itself from the parent stock, so much so that in the case of a habitual purpose, instead of willing the thing because we desire it, we often desire it only because we will it. This, however, is but an instance of that familiar fact, the power of habit, and is nowise confined to the case of virtuous actions. Many indifferent things which men originally did from a motive of some sort they continue to do from habit. Sometimes this is done unconsciously, the consciousness coming only after the action; at other times with conscious volition, but volition which has become habitual and is put in operation by the force of habit, in opposition perhaps to the deliberate preference, as often happens with those who have contracted habits of vicious or hurtful indulgence. Third and last comes the case in which the habitual act of will in the individual instance is not in contradiction to the general intention prevailing at other times, but in fulfillment of it, as in the case of the person of confirmed virtue and of all who pursue deliberately and consistently any determinate end. The distinction between will and desire thus understood is an authentic and highly important psychological fact; but the fact consists solely in this—that will, like all other parts of our constitution, is amenable to habit, and that we may will from habit what we no longer desire for itself, or desire only because we will it. It is not the less true that will, in the beginning, is entirely produced by desire, including in that term the repelling influence of pain as well as the attractive one of pleasure. Let us take into consideration no longer the person who has a confirmed will to do right, but him in whom that virtuous will is still feeble, conquerable by temptation, and not to be fully relied on; by what means can it be strengthened? How can the will to be virtuous, where it does not exist in sufficient force, be implanted or awakened? Only by making the person *desire* virtue—by making him think of it in a pleasurable light, or of its absence in a painful one. It is by associating the doing right with pleasure, or the wrong with pain, or by eliciting and impressing and bringing home to the person's experience the pleasure naturally involved in the one or the pain in the other, that it is possible to call forth that will to be virtuous which, when confirmed, acts without any thought of either pleasure or pain. Will is the child of desire, and passes out of the dominion of its parent only to come under that of habit. That which is the result of habit affords no presumption of being intrinsically good; and there would be no reason for wishing that the purpose of virtue should become independent of pleasure and pain were it not that the influence of the pleasurable and painful associations which prompt to virtue is not sufficiently to be depended on for unerring constancy of action until it has acquired the support of habit. Both in feeling and in conduct, habit is the only thing which imparts certainty; and it is because of the importance to others of being able to rely absolutely on one's feelings and conduct, and to oneself of being able to rely on one's own, that the will to do right ought to be cultivated into this habitual independence. In other words, this state of the will is a means to good, not intrinsically a good; and does not contradict the doctrine that nothing is a good to human beings but in so far as it is either itself pleasurable or a means of attaining pleasure or averting pain.

But if this doctrine be true, the principle of utility is proved. Whether it is so or not must now be left to the consideration of the thoughtful reader.

CHAPTER V

On the Connection Between Justice and Utility

In all ages of speculation one of the strongest obstacles to the reception of the doctrine that utility or happiness is the criterion of right and wrong has been drawn from the idea of justice. The powerful sentiment and apparently clear perception which that word recalls with a rapidity and certainty resembling an instinct have seemed to the majority of thinkers to point to an inherent quality in things; to show that the just must have an existence in nature as something absolute, generically distinct from every variety of the expedient and, in idea, opposed to it, though (as is commonly acknowledged) never, in the long run, disjoined from it in fact.

In the case of this, as of our other moral sentiments, there is no necessary connection between the question of its origin and that of its binding force. That a feeling is bestowed on us by nature does not necessarily legitimate all its promptings. The feeling of justice might be a peculiar instinct, and might yet require, like our other instincts, to be controlled and enlightened by a higher reason. If we have intellectual instincts leading us to judge in a particular way, as well as animal instincts that prompt us to act in a particular way, there is no necessity that the former should be more infallible in their sphere than the latter in theirs; it may as well happen that wrong judgments are occasionally suggested by those, as wrong actions by these. But though it is one thing to believe that we have natural feelings of justice, and another to acknowledge them as an ultimate criterion of conduct, these two opinions are very closely connected in point of fact. Mankind are always predisposed to believe that any subjective feeling, not otherwise accounted for, is a revelation of some objective reality. Our present object is to determine whether the reality to which the feeling of justice corresponds is one which needs any such special revelation, whether the justice or injustice of an action is a thing intrinsically peculiar and distinct from all its other qualities or only a combination of certain of those qualities presented under a peculiar aspect. For the purpose of this inquiry it is practically important to consider whether the feeling itself, of justice and injustice, is *sui generis* like our sensations of color and taste or a derivative feeling formed by a combination of others. And this it is the more essential to examine, as people are in general willing enough to allow that objectively the dictates of justice coincide with a part of the field of general expediency; but inasmuch as the subjective mental feeling of justice is different from that which commonly attaches to simple expediency, and, except in the extreme cases of the latter, is far more imperative in its demands, people find it difficult to see in justice only a particular kind or branch of general utility, and think that its superior binding force requires a totally different origin.

To throw light upon this question, it is necessary to attempt to ascertain what is the distinguishing character of justice, or of injustice; what is the quality, or whether there is any quality, attributed in common to all modes of conduct designated as unjust (for justice, like many other moral attributes, is best defined by its opposite), and distinguishing them from such modes of conduct as are disapproved, but without having that particular epithet of disapprobation applied to them. If in everything which men are accustomed to characterize as just or unjust some one common attribute or collection of attributes is always present, we may judge whether this particular attribute or combination of attributes would be capable of gathering round it a sentiment of that peculiar character and intensity by virtue of the general laws of our emotional constitution, or whether the sentiment is inexplicable and requires to be regarded as a special provision of nature. If we find the former to be the case, we shall, in resolving this question, have resolved also the main problem; if the latter, we shall have to seek for some other mode of investigating it.

To find the common attributes of a variety of ob-

jects, it is necessary to begin by surveying the objects themselves in the concrete. Let us therefore advert successively to the various modes of action and arrangements of human affairs which are classed, by universal or widely spread opinion, as just or as unjust. The things well known to excite the sentiments associated with those names are of a very multifarious character. I shall pass them rapidly in review, without studying any particular arrangement.

In the first place, it is mostly considered unjust to deprive anyone of his personal liberty, his property, or any other thing which belongs to him by law. Here, therefore, is one instance of the application of the terms "just" and "unjust" in a perfectly definite sense, namely, that it is just to respect, unjust to violate, the *legal rights* of anyone. But this judgment admits of several exceptions, arising from the other forms in which the notions of justice and injustice present themselves. For example, the person who suffers the deprivation may (as the phrase is) have *forfeited* the rights which he is so deprived of—a case to which we shall return presently. But also—

Secondly, the legal rights of which he is deprived may be rights which *ought* not to have belonged to him; in other words, the law which confers on him these rights may be a bad law. When it is so or when (which is the same thing for our purpose) it is supposed to be so, opinions will differ as to the justice or injustice of infringing it. Some maintain that no law, however bad, ought to be disobeyed by an individual citizen; that his opposition to it, if shown at all, should only be shown in endeavoring to get it altered by competent authority. This opinion (which condemns many of the most illustrious benefactors of mankind, and would often protect pernicious institutions against the only weapons which, in the state of things existing at the time, have any chance of succeeding against them) is defended by those tho hold it on grounds of expediency, principally on that of the importance to the common interest of mankind, of maintaining inviolate the sentiment of submission to law. Other persons, again, hold the directly contrary opinion that any law, judged to be bad, may blamelessly be disobeyed, even though it be not judged to be unjust but only inexpedient, while others would confine the license of disobedience to the case of unjust laws; but, again, some say that all laws which are inexpedient are unjust, since every law imposes some restriction on the natural liberty of mankind, which restriction is an injustice unless legitimated by tending to their good. Among these diversities of opinion it seems to be universally admitted that there may be unjust laws, and that law, consequently, is not the ultimate criterion of justice, but may give to one person a benefit, or impose on another an evil, which justice condemns. When, however, a law is thought to be unjust, it seems always to be regarded as being so in the same way in which a breach of law is unjust, namely, by infringing somebody's right, which, as it cannot in this case be a legal right, receives a different appellation and is called a moral right. We may say, therefore, that a second case of injustice consists in taking or withholding from any person that to which he has a *moral right*.

Thirdly, it is universally considered just that each person should obtain that (whether good or evil) which he *deserves*, and unjust that he should obtain a good or be made to undergo an evil which he does not deserve. This is, perhaps, the clearest and most emphatic form in which the idea of justice is conceived by the general mind. As it involves the notion of desert, the question arises what constitutes desert? Speaking in a general way, a person is understood to deserve good if he does right, evil if he does wrong; and in a more particular sense, to deserve good from those to whom he does or has done good, and evil from those to whom he does or has done evil. The precept of returning good for evil has never been regarded as a case of the fulfillment of justice, but as one in which the claims of justice are waived, in obedience to other considerations.

Fourthly, it is confessedly unjust to *break faith* with anyone: to violate an engagement, either express or implied, or disappoint expectations raised by our own conduct, at least if we have raised those expectations knowingly and voluntarily. Like the other obligations of justice already spoken of, this one is not regarded as absolute, but as capable of being overruled by a stronger obligation of justice on the other side, or by such conduct on the part of the person concerned as is deemed to absolve us from our obligation to him and to constitute a *forfeiture* of the benefit which he has been led to expect.

Fifthly, it is, by universal admission, inconsistent with justice to be *partial*—to show favor or preference to one person over another in matters to which favor

and preference do not properly apply. Impartiality, however, does not seem to be regarded as a duty in itself, but rather as instrumental to some other duty; for it is admitted that favor and preference are not always censurable, and, indeed, the cases in which they are condemned are rather the exception than the rule. A person would be more likely to be blamed than applauded for giving his family or friends no superiority in good offices over strangers when he could do so without violating any other duty; and no one thinks it unjust to seek one person in preference to another as a friend, connection, or companion. Impartiality where rights are concerned is of course obligatory, but this is involved in the more general obligation of giving to everyone his right. A tribunal, for example, must be impartial because it is bound to award, without regard to any other consideration, a disputed object to the one of two parties who has the right to it. There are other cases in which impartiality means being solely influenced by desert, as with those who, in the capacity of judges, preceptors, or parents, administer reward and punishment as such. There are cases, again, in which it means being solely influenced by consideration for the public interest, as in making a selection among candidates for a government employment. Impartiality, in short, as an obligation of justice, may be said to mean being exclusively influenced by the considerations which it is supposed ought to influence the particular case in hand, and resisting solicitation of any motives which prompt to conduct different from what those considerations would dictate.

Nearly allied to the idea of impartiality is that of *equality*, which often enters as a component part both into the conception of justice and into the practice of it, and, in the eyes of many persons, constitutes its essence. But in this, still more than in any other case, the notion of justice varies in different persons, and always conforms in its variations to their notion of utility. Each person maintains that equality is the dictate of justice, except where he thinks that expediency requires inequality. The justice of giving equal protection to the rights of all is maintained by those who support the most outrageous inequality in the rights themselves. Even in slave countries it is theoretically admitted that the rights of the slave, such as they are, ought to be as sacred as those of the master, and that a tribunal which fails to enforce them with equal strictness is wanting in justice; while, at the same time, institutions which leave to the slave scarcely any rights to enforce are not deemed unjust because they are not deemed inexpedient. Those who think that utility requires distinctions of rank do not consider it unjust that riches and social privileges should be unequally dispensed; but those who think this inequality inexpedient think it unjust also. Whoever thinks that government is necessary sees no injustice in as much inequality as is constituted by giving to the magistrate powers not granted to other people. Even among those who hold leveling doctrines, there are differences of opinion about expediency. Some communists consider it unjust that the produce of the labor of the community should be shared on any other principle than that of exact equality; others think it just that those should receive most whose wants are greatest; while others hold that those who work harder, or who produce more, or whose services are more valuable to the community, may justly claim a larger quota in the division of the produce. And the sense of natural justice may be plausibly appealed to in behalf of every one of these opinions.

Among so many diverse applications of the term "justice," which yet is not regarded as ambiguous, it is a matter of some difficulty to seize the mental link which holds them together, and on which the moral sentiment adhering to the term essentially depends. Perhaps, in this embarrassment, some help may be derived from the history of the word, as indicated by its etymology.

In most if not in all languages, the etymology of the word which corresponds to "just" points distinctly to an origin connected with the ordinances of law. *Justum* is a form of *jussum*, that which has been ordered. *Dikaion* comes directly from *dike*, a suit at law. *Recht*, from which came *right* and *righteous*, is synonymous with law. The courts of justice, the administration of justice, are the courts and the administration of law. *La justice*, in French, is the established term for judicature. I am not committing the fallacy, imputed with some show of truth to Horne Tooke,[8] of assuming that a word must still continue to mean what it originally meant. Etymology is slight

evidence of what the idea now signified is, but the very best evidence of how it sprang up. There can, I think, be no doubt that the *idée mère*, the primitive element, in the formation of the notion of justice was conformity to law. It constituted the entire idea among the Hebrews, up to the birth of Christianity; as might be expected in the case of a people whose laws attempted to embrace all subjects on which precepts were required, and who believed those laws to be a direct emanation from the Supreme Being. But other nations, and in particular the Greeks and Romans, who knew that their laws had been made originally, and still continued to be made, by men, were not afraid to admit that those men might make bad laws; might do, by law, the same things, and from the same motives, which if done by individuals without the sanction of law would be called unjust. And hence the sentiment of injustice came to be attached, not to all violations of law, but only to violations of such laws as *ought* to exist, including such as ought to exist but do not, and to laws themselves if supposed to be contrary to what ought to be law. In this manner the idea of law and of its injunctions was still predominant in the notion of justice, even when the laws actually in force ceased to be accepted as the standard of it.

It is true that mankind consider the idea of justice and its obligations as applicable to many things which neither are, nor is it desired that they should be, regulated by law. Nobody desires that laws should interfere with the whole detail of private life; yet everyone allows that in all daily conduct a person may and does show himself to be either just or unjust. But even here, the idea of the breach of what ought to be law still lingers in a modified shape. It would always give us pleasure, and chime in with our feelings of fitness, that acts which we deem unjust should be punished, though we do not always think it expedient that this should be done by the tribunals. We forego that gratification on account of incidental inconveniences. We should be glad to see just conduct enforced and injustice repressed, even in the minutest details, if we were not, with reason, afraid of trusting the magistrate with so unlimited an amount of power over individuals. When we think that a person is bound in justice to do a thing, it is an ordinary form of language to say that he ought to be compelled to do it. We should be gratified to see the obligation

---

8. [John Horne Tooke (1736–1812) was an English politician and philologist who supported both the American and French Revolutions.]

enforced by anybody who had the power. If we see that its enforcement by law would be inexpedient, we lament the impossibility, we consider the impunity given to injustice as an evil, and strive to make amends for it by bringing a strong expression of our own and the public disapprobation to bear upon the offender. Thus the idea of legal constraint is still the generating idea of the notion of justice, though undergoing several transformations before that notion as it exists in an advanced state of society becomes complete.

The above is, I think, a true account, as far as it goes, of the origin and progressive growth of the idea of justice. But we must observe that it contains as yet nothing to distinguish that obligation from moral obligation in general. For the truth is that the idea of penal sanction, which is the essence of law, enters not only into the conception of injustice, but into that of any kind of wrong. We do not call anything wrong unless we mean to imply that a person ought to be punished in some way or other for doing it— if not by law, by the opinion of his fellow creatures; if not by opinion, by the reproaches of his own conscience. This seems the real turning point of the distinction between morality and simple expediency. It is a part of the notion of duty in every one of its forms that a person may rightfully be compelled to fulfill it. Duty is a thing which may be *exacted* from a person, as one exacts a debt. Unless we think that it may be exacted from him, we do not call it his duty. Reasons of prudence, or the interest of other people, may militate against actually exacting it, but the person himself, it is clearly understood, would not be entitled to complain. There are other things, on the contrary, which we wish that people should do, which we like or admire them for doing, perhaps dislike or despise them for not doing, but yet admit that they are not bound to do; it is not a case of moral obligation; we do not blame them, that is, we do not think that they are proper objects of punishment. How we come by these ideas of deserving and not deserving punishment will appear, perhaps, in the sequel; but I think there is no doubt that this distinction lies at the bottom of the notions of right and wrong; that we call any conduct wrong, or employ, instead, some other term of dislike or disparagement, according as we think that the person ought, or ought not, to be punished for it; and we say it would be right to do so and so, or merely that it would be

desirable or laudable, according as we would wish to see the person whom it concerns compelled, or only persuaded and exhorted, to act in that manner.[9]

This, therefore, being the characteristic difference which marks off, not justice, but morality in general from the remaining provinces of expediency and worthiness, the character is still to be sought which distinguishes justice from other branches of morality. Now it is known that ethical writers divide moral duties into two classes, denoted by the ill-chosen expressions, duties of perfect and of imperfect obligation; the latter being those in which, though the act is obligatory, the particular occasions of performing it are left to our choice, as in the case of charity or beneficence, which we are indeed bound to practice but not toward any definite person, nor at any prescribed time. In the more precise language of philosophic jurists, duties of perfect obligation are those duties in virtue of which a correlative *right* resides in some person or persons; duties of imperfect obligation are those moral obligations which do not give birth to any right. I think it will be found that this distinction exactly coincides with that which exists between justice and the other obligations of morality. In our survey of the various popular acceptations of justice, the term appeared generally to involve the idea of a personal right—a claim on the part of one or more individuals, like that which the law gives when it confers a proprietary or other legal right. Whether the injustice consists in depriving a person of a possession, or in breaking faith with him, or in treating him worse than he deserves, or worse than other people who have no greater claims—in each case the supposition implies two things: a wrong done, and some assignable person who is wronged. Injustice may also be done by treating a person better than others; but the wrong in this case is to his competitors, who are also assignable persons. It seems to me that this feature in the case—a right in some person, correlative to the moral obligation— constitutes the specific difference between justice and

9. See this point enforced and illustrated by Professor Bain, in an admirable chapter (entitled "The Ethical Emotions, or the Moral Sense"), of the second of the two treatises composing his elaborate and profound work on the Mind. [Alexander Bain (1818–1903) was a Scottish philosopher and psychologist. The work referred to is his *The Emotions and the Will.*]

generosity of beneficence. Justice implies something which it is not only right to do, and wrong not to do, but which some individual person can claim from us as his moral right. No one has a moral right to our generosity or beneficence because we are not morally bound to practice those virtues toward any given individual. And it will be found with respect to this as to every correct definition that the instances which seem to conflict with it are those which most confirm it. For if a moralist attempts, as some have done, to make out that mankind generally, though not any given individual, have a right to all the good we can do them, he at once, by that thesis, includes generosity and beneficence within the category of justice. He is obliged to say that our utmost exertions are *due* to our fellow creatures, thus assimilating them to a debt; or that nothing less can be a sufficient *return* for what society does for us, thus classing the case as one of gratitude; both of which are acknowledged cases of justice, and not of the virtue of beneficence; and whoever does not place the distinction between justice and morality in general, where we have now placed it, will be found to make no distinction between them at all, but to merge all morality in justice.

Having thus endeavored to determine the distinctive elements which enter into the composition of the idea of justice, we are ready to enter on the inquiry whether the feeling which accompanies the idea is attached to it by a special dispensation of nature, or whether it could have grown up, by any known laws, out of the idea itself; and, in particular, whether it can have originated in considerations of general expediency.

I conceive that the sentiment itself does not arise from anything which would commonly or correctly be termed an idea of expediency, but that, though the sentiment does not, whatever is moral in it does.

We have seen that the two essential ingredients in the sentiment of justice are the desire to punish a person who has done harm and the knowledge or belief that there is some definite individual or individuals to whom harm has been done.

Now it appears to me that the desire to punish a person who has done harm to some individual is a spontaneous outgrowth from two sentiments, both in the highest degree natural and which either are or resemble instincts: the impulse of self-defense and the feeling of sympathy.

It is natural to resent and to repel or retaliate any harm done or attempted against ourselves or against those with whom we sympathize. The origin of this sentiment it is not necessary here to discuss. Whether it be an instinct or a result of intelligence, it is, we know, common to all animal nature; for every animal tries to hurt those who have hurt, or who it thinks are about to hurt, itself or its young. Human beings, on this point, only differ from other animals in two particulars. First, in being capable of sympathizing, not solely with their offspring, or, like some of the more noble animals, with some superior animal who is kind to them, but with all human, and even with all sentient, beings; secondly, in having a more developed intelligence, which gives a wider range to the whole of their sentiments, whether self-regarding or sympathetic. By virtue of his superior intelligence, even apart from his superior range of sympathy, a human being is capable of apprehending a community of interest between himself and the human society of which he forms a part, such that any conduct which threatens the security of the society generally is threatening to his own, and calls forth his instinct (if instinct it be) of self-defense. The same superiority of intelligence, joined to the power of sympathizing with human beings generally, enables him to attach himself to the collective idea of his tribe, his country, or mankind in such a manner that any act hurtful to them raises his instinct of sympathy and urges him to resistance.

The sentiment of justice, in that one of its elements which consists of the desire to punish, is thus, I conceive, the natural feeling of retaliation or vengeance, rendered by intellect and sympathy applicable to those injuries, that is, to those hurts, which wound us through, or in common with, society at large. This sentiment, in itself, has nothing moral in it; what is moral is the exclusive subordination of it to the social sympathies, so as to wait on and obey their call. For the natural feeling would make us resent indiscriminately whatever anyone does that is disagreeable to us; but, when moralized by the social feeling, it only acts in the directions conformable to the general good: just persons resenting a hurt to society, though not otherwise a hurt to themselves, and not resenting a hurt to themselves, however painful, unless it be of the kind which society has a common interest with them in the repression of.

It is no objection against this doctrine to say that, when we feel our sentiment of justice outraged, we are not thinking of society at large or of any collective interest, but only of the individual case. It is common enough, certainly, though the reverse of commendable, to feel resentment merely because we have suffered pain; but a person whose resentment is really a moral feeling, that is, who considers whether an act is blamable before he allows himself to resent it— such a person, though he may not say expressly to himself that he is standing up for the interest of society, certainly does feel that he is asserting a rule which is for the benefit of others as well as for his own. If he is not feeling this, if he is regarding the act solely as it affects him individually, he is not consciously just; he is not concerning himself about the justice of his actions. This is admitted even by anti-utilitarian moralists. When Kant (as before remarked) propounds as the fundamental principle of morals, "So act that thy rule of conduct might be adopted as a law by all rational beings," he virtually acknowledges that the interest of mankind collectively, or at least of mankind indiscriminately, must be in the mind of the agent when conscientiously deciding on the morality of the act. Otherwise he uses words without a meaning; for that a rule even of utter selfishness could not *possibly* be adopted by all rational beings— that there is any insuperable obstacle in the nature of things to its adoption—cannot be even plausibly maintained. To give any meaning to Kant's principle, the sense put upon it must be that we ought to shape our conduct by a rule which all rational beings might adopt *with benefit to their collective interest.*

To recapitulate: the idea of justice supposes two things—a rule of conduct and a sentiment which sanctions the rule. The first must be supposed common to all mankind and intended for their good. The other (the sentiment) is a desire that punishment may be suffered by those who infringe the rule. There is involved, in addition, the conception of some definite person who suffers by the infringement, whose rights (to use the expression appropriated to the case) are violated by it. And the sentiment of justice appears to me to be the animal desire to repel or retaliate a hurt or damage to oneself or to those with whom one sympathizes, widened so as to include all persons, by the human capacity of enlarged sympathy and the human conception of intelligent self-interest. From

the latter elements the feeling derives its morality; from the former, its peculiar impressiveness and energy of self-assertion.

I have, throughout, treated the idea of a *right* residing in the injured person and violated by the injury, not as a separate element in the composition of the idea and sentiment, but as one of the forms in which the other two elements clothe themselves. These elements are a hurt to some assignable person or persons, on the one hand, and a demand for punishment, on the other. An examination of our own minds, I think, will show that these two things include all that we mean when we speak of violation of a right. When we call anything a person's right, we mean that he has a valid claim on society to protect him in the possession of it, either by the force of law or by that of education and opinion. If he has what we consider a sufficient claim, on whatever account, to have something guaranteed to him by society, we say that he has a right to it. If we desire to prove that anything does not belong to him by right, we think this done as soon as it is admitted that society ought not to take measure for securing it to him, but should leave him to chance or to his own exertions. Thus a person is said to have a right to what he can earn in fair professional competition, because society ought not to allow any other person to hinder him from endeavoring to earn in that manner as much as he can. But he has not a right to three hundred a year, though he may happen to be earning it; because society is not called on to provide that he shall earn that sum. On the contrary, if he owns ten thousand pounds three-per-cent stock, he *has* a right to three hundred a year because society has come under an obligation to provide him with an income of that amount.

To have a right, then, is, I conceive, to have something which society ought to defend me in the possession of. If the objector goes on to ask why it ought, I can give him no other reason than general utility. If that expression does not seem to convey a sufficient feeling of the strength of the obligation, nor to account for the peculiar energy of the feeling, it is because there goes to the composition of the sentiment, not a rational only but also an animal element—the thirst for retaliation; and this thirst derives its intensity, as well as its moral justification, from the extraordinarily important and impressive kind of utility which is concerned. The interest involved is that of security, to everyone's feelings the most vital of all interests. All other earthly benefits are needed by one person, not needed by another; and many of them can, if necessary, be cheerfully foregone or replaced by something else; but security no human being can possibly do without; on it we depend for all our immunity from evil and for the whole value of all and every good, beyond the passing moment, since nothing but the gratification of the instant could be of any worth to us if we could be deprived of everything the next instant by whoever was momentarily stronger than ourselves. Now this most indispensable of all necessaries, after physical nutriment, cannot be had unless the machinery for providing it ks kept unintermittedly in active play. Our notion, therefore, of the claim we have on our fellow creatures to join in making safe for us the very groundwork of our existence gathers feelings around it so much more intense than those concerned in any of the more common cases of utility that the difference in degree (as is often the case in psychology) becomes a real difference in kind. The claim assumes that character of absoluteness, that apparent infinity and incommensurability with all other considerations which constitute the distinction between the feeling of right and wrong and that of ordinary expediency and inexpediency. The feelings concerned are so powerful, and we count so positively on finding a responsive feeling in others (all being alike interested) that *ought* and *should* grow into *must*, and recognized indispensability becomes a moral necessity, analogous to physical, and often not inferior to it in binding force.

If the preceding analysis, or something resembling it, be not the correct account of the notion of justice — if justice be totally independent of utility, and be a standard *per se*, which the mind can recognize by simple introspection of itself — it is hard to understand why that internal oracle is so ambiguous, and why so many things appear either just or unjust, according to the light in which they are regarded.

We are continually informed that utility is an uncertain standard, which every different person interprets differently, and that there is no safety but in the immutable, ineffaceable, and unmistakable dictates of justice, which carry their evidence in themselves and are independent of the fluctuations of opinion. One would suppose from this that on questions of justice there could be no controversy; that, if we take

that for our rule, its application to any given case could leave us in as little doubt as a mathematical demonstration. So far is this from being the fact that there is as much difference of opinion, and as much discussion, about what is just as about what is useful to society. Not only have different nations and individuals different notions of justice, but in the mind of one and the same individual, justice is not some one rule, principle, or maxim, but many which do not always coincide in their dictates, and, in choosing between which, he is guided either by some extraneous standard or by his own personal predilections.

For instance, there are some who say that it is unjust to punish anyone for the sake of example to others, that punishment is just only when intended for the good of the sufferer himself. Others maintain the extreme reverse, contending that to punish persons who have attained years of discretion, for their own benefit, is despotism and injustice, since, if the matter at issue is solely their own good, no one has a right to control their own judgment of it; but that they may justly be punished to prevent evil to others, this being the exercise of the legitimate right of self-defense. Mr. Owen,[10] again, affirms that it is unjust to punish at all, for the criminal did not make his own character; his education and the circumstances which surrounded him have made him a criminal, and for these he is not responsible. All these opinions are extremely plausible; and so long as the question is argued as one of justice simply, without going down to the principles which lie under justice and are the source of its authority, I am unable to see how any of these reasoners cam be refuted. For in truth every one of the three builds upon rules of justice confessedly true. The first appeals to the acknowledged injustice of singling out an individual and making him a sacrifice, without his consent, for other people's benefit. The second relies on the acknowledged justice of self-defense and the admitted injustice of forcing one person to conform to another's notions of what constitutes his good. The Owenite invokes the admitted principle that it is unjust to punish anyone

10. [Robert Owen (1771–1858) was a British social reformer who believed that individual character is determined by environment. He proposed the formation of self-sufficient cooperative communities, one of which was established in 1825 in New Harmony, Indiana, but lasted only a few years.]

for what he cannot help. Each is triumphant so long as he is not compelled to take into consideration any other maxims of justice than the one he has selected; but as soon as their several maxims are brought face to face, each disputant seems to have exactly as much to say for himself as the others. No one of them can carry out his own notion of justice without trampling upon another equally binding. These are difficulties; they have always been felt to be such; and many devices have been invented to turn rather than to overcome them. As a refuge from the last of the three, men imagined what they called the freedom of the will—fancying that they could not justify punishing a man whose will is in a thoroughly hateful state unless it be supposed to have come into that state through no influence of anterior circumstances. To escape from the other difficulties, a favorite contrivance has been the fiction of a contract whereby at some unknown period all the members of society engaged to obey the laws and consented to be punished for any disobedience to them, thereby giving to their legislators the right, which it is assumed they would not otherwise have had, of punishing them, either for their own good or for that of society. This happy thought was considered to get rid of the whole difficulty and to legitimate the infliction of punishment, in virtue of another received maxim of justice, *volenti non fit injuria*—that is not unjust which is done with the consent of the person who is supposed to be hurt by it. I need hardly remark that, even if the consent were not mere fiction, this maxim is not superior in authority to the others which it is brought in to supersede. It is, on the contrary, an instructive specimen of the loose and irregular manner in which supposed principles of justice grow up. This particular one evidently came into use as a help to the coarse exigencies of courts of law, which are sometimes obliged to be content with very uncertain presumptions, on account of the greater evils which would often arise from any attempt on their part to cut finer. But even courts of law are not able to adhere consistently to the maxim, for they allow voluntary engagements to be set aside on the ground of fraud, and sometimes on that of mere mistake or misinformation.

Again, when the legitimacy of inflicting punishment is admitted, how many conflicting conceptions of justice come to light in discussing the proper appor-

tionment of punishments to offenses. No rule on the subject recommends itself so strongly to the primitive and spontaneous sentiment of justice as the *lex talionis*, an eye for an eye and a tooth for a tooth. Though this principle of the Jewish and of the Mohammedan law has been generally abandoned in Europe as a practical maxim, there is, I suspect, in most minds, a secret hankering after it; and when retribution accidentally falls on an offender in that precise shape, the general feeling of satisfaction evinced bears witness how natural is the sentiment to which this repayment in kind is acceptable. With many, the test of justice in penal infliction is that the punishment should be proportioned to the offense, meaning that it should be exactly measured by the moral guilt of the culprit (whatever be their standard for measuring moral guilt), the consideration what amount of punishment is necessary to deter from the offense having nothing to do with the question of justice, in their estimation; while there are others to whom that consideration is all in all, who maintain that it is not just, at least for man, to inflict on a fellow creature, whatever may be his offenses, any amount of suffering beyond the least that will suffice to prevent him from repeating, and others from imitating, his misconduct.

To take another example from a subject already once referred to. In co-operative industrial associations, is it just or not that talent or skill should give a title to superior remuneration? On the negative side of the question it is argued that whoever does the best he can deserves equally well, and ought not in justice to be put in a position of inferiority for no fault of his own; that superior abilities have already advantages more than enough, in the admiration they excite, the personal influence they command, and the internal sources of satisfaction attending them, without adding to these a superior share of the world's goods; and that society is bound in justice rather to make compensation to the less favored for this unmerited inequality of advantages than to aggravate it. On the contrary side it is contended that society receives more from the efficient laborer; that, his services being more useful, society owes him a larger return for them; that a greater share of the joint result is actually his work, and not to allow his claim to it is a kind of robbery; that, if he is only to receive as much as others, he can only be justly required to produce as much, and to give a smaller amount of time and exertion, proportioned to his superior efficiency. Who shall decide between these appeals to conflicting principles of justice? Justice has in this case two sides to it, which it is impossible to bring into harmony, and the two disputants have chosen opposite sides; the one looks to what it is just that the individual should receive, the other to what it is just that the community should give. Each, from his own point of view, is unanswerable; and any choice between them, on grounds of justice, must be perfectly arbitrary. Social utility alone can decide the preference.

How many, again, and how irreconcilable are the standards of justice to which reference is made in discussing the repartition of taxation. One opinion is that payment to the state should be in numerical proportion to pecuniary means. Others think that justice dictates what they term graduated taxation—taking a higher percentage from those who have more to spare. In point of natural justice a strong case might be made for disregarding means altogether, and taking the same absolute sum (whenever it could be got) from everyone; as the subscribers to a mess or to a club all pay the same sum for the same privileges, whether they can all equally afford it or not. Since the protection (it might be said) of law and government is afforded to and is equally required by all, there is no injustice in making all buy it at the same price. It is reckoned justice, not injustice, that a dealer should charge to all customers the same price for the same article, not a price varying according to their means of payment. This doctrine, as applied to taxation, finds no advocates because it conflicts so strongly with man's feelings of humanity and of social expediency; but the principle of justice which it invokes is as true and as binding as those which can be appealed to against it. Accordingly it exerts a tacit influence on the line of defense employed for other modes of assessing taxation. People feel obliged to argue that the state does more for the rich man than for the poor, as a justification for its taking more from them, though this is in reality not true, for the rich would be far better able to protect themselves, in the absence of law or government, than the poor, and indeed would probably be successful in converting the poor into their slaves. Others, again, so far defer to the same conception of justice as to maintain that all should pay an equal capitation tax for the protection of their persons (these being of equal value to all), and an unequal tax for the protection of their property, which is unequal. To this others reply that the all of one man is as valuable to him as the all of another. From these confusions there is no other mode of extrication than the utilitarian.

Is, then, the difference between the just and the expedient a merely imaginary distinction? Have mankind been under a delusion in thinking that justice is a more sacred thing than policy, and that the latter ought only to be listened to after the former has been satisfied? By no means. The exposition we have given of the nature and origin of the sentiment recognizes a real distinction; and no one of those who profess the most sublime contempt for the consequences of actions as an element in their morality attaches more importance to the distinction than I do. While I dispute the pretensions of any theory which sets up an imaginary standard of justice not grounded on utility, I account the justice which is grounded on utility to be the chief part, and incomparably the most sacred and binding part, of all morality. Justice is a name for certain classes of moral rules which concern the essentials of human well-being more nearly, and are therefore of more absolute obligation, than any other rules for the guidance of life; and the notion which we have found to be of the essence of the idea of justice—that of a right residing in an individual—implies and testifies to this more binding obligation.

The moral rules which forbid mankind to hurt one another (in which we must never forget to include a wrongful interference with each other's freedom) are more vital to human well-being than any maxims, however important, which only point out the best mode of managing some department of human affairs. They have also the peculiarity that they are the main element in determining the whole of the social feelings of mankind. It is their observance which alone preserves peace among human beings; if obedience to them were not the rule, and disobedience the exception, everyone would see in everyone else an enemy against whom he must be perpetually guarding himself. What is hardly less important, these are the precepts which mankind have the strongest and the most direct inducements for impressing upon one another. By merely giving to each other prudential instruction or exhortation, they may gain, or think they gain, nothing; in inculcating on each other the duty of positive beneficence, they have an unmistakable interest, but far less in degree; a person may possibly not need the benefits of others, but he always needs that they should not do him hurt. Thus the moralities which protect every individual from being harmed by others, either directly or by being hindered in his freedom of pursuing his own good, are at once those which he himself has most at heart and those which he has the strongest interest in publishing and enforcing by word and deed. It is by a person's observance of these that his fitness to exist as one of the fellowship of human beings is tested and decided; for on that depends his being a nuisance or not to those with whom he is in contact. Now it is these moralities primarily which compose the obligation of justice. The most marked cases of injustice, and those which give the tone to the feeling of repugnance which characterizes the sentiment, are acts of wrongful aggression or wrongful exercise of power over someone; the next are those which consist in wrongfully withholding from him something which is his due — in both cases inflicting on him a positive hurt, either in the form of direct suffering or of the privation of some good which he had reasonable ground, either of a physical or of a social kind, for counting upon.

The same powerful motives which command the observance of these primary moralities enjoin the punishment of those who violate them; and as the impulses of self-defense, of defense of others, and of vengeance are all called forth against such persons, retribution, or evil for evil, becomes closely connected with the sentiment of justice, and is universally included in the idea. Good for good is also one of the dictates of justice; and this, though its social utility is evident, and though it carries with it a natural human feeling, has not at first sight that obvious connection with hurt or injury which, existing in the most elementary cases of just and unjust, is the source of the characteristic intensity of the sentiment. But the connection, though less obvious, is not less real. He who accepts benefits and denies a return of them when needed inflicts a real hurt by disappointing one of the most natural and reasonable of expectations, and one which he must at least tacitly have encouraged, otherwise the benefits would seldom have been conferred. The important rank, among human evils and wrongs, of the disappointment of expectation is shown in the fact that it constitutes the principal

criminality of two such highly immoral acts as a breach of friendship and a breach of promise. Few hurts which human beings can sustain are greater, and none wound more, than when that on which they habitually and with full assurance relied fails them in the hour of need; and few wrongs are greater than this mere withholding of good; none excite more resentment, either in the person suffering or in a sympathizing spectator. The principle, therefore, of giving to each what they deserve, that is, good for good as well as evil for evil, is not only included within the idea of justice as we have defined it, but is a proper object of that intensity of sentiment which places the just human estimation above the simply expedient.

Most of the maxims of justice current in the world, and commonly appealed to in its transactions, are simply instrumental to carrying into effect the principles of justice which we have now spoken of. That a person is only responsible for what he has done voluntarily, or could voluntarily have avoided, that it is unjust to condemn any person unheard; that the punishment ought to be proportioned to the offense, and the like, are maxims intended to prevent the just principle of evil for evil from being perverted to the infliction of evil without that justification. The greater part of these common maxims have come into use from the practice of courts of justice, which have been naturally led to a more complete recognition and elaboration than was likely to suggest itself to others, of the rules necessary to enable them to fulfill their double function — of inflicting punishment when due, and of awarding to each person his right.

That first of judicial virtues, impartiality, is an obligation of justice, partly for the reason last mentioned, as being a necessary condition of the fulfillment of other obligations of justice. But this is not the only source of the exalted rank, among human obligations, of those maxims of equality and impartiality, which, both in popular estimation and in that of the most enlightened, are included among the precepts of justice. In one point of view, they may be considered as corollaries from the principles already laid down. If it is a duty to do to each according to his deserts, returning good for good, as well as repressing evil by evil, it necessarily follows that we should treat all equally well (when no higher duty forbids) who have deserved equally well of *us*, and that society should treat all equally well who have deserved equally well of *it*, that is, who have deserved equally well absolutely. This is the highest abstract standard of social and distributive justice, toward which all institutions and the efforts of all virtuous citizens should be made in the utmost possible degree to converge. But this great moral duty rests upon a still deeper foundation, being a direct emanation from the first principle of morals, and not a mere logical corollary from secondary or derivative doctrines. It is involved in the very meaning of utility, or the greatest happiness principle. That principle is a mere form of words without rational signification unless one person's happiness, supposed equal in degree (with the proper allowance made for kind), is counted for exactly as much as another's. Those conditions being supplied, Bentham's dictum "everybody to count for one, nobody for more than one," might be written under the principle of utility as an explanatory commentary.[11] The equal claim of everybody to happiness, in the estimation of the moralist and of the legislator, involves an equal claim to all the means of happiness except in so far as the inevitable conditions of human life and the general interest in which that of every individual is included set limits to the maxim; and those limits ought to be strictly construed. As every other maxim of justice, so this is by no means applied or held applicable universally; on the contrary, as I have already remarked, it bends to every person's ideas of social expediency. But in whatever case it is deemed applicable at all, it is held to be the dictate of justice. All persons are deemed to have a *right* to equality of treatment, except when some recognized social expediency requires the reverse. And hence all social inequalities which have ceased to be considered expedient assume the character, not of simple inexpediency, but of injustice, and appear so tyrannical that people are apt to wonder how they ever could have been tolerated—forgetful that they themselves, perhaps, tolerate other inequalities under an equally mistaken notion of expediency, the correction of which would make that which they approve seem quite as monstrous as what they have at last learned to condemn. The entire history of social improvement has been a series of transitions by which one custom or institution after another, from being a supposed primary necessity of social existence, has passed into the rank of a universally stigmatized injustice and tyranny. So it has been with the distinctions of slaves and freemen, nobles and serfs, patricians and plebeians; and so it will be, and in part already is, with the aristocracies of color, race, and sex.

It appears from what has been said that justice is a name for certain moral requirements which, regarded

---

11. This implication, in the first principle of the utilitarian scheme, of perfect impartiality between persons is regarded by Mr. Herbert Spencer (in his *Social Statics*) as a disproof of the pretensions of utility to be a sufficient guide to right; since (he says) the principle of utility presupposes the anterior principle that everybody has an equal right to happiness. It may be more correctly described as supposing that equal amounts of happiness are equally desirable, whether felt by the same or different persons. This, however, is not a *pre*supposition, not a premise needful to support the principle of utility, but the very principle itself; for what is the principle of utility if it be not that "happiness" and "desirable" are synonymous terms? If there is any anterior principle implied, it can be no other than this, that the truths of arithmetic are applicable to the valuation of happiness, as of all other measurable quantities.

(Mr. Herbert Spencer, in a private communication on the subject of the preceding note, objects to being considered an opponent of utilitarianism and states that he regards happiness as the ultimate end of morality; but deems that end only partially attainable by empirical generalizations from the observed results of conduct, and completely attainable only by deducing, from the laws of life and the conditions of existence, what kinds of action necessarily tend to produce happiness, and what kinds to produce unhappiness. With the exception of the word "necessarily," I have no dissent to express from this doctrine; and (omitting that word) I am not aware that any modern advocate of utilitarianism is of a different opinion. Bentham, certainly, to whom in the *Social Statics* Mr. Spencer particularly referred, is, least of all writers, chargeable with unwillingness to deduce the effect of actions on happiness from the laws of human nature and the universal conditions of human life. The common charge against him is of relying too exclusively upon such deductions and declining altogether to be bound by the generalizations from specific experience which Mr. Spencer thinks that utilitarians generally confine themselves to. My own opinion (and, as I collect, Mr. Spencer's) is that in ethics, as in all other branches of scientific study, the consilience of the results of both these processes, each corroborating and verifying the other, is requisite to give to any general proposition the kind and degree of evidence which constitutes scientific proof.)

collectively, stand higher in the scale of social utility, and are therefore of more paramount obligation, than any others, though particular cases may occur in which some other social duty is so important as to overrule any one of the general maxims of justice. Thus, to save a life, it may not only be allowable, but a duty, to steal or take by force the necessary food or medicine, or to kidnap and compel to officiate the only qualified medical practitioner. In such cases, as we do not call anything justice which is not a virtue, we usually say, not that justice must give way to some other moral principle, but that what is just in ordinary cases is, by reason of that other principle, not just in the particular case. By this useful accommodation of language, the character of indefeasibility attributed to justice is kept up, and we are saved from the necessity of maintaining that there can be laudable injustice.

The considerations which have not been adduced resolve, I conceive, the only real difficulty in the utilitarian theory of morals. It has always been evident that all cases of justice are also cases of expediency; the difference is in the peculiar sentiment which attaches to the former, as contradistinguished from the latter. If this characteristic sentiment has been sufficiently accounted for; if there is no necessity to assume for it any peculiarity of origin; if it is simply the natural feeling of resentment, moralized by being made co-extensive with the demands of social good; and if this feeling not only does but ought to exist in all the classes of cases to which the idea of justice corresponds—that idea no longer presents itself as a stumbling block to the utilitarian ethics. Justice remains the appropriate name for certain social utilities which are vastly more important, and therefore more absolute and imperative, than any others are as a class (though not more so than others may be in particular cases); and which, therefore, ought to be, as well as naturally are, guarded by a sentiment, not only different in degree, but also in kind; distinguished from the milder feeling which attaches to the mere idea of promoting human pleasure or convenience at once by the more definite nature of its commands and by the sterner character of its sanctions.

On Liberty

*The grand, leading principle, towards which every argument unfolded in these pages directly
converges, is the absolute and essential importance of human development in its richest diversity
—Wilhelm von Humboldt: Sphere and Duties of Government.*[1]

*To the beloved and deplored memory of her who was
the inspirer, and in part the author, of all that is best
in my writings—the friend and wife whose exalted
sense of truth and right was my strongest incitement,
and whose approbation was my chief reward—I dedi-
cate this volume. Like all that I have written for many
years, it belongs as much to her as to me; but the work
as it stands has had, in a very insufficient degree, the
inestimable advantage of her revision; some of the most
important portions having been reserved for a more
careful re-examination, which they are now never destined to receive. Were I but capable of interpreting to
the world one half the great thoughts and noble feelings
which are buried in her grave, I should be the medium
of a greater benefit to it, than is ever likely to arise
from anything that I can write, unprompted and unassisted by her all but unrivaled wisdom.*

CHAPTER I

Introductory

The subject of this essay is not the so-called "liberty of
the will," so unfortunately opposed to the misnamed
doctrine of philosophical necessity; but civil, or social
liberty: the nature and limits of the power which can
be legitimately exercised by society over the individual. A question seldom stated, and hardly ever discussed in general terms, but which profoundly influences the practical controversies of the age by its
latent presence, and is likely soon to make itself recognized as the vital question of the future. It is so far

1. [Wilhelm Freiherr von Humboldt (1767–1835), German statesman and philologist, was a liberal reformer and
a founder of the University of Berlin.—S.M.C.]

from being new that, in a certain sense, it has divided
mankind almost from the remotest ages; but in the
stage of progress into which the more civilized portions of the species have now entered, it presents itself
under new conditions and requires a different and
more fundamental treatment.

The struggle between liberty and authority is the
most conspicuous feature in the portions of history
with which we are earliest familiar, particularly in
that of Greece, Rome, and England. But in old times
this contest was between subjects, or some classes of
subjects, and the government. By liberty was meant
protection against the tyranny of the political rulers.
The rulers were conceived (except in some of the
popular governments of Greece) as in a necessarily
antagonistic position to the people whom they ruled.
They consisted of a governing One, or a governing
tribe or caste, who derived their authority from inheritance or conquest, who, at all events, did not hold it
at the pleasure of the governed, and whose supremacy
men did not venture, perhaps did not desire, to contest, whatever precautions might be taken against its
oppressive exercise. Their power was regarded as necessary, but also as highly dangerous; as a weapon
which they would attempt to use against their subjects, no less than against external enemies. To prevent the weaker members of the community from
being preyed upon by innumerable vultures, it was
needful that there should be an animal of prey
stronger than the rest, commissioned to keep them
down. But as the king of the vultures would be no
less bent upon preying on the flock than any of the
minor harpies, it was indispensable to be in a perpetual attitude of defense against his beak and claws.
The aim, therefore, of patriots was to set limits to the
power which the ruler should be suffered to exercise

over the community; and this limitation was what they meant by liberty. It was attempted in two ways. First, by obtaining a recognition of certain immunities, called political liberties or rights, which it was to be regarded as a breach of duty in the ruler to infringe, and which if he did infringe, specific resistance or general rebellion was held to be justifiable. A second, and generally a later, expedient was the establishment of constitutional checks by which the consent of the community, or of a body of some sort, supposed to represent its interests, was made a necessary condition to some of the more important acts of the governing power. To the first of these modes of limitation, the ruling power, in most European countries, was compelled, more or less, to submit. It was not so with the second; and, to attain this, or, when already in some degree possessed, to attain it more completely, became everywhere the principal object of the lovers of liberty. And so long as mankind were content to combat one enemy by another, and to be ruled by a master on condition of being guaranteed more or less efficaciously against his tyranny, they did not carry their aspirations beyond this point.

A time, however, came, in the progress of human affairs, when men ceased to think it a necessity of nature that their governors should be an independent power opposed in interest to themselves. It appeared to them much better that the various magistrates of the state should be their tenants or delegates, revocable at their pleasure. In that way alone, it seemed, could they have complete security that the powers of government would never be abused to their disadvantage. By degrees this new demand for elective and temporary rulers became the prominent object of the exertions of the popular party wherever any such party existed, and superseded, to a considerable extent, the previous efforts to limit the power of rulers. As the struggle proceeded for making the ruling power emanate from the periodical choice of the ruled, some persons began to think that too much importance had been attached to the limitation of the power itself. *That* (it might seem) was a resource against rulers whose interests were habitually opposed to those of the people. What was now wanted was that the rulers should be identified with the people, that their interest and will should be the interest and will of the nation. The nation did not need to be protected against its own will. There was no fear of its tyrannizing over itself.

Let the rulers be effectually responsible to it, promptly removable by it, and it could afford to trust them with power of which it could itself dictate the use to be made. Their power was but the nation's own power, concentrated and in a form convenient for exercise. This mode of thought, or rather perhaps of feeling, was common among the last generation of European liberalism, in the Continental section of which it still apparently predominates. Those who admit any limit to what a government may do, except in the case of such governments as they think ought not to exist, stand out as brilliant exceptions among the political thinkers of the Continent. A similar tone of sentiment might by this time have been prevalent in our own country if the circumstances which for a time encouraged it had continued unaltered.

But, in political and philosophical theories as well as in persons, success discloses faults and infirmities which failure might have concealed from observation. The notion that the people have no need to limit their power over themselves might seem axiomatic, when popular government was a thing only dreamed about, or read of as having existed at some distant period of the past. Neither was that notion necessarily disturbed by such temporary aberrations as those of the French Revolution, the worst of which were the work of a usurping few, and which, in any case, belonged, not to the permanent working of popular institutions, but to a sudden and convulsive outbreak against monarchical and aristocratic despotism. In time, however, a democratic republic came to occupy a large portion of the earth's surface and made itself felt as one of the most powerful members of the community of nations;[2] and elective and responsible government became subject to the observations and criticisms which wait upon a great existing fact. It was now perceived that such phrases as "self-government," and "the power of the people over themselves," do not express the true state of the case. The "people" who exercise the power are not always the same people with those over whom it is exercised; and the "self-government" spoken of is not the government of each by himself, but of each by all the rest. The will of the people, moreover, practically means the will of the most numerous or the most active *part* of

---

2. [The reference is to the United States.]

the people—the majority, or those who succeed in making themselves accepted as the majority; the people, consequently, *may* desire to oppress a part of their number, and precautions are as much needed against this as against any other abuse of power. The limitation, therefore, of the power of government over individuals loses none of its importance when the holders of power are regularly accountable to the community, that is, to the strongest party therein. This view of things, recommending itself equally to the intelligence of thinkers and to the inclination of those important classes in European society to whose real or supposed interests democracy is adverse, has had no difficulty in establishing itself; and in political speculations "the tyranny of the majority" is now generally included among the evils against which society requires to be on its guard.

Like other tyrannies, the tyranny of the majority was at first, and is still vulgarly, held in dread, chiefly as operating through the acts of the public authorities. But reflecting persons perceived that when society is itself the tyrant—society collectively over the separate individuals who compose it—its means of tyrannizing are not restricted to the acts which it may do by the hands of its political functionaries. Society can and does execute its own mandates; and if it issues wrong mandates instead of right, or any mandates at all in things with which it ought not to meddle, it practices a social tyranny more formidable than many kinds of political oppression, since, though not usually upheld by such extreme penalties, it leaves fewer means of escape, penetrating much more deeply into the details of life, and enslaving the soul itself. Protection, therefore, against the tyranny of the magistrate is not enough; there needs protection also against the tyranny of the prevailing opinion and feeling, against the tendency of society to impose, by other means than civil penalties, its own ideas and practices as rules of conduct on those who dissent from them; to fetter the development and, if possible, prevent the formation of any individuality not in harmony with its ways, and compel all characters to fashion themselves upon the model of its own. There is a limit to the legitimate interference of collective opinion with individual independence; and to find that limit, and maintain it against encroachment, is as indispensable to a good condition of human affairs as protection against political despotism.

But though this proposition is not likely to be contested in general terms, the practical question where to place the limit—how to make the fitting adjustment between individual independence and social control—is a subject on which nearly everything remains to be done. All that makes existence valuable to anyone depends on the enforcement of restraints upon the actions of other people. Some rules of conduct, therefore, must be imposed—by law in the first place, and by opinion on many things which are not fit subjects for the operation of law. What these rules should be is the principal question in human affairs; but if we except a few of the most obvious cases, it is one of those which least progress has been made in resolving. No two ages, and scarcely any two countries, have decided it alike; and the decision of one age or country is a wonder to another. Yet the people of any given age and country no more suspect any difficulty in it than if it were a subject on which mankind had always been agreed. The rules which obtain among themselves appear to them self-evident and self-justifying. This all but universal illusion is one of the examples of the magical influence of custom, which is not only, as the proverb says, a second nature but is continually mistaken for the first. The effect of custom, in preventing any misgiving respecting the rules of conduct which mankind impose on one another, is all the more complete because the subject is one on which it is not generally considered necessary that reasons should be given, either by one person to others or by each to himself. People are accustomed to believe, and have been encouraged in the belief by some who aspire to the character of philosophers, that their feelings on subjects of this nature are better than reasons and render reasons unnecessary. The practical principle which guides them to their opinions on the regulation of human conduct is the feeling in each person's mind that everybody should be required to act as he, and those with whom he sympathizes, would like them to act. No one, indeed, acknowledges to himself that his standard of judgment is his own liking; but an opinion on a point of conduct, not supported by reasons, can only count as one person's preference; and if the reasons, when given, are a mere appeal to a similar preference felt by other people, it is still only many people's liking instead of one. To an ordinary man, however, his own preference, thus supported, is not only a perfectly satisfactory reason but the only one he generally has for any of his notions of morality, taste, or propriety, which are not expressly written in his religious creed, and his chief guide in the interpretation even of that. Men's opinions, accordingly, on what is laudable or blamable are affected by all the multifarious causes which influence their wishes in regard to the conduct of others, and which are as numerous as those which determine their wishes on any other subject. Sometimes their reason; at other times their prejudices or superstitions; often their social affections, not seldom their antisocial ones, their envy or jealousy, their arrogance or contemptuousness; but most commonly their desires or fears for themselves—their legitimate or illegitimate self-interest. Wherever there is an ascendant class, a large portion of the morality of the country emanates from its class interests and its feelings of class superiority. The morality between Spartans and Helots,[3] between planters and Negroes, between princes and subjects, between nobles and roturiers,[4] between men and women has been for the most part the creation of these class interests and feelings; and the sentiments thus generated react in turn upon the moral feelings of the members of the ascendant class, in their relations among themselves. Where, on the other hand, a class, formerly ascendant, has lost its ascendancy, or where its ascendancy is unpopular, the prevailing moral sentiments frequently bear the impress of an impatient dislike of superiority. Another grand determining principle of the rules of conduct, both in act and forbearance, which have been enforced by law or opinion, has been the servility of mankind toward the supposed preferences or aversions of their temporal masters or of their gods. This servility, though essentially selfish, is not hypocrisy; it gives rise to perfectly genuine sentiments of abhorrence; it made men burn magicians and heretics. Among so many baser influences, the general and obvious interests of society have, of course, had a share, and a large one, in the direction of the moral sentiments; less, however, as a matter of reason, and on their own account, than as a consequence of the sympathies and antipathies which grew out of them; and sympathies and antipathies which had little or nothing to do with the interests of society have made themselves felt in the establishment of moralities with quite as great force.

The likings and dislikings of society, or of some powerful portion of it, are thus the main thing which has practically determined the rules laid down for general observance, under the penalties of law or opinion. And in general, those who have been in advance of society in thought and feeling have left this condition of things unassailed in principle, however they may have come into conflict with it in some of its details. They have occupied themselves rather in inquiring what things society ought to like or dislike than in questioning whether its likings or dislikings should be a law to individuals. They preferred endeavoring to alter the feelings of mankind on the particular points on which they were themselves heretical rather than make common cause in defense of freedom with heretics generally. The only case in which the higher ground has been taken on principle and maintained with consistency, by any but an individual here and there, is that of religious belief: a case instructive in many ways, and not least so as forming a most striking instance of the fallibility of what is called the moral sense; for the *odium theologicum*,[5] in a sincere bigot, is one of the most unequivocal cases of moral feeling. Those who first broke the yoke of what called itself the Universal Church were in general as little willing to permit difference of religious opinion as that church itself. But when the heat of the conflict was over, without giving a complete victory to any party, and each church or sect was reduced to limit its hopes to retaining possession of the ground it already occupied, minorities, seeing that they had no chance of becoming majorities, were under the necessity of pleading to those whom they could not convert for permission to differ. It is accordingly on this battlefield, almost solely, that the rights of the individual against society have been asserted on broad grounds of principle, and the claim of society to exercise authority over dissentients openly controverted. The great writers to whom the world owes what religious liberty it possesses have mostly asserted freedom of conscience as an indefeasible right, and denied absolutely that a human being is accountable to others

---

3. [Helots were Spartan state serfs alloted to landowners.]

4. [Roturiers are plebeians, persons of low rank.]

5. [Hatred engendered by bitter theological controversy.]

for his religious belief. Yet so natural to mankind is intolerance in whatever they really care about that religious freedom has hardly anywhere been practically realized, except where religious indifference, which dislikes to have its peace disturbed by theological quarrels, has added its weight to the scale. In the minds of almost all religious persons, even in the most tolerant countries, the duty of toleration is admitted with tacit reserves. One person will bear with dissent in matters of church government, but not of dogma; another can tolerate everybody, short of a Papist or a Unitarian; another, everyone who believes in revealed religion; a few extend their charity a little further, but stop at the belief in a God and in a future state. Wherever the sentiment of the majority is still genuine and intense, it is found to have abated little of its claim to be obeyed.

In England, from the peculiar circumstances of our political history, though the yoke of opinion is perhaps heavier, that of law is lighter than in most other countries of Europe; and there is considerable jealousy of direct interference by the legislative or the executive power with private conduct, not so much from any just regard for the independence of the individual as from the still subsisting habit of looking on the government as representing an opposite interest to the public. The majority have not yet learned to feel the power of the government their power, or its opinions their opinions. When they do so, individual liberty will probably be as much exposed to invasion from the government as it already is from public opinion. But, as yet, there is a considerable amount of feeling ready to be called forth against any attempt of the law to control individuals in things in which they have not hitherto been accustomed to be controlled by it; and this with very little discrimination as to whether the matter is, or is not, within the legitimate sphere of legal control; insomuch that the feeling, highly salutary on the whole, is perhaps quite as often misplaced as well grounded in the particular instances of its application. There is, in fact, no recognized principle by which the propriety or impropriety of government interference is customarily tested. People decide according to their personal preferences. Some, whenever they see any good to be done, or evil to be remedied, would willingly instigate the government to undertake the business, while others prefer to bear almost any amount of social evil rather than add one to the departments of human interests amenable to governmental control. And men range themselves on one or the other side in any particular case, according to this general direction of their sentiments, or according to the degree of interest which they feel in the particular thing which it is proposed that the government should do, or according to the belief they entertain that the government would, or would not, do it in the manner they prefer; but very rarely on account of any opinion to which they consistently adhere, as to what things are fit to be done by a government. And it seems to me that in consequence of this absence of rule or principle, one side is at present as often wrong as the other; the interference of government is, with about equal frequency, improperly invoked and improperly condemned.

The object of this essay is to assert one very simple principle, as entitled to govern absolutely the dealings of society with the individual in the way of compulsion and control, whether the means used be physical force in the form of legal penalties or the moral coercion of public opinion. That principle is that the sole end for which mankind are warranted, individually or collectively, in interfering with the liberty of action of any of their number is self-protection. That the only purpose for which power can be rightfully exercised over any member of a civilized community, against his will, is to prevent harm to others. His own good, either physical or moral, is not a sufficient warrant. He cannot rightfully be compelled to do or forbear because it will be better for him to do so, because it will make him happier, because, in the opinions of others, to do so would be wise or even right. These are good reasons for remonstrating with him, or reasoning with him, or persuading him, or entreating him, but not for compelling him or visiting him with any evil in case he do otherwise. To justify that, the conduct from which it is desired to deter him must be calculated to produce evil to someone else. The only part of the conduct of anyone for which he is amenable to society is that which concerns others. In the part which merely concerns himself, his independence is, of right, absolute. Over himself, over his own body and mind, the individual is sovereign.

It is, perhaps, hardly necessary to say that this doctrine is meant to apply only to human beings in the maturity of their faculties. We are not speaking of children or of young persons below the age which the law may fix as that of manhood or womanhood. Those who are still in a state to require being taken care of by others must be protected against their own actions as well as against external injury. For the same reason we may leave out of consideration those backward states of society in which the race itself may be considered as in its nonage. The early difficulties in the way of spontaneous progress are so great that there is seldom any choice of means for overcoming them; and a ruler full of the spirit of improvement is warranted in the use of any expedients that will attain an end perhaps otherwise unattainable. Despotism is a legitimate mode of government in dealing with barbarians, provided the end be their improvement and the means justified by actually effecting that end. Liberty, as a principle, has no application to any state of things anterior to the time when mankind have become capable of being improved by free and equal discussion. Until then, there is nothing for them but implicit obedience to an Akbar[6] or a Charlemagne, if they are so fortunate as to find one. But as soon as mankind have attained the capacity of being guided to their own improvement by conviction or persuasion (a period long since reached in all nations with whom we need here concern ourselves), compulsion, either in the direct form or in that of pains and penalties for noncompliance, is no longer admissible as a means to their own good, and justifiable only for the security of others.

It is proper to state that I forego any advantage which could be derived to my argument from the idea of abstract right as a thing independent of utility. I regard utility as the ultimate appeal on all ethical questions; but it must be utility in the largest sense, grounded on the permanent interests of man as a progressive being. Those interests, I contend, authorize the subjection of individual spontaneity to external control only in respect to those actions of each which concern the interest of other people. If anyone does an act hurtful to others, there is a *prima facie* case for punishing him by law or, where legal penalties are not safely applicable, by general disapprobation. There are also many positive acts for the benefit of others which he may rightfully be compelled to per-

form, such as to give evidence in a court of justice, to bear his fair share in the common defense or in any other joint work necessary to the interest of the society of which he enjoys the protection, and to perform certain acts of individual beneficence, such as saving a fellow creature's life or interposing to protect the defenseless against ill usage—things which whenever it is obviously a man's duty to do he may rightfully be made responsible to society for not doing. A person may cause evil to others not only by his actions but by his inaction, and in either case he is justly accountable to them for the injury. The latter case, it is true, requires a much more cautious exercise of compulsion than the former. To make anyone answerable for doing evil to others is the rule; to make him answerable for not preventing evil is, comparatively speaking, the exception. Yet there are many cases clear enough and grave enough to justify that exception. In all things which regard the external relations of the individual, he is *de jure* amenable to those whose interests are concerned, and, if need be, to society as their protector. There are often good reasons for not holding him to the responsibility; but these reasons must arise from the special expediences of the case: either because it is a kind of case in which he is on the whole likely to act better when left to his own discretion than when controlled in any way in which society have it in their power to control him; or because the attempt to exercise control would produce other evils, greater than those which it would prevent. When such reasons as these preclude the enforcement of responsibility, the conscience of the agent himself should step into the vacant judgment seat and protect those interests of others which have no external protection; judging himself all the more rigidly, because the case does not admit of his being made accountable to the judgment of his fellow creatures.

But there is a sphere of action in which society, as distinguished from the individual, has, if any, only an indirect interest: comprehending all that portion of a person's life and conduct which affects only himself or, if it also affects others, only with their free, voluntary, and undeceived consent and participation. When I say only himself, I mean directly and in the first instance; for whatever affects himself may affect others through himself: and the objection which may be grounded on this contingency will receive consid-

6. [Akbar (1542–1605) was a Mogul emperor of India.]

eration in the sequel. This, then, is the appropriate region of human liberty. It comprises, first, the inward domain of consciousness, demanding liberty of conscience in the most comprehensive sense, liberty of thought and feeling, absolute freedom of opinion and sentiment on all subjects, practical or speculative, scientific, moral, or theological. The liberty of expressing and publishing opinions may seem to fall under a different principle, since it belongs to that part of the conduct of an individual which concerns other people, but, being almost of as much importance as the liberty of thought itself and resting in great part on the same reasons, is practically inseparable from it. Secondly, the principle requires liberty of tastes and pursuits, of framing the plan of our life to suit our own character, of doing as we like, subject to such consequences as may follow, without impediment from our fellow creatures, so long as what we do does not harm them, even though they should think our conduct foolish, perverse, or wrong. Thirdly, from this liberty of each individual follows the liberty, within the same limits, of combination among individuals; freedom to unite for any purpose not involving harm to others: the persons combining being supposed to be of full age and not forced or deceived.

No society in which these liberties are not, on the whole, respected is free, whatever may be its form of government; and none is completely free in which they do not exist absolute and unqualified. The only freedom which deserves the name is that of pursuing our own good in our own way, so long as we do not attempt to deprive others of theirs or impede their efforts to obtain it. Each is the proper guardian of his own health, whether bodily *or* mental and spiritual. Mankind are greater gainers by suffering each other to live as seems good to themselves than by compelling each to live as seems good to the rest.

Though this doctrine is anything but new and, to some persons, may have the air of a truism, there is no doctrine which stands more directly opposed to the general tendency of existing opinion and practice. Society has expended fully as much effort in the attempt (according to its lights) to compel people to conform to its notions of personal as of social excellence. The ancient commonwealths thought themselves entitled to practice, and the ancient philosophers countenanced, the regulation of every part of private conduct by public authority, on the ground that the State had a deep interest in the whole bodily and mental discipline of every one of its citizens—a mode of thinking which may have been admissible in small republics surrounded by powerful enemies, in constant peril of being subverted by foreign attack or internal commotion, and to which even a short interval of relaxed energy and self-command might so easily be fatal that they could not afford to wait for the salutary permanent effects of freedom. In the modern world, the greater size of political communities and, above all, the separation between spiritual and temporal authority (which placed the direction of men's consciences in other hands than those which controlled their worldly affairs) prevented so great an interference by law in the details of private life; but the engines of moral repression have been wielded more strenuously against divergence from the reigning opinion in self-regarding than even in social matters; religion, the most powerful of the elements which have entered into the formation of moral feeling, having almost always been governed either by the ambition of a hierarchy seeking control over every department of human conduct, or by the spirit of Puritanism. And some of those modern reformers who have placed themselves in strongest opposition to the religions of the past have been noway behind either churches or sects in their assertion of the right of spiritual domination: M. Comte,[7] in particular, whose social system, as unfolded in his *Système de Politique Positive*, aims at establishing (though by moral more than by legal appliances) a despotism of society over the individual surpassing anything contemplated in the political ideal of the most rigid disciplinarian among the ancient philosophers.

Apart from the peculiar tenets of individual thinkers, there is also in the world at large an increasing inclination to stretch unduly the powers of society over the individual both by the force of opinion and even by that of legislation; and as the tendency of all the changes taking place in the world is to strengthen society and diminish the power of the individual, this encroachment is not one of the evils which tend spontaneously to disappear, but, on the contrary, to grow more and more formidable. The disposition of

7. [Regarding Comte, see Mill's *Utilitarianism*, n. 7. The work referred to is the *System of Positive Polity*.]

mankind, whether as rulers or as fellow citizens, to impose their own opinions and inclinations as a rule of conduct on others is so energetically supported by some of the best and by some of the worst feelings incident to human nature that it is hardly ever kept under restraint by anything but want of power; and as the power is not declining, but growing, unless a strong barrier of moral conviction can be raised against the mischief, we must expect, in the present circumstances of the world, to see it increase.

It will be convenient for the argument if, instead of at once entering upon the general thesis, we confine ourselves in the first instance to a single branch of it on which the principle here stated is, if not fully, yet to a certain point, recognized by the current opinions. This one branch is the Liberty of Thought, from which it is impossible to separate the cognate liberty of speaking and of writing. Although these liberties, to some considerable amount, form part of the political morality of all countries which profess religious toleration and free institutions, the grounds, both philosophical and practical, on which they rest are perhaps not so familiar to the general mind, nor so thoroughly appreciated by many, even of the leaders of opinion, as might have been expected. Those grounds, when rightly understood, are of much wider application than to only one division of the subject, and a thorough consideration of this part of the question will be found the best introduction to the remainder. Those to whom nothing which I am about to say will be new may therefore, I hope, excuse me if on a subject which for now three centuries has been so often discussed I venture on one discussion more.

CHAPTER II
Of the Liberty of Thought and Discussion

The time, it is to be hoped, is gone by when any defense would be necessary of the "liberty of the press" as one of the securities against corrupt or tyrannical government. No argument, we may suppose, can now be needed against permitting a legislature or an executive, not identified in interest with the people, to prescribe opinions to them and determine what doctrines or what arguments they shall be allowed to hear. This aspect of the question, besides, has been

so often and so triumphantly enforced by preceding writers that it needs not be specially insisted on in this place. Though the law of England, on the subject of the press, is as servile to this day as it was in the time of the Tudors, there is little danger of its being actually put in force against political discussion except during some temporary panic when fear of insurrection drives ministers and judges from their propriety;[8] and, speaking generally, it is not, in constitutional countries, to be apprehended that the government, whether completely responsible to the people or not, will often attempt to control the expression of opinion, except when in doing so it makes itself the organ of the general intolerance of the public. Let us suppose,

8. These words had scarcely been written when, as if to give them an emphatic contradiction, occurred the Government Press Prosecutions of 1858. That ill-judged interference with the liberty of public discussion has not, however, induced me to alter a single word in the text, nor has it at all weakened my conviction that, moments of panic excepted, the era of pains and penalties for political discussion has, in our own country, passed away. For, in the first place, the prosecutions were not persisted in; and, in the second, they were never, properly speaking, political prosecutions. The offense charged was not that of criticizing institutions or the acts or persons of rulers, but of circulating what was deemed as immoral doctrine, the lawfulness of tyrannicide.

If the arguments of the present chapter are of any validity, there ought to exist the fullest liberty of professing and discussing, as a matter of ethical conviction, any doctrine, however immoral it may be considered. It would, therefore, be irrelevant and out of place to examine here whether the doctrine of tyrannicide deserves that title. I shall content myself with saying that the subject has been at all times one of the open questions of morals; that the act of a private citizen in striking down a criminal who, by raising himself above the law, has placed himself beyond the reach of legal punishment or control has been accounted by whole nations, and by some of the best and wisest of men, not a crime but an act of exalted virtue; and that, right or wrong, it is not of the nature of assassination, but of civil war. As such, I hold that the instigation to it, in a specific case, may be a proper subject of punishment, but only if an overt act has followed, and at least a probable connection can be established between the act and the instigation. Even then it is not a foreign government but the very government assailed which alone, in the exercise of self-defense, can legitimately punish attacks directed against its own existence.

therefore, that the government is entirely at one with the people, and never thinks of exerting any power of coercion unless in agreement with what it conceives to be their voice. But I deny the right of the people to exercise such coercion, either by themselves or by their government. The power itself is illegitimate. The best government has no more title to it than the worst. It is as noxious, or more noxious, when exerted in accordance with public opinion than when in opposition to it. If all mankind minus one were of one opinion, mankind would be no more justified in silencing that one person than he, if he had the power, would be justified in silencing mankind. Were an opinion a personal possession of no value except to the owner, if to be obstructed in the enjoyment of it were simply a private injury, it would make some difference whether the injury was inflicted only on a few persons or on many. But the peculiar evil of silencing the expression of an opinion is that it is robbing the human race, posterity as well as the existing generation—those who dissent from the opinion, still more than those who hold it. If the opinion is right, they are deprived of the opportunity of exchanging error for truth; if wrong, they lose, what is almost as great a benefit, the clearer perception and livelier impression of truth produced by its collision with error.

It is necessary to consider separately these two hypotheses, each of which has a distinct branch of the argument corresponding to it. We can never be sure that the opinion we are endeavoring to stifle is a false opinion; and if we were sure, stifling it would be an evil still.

First, the opinion which it is attempted to suppress by authority may possibly be true. Those who desire to suppress it, of course, deny its truth; but they are not infallible. They have no authority to decide the question for all mankind and exclude every other person from the means of judging. To refuse a hearing to an opinion because they are sure that it is false is to assume that *their* certainty is the same thing as *absolute* certainty. All silencing of discussion is an assumption of infallibility. Its condemnation may be allowed to rest on this common argument, not the worse for being common.

Unfortunately for the good sense of mankind, the fact of their fallibility is far from carrying the weight in their practical judgment which is always allowed

to it in theory; for while everyone well knows himself to be fallible, few think it necessary to take any precautions against their own fallibility, or admit the supposition that any opinion of which they feel very certain may be one of the examples of the error to which they acknowledge themselves to be liable. Absolute princes, or others who are accustomed to unlimited deference, usually feel this complete confidence in their own opinions on nearly all subjects. People more happily situated, who sometimes hear their opinions disputed and are not wholly unused to be set right when they are wrong, place the same unbounded reliance only on such of their opinions as are shared by all who surround them, or to whom they habitually defer; for in proportion to a man's want of confidence in his own solitary judgment does he usually repose, with implicit trust, on the infallibility of "the world" in general. And the world, to each individual, means the part of it with which he comes in contact: his party, his sect, his church, his class of society; the man may be called, by comparison, almost liberal and large-minded to whom it means anything so comprehensive as his own country or his own age. Nor is his faith in this collective authority at all shaken by his being aware that other ages, countries, sects, churches, classes, and parties have thought, and even now think, the exact reverse. He devolves upon his own world the responsibility of being in the right against the dissentient worlds of other people; and it never troubles him that mere accident has decided which of these numerous worlds is the object of his reliance, and that the same causes which make him a churchman in London would have made him a Buddhist or a Confucian in Peking. Yet it is as evident in itself, as any amount of argument can make it, that ages are no more infallible than individuals—every age having held many opinions which subsequent ages have deemed not only false but absurd; and it is as certain that many opinions, now general, will be rejected by future ages, as it is that many, once general, are rejected by the present.

The objection likely to be made to this argument would probably take some such form as the following. There is no greater assumption of infallibility in forbidding the propagation of error than in any other thing which is done by public authority on its own judgment and responsibility. Judgment is given to men that they may use it. Because it may be used erroneously, are men to be told that they ought not to use it at all? To prohibit what they think pernicious is not claiming exemption from error, but fulfilling the duty incumbent on them, although fallible, of acting on their conscientious conviction. If we were never to act on our opinions, because those opinions may be wrong, we should leave all our interests uncared for, and all our duties unperformed. An objection which applies to all conduct can be no valid objection to any conduct in particular. It is the duty of governments, and of individuals, to form the truest opinions they can; to form them carefully, and never impose them upon others unless they are quite sure of being right. But when they are sure (such reasoners may say), it is not conscientiousness but cowardice to shrink from acting on their opinions and allow doctrines which they honestly think dangerous to the welfare of mankind, either in this life or in another, to be scattered abroad without restraint, because other people, in less enlightened times, have persecuted opinions now believed to be true. Let us take care, it may be said, not to make the same mistake; but governments and nations have made mistakes in other things which are not denied to be fit subjects for the exercise of authority: they have laid on bad taxes, made unjust wars. Ought we therefore to lay on no taxes and, under whatever provocation, make no wars? Men and governments must act to the best of their ability. There is no such thing as absolute certainty, but there is assurance sufficient for the purposes of human life. We may, and must, assume our opinion to be true for the guidance of our own conduct; and it is assuming no more when we forbid bad men to pervert society by the propagation of opinions which we regard as false and pernicious.

I answer, that it is assuming very much more. There is the greatest difference between presuming an opinion to be true because, with every opportunity for contesting it, it has not been refuted, and assuming its truth for the purpose of not permitting its refutation. Complete liberty of contradicting and disproving our opinion is the very condition which justifies us in assuming its truth for purposes of action; and on no other terms can a being with human faculties have any rational assurance of being right.

When we consider either the history of opinion or the ordinary conduct of human life, to what is it to be ascribed that the one and the other are no worse than they are? Not certainly to the inherent force of the human understanding, for on any matter not self-evident there are ninety-nine persons totally incapable of judging of it for one who is capable; and the capacity of the hundredth person is only comparative, for the majority of the eminent men of every past generation held many opinions now known to be erroneous, and did or approved numerous things which no one will now justify. Why is it, then, that there is on the whole a preponderance among mankind of rational opinions and rational conduct? If there really is this preponderance — which there must be unless human affairs are, and have always been, in an almost desperate state — it is owing to a quality of the human mind, the source of everything respectable in man either as an intellectual or as a moral being, namely, that his errors are corrigible. He is capable of rectifying his mistakes by discussion and experience. Not by experience alone. There must be discussion to show how experience is to be interpreted. Wrong opinions and practices gradually yield to fact and argument; but facts and arguments, to produce any effect on the mind, must be brought before it. Very few facts are able to tell their own story, without comments to bring out their meaning. The whole strength and value, then, of human judgment depending on the one property, that it can be set right when it is wrong, reliance can be placed on it only when the means of setting it right are kept constantly at hand. In the case of any person whose judgment is really deserving of confidence, how has it become so? Because he has kept his mind open to criticism of his opinions and conduct. Because it has been his practice to listen to all that could be said against him; to profit by as much of it as was just, and to expound to himself, and upon occasion to others, the fallacy of what was fallacious. Because he has felt that the only way in which a human being can make some approach to knowing the whole of a subject is by hearing what can be said about it by persons of every variety of opinion, and studying all modes in which it can be looked at by every character of mind. No wise man ever acquired his wisdom in any mode but this; nor is it in the nature of human intellect to become wise in any other manner. The steady habit of correcting and completing his own opinion by collating it with those of others, so far from causing doubt and hesitation in carrying it into practice, is the only stable foundation for a just reliance on it; for, being cognizant of all that can, at least obviously, be said against him, and having taken up his position against all gain-sayers—knowing that he has sought for objections and difficulties instead of avoiding them, and has shut out no light which can be thrown upon the subject from any quarter—he has a right to think his judgment better than that of any person, or any multitude, who have not gone through a similar process.

It is not too much to require that what the wisest of mankind, those who are best entitled to trust their own judgment, find necessary to warrant their relying on it, should be submitted to by that miscellaneous collection of a few wise and many foolish individuals called the public. The most intolerant of churches, the Roman Catholic Church, even at the canonization of a saint admits, and listens patiently to, a "devil's advocate." The holiest of men, it appears, cannot be admitted to posthumous honors until all that the devil could say against him is known and weighed. If even the Newtonian philosophy were not permitted to be questioned, mankind could not feel as complete assurance of its truth as they now do. The beliefs which we have most warrant for have no safeguard to rest on but a standing invitation to the whole world to prove them unfounded. If the challenge is not accepted, or is accepted and the attempt fails, we are far enough from certainty still, but we have done the best that the existing state of human reason admits of: we have neglected nothing that could give the truth a chance of reaching us; if the lists are kept open, we may hope that, if there be a better truth, it will be found when the human mind is capable of receiving it; and in the meantime we may rely on having attained such approach to truth as is possible in our own day. This is the amount of certainty attainable by a fallible being, and this the sole way of attaining it.

Strange it is that men should admit the validity of the arguments for free discussion, but object to their being "pushed to an extreme," not seeing that unless the reasons are good for an extreme case, they are not good for any case. Strange that they should imagine that they are not assuming infallibility when they acknowledge that there should be free discussion on all subjects which can possibly be *doubtful*, but think that some particular principle or doctrine should be

forbidden to be questioned because it is so *certain*, that is, because *they are certain* that it is certain. To call any proposition certain, while there is anyone who would deny its certainty if permitted, but who is not permitted, is to assume that we ourselves, and those who agree with us, are the judges of certainty, and judges without hearing the other side.

In the present age—which has been described as "destitute of faith, but terrified at skepticism"[9]—in which people feel sure, not so much that their opinions are true as that they should not know what to do without them—the claims of an opinion to be protected from public attack are rested not so much on its truth as on its importance to society. There are, it is alleged, certain beliefs so useful, not to say indispensable, to well-being that it is as much the duty of governments to uphold those beliefs as to protect any other of the interests of society. In a case of such necessity, and so directly in the line of their duty, something less than infallibility may, it is maintained, warrant, and even bind, governments to act on their own opinion confirmed by the general opinion of mankind. It is also often argued, and still oftener thought, that none but bad men would desire to weaken these salutary beliefs; and there can be nothing wrong, it is thought, in restraining bad men and prohibiting what only such men would wish to practice. This mode of thinking makes the justification of restraints on discussion not a question of the truth of doctrines but of their usefulness, and flatters itself by that means to escape the responsibility of claiming to be an infallible judge of opinions. But those who thus satisfy themselves do not perceive that the assumption of infallibility is merely shifted from one point to another. The usefulness of an opinion is itself matter of opinion—as disputable, as open to discussion, and requiring discussion as much as the opinion itself. There is the same need of an infallible judge of opinions to decide an opinion to be noxious as to decide it to be false, unless the opinion condemned has full opportunity of defending itself. And it will not do to say that the heretic may be allowed to maintain the utility or harmlessness of his opinion, though forbidden to maintain its truth. The truth of

9. [The quotation is from Thomas Carlyle's "Memoirs of the Life of Scott," reprinted in his *Critical and Miscellaneous Essays*. Regarding Carlyle, see Mill's *Utilitarianism*, n. 3.]

an opinion is part of its utility. If we would know whether or not it is desirable that a proposition should be believed, is it possible to exclude the consideration of whether or not it is true? In the opinion, not of bad men, but of the best men, no belief which is contrary to truth can be really useful; and can you prevent such men from urging that plea when they are charged with culpability for denying some doctrine which they are told is useful, but which they believe to be false? Those who are on the side of received opinions never fail to take all possible advantage of this plea; you do not find *them* handling the question of utility as if it could be completely abstracted from that of truth; on the contrary, it is, above all, because their doctrine is "the truth" that the knowledge or the belief of it is held to be so indispensable. There can be no fair discussion of the question of usefulness when an argument so vital may be employed on one side, but not on the other. And in point of fact, when law or public feeling do not permit the truth of an opinion to be disputed, they are just as little tolerant of a denial of its usefulness. The utmost they allow is an extenuation of its absolute necessity, or of the positive guilt of rejecting it.

In order more fully to illustrate the mischief of denying a hearing to opinions because we, in our own judgment, have condemned them, it will be desirable to fix down the discussion to a concrete case; and I choose, by preference, the cases which are least favorable to me—in which the argument against freedom of opinion, both on the score of truth and on that of utility, is considered the strongest. Let the opinions impugned be the belief in a God and in a future state, or any of the commonly received doctrines of morality. To fight the battle on such ground gives a great advantage to an unfair antagonist, since he will be sure to say (and many who have no desire to be unfair will say it internally), Are these the doctrines which you do not deem sufficiently certain to be taken under the protection of law? Is the belief in a God one of the opinions to feel sure of which you hold to be assuming infallibility? But I must be permitted to observe that it is not the feeling sure of a doctrine (be it what it may) which I call an assumption of infallibility. It is the undertaking to decide that question *for others*, without allowing them to hear what can be said on the contrary side. And I denounce and reprobate this pretension not the less

if put forth on the side of my most solemn convictions. However positive anyone's persuasion may be, not only of the falsity but of the pernicious consequences—not only of the pernicious consequences, but (to adopt expressions which I altogether condemn) the immorality and impiety of an opinion—yet if, in pursuance of that private judgment, though backed by the public judgment of his country or his contemporaries, he prevents the opinion from being heard in its defense, he assumes infallibility. And so far from the assumption being less objectionable or less dangerous because the opinion is called immoral or impious, this is the case of all others in which it is most fatal. These are exactly the occasions on which the men of one generation commit those dreadful mistakes which excite the astonishment and horror of posterity. It is among such that we find the instances memorable in history, when the arm of the law has been employed to root out the best men and the noblest doctrines; with deplorable success as to the men, though some of the doctrines have survived to be (as if in mockery) invoked in defense of similar conduct toward those who dissent from *them*, or from their received interpretation.

Mankind can hardly be too often reminded that there was once a man called Socrates, between whom and the legal authorities and public opinion of his time there took place a memorable collision. Born in an age and country abounding in individual greatness, this man has been handed down to us by those who best knew both him and the age as the most virtuous man in it; while *we* know him as the head and prototype of all subsequent teachers of virtue, the source equally of the lofty inspiration of Plato and the judicious utilitarianism of Aristotle, "*i maestri di color che sanno*,"[10] the two headsprings of ethical as of all other philosophy. This acknowledged master of all the eminent thinkers who have since lived—whose fame, still growing after more than two thousand years, all but outweighs the whole remainder of the names which make his native city illustrious—was put to death by his countrymen, after a judicial conviction, for impiety and immorality. Impiety, in denying the gods recognized by the State; indeed, his accuser asserted (see the *Apologia*) that he believed in no gods at all.

10. [The master of them that know.]

Immorality, in being, by his doctrines and instructions, a "corruptor of youth." Of these charges the tribunal, there is every ground for believing, honestly found him guilty, and condemned the man who probably of all then born had deserved best of mankind to be put to death as a criminal.

To pass from this to the only other instance of judicial iniquity, the mention of which, after the condemnation of Socrates, would not be an anticlimax: the event which took place on Calvary rather more than eighteen hundred years ago. The man who left on the memory of those who witnessed his life and conversation such an impression of his moral grandeur that eighteen subsequent centuries have done homage to him as the Almighty in person, was ignominiously put to death, as what? As a blasphemer. Men did not merely mistake their benefactor, they mistook him for the exact contrary of what he was and treated him as that prodigy of impiety which they themselves are now held to be for their treatment of him. The feelings with which mankind now regard these lamentable transactions, especially the later of the two, render them extremely unjust in their judgment of the unhappy actors. These were, to all appearance, not bad men—not worse than men commonly are, but rather the contrary; men who possessed in a full, or somewhat more than a full measure, the religious, moral, and patriotic feelings of their time and people: the very kind of men who, in all times, our own included, have every chance of passing through life blameless and respected. The high priest who rent his garments when the words were pronounced, which, according to all the ideas of his country, constituted the blackest guilt, was in all probability quite as sincere in his horror and indignation as the generality of respectable and pious men now are in the religious and moral sentiments they profess; and most of those who now shudder at his conduct, if they had lived in his time, and been born Jews, would have acted precisely as he did. Orthodox Christians who are tempted to think that those who stoned to death the first martyrs must have been worse men than they themselves are ought to remember that one of those persecutors was Saint Paul.

Let us add one more example, the most striking of all, if the impressiveness of an error is measured by the wisdom and virtue of him who falls into it. If ever anyone possessed of power had grounds for thinking himself the best and most enlightened among his contemporaries, it was the Emperor Marcus Aurelius.[11] Absolute monarch of the whole civilized world, he preserved through life not only the most unblemished justice, but what was less to be expected from his Stoical breeding, the tenderest heart. The few failings which are attributed to him were all on the side of indulgence, while his writings, the highest ethical product of the ancient mind, differ scarcely perceptibly, if they differ at all, from the most characteristic teachings of Christ. This man, a better Christian in all but the dogmatic sense of the word than almost any of the ostensibly Christian sovereigns who have since reigned, persecuted Christianity. Placed at the summit of all the previous attainments of humanity, with an open, unfettered intellect, and a character which led him of himself to embody in his moral writings the Christian ideal, he yet failed to see that Christianity was to be a good and not an evil to the world, with his duties to which he was so deeply penetrated. Existing society he knew to be in a deplorable state. But such as it was, he saw, or thought he saw, that it was held together, and prevented from being worse, by belief and reverence of the received divinities. As a ruler of mankind, he deemed it his duty not to suffer society to fall in pieces; and saw not how, if its existing ties were removed, any others could be formed which could again knit it together. The new religion openly aimed at dissolving these ties; unless, therefore, it was his duty to adopt that religion, it seemed to be his duty to put it down. Inasmuch then as the theology of Christianity did not appear to him true or of divine origin, inasmuch as this strange history of a crucified God was not credible to him, and a system which purported to rest entirely upon a foundation to him so wholly unbelievable, could not be foreseen by him to be that renovating agency which, after all abatements, it has in fact proved to be; the gentlest and most amiable of philosophers and rulers, under a solemn sense of duty, authorized the persecution of Christianity. To my mind this is one of the most tragical facts in all history. It is a bitter thought how different a thing the Christianity of the world might have been if the Christian faith had been adopted as the religion

11. [Regarding Marcus Aurelius, see Hume's *Enquiry*, n. 58.]

of the empire under the auspices of Marcus Aurelius instead of those of Constantine. But it would be equally unjust to him and false to truth to deny that no one plea which can be urged for punishing anti-Christian teaching was wanting to Marcus Aurelius for punishing, as he did, the propagation of Christianity. No Christian more firmly believes that atheism is false and tends to the dissolution of society than Marcus Aurelius believed the same things of Christianity; he who, of all men then living, might have been thought the most capable of appreciating it. Unless anyone who approves of punishment for the promulgation of opinions flatters himself that he is a wiser and better man than Marcus Aurelius—more deeply versed in the wisdom of his time, more elevated in his intellect above it, more earnest in his search for truth, or more single-minded in his devotion to it when found—let him abstain from that assumption of the joint infallibility of himself and the multitude which the great Antoninus made with so unfortunate a result.

Aware of the impossibility of defending the use of punishment for restraining irreligious opinions by any argument which will not justify Marcus Antoninus, the enemies of religious freedom, when hard pressed, occasionally accept this consequence and say, with Dr. Johnson,[12] that the persecutors of Christianity were in the right, that persecution is an ordeal through which truth ought to pass, and always passes successfully, legal penalties being, in the end, powerless against truth, though sometimes beneficially effective against mischievous errors. This is a form of the argument for religious intolerance sufficiently remarkable not to be passed without notice.

A theory which maintains that truth may justifiably be persecuted because persecution cannot possibly do it any harm cannot be charged with being intentionally hostile to the reception of new truths; but we cannot commend the generosity of its dealing with the persons to whom mankind are indebted for them. To discover to the world something which deeply concerns it, and of which it was previously ignorant, to prove to it that it had been mistaken on some vital point of temporal or spiritual interest, is as important a service as a human being can render to his fellow creatures, and in certain cases, as in those of the early Christians and of the Reformers, those who think with Dr. Johnson believe it to have been the most precious gift which could be bestowed on mankind. That the authors of such splendid benefits should be requited by martyrdom, that their reward should be to be dealt with as the vilest of criminals, is not, upon this theory, a deplorable error and misfortune for which humanity should mourn in sackcloth and ashes, but the normal and justifiable state of things. The propounder of a new truth, according to this doctrine, should stand, as stood, in the legislation of the Locrians,[13] the proposer of a new law, with a halter round his neck, to be instantly tightened if the public assembly did not, on hearing his reasons, then and there adopt his proposition. People who defend this mode of treating benefactors cannot be supposed to set much value on the benefit; and I believe this view of the subject is mostly confined to the sort of persons who think that new truths may have been desirable once, but that we have had enough of them now.

But, indeed, the dictum that truth always triumphs over persecution is one of those pleasant falsehoods which men repeat after one another till they pass into commonplaces, but which all experience refutes. History teems with instances of truth put down by persecution. If not suppressed forever, it may be thrown back for centuries. To speak only of religious opinion: the Reformation broke out at least twenty times before Luther, and was put down. Arnold of Brescia[14] was put down. Fra Dolcino[15] was put down.

12. [Samuel Johnson (1709–1784) was the leading literary critic of his time and author of the *Dictionary of the English Language* (1755).]

13. [The Locrians, Greek colonists in southern Italy, adopted in the seventh century, B.C. the earliest written legal code in Europe. It was drafted by the lawgiver Zaleucus and was known for its extreme severity.]

14. [Arnold of Brescia (c.1090–1155), Italian monk and reformer, was exiled and his books burned for opposing the Church's possession of property. He defended the people of Rome who wished liberty and other democratic rights. He was executed as a political rebel.]

15. [Fra Dolcino of Novario (d. 1307), leader of an ascetic religious sect that urged purification of the Church, was tortured to death.]

Savonarola[16] was put down. The Albigeois[17] were put down. The Vaudois[18] were put down. The Lollards[19] were put down. The Hussites[20] were put down. Even after the era of Luther, wherever persecution was persisted in, it was successful. In Spain, Italy, Flanders, the Austrian empire, Protestantism was rooted out; and, most likely, would have been so in England had Queen Mary lived or Queen Elizabeth died. Persecution has always succeeded save where the heretics were too strong a party to be effactually persecuted. No reasonable person can doubt that Christianity might have been extirpated in the Roman Empire. It spread and became predominant because the persecutions were only occasional, lasting but a short time, and separated by long intervals of almost undisturbed propagandism. It is a piece of idle sentimentality that truth, merely as truth, has any inherent power denied to error of prevailing against the dungeon and the stake. Men are not more zealous for truth than they often are for error, and a sufficient application of legal or even of social penalties will generally succeed in stopping the propagation of either. The real advantage which truth has consists in this, that when an opinion is true, it may be extinguished once, twice, or many times, but in the course of ages there will generally be found persons to rediscover it, until some one of its reappearances falls on a time when from favorable circumstances it escapes persecution until it has made such head as to withstand all subsequent attempts to suppress it.

It will be said that we do not now put to death the introducers of new opinions: we are not like our fathers who slew the prophets; we even build sepulchers to them. It is true we no longer put heretics to death; and the amount of penal infliction which modern feeling would probably tolerate, even against the most obnoxious opinions, is not sufficient to extirpate them. But let us not flatter ourselves that we are yet free from the stain even of legal persecution. Penalties for opinion, or at least for its expression, still exist by law; and their enforcement is not, even in these times, so unexampled as to make it at all incredible that they may some day be revived in full force. In the year 1857, at the summer assizes[21] of the county of Cornwall, an unfortunate man, said to be of unexceptionable conduct in all relations of life, was sentenced to twenty-one months' imprisonment for uttering, and writing on a gate, some offensive words concerning Christianity.[22] Within a month of the same time, at the Old Bailey, two persons, on two separate occasions,[23] were rejected as jurymen, and one of them grossly insulted by the judge and by one of the counsel, because they honestly declared that they had no theological belief; and a third, a foreigner,[24] for the same reason, was denied justice against a thief. This refusal of redress took place in virtue of the legal

16. [Girolamo Savonarola (1452–1498), Italian religious reformer, severely condemned what he considered the degeneration of spiritual and moral values in his time. He was hanged for schism and heresy.]

17. [Albigensianism, a medieval French religious movement which maintained the existence of both God and the Evil One, was condemned as heretical by the Church and stamped out in the thirteenth century by the papal Inquisition.]

18. [The Waldensians, known in French as "Vaudois," were a medieval religious sect who proclaimed the Bible as the sole guide of life and rejected the claims of the papacy. In 1184 the Church condemned them as heretics, and many were burned at the stake, but the group survived in weakened form and became affiliated with Protestantism.]

19. [Lollardy, a medieval English movement for ecclesiastical reform led by John Wycliff (1320–1384), considered the Bible, as interpreted by each person for himself, the standard of holiness. Severe repressive measures were begun against it by the Church about 1400, but surviving remnants contributed to the development of Protestantism.]

20. [The Hussites, followers of the Czech religious reformer John Huss (c. 1369–1415), demanded the abolition of the feudal system and limitations on the powers of the Church. Huss, a champion of his countrymen, was burned at the stake for heresy, but the movement helped pave the way for the Protestant Reformation and the rise of modern nationalism.]

21. [Assizes are civil or criminal courts held periodically in English counties.]

22. [Thomas Pooley, Bodmin Assizes, July 31, 1857. In December following, he received a free pardon from the Crown.]

23. [George Jacob Holyoake, August 17, 1857; Edward Truelove, July, 1857.]

24. [Baron de Gleichen, Marlborough Street Police Court, August 4, 1857.]

doctrine that no person can be allowed to give evidence in a court of justice who does not profess belief in a God (any god is sufficient) and in a future state, which is equivalent to declaring such persons to be outlaws, excluded from the protection of the tribunals; who may not only be robbed or assaulted with impunity, if no one but themselves, or persons of similar opinions, be present, but anyone else may be robbed or assaulted with impunity if the proof of the fact depends on their evidence. The assumption on which this is grounded is that the oath is worthless of a person who does not believe in a future state—a proposition which betokens much ignorance of history in those who assent to it (since it is historically true that a large proportion of infidels in all ages have been persons of distinguished integrity and honor), and would be maintained by no one who had the smallest conception how many of the persons in greatest repute with the world, both for virtues and attainments, are well known, at least to their intimates, to be unbelievers. The rule, besides, is suicidal and cuts away its own foundation. Under pretense that atheists must be liars, it admits the testimony of all atheists who are willing to lie, and rejects only those who brave the obloquy of publicly confessing a detested creed rather than affirm a falsehood. A rule thus self-convicted of absurdity so far as regards its professed purpose can be kept in force only as a badge of hatred, a relic of persecution—a persecution, too, having the peculiarity that the qualification for undergoing it is the being clearly proved not to deserve it. The rule and the theory it implies are hardly less insulting to believers than to infidels. For if he who does not believe in a future state necessarily lies, it follows that they who do believe are only prevented from lying, if prevented they are, by the fear of hell. We will not do the authors and abettors of the rule the injury of supposing that the conception which they have formed of Christian virtue is drawn from their own consciousness.

These, indeed, are but rags and remnants of persecution, and may be thought to be not so much an indication of the wish to persecute, as an example of that very frequent infirmity of English minds, which makes them take a preposterous pleasure in the assertion of a bad principle, when they are no longer bad enough to desire to carry it really into practice. But unhappily there is no security in the state of the public mind that the suspension of worse forms of legal persecution, which has lasted for about the space of a generation, will continue. In this age the quiet surface of routine is as often ruffled by attempts to resuscitate past evils as to introduce new benefits. What is boasted of at the present time as the revival of religion is always, in narrow and uncultivated minds, at least as much the revival of bigotry; and where there is the strong permanent leaven of intolerance in the feelings of a people, which at all times abides in the middle classes of this country, it needs but little to provoke them into actively persecuting those whom they have never ceased to think proper objects of persecution.[25] For it is this—it is the opinions men entertain, and the feelings they cherish, respecting those who disown the beliefs they deem important which makes this country not a place of mental freedom. For a long time past, the chief mis-

---

25. Ample warning may be drawn from the large infusion of the passions of a persecutor, which mingled with the general display of the worst parts of our national character on the occasion of the Sepoy insurrection. The ravings of fanatics or charlatans from the pulpit may be unworthy of notice; but the heads of the Evangelical party have announced as their principle for the government of Hindus and Mohammedans that no schools be supported by public money in which the Bible is not taught, and by necessary consequence that no public employment be given to any but real or pretended Christians. An Undersecretary of State, in a speech delivered to his constituents on the 12th of November, 1857, is reported to have said: "Toleration of their faith" (the faith of a hundred millions of British subjects), "the superstition which they call religion, by the British Government, had had the effect of retarding the ascendancy of the British name, and preventing the salutary growth of Christianity ... Toleration was the great cornerstone of the religious liberties of this country; but do not let them abuse that precious word 'toleration.'" As he understood it, it meant the complete liberty to all, freedom of worship, *among Christians, who worshiped upon the same foundation*. It meant toleration of all sects and denominations of *Christians who believed in the one mediation*." I desire to call attention to the fact that a man who has been deemed fit to fill a high office in the government of this country under a liberal ministry maintains the doctrine that all who do not believe in the divinity of Christ are beyond the pale of toleration. Who, after this imbecile display, can indulge the illusion that religious persecution has passed away, never to return?

chief of the legal penalties is that they strengthen the social stigma. It is that stigma which is really effective, and so effective is it that the profession of opinions which are under the ban of society is much less common in England than is, in many other countries, the avowal of those which incur risk of judicial punishment. In respect to all persons but those whose pecuniary circumstances make them independent of the good will of other people, opinion, on this subject, is as efficacious as law; men might as well be imprisoned as excluded from the means of earning their bread. Those whose bread is already secured, and who desire no favors from men in power, or from bodies of men, or from the public, have nothing to fear from the open avowal of any opinions but to be ill-thought of and ill-spoken of, and this it ought not to require a very heroic mold to enable them to bear. There is no room for any appeal *ad misericordiam* in behalf of such persons. But though we do not now inflict so much evil on those who think differently from us as it was formerly our custom to do, it may be that we do ourselves as much evil as ever by our treatment of them. Socrates was put to death, but the Socratic philosophy rose like the sun in heaven and spread its illumination over the whole intellectual firmament. Christians were cast to the lions, but the Christian church grew up a stately and spreading tree, overtopping the older and less vigorous growths, and stifling them by its shade. Our merely social intolerance kills no one, roots out no opinions, but induces men to disguise them or to abstain from any active effort for their diffusion. With us, heretical opinions do not perceptibly gain, or even lose, ground in each decade or generation; they never blaze out far and wide, but continue to smolder in the narrow circles of thinking and studious persons among whom they originate, without ever lighting up the general affairs of mankind with either a true or a deceptive light. And thus is kept up a state of things very satisfactory to some minds, because, without the unpleasant process of fining or imprisoning anybody, it maintains all prevailing opinions outwardly undisturbed, while it does not absolutely interdict the exercise of reason by dissentients afflicted with the malady of thought. A convenient plan for having peace in the intellectual world, and keeping all things going on therein very much as they do already. But the price paid for this sort of intellectual pacification is the sacrifice of the entire moral courage of the human mind. A state of things in which a large portion of the most active and inquiring intellects find it advisable to keep the general principles and grounds of their convictions within their own breasts, and attempt, in what they address to the public, to fit as much as they can of their own conclusions to premises which they have internally renounced, cannot send forth the open, fearless characters and logical, consistent intellects who once adorned the thinking world. The sort of men who can be looked for under it are either mere conformers to commonplace, or timeservers for truth, whose arguments on all great subjects are meant for their hearers, and are not those which have convinced themselves. Those who avoid this alternative do so by narrowing their thoughts and interest to things which can be spoken of without venturing within the region of principles, that is, to small practical matters which would come right of themselves, if but the minds of mankind were strengthened and enlarged, and which will never be made effectually right until then, while that which would strengthen and enlarge men's minds—free and daring speculation on the highest subjects—is abandoned.

Those in whose eyes this reticence on the part of heretics is no evil should consider, in the first place, that in consequence of it there is never any fair and thorough discussion of heretical opinions; and that such of them as could not stand such a discussion, though they may be prevented from spreading, do not disappear. But it is not the minds of heretics that are deteriorated most by the ban placed on all inquiry which does not end in the orthodox conclusions. The greatest harm done is to those who are not heretics, and whose whole mental development is cramped and their reason cowed by the fear of heresy. Who can compute what the world loses in the multitude of promising intellects combined with timid characters, who dare not follow out any bold, vigorous, independent train of thought, lest it should land them in something which would admit of being considered irreligious or immoral? Among them we may occasionally see some man of deep conscientiousness and subtle and refined understanding, who spends a life in sophisticating with an intellect which he cannot silence, and exhausts the resources of ingenuity in attempting to reconcile the promptings of his conscience and reason with orthodoxy, which yet he does not, perhaps, to the end succeed in doing. No one can be a great thinker who does not recognize that as a thinker it is his first duty to follow his intellect to whatever conclusions it may lead. Truth gains more even by the errors of one who, with due study and preparation, thinks for himself than by the true opinions of those who only hold them because they do not suffer themselves to think. Not that it is solely, or chiefly, to form great thinkers that freedom of thinking is required. On the contrary, it is as much and even more indispensable to enable average human beings to attain the mental stature which they are capable of. There have been, and may again be, great individual thinkers in a general atmosphere of mental slavery. But there never has been, nor ever will be, in that atmosphere an intellectually active people. Where any people has made a temporary approach to such a character, it has been because the dread of heterodox speculation was for a time suspended. Where there is a tacit convention that principles are not to be disputed, where the discussion of the greatest questions which can occupy humanity is considered to be closed, we cannot hope to find that generally high scale of mental activity which has made some periods of history so remarkable. Never when controversy avoided the subjects which are large and important enough to kindle enthusiasm was the mind of a people stirred up from its foundations, and the impulse given which raised even persons of the most ordinary intellect to something of the dignity of thinking beings. Of such we have had an example in the condition of Europe during the times immediately following the Reformation; another, though limited to the Continent and to a more cultivated class, in the speculative movement of the latter half of the eighteenth century; and a third, of still briefer duration, in the intellectual fermentation of Germany during the Goethian and Fichtean period.[26] These periods differed widely in the particular opinions which they developed, but were alike in this, that during all three the yoke of authority was broken. In each, an old mental despotism had been thrown off, and no new one had yet taken its place. The impulse given at these three periods has made Europe what it now is. Every single improvement which has taken

26. [Johann Fichte (1762–1814) was a post-Kantian German philosopher.]

place either in the human mind or in institutions may be traced distinctly to one or other of them. Appearances have for some time indicated that all three impulses are well-nigh spent; and we can expect no fresh start until we again assert our mental freedom.

Let us now pass to the second division of the argument, and dismissing the supposition that any of the received opinions may be false, let us assume them to be true and examine into the worth of the manner in which they are likely to be held when their truth is not freely and openly canvassed. However unwillingly a person who has a strong opinion may admit the possibility that his opinion may be false, he ought to be moved by the consideration that, however true it may be, if it is not fully, frequently, and fearlessly discussed, it will be held as a dead dogma, not a living truth.

There is a class of persons (happily not quite so numerous as formerly) who think it enough if a person assents undoubtingly to what they think true, though he has no knowledge whatever of the grounds of the opinion and could not make a tenable defense of it against the most superficial objections. Such persons, if they can once get their creed taught from authority, naturally think that no good, and some harm, comes of its being allowed to be questioned. Where their influence prevails, they make it nearly impossible for the received opinion to be rejected wisely and considerately, though it may still be rejected rashly and ignorantly; for to shut out discussion entirely is seldom possible, and when it once gets in, beliefs not grounded on conviction are apt to give way before the slightest semblance of an argument. Waiving, however, this possibility—assuming that the true opinion abides in the mind, but abides as a prejudice, a belief independent of, and proof against, argument—this is not the way in which truth ought to be held by a rational being. This is not knowing the truth. Truth, thus held, is but one superstition the more, accidentally clinging to the words which enunciate a truth.

If the intellect and judgment of mankind ought to be cultivated, a thing which Protestants at least do not deny, on what can these faculties be more appropriately exercised by anyone than on the things which concern him so much that it is considered necessary for him to hold opinions on them? If the cultivation of the understanding consists in one thing more than in another, it is surely in learning the grounds of one's own opinions. Whatever people believe, on subjects on which it is of the first importance to believe rightly, they ought to be able to defend against at least the common objections. But, someone may say, "Let them be *taught* the grounds of their opinions. It does not follow that opinions must be merely parroted because they are never heard controverted. Persons who learn geometry do not simply commit the theorems to memory, but understand and learn likewise the demonstrations; and it would be absurd to say that they remain ignorant of the grounds of geometrical truths because they never hear anyone deny and attempt to disprove them." Undoubtedly: and such teaching suffices on a subject like mathematics, where there is nothing at all to be said on the wrong side of the question. The peculiarity of the evidence of mathematical truths is that all the argument is on one side. There are no objections, and no answers to objections. But on every subject on which difference of opinion is possible, the truth depends on a balance to be struck between two sets of conflicting reasons. Even in natural philosophy, there is always some other explanation possible of the same facts; some geocentric theory instead of heliocentric, some phlogiston instead of oxygen; and it has to be shown why that other theory cannot be the true one; and until this is shown, and until we know how it is shown, we do not understand the grounds of our opinion. But when we turn to subjects infinitely more complicated, to morals, religion, politics, social relations, and the business of life, three-fourths of the arguments for every disputed opinion consist in dispelling the appearance which favor some opinion different from it. The greatest orator, save one, of antiquity, has left it on record that he always studied his adversary's case with as great, if not still greater, intensity than even his own. What Cicero[27] practiced as the means of forensic success requires to be imitated by all who study any subject in order to arrive at the truth. He who knows only his own side of the case knows little of that. His reasons may be good, and no one may have been able to refute them. But if he is equally unable to refute the reasons on the opposite side, if

he does not so much as know what they are, he has no ground for preferring either opinion. The rational position for him would be suspension of judgment, and unless he contents himself with that, he is either led by authority or adopts, like the generality of the world, the side to which he feels most inclination. Nor is it enough that he should hear the arguments of adversaries from his own teachers, presented as they state them, and accompanied by what they offer as refutations. That is not the way to do justice to the arguments or bring them into real contact with his own mind. He must be able to hear them from persons who actually believe them, who defend them in earnest and do their very utmost for them. He must know them in their most plausible and persuasive form; he must feel the whole force of the difficulty which the true view of the subject has to encounter and dispose of, else he will never really possess himself of the portion of truth which meets and removes that difficulty. Ninety-nine in a hundred of what are called educated men are in this condition, even of those who can argue fluently for their opinions. Their conclusion may be true, but it might be false for anything they know; they have never thrown themselves into the mental position of those who think differently from them, and considered what such persons may have to say; and, consequently, they do not, in any proper sense of the word, know the doctrine which they themselves profess. They do not know those parts of it which explain and justify the remainder—the considerations which show that a fact which seemingly conflicts with another is reconcilable with it, or that, of two apparently strong reasons, one and not the other ought to be preferred. All that part of the truth which turns the scale and decides the judgment of a completely informed mind, they are strangers to; nor is it ever really known but to those who have attended equally and impartially to both sides and endeavored to see the reasons of both in the strongest light. So essential is this discipline to a real understanding of moral and human subjects that, if opponents of all-important truths do not exist, it is indispensable to imagine them and supply them with the strongest arguments which the most skillful devil's advocate can conjure up.

To abate the force of these considerations, an enemy of free discussion may be supposed to say that there is no necessity for mankind in general to know

27. [Regarding Cicero, see Locke's *Essay*, n.8.]

and understand all that can be said against or for their opinions by philosophers and theologians. That it is not needful for common men to be able to expose all the misstatements or fallacies of an ingenious opponent. That it is enough if there is always somebody capable of answering them, so that nothing likely to mislead uninstructed persons remains unrefuted. That simple minds, having been taught the obvious grounds of the truths inculcated in them, may trust to authority for the rest and, being aware that they have neither knowledge nor talent to resolve every difficulty which can be raised, may repose in the assurance that all those which have been raised have been or can be answered by those who are specially trained to the task.

Conceding to this view of the subject the utmost that can be claimed for it by those most easily satisfied with the amount of understanding of truth which ought to accompany the belief of it, even so, the argument for free discussion is noway weakened. For even this doctrine acknowledges that mankind ought to have a rational assurance that all objections have been satisfactorily answered; and how are they to be answered if that which requires to be answered is not spoken? Or how can the answer be known to be satisfactory if the objectors have no opportunity of showing that it is unsatisfactory? If not the public, at least the philosophers and theologians who are to resolve the difficulties must make themselves familiar with those difficulties in their most puzzling form; and this cannot be accomplished unless they are freely stated and placed in the most advantageous light which they admit of. The Catholic Church has its own way of dealing with this embarrassing problem. It makes a broad separation between those who can be permitted to receive its doctrines on conviction and those who must accept them on trust. Neither, indeed, are allowed any choice as to what they will accept; but the clergy, such at least as can be fully confided in, may admissibly and meritoriously make themselves acquainted with the arguments of opponents, in order to answer them, and may, therefore, read heretical books; the laity, not unless by special permission, hard to be obtained. This discipline recognizes a knowledge of the enemy's case as beneficial to the teachers, but finds means, consistent with this, of denying it to the rest of the world, thus giving to the *élite* more mental culture, though not more mental

freedom, than it allows to the mass. By this device it succeeds in obtaining the kind of mental superiority which its purposes require; for though culture without freedom never made a large and liberal mind, it can make a clever *nisi prius*[28] advocate of a cause. But in countries professing Protestantism, this resource is denied, since Protestants hold, at least in theory, that the responsibility for the choice of a religion must be borne by each for himself and cannot be thrown off upon teachers. Besides, in the present state of the world, it is practically impossible that writings which are read by the instructed can be kept from the uninstructed. If the teachers of mankind are to be cognizant of all that they ought to know, everything must be free to be written and published without restraint.

If, however, the mischievous operation of the absence of free discussion, when the received opinions are true, were confined to leaving men ignorant of the grounds of those opinions, it might be thought that this, if an intellectual, is no moral evil and does not affect the worth of the opinions, regarded in their influence on the character. The fact, however, is that not only the grounds of the opinion are forgotten in the absence of discussion, but too often the meaning of the opinion itself. The words which convey it cease to suggest ideas, or suggest only a small portion of those they were originally employed to communicate. Instead of a vivid conception and a living belief, there remain only a few phrases retained by rote; or, if any part, the shell and husk only of the meaning is retained, the finer essence being lost. The great chapter in human history which this fact occupies and fills cannot be too earnestly studied and meditated on.

It is illustrated in the experience of almost all ethical doctrines and religious creeds. They are all full of meaning and vitality to those who originate them, and to the direct disciples of the originators. Their meaning continues to be felt in undiminished strength, and is perhaps brought out into even fuller consciousness, so long as the struggle lasts to give the doctrine or creed an ascendancy over other creeds. At last it either prevails and becomes the general opinion, or its progress stops; it keeps possession of the ground it has gained, but ceases to spread further.

28. [A term, adopted from English legal proceedings, meaning that existing law is to be presumed valid until demonstrated otherwise.]

When either of these results has become apparent, controversy on the subject flags, and gradually dies away. The doctrine has taken its place, if not as a received opinion, as one of the admitted sects or divisions of opinion; those who hold it have generally inherited, not adopted it; and conversion from one of these doctrines to another, being now an exceptional fact, occupies little place in the thoughts of their professors. Instead of being, as at first, constantly on the alert either to defend themselves against the world or to bring the world over to them, they have subsided into acquiescence and neither listen, when they can help it, to arguments against their creed, nor trouble dissentients (if there be such) with arguments in its favor. From this time may usually be dated the decline in the living power of the doctrine. We often hear the teachers of all creeds lamenting the difficulty of keeping up in the minds of believers a lively apprehension of the truth which they nominally recognize, so that it may penetrate the feelings and acquire a real mastery over the conduct. No such difficulty is complained of while the creed is still fighting for its existence; even the weaker combatants then know and feel what they are fighting for, and the difference between it and other doctrines; and in that period of every creed's existence not a few persons may be found who have realized its fundamental principles in all the forms of thought, have weighed and considered them in all their important bearings, and have experienced the full effect on the character which belief in that creed ought to produce in a mind thoroughly imbued with it. But when it has come to be an hereditary creed, and to be received passively, not actively — when the mind is no longer compelled, in the same degree as at first, to exercise its vital powers on the questions which its belief presents to it, there is a progressive tendency to forget all of the belief except the formularies, or to give it a dull and torpid assent, as if accepting it on trust dispensed with the necessity of realizing it in consciousness, or testing it by personal experience, until it almost ceases to connect itself at all with the inner life of the human being. Then are seen the cases, so frequent in this age of the world as almost to form the majority, in which the creed remains as it were outside the mind, incrusting and petrifying it against all other influences addressed to the higher parts of our nature; manifesting its power by not suffering any fresh and living

conviction to get in, but itself doing nothing for the mind or heart except standing sentinel over them to keep them vacant.

To what an extent doctrines intrinsically fitted to make the deepest impression upon the mind may remain in it as dead beliefs, without being ever realized in the imagination, the feelings, or the understanding, is exemplified by the manner in which the majority of believers hold the doctrines of Christianity. By Christianity, I here mean what is accounted such by all churches and sects — the maxims and precepts contained in the New Testament. These are considered sacred, and accepted as laws, by all professing Christians. Yet it is scarcely too much to say that not one Christian in a thousand guides or tests his individual conduct by reference to those laws. The standard to which he does refer it is the custom of his nation, his class, or his religious profession. He has thus, on the one hand, a collection of ethical maxims which he believes to have been vouchsafed to him by infallible wisdom as rules for his government; and, on the other, a set of everyday judgments and practices which go a certain length with some of those maxims, not so great a length with others, stand in direct opposition to some, and are, on the whole, a compromise between the Christian creed and the interests and suggestions of worldly life. To the first of these standards he gives his homage; to the other his real allegiance. All Christians believe that the blessed are the poor and humble, and those who are ill-used by the world; that it is easier for a camel to pass through the eye of a needle than for a rich man to enter the kingdom of heaven; that they should judge not, lest they be judged; that they should swear not at all; that they should love their neighbor as themselves; that if one take their cloak, they should give him their coat also; that they should take no thought for the morrow; that if they would be perfect they should sell all that they have and give it to the poor. They are not insincere when they say that they believe these things. They do believe them, as people believe what they have always heard lauded and never discussed. But in the sense of that living belief which regulates conduct, they believe these doctrines just up to the point to which it is usual to act upon them. The doctrines in their integrity are serviceable to pelt adversaries with; and it is understood that they are to be put forward (when possible) as the reasons for whatever people do that they think laudable. But anyone who reminded them that the maxims require an infinity of things which they never even think of doing would gain nothing but to be classed among those very unpopular characters who affect to be better than other people. The doctrines have no hold on ordinary believers—are not a power in their minds. They have an habitual respect for the sound of them, but no feeling which spreads from the words to the things signified and forces the mind to take *them* in and make them conform to the formula. Whenever conduct is concerned, they look round for Mr. A and B to direct them how far to go in obeying Christ.

Now we may be well assured that the case was not thus, but far otherwise, with the early Christians. Had it been thus, Christianity never would have expanded from an obscure sect of the despised Hebrews into the religion of the Roman empire. When their enemies said, "See how these Christians love one another" (a remark not likely to be made by anybody now), they assuredly had a much livelier feeling of the meaning of their creed than they have ever had since. And to this cause, probably, it is chiefly owing that Christianity now makes so little progress in extending its domain, and after eighteen centuries is still nearly confined to Europeans and the descendants of Europeans. Even with the strictly religious, who are much in earnest about their doctrines and attach a greater amount of meaning to many of them than people in general, it commonly happens that the part which is thus comparatively active in their minds is that which was made by Calvin, or Knox,[29] or some such person much nearer in character to themselves. The sayings of Christ coexist passively in their minds, producing hardly any effect beyond what is caused by mere listening to words so amiable and bland. There are many reasons, doubtless, why doctrines which are the badge of a sect retain more of their vitality than those common to all recognized sects, and why more pains are taken by teachers to keep their meaning alive; but one reason certainly is that the peculiar doctrines are more questioned and have to be oftener defended against open gainsayers. Both teachers and learners go to sleep at their post as soon as there is no enemy in the field.

29. [John Knox (c. 1514–1572) was the religious reformer who founded Scottish Presbyterianism.]

The same thing holds true, generally speaking, of all traditional doctrines—those of prudence and knowledge of life as well as of morals or religion. All languages and literatures are full of general observations on life, both as to what it is and how to conduct oneself in it—observations which everybody knows, which everybody repeats or hears with acquiescence, which are received as truisms, yet of which most people first truly learn the meaning when experience, generally of a painful kind, has made it a reality to them. How often, when smarting under some unforeseen misfortune or disappointment, does a person call to mind some proverb or common saying, familiar to him all his life, the meaning of which, if he had ever before felt it as he does now, would have saved him from the calamity. There are indeed reasons for this, other than the absence of discussion; there are many truths of which the full meaning *cannot* be realized until personal experience has brought it home. But much more of the meaning even of these would have been understood, and what was understood would have been far more deeply impressed on the mind, if the man had been accustomed to hear it argued *pro* and *con* by people who did understand it. The fatal tendency of mankind to leave off thinking about a thing when it is no longer doubtful is the cause of half their errors. A contemporary author has well spoken of "the deep slumber of a decided opinion."

But what! (it may be asked), Is the absence of unanimity an indispensable condition of true knowledge? Is it necessary that some part of mankind should persist in error to enable any to realize the truth? Does a belief cease to be real and vital as soon as it is generally received—and is a proposition never thoroughly understood and felt unless some doubt of it remains? As soon as mankind have unanimously accepted a truth, does the truth perish within them? The highest aim and best result of improved intelligence, it has hitherto been thought, is to unite mankind more and more in the acknowledgment of all-important truths; and does the intelligence only last as long as it has not achieved its object? Do the fruits of conquest perish by the very completeness of the victory?

I affirm no such thing. As mankind improve, the number of doctrines which are no longer disputed or doubted will be constantly on the increase; and the well-being of mankind may almost be measured by the number and gravity of the truths which have reached the point of being uncontested. The cessation, on one question after another, of serious controversy is one of the necessary incidents of the consolidation of opinion—a consolidation as salutary in the case of true opinions as it is dangerous and noxious when the opinions are erroneous. But though this gradual narrowing of the bounds of diversity of opinion is necessary in both senses of the term, being at once inevitable and indispensable, we are not therefore obliged to conclude that all its consequences must be beneficial. The loss of so important an aid to the intelligent and living apprehension of a truth as is afforded by the necessity of explaining it to, or defending it against, opponents, though not sufficient to outweigh, is no trifling drawback from the benefit of its universal recognition. Where this advantage can no longer be had, I confess I should like to see the teachers of mankind endeavoring to provide a substitute for it—some contrivance for making the difficulties of the question as present to the learner's consciousness as if they were pressed upon him by a dissentient champion, eager for his conversion.

But instead of seeking contrivances for this purpose, they have lost those they formerly had. The Socratic dialectics, so magnificently exemplified in the dialogues of Plato, were a contrivance of this description. They were essentially a negative discussion of the great questions of philosophy and life, directed with consummate skill to the purpose of convincing anyone who had merely adopted the commonplaces of received opinion that he did not understand the subject—that he as yet attached no definite meaning to the doctrines he professed; in order that, becoming aware of his ignorance, he might be put in the way to obtain a stable belief, resting on a clear apprehension both of the meaning of doctrines and of their evidence. The school disputations of the Middle Ages had a somewhat similar object. They were intended to make sure that the pupil understood his own opinion, and (by necessary correlation) the opinion opposed to it, and could enforce the grounds of the one and confute those of the other. These last-mentioned contests had indeed the incurable defect that the premises appealed to were taken from authority, not from reason; and, as a discipline to the mind, they were in every respect inferior to the powerful dialec-

tics which formed the intellects of the "*Socratici viri*";[30] but the modern mind owes far more to both than it is generally willing to admit, and the present modes of education contain nothing which in the smallest degree supplies the place either of the one or of the other. A person who derives all his instruction from teachers or books, even if he escape the besetting temptation of contenting himself with cram, is under no compulsion to hear both sides; accordingly it is far from a frequent accomplishment, even among thinkers, to know both sides; and the weakest part of what everybody says in defense of his opinion is what he intends as a reply to antagonists. It is the fashion of the present time to disparage negative logic—that which points out weaknesses in theory or errors in practice without establishing positive truths. Such negative criticism would indeed be poor enough as an ultimate result, but as a means to attaining any positive knowledge or conviction worthy the name it cannot be valued too highly; and until people are again systematically trained to it, there will be few great thinkers and a low general average of intellect in any but the mathematical and physical departments of speculation. On any other subject no one's opinions deserve the name of knowledge, except so far as he has either had forced upon him by others or gone through of himself the same mental process which would have been required of him in carrying on an active controversy with opponents. That, therefore, which, when absent, it is so indispensable, but so difficult, to create, how worse than absurd it is to forego when spontaneously offering itself! If there are any persons who contest a received opinion, or who will do so if law or opinion will let them, let us thank them for it, open our minds to listen to them, and rejoice that there is someone to do for us what we otherwise ought, if we have any regard for either the certainty or the vitality of our convictions, to do with much greater labor for ourselves.

It still remains to speak of one of the principal causes which make diversity of opinion advantageous, and will continue to do so until mankind shall have entered a stage of intellectual advancement which at present seems at an incalculable distance. We have hitherto considered only two possibilities: that the

30. [The pupils and followers of Socrates.]

received opinion may be false, and some other opinion, consequently, true; or that, the received opinion being true, a conflict with the opposite error is essential to a clear apprehension and deep feeling of its truth. But there is a commoner case than either of these: when the conflicting doctrines, instead of being one true and the other false, share the truth between them, and the nonconforming opinion is needed to supply the remainder of the truth of which the received doctrine embodies only a part. Popular opinions, on subjects not palpable to sense, are often true, but seldom or never the whole truth. They are a part of the truth, sometimes a greater, sometimes a smaller part, but exaggerated, distorted, and disjointed from the truths by which they ought to be accompanied and limited. Heretical opinions, on the other hand, are generally some of these suppressed and neglected truths, bursting the bonds which kept them down, and either seeking reconciliation with the truth contained in the common opinion, or fronting it as enemies, and setting themselves up, with similar exclusiveness, as the whole truth. The latter case is hitherto the most frequent, as, in the human mind, one-sidedness has always been the rule, and many-sidedness the exception. Hence, even in revolutions of opinion, one part of the truth usually sets while another rises. Even progress, which ought to superadd, for the most part only substitutes one partial and incomplete truth for another; improvement consisting chiefly in this, that the new fragment of truth is more wanted, more adapted to the needs of the time than that which it displaces. Such being the partial character of prevailing opinions, even when resting on a true foundation, every opinion which embodies somewhat of the portion of truth which the common opinion omits ought to be considered precious, with whatever amount of error and confusion that truth may be blended. No sober judge of human affairs will feel bound to be indignant because those who force on our notice truths which we should otherwise have overlooked, overlook some of those which we see. Rather, he will think that so long as popular truth is one-sided, it is more desirable than otherwise that unpopular truth should have one-sided assertors, too, such being usually the most energetic and the most likely to compel reluctant attention to the fragment of wisdom which they proclaim as if it were the whole.

Thus, in the eighteenth century, when nearly all the instructed, and all those of the uninstructed who were led by them, were lost in admiration of what is called civilization, and of the marvels of modern science, literature, and philosophy, and while greatly overrating the amount of unlikeness between the men of modern and those of ancient times, indulged the belief that the whole of the difference was in their own favor; with what a salutary shock did the paradoxes of Rousseau explode like bombshells in the midst, dislocating the compact mass of one-sided opinion and forcing its elements to recombine in a better form and with additional ingredients. Not that the current opinions were on the whole farther from the truth than Rousseau's were; on the contrary, they were nearer to it; they contained more of positive truth, and very much less of error. Nevertheless there lay in Rousseau's doctrine, and has floated down the stream of opinion along with it, a considerable amount of exactly those truths which the popular opinion wanted; and these are the deposit which was left behind them when the flood subsided. The superior worth of simplicity of life, the enervating and demoralizing effect of the trammels and hypocrisies of artificial society are ideas which have never been entirely absent from cultivated minds since Rousseau wrote; and they will in time produce their due effect, though at present needing to be asserted as much as ever, and to be asserted by deeds; for words, on this subject, have nearly exhausted their power.

In politics, again, it is almost a commonplace that a party of order or stability and a party of progress or reform are both necessary elements of a healthy state of political life, until the one or the other shall have so enlarged its mental grasp as to be a party equally of order and of progress, knowing and distinguishing what is fit to be preserved from what ought to be swept away. Each of these modes of thinking derives its utility from the deficiencies of the other; but it is in a great measure the opposition of the other that keeps each within the limits of reason and sanity. Unless opinions favorable to democracy and to aristocracy, to property and to equality, to co-operation and to competition, to luxury and to abstinence, to sociality and individuality, to liberty and discipline, and all the other standing antagonisms of practical life, are expressed with equal freedom and enforced and defended with equal talent and energy, there is no chance of both elements obtaining their due; one scale is sure to go up, and the other down. Truth, in the great practical concerns of life, is so much a question of the reconciling and combining of opposites that very few have minds sufficiently capacious and impartial to make the adjustment with an approach to correctness, and it has to be made by the rough process of a struggle between combatants fighting under hostile banners. On any of the great open questions just enumerated, if either of the two opinions has a better claim than the other, not merely to be tolerated, but to be encouraged and countenanced, it is the one which happens at the particular time and place to be in a minority. That is the opinion which, for the time being, represents the neglected interests, the side of human well-being which is in danger of obtaining less than its share. I am aware that there is not, in this country, any intolerance of differences of opinion on most of these topics. They are adduced to show, by admitted and multiplied examples, the universality of the fact that only through diversity of opinion is there, in the existing state of human intellect, a chance of fair play to all sides of the truth. When there are persons to be found who form an exception to the apparent unanimity of the world on any subject, even if the world is in the right, it is always probable that dissentients have something worth hearing to say for themselves, and that truth would lose something by their silence.

It may be objected, "But *some* received principles, especially on the highest and most vital subjects, are more than half-truths. The Christian morality, for instance, is the whole truth on that subject, and if anyone teaches a morality which varies from it, he is wholly in error." As this is of all cases the most important in practice, none can be fitter to test the general maxim. But before pronouncing what Christian morality is or is not, it would be desirable to decide what is meant by Christian morality. If it means the morality of the New Testament, I wonder that any one who derives his knowledge of this from the book itself can suppose that it was announced, or intended, as a complete doctrine of morals. The Gospel always refers to a pre-existing morality and confines its precepts to the particulars in which that morality was to be corrected or superseded by a wider and higher, expressing itself, moreover, in terms most general, often impossible to be interpreted literally, and possessing rather the impressiveness of poetry or elo-

quence than the precision of legislation. To extract from it a body of ethical doctrine has never been possible without eking it out from the Old Testament, that is, from a system elaborate indeed, but in many respects barbarous, and intended only for a barbarous people. St. Paul, a declared enemy to this Judaical mode of interpreting the doctrine and filling up the scheme of his Master, equally assumes a pre-existing morality, namely that of the Greeks and Romans; and his advice to Christians is in a great measure a system of accommodation to that, even to the extent of giving an apparent sanction to slavery. What is called Christian, but should rather be termed theological, morality was not the work of Christ or the Apostles, but is of much later origin, having been gradually built up by the Catholic Church of the first five centuries, and though not implicitly adopted by moderns and Protestants, has been much less modified by them than might have been expected. For the most part, indeed, they have contented themselves with cutting off the additions which had been made to it in the Middle Ages, each sect supplying the place by fresh additions, adapted to its own character and tendencies. That mankind owe a great debt to this morality, and to its early teachers, I should be the last person to deny, but I do not scruple to say of it that it is, in many important points, incomplete and one-sided, and that, unless ideas and feelings not sanctioned by it had contributed to the formation of European life and character, human affairs would have been in a worse condition than they now are. Christian morality (so called) has all the characters of a reaction; it is, in great part, a protest against paganism. Its ideal is negative rather than positive; passive rather than active; innocence rather than nobleness; abstinence from evil rather than energetic pursuit of good; in its precepts (as has been well said) "thou shalt not" predominates unduly over "though shalt." In its horror of sensuality, it made an idol of asceticism which has been gradually compromised away into one of legality. It holds out the hope of heaven and the threat of hell as the appointed and appropriate motives to a virtuous life: in this falling far below the best of the ancients, and doing what lies in it to give to human morality an essentially selfish character, by disconnecting each man's feelings of duty from the interests of his fellow creatures, except so far as a self-interested inducement is offered to him for consulting them.

It is essentially a doctrine of passive obedience; it inculcates submission to all authorities found established; who indeed are not to be actively obeyed when they command what religion forbids, but who are not to be resisted, far less rebelled against, for any amount of wrong to ourselves. And while, in the morality of the best pagan nations, duty to the State holds even a disproportionate place, infringing on the just liberty of the individual, in purely Christian ethics that grand department of duty is scarcely noticed or acknowledged. It is in the Koran, not the New Testament, that we read the maxim: "A ruler who appoints any man to an office, when there is in his dominions another man better qualified for it, sins against God and against the State." What little recognition the idea of obligation to the public obtains in modern morality is derived from Greek and Roman sources, not from Christian; as, even in the morality of private life, whatever exists of magnanimity, high-mindedness, personal dignity, even the sense of honor, is derived from the purely human, not the religious part of our education, and never could have grown out of a standard of ethics in which the only worth, professedly recognized, is that of obedience.

I am as far as anyone from pretending that these defects are necessarily inherent in the Christian ethics in every manner in which it can be conceived, or that the many requisites of a complete moral doctrine which it does not contain do not admit of being reconciled with it. Far less would I insinuate this out of the doctrines and precepts of Christ himself. I believe that the sayings of Christ are all that I can see any evidence of their having been intended to be; that they are irreconcilable with nothing which a comprehensive morality requires; that everything which is excellent in ethics may be brought within them, with no greater violence to their language than has been done to it by all who have attempted to deduce from them any practical system of conduct whatever. But it is quite consistent with this to believe that they contain, and were meant to contain, only a part of the truth; that many essential elements of the highest morality are among the things which are not provided for, nor intended to be provided for, in the recorded deliverances of the Founder of Christianity, and which have been entirely thrown aside in the system of ethics erected on the basis of those deliverances by the Christian Church. And this being

so, I think it a great error to persist in attempting to find in the Christian doctrine that complete rule for our guidance which its Author intended it to sanction and enforce, but only partially to provide. I believe, too, that this narrow theory is becoming a grave practical evil, detracting greatly from the moral training and instruction which so many well-meaning persons are now at length exerting themselves to promote. I much fear that by attempting to form the mind and feelings on an exclusively religious type, and discarding those secular standards (as for want of a better name they may be called) which heretofore coexisted with and supplemented the Christian ethics, receiving some of its spirit, and infusing into it some of theirs, there will result, and is even now resulting, a low, abject, servile type of character which, submit itself as it may to what it deems the Supreme Will, is incapable of rising to or sympathizing in the conception of Supreme Goodness. I believe that other ethics than any which can be evolved from exclusively Christian sources must exist side by side with Christian ethics to produce the moral regeneration of mankind; and that the Christian system is no exception to the rule that in an imperfect state of the human mind the interests of truth require a diversity of opinions. It is not necessary that in ceasing to ignore the moral truths not contained in Christianity men should ignore any of those which it does contain. Such prejudice or oversight, when it occurs, is altogether an evil, but it is one from which we cannot hope to be always exempt, and must be regarded as the price paid for an inestimable good. The exclusive pretension made by a part of the truth to be the whole must and ought to be protested against; and if a reactionary impulse should make the protestors unjust in their turn, this one-sidedness, like the other, may be lamented but must be tolerated. If Christians would teach infidels to be just to Christianity, they should themselves be just to infidelity. It can do truth no service to blink the fact, known to all who have the most ordinary acquaintance with literary history, that a large portion of the noblest and most valuable moral teaching has been the work, not only of men who did not know, but of men who knew and rejected, the Christian faith.

I do not pretend that the most unlimited use of the freedom of enunciating all possible opinions would put an end to the evils of religious or philosophical sectarianism. Every truth which men of narrow capacity are in earnest about is sure to be asserted, inculcated, and in many ways even acted on, as if no other truth existed in the world, or at all events none that could limit or qualify the first. I acknowledge that the tendency of all opinions to become sectarian is not cured by the freest discussion, but is often heightened and exacerbated thereby; the truth which ought to have been, but was not, seen, being rejected all the more violently because proclaimed by persons regarded as opponents. But it is not on the impassioned partisan, it is on the calmer and more disinterested bystander, that this collision of opinions works its salutary effect. Not the violent conflict between parts of the truth, but the quiet suppression of half of it, is the formidable evil; there is always hope when people are forced to listen to both sides; it is when they attend only to one that errors harden into prejudices, and truth itself ceases to have the effect of truth by being exaggerated into falsehood. And since there are few mental attributes more rare than that judicial faculty which can sit in intelligent judgment between two sides of a question, of which only one is represented by an advocate before it, truth has no chance but in proportion as every side of it, every opinion which embodies any fraction of the truth, not only finds advocates, but is so advocated as to be listened to.

We have now recognized the necessity to the mental well-being of mankind (on which all their other well-being depends) of freedom of opinion, and freedom of the expression of opinion, on four distinct grounds, which we will now briefly recapitulate:

First, if any opinion is compelled to silence, that opinion may, for aught we can certainly know, be true. To deny this is to assume our own infallibility.

Secondly, though the silenced opinion be an error, it may, and very commonly does, contain a portion of truth; and since the general or prevailing opinion on any subject is rarely or never the whole truth, it is only by the collision of adverse opinions that the remainder of the truth has any chance of being supplied.

Thirdly, even if the received opinion be not only true, but the whole truth; unless it is suffered to be, and actually is, vigorously and earnestly contested, it will, by most of those who receive it, be held in the manner of a prejudice, with little comprehension or feeling of its rational grounds. And not only this, but,

fourthly, the meaning of the doctrine itself will be in danger of being lost or enfeebled, and deprived of its vital effect on the character and conduct: the dogma becoming a mere formal profession, inefficacious for good, but cumbering the ground and preventing the growth of any real and heartfelt conviction from reason or personal experience.

Before quitting the subject of freedom of opinion, it is fit to take some notice of those who say that the free expression of all opinions should be permitted on condition that the manner be temperate, and do not pass the bounds of fair discussion. Much might be said on the impossibility of fixing where these supposed bounds are to be placed; for if the test be offense to those whose opinions are attacked, I think experience testifies that this offense is given whenever the attack is telling and powerful, and that every opponent who pushes them hard, and whom they find it difficult to answer, appears to them, if he shows any strong feeling on the subject, an intemperate opponent. But this, though an important consideration in a practical point of view, merges in a more fundamental objection. Undoubtedly, the manner of asserting an opinion, even though it be a true one, may be very objectionable and may justly incur severe censure. But the principal offenses of the kind are such as it is mostly impossible, unless by accidental self-betrayal, to bring home to conviction. The gravest of them is, to argue sophistically, to suppress facts or arguments, to mistake the elements of the case, or misrepresent the opposite opinion. But all this, even to the most aggravated degree, is so continually done in perfect good faith by persons who are not considered, and in many other respects may not deserve to be considered, ignorant or incompetent, that it is rarely possible, on adequate grounds, conscientiously to stamp the misrepresentation as morally culpable, and still less could law presume to interfere with this kind of controversial misconduct. With regard to what is commonly meant by intemperate discussion, namely invective, sarcasm, personality, and the like, the denunciation of these weapons would deserve more sympathy if it were ever proposed to interdict them equally to both sides; but it is only desired to restrain the employment of them against the prevailing opinion; against the unprevailing they may not only be used without general disapproval, but will be likely to obtain for him who uses them the praise of honest zeal and righteous indignation. Yet whatever mischief arises from their use is greatest when they are employed against the comparatively defenseless; and whatever unfair advantage can be derived by any opinion from this mode of asserting it accrues almost exclusively to received opinions. The worst offense of this kind which can be committed by a polemic is to stigmatize those who hold the contrary opinion as bad and immoral men. To calumny of this sort, those who hold any unpopular opinion are peculiarly exposed, because they are in general few and uninfluential, and nobody but themselves feels much interested in seeing justice done them; but this weapon is, from the nature of the case, denied to those who attack a prevailing opinion: they can neither use it with safety to themselves, nor, if they could, would it do anything but recoil on their own cause. In general, opinions contrary to those commonly received can only obtain a hearing by studied moderation of language and the most cautious avoidance of unnecessary offense, from which they hardly ever deviate even in a slight degree without losing ground, while unmeasured vituperation employed on the side of the prevailing opinion really does deter people from professing contrary opinions and from listening to those who profess them. For the interest, therefore, of truth and justice it is far more important to restrain this employment of vituperative language than the other; and, for example, if it were necessary to choose, there would be much more need to discourage offensive attacks on infidelity than on religion. It is, however, obvious that law and authority have no business with restraining either, while opinion ought, in every instance, to determine its verdict by the circumstances of the individual case — condemning everyone, on whichever side of the argument he places himself, in whose mode of advocacy either want of candor, or malignity, bigotry, or intolerance of feeling manifest themselves; but not inferring these vices from the side which a person takes, though it be the contrary side of the question to our own; and giving merited honor to everyone, whatever opinion he may hold, who has calmness to see and honesty to state what his opponents and their opinions really are, exaggerating nothing to their discredit, keeping nothing back which tells, or can be supposed to tell, in their favor. This is the real morality of public discussion; and if often violated, I am happy to think that there are many controversialists who to a great extent observe it, and a still greater number who conscientiously strive toward it.

CHAPTER III

Of Individuality, as One of the Elements of Well-Being

Such being the reasons which make it imperative that human beings should be free to form opinions and to express their opinions without reserve; and such the baneful consequences to the intellectual, and through that to the moral nature of man, unless this liberty is either conceded or asserted in spite of prohibition; let us next examine whether the same reasons do not require that men should be free to act upon their opinions — to carry these out in their lives without hindrance, either physical or moral, from their fellow men, so long as it is at their own risk and peril. This last proviso is of course indispensable. No one pretends that actions should be as free as opinions. On the contrary, even opinions lose their immunity when the circumstances in which they are expressed are such as to constitute their expression a positive instigation to some mischievous act. An opinion that corn dealers are starvers of the poor, or that private property is robbery, ought to be unmolested when simply circulated through the press, but may justly incur punishment when delivered orally to an excited mob assembled before the house of a corn dealer, or when handed about among the same mob in the form of a placard. Acts, of whatever kind, which without justifiable cause do harm to others may be, and in the more important cases absolutely require to be, controlled by the unfavorable sentiments, and, when needful, by the active interference of mankind. The liberty of the individual must be thus far limited; he must not make himself a nuisance to other people. But if he refrains from molesting others in what concerns them, and merely acts according to his own inclination and judgment in things which concern himself, the same reasons which show that opinion should be free prove also that he should be allowed, without molestation, to carry his opinions into practice at his own cost. That mankind are not infallible; that their truths, for the most part, are only half-truths; that unity of opinion, unless resulting from the fullest and freest comparison of opposite opinions, is not desirable, and diversity not an evil, but a good, until mankind are much more capable than at present of recognizing all sides of the truth, are principles applicable to men's modes of action not less than to their opinions. As it is useful that while mankind are imperfect there should be different opinions, so it is that there should be different experiments of living; that free scope should be given to varieties of character, short of injury to others; and that the worth of different modes of life should be proved practically, when anyone thinks fit to try them. It is desirable, in short, that in things which do not primarily concern others individuality should assert itself. Where not the person's own character but the traditions or customs of other people are the rule of conduct, there is wanting one of the principal ingredients of human happiness, and quite the chief ingredient of individual and social progress.

In maintaining this principle, the greatest difficulty to be encountered does not lie in the appreciation of means toward an acknowledged end, but in the indifference of persons in general to the end itself. If it were felt that the free development of individuality is one of the leading essentials of well-being; that it is not only a co-ordinate element with all that is designated by the terms civilization, instruction, education, culture, but is itself a necessary part and condition of all those things, there would be no danger that liberty should be undervalued, and the adjustment of the boundaries between it and social control would present no extraordinary difficulty. But the evil is that individual spontaneity is hardly recognized by the common modes of thinking as having any intrinsic worth, or deserving any regard on its own account. The majority, being satisfied with the ways of mankind as they now are (for it is they who make them what they are), cannot comprehend why those ways should not be good enough for everybody; and what is more, spontaneity forms no part of the ideal of the majority of moral and social reformers, but is rather looked on with jealousy, as a troublesome and perhaps rebellious obstruction to the general acceptance of what these reformers, in their own judgment, think would be best for mankind. Few persons, out of Germany, even comprehend the meaning of the doctrine which Wilhelm von Humboldt, so eminent both as a *savant* and as a politician, made the text of a treatise—that "the end of man, or that which is prescribed by the eternal or immutable dictates of reason, and not suggested by vague and transient desires, is the highest and most harmonious development of his powers to a complete and consistent whole"; that, therefore, the object "toward which every human being must ceaselessly direct his efforts, and on which especially those who design to influence their fellow men must ever keep their eyes, is the individuality of power and development"; that for this there are two requisites, "freedom, and variety of situations"; and that from the union of these arise "individual vigor and manifold diversity," which combine themselves in "originality."[31]

Little, however, as people are accustomed to a doctrine like that of von Humboldt, and surprising as it may be to them to find so high a value attached to individuality, the question, one must nevertheless think, can only be one of degree. No one's idea of excellence in conduct is that people should do absolutely nothing but copy one another. No one would assert that people ought not to put into their mode of life, and into the conduct of their concerns, any impress whatever of their own judgment or of their own individual character. On the other hand, it would be absurd to pretend that people ought to live as if nothing whatever had been known in the world before they came into it; as if experience had as yet done nothing toward showing that one mode of existence, or of conduct, is preferable to another. Nobody denies that people should be so taught and trained in youth as to know and benefit by the ascertained results of human experience. But it is the privilege and proper condition of a human being, arrived at the maturity of his faculties, to use and interpret experience in his own way. It is for him to find out what part of recorded experience is properly applicable to his own circumstances and character. The traditions and customs of other people are, to a certain extent, evidence of what their experience has taught *them*—presumptive evidence, and as such, have a claim to his deference: but, in the first place, their experience may be too narrow, or they may have not interpreted it rightly. Secondly, their interpretation of experience may be correct, but unsuitable to him. Customs are made for

31. [*The Sphere and Duties of Government*, from the German of Baron Wilhelm von Humboldt, pp. 11–13.]

customary circumstances and customary characters; and his circumstances or his character may be uncustomary. Thirdly, though the customs be both good as customs and suitable to him, yet to conform to custom merely *as* custom does not educate or develop in him any of the qualities which are the distinctive endowment of a human being. The human faculties of perception, judgment, discriminative feeling, mental activity, and even moral preference are exercised only in making a choice. He who does anything because it is the custom makes no choice. He gains no practice either in discerning or in desiring what is best. The mental and moral, like the muscular, powers are improved only by being used. The faculties are called into no exercise by doing a thing merely because others do it, no more than by believing a thing only because others believe it. If the grounds of an opinion are not conclusive to the person's own reason, his reason cannot be strengthened, but is likely to be weakened, by his adopting it: and if the inducements to an act are not such as are consentaneous to his own feelings and character (where affection, or the rights of others, are not concerned), it is so much done toward rendering his feelings and character inert and torpid instead of active and energetic.

He who lets the world, or his own portion of it, choose his plan of life for him has no need of any other faculty than the ape-like one of imitation. He who chooses his plan for himself employs all his faculties. He must use observation to see, reasoning and judgment to foresee, activity to gather materials for decision, discrimination to decide, and when he has decided, firmness and self-control to hold to his deliberate decision. And these qualities he requires and exercises exactly in proportion as the part of his conduct which he determines according to his own judgment and feelings is a large one. It is possible that he might be guided in some good path, and kept out of harm's way, without any of these things. But what will be his comparative worth as a human being? It really is of importance, not only what men do, but also what manner of men they are that do it. Among the works of man which human life is rightly employed in perfecting and beautifying, the first in importance surely is man himself. Supposing it were possible to get houses built, corn grown, battles fought, causes tried, and even churches erected and prayers said by machinery — by automatons in human

form — it would be a considerable loss to exchange for these automatons even the men and women who at present inhabit the more civilized parts of the world, and who assuredly are but starved specimens of what nature can and will produce. Human nature is not a machine to be built after a model, and set to do exactly the work prescribed for it, but a tree, which requires to grow and develop itself on all sides, according to the tendency of the inward forces which make it a living thing.

It will probably be conceded that it is desirable people should exercise understandings, and that an intelligent following of custom, or even occasionally an intelligent deviation from custom, is better than a blind and simply mechanical adhesion to it. To a certain extent it is admitted that our understanding should be our own; but there is not the same willingness to admit that our desires and impulses should be our own likewise, or that to possess impulses of our own, and of any strength, is anything but a peril and a snare. Yet desires and impulses are as much a part of a perfect human being as beliefs and restraints; and strong impulses are only perilous when not properly balanced, when one set of aims and inclinations is developed into strength, while others, which ought to coexist with them, remain weak and inactive. It is not because men's desires are strong that they act ill; it is because their consciences are weak. There is no natural connection between strong impulses and a weak conscience. The natural connection is the other way. To say that one person's desires and feelings are stronger and more various than those of another is merely to say that he has more of the raw material of human nature and is therefore capable, perhaps of more evil, but certainly of more good. Strong impulses are but another name for energy. Energy may be turned to bad uses; but more good may always be made of an energetic nature than of an indolent and impassive one. Those who have most natural feeling are always those whose cultivated feelings may be made the strongest. The same strong susceptibilities which make the personal impulses vivid and powerful are also the source from whence are generated the most passionate love of virtue and the sternest self-control. It is through the cultivation of these that society both does its duty and protects its interests, not by rejecting the stuff of which heroes are made, because it knows not how to make them. A person whose desires and impulses are his own—are the expression of his own nature, as it has been developed and modified by his own culture—is said to have a character. One whose desires and impulses are not his own has no character, no more than a steam engine has a character. If, in addition to being his own, his impulses are strong and are under the government of a strong will, he has an energetic character. Whoever thinks that individuality of desires and impulses should not be encouraged to unfold itself must maintain that society has no need of strong natures—is not the better for containing many persons who have much character—and that a high general average of energy is not desirable.

In some early states of society, these forces might be, and were, too much ahead of the power which society then possessed of disciplining and controlling them. There has been a time when the element of spontaneity and individuality was in excess, and the social principle had a hard struggle with it. The difficulty then was to induce men of strong bodies or minds to pay obedience to any rules which required them to control their impulses. To overcome this difficulty, law and discipline, like the Popes struggling against the Emperors, asserted a power over the whole man, claiming to control all his life in order to control his character—which society had not found any other sufficient means of binding. But society has now fairly got the better of individuality; and the danger which threatens human nature is not the excess, but the deficiency, of personal impulses and preferences. Things are vastly changed since the passions of those who were strong by station or by personal endowment were in a state of habitual rebellion against laws and ordinances, and required to be rigorously chained up to enable the persons within their reach to enjoy any particle of security. In our times, from the highest class of society down to the lowest, everyone lives as under the eye of a hostile and dreaded censorship. Not only in what concerns others, but in what concerns only themselves, the individual or the family do not ask themselves, what do I prefer? or, what would suit my character and disposition? or, what would allow the best and highest in me to have fair play and enable it to grow and thrive? They ask themselves, what is suitable to my position? what is usually done by persons of my station and pecuniary circumstances? or (worse still) what is usually done by persons

of a station and circumstances superior to mine? I do not mean that they choose what is customary in preference to what suits their own inclination. It does not occur to them to have any inclination except for what is customary. Thus the mind itself is bowed to the yoke: even in what people do for pleasure, conformity is the first thing thought of; they like in crowds; they exercise choice only among things commonly done; peculiarity of taste, eccentricity of conduct are shunned equally with crimes, until by dint of not following their own nature they have no nature to follow: their human capacities are withered and starved; they become incapable of any strong wishes or native pleasures, and are generally without either opinions or feelings of home growth, or properly their own. Now is this, or is it not, the desirable condition of human nature?

It is so, on the Calvinistic theory. According to that, the one great offense of man is self-will. All the good of which humanity is capable is comprised in obedience. You have no choice; thus you must do, and no otherwise: "Whatever is not a duty is a sin." Human nature being radically corrupt, there is no redemption for anyone until human nature is killed within him. To one holding this theory of life, crushing out any of the human faculties, capacities, and susceptibilities is no evil: man needs no capacity but that of surrendering himself to the will of God; and if he uses any of his faculties for any other purpose but to do that supposed will more effectually, he is better without them. This is the theory of Calvinism; and it is held, in a mitigated form, by many who do not consider themselves Calvinists; the mitigation consisting in giving a less ascetic interpretation to the alleged will of God, asserting it to be his will that mankind should gratify some of their inclinations, of course not in the manner they themselves prefer, but in the way of obedience, that is, in a way prescribed to them by authority, and, therefore, by the necessary condition of the case, the same for all.

In some such insidious form there is at present a strong tendency to this narrow theory of life, and to the pinched and hidebound type of human character which it patronizes. Many persons, no doubt, sincerely think that human beings thus cramped and dwarfed are as their Maker designed them to be, just as many have thought that trees are a much finer thing when clipped into pollards, or cut out into figures of animals, than as nature made them. But if it be any part of religion to believe that man was made by a good Being, it is more consistent with that faith to believe that this Being gave all human faculties that they might be cultivated and unfolded, not rooted out and consumed, and that he takes delight in every nearer approach made by his creatures to the ideal conception embodied in them, every increase in any of their capabilities of comprehension, of action, or of enjoyment. There is a different type of human excellence from the Calvinistic: a conception of humanity as having its nature bestowed on it for other purposes than merely to be abnegated. "Pagan self-assertion" is one of the elements of human worth, as well as "Christian self-denial."[32] There is a Greek ideal of self-development, which the Platonic and Christian ideal of self-government blends with, but does not supersede. It may be better to be a John Knox than an Alcibiades,[33] but it is better to be a Pericles[34] than either; nor would a Pericles, if we had one in these days, be without anything good which belonged to John Knox.

It is not by wearing down into uniformity all that is individual in themselves, but by cultivating it and calling it forth, within the limits imposed by the rights and interests of others, that human beings become a noble and beautiful object of contemplation; and as the works partake the character of those who do them, by the same process human life also becomes rich, diversified, and animating, furnishing more abundant aliment to high thoughts and elevating feelings, and strengthening the tie which binds every individual to the race, by making the race infinitely better worth belonging to. In proportion to the development of his individuality, each person becomes more valuable to himself, and is, therefore, capable of being more valuable to others. There is a greater fullness of life about his own existence, and when there is more life in the units there is more in the mass which is composed of them. As much compression as is

necessary to prevent the stronger specimens of human nature from encroaching on the rights of others cannot be dispensed with; but for this there is ample compensation even in the point of view of human development. The means of development which the individual loses by being prevented from gratifying his inclination to the injury of others are chiefly obtained at the expense of the development of other people. And even to himself there is a full equivalent in the better development of the social part of his nature, rendered possible by the restraint put upon the selfish part. To be held to rigid rules of justice for the sake of others develops the feelings and capacities which have the good of others for their object. But to be restrained in things not affecting their good, by their mere displeasure, develops nothing valuable except such force of character as may unfold itself in resisting the restraint. If acquiesced in, it dulls and blunts the whole nature. To give any fair play to the nature of each, it is essential that different persons should be allowed to lead different lives. In proportion as this latitude has been exercised in any age has that age been noteworthy to posterity. Even despotism does not produce its worst effects so long as individuality exists under it; and whatever crushes individuality is despotism, by whatever name it may be called and whether it professes to be enforcing the will of God or the injunctions of men.

Having said that the individuality is the same thing with development, and that it is only the cultivation of individuality which produces, or can produce, well-developed human beings, I might here close the argument; for what more or better can be said of any condition of human affairs than that it brings human beings themselves nearer to the best thing they can be? Or what worse can be said of any obstruction to good than that it prevents this? Doubtless, however, these considerations will not suffice to convince those who most need convincing; and it is necessary further to show that these developed human beings are of some use to the undeveloped—to point out to those who do not desire liberty, and would not avail themselves of it, that they may be in some intelligible manner rewarded for allowing other people to make use of it without hindrance.

In the first place, then, I would suggest that they might possibly learn something from them. It will not be denied by anybody that originality is a valuable

---

32. Sterling's *Essays.* [John Sterling (1806–1844) was a British essayist and poet. The reference is to his *Essays and Tales.*]

33. [Alcibiades (c. 450–404 B.C.) was an ambitious Athenian general who, according to some historians, was largely responsible for the decline of Athens.]

34. [Regarding Pericles, see Aristotle's *Ethics*, n. 13.]

element in human affairs. There is always need of persons not only to discover new truths and point out when what were once truths are true no longer, but also to commence new practices and set the example of more enlightened conduct and better taste and sense in human life. This cannot well be gainsaid by anybody who does not believe that the world has already attained perfection in all its ways and practices. It is true that this benefit is not capable of being rendered by everybody alike; there are but few persons, in comparison with the whole of mankind, whose experiments, if adopted by others, would be likely to be any improvement on established practice. But these few are the salt of the earth; without them, human life would become a stagnant pool. Not only is it they who introduce good things which did not before exist; it is they who keep the life in those which already exist. If there were nothing new to be done, would human intellect cease to be necessary? Would it be a reason why those who do the old things should forget why they are done, and do them like cattle, not like human beings? There is only too great a tendency in the best beliefs and practices to degenerate into the mechanical; and unless there were a succession of persons whose ever-recurring originality prevents the grounds of those beliefs and practices from becoming merely traditional, such dead matter would not resist the smallest shock from anything really alive, and there would be no reason why civilization should not die out, as in the Byzantine Empire. Persons of genius, it is true, are, and are always likely to be, a small minority; but in order to have them, it is necessary to preserve the soil in which they grow. Genius can only breathe freely in an *atmosphere* of freedom. Persons of genius are, *ex vi termini*,[35] more individual than any other people—less capable, consequently, of fitting themselves, without hurtful compression, into any of the small number of molds which society provides in order to save its members the trouble of forming their own character. If from timidity they consent to be forced into one of these molds, and to let all that part of themselves which cannot expand under the pressure remain unexpanded, society will be little the better for their genius. If they are of a strong character and break their fetters, they become a mark for the society which has not succeeded in reducing them to commonplace, to point out with solemn warnings as "wild," "erratic," and the like—much as if one should complain of the Niagara river for not flowing smoothly between its banks like a Dutch canal.

I insist thus emphatically on the importance of genius and the necessity of allowing it to unfold itself freely both in thought and in practice, being well aware that no one will deny the position in theory, but knowing also that almost everyone, in reality, is totally indifferent to it. People think genius a fine thing if it enables a man to write an exciting poem or paint a picture. But in its true sense, that of originality in thought and action, though no one says that it is not a thing to be admired, nearly all, at heart, think that they can do very well without it. Unhappily this is too natural to be wondered at. Originality is the one thing which unoriginal minds cannot feel the use of. They cannot see what it is to do for them: how should they? If they could see what it would do for them, it would not be originality. The first service which originality has to render them is that of opening their eyes: which being once fully done, they would have a chance of being themselves original. Meanwhile, recollecting that nothing was ever done which someone was not the first to do, and that all good things which exist are the fruits of originality, let them be modest enough to believe that there is something still left for it to accomplish, and assure themselves that they are more in need of originality, the less they are conscious of the want.

In sober truth, whatever homage may be professed, or even paid, to real or supposed mental superiority, the general tendency of things throughout the world is to render mediocrity the ascendant power among mankind. In ancient history, in the Middle Ages, and in a diminishing degree through the long transition from feudality to the present time, the individual was a power in himself; and if he had either great talents or a high social position, he was a considerable power. At present individuals are lost in the crowd. In politics it is almost a triviality to say that public opinion now rules the world. The only power deserving the name is that of masses, and of governments while they make themselves the organ of the tendencies and instincts of masses. This is as true in the moral and social relations of private life as in public transactions. Those

35. [By definition.]

whose opinions go by the name of public opinion are not always the same sort of public: in America, they are the whole white population; in England, chiefly the middle class. But they are always a mass, that is to say, collective mediocrity. And what is a still greater novelty, the mass do not now take their opinions from dignitaries in Church or State, from ostensible leaders, or from books. Their thinking is done for them by men much like themselves, addressing them or speaking in their name, on the spur of the moment, through the newspapers. I am not complaining of all this. I do not assert that anything better is compatible, as a general rule, with the present low state of the human mind. But that does not hinder the government of mediocrity from being mediocre government. No government by a democracy or a numerous aristocracy, either in its political acts or in the opinions, qualities, and tone of mind which it fosters, ever did or could rise above mediocrity except in so far as the sovereign. Many have let themselves be guided (which in their best times they always have done) by the counsels and influence of a more highly gifted and instructed *one* or *few*. The initiation of all wise or noble things comes and must come from individuals; generally at first from some one individual. The honor and glory of the average man is that he is capable of following that initiative; that he can respond internally to wise and noble things, and be led to them with his eyes open. I am not countenancing the sort of "hero-worship" which applauds the strong man of genius for forcibly seizing on the government of the world and making it do his bidding in spite of itself. All he can claim is freedom to point out the way. The power of compelling others into it is not only inconsistent with the freedom and development of all the rest, but corrupting to the strong man himself. It does seem, however, that when the opinions of masses of merely average men are everywhere become or becoming the dominant power, the counterpoise and corrective to that tendency would be the more and more pronounced individuality of those who stand on the higher eminences of thought. It is in these circumstances most especially that exceptional individuals, instead of being deterred, should be encouraged in acting differently from the mass. In other times there was no advantage in their doing so, unless they acted not only differently but better. In this age, the mere example of nonconformity, the

mere refusal to bend the knee to custom, is itself a service. Precisely because the tyranny of opinion is such as to make eccentricity a reproach, it is desirable, in order to break through that tyranny, that people should be eccentric. Eccentricity has always abounded when and where strength of character has abounded; and the amount of eccentricity in a society has generally been proportional to the amount of genius, mental vigor, and moral courage it contained. That so few now dare to be eccentric marks the chief danger of the time.

I have said that it is important to give the freest scope possible to uncustomary things, in order that it may in time appear which of these are fit to be converted into customs. But independence of action and disregard of custom are not solely deserving of encouragement for the chance they afford that better modes of action, and customs more worthy of general adoption, may be struck out; nor is it only persons of decided mental superiority who have a just claim to carry on their lives in their own way. There is no reason that all human existence should be constructed on some one or some small number of patterns. If a person possesses any tolerable amount of common sense and experience, his own mode of laying out his existence is the best, not because it is the best in itself, but because it is his own mode. Human beings are not like sheep; and even sheep are not undistinguishably alike. A man cannot get a coat or a pair of boots to fit him unless they are either made to his measure or he has a whole warehouseful to choose from; and is it easier to fit him with a life than with a coat, or are human beings more like one another in their whole physical and spiritual conformation than in the shape of their feet? If it were only that people have diversities of taste, that is reason enough for not attempting to shape them all after one model. But different persons also require different conditions for their spiritual development; and can no more exist healthily in the same moral than all the variety of plants can in the same physical atmosphere and climate. The same things which are helps to one person toward the cultivation of his higher nature are hindrances to another. The same mode of life is a healthy excitement to one, keeping all his faculties of action and enjoyment in their best order, while to another it is a distracting burden which suspends or crushes all internal life. Such are the differences among human beings in their sources of pleasure, their susceptibilities of pain, and the operation on them of different physical and moral agencies that, unless there is a corresponding diversity in their modes of life, they neither obtain their fair share of happiness, nor grow up to the mental, moral, and aesthetic stature of which their nature is capable. Why then should tolerance, as far as the public sentiment is concerned, extend only to tastes and modes of life which extort acquiescence by the multitude of their adherents? Nowhere (except in some monastic institutions) is diversity of taste entirely unrecognized; a person may, without blame, either like or dislike rowing, or smoking, or music, or athletic exercises, or chess, or cards, or study, because both those who like each of these things and those who dislike them are too numerous to be put down. But the man, and still more the woman, who can be accused either of doing "what nobody does," or of not doing "what everybody does," is the subject of as much depreciatory remark as if he or she had committed some grave moral delinquency. Persons require to possess a title, or some other badge of rank, or of the consideration of people of rank, to be able to indulge somewhat in the luxury of doing as they like without detriment to their estimation. To indulge somewhat, I repeat: for whoever allow themselves much of that indulgence incur the risk of something worse than disparaging speeches—they are in peril of a commission *de lunatico* and of having their property taken from them and given to their relations.[36]

36. There is something both contemptible and frightful in the sort of evidence on which, of late years, any person can be judicially declared unfit for the management of his affairs; and after his death, his disposal of his property can be set aside if there is enough of it to pay the expenses of litigation—which are charged on the property itself. All the minute details of his daily life are pried into, and whatever is found which, seen through the medium of the perceiving and describing faculties of the lowest of the low, bears an appearance unlike absolute commonplace, is laid before the jury as evidence of insanity, and often with success; the jurors being little, if at all, less vulgar and ignorant than the witnesses, while the judges, with that extraordinary want of knowledge of human nature and life which continually astonishes us in English lawyers, often help to mislead them. These trials speak volumes as to the state of feeling and opinion among the vulgar with regard to human liberty. So

There is one characteristic of the present direction of public opinion peculiarly calculated to make it intolerant of any marked demonstrations of individuality. The general average of mankind are not only moderate in intellect, but also moderate in inclinations; they have no tastes or wishes strong enough to incline them to do anything unusual, and they consequently do not understand those who have, and class all such with the wild and intemperate whom they are accustomed to look down upon. Now, in addition to this fact which is general, we have only to suppose that a strong movement has set in toward the improvement of morals, and it is evident what we have to expect. In these days such a movement has set in; much has actually been effected in the way of increased regularity of conduct and discouragement of excesses; and there is a philanthropic spirit abroad for the exercise of which there is no more inviting field than the moral and prudential improvement of our fellow creatures. These tendencies of the times cause the public to be more disposed than at most former periods to prescribe general rules of conduct and endeavor to make everyone conform to the approved standard. And that standard, express or tacit, is to desire nothing strongly. Its ideal of character is to be without any marked character—to maim by compression, like a Chinese lady's foot, every part of human nature which stands out prominently and tends to make the person markedly dissimilar in outline to commonplace humanity.

As is usually the case with ideals which exclude one-half of what is desirable, the present standard of approbation produces only an inferior imitation of the other half. Instead of great energies guided by vigorous reason and strong feelings strongly controlled

far from setting any value on individuality—so far from respecting the right of each individual to act, in things indifferent, as seems good to his own judgment and inclinations, judges and juries cannot even conceive that a person in a state of sanity can desire such freedom. In former days, when it was proposed to burn atheists, charitable people used to suggest putting them in a madhouse instead; it would be nothing surprising nowadays were we to see this done, and the doers applauding themselves because, instead of persecuting for religion, they had adopted so humane and Christian a mode of treating these unfortunates, not without a silent satisfaction at their having thereby obtained their deserts.

by a conscientious will, its result is weak feelings and weak energies, which therefore can be kept in outward conformity to rule without any strength either of will or of reason. Already energetic characters on any large scale are becoming merely traditional. There is now scarcely any outlet for energy in this country except business. The energy expended in this may still be regarded as considerable. What little is left from that employment is expended on some hobby, which may be a useful, even a philanthropic, hobby, but is always some one thing, and generally a thing of small dimensions. The greatness of England is now all collective; individually small, we only appear capable of anything great by our habit of combining; and with this our moral and religious philanthropists are perfectly contented. But it was men of another stamp than this that made England what it has been; and men of another stamp will be needed to prevent its decline.

The despotism of custom is everywhere the standing hindrance to human advancement, being in unceasing antagonism to that disposition to aim at something better than customary, which is called, according to circumstances, the spirit of liberty, or that of progress or improvement. The spirit of improvement is not always a spirit of liberty, for it may aim at forcing improvements on an unwilling people; and the spirit of liberty, in so far as it resists such attempts, may ally itself locally and temporarily with the opponents of improvement; but the only unfailing and permanent source of improvement is liberty, since by it there are as many possible independent centers of improvement as there are individuals. The progressive principle, however, in either shape, whether as the love of liberty or of improvement, is antagonistic to the sway of custom, involving at least emancipation from that yoke; and the contest between the two constitutes the chief interest of the history of mankind. The greater part of the world has, properly speaking, no history, because the despotism of Custom is complete. This is the case over the whole East. Custom is there, in all things, the final appeal; justice and right mean conformity to custom; the argument of custom no one, unless some tyrant intoxicated with power, thinks of resisting. And we see the result. Those nations must once have had originality; they did not start out of the ground populous, lettered, and versed in many of the arts of life; they made themselves all this, and were then the

greatest and most powerful nations of the world. What are they now? The subjects or dependents of tribes whose forefathers wandered in the forests when theirs had magnificent palaces and gorgeous temples, but over whom custom exercised only a divided rule with liberty and progress. A people, it appears, may be progressive for a certain length of time, and then stop: when does it stop? When it ceases to possess individuality. If a similar change should befall the nations of Europe, it will not be in exactly the same shape: the despotism of custom with which these nations are threatened is not precisely stationariness. It proscribes singularity, but it does not preclude change, provided all change together. We have discarded the fixed costumes of our forefathers; everyone must still dress like other people, but the fashion may change once or twice a year. We thus take care that when there is a change, it shall be for change's sake, and not from any idea of beauty or convenience; for the same idea of beauty or convenience would not strike all the world at the same moment, and be simultaneously thrown aside by all at another moment. But we are progressive as well as changeable: we continually make new inventions in mechanical things, and keep them until they are again superseded by better; we are eager for improvement in politics, in education, even in morals, though in this last our idea of improvement chiefly consists in persuading or forcing other people to be as good as ourselves. It is not progress that we object to; on the contrary, we flatter ourselves that we are the most progressive people who ever lived. It is individuality that we war against: we should think we had done wonders if we had made ourselves all alike, forgetting that the unlikeness of one person to another is generally the first thing which draws the attention of either to the imperfection of his own type and the superiority of another, or the possibility, by combining the advantages of both, of producing something better than either. We have a warning example in China—a nation of much talent and, in some respects, even wisdom, owing to the rare good fortune of having been provided at an early period with a particularly good set of customs, the work, in some measure, of men to whom even the most enlightened European must accord, under certain limitations, the title of sages and philosophers. They are remarkable, too, in the excellence of their apparatus for impressing, as far as possible, the best wisdom they possess upon every mind in the community, and securing that those who have appropriated most of it shall occupy the posts of honor and power. Surely the people who did this have discovered the secret of human progressiveness and must have kept themselves steadily at the head of the movement of the world. On the contrary, they have become stationary—have remained so for thousands of years; and if they are ever to be further improved, it must be by foreigners. They have succeeded beyond all hope in what English philanthropists are so industriously working at—in making a people all alike, all governing their thoughts and conduct by the same maxims and rules; and these are the fruits. The modern *régime* of public opinion is, in an unorganized form, what the Chinese educational and political systems are in an organized; and unless individuality shall be able successfully to assert itself against this yoke, Europe, not-withstanding its noble antecedents and its professed Christianity, will tend to become another China.

What is it that has hitherto preserved Europe from this lot? What has made the European family of nations an improving, instead of a stationary, portion of mankind? Not any superior excellence in them, which, when it exists, exists as the effect, not as the cause, but their remarkable diversity of character and culture. Individuals, classes, nations have been extremely unlike one another: they have struck out a great variety of paths, each leading to something valuable; and although at every period those who traveled in different paths have been intolerant of one another, and each would have thought it an excellent thing if all the rest could have been compelled to travel his road, their attempts to thwart each other's development have rarely had any permanent success, and each has in time endured to receive the good which the others have offered. Europe is, in my judgment, wholly indebted to this plurality of paths for its progressive and many-sided development. But it already begins to possess this benefit in a considerably less degree. It is decidedly advancing toward the Chinese ideal of making all people alike. M. de Tocqueville,[37] in his last important work, remarks

how much more the Frenchmen of the present day resemble one another than did those even of the last generation. The same remark might be made of Englishmen in a far greater degree. In a passage already quoted from Wilhelm von Humboldt, he points out two things as necessary conditions of human development—because necessary to render people unlike one another—namely, freedom and variety of situations. The second of these two conditions is in this country every day diminishing. The circumstances which surround different classes and individuals, and shape their characters, are daily becoming more assimilated. Formerly, different ranks, different neighborhoods, different trades and professions lived in what might be called different worlds; at present, to a great degree in the same. Comparatively speaking, they now read the same things, listen to the same things, see the same things, go to the same places, have their hopes and fears directed to the same objects, have the same rights and liberties, and the same means of asserting them. Great as are the differences of position which remain, they are nothing to those which have ceased. And the assimilation is still proceeding. All the political changes of the age promote it, since they all tend to raise the low and to lower the high. Every extension of education promotes it, because education brings people under common influences and gives them access to the general stock of facts and sentiments. Improvement in the means of communication promotes it, by bringing the inhabitants of distant places into personal contact, and keeping up a rapid flow of changes of residence between one place and another. The increase of commerce and manufactures promotes it, by diffusing more widely the advantages of easy circumstances and opening all objects of ambition, even the highest, to general competition, whereby the desire of rising becomes no longer the character of a particular class, but of all classes. A more powerful agency than even all these, in bringing about a general similarity among mankind, is the complete establishment, in this and other free countries, of the ascendancy of public opinion in the State. As the various social eminences which enabled persons entrenched on them to disregard the opinion of the multitude gradually become

37. [Alexis de Tocqueville (1805–1859) was the French writer who authored *Democracy in America*, perhaps the single most impressive sociological study of American democratic life. The work referred to is *The Old Régime and the French Revolution*.]

leveled; as the very idea of resisting the will of the public, when it is positively known that they have a will, disappears more and more from the minds of practical politicians, there ceases to be any social support for nonconformity—any substantive power in society which, itself opposed to the ascendancy of numbers, is interested in taking under its protection opinions and tendencies at variance with those of the public.

The combination of all these causes forms so great a mass of influences hostile to individuality that it is not easy to see how it can stand its ground. It will do so with increasing difficulty unless the intelligent part of the public can be made to feel its value—to see that it is good there should be differences, even though not for the better, even though, as it may appear to them, some should be for the worse. If the claims of individuality are ever to be asserted, the time is now while much is still wanting to complete the enforced assimilation. It is only in the earlier stages that any stand can be successfully made against the encroachment. The demand that all other people shall resemble ourselves grows by what it feeds on. If resistance waits till life is reduced *nearly* to one uniform type, all deviations from that type will come to be considered impious, immoral, even monstrous and contrary to nature. Mankind speedily become unable to conceive diversity when they have been for some time unaccustomed to see it.

CHAPTER IV

Of the Limits to the Authority of Society over the Individual

What, then, is the rightful limit to the sovereignty of the individual over himself? Where does the authority of society begin? How much of human life should be assigned to individuality, and how much to society?

Each will receive its proper share if each has that which more particularly concerns it. To individuality should belong the part of life in which it is chiefly the individual that is interested; to society, the part which chiefly interests society.

Though society is not founded on a contract, and though no good purpose is answered by inventing a contract in order to deduce social obligations from it, everyone who receives the protection of society

owes a return for the benefit, and the fact of living in society renders it indispensable that each should be bound to observe a certain line of conduct toward the rest. This conduct consists, first, in not injuring the interests of one another, or rather certain interests which, either by express legal provision or by tacit understanding, ought to be considered as rights; and secondly, in each person's bearing his share (to be fixed on some equitable principle) of the labors and sacrifices incurred for defending the society or its members from injury and molestation. These conditions society is justified in enforcing at all costs to those who endeavor to withhold fulfillment. Nor is this all that society may do. The acts of an individual may be hurtful to others or wanting in due consideration for their welfare, without going to the length of violating any of their constituted rights. The offender may then be justly punished by opinion, though not by law. As soon as any part of a person's conduct affects prejudicially the interests of others, society has jurisdiction over it, and the question whether the general welfare will or will not be promoted by interfering with it becomes open to discussion. But there is no room for entertaining any such question when a person's conduct affects the interests of no persons besides himself, or needs not affect them unless they like (all the persons concerned being of full age and the ordinary amount of understanding). In all such cases, there should be perfect freedom, legal and social, to do the action and stand the consequences.

It would be a great misunderstanding of this doctrine to suppose that it is one of selfish indifference which pretends that human beings have no business with each other's conduct in life, and that they should not concern themselves about the well-doing or well-being of one another, unless their own interest is involved. Instead of any diminution, there is need of a great increase of disinterested exertion to promote the good of others. But disinterested benevolence can find other instruments to persuade people to their good than whips and scourges, either of the literal or the metaphorical sort. I am the last person to undervalue the self-regarding virtues; they are only second in importance, if even second, to the social. It is equally the business of education to cultivate both. But even education works by conviction and persuasion as well as by compulsion, and it is by the former only that, when the period of education is passed, the self-regarding virtues should be inculcated. Human beings owe to each other help to distinguish the better from the worse, and encouragement to choose the former and avoid the latter. They should be forever stimulating each other to increased exercise of their higher faculties and increased direction of their feelings and aims toward wise instead of foolish, elevating instead of degrading, objects and contemplations. But neither one person, nor any number of persons, is warranted in saying to another human creature of ripe years that he shall not do with his life for his own benefit what he chooses to do with it. He is the person most interested in his own wellbeing: the interest which any other person, except in cases of strong personal attachment, can have in it is trifling compared with that which he himself has; the interest which society has in him individually (except as to his conduct to others) is fractional and altogether indirect, while with respect to his own feelings and circumstances the most ordinary man or woman has means of knowledge immeasurably surpassing those that can be possessed by anyone else. The interference of society to overrule his judgment and purposes in what only regards himself must be grounded on general presumptions which may be altogether wrong and, even if right, are as likely as not to be misapplied to individual cases, by persons no better acquainted with the circumstances of such cases than those are who look at them merely from without. In this department, therefore, of human affairs, individuality has its proper field of action. In the conduct of human beings toward one another it is necessary that general rules should for the most part be observed in order that people may know what they have to expect; but in each person's own concerns his individual spontaneity is entitled to free exercise. Considerations to aid his judgment, exhortations to strengthen his will may be offered to him, even obtruded on him, by others; but he himself is the final judge. All errors which he is likely to commit against advice and warning are far outweighed by the evil of allowing others to constrain him to what they deem his good.

I do not mean that the feelings with which a person is regarded by others ought not to be in any way affected by his self-regarding qualities or deficiencies. This is neither possible nor desirable. If he is eminent in any of the qualities which conduce to his own good, he is, so far, a proper object of admiration. He is so much the nearer to the ideal perfection of human nature. If he is grossly deficient in those qualities, a sentiment the opposite of admiration will follow. There is a degree of folly, and a degree of what may be called (though the phrase is not unobjectionable) lowness or depravation of taste, which, though it cannot justify doing harm to the person who manifests it, renders him necessarily and properly a subject of distaste, or, in extreme cases, even of contempt: a person could not have the opposite qualities in due strength without entertaining these feelings. Though doing no wrong to anyone, a person may so act as to compel us to judge him, and feel to him, as a fool or as a being of an inferior order; and since this judgment and feeling are a fact which he would prefer to avoid, it is doing him a service to warn him of it beforehand, as of any other disagreeable consequence to which he exposes himself. It would be well, indeed, if this good office were much more freely rendered than the common notions of politeness at present permit, and if one person could honestly point out to another that he thinks him in fault, without being considered unmannerly or presuming. We have a right, also, in various ways, to act upon our unfavorable opinion of anyone, not to the oppression of his individuality, but in the exercise of ours. We are not bound, for example, to seek his society; we have a right to avoid it (though not to parade the avoidance), for we have a right to choose the society most acceptable to us. We have a right, and it may be our duty, to caution others against him if we think his example or conversation likely to have a pernicious effect on those with whom he associates. We may give others a preference over him in optional good offices, except those which tend to his improvement. In these various modes a person may suffer very severe penalties at the hands of others for faults which directly concern only himself; but he suffers these penalties only in so far as they are the natural and, as it were, the spontaneous consequences of the faults themselves, not because they are purposely inflicted on him for the sake of punishment. A person who shows rashness, obstinacy, self-conceit—who cannot live within moderate means; who cannot restrain himself from hurtful indulgence; who pursues animal pleasures at the expense of those of feeling and intellect—must expect to be lowered in the opinion of others, and to have a less share of their favorable sentiments; but of this he has no right to complain unless he has merited their favor by special excellence in his social relations and has thus established a title to their good offices, which is not affected by his demerits toward himself.

What I contend for is that the inconveniences which are strictly inseparable from the unfavorable judgment of others are the only ones to which a person should ever be subjected for that portion of his conduct and character which concerns his own good, but which does not affect the interest of others in their relations with him. Acts injurious to others require a totally different treatment. Encroachment on their rights; infliction on them of any loss or damage not justified by his own rights; falsehood or duplicity in dealing with them; unfair or ungenerous use of advantages over them; even selfish abstinence from defending them against injury—these are fit objects of moral reprobation and, in grave cases, of moral retribution and punishment. And not only these acts, but the dispositions which lead to them, are properly immoral and fit subjects of disapprobation which may rise to abhorrence. Cruelty of disposition; malice and ill-nature; that most antisocial and odious of all passions, envy; dissimulation and insincerity, irascibility on insufficient cause, and resentment disproportioned to the provocation; the love of domineering over others; the desire to engross more than one's share of advantages (the *pleonexia*[38] of the Greeks); the pride which derives gratification from the abasement of others; the egotism which thinks self and its concerns more important than everything else, and decides all doubtful questions in its own favor—these are moral vices and constitute a bad and odious moral character; unlike the self-regarding faults previously mentioned, which are not properly immoralities and, to whatever pitch they may be carried, do not constitute wickedness. They may be proofs of any amount of folly or want of personal dignity and self-respect, but they are only a subject of moral reprobation when they involve a breach of duty to others, for whose sake the individual is bound to have care for himself. What are called duties to ourselves are not socially obligatory unless circumstances render them at the same time duties to others. The term duty to oneself,

when it means anything more than prudence, means self-respect or self-development, and for none of these is anyone accountable to his fellow creatures, because for none of them is it for the good of mankind that he be held accountable to them.

The distinction between the loss of consideration which a person may rightly incur by defect of prudence or of personal dignity, and the reprobation which is due to him for an offense against the rights of others, is not a merely nominal distinction. It makes a vast difference both in our feelings and in our conduct toward him whether he displeases us in things in which we think we have a right to control him or in things in which we know that we have not. If he displeases us, we may express our distaste, and we may stand aloof from a person as well as from a thing that displeases us; but we shall not therefore feel called on to make his life uncomfortable. We shall reflect that he already bears, or will bear, the whole penalty of his error; if he spoils his life by mismanagement, we shall not, for that reason, desire to spoil it still further; instead of wishing to punish him, we shall rather endeavor to alleviate his punishment by showing him how he may avoid or cure the evils his conduct tends to bring upon him. He may be to us an object of pity, perhaps of dislike, but not of anger or resentment; we shall not treat him like an enemy of society; the worst we shall think ourselves justified in doing is leaving him to himself, if we do not interfere benevolently by showing interest or concern for him. It is far otherwise if he has infringed the rules necessary for the protection of his fellow creatures, individually or collectively. The evil consequences of his acts do not then fall on himself, but on others; and society, as the protector of all its members, must retaliate on him, must inflict pain on him for the express purpose of punishment, and must take care that it be sufficiently severe. In the one case, he is an offender at our bar, and we are called on not only to sit in judgment on him, but, in one shape or another, to execute our own sentence; in the other case, it is not our part to inflict any suffering on him, except what may incidentally follow from our using the same liberty in the regulation of our own affairs which we allow to him in his.

The distinction here pointed out between the part of a person's life which concerns only himself and that which concerns others, many persons will refuse

38. [Greed.]

to admit. How (it may be asked) can any part of the conduct of a member of society be a matter of indifference to the other members? No person is an entirely isolated being; it is impossible for a person to do anything seriously or permanently hurtful to himself without mischief reaching at least to his near connections, and often far beyond them. If he injures his property, he does harm to those who directly or indirectly derived support from it, and usually diminishes, by a greater or less amount, the general resources of the community. If he deteriorates his bodily or mental faculties, he not only brings evil upon all who depended on him for any portion of their happiness, but disqualifies himself for rendering the services which he owes to his fellow creatures generally, perhaps becomes a burden on their affection or benevolence; and if such conduct were very frequent hardly any offense that is committed would detract more from the general sum of good. Finally, if by his vices or follies a person does no direct harm to others, he is nevertheless (it may be said) injurious by his example, and ought to be compelled to control himself for the sake of those whom the sight or knowledge of his conduct might corrupt or mislead.

And even (it will be added) if the consequences of misconduct could be confined to the vicious or thoughtless individual, ought society to abandon to their own guidance those who are manifestly unfit for it? If protection against themselves is confessedly due to children and persons under age, is not society equally bound to afford it to persons of mature years who are equally incapable of self-government? If gambling, or drunkenness, or incontinence, or idleness, or uncleanliness are as injurious to happiness, and as great a hindrance to improvement, as many or most of the acts prohibited by law, why (it may be asked) should not law, so far as is consistent with practicability and social convenience, endeavor to repress these also? And as a supplement to the unavoidable imperfections of law, ought not opinion at least to organize a powerful police against these vices and visit rigidly with social penalties those who are known to practice them? There is no question here (it may be said) about restricting individuality, or impeding the trial of new and original experiments in living. The only things it is sought to prevent are things which have been tried and condemned from the beginning of the world until now—things which

experience has shown not to be useful or suitable to any person's individuality. There must be some length of time and amount of experience after which a moral or prudential truth may be regarded as established; and it is merely desired to prevent generation after generation from falling over the same precipice which has been fatal to their predecessors.

I fully admit that the mischief which a person does to himself may seriously affect, both through their sympathies and their interests, those nearly connected with him and, in a minor degree, society at large. When, by conduct of this sort, a person is led to violate a distinct and assignable obligation to any other person or persons, the case is taken out of the self-regarding class and becomes amenable to moral disapprobation in the proper sense of the term. If, for example, a man, through intemperance or extravagance, becomes unable to pay his debts, or, having undertaken the moral responsibility of a family, becomes from the same cause incapable of supporting or educating them, he is deservedly reprobated and might be justly punished; but it is for the breach of duty to his family or creditors, not for the extravagance. If the resources which ought to have been devoted to them had been diverted from them for the most prudent investment, the moral culpability would have been the same. George Barnwell[39] murdered his uncle to get money for his mistress, but if he had done it to set himself up in business, he would equally have been hanged. Again, in the frequent case of a man who causes grief to his family by addiction to bad habits, he deserves reproach for his unkindness or ingratitude; but so he may for cultivating habits not in themselves vicious, if they are painful to those with whom he passes his life, or who from personal ties are dependent on him for their comfort. Whoever fails in the consideration generally due to the interests and feelings of others, not being compelled by some more imperative duty, or justified by allowable self-preference, is a subject of moral disapprobation for that failure, but not for the cause of it, nor for the errors, merely personal to himself, which may have remotely led to it. In like manner, when a person disables himself, by conduct purely self-regarding, from the performance of some definite duty incum-

39. [A character in an English ballad.]

bent on him to the public, he is guilty of a social offense. No person ought to be punished simply for being drunk; but a soldier or a policeman should be punished for being drunk on duty. Whenever, in short, there is a definite damage, or a definite risk of damage, either to an individual or to the public, the case is taken out of the province of liberty and placed in that of morality or law.

But with regard to the merely contingent or, as it may be called, constructive injury which a person causes to society by conduct which neither violates any specific duty to the public, nor occasions perceptible hurt to any assignable individual except himself, the inconvenience is one which society can afford to bear, for the sake of the greater good of human freedom. If grown persons are to be punished for not taking proper care of themselves, I would rather it were for their own sake than under pretense of preventing them from impairing their capacity or rendering to society benefits which society does not pretend it has a right to exact. But I cannot consent to argue the point as if society had no means of bringing its weaker members up to its ordinary standard of rational conduct, except waiting till they do something irrational, and then punishing them, legally or morally, for it. Society has had absolute power over them during all the early portion of their existence; it has had the whole period of childhood and nonage in which to try whether it could make them capable of rational conduct in life. The existing generation is master both of the training and the entire circumstances of the generation to come; it cannot indeed make them perfectly wise and good, because it is itself so lamentably deficient in goodness and wisdom; and its best efforts are not always, in individual cases, its most successful ones; but it is perfectly well able to make the rising generation, as a whole, as good as, and a little better than, itself. If society lets any considerable number of its members grow up mere children, incapable of being acted on by rational consideration of distant motives, society has itself to blame for the consequences. Armed not only with all the powers of education, but with the ascendancy which the authority of a received opinion always exercises over the minds who are least fitted to judge for themselves, and aided by the *natural* penalties which cannot be prevented from falling on those who incur the distaste or the contempt of those who know them—let not

society pretend that it needs, besides all this, the power to issue commands and enforce obedience in the personal concerns of individuals in which, on all principles of justice and policy, the decision ought to rest with those who are to abide the consequences. Nor is there anything which tends more to discredit and frustrate the better means of influencing conduct than a resort to the worse. If there be among those whom it is attempted to coerce into prudence or temperance any of the material of which vigorous and independent characters are made, they will infallibly rebel against the yoke. No such person will ever feel that others have a right to control him in his concerns, such as they have to prevent him from injuring them in theirs; and it easily comes to be considered a mark of spirit and courage to fly in the face of such usurped authority and do with ostentation the exact opposite of what it enjoins, as in the fashion of grossness which succeeded, in the time of Charles II, to the fanatical moral intolerance of the Puritans. With respect to what is said of the necessity of protecting society from the bad example set to others by the vicious or the self-indulgent, it is true that bad example may have a pernicious effect, especially the example of doing wrong to others with impunity to the wrong-doer. But we are now speaking of conduct which, while it does no wrong to others, is supposed to do great harm to the agent himself; and I do not see how those who believe this can think otherwise than that the example, on the whole, must be more salutary than hurtful, since, if it displays the misconduct, it displays also the painful or degrading consequences which, if the conduct is justly censured, must be supposed to be in all or most cases attendant on it.

But the strongest of all the arguments against the interference of the public with purely personal conduct is that, when it does interfere, the odds are that it interferes wrongly and in the wrong place. On questions of social morality, of duty to others, the opinion of the public, that is, of an over-ruling majority, though often wrong, is likely to be still oftener right, because on such questions they are only required to judge of their own interests, of the manner in which some mode of conduct, if allowed to be practiced, would affect themselves. But the opinion of a similar majority, imposed as a law on the minority, on questions of self-regarding conduct is quite as likely to be wrong as right, for in these cases public opinion means, at the best, some people's opinion of what is good or bad for other people, while very often it does not even mean that—the public, with the most perfect indifference, passing over the pleasure or convenience of those whose conduct they censure and considering their own preference. There are many who consider as an injury to themselves any conduct which they have a distaste for, and resent it as an outrage to their feelings; as a religious bigot, when charged with disregarding the religious feelings of others, has been known to retort that they disregard his feelings by persisting in their abominable worship or creed. But there is no parity between the feeling of a person for his own opinion and the feeling of another who is offended at his holding it, no more than between the desire of a thief to take a purse and the desire of the right owner to keep it. And a person's taste is as much his own peculiar concern as his opinion or his purse.

Charles Sanders Peirce

Widely esteemed as America's most versatile and original philosopher, and renowned as the founder of pragmatism, Charles Sanders Peirce was born in Cambridge, Massachusetts in 1839. He was the second son of Benjamin Peirce, one of America's leading mathematicians, from whom he received much of his early education and acquired an intensely intellectual discipline. He was educated at Harvard College, graduating in 1859 and thereafter receiving the M.A. at Harvard in 1862, and the Sc.B. degree in chemistry, *summa cum laude*, in 1863. In 1861, he began work as a physical scientist with the U.S. Coast and Geodetic Survey, a relationship that continued intermittently until 1891.

Despite his brilliance and his pioneering contributions to metaphysics, the history and philosophy of science, the theory of signs, and the development of symbolic logic, Peirce never succeeded in gaining a permanent university position, the only extended teaching he did having been on a logic lectureship at the Johns Hopkins University from 1879 to 1884.

In 1887 Peirce retired to Milford, Pennsylvania, where he spent the rest of his life in almost complete isolation, striving to complete a comprehensive work of philosophy. But he never produced any systematic philosophical books, although he continued to labor on difficult theoretical problems and to write prolifically on specialized topics. He died in 1914, "a frustrated, isolated man, still working on his logic, without a publisher, with scarcely a disciple, unknown to the public at large" (*Dictionary of American Biography*).

Nevertheless, his fame and influence have continue to grow with the years, stimulated by the continuing study of the huge collection of manuscripts left at his death. The study of Peirce has indeed by now become a worldwide scholarly industry, ramifying into virtually every academic discipline.

The first of the papers to follow, "The Fixation of Belief," appeared in 1877. It presents Peirce's theory of inquiry. Doubt, for him, is not the mere absence of belief. Rather, it is "an uneasy and dissatisfied state from which we struggle to free ourselves and pass into the state of belief . . . a calm and satisfactory state which we do not wish to avoid, or to change to a belief in anything else." Belief is in the nature of habit, representing a regular association between our circumstances and our actions. Inquiry is, for Peirce, the struggle to overcome the irritation of doubt and to attain belief. Peirce compares four methods for the fixation of belief: the method of tenacity, the method of authority, the *a priori* method, and the method of science.

Tenacity is largely a matter of reiterating the belief in question and turning away from all contrary evidence. It is, however, he argues, ineffective for when confronted with the contrary beliefs of others, our confidence in our own tenaciously held beliefs is shaken, unsettling our beliefs. The method of authority, essentially adoption of tenacity by a whole group using the group's institutions to enforce the preferred doctrines, is more effective than the previous method but is also ineffective since no society can regulate all opinion within, nor prevent awareness of contrary opinions without. Again unsettlement ensues.

The *a priori* method rejects both the "willful adherence to a belief, and the arbitrary forcing of it upon others," allowing beliefs to form through the natural inclination to adopt whatever seems "agreeable to reason." This method assimilates inquiry to the development of taste, subject to pendulum swings and never reaching a stable agreement. Peirce considers, finally, the method of science, which settles opinion not by willfulness, force, or taste, but by reference to external permanencies with properties "independent of our opinions about them." It is the only method of the four that is self-corrective, allowing the possibility of errors in application corrigible by the very use of the method in question, whereas the pursuit of any of the other methods is necessarily correct by the method itself, so that errors cannot even be admitted, much less be open to correction.

Peirce's argument for the method of science is open to the charge that it is science itself that unsettles belief more rapidly than any of the other methods, holding all its theories to be provisional and subjecting all to the test of continuing experience. Indeed Peirce's essay seems to shift ground from considering the unsettlement of *beliefs* to the unsettlement of *methods*. He seems in the end to be arguing that because science is self-corrective, it is itself, as a method, capable of remaining firm while continuing to enable us to learn from experience.

"How to Make Our Ideas Clear" appeared in 1878. It applies his theory of inquiry to the development of what has been called his pragmatic maxim, as a method for the clarification of ideas. Since, as Peirce argues, the function of thought is to attain belief, the essence of which is "the establishment of a habit," we develop the meaning of an idea by determining "what habits it involves."

The pragmatic maxim, appearing at the end of Section II of the paper, thus reads: "Consider what effects, which might conceivably have practical bearings, we conceive the object of our conception to have. Then our conception of these effects is the whole of our conception of the object." An *effect with practical bearings* being, more precisely, a perceptible consequence contingent on our action, Peirce's idea is now to sum up all such action-contingent consequences of the object. Our conception of these consequences, he concludes, is our very conception of the object.

To clarify the notion of hardness, we are thus instructed not to seek some image of this property by introspection, nor to construct some abstract definition of it. Rather, we are to ask what perceptible effects habitually result from various operations upon hard things: A hard thing will, for example, "not be scratched by other substances," will make a noise if struck, will offer a certain resistance if pushed, etc. The idea of hardness is then nothing more than the idea of these action-contingent affects. Moreover, in believing an object is to be hard, we are set habitually to act toward it in accordance with its supposed trait of hardness, in pursuit of our purposes. Our belief in its hardness embodies a conditional prediction of its behavior, testable by the senses.

The meaning of an idea is, of course, independent of its truth; both false and true statements have meaning. But Peirce believes that the processes of inquiry, carried on by an open and ideal community of scientific investigators, continually weed out the false beliefs and in the long run converge on the true. In a celebrated passage he defines truth and reality in terms of such ultimate convergence: "The opinion which is fated to be ultimately agreed to by all who investigate is what we mean by the truth, and the object represented in this opinion is the real."

• • •

A biography of Peirce is available in Joseph Brent, *Charles Sanders Peirce: A Life* (Bloomington: Indiana University Press, 1993). Useful interpretive discussions of Peirce are Murray G. Murphey, *The Development of Peirce's Philosophy* (Cambridge, Mass.: Harvard University Press, 1961); W. B. Gallie, *Peirce and Pragmatism* (New York: Dover, 1966); and Peter Skagestad, *The Road of Inquiry: Charles Peirce's Pragmatic Realism* (New York: Columbia University Press, 1981). For a general discussion of Peirce as well as the other pragmatic philosophers, see H. S. Thayer, *Meaning and Action: A Critical History of Pragmatism* (Indianapolis: Bobbs-Merrill, 1968) and Israel Scheffler, *Four Pragmatists* (London: Routledge, 1974). A collection of critical articles on Peirce by the dean of American Peirce scholars is K. L. Ketner and C. Kloesel, eds., *Peirce, Semeiotic, and Pragmatism: Essays by Max H. Fisch* (Bloomington: Indiana University Press, 1986).

I.S.

The Fixation of Belief

I

Few persons care to study logic, because everybody conceives himself to be proficient enough in the art of reasoning already. But I observe that this satisfaction is limited to one's own ratiocination, and does not extend to that of other men.

We come to the full possession of our power of drawing inferences the last of all our faculties, for it is not so much a natural gift as a long and difficult art. The history of its practice would make a grand subject for a book. The mediæval schoolman, following the Romans, made logic the earliest of a boy's studies after grammar, as being very easy. So it was as they understood it. Its fundamental principle, according to them, was that all knowledge rests on either authority or reason; but that whatever is deduced by reason depends ultimately on a premise derived from authority. Accordingly, as soon as a boy was perfect in the syllogistic procedure, his intellectual kit of tools was held to be complete.

To Roger Bacon,[1] that remarkable mind who in the middle of the thirteenth century was almost a scientific man, the schoolmen's conception of reasoning appeared only an obstacle to truth. He saw that experience alone teaches anything—a proposition which to us seems easy to understand, because a distinct conception of experience has been handed down to us from former generations; which to him also seemed perfectly clear, because its difficulties had not yet unfolded themselves. Of all kinds of experience, the best, he thought, was interior illumination, which teaches many things about nature which the external senses could never discover, such as the transubstantiation of bread.

Four centuries later, the more celebrated Bacon,[2] in the first book of his *Novum Organum*, gave his clear account of experience as something which must be opened to verification and re-examination. But, superior as Lord Bacon's conception is to earlier notions, a modern reader who is not in awe of his grandiloquence is chiefly struck by the inadequacy of his view of scientific procedure. That we have only to make some crude experiments, to draw up briefs of the results in certain blank forms, to go through these by rule, checking off everything disproved and setting down the alternatives, and that thus in a few years physical science would be finished up—what an idea! "He wrote on science like a Lord Chancellor," indeed, as Harvey,[3] a genuine man of science, said.

The early scientists, Copernicus,[4] Tycho Brahe,[5] Kepler,[6] Galileo,[7] Harvey,[8] and Gilbert,[9] had methods more like those of their modern brethren. Kepler undertook to draw a curve through the places of Mars; and his greatest service to science was in impressing

Reprinted from the *Collected Papers of Charles Sanders Peirce*, ed. Charles Hartshorne and Paul Weiss. Cambridge, Mass.: The Belknap Press of Harvard University Press; 1934. Vol. V. Copyright 1934 by the President and Fellows of Harvard College. Reprinted by permission of the publishers.

1. [The reference is to the English philosopher and scientist (c. 1214–1292).—S.M.C.]

2. [The reference is to the English philosopher and Lord Chancellor Francis Bacon (1561–1626).]

3. [The reference is to William Harvey (1578–1657), the English physician widely credited with laying the foundation of modern medicine.]

4. [The reference is to Nicholas Copernicus (1473–1543), the Polish astronomer who developed the theory that the planets revolve around the sun.]

5. [The reference is to the Danish astronomer (1546–1601), who calculated the position of planets and stars.]

6. [The reference is to the German astronomer Johannes Kepler (1571–1630), whose three laws describe the revolution of the planets around the sun.]

7. [The reference is to Galileo Galilei (1564–1642), the renowned Italian astronomer, mathematician, and physicist.]

8. [The reference is to William Harvey (see note 3 above).]

9. [The reference is to William Gilbert (1544–1603), the English scientist and physician, best known for his studies of electricity and magnetism.]

on men's minds that this was the thing to be done if they wished to improve astronomy; that they were not to content themselves with inquiring whether one system of epicycles was better than another but that they were to sit down by the figures and find out what the curve, in truth, was. He accomplished this by his incomparable energy and courage, blundering along in the most inconceivable way (to us), from one irrational hypothesis to another, until, after trying twenty-two of these, he fell, by the mere exhaustion of his invention, upon the orbit which a mind well furnished with the weapons of modern logic would have tried almost at the outset.

In the same way, every work of science great enough to be remembered for a few generations affords some exemplification of the defective state of the art of reasoning of the time when it was written; and each chief step in science has been a lesson in logic. It was so when Lavoisier[10] and his contemporaries took up the study of Chemistry. The old chemist's maxim had been *Lege, lege, lege, labora, ora, et relege.*[11] Lavoisier's method was not to read and pray, not to dream that some long and complicated chemical process would have a certain effect, to put it into practice with dull patience, after its inevitable failure to dream that with some modification it would have another result, and to end by publishing the last dream as a fact: his way was to carry his mind into his laboratory, and to make of his alembics and cucurbits instruments of thought, giving a new conception of reasoning as something which was to be done with one's eyes open, by manipulating real things instead of words and fancies.

The Darwinian controversy is, in large part, a question of logic. Mr. Darwin[12] proposed to apply the statistical method to biology. The same thing has been done in a widely different branch of science, the theory of gases. Though unable to say what the movement of any particular molecule of gas would be on a certain hypothesis regarding the constitution of this class of bodies, Clausius[13] and Maxwell[14] were yet able, by the application of the doctrine of probabilities, to predict that in the long run such and such a proportion of the molecules would, under given circumstances, acquire such and such velocities; that there would take place, every second, such and such a number of collisions, etc.; and from these propositions they were able to deduce certain properties of gases, especially in regard to their heat-relations. In like manner, Darwin, while unable to say what the operation of variation and natural selection in every individual case will be, demonstrates that in the long run they will adapt animals to their circumstances. Whether or not existing animal forms are due to such action, or what position the theory ought to take, forms the subject of a discussion in which questions of fact and questions of logic are curiously interlaced.

II

The object of reasoning is to find out, from the consideration of what we already know, something else which we do not know. Consequently, reasoning is good if it be such as to give a true conclusion from true premises, and not otherwise. Thus, the question of validity is purely one of fact and not of thinking. A being the premises and B being the conclusion, the question is, whether these facts are really so related that if A is, B is. If so, the inference is valid; if not, not. It is not in the least the question whether, when the premises are accepted by the mind, we feel an impulse to accept the conclusion also. It is true that we do generally reason correctly by nature. But that is an accident; the true conclusion would remain true if we had no impulse to accept it; and the false one would remain false, though we could not resist the tendency to believe in it.

We are, doubtless, in the main logical animals, but we are not perfectly so. Most of us, for example, are naturally more sanguine and hopeful than logic would justify. We seem to be so constituted that in

10. [The reference is to Antoine Laurent Lavoisier (1743–1794), a founder of modern chemistry.]

11. [Look, look, look, work, speak, and look again.]

12. [The reference is to the celebrated English naturalist Charles Darwin (1809–1882), who developed the theory of evolution.]

13. [The reference is to the German mathematical physicist Rudolf Julius Emanuel Clausius (1822–1888), a pioneer in the field of thermodynamics.]

14. [The reference is to the Scottish physicist James Clark Maxwell (1831–1879), who developed the theory of the electromagnetic field.]

the absence of any facts to go upon we are happy and self-satisfied; so that the effect of experience is continually to counteract our hopes and aspirations. Yet a lifetime of the application of this corrective does not usually eradicate our sanguine disposition. Where hope is unchecked by any experience, it is likely that our optimism is extravagant. Logicality in regard to practical matters is the most useful quality an animal can possess, and might, therefore, result from the action of natural selection; but outside of these it is probably of more advantage to the animal to have his mind filled with pleasing and encouraging visions, independently of their truth; and thus, upon unpractical subjects, natural selection might occasion a fallacious tendency of thought.

That which determines us, from given premises, to draw one inference rather than another is some habit of mind, whether it be constitutional or acquired. The habit is good or otherwise, according as it produces true conclusions from true premises or not; and an inference is regarded as valid or not, without reference to the truth or falsity of its conclusion specially, but according as the habit which determines it is such as to produce true conclusions in general or not. The particular habit of mind which governs this or that inference may be formulated in a proposition whose truth depends on the validity of the inferences which the habit determines; and such a formula is called a *guiding principle* of inference. Suppose, for example, that we observe that a rotating disk of copper quickly comes to rest when placed between the poles of a magnet, and we infer that this will happen with every disk of copper. The guiding principle is that what is true of one piece of copper is true of another. Such a guiding principle with regard to copper would be much safer than with regard to many other substances—brass, for example.

A book might be written to signalize all the most important of these guiding principles of reasoning. It would probably be, we must confess, of no service to a person whose thought is directed wholly to practical subjects, and whose activity moves along thoroughly beaten paths. The problems which present themselves to such a mind are matters of routine which he has learned once for all to handle in learning his business. But let a man venture into an unfamiliar field, or where his results are not continually checked by experience, and all history shows that the most masculine

intellect will ofttimes lose his orientation and waste his efforts in directions which bring him no nearer to his goal, or even carry him entirely astray. He is like a ship on the open sea, with no one on board who understands the rules of navigation. And in such a case some general study of the guiding principles of reasoning would be sure to be found useful.

The subject could hardly be treated, however, without being first limited; since almost any fact may serve as a guiding principle. But it so happens that there exists a division among facts, such that in one class are all those which are absolutely essential as guiding principles, while in the other are all those which have any other interest as objects of research. This division is between those which are necessarily taken for granted in asking whether a certain conclusion follows from certain premises, and those which are not implied in that question. A moment's thought will show that a variety of facts are already assumed when the logical question is first asked. It is implied, for instance, that there are such states of mind as doubt and belief—that a passage from one to the other is possible, the object of thought remaining the same, and that this transition is subject to some rules which all minds are alike bound by. As these are facts which we must already know before we can have any clear conception of reasoning at all, it cannot be supposed to be any longer of much interest to inquire into their truth or falsity. On the other hand, it is easy to believe that those rules of reasoning which are deduced from the very idea of the process are the ones which are the most essential; and, indeed, that so long as it conforms to these it will, at least, not lead to false conclusions from true premises. In point of fact, the importance of what may be deduced from the assumptions involved in the logical question turns out to be greater than might be supposed, and this for reasons which it is difficult to exhibit at the outset. The only one which I shall here mention is that conceptions which are really products of logical reflections, without being readily seen to be so, mingle with our ordinary thoughts, and are frequently the causes of great confusion. This is the case, for example, with the conception of quality. A quality as such is never an object of observation. We can see that a thing is blue or green, but the quality of being blue and the quality of being green are not things which we see; they are products of logical reflections. The truth is that common sense, or thought as it first emerges above the level of the narrowly practical, is deeply imbued with that bad logical quality to which the epithet *metaphysical* is commonly applied; and nothing can clear it up but a severe course of logic.

III

We generally know when we wish to ask a question and when we wish to pronounce a judgment, for there is a dissimilarity between the sensation of doubting and that of believing.

But this is not all which distinguishes doubt from belief. There is a practical difference. Our beliefs guide our desires and shape our actions. The Assassins, or followers of the Old Man of the Mountain, used to rush into death at his least command, because they believed that obedience to him would insure everlasting felicity. Had they doubted this, they would not have acted as they did. So it is with every belief, according to its degree. The feeling of believing is a more or less sure indication of there being established in our nature some habit which will determine our actions. Doubt never has such an effect.

Nor must we overlook a third point of difference. Doubt is an uneasy and dissatisfied state from which we struggle to free ourselves and pass into the state of belief; while the latter is a calm and satisfactory state which we do not wish to avoid, or to change to a belief in anything else. On the contrary, we cling tenaciously, not merely to believing, but to believing just what we do believe.

Thus, both doubt and belief have positive effects upon us, though very different ones. Belief does not make us act at once, but puts us into such a condition that we shall behave in a certain way, when the occasion arises. Doubt has not the least effect of this sort, but stimulates us to action until it is destroyed. This reminds us of the irritation of a nerve and the reflex action produced thereby; while for the analogue of belief, in the nervous system, we must look to what are called nervous associations—for example, to that habit of the nerves in consequence of which the smell of a peach will make the mouth water.

IV

The irritation of doubt causes a struggle to attain a state of belief. I shall term this struggle *inquiry*, though it must be admitted that this is sometimes not a very apt designation.

The irritation of doubt is the only immediate motive for the struggle to attain belief. It is certainly best for us that our beliefs should be such as may truly guide our actions so as to satisfy our desires; and this reflection will make us reject any belief which does not seem to have been so formed as to insure this result. But it will only do so by creating a doubt in the place of that belief. With the doubt, therefore, the struggle begins, and with the cessation of doubt it ends. Hence, the sole object of inquiry is the settlement of opinion. We may fancy that this is not enough for us, and that we seek not merely an opinion, but a true opinion. But put this fancy to the test, and it proves groundless; for as soon as a firm belief is reached we are entirely satisfied, whether the belief be false or true. And it is clear that nothing out of the sphere of our knowledge can be our object, for nothing which does not affect the mind can be a motive for a mental effort. The most that can be maintained is that we seek for a belief that we shall *think* to be true. But we think each one of our beliefs to be true, and, indeed, it is mere tautology to say so.

That the settlement of opinion is the sole end of inquiry is a very important proposition. It sweeps away, at once, various vague and erroneous conceptions of proof. A few of these may be noticed here.

1. Some philosophers have imagined that to start an inquiry it was only necessary to utter a question or set it down on paper, and have even recommended us to begin our studies with questioning everything! But the mere putting of a proposition into the interrogative form does not stimulate the mind to any struggle after belief. There must be a real and living doubt, and without all this, discussion is idle.

2. It is a very common idea that a demonstration must rest on some ultimate and absolutely indubitable propositions. These, according to one school, are first principles of a general nature; according to another, are first sensations. But, in point of fact, an inquiry, to have that completely satisfactory result called demonstration, has only to start with propositions perfectly free from all actual doubt. If the premises are not in fact doubted at all, they cannot be more satisfactory than they are.

3. Some people seem to love to argue a point after all the world is fully convinced of it. But no further advance can be made. When doubt ceases, mental action on the subject comes to an end; and, if it did go on, it would be without a purpose, except that of self-criticism.

V

If the settlement of opinion is the sole object of inquiry, and if belief is of the nature of a habit, why should we not attain the desired end, by taking any answer to a question, which we may fancy, and constantly reiterating it to ourselves, dwelling on all which may conduce to that belief, and learning to turn with contempt and hatred from anything which might disturb it? This simple and direct method is really pursued by many men. I remember once being entreated not to read a certain newspaper lest it might change my opinion upon free-trade. "Lest I might be entrapped by its fallacies and misstatements" was the form of expression. "You are not," my friend said, "a special student of political economy. You might, therefore, easily be deceived by fallacious arguments upon the subject. You might, then, if you read this paper, be led to believe in protection. But you admit that free-trade is the true doctrine; and you do not wish to believe what is not true." I have often known this system to be deliberately adopted. Still oftener, the instinctive dislike of an undecided state of mind, exaggerated into a vague dread of doubt, makes men cling spasmodically to the views they already take. The man feels that if he only holds to his belief without wavering, it will be entirely satisfactory. Nor can it be denied that a steady and immovable faith yields great peace of mind. It may, indeed, give rise to inconveniences, as if a man should resolutely continue to believe that fire would not burn him, or that he would be eternally damned if he received his *ingesta* otherwise than through a stomach-pump. But then the man who adopts this method will not allow that its inconveniences are greater than its advantages. He will say, "I hold steadfastly to the truth and the truth is always wholesome." And in many cases it may very well be that the pleasure he derives from his calm faith overbalances any inconveniences resulting from its deceptive character. Thus, if it be true that death is annihilation, then the man who believes that

he will certainly go straight to heaven when he dies, provided he have fulfilled certain simple observances in this life, has a cheap pleasure which will not be followed by the least disappointment. A similar consideration seems to have weight with many persons in religious topics, for we frequently hear it said, "Oh, I could not believe so-and-so, because I should be wretched if I did." When an ostrich buries its head in the sand as danger approaches, it very likely takes the happiest course. It hides the danger, and then calmly says there is no danger; and, if it feels perfectly sure there is none, why should it raise its head to see? A man may go through life, systematically keeping out of view all that might cause a change in his opinions, and if he only succeeds—basing his method, as he does, on two fundamental psychological laws—I do not see what can be said against his doing so. It would be an egotistical impertinence to object that his procedure is irrational, for that only amounts to saying that his method of settling belief is not ours. He does not propose to himself to be rational, and indeed, will often talk with scorn of man's weak and illusive reason. So let him think as he pleases.

But this method of fixing belief, which may be called the *method of tenacity*, will be unable to hold its ground in practice. The social impulse is against it. The man who adopts it will find that other men think differently from him, and it will be apt to occur to him in some saner moment that their opinions are quite as good as his own, and this will shake his confidence in his belief. This conception, that another man's thought or sentiment may be equivalent to one's own, is a distinctly new step, and a highly important one. It arises from an impulse too strong in man to be suppressed, without danger of destroying the human species. Unless we make ourselves hermits, we shall necessarily influence each other's opinions; so that the problem becomes how to fix belief, not in the individual merely, but in the community.

Let the will of the state act, then, instead of that of the individual. Let an institution be created which shall have for its object to keep correct doctrines before the attention of the people, to reiterate them perpetually, and to teach them to the young; having at the same time power to prevent contrary doctrines from being taught, advocated, or expressed. Let all possible causes of a change of mind be removed from men's apprehensions. Let them be kept ignorant, lest they should learn of some reason to think otherwise than they do. Let their passions be enlisted, so that they may regard private and unusual opinions with hatred and horror. Then, let all men who reject the established belief be terrified into silence. Let the people turn out and tar-and-feather such men, or let inquisitions be made into the manner of thinking of suspected persons, and, when they are found guilty of forbidden beliefs, let them be subjected to some signal punishment. When complete agreement could not otherwise be reached, a general massacre of all who have not thought in a certain way has proved a very effective means of settling opinion in a country. If the power to do this be wanting, let a list of opinions be drawn up, to which no man of the least independence of thought can assent, and let the faithful be required to accept all these propositions, in order to segregate them as radically as possible from the influence of the rest of the world.

This method has, from the earliest times, been one of the chief means of upholding correct theological and political doctrines, and of preserving their universal or catholic character. In Rome, especially, it has been practiced from the days of Numa Pompilius[15] to those of Pius Nonus.[16] This is the most perfect example in history; but wherever there is a priesthood—and no religion has been without one—this method has been more or less made use of. Wherever there is aristocracy, or a guild, or any association of a class of men whose interests depend or are supposed to depend on certain propositions, there will be inevitably found some traces of this natural product of social feeling. Cruelties always accompany this system; and when it is consistently carried out, they become atrocities of the most horrible kind in the eyes of any rational man. Nor should this occasion surprise, for the officer of a society does not feel justified in surrendering the interests of that society for the sake of mercy, as he might his own private

15. [According to legend, Numa Pompilius was the king of Rome who succeeded its founder, Romulus.]

16. [The reference is to Pope Pius IX (1792–1878), the Italian whose pontificate (1846–1878) was the longest in history, during which he convened the First Vatican Council, whose principal work was the enunciation of papal infallibility.]

interests. It is natural, therefore, that sympathy and fellowship should thus produce a most ruthless power.

In judging this method of fixing belief, which may be called the *method of authority*, we must, in the first place, allow its immeasurable mental and moral superiority to the method of tenacity. Its success is proportionally greater; and in fact it has over and over again worked the most majestic results. The mere structures of stone which it has caused to be put together—in Siam, for example, in Egypt, and in Europe—have many of them a sublimity hardly more than rivaled by the greatest works of nature. And, except the geological epochs, there are no periods of time so vast as those which are measured by some of these organized faiths. If we scrutinize the matter closely, we shall find that there has not been one of their creeds which has remained always the same; yet the change is so slow as to be imperceptible during one person's life, so that individual belief remains sensibly fixed. For the mass of mankind, then, there is perhaps no better method than this. If it is their highest impulse to be intellectual slaves, then slaves they ought to remain.

But no institution can undertake to regulate opinions upon every subject. Only the most important ones can be attended to, and on the rest men's minds must be left to the action of natural causes. This imperfection will be no source of weakness so long as men are in such a state of culture that one opinion does not influence another—that is, so long as they cannot put two and two together. But in the most priest-ridden states some individuals will be found who are raised above that condition. These men possess a wider sort of social feeling; they see that men in other countries and in other ages have held to very different doctrines from those which they themselves have been brought up to believe; and they cannot help seeing that it is the mere accident of their having been taught as they have, and of their having been surrounded with the manners and associations they have, that has caused them to believe as they do and not far differently. And their candor cannot resist the reflection that there is no reason to rate their own views at a higher value than those of other nations and other centuries; and this gives rise to doubts in their minds.

They will further perceive that such doubts as these must exist in their minds with reference to every belief which seems to be determined by the caprice either of themselves or of those who originated the popular opinions. The willful adherence to a belief, and the arbitrary forcing of it upon others, must, therefore, both be given up and a new method of settling opinions must be adopted, which shall not only produce an impulse to believe, but shall also decide what proposition it is which is to be believed. Let the action of natural preferences be unimpeded, then, and under their influence let men conversing together and regarding matters in different lights, gradually develop beliefs in harmony with natural causes. This method resembles that by which conceptions of art have been brought to maturity. The most perfect example of it is to be found in the history of metaphysical philosophy. Systems of this sort have not usually rested upon observed facts, at least not in any great degree. They have been chiefly adopted because their fundamental proposition seemed "agreeable to reason." This is an apt expression; it does not mean that which agrees with experience, but that which we find ourselves inclined to believe. Plato, for example, finds it agreeable to reason that the distances of the celestial spheres from one another should be proportional to the different lengths of strings which produce harmonious chords. Many philosophers have been led to their main conclusions by considerations like this; but this is the lowest and least developed form which the method takes, for it is clear that another man might find Kepler's theory, that the celestial spheres are proportional to the inscribed and circumscribed spheres of the different regular solids, more agreeable to *his* reason. But the shock of opinions will soon lead men to rest on preferences of a far more universal nature. Take, for example, the doctrine that man only acts selfishly—that is, from the consideration that acting one way will afford him more pleasure than acting in another. This rests on no fact in the world, but it has had a wide acceptance as being the only reasonable theory.

This method is far more intellectual and respectable from the point of view of reason than either of the others which we have noticed. But its failure has been the most manifest. It makes of inquiry something similar to the development of taste; but taste, unfortunately, is always more or less a matter of fashion, and accordingly, metaphysicians have never come to any fixed agreement, but the pendulum has swung backward and forward between a more material and a more spiritual philosophy, from the earliest times to the latest. And so from this, which has been called the *a priori method*, we are driven, in Lord Bacon's phrase, to a true induction. We have examined into this *a priori* method as something which promised to deliver our opinions from their accidental and capricious element. But development, while it is a process which eliminates the effect of some casual circumstances, only magnifies that of others. This method, therefore, does not differ in a very essential way from that of authority. The government may not have lifted its finger to influence my convictions; I may have been left outwardly quite free to choose, we will say, between monogamy and polygamy, and appealing to my conscience only, I may have concluded that the latter practice is in itself licentious. But when I come to see that the chief obstacle to the spread of Christianity among a people of as high culture as the Hindoos has been a conviction of the immorality of our way of treating women, I cannot help seeing that, though governments do not interfere, sentiments in their development will be very greatly determined by accidental causes. Now, there are some people, among whom I must suppose that my reader is to be found, who, when they see that any belief of theirs is determined by any circumstance extraneous to the facts, will from that moment not merely admit in words that that belief is doubtful, but will experience a real doubt of it, so that it ceases in some degree at least to be a belief.

To satisfy our doubts, therefore, it is necessary that a method should be found by which our beliefs may be caused by nothing human, but by some external permanency—by something upon which our thinking has no effect. Some mystics imagine that they have such a method in a private inspiration from on high. But that is only a form of the method of tenacity, in which the conception of truth as something public is not yet developed. Our external permanency would not be external, in our sense, if it was restricted in its influence to one individual. It must be something which affects, or might affect, every man. And, though these affections are necessarily as various as are individual conditions, yet the method must be such that the ultimate conclusion of every man shall be the same, or would be the same if inquiry were sufficiently persisted in. Such is the method of science. Its fundamental hypothesis, restated in more familiar language, is this: There are real things, whose characters are entirely independent of our opinions about them; those realities affect our senses according to regular laws, and, though our sensations are as different as our relations to the objects, yet, by taking advantage of the laws of perception, we can ascertain by reasoning how things really are, and any man, if he have sufficient experience and reason enough about it, will be led to the one true conclusion. The new conception here involved is that of reality. It may be asked how I know that there any realities. If this hypothesis is the sole support of my method of inquiry, my method of inquiry must not be used to support my hypothesis. The reply is this: (1) If investigation cannot be regarded as proving that there are real things, it at least does not lead to a contrary conclusion; but the method and the conception on which it is based remain ever in harmony. No doubts of the method, therefore, necessarily arise from its practice, as is the case with all the others. (2) The feeling which gives rise to any method of fixing belief is a dissatisfaction at two repugnant propositions. But here already is a vague concession that there is some *one* thing to which a proposition should conform. Nobody, therefore, can really doubt that there are realities, or, if he did, doubt would not be a source of dissatisfaction. The hypothesis, therefore, is one which every mind admits. So that the social impulse does not cause men to doubt it. (3) Everybody uses the scientific method about a great many things, and only ceases to use it when he does not know how to apply it. (4) Experience of the method has not led us to doubt it, but, on the contrary, scientific investigation has had the most wonderful triumphs in the way of settling opinion. These afford the explanation of my not doubting the method or the hypothesis which it supposes; and not having any doubt, nor believing that anybody else whom I could influence has, it would be the merest babble for me to say more about it. If there be anybody with a living doubt upon the subject, let him consider it.

To describe the method of scientific investigation is the object of this series of papers. At present I have only room to notice some points of contrast between it and other methods of fixing belief.

This is the only one of the four methods which presents any distinction of a right and a wrong way.

If I adopt the method of tenacity and shut myself out from all influences, whatever I think necessary to doing this is necessary according to that method. So with the method of authority: the state may try to put down heresy by means which, from a scientific point of view, seem very ill-calculated to accomplish its purposes; but the only test *on that method* is what the state thinks, so that it cannot pursue the method wrongly. So with the *a priori* method. The very essence of it is to think as one is inclined to think. All metaphysicians will be sure to do that, however they may be inclined to judge each other to be perversely wrong. The Hegelian system recognizes every natural tendency of thought as logical, although it is certain to be abolished by countertendencies. Hegel thinks there is a regular system in the succession of these tendencies, in consequence of which, after drifting one way and the other for a long time, opinion will at last go right. And it is true that metaphysicians get the right ideas at last; Hegel's system of Nature represents tolerably the science of his day; and one may be sure that whatever scientific investigation has put out of doubt will presently receive *a priori* demonstration on the part of the metaphysicians. But with the scientific method the case is different. I may start with known and observed facts to proceed to the unknown; and yet the rules which I follow in doing so may not be such as investigation would approve. The test of whether I am truly following the method is not an immediate appeal to my feelings and purposes, but, on the contrary, itself involves the application of the method. Hence it is that bad reasoning as well as good reasoning is possible; and this fact is the foundation of the practical side of logic.

It is not to be supposed that the first three methods of settling opinion present no advantage whatever over the scientific method. On the contrary, each has some peculiar convenience of its own. The *a priori* method is distinguished for its comfortable conclusions. It is the nature of the process to adopt whatever belief we are inclined to, and there are certain flatteries to one's vanities which we all believe by nature, until we are awakened from our pleasing dream by rough facts. The method of authority will always govern the mass of mankind; and those who wield the various forms of organized force in the state will never be convinced that dangerous reasoning ought not to be suppressed in some way. If liberty of speech is to be untrammeled from the grosser forms of constraint, then uniformity of opinion will be secured by a moral terrorism to which the respectability of society will give its thorough approval. Following the method of authority is the path of peace. Certain non-conformities are permitted; certain others (considered unsafe) are forbidden. These are different in different countries and in different ages; but, wherever you are let it be known that you seriously hold a tabooed belief, and you may be perfectly sure of being treated with a cruelty no less brutal but more refined than hunting you like a wolf. Thus, the greatest intellectual benefactors of mankind have never dared, and dare not now, to utter the whole of their thought; and thus a shade of *prima facie* doubt is cast upon every proposition which is considered essential to the security of society. Singularly enough, the persecution does not all come from without; but a man torments himself and is oftentimes most distressed at finding himself believing propositions which he has been brought up to regard with aversion. The peaceful and sympathetic man will, therefore, find it hard to resist the temptation to submit his opinions to authority. But most of all I admire the method of tenacity for its strength, simplicity, and directness. Men who pursue it are distinguished for their decision of character, which becomes very easy with such a mental rule. They do not waste time in trying to make up their minds to what they want, but, fastening like lightning upon whatever alternative comes first, they hold to it to the end, whatever happens, without an instant's irresolution. This is one of the splendid qualities which generally accompany brilliant, unlasting success. It is impossible not to envy the man who can dismiss reason, although we know how it must turn out at last.

Such are the advantages which the other methods of settling opinions have over scientific investigation. A man should consider well of them; and then he should consider that, after all, he wishes his opinions to coincide with the fact, and that there is no reason why the results of those first three methods should do so. To bring about this effect is the prerogative of the method of science. Upon such considerations he has to make his choice—a choice which is far more than the adoption of any intellectual opinion, which is one of the ruling decisions of his life, to which

when once made he is bound to adhere. The force of habit will sometimes cause a man to hold on to old beliefs after he is in a condition to see that they have no sound basis. But reflection upon the state of the case will overcome these habits, and he ought to allow reflection full weight. People sometimes shrink from doing this, having an idea that beliefs are wholesome which they cannot help feeling rest on nothing. But let such persons suppose an analogous though different case from their own. Let them ask themselves what they would say to a reformed Mussulman who should hesitate to give up his old notions in regard to the relations of the sexes; or to a reformed Catholic who should still shrink from the Bible. Would they not say that these persons ought to consider the matter fully, and clearly understand the new doctrine, and then ought to embrace it in its entirety? But, above all, let it be considered that what is more wholesome than any particular belief is integrity of belief; and that to avoid looking into the support of any belief from a fear that it may turn out rotten is quite as immoral as it is disadvantageous. The person who confesses that there is such a thing as truth, which is distinguished from falsehood simply by this, that if acted on it should, on full consideration, carry us to the point we aim at and not astray, and then, though convinced of this, dares not know the truth and seeks to avoid it, is in a sorry state of mind, indeed.

Yes, the other methods do have their merits: a clear logical conscience does cost something—just as any virtue, just as all that we cherish, costs us dear. But, we should not desire it to be otherwise. The genius of a man's logical method should be loved and reverenced as his bride, whom he has chosen from all the world. He need not condemn the others; on the contrary, he may honor them deeply, and in doing so he only honors her the more. But she is the one that he has chosen, and he knows that he was right in making that choice. And having made it, he will work and fight for her, and will not complain that there are blows to take, hoping that there may be as many and as hard to give, and will strive to be the worthy knight and champion of her from the blaze of whose splendors he draws his inspiration and his courage.

How to Make Our Ideas Clear

I

Whoever has looked into a modern treatise on logic of the common sort, will doubtless remember the two distinctions between *clear* and *obscure* conceptions, and between *distinct* and *confused* conceptions. They have lain in the books now for nigh two centuries, unimproved and unmodified, and are generally reckoned by logicians as among the gems of their doctrine.

A clear idea is defined as one which is so apprehended that it will be recognized wherever it is met with, and so that no other will be mistaken for it. If it fails of this clearness, it is said to be obscure.

This is rather a neat bit of philosophical terminology; yet, since it is clearness that they were defining, I wish the logicians had made their definition a little more plain. Never to fail to recognize an idea, and under no circumstances to mistake another for it, let it come in how recondite a form it may, would indeed imply such prodigious force and clearness of intellect as is seldom met with in this world. On the other hand, merely to have such an acquaintance with the idea as to have become familiar with it, and to have lost all hesitancy in recognizing it in ordinary cases, hardly seems to deserve the name of clearness of apprehension, since after all it only amounts to a subjective feeling of mastery which may be entirely mistaken. I take it, however, that when the logicians speak of "clearness," they mean nothing more than such a familiarity with an idea, since they regard the quality as but a small merit, which needs to be supplemented by another, which they call *distinctness*.

A distinct idea is defined as one which contains nothing which is not clear. This is technical language; by the *contents* of an idea logicians understand whatever is contained in its definition. So that an idea is *distinctly* apprehended, according to them, when we can give a precise definition of it, in abstract terms. Here the professional logicians leave the subject; and I would not have troubled the reader with what they have to say if it were not such a striking example of how they have been slumbering through ages of intellectual activity, listlessly disregarding the enginery of modern thought, and never dreaming of applying its lessons to the improvement of logic. It is easy to show that the doctrine that familiar use and abstract distinctness make the perfection of apprehension, has its only true place in philosophies which have long been extinct; and it is now time to formulate the method of attaining to a more perfect clearness of thought, such as we see and admire in the thinkers of our own time.

When Descartes set about the reconstruction of philosophy, his first step was to (theoretically) permit skepticism and to discard the practice of the schoolmen of looking to authority as the ultimate source of truth. That done, he sought a more natural fountain of true principles, and professed to find it in the human mind; thus passing, in the directest way, from the method of authority to that of apriority, as described in my first paper. Self-consciousness was to furnish us with our fundamental truths, and to decide what was agreeable to reason. But since, evidently, not all ideas are true, he was led to note, as the first condition of infallibility, that they must be clear. The distinction between an idea *seeming* clear and really being so, never occurred to him. Trusting to introspection, as he did, even for a knowledge of external things, why should he question its testimony in respect to the contents of our own minds? But then, I suppose, seeing men, who seemed to be quite clear and positive, holding opposite opinions upon fundamental principles, he was further led to say that clearness of ideas is not sufficient, but that they need also to be distinct, i.e., to have nothing unclear about them. What he probably meant by this (for he did not explain himself with precision) was that they must sustain the test of dialectical examination; that they must not only seem clear at the outset, but that discussion must never be able to bring to light points of obscurity connected with them.

Such was the distinction of Descartes, and one sees that it was precisely on the level of his philosophy.

It was somewhat developed by Leibniz. This great and singular genius was as remarkable for what he failed to see as for what he saw. That a piece of mechanism could not do work perpetually without being fed with power in some form, was a thing perfectly apparent to him; yet he did not understand that the machinery of the mind can only transform knowledge, but never originate it, unless it be fed with facts of observation. He thus missed the most essential point of the Cartesian philosophy, which is, that to accept propositions which seem perfectly evident to us is a thing which, whether it be logical or illogical, we cannot help doing. Instead of regarding the matter in this way, he sought to reduce the first principles of science to formulas which cannot be denied without self-contradiction, and was apparently unaware of the great difference between his position and that of Descartes. So he reverted to the old formalities of logic, and, above all, abstract definitions played a great part in his philosophy. It was quite natural, therefore, that on observing that the method of Descartes labored under the difficulty that we may seem to ourselves to have clear apprehensions of ideas which in truth are very hazy, no better remedy occurred to him than to require an abstract definition of every important term. Accordingly, in adopting the distinction of *clear* and *distinct* notions, he described the latter quality as the clear apprehension of everything contained in the definition; and the books have ever since copied his words. There is no danger that his chimerical scheme will ever again be overvalued. Nothing new can ever be learned by analyzing definitions. Nevertheless, our existing beliefs can be set in order by this process, and order is an essential element of intellectual economy, as of every other. It may be acknowledged, therefore, that the books are right in making familiarity with a notion the first step toward clearness of apprehension, and the defining of it the second. But in omitting all mention of any higher perspicuity of thought, they simply mirror a philosophy which was exploded a hundred years ago. That much-admired "ornament of logic"—the doctrine of clearness and distinctness—may be pretty enough, but it is high time to relegate to our cabinet of curiosities the antique *bijou*, and to wear about us something better adapted to modern uses.

The very first lesson that we have a right to demand that logic shall teach us is how to make our ideas clear; and a most important one it is, depreciated only by minds who stand in need of it. To know what we think, to be masters of our own meaning, will make a solid foundation for great and weighty thought. It is most easily learned by those whose ideas are meager and restricted; and far happier they than such as wallow helplessly in a rich mud of conceptions. A nation, it is true, may, in the course of generations, overcome the disadvantage of an excessive wealth of language and its natural concomitant, a vast, unfathomable deep of ideas. We may see it in history, slowly perfecting its literary forms, sloughing at length its metaphysics, and, by virtue of the untirable patience which is often a compensation, attaining great excellence in every branch of mental acquirement. The page of history is not yet unrolled which is to tell us whether such a people will or will not in the long run prevail over one whose ideas (like the words of their language) are few, but which possesses a wonderful mastery over those which it has. For an individual, however, there can be no question that a few clear ideas are worth more than many confused ones. A young man would hardly be persuaded to sacrifice the greater part of his thoughts to save the rest; and the muddled head is the least apt to see the necessity of such a sacrifice. Him we can usually only commiserate, as a person with a congenital defect. Time will help him, but intellectual maturity with regard to clearness comes rather late, an unfortunate arrangement of nature, inasmuch as clearness is of less use to a man settled in life, whose errors have in great measure had their effect, than it would be to one whose path lies before him. It is terrible to see how a single unclear idea, a single formula without meaning, lurking in a young man's head, will sometimes act like an obstruction of inert matter in an artery, hindering the nutrition of the brain, and condemning its victim to pine away in the fullness of his intellectual vigor and in the midst of intellectual plenty. Many a man has cherished for years as his hobby some vague shadow of an idea, too meaningless to be positively false; he has, nevertheless, passionately loved it, has made it his companion by day and by night, and has given to it his strength and his life, leaving all other occupations for its sake, and in short has lived with it and for it, until it has become, as it were, flesh of his flesh and bone of his bone; and then he has waked up some bright morning to find it gone, clean vanished away like the beautiful Melusina of the fable,[1] and the essence of his life gone with it. I have myself known such a man; and who can tell how many histories of circle-squarers, metaphysicians, astrologers, and what not, may not be told in the old German story?

II

The principles set forth in the first of these papers lead, at once, to a method of reaching a clearness of thought of a far higher grade than the "distinctness" of the logicians. We have there found that the action of thought is excited by the irritation of doubt, and ceases when belief is attained; so that the production of belief is the sole function of thought. All these words, however, are too strong for my purpose. It is as if I had described the phenomena as they appear under a mental microscope. Doubt and Belief, as the words are commonly employed, relate to religious or other grave discussions. But here I use them to designate the starting of any question, no matter how small or how great, and the resolution of it. If, for instance, in a horsecar, I pull out my purse and find a five-cent nickel and five coppers, I decide, while my hand is going to the purse, in which way I will pay my fare. To call such a question Doubt, and my decision Belief, is certainly to use words very disproportionate to the occasion. To speak of such a doubt as causing an irritation which needs to be appeased, suggests a temper which is uncomfortable to the verge of insanity. Yet, looking at the matter minutely, it must be admitted that, if there is the least hesitation as to whether I shall pay the five coppers or the nickel (as there will be sure to be, unless I act from some previously contracted habit in the matter), though irritation is too strong a word, yet I am excited to such small mental activity as may be necessary to deciding how I shall act. Most frequently doubts arise from some indecision, however momentary, in our action. Sometimes it is not so. I have, for example, to wait in a railway-station, and to pass the time I read the advertisements on the

walls. I compare the advantages of different trains and different routes which I never expect to take, merely fancying myself to be in a state of hesitancy, because I am bored with having nothing to trouble me. Feigned hesitancy, whether feigned for mere amusement or with a lofty purpose, plays a great part in the production of scientific inquiry. However the doubt may originate, it stimulates the mind to an activity which may be slight or energetic, calm or turbulent. Images pass rapidly through consciousness, one incessantly melting into another, until at last, when all is over—it may be in a fraction of a second, in an hour, or after long years—we find ourselves decided as to how we should act under such circumstances as those which occasioned our hesitation. In other words, we have attained belief.

In this process we observe two sorts of elements of consciousness, the distinction between which may best be made clear by means of an illustration. In a piece of music there are the separate notes, and there is the air. A single tone may be prolonged for an hour or a day, and it exists as perfectly in each second of that time as in the whole taken together; so that, as long as it is sounding, it might be present to a sense from which everything in the past was as completely absent as the future itself. But it is different with the air, the performance of which occupies a certain time, during the portions of which only portions of it are played. It consists in an orderliness in the succession of sounds which strike the ear at different times; and to perceive it there must be some continuity of consciousness which makes the events of a lapse of time present to us. We certainly only perceive the air by hearing the separate notes; yet we cannot be said to directly hear it, for we hear only what is present at the instant, and an orderliness of succession cannot exist in an instant. These two sorts of objects, what we are *immediately* conscious of and what we are *mediately* conscious of, are found in all consciousness. Some elements (the sensations) are completely present at every instant so long as they last, while others (like thought) are actions having beginning, middle, and end, and consist in a congruence in the succession of sensations which flow through the mind. They cannot be immediately present to us, but must cover some portion of the past or future. Thought is a thread of melody running through the succession of our sensations.

---

1. [According to legend, Melusina, a fairy who changed into a serpent from the waist down every Saturday, married a mortal, made him promise not to visit her on that day, and, on his breaking that agreement, fled from him.]

We may add that just as a piece of music may be written in parts, each part having its own air, so various systems of relationship of succession subsist together between the same sensations. These different systems are distinguished by having different motives, ideas, or functions. Thought is only one such system; for its sole motive, idea, and function is to produce belief, and whatever does not concern that purpose belongs to some other system of relations. The action of thinking may incidentally have other results. It may serve to amuse us, for example, and among *dilettanti* it is not rare to find those who have so perverted thought to the purposes of pleasure that it seems to vex them to think that the questions upon which they delight to exercise it may ever get finally settled; and a positive discovery which takes a favorite subject out of the arena of literary debate is met with ill-concealed dislike. This disposition is the very debauchery of thought. But the soul and meaning of thought, abstracted from the other elements which accompany it, though it may be voluntarily thwarted, can never be made to direct itself toward anything but the production of belief. Thought in action has for its only possible motive the attainment of thought at rest; and whatever does not refer to belief is no part of the thought itself.

And what, then, is belief? It is the demi-cadence which closes a musical phrase in the symphony of our intellectual life. We have seen that it has just three properties: first, it is something that we are aware of; second, it appeases the irritation of doubt; and, third, it involves the establishment in our nature of a rule of action, or, say for short, a *habit*. As it appeases the irritation of doubt, which is the motive for thinking, thought relaxes, and comes to rest for a moment when belief is reached. But, since belief is a rule for action, the application of which involves further doubt and further thought, at the same time that it is a stopping-place, it is also a new starting-place for thought. That is why I have permitted myself to call it thought at rest, although thought is essentially an action. The *final* upshot of thinking is the exercise of volition, and of this thought no longer forms a part; but belief is only a stadium of mental action, an effect upon our nature due to thought, which will influence future thinking.

The essence of belief is the establishment of a habit, and different beliefs are distinguished by the different modes of action to which they give rise. If beliefs do not differ in this respect, if they appease the same doubt by producing the same rule of action, then no mere differences in the manner of consciousness of them can make them different beliefs, any more than playing a tune in different keys is playing different tunes. Imaginary distinctions are often drawn between beliefs which differ only in their mode of expression—the wrangling which ensues is real enough, however. To believe that any objects are arranged among themselves as in Fig. 1, and to believe

FIG. 1

FIG. 2

that they are arranged as in Fig. 2, are one and the same belief; yet it is conceivable that a man should assert one proposition and deny the other. Such false distinctions do as much harm as the confusion of beliefs really different, and are among the pitfalls of which we ought constantly to beware, especially when we are upon metaphysical ground. One singular deception of this sort, which often occurs, is to mistake the sensation produced by our own unclearness of thought for a character of the object we are thinking. Instead of perceiving that the obscurity is purely subjective, we fancy that we contemplate a quality of the object which is essentially mysterious; and if our conception be afterward presented to us in a clear form we do not recognize it as the same, owing to the absence of the feeling of unintelligibility. So long as this deception lasts, it obviously puts an impassable barrier in the way of perspicuous thinking; so that it equally interests the opponents of rational thought to perpetuate it, and its adherents to guard against it.

Another such deception is to mistake a mere difference in the grammatical construction of two words for a distinction between the ideas they express. In this pedantic age, when the general mob of writers attend so much more to words than to things, this error is common enough. When I just said that thought is an *action*, and that it consists in a *relation*, although a person performs an action but not a relation, which can only be the result of an action, yet there was no inconsistency in what I said, but only a grammatical vagueness.

From all these sophisms we shall be perfectly safe so long as we reflect that the whole function of thought is to produce habits of action; and that whatever there is connected with a thought, but irrelevant to its purpose, is an accretion to it, but no part of it. If there be a unity among our sensations which has no reference to how we shall act on a given occasion, as when we listen to a piece of music, why, we do not call that thinking. To develop its meaning, we have, therefore, simply to determine what habits it produces, for what a thing means is simply what habits it involves. Now, the identity of a habit depends on how it might lead us to act, not merely under such circumstances as are likely to arise, but under such as might possibly occur, no matter how improbable they may be. What the habit is depends on *when* and *how* it causes us to act. As for the *when*, every stimulus to action is derived from perception; as for the *how*, every purpose of action is to produce some sensible result. Thus, we come down to what is tangible and practical as the root of every real distinction of thought, no matter how subtle it may be; and there is no distinction of meaning so fine as to consist in anything but a possible difference of practice.

To see what this principle leads to, consider in the light of it such a doctrine as that of transubstantiation. The Protestant churches generally hold that the elements of the sacrament are flesh and blood only in a tropical sense; they nourish our souls as meat and the juice of it would our bodies. But the Catholics maintain that they are literally just that, meat and

blood; although they possess all the sensible qualities of wafer-cakes and diluted wine. But we can have no conception of wine except what may enter into a belief, either—

1. That this, that, or the other, is wine; or,

2. That wine possesses certain properties.

Such beliefs are nothing but self-notifications that we should, upon occasion, act in regard to such things as we believe to be wine according to the qualities which we believe wine to possess. The occasion of such action would be some sensible perception, the motive of it to produce some sensible result. Thus our action has exclusive reference to what affects the senses, our habit has the same bearing as our action, our belief the same as our habit, our conception the same as our belief; and we can consequently mean nothing by wine but what has certain effects, direct or indirect, upon our senses; and to talk of something as having all the sensible characters of wine, yet being in reality blood, is senseless jargon. Now, it is not my object to pursue the theological question; and having used it as a logical example I drop it, without caring to anticipate the theologian's reply. I only desire to point out how impossible it is that we should have an idea in our minds which relates to anything but conceived sensible effects of things. Our idea of anything *is* our idea of its sensible effects; and if we fancy that we have any other we deceive ourselves, and mistake a mere sensation accompanying the thought for a part of the thought itself. It is absurd to say that thought has any meaning unrelated to its only function. It is foolish for Catholics and Protestants to fancy themselves in disagreement about the elements of the sacrament, if they agree in regard to all their sensible effects, here or hereafter.

It appears, then, that the rule for attaining the third grade of clearness of apprehension is as follows: consider what effects, which might conceivably have practical bearings, we conceive the object of our conception to have. Then, our conception of these effects is the whole of our conception of the object.

III

Let us illustrate this rule by some examples; and, to begin with the simplest one possible, let us ask what we mean by calling a thing *hard*. Evidently that it will not be scratched by many other substances. The whole conception of this quality, as of every other, lies in its conceived effects. There is absolutely no difference between a hard thing and a soft thing so long as they are not brought to the test. Suppose, then, that a diamond could be crystallized in the midst of a cushion of soft cotton, and should remain there until it was finally burned up. Would it be false to say that that diamond was soft? This seems a foolish question, and would be so, in fact, except in the realm of logic. There such questions are often of the greatest utility as serving to bring logical principles into sharper relief than real discussions ever could. In studying logic we must not put them aside with hasty answers, but must consider them with attentive care, in order to make out the principles involved. We may, in the present case, modify our question, and ask what prevents us from saying that all hard bodies remain perfectly soft until they are touched, when their hardness increases with the pressure until they are scratched. Reflection will show that the reply is this: there would be no *falsity* in such modes of speech. They would involve a modification of our present usage of speech with regard to the words "hard" and "soft," but not of their meanings. For they represent no fact to be different from what it is; only they involve arrangements of facts which would be exceedingly maladroit. This leads us to remark that the question of what would occur under circumstances which do not actually arise is not a question of fact, but only of the most perspicuous arrangement of them. For example, the question of free-will and fate in its simplest form, stripped of verbiage, is something like this: I have done something of which I am ashamed; could I, by an effort of the will, have resisted the temptation, and done otherwise? The philosophical reply is that this is not a question of fact, but only of the [possible] arrangement of facts. Arranging them so as to exhibit what is particularly pertinent to my question—namely, that I ought to blame myself for having done wrong—it is perfectly true to say that, if I had willed to do otherwise than I did, I should have done otherwise. On the other hand, arranging the facts so as to exhibit another important consideration, it is equally true that when a temptation has once been allowed to work, it will, if it has a certain force, produce its effect, let me struggle how I may. There is no objection to a contradiction in what would

result from a false supposition. The *reductio ad absurdum* consists in showing that contradictory results would follow from a hypothesis which is consequently judged to be false. Many questions are involved in the free-will discussion, and I am far from desiring to say that both sides are equally right. On the contrary, I am of opinion that one side [determinism] denies important facts, and that the other does not. But what I do say is that the above single question was the origin of the whole doubt; that, had it not been for this question, the controversy would never have arisen; and that this question is perfectly solved in the manner which I have indicated.

Let us next seek a clear idea of Weight. This is another very easy case. To say that a body is heavy means simply that, in the absence of opposing force, it will fall. This (neglecting certain specifications of how it will fall, etc., which exist in the mind of the physicist who uses the word) is evidently the whole conception of weight. It is a fair question whether some particular facts may not *account* for gravity; but what we mean by the force itself is completely involved in its effects.

This leads us to undertake an account of the idea of Force in general. This is the great conception which, developed in the early part of the seventeenth century from the rude idea of a cause, and, constantly improved upon since, has shown us how to explain all the changes of motion which bodies experience, and how to think about all physical phenomena; which has given birth to modern science, and changed the face of the globe; and which, aside from its more special uses, has played a principal part in directing the course of modern thought, and in furthering modern social development. It is, therefore, worth some pains to comprehend it. According to our rule, we must begin by asking what is the immediate use of thinking about force; and the answer is that we thus account for changes of motion. If bodies were left to themselves, without the intervention of forces, every motion would continue unchanged both in velocity and in direction. Furthermore, change of motion never takes place abruptly; if its direction is changed, it is always through a curve without angles; if its velocity alters, it is by degrees. The gradual changes which are constantly taking place are conceived by geometers to be compounded together according to the rules of the parallelogram of forces. If the reader does not already know what this is, he will find it, I hope, to his advantage to endeavor to follow the following explanation; but if mathematics are insupportable to him, pray let him skip three paragraphs rather than that we should part company here.

A *path* is a line whose beginning and end are distinguished. Two paths are considered to be equivalent, which, beginning at the same point, lead to the same point. Thus the two paths, $A B C D E$ and $A F G H E$ (Fig. 3), are equivalent. Paths which do *not* begin at the same point are considered to be equivalent, provided that, on moving either of them without turning it, but keeping it always parallel to its original position, [so that] when its beginning coincides with that of the other path, the ends also coincide. Paths are considered as geometrically added together, when one begins where the other ends; thus the path $A E$ is conceived to be a sum of $A B$, $B C$, $C D$, and $D E$. In the parallelogram of Fig. 4 the diagonal $A C$ is the sum of $A B$ and $B C$; or, since $A D$ is geometrically equivalent to $B C$, $A C$ is the geometrical sum of $A B$ and $A D$.

FIG. 3   FIG. 4

All this is purely conventional. It simply amounts to this: that we choose to call paths having the relations I have described equal or added. But, though it is a convention, it is a convention with a good reason. The rule for geometrical addition may be applied not only to paths, but to any other things which can be represented by paths. Now, as a path is determined by the varying direction and distance of the point which moves over it from the starting-point, it follows that anything which from its beginning to its end is determined by a varying direction and a varying magnitude is capable of being represented by a line. Accordingly, *velocities* may be represented by lines, for they have only directions and rates. The same thing is true of *accelerations*, or changes of velocities. This is evident enough in the case of velocities; and it becomes evident for accelerations if we consider that precisely what velocities are to positions—

namely, states of change of them—that accelerations are to velocities.

The so-called "parallelogram of forces" is simply a rule for compounding accelerations. The rule is, to represent the accelerations by paths, and then to geometrically add the paths. The geometers, however, not only use the "parallelogram of forces" to compound different accelerations, but also to resolve one acceleration into a sum of several. Let $A B$ (Fig. 5) be the path which represents a certain acceleration—say, such a change in the motion of a body that at the end of one second the body will, under the influence of that change, be in a position different from what it would have had if its motion had continued unchanged, such that a path equivalent to $A B$ would lead from the latter position to the former. This acceleration may be considered as the sum of the accelerations represented by $A C$ and $C B$. It may also be considered as the sum of the very different accelerations represented by $A D$ and $D B$, where $A D$ is almost the opposite of $A C$. And it is clear that there is an immense variety of ways in which $A B$ might be resolved into the sum of two accelerations.

FIG. 5

After this tedious explanation, which I hope, in view of the extraordinary interest of the conception of force, may not have exhausted the reader's patience, we are prepared at last to state the grand fact which this conception embodies. This fact is that if the actual changes of motion which the different particles of bodies experience are each resolved in its appropriate way, each component acceleration is precisely such as is prescribed by a certain law of Nature, according to which bodies in the relative positions which the bodies in question actually have at the moment always receive certain accelerations, which, being compounded by geometrical addition, give the acceleration which the body actually experiences.

This is the only fact which the idea of force represents and whoever will take the trouble clearly to apprehend what this fact is perfectly comprehends what force is. Whether we ought to say that a force *is* an acceleration, or that it *causes* an acceleration, is a mere question of propriety of language, which has no more to do with our real meaning than the difference between the French idiom "*Il fait froid*" and its English equivalent "*It is cold.*" Yet it is surprising to see how this simple affair has muddled men's minds. In how many profound treatises is not force spoken of as a "mysterious entity," which seems to be only a way of confessing that the author despairs of ever getting a clear notion of what the word means! In a recent, admired work on *Analytic Mechanics*[2] it is stated that we understand precisely the effect of force, but what force itself is we do not understand! This is simply a self-contradiction. The idea which the word "force" excites in our minds has no other function than to affect our actions, and these actions can have no reference to force otherwise than through its effects. Consequently, if we know what the effects of force are, we are acquainted with every fact which is implied in saying that a force exists, and there is nothing more to know. The truth is, there is some vague notion afloat that a question may mean something which the mind cannot conceive; and when some hair-splitting philosophers have been confronted with the absurdity of such a view, they have invented an empty distinction between positive and negative conceptions, in the attempt to give their non-idea a form not obviously nonsensical. The nullity of it is sufficiently plain from the considerations given a few pages back; and, apart from those considerations, the quibbling character of the distinction must have struck every mind accustomed to real thinking.

IV

Let us now approach the subject of logic, and consider a conception which particularly concerns it, that of *reality*. Taking clearness in the sense of familiarity, no idea could be clearer than this. Every child uses it with perfect confidence, never dreaming that he does not understand it. As for clearness in its second grade, however, it would probably puzzle most men,

even among those of a reflective turn of mind, to give an abstract definition of the real. Yet such a definition may perhaps be reached by considering the points of difference between reality and its opposite, fiction. A figment is a product of somebody's imagination; it has such characters as his thought impresses upon it. That those characters are independent of how you or I think is an external reality. There are, however, phenomena within our own minds, dependent upon our thought, which are at the same time real in the sense that we really think them. But though their characters depend on how we think, they do not depend on what we think those characters to be. Thus, a dream has a real existence as a mental phenomenon, if somebody has really dreamt it; that he dreamt so and so, does not depend on what anybody thinks was dreamt, but is completely independent of all opinion on the subject. On the other hand, considering, not the fact of dreaming, but the thing dreamt, it retains its peculiarities by virtue of no other fact than that it was dreamt to possess them. Thus we may define the real as that whose characters are independent of what anybody may think them to be.

But, however satisfactory such a definition may be found, it would be a great mistake to suppose that it makes the idea of reality perfectly clear. Here, then, let us apply our rules. According to them, reality, like every other quality, consists in the peculiar, sensible effects which things partaking of it produce. The only effect which real things have is to cause belief, for all the sensations which they excite emerge into consciousness in the form of beliefs. The question, therefore, is, how is true belief (or belief in the real) distinguished from false belief (or belief in fiction). Now, as we have seen in the former paper, the ideas of truth and falsehood, in their full development, appertain exclusively to the scientific method of settling opinion. A person who arbitrarily chooses the propositions which he will adopt can use the word truth only to emphasize the expression of his determination to hold on to his choice. Of course, the method of tenacity never prevailed exclusively; reason is too natural to men for that. But in the literature of the Dark Ages we find some fine examples of it. When Scotus Erigena[3] is commenting upon a poetical passage in

2. [The reference is to a book by the German physicist Gustav Robert Kirchhoff (1824–1887).]

3. [The reference is the John Scotus Erigena (c. 810–c.877), born in Ireland, a leading philosopher of his time.]

which hellebore is spoken of as having caused the death of Socrates, he does not hesitate to inform the inquiring reader that Helleborus and Socrates were two eminent Greek philosophers, and that the latter having been overcome in argument by the former took the matter to heart and died of it! What sort of an idea of truth could a man have who could adopt and teach, without the qualification of a "perhaps," an opinion taken so entirely at random? The real spirit of Socrates, who I hope would have been delighted to have been "overcome in argument," because he would have learned something by it, is in curious contrast with the naïve idea of the glossist, for whom (as for the "born missionary" of today) discussion would seem to have been simply a struggle. When philosophy began to awake from its long slumber, and before theology completely dominated it, the practice seems to have been for each professor to seize upon any philosophical position he found unoccupied and which seemed a strong one, to intrench himself in it, and to sally forth from time to time to give battle to the others. Thus, even the scanty records we possess of those disputes enable us to make out a dozen or more opinions held by different teachers at one time concerning the question of nominalism and realism. Read the opening part of the *Historia Calamitatum* of Abélard,[4] who was certainly as philosophical as any of his contemporaries, and see the spirit of combat which it breathes. For him, the truth is simply his particular stronghold. When the method of authority prevailed, the truth meant little more than the Catholic faith. All the efforts of the scholastic doctors are directed toward harmonizing their faith in Aristotle and their faith in the Church, and one may search their ponderous folios through without finding an argument which goes any further. It is noticeable that where different faiths flourish side by side, renegades are looked upon with contempt even by the party whose belief they adopt; so completely has the idea of loyalty replaced that of truth-seeking. Since the time of Descartes, the defect in the conception of truth has been less apparent. Still, it will sometimes strike a scientific man that the philosophers have been less intent on finding out what the facts are than on inquiring what belief is most in harmony with their

system. It is hard to convince a follower of the *a priori* method by adducing facts; but show him that an opinion he is defending is inconsistent with what he has laid down elsewhere, and he will be very apt to retract it. These minds do not seem to believe that disputation is ever to cease; they seem to think that the opinion which is natural for one man is not so for another, and that belief will, consequently, never be settled. In contenting themselves with fixing their own opinions by a method which would lead another man to a different result, they betray their feeble hold of the conception of what truth is.

On the other hand, all the followers of science are fully persuaded that the processes of investigation, if only pushed far enough, will give one certain solution to each question to which they can be applied. One man may investigate the velocity of light by studying the transits of Venus and the aberration of the stars; another by the oppositions of Mars and the eclipses of Jupiter's satellites; a third by the method of Fizeau;[5] a fourth by that of Foucault;[6] a fifth by the motions of the curves of Lissajous;[7] a sixth, a seventh, an eighth, and a ninth, may follow the different methods of comparing the measures of statical and dynamical electricity. They may at first obtain different results, but, as each perfects his method and his processes, the results will move steadily together toward a destined center. So with all scientific research. Different minds may set out with the most antagonistic views, but the progress of investigation carries them by a force outside of themselves to one and the same conclusion. This activity of thought by which we are carried, not where we wish, but to a foreordained goal, is like the operation of destiny. No modification of the point of view taken, no selection of other facts for study, no natural bent of mind even, can enable a man to escape the predestinate opinion. This great law is embodied in the conception of truth and reality. The opinion which is fated to be ultimately agreed to by all who investigate is what we mean by the truth, and

4. [The reference is to the French philosopher Peter Abelard (1079–1142).]

5. [The reference is to the French physicist Armand Hippolyte Louis Fizeau (1819–1896).]

6. [The reference is to the French physicist Jean Bernard Léon Foucault (1819–1868).]

7. [The reference is to the French physicist Jules Antoine Lissajous (1822–1880).]

the object represented in this opinion is the real. That is the way I would explain reality.

But it may be said that this view is directly opposed to the abstract definition which we have given of reality, inasmuch as it makes the characters of the real depend on what is ultimately thought about them. But the answer to this is that, on the one hand, reality is independent, not necessarily of thought in general, but only of what you or I or any finite number of men may think about it; and that, on the other hand, though the object of the final opinion depends on what that opinion is, yet what that opinion is does not depend on what you or I or any man thinks. Our perversity and that of others may indefinitely postpone the settlement of opinion; it might even conceivably cause an arbitrary proposition to be universally accepted as long as the human race should last. Yet even that would not change the nature of the belief, which alone could be the result of investigation carried sufficiently far; and if, after the extinction of our race, another should arise with faculties and disposition for investigation, that true opinion must be the one which they would ultimately come to. "Truth crushed to earth shall rise again," and the opinion which would finally result from investigation does not depend on how anybody may actually think. But the reality of that which is real does depend on the real fact that investigation is destined to lead, at last, if continued long enough, to a belief in it.

But I may be asked what I have to say to all the minute facts of history, forgotten never to be recovered, to the lost books of the ancients, to the buried secrets.

> Full many a gem of purest ray serene
> The dark, unfathomed caves of ocean bear;
> Full many a flower is born to blush unseen,
> And waste its sweetness on the desert air.[8]

Do these things not really exist because they are hopelessly beyond the reach of our knowledge? And then, after the universe is dead (according to the prediction of some scientists), and all life has ceased forever, will not the shock of atoms continue though there

will be no mind to know it? To this I reply that, though in no possible state of knowledge can any number be great enough to express the relation between the amount of what rests unknown to the amount of the known, yet it is unphilosophical to suppose that, with regard to any given question (which has any clear meaning), investigation would not bring forth a solution of it, if it were carried far enough. Who would have said, a few years ago, that we could ever know of what substances stars are made whose light may have been longer in reaching us than the human race has existed? Who can be sure of what we shall not know in a few hundred years? Who can guess what would be the result of continuing the pursuit of science for ten thousand years, with the activity of the last hundred? And if it were to go on for a million, or a billion, or any number of years you please, how is it possible to say that there is any question which might not ultimately be solved?

But it may be objected, "Why make so much of these remote considerations, especially when it is your principle that only practical distinctions have a meaning?" Well, I must confess that it makes very little difference whether we say that a stone on the bottom of the ocean, in complete darkness, is brilliant or not—that is to say, that it *probably* makes no difference, remembering always that that stone *may* be fished up tomorrow. But that there are gems at the bottom of the sea, flowers in the untraveled desert, etc., are propositions which, like that about a diamond being hard when it is not pressed, concern much more the arrangement of our language than they do the meaning of our ideas.

It seems to me, however, that we have, by the application of our rule, reached so clear an apprehension of what we mean by reality, and of the fact which the idea rests on, that we should not, perhaps, be making a pretension so presumptuous as it would be singular, if we were to offer a metaphysical theory of existence for universal acceptance among those who employ the scientific method of fixing belief. However, as metaphysics is a subject much more curious than useful, the knowledge of which, like that of a sunken reef, serves chiefly to enable us to keep clear of it, I will not trouble the reader with any more Ontology at this moment. I have already been led much further into that path than I should have desired; and I have given the reader such a dose of

---

8. [The quotation is from "Elegy Written in a Country Churchyard," by the English poet Thomas Gray (1716–1771).

mathematics, psychology, and all that is most abstruse, that I fear he may already have left me, and that what I am now writing is for the compositor and proofreader exclusively. I trusted to the importance of the subject. There is no royal road to logic, and really valuable ideas can only be had at the price of close attention. But I know that in the matter of ideas the public prefer the cheap and nasty; and in my next paper I am going to return to the easily intelligible, and not wander from it again. The reader who has been at the pains of wading through this paper shall be rewarded in the next one by seeing how beautifully what has been developed in this tedious way can be applied to the ascertainment of the rules of scientific reasoning.

We have, hitherto, not crossed the threshold of scientific logic. It is certainly important to know how to make our ideas clear, but they may be ever so clear without being true. How to make them so, we have next to study. How to give birth to those vital and procreative ideas which multiply into a thousand forms and diffuse themselves everywhere, advancing civilization and making the dignity of man, is an art not yet reduced to rules, but of the secret of which the history of science affords some hints.

Friedrich Nietzsche

F riedrich Nietzsche was born in 1844 in a small town in Prussia. He studied classical philology at the universities of Bonn and Leipzig, where he proved to be such an extraordinary student that, even without a completed doctoral thesis, he was appointed professor of classical philology at the University of Basel at the age of twenty-five. At Basel, he read Schopenhauer and Greek philosophy, and for a few years he was enthralled by the composer Richard Wagner. Somewhat shy and withdrawn by nature, Nietzsche was severely myopic and subject to migraine headaches. By 1879 his poor health led him to resign his professorship, and he spent the next ten years composing the works that make up his mature philosophy (five books, including *Twilight of the Idols* and *The Antichrist,* appeared in the last year of his productive life, 1888). At the age of forty-four he suffered a complete mental collapse that left him a helpless invalid until his death in 1900.

The key to Nietzsche's philosophy is his most famous one-liner, "God is dead." What this means is not that people are living more secular lives, but that all the traditional ideas of an "absolute" in Western civilization—ideas about a transcendent basis for finding direction and meaning in life—have collapsed, and there are no prospects of new absolutes arising in the future. So the term "God" in this remark refers not just to the deity of the Judeo-Christian tradition, but also to such god-terms as the Greek *cosmos,* the Enlightenment concept of Reason, and even our scientific idea of a law-governed nature.

Much of Nietzsche's thought is devoted to working out the consequences of this recognition of the loss of absolutes. If God is dead, then there is no way we can arrive at a "God's-eye view" of reality as it is in itself, independent of any perspective or interpretation. Nietzsche rejects the "doctrine of immaculate perception," the assumption that we can perceive things as they are in themselves. Instead, he holds that our beliefs about the world are always conditioned by our own point of view as specific sorts of creatures located in a particular place and time. This "perspectivism" in turn implies that we have no access to any timeless truths about our own essence as humans. It is pointless to try to find a "proper way to be human" or a fixed table of values that determines good or evil for all people at all times. In the end, it is up to us to create our own values in life. In Nietzsche's view, the ideal person is one who is freed from the old "craving for metaphysical comfort," one who understands that "truth" is nothing but "a mobile army of metaphors" that is always subject to revision.

Twilight of the Idols presents a vivid overview of Nietzsche's mature philosophy. A central aim of *Twilight* is to attack what Nietzsche sees as one of the chief enemies of life-affirmation in the West: the Platonic dream of an "other," better world—a world of transcendent Forms—beyond the sensory, material world in which we find ourselves. In Nietzsche's view, the belief in a "true world" distinct from our familiar material world arises because of Plato's fascination with reason and his distaste for our "animal" appetites and drives. To help shake us out of the unquestioning assumption that reason is the highest good for humans, Nietzsche employs a sort of thought-experiment about what might have motivated Platonism at its inception. Suppose it were the case, he suggests, that Socrates and Plato, far from embodying everything fine and noble about the Greeks, were in fact misfits and decadents who were unable to enjoy the sensuous, spontaneous life of the more "noble" Greeks described by Homer. On this supposition, their prejudice in favor of reason would be a form of sour grapes, a symptom of sickly, bitter minds who are incapable of fulfilling their natural, healthy drives. Rationalism would then be a symptom of decline and decadence, not a step toward the improvement of the human race.

Nietzsche toys with the idea that the Platonic glorification of reason results from a peculiarity of philosophers: their fear of change. Unable to stomach the uncertainties of a world of "becoming," philosophers turn away from the transient material objects that make up the actual world and instead focus on their own concepts of things. The fateful move comes when philosophers assume that their abstract concepts (for example, "being," "substance," "God") actually correspond to entities that exist in reality—things that are more real than the concrete, changing items in the material world we see around us.

The criticisms of Platonism carry consequences for all Western thought. Christianity, which Nietzsche calls "Platonism for the masses," reproduces Plato's "two-world" view in its distinction between heaven and earth. And even modern science presupposes Platonic dualism in its distinction between observable phenomena and underlying forces. These different conceptions of a distinction between "appearance" and "reality" are deposited in our language, and they make up a hardened "mythology" we pass along from generation to generation. Nietzsche's aim is to destabilize and undercut these assumptions. In his view, there is only *one* world—the world we find around us—and calling that world an "apparent" world just buys into the kind of invidious contrast that got Platonism going in the first place.

• • •

Valuable early works on Nietzsche include Arthur C. Danto, *Nietzsche as Philosopher* (New York: Macmillan, 1965) and Walter Kaufmann, *Nietzsche: Philosopher, Psychologist, Antichrist* (Princeton: Princeton University Press, 1974). Some especially helpful recent studies are Richard Schacht, *Nietzsche* (London: Routledge, 1983); Alexander Nehamas, *Nietzsche: Life as Literature* (Cambridge, Mass.: Harvard University Press, 1983); and Graham Parke, *Composing the Soul* (Chicago: University of Chicago Press, 1994). For Nietzsche's impact on current postmodern movements, see David B. Allison, ed., *The New Nietzsche* (Cambridge, Mass.: MIT Press, 1985). Good recent collections of essays are Robert C. Solomon and Kathleen M. Higgins, eds., *Reading Nietzsche* (New York: Oxford University Press, 1988) and Bernd Magnus and Kathleen Higgins, eds., *The Cambridge Companion to Nietzsche* (Cambridge: Cambridge University Press, 1996).

C.G.

Twilight of the Idols: Or, How to Philosophize with the Hammer

(abridged)

The Problem of Socrates

1

The wisest sages of all times have come to the same judgment about life: *it is good for nothing*. Always and everywhere we have heard the same sound escape their mouths—a sound full of diffidence, full of melancholy, full of fatigue with life, full of hostility to life. Even Socrates said, as he died, "Living—that means being sick a long time. I owe a rooster to the savior Asclepius."[1] Even Socrates had had enough.

What does that *demonstrate*? What does that *indicate*? In the past one would have said (oh, one has said it, and loud enough, especially our pessimists!): "Here there must be something true in any case! The *consensus sapientium* [agreement of the wise] demonstrates the truth." Shall we still speak this way today? *May* we do so? "Here there must be some *sickness* in any case"—that's *our* answer; these wisest sages of all times, one should first take a close look at them! Were they perhaps, all of them, no longer steady on their legs? Worn out? Shaky? *Décadents*? Does wisdom perhaps appear on Earth as a scavenger bird, excited by the scent of rotting meat?

2

In my own case this disrespectful thought—that the great sages are *declining types*—first occurred to me precisely in regards to an instance where learned

and unlearned prejudice most strongly opposes it. I recognized Socrates and Plato as symptoms of decay, as instruments of the Greek dissolution, as pseudo-Greek, as anti-Greek (*Birth of Tragedy*, 1872). That *consensus sapientium*—this I grasped better and better—demonstrates least of all that they were right about what they agreed on. Rather, it demonstrates that they themselves, these wisest ones, were somehow in *physiological* agreement, so that they took the same negative stance toward life—and *had* to take it.

Judgments, value judgments about life, for or against, can in the final analysis never be true; they have value only as symptoms, they come into consideration only as symptoms—in themselves, such judgments are stupidities. One absolutely must reach out and try to grasp this astounding *finesse, that the value of life cannot be assessed*. Not by the living, since they are parties to the dispute—in fact, they are the objects of contention, and not the judges; not by the dead, for another reason. Thus, when philosophers see a problem in the *value* of life, this even amounts to an objection to them, a question mark attached to their wisdom, an unwisdom.—What? And all these great sages—are we saying they were not only *décadents*, but they were not even wise to begin with? But here I come back to the problem of Socrates.

3

Socrates belonged by origin to the lowest folk; Socrates was rabble. One knows, one can still see for oneself, how ugly he was. But ugliness, which in itself is an objection, was among the Greeks virtually a refutation. Was Socrates a Greek at all? Ugliness is often enough the expression of a blocked development, a development *hampered* by interbreeding. Otherwise, it comes to light as a development in

From *Twilight of the Idols: Or, How to Philosophize with the Hammer*. Translated by Richard Polt. Copyright 1995. Reprinted with permission.

1. [Asclepius was the god of medicine. See Plato, *Phaedo* 118a.—R.P.]

decline. Forensic anthropologists tell us that the typical criminal is ugly: *monstrum in fronte, monstrum in animo* [monster in the face, monster in the soul]. But the criminal is a *décadent*. Was Socrates a typical criminal? — At any rate this would not clash with that well-known judgment of a physiognomist which sounded so offensive to Socrates' friends. A visitor who knew about faces, when he passed through Athens, said to Socrates' face that he *was* a *monstrum* — that he contained all bad vices and cravings within him. And Socrates simply answered: "You know me, sir!"

4

Socrates' *décadence* is signaled not only by the confessed depravity and anarchy of his instincts, but also by the overdevelopment of the logical and that *arthritic nastiness* that characterizes him. And let us not forget those auditory hallucinations which have been interpreted in religious terms as "Socrates' *daimonion* [divine sign]." Everything about him is exaggerated, *buffo*, a caricature; everything is at the same time covert, subliminal, ulterior. — I am trying to grasp from what idiosyncrasy that Socratic equation — reason = virtue = happiness — stems, the most bizarre equation that there is, and one which in particular has all the instincts of the older Hellenes against it.

5

With Socrates, Greek taste takes a turn in favor of dialectic. What is actually happening there? Primarily, a *noble* taste is thereby defeated; with dialectic, the rabble rises to the top. Before Socrates, dialectical manners were rejected in good society. They were taken to be bad manners, they were a compromising exposure. One warned the youth against them. And all such presentation of one's reasons was mistrusted. Respectable things, like respectable people, just don't carry their reasons around on their sleeves like that. It is improper to show your whole hand. Whatever has to get itself proved in advance is not worth much. Wherever authority is still considered good form, so that one does not "give reasons" but commands, the dialectician is a sort of clown. One laughs at him; one does not take him seriously. — Socrates was the clown who *succeeded in making people take him seriously*; what actually happened there?

6

Dialectic is chosen only as a last resort. It is well-known that it creates mistrust, that it is not very convincing. Nothing can be wiped away more easily than a dialectician's effect; this is proven by the experience of every gathering where people speak. It can only be a *last resort* deployed by those who have no other weapons. One needs to get one's rights by *force*; otherwise, one makes no use of it. This is why the Jews were dialecticians. Reynard the Fox was one. What? And Socrates was one too?

7

Is Socrates' irony an expression of revolt? Of the rabble's *ressentiment*?[2] Does he, as one of the oppressed, relish his own ferocity in the knife-thrusts of the syllogism? Does he take *revenge* on the nobles whom he fascinates? As dialectician, one has a merciless instrument at hand; one can play the tyrant with it; one compromises by conquering. The dialectician lays on his opponent the burden of proving that he is not an idiot. He infuriates, and at the same time paralyzes. The dialectician *disempowers* the intellect of his opponent. — What? Is dialectic just a form of *revenge* in Socrates?

8

I have made it understandable how Socrates could be repulsive. Now it is all the more necessary to explain why he was *fascinating*. — The fact that he discovered a new kind of *agon* [contest], that in this contest he served as the first fencing master for the noble circles of Athens, is the first point. He fascinated by stimulating the combative drive of the Hellenes: he introduced a variant into the wrestling match between young men and youths. Socrates was also a great *erotic*.

9

But Socrates surmised even more. He saw *past* his noble Athenians; he grasped that *his* case, his idiosyncratic case, was already not exceptional. The same kind of degeneration was silently preparing itself everywhere; the old Athens was coming to an end. And

2. [Resentful vengefulness (French). Nietzsche develops this concept at length in *On the Genealogy of Morals* (1887).]

Socrates understood that all the world had *need* of him—his means, his cure, his personal device for self-preservation. Everywhere, the instincts were in anarchy; everywhere, one was five steps away from excess; the *monstrum in animo* was the general threat. "The drives want to play the tyrant; a *counter-tyrant* who is stronger must be invented."

When that physiognomist had exposed to Socrates who he was, a cave of all bad cravings, the great ironist allowed himself another word that gives us the key to him. "That is true," he said, "but I became the master of them all." *How* did Socrates become master of *himself*? His case was at bottom only the extreme case, only the most striking example of what began at that time to be the general emergency: the fact that no one was master of himself any more, that the instincts were turning *against* each other. He was fascinating as this extreme case—his fearsome ugliness displayed him as such to every eye. He was even more fascinating, of course, as an answer, as a solution, as the semblance of a *cure* for this case.

10

When one finds it necessary to make a tyrant out of *reason*, as Socrates did, then there must be no small danger that something else should play the tyrant. Rationality was at that time surmised to be a *savior*; neither Socrates nor his "sick patients" were rational by free choice—it was *de rigueur*, it was their *final* means. The fanaticism with which all Greek speculation throws itself at rationality betrays a situation of emergency—they were in danger, they had to make *this* choice: either to be destroyed, or—to be *absurdly rational*.

The moralism of the Greek philosophers from Plato on is pathologically conditioned; likewise their assessment of dialectic. Reason = virtue = happiness simply means: one must imitate Socrates and produce a permanent *daylight* against the dark desires—the daylight of reason. One must be cunning, sharp, clear at all costs; every acquiescence to the instincts, to the unconscious, leads *downward*.

11

I have made it understandable how Socrates was fascinating: he appeared to be a doctor, a savior. Is it necessary to go on to point out the error which lay in his belief in "rationality at all costs"?—It is a self-deception on the part of philosophers and moralists to think that they can escape from *décadence* merely by making war against it. Such an escape is beyond their strength. What they choose as a means, as salvation, is itself just another expression of *décadence*— they *alter* its expression, they do not do away with it itself. Socrates was a misunderstanding; *the whole morality of betterment, that of Christianity included, was a misunderstanding*. The most glaring daylight, rationality at all costs, a life bright, cold, careful, aware, without instinct, in resistance to the instincts, was itself just a sickness, another sickness—and not at all a way back to "virtue," to "health," to happiness. To *have* to fight the instincts—that is the formula for *décadence*. As long as life *is ascending*, happiness is the same as instinct.

12

Did he himself still grasp that, this most cunning of all self-outwitters? Did he tell himself this in the end, in the *wisdom* of his courage in the face of death? Socrates *wanted* to die—not Athens, but *he* gave himself the poison cup, he forced Athens to give him the poison cup. "Socrates is no doctor," he said to himself softly, "death is the only doctor here . . . Socrates himself has just been sick for a long time. . . ."

"Reason" in Philosophy

1

You ask me what is idiosyncratic about philosophers? . . . There is, for instance, their lack of a sense of history, their hatred for the very notion of becoming, their Egyptianism. They think they are *honoring* a thing if they de-historicize it, see it *sub specie aeterni*[3]—if they make a mummy out of it. Everything that philosophers have handled, for thousands of years now, has been a conceptual mummy; nothing real escaped their hands alive. They kill and stuff whatever they worship, these gentlemen who idolize concepts; they endanger the life of whatever they worship. In

3. ["From the perspective of the eternal"—an expression used by Spinoza.]

their view, death, change, and age, like procreation and growth, are objections—refutations, even. That which is, does not *become*; that which becomes, *is* not.

Now, they all believe, desperately even, in that which *is*. But since they fail to get it into their grasp, they look for the reason why it withholds itself from them. "There must be an illusion, a trick, at work that prevents us from perceiving that which *is*; where's the trickster?"—"We've got the trickster!" they cry happily, "it's sensation! These senses, *which are so immoral anyway*, trick us about the *true* world. The moral is: free yourself from the senses' trickery, from becoming, from history, from the lie; history is nothing but belief in the senses, belief in the lie. The moral is: say No to everything that lends credence to the senses, to all the rest of humanity; all that is merely 'the masses.' Be a philosopher, be a mummy, portray monotono-theism with a gravedigger's pantomime!—And above all, away with the *body*, this pathetic *idée fixe* [pet idea] of the senses, afflicted with every logical error there is, refuted, even impossible—although it has the nerve to behave as if it were real!" . . .

2

I set aside with great respect the name of *Heraclitus*. While the rest of the mass of philosophers were rejecting the testimony of their senses, because they displayed plurality and change, he rejected the testimony of the senses because they displayed things as if they had duration and unity. Heraclitus did not do justice to the senses either. They do not lie either in the way the Eleatics[4] thought, or in the way that he thought—they do not lie at all. What we *make* of their testimony is what first introduces the lie—for instance, the lie of unity, the lie of thinghood, of substance, of duration. . . . "Reason" is what causes us to falsify the testimony of the senses. Insofar as the senses display becoming, passing away, and change, they do not lie. But Heraclitus will always be in the right for saying that being is an empty fiction. The "apparent" world is the only world; the "true world" is merely *added to it by a lie.*

4. [Followers of Parmenides of Elea (c. 475 B.C.), who asserted that that which is, is unchangeable, uniform, and unitary.]

3

And what fine tools of observation we have in our senses! This nose, for instance, of which no philosopher has yet spoken with admiration and gratitude, is in fact the most delicate instrument at our disposal; it can register minimal differences in motion which even the spectroscope fails to register. The extent to which we possess science today is precisely the extent to which we have decided to *accept* the testimony of the senses—and learned to sharpen them, arm them, and think them through to their end. The rest is a miscarriage and not-yet-science—that is, metaphysics, theology, psychology, epistemology. *Or* it is formal science, a theory of signs, such as logic and that applied logic, mathematics. In these formal sciences, reality makes no appearance at all, not even as a problem; nor is there any hint of the question of what value such a convention of signs has in the first place.

4

The *other* idiosyncrasy of philosophers, which is no less dangerous, consists in confusing what is first with what is last. They posit what comes at the end—unfortunately, for it should never come at all!—the "highest concepts," that is, the most universal and emptiest concepts, the final wisp of evaporating reality—these they posit at the beginning *as* the beginning. This, again, just expresses their way of honoring something: the higher is not *permitted* to grow out of the lower, is not *permitted* to have grown at all.

The moral is: everything that is of the first rank must be *causa sui* [cause of itself]. Origination from something else counts as an objection that casts doubt on the value of what has so originated. All the supreme values are of the first rank; all the highest concepts—that which *is*, the unconditional, the good, the true, the perfect—all this cannot have become, and *must* consequently be *causa sui*. But all this cannot be at odds with itself either, cannot contradict itself. That's where they get their stupendous concept "God." The last, the thinnest, the emptiest concept is posited as the first, as a cause in itself, as *ens realissimum* [the most real being]. To think that humanity has had to take seriously the mental distortions of sickly web-spinners!—And it has paid dearly for having done so!

5

Let us, finally, present the opposing way in which *we* (I politely say we) view the problem of error and illusion. It used to be that one took alteration, change, becoming in general as a proof of illusion, as a sign that something must be there, leading us astray. Today, in contrast, it is precisely to the extent that we are compelled by the prejudice of reason to posit unity, identity, duration, substance, cause, thinghood, being, that we see ourselves, as it were, entangled in error, *forced* into error—so sure are we, on the basis of a rigorous self-examination, that it is here that the error lies.

This case is just like the supposed motions of our great star. In that case, error has our eyes as its constant advocates, whereas in the first case, its advocate is our *language*. In its origin, language belongs to the time of the most rudimentary type of psychology; we encounter a crude set of fetishes when we pay attention to the basic presuppositions of the metaphysics of language—or, to put it plainly, *reason. Reason* sees actors and actions everywhere; it believes in the will as an absolute cause; it believes in the "I," in the I as a being, in the I as a substance, and *projects* its belief in the I-substance onto all things—that is how it first *creates* the concept "thing." Being is thought into things everywhere as a cause, is *imputed* to things; from the conception "I" there follows the derivative concept "being." At the beginning there stands the great and fatal error of thinking that the will is something that *acts*—that will is an *ability*. Today we know that it is merely a word.

Much, much later, in a world that was more enlightened by a thousandfold, philosophers were startled to become aware of their *certitude*, their subjective *certainty* in manipulating the categories of reason; they concluded that these categories could not come from experience—all experience stands in contradiction to them, after all. *So where did they come from?*—And in India, as in Greece, they made the same mistake: "We must already have been at home in a higher world"—instead of *in a far lower one*, which would have been the truth!—"we must have been divine, *since* we have reason!"

In fact, nothing up to now has been more naively persuasive than the error of being, as it was formulated by the Eleatics, for instance; after all, it has on its side every word, every sentence we speak! Even the opponents of the Eleatics fell prey to the seduction of their concept of being—among others, Democritus did so in inventing his *atom*. "Reason" in language: oh, what a tricky old woman she is! I'm afraid we're not rid of God because we still believe in grammar.

6

One will be thankful to me if I condense such an essential and new insight into four theses; I thus make it easier to understand, and I challenge you to argue against it.

First proposition. The grounds on which "this" world has been designated as apparent are, rather, grounds for its reality; *another* kind of reality is absolutely indemonstrable.

Second proposition. The distinguishing marks which one has given to the "true being" of things are the distinguishing marks of nonbeing, of *nothing*. The "true world" has been constructed by contradicting the actual world—this "true world" is in fact an apparent world, insofar as it is merely a *moral-optical* illusion.

Third proposition. It makes no sense whatsoever to tell fables about "another" world than this one, provided that the instinct to slander, trivialize, and look down upon life is not powerful in us; in that case, we *revenge* ourselves on life with the phantasmagorias of "another," "better" life.

Fourth proposition. To divide the world into a "true" and an "apparent" world, whether in the style of Christianity or in the style of Kant (a *sneaky* Christian to the end) is merely a sign of *décadence*—a symptom of *declining* life.—The fact that the artist prizes appearance over reality is no objection to this proposition. For "appearance" here means reality *once again*, but in the form of a selection, an emphasis, and a correction. Tragic artists are *not* pessimists—in fact, they say *Yes* to everything questionable and terrible itself; they are *Dionysian*.

How the "True World" Finally Became a Fiction
History of an Error

1. The true world, attainable for those who are wise, devout, virtuous—they live in it, *they are it*.

(Oldest form of the idea, relatively clever, simple, convincing. Paraphrase of the assertion, "I, Plato, *am* the truth.")

2. The true world, unattainable for now, but promised to those who are wise, devout, virtuous ("to the sinner who does penance").

(Progress of the idea: it becomes more refined, more devious, more mystifying—*it becomes woman*, it becomes Christian.)

3. The true world, unattainable, unprovable, unpromisable, but a consolation, an obligation, an imperative, merely by virtue of being thought.

(The old sun basically, but glimpsed through fog and skepticism; the idea become sublime, pallid, Nordic, Königsbergian.[5])

4. The true world—unattainable? In any case, unattained. And if it is unattained, it is also *unknown*. Hence it is also not consoling, redeeming, obligating; to what could something unknown obligate us?

(Grey dawn. First yawnings of reason. Rooster's crow of positivism.)

5. The "true world"—an idea that is useful for nothing anymore, no longer even obligating—an idea become useless, superfluous, *hence* a refuted idea; let us do away with it!

(Bright day; breakfast; return of *bon sens* [good sense] and cheerfulness; Plato's blush; pandemonium of all free spirits.)

6. We have done away with the true world; what world is left over? The apparent one, maybe? ... But no! *Along with the true world, we have also done away with the apparent!*

(Midday; moment of the shortest shadow; end of the longest error; high point of humanity; INCIPIT ZARATHUSTRA [here begins Zarathustra].)

Morality as Anti-Nature

1

All passions have a time when they are merely fatal, when they drag their victim down with the heaviness of their stupidity—and a later, much later time when they marry the spirit, they "spiritualize" themselves. It used to be that on account of the stupidity in passion, one made war against passion itself; one conspired to destroy it. All the old moral monsters are of one mind on this point: "*il faut tuer les passions*" [the passions must be killed]. The best-known formula for this is in the New Testament, in that Sermon on the Mount in which, by the way, things are not contemplated *from a height* at all. For instance, there it is said with reference to sexuality, "if your eye offends you, pluck it out." Fortunately, no Christian acts according to this prescription.

To *destroy* the passions and desires, merely in order to protect oneself against their stupidity and the disagreeable consequences of their stupidity, seems to us today to be itself an acute form of stupidity. We no longer admire dentists who *pull out* teeth so that they won't hurt anymore. But on the other hand, it is only fair to concede that on the soil from which Christianity grew, the concept of "*spiritualizing* the passions" was simply inconceivable. After all, the early Church fought, as is known, *against* the "intellectuals," on behalf of those who were "poor in spirit"; how could one expect the Church to wage an intelligent war against passion? The Church fights passion by cutting it out, in every sense; its practice, its "therapy" is *castration*. It never asks, "How does one spiritualize, beautify, deify a desire?"—its discipline has always emphasized eradication—eradication of sensuality, pride, ambition to rule, covetousness, vengefulness. But ripping out the passions by the root means ripping out life by the root; the practice of the Church is *hostile to life*.

2

The same means—castration, eradication—is instinctively chosen in the struggle against a desire by those who are too weak-willed, too degenerate to moderate their own desire—by those natures who need La Trappe,[6] to use a metaphor (and not to use one), some ultimate declaration of war, an *abyss* between themselves and a passion. Radical means are indis-

_____

5. [An allusion to Kant, who lived all his life in Königsberg. For Kant, it is impossible for us to know about "things in themselves"—including God, free will, and an immortal soul; however, rational morality obliges us to "postulate" such things.]

6. [The original abbey of the highly disciplined Trappist monks.]

pensable only for degenerates; to have a weak will, or, put more precisely, to be incapable of *not* reacting to a stimulus, is itself just another form of degeneration. Radical enmity, enmity to the death against sensuality, is always a symptom that repays reflection; it justifies one's suspicions about the general condition of one who goes to this type of extreme.

By the way, this enmity, this hatred reaches its peak only when such natures no longer have enough stamina even for the radical therapy, for the repudiation of their "devil." Survey the whole history of priests and philosophers, and artists too: the most poisonous words against the senses have come *not* from the impotent, *not* even from the ascetics, but from the impossible ascetics, from those who were in need of being ascetics.

3

The spiritualization of sensuality is known as *love*; it is a great triumph over Christianity. Another triumph is our spiritualization of *enmity*. It consists in a deep grasp of the value of having enemies; in short, our way of acting and drawing conclusions is the reverse of what it used to be. In every age, the Church wanted its enemies to be destroyed; we, we immoralists and anti-Christians, see our own advantage in the Church's continued existence. In the political sphere, too, enmity has now become more spiritual—much more clever, much more reflective, much more *considerate*. Almost every party grasps that its own interest, its own self-preservation, depends on the opposing party's not losing its strength. The same applies to politics on the large scale. Above all, a new creation, such as the new *Reich*,[7] needs enemies more than it needs friends; only in opposition does it feel that it is necessary, only in opposition does it *become* necessary.

We conduct ourselves no differently as regards the "inner enemy": here, too, we have spiritualized enmity; here, too, we have realized its *value*. One is *fruitful* only at the price of being rich in oppositions; one remains *young* only under the condition that the soul not slacken, not yearn for peace. Nothing has become more alien to us than that former object of

desire, "peace of the soul," the *Christian* object of desire; nothing makes us less envious than the morality-cow and the fat contentment of good conscience. One has relinquished *great* life when one relinquishes war.

In many cases, of course, "peace of the soul" is just a misunderstanding—something *else* which simply does not know how to call itself by a more honest name. Without delay and without prejudice, here are a couple of cases. For instance, "peace of the soul" can be an animal richness, gently radiating into the moral (or the religious) realm. Or the beginning of fatigue, the first shadow cast by the evening, every sort of evening. Or a sign that the air is humid, that southern winds are on their way. Or unconscious thankfulness for good digestion (sometimes called "love of humanity"). Or the growing calm of the convalescent to whom all things taste new, and who is awaiting. . . . Or the condition that follows a powerful gratification of our dominant passion, the good feeling of a rare satisfaction. Or the senile feebleness of our will, our desires, our vices. Or laziness, convinced by vanity to dress itself up in morality. Or the arrival of a certainty, even a terrible certainty, after a long, suspenseful period of being tortured by uncertainty. Or the expression of ripeness and mastery in the midst of doing, creating, working, willing—unhurried breathing, the *attained* "freedom of the will". . . . *Twilight of the Idols*: who knows? Maybe this, too, is just a kind of "peace of the soul."

4

I shall put a principle into a formula. All naturalism in morality, that is, all *healthy* morality, is ruled by an instinct of life; some decree of life is fulfilled by a particular canon of "shall" and "shall not," some restriction and hostility on life's path is thereby shoved aside. *Anti-natural* morality—that is, almost every morality that has been taught, honored and preached up to now—turns, in contrast, precisely *against* the instincts of life; it is a sometimes stealthy, sometimes loud and bold *condemnation* of these instincts. By saying, "God looks into the heart," it says No to the lowest and highest desires of life, and takes God to be the *enemy of life*. The saint in whom God takes delight is the ideal eunuch. Life ends where the "kingdom of God" *begins*.

---

7. [The new German Empire, proclaimed by Bismarck in 1871.]

5

Once one has grasped the impiety of a revolt against life such as has become nearly sacrosanct in Christian morality, one has, fortunately, also grasped something else: the uselessness, illusiveness, absurdity, and *mendacity* of such a revolt. A condemnation of life by one who is alive is, in the end, just a symptom of a particular kind of life; the question of whether the condemnation is justified or unjustified has not been raised here at all. One would have to occupy a position *outside* life, and on the other hand, to know life as well as one who has lived it—as many, as all who have lived it—in order to be allowed even to touch upon the problem of the *value* of life. These are reasons enough to grasp that this problem is, for us, an inaccessible problem. When we speak of values, we speak under the inspiration and optics of life; life itself is forcing us to posit values, life itself is valuing by means of us, *when* we posit values.

It follows from this that even that *anti-nature of a morality* that takes God as the counter-concept and condemnation of life is itself just one of the value judgments of life.—A judgment of *which* life? Of *which* kind of life?—But I already gave the answer: of declining, weakened, tired, and condemned life. Morality as it has been understood up to now—as it was finally formulated once more by Schopenhauer,[8] as "negation of the will to life"—is the *décadence-instinct* itself, making itself into an imperative. "*Perish!*" it says—it is the condemnation decreed by the condemned.

6

Finally, let us consider how naive it is in the first place to say, "Human beings *should* be such and such!" Reality shows us a captivating treasury of types, the exuberance of an evanescent play and alteration of forms. And some pathetic bystander of a moralist says to all this, "No! Human beings should be *differ-*

ent"? He even knows *how* human beings should be, this sniveling bigot; he paints himself on the wall and pronounces, "*Ecce homo!*"[9]

But even if the moralist simply turns to the individual and says, "*You* should be such and such!" he does not stop making himself ridiculous. The individual is a slice of fate, both ahead and behind—one more law, one more necessity for everything that is coming and will be. To say to the individual, "change yourself," means wishing that everything should change itself, even retroactively. And there really have been consistent moralists; they wanted human beings to be different, namely virtuous, they wanted them made in their own image, namely as bigots. To this end, they *denied* the world! No small lunacy! No modest sort of immodesty!

Morality, insofar as it *condemns* on its own grounds, and *not* from the point of view of life's perspectives and objectives, is a specific error for which one should have no sympathy, an *idiosyncrasy of degenerates* which has done an unspeakable amount of harm! In contrast, we others, we immoralists, have opened our hearts wide to every form of understanding, comprehending, *approving*. We do not easily deny, we seek our honor in being those who *affirm*. Our eyes have been opened more and more to that economy that needs and knows how to use all that the holy craziness of the priest, the *sick* reason in the priest rejects—that economy in the law of life that draws its advantage even from the repulsive species of the bigot, the priest, the virtuous. *What* advantage?—But we ourselves, we immoralists, are the answer here.

The Four Great Errors

1

Error of confusing cause and effect

There is no error more dangerous than *confusing the effect with the cause*; I call it the genuine ruination of reason. Nevertheless, this error belongs among both the oldest and most contemporary customs of humanity; it has even been made sacred among us, it bears the names of "religion" and "morality." *Every* state-

8. [Arthur Schopenhauer (1788–1869) was a German philosopher who, drawing on the work of Kant and opposing the views of Hegel, maintained that the essence of the world is will, that each individual is identical with that will, that the will is without purpose, and that our lives of blind willing are doomed to misery.—S.M.C.]

9. ["Behold the man" (John 19:5); but also, "behold man," behold what it is to be human.]

ment formulated by religion and morality contains it; priests and moral lawgivers are the ones who originated this ruination of reason.

I offer an example. Everyone knows the book of the famous Cornaro[10] in which he promotes his skimpy diet as a prescription for a long, happy life — and a virtuous one. Few books have been read so widely; still today, in England, it is printed by the thousands of copies every year. I have no doubt that hardly any book (the Bible excepted, as is only fair) has done as much damage, has *shortened* as many lives as this curiosity which was so well-meaning. The reason: confusing effect and cause. The honorable Italian saw in his diet the *cause* of his long life, whereas in fact, the preconditions of his long life — extraordinary metabolic slowness, low expenditure of energy — were the cause of his skimpy diet. He was not at liberty to eat a little *or* a lot, his frugality was *not* "freely willed"; he got sick if he ate more. But for whoever is not a cold fish, not only does it do good, but it is necessary to eat *properly*. Scholars of *our* day, with their rapid expenditure of nervous energy, would destroy themselves if they followed Cornaro's regimen. *Crede experto* [believe the one with experience].

2

The most general formula that lies at the basis of every religion and morality is, "Do such and such, don't do such and such — that will make you happy! Or else. . . ." Every morality, every religion *is* this imperative; I call it the great original sin of reason, the *immortal unreason*. In my mouth, this formula changes into its opposite — *first* example of my "revaluation of all values": well-constituted people, "happy" ones, *must* do certain acts and instinctively shrink away from other acts; they import their characteristic physiological order into their relations to people and things. In a formula: their virtue is the *effect* of their happiness.

Long life and many offspring are *not* the reward of virtue; virtue itself is rather that slow metabolism that, among other things, also has a long life, many

10. [Luigi Cornaro (1467?–1566) was a Venetian nobleman who wrote the widely translated *Discourse on the Sober Life*, published in 1558.]

offspring, and, in short, *Cornarism* as its consequence. The Church and morality say, "A race, a people is destroyed by vice and luxury." My *reconstituted* reason says: when a people is perishing, physiologically degenerating, the *effects* of this are vice and luxury (that is, the need for ever stronger and ever more frequent stimuli, of the sort that is familiar to every exhausted nature). This young man becomes prematurely pale and flabby. His friends say: such and such a sickness is responsible for this. I say: the fact *that* he got sick, *that* he did not resist the sickness, was already the effect of an impoverished life, an inherited exhaustion. The newspaper reader says: this party is destroying itself by making such a mistake. My *higher* politics says: a party that makes such mistakes is over — it no longer has sure instincts.

Every mistake, in every sense, is the effect of degenerate instincts, of a disintegrated will; this virtually defines the *bad*. Everything *good* is instinct — and consequently is easy, necessary, free. Exertion is an objection; the *god* is typically different from the hero (in my language: *light* feet are the first attribute of godliness).

3

Error of a false causality

In every age we have believed that we know what a cause is. But where did we get our knowledge, or more precisely, our belief that we know about this? From the realm of the famous "internal facts," none of which has up to now proved to be factual. We believed that we ourselves were causal in the act of willing; there, at least, we thought that we were *catching causality in the act*.

Likewise, we never doubted that all the antecedents of an action, its causes, were to be sought in consciousness, and could be discovered there if we looked for them — discovered as "motives"; otherwise, one would not have been free *for* the action, responsible *for* it. Finally, who would have disputed the claim that a thought is caused? That the "I" causes the thought? — Of these three "interior facts" by which causality seemed to vouch for itself, the first and most convincing is the "fact" of *will as cause*; the conception of a consciousness ("mind") as cause, and still later of the "I" (the "subject") as cause were merely born later, after the will had firmly established causality as given, as an *empirical fact*.

In the meantime, we have thought better of this. Today we believe not a word of all that anymore. The "internal world" is full of optical illusions and false flashes; the will is one of them. The will no longer moves anything, and consequently no longer explains anything either; it merely accompanies events, and can even be absent. The so-called "motive": another error—just a surface phenomenon of consciousness, an accessory to the act, which rather conceals the antecedents of an act than represents them. And as for the "I"! That has become a fable, a fiction, a play on words; it has completely and utterly ceased to think, to feel, and to will! What is the consequence of this? There are no mental causes at all! The whole supposed empirical evidence for them has gone to the devil! *That's* the consequence!

And we had made a fine misuse of this "evidence"; we had *created* the world on that basis as a world of causes, a world of wills, a world of minds. The oldest and most long-standing psychology was at work here, and it did nothing else at all; all happening was for it a doing, all doing the effect of a willing; the world became for it a plurality of doers, a doer (a "subject") was imputed to all that happened. Human beings projected their three "internal facts," the objects of their firmest belief—will, mind, "I"—beyond themselves; they first derived the concept of being from the concept "I," they posited "things" as existing in their own image, according to their concept of the "I" as a cause. No wonder that they later rediscovered in things only *what they had put into them!*—The thing itself—to say it once again—the concept of a thing is a mere reflex of the belief in the "I" as a cause. And even your atom, my dear mechanists and physicists—how much error, how much rudimentary psychology remains in your atom!—Not to mention the "thing in itself," the *horrendum pudendum* [horrible, shameful thing] of the metaphysicians! The error of mind as cause confused with reality! And made into the measure of reality! And called *God!*

4

Error of imaginary causes

I begin from dreams: a particular sensation—for instance, the result of a distant cannon shot—subsequently has a cause imputed to it (often a whole little story in which precisely the dreamer is the protagonist). Meanwhile, the sensation persists in a kind of resonance; it waits, as it were, until the drive for causes allows it to come into the foreground—not as an accident anymore, but as "meaning." The cannon shot shows up in a *causal* way, in an apparent reversal of time. What is later, the motivation, is experienced first, often with a hundred particularities which flash by like lightning; the shot *follows.*—What has happened? The representations *generated* by a certain state of affairs were misunderstood as the cause of this state of affairs.

In fact, we do just the same thing when we are awake. Most of our common feelings—every sort of inhibition, pressure, tension, explosion in the play and counter-play of the organs, particularly including the state of our sympathetic nervous system—arouse our drive to find causes; we want to have a *reason* for finding ourselves in *such and such* a state—a bad state or a good state. It is never enough for us simply to ascertain the mere fact *that* we find ourselves in such and such a state; we admit this fact—become *conscious* of it—*if* we have given it some kind of motivation. Memory, which is activated in such cases without our knowing it, calls up earlier states of the same kind, and the causal interpretations that are rooted in them—but *not* their causation. To be sure, the belief that the representations, the accompanying occurrences in consciousness, were the causes is also called up by the memory. Thus we become *accustomed* to a particular interpretation of causes that in fact inhibits and even excludes an *investigation* of the cause.

5

A *psychological explanation of this error*

Tracing something unfamiliar back to something familiar alleviates us, calms us, pacifies us, and furthermore provides a feeling of power. The unfamiliar brings with it danger, unrest, and care; our first instinct is directed at *doing away with* these painful conditions. First principle: some explanation is better than none. Since at bottom it is only a matter of wanting to free oneself from oppressive representations, one is not exactly stringent about the means of freeing oneself from them; the first representation that serves to explain the unfamiliar as familiar is so beneficial that one "takes it to be true." Proof of *pleasure* ("strength") as criterion of truth.

The drive to find causes is thus conditioned and aroused by the feeling of fear. The "why?" should, whenever possible, not so much provide the cause for its own sake, but rather provide a *type of cause*— a calming, pacifying, alleviating cause. The fact that something already *familiar*, experienced, inscribed in memory, is posited as the cause, is the first consequence of this requirement. The new, the unexperienced, the alien, is excluded as a cause. Thus, not only is one type of explanation sought as the cause, but there is a type of explanation that is *singled out* and *preferred*, the type which does away with the feeling of the alien, new, and unexperienced, as quickly and as frequently as possible—the most *customary* explanations.

Consequence: one kind of cause-positing becomes more and more prevalent, concentrates itself into a system, and finally comes to the fore as *dominant*, that is, as simply *excluding* any *other* causes and explanations. The banker thinks right away about "business," the Christian about "sin," the girl about her love.

6

The entire realm of morality and religion belongs under this concept of imaginary causes

"Explanation" of the *unpleasant* common feelings. These feelings are brought about by beings that are our enemies (evil spirits—the most famous case— misunderstanding of hysterics as witches). They are brought about by unacceptable actions (the feeling of "sin," of "sinfulness," is imputed to a physiological unease—one always finds reasons to be dissatisfied with oneself). They are brought about as punishments, as payment for something that we ought not to have done, that we ought not to have *been*. (Impudently generalized by Schopenhauer into a statement in which morality appears as what it is, as something that really poisons and despises life: "every great pain, be it bodily or spiritual, expresses what we deserve, for it could not come to us if we did not deserve it."—*The World as Will and Representation*, II.) They are brought about as the effects of thoughtless actions that turned out badly (the emotions, the senses, are

posited as a cause, as "responsible"; physiological crises are interpreted as "deserved" with the help of *other* crises).

"Explanation" of the *pleasant* common feelings. These feelings are brought about by trust in God. They are brought about by our awareness of good actions (the so-called "good conscience," a physiological condition that sometimes looks so similar to a good digestion that it might be confused with it). They are brought about by the successful outcome of our enterprises (naively false conclusion: the successful outcome of an enterprise does not at all create pleasant common feelings for a hypochondriac or a Pascal[11]). They are brought about by faith, love, hope—the Christian virtues.

In truth, all these supposed explanations are *subsequent* states and translations, so to speak, of feelings of pleasure or displeasure into a false dialect. One is in a state of hope *because* the basic physiological feeling is once again strong and rich; one trusts in God *because* the feeling of fullness and strength gives one calm. Morality and religion totally belong to the *psychology of error*: in every single case, cause and effect are confused, or truth is confused with the effect of what is *believed* to be true, or a state of consciousness is confused with the causation of this state.

7

Error of free will

Today we no longer have any sympathy for the concept of "free will." We know only too well what it is: the most disreputable of all the theologians' artifices, the aim of which is to make humanity "responsible" in the theologians' sense, that is, *to make it dependent on them.*—Here, I am simply offering the psychology of all making-responsible. Wherever responsibilities are sought, what tends to be doing the seeking is the instinct of *wanting to punish and rule.* One has stripped becoming of its innocence when some state of being-such-and-such is traced back to will, to intentions, to acts; the doctrine of the will was essentially invented for the purpose of punishment, that is, for

---

11. [In his *Pensées*, Blaise Pascal (1623–1662) stresses the fragility and wretchedness of human life.]

the purpose of *wanting to find people guilty*. All the old psychology, the psychology of will, has its precondition in the fact that its originators, the priests in the elites of old communities, wanted to create a *right* for themselves to inflict punishments—or wanted to create a right for God to do so. Human beings were thought to be "free" so that they could be ruled, so that they could be punished—so that they could become *guilty*.

Consequently, every action *had* to be thought as willed, the origin of every action *had* to be thought to lie in consciousness (and thus the *most fundamental* act of counterfeiting *in psychologicis* [in psychological matters] was itself made into the principle of psychology). Today, when we have initiated the *reverse* movement, when we immoralists seek with all our strength to get the concepts of guilt and punishment back out of the world, and to purge psychology, history, nature, social institutions, and sanctions of these concepts, there is in our eyes no opposition more radical than that of the theologians, who, with the concept of the "moral order of the world," go on infecting the innocence of becoming by means of "punishment" and "guilt." Christianity is a metaphysics of the hangman.

8

What is the only doctrine that can be *ours?*—That nobody *gives* human beings their qualities, neither God, nor society, nor their parents and ancestors, nor *they themselves* (the nonsense of the last notion we have rejected was taught by Kant as "intelligible freedom," and perhaps already taught by Plato as well). *Nobody* is responsible for the fact that we are here at all, that we are constituted in such and such a way, that we are in these circumstances, in this environment. The fatality of our essence is not to be resolved by the fatality of all that was and that will be. We are *not* the consequence of a special intention, a will, a goal; we are *not* being used in an attempt to reach an "ideal of humanity," or an "ideal of happiness," or an "ideal of morality"—it is absurd to want to *divert* our essence towards some goal. We have invented the concept "goal"; in reality, goals are *absent*.

One is necessary, one is a piece of fate, one belongs to the whole, one *is* in the whole. There is nothing that could rule, measure, compare, judge our being,

for that would mean ruling, measuring, comparing, and judging the whole—*but there is nothing outside the whole!*—That nobody is made responsible anymore, that no way of being may be traced back to a *causa prima* [first cause], that the world is not a unity either as sensorium or as "spirit," *this alone is the great liberation*—thus the *innocence* of becoming is restored.—The concept "God" was up to now the greatest *objection* against existence. We deny God, and in denying God we deny responsibility; only *thus* do we redeem the world.

What I Owe to the Ancients

1

In closing, a word about that world to which I have sought access, to which I have perhaps found a new access—the ancient world. My taste, which may be the opposite of a tolerant taste, is far, here too, from saying Yes to just anything; it does not like to say Yes at all, it prefers to say No, and what it likes best is to say nothing at all. . . . This applies to entire cultures, it applies to books—it also applies to places and landscapes.

Ultimately it is a very small number of ancient books that count in my life; the most famous are not among them. My feeling for style, for the epigram as a style, awoke almost instantly when I came into contact with Sallust. I have not forgotten the amazement of my honored teacher Corssen when he had to give the very first grade to the worst of his Latin students—I had finished in one blow. Concise, severe, founded on as much substance as possible, with a cold spite against the "beautiful word" and the "beautiful feeling"—I discovered myself in this. One will recognize in me, even in my *Zarathustra*, a very earnest ambition for the *Roman* style, for the "*aere perennius*"[12] in style.

It was no different upon my first contact with Horace. Even today I have never derived as much artistic delight from any poet as I got from the start from a

---

12. [More lasting than bronze. "I have erected a monument more lasting than bronze" (i.e. my poetry): Horace, *Odes* III, 30.]

Horatian Ode. In certain languages, what is attained here is not even *desirable*. This mosaic of words in which every word pours out its force as sound, as place, as concept to the right and to the left and over the whole, this minimum in the range and number of signs, this maximum in the energy of the signs which is thus achieved—all that is Roman, and, if one wishes to believe me, *noble par excellence*. All remaining verse is, as compared to this, somewhat too popular—just emotional verbosity.

2

To the Greeks I owe no impressions that are comparably strong. And, to come right out and say it, they *cannot* be for us what the Romans are. One does not *learn* from the Greeks—their way is too alien, and also too fluid, to have an imperative effect, a "classical" effect. Who would ever have learned to write from a Greek! Who would ever have learned it *without* the Romans!

Please do not bring up Plato as an objection to me. In relation to Plato I am fundamentally a skeptic, and was always incapable of joining in the admiration for Plato the *artist* which is traditional among scholars. In this case, I ultimately have on my side the most refined arbiters of taste among the ancients themselves. As it seems to me, Plato mixes all the stylistic forms together; thus he is one of the *first décadents* in style. He has something similar on his conscience to what the Cynics[13] had, who invented the *satura Menippea*.[14] In order for the Platonic dialogue, this repulsively self-satisfied and childish kind of dialectic, to exert its charm, one must never have read good French authors—for instance, Fontenelle.[15] Plato is boring. Ultimately, my mistrust in the case of Plato reaches into the depths; I find him so divergent from

all the fundamental instincts of the Hellenes, so over-moralized, such a Christian before his time—he already takes the concept "good" to be the highest concept—that in regards to the whole Plato phenomenon I would rather use the harsh expression "exalted swindle"—or if it sounds better, idealism—than any other. We have paid dearly for the fact that this Athenian went to school with the Egyptians (or with the Jews in Egypt? . . .). In the great disaster of Christianity, Plato is that ambiguity and fascination called the "ideal" which made it possible for the nobler natures of antiquity to misunderstand themselves and to step on the *bridge* that led to the "cross."—And how much Plato there still is in the concept "Church," in the structure, system, and practice of the Church!

My recreation, my predilection, my *cure* for all Platonism has always been *Thucydides*.[16] Thucydides and, perhaps, Machiavelli's[17] *Prince* are most closely related to me by their unconditional will to fabricate nothing and to see reason in *reality*—*not* in "reason," and still less in "morality." There is no cure more fundamental than Thucydides for the Greeks' miserable prettification of things into the ideal, a prettification which the "classically educated" youth brings with him into life as the reward for his school training. One must turn Thucydides over line by line and read his background thoughts as clearly as his words; there are few thinkers so rich in background thoughts. In him, the *culture of the sophists*, which means the *culture of the realists*, reaches its perfect expression—this invaluable movement in the midst of the Socratic schools' moralistic and idealistic swindle, which was then breaking out on every side. Greek philosophy as the *décadence* of Greek instinct; Thucydides as the great summation, the final appearance of that strong, strict, hard factuality that was a matter of instinct for the older Hellenes. *Courage* in the face of reality is, in the final analysis, the point of difference between natures such as Thucydides and Plato. Plato is a coward in the face of reality—*consequently* he flees into the ideal; Thucydides has control over *himself*—consequently he also has control over things.

---

13. [The Cynics were members of an Athenian philosophical school who, considering themselves followers of Socrates, maintained that virtue is self-sufficiency and the suppression of desires.]

14. [Menippus the Cynic originated this genre, which expresses philosophical views in a humorous way, mixing verse and prose.]

15. [Bernard le Bovier de Fontenelle (1657–1757) was a French writer who attacked supersitition and popularized developments in science.]

16. [Regarding Thucydides, see Hume's *Dialogues Concerning Natural Religion*, n. 34.]

17. [Niccolò Machiavelli (1469–1527) was an Italian author and statesman whose best-known work, *The Prince*, describes how a ruler gains and maintains power.]

3

Smelling out "beautiful souls" in the Greeks, "golden means" and other perfections, admiring in them, for instance, calm in grandeur, an ideal disposition, elevated simplicity—I was protected from this "elevated simplicity," which is in the end *niaiserie allemande* [German foolishness], by the psychologist in me. I saw their strongest instinct, the will to power; I saw them tremble before the boundless force of this drive; I saw all their institutions arise from rules of security, in order to make themselves safe in the face of each other's inner *explosives*. The immense internal tension then discharged itself in frightful and ruthless external hostility; the city-states ripped each other to shreds so that the citizens might, each of them, attain peace with themselves. It was necessary to be strong; danger was nearby—it lay in ambush everywhere. The wonderfully supple bodily character, the bold realism and immoralism that characterizes the Hellenes was a *necessity*, not their "nature." It was a consequence to begin with, it was not there from the start. And with their festivals and arts, they wanted nothing but to feel *superior*, to *show* that they were superior; these were means of glorifying themselves, and in certain circumstances, of making themselves frightening.

To judge the Greeks, in the German fashion, by their philosophers, to use, say, the simpleminded uprightness of the Socratic schools to elucidate *what* is essentially Hellenic—! After all, the philosophers are the *décadents* of the Greek world, the counter-movement against the old, noble taste (against the combative instinct, against the polis, against the value of the race, against the authority of tradition). The Socratic virtues were preached *because* the Greeks had lost them; excitable, fearful, inconstant comedians all of them, they had a couple of reasons too many to let morality be preached at them. Not that it was any help—but big words and attitudes suit *décadents* so well.

4

For the sake of understanding the older, the still rich and even overflowing Hellenic instinct, I was the first to take seriously that wonderful phenomenon that bears the name of Dionysus;[18] it is explainable only in terms of *too much* energy. Whoever investigated the Greeks—such as that deepest living connoisseur of their culture, Jacob Burckhardt of Basel[19]—knew right away that I had achieved something; Burckhardt included a special section on this phenomenon in his *Civilization of the Greeks*. If one wants to see the opposite, one should look at the almost amusing poverty of instinct of the German philologists when they come close to the Dionysian. The famous Lobeck,[20] in particular, who crept into this world of enigmas with the respectable self-assurance of a worm dried out between books, and convinced himself that being nauseatingly flippant and childish made him scientific—Lobeck made it known, sparing no expense on learned accoutrements, that there was really nothing to all these curiosities. Of course, the priests might have communicated to the participants in such orgies some things not devoid of value—for instance, that wine excites desire, that people can survive eating fruit under certain circumstances, that plants bloom in the spring and wither in the fall. As for the bewildering wealth of rites, symbols, and myths of orgiastic origin with which the ancient world was quite literally overgrown, Lobeck finds an opportunity here to increase his cleverness by another notch. "The Greeks," he says (*Aglaophamus* I, 672), "when they had nothing else to do, used to laugh, jump, and race around—or, since people sometimes have this desire too, they sat down, wept and wailed. *Others* then came along and sought some reason for this remarkable activity. And thus, as explanations of these customs, arose those countless sagas and myths. On the other hand, one believed that this *comical behavior* which now took place on festival days also necessarily belonged to the festivities, and took it to be an indispensable part of the worship."

That is despicable blather; one will not for a single moment take a Lobeck seriously. We are affected quite differently when we test the concept "Greek"

18. [Dionysus was the Greek god of fertility and wine who came to symbolize divine creativity.]
19. [Jacob Burckhardt (1818–1897) was a noted Swiss cultural historian.]
20. [Christian August Lobeck (1781–1860) was a German classical scholar.]

that Winckelmann[21] and Goethe[22] developed, and find it incompatible with that element out of which grows Dionysian art—the orgy. In fact, I have no doubt that Goethe would have excluded anything of the sort in principle from the possibilities of the Greek soul. *Consequently, Goethe did not understand the Greeks.* For only in the Dionysian mysteries, in the psychology of the Dionysian condition, does the *fundamental fact* of the Hellenic instinct express itself— its "will to life." *What* did the Hellene procure in these mysteries? *Eternal* life, the eternal recurrence of life; the future promised and made sacred in the past; the triumphant Yes to life beyond death and change; *true* life as collective survival through procreation, through the mysteries of sexuality. Thus, for the Greeks the *sexual* symbol was the ultimate revered symbol, the authentic, deep meaning in all ancient piety. Every element of the act of procreation, of pregnancy and birth, awoke the highest and most festive feelings. In the teachings of the mysteries, *pain* is declared holy; the "pangs of the childbearer" make pain in general holy—all becoming and growth, everything that vouches for the future *requires* pain. For there to be the eternal joy of creation, for the will to life to affirm itself eternally, there *must* also eternally be the "torment of the childbearer." . . . All this is signified by the name Dionysus; I know no higher symbolism than this *Greek* symbolism, the symbolism

21. [Johann Joachim Winckelmann (1717–1768) was a German classical archeologist, art critic, and historian of ancient art.]

22. [Johann Wolfgang von Goethe (1749–1832), poet, dramatist, novelist, and scientist, was an intellectual titan of the modern world.]

of the Dionysian rites. In them, the deepest instinct of life, the instinct for the future of life, for the eternity of life, is religiously experienced—the very way to life, procreation, as the *holy way*. It was Christianity, on the basis of its *ressentiment against* life, that first made something unclean out of sexuality; it threw *filth* on the beginning, on the precondition of our life.

5

The psychology of the orgy as an overflowing feeling of life and energy, within which even pain works as a stimulant, gave me the key to the concept of the *tragic* feeling, which was misunderstood as much by Aristotle as, especially, by our pessimists. Tragedy is so far from giving any evidence for the pessimism of the Hellenes in Schopenhauer's sense that it rather has to count as the decisive rejection of and *counterauthority* to such pessimism. Saying Yes to life even in its most strange and intractable problems, the will to life, celebrating its own inexhaustibility by *sacrificing* its highest types—*that* is what I called Dionysian, *that* is what I found as the bridge to the psychology of the *tragic* poet. *Not* in order to be released from terror and pity, not in order to purify oneself of a dangerous emotion through its vehement discharge— thus Aristotle understood it—but rather, beyond terror and pity, to *be* oneself the eternal joy of becoming, that joy that also includes in itself the *joy of destruction.* . . . And thus I touch again upon the spot from which I first set out—*The Birth of Tragedy* was my first revaluation of all values. Thus I take my stand again upon the ground from which grows my willing, my being *able*—I, the final follower of the philosopher Dionysus—I, the teacher of the eternal recurrence. . . .

Bertrand Russell

Bertrand Russell (1872–1970) was one of the leading thinkers of the twentieth century. He was born into a prominent English family and inherited the title of Earl Russell from his brother. John Stuart Mill was his godfather. Russell received degrees in mathematics and philosophy from Cambridge University in 1893–94, returning to Cambridge shortly afterwards. He took up the project of showing that mathematics could be derived from logic; to this end, he collaborated with Alfred North Whitehead on the development of modern symbolic logic, which was an achievement of signal importance. At Cambridge, Russell was also closely associated with G.E. Moore and Ludwig Wittgenstein, themselves major twentieth-century philosophers.

Russell did not confine his activities to the academy. He was on familiar terms with many of the leading intellectuals and writers of his day, including D.H. Lawrence, Joseph Conrad, Virginia Woolf, and T.S. Eliot (who wrote a poem about him). Russell spent the period from 1938 to 1944 in the United States, where his liberal views about marriage and religion aroused controversy. Russell was an important and courageous public figure, who was willing to go to jail for what he believed in. He was tried and convicted for an article he wrote in opposition to Britain's role in World War I, and at age 88 he was arrested for his role in civil disobedience to promote nuclear disarmament.

Russell's philosophy combined the resources of modern logic with a staunch commitment to empiricism (the view that all knowledge of the world is derived from sense experience). Thus, Russell did much to set the pattern for the way philosophy has been done in English-speaking countries, and as it is practiced today. His contributions were honored with the award of a Nobel Prize for Literature in 1950.

Some of Russell's most important philosophical works are *The Philosophy of Leibniz* (1900), *The Principles of Mathematics* (1903), *Principia Mathematica* with Whitehead (1910–13), *The Problems of Philosophy* (1912), *Introduction to Mathematical Philosophy* (1919), *The Analysis of Mind* (1921), *The Analysis of Matter* (1927), *An Inquiry Into Meaning and Truth* (1940), and *Human Knowledge, Its Scope and Limits* (1948).

The Problems of Philosophy is an introduction to some central questions about the nature of knowledge and reality. In this book Russell undertakes to set out what the issues are, outlining his own views simply and briefly. (He pursues these matters much more fully in his other writings.) Russell's starting point is the natural supposition that what is real are physical objects, and that we gain knowledge about these things by perceiving them. This outlook is not wrong, but it needs to be examined and spelled out with care. For example, depending on where we are, the shape of a coin may look oval to you and circular to me. So, strictly speaking, you and I are experiencing different things: your experience confronts you with something oval, while my experience confronts me with something circular. Since one and the same thing can't be both oval and circular, the items we experience must be different from one another, and different from the coin as well. Russell calls these items *sense-data*.

If experience informs us directly about our own sense-data, and not about physical objects, why should we suppose that there are any physical objects at all? Why not say that all there is, and all we know about, are our sense-data? A view like this one, which Russell calls "idealism," was adopted by Berkeley in the eighteenth century, and versions of idealism were prevalent in Britain when Russell came upon the philosophical scene. Russell presents some telling criticisms of the idealists' position. He also makes the positive point that our sense-data exhibit various patterns and regularities. A good explanation of the order in our sense-data is that they are caused by physical objects that exist independently of them. Russell's overthrow of idealism was a turning point in twentieth-century philosophy.

Although Russell maintains that we can have knowledge pertaining to physical objects as well as to sense-data, he distinguishes two different sorts of knowledge, namely *knowledge by acquaintance* and *knowledge by description*. The former is knowledge of *things*, the latter is knowledge of *truths*. All knowledge by description depends upon or is derived from knowledge by acquaintance. Russell holds that we may know sense-data by acquaintance, since we experience them directly, but we know physical objects only by description. The scope of our acquaintance not only determines what we can know, it also sets the limits of what we can say or think. Russell writes, "Every proposition which we can understand must be composed wholly of constituents with which we are acquainted."

For Russell, philosophy begins with our ordinary beliefs and tries to clear away vagueness and confusion. Whatever insight we achieve is obtained by thinking as closely, precisely, and rigorously as we can, making use of the resources of logic and science. This conception of philosophy is itself among Russell's most significant and lasting contributions.

• • •

An excellent introduction is A. J. Ayer, *Russell* (New York: Viking Press, 1972). At a more advanced level are A. J. Ayer, *Russell and Moore: The Analytical Heritage* (Cambridge, Mass.: Harvard University Press, 1971); David Pears, *Bertrand Russell and the British Tradition in Philosophy* (New York: Random House, 1967); R. M. Sainsbury, *Russell* (London: Routledge and Kegan Paul, 1979); and Peter Hylton, *Russell, Idealism, and the Emergence of Analytical Philosophy* (New York: Oxford University Press, 1990). An important contemporary critique of the theory of sense-data is J. L. Austin, *Sense and Sensibilia* (Oxford: Clarendon Press, 1962).

J.V.

The Problems of Philosophy

CHAPTER I

Appearance and Reality

Is there any knowledge in the world which is so certain that no reasonable man could doubt it? This question, which at first sight might not seem difficult, is really one of the most difficult that can be asked. When we have realized the obstacles in the way of a straightforward and confident answer, we shall be well launched on the study of philosophy—for philosophy is merely the attempt to answer such ultimate questions, not carelessly and dogmatically, as we do in ordinary life and even in the sciences, but critically, after exploring all that makes such questions puzzling, and after realizing all the vagueness and confusion that underlie our ordinary ideas.

In daily life, we assume as certain many things which, on a closer scrutiny, are found to be so full of apparent contradictions that only a great amount of thought enables us to know what it is that we really may believe. In the search for certainty, it is natural to begin with our present experiences, and in some sense, no doubt, knowledge is to be derived from them. But any statement as to what it is that our immediate experiences make us know is very likely to be wrong. It seems to me that I am now sitting in a chair, at a table of a certain shape, on which I see sheets of paper with writing or print. By turning my head I see out of the window buildings and clouds and the sun. I believe that the sun is about ninety-three million miles from the earth; that it is a hot globe many times bigger than the earth; that, owing to the earth's rotation, it rises every morning, and will continue to do so for an indefinite time in the future. I believe that, if any other normal person comes into my room, he will see the same chairs and tables and books and papers as I see, and that the table which I see is the same as the table which I feel pressing

Reprinted from *The Problems of Philosophy* by Bertrand Russell (1912) by permission of Oxford University Press.

against my arm. All this seems to be so evident as to be hardly worth stating, except in answer to a man who doubts whether I know anything. Yet all this may be reasonably doubted, and all of it requires much careful discussion before we can be sure that we have stated it in a form that is wholly true.

To make our difficulties plain, let us concentrate attention on the table. To the eye it is oblong, brown and shiny, to the touch it is smooth and cool and hard; when I tap it, it gives out a wooden sound. Any one else who sees and feels and hears the table will agree with this description, so that it might seem as if no difficulty would arise; but as soon as we try to be more precise our troubles begin. Although I believe that the table is 'really' of the same colour all over, the parts that reflect the light look much brighter than the other parts, and some parts look white because of reflected light. I know that, if I move, the parts that reflect the light will be different, so that the apparent distribution of colours on the table will change. It follows that if several people are looking at the table at the same moment, no two of them will see exactly the same distribution of colours, because no two can see it from exactly the same point of view, and any change in the point of view makes some change in the way the light is reflected.

For most practical purposes these differences are unimportant, but to the painter they are all-important: the painter has to unlearn the habit of thinking that things seem to have the colour which common sense says they 'really' have, and to learn the habit of seeing things as they appear. Here we have already the beginning of one of the distinctions that cause most trouble in philosophy—the distinction between 'appearance' and 'reality', between what things seem to be and what they are. The painter wants to know what things seem to be, the practical man and the philosopher want to know what they are; but the philosopher's wish to know this is stronger than the practical man's, and is more troubled by knowledge as to the difficulties of answering the question.

To return to the table. It is evident from what we

have found, that there is no colour which preeminently appears to be *the* colour of the table, or even of any one particular part of the table — it appears to be of different colours from different points of view, and there is no reason for regarding some of these as more really its colour than others. And we know that even from a given point of view the colour will seem different by artificial light, or to a colour-blind man, or to a man wearing blue spectacles, while in the dark there will be no colour at all, though to touch and hearing the table will be unchanged. This colour is not something which is inherent in the table, but something depending upon the table and the spectator and the way the light falls on the table. When, in ordinary life, we speak of *the* colour of the table, we only mean the sort of colour which it will seem to have to a normal spectator from an ordinary point of view under usual conditions of light. But the other colours which appear under other conditions have just as good a right to be considered real; and therefore, to avoid favouritism, we are compelled to deny that, in itself, the table has any one particular colour.

The same thing applies to the texture. With the naked eye one can see the grain, but otherwise the table looks smooth and even. If we looked at it through a microscope, we should see roughnesses and hills and valleys, and all sorts of differences that are imperceptible to the naked eye. Which of these is the 'real' table? We are naturally tempted to say that what we see through the microscope is more real, but that in turn would be changed by a still more powerful microscope. If, then, we cannot trust what we see with the naked eye, why should we trust what we see through a microscope? Thus, again, the confidence in our senses with which we began deserts us.

The *shape* of the table is no better. We are all in the habit of judging as to the 'real' shapes of things, and we do this so unreflectingly that we come to think we actually see the real shapes. But, in fact, as we all have to learn if we try to draw, a given thing looks different in shape from every different point of view. If our table is 'really' rectangular, it will look, from almost all points of view, as if it had two acute angles and two obtuse angles. If opposite sides are parallel, they will look as if they converged to a point away from the spectator; if they are of equal length, they will look as if the nearer side were longer. All these things are not commonly noticed in looking at a table, because experience has taught us to construct the 'real' shape from the apparent shape, and the 'real' shape is what interests us as practical men. But the 'real' shape is not what we see; it is something inferred from what we see. And what we see is constantly changing in shape as we move about the room; so that here again the senses seem not to give us the truth about the table itself, but only about the appearance of the table.

Similar difficulties arise when we consider the sense of touch. It is true that the table always gives us a sensation of hardness, and we feel that it resists pressure. But the sensation we obtain depends upon how hard we press the table and also upon what part of the body we press with; thus the various sensations due to various pressures or various parts of the body cannot be supposed to reveal *directly* any definite property of the table, but at most to be *signs* of some property which perhaps *causes* all the sensations, but is not actually apparent in any of them. And the same applies still more obviously to the sounds which can be elicited by rapping the table.

Thus it becomes evident that the real table, if there is one, is not the same as what we immediately experience by sight or touch or hearing. The real table, if there is one, is not *immediately* known to us at all, but must be an inference from what is immediately known. Hence, two very difficult questions at once arise; namely, (1) Is there a real table at all? (2) If so, what sort of object can it be?

It will help us in considering these questions to have a few simple terms of which the meaning is definite and clear. Let us give the name of 'sense-data' to the things that are immediately known in sensation: such things as colours, sounds, smells, hardnesses, roughnesses, and so on. We shall give the name 'sensation' to the experience of being immediately aware of these things. Thus, whenever we see a colour, we have a sensation *of* colour, but the colour itself is a sense-datum, not a sensation. The colour is that *of* which we are immediately aware, and the awareness itself is the sensation. It is plain that if we are to know anything about the table, it must be by means of the sense-data — brown colour, oblong shape, smoothness, etc. — which we associate with the table; but, for the reasons which have been given, we cannot say that the table *is* the sense-data, or even that the sense-data are directly properties of the table.

Thus a problem arises as to the relation of the sense-data to the real table, supposing there is such a thing.

The real table, if it exists, we will call a 'physical object'. Thus we have to consider the relation of sense-data to physical objects. The collection of all physical objects is called 'matter'. Thus our two questions may be re-stated as follows: (1) Is there any such thing as matter? (2) If so, what is its nature?

The philosopher who first brought prominently forward the reasons for regarding the immediate objects of our senses as not existing independently of us was Bishop Berkeley (1685–1753). His *Three Dialogues between Hylas and Philonous, in Opposition to Sceptics and Atheists*, undertake to prove that there is no such thing as matter at all, and that the world consists of nothing but minds and their ideas. Hylas has hitherto believed in matter, but he is no match for Philonous, who mercilessly drives him into contradictions and paradoxes, and makes his own denial of matter seem, in the end, as if it were almost common sense. The arguments employed are of very different value: some are important and sound, others are confused or quibbling. But Berkeley retains the merit of having shown that the existence of matter is capable of being denied without absurdity, and that if there are any things that exist independently of us they cannot be the immediate objects of our sensations.

There are two different questions involved when we ask whether matter exists, and it is important to keep them clear. We commonly mean by 'matter' something which is opposed to 'mind', something which we think of as occupying space and as radically incapable of any sort of thought or consciousness. It is chiefly in this sense that Berkeley denies matter; that is to say, he does not deny that the sense-data which we commonly take as signs of the existence of the table are really signs of the existence of *something* independent of us, but he does deny that this something is non-mental, that it is neither mind nor ideas entertained by some mind. He admits that there must be something which continues to exist when we go out of the room or shut our eyes, and that what we call seeing the table does really give us reason for believing in something which persists even when we are not seeing it. But he thinks that this something cannot be radically different in nature from what we see, and cannot be independent of seeing altogether,

though it must be independent of *our* seeing. He is thus led to regard the 'real' table as an idea in the mind of God. Such an idea has the required permanence and independence of ourselves, without being — as matter would otherwise be — something quite unknowable, in the sense that we can only infer it, and can never be directly and immediately aware of it.

Other philosophers since Berkeley have also held that, although the table does not depend for its existence upon being seen by me, it does depend upon being seen (or otherwise apprehended in sensation) by *some* mind — not necessarily the mind of God, but more often the whole collective mind of the universe. This they hold, as Berkeley does, chiefly because they think there can be nothing real — or at any rate nothing known to be real — except minds and their thoughts and feelings. We might state the argument by which they support their view in some such way as this: 'Whatever can be thought of is an idea in the mind of the person thinking of it; therefore nothing can be thought of except ideas in minds; therefore anything else is inconceivable, and what is inconceivable cannot exist.'

Such an argument, in my opinion, is fallacious; and of course those who advance it do not put it so shortly or so crudely. But whether valid or not, the argument has been very widely advanced in one form or another; and very many philosophers, perhaps a majority, have held that there is nothing real except minds and their ideas. Such philosophers are called 'idealists'. When they come to explaining matter, they either say, like Berkeley, that matter is really nothing but a collection of ideas, or they say, like Leibniz (1646–1716), that what appears as matter is really a collection of more or less rudimentary minds.

But these philosophers, though they deny matter as opposed to mind, nevertheless, in another sense, admit matter. It will be remembered that we asked two questions; namely, (1) Is there a real table at all? (2) If so, what sort of object can it be? Now both Berkeley and Leibniz admit that there is a real table, but Berkeley says it is certain ideas in the mind of God, and Leibniz says it is a colony of souls. Thus both of them answer our first question in the affirmative, and only diverge from the views of ordinary mortals in their answer to our second question. In fact, almost all philosophers seem to be agreed that there is a real table: they almost all agree that, however much our sense-data—colour, shape, smoothness, etc.—may depend upon us, yet their occurrence is a sign of something existing independently of us, something differing, perhaps, completely from our sense-data, and yet to be regarded as causing those sense-data whenever we are in a suitable relation to the real table.

Now obviously this point in which the philosophers are agreed—the view that there *is* a real table, whatever its nature may be—is vitally important, and it will be worth while to consider what reasons there are for accepting this view before we go on to the further question as to the nature of the real table. Our next chapter, therefore, will be concerned with the reasons for supposing that there is a real table at all.

Before we go farther it will be well to consider for a moment what it is that we have discovered so far. It has appeared that, if we take any common object of the sort that is supposed to be known by the senses, what the senses *immediately* tell us is not the truth about the object as it is apart from us, but only the truth about certain sense-data which, so far as we can see, depend upon the relations between us and the object. Thus what we directly see and feel is merely 'appearance', which we believe to be a sign of some 'reality' behind. But if the reality is not what appears, have we any means of knowing whether there is any reality at all? And if so, have we any means of finding out what it is like?

Such questions are bewildering, and it is difficult to know that even the strangest hypotheses may not be true. Thus our familiar table, which has roused but the slightest thoughts in us hitherto, has become a problem full of surprising possibilities. The one thing we know about it is that it is not what it seems. Beyond this modest result, so far, we have the most complete liberty of conjecture. Leibniz tells us it is a community of souls: Berkeley tells us it is an idea in the mind of God; sober science, scarcely less wonderful, tells us it is a vast collection of electric charges in violent motion.

Among these surprising possibilities, doubt suggests that perhaps there is no table at all. Philosophy, if it cannot *answer* so many questions as we could wish, has at least the power of *asking* questions which increase the interest of the world, and show the strangeness and wonder lying just below the surface even in the commonest things of daily life.

CHAPTER II
The Existence of Matter

IN this chapter we have to ask ourselves whether, in any sense at all, there is such a thing as matter. Is there a table which has a certain intrinsic nature, and continues to exist when I am not looking, or is the table merely a product of my imagination, a dream-table in a very prolonged dream? This question is of the greatest importance. For if we cannot be sure of the independent existence of the objects, we cannot be sure of the independent existence of other people's bodies, and therefore still less of other people's minds, since we have no grounds for believing in their minds except such as are derived from observing their bodies. Thus if we cannot be sure of the independent existence of objects, we shall be left alone in a desert—it may be that the whole outer world is nothing but a dream, and that we alone exist. This is an uncomfortable possibility; but although it cannot be strictly *proved* to be false, there is not the slightest reason to suppose that it is true. In this chapter we have to see why this is the case.

Before we embark upon doubtful matters, let us try to find some more or less fixed point from which to start. Although we are doubting the physical existence of the table, we are not doubting the existence of the sense-data which made us think there was a table; we are not doubting that, while we look, a certain colour and shape appear to us, and while we press, a certain sensation of hardness is experienced by us. All this, which is psychological, we are not calling in question. In fact, whatever else may be doubtful, some at least of our immediate experiences seem absolutely certain.

Descartes (1596–1650), the founder of modern philosophy, invented a method which may still be used with profit—the method of systematic doubt. He determined that he would believe nothing which he did not see quite clearly and distinctly to be true. Whatever he could bring himself to doubt, he would doubt, until he saw reason for not doubting it. By applying this method he gradually became convinced that the only existence of which he could be *quite* certain was his own. He imagined a deceitful demon, who presented unreal things to his senses in a perpetual phantasmagoria; it might be very improbable that such a demon existed, but still it was possible, and therefore doubt concerning things perceived by the senses was possible.

But doubt concerning his own existence was not possible, for if he did not exist, no demon could deceive him. If he doubted, he must exist; if he had any experiences whatever, he must exist. Thus, his own existence was an absolute certainty to him. 'I think, therefore I am,' he said (*Cogito, ergo sum*); and on the basis of this certainty he set to work to build up again the world of knowledge which his doubt had laid in ruins. By inventing the method of doubt, and by showing that subjective things are the most certain, Descartes performed a great service to philosophy, and one which makes him still useful to all students of the subject.

But some care is needed in using Descartes' argument. '*I* think, therefore *I* am' says rather more than is strictly certain. It might seem as though we were quite sure of being the same person to-day as we were yesterday, and this is no doubt true in some sense. But the real Self is as hard to arrive at as the real table, and does not seem to have that absolute, convincing certainty that belongs to particular experiences. When I look at my table and see a certain brown colour, what is quite certain at once is not '*I* am seeing a brown colour', but rather, 'a brown colour is being seen'. This of course involves something (or somebody) which (or who) sees the brown colour; but it does not of itself involve that more or less permanent person whom we call '*I*'. So far as immediate certainty goes, it might be that the something which sees the brown colour is quite momentary, and not the same as the something which has some different experience the next moment.

Thus it is our particular thoughts and feelings that have primitive certainty. And this applies to dreams and hallucinations as well as to normal perceptions: when we dream or see a ghost, we certainly do have the sensations we think we have, but for various reasons it is held that no physical object corresponds to these sensations. Thus the certainty of our knowledge of our own experiences does not have to be limited in any way to allow for exceptional cases. Here, therefore, we have, for what it is worth, a solid basis from which to begin our pursuit of knowledge.

The problem we have to consider is this: Granted that we are certain of our own sense-data, have we any reason for regarding them as signs of the existence of something else, which we can call the physical object? When we have enumerated all the sense-data which we should naturally regard as connected with the table, have we said all there is to say about the table, or is there still something else — something not a sense-datum, something which persists when we go out of the room? Common sense unhesitatingly answers that there is. What can be bought and sold and pushed about and have a cloth laid on it, and so on, cannot be a *mere* collection of sense-data. If the cloth completely hides the table, we shall derive no sense-data from the table, and therefore, if the table were merely sense-data, it would have ceased to exist, and the cloth would be suspended in empty air, resting, by a miracle, in the place where the table formerly was. This seems plainly absurd; but whoever wishes to become a philosopher must learn not to be frightened by absurdities.

One great reason why it is felt that we must secure a physical object in addition to the sense-data, is that we want the *same* object for different people. When ten people are sitting round a dinner-table, it seems preposterous to maintain that they are not seeing the same tablecloth, the same knives and forks and spoons and glasses. But the sense-data are private to each separate person; what is immediately present to the sight of one is not immediately present to the sight of another: they all see things from slightly different points of view, and therefore see them slightly differently. Thus, if there are to be public neutral objects, which can be in some sense known to many different people, there must be something over and above the private and particular sense-data which appear to various people. What reason, then, have we for believing that there are such public neutral objects?

The first answer that naturally occurs to one is that, although different people may see the table slightly differently, still they all see more or less similar things when they look at the table, and the variations in what they see follow the laws of perspective and reflection of light, so that it is easy to arrive at a permanent object underlying all the different people's sense-data. I bought my table from the former occupant of my room; I could not buy *his* sense-data, which died when he went away, but I could and did buy the confident expectation of more or less similar sense-data. Thus it is the fact that different people have similar sense-data, and that one person in a given place at different times has similar sense-data, which makes us suppose that over and above the sense-data there is a permanent public object which underlies or causes the sense-data of various people at various times.

Now in so far as the above considerations depend upon supposing that there are other people besides ourselves, they beg the very question at issue. Other people are represented to me by certain sense-data, such as the sight of them or the sound of their voices, and if I had no reason to believe that there were physical objects independent of my sense-data, I should have no reason to believe that other people exist except as part of my dream. Thus, when we are trying to show that there must be objects independent of our own sense-data, we cannot appeal to the testimony of other people, since this testimony itself consists of sense-data, and does not reveal other people's experiences unless our own sense-data are signs of things existing independently of us. We must therefore, if possible, find, in our own purely private experiences, characteristics which show, or tend to show, that there are in the world things other than ourselves and our private experiences.

In one sense it must be admitted that we can never *prove* the existence of things other than ourselves and our experiences. No logical absurdity results from the hypothesis that the world consists of myself and my thoughts and feelings and sensations, and that everything else is mere fancy. In dreams a very complicated world may seem to be present, and yet on waking we find it was a delusion; that is to say, we find that the sense-data in the dream do not appear to have corresponded with such physical objects as we should naturally infer from our sense-data. (It is true that, when the physical world is assumed, it is possible to find physical causes for the sense-data in dreams: a door banging, for instance, may cause us to dream of a naval engagement. But although, in this case, there is a physical *cause* for the sense-data, there is not a physical object *corresponding* to the sense-data in the way in which an actual naval battle would correspond.) There is no logical impossibility in the supposition that the whole of life is a dream, in which we ourselves create all the objects that come before us. But although this is not logically impossible, there is no reason whatever to suppose that it is true; and it is, in fact, a less simple hypothesis, viewed as a

means of accounting for the facts of our own life, than the common-sense hypothesis that there really are objects independent of us, whose action on us causes our sensations.

The way in which simplicity comes in from supposing that there really are physical objects is easily seen. If the cat appears at one moment in one part of the room, and at another in another part, it is natural to suppose that it has moved from the one to the other, passing over a series of intermediate positions. But if it is merely a set of sense-data, it cannot have ever been in any place where I did not see it; thus we shall have to suppose that it did not exist at all while I was not looking, but suddenly sprang into being in a new place. If the cat exists whether I see it or not, we can understand from our own experience how it gets hungry between one meal and the next; but if it does not exist when I am not seeing it, it seems odd that appetite should grow during non-existence as fast as during existence. And if the cat consists only of sense-data, it cannot be *hungry*, since no hunger but my own can be a sense-datum to me. Thus the behaviour of the sense-data which represent the cat to me, though it seems quite natural when regarded as an expression of hunger, becomes utterly inexplicable when regarded as mere movements and changes of patches of colour, which are as incapable of hunger as a triangle is of playing football.

But the difficulty in the case of the cat is nothing compared to the difficulty in the case of human beings. When human beings speak—that is, when we hear certain noises which we associate with ideas, and simultaneously see certain motions of lips and expressions of face—it is very difficult to suppose that what we hear is not the expression of a thought, as we know it would be if we emitted the same sounds. Of course similar things happen in dreams, where we are mistaken as to the existence of other people. But dreams are more or less suggested by what we call waking life, and are capable of being more or less accounted for on scientific principles if we assume that there really is a physical world. Thus every principle of simplicity urges us to adopt the natural view, that there really are objects other than ourselves and our sense-data which have an existence not dependent upon our perceiving them.

Of course it is not by argument that we originally come by our belief in an independent external world.

We find this belief ready in ourselves as soon as we being to reflect: it is what may be called an *instinctive* belief. We should never have been led to question this belief but for the fact that, at any rate in the case of sight, it seems as if the sense-datum itself were instinctively believed to be the independent object, whereas argument shows that the object cannot be identical with the sense-datum. This discovery, however—which is not at all paradoxical in the case of taste and smell and sound, and only slightly so in the case of touch—leaves undiminished our instinctive belief that there *are* objects *corresponding* to our sense-data. Since this belief does not lead to any difficulties, but on the contrary tends to simplify and systematize our account of our experiences, there seems no good reason for rejecting it. We may therefore admit—though with a slight doubt derived from dreams—that the external world does really exist, and is not wholly dependent for its existence upon our continuing to perceive it.

The argument which has led us to this conclusion is doubtless less strong than we could wish, but it is typical of many philosophical arguments, and it is therefore worth while to consider briefly its general character and validity. All knowledge, we find, must be built up upon our instinctive beliefs, and if these are rejected, nothing is left. But among our instinctive beliefs some are much stronger than others, while many have, by habit and association, become entangled with other beliefs, not really instinctive, but falsely supposed to be part of what is believed instinctively.

Philosophy should show us the hierarchy of our instinctive beliefs, beginning with those we hold most strongly, and presenting each as much isolated and as free from irrelevant additions as possible. It should take care to show that, in the form in which they are finally set forth, our instinctive beliefs do not clash, but form a harmonious system. There can never be any reason for rejecting one instinctive belief except that it clashes with others; thus, if they are found to harmonize, the whole system becomes worthy of acceptance.

It is of course *possible* that all or any of our beliefs may be mistaken, and therefore all ought to be held with at least some slight element of doubt. But we cannot have *reason* to reject a belief except on the ground of some other belief. Hence, by organizing our instinctive beliefs and their consequences, by considering which among them is most possible, if necessary, to modify or abandon, we can arrive, on the basis of accepting as our sole data what we instinctively believe, at an orderly systematic organization of our knowledge, in which, though the *possibility* of error remains, its likelihood is diminished by the interrelation of the parts and by the critical scrutiny which has preceded acquiescence.

This function, at least, philosophy can perform. Most philosophers, rightly or wrongly, believe that philosophy can do much more than this—that it can give us knowledge, not otherwise attainable, concerning the universe as a whole, and concerning the nature of ultimate reality. Whether this be the case or not, the more modest function we have spoken of can certainly be performed by philosophy, and certainly suffices, for those who have once begun to doubt the adequacy of common sense, to justify the arduous and difficult labours that philosophical problems involve.

CHAPTER III

The Nature of Matter

In the preceding chapter we agreed, though without being able to find demonstrative reasons, that it is rational to believe that our sense-data—for example, those which we regard as associated with my table—are really signs of the existence of something independent of us and our perceptions. That is to say, over and above the sensations of colour, hardness, noise, and so on, which make up the appearance of the table to me, I assume that there is something else, *of* which these things are appearances. The colour ceases to exist if I shut my eyes, the sensation of hardness ceases to exist if I remove my arm from contact with the table, the sound ceases to exist if I cease to rap the table with my knuckles. But I do not believe that when all these things cease the table ceases. On the contrary, I believe that it is because the table exists continuously that all these sense-data will reappear when I open my eyes, replace my arm, and begin again to rap with my knuckles. The question we have to consider in this chapter is: What is the nature of this real table, which persists independently of my perception of it?

To this question physical science gives an answer,

somewhat incomplete it is true, and in part still very hypothetical, but yet deserving of respect so far as it goes. Physical science, more or less unconsciously, has drifted into the view that all natural phenomena ought to be reduced to motions. Light and heat and sound are all due to wave-motions, which travel from the body emitting them to the person who sees light or feels heat or hears sound. That which has the wave-motion is either aether or 'gross matter', but in either case is what the philosopher would call matter. The only properties which science assigns to it are position in space, and the power of motion according to the laws of motion. Science does not deny that it *may* have other properties; but if so, such other properties are not useful to the man of science, and in no way assist him in explaining the phenomena.

It is sometimes said that 'light *is* a form of wave-motion', but this is misleading, for the light which we immediately see, which we know directly by means of our senses, is *not* a form of wave-motion, but something quite different—something which we all know if we are not blind, though we cannot describe it so as to convey our knowledge to a man who is blind. A wave-motion, on the contrary, could quite well be described to a blind man, since he can acquire a knowledge of space by the sense of touch; and he can experience a wave-motion by a sea voyage almost as well as we can. But this, which a blind man can understand, is not what we mean by *light*: we mean by *light* just that which a blind man can never understand, and which we can never describe to him.

Now this something, which all of us who are not blind know, is not, according to science, really to be found in the outer world: it is something caused by the action of certain waves upon the eyes and nerves and brain of the person who sees the light. When it is said that light *is* waves, what is really meant is that waves are the physical cause of our sensations of light. But light itself, the thing which seeing people experience and blind people do not, is not supposed by science to form any part of the world that is independent of us and our senses. And very similar remarks would apply to other kinds of sensations.

It is not only colours and sounds and so on that are absent from the scientific world of matter, but also *space* as we get it through sight or touch. It is essential to science that its matter should be in *a* space, but the space in which it is cannot be exactly the space we see or feel. To begin with, space as we see it is not the same as space as we get it by the sense of touch; it is only by experience in infancy that we learn how to touch things we see, or how to get a sight of things which we feel touching us. But the space of science is neutral as between touch and sight; thus it cannot be either the space of touch or the space of sight.

Again, different people see the same object as of different shapes, according to their point of view. A circular coin, for example, though we should always *judge* it to be circular, will *look* oval unless we are straight in front of it. When we judge that it *is* circular, we are judging that it has a real shape which is not its apparent shape, but belongs to it intrinsically apart from its appearance. But this real shape, which is what concerns science, must be in a real space, not the same as anybody's *apparent* space. The real space is public, the apparent space is private to the percipient. In different people's *private* spaces the same object seems to have different shapes; thus the real space, in which it has its real shape, must be different from the private spaces. The space of science, therefore, though *connected* with the spaces we see and feel, is not identical with them, and the manner of its connexion requires investigation.

We agreed provisionally that physical objects cannot be quite like our sense-data, but may be regarded as *causing* our sensations. These physical objects are in the space of science, which we may call 'physical' space. It is important to notice that, if our sensations are to be caused by physical objects, there must be a physical space containing these objects and our sense-organs and nerves and brain. We get a sensation of touch from an object when we are in contact with it; that is to say, when some part of our body occupies a place in physical space quite close to the space occupied by the object. We see an object (roughly speaking) when no opaque body is between the object and our eyes in physical space. Similarly, we only hear or smell or taste an object when we are sufficiently near to it, or when it touches the tongue, or has some suitable position in physical space relatively to our body. We cannot begin to state what different sensations we shall derive from a given object under different circumstances unless we regard the object and our body as both in one physical space, for it is mainly the relative positions of the object and our body that determine what sensations we shall derive from the object.

Now our sense-data are situated in our private spaces, either the space of sight or the space of touch or such vaguer spaces as other senses may give us. If, as science and common sense assume, there is one public all-embracing physical space in which physical objects are, the relative positions of physical objects in physical space must more or less correspond to the relative positions of sense-data in our private spaces. There is no difficulty in supposing this to be the case. If we see on a road one house nearer to us than another, our other senses will bear out the view that it is nearer; for example, it will be reached sooner if we walk along the road. Other people will agree that the house which looks nearer to us is nearer; the ordnance map will take the same view; and thus everything points to a spatial relation between the houses corresponding to the relation between the sense-data which we see when we look at the houses. Thus we may assume that there is a physical space in which physical objects have spatial relations corresponding to those which the corresponding sense-data have in our private spaces. It is this physical space which is dealt with in geometry and assumed in physics and astronomy.

Assuming that there is physical space, and that it does thus correspond to private spaces, what can be know about it? We can know *only* what is required in order to secure the correspondence. That is to say, we can know nothing of what it is like in itself, but we can know the sort of arrangement of physical objects which results from their spatial relations. We can know, for example, that the earth and moon and sun are in one straight line during an eclipse, though we cannot know what a physical straight line is in itself, as we know the look of a straight line in our visual space. Thus we come to know much more about the *relations* of distances in physical space than about the distances themselves; we may know that one distance is greater than another, or that it is along the same straight line as the other, but we cannot have that immediate acquaintance with physical distances that we have with distances in our private spaces, or with colours or sounds or other sense-data. We can know all those things about physical space which a man born blind might know through other people about the space of sight; but the kind of things which

a man born blind could never know about the space of sight we also cannot know about physical space. We can know the properties of the relations required to preserve the correspondence with sense-data, but we cannot know the nature of the terms between which the relations hold.

With regard to time, our *feeling* of duration or of the lapse of time is notoriously an unsafe guide as to the time that has elapsed by the clock. Times when we are bored or suffering pain pass slowly, times when we are agreeably occupied pass quickly, and times when we are sleeping pass almost as if they did not exist. Thus, in so far as time is constituted by duration, there is the same necessity for distinguishing a public and a private time as there was in the case of space. But in so far as time consists in an *order* of before and after, there is no need to make such a distinction; the time-order which events seem to have is, so far as we can see, the same as the time-order which they do have. At any rate no reason can be given for supposing that the two orders are not the same. The same is usually true of space: if a regiment of men are marching along a road, the *shape* of the regiment will look different from different points of view, but the men will appear arranged in the same *order* from all points of view. Hence we regard the *order* as true also in physical space, whereas the shape is only supposed to correspond to the physical space so far as is required for the preservation of the order.

In saying that the time-order which events *seem to have* is the same as the time-order which they *really have*, it is necessary to guard against a possible misunderstanding. It must not be supposed that the various states of different physical objects have the same time-order as the sense-data which constitute the perceptions of those objects. Considered as physical objects, the thunder and lightning are simultaneous; that is to say, the lightning is simultaneous with the disturbance of the air in the place where the disturbance begins, namely, where the lightning is. But the sense-datum which we call hearing the thunder does not take place until the disturbance of the air has travelled as far as to where we are. Similarly, it takes about eight minutes for the sun's light to reach us; thus, when we see the sun we are seeing the sun of eight minutes ago. So far as our sense-data afford evidence as to the physical sun they afford evidence as to the physical sun of eight minutes ago; if the physical sun had ceased to exist within the last eight minutes, that would make no difference to the sense-data which we call 'seeing the sun'. This affords a fresh illustration of the necessity of distinguishing between sense-data and physical objects.

What we have found as regards space is much the same as what we find in relation to the correspondence of the sense-data with their physical counterparts. If one object looks blue and another red, we may reasonably presume that there is some corresponding difference between the physical objects; if two objects both look blue, we may presume a corresponding similarity. But we cannot hope to be acquainted directly with the quality in the physical object which makes it look blue or red. Science tells us that this quality is a certain sort of wave-motion, and this sounds familiar, because we think of wave-motions in the space we see. But the wave-motions must really be in physical space, with which we have no direct acquaintance; thus the real wave-motions have not that familiarity which we might have supposed them to have. And what holds for colours is closely similar to what holds for other sense-data. Thus we find that, although the *relations* of physical objects have all sorts of knowable properties, derived from their correspondence with the relations of sense-data, the physical objects themselves remain unknown in their intrinsic nature, so far at least as can be discovered by means of the senses. The question remains whether there is any other method of discovering the intrinsic nature of physical objects.

The most natural, though not ultimately the most defensible, hypothesis to adopt in the first instance, at any rate as regards visual sense-data, would be that, though physical objects cannot, for the reasons we have been considering, be *exactly* like sense-data, yet they may be more or less like. According to this view, physical objects will, for example, really have colours, and we might, by good luck, see an object as of the colour it really is. The colour which an object seems to have at any given moment will in general be very similar, though not quite the same, from many different points of view; we might thus suppose the 'real' colour to be a sort of medium colour, intermediate between the various shades which appear from the different points of view.

Such a theory is perhaps not capable of being definitely refuted, but it can be shown to be ground-less. To begin with, it is plain that the colour we see depends only upon the nature of the light-waves that strike the eye, and is therefore modified by the medium intervening between us and the object, as well as by the manner in which light is reflected from the object in the direction of the eye. The intervening air alters colours unless it is perfectly clear, and any strong reflection will alter them completely. Thus the colour we see is a result of the ray as it reaches the eye, and not simply a property of the object from which the ray comes. Hence, also, provided certain waves reach the eye, we shall see a certain colour, whether the object from which the waves start has any colour or not. Thus it is quite gratuitous to suppose that physical objects have colours, and therefore there is no justification for making such a supposition. Exactly similar arguments will apply to other sense-data.

It remains to ask whether there are any general philosophical arguments enabling us to say that, if matter is real, it *must* be of such and such a nature. As explained above, very many philosophers, perhaps most, have held that whatever is real must be in some sense mental, or at any rate that whatever we can know anything about must be in some sense mental. Such philosophers are called 'idealists'. Idealists tell us that what appears as matter is really something mental; namely, either (as Leibniz held) more or less rudimentary minds, or (as Berkeley contended) ideas in the minds which, as we should commonly say, 'perceive' the matter. Thus idealists deny the existence of matter as something intrinsically different from mind, though they do not deny that our sense-data are signs of something which exists independently of our private sensations. In the following chapter we shall consider briefly the reasons—in my opinion fallacious—which idealists advance in favour of their theory.

CHAPTER IV
Idealism

THE word 'idealism' is used by different philosophers in somewhat different senses. We shall understand by it the doctrine that whatever exists, or at any rate whatever can be known to exist, must be in some sense mental. This doctrine, which is very widely held among philosophers, has several forms, and is advocated on several different grounds. The doctrine is so widely held, and so interesting in itself, that even the briefest survey of philosophy must give some account of it.

Those who are unaccustomed to philosophical speculation may be inclined to dismiss such a doctrine as obviously absurd. There is no doubt that common sense regards tables and chairs and the sun and moon and material objects generally as something radically different from minds and the contents of minds, and as having an existence which might continue if minds ceased. We think of matter as having existed long before there were any minds, and it is hard to think of it as a mere product of mental activity. But whether true or false, idealism is not to be dismissed as obviously absurd.

We have seen that, even if physical objects do have an independent existence, they must differ very widely from sense-data, and can only have a *correspondence* with sense-data, in the same sort of way in which a catalogue has a correspondence with the things catalogued. Hence common sense leaves us completely in the dark as to the true intrinsic nature of physical objects, and if there were good reason to regard them as mental, we could not legitimately reject this opinion merely because it strikes us as strange. The truth about physical objects *must* be strange. It *may* be unattainable, but if any philosopher believes that he has attained it, the fact that what he offers as the truth is strange ought not to be made a ground of objection to his opinion.

The grounds on which idealism is advocated are generally grounds derived from the theory of knowledge, that is to say, from a discussion of the conditions which things must satisfy in order that we may be able to know them. The first serious attempt to establish idealism on such grounds was that of Bishop Berkeley. He proved first, by arguments which were largely valid, that our sense-data cannot be supposed to have an existence independent of us, but must be, in part at least, 'in' the mind, in the sense that their existence would not continue if there were no seeing or hearing or touching or smelling or tasting. So far, his contention was almost certainly valid, even if some of his arguments were not so. But he went on to argue that sense-data were the only things of whose existence our perceptions could assure us, and that to be known

is to be 'in' a mind, and therefore to be mental. Hence he concluded that nothing can ever be known except what is in some mind, and that whatever is known without being in my mind must be in some other mind.

In order to understand his argument, it is necessary to understand his use of the word 'idea'. He gives the name 'idea' to anything which is *immediately* known, as, for example, sense-data are known. Thus a particular colour which we see is an idea; so is a voice which we hear, and so on. But the term is not wholly confined to sense-data. There will also be things remembered or imagined, for with such things also we have immediate acquaintance at the moment of remembering or imaging. All such immediate data he calls 'ideas'.

He then proceeds to consider common objects, such as a tree, for instance. He shows that all we know immediately when we 'perceive' the tree consists of ideas in his sense of the word, and he argues that there is not the slightest ground for supposing that there is anything real about the tree except what is perceived. Its being, he says, consists in being perceived: in the Latin of the schoolmen its *'esse'* is *'percipi'*. He fully admits that the tree must continue to exist even when we shut our eyes or when no human being is near it. But this continued existence, he says, is due to the fact that God continues to perceive it; the 'real' tree, which corresponds to what we call the physical object, consists of ideas in the mind of God, ideas more or less like those we have when we see the tree, but differing in the fact that they are permanent in God's mind so long as the tree continues to exist. All our perceptions, according to him, consist in a partial participation in God's perceptions, and it is because of this participation that different people see more or less the same tree. Thus apart from minds and their ideas there is nothing in the world, nor is it possible that anything else should ever be known, since whatever is known is necessarily an idea.

There are in this argument a good many fallacies which have been important in the history of philosophy, and which it will be as well to bring to light. In the first place, there is a confusion engendered by the use of the word 'idea'. We think of an idea as essentially something *in* somebody's mind, and thus when we are told a tree consists entirely of ideas, it is natural to suppose that, if so, the tree must be entirely in minds. But the notion of being 'in' the mind is ambiguous. We speak of bearing a person in mind, not meaning that the person is in our minds, but that a thought of him is in our minds. When a man says that some business he had to arrange went clean out of his mind, he does not mean to imply that the business itself was ever in his mind, but only that a thought of the business was formerly in his mind, but afterwards ceased to be in his mind. And so when Berkeley says that the tree must be in our minds if we can know it, all that he really has a right to say is that a thought of the tree must be in our minds. To argue that the tree itself must be in our minds is like arguing that a person whom we bear in mind is himself in our minds. This confusion may seem too gross to have been really committed by any competent philosopher, but various attendant circumstances rendered it possible. In order to see how it was possible, we must go more deeply into the question as to the nature of ideas.

Before taking up the general question of the nature of ideas, we must disentangle two entirely separate questions which arise concerning sense-data and physical objects. We saw that, for various reasons of detail, Berkeley was right in treating the sense-data which constitute our perception of the tree as more or less subjective, in the sense that they depend upon us as much as upon the tree, and would not exist if the tree were not being perceived. But this is an entirely different point from the one by which Berkeley seeks to prove that whatever can be immediately known *must* be in a mind. For this purpose arguments of detail as to the dependence of sense-data upon us are useless. It is necessary to prove, generally, that by being known, things are shown to be mental. This is what Berkeley believes himself to have done. It is this question, and not our previous question as to the difference between sense-data and the physical object, that must now concern us.

Taking the word 'idea' in Berkeley's sense, there are two quite distinct things to be considered whenever an idea is before the mind. There is on the one hand the thing of which we are aware — say the colour of my table — and on the other hand the actual awareness itself, the mental act of apprehending the thing. The mental act is undoubtedly mental, but is there any reason to suppose that the thing apprehended is

in any sense mental? Our previous arguments concerning the colour did not prove it to be mental; they only proved that its existence depends upon the relation of our sense organs to the physical object — in our case, the table. That is to say, they proved that a certain colour will exist, in a certain light, if a normal eye is placed at a certain point relatively to the table. They did not prove that the colour is in the mind of the percipient.

Berkeley's view, that obviously the colour *must* be in the mind, seems to depend for its plausibility upon confusing the thing apprehended with the act of apprehension. Either of these might be called an apprehension. Either of these might be called an 'idea'; probably either would have been called an idea by Berkeley. The act is undoubtedly in the mind; hence, when we are thinking of the act, we readily assent to the view that ideas must be in the mind. Then, forgetting that this was only true when ideas were taken as acts of apprehension, we transfer the proposition that 'ideas are in the mind' to ideas in the other sense, i.e. to the things apprehended by our acts of apprehension. Thus, by an unconscious equivocation, we arrive at the conclusion that whatever we can apprehend must be in our minds. This seems to be the true analysis of Berkeley's argument, and the ultimate fallacy upon which it rests.

This question of the distinction between act and object in our apprehending of things is vitally important, since our whole power of acquiring knowledge is bound up with it. The faculty of being acquainted with things other than itself is the main characteristic of a mind. Acquaintance with objects essentially consists in a relation between the mind and something other than the mind; it is this that constitutes the mind's power of knowing things. If we say that the things known must be in the mind, we are either unduly limiting the mind's power of knowing, or we are uttering a mere tautology. We are uttering a mere tautology if we mean by '*in* the mind' the same as by '*before* the mind', i.e. if we mean merely being apprehended by the mind. But if we mean this, we shall have to admit that what, *in this sense*, is in the mind, may nevertheless be not mental. Thus when we realize the nature of knowledge, Berkeley's argument is seen to be wrong in substance as well as in form, and his grounds for supposing that 'ideas' — i.e. the objects apprehended — must be mental, are found to have no validity whatever. Hence his grounds in favour of idealism may be dismissed. It remains to see whether there are any other grounds.

It is often said, as though it were a self-evident truism, that we cannot know that anything exists which we do not know. It is inferred that whatever can in any way be relevant to our experience must be at least capable of being known by us; whence it follows that if matter were essentially something with which we could not become acquainted, matter would be something which we could not know to exist, and which could have for us no importance whatever. It is generally also implied, for reasons which remain obscure, that what can have no importance for us cannot be real, and that therefore matter, if it is not composed of minds or of mental ideas, is impossible and a mere chimaera.

To go into this argument fully at our present stage would be impossible, since it raises points requiring a considerable preliminary discussion; but certain reasons for rejecting the argument may be noticed at once. To begin at the end: there is no reason why what cannot have any *practical* importance for us should not be real. It is true that, if *theoretical* importance is included, everything real is of *some* importance to us, since, as persons desirous of knowing the truth about the universe, we have some interest in everything that the universe contains. But if this sort of interest is included, it is not the case that matter has no importance for us, provided it exists, even if we cannot know that it exists. We can, obviously, suspect that it may exist, and wonder whether it does; hence it is connected with our desire for knowledge, and has the importance of either satisfying or thwarting this desire.

Again, it is by no means a truism, and is in fact false, that we cannot know that anything exists which we do not know. The word 'know' is here used in two different senses. (1) In its first use it is applicable to the sort of knowledge which is opposed to error, the sense in which what we know is *true*, the sense which applies to our beliefs and convictions, i.e. to what are called *judgments*. In this sense of the word we know *that* something is the case. This sort of knowledge may be described as knowledge of *truths*. (2) In the second use of the word 'know' above, the word applies to our knowledge of *things*, which we may call *acquaintance*. This is the sense in which we

know sense data. (The distinction involved is roughly that between *savoir* and *connaître* in French, or between *wissen* and *kennen* in German.)

Thus the statement which seemed like a truism becomes, when re-stated, the following: 'We can never truly judge that something with which we are not acquainted exists.' This is by no means a truism, but on the contrary a palpable falsehood. I have not the honour to be acquainted with the Emperor of China, but I truly judge that he exists. It may be said, of course, that I judge this because of other people's acquaintance with him. This, however, would be an irrelevant retort, since, if the principle were true, I could not know that any one else is acquainted with him. But further: there is no reason why I should not know of the existence of something with which *nobody* is acquainted. This point is important, and demands elucidation.

If I am acquainted with a thing which exists, my acquaintance gives me the knowledge that it exists. But it is not true that, conversely, whenever I can know that a thing of a certain sort exists, I or some one else must be acquainted with the thing. What happens, in cases where I have true judgement without acquaintance, is that the thing is known to me by *description*, and that, in virtue of some general principle, the existence of a thing answering to this description can be inferred from the existence of something with which I am acquainted. In order to understand this point fully, it will be well first to deal with the difference between knowledge by acquaintance and knowledge by description, and then to consider what knowledge of general principles, if any, has the same kind of certainty as our knowledge of the existence of our own experiences. These subjects will be dealt with in the following chapters.

Chapter V

Knowledge by Acquaintance and Knowledge by Description

In the preceding chapter we saw that there are two sorts of knowledge: knowledge of things, and knowledge of truths. In this chapter we shall be concerned exclusively with knowledge of things, of which in turn we shall have to distinguish two kinds. Knowledge of things, when it is of the kind we call knowledge by *acquaintance*, is essentially simpler than any knowledge of truths, and logically independent of knowledge of truths, though it would be rash to assume that human beings ever, in fact, have acquaintance with things without at the same time knowing some truth about them. Knowledge of things by *description*, on the contrary, always involves, as we shall find in the course of the present chapter, some knowledge of truths as its source and ground. But first of all we must make clear what we mean by 'acquaintance' and what we mean by 'description'.

We shall say that we have *acquaintance* with anything of which we are directly aware, without the intermediary of any process of inference or any knowledge of truths. Thus in the presence of my table I am acquainted with the sense-data that make up the appearance of my table — its colour, shape, hardness, smoothness, etc.; all these are things of which I am immediately conscious when I am seeing and touching my table. The particular shade of colour that I am seeing may have many things said about it — I may say that it is brown, that it is rather dark, and so on. But such statements, though they make me know truths *about* the colour, do not make me know the colour itself any better than I did before: so far as concerns knowledge of the colour itself, as opposed to knowledge of truths about it, I know the colour perfectly and completely when I see it, and no further knowledge of it itself is even theoretically possible. Thus the sense-data which make up the appearance of my table are things with which I have acquaintance, things immediately known to me just as they are.

My knowledge of the table as a physical object, on the contrary, is not direct knowledge. Such as it is, it is obtained through acquaintance with the sense-data that make up the appearance of the table. We have seen that it is possible, without absurdity, to doubt whether there is a table at all, whereas it is not possible to doubt the sense-data. My knowledge of the table is of the kind which we shall call 'knowledge by description'. The table is 'the physical object which causes such-and-such sense-data'. This *describes* the table by means of the sense-data. In order to know anything at all about the table, we must know truths connecting it with things with which we have acquaintance: we must know that 'such-and-such sense-data are caused by a physical object'. There is no

state of mind in which we are directly aware of the table; all our knowledge of the table is really knowledge of *truths*, and the actual thing which is the table is not, strictly speaking, known to us at all. We know a description, and we know that there is just one object to which this description applies, though the object itself is not directly known to us. In such a case, we say that our knowledge of the object is knowledge by description.

All our knowledge, both knowledge of things and knowledge of truths, rests upon acquaintance as its foundation. It is therefore important to consider what kinds of things there are with which we have acquaintance.

Sense-data, as we have already seen, are among the things with which we are acquainted; in fact, they supply the most obvious and striking example of knowledge by acquaintance. But if they were the sole example, our knowledge would be very much more restricted than it is. We should only know what is now present to our senses: we could not know anything about the past — not even that there was a past — nor could we know any truths about our sense-data, for all knowledge of truths, as we shall show, demands acquaintance with things which are of an essentially different character from sense-data, the things which are sometimes called 'abstract ideas', but which we shall call 'universals'. We have therefore to consider acquaintance with other things besides sense-data if we are to obtain any tolerably adequate analysis of our knowledge.

The first extension beyond sense-data to be considered is acquaintance by *memory*. It is obvious that we often remember what we have seen or heard or had otherwise present to our senses, and that in such cases we are still immediately aware of what we remember, in spite of the fact that it appears as past and not as present. This immediate knowledge by memory is the source of all our knowledge concerning the past: without it, there could be no knowledge of the past by inference, since we should never know that there was anything past to be inferred.

The next extension to be considered is acquaintance by *introspection*. We are not only aware of things, but we are often aware of being aware of them. When I see the sun, I am often aware of my seeing the sun; thus 'my seeing the sun' is an object with which I have acquaintance. When I desire food, I may be aware of my desire for food; thus 'my desiring food' is an object with which I am acquainted. Similarly we may be aware of our feeling pleasure or pain, and generally of the events which happen in our minds. This kind of acquaintance, which may be called self-consciousness, is the source of all our knowledge of mental things. It is obvious that it is only what goes on in our own minds that can be thus known immediately. What goes on in the minds of others is known to us through our perception of their bodies, that is, through the sense-data in us which are associated with their bodies. But for our acquaintance with the contents of our own minds, we should be unable to imagine the minds of others, and therefore we could never arrive at the knowledge that they have minds. It seems natural to suppose that self-consciousness is one of the things that distinguish men from animals: animals, we may suppose, though they have acquaintance with sense-data, never become aware of this acquaintance. I do not mean that they *doubt* whether they exist, but that they have never become conscious of the fact that they have sensations and feelings, nor therefore of the fact that they, the subjects of their sensations and feelings, exist.

We have spoken of acquaintance with the contents of our minds as *self*-consciousness, but it is not, of course, consciousness of our *self*: it is consciousness of particular thoughts and feelings. The question whether we are also acquainted with our bare selves, as opposed to particular thoughts and feelings, is a very difficult one, upon which it would be rash to speak positively. When we try to look into ourselves we always seem to come upon some particular thought or feeling, and not upon the 'I' which has the thought or feeling. Nevertheless there are some reasons for thinking that we are acquainted with the 'I', though the acquaintance is hard to disentangle from other things. To make clear what sort of reason there is, let us consider for a moment what our acquaintance with particular thoughts really involves.

When I am acquainted with 'my seeing the sun', it seems plain that I am acquainted with two different things in relation to each other. On the one hand there is the sense-datum which represents the sun to me, on the other hand there is that which sees this sense-datum. All acquaintance, such as my acquaintance with the sense-datum which represents the sun, seems obviously a relation between the person ac-

quainted and the object with which the person is acquainted. When a case of acquaintance is one with which I can be acquainted (as I am acquainted with my acquaintance with the sense-datum representing the sun), it is plain that the person acquainted is myself. Thus, when I am acquainted with my seeing the sun, the whole fact with which I am acquainted is 'Self-acquainted-with-sense-datum'.

Further, we know the truth 'I am acquainted with this sense-datum'. It is hard to see how we could know this truth, or even understand what is meant by it, unless we were acquainted with something which we call 'I'. It does not seem necessary to suppose that we are acquainted with a more or less permanent person, the same to-day as yesterday, but it does seem as though we must be acquainted with that thing, whatever its nature, which sees the sun and has acquaintance with sense-data. Thus, in some sense it would seem we must be acquainted with our Selves as opposed to our particular experiences. But the question is difficult, and complicated arguments can be adduced on either side. Hence, although acquaintance with ourselves seems *probably* to occur, it is not wise to assert that it undoubtedly does occur.

We may therefore sum up as follows what has been said concerning acquaintance with things that exist. We have acquaintance in sensation with the data of the outer senses, and in introspection with the data of what may be called the inner sense—thoughts, feelings, desires, etc.; we have acquaintance in memory with things which have been data either of the outer senses or of the inner sense. Further, it is probable, though not certain, that we have acquaintance with Self, as that which is aware of things or has desires towards things.

In addition to our acquaintance with particular existing things, we also have acquaintance with what we shall call *universals*, that is to say, general ideas, such as *whiteness, diversity, brotherhood,* and so on. Every complete sentence must contain at least one word which stands for a universal, since all verbs have a meaning which is universal. We shall return to universals later on, in Chapter IX; for the present, it is only necessary to guard against the supposition that whatever we can be acquainted with must be something particular and existent. Awareness of universals is called *conceiving*, and a universal of which we are aware is called a *concept*.

It will be seen that among the objects with which we are acquainted are not included physical objects (as opposed to sense-data), nor other people's minds. These things are known to us by what I call 'knowledge by description', which we must now consider.

By a 'description' I mean any phrase of the form 'a so-and-so' or 'the so-and-so'. A phrase of the form 'a so-and-so' I shall call an 'ambiguous' description; a phrase of the form 'the so-and-so' (in the singular) I shall call a 'definite' description. Thus 'a man' is an ambiguous description, and 'the man with the iron mask' is a definite description. There are various problems connected with ambiguous descriptions, but I pass them by, since they do not directly concern the matter we are discussing, which is the nature of our knowledge concerning objects in cases where we know that there is an object answering to a definite description, though we are not *acquainted* with any such object. This is a matter which is concerned exclusively with *definite* descriptions. I shall therefore, in the sequel, speak simply of 'descriptions' when I mean 'definite descriptions'. Thus a description will mean any phrase of the form 'the so-and-so' in the singular.

We shall say that an object is 'known by description' when we know that it is 'the so-and-so', i.e. when we know that there is one object, and no more, having a certain property; and it will generally be implied that we do not have knowledge of the same object by acquaintance. We know that the man with the iron mask existed, and many propositions are known about him; but we do not know who he was. We know that the candidate who gets the most votes will be elected, and in this case we are very likely also acquainted (in the only sense in which one can be acquainted with some one else) with the man who is, in fact, the candidate who will get most votes; but we do not know which of the candidates he is, i.e. we do not know any proposition of the form 'A is the candidate who will get most votes' where A is one of the candidates by name. We shall say that we have 'merely descriptive knowledge' of the so-and-so when, although we know that the so-and-so exists, and although we may possibly be acquainted with the object which is, in fact, the so-and-so, yet we do not know any proposition '*a* is the so-and-so', where *a* is something with which we are acquainted.

When we say 'the so-and-so exists', we mean that there is just one object which is the so-and-so. The proposition '*a* is the so-and-so' means that *a* has the property so-and-so, and nothing else has. 'Mr. A. is the Unionist candidate for this constituency' means 'Mr. A. is a Unionist candidate for this constituency, and no one else is'. 'The Unionist candidate for this constituency exists' means 'some one is a Unionist candidate for this constituency, and no one else is'. Thus, when we are acquainted with an object which is the so-and-so, we know that the so-and-so exists; but we may know that the so-and-so exists when we are not acquainted with any object which we know to be the so-and-so, and even when we are not acquainted with any object which, in fact, is the so-and-so.

Common words, even proper names, are usually really descriptions. That is to say, the thought in the mind of a person using a proper name correctly can generally only be expressed explicitly if we replace the proper name by a description. Moreover, the description required to express the thought will vary for different people, or for the same person at different times. The only thing constant (so long as the name is rightly used) is the object to which the name applies. But so long as this remains constant, the particular description involved usually makes no difference to the truth or falsehood of the proposition in which the name appears.

Let us take some illustrations. Suppose some statement made about Bismarck. Assuming that there is such a thing as direct acquaintance with oneself, Bismarck himself might have used his name directly to designate the particular person with whom he was acquainted. In this case, if he made a judgement about himself, he himself might be a constituent of the judgement. Here the proper name has the direct use which it always wishes to have, as simply standing for a certain object, and not for a description of the object. But if a person who knew Bismarck made a judgement about him, the case is different. What this person was acquainted with were certain sense-data which he connected (rightly, we will suppose) with Bismarck's body. His body, as a physical object, and still more his mind, were only known as the body and the mind connected with these sense-data. That is, they were known by description. It is, of course, very much a matter of chance which characteristics of a man's appearance will come into a friend's mind when he thinks of him; thus the description actually in the friend's mind is accidental. The essential point is that he knows that the various descriptions all apply to the same entity, in spite of not being acquainted with the entity in question.

When we, who did not know Bismarck, make a judgement about him, the description in our minds will probably be some more or less vague mass of historical knowledge—far more, in most cases, than is required to identify him. But, for the sake of illustration, let us assume that we think of him as 'the first Chancellor of the German Empire'. Here all the words are abstract except 'German'. The word 'German' will, again, have different meanings for different people. To some it will recall travels in Germany, to some the look of Germany on the map, and so on. But if we are to obtain a description which we know to be applicable, we shall be compelled, at some point, to bring in a reference to a particular with which we are acquainted. Such reference is involved in any mention of past, present, and future (as opposed to definite dates), or of here and there, or of what others have told us. Thus it would seem that, in some way or other, a description known to be applicable to a particular must involve some reference to a particular with which we are acquainted, if our knowledge about the thing described is not to be merely what follows *logically* from the description. For example, 'the most long-lived of men' is a description involving only universals, which must apply to some man, but we can make no judgements concerning this man which involve knowledge about him beyond what the description gives. If, however, we say, 'The first Chancellor of the German Empire was an astute diplomatist', we can only be assured of the truth of our judgement in virtue of something with which we are acquainted—usually a testimony heard or read. Apart from the information we convey to others, apart from the fact about the actual Bismarck, which gives importance to our judgement, the thought we really have contains the one or more particulars involved, and otherwise consists wholly of concepts.

All names of places—London, England, Europe, the Earth, the Solar System—similarly involve, when used, descriptions which start from some one or more particulars with which we are acquainted. I suspect that even the Universe, as considered by metaphysics, involves such a connexion with particulars. In logic, on the contrary, where we are concerned not merely with what does exist, but with whatever might or could exist or be, no reference to actual particulars is involved.

It would seem that, when we make a statement about something only known by description, we often *intend* to make our statement, not in the form involving the description, but about the actual thing described. That is to say, when we say anything about Bismarck, we should like, if we could, to make the judgement which Bismarck alone can make, namely, the judgment of which he himself is a constituent. In this we are necessarily defeated, since the actual Bismarck is unknown to us. But we know that there is an object B, called Bismarck, and that B was an astute diplomatist. We can thus *describe* the proposition we should like to affirm, namely, 'B was an astute diplomatist', where B is the object which was Bismarck. If we are describing Bismarck as 'the first Chancellor of the German Empire', the proposition we should like to affirm may be described as 'the proposition asserting, concerning the actual object which was the first Chancellor of the German Empire, that this object was an astute diplomatist'. What enables us to communicate in spite of the varying descriptions we employ is that we know there is a true proposition concerning the actual Bismarck, and that however we may vary the description (so long as the description is correct) the proposition described is still the same. This proposition , which is described and is known to be true, is what interests us; but we are not acquainted with the proposition itself, and do not know *it*, though we know it is true.

It will be seen that there are various stages in the removal from acquaintance with particulars: there is Bismarck to people who knew him; Bismarck to those who only know of him through history; the man with the iron mask; the longest-lived of men. These are progressively further removed from acquaintance with particulars; the first comes as near to acquaintance as is possible in regard to another person; in the second, we shall still be said to know 'who Bismarck was'; in the third, we do not know who was the man with the iron mask, though we can know many propositions about him which are not logically deducible from the fact that he wore an iron mask; in the fourth, finally, we know nothing beyond what is logically deducible from the definition of the man. There is a similar hierarchy in the region of universals. Many universals, like many particulars, are only known to us by description. But here, as in the case of particulars, knowledge concerning what is known by description is ultimately reducible to knowledge concerning what is known by acquaintance.

The fundamental principle in the analysis of propositions containing descriptions is this: *Every proposition which we can understand must be composed wholly of constituents with which we are acquainted.*

We shall not at this stage attempt to answer all the objections which may be urged against this fundamental principle. For the present, we shall merely point out that, in some way or other, it must be possible to meet these objections, for it is scarcely conceivable that we can make a judgement or entertain a supposition without knowing what it is that we are judging or supposing about. We must attach *some* meaning to the words we use, if we are to speak significantly and not utter mere noise; and the meaning we attach to our words must be something with which we are acquainted. Thus when, for example,

we make a statement about Julius Caesar, it is plain that Julius Caesar himself is not before our minds, since we are not acquainted with him. We have in mind some *description* of Julius Caesar: 'the man who was assassinated on the Ides of March', 'the founder of the Roman Empire', or, perhaps, merely 'the man whose name was *Julius Caesar*'. (In this last description, *Julius Caesar* is a noise or shape with which we are acquainted.) Thus our statement does not mean quite what it seems to mean, but means something involving, instead of Julius Caesar, some description of him which is composed wholly of particulars and universals with which we are acquainted.

The chief importance of knowledge by description is that it enables us to pass beyond the limits of our private experience. In spite of the fact that we can only know truths which are wholly composed of terms which we have experienced in acquaintance, we can yet have knowledge by description of things which we have never experienced. In view of the very narrow range of our immediate experience, this result is vital, and until it is understood, much of our knowledge must remain mysterious and therefore, doubtful.

Jean-Paul Sartre

Born in Paris in 1905, Jean-Paul Sartre spent a number of years after graduating from the École Normale Supérieure teaching in *lycées* (roughly equivalent to high schools). His study of phenomenology in Berlin in 1933–34 led to his early works, *Nausea, Transcendence of the Ego,* and his greatest work, *Being and Nothingness* (1943). His 1945 lecture, "The Humanism of Existentialism" (published in 1946), contributed to the worldwide vogue of existentialism in the fifties and sixties. Sartre also wrote novels and plays, including *No Exit, The Age of Reason, The Wall,* and *The Flies,* and he edited *Les Temps Modernes,* the most influential literary journal in France for many years. One of the greatest intellectuals in French history, he was mourned in the streets of Paris by tens of thousands of people when he died in 1980.

"The Humanism of Existentialism" was a popular lecture designed to answer critics and present a rough outline of Sartre's views. In response to charges that existentialism paints a dreary picture of human existence, Sartre claims that this philosophy is the most humanistic of all, for it starts out from a description of how things appear to us prior to reflection and theorizing, and it rejects the idea that there is any transcendent basis for values or truth to which humans must submit themselves. This is part of what it means to say that "subjectivity" is the starting point: we have no choice but to begin with a phenomenological account of how things present themselves to us in our ordinary experience.

Sartre defines existentialism as the view that, for humans, "existence precedes essence." This succinct formula is best understood by contrasting it with "essentialism," the view that, for any type of thing in the world, there is an essence (e.g., a Platonic Form) which determines in advance what things of that type are and what they ought to be. Sartre diagnoses essentialism by suggesting that such a view only makes sense if people assume that there is a Creator who has created things in the world in a way similar to that in which human artisans create tools. In other words, essentialism assumes that, just as the craftsperson has a concept of what a tool should be before he or she creates it, so God also has a plan for creation and has created things with particular ideas about what things should be. It would follow, then, that whatever exists is derived from, and should strive to be like, the essences that existed in the mind of God before creation.

Existentialism, in Sartre's definition, holds the exact opposite view. If "God is dead" (as Nietzsche claimed) and there are no transcendent Absolutes that determine what things are and ought to be, then for one type of entity at least, for humans, existence precedes essence. This means that humans first exist—they just show up one day; they are there, involved in the world and trying to accomplish something—and only afterward do they create their own identity (or essence) through what they do. If there is no essence or human nature given in advance, it follows that humans are self-creating beings: they make themselves in the course of living out their lives. In this sense, you *are* what you *do*—you fashion your own identity through the choices you make as an agent in the world. For example, if you generally run away whenever you are faced with a frightening situation, then you are making yourself into a coward. Being a coward is something you are choosing for yourself, though you are probably quite unaware that you are doing so. Since each of us creates a configuration of possibilities for ourselves in the choices we make in our lives, Sartre can say that we are nothing other than the "ensemble" of our actions over a lifetime.

If there is no pregiven human nature that determines in advance how we act, then we are free in the sense that we are the ultimate causes of our actions. To say that we are free is not to say that environmental and genetic factors have no influence on what we are and do. Sartre insists that, as living organisms in the causal order of the world, we are *en soi* or "in itself," as much a part of the causal order as a lectern or a cauliflower. But he holds that, as self-conscious—as *pour soi* or "for itself"—we can become aware of these causal factors and reflect on them, and through this reflection we can decide what these factors mean to us and interfere with their influence if we wish. In this respect, we always "surpass" or "transcend" our causal conditioning: we can step back from the causal context in which we find ourselves and redefine it through our choices. We are therefore fully responsible for everything we do.

On what basis do we make our choices? Sartre argues that there is no basis for choice. Ethical principles are always too general and broad to provide guidance in dealing with concrete moral dilemmas. Moreover, our ethical principles are just as much a matter of free choice as the actions themselves. If we turn to an advisor, we usually know in advance what they will say, so choosing an advisor is choosing the advice. Even our feelings can't be a guide, because as a rule we don't know how we really feel about things until after we have acted. In the end, making a choice comes down to just taking a leap in one direction rather than another. You just "invent" or "create," in the same way a painter might decide to splash a little red in the corner of a painting. There are no rules or directives that compel us to act in one way rather than another. We are alone, with neither excuses behind us nor justifications before us.

"The Humanism of Existentialism" tries to respond to charges that existentialism undermines ethics by leaving individuals with no basis for deliberation or choice in deciding how to act. Though Sartre's reasoning is not easy to follow here, he seems to be saying that, since phenomenology shows that the individual is only an instance of the human, with no morally relevant differences from other humans, one should see that, in making choices, one is always choosing for all humans. Sartre seems to be looking for something like Kant's "principle of universalizability" here. In choosing to act in a specific way, I commit myself to the position that all people should act, or are entitled to act, in the same way. This attempt to save ethics has been subjected to some powerful criticisms over the years, and the jury is still out on whether existentialism makes room for ethics.

● ● ●

A clear summary and criticism of Sartre is found in Richard Bernstein, *Praxis and Action* (Philadelphia: University of Pennsylvania Press, 1971). Good studies dealing with the topics of freedom and ethics are Thomas C. Anderson, *Sartre's Two Ethics: From Authenticity to Integral Humanity* (La Salle: Open Court, 1993); David Detmer, *Freedom as a Value: A Critique of the Ethical Theory of Jean-Paul Sartre* (La Salle: Open Court, 1988); and Thomas Busch, *The Power of Consciousness and the Force of Circumstances in Sartre's Philosophy* (Bloomington: Indiana University Press, 1990).

C.G.

The Humanism of Existentialism

I should like on this occasion to defend existentialism against some charges which have been brought against it.

First, it has been charged with inviting people to remain in a kind of desperate quietism because, since no solutions are possible, we should have to consider action in this world as quite impossible. We should then end up in a philosophy of contemplation; and since contemplation is a luxury, we come in the end to a bourgeois philosophy. The communists in particular have made these charges.

On the other hand, we have been charged with dwelling on human degradation, with pointing up everywhere the sordid, shady, and slimy, and neglecting the gracious and beautiful, the bright side of human nature; for example, according to Mlle. Mercier, a Catholic critic, with forgetting the smile of the child. Both sides charge us with having ignored human solidarity, with considering man as an isolated being. The communists say that the main reason for this is that we take pure subjectivity, the *Cartesian I think*, as our starting point, in other words, the moment in which man becomes fully aware of what it means to him to be an isolated being; as a result, we are unable to return to a state of solidarity with the men who are not ourselves, a state which we can never reach in the *cogito*.

From the Christian standpoint, we are charged with denying the reality and seriousness of human undertakings, since, if we reject God's commandments and the eternal verities, there no longer remains anything but pure caprice, with everyone permitted to do as he pleases and incapable, from his own point of view, of condemning the points of view and acts of others.

I shall try today to answer these different charges. Many people are going to be surprised at what is said here about humanism. We shall try to see in what

sense it is to be understood. In any case, what can be said from the very beginning is that by existentialism we mean a doctrine which makes human life possible and, in addition, declares that every truth and every action implies a human setting and a human subjectivity.

As is generally known, the basic charge against us is that we put the emphasis on the dark side of human life. Someone recently told me of a lady who, when she let slip a vulgar word in a moment of irritation, excused herself by saying, "I guess I'm becoming an existentialist." Consequently, existentialism is regarded as something ugly; that is why we are said to be naturalists; and if we are, it is rather surprising that in this day and age we cause so much more alarm and scandal than does naturalism, properly so called. The kind of person who can take in his stride such a novel as Zola's *The Earth*[1] is disgusted as soon as he starts reading an existentialist novel; the kind of person who is resigned to the wisdom of the ages— which is pretty sad—finds us even sadder. Yet, what can be more disillusioning than saying "true charity begins at home" or "a scoundrel will always return evil for good?"

We know the commonplace remarks made when this subject comes up, remarks which always add up to the same thing: we shouldn't struggle against the powers-that-be; we shouldn't resist authority; we shouldn't try to rise above our station; any action which doesn't conform to authority is romantic; any effort not based on past experience is doomed to failure; experience shows that man's bent is always toward trouble, that there must be a strong hand to hold him in check, if not, there will be anarchy. There are still people who go on mumbling these melancholy old saws, the people who say, "It's only human!" whenever a more or less repugnant act is pointed out to them, the people who glut themselves on *chansons réalistes*; these are the people who accuse

From *Existentialism and Human Emotion* by Jean-Paul Sartre, translated by Bernard Frechtman, © 1957 by Philosophical Library. Reprinted with permission.

1. [The reference is to the French novelist Émile Zola (1840–1902).—S.M.C.]

existentialism of being too gloomy; and to such an extent that I wonder whether they are complaining about it, not for its pessimism, but much rather its optimism. Can it be that what really scares them in the doctrine I shall try to present here is that it leaves to man a possibility of choice? To answer this question, we must re-examine it on a strictly philosophical plane. What is meant by the term *existentialism*?

Most people who use the word would be rather embarrassed if they had to explain it, since, now that the word is all the rage, even the work of a musician or painter is being called existentialist. A gossip columnist in *Clartés* signs himself *The Existentialist,* so that by this time the word has been so stretched and has taken on so broad a meaning, that it no longer means anything at all. It seems that for want of an advance-guard doctrine analogous to surrealism, the kind of people who are eager for scandal and flurry turn to this philosophy which in other respects does not at all serve their purposes in this sphere.

Actually, it is the least scandalous, the most austere of doctrines. It is intended strictly for specialists and philosophers. Yet it can be defined easily. What complicates matters is that there are two kinds of existentialist; first, those who are Christian, among whom I would include Jaspers[2] and Gabriel Marcel,[3] both Catholic; and on the other hand the atheistic existentialists, among whom I class Heidegger,[4] and then the French existentialists and myself. What they have in common is that they think that existence precedes essence, or, if you prefer, that subjectivity must be the starting point.

Just what does that mean? Let us consider some object that is manufactured, for example, a book or a paper-cutter: here is an object which has been made by an artisan whose inspiration came from a concept. He referred to the concept of what a paper-cutter is and likewise to a known method of production, which is part of the concept, something which is, by and large, a routine. Thus, the paper-cutter is at once an object produced in a certain way and, on the other hand, one having a specific use; and one cannot postulate a man who produces a paper-cutter but does not know what it is used for. Therefore, let us say that, for the paper-cutter, essence — that is, the ensemble of both the production routines and the properties which enable it to be both produced and defined — precedes existence. Thus, the presence of the paper-cutter or book in front of me is determined. Therefore, we have here a technical view of the world whereby it can be said that production precedes existence.

When we conceive God as the Creator, He is generally thought of as a superior sort of artisan. Whatever doctrine we may be considering, whether one like that of Descartes or that of Leibniz, we always grant that will more or less follows understanding or, at the very least, accompanies it, and that when God creates He knows exactly what He is creating. Thus, the concept of man in the mind of God is comparable to the concept of paper-cutter in the mind of the manufacturer, and, following certain techniques and a conception, God produces man, just as the artisan, following a definition and a technique, makes a paper-cutter. Thus, the individual man is the realization of a certain concept in the divine intelligence.

In the eighteenth century, the atheism of the *philosophes* discarded the idea of God, but not so much for the notion that essence precedes existence. To a certain extent, this idea is found everywhere; we find it in Diderot,[5] in Voltaire,[6] and even in Kant. Man has a human nature; this human nature, which is the concept of the human, is found in all men, which means that each man is a particular example of a universal concept, man. In Kant, the result of this universality is that the wild-man, the natural man, as well as the bourgeois, are circumscribed by the same definition and have the same basic qualities. Thus, here too the essence of man precedes the historical existence that we find in nature.

Atheistic existentialism, which I represent, is more coherent. It states that if God does not exist, there is at least one being in whom existence precedes essence, a being who exists before he can be defined by any

2. [The reference is to the German philosopher Karl Jaspers (1883–1969).]

3. [The reference is to the French philosopher and dramatist (1889–1973).]

4. [The reference is to the German philosopher Martin Heidegger (1889–1976).]

5. [The reference is to the French philosopher, playwright, and critic Denis Diderot (1713–1784).]

6. [The reference is to the influential French philosopher, historian, writer, and critic François Marie Arouet de Voltaire (1694–1778).]

concept, and that this being is man, or, as Heidegger says, human reality. What is meant here by saying that existence precedes essence? It means that, first of all, man exists, turns up, appears on the scene, and, only afterwards, defines himself. If man, as the existentialist conceives him, is indefinable, it is because at first he is nothing. Only afterward will he be something, and he himself will have made what he will be. Thus, there is no human nature, since there is no God to conceive it. Not only is man what he conceives himself to be, but he is also only what he wills himself to be after this thrust toward existence.

Man is nothing else but what he makes of himself. Such is the first principle of existentialism. It is also what is called subjectivity, the name we are labeled with when charges are brought against us. But what do we mean by this, if not that man has a greater dignity than a stone or table? For we mean that man first exists, that is, that man first of all is the being who hurls himself toward a future and who is conscious of imagining himself as being in the future. Man is at the start a plan which is aware of itself, rather than a patch of moss, a piece of garbage, or a cauliflower; nothing exists prior to this plan; there is nothing in heaven; man will be what he will have planned to be. Not what he will want to be. Because by the word "will" we generally mean a conscious decision, which is subsequent to what we have already made of ourselves. I may want to belong to a political party, write a book, get married; but all that is only a manifestation of an earlier, more spontaneous choice that is called "will." But if existence really does precede essence, man is responsible for what he is. Thus, existentialism's first move is to make every man aware of what he is and to make the full responsibility of his existence rest on him. And when we say that a man is responsible for himself, we do not only mean that he is responsible for his own individuality, but that he is responsible for all men.

The word subjectivism has two meanings, and our opponents play on the two. Subjectivism means, on the one hand, that an individual chooses and makes himself; and, on the other, that it is impossible for man to transcend human subjectivity. The second of these is the essential meaning of existentialism. When we say that man chooses his own self, we mean that every one of us does likewise; but we also mean by that that in making this choice he also chooses all

men. In fact, in creating the man that we want to be, there is not a single one of our acts which does not at the same time create an image of man as we think he ought to be. To choose to be this or that is to affirm at the same time the value of what we choose, because we can never choose evil. We always choose the good, and nothing can be good for us without being good for all.

If, on the other hand, existence precedes essence, and if we grant that we exist and fashion our image at one and the same time, the image is valid for everybody and for our whole age. Thus, our responsibility is much greater than we might have supposed, because it involves all mankind. If I am a workingman and choose to join a Christian trade-union rather than be a communist, and if by being a member I want to show that the best thing for man is resignation, that the kingdom of man is not of this world, I am not only involving my own case—I want to be resigned for everyone. As a result, my action has involved all humanity. To take a more individual matter, if I want to marry, to have children; even if this marriage depends solely on my own circumstances or passion or wish, I am involving all humanity in monogamy and not merely myself. Therefore, I am responsible for myself and for everyone else. I am creating a certain image of man of my own choosing. In choosing myself, I choose man.

This helps us understand what the actual content is of such rather grandiloquent words as anguish, forlornness, despair. As you will see, it's all quite simple.

First, what is meant by anguish? The existentialists say at once that man is anguish. What that means is this: the man who involves himself and who realizes that he is not only the person he chooses to be, but also a lawmaker who is, at the same time, choosing all mankind as well as himself, cannot help escape the feeling of his total and deep responsibility. Of course, there are many people who are not anxious; but we claim that they are hiding their anxiety, that they are fleeing from it. Certainly, many people believe that when they do something, they themselves are the only ones involved, and when someone says to them, "What if everyone acted that way?" they shrug their shoulders and answer, "Everyone doesn't act that way." But really, one should always ask himself, "What would happen if everybody looked at things that way?" There is no escaping this disturbing thought except by a kind of double-dealing. A man who lies and makes excuses for himself by saying "not everybody does that," is someone with an uneasy conscience, because the act of lying implies that a universal value is conferred upon the lie.

Anguish is evident even when it conceals itself. This is the anguish that Kierkegaard called the anguish of Abraham. You know the story: an angel has ordered Abraham to sacrifice his son; if it really were an angel who has come and said, "You are Abraham, you shall sacrifice your son," everything would be all right. But everyone might first wonder, "Is it really an angel, and am I really Abraham? What proof do I have?"

There was a madwoman who had hallucinations; someone used to speak to her on the telephone and give her orders. Her doctor asked her, "Who is it who talks to you?" She answered, "He says it's God." What proof did she really have that it was God? If an angel comes to me, what proof is there that it's an angel? And if I hear voices, what proof is there that they come from heaven and not from hell, or from the subconscious, or a pathological condition? What proves that they are addressed to me? What proof is there that I have been appointed to impose my choice and my conception of man on humanity? I'll never find any proof or sign to convince me of that. If a voice addresses me, it is always for me to decide that this is the angel's voice; if I consider that such an act is a good one, it is I who will choose to say that it is good rather than bad.

Now, I'm not being singled out as an Abraham, and yet at every moment I'm obliged to perform exemplary acts. For every man, everything happens as if all mankind had its eyes fixed on him and were guiding itself by what he does. And every man ought to say to himself, "Am I really the kind of man who has the right to act in such a way that humanity might guide itself by my actions?" And if he does not say that to himself, he is masking his anguish.

There is no question here of the kind of anguish which would lead to quietism, to inaction. It is a matter of a simple sort of anguish that anybody who has had responsibilities is familiar with. For example, when a military officer takes the responsibility for an attack and sends a certain number of men to death, he chooses to do so, and in the main he alone makes the choice. Doubtless, orders come from above, but they are too broad; he interprets them, and on this interpretation depend the lives of ten or fourteen or twenty men. In making a decision he cannot help having a certain anguish. All leaders know this anguish. That doesn't keep them from acting; on the contrary, it is the very condition of their action. For it implies that they envisage a number of possibilities, and when they choose one, they realize that it has value only because it is chosen. We shall see that this kind of anguish, which is the kind that existentialism describes, is explained, in addition, by a direct responsibility to the other men whom it involves. It is not a curtain separating us from action, but is part of action itself.

When we speak of forlornness, a term Heidegger was fond of, we mean only that God does not exist and that we have to face all the consequences of this. The existentialist is strongly opposed to a certain kind of secular ethics which would like to abolish God with the least possible expense. About 1880, some French teachers tried to set up a secular ethics which went something like this: God is a useless and costly hypothesis; we are discarding it; but, meanwhile, in order for there to be an ethics, a society, a civilization, it is essential that certain values be taken seriously and that they be considered as having an a priori existence. It must be obligatory, a priori, to be honest, not to lie, not to beat your wife, to have children, etc., etc. So we're going to try a little device which will make it possible to show that values exist all the same, inscribed in a heaven of ideas, though otherwise God does not exist. In other words—and this, I believe, is the tendency of everything called reformism in France—nothing will be changed if God does not exist. We shall find ourselves with the same norms of honesty, progress, and humanism, and we shall have made of God an outdated hypothesis which will peacefully die off by itself.

The existentialist, on the contrary, thinks it very distressing that God does not exist, because all possibility of finding values in a heaven of ideas disappears along with Him; there can no longer be an a priori Good, since there is no infinite and perfect consciousness to think it. Nowhere is it written that the Good exists, that we must be honest, that we must not lie; because the fact is we are on a plane where there are only men. Dostoyevsky said, "If God didn't exist, everything would be possible." That is the very starting point of existentialism. Indeed, everything is permissible if God does not exist, and as a result man is forlorn, because neither within him nor without does he find anything to cling to. He can't start making excuses for himself.

If existence really does precede essence, there is no explaining things away by reference to a fixed and given human nature. In other words, there is no determinism, man is free, man is freedom. On the other hand, if God does not exist, we find no values or commands to turn to which legitimize our conduct. So, in the bright realm of values, we have no excuse behind us, nor justification before us. We are alone, with no excuses.

That is the idea I shall try to convey when I say that man is condemned to be free. Condemned, because he did not create himself, yet, in other respects is free; because, once thrown into the world, he is responsible for everything he does. The existentialist does not believe in the power of passion. He will never agree that a sweeping passion is a ravaging torrent which fatally leads a man to certain acts and is therefore an excuse. He thinks that man is responsible for his passion.

The existentialist does not think that man is going to help himself by finding in the world some omen by which to orient himself. Because he thinks that man will interpret the omen to suit himself. Therefore, he thinks that man, with no support and no aid, is condemned every moment to invent man. Ponge,[7] in a very fine article, has said, "Man is the future of man." That's exactly it. But if it is taken to mean that this future is recorded in heaven, that God sees it, then it is false, because it would really no longer be a future. If it is taken to mean that, whatever a man may be, there is a future to be forged, a virgin future before him, then this remark is sound. But then we are forlorn.

To give you an example which will enable you to understand forlornness better, I shall cite the case of one of my students who came to see me under the following circumstances: his father was on bad terms with his mother, and, moreover, was inclined to be a collaborationist; his older brother had been killed

in the German offensive of 1940, and the young man, with somewhat immature but generous feelings, wanted to avenge him. His mother lived alone with him, very much upset by the half-treason of her husband and the death of her older son; the boy was her only consolation.

The boy was faced with the choice of leaving for England and joining the Free French Forces—that is, leaving his mother behind—or remaining with his mother and helping her to carry on. He was fully aware that the woman lived only for him and that his going-off—perhaps his death—would plunge her into despair. He was also aware that every act that he did for his mother's sake was a sure thing, in the sense that it was helping her to carry on, whereas every effort he made toward going off and fighting was an uncertain move which might run aground and prove completely useless; for example, on his way to England he might, while passing through Spain, be detained indefinitely in a Spanish camp; he might reach England or Algiers and be stuck in an office at a desk job. As a result, he was faced with two very different kinds of action: one, concrete, immediate, but concerning only one individual; the other concerned an incomparably vaster group, a national collectivity, but for that very reason was dubious, and might be interrupted en route. And, at the same time, he was wavering between two kinds of ethics. On the one hand, an ethics of sympathy, of personal devotion; on the other, a broader ethics, but one whose efficacy was more dubious. He had to choose between the two.

Who could help him choose? Christian doctrine? No. Christian doctrine says, "Be charitable, love your neighbor, take the more rugged path, etc., etc." But which is the more rugged path? Whom should he love as a brother? The fighting man or his mother? Which does the greater good, the vague act of fighting in a group, or the concrete one of helping a particular human being to go on living? Who can decide a priori? Nobody. No book of ethics can tell him. The Kantian ethics says, "Never treat any person as a means, but as an end." Very well, if I stay with my mother, I'll treat her as an end and not as a means; but by virtue of this very fact, I'm running the risk of treating the people around me who are fighting, as means; and, conversely, if I go to join those who are fighting, I'll be treating them as an end, and, by doing that, I run the risk of treating my mother as a means.

7. [The reference is to the French essayist and poet Francis Ponge (1899–1988).]

If values are vague, and if they are always too broad for the concrete and specific case that we are considering, the only thing left for us is to trust our instincts. That's what this young man tried to do; and when I saw him, he said, "In the end, feeling is what counts. I ought to choose whichever pushes me in one direction. If I feel that I love my mother enough to sacrifice everything else for her—my desire for vengeance, for action, for adventure—then I'll stay with her. If, on the contrary, I feel that my love for my mother isn't enough, I'll leave."

But how is the value of a feeling determined? What gives his feeling for his mother value? Precisely the fact that he remained with her. I may say that I like so-and-so well enough to sacrifice a certain amount of money for him, but I may say so only if I've done it. I may say "I love my mother well enough to remain with her" if I have remained with her. The only way to determine the value of this affection is, precisely, to perform an act which confirms and defines it. But, since I require this affection to justify my act, I find myself caught in a vicious circle.

On the other hand, Gide[8] has well said that a mock feeling and a true feeling are almost indistinguishable; to decide that I love my mother and will remain with her, or to remain with her by putting on an act, amount somewhat to the same thing. In other words, the feeling is formed by the acts one performs; so, I cannot refer to it in order to act upon it. Which means that I can neither seek within myself the true condition which will impel me to act, nor apply to a system of ethics for concepts which will permit me to act. You will say, "At least, he did go to a teacher for advice." But if you seek advice from a priest, for example, you have chosen this priest; you already knew, more or less, just about what advice he was going to give you. In other words, choosing your adviser is involving yourself. The proof of this is that if you are a Christian, you will say, "Consult a priest." But some priests are collaborating, some are just marking time, some are resisting. Which to choose? If the young man chooses a priest who is resisting or collaborating, he has already decided on the kind of advice he's going to get. Therefore, in coming to see me he knew the answer I was going to give him, and

I had only one answer to give: "You're free, choose, that is, invent." No general ethics can show you what is to be done; there are no omens in the world. The Catholics will reply, "But there are." Granted—but, in any case, I myself choose the meaning they have.

When I was a prisoner, I knew a rather remarkable young man who was a Jesuit. He had entered the Jesuit order in the following way: he had had a number of very bad breaks; in childhood, his father died, leaving him in poverty, and he was a scholarship student at a religious institution where he was constantly made to feel that he was being kept out of charity; then, he failed to get any of the honors and distinctions that children like; later on, at about eighteen, he bungled a love affair; finally, at twenty-two, he failed in military training, a childish enough matter, but it was the last straw.

This young fellow might well have felt that he had botched everything. It was a sign of something, but of what? He might have taken refuge in bitterness or despair. But he very wisely looked upon all this as a sign that he was not made for secular triumphs, and that only the triumphs of religion, holiness, and faith were open to him. He saw the hand of God in all this, and so he entered the order. Who can help seeing that he alone decided what the sign meant?

Some other interpretation might have been drawn from this series of setbacks; for example, that he might have done better to turn carpenter or revolutionist. Therefore, he is fully responsible for the interpretation. Forlornness implies that we ourselves choose our being. Forlornness and anguish go together.

As for despair, the term has a very simple meaning. It means that we shall confine ourselves to reckoning only with what depends upon our will, or on the ensemble of probabilities which make our action possible. When we want something, we always have to reckon with probabilities. I may be counting on the arrival of a friend. The friend is coming by rail or streetcar; this supposes that the train will arrive on schedule, or that the street-car will not jump the track. I am left in the realm of possibility; but possibilities are to be reckoned with only to the point where my action comports with the ensemble of these possibilities, and no further. The moment the possibilities I am considering are not rigorously involved by my action, I ought to disengage myself from them, because no God, no scheme, can adapt the world and

8. [The reference is to the French writer André Gide (1869–1951).]

its possibilities to my will. When Descartes said, "Conquer yourself rather than the world," he meant essentially the same thing.

The Marxists to whom I have spoken reply, "You can rely on the support of others in your action, which obviously has certain limits because you're not going to live forever. That means: rely on both what others are doing elsewhere to help you, in China, in Russia, and what they will do later on, after your death, to carry on the action and lead it to its fulfillment, which will be the revolution. You even *have* to rely upon that, otherwise you're immoral." I reply at once that I will always rely on fellow-fighters insofar as these comrades are involved with me in a common struggle, in the unity of a party or a group in which I can more or less make my weight felt; that is, one whose ranks I am in as a fighter and whose movements I am aware of at every moment. In such a situation, relying on the unity and will of the party is exactly like counting on the fact that the train will arrive on time or that the car won't jump the track. But, given that man is free and that there is no human nature for me to depend on, I cannot count on men whom I do not know by relying on human goodness or man's concern for the good of society. I don't know what will become of the Russian revolution; I may make an example of it to the extent that at the present time it is apparent that the proletariat plays a part in Russia that it plays in no other nation. But I can't swear that this will inevitably lead to a triumph of the proletariat. I've got to limit myself to what I see.

Given that men are free and that tomorrow they will freely decide what man will be, I cannot be sure that, after my death, fellow-fighters will carry on my work to bring it to its maximum perfection. Tomorrow, after my death, some men may decide to set up Fascism, and the others may be cowardly and muddled enough to let them do it. Fascism will then be the human reality, so much the worse for us.

Actually, things will be as man will have decided they are to be. Does that mean that I should abandon myself to quietism? No. First, I should involve myself; then, act on the old saw, "Nothing ventured, nothing gained." Nor does it mean that I shouldn't belong to a party, but rather that I shall have no illusions and shall do what I can. For example, suppose I ask myself, "Will socialization, as such, ever come about?" I know nothing about it. All I know is that I'm going to do everything in my power to bring it about. Beyond that, I can't count on anything. Quietism is the attitude of people who say, "Let others do what I can't do." The doctrine I am presenting is the very opposite of quietism, since it declares, "There is no reality except in action." Moreover, it goes further, since it adds, "Man is nothing else than his plan; he exists only to the extent that he fulfills himself; he is therefore nothing else than the ensemble of his acts, nothing else than his life."

According to this, we can understand why our doctrine horrifies certain people. Because often the only way they can bear their wretchedness is to think, "Circumstances have been against me. What I've been and done doesn't show my true worth. To be sure, I've had no great love, no great friendship, but that's because I haven't met a man or woman who was worthy. The books I've written haven't been very good because I haven't had the proper leisure. I haven't had children to devote myself to because I didn't find a man with whom I could have spent my life. So there remains within me, unused and quite viable, a host of propensities, inclinations, possibilities, that one wouldn't guess from the mere series of things I've done."

Now, for the existentialist there is really no love other than one which manifests itself in a person's being in love. There is no genius other than one which is expressed in works of art; the genius of Proust[9] is the sum of Proust's works; the genius of Racine[10] is his series of tragedies. Outside of that, there is nothing. Why say that Racine could have written another tragedy, when he didn't write it? A man is involved in life, leaves his impress on it, and outside of that there is nothing. To be sure, this may seem a harsh thought to someone whose life hasn't been a success. But, on the other hand, it prompts people to understand that reality alone is what counts, that dreams, expectations, and hopes warrant no more than to define a man as a disappointed dream, as miscarried hopes, as vain expectations. In other words, to define him negatively and not positively. However,

9. [The reference is to the French novelist Marcel Proust (1871–1922), a leading figure in twentieth-century literature.]

10. [The reference is to the French dramatist Jean Racine (1639–1699).]

when we say, "You are nothing else than your life," that does not imply that the artist will be judged solely on the basis of his works of art; a thousand other things will contribute toward summing him up. What we mean is that a man is nothing else than a series of undertakings, that he is the sum, the organization, the ensemble of the relationships which make up these undertakings.

When all is said and done, what we are accused of, at bottom, is not our pessimism, but an optimistic toughness. If people throw up to us our works of fiction in which we write about people who are soft, weak, cowardly, and sometimes even downright bad, it's not because these people are soft, weak, cowardly, or bad; because if we were to say, as Zola did, that they are that way because of heredity, the workings of environment, society, because of biological or psychological determinism, people would be reassured. They would say, "Well, that's what we're like, no one can do anything about it." But when the existentialist writes about a coward, he says that this coward is responsible for his cowardice. He's not like that because he has a cowardly heart or lung or brain; he's not like that on account of his physiological make-up; but he's like that because he has made himself a coward by his acts. There's no such thing as a cowardly constitution; there are nervous constitutions; there is poor blood, as the common people say, or strong constitutions. But the man whose blood is poor is not a coward on that account, for what makes cowardice is the act of renouncing or yielding. A constitution is not an act; the coward is defined on the basis of the acts he performs. People feel, in a vague sort of way, that this coward we're talking about is guilty of being a coward, and the thought frightens them. What people would like is that a coward or a hero be born that way.

One of the complaints most frequently made about *The Ways of Freedom*[11] can be summed up as follows: "After all, these people are so spineless, how are you going to make heroes out of them?" This objection almost makes me laugh, for it assumes that people are born heroes. That's what people really want to think. If you're born cowardly, you may set your mind

perfectly at rest; there's nothing you can do about it; you'll be cowardly all your life, whatever you may do. If you're born a hero, you may set your mind just as much at rest; you'll be a hero all your life; you'll drink like a hero and eat like a hero. What the existentialist says is that the coward makes himself cowardly, that the hero makes himself heroic. There's always a possibility for the coward not to be cowardly any more and for the hero to stop being heroic. What counts is total involvement; some one particular action or set of circumstances is not total involvement.

Thus, I think we have answered a number of the charges concerning existentialism. You see that it cannot be taken for a philosophy of quietism, since it defines man in terms of action; nor for a pessimistic description of man—there is no doctrine more optimistic, since man's destiny is within himself; nor for an attempt to discourage man from acting, since it tells him that the only hope is in his acting and that action is the only thing that enables a man to live. Consequently, we are dealing here with an ethics of action and involvement.

Nevertheless, on the basis of a few notions like these, we are still charged with immuring man in his private subjectivity. There again we're very much misunderstood. Subjectivity of the individual is indeed our point of departure, and this for strictly philosophic reasons. Not because we are bourgeois, but because we want a doctrine based on truth and not a lot of fine theories, full of hope but with no real basis. There can be no other truth to take off from than this: *I think; therefore, I exist*. There we have the absolute truth of consciousness becoming aware of itself. Every theory which takes man out of the moment in which he becomes aware of himself is, at its very beginning, a theory which confounds truth, for outside the Cartesian *cogito*, all views are only probable, and a doctrine of probability which is not bound to a truth dissolves into thin air. In order to describe the probable, you must have a firm hold on the true. Therefore, before there can be any truth whatsoever, there must be an absolute truth; and this one is simple and easily arrived at; it's on everyone's doorstep; it's a matter of grasping it directly.

Secondly, this theory is the only one which gives man dignity, the only one which does not reduce him to an object. The effect of all materialism is to treat all men, including the one philosophizing, as

11. [The reference is to Sartre's trilogy of novels, *The Age of Reason, The Reprieve*, and the subsequently published *Troubled Sleep*.]

objects, that is, as an ensemble of determined reactions in no way distinguished from the ensemble of qualities and phenomena which constitute a table or a chair or a stone. We definitely wish to establish the human realm as an ensemble of values distinct from the material realm. But the subjectivity that we have thus arrived at, and which we have claimed to be truth, is not a strictly individual subjectivity, for we have demonstrated that one discovers in the *cogito* not only himself, but others as well.

The philosophies of Descartes and Kant to the contrary, through the *I think* we reach our own self in the presence of others, and the others are just as real to us as our own self. Thus, the man who becomes aware of himself through the *cogito* also perceives all others, and he perceives them as the condition of his own existence. He realizes that he cannot be anything (in the sense that we say that someone is witty or nasty or jealous) unless others recognize it as such. In order to get any truth about myself, I must have contact with another person. The other is indispensable to my own existence, as well as my knowledge about myself. This being so, in discovering my inner being I discover the other person at the same time, like a freedom placed in front of me which thinks and wills only for or against me. Hence, let us at once announce the discovery of a world which we shall call intersubjectivity; this is the world in which man decides what he is and what others are.

Besides, if it is impossible to find in every man some universal essence which would be human nature, yet there does exist a universal human condition. It's not by chance that today's thinkers speak more readily of man's condition than of his nature. By condition they mean, more or less definitely, the a priori limits which outline man's fundamental situation in the universe. Historical situations vary; a man may be born a slave in a pagan society or a feudal lord or a proletarian. What does not vary is the necessity for him to exist in the world, to be at work there, to be there in the midst of other people, and to be mortal there. The limits are neither subjective nor objective, or, rather, they have an objective and a subjective side. Objective because they are to be found everywhere and are recognizable everywhere; subjective because they are *lived* and are nothing if man does not live them, that is, freely determine his existence with reference to them. And though the configurations may differ, at

least none of them are completely strange to me, because they all appear as attempts either to pass beyond these limits or recede from them or deny them or adapt to them. Consequently, every configuration, however individual it may be, has a universal value.

Every configuration, even the Chinese, the Indian, or the Negro, can be understood by a Westerner. "Can be understood" means that by virtue of a situation that he can imagine, a European of 1945 can, in like manner, push himself to his limits and reconstitute within himself the configuration of the Chinese, the Indian, or the African. Every configuration has universality in the sense that every configuration can be understood by every man. This does not at all mean that this configuration defines man forever, but that it can be met with again. There is always a way to understand the idiot, the child, the savage, the foreigner, provided one has the necessary information.

In this sense we may say that there is a universality of man; but it is not given, it is perpetually being made. I build the universal in choosing myself; I build it in understanding the configuration of every other man, whatever age he might have lived in. This absoluteness of choice does not do away with the relativeness of each epoch. At heart, what existentialism shows is the connection between the absolute character of free involvement, by virtue of which every man realizes himself in realizing a type of mankind, an involvement always comprehensible in any age whatsoever and by any person whosoever, and the relativeness of the cultural ensemble which may result from such a choice; it must be stressed that the relativity of Cartesianism and the absolute character of Cartesian involvement go together. In this sense, you may, if you like, say that each of us performs an absolute act in breathing, eating, sleeping, or behaving in any way whatever. There is no difference between being free, like a configuration, like an existence which chooses its essence, and being absolute. There is no difference between being an absolute temporarily localized, that is, localized in history, and being universally comprehensible.

This does not entirely settle the objection to subjectivism. In fact, the objection still takes several forms. First, there is the following: we are told, "So you're able to do anything, no matter what!" This is expressed in various ways. First we are accused of anarchy; then they say, "You're unable to pass judgment on others, because there's no reason to prefer one configuration to another"; finally they tell us, "Everything is arbitrary in this choosing of yours. You take something from one pocket and pretend you're putting it into the other."

These three objections aren't very serious. Take the first objection. "You're able to do anything, no matter what" is not to the point. In one sense choice is possible, but what is not possible is not to choose. I can always choose, but I ought to know that if I do not choose, I am still choosing. Though this may seem purely formal, it is highly important for keeping fantasy and caprice within bounds. If it is true that in facing a situation, for example, one in which, as a person capable of having sexual relations, of having children, I am obliged to choose an attitude, and if I in any way assume responsibility for a choice which, in involving myself, also involves all mankind, this has nothing to do with caprice, even if no a priori value determines my choice.

If anybody thinks that he recognizes here Gide's theory of the arbitrary act, he fails to see the enormous difference between this doctrine and Gide's. Gide does not know what a situation is. He acts out of pure caprice. For us, on the contrary, man is in an organized situation in which he himself is involved. Through his choice, he involves all mankind, and he cannot avoid making a choice; either he will remain chaste, or he will marry without having children, or he will marry and have children; anyhow, whatever he may do, it is impossible for him not to take full responsibility for the way he handles this problem. Doubtless, he chooses without referring to preestablished values, but it is unfair to accuse him of caprice. Instead, let us say that moral choice is to be compared to the making of a work of art. And before going any further, let it be said at once that we are not dealing here with an aesthetic ethics, because our opponents are so dishonest that they even accuse us of that. The example I've chosen is a comparison only.

Having said that, may I ask whether anyone has ever accused an artist who has painted a picture of not having drawn his inspiration from rules set up a priori? Has anyone ever asked, "What painting ought he to make?" It is clearly understood that there is no definite painting to be made, that the artist is engaged in the making of his painting, and that the painting to be made is precisely the painting he will have made. It is clearly understood that there are no a priori aesthetic values, but that there are values which appear subsequently in the coherence of the painting, in the correspondence between what the artist intended and the result. Nobody can tell what the painting of tomorrow will be like. Painting can be judged only after it has once been made. What connection does that have with ethics? We are in the same creative situation. We never say that a work of art is arbitrary. When we speak of a canvas of Picasso[12] we never say that it is arbitrary; we understand quite well that he was making himself what he is at the very time he was painting, that the ensemble of his work is embodied in his life.

The same holds on the ethical plane. What art and ethics have in common is that we have creation and invention in both cases. We cannot decide a priori what there is to be done. I think that I pointed that out quite sufficiently when I mentioned the case of the student who came to see me, and who might have applied to all the ethical systems, Kantian or otherwise, without getting any sort of guidance. He was obliged to devise his law himself. Never let it be said by us that this man—who, taking affection, individual action, and kind-heartedness toward a specific person as his ethical first principle, chooses to remain with his mother, or who, preferring to make a sacrifice, chooses to go to England—has made an arbitrary choice. Man makes himself. He isn't ready made at the start. In choosing his ethics, he makes himself, and force of circumstances is such that he cannot abstain from choosing one. We define man only in relationship to involvement. It is therefore absurd to charge us with arbitrariness of choice.

In the second place, it is said that we are unable to pass judgment on others. In a way this is true, and in another way, false. It is true in this sense, that, whenever a man sanely and sincerely involves himself and chooses his configuration, it is impossible for him to prefer another configuration, regardless of what his own may be in other respects. It is true in this sense, that we do not believe in progress. Progress is betterment. Man is always the same. The situation confronting him varies. Choice always remains a

12. [The reference is to the renowned Spanish artist Pablo Picasso (1881–1973).]

choice in a situation. The problem has not changed since the time one could choose between those for and those against slavery, for example, at the time of the Civil War, and the present time, when one can side with the Maquis Resistance Party, or with the Communists.

But, nevertheless, one can still pass judgment, for, as I have said, one makes a choice in relationship to others. First, one can judge (and this is perhaps not a judgment of value, but a logical judgment) that certain choices are based on error and others on truth. If we have defined man's situation as a free choice, with no excuses and no recourse, every man who takes refuge behind the excuse of his passions, every man who sets up a determinism, is a dishonest man.

The objection may be raised, "But why mayn't he choose himself dishonestly?" I reply that I am not obliged to pass moral judgment on him, but that I do define his dishonesty as an error. One cannot help considering the truth of the matter. Dishonesty is obviously a falsehood because it belies the complete freedom of involvement. On the same grounds, I maintain that there is also dishonesty if I choose to state that certain values exist prior to me; it is self-contradictory for me to want them and at the same state that they are imposed on me. Suppose someone says to me, "What if I want to be dishonest?" I'll answer, "There's no reason for you not to be, but I'm saying that that's what you are, and that the strictly coherent attitude is that of honesty."

Besides, I can bring moral judgment to bear. When I declare that freedom in every concrete circumstance can have no other aim than to want itself, if man has once become aware that in his forlornness he imposes values, he can no longer want but one thing, and that is freedom, as the basis of all values. That doesn't mean that he wants it in the abstract. It means simply that the ultimate meaning of the acts of honest men is the quest for freedom as such. A man who belongs to a communist or revolutionary union wants concrete goals; these goals imply an abstract desire for freedom; but this freedom is wanted in something concrete. We want freedom for freedom's sake and in every particular circumstance. And in wanting freedom we discover that it depends entirely on the freedom of others, and that the freedom of others depends on ours. Of course, freedom as the definition of man does not depend on others, but as soon as there is

involvement, I am obliged to want others to have freedom at the same time that I want my own freedom. I can take freedom as my goal only if I take that of others as a goal as well. Consequently, when, in all honesty, I've recognized that man is a being in whom existence precedes essence, that he is a free being who, in various circumstances, can want only his freedom, I have at the same time recognized that I can want only the freedom of others.

Therefore, in the name of this will for freedom, which freedom itself implies, I may pass judgment on those who seek to hide from themselves the complete arbitrariness and the complete freedom of their existence. Those who hide their complete freedom from themselves out of a spirit of seriousness or by means of deterministic excuses, I shall call cowards; those who try to show that their existence was necessary, when it is the very contingency of man's appearance on earth, I shall call stinkers. But cowards or stinkers can be judged only from a strictly unbiased point of view.

Therefore though the content of ethics is variable, a certain form of it is universal. Kant says that freedom desires both itself and the freedom of others. Granted. But he believes that the formal and the universal are enough to constitute an ethics. We, on the other hand, think that principles which are too abstract run aground in trying to decide action. Once again, take the case of the student. In the name of what, in the name of what great moral maxim do you think he could have decided, in perfect peace of mind, to abandon his mother or to stay with her? There is no way of judging. The content is always concrete and thereby unforeseeable; there is always the element of invention. The one thing that counts is knowing whether the inventing that has been done, has been done in the name of freedom.

For example, let us look at the following two cases. You will see to what extent they correspond, yet differ. Take *The Mill on the Floss.*[13] We find a certain young girl, Maggie Tulliver, who is an embodiment of the value of passion and who is aware of it. She is in love with a young man, Stephen, who is engaged to an

13. [The reference is to a novel by the remarkable Englishwoman, born Mary Ann Evans (1819–1880), who, writing under the pseudonym George Eliot, became one of the nineteenth century's leading literary figures.]

insignificant young girl. This Maggie Tulliver, instead of heedlessly preferring her own happiness, chooses, in the name of human solidarity, to sacrifice herself and give up the man she loves. On the other hand, Sanseverina, in *The Charterhouse of Parma*,[14] believing that passion is man's true value, would say that a great love deserves sacrifices; that it is to be preferred to the banality of the conjugal love that would tie Stephen to the young ninny he had to marry. She would choose to sacrifice the girl and fulfill her happiness; and, as Stendahl shows, she is even ready to sacrifice herself for the sake of passion, if this life demands it. Here we are in the presence of two strictly opposed moralities. I claim that they are much the same thing; in both cases what has been set up as the goal is freedom.

You can imagine two highly similar attitudes: one girl prefers to renounce her love out of resignation; another prefers to disregard the prior attachment of the man she loves out of sexual desire. On the surface these two actions resemble those we've just described. However, they are completely different. Sanseverina's attitude is much nearer that of Maggie Tulliver, one of heedless rapacity.

Thus, you see that the second charge is true and, at the same time, false. One may choose anything if it is on the grounds of free involvement.

The third objection is the following: "You take something from one pocket and put it into the other. That is, fundamentally, values aren't serious, since you choose them." My answer to this is that I'm quite vexed that that's the way it is; but if I've discarded God the Father, there has to be someone to invent values. You've got to take things as they are. Moreover, to say that we invent values means nothing else but this: life has no meaning a priori. Before you come alive, life is nothing; it's up to you to give it a meaning, and value is nothing else but the meaning that you choose. In that way, you see, there is a possibility of creating a human community.

I've been reproached for asking whether existentialism is humanistic. It's been said, "But you said in *Nausea* that the humanists were all wrong. You made fun of a certain kind of humanist. Why come back

to it now?" Actually, the word humanism has two very different meanings. By humanism one can mean a theory which takes man as an end and as a higher value. Humanism in this sense can be found in Cocteau's tale *Around the World in Eighty Hours*[15] when a character, because he is flying over some mountains in an airplane, declares, "Man is simply amazing." That means that I, who did not build the airplanes, shall personally benefit from these particular inventions, and that I, as man, shall personally consider myself responsible for, and honored by, acts of a few particular men. This would imply that we ascribe a value to man on the basis of the highest deeds of certain men. This humanism is absurd, because only the dog or the horse would be able to make such an over-all judgment about man, which they are careful not to do, at least to my knowledge.

But it cannot be granted that a man may make a judgment about man. Existentialism spares him from any such judgment. The existentialist will never consider man as an end because he is always in the making. Nor should we believe that there is a mankind to which we might set up a cult in the manner of Auguste Comte.[16] The cult of mankind ends in the self-enclosed humanism of Comte, and, let it be said, of fascism. This kind of humanism we can do without.

But there is another meaning of humanism. Fundamentally it is this: man is constantly outside of himself; in projecting himself, in losing himself outside of himself, he makes for man's existing; and, on the other hand, it is by pursuing transcendent goals that he is able to exist; man, being this state of passing-beyond, and seizing upon things only as they bear upon this passing-beyond, is at the heart, at the center of this passing-beyond. There is no universe other than a human universe, the universe of human subjectivity. This connection between transcendency, as a constituent element of man—not in the sense that God is transcendent, but in the sense of passing beyond—and subjectivity, in the sense that man is

14. [The reference is to the influential novel by the French author Marie Henri Beyle (1783–1842), who used the pseudonym Stendhal.]

15. [The reference is to the French writer Jean Cocteau (1889–1963).]

16. [The reference is to the French philosopher and social theorist Auguste Comte (1798–1857), whose study of the nature of social change led to the development of the field of sociology.]

not closed in on himself but is always present in a human universe, is what we call existentialism humanism. Humanism, because we remind man that there is no law-maker other than himself, and that in his forlornness he will decide by himself; because we point out that man will fulfill himself as man, not in turning toward himself, but in seeking outside of himself a goal which is just this liberation, just this particular fulfillment.

From these few reflections it is evident that nothing is more unjust than the objections that have been raised against us. Existentialism is nothing else than an attempt to draw all the consequences of a coherent atheistic position. It isn't trying to plunge man into despair at all. But if one calls every attitude of unbelief despair, like the Christians, then the word is not being used in its original sense. Existentialism isn't so atheistic that it wears itself out showing that God doesn't exist. Rather, it declares that even if God did exist, that would change nothing. There you've got our point of view. Not that we believe that God exists, but we think that the problem of His existence is not the issue. In this sense existentialism is optimistic, a doctrine of action, and it is plain dishonesty for Christians to make no distinction between their own despair and ours and then to call us despairing.